THE COMPLETE CHRISTIAN
DICTIONARY
FOR HOME AND SCHOOL

A complete dictionary of the English
language that includes biblical definitions
of words and phrases including God,
man, sin, grace, wisdom, truth
and hundreds of others.

Over 45,000 entries, including 2,100
Bible verses and 700 references to Jesus.

Gospel Light

ALL NATIONS
LITERATURE

EDITORIAL STAFF

SENIOR EDITORS: Morris G. Watkins; Lois I. Watkins

ASSOCIATE EDITORS: Mae Johnson; Jane Mees

SPECIAL CONSULTANT: Eugene W. Bunkowske

EDITORIAL ASSISTANTS: Lois Albrecht; Imogene Bishop; Clair Dewey; Elfrieda Frueh; Enid Miller; Belva Nerlien; Rebecca L. O'Shell; Amy Person; Sharon Watkins

CLERKS AND TYPISTS: Sharon Mather; Rani Khin Mar Nwe; Roland Octavianus; Yvonne Pitcher; Jeannie Sindlinger; Lisa Zamar

TECHNICAL ASSISTANTS: Robby Butler; Robert C. Law; Claire Mellis; John Pitcher; David Ritchey

GENERAL CONSULTANTS: Frank Brenner; Warwick Cooper; Elmer Eggen; Albert Hennig; Dan Marshall; Nancy Nemoyer; Lauren Peppler; Mary Peppler; Orvil Roetman; Robert Schmitt; Ian Stanley; John Westra; Waldo Werning; Edwin Zehnder

IPA FONTS: The IPA font(s) used to print this work is(are) available from Linguist's Software, Inc., PO Box 580, Edmonds, WA 98020-0580 tel (206) 775-1130.

ISBN: 0-8307-1736-6 (HC)
ISBN: 0-8307-1737-4 (PB)
Distributed by Gospel Light
Ventura, California, U.S.A.

CONTENTS

Parts of a Dictionary Entry	ii
Your Guide to the All Nations Dictionary	iii
Words and Meanings	iii
Kinds of Entries	iv
Other Kinds of Entries	v
Sounds and Spellings	vi
Practice Using the All Nations Dictionary	xi
Pronunciation Key	xvii
Various Spellings of English Sounds	xix
Abbreviations Used in This Dictionary	xx
Dictionary	23
Key Language Points	806
Weights and Measures	826

PARTS OF A DICTIONARY ENTRY

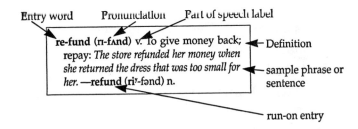

Entry word   Pronunciation   Part of speech label

re-fund (rĭ-fŭnd) v. To give money back; — Definition
repay: *The store refunded her money when
she returned the dress that was too small for* — sample phrase or
her. —**refund** (rĭ'-fənd) n.   sentence

run-on entry

---

irregular ending   definition number

tell (tĕl) v. **told** (tō^wld), **telling 1.** To express by speech or writing **2.**
To show, make known: *This green light tells us we can go now.* **3.** To
recognize; know: *It was so dark I couldn't tell it was you.* **4.** To be — idiom
noticeable; have an effect: *In the last days of the campaign, his
tiredness began to tell on him.* **5. all told** Altogether; when all have
been counted **6. tell the time** To read the time from a clock or
watch **7. tell off** To rebuke severely **8. there's no telling** It's
impossible to know **9. you can never tell** Who knows for sure?
One can not be sure about something

---

irregular endings   British or American English

tar-dy (tär-dĭ^y) adj. **-dier, -diest 1.** *AmE.*
Late **2.** Slow in acting or happening
—**tardily** adv. —**tardiness** n.

word family

---

take-off (tē^yk-ôf) n. **1.** The beginning of
an airplane flight: *a smooth takeoff* **2.** — usage
infml. An amusing copy of someone's
behavior: *an amusing takeoff on a famous
movie star* —see also TAKE OFF — cross reference

YOUR GUIDE TO THE ALL NATIONS DICTIONARY

Inside the dictionary there are about 45,000 carefully chosen words with their definitions and other facts about them. Definitions are given in clear, easily understood words. There are also many examples that show the entry words in context.

Inside the front cover of your dictionary are the complete Pronunciation Key and the chart of Parts of a Dictionary Entry. Inside the back cover is a chart showing the most common spellings of English sounds. Remember to use these charts whenever you need their help.

WORDS AND MEANINGS

Finding An Entry

Each word that is explained or defined in a dictionary is called an entry word. Everything that is said about the entry word makes up a complete entry.

All the entry words in this dictionary are arranged in **alphabetical order:**

a	b	c	d	e	f	g	h	i
j	k	l	m	n	o	p	q	r
s	t	u	v	w	x	y	z	

When a group of words begin with the same first letter, they have to be arranged according to the second letter. If the first two letters are the same, they have to be alphabetized by the third letter, and so on.

To help you further, at the top of each page there is a **guideword** in heavy, bold print. The guideword at the top, left hand side of the left hand page is the first word on the left hand page. The guideword at the top, right hand side of the right hand page is the last word on that page.

Reading An Entry

Here is a sample of a dictionary entry:

There are two definitions for the word, "amuse." The first definition

> **a-muse** (ə-myuᵂz) v. -mused, -musing **1.** To make one laugh or smile: *The monkey's antics amused everyone.* **2.** To make time pass pleasantly: *The children amused themselves by gathering sea shells.*

tells you that it means "to make one laugh or smile." The second meaning is "to make time pass pleasantly."

These statements of meaning are given in regular type style.

Both of these definitions are followed by sentences printed in italics. These are examples to help you learn how the word is used in phrases and sentences.

Finding A Meaning

If there is more than one meaning for the word, the different meanings are separated by numbers in bold print. Where a word has two or more closely related meanings, they are included under one number and separated by letters in bold print. You may have to look through several meanings to find the meaning you want.

KINDS OF ENTRIES

Root Words and Entries

In many cases the word you want to look up is not itself an entry word. You will need to find its root word. For example, if you wanted the words "poked" or "poking" you would look for the root word "poke."

If a verb, noun, adjective, or adverb has regular endings, the endings are not shown in the dictionary. However, if these words have special forms, the changes are shown with the entry word, following the pronunciation and the part of speech.

Examples:

Verbs with irregular past tense and past participle

---

fiddle (fɪd-əl) v. **-dled, -dling** *infml.* **1.** To play the fiddle **2.** To spend time aimlessly and restlessly, esp. to play with something in the hands: *Quit fiddling around and get to work. / Stop fiddling with that knife. You might cut yourself!* —**fiddler** (fɪd-lər) n.

---

flap (flæp) **-pp-** To move up and down or from side to side, usu. making a noise: *curtains flapping in the breeze*

---

fight (faɪt) v. **fought** (fɔt), **fighting 1.** To participate in battle: *Britain fought against Germany in World Wars I and II.* **2.** To prevent or oppose: *to fight crime / a fire* **3.** To quarrel: *The two men had a fight ten years ago and haven't spoken to each other since.* **4.** To box or wrestle **5.** To make one's way, as if by combat: *We fought our way through the crowd.* —**fighter** n.

Nouns with irregular plurals

foot (fʊt) n. **feet** (fiʸt) **1.** The lowest part of the leg, below the ankle, on which a person or animal stands **2.** A measure of length equal to 12 inches: *Twelve inches make one foot.* | *The board is six feet long.* **3.** The base or lowest part of sthg.: *Our kitten likes to sleep at the foot of my bed.* | *the foot of the stairs*

fu-ry (fyʊ-riʸ) n. **-ries 1.** Very great anger; rage: *She flew into a fury because her parents wouldn't let her go to the party.* **2.** Extreme fierceness: *The fury of the storm leveled almost everything on the island.*

fly (flaɪ) n. **flies 1.** A type of small insect with two wings, esp. the housefly **2.** **fly in the ointment** A person or thing that spoils an otherwise perfect situation, occasion, etc.

Adjectives and Adverbs with irregular comparative and superlative forms

fat (fæt) adj. **-tt- 1.** Fleshy; plump; overweight: *I'll have to go on a diet. I've gotten fat from sitting so much.* **2.** Thick; well-filled out; big: *We made a fat profit on the sale of our house.*

fee-ble (fiʸ-bəl) adj. **-bler, -blest** Weak; having little strength: *a feeble old woman*

far (fɑr) adv. **farther** (fɑr-ðər) or **further** (fɜr-ðər), **farthest** (fɑr-ðɪst) or furthest (fɜr-ðɪst) **1.** Long way: *We drove far up the coast.* **2.** Very much: *far prettier* | *far wiser* **3.** **so far** (a) Up to now: *So far I'm enjoying my job, but I've only been here two days.* (b) Up to a certain degree, distance, etc.: *She can only walk so far before she has to stop and rest.* | *to trust someone so far and no further* **4.** **far and wide** Everywhere **5.** **so far, so good** Things are successful up to now: *Our old car has made it half way home. So far, so good!* —see FURTHER

OTHER KINDS OF ENTRIES

Prefixes, Suffixes, and Combining Forms

Prefixes are parts of words that are added at the beginnings of words to add to or change the meaning. Examples: un- as in **un**able, re- as in **re**possess, in- as in **in**complete

Suffixes are parts of words that are added to the ends of words to add to or change the meaning. Examples: -ful as in beauti**ful**, -ly as in man**ly**, -able as in work**able**, -like as in child**like**, -hood as in brother**hood**

Combining forms are whole words that are added to other words to add to or change the meaning. Example: -boy as in cow**boy**

Simple prefixes, suffixes, and combining forms are listed in the dictionary as separate entries. However, if there is a change in the spelling

or if the meaning is not clear, some words made by adding a prefix or suffix to the root word are listed as separate entries.

If the spelling is not changed and the meaning is clear without a special explanation, words with suffixes are shown as "run-ons" in bold type at the end of the entries for root words. Examples: —**fully** adj., —**fullness** n., —**educational** adj., —**electrical** adj., —**electrically** adv.

Compounds

Compounds are words in which two or more separate words are put together to make one. **Examples:**
airmail, baseball, bathtub, background

Some compounds are usually spelled with a hyphen separating the parts. **Examples:**
mother-in-law, cold-hearted, double-talk, absent-minded

Some words that seem like compounds are written as separate words. **Examples:**
black eye, checking account, hot dog, post office

Idioms

Idioms are words, phrases, or sentences that have a special meaning beyond the meaning of the separate words. **Examples:**
The sentences, *"Our new principal is standing on the wall,"* and *"Our new principal is really on the ball,"* have quite different meanings. We can easily tell the meaning of the first sentence, but the meaning of the second is quite different from the meanings of the separate words. In this sentence, *"on the ball"* means that he is *"efficient, up-to-date, and ready to act."*

SOUNDS AND SPELLING

When you look up a word in the dictionary to check its spelling or meaning, you often need to find out its pronunciation to make sure you have found the right entry. Also, you often need to use the dictionary to find out how to pronounce a new word that you have seen in reading.

Pronunciation Symbols

Immediately after the entry word in the dictionary the pronunciation is shown in parentheses. The symbols used are based on the International Phonetic Alphabet with a few changes to make it easier for the learner to know how the sounds are said. Sometimes the pronunciation looks very similar to the

spelling of the word as in the following examples:

bend (bɛnd); lip (lɪp); grow (groʷ); glue (gluʷ); bay (beʸ); stress (strɛs)

In many cases English words are not pronounced exactly as they are spelled, so the pronunciations in the dictionary make use of the special symbols of the International Phonetic Alphabet.

jet (dʒɛt); gem (dʒɛm); phone (foʷn); know (noʷ)

In English the vowels /i/, /e/, /o/, and /u/ tend to be longer than in other languages and to end with a short glide. This is indicated by the use of the symbols /iʸ/, /eʸ/, /oʷ/, and uʷ/. Examples: biʸ, beʸ, gloʷ, gluʷ

The symbol /y/ has been used for the beginning sound in "you" (yuʷ).

Schwa (ə)

In a large number of English words, the vowel in an unaccented syllable tends to become more neutral. This sound is represented by the symbol (ə). It is the sound heard in the first syllable of "above" and "collect," and the second syllable of "hundred," "circus," and "criminal."

In rapid speech the schwa sound itself may be dropped so that only the consonants are heard in the syllable. Example: The word "battle" (bæt-əl) in rapid speech could sound like (bæt-l), or even (bæ-l). We have not made an attempt to represent these possible changes in the dictionary.

Pronunciation Keys

In this dictionary each pronunciation symbol stands for one sound and each symbol always stands for the same sound. A complete pronunciation key is placed inside the front cover so that you can easily turn to it for help.

Stress

Many English words are very short and have only one vowel sound. These are one syllable words. However, there are also many words with two or more syllables. In these words, one syllable is said with more force, or stress, than the other syllables. The pronunciation guides for each word in the dictionary show which is the stressed syllable by using bold print.

Syllables that do not have stress are called unstressed syllables. In unstressed syllables the vowel sound is often pronounced as a schwa.

Varieties of Pronunciation

Some words can be pronounced in more than one way. For example:

route (raʊt / ruʷt); either (iʸ-ðər / aɪ-ðər); root (rʊt / ruʷt)

In such cases both pronunciations are correct and both are given in this dictionary. The pronunciation given first is the more common, so it is given first.

Some types of variation in pronunciation are quite common. For example, **general** is pronounced (dʒɛn-ə-rəl) or (dʒɛn rəl). Though both are common and acceptable, this dictionary gives only the first, more careful pronunciation of such words.

Sometimes when a word has more than one pronunciation, it is important that you use the right one. These words change their stress pattern when they change their use in a sentence. For example...

The movie was pro**duced** by MGM Studios.

You'll find the carrots in the **pro**duce department.

In the following examples, the changes in pronunciation are used to distinguish homographs (words that have the same spelling but different origins and meaning).

wind (wɪnd/ waɪnd); wound (wuʷnd/ waʊnd); bow (baʊ/ boʷ)

Varieties of Spelling

Some words can be spelled in two different ways, as follows:

color, colour / honor, honour / marvelous, marvellous / practice, practise / glamor, glamour

Either of the two forms given for each of these pairs is correct and both are given in the dictionary. The form given first is the more common one, but you should use the one that is accepted in your country or area. In addition, use the same form all the time. Don't change from one to the other. Such words are entered in the dictionary in the following way:

col-or *AmE.;* col-our *BrE.* (kʌ-lər) adj. Definition: *AmE.* means American English; *BrE.* means British English.

Spelling Problems

How do you look up a word in the dictionary if you don't know how to spell it? How would you find the spelling of the following words, for example? They all start with an (n) sound, but with a different letter before the (n).

gnat, know, pneumonia

Other words begin with an (s) sound, but actually begin with a (p) as in psychic, or (c) as in city. Some words begin with a (k) sound, but actually begin with a (c) as in cat or a (q) as in quick. Some words begin with an (r) sound, but actually begin with (w) as in write, and some words beginning with a (j) sound, actually begin with (g) as in general.

To help you make good guesses, use the spelling chart on the inside of the back cover. The words shown in pronunciation symbols at the bottom of the previous page all start with the sound (n), and the chart says that this sound at the beginning of words can be spelled as "gn", "kn", or "pn"

Now look at the second sound in the word (by). The chart shows that at the end of a word this sound can be spelled as with (ye) as in dye, or with (ie) as in die, with (igh) as in sigh, or (uy) as in buy.

Special Features
Part-of-Speech Labels

Words like noun, adjective, and verb are names for parts of speech. The parts of speech used in this dictionary, together with their abbreviations, are listed below.

noun	n.
verb	v.
adverb	adv.
adjective	adj.
pronoun	pron.
preposition	prep.
conjunction	conj.
interjection	interj.
determiner	determ.

Sometimes the same word (same spelling) can be used as a noun or a verb or an adjective, as in the following examples:

We are going to dinner with Mr. and Mrs. Long.

He has long legs.

John and Mary both long to go home.

In the first sentence, **Long** is a noun.

In the second sentence, **long** is an adjective describing legs.

In the third sentence, **long** is a verb meaning "to yearn". *They were longing or yearning (= had a strong desire) to go back home.*

Immediately following the pronunciation of a word the part of speech is given as follows:

long (loŋ) n. (Definition)

Looking at the part-of-speech label can help you understand the definition of a word. For example, you may not be sure from the entry for "creation" whether it should be used as a noun or adjective. However, by looking at the part-of-speech label you can see that the word is a noun. Part -of-speech labels can also help you to find the right meaning of a word.

Usage Labels

Some words may be good English words in some situations but not in all situations: For example, the word 'kid' often refers to children. We might say, "How are your kids?" meaning, "How are your children?" In this case, we put *infml.* for informal before the definition of **kid.** This means that it is all right to use this word in this way in informal situations, but may not be appropriate in formal settings. Other USAGE LABELS include *spir.* (spiritual), *fig.* (figurative), *fml.* (formal), *derog.* (derogative), *tech.* (technical) and *slang.*

The label "slang" refers to a word or to a word usage that is not yet considered part of the general language. Slang terms can often be very expressive, and some slang may be especially popular at a particular time or with a particular group of people. Slang terms are used more in speech than in writing, and some teachers object to the use of any slang words in writing (in any written composition).

PRACTICE USING THE
ALL NATIONS DICTIONARY

A dictionary is a special kind of reference book with words listed in alphabetical order. In order to use a dictionary effectively you must know how to find the words you want to use, what information is given in the dictionary about those words, and how the information is organized. This section of the *All Nations Dictionary* is intended to give you practice in using the dictionary.

Finding An Entry

1. Remember that all the entry words are arranged in alphabetical order. Arrange the following words in alphabetical order, then look them up in the dictionary.

child, apple, ivory, money, goat, feather, sugar, zipper, roar, vase

2. When a group of words begin with the same letter, they have to be arranged according to the second letter. Arrange the following group of words in alphabetical order, then look them up in the dictionary.

chair, cackle, clarinet, circus, curfew, crumb, cozy, cement, cyclone

3. When the first two letters are the same in a group of words, they are arranged according to the third letter, and so on. Arrange the following words in alphabetical order, then look them up in the dictionary.

shovel, shadow, shriek, shy, shepherd, shudder, shirt

Guide Words

At the top of every page in this dictionary there is a guide word in heavy type. Find the guide word at the top left-hand side of page 96, and the guide word at the top right-hand side of page 97. Find three words that can be found between these two guide words in the dictionary.

Finding A Meaning

Look up the following words and find at least two different meanings for each word.

attend, counter, finger, mint, soft

Finding Root Words

Many times the word you want to use will not be an entry word itself. You will need to find the root word from which it comes. Think of the root word for each of the words below.

apples, pennies, prettiest, fought, jumping, originally, copied

Finding Other Kinds Of Entries

1. Find the prefix **un-** among the entries in the dictionary. Think of five words you can form by using the prefix **un-**. See if you can find them in the dictionary. You may need to look at one of the "run-on"s in bold type at the end of the root word entry.

2. Find the suffix **-ful** in the dictionary. Think of five words you can form by using the suffix **-ful**. See if you can find them in the dictionary.

3. Find two other prefixes and two other suffixes in the dictionary that you could use to form new words. Form two new words from each prefix and suffix. Find the words you formed in the dictionary.

Learning About Special Features of a Word

Many times it will be helpful for you to know the part-of-speech label for a word that you want to use. Some words can be used in more than one way. In the *All Nations Dictionary* the part-of-speech

label is given in its abbreviated form right after the entry word. Look up the following words in the dictionary and find out what part of speech they are. Then use the word in a sentence.

charade, embrace, idealize, nautical, narrow

Using The Pronunciation Key

One of the special features of the *All Nations Dictionary* is the use of the International Phonetic Alphabet (IPA) to help you in pronunciation. The symbols in the IPA are used by language students all over the world to learn a language other than their own. They are even used by linguists who are writing a language down for the first time.

For those who are not familiar with the IPA we are including an opportunity for you to practice it so that you can tell more easily how a word should be pronounced. Please take time now to study the pronunciation key given on page xvi. Pay special attention to the symbols you don't already know.

1. Say each word in the box below. Then circle the correct pronunciation next to it. Look up the word in the dictionary to see if you guessed correctly.

nest [nəst] [nɛst]	pat [pæt] [pɑt]
hid [hiʸd] [hɪd]	see [sɪ] [siʸ]
sun [sʌn] [suʷn]	cool [kuʷl] [kʊl]
cot [kʊt] [kɑt]	take [teʸk] [tæk]
roll [roʷl] [rɔl]	cough [kʌf] [kɔf]

In some of the words above you noticed that the pronunciation key showed a small letter "y" or "w" above the line. These symbols show us that the vowel is longer than usual and that it ends in a glide. Try saying the words "see," "roll," "cool," and "take." Can you feel your tongue changing positions at the end of the sound?

2. Some English vowel sounds are really a combination of two sounds. These are called diphthongs and they are represented in the IPA by a combination of two symbols. Say each word in the box below and then circle the correct pronunciation. Look the word up in the dictionary to see if you guessed correctly.

round [raʊnd] [raɪmd]	loud [lɔɪd] [laʊd]
toy [taɪ] [tɔɪ]	smile [smaɪl] [smiʸl]
high [haɪ] [haʊ]	foot [fɔɪt] [fʊt]
find [faɪmd] [faʊnd]	boil [bɔɪl] [baɪl]
cow [kaʊ] [koʷ]	crowd [kraɪd] [kraʊd]

3. In many English words, the vowel in an <u>unstressed</u> syllable tends to become more neutral. This sound is represented by the schwa (ə). In rapid speech the schwa sound may disappear altogether. When the same neutral sound occurs in a <u>stressed</u> syllable it is represented by the (ʌ) symbol. Say each word in the box below and fill in the blank spaces with the correct symbol (ʌ) or (ə). Look the words up in the dictionary to see if you are correct.

above __- b__v	tub t__b
love l__v	funny f__n - iʸ
commit k__- mɪt	drug dr__g

4. When a vowel sound is followed by an [r] sound, the sound of the vowel is changed somewhat. In words like "turn" and "fern" we have used a special symbol [ɜ] for the vowel before the [r]. In words like "care" [kɛər] and "hair" [hɛər] we have used the same symbol as in words like "pet" [pɛt], followed by the schwa [ə] and the [r]. Notice these symbols in the pronunciation key. Say each word in the box below and circle the correct pronunciation. Check the dictionary to see if you are correct.

clear [klɪər] [klɪr]	tour [tʊər] [tɜər]
burn [bɜrn] [bɛərn]	deer [dɪər] [dɛər]
bear [bɪər] [bɛər]	learn [lɛərn] [lɜrn]

5. Many of the symbols for consonants are the same as in the English alphabet. There are only five new symbols you will need to learn. In spelling the words "think" and "this" we use the letters "th" for both, but these are two different sounds. So, in the IPA we use two different symbols. Say each word in the box below and circle the correct pronunciation. Check in the dictionary to see if you are correct.

thee [θiʸ] [ðiʸ]	thin [θm] [ðm]
throne [θroʷn] [ðroʷn]	thump [θʌmp] [ðʌmp]
thus [θʌs] [ðʌs]	these [θiʸz] [ðiʸz]

6. Say each word in the box below and circle the correct pronunciation. Check in the dictionary to see if you are correct.

shoe [ʒuʷ] [ʃuʷ]	wish [wɪʒ] [wɪʃ]
azure [æʒ-ər] [æʃ-ər]	leisure [liʸ-ʒər] [liʸ-ʃər]
pleasure [plɛʒ-ər] [plɛʃ-ər] shelf [ʒɛlf] [ʃɛlf]	

7. The sound of the "ch" in "chew" [tʃuʷ] and of the "j" in "jump" [dʒʌmp] are really combinations of two sounds said very close together. Say each of the words in the box below and circle the correct pronunciation. Check in the dictionary to see if you are correct.

church [tʃɜrtʃ] [dʒɜrdʒ]	catch [kætʃ] [kædʒ]
judge [tʃʌtʃ] [dʒʌdʒ]	cage [keʸtʃ] [keʸdʒ]
chin [tʃm] [dʒm]	gentle [tʃen-təl] [dʒen-təl]

8. The sound at the end of the word "sing" is represented by the symbol [ŋ]. This sound is made by saying the [n] and [g] sounds close together. Say the words in the box below and circle the correct pronunciation. Check in the dictionary to see if you are correct.

ink [ɪnk] [ɪŋk]	monkey [mʌn-kiʸ] [mʌŋ-kiʸ]
thing [θm] [θɪŋ]	money [mʌn-iʸ] [mʌŋ-iʸ]
finger [fɪn-gər] [fɪŋ-gər]	banker [bæŋk-ər] [bæŋ-ər]

9. Many words in English have two or more syllables. In these words one syllable is said with more stress than the other syllables. In the *All Nations Dictionary* we have marked the stressed syllables by using bold type. In the box below, circle the stressed syllable in each word.

chipmunk [tʃɪp-mʌŋk]	airplane [ɛər-pleʸn]
grandmother [grænd-mə-ðər]	button [bʌt-ɔn]
understand [ən-dər-stænd]	elephant [ɛl-ə-fənt]

10. Now, try your skill at using the International Phonetic Alphabet. In the blank space after each word, write the correct pronunciation using the symbols we have just practiced. Check the words in the dictionary to see if you are correct.

apple _____   lamb _____

pet _____   kitten _____

fish _____   head _____

birthday _____   foot _____

Finding The Meanings Of Bible Words

Many words are important in the English language because of the way they are used in the Bible. In the *All Nations Dictionary* we have included definitions of terms used in the Bible. The definition is given first and then one or more Bible verses are given to help you better understand the meaning. If you speak another language besides English, it will be helpful for you to find the same verses in the Bible in your own language.

At the end of an entry there may be additional words in capital letters. You may also find it helpful to look up each of these words in the dictionary.

Try looking up a few of the Bible terms below.

life, heaven, God, man, truth, Jesus

PRONUNCIATION KEY

The pronunciation of each word is shown in parenthesis following the entry word. The syllable that is stressed is printed in bold type.

ɑ	hot, father	p	pie
æ	hat, can	b	big
aɪ	my, p**ie**	t	top
aʊ	found, about	d	dig
		k	king, cap
ɛ	pet, best	g	go
eʸ	play, date		
		tʃ	chew
ɪ	hit, pin	dʒ	jet
iʸ	be, wheel		
		f	fine
oʷ	no, home	v	vine
ɔ	bought, horse	θ	thin
ɔɪ	boy, oil	ð	then
		s	see
uʷ	boot, pool	z	zoo
ʊ	put, book	ʃ	shop
		ʒ	treasure
ɜr	turn, fern	h	house
ɛər	care, hair		
ɪər	here, fear	m	man
ʊər	tour, sure	n	now
		ŋ	sing
ʌ	but, cup		
ə	about, sister	w	we
		l	long

In many words having the schwa (ə) sound, the sound may not be heard, especially in rapid speech.

r	row
y	yes

VARIOUS SPELLINGS OF ENGLISH SOUNDS

Sound	Spellings
ɑ	hot, father, sorrow, bark, **ah**, calm, heart, guard, knowledge, watch, sergeant, honest
æ	hat, can, plaid, laugh, meringue, half
aɪ	my, pie, child, alkali, ice, ride, high, aisle, aye, eye, choir, guile, buy, eider, geyser, sign, isle, island, guidance, height
aʊ	found, about, owl, powder, sauerkraut, house, bough, hour
ɛ	pet, best, berry, very, any, said, head, heifer, guest, bury, there, says, leopard, friend
e^y	play, date, braid, may, eight, gauge, fete, matinee, break, grey, gaol, weigh, dossier, bouquet, chalet, straight
ɪ	hit, pin, fish, physics, mirror, been, carriage, hymn, mischief, women, busy, build, pretty
i^y	be, wheel, eel, mete, weak, easy, key, algae, ceiling, ski, machine, Marie, chief, suite, people, amoeba, quay, pity
o^w	no, home, hold, so, blow, toe, boat, oh, owe, chauffeur, sew, yeoman, folks, brooch, soul, beau, though, apropos, depot
ɔ	bought, horse, auto, awl, awe, cloth, all, broad, taught, talk, ought, reservoir, Arkansas, Utah, floor, appal
ɔɪ	boy, oil, buoyant, Illinois, Freud, lawyer
u^w	boot, pool, ooze, tomb, who, group, canoe, cruise, lieutenant, studious, true, rule, neutral, threw, move, through, two, Sioux, suit, rendevous, coup, pooh-pooh, wooed
ʊ	put, book, wolf, woman, worsted, could
ɚ	turn, fern, sir, early, world, journey, myrtle, colonel, burr
ɛɚ	care, hair, berry, very, bury, there, Mary
ɪɚ	here, fear, sheer, mirror
ʊɚ	tour, sure, entrepreneur
ʌ	but, cup, was, the, oven, blood, come, rough, does, double
ə	about, sister, sofa, pencil, effect, upon, ethyl, forfeit, fountain, cautious, pariah, chauffeur, augur, zephyr, liar, occasion

VARIOUS SPELLINGS OF
ENGLISH SOUNDS (continued)

Sound	Spellings
p	pie, happy, hiccough
b	big, ebb, rabbit
t	top, button, Thomas, bought, yacht, ptomaine, talked, debt,
d	dig, add, ladder
k	king, cap, chemistry, bucket, account, acquire, Bacchus, ache, sacque, folk, queue, quay
g	go, egg, guest, rogue, ghost
tʃ	chew, righteous, question, future, avalanche, watch
dʒ	jet, gem, allegiance, avenge, lodging, soldier, adjoin, verdure, exaggerate, bridge
f	fine, off, phrase, laugh
v	vine, flivver, of, have
θ	thin, absinthe
ð	then, smooth, breathe
s	see, glass, cent, nice, scent, acquiesce, schism, psychology
z	zoo, buzz, Xerox, easy, scissors, rose
ʃ	shop, chauffeur, sure, pshaw, schist, ocean, special, conscience, nauseous, tension, issue, nation, douche
ʒ	treasure, regime, garage, decision, azure, brazier
h	house, who
hw	where, white
m	man, common, comb, paradigm, calm, solemn
n	now, Ann, sign, knife, mnemonic, cologne, gnat, pneumonia
ŋ	sing, tongue, ink
w	we, choir, quick
l	long, Lloyd, tell
r	row, burr, rhythm, catarrh, wrong
y	yes, hallelujah, azalea, opinion

ABBREVIATIONS USED IN THIS DICTIONARY

abbr.	abbreviation, abbreviated
A.D.	Anno Domini
adj.	adjective
adv.	adverb
a.m.	Ante Meridium (before midday)
AmE.	American English
B.C.	Before Christ
BrE.	British English
cap.	capital, capitalized
comb. form	combining form
derog.	derogative
determ.	determiner
esp.	especially
etc.	etcetera
euph.	euphemism
fem.	feminine
fig.	figurative
fml.	formal
gen.	general
imper.	imperative
infml.	informal
interj.	interjection
IPA	International Phonetic Alphabet
irreg.	irregular
lit.	literary, literally
masc.	masculine
n.	noun
part.	participle
pl.	plural
p.m.	Post Meridium (after midday)
prep.	preposition
pres.	present
pron.	pronoun
sbdy.	somebody
sing.	singular
spir.	spiritual
sthg.	something
superl.	superlative
tech.	technical
US	United States
usu.	usually
v.	verb
var.	variant

A, a (eʸ) n. **1.** The first letter of the English alphabet **2.** The first in a series **3.** The best grade in quality (always capitalized): *grade A milk* **4.** "A," a grade rating for excellent school work

a (ə) prep. For each; per: *twice a day/$3.00 a hundred*

a (ə); emphatic (eʸ) determ. , indef. art. **1.** A form of **an** used before a noun or adjective that begins with a consonant, in a nonspecific way: *a book/a pretty girl* **2.** One: *a pair of shoes* **3.** Any: *Do you have a pen?* **4.** The same: *three of a kind*

aard-vark (ɑrd–vark) n. A large burrowing African animal that looks like a pig, but has a long tail, strong claws and a long sticky tongue

ab- (æb–/əb–) (also **a–** before **m, p,** and **v** as in **avocation** and **abs–** before **c** and **t** as in **abstract**) prefix Off; from; away

a-back (ə–bæk) adv. **taken aback** To be surprised or startled

ab-a-cus (æb–ə–kəs) n. *pl.* **-cusses** or **-ci** A device consisting of a frame holding parallel rods that are strung with movable beads, used for counting

a-ban-don (ə–bæn–dən) v. To give up, leave, forsake: *The crew had to abandon the sinking ship.* —**abandonment** n.

a-base (ə–beʸs) v. To humble: *Everyone who exalts himself will be abased* (Luke 18:14).

a-bate (ə–beʸt) v. **-bated, -bating** To decrease or become less —**abatement** n.

ab-bess (æb–əs) n. A nun who is the head of a convent

ab-bey (æ–biʸ) n. **1.** A monastery or convent ruled by an abbot or abbess **2.** The entire number of monks or nuns in an abbey **3.** A church that was formerly an abbey: *Westminster Abbey is in London.*

ab-bot (æb–ət) n. The male head of an abbey

abbr.; also **abbrev.** n. Short form of **abbreviation**

ab-bre-vi-ate (ə–briʸ–viʸ–eʸt) v. **-ated, -ating** To make shorter

ab-bre-vi-a-tion (ə–briʸ–viʸ–eʸ–ʃən) n. **1.** The act or state of shortening **2.** A shortened form of a word or phrase: *"Apr." for "April," "Dr." for "doctor"*

ab-di-cate (æb–də–keʸt) v. **1.** To formally give up or relinquish power and authority as of a king or queen **2.** To give up authority or responsibility: *The father abdicated all responsibility to his son.*

ab-do-men (æb–də–mən) n. The part of the body below the chest containing most of the digestive organs —**ab-dom-i-nal** (æb–dɑm–ə–nəl) adj.

ab-duct (æb–dʌkt) v. To take a person away illegally by force or fraud; to kidnap —**abduction** n.

ab-duc-tor (æb–dʌk–tər) n. One who abducts someone

a-bet (ə–bet) v. **-tt-** To help or encourage, usually to do sthg. wrong

a-bey-ance (ə–beʸ–əns) n. The condition of being temporarily suspended: *The decision was left in abeyance for weeks.*

ab-hor (əb–hor/ æb–) v. **-rr-** To loathe; detest; hate very much

ab-hor-rent (əb–hor–ənt/ æb–) adj. Detestable

a-bide (ə–baɪd) v. **abode** (ə–boʷd) or **abided, abiding 1.** To dwell; remain; last **2.** To bear; endure

a-bil-i-ty (ə–bɪl–ə–tiʸ) n. **-ties** Skill and power to make, do, or think, etc.: *athletic ability/He has the ability to become a great artist.*

ab-ject (æb–dʒɛkt/ æb–dʒɛkt) adj. Miserable; wretched; extreme: *abject poverty*

a-blaze (ə–bleʸz) adj. Being on fire; blazing

a-ble (eʸ–bəl) adj. **abler, ablest 1.** Having ability **2.** Talented; capable

–able (–ə–bəl); **–ible** adj. suffix **1.** Having enough ability or worthy of the action of the verb: *adaptable* **2.** Having the characteristic of a stated noun: *changeable/accessible*

ab-lu-tions (æb–luʷ–ʃən) n. *pl.* A washing or cleansing of the body or a part of the body

ab-nor-mal (æb–nor–məl) adj. Different, often in an undesirable way; not normal —**abnormally** adv.

a-board (ə–bord) adv., prep. On board a train, ship, plane or bus: *There were 60 people aboard the plane.*

a-bode (ə–boʷd) n. **1.** Dwelling place; residence **2.** Sojourn

a-bol-ish (ə–bɑl–ɪʃ) v. To put an end to, esp. by law: *It would be wonderful if war could be*

abolished. —**ab-o-li-tion** (æ–bə–lɪʃ–ən) n. *the abolition of slavery*

a-bom-i-na-ble (ə–bɑm–ə–nə–bəl) adj. Loathsome; detestable

a-bom-i-na-tion (ə–bɑm–ə–neʸ–ʃən) n. Sthg. loathed

ab-o-rig-i-ne (æb–ə–rɪdʒ–ə–niʸ) n. -nes 1. Any of the first or original known inhabitants of an area 2. aborigines The native people, animals, or plants of a region —**aboriginal** adj.

a-bort (ə–bɔrt) v. 1. To end a pregnancy too soon so that the child cannot live 2. To give birth too early (to a dead child) —compare MISCARRIAGE 3. To end before the expected time due to some trouble: *The planned summer program had to be aborted due to extremely hot weather.*

a-bor-tion (ə–bɔr–ʃən) n. The act of giving birth or causing to give birth before time so that the child cannot live, esp. when done intentionally NOTE: The intentional ending of another's life, except in self-defense, is a sin against God's commandment, "You shall not kill." While God hates sin, and all people are sinners, he nevertheless loves the sinner. In his grace and mercy he has provided a way of forgiveness. "The gift of God is eternal life through Jesus Christ our Lord" (Romans 6:23).

a-bor-tive (ə–bɔrt–ɪv) adj. Useless: *an abortive attempt*

a-bound (ə–baʊnd) v. 1. To exist in large amounts 2. To be fully supplied: *God is able to make all grace abound to you, so that in all things at all times, having all that you need, you will abound in every good work* (2 Corinthians 9:8).

a-bound-ing (ə–baʊnd–ɪŋ) adj. *The Lord is compassionate and gracious, slow to anger, abounding in love* (Psalm 103:8).

a-bout (ə–baʊt) adv. 1. Near the amount; almost: *We have about three bushels of apples.* 2. In the opposite direction: *The car spun about into the oncoming traffic.* 3. Aimlessly: *He was found wandering about in the desert.*

about prep. 1. Concerning: *I'd like to talk to you about that problem.* 2. Almost ready to start: *The meeting is about to begin.* 3. **how**

about (used in making a suggestion): *How about going to the movies with me?*

a-bove (ə–bʌv) adv. 1. In, at, or to a higher place; overhead: *the floor above* 2. In heaven: *St. Paul, writing to Christians, says, "Since you have been raised with Christ, set your hearts on things above, where Christ is seated at the right hand of God. Set your minds on things above, not on earthly things"* (Colossians 3:1,2). 3. Upstairs

above prep. 1. Higher than; on top of; over: *His office is above ours./ fig. She's above any kind of dishonesty.* 2. More than: *God values moral character above sacrifice* (1 Samuel 15:22). 3. Higher in position or authority: *The department head is above all the other employees.* 4. **above all** Most important 5. **above board** Honest; straightforward

A-bra-ham (eʸ–brə–hæm) n. 1. A masculine name meaning "Father of a multitude" 2. The man called of God some 2000 years B.C. to be the father of many nations both physically and spiritually. NOTE: Abraham was born in Ur of the Chaldees, near the north end of the Persian Gulf. Most of the people there, including Abraham's father, were idolaters (Joshua 24:2). God spoke to Abraham, saying, "Leave your country, your people, and your father's household and go to a land I will show you, and I will make your name great, and you will be a blessing. I will bless those who bless you and whoever curses you I will curse, and all peoples on earth will be blessed through you" (Genesis 12:1-3). Later God said, "Through your offspring (or seed) all nations of the earth will be blessed" (Gen. 22:18). This promise was repeated to Abraham's son Isaac (Gen. 26:4) and to his grandson Jacob (Gen. 28:14). Abraham was also told by God that he would be the father of many nations (Gen. 17:4,5) and that his descendants would be as numerous as the dust of the earth (Gen. 13:16), the stars in the sky (Gen. 15:5), and the sand on the seashore (Gen. 22:17). All of these prophecies have been fulfilled. But the most significant prophecy was that through Abraham's offspring, all nations of

the earth would be blessed. The word "off-spring" here refers to Jesus Christ, who, according to his human nature was a decendant of Abraham, born 2000 years after the promise was given. The Bible says that he [Abraham] is the father of all who believe [in Jesus] (Romans 4:11). If you belong to Christ, then you are Abraham's seed, and heirs [of eternal life] according to the promise (Galatians 3: 29). —see JESUS

a-bra-sive (ə–breˠ-sɪv) adj. **1.** Causing to wear away by rubbing or erosion **2.** Causing friction or irritation: *an abrasive personality* —**a-bra-sion** (ə–breˠ–ʒən) n. ...

abrasive n. A substance for grinding, smoothing, or polishing

a-breast (ə–brɛst) adj., adv. **1.** Side by side and facing the same way **2.** Keeping up with: *abreast of the times*

a-bridge (ə–brɪdʒ) v. To shorten —**abridge-ment** or **abridgment** n.

a-broad (ə–brɔd) adv. **1.** To or in another country, esp. overseas: *They take a vacation abroad every year.* **2.** Covering a wide area: *There's a rumor abroad that ...*

ab-ro-gate (æb–rə–geˠt) v. -**gated**, -**gating** To abolish by authority —**ab-ro-ga-tion** (æb–rə–geˠ–ʃən) n.

a-brupt (ə–brʌpt) adj. **1.** Sudden: *an abrupt stop* **2.** Disconnected; not smooth: *short, abrupt sentences* **3.** Steep: *an abrupt drop or incline* **4.** So quick as to seem rude —**abruptly** adv.

ab-scess (æb–sɛs) n. A collection of pus surrounded by inflamed tissue —**abscessed** adj.

ab-scond (əb–skɑnd/ æb–) v. To run away secretly

ab-sence (æb–səns) n. **1.** The state of being away **2.** The time during which a person is away: *Someone will have to do your work during your absence.* **3.** Lack: *an absence of proof*

ab-sent (æb–sənt) adj. **1.** Away; not present **2.** Not existing **3.** Not attentive

ab-sent (æb–sɛnt) v. To stay away from: *He absented himself from the meeting.*

ab-sent–mind-ed (æb–sənt–maɪmd–ɪd) adj. **1.** Forgetful **2.** Unaware of one's surroundings or action; not paying attention

ab-so-lute (æb–sə–luˠt) adj. **1.** Complete; per-fect: *God's Word is the [absolute] truth* (John 17 17). **1.** Having complete power; not limited: *The emperor had absolute power to do anything he chose to do.*

ab-so-lute-ly (æb–sə–luˠt–liˠ) adv. Complete-ly: *The Bible is absolutely true. There's no question about it.*

ab-solve (əb–sɑlv) v. -**solved**, -**solving** **1.** To free from the consequences or penalties resulting from actions **2.** To grant remission of sins to sbdy.

ab-sorb (æb–zɔrb) v. **1.** To soak up: *Dry sand absorbs water quickly./Some students absorb ideas much more quickly than others.* **2.** To take one's complete attention: *He was so absorbed in his work, he didn't want to go to the party.*

ab-sor-bent (əb–sɔr–bənt /–zɔr–) adj. Absorb-ing or tending to absorb

absorbent n. A substance that absorbs

ab-sorp-tion (əb–sɔrp–ʃən/ æb–/ –zɔrp–) n. **1.** A process of absorbing or being absorbed **2.** Concentration; attention

ab-stain (æb–steˠn/ əb–) v. To hold oneself back from doing sthg.; to refrain from sthg.: *I urge you ... to abstain from sinful desires which war against your soul* (1 Peter 2:11).

ab-sti-nence (æb–stə–nəns) n. Abstaining, esp. from food or alcohol

ab-stract (æb–strækt) v. To remove or separate sthg.: *The metal was abstracted from the ore.*

ab-stract (æb–strækt) n. **1.** A shortened form of an article, speech, etc. **2.** In art, a drawing, painting, etc. that expresses the artist's ideas, attitudes, and emotions rather than showing an actual likeness of an object, scene, etc.

ab-stract (æb–strækt/əb–) adj. Thought of as a quality rather than sthg. observable, such as an idea or thought: *An abstract idea like justice is very hard to define.*

ab-strac-tion (æb–stræk–ʃən) n. **1.** The state of being inattentive; absent-mindedness **2.** An idea or a quality rather than an object **3.** The act or process of taking sthg. out: *the abstraction of a tooth* **4.** An abstract work of art, one that does not try to show an object or scene (as it would be seen by a camera), but an idea

ab-surd (əb–zɜrd) adj. Ridiculous; unreasonable

a-bun-dance (ə–bʌn–dəns) n. A quantity that is more than enough: *Beware of covetousness; for a man's life consists not in the abundance of the things which he possesses* (Luke 12:15).

a-bun-dant (ə–bʌn–dənt) adj. **1.** Plentiful; more than enough: *The country has an abundant supply of wheat./ ...the Lord God, merciful and gracious, long-suffering, and abundant in goodness and truth* (Exodus 34:6 KJV). **2.** Having plenty of sthg.

a-buse (ə–byuᵂz) v. abused, abusing **1.** To use wrongly, improperly, or cruelly, esp. people or animals **2.** To say hurtful or rude things to or about someone **3.** To put to wrong use: *to abuse one's privileges* —abuse (ə–byuᵂs) n. —abusive adj.

a-byss (ə–bɪs) n. A deep hole that seems to have no bottom

ac-a-dem-ic (æk–ə–dɛm–ɪk) adj. **1.** Concerning studying or teaching, esp. in a college or university **2.** Subjects taught to teach one's mind rather than train one's hands

a-cad-e-my (ə–kæd–ə–miʸ) n. -mies **1.** A school for training for a special purpose or skill: *a music academy* **2.** A group of people interested in art, science, or literature **3.** An association of scholars

a cap-pel-la (ɑk–ə–pɛl–ə) n. Music sung without accompaniment —a cappella adj.

ac-cel-er-ate (æk–sɛl–ər–eʸt) v. -ated, -ating **1.** To make or become faster **2.** To cause to happen sooner —ac-celeration n.

accelerator (æk–sɛl–ə–reʸ–tər) n. **1.** A mechanical device, esp. on an automobile, for increasing the speed **2.** A person that causes sthg. to go faster

ac-cent (æk–sɛnt) n. **1.** A particular way of speaking, esp. in a certain country or area of a country: *He speaks with an accent.* **2.** Stress placed on a word or part of a word (syllable): *The accent in the word "dictionary" is on the first syllable.* **3.** The mark or symbol (') used to show which syllable is stressed: *The accent in* (æk'–sɛnt) *is on the first syllable.*

accent v. **1.** To stress the pronunciation **2.** To mark with a printed accent

ac-cen-tu-ate (ə–sɛn–tʃuᵂ–eʸt) v. **1.** To pronounce or mark a word with its accent **2.** To emphasize: *That blue dress accentuates her blue eyes.*

ac-cept (æk–sɛpt/ ək–) v. **1.** To receive: *He accepted the award on behalf of the mayor.* **2.** To agree or believe: *Do you accept your friend's beliefs on nuclear warfare?*

ac-cept-a-ble (æk–sɛpt–ə–bəl/ ək–) adj. Good enough to be accepted; suitable: *His work is not outstanding but it's acceptable.* —opposite UNACCEPTABLE

acceptance (æk–sɛpt–əns/ ək–) n. The act of accepting: *Here is a trustworthy saying that deserves full acceptance: "Christ Jesus came into the world to save sinners — of whom I am the worst"* (1 Timothy 1:15).

ac-cess (æk–sɛs) n. **1.** A means of entering: *They found access to the house through an unlocked window.* **2.** The right to use something: *Young people need to have access to good books and music.*

ac-ces-si-ble (ək–sɛs–ə–bəl/ æk–) adj. Easily reached or entered: *The house is only accessible through this heavy gate.* —opposite INACCESSIBLE

ac-ces-so-ry (ək–sɛs–ə–riʸ) n. **1.** Sthg. useful but nonessential: *A radio is an accessory in an automobile.* **2.** One who, though absent, assists in committing a crime

ac-ci-dent (æk–sə–dənt) n. **1.** A chance event, usu. unpleasant: *There was a terrible car accident on the freeway.* **2. by accident** By chance; not intentionally

ac-ci-den-tal (æk–sə–dɛn–təl) adj. Happening by chance; not by intention —accidentally adv.

ac-claim (ə–kleʸm) v. To praise; to applaud enthusiastically

acclaim n. Applause —ac-cla-ma-tion (æk–lə–meʸ–ʃən) n.

ac-cli-mate (æk–lə–meʸt/ ə–klaɪ–mət) v. -mated, -mating To adjust to a new climate or situation

ac-cli-ma-tize (ə–klaɪ–mə–taɪz) v. -tized, -tizing To become accustomed to another climate

ac-co-lade (æk–ə–leʸd) n. An award, honor, or lauditory notice

ac-com-mo-date (ə–kɑm–ə–deʸt) v. -dated,

-dating 1. To provide or supply with a room in which to stay **2.** To do a favor for **3.** To adapt; to adjust

ac·com·mo·dat·ing (ə–kɑm–ə–deʸt–ɪŋ) adj. Willing to do as one is asked

ac·com·mo·da·tion (ə–kɑm–ə–deʸ–ʃən) n. **1.** The act of accommodating or of being accommodated **2.** Sthg. that meets a need **3. accommodations** pl. Lodgings

ac·com·pa·ni·ment (ə–kʌm–pə–niʸ–mənt) n. **1.** Anything that goes along with or adds to sthg. else **2.** Music that is played to go along with any other activity

ac·com·pa·ny (ə–kʌm–pə–niʸ) v. **-nied, -nying 1.** To go with someone: *Her friend accompanied her to Paris.* **2.** To exist at the same time: *Disease often accompanies other disasters.* **3.** To play supporting music in a performance: *Ann sings and Mary accompanies her on the guitar.*

ac·com·plice (ə–kɑm–plis) n. Sbdy. who helps another, esp. in a crime

ac·com·plish (ə–kɑm–plɪʃ) v. To get sthg. done: *What does he expect to accomplish in such a short time?*

ac·com·plished (ə–kɑm–plɪʃt) adj. Skillful; very talented and capable: *an accomplished writer*

ac·com·plish·ment (ə–kɑm–plɪʃ–mənt) n. **1.** The act of accomplishing sthg. completely and successfully: *Riding your bicycle across the country was quite an accomplishment.* **2.** A skill: *Playing the violin, writing stories for children, and cooking Chinese food are a few of her many accomplishments.*

ac·cord (ə–kɔrd) n. **1.** Agreement: *Are the two political parties in accord on this issue?* **2. of one's own accord** Willing **3. with one accord** With everyone in agreement

ac·cord·ance (ə–kɔrd–əns) n. In agreement with: *I bought the supplies in accordance with the committee's decision.*

ac·cord·ing·ly (ə–kɔrd–ɪŋ–liʸ) adv. In a suitable manner; appropriately

ac·cord·ing to (ə–kɔrd–ɪŋ tuʷ) prep. **1.** In the manner said or shown: *According to my instructions I will send the order today.* **2.** In a way that agrees with: *You will be punished according to the seriousness of your crime.*

ac·cor·di·on (ə–kɔr–diʸ–ən) n. A portable musical instrument with bellows, a key board, and metal reeds

ac·cost (ə–kɔst/ –kɑst) v. To approach and speak to sbdy., esp. in an unfriendly or sexual way

ac·count (ə–kaʊnt) n. **1.** A written or spoken report or description: *The newspaper account of the meeting was accurate.* **2.** Consideration: *Have you taken everything into account?* **3.** A record or statement of money received and paid out: *The company kept detailed accounts of all their business dealings.* **4.** An arrangement for buying now and paying later: *I'd like to put this purchase on my account.* **5.** A statement of money owed: *My account is due today. Here is my check.* **6.** Money kept in a bank: *a checking account*

ac·count·a·ble (ə–kaʊnt–ə–bəl) adj. Responsible; required to give an explanation

ac·count·ant (ə–kaʊnt–ənt) n. One whose job it is to keep and examine the money accounts for businesses or individuals

ac·count·ing (ə–kaʊnt–ɪŋ) n. **1.** The art and system of keeping and analyzing financial records **2.** An explanation of one's behavior

ac·cred·it (ə–kred–ət) v. **1.** To endorse or approve officially **2.** To credit —**ac·cred·i·ta·tion** (ə–kred–ə–teʸ–ʃən) n.

ac·crue (ə–kruʷ) v. To be given or added to: *Interest accrues to the money in our savings account.*

ac·cu·mu·late (ə–kyuʷ–myə–leʸt) v. **-lated, -lating** To add to: *He accumulated a small fortune through investing in rare coins.* —**ac·cu·mu·la·tion** (ə–kyuʷ–myə–leʸ–ʃən) n.

ac·cu·ra·cy (æk–yər–ə–siʸ) n. The quality of being accurate or exact —opposite INACCURACY

ac·cu·rate (æk–yər–ɪt) adj. Correct; exact

ac·cursed (ə–kɜr–səd/ ə–kɜrst) adj. Under a curse: *No one speaking by the Spirit of God calls Jesus accursed, and no one can say that Jesus is Lord except by the Holy Spirit* (1 Corinthians 12:3).

ac·cu·sa·tion (æk–yə–zeʸ–ʃən) n. A charge of doing wrong

ac·cuse (ə–kyuʷz) v. **-cused, -cusing** To charge someone with doing wrong or breaking the

law; to blame: *The police accused him of stealing the car.*

ac·cus·tom (ə–kʌs–təm) v. To cause to become used to: *They accustomed themselves to a simple lifestyle.*

ac·cus·tomed (ə–kʌs–təmd) adj. **1.** Used to: *Are you accustomed to this warm climate yet?* **2.** Usual: *I am going on my accustomed walk this morning.*

ace (eʸs) n. **1.** A playing card with a single mark: *an ace of spades* **2.** An expert in sthg.: *a World War II ace (=a skilled pilot)*

ache (eʸk) v. **ached, aching** To have a steady pain: *My tooth has been aching for a week./fig. She was aching to become an actress.*

ache n. A continuous pain: *I feel a dull ache in my chest.*

a·chieve (ə–tʃiʸv) v. **-chieved, -chieving** To accomplish or complete sthg. successfully: *He achieved his goal of making a million dollars before he reached the age of thirty.*

a·chieve·ment (ə–tʃiʸv–mənt) n. The successful accomplishment of a task: *Swimming the English Channel is quite an achievement.*

ac·id (æs–əd) n. **1.** A type of chemical substance which may destroy things it touches: *The battery acid burned a hole in my jeans.* **2. acid test** A final test which will prove the quality or value of sthg.

acid adj. **1.** Having a sour, sharp, or bitter taste: *Vinegar gives an acid taste to the salad.* **2.** Hurtful in speech —compare SARCASTIC

ac·knowl·edge (æk–nɑ–lɪdʒ/ ək–) v. **1.** To admit the truth of: *The sales lady acknowledged her mistake and refunded the money she had overcharged me./ spir. If anyone acknowledges that Jesus is the Son of God, God lives in him and he in God (1 John 4:15). —see JESUS* **2.** To write to say that one has received sthg.: *Mr. Smith acknowledged my letter.* **—acknowledgment** n.

ac·me (æk–miʸ) n. The highest point; the peak of perfection

ac·ne (**æk**–niʸ) n. A skin disorder, marked by inflammation of the oil glands, producing pimples, esp. on the face

ac·o·lyte (æk–ə–laɪt) n. An altar attendant in a Christian church

a·corn (eʸ–kɔrn) n. The nut of the oak tree

a·cous·tic (ə–kuʷs–tɪk) adj. Concerning sound or the sense of hearing

acoustics (ə–kuʷs–tɪks) n. *pl.* **1.** The qualities of a room or hall that make it good or bad for carrying sound: *The acoustics in this room are bad. I couldn't understand a word the speaker said.* **2.** The science dealing with sound

ac·quaint (ə–kweʸnt) v. **1.** To inform sbdy. about sthg.: *I'm not acquainted with the facts on this matter. I'd better read your brochure.* **2. be acquainted with** To have met socially: *Yes, I'm acquainted with Mr. Jones. He has just moved into the office next to ours.*

ac·quaint·ance (ə–kweʸnt–əns) n. **1.** Personal knowledge **2.** A person with whom one is acquainted

ac·qui·esce (æk–wiʸ–ɛs) v. **-esced, -esc·ing** To agree without protest **—acquiescence** n.

ac·quire (ə–kwaɪ–ər) v. **-quired, -quiring 1.** To gain or come to possess sthg.: *She acquired a lot of experience in her travels.* **2. acquire a taste** To learn to like sthg.: *I acquired a taste for avocados from my sister who raises them in her back yard.*

ac·qui·si·tion (æk–wə–zɪ–ʃən) n. **1.** The act of acquiring sthg. **2.** Sthg. acquired

ac·quit (ə–kwɪt) v. **-tt-** To declare someone innocent of a crime: *The jury acquitted her of the crime of murder and she was set free./ spir. Acquitting the guilty and condemning the innocent — the Lord detests [hates] them both (Proverbs 17:15).*

ac·quit·tal (ə–kwɪt–əl) n. A legal judgment of "not guilty"

a·cre (eʸ–kər) n. A measure of land; 4,840 square yards or about 4,047 square meters; 43,560 square feet

a·cre·age (eʸ–kər–ɪdʒ) n. Land measured by acres

ac·rid (æk–rid) adj. Harsh or bitter in taste or smell

ac·ri·mo·ny (æk–rə–moʷ–niʸ) n. Bitterness of feeling or speech **—ac·ri·mon·i·ous** (æk–rə–moʷ–niʸ–əs) n.

ac·ro·bat (æk–rə–bæt) n. One who performs spectacular gymnastic feats

ac·ro·nym (æk–rə–nɪm) n. A word formed from the initial letters of a name: *WHO is an acronym for World Health Organization.*

ac·ro·pho·bi·a (æk-rə-fo^w-bi^y-ə) n. An abnormal fear of being in high places

a·cross (ə-krɔs) prep., adv. **1.** From one side to the other: *The tree was lying across the road.* **2.** On or to the opposite side: *She lived across the street from us.* **3.** So as to cross: *The two lines cut across each other.*

act (ækt) v. **1.** To perform a deed; take action: *He acted quickly to save the child's life.* **2.** To behave in the stated manner: *He acts like a gentleman.* **3.** To be an actor: *He hopes to act in the new play on Broadway.* **4.** To appear to be: *He acts greedy.* **5.** To function in a certain way: *This wall acts as a barrier between us.*

act n. **1.** The process of doing sthg.: *He was caught in the act of stealing a car.* **2.** A deed; sthg. that is done: *Giving all that food to the hungry was an act of kindness.* **3.** An enactment by a legislative body: *an act of congress* **4.** A major part of a play or opera: *The villain was captured in the third act.* **5.** A performance in a variety show: *Our play follows the magic act.* **6.** A pose: *He's not as innocent as he seems. He's putting on an act.*

act·ing (ækt-ɪŋ) adj. Temporarily taking the responsibilities of another: *He was the acting director while the executive director was out of the country.*

acting n. The occupation or performance of an actor

ac·tion (æk-ʃən) n. **1.** Process of doing things: *The Council needs to take action (=begin to act) against all the crime in our city.* **2.** Sthg. done: *The decision was followed immediately by action.* **3.** The main events in a movie, play, book, etc.: *The action takes place during the Civil War.* **4.** Military battle: *My friend's brother was killed in action during the war.*

ac·ti·vate (æk-tə-ve^yt) v. -vated, -vating **1.** To spur into action **2.** To make active **3.** To call to active duty, as in the military

ac·tive (æk-tɪv) adj. Doing things, or able and ready to take action: *He's not in good health, but he's still an active church member.* —opposite INACTIVE —**ac·tivism** n.

ac·tiv·i·ty (æk-tɪv-ə-ti^y) n. -ties **1.** A lot of things happening; a state of being active **2.** Any specific action: *sports activities*

ac·tor (æk-tər) n. A person, esp. a man who

acts in a play or movie

ac·tress (æk-trɪs) n. A woman who acts in a play or movie

Acts (ækts) n. One of the 27 books of the New Testament. The full title is "The Acts of the Apostles." It is a history of the early Christian church from the time of Christ's ascension into heaven to about the year 64 A.D. The latter half of the book is primarily about the Apostle Paul, his missionary journeys and the planting of churches in Greece and what is now called Turkey. —see NEW TESTAMENT

ac·tu·al (æk-tʃu^w-əl) adj. Real; existing in fact: *This is an actual story of what really happened.*

ac·tu·al·ly (æk-tʃu^w-əl-i^y) adv. Really: *The mayor is actually letting us use this house for the project.*

ac·tu·ate (æk-tʃə-we^yt) v. -ated, -ating To put into action

a·cu·men (ə-kyu^w-mən/ æk-yə-mən) n. Sharpness of mind; keenness of insight or judgment

ac·u·punc·ture (æk-yə-pəŋk-tʃər) n. A traditional Chinese method of treating illness by piercing the skin with fine needles

a·cute (ə-kyu^wt) adj. **1.** Of the mind or senses, able to sense small differences: *an acute sense of smell* **2.** Severe: *Africa has faced an acute shortage of food many times.* **3.** Of an angle, less than 90 degrees

ad (æd) n. Advertisement

A.D. (e^y-di^y) Short for Latin Anno Domini; in the year since the birth of Jesus Christ: *World War II ended in 1945 A.D.* —compare B.C.

ad·age (æd-ɪdʒ) n. An old familiar saying

Ad·am (æd-əm) n. **1.** A masculine name **2.** The first man that God created —see MAN, ORIGINAL SIN

ad·a·mant (æd-ə-mənt) adj. Inflexible; unyielding —**adamantly** adv. *He adamantly refused to go.*

a·dapt (ə-dæpt) v. To make or become suitable or fit for a new use or situation: *The children have adapted quickly to their new school.* — **adaptive** adj.

a·dapt·a·ble (ə-dæpt-ə-bəl) adj. Able to change or be changed so as to be suitable

for different conditions, new needs, etc.
—a·dapt·a·bil·i·ty (ə–dæpt–ə–bɪl–ə–ti^y) n.

a·dap·ta·tion (æd–əp–te^y–ʃən) n. The state of being adapted

a·dapt·er (ə–dæpt–ər) n. **1.** One that adapts **2.** A device for connecting two dissimilar parts of an apparatus: *We need an adapter in order to plug this projector into that electric outlet.*

add (æd) v. **1.** To put together with something else so as to increase the amount or number: *Let's add some more names to the list.* **2.** To join numbers to get the total: *If we add eight and nine we get 17.* —opposite SUBTRACT **3.** To say also: *I'd like to add that we really enjoyed the dinner.* **4. add insult to injury** To make matters worse

ad·dend (æd–ɛnd) n. Any one of a set of numbers that are to be added

ad·den·dum (ə–dɛn–dəm) n. *pl.* **addenda** Something added

ad·der (æd–ər) n. A poisonous snake

ad·dict (ə–dɪkt) v. **1.** To devote or surrender oneself to something (drugs, tobacco, alcohol, etc.) habitually or excessively **2.** To become physiologically dependent on a drug **addict** (æd–ɪkt) n. One who is addicted (to a drug, etc.) —**ad·dic·tion** (ə–dɪk–ʃən) n.

ad·di·tion (ə–dɪ–ʃən) n. **1.** The act or process of adding **2.** A thing added to sthg. else: *We have just built an addition onto our house.*

ad·di·tion·al (ə–dɪ–ʃən–əl) adj. Added extra —**additionally** adv.

ad·di·tive (æd–ə–tɪv) n. A substance added in small amounts for a special purpose: *a gasoline additive*

ad·dress (ə–drɛs) v. **1.** To speak to: *The senator will address the audience.* **2.** To indicate the destination of mail: *He addressed the envelope to his office in Washington.*

ad·dress (ə–drɛs/ æ–drɛs) n. **1.** A formal written or spoken speech: *Hundreds of people heard the university president's address.* **2.** The indication of where mail is to be sent: *Be sure to put the complete address on the envelope.* **3.** The location at which a person can be reached: *My address is 123 S. Kirby Street.*

ad·e·noids (æd–ən–ɔɪdz) n. Swellings between the back of the nose and the throat

may which hinder breathing

a·dept (ə–dɛpt) adj. Highly skilled; expert

ad·e·quate (æd–ə–kwɪt) adj. Enough, but not more than is needed: *Is your salary adequate for a family of four?*

ad·here (æd–hɪər/ əd–) v. **-hered, -hering 1.** To stick fast to sthg.: *Do you think this tape will adhere to the package?* **2.** To remain faithful and continue to give support to a person or cause **3.** To stick to a plan or course of action

ad·he·sion (æd–hi^y–ʒən/ əd–) n. **1.** The act of adhering **2.** Bodily tissues that are abnormally joined together

ad·he·sive (æd–hi^y–sɪv/ əd–) adj. **1.** To tend to adhere; sticky **2.** Prepared for adhering

a·dieu (ə–du^w/ə–dyu^w) n., interj. Farewell

ad·ja·cent (ə–dʒe^y–sənt) adj. Near or very close; joining or almost joining: *Spain and Portugal are adjacent countries.*

ad·jec·tive (æ–dʒɪk–tɪv) n. A word used to describe or limit a noun, such as "funny" in "a funny hat," or a pronoun, such as "big " in "She is big."

ad·join (ə–dʒɔɪn) v. To be situated next to

ad·join·ing (ə–dʒɔɪn–ɪŋ) adj. Touching or bordering

ad·journ (ə–dʒɜrn) v. To end a meeting or to stop for a particular period of time

ad·ju·di·cate (ə–dʒu^w–də–ke^yt) v. **-cated, -cating** To act as a judge (in an artistic competition, etc.)

ad·junct (æd–ənkt) n., adj. **1.** One attached to another in a subordinate position: *an adjunct professor at the university* **2.** *Gram.* Adverb or adverbial phrase added to a clause or sentence to modify the meaning of a verb

ad·jure (ə–dʒʊər) v. **-jured, -juring** To command or entreat solemnly: *I adjure you to tell the truth.*

ad·just (ə–dʒʌst) v. To change slightly: *He had to adjust the seat (=raise it or lower it) before he could ride his brother's bicycle.* —**adjustable** adj. —**adjustment** n.

ad–lib (æd–lɪb) v. **-bb-** To speak without preparation —**ad–lib** adj. —**ad lib** adv.

ad·min·is·ter (æd–mɪn–ə–stər/ əd–) v. **1.** To direct or control the affairs of a person or group **2.** To give or apply: *A passerby admin-*

istered first aid to the accident victims.

ad-min-is-tra-tion (æd–mɪn–ə–streˠ–ʃən/ əd–) n. The control or direction of affairs of a business, school, etc.

ad-min-is-tra-tive (æd–mɪn–ə–streˠ–trɪv/ əd–) adj. Concerning the control and direction of a business: *He's the administrative director of the company.*

ad-min-is-tra-tor (æd–mɪn–ə–streˠ–tər/ əd–) n. A person who controls or directs the affairs of a school or business

ad-mir-a-ble (æd–mər–ə–bəl) adj. Worthy of respect:*Whatever is admirable ... think about such things* (Philippians 4:8).

ad-mir-al (æd–mə–rəl) n. The Commander in Chief of a navy or fleet

ad-mi-ra-tion (æd–mə–reˠ–ʃən) n. A feeling of respect: *I have a lot of admiration for him.*

ad-mire (æd–maɪ–ər/ əd–) v. -mired, -miring To regard with pleasure and respect: *She was admired for her honesty.*

ad-mis-si-ble (æd–mɪs–ə–bəl/ əd–) adj. That which can be, or is worthy to be admitted or allowed; allowable

ad-mis-sion (æd–mɪ–ʃən/ əd–) n. 1. Allowing or being allowed to enter or enroll in a school or join a club 2. Sthg. admitted or confessed: *an admission of guilt* 3. An entrance fee

ad-mit (æd–mɪt/ əd–) v. -mitted, -mit-ting 1. To permit to enter 2. To confess to doing sthg. wrong: *He admitted that he had taken the book without asking.* 3. To concede: *Mr. Jones had to admit defeat in the election.*

ad-mit-tance (æd–mɪt–əns/ əd–) n. Right of entrance: *We gained admittance to the meeting when we showed the doorkeeper our badges.*

ad-mit-ted-ly (æd–mɪt–əd–liˠ/ əd–) adv. By general admission: *She was admittedly the best qualified for the job.*

ad-mon-ish (æd–man–ɪʃ/ əd–) v. 1. To reprove mildly 2. To warn, urge, or caution against specific faults: *Mr. Jones always gave us the admonition to be careful crossing the street before we went home from school. / Let the word of Christ dwell in you richly, teaching and admonishing one another in psalms, hymns, and spiritual songs, singing with grace in your hearts to the Lord* (Colossians 3:16 NKJV).

ad-mo-ni-tion (æd–mə–nɪ–ʃən) n. 1. Mild reproof 2. Caution or warning against fault or oversight: *And you fathers, do not provoke your children to wrath, but bring them up in the training and admonition of the Lord* (Ephesians 6:4 NKJV).

ad nau-se-am (æd nɔ–ziˠ–əm) adv. To a sickening degree

a-do (ə–duʷ) n. 1. Excitement; fuss 2. Trouble

a-do-be (ə–doʷ–biˠ) n. 1. Sun-dried brick 2. A structure made of adobe bricks —**adobe** adj.

ad-o-les-cent (æ–də–lɛs–ənt) n., adj. A person in the early teenage years —**adolescence** n.

a-dopt (ə–dapt) v. 1. To take a child into one's family legally and raise as one's own 2. To take up and use as one's own: *We adopted his new method of teaching math.* 3. To vote to accept: *They decided to adopt the resolution.*

a-dop-tion (ə–dap–ʃən) n., adj. 1. The act of adopting: *Couples who can't have children of their own may wish to consider adoption./Our attorney is preparing adoption papers for little Jimmy.* 2. A vote to accept: *I am in favor of adoption of the resolution.*

a-dop-tive (ə–dap–trɪv) adj. Having acquired by adoption NOTE: We speak of **adopted** children, but **adoptive** parents.

a-dor-a-ble (ə–dɔr–ə–bəl) adj. Worthy of one's love: *Your baby is adorable.*

ad-or-a-tion (æ–də–reˠ–ʃən) n. 1. Religious worship: *God alone is worthy of our adoration* (Revelations 22:8,9). 2. Deep love and respect

a-dore (ə–dɔr) v. -dored, -doring To worship; love deeply and respect deeply

a-dorn (ə–dɔrn) v. To decorate with ornaments —**adornment** n.

a-drift (ə–drɪft) adj., adv. 1. Afloat without power or moorings; drifting 2. *fig.*Without guidance or purpose

a-droit (ə–drɔɪt) adj. 1. Skillful with one's hands 2. Shrewd; clever; resourceful —**adroitly** adv.

a-dult (ə–dʌlt/ æ–dəlt) adj., n. A fully grown person, esp. a person over an age stated by law, usu. 18 or 21 —**adulthood** n.

a-dul-ter-ate (ə–dʌl–tə–reˠt) v. -ated, -ating To make impure by adding an inferior substance and mixing it in

a-dul-ter-y (ə–dʌl–tə–ri^y) n. Sexual intercourse between a married person and a person who is not the lawful spouse: *Adultery is a sin against the commandment of God, "You shall not commit adultery"* (Exodus 20:14). *Whoever looks at a woman [any woman] to lust for her has already committed adultery with her in his heart* (Matthew 5:28). NOTE: Adultery was punishable by death in Bible times (Leviticus 20:10). In some countries, even today, the punishment for adultery is very severe. God hates this sin and all sin, but he is also a God of love and mercy and forgiveness. If we truly repent of our sins and put our trust in Jesus Christ for our salvation, we will have eternal life. For the wages of sin is (eternal) death, but the gift of God is eternal life through Jesus Christ our Lord (Romans 6:23). —see JESUS, SIN, REPENT, FORGIVENESS —adulterer n. —adulteress n.

a-dul-ter-ous (ə–dʌl–tə–rəs) adj. **1.** Unfaithful to one's spouse **2.** *spir.* Unfaithful to God, worshiping false gods.

ad-vance (əd–væns) n. **1.** Forward movement: *We watched the advance of the army up the hill.* **2.** Money that is paid before the proper time or lent to someone **3. in advance** Before the expected time —advancement n.

advance v. **1.** Move forward: *The enemy is advancing toward the city.* **2.** Give or pay money ahead of time: *Please advance me $10 to cover my expenses.*

ad-vanced (əd–vænst) adj. Ahead in development: *advanced industrial nations*

ad-van-tage (əd–væn–tɪdʒ) n. **1.** Sthg. that may help one to gain a desired result: *He has the advantage of an excellent education.* **2.** Profit; gain; benefit: *What are the advantages of this job over that one?* —opposite DISADVANTAGE **3. take advantage of** To make use of, esp. by deceiving someone or using wrongly

ad-van-ta-geous (æd–væn–te^y–dʒəs) adj. Helpful; resulting in benefits —op-posite DISADVANTAGEOUS —advantageously adv.

ad-vent (æd–vent) n. The arrival of an important person or event

Ad-vent n. **1.** The second coming of Christ **2.** The period including four Sundays before Christmas —see CHRISTMAS

ad-ven-ture (əd–ven–tʃər) n. **1.** An experience, journey, etc. that is unusual, exciting, and sometimes dangerous **2.** Excitement in some activity; risk: *He enjoyed the adventure of traveling about the world.* —adventurer *masc.*, adventuress *fem.* n.

ad-ven-tur-ous (æd–ven–tʃər–əs) adj. **1.** Willing to take risks **2.** Full of danger or excitement

ad-verb (æd–vərb) n. Any word used to describe or add to the meaning of a verb, an adjective, another adverb, or a sentence, and which answers such questions as, "How?", "When?", or "Where?", as in "The sun shone **brightly.**" and "The campus of the university is **quite large.**"

ad-ver-sar-y (æd–vər–sɛər–i^y) n. **-ies** An enemy: *Be sober, be vigilant; because your adversary the devil walks about as a roaring lion, seeking whom he may devour* (1 Peter 5:8 NKJV).

ad-verse (æd–vərs/ æd–vɜrs) adj. Unfavorable; working against; opposing: *adverse reaction*

ad-ver-si-ty (æd–vɜr–sə–ti^y/ əd–) n. **-ties** Difficulty; trouble: *He had many adversities, but he didn't let himself be overcome.*

ad-ver-tise (æd–vər–taɪz) v. **-tised, -tising 1.** To make known to the public sthg. that is for sale, for rent, etc. as in a newspaper, or on television: *I advertised my house in the newspaper.* **2.** To make known a need for someone or sthg. by placing an advertisement in a newspaper, store window, etc.: *We should advertise for a tutor to help Johnny learn math.* —advertiser n.

ad-ver-tise-ment (əd–vɜr–tɪz–mənt/ æd–vər–taɪz–mənt/ əd–) n. also **ad** *infml.* A notice of sthg. for sale, for rent, etc., given in a newspaper, on television, or pasted on a wall

ad-ver-tis-ing (æd–vər–taɪz–ɪŋ) n. The business of making known to people what is for sale or for rent, what is needed by someone, etc. and encouraging them to respond

ad-vice (əd–vaɪs) n. Opinion given on how to behave or act: *My friend gave me some good advice on where to spend my vacation./ A wise*

man listens to advice (Proverbs 12:15).

ad-vis-a-ble (әd–vaɪz–ә–bәl) adj. Reasonable or sensible under the circumstances —opposite INADVISABLE —ad-vis-a-bil-i-ty (әd–vaɪz–ә–bɪl–ә–tiʸ) n.

ad-vise (әd–vaɪz) v. -vised, -vising 1. To tell sbdy. what should be done; give counsel: *The doctor advised me to get more exercise.* 2. To notify; inform: *We wish to advise you that your phone bill is overdue.*

ad-vis-er (әd–vaɪz–әr); also advisor n. A person who gives advice, esp. to government or business leaders or to students: *For lack of guidance a nation falls, but many advisers make victory sure* (Proverbs 11:14).

ad-vi-so-ry (әd–vaɪz–ә–riʸ) adj. Having or exercising power to advise: *He's an advisory member of the board of directors.*

ad-vo-cate (æd–vә–keʸt) v. -cated, -cat-ing To plead in favor of

ad-vo-cate (æd–vә–kɪt) n. 1. One who pleads another's cause: *the advocate for the defense/If anyone sins, we have an Advocate with the Father, Jesus Christ the righteous. And he himself is the propitiation [atoning sacrifice] for our sins, and not for ours only but also for the whole world* (1 John 2:1,2 NKJV). —see JESUS 2. One who argues or pleads for a cause or proposal

adz or adze (ædz) n. A type of ax used for shaping wood

ae-gis (iʸ–dʒәs) n. 1. Protection 2. Patronage

ae-on (iʸ–ən/ –ɑn) n. A variation of eon: A long period of time.

aer-ate (ɛәr–eʸt) v. -ated, -ating 1. To supply liquid with air or other gas 2. To expose to the circulation of air 3. To supply blood with oxygen

aer-i-al (ɛәr–iʸ–әl) adj. Inhabiting or occurring in the air: *aerial photography*

aer-o-bics (ær–oʷ–bɪks/ɛәr–) n. *pl.* Exercise emphasizing increased oxygen consumption without muscle strain

aer-o-nau-tics (ɛәr–ә–nɑ–tɪks) n. The scientific study dealing with the operation of aircraft or with their design and manufacture

aer-o-plane (ɛәr–ә–pleʸn) n. *BrE.* for airplane

aer-o-sol (ɛәr–ә–sɑl/–sɔl) n. A substance sealed in a container under pressure, with a device for releasing it as a fine spray: *Many deodorants come in the form of aerosols.*

aer-o-space (ɛәr–oʷ–speʸs) n. 1. The earth's atmosphere and outer space 2. The science of the flight of aircraft and spacecraft in earth's atmosphere and in outer space

aes-thet-ic (ɛs–θɛt–ɪk) adj. 1. Artistic and pleasing to the eye 2. Appreciative of the beautiful: *Some people have no aesthetic sense.*

a-far (ә–fɑr) adv. Far away

af-fa-ble (æf–ә–bәl) adj. Pleasant; friendly; easy to speak to

af-fair (ә–fɛәr) n. 1. An event; a happening 2. Sthg. that has been done or needs to be taken care of; business: *All our business affairs need to be in order before we leave on vacation.*

af-fect (ә–fɛkt) v. 1. To influence; to produce a change in: *Being overweight affects the heart.* 2. To move one's feelings: *She was deeply affected by the sad news.*

af-fec-ta-tion (æf–ɛk–teʸ–ʃən) n. Pretense

af-fec-tion (ә–fɛk–ʃən) n. A tender, lasting love or fondness

af-fec-tion-ate (ә–fɛk–ʃәn–әt) adj. Showing gentle love —affectionately adv.

af-fi-da-vit (æf–ә–deʸ–vәt) n. A written statement for use as legal evidence, sworn on oath to be true

af-fil-i-ate (ә–fɪl–iʸ–eʸt) v. -ated, -ating To associate as a member or branch

af-fil-i-ate (ә–fɪl–iʸ–әt) n. An affiliated person or organization —af-fil-i-a-tion (ә–fɪl–iʸ–eʸ–ʃən) n.

af-fin-i-ty (ә–fɪn–ә–tiʸ) n. -ties 1. A feeling of attraction toward sbdy. or sthg. 2. Closeness in relationship

af-firm (ә–fɜrm) v. 1. Confirm; ratify 2. To assert positively

af-fir-ma-tion (æ–fәr–meʸ–ʃən) n. 1. An act of affirming 2. A solemn declaration

af-firm-a-tive (ә–fɜrm–ә–tɪv) n., adj. Saying or indicating "yes" to a question: *She gave an affirmative nod to the question./ She answered in the affirmative.*

af-fix (æ–fɪks) n. One or more sounds or letters attached to the beginning or end of a word; a prefix or suffix: *In the word "unfinished," "un" is an affix meaning "not."*

af-fix (ә–fɪks) v. To attach; add: *Affix this*

stamp to the envelope.

af-flict (ə-flɪkt) v. To cause pain or suffering; to trouble: *afflicted with disease/Before I was afflicted I went astray, but now [O Lord] I obey your word* (Psalm 119:67).

af-flic-tion (ə-flɪk-ʃən) n. Sthg. causing pain or grief: *Be joyful in hope, patient in affliction, faithful in prayer* (Romans 12:12).

af-flu-ence (æf-luʷ-əns) n. Abundant supply; wealth

af-flu-ent (æf-luʷ-ənt) adj. Wealthy

af-ford (ə-fɔrd) v. To be able to do, spend, buy, etc.: *She can't afford a car.*

af-front (ə-frʌnt) v. To insult deliberately

affront n. A deliberate insult or show of disrespect

a-fire (ə-faɪ-ər) adj., adv. Burning; being on fire

a-flame (ə-fleʸm) adj., adv. Flaming

a-float (ə-floʷt) adj., adv. 1. Floating; drifting 2. At sea 3. Flooded

a-foot (ə-fʊt) adv. Happening or about to happen: *There's a scheme afoot to oust the prime minister.*

a-fraid (ə-freʸd) adj. 1. Feeling fear; frightened: *My grandson is afraid of the dark./The Lord is the stronghold of my life — of whom shall I be afraid* (Psalm 27:1). 2. afraid that *pol.* Sorry for sthg. that has happened or will happen: *I'm afraid that I've broken your window.*

a-fresh (ə-freʃ) adv. Anew; again

Af-ri-ca (æf-rɪ-kə) n. A large continent south of Europe (11,600,000 square miles)

Af-ri-can (æf-rɪ-kən) adj. Concerning Africa

African n. A person from Africa

aft (æft) adv. Near or in the back of the ship or aircraft

af-ter (æf-tər) prep. 1. Following sthg. in time; later than: *We'll have lunch after English class.* 2. Following continuously: *month after month* 3. Following in place or order: *Your name comes after John's on the list.* 4. As a result of: *After the way my parents cared for me, I owe them a lot.* 5. Searching for: *The police are after two men in a yellow pickup truck.* 6. With the name of: *Mark named his son after his great-grandfather.*

after adv. At a later time; afterwards: *I'll work on Tuesday and you can work on the day after.* —compare BEFORE

after conj. At a later time: *John arrived after I left.* —compare BEFORE

af-ter-math (æf-tər-mæθ) n. Consequences; effects; outcome

af-ter-noon (æf-tər-nuʷn) adj., n. The time between noon and sunset: *We often have afternoon tea.*

af-ter-thought (æf-tər-θɔt) n. A thought or idea that occurs to sbdy. after an event or decision

af-ter-wards (æf-tər-wərdz) also **afterward** adv. Later: *I had supper and watched a movie afterwards.*

a-gain (ə-gen) adv. 1. Another time: *Let me see that again.* 2. Back to the same place or condition as before: *She had a broken leg, but she is well again.* 3. **again and again** Over and over; repeatedly: *We tried again and again to reach her by phone but her line was busy.*

a-gainst (ə-genst) prep. 1. In the direction of sthg. so as to touch or strike it: *The waves splashed against the shore.* 2. In an opposite direction to: *We drove against the traffic.* 3. Unfavorable or hostile toward: *If God is for us, who can be against us?* (Romans 8:31). 4. Having as a background: *The mountains looked beautiful against the blue sky.* 5. Touching, or near: *The tree was leaning against the house.*

a-gape (ə-geʸp) adj., adv. With the mouth wide open as in amazement

ag-ate (æg-ət) n. A semi-precious stone having layers of various colors

–age (–ɪdʒ/–ədʒ) suffix 1. Collection; sum: *mileage* 2. Act or process: *passage* 3. Fees for the cost of: *postage* 4. Condition; rank: *peonage*

age (eʸdʒ) n. 1. The number of years in a person's life or that a thing has existed: *My son's age is nine.* 2. A period of years in a person's life: *middle age/old age* 3. The years when one is old: *His eyesight had dimmed with age.* 4. A time period in history: *the Iron Age/Great and marvelous are your deeds, Lord God Almighty. Just and true are your ways, King of the ages. ... All nations will come and worship before you* (Revelation 15:3,4). 5.

infml. A period of a few months or years: *I haven't seen her for ages.* 6 **under/ over age** The time of life at which a person may or may not do sthg.: *Young people who are under age may not buy liquor.* 7. **(be)come of age** The age at which a person may legally vote, get married without his parents' consent, and be held responsible for his own actions, etc.

age v. To get old: *His illness caused him to age quickly.* —**aging/ ageing** (e^y–dʒɪŋ) n., adj.

a-ged (e^y–dʒɪd) adj. Very old: *an aged man*

age-less (e^ydʒ–lɪs) adj. Never growing old or never looking old: *His talent seemed ageless.*

a-gen-cy (e^y–dʒən–si^y) n. 1. A business or service acting for others: *a travel agency* 2. A government office serving a specific purpose: *the Environmental Protection Agency* 3. A mode of action through which something is done

a-gen-da (ə–dʒɛn–də) n. **-das** 1. Items of business to be dealt with at a meeting 2. A list of things to be done

a-gent (e^y–dʒənt) n. 1. One who acts on behalf of another: *a publicity agent* 2. A person who instigates some activity 3. Sthg. that produces an effect or change: *a cleansing agent*

ag-gran-dize (ə–græn–daɪz) v. **-dized, -dizing** To make greater; increase —**aggrandizement** n.

ag-gra-vate (æg–rə–ve^yt) v. **-vated, -vating** 1. To make worse: *His rude behavior aggravated the situation.* 2. To annoy; irritate —**ag-gra-va-tion** (æg–rə–ve^y–ʃən) n.

ag-gre-gate (æg–rə–gət) adj. Total; gathered together so as to constitute a whole

ag-gre-gate (æg–rə–gət) n. An assemblage or group

ag-gre-gate (æg–rə–ge^yt) v. **-gated, -gat-ing** To gather into a mass or whole

ag-gres-sion (ə–grɛʃ–ən) n. 1. An unprovoked attack on another 2. Hostile action or behavior

ag-gres-sive (ə–grɛs–ɪv) adj. 1. Ready to oppose or attack; quarrelsome: *That boy is so aggressive, he's always fighting in school.* 2. Self-assertive; forceful: *One has to be somewhat aggressive to succeed in this competitive world.*

a-ghast (ə–gæst) adj. Struck with horror; terrified

ag-ile (ædʒ–əl) adj. Able to move quickly and easily —**a-gil-i-ty** (ə–dʒɪl–ət–i^y) n.

ag-i-tate (ædʒ–ə–te^yt) v. **-tated, -tating** 1. To upset; disturb 2. To move or stir violently 3. To arouse or try to arouse public interest: *That group is agitating for prison reform.* —**ag-i-ta-tion** (ædʒ–ə–te^y–ʃən) n. —**ag-i-ta-tor** (ædʒ–ə–te^yt–ər) n.

a-glow (ə–glo^w) adj. , adv. Glowing

ag-nos-tic (æg–nɑs–tɪk) n. A person who believes that nothing can be known about the existence of God or of anything except material things —**agnos-ticism** (æg–nɑs–tə–sɪz–əm) n. NOTE: God, however, has revealed himself clearly to us in his Holy Word, the Bible. —see BIBLE, GOD, JESUS, HOLY SPIRIT

a-go (ə–go^w) adv., adj. Back in time from now; before now: *He graduated from high school 50 years ago.*

a-gog (ə–gɑg) adj. Eager and excited

ag-o-nize (æg–ə–naɪz) v. **-nized, -nizing** 1. To cause agony; to pain greatly 2. To worry intensely: *He agonized over his mistakes.*

ag-o-ny (æg–ə–ni^y) n. Extreme physical or mental suffering

ag-o-ra-pho-bi-a (æg–ər–ə–fo^w–bi^y–ə) n. An abnormal fear of open spaces —**ag-oraphobic** adj.

a-grar-i-an (ə–grɛər–i^y–ən) adj. Having to do with farm land or farming

a-gree (ə–gri^y) v. **-greed, -greeing** 1. To be of the same opinion: *The two agreed on a plan of action.* —opposite DISAGREE 2. To accept an idea or opinion; approve: *He agreed to take the position.* 3. To be in accord: *Your report agrees with his.* 4. *infml.* To be suitable to one's health: *This climate doesn't agree with me. I'm sick all the time.*

a-gree-a-ble (ə–gri^y–ə–bəl) adj. 1. Pleasing; enjoyable: *I like to be with Mary, as she is an agreeable person.* —opposite DISAGREEABLE 2. Willing to agree

a-gree-a-bly (ə–gri^y–ə–bli^y) adv. Pleasantly: *We settled the matter agreeably.*

a-gree-ment (ə–gri^y–mənt) n. 1. An act or fact of agreeing 2. An understanding or arrange-

ment made between two or more people, countries, etc.: *Our agreement with the company gives us the right to use this computer for one month.*

ag·ri·cul·ture (æg–ɹɪ–kʌl–tʃəɹ) n. The science or art of farming, esp. of growing crops —**ag·ri·cul·tur·al** (æg–ɹɪ–kʌl–tʃəɹ–əl) adj.

a·gron·o·my (ə–grɑn–ə–miʸ) n. The science of soil management and the production of field crops —**agrono-mist** n.

a·ground (ə–graʊnd) adj., adv. Of a boat or ship, stuck on the shore, the bottom, a reef, etc. of a body of water

a·head (ə–hɛd) adv., adj. **1.** In or to the front; in advance: *We drove ahead, hoping to reach home by five.* **2.** In or into the future: *to look ahead* **3.** In front of; having more success: *Mary is ahead of John in science.* **4. get ahead** To succeed

aid (eʸd) n. **1.** Assistance; help: *The relief agency brought aid to the starving children.* **2.** Sthg. or someone that supports or helps: *a hearing aid*

aid v. To help or support

aide (eʸd) n. An assistant, esp. an assistant to a government official

AIDS (eʸdz) n. Acquired immune deficiency syndrome, a viral disease that attacks and breaks down the body's immune system, leading to serious and usu. fatal infections: *AIDS can be transmitted by intimate sexual contact with a carrier or through the blood.*

ail (eʸl) v. *infml.* To be sick and become weak

ail·ment (eʸl–mənt) n. An illness, esp. one that is not very serious

aim (eʸm) v. **1.** To direct a weapon, shot, remark, etc. towards some person or object **2.** To try to do, be, or obtain something; intend to: *I aim to please./St. Paul, writing to believers in Corinth (in Greece), said, "Aim for perfection, ... be of one mind, live in peace. And the God of love and peace will be with you"* (2 Corinthians 13:11).

aim n. **1.** The act of pointing or directing a weapon, remark, etc.: *The hunter's aim was good.* **2.** The desired outcome

aim·less (eʸm–ləs) adj. Without purpose: *aimless wandering* —**aimlessly** adv.

ain't (eʸnt) v. Nonstandard short form for am

not, is not, are not, has not, and have not: *That ain't mine.*

air (ɛəɹ) n. **1.** The mixture of gases that we breathe, that surrounds the earth: *a breath of fresh air* **2.** The space above the earth; the sky: *He threw the ball up in the air. / Jesus said, "Look at the birds of the air; they do not sow or reap or store away in barns, and yet your heavenly Father feeds them. Are you not much more valuable than they?"* (Matthew 6:26). **3.** The general feeling in a place or around a person: *There was an air of expectation in the crowd.* **4. on/ off the air** Broadcasting/ not broadcasting

air v. **1.** To let air into or through in order to freshen: *We aired out the building before we moved the furniture in.* **2.** To make known to others one's opinions, ideas, complaints, etc., often in an unpleasant way: *He's always airing his opinions.* —**airing** n.

air-borne (ɛəɹ–bɔrn) adj. **1.** Carried or transported by air **2.** In flight

air-con·di·tioned (ɛəɹ–kən–dɪ–ʃənd) adj. Having the air in a room, car, plane, etc. brought to the desired temperature and humidity: *Is your classroom air-conditioned?*

air-craft (ɛəɹ–kræft) n. **1.** A machine capable of flight in the air and regarded as a carrier of passengers and/ or cargo **2.** Such craft collectively, including airplanes, gliders, and helicopters

aircraft carrier (ɛəɹ–kræft kɛəɹ–iʸ–əɹ) n. A ship that carries aircraft and is a base for airplanes

air-field (ɛəɹ–fiʸld) n. A level field equipped with hangars and runways for aircraft

air force (ɛəɹ–fɔrs) n. A military branch that uses aircraft in fighting

air-lift (ɛəɹ–lɪft) n. A large-scale transport of goods or troops, esp. in times of emergency **airlift** v. To transport goods, troops, etc. on a large scale

air-line (ɛəɹ–laɪn) n. A regular service for carrying passengers and goods by air

air mail (ɛəɹ–meʸl) n. Mail carried by aircraft —**air-mail** adj. *an air-mail stamp*

air-plane (ɛəɹ–pleʸn) n. A winged vehicle, heavier than air, capable of flight, and propelled by jet engines or propellers

air-port (εər–pɔrt) n. A place where aircraft land and take off

air-ship (εər–ʃɪp) n. A self-propelled, lighter-than-air craft, that carries passengers; dirigible

air-sick (εər–sɪk) adj. Sick because of the motion of an aircraft —airsickness n.

air-strip (εər–strɪp) n. A runway without normal airport facilities

air-tight (εər–taɪt) adj. Not letting air in or out: *airtight can/ fig. an airtight alibi (=an alibi that cannot be broken)*

air-y (εər–iʸ) adj. **airier, airiest 1.** Open to a free current of air **2.** Of air

aisle (aɪl) n. A passage between rows of seats, as in a theater or a church or on a bus, train or plane

a-jar (ə–dʒɑr) adv., adj. Of a door, slightly open

a-kin (ə–kɪn) adj. **1.** Related **2.** Similar

–al (–əl) suffix adj. Of; pertaining to; like: *fatal/ lethal*

–al suffix n. That which pertains to: *withdrawal*

al-a-bas-ter (æl–ə–bæs–tər) n., adj. A white semi-transparent stone, often carved into ornaments

a la carte (ɑ–lə–kɑrt) adv., adj. Having a separate price for each item on the menu

a-lac-ri-ty (ə–læk–rɪ–tiʸ) n. Cheerful eagerness to do sthg.: *He obeyed with alacrity.*

a la mode (ɑ–lə–moʷd) adv., adj. **1.** Fashionable **2.** Served with ice cream

a-larm (ə–lɑrm) n. **1.** Sudden fear and anxiety caused by the approach of possible danger **2.** A signal warning of danger: *I rang the alarm as soon as I smelled the smoke.* **3.** Any device, such as a bell, noise, or flag, by which a warning is given

alarm v. To stir up sudden fear and anxiety

al-ba-core (æl–bə–kɔr) n. A large species of fish off the coast of North America, related to the tuna

al-ba-tross (æl–bə–trɔs) n. A large, long-winged seabird

al-bi-no (æl–baɪ–noʷ) n. **-nos** A person or animal having unusually pale skin, very light hair, and lacking normal eye coloring

al-bum (æl–bəm) n. A book used for keeping photographs, stamps, etc.

al-bu-men (æl–byuʷ–mən) n. The white of eggs

al-bu-min (æl–byuʷ–mən) n. Any of a class of water-soluble proteins including the main constituent of the white of eggs

al-bu-mi-nous (æl–byuʷ–mə–nəs) adj. Of or like albumin

al-che-my (æl–kə–miʸ) n. An early form of chemistry, the chief aim of which was to turn other metals into gold

alchemist (æl–kə–məst) n. One who practices alchemy

al-co-hol (æl–kə–hɔl) n. **1.** The colorless liquid present in wine, beer, and other liquor that can make one drunk **2.** The drinks containing alcohol

al-co-hol-ic (æl–kə–hɔl–ɪk) n. One who has the condition of alcoholism

alcoholic adj. Concerning, caused by, or containing alcohol —opposite NON-ALCOHOLIC

al-co-hol-ism (æl–kə–hɔl–ɪzm) n. The continued excessive and usu. uncontrollable use of alcoholic drinks; also the abnormal state associated with such use; repeated drunkenness over a long period of time: *Alcoholism is the fourth biggest killer in the US and also the destroyer of countless homes and families every year.* NOTE: The acts of the sinful nature are obvious: sexual immorality, ... drunkenness and the like. Those who live like this will not inherit the kingdom of God (Galatians 5:19-21). While alcoholism is a sin, and all people are sinners, he nevertheless loves the sinner. In his grace and mercy he has provided a way of forgiveness. "The gift of God is eternal life through Jesus Christ our Lord" (Romans 6:23).

al-cove (æl–koʷv) n. A small room or space opening into a larger one

ale (eʸl) n. An alcoholic beverage brewed from malt and hops, usu. more bitter than beer

a-lert (ə–lɜrt) n. **1.** A warning signal to be ready for danger **2. on the alert** On guard; watching for danger, as after a warning

alert v. To warn: *The doctor alerted me to the danger of smoking.*

alert adj. **1.** Quick to see and act: *He is very alert.* **2.** On guard; watchful: *Be self controlled and alert. Your enemy the devil prowls around like a roaring lion looking for someone to devour* (1 Peter 5:8). —**alertness** n.

al·fal·fa (æl–fæl–fə) n. A plant with clover-like leaves, widely grown for hay and forage

al·ga (æl–gə) n. *pl.* **algae** (æl–dʒiʸ) A water plant with no true stems or leaves, such as seaweed

al·ge·bra (æl–dʒə–brə) n. A branch of mathematics using symbols (such as letters) in calculating

a·li·as (eʸ–liʸ–əs) n. *pl.* **a·li·as·es** A false name; an assumed name

alias adv. Also known as: *The police know him as Tom Jones, alias Bob Smith, alias Bill Brown.*

al·i·bi (æl–ə–baɪ) n. **1.** An excuse **2.** A defense given by one accused of a crime

al·ien (eʸ–liʸ–ən) n. **1.** One owing allegiance to another country or government **2.** Not one's own; unfamiliar: *an alien culture* **3.** Contrary; against: *Cheating was alien to his nature.*

alien n. **1.** An unnaturalized resident of a country, not a citizen of the country in which he is residing: *Since he was an alien in the country he was not allowed to vote./ Do not mistreat an alien or oppress him* (Exodus 22:21). **2.** A member of another group or region **3.** Someone excluded from a group; an outsider: *The Lord watches over the alien and sustains the fatherless and the widow* (Psalm 146:9).

al·ien·a·ble (eʸɪ–yən–ə–bəl) adj. Capable of being transferred to the ownership of another —opposite INALIENABLE

al·ien·ate (eʸl–yən–eʸt/ eʸ–liʸ–ən–eʸt) v. **-ated, -ating** **1.** To cause to become unfriendly; estrange: *John alienated his son by his constant criticism./ You who are trying to be justified by [keeping] the law have been alienated from Christ: you have fallen away from grace* (Galatians 5:4). *For it is by grace you have been saved, through faith [in Christ our Savior]... not by works [of the law], so that no one can boast* (Ephesians 2:8,9). —see JESUS **2.** To transfer property to the ownership of another —**al·i-**

en·a·tion (eʸ–liʸ–ə–neʸ–ʃən) n.

a·light (ə–laɪt) v. **1.** To get down, as from a horse **2.** To descend and settle: *The robin alighted on the branch*

alight adj., adv. On fire; burning

a·lign (ə–laɪn) v. **1.** To place in line **2.** To take sides with; to join as an ally —**alignment** n. The act of placing in line: *My car needs a wheel alignment*

a·like (ə–laɪk) adj., adv. Like one another; similar: *The three sisters look very much alike.*

al·i·men·ta·ry (æl–ə–mɛn–tə–riʸ) adj. Of or pertaining to food or nutrition

al·i·men·ta·ry ca·nal (æl–ə–mɛn–tə–riʸ kə–næl) n. The passageway for food from the mouth to the anus

al·i·mo·ny (æl–ə–moʷ–niʸ) n. **-nies** An allowance for support paid by one spouse to the other spouse after a divorce or legal separation

a·live (ə–laɪv) adj. **1.** Having life; living: *It's wonderful to be alive after such a close call in the car accident yesterday./ Early in the morning the women came to the tomb where Jesus had been laid after his death on the cross, and they saw a vision of angels who said he [Jesus] was alive* (Luke 24:22,23). **2.** Full of life; active: *For an eighty-year-old, he's still very much alive.*

al·ka·li (æl–kə–laɪ) n. **-lis** or **-lies** **1.** A substance (such as carbonate of sodium) that has marked basic properties **2.** A mixture of salts in the soil of some dry regions

all (ɔl) determ. **1.** The entire amount of: *Who drank all the the milk? There's none left./ If we walk in the light [of God's word], as he [God] is in the light, we have fellowship with one another, and the blood of Jesus, his Son, purifies us from all sin* (1 John 1:7). **2.** Every one: *We're all going./All have sinned and fall short of the glory of God* (Romans 3:23). *He [Christ] died for all, that those who live should no longer live for themselves but for him who died for them and was raised again* (2 Corinthians 5:15).

all adv. **1.** Completely; entirely: *She lived all alone.* **2.** For each side; apiece: *The score of the game was five all; nobody won.* **3. all but** Almost; nearly: *Dinner is all but ready.* **4. all over (a)** Everywhere: *She has flowers all over*

— *in every room.* (b) Everywhere in a place: *We've searched all over for your wallet.* (c) To every part of a place: *to send letters all over Europe* (d) Finished: *The party is all over.*

all pron. **1.** Everybody, everything, or everyone: *One piece of bread was all he had.* **2. at all** (used in negatives, questions, etc.) (Not) in the least; in any way: *Do you understand this at all?/I don't like her at all.* —see also NOT AT ALL

Al·lah (ɑ–lə/ æ–lə) n. In Islam, the one supreme being; God

al·lay (ə–le^y) v. **1.** To put to rest: *to allay one's fears* **2.** To reduce in severity; alleviate; lighten

al·lege (ə–lɛdʒ) v. **-leged, -leging 1.** To state as a fact without proof **2.** To bring forward as a reason or excuse —**al·le·ga·tion** (æl–ə–ge^y–ʃən) n.

al·leged (ə–lɛdʒd) adj. Declared true, though without proof —**al·leg·ed·ly** (ə–lɛdʒ–ɪd–li^y) adv.

al·le·giance (ə–li^y–dʒəns) n. Loyalty owed to a person or cause, esp. to one's government

al·le·go·ry (æl–ə–gɔr–i^y) n. **-ries** A story in which the characters and events symbolize a deeper underlying meaning —**al·le·go·ri·cal** (æl–ə–gɔr–ɪ–kəl) adj. —**allegorically** adv.

al·le·lu·ia (ɑl–ə–lu^w–yə) interj. "Hallelujah!" "Praise the Lord!" (An expression from the Hebrew language, used to express praise, thanks, and joy)

al·ler·gic (ə–lɜr–dʒɪk) adj. Having an unfavorable reaction to pollen, foods, etc.: *She's allergic to cats.*

al·ler·gy (æl–ər–dʒi^y) n. **-gies** A physical condition producing an unfavorable reaction to certain foods, pollen, etc.: *The rash on her face is caused by an allergy to eggs.*

al·le·vi·ate (ə–li^y–vi^y–e^yt) v. **-ated, -ating** To lessen; to make less severe

al·ley (æl–i^y) n. **-leys 1.** A narrow passage or street between or behind buildings **2.** A bowling alley

al·li·ance (ə–laɪ–əns) n. An agreement or treaty by which people or nations ally themselves with one another —see ALLY

al·lied (ə–laɪd/ æl–aɪd) adj. **1.** Of countries or forces that are in alliance **2.** Similar: *asthma and allied illnesses*

al·li·ga·tor (æl–ə–ge^y–tər) n. A large reptile of the crocodile family, found in the SE United States and in China, living in marshes and rivers

al·lo·cate (æl–ə–ke^yt) v. **-cated, -cating** To allot; to assign; to give to someone for his own use: *A room was allocated to each student.*

al·lo·ca·tion (æl–ə–ke^y–ʃən) n. The act of allocating: *The allocation of money is the responsibility of the scholarship committee.*

al·lot (ə–lɑt) v. **-tt-** To distribute as a share or portion; assign; allocate —**allotment** n.

al·lo·saur·us (æl–ə–sɔr–əs) n. **-sauri** (–sɔr–i^y) A large meat-eating dinosaur that looked like a tyrannosaurus. It had short front legs and walked upright on its hind legs.

al·low (ə–laʊ) v. **1.** Permit: *How many books are we allowed to borrow?* **2.** To permit to enter or to stay: *They won't allow children in the pool without an adult.* **3.** To admit: *The speaker allowed there were some flaws in his speech.* —opposite DISALLOW **4.** To provide, esp. money or time: *The company allowed extra funds for the job.*

al·low·a·ble (ə–laʊ–ə–bəl) adj. That may be permitted

al·low·ance (ə–laʊ–əns) n. **1.** Sthg. provided regularly, esp. money: *a grocery allowance of $150 a week* **2.** AmE. Money given regularly (usu. weekly) to a child **3.** The taking into account of facts that may change an opinion, judgment, etc. (esp.in the phrase **make allowances for**)

al·loy (æl–ɔɪ) n. **1.** A metal formed by a mixture of metals or by a metal and some other substance **2.** An inferior metal mixed with one of greater value —**alloy** (ə–lɔɪ/ æl–ɔɪ) v.

all right (ɔl raɪt) adj. **1.** Correct; without mistakes: *His spelling words were all right.* **2.** Safe; healthy; unhurt: *Are you all right since your operation?* **3.** *infml.* Acceptable; in a satisfactory manner: *His paintings are all right but I like the other artist better.*

all right adv. I/ we agree: *Let's get to work now. All right, we will.*

All Saints Day A Christian feast observed on November first in honor of all the saints

al·lude (ə–lu^wd) v. **luded, -luding** To make

an indirect reference to sthg. —**allusion** n.

al-lure (ə-lʋər) v. -**lured**, -**luring** To entice; to attract

al-lur-ing (ə-lʋər-iŋ) adj. Attractive; enticing

al-lu-sion (ə-lu^w-ʒən) n. *fml.* Sthg. spoken of in an indirect way

al-lu-vi-um (ə-lu^w-vi^y-əm) n. Earth, sand, etc. brought down to low lands by rivers —**alluvial** adj.

al-ly (æl-aɪ) n. -**lies** One united with another in an alliance

al-ly (ə-laɪ) v. -**lied**, -**lying** To unite in an alliance

al-ma ma-ter (æl-mə mɑ-tər) n. College or other school in which one has been educated

al-ma-nac (ɔl-mə-næk) n. An annual publication containing a calendar with times of sunrise and sunset, astronomical data, and much other information

al-might-y (ɔl-maɪt-i^y) adj. Having the power to do anything: *Almighty God / Holy, holy, holy is the Lord God Almighty* (Isaiah 6:3). —see GOD

al-mond (ɑ-mənd/ æm-ənd/ æl-mənd/ ɑl-) n. **1.** A tree, the seeds of whose fruit are eaten as nuts **2.** The nut itself

al-most (ɔl-mo^wst) adv. Nearly but not quite: *I almost made it to work on time.*

alms (ɑmz) n. Money, food, clothes, etc., given to poor people

a-loft (ə-lɔft) adv. **1.** On high **2.** In the air

a-lo-ha (ə-lo^w-ə/ɑ-lo^w-hɑ) interj. **1.** Greetings **2.** Farewell

a-lone (ə-lo^wn) adv., adj. **1.** Without anyone else: *He sat at home alone.* **2.** Only: *You alone know the answer to your question.* (=you are the only person who can answer it) **3. leave/ let alone (a)** To permit to be by oneself **(b)** To let sthg. remain untouched or unchanged: *Let it alone. It doesn't need fixing.*

a-long (ə-lɔŋ) prep. By the side of: *We planted roses along the fence./Their house is along this road some place.*

along adv. **1.** Onwards; on: *She walked along the path.* **2.** With others or oneself: *I took my sister along on the trip.* **3.** Here or there: *Stephen will be along soon. He's just leaving the house.* **4. alongside** adv., prep. By the side of

a-loof (ə-lu^wf) adj. Keeping oneself apart or at a distance from other people —**aloofness** n.

a-loud (ə-laʋd) also **out loud** adv. **1.** Loud enough to be heard: *Please read the next paragraph aloud for the class.* **2.** In a loud voice: *He cried aloud when the heavy book fell on his foot.*

al-pac-a (æl-pæk-ə) n. **1.** A type of South American llama with long silk-like wool **2.** The wool of this animal

al-pha-bet (æl-fə-bɛt) n. The letters used in writing a language, esp. when arranged in order

al-pha-bet-i-cal (æl-fə-bɛt-ɪ-kəl) adj. Of the alphabet: *Names in the telephone book are arranged in alphabetical order.* —**alphabetically** adv.

al-pha-bet-ize (æl-fə-bə-taɪz) v. -**ized**, -**izing** **1.** To arrange in alphabetical order **2.** To supply with an alphabet —**al-pha-bet-i-za-tion** (æl-fə-bɛt-ɪ-ze^y-ʃən) n.

al-read-y (ɔl-rɛd-i^y) adv. **1.** By or before a point in time: *The plane had already taken off.* (=before I arrived) **2.** Before: *I've already seen that movie and don't care to see it again.* NOTE: Compare the meanings of **already** and **all ready**: We're **all ready** can mean either that everyone is ready or that we are (completely) ready; **already** could not be used in this way.

al-so (ɔl-so^w) adv. Besides; too; in addition: *I'm going to Manila, and afterwards I will also visit Honolulu.*

al-tar (ɔl-tər) n. **1.** A structure on which sacrifices are offered or incense is burned in worship **2.** A raised level surface or table used in a religious ceremony, as in the Christian Service of Communion

al-ter (ɔl-tər) v. To cause to become different; to change: *The seamstress can alter your skirt while you wait. It's only a little too long.* —**al-ter-a-tion** (ɔl-tə-re^y-ʃən) n.

al-ter-ca-tion (ɔl-tər-ke^y-ʃən) n. A noisy or angry dispute

al-ter-nate (ɔl-tər-nət) adj. **1.** Arranged or succeeding by turns **2.** Every second day, week, etc.: *The committee meets on alternate Tuesdays./My wife and I take the children to school on alternate days.* —**alternately** adv.

al-ter-nate (ɔl-tər-nət) n. A substitute: *John is*

a delegate to the convention and Tom is his alternate (=in case John is unable to attend for any reason).

al-ter-nate (ɔl–tər–ne^yt) v. **-nated, -nating** Happening by turns, one after the other, repeatedly: *Tom alternates between studying and teaching.*

al-ter-na-tive (ɔl–tər–nə–tɪv) adj. That which may be chosen instead of sthg. else: *An alternative arrangement can be made if this plan doesn't meet with your approval.*

alternative n. A choice: *I didn't want to drive so far, but the airlines were on strike, so I had no alternative.*

al-though (ɔl–ðo^w) conj. In spite of the fact that; even though: *Although she didn't feel well, she went to work as usual.*

al-ti-me-ter (æl–tɪ–mə–tər) n. An instrument for measuring height above sea level

al-ti-tude (æl–tə–tu^wd) n. Height above sea level: *The captain said that we are flying at an altitude of 37,000 feet.*

al-to (æl–to^w) n. **-tos 1.** A low female singing voice **2.** A singer having an alto voice **3.** A part written in the range of the alto voice

al-to-geth-er (ɔl–tə–ge–ðər) adv. **1.** Entirely; thoroughly: *The excuse she made was not altogether true. She just didn't want to go out tonight.* **2.** Considering everything; on the whole: *It was hard work, but altogether we enjoyed being on the committee.* —see ABSOLUTELY

al-tru-ism (æl–tru^w–ɪz–əm) n. Unselfish concern for the welfare of others —**al-tru-is-tic** (æl–tru^w–ɪs–tɪk) adj. —**altruistically** adv.

al-u-min-i-um (æl–yu^w–mɪn–i^y–əm) n. *BrE.* for **aluminum**

a-lu-mi-nize (ə–lu^w–mə–naɪz) v. **-nized, -nizing** To coat with aluminum

a-lum-i-num (ə–lu^w–mə–nəm) n. A lightweight silvery metal, used either pure or as an alloy for making utensils or fittings where lightness is an advantage

a-lum-na (ə–lʌm–nə) n. *pl.* **-nae** (–ni^y) A female former student of a school or college

a-lum-nus (ə–lʌm–nəs) n. *pl.* **-ni** (–naɪ) A male former student of a school or college

al-ways (ɔl–we^yz/ –wi^yz) adv. **1.** Without exception; again and again: *The bus always*

leaves on time./He's always complaining. **2.** Without end: *I will always remember this day./ Jesus promised his disciples, "Surely I will be with you always, to the very end of the age"* (Matthew 28:20).

am strong (æm) v. Contraction of **I am: I'm** (aɪm or əm) 1st person sing. pres. tense of **be:** *I'm working at a new job now./ Are you going to the concert tonight? Yes, I am.* —see AREN'T

a.m. (e^y–em) Latin *abbr.* for **ante meridiem** (=before midday) (used in telling the time): *The traffic on the freeway is the worst around 8:00 a.m. when people are going to work.* —compare P. M.

a-mal-ga-mate (ə–mæl–gə–me^yt) v. **-mated, -mating** To mix; to combine —**a-mal-ga-ma-tion** (ə–mæl–gə–me^y–ʃən) n.

a-mass (ə–mæs) v. To accumulate

am-a-teur (æm–ə–tər/ –tʃər/ –tʃʊər) n. A person who does sthg. as a pastime rather than as a profession —**ama-teurish**

a-maze (ə–me^yz) v. **-mazed, -mazing** To fill with great surprise or wonder: *We were amazed at the beautiful scenery./ The crowds were amazed at his [Jesus'] teaching* (Matthew 7:28). —**amazement** n.

a-maz-ing (ə–me^y–zɪŋ) adj. Causing astonishment or wonder: *He is an amazing person! He goes out of his way to help everyone./What amazing news!* —**amazingly** adv.

am-bas-sa-dor (æm–bæs–ə–dər) n. **1.** An official of high rank appointed to represent his/ her country in the capital city of another country in an embassy **2.** *fig.* One who represents God or godly qualities: *He is an ambassador of good will./One who represents Jesus Christ can be called an "ambassador for Christ."*

am-ber (æm–bər) n. **1.** A yellow traffic light shown alone as a cautionary signal or between green (=go) and red (=stop) lights **2.** A yellow or brownish-yellow resin used for making ornamental objects **3.** A brownish yellow color —**amber** adj.

am-bi-dex-trous (æm–bɪ–dek–strəs) adj. Able to use either hand equally well

am-big-u-ous (æm–bɪg–yu^w–əs) adj. **1.** Capable of being interpreted in more than one way **2.** Doubtful or uncertain —**am-**

biguously adv. —**am-bi-gu-i-ty** (æm–bə–gyu^w–ə–ti^y) n.

am-bi-tion (æm–bɪ–ʃən) n. **1.** Strong desire for riches, power, success, etc.: *He should go far in the business world; he has a lot of ambition./ Do nothing out of selfish ambition or vain conceit, but in humility consider others better than yourselves* (Philippians 2:3). *For where you have envy and selfish ambition in your hearts, there you find disorder and every evil practice* (James 3:16). **2.** Strong desire to do or be sthg.: *It was her ambition to be a concert pianist.*

am-bi-tious (æm–bɪ–ʃəs) adj. **1.** Full of desire for success, power, riches, etc.: *He's ambitious to help other people spiritually and physically. I hope he succeeds.* **2.** Demanding a strong desire for success, great effort, great skill, etc.: *an ambitious attempt to sell the new products* —**ambitiously** adv.

am-biv-a-lence (æm–bɪv–ə–ləns) n. A simultaneous attraction toward, and repulsion from, a certain person or thing

am-biv-a-lent (æm–bɪv–ə–lənt) adj. Having mixed feelings toward a certain person, object, or situation

am-ble (**æm**–bəl) v. **-bled, -bling** To walk at a slow, leisurely pace

amble n. A gentle pace —**ambler** n.

am-bu-lance (æm–byə–ləns) n. A motor vehicle for carrying the ill or wounded, esp. to a hospital

am-bu-la-to-ry (æm–byə–lə–tɔr–i^y) adj. Able to walk about

am-bush (æm–bʊʃ) n. A trap by which hidden people attack an enemy by surprise

ambush v. To make a surprise attack on someone from a place of hiding: *We were ambushed after we entered the canyon.*

a-me-ba or **a-moe-ba** (ə–mi^y–bə) n. A microscopic one-celled animal that changes shape constantly

a-men (e^y–mɛn/ ɑ–mɛn) interj. (used at the close of a prayer or hymn) May it be so.

a-men-a-ble (ə–mɛn–ə–bəl) adj. Responsive; open to advice or suggestion

a-mend (ə–mɛnd) v. To make changes in the words of a rule or law

a-mend-ment (ə–mɛnd–mənt) n. An addition to, or correction of, a document, resolution, constitution, etc.

a-mends (ə–mɛndz) n. pl. **1.** Repayment for a loss or injury **2. make amends** To repair or repay for some harm or damage, etc.: *I'm sorry I lost your book. I'd like to make amends by buying you a new one.*

a-men-i-ty (ə–mɛn–ə–ti^y) n. **-ties 1.** Agreeableness **2.** Sthg. that provides or increases comfort or convenience

a-men-i-ties (ə–mɛn–ə–ti^{y}z) n. pl. **1.** Social courtesies **2.** Things that make life easier and more pleasant: *Telephones, televisions, and microwaves were amenities in the apartment.*

A-mer-i-ca (ə–mɛər–ɪ–kə) n. **1.** The United States **2.** North or South America **3. the Americas** The Western Hemisphere

A-mer-i-can (ə–mɛər–ɪ–kən) adj. Of North, Central, or South America, esp. the United States of America: *A Ford is an American car.*

American n. A native or inhabitant of N. or S. America, esp. of the US: *Most Americans are interested in traveling in other countries.*

am-e-thyst (æm–ə–θɪst) n. A precious stone of bluish-violet color

a-mi-a-ble (e^y–mi^y–ə–bəl) adj. **1.** Agreeable **2.** Having a friendly and sociable disposition —**a-mi-a-bil-i-ty** (e^y–mi^y–ə–bɪl–ə–ti^y) n. —**a-miably** adv.

am-i-ca-ble (æm–ɪ–kə–bəl) adj. Friendly; peaceable —**amicably** adv.

a-mid (ə–mɪd) or **amidst** (ə–mɪdst) prep. In or into the middle of; among

a-miss (ə–mɪs) adj., adv. Out of proper order; wrong

am-i-ty (æm–ə–ti^y) n. **-ties** Friendly relations

am-mo-nia (ə–mo^w–nyə) n. **1.** A colorless gaseous compound of nitrogen and hydrogen used in refrigeration and in the making of fertilizers and explosives **2.** A solution of ammonia in water

am-mu-ni-tion (æm–yə–nɪ–ʃən) n. Explosive weapons, esp. for use in a war: *Our store of ammunition included bullets, bombs, and grenades.*

am-ne-sia (æm–ni^y–ʒə) n. Memory loss

am-nes-ty (æm–nəs–ti^y) n. **-ties** An act granting pardon to a group of individuals

a-moe-ba (ə–mi^y–bə) n. -bas A microscopic organism consisting of a single cell that changes shape constantly

a-mok (ə–mʌk) adv. In a frenzied manner

a-mong (ə–mʌŋ) also a-mongst (ə–mʌŋst) prep. 1. Surrounded by: *hidden among the bushes* 2. One of the group of: *His company is among the top ten in the US.* 3. (Speaking of things divided out to more than two people): *Share the candy among the four of you.* —compare BETWEEN

a-mor-al (e^y–mɔr–əl) adj. Neither moral nor immoral; not based on moral standards

am-o-rous (æm–ə–rəs) adj. Of, showing, or feeling sexual love —amorously adv. —amorousness n.

A-mos (e^y–məs) n. 1. Masculine name 2. Hebrew shepherd who became a prophet 3. A book of the Old Testament that contains his prophecies

a-mount (ə–maʊnt) n. 1. A quantity: *We'll need a large amount of food for the weekend.* NOTE: Amount is used with non-count nouns (nouns for which you cannot use a plural) as in "the amount of money." With plurals it is better to use number as in "the number of people." 2. amount to Add up to; to be equal to: *The repairs on your old car will amount to about $500.*

amp (æmp) *abbr.* for ampere

am-pere (æm–pɪər) n. A unit of electricity

am-phib-i-an (æm–fɪb–i^y–ən) n. 1. Any of a group of animals (such as frogs) intermediate between fishes and reptiles 2. A vehicle designed to operate on both land and water

am-phib-i-ous (æm–fɪb–i^y–əs) adj. 1. Able to live on land and in the water 2. Adapted for both land and water

am-phi-the-a-ter (æm–fɪ–θi^y–ə–tər) n. 1. An elliptical or circular building with rows of seats sloping upward and backward around a central open space 2. Anything resembling such a structure, indoors or outdoors

am-ple (æm–pəl) adj. Plenty; more than enough: *There will be ample money for a family vacation.*

am-pli-fy (æm–plə–faɪ) v. -fied, -fying 1. To make larger 2. To make louder —am-pli-fi-ca-tion (æm–plə–fə–ke^y–ʃən) n. —am-pli-fi-er (æm–plə–faɪ–ər) n.

am-pu-tate (æm–pyə–te^yt) v. -tated, -tating To cut off an arm, leg or other part of the body, esp. for medical reasons: *The doctor will have to amputate her badly infected arm.*

am-pu-tee (æm–pyə–ti^y) n. One who has had an arm or leg amputated

a-muck or a-mok (ə–mʌk) adv. run amuck To become furious and do a lot of damage

am-u-let (æm–yə–lət) n. An object worn as a charm against evil

a-muse (ə–myu^wz) v. -mused, -musing 1. To make one laugh or smile: *The monkey's antics amused everyone.* 2. To make time pass pleasantly: *The children amused themselves by gathering sea shells.*

a-muse-ment (ə–myu^wz–mənt) n. 1. The state of being amused; enjoyment: *To our amusement the actor's wig blew off just as he was kissing the leading lady.* 2. Entertainment; sthg. that causes one's time to pass pleasantly: *Our city has many amusements for young people.*

a-muse-ment park (ə–myu^wz–mənt pɑrk) n. *AmE.* A park with rides, games of skill, and other amusements

–an (–ən) also –ian or –ean (i^y–ən) suffix n. Inhabitant of: *North American/Bostonian*

–an (–ən) also –ian or –ean (i^y–ən) suffix adj. 1. Pertaining to: *Asian plants and animals* 2. Resembling: *Mozartean*

an weak (ən); strong (æn) determ. , indef. art. (Used when the following word starts with a vowel sound): *an old man, not a young one/ an apple, not a pear*

–ana (–æn–ə/–ɑn–/–e^yn–) also –iana (i^y–æn–ə) suffix n. Things pertaining to; sayings or anecdotes of; information about: *Americana*

a-nach-ro-nism (ə–næk–rə–nɪz–əm) n. 1. A person or idea regarded as out of date 2. A mistake in placing sthg. into a particular historical period 3. The thing wrongly placed

an-a-con-da (æn–ə–kɑn–də) n. A large S. American water snake that crushes its prey

a-nae-mi-a (ə–ni^y–mi^y–ə) n. Var. of anemia

an-aes-the-sia (æn–əs–θi^y–ʒə) n. Var. of anes-

thesia

an-aes-thet-ic (æn–əs–θɛt–ɪk) adj., n. Var. of anesthetic

an-a-gram (æn–ə–græm) n. A word or sentence obtained by changing the order of the letters in another word or sentence

a-nal (eʸ–nəl) adj. Of the anus

a-nal-o-gous (ə–næl–ə–gəs) adj. Similar in certain respects —**analogously** adv.

a-nal-o-gy (ə–næl–ə–dʒiʸ) n. **-gies** A partial likeness between two things that are compared: *the analogy between the human heart and a pump* —**an-a-log-i-cal** (æn–əl–ɑdj–ɪ–kəl) adj.

a-nal-y-sis (ə–næl–ə–sɪs) n. **-ses** (–siʸz) **1.** An act of analyzing **2.** A statement of the result of this

an-a-lyst (æn–ə–ləst) n. **1.** One skilled in analysis **2.** A psychoanalyst

an-a-lyt-ic (æn–ə–lɪt–ɪk) **an-a-lyt-i-cal** (æn–ə–lɪt–ɪ–kəl) adj. Of or using analysis —**analytically** adv.

an-a-lyze (æn–ə–laɪz) v. **-lyzed, -lyzing 1.** To separate a substance into its parts in order to identify it or study its structure **2.** To examine and interpret: *They tried to analyze the reason for their failure.*

an-ar-chism (æn–ər–kɪz–əm) n. The theory that all forms of government are oppressive and should be abolished —**anarchist** n.

an-ar-chy (æn–ər–kiʸ) n. **-chies 1.** The absence of government or control, resulting in lawlessness **2.** Disorder; confusion

a-nath-e-ma (ə–næθ–ə–mə) n. **1.** A person or thing detested **2.** A person or thing accused or condemned **3.** A formal curse involving excommunication from the church: *If any man love not the Lord Jesus Christ, let him be Anathema* (1 Corinthians 16:22KJV). —see JESUS, SALVATION

a-nat-o-my (ə–næt–ə–miʸ) n. **-mies 1.** The scientific study of bodily structures **2.** The structure of the body: *He was in pain from head to toe, in every part of his anatomy.* —**a-na-tom-ic** (æn–ə–tɑm–ɪk) adj. —**anatomical** adj. —**anatomically** adv. —**anatomist** (ə–næt–ə–məst) n.

a-nat-o-saur-us (ə–næt–ə–sɔr–əs) n. **-sauri** (–sɔr–iʸ) A plant-eating dinosaur with a duck-like head, short forelegs, and long hind legs on which it walked upright

–ance (–əns) Denotes action, process, quality, or state: *attendance*

an-ces-tor (æn–sɛs–tər) n. Any one of those persons, esp. one living a long time ago, from whom another is descended

an-ces-try (æn–sɛs–triʸ) n. **-tries 1.** Descent or lineage **2.** One's ancestors

an-chor (æŋ–kər) n. A heavy metal device, usu. hooked, at the end of a chain or rope, let down into the water to keep a ship from moving

anchor v. **1.** To stop sailing and let down the anchor **2.** To fix firmly

anchor-man (æŋ–kər–mæn) n. **1.** A broadcaster who participates in and coordinates the work of other broadcasters **2.** The strongest member of a relay team or other athletic team, who competes last

an-cient (eʸn–tʃənt/ eʸn–ʃənt) adj. **1.** Belonging to times long ago: *ancient civilization of Rome* **2.** *often humor.* Very old: *He's driving that ancient car again.* —see OLD

an-cil-lar-y (æn–sə–lɛər–iʸ) adj. Serving or supporting sthg. more important

and (ænd/ ənd/ ən) conj. **1.** (joining two things of the same type or importance — words, phrases, or clauses) Meaning **as well as, also, plus:** *a hat and coat/a tall man and a short lady* **2.** Then; afterwards: *I opened the book and began to read.* **3.** Expressing a reason or result: *Work hard and you will succeed.* (=if you work hard, you will succeed) **4.** Used instead of **to** after certain verbs, esp. **come, go, try,** etc.: *Try and catch me if you can.*

and-i-ron (ænd–aɪ–ərn) n. A metal piece for holding up logs in a fireplace

an-ec-dote (æn–ɪk–doʷt) n. A short, amusing, or interesting story about a real person or event —**anecdotal** adj.

a-ne-mi-a (ə–niʸ–miʸ–ə) n. A condition in which the blood is lacking in quantity or in red cells, or in hemoglobin, and which is marked by paleness, weakness, and irregular heart action —**anemic** adj.

an-es-the-sia (æn–əs–θiʸ–ʒə) n. **1.** Loss of bodily sensation **2.** Insensibility to pain, induced by certain drugs

an-es-thet-ic (æn–əs–θɛt–ɪk) n. A substance that produces loss of sensation and of ability to feel pain

an-es-the-tist (ə–nɛs–θə–təst) n. A person trained to administer anesthetics

a-new (ə–nuʷ) adv. Again; in a new or different way

an-gel (eʸn–dʒəl) n. A spiritual and supernatural being who continually worships and serves God in heaven and who is sent into the world from time to time as his messenger to inform God's people and to comfort and minister to them NOTE: Angels appeared to shepherds in the fields, announcing the birth of Jesus (Luke 2:8-14). Angels also announced his resurrection (rising from the dead) (Luke 24:5-7). They announced that Jesus would return again (Acts 1:10,11). They are personal, sinless, immortal beings, existing in great numbers, and in close relation with individual men and women throughout the history of God's kingdom. They have great strength, intelligence, and wisdom, far superior to that of human beings. They are "ministering spirits sent to serve those who will inherit salvation" (Hebrews 1:14).

an-gel-ic (æn–dʒɛl–ɪk) adj. Having qualities of an angel; without sin or fault

an-ger (æŋ–gər) n. A fierce feeling of displeasure, usu. leading to a desire to fight against the person or thing causing the feeling: *She shouted in anger at the reckless driver who hit her car./ A gentle answer turns away wrath, but a harsh word stirs up anger* (Proverbs 15:1). *God is slow to anger, abounding in love* (Psalm 103:8).

anger v. To make angry: *Do not associate with one who is easily angered* (Proverbs 22:24). —see ANGRY

an-gi-na (æn–dʒaɪ–nə) n. **1.** A localized spasm of pain or any condition marked by such spasms, esp. chestpain, specifically same as angina pectoris **2.** A disease, esp. of the throat, characterized by spasmodic suffocating attacks

an-gi-na pec-to-ris (æn–dʒaɪ–nə pɛk–tə–rɪs) n. A severely painful muscular spasm of the chest, due to an insufficient flow of blood to the heart

an-gle (æŋ–gəl) n. **1.** The space between two lines or surfaces that meet or cross each other: *a right angle* **2.** The position or direction from which an object is viewed: *fig. Look at the problem from all angles.*

an-gli-cize (æŋ–glə–saɪz) v. **-cized, -cizing** To change to English pronunciation, customs, manner, character, etc.: *After living in England for many years, he had become anglicized.*

an-gry (æŋ–griʸ) adj. **-grier, -griest 1.** Full of anger: *My neighbor was very angry about the damage to his property./ Everyone should be quick to listen, slow to speak and slow to become angry* (James 1:19). **2.** Of the sky or clouds, stormy —**angrily** adv. NOTE: **To bother** means **to displease.**: *Will it bother you if I turn the radio on?* Things can **annoy** or irritate one and yet not be bad enough to make one **angry**. *The donkey was annoyed by a fly buzzing around his ears./ The man was angry because the vandals had damaged his car.*

an-guish (æŋ–gwɪʃ) n. Extreme pain or distress, esp. of the mind

an-guished (æŋ–gwɪʃt) adj. Full of anguish; tormented

an-gu-lar (æŋ–gyə–lər) adj. **1.** Having an angle or angles **2.** Measured by an angle **3.** Sharp-cornered **4.** Thin, bony

an-i-mal (æn–ə–məl) n. A living creature, capable of feeling and moving itself when it wants to: *A deer is a very quick, graceful animal.*

an-i-mate (æn–ə–mət) adj. Having life —opposite INANIMATE

an-i-mate (æn–ə–meʸt) v. **-mated, -mating 1.** To impart life to **2.** To give spirit and vigor to **3.** To make sth. appear to move —**animated** adj.

an-i-ma-tion (æn–ə–meʸ–ʃən) n. **1.** Liveliness **2.** An animated cartoon

an-i-mism (æn–ə–mɪz–əm) n. Belief that all natural objects and phenomena (trees, stones, the wind, etc.) have souls —**animist** n. —**an-i-mis-tic** (æn–ə–mɪs–tɪk) adj.

an-i-mos-i-ty (æn–ə–mɑs–ə–tiʸ) n. **-ties** Bitter hostility or hatred

an-kle (æŋ–kəl) n. **1.** The joint connecting the foot and the leg **2.** The thin part of the leg

between the foot and the calf

ank-let (æŋk–lət) n. **1.** A short sock covering the ankle **2.** An ornament worn around the ankle

an-ky-lo-saur-us (æŋ–kə–loᵂ–sɔr–əs) n. -sauri (–sɔr–iʸ) A medium-sized dinosaur with a long, low, thick body covered with bony plates and spikes

an-nals (æn–əlz) n. *pl.* A historical record of events

an-nex (ə–nɛks/ æn–) v. **1.** To add or join to, esp. a larger thing **2.** To incorporate a territory into an existing country or state

an-nex (æn–ɛks) n. A building added on to a larger one or situated nearby

an-ni-hi-late (ə–naɪ–ə–leʸt) v. -lated, -lating To completely destroy —**an-ni-hi-la-tion** (ə–naɪ–ə–leʸ–ʃən) n.

an-ni-ver-sa-ry (æn–ə–vɜr–sə–riʸ) n. -ries A day which is exactly one year or an exact number of years after a birth, wedding, or other event: *Today is our fortieth wedding anniversary.*

an-no Do-mi-ni (æn–oᵂ dɑm–ə–naɪ/ –niʸ) n. *Latin* In the year of our Lord (usu. shortened to A.D.): *The year 2000 A.D. will be 2,000 years since the birth of our Lord and Savior Jesus Christ.*

an-no-tate (æn–ə–teʸt) v. -tated, -tating To supply a literary work with explanatory notes —**an-no-ta-tion** (æn–ə–teʸ–ʃən) n. —**an-no-ta-tive** (æn–ə–teʸ–tɪv) adj.

an-nounce (ə–naʊns) v. -nounced, -nouncing **1.** To state aloud: *The judge announced the winner of the contest.* **2.** To make known publicly: *The company manager announced that there would be a meeting of all employees at three o'clock on Tuesday.* —announcement n.

an-nounc-er (ə–naʊns–ər) n. A person who reads news or commercials or introduces people, acts, etc., esp. on a radio or television program

an-noy (ə–nɔɪ) v. -noyed, -noying To cause trouble; make someone a little angry: *The noise of the traffic at night is very annoying to me.* —see ANGRY

an-noy-ance (ə–nɔɪ–əns) n. **1.** Sthg. which annoys **2.** The state of being annoyed: *The donkey showed his annoyance at the fly buzzing*

around his ears by stamping his feet. / *A fool shows his annoyance at once, but a prudent man overlooks an insult* (Proverbs 12:16).

an-nu-al (æn–yuᵂ–əl) adj. Happening, appearing, etc. every year or once a year: *an annual meeting* —annually adv.

annual n. **1.** A plant that lives for one year or season or less —compare BIENNIAL **2.** A book that comes out every year, having the same title but with different contents

an-nu-i-ty (ə–nuᵂ–ət–iʸ) n. -ties A fixed annual allowance, esp. one provided by a form of investment

an-nul (ə–nʌl) v. -ll- To make null and void; to destroy the validity of: *Their marriage was annulled.*

an-nun-ci-ate (ə–nʌn–siʸ–eʸt) v. -ated, -ating To announce

an-nun-ci-a-tion (ə–nʌn–siʸ–eʸ–ʃən) n. **1.** The act of announcing. The announcement by the angel Gabriel to the Virgin Mary that she was to be the mother of the Christ, and that she would conceive by the power of the Holy Spirit, saying, "The Holy Spirit will come upon you, and the power of the Most High will overshadow you. So the holy one to be born will be called the Son of God" (Luke 1:35). —see JESUS

a-noint (ə–nɔɪnt) v. **1.** To apply oil to a person, esp. in a religious ceremony **2.** To consecrate or set apart: *God anointed Jesus ... with the Holy Spirit and power, and ... he went around doing good and healing all who were under the power of the devil, because God was with him* (Acts 10:38). —anointment n.

a-nom-a-ly (ə–nɑm–ə–liʸ) n. -lies Sthg. unusual; irregular; abnormal —anom-alous adj.

a-non (ə–nɑn) adv. **1.** Soon **2.** At another time

an-o-nym-i-ty (æn–ə–nɪm–ə–tiʸ) n. The quality or state of being anonymous

a-non-y-mous (ə–nɑn–ə–məs) adj. Of unknown or undeclared origin or authorship —anonymously adv.

an-o-rex-i-a (æn–ə–rɛk–siʸ–ə) n. An abnormal lack of appetite, esp. when prolonged

an-oth-er (ə–nʌ–ðər) determ., adj., pron. **1.** An additional similar one: *Would you like another cup of coffee?* **2.** A different one: *Let's go to another place for our vacation next time.* **3.**

Some other or any other: *We should love one another* (1 John 3:11).

an·swer (æn–sər) v. **1.** To say, write, or do sthg. in response to; reply to: *Why didn't you answer my letter?* **2. answer to (a)** Be as described in; fit: *She answers to the description in the ad.* **(b)** Be accountable to: *If you disobey, you'll have to answer to me.*

answer n. **1.** Sthg. that is said or written when one is asked a question, sent a letter, etc.; reply: *I have to send him an answer to his letter today./ A gentle answer turns away wrath, but a harsh word stirs up wrath* (Proverbs 15:1). **2. in answer to** As a result: *Help came in answer to her screams.* **3.** Solution: *What is the answer to this math problem? It's 233./ fig. We don't have the money to buy another computer. The only answer is to rent one.*

an·swer·a·ble (æn–sər–ə–bəl) adj. **1.** Having to account for sthg.; to have the responsibility: *We are answerable to the company for the use of this equipment.* **2.** Capable of being answered: *Some questions are not answerable.*

–ant (–ənt) suffix adj. Equivalent of English **–ing:** *defiant (=defying)*

–ant suffix n. Doer: *defendant*

ant (ænt) n. Any of a family of small, usu. wingless insects living in colonies on the ground

ant·ac·id (ænt–æs–əd) n. An agent that neutralizes acid, esp. excess stomach acid —**antacid** adj.

an·tag·o·nism (æn–tæg–ə–nɪz–əm) n. Active opposition or hostility —**antagonist** n. —**antag·o·nis·tic** (æn–tæg–ə–nɪs–tɪk) adj.

an·tag·o·nize (æn–tæg–ə–naɪz) v. To arouse hostility in others; annoy

ant·arc·tic (ænt–ɑr–tɪk) adj. Of or related to the South Pole and the region around it —**Antarctic** n.

an·te– (ænt–ɪ–/–iʸ–/–ə–) prefix **1.** Before: *antecedent* **2.** In front of: *antechamber*

ant·eat·er (ænt–iʸ–tər) n. An animal with a long snout and a long sticky tongue that feeds on ants and other insects

an·te·bel·lum (ænt–ɪ–bɛl–əm) adj. Before the war, specifically before the American Civil War

an·te·ced·ent (ænt–ə–siʸd–ənt) n. **1.** A noun, pronoun, phrase, or clause referred to by a personal or relative pronoun **2.** A preceding event or cause **3. antecedents** *pl.* Ancestors —**antecedent** adj.

an·te·cham·ber (æn–tɪ–tʃeʸm–bər) n. A room that serves as a waiting room and entrance to a larger room

an·te·date (æn–tɪ–deʸt) v. **-dated, -dating 1.** To date before the true time: *Mr. Smith must have antedated his check.* **2.** To be earlier in date than sthg. else: *The writings of Moses antedate those of Isaiah.*

an·te·di·lu·vi·an (æn–tɪ–də–luʷ–viʸ–ən) adj. *usu. fig.* Old enough to have existed before the great Flood in the days of Noah: *His ideas are antediluvian.*

an·te·lope (æn–tə–loʷp) n. A swift-running animal resembling a deer, found esp. in Africa

an·te me·ri·di·em (æn–tɪ mə–rɪd–iʸ–əm) adj. **1.** Of or pertaining to the morning **2.** Occurring before noon

an·ten·na (æn–tɛn–ə) also **feeler** n. **-nae** (–niʸ) A long, sensitive, hair-like organ, usu. in pairs, on the head of an insect, crab, lobster, etc.; a feeler

antenna n. **-nas** A wire rod or framework put up to receive radio or television broadcasts; aerial

an·te·ri·or (æn–trər–iʸ–ər) adj. **1.** At or toward the front **2.** Earlier

an·te·room (æn–tɪ–ruʷm) n. A room leading to a more important room

an·them (æn–θəm) n. A song of praise or loyalty: *What is the national anthem of your country?*

an·ther (æn–θər) n. The pollen-bearing organ at the end of a stamen

an·thol·o·gy (æn–θɑl–ə–dʒiʸ) **-gies** n. A collection of literary selections, esp. poems

an·thro·pol·o·gy (æn–θrə–pɑl–ə–dʒiʸ) n. The scientific study of mankind, dealing esp. with his origin, development, customs and beliefs —**anthropologist** n.

an·ti– (æn–taɪ–/ –tiʸ–) prefix **1.** Against, opposed to: *antislavery* **2.** Preventing; counteracting: *antiperspirant* NOTE: Do not confuse **anti–** with **ante–**.

an·ti·bi·ot·ic (æn–tɪ–baɪ–ɑt–ɪk) n. A medicine

which is used to kill the bacteria that cause disease: *Penicillin is an antibiotic.*

an-ti-bod-y (æn–tɪ–bɑd–iʸ) **-ies** n. A substance produced in the body which attacks and destroys bacteria: *Babies have few antibodies against infection.*

an-ti-christ (æn–tɪ–kraɪst) n. An enemy of Jesus Christ and his teachings: *Who is the liar? It is the man who denies that Jesus is the Christ. Such a man is the antichrist — he denies the Father and the Son (1 John 2:22). Every spirit that does not acknowledge Jesus is not from God. This is the spirit of the antichrist (1 John 4:3).*

an-tic-i-pate (æn–tɪs–ə–peʸt) v. **-pated, -pating** To expect: *We anticipate a large crowd at the opening of the new musical.*

an-tic-i-pa-tion (æn–tɪs–ə–peʸ–ʃən) n. The act of anticipating, esp. with pleasure: *The children were joyous in their anticipation of Christmas.*

an-ti-cli-max (æn–tɪ–klaɪ–mæks) n. **1.** An event or statement that is strikingly less important than what has preceded it **2.** A dull or disappointing ending to a play, e.g., after increasing excitement or interest

an-tics (æn–tɪks) n. Odd, silly, or amusing behavior

an-ti-dote (æn–tɪ–doʷt) n. A medicine which is given to a person to prevent a poison from taking effect: *If you are bitten by a poisonous snake, you have to take an antidote for it.*

an-ti-freeze (æn–tɪ–friʸz) n. A substance added to water to lower its freezing point

an-ti-his-ta-mine (æn–tɪ–hɪs–tə–mən) n. Any of various medicines used to treat allergies

an-tip-athy (æn–tɪp–ə–θi) n. **1.** A strong dislike **2.** The object of this

an-ti-quat-ed (æn–tɪ–kweʸt–əd) adj. Old fashioned; out-of-date

an-tique (æn–tiʸk) n. A piece of china, furniture, jewelry, etc., that is old, esp. one that is rare and valuable **—antique** adj. *an antique rocking chair*

an-tiq-ui-ty (æn–tɪk–wə–tiʸ) n. **-ties 1.** Ancient times, esp. before the Middle Ages **2.** An object dating from ancient times

an-ti-sep-tic (æn–tɪ–sep–tɪk) adj. Preventing the growth of disease germs

antiseptic n. A substance with an antiseptic effect

an-ti-so-cial (æn–tɪ–soʷ–ʃəl) adj. **1.** Not sociable **2.** Hostile toward others **3.** Opposed to the social system

an-tith-e-sis (æn–tɪθ–ə–sɪs) n. **-ses** (–siʸz) **1.** The direct opposite of: *Good is the antithesis of evil.* **2.** The contrasting of two ideas, words, etc. in a sentence: "*To err is human, to forgive is divine,*" is an example of an antithesis. **—anti-thet-i-cal** (ænt–ə–θət–ɪ–kəl) adj.

ant-ler (ænt–lər) n. The branched horn of a deer

an-to-nym (æn–tə–nɪm) n. A word that is opposite in meaning to another word **—compare SYNONYM**

a-nus (eʸ–nəs) n. pl. **a-nus-es, a-ni** The opening at the lower end of the alimentary canal through which waste material passes out of the body

an-vil (æn–vɪl) n. A heavy iron block on which metal is shaped by hammering

anx-i-e-ty (æŋ–zaɪ–ə–tiʸ) n. **-ties 1.** Fear and worry, esp. about what is going to happen: *Mary's parents felt great anxiety for her safety after she started on her long trip alone./ Cast all your anxiety on him [Jesus], because he cares for you (1 Peter 5:7).* **2.** A strong but often uneasy desire to do sthg. **—see NERVOUS**

anx-ious (æŋ–ʃəs/ æŋk–ʃəs) adj. **1.** Feeling or showing anxiety; uneasy: *I was anxious about the doctor's diagnosis of my mother's illness./Do not be anxious about anything, but in everything, by prayer and petition, with thanksgiving, present your requests to God (Philippians 4:6).* **2.** Having a strong desire to do sthg.: *He was anxious to please his teacher.* **—anxiously** adv.

an-y (ɛn–iʸ) determ., adj., pron. **1.** Every; one, no matter which (of more than two): *Any taxi driver will know where the airport is.* **2.** (used only in negatives, questions, etc.) Some; no matter how much or how little: *He didn't have any money at all.* **3.** All; as much as possible: *The people in the flood area will take any help you can give them.* **4. in any case (a)** also **at any rate** Whatever happens: *I may lose my job, but in any case my family will have enough to live on for a while.* **(b)** In addition; also: *We can't afford to go to the movies, and in*

any case we have too much work to do.

any adv. To the least degree; at all; *I can't stay awake any longer.*

an-y-bod-y (ɛn–iʸ–bəd–iʸ) also **anyone** pron. All people; any person, no matter who: *Does anybody know whose book this is?*

an-y-how (ɛn–iʸ–haʊ) adv. *infml.* Also **anyway** 1. No matter what else may be true; in any case: *I'll have to drive a long way to work, but I'll take the job anyhow.* 2. In a careless way; haphazardly

an-y-more (ɛn–iʸ–mɔr) adv. Now; from now on: *I never go there anymore.* NOTE: Do not confuse **anymore** with **any more.** "I don't want any more pie right now," is quite different from, "I don't want pie anymore."

an-y-place (ɛn–iʸ–pleʸs) adv. Anywhere

an-y-one (ɛn–iʸ–wən) pron. Anybody; any person NOTE: Compare **anyone** and **any one:** "**Anyone** can come to the party." "There are three salesladies free at the moment. **Any one** of them will be able to help you."

an-y-thing (ɛn–iʸ–θɪŋ) pron. 1. Any one object, event, fact, etc.; sthg.: *He doesn't have anything to say in the matter. It's all decided./ Do you want to take anything along to eat?* 2. **anything but** By no means; not at all: *That car is anything but reliable. (=It's not reliable.)*

an-y-time (ɛn–iʸ–taɪm) adv. At any time whatever

an-y-way (ɛn–iʸ–weʸ) adv. Anyhow

an-y-where (ɛn–iʸ–wɛər/ –hwɛər) adv. 1. In, at, or to any place: *Shop anywhere you like, but this store has the best prices.* 2. Any place at all: *Are you going anywhere for your vacation?*

an-y-wise (ɛn–iʸ–waɪz) adv. In any way whatever

a-or-ta (eʸ–ɔr–tə) n. **-tas** or **-tae** The main artery that carries blood from the heart

a-part (ə–pɑrt) adv. 1. Separated in place or time: *The two buses arrived thirty minutes apart.* 2. Into pieces: *He took the car apart to find out what was wrong with it.* 3. **tell/ know apart** To be able to tell the difference between: *How do you tell the twins apart?*

a-part-heid (ə–pɑr–taɪd/ –taɪt/ –teʸt) n. The separation of races of people in a country

a-part-ment (ə–pɑrt–mənt) n. One or more

rooms, usu. including a kitchen and bathroom, esp. one such set in a building

ap-a-thy (æ–pə–θiʸ) n. **-thies** Lack of feeling or interest in things; lack of interest or ability to act in any way —**ap-a-thet-ic** (æp–ə–θɛt–ɪk) adj.

ape (eʸp) v. **aped, aping** To copy another person's behavior, manners, speech, etc.; imitate

ape n. Any of a family of large monkeys with a very short tail or no tail at all, such as a gorilla or chimpanzee

ap-er-ture (æp–ər–tʃər) n. An opening; a hole

a-pex (eʸ–pɛks) n. The highest point of anything

a-piece (ə–piʸs) adv. Each: *The three of you may have one apple apiece.*

a-poc-a-lypse (ə–pɑk–ə–lɪps) n. 1. A prophecy or revelation 2. **Apocalypse** The Book of Revelation, the last book of the New Testament which tells of the end times and the return of Jesus Christ

a-poc-a-lyp-tic (ə–pɑk–ə–lɪp–tɪk) adj. Prophesying dramatic events such as those recorded in the Apocalypse

A-poc-ry-pha (ə–pɑk–rə–fə) n. *pl.* Those 14 books of the Old Testament that were not accepted by the Jews as part of the Hebrew Scriptures and have never been accepted as a part of the Protestant Bible

a-poc-ry-phal (ə–pɑk–rə–fəl) adj. 1. Any writings of doubtful authenticity 2. False; counterfeit

a-pol-o-get-ic (ə–pɑl–ə–dʒɛt–ɪk) adj. Expressing sorrow or regret —**apologetically** adv.

a-pol-o-gize (ə–pɑl–ə–dʒaɪz) v. **-gized, -gizing** To say one is sorry for a fault, for causing pain, etc.: *You'd better apologize to your brother for bumping his arm. You made him spill his food.*

a-pol-o-gy (ə–pɑl–ə–dʒiʸ) n. **-gies** A statement expressing regret for causing trouble, pain, etc.

ap-o-plex-y (æp–ə–plɛk–siʸ) n. A sudden loss of bodily function due to rupture or blockage of a blood vessel in the brain

a-pos-ta-sy (ə–pɑs–tə–siʸ) n. **-sies** Desertion of one's faith, religion, party or principles

a-pos-tate (ə–pɑs–teʸt) n. One who renounces

his religion, principles, political party, etc.

a-pos-tle (ə–**pɑs**–əl) n. **1.** One of the followers of Jesus Christ, chosen by him to go and preach the Gospel of salvation through faith in him and to teach the believers to observe all that he (Christ) had commanded **2.** Anyone who leads a new cause —**ap-os-tol-ic** (æp–ə–**stɑl**–ɪk) adj.

a-pos-tro-phe (ə–**pɑs**–trə–fiʸ) n. The sign (') used in writing **(a)** To show that one or more letters or figures have been left out (as in can't for "cannot" and '06 for "1906") **(b)** With "s" to show possession (as in "Mary's shoe," "teachers' desks," etc.) **(c)** Before "s" for the plural of letters and figures: *There are four i's in "Mississippi."*

a-poth-e-car-y (ə–pɑθ–ə–kɛər–iʸ) n. **-ies** A person who prepares and sells medicines; druggist; pharmacist

ap-pall *AmE.* **appal** *BrE.* (ə–**pɔl**) v. To fill with dismay, fear, terror, hatred, etc.; shock greatly: *We were appalled at the news of the massacre.*

ap-pal-ling (ə–**pɔl**–ɪŋ) adj. **1.** Shocking; terrible **2.** *infml.* Very bad: *an appalling state of affairs*

ap-pa-ra-tus (æp–ə–**ræ**–təs/ æp–ə–**reʸ**–təs) n. **1.** A set of materials or equipment for a particular use **2.** The equipment used in gymnastics

ap-par-el (ə–**pɛər**–əl) n. Clothing

ap-par-ent (ə–**pɛər**–ənt) adj. **1.** Clearly seen or understood: *His interest in music was apparent from the time he was three years old.* **2.** Seeming to be sthg. that it is not: *His apparent boldness covered his fear.*

ap-par-ent-ly (ə–**pɛər**–ənt–liʸ) adv. As it appears: *I was 30 minutes late for our appointment. Apparently my watch was wrong.*

ap-pa-ri-tion (æp–ə–rɪʃ–ən) n. **1.** A supernatural appearance; a ghost **2.** A sudden, unusual sight

ap-peal (ə–**piʸl**) v. **1.** To request help, support, money, mercy, etc.: *The accused man appealed to the jury for mercy.* **2.** To be pleasing, attractive, or interesting: *A vacation in Hawaii certainly appeals to me. Would you like to go with me?* **3.** To ask a higher law court to change the decision of a lower court **4. appeal to**

sbdy./ sthg. To try to get support: *By appealing to his love of good books, we persuaded him to help us raise funds for the new library.*

appeal n. **1.** A strong, often urgent request: *His appeal for food and clothing was answered very quickly.* **2.** A quality that attracts or interests: *Adventure stories have a great appeal for children.* **3.** A request to a higher court to change the decision of a lower court: *an appeal for a new trial*

ap-peal-ing (ə–**piʸl**–ɪŋ) adj. **1.** Able to move a person's feelings: *the appealing eyes of a lonely child* **2.** Attractive or interesting: *What an appealing basket of fruit!* —opposite UNAPPEALING

ap-pear (ə–**prɪər**) v. **1.** To show up so as to be seen; come into sight: *After several weeks at sea, land finally appeared on the horizon.* —opposite DISAPPEAR **2.** To seem; look like: *It appears the meeting is ready to begin.* **3.** To be present formally, as in a court of law: *He received a summons to appear in court./ We must all appear before the judgment seat of Christ (2 Corinthians 5:10).*

ap-pear-ance (ə–**prɪər**–əns) n. **1.** The act of appearing: *Spring will make her appearance soon.* —opposite DISAPPEARANCE **2.** That which can be seen; outward qualities; look: *He had an unhealthy appearance./ Man looks at the outward appearance [of what someone does], but God looks at the heart (1 Samuel 16:7). Jesus said, "Don't judge by mere appearances, but make a right judgment" (John 7:24).*

ap-pease (ə–**piʸz**) v. **-peased, -peasing** To calm or satisfy (a person, desire, etc.) by supplying what is needed or requested: *His thirst was soon appeased after he reached the oasis.* —**appeasement** n.

ap-pel-la-tion (æp–ə–leʸ–ʃən) n. **1.** The act of calling by a name **2.** A name or title that identifies or describes one

ap-pend (ə–**pend**) v. To attach, esp. as something additional

ap-pend-age (ə–**pend**–ɪdʒ) n. **1.** Sthg. attached to a larger entity **2.** A subordinate bodily part, as a finger or toe

ap-pen-dec-to-my (æp–ən–**dek**–tə–miʸ) n. **-mies** Surgical removal of the intestinal appendix

ap·pen·di·ci·tis (ə–pɛn–də–saɪ–tɪs) n. The diseased state of the appendix, often requiring surgical removal

ap·pen·dix (ə–pɛn–dɪks) n. **-dixes** or **-dices** (–dɪs–əz) **1.** A small worm-like organ leading off the bowel, which has no known use **2.** Something additional, esp. information at the end of a book

ap·pe·tite (æp–ə–taɪt) n. A physical desire, esp. for food: *Football players generally have hearty appetites./ fig. He has no appetite for reading good books.*

ap·pe·tiz·er (æp–ə–taɪ–zər) n. A food or drink just before a meal to stimulate the appetite

ap·pe·tiz·ing (æp–ə–taɪz–ɪŋ) adj. Tempting to the appetite —**appetizingly** adv.

ap·plaud (ə–plɔd) v. **1.** To show approval of a speaker, performer, etc., esp. by clapping **2.** To show strong approval of a person, idea, etc.: *You are to be applauded for taking an honest, though unpopular stand on the matter.*

ap·plause (ə–plɔz) n. Approval or praise for a performance or performer, esp. by striking the hands together (clapping)

ap·ple (æp–əl) n. **1.** A firm, round fruit with white, juicy flesh and usu. a red, green, or yellow skin and small seeds **2. apple of someone's eye** *infml.* Sbdy. or sthg. that is especially well liked

ap·pli·ance (ə–plaɪ–əns) n. A machine run by electricity and used in the house for a certain task: *We bought all new appliances when we moved into this house — a washer, dryer, dishwasher, and refrigerator.*

ap·pli·ca·ble (æp–lɪ–kə–bəl/ ə–plɪk–ə–bəl) adj. Capable of being applied; relevant

ap·pli·cant (æp–lɪ–kənt) n. A person who makes a request, esp. officially and in writing, for a job, etc.

ap·pli·ca·tion (æp–lɪ–keʸ–ʃən) n. **1.** The act of making a request, esp. in writing: *I made five applications for jobs but didn't get one yet.* **2.** The act of putting sthg. to use: *the application of good common sense*

ap·pli·ca·tor (æp–lə–keʸt–ər) n. A device for applying a substance

ap·plied (ə–plaɪd) adj. Put to practical use

ap·ply (ə–plaɪ) v. **-plied, -plying 1.** To request sthg., esp. in writing, such as a job, loan,

etc.: *Did you apply for the job yet?* **2.** To put into use: *We'll need to apply two coats of fresh paint to cover the old paint.* **3.** To give careful and continuous attention or effort: *You'd better apply yourself if you expect to keep this job./Apply your heart to instruction and your ears to words of knowledge* (Proverbs 23:12).

ap·point (ə–pɔɪnt) v. **1.** To name someone for a position, job, etc.: *He was appointed chairman of the committee.* **2.** *fml.* To arrange; set; decide: *Will you be able to come at the appointed time?*

ap·point·ment (ə–pɔɪnt–mənt) n. **1.** A meeting at a time and place that has been arranged: *I have an appointment at the dentist's office at 3:00.* **2.** The agreement to meet at a certain time and place: *The realtor will show this house by appointment only.* **3.** The selecting of someone for a position or job: *His appointment to the position will be announced soon.*

ap·por·tion (ə–por–ʃən) v. To distribute proportionately

ap·praise (ə–preʸz) v. **-praised, -praising** *fml.* To judge the value, condition, etc. of sthg.; find out what sthg. is worth: *The house was appraised at over $500,000.* —**appraisal** n.

ap·pre·cia·ble (ə–priʸ–ʃə–bəl) adj. Large enough to be recognized and appreciated —**appreciably** adv.

ap·pre·ci·ate (ə–priʸ–ʃiʸ–eʸt) v. **-ated, -ating 1.** To enjoy the good qualities of; think well of: *to appreciate good music/ I appreciate your thoughtfulness.* **2.** To rise in value: *Houses in this area have appreciated 27% in the last year.* —opposite DEPRECIATE

ap·pre·ci·a·tion (ə–priʸ–ʃiʸ–eʸ–ʃən) n. **1.** The act or fact of appreciating **2.** A rise in value or price

ap·pre·ci·a·tive (ə–priʸ–ʃiʸ–ə–tɪv) adj. Grateful; thankful —opposite UNAPPRECIATIVE —**appreciatively** adv.

ap·pre·hend (æp–riʸ–hɛnd) v. **1.** To arrest **2.** To become aware of **3.** To understand

ap·pre·hen·sion (æp–riʸ–hɛn–ʃən) n. Fear and anxiety

ap·pre·hen·sive (æp–riʸ–hɛn–sɪv) adj. Viewing the future with anxiety —**apprehensively** adv.

ap·pren·tice (ə–prɛnt–əs) n. A person learn-

ing a craft under a skilled worker

ap-prise (ə-**praɪz**) v. -prised, -prising Inform

ap-proach (ə-**proʷtʃ**) v. **1.** To come near or nearer to: *The train was approaching the station./In him [Jesus] and through faith in him, we may approach God with freedom and confidence* (Ephesians 3:12). *This is the assurance we have in approaching God: that if we ask anything according to his will, he hears us* (1 John 5:14). **2.** To speak to or make a request, esp. about sthg. for the first time: *He approached me this morning about lending him some money.*

approach n. **1.** The act of coming near: *We could hear the approach of the train for miles.* **2.** A way of entering: *The enemy has cut off the approach to the city.* **3.** A method of doing sthg. or way of thinking: *a new approach to automobile design*

ap-proach-a-ble (ə-**proʷtʃ**-ə-bəl) adj. **1.** Capable of being reached **2.** Friendly; easy to speak to: *Your friend seems to be a very approachable person.* —opposite UNAPPROACHABLE

ap-pro-ba-tion (æp-rə-beʸ-ʃən) n. Approval

ap-pro-pri-ate (ə-**proʷ**-priʸ-eʸt) v. -ated, -ating **1.** To set aside for a certain purpose: *Six thousand dollars has been appropriated for our trip to China.* **2.** To steal

ap-pro-pri-ate (ə-**proʷ**-priʸ-ət) adj. Proper or suitable: *His faded jeans were not appropriate for an important business meeting./Women should dress modestly, with decency and propriety, not with ... expensive clothes, but with good deeds, appropriate for women who profess to worship God* (1 Timothy 2:9-10). —opposite INAPPROPRIATE —appropriately adv.

ap-prov-al (ə-**pruʷ**-vəl) n. **1.** The act of agreeing that sthg. is good —opposite DISAPPROVAL **2. on approval** *infml.* Of goods bought at a store, on a trial basis, to be returned for the refund of one's money, if not found satisfactory

ap-prove (ə-**pruʷ**v) v. -proved, -proving **1.** To give official agreement to: *Our application for a loan has been approved.* **2. approve of** sbdy./ sthg. To agree that sthg. is good, right, wise, etc.: *I don't approve of smoking.*

It's very harmful to one's health. —**approvingly** adv.

ap-prox-i-mate (ə-**praks**-ə-mət) adj. Nearly correct but not exact: *The approximate area of Nigeria is 357,000 square miles.* —**approximately** adv.

ap-prox-i-mate (ə-**praks**-ə-meʸt) v. -mated, -mating **1.** To come near to **2.** To be almost the same as sthg.

ap-ri-cot (eʸ-prɪ-kɑt/ æp-rɪ-kɑt) n. A juicy, oval fruit with a pit, related to the plum and peach, having an orange-pink color when ripe

A-pril (eʸ-prəl) Also **Apr.** *written abbr.* n. **1.** The fourth month of the year **2. April Fool's Day** *AmE.* The first day of April, a day marked by the playing of practical jokes

a-pron (eʸ-prən) n. A garment worn over one's clothes to keep them clean, for example, while cooking

ap-ro-pos (æp-rə-poʷ) adv. Appropriately; to the point

apropos adj. Suitable or relevant to what is being said or done

apt (æpt) adj. **1.** Tending to do sthg.; likely: *The weather is apt to be changeable at that time of the year in London.* **2.** Exactly fitting: *an apt statement* —**aptly** adv. —**aptness** n.

ap-ti-tude (æp-tə-tuʷd) n. Natural ability or talent, esp. in learning: *She showed great aptitude for learning music.*

aq-ua (ɑk-wə/ æk-wə) n. **1.** Water **2.** The color aquamarine, a light greenish-blue —**aqua** adj. Of a light greenish color

a-quar-i-um (ə-**kweər**-iʸ-əm) n. **1.** An artificial pool or tank for keeping living fish and water animals and plants **2.** A building containing such ponds and tanks

a-quat-ic (ə-**kwɑt**-ɪk) adj. **1.** Growing or living in or near water **2.** Performed in or on water

aq-ue-duct (æk-wə-dəkt) n. An artificial channel for carrying water, esp. one built like a bridge above low ground

ar-a-ble (eər-ə-bəl) adj. Suitable for plowing and for raising crops

ar-bi-ter (ɑr-bɪ-tər) n. One having power to decide; a judge

ar-bi-trar-y (ɑr-bə-treər-iʸ) adj. **1.** Based on random choice or impulse **2.** Despotic; un-

restrained; making decisions without consulting others: *An arbitrary ruler is unpopular with his subjects.* —**ar-bi-trar-i-ly** (ɑr-bə-trɛər-ə-liʸ) adv.

ar-bi-trate (ɑr-bə-treʸt) v. **-trated, -trating** To act as an arbitrator

ar-bi-trat-or (ɑr-bə-treʸt-ər) n. An impartial person who is appointed to settle a dispute between two or more others

ar-bor (ɑr-bər) n. A shady place among trees, usu. with a seat, esp. in a garden

ar-bo-re-tum (ɑr-bə-reʸ-təm) n. **-retums** or **-reta** A place where trees and other plants are grown for scientific and educational purposes

arc (ɑrk) n. Part of a circle or any curved line: *an arc of 90 degrees, or one-fourth of a complete circle*

ar-cade (ɑr-keʸd) n. **1.** An arched or covered passageway, esp. one lined with shops **2.** A series of arches supporting, or along a wall

arch (ɑrtʃ) n. **1.** The top curved part over an open space in a bridge, doorway, window, etc. **2.** Sthg. with this shape, esp. the middle of the bottom of the foot

arch v. To form into an arch

ar-chae-ol-o-gy or **ar-che-ol-o-gy** (ɑr-kiʸ-ɑl-ə-dʒiʸ) n. The study of past human life as revealed by relics left by ancient peoples —**ar-che-o-log-i-cal** (ɑr-kiʸ-ə-lɑdʒ-ɪ-kəl) adj. —**ar-che-ol-o-gist** (ɑr-kiʸ-ɑl-ə-dʒɪst) n.

ar-cha-ic (ɑr-keʸ-ɪk) adj. **1.** Belonging to an earlier time **2.** Antiquated **3.** A word or expression characteristic of the past and surviving in some special uses: *"Thou art" is an archaic form of "you are."*

arch-an-gel (ɑrk-eʸn-dʒəl) n. An angel of the highest rank: *Gabriel and Michael are archangels.* —see ANGEL

arch-bish-op (ɑrtʃ-bɪʃ-əp) n. A bishop of the highest rank

arch-er (ɑrtʃ-ər) n. One who shoots with a bow and arrows

arch-er-y (ɑr-tʃə-riʸ) n. The art of shooting with bows and arrows

arch-i-pel-a-go (ɑr-kə-pɛl-ə-goʷ) n. **1.** A large group of islands **2.** A sea containing a large group of islands

ar-chi-tect (ɑr-kə-tɛkt) n. A person who designs new buildings and oversees their building

ar-chi-tec-ture (ɑr-kə-tɛk-tʃər) n. **1.** The art or practice of designing buildings and supervising their construction **2.** The style or manner of building: *Gothic architecture* —**ar-chi-tec-tur-al** (ɑr-kə-tɛk-tʃər-əl) adj.

ar-chives (ɑr-kaɪvz) n. *pl.* **1.** The records or historical documents of an institution or community **2.** A place where such records or documents are kept

arch-way (ɑrtʃ-weʸ) n. **1.** A passageway under an arch **2.** An arch framing a passage

arc-tic (ɑrk-tɪk/ ɑr-tɪk) adj. **1.** Of the regions around the North Pole **2.** Very cold

Arc-tic (ɑrk-tɪk/ ɑr-tɪk) n. **1.** The Arctic regions **2.** The Arctic Ocean

Arc-tic Circle (ɑrk-tɪk sɜr-kəl/ ɑr-) n. The line of latitude 66.5 degrees north of the equator and 23.5 degrees south of the North Pole

ar-dent (ɑr-dənt) adj. Strong in feeling; eager; fierce: *an ardent baseball fan* —**ardently** adv.

ar-dor (ɑr-dər) n. Warmth of feeling; zeal

ar-du-ous (ɑr-dʒuʷ-əs) adj. Difficult; laborious —**arduously** adv. —**ardu-ousness** n.

are strong (ɑr); weak (ər) v. Pres. tense *pl.* of **be**

ar-e-a (ɛər-iʸ-ə) n. **1.** The measure of a flat surface obtained by multiplying the length by the width: *What's the area of this classroom?* —compare VOLUME **2.** A part or division of a town, region, country, the world, etc.: *This area of Africa is all jungle.* **3.** A space or surface used for a specific purpose: *the parking area behind the building* **4.** A subject, special field of work, etc.: *research in the area of marine biology*

ar-e-a code (ɛər-iʸ-ə koʷd) n. In the US and Canada, the three numbers used before a telephone number when making a long-distance call: *My area code is eight-one-eight (818).*

a-re-na (ə-riʸ-nə) n. **1.** A building or enclosed area used for sports, public amusements, etc. **2.** *fig.* Any sphere of struggle or conflict: *the arena of war*

aren't (ɑrnt/ ɑr-ənt) v. Short for **are not**: *These aren't my books.*

ar-gu-a-ble (ɑr-gyuʷ-ə-bəl) adj. **1.** That can be supported with reasons **2.** Doubtful to some

extent

ar-gue (ɑr–gyu^w) v. -gued, -guing To have a disagreement; quarrel: *Why do you and your brother argue so much?*

ar-gu-ment (ɑr–gyə–mənt) n. **1.** A disagreement; quarrel **2.** A reason given to prove or disprove sthg.: *She listed all the arguments she could find against the use of nuclear energy.*

a-ri-a (ɑ–ri^y–ə) n. A song for a solo piece in an opera

ar-id (ɛər–əd) adj. Of an area or a country, very dry and unproductive: *the arid wastelands*

a-rise (ə–raɪz) v. arose (ə–ro^wz), arisen (ə–rɪz–ən), arising To come into being; appear: *A storm arose before we could finish painting the porch.*

ar-is-toc-ra-cy (ɛər–ə–stɑk–rə–si^y) n. -cies **1.** Government by a noble or privileged class **2.** The governing class of such a government —**ar-is-to-crat** (ə–rɪs–tə–kræt) n. —**ar-is-to-crat-ic** (ə–rɪs–tə–kræt–ɪk) adj.

a-rith-me-tic (ə–rɪθ–mə–tɪk) n. The science or art of numbers; calculation by numbers —compare MATHEMATICS

ark (ɑrk) n. A boat resembling that of Noah at the time of the Great Flood NOTE: The Great Flood covered the entire earth, destroying all mankind except for the four men and four women on Noah's Ark (Genesis 6-9).

arm (ɑrm) n. **1.** Either of the two upper limbs of a person **2.** Sthg. that is shaped like or moves like an arm or is thought of like an arm: *the arm of the law* **3.** The part of a garment that covers the arm; sleeve **4. keep somebody at arm's length** To keep at a distance; to not be friendly with somebody

arm v. To supply with or have weapons or armor: *The criminal is armed (=with a gun) and dangerous./ armed for war/fig. He was armed with many facts to answer all our questions.* —opposite DISARM —see also UNARMED

ar-mad-a (ɑr–mɑ–də) n. A fleet of warships

ar-ma-dil-lo (ɑr–mə–dɪl–o^w) n. Any of a family of burrowing animals of North and South America that has a bony covering that looks like armor

ar-ma-ment (ɑr–mə–mənt) n. **1.** Military strength **2.** Arms and equipment **3.** The process of preparing for war

ar-mi-stice (ɑr–mə–stəs) n. An agreement to stop fighting a war for a period of time

ar-mor *AmE.* **ar-mour** *BrE.* (ɑr–mər) n. **1.** Protective covering of metal or strong leather, formerly worn in battle by fighting men and their horses **2.** Strong protective metal covering on ships, aircraft, and other fighting vehicles **3.** *spir.* The word of God: *Put on the full armor of God so that you can take your stand against the devil's schemes* (Ephesians 6:11).

ar-mored *AmE.* **ar-moured** *BrE.* (ɑr–mərd) adj. **1.** Covered with armor: *an armored truck* **2.** Having fighting vehicles protected by armor: *an armored division*

ar-mor-y *AmE.* **ar-mour-y** *BrE.* (ɑr–mər–i^y) n. -ies A place for storing weapons and other instruments of war

arms (ɑrmz) n. **1.** Weapons **2. up in arms** *infml.* Very angry and ready to argue strongly: *Everybody was up in arms over the new tax law.*

ar-my (ɑr–mi^y) n. -mies **1.** The military forces of a country, esp. those who fight on land **2.** Any large group, esp. one joined together for some specific purpose: *an army of truck drivers*

a-ro-ma (ə–ro^w–mə) n. A strong pleasant smell: *the aroma of freshly baked bread* —**ar-o-mat-ic** (ɛər–ə–mæt–ɪk) adj.

a-rose (ə–ro^wz) v. Past tense of **arise**

a-round (ə–raʊnd) prep. **1.** On all sides of: *The children gathered around the campfire.* **2.** (a) In various places in: *They traveled around Europe.* (b) Near: *I'd like to live around Chicago somewhere.* **3.** Along the edge or border of: *Please walk around the flower bed, not through it.*

around adv. **1.** Also **about** (a) From one place to another; here and there: *They move around a lot./ They traveled around in Europe.* (b) Nearby: *My brother is around somewhere.* **2.** Facing the other way: *Turn around and look behind you.* **3.** (a) Going in a circle: *The merry-go-round went around and around.* (b) On all sides: *There are mountains all around.*

a-rouse (ə-rauz) v. -roused, -rousing 1. To awaken; rouse: *We were aroused early in the morning by the sound of the siren.* 2. To stir up feelings or action: *The sight of the lame child aroused his pity.*

ar-raign (ə-rey̆n) v. 1. To call before a court to answer to an indictment 2. To accuse or denounce —**arraignment** n.

ar-range (ə-rey̆ndʒ) v. -ranged, -ranging 1. To set in a suitable order: *to arrange pictures on the wall* 2. Make ready; plan in advance: *We arranged to rent a car at the airport.* 3. To set out or adapt a piece of music in a certain way, as for different instruments: *to arrange a piece of music*

ar-range-ment (ə-rey̆ndʒ-mənt) n. 1. A plan or agreement: *We made all the arrangements for our trip by telephone.* 2. The act of putting into order: *She was very careful about the arrangement of the books on the shelves.* 3. Sthg. that has been put in order: *a beautiful arrangement of flowers* 4. A piece of music set out in a certain way, as for different instruments

ar-ray (ə-rey̆) v. 1. To arrange in order 2. To dress splendidly 3. To adorn

array n. 1. A regular arrangement —opposite DISARRAY 2. An imposing group 3. Rich apparel

ar-rears (ə-rɪərz) n. pl. 1. Money that is owing and ought to have been paid earlier 2. Work that should have been finished but is still waiting to be done

ar-rest (ə-rest) v. 1. To take someone in the name of the law and usu. put in prison: *He was arrested for armed robbery.* 2. *fml.* To bring to an end; stop: *The spread of the disease was arrested by the work of the health department.*

arrest n. The act of arresting or of being arrested

ar-ri-val (ə-raɪv-əl) n. 1. The act of arriving 2. A thing or person that has arrived: *This book is a new arrival in our library.*

ar-rive (ə-raɪv) v. -rived, -riving 1. To reach a place, esp. after traveling some distance: *The plane arrived on time.* 2. To happen; come: *The time for our vacation has arrived.* 3. **arrive at sthg.** To reach: *How did you arrive at that answer?*

ar-ro-gance (ɛər-ə-gəns) n. Pride; haughtiness: *From within, out of men's hearts, come evil thoughts, sexual immorality, theft, murder, adultery, greed ... arrogance and folly. All these evils come from inside and make a man "unclean"* (Mark 7:21-23).

ar-ro-gant (ɛər-ə-gənt) adj. Full of pride and self-importance, esp. in a way that shows no respect for other people —**arrogantly** adv.

ar-row (ɛər-oʷ) n. 1. A thin straight stick with a point at one end and usually feathers at the other, which is shot from a long piece of bent wood (bow), used in sport, hunting, or war 2. A sign shaped like an arrow used for showing direction

ar-se-nal (ɑr-sə-nəl) n. A place for making and storing arms and military equipment

ar-se-nic (ɑr-sə-nɪk) n. 1. An element which is used to make certain poisons 2. A poison made with arsenic: *He was poisoned with arsenic.*

ar-son (ɑr-sən) n. The crime of setting fire to a building on purpose

art (ɑrt) n. 1. The making or expression of what is beautiful or true, in painting, music, drama, etc. 2. Things created in this way: *The gallery is full of works of art — sculptures, paintings, and other beautiful objects.* 3. Fine skill in making or doing anything: *She has skating down to an art.*

ar-ter-y (ɑr-tər-iʸ) n. -ies 1. Any of the thick-walled tubes that carry blood from the heart to the rest of the body —compare VEIN 2. A main road, railroad, etc.

art-ful (ɑrt-fəl) adj. 1. Clever, esp. in reaching a goal 2. Cunning; crafty 3. Done with or showing considerable art or skill —**artfully** adv.

art gal-ler-y (ɑrt gæl-ə-riʸ) n. -ies A room or building in which statues, paintings, etc. are displayed

ar-thri-tis (ɑrθ-raɪ-təs) n. A disease of the human body which causes pain and swelling in the joints —**ar-thrit-ic** (ɑrθ-rɪt-ɪk) adj. , n.

ar-ti-choke (ɑr-tɪ-tʃoʷk) n. 1. A thistle-like plant 2. The flower of this plant cooked as a vegetable

ar-ti-cle (ɑr-tɪ-kəl) n. 1. A thing or object, esp.

a particular one of a group: *I bought three articles for my tool box at the hardware store.* **2.** A complete piece of writing such as an essay, report, etc. in a newspaper or magazine **3.** *tech.* The words **a** or **an** (indefinite articles) and **the** (definite article)

ar-tic-u-late (ɑr–tɪk–yə–lət) adj. **1.** Able to express clearly: *a very articulate person* —opposite INARTICULATE **2.** Pronounced clearly and distinctly: *Articulate speech is essential for a teacher.*

ar-tic-u-late (ɑr–tɪk–yə–le^{y}t) v. **-lated, -lating 1.** To pronounce words distinctly **2.** To express in words —**ar-tic-u-la-tion** (ɑr–tɪk–yə–le^y–ʃən) n.

ar-ti-fact (ɑr–tə–fækt) n. An object, esp. a tool or weapon, produced by human workmanship

ar-ti-fice (ɑr–tə–fəs) n. **1.** Trick; trickery **2.** An ingenious device; ingenuity; cleverness —**artificer** n. A skilled worker

ar-ti-fi-cial (ɑr–tə–fɪ–ʃəl) adj. **1.** Not made by nature; man-made: *artificial plants/ artificial fur* —compare NATURAL, MAN–MADE **2.** Pretended; unreal: *He always seemed to wear an artificial smile.* —**artificially** adv.

ar-til-ler-y (ɑr–tɪl–ə–ri^y) n. **1.** Large guns used in fighting on land **2.** The branch of an army that uses these

ar-ti-san (ɑr–tə–zən/ –sən) n. A person skilled in working with the hands or in a trade

art-ist (ɑr–tɪst) n. **1.** One who is skilled in any of the fine arts, such as painting, sculpture, or music **2.** One whose work shows skill: *The cook was a real artist when it came to making a cheap meal look expensive.* —**ar-tis-tic** (ɑr–tɪs–tɪk) adj. **artistically** adv.

arts (ɑrts) n. Those fields of study that are not thought of as part of science, esp. as taught at a university: *I'm majoring in the arts: history of music, literature, and English.* —compare THE SCIENCES

as (æz) conj. **1.** (Used in comparisons): *She's as pretty as her sister.* **2.** In the same manner that: *Do as you are told!* **3.** While; when: *My mother always sang as she worked.* **4.** Because; since: *As he had no car, he had to take a bus.* **5.** Though: *Worn as they were, we used the old curtains in the office.* **6. as it is** In reality: *I wanted to buy my own car, but as it is I can't afford one.* **7. as it were** So to speak; as if it were true: *My aunt has cared for me since I was young. She's my mother, as it were.* **8. as for** With regard to: *I don't like driving so far, but as for my job, I like it a lot.*

as adv., prep. **1.** To the same degree: *just as old/ intelligent/ talented* **2.** In the manner or condition of: *I use sugar as a sweetener in my coffee.*

a.s.a.p. Short for **as soon as possible**

as if; also **as though** conj. **1.** The way it would be if something were true: *She said it as if she meant it, but I don't think she did.* **2.** In a way that suggests that sthg. may be true: *She looked as if she would cry.*

as of prep. Up to, on, or from a stated time: *He was the new director as of last Thursday at 8:00 a.m.*

as to prep. About; concerning: *She was very clear as to one thing. She wanted a successful career in modeling.*

as-bes-tos (æs–bes–təs) n. A soft fibrous mineral, made into fireproof material or used as insulation

as-cend (ə–send) v. *often fml.* To climb; go, come, or move up: *She ascended the stairs gracefully./ He [Jesus] who descended is the very one who ascended higher than all the heavens* (Ephesians 4:10). —opposite DESCEND

as-cen-sion (ə–sen–ʃən) n. Ascent; the act of going up

Ascension Day n. The fortieth day after Easter commemorating the ascension of our Lord and Savior Jesus Christ which occurred 40 days after his resurrection from the dead and was witnessed by the Apostle (Acts 1:9-10).

as-cent (ə–sent) n. **1.** The act of climbing, going up, or rising; ascending **2.** A steep slope upward: *It was quite an ascent to his house at the top of the hill.* NOTE: Do not confuse **ascent** with **assent**

as-cer-tain (æs–ər–te^{y}n) v. To find out by inquiring

as-cet-ic (ə–set–ɪk) adj. Practicing self-denial, avoiding pleasures and comfort, esp. for religious reasons: *He led a very ascetic life.* —**ascetic** n.

as-cribe (ə–skraɪb) v. -cribed, -cribing To attribute to a specific cause, source, or origin; to think of as belonging to: *To what do you ascribe your success?*/ *Ascribe to the Lord the glory due his name; worship the Lord in the splendor of his holiness* (Psalm 29:2).

ash (æʃ) n. **1.** The hard wood of a forest tree or the tree itself **2.** The soft gray powder remaining after sthg. has been burned: *We found the ring in the ashes of the house that had burned.*

a-shamed (ə–ʃeʸmd) adj. Feeling shame, guilt, sorrow, or unwillingness because of fear or shame: *I am ashamed of myself for being so rude.*/ *Jesus said, "If anyone is ashamed of me and of my words in this adulterous and sinful generation, the Son of Man will be ashamed of him when he comes in his Father's glory with the holy angels"* (Mark 8:38). *I am not ashamed of the gospel [of Jesus Christ], because it is the power of God for the salvation of everyone who believes* (Romans 1:16).

ash-en (æʃ–ən) adj. **1.** Of or resembling ashes **2.** Deadly pale: *She looked ashen after hearing the news of his death.*

a-shore (ə–ʃɔr) adv. On, onto, or to the shore or land: *We swam ashore.*

ash-ram (æsh–rəm) n. A place of religious retreat, esp. in India

Ash Wednes-day n. The first day of Lent, called such because of the custom in the early church of sprinkling ashes on the heads of penitent sinners. Lent is a period of forty days before Easter, the day of our Lord's resurrection. It is a period of fasting for many Christians in commemoration of the suffering and death of our Savior for the sins of the world on Good Friday, the Friday before Easter. —see LENT, GOOD FRIDAY, EASTER, JESUS

A-sia (eʸ–ʒə) n. The world's largest continent, extending from the Ural Mountains and the Aegean Sea to the Pacific Ocean and from the Arctic to the Indian Ocean, approximately 16,500,000 sq. mi.

A-sian (eʸ–ʒən) adj. Concerning Asia

Asian n. A person from Asia

a-side (ə–saɪd) adv. **1.** To or toward the side **2.** Out of the way **3.** aside from **(a)** Besides; in addition to: *Aside from being pretty, she's also very talented.* **(b)** With the exception of: *Aside from poor eyesight, he's in perfect health.*

as-i-nine (æs–ə–nam) adj. Stupid; silly

ask (æsk) v. **1.** To call on a person for an answer; inquire: *The man asked the stranger what his name was.* **2.** Request: *It's difficult for me to ask anyone for money.*/ *If any of you lacks wisdom, he should ask God who gives generously to all without finding fault and it will be given to him* (James 1:5). *Jesus said to his disciples, "I will do whatever you ask in my name, so that the Son [Jesus] may bring glory to the Father. You may ask me for anything in my name, and I will do it"* (John 14:13-14). —see PRAYER

a-skance (əs–kæns) adv. **1.** With a side glance **2.** With distrust: *She looked askance at his offer to help.*

a-skew (ə–skyuʷ) adj. Not straight

a-sleep (ə–sliʸp) adj. **1.** Sleeping —opposite AWAKE **2.** Of an arm or leg that has been in one position too long, not able to feel; numb

asp (æsp) n. A small poisonous snake

as-par-a-gus (ə–speər–ə–gəs) n. A type of plant whose young shoots are eaten as a vegetable

as-pect (æs–pɛkt) n. A particular side of a many-sided idea, plan, proposal, etc.: *You need to consider every aspect of your plan to avoid problems.*

as-pen (æs–pən) n. A kind of poplar tree with leaves that flutter in the slightest breeze

as-per-sion (ə–spɜr–ʒən) n. A malicious or slanderous statement

as-phalt (æs–fɔlt) n. **1.** A black, sticky substance, which, when mixed with gravel, is used for paving streets, driveways, etc. **2.** asphalt jungle A part of a big city where people feel threatened by violence and crime

as-phyx-i-ate (æs–fɪk–siʸ–eʸt) v. -ated, -ating To suffocate; smother —**as-phyx-i-a-tion** (æs–fɪk–siʸ–eʸ–ʃən) n.

as-pi-rate (æs–pə–rət) n. **1.** The speech sound represented in English by the "h" in "hat" **2.** A speech sound that has a puff of breath as its final element

as-pi-rate (æs–pə–reʸt) v. To suck in or draw in, as by inhaling

as-pi-ra-tion (æs–pə–re^y–ʃən) n. **1.** A strong desire to achieve sthg. noble **2.** The object of this desire **3.** The pronunciation of a consonant with an aspirate, such as the "h" in "hat"

as-pire (ə–spaɪ–ər) v. **-spired, -spiring** To have a noble desire or ambition: *He aspires to be a great leader of men.* —**as-pir-ant** (æs–pə–rənt/ ə–spaɪ–rənt) n. —**as-piring** adj.

as-pi-rin (æs–pə–rən) n. **-rin** or **-rins** A medicine that lessens pain and fever

ass (æs) n. **1.** An animal like a horse but smaller and with longer ears: *Donkeys and burros are domesticated asses.* **2.** *infml.* A stupid, foolish person **3.** *AmE. infml.* Vulgar for **buttocks**

as-sail (ə–se^yl) v. To attack: *He was assailed by questions from all sides.*

as-sail-ant (ə–se^yl–ənt) n. A person who attacks: *His assailant came up behind him in the dark.*

as-sas-sin (ə–sæs–ən) n. A murderer, esp. of a political figure

as-sas-sin-ate (ə–sæs–ən–e^yt) v. **-ated, -ating** To murder by sudden or secret attack, esp. someone who is important politically —**as-sas-si-na-tion** (ə–sæs–ə–ne^y–ʃən) n.

as-sault (ə–sɔlt) n. A violent attack, usu. sudden: *They began their assault on the fortress at midnight.* —**assault** v. *He was imprisoned for assaulting a fifteen year old girl.*

as-sem-blage (ə–sɛm–blɪdʒ) n. **1.** A collection of persons or things **2.** The act or process of assembling **3.** The fitting together, as of the parts of a machine

as-sem-ble (ə–sɛm–bəl) v. **-bled, -bling 1.** To gather people together: *A large crowd assembled in front of the governor's office.* **2.** To put together: *to assemble a bicycle*

as-sem-bly (ə–sɛm–bli^y) n. **-blies 1.** The meeting of a group of people for a special purpose: *There was a special speaker at our high school assembly.* **2.** In some states of the US, a law-making body, esp. the lower of two such bodies: *the California State Assembly*

as-sem-bly line (ə–sɛm–bli^y lam) n. A line of factory workers and equipment on which the work passes consecutively from worker to worker until completed

as-sent (ə–sɛnt) v. To express agreement

NOTE: Do not confuse **assent** with **ascent**

as-sert (ə–sɜrt) v. **1.** To state positively: *She asserted that she would not go.* **2.** To defend or maintain: *They asserted their right to disagree.* **3. assert oneself** To insist on one's rights or on being recognized —**assertion** n. —**assertive** adj. —**assertively** adv.

as-sess (ə–sɛs) v. **1.** To set the value on property for some special purpose: *For taxation purposes the house was assessed at $90,000.* **2.** To decide on the quality or worth of: *The driver assessed the damages done by the accident.* —**assessment** n.

as-set (æ–sɛt) n. Anything owned, such as a building or furniture, that has value and that may be sold to pay a debt: *It's a large company with many assets.*

as-sid-u-ous (ə–sɪdʒ–u^w–əs) adj. **1.** Diligent; attentive **2.** Persistent

as-sign (ə–saɪn) v. **1.** To give as a share or for one's use: *Each student was assigned a book for use in the class.* **2.** To appoint; decide on

as-sign-ment (ə–saɪn–mənt) n. A job which one is given or to which one is being sent: *a classroom assignment*

as-sim-i-late (ə–sɪm–ə–le^yt) v. **-lated, -lating 1.** To take in, digest, and change food into living tissue: *Plants assimilate food from the earth.* **2.** To take in; to understand: *I can't assimilate all this information at once.* **3.** To make or become similar —**as-sim-i-la-tion** (ə–sɪm–ə–le^y–ʃən) n.

as-sist (ə–sɪst) v. To help or give support: *They assisted the elderly lady across the street.*

as-sist-ance (ə–sɪst–əns) n. Help; support: *Can I be of any assistance?*

as-sist-ant (ə–sɪst–ənt) n. A person who helps another, as in a job, and is under that person's direction

as-so-ci-ate (ə–so^w–ʃi^y–e^yt) v. **-ated, -ating 1.** To join socially or in business: *He associates with many important people in his job./ Do not associate with one who is easily angered, or you may learn his ways and get yourself ensnared* (Proverbs 22:24,25). *On the other hand, "Do not be proud, but be willing to associate with people of low position. Do not be conceited"* (Romans 12:16). **2.** To connect in one's thoughts: *What do you associate with vacation?*

as-so-ci-ate (ə-soʷ-ʃiʸ-ət) n. **1.** A person connected with another as a friend, business partner, fellow student, etc.: *The two were business associates until they had an argument.* **2. associate degree** A degree given after two years' study, usu. at a junior college or a community college

as-so-ci-a-tion (ə-soʷ-ʃiʸ-eʸ-ʃən) n. **1.** An organization formed for a particular purpose: *an association of artists* **2.** Joining or being joined with sbdy. or sthg.: *They are working in association with each other.* **3.** The act of connecting things, esp. in the thoughts —opposite DISSOCIATION

as-sort (ə-sɔrt) v. To distribute into like groups; to classify

as-sort-ed (ə-sɔrt-əd) adj. Consisting of various kinds: *He gave his wife a box of assorted chocolates.*

as-suage (ə-sweʸdʒ) v. -suaged, -suag-ing **1.** To make less severe **2.** To satisfy

as-sume (ə-suʷm) v. -sumed, -suming **1.** To take as a fact though not proved: *I assumed he was telling the truth.* **2.** To take upon oneself: *He assumed full responsibility for the accident.* **3.** To pretend to have: *She is going under an assumed name.*

as-sump-tion (ə-sʌmp-ʃən) n. **1.** Sthg. assumed: *I was under the assumption that you were coming tomorrow.* **2.** The act of assuming: *His assumption of leadership proved disastrous.*

as-sur-ance (ə-ʃʊər-əns) n. **1.** Confidence: *He has great assurance in his own ability.* **2.** A promise: *He gave me his assurance that he'd be here tomorrow.*

as-sure (ə-ʃʊər) v. -sured, -suring **1.** To make sthg. certain: *That field goal with less than a minute to play assured our victory.* **2.** To state positively: *I assured him that I'd be there.* **3.** To give confidence to: *He assured me that my application would be accepted.*

as-ter-isk (æs-tə-rɪsk) n. A star-shaped character (*) used as a reference mark or as an indication of the omission of letters or words

a-stern (ə-stɜrn) adj., adv. **1.** At or near the rear of a ship or airplane **2.** Behind a vessel

asth-ma (æz-mə) n. A respiratory disease, often arising from allergies, characterized by difficulty in breathing, tightness of the chest, and coughing —**asthmatic** is (æz-mæt-ɪk) adj., n.

a-stir (ə-stɜr) adj. Being in action; moving

as-ton-ish (ə-stɑn-ɪʃ) v. To fill with sudden wonder or amazement —**astonishing** adj. —**astonishment** n.

as-tound (ə-staʊnd) v. To fill with bewildered wonder —**astounding** adj. —**astoundingly** adv.

as-tral (æs-trəl) adj. Of or relating to the stars

a-stray (ə-streʸ) adj., adv. Off the right way, esp. so as to be in error: *Our dog isn't here; he must have gone astray./ spir. All we like sheep have gone astray ... and the Lord laid on him [Jesus] the iniquity of us all* (Isaiah 53:6).

a-stride (ə-straɪd) prep. With a leg on each side of

as-trin-gent (ə-strɪn-dʒənt) adj. **1.** Able or tending to shrink body tissues **2.** Harsh; severe

as-trol-o-gy (ə-strɑl-ə-dʒiʸ) n. The study of the supposed influence of the stars and other heavenly bodies on human affairs. NOTE: Astrologers claim they can foretell, from the movements of the heavenly bodies, both the fate of nations and the characters and fortunes of individuals. Astrology is a type of divination and as such is strongly condemned by God in His Holy Word, the Bible: "Let no one be found among you who...practices divination..." (Deuteronomy 18:10). God also speaks out concerning the futility (uselessness) of such a practice, saying: "*Let your astrologers come forward, those stargazers who make predictions month by month,... They cannot even save themselves*" (Isaiah 47:13,14). Astrology is a sin, and the wages of sin is death. God hates sin, and all people are sinners, but he is also a God of love and mercy and forgiveness, and if we truly repent and turn from our sinful ways and put our trust in Jesus for salvation, we shall have eternal life. In his grace and mercy he has provided the way of forgiveness. "The wages of sin is death, but the gift of God is eternal life through Jesus Christ our Lord" (Romans 6:23). —see JESUS, SIN,

GRACE, FORGIVENESS

as-tro-naut (æs-trə-nɔt) n. A traveler in a spacecraft, esp. as a crew member

as-tro-nau-tics (æs-trə-nɔt-ɪks) n. *pl.* The science of the construction and operation of spacecraft

as-tro-nom-i-cal (æs-trə-nɑm-ɪ-kəl) adj. 1. Of or relating to astronomy 2. Extremely large: *an astronomical amount of money*

as-tron-o-my (ə-strɑn-ə-miᵞ) n. The scientific study of the positions, distribution, motion, and compositions of the stars and other heavenly bodies, not to be confused with astrology which is not scientific —**astronomer** n.

as-tute (ə-stuʷt) adj. Shrewdly discerning; cunning; clever; keen in judgment

a-sun-der (ə-sʌn-dər) adv. 1. Into parts or pieces 2. Apart in direction

a-sy-lum (ə-saɪ-ləm) n. 1. A place of refuge 2. Protection given esp. to political figures 3. An institution for the care of the needy, esp. for the insane

at (ət) strong (æt) prep. 1. Shows a point in time or space: *She arrives at the office every day at 8:00 ᴀ.m.* 2. Shows an intended aim or object in the direction of: *He shot at the bear.* 3. Used when one acts or feels in answer to sthg.: *I smiled at the memory of such good times.* 4. Shows that sbdy. does sthg. well, badly, etc.: *He's good at music.* 5. Shows what one is doing or one's state of being: *He was hard at work./at peace with himself*

ate (eᵞt) v. Past tense of eat

a-the-ism (eᵞ-θiᵞ-ɪzm) n. Disbelief in the existence of God

a-the-ist (eᵞ-θiᵞ-əst) n. A person who believes that there is no God. God, however, has revealed himself very clearly in his Holy Word, the Bible. —see GOD, BIBLE

ath-lete (æθ-liᵞt) n. A person who practices bodily exercises and games that need strength and speed such as running and jumping

ath-let-ic (æθ-lɛt-ɪk) adj. 1. Of or concerning athletes or athletics 2. Strong in body, skillful, active, etc., with plenty of muscle

ath-let-ics (æθ-lɛt-ɪks) n. The practice of bodily exercises and of sports demanding strength and speed

at-las (æt-ləs) n. A book of maps

at-mos-phere (æt-məs-frər) n. 1. The air around the earth 2. Any surrounding feeling: *a friendly atmosphere* —**atmospheric** adj.

at-oll (æ-tɔl/eᵞ-) n. A ring-shaped coral reef enclosing a lagoon

at-om (æt-əm) n. The smallest particle of a chemical element that can exist alone or in combination

a-tom-ic (ə-tɑm-ɪk) adj. Of or related to atoms: *atomic energy/ atomic bombs*

at-om-iz-er (æt-ə-maɪ-zər) n. A device for reducing a liquid to a very fine spray: *the atomizer on the perfume bottle* —**atomize** v.

a-tone (ə-toʷn) v. -toned, -toning 1. To make payment for sins, crime, etc.: *She tried to atone for her neglect of the children by buying them lots of toys.* 2. To provide or make possible man's salvation and reconciliation to God: *He [Jesus] is the atoning sacrifice for our sins, and not only for ours, but for the sins of the whole world* (1 John 2:2). —see JESUS

a-tone-ment (ə-toʷn-mənt) n. The act that provides or makes possible salvation and reconciliation between man and God. Jesus Christ suffered and died as the one true sacrifice, making complete satisfaction for the sin of the world: *We rejoice in God through our Lord Jesus Christ, by whom we have now received the atonement (Romans 5:11).* —see JESUS

at-ri-um (eᵞ-triᵞ-əm) n. 1. Either of the two upper cavities of the heart into which the veins pour blood 2. The central court of a Roman house

a-tro-cious (ə-troʷ-ʃəs) adj. 1. Savagely cruel; brutal; wicked 2. Very bad: *These prices are atrocious.* —**atrociousness** n.

a-troc-i-ty (ə-trɑs-ət-iᵞ) n. -ties 1. The quality or state of being atrocious 2. An atrocious act or object: *The invading army committed many atrocities on innocent women and children.*

at-ro-phy (æ-trə-fiᵞ) n. -phies Decrease in size or the wasting away of a bodily part or tissue

atrophy v. -phied, -phying To cause or to

undergo atrophy

at-tach (ə-tætʃ) v. To fix, to fasten by sticking, tying, etc.; join: *We attached a padlock to the trunk to prevent its being opened.*

at-tached (ə-tætʃt) adj. To be fond of someone or something: *She was very attached to her old doll even though it was cracked and dirty.*

at-tach-ment (ə-tætʃ-mənt) n. **1.** Connection by ties of affection or regard **2.** A device attached to a machine or instrument **3.** A connection by which one thing is attached to another **4.** Legal seizure of property

at-tack (ə-tæk) v. **1.** To use force against in order to harm, esp. with weapons: *He was attacked by a robber.* **2.** To speak or write against: *The president's views on foreign policy were attacked by the newspapers.* **3.** To hurt, damage, etc., esp. by a continuing action: *The disease attacked the pine trees, causing great damage to the forest.* **4.** To begin with eagerness in a forceful way: *We attacked the problem at once and soon found an answer.* —**attacker** n.

attack n. **1.** An act of violence intended to cause damage: *Enemy attacks often come at night.* **2.** Written or spoken words intended to damage: *an attack on the senator's policies* **3.** A sudden, serious illness, esp. one which tends to return: *a heart attack*

at-tain (ə-teⁿ) v. **1.** Achieve; accomplish: *He attained great success as an author.* **2.** To arrive at; reach: *He attained the age of 96.*

at-tain-ment (ə-teⁿ-mənt) n. **1.** The act of attaining: *The attainment of wealth did not make him happy.* **2.** Sthg. one has attained: *a woman of many attainments*

at-tempt (ə-tempt) v. To make an effort at; try: *I attempted to learn to speak Navajo but was not very successful.*

attempt n. An effort made to do sthg.

at-tend (ə-tend) v. **1.** To be present at; go to: *Do you plan to attend the concert?* **2.** To look after; care for **3.** To pay attention to **4.** To accompany as a result: *Success attended his efforts.*

at-ten-dance (ə-tend-əns) n. **1.** The act of being present, esp. regularly: *She had perfect attendance all through school.* **2.** The number of those present: *The attendance at the meeting was about 200.*

at-ten-dant (ə-ten-dənt) n. A person who takes care of a place or person: *a service station attendant*

at-ten-tion (ə-ten-ʃən) n. **1.** The act of keeping the mind closely on sthg., esp. by watching or listening; complete and careful thought: *Please pay attention. This is an important matter.* —opposite INATTENTION **2.** Particular care and action: *Young children need a lot of attention.* **3.** at/ to attention A military position in which a soldier stands straight and still

at-ten-tive (ə-ten-tɪv) adj. Taking careful notice: *The eyes of the Lord are on the righteous and his ears are attentive to their prayer* (1 Peter 3:12). —opposite INATTENTIVE —**attentively** adv. —**atten-tiveness** n.

at-test (ə-test) v. **1.** To testify: *The witness attested as to the good character of the accused.* **2.** To certify as genuine by signing as a witness —**at-tes-ta-tion** (æ-tɛs-teⁿ-ʃən) n.

at-tic (æt-ɪk) n. The room or space in a building just below the roof

at-tire (ə-taɪ-ər) n. Clothing

at-ti-tude (æt-ə-tuʷd) n. A manner of acting that shows one's inward thoughts and feelings: *His friendly attitude showed his concern for others./ Your attitude should be the same as that of Jesus Christ, who, being in very nature God ... made himself nothing ... (and) humbled himself and became obedient unto death — even death on a cross* (Philippians 2:5-8). —see HOLY SPIRIT, JESUS

at-tor-ney (ə-tɜr-niʸ) n. -neys One who has legal power to act for another, esp. a lawyer

at-tor-ney at law (ə-tɜr-niʸ æt lɔ) n. A lawyer

at-tract (ə-trækt) v. To draw to itself or oneself; to cause to like, notice, or turn towards: *She was attracted by his friendly smile.*

at-trac-tion (ə-træk-ʃən) n. **1.** The capability or act of attracting: *The idea of a vacation in Hawaii has a lot of attraction for me.* **2.** Sthg. which attracts: *Major league baseball games are sometimes called "sports attractions."*

at-trac-tive (ə-træk-tɪv) adj. **1.** Able to attract: *The offer of such a position is very attractive.* **2.** Pretty or handsome: *an attractive child/ book*

cover —opposite UNATTRACTIVE —see BEAUTIFUL

at-trib-ute (ə–trɪb–yuᵂt) v. **-uted, -uting 1.** To think of as being written or produced by: *This play has been attributed to Shakespeare.* **2.** To think of as being caused by: *His illness was attributed to his long exposure to the cold weather.* **—at-trib-u-tion** (æ–trə–byuᵂ–ʃən) n.

at-tri-bute (æ–trə–byuᵂt) n. An inherent characteristic: *The attributes of God include holiness, love, mercy, compassion, forgiveness, faithfulness and justice. He is also eternal, all-knowing, all-powerful, and ever-present.*

at-trib-u-tive (ə–trɪb–yuᵂ–tɪv) adj. **1.** Of or like an attribute **2.** *gram.* (of adjectives or nouns) Used directly before a noun, to describe it

at-tri-tion (ə–trɪ–ʃən) n. **1.** The act or process of wearing away or grinding down by friction **2.** The loss in the personnel of an organization in the normal course of events

at-tune (ə–tuᵂn) v. To bring into harmony

au-burn (ɔ–bərn) adj. Reddish brown

auc-tion (ɔk–ʃən) also **sale** n. A public sale where goods are sold to the person who offers the most money: *a book auction*

auction v. To sell by auction

au-da-cious (ɔ–deʸ–ʃəs) adj. **1.** Daring; bold **2.** Insolent **—audaciously** adv. **—audaciousness** n.

au-da-ci-ty (ɔ–dæ–sə–tiʸ) n. Impudence: *He had the audacity to tell me I was fat.*

au-di-ble (ɔ–də–bəl) adj. Capable of being heard **—au-di-bil-i-ty** (ɔd–ə–bɪl–ət–iʸ) n. **—audibly** adv.

au-di-ence (ɔ–diʸ–əns) n. All the people listening to or watching a performance, speech, radio program, television show, etc.

au-di-o (ɔ–diʸ–oᵂ) adj. Of or relating to sound or its reproduction

au-di-o-vis-u-al (ɔ–diʸ–oᵂ–vɪ–ʒyuᵂ–əl) adj. Of or concerning both sight and sound

au-dit (ɔd–ɪt) n. A formal examination and verification of financial records

audit v. **1.** To make an audit of: *A Certified Public Accountant audited our books.* **2.** To attend a course (e.g., in college) without expecting credit

au-di-tion (ɔ–dɪ–ʃən) n. A trial performance to appraise an entertainer's merits

au-di-tor (ɔd–ət–ər) n. **1.** A listener **2.** One who audits

au-di-to-ri-um (ɔ–də–tɔ–riʸ–əm) n. The room or space in a theater, hall, etc., for people to sit when listening to or watching a performance

au-di-to-ry (ɔ–də–tɔ–riʸ) adj. Of hearing

au-ger (ɔ–gər) v. A tool with a spiral cutting edge for boring holes

aug-ment (ɔg–mɛnt) v. To enlarge; increase **—aug-men-ta-tion** (ɔg–mən–teʸ–ʃən) n.

Au-gust (ɔ–gəst) also **Aug.** *written abbr.* n. The eighth month of the year

au-gust (ɔ–gʌst) adj. Full of dignity; imposing

aunt (ænt/ ɑnt) n. The sister of one's father or mother or the wife of one's uncle

au-ra (ɔr–ə) n. *pl.* **-ras, rae** (–reʸ) A distinctive air or atmosphere surrounding a person: *an aura of happiness*

au-ral (ɔr–əl) adj. Pertaining to the ear or sense of hearing

au-ri-cle (ɔr–ə–kəl) n. **1.** The outer portion of the ear **2.** An ear-like part or appendage **3.** A small appendage to the atrium of the heart

au-ric-u-lar (ɔ–rɪk–yʊ–lər) adj. **1.** Aural **2.** Perceived by the ear **3.** Shaped like an ear **4.** Pertaining to an auricle of the heart

au-ro-ra bo-re-a-lis (ɔ–rɔr–ə bɔr–iʸ–æl–ɪs) n. Bands of colored light seen in the night sky near the North Pole, thought to be of electrical origin

aus-pi-ces (ɔs–pə–səs) n. *pl.* Control or supervision

aus-pi-cious (ɔ–spɪʃ–əs) adj. Showing signs that promise success **—auspi-ciously** adv.

aus-tere (ɔ–stɪər) adj. **1.** Stern; severe; strict **2.** Severely simple and plain, without adornment or comfort

aus-ter-i-ty (ɔs–tɛɑr–ə–tiʸ) n. **-ties** An austere condition

Aus-tra-lia (ɔs–treʸ–lyə) n. An English-speaking continent and country southeast of Asia, about the size of the US, area 2,967,909 sq. mi.

Aus-tra-lian (ɔs–treʸ–lyən) adj. Pertaining to Australia

au-then-tic (ɔ–θɛn–tɪk) adj. That has in fact

been made, painted, written, etc. by the person who is claimed to have done it; gen uine —**authentically** adv. —**au-then-tic-i-ty** (ɔ-θɛn-tɪs-ə-tiʸ) n.

au-then-ti-cate (ɔ-θɛn-tə-keʸt) v. -**cated,** -**cating** To prove the authenticity of sthg. —**au-then-ti-ca-tion** (ɔ-θɛn-tə-keʸ-ʃən) n.

au-thor (ɔ-θər) n. The person who wrote a book, newspaper article, play, poem, etc.

au-thor-i-tar-i-an (ɔ-θɔr-ə-teər-iʸ-ən) adj. **1.** Characterized by or favoring blind obedience to authority **2.** Characterized by or favoring concentration of political power in an authority that is not responsible to the people

au-thor-i-ta-tive (ɔ-θɔr-ə-teʸ-tɪv) adj. Being an authority; trustworthy

au-thor-i-ty (ə-θɔr-ə-tiʸ) n. -**ties 1.** A person or group holding the ability, power, or right, to control and command: *The president is the top authority in some countries.* **2.** Power to influence, esp. resulting from experience, knowledge, etc.: *to speak with authority/Jesus said, "All authority in heaven and on earth has been given to me"* (Matthew 28:18).

au-thor-i-za-tion (ɔ-θər-ə-zeʸ-ʃən) n. The ability, power, right, etc. to control: *Where did you get the authorization to enter this building?*

au-thor-ize (ɔ-θə-raɪz) v. -**ized, -izing 1.** To give legal power to **2.** To sanction **3.** To justify —**authorized** adj. —op-posite UNAUTHORIZED

au-tism (ɔ-tɪzm) n. A state of mind characterized by daydreaming and disregard of reality

au-to (ɔt-oʷ- /ɑt-) n. *infml.* Automobile

au-to- (ɔt-oʷ- /ɑt-/ -ə-) prefix By oneself or itself

au-to-bi-og-ra-phy (ɔ-tə-baɪ-ɑg-rə-fiʸ) n. A book written about oneself —**au-to-bi-o-graph-i-cal** (ɔ-toʷ-baɪ-ə-græf-ɪ-kəl) adj.

au-to-cra-cy (ɔ-tɑ-krə-siʸ) n. -**cies** Government by one person having unlimited power

au-to-crat (ɔt-ə-kræt) n. A ruler with unlimited power; a dictator —**au-to-crat-ic** (ɔt-ə-kræt-ɪk) adj.

au-to-graph (ɔ-tə-græf) n. **1.** An original manuscript **2.** A person's signature, written by hand

autograph v. To write one's signature on something: *Will you autograph this picture for me please?*

au-to-mat-ic (ɔ-tə-mæt-ɪk) adj. **1.** Able to work or move without needing a person to operate it: *The air-conditioner is automatic. It turns itself off and on.* **2.** Done as a habit, without thought: *With practice, hitting the right keys when typing can become automatic to you.* **3.** Sure to happen: *Your yearly vacation is automatic.* —**automatically** adv.

au-to-ma-tion (ɔt-ə-meʸ-ʃən) n. The use of automatic equipment

au-to-mo-bile (ɔ-tə-mə-biʸl/ ɔ-tə-mə-biʸl) adj. *AmE. fml.* Car; having to do with cars: *Automobile production goes up every year.*

au-to-mo-tive (ɔt-ə-moʷ-tɪv) adj. Of or relating to motor vehicles

au-ton-o-mous (ɔ-tɑn-ə-məs) adj. Having the right or power of self-gov-ernment

au-top-sy (ɔ-tɑp-siʸ) n. -**sies** Examination of a dead body to determine the cause of death

au-tumn (ɔ-təm) n. Fall; September to December 21st in the Northern Hemisphere

aux-il-ia-ry (ɔg-zɪl-yə-riʸ) adj. **1.** Providing help **2.** Functioning in a subsidiary way

auxiliary n. -**ries 1.** An auxiliary person, group, or device **2.** An auxiliary verb: *In the sentence, "He has gone," the word "has" is an auxiliary.* **3. Auxiliaries** Auxiliary troops

a-vail (ə-veʸl) v. To be of help or advantage: *He availed himself of the opportunity.* (= made use of it)

avail n. Effectiveness; advantage: *He tried to revive her, but it was to no avail.*

a-vail-a-ble (ə-veʸl-ə-bəl) adj. Capable of being gotten, obtained, used, seen, etc.: *Is this coat available in size 12?* —opposite UNAVAILABLE —**a-vail-a-bil-i-ty** (ə-veʸl-ə-bɪl-ə-tiʸ) n.

av-a-lanche (æv-ə-læntʃ) n. **1.** A mass of snow or rock pouring down a mountainside **2.** A great amount suddenly: *an avalanche of mail*

a-vant-garde (ə-vɑnt-gɑrd) n. The leaders in new or unconventional movements —**avant-garde** adj.

av-a-rice (æv-ə-rɪs) n. Greed for gain —**av-a-**

ri-cious (æv–ə–ɪʃ–əs) —avari-ciously adv.

a-venge (ə–vɛndʒ) v. avenged, avenging **1.** To take revenge: *He felt that he had to avenge the wrong./ Do not take revenge, my friends, but leave room for God's wrath, for it is written: "It is mine to avenge; I will repay," says the Lord* (Romans 12:19). **2.** To take vengeance on behalf of someone: *He avenged his father's death.*

av-e-nue (æv–ə–nuʷ) also **Ave.** *written abbr.* n. Part of the name of a wide street in a city: *Fifth Avenue/ fig.* They explored every avenue (=tried every possible way) but could not find a way to cut expenses.

av-er-age (æv–ər–ɪdʒ/ æv–rɪdʒ) n. **1.** The amount reached when one adds together several quantities and then divides by the number of quantities: *The average of 4, 6, and 11 is 7.* **2.** A level thought of as usual or ordinary: *The boy's intelligence is far above average.* —**average** adj. *My weight is average for my height and age.*

average v. **-aged, -aging 1.** To be or amount to an average: *The number of books I read averages about just one per month.* **2.** To figure out the average of figures

a-verse (ə–vɜrs) adj. Opposed

a-ver-sion (ə–vɜr–ʒən) n. **1.** A strong dislike **2.** Something disliked

a-vert (ə–vɜrt) v. To prevent; to ward off: *They turned just in time to avert disaster.*

a-vi-ar-y (eʸ–viʸ–ɛər–iʸ) n. **-ies** A place for keeping birds

a-vi-a-tion (eʸ–viʸ–eʸ–ʃən) n. **1.** The science or practice of flying airplanes **2.** The aircraft industry

a-vi-a-tor (eʸ–viʸ–eʸ–tər) n. The pilot of some type of aircraft

av-id (æv–əd) adj. **1.** Craving eagerly **2.** Enthusiastic in pursuit of an interest —**avidly** adv.

av-o-ca-do (æv–ə–kɑ–doʷ) n. **1.** A tropical American tree **2.** The soft, oily fruit of this tree

av-o-ca-tion (æv–ə–keʸ–ʃən) n. A hobby or minor occupation

a-void (ə–vɔɪd) v. To stay away from, esp. on purpose: *I try to avoid too much fat in my diet./ Avoid every kind of evil* (1 Thessalonians 5:22). —**avoidable** adj. —**avoidance** n.

av-oir-du-pois (æv–ər–də–pɔɪ) n. **1.** The system of weights in Britain and the US based on 16 ounces in the pound **2.** *infml.* Bodily weight, esp. personal weight

a-vow (ə–vaʊ) v. To declare openly

a-wait (ə–weʸt) v. To wait for; expect

a-wake (ə–weʸk) adj. Not asleep; having awoken: *I have trouble staying awake when I drive long distances.*

awake (ə–weʸk) v. also **awaken** (ə–weʸk–ən) v. **awoke** (ə–woʷk) or **awaked, awakened** or **awoken** (ə–woʷk–ən) To cause to be no longer asleep

a-wak-en-ing (ə–weʸk–ən–ɪŋ) n. The act of waking from sleep

a-ward (ə–wɔrd) n. Sthg. granted as the result of an official decision, esp. money or a prize

award v. To give, esp. as the result of an official decision

a-ware (ə–wɛər) adj. Having knowl- edge of or understanding about: *aware of the facts* —opposite UNAWARE —**awareness** n.

a-way (ə–weʸ) adv. **1.** From any given place; in another direction: *She said she was going away but she didn't tell us where./ He drove away from the house.* **2.** At a stated distance: *How far away do you live?* **3.** In a secure place: *Put your books away, please.* (=in your desk) **4.** So as to be all used up: *We gave all the food away to the hungry children.* **5. right away** At once: *We are leaving right away!*

awe (ɔ) n. A mixed feeling of reverence, fear, and wonder, inspired by God or caused by something sacred, majestic, or mysterious: *When the crowd saw Jesus heal the paralytic man, they were filled with awe; and they praised God, who had given such authority to men* (Matthew 9:8).

awe-some (ɔ–səm) adj. Worthy of awe, wonder, reverence, etc.: *How awesome is the Lord Most High, the great King over all the earth!* (Psalm 47:2).

awe-struck (ɔ–strʌk) **awe-strick-en** (ɔ–strɪk–ən) adj. Suddenly struck or filled with awe

aw-ful (ɔ–fəl) adj. **1.** Terrible; shocking: *The accident was awful.* **2.** *infml.* Very bad; very great: *an awful storm*

aw-ful-ly (ɔf–ə–liʸ) adv. Very: *awfully pretty/*

awfully old

a-while (ə–waɪl) adv. *esp. lit.* For a short period of time: *We waited awhile before calling a second time.*

awk-ward (ɔk–wərd) adj. **1.** Not skillful in moving the body or parts of the body easily; clumsy: *The dancer's movements were quite awkward. He was a poor dancer.* **2.** Not well made for easy use: *an awkward place to reach* **3.** Hard to deal with; not convenient; embarrassing: *Six o'clock would be an awkward time for us to meet. We're having guests for dinner at six thirty.* —**awkwardly** adv. —**awkwardness** n.

awl (ɔl) n. A pointed tool for boring small holes

awn-ing (ɔ–nɪŋ) n. A canvas cover to give shelter

a-woke (ə–woʷk) v. Past tense of **awake**

a-wry (ə–raɪ) adv. **1.** Twisted to one side **2.** Amiss: *Our plans went awry.* —**awry** adj. Crooked; wrong

ax; also **axe** (æks) n. **axes** (æks–ɪz) A long handled tool with a heavy metal blade, used to cut down trees, etc.

ax; also **axe** (æks) v. **axed, axing** *infml.* To remove suddenly and usu. without warning: *His job was axed when the company decided to close the art department.*

ax-i-om (æk–siʸ–əm) n. **1.** A statement generally accepted as true; maxim **2.** A statement regarded as an evident truth

ax-is (æk–sɪs) n. *pl.* **axes** (æk–siʸz) **1.** A real or imaginary straight line that passes through the center of a body that actually or supposedly revolves upon it: *the earth's axis* **2.** An alliance between major world powers

ax-le (æks–əl) n. A bar usu. with a wheel on either end, around which the wheels turn: *The rear axle of our car was broken in the accident.*

aye (aɪ) adv. Yes —**aye** n. A vote in favor of a proposal

a-zal-ea (ə–zeʸl–yə) n. A shrub-like flowering plant

az-ure (æʒ–ər) n. The blue of the clear sky —**azure** adj.

B, b (bi^y) n. The second letter of the English alphabet

bab-ble (bæb–əl) v. **1.** To talk in a confused, meaningless way **2.** To make a low, bubbling sound, such as a brook does when flowing over rocks —**babbling** adj. *a babbling brook*

babe (be^yb) n. **1.** A baby **2.** *slang* A girl or woman

ba-bel (be^y–bəl) n. **1.** A confused mixture of voices **2. Babel** The place where men tried to build a tower to heaven but had to stop building when God confused their languages (Genesis 11: 1-9). Until that time, all people on earth spoke the same language and lived in the same general area, but when they could no longer understand one another, they were scattered over the face of the earth.

ba-boon (bæ–bu^wn) n. A large African monkey

ba-by (be^y–bi^y) n. **-bies 1.** A newly-born child; infant **2.** A newly-born animal: *When an elephant has a baby, it is called a "calf."* **3.** The youngest of a group: *Johnny is the baby of the class.*

bac-ca-lau-re-ate (bæk–ə–lɔ–ri^y–ət) n. **1.** A college degree **2.** A speech addressed to a graduating class at a college commencement

bach-e-lor (bætʃ–ə–lər) n. **1.** An unmarried man **2.** A person who holds a first university degree: *Bachelor of Science (abbr.: B.S.) Bachelor of Arts (abbr.: B.A.)*

back (bæk) n. **1.** The part of the body that is opposite to the front, reaching from the neck to the end of the spine: *The man was carrying a load on his back.* **2.** The part opposite the front: *the back of the building* **3.** The part of a chair that supports one's back when sitting **4. behind someone's back** Secretly; unknown to the person concerned: *The girls criticized their teacher behind her back.* **5. have one's back to/ against the wall** *infml.* To be in a desperate position, requiring a lot of hard work to overcome

back adv. **1.** Place where someone or something was before: *She put the dishes back in the cupboard.* **2.** Towards or at the rear; away

from the front: *She pulled her hair back off her face.* **3.** Away from the speaker: *Please stand back. I need to mop the floor where you're standing.* **4.** At an earlier date: *We first met back in 1959.* **5.** In reply: *Call me back at ten o'clock.* **6. back and forth** A movement backwards and forwards

back v. **1.** To go or cause to go in reverse: *The car backed down the street.* **2.** To encourage and support, esp. with financial help **3. back down** also **back off** To give in to an argument, opinion, or claim; admit defeat: *I had to back down when I saw that my grandfather was right.* **4. back out** To refuse to keep a promise, contract, etc.: *It will make it very difficult for everyone if you back out of your contract now.* **5. back sbdy. up** To support: *I'm really glad you backed up my story. Otherwise, I might have been in trouble.*

back adj. **1.** At the rear: *the back entrance/the backyard* **2.** Overdue: *back wages*

back-ache (bæk–e^yk) n. A pain in the back

back-bite (bæk–baɪt) v. **-bit, -bitten, -biting** To slander sbdy. who is not present

back-fire (bæk–faɪr) n. An explosion of prematurely ignited fuel, esp. from the exhaust of a motor vehicle

backfire v. **-fired, -firing** To explode in a backfire: *The car backfired.*

back-ground (bæk–graʊnd) n. **1.** The part of the scene that is behind the main object or event: *This is a picture of my boat. In the background, you can see an island.* **2.** The conditions surrounding an event: *The revolution took place against a background of financial and political difficulties.* **3.** A person's family, education, and experience: *a young man with a good family background*

back-lash (bæk–læʃ) n. **1.** A sudden backward movement **2.** A strong hostile reaction

back-log (bæk–lɔg) n. **1.** An accumulation, esp. of unfinished work **2.** A reserve supply

back-pack (bæk–pæk) n. A camping pack carried on the back

back-slap (bæk–slæp) v. **-slapped, -slapping** To display excessive cordiality —**backslapper** n.

back-slide (bæk–slaɪd) v. **-slid** or **-slid-den, -sliding** To go backward morally or in relig-

ious practice: *O Lord, do something for the sake of your name. For our backsliding is great; we have sinned against you* (Jeremiah 14:7).

back-talk (bæk–tɔk) n. A sarcastic or argumentative reply

back-ward (bæk–wərd) adj. **1.** Towards the back or the past: *a backward glance* **2.** Slow in development: *I have visited some very backward countries on this trip. Some places didn't even have electricity.*

back-wards (bæk–wərdz) also **backward** adv. **1.** Towards the beginning, the back, or the past: *"Was " spelled backwards is "saw."/ to jump backwards* **2.** With the back part in front: *The child put his shirt on backwards.* —see also FORWARDS

back-yard (bæk–yɑrd) n. An area behind a house, often covered with grass: *All the neighborhood children like to play in our backyard.*

ba-con (be^y–kən) n. Salted and smoked meat from the back or sides of a hog

bac-te-ri-a (bæk–trər–i^y–ə) n. The smallest forms of plant life, existing in water, soil, air, plants, and in the bodies of people and animals (Some of them cause disease, and some of them are necessary for fermentation and other useful processes.) —compare GERM

bac-te-ri-ol-o-gy (bæk–trər–i^y–ɑl–ə–dʒi^y) n. The scientific study of bacteria —**bacteriologist** n.

bad (bæd) adj. **worse** (wɜrs), **worst** (wɜrst) **1.** Not good; harmful: *Overeating is bad for your health./ I felt bad about missing your party last week.* **2.** Naughty; wicked; evil; sinful: *Sad to say, we have some very bad neighbors.* **3.** Disagreeable: *a bad taste* **4.** Serious; severe: *a bad cold* **5.** Defective; below standard: *bad plumbing* **6. a bad name** A poor reputation **7. That's too bad!** I'm sorry!: *You had to work on a holiday? That's too bad!*

badge (bædʒ) n. A small piece of material made of metal or plastic, to show a person's authority, employment, rank, or membership of a group

bad-ly (bæd–li^y) adv. **1.** In a poor manner: *badly–made toys/ to dance badly* —opposite WELL **2.** Greatly: *She was badly in need of*

some new shoes.

bad-min-ton (bæd–mɪnt–ən) n. A game similar to tennis in which a feathered cork, called a shuttlecock, is hit over a net with a racket

baf-fle (bæf–əl) v. **-fled, -fling 1.** To puzzle; to perplex **2.** To frustrate

bag (bæg) n. **1.** A soft–sided container made of paper, cloth, leather, etc., with an opening at the top that can be closed: *a paper bag/ a bag of apples* **2. in the bag** *infml.* Certain: *Our team is leading by a score of 19 to 2. The game is in the bag.*

ba-gel (be^y–gəl) n. A hard, doughnut–shaped roll, often eaten for breakfast

bag-gage (bæg–ɪdʒ) also **luggage** n. All the trunks, suitcases, and other containers used when a person travels

bail (be^yl) n. **1.** Money or property pledged as security by a person accused of a crime, guaranteeing that, if he is released temporarily, he will return to stand trial **2.** Permission for a person's release on such security

bail v. To allow or obtain the release of a person on bail

bail v. **1.** To scoop water out of a boat **2. bail out (a)** To relieve someone of financial difficulty in an emergency **(b)** To jump from an airplane in flight

bait (be^yt) v. **1.** To place bait on a hook to catch fish, or in a trap to catch animals **2.** To torment; harass **3.** To entice

bait n. **1.** Pieces of food used to attract and catch fish, animals, or birds: *He put some bait on a hook at the end of a line, and threw it into the water to try to catch a fish.* **2.** Anything used to tempt or entice

bake (be^yk) v. **baked, baking 1.** To cook with dry heat in an oven: *to bake a cake* **2.** To harden by heating: *In some parts of the world bricks are still baked in the sun to harden them.*

bak-er (be^yk–ər) n. A person who bakes bread, cakes, pies, etc., usu. as a profession

bak-er-y (be^yk–ər–i^y) n. **-ies** A place for baking and/or selling pies, cakes, bread, etc.

bal-ance (bæl–əns) v. **-anced, -ancing 1.** To bring into or keep in a state of balance: *The trained seal balanced a ball on its nose.* **2.** To show expenses to be equal to income: *The*

store's accounts balanced at the end of the first month.

balance n. **1.** An even distribution of weight; steadiness; not falling: *It's hard to keep your balance when walking on ice.* —opposite IM-BALANCE **2.** Something on one side which equals something on the other: *Try to keep a good balance in your diet between the different food groups.* **3.** An instrument for weighing things, esp. by comparing the amounts in two hanging pans: *fig. The man is very ill. His life hangs in the balance. (=is uncertain)* **4.** An amount which remains: *I will have to check my bank balance. (=see how much money I have in the bank)*

bal-co-ny (bǽl–kə–niʸ) n. -nies **1.** A place for people to stand or sit on, above street level, built onto the outside wall of a building, and entered through a door from an upper room: *We love sitting out on the balcony in the evenings.* **2.** The seats on an upper floor of a theater

bald (bɔld) adj. With no hair on all or part of the head: *The bald man wore a hat to protect his head from the hot sun.* —baldness n.

bale (beʸl) n. A large bundle of goods or material, tightly tied together: *a bale of hay* —bale v.

bale-ful (beʸl–fəl) adj. Harmful or threatening harm

balk (bɔk) v. **1.** To refuse to proceed **2.** To hinder or discourage **3.** In baseball, to make an illegal motion before pitching the ball, allowing all base runners to advance one base automatically

ball (bɔl) n. **1.** A solid or hollow sphere; a round or oval object used in play; anything of like shape: *tennis ball/ football/ ping-pong ball/ The children's ball rolled into the street.* **2.** An object that has been formed into a round shape by pressing or winding: *a ball of yarn/ a snowball* **3.** A rounded part of the body: *ball of the foot/ eyeball* **4.** A large formal social dance **5.** *infml.* A time of having fun: *We had a ball at the birthday party.* **6. on the ball** *infml.* Up-to-date, efficient, and ready to act: *Our new principal is really on the ball.* **7. play ball** *infml.* Cooperate: *You'd better play ball with me if you expect to keep your job.* **8.**

start/ keep the ball rolling To begin an activity, project, etc., or see that it continues

bal-lad (bǽl–əd) n. **1.** A slow, romantic popular song **2.** A simple song or poem, esp. one telling a story

bal-le-ri-na (bæl–ə–riʸ–nə) n. A female ballet dancer

bal-let (bæ–leʸ) n. Dancing in which steps are combined with posing and light, flowing movements to present a story

bal-loon (bə–luʷn) n. **1.** A large airtight bag that can be filled with gas or heated air so that it will float in the air **2.** A small, light, colored, rubber bag that can be blown up, used as a toy

bal-lot (bǽl–ət) n. **1.** A piece of paper used to make a vote in an election **2.** Act of voting by ballot or voting machine

balm (bɑm) n. **1.** An ointment that soothes or heals **2.** Anything that has a soothing or healing influence **3.** A fragrant herb

balm-y (bɑm–iʸ) adj. -ier, -iest **1.** Of air, soft and warm: *a balmy breeze* **2.** Of weather, mild: *a balmy summer evening*

ba-lo-ney (bə–loʷ–niʸ) n. **1.** Nonsense **2.** Bologna

bam-boo (bæm–buʷ) n. -boos A tall, tropical plant of the grass family, or its hollow, hard, jointed stems

bamboo adj. Made of the stem of this plant: *a bamboo chair*

ban (bæn) v. -nn- To forbid, esp. by an order or law: *They have banned smoking in theaters as a safety measure.* —ban n.

ba-nal (beʸ–nəl) adj. **1.** Lacking originality or freshness **2.** Common; ordinary

ba-nan-a (bə–næn–ə) n. A long tropical fruit, with a thick, yellow skin and a soft, white, sweet inner part

band (bænd) v. **1.** To put a band or bands around something to hold it together or strengthen it **2. band together** To unite for some special purpose

band n. **1.** A thin flat strip of material **(a)** For holding things together, or for putting around something to make it stronger **(b)** Used as part of an article of clothing: *arm band/ hat band* **2.** A strip or stripe of a color or pattern that is different from the back-

baptism

ground on which it is placed: *She sewed a band of blue cloth at the bottom of the white skirt.*

band n. **1.** A group of people joined for some common purpose, usu. with a leader: *a band of artists* **2.** A group of musicians that play together, usu. playing popular music or music for marching —compare ORCHESTRA

ban·dage (bæn–dɪdʒ) n. A piece of cloth or long strip of cloth for covering a wound or other injury —bandage v.

ban·dan·na or **ban·dan·a** (bæn–dæn–ə) n. A large handkerchief, usu. colored, used as a head scarf

ban·dit (bæn–dɪt) n. A robber, esp. one of an armed band of robbers

band·wag·on (bænd–wæg–ən) n. **1.** A wagon carrying musicians in a parade **2.** A person, idea, or movement that attracts open support because it is winning or gaining in popularity (used in phrases like "climb on the band wagon")

bang (bæŋ) n. **1.** A strong, sharp blow **2.** A sudden loud sound: *I heard the bang of a gun in the street.* **3. bangs** Locks of hair cut across the forehead

bang v. **1.** To bump; hit: *He fell and banged his head on the edge of the table.* **2.** To hit or strike forcefully, often with a loud noise: *She banged her books on the table and walked out angrily.* **3.** To make a loud sound: *Someone is banging on the door.* **4. bang sthg. up** *AmE. infml.* To damage: *I banged up my sister's car in the accident.*

ban·ish (bæn–ɪʃ) v. **1.** To condemn to exile **2.** To dismiss from one's presence or mind: *banish the thought* —banishment n.

ban·is·ter (bæn–əs–tər) n. **1.** The handrail of a staircase **2.** One of the uprights supporting this handrail **3.** The uprights and the rail together

ban·jo (bæn–dʒoʷ) n. **-jos** or **-joes** A stringed musical instrument, something like a guitar, having a round body

bank (bæŋk) n. **1.** A business where money is put by individuals, corporations, etc., for safekeeping, to be paid out of their account on demand, and where money is handled in other ways to make the exchange of funds by checks, notes, loans, etc. easier **2.** A place for the storage of organic products of human origin for medical use: *a blood bank*

bank n. **1.** Sloping land along the sides of a river, lake, etc.: *The heavy rains caused the river to overflow its banks.* **2.** A long mass of clouds or snow or other soft substance

bank v. **1.** To form into a bank or banks: *The earth was banked up along the garden wall.* **2.** To cover a fire with a large amount of coal, to prevent much air from getting in and to keep it burning **3.** To tilt (an aircraft, etc.) while turning

bank·er (bæŋk–ər) n. A person who owns or manages a bank

bank·rupt (bæŋk–rəpt) adj. **1.** Not having funds for paying one's debts: *The business may go bankrupt if it can't get financial backing for its new product.* **2. morally bankrupt** *fig.* Having no morals —bankruptcy n.

ban·ner (bæn–ər) n. **1.** A military flag **2.** A large strip of cloth, usu. hung between two poles, bearing a slogan: *Many of the demonstrators were carrying banners.*

ban·quet (bæŋ–kwət) n. A formal dinner with many guests in honor of a particular person or occasion

bap·tism (bæp–tɪz–əm) n. **1.** The application of water to a person as a sacrament or religious ceremony by which he is initiated into the visible church of Christ. This is usu. performed by sprinkling or immersion: *Jesus commanded baptism, saying, "Make disciples of all nations, baptizing them in the name of the Father and of the Son and of the Holy Spirit..."* (Matthew 28:19). *"Whoever believes [in Jesus] and is baptized will be saved, but whoever does not believe will be condemned"* (Mark 16:16). Saint Paul wrote, *". . . all of us who were baptized into Christ Jesus were baptized into his death? (That is, our old sinful nature was buried) . . . in order that, just as Christ was raised from the dead through the glory of the Father, we too may live a new[spiritual] life"* (Romans 6:3,4). *Having been buried with him in baptism and raised [spiritually] with him through your faith in the power of God,*

who raised him from the dead" (Colossians 2:12). —see BAPTIZE 2. An outpouring of the Holy Spirit. NOTE: Jesus told his disciples: "In a few days you will be baptized with the Holy Spirit...You will receive power when the Holy Spirit comes on you; and you will be my witnesses...to the ends of the earth" (Acts 1:5,8). This promise was fulfilled ten days later, on the day of Pentecost (Acts 2:1-4). **3.** The sufferings of our Savior Jesus Christ: *Immediately after predicting his suffering and death, Jesus asked two of his disciples, "Can you. . . be baptized with the baptism I am baptized with?"* (Mark 10:38). **4.** An act, experience, or ordeal by which one is purified, sanctified, initiated, or named, such as a soldier's first experience under enemy fire

bap·tis·mal (bæp–tɪz–məl) adj. Of or related to baptism: *a baptismal font*

Baptist (bæp–tɪst) n. **1.** One who administers baptism **2.** A name appropriately given to John, the forerunner of Jesus Christ **3.** A member of a Protestant Church that believes in baptism by immersion at an age when a person is old enough to understand what baptism means

bap·tist·ry (bæp–tɪs–triʸ) n. A place where the sacrament of baptism is administered

bap·tize also **-tise** *BrE.* (bæp–taɪz/ bæp–taɪz) v. **-tized, -tizing** To perform the sacrament of baptism; to christen. NOTE: By some denominations of Christians, baptism is performed by immersing the whole body in water, and this is done only to adults. More generally the ceremony is performed by sprinkling water on the head of a person, whether an infant or an adult, and in the case of an infant, by giving him a name: *Peter replied, "Repent and be baptized, every one of you, in the name of Jesus Christ so that your sins may be forgiven. And you will receive the gift of the Holy Spirit. The promise is for you and your children and for all who are far off, for all whom the Lord our God will call"* (Acts 2:38,39). *Ananias said to Paul, "Get up, be baptized and wash your sins away"* (Acts 22:16).—see JESUS, REPENT, FORGIVENESS

bar (bɑr) n. **1.** Any piece of wood, metal, etc., that is longer than it is wide: *a candy bar/ a bar of soap* **2.** A long piece of wood or metal across a door, gate, or window that keeps it closed: *There were metal bars across the windows to keep out any robbers.* **3.** An underwater sand bank, parallel to the shore, at the entrance to a bay, etc. **4.** A short series of notes in music **5.** A place with a counter where **(a)** food is sold: *snack bar/salad bar* **(b)** alcoholic drinks are sold

bar v. **-rr- 1.** To lock or close firmly with a bar: *to bar the gate* —opposite UNBAR **2.** To keep in or out by tightly closing a door, gate, etc.: *The gates were locked to bar any thieves from the property.* **3.** To forbid; ban: *The police have barred the use of handguns in the city.*

Bar n. **1.** The members of the profession of law *BrE.* **barrister 2. be called to the bar** To become a lawyer

bar·bar·i·an (bɑr–beər–iʸ–ən) n. An uncultured and uncivilized person

bar·bar·ic (bɑr–beər–ɪk) adj. Barbarous

bar·ba·rism (bɑr–bər–ɪzm) n. **1.** The state of being uncivilized **2.** Barbarous behavior, esp. an incorrect use of one's language

bar·bar·i·ty (bɑr–beər–ə–tiʸ) n. **-ties 1.** The state of being barbarous **2.** A barbarous act

bar·ba·rous (bɑr–bə–rəs) adj. **1.** Uncivilized; uncultured **2.** Brutal

bar·be·cue (bɑr–bə–kyuʷ) n. **1.** A frame for grilling meat over an open fire **2.** A social gathering in the open air, at which food is barbecued

barbecue v. **-cued, -cuing** To cook on a barbecue: *She barbecued enough steak for 17 people.*

bar·ber (bɑr–bər) n. A person whose trade is cutting the hair, shaving and trimming beards, etc. —compare HAIRDRESSER

bare (beər) adj. **1.** Without covering; empty: *bareheaded (=without a hat)/bare land (=without buildings)* **2.** Only just enough: *He gave only the bare facts.* —**barely** adv, —**bareness** n.

bare (beər) v. To reveal

bar·gain (bɑr–gɪn) v. To discuss the terms of a sale, agreement, or contract, trying to get the best price possible: *We couldn't bargain*

with her, because she was determined to get her price.

bargain n. **1.** An agreement to do something for each other: *The two boys made a bargain; Bill would help Joe paint the fence, and Joe would help Bill weed the garden.* **2.** Something of good quality bought at a low price: *I got a real bargain on this dress. It was fifty per cent off its regular price.*

barge (bɑrdʒ) n. A flat-bottomed boat used on rivers and canals

barge v. **barged, barging 1.** To move clumsily: *He's always barging about the room, knocking things over.* **2.** To bump into: *He barged right into Mary and didn't even apologize.* **3.** To enter a room or push one's way into a group rudely: *He barged into the room without knocking.*

bar-i-tone (bear–ɪ–to^wn) n. **1.** A male singing voice, lower than a tenor but higher than a bass **2.** A singer with a baritone voice **3.** A singing part written for a baritone voice

bark (bɑrk) v. **1.** To make the sound made by a dog when it is excited: *The dog barked when it saw the stranger approach the house.* —compare GROWL **2.** To speak in a loud sharp voice: *I don't like it when someone barks orders at me.*

bark n. **1.** The sound made by a dog when it is excited **2. his bark is worse than his bite** *infml.* His actions are not as bad as the way he sounds. **3.** The outer covering of the trunk and branches of a tree

bar-ley (bɑr–li^y) n. A type of grain used for food and for making beer and whiskey

bar-maid (bɑr–me^yd) n. A woman who serves drinks in a bar

bar-man (bɑr–mən) n. A man who serves drinks in a bar

barn (bɑrn) n. A farm building for keeping animals in, esp. horses or cows, also for storing hay, grain, etc., and equipment

bar-na-cle (bɑr–nə–kəl) n. A kind of small shellfish that attaches itself to the bottom of boats and to other things under water

ba-rom-e-ter (bə–rɑm–ə–tər) n. An instrument that measures the weight and the pressure of the atmosphere and indicates changes of weather —**ba-ro-met-ric** (bear–ə–met–rɪk)

adj.

bar-racks (bear–əks) n. A building or group of buildings used as living quarters for soldiers

bar-rage (bə–rɑʒ) n. **1.** A heavy, continuous bombardment by artillery **2.** *fig.* An overwhelming and rapid fire of questions: *The president was met with a barrage of questions from the news media.* **3.** A man–made barrier across a river

bar-rel (bear–əl) n. **1.** A large container of greater height than breadth, usu. of wood, with curved sides and a flat round top and bottom, used for storing or shipping things **2.** Also **barrelful** The amount of something contained in a barrel **3.** A long hollow tube or cylinder: *the barrel of a gun*

bar-ren (bear–ən) adj. **1.** Of female animals and women, not able to bear young: *They had no children because Elizabeth was barren* (Luke 1:7). **2.** Of plants, having no fruit or seed **3.** Of land, unproductive: *That country has a lot of barren land.*

bar-ri-cade (bear–ə–ke^yd) n. A barrier, often quickly constructed, put up to block traffic on a street, etc.

barricade v. **-caded, -cading 1.** To block something (a street, etc.) with a barricade **2.** To shut oneself away behind a barrier: *He felt that he had to barricade himself into his room so that he wouldn't be interrupted while writing his speech.*

bar-ri-er (bear–i^y–ər) n. **1.** Something like a fence used to keep people or animals from moving about freely: *The guards put up barriers to control the prisoners.* **2.** A natural formation of land or water which limits the movement of people or animals: *Until Columbus crossed it in 1492, the Atlantic Ocean was a barrier between the eastern and western hemispheres.* **3.** Hindrance: *language barrier/ cultural or social barrier*

bar-ter (bɑr–tər) v. To trade by exchanging goods or services, without using money

base (be^ys) n. **1.** The bottom of a thing or the part on which it stands: *The base of that statue is made of marble./Our house is at the base of the mountain.* **2.** A center of business or military operations; headquarters: *Our compa-*

ny's base is in Fort Wayne, but we have a western regional office in San Francisco. **3.** A permanent military camp **4.** Any of the four points of a baseball diamond **5. not get to first base (with)** infml. Not to succeed in trying to do something: I never got to first base in my attempt to become mayor.

base sthg. on/upon sthg. v. based, basing To use something as the starting point or reason: I try to base my conclusions on well-known facts.

base-ball (beᵞs–bɔl) n. **1.** A game played with a bat and a hard ball between two teams of nine players each on a large diamond-shaped field **2.** The ball used in this game

base-less (beᵞs–lıs) adj. Unfounded; having no basis in fact

base-ment (beᵞs–mənt) n. The lowest level of a house, partially or wholly underground: The furnace which provides the heating for this house is in the basement. —compare CELLAR

bash (bæʃ) v. **1.** To beat or to smash: The robbers bashed in the windows of the store. **2.** infml. AmE. To criticize severely, esp. out of prejudice

bash-ful (bæʃ–fəl) adj. Shy; timid: As a child, I was very bashful and afraid of strangers.

ba-sic (beᵞ–sık) adj. Essential; fundamental: basic education/ basic principles —**basically** adv.

ba-sin (beᵞ–sən) n. **1.** A round, shallow container for holding liquids or food; large bowl: She poured water into the basin and washed her hands. **2.** The area drained by a river: the basin of the Mississippi **3.** A bowl-shaped valley: the Los Angeles Basin

ba-sis (beᵞ–sıs) n. -ses (–siᵞz) The fundamental principle from which something is made, started, built, developed, or calculated: On what basis did you reach your decision?

bask (bæsk) v. To enjoy a pleasant warmth and light: basking in the California sunshine

bas-ket (bæs–kət) n. **1.** A container which is woven of bent sticks, stems of certain plants, etc., which will hold solid things but not liquids: a basket of fruit **2.** A round net which is open at the bottom and is fixed to a metal ring, used as the goal in the game of basketball

bas-ket-ball (bæs–kət–bɔl) n. **1.** An indoor game in which each of two teams of usu. five players each, tries to throw a large ball through the other team's basket **2.** The ball used in playing basketball

bass (beᵞs) n. **1.** A man with the lowest male singing voice —compare TENOR **2.** The part in written music for the lowest voice or instrument

bass adj. Of the deepest male singing voice or musical instrument: a bass horn

bass (bæs) n. **bass** or **basses** Any of various families of food and game fishes found in fresh or salt water

baste (beᵞst) v. basted, basting **1.** To sew with long stitches to keep something in place for only a short time **2.** To moisten food with liquid at intervals as it cooks: The turkey needs to be basted every 20 minutes as it is roasting.

bas-tion (bæs–tʃən) n. **1.** A part of a fortification that sticks out **2.** A person, place, or thing that serves as a defense

bat (bæt) n. **1.** A stick made of wood, specially shaped, and used for hitting the ball in various games —see BASEBALL **2. at bat** In baseball, taking a turn at batting the ball **3. right off the bat** infml. Immediately: He was hired yesterday and began working right off the bat.

bat v. -tt- **1.** To hit **2.** To have a turn at bat in baseball

bat n. **1.** A small, flying, mouse-like, night animal that usu. eats insects or fruit **2. as blind as a bat** infml. Quite blind

batch (bætʃ) n. A quantity of something produced at one time or used at one time: Let's bake a batch of cookies for Christmas.

bath (bæθ) n. **baths** (bæðz) An act of washing one's whole body: AmE. to take a bath /BrE. to have a bath

bathe (beᵞð) v. bathed, bathing **1.** AmE. To take a bath BrE. To have a bath: She can't come to the phone right now; she's bathing. **2.** To give someone a bath: Mrs. Johnson is bathing her new baby for the first time. **3.** To cover as if with liquid: The kitchen was bathed in sunlight. **4.** Esp. BrE. To go swimming or to enter a body of water for pleasure: The chil-

dren love to bathe in the cool lake water. —bather n

bath-robe (bæθ–ro^wb) n. A loose-fitting garment worn to and from the bath

bath-room (bæθ–ru^wm) n. A room having a bathtub and/ or a toilet, and usu. a wash basin

bath-tub (bæθ–tʌb) n. A tub in which one bathes, now usu. oblong and fixed in the bathroom

ba-ton (bə–tɑn) n. **1.** A thin stick used by the conductor of an orchestra for beating time **2.** A staff carried and twirled by a drum major or drum majorette

bat-tal-ion (bə–tæl–yən) n. **1.** A large number of troops organized to act together **2.** A military unit composed of a headquarters and two or more units

bat-ten (bæt–ən) n. **1.** A piece of wood used for keeping other pieces in place **2.** On ships, a strip of wood used to fasten down the hatches **3. batten down** v. To fasten with battens: *They battened down the hatches at the first sign of the storm.*

bat-ter (bæt–ər) n. **1.** A mixture of flour, eggs, and milk, for making pancakes, cakes, etc. **2.** The baseball player who is at bat

batter v. **1.** To beat hard again and again: *Hail battered against the windows.* **2.** To damage, break, or knock out of shape: *The little boat was battered to pieces against the rocks.* —**battered** adj. *a battered old car*

bat-ter-y (bæt–ər–i^y) n. **-ies 1.** A connected group of cells that produce electricity **2.** A set of big guns with the men and officers who operate them **3.** A set of guns placed in position on a warship or fort

bat-tle (bæt–əl) n. A fight between enemy armed forces or opposing groups; a struggle: *He was wounded in battle.* —compare WAR

battle v. **-tled, -tling** To carry on a fight or struggle

bat-tle-field (bæt–əl–fi^yld) also **battleground** (–graʊnd) n. An area where a battle is being or has been fought

bat-tle-ship (bæt–əl–ʃɪp) n. A very large kind of warship, with very big guns and heavy armor

bau-ble (bɔ–bəl) n. A thing that is showy but worthless or useless

bawl (bɔl) v. To cry loudly

bay (be^y) n. **1.** A narrow part of the sea or of a large lake extending into the land: *the Bay of Bengal* **2.** A compartment or space for storage in a barn, aircraft, etc.

bay-o-net (be^y–ə–nɛt/be^y–ə–nɛt) n. A knife-like blade that can be fastened to the muzzle of a gun to be used in hand-to-hand fighting

ba-zaar (bə–zɑr) n. **1.** A group of shops in a marketplace **2.** A fair for the sale of articles, usu. for charity

B.C. adv. *abbr.* for **Before Christ:** *Confucius lived from 551 to 479 B.C.* —com-pare A.D.

be- (bɪ–/bə–/bi^y–) prefix **1.** To cause to be; to make **2.** Completely; all over: *besmear* **3.** To treat as: *befriend* **4.** To cut off: *behead*

be (bi^y) v. To exist: *There seems to be a hole in my sock.* —see also BEEN

be v. **1.** Shows that something or someone is the same as the subject: *Today is Wednesday./ The girl in the first row is my friend.* **2.** Shows time or position: *Tomorrow is the first day of school. /The pencil is on the floor.* **3.** Showing identity or a quality: *Elephants are very large./ The sky is blue.* —see also BEEN

be v. Used as a helping verb with another verb

Present tense singular:
 I am, I'm; You are, you're; He/She/It is; He's/She's/It's
Present tense plural:
 We are, we're; You are, you're; They are, they're
Past tense singular:
 I was, You were, He/She/It was
Past tense plural:
 We were, You were, They were
Past participle: been
Present participle: being
Negative short forms: aren't, isn't, wasn't , weren't

1. BE + VERB + –ing forms the continuous tenses of verbs: *The baby is crying now./ He was sleeping./ We're going for a walk after his bath. (=it has been planned and arranged)* **2.** BE + the past part. forms the passive of verbs:

This song is sung at Christmas time./ The broken toy was fixed. **3.** BE + TO + VERB: **(a)** (Shows what must happen): *All papers are to be (=must be) on my desk by September 30th./ You are not to (=you must not) speak to your father in that tone of voice.* **(b)** (Shows something planned for the future): *Our vacation is to begin next week.* **(c)** (Shows something that may happen in the future): *If you were to miss the bus, what would you do?* —see also BEEN

beach (biᵞtʃ) n. The part of the shore of an ocean, sea, or lake or the bank of a river which is covered by sand or pebbles

bea-con (biᵞ–kən) n. A flashing light for helping sailors or airmen find their way

bead (biᵞd) n. A small hard piece of material with a hole through it so that it can be strung with others on a wire or thread to be worn for decoration around the neck, arm, etc.: *a string of white beads*

beak (biᵞk) n. The horny jaws of a bird, usu. coming to a point; bill

beam (biᵞm) n. **1.** A ray of light **2.** Radio signals sent out in one direction only, often to guide pilots **3.** A long, heavy piece of wood or metal used to support a building

beam (biᵞm) v. **1.** To send out light: *The sun beamed brightly in the summer sky.* **2.** To wear a bright, happy smile: *She was beaming with delight.* **3.** To send out radio beams in a certain direction: *The news was beamed (by radio) to the Far East.*

bean (biᵞn) n. **1.** The seed of any of various climbing plants, used for food **2.** A plant that produces these seeds **3.** A seed of certain plants, such as the coffee plant, from which food or drink is made: *vanilla beans* **4.** **spill the beans** *infml.* To give away a secret without meaning to

bear (beər) v. **bore** (bɔr), **borne** (bɔrn), **bearing 1.** To hold up: *Will these beams bear the weight of the roof? /fig. The company will bear the cost of your travel.* **2.** *fml.* To carry: *He bore the whole load by himself./ spir. Praise be to the Lord, to God our Savior, who daily bears our burden* (Psalm 68:19). **3.** To show or display; be visible: *The contract bears the signatures of both parties.* **4.** To endure with patience: *God*

is faithful; he will not let you be tempted beyond what you can bear (1 Corinthians 10:13). **5.** To give birth to: *She has borne two sons and a daughter.* **6.** To bring forth a crop, fruit, etc.: *The garden is bearing a lot of vegetables this summer./ spir. Jesus said to his disciples "This is to my Father's glory, that you bear much fruit [=produce good deeds], showing yourselves to be my disciples"* (John 15:8). **7.** To move in a given direction: *Bear left after you cross the bridge, and you shouldn't have any trouble finding our house.* **8. bear with sbdy./ sthg.** To show patience with: *Bear with each other and forgive whatever grievances you may have against one another* (Colossians 3:13). *Be patient, bearing with one another in love* (Ephesians 4:2).

bear n. A large, heavy four-legged animal with shaggy hair and a short tail

bear-a-ble (beər–ə–bəl) adj. That can be endured

beard (biərd) n. The hair that grows on the face of a man —**bearded** adj. *a kindly, bearded gentleman*

bear-er (beər–ər) n. **1.** A person who carries something: *I always like to be the bearer of good news.* **2. pallbearer** *AmE.* One who helps to carry the coffin at a funeral

bear-ing (beər–ŋ) n. **1.** Manner of acting and of holding one's body: *humble bearing* **2.** Application or meaning: *Her arguments had a lot of bearing on the final decision.* **3.** The position or direction of one point with regard to another on the compass: *The captain took a compass bearing.* **4. lose one's bearings** Become confused: *The hikers lost their bearings in the woods and had to camp on the trail until someone came to rescue them.*

beast (biᵞst) n. **1.** Any large four-footed animal **2.** *derog.* A mean person; brute: *The killer was a real beast.*

beast-ly (biᵞst–liᵞ) adj. **1.** Of or like a beast **2.** Nasty or disagreeable

beastly adv. *BrE.* Very: *The weather is beastly hot today.*

beat (biᵞt) v. **beat, beaten** (biᵞt–ən) or **beat; beating 1.** To punish by hitting with hard blows; to whip **2.** To hit again and again: *The man was beating on the door to get in from the*

rain. **3.** To mix cream, eggs, etc., rapidly with a fork, spoon, or beater: *to beat eggs and sugar together* **4.** To outdo someone in a race, contest, etc.: *The third grade beat the fourth grade in number of books read./ fig. "How does he get so much done in a day?" "It beats me." (=I don't understand it)* **5.** To move at a regular pace: *II was so scared could feel my heart beating.* **6. beat about/ around the bush** To put off talking about the most important part of a topic of discussion **7. beat time** To mark time in music by regular movements or noises **8. beat sbdy. up** *infml.* To hurt someone badly by hitting: *The robbers took the old man's wallet and then beat him up.*

beat n. **1.** A single stroke of a series: *His heart missed a beat.* **2.** Time in music or poetry: *the beat of the music* **3.** A rhythm made by, or as if by, repeated beating: *the beat of a drum* **4.** The regular route taken by someone on duty: *the policeman's beat*

beat adj. *infml.* Extremely tired: *We were really beat after that long hike!*

beat-er (bi^y t–ər) n. A kitchen utensil used for beating: *an egg beater*

be-at-i-tude (bi^y–æt–ɪ–tu^w d) n. **1.** Supreme blessedness or happiness **2. the Beatitudes** Any of the statements made at the beginning of the Sermon on the Mount (Matthew 5:3-12) beginning "Blessed are..."

beau (bo^w) n. **-beaus, beaux** A man who is the sweetheart or courter of a girl or woman

beau-ti-cian (byu^w–tɪʃ–ən) n. A person who does hair styles, gives manicures, etc. in a beauty shop

beau-ti-ful (byu^w–tə–fəl) adj. Very pleasing to the eye, ear, mind, etc.; having beauty: *The girl [Rebekah] was very beautiful* (Genesis 24:6). **2.** *spir.* Pleasing and satisfying to the spirit: *How beautiful on the mountains are the feet of those who bring good news, who proclaim peace, who bring good tidings, who proclaim salvation* (Isaiah 52:7). —**beautifully** adv. NOTE: **Beautiful** is a very strong word for describing one's physical appearance. It means "giving great pleasure to the senses." **Pretty, handsome, good-looking,** and **attractive** all mean "pleasant to the eye," but **pretty** is only used of women and chil-

dren, and **handsome** is usu. only used of men. **Good-looking, handsome,** and **plain** are generally used of people, and the other words are also used of things: *a pretty picture*

beau-ti-fy (byu^w–tə–faɪ) v. **-fied, -fying** To make beautiful

beau-ty (byu^w–ti^y) n. **-ties 1.** Qualities that are pleasing to the senses or that satisfy the mind or spirit: *a painting of great beauty/ spir. Wives... Your beauty should not come from outward adornment... Instead, it should be that of your inner self, the unfading beauty of a gentle and quiet spirit, which is of great worth in God's sight* (1 Peter 3:4,5). **2.** Someone (usu. female) or sthg. having such qualities: *That girl is a real beauty.* **3.** *infml.* Someone or sthg. very good or very bad: *That black eye is a real beauty.* **4. the beauty of sthg.** The good of sthg.: *The beauty of this plan is its simplicity!*

bea-ver (bi^y–vər) n. **1.** A brown, furry animal with strong chisel-like teeth, that is at home both on land and in water, where it builds dams of mud and twigs **2.** The fur of this animal **3.** *infml.* A hardworking person

be-cause (bi^y–kɔz/ –kʌz) conj. On account of; for the reason that: *I am leaving early, because I have another meeting.*

because of prep. On account of; due to: *He was sent to the principal's office because of his bad behavior.*

beck-on (bɛk–ən) v. **1.** To signal or call by a gesture of the head or hand **2.** To appear inviting; to attract

be-come (bi^y–kʌm) v. **-came** (–ke^y m), **-come, -coming 1.** To come to be: *My sister became a teacher./ The sky became dark with clouds./ To all who received him [Jesus], to those who believed in his name [for salvation], he gave the right to become children of God* (John 1:12). —see JESUS **2. become of sbdy./ sthg.** To happen to: *Whatever became of Roger? When we were in college, he was voted the most likely to succeed.*

be-com-ing (bɪ–kʌm–ɪŋ) adj. *fml.* **1.** Suitable; proper: *His dirty jeans were not becoming at the business meeting.* **2.** Of clothing, jewelry, makeup, etc., suitable for the wearer: *Your hat is very becoming to you.* —opposite UN-

BECOMING —becomingly adv.

bed (bɛd) n. 1. Any piece of furniture for sleeping on 2. An area of ground where flowers, vegetables, etc., are planted: *a flower bed* 3. Any surface that is the base or foundation of sthg.: *the railroad bed* 4. A layer of rock of a certain kind: *The house was built on a bed of shale.* 5. **a bed of roses** *infml.* An easy, soft state of being 6. **get up on the wrong side of the bed** *infml.* To be in a bad mood

bed-ding (bɛd–ɪŋ) n. 1. Mattresses, blankets, pillows, etc. 2. Litter, straw, etc. used as a bed for animals

bed-lam (bɛd–ləm) n. A scene of wild uproar and confusion

be-drag-gle (bɪ–dræg–əl) v. -gled, -gling To make wet and dirty by dragging in the mud —bedraggled adj.

bed-rid-den (bɛd–rɪd–ən) adj. Confined to bed

bed-roll (bɛd–roʷl) n. Bedding rolled for portability, for use esp. out-of-doors

bed-room (bɛd–ruʷm) n. A room with a bed, esp. for sleeping

bed-spread (bɛd–sprɛd) n. A cover that is placed over the blankets and pillows on a bed

bee (biʸ) n. A four-winged insect with a sting, that lives in a colony and collects pollen and nectar from flowers for making wax and honey, often kept in hives for the honey

beef (biʸf) n. 1. A full-grown cow, bull, or steer 2. The meat of such an animal —see MEAT

beef v. *infml., often derog.* To complain: *Stop beefing about your kids and start encouraging them!*

bee-hive (biʸ–haɪv) n. 1. A box or other structure for keeping bees 2. A colony of bees; swarm 3. *fig.* A very busy place: *a beehive of activity*

bee-line (biʸ–laɪn) n. A straight, direct course: *As soon as class was out, he made a beeline for the football field.*

been *AmE.* (bɪn) *BrE.* (biʸn) v. 1. Past part. of **be** 2. To have gone somewhere and returned: *Has he ever been to Chicago?*

beer (bɪər) n. An alcoholic drink made from grain

beet (biʸt) n. 1. A large, round, red, root vegetable 2. **sugar beet** A plant with white roots from which sugar is obtained —see also SUGAR

bee-tle (biʸ–təl) n. An insect with four wings of which the stiff outer pair covers the inner pair when not in flight

be-fore (bɪ–fɔr) adv. Earlier; at an earlier time: *Have you been here before?*

before prep. 1. Earlier than: *before 1860/We arrived before anyone else./Jesus said, "Before Abraham was, I am"* (John 8:58). 2. Ahead of: *She was before me in the line.*

before conj. 1. Prior to; earlier than some other time or event: *Eat your breakfast before you leave.* 2. Rather than: *I'd choose this one before that one.*

be-fore-hand (bɪ–fɔr–hænd/ –foʷr–) adv. Ahead of time: *We had been warned beforehand, so the exam did not take us by surprise.*

be-fud-dle (bɪ–fʌd–əl) v. -dled, -dling 1. To confuse 2. To stupefy, as with liquor or drugs —befuddled adj.

be-friend (bɪ–frɛnd) v. To act as a friend to someone

beg (bɛg) v. -gg- 1. To ask for food, money, or other necessary things as a gift because a person has no money: *She used to live by begging on the streets of Los Angeles./He begged for mercy.* 2. To ask earnestly: *He begged me to stay.* 3. *fml.* To ask to be allowed to speak: *I beg to differ. You are mistaken on that point.*

beg-gar (bɛg–ər) n. 1. A person who lives by begging 2. **beggars can't be choosers** *infml.* One who begs must take what he is offered

be-gin (bɪ–gɪn) v. began (bɪ–gæn), begun (bɪ–gʌn) To start doing, acting, going, etc.: *This class begins at 8:00 A.M.*

be-gin-ner (bɪ–gɪn–ər) n. A person who has just started to learn something or to do something

be-gin-ning (bɪ–gɪn–ɪŋ) n. The starting point; origin; the time and place of starting: *In the beginning God created the heavens and the earth* (Genesis 1:1). *In the beginning was the Word, and the Word was with God, and the Word was God ... And the Word became flesh and made his dwelling among us* (John 1:1,14). —see JESUS

be-grudge (bɪ-grʌdʒ) v. 1. To envy another's enjoyment or pleasure 2. To give unwillingly or with ill will 3. To look upon with disapproval

be-guile (bɪ-gaɪl) v. -guiled, -guiling 1. To deceive 2. To harm or divert

be-half (bɪ-hæf) n. 1. Support; interest; benefit 2. on/ in behalf of someone/ someone's behalf AmE. Acting, speaking, etc., for someone else; in the interest of another: *She's speaking on behalf of her husband who can't be here today.*

be-have (bɪ-heʸv) v. -haved, -having 1. To act; conduct oneself: *The children behaved with great maturity when their father died.* 2. To act in a socially acceptable or polite way: *Behave yourself!*

be-hav-ior AmE. be-hav-iour BrE.(bɪ-heʸv-yər) n. 1. The way a person behaves 2. be on one's best behavior To show one's best conduct and manners: *The children were on their best behavior when their grandmother came to visit them.*

be-hind (bɪ-haɪnd) prep. 1. Towards or in the rear of: *We parked our car behind the office.* 2. Not as good as; below: *Mary is a little behind other children of her age.* 3. Supporting; encouraging: *Is the owner of the business behind (=agreeing with) this plan?*

behind adv. 1. In a former location: *I left my glasses behind when I came to work this morning.* 2. Late: *They're always behind with their car payment.*

be-hold (bɪ-hoʷld) v. beheld, beholding To have in view; to see: *We beheld his [Jesus'] glory... full of grace and truth* (John 1:14).

beige (beʸʒ) n., adj. A dull, pale brown

be-ing (biʸ-ɪŋ) n. 1. The fact of living; existence: *The city came into being over a hundred years ago.* 2. Something living, esp. a person: *a human being/a divine being*

be-lat-ed (bɪ-leʸt-əd) adj. Late, or too late —belatedly adv. —belatedness n.

belch (bɛltʃ) v. 1. To send out wind noisily from the mouth 2. To gush; to send out smoke from a smokestack or other opening: *The steam engine was belching black smoke.* —belch n. The act or sound of belching

be-lief (bə-liʸf/ biʸ-liʸf) n. 1. The conviction that something is true or real: *Few people shared Columbus' belief that the world is round.* 2. Trust, confidence; faith in someone or something as good: *a belief in medicine* 3. An idea that is thought to be true and that is a part of a system of ideas: *religious beliefs*

be-liev-a-ble (bə-liʸv-ə-bəl) adj. Able to be believed —see also UNBELIEVABLE —believably adv.

be-lieve (bə-liʸv/ biʸ-liʸv) v. -lieved, -lieving 1. To think of sbdy. or sthg. as true or honest: *I believe he's telling the truth.* 2. To have faith in; to consider true: *Whoever believes in him [Jesus] shall not perish but have eternal life* (John 3:16). *Believe in the Lord Jesus, and you will be saved* (Acts 16:31). —see JESUS 3. To have as an opinion; suppose: *I believe John is well qualified for the position.* 4. To think: *Do you think it will rain? Yes, I believe so.*

be-liev-er (bə-liʸv-ər/ biʸ-liʸv-ər) n. One who has faith in sbdy., sthg., or a system of ideas

be-lit-tle (bɪ-lɪt-əl) v. -littled, -littling To say or imply that sthg. is of little value

bell (bɛl) n. A hollow metal object, usu. round and open at the bottom, which rings when struck by another metal object

bel-lig-er-en-cy (bə-lɪdʒ-ər-ən-siʸ) n. The status of a nation engaged in war

bel-lig-er-ent (bə-lɪdʒ-ər-ənt) adj. Aggressively hostile

bel-low (bɛl-oʷ) v. 1. To make a loud, deep, hollow sound like that of a bull 2. To shout loudly

bel-ly (bɛl-iʸ) n. -lies 1. infml. The front part of the human body, between the waist and the legs, containing the stomach and bowels 2. Any surface or object that curves out like this part of the body: *the belly of a ship*

be-long (bɪ-lɔŋ) v. To be in the right or suitable place: *Where do these dishes belong?*

belong to sbdy./ sthg. v. 1. To be owned by: *The gray Buick belongs to me./The Lord said,..."Everything under heaven belongs to me"* (Job 41:11). *Jesus said, "He who belongs to God hears what God says"* (John 8:47). 2. To be a member of; be associated with: *My brother belongs to a health club.*

be-long-ings (bɪ-lɔŋ-ɪŋz) n. One's possessions; the goods that belong to a person: *He*

piled all his belongings on the truck and drove away.

be-loved (bɪ–lʌvd/ bɪ–lʌv–əd) adj. Dearly loved: *Her beloved (husband) was by her side./ A voice came out of the cloud, saying, "This [Jesus] is my beloved Son, in whom I am well-pleased. Hear him!"* (Matthew 17:5 NKJV). —see JESUS —**beloved** n.

be-low (bɪ–loʷ) adv. **1.** In a lower place; beneath: *I looked on the top shelf. Did you look below?* —opposite ABOVE —com-pare UNDER **2.** Under the surface: *The miners were trapped below. (=under-ground)/ At the captain's command, the sailors went below. (=to a lower deck of the ship)* **3.** In a book or other printed material, farther down on the same page or on a later page

below prep. Lower than, in position, rank, or worth: *His salary this year was below last year's./ Are you below the age of 65?* —opposite ABOVE

belt (bɛlt) n. **1.** A strip of leather or other material worn around the waist: *a leather belt* **2.** An endless strap of leather or other material used for carrying materials or driving a machine **3.** An area of the country that has some special quality: *the corn belt (=where corn is the major crop)* **4. tighten one's belt** *infml.* To live more economically: *We really had to tighten our belts when my father lost his job.*

belt v. **1.** To strike a hard blow, esp. with the hand: *He belted the big man on the chin and knocked him down.* **2.** To strike with a belt

bench (bɛntʃ) n. **1.** A long hard seat for two or more people: *a picnic bench* **2.** A judge or his position in court **3.** A worktable

bend (bɛnd) v. bent, bending **1.** To force a change in shape: *He bent the coat hanger until it was straight.* **2.** To lean down, back, forward, etc., away from an upright position: *She bent down to pick up the child.* **3.** To turn from a straight line: *The river bends to the south just outside the town.*

bend n. **1.** A bending or being bent **2.** Something that is bent: *We came to a bend in the path.*

be-neath (biʸ–niʸθ) adv. Underneath; below: *They stood on the balcony watching the cars go*

by on the street beneath. —compare UNDER, BELOW

beneath prep. **1.** Below; underneath: *The sun sank beneath the horizon.* **2.** *fml.* Unworthy of: *He thought the job was beneath him.* —compare UNDER, BELOW

ben-e-dic-tion (bɛn–ə–dɪk–ʃən) n. A blessing or the act of giving a blessing: *"May the grace of the Lord Jesus Christ, and the love of God, and the fellowship of the Holy Spirit be with you all,"* is a benediction (2 Corinthians 13:14).

ben-e-fac-tion (bɛn–ə–fæk–ʃən) n. **1.** The act of doing good **2.** A charitable gift

ben-e-fac-tor (bɛn–ə–fæk–tər) n. One who gives financial or other help

ben-e-fi-cial (bɛn–ə–fɪ–ʃəl) adj. Helpful; advantageous

ben-e-fi-ci-ar-y (bɛn–ə–fɪ–ʃiʸ–ɛər–iʸ/ bɛn–ə–fɪ–ʃər–iʸ) n. **-ies** A person who receives a benefit, esp. one who receives money or property left by someone who has died

ben-e-fit (bɛn–ə–fɪt) n. **1.** Any advantage, profit, or helpful effect: *Dr. Brown had the benefit of attending the best medical school./ Praise the Lord, O my soul, and forget not all his benefits — who forgives all your sins ...* (Psalm 103:2,3). **2.** Money given to someone by the government as a right, esp. in disability or unemployment: *veterans' benefits*

benefit v. **-fited, -fiting 1.** To be helpful or useful to others **2.** To profit; gain advantage

be-nev-o-lent (bə–nɛv–ə–lənt) adj. **1.** Wishing to do good to others; kindly and helpful **2.** Charitable —**benevolently** adv. —**benevolence** n.

be-nign (bɪ–nam) adj. **1.** Kind and gentle **2.** Mild and gentle in its effect **3. a benign tumor** One that is not malignant

bent (bɛnt) v. **1.** Past tense and part. of **bend**: *The fender was bent in an accident last night.* **2. bent on** Determined: *He was bent on self-destruction.*

bent n. Natural tendency

be-queath (bɪ–kwiʸθ) v. **1.** To leave by will **2.** To hand down

be-quest (bɪ–kwɛst) n. **1.** The action of bequeathing **2.** That which is bequeathed

be-rate (bɪ–reʸt) v. **-rated, -rating** To scold se-

verely

be-reave (bə-riʸv) v. -reaved, -reaving To deprive, esp. ol a relative, by death —**bereavement** n.

be-reft (bɪ-rɛft) v. Deprived of or lacking sthg.

be-ret (bə-reʸ) n. A round, soft cap made of felt

ber-ry (bɛər-iʸ) n. -ries A small, usu. round, soft, juicy fruit: *There are strawberries, blueberries, raspberries, and many other kinds of delicious berries.*

ber-serk *AmE.* **ber-zerk** *BrE.* (bər-zɜrk) adj. Crazy; frenzied; in an uncontrollable and destructive rage: *He went berserk and shot and killed 22 people at the shopping mall.*

berth (bɜrθ) n. 1. A place for anchoring a ship, as in a harbor 2. A small bed for sleeping on a ship or train

be-seech (bɪ-siʸtʃ) v. -sought (bɪ-sɔt) or -seeched, -seeching To ask earnestly; entreat; implore

be-set (bɪ-sɛt) v. -set, -setting 1.To harass 2. To hem in; to encircle 3. To set, as with gems

be-side (bɪ-saɪd) prep. 1. Alongside; next to: *standing beside the river* 2. In comparison with: *My old car looks pretty shabby beside your new one.* 3. **beside oneself (with)** Wildly upset or excited: *The lady was beside herself with joy when she heard she'd won the sweepstakes.* 4. **beside the point** Not related to the main point or question: *They were happy to find the house they were looking for; the fact that it was old was beside the point.* —see BESIDES

be-sides (bɪ-saɪdz) adv. In addition; also: *I don't need this bicycle anymore, and besides I can buy another one.*

be-siege (bɪ-siʸdʒ) v. To lay siege to

best (bɛst) adj. Superlative of **good** 1. The highest in quality; better than all others: *This is the best coffee I've ever tasted.* —compare WORST 2. **the best part of** Most of: *They've been away for the best part of a month.*

best adv. Superlative of **well** 1. In a better way than all others: *Of all the pianists, he plays the piano best.* 2. To the highest degree; most: *the best-loved songs*

best n. 1. Something better than all others;

the greatest, prettiest, biggest, etc.; the greatest degree of good: *Only the best will do for the king.* 2. A person's best effort or state: *He expects the best from all his employees.* 3. **make the best of** To do as well as possible with something that is not very good: *This room is terrible but we'll have to make the best of it.* —compare WORST

best seller (bɛst sɛl-ər) n. Something, esp. a book, that is currently outselling others: *The Bible is the best seller in America, year after year.* —see BIBLE

be-stow (bɪ-stoʷ) v. 1. To present as a gift 2. To apply; expend, as time 3. To give in marriage —**bestowal, bestowment** n.

bet (bɛt) n. 1. An agreement to risk money, taking a chance on the result of a future event: *He placed a bet on a horse named "Ginger" in the fifth race.* 2. Money risked in this way: *a $10 bet*

bet v. bet, betting 1. To make a bet on the outcome of a future event: *I bet you $5 that they'll win the next election.* 2. **I bet** *infml.* "I strongly believe it will..." : *I bet you'll find a job tomorrow. I feel it in my bones!*

be-tray (bɪ-treʸ) v. -trayed, -traying 1. To be disloyal to; to break faith with: *The soldier betrayed his country by giving information to the enemy./Judas Iscariot, who betrayed Jesus, said, "I have betrayed innocent blood"* (Matthew 27:4). 2. *fml.* To reveal, esp. a secret: *He betrayed the confidence of his friend.* 3. To reveal the true feelings or intentions of: *Her downward glance betrayed her guilt.* —**betrayer** n.

be-tray-al (bɪ-treʸ-əl) n. The act of betraying: *The betrayal of Jesus Christ by Judas Iscariot is probably the best known betrayal on record.*

bet-ter (bɛt-ər) v. To improve on: *He tried to better his tennis game before the match.* —opposite WORSEN

better adj. 1. Comparative of **good**; higher in quality; more than good: *Their car is newer and better than your old one.* 2. Comparative of **well** (=healthy) (a) Improved physically: *Do you feel better today than yesterday?* (b) Healthy again after an illness: *Now that her back is better she can go back to work.* —opposite WORSE 3. **better than** *infml.* A

larger number than: *We'll need food for better than a hundred guests.* **4. one's better half** *infml. humor.* One's wife or husband **5. the better part of** More than half: *I spent the better part of $50 on groceries. The bill came to $41.98.*

better adv. Comparative of well **1.** In a better way: *He plays tennis better than his brother.* **2.** To a greater degree; more: *She understands computers better than I do.* —opposite WORSE **3. had better** Should; ought to: *I had better get to work now.*

better n. **1.** The part or thing that is more than good: *Don't settle for "better" when "best" is within reach.* **2. a change for the better** An improvement **3. get the better of** To defeat someone or overcome a difficulty: *Billy and Johnny had a fight, and Billy got the better of Johnny and won the fight.* —opposite WORSE

bet-ween (bi^y–twi^yn) prep. **1.** (Used when two things are separated): *My car was parked between the two buildings.* **2.** (Used when things are shared by two): *The two girls divided an apple between them.* **3. between you and me** As a secret; privately: *Between you and me, I think this business may fail soon.* Compare **among** and **between: Between** should only be used with two people or things, and **among** with three or more: *Divide the work between the two men. Divide the work among all of the workers.*

between adv. **1.** In or into a space, or length of time, separating two points: *There's a house on each corner, but nothing between.* **2. few and far between** *infml.* Infrequent

bev-el (bɛv–əl) n. **1.** The angle that one line or surface makes with another when they are not at right angles **2.** A tool for adjusting the slant of the surfaces of a piece of work

bev-er-age (bɛv–ə–rɪdʒ) n. *fml.* Any liquid for drinking, other than water: *I enjoy hot beverages (=tea, coffee, etc.) more in cold weather.*

bev-y (bɛv–i^y) n. **1.** A large collection or group **2.** A group of animals together, esp. a group of quail

be-wail (bɪ–we^yl) v. To complain about

be-ware (bɪ–wɛər) v. To be careful; watch out for; be on your guard against: *Beware of the*

dog./ spir. Beware of false prophets* (Matthew 7:15). *Beware of covetousness [the evil desire to have something that belongs to someone else] for a man's life does not consist in the abundance of the things he possesses* (Luke 12:15 NKJV).

be-wil-der (bɪ–wɪl–dər) v. To perplex; confuse

be-witch (bɪ–wɪtʃ) v. **1.** To affect by witchcraft **2.** To fascinate; charm

be-yond (bɪ–yɑnd) prep. **1.** Farther on in space: *Beyond those mountains lies another range of mountains.* **2.** Farther on in time: *It's beyond quitting time already.* **3.** Past the limits of: *The poor child is beyond hope. He may not live through the night.* **4.** More than; except for: *I don't know anything beyond what I have told you.*

beyond adv. Farther on in space or time: *I can work until five, but not a minute beyond.*

bi– (baɪ–) prefix Two, as in **bicycle, bifocal**

bi-an-nu-al (baɪ–æn–yu^w–əl) adj. Occurring twice a year —**biannually** adv.

bi-as (baɪ–əs) n. **1.** Prejudice **2.** A line diagonal to the grain of a fabric

bias adv. Diagonally

bias v. **biased** or **biassed, biasing** or **biassing** To give a prejudiced outlook

bib (bɪb) n. A protective cloth placed under a child's chin to protect his clothing from spilled food and drink

Bi-ble (baɪ–bəl) n. A copy of the holy book of the Christians and the Jews; the word of God recorded by holy men of God inspired by the Holy Spirit, written over a period of 1600 years, from 1500 B.C. to 100 A.D. NOTE: There are two chief parts: The Old Testament which was written between 1500 and 400 B.C., and the New Testament, written during the second half of the first century A.D. The first book of the Bible, Genesis, tells of the creation of the world and all that is in it, including the first man and woman, created in the image of God, in true holiness and righteousness. Genesis tells of their fall into sin and the promise of a Savior. While much of the Old Testament relates the history of Israel and her neighbors and tells of many great men and women of faith, there are also many prophecies concerning the promised Savior. The New Tes-

tament tells about the fulfillment of those prophecies by Jesus Christ, true God and true man, who left all the glory and splendor of his heavenly home to come into the world to save sinful mankind by his innocent suffering and death on the cross. It tells how he conquered death for us by rising from the dead and returning to heaven to prepare a place for all those who put their trust in him: *The Bible not only shows us our Savior, but it shows us how to live holy lives to his glory. Saint John said that his gospel [good news about Jesus] was written that you might "believe that Jesus is the Christ, the Son of God, and that believing you may have life [eternal life] in his name"* (John 20:31). —**Bib-li-cal** (bɪb–lɪ–kəl) adj. —see GOSPEL, OLD TESTAMENT, NEW TESTAMENT

bib-li-og-ra-phy (bɪb–liy–ɑg–rə–fiy) n. –phies A list of books, magazine articles, etc., on a given topic, esp. a list of all such printed materials used as resources in writing a book or an article

bi-cen-ten-ni-al (baɪ–sɛn–tɛn–iy–əl) n. A 200th anniversary or its celebration

bi-ceps (baɪ–sɛps) n. The muscle in the front of the upper part of the arm

bick-er (bɪk–ər) v. To quarrel, usu. over small matters

bi-cy-cle (baɪ–sɪk–əl) n. A two-wheeled vehicle which one rides by sitting on a saddle and pedaling with the feet: *My son rode his bicycle all the way across the country.*

bicycle (baɪ–sɪk–əl) also **bike, cycle** *infml.* v. -cled, -cling To ride a bicycle: *My brother and I bicycled/ cycled to school every day when we were young.*

bid (bɪd) v. **bade,** (bæd/ beyd) or **bid, bidden** (bɪd–ən) or **bid, bidding 1.** To offer a price, whether for payment or acceptance, as at an auction: *She bid $100 for the antique table.* **2.** *old use or lit.* To give a greeting or order to someone: *We have just bid good-bye to some very good friends.*

bid n. **1.** An offer to pay a certain price for something: *a bid of $60,000 for that old house* **2.** An offer to do a job at a certain price: *The company accepted our bid to run their advertising campaign.* **3.** An attempt to obtain some-

thing: *The candidate made a bid for the presidency.*

bi-en-ni-al (baɪ–ɛn–iy–əl) n. **1.** Taking place once every two years **2.** Lasting two years **3.** Of plants, producing leaves the first year, and bearing fruit and dying the second year

bi-en-ni-um (baɪ–ɛn–iy–əm) n. A period of two years

bi-fo-cals (baɪ–fow–kəlz) n. pl. A pair of glasses having lenses with one part ground for close focus as for reading, and the other part ground for focus farther away

big (bɪg) adj. **-gg- 1.** More than average in weight, size, force, importance, etc.: *We had a big storm yesterday.* —opposite LITTLE, SMALL **2.** *infml.* Very important and popular: *He's a big name in radio.* **3. that's big of (you, him, etc.)** *infml.* That's good of (you, him, etc.) **4. big mouth** *AmE. infml.* A person who talks too much, esp. in an opinionated and gossipy way: *John's such a big mouth. He told everybody about my poor grades.* **5. big shot** *AmE. infml.* Someone powerful and important: *He's a big shot in the company; he's the vice–president.*

big-a-my (bɪg–ə–miy) n. The act of marrying one person while still legally married to another

big-ot (bɪg–ət) n. One who is intolerantly devoted to his own political party, race, church, or opinion —**bigotry** n. —**bigoted** adj.

bike (baɪk) n. Short for **bicycle**

bi-ki-ni (bɪ–kiy–niy) n. A woman's brief two-piece bathing suit

bi-lat-er-al (baɪ–læt–ər–əl) adj. **1.** Of or having two sides **2.** Affecting or undertaken by two sides equally: *A bilateral agreement is one made between two persons or groups.*

bile (baɪl) n. **1.** Bitter yellowish or greenish fluid secreted by the liver **2.** Bitterness of spirit

bi-lin-gual (baɪ–lɪŋ–gwəl) adj. Expressed in, or able to speak two languages

bill (bɪl) n. **1.** A statement of things bought and their price: *He doesn't like to pay cash, so he has a charge account at the store. At the end of the month, he receives a bill for all the purchases he made during the month.* **2.** A

printed notice or advertisement: *They distributed handbills about the new store throughout the neighborhood.* **3.** *AmE.* A piece of paper money: *a hundred-dollar bill* **4.** A written proposal for a law for the government to consider: *The senators were debating the bill which proposed spending one million dollars for new schools.* **5.** The beak of a bird

bill v. To present a statement of charges to sbdy.

bill-board (bɪl–bɔrd) n. *AmE.* A large, usu. high, flat surface on which advertisements are placed

bill-fold (bɪl–foᵂld) n. A wallet

bil-lion (bɪl–yən) adj., n., pron. *AmE.* Thousand million: *1,000,000,000*

bil-lion-aire (bɪl–yə–nɛɛr) n. A person who has wealth of at least one billion dollars, pounds, etc.

bi-month-ly (baɪ–mʌnθ–liʸ) adj. **1.** Happening every two months **2.** Happening twice a month

bin (bɪn) n. A storage receptacle or container

bi-na-ry (baɪ–nə–riʸ) adj. **1.** Pertaining to two; double; paired **2.** Permitting only two possibilities, as in a computer bit **3. binary system** A way of writing numbers using only the numbers 0 and 1. These two binary digits can be used in combinations to stand for any amount. The binary system is often used in computers. **4. binary star** A pair of stars revolving about a common center of gravity

binary n. -ries A combination of two things

bind (baɪnd) v. **bound** (baʊnd), **binding 1.** To tie together: *These sticks will be easier to carry if they are bound together.* **2.** To wrap in a bandage: *to bind wounds* **3.** To fasten together the printed pages of a book and enclose them within a protective cover: *bind a book* **4.** To strengthen or decorate the edges of something with a band of material: *to bind a seam* **5.** To cause to stick together: *This glue doesn't bind very well.* **6.** To do something because of a promise or legal agreement: *I am bound to pay off the debt before the end of the year.*

bind-er (baɪn–dər) n. **1.** A cover for loose

papers **2.** A person or anything that binds sthg. **3.** Anything used to bind, such as **glue 4.** A written statement binding parties to an agreement **5.** A machine that cuts and ties grain

bind-er-y (baɪnd–ər–iʸ) n. -ies A place where books are bound

bind-ing (baɪnd–ɪŋ) n. **1.** The cover on a book: *The leather binding on this book is beautiful.* **2.** A band of material sewn or stuck along the edge of something for decoration or for strength: *seam bind-ing*

binge (bɪndʒ) n. A period of un-controlled self-indulgence; a wild spree; eating, drinking, and making merry

bin-go (bɪŋ–goᵂ) n. A game of chance played with cards having numbered squares, won by covering five squares in a row

bin-oc-u-lars (bɪn–ɑk–yə–lərz) n. A hand-held telescope adapted for use with both eyes; field glasses

bio- (baɪ–oᵂ–) prefix Life; living organisms

bi-og-ra-phy (baɪ–ɑg–rə–fiʸ) n. -phies An account of the life of a person, usu. written —**biographer** n. —**bi-og-raph-i-cal** (baɪ–ə–græ–fɪ–kəl) adj.

bi-ol-o-gy (baɪ–ɑl–ə–dʒiʸ) n. The branch of science that deals with the study of living plants and animals —**biologist** n. —**bi-o-log-i-cal** (baɪ–ə–lɑdʒ–ɪ–kəl) adj. —**biolog-ically** adv.

birch (bɜrtʃ) n. **1.** Any of a kind of tree or shrub having light-grained wood and bark that can be separated from the wood in sheets **2.** The wood of this tree

bird (bɜrd) n. **1.** Any of a class of animals with two wings and a body covered with feathers, which can usu. fly in the air **2. early bird** *infml.* One who gets up or arrives ahead of others **3. kill two birds with one stone** *infml.* To obtain two benefits with one action **4. (strictly) for the birds** *AmE. infml.* Of no value; silly

birth (bɜrθ) n. **1.** The act or time of being born: *the birth of a baby/Surely I was sinful at birth, sinful from the time my mother conceived me* (Psalm 51:5). *Even from birth the wicked go astray* (Psalm 58:3). **2.** Family background: *of royal birth* **3. birthmark** A mark or blemish

on the skin at birth **4. birthplace** The place of one's birth **5. birthright** A privilege or possession to which one is entitled by birth **6. birthstone** A gem associated symbolically with the month of one's birth

birth-day (bɜrθ–de^y) n. **1.** The date on which a person was born **2.** The day each year on which this date falls: *Best wishes for a Happy Birthday!* —compare ANNIVERSARY

birth-right (bɜrθ–raɪt) n. **1.** Any privilege or possession to which a person is entitled by birth **2.** Right of the first-born

bis (bɪs) adv. Twice

bis interj. Encore

bis-cuit (bɪs–kət) n. **1.** *AmE.* A small, soft type of bread, usu. round, for one person **2.** *BrE.* for **cookie**

bi-sect (baɪ–sɛkt/ baɪ–sɛkt) v. *tech.* To cut or divide into two equal parts —**bi-sec-tion** (baɪ–sɛk-ʃən/ baɪ–sɛk-ʃən) n.

bish-op (bɪʃ–əp) n. **1.** A high ranking Christian clergyman **2.** In the game of chess, the two pieces that move diagonally across any number of unoccupied spaces of the same color

bi-son (baɪ–sən) n. A large, wild ox, esp. with a shaggy mane and hump shoulders, found on the plains of the western US

bit (bɪt) n. **1.** A small amount: *We did a bit of work before breakfast this morning./a bit of advice* **2.** A short time: *I'll be ready in just a bit.* **3.** To some degree: *a bit hungry* **4.** The part of a bridle that is put in a horse's mouth for controlling its movements **5.** A part of a tool for drilling holes **6.** The standard measure of computer information

bite (baɪt) v. **bit** (bɪt), **bitten** (bɪt–ən), biting **1.** To seize, tear, cut, or crush something with the teeth: *Does your dog bite?* **2.** Of insects and snakes, to break the skin and draw blood: *Be careful not to get bitten by a snake.*

bite n. **1.** The act or manner of biting: *Someone has taken a bite out of the candy.* **2.** *infml.* Some food, esp. a small amount of food: *Could we get a bite to eat? I'm really hungry.*

bit-ing (baɪt–ɪŋ) adj. Cutting and painful: *a cold, biting wind/ biting criticism*

bit-ter (bɪt–ər) adj. **1.** Having a sharp, unpleasant taste —opposite SWEET **2.** Of weather, wind, etc., strong, sharp, cutting, biting, etc.: *a bitter winter snowstorm* **3.** Strongly unpleasant, as caused by hatred, anger, sorrow, etc.: *bitter shame/ bitter failure* —**bitterly** adv.

bit-ter-ness (bɪt–ər–nəs) n. **1.** A biting, disagreeable sensation on the tongue **2.** *fig.* Extreme enmity or hatred: *Get rid of all bitterness, rage and anger...* (Ephe-sians 4:31). **3.** Keen sorrow, painful affliction, deep distress of mind: *A foolish son brings grief to his father and bitterness to the one who bore him* (Proverbs 17:25).

biv-ou-ac (bɪv–wæk/ bɪv–u^w–wæk) n. A usu. temporary encampment, esp. of soldiers, with little or no shelter

bi-week-ly (baɪ–wi^yk–li^y) adj., adv. **1.** Happening every two weeks **2.** Happening twice a week

bi-zarre (bɪ–zɑr) adj. Very strange; odd

blab (blæb) v. **-bb- 1.** To talk a lot **2.** To let out a secret

black (blæk) adj. **1.** The very darkest color like coal or soot; the opposite of white: *It was such a black night, I couldn't see my hand in front of my face./ I like my coffee black.* (=without milk or cream) **2.** Of feelings, behavior, news, etc., sad, evil, or bad: *a black deed/The future certainly looked black for them after their father died.* **3.** A very dark skin color: *Black people from West Africa were brought to the Western Hemisphere as slaves in the 1700's.* —compare WHITE **4. black sheep** One who is looked down upon by other members of a respectable group: *He was the black sheep of the family, because he was always in trouble with the law or with sbdy.*

black or **blacken** v. **1.** To make sthg. black **2. black out** To faint: *The blow on the head caused him to black out.* **3. black sthg. out** To darken so that no light can be seen: *We had to black out the windows so we could watch the movie.* —**blackness** n.

black n. **1.** The darkest color: *She looked striking dressed in black with diamond jewelry.* **2.** A person of a black-skinned race: *More than 12% of the people in America are blacks.* **3. in the black** The state of making a profit:

Our company is in the black this month.
—opposite IN THE RED

black-board (blæk–bord) also **chalkboard, board** n. A dark, smooth surface used in classrooms to write on with chalk

black-en (blæk–ən) v. To make or become black or dark: *Thick, dark smoke blackened the sky./ fig. His good name was blackened by terrible rumors.*

black eye (blæk aɪ) n. A bruised discoloration of the flesh surrounding the eye

black-list (blæk–lɪst) n. A list of disapproved persons or organizations, etc.

black magic (blæk mædʒ–ɪk) n. Magic in league with the devil; witchcraft

black-mail (blæk–meʸl) v. To get money or some advantage from people by threatening to tell secret information about them —blackmailer n.

black market (blæk mɑr–kət) n. Illegal buying or selling of goods

black-out (blæk–aʊt) n. 1. Total darkness due to putting out all the lights, esp. lights that might be seen by enemy aircraft during an air raid 2. A temporary loss of consciousness 3. A stoppage, as of electricity

black-smith (blæk–smɪθ) n. One who makes and repairs articles of iron

black widow (blæk wɪd–oʷ) n. A very poisonous spider, the female having an hourglass-shaped red mark on the underside of the abdomen

blad-der (blæd–ər) n. 1. A bag of skin inside a person's body in which waste liquid collects and from there is passed out 2. A bag of skin, leather, plastic, rubber, etc. which can be filled with gas or liquid

blade (bleʸd) n. 1. The sharp, cutting part of a knife or other tool or weapon 2. The flat wide part of a propeller, oar, etc. 3. A thin, long leaf of grass

blame (bleʸm) n. Responsibility for sthg. bad or the accusation that one is responsible: *Blame for the accident was put on John and me.* —blame v.

blame-less (bleʸm–ləs) adj. Free from guilt; without blame: *a blameless life/ Such a high priest [Jesus]... is holy, blameless, pure, set apart from sinners, exalted above the heavens*

(Hebrews 7:26). —**blamelessly** adv.

blanch (blæntʃ) v. 1. To bleach or whiten 2. To scald by the use of boiling water 3. To become pale

bland (blænd) adj. 1. Of food, mild and without much flavor 2. Of people and behavior, lacking any special character; not showing strong feelings

blank (blæŋk) adj. 1. Without writing or marks of any kind: *a blank sheet of paper/ blank walls* 2. Lacking in expression: *I explained the lesson three times, but he still sat there with a blank look on his face.*

blank n. An empty space: *Please fill in all the blanks on this form.*

blan-ket (blæŋ–kət) n., adj. 1. A large piece of woven fabric used as a covering on a bed to keep one warm 2. *fig.* Any covering layer: *The furniture was covered with a blanket of dust.* 3. Covering all cases, persons, or possible happenings; without limits: *a blanket retirement plan*

blare (blɛəɪ) v. blared, blaring To make a loud harsh sound —blare n.

blas-pheme (blæs–fiʸm) v. -phemed, -pheming (against) To speak in a way that shows lack of respect for God or religious matters: *Blasphemy against the true God is a sin that was punishable by death in olden times. God commanded, "Anyone who blasphemes the name of the Lord must be put to death"* (Leviticus 24:16). NOTE: God hates all sin. Nevertheless, he loves those who sin and wants them to have eternal life. Because of his great love and mercy, he forgives all those who repent of their sins and put their trust in Jesus. —see FORGIVENESS, JESUS —**blas-phem-er** (blæs–fiʸm–ər) n. —**blas-phe-mous** (blæs–fəm–əs) adj. —**blasphemously** adv.

blas-phe-my (blæs–fəm–iʸ) n. -mies Lack of respect shown in language or behavior toward God or holy things

blast (blæst) v. To destroy or break up by an explosion, esp. rock: *The road builders have blasted away the rock in order to make a tunnel.*

blast n. 1. An explosion 2. A sudden forceful movement of the air: *a cold blast of wind* 3. A loud sound such as that made by blowing a

brass wind instrument **4. blast off** The moment of the launching of a rocket

bla-tant (ble^yt–ənt) adj. **1.** Attracting attention in a very obvious way **2.** Very obvious and unashamed: *a blatant lie*

blaze (ble^yz) n. (*usu. sing.*) **1.** The sudden, very bright shooting up of a fire: *We saw the fire suddenly burst into a blaze.* **2.** A large dangerous fire: *The firemen fought bravely to control the blaze.*

blaze v. **blazed, blazing** To burn brightly: *The fire blazed brightly in the fireplace./fig. Her eyes blazed with hatred.* —**blazing** adj.

bleach (bli^ytʃ) v. To make white or become white —**bleach** n.

bleak (bli^yk) adj. Cold, dreary, and uninviting: *My father's funeral was on a bleak day in early December./fig. The outlook for jobs is bleak in our city right now.*

blear-y (blıər–i^y) adj. **-ier, -iest 1.** Dull or dimmed, esp. from lack of sleep: *blear-y-eyed* **2.** Poorly outlined or defined

bleed (bli^yd) v. **bled** (blɛd), **bleeding 1.** To lose blood: *The knife slipped and cut his hand, causing it to bleed./fig. The thought of all the suffering children makes my heart bleed.* (=I feel very sorry for them) **2.** *fig.* To take advantage of someone by making them pay too much money: *The blackmailer bled them for thousands of dollars.*

blem-ish (blɛm–ıʃ) v. To spoil the perfection of someone or sthg.: *His handsome features were blemished by a big scar on his left cheek.*

blemish n. A flaw that spoils beauty or perfection: *fig. a blemish on his good name/ spir. You were redeemed... with the precious blood of Christ, a lamb without blemish or defect [sinless]* (1 Peter 1:18,19). —see JESUS —also LAMB OF GOD

blend (blɛnd) v. **1.** To mix together; produce by mixing: *Blend the sugar, flour, butter and eggs.* **2.** To look nice together; be in harmony: *The color of the sofa and chairs blends well with the carpet.* —**blend** n.

bless (blɛs) v. **blessed** or **blest** (blɛst), **blessing 1.** To pray for God's favor upon someone or sthg.: *The minister blessed the congregation at the close of the service.* **2.** To praise God or call him holy: *Bless the Lord, O my soul;... bless his*

holy name (Psalm 103:1 KJV). **3. be blessed with** To have the stated benefit: *blessed with long life* —opposite DAMN

bless-ed (blɛs–əd) adj. Enjoying happiness; favored by God: *Blessed are the pure in heart, for they will see God. Blessed are the peacemakers, for they will be called sons of God* (Matthew 5:8,9). *Blessed... are those who hear the word of God and obey it* (Luke 11:28). —opposite DAMNED —**blessedness** n.

bless-ing (blɛs–m̩) n. **1.** An act of asking or receiving divine help, favor, protection, etc.: *The blessing of the Lord be upon you all.* **2.** Encouragement; approval: *The young couple had the blessing of their parents on their wedding.*

blew (blu^w) v. Past tense of **blow**

blight (blaıt) n. **1.** A disease or injury of plants that causes them to wither, stop growing, or die **2.** Anything that de-stroys, prevents growth, etc. —**blight** v.

blind (blaınd) n. (*usu. sing.*) —also **window shade** *AmE.* **1.** A wide strip of cloth or other material pulled down from a roller to cover a window **2.** Also **blinds, venetian blinds** A window covering made of long, thin, flat strips of metal, plastic, or wood fastened with heavy string in such a way that the strips can be raised and lowered, or turned to let in air and light or shut them out

blind adj. **1.** Not able to see: *Our grandson has never been able to see; he was born blind./ Can a blind man lead a blind man? Will they not both fall into a pit?* (Luke 6:39). **2.** Having poor understanding or judgment: *John was blind to his wife's emotional needs.* **3. spiritually blind** Unable to see (=understand) spiritual truths: *The world is full of spiritually blind people, because "the god of this age [Satan] has blinded the minds of unbelievers, so that they cannot see the light of the gospel of the glory of Christ, who is the image of God"* (2 Corinthians 4:4). —**blindly** adv. —**blindness** n.

blind v. To cause someone to be unable to see: *He was blinded by the lights of the oncoming traffic./fig. His love for her blinded him to all the problems that lay ahead.*

blink (blıŋk) v. **1.** To shut the eyes and quick-

ly open them again, once or many times: *She blinked her eyes when he shined the light in her face.* **2.** Of lights, to go off and on, again and again, rapidly: *The lights on the Christmas tree were blinking.* —compare WINK

blink n. An act of blinking

bliss (blɪs) n. Extreme happiness —**blissful** adj. —**blissfully** adv.

blis-ter (blɪs-tər) n. A bump under the skin filled with a thin, watery liquid, caused by rubbing, burning, etc.: *While he was digging in the garden the shovel caused blisters on his hands.*

blister v. To cause blisters to form: *The hot sun blistered the fresh paint on the fence.*

blithe (blaɪθ) adj. Carefree; cheerful —**blithely** adv.

bliz-zard (blɪz-zərd) n. A severe snowstorm, usu. with strong winds and lasting for several hours

bloat (bloʷt) v. To swell by air or as if by water or air —**bloated** (bloʷt-əd) adj. *His stomach was bloated.*

blob (blɑb) n. A drop of liquid, a round spot

bloc (blɑk) n. A group of countries, political parties, etc., that act together because of a common interest: *the Western bloc of nations* —compare BLOCK

block (blɑk) n. **1.** A large, solid, usu. flat-sided, piece of wood, stone, etc., cut to be used for a particular purpose: *The walls of the house were made of mud blocks.* **2.** The distance from one street to the next one in a city: *It's six blocks from here to the library.* **3. a city block** An area between two streets that run east and west and two others that run north and south; for example, an area of some two to three acres, sometimes more: *The huge explosion and the fire that followed destroyed all the buildings in six city blocks.* **4.** A quantity of things taken together as a single whole: *a block of tickets to the concert* **5.** Sthg. that cuts off movement: *Please clear the block out of the pipe so we can get the water running again.* **6.** A small piece of wood, plastic, etc., usu. shaped like a cube, used as a child's toy: *The children are playing with their blocks.* —compare BLOC

block v. To stop the movement, activity, or

success of sthg. by putting a hindrance in the way: *The road was blocked by a fallen tree./ The senator was trying to block passage of the bill into law.*

block-ade (blɑ-keʸd) n. The surrounding of a place, usu. by troops or ships, to prevent entrance or exit

block-head (blɑk-hɛd) n. A stupid person

blond (blɑnd) adj. Of hair, of a light brown or yellowish color

blonde (blɑnd) n. A person of fair skin and light-colored hair

blood (blʌd) n. **1.** The red fluid that flows through the body, bringing food and oxygen to all parts of the body: *The heart pumps blood through the body./ spir. For you know that it was not with perishable things such as silver or gold that you were redeemed from the empty way of life handed down to you from your fathers, but with the precious blood of Christ, a lamb without blemish or defect [when he suffered and died for us on the cross]* (1Peter 1: 18,19). —see JESUS **2.** Family relationship: *The circus is in their blood; they've been in the circus for four generations.* **3. make one's blood run cold** To fill one with fear: *The sound of gunfire in the street made his blood run cold.* **4. in cold blood** Without mercy and on purpose: *The six youths killed the old man in cold blood.* —**bloody** adj.

bloom (bluʷm) v. To bring forth flowers or be in flower: *The cherry trees should bloom soon./ fig. The bride was blooming with beauty and happiness.* —compare BLOSSOM, FLOWER —**bloom** n.

blos-som (blɑs-əm) v. **1.** To yield flowers; bloom: *The plum trees are blossoming.* **2.** To develop: *Their romance blossomed./ Debbie is blossoming into quite an artist.*

blossom n. The flower of a tree or bush: *apple blossoms* —compare BLOOM, FLOWER

blot (blɑt) v. -tt- **1.** To make one or more spots, stains, etc. on sthg.: *Because of the ink blot on his paper he had to take a clean sheet./ fig. She blotted her driving record by getting a ticket for speeding.* **2.** To cause to dry with blotting paper **3. blot sthg. out** To hide or cover: *God said, "I, even I, am he who blots out your transgressions, for my own sake, and remembers*

your sins no more" (Isaiah 43:25).

blot n. 1. A block or dirty spot, esp. made by ink dropped accidentally from a pen: *a blot of ink on my shirt pocket* 2. A character flaw or shameful act, esp. by someone thought to be of good character: *Cheating on the exam was a terrible blot on Ed's character!*

blotch (blɑtʃ) n. A large and usu. irregular spot or patch of color, as of ink

blot-ting pa-per (blɑt–ŋ peʸ–pər) n. Special soft paper that is used for drying wet ink on paper

blouse (blaʊs) n. A piece of women's clothing which covers the body from the neck to the waist, worn with either a skirt or pants

blow (bloʷ) v. blew (bluʷ), blown, blowing 1. To force out air through the lips: *She blew out the candle./The policeman blew his whistle./The boy blew up a balloon.* 2. To move or be carried as by the wind: *The wind's hardly blowing at all right now./The wind has blown down all the trees in our yard.* 3. To make a sound on a horn or other device: *The engineer blew the whistle as the train came into the station.* 4. (a) Of an electrical fuse, to melt when overloaded: *The fuse blew, causing all the lights to go out.* (b) To cause a fuse to do this by over-loading it: *I turned on the electric coffee maker, the microwave oven, and the toaster, all at the same time. No wonder I blew a fuse!* (c) fig. To become suddenly very angry: *Dad blew a fuse when I showed him my poor grades.* 5. infml. To lose sthg., esp. money, as the result of foolishness: *My son just blew $100 on a radio that doesn't work.* 6. **blow one's nose** To clean the nose by blowing through it into a handkerchief 7. **blow one's top** infml. To get extremely angry 8. **blow out** (a) Of a tire, to burst: *The tire blew out while he was driving on the freeway.* (b) **blow sthg. out** To cause to be forced out by the movement of air or other gas: *The wind blew the windows out of the house.* —compare BLOWOUT 9. **blow over** Of bad weather, to pass away without damage: *The rain has blown over./fig. Let's just wait. Maybe our troubles will blow over.* 10. **blow up/ blow sthg. up** (a) To cause to explode: *The enemy blew up the train.* (b) To get very angry: *My*

brother blew up when I put a dent in the fender of his new car. (c) To enlarge a photograph

blow n. 1. A forceful stroke with the hand, a weapon, etc.: *The guard hit the robber with such a hard blow that he fell to the ground.* 2. A shock or disaster: *The news of her mother's illness was a great blow to her.*

blown (bloʷn) v. Past part. of **blow**

blow-out (bloʷ–aʊt) n. 1. The bursting of a tire or some type of container: *We had a blowout just as we drove off the freeway.* 2. infml. A very noisy, festive party: *My birthday party was a real blowout.* —see also BLOW OUT

blow-up (bloʷ–əp) n. 1. An enlargement of a photograph 2. A sudden burst of anger

blub-ber (blʌb–ər) n. 1. The fat of large sea mammals, such as whales 2. A noisy crying

blubber v. To cry noisily

blud-geon (blʌdʒ–ən) n. A short heavy club

bludgeon v. To strike with, or as if with, a bludgeon

blue (bluʷ) n. 1. The color of the sky or of a lake or sea on a clear day: *She decorated her room in blue.* 2. **out of the blue** Unplanned; not expected: *We didn't invite John. He just arrived out of the blue.*

blue adj. 1. Of the color blue: *She bought blue shoes and a blue purse to match her dress.* 2. infml. Sad: *Jill was feeling kind of blue because it was the first day of school for her youngest son.* 3. **till one is blue in the face** Keeping on without success: *You can plead with him till you're blue in the face but he'll never let you go to the party.* —blueness n. —bluish adj.

blue-ber-ry (bluʷ–bɛər–iʸ) n. -ries 1. A small bush which grows in North America 2. The small round fruit of this bush

blues (bluʷz) n. 1. A style of slow, sad music of black American origin 2. infml. The state of being in low spirits: *I seem to get the blues easily when the weather is so gloomy.*

bluff (blʌf) v. To try to deceive (by a display of self-confidence)

bluff n. 1. A high, steep bank overlooking a river or the sea 2. Deception; trickery

blun-der (blʌn–dər) n. A stupid, careless, or unnecessary mistake: *Selling his house so cheaply was a real blunder.*

blunder v. 1. To make a blunder 2. To move

unsteadily, as if blind or confused: *He blundered along the rough path.* —**blunderer** n.

blunt (blʌnt) adj. **1.** Having an edge or a point that is not sharp **2.** Rough in manner

blunt v. To make less sharp or painful —**bluntly** adv.

blur (blɜr) v. **-rr-** To cause to become vague or unclear: *The words on the page blurred as tears filled her eyes.*

blur n. A shape that is not clearly seen: *The trees in the distance are only a blur./ fig. My understanding of electronics is only a blur.*

blurt (blɜrt) v. To utter suddenly and without thinking

blush (blʌʃ) v. To get red in the face, from shame or embarrassment: *He blushed when he saw everyone watching his clumsy attempts to learn how to play tennis.* —**blushingly** adv.

blus-ter (blʌs-tər) v. **1.** To blow gustily, as the wind **2.** To talk in a noisy, threatening manner —**blustery** adv. —**blusterer** n.

bo-a (boʷ-ə) n. A large snake that crushes its prey

boar (bɔr) n. **1.** An uncastrated male pig **2.** A wild pig

board (bɔrd) n. **1.** A large, flat, narrow piece of cut wood; plank: *The carpenter used four boards to make the shelves for the bookcase.* **2.** A flat piece of hard material used for a special purpose: *He put the announcement on the bulletin board.* **3.** The cost of meals: *He pays $70 a week for room and board at the boarding house.* **4.** A group of persons responsible for making decisions and giving advice for a company, government agency, etc.: *board of directors/ board of governors/ advisory board* **5. above board** Of an action in business, open, honest, trustworthy **6. across the board** Involving all groups or members, as in an industry, company, society, etc.: *a seven percent wage increase across the board (=everyone received a seven percent increase in wages)* **7. on board** In or on a ship, airplane, etc.: *After the passengers were all on board, the train left the station.* —compare ABOARD

board v. **1.** To cover with boards: *Because the old house was empty, they boarded up the doors and windows.* **2.** To go on board a ship,

airplane, train, etc.: *Passengers must board the train through Gate 15.* **3.** To provide room and meals for payment: *They have a big house and enjoy boarding college students.*

board-er (bɔrd-ər) n. A person who pays for his room and board

boast (boʷst) v. **1.** *usu. derog.* To talk about one's own accomplishments or abilities with too much pride: *She's always boasting about how intelligent her children are./ Do not boast about tomorrow, for you do not know what a day may bring forth (Proverbs 27:1). Like clouds and wind without rain is a man who boasts of gifts he does not give (Proverbs 25:14). All the evildoers are full of boasting (Psalm 94:4).* **2.** *not derog.* To own or possess sthg. of real value (usu. not said of people): *This city boasts that it has less crime than any other city in the country. / May I never boast except in the cross of our Lord Jesus Christ, through which the world has been crucified to me, and I to the world (Galatians 6:14).* —**boast** n. —**boastful** adj. —**boastfully** adv. —**boastfulness** n.

boat (boʷt) n. **1.** A small, open vessel used on water, moved by oars, sails, or a motor: *They went fishing on the lake in a rowboat.* **2.** A large, enclosed vessel for crossing the ocean or taking long trips on the water: *Before there were airplanes, people traveled between Europe and America by boat.* —compare SHIP **3. in the same boat** *infml.* Having the same difficulty: *We've both lost our jobs, so now we're in the same boat.* **4. rock the boat** *infml.* To disturb matters by suggesting changes

bob (bɑb) v. **-bb-** **1.** To move up and down jerkily or repeatedly, esp. in the water **2.** To cut a woman's hair to about neck level

bob-bin (bɑb-ən) n. A small, cylindrical piece of wood or other material on which thread is wound

bod-i-ly (bɑd-ɪ-liʸ) adj. Of the human body: *Bodily exercise is of some value, but godliness has value for all things, holding promise for the present life and the life to come (1 Timothy 4:8). In Christ all the fullness of the Deity lives in bodily form (Colossians 2:9).* —**bodily** adv.

bod-y (bɑd-iʸ) n. **-ies** **1.** The whole physical part of a person or animal, including the

flesh and bones but not the mind or soul: *The dead man's body was buried in the cemetery./ You are not your own; you were bought at a price. Therefore, honor God with your body* (1 Corinthians 6:19-20). *Jesus said, "Don't be afraid of those who kill the body but cannot kill the soul. Rather, be afraid of the One who can destroy both soul and body in hell"* (Matthew 10:28). **2.** An area or amount: *The Great Lakes are large bodies of fresh water along the border between the United States and Canada.* **3.** A number of people who meet or work together: *The student body of the university holds a monthly meeting.* **4.** The central part of a motor vehicle, aircraft, etc.: *When the airplane made an emergency landing, one wing was broken off, but the other wing and the body were not damaged.* **5. heavenly bodies** *tech.* The sun, moon, and stars

bog (bɑg/ bɔg) n. A marsh; wet, spongy ground

bog v. **-gg- 1.** To sink into, as if in a bog **2. bogged down** Hindered, unable to make any progress

bog-gle (**bɑg**–əl) v. **-gled, -gling** To be astonished at: *It boggles the mind.*

bo-gus (bo**ʷ**–gəs) adj. False

boil (bɔɪl) v. **1.** To heat water or other liquid to the point where it forms bubbles and turns to steam: *Water boils at 212°F, or 100°C, at sea level.* **2.** To cook in boiling water: *Please boil my egg for three minutes.* **3. make one's blood boil** To become very angry —**boil** n. *Bring the water to a boil before putting the egg in it.*

boil n. An infected pus-filled swelling on the skin, usu. painful

bois-ter-ous (bɔɪst–ə–rəs/ bɔɪs–trəs) adj. **1.** Wild; noisy **2.** Of weather, stormy

bold (bo**ʷ**ld) adj. **1.** Brave; fearless; courageous: *The policeman was a bold man; he rescued the child from the building just before it collapsed./ The wicked man flees though no one pursues, but the righteous are as bold as a lion* (Proverbs 28:1). **2.** Printed in type that is darker and heavier than normal: *Each new word in this dictionary is in bold type.* —**boldness** n. —**boldly** adv. *They were all filled with the Holy Spirit and spoke the Word*

of God boldly (Acts 4:31).

bo-lo-gna (bə–lo**ʷ**–nə) n. A large type of meat nouçəɲə

bol-ster (bo**ʷ**l–stər) n. A long pillow or cushion extending from one side of a bed to the other

bolster v. To support with, or as if with, a bolster; to reinforce: *We're getting a loan to bolster the financial status of the company.*

bolt (bo**ʷ**lt) n. **1.** A rod with a head at one end and a screw thread at the other used to hold objects in place: *The two pieces of metal were held together with six bolts.* **2.** A sliding bar used to fasten a door shut **3.** A flash of lightning **4.** A roll of cloth or wallpaper

bolt v. **1.** To secure or fasten with a bolt: *She bolted the door shut.* **2.** To move suddenly, as in fright or in a hurry: *The horse bolted when it saw the oncoming train.*

bomb (bɑm) n. A metal device filled with explosives that can be set off by throwing, dropping, lighting a fuse, etc.: *They planted a bomb in the train station.*

bomb v. To attack, damage, or destroy with a bomb or bombs

bom-bard (bɑm–bɑrd) v. **1.** To attack continually with bombs or shells: *The big guns bombarded the city, destroying many buildings.* **2.** *fig.* To attack sbdy. with many questions, etc.: *The reporters bombarded the senator with questions about his new proposal.* —**bombardment** n.

bomb-er (bɑm–ər) n. **1.** An airplane made for carrying and dropping bombs **2.** A person who plants bombs in buildings and other places which he or she wants to destroy

bona fide (bo**ʷ**–nə faɪd/ bɑn–ə/ faɪd–i**ʸ**/ faɪd–ə) adj. Genuine; without fraud

bond (bɑnd) n. **1.** Any kind of tie, agreement, feeling, etc., that unites people or groups: *During their college years, the two young men developed a bond of friendship which was never broken.* **2.** An interest-bearing certificate in which a government or a company promises to pay back money that has been lent to it: *a United States Treasury Bond* **3.** Money paid as a promise or surety: *His father paid his bail bond so that he could get out of jail.*

bond-age (bɑn–dɪdʒ) n. **1.** Slavery; subjection

to some outside force or influence **2. spiritual bondage** Slavery to sin

bone (boʷn) n. **1.** One of the solid parts of the body which make up the skeleton and around which are the flesh and skin: *There are supposed to be 212 separate bones in the human body.* **2. cut to the bone** To lower costs, services, etc., as much as possible: *We have cut our entertainment expenses to the bone.* **3. feel in one's bones** To believe sthg. through intuition, not by facts or proof: *I'm going to get this job! I can feel it in my bones.* **4. bone up** *infml.* To study hard and briefly, usu. for a special purpose: *He's boning up on Europe in preparation for his trip there next month.*

bone-less (boʷn–ləs) adj. Having no bones

bon-net (bɑn–ət) n. A hat or covering for the head, tied under the chin and worn by women or small children

bo-nus (boʷ–nəs) n. **1.** An extra payment beyond what is usual, necessary, or expected: *The famous boxer got a new car as a bonus for winning the fight.* **2.** *infml.* Sthg. pleasant besides what is expected: *Having a vacation in Hawaii was wonderful, but having an extra week there was an added bonus.*

bon-y (boʷn–iʸ) adj. **-ier, -iest 1.** Very thin: *You need to gain a few pounds. You're getting too bony.* **2.** Full of bones: *Some kinds of fish are bonier than others.*

boo (buʷ) interj. A shout of disapproval or contempt

boo v. To shout disapproval: *The audience booed him right off the stage.*

boo-by (buʷ–biʸ) n. A stupid person

boo-by prize (buʷ–biʸ praɪz) n. A prize for the poorest performance in a contest

boo-by trap (buʷ–biʸ træp) n. **1.** A harmless-looking device which may explode or ensnare someone when it is touched or approached, causing the person harm **2.** A hidden trap rigged up for a practical joke

book (bʊk) n. **1.** A number of sheets of paper, blank or with sthg. printed on them, fastened together to be written in or to be read: *This dictionary is one example of a book./ St. John, writing about a vision of heaven, said, "I saw the dead, great and small, standing before the throne, and books were opened. Another book was opened, which is the book of life. The dead were judged according to what they had done, as recorded in the books. If anyone's name was not found written in the book of life, he was thrown into the lake of fire"* (Revelation 20:12,15). NOTE: Those whose names are written in the book of life are those who put their trust in Jesus for their salvation rather than in their own works. *...whoever believes in him shall not perish but have eternal life* (John 3:16). —see JESUS **2.** A collection of similar things attached together, esp. a small one with its own paper or cardboard cover: *a book of matches/ I'd like a book of stamps, please.* **3. books** In a business, written records of accounts, names, etc.: *We have over six hundred customers on our books.* **4. the Good Book** The Bible: *Mother reads from the Good Book every morning.*

book v. **1.** *infml.* To enter formal charges against sbdy. in police records: *The police booked him for robbery.* **2.** To reserve a hotel room, a plane ticket, a seat at a concert, etc., in advance

book-case (bʊk–keʸs) n. A set of shelves for holding books

book-keep-er (bʊk–kiʸp–ər) n. A person who does bookkeeping

book-keep-ing (bʊk–kiʸp–ɪŋ) n. The act of keeping records of the accounts of money of a business company, a government office, etc.

book-mark (bʊk–mɑrk) n. Sthg. placed between the pages of a book to keep one's place

book-shelf (bʊk–ʃɛlf) n. A shelf for books

book-worm (bʊk–wɜrm) n. A person who spends a lot of time reading books

boom (buʷm) v. **1.** To make a loud, long, hollow sound, as of a heavy gun **2.** To increase suddenly, esp. in value: *The tourist business is booming in Switzerland.* —**boom** n.

boo-mer-ang (buʷ–mə–ræŋ) n. **1.** A curved piece of wood, which, when thrown, returns to the thrower, used as a hunting weapon by Australian aborigines **2.** Sthg. that causes unexpected harm to its originator

boomerang v. To act as a boomerang: *Unfortunately, his plan boomeranged on him.*

boon (buᵂn) n. A blessing; a benefit

boon-docks (buᵂn–daks) n. **1.** Rough or isolated country **2.** A rural area

boor (bʊər) n. A rude, ill-mannered person — **boorish** adj. —**boorishly** adv.

boost (buᵂst) v. **1.** To push up; lift up: *Could you boost me up so I can reach the top shelf, please?* **2.** To raise or increase in amount: *to boost taxes* **3.** To help or encourage: *His praise boosted her spirits.* —**boost** n.

boot (buᵂt) n. **1.** A covering for the foot and ankle, and sometimes the upper part of the leg, usu. made of leather or rubber and heavier and thicker than a shoe: *hiking boots/ snow boots/hip boots* **2.** *BrE.* Trunk of a car; the compartment for baggage, usu. at the back of a car **3.** *infml.* The act of dismissing sbdy., esp. from a job: *They gave him the boot for failing to do the work expected of him.* (=he lost his job)

booth (buᵂθ) n. **booths** (buᵂðz) **1.** A small tent or open-fronted building where goods are sold or games are played at a fair or market; a table where goods are exhibited at a convention **2.** A small enclosed space, big enough for only one person, used for a special purpose: *a telephone booth/a voting booth* **3.** A partly enclosed place in a restaurant, usu. along the wall, with a table and seats

boot-leg (buᵂt–lɛg) v. To make, transport, or sell (as liquor) illegally —**boot-legger** n.

boot-y (buᵂt–iʸ) n. **-ies** Plunder; spoil

booze (buᵂz) n. Intoxicating liquor

bor-der (bɔr–dər) n. **1.** The line separating two countries **2.** Edge: *There was a border of shrubs along the sidewalk.*

border v. **1.** To form a border **2.** **border on/ upon sthg.** To be almost the same as sthg.: *Her comments bordered on stupidity.*

border-line (bɔr–dər–laɪn) adj. Between two different types or categories: *We don't know whether to hire her for the job or not; she's a borderline case.*

bore (bɔr) v. Past tense of **bear**

bore v. To make sbdy. lose interest, esp. by speaking in a dull way: *Because the lesson was too easy, the students were bored by it.*

—**boredom** (bɔr–dəm) n.

bore n. **1.** *derog.* A person who continually speaks in a dull way, causing others to lose interest **2.** Sthg. dull and uninteresting: *He wasn't a good teacher, and his classes were a bore.*

bore v. To make a round hole, tunnel, etc., by using a drilling tool or by digging: *The plumber bored a hole through the wall for the pipe.* —**borer** n.

born (bɔrn) v. Brought into life or being by birth: *Abraham Lincoln was born in 1809./fig. The organization was born fifty years ago at a small meeting.*

born adj. **1.** Having a certain quality as if from birth: *a born leader/ Mary was born blind.* **2.** **born again** Having received new life, or spiritual birth: *For you have been born again, not of perishable seed, but of imperishable, through the living and enduring word of God* (1 Peter 1:23). NOTE: "Born again" is a phrase used to describe someone who is a Christian, one who not only has a knowledge of Jesus Christ, but whose life has been changed by God. One who has been "born again" does not rely on his own "works of righteous-ness" for eternal life, but puts his trust completely in Jesus who came into the world to save sinners, suffered and died on Calvary's cross to pay for our sins, and rose again, conquering sin, death, and the devil, proving that he is who he claimed to be—true God and Savior of the world. The "born again" Christian no longer lives unto himself (his own selfish interests) but unto him who died for us and rose again (2 Corinthians 5:15). A person is born again by the power of the Holy Spirit working through the Word of God.

bor-row (bar–oᵂ) v. **1.** To take or receive sthg. temporarily, with the understanding that it will be returned **2.** To take over certain words, ideas, etc. as one's own: *Many English words are borrowed from French.* —**borrower** n.

bo-som (bʊz–əm/ buᵂ–zəm) n. **1.** The front of the human chest, esp. the female breasts **2.** The seat of secret thoughts and feelings

boss (bɔs) n. An employer; manager; person

who gives orders to others: *She likes her boss, because he is always thoughtful and courteous.*

boss v. *infml.* To give orders in an unpleasant, rude way: *No one likes him, because he bosses people around.* —**bossy** adj.

bot-a-ny (bɑt–ni^y/ bɑt–ə–ni^y) n. -nies A branch of biology dealing with plants and plant life —**bo-tan-i-cal** (bə–tæn–ɪ–kəl) or **bo-tan-ic** (bə–**tæn**–ɪk) adj.

botch (bɑtʃ) v. **1.** To patch clumsily **2.** To bungle: *We really botched up that job. We'd better do it over!*

both (bo^wθ) adj., pron. The two; the one and the other together: *My husband and I both work for the same company.*

both-er (bɑð–ər) n. Trouble, inconvenience, or nuisance, usu. minor and lasting a short time: *I hate to be a bother to you, but may I borrow your pen for a minute?*

bother v. **1.** To cause sbdy. to be slightly upset; to annoy or trouble, esp. in small ways: *Please don't bother me while I'm eating my lunch!/ pol. We're sorry to bother you, but could you tell us how to find the Royal Hotel?* **2.** To cause inconvenience to oneself: *I don't have time to bother with that job today.*

bot-tle (bɑt–əl) n. A glass or plastic container for liquids, with a narrow neck or mouth and usu. no handle

bot-tle-neck (bɑt–əl–nɛk) n. **1.** The neck of a bottle **2.** Any route where traffic is slowed or stopped **3.** Any point at which movement or progress is hindered because much must be passed through it

bot-tom (bɑt–əm) n. **1.** The lowest part or place: *at the bottom of the hill / the bottom of the dish* **2.** The land surface under a lake, river, etc.: *They dropped the boat's anchor over the side, and it sank to the bottom of the lake.* **3.** The lowest place in a group or situation: *He was a poor salesman, and was always at the bottom of the list of salesmen each month.* **4.** The part of the body on which a person sits; buttocks **5.** *often derog.* The cause on which everything else rests: *The police finally found who was at the bottom of the series of robberies.* **6. from the bottom of one's heart** With deep feeling: *She thanked them from the bottom of her heart for their help.* —**bottom** adj.

bough (baʊ) n. A main branch of a tree

bought (bɔt) v. Past tense and part. of **buy**

bouil-lon (bu^w–yɑn/bʊl–yɑn/–yən) n. Clear broth made from beef or other meat

boul-der (bo^wl–dər) n. A very large stone or rock: *A boulder fell down the hillside and blocked the road.*

boul-e-vard (bʊl–ə–vɑrd) n. A wide, well-made street, often with trees on each side: *Wilshire Boulevard*

bounce (baʊns/baʊnts) v. **bounced, bouncing** Bound; rebound: *The ball bounced over the fence./ fig. He bounced out of bed (=got out of bed quickly).* —**bounce** n.

boun-cing (baʊn–sɪŋ/ baʊnt–sɪŋ) adj. Esp. of babies, healthy and active: *a bouncing baby boy*

bound (baʊnd) v. **1.** To mark the boundary of; to limit within a certain space: *Spain is bounded on the north by France.* **2.** To leap; jump

bound n. A leap; jump

bound v. Past tense and past part. of **bind**

bound adj. **1.** Held; limited: *Because of the snowstorm, they were house-bound for three days.* **2.** Constrained; obliged; obligated: *He felt bound to keep his promise.* **3.** Certain; very likely: *Our team is bound to lose at least one game this season.* **4.** Of the pages of a book, fastened together between covers: *There was a beautifully bound Bible on the table.* **5.** Ready to go; going: *He boarded a ship bound for New York.*

bound-a-ry (baʊn–də–ri^y) n. -ries **1.** A line or other thing marking a limit: *That fence marks the boundary between our farm and our neighbor's.* —compare BORDER **2.** *fig.* The outer limit of sthg.: *the boundaries of scientific investigation*

bound-less (baʊnd–ləs) adj. Having no limit: *boundless energy* —**boundlessness** n. —**boundlessly** adv.

boun-te-ous (baʊn–ti^y–əs) adj. **1.** Generous **2.** Plentiful

boun-ti-ful (baʊn–tɪ–fəl) adj. **1.** Bounteous **2.** Abundant; plentiful —**boun-tifully** adv.

boun-ty (baʊn–ti^y) n. **1.** Generosity **2.** Sthg. that is given liberally **3.** A reward, esp. one given by a government for performing a service

bou-quet (bo^w–ke^y/ bu^w–) n. A bunch of flow-ers

bour-geois (bʊər–ʒwɑ/ bər–ʒwɑ) n. 1. One who belongs to the middle class 2. A capitalist

bourgeois adj. 1. Of or typical of the middle class 2. Overly concerned with respectability and possessions

bour-geoi-sie (bʊər–ʒwɑ–zi^y/ bɜrʒ–wɑ–zi^y) n. The middle class as opposed to the aristoc-racy or the working class

bout (baʊt) n. 1. Contest; match 2. Session: *She had quite a bout with the manager.*

bou-tique (bu^w–ti^{y}k)n. A small retail store, esp. a shop for women's clothing

bo-vine (bo^w–vaɪn/ –vi^{y}n) adj. 1. Of or like an ox or a cow 2. Stupid

bow (baʊ) v. 1. To bend the head or upper part of the body forward (or bend the knees) to show respect, reverence, etc.: *At the name of Jesus every knee should bow... and every tongue confess that Jesus Christ is Lord* (Philippians 2:10,11). 2. **bow out** To leave, or stop doing sthg.: *The mayor bowed out of the campaign, because he knew he would lose the election.*

bow n. 1. The act of bowing 2. **take a bow** Of actors or soloists, to come back on stage af-ter a performance to acknowledge the ap-plause of the audience 3. The front end of a boat —compare STERN

bow (bo^w) n. 1. A long strip of wood shaped into a curve and held by a tight string be-tween its ends, used for shooting arrows 2. A long, thin, straight piece of wood with a band of horsehairs between its ends, used for playing a violin and other similar stringed instruments 3. A knot formed by doubling a string, ribbon, etc., into two or more loops, such as used in tying shoes, in decorations, etc.: *After wrapping the package, she tied it with a beautiful bow.*

bow-els (baʊ–əlz) n. 1. Tubes from the stom-ach which carry waste matter out of the body; intestines 2. The interior part of sthg.: *bowels of the earth*

bow-er (baʊ–ər) n. A place in a garden made shady by overhanging plants

bowl (bo^{w}l) n. A deep, round container or dish, open at the top, for holding food, liq-uids, etc.: *soup bowl/ sugar bowl/ salad bowl*

bowl-ing (bo^{w}l–ɪŋ) n. Any of various games in which a ball is rolled at an object or group of objects, played on a green or an alley

box (bɑks) n. 1. A container for solids, usu. square or rectangular and with stiff sides and often a lid: *a cardboard box/ a jewelry box* 2. A small room or enclosed space, usu. for a special purpose: *a press box at the football stadium*

box-ing (bɑk–sɪŋ) n. The sport of fighting with tightly closed hands (fists), usu. cov-ered with padded gloves —compare WRES-TLING —box v.

boy (bɔɪ) n. 1. A male child; son: *Our boy was five years old when he started school./The Mar-tins have two boys and two girls, all under the age of twelve.* 2. **–boy** A boy or man who does a certain job: *a cowboy* —**boyhood** n. —**boy-ish** adj.

boy interj. AmE. infml. An expression of ex-citement, surprise, joy, etc.: *Boy! How nice to see you! I thought you were out of the country.*

boy-cott (bɔɪ–kɑt) v. To stop buying things or dealing with a company or store as a means of protest —**boycott** n.

boy-friend (bɔɪ–frɛnd) n. A regular male companion of a woman, esp. with romantic interest —compare GIRLFRIEND

bra (brɑ) n. Short for **brassiere**

brace (bre^{y}s) v. **braced, bracing** 1. To strength-en: *We braced the roof with iron poles.* 2. To provide support: *Her weak leg had to be braced.* 3. To prepare oneself, usu. for a diffi-culty, shock, disappointment, etc.: *The na-tion was braced for war even though there was no official declaration.*

brace n. 1. A device that supports or steadies a weight 2. A device worn on a part of the body for support 3. **braces (a)** Wire devices worn inside the mouth to straighten une-ven teeth **(b)** BrE. for **suspenders**

brace-let (bre^{y}s–lət) n. A decorative band or ring worn round the wrist

brack-et (bræk–ət) n. 1. A metal or wood fix-ture put in or on a wall to support sthg.: *a shelf bracket* 2. Either of a pair of punctuation marks [ ], used for enclosing certain infor-mation: *[This sentence is enclosed in brackets.]*

—compare PARENTHESIS **3**. A group of people within stated limits: *the 20 to 30 age bracket*

brad (bræd) n. A thin wire nail with a small head, sometimes off center

brag (bræg) v. *-gg- derog*. To speak with too much praise of oneself; boast

Brah-man, Brah-min (brɑ–mən) n. **1**. A member of the highest or priestly caste among Hindus **2**. A breed of cattle native to India and developed in the US

Brah-man-ism, Brah-min-ism (brɑ–mən–ɪz–əm) n. Orthodox Hinduism

braid (breʸd) v. **1**. To interweave strands of hair, thread, etc. **2**. To decorate with an interwoven trim **3**. To make by weaving strands together

braid n. **1**. **(a)** A length of hair that has been braided **(b)** A narrow length of interwoven or braided material **2**. An ornamental strip of braided material

braille (breʸl) n. A system of writing using characters made up of raised dots, enabling the blind to read

brain (breʸn) n. **1**. The organ in the head which controls and coordinates mental and physical activities: *His brain was damaged in the accident so that he could no longer control his movements.* **2**. Mental ability; intelligence: *He has a good brain, and he works hard. He should do well.* **3**. *infml*. A person of high intelligence: *He's a real brain when it comes to computers.*

brain-child (breʸn–tʃaɪld) n. The product of one's imagination

brains (breʸnz) n. **1**. The material which the brain is made of **2**. *infml*. Mental ability: *John's got brains. He figured out the answer in record time.* **3**. **rack one's brains** *infml*. To try hard to remember, understand, or solve a problem

brain-storm (breʸn–stɔrm) n. *infml*. A sudden clever idea

brain-storm-ing (breʸn–stɔrm–ɪŋ) n. A technique by which a group of people present and discuss different possibilities in order to find a solution to a problem

brain-wash (breʸn–wɒʃ) v. **1**. To indoctrinate so completely as to cause a change of be-

liefs and mental attitudes **2**. To persuade by propaganda or salesmanship

brake (breʸk) n. An apparatus for reducing the speed or stopping a wheel, car, etc.: *He put on the brake to keep the car from rolling down the hill.* —**brake** v.

bran (bræn) n. The inner husks of wheat, usu. separated from flour after grinding

branch (bræntʃ) v. **1**. To divide into or form branches: *That railroad branches about 100 miles from here, one branch going north and the other going south.* **2**. **branch out** To add to one's interests or activities: *Our company has branched out and opened an office in another city.*

branch n. **1**. The part of a tree which grows out of the trunk and has smaller branches and leaves on it: *The cat climbed up the tree and sat on a branch.* **2**. A similar division of sthg. other than a tree: *a branch of a river/ railroad* **3**. *fig*. A subdivision of sthg.: *One branch of our family came from Germany to the US in 1850./ That bank has ten branches throughout the city.*

brand (brænd) n. **1**. Goods which are the product of a particular firm or producer: *What is your favorite brand of soap?* **2**. A mark made by burning, to show ownership: *These cattle have the Lazy R brand on them.* **3**. A piece of burning wood

brand v. To mark by or as if by burning, esp. to show ownership: *The cowboys will be branding our cattle next week./ fig. He is branded as a coward.* (=*everyone knows or believes that he's a coward*)

brand-ish (bræn–dɪʃ) v. To wave or shake, as a sword

brash (bræʃ) adj. **1**. Brittle or fragile **2**. Reckless; hasty **3**. Offensively bold

brass (bræs) n. A mixture of copper and zinc, making a very hard, bright yellow metal: *a brass band* (=*a band made up mostly of brass musical instruments*)

bras-siere (brə–zɪər) n. A woman's undergarment worn to support the breasts

bras-sy (bræs–iʸ) adj. **-sier, -siest 1**. Cheap and showy **2**. Like brass in color **3**. Like the sound of a brass instrument **4**. Insolently bold

brat (bræt) n. An obnoxious, badly behaved child

bra-va-do (brə–va–do") n. -does A show of bravery; a bold pretense

brave (bre^y v) adj. *apprec.* Full of courage and ready to suffer danger or pain: *brave soldiers/ actions* —**bravely** adv. —**bravery** n.

brave v. **braved, braving** To act in the face of danger, pain, or trouble without showing fear

bra-vo (bra–vo^w) interj. Well done!

brawl (brɔl) n. A noisy quarrel —**brawl** v.

brawn (brɔn) n. Muscle power

brawn-y (brɔn–i^y) adj. Big and strong

bray (bre^y) n. The loud, harsh cry of a donkey —**bray** v.

bra-zen (bre^y–zən) adj. **1.** Made of brass **2.** Sounding loud and harsh **3.** Of the color of brass **4.** Full of contempt and boldness —**brazenness** n.

bra-zier (bre^y–ʒər) n. A kind of metal pan for holding burning coals or charcoal

breach (bri^y tʃ) n. **1.** A breaking of a law or obligation **2.** A hole in a solid structure **3.** The disrupting of a friendship or relationship

bread (brɛd) n. **1.** A common food made mainly of flour, usu. baked: *a loaf of bread* **2.** Food as one's means of staying alive: *our daily bread/Who is the breadwinner in your family? (=who earns the money, food, etc.?)* **3.** *infml.* Money **4. bread and butter** *infml.* Means of earning money: *Acting is his bread and butter.* **5. bread** *spir.* Spiritual food; the Word of God: *Jesus said, "Man does not live on bread alone, but on every word that comes from the mouth of God"* (Matthew 4:4). *Jesus also said, "I am the bread of life. He who comes to me will never go hungry, and he who believes in me will never thirst. I am the living bread that came down from heaven. He who feeds on this bread will live forever"* (John 6:35, 51, 58). Jesus meant that whoever believes that he came down from heaven to give his body and blood (to suffer and die on the cross) for our sins will have everlasting life (John 3:16; John 14:6).

breadth (brɛdθ) n. **1.** *fml.* Width; the distance from side to side: *He has traveled the breadth of the country in his search for happiness.* —compare LENGTH **2.** A broad stretch: *He has great breadth of understanding.*

break (bre^yk) v. **broke** (bro^wk), **broken** (bro^w–kən), **breaking 1.** To separate into pieces, esp. suddenly or violently: *The cup broke when it fell on the floor.* **2.** To start suddenly: *War broke out./An epidemic broke out.* **3.** To disobey; not keep: *Everyone who sins breaks the law; in fact, sin is lawlessness* (1 John 3:4)./ *Whoever keeps the whole law and yet stumbles at just one point is guilty of breaking all of it* (James 2:10)./ *She broke her promise.* **4.** To force a way into or out of: *He broke into the store and stole some jewelry./ The prisoners broke out of prison.* **5.** To bring under control: *After 20 years of smoking, he finally broke the habit.* **6.** To do better than: *He broke the high jump record./ Mr. Smith broke all the sales records for the month of April.* **7.** To interrupt an activity: *Pardon me for breaking in (=interrupting a conversation), but there's an urgent telephone call for you on line two./ Let's break for lunch and continue the meeting at one o'clock.* **8.** To cause to come to an end: *The train whistle broke the silence of the night.* **9.** To cause to come into being or notice, esp. suddenly: *Their car broke into view.* **10.** To find the secret of: *She broke their code. (=secret writing)* **11. break away** To escape **12. break down (a) break sthg. down** To destroy; reduce or be reduced to pieces: *They broke down the wall.* **(b)** Of machinery, to stop working: *Our car broke down on the way to work.* **(c)** Of a person, to lose control of one's feelings: *Jimmy broke down and cried when he heard the sad news.* —see also BREAKDOWN **13. break even** In a business, making neither a profit nor a loss **14. break in (a)** Using force to enter a building: *He broke in and stole a typewriter.* **(b)** To interrupt a conversation: *He broke in with an angry denial when he was accused of failing to do his job.* **(c) break sthg. in** To gradually accustom sthg. to full use: *I'm breaking in a new pair of shoes. (=wearing them to make them comfortable)* **15. break into sthg.** also **burst into sthg.** To start suddenly: *to break into song/laughter* **16. break sbdy. of sthg.** To cause sbdy. to give up a bad habit: *Doctors are trying to break him of his de-*

pendence on alcohol. **17. break off** To end: *Mary and Joe have broken off their relationship.* **18. break out (a)** To come about suddenly: *A fight broke out./His face broke out (=became covered) with a rash.* **(b)** To escape from: *to break out of prison* **19. break through sthg.** To make a way through: *He broke through the enemy lines and escaped./The scientists have broken through in their study of communicable diseases and now have ways of preventing many of them.* —see also BREAKTHROUGH **20. break up (a) break sthg. up** To end: *The party broke up at midnight/Their marriage broke up after 17 years. AmE.* **(b) break sbdy. up** To cause great amusement: *His funny story broke everyone up.* —see also BREAK DOWN, BREAKUP **21. break with sbdy./ sthg.** To end one's relationship with: *to break with one's former teammates*

break n. **1.** An opening made by breaking or being broken: *a break in the clouds* **2.** A pause between activities: *a coffee break* **3.** A change from the usual: *a break in the weather* **4.** The time just before sunrise when daylight first appears: *at break of day/at daybreak* **5.** *infml.* A chance; opportunity: *Give him a break and he'll do a good job.* **6.** Fate, esp. in the phrase "those are the breaks"

break-down (breᵏk–daʊn) n. **1.** A failure in function, esp. a physical, mental, or nervous collapse: *He had a nervous breakdown, and was unable to continue his work or serve on the committee.* **2.** A division showing a more detailed explanation: *Please give me a breakdown of our expenses for the month.* —see also BREAK DOWN, BREAKUP

break-fast (brek–fəst) n. The first meal of the day

break-in (breᵏk–ɪn) n. The forcible entering of a building —see BREAK IN

break-through (breᵏk–θruʷ) n. A major discovery, often made suddenly following repeated failures, esp. one that will lead to other discoveries: *Madame Curie made a major breakthrough in the treatment of cancer when she discovered radium.* —see also BREAK THROUGH

break-up (breᵏk–əp) n. **1.** A coming to an end, esp. of a relationship: *the breakup of a marri-*

age **2.** A separation into smaller parts: *the breakup of a large company* —see also BREAK UP, BREAKDOWN

breast (brest) n. **1.** Either of the two parts of a woman's body that produces milk: *She nestled her baby to her breast.* **2.** The smaller part like this on a man's body **3.** The front part of the human body from the shoulders to the abdomen

breath (brɛθ) n. **1.** Air taken into and breathed out of the lungs: *After all that running I'm all out of breath./fig. Let's go out for a breath of fresh air.* **2. catch one's breath** To return to one's normal rate of breathing after some activity such as running **3. take one's breath away** To cause sbdy. such great surprise, pleasure, etc. that they are unable to speak: *The Grand Canyon was so awesome that it took my breath away.* **4. save one's breath** To stop speaking because it is useless: *Save your breath; they won't believe you anyway.*

breathe (briʸð) v. **breathed, breathing 1.** To take air, gas, etc. into the lungs and let it out again: *It's wonderful to be able to breathe this clear mountain air.* **2. breathe down someone's neck** *infml.* To annoy sbdy. by following or watching them too closely

breath-tak-ing (brɛθ–teʸk–m̩) adj. **1.** Taking one's breath away **2.** Exciting; awe-inspiring

bred (brɛd) v. Past tense and past part. of **breed**

breech (briʸtʃ) n. The back part of a gun

breech-es (brɪtʃ–əz) n. Trousers

breed (briʸd) v. **bred, breeding 1.** To produce offspring: *Rabbits breed often.* **2.** To cause to be born **3.** To raise (cattle, etc.) **4.** To rear or bring up children **5.** To cause; to produce or be produced: *This sort of thing breeds trouble.*

breed n. **1.** A homogeneous group of animals within a species, developed by humans **2.** *fig.* A sort or kind: *a new breed of salesman*

breeze (briʸz) n. **1.** A light gentle gust of air —see WEATHER **2.** *infml.* Sthg. done with ease: *Learning Chinese is no breeze!*

breez-y (briʸz–iʸ) **-ier, -iest** adj. Of or having fairly strong breezes

breth-ren (brɛð–rən) n. Plural of **brother**, esp. in formal address

brev-i-ty (brev–ə–ti^y) n. Shortness

brew (hru^w) v. 1. To make beer by boiling and fermentation; to make tea by steeping 2. To be under preparation in this way: *The tea is brewing.* 3. To bring about; to develop: *Trouble is brewing.*

brew n. 1. A liquid made by brewing 2. *infml.* A glass of beer

bribe (braɪb) v. **bribed, bribing** To influence, esp. someone in a position of trust, by favors or gifts

bribe n. Sthg. offered or given to someone to get them to grant a favor: *Do not accept a bribe, for a bribe blinds the eyes of the wise and twists the words of the righteous* (Deuteronomy 16:19). *Cursed is the man who accepts a bribe to kill an innocent person* (Deuteronomy 27:25).

brib-er-y (braɪ–bər–i^y) n. Giving or taking of a bribe

brick (brɪk) n. A hard block of baked clay used for building: *The house was built out of yellow bricks.*

bride (braɪd) n. A woman just married or about to be married —see also BRIDE-GROOM —**bridal** adj.

bride-groom (braɪd–gru^wm) also **groom** n. A man just married or about to be married —see also BRIDE

brides-maid (braɪdz–me^yd) n. An unmarried woman who attends the bride at the wedding

bridge (brɪdʒ) n. 1. A structure built over a road, railway, valley, river, etc. 2. The raised part of a ship on which the captain and other officers stand to control the ship

bri-dle (braɪd–əl) n. The straps and reins worn on a horse's head by which it is controlled —**bridle** v.

brief (bri^yf) adj. Short, esp. in time: *a brief look at the report/ a brief letter*

brief v. To give final instructions or necessary information to: *The officer briefed his men before the attack.* —see also DEBRIEF —**briefing** n.

brief-case (bri^yf–ke^ys) n. A flat, usu. soft, leather case which opens at the top for carrying papers or books

bri-er (braɪ–ər) n. 1. Any thorny or prickly bush 2. A growth of such plants

brig (brɪg) n. 1. A ship's prison 2. A two-masted sailing vessel

bri-gade (brɪ–ge^yd) n. 1. An army unit forming part of a division 2. A group of people organized for a specific purpose: *a fire brigade*

bright (braɪt) adj. 1. Shining; radiant; giving out or reflecting light very strongly: *The light of the sun is very bright./ fig. one of the brightest days of my life/ bright eyes* 2. Of a strong, clear, color that is easily seen: *bright red/ yellow* 3. Intelligent: *a bright child/ idea* 4. Showing hope of future success: *He has a bright future ahead of him!* 5. **look at the bright side of things** To be cheerful and hopeful in spite of problems —**brightly** adv.

bright-en (braɪt–ən) v. To cause to become bright

bright-ness (braɪt–nəs) n. The quality of being bright: *Those who are wise [unto salvation] will shine like the brightness of the heavens, and those who lead many to righteousness, like the stars for ever and ever* (Daniel 12:3).

bril-liant (brɪl–yənt) adj. 1. Very bright: *a brilliant sun* 2. Very intelligent: *a brilliant speaker/ scientist* —**brilliance, -cy** n. —**brilliantly** adv.

brim (brɪm) n. Edge; rim; border

brim-stone (brɪm–sto^wn) n. Sulphur

brine (braɪn) n. Salt water —**brin-y** (braɪn–i^y) adj.

bring (brɪŋ) v. **brought** (brɔt), **bringing** 1. To carry or cause to come with one to or towards someone: *Father brought gifts for all the children.* 2. To lead to or cause: *April showers bring May flowers.* 3. To sell for: *This house should bring a pretty good price.* 4. To make official charges: *The policeman brought charges against the thief.* 5. To cause to come to a certain place or condition: *Their noisy partying brought a lot of complaints from the neighbors.* 6. **bring sthg. about** To cause: *The automobile has brought about many changes in our lives.* 7. **bring sbdy. around/ over** To convince sbdy.; to change their thinking: *I hope we can bring him around to our way of thinking.* 8. **bring sbdy./ sthg. back (a)** To cause the return of sthg. or sbdy.: *Do you think*

they'll ever bring back the old songs we used to enjoy? **(b)** To get sthg. and return with it: *Would you please bring back some milk from the store for me?* **9. bring sbdy./ sthg. out (a)** To produce: *to bring out a new product/fig. to bring out the best in someone* **(b)** To cause to be produced earlier: *This warm weather should bring the blossoms out.* **10. bring sbdy. to** Also **bring sbdy. around** *AmE.* **bring sbdy. round** *BrE.* To revive someone who has fainted or become unconscious: *They tried to bring her around after she fainted.* **11. bring sbdy. through sthg.** To save sbdy. from sthg.: *The doctor brought Mother through a serious illness.* **12. bring sbdy./ sthg. up (a)** To take care of in the family until grown: *to bring up children* —com-pare RAISE **(b)** To introduce a subject: *to bring up the matter of...* —compare COME UP

brink (brɪŋk) n. **1.** The edge (of a cliff, etc.) **2. on the brink of** On the verge of; almost to the point of: *on the brink of war*

brisk (brɪsk) adj. Moving quickly; lively: *a brisk walk* —**briskness** n.

bris-tle (brɪs-əl) n. **1.** A short, stiff hair **2.** One of the short, stiff pieces of hair or wire in a brush

bristle v. **-tled, -tling 1.** To raise the bristles in anger or fear **2.** To show indignation **3.** To be thickly set with bristles

brit-tle (brɪt-əl) adj. Hard, but easily broken

broad (brɔd) adj. **1.** Wide: *broad shoulders/ the broad horizon* **2.** Not limited; broad-minded **3.** Full and clear, esp. in the phrase "broad daylight"

broad-cast (brɔd-kæst) n. A single radio or television presentation: *We all paid close attention to the radio broadcasts from the war zone.*

broadcast v. **-cast** also **-casted** *AmE.* **-casting 1.** To send out or speak or perform on a radio or television presentation **2.** To make widely known: *Mary broadcast the news to all her friends.* —**broadcaster** n. —**broadcasting** n.

broad-en (brɔd-ən) v. To make broad or broader: *The workmen were broadening the road.*

broad–mind-ed (brɔd–maɪn-dəd) adj. Respectful of the opinions and actions of oth-

ers even if not the same as one's own —opposite NARROW–MINDED —**broad-mindedness** n.

bro-cade (broʷ-keʸd) n. A fabric woven with raised designs

broc-co-li (brɑk-ə-liʸ) n. A plant with thickly clustered bud and stalks, eaten as a vegetable

bro-chure (broʷ-ʃʊər/ -ʃyʊər) n. A small folder or pamphlet

broil (brɔɪl) v. To cook by exposure to direct heat; to grill

broke (broʷk) adj. *infml.* Having no money at all: *He is (flat) broke.*

broke (broʷk) v. Past tense of **break**

brok-en (broʷ-kən) adj. **1.** Forcibly separated into smaller pieces; damaged: *a broken window* **2.** (of a vow or promise) Not kept: *a broken law/ promise/ a broken marriage* **3.** Poorly spoken or written: *broken English*

broken v. Past part. of **break**

bro-ken–heart-ed (broʷ-kən-hɑrt-əd) adj. Overcome by grief or despair: *The Lord is close to the broken-hearted and saves those who are crushed in spirit* (Psalm 34:18).

bron-chi-tis (brɑŋ-kaɪ-tɪs) n. The inflammation of the bronchi, causing difficulty in breathing

bron-chus (brɑŋ-kəs) n. **-chi** The air passages in the lungs —**bron-chi-al** (brɑŋ-kiʸ-əl) adj. *bronchial pneumonia* —**bron-chi-tic** (brɑŋ-kɪt-ɪk) adj. *a bronchitic cough*

bron-co (brɑŋ-koʷ) n. A small, wild, or half-tamed horse of western North America

bron-to-sau-rus (brɑn-tə-saʊr-əs) n. **-sau-ri** (-saʊ-riʸ) A very large dinosaur with a long neck and a long powerful tail for defending itself, that lived in swamps and streams

bronze (brɑnz) n. A reddish-brown mixture of copper and tin

brooch (broʷtʃ) n. Any decorative pin or clasp for the clothing

brood (bruʷd) v. **1.** Of hens, to sit on eggs **2.** To think anxiously for some time

brood n. A number of young birds hatched at one time; young animals or children of the same family

brook (brʊk) n. A small stream

broom (bruʷm) n. A brush used for sweeping

broth (brɔθ) n. Liquid in which meat or vegetables have been cooked

broth-er (brʌð–ər) n. **1.** A male relative with the same parents: *Peter and Andrew were brothers.* **2.** A male member of the same faith or group: *a brother in the church/ Jesus said, "Whoever does the will of my Father in heaven is my brother and sister and mother"* (Matthew 12:50). **3.** A title for a male member of a religious group: *Brother John will read the Scripture lesson.* —compare SISTER —**broth-erly** adj. *brotherly love* —**brotherliness** n.

broth-er-in-law n. —**broth-ers-in-law 1.** The brother of one's husband or wife **2.** The husband of one's sister **3.** The husband of the sister of one's husband or wife —see also SISTER–IN–LAW

brought (brɔt) v. Past tense and part. of **bring**

brow (braʊ) n. **1.** An eyebrow **2.** The forehead **3.** A projecting or overhanging part: *the brow of a hill*

brown (braʊn) n., adj. The color of earth or of chocolate or coffee: *He is very brown after lying in the sun all summer.*

brown v. To make or become brown or browner: *The turkey browned as it roasted in the oven.*

browse (braʊz) v. **browsed, browsing** To look through a book or at items on sale, in a casual, leisurely way

bruise (bruʷz) n. A discolored place on the skin of a human, animal, or fruit where it has been injured by a blow but not broken

bruise v. **bruised, bruising** To cause one or more bruises on sthg.

bru-nette (bruʷ–nɛt) adj. Having dark or brown hair

brunette n. A person with dark or brown hair

brush (brʌʃ) n. An instrument made of stiff hair, nylon, etc., used esp. for grooming, cleaning, or painting: *a clothes brush/ a toothbrush/ a paintbrush*

brush n. **1.** Small branches from trees or bushes **2.** Land covered by small rough trees and bushes **3.** A skirmish; a slight encounter: *a brush with the law/ police*

brush up v. To study sthg. that is known but has been partly forgotten: *I have to brush up on my Spanish before I go to Madrid.* —**brush-up** n.

brusque (brʌsk) adj. Blunt; abrupt; curt

bru-tal (bruʷt–əl) adj. Very cruel; merciless —**bru-tal-i-ty** (bruʷ–tæl–ɪ–tiʸ) n. —**bru-tal-ize** (bruʷt–əl–aɪz) v. **-ized, -izing**

brute (bruʷt) n. **1.** An animal **2.** A brutal person **3.** An unpleasant or difficult person or thing

brute adj. **1.** Like a brute **2.** Cruel **3.** Unreasoning —**brutish** adj.

bub-ble (bʌb–əl) n. A thin ball of liquid enclosing gas or air: *Children love blowing bubbles.*

bubble v. **-bled, -bling** To form or rise in bubbles: *The soda bubbled in the glass.*

buck (bʌk) n. **1.** The male of the deer, rabbit, etc. **2.** *fml.* A robust or high-spirited young man **3.** *AmE. infml.* An American dollar: *Can you lend me five bucks?* **4. pass the buck** *infml.* To pass on the responsibility to someone else

buck v. Of a horse or a mule, to make a series of rapid jumps into the air, sometimes in an attempt to throw the rider off

buck-et (bʌk–ət) n. **1.** A container for carrying liquids, made of metal, plastic, or wood and having an open top and a handle; a pail **2. kick the bucket** *infml.* To die

buck-le (bʌk–əl) n. **1.** A clasp, esp. one with a movable tongue for fastening two belt or strap ends **2.** An ornament that resembles a buckle

buckle v. **-led, -ling 1.** To fasten or secure with a buckle: *Make sure your seat belts are buckled.* **2. buckle down** To begin working hard **3.** To bend, warp, or crumple under pressure or heat: *The intensive heat caused the sidewalk to buckle.* **4.** To collapse or yield: *Strong winds caused the bridge to buckle and fall into the river.*

bu-col-ic (buʷ–kɑl–ɪk) adj. Pastoral; rustic

bud (bʌd) n. **1.** A small knob that will develop into a branch, leaf, or flower **2.** A flower or leaf not fully open

bud v. **budded, budding 1.** To be in bud **2.** To graft a bud on a plant

Bud-dhism (buʷ–dɪz–əm) n. A religion of eastern and southern Asia growing out of

the teachings of Gautama Buddha; the doctrine that suffering is inseparable from existence, but that inward extinction of the self and of the senses culminates in a state of illumination called Nirvana —**Bud-dhist** (buᵂ–dɪst) n.

budge (bʌdʒ) v. **budged, budging** To cause to move slightly: *I can't budge this rock.*

budg-et (bʌdʒ–ət) n. **1.** Any plan showing how money is to be spent: *a family/ business/ weekly budget/ To balance the budget we must make sure that we do not spend more money than is earned.* **2.** The quantity of money stated in these plans

budget v. To plan private or public spending within the limits of a certain amount of money: *They budgeted $2,000,000 for a new city library.*

buff (bʌf) n. **1.** A dull, brownish-yellow color **2.** A heavy, soft, brownish-yellow leather made from the skin of the buffalo or from other animal hides **3.** A military coat made of leather **4.** A small block covered with this leather or with cloth, used for cleaning or shining

buff adj. **1.** Made of buff **2.** Of the color of buff

buff v. **1.** To clean or polish with a buff **2.** To make clean or soft like buff

buf-fa-lo (bʌf–ə–loᵂ) n. **-loes** or **-lo 1.** A kind of ox found in Asia and South Africa **2.** The North American bison, a large animal with a very large head and shoulders, covered with lots of hair

buf-fer (bʌf–ər) n. **1.** Sthg. used to shine or polish **2.** A person, thing, or country that protects against the shock of an impact or lessens an unpleasant effect

buf-fet (bʌf–ət) v. To hit sharply and repeatedly: *We were buffeted about by the strong wind.*

buf-fet (bə–feʸ) n. **1.** A cabinet for holding china **2.** Provision of food where guests serve themselves: *a buffet luncheon* **3.** A counter where food and drink may be bought and consumed

bug (bʌg) n. **1.** Any small flying or creeping insect **2.** A germ that causes disease: *I must have picked up a "flu" bug; I'm not feeling very well.* **3.** A tiny device which may be hidden in a room to record conversations

bug v. **-gg-** *infml.* **1.** To hide a secret listening device in someone's room, office, etc.: *The spies have bugged her office.* **2.** *AmE.* To keep annoying someone: *Stop bugging me.*

bug-gy (bʌg iʸ) n. **-gies 1.** A light horse-drawn carriage **2.** A baby carriage

bu-gle (byuᵂ–gəl) n. A type of small trumpet

bu-gler (byuᵂ–glər) n. One who plays the bugle

build (bɪld) n. A person's physical size and shape: *What a great build he has! He must be a football star!*

build (bɪld) v. **built** (bɪlt), **building 1.** To make one or more things by putting pieces together: *That house is built out of brick(s)./ Every house is built by someone, but God is the builder of everything* (Hebrews 3:4)./ *They're building a shopping mall there now./ fig. Hard work builds character./ We are building for the future.* **2. build up** (=build sthg. up) To cause to become larger, stronger — physically, financially, spiritually, academically, etc.: *They gradually built up a good business./ Now I commit you to God and the word of his grace, which can build you up [spiritually]* (Acts 20:32). *But you dear friends, build yourselves up in your most holy faith* (Jude 20). *Encourage one another and build each other up* (1 Thessalonians 5:11). —see also BUILDUP

builder (bɪld–ər) n. One who builds: *He [Abraham] was looking forward to the city with foundations, whose architect and builder is God* (Hebrews 11:10).

build-ing (bɪld–ɱ) n. A structure with a roof and walls that is intended to stay in one place and not to be moved or taken down again: *Houses and churches are buildings.*

build-up (bɪld–əp) n. An increase: *There has been quite a buildup of traffic in the past couple of hours.*

bulb (bʌlb) n. **1.** The round root of certain plants: *a tulip bulb* **2.** Any object having a similar shape, for example, the glass part of an electric lamp: *a light bulb*

bulge (bʌldʒ) n. A rounded swelling; an outward curve

bulge v. **-bulged, bulging 1.** To form a bulge

2. To swell or bend outward

bulk (bʌlk) n. **1.** Great size or quantity ? An unusually large body: *The elephant lowered its great bulk.* **3.** The greater part of: *The bulk of the stock has already been sold.* **4. in bulk** In large quantities rather than in separate packages: *to buy/sell in bulk*

bulk-y (bʌlk–iʸ) adj. **-ier, -iest 1.** Having bulk, esp. if large for its kind, or fat **2.** Having great size or mass compared with weight: *a bulky, woolen garment*

bull (bʊl) n. The adult male of the cattle family or of various other large animals, such as the elephant, elk, moose, whale, walrus, etc.

bull-doze (bʊl–doʷz) v. **-dozed, -dozing 1.** To clear the land with a bulldozer **2.** *infml.* To force people to do sthg.: *He bulldozed the board of directors into accepting his proposal.*

bull-doz-er (bʊl–doʷ–zər) n. A powerful tractor with a broad steel blade mounted in front, used for moving earth or clearing the ground

bul-let (bʊl–ət) n. A small, round or cone-shaped missile to be shot from a gun

bul-le-tin (bʊl–ə–tən) n. **1.** A short, public, usu. official, notice or news report intended for immediate release: *Here is the latest bulletin about the war.* **2.** A periodical, esp. one produced by an association or group

bull-head-ed (bʊl–hed–əd) adj. Very stubborn; headstrong; obstinate

bull's-eye (bʊlz–aɪ) n. **1.** The center of a target **2.** A shot that hits this

bull's-eye interj. Perfect; just the thing; exactly right

bul-ly (bʊl–iʸ) n. **-lies** A person who uses his strength or power to hurt or frighten others into doing what he wants

bully v. **bullied, bullying** To behave as a bully; to intimidate: *The older boys bullied the younger ones.*

bum (bʌm) n. *infml. derog. esp. AmE.* **1.** A loafer; tramp **2.** One who spends a lot of time on a certain game or amusement: *a tennis bum*

bump (bʌmp) n. **1.** A knock or blow **2.** A swelling, lump, or bulge: *He fell off the porch and got a bump on his head.* —**bumpy** adj. *a rough, bumpy road* —**bumpiness** n.

bump (bʌmp) v. **1.** To strike or knock with force or violence: *The car bumped into the tree.* **2.** To move along with much sudden shaking, as of a wheeled vehicle over uneven ground: *We bumped along the road.* **3. bump into sbdy.** *infml.* To meet by chance: *I bumped into an old friend at the mall last night.* **4. bump sbdy. off** *infml.* To kill; murder

bump-er (bʌmp–ər) n. A bar fixed on the front or back of a vehicle to protect it when it knocks against anything

bumper adj. Very large: *a bumper crop*

bun (bʌn) n. A small bread roll, often sweetened

bunch (bʌntʃ) n. **1.** A number of things of the same kind, held together in some way: *a bunch of flowers/ bananas* **2.** *infml.* A group: *This bunch of girls is going on a picnic.*

bun-dle (bʌn–dəl) n. **1.** A number of things loosely bound together **2.** Sthg. wrapped for carrying **3.** *infml.* A mass of: *I'm so excited, I'm just a bundle of nerves./ He made a bundle in real estate.*

bundle v. **bundled, bundling 1.** To make into a bundle **2. bundle up** To dress warmly: *You'd better bundle up. It's cold outside.*

bun-ga-low (bʌŋ–gə–loʷ) n. A small one-story house

bun-gle (bʌŋ–gəl) v. **-gled, -gling** To do sthg. poorly: *They really bungled that job.*

bun-ion (bʌn–yən) n. A painful lump or swelling on the joint of the big toe

bunk (bʌŋk) n. A narrow bed that is often one of two or more placed one above the other: *Bunk beds are useful, esp. when many people must sleep in the same small room.*

bunt (bʌnt) v. In baseball, to bat a pitched ball lightly so it does not go beyond the infield —**bunt** n.

buoy (bɔɪ/ buʷ–iʸ) n. **1.** A floating object which serves as a guide or as a warning for ships **2.** Sthg. which acts as a float (e.g., a life buoy)

buoy-an-cy (bɔɪ–ən–siʸ) n. Ability to float

buoy-ant (bɔɪ–ənt) adj. Light; cheerful

bur-den (bər–dən) n. *fml.* **1.** A heavy load: *The camel carried a very heavy burden.* **2.** Care; responsibility: *Taking care of her aged mother has been quite a burden for her.* **3.** A strong

feeling of guilt and shame: *My guilt has overwhelmed me like a burden too heavy to bear* (Psalm 38:4).

bur-den v. **-dened, -dening 1.** To worry or trouble someone: *I don't want to burden you with a lengthy report of what happened.* **2.** To load someone down with financial or other responsibilities: *The people were burdened with heavy taxation.*

bu-reau (byʊr–o^w) n. **bureaus, bureaux** (byʊr–o^wz) **1.** *AmE.* A chest of drawers for storing clothing and personal items **2.** A government department: *The Bureau of Streets and Roads* **3.** A business office, esp. one that collects and/ or keeps records

bu-reau-cra-cy (byʊ–rɑk–rə–si^y) n. **-cies 1.** A group of government-appointed officials **2.** An unwieldy administrative system having little initiative or flexibility

bu-reau-crat (byʊr–ə–kræt) n. One who practices or favors bureaucracy —**bu-reau-crat-ic** (byʊr–ə–kræt–ɪk) adj.

bur-glar (bɜr–glər) n. One who breaks into houses, stores, churches, schools, etc., esp. during the night in order to rob them —see THIEF

bur-gla-ry (bɜr–glər–i^y) n. **-ries** The crime of forcibly entering a building with the intention of stealing

bur-i-al (beər–i^y–əl) n. The act or process of putting a dead body into a grave —see BURY

bur-lap (bɜr–læp) n. A coarse, heavy, plain-woven cloth, usu. of hemp or jute

bur-ly (bɜr–li^y) adj. **-lier, -liest** Strong and heavily built; husky; muscular

burn (bɜrn) v. **burned** or **burnt** (bɜrnt), **burning 1.** To be or become on fire: *This kind of coal doesn't burn very easily.* **2.** To destroy by fire: *The building was burned to the ground.* **3.** To use for power, heating, or lighting: *Those lamps burn kerosene.* **4.** To produce an unpleasant hot feeling: *The hot sands burned my feet. / fig. He's burning with fever.* **5. burn sbdy. up** *fig.* To make someone very angry: *He really burns me up.*

burn n. An injury or effect produced by burning: *His life was spared, but he is suffering from many second and third degree burns.*

burn-er (bɜr–nər) n. The part of a fuel-burning device that produces the flames

burn-ing (bɜr–nɪŋ) adj. **1.** Being on fire: *a burning bush* **2.** Producing a feeling of great heat or fire: *a burning fever* **3.** Very important; urgent: *The war on drugs is one of the burning issues of our time.* **4.** Intense: *a burning desire*

bur-ro (bɜr–o^w/bu^w–ro^w) n. A donkey, esp. a small one used as a pack animal

bur-row (bɜr–o^w) n. A hole in the ground made by an animal, such as a rabbit

burrow v. **1.** To form by tunneling: *He burrowed his way through the snow.* **2.** T o progress by, or as if by digging

burst (bɜrst) n. **1.** A sudden outbreak: *a burst of laughter/ a burst of speed* **2.** Explosion: *The burst of dynamite a mile away shook our house and rattled our windows.*

burst (bɜrst) v. **burst, bursting 1.** To break suddenly: *The balloon burst.* **2.** To enter suddenly: *She burst into my room.* **3.** To be filled to the breaking point: *If I eat another bite, I'll burst./ fig. She's bursting to tell you the news.* (=*She can hardly wait*) **4.** To come into the stated condition suddenly: *She burst into tears when she heard the news of her husband's death.*

bur-y (beər–i^y) v. **-ied, -ying 1.** To put into the grave: *She was buried at Forest Lawn Memorial Park.* **2.** To hide sthg., esp. in the ground: *The thieves buried the stolen goods under the old oak tree.* **3.** To hide: *fig. The facts are buried in a few old books.* **4. to bury the hatchet** *infml.* To stop fighting and forget the quarrels of the past and become friends again

bus (bʌs) n. A large motor-driven passenger vehicle

bus-boy (bʌs-bɔɪ) n. A waiter's assistant in a restaurant

bush (bʊʃ) n. **1.** A shrub: *a rose bush* **2. the bush** Rough uncleared country **3. to beat around the bush** In speaking, to waste time on unimportant details and not get to the main point: *Stop beating around the bush and give us your decision.*

bush-el (bʊʃ–əl) n. A unit of measurement for dry things such as vegetables, grains, and fruits, equal to 4 pecks or 32 quarts

bush-y (bʊʃ–i^y) adj. **-ier, -iest** Of hair or plants,

growing thickly: *a bushy head of hair*

busi-ness (bɪz-nɪs) n. **1.** One's work, employment, or mission: *I'm in the clothing business.* **2.** Trade and the making of money: *Business is booming! (=it's very good)* **3.** Personal concerns: *Make it your ambition to lead a quiet life, to mind your own business and to work with your hands... so that your daily life may win the respect of outsiders and so that you will not be dependent on anybody* (1 Thessalonians 4:11,12). **4.** An event or matter: *I don't like this business of having to fight traffic on the way to work every morning.* **5. have no business doing sthg.** Should not do sthg. **6. Mind your own business/ none of your business** *infml. It's none of your business so keep out of it.*

busi-ness-man (bɪz-nəs-mæn) n. **-men** A man engaged in commercial or industrial activity

busi-ness-wom-an (bɪz-nəs-wʊm-ən) n. **-wom-en** A woman engaged in commercial or industrial activity

bust (bʌst) n. **1.** A sculpture of the head and shoulders of a human being **2.** The measurement around a woman's chest

bus-tle (bʌs-əl) v. **-tled, -tling** To move or work in a brisk, energetic way

bustle n. Briskly energetic activity

bus-y (bɪz-iʸ) adj. **-ier, -iest 1.** Active; not idle: *They [the older women] can train the younger women to love their husbands and children, to be self-controlled and pure, to be busy at home, to be kind...* (Titus 2:4-5). **2.** *AmE.* Of telephones, in use: *I'm sorry, the line is busy.* **3. busy signal** *AmE.* The sound made by a telephone when it is in use: *I tried to call you many times yesterday, but I always got a busy signal.* **—busily** adv.

but (bʌt) prep. Other than; except: *There's no one here but me.*

but conj. **1.** Yet; nevertheless: *He would like to go fishing, but he can't go today.* **2.** Except that: *We were going to the ball game, but it rained (so we didn't.)* **3.** Instead; on the contrary: *I had not just one, but three job offers today.* **4.** Although; nevertheless: *He came home poorer but wiser.*

butch-er (bʊtʃ-ər) n. A person who kills animals for food or one who sells meat

butcher v. To kill cruelly: *They butchered many people.*

but-ler (bʌt-lər) n. The head male servant of a house who is in charge of other servants

butt (bʌt) v. **1.** To strike someone or sthg. with the head or horns, as a goat does **2. butt in** To interrupt or interfere: *Stop butting in while I'm talking.*

butt n. **1.** The thick, heavy end, esp. of a rifle **2.** The end of a finished cigar or cigarette: *a cigarette butt* **3.** A person whom others criticize or tell jokes about: *John was the butt of most of their jokes.* **4.** *AmE. infml.* The buttocks

but-ter (bʌt-ər) n. Yellow fat made from milk, used to spread on bread and in cooking, baking, etc.

butter v. To spread with butter: *He buttered his toast.*

but-ter-fly (bʌt-ər-flaɪ) n. **-flies** Any of several flying insects that fly by day and often have beautifully-colored wings

but-tock (bʌt-ək) n. **1.** Either of the two parts of the body on which a person sits **2.** The corresponding part of an animal

but-ton (bʌt-ən) n. **1.** A small, usu. round or flat object which is passed through an opening (buttonhole) to act as a fastener **2.** A button-like object or device, esp. one which is pressed to start a machine or ring a bell: *I pressed the button for the elevator.*

but-ton-hole (bʌt-ən howˡl) v. **-holed, -holing** *infml.* To stop someone and force him/ her to listen: *She buttonholed me in the hall and told me all her problems.*

buttonhole n. An opening through which a button is passed to form a fastener

buy (baɪ) v. **bought** (bɔt), **buying 1.** To obtain sthg. in exchange for money (or for sthg. else); to purchase: *He bought a new book, and she bought a new dress./ The Bible says, "You are not your own; you are bought with a price [the blood of Christ]. Therefore honor God with your body"* (1 Corinthians 6:19,20). **—opposite SELL 2.** *infml.* To accept as true: *I don't buy your story. You'd better tell the truth.*

buy n. *infml.* **1.** An act of buying sthg. **2.** Sthg. worth more than the price asked: *That dress is a good buy. It was twice as much last week!*

buy-er (baɪ–ər) n. A person who buys products, esp. for a company or large store for re-sale

buzz (bʌz) v. **1.** To make a low humming noise, as bees do: *The room was buzzing with excitement* **2.** To call for someone by using an electric signaling device: *He buzzed his secretary for some information.*

buzz n. A call on the telephone: *Give me a buzz the next time you're in town.*

buz-zard (bʌz–ərd) n. A large, slow-flying bird of prey; a kind of hawk

buz-zer (bʌz–ər) n. A device with which to buzz someone: *He called his secretary on the buzzer.*

by (baɪ) prep. **1.** Near; next to: *She was sitting by the table.* **2.** Past: *They drove right by me without stopping.* **3.** Through; with the use of: *He entered by the back door./ He came by train.* **4.** (Shows the performer of the action): *a song by George Gershwin* **5.** Not later than: *I need it by noon tomorrow.* **6.** According to: *We've got to do this by the rules.* **7.** According to the amount of: *He won the race by ten yards.* **8.** (In numbers and measurements): *I need a box about two inches by six inches by nine.* **9.** During: *Some people work by night and sleep by day.* **10.** With regard to: *a carpenter by trade* **11.** Entirely on

one's own: *I drove all the way from New York to San Francisco by myself.* **12. by the way** *infml.* (Introducing a new subject): *By the way, what are you going to do tomorrow?*

by (baɪ) adv. **1.** Past: *May I get by, please?* **2.** Near: *There were several people standing by.* **3. by and by** Sooner or later **4. by and large** Generally speaking

bye–bye (baɪ–baɪ) interj. Goodbye; farewell

by-gone (baɪ–gɔn) adj. Past or gone by

bygone n. **1.** A past event **2. let bygones be bygones** To forget past disagreements

by-law (baɪ–lɔ) n. A rule governing a society's or a corporation's affairs

by-pass (baɪ–pæs) n. A way around sthg.; an alternate route

by-pass v. To avoid sthg.

by-stand-er (baɪ–stæn–dər) n. A person standing near, but not taking part in whatever is happening: *My sister was shot during the robbery, and she was just an innocent bystander.*

byte (baɪt) n. A unit of computer memory, usu. made up of eight bits: *One letter on the computer keyboard takes up one byte of memory.*

by-way (baɪ–weʸ) n. A small path or road which is not well known

C **C, c** (si⁀ʸ) n. **1.** The third letter of the English alphabet **2.** *C written abbr.* said as: CENTIGRADE(=Celsius): *100 C*

cab (kæb) n. **1.** A taxi: *When we are in New York, we go almost everywhere by cab or on the subway.* **2.** The part of a truck, crane, etc. in which the driver stands or sits

cab-bage (kæb–ɪdʒ) n. A round vegetable, similar in appearance to a head of lettuce, having thick green leaves

cab-in (kæb–ən) n. **1.** A small cottage, usu. of simple design and construction: *Abraham Lincoln lived in a log cabin for many years.* **2.** The area at the front of an airplane in which the pilot sits **3.** A small room on a ship used for sleeping or as living space

cab-i-net (kæb–ə–nət/ kæb–nət) n. **1.** A piece of furniture with shelves and doors **2.** A wooden or metal case with shelves or drawers: *a storage cabinet/ a filing cabinet* **3.** A case for displaying articles such as jewelry, historic documents, etc. **4.** An upright case housing a radio or TV set **5.** An advisory council of a head of state: *The Secretary of Education is an important member of the president's cabinet.*

ca-ble (keʸ–bəl) v. **-bled, -bling** To send someone money, a message, etc. by telegraph: *My mother cabled some money to me.*

cable n. **1.** A very strong rope or thick metal line used on board ships, to support bridges, etc. —compare WIRE **2.** A line of covered telegraph wires laid underground or under the sea for carrying electricity or telephone and telegraph messages: *Telegrams go from the US to Europe by cable.* **3.** Also **ca-ble-gram** (keʸ–bəl–græm) *fml.* A telegram

ca-ca-o (kə–kaʊ/ kə–keʸ–oʷ) n. A tropical tree whose seeds (cacao beans) are the source of cocoa and chocolate

SPELLING NOTE:
Words having the sound /k/, like *cat*, may be spelled with k-, like **king**, or qu-, like **queen**. Words having the sound /s/, like *city*, may be spelled with s-, like **see**, or ps-, like **psychologist**.

cache (kæʃ) n. **1.** A hiding place for provisions and other valuables **2.** A quantity of such hidden things

cack-le (kæk–əl) n. **1.** The loud clucking sound made by a hen after laying an egg **2.** A loud, silly laugh

cackle v. **-led, -ling** To give a cackle

cac-tus (kæk–təs) n. **cac-ti** (kæk–taɪ) or **cactuses** A prickly plant that lives in hot, dry climates, having no leaves but fleshy stems that do the work of leaves

cad (kæd) n. A dishonorable person

ca-dence (keʸd–əns) n. **1.** The fall of the voice, as at the end of a sentence **2.** Rhythm **3.** A group of chords that end a piece of music

ca-det (kə–dɛt) n. **1.** One who is training to be an officer in the armed forces or to be a police officer **2.** A schoolboy who takes military training

ca-fé (kə–feʸ) n. A small restaurant that serves light meals and drinks —compare RESTAURANT

caf-e-te-ri-a (kæf–ə–tɪər–iʸ–ə) n. A restaurant where people serve themselves, often in a school, factory, etc.

caf-feine (kæ–fiʸn/ kæ–fiʸn) n. A chemical substance found in coffee and tea, used also as a stimulant in some medicines

cage (keʸdʒ) n. An enclosure for keeping animals or birds, often having a wire or metal framework

cage v. **caged, caging** To put into a cage: *fig. The young housewife felt caged in because of staying at home all day.*

cake (keʸk) n. **1.** A food, usu. sweet, made by baking a mixture of flour, eggs, etc., often coated with icing **2.** A flat shaped piece of sthg.: *a cake of soap*

ca-jole (kə–dʒoʷl) v. **-joled, -joling** To coax

cake v. **caked, caking** To be encrusted: *My shoes were caked with mud after walking down that muddy path.*

cal-a-mine (kæl–ə–maɪn) n. A pink powder used to soothe inflamed or sore skin

ca-lam-i-ty (kə–læm–ə–tiʸ) n. **-ties** A great disaster

cal-ci-um (kæl–siʸ–əm) n. A silver-white metallic element that is found in bones, teeth, shells, and limestone

cal·cu·late (kæl–kyə–le^yt) v. -lated, -lating **1.** To work out or find out sthg. mathematically **2.** To estimate **3.** To intend; plan

cal·cu·la·ted (kæl–kyə–le^y–təd) adj. Estimated with careful forethought: *a calculated risk*

cal·cu·la·ting (kæl–kyə–le^y–tɪŋ) adj. Coldly planning future actions; scheming; conniving

cal·cu·la·tion (kæl–kyə–le^y–ʃən) n. **1.** The act, process or result of calculating **2.** Deliberation; foresight

cal·cu·la·tor (kæl–kyə–le^y–tər) n. **1.** One who performs calculations **2.** A machine that makes mathematical calculations

cal·cu·lus (kæl–kyə–ləs) n. **-li** (li^y) **-lus-es** A mathematical system of calculation that studies variable quantities

cal·en·dar (kæl–ən–dər) n. A sheet or folder showing a list of the days and months of the year: *We looked up the date on the calendar.*

calf (kæf) n. **calves** (kævz) **1.** The fleshy back part of the human leg below the knee **2.** The young of the cow, elephant, or other large animals

cal·i·ber *see* **calibre**

cal·i·brate (kæl–ə–bre^yt) v. **1.** To check or adjust the scale of a measuring instrument **2.** To mark out the scale of a measuring instrument

cal·i·bre (kæl–ə–bər) n. **1.** The inner diameter of a gun barrel **2.** Ability; quality of character: *a man of high calibre*

cal·i·co (kæl–ɪ–ko^w) n. **-coes** or **-cos** Cotton cloth printed in a figured pattern of bright colors

calico adj. **1.** Made of calico **2.** Spotted or streaked: *a calico cat*

cal·i·pers *also* **cal·li·pers** (kæl–ə–pərz) n. An instrument used to measure the inside or outside diameter of objects

ca·liph (ke^y–lɪf) n. A chief civil and religious leader in some Muslim countries —**ca·liph·ate** (kæ–lɪ–fe^yt) n.

cal·is·then·ics *also* **cal·lis·then·ics** (kæl–əs–θɛn–ɪks) n. Light, repeated exercises for the development of strong and graceful bodies

call (kɔl) v. **1.** To say, speak or shout in a loud clear voice: *They were calling for help./ God says, "Call upon me in the day of trouble. I will deliver you, and you shall honor me"* (Psalm 50:15). **2.** To speak loudly or officially or send a message to try to get someone to come to you: *Your mother is calling you.* **3.** To cause to happen: *The chairman called a meeting.* **4.** To pay a visit to someone: *The Smiths called on us last night.* **5.** To telephone someone: *I tried to call him last night but his line was always busy.* **6.** To name: *They called him John.* **7.** To say that someone is sthg.: *She called him a bum.* **8. call off** To cause not to happen: *The baseball game was called off because of rain.*

call n. **1.** A cry; shout: *Mrs. Jones heard her child's call for help.* **2.** A try to reach someone on the telephone; a telephone conversation: *I have a call for you from your wife.* **3.** A short usu. formal or professional visit: *The doctor is making a call on Mr. Jones.* **4.** A request or summons to meet, come, or do sthg.: *He felt a call (from God) to preach the Good News about Jesus Christ.* **5. close call** Sthg. bad that almost happened but didn't: *That was a close call! That bus nearly hit us!* **6. no call for** No reason for: *There's no call for you to get angry.* **7. on call** Ready to work if needed: *The doctor will be on call all night.*

cal·lig·ra·phy (kə–lɪg–rə–fi^y) n. **1.** The art of decorative handwriting **2.** Penmanship; handwriting —**caligrapher** n.

call·ing (kɔl–ɪŋ) n. **1.** A strong feeling of duty or a desire to do a particular job; vocation: *My son had a calling to become a minister of the Gospel of Jesus Christ.* **2.** *fml.* Trade or profession: *What was his calling? He was a college professor.*

cal·li·o·pe (kə–laɪ–ə–pi^y) n. A mechanical organ in which the notes are produced by steam whistles sounded from a keyboard

cal·lous (kæl–əs) adj. **1.** Having calluses **2.** A hardened, insensitive attitude

callous v. To make or become callous

cal·lus (kæl–əs) **-lus-es** n. A localized thickening and toughening of the skin, esp. of the hands: *The wood chopper had many calluses on his hands.*

callus v. To form or develop a callus

calm (kɑm) v. **1.** To soothe: *She calmed the frightened child by singing softly to her.* **2.** *also*

calm down To become or make calm: *The hungry man quickly calmed down when I said I'd pay the damages.*

calm n. **1.** A quiet, peaceful time, without worry or excitement **2.** Quiet weather

calm adj. **1.** Not excited; quiet; untroubled: *Even during the robbery, my mother remained calm.* **2. (a)** Not windy: *Today was very calm after yesterday's wind.* **(b)** Still; smooth: *The lake was very calm.* —**calmly** adv.

cal-o-rie (kæl–ə–ri^y) n. A measure for the amount of heat or energy that a food will produce: *One small apple has 90 calories.* —**ca-lo-ric** (kə–lɔr–ɪk) adj.

Cal-va-ry (kæl–və–ri^y) n. The hill on which Jesus Christ was crucified for the sins of mankind, near the place where he rose again three days later NOTE: Do not confuse Calvary with cavalry. —see JESUS

calves (kævz) n. Plural of **calf**

came (ke^{y}m) v. Past tense of **come**

cam-el (kæm–əl) n. A large animal with a long neck and one or two large humps on its back, used for riding or carrying goods, esp. in desert lands

cam-er-a (kæm–ər–ə) n. A closed light-proof box for taking photographs or moving pictures

cam-ou-flage (kæm–ə–flɑʒ) n. **1.** A method of hiding people or things by disguising them or covering them so as to look like the surroundings **2.** The concealment itself

camouflage v. **-flaged, -flaging** To conceal in this way

camp (kæmp) n. A place where people live for short periods of time, usu. in tents: *The fishermen had a camp just a few feet from the stream.*

camp v. To set up or live in a camp: *Many families enjoy camping during the summer.*

cam-paign (kæm–pe^{y}n) n. **1.** An organized action in support of a cause or movement: *a presidential campaign* **2.** A war or a part of a war: *a military campaign*

campaign v. **1.** To organize support **2.** To serve in a military campaign

camp-er (kæmp–ər) n. **1.** A person who camps **2.** A vehicle equipped as a living quarters for camping or long trips

cam-phor (kæm–fər) n. A strong-smelling substance used in medicine and moth balls and in making plastics

cam-pus (kæm–pəs) n. **-puses** The grounds of a school, college, or university

can (kæn) n. **1.** Also **tin** esp. *BrE*. A closed metal container in which food or liquid is preserved without air: *She opened a can of peaches.* **2.** A metal container with an open or removable top, used for holding milk, coffee, oil, etc. **3.** The food or drink of such a container: *One can of soup will serve two people if they aren't too hungry.*

can v. **-nn-** To preserve food by putting it in a closed container, usu. metal, without air: *canned salmon/ canned fruit*

can (kən) strong (kæn) v. **could;** Neg. contraction **can't** (kænt) or **cannot** (kæ–nɑt/ kə–nɑt); Past tense negative contraction **couldn't** (kʊd–ənt) **1.** To know how to or be able to: *Can you speak German?/ Can you ride a horse?* **2.** To be allowed to do sthg. or have permission to: *You can't play here. Go to the park./ Can we eat now, please?* NOTE: In asking permission to do sthg. or take sthg., the use of can is now more common than may. *Can I have a piece of cake, please?*

ca-nal (kə–næl) n. A man-made waterway for ships or boats: *Boats can pass from the Red Sea to the Mediterranean through the Suez Canal.*

ca-nar-y (kə–neər–i^y) n. *pl.* **-ies 1.** A small yellow songbird **2.** A bright yellow color

can-cel (kæn–səl) v. **-celed** or **-celled, -cel-ing** or **-cel-ling** To call off a planned activity, idea, etc.: *The summer program was canceled because of a lack of interest.*

can-cel-la-tion (kæn–sə–le^y–ʃən) n. The act of canceling sthg.

can-cer (kæn–sər) n. A diseased growth anywhere in the body of a person or animal, which may cause death: *Smoking causes lung cancer.* —**cancerous** adj.

can-de-la-brum (kæn–də–lɑ–brəm) n. **-bra** A large candlestick with arms for holding several candles, usu. seven

can-did (kæn–dəd) adj. Honest; frank; not hiding one's thoughts —**candidly** adv. —**candidness** n.

can-di-da-cy (kæn–dɪ–də–si^y) n. **-cies** The fact

or state of being a candidate

can-di-date (kæn–də–de^{y}t/ –dət) n. A person who is seeking a certain position, esp. in an election: *He was a candidate for mayor, but he lost.*

can-dle (kæn–dəl) n. A stick of wax containing a length of string which gives light when burned: *It is better to light one candle than to curse the darkness.*

can-dor (kæn–dər) n. Frankness; honesty; straightforwardness

can-dy (kæn–di^y) n. -dies Various types of a sweet food made mainly from sugar with flavoring, chocolate, nuts, etc.

cane (ke^{y}n) n. **1.** The stem of certain kinds of plants, such as bamboo and sugar cane **2.** A stick used for aid in walking

ca-nine (ke^y–nam) n. **1.** Any member of the dog family, including wolves and foxes **2.** A dog **3.** In man, one of the four sharp, pointed teeth

canine adj. Of or like a dog: *canine characteristics*

can-is-ter (kæn–əs–tər) n. **1.** A metal box or other container with a cover, used for storage: *a set of canisters for coffee, tea, sugar, flour, etc.* **2.** A metallic cylinder filled with shot or tear gas that, when fired from a gun, bursts and scatters its contents

can-ker (kæŋ–kər) *also* **canker sore** (sɔr) n. An ulcerous sore in the mouth or on the lip

canned (kænd) adj. **1.** Preserved by sealing in an airtight can or jar **2.** *infml.* Recorded or taped: *a canned message*

can-ner-y (kæn–ə–ri^y) n. -ies A factory where fish, meat, or vegetables are canned

can-ni-bal (kæn–ə–bəl) n. **1.** A person who eats the flesh of other human beings **2.** An animal that eats the flesh of its own kind

can-non (kæn–ən) n. **cannons** or **cannon** A very large gun, often fixed to the ground or to a ship

can-not (kæn–ɑt/ kə–nɑt) v. Can not

can-ny (kæn–i^y) adj. -nier, -niest Shrewd

ca-noe (kə–nu^w) n. A narrow boat, pointed at both ends, moved by paddles held in the hands

canoe v. -noed, -noeing To travel by canoe

can-on (kæn–ən) n. **1.** A law or code of laws established by a church council **2.** The books of the Bible officially recognized by a Christian church **3.** A basic principle or standard

can-on-ize (kæn–ə–naɪz) v. -ized, -izing **1.** Officially declare sbdy. to be a saint **2.** To put in the Biblical canon **3.** To give church sanction to

can-o-py (kæn–ə–pi^y) n. -pies A cloth covering fastened or held horizontally over an entrance, a bed, a throne, etc. or carried over an important person

can't (kænt) v. Short for **cannot**

can-ta-loupe (kæn–tə–lo^{w}p) n. A melon with a ribbed, rough rind and orange flesh

can-tan-ker-ous (kæn–tæŋ–kər–əs) adj. Bad-tempered; quarrelsome

can-ta-ta (kən–tɑt–ə) n. A vocal and instrumental composition consisting of solos, choruses, and recitatives

can-teen (kæn–ti^{y}n) n. **1.** A water flask for campers, soldiers, etc. **2.** A restaurant for the employees of a factory **3.** A place of entertainment for men in the armed forces

can-ter (kæn–tər) n. Of a horse, smooth, easy movement that is faster than a trot, but slower than a gallop

canter v. To ride or move at this pace

can-tor (kæn–tər) n. Leader of the singing in a church or synagogue

can-vas (kæn–vəs) n. **1.** Strong rough cloth used for covering boats and cars, and for making sails, tents, etc. **2.** A surface prepared to receive oil paint **3.** An oil painting **4.** The floor of a boxing or wrestling ring

can-vass, -vas (kæn–vəs) v. To go to people to ask their opinions or request support or invite them to church, etc.

can-yon (kæn–yən) n. A deep, narrow valley between high cliffs, usu. with a river flowing through it

cap (kæp) n. **1.** A soft, closely fitting head-covering of various styles, worn by nurses, soldiers, sailors, etc. or by anyone in cold weather —compare HAT **2.** A covering for the top of a container: *a bottle cap*

cap v. -pp- To put a lid on sthg.: *They capped the jars of jam.*

ca-pa-bil-i-ty (ke^y–pə–bɪl–ə–ti^y) n. -ties Having

ability

ca-pa-ble (ke^y-pə-həl) adj. Having the ability or the power to do sthg.

ca-pac-i-ty (kə-pæs-ə-ti^y) n. -ties 1. The amount that sthg. can hold: *The seating capacity of this restaurant is 210.* 2. The amount that sthg. can produce: *working at full capacity (=producing the greatest amount possible)* 3. A person's ability or power to do sthg.: *John does not have the capacity to handle the responsibility for leadership in the company.* 4. Position: *I am speaking in my capacity as assistant to the director of the library.*

cape (ke^yp) n. 1. A piece of land jutting out into the water: *Cape Cod* 2. A loose, sleeveless garment fastened at the neck and hanging from the shoulders

ca-per (ke^y-pər) v. To run about playfully

caper n. 1. A prank; child-like mischief 2. *slang* An illegal escapade

cap-il-lar-y (kæp-ə-lɛər-i^y) n. 1. Any of the tiny blood vessels that connect the arteries and veins 2. A tube with a small internal diameter

cap-i-tal (kæp-ə-təl) n. 1. A city where the center of government is located: *New Delhi is the capital of India.* —com-pare CAPITOL 2. Of or involving wealth or money, esp. used to produce more wealth: *We have put a lot of capital into this project.* 3. A capital letter (such as A, B, C): *The title on the front cover of a book is often written entirely in capital letters, for example: DICTIONARY.*

capital adj. 1. Involving or punishable by death: *In my opinion, the selling of cocaine ought to be a capital offense.* —see CAPITAL PUNISHMENT 2. Of a letter, written or printed in its large form (such as A, B, C), used at the beginning of a sentence, a person's name, etc. —also UPPER CASE

cap-i-tal-ism (kæp-ə-təl-ɪz-əm) n. The economic system in which production and trade are based on the private ownership of wealth —compare COMMUNISM

cap-i-tal-ist (kæp-ə-təl-əst) n. A person who owns or controls much wealth, esp. one who has wealth invested in business —cap-i-tal-is-tic (kæp-ə-təl-ɪs-tɪk) adj.

cap-i-tal-ize (kæp-ə-təl-aɪz) v. -ized, -izing 1. To write or print in capital letters: *Capitalize the first letter of every word in the title of the book.* 2. capitalize on sthg. To use to one's advantage or profit: *The Trojans capitalized on the other team's mistakes and won the game.* —cap-i-tal-i-za-tion (kæp-ə-təl-ə-ze^y-ʃən) n.

cap-i-tal pun-ish-ment (kæp-ə-təl pʌn-ɪʃ-mənt) n. The death penalty for a crime

cap-i-tol (kæp-ə-təl) n. The building in which the state or national lawmaking body meets —compare CAPITAL

ca-pit-u-late (kə-pɪtʃ-ə-le^yt) v. -lated, -lating To surrender —ca-pit-u-la-tion (kə-pɪtʃ-ə-le^y-ʃən) n.

ca-price (kə-pri^ys) n. 1. A whim 2. Music in a lively, fanciful style

ca-pri-cious (kə-pri^y-ʃəs/ -prɪʃ-) adj. 1. Impulsive 2. Changeable: *a capricious breeze* —capriciously adv.

cap-size (kæp-saɪz) v. -sized, -sizing To overturn: *The boat capsized.*

cap-sule (kæp-səl) n. 1. A small, soluble case filled with medicine for swallowing 2. A seed case that splits open when ripe 3. A pressurized compartment of a spacecraft or aircraft

cap-tain (kæp-tən) n. 1. The leader of a group or team 2. The one in command of a ship or aircraft 3. A middle rank officer in the armed forces

captain v. To serve as captain or leader

cap-tion (kæp-ʃən) n. 1. A short description, as of a photograph 2. A subtitle of a motion picture 3. A title, as of a chapter or document

caption v. To supply a caption for sthg.

cap-tiv-ate (kæp-tə-ve^yt) v. -vated, -vating To charm, fascinate

cap-tive (kæp-tɪv) n. A person taken as a prisoner, esp. in war

captive adj. 1. Taken and held prisoner, esp. in war: *The rebels held their prisoners captive for two years./ spir. We take captive every thought to make it obedient to Christ. (=observing all that he has commanded and doing all to the glory of God)* (2 Corinthians 10:5). 2. a captive audience A person or persons who must listen because they cannot leave easily: *Lying there with my broken leg I*

became a captive audience to all my roommate's boring stories.

cap-tiv-i-ty (kæp–trv–ə–ti^y) n. -ties The state of being captive: *Some birds thrive when in captivity.*

cap-tor (kæp–tər) n. A person who captures

cap-ture (kæp–tʃər) v. -tured, -turing **1.** To take or be taken prisoner by force **2.** To take control of sthg. by force: *They captured the bridge and held it until all the troops and equipment had crossed the river.* **3.** To preserve on film, in words, or other more permanent form: *He tried to capture the power of the sea on canvas.*

capture n. The act of taking or being taken by force: *The gorilla's capture came after a long chase.*

car (kɑr) n. **1.** A motor-driven vehicle with wheels, used for carrying people: *He walks to work, but his wife drives her car.* **2.** A carriage of the stated kind for use on railroads, cables, etc.: *He was too late for dinner on the train. The dining car was closed.*

car-a-mel (kɛər–ə–məl/ –mɛl/ kɑr–) n. **1.** Burnt sugar, used for coloring and flavoring food **2.** A chewy candy

car-at (kɛər–ət) n. A measure of weight for precious stones, equal to 200 milligrams (seven-thousandths of an ounce): *A 14 carat diamond weighs about 1/10th of an ounce.*

car-a-van (kɛər–ə–væn) n. **1.** A number of travelers, crossing the desert together: *a camel caravan* **2.** Any groups, such as vehicles, traveling together in a file, one after the other

car-bine (kɑr–bam/ –bi^{y}n) n. A light, semiautomatic rifle

car-bo-hy-drate (kɑr–bo^w–har–dre^{y}t/ –drət) n. One of a group of substances containing carbon, hydrogen, and oxygen, which provide the body with heat and energy

car-bon (kɑr–bən) n. An element that appears in the pure state as the diamond or graphite, and in an impure state as charcoal

car-bon-at-ed (kɑr–bən–e^{y}t–əd) adj. Containing carbon dioxide: *A carbonated drink has small bubbles.*

car-bon di-ox-ide (kɑr–bən dar–ɑks–aɪd) n. A gas present in the air and exhaled by human beings and animals

car-bon mo-nox-ide (kɑr–bən mə–nɑks–aɪd) n. A poisonous gas with no smell

car-bu-re-tor *AmE.* **carburettor** *BrE.* (kɑr–bə–re^y–tər) n. The part of an automobile engine that changes gasoline (petrol) into vapor

car-cass *AmE.* **car-case** *BrE.* (kɑr–kəs) n. The dead body of an animal

car-cin-o-gen (kɑr–sɪn–ə–dʒən/ –dʒɛn) n. Anything that produces cancer

card (kɑrd) n. **1.** A small sheet of stiff paper or plastic for various uses **2.** A small sheet of stiff paper or plastic with information printed on it, such as the name and address and the identification number of the user, for various uses: *a credit card (=for making purchases on credit)/ a business card (=for giving information to customers, clients, etc.)* **3.** **greeting card** A sheet of stiff paper, usu. folded with a picture on the front and a message inside, mailed or handed to someone on a special occasion, such as a birthday, anniversary, Christmas, etc. **4. playing card** One of a set (deck) of 52 small sheets of plastic or stiff paper specially marked to be used for various games **5. postcard** A card on which a message may be written for sending by mail and which must have a postage stamp on it: *My friend in Paris sent me a picture postcard of the French countryside.*

card-board (kɑrd–bɔrd) n. A thick, stiff, paperlike, brownish, material used for making boxes, etc.

car-di-ac (kɑr–di^y–æk) adj. Pertaining to the heart: *a cardiac failure*

car-di-gan (kɑr–də–gən) n. A sweater or jacket, usu. knitted, that opens down the front, usu. with long sleeves and no collar

car-di-nal (kɑrd–ən–əl) n. **1.** A priest of high rank in the Roman Catholic church **2.** A North American bird, the male of which is bright red in color

cardinal adj. Most important; chief; main: *a cardinal sin*

car-di-nal num-ber (kɑrd–ən–əl nʌm–bər) n. One of the numbers 1, 2, 3, etc. —compare ORDINAL NUMBER (first, second, third, etc.)

care (kɛər) n. **1.** Worry; anxiety; a troubled

state of the mind: *Cast your cares on the Lord and he will sustain you: he will never let the righteous fall* (Psalm 55:22). **2.** Responsibility; charge: *under the doctor's care* **3.** Serious attention; effort: *You'd better give more care to your family if you want them to turn out well.*

care v. **cared, caring 1.** To be worried or concerned about: *Cast all your anxiety upon him [Jesus] because he cares for you* (1 Peter 5:7). **2.** To like; want: *Would you care for more coffee?* **3. care for sbdy./ sthg. (a)** To nurse, look after, or attend: *He's cared for his parents ever since his father became ill.* **(b)** To like or want: *I really don't care for a piece of pie right now.*

ca-reen (kə–ri^{y}n) v. **1.** To lurch or twist from side to side while moving, in an uncontrolled fashion **2.** To lean sideways **3.** To turn (a ship, e.g.) on its side, as for repairs

ca-reer (kə–nɪr) n. **1.** A job or profession which one trains for and follows as his life's work **2.** A way of making a living: *He spent most of his career as an army helicopter pilot.* —see JOB

care-free (kɛər–fri^y) adj. **1.** Having no worries **2.** Requiring little attention or care, esp. with regard to laundry: *carefree fabrics*

care-ful (kɛər–fəl) adj. **1.** Taking care to avoid danger: *Be careful! Don't drop the baby!* **2.** Paying close attention to details: *So be careful to do what the Lord your God has commanded you: do not turn aside to the right or to the left* (Deuteron-omy 5:32). **3.** Done with care: *The committee made a careful study of the problem before giving us their report.*

care-ful-ly (kɛər–fəl–i^y) adv. *Carry this vase carefully. Don't break it.* —see also CARELESS —carefulness n.

care-less (kɛər–ləs) adj. **1.** Inattentive **2.** Not exact or thorough **3.** Done or said heedlessly **4.** Having no care or concern —carelessly adv. —carelessness n.

ca-ress (kə–rɛs) n. A gentle, affectionate touch or stroking

caress v. To touch or stroke gently with affection

care-tak-er (kɛər–te^{y}k–ər) n. **1.** A person in charge of the maintenance of a building or property **2.** A person or a group that performs the duties of an office temporarily

car-go (kɑr–go^w) n. **-goes** Goods carried by a ship, plane, or truck, etc.: *The old pirate ship had carried many a cargo of gold and jewels*

car-i-ca-ture (kɛər–ə–kə–tʃər) n. A picture that greatly exaggerates the peculiarities of a person, so as to be ridiculous

caricature v. **-tured, -turing** Drawing or painting caricatures: *He is always caricaturing politicians.*

car-ies (kɛər–i^{y}z) n. Decay in bones or teeth

car-nage (kɑr–nɪdʒ) n. The slaughter of many people

car-nal (kɑr–nəl) adj. **1.** Relating to the desires of the flesh **2.** Not spiritual

car-na-tion (kɑr–ne^y–ʃən) n. A type of garden flower, usu. pink, red, or white

car-ni-val (kɑr–nə–vəl) n. **1.** A public entertainment, often involving a lot of people in various costumes **2.** A traveling amusement show, having various rides, sideshows, and games where one can win prizes **3.** A time of merrymaking and feasting

car-ni-vore (kɑr–nə–vɔr) n. A flesh-eating animal: *A tiger is a carnivore.* —**car-ni-vor-ous** (kɑr-nɪv-ə-rəs) adj. *A tiger is a carnivorous animal.*

car-ol (kɛər–əl) n. A song of joy and praise, esp. sung at Christmas

ca-rouse (kə–raʊz) v. **-roused, -rousing** To take part in a noisy drinking session

car-ou-sel (kɛər–ə–sɛl) n. **1.** A merry-go-round (a popular ride with children) **2.** A delivery system that rotates like a merry-go-round: *Passengers of Flight 316 can claim their baggage at carousel number 2.*

car-pen-ter (kɑr–pən–tər) n. A workman who makes and repairs wooden objects

car-pen-try (kɑr–pən–tri^y) n. The skill or work of a carpenter

car-pet (kɑr–pət) n. Heavy, woven material for covering floors, made of woolen, cotton, or synthetic fibers, etc.

carpet v. To cover with a carpet

car-riage (kɛər–ɪdʒ) n. A wheeled passenger vehicle, esp. a horse-drawn one

car-ri-er (kɛər–i^y–ər) n. **1.** A person or a company that can be hired to carry goods or passengers from one place to another **2.** A person, animal, or thing that carries and

spreads diseases, esp. without catching the disease 3. An aircraft carrier

car-ri-on (keər–i^y–ən) n. Dead, decaying flesh

car-rot (keər–ət) n. A long, orange, pointed root, eaten as a vegetable

car-ry (keər–i^y) v. **-ried, -rying 1.** To move while holding sthg.: *He carried the groceries into the house.* **2.** To bear the weight of: *These four pillars carry the weight of the whole roof.* **3.** To include as part of its contents: *The newspaper carried the whole story of the invasion.* **4.** To influence: *His opinion carries a lot of weight with the committee.* (=*influences them greatly*) **5.** To spread: *Flies and mosquitoes carry many serious diseases.* **6.** To result in: *Such ambition will carry him to the top.* **7.** To be able to cover a certain distance: *His powerful voice carried for a whole mile across the hillsides.* **8.** To be approved: *The motion was carried by 617 votes to 254.* **9.** To win the support of: *The President carried almost every state and easily won the election.* **10. carry on** *infml.* (a) To behave in a wild, excited, and anxious manner (b) To continue

cart (kart) n. **1.** Any of various small, strong, usu. two-wheeled wooden vehicles pulled by an animal, esp. a horse, or by hand, and used for carrying things **2. put the cart before the horse** To do or put things in the wrong order

cart v. To carry or deliver in a cart or as if in a cart: *We carted all our belongings up the stairs to our new apartment.*

carte blanche (kart blanʃ/ blantʃ) n. *pl.* **cartes blanches** (karts blanʃ/ kart blan–ʃəz) **1.** Full authority **2.** Freedom to do as one wishes

car-ti-lage (kar–tə–lɪdʒ) n. A firm but flexible type of connective tissue in people and animals

car-tog-ra-pher (kar–tag–rə–fər) n. One who draws maps

car-tog-ra-phy (kar–tag–rə–fi^y) n. The production of maps

car-ton (kar–tən) n. A box made from stiff paper or cardboard

car-toon (kar–tu^{w}n) n. **1.** A humorous drawing **2.** A comic strip

car-tridge (kar–trɪdʒ) n. **1.** A metal or paper case containing an explosive and a bullet **2.**

A small case in a record player containing the needle that picks up sound signals from a record **3.** A plastic case containing magnetic tape for recording or a roll of film

carve (karv) v. **carved, carving 1.** To cut out of a piece of wood or stone with care and precision: *He carved a beautiful eagle out of a piece of rosewood.* **2.** To slice and serve cooked meat at the dinner table: *At our house, father always carves the Thanksgiving turkey.*

carv-ing (kar–vɪŋ) n. **1.** Sthg. made by carving: *an ivory carving of an elephant* **2.** The work of art of a person who carves

cas-cade (kæs–ke^{y}d) n. **1.** A waterfall over a steep, rocky surface **2.** A series of shallow waterfalls, either natural or artificial

cascade v. **-caded, -cading** To fall like a waterfall

case (ke^{y}s) n. **1.** An example: *It was a case of neglect on his part.* **2.** A particular situation: *It might rain. In that case, we'll have to postpone the game.* **3.** The form of a word (esp. of a noun, or pronoun) showing its relationship with other words in a sentence: *the objective case, possessive case, etc.* **4.** A convincing argument: *The police have a clear-cut case against him.* **5.** An instance of disease: *a case of measles* **6.** Events needing police or other action: *This is a case for the F.B.I.* **7. in any case** Whatever happens: *In any case, we'll be there when you arrive.* **8. (just) in case** So as to be prepared if: *I don't think it will rain, but I'm taking my umbrella just in case (it does).*

case n. **1.** A large box for storing or moving goods: *a case of Pepsi Cola* (=24 *bottles*) **2.** The quantity that such a box holds **3. lower case/ upper case** Of small/ large letters of the alphabet: *The letter 'm' is lower case and the letter 'M' is upper case.*

cash (kæʃ) n. **1.** Money in coins and bills **2.** Money that a person actually has, including money on deposit at the bank

cash v. To exchange a personal check, travelers check, or money order for cash: *Can you cash this check for $200?*

cash-ew (kæʃ–u^w/ kə–ʃu^w) n. **1.** A tropical American tree that bears kidney-shaped nuts **2.** The nuts it bears

cash-ier (kæʃ–ɪər) n. A person working in a

bank, hotel, restaurant, store, etc., who receive money and records payments

cash-mere (kæʒ–mɪər/ kæʃ–) n. **1.** Fine, downy wool from goats of North India **2.** A fabric made from this wool

cas-ing (keʸs–ɪŋ) n. **1.** A framework, as around a door **2.** The outer covering of an automobile tire

ca-si-no (kə–siʸ–noʷ) n. A building with gambling tables

cas-ket (kæs–kət) n. *AmE.* for **coffin**

cas-sa-va (kə–sɑ–və) n. A tropical plant with a starchy root from which tapioca is obtained

cas-se-role (kæs–ə–roʷl) n. **1.** A dish in which food is baked and served **2.** Food baked and served in such a dish

cas-sette (kə–set) n. **1.** A case containing magnetic tape, which can be fitted into a cassette player (=a machine for playing a cassette) or video —compare CARTRIDGE **2.** A container with film already in it which can be placed into a camera

cast (kæst) n. **1.** The actors in a play, film, etc.: *The cast is ready for rehearsal.* **2.** An act of throwing, esp. a fishing line **3.** A hard, stiff covering for holding a broken bone in place until it gets better

cast v. **cast, casting 1.** *fml.* To throw: *He that is without sin among you, let him first cast a stone at her [at the woman caught in the sinful act of adultery]* (John 8:7 KJV). **2.** To throw off; remove quickly: *He cast off his coat and jumped into the water to save the drowning child.* **3.** To make an object by pouring hot metal or plastic into a mold **4.** To give an acting part to someone in a movie or a play: *The director cast Charlton Heston as Moses.* **5. cast sbdy./ sthg. out** To force to get out or away; expel: *Jesus commanded his disciples [followers] to preach, heal the sick, raise the dead, and cast out devils* (Matthew 10:7,8).

caste (kæst) n. **1.** One of the hereditary social classes in Hinduism that restrict the occupation of their members and their association with the members of other castes **2.** Any class distinction based on differences of wealth, inherited rank or privilege, profession, or occupation

cast-er (kæst–ər) n. A small wheel on a swivel,

set under a piece of furniture, to make it easier to move

cas-ti-gate (kæs–tʊ–geʸt) v. **-gated, -gating** To punish or criticize severely

cas-tle (kæs–əl) n. A large fortified building or set of buildings made in former times

cas-trate (kæs–treʸt) v. **-trated, -trating** To remove the testicles or ovaries of —**cas-tra-tion** (kæs–treʸ–ʃən) n.

cas-u-al (kæʒ–yuʷ–əl) adj. **1.** Happening by chance; not intentional: *a casual meeting* **2.** Informal: *casual dress* **3.** Relaxed; leisurely: *a casual stroll around the park* **4.** Not serious or thorough: *I thought the author's treatment of the subject was rather casual. He didn't seem to know much about it.*

ca-su-al-ty (kæʒ–uʷ–əl–tiʸ) n. **-ties 1.** One injured or killed, captured, or missing in action against an enemy **2.** One killed or injured in an accident

cat (kæt) n. **1.** A small, domesticated animal with soft fur, often kept as a pet or to catch rats and mice **2.** Any of various related animals, such as the lion or tiger **3. let the cat out of the bag** *infml.* To reveal a secret, usu. without meaning to do so **4. rain cats and dogs** *infml.* To rain very hard

cat-a– (kæt–ə–) prefix **1.** Down; downward **2.** Against: *catapult* (= *a weapon for shooting darts or missiles against a target*) **3.** Wrongly: *catachresis* (kæt–ə–kriʸ–səs) (=*use of the wrong word for the context*)

cat-a-clysm (kæt–ə–klɪz–əm) n. **1.** A great flood; a deluge **2.** A sudden or violent disaster or disturbance

cat-a-comb (kæt–ə–koʷm) n. An underground place of burial, consisting of passages, small rooms, and recesses for tombs

cat-a-log (kæt–ə–lɔg/ –lɑg) n. A list of places, names, goods, services, etc., usu. with information about them; a book containing such a list: *There are college catalogs, publishers' catalogs, department store catalogs, etc.*

catalog v. **-loged** or **-logued** To enter an article, book, etc. into a catalog

cat-a-lyst (kæt–ə–ləst) n. **1.** A substance that aids or speeds up a chemical reaction while remaining unchanged itself **2.** A person or thing that precipitates change —**ca-tal-y-sis**

(kə–**tæl**–ə–səs) n.

cat-a-lyt-ic (kæt–ə–lɪt–ɪk) n. Causing catalysis

cat-a-pult (**kæt**–ə–pʌlt) n. **1.** A device with elastic for shooting small stones **2.** A mechanism for launching aircraft from the deck of a ship

catapult v. **1.** To fling forcibly **2.** To rush violently

cat-a-ract (**kæt**–ə–rækt) n. **1.** A waterfall **2.** An abnormal growth on the eye causing a gradual loss of sight

ca-tas-tro-phe (kə–tæs–trə–fiʸ) n. A disaster; a great and sudden calamity

catch (kætʃ/ ketʃ) v. **caught** (kɔt), **catching 1.** To capture, esp. after a chase: *They caught the criminals after a wild chase.* **2.** To discover, sometimes unexpectedly: *They caught him in the act of stealing.* **3.** To trap: *They caught the rat in a trap.* **4.** To get hold of sthg. moving in the air: *The center fielder jumped high to catch the ball off the top of the fence, robbing the batter of a home run.* **5.** To be in time for: *We had to run to catch the bus.* —opposite MISS **6.** To get sick; to become infected with: *Bundle up or you'll catch a cold.* **7.** To become hooked or stuck: *Her skirt got caught in the car door.* **8.** To attract someone's attention: *See if you can catch the waitress's eye. I'd like some more coffee.* **9.** To see momentarily: *I caught a glimpse of the other car a split second before the crash.* **10.** To hear; understand: *I didn't catch what she said. Would you ask her to repeat it, please.* **11.** To begin to burn: *The house caught fire.* **12. catch on (a)** To understand: *That was a very funny joke, but it took me a while to catch on.* **(b)** To become popular: *Do you think the new T.V. program will catch on?* **13. catch up (a)** To come up from behind and draw even with: *Mary was ahead in the race, but Susan was able to catch up.* **(b)** To come up to date: *I'm two weeks behind in my homework. I just have to catch up tonight.*

catch n. **1.** An act of seizing and holding sthg. that was moving in the air: *Nice catch! That ball was thrown hard.* **2.** The amount of sthg. caught: *a big catch of fish* **3.** A hook or fastener: *The catch on this necklace is broken. Can you fix it?* **4.** *infml.* Sthg. wrong, a hidden problem: *He agreed so quickly on the price; I*

thought there must be a catch somewhere! **5.** A simple game played by two or more in which a ball is thrown back and forth: *How would you children like to play catch?*

catch-er (kætʃ–ər/ketʃ–) n. **1.** One who or that which catches. In baseball, the player behind home plate, who catches the ball thrown by the pitcher unless it is hit by the batter

catch-ing (kætʃ–ɪŋ/ ketʃ–ɪŋ) adj. *infml.* Infectious

cat-e-chism (**kæt**–ə–kɪz–əm) n. A summary of the principles of a religion in the form of questions and answers —**catechist** n. —**catechize** v.

cat-e-chu-men (kæt–ə–**kyu**ʷ–mən) n. A convert receiving religious instruction before baptism or membership in a church

cat-e-gor-i-cal (kæt–ə–**gor**–ɪ–kəl) adj. Allowing of no doubt or argument

cat-e-go-rize (kæt–ə–gə–raiz) v. **-rized, -rizing** To put in a category or a class

cat-e-go-ry (kæt–ə–gor–iʸ) n. **-ries** A division used in classification; a class, group, or kind

ca-ter (keʸ–tər) v. To provide what is needed or wanted, esp. food or entertainment

ca-ter-er (keʸ–tər–ər) n. Someone whose business it is to supply food

cat-er-pil-lar (**kæt**–ər–pɪl–ər) n. The worm-like larva of a butterfly or moth

ca-the-dral (kə–θiʸ–drəl) n. **1.** The chief church of a district ruled by a bishop **2.** Loosely, any large, imposing church

cath-o-lic (kæθ–lɪk/ **kæθ**–ə–lɪk) adj. Broad; widespread; universal: *The catholic Church is the Church in all places; it includes all people who say Jesus is Lord.*

Catholic adj., n. also **Roman Catholic** A member of the Roman Catholic church

Ca-thol-i-cism (kə–θɑl–ə–sɪz–əm) n. The faith, doctrine, system and practice of the Roman Catholic Church

cat-nap (**kæt**–næp) n. A short nap

cat-sup (**kæt**–səp) n. also **ketchup** A thick sauce made from tomatoes and vinegar, etc., used as a seasoning

cat-tle (**kæt**–əl) n. Large farm animals kept for their meat or milk, esp. cows

cat-walk (kæt–wɔk) n. A narrow walk, esp. one that is high above the surrounding area

cau-cus (kɔ–kəs) n. A meeting of local members of a political party to nominate candidates, determine policies, etc.

caucus v. To meet in a caucus

caught (kɔt) v. Past tense & part. of **catch**

caul-dron (kɔl–drən) n. A large, deep pot for boiling things

cau-li-flow-er (kɔ–lɪ–flaʊ–ər/ kɑ–) n. A type of cabbage with a large white flower head

caulk (kɔk) also **calk** v. **1.** To make watertight by filling the seams or cracks with waterproof material **2.** To fill cracks or seams with filler

cause (kɔz) n. **1.** That which produces an effect **2.** Reason: *There's no cause for complaint.* **3.** An aim for which a person or a group works: *He's been fighting for the cause of freedom all his life.*

cause v. **caused, causing** To be the reason for; to lead to: *What caused the accident?*

caus-tic (kɔs–tɪk) adj. **1.** Able to burn or corrode things by chemical action **2.** Sarcastic: *a caustic remark/ speech*

cau-tion (kɔ–ʃən) n. **1.** Great care; taking care to minimize risk **2.** A spoken warning: *The policeman gave him a caution rather than a ticket for speeding.*

caution v. To warn: *The police officer cautioned him against using the mountain road because of the landslide.*

cau-tious (kɔ–ʃəs) adj. Careful to avoid danger; paying attention —**cautiously** adv. *We should drive cautiously all the time.*

cav-al-cade (kæv–əl–keɪd) n. **1.** A procession, esp. of persons riding on horses or in horse-drawn carriages **2.** A pag-eant or pageant-like sequence

cav-a-lier (kæv–ə–lɪər) n. **1.** Formerly an armed horseman; a knight **2.** A gallant gentleman

cavalier adj. **1.** Haughty **2.** Carefree and gay; lighthearted

cav-al-ry (kæv–əl–riʸ) n. **-ries** Troops who fight on horseback —**cavalryman** n. NOTE: Do not confuse cavalry with Calvary

cave (keʸv) n. A hollow place underground or in the side of a hill

cave in v. To fall in: *The weight of the snow caused the roof to cave in.*

cav-ern (kæv–ərn) n. A large cave —**cav-ernous** adj.

cav-i-ar (kæv–iʸ–ɑr) n. The pickled eggs (roe) of the sturgeon, used as food, usu. served as a delicacy

cav-i-ty (kæv–ə–tiʸ) n. **-ties** A hole in sthg. solid: *a cavity in a tooth*

ca-vort (kə–vɔrt) v. To prance about

cc abbr. for cubic centimeter: *a 180 cc engine*

cease (siʸs) v. **ceased, ceasing** To stop; bring to an end: *Cease fire! (=Stop shooting!)*

cease-less (siʸs–ləs) adj. Without a pause; continuous

cease-less-ly (siʸs–ləs–liʸ) adv. Continuously; without ceasing: *The dog barked ceaselessly.*

ce-dar (siʸ–dər) n. **1.** A large evergreen tree with sweet smelling wood **2.** Its wood

cede (siʸd) v. **ceded, ceding** To give up one's rights or possessions: *They had to cede much territory to the conquering country.*

ceil-ing (siʸl–ɪŋ) n. **1.** The top inner surface of a room **2.** Upper limit on prices, rent, wages, etc.

cel-e-brate (sɛl–ə–breʸt) v. **-brated, -brating 1.** To observe a notable occasion with public or private festivities and rejoicing: *They celebrated their anniversary.* **2.** To honor a holy day with appropriate ceremonies and/ or refraining from ordinary business: *On Easter Sunday we celebrate the day that Jesus rose from the dead.*

cel-e-brat-ed (sɛl–ə–breʸt–əd) adj. Well-known; much spoken of; famous: *Michaelangelo is a celebrated artist.*

cel-e-bra-tion (sɛl–ə–breʸ–ʃən) n. The act of celebrating: *This joyous occasion calls for a celebration.*

ce-leb-ri-ty (sə–lɛb–rə–tiʸ) n. A well-known person

cel-e-ry (sɛl–ə–riʸ) n. A garden plant with crisp stems, used in salads, soup, etc.

ce-les-tial (sə–lɛs–tʃəl) adj. **1.** Of the sky: *celestial bodies (=the sun, moon, and stars)* **2.** Of heaven; divine: *celestial beings*

cel-i-ba-cy (sɛl–ə–bə–siʸ) n. The state of remaining celibate

cel-i-bate (sɛl–ə–bət) n. **1.** One who remains

unmarried, esp. for religious reasons **2.** One who does not have sexual relations

cell (sɛl) n. **1.** A small room, as in a prison or a monastery or convent, usu. for one person **2.** One small unit of a larger whole **3.** A microscopic unit of living matter, with one center of activity (nucleus) that can perform all the life functions: *All plants and animals are made up of cells.* **4.** A device for making a current of electricity by chemical action

cel-lar (sɛl–ər) n. **1.** An underground room for storing things, usu. beneath a building **2.** A stock of wine kept in such a room

cel-list (tʃɛl–ɪst) n. A person who plays a cello

cel-lo (tʃɛl–o͞ʷ) n. An instrument like a very large violin, played by a seated player who holds the cello between his knees

cel-lo-phane (sɛl–ə–fe͞ʸn) n. A thin, flexible, transparent paper used for moisture-proof wrapping

cel-lu-lar (sɛl–yə–lər) adj. **1.** Composed of cells **2.** Woven with an open mesh

cel-lu-lose (sɛl–yə–lo͞ʷs) n. An organic substance found in all plant tissues, used in making plastics

Cel-si-us (sɛl–si͞ʸ–əs) n. also **Centigrade** The temperature scale that registers the freezing point of water at 0 (zero) degrees and the boiling point of water at 100 degrees, named after Anders Celsius (1701-44), the Swedish astronomer who devised the centigrade scale

ce-ment (sɪ–mɛnt) n. A mixture of clay and limestone which, when mixed with water and allowed to dry, becomes hard like stone: *Cement is used widely in making concrete roads, sidewalks, foundations, and sometimes entire buildings.*

cement v. To bind together or make firm with or as if with cement: *fig. Working together for a common cause has cemented our friendship.*

cem-e-ter-y (sɛm–ə–tɛər–i͞ʸ) n. **-ies** A burial place, often called a memorial park; graveyard

cen-sor (sɛn–sər) n. An official who has the authority to examine printed matter, films, or sometimes private letters, and remove whatever might be objectionable or (in war)

helpful to the enemy —**censor** v. —**censorship** n.

cen-sure (sɛn–tʃər) n. **1.** The act of blaming or condemning sternly **2.** An official reprimand

censure v. **-sured, -suring** To find fault with; to criticize

cen-sus (sɛn–səs) n. **-suses** An official count of a country's population and the recording of age, sex, economic status, etc.

cent (sɛnt) n. **1.** A 100th part of a dollar, or a coin of this value; a penny: *A cent is 1/100th of a dollar.* **2.** A 100th part of certain other money standards

cen-te-nar-y (sɛn–tɛn–ər–i͞ʸ/ sɛn–tə–nɛər–i͞ʸ) n. **-ies 1.** A centennial **2.** A century

centenary adj. **1.** Of a centennial **2.** Of a century

cen-ten-ni-al (sɛn–tɛn–i͞ʸ–əl) n., adj. A 100th anniversary or its celebration

cen-ter *AmE.* **centre** *BrE.* (sɛn–tər) n. **1.** A point equally distant from all sides; the point around which a circle is drawn **2.** The middle part: *Midway Island is in the center of the Pacific Ocean.* **3.** A place of concentrated activity: *a shopping center* **4.** An area, person, or thing that is of the most importance or interest: *Wherever she goes, she is the center of attention.*

center (sɛn–tər) v. **1.** To draw to one place; to focus on: *Our thoughts centered on the little girl who had fallen down the well.* **2.** To place sthg. in or at the center: *Center this letter on the page please.*

Cen-ti-grade (sɛn–tə–gre͞ʸd) also **Celsius** n. The temperature scale in which water freezes at zero degrees and boils at l00 degrees

cen-ti-me-ter (sɛn–tə–mi͞ʸ–tər) n. A measure of length equal to one hundredth of a meter (about four-tenths of an inch)

cen-ti-pede (sɛn–tɪ–pi͞ʸd) n. A small worm-like animal with many legs

cen-tral (sɛn–trəl) adj. Being the center: *the central part of the city*

cen-tral-ize (sɛn–trəl–aɪz) v. **-ized, -izing** To bring to a central point or under central control

cen-tre (sɛn–tər) n. *BrE. variation of* **center**

cen-trif-u-gal (sɛn–trɪf–ə–gəl) adj. Proceeding or acting in a direction away from the center or axis

cen-trip-e-tal (sɛn–trɪp–ə–təl) adj. Proceeding or acting in a direction toward the center or axis

cen-tu-ry (sɛn–tʃər–iʸ) n. -ries 1. A period of 100 years 2. One of the 100-year periods before or since the birth of Christ: *This is the twentieth century.*

ce-ram-ic (sə–ræm–ɪk) n. 1. *usu. pl.* The art or process of making articles from clay by shaping and firing them 2. The art of making any product (such as brick, tile, or glass) from a non-metallic mineral by firing —ceramic adj.

ce-re-al (sɪər–iʸ–əl) n. 1. A plant grown for the production of grain for food, such as wheat, rice, corn, oats, etc. 2. Food made from these grains, eaten esp. at breakfast

ce-re-bral (sə–riʸ–brəl/ sɛər–ə–) adj. 1. Of the brain 2. Intellectual

ce-re-brum (sə–riʸ–brəm/ sɛər–ə–) n. -brums or -bra The enlarged front and upper part of the brain that acts as the center for conscious thought —cere-bral adj.

cer-e-mo-ny (sɛər–ə–moʷ–niʸ) n. -nies A formal action used for marking an important public or social event, esp. a religious event: *a wedding ceremony* —cer-e-mo-ni-ous (sɛər–ə–moʷ–niʸ–əs) adj. —ceremonial n., adj. —ceremo-nially adv.

cer-tain (sɜr–tən) adj. 1. To know for sure; having no doubt: *I'm certain that all of us are getting older.* 2. Fixed; settled: *We agreed that I would get a certain percentage of the profit.* 3. Of a specific but unspecified character: *That old house has a certain charm about it.* 4. make certain To do whatever is necessary to be sure of sthg.: *Make certain you know what time his plane arrives.* —opposite UNCERTAIN —see SURE

certain determ., pron. (Used like some when it is not clear who you are talking about): *Certain people are waiting to see you.*

cer-tain-ly (sɜr–tən–liʸ) adv. 1. Beyond a doubt; surely 2. Yes, of course

cer-tain-ty (sɜr–tən–tiʸ) n. -ties 1. The state of being sure; without doubt: *Can you say with certainty where you will be next year on this date?* 2. A definite fact: *Our acceptance at the university is a certainty.* —see also UNCERTAINTY*

cer-tif-i-cate (sər–tɪf–ə–kət) n. 1. An official paper (document) stating that certain facts are true: *birth/ marriage/ health certificate* 2. A document stating that one has completed certain course requirements: *Mary has a certificate in teaching English as a second language.*

cer-ti-fi-ca-tion (sɜrt–ə–fə–keʸ–ʃən) n. An act or statement of certifying:*He received his certification as a high school history teacher.*

cer-ti-fy (sɜrt–ə–faɪ) v. -fied, -fying 1. To verify, confirm; to declare sthg. to be correct or true 2. To guarantee a bank check to be good with a statement to that effect stamped on its face: *This check was certified by the bank.* 3. To give a certificate to someone, verifying successful completion of a course of training for a particular profession: *She's been certified to teach English.*

Ce-sar-e-an or **Ce-sar-i-an sec-tion** also **Cae-sar-e-an** (siʸ–zɛər–iʸ–ən sɛk–ʃen) n. A surgical operation for delivering a baby by cutting through the walls of the mother's abdomen and uterus

cess-pool (sɛs–puʷl) n. A covered pit for receiving waste or sewage

chafe (tʃeʸf) v. chafed, chafing 1. To become angry or irritated 2. To make or become sore by rubbing 3. To make warm by rubbing

chaff (tʃæf) n. 1. Grain husks that have been separated from the seed 2. Worthless matter

cha-grin (ʃə–grɪn) n. Mental uneasiness or annoyance caused by disappointment or humiliation

chagrin v. To cause to feel chagrin

chain (tʃeʸn) n. 1. A flexible length of usu. metal links, joined to or fitted into one another, used for fastening, decorating, etc.: *A ship's anchor is held by a very heavy chain.* 2. A number of things that are connected, such as events, res-taurants, mountains, etc.: *a chain store (=group of shops under one ownership)/chain of events/ a mountain chain* 3. in

chains Held in prison or as a slave

chain v. **1.** To limit the freedom of someone or sthg. with chains or as if with chains: *That vicious dog should be chained up before he hurts sbdy./fig. He never takes a vacation. He's chained to his job.* **2.** To lock sthg. with a chain to prevent theft: *He chained his bicycle to a tree.* —opposite UNCHAIN

chair (tʃɛər) n. **1.** A piece of furniture for one person to sit on, usu. with a back, a seat, four legs, and sometimes arms **2.** An office or a position of authority or dignity: *He holds the chair of linguistics in that university.*

chair v. To act as chairman of a meeting: *John chaired the meeting of the board of directors.*

chair-man (tʃɛr-mən) also **chairperson** n. **-men 1.** A person who presides or is in charge of a meeting **2.** The person who directs the work of a committee

cha-let (ʃæ-leʸ) n. **1.** A herdsman's cabin in the Swiss mountains **2.** A building in the style of a Swiss cottage

chalk (tʃɔk) n. **1.** A type of limestone, used for making lime and various writing materials **2.** A piece of this material used for writing or drawing, usu. on a blackboard: *The teacher wrote the Spanish words on the blackboard with white chalk and their meanings in English with yellow chalk.* —**chalky** adj. **-ier, -iest**

chalk-board (tʃɔk-bɔrd) n. A colored writing slate (usu. black or green) on which chalk is used

chal-lenge (tʃæl-əndʒ) n. **1.** An invitation to compete in a fight, contest, game, etc.: *He accepted his friend's challenge to race across the lake.* **2.** A dare: *Fred ignored my challenge to jump off the roof into a pile of sand because it was too dangerous.* **3.** Sthg. that demands a lot of attention and hard work: *Learning a foreign language well in six months is quite a challenge.*

challenge v. **-lenged, -lenging 1.** To call or dare someone to compete against one in some kind of game or contest: *The old man challenged his friend to a game of Chinese checkers.* **2.** To call into question the lawfulness or rightness of sthg.: *We challenged the ruling of the court.* —**challenger** n.

cham-ber (tʃeʸm-bər) n. **1.** A room **2.** A large

meeting hall, esp. one for the meeting of a legislative assembly **3.** An enclosed space at the bore of a gun, for holding a charge

cha-me-le-on (kə-miʸl-yən) n. **1.** A lizard that is capable of changing color **2.** A person of changeable disposition

cham-pagne (ʃæm-peʸn) n. A sparkling white wine, originally produced in Champagne, France

cham-pi-on (tʃæm-piʸ-ən) n. **1.** One who has won a contest of courage, strength, or skill: *a golf champion* **2.** One who fights for or defends a principle, a cause, or a person: *a champion of human rights*

champion v. To fight for or defend a principle, cause, person, etc.

cham-pi-on-ship (tʃæm-piʸ-ən-ʃɪp) n. **1.** The position, title, or rank of a champion **2.** A competition held to determine the champion

chance (tʃæns) n. **1.** An event happening without apparent cause **2.** An unpredictable or unplanned event: *I met an old friend of mine at the shopping mall, purely by chance.* **3.** A risk: *Don't take foolish chances.* **4.** An opportunity: *I hope I get a chance to read his new book soon.* **5.** A possibility: *There's a good chance we will get the contract to build the new bridge.*

chance adj. Unplanned: *a chance meeting*

chance v. **chanced, chancing 1.** To happen upon: *They just chanced upon an abandoned gold mine.* **2.** To leave to chance: *That bridge looks pretty weak. I don't feel like chancing it.*

chan-cel (tʃæn-səl) n. A space around the altar of a church

chan-cel-lor (tʃæn-sə-lər/ -slər) n. **1.** A state or legal official of various kinds **2.** The head of a university

chan-de-lier (ʃæn-də-lɪər) n. An ornamental hanging fixture, often very elaborate, with supports for several lights

change (tʃeʸndʒ) v. **changed, changing 1.** To be or to become different: *I the Lord do not change (Malachi 3:6)./It's beautiful in the autumn when the leaves change colors, from green to red, yellow, and brown.* **2.** To transfer from one to another: *He changed trains in Chicago.* **3.** To put fresh clothes or a covering on someone or sthg.: *Have you changed the*

sheets on the bed lately? **4.** To put on different clothes: *He changed his shirt.* **5.** To give money in exchange for other money: *Pardon me, could you change this five dollar bill for me? (=give me change for five dollars)*

change n. **1.** The act or result of becoming different: *If we are going to win this contest, we need a change of strategy.* **2.** Sth. done differently for variety, excitement, etc.: *Let's take our vacation in France for a change.* **3.** Sth. clean to replace what is being used: *He took a change of clothing with him, as he planned to stay overnight.* **4.** Money returned to one when the amount given is more than the cost of the goods purchased: *This food cost $4.50, and I gave you a $5.00 bill, so I should get 50 cents change.* **5. (a)** Coins: *How much change do you have in your pocket?* **(b)** Money exchanged for money of higher or lower value: *Can you give me change for a twenty dollar bill?*

change-a-ble (tʃeʸndʒ–ə–bəl) adj. Likely to change; variable —**change-a-bil-i-ty** (tʃeʸndʒ–ə–bɪl–ə–tiʸ) n.

chan-nel (tʃæn–əl) n. **1.** The deeper part of a river or other waterway **2.** A passage for liquids **3.** A narrow sea passage connecting two bodies of water: *the English Channel* **4.** A TV station **5.** Any course along which information is passed: *You must go through the proper channels to get help.*

channel v. To direct: *I decided to channel my support for the orphanage through a reliable agency.*

chant (tʃænt) n. **1.** A repetitive song with several words sung on a single tone **2.** A manner of singing or speaking in musical monotones

chant v. **1.** To sing a chant **2.** To sing or speak in the manner of a chant

cha-os (keʸ–ɑs) n. A state of complete disorder and confusion —**cha-ot-ic** (keʸ–ɑt–ɪk) adj. —**chaotically** adv.

chap (tʃæp) n. Fellow: *He's a nice chap.*

chap v. **-pp-** (esp. of the lips) To dry and crack open, usually from the wind and cold weather

chap-el (tʃæp–əl) n. **1.** A small place of Christian worship **2.** The worship services held in

such a place: *We go to chapel on Sunday and Wednesday evenings.*

chap-er-on (ʃæp–ə–roʷn) n. **1.** An older person who accompanies young people at a social gathering to ensure proper behavior **2.** An older woman who accompanies young unmarried women in public for the sake of propriety

chap-lain (tʃæp–lən) n. A clergyman who is officially attached to a military unit, a hospital, a prison, etc.

chap-ter (tʃæp–tər) n. **1.** One of the main divisions of a book **2.** *esp. AmE.* A local branch of a club or organization

char (tʃɑr) v. **-rr-** To scorch or become scorched; to blacken by burning: *The wood was charred by the intense heat.*

char-ac-ter (kɛər–ɪk–tər) n. **1.** The part of a person that makes one different from anyone else: *Its interesting to watch the development of a child's character.* **2.** Honesty; integrity, morals, etc.: *A wife of noble character is her husband's crown, but a disgraceful wife is like decay in his bones* (Proverbs 12:4). **3.** A person in a story, play, etc.: *The characters in this play are all rather strange.* **4.** *infml.* A person as stated: *Some foolhardy character (=he was a reckless character) just jumped off that tall building with a parachute.* **5.** *infml.* A person who behaves in an odd or humorous manner: *Frank's quite a character; you should see him at a party!* **6.** A symbol in a writing system: *Chinese characters*

char-ac-ter-is-tic (kɛər–ɪk–tər–ɪs–tɪk) n. A special and easily recognized quality of someone or sth.: *A characteristic of the giraffe is its long neck.*

char-ac-ter-ize (kɛər–ɪk–tər–aɪz) v. **-ized, -izing** **1.** To describe the character of: *She characterized him as being lazy and irresponsible.* **2.** To be characteristic of: *Venice, Italy, is characterized by its many canals.* —**char-ac-ter-i-za-tion** (kɛər–ɪk–tər–ə–zeʸ–ʃən) n.

cha-rade (ʃə–reʸd) n. **1.** A ridiculous pretense, so obvious that it doesn't deceive anyone **2.** *pl.* A game in which words or phrases are acted out in pantomime until guessed by other players

char-coal (tʃɑr–koʷl) n. **1.** A dark, porous, car-

bon-containing material made by the distillation of wood, used as a fuel or a filter 2. A dark gray 3. A drawing pencil made from charcoal

charge (t∫ɑrdʒ) n. 1. Money you must pay for goods or services: *This store has a charge for delivery service.* 2. Control; responsibility: *Mr. Smith is in charge of this department.* 3. Blame; accusation: *Who will bring any charge against those whom God has chosen? It is God who justifies* (Romans 8:33). 4. A rushing, forceful attack: *The young officer led his men in a charge against the enemy stronghold.* 5. Electricity put into a battery or other electrical device

charge v. **charged, charging** 1. To entrust with a duty, responsibility, etc. 2. To set as a price: *How much do you charge to clean a suit?* 3. To make a note (of a sum of money) as being owed: *Charge this dinner to my hotel room number.* 4. To rush in or out: *The children charged out of the school building at the end of the day.* 5. To accuse: *He was charged with stealing the car.* 6. To cause to take in electricity: *Your car battery needs charging.*

char-i-ot (t∫ɛər-iʸ-ət) n. In ancient times, a light two-wheeled vehicle, drawn by horses, used in warfare, races, and parades

char-is-ma (kɛər-ɪz-mə) n. The special quality that gives an individual influence, charm, or inspiration over large numbers of people

char-is-mat-ic (kɛər-ɪz-mæt-ɪk) adj. 1. Having the special quality of charisma 2. Gifted by the Holy Spirit. Charismatic is from the Greek word which means "gift."

charismatic n. A person who is part of the Charismatic Movement

Charismatic Movement (kɛər-ɪz-mæt-ɪk muʷv-mənt) A movement that began in the United States in the 1950s as a revival of the gifts of the Spirit. NOTE: The Charismatic Movement stresses baptism in the Holy Spirit, that this is the beginning of the Spirit-filled life. The baptism in the Spirit gives power for witness and ministry. Some Charismatics greatly stress the gift of speaking in tongues, believing that this is a way of speaking to God in a language given by the Holy Spirit. They especially practice speaking in tongues in times of prayer. They believe it is a form of praise to God. But they also stress other gifts of the Spirit such as healing and prophecy. Some members of the Charismatic Movement do not stress speaking in tongues. They see it as only one sign of the baptism with the Holy Spirit.

char-i-ta-ble (t∫ɛər-ɪ-tə-bəl) adj. 1. Generous to the needy 2. Tolerant of the judgment of others —**charitableness** n. —**charitably** adv.

char-i-ty (t∫ɛər-ə-tiʸ) n. **-ties** 1. Kindness, esp. in giving money, food, clothing, etc. to poor people 2. An organization or fund established to collect funds, food, etc. for the poor and needy: *Many charities sent money and supplies to help the flood victims.*

char-la-tan (∫ɑr-lə-tən) n. A fraud; one who deceives others by claiming to know more than he does know

charm (t∫ɑrm) n. 1. The power or ability to attract or please someone: *This little village has a lot of charm that you won't find in a big city.* 2. An object worn by some non-Christians to keep away evil or bring good luck: *Christians trust in Jesus to supply all their needs, so they don't wear charms.* 3. An object, act, or phrase believed to have supernatural powers 4. **to work like a charm** Be completely successful

charm v. 1. To please; delight: *Maria charms everyone with her friendly smile.* 2. To control as if by magic —**charmer** n.

charm-ing (t∫ɑrm-ɪŋ) adj. Very pleasing; delightful: *What a charming young lady!* —**charmingly** adv.

chart (t∫ɑrt) n. 1. Information presented in the form of a picture, graph, etc.: *a population chart* 2. A map

chart v. 1. To make a map or a chart; to show or mark on a chart: *fig. The TV documentary charts the growth of our nation.* 2. To plan a course of action: *They charted their course before they began their trip.*

char-ter (t∫ɑr-tər) n. A formal document giving rights, privileges, etc.

charter v. To rent or hire: *They chartered a bus for their trip.*

charter adj. **1.** Hired: *a charter bus* **2.** (of an air journey made in a hired aircraft): *a charter flight*

chase (tʃeʸs) v. **chased, chasing 1.** To follow quickly and try to catch: *The cat was chasing the rat.* **2.** To drive away: *The barking of the dogs chased the prowler away.* **3.** To run; hurry: *The children keep chasing in and out.*

chase n. An act of going after someone or sthg.: *They caught the thief after a 30 minute chase.*

chasm (kæz–əm) n. **1.** A deep crack or opening in the earth's surface **2.** A significant difference of opinion or interests

chas-sis (tʃæs–iʸ / ʃæs–) n. *pl.* **chassis** (–iʸz) **1.** The steel frame that supports the body and motor of an automobile vehicle **2.** The landing gear of an aircraft **3.** The framework that holds the functioning parts of a radio, TV, etc.

chaste (tʃeʸst) adj. **1.** Virtuous; morally pure **2.** Not having sexual intercourse except with the person to whom one is married

chas-ten (tʃeʸ–sən) v. To discipline; to correct through punishment or suffering

chas-tise (tʃæs–taɪz) v. **-tised, -tising** To punish, esp. bodily —**chas-tise-ment** (tʃæs–taɪz–mənt/tʃæs–təz–mənt) n.

chas-ti-ty (tʃæs–tə–tiʸ) n. The quality or state of being chaste; sexual purity

chat (tʃæt) v. To talk in an easy, friendly way, usu. about unimportant matters

chat n. An informal conversation

chat-ter (tʃæt–ər) v. **1.** To talk quickly and continually about unimportant matters **2.** To knock together, esp. the teeth, due to fear or cold weather —**chatter** n. *Turn away from godless chatter* (1 Timothy 6:20). *Avoid godless chatter, because those who indulge in it will become more and more ungodly* (2 Timothy 2:16). —**chattering** adj. *A chattering fool comes to ruin* (Proverbs 10:8,10).

chat-ter-box (tʃæt–ər–baks) n. A person who talks all the time: *Some teenage girls are real chatterboxes.*

chauf-feur (ʃoʷ–fər) n. A person hired to drive someone's car

cheap (tʃiʸp) adv. **1.** Very low in price: *I was surprised that I got this car so cheap.* **2.** *infml.*

Behaving in a way that lowers one's worth: *She always acts so cheap.*

cheap adj. **1.** Low priced, costing little: *Nothing is very cheap these days.* **2.** Charging low prices: *This is the cheapest beauty parlor in town.* **3.** Of little value or poor quality: *Don't buy those cheap shoes. They won't last very long.* **4.** *infml.* Selfish with one's money; stingy: *That guy is really cheap. He never leaves a tip in the restaurant.*

cheat (tʃiʸt) v. **-ed, -ing 1.** To act dishonestly to gain an advantage: *The teacher caught him cheating on the test.* **2.** To trick; to deceive; to deprive someone of sthg. by deceit; to swindle: *He cheated the old lady out of thousands of dollars by persuading her to sign a paper that she didn't understand.* **3.** To win, or attempt to win, a game or contest by breaking the rules: *It's no wonder that Tom always wins at checkers; he cheats.* **4.** To avoid or escape as if by trickery: *The mountain climbers cheated death.*

cheat n. A dishonest person

check (tʃɛk) n. **1.** A test, comparison, or examination to make sure that sthg. is all right: *I made a thorough check of my purchases before leaving the store.* **2.** A restraint or control: *The government is putting forth great effort to bring the use of drugs in check.* **3.** A mark to show that sthg. is correct or the one chosen: *Put a check in front of each correct answer.* **4.** A bill at a restaurant **5.** A ticket or card for claiming sthg. that has been left for safekeeping: *Here's the check for my coat.* **6.** *BrE.* **cheque** A written order, usu. supplied by the bank, to pay someone the stated amount of money from one's account: *I usually pay my bills by check.*

check v. **1.** To examine as to accuracy: *Have you checked the spelling of all the words in your letter?* **2.** To leave sthg. for safekeeping: *He checked his hat and coat before being seated.* **3.** To find out: *He checked the air pressure in his car tires.* **4.** To mark sthg. to show if it is correct **5.** To block the progress of **6. check in** To report one's arrival, as at an airport, hotel desk, etc. **7. check out (a)** To leave a hotel, motel, etc. after paying the bill **(b) (i)** To find out if sthg. is true or not by asking ques-

tions: *Check out his story to see if he's lying or exaggerating.* (ii) To prove to be true after inquiries have been made: *The police found that his story checked out with the facts.* (c) To take sthg. after having its removal recorded: *Before leaving the library, Mary checked out three books.* **8. check up on sbdy./ sthg.** To make a thorough examination into sbdy./ sthg.: *The police are checking up on all known drug offenders in the area.*

check-er *AmE.* **cheq-uer** *BrE.* (tʃɛk–ər) n. **1.** A person who receives items for temporary storage **2.** One of the pieces used in a game of checkers

check-ers (tʃɛk–ərz) n. A game played on a checkerboard by two players, each starting with twelve checkers

check-ing ac-count (tʃɛk–ɪŋ ə–kaʊnt) n. A bank account from which money can be taken out by check at any time

check-mate (tʃɛk–meʸt) v. **1.** To arrest or counter completely **2.** To check a chess opponent's king so that escape is impossible —**checkmate** n.

check-up (tʃɛk–ʌp) n. A general medical examination: *You're having chest pains? You'd better see your doctor for a checkup.*

cheek (tʃiʸk) n. **1.** A fleshy part on either side of the face above the jaw and below the eyes: *spir. When Jesus said, "If someone strikes you on the right cheek, turn to him your other also," he meant we should not seek revenge* (Matthew 5:39). **2.** Insolent boldness **3.** Buttock

cheer (tʃɪər) n. **1.** A glad excited shout of praise, encouragement, etc.: *The crowd broke into cheers as the first runner crossed the finish line.* **2.** State of mind or of feeling: *Jesus said to the paralyzed man, "Be of good cheer, your sins are forgiven"* (Matthew 9:2). *Then he healed him.*

cheer v. **1.** To shout excitedly in approval or support **2.** To give someone encouragement or hope: *An anxious heart weighs a man down, but a kind word cheers him up* (Proverbs 12:25). **3. cheer up** *infml.* To become more cheerful: *Cheer up! Things could be a lot worse.*

cheer-ful (tʃɪər–fəl) adj. Full of happiness; in

good spirits: *A cheerful look brings joy to the heart* (Proverbs 15:30). —**cheerfully** adv. —**cheerfulness** n.

cheer-less (tʃɪər–ləs) adj. Dull; dreary; depressing: *a cheerless, dismal report*

cheese (tʃiʸz) n. A solid food made from milk: *A grilled cheese sandwich, please.*

cheese-bur-ger (tʃiʸz bər–gər) n. A hamburger with a slice of cheese on top

chef (ʃɛf) n. A skilled cook, esp. the chief cook in a restaurant

chem-i-cal (kɛm–ɪ–kəl) n. Any substance used in or obtained by a chemical process: *Some chemicals give off poisonous fumes when burned.*

chemical adj. **1.** Of or relating to chemistry: *a chemical reaction/ chemical warfare* **2.** Acting, operated, or produced by chemicals —**chemically** adv.

chem-ist (kɛm–əst) n. **1.** One who is trained in chemistry **2.** *BrE.* pharmacist

chem-is-try (kɛm–əs–triʸ) n. **-tries** The science dealing with the nature of substances which make up the earth, universe, and living things, and the ways in which they act on, or combine with, each other

che-mo-ther-a-py (kiʸ–moʷ–θɛr–ə–piʸ) n. The use of chemicals in treating diseases

cheque (tʃɛk) n. *BrE.* for **check**

cher-ish (tʃɛər–ɪʃ) v. *fml.* To hold dear; love: *The little girl cherished the picture of her grandfather. / He who cherishes understanding prospers* (Proverbs 19:8).

cher-ry (tʃɛər–iʸ) n. **-ries 1.** A small, fleshy, round fruit with a stone-like seed, usu. red in color **2.** The wood of the tree on which this fruit grows

cherry adj. A shade of red, usu. middle red

cher-ub (tʃɛər–əb) pl. **cherubim** (tʃɛər–ə–bɪm) n. A kind of angel; a heavenly creature belonging to the spiritual realm

chess (tʃɛs) n. A game of skill played on a special board by two players, each having 16 pieces that are moved in an attempt to checkmate the opponent's king

chest (tʃɛst) n. **1.** The upper front part of the body enclosed by the ribs and breastbone, containing the heart and lungs **2.** A large, strong box for keeping valuable objects,

packing goods, etc.: *a treasure chest* **3.** A bureau or dresser; a piece of furniture with several drawers for clothing

chest-nut (tʃest–nət) n. **1.** Either of two types of reddish-brown nut, one of which is edible, the other not **2.** The wood of the trees that bear these nuts

chestnut adj. The reddish-brown color of this nut: *chestnut hair*

chev-ron (ʃɛv–rən) n. A V-shaped sign, as on the sleeve of an army sergeant

chew (tʃuʷ) v. **1.** To crush food with the teeth **2. bite off more than one can chew** *infml.* To try to do more than one can deal with successfully **3. chew the fat** *infml.* To chat; talk idly or casually

chic (ʃiʸk) adj. Stylish; fashionable

chi-can-er-y (ʃɪ-keʸn–ər–iʸ /tʃɪ–) n. **-ies** Dishonest trickery

Chi-ca-no (tʃɪ–kɑ–noʷ) n. **-nos** A Mexican-American

Chicano adj. Of or pertaining to Mexican-Americans

chick-en (tʃɪk–ən) n. **1.** A common farm bird raised for its eggs and meat, esp. when young; fowl: *He raises chickens on his farm.* **2.** The meat of this bird: *We had chicken for dinner.* NOTE: A baby chicken is called a **chick**, a male chicken is a **rooster**, and a female chicken is a **hen**. **3.** *infml.* A cowardly person

chide (tʃaɪd) v. To give a scolding to

chief (tʃiʸf) n. **1.** The head or leader of a group; person with highest rank, etc.: *The chief of police announced a severe crackdown on crime in the city.* **2. chief of staff** The commander of the US army or air force

chief adj. **1.** Most important or highest in rank: *What is the chief product produced in this factory?* **2. Chief Executive** *AmE.* President of the United States

chief-ly (tʃiʸf–liʸ) adv. Mainly; mostly: *The president talked chiefly about foreign policy.*

child (tʃaɪld) n. **chil-dren** (tʃɪl–drən) **1.** A young human being, between birth and puberty **2.** A son or daughter: *Our new neighbors have four children./ We are all children of God through faith in Christ Jesus* (Galatians 3:26). **3. child's play** Sth. easy to do: *Painting a*

picture of a tree is child's play for him. He's a trained artist.* **4. be with child** *lit.* To be pregnant

child-hood (tʃaɪld–hʊd) n. **1.** The time when one was or is a child **2. second childhood** Weakness of mind caused by old age

child-ish (tʃaɪld–ɪʃ) adj. **1.** Of, typical of, or suitable for a child: *The children were playing childish games on the front porch while the adults were busy doing the yard work.* **2.** *derog.* Immature in behavior: *a childish remark* —compare CHILDLIKE —**childishly** adv.

child-like (tʃaɪld–laɪk) adj. Characteristic of a child, esp. having a natural lovable and trusting quality —compare CHILDISH

Child of God (tʃaɪld əv gɑd) n. Every person in the world NOTE: Everyone is a child of God because God created all people. However, sin has separated people from God and made them children of Satan. Only by being born again through the Spirit of God can one be received back into the family of God and become his child in a special way: *Jesus said, "Let the little children come to me and do not hinder them, for the Kingdom of God belongs to such as these"* (Matthew 19:14). *Unless you change and become like little children [trusting completely in Jesus Christ for eternal life] you will never enter the kingdom of God* (Matthew 18:3).

chil-i or **chil-e** (tʃɪl–iʸ) n. **-ies, -es, -lies 1.** The very pungent pod of the red pepper **2.** A condiment made from the dried fruit of this plant

chill (tʃɪl) v. To cause sth. to become cold, esp. without freezing

chill n. **1.** A moderate coldness: *There is a chill in the air on a November morning.* **2.** A sensation of coldness or a similar feeling as from a fever or from fear: *That scream sent a chill up my spine.*

chill-y (tʃɪl–iʸ) adj. **-ier, -iest 1.** Rather cold; cold enough to make one feel uncomfortable: *It's getting chilly; where's my sweater?* **2.** Unfriendly: *The unpopular governor received a chilly welcome when he arrived in this city.*

chime (tʃaɪm) n. **1.** The sound of bells ringing **2.** *pl.* A set of bells, as in a clock —**chime** v. To ring

chim-ney (tʃɪm–niʸ) n. **-neys 1.** The hollow passage often rising above the roof of a building, through which smoke passes from a fire **2.** A glass tube for enclosing the flame of a lamp

chim-pan-zee (tʃɪm–pæn–ziʸ) n. A dark-haired, friendly African ape

chin (tʃɪn) n. **1.** The front part of the face below the mouth; the central forward portion of the lower jaw **2. (keep your) chin up!** *infml.* Keep up your courage

chi-na (tʃaɪ–nə) n. **1.** A hard, white substance made by baking fine clay at high temperatures, originally made in China —compare PORCELAIN **2.** Plates, bowls, cups, etc., made from this **3.** Any earthenware dishes or crockery

chin-chil-la (tʃɪn–tʃɪl–ə) n. A small South American animal valued for its soft gray fur

chip (tʃɪp) n. **1.** A small piece of paint, wood, or rock, etc., broken off sthg. **2.** A mark made when a small piece is broken off of sthg. **3.** *AmE.* Potato chip **4.** *BrE.* French fry: *fish and chips* **5. a chip off the old block** *infml.* One who is like his father **6. have a chip on one's shoulder** *infml.* Wanting to fight or quarrel, as a result of feeling badly treated

chip v. **-pp-** To break or cut so as to form chips

chip-munk (tʃɪp–mənk) n. A kind of North American squirrel

chir-op-o-dist (kə–rɑp–ə–dɪst/ʃə–/kaɪ–) n. One who treats minor disorders and diseases of the feet —**chiropody** (kə–rɑp–ə–diʸ/ʃə–/kaɪ–) n. The treatment of these disorders

chi-ro-prac-tic (kaɪ–rə–præk–tɪk/ kaɪ–rə–præk–tɪk) n. A method of treating disease by manipulating people's joints, esp. those of the spine

chirp (tʃɜrp) v. To make the sharp sound(s) that small birds make —**chirp** n.

chis-el (tʃɪz–əl) n. A metal tool with a sharp edge, used for cutting into or shaping wood, stone, etc.

chisel v. **1.** To cut or shape with a chisel: *He chiseled the wood into the figure of a horse.* —compare CARVE **2.** *infml.* To get sthg.

through deceit: *He chiseled us out of a lot of money!*

chiv-al-rous (ʃɪv–əl–rəs) adj. Generous; courteous

chiv-al-ry (ʃɪv–əl–riʸ) n. Kindness, esp. toward women or to the weak

chive (tʃaɪv) n. A small bulbous plant related to the onion, used as seasoning in cooking

chlor-i-nate (klɔr–ə–neʸt) v. **-nated, -nating** To treat or combine with chlorine: *They chlorinated the swimming pool.*

chlor-ine (klɔr–iʸn) n. A chemical element used in purifying water, as a disinfectant, as a bleaching agent, and in the manufacture of chloroform

chlor-o-form (klɔr–ə–fɔrm) n. A clear, colorless substance that causes unconsciousness when breathed

chloroform v. To put to sleep (anesthetize) or kill with chloroform

chlor-o-phyll (klɔr–ə–fɪl) n. A green coloring matter in plants

choc-o-late (tʃɑk–lɪt) n. **1.** Roasted and crushed seeds of a tropical tree (cacao) **2.** Candy made with this substance **3.** A brown powder made by crushing this substance, used for flavoring foods and drinks **4. hot chocolate** A drink made by mixing this powder into hot milk

choice (tʃɔɪs) n. **1.** The act or result of choosing or selecting **2.** The power, right, or chance to make a decision: *I had no choice but to do as my captors demanded.* **3.** A variety from which to choose: *There was a huge choice of dresses in the clothing department.*

choice adj. The highest quality: *choice oranges*

choir (kwaɪ–ər/ kwaɪr) n. A group of people who sing together during worship services: *The choir sings every Sunday.*

choke (tʃoʷk) v. **choked, choking 1.** To prevent or be prevented from breathing because of blocking or squeezing the windpipe: *He started to choke on a piece of meat that got stuck in his windpipe.* **2.** To fill a passage completely: *The gutter was choked with leaves and had to be cleaned.*

chol-er-a (kɑl–ər–ə) n. An infectious and often fatal disease, causing severe diarrhea

cho-les-ter-ol (kə–lɛs–tə–rɔl/ –roʷl) n. A fatty substance found in many foods, believed to cause hardening of the arteries

choose (tʃuʷz) v. **chose** (tʃoʷz), **chosen** (tʃoʷz–ən), **choosing** To decide to take sthg. or do sthg. or buy sthg.; to make a decision: *Choose for yourselves whom you will serve, whether the gods your forefathers served beyond the river, or the gods of the Amorites... But as for me and my household, we will serve the Lord* (Joshua 24:15).

choos-y (tʃuʷz–iʸ) adj. **-ier, -iest 1.** Careful and cautious in choosing **2.** Hard to please

chop (tʃɑp) v. **-pp- 1.** To cut by repeatedly striking with an axe or other heavy sharp-ended tool: *He is chopping wood for the fireplace.* **2.** To cut into small bits: *She's chopping celery for the salad.*

chop n. **1.** A short, sharp, downward blow with a knife or an axe **2.** A slice of meat, esp. lamb or pork, cut along with a piece of bone

chop-py (tʃɑp–iʸ) adj. **-pier, -piest** Rough, with short, broken waves, as of the sea: *A storm was coming up and the sea was getting choppy.* —**choppiness** n.

chor-al (kɔr–əl) adj. Of or for a choir

chord (kɔrd) n. **1.** A combination of three or more tones sounded at the same time **2.** A straight line joining any two points on a curve

chore (tʃɔr) n. **1.** A small job **2.** A difficult task **3. chores** Routine household tasks

chor-e-og-ra-phy (kɔr–iʸ–**ɑg**–rə–fiʸ) n. The art of designing and arranging the movements of a dance, esp. a ballet

cho-rus (kɔ–rəs) n. **1.** A group of singers who perform together **2.** A piece of music played or sung after each group of lines of a song; a refrain **3.** A group of dancers performing in a musical comedy or revue **4.** Sthg. said by a lot of people together: *The decision of the judges was greeted by a chorus of cheers.*

chorus v. To sing or speak at the same time

chose (tʃoʷz) v. Past tense of **choose**

cho-sen (tʃoʷz–ən) v. Past part. of **choose**

Christ (kraɪst) n. also **Jesus Christ** The title, "Christ" is from the Greek word "Christos" which means "Messiah." In Hebrew, "Messiah" means "the Anointed One."

NOTE: Christians believe that Jesus of Nazareth is the Christ. Therefore, he is called "Jesus Christ." Kings and priests were anointed with oil (olive oil) in a special ceremony, which signified their power and authority to carry out their office: *Jesus (meaning "Savior") "was anointed by God with the Holy Spirit and with power to preach good news [the Gospel] to the poor,"* (Luke 4:18) *"and he went around doing good and healing all who were under the power of the devil, because God was with him"* (Acts 10:38). —see ANOINT, GOSPEL, JESUS CHRIST

Chris-tian (krɪs–tʃən) n. A person who believes in Jesus Christ as his personal Savior from sin, eternal death, and the devil; one who knows that he has eternal life through faith in Jesus Christ who died for him and rose again: *The disciples of Jesus were first called Christians at Antioch [in Syria]* (Acts 11:26). NOTE: Out of love and gratitude for all God has done for him, a Christian does good works to please and glorify God, but he does not trust in his own works for salvation. A Christian knows that the wages of sin is death, but the gift of God is eternal life in Christ Jesus our Lord (Romans 6:23). He knows that it is by grace (unmerited love and favor of God) that we have been saved through faith, and not of ourselves, "it's a gift of God, not of works lest anyone should boast" (Ephesians 2:8,9 KJV). A person may become a Christian, no matter who he is or what evil he has done if he repents (turns from his evil ways) and believes (puts his trust in) Jesus for salvation. "Whoever calls on the name of the Lord [Jesus] will be saved" (Romans 10:13). —see JESUS CHRIST

Chris-tian (krɪs–tʃən) adj. **1.** Believing in or belonging to any of the various branches of Christianity. A true Christian church is a church in which the members worship Jesus Christ as their Lord and Savior. A Christian wedding is one in which both bride and groom are followers of Jesus Christ, putting their trust in him for salvation and living unto him who died for them and rose again (2 Corinthians 5:15). **2.** Of or

related to Christ, Christianity, or Christians: *He behaved in a Christian (=kind and generous) way toward his enemies.* —opposite UNCHRISTIAN

Chris-ti-an-i-ty (krɪs–tʃiʸ–æn–ə–tiʸ) n. The Christian religion founded on the teachings of Jesus Christ. NOTE: Christianity spread throughout the Mediterranean world and as far east as India within 70 years after the death and resurrection of Jesus Christ. Today approximately 33% of the world's population are at least nominal members of the Christian church. Christianity is growing rapidly in Africa and in some Asian countries today. —see CHRIST, CHRISTIAN, JESUS

Christ-like (kraɪst–laɪk) adj. Loving, kind, gentle, holy, and humble, like Jesus Christ, our Savior —see JESUS CHRIST

Christ-mas (krɪs–məs) n. also **Christmas Day** December 25, a holiday celebrated by Christians as the anniversary of the birth of Jesus Christ our Lord and Savior. The true spirit of Christmas is one of joy and the expression of love through greetings, gift-giving, and time spent with loved ones. For Christians it is a special time of worship in the church. Many non-Christians also celebrate the holiday, following the many secular traditions that have developed over the centuries. The season from Christmas Eve (December 24) until Epiphany (January 6) is called "Christmastide" or "Yuletide."

chro-mi-um (kroʷ–miʸ–əm) n. A lustrous, hard, metallic element used in hardening steel alloys to produce stainless steels, and in other ways

chro-mo-some (kroʷ–mə–soʷm) n. One of the tiny threads or rods in plant and animal cells, containing the genes

chron-ic (krɑn–ɪk) adj. Esp. of a disease, lasting a long time

chron-i-cle (krɑn–ɪ–kəl) n. A record of events in order of time

Chron-i-cles (krɑn–ɪ–kəlz) n. First and Second Chronicles are books of the Old Testament. They tell of the kings of the united Israel and of the kings of the Southern Kingdom of Judah (from about 1040 to 606 B.C.). King David and King Solomon and the building of the Temple are very important in Chronicles. —see BIBLE, OLD TESTAMENT

chron-o-lo-gy (krə–nɑl–ə–dʒiʸ) n. **-gies 1.** The arrangement of events according to the order in which they occurred **2.** A list illustrating the relative order of events in time —**chron-o-log-i-cal** (krɑn–ə–lɑ–dʒɪ–kəl) adj. *He wrote the dates of the events in chronological order.*

chrys-a-lis (krɪs–ə–lɪs) n. The stage in an insect's life when it forms a sheath inside which it changes from a grub (larva) to an adult insect, esp. a butterfly or moth

chrys-an-the-mum (krɪs–æn–thə–məm) n. Any of a variety of plants noted for the size and variety of colors of its flowers

chub-by (tʃʌb–iʸ) adj. **-bier, -biest** *infml.* Round and plump; slightly fat —opposite THIN —**chubbiness** n.

chuck (tʃʌk) v. To throw: *Don chucked the ball to Bill.*

chuck-le (tʃʌk–əl) v. **-led, -ling** To laugh quietly

chug (tʃʌg) n. A short, dull, explosive sound **chug** v. **chugged, chugging 1.** To make this sound **2.** To move with this sound

chum (tʃʌm) n. A close friend

chum-my (tʃʌm–iʸ) adj. Intimately friendly

chunk (tʃʌŋk) n. **1.** A thick mass or lump of anything **2.** A large amount

chunk-y (tʃʌŋ–kiʸ) adj. **1.** Thick and stout **2.** In a chunk or chunks: *I like chunky peanut butter.*

church (tʃɜrtʃ) n. **1.** The Biblical meaning of the word "church" is the whole number of true believers, and only the true believers throughout the world. It is called the invisible church because one can't see it. Only God can look into a person's heart and know if he or she is a true believer in Jesus. **2.** All of those people who profess to be Christians **3.** A denomination or fellowship of churches: *The Church of England/ The Church of Scotland* **4.** A building made for public Christian worship: *My friends go to church every Sunday.* **5.** A local group of worshipers (congregation) in a particular place: *John is a member of the Lake Avenue*

Church. **6.** Ecclesiastical (church) power, as distinguished from the secular: *We speak of the separation of church and state.*

church-go-er (tʃɜrtʃ–goʷ–ər) n. One who attends a Christian church regularly

churl-ish (tʃɜrl–ɪʃ) adj. Rude, ill-mannered

churn (tʃɜrn) n. A device in which milk or cream is agitated to make butter

churn v. **1.** To stir or agitate in a churn **2.** To make butter by churning **3.** To move or be moved violently: *The sea churned violently during a storm.*

ci-der (saɪ–dər) n. The juice made from apples, used as a beverage or in making vinegar

ci-gar (sɪ–gɑr) n. A roll of tobacco for smoking

ci-gar-ette (sɪ–gə–rɛt) n. A short roll of finely cut tobacco, wrapped in paper for smoking

cin-der (sɪn–dər) n. A piece of coal which has been burned, but not reduced to ashes

cin-e-ma (sɪn–ə–mə) n. **1.** Also **movies** *AmE.* The art or industry of making moving pictures **2.** Esp. *BrE.* Movie theater

cin-na-mon (sɪn–ə–mən) n. A brownish, sweet-smelling powder obtained from the bark of a tropical Asian tree, used for giving a special taste to food

ci-pher (saɪ–fər) n. **1.** A secret method of writing coded symbols **2.** The key to such a method

cir-ca (sɜr–kə) prep. About (Used with approximate dates, figures, etc.)

cir-cle (sɜr–kəl) n. A round area enclosed by a curved line that is everywhere equally distant from one fixed point

circle v. **-cled, -cling** To draw or move in a circle: *The airplane circled the airport three times before landing.*

cir-cuit (sɜr–kət) n. **1.** A closed curve; a complete ring: *We made a circuit of the entire city.* **2.** The establishments on a regular journey from place to place: *The salesman has a regular circuit which he follows several times each year.* **3.** The complete path of an electric current

cir-cu-lar (sɜr–kyə–lər) n. A printed advertisement for public distribution

circular adj. **1.** Round; shaped like or nearly like a circle **2.** Forming or moving in a circle

cir-cu-late (sɜr–kyə–leʸt) v. **-lated, -lating 1.** To cause to move or flow along a closed path: *Blood circulates through our bodies.* **2.** To move about freely: *The fan in the room caused the air to circulate.* **—cir-cu-la-to-ry** (sɜr–kyə–lə–tɔr–iʸ) adj. **cir-cu-la-tion** (sɜr–kyə–leʸ–ʃən) n. **1.** The flow of liquid around a closed system, esp. the movement of blood through the body **2.** The movement of money from person to person: *This dime has been in circulation for 30 years.* **3.** The number of copies of a newspaper or magazine sold or read over a certain time: *This newspaper has a circulation of more than a million daily and 1.5 million on Sundays.*

cir-cum– (sɜr–kəm–) prefix Around; about; surrounding

cir-cum-cise (sɜr–kəm–saɪz) v. **-cised, -cising** To cut off the foreskin of the male sex organ, often as a religious rite **—cir-cum-ci-sion** (sɜr–kəm–sɪ–ʒən) n. *For in Christ Jesus neither circumcision nor uncircumcision has any value. The only thing that counts is faith [in Jesus] expressing itself in love* (Galatians 5:6).

cir-cum-fer-ence (sɜr–kʌm–fər–əns) n. The length around the outside of a circle: *The circumference of the earth is nearly 25,000 miles.*

cir-cum-flex (sɜr–kəm–flɛks) n. A mark placed over a vowel in some alphabets to denote quality, stress, nasalization, etc.

cir-cum-nav-i-gate (sɜr–kəm–**næv**–ə–geʸt) v. **-gated, -gating** To go completely around, esp. by water: *to circumnavigate the globe (=go around the world)*

cir-cum-spect (sɜr–kəm–spɛkt) adj. Cautious and watchful **—circumspectly** adv. *See then that you walk circumspectly, not as fools, but as wise, redeeming the time [making the most of every opportunity], because the days are evil* (Ephesians 5:15;16 KJV).

cir-cum-stance (sɜr–kəm–stæns) n. **1.** usu. pl. Condition, or event influencing other events, persons, or courses of action: *Be joyful always, pray continually; give thanks in all circumstances, for this is God's will for you in Christ Jesus* (1 Thessalonians 5:16-18). **2. in/ under the circumstances** Because of the

way things are or were: *I wanted to start home, but under the circumstances (a bad storm), I decided to wait until morning.*

cir·cum·stan·tial (sər–kəm–**stæn**–ʃəl) adj. **1.** Of or depending on the circumstances **2.** Incidental; not very important **3.** Complete and detailed **4. circumstantial evidence** Evidence that points to a conclusion but does not give proof of it

cir·cum·stan·ti·ate (sər–kəm–**stæn**–ʃiʸ–eʸt) v. **-ated, -ating** To give detailed proof

cir·cum·vent (sər–kəm–**vɛnt**) v. **1.** To get around (a difficulty) **2.** To outwit

cir·cus (**sɜr**–kəs) n. **1.** A traveling company of animals, acrobats, clowns, and other performers **2.** The tent-covered place where these performances usu. take place

cir·rus (**sɪər**–əs) n. **-ri** (–riʸ) A fleecy kind of cloud

cis·tern (**sɪs**–tərn) n. A very large container for storing water, esp. rainwater

cit·a·del (**sɪt**–ə–dəl/ –dɛl) n. A fortress

cite (saɪt) v. **cit·ed, cit·ing** **1.** To quote as an example or as proof **2.** To summon a person to appear in court

cit·i·zen (**sɪt**–ə–zən) n. **1.** One who has full rights as a member of a particular country, either by birth or by becoming naturalized (=being officially allowed to become a member) **2.** A person who lives in a town or city: *a citizen of Rome* —compare ALIEN, NATIONAL

cit·i·zen·ship (**sɪt**–ə–zən–ʃɪp) n. The state of being a citizen: *St. Paul, writing to the Christians in Philippi, said, "Our citizenship is in heaven. And we eagerly await a Savior from there, the Lord Jesus Christ... who will transform our lowly bodies so that they will be like his glorious body"* (Philippians 3:20-21).

cit·rus (**sɪt**–rəs) adj. Of or pertaining to trees and their fruit, such as oranges, lemons, and grapefruit

cit·y (**sɪt**–iʸ) n. **-ies** An inhabited place, usu. larger and more important than a town: *New York is the largest city in the United States.* —compare TOWN, VILLAGE

civ·ic (**sɪv**–ɪk) adj. Of a city or its citizens: *All citizens of a city have certain civic responsibilities.*

civ·ics (**sɪv**–ɪks) n. The study of government and the rights and duties of citizenship, etc.

civ·il (**sɪv**–əl) adj. **1.** Of or relating to the general population; not military **2.** Of law, dealing with the rights of private citizens; concerned with judging private disputes between people rather than with criminal offenses: *Divorce cases are decided by civil law.* **3.** Polite, courteous: *Keep a civil tongue in your head! (=Don't speak rudely.)*

ci·vil·ian (sə–**vɪl**–yən) n. One not serving in the armed forces

civ·i·li·za·tion also **-sation** BrE. (sɪv–ə–lə–**zeʸ**–ʃən) n. **1.** A stage of human social development, esp. one with a high level of cultural and technological development **2.** The cultural characteristics of an advanced society of a particular time or place: *the civilization of ancient Greece*

civ·i·lize **-lized, -lizing** also **-lise** BrE. (**sɪv**–ə–laɪz) v. To bring out of a primitive or uneducated state: *The Romans hoped to civilize the ancient Britons.*

clad (klæd) v. Past part. of **clothe**

claim (kleʸm) n. **1.** A demand as a right: *They put in an insurance claim after their house burned down.* **2.** A declaration that one is the owner of a piece of property: *He said he had a claim to his parent's house, as he was their only child.* **3.** A statement of fact: *His claim about the number of people involved in the fight was greatly exaggerated.* **4.** Sthg. claimed, esp. a piece of land: *His great grandfather staked out a claim of many acres during the gold rush days in California.*

claim v. **1.** To ask for or demand one's own property, money, etc.: *Did you claim your insurance after the fire?* **2.** To declare to be true, esp. in the face of opposition; maintain: *If we claim to be without sin, we deceive ourselves and the truth is not in us. If we confess our sins [trusting in Jesus for forgiveness and salvation], he is faithful and just and will forgive us our sins and purify us from all unrighteousness* (1 John 1:8,9). *Anyone who claims to be in the light [spiritual light] but hates his brother is still in the darkness* (1 John 2:9).

clair·voy·ance (klɛər–**vɔɪ**–əns) n. The supposed power to see into the future or into

the spirit world

clam (klæm) n. A shellfish with a hinged shell

clam, clammed, clamming v. **1.** To fish for clams **2. clam up** *fig.* To refuse to talk

clam-my (klæm-iʸ) adj. **-mier, -miest** Unpleasantly moist and sticky —**clam-miness** n.

clam-or (klæm-ər) n. **1.** A loud, confused noise, esp. of shouting **2.** A loud protest —**clamor** v. *The prisoners were clam-oring for more food.*

clamp (klæmp) n. A device for fastening or holding things together

clamp v. **1.** To fasten with a clamp: *Clamp these two pieces of wood together.* **2. clamp down** *infml.* To become stricter; put a stop to: *The police are clamping down on organized crime.*

clan (klæn) n. **1.** A group with a common ancestor **2.** A large family forming a close group

clan-des-tine (klæn-dɛs-tən) adj. Hidden; secret

clang (klæŋ) n. A loud ringing sound

clang v. To make a clang

clank (klæŋk) n. A metallic sound like that of metal striking metal

clan-nish (klæn-ɪʃ) adj. Clinging together and excluding all others

clap (klæp) v. **-pp-** To strike the palms of one's hands together several times to show approval of a performance: *The crowd clapped many times during the president's speech.*

clap n. **1.** A very loud, explosive sound: *a clap of thunder* **2.** An act of clapping: *When she had finished singing, there wasn't a single clap from anyone in the theatre.*

clar-i-fy (klɛər-ə-faɪ) v. **-fied, -fying** To make or become more clear: *We asked the candidate to clarify his position on equal pay for women.* —**clar-i-fi-ca-tion** (klær-ə-fə-keʸ-ʃən) n.

clar-i-net (klɛər-ɪ-nɛt) n. A woodwind musical instrument

clar-ion (klɛər-iʸ-ən) adj. Clear, sharp, and rousing

clar-i-ty (klɛər-ə-tiʸ) n. Clearness

clash (klæʃ) v. **1.** To fight: *The two armies clashed on the seashore.* **2.** To come into opposition; conflict; collide: *The green of your blouse clashes with the red of your skirt.*

clash n. **1.** A loud, usu. metallic sound of a collision: *We were awakened by the clash of sthg. outside.* **2.** A disagreement: *a clash of interests* **3.** A hostile encounter: *a border clash*

clasp (klæsp) v. To hold tightly: *He clasped the money in his right hand.*

clasp n. **1.** A fastener (usu. metal) for holding two things or parts of one thing together: *the clasp on a belt* **2.** A tight firm grip, esp. by the hand

class (klæs) n. **1.** A group whose members are of the same general nature: *the ruling class/ the working class* **2.** A group of pupils or students who are taught together: *John was in my Spanish class.* **3.** A period of time during which students are taught: *What time does your next class begin?* **4.** A number of students in a school or university, graduating in the same year: *She was in the class of 1968.* **5.** A division according to quality: *A first-class ticket (on a ship or a plane) usu. costs much more than a second-class ticket.*

clas-sic (klæs-ɪk) adj. **1.** Of the highest quality **2.** Belonging to an established set of standards; well known: *a classic example* —compare CLASSICAL

classic n. A piece of literature or art of enduring excellence: *That painting is an 18th century classic.*

clas-si-cal (klæs-ɪ-kəl) adj. **1.** Of or relating to ancient Greek or Roman models in literature or art: *classical literature / a classical education* **2.** Of music, arranged (composed) with serious artistic intentions: *Mozart wrote classical music.* —compare CLASSIC

clas-si-fi-a-ble (klæs-ə-faɪ-ə-bəl) adj. Able to be classified

clas-si-fi-ca-tion (klæs-ə-fə-keʸ-ʃən) n. The result of classifying (plants, animals, books, etc.)

clas-si-fied (klæs-ə-faɪd) adj. **1.** Of advertising, arranged according to subject matter **2.** Of information, officially secret and available only to certain people

clas-si-fied ad (klæs-ə-faɪd æd) n. A usu. small advertisement placed in a newspaper by a person wishing to buy or sell sthg. or to offer or get employment, etc.

clas-si-fy (klæs-ə-faɪ) v. **-fied, -fying 1.** To ar-

range systematically into classes or groups: *Librarians spend a lot of time classifying books.* **2.** To officially mark or declare information top secret: *The State Department has classified this information as secret.*

class-y (klæs–i^y) adj. -ier, -iest Stylish; fashionable

clat-ter (klæt–ər) n. 1. A sound like that of dishes rattling together **2.** Noisy talking

clatter v. To make a clatter: *Stop clattering those dishes.*

clause (klɔz) n. 1. A group of words with a subject and a verb, forming a complete sentence or only part of a sentence NOTE: In the sentence, "He quit work when he was tired," "He quit work" and "when he was tired" are two separate clauses. —compare PHRASE, SENTENCE **2.** A separate part of a written agreement or a will or other document

claus-tro-pho-bi-a (klɔs–trə–fo^w–bi^y–ə) n. A fear of being in a closed space —**claustrophobic adj.**

claw (klɔ) n. 1. A sharp usu. curved nail on the toe of an animal **2.** The pincers of a shellfish: *a lobster claw*

claw v. To scratch, tear, or dig with or as if with claws: *That cat keeps clawing the furniture.*

clay (kle^y) n. 1. Firm, heavy earth, soft when wet, becoming hard when baked at a high temperature, and from which bricks and pottery are made **2.** Earth or mud **3.** The mortal human body: *O Lord, you are our Father. We are the clay, you are the potter; we are all the work of your hand* (Isaiah 64:8).

clean (kli^{y}n) adj. 1. Not dirty: *Are your hands clean?* **2.** Not yet used; fresh: *a clean sheet of paper* **3.** Morally or sexually pure: *Who can say, "I have kept my heart pure; I am clean and without sin?"* (Proverbs 20:9). *All of us have become like one who is unclean, and all our righteous acts are like filthy rags* (Isaiah 64:6). *But if we walk in the light [of God's word] as he [God] is in the light, we have fellowship with one another, and the blood of Jesus, his Son, purifies [cleanses] us from all sin. If we confess our sins, he is faithful and just and will forgive us our sins and purify [cleanse] us from all un-*

righteousness (1 John 1:7,9). —see JESUS **4.**

come clean To admit one's guilt; tell the unpleasant truth: *Why don't you come clean and tell us the whole story?* —**cleanness n.**

clean v. To cause to become clean; to make tidy: *He's cleaning his room.* —**cleaning n.** *Ann is doing the spring cleaning.*

clean-er (kli^{y}n–ər) n. 1. A person whose job is cleaning offices, houses, etc. **2.** A machine, device, or substance used in cleaning

clean-li-ness (klɛn–li^y–nəs) n. Habitual cleanness

cleanse (klɛnz) v. cleansed, cleansing 1. To make a wound clean or pure: *The nurse cleansed the wound before stitching it.* **2.** *fig.* To make someone clean of sin: *The blood of Jesus Christ his Son cleanses us from all sin* (1 John 1:7 NKJV).

cleans-er (klɛnz–ər) n. A substance used for cleaning

clear (klɪər) adj. 1. Free from smog, fog, or cloudiness: *a clear day* **2.** Easy to see through: *clear glass* **3.** Free from blemishes: *clear skin* **4.** Easily heard, seen, read, or understood: *a clear style of writing* **5.** Free from doubt; not confused: *a clear thinker* **6.** Definite; feeling or showing confidence: *He was very clear about his intentions.* **7.** Open; free from any hindrance or obstruction: *a clear road/ a clear view* **8.** Free from guilt or blame: *a clear conscience* **9.** Obvious: *a clear case of cheating* **10. in the clear** *infml.* Free from danger, blame, guilt, etc. —see also CLARITY

clear v. 1. To make or become clear: *After the blizzard, the sky cleared.* **2.** To remove sthg. from an area: *We finally cleared all that junk out of the basement.* **3.** To declare someone to be free from blame: *The judge cleared the prisoner of all criminal charges.* **4.** To give official permission to or for: *The plans for the new highway have to be cleared by the town council.* **5.** To pass over sthg. without touching: *The high-jumper easily cleared six feet, ten inches.* **6. clear up (a)** To find an answer to; explain: *to clear up the mystery* **(b)** To improve: *I hope the weather clears up by tomorrow night.*

clear adv. 1. In a distinct manner: *We hear you loud and clear.* **2.** Out of the way: *He jumped clear of the oncoming train.* **3.** All the way: *You*

can see clear to Pike's Peak, a hundred miles away, on a day like this

clear-ing (klɪər–ɪŋ) n. An area of land that has been cleared of trees and brush

clear-ly (klɪər–liʸ) adv. **1.** Distinctly: *He spoke very clearly.* **2.** Undoubtedly: *She's clearly the most efficient secretary in the office.*

cleave (kliʸv) v. **cleaved, cleft** (klɛft) or **clove** (kloʷv); **cleaved, cleft,** or **cloven; cleaving 1.** To cut open or through **2.** To split **3.** To chop off

cleav-er (kliʸv–ər) n. A heavy knife, esp. one used by butchers

cleft (klɛft) n. A crack or split made by, or as if by, cleaving: *a cleft in the rock*

clem-en-cy (klɛm–ən–siʸ) n. **-cies 1.** Showing mercy **2.** Esp. of weather, mild

clench (klɛntʃ) v. To grasp or hold tightly: *He clenched the coin in his hand.*

cler-gy (klɜr–dʒiʸ) n. **-gies** Ministers in the Christian church

cler-gy-man (klɜr–dʒiʸ–mən) n. **-men** (–mɛn) A Christian minister

cler-i-cal (klɛr–ɪ–kəl) adj. **1.** Of or pertaining to clerks **2.** Of or pertaining to the clergy

clerk (klɜrk) n. **1.** Someone employed to keep records, accounts, etc. **2.** A salesclerk **3.** An official in charge of court records, etc. —**clerk** v.

clev-er (klɛv–ər) adj. **1.** Mentally bright; quick to learn: *a clever student* **2.** The result of a quick, able mind: *a clever idea* —**cleverly** adv. —**cleverness** n.

cli-che (kliʸ–ʃeʸ) n. A remark that has been used so much that it has lost much of its meaning

click (klɪk) n. A slight, sharp sound: *the click of the light switch*

click v. **1.** To make a click or series of clicks **2.** *infml.* (a) To succeed: *His business clicked.* (b) To work well together: *That's a team that really clicks.*

cli-ent (klaɪ–ənt) n. A person using the services of a lawyer, architect, or other professional person other than a doctor —see CUSTOMER

cli-en-tele (klaɪ–ən–tɛl) n. All one's clients or customers, collectively

cliff (klɪf) n. A high, very steep face of rock or earth: *The house was on a cliff overlooking the ocean.*

cli-mac-tic (klaɪ–mæk–tɪk) adj. Of or having a climax NOTE: Do not confuse climactic with climatic

cli-mate (klaɪ–mət) n. **1.** The average weather conditions of an area: *a subtropical climate* **2.** *fig.* A general attitude or feeling: *the present political climate*

cli-mat-ic (klaɪ–mæt–ɪk) adj. Of or related to climate —**climatically** adv.

cli-max (klaɪ–mæks) n. The most interesting part of a book, film, etc., usu. near the end of the story

climax v. To reach a climax —**climactic** adj.

climb (klaɪm) v. **climbed, climbing 1.** To move, esp. from a lower to a higher position, using the feet only, hands only, or by using the hands and feet: *John can climb a rope faster than anyone in school./ Can you climb that palm tree?/ Bill climbed 17 flights of stairs to the top of the building.* **2.** To rise to a higher point; go higher: *The temperature climbed as the sun climbed higher in the sky.* **3. climb down** To go down, esp. by using the hands and feet: *He climbed down the ladder.*

climb n. **1.** The act of climbing: *After a climb of six hours, they reached their destination.* **2.** A place to be climbed; very steep slope: *The north slope of the mountain has quite a climb.*

climb-er (klaɪm–ər) n. Someone or sthg. that climbs

clinch (klɪntʃ) v. **1.** To come to an agreement: *The salesman clinched the deal.* **2.** *infml.* To embrace

clinch n. **1.** A tight grip **2.** *infml.* A lovers' embrace

cling (klɪŋ) v. **clung** (klʌŋ), **clinging 1.** To grip tightly, refusing to let go: *Hate what is evil; cling to what is good* (Romans 12:9). **2.** To remain or linger; to be difficult to get rid of: *The odor clung to the room for hours.*

cling-ing (klɪŋ–ɪŋ) adj. **1.** Tight-fitting; sticking closely to the body: *a clinging shirt* **2.** Too dependent upon another person: *The clinging child would not leave her mother.*

clin-ic (klɪn–ɪk) n. A small building or part of a hospital where specialized medical treatment and advice is given to outpatients: *an*

eye clinic —**clinical** adj.

clink (klıŋk) v. To make a slight sound like that of pieces of glass lightly hitting each other

clip (klıp) n. **1.** A small plastic or metal device for holding things together: *a paper clip* **2.** A fast speed: *He was moving along at a pretty good clip.*

clip v. **-pp- 1.** To fasten onto sthg. with a clip: *Clip these sheets of paper together, please.* **2.** To cut with scissors or another sharp instrument, esp. to cut small parts off sthg.: *He clipped a news article out of the paper.* **3.** *infml.* To be overcharged for sthg.: *We really got clipped at that restaurant.*

clip-per (klıp–ər) n. A sailing vessel built for great speed

clip-pers (klıp–ərz) n. A usu. scissor-like tool used for clipping or trimming: *hair/ fingernail/ hedge clippers*

clip-ping (klıp–ıŋ) n. **1.** A piece cut off of sthg.: *fingernail clippings* **2.** A piece cut out of a newspaper, magazine, etc., such as an article, advertisement, or photograph: *newspaper clippings*

clique (klık) n. A group of people who are friendly with each other but who exclude others

cloak (kloʷk) n. **1.** A loose outer garment **2.** A disguise or pretense

cloak v. To hide; keep secret: *cloaked in secrecy*

clob-ber (klab–ər) v. **1.** To beat severely: *The boxer clobbered his opponent.* **2.** To hit hard: *The batter clobbered the ball.* **3.** *infml.* To defeat decisively: *Their football team clobbered us, 49 to 0.*

clock (klak) n. **1.** An instrument for measuring and showing time, unlike a watch, not meant for being carried about: *According to the clock on the wall, it's time for recess.* **2. around the clock** Twenty-four hours a day without stopping: *We worked around the clock during the flood to protect our houses.*

clock v. To time someone: *I clocked him while he ran a mile.*

clock-wise (klak–waız) adj., adv. In the direction in which the hands of a clock move: *Turn the lid clockwise if you want to tighten it.*

—opposite COUNTERCLOCKWISE

clod (klad) n. **1.** A lump, esp. of earth **2.** *infml.* A stupid person

clog (klag) v. **-gg-** To cause to become blocked: *The sink would not drain because the drain pipe was clogged.*

clois-ter (klɔıs–tər) n. **1.** A place of religious seclusion, such as a monastery or convent **2.** Any covered walk with an open arcade facing a garden or courtyard, as in a college, church, or monastery

cloister v. To confine, as in a cloister —**cloistered** adj. *a cloistered existence*

clone (kloʷn) n. **1.** A group of genetically identical cells that have descended from a single ancestor **2.** A group of organisms that have descended from a single individual **3.** A computer designed to duplicate the functions of another model

close (kloʷz) n. The end, esp. of an activity or of a period of time: *He brought the meeting to a close.*

close v. **closed, closing 1.** To shut: *Please close the window./ He who gives to the poor will lack nothing, but he who closes his eyes to them receives many curses* (Proverbs 28:27). **2.** To bring to an end: *He closed his speech with a stirring challenge.* —see OPEN **3. close down** To stop operation: *The company decided to close down the factory.* **4. close in** To encircle and gradually move in, usu. from all sides: *The people panicked when the enemy army closed in.*

close (kloʷs) adv. **1.** Near: *We live close to the church.* **2. close to** Almost: *It happened close to 20 years ago.*

close adj. **1.** Near: *The buildings are close together.* **2.** Near in relationship: *The Lord is close to the brokenhearted and saves those who are crushed in spirit* (Psalm 34:18). —opposite DISTANT **3.** Thorough; careful: *The guards kept a close watch on the prisoners.* **4.** Decided by a very small margin: *a close game* —compare NARROW **5. a close call/ shave** *infml.* Sthg. bad that almost happened but didn't: *That was a close call! We almost got hit by that bus!* —see NEAR —**closely** adv. —**closeness** n.

closed (kloʷzd) adj. Not open to the public:

clutch

Many stores are closed on Sundays.

clos-et (**klɒz-ət**/ **klɑn**) n. A very small room for storing supplies or clothing

clo-sure (**klo**^w**–ʒər**) n. 1. The condition of being closed 2. A conclusion or end

clot (**klɑt**) n. A thick or solid mass or lump formed from liquid: *a blood clot*

clot v. **-tt-** To cause to form into clots

cloth (**klɔθ**) n. cloths (**klɔðz**) A piece of material made from wool, cotton, silk, etc.: *Mother bought some cloth for a new dress.*

clothe (**klo**^w**ð**) v. clothed or clad (**klæd**), clothing 1. To provide clothes for: *John has to work at two jobs to feed and clothe his family.* 2. spir. (a) To become like: *Clothe yourselves with the Lord Jesus Christ, and do not think about how to gratify the desires of the sinful nature* (Romans 13:14). (b) To be filled with: *Clothe yourselves with compassion, kindness, humility, gentleness, and patience* (Colossians 3:12).

clothes (**klo**^w**z**/ **klo**^w**ðz**) n. also clothing (**klo**^w**–ðɪŋ**) Garments, such as pants, shirts, skirts, blouses, coats, hats, etc., worn on the body

cloud (**klaʊd**) n. 1. A mass of tiny drops of water floating high in the sky: *a beautiful sunny day with hardly a cloud in the sky/ fig. Clouds of smoke rose above the stricken city.* 2. Sthg. that causes unhappiness or fear: *War clouds were gathering.* 3. **under a cloud** Out of favor; looked upon with suspicion: *He left his teaching job under a cloud.* 4. **on cloud nine** AmE. infml. Very, very happy

cloud v. 1. To cover or hide with, or as if with, clouds: *The sky clouded over and we knew it would rain.* 2. To make or become gloomy or troubled 3. To confuse: *Stick to the subject. Don't cloud the issue by bringing in all these unrelated matters.*

cloud-y (**klaʊd–i**^y) adj. **-ier, -iest** 1. Full of clouds, overcast 2. Not clear: *cloudy water/ a cloudy memory*

clout (**klaʊt**) n. A hard blow: *He hit the ball 500 feet; that was quite a clout.*

clout v. To strike or hit hard

clove (**klo**^w**v**) n. 1. A flower bud of the clove tree, used as a spice 2. A small section of a bulb, as of garlic

clo-ver (**klo**^w**–vər**) n. 1. A small, usu. three-leafed plant often grown as food for cattle 2. **in clover** infml. Living in comfort

clown (**klaʊn**) n. A performer who dresses in a funny way and tries to make people laugh

clown v. often derog. To behave like a clown; act stupidly: *Stop clowning around and get to work.*

club (**klʌb**) n. 1. A group of people who join together for a certain purpose: *a health club* 2. The place where these people meet: *a country club* 3. A heavy stick that can be used for a weapon 4. A specially shaped stick for hitting a ball in certain sports, esp. golf: *a golf club*

club v. **-bb-** To beat with a heavy stick (club): *He clubbed the snake to death.*

cluck (**klʌk**) n. 1. The noise made by a hen 2. **dumb cluck** A stupid person

cluck v. To make the sound of a hen

clue (**klu**^w) n. 1. Evidence that helps find an answer to a question, puzzle, mystery, difficulty, etc.: *Have the police found any clues in that railway station murder case?* 2. **not to have a clue** infml. Unable to understand: *I don't have a clue as to what he's talking about.*

clump (**klʌmp**) n. 1. A group of trees, bushes, shrubs, etc., growing together 2. A heavy, solid lump or mass of dirt, mud, etc. 3. A heavy, dull sound

clump v. 1. To walk with a heavy, dull sound 2. To form clumps

clum-sy (**klʌm–zi**^y) adj. **-sier, -siest** derog. 1. Awkward: *He's too clumsy ever to be a dancer.* 2. Difficult to handle or control: *This large, soft mattress is a clumsy thing for one person to carry.* —clumsily adv. —clumsiness n.

clung (**klʌŋ**) v. Past tense and part. of cling

clus-ter (**klʌs–tər**) n. A number of similar things growing or being close together in a group; a bunch: *a cluster of grapes*

cluster v. To gather or grow in one or more clusters: *The girls clustered together around the fire.*

clutch (**klʌtʃ**) v. To hold tightly: *He clutched the steering wheel as the car went into a spin.*

clutch n. 1. A tight hold: *His clutch was not tight enough, and he fell.* 2. A device, esp. in a car, which allows working parts of an en-

gine to be connected or disconnected: *Push in the clutch to change gears.* **3. in the clutches of** In the control of **4. in the clutch** A critical situation: *He is a good hitter (in baseball), esp. in a clutch.*

clut-ter (klʌt–ər) n. Things scattered about in a disorderly manner: *What a terrible clutter! It looks like a tornado hit this room.*

clutter v. To make untidy: *The garage was cluttered with junk.*

cm *written abbr.* said as: centimeter(s) (sɛn–tɪ–miᵞ–tər/z)

Co. *Written abbr.* **1.** Said as **company** (kʌm–pən–iᵞ): *James Smith & Co.* **2.** Said as **county** (kaʊn–tiᵞ): *Los Angeles Co.*

c/o *abbr.* for in care of

co– (koʷ–) prefix With; together; jointly: *coeducation/ co-author/ copilot*

coach (koʷtʃ) n. **1.** A person who trains individuals or a team of performers: *a football coach* **2.** A railway passenger car **3.** *BrE.* Motorbus **4.** An enclosed four-wheeled, horse-drawn carriage used in former times, but now used only in official ceremonies **5.** Economy class on a plane or train

coach v. To train or teach a person or a group: *Mr. Nelson coaches athletes in track and field events.*

co-ag-u-late (koʷ–æg–yə–leʸt) v. -lated, -lating To change from a fluid into a thickened mass: *Milk coagulates.* —**co-ag-u-la-tion** (koʷ–æg–yə–leʸ–shən) n.

coal (koʷl) n. **1.** A piece of a black mineral, which can be burned to give heat, and from which gas and many other products can be made **2. rake over the coals** *infml.* To severely scold someone for doing sth. wrong

co-a-lesce (koʷ–ə–lɛs) v. -lesced, -lescing To grow or come together so as to become one; to fuse; to unite —**coa-lescence** n.

co-a-li-tion (koʷ–ə–lɪ–ʃən) n. Any political alliance or union, esp. a temporary one

coarse (kɔrs) adj. **1.** Rough, not smooth **2.** Rough in manner, speech, etc.: *Nor should there be obscenity, foolish talk or coarse joking* (Ephesians 5:4). —**coarsen** v.

coast (koʷst) n. The land next to the sea; seashore

coast v. To keep rolling, esp. down a hill,

without any effort: *We ran out of gas but were able to coast into a gas station.*

coast-al (koʷst–əl) adj. Of or near the coast: *coastal fishing*

coast-er (koʷst–ər) n. **1.** Sth. that coasts **2.** A small disk or mat for placing under a drinking glass to protect the table or other surface

coast guard (koʷst gɑrd) n. The military or naval coastal patrol of a nation

coast-line (koʷst–laɪn) n. The shape or outline of a coast: *The Atlantic coastline of the United States is very irregular, with many bays and inlets.*

coat (koʷt) n. **1.** An outer garment with long sleeves, usu. fastened in front with buttons **2.** An animal's fur, wool, hair, etc. **3.** also **coating** A covering spread over a surface: *a coat of paint/ of dust*

coat v. To cover with a coat: *A thick layer of dust coated the furniture.*

coax (koʷks) v. **1.** To gently persuade someone to do sth. **2.** To obtain in this way: *He coaxed a smile from her.*

cob (kab) also **corncob** n. The long hard central part of an ear of corn

co-balt (koʷ–bɔlt) n. **1.** A silver-white metallic element **2.** A blue coloring obtained from it

co-bra (koʷ–brə) n. A very poisonous snake of India and Africa

cob-web (kab–wɛb) n. The fine network spun by a spider

co-caine (koʷ–keʸn) n. A drug obtained from the leaves of a South American shrub, used as an anesthetic, also taken illegally for pleasure: *His life and his usefulness to society were destroyed by his addiction to cocaine.*

cock (kak) n. **1.** A rooster or other male bird **2.** A hand-operated valve or faucet **3. (a)** A lever in a gun **(b)** Its position when ready to be fired

cock v. To pull back and set the cock of a gun: *The gun was cocked.*

cock v. To tilt or turn upward: *The dog cocked his ears.* (=raised them attentively)

cock–and–bull sto-ry (kak–ən–bʊl stɔr–iᵞ) n. A foolish story that one should not believe

cock-pit (kak–pɪt) n. **1.** The compartment for the pilot and crew of an aircraft **2.** The driv-

er's seat in a racing car

cock·roach (kɑk–roʷtʃ) n. A beetle-like insect that infests kitchens, cellars, etc.

cock·tail (kɑk–teʸl) n. **1.** A mixed alcoholic drink **2. fruit cocktail** Small pieces of fruit, served as an appetizer

cock·y (kɑk–iʸ) adj. -ier, -iest Conceited; arrogant

co·coa (koʷ–koʷ) n. **1.** A dark brown powder made from crushed cacao seeds, used in making chocolate **2.** A drink made from this powder

co·co·nut (koʷ–kə–nət) n. **1.** The large hard-shelled seed of a tropical palm tree, containing a milky juice **2.** Its edible, white lining

co·coon (kə–kuʷn) n. **1.** The silky sheath around a chrysalis **2.** A protective wrapping

cod (kɑd) n. A popular food fish found in the colder waters of the North Atlantic Ocean

C.O.D. (siʸ oʷ diʸ)**1.** Cash on delivery **2.** Collect on delivery

cod·dle (kɑd–əl) v. -dled, -dling To treat too protectively; to pamper

code (koʷd) n. **1.** A way of signalling or sending secret messages, using words, letters, numbers, etc. agreed on beforehand **2.** A system of signals (such as the dots and dashes of the Morse Code) used instead of letters and numbers in a message that is to be telegraphed **3.** A system of principles or rules: *a moral code*

code v. **coded, coding** also **encode** *fml.* To put into a code

cod·i·fy (kɑd–ə–faɪ) v. -fied, -fying To arrange laws or rules systematically into a code

co·ed (koʷ–ɛd/ koʷ–ɛd) adj. *infml.* Coeducational

coed n. *infml.* A girl or young woman at a coeducational school or college

co·ed·u·ca·tion (koʷ–ɛdʒ–ə–keʸ–ʃən) n. The educating of boys and girls together —**coeducational** adj.

co·e·qual (koʷ–iʸ–kwəl) adj. Equal

coequal n. A person who is the equal of another —**coequally** adv.

co·erce (koʷ–ɜrs) v. -erced, -ercing To compel by threats or force —**co·er·cion** (koʷ–ɜr–ʒən/ –ʃən) n.

co·erc·ive (koʷ–ɜrs–ɪv) adj. Using coercion

co·ex·ist (koʷ–ɪg–zɪst) v. To exist together

co·ex·ist·ence (koʷ ɪg zɪst–əns) n **1.** Coexisting **2. peaceful coexistence** Tolerance of each other by countries having different social or political systems

cof·fee (kɔ–fiʸ) n. **1.** An aromatic, mildly stimulating beverage made from the bean-like seeds of a tropical tree **2.** A cup of this drink: *One coffee please!* **3.** The seeds themselves **4.** The tree itself

coffee adj. **1.** The flavor: *coffee (flavored) ice cream* **2.** The color: *a coffee (colored) dress*

coffee break (kɔ–fiʸ breʸk) n. A short intermission from work for coffee or other refreshments

coffee cake (kɔ–fiʸ keʸk) n. A cake made of sweetened yeast dough, often containing nuts and/or raisins

coffee pot (kɔ–fiʸ pɑt) n. A covered utensil with a spout, used for making coffee

coffee shop (kɔ–fiʸ ʃɑp) n. A small restaurant

coffee table (kɔ–fiʸ teʸ–bəl) n. A low table for putting cups, glasses, etc. on

cof·fin (kɔf–ən) n. The box in which a dead person is buried

cog (kɑg) n. **1.** A tooth or notch on the rim of a wheel or gear: *The chain came off his bicycle because some of the cogs were broken.* **2.** A person having a small part in a big organization: *He's just one small cog in the city government.*

co·gent (koʷ–dʒənt) adj. Convincing: *a cogent argument*

cog·i·tate (kɑdʒ–ə–teʸt) v. -tated, -tating **1.** To think carefully **2.** To ponder; meditate

cog·nate (kɑg–neʸt) adj. **1.** Having a common origin, esp. with regard to culture or linguistics **2.** Similar in nature

cog·ni·tion (kɑg–nɪ–ʃən) n. **1.** The mental process by which knowledge is acquired **2.** Knowledge —**cognitive** adj.

cog·ni·zance (kɑg–nɪ–zəns) n. **1.** Conscious knowledge or recognition; awareness **2.** Observance; notice **3. take cognizance of** To acknowledge; to take into consideration —**cognizant** adj.

co·here (koʷ–hɪər) v. -hered, -hering **1.** To stick together; be united **2.** To be reasonably con-

nected, esp. in thought

co-her-ent (ko^w–hɪər–ənt) adj. Naturally or reasonably connected; easily understood —opposite INCOHERENT —**coherently** adv. —**coherence** n.

co-he-sion (ko^w–hi^y–ʒən) n. The act or state of sticking together —**cohesive** adj. —**cohesively** adv. —**cohesiveness** n.

coil (kɔɪl) v. To wind into rings or loops: *The snake coiled itself around the tree.* —opposite UNCOIL

coil n. **1.** A length of sthg. wound into rings or loops: *a coil of rope* **2.** *tech.* A length of wire, wound and used for conducting electricity

coin (kɔɪn) n. A piece of flat and usu. round metal, used as money

coin v. **1.** To make coins from metal: *When will the government coin more silver dollars?* **2.** To invent a word or phrase: *Who coined the word "Funology"?*

co-in-cide (ko^w–ɪn–saɪd) v. -cided, -ciding **1.** To happen at the same time **2.** To agree: *My ideas and beliefs don't coincide with his.*

co-in-ci-dence (ko^w–ɪn–sə–dəns) n. A combination of events, happening at the same time, but not planned that way

co-in-ci-den-tal (ko^w–ɪn–sə–den–təl) adj. Resulting from a coincidence: *a coincidental meeting* —**coincidentally** adv.

co-la (ko^w–lə) n. **1.** An African tree **2.** A carbonated, non-alcoholic drink flavored with the seeds of this tree

cold (ko^wld) adj. **1.** Having a low or lower than usual temperature; not warm: *a cold day* **2.** Of people or their actions, showing unfriendly feelings: *Mary was given a cold reception from her former friends because of what she said about them.* —**coldness** n. —**coldly** adv.

cold n. **1.** Low temperature; not warm or hot: *Don't go out in the cold without a sweater!* **2.** An illness with running nose, coughing, a slight fever, and general discomfort **3.** **out in the cold** *infml.* Seemingly unwanted; rejected: *He was left out in the cold at the party because he didn't know how to play any of the games.*

cold–blood-ed (ko^wld–blʌd–əd) adj. **1.** Having

blood that is the same temperature as the surroundings of the body: *Fish are cold-blooded animals.* **2.** Cruel; ruthless: *cold-blooded murder*

cold cream (ko^wld kri^ym) n. A cosmetic for cleansing and softening the skin

cold feet (ko^wld fi^yt) n. Lack of courage: *He got cold feet and wouldn't dive from the ten meter platform.*

cold–heart-ed (ko^wld hɑrt–əd)adj. Lacking sympathy

cold shoulder (ko^wld ʃo^wl–dər) n. Deliberate and extreme coldness in attitude: *She gave him the cold shoulder. (=she was very unfriendly toward him)*

cold sore (ko^wld sɔr) n. A sore on the lips that often accompanies a cold or fever

cold turkey (ko^wld tɜr–ki^y) adv. *slang* Immediate and complete withdrawal from the use of sthg., such as tobacco or alcohol: *He quit smoking, cold turkey.*

col-i-se-um (kɑl–ə–si^y–əm) n. A large building or stadium for sports events, shows, etc.

col-lab-o-rate (kə–læb–ə–re^yt) v. -rated, -rating **1.** To work together with someone else **2.** *derog.* To work with an enemy to betray one's own country —**collaborator** n. —**col-lab-o-ra-tion** (kə–læb–ə–re^y–ʃən) n. *Our two organizations are working in close collaboration with each other.*

col-lage (kə–lɑʒ/kɔ–/ko^w–) n. **1.** An art composition made of paper, cloth, wood, etc. glued onto a flat surface, usu. framed like a picture **2.** A film showing a series of unconnected shots in rapid succession

col-lapse (kə–læps) v. -lapsed, -lapsing **1.** To fall down suddenly; cave in: *The roof collapsed under the weight of the snow.* **2.** *fig.* To cease suddenly: *All open opposition to the government collapsed due to the enemy invasion.* **3.** To fall down, helpless or unconscious: *He collapsed due to a heart attack.* **4.** To fold into a shape that takes up less space: *These tables collapse, so they can be stored easily when not in use.*

collapse n. **1.** The act of falling down: *The snow caused the collapse of the roof./fig. There's been a complete collapse of law and order in this city in recent years.* **2.** Sudden and complete

loss of strength and/ or will: *Tom suffered from a nervous collapse.*

col·laps·i·ble (kə–læps–ə–bəl) adj. *Stlg.* that can be collapsed for easy storing

col·lar (kɑl–ər) n. **1.** The part of a shirt, coat, dress, or blouse, etc. that fits around one's neck **2.** A leather or metal band put around an animal's neck: *a dog collar*

col·lar·bone (kɑl–ər–boʷn) n. Either of a pair of bones joining the breastbone and shoulder blade

col·late (kə–leʸt) v. **-lated, -lating 1.** To collect or arrange in proper order **2.** To compare texts critically

col·la·tion (kə–leʸ–ʃən) n. The act of collating

col·lat·er·al (kə–læt–ər–əl) adj. **1.** Situated or running side by side **2.** Accompanying **3.** Additional **4.** Secondary or indirect

collateral n. Security pledged for the payment of a loan

col·league (kɑ–liʸg) n. A co-worker; one who works in the same profession or for the same firm or office

col·lect (kə–lɛkt) v. **1.** To bring or gather together: *Bob collects stamps for a hobby; Jim collects rare coins.* **2.** To receive payment: *The landlord came to collect the rent.* **3.** To pick up and take away: *He collected the trash.* —**collection** n.

col·lect·ed (kə–lɛkt–əd) adj. Having control of one's emotions: *In spite of all the trouble, Jim remained calm and collected.*

col·lect·or (kə–lɛk–tər) n. **1.** A person employed to collect taxes, tickets, etc. **2.** A person who collects stamps, rare coins, etc. as a hobby

col·lege (kɑl–ɪdʒ) n. **1.** A school of higher learning, granting a bachelor's degree **2.** An institution offering instruction in a vocational field: *a barber college* **3.** *fml.* A body of people with a common profession, purpose, duties, or rights

col·lide (kə–laɪd) v. **-lided, -liding** To come together with sudden impact; to crash: *Many people were badly hurt when the truck and bus collided.*

col·li·sion (kə–lɪ–ʒən) n. The act of colliding

col·lo·qui·al (kə–loʷ–kwiʸ–əl) adj. Suitable for ordinary conversation, but not for formal speech —**colloquialism** n.

col·lu·sion (kə–luʷ–ʒən) n. An agreement between two or more people for a deceitful or fraudulent purpose

co·logne (kə–loʷn) n. A lightly scented liquid, used for cooling and scenting the skin

co·lon (koʷ–lən) n. **1.** A mark (:) used to show a break in a sentence **2.** A part of the bowel

colo·nel (kɜr–nəl) n. An officer of middle rank in the army or air force

co·lo·ni·al (kə–loʷ–niʸ–əl) adj. Of or related to colonies

co·lo·ni·al·ism (kə–loʷ–niʸ–əl–ɪz–əm) n. A governmental policy of acquiring and controlling a foreign territory

col·o·nist (kɑl–ə–nəst) n. One who takes part in founding a colony

col·o·nize (kɑl–ə–naɪz) v. **-nized, -nizing 1.** To establish a colony **2.** To settle in a colony —**col·o·ni·za·tion** (kɑl–ə–nə–zeʸ–ʃən) n.

col·o·ny (kɑl–ə–niʸ) n. **-nies 1.** A country or area under the control of another country, often settled by people from that other country **2.** Any group of people or animals of the same type living together

col·or *AmE.* **col·our** *BrE.* (kʌl–ər) n. **1.** The quality which allows one to see the difference between two things which are exactly the same shape and size: *The primary colors are red, yellow, and blue. There are many other colors and many shades of each color.* **2. with flying colors** Great success; high marks: *He passed the exam with "flying colors."*

color v. **1.** To cause sthg. to have color, esp. with a crayon or pencil: *The child is coloring the picture.* **2.** To take on or change color: *Autumn is here; the leaves have started to color.*

col·or·blind (kʌl–ər–blaɪnd) adj. Partially or totally unable to see differences in color

col·ored (kʌl–ərd) adj. **1.** Having color **2.** Not white skinned

col·or·ful *AmE.* **colourful** *BrE.* (kʌl–ər–fəl) adj. **1.** Full of color; bright: *a butterfly with colorful wings* **2.** Rich in variety or vivid detail: *a colorful career*

col·or·less (kʌl–ər–ləs) adj. **1.** Without color: *Pure air is colorless.* **2.** Dull; not interesting; lacking variety or excitement

col·ors (kʌl–ərz) n. **1.** A flag: *The soldiers salut-*

ed the colors when they were on parade. **2.** Certain colors worn by a jockey to show that his racehorse belongs to a certain person: *Eddie raced under the same colors for many years.* **3.** An attitude of personality: *By doing that, he revealed his true colors.*

co-los-sal (kə–lɑs–əl) adj. Very great in size, degree, or achievement: *a colossal success*

Co-los-sians (kə–lɑ–ʃənz) n. A book of the New Testament. NOTE: It is a letter from the Apostle Paul to the church of Colosse in what is now southwestern Turkey. It speaks strongly of the supremacy and deity of Jesus Christ and contains rules for holy living and warnings against false teachers. —see BIBLE, JESUS, NEW TESTAMENT

colt (koʷlt) n. A young male horse or related animal

col-umn (kɑl–əm) n. **1.** A pillar used in a building as a support or decoration **2.** Anything that looks like a pillar in shape or use: *a spinal column* **3.** A vertical section on a page: *This dictionary is arranged in two columns.* **4.** An article that appears regularly in a newspaper or magazine

col-um-nist (kɑl–əm–nəst) n. A journalist who regularly writes for a magazine or newspaper

com– (kʌm–) prefix also **co–** before gn, h, and vowels, as in cooperate, cohabitate; **col–** before l, as in collide; **con–** before c, d, f, g, j, n, g, s, t, and v, as in concur and conspire With; together: *compare/combine*

co-ma (koʷ–mə) n. A state of unconsciousness due to an illness, injury or poison

co-ma-tose (koʷ–mə–toʷs/ kɑ–) adj. In a coma

comb (koʷm) n. A toothed instrument used for arranging the hair

comb v. **1.** To tidy, straighten, or arrange the hair with a comb: *He ought to comb his hair.* **2.** To search a place thoroughly: *The police combed the whole area, searching for the missing girl.*

com-bat (kəm–bæt/ kɑm–bæt) v. **-t-,** or **-tt-** To fight or struggle against: *to combat evil/ The police chief has spent a lifetime combating crime.*

combat (kɑm–bæt) n. **1.** Active fighting between enemy forces **2.** Any fight or struggle

com-bat-ant (kəm–bæt–ənt) n. One who is fighting —**combative** adj.

com-bi-na-tion (kɑm–bə–neʸ–ʃən) n. **1.** The process of combining or of being combined **2.** A number of people or groups united for a common purpose: *This organization is supported by a combination of people from various races and all walks of life.* **3.** A sequence of numbers or letters needed to open a combination lock

com-bine (kəm–bɑm) v. **-bined, -bining** To come together, unite, or join together

com-bine (kɑm–bɑm) n. **1.** *infml.* A business combination **2.** A machine for cutting and threshing grain in the field

com-bus-ti-ble (kəm–bʌs–tə–bəl) adj.. Capable of catching fire and burning: *Gasoline is a combustible substance.*

com-bus-tion (kəm–bʌs–tʃən) n. The act or process of burning —**combustive** adj.

come (kʌm) v. **came** (keʸm) **come, coming** **1.** To move towards the speaker or a particular place: *Jesus Christ came into the world to save sinners* (1 Timothy 1:15). *At that time they will see the Son of Man [Jesus] coming in a cloud with power and great glory* (Luke 21:27). *Look, he [Jesus] is coming with the clouds and every eye will see him* (Revelation 1:7). **2.** To arrive: *We'll be home when you come.* **3.** To reach: *Her hair comes down to her waist.* **4.** To be in a particular place or position: *The letter "X" comes after "W" in the English alphabet.* **5.** To happen: *How did you come to know so much about that?* **6.** To begin: *Sooner or later you will come to like this job.* **7.** To become: *The sign on my office door came loose.* **8.** To be available: *Cars come in many shapes, sizes, and colors.* **9.** To be produced by: *Milk comes from cows.* **10. come and go** To pass or disappear quickly; change: *Ideas and opinions come and go, "but the Word of our God shall stand forever"* (Isaiah 40:8). **11. how come?** *infml.* Why did it happen (that)...?: *How come you didn't go to work today?* **12. come about** To happen: *How did this state of affairs come about?* **13. come across (a)** To find: *I've just come across some old photos that I thought were lost.* **(b)** To produce an impression: *How did my speech*

come across? What are people saying about it?
14. come along (a) To advance or improve:
She's coming along just fine after her operation.
(b) To happen: *He took advantage of every sale
that came along.* **15. come apart** To break
without force; to fall apart: *I tried to pick up
this puzzle and it just came apart.* **16. come
around** (a) To regain consciousness (b) To
change one's mind: *He'll soon come around to
our way of thinking.* (c) To happen regularly:
The mailman comes around every day. **17.
come at** To advance in a threatening way:
He came at her with a knife. **18. come back** (a)
To return: *Jesus said, "I am going there [to
heaven] to prepare a place for you. I will come
back and take you to be with me"* (John 14:2,3).
(b) To return to one's memory: *Now I remember. It all comes back to me now.* (c) To become fashionable again **19. come between**
To separate: *They are inseparable; nothing can
come between them.* **20. come by** To obtain:
Bargains are hard to come by these days. **21.
come down** (a) To decline: *Do you think prices will ever come down?* (b) To be passed
down from one generation or from one period of history to another: *This literature has
come down to us from the 17th century.* **22.
come down with sthg.** *infml.* To catch an infectious disease/ illness: *She came down with
the flu.* **23. come forward** To offer oneself to
fill a position, to help someone, etc.: *Has
anyone come forward with information about
the accident?* **24. come from** A place of origin: *I come from London but have spent most of
my life in Hong Kong.* **25. come in** To arrive
as expected: *When does the train come in?* **26.
come in handy** To be useful: *This strange
tool may come in handy one day, so don't lose it.*
27. come into sthg. (a) To gain a sum of money, esp. to inherit it after someone's death:
She came into a fortune when her uncle died. (b)
To begin to be: *The men were excited when
land finally came into view after two months at
sea.* **28. come of sthg.** To result from: *Do you
think that any good will come of your letter?* **29.
come of age** To reach an age when one is
qualified for full legal rights **30. come on**
infml. To start: *The movie comes on at nine
o'clock.* **31. come out** (a) To appear: *The storm*

clouds passed and the stars came out.* (b) To become known: *The news came out that the president had been shot.* (9) Of stains, dirt, etc., to
be removed; disappear: *The ugly stains won't
come out, no matter what I do.* **32. come out
against sthg.** To declare one's opposition:
The senator came out against the new proposal.
33. come over sbdy. To trouble someone: *A
feeling of dizziness came over her and she fell
down.* **34. come through** (a) To do what is
needed or expected: *I knew Steve would come
through when we really needed him.* (b) To continue to live after sthg. dangerous happens:
John came through the surgery very well. **35.
come to sbdy./ sthg.** (a) To arrive: *It has come
to my attention that you lied about your age.* (b)
To concern: *When it comes to nuclear physics,
I know nothing.* (c) To suddenly remember:
Suddenly his name came to me. **36. come to
pass** *fml.* To happen **37. come under sthg.** (a)
To be governed or controlled by: *This committee will come under the Department of
Highways.* (b) To receive: *We came under attack at dawn.* **38. come up** (a) To come to attention or consideration: *Your recommendation came up at the committee meeting.* (b) To
happen: *Let me know if anything comes up.* **39.
come up in the world** To reach a higher position, social status, or standard of living

come-back (kʌm–bæk) *n.* A return to a former
position of strength or importance: *Due to
an accident the former champion hadn't fought
in years, but now he's making a comeback.*

co-me-di-an (kə–miˠ–diˠ–ən) *n.* A professional
entertainer who tells jokes or does funny
things to amuse —**co-me-di-enne** (kə–miˠ–
diˠ–**en**) *n. fem.*

come–down (kʌm–daʊn) *n.* A descent from
dignity, importance, or prosperity: *She was
once a movie star, now she can hardly get a supporting role. What a comedown!*

co-me-dy (kɑ–mə–diˠ) *n.* **-dies 1.** A comical
play, movie, or TV show **2.** An amusing incident **3.** Humor

come-ly (kʌm–liˠ) *adj.* **-lier, -liest** Pleasing in
appearance —**comeliness** *n.*

com-et (kɑm–ɪt) *n.* A celestial body having a
solid head and an elongated, curved vapor
tail, moving about the sun: *Halley's Comet*

appeared in 1986 and will appear again in 2062.

com-fort (kʌm–fərt) n. **1.** The state of ease and contentment, being free from anxiety, pain, or suffering, and having all bodily wants satisfied: *It was such a comfort to learn that you were safe.* **2.** A person or thing that gives strength, hope, or sympathy: *Praise be to the God and Father of our Lord Jesus Christ, the Father of compassion and the God of all comfort* (2 Corinthians 1:3). —see also DISCOMFORT

comfort v. To give comfort to; to make someone feel better: *God comforts us in all our troubles, so that we can comfort those in any trouble with the comfort we ourselves have received from God* (2 Corinthians 1:4). —comforter n.

com-fort-a-ble (kʌmf–tər–bəl/ kʌm–fərt–ə–bəl) adj. **1.** Having or providing comfort: *a comfortable bed* **2.** Not experiencing too much pain, grief, anxiety, etc.: *The doctor said that Dad was comfortable after his operation.* —see also UNCOMFORTABLE —comfortably adv.

com-fort-er (kəm–fər–tər) n. **1.** A person or thing that comforts **2.** A thick quilt

com-ic (kɑm–ɪk) adj. Causing amusement and laughter

comic n. **1.** A comedian **2.** A comic book —comical adj. —comically adv.

com-ing (kʌm–ɪŋ) adj. That which is coming or will come: *the coming election*

coming n. Arrival: *With the coming of winter, nights get longer and colder.*

com-ma (kɑm–ə) n. The mark (,) used in writing and printing for showing a short pause: *For supper we had salad, spaghetti with tomato sauce, and chocolate ice cream.*

com-mand (kə–mænd) v. **1.** To order with authority, expecting people to obey: *Noah did all that the Lord commanded him* (Genesis 7:5). —see ORDER **2.** To deserve and get: *This great man of God is able to command everyone's respect.*

command n. **1.** An order: *By faith we understand that the universe was formed at God's command* (Hebrews 11:3). **2.** Control: *Who is in command of Company B?* **3.** The ability to control and use: *Do you have a good command*

of the English language?

com-man-deer (kɑm–ən–**dɪər**) v. To seize arbitrarily, esp. for public use; confiscate

com-mand-er (kə–mæn–dər) n. **1.** One who commands **2.** A leader or chief officer **3.** A commissioned officer in command of a military unit **4.** A naval officer ranking just below a captain **5. commander in chief (a)** The supreme commander of the armed forces of a nation **(b)** The commander of a major force

com-mand-ing (kə–mænd–ɪŋ) adj. **1.** Having command; being in charge: *Captain Smith is our commanding officer.* **2.** Deserving or expecting respect and obedience: *The school principal has such a commanding voice that everyone obeys him.*

com-mand-ment (kə–mænd–mənt) n. **1.** An edict; order; law **2.** Any of the Ten Commandments which were given by God on Mount Sinai, as follows: *"You shall have no other gods before me. You shall not make for yourself an idol in the form of anything in heaven above or on the earth beneath or in the waters below. You shall not bow down to them or worship them;... You shall not misuse the name of the Lord your God, for the Lord will not hold anyone guiltless who misuses his name. Remember the Sabbath day by keeping it holy. Six days you shall labor and do all your work, but the seventh day is a Sabbath to the Lord your God. On it you shall not do any work. Honor your father and your mother, so that you may live long in the land the Lord your God is giving you. You shall not murder. You shall not commit adultery. You shall not steal. You shall not give false testimony against your neighbor. You shall not covet your neighbor's house. You shall not covet your neighbor's wife, or his manservant or maidservant, his ox or donkey, or anything that belongs to your neighbor"* (Exodus 20:1-17).*When asked which was the greatest commandment in the Law, Jesus replied, "Love the Lord your God with all your heart and with all your soul and with all your mind. This is the first and greatest commandment. And the second is like it: Love your neighbor as yourself"* (Matthew 22: 37-40). NOTE: The breaking of any of these commandments is called sin.

God hates sin, (Hebrews 1:9) and the wages of sin (what we deserve) is (eternal) death (Romans 6:23). Nevertheless, God loves sinners and has provided salvation for penitent sinners (those who are sorry for their sins and turn from their evil ways), who put their trust in Jesus for eternal life. "The gift of God is eternal life through Jesus Christ our Lord" (Romans 6:23). —see FORGIVENESS, JESUS, SIN

com-man-do (kə–**mæn**–do^w) n. -dos or -does A member of a small military unit esp. trained for tasks requiring courage and skill

com-mem-o-rate (kə–**mem**–ə–re^{y}t) v. -rated, -rating 1. To give honor to the memory of someone by a solemn celebration: *We commemorate our Savior's resurrection on Easter Sunday.* 2. To be a memorial to —**com-mem-o-ra-tion** (kə–mεm–ə–re^y–ʃən) n. —**com-mem-o-ra-tive** (kə–mεm–ə–rə–tɪv) adj.

com-mence (kə–**mεns**) v. -menced, -mencing *fml.* To begin

com-mence-ment (kə–**mεns**–mənt) n. 1. The act of commencing 2. *AmE.* A graduation ceremony, as of a college

com-mend (kə–**mεnd**) v. 1. To recommend; speak favorably of 2. To commit to one's care 3. Praise

com-men-da-ble (kə–**mεn**–də–bəl) adj. Worthy of praise —**commendably** adv. —**com-men-da-tion** (kɑ–mən–**de**^{y}–ʃən) n.

com-men-su-rate (kə–**mεns**–ə–rət/ –mεntʃ–) adj. 1. Having the same measure 2. Corresponding in amount or degree: *The salary was commensurate with the output.*

com-ment (**kɑ**–mεnt) n. A remark; an opinion, explanation, or judgment, written or spoken

comment v. To remark or give an opinion: *The candidate refused to comment on several crucial issues.*

com-men-tar-y (**kɑm**–ən–tεɑr–i^y) n. -ies A systematic series of comments: *a Bible commentary*

com-men-ta-tor (**kɑm**–ən–te^y–tər) n. One who makes comments, esp. one who gives comments on the news on radio or television

com-merce (**kɑ**–mərs) n. The buying and selling of goods; trade

com-mer-cial (kə–**mɜr**–ʃəl) adj. 1. Of, related to, or used in commerce 2. Likely to produce profit: *Oil has been found in commercial quantities on our property.*

commercial n. An advertisement on radio or TV

com-mer-cial-ize also -ise *BrE.* (kə–**mɜr**–ʃəl–aɪz) v. -ized, -izing *often derog.* To make sthg. a matter of profit: *Christmas has become much too commercialized.* —**commercially** adv. —**commercialism** n.

com-mis-sar-y (**kɑm**–ə–sεɑr–i^y) n. -ies 1. A store for equipment and provisions, esp. for military personnel 2. A lunchroom, esp. in a motion picture studio 3. A person to whom some duty is given by authority

com-mis-sion (kə–**mɪʃ**–ən) n. 1. An amount of money paid to a salesman or agent for goods sold or services rendered 2. A warrant or document giving authority to an officer in the armed forces 3. A group specially appointed to investigate sthg. or perform certain duties 4. **The Great Commission** The commission of our Lord and Savior Jesus Christ, after his resurrection and shortly before his ascension into heaven, to make disciples of all nations, baptizing them, teaching them to observe all that he had commanded (Matthew 28:18-20). 5. **out of commission** Not working properly; waiting for repair; out of order: *My car is out of commission.* 6. The act of actually doing sthg. NOTE: Actually shooting or stabbing someone would be a **sin of commission**. Letting someone suffer and die and doing nothing to help the person, when it was within one's power to help, would be a **sin of omission** (James 4:17).

commission v. To give a commission to a person or group of people: *Jesus commissioned his followers to go and make disciples of all nations* (Matthew 28:19).

com-mis-sion-er (kə–**mɪʃ**–ə–nər) n. 1. A person with a commission 2. The representative of governmental authority in a district or unit of government

com-mit (kə–**mɪt**) v. -tt- 1. To do sthg. wrong, sinful, or unlawful: *He committed suicide.* 2.

To order someone to be placed under the control or supervision of another, esp. in a mental hospital: *She was committed to a mental institution.* **3.** To bind as by a promise; pledge oneself to a certain cause or course of action: *Commit your way unto the Lord; trust also in him, and he shall bring it to pass* (Psalm 37:5). *Commit to the Lord whatever you do, and your plans will succeed* (Proverbs 16:3). **4. commit to memory** *fml.* Memorize: *He committed much of God's word to memory.* —**committed** adj.

com-mit-ment (kə-mɪt-mənt) n. **1.** An act of committing **2.** An obligation or promise: *He couldn't accept the dinner invitation because of a previous commitment.*

com-mit-tal (kə-mɪt-əl) n. **1.** Committing to a prison or other place of confinement **2.** Committing a body at burial or cremation

com-mit-ted (kə-mɪt-əd) adj. Dedicated or pledged, esp. to support a doctrine or cause

com-mit-tee (kə-mɪt-iʸ) n. A group of people chosen or appointed to plan, study, propose or do a particular job or for special duties: *The building committee will meet Thursday evening to discuss plans for the new school.* —compare COMMISSION

com-mode (kə-moʷd) n. **1.** A chest of drawers **2.** A portable toilet, as for an invalid **3.** A movable stand containing a washbowl

com-mod-i-ty (kə-mɑd-ə-tiʸ) n. -ties **1.** A product of agriculture or mining **2.** An article of commerce: *Perfume is one of the many commodities that France sells abroad.*

com-mod-i-us (kə-moʷ-diʸ-əs) adj. Roomy

com-mo-dore (kɑm-ə-dɔr) n. **1.** A commissioned officer in the US Navy, ranking above a captain and below a rear admiral **2.** The senior captain of a fleet of merchant vessels **3.** The president of a yacht club

com-mon (kɑ-mən) adj. **1.** Found or happening often and in many places; usual: *Wheat fields are common in Kansas.* **2.** Ordinary; of no special quality: *the common man/ woman/ the common cold* **3.** Belonging to or shared equally by two or more: *Rich and poor have this in common: The Lord is the Maker of them all* (Proverbs 22:2). **4. in common (a)** In shared possession: *All the believers were to-*gether and had everything in common. Selling their possessions and goods, they gave to anyone as he had need* (Acts 2:44,45). **(b)** Having the same likes and dislikes, the same convictions, etc.: *They should get along well together; they have much in common.*

com-mon-er (kɑm-ə-nər) n. One of the common people; not a member of the nobility

com-mon-ly (kɑ-mən-liʸ) adj. Usually; generally; ordinarily —opposite UNCOMMONLY

Common Market (kɑm-ən mɑr-kət) n. The European Economic Community, an association of certain European countries with internal free trade and common tariffs on their imports from countries outside the community

com-mon-place (kɑm-ən-pleʸs) adj. Ordinary; usual; lacking originality —**commonplace** n. *Air travel is now commonplace.*

common sense (kɑm-ən sɛns) n. **1.** Normal good sense in practical matters, gained by experiences in life, not by special study **2.** Sound and prudent judgment

com-mon-wealth (kɑm-ən-wɛlθ) n. **1.** A group of sovereign states and their dependencies **2.** A republic **3.** A federation of states: *The Commonwealth of Australia*

com-mo-tion (kə-moʷ-ʃən) n. Violent or turbulent motion; great and noisy confusion or excitement: *What is all that commotion in the next room?*

com-mun-al (kə-myuʷn-əl) adj. **1.** Pertaining to a commune or an organization of communes **2.** Of or belonging to a community **3.** Marked by collective ownership and use of property

com-mune (kɑm-yuʷn) n. **1.** A group of people living together and sharing everything they own **2.** The common people **3.** The smallest administrative districts in some European countries

com-mune (kə-myuʷn) v. -muned, -muning **1.** To receive the sacrament of Holy Communion **2.** To talk together intimately **3.** To communicate mentally or spiritually

com-mu-ni-ca-ble (kə-myuʷ-nɪ-kə-bəl) adj. **1.** That can be communicated, as an idea **2.** That can be passed from one person to an-

other, as a disease

com·mu·ni·cant (kə–myu^w–nɪ–kənt) n. **1.** A person who receives Holy Communion **2.** One who does this regularly

com·mu·ni·cate (kə–myu^w–nə–ke^yt) v. -cated, -cating *fml.* **1.** To make known; impart: *Some people communicate their thoughts and ideas clearly; others do not.* **2.** To share or exchange news, information, opinions, etc.: *Have you communicated with anyone back home since you left on your vacation?*

com·mun·i·ca·tion (kə–myu^w–nə–ke^y–ʃən) n. **1.** The act of communicating: *Radio and television are important means of communication.* **2.** Sthg. communicated: *This communication is intended for merchant ships only.* **3. communications** Various ways of traveling and sending information from place to place

com·mun·i·ca·tive (kə–myu^w–nɪ–kə–tɪv) adj. Ready and willing to talk and give information

com·mu·nion (kə–myu^wn–yən) n. **1.** The sharing or exchange of beliefs, ideas, feelings, etc. **2.** A religious or spiritual fellowship

Communion also **Holy Communion** n. The religious service in Christian churches in which bread and wine are shared in a solemn ceremony as a commemoration of the suffering and death of Jesus Christ to pay for our sins. NOTE: Saint Matthew tells us, "While they were eating, Jesus took bread, gave thanks and broke it, and gave it to his disciples, saying, 'Take and eat; this is my body,' Then he took the cup, gave thanks, and offered it to them, saying, 'Drink from it, all of you. This is my blood of the covenant, which is poured out for many for the forgiveness of sins. I tell you, I will not drink of this fruit of the vine from now on until that day when I drink it anew with you in my Father's kingdom'"(Matthew 26:26-29).

com·mu·ni·que (kə–myu^w–nə–ke^y/–nə–ke^y) n. An official bulletin

com·mun·ism (kɑm–yə–nɪz–əm) n. **1.** Social organization in which goods are held in common **2.** A theory of social organization advocating common ownership of the means of production and distribution of products of industry based on need —**communist** n. —**com·mu·nis·tic** (kɑm–yə–nɪs–tɪk) adj.

Communism n. A system of social organization in which all economic and social activity is controlled by a totalitarian state. NOTE: The Communist Party is atheistic, that is, it denies the existence of God. Karl Marx stated that religion is the opiate of the people. Lenin wrote, "Millions of epidemics and natural catastrophes are preferable to the slightest notion of God." NOTE: Even though unbelief in Jesus is the worst of sins, atheists, including Com-munists, can be saved if they repent and believe the Good News that Jesus suffered and died for our sins and rose again that we might have eternal life. —**Communist** n. —see JESUS

com·mu·ni·ty (kə–myu^w–nə–ti^y) n. -ties **1.** A group of people living in one place or district **2.** The public; people in general: *Police officers, firemen, and many others serve in the best interest of the community.* **3.** A social class

community college (kə–myu^w–nə–ti^y kɑl–ɪdʒ) n. A junior college without residential facilities, which is often government funded

community property (kə–myu^w–nə–ti^y prɑp–ər–ti^y) n. Property held jointly by a husband and wife

com·mute (kə–myu^wt) v. -muted, -muting **1.** To travel daily by car, bus, or train from home to one's place of work **2.** To change a criminal sentence to one less severe: *His death sentence was commuted to life imprisonment.*

commute n. The distance traveled by a commuter: *It's a long commute from Los Angeles to San Francisco.*

com·mut·er (kə–myu^wt–ər) n. A person who travels regularly back and forth to work

com·pact (kɑm–pækt) n. **1.** A small car **2.** A small case, usually containing face powder and a mirror

compact adj. (kəm–pækt/ kam–pækt) **1.** Firmly and closely united or packed **2.** Arranged within a small space: *a compact little apartment* —**compactly** adv.

com·pan·ion (kəm–pæn–yən) n. A person who spends time with another by choice, because he or she is a friend, or by chance,

as when traveling: *He was my traveling companion on my bus trip to Miami.* —**companionship** n.

com-pa-ny (kʌm–pə–niʸ) n. -nies 1. A business enterprise: *a bus company/ an oil company* 2. Companionship; fellowship: *I was grateful for Tom's company on the trip across the country.* 3. One or more guests: *We're expecting company tonight.* 4. A body of soldiers, usu. part of a regiment or battalion: *What company are you in?* 5. A troupe of dramatic or musical performers

com-par-a-ble (kɑm–pə–rə–bəl) adj. Capable of being compared —**com-par-a-bil-i-ty** (kɑm–pə–rə–bɪl–ə–tiʸ) n.

com-par-a-tive (kəm–peɑr–ə–tɪv) n. 1. The form of an adjective or adverb which compares: *"Bigger" is the comparative of "big;" "slower" is the comparative of "slow."* 2. Sthg. or sbdy. judged by comparison 3. Making a comparison —**comparatively** adv.

com-pare (kəm–peɑr) v. -pared, -paring To examine two things to see how they are different: *If you compare our two cars, you'll find that one is much newer than the other.*

com-par-i-son (kəm–peɑr–ə–sən) n. 1. The act of comparing: *In comparison with New York, Portland is small.* 2. Likeness: *There's no comparison between your brand new car and my old wreck.*

com-part-ment (kəm–pɑrt–mənt) n. 1. A section of an enclosed space; a room 2. A separate division

com-part-ment-a-lize (kəm–pɑrt–mɛnt–əl–aɪz) v. -lized, -lizing To separate into compartments

com-pass (kʌm–pəs/ kɑm–) n. 1. A device for determining direction, having a magnetic needle that always points north 2. A V-shaped device used for drawing circles

compass v. 1. To go round sthg. 2. To surround completely 3. To understand

com-pas-sion (kəm–pæ–ʃən) n. Pity or sympathy for the sufferings and misfortunes of others and a desire to give help or show mercy: *The Lord is good to all and has compassion on all he has made* (Psalm 145:9). *As God's chosen people... clothe yourselves with compassion, kindness, humility, gentleness and pa-*

tience (Colossians 3:12).

com-pas-sion-ate (kəm–pæ–ʃən–ɪt) adj. Feeling or showing compassion: *The Lord is gracious and compassionate, slow to anger and rich in love* (Psalm 145:8). —**compassionately** adv.

com-pat-i-ble (kəm–pæt–ə–bəl) adj. 1. Capable of living and working together in close harmony: *The business failed because the goals of the two owners were not compatible.* 2. Of equipment, capable of being used together: *The two computers are fully compatible.* —opposite INCOMPATIBLE —**compatibly** adv. —**com-pat-i-bil-i-ty** (kəm–pæt–ə–bɪl–ə–tiʸ) n.

com-pel (kəm–pɛl) v. -ll- To force someone to do sthg.: *The storm compelled us to change our plans./fig. Her wisdom and great ability compel our admiration.* (=compel us to admire her) —**compelling** adj. —**compellingly** adv.

com-pen-sate (kɑm–pən–seʸt) v. -sated, -sating To make up for wrong or damage done, esp. by giving money —**com-pen-sa-to-ry** (kəm–pɛns–ə–tɔr–iʸ) adj.

com-pen-sa-tion (kɑm–pən–seʸ–ʃən) n. Sthg. (usu. money) given to make up for wrong or damage

com-pete (kəm–piʸt) v. -peted, -peting To try to beat others, as in an athletic event or other contest: *If anyone competes as an athlete, he does not receive the victor's crown [or a medal] unless he competes according to the rules* (2 Timothy 2:5).

com-pe-tence (kɑm–pə–təns) n. The condition of being competent

com-pe-tent (kɑm–pə–tənt) adj. 1. Properly or well qualified; capable; skilled 2. Adequate for a purpose 3. Legally qualified

com-pe-ti-tion (kɑm–pə–tɪ–ʃən) n. 1. The act of competing 2. A contest: *athletic competition* 3. The people competing: *There was a lot of competition for the job.*

com-pet-i-tive (kəm–pɛt–ət–ɪv) adj. 1. Of a person, enjoying competition 2. Of a price, product, etc., able to compete successfully with prices, etc. of competitors —**competitively** adv. —**competitiveness** n.

com-pet-i-tor (kəm–pɛt–ət–ər) n. A person, team, firm, etc. competing with another or

others; a rival

com·pile (kəm–paɪl) v. -piled, -piling To gather into a single volume facts found in various places: *It takes years of hard work to compile a good dictionary.* —compiler n.

com·pla·cen·cy (kəm–pleˠ–sən–siˠ) -cies Also com·pla·cence (kəm–pleˠ–səns) n. Self-satisfaction; smugness; indifference: *The complacency of fools will destroy them* (Proverbs 1:32). —complacent adj. —complacently adv.

com·plain (kəm–pleˠn) v. To express feelings of pain, annoyance, resentment, discontent, etc.: *An old Arabian proverb says: "I had no shoes and complained, until I met a man who had no feet."/ Do everything without complaining or arguing* (Philippians 2:14). —complainingly adv.

com·plaint (kəm–pleˠnt) n. 1. A cause or reason for complaining: *They gave their employer a list of their complaints.* 2. A statement expressing annoyance, unhappiness, grief, etc.: *The police received many complaints about the cars racing up and down our street.* 3. The act of complaining

com·plai·sant (kəm–pleˠs–ənt/–pleˠz–) adj. Desiring to please; compliant

com·ple·ment (kɑm–plə–mənt) n. 1. Sthg. that completes or brings to perfection: *The apple pie á la mode was a nice complement to a delicious dinner.* 2. The amount necessary to make sthg. complete —compare COMPLIMENT

complement v. To make sthg. complete: *This pie complements the dinner perfectly.* —com·ple·men·ta·ry (kɑm–plə–mɛn–tə–riˠ) adj.

com·plete (kəm–pliˠt) adj. 1. Having all that is needed or wanted; lacking nothing: *If anyone obeys his [Jesus'] word, God's love is truly made complete in him* (1 John 2:5). *This is love: not that we loved God, but that he loved us and sent his Son as an atoning sacrifice for our sins... Since God so loved us, we also ought to love one another... If we love each other, God lives in us and his love is made complete in us* (1 John 4:10-12). —opposite INCOMPLETE 2. Finished; ended: *When will work on the new house be complete?* 3. Thorough; full: *It was a complete surprise to hear of your recent illness.*

—completeness n.

complete v. -pleted, -pleting To finish; to add what is missing or needed to sthg, to form a finished whole: *See to it that you complete the work you have to do.* —completely adv.

com·ple·tion (kəm–pliˠ–ʃən) n. Finished or the state of being finished

com·plex (kɑm–plɛks) n. 1. Sthg. that is composed of two or more parts: *a sports complex/ a shopping complex* 2. A number of repressed emotions, desires, fears, feelings, etc. that influence one's personality and behavior: *an inferiority complex*

complex (kəm–plɛks/ kɑm–plɛks/ kɑm–plɛks) adj. 1. Difficult to understand or explain: *His political ideas were too complex for the average working man.* —opposite SIMPLE 2. Consisting of many closely connected parts: *There's a complex network of freeways in Los Angeles.* —com·plex·i·ty (kəm–plɛks–ə–tiˠ) n. -ties

com·plex·ion (kəm–plɛk–ʃən) n. 1. The natural color, texture, and appearance of the skin, esp. of the face: *a good/ dark/ fair/ pale complexion* 2. General character or appearance: *By changing the complexion of the Board of Directors (by adding new members), we could see a number of policy changes.*

complex sentence (kɑm–plɛks sɛn–təns) n. A sentence containing an independent clause and one or more dependent clauses

com·pli·ance (kəm–plaɪ–əns) n. Complying with the way someone else may have commanded or wished —com·pli·ant adj. Willing to comply

com·pli·cate (kɑm–plə–keˠt) v. -cated, -cating To make sthg. difficult to understand or deal with —opposite SIMPLIFY —complicated adj. —com·pli·ca·tion (kɑm–plə–keˠ–ʃən) n.

com·pli·ci·ty (kəm–plɪ–sə–tiˠ) n. The state of having a share in the committing of a crime

com·pli·ment (kɑm–plə–mənt) n. An expression of praise or flattery: *He received many compliments for his graduation speech.*

compliment v. To praise or congratulate: *I complimented her for her beautiful singing.* NOTE: Do not confuse **compliment** with **complement**

com-pli-men-ta-ry (kɑm–plə–**men**–tə–riʸ) adj. **1.** Expressing a compliment **2.** Freely given as a courtesy: *complimentary tickets to the theatre*

com-ply (kəm–plaɪ) v. -plied, -plying *fml.* To do sthg. that someone else orders, requests, or wishes: *Those who do not comply with the law will be punished.* —compliance n. —compliant adj.

com-po-nent (kəm–po**ʷ**–nənt) n. A constituent part of a machine, such as a car, or an instrument, like a radio

component adj. Serving to form part of

com-pose (kəm–po**ʷ**z) v. -posed, -posing **1.** To make up or constitute: *Water is composed of hydrogen and oxygen.* **2.** To make by putting together parts or elements **3.** To write music, poetry, etc.: *Charles Wesley composed more than 6,500 hymns.* **4.** To make oneself calm, quiet, etc.: *Henry was frantic at first but soon composed himself.*

com-posed (kəm–po**ʷ**zd) adj. Calm, quiet, etc.

com-pos-er (kəm–po**ʷ**z–ər) n. A person who writes music

com-pos-ite (kəm–**paz**–ət) adj. Made up of several different parts or materials

composite n. A thing of distinct parts; a compound

com-po-si-tion (kɑm–pə–zɪ–ʃən) n. **1.** A literary, musical, or artistic product: *One of Wesley's better known compositions is, "O for a Thousand Tongues to Sing."* **2.** The arrangement of the various parts of which sthg. is made up: *the composition of a committee* **3.** The art of writing, esp. creative writing: *He's taking a course in English composition.* **4.** A short piece of writing (essay) done as an educational exercise **5.** A mixture of various substances: *a composition of various chemicals*

com-post (kɑm–po**ʷ**st) n. A mixture of decaying organic substances for fertilizing the land

com-po-sure (kəm–po**ʷ**–ʒər) n. Calmness of mind or manner

com-pound (kɑm–paʊnd) v. **1.** To add to or increase, usu. negative: *Our difficulties were compounded when our car broke down at midnight during the blizzard, and we had no idea where we were.* **2.** To increase, as interest on money in a savings account, by an amount that itself increases: *Money in my savings account is compounded daily.*

com-pound (**kɑm**–paʊnd) adj., n. **1.** Sthg. consisting of a combination of two or more parts: *"Mary sang and Alice accompanied her on the piano" is a compound sentence.* **2.** A substance formed by the union of two or more chemical elements: *Water is a compound consisting of hydrogen and oxygen.* —compare ELEMENT

compound n. A group of buildings enclosed by a wall, fence, etc.

com-pre-hend (kɑm–prɪ–**hend**) v. *fml.* To understand: *Have you comprehended the vast expanses of the earth?* (Job 38:18). —com-pre-hen-sion (kɑm–prɪ–hen–ʃən) n.

com-pre-hen-si-ble (kɑm–prɪ–**hens**–ə–bəl) adj. Able to be understood —opposite INCOMPREHENSIBLE

com-pre-hen-sive (kɑm–prə–**hen**–sɪv) adj. Including or comprehending much; large in scope or content: *a comprehensive examination*

com-press (kəm–**pres**) v. To press together; to force into less space

com-pres-sion (kəm–**preʃ**–ən) n. The act or state of being compressed

com-prise (kəm–praɪz) v. -prised, -pris-ing **1.** To consist of **2.** To include or contain NOTE: The whole **comprises** the parts; the parts **compose** the whole: *The family comprises four sons and four daughters. The family is composed of four sons and four daughters.*

com-pro-mise (kɑm–prə–maɪz) v. -mised, -mising **1.** To reach a settlement by each side giving up some of its demands **2.** To make someone or sthg. open to dishonor: *John knew that he had compromised his faith by working for a company that produced gambling devices.* —compromise n. *The president and the congress reached a compromise on taxes.*

com-pul-sion (kəm–pʌl–ʃən) n. **1.** A force that drives a person to do sthg.; coercion **2.** A strong desire that is difficult to control: *a compulsion to drink/ gamble*

com-pul-sive (kəm–pʌl–sɪv) adj. Caused by or subject to psychological compulsion: *a compulsive gambler*

com-puls-o-ry (kəm–pʌls–ə–riʸ) adj. Sthg. that must be done; mandatory: *Education in the US is compulsory through age 16./ In many countries two years of military service is compulsory for all young people.*

com-punc-tion (kəm–pʌŋk–ʃən) n. Guilt; shame; a pricking of the conscience: *He had no compunctions about taking money from a blind man.*

com-pute (kəm–pyuʷt) v. **-puted, -puting** To calculate a result by means of arithmetic—**com-pu-ta-tion** (kam–pyuʷ–teʸ–ʃən) n.

com-put-er (kəm–pyuʷt–ər) n. An electronic machine for making calculations, storing and analyzing information fed into it, and controlling machinery automatically

com-put-er-ize (kəm–pyuʷt–ər–aız) v. **-ized, -izing 1.** To equip with one or more computers **2.** To perform by means of one or more computers

com-put-er pro-gram-mer (kəm–pyuʷt–ər proʷ–græm–ər) n. One who prepares and tests programs for computers

com-rade (kam–ræd) n. **1.** A close companion who shares one's activities **2.** A fellow Socialist or Communist

com-rade-ship (kam–ræd–ʃɪp) n. Companionship; friendship

con- (kən–) prefix Variation of **com–**

con (kən) adv. Opposing; against

con n. That which opposes: *They discussed the pros and cons of the issue.*

con n. *slang* Short for **convict**

con v. **-nn-** To persuade or swindle after gaining one's confidence: *They conned the poor woman out of all her money.*

con-cave (kən–keʸv) adj. Curving like the surface of a ball as seen from the inside

con-ceal (kən–siʸl) v. To hide or keep secret: *God says, "My eyes are on all their ways; they are not hidden from me, nor is their sin concealed from my eyes"* (Jeremiah 16:17). —**concealment** n.

con-cede (kən–siʸd) v. **-cede, -ceding 1.** To admit as true, often unwillingly: *The senator conceded defeat before half the votes were counted.* **2.** To give as a right; allow; yield: *They conceded us the right to cross their land.*

con-ceit (kən–siʸt) n. Too high an opinion of one's own abilities: *Do nothing out of selfish ambition or vain conceit, but in humility consider others better than yourselves* (Philippians 2:3). *Do you see a man that is wise in his own conceit? There is more hope for a fool than for him* (Proverbs 26:12). —**conceited** adj.

con-ceiv-a-ble (kən–siʸv–ə–bəl) adj. Imaginable; possible: *It is conceivable that there will be a third world war, but we certainly pray that it will never happen.* —opposite INCONCEIVABLE —**conceivably** adv.

con-ceive (kən–siʸv) v. **-ceived, -ceiving 1.** To think of; imagine; consider: *Scientists first conceived the idea of television in the 1920s.* **2.** *tech.* To become pregnant with a child: *Jesus was conceived by the Holy Spirit and born of the Virgin Mary.* **3. conceive of** sbdy./ sthg. To think of; imagine: *It's difficult to conceive of traveling to another planet.*

con-cen-trate (kan–sən–treʸt) v. **-trated, -trating 1.** To direct all one's attention on sthg.; focus on: *You had better concentrate on your studies if you expect to pass this course.* **2.** To gather in or around one place: *Industrial development is concentrated in this area.*

con-cen-trat-ed (kan–sən–treʸt–əd) adj. **1.** More intense: *concentrated effort* **2.** Less diluted; denser; stronger: *concentrated lemon juice*

con-cen-tra-tion (kan–sən–treʸ–ʃən) n. **1.** Close attention: *Operating this complicated machine will require all your concentration.* **2.** A close gathering: *There is a concentration of restaurants and motels in this part of town.*

concentration camp (kan–sən–treʸ–ʃən kæmp) n. A camp where prisoners of war, enemy aliens, or political prisoners are confined

con-cen-tric (kən–sen–trɪk/ kan–) adj. Having the same center: *concentric circles, like those of a target*

con-cept (kan–sɛpt) n. A general idea about sthg.: *His concept about a woman's place in society is somewhat out of date.*

con-cep-tu-al (kən–sɛp–tʃuʷ–əl/ –sɛp–tʃəl) adj. Of or pertaining to conception or concepts

con-cep-tion (kən–sɛp–ʃən) n. **1.** The act of conceiving or being conceived **2.** The power to form ideas or concepts **3.** The starting of a new life by the union of a male and a female sex cell

con-cep-tu-a-lize (kən–sɛp–tʃuʷ–ə–laɪz) v. To form an idea —con-cep-tu-a-li-za-tion (kən–sɛp–tʃuʷ–ə–lə–zeʸ–ʃən) n.

con-cern (kən–sɜrn) v. 1. To have to do with: *This story concerns a man who gave up a fortune in order to preach the Good News about Jesus to poor people and heal the sick.* 2. To be of importance or interest to: *We are all concerned about the well-being of our loved ones, and we are all concerned about the future.* 3. To worry; be anxious: *Do not be anxious [=don't worry, don't be too concerned] about anything, but in everything, by prayer and petition, with thanksgiving, present your requests to God* (Philippians 4:6).

concern n. 1. A matter that is of interest to someone: *The righteous care about justice for the poor, but the wicked have no such concern* (Proverbs 29:7). 2. Worry; anxiety: *Cast all your anxiety [=worries, concerns] on him [God], because he cares for you* (1 Peter 5:7). 3. A business; firm: *Our concern makes men's clothing.*

con-cerned (kən–sɜrnd) adj. Worried; anxious: *concerned people*

con-cern-ing (kən–sɜrn–ɪŋ) prep. With regard to: *Concerning your letter, I'm happy to say that we are in perfect agreement with you.*

con-cert (kɑn–sərt) n. 1. A musical performance given by a number of musicians or singers or both 2. Agreement; cooperation

con-cert-ed (kən–sɜrt–əd) adj. 1. Done together by agreement 2. Very strong: *They made a concerted effort to complete the job before sunset.*

con-cer-to (kən–tʃeɑr–toʷ) n. A piece of music for one or more solo instruments and an orchestra

con-ces-sion (kən–sɛʃ–ən) n. 1. The act of conceding or yielding sthg., esp. after a disagreement 2. Sthg. conceded 3. A right given by the owner of a piece of land to extract minerals from it, or to sell goods there: *the food concessions at the fairgrounds*

con-cil-i-ate (kən–sɪl–iʸ–eʸt) v. -ated, -ating 1. To overcome the anger or hostility of someone 2. To gain the good will of —con-cil-i-a-tion (kən–sɪl–iʸ–eʸ–ʃən) n. —con-cil-i-a-to-ry (kən–sɪl–iʸ–ə–tɔr–iʸ) adj.

con-cise (kən–saɪs) adj. Expressing much in just a few words —concisely adj.

con-clude (kən–kluʷd) v. -cluded, -clud-ing 1. To bring or come to an end: *We concluded the meeting at ten p.m.* 2. To bring to a settlement: *We concluded an agreement with all the people concerned.* 3. To decide; to come to believe sthg.: *You were so late, we concluded that you weren't coming.*

con-clu-sion (kən–kluʷ–ʒən) n. 1. A judgment or decision: *What conclusion did you come to, after hearing all the facts?/ Be careful not to jump to conclusions. (=to form a judgment too quickly)* 2. The closing part of sthg.; the end: *The conclusion of the program was boring.* 3. **a foregone conclusion (a)** Sthg. decided in advance **(b)** Sthg. very likely to happen

con-clu-sive (kən–kluʷ–sɪv) adj. Sthg. that puts an end to all doubt; deciding: *conclusive proof*

con-coct (kən–kɑkt) v. 1. To make sthg. by mixing or combining parts 2. To devise; invent: *He concocted a wild story.* —con-coc-tion (kən–kɑk–ʃən) n.

con-com-i-tant (kən–kɑm–ə–tənt/ kɑn–) adj. Accompanying

concomitant n. An accompanying thing: *Misery is a concomitant of war.*

con-cord (kɑn–kɔrd) n. Complete peace and agreement

con-cord-ance (kən–kɔr–dəns) n. 1. Agreement; harmony 2. An alphabetical list of all the words used in a book or the works of an author, together with references to the passages in which they occur

con-course (kɑn–kɔrs) n. A large hall or passageway, as at an airport: *My plane departs from Gate 12 on Concourse A.*

con-crete (kɑn–kriʸt/ kɑn–kriʸt) n. A hard building material made by mixing sand, very small stones, cement, and water

concrete adj. *fml.* Sthg. real; actual; specific: *Her desire to help became a concrete action when she donated a million dollars to the cause.* —concretely adv.

con-cu-bine (kɑŋ–kyə–baɪn) n. 1. A woman who is not legally married to a man, but has a recognized position in his household 2. In some polygamous societies, a secondary

wife, of lower social and legal status

con-cu-pis-cence (kɑn–kyuᵂp–ə–səns) n. Strong or abnormal desire, esp. sexual de sire

con-cur (kən–kɜr) v. -rr- **1.** To agree **2.** To act together **3.** To coincide

con-cur-rence (kən–kɜr–əns) n. Agreement in action or opinion

con-cur-rent (kən–kɜr–ənt) adj. **1.** Occurring at the same time **2.** Joint and equal in authori ty

con-cus-sion (kən–kʌʃ–ən) n. **1.** A violent shock or blow **2.** Jarring of the brain, spinal cord, etc. from a violent blow

con-demn (kən–dɛm) v. **1.** To say that one disapproves of sthg.: *We all condemn cruelty to children.* **2.** To say officially that sthg. is not fit for use or consumption: *The building was condemned.* **3.** To say officially what someone's punishment is to be: *The prisoner was condemned to death.* **4.** To take or accept sthg. that one does not want: *John was con demned to a job he hates.* **5.** (in the Bible) Re fers to the final condemnation and judg ment: *God did not send his Son into the world to condemn the world, but to save the world through him. Whoever believes in him is not condemned, but whoever does not believe stands condemned already [to eternal death], because he has not believed in the name of God's one and only Son* (John 3:17,18). *Whoever believes [the Good News about Jesus Christ] and is baptized will be saved., but whoever does not believe will be condemned* (Mark 16:16). *Jesus said, "Who ever hears my Word and believes him who sent me has eternal life and will not be condemned; he has crossed over from death to life"* (John 5:24). —see CONDEMNATION, FORGIVE NESS, GOSPEL, JESUS, JUSTIFICATION

con-dem-na-tion (kɑn–dɛm–neʸ–ʃən) n. The act of being condemned: *There is no condem nation for those who are in Christ Jesus [=those who put their trust in Jesus for their salvation]* (Romans 8:1). —see CONDEMN, JESUS

con-den-sa-tion (kɑn–dɛn–seʸ–ʃən) n. **1.** The act of condensing **2.** Liquid formed from va por

con-dense (kən–dɛns) v. -densed, -densing **1.** To shorten or make smaller: *He condensed his report from 20 pages to 15.* **2.** To cause to become liquid, stronger, or more concen trated. *condensed milk*

con-de-scend (kɑn–dɪ–sɛnd) v. **1.** To act gra ciously to do sthg.: *The president condescend ed to visit our small factory in our small town.* **2.** To behave in a way that shows one's feel ings of superiority —**condescending** adj. —**condescendingly** adv. —**condescension** n.

con-di-ment (kɑn–də–mənt) n. Sthg. that sea sons or flavors food: *Salt and pepper are cond iments.*

con-di-tion (kən–dɪ–ʃən) n. **1.** A state of being or existence; state of affairs; circumstances: *It must be difficult to get used to the condition of weightlessness.* **2.** The state of general health, fitness, or readiness for use: *Before you buy a car, make sure it is in good condition.* **3.** An abnormality: *She has a heart condition.* **4.** Sthg. required as part of an agreement: *She said she would go with us on condition that she pay her share of the expenses.* **5. conditions** The situation or the surroundings that af fect sthg.: *This company provides good work ing conditions.*

condition v. **1.** To bring into the desired con dition; to make physically fit **2.** To have a strong effect: *The amount of money I spend on my vacation will be conditioned by the amount I'm able to save between now and then.*

con-di-tion-al (kən–dɪ–ʃən–əl) adj. Pertaining to or dependent upon certain conditions

con-do (kɑn–doᵂ) n. *infml.* Short for **condo minium**

con-do-lence (kən–doᵂ–ləns) n. Sympathy for someone who has suffered great loss

con-dom (kɑn–dəm) n. A sheath usu. of rub ber or plastic used by men as a contracep tive or to prevent venereal disease

con-do-min-i-um (kɑn–də–mm–iʸ–əm) n. An apartment building that is owned by the people who live in those apartments

con-done (kən–doᵂn) v. -doned, -don-ing To overlook an offense with relative tolerance, treating the offender as though he had done nothing wrong: *We cannot condone vio lence, perversion, and sexual immorality.*

con-du-cive (kən–duᵂ–sɪv) adj. Favorable;

likely to produce: *Fresh air and sunshine are conducive to good health.*

con-duct (**kɑn**–dəkt) n. Behavior: *Even a child is known by his actions, by whether his conduct is pure and right* (Proverbs 20:11).

con-duct (kən–**dʌkt**) v. **1.** To direct or lead: *Good will come to him… who conducts his affairs with justice* (Psalm 112:5). **2.** *fml.* To behave oneself: *Whatever happens, conduct yourselves in a manner worthy of the gospel of Christ* (Philippians 1:27). **3.** To direct the playing of musicians **4.** To act as the path for electricity, heat, etc.: *Most metals conduct electricity.* **5.** To manage or carry on: *to conduct a meeting* **6.** To serve as a channel for water: *These pipes conduct water to the kitchen.* —**conductible** adj. —**con-duct-i-bil-i-ty** (kən–dʌk–tə–bɪl–ət–iʸ) n.

con-duc-tion (kən–**dʌk**–ʃən) n. The conveying (passing on) of electric current along wires or of heat by contact

con-duc-tiv-i-ty (kən–dʌk–**tɪv**–ə–tiʸ) n. Property or power of conducting heat, electricty, etc.

con-duc-tor (kən–**dʌk**–tər) n. **1.** One who directs the playing of a group of musicians **2.** One employed to collect payment from passengers on a public means of transportation: *a train conductor* **3.** A substance that acts as a path for electricity, heat, etc.: *Copper is a good conductor of electricity.*

con-du-it (**kɑn**–dwɪt / –duʷ–wɪt) n. **1.** A pipe or channel for water or other fluid **2.** A pipe or tube for protecting electric wires

cone (koʷn) n. **1.** A solid figure having a round base and a pointed top **2.** Sthg. having a similar shape: *an ice cream cone* **3.** The fruit of a pine or fir tree

con-fec-tion (kən–**fɛk**–ʃən) n. **1.** A fancy dish or sweet **2.** Candy

con-fed-er-a-cy (kən–**fɛd**–ər–ə–siʸ) n. -cies A united alliance

con-fed-er-ate (kən–**fɛd**–ər–ət) adj., n. -ated, -ating **1.** United in an alliance **2.** A person, group, nation, etc. in a confederacy **3.** An accomplice **4.** An adherent of the Confederate States of America **5. Confederate States of America** The group of eleven states that seceded from the United States in 1860-61

con-fer (kən–**fɜr**) v. -rr- **1.** To bestow sthg. upon someone, such as an honor **2.** To consult together: *The referees conferred with one another.*

con-fer-ence (**kɑn**–fər–əns) n. **1.** A meeting held so that opinions and ideas can be exchanged **2.** An association of athletic teams, schools, or churches

con-fess (kən–**fɛs**) v. **1.** To admit a sin, crime, mistake, sthg. wrong: *Johnny confessed that he was the one who had broken the lamp.* **2.** To make one's sins known to God: *If we confess our sins [to God] he is faithful and just and will forgive us our sins and purify us from all unrighteousness* (1 John 1:9). *Confess your sins to each other and pray for each other so that you may be healed* (James 5:16).

con-fes-sion (kən–**fe**–ʃən) n. **1.** The act of admitting one's guilt **2.** A declaration of one's faith: *If you confess with your mouth, "Jesus is Lord", and believe in your heart that God has raised him from the dead, you will be saved* (Romans 10:9). **3.** A formal declaration of religious beliefs; creed —compare CREED **4. confession of sins** *"O almighty God, merciful Father, I, a poor, miserable sinner, confess unto you all my sins and iniquities with which I have ever offended you and justly deserved your punishment, now and eternally. But I am truly sorry for my sins and sincerely repent of them, and I pray Lord, that because of your boundless mercy, and for the sake of the holy, innocent, bitter suffering and death of your beloved Son, Jesus Christ, you will be gracious and merciful to me, a poor sinful being."* If this is your true confession, you can rest assured that your sins are forgiven, as God promised in the verse under number 2 above. —see JESUS, SIN, FORGIVENESS

con-fet-ti (kən–**fɛt**–iʸ) n. Small pieces of colored paper thrown at weddings, parades, and on many happy occasions

con-fi-dant (**kɑn**–fə–dænt / –dɑnt) n. One trusted with a secret

con-fide (kən–**faɪd**) v. -fided, -fiding **1.** To have a show of faith; to trust **2.** To tell confidentially: *The Lord confides in those who fear him. He makes his covenant known to them* (Psalm 25:14).

con-fi-dence (kɑn–fə–dəns) n. **1.** Complete trust; belief in one's own or another's ability: *In him [Jesus] and through him we may approach God with freedom and confidence* (Ephesians 3:12). **2.** A secret; a personal matter told secretly to a person: *A gossip betrays a confidence, but a trustworthy man keeps a secret* (Proverbs 11:13). **3. in confidence** Privately; secretly

con-fi-dent (kɑn–fə–dənt) adj. A feeling of confidence: *Tom was confident that he'd win the race.* —**confidently** adv.

con-fi-den-tial (kɑn–fə–**den**–ʃəl) adj. To be kept secret: *a confidential matter* —**confidentially** adv.

con-fig-u-ra-tion (kən–fig–yə–**re**ʸ–ʃən) n. Arrangement of parts of sthg.; shape

con-fine (kən–faɪn) v. **-fined, -fining** To keep in a small space: *We were confined in a very small room.* —**confinement** n. *The mass murderer was kept in solitary confinement.* (=kept completely alone)

con-fines (kɑn–faɪnz) n. Limits; borders: *They were kept within the confines of the prison walls.*

con-firm (kən–fɜrm) v. **1.** To give proof of: *His confession confirmed what we already believed.* **2.** *tech.* To admit a person to full membership of a church

con-fir-ma-tion (kɑn–fər–**me**ʸ–ʃən) n. **1.** Proof; sthg. that confirms: *The new evidence was further confirmation for my beliefs.* **2.** *tech.* A religious service practiced in many churches in which a person confirms his belief in the Christian faith and is made a full member of the church —**confirmation** adj. *confirmation certificate*

con-firmed (kən–fɜrmd) adj. **1.** A full member of a Christian church: *He's a confirmed member at Trinity Church.* **2.** Firmly entrenched in a way of life: *a confirmed bachelor* **3.** Established; verified: *a confirmed reservation*

con-fis-cate (kɑn–fəs–keʸt) v. **-cated, -cating** To seize private property officially and without payment: *His car was confiscated for parking in a "No Parking Zone."* —**con-fis-ca-tion** (kɑn–fəs–**ke**ʸ–ʃən) n.

con-fla-gra-tion (kɑn–flə–**gre**ʸ–ʃən) n. A large and destructive fire

con-flict (kən–flɪkt) v. To be in opposition to another or each other; disagree: *The senator's ideas conflicted with those of the president.* —**conflicting** adj.

con-flict (kɑn–flɪkt) n. **1.** A disagreement; quarrel **2.** A war: *Armed conflict could begin today.*

con-flu-ence (kɑn–flu ͭ–əns/ kən–flu ͭ–əns) n. The flowing together of two or more rivers: *Manaus is at the confluence of the Amazon and Negros Rivers.*

con-form (kən–fɔrm) v. *fml.* To obey or act in accordance with established patterns, rules, etc.: *Do not conform to the pattern of this world but be transformed by the renewing of your mind* (Romans 12:2). —**conformity** n. —**conformist** n.

con-found (kən–faʊnd) v. To throw into confusion and disorder; to puzzle; bewilder —**confounded** adj.

con-front (kən–frʌnt) v. To face boldly: *They confronted him with the evidence.*

con-fron-ta-tion (kɑn–frən–te ͭ–ʃən) n. The act of confronting

Con-fu-cian-ism (kən–fyu ͭ–ʃən–ɪz–əm) n. The system of morality growing out of the teachings of the Chinese philosopher Confucius (551?-479 B.C.) —**Confucian** n., adj.

con-fuse (kən–fyu ͭz) v. **-fused, -fusing 1.** To mislead; to make mentally unclear or uncertain: *I was confused by all the flashing colored lights.* **2.** To mix up in the mind; fail to tell the difference between two things: *I'm confused. Which of the twins is Melody and which one is Joy?* —**confused** adj. —**con-fus-ed-ly** (kən–fyu ͭz–əd–li ͭ) adv. —**confusing** adj. —**con-fu-sion** (kən–fyu ͭ–ʒən) n. *To avoid confusion, the teams wore different colored uniforms.*

con game (kɑn geʸm) n. *slang* An act of swindling sbdy. by first gaining his trust

con-geal (kən–dʒi ͭl) v. To become solid, esp. by cooling or freezing

con-gen-ial (kən–dʒi ͭn–yəl) adj. Pleasant; agreeable in nature or character: *a very congenial fellow* —**con-gen-i-al-i-ty** (kən–dʒi ͭ–ni ͭ–æl–ə–ti ͭ) n. —**congenially** adv.

con-gen-i-tal (kən–dʒen–ə–təl) adj. Existing since one's birth: *The child's brain disorder*

was congenital.

con-gest-ed (kən–dʒɛst–əd) adj. Very crowded or full, esp. because of traffic: *The freeways are always very congested between three and six p.m.* —**con-ges-tion** (kən–dʒɛs–tʃən) n. *I don't like driving through any big city because there's too much congestion.*

con-glom-er-ate (kən–glɑm–ər–rət) adj. **1.** Composed of parts from a number of sources **2.** Densely clustered

conglomerate n. A company formed by merging or acquiring several other companies in different branches of industry

con-glom-er-a-tion (kən–glɑm–ər–eʸ–ʃən) n. A mass of different things put together: *What a conglomeration of old toys!*

con-grat-u-late (kən–græ–tʃə–leʸt) v. -lated, -lating To praise and tell a person that one is pleased with his achievement or good fortune: *We congratulated them on their golden (50th) wedding anniversary.* —**con-grat-u-la-tion** (kən–græ–tʃə–leʸ–ʃən) n.

con-grat-u-la-tions (kən–græ–tʃə–leʸ–ʃənz) n. *also* **congrats** (kən–**græts**) *infml.* n. An expression of happiness for someone's success: *Congratulations! I hear that you've been promoted.* —**con-grat-u-la-to-ry** (kən–græt ʃ–yə–lə–tɔr–iʸ) adj.

con-gre-gate (kɑŋ–grə–geʸt) v. -gated, -gating To gather in a body or crowd

con-gre-ga-tion (kɑŋ–grə–geʸ–ʃən) n. **1.** The members of a particular place of worship **2.** A group of people gathered together, esp. in a church for a worship service or instruction

con-gress (kɑŋ–grəs) n. **1.** A formal meeting or assembly of representatives of societies, church bodies, countries, etc. to discuss problems **2.** The elected law-making body of certain countries **3. Congress** The US legislature, consisting of the Senate and the House of Representatives —**con-gres-sio-nal** (kən–**grɛʃ**–ən–əl) adj.

con-gress-man (kɑŋ–grəs–mən) n. **con-gress-wo-man** (kɑŋ–grəs–wʊ–mən) *fem.* Member of the US Congress

con-gru-ent (kɑŋ–gruʷ–ənt/ kən–**gruʷ**–ənt) adj. **1.** Corresponding; congruous **2.** Coinciding exactly when superimposed: *congruent triangles*

con-gru-ous (kɑŋ–gruʷ–əs) adj. **1.** Harmonious; corresponding in character or kind **2.** Congruent

con-i-cal (kɑn–ɪ–kəl) adj. Shaped like a cone: *a conical roof*

con-i-fer (kɑn–ə–fər) n. A tree that bears cones and usu. keeps its leaves or needles during the winter

co-nif-er-ous (koʷ–nɪf–ər–əs) adj. Having cones: *Pine trees are coniferous, and their cones are often used for decorations at Christmas time.*

con-jec-ture (kən–dʒɛk–tʃər) n. A guess, based on insufficient information

con-ju-gal (kɑn–dʒɪ–gəl/ kən–dʒuʷ–gəl) adj. Pertaining to marriage: *conjugal rights*

con-ju-gate (kɑn–dʒə–geʸt) v. -gated, -gating To give the various forms of a verb that show number, person, tense, etc. —**con-ju-ga-tion** (kɑn–dʒə–geʸ–ʃən) n.

con-junc-tion (kən–dʒʌŋk–ʃən) n. **1.** A word such as "but" or "and" that connects parts of sentences, phrases, etc. **2. in conjunction with** In combination with; together with: *The army is acting in conjunction with the police to put an end to the drug traffic and terrorism.*

con-junc-ti-vi-tis (kən–dʒʌŋk–tə–vaɪt–əs) n. Inflammation of the mucous membrane lining the inner eyelid and part of the eyeball

con-jure (kɑn–dʒər) v. -jured -juring **1.** To perform tricks that appear to be magical **2.** To summon a spirit to appear **3.** To produce as if from nothing: *Mother conjured up a meal.* **4.** To produce in the mind: *The mention of Central Africa conjures up visions of lions and elephants.* —**conjuror** or **conjurer** n.

con man (kɑn mæn) n. *slang* A person who swindles people by first gaining their trust

con-nect (kə–nɛkt) v. **1.** To join; unite; link: *The electrician connected the wires.* **2.** Related to sthg. in some way: *He was connected with the university.* **3.** To join by telephone: *Mary was connected with the wrong number.* **4.** To join to an electricity supply: *Make sure that the TV is connected properly.* —opposite DIS-

CONNECT 5. Concerning buses, trains, planes, etc., scheduled so that passengers can change from one to the others *This flight connects with flight 313 to Dallas.* —**connective** adj.

con-nec-tion also **connexion** BrE. (kə–nɛk–ʃən) n. 1. The act of connecting 2. An association or relation: *Don't you know there's a connection between smoking and lung cancer?* 3. A transfer from one plane, train, or bus to another: *At the Chicago Airport one can make connections with flights to almost anywhere in the world.* 4. in connection with Concerning

con-nip-tion (kə–nɪp–ʃən) n. *infml.* A fit of rage; hysteria

con-nive (kə–naɪv) v. -nived, -niving 1. To cooperate secretly 2. To make no attempt to prevent (sthg. illegal)

con-nois-seur (kɑn–ə–sɜr) n. A critical judge in matters of art or taste

con-no-ta-tion (kɑn–ə–teʸ–ʃən) n. The implied meaning of an expression in addition to the one clearly stated

con-no-ta-tive (kɑn–ə–teʸ–tɪv) adj. Connoting; suggesting

con-note (kə–noʷt) v. -noted, -noting To imply sthg. in addition to the literal meaning

con-nu-bi-al (kə–nuʷ–biʸ–əl) adj. Of or relating to marriage

con-quer (kɑŋ–kər) v. 1. To defeat an enemy 2. To take by force 3. To gain control over a bad habit or some difficulty: *After many attempts to quit smoking, he finally conquered the habit.*

con-quer-or (kɑŋ–kər–ər) n. One who is victorious: *Who shall separate us from the love of Christ? Shall trouble or hardship or persecution or famine or nakedness or danger or sword? No, in all these things we are more than conquerors through him who loved us. [Nothing] will be able to separate us from the love of God that is in Christ Jesus our Lord* (Romans 8:35-39).

con-quest (kɑn–kwɛst) n. 1. The act or process of conquering 2. Sthg. acquired by conquering

con-science (kɑn–ʃəns) n. 1. A knowledge or sense of right and wrong, with a compulsion to do right; moral judgment that opposes the violation of a previously recognized ethical principle NOTE: In order that our conscience may guide us correctly, we must first have the right moral convictions, and these can only be obtained from the Word of God. But whether we know the Word of God with regard to a certain act or not, if we disregard the voice of conscience and do what we believe to be wrong, we are guilty of sin. Everything that does not come from faith [conviction] is sin (Romans 14:23). While the witness of conscience must not be ignored, it is not, in itself, an infallible guide. God does not forbid the eating of meat on Friday, for example. But if a person believes it to be a sin, and eats meat on Friday anyway, he is sinning against his conscience. We must never urge anyone to do sthg. that he believes to be morally wrong, even though he is mistaken in such belief. 2. **doubting conscience** There is really no such thing as a doubting conscience. The doubt is in the mind; we do not know whether a thing is right or wrong. In such cases, we should suspend action until the Word of God makes it clear to us. 3. **guilty conscience** If we do or say sthg. that we know or believe to be wrong, or if we fail to do what we believe to be right, our conscience will trouble us. We will have a sense of guilt, a guilty conscience. The cure for a guilty conscience is faith in the forgiving grace of God. "Let us draw near [to God] with true hearts and fullest confidence, knowing that our inmost souls have been sprinkled with his blood [the blood of Christ shed for our sins on Calvary's cross], just as our bodies are cleansed by the washing of clean water" (Hebrews 10:22). "If we confess our sins [including our sins against our conscience] he [God] is faithful and just and will forgive us our sins and purify us from all unrighteousness" (1 John 1:9). —see CONFESS, FORGIVENESS, GOSPEL, JESUS

con-sci-en-tious (kɑn–tʃiʸ–ɛn–ʃəs) adj. 1. Honest 2. Hardworking; thorough and painstaking; showing or done with careful attention —**conscientiously** adv. —**conscientiousness** n.

con-scious (kɑn-ʃəs) adj. 1. Awake; having one's mind and senses working; able to think, feel, etc.: *He had a bad fall on his head, but he's still conscious.* 2. Aware of: *Bob isn't conscious of his bad manners.* 3. Deliberate; intentional —consciousness n.

con-script (kən-skrɪpt) v. To enroll by compulsion for military service

con-se-crate (kɑn-sə-kreʸt) v. -crated, -crating To set apart solemnly for a particular purpose; esp. a sacred purpose: *Consecrate yourselves and be holy, because I am the Lord your God. Keep my decrees [laws] and follow them: I am the Lord who makes you holy* (Leviticus 20:7,8). —con-se-cra-tion (kɑn-sə-kreʸ-ʃən) n.

con-sec-u-tive (kən-sɛk-yə-tɪv) adj. Following in an unbroken order: *Monday, Tuesday, and Wednesday are consecutive days of the week.* —consecutively adv.

con-sen-sus (kən-sɛn-səs) n. General agreement in opinion

con-sent (kən-sɛnt) n. 1. Agreement; permission: *Mary's parents gave their consent to her marriage.* 2. age of consent The age at which one may lawfully marry

consent v. To agree; give permission: *My son, if sinners entice [tempt] you, do not consent [=do not give in to them]* (Proverbs 1:10 KJV).

con-se-quence (kɑn-sə-kwɛns/ kɑn-siʸ-kwɛns) n. 1. Result; sthg. that follows from an action or condition: *People who eat, drink, and/ or smoke too much will, sooner or later, suffer the consequences.* 2. fml. Importance: *a matter of little consequence* —con-se-quen-tial (kæn-sə-kwɛn-tʃəl) adj. —consequently adv.

con-ser-va-tion (kɑn-sər-veʸ-ʃən) n. The act of conserving; preservation: *The conservation of water is very important in desert lands.*

con-serv-a-tive (kən-sɜrv-ə-tɪv) adj. 1. Favoring existing views, policies, and conditions of the established order of society NOTE: We should be very liberal when it comes to giving to others or helping them in any way, but very conservative when it comes to the word of God, not changing a single word. "Do not add to his [God's] words, or he will rebuke you and prove you a liar"

(Proverbs 30:6). "Do not add to what I [God] command you and do not subtract from it..." (Deuteronomy 4:2). 2. Modest: *She always dresses in a conservative way.* 3. Careful; kept within reasonable limits: *She made a conservative guess at the population of Nigeria.* —conservatively adv. —conservative n. *Mr. Brown is a real conservative. He doesn't like any kind of change at all.* —conservativism n.

con-serv-a-tor-y (kən-sɜrv-ə-tɔr-iʸ) n. -ies A place of instruction in one of the fine arts (as music)

con-serve (kən-sɜrv) v. -served, -serving To keep from change or destruction; to use carefully; preserve: *We must conserve our forests and other natural resources for future generations.*

con-sid-er (kən-sɪd-ər) v. 1. To think about: *Oh, Lord... when I consider your heavens, the work of your fingers, the moon and the stars, which you have set in place, what is man that you care for him?* (Psalm 8:3,4). 2. To think about others or sthg. in a stated way: *In humility consider others better than yourselves* (Philippians 2:3). 3. To take into account; remember: *Considering the fact that Roger has only been studying English for six months, he speaks it quite well.*

con-sid-er-a-ble (kən-sɪd-ər-ə-bəl) adj. A fairly large amount; great in quantity or importance: *a man of considerable wealth/ influence* —considerably adv. *Our car is considerably smaller than his.*

con-sid-er-ate (kən-sɪd-ər-ət) adj. Thoughtful of the rights and feelings of others: *Remind the people to be... peaceable and considerate, and to show true humility toward all men* (Titus 3:1,2). —opposite INCONSIDERATE —considerately adv.

con-sid-er-a-tion (kən-sɪd-ə-reʸ-ʃən) n. 1. Attention: *We'll give your request our careful consideration.* 2. Concern for the wishes and feelings of others: *John stayed home out of consideration for his mother.* 3. A fact to be taken into account when making a decision: *The weather must certainly be taken into consideration when planning a vacation.*

con-sign (kən-saɪn) v. 1. To give over to the

care of another person **2.** To assign to a less important position

con-sign-ment (kən–sam–mənt) n. A shipment of goods to an agent for sale or custody

con-sist (kən–sɪst) v. To be made up of: *Be on your guard against all kinds of greed; a man's life does not consist in the abundance of his possessions* (Luke 12:15).

con-sist-en-cy (kən–sɪst–ən–si^y) n. -cies **1.** Keeping to the same principles or course of action: *Her actions lack consistency; she says one thing and does sthg. altogether different.* —opposite INCONSISTENCY **2.** Degree of firmness: *Mix the cement to the right consistency.* —consistent adj. —consistently adv.

con-so-la-tion (kɑn–sə–le^y–ʃən) n. Comfort during a time of sadness or disappointment: *When anxiety was great within me, [O Lord] your consolation brought joy to my soul* (Psalm 94:19).

con-sole (kən–so^wl) v. -soled, -soling To give comfort to someone in times of sadness or discouragement

con-sol-i-date (kən–sɑl–ə–de^yt) v. -dated, -dating To combine into fewer or one: *Several small businesses consolidated to form one large company.* —con-sol-i-da-tion (kən–sɑl–ɪ–de^y–ʃən) n. *the consolidation of four small companies into one large one*

con-so-nant (kɑn–sə–nənt) n. A letter representing any of the speech sounds made partly or completely by stopping the flow of air: *All the letters of the English alphabet except a, e, i, o, and u are consonants.* —compare VOWEL

con-sort (kɑn–sɔrt) n. A husband or wife, esp. of a monarch

consort (kən–sɔrt) v. To associate with

con-sor-ti-um (kən–sɔr–ʃi^y–əm) n. **1.** An international business or banking agreement **2.** Association; society **3.** *law* The companionship and support provided by marriage

con-spic-u-ous (kən–spɪk–yu^w–əs) adj. Attracting much attention; not easy to overlook: *She's very conspicuous because of her weird clothing.* —opposite INCONSPICUOUS —conspicuously adv.

con-spir-a-cy (kən–spɪər–ə–si^y) n. -cies A secret plan to do sthg. unlawful: *a conspiracy*

by some army officers to seize control of the government —conspirator n.

con-spire (kən–spaɪ–ər/–spaɪr) v. -spired, -spiring To plan sthg. together secretly, esp. sthg. illegal or sinful

con-sta-ble (kɑn–stə–bəl) n. A police officer in a small town

con-stab-u-lar-y (kən–stæb–yə–lɛər–i^y) n. -ies A police force

con-stan-cy (kɑn–stən–si^y) n. Freedom from change; faithfulness; stability

con-stant (kɑn–stənt) adj. **1.** Never stopping; never changing: *The plane flew at a constant speed.* —opposite INCONSTANT **2.** *lit.* Steadfast; faithful; loyal: *a constant friend* **3.** Happening all the time: *A quarrelsome wife is like a constant dripping on a rainy day* (Proverbs 27:15). —constantly adv.

con-stel-la-tion (kɑn–stə–le^y–ʃən) n. Any of 88 groups of stars considered to resemble an animal, an inanimate object, or some mythological character: *The Big Dipper is a constellation.*

con-ster-na-tion (kɑn–stər–ne^y–ʃən) n. Great confusion or dismay: *After shopping all day in the big city, to our consternation, we couldn't find our car.*

con-sti-pat-ed (kɑn–stə–pe^y–təd) adj. Having difficulty passing waste matter from the bowels

con-sti-pa-tion (kɑn–stə–pe^y–ʃən) n. Difficult, delayed, or infrequent movement of the bowels

con-stit-u-en-cy (kən–stɪtʃ–u^w–ən–si^y) n. -cies **1.** The voters of a district, represented by an elected officer **2.** The district itself **3.** A group of supporters

con-stit-u-ent (kən–stɪtʃ–u^w–ənt) n. **1.** A part of a whole; a component **2.** A member of a constituency **3.** A supporter

constituent adj. Forming part of a whole: *a constituent part*

con-sti-tute (kɑn–stə–tu^wt) v. -tuted, -tuting *fml.* To make up; compose: *Twelve months constitute a year.*

con-sti-tu-tion (kɑn–stə–tu^w–ʃən) n. **1.** The principles according to which a country is governed: *The Constitution of the US was adopted in 1787 and put into effect in 1789.* **2.**

The physical make-up of an individual **3.** The make-up or composition of sthg.: *the constitution of the moon*

con·sti·tu·tion·al (kən–stə–tu^w–ʃən–əl) adj. **1.** Allowed or limited by the constitution; in agreement with the constitution: *Is the senator's proposal constitutional?* **2.** Of or relating to the con-stitution of body or mind —**con·sti·tu·tion·al·i·ty** (kən–stə–tu^w–ʃə–næl–ət–i^y) n.

con·strain (kən–stre^yn) v. To force someone to do sthg.

constraint (kən–stre^ynt) n. Compulsion: *He agreed to do it, but only under constraint.*

con·strict (kən–strɪkt) v. To press together tightly; to make smaller or tighter —**con·striction** n. *constriction of the blood vessels* —**constrictive** adj.

con·struct (kən–strʌkt) v. To build; to put together by combining parts: *a difficult sentence to construct*

con·struc·tion (kən–strʌk–ʃən) n., adj. **1.** The business or process of building: *My father is in the construction business./The construction of the dam took several years.* **2.** The act of construction: *There's a new shopping center under construction near here.* **3.** Sthg. constructed, esp. a building, bridge, highway, or dam: *The Pentagon is a five-sided construction.*

con·struc·tive (kən–strʌk–tɪv) adj. Helpful: *constructive criticism* —opposite NONCONSTRUCTIVE —**constructively** adv.

con·strue (kən–stru^w) v. **construed, construing** To interpret; to explain: *His words could be construed either as a promise or a threat.*

con·sul (kɑn–səl) n. An official appointed to live in a foreign city in order to assist his countrymen there and to help commercial relations between the two countries

con·sul·ate (kɑn–səl–ət) n. **1.** The official premises of a consul **2.** A consul's position

con·sult (kən–sʌlt) v. To go to a person or a book to seek advice or information: *Have you consulted your doctor about those chest pains?/ A mocker resents correction; he will not consult the wise* (Proverbs 15:12). —**con·sul·ta·tion** (kɑn–səl–te^y–ʃən) n.

con·sult·ant (kən–sʌl–tənt) n. A person who gives professional advice: *a linguistics con-*

sultant

con·sume (kən–su^wm/ kən–syu^wm) v. **-sumed, -suming 1.** To eat or drink **2.** To use: *The controversy consumed several hours of the committee's time.* **3.** To destroy: *The fire soon consumed 40 houses in the foothills.*

con·sum·er (kən–su^wm–ər/ kən–syu^wm–ər) n. One who buys and uses goods and services: *The consumers must be protected against the sale of inferior products.*

con·sum·mate (kɑn–sə–me^yt) v. **-mated, mating 1.** To complete or perfect **2.** To fulfill a marriage by sexual intercourse —**con·sum·ma·tion** (kɑn–sə–me^y–ʃən) n.

consummate (kən–sʌm–ət/kɑn–sə–mət) adj. Perfect or complete

con·sump·tion (kən–sʌmp–ʃən) n. The act of consuming or using up: *This nation's consumption of oil is increasing.*

con·tact (kɑn–tækt) n. **1.** In touch with; receiving information from: *Have you kept in contact with your old classmates?* **2.** *infml.* Association or relationship **3.** A friend or acquaintance through whom one can get help: *I have a contact at the embassy; perhaps he can help us.* **4.** A junction of electrical conductors

contact v. To communicate with: *I've been trying to contact my brother by telephone, but he's apparently out of town.*

con·ta·gious (kən–te^y–dʒəs) adj. **1.** Spreading from one person to another by physical contact **2.** Bearing a contagious disease —compare INFECTIOUS **3.** *fig.* Spreading or tending to spread from person to person: *Enthusiasm is contagious.* —**contagiously** adv.

con·tain (kən–te^yn) v. **1.** To hold; have within itself: *This can contains five gallons of gasoline./ His letters contain some real gems of wisdom./ But who is able to build a temple for him [God], since the heavens, even the highest heavens, cannot contain him?* (2 Chronicles 2:6). **2.** To get or keep under control: *The fire fighters have finally contained the forest fire.*

con·tain·er (kən–te^yn–ər) n. Sthg. used for holding things, such as a box, bottle, jar, can, etc.

con·tam·i·nate (kən–tæm–ə–ne^yt) v. **-nated,**

-**nating** To make impure or dirty: *The town's water supply has been contaminated by chemicals from the factory.* / spir. *Let us purify ourselves from everything that contaminates body and spirit, perfecting holiness out of reverence for God* (2 Corinthians 7:1).

con-tem-plate (kən–təm–ple^{y}t) v. **-plated, -plating** To think seriously; consider

con-tem-pla-tion (kan–təm–ple^y–ʃən) n. Deep and serious thought

con-tem-po-ra-ne-ous (kən–tɛm–pə–re^y–ni^y–əs) adj. (esp. of events) Contemporary —**contemporaneously** adv.

con-tem-po-rar-y (kən–tɛm–pə–rɛər–i^y) adj. **1.** Living or happening during the same period of time **2.** Current; modern

contemporary n. **-ies 1.** One who lived or is living at the same time as another **2.** A person of the present time

con-tempt (kən–tɛmpt) n. A lack of respect; the act of despising: *He who oppresses the poor shows contempt for their Maker* (Proverbs 14:31). —compare SCORN

con-tempt-i-ble (kən–tɛmpt–ə–bəl) adj. Deserving contempt; despicable: *His behavior was contemptible.*

con-temp-tu-ous (kən–tɛmp–tʃu^w–əs) adj. Showing contempt; scornful —**contemptuously** adv. *She laughed contemptuously at the prophecy.*

con-tend (kən–tɛnd) v. **1.** To compete: *He contended for a gold medal in the marathon at the Olympics.* **2.** To strive with difficulty; to struggle: *Help these women who have contended at my side in the cause of the gospel, whose names are in the book of life* (Philippians 4:3).

con-tend-er (kən–tɛnd–ər) n. A person who has entered into a competition

con-tent (kan–tɛnt) n. **1.** The subject matter of a book, paper, etc.: *The content of his speech was interesting, but he wasn't a very good speaker.* **2.** The amount of a substance contained in sthg.: *Watermelons have a high water content.*

con-tent (kən–tɛnt) adj. Satisfied; happy: *If we have food and clothing we will be content with that* (1 Timothy 6:8). *Even in prison because of his faith, the apostle Paul wrote, "I have learned to be content whatever the circumstances. I*

know what it is to be in need and what it is to have plenty. I have learned the secret of being content in any and every situation, whether well fed or hungry, whether living in plenty or in want. I can do everything through him [Jesus] who gives me strength* (Philippians 4:11-13). —opposite DISCONTENT

con-tent-ed (kən–tɛnt–əd) adj. Satisfied, happy —opposite DISCONTENTED —**contentedly** adv. —**contentment** n. *Godliness with contentment is great gain* (1 Timothy 6:6).

con-ten-tion (kən–tɛn–ʃən) n. **1.** An opinion supported by debate: *It is my contention that we must declare all-out war on drugs.* **2.** Argument or debate: *There's much contention in town regarding the newly proposed highway.*

con-ten-tious (kən–tɛn–ʃəs) adj. Likely to start an argument

con-tents (kan–tɛnts) n. **1.** That which is contained in a box, can, bottle, etc. **2. table of contents** A list at the front of a book showing what that book contains —compare CONTENT

con-test (kan–tɛst) n. A competition: *a beauty contest*

contest (kən–tɛst/ kan–tɛst) v. fml. **1.** To compete for; to try to win: *Many people are contesting his seat on the counsel.* **2.** To dispute: *His lawyer intends to contest the judge's decision in another court.*

con-test-ant (kən–tɛst–ənt) n. A person competing in a contest

con-text (kan–tɛkst) n. **1.** The words that come before and after a particular word or phrase that help to determine its meaning: *To properly understand a Bible verse or anything that is written, we need to take the context into account.* **2.** The circumstances surrounding an act or event

con-tig-u-ous (kən–tɪg–yu^w–wəs) adj. Touching; adjoining: *The United States is contiguous to Canada.* —**contigu-ously** adv. —**con-ti-gu-i-ty** (kan–tə–gyu^w–ət–i^y) n.

con-ti-nent (kan–tə–nənt) n. One of the major land masses of the globe: *Africa is a continent.* —**con-ti-nen-tal** (kant–ən–ɛnt–əl) adj.

con-tin-gen-cy (kən–tɪn–dʒən–si^y) n. **-cies 1.** Sthg. unforeseen; a possibility, esp. one that could cause problems: *prepared for all contin-*

gencies. **2. contingency plans** Alternate plans; plans made in case sthg. unforeseen happens

con-tin-gent (kən-tin-dʒənt) *adj.* Dependent on some other happening or circumstance: *Our ability to go is contingent on our employer's willingness to give us time off from work.*

contingent *n.* **1.** A body of ships or troops, etc. supplied to form part of a force **2.** A group of people forming a part of a gathering: *the Scottish contingent*

con-tin-u-al (kən-tin-yu^w-əl) *adj.* Repeated often; frequent: *The cheerful heart has a continual feast* (Proverbs 15:15). **—continually** *adv. Pray continually* (1 Thessalonians 5:17). *I will bless the Lord at all times. His praise shall continually be in my mouth* (Psalm 34:1 KJV). NOTE: **Continual** means "happening again and again over a long period of time." **Continuous** means "continuing without interruption."

con-tin-u-a-tion (kən-tin-yu^w-e^y-ʃən) *n.* **1.** The act of continuing: *The continuation of his studies is very important to him.* **2.** Sthg. which continues from sthg. else: *This is a continuation of the story we heard last week.*

con-tin-ue (kən-tin-yu^w) *v.* **-ued, -uing 1.** To go on happening: *Anyone who runs ahead and does not continue in the teaching of Christ does not have God; whoever continues in the teaching has both the Father and the Son* (2 John:9). **2.** To cause to start again after an interruption: *The movie will continue after these commercials.* **—opposite DISCONTINUE**

con-ti-nu-i-ty (kən-tə-nu^w-ə-ti^y) *n.* The state of being continuous or logically related

con-tin-u-ous (kən-tin-yu^w-əs) *adj.* Continuing without interruption: *The brain needs a continuous supply of blood.* **—see CONTINUAL —continuously** *adv.*

con-tin-u-um (kən-tin-yu^w-əm) *n. pl.* **-ums, -ua 1.** A continuous whole, quantity, or series **2.** A thing whose parts cannot be separated or thought of as separate

con-tort (kən-tɔrt) *v.* To twist out of shape **—contortion** *n.* **—contortionist** *n.*

con-tour (kɒn-tʊər) *n.* **1.** The outline of a figure, body, or mass **2.** A line drawn on a map connecting all the places having the same

height above sea level

con-tra- (kɒn-trə-) *prefix* Against; opposing; contrary

con-tra-band (kɒn-trə-bænd) *n., adj.* **1.** Unlawful or prohibited trade **2.** Goods forbidden by law to be imported or exported

con-tra-cep-tion (kɒn-trə-sɛp-ʃən) *n.* The deliberate prevention of the fertilization of the human ovum **—contraceptive** *n., adj.*

con-tract (kɒn-trakt/kən-trækt) *v.* **1.** To reduce in size: *Metal contracts as it becomes cool.* **—opposite EXPAND 2.** To get an illness: *I'm afraid I've contracted malaria.* **3.** To make formal agreement: *They have contracted to build a skyscraper that will be the tallest building in the world.* **—contractor** *n.*

con-tract (kɒn-trækt) *n.* A legal written agreement **—con-trac-tu-al** (kən-træk-tʃu^w-əl) *adj.* **—contractually** *adv.*

con-trac-tion (kən-træk-ʃən) *n.* **1.** The act of contracting **2.** The shortened form of a word or words: *"Doesn't" is a contraction of "does not."*

con-tra-dict (kɒn-trə-dıkt) *v.* **1.** To say the opposite of: *Stop contradicting your mother.* **2.** To disagree with: *His words are contradicted by his actions, that is, he doesn't practice what he preaches.* **—contradictory** *adj.* **—contradiction** *n.*

con-tral-to (kən-træl-to^w) *n.* **1.** The lowest female voice **2.** A singer having such a voice

con-trap-tion (kən-træp-ʃən) *n. infml.* A strange machine or apparatus

con-tra-pun-tal (kɒn-trə-pʌn-təl) *adj.* Of or relating to counterpoint

con-tra-ri-wise (kɒn-trɛər-i^y-waız) *adv.* On the contrary; conversely; on the other hand

con-trar-y (kɒn-trɛər-i^y / kən-trɛər-i^y) *adj.* Opposite in character or direction: *They had difficulty sailing across the lake because the wind was contrary./ The captain was a very contrary person, seldom agreeing with anyone about anything.*

contrary (kɒn-trɛər-i^y) *n.* **1.** The opposite: *Most people think he's guilty, but I believe the contrary.* **2. on the contrary** Used to express opposition to what has just been said: *I hear you like this cold weather. On the contrary; I prefer it hot.* **3. to the contrary** To the oppo-

site effect; differently: *If you don't hear anything to the contrary, I'll pick you up at noon.*

con-trast (**kɑn–træst**) n. **1.** Unlikeness shown when things are compared: *It's difficult to see the contrast between these two pictures until they are viewed side by side.* **2.** A marked difference or unlikeness: *What a contrast between sisters! Mary talks all the time, and Martha hardly says anything.*

con-trast (kən–træst) v. To compare two people or things in order to make the differences obvious: *To contrast the goodness of God with our rebellion, will tend to make us humble and thankful.*

con-tra-vene (kɑn–trə–viᵛn) v. **-vened, -vening** To act contrary to; to come into conflict with —**con-tra-ven-tion** (kɑn–trə–vɛn–ʃən) n.

con-trib-ute (kən–trɪb–yuᵂt/ –yət) v. **-uted, -uting 1.** To join others in giving help, money, etc.: *Tens of thousands of people contributed money, food, clothing and blankets to the earthquake victims in Mexico.* **2.** To help in bringing about sth. good or bad: *Fresh air contributes to good health./ Drug peddlers and users are contributing to the moral decay of our country.* **3.** To write articles for a magazine or newspaper: *Last year he contributed 50 articles to the local newspaper.* —**con-tri-bu-tion** (kɑn–trə–byuᵂ–ʃən) n. —**con-trib-u-tor** (kən–trɪb–yə–tər) n. *He's a regular contributor to our orphanage.*

con-trite (kɑn–traɪt/ kən–traɪt) adj. Penitent; repentant: *"This is the one I esteem," declares the Lord, "he who is humble and contrite in spirit, and trembles at my word"* (Isaiah 66:2).

con-triv-ance (kən–traɪv–əns) n. **1.** Act of contriving **2.** Sth. contrived; a plan; a scheme **3.** A mechanical device

con-trive (kən–traɪv) v. **-trived, -triving 1.** To plan cleverly **2.** To achieve in a clever, resourceful way **3.** To manage

con-trol (kən–troᵂl) v. **-trolled, -trolling** To direct influence over; to exercise authority over: *Better... a man who controls his temper than one who takes a city* (Proverbs 16:32).

control n. **1.** The power to direct or restrain sth.: *A fool gives full vent to his anger, but a wise man keeps himself under control* (Pro-

verbs 29:11). **2.** The act of controlling: *price controls* **3.** The place from which sth. (a train, plane, etc.) is controlled **4. in control** In command; in charge

con-tro-ver-sial (kɑn–trə–vɜr–ʃəl) adj. Causing much argument or disagreement: *a controversial person* —**con-troversially** adv.

con-tro-ver-sy (kɑn–trə–vɜr–siᵛ) n. **-sies** A disagreement; argument

co-nun-drum (kə–nʌn–drəm) n. A riddle

con-va-lesce (kɑn–və–lɛs) v. **-lesced, -lescing** To recover health gradually after an illness

con-va-les-cence (kɑn–və–lɛs–əns) n. The period of time spent recovering from an illness

con-va-les-cent (kɑn–və–lɛs–ənt) n. A person who is convalescing

con-vec-tion (kən–vɛk–ʃən) n. The transmission of heat within a gas or liquid by movement of the heated parts

con-vene (kən–viᵛn) v. **-vened, -vening** To call or come together for a meeting

con-ven-ience (kən–viᵛn–yəns) n. **1.** Suitableness: *Please answer this letter at your earliest convenience.* **2.** Any labor-saving device: *This new mixer is quite a convenience.*

con-ven-ient (kən–viᵛn–yənt) adj. Suited to one's comfort or needs: *a convenient location/ time* —opposite INCONVENIENT —**conveniently** adv.

con-vent (kɑn–vɛnt) n. **1.** A religious community, esp. of nuns **2.** The buildings of such a community

con-ven-tion (kən–vɛn–tʃən) n. **1.** A group of people convened for some purpose: *a teachers' convention* **2.** Generally accepted social behavior; a custom

con-ven-tion-al (kən–vɛn–tʃən–əl) adj. **1.** Following accepted customs and standards, sometimes too closely; done by habit **2.** Commonplace; ordinary —opposite UNCONVENTIONAL

con-verge (kən–vɜrdʒ) v. **-verged, -verging** To come together; meet at a point: *The two roads converged near the entrance to the canyon.*

con-ver-sa-tion (kɑn–vər–seᵛ–ʃən) n. An informal talk: *Let your conversation be always full of grace, seasoned with salt [adding flavor], so that you may know how to answer everyone*

(Colossians 4:6).

con-verse (kən–**vɜrs**) v. **-versed, -versing** To talk informally

con-verse (**kɑn**–vərs) adj. Opposite: *I'm sorry, but I am of the converse opinion.* —**converse** n. Opposite

con-ver-sion (kən–**vɜr**–ʒən) n. **1.** The act of changing from one purpose, system, etc. to another: *The conversion of this old mansion to a library took place in 1923.* **2.** *spir.* A turning from spiritual darkness to light and from the power of Satan to God: *Jesus told Paul, "I am sending you to open their eyes and turn them from darkness to light and from the power of Satan to God, so that they may receive forgiveness of sins and a place among those who are sanctified [made holy] by faith in me"* (Acts 26:18). NOTE: Man is by nature spiritually dead in transgressions (Ephesians 2:1,5). He cannot by his own reason or strength be converted from spiritual death to spiritual life. Man's conversion from unbelief to saving faith in Jesus Christ is entirely the work of the Holy Spirit. No one can say, "Jesus is Lord," except by the Holy Spirit (1 Corinthians 12:3). However, Christians, like St. Paul himself, can help to open people's eyes and turn (convert) them from darkness to light and from the power of Satan to God through the Word of God -- the Law which shows them their sins and their need for a Savior, and the Gospel [Good News] of our Savior Jesus Christ, who died for us and rose again. Paul said, "I am not ashamed of the Gospel, because it is the power of God for the salvation of everyone who believes" (Romans 1:16).

con-vert (kən–**vɜrt**) v. **1.** To change from one thing into another: *I converted my US dollars into yen.* **2.** To change from one religious or political persuasion to another: *John was converted to Christianity when he was 17.*

con-vert (**kɑn**–vərt) n. A person who has changed religious or political beliefs, etc.

con-vert-i-ble (kən–**vɜrt**–ə–bəl) adj. **1.** Able to be converted **2.** Of money, that can be freely exchanged for other types of money

convertible n. An automobile with a roof that can be folded back

con-vex (kən–**vɛks**) adj. Curved on the outer side, like the outside of a ball —opposite CONCAVE

con-vey (kən–**veʸ**) v. **-veyed, -veying 1.** To carry from one place to another **2.** To transmit; make known feelings, thoughts, etc.: *Words convey meaning.*

con-vict (kən–**vɪkt**) v. To prove or find guilty: *See, the Lord is coming with thousands upon thousands of his holy ones to judge everyone, and to convict all the ungodly of all the ungodly acts they have done... and of all the harsh words ungodly sinners have spoken against him* (Jude 14,15). —opposite ACQUIT

con-vict (**kɑn**–vɪkt) n. A person found guilty of a crime and sent to prison

con-vic-tion (kən–**vɪk**–ʃən) n. **1.** The act of convicting: *This was his fourth conviction for drunk driving.* —opposite ACQUITTAL **2.** A very firm and sincere belief: *I'm of the steadfast conviction that the Bible is the inspired word of God.*

con-vince (kən–**vɪns**) v. **-vinced, -vincing** To be persuaded or to persuade someone else that sthg. is true; to cause someone to believe: *I am convinced that neither life nor death... nor any powers... nor anything else in all creation will be able to separate us from the love of God that is in Christ Jesus our Lord* (Romans 8:38,39). —**convincing** adj. —opposite UNCONVINCING —**convincingly** adv.

con-vi-vi-al (kən–**vɪv**–iʸ–əl) adj. **1.** Fond of feasting and good fellowship **2.** Festive

con-vo-ca-tion (kɑn–voʷ–**keʸ**–ʃən) n. **1.** An act of calling together for a meeting **2.** A group that has been called together, esp. an ecclesiastical or academic assembly

con-voke (kən–**voʷk**) v. **-voked, -voking** To call together for a meeting; summon to assemble; convene

con-voy (**kɑn**–vɔɪ) n. A number of ships or vehicles traveling with the protection of armed ships, vehicles, etc.

convoy v. **-voyed, -voying** To escort and protect a group of ships, vehicles, etc.

con-vulse (kən–**vʌls**) v. **-vulsed, -vulsing** To shake violently

con-vul-sion (kən–**vʌl**–ʃən) n. **1.** A sudden stiffening or jerking of the muscles **2.** A vio-

lent disturbance

cook (kʊk) v. To prepare food for eating by using heat; make a dish of some kind of food

cook n. A person who prepares and cooks food

cook-ie (kʊk-iʸ) n. 1. A small cake made from stiff, sweet dough 2. *slang* A person: *He's a smart cookie.*

cool (kuʷl) adj. 1. Neither warm nor cold: *a cool breeze* 2. Calm; unexcited: *Even when you strongly disagree with people, try to keep cool.* 3. Not very friendly: *Ann seemed very cool towards me today.* —**cool** n. *the cool of the evening*

cool v. 1. To make or become cool: *He opened all the windows to cool the room.* 2. **cool down** also **cool off** To become calmer and less excited or less angry: *It took Tom a long time to cool off after the argument.*

cool-er (kuʷl-ər) n. A container or device that makes or keeps sthg. cool

coop (kuʷp) n. A cage for poultry

coop v. To confine or shut in: *He was cooped up in his room for several days, trying to finish the book he was writing.*

co-op-er-ate (koʷ-ɑp-ə-reʸt) v. -ated, -ating To work together for a common purpose: *If we all cooperate, we'll get the work done quickly.* —**co-op-er-a-tion** (koʷ-ɑp-ə-reʸ-ʃən) n.

co-op-er-a-tive (koʷ-ɑp-ər-ə-tɪv) adj. 1. Helpful; willing to cooperate: *Mom thanked all the children for being so cooperative in helping with the cleaning.* —opposite UNCOOPERATIVE 2. Engaged in joint economic activity —**cooperatively** adv.

cooperative n. An enterprise owned and operated jointly by those who use its facilities and services

co-or-di-nate (koʷ-ɔr-də-neʸt) v. -nated, -nating To work together harmoniously, esp. to increase effectiveness: *We can get more done if we coordinate our efforts.*

co-or-di-na-tion (koʷ-ɔr-də-neʸ-ʃən) n. 1. The act of coordinating 2. The organized action of muscles, esp. in performing complicated movements: *Dancers, figure skaters, and gymnasts need good coordination.*

cop (kɑp) n. *infml.* A policeman or police-woman

cope (koʷp) v. coped, coping To contend with sthg. successfully

co-pi-ous (koʷ-piʸ-əs) adj. Plentiful. *Irving Berlin was a copious song writer.*

cop-per (kɑp-ər) n. 1. A malleable reddish-brown metallic element that is an excellent conductor of heat and electricity 2. A reddish-brown color —**cop-per-y** (kɑp-ər-iʸ) adj.

cop-ra (koʷp-rə) n. The dried kernel of the coconut, yielding coconut oil

cop-u-la (kɑp-yə-lə) n. A verb such as **be**, **seem**, **feel**, that links the subject with its predicate

cop-u-late (kɑp-yə-leʸt) v. -lated, -lating To engage in sexual intercourse —**cop-u-la-tion** (kɑp-yə-leʸ-ʃən) n.

cop-y (kɑp-iʸ) n. -ies 1. Sthg. that is an exact duplicate of another: *I made three copies of the letter.* 2. A single example of a magazine or newspaper: *I picked up a copy of "The Daily News" on the way home tonight.*

copy v. -ied, -ying 1. To make a duplicate of sthg. 2. To do what someone else does: *Mary always copies everything I do.* 3. To cheat on an examination by looking at someone else's paper and writing what that person wrote

cop-y-right (kɑp-iʸ-raɪt) n. The exclusive right to reproduce, publish, and sell an original work, or any part of it, for a certain number of years

co-quette (koʷ-kɛt) n. A woman who flirts —**co-quet-tish** (koʷ-kɛt-ɪʃ) adj.

cor-al (kɔr-əl) n. A hard substance made up of the skeletons of certain tiny marine animals, gradually building up from the bottom of the sea to form a rock-like mass, a coral reef

cord (kɔrd) n. 1. A strong, heavy string or a thin rope 2. An insulated, flexible wire for joining an electrical appliance to a supply of electricity 3. Anything of cord-like appearance: *vocal cords/spinal cord*

cor-dial (kɔr-dʒəl) adj. Very friendly —**cor-di-al-i-ty** (kɔr-dʒiʸ-æl-ət-iʸ) n.

cor-dial-ly (kɔr-dʒəl-iʸ) adv. In a cordial manner: *You are cordially invited to the wedding.*

cor-don (kɔr–dən) n. 1. A ring of people or ships, e.g., enclosing or guarding sthg. 2. A ribbon or cord worn as a sign of honor —cordon adj., v.

cor-du-roy (kɔr–də–rɔi) n. A heavy, ribbed fabric, usu. of cotton

core (kɔr) n. 1. The central part of certain fruits, such as the apple 2. The most important part of sthg. 3. to the core Thoroughly; completely: *That wicked person is rotten to the core.*

Co-rin-thi-ans (kə–rm–θiʸ–ənz) n. First and Second Corinthians are the names of two books in the New Testament. NOTE: The two books are letters that the Apostle Paul wrote to Christians in the city of Corinth in Southern Greece. First Corinthians was written to help solve problems in the young church. It also discusses spiritual gifts, the meaning of Christian love, and the importance of the resurrection of Jesus Christ. In Second Corinthians, Paul dwells largely upon his own ministry, disclosing his motives, his spiritual passion, and his tender love for the church. It also includes many great doctrinal verses. —see BIBLE, NEW TESTAMENT

cork (kɔrk) n. 1. The lightweight, outer covering (bark) of a Mediterranean tree, the cork oak 2. A round piece of this material which fits into the neck of a bottle to keep it tightly closed

corn (kɔrn) n. 1. *AmE.* also maize, sweet corn *BrE.* A type of cereal crop with big, usu. yellow seeds: *Corn is grown throughout the United States, esp. in the Midwest.* 2. A thickening of the skin, usu. on or near a toe, caused by friction or pressure

cor-ne-a (kɔr–niʸ–ə) n. The transparent covering of the eyeball

cor-ner (kɔr–nər) n. 1. The point at which two lines, walls, edges, etc., meet: *She put the floor lamp in the corner of the room.* 2. The place where two roads or streets meet: *He lives at the corner of Sixth and Elm streets.* 3. A distant part of the world: *People from all corners of the world came to the university to study.*

corner v. 1. To trap a person by forcing him into a place from which it is difficult to escape: *The police had the criminal cornered in an old warehouse.* 2. to corner the market To gain control of the market

cor-ner-stone (kɔr–nər–stoʷn) n. 1. A stone representing the starting place in the construction of a building 2. Sthg. essential or basic: *Hard work is the cornerstone of success.*

cor-net (kɔr–net) n. A small musical wind instrument like a trumpet

cor-nice (kɔr–nəs) n. 1. An ornamental moulding around the wall or a room just below the ceiling 2. The horizontal projecting part crowning the wall of a building

corn-y (kɔrn–iʸ) adj. -ier, -iest Trite; tiresomely simple

co-rol-la (kə–rɑl–ə) n. The petals of a flower

cor-ol-lar-y (kɔr–ə–lɛər–iʸ) n. -ies 1. Sthg. that may be taken for granted when sthg. else is proven true 2. A consequence or result

co-ro-na (kə–roʷ–nə) n. *pl.* -nas, -nae (neʸ) 1. A colored ring of light around the sun or moon, e.g. during an eclipse 2. A faint glow around the surface of an electrical conductor at high voltage

cor-o-nar-y (kɔr–ə–nɛər–iʸ) n. Short for coronary thrombosis A heart disease caused by blockage of one of the arteries supplying the heart

cor-o-na-tion (kɔr–ə–neʸ–ʃən) n. The crowning of a king or queen

cor-o-ner (kɔr–ə–nər) n. A public official whose chief duty is to investigate the causes of sudden or accidental death

cor-o-net (kɔr–ə–net) n. 1. A small crown, indicating rank lower than a sovereign 2. A crown-like head-dress

cor-po-ral (kɔr–prəl/ kɔr–pə–rəl) n. A noncommissioned officer, as in the army, ranking next below a sergeant

corporal adj. Bodily; physical: *corporal punishment*

cor-po-rate (kɔr–pər–ət) adj. 1. Of or forming a whole; united 2. Formed into a corporation; incorporated 3. Of or belonging to a corporation

cor-po-ra-tion (kɔr–pə–reʸ–ʃən) n. A large business organization

cor-po-re-al (kɔr–pɔr–iʸ–əl) adj. 1. Of the body

2. Material, not spiritual

corps (kɔr) n. **1.** A specialized branch of the armed forces: *the medical corps* **2.** A group of persons united in a special activity: *the diplomatic corps*

corpse (kɔrps) n. A dead body, esp. of a person

cor-pu-lent (kɔr-pyə-lənt) adj. Fat; stout —corpulence n.

cor-pus-cle (kɔr-pʌs-əl) n. One of the red or white cells in the blood

cor-ral (kə-ræl) n. An enclosure for horses, cattle, etc.

cor-rect (kə-rɛkt) adj. **1.** Right; true; accurate; without mistakes **2.** Proper in accordance with an approved form of behavior —opposite INCORRECT —correctly adv. —correctness n.

correct v. **1.** To make right or better: *He made several mistakes in spelling and had to correct them.* **2.** To point out faults in a person, to discipline someone: *Blessed is the man whom God corrects* (Job 5:17).

cor-rec-tion (kə-rɛk-ʃən) n. **1.** The act of correcting: *He who hates correction is stupid* (Proverbs 12:1). *He who heeds correction gains understanding* (Proverbs 15:32 KJV). **2.** A change that corrects sthg. **3.** Discipline: *The rod of correction imparts wisdom, but a child left to itself disgraces his mother* (Proverbs 29:15). —corrective adj. , n.

cor-re-late (kɔr-ə-leyt) v. To connect in a systematic way —cor-rel-a-tive (kə-rɛl-ət-ɪv) adj.

cor-re-la-tion (kɔr-ə-ley-ʃən) n. A shared relationship: *There's a high correlation between illiteracy and poverty.*

cor-re-spond (kɔr-ə-spand) v. **1.** To write letters to each other: *Jim corresponds with people all over the world.* **2.** To match; to agree with: *These tools don't correspond with the list of those I ordered.*

cor-re-spond-ence (kɔr-ə-span-dəns) n. **1.** Communication by letters **2.** The letters exchanged **3.** correspondence course A course of lessons sent by mail: *Carlos is taking a Bible Correspondence Course.*

cor-re-spond-ent (kɔr-ə-span-dənt) n. **1.** A person who writes letters **2.** Someone employed by a newspaper, news magazine, radio, TV, etc., to report the news from a certain area: *a foreign correspondent*

cor-re-spond-ing (kɔr-ə-spand-ɪŋ) adj. Related: *All privileges carry corresponding responsibilities.* —correspondingly adv.

cor-ri-dor (kɔr-ə-dər) n. A long main passageway in a building providing access to separate rooms

cor-ri-gi-ble (kɔr-ə-dʒə-bəl) adj. Capable of being corrected —opposite INCORRIGIBLE

cor-rob-o-rate (kə-rab-ə-reyt) v. -rated, -rating To support with additional evidence; confirm —cor-rob-o-ra-tion (kə-rab-ə-rey-ʃən) n. —cor-rob-o-ra-tive (kə-rab-ə-rə-tɪv) —cor-rob-o-ra-to-ry (kə-rab-ə-rə-tɔr-iy) adj.

cor-rode (kə-rowd) v. -roded, -roding To eat or be eaten away gradually (as by rust or a chemical): *Rust corrodes metal.* —corrosion n. —corrosive adj. , n.

cor-ru-gate (kɔr-ə-geyt) v. -gated, -gating Shaped into alternate ridges and grooves —corrugated adj. *The house has a corrugated metal roof.* —cor-ru-ga-tion (kɔr-ə-gey-ʃən) n.

cor-rupt (kə-rʌpt) adj. **1.** Immoral; wicked: *Keep corrupt talk far from your lips* (Proverbs 4:24). **2.** Dishonest; accepting bribes: *A corrupt witness mocks at justice* (Proverbs 19:28). *Everyone has turned away, they have become corrupt; there is no one who does good, not even one* (Psalm 53:3). —see also INCORRUPTIBLE **3.** Containing mistakes; not like the original: *They spoke a corrupt form of French.* **4.** Decaying; putrid —corruptly adv. —corruptness n.

cor-rupt (kə-rʌpt) v. **1.** To make morally bad: *Bad company corrupts good character* (1 Corinthians 15:33). **2.** To influence, esp. a public official, to do sthg. bad; bribe: *A bribe corrupts the heart* (Ecclesiastes 7:7). **3.** To change a language in a bad way: *The language has been corrupted by the introduction of foreign words.* —corruptible adj. —cor-rupt-i-bil-i-ty (kə-rʌp-tə-bɪl-ət-iy) n.

cor-rup-tion (kə-rʌp-ʃən) n. **1.** The act of corrupting **2.** Immoral behavior: *If they have escaped the corruption of the world by knowing our Lord and Savior Jesus Christ and are again entangled in it and overcome by it, they are*

worse off at the end than they were at the beginning (2 Peter 2:20). **3.** Decay: *the corruption of the body after death.*

cor·sage (kɔr–**saʒ**/ –**sadʒ**) n. A small arrangement of flowers to be worn by a woman, usu. on the upper part of the dress

cor·vette (kɔr–**vet**) n. A fast, lightly armed warship, slightly smaller than a destroyer

co·sign (**koʷ**–saɪn) v. To sign a note or other document jointly with others

cos·met·ic (kɑz–**met**–ɪk) n. A substance for beautifying the body, esp. the face

cosmetic adj. Used for beautifying the appearance, esp. the skin

cos·me·tol·o·gist (kɑz–mə–**tɑl**–ə–dʒɪst) n. A beautician

cos·mic (kɑz–mɪk) adj. **1.** Of the universe **2. cosmic rays** High energy radiation that reaches the earth from outer space

cos·mo·pol·i·tan (kɑz–mə–**pɑl**–ə–tən) adj. **1.** Containing people from many parts of the world: *a cosmopolitan city* **2.** Free from national prejudices and feeling at home in any part of the world: *a cosmopolitan outlook*

cos·mos (kɑz–məs) n. The universe seen as a whole; all space

cost (kɔst) n. **1.** The amount you have to pay for sthg.; price: *The cost of living keeps going up and up./They sinned at the cost of their lives* (Numbers 16:38). **2.** The price of producing sthg.: *Production costs are getting higher and higher.*

cost v. **cost, costing** To require a certain amount in payment as a price: *Though it cost all you have, get understanding* (Proverbs 4:7). *fig. His fight for freedom cost him his life.*

cost·ly (kɔst–liʸ) adj. **-lier, -liest 1.** Expensive **2.** Sthg. gained or won at a great expense: *the costliest war in history*

cos·tume (kɑs–tuʷm) n. A style of dress, esp. that typical of a nation, period of history, or social class, or suitable for a particular activity: *They went to the party in 18th century costume.*

costume v. To furnish with a costume

co·sy or **co·zy** (koʷ–ziʸ) adj. Warm and comfortable

cot (kɑt) n. A small, collapsible bed, light in weight, easy to carry

co·te·rie (koʷ–tə–reʸ) n. A group of persons with a common interest

cot·tage (kɑt–ɪdʒ) n. A small, simple house, esp. in the country

cot·ton (kɑt–ən) n. **1.** A soft, fluffy white substance around the seeds of the cotton plant **2.** The plant itself **3.** Thread or cloth made from this

couch (kaʊtʃ) n. A piece of furniture, usu. upholstered, with a back and arms, on which more than one person may sit

couch v. To express in words of a certain kind; to phrase: *He couched his request in very polite terms.*

cou·gar (kuʷ–ger) n. A large American cat; a puma; a mountain lion

cough (kɔf) v. **1.** To push air out from the lungs suddenly and noisily, usu. due to discomfort in the throat **2.** To clear something from the throat in this manner: *When he began to cough up blood, I called the doctor.*

cough n. **1.** An act of coughing **2.** An illness marked by frequent coughing: *He has had a bad cough for a long time.*

could (kʊd) v. **1.** Past tense of **can**: *I can't lift very much now, but I could when I was young.* **2.** (Used to show a possibility): *I could have driven all night, but I didn't.* **3.** (Used when making a polite request): *Could you help me move this desk, please?*

could·n't (kʊd–ənt) v. Short for **could not**: *I couldn't hear you.*

coun·cil (kaʊn–səl) n. An official body of people appointed or elected to make laws or decisions, for a town, church, etc., or to give advice: *the city council*

coun·cil·or (kaʊn–səl–ər) n. A member of a council

coun·sel (kaʊn–səl) n. **1.** The lawyer(s) who speak for someone in a court of law **2.** Advice: *Blessed is the man who does not walk in the counsel of the wicked...* (Psalm 1:1). *Plans fail for lack of counsel, but with many advisors, they succeed* (Proverbs 15:22).

counsel v. To advise: *They counseled us not to try to cross the desert in the daytime.* —compare COUNCIL

coun·sel·or (kaʊn–səl–ər) n. **1.** An adviser: *a marriage counselor* **2.** A lawyer

Coun-sel-or (kaʊn–səl–ər) n. One of the titles for the Holy Spirit; *Jesus said, "If you love me, you will obey what I command, and I will ask the Father, and he will give you another Counselor to be with you forever. The Counselor, the Holy Spirit, whom the Father will send in my name, will teach you all things and will remind you of everything I have said to you. When the Counselor comes... he will testify about me"* (John 14:15,16,26 and 15:26). —see also HOLY SPIRIT

count (kaʊnt) v. **1.** To say or name the numbers in order **2.** To find the total of **3.** To consider; regard: *We count our health as a great blessing.* **4.** To have value: *The only thing that counts is faith [in Jesus Christ] expressing itself through love* (Galatians 5:6). **5. count on/ upon sbdy./ sthg.** To depend on: *You can count on him to get the job done.* **6. count sbdy. out** To leave out: *If you're going hiking in this kind of weather, count me out.* —opposite COUNT IN

count n. **1.** The act of counting **2.** The total reached by counting **3.** A nobleman in some European countries

coun-te-nance (kaʊn–tə–nəns) n. **1.** The expression on a person's face **2.** Favor or approval

countenance v. **-nanced, -nancing** To allow or encourage

coun-ter (kaʊn–tər) n. **1.** A table or other flat surface at which people in a shop, restaurant, etc. are served or other business is transacted **2.** A person or a device that counts something

counter– prefix Against; opposite, as in **counterattack** or **counterclockwise**

count-er-act (kaʊn–tər–ækt) v. To reduce or prevent the effects of something

count-er-at-tack (kaʊn–tər–ə–tæk) n. The attack made by the defenders after being attacked by the enemy

count-er-clock-wise (kaʊn–tər–klɑk–waɪz) adv. Opposite the movement of the hands on the clock: *They ran counterclockwise around the track.*

count-er-feit (kaʊn–tər–fɪt) v. To make a copy of something, usu. with the intent to defraud —**counterfeiter** n.

counterfeit adj. Likely to be mistaken for something of higher value, esp. when presented as the real thing: *counterfeit money*

counterfeit n. An imitation; phony. *This twenty dollar bill is a counterfeit.*

count-er-part (kaʊn–tər–part) n. A person or thing corresponding to another in position or use

count-er-point (kaʊn–tər–point) n. **1.** One melody added as an accompaniment to another **2.** Art or practice of combining melodies according to fixed rules

count-er-pro-duc-tive (kaʊn–tər–proʷ–dʌk–tɪv) adj. Having the opposite of the desired effect

count-ess (kaʊnt–əs) n. The wife or widow of a count

count-less (kaʊnt–ləs) adj. **1.** Too many to be counted **2.** A large number

coun-try (kʌn–triʸ) n. **-tries 1.** A populated area which is separate and which governs itself: *By justice a king gives a country stability, but one who is greedy for bribes tears it down* (Proverbs 29:4)./ *Spain is a country in Europe.* **2.** The inhabitants of a nation or state **3.** The land outside cities or towns: *We're going for a ride in the country today.*

coun-try-man (kʌn–triʸ–mən) n. A citizen of one's own country

coun-try-side (kʌn–triʸ–saɪd) n. A rural area

coun-ty (kaʊn–tiʸ) n. **-ties** An area of land divided from others for purposes of local government: *The state where I live is divided into many counties.*

coup (kuʷ) n. A sudden action taken to obtain power or to achieve a desired result: *a military coup*

coupe (kuʷp) n. A small, closed, two-door automobile

cou-ple (kʌ–pəl) n. **1.** Two people or things considered together: *If you have a couple minutes, there are a couple of questions I'd like to ask you.* **2.** Two people together, esp. if they are married, engaged, or on a date: *Bob and Alice are a nice couple.*

couple v. **-pled, -pling** To join two things together: *They coupled the cars of the train together.*

cou-pon (kuʷ–pan/ kyuʷ–) n. A ticket that

shows the right of the holder to receive a re-fund or some service or other benefit: *This coupon is worth 40 cents off our next jar of cof-fee.*

cour·age (kɜr-ɪdʒ) n. **1.** Bravery; ability to con-trol fear in the face of danger, pain, etc.: *When the disciples saw Jesus walking on the lake, they were terrified. "It's a ghost," they said, and cried out in fear. But Jesus immediate-ly said to them, "Take courage! It is I. Don't be afraid"* (Matthew 14:26,27). **2. have the cou-rage of one's (own) convictions** To be brave enough to do or say what one be-lieves to be right

cou·ra·geous (kə-reʸ-dʒəs) adj. Having or showing courage; brave; fearless —**coura-geously** adv.

cou·ri·er (kɜr-iʸ-ər) n. A messenger carrying news or important papers

course (kɔrs) n. **1.** Onward movement in space or time: *In his heart a man plans his course, but the Lord determines his steps* (Pro-verbs 16:9). **2.** Direction of movement taken by someone or something: *the course of a stream* **3.** A series of instruction lessons dealing with a particular subject: *a three-unit history course* **4.** A series of studies lead-ing to a college degree: *a four-year course in engineering* **5.** Any of the parts of a meal: *a seven-course dinner.* **6.** The land on which a race is held or certain sports played: *a golf course* **7. of course** Obviously; naturally: *Do you want to lose all your money? Of course not!*

court (kɔrt) n. **1.** A place where justice is ad-ministered **2.** Those gathered to hear and judge a law case: *The court stood when the judge entered.* **3.** An area prepared and marked off for various ball games, such as tennis, basketball, volleyball, etc. **4.** A short street **5.** An open space enclosed by a build-ing or buildings

court v. **1.** To try to win someone's favor or support **2.** To attempt to gain the love of; to woo **3.** To invite, often unknowingly: *They were courting disaster by leaving port when a hurricane was heading their way.*

cour·te·ous (kɜrt-iʸ-əs) adj. Polite and kind; having good manners and respect for oth-ers —**cour·te·sy** (kɜrt-ə-siʸ) n. -sies

court-house (kɔrt-haʊs) n. **1.** A building that houses courts of law and usu. administra-tive offices of a county **2.** The county seat

court-mar·tial (kɔrt-mɑr-ʃəl) n. **1.** A court for trying offenses against military law **2.** A trial by such a court

court-martial v. To try by such a court

court-room (kɔrt-ruʷm) n. A room in which judicial proceedings are held

court-ship (kɔrt-ʃɪp) n. **1.** Courting; wooing **2.** The period during which this takes place

court-yard (kɔrt-yɑrd) n. An area enclosed by walls or buildings, often with grass and flowers and other plants

cous·in (kʌz-ən) n. The child of one's uncle or aunt

cove (koʷv) n. A small bay

cov·e·nant (kʌv-ə-nənt) n. A formal, binding agreement between two or more people or groups

Cov·e·nant n. In the New Testament of the Holy Bible we read of only two covenants, the old and the new. The New Covenant, the covenant of grace, was established by Christ and supersedes the old covenant of the law with all its animal sacrifices and rit-ualistic practices in the sense that through the new covenant the old is fulfilled and its purpose achieved: *...because by one sacri-fice, he [Jesus] has perfected forever those who are being made holy* (Hebrews 10:14). *"This is the covenant I will make with them af-ter that time," says the Lord. "I will put my law in their hearts, and I will write them on their minds." Then he adds, "Their sins and lawless acts I will remember no more. And where these have been forgiven, there is no longer any sacri-fice for sin"* (Hebrews 10:16-18). —see JESUS

cov·er (kʌv-ər) v. **1.** To place or spread some-thing over, upon, or in front of in order to hide or protect —opposite UNCOVER **2.** To clothe **3.** To shelter or protect **4.** To extend over: *The car was covered with snow.* **5.** To consist of: *The senator's speech covered many subjects.* **6.** To travel a distance: *We covered 700 miles yesterday in our new car.* **7.** To re-port the details of a news event: *One of our best reporters covered the disaster.* **8.** To be enough money for: *Will $50 cover the cost of*

the broken window? **9.** To protect from loss; to insure: *Are we covered against earthquakes?* **10.** To forgive: *Blessed is he whose transgressions are forgiven, whose sins are covered* (Psalm 32:1). *Love covers over all wrongs* (Proverbs 10:12). **11. cover up for sbdy.** To hide something shameful in order to protect someone else from disgrace, punishment, etc.: *George took the blame for the car accident in order to cover up for his son who had no driver's license.*

cover n. **1.** Something that protects by covering: *Put a cover over that hole before someone falls in it.* **2.** The outer front or back page of a magazine or book **3.** Shelter: *If it starts to rain, where can we take cover?* **4.** Something that conceals or disguises: *This business is a cover for unlawful activity.* **5. under separate cover** In a separate envelope or package: *Enclosed is a receipt. Your order is being sent under separate cover.*

co-vert (ko^w–vərt/kə–) adj. Concealed; hidden; disguised

covert n. **1.** A shelter or hiding place **2.** A thicket giving shelter to wild animals

cov-et (kʌv–ət) v. *derog.* To desire eagerly to have something or someone belonging to another person: *Covetousness is a grievous sin against God's Law. The Bible says, "You shall not covet your neighbor's house. You shall not covet your neighbor's wife,... or anything that belongs to your neighbor"* (Exodus 20:17). —see COVETOUS

cov-et-ous (kʌv–ət–əs) adj. Desiring something that belongs to someone else: *No covetous man, who is an idolater, has any inheritance in the kingdom of Christ and God* (Ephesians 5:5). NOTE: God hates the sin of covetousness and all other sins. But because of his great love and mercy, he forgives those who repent of their sins and put their trust in Jesus for eternal life. —covetousness n. —see SIN, REPENT, FORGIVENESS, JESUS

cow (kaʊ) n. **1.** The mature female of cattle, kept on farms esp. to provide milk **2.** The female form of some other animals, such as the moose or the elephant, of which the male is called a bull

cow-ard (kaʊ–ərd) n. One who lacks courage in the face of danger, pain, or difficulty —cowardly adj —cowardice also cowardliness n.

cow-boy (kaʊ–bɔɪ) n. A man who is hired to tend or drive cattle

cow-er (kaʊ–ər) v. To crouch in fear

co-work-er (ko^w–wɜrk–ər) n. A fellow worker

coy (kɔɪ) adj. **1.** Falsely modest **2.** Artfully shy or reserved

coy-o-te (kaɪ–o^w–ti^y / kaɪ–o^{w}t) n. A carnivorous wolf-like animal of western North America

co-zy also **co-sy** (ko^w–zi^y) adj. -zier, -ziest Comfortable: *a cozy armchair* —cozily adv. —coziness n.

crab (kræb) n. An edible sea animal with a shell and five pairs of legs, the first pair having claws

crab n. A grouchy, irritable person: *He's such an old crab, always complaining about something!*

crab-by (kræb–i^y) adj. -bier, -biest Ill-natured, grouchy

crack (kræk) v. **1.** To break partly, without falling to pieces: *A rock cracked our window.* **2.** To cause to make a sudden sharp sound: *Thunder cracked threateningly.* **3.** To break open: *Al cracked the walnuts with the nutcracker.* **4.** To make a joke: *He cracked a joke* **5.** To discover or solve: *to crack a safe / a code* **6.** To strike with a sudden blow: *He fell and cracked his head on the sidewalk.* **7.** To fail in tone: *His voice cracked.* **8.** To give in to torture: *The spy cracked under pressure and told everything he knew.* **9. crack down** To become more severe: *The government is cracking down on drugs.* **10. crack up** *infml.* **(a)** To cause to laugh, almost uncontrollably: *His jokes always crack me up.* **(b)** To lose control of one's feelings; to have a nervous breakdown: *Mary cracked up after her husband died.* **(c)** To have an accident: *He was leading the auto race until he cracked up.*

crack n. **1.** A line of division caused by splitting: *a crack in the cup* **2.** A narrow opening: *The window was opened just a crack.* **3.** An explosive sound: *a crack of thunder* **4.** A sudden sharp blow: *He got a crack on his head from the fall.* **5.** *infml.* An attempt: *It was her*

first crack at writing an article for a magazine **6.** A sarcastic remark: *Bob's always making cracks about my big ears.* **7. crack of dawn** The first light of day **8. crack-down (kræk-daʊn)** Greater strictness: *There will also be a crackdown on drunken driving.*

cracked (krækt) adj. **1.** Damaged by cracks: *a cracked dish* **2.** *slang* Crazy

crack·er (kræk-ər) n. A flat, thin, dry cake, round or square, and usu. unsweetened: *soda/graham crackers*

crack-le (kræk-əl) v. **-led, -ling** To make rapidly repeating sharp noises: *The fire crackled in the fireplace.*

crack-pot (kræk-pɑt) n. An eccentric person

cra-dle (kreʸ-dəl) n. **1.** A small bed for a baby, esp. one that can be rocked gently **2.** The place where something begins; origin: *the cradle of civilization* **3.** A support for a telephone receiver

cradle v. **-dled, -dling** To place in or as if into a cradle

craft (kræft) n. **1.** A job or trade requiring skill, esp. with one's hands **2.** A boat, ship, or aircraft

crafts-man (kræfts-mən) n. **-men (-mɛn)** A skilled worker who practices a craft —**craftsmanship** n.

craft-y (kræf-tiʸ) adj. **-ier, -iest** Cleverly deceitful: *The Lord condemns a crafty man* (Proverbs 12:2). *A quick-tempered man does foolish things, and a crafty man is hated* (Proverbs 14:17). —**craftily** adv. —**craftiness** n.

crag (kræg) n. A steep or rugged rock —**craggy** adj. **-gier, -giest**

cram (kræm) v. **-mm- 1.** To force people or things into a small space: *They crammed 90 people into a bus that seats only 45.* **2.** To study hard for a short time in preparation for a test: *Betty sat up all night cramming for her chemistry test.*

cramp (kræmp) n. **1.** A painful stiffening of a muscle: *I got a cramp in my leg and had to be pulled out of the swimming pool.* **2.** Sharp abdominal pains

cramp v. To restrict from free action; to hinder: *That little apartment really cramped us.*

cramped (kræmpt) adj. Limited in space: *a cramped apartment*

cran-berry (kræn-bɛər-iʸ) n. **1.** The edible, small, tart, red berry of a kind of shrub, used for making jelly and sauce **2.** The shrub itself

crane (kreʸn) n. **1.** A machine for lifting and moving heavy objects **2.** A tall water bird with very long legs and neck

cra-ni-um (kreʸ-niʸ-əm) n. **-nia** or **-niums** The skull —**cranial** adj.

crank (kræŋk) n. **1.** A handle with which something can be made to turn: *In the old days we had to start the car with a crank.* **2.** A person with strange ideas **3.** An ill-tempered person: *He's such an old crank!*

crank-y (kræŋk-iʸ) adj. **-ier, -iest** Bad tempered: *a cranky, unfriendly old man*

crash (kræʃ) v. **1.** To collide in a violent and noisy accident: *The plane crashed.* **2.** To strike something noisily and violently: *The vase fell and crashed on the floor.* **3.** To move violently and noisily: *The army tank crashed through the barricade.* **4.** To make a sudden loud noise: *The thunder crashed above our house.* **5.** To enter and attend without invitation and without paying: *They crashed the party.* **6.** In the financial world, to fail suddenly; come to ruin: *The stock market crashed in 1929.*

crash n. **1.** A violent automobile or airplane accident: *a terrible crash at the corner of 6th and Main* **2.** A sudden loud noise: *a crash of thunder* **3.** A severe business failure: *the Stock Market crash*

crash adj. Marked by an intensive effort to reach the desired results in the shortest possible time: *a crash diet*

crass (kræs) adj. **1.** Very vulgar or stupid **2.** Coarse or thick —**crassness** n.

crate (kreʸt) n. A box made of wood for holding fruit, bottles, etc.

cra-ter (kreʸt-ər) n. **1.** A bowl-shaped depression at the mouth of a volcano **2.** A hole made in the ground by a falling meteor or the explosion of a shell

crave (kreʸv) v. **craved, craving 1.** To have an intense desire for: *Like newborn babies, crave pure spiritual milk, so that by it you may grow up in your salvation* (1 Peter 2:2). *The wicked man craves evil* (Proverbs 21:10). **2.** To beg earnestly for

cra-ving (kre^y-vɪŋ) n. An intense desire for something; a longing: *The Lord does not let the righteous go hungry, but he thwarts the craving of the wicked* (Proverbs 10:3).

crawl (krɔl) v. **1.** To move slowly by drawing the body along the ground or floor: *John crawled under the car to work on it.* **2.** To move very slowly: *The traffic was crawling along at a snail's pace.* **3.** *fig.* To be covered by insects, etc.: *The room was crawling with ants.*

cray-on (kre^y-ən) n. A stick of colored wax used for writing or drawing

craze (kre^{y}z) n. **1.** Fashion **2.** Great but temporary enthusiasm

cra-zy (kre^y-zi^y) adj. -zier, -ziest **1.** Not mentally sound; insane; mad: *The crazy man was running around, screaming, and cutting himself with stones.* **2.** *fig.* Foolish: *He's crazy to go out in a storm like this!* **3.** Wildly excited; very fond of or interested in: *Jim is crazy about Janet.* **4. like crazy** Extremely fast, busy, active, etc.: *He'll have to drive like crazy to get there in time.* —**crazily** adv. —**craziness** n.

creak (kri^{y}k) v. To make a squeaking sound, like that of a badly-oiled door when it opens —**creaky** adj. -ier, -iest

cream (kri^{y}m) n. **1.** The yellowish, fatty liquid that rises to the top of milk **2.** Something similar to this: *cream of tomato soup* **3.** A cosmetic: *face cream* **4.** The best: *Our students are the best in the country, the cream of the crop.* —**creamy** adj.

crease (kri^{y}s) n. A line or mark made on cloth or paper by folding, pressing, or wrinkling: *My mother put a crease in my pants with her iron.*

crease v. **creased, creasing** To make a crease by folding or pressing with an iron

cre-ate (kri^y-e^{y}t) v. **-ated, -ating** To make something new: *In the beginning God created the heaven and the earth* (Genesis 1:1).

cre-a-tion (kri^y-e^y-ʃən) n. **1.** The act of creating or the fact of being created **2.** Anything created

Cre-a-tion n. The universe, the world, and all living things: *Nothing in all creation is hidden from God's sight* (Hebrews 4:13). NOTE: We are told clearly in the Scriptures, time and time again, that God created heaven and earth and all that they contain. But even apart from God's Word, the tremendous complexity and order of the world and its plants and animals can only be explained by intelligent planning. "The heavens declare the glory of God and the sky shows his handiwork" (Psalm 19:1). "Since the creation of the world, God's invisible qualities - his eternal power and divine nature - have been clearly seen, being understood from what has been made, so that men [who don't believe in God] are without excuse" (Romans 1:20). Nevertheless, some people prefer to believe that the universe came into existence purely by chance. Why is this? There is only one possible explanation. It is simply that, as the Bible says, "they did not like to retain God in their knowledge" (Romans 1:28). "The fool has said in his heart, There is no God" (Psalm 14:1). —see GOD, JESUS, EVOLUTION

cre-a-tive (kri^y-e^y-tɪv) adj. **1.** Producing new and original ideas and things **2.** Resulting from newness of thought or expression —**creatively** adv. —**cre-a-tiv-i-ty** (kri^y-e^y-tɪv-ə-ti^y) n. also —**cre-a-tive-ness** (kri^y-e^y-tɪv-nɪs) n. *Someone with a lot of creativity is needed around here.*

cre-a-tor (kri^y-e^y-tər) n. **1.** A person who creates **2. Creator** God; the creator of the universe: *The Lord is the everlasting God, the Creator of the ends of the earth* (Isaiah 40:28). —see GOD, CREATION

crea-ture (kri^y-tʃər) n. **1.** Anything created **2.** An animal **3.** A human being: *O give thanks unto the Lord... who gives food to every creature* (Psalm 136:1,25).

creche (krɛʃ/kre^{y}ʃ) n. A representation of the birth of our Lord and Savior Jesus Christ —see JESUS

cre-dence (kri^y-dəns) n. Belief

cre-den-tial (krə-dɛn-ʃəl) n. **1.** That which entitles one to confidence **2.** *usu. pl.* A document giving evidence of one's authority, position, or trustworthiness

cred-i-ble (krɛd-ə-bəl) adj. Trustworthy; believable —**cred-i-bil-i-ty** (krɛd-ə-bɪl-ət-i^y) n.

cred·it (krɛd–ət) n. **1.** Honor given someone for good work or good performance: *She shared the credit with her co-workers.* **2.** A source of honor: *He was a credit to his country and to his profession.* **3.** A system of purchasing services or goods when wanted and paying for them later **4.** The quality of being likely to repay debts: *Her credit is good. You can depend on her to pay her bills.* **5.** The amount of money in a person's account in a bank: *a credit balance (=money in the bank)* —compare DEBIT **6.** Confidence: *I place full credit in the administration's abilities.* **7.** Public recognition; praise: *I was given no credit for my discovery.* **8.** (esp. in the US) A measure of work completed by a student at a college or university: *She has almost enough credits to graduate.* **9. to someone's credit (a)** In someone's favor: *It is to his credit that he overcame such a handicap to win the race.* **(b)** Something produced or belonging to one: *She's only 29 years old, and she already has four books to her credit! (=she's written four books)*

credit v. To place an amount of money in an account: *Please credit this $500 to my account.*

cred·i·tor (krɛd–ə–tər) n. A person to whom money is due —compare DEBTOR

cre·do (kriʸ–doʷ/kreʸ–) n. A set of beliefs —see CREED

cred·u·li·ty (krə–duʷ–lə–tiʸ) n. Gullibility; readiness to believe

cred·u·lous (krɛ–dʒuʷ–ləs) adj. Likely to believe sthg. on very slight evidence

creed (kriʸd) n. A system of religious beliefs NOTE: Following is an example of a Christian creed used throughout the Christian world since 325 A.D.:

I believe in one God, the Father Almighty, Maker of heaven and earth and of all things visible and invisible.

And in one Lord Jesus Christ, the only begotten Son of God, begotten of his Father before all worlds, God of God, Light of Light, Very God of Very God, Begotten, not made, being of one substance with the Father, by whom all things were made; who for us men and for our salvation came down from heaven and was incarnate by the Holy Ghost of the Virgin Mary and was

made man; and was crucified also for us under Pontius Pilate. He suffered and was buried; and the third day he rose again according to the Scriptures; and ascended into heaven, and sits on the right hand of the Father; and he shall come again with glory to judge both the living and the dead; whose kingdom shall have no end.

And I believe in the Holy Spirit, the Lord and Giver of Life, who proceeds from the Father and the Son, who with the Father and the Son is worshiped and glorified, who spoke by the Prophets. And I believe one holy Christian and Apostolic church. I acknowledge one Baptism for the remission of sins, and I look for the resurrection of the dead; and the life of the world to come. Amen. —see GOD, JESUS, HOLY SPIRIT

creek (kriʸk/ krɪk) n. **1.** A small stream **2. up a/ the creek** *infml.* In trouble: *I missed my flight to Chicago for an important job interview. Now I'm really up a creek.*

creep (kriʸp) v. **crept** (krɛpt) **creeping 1.** To move slowly and stealthily, esp. with the body close to the ground: *The burglar crept in the shadows toward the house.* **2.** To grow along the surface of the ground or a wall, like ivy: *A lovely vine crept along the wall.*

creep·y (kriʸp–iʸ) adj. **-ier, -iest** An unpleasant sensation of horror or fear: *This empty old house with its squeaking doors gives her a creepy feeling.*

cre·mate (kriʸ–meʸt) v. **-mated, -mating** To burn a dead body to ashes —**cre·ma·tion** (krɪ–meʸ–ʃən/kriʸ–) n.

cre·ma·to·ry (kriʸ–mə–tɔr–iʸ) n. A place or furnace for cremating

cre·o·sote (kriʸ–ə–soʷt) n. An oily liquid made from wood tar, used to keep wood from rotting

crepe (kreʸp) n. **1.** A thin crinkled fabric **2.** Rubber with a crinkled texture, used for the soles of shoes **3. crepe paper** Thin, crepe-like paper

crept (krɛpt) v. Past tense and past part. of creep

cre·scen·do (krə–ʃɛn–doʷ) n. **-dos** Of sound, a gradual increase in volume

crescendo v. **-doed, -doing** To increase grad-

ually in volume

cres·cent (krɛs–ənt) n. **1.** The figure of the moon during its first or last quarter **2.** Any object shaped like this

cress (krɛs) n. One of various plants of the mustard family, with pungent leaves, often used in salad

crest (krɛst) n. The top of something, esp. of a hill or a wave

cre·vasse (krɪ–væs) n. A deep crack, esp. in a glacier

crev·ice (krɛv–ɪs) n. A crack forming a narrow opening

crew (kruʷ) n. **1.** The personnel manning a plane or a ship **2.** A group of people working together: *the flight crew*

crib (krɪb) n. **1.** A small child's bed, usu. with movable sides **2.** A small building for storing corn **3.** A manger for feeding animals

crib·bage (krɪb–ɪdʒ) n. A card game scored on a small board having holes for pegs

crick (krɪk) n. A sharp pain (in the neck)

crick·et (krɪk–ət) n. A leaping insect, the male of which makes a sharp, chirping sound

cricket n. An outdoor game played with a bat and ball by two teams of eleven players, using wickets

cried (kraɪd) v. Past tense and part. of **cry**

cri·er (kraɪ–ər) n. **1.** Anyone who cries **2.** (formerly) One who publicly proclaims an announcement; a town crier

cries (kraɪz) v. 3rd person sing., pres. tense of **cry**

crime (kraɪm) n. **1.** An act committed or omitted in violation of the law **2.** *fig.* A shame: *It's a crime that this food will be wasted.* —compare SIN

crim·i·nal (krɪm–ə–nəl) n. One who has committed a crime —criminal adj. —criminally adv.

crimson (krɪm–zən) adj. A deep, purplish-red color

cringe (krɪndʒ) v. cringed, cringing To shrink back or crouch from fear; to cower

crin·kle (krɪŋ–kəl) v. -kled, -kling To make or become wrinkled —crinkle n. A wrinkle or crease

crip·ple (krɪp–əl) n. **1.** A lame person or ani-

mal **2.** One who is disabled in any way

cripple v. -pled, -pling **1.** To make a cripple of someone, esp. by making it difficult or impossible to use one of his arms or legs **2.** To disable someone in any way

cri·sis (kraɪ–sɪs) n. -ses (–siʸz) **1.** A turning point for better or worse of an acute disease or fever **2.** A decisive or critical moment: *a financial crisis*

crisp (krɪsp) adj. **1.** Hard and dry but easily broken: *crisp toast* **2.** Firm; fresh: *crisp lettuce* **3.** Brisk, invigorating: *a crisp autumn breeze* —crispy, -ier, -iest adj. *crispy potato chips*

criss-cross (krɪs–krɔs) v. **1.** To mark with crossing lines **2.** To move crosswise through or over

crisscross n. A pattern made of crossing lines

cri·te·ri·on (kraɪ–tɪər–iʸ–ən) n. -ria or -ons A standard on which a judgment may be based

crit·ic (krɪt–ɪk) n. **1.** One who forms and expresses judgments, esp. regarding literary or artistic works **2.** One who habitually finds fault

crit·i·cal (krɪt–ɪ–kəl) adj. **1.** Finding fault: *Why are you so critical of the administration?* **2.** In the nature of a crisis: *His heart condition is reported as being critical.*

crit·i·cism (krɪt–ə–sɪz–əm) n. **1.** The act or art of judging the quality of literature or a work of art **2.** Faultfinding **3.** Helpful suggestions: *The students gave constructive criticism regarding the course they had just completed.*

crit·i·cize (krɪt–ə–saɪz) v. -cized, -cizing **1.** To find fault with **2.** To evaluate; make a judgment about the good and bad points of something

croak (kroʷk) v. **1.** To utter a low, hoarse sound, like a frog **2.** *slang* To die

croak n. A croaking sound: *I heard the deep, loud croak of a big frog.*

cro·chet (kroʷ–ʃeʸ) v. -cheted (–ʃeʸd), -cheting (–ʃeʸ–ɪŋ) To make a piece of needlework using a special needle that has a small hook at one end

crochet n. Needlework made by crocheting

crock (krɔk) n. An earthenware pot or jar

crock-er-y (krɑk–ər–i^y) n. Earthenware; cups, plates, pots, etc. , collectively

croc-o-dile (krɑk–ə–daɪl) n. A large thick-skinned reptile found in sluggish waters and swamps in the tropics

cro-cus (kro^w–kəs) n. -cuses A small plant, related to the irises, with purple, yellow, or white flowers that bloom early in the spring

crois-sant (krɑ–sɑnt/ kwɑ–sɑn) n. A rich, crescent-shaped roll

crook (krʊk) n. *slang* A thief

crook-ed (krʊk–əd) adj. **1.** Not straight; bent; twisted **2.** Dishonest

croon (kru^wn) v. To sing or hum in a low voice —**crooner** n.

crop (krɑp) n. **1.** A plant which is farmed and harvested, such as fruit, vegetables, or grain: *Rice and tea are two of China's chief crops.* **2.** The yield at harvest: *This year's corn crop was the biggest ever.*

cro-quet (kro^w–ke^y) n. An outdoor game in which mallets are used to drive wooden balls through a series of wickets

cross (krɔs) v. **1.** To go over to the other side: *It took us three days to cross the desert./ The bridge crossed the river.* **2.** To place two things across each other: *He crossed his legs.* **3.** To go or be placed across each other: *Broadway and 5th Avenue cross near the center of town.* **4.** To oppose someone or their wishes: *Jack really hates to be crossed. He's difficult to get along with.* **5.** To make a movement of the hand forming a cross on oneself as a religious act: *She crossed herself as she left the church.* **6.** To cause an animal or plant to breed with one of another kind: *Is it possible to cross a donkey with a horse?* **7. cross sbdy./ sthg. off** To remove from a list by drawing a line through: *He moved and left no forwarding address, so we crossed his name off the mailing list.* **8. cross sthg. out** To draw a line through something that is written: *I crossed out the mistakes in my composition and wrote it again.*

cross n. **1.** A mark (X) often used to show where something is or where it ought to be **2.** A mark to show that something is incorrect **3.** An upright post with another piece of wood across it near the top of which people were bound or nailed in ancient times and left to die as a punishment NOTE: Jesus Christ, though innocent, was nailed to a cross and left to die (crucified). He died and was buried. The third day he rose again from the dead. Forty days later he returned to his heavenly throne. Today the cross is used as a sign of the Christian religion (on and inside church buildings, as jewelry, etc.) —see JESUS, CRUCIFY **4.** The cross (+) is often used to mark a person's grave even though that person may not have been a Christian **5.** Sometimes a cross is used to mark the place where a person died (in a car accident, for example) even though that person may not have been a Christian **6.** Self-sacrifice; self-denial; the sacrifice of earthly goods and pleasures in order to save others: *Jesus said: "If anyone desires to come after me, let him deny himself, and take up his cross daily and follow me"* (Luke 9:23). **7.** A trial or affliction: *He has a terrible cross to bear.* **8.** A combination of two different things: *A mule is a cross between a horse and a donkey.*

cross adj. Angry; bad-tempered: *Grandma was really cross when the boys trampled on her flowers.*

cross–ex-am-ine v. (krɔs–ɪg–zæm–ən) -ined, -ining To question someone closely in order to compare the resulting answers with former responses —**cross–examination** n.

cross-ing (krɔs–ɪŋ) n. **1.** A journey across the water: *We had a smooth crossing.* **2.** A place marked off for pedestrians to cross the street: *a pedestrian crossing* **3.** A place where railroad tracks cross the street: *a railroad crossing* **4.** The act of crossing: *The old ship had made many crossings of the Atlantic.*

cross–ref-er-ence (krɔs–ref–ər–əns) n. A note directing readers to another part of the book for further information: *Cross-references in this dictionary are in capital letters.* —**cross–reference** v.

cross-walk (krɔs–wɔk) n. A lane marked off for pedestrians for crossing a street

crotch (krɑtʃ) n. **1.** A place where things fork **2.** The part of the human body or of a gar-

ment where the legs fork

crotch-et-y (krɑtʃ-ə-ti^y) adj. Bad-tempered

crouch (krɑutʃ) v. **1.** Of humans, to squat to stand with the knees well bent **2.** Of animals, to lie close to the ground, hiding or in readiness for action: *The leopard crouched, ready to spring on its prey.*

crouch n. A squatting position

croup (kru^wp) n. A children's disease characterized by hoarse coughing and difficult breathing

crow (kro^w) v. **1.** To make the loud shrill cry of a rooster **2.** To speak proudly: *I'm tired of listening to Tom crow about his athletic achievements.*

crow n. **1.** The cry of a rooster **2.** A large, shiny black bird **3. as the crow flies** In a straight line **4. to eat crow** To be forced to admit that one was wrong

crowd (krɑud) v. **1.** To crowd together in large numbers: *People crowded into the sports arena.* **2.** To fill: *Shoppers crowded the streets.*

crowd n. **1.** Many people crowded together: *an overflow crowd at the baseball game* **2.** A particular group: *the college crowd*

crowd-ed (krɑud-əd) adj. Completely full: *a crowded room*

crown (krɑun) n. **1.** A head covering, usu. made of gold with jewels in it, worn by a king or queen as a sign of royal power **2.** The top of the head, a hat, a hill, etc.: *the crown of a hill* **3.** The governing power of a monarch: *land belonging to the Crown* **4.** A symbol of victory and reward; championship title: *He won the boxing crown in 1981.* **5.** *fig. and spir.* Crowns were used all over the world by priests and in religious services. In Grecian athletic games the victors were given crowns of leaves. In contrast to these leaves which wither, there is the incorruptible crown that will last forever — a crown of righteousness and glory and life: *Shortly before his death, St. Paul wrote, "I have fought the good fight, I have finished the race, I have kept the faith. Now there is in store for me the crown of righteousness, which the Lord, the righteous Judge, will award to me on that day — and not only to me, but also to all who have longed for his appearing"* (2 Timothy 4:7,8).

Blessed is the man who perseveres under trial, because when he has stood the test, he will receive the crown of life that God has promised to those who love him (James 1:12). *And when the Chief Shepherd [Jesus] appears, you will receive the crown of glory that will never fade away* (1 Peter 5:4).

crown v. **1.** To put a crown on a person's head as a sign of royal power **2.** To confer honor upon someone **3.** To cover the top of something: *Snow crowned the mountain peaks.* **4.** To reach a successful conclusion: *Her efforts were crowned with success.* **5.** To hit someone on the head: *She crowned the burglar with a lamp.*

cru-cial (cru^w-ʃəl) adj. Critical; vital; of the utmost importance: *Literacy is crucial for a better informed, healthier, more productive society.* —**crucially** adv.

cru-ci-ble (kru^w-sə-bəl) n. **1.** A heat resistant vessel for melting metals **2.** A severely trying experience

cru-ci-fix (kru^w-sə-fiks) n. **1.** A Christian symbol consisting of the cross with the figure of Jesus on it **2.** The cross as a Christian symbol

cru-ci-fix-ion (kru^w-sə-fik-ʃən) n. The act of crucifying —see JESUS, CREED

cru-ci-fy (kru^w-sə-fai) v. **-fied, -fying 1.** To kill someone by nailing or binding to a cross and leaving him to die: *Jesus, speaking of himself, told his disciples, "They [the chief priests and teachers of the law] will condemn him to death and will turn him over to the Gentiles to be mocked and flogged and crucified. On the third day he will be raised to life!"* (Matthew 20:18,19). *And they crucified him* (Mark 15:24). *The angel said to the women [who came to the tomb to anoint the body of Jesus], "Do not be afraid, for I know that you are looking for Jesus, who was crucified. He is not here; he has risen, just as he said"* (Matthew 28:5,6). —see CROSS **2.** *spir.* To stop sinning; to put to death any sinful desires: *Those who belong to Jesus Christ [those who trust in him for eternal life] have crucified the sinful nature with its passions and desires* (Galatians 5:24). **3.** To ruin a person's reputation and career: *He crucified his political opponents with his verbal*

attacks.

crude (kruᵂd) adj. **1.** In an unrefined or natural state; untreated: *crude oil* **2.** Lacking tact or sensitive feeling: *crude behavior* **3.** Roughly, unskillfully made: *a crude hut* —**crudely** adv.

cru-el (kruᵂ–əl) adj. -ll- **1.** Causing pain or suffering to others; taking pleasure in the pain of another; merciless **2.** Painful; causing suffering: *a cruel war/ wind/ disease* —**cruelly** adv.

cru-el-ty (kruᵂ–əl–tiʸ) n. -ties The quality of being cruel

cruise (kruᵂz) v. cruised, cruising **1.** To sail in an unhurried way, for pleasure **2.** Of a car, boat, plane, etc., to move at a fairly high but steady speed, esp. on a long journey: *He cruised along the long, flat road at 60 miles per hour.*

cruise n. A sea voyage for pleasure

crumb (krʌm) n. A tiny piece of dry food, esp. of crackers, cookies, bread, or cake

crum-ble (krʌm–bəl) v. -bled, -bling To break into very small pieces: *He crumbled the cookie in his fingers./ fig. In the end, the Roman Empire crumbled.*

crum-my (krʌm–iʸ) adj. -mier, -miest Of very poor quality

crum-ple (krʌm–pəl) v. -pled, -pling **1.** To crush together; to make or become wrinkled **2.** To collapse loosely NOTE: Do not confuse **crumple** with **crumble**

crunch (krʌntʃ) v. **1.** To crush something, usu. using the teeth: *She annoyed people by crunching potato chips during the movie.* **2.** To make a harsh sound as though being crushed: *The gravel crunched under his feet.*

crunch n. **1.** A sound like that of something being crushed: *the crunch of ice under his feet* **2.** A tight or critical situation: *a financial crunch*

cru-sade (kruᵂ–seʸd) n. **1.** A reforming enterprise undertaken with zeal: *a crusade to improve education* **2.** A campaign against something believed to be bad: *a crusade against drugs*

crush (krʌʃ) v. **1.** To press with great force so as to destroy the natural shape of something; to pound or grind something to pow-

der: *This machine crushes wheat grain to make flour.* **2.** To put down; subdue: *The government has crushed the rebellion.* **3.** To be brokenhearted: *The Lord is close to the brokenhearted and saves those who are crushed in spirit* (Psalm 34:18). **4.** To defeat or be defeated thoroughly: *Our football team was crushed by the visiting team last Saturday, 54 to 6.*

crust (krʌst) n. **1.** A hard, usu. brown outer layer of baked bread **2.** The baked shell of a pie **3.** The outer layer of the earth: *the earth's crust* —**crusty** adj.

crus-ta-cean (krʌs–teʸ– ʃən) n. Any of various types of animals that have a hard outer shell and live mostly in the water, such as crabs, lobsters, and shrimp

crutch (krʌtʃ) n. **1.** A support to assist a lame person in walking, usu. with a crosspiece fitting under the armpit **2.** Something depended on for support or to help remember

crux (krʌks) n. *pl.* **cruxes** The basic or central part of a problem: *The crux of the matter is ...*

cry (kraı) v. cried, crying **1.** To weep; to shed tears as a sign of sorrow, grief, pain, etc. **2.** To make a loud sound expressing fear or pain: *Susan cried out with pain when she cut her finger.* **3.** To shout; to call loudly: *John the Baptist was the voice of one crying in the wilderness, "Prepare the way of the Lord, make his paths straight"* (Matthew 3:3 NKJV). **4.** To make the sound of certain animals

cry n. **cries** **1.** Any loud sound expressing fear, pain, etc. **2.** A call or plea for help: *The eyes of the Lord are on the righteous, and his ears are attentive to their cry* (Psalm 34:15). **3.** The natural sound of certain animals or birds **4.** **battle cry** A cry to show or encourage bravery in a battle

cry-ing (kraı–ıŋ) adj. *infml.* Something that demands attention: *a crying need/ shame*

crypt (krıpt) n. An underground cell or chapel, esp. beneath a church, used as a burial place

cryp-tic (krıp–tık) adj. Intentionally very difficult to understand: *a cryptic message*

crys-tal (krıs–təl) n. **1.** A small part of a solid substance, such as ice or salt, having a regular shape **2.** A special kind of very clear

glass often used for ornaments 3. Things made of cut glass

crystal adj. Clear as crystal

cub (kʌb) n. The young of certain wild animals such as the bear, lion, etc.

cube (kyuᵂb) n. **1.** A solid object with six equal square sides: *a sugar cube* **2.** The number made by multiplying a number by itself twice: *The cube of two is eight: (2x2x2=8)*

cu-bic (kyuᵂ–bɪk) adj. **1.** Of three dimensions: *There are 1,728 cubic inches in one cubic foot.* **2.** Shaped like a cube: *This box is a perfect cube, 12 inches high, 12 inches long, and 12 inches wide. It is one cubic foot.*

cu-bi-cle (kyuᵂ–bɪ–kəl) n. A small division of a large room, screened for privacy —**cubicle** adj. Cube-shaped

cub-it (kyuᵂ–bət) n. An ancient linear measurement, approximately 18 inches

cu-ckoo (kuᵂ–kuᵂ) n. A European bird that lays its eggs in the nests of other birds for them to hatch

cu-ckoo adj. Foolish; stupid

cu-cum-ber (kyuᵂ–kʌm–bər) n. **1.** A long, green-skinned fruit related to the gourds and eaten as a vegetable **2.** The plant producing this

cud (kʌd) n. Food brought from the first stomach of certain animals, such as the cow, back into the mouth and chewed again

cud-dle (kʌd–əl) v. -**dled**, -**dling 1.** To hug tenderly **2.** To lie close and snug —**cuddlesome** adj.

cud-dly (kʌd–liʸ) adj. -**dlier,** -**dliest** Pleasant to cuddle: *a cuddly little puppy*

cud-gel (kʌdʒ–əl) n. A heavy stick or club

cue (kyuᵂ) n. **1.** *theatrical* Anything said or done that is followed by a specific action **2.** A hint **3.** A long rod, tapered at one end, used in playing pool or billiards

cue v. **cued, cuing** To give a cue to

cuff (kʌf) n. **1.** A fold at the end of a sleeve **2.** A band of cloth turned upwards at the bottom of a trouser leg **3. off the cuff** Without rehearsal or preparation **4. on the cuff** On credit

cui-sine (kwɪ–ziʸn) n. A style of cooking

cul-de-sac (kʌl–də–sæk) n. A street that is closed at one end

cul-i-na-ry (kyuᵂ–lə–nɛər–iʸ) adj. Of or relating to cookery

cull (kʌl) v. To choose; pick out from a group

cull n. Sthg. rejected from a group or lot as useless or inferior

cul-mi-nate (kʌl–mə–neʸt) v. -**nated,** -**nating 1.** To end or conclude **2.** To reach its highest point or degree: *The argument culminated in a fist fight.* —**cul-mi-na-tion** (kʌl–mə–neʸ–ʃən) n.

cu-lotte (kuᵂ–lɑt/kyuᵂ–) n. A woman's trouser-like garment, cut to resemble a skirt

cul-pa-ble (kʌl–pə–bəl) adj. Deserving blame; guilty

cul-prit (kʌl–prət) n. Someone guilty of a crime or offense

cult (kʌlt) n. **1.** A system or community of religious worship and ritual **2. (a)** Obsessive devotion to a person or ideal **(b)** A group of persons sharing such devotion

cul-ti-vate (kʌl–tə–veʸt) v. -**vated,** -**vating 1.** To prepare land for the growing of crops **2.** To produce by preparing the soil, planting, watering, weeding, etc. **3.** To spend time and care in developing something: *to cultivate a love of classical music* **4.** To encourage the growth of friendship with a person

cul-ti-va-tion (kʌl–tə–veʸ–ʃən) n. The act of cultivating

cul-ture (kʌl–tʃər) n. **1.** The beliefs, customs, institutions, arts and all the other products of human work and thought created by a people or group at a particular time: *ancient Chinese culture/ a tribal culture* **2.** Refinement of intellectual and artistic tastes **3.** The act of developing by education and training **4.** The growing of a particular crop: *grape culture* —**cultural** adj. —**culturally** adv.

cul-vert (kʌl–vərt) n. A drain crossing under a road or railroad

cum-ber-some (kʌm–bər–səm) adj. **1.** Heavy and awkward to carry **2.** Unwieldy or clumsy

cum lau-de (kuᵂm–lau–dɛ/ –lɔ–deʸ) adj., adv. With academic distinction: *He graduated cum laude.*

cu-mu-la-tive (kyuᵂ–myə–lə–tɪv) adj. Increasing by successive additions

cu-mu-lus (kyuᵂm–yə–ləs) adj. A massive white cloud having a flat base and rounded outlines

cun-ning (kʌn–ıŋ) adj. 1. Shrewd; skilled at deceiving people; crafty; sly 2. Exhibiting ingenuity 3. *infml.* Charming; delicately pleasing

cup (kʌp) n. 1. A small, round container, usu. with a handle, from which liquids are drunk 2. Also **cupful** (kʌp–fəl) The amount held by one cup

cup v. **-pp-** To form (esp. the hands) into the shape of a cup

cup-board (kʌb–ərd) n. A cabinet or closet, esp. in the kitchen, where plates, food, etc. may be stored

cup-ful (kʌp–fʊl) n. **-fuls** The quantity held by a cup

cu-rate (kyʊər–ət) n. A clergyman assisting a parish priest, rector, or vicar

cur-a-tive (kyʊər–ə–tıv) adj. Having the power to cure

curative n. A remedy

cur-a-tor (kyʊər–ə–tər) n. A person in charge of a museum or similar institution

curb (kɜrb) n. 1. The edging of a sidewalk, usu. made of cement 2. A controlling influence: *Keep a curb on your temper*

curb v. To control one's feelings, hunger, temper, spending, etc.: *Ann has a hard time curbing her appetite.*

curd (kɜrd) n. The coagulated portion of milk, from which cheese is made —**curdy** adj.

cur-dle (kɜr–dəl) v. **-dled, -dling** To make or become curdy; coagulate

cure (kyʊər) v. **cured, curing** To heal someone of a sickness or disease: *Mary was cured of ulcers./ fig.* Parents try to cure their children of bad habits.

cure n. 1. A remedy; a medicine that helps people recover from an illness, disease, etc. 2. Medical treatment: *She went for a cure at a health spa.* 3. A return to health after illness: *This new drug should bring about a cure.*

cur-few (kɜr–fyuᵂ) n. A signal or time after which designated people must remain indoors until the next day

cu-ri-o (kyʊər–iʸ–oᵂ) n. A rare or curious object

cu-ri-os-i-ty (kyʊər–iʸ–ɑs–ı–tiʸ) n. **-ties** 1. The desire to find out and know things 2. Something that is interesting because it is rare and strange

cu-ri-ous (kyʊər–iʸ–əs) adj. 1. Eager to know or learn 2. Odd; strange; peculiar —**curiously** adv.

curl (kɜrl) v. (esp. of hair) 1. To twist into or form a curl or curls 2. To lie or sit with the knees drawn up comfortably: *She curled up by the fire to read her book*

curl n. A piece of hair that twists into a small ring —**curly** adj. *She has curly blond hair.*

cur-rant (kɜr–ənt) n. 1. A small, round, acid berry for making jelly 2. The bush producing this berry

cur-ren-cy (kɜr–ən–siʸ) n. **-cies** 1. Money in actual use in a country 2. The state of being in general acceptance: *Reports of corruption in the local government are gaining currency among reporters.*

cur-rent (kɜr–ənt) adj. Belonging to the present time; present day: *current events*

current n. 1. A continuous, onward flow of fluid or gas: *The current is strongest in the middle of the river.* 2. The flow of electricity

cur-ric-u-lum (kə–rık–yə–ləm) n. **-la** or **-lums** A course of study offered in a school or one of its divisions

cur-ry (kɜr–iʸ) n. 1. A condiment; a seasoning made with hot-tasting spices 2. A dish flavored with this: *I like chicken curry.*

curse (kɜrs) v. **cursed, cursing** 1. To call down evil or misfortune upon someone: *Whoever says to the guilty, "You are innocent," people will curse him and nations denounce him* (Proverbs 24:24). 2. To swear at; use blasphemous, profane, or obscene language against: *Jesus said, "Bless those who curse you"* (Luke 6:28). *Bless those who persecute you. Bless and do not curse* (Romans 12:14). 3. **cursed** Suffering misfortune or great harm because of: *Cursed is ev-eryone who does not continue to do everything written in the Book of law. Christ redeemed us from the curse of the law by becoming a curse for us, for it is written: "Cursed is everyone who is hung on a tree"* (Galatians 3:10,13). —see CRUCIFY

curse n. 1. A calling on God to send evil

down on some person or thing 2. A profane, obscene, or blasphemous oath, expressing hatred, anger, etc. 3. A person or thing that has been cursed 4. Evil or injury that seems to come in answer to a curse: *He who gives to the poor will lack nothing, but he who closes his eyes to them receives many curses* (Proverbs 28:27). *The Lord's curse is on the house of the wicked, but he blesses the home of the righteous* (Proverbs 3:33).

cur-sive (kɜr–sɪv) adj. Writing in which the letters are joined

cur-sor (kɜr–sər) n. A flashing, movable dot of light on a computer screen that shows where data may be inserted or moved

cur-so-ry (kɜr–sə–riʸ) adj. Hasty and superficial; not thorough

curt (kɜrt) adj. Rudely brief: *a curt reply*

cur-tail (kər–teʸl) v. To cut short; to make less; to make (e.g., a visit) shorter than originally intended —**curtailment** n.

cur-tain (kɜr–tən) n. 1. A piece of hanging cloth that can be drawn back, esp. at a window 2. The screen hanging between the stage and the auditorium of a theatre

curt-sy (kɜrt–siʸ) n. -sies A movement of respect, bending the knees and lowering the body with one foot forward, done by women and girls

cur-va-ceous (kər–veʸ–ʃəs) adj. Of a woman, having attractive curves of the body

cur-va-ture (kɜr–və–tʃər) n. 1. The condition of being curved, esp. abnormally: *curvature of the spine* 2. The extent to which something is curved: *the curvature of the earth*

curve (kɜrv) n. A line that is not straight at any point, like the edge of a circle

cush-ion (kʊʃ–ən) n. A soft pillow or pad to rest on or against

cushion v. To lessen or soften the force of shock: *The snow cushioned his fall from the roof.*

cus-tard (kʌs–tərd) n. A dish or sauce made with beaten eggs and milk

cus-to-di-an (kəs–toʷ–diʸ–ən) n. 1. A guardian or keeper of a public building; keeper of an office building, library, apartment, etc. 2. A janitor

cus-to-dy (kʌs–tə–diʸ) n. 1. The act or right of

caring for someone: *After the divorce, the mother was given custody of the children.* 2. Imprisonment: *The thief was taken into custody.*

cus-tom (kʌs–təm) n. 1. An established, socially accepted practice: *Social customs vary greatly from country to country.* 2. A habit of an individual: *His custom was to get up early and run two miles before breakfast.* 3. **custom**—Built or made in accordance with the customer's wishes: *a custom-built car*

cus-tom-ar-y (kʌs–təm–ɛr–iʸ) adj. Established by custom; usual: *It is customary to give people gifts on their birthdays.* —**cus-tom-ar-i-ly** (kəs–tə–**mɛɔr**–ɪ–liʸ) adv.

cus-tom-er (kʌs–təm–ər) n. A person who buys goods or services from a store, esp. on a regular basis

cus-tom-ize (kʌs–təm–aɪz) v. To make, build, or change according to the buyer's or owner's wishes

cus-toms (kʌs–təmz) n. 1. The area at a port or airport where officials examine goods and baggage brought into a country 2. Taxes (duty) paid on imported goods

cut (kʌt) v. cut, cutting 1. To injure or wound with something sharp: *He cut his finger with a knife* 2. To make a hole in something with a sharp instrument: *That sharp corner cut a hole in my skirt.* 3. To detach something with a knife or a pair of scissors: *She cut the coupons out of the newspaper.* 4. To clear the way: *They cut a path through the jungle.* 5. To make shorter: *He cut the grass.* 6. *fig.* To hurt someone's feeling by saying something hurtful: *His remark cut me deeply.* 7. To make something less frequent: *They're cutting back train services between here and San Francisco.* 8. To grow a tooth: *Our baby's cutting her first teeth.* 9. To interrupt a supply of water, gas, electricity, etc.: *The water was cut off today for two hours.* 10. To cross: *Don't cut across the lawn; use the sidewalk* 11. To stay away from deliberately: *He cut classes yesterday* 12. To reduce by removing part: *to cut taxes* 13. To be able to be cut: *This hard wood is difficult to cut.* 14. **cut back (a)** To cut a plant close to the stem; to prune **(b)** To reduce in size or amount: *to cut back on production* 15. **cut corners** To do something in a less than perfect

way in order to save time, money, etc. **16. cut it out** *infml.* To stop it: *Bob and Jimmy were arguing, so their mother told them to cut it out or go to bed.* **17. cut it thin** To leave oneself little time or money to do what is needed: *After a trip of 4,000 miles, we arrived home with just 50 cents. That's really cutting it thin.* **18. cut off** To disconnect: *I was talking to my brother on the phone and we got cut off.* **19. cut out for...** Well-suited for...: *I'm not cut out for this kind of work.* **20. cut up** *infml.* To behave in an amusing or annoying way: *Tom's always cutting up in class and making the other kids laugh.*

cut n. **1.** A wound: *How did you get that cut on your forehead?* **2.** Pieces of meat: *We're having cold cuts for lunch.* **3.** A reduction in size or amount: *cuts in spending* **4.** A share: *George hopes to get a 50% cut of the profits.*

cut–and–dried (kʌt–ən–draɪd) adj. **1.** Determined beforehand **2.** Routine

cu‑ta‑ne‑ous (kyuʷ–teʸ–niʸ–əs) adj. Of or affecting the skin

cute (kyuʷt) adj. **cuter, cutest 1.** Daintily pretty: *a cute baby* **2.** Clever; shrewd —**cutely** adv. —**cuteness** n.

cu‑ti‑cle (kyuʷt–ɪ–kəl) n. The skin at the bottom and edges of the finger and toenails

cut‑lass (kʌt–ləs) n. A short sword with a wide, slightly curved blade

cut‑ler‑y (kʌt–lə–riʸ) n. Cutting instruments collectively, esp. those used in cutting and eating food

cut‑let (kʌt–lət) n. A thin slice of meat, esp. of veal or lamb

cut‑off (kʌt–ɔf) n. **1.** A road or path used as a short‑cut or bypass **2.** A device for turning off a flow, as of water or natural gas

cut‑rate (kʌt–reʸt) adj. On sale at a reduced price

cut‑ter (kʌt–ər) n. **1.** A person or thing that cuts **2.** A single‑masted sailing vessel **3.** A lightly armed vessel, used by a government to enforce regulations **4.** A ship's boat for transporting passengers and supplies **5.** A light sleigh

cut‑throat (kʌt–θroʷt) adj. **1.** Ruthless; merciless: *cut‑throat competition* **2.** Cruel or murderous

cut‑ting (kʌt–ɪŋ) n. A root or stem cut from a plant and used to grow new plants

cutting adj. **1.** Wounding the feelings severely; sarcastic: *a cutting remark* **2.** Piercing and very cold: *a cutting wind*

cut‑up (kʌt–əp) n. A person who is always clowning around

–cy (–siʸ) suffix **1.** A quality or state, as in *normalcy, infancy* **2.** Rank or office: *presidency*

cy‑a‑nide (saɪ–ə–naɪd) n. A very strong poison

cy‑cle (saɪ–kəl) n. **1.** A number of related events happening in a regularly repeated order: *the cycle of the seasons* **2.** The period of time needed for this to be completed **3.** Bicycle **4.** Motorcycle

cycle v. **cycled, cycling** To ride a cycle (bicycle or motorcycle): *They cycled (=bicycled) all the way across the United States in 30 days.*

cy‑clist (saɪ–klɪst) n. One who rides a bicycle

cy‑clone (saɪ–kloʷn) n. A very violent wind moving rapidly in a circle around a calm central area

cyl‑in‑der (sɪl–ən–dər) n. **1.** A hollow or solid body with a circular base and straight sides **2.** A vessel within which a piston moves backwards and forwards as in an engine

cy‑lin‑dri‑cal (sɪ–lɪn–drɪ–kəl) adj. Having the shape of a cylinder: *a cylindrical rod*

cym‑bal (sɪm–bəl) n. A brass, plate‑like musical percussion instrument, beaten together in pairs, causing a sharp ringing sound —**cymbalist** n. One who plays the cymbals

cyn‑ic (sɪn–ɪk) n. A person who believes that all people are motivated only by selfishness and who shows this by making unkind remarks about people

cy‑press (saɪ–prəs) n. An evergreen tree, related to the pines

cyst (sɪst) n. A growth in or on the body, containing liquid matter

cys‑tic fi‑bro‑sis (sɪs–tɪk faɪ–broʷ–səs) n. A hereditary disease of the pancreas, lungs, etc. in which there is difficulty in breathing and digestion

czar (zɑr) n. **1.** An emperor; title of any of the former emperors of Russia, and at various times, the rulers of other Slavik nations **2.** One having great power or authority

D, d (di^y) n. The fourth letter of the English alphabet
d. Written abbr. Said as *li. di d. 1901*

dab (dæb) v. **-bb- 1.** To apply with short, light strokes **2.** To touch or strike gently
dab n. **1.** A small amount **2.** A quick or light pat
dab-ble (dæb–əl) v. **-bled, -bling 1.** To work at sthg. in a superficial manner **2.** To play in water or as if in water
dachs-hund (daks-hunt/dak–sənt) n. **-hunds** or **-hunde** German for badger hound, one of a breed of dogs with a long, low body, short legs, and long, droopy ears, originally used in hunting
dad (dæd) also **daddy** (dæd–i^y) n. *infml.* (used esp. by children or in speaking to children) Father
daf-fo-dil (dæf–ə–dil) n. A plant having yellow flowers that bloom in the spring
daf-fy (dæf–i^y) adj. **-fier, -fiest** Silly or crazy
dag-ger (dæg–ər) n. **1.** A short, pointed weapon with sharp edges, used for stabbing **2.** A reference mark
dahl-ia (dæl–yə/dal–) n. A plant cultivated for its various colored flowers
dai-ly (de^y–li^y) adj., adv. Every day, or every day except Saturday and Sunday: *Take this medicine three times daily.*
daily n. **-lies** A daily newspaper
dain-ty (de^yn–ti^y) adj. **-tier, -tiest** Small; delicate; fragile: *a dainty flower* **—daintily** adv. **—daintiness** n.
dair-y (dɛər–i^y) n. **-ies 1.** A place where milk is kept and butter and cheese are made **2.** A store that sells milk and milk products
dai-sy (de^y–zi^y) n. **-sies** A type of small common flower with white petals
Da-lai La-ma (da–li^y la–mə) n. The spiritual leader of Tibetan Lamaism and, traditionally, the political leader of Tibet
dale (de^yl) n. A valley
dal-ly (dæl–i^y) v. **-lied, -lying** To waste time
dam (dæm) n. A barrier across a stream to prevent the flow of water for flood control and/or to provide water for drinking, irrigation, power generation, recreation, etc.
dam (dæm) v. **-mm-** To construct a dam across: *They dammed up the Colorado River in*

1930 *to provide water and power for Arizona, Southern Nevada and Southern California.*
dam-age (dæm–idʒ) n. Harm or loss due to injury to a person's reputation or to property: *The fire caused great damage.*
damage v. **-aged, -aging** To cause damage
dam-ag-es (dæm–idʒ–əz) n. Money that must be paid for damage caused: *The man was ordered to pay damages to the owner of the house after he ran into it.*
dame (de^ym) n. *infml.* A woman
damn (dæm) v. **1.** To criticize adversely; condemn **2.** To condemn to everlasting punishment: *Jesus said, "Go into all the world and preach the gospel to every creature. He that believes and is baptized will be saved. He that does not believe will be damned"* (Mark 16:16). **—see** DAMNATION **3.** To swear at someone by saying, *"Damn you!"* **4. damn it!** interj. An expression of anger or disappointment NOTE: Such language is sinful. A Christian will not use this word in speaking to anyone. We are told to love everyone, even our enemies: *Let no corrupt communication proceed out of your mouth, but that which is edifying, that it may minister grace unto the hearers. Let all bitterness, wrath, anger, clamor and evil speaking be put away from you... and be kind to one another, tenderhearted, forgiving one another, just as God in Christ also forgave you* (Ephesians 4:29, 31-32).
dam-na-ble (dæm–nə–bəl) adj. **1.** Liable to or deserving punishment **2.** Detestable: *There shall be false teachers among you who ... shall bring in damnable heresies [false teachings], even denying the Lord that bought them, and bring upon themselves swift destruction* (2 Peter 2:1 KJV). **—see** DAMNATION
dam-na-tion (dæm–ne^y–ʃən) n. Condemnation: *Woe to you, Scribes and Pharisees, hypocrites!... you shall receive the greater damnation [in hell, a place of torment, forever and ever]* (Matthew 23:14). *That they all might be damned who believed not the truth, but had pleasure in unrighteousness* (2 Thessalonians 2:12 KJV). NOTE: *The wages [what we deserve] of sin is death [eternal damnation] but the gift of God is eternal life through Je-*

sus Christ our Lord (Romans 6:23). God hates sin but because of his great love and mercy he forgives sinners who repent of their sins and put their trust in Jesus for eternal life. —see FORGIVE-NESS, JESUS

damp (dæmp) adj. Somewhat wet; moist: *damp weather* —**damply** adv. —**dampness** n. *The dampness made the air feel colder than it actually was.*

damp-en (dæmp–ən) v. **1.** To make sthg. damp: *That light shower hardly dampened the ground.* **2.** To cause feelings of happiness, eagerness, etc. to be weakened: *Nothing can dampen my spirits on such a beautiful day!*

dam-per (dæm–pər) n. **1.** An adjustable plate for regulating the draft in a stove or furnace, etc. **2.** A thing or person that dampens, depresses, or checks

dam-sel (dæm–zəl) n. A young, unmarried woman

dance (dæns) v. **danced, dancing** To move one's body in time to music: *Fred Astaire danced his way to fame./fig. The daisies danced in the breeze.* —**dancer** n.

dance n. **1.** An act of dancing **2.** A particular set of movements performed to music: *The waltz is a beautiful dance.* **3.** A social gathering for dancing: *The dance continued until midnight.*

dan-de-li-on (dæn–də–laɪ–ən) n. A common weed with yellow flowers

dan-der (dæn–dər) n. *infml.* Anger or temper

dan-druff (dæn–drəf) n. A whitish dead skin on the scalp that comes off in small flakes

dan-dy (dæn–diʸ) adj. **-dier, -diest** Very good, first rate

dandy n. **1.** Sthg. excellent in its class **2.** A man who is unduly attentive to dress

dan-ger (deʸn–dʒər) n. **1.** The probability or possibility of harm or loss: *The children were not aware of the danger of falling through the thin ice./ A prudent man sees danger and takes refuge, but the simple keep going and suffer because of it* (Proverbs 22:3). **2.** A case or cause of harm: *the dangers of a plane crash*

dan-ger-ous (deʸn–dʒər–əs) adj. Hazardous: *a dangerous animal/ Smoking is dangerous to one's health.* —**dangerously** adv.

dan-gle (dæŋ–gəl) v. **-gled, -gling 1.** To hang

loosely, esp. with a swinging motion **2.** To be left without proper grammatical connection in a sentence

Dan-iel (dæn–yəl) n. A book of the Old Testament written by the prophet Daniel during the Babylonian Captivity of Judah (606 - 536 B.C.) NOTE: The main theme is the Sovereignty of God over the affairs of men in all ages. The first part is largely a narrative of Daniel's personal life and local history. Part two contains visions and prophecies relating to the controlling hand of God, resulting in the ultimate triumph of God's Kingdom over all satanic world powers. —see BIBLE, OLD TESTAMENT

dap-per (dæp–ər) adj. **1.** Small and neat **2.** Alert and lively in movement and manners

dare (dɛər) v. **dared, daring 1.** To be bold enough to do a certain thing: *He dared to contradict his boss.* **2.** To try to get someone to do sthg. dangerous: *I dared him to jump off the roof.* —**dare** n.

dare-devil (dɛər–dɛv–ɪl) n. A recklessly bold person

dar-ing (dɛər–ɪŋ) adj. Bold, fearless, courageous

dark (dɑrk) adj. **1.** Partly or completely without light: *a very dark night* **2.** Tending towards black: *a dark color* **3.** Gloomy or dismal: *A pessimist looks at the dark side of everything.* **4.** Evil or wicked **5.** Ignorant or unenlightened **6.** Hidden or secret

dark n. **1.** The absence of light; darkness: *It's hard to find anything in the dark.* **2. in the dark** Ignorant of the facts

dark-en (dɑrk–ən) v. To become dark or cause to become dark: *Smoke from the forest fire darkened the sky.*

dark-ness (dɑrk–nəs) n. The state of being dark: *After the power failure, the town was in total darkness./ spir. When Jesus returns, he will bring to light what is hidden in darkness and will expose the motives of men's hearts* (1 Corinthians 4:5). *Writing to believers in Ephesus, Paul says, "Have nothing to do with the fruitless deeds of darkness but rather expose them"* (Ephesians 5:11). *To the Christians in Colosse he writes, "God has rescued us from the dominion of darkness and brought us into the kingdom*

of the Son he loves, in whom we have redemption, the forgiveness of sins" (Colossians 1:13,14). *Peter says, "You [Christians] are a people belonging to God, that you may declare the praises of him who called you out of darkness into his wonderful light"* (1 Peter 2:9).

dar-ling (dar-lĭŋ) n. One dearly loved

darling adj. **1.** Dearly loved **2.** Very nice; charming NOTE: This word is used much more frequently by women than by men.

darn (darn) v. To mend clothes with interlacing stitches

darn interj. A mild form of cursing

dart (dart) n. A small sharp-pointed object to be thrown or shot, used as a weapon or in games

dart v. To move quickly and suddenly: *He darted right out in front of the car.*

dash (dæʃ) v. **1.** To start suddenly and run fast: *He dashed out of the house and into the car.* **2.** To hit or cause to hit with force: *The waves dashed the raft against the rocks.* **3.** To cause to lose hopes, aspirations, etc.: *His hopes of breaking the record in the long jump were dashed when he broke his foot.*

dash n. **1.** A sudden, quick, usu. short, run: *The horse saw the open gate and made a dash for freedom.* **2.** A short foot race: *a hundred yard dash* **3.** A small amount of sthg., esp. a flavoring: *a dash of salt* **4.** A mark (—) used in writing and printing, used to indicate a break or omission

dash-board (dæʃ–bord) n. An instrument panel beneath the windshield of an automobile containing dials and controls

dash-ing (dæʃ–ĭŋ) adj. **1.** Bold, brave, daring **2.** Showy or stylish —**dashingly** adv.

das-tard (dæs–tərd) n. A mean, cowardly person —**dastardly** adj.

da-ta (deʸ–tə/ dæ–tə) n. *sing.* or *pl.* Factual information such as measurements or statistics

da-ta base (deʸ–tə beʸs/dæ–tə) also **data bank** n. A large collection of data in a computer, arranged so that it can be retrieved, expanded, and updated quickly for various uses

date (deʸt) n. **1.** The particular time at which sthg. happened or happens: *The date of the*

first airplane flight was December 17, 1903. **2.** The day of the month: *Today's date is November 25th.* **3.** An appointment **4.** *infml.* A special social meeting between two persons of the opposite sex **5.** **out of date (a)** Old fashioned **(b)** No longer able to be used because the time for use has ended: *This newspaper is out of date.* **6.** **up-to-date** Modern —**datable** adj. Able to be dated

date v. **dated, dating 1.** To estimate or show the date of: *I believe this pottery dates from the 17th century.* **2.** To mark the date on: *Please date your check and sign it.*

dat-ive (deʸt–ĭv) n. Belonging to a grammatical case that marks the indirect object of the verb

daub (dɔb) v. **-bb- 1.** To smear **2.** To paint carelessly or without skill —**daub** n.

daugh-ter (dɔ–tər) n. One's female child

daughter–in–law (dɔ–tər–ĭn–lɔ) n. *pl.* **daughters–in–law** The wife of one's son

daunt (dɔnt/dɑnt) v. **1.** To discriminate **2.** To discourage

daunt-less (dɔnt–ləs/**dɑnt**–) adj. Fearless —**dauntlessly** adv. —**dauntlessness** n.

daw-dle (dɔd–əl) v. **-dled, -dling** To move slowly —**dawdler** n.

dawn (dɔn) n. **1.** The beginning of day when light first appears: *I always awaken before dawn in the summer.* **2.** The beginning: *the dawn of civilization*

dawn v. **1.** Of the morning, to begin to grow light as the sun is just rising: *A new day has dawned.* **2.** **dawn on/ upon someone** To become known: *It suddenly dawned on me that I had forgotten my appointment.*

day (deʸ) n. **1.** A time period of 24 hours: *There are seven days in a week./ Better is one day in your courts, O Lord, than a thousand anywhere else* (Psalm 84:10). *Teach us to number our days, [O Lord], that we may apply our hearts unto wisdom* (Psalm 90:12 KJV). *This is the day the Lord has made; let us rejoice and be glad in it* (Psalm 118:24). **2.** The time from sunrise to sunset: *Call me in the evening, because I am seldom at home during the day.* **3.** A time for working within a 24-hour period: *She works an eight-hour day.* **4.** A period or point of time: *God says, "Call upon me in the*

day of trouble; I will deliver you, and you will honor me" (Psalm 50:15). **5. call it a day** *infml.* To stop working for the day: *Everyone was tired and ready to call it a day.* **6. make someone's day** *infml.* To cause someone pleasure or happiness **7. Day of the Lord** Judgment Day: *For God has set a day when he will judge the world with justice by the man he has appointed. He has given proof of this to all men by raising him [Jesus] from the dead* (Acts 17:31). *On that day "God will judge men's secrets through Jesus Christ"* (Romans 2:16). *The day of the Lord will come [suddenly and unexpectedly] like a thief in the night* (1 Thessalonians 5:2).

day-break (deʸ–breʸk) n. Dawn

day-dream (deʸ–driʸm) n. Idle and pleasant thought

day-dream v. To allow one's thoughts to wander: *No wonder he does so poorly in school; he's always daydreaming instead of listening to the teacher.*

day-light (deʸ–laıt) n. The time of day when there is light: *There is more daylight during the summer than in the winter.*

daze (deʸz) v. **dazed, dazing** To cause to be unable to think or feel clearly: *The blow on the head dazed him for a moment.* **—daze** n. *He was in a daze for several hours after the accident.* **— dazedly** adv.

daz-zle (dæ–zəl) v. **-zled, -zling 1.** To shine brightly **2.** To impress greatly **—dazzling** adj. Brilliant; outstanding; fascinating: *a dazzling performance*

DC abbr. **1.** Direct current; electricity moving in one direction only **—com-pare AC 2.** District of Columbia (dıs–trıkt əv kə–lʌm–bı–yə) n. (the area of the US where the capital is located): *Washington, DC*

DD n. Doctor of Divinity

DDS n. **1.** Doctor of Dental Science **2.** Doctor of Dental Surgery

DDT n. A water insoluble substance used as an insecticide

de– (dı–/ də–/diʸ–) prefix **1.** Remove: *dehumidify* **2.** Negate: *demerit* **3.** Reverse: *decode*

dea-con (diʸ–kən) n. **1.** A member of the clergy ranking just below a priest **2.** A lay official assistant to a minister in some Protest-

ant churches

dea-con-ess (diʸ–kən–əs) n. A woman appointed or elected to serve as an assistant in the church

de-ac-ti-vate (diʸ–æk–tə–veʸt) v. **-vated, -vating** To cause to be inactive

dead (dɛd) adj. **1.** No longer alive; lifeless **2.** Spiritually dead: *You [all of us] were dead in transgressions and sins "gratifying the cravings of our sinful nature and following its desires and thoughts." But because of his great love for us, God who is rich in mercy, made us [believers] alive with Christ, even when we were dead in transgressions* (Ephesians 2:1-5). **—see JESUS 3.** Unresponsive: *There was a dead silence in the audience.* **4.** No longer in existence or use: *The phone is dead.* **5.** Weary and worn out: *He is dead tired after working hard all day.* **6.** Exact or complete, as in **dead center** or **dead end**

dead n. **1.** Those who have died: *The angel said to the women who came to the tomb looking for Jesus, "Why do you seek the living among the dead? He is not here, but is risen"* (Luke 24:5). *Jesus said, "Follow me and let the dead [spiritually dead] bury their dead [physically dead]"* (Matthew 8:22). **2. in the dead of** In the least active part of: *in the dead of winter*

dead adv. **1.** *infml.* Entirely: *dead wrong* **2.** *infml.* Immediately: *dead ahead*

dead-beat (dɛd–biʸt) n. **1.** One who doesn't pay his debts **2.** A lazy person

dead-en (dɛd–ən) v. To make weaker or less intense: *medicine to deaden the feeling*

dead-line (dɛd–laın) n. A time or date by which sthg. must be done: *I hope to finish this assignment before the deadline on December 15th.*

dead-lock (dɛd–lɑk) n. A disagreement which cannot be overcome; standstill

dead-ly (dɛd–liʸ) adj. **-lier, -liest** Likely to cause, or capable of causing death: *a deadly disease/weapon* **—deadliness** n.

deaf (dɛf) adj. **1.** Not able to hear at all or to hear well **2. turn a deaf ear** Unwilling to hear or listen: *The villain turned a deaf ear to her pleas for mercy.* **—deafness** n.

deaf-en (dɛf–ən) v. To cause to become deaf: *The mine worker had been deafened by an explo-*

sion in the mine.

deaf mute (def-mu^wt) n. One who can neither hear nor speak

deal (di^yl) v. **dealt** (dɛlt), **dealing 1.** To distribute playing cards to players in a game **2.** To give each person a share of sthg.: *Who's going to deal out the money?* **3. deal a blow** To strike: *He dealt her a blow that knocked her down.* **4. deal with sbdy./ sthg. (a)** To do business with: *This company has always dealt honestly with me.* **(b)** To take action concerning: *How do you deal with this problem?* **5.** To be concerned with: *This magazine article deals with the prevention of cancer.*

deal n. **1.** Any business or other arrangement that works to the advantage of both sides: *Now is the time to get a good deal on a used car.* **2.** An amount or degree, usu. large: *A great deal of money is spent each year on fighting crime.* **3.** The act of dealing cards to players in a card game **4. dirty/ raw deal** *infml.* Unfair treatment received

deal-er (di^yl–ər) n. **1.** One who is in a stated type of business: *a used-car dealer* **2.** A person who gives out playing cards in a game

deal-er-ship (di^yl–ər–ʃɪp) n. An agency that has authorization to sell a particular item in a certain area

dean (di^yn) n. An important officer in a school **(a)** Head of a faculty, division, college, or school in some universities: *Academic Dean* **(b)** A college or secondary school administrator in charge of counseling and disciplining students

dear (dɪər) adj. **1.** Greatly loved: *a dear mother* **2.** Highly esteemed or regarded **3.** Used at the beginning of a letter: *Dear Friends/ Dear Sir* **4.** BrE. Expensive: *It's much too dear. Do you have one that's less costly?* —compare CHEAP

dear n. One who is loved or has lovable characteristics: *She's always helping people. She's such a dear.*

dear-ly (dɪər–li^y) adv. **1.** With deep feeling, usu. loving feeling: *Mr. and Mrs. Wilson love each other dearly.* **2.** At extremely high cost in time, effort, pain, etc.: *He suffered dearly because of his crime.*

death (dɛθ) n. **1.** The end of life NOTE: There

are three kinds of death: physical, eternal and spiritual. **(a)** Physical/ temporal: *Yes, though I walk through the valley of the shadow of death, I will fear no evil, for you [Lord] are with me* (Psalm 23:4). *Jesus says, "Be faithful until death, and I will give you a crown of life"* (Revelation 2:10). **(b)** Spiritual: *Jesus said, "He who hears my word and believes in him who sent me has everlasting life, and shall not come into judgment, but is passed from death unto life"* (John 5:24). **(c)** Eternal: *The wages of sin is death [eternal death or eternal separation from God]* (Romans 6:23). **2. sudden death** *fig.* In football, if the score is tied at the end of the regulation time, the game goes into overtime. Whoever scores first is the winner. It is "sudden death" for the losing team.

death-bed (dɛθ–bɛd) n. The bed on which a person dies

death trap (dɛθ træp) A building, car, or a situation that is very dangerous: *The old mine was a real death trap.*

de-ba-cle (dɪ–bɑ–kəl) n. A sudden disastrous collapse or defeat

de-base (dɪ–be^ys) v. **-based, -basing** To lower in value or character; to degrade

de-bat-able (di^y–be^yt–ə–bəl) adj. Doubtful; questionable

de-bate (di^y–be^yt) v. **-bated, -bating 1.** To discuss opposing points **2.** To discuss or argue formally **3.** To consider

debate n. **1.** The act of debating: *The two presidential candidates will have a debate on TV next week.* **2.** A formal contest of argumentation in which two opposing teams defend and attack a given proposition

de-bauch (di^y–bɔtʃ) v. To lead into sinful forms of behavior, esp. in relation to sex and alcohol

de-bauch-er-y (di^y–bɔtʃ–ə–ri^y) n. Sinful behavior, esp. with regard to sex and alcohol: *Do not get drunk on wine, which leads to debauchery...* (Ephesians 5:18). *The acts of the sinful nature are obvious: sexual immorality, impurity and debauchery ... those who live like this will not inherit the kingdom of God* (Galatians 5:19-21). NOTE: God hates sin, but loves those who sin and wants all people to be

saved. He does not want anyone to perish. Because of his great love and mercy, he forgives those who repent of their sins and put their trust in Jesus for eternal life (Mark 1:15, Acts 16:31). —see FORGIVENESS, JESUS

de-bil-i-tate (dɪ–bɪl–ə–te^yt) v. -tated, -tating To make feeble or weak —**debilitating** adj. *a debilitating disease*

de-bil-i-ty (dɪ–bɪl–ə–ti^y) n. Feebleness

deb-it (dɛb–ət) n. An item of debt —**debit** To charge with a debt

deb-o-nair (dɛb–ə–neər) adj. **1.** Courteous and charming **2.** Pleasant and cheerful in dress and manners

de-brief (di^y –bri^yf) v. To gather information from one or more persons returning from a mission

de-bris (də–bri^y) n. Rubbish; the remains of sthg. broken or destroyed

debt (dɛt) n. Sthg. that is owed to sbdy.: *a debt of $500/ Let no debt remain outstanding, except the continuing debt to love one another* (Romans 13:8).

debt-or (dɛt–ər) n. One who owes money —compare CREDITOR

de-but (dɪ–byu^w/ de^y–byu^w/ de^y–byu^w) n. The first public appearance

deb-u-tante (dɛb–yu^w–tɑnt/ dɛb–yu^w–tɑnt) n. A young lady making her first public appearance in upper-class society

dec-ade (dɛk–e^yd) n. A period of ten years

dec-a-dence (dɛk–ə–dəns) n. A falling from a higher to a lower state; deterioration —**decadent** adj.

de-caf-fein-a-ted (dɪ–kæf–ɪ–ne^yt–əd) adj. Having the caffeine extracted: *decaffeinated coffee*

de-cal (dɪ–kæl/ di^y–kæl) n. **1.** The art or process of transferring pictures from specially prepared paper to glass, metal, etc. **2.** The paper bearing such a design

de-cal-ci-fy (dɪ–kæl–sə–faɪ) v. -fied, -fying To deprive of lime —**de-cal-ci-fi-ca-tion** (dɪ–kæl–sə–fə–ke^y–ʃən) n.

Dec-a-logue (dɛk–ə–lɔg/ –lɑg) n. see Ten Commandments

de-camp (dɪ–kæmp) v. **1.** To break up camp and depart **2.** To depart quickly and secretly

de-cant (dɪ–kænt) v. To pour gently so as not to disturb the sediment

de-can-ter (dɪ–kænt–ər) n. An ornamental bottle for wine, brandy, etc.

de-cap-i-tate (dɪ–kæp–ə–te^yt) v. -tated, -tating To behead —**de-cap-i-ta-tion** (dɪ–kæp–ə–te^y–ʃən) n.

de-cath-lon (dɪ–kæθ–lɑn/ –lən) n. An athletic contest in which the athletes compete in ten track and field events

de-cay (di^y–ke^y) v. **1.** To become or cause to become bad: *The old tree had begun to decay.* **2.** To decrease in health, power, etc.: *Most nations seem to decay by the end of two hundred years of their history.*

decay n. The condition, action, or result of decaying: *We could see decay all around us in the old house.*

de-cease (dɪ–si^ys) v. -ceased, -ceasing To die —**decease** n. Death

de-ceased (dɪ–si^yst) adj. **1.** Dead **2.** the deceased The dead person or persons

de-ce-dent (dɪ–si^yd–ənt) n. A dead person

de-ceit (dɪ–si^yt) n. *derog.* The quality of being dishonest

de-ceit-ful (dɪ–si^yt–fəl) adj. *derog.* Deceptive; dishonest —**deceitfully** adv. —**deceitfulness** n.

de-ceive (dɪ–si^yv) v. -ceive, -ceiving To trick someone into believing what is false or bad: *The shopkeeper deceived me. He told me this was a genuine diamond.* —**deceiver** n.

de-cel-er-ate (di^y–sɛl–ə–re^yt) v. -rated, -rating To slow down —**de-cel-er-a-tion** n. (di^y–sɛl–ə–re^y–ʃən)

De-cem-ber (dɪ–sɛm–bər) also **Dec.** *written abbr.* n. The 12th month of the year

de-cen-cy (di^y–sən–si^y) n. The quality of being socially proper

de-cent (di^y–sənt) adj. **1.** Socially acceptable; showing good taste in dress and behavior: *He and his friends are all decent young people./ decent behavior* —op-posite INDECENT **2.** *infml.* Good: *I hope you had a decent breakfast before coming to work.* **3.** *infml.* Helpful; kind: *It was really very decent of him to buy us all lunch.* —**decently** adv.

de-cen-tral-ize (di^y–sɛn–trə–laɪz) v. -ized, -izing **1.** To distribute authority and func-

tions over a wider area **2.** To redistribute population and industry from urban centers to outlying areas —**de-cen-tral-i-za-tion** (di^y–sɛn–trəl–ɪ–ze^y–ʃən/ –aɪ–ze^y–ʃən) n.

de-cep-tion (dɪ–sɛp–ʃən) n. An act of deceiving; a trick

de-cep-tive (dɪ–sɛp–tɪv) adj. Causing someone to be deceived; misleading

de-ci-bel (dɛs–ə–bəl) n. A unit of loudness of sound

de-cide (dɪ–saɪd) v. -**cided**, -**ciding** **1.** To reach an answer: *We decided to buy the house on the corner.* **2.** To choose or make a judgment: *The jury must decide whether he is guilty or not.* **3.** To cause a clear or definite end: *One touchdown in the fourth quarter decided the victory for our team.*

de-cid-u-ous (dɪ–sɪdʒ–u^w–əs) adj. **1.** Shedding leaves annually **2.** Falling off at a particular season or state of growth, as leaves, horns, etc.

dec-i-mal (dɛs–ə–məl) n. Numbers like .395, .02, 1.06, etc., based on the number ten: *A decimal always has a decimal point in it.*

dec-i-mate (dɛs–ə–me^{y}t) v. -**mated**, -**mating** To destroy a great number of

dec-i-me-ter (dɛs–ə–mi^{y}t–ər) n. A metric unit of length equal to one-tenth of a meter

de-ci-pher (dɪ–saɪ–fər) v. **1.** To make out the meaning of sthg. difficult to read **2.** To translate sthg. such as a code into understandable language

de-ci-sion (dɪ–sɪʒ–ən) n. A conclusion; a choice or judgment

de-ci-sive (dɪ–saɪ–sɪv) adj. **1.** Showing firmness in making decisions and sticking to them: *A successful businessman must be decisive in his actions.* **2.** Leading to a definite outcome: *It was a decisive victory which gave us the championship.* **3.** Unquestionable; unmistakable —opposite INDECISIVE —**decisively** adv. —**decisiveness** n.

deck (dɛk) n. **1.** The floor of a ship, usu. made of wood **2.** A surface similar to this: *the top deck of a double-deck bus* **3.** AmE. A pack of playing cards

dec-la-ra-tion (dɛk–lə–re^y–ʃən) n. The act of declaring: *a declaration of war*

de-clar-a-tive (dɪ–klær–ə–tɪv/ –klɛər–) adj.

Serving to declare: *a declarative sentence* Also **de-clar-a-to-ry** (dɪ–klær–ə–tɔr–i^y / klɛor–)

de-clare (dɪ–klɛər) v. -**clared**, -**claring** **1.** To announce publicly and officially: *England and France declared war on Germany in 1939.* **2.** To state or show emphatically so that there is no doubt: *Jesus was declared with power to be the Son of God by his resurrection from the dead* (Romans 1:4). **3.** To give a full listing of property for which one may owe tax or duty: *You will have to declare these items at Customs.*

de-clas-si-fy (di^y–klæs–ə–faɪ) v. -**fied**, -**fying** To remove the security classification from —**de-clas-si-fi-ca-tion** (di^y–klæs–ə–fɪ–ke^y–ʃən) n.

de-clen-sion (dɪ–klɛn–ʃən) n. **1.** The inflection of nouns, pronouns, and adjectives **2.** A slope **3.** Deterioration

de-cline (dɪ–klaɪn) v. -**clined**, -**clining** **1.** To move downward in position, influence, financial worth etc.: *The price of gold has declined steadily for the past year.* **2.** *fml.* To refuse an invitation, offer, etc., politely: *We offered them the use of our car for the weekend, but they declined the offer.*

decline n. A period of time during which sthg. is nearing its end: *the decline and fall of the Roman Empire*

de-cliv-i-ty (dɪ–klɪv–ə–ti^y) n. -**ties** A downward slope, as of the ground

de-code (di^y–ko^{w}d) v. -**coded**, -**coding** To translate a coded message into plain, ordinary language

de-com-mis-sion (di^y–kə–mɪʃ–ən) v. To retire (a ship) from active service

de-com-pose (di^y–kəm–po^{w}z) v. -**posed**, -**posing** **1.** To rot or decay **2.** To separate into parts or elements —**decomposed** adj. *decomposed granite*

de-con-ges-tant (di^y–kən–dʒɛs–tənt) n. An agent that relieves congestion, esp. in the nose

de-cor (de^y–kɔr) n. A style of decoration, as of a room or building

dec-o-rate (dɛk–ə–re^{y}t) v. -**rated**, -**rating** **1.** To adorn with sthg. beautiful or becoming, esp. for a special occasion: *We always deco-*

rate our Christmas tree with silver and gold ornaments. **2.** To paint or wallpaper the walls of a house and add other furnishings to make it more attractive: *It will be a challenge to decorate this old house.* **3.** To honor someone with an official medal or other mark

dec-o-ra-tion (dɛk–ə–reʸ–ʃən) n. **1.** The act of decorating **2.** An ornament; sthg. that adorns **3.** A medal or other sign of honor given to someone, esp. a military honor

dec-o-ra-tive (dɛk–ə–rə–tɪv) adj. Ornamental

dec-o-ra-tor (dɛk–ə–reʸ–tər) n. One who plans the decoration of a house, office, etc.: *We need an interior decorator for our office.*

de-cor-um (dɪ–kɔr–əm) n. **1.** Conformity to accepted standards of conduct **2.** Orderliness

de-cou-page also **dé-cou-page** (deʸ–kuʷ–paʒ) n. The art and craft of decorating surfaces by gluing paper cutouts on them

de-coy (diʸ–kɔɪ) n. **-coys 1.** A living or artificial animal used to entice game **2.** One who leads others into danger or a trap

de-crease (dɪ–kriʸs/ diʸ–kriʸs) v. **-creased, -creasing** To become or cause to become less in size, number, strength, value, etc.: *Our sales are decreasing.* —opposite IN-CREASE —decrease (diʸ–kriʸs) n.

de-cree (dɪ–kriʸ) n. **1.** An official command or order **2.** The judgment of a court

decree v. **-creed, -creeing** To give an official order which has the force of law

de-crep-it (dɪ–krɛp–ət) adj. Weakened by old age, illness or hard use

de-cry (dɪ–kraɪ) v. **-cried, -crying 1.** To express disapproval **2.** To condemn; find fault with

ded-i-cate (dɛd–ɪ–keʸt) v. **-cated, -cating 1.** To set apart for a special purpose: *They will dedicate the new church next Sunday.* **2.** To commit oneself fully to a particular task: *The doctor dedicated his life to finding a cure for that dreaded disease.* **3.** To inscribe (e.g. a book) to sbdy.

ded-i-cat-ed (dɛd–ɪ–keʸt–əd) adj. Committed to the fulfillment of an idea, purpose, etc.

ded-i-ca-tion (dɛd–ɪ–keʸ–ʃən) n. **1.** The act of dedicating **2.** The condition of being dedicated

de-duce (diʸ–duʷs) v. **-duced, -ducing 1.** To find out sthg. by putting together all that is known **2.** To trace the course of sthg. —de-du-ci-ble (dɪ–duʷ–sə–bəl) adj.

de-duct (dɪ–dʌkt) v. To subtract —deductible adj.

de-duc-tion (dɪ–dʌk–ʃən) n. **1.** The act of deducting; subtracting **2.** Sthg. that is or may be deducted **3. (a)** Reaching a conclusion by reasoning **(b)** The conclusion reached —deductive adj.

deed (diʸd) n. **1.** Sthg. that is done on purpose: *good deeds/ Let your light shine before men, that they may see your good deeds and praise your Father in heaven* (Matthew 5:16). *Command the rich ... to do good, to be rich in good deeds and to be generous and willing to share* (1 Timothy 6:17,18). **2.** A document or paper that is an official record of an agreement, esp. concerning ownership of land or a building: *Keep the deed to your house in a safe place.*

deem (diʸm) v. To think; judge

deep (diʸp) adj., adv. **1.** Going far down from the surface: *How deep is the swimming pool at this end?* **2.** Going a long way in from the outside or the front edge of sthg.: *a deep wound* **3.** Of a color, strong and definite: *Her eyes were a deep blue like the sky.* **4.** Strong and hard to change: *deep convictions* **5.** Severely damaging: *deep in trouble* **6.** Wise and serious: *a deep thinker* **7.** Very hard to understand and solve: *a deep mystery* **8. go off the deep end** *infml.* To carry one's ideas or actions to the extreme —deeply adv.

deep-en (diʸ–pən) v. To make deeper: *They had to deepen the well.*

deer (dɪər) n. *pl.* deer A four-footed animal known for its speed and grace, most types, esp. the males, having wide branching horns —sounds like DEAR

de-face (diʸ–feʸs) v. **-faced, -facing** To destroy or mar the surface of

de fac-to (diʸ fæk–toʷ/ deʸ–) adj. **1.** Actually exercising power **2.** Actually existing

de-fame (diʸ–feʸm) v. **-famed, -faming** To destroy or injure the reputation of sbdy. by slander —def-a-ma-tion (dɛf–ə–meʸ–ʃən) n. —de-fam-a-to-ry (dɪ–fæm–ə–tɔr–iʸ) adj.

de-fault (dɪ–fɔlt) n. **1.** Failure to do sthg. required by duty or by law **2.** Failure to com-

pete in a contest or game: *North High School didn't show up for the track meet, so our team won by default.*

de-feat (dɪ-fiᵞt) v. **1.** To win victory over; to beat **2.** To prevent the success of: *By saying the wrong thing, he defeated his own purpose.*

defeat n. **1.** The act of winning a victory over another: *Our team scored its final defeat this week, giving us the championship.* **2.** The act or state of being beaten by another: *This is our second defeat of the season. I hope we start winning a few games soon.* —compare VICTORY

de-fect (diᵞ-fɛkt/ dɪ-fɛkt) n. **1.** Lack of sthg. necessary or desirable **2.** An imperfection; a fault

de-fect (dɪ-fɛkt) v. To desert one's country, party, etc. in order to adopt another —**defector** n.

de-fec-tive (dɪ-fɛk-tɪv) adj. Having some imperfection; faulty

de-fend (dɪ-fɛnd) v. **1.** To protect from harm or attack: *The bridge is difficult to defend against an air attack./ Defend the cause of the poor and needy* (Proverbs 31:9). **2.** To argue in favor of sthg. which is being criticized: *to defend one's values* **3.** To act as a lawyer for sbdy. who has been accused and charged with a crime —compare PROSECUTE —**defen-si-ble** (dɪ-fɛn-sə-bəl) adj.

de-fend-ant (dɪ-fɛn-dənt) n. A person charged with a crime

de-fense *AmE.* **defence** *BrE.* (diᵞ-fɛns) n. **1.** The act of defending: *the defense of one's property* **2.** Weapons, methods, or other things used in defending sbdy. or sthg. **3.** The system of arguments used in defending a person charged with a crime: *The lawyer's defense of the defendant was well prepared.* **4.** In sports, the team that is trying to prevent the other team from scoring —**defenseless** adj. —**defensible** adj.

de-fen-sive (dɪ-fɛns-ɪv) adj. Of, intended, or done for defense: *defensive weapons* —opposite OFFENSIVE

defensive n. A position of being able to defend oneself against attack: *on the defensive* —**defensively** adv. —**defensiveness** n.

de-fer (dɪ-fɜr) v. **-ferred, -ferring 1.** To postpone; put off; delay: *Hope deferred makes the heart sick* (Proverbs 13:12). **2.** To yield to the opinion or wishes of another

def-er-ence (def-ər-əns) n. Courteous or respectful regard for another's wishes

de-fi-ance (dɪ-faɪ-əns) n. Willingness to resist; contempt of opposition

de-fi-ant (dɪ-faɪ-ənt) adj. Full of contempt; fearless and disrespectful —see DEFY

de-fi-cien-cy (dɪ-fɪʃ-ən-siᵞ) n. **-cies** A lack of sthg. necessary; the quality or state of being deficient: *a vitamin deficiency*

de-fi-cient (dɪ-fɪʃ-ənt) adj. Lacking sthg. necessary or important; insufficient; not having enough —**deficiently** adv.

def-i-cit (def-ə-sət) n. **1.** The amount by which a total falls short of what is needed **2.** An excess of expenditures over income

de-file (dɪ-faɪl) v. **-filed, -filing** To make dirty; to pollute: *Out of the heart proceed evil thoughts, murders, adulteries, fornications, thefts, false witness, blasphemies. These are the things which defile a man...* (Matthew 15:19,20 NKJV). —**defilement** n.

de-fine (dɪ-faɪn) v. **-fined, -fining 1.** To give the meaning(s) of a word or idea; describe exactly: *Many words are defined in this dictionary.* **2.** To indicate the edges or shape of: *a clearly defined shape* **3.** To describe the boundaries of —**definable** adj.

def-i-nite (def-ə-nət) adj. Clear in meaning, without any uncertainty: *We have set a definite time for our next meeting; it's Friday at two o'clock.* —opposite INDEFINITE —**definitely** adv.

def-i-ni-tion (def-ə-nɪ-ʃən) n. **1.** A precise statement of the meaning of sthg., esp. a word or phrase **2.** Distinctness of shape, color, or sound

de-fin-i-tive (dɪ-fɪn-ə-tɪv) adj. Quite fixed; final

de-flate (dɪ-fleᵞt) v. **-flated, -flating 1.** To release the air or gas from **2.** To reduce prices, etc. from an inflated condition **3.** To reduce a person's ego, hopes, etc. —**deflation** n.

de-flect (dɪ-flɛkt) v. To cause to turn aside: *He could have caught the ball if it hadn't been deflected.*

de-form (dɪ-fɔrm) v. **1.** To spoil the natural form or appearance of; disfigure **2.** To be-

come changed in shape —**deformed** adj.

de-form-i-ty (dɪ–fɔr–mə–ti^y) n. **1.** The condition of being deformed **2.** A part of the body that is deformed

de-fraud (dɪ–frɔd) v. To swindle; to cheat; to deceive so as to get or keep sthg. wrongly and usu. unlawfully: *The Bible says, "Do not defraud your neighbor or rob him"* (Leviticus 19:13). To defraud sbdy. is a sin, and God hates sin, and the wages of sin is eternal death. But God is rich in mercy, and because of his great love and mercy, he forgives those who repent of their sins and who trust in Jesus for eternal life. —see FORGIVENESS, JESUS

de-frost (dɪ–frɔst) v. To remove ice from; to thaw out: *She defrosted the meat by placing it in the microwave oven for a time.*

deft (dɛft) adj. Skillful —**deftly** adv. —**deftness** n.

de-funct (dɪ–fʌŋkt) adj. No longer in existence, operation, or use

de-fuse (di^y–fyu^wz) v. **-fused, -fusing 1.** To remove the fuse (as from a bomb) **2.** To make less harmful

de-fy (dɪ–faɪ) v. **-fied, -fying 1.** To show no fear of nor respect for: *Criminals defy the law./fig. The airplane seems to defy the law of gravity.* **2.** To urge someone, very strongly, to do sthg. thought to be impossible; dare; challenge: *I defy you to find a better typewriter for the price.*

deg. (dɪ–gri^yz) n. Short for degrees

de-gen-er-ate (dɪ–dʒɛn–ə–rət) adj. Having become worse in character, quality, etc. —**degen-e-ra-cy** (dɪ–dʒɛn–ə–rə–si^y) n.

degenerate (dɪ–dʒɛn–ə–rət) n. A degenerate person, esp. a sexual pervert

de-gen-e-rate (dɪ–dʒɛn–ə–re^yt) v. **-rated, -rating 1.** To pass from a higher to a lower condition; to deteriorate **2.** To become lower and lower mentally and morally —**de-gen-er-a-tion** (dɪ–dʒɛn–ər–e^y–ʃən) n.

de-grade (dɪ–gre^yd) v. **-graded, -grading** To lower in the opinion of others, in self-respect, or in behavior: *It was very degrading to be punished in front of the whole class.* —**degradable** adj. —**deg-ra-da-tion** (dɛ–grə–de^y–ʃən) n.

deg-ree (dɪ–gri^y) n. **1.** Any of various measures: *Water freezes at 32 degrees Fahrenheit (32°F) and boils at 212 degrees Fahrenheit.* **2.** Relative intensity: *third degree burns* **3.** 1/360th of a circle **4.** A unit of latitude or longitude: *The equator is zero degrees latitude, and Los Angeles is about 32 degrees north latitude.* **5.** A step or stage in an order of measuring ability, progress, etc.: *The class has reached a high degree of achievement in science.* **6.** A classification of a crime, according to its seriousness: *murder in the first degree* **7.** A title given by a university: *He has a Master's Degree in Education.*

de-hy-drate (di^y–haɪ–dre^yt) v. **-drated, -drating** To dry; to remove or lose water: *He was very dehydrated and near death after crossing the desert.* —**de-hy-dra-tion** (dɪ–haɪ–dre^y–ʃən) n.

de-ice (di^y–aɪs) v. **-iced, -icing** To remove the ice from sthg.

de-i-fy (di^y–ə–faɪ) v. **-fied, -fying 1.** To make a god of **2.** To worship; glorify

deign (de^yn) v. To do as a favor or to act as if doing a favor; condescend

de-ism (de^y–ɪz–əm) n. A system of thought advocating natural religion based on reason rather than divine revelation NOTE: God's word, the Bible, warns us against this, saying, "See to it that no one takes you captive through hollow and deceptive philosophy, which depends on human tradition and the basic principles of this world rather than on Christ" (Colossians 2:8). —see BIBLE, JESUS CHRIST, DEITY

de-i-ty (di^y–ə–ti^y) n. **-ties** A god or goddess: *Christians believe in the deity of Christ, that he is true God and Savior of the world./ For in Christ all the fullness of the Deity lives in bodily form* (Colossians 2:9). —see JESUS

de-ject-ed (dɪ–dʒɛk–təd) adj. Sad; depressed; disheartened —**dejectedly** adv. —**dejection** n.

de-lay (dɪ–le^y) v. **-layed, -laying 1.** To put off to a later time: *We decided to delay going on our vacation./ When you make a vow to God, do not delay in fulfilling it* (Ecclesiastes 5:4). **2.** To stop for a while, move slowly, or in some other way cause lateness: *We were delayed by the snow blocking the road.*

delay n. **-lays** The act of delaying or the state

of being delayed: *Let's not have any delay get-ling this job done*

de-lec-ta-ble (dɪ-**lek**-tə-bəl) adj. **1.** Delightful **2.** Delicious

del-e-gate (**del**-ə-gət) n. A person acting as a representative for one or more others at a meeting or in an organization

del-e-gate (**del**-ə-ge^{y}t) v. **-gated, -gating** To entrust a task, power, responsibility, etc. to another person

del-e-ga-tion (del-ə-**ge**^{y}-ʃən) n. **1.** The act of delegating or the state of being delegated **2.** A group of delegates

de-lete (dɪ-**li**^{y}t) v. **-leted, -leting** To take or cut out sthg. written or printed —**deletion** n.

del-e-te-ri-ous (del-ə-**trər**-i^y-əs) adj. Harmful

del-i (**del**-i^y) n. **-is** *AmE*. **1.** Short for **delicatessen 2.** The food sold in a delicatessen

de-lib-er-ate (dɪ-**lɪb**-ər-ət) adj. **1.** On purpose **2.** Of speech or movement, slow, unhurried, and steady —**deliberately** adv.

de-lib-er-ate (dɪ-**lɪb**-ə-re^{y}t) v. **-ated, -ating** To think over or discuss carefully before reaching a decision —**de-lib-er-a-tion** (dɪ-lɪb-ə-**re**^{y}-ʃən) n. —**de-lib-er-a-tive** (dɪ-**lɪb**-ə-re^y-trv) adj.

del-i-ca-cy (**del**-ɪ-kə-si^y) n. **-cies 1.** The quality of being delicate **2.** A choice food

del-i-cate (**del**-ɪ-kət) adj. **1.** Finely made: *My grandmother's china dishes were very delicate.* **2.** Needing careful treatment because of being easily broken or hurt: *a delicate child/ a delicate situation* **3.** Pleasing to the senses but not strong and not easy to recognize: *a delicate flavor* **4.** Sensitive; able to distinguish very slight changes: *a delicate instrument* —**delicately** adv.

del-i-ca-tes-sen (del-ɪ-kə-**tes**-ən) n. A shop that sells freshly prepared foods ready for serving

de-li-cious (dɪ-**lɪʃ**-əs) adj. Giving pleasure to one's senses, esp. the sense of taste: *What a delicious dessert!* —**deliciously** adv.

de-light (dɪ-**lart**) v. To bring deep satisfaction and joy: *Delight yourself in the Lord and he will give you the desires of your heart* (Psalm 37:4). *The Lord detests lying lips, but he delights in men who are truthful* (Proverbs 12:22). —**delighted** adj.

delight n. Sthg. that gives great pleasure or enjoyment: *Blessed is the man who does not walk in the counsel of the wicked... but his delight is in the law of the Lord* (Psalm 1:1,2). —**delightful** adj. —**delightfully** adv. —**delightfulness** n.

de-lim-it (dɪ-**lɪm**-ət) v. To fix the limits of sthg.

de-lin-e-ate (dɪ-**lɪ**^{y}n-i^y-e^{y}t) v. **-ated, -ating 1.** To sketch in outline **2.** To describe precisely in words

de-lin-quent (dɪ-**lɪŋ**-kwənt) adj. **1.** Having committed an offense or having failed to perform a duty **2.** Past due, such as a debt

delinquent n. A delinquent person —**de-lin-quen-cy** (dɪ-**lɪŋ**-kwən-si^y) n.

de-lir-i-ous (dɪ-**lɪər**-i^y-əs) adj. **1.** Suffering from or caused by delirium **2.** Wildly excited

de-lir-i-um (dɪ-**lɪər**-i^y-əm) n. Violent restlessness, often caused by fever, characterized by wandering speech and hallucinations

de-lir-i-um tre-mens (dɪ-**lɪər**-i^y-əm **tri**^{y}-mənz) n. A form of acute insanity caused by excessive use of alcohol and characterized by terrifying delusions and trembling

de-liv-er (dɪ-**lɪv**-ər) v. **1.** To take things to someone's house or business: *We will deliver your living room furniture today.* **2.** To give; hand over: *He [Jesus] was delivered over to death for our sins and raised to life for our justification* (Romans 4:25). **3.** To free from; rescue: *I sought the Lord and he heard me; he delivered me from all my fears* (Psalm 34:4). **4.** To assist in the birth of: *The policeman had to deliver the baby; the mother couldn't make it to the hospital.* **5.** To read or give a speech: *The speaker delivered his speech eloquently.*

de-liv-er-ance (dɪ-**lɪv**-rəns/ dɪ-**lɪv**-ə-rəns) n. *fml.* The act of saving from danger or freeing from a bad situation; the state of being saved from danger: *A horse is a vain hope for deliverance... But the eyes of the Lord are on those who fear him, on those who hope in his unfailing love, to deliver them from death and keep them alive in famine* (Psalm 33:17).

de-liv-er-y (dɪ-**lɪv**-ər-i^y) n. **-ies 1.** The act of taking sthg. to somebody's house or business: *We offer free delivery to all our regular custom-*

ers. **2.** The birth of a child: *The mother had a difficult delivery.* **3.** The act or style of giving a speech or of throwing a ball in a game

dell (dɛl) n. A small valley

del-phin-i-um (dɛl–fɪn–ɪ–əm) n. A garden plant cultivated for its showy blue flowers

del-ta (dɛl–tə) n. **1.** The fourth letter of the Greek alphabet **2.** A triangular patch of land accumulated at the mouth of a river between two or more of its branches

de-lude (dɪ–luᵂd) v. **-luded, -luding** To deceive

del-uge (dɛl–uᵂdʒ) n. **1.** A great flood **2. the Deluge** The great flood in the days of Noah when, because of the corruption and violence that filled the earth, God destroyed the earth and all human life except for Noah, who walked with God, and his family, eight people in all (Genesis 6:1-8:19). **3.** Anything coming in a great rush: *a deluge of questions*

de-lu-sion (dɪ–luᵂ–ʒən) n. **1.** A false belief or opinion **2.** A persistent false belief that is a symptom or form of madness

de-luxe (dɪ–lʌks) adj. Exceptionally luxurious or elegant

delve (dɛlv) v. **delved, delving** To search deeply and laboriously

de-mag-ne-tize (diʸ–mæg–nə–taɪz) v. To deprive of magnetism

dem-a-gogue or **dem-a-gog** (dɛm–ə–gɑg) n. A political leader who appeals to the passions and prejudices of the people for his own political advancement

de-mand (dɪ–mænd) n. **1.** An act of demanding or asking, esp. with authority **2.** The desire of people for goods or services: *Is there much demand for teachers in this city?* **3.** A seeking or being sought after: *That speaker is in great demand.*

demand v. To claim very strongly: *I demand an answer.*

de-mand-ing (dɪ–mæn–dɪŋ) adj. Needing a lot of effort or attention: *This is a very demanding job.*

de-mean (dɪ–miʸn) v. To lower in dignity or standing

de-mean-or (dɪ–miʸ–nər) n. Conduct —compare MISDEMEANOR

de-ment-ed (dɪ–mɛn–təd) adj. Crazy; mad; of unbalanced mind

de-mer-it (dɪ–mɛr–ət) n. **1.** A fault; a defect **2.** A mark against a person's school record

dem-i-god (dɛm–ɪ–gɑd) n. **1.** An inferior god **2.** A deified human being NOTE: There is only one true God and we are to worship and serve only him (Matthew 4:10). —see GOD, JESUS, HOLY SPIRIT

de-mise (dɪ–maɪz) n. *fml.* Death

de-mo-bi-lize (diʸ–moᵂ–bɪ–laɪz) v. **-lized, -lizing 1.** To disband troops **2.** To change from a state of war to a state of peace

de-moc-ra-cy (dɪ–mɑk–rə–siʸ) n. **-cies 1.** A government that has elected representatives **2.** A country that is governed by its people or their elected representatives

dem-o-crat (dɛm–ə–kræt) n. **1.** A person who believes in or works for democracy **2. Democrat** A member of the Democratic party in the US

dem-o-crat-ic (dɛm–ə–kræt–ɪk) adj. **1.** Of, like, or supporting democracy **2.** In accordance with the principle of equal rights for all —**democratically** adv.

de-mol-ish (dɪ–mɑl–ɪʃ) v. To destroy; knock down: *They plan to demolish all the old buildings and build a new mall./ spir.The weapons we fight with [in this spiritual warfare] have divine power to demolish strongholds. We demolish arguments and every pretension [such as evolution] that sets itself up against the knowledge of God, and we take captive ev-ery thought and make it obedient to Christ* (2 Corinthians 10:4,5). —**de-mo-li-tion** (dɛm–əl–ɪ–ʃən) n.

de-mon (diʸ–mən) n. **1.** A devil or evil spirit NOTE: This word, in the Bible, usually refers to inferior spiritual beings, angels who rebelled against God and kept not their first estate (Matthew 25:41; Revelation 12:7,9), the ministers of the devil (Luke 4:35; 9:1; John 10:21). Satan is called the prince of devils (Matthew 9:34; 12:24; Mark 3:22; Luke 11:15). Demons (evil spirits) sometimes enter the body of a person to torment him (Matthew 9:33; 17:14-18). Jesus Christ drove out many demons (Mark 1:34) and gave his apostles authority to do likewise

(Mark 3:15), and they did so (Mark 6:13). **see** DEVIL, —**de-mon-ic** (dɪ-**man**-ɪk) adj. **2.** One who is very zealous in a particular skill: *He works/plays ball/fights like a demon.*

de-mo-ni-ac (dɪ-**mo**ʷ-niʸ-æk) n. Someone under the influence of one or more demons

de-mon-stra-ble (dɪ-**man**-strə-bəl) adj. That which can be demonstrated —**demonstrably** adv.

de-mon-strate (**dɛm**-ən-streʸt) v. -**strated**, -**strating** **1.** To show exactly: *Could you please demonstrate how to put this bicycle together?* **2.** To prove or clarify, esp. by giving many reasons and examples: *It can be demonstrated that the earth is round simply by looking at the horizon from the shore of the ocean.* **3.** To participate in a public show of strong feeling, esp. by marching, shouting, carrying banners, etc.: *They demonstrated against the use of pesticides.* —**demonstrator** n.

dem-on-stra-tion (dɛm-ən-**stre**ʸ-ʃən) n. **1.** The act of demonstrating **2.** A public show of strong feeling, often with marching, big signs, etc.: *a demonstration in favor of aid for the homeless*

de-mon-stra-tive (dɪ-**man**-strə-tɪv) adj. **1.** Showing one's feeling openly: *a demonstrative child* **2.** Serving to show, prove, or illustrate **3.** *Gram.* A word indicating the thing referred to: *In the sentence, "This is my book, that is yours," "this" and "that"are demonstratives.*

de-mor-al-ize (dɪ-**mor**-ə-laɪz) v. -**ized**, -**izing** To take away the confidence of

de-mote (dɪ-**mo**ʷt) v. -**moted**, **moting** To reduce to a lower rank or grade —**demotion** n.

de-mur (dɪ-**mər**) v. -**rr**- To object

de-mure (dɪ-**myvər**) adj. **1.** Shy and modest **2.** Quiet and serious or pretending to be so —**demurely** adv.

den (dɛn) n. **1.** The home of a fierce wild animal, esp. a lion: *fig. a den of thieves* **2.** *AmE.* A room in a house specially arranged for studying, resting, watching TV, etc. **3.** A small secluded room used as a hide-out for an illegal activity **4.** A unit of about 8 to 10 Boy Scouts

de-ni-al (dɪ-**naɪ**-əl) n. **1.** A negative reply, as to a request **2.** Refusal to grant the truth of a statement **3.** **self-denial** Sacrifice of one's own comfort or gratification —**see** DENY

den-i-grate (**dɛn**-ə-greʸt) v. -**grated**, -**grating** **1.** To attack one's reputation **2.** To belittle

den-im (**dɛn**-əm) n. **1.** A strong cotton fabric used for making clothes **2. denims** Trousers made of denim

den-i-zen (**dɛn**-ɪ-zən) n. An inhabitant

de-nom-i-na-tion (dɪ-nam-ə-neʸ-ʃən) n. **1.** A name or title **2.** A value, as of a coin **3.** A group of people having the same religious beliefs —**denominational** adj.

de-nom-i-na-tor (dɪ-**nam**-ə-neʸ-tər) n. **1.** The part of a fraction that is below the line **2.** A characteristic or quality held in common

de-note (dɪ-**no**ʷt) v. To mean; be a sign of —**de-no-ta-tion** (diʸ-noʷ-teʸ-ʃən) n.

de-nounce (dɪ-**naʊns**) v. -**nounced**, -**nouncing** **1.** To speak publicly against **2.** To give information against **3.** To announce that one is ending a treaty or agreement

dense (dɛns) adj. **1.** Closely packed or crowded: *dense traffic* **2.** Hard to see through: *a dense fog/ fig. a dense book* **3.** Stupid: *He's a rather dense person.* —**densely** adv. *a densely populated area* —**denseness** n.

den-si-ty (**dɛn**-sɪ-tiʸ) n. -**ties** **1.** The quality or state of being dense **2.** The quantity of sthg. per unit of area, volume, or length: *Hong Kong has a population density of more than 14,000 per square mile.*

dent (dɛnt) n. A depression or hollow place in the surface of sthg., caused by a blow or pressure: *a dent in a car*

den-tal (**dɛn**-təl) adj. Having to do with teeth: *dental technician*

den-ti-frice (**dɛn**-tɪ-frəs) n. A powder, paste, or liquid for cleaning the teeth

den-tist (**dɛn**-təst) n. A person who is professionally trained to treat the teeth and gums —**dentistry** n.

den-ture (**dɛn**-tʃər) n. often plural Set of false teeth

de-nude (diʸ-**nu**ʷd) v. -**nuded**, -**nuding** To make bare; to strip: *The fields of grain were denuded by the locusts.*

de-nun-ci-a-tion (diʸ-nʌn-sɪ-eʸ-ʃən) n. —**see** DENOUNCE

de-ny (dɪ-**naɪ**) v. -nied, -nying 1. To answer in the negative: *A servant girl saw him [Peter] ...and said, "This man was with him [Jesus]," But he denied it. "Woman, I don't know him," he said* (Luke 22:56,57). 2. To refuse to accept as true: *Who is the liar? It is the man who denies that Jesus is the Christ — he denies the Father and the Son. No one who denies the Son has the Father; whoever acknowledges the Son has the Father also* (1 John 2:22,23). —compare AFFIRM, ADMIT 3. To keep sthg. from sbdy.: *Do not deny justice to your poor people in their law suits* (Exodus 23:6). 4. *fml.* To refuse to accept connection with or responsibility for: *Jesus said, "Whoever denies me before men, him will I also deny before my Father in heaven"* (Matthew 10:33). 5. **to deny oneself** To sacrifice one's own comfort or gratification: *Jesus said, "If anyone would come after me, he must deny himself and take up his cross [of self-sacrifice] daily and follow me"* (Luke 9:23). —see DENIAL

de-o-dor-ant (diᵞ-**o**ʷd-ə-rənt) n. A preparation that removes or hides unpleasant odors

de-o-dor-ize (diᵞ-**o**ʷd-ə-raɪz) v. -ized, -izing To rid of unpleasant odor

de-part (dɪ-**part**) v. 1. To leave; go away: *The train departed from the station at 12 noon.* 2. *spir.* To leave this world: *St. Paul wrote: "I desire to depart and be with Christ [in heaven], which is better by far [than remaining on earth]"* (Philippians 1:23).

de-part-ment (dɪ-**part**-mənt) n. A major division or branch of a government, business, etc.: *the English department of a university/ the furniture department at the department store* —**de-part-men-tal** (dɪ-part-**men**-təl) adj.

de-par-ture (dɪ-**par**-tʃər) n. The action of departing: *What is the departure time of flight 602?*

de-pend (dɪ-**pend**) v. 1. To trust: *We're depending on you to finish the job by sunset.* 2. **depend on/ upon (a)** To be supported by: *She depends on her children for support.* (b) To happen because of sthg. else: *My plans for the summer depend on whether or not I am accepted by the university.*

de-pend-a-ble (dɪ-**pen**-də-bəl) adj. Reliable; able to be depended on —**dependably** adv. —**de-pend-a-bil-i-ty** (dɪ-pen-də-**bil**-ə-tiᵞ) n.

de-pend-ence (dɪ-**pen**-dəns) n. 1. The quality or state of being materially supported by another person 2. The need to have sthg., esp. certain drugs regularly

de-pen-dent (dɪ-**pen**-dənt) n. Someone who depends on another for food, clothing, shelter, etc.: *How many dependents do you have?*

dependent adj. Depending on sthg. else: *Her finishing college is dependent on the grades she gets.*

de-pict (dɪ-**pɪkt**) v. 1. To represent by a picture 2. To describe —depiction n.

de-plane (diᵞ-**ple**ᵞn) v. -planed, -planing To get off an airplane

de-plete (dɪ-**pli**ᵞt) v. -pleted, -pleting To make smaller in amount: *After a few days in the hospital, his funds were completely depleted.*

de-plore (dɪ-**plɔr**) v. -plored, -ploring 1. To feel or express strong disapproval of 2. To feel or express deep sorrow over —**deplorable** adj. Regrettable; very bad

de-ploy (dɪ-**plɔɪ**) v. -ployed, -ploying To place in position ready for action

de-pop-u-late (diᵞ-**pap**-yə-leᵞt) v. -lated, -lating To reduce greatly the number of people in an area —depopulated adj.

de-port (dɪ-**pɔrt**) v. To force someone out of the country by legal action —**de-por-ta-tion** (diᵞ-pɔr-teᵞ-ʃən) n.

de-port-ment (dɪ-**pɔrt**-mənt) n. 1. Behavior 2. The way of carrying or holding oneself; bearing

de-pose (dɪ-**po**ʷz) v. -posed, -posing To remove from a high position, esp. a king from his throne

de-pos-it (dɪ-**paz**-ɪt) v. 1. To place in a bank or safe: *He deposited a lot of money in the bank yesterday.* 2. To put down or unload: *Mud and sand are being deposited at the mouth of the river all the time.* 3. To give money as partial payment or security

deposit n. 1. Sthg. deposited by a natural process: *We discovered that there was a rich deposit of oil under our land.* 2. Partial payment of money to hold sthg. for purchase so it can't be sold to someone else: *We paid a $1,000 deposit on the house at the corner of Elm*

and Main.

de·po·si·tion (dɛp–ə–zɪʃ–ən) n. **1.** Removal from an office or position **2.** The act or process of depositing **3.** Sthg. deposited

de·pos·i·to·ry (dɪ–pɑz–ə–tɔr–iʸ) n. **-ries** A place where anything is deposited

de·pot (diʸ–poʷ) n. A railroad or bus station

de·praved (dɪ–preʸvd) adj. Spiritually corrupt; wicked: *Since the first man, Adam, fell into sin and lost the image of God, (the holy nature with which he was created), all people have been born in sin. By nature we are evil and corrupt, depraved, worthy of nothing but everlasting punishment. "Since they [people] did not think it worthwhile to retain the knowledge of God, he gave them over to a depraved mind, to do what ought not to be done"* (Romans 1:28). NOTE: Nevertheless, God loves us so much that he sent his one and only Son into the world to suffer and die for us and to pay for all our sins with his own blood. He died and was buried. But, the third day he rose again from the dead. Forty days later he returned to heaven to prepare a place for all those who turn from their evil ways and put their trust in him for everlasting life. —see JESUS, MAN, SIN

de·prav·i·ty (dɪ–præv–ə–tiʸ) n. **-ties** Spiritual corruption: *They [people] have become filled with every kind of wickedness, evil, greed and depravity* (Romans 1:29). —see SIN, DEPRAVED

de·pre·ci·ate (dɪ–priʸ–ʃiʸ–eʸt) v. **-ated, -ating** (esp. of money, property, possessions, etc.) To go down in value —opposite APPRECIATE —**de·pre·ci·a·tion** (dɪ–priʸ–ʃiʸ–eʸ–ʃən) n.

de·press (dɪ–prɛs) v. **1.** To cause to become sad or discouraged: *Rainy weather always depresses me.* **2.** To weaken: *This part of the city has been depressed because of industries moving out of the area.* **3.** *fml.* To press down —**depressing** adj. —**depressingly** adv.

de·pressed (dɪ–prɛst) adj. **1.** Saddened and discouraged **2.** Experiencing a bad economy: *depressed nations*

de·pres·sion (dɪ–prɛʃ–ən) n. **1.** Dejection; a deep feeling of discouragement: *She suffered a deep depression after the loss of her mother.* **2.**

A period of low general economic activity, esp. with high unemployment: *There was a great depression in the 1930s.*

de·prive (dɪ–praɪv) v. **-prived, -priving** To withhold sthg. or take it away from someone: *They deprived the immigrants of their rights.* —**de·pri·va·tion** (dɛp–rə–veʸ–ʃən) n.

de·prived (dɪ–praɪvd) adj. (esp. of people) Lacking the essentials of life such as food, money, etc.

depth (dɛpθ) n. **1.** The state of being deep; distance from the top of sthg. to the bottom or from front to back: *The depth of the pool at this end is eight feet.* **2. in depth** Done very thoroughly: *an in-depth study of the subject*

dep·u·ta·tion (dɛp–yə–teʸ–ʃən) n. Persons chosen and sent to speak and act for others

dep·u·tize (dɛp–yə–taɪz) v. **-tized, -tizing** To act as a deputy; to take another's place for a time

dep·u·ty (dɛp–yə–tiʸ) n. **-ties** A person who has been authorized to act for another: *While the sheriff was ill, his deputy handled the job very well.*

de·rail (dɪ–reʸl/ diʸ–) v. To cause a railroad train to leave the rails —**derailment** n.

de·range (dɪ–reʸndʒ) v. **-ranged, -ranging** To put out of place or out of working order

de·ranged (dɪ–reʸndʒd) adj. Out of one's mind; insane

der·by (dɑr–biʸ) n. **-bies 1.** A horse race, usu. for three-year-olds, held annually: *The Kentucky Derby* **2.** A race open to all contestants **3.** A stiff felt hat with a round crown and a narrow brim

der·e·lict (dɛər–ə–lɪkt) adj. **1.** Left or abandoned, as by the owner: *a derelict ship* **2.** Negligent of duty

derelict n. A homeless or jobless person

der·e·lic·tion (dɛər–ə–lɪk–ʃən) n. **1.** Willful failure or neglect, as of duty **2.** Abandonment

de·ride (dɪ–raɪd) v. **-rided, -riding** To laugh at; mock; make fun of, as having no value: *A man who lacks judgment derides his neighbor, but a man of understanding holds his tongue* (Proverbs 11:12).

de·ri·sion (dɪ–rɪʒ–ən) n. The act of deriding, or the state of being derided —**de·ri·sive** (dɪ–

rar–srv) adj.

de-rive (dɪ–**rarv**) v. **-rived, -riving 1.** To receive or obtain from: *to derive satisfaction* **2.** To trace back to the beginning of its existence —**der-i-va-tion** (dɛər–ə–**ve**ʸ–ʃən) n.

de-riv-a-tive (dɪ–**rɪv**–ə–tɪv) n., adj. Sthg. that has its origin in sthg. else: *"Monotonous" is a derivative of the Greek word "monotonos."*

der-ma-ti-tis (dɔr–mə–**taɪt**–ɪs) n. Inflammation of the skin

de-rog-a-to-ry (dɪ–**rɑg**–ə–tɔr–iʸ) adj. Disrespectful; causing harm to one's reputation

der-rick (**dɛər**–ɪk) n. **1.** A large crane for lifting and moving heavy objects **2.** A tall framework over the opening of an oil well, used to support equipment

der-vish (**dɔr**–vɪʃ) n. A member of any of various Muslim orders, some of whom express their devotion by whirling, howling, etc.

des-cant (**dɛs**–kænt) n. **1.** A discussion or a series of remarks **2.** *Music* **(a)** A counterpoint above the basic melody **(b)** The upper part in part music

de-scend (dɪ–**sɛnd**) v. To move from a higher to a lower level; go down: *We reached our destination just as the sun descended behind the hills./ He had difficulty descending the shaky ladder.* —opposite ASCEND

de-scend-ant (dɪ–**sɛn**–dənt) n. **1.** A person who has another as grandfather or grandmother, great-grandfather, etc.: *He's a descendant of William Penn.* **2. descended from** Having another as a parent, grandparent, etc. —compare ANCESTOR

de-scent (dɪ–**sɛnt**) n. **1.** The act of going or coming down: *The road makes a sharp descent just before reaching the river.* —opposite ASCENT **2.** Family origin; lineage: *She's of Spanish descent.*

de-scribe (dɪ–**skraɪb**) v. **-scribed, -scribing** To tell in oral or written form what sthg. is like: *Can you describe what the thief looked like?*

de-scrip-tion (dɪ–**skrɪp**–ʃən) n. **1.** An account that describes **2.** The act of describing: *The latest issue of the magazine gave a good description on the rain forests of Brazil.* —**descriptive** adj.

des-e-crate (**dɛs**–ə–kreʸt) v. **-crated, -crating** To treat sthg. sacred with contempt or disrespect: *They desecrated the temple.*

des-ert (**dɛz**–ərt) n. A large sandy piece of land where there is very little rain and few, if any, plants: *the Sahara Desert/ Better to live in a desert than with a quarrelsome and ill-tempered wife* (Proverbs 21:19).

de-sert (dɪ–**zɜrt**) v. **1.** To leave without intending to return: *He deserted his wife two years ago, and she hasn't seen or heard from him since then.* **2.** To be absent from military service without permission: *He deserted the army.*

de-sert-er (dɪ–**zɜr**–tər) n. A person who leaves military service without permission

de-serve (dɪ–**zɜrv**) v. **-served, -serving** To be worthy of or suitable for: *You've been working all night. You deserve a rest./ He [God] does not treat us as our sins deserve or repay us according to our iniquities. As far as the east is from the west, so far has he removed our transgressions from us* (Psalm 103:10,12).

de-sign (dɪ–**zaɪn**) n. **1.** A plan for doing or making sthg., etc. **2.** A drawing showing how sthg. is to be made **3.** The art of making such drawings: *She had hoped to attend a school of dress design.*

design v. **1.** To draw the plans for sthg.: *He designs office buildings.* **2.** To conceive and develop for a certain use: *a house designed for a large family* —**designer** n. *She's a dress designer.*

des-ig-nate (**dɛz**–ɪg–neʸt) v. **-nated, -nating 1.** To point out the location of: *These marks on the drawing designate all the electrical outlets in the building.* **2.** To set apart for special work: *I've been designated by the principal to act for him while he is away.* —**des-ig-na-tion** (dɛz–ɪg–**ne**ʸ–ʃən) n.

de-sir-a-ble (dɪ–**zaɪr**–ə–bəl/ –**zaɪ**–ər–) adj. Having pleasing characteristics; worthy: *A good name [reputation] is more desirable than great riches; to be esteemed is better than silver or gold* (Proverbs 22:1). —opposite UNDESIRABLE —**de-sir-a-bil-i-ty** (dɪ–zaɪr–ə–**bɪl**–ə–tiʸ/ –zaɪ–ər–) n.

de-sire (dɪ–**zaɪr**/ –**zaɪ**–ər–) v. **-sired, -siring** To long for: *Wisdom is more precious than rubies, and nothing you desire can compare with her* (Proverbs 8:11).

desire n. A strong wish for sthg.: *Delight yourself in the Lord and he will give you the desires of your heart* (Psalm 37:4). *The desire of the righteous ends only in good* (Proverbs 11:23). —**de-sir-ous** (dɪ–zaɪr–əs/–zaɪ–ər–) adj.

desk (dɛsk) n. A table, often with drawers, at which one writes, studies or does business

des-o-late (dɛs–ə–lət) adj. **1.** Deserted; abandoned; empty of people **2.** Forsaken; lonely **3.** Barren; lifeless **4.** Cheerless; gloomy

des-o-la-tion (dɛs–ə–leʸ–ʃən) n. **1.** Ruin; devastation **2.** A barren wasteland **3.** Grief; sadness **4.** Loneliness

de-spair (dɪ–speər) v. To lose all hope or confidence: *He despaired of finishing his work before the weekend.* —**despairing** adj. —**despairingly** adv.

despair n. Complete hopelessness: *filled with despair over the loss of a loved one*

des-per-ate (dɛs–pər–ət) adj. **1.** Having become hopeless or almost beyond all hope: *He was desperate for work to provide food for his family.* **2.** Of an action, using extreme measures as a last attempt: *a last desperate effort to save the drowning man* **3.** Of a state of affairs, extremely difficult: *The family was in a desperate state after their home was destroyed.* —**desperately** adv. —**des-per-a-tion** (dɛs–pə–reʸ–ʃən) n.

des-pi-ca-ble (dɛs–pɪk–ə–bəl) adj. That which is to be despised; contemptible

de-spise (dɪ–spaɪz) v. -spised, -spising To look down on with contempt; to hate; detest; regard as worthless: *Fools despise wisdom and discipline* (Proverbs 1:7).

de-spite (dɪ–spaɪt) prep. Even though; in spite of: *He went to school despite his illness.* (=*even though he was ill*)

de-spond-en-cy (dɪ–spɑn–dən–siʸ) n. -cies Depression from loss of courage or hope

de-spond-ent (dɪ–spɑn–dənt) adj. Downhearted; dejected

des-pot (dɛs–pət) n. **1.** A ruler who uses power unjustly or cruelly **2.** Any tyrant or oppressor —**des-pot-ic** (dɛs–pɑt–ɪk) adj. —**des-po-tism** (dɛs–pə–tɪz–əm) n.

des-sert (dɪ–zɜrt) n. Food served at the end of a meal, usu. sweet: *I'd like a big piece of chocolate cake for dessert, please.*

des-ti-na-tion (dɛs–tə–neʸ–ʃən) n. A place to which a person or thing is traveling or is sent: the end of a journey: *The destination of Flight 777 is Paris, France.*

des-tine (dɛs–tɪn) v. To set apart for a certain use

des-tined (dɛs–tɪnd) adj. **1.** Intended for some special purpose: *He was destined by his parents for a life on the stage.* **2.** To be directed toward or headed for; certain to happen: *Just as man is destined to die once, and after that to face judgment, so Christ was sacrificed once to take away the sins of many people; and he will appear a second time... to bring salvation to those who are waiting for him* (Hebrews 9:27,28).

des-ti-ny (dɛs–tə–niʸ) n. -nies That which must or had to happen: *Death is the destiny of every man* (Ecclesiastes 7:2). *Many live as the enemies of the cross of Christ. Their destiny is destruction, their god is their stomach, and their glory is in their shame* (Philippians 3:19). *But those who repent of their sins and put their trust in Jesus for eternal life will be saved* (Mark 1:15 ; Acts 16:31).

des-ti-tute (dɛs–tə–tuʷt) adj. **1.** Having no food, clothing, shelter, or money **2.** Deprived or lacking: *Speak up for those who cannot speak for themselves, for the rights of all who are destitute* (Proverbs 31:8).

de-stroy (dɪ–strɔɪ) v. -stroyed, -stroying To ruin entirely; put sthg. out of existence: *The fire destroyed six homes./ fig. All hopes of a peaceful settlement were destroyed by his angry speech./ Job said, "I know that my Redeemer lives, and that in the end he will stand upon the earth. And after my skin has been destroyed, yet in my flesh I will see God"* (Job 19:25,26). *[Jesus] has destroyed death and has brought life and immortality to light through the gospel* (2 Timothy 1:10).

de-stroy-er (dɪ–strɔɪ–ər) n. **1.** A person who destroys sthg. **2.** A small, very fast warship

de-struc-tion (dɪ–strʌk–ʃən) n. The act of destroying or state of being destroyed: *the destruction of the forest by fire/ Pride goes before destruction, a haughty spirit before a fall* (Proverbs 16:18). *They [those who do not know God and do not obey the gospel of our Lord Jesus*

Christ] will be punished with everlasting destruction and shut out from the presence of the Lord... on the day he comes to be glorified in his holy people and to be marveled at among all those who have believed (2 Thessalonians 1:9).

de-struc-tive (dɪ–strʌk–tɪv) adj. Causing, or designed to cause, destruction: *a destructive storm*

des-ul-to-ry (dɛs–əl–tɔr–iʸ) 1. Passing from one thing to another 2. Occurring by chance —**des-ul-to-ri-ly** (dɛs–əl–tɔr–ə–liʸ) adv.

de-tach (dɪ–tætʃ) v. To unfasten; remove; separate: *Several railway cars were detached from the rest of the train at Pittsburgh.* —**detachable** adj. —**detached** adj.

de-tach-ment (diʸ–tætʃ–mənt) n. 1. A group of ships or troops detached from a larger group for a special duty 2. Freedom from bias or emotion; lack of concern

de-tail (diʸ–teʸl) n. 1. A small point or fact: *He told us every little detail of their vacation trip.* 2. Lengthy treatment of all the small points in a whole: *The article went into detail about the health benefits of physical exercise.* —**detailed** adj. *a detailed account*

de-tain (dɪ–teʸn) v. 1. To delay and keep from continuing on 2. To hold a person somewhere for a specific amount of time: *The suspects were detained for questioning.*

de-tect (dɪ–tɛkt) v. To discover; notice: *Steroids were detected in the athlete's blood stream and he was disqualified from the race.* —**detection** n. *The theft of the jewels escaped detection (=was not discovered) until the next day.* —**detectable** adj.

de-tec-tive (dɪ–tɛk–tɪv) n. A person, esp. a member of the police force, whose job it is to investigate crimes and find the criminals

de-tente (deʸ–tɑnt) n. A less troubled state of political relations between countries

de-ten-tion (dɪ–tɛn–ʃən) n. The act or fact of detaining or holding back —see DETAIN

de-ter (dɪ–tɜr) v. -rr- To keep someone from acting

de-ter-gent (dɪ–tɜr–dʒənt) n. A cleansing agent, esp. one that is chemically different from soap

de-te-ri-o-rate (dɪ–tɪər–iʸ–ə–reʸt) v. -rated, -rating To worsen: *His health deteriorated rapidly.* —compare IMPROVE —**de-te-ri-o-ra-tion** (dɪ–tɪər–iʸ–ə–reʸ–ʃən) n.

de-ter-mi-nate (dɪ–tɜrm–ə–nət) adj. 1. Definitely limited or fixed 2. Settled and conclusive; final

de-ter-mi-na-tion (dɪ–tɜr–mə–neʸ–ʃən) n. 1. Firm intention; strength of will: *The president announced his determination to put an end to terrorism.* 2. The act of coming to a decision: *In their hasty determination to sell the house, they overlooked other possibilities for raising the money they needed.*

de-ter-mine (dɪ–tɜr–mɪn) v. -mined, -mining 1. *fml.* To find out: *He set out to determine the rights and wrongs of the case.* 2. To reach a firm decision: *He determined to complete his assignment successfully.* 3. To fix conclusively or authoritatively: *He [God] determined the number of the stars and calls them each by name* (Psalm 147:4). 4. To regulate: *In his heart a man plans his course, but the Lord determines his steps* (Proverbs 16:9).

de-ter-mined (dɪ–tɜr–mɪnd) adj. Strong-willed: *He's determined to reach his goal of losing twenty pounds.*

de-ter-min-er (dɪ–tɜr–mə–nər) n. *tech.* A word that limits the meaning of a noun and comes before an adjective that describes the same noun: *"my " in "my old sweater"*

de-ter-rent (dɪ–tɜr–ənt) n. Sthg. that serves to deter

de-test (dɪ–tɛst) v. To feel a very strong hatred: *The Lord detests lying lips* (Proverbs 12:22). *The Lord detests the thoughts of the wicked* (Proverbs 15:26).

de-test-a-ble (dɪ–tɛst–ə–bəl) adj. Intensely disliked; hateful: *The sacrifice of the wicked is detestable* (Proverbs 21:27). *If anyone turns a deaf ear [does not listen] to the law, even his prayers are detestable* (Proverbs 28:9). —NOTE: Although God detests all sin, he is also a God of love, mercy and forgiveness, and if we repent and put our trust in Jesus for our salvation, we will have eternal life(Mark 1:15 ; Acts 16:31). The wages of sin is death, but the gift of God is eternal life through Jesus Christ our Lord (Romans 6:23).

de-throne (diʸ–θroʷn) v. -throned, -throning
To remove from the throne, to depose
—dethronement n.

det-o-nate (dɛt–ə–neʸt) v. -nated, -nating To
(cause to) explode

det-o-na-tion (dɛt–ə–neʸ–ʃən) n. An explosion

det-o-na-tor (dɛt–ə–neʸ–tər) n. A device that
detonates an explosive

de-tour (diʸ–tʊər) n. A roundabout way to get
past sth.: *We had to make a detour because the
bridge was washed out.*

de-tract (dɪ–trækt) v. To take away from: *The
cold weather did not detract from our enjoyment of the occasion.*

det-ri-ment (dɛt–rə–mənt) n. Sthg. harmful:
Heavy smoking is a detriment to one's health.
—det-ri-men-tal (dɛt–rə–men–təl) adj.

deuce (duʷs) n. 1. (in tennis) The score of 40
all 2. The two on a playing card or on dice 3.
slang A two-dollar bill

Deu-ter-on-o-my (duʷ–tər–an–ə–miʸ) n. The
fifth book of the Old Testament giving a
repetition of the Law of Moses —see OLD
TESTAMENT

de-val-ue (diʸ–væl–yuʷ) v. -ued, -uing To lower the exchange value of money —de-val-u-
a-tion (diʸ–væl–yuʷ–eʸ–ʃən) n.

dev-as-tate (dɛv–ə–steʸt) v. 1. To cause complete destruction 2. To overwhelm with
grief —dev-as-ta-tion (dɛv–ə–steʸ–ʃən) n.

dev-as-tat-ing (dɛv–ə–steʸt–ɪŋ) adj. 1. Destroying completely 2. *infml.* Having great beauty: *She's a devastating redhead.* —**devas-
tatingly** adv.

de-vel-op (dɪ–vɛl–əp) v. 1. To cause to grow,
expand, or become more complete: *to develop one's business* 2. To begin to be seen or become active: *Trouble is developing at the border.* 3. To put sthg. through various stages of
production

de-vel-op-er (dɪ–vɛl–əp–ər) n. 1. One who develops 2. A person or firm that develops
land, constructs new houses, etc. 3. A substance used for developing photographic
film

development (dɪ–vɛl–əp–mənt) n. 1. Developing; being developed 2. Sthg. that has been
developed or is being developed —de-vel-
op-men-tal (dɪ–vɛl–əp–men–təl) adj.

de-vi-ant (diʸ–viʸ–ənt) adj. Deviating from
what is accepted as normal
deviant n. A person who deviates from accepted standards

de-vi-ate (diʸ–viʸ–eʸt) v. -ated, -ating To turn
aside, esp. from the normal or standard
course —de-vi-a-tion (diʸ–viʸ–eʸ–ʃən) n.

de-vice (dɪ–vais) n. 1. A tool or instrument,
esp. one that is cleverly thought out: *a device
for opening doors electronically* 2. A plan, esp.
a deceptive plan 3. **leave someone to his
own devices** To leave someone to do as he
pleases: *God said, "My people would not listen
to me... so I gave them over to their own stubborn hearts to follow their own devices"* (Psalm
81:11,12).

dev-il (dɛv–əl) n. 1. The most powerful evil
spirit; Satan: *The devil is the external cause of
sin in the world. Created good and holy, the
devil soon rebelled against God. "The devil has
sinned from the beginning"* (1 John 3:8).
NOTE: How it was possible for a perfectly
good and holy angel to sin, we do not
know. But he did rebel against God and
was cast out of heaven. "Jesus said, 'I saw
Satan like lightning fall from heaven'"
(Luke 10:18). Ever since that time Satan has
been determined to destroy the work of
God, especially man, God's foremost visible creation. He is to this day the driving
force in the children of unbelief and is
tempting the Christians to evil. He is very
clever, often disguising himself as an "angel of light" (2 Corinthians 11:14). "But he is
a liar and the father of lies" (John 8:44). He
offers people power, fame and fortune, gla-
mour and fun, and whatever it takes to get
them to rebel against God. He is described
as a "roaring lion seeking whom he may
devour" (1 Peter 5:8). "But Jesus Christ
came into the world to destroy the works of
the devil" (1 John 3:8). Christians can resist
the devil with the Word of God. The Bible
says, "Resist the devil and he will flee from
you" (James 4:7). Jesus also tells Christians,
"Greater is he that is in you [the Holy Spir-
it], than he that is in the world [Satan]" (1
John 4:4). Jesus has redeemed us from the
power of the devil. He did this when, as our

substitute, he successfully resisted the temptations of the devil and when, by his death on the cross he fully paid the penalty of our guilt (Matthew 4:3-11; Genesis 3:15; Hebrews 2:14). While this deliverance from the power of the devil was obtained for all people, only they enjoy it who personally believe in Jesus as their Lord and Savior. They are able in the strength of faith to resist and to overcome the temptations of the devil (1 Peter 5:8; Ephesians 6:11; James 4:7). Though Christians can still fall into sin, because of the weakness of their flesh, the devil cannot successfully accuse them before God, because Christ pleads for them (1 John 2:2). It was by sin that man brought upon himself guilt and punishment and became subject to spiritual, temporal, and eternal death, thereby putting himself under the power of the devil. By redeeming us from sin, Christ delivered us from all of these. "Believe in the Lord Jesus Christ and you will be saved" (Acts 16:31). **2.** An evil spirit or demon, of which the world is full; an agent of Satan **3.** A wicked or mischievous person **4.** A dashing or daring person **5.** An unfortunate person: *the poor devil* **6.** One who likes to play tricks on people: *You little devil!*

dev-il-ish (dɛv–əl–ɪʃ) adj. Like the devil

dev-il-try (dɛv–əl–triʸ) n. -tries **1.** Wickedness **2.** Mischief

de-vi-ous (diʸ–viʸ–əs) adj. **1.** Not direct; roundabout **2.** Deceitful: *The way of the guilty is devious, but the conduct of the innocent is upright* (Proverbs 21:8).

de-vise (dɪ–vaɪz) v. -vised, -vising To plan or plot; to create from existing ideas

de-vi-tal-ize (diʸ–vaɪt–əl–aɪz) v. -ized, -izing To remove vitality from

de-void (dɪ–vɔɪd) adj. Empty; lacking: *He seems to be devoid of all feeling or emotion.*

de-volve (diʸ–vɑlv) v. -volved, -volving To fall as a duty on someone

de-vote (dɪ–voʷt) v. -voted, -voting To set apart to be given wholly or completely to a particular purpose: *His life was devoted to helping other people./ Devote yourselves to prayer* (Colossians 4:2). *Devote your heart and*

soul to seeking the Lord your God (1 Chronicles 22:19).

de-vot-ed (dɪ–voʷt–əd) adj. Feeling or showing great loyalty and fondness: *She is very devoted to her family./ Be devoted to one another in brotherly love* (Romans 12:10). —**devotedly** adv.

de-vo-tion (dɪ–voʷ–ʃən) n. **1.** The act of committing oneself for some purpose or to some person **2.** The condition of being devoted to someone or sthg.: *I am saying this... that you may live in a right way in undivided devotion to the Lord* (1 Corinthians 7:35).

de-vour (dɪ–vaʊr/ –aʊ–ər) v. **1.** To eat greedily: *The hungry children devoured all the food./fig. Be self-controlled and alert. Your enemy the devil prowls around like a roaring lion looking for someone to devour* (1 Peter 5:8). **2.** To take in eagerly and quickly by the senses or mind: *He devoured that big book in two days.*

de-vout (dɪ–vaʊt) adj. **1.** Deeply concerned with religion **2.** Very serious about: *He and all his family were devout and God-fearing; he gave generously to those in need and prayed to God regularly* (Acts 10:2). —**devoutly** adv.

dew (duʷ) n. Moisture which forms on cold surfaces during the night —compare RAIN

dew-y (duʷ–iʸ) adj. Wet with dew

dex-ter-i-ty (dɛk–stɛər–ə–tiʸ) n. Skill; cleverness, esp. in the use of the hands —**dexterous** or **dextrous** (dɛk–strəs) adj.

dia. abbr. Diameter

di-a- (daɪ–ə–) before vowels, also **di–** prefix **1.** Through; across; between; apart **2.** Thoroughly

di-a-be-tes (daɪ–ə–biʸ–tɪs/ –tiʸz) n. A disease marked by too much sugar in the blood —**di-a-bet-ic** (daɪ–ə–bet–ɪk) adj. , n.

di-a-bol-i-cal (daɪ–ə–bɑl–ɪ–kəl) adj. derog. Relating to the devil; wicked: *a diabolical plot*

di-a-crit-i-cal mark (daɪ–ə–krɪt–ɪ–kəl mɑrk) adj. A mark added to a letter to indicate its pronunciation or distinguish it in some way

di-a-dem (daɪ–ə–dɛm) n. **1.** A crown worn as a sign of sovereignty **2.** Royal authority or status

di-ag-nose (daɪ–əg–noʷs/ daɪ–əg–noʷs) v. -nosed, -nosing To recognize a disease by

its signs and symptoms

di-ag-no-sis (daɪ-əg-no^w-səs) n. *pl.* -noses
(-no^w-si^yz) n. The act of identifying a disease
—di-ag-nos-tic (daɪ-əg-**nas**-tɪk) adj.

di-ag-o-nal (daɪ-**æg**-ə-nəl) n., adj. **1.** A
straight line from one corner across to the
opposite corner of a four-sided figure **2.**
Any straight line which runs in a slanted
direction —diagonally adv.

di-a-gram (daɪ-ə-græm) n. A plan or figure
drawn to explain sthg. —di-a-gram-matic
(daɪ-ə-grə-**mæt**-ɪk) adj.

di-al (daɪ-əl) n. **1.** The face of an instrument
such as a watch or a clock, which shows
measurements by means of a pointer and
numbers or figures **2.** The disk on a telephone with numbered holes for the fingers,
which is moved when one makes a telephone call **3.** The plate or disk on a radio or
television set that shows the station or
channel selected

dial v. To make a telephone call: *He dialed the
wrong number.*

di-a-lect (daɪ-ə-lɛkt) n. A regional variety of a
language, which is different from other
forms of the same language: *the Midwestern
dialect*

di-a-logue (daɪ-ə-lɔg/-lɑg) also dialog n. **1.** A
conversation or discussion **2.** The words
spoken by the actors in a play or story

di-am-e-ter (daɪ-**æm**-ə-tər) n. The distance
across a circle, passing through the center
—compare RADIUS

di-a-mond (daɪ-mənd/daɪ-ə-mənd) n. **1.** A
very hard, brilliant, precious stone, which
is used esp. in jewelry **2.** A four-sided figure
with sides of equal length that stands on
one of its points **3.** A playing card with one
or more figures like this in red: *the ten of diamonds*

di-a-per (daɪ-pər/daɪ-ə-pər) n. A piece of soft
cloth or paper worn by a baby to serve as
underpants

di-a-phragm (daɪ-ə-fræm) n. **1.** The muscle
that separates the lower part of the body
from the chest **2.** Any thin dividing layer

di-ar-rhe-a (daɪ-ə-ri^y-ə) n. -rhoea A condition
characterized by too frequent emptying of
the bowels in liquid form

di-a-ry (daɪ-ə-ri^y) n. -ries **1.** A daily record of
the events or thoughts in a person's life **2.**
The book in which such a record is kept

di-a-tribe (daɪ-ə-traɪb) n. A violent attack in
words, very abusive criticism

dice (daɪs) n. *pl.* (*sing.* die) A small cube (six-
sided block) with numbered sides, used in
games of chance

dice v. diced, dicing To cut into small cubes:
She diced the carrots.

dic-tate (dɪk-te^yt) v. -tated, -tating **1.** To say or
read aloud for transcription **2.** To command
with authority —dic-ta-tion (dɪk-te^y-ʃən) n.

dic-ta-tor (dɪk-te^y-tər) n. **1.** A ruler having
complete authority and unlimited power **2.**
One who dictates —dic-ta-to-ri-al (dɪk-tə-
tɔr-i^y-əl) adj.

dic-tion (dɪk-ʃən) n. The way one pronounces
words: *Our teacher insisted that we practice
good diction in her class.*

dic-tion-ar-y (dɪk-ʃə-**nɛər**-i^y) n. -ies A book
that lists words in alphabetical order with
their meanings in the same or another language: *a Chinese-English dictionary/a medical
dictionary* (=a dictionary of medical terms)

did (dɪd) v. Past tense of do

did-n't (dɪd-ənt/ dɪd-nt) Short for did not

die (daɪ) v. died, dying (daɪ-ɪŋ) **1.** To cease living **2.** To pass out of existence NOTE: There
are three kinds of death: physical death
which is separation of the body and soul;
spiritual death, which is separation from
God while here on earth; and eternal death
which is eternal separation from God. —see
also DEATH When a Christian dies, his or
her soul immediately goes to heaven. Jesus
told the repentant thief on the cross, "Today you shall be with me in paradise"
(Luke 23:43). When an unbeliever dies, his
soul goes to hell, a place of eternal punishment prepared for the devil and his angels
(Luke 16:23; John 3:36; Matthew 25:41,46).
"It is appointed unto men to die once, but
after this the judgment" (Hebrews 9:27
KJV). "Jesus said, 'I am the resurrection and
the life. He who believes in me, though he
may die, he shall live. And whoever lives
and believes in me shall never die'" (John
11:25, 26). If a person is born again (born

spiritually) through faith in Jesus Christ, he will die a physical death, but he will not suffer eternal death. His physical death will be the gateway to heaven. **3.** *fig.* To desire sth. greatly: *He is dying to meet the President.* **4. die down** To weaken: *The wind is dying down.* **5. die out** To disappear completely: *Some Indian tribes in South America have died out.*

die n. A metal block used for shaping metal, plastic, etc.

die-sel (diᵞ–zəl/–səl) n. **1.** A diesel engine **2.** A vehicle driven by a diesel engine —**diesel** adj.

die-sel en-gine (diᵞ–zəl **en**–dʒən/–səl) n. An internal combustion engine in which heavy oil is ignited by heat generated by highly compressed air

di-et (dar–ət) n. **1.** The usual food and drink taken by a person or group: *I like to have a lot of vegetables in my diet.* **2.** Certain foods and drink that one is allowed, esp. for weight loss or other health problems: *He is on a salt-free diet.*

diet v. To eat only those foods that are allowed: *No cake for me, please; I'm dieting.*

di-e-ti-tian or **di-e-ti-cian** (dar–ə–tʃ–ən) n. A person trained to plan meals that provide good nutrition or meet a specific need

dif-fer (dɪf–ər) v. **1.** To be unlike: *Your school differs from mine in many ways.* **2.** To hold opinions that are not the same

dif-fer-ence (dɪf–rəns/ –ər–əns) n. **1.** A point where sth. is not the same as sth. else: *There is no difference, for all have sinned and fall short of the glory of God; and are justified freely by his grace through the redemption that came by Christ Jesus* (Romans 3:23,24). **2.** An amount or way in which things are not the same: *The difference between 9 and 12 is 3.* **3.** A slight disagreement: *They settled their differences and are friends again.*

dif-fer-ent (dɪf–rənt/ –ər–ənt) adj. **1.** Partly or completely unlike: *Copper and silver are quite different.* **2.** Not the same one or ones: *There will be three different kinds of cake for the party.* —**differently** adv.

dif-fer-en-tial (dɪf–ər–**en**–ʃəl) n. **1.** The difference between different individuals, wages,

etc.: *a wage differential* **2. differential gear** An arrangement of gears that allows one turning shaft to turn two others at different speeds

dif-fer-en-ti-ate (dɪf–ər–**en**–ʃiᵞ–eᵞt) v. **-ated, -ating 1.** To make a distinction **2.** To recognize as different

dif-fi-cult (dɪf–ɪ–kəlt) adj. Not easy; hard to do, make, or understand: *Navajo is a difficult language to learn.*

dif-fi-cul-ty (dɪf–ɪ–kəl–tiᵞ) n. **-ties 1.** The quality or state of being difficult; trouble: *She had great difficulty in learning Chinese.* **2.** Sth. difficult; some type of trouble: *He's having financial (=money) difficulties.*

dif-fi-dent (dɪf–ə–dənt) adj. Lacking self-confidence; shy; retiring

dif-fuse (dɪ–fuᵂz) v. **-fused, -fusing 1.** To spread in all directions: *to diffuse light or knowledge* **2.** To mix liquids or gases; to become intermingled

dif-fuse (dɪ–fuᵂs) adj. **1.** Spread out; not concentrated **2.** Too wordy; not concise

dig (dɪg) v. **dug** (dʌg), **digging 1.** To turn up, loosen, and move earth **2.** To make a hole by removing the earth **3.** *fig.* To search for and discover: *to dig up information* **4.** *fig.* To work very hard: *We'll finish this job by sunset if we really dig in.*

di-gest (dar–dʒest) v. **1.** To be broken down into a form that the body can use: *Milk is not easy to digest.* **2.** To think over and organize in the mind: *It'll take me a while to digest everything we learned in class today.* —**digestible** adj. —**digestive** adj.

di-gest (dar–dʒest) n. A short piece of writing that gives the most important facts: *a science digest*

di-ges-tion (dɪ–dʒes–tʃən) n. The act of digesting food: *Chewing your food well is an aid to digestion.*

dig-ger (dɪg–ər) n. **1.** One who digs **2.** A machine for digging

dig-it (dɪdʒ–ət) n. **1.** Any numeral from 0 to 9 **2.** A finger or a toe

dig-it-al (dɪdʒ–ə–təl) adj. Using numbers that are digits to represent all the variables involved in calculation: *digital clock*

dig-i-tal-is (dɪdʒ–ə–**tæl**–əs) n. A drug used as

a heart stimulant

dig-ni-fied (dɪg-nə-faɪd) adj. Having or expressing dignity —opposite UNDIGNIFIED

dig-ni-fy (dɪg-nə-faɪ) v. 1. To make sthg. seem worthy; give dignity to: *a meeting dignified by the presence of the mayor* 2. To give an important-sounding name to sbdy. or sthg.: *I wouldn't dignify that trashy painting by calling it art.*

dig-ni-ty (dɪg-nə-tiʸ) n. 1. The state of being worthy, noble, and excellent in character: *A wife of noble character who can find? She is clothed with strength and dignity* (Proverbs 31:10,25). 2. A reserved and formal manner: *The queen entered the room with great dignity.*

di-graph (daɪ-græf) n. A combination of two letters to represent a single sound

di-gress (daɪ-grɛs) v. To wander from the main point in speaking or writing

dike (daɪk) n. A bank of earth to control water; a levee

di-lap-i-dat-ed (də-læp-ə-deʸt-əd) adj. Fallen into ruin or decay: *a dilapidated old car*

di-late (daɪ-leʸt) v. -lated, -lating To make or become wider or larger —di-la-tion (daɪ-leʸ-ʃən) n.

dil-a-to-ry (dɪl-ə-tɔr-iʸ) adj. Slow in doing sthg.; not prompt

di-lem-ma (də-lɛm-ə) n. A choice between two courses of action which are equally undesirable

dil-i-gent (dɪl-ə-dʒənt) adj. Hardworking; industrious; putting care and effort into what one does: *The plans of the diligent lead to profit as surely as haste leads to poverty* (Proverbs 21:5). —diligently adv. —diligence n.

dill (dɪl) n. An herb with aromatic leaves and seeds used as a seasoning

dil-ly (dɪl-iʸ) adj. *slang* Sthg. very good: *That's a real dilly.*

dil-ly-dal-ly (dɪl-iʸ-dæl-iʸ) v. -lied, -lying To waste time: *Stop dillydallying and get to work.*

di-lute (daɪ-luʷt) v. -luted, -luting To make a liquid thinner by mixing another liquid with it: *She diluted the lemon juice with water.*

dim (dɪm) adj. -mm- 1. Not bright; not clear: *The lights in the best restaurants are usually dim.* 2. *fig.* Negative: *He took a dim view of*

what the chairman proposed.

dim v. -mm- To become dim or cause to become dim: *They dimmed the theater lights.* —dimly adv. —dimness n.

dime (daɪm) n. A coin of the US and Canada, worth ten cents or one-tenth of a dollar

di-men-sion (dɪ-mɛn-ʃən) n. A measurement in one direction only: *A box has three dimensions: length, width, and height.*/*fig.* *We need to consider another dimension of this problem before we make a decision.*

di-men-sions (dɪ-mɛn-ʃənz) n. Measurements of size: *What are the dimensions of this room?* (=its height, length, and width)

di-min-ish (dɪ-mɪn-ɪʃ) v. To make or become smaller or less important

di-min-u-tive (dɪ-mɪn-yə-tɪv) adj. 1. Tiny; of very small size 2. Expressing smallness as in the suffix "-let" in "booklet"

dim-ple (dɪm-pəl) n. A small hollow place in the face, esp. on the cheek

dim-wit (dɪm-wɪt) n. A stupid person —dim-witted adj. Stupid

din (dɪn) n. A loud, continuous, unpleasant noise: *The din of the downtown traffic gave me a severe headache.*

dine (daɪn) v. -dined, dining *fml.* To eat dinner: *We are dining out tonight.*

din-er (daɪ-nər) n. 1. A small restaurant 2. A car on a train where meals are served 3. A person who dines, esp. in a restaurant

di-nette (daɪ-nɛt) n. 1. A small room used for meals 2. A set of furniture for dining

ding (dɪŋ) n. The sound a bell makes

ding-a-ling (dɪŋ-ə-lɪŋ) n. A stupid person

din-ghy (dɪŋ-giʸ/dɪŋ-iʸ) n. A small open boat driven by sails or oars

din-gy (dɪm-dʒiʸ) adj. -gier, -giest Dirty; grimy: *a dingy old building*

din-ky (dɪŋ-kiʸ) adj. Very small: *a dinky little car*

din-ner (dɪm-ər) n. 1. The main meal of the day, eaten either at noon or in the evening 2. A formal feast or banquet: *The guests are wearing formal dress to the dinner tonight.* NOTE: If dinner is in the evening, the noon meal is called **lunch**; if dinner is at noon, the evening meal is called **supper**.

di-no-saur (daɪ-nə-sɔr) n. Any of various

types of giant reptiles that probably became extinct at the time of the Great Flood that covered the entire earth during the time of Noah, referred to in Genesis 6 to 9. NOTE: Scientists have discovered more than 800 different kinds of dinosaurs and have found them on every continent. Seven kinds of dinosaurs are described in this dictionary: allosaurus, anatosaurus, ankylosaurus, brontosaurus, stegosaurus, triceratops, and tyrannosaurus. The word "dinosaur" comes from two Greek words meaning "terrible lizard." The first dinosaur fossils discovered were huge and scientists believed they must be fierce creatures. But some dinosaurs were small, plant-eating animals and no dinosaurs were actually lizards, so the name "dinosaur" is really a misnomer.

dint (dɪnt) n. **by dint of** By means of

di-o-cese (daɪ-ə-sɪs/ -siᵞs/ -siᵞz) n. The district or churches under the leadership of a bishop

di-ox-ide (daɪ-ɑk-saɪd) n. An oxide with two atoms of oxygen and one of some other element

dip (dɪp) v. **-pp- 1.** To put sthg. into a liquid for a moment and then take it out: *He dipped his foot into the water to see how cold it was.* **2.** To go down slightly: *The path dips a little just before the footbridge.*

dip n. **1.** A slight drop down; gentle slope: *a dip in the road* **2.** *infml.* A short, quick swim

diph-the-ri-a (dɪf-θɪər-iᵞ-ə/ dɪp-) n. An infectious disease that causes severe inflammation of the mucous membrane, esp. in the throat

diph-thong (dɪf-θɔŋ/ dɪp-) n. A compound vowel sound produced by combining two simple ones, such as the **ou** in **sound** or the **oi** in **boil**

di-plo-ma (dɪ-ploʷ-mə) n. An official paper showing that a person has successfully completed a course of study: *a high school diploma*

di-plo-ma-cy (dɪ-ploʷ-mə-siᵞ) n. **1.** The art and practice of starting good relations between nations and keeping them going **2.** Ability in dealing with other people

dip-lo-mat (dɪp-lə-mæt) n. One whose job is to deal with other people, especially as a representative of his country

dip-lo-mat-ic (dɪp-lə-mæt-ɪk) adj. **1.** Concerning diplomacy: *Henry did very well as a member of the diplomatic corps.* **2.** Able to deal well with people; tactful: *Mary is always so diplomatic; she never seems to hurt anybody's feelings.* —opposite UNDIPLOMATIC —**dip-lo-mat-i-cal-ly** (dɪp-lə-mæt-ɪ-kə-liᵞ) adv.

dip-per (dɪp-ər) n. **1.** Sthg. that dips or is used for dipping **2. Big Dipper** A constellation consisting of seven bright stars resembling a water dipper

dip-so-ma-ni-a (dɪp-sə-meᵞ-niᵞ-ə/ -nyə) n. An uncontrollable craving for alcohol —**dipsomaniac** n.

dir. *abbr.* director

dire (daɪr/ daɪ-ər) adj. Very great; severe; dreadful: *in dire need*

di-rect (də-rɛkt/ daɪ-) v. **1.** To show or point out the way to a place: *Can you direct me to the post office?* **2.** To supervise the way sthg. is done: *He directed the building of the new bridge./ May the Lord direct your hearts into God's love and Christ's perseverance* (2 Thessalonians 3:5). **3.** *fml.* To give orders: *The policeman directed traffic around the accident.*

direct adj. **1.** Going from one point straight to another without turning aside **2.** Leading from one thing to another as an immediate result: *His death from lung cancer was a direct result of his heavy smoking.* **3.** Honest and clear: *a direct answer* —opposite INDIRECT **4.** Exact: *Debbie and Joan are direct opposites in appearance and personality.* —**directness** n.

di-rec-tion (də-rɛk-ʃən) n. **1.** The action of directing; control: *The planning of the campaign is under the direction of Mrs. Johnson.* **2.** The line or course on which a person or thing moves or is pointed toward: *The plane was headed east in the direction of Chicago.* **3.** The place or point towards which a person or thing faces: *What direction are we going?* **4.** Instructions on how to do sthg.: *My son's tricycle came with a set of directions for putting it together.*

di-rect-ly (də-rɛkt-liᵞ/ daɪ-) adv. **1.** Exactly; in a direct manner: *The bank is directly across*

the street from the post office. —opposite IN-
DIRECTLY **2.** Immediately; very soon:
infml. We'll be ready to go directly.

di·rec·tor (də–rɛk–tər/ daɪ–) n. **1.** One who
controls a group or an organization or company **2.** One who directs a movie or a play
or an orchestra, etc. —compare PRODUC-
ER

di·rec·to·ry (də–rɛk–tə–riʸ/ daɪ–) n. -ries An alphabetical or classified list of names and
addresses: *the telephone directory*

dirge (dərdʒ) n. A slow mournful song; a
hymn of lamentation

di·ri·gi·ble (dɪr–ə–dʒə–bəl) n. An airship that
can be directed or steered

dirt (dərt) n. **1.** Sthg. that causes things to become soiled: *Wash the dirt off your face.* **2.**
Dust; soil; loose earth: *I just dropped my hot
dog in the dirt!* **3.** Foul languag; scandal: *I de-
test magazines that print all the dirt they can
find about someone.*

dirt·y (dərt–iʸ) adj. -ier, -iest **1.** Not clean: *Sbdy.
needs to do the laundry; all our clothes are dirty.*
2. (of thoughts or words) Concerned with
sex in an indecent way: *Some people seem to
enjoy telling dirty stories.* **3. dirty trick** A
mean trick **4. a dirty look** *infml.* A look of
disgust or disapproval

dirty v. -ied, -ying To make dirty: *The child fell
in the mud and dirtied his new white sweater.*

dis– (dɪs–) Prefix meaning **not** when used at
the beginning of such words as **disability,
disabuse, disadvantage, disagree, disallow,
disappear, disapprove, disarm, disarrange,
disarray, disassociate;** but *not* at the beginning of the following words: **disappoint,
distance, distribute, dispel, distinguish,
disaster, dish, disk, dismal, discount, disease, discourse, discussion, discord, discern, discharge, discipline, disciple**

dis·a·ble (dɪs–eʸ–bəl) v. -abled, -abling To
cause to be unable to do sthg., esp. by making a limb useless

dis·a·gree (dɪs–ə–griʸ) v. **1.** To have a different opinion **2.** To be unlike: *What you said
just now disagrees with what you said earlier.*
3. To quarrel **4.** To have bad effects: *This food
disagrees with me.* —disagreeable adj. —disagreement n.

dis·ap·pear (dɪs–ə–pɪər) v. **1.** To go out of
sight; vanish **2.** To cease to exist —disappearance n.

dis·ap·point (dɪs–ə–pɔɪnt) v. To fail to live up
to someone's expectations: *I know this will
disappoint you, but you can't play in the game
this week; your grades are too low.*

dis·ap·point·ed (dɪs–ə–pɔɪnt–əd) adj. Unhappy at not seeing hopes fulfilled: *I am really
disappointed that I won't be able to go to the
game with you.*

dis·ap·point·ment (dɪs–ə–pɔɪnt–mənt) n. **1.**
Failure of expectation **2.** Depression caused
by failure

dis·ap·prove (dɪs–ə–pruʷv) v. -proved,
-proving To have or to express an unfavorable opinion —disapproval n.

dis·arm (dɪs–ɑrm) v. **1.** To deprive of weapons **2.** To reduce armed forces **3.** To defuse a
bomb **4.** To do or say sthg. to make it difficult for sbdy. to feel anger, doubt, or suspicion —disarmament n.

dis·ar·ray (dɪs–ə–reʸ) v. To disarrange —disarray n. Disorder

dis·as·ter (dɪz–æs–tər) n. **1.** Sthg. terrible that
happens unexpectedly: *The flood caused great
disaster.* **2.** A complete failure: *The performance was a disaster.*

dis·as·trous (dɪz–æs–trəs) adj. Terrible; very
bad; causing a disaster: *a disastrous earthquake*

dis·a·vow (dɪs–ə–vaʊ) v. To disclaim; to deny
responsibility for

dis·band (dɪs–bænd) v. To break up; to separate

dis·bar (dɪs–bɑr) v. To expel from membership in a legal profession

dis·be·lieve (dɪs–bə–liʸv) v. -lieved, -lieving
To refuse to believe or be unable to believe
—disbelief n. —disbeliever n.

dis·burse (dɪs–bərs) v. To pay out money
NOTE: Do not confuse with disperse

disc (dɪsk) n. **1.** A disk **2.** A phonograph
record **3.** A plate covered with magnetic
material on which computer data is stored

dis·card (dɪs–kɑrd) v. To throw away as useless

disc jock·ey (dɪsk dʒɑk–iʸ) n. *infml.* A person
who conducts a broadcast program of

records of popular music

dis-cern (dɪs-**ɜrn**) v. *fml.* **1.** To see, notice, esp. with difficulty: *He was hardly able to discern the road in the dark.* **2.** To understand: *The man without the [Holy] Spirit does not accept the things that come from the Spirit of God... and he cannot understand them, because they are spiritually discerned* (1 Corinthians 2:14). —**discernible** adj.

dis-cern-ing (dɪ-**sɜrn-ŋ**) adj. Showing insight and understanding: *Wisdom is found on the lips of the discerning...* (Proverbs 10:13). —**discernment** n.

dis-charge (dɪs-**tʃɑrdʒ**) v. -**charged, -charging 1.** To release or dismiss someone: *He was discharged from the army last year./ She was discharged from the hospital yesterday.* **2.** To give off or send out: *A lot of black smoke was being discharged from the chimney.* **3.** To perform a duty **4.** To fire a gun **5.** To unload cargo

dis-charge (dɪs-**tʃɑrdʒ**) n. **1.** The action of discharging **2.** The result of being discharged: *After his discharge from the navy he went to college.*

dis-ci-ple (dɪ-**saɪ-pəl**) n. A follower of any great teacher: *Jesus commanded his disciples to make disciples of all nations. A good disciple is more than just a follower. Jesus said, "All men will know that you are my disciples if you love one another"* (John 13:35). *He also said, "...any of you who does not give up everything he has cannot be my disciple"* (Luke 14:33). *Obviously he must also be obedient to his word. "If you abide in my word, you are my disciples in deed"* (John 8:31). *A true disciple does good works that glorify God. Jesus said, "By this my Father is glorified, that you bear much fruit; so shall you be my disciples"* (John 15:8). —**discipleship** n.

dis-ci-pline (dɪs-ə-plɪn) n. **1.** Training that produces obedience, self-control, or a particular skill **2.** Control gained as a result of this training: *The teacher had very good discipline in her classroom because of the excellent training she gave her students.* **3.** Training (sometimes painful) that corrects, molds, or perfects: *My son, do not despise the Lord's discipline... because the Lord disciplines those he*

loves (Proverbs 3:11,12). —**disciplinary** adj. —**disciplinarian** (dɪs-ə-plə-**neər**-iʸ-ən) n.

discipline v. -**plined, -plining 1.** To train and develop by instruction and exercise, esp. in self-control: *You must learn to discipline yourself.* **2.** To punish: *Discipline your son, and he will give you peace; he will bring delight to your soul* (Proverbs 29:17).

dis-claim (dɪs-**kleʸm**) v. To deny having any connection with or a responsibility for

dis-close (dɪs-**kloʷz**) v. -**closed, -closing** To reveal; to make known

dis-co (dɪs-**koʷ**) n. -**cos** A discotheque

dis-col-or (dɪs-**kʌl**-ər) v. **1.** To spoil the color of sthg. **2.** To become changed in color —**dis-col-or-a-tion** (dɪs-kʌl-ər-**eʸ**-ʃən) n.

dis-com-bob-u-late (dɪs-kəm-**bɑb**-yuʷ-leʸt) v. -**lated, -lating** To disturb or confuse

dis-com-fit (dɪs-**kʌm**-frt) v. To disconcert, upset, frustrate —**dis-com-fi-ture** (dɪs-**kʌm**-fɪ-tʃər) n. Embarrassment

dis-com-fort (dɪs-**kʌm**-fərt) n. **1.** Lack of comfort in body or mind **2.** Sthg. that causes this

dis-con-cert (dɪs-kən-**sɜrt**) v. To perturb; to upset

dis-con-nect (dɪs-kə-**nɛkt**) v. To break the connection between things

dis-con-nec-ted (dɪs-kə-**nɛkt**-əd) adj. **1.** Not connected **2.** Rambling; incoherent

dis-con-so-late (dɪs-**kɑn**-sə-lət) adj. Hopelessly sad; cheerless

dis-con-tent (dɪs-kən-**tɛnt**) n. Dissatisfaction; uneasiness of mind —**discontented** adj.

dis-con-tin-ue (dɪs-kən-**tɪn**-yuʷ) v. -**tinued, -tinuing** To stop operating or using or doing sthg. —**discontinuance** n. —**discontinuous** adj.

dis-cord (dɪs-kɔrd) n. *fml.* Dissension; disagreement between people: *The acts of the sinful nature are obvious: sexual immorality... idolatry and witchcraft, hatred, discord, jealousy...* (Galatians 5:19,20). *God hates it when we sow discord among brothers* (Proverbs 6:16,19 KJV). NOTE: God hates all sin for he is perfectly holy. But he is also a God of love, and because of his love and mercy, he forgives all sinners who turn from their wicked ways (who repent) and trust in Je-

sus for eternal life (Acts 3:19; Acts 16:31).

dis-co-theque (dɪs–kə–tɛk) n. A nightclub where amplified music is played for dancing

dis-count (dɪs–kaʊnt) n. A lowering of the cost of buying goods in a shop: *a discount of ten percent for paying cash*

dis-count (dɪs–kaʊnt/ dɪs–**kaʊnt**) v. **1.** To lower the price of goods **2.** To pay little or no attention to: *Some of what he says must be discounted; he exaggerates.*

dis-cour-age (dɪs–kɜr–ɪdʒ) v. -aged -aging **1.** To cause to lose courage and enthusiasm: *Fathers, do not embitter your children or they will become discouraged* (Colossians 3:21). **2.** To try to keep someone from doing sthg., esp. by letting them know that their action is not approved: *We discourage smoking in this office.* —opposite ENCOURAGE —**discouraged** adj. —**discouragement** n.

dis-course (dɪs–kɔrs) n. **1.** Conversation **2.** Extended expression of thought on a subject

dis-cov-er (dɪs–kʌv–ər) v. **1.** To find sthg. that was in existence before, but not known: *Gold was discovered in California in 1849.* —compare INVENT **2.** To learn of sthg. previously unknown: *Sbdy. needs to discover a cure for the common cold.* —**discoverer** n.

dis-cov-er-y (dɪs–kʌv–riʸ/ dɪs–kʌv–ə–riʸ) n. -ies **1.** The act of discovering: *The discovery of gold at Sutter's Creek led to the Gold Rush in California.* **2.** Sthg. that is discovered

dis-cred-it (dɪs–krɛd–ət) v. **1.** To damage the good reputation of **2.** To refuse to believe **3.** To cause to be disbelieved

discredit n. **1.** Loss of good reputation **2.** Disgrace **3.** Disbelief —**discreditable** adj.

dis-creet (dɪs–kriʸt) adj. Having or showing good judgment and self-restraint in speech and behavior; cautious; tactful —opposite INDISCREET —**discreetly** adv.

dis-crep-an-cy (dɪs–krɛp–ən–siʸ) n. -cies Difference; lack of agreement between two stories, two amounts of money, etc.

dis-cre-tion (dɪs–krɛʃ–ən) n. **1.** The quality of being discreet in one's speech or actions **2.** Good judgment: *I, wisdom... possess knowledge and discretion* (Proverbs 8:12). **3.** Freedom to act according to one's own judg-

ment

dis-cre-tion-ar-y (dɪs–krɛʃ–ə–nɛər–iʸ) adj. Done or used at a person's discretion

dis-crim-i-nate (dɪs–krɪm–ə–neʸt) v. -nated, -nating **1.** To have good taste or judgment: *We must be able to discriminate between right and wrong.* **2.** To make a distinction; to give unfair treatment, esp. because of prejudice: *We should not discriminate against people because of their race, color, social status, or religion.* —**discriminating** adj. —**dis-crim-i-na-tion** (dɪs–krɪm–ə–neʸ–ʃən) n.

dis-crim-i-na-tor-y (dɪs–krɪm–ə–nə–tɔr–iʸ) adj. Characterized by discrimination and unfair treatment

dis-cus (dɪs–kəs) n. A heavy disc thrown by a discus thrower in a track-and-field meet

dis-cuss (dɪs–kʌs) v. To talk about sthg. with someone, considering it from several points of view, esp. formally: *The staff discussed the plans for the new hospital.*

dis-cus-sion (dɪs–kʌʃ–ən) n. An act of discussing

dis-dain (dɪs–deʸn) n. Scorn; contempt

disdain v. To regard with disdain; to treat as though unworthy of notice —**disdainful** adj. —**disdainfully** adv.

dis-ease (dɪ–ziʸz) n. An illness or disorder caused by infection, diet, condition of life, or that is inherited, not by an accident —**diseased** adj. NOTE: Illness is a state of being unwell, which may be caused by a disease. Diseases that can be caught and passed on are called infectious or contagious. A person who has a disease is ill or sick. *Jesus went through all the towns and villages... preaching the good news of the kingdom and healing every disease and sickness* (Matthew 9:35).

dis-em-bark (dɪs–əm–bɑrk) v. To put or go ashore —**dis-em-bar-ka-tion** (dɪs–ɛm–bɑr–keʸ–ʃən) n.

dis-em-bod-ied (dɪs–ɪm–bɑd–iʸd) adj. Of the soul or spirit, freed from the body

dis-en-chant (dɪs–ɪn–tʃænt) v. To free from enchantment; to disillusion —**disenchant-ment** n.

dis-en-tan-gle (dɪs–ən–tæŋ–gəl) v. -gled, -gling To untangle; to rid of entanglement

dis-fa-vor (dɪs-feʸ-vər) n. Dislike; disapproval

dis-fig-ure (dɪs-fɪg-yər) v. -ured, -uring To spoil the appearance or shape of —**disfigured** adj.

dis-fran-chise (dɪs-fræn-tʃaɪz) v. -chised, -chising To deprive of the right to vote —**disfranchisement** n.

dis-gorge (dɪs-ɡɔrdʒ) v. -gorged, -gorging 1. To throw out from the gorge or throat 2. To pour forth: *The river disgorged itself into the sea.*

dis-grace (dɪs-ɡreʸs) v. -graced, -gracing To bring shame to: *John disgraced himself last night by drinking too much and starting a fight.*

disgrace n. Sthg. that causes shame or lack of respect: *Righteousness exalts a nation, but sin is a disgrace to any people* (Proverbs 14:34). *Being poor is no disgrace.* —**disgraceful** adj. *A son who sleeps through the harvest is a disgraceful son* (Proverbs 10:5). —**disgracefully** adv.

dis-grun-tled (dɪs-ɡrʌn-təld) adj. Discontented; unhappy; upset

dis-guise (dɪs-ɡaɪz) v. -guised, -guising 1. To change one's usual appearance so as to hide the true identity: *The thief disguised himself as a woman.* 2. To cover up the truth: *She tried in vain to disguise her disappointment at not being able to go to the game.*

disguise n. 1. Sthg. that is worn in order to hide who one really is: *He wore a false beard and a wig as a disguise.* 2. The condition of being disguised: *She came to the party in disguise and fooled everyone.*

dis-gust (dɪs-ɡʌst/ dɪs-kʌst) n. Strong feeling of disapproval: *His drunken behavior filled her with disgust.*

dis-gust (dɪs-ɡʌst) v. To cause someone to feel disgust: *His rude behavior disgusted his friends.* —**disgusted** adj.

dish (dɪʃ) n. 1. A flat or shallow, usu. round, container for holding or serving food 2. A particular food of one kind: *Roast beef is his favorite dish.*

dish v. 1. Used with **up** or **out** (a) To put into a dish, as when serving food: *She dished out the potatoes and vegetables.* (b) *derog.* To give unwanted advice: *He thinks he knows everything, and he's always dishing out advice.* 2. To

make into the shape of a dish

dish-cloth (dɪʃ-klɔθ) n. A cloth for washing dishes

dis-heart-en (dɪs-hɑrt-ən) v. To discourage; to cause to lose hope —**disheartening** adj. *a disheartening experience*

dish-es (dɪʃ-əz) n. All the plates, cups, knives, forks, etc., used for a meal: *It won't take long to wash the dishes; there aren't many.*

di-shev-eled (dɪ-ʃɛv-əld) adj. Untidy

dis-hon-est (dɪs-ɑn-əst) adj. Not honest; untrustworthy; deceitful: *The Lord hates dishonest scales* (Proverbs 11:1). *Whoever is dishonest with very little will also be dishonest with much* (Luke 16:10).

dis-hon-or (dɪs-ɑn-ər) n. 1. Loss of honor or respect 2. Sthg. that causes this —**dishonor** v. —**dishonorable** adj.

dis-il-lu-sion (dɪs-ə-luʷ-ʒən) v. To free from pleasant but mistaken beliefs

dis-il-lu-sion-ment (dɪs-ə-luʷ-ʒən-mənt) n. The state of being disillusioned

dis-in-cli-na-tion (dɪs-ɪn-klə-neʸ-ʃən) n. Unwillingness

dis-in-cline (dɪs-ɪn-klaɪn) v. -clined, -clining To make or to be unwilling

dis-in-fect (dɪs-ɪn-fɛkt) v. To clean by destroying bacteria that may cause disease

dis-in-fect-ant (dɪs-ɪn-fɛkt-ənt) n. A substance used for disinfecting things

dis-in-her-it (dɪs-ɪn-hɛr-ɪt) v. To deprive a person of an inheritance by making a will naming another or others as one's heir(s)

dis-in-te-grate (dɪs-ɪn-tə-ɡreʸt) v. -grated, -grating To break or cause to break into small parts —**disintegrated** adj. —**dis-in-te-gra-tion** (dɪs-ɪn-tə-ɡreʸ-ʃən) n.

dis-in-ter-est-ed (dɪs-ɪn-trɪst-əd/ -tər-ɪst-əd) adj. Unbiased; not influenced by self-interest

dis-joint-ed (dɪs-dʒɔɪnt-əd) adj. 1. Separated at or as if at the joint 2. Of speech, incoherent; disconnected

disk (dɪsk) n. also **disc** 1. A thin circular object 2. A phonograph record 3. A computer diskette

dis-kette (dɪs-kɛt) n. A small flexible plastic disk on which computer data is stored

dis-like (dɪs-laɪk) v. -liked, -liking To not like

sthg.

dislike n. A feeling of not liking sthg.

dis-lo-cate (dıs-loᵂ-keˈt/ dıs-loᵂ-koᵛt) v. **-cated, -cating 1.** To put a bone out of place: *He dislocated his shoulder in the football game.* **2.** Disrupt —**dis-lo-ca-tion** (dıs-loᵂ-keʸ-ʃən) n.

dis-lodge (dıs-lɑdʒ) v. **-lodged, -lodging** To move or force from an established position

dis-loy-al (dıs-lɔɪ-əl) adj. Not loyal; unfaithful —**disloyalty** n.

dis-mal (dız-məl) adj. **1.** Bleak; cheerless; dreary **2.** Feeble: *a dismal attempt at humor* —**dismally** adv.

dis-man-tle (dıs-mæn-təl) v. **-tled, -tling** To take apart: *They dismantled the machinery before moving it to the other factory.*

dis-may (dıs-meʸ) v. To cause to lose courage: *The one who trusts [in Jesus] will never be dismayed* (Isaiah 28:16). —**dismay** n.

dis-mem-ber (dıs-mem-bər) v. To take or tear a body apart, limb from limb —**dismembered** adj. *the man's dismembered body*

dis-miss (dıs-mıs) v. **1.** *fml.* To remove from a job: *Bill was dismissed from his job for no good reason.* **2.** To direct or permit to leave: *The teacher dismissed the class early.* **3.** To reject: *He just laughed and dismissed the idea as impossible.*

dis-mis-sal (dıs-mıs-əl) n. **1.** The act of dismissing sbdy. or of being dismissed **2.** An order for the dismissal of sbdy.

dis-mount (dıs-maʊnt) v. To get down from a horse or a bicycle

dis-o-be-di-ence (dıs-ə-biʸ-diʸ-əns) n. Neglect or refusal to obey: *Just as through the disobedience of one man [the first man, Adam], the many were made sinners, so also through the obedience of one man [Jesus Christ] the many were made righteous* (Romans 5:19). —see JESUS, MAN, SIN

dis-o-be-di-ent (dıs-ə-biʸ-diʸ-ənt) n., adj. Not obedient; refusing to obey: *It is shameful even to mention what the disobedient do in secret* (Ephesians 5:12). *God's wrath comes on those who are disobedient* (Ephesians 5:6). —see JESUS, MAN, SIN —**disobedience** n.

dis-o-bey (dıs-oᵂ-beʸ) v. **-beyed, -beying** To refuse or fail to obey

dis-or-der (dıs-ɔr-dər) n. **1.** A lack of order: *For where you have envy and selfish ambition, there you find disorder and ev-ery evil practice* (James 3:16). **2.** A public disturbance, riot ing **3.** A disturbance of the normal functioning of the body or mind: *a nervous disorder* —**disorderly** adj.

dis-or-gan-ize (dıs-ɔr-gə-naɪz) v. **-ized, -izing** To throw into confusion

dis-or-gan-ized (dıs-ɔr-gə-naɪzd) adj. Lacking organization

dis-o-ri-ent (dıs-ɔr-iʸ-ənt) v. To confuse sbdy., causing him to lose his bearings

dis-o-ri-en-tate (dıs-ɔr-iʸ-ən-teʸt) v. **-tated, -tating** To disorient —**dis-o-ri-en-ta-tion** (dıs-ɔr-iʸ-ən-teʸ-ʃən) n.

dis-own (dıs-oᵂn) v. To refuse to accept or acknowledge as one's own: *Jesus said, "Whoever acknowledges me before men, I will also acknowledge him before my Father in heaven. But whoever disowns me before men, I will disown him before my Father in heaven"* (Matthew 10:33).

dis-par-age (dıs-peər-ıdʒ/ -pær-) v. **-aged, -aging** To belittle —**disparagement** n. —**disparagingly** adv.

dis-pa-rate (dıs-peər-ət/-pær-/dıs-pə-rət) adj. Different in kind —**disparately** adv.

dis-par-i-ty (dıs-peər-ə-tiʸ/-pær-) n. Great difference; inequality

dis-pas-sion (dıs-pæʃ-ən) n. Freedom from emotion

dis-pas-sion-ate (dıs-pæʃ-ən-ət) adj. Unbiased; favoring no one; not influenced by strong feeling —**dispassionately** adv.

dis-patch (dıs-pætʃ) v. **1.** To send, esp. with speed: *This telegram has to be dispatched today.* **2.** To finish a task quickly and well

dispatch n. **1.** An important, official message carried by a government official, or sent to a newspaper by one of its writers, etc. **2.** *fml.* Efficiency and quickness: *The ambulance reached the accident scene with great dispatch.*

dis-pel (dıs-pel) v. **-ll-** To scatter; drive away: *Her mother's soft singing dispelled the child's fears.*

dis-pens-a-ble (dıs-pen-sə-bəl) adj. Not needed; that which can be dispensed with —opposite INDISPENSABLE

dis-pen-sa-ry (dɪs–pɛns–ə–riʸ) n. -ries A place for dispensing medicine, esp. in a hospital or clinic

dis-pen-sa-tion (dɪs–pɛn–seʸ–ʃən) n. **1.** Dispensing; distributing **2.** Ordering of the world by divine authority **3.** Exemption from a penalty or duty

Dis-pen-sa-tion-al-ism (dɪs–pɛn–seʸ–ʃən–əl–ɪzɪn) n. The teaching that God acts in different ways at different times in history. It is a way of interpreting the Bible that began in the 1800s. It usually divides history into seven periods or dispensations. It is known for its special teaching about the second coming of Christ. It teaches that the Rapture of the Church will be a secret event and Christ will return openly after that. —see BIBLE, JESUS, RAPTURE

dis-pense (dɪs–pɛns) v. -pensed, -pens-ing **1.** To give out to people, usu. many people: *to dispense justice/ There is a machine in the hall that dispenses hot soup.* **2.** To prepare and distribute medicine **3. dispense with** Do without —**dispenser** n. *a soap dispenser*

dis-perse (dɪs–pɜrs) v. -persed, -persing To cause to break up in different directions: *The crowd dispersed when the storm approached.* —**dispersion** n.

dis-place (dɪs–pleʸs) v. -placed, -placing **1.** To shift from its place **2.** To take the place of

dis-place-ment (dɪs–pleʸs–mənt) n. **1.** The act of displacing **2.** The amount of fluid displaced by a floating body: *What is the displacement of water by that huge ocean liner, the Queen Mary?*

dis-play (dɪs–pleʸ) v. -played, -playing To show or exhibit: *They displayed the goods in the store window./ The Apostle Paul said, "I was shown mercy so that in me, the worst of sinners, Christ Jesus might display his unlimited patience as an example for those who would believe on him and receive eternal life"* (1 Timothy 1:16).

display n. The act or result of displaying: *The books were on display at the county fair.*

dis-please (dɪs–pliʸz) v. -pleased, -pleasing To annoy or irritate

dis-pleas-ure (dɪs–plɛʒ–ər) n. A feeling of annoyance and dislike

dis-pos-a-ble (dɪs–poʷz–ə–bəl) adj. Designed to be used once and then discarded: *disposable towels*

dis-pos-al (dɪs–poʷz–əl) n. **1.** The act of removing or getting rid of sthg.: *disposal of property/ garbage* **2. at someone's disposal** Available for someone's use: *My pickup truck is at your disposal any time you need it.*

dis-pose (dɪs–poʷz) v. -posed, -posing **1.** To be inclined to: *He was disposed to accept the offer.* **2.** To place in a certain order; to arrange **3.** To prepare **4.** To settle **5. dispose of** To get rid of sthg. that is no longer needed: *Dispose of this garbage for us, please.*

dis-po-si-tion (dɪs–pə–zɪ–ʃən) n. **1.** A person's general nature, characteristics, etc.: *a cheerful disposition* **2.** The act or power of disposing: *funds at their disposition* **3.** Tendency; inclination **4.** Arrangement

dis-pos-sess (dɪs–pə–zɛs) v. To deprive of possessions —**dispossession** n.

dis-pro-por-tion (dɪs–prə–por–ʃən) n. A lack of proper proportion —**disproportionate** adj. —**disproportionately** adv.

dis-prove (dɪs–pruʷv) v. -proved, -proving To prove sthg. to be false

dis-put-a-ble (dɪs–pyuʷ–tə–bəl) adj. Not necessarily true; sthg. that can be argued against —opposite INDISPUTABLE

dis-pu-ta-tion (dɪs–pyuʷ– teʸ–ʃən) n. An argument or debate —**disputatious** adj.

dis-pute (dɪs–pyuʷt) v. -puted, -puting **1.** To argue about, esp. for a long time: *They disputed for weeks about the location of the new prison.* **2.** To question the truth of sthg.; doubt: *Henry disputed the validity of the salesman's claim.*

dispute n. An argument or quarrel, esp. a long, angry disagreement: *A dispute arose over the boundary between the two countries.*

dis-qual-i-fy (dɪs–kwɑl–ə–faɪ) v. -fied, -fying To put out of a competition for breaking the rules or because of age, weight, etc.: *He won the race but was later disqualified because of his use of drugs.*

dis-qui-et (dɪs–kwaɪ–ət) v. To make uneasy; to disturb

dis-re-gard (dɪs–riʸ–gɑrd) v. To ignore; pay no attention to —**disregard** n.

dis-re-pair (dɪs-rɪ-peər) n. A state of being out of repair

dis-rep-u-ta-ble (dɪs-rep-yət-ə bəl) adj. Having a bad reputation; not respectable

dis-re-pute (dɪs-rɪ-pyuʷt) n. Loss or lack of reputation; low esteem: *Many will follow their shameful ways [of their false teachers] and will bring the way of truth into disrepute* (2 Peter 2:2).

dis-re-spect (dɪs-rɪ-spɛkt) n. Lack of respect —disrespectful adj. —disrespectfully adv.

dis-robe (dɪs-roʷb) v. To undress

dis-rupt (dɪs-rʌpt) v. To stop or throw into disorder: *Our electricity was disrupted for hours because of the terrible snowstorm.* —disruption n. —disruptive adj. *a disruptive influence*

dis-sat-is-fac-tion (dɪs-sæt-ɪs-fæk-ʃən) n. Discontent

dis-sat-is-fy (dɪs-sæt-ɪs-faɪ) v. -fied, -fying To fail to meet one's expectations or desires

dis-sect (daɪ-sɛkt) v. To cut into parts, esp. a plant or animal, in order to study the parts —dis-sec-tion (dɪ-sɛk-ʃən) n.

dis-sem-ble (dɪs-ɛm-bəl) v. -bled, -bling Hide or cover up one's true thoughts or feelings

dis-sem-i-nate (dɪ-sɛm-ə-neʸt) v. -nated, -nating To scatter; to spread widely; distribute —dis-sem-i-na-tion (dɪ-sɛm-ə-neʸ-ʃən) n.

dis-sen-sion (dɪ-sɛn-ʃən) n. Strong difference of opinion, esp. leading to angry quarreling: *There has always been a lot of dissension between the two parties.*

dis-sent (dɪ-sɛnt) v. To have a different opinion; to refuse to agree —dissent n. Disagreement

dis-sent-er (dɪ-sɛnt-ər) n. One who dissents

dis-ser-ta-tion (dɪs-ər-teʸ-ʃən) n. 1. A treatise, esp. one written as a doctoral thesis 2. A long piece of writing or talk on a particular (usu. scholarly) subject

dis-ser-vice (dɪs-ər-vɪs) n. A harmful action

dis-si-dent (dɪs-ə-dənt) n. A person who is often and openly in disagreement with others

dis-sim-u-late (dɪs-ɪm-ə-leʸt) v. -lated, -lating To dissemble; to hide one's true feelings; to pretend —dis-sim-u-la-tion (dɪs-ɪm-ə-leʸ-ʃən) n.

dis-si-pate (dɪs-ə-peʸt) v. -pated, -pating 1. To cause to disappear; *A strong breeze dissipated the smoke.* 2. To waste; squander; use foolishly 3. To lose and not be able to recover: *the heat dissipated*

dis-si-pat-ed (dɪs-ə-peʸt-əd) adj. Having wasted one's money, energy, etc. on the pleasures of this world: *He lived a dissipated life.* —dis-si-pa-tion (dɪs-ə-peʸ-ʃən) n.

dis-so-ci-ate (dɪs-oʷ-ʃiʸ-eʸt) v. -ated, -ating To separate in one's thoughts: *It is difficult to dissociate the famous author from his books* —dissociation n.

dis-so-lu-tion (dɪs-ə-luʷ-ʃən) n. 1. Decomposition; disintegration 2. The dissolving or terminating of an association or partnership

dis-solve (dɪ-zɑlv) v. -solved, -solving 1. To make or become liquid; to melt: *Sugar dissolves easily in water but salt does not.* 2. To put an end to a company, organization, etc.: *They decided to dissolve the corporation after 85 years in business.*

dis-so-nant (dɪs-ə-nənt) adj. Discordant —dissonance n.

dis-suade (dɪ-sweʸd) v. -suaded, -suading To persuade against a course of action —dissuasion n.

dis-taff (dɪs-tæf) n. 1. The stick that holds the bunch of flax or wool in spinning 2. Woman or women in general

dis-tance (dɪs-təns) n. The amount of separation in space or time: *The distance between Los Angeles and Hong Kong is about 17 hours by plane./ The distance between my house and my office is about 17 miles./ fig. There seems to be a bit of distance between us lately. Can you tell me why you're upset with me?*

dis-tant (dɪs-tənt) adj. 1. Far away in time or space: *distant lands/ the distant past* 2. Separated in relationship: *I just found out about one of my distant relatives. It turns out we are second cousins.* —distantly adv. *to be distantly related*

dis-taste (dɪs-teʸst) n. Dislike

dis-taste-ful (dɪs-teʸst-fəl) adj. Unpleasant; disagreeable: *The job of scrubbing floors was distasteful to him.*

dis-tem-per (dɪs–tɛm–pər) n. A contagious, often fatal disease of dogs and certain other animals, with coughing and weakness

dis-tend (dɪs–tɛnd) v. To swell or become swollen by pressure from within —**distension** n.

dis-till (dɪs–tɪl) v. *AmE.* **distil** *BrE* . **-ll-** To go through the chemical process of turning a liquid into gas and then back into liquid, as when separating alcohol from water: *distilled water* —**dis-til-la-tion** (dɪs–tə–leʸ–ʃən) n.

dis-till-er-y (dɪs–tɪl–ər–iʸ) n. **-ies** A place where whiskey and certain other alcoholic liquors are produced

dis-tinct (dɪs–tɪŋt/–tɪŋkt) adj. **1.** Clearly different: *Each of our children has his own distinct personality.* **2.** Able to be seen, heard, understood, etc. clearly; noticeable: *There's a distinct fragrance of orange blossoms in the air.* —opposite INDISTINCT —**distinctly** adv. *I could hear him distinctly over the phone, even though he was 10,000 miles away.* —**distinctness** n.

dis-tinc-tion (dɪs–tɪŋ–ʃən/ –tɪŋk–) n. **1.** Difference: *Can you make a distinction between these two sounds?* **2.** The quality or state of being unusual, esp. of being worthy: *She has earned distinction as a great singer.* **3.** An honor: *She had the distinction of being the first woman to fly across the United States.*

dis-tinc-tive (dɪs–tɪŋk–tɪv) adj. Serving to mark a person or thing as unusual: *She had a distinctive voice.* —**distinctively** adv. —**distinctiveness** n.

dis-tin-guish (dɪs–tɪŋ–gwɪʃ) v. **1.** To hear, see, or recognize because of some special difference: *I can easily distinguish my bright yellow van in the parking lot.* **2.** To make differences between or recognize as different: *to distinguish between right and wrong* **3.** To set apart into kinds, classes, etc.: *Zebras are distinguished by their black and white stripes.* **4.** To behave oneself in a manner that is noticed: *The team distinguished themselves by winning every game.*

dis-tin-guish-a-ble (dɪs–tɪŋ–gwɪʃ–ə–bəl) adj. That which can be seen, heard, or recognized as clearly different: *The words "fifty" and "fifteen" are not clearly distinguishable;* they sound too much alike. —opposite INDISTINGUISHABLE

dis-tin-guished (dɪs–tɪŋ–gwɪʃt) adj. Noticeable because of excellent quality or deserved fame: *a distinguished performance/ author* —see FAMOUS

dis-tort (dɪs–tɔrt) v. **1.** To twist out of the true meaning: *Why are you distorting the truth? Why don't you tell us what really happened?* **2.** To twist sthg. out of its usual shape or condition: *Extreme pain distorted her beautiful face.* **3.** To reproduce improperly: *The station isn't coming in very well; the sound is distorted.* —**distortion** n.

dis-tract (dɪs–trækt) v. To take a person's mind off what he/ she is doing: *Homesickness distracted her from studying for her exams.* —**distractible** adj.

dis-tract-ed (dɪs–trækt–əd) adj. Troubled about many things; distraught

dis-trac-tion (dɪs–træk–ʃən) n. **1.** Sthg. that distracts or makes it difficult for one to concentrate **2.** An amusement or entertainment **3.** Mental distress

dis-traught (dɪs–trɔt) adj. Greatly upset; nearly crazy with grief or worry

dis-tress (dɪs–trɛs) n., adj. **1.** Great suffering, pain, or discomfort: *They were in great distress without food or water.* **2.** A state of great danger or trouble: *The plane had sent a message of distress just before the crash.*

distress v. To afflict with great pain, anxiety, strain, or grief: *The whole nation was distressed by the news of the assassination.*

dis-tres-sing (dɪs–trɛs–ɪŋ) adj. Causing great concern: *a distressing phone call*

dis-trib-ute (dɪs–trɪ–byuʷt) v. **-uted, -uting 1.** To give out; divide among: *Uncle Bill distributed Christmas gifts to all the children.* **2.** To spread out in order to cover; scatter widely: *Food was distributed throughout the country to all the starving population.*

dis-tri-bu-tion (dɪs–trə–byuʷ–ʃən) n. **1.** An act of distributing **2.** The state of being distributed

dis-tri-bu-tor (dɪs–trɪ–byuʷ–tər) n. **1.** One who distributes things **2.** A device for distributing a current to the spark plugs in an engine

dis-trict (dɪs-trɪkt) n. A division of a country, city, etc., esp. made for purposes of governing, education, etc.: *a school district / District of Columbia*

dis-trust (dɪs-trʌst) v. To lack trust in; doubt
distrust n. Lack of trust; suspicion

dis-turb (dɪs-tɜrb) v. 1. To interrupt, esp. a person who is working, engaged in conversation, etc.: *May I disturb you for a moment? I have sthg. important to ask you.* 2. To upset; worry: *They were disturbed by the bad news from home.* 3. To upset the usual order or natural condition of: *A breakdown in the computer disturbed our schedule for the day.* —disturbing adj.

dis-turb-ance (dɪs-tɜr-bəns) n. 1. An act of disturbing or the state of being disturbed: *The mob on the street created quite a disturbance.* 2. Sthg. that disturbs: *The disturbance down on the street kept me awake.*

dis-turbed (dɪ-stɜrbd) adj. Showing signs of emotional illness: *emotionally disturbed*

dis-u-nite (dɪs-yuʷ-naɪt) v. -nited, -niting To separate; to divide

dis-u-ni-ty (dɪs-yuʷ-nə-tiʸ) n. A lack of unity

dis-use (dɪs-yuʷs) n. The state of being no longer in use or practice

ditch (dɪtʃ) n. A long, narrow trench dug in the ground, esp. for water to flow through

dith-er (dɪð-ər) v. 1. To tremble or quiver 2. To hesitate indecisively —dither n. A very nervous state

dit-to (dɪt-oʷ) n. -toes The same as sthg. already written or said —ditto marks A mark composed of a pair of inverted commas representing the word "ditto"

dit-ty (dɪt-iʸ) n. A short simple song

di-ur-nal (daɪ-ɜr-nəl) adj. 1. Of the day, not nocturnal 2. Occupying a day

di-van (dɪ-væn) n. A couch; sofa

dive (daɪv) v. dived also dove (doʷv) dived, diving 1. To jump into the water headfirst: *She dived off the diving board into the pool.* 2. To go underwater; submerge: *They went deep-sea diving.* 3. To dart downward or out of sight: *The thief dived behind the corner of the building.*

dive n. 1. An act of diving: *He just did a beautiful dive off the three meter board.* 2. infml. A restaurant or place for amusement that is not very respectable: *I don't want to be seen in that dive!*

div-er (daɪv-ər) n. A person who dives, esp. one who does deep-sea diving with special equipment

di-verge (də-vɜrdʒ/ daɪ-) v. -verged, -verging 1. To go in different directions 2. To differ; to go away from: *to diverge from the truth* —divergent adj. —divergence n.

di-verse (də-vɜrs/ daɪ-) adj. Of differing kinds —diversely adv.

di-ver-si-fy (də-vɜr-sɪ-faɪ) v. -fied, -fying 1. To make or become different or varied 2. To spread out activities or investments, esp. in business

di-ver-sion (də-vɜr-ʃən/ daɪ-) n. 1. An act of turning from the usual course, activity, or use 2. An amusement or sthg. that diverts

di-ver-si-ty (də-vɜr-sɪ-tiʸ/ daɪ-) n. -ties Variety

di-vert (də-vɜrt/daɪ-) v. 1. To turn a thing from its course: *They diverted the traffic because of the accident.* 2. To distract: *They diverted our attention.* 3. To entertain or amuse

di-vest (də-vɛst/daɪ-) v. To take away; to deprive: *The governor was divested of his authority.*

di-vide (də-vaɪd) v. -vided, -viding 1. To distribute the pieces of: *The children divided the candy among themselves.* 2. To separate into parts: *Lesson one is too long; I'm going to divide it.* 3. To figure out how many times one number contains or is contained in another number: *100 divided by 5 is 20.* —compare MULTIPLY

div-i-dend (dɪv-ə-dɛnd/ -dənd) n. 1. A number that is to be divided 2. A benefit from an action: *Ann's hard work paid great dividends.* 3. A sum of money to be distributed to stockholders

di-vid-er (də-vaɪd-ər) n. 1. Sthg. that divides, as a partition in a room 2. dividers An instrument resembling a compass, used for dividing lines and transferring measurements

div-i-na-tion (dɪv-ə-neʸ-ʃən) n. The art of obtaining secret knowledge, esp. of the future: *Divination is a pagan counterpart of prophecy. Divination is by demon power, whereas genuine*

prophecy is by the Spirit of God. God, therefore, detests divination of any kind. "Let no one be found among you who... practices divination or sorcery, interprets omens, engages in witchcraft, or casts spells, or who is a medium or spiritist or who consults the dead. Anyone who does these things is detestable to the Lord" (Deuteronomy 18:10-12). NOTE: God hates all sin. But he is also a God of love and is not willing that any should perish but to come to repentance and put their trust in Jesus for eternal salvation (2Peter 3:9; Mark 1:15; Acts 16:31). —see JESUS

di-vine (dɪ-**vaɪn**) adj. **1.** Being or having the nature of God: *Jesus Christ has both a divine and human nature. He is true God and true man.* —see CREED *His [Jesus'] divine power has given us everything we need for life and godliness through our knowledge of him who called us by his own glory and goodness* (2 Peter 1:3). **2.** Coming from God: *the divine right of kings* **3.** Very, very, good: *The banquet was simply divine.* NOTE: This use of the word **divine** is common among women, but is seldom if ever used by men or boys.

divine v. **-vined, -vining 1.** *fml.* To discover or guess the unknown, esp. the future, by occult means. NOTE: This is a sin against the commandment of God: *There shall not be found among you anyone... that uses divination. For all who do these things are an abomination [are hateful] unto the Lord* (Deuteronomy 18:10, 12). —see DIVINATION **2.** To locate water underground, esp. by using a Y-shaped stick (a divining rod)

di-vine-ly (dɪ-**vaɪn**-liʸ) adv. Beautifully; gracefully: *She danced divinely.*

di-vin-i-ty (də-**vɪn**-ə-tiʸ) n. **-ties** The quality or state of being divine

di-vis-i-ble (də-**vɪz**-ə-bəl) adj. That which can be divided: *15 is divisible by 3.*

di-vi-sion (də-**vɪ**-ʒən) n. **1.** Separation or distribution: *a division of authority* **2.** One of the parts into which sthg. is divided: *He works for the Division of Bridges of the Department of Highways.* **3.** Sthg. that divides or separates: *The Mississippi River forms the division between Iowa and Illinois.* **4.** Disagreement; discord **5.** The operation of finding out how many times one number is contained in another: *the division of 56 by 7*

di-vi-sive (də-**vaɪ**-sɪv/-**vɪ**-) adj. Causing division, dissension, or strife: *That group is a divisive influence on campus.* —**divisively** adv.

di-vorce (də-**vɔrs**) n. The ending of a marriage as declared by a court of law: *She got a divorce after years of unhappiness.*

divorce v. **-vorced, -vorcing 1.** To end a marriage: *John and Mary divorced each other.*/ *Jesus said, "Anyone who divorces his wife, except for marital unfaithfulness, causes her to commit adultery, and anyone who marries a woman so divorced commits adultery"* (Matthew 5:32). —see ADULTERY **2.** *fml.* To separate: *It is sometimes difficult to divorce certain concepts from others in one's mind.*

di-vor-cée (dɪ-vɔr-se**ʸ**) n. A divorced woman

di-vulge (dar-**vʌldʒ**) v. **-vulged, -vulg-ing** To reveal; tell; to make known a secret

diz-zy (**dɪz**-iʸ) adj. **-zier, -ziest 1.** Having a whirling sensation in the head; having a feeling of loss of balance, as if things are spinning round and round: *He became so dizzy from whirling around so long, that he fell down.* **2.** Causing this feeling: *a dizzy height* **3.** *infml.* Foolish or stupid —**dizzily** adv. —**dizziness** n.

do (duʷ/də) v. **did, done, doing**

Present tense singular:
I **do,** You **do,** He/She/It **does**
Present tense plural:
We **do,** You **do,** They **do**
Past tense singular:
I **did,** You **did,** He/She/It **did**
Past tense plural:
We **did,** You **did,** They **did**
Past participle: **done**
Present participle: **done**
Negative short forms: **don't** (doʷnt), **doesn't** (dʌz-ənt), **didn't** (dɪd-ənt)

1. (a) Used as a helping verb with another verb: *Do you like tea?* **(b)** Used to make another verb stronger: *I really do like her!* **2.** Used instead of another verb: *He likes coffee, and so do I. He speaks English better than she does.*(=better than she speaks English) **3.** Used of actions: *to do repairs/ to do the cooking/ to do the dishes* (=clean them)/ *to do one's hair*

(=*arrange it*) **4.** Used in certain expressions: *I did my best to get her by six, but the traffic prevented me.* **5.** To be sufficient! *$50 will do.* **6.** To behave: *Do as you're told!* **7.** To advance: *They did well in the examination.* **8. How are you doing?** *infml. esp. AmE.* (An informal greeting) **9. How do you do?** (Used when one is introduced to someone) **10. What do you do (for a living)?** What is your work? **11. do away with sbdy./ sthg. (a)** To put an end to; abolish: *The company did away with some old-fashioned policies.* **(b)** *infml.* To kill or murder someone or oneself **12. do sbdy. in** *infml.* **(a)** To kill: *They did her in with an ax!* **(b)** To tire completely: *That long walk really did me in!* **13. do sthg. over (a)** To repaint a room, wall, etc. **(b)** *AmE.* To do again: *This composition has many mistakes. You'll have to do it over.* **14. do with sthg. (a)** To need or want: *I could do with a cup of coffee.* **(b) have to do with** To have a connection with: *His job has to do with forestry.* **(c) have sthg./ nothing/ anything to do with** To have some/ no/ any connection with: *Have nothing to do with the fruitless deeds of darkness but rather expose them* (Ephesians 5:11). **15. do without (sbdy./ sthg.)** To continue to live without: *I don't have money to buy a new car, so I'll just have to do without.*

doc-ile (dɑs–əl) adj. A person or animal that is easy to manage —**do-cil-i-ty** (dɑ–sɪl–ə–ti^y) n.

dock (dɑk) n. A place where ships are loaded and unloaded

dock v. To cause to arrive at, or remain at, a dock: *The ship was docked at Pier 15.*

dock-age (dɑk–ɪdʒ) n. **1.** The provision or use of a dock **2.** The charge for using a dock

dock-et (dɑk–ət) n. **1.** A label giving the contents of sthg. **2.** A list of things to be done **3.** A calendar of cases awaiting court action **4.** A record of the proceedings in a legal action

dock-yard (dɑk–yɑrd) n. A shipyard; an area where ships are built and repaired

doc-tor (dɑk–tər) n. **1.** A person whose profession is to treat sick or injured people or animals **2.** A person holding one of the highest degrees given by a university, such as a

Doctor of Philosophy degree (Ph.D.)

doctor v. **1.** To give professional medical treatment to sbdy. **2.** *derog.* To change, esp. in a dishonest way: *They were charged with doctoring the election results.*

doc-tor-ate (dɑk–tər–ət) n. The degree or status of a doctor

doc-tri-naire (dɑk–trə–**nεər**) adj. Sbdy. who attempts to put an abstract theory into effect without consideration of practical difficulties

doc-trine (dɑk–trɪn) n. **1.** A belief or set of beliefs that is taught: *church doctrine* —see CREED **2.** A statement of official government opinions and intentions, esp. in international relations: *the Monroe Doctrine* —**doctrinal** (dɑk–trɪ–nəl) adj.

doc-u-ment (dɑk–yə–mənt) n. A written statement that gives information, proof, or evidence of sthg.

document v. To prove or support with documents: *The history of the war is well documented.* —**doc-u-men-ta-tion** (dɑk–yə–mən–te^y–ʃən) n.

doc-u-men-ta-ry (dɑk–yə–**men**–tə–ri^y) n. **1.** A factual presentation in artistic form: *a documentary movie* **2.** Of or relating to documents —**documentary** adj.

dod-der (dɑd–ər) v. -dered, -dering To become feeble and shaky, esp. from old age

dodge (dɑdʒ) v. dodged, dodging **1.** To avoid sthg. by suddenly moving aside: *He dodged the car and escaped unharmed.* **2.** *infml.* To avoid by some unlawful or dishonest act: *He dodged the draft by leaving the country.* —**dodge** n. —**dodger** n.

do-do (do^w–do^w) n. -does **1.** A stupid person **2.** A heavy, flightless extinct bird related to the pigeon

doe (do^w) n. An adult female of the deer family and some other animals

do-er (du^w–ər) n. One who does things; one who takes an active part

does (dʌz) v. Third person singular, pres. of do: *He/ She/ It does*

does-n't (dʌz–ənt/ dʌznt) Short for **does not**

doff (dɑf/ dɔf) v. To take off and lift up: *He doffed his hat.*

dog (dɔg/ dɑg) n. **1.** A common four-legged,

domestic animal related to wolves: *A young dog is called a puppy.* 2. **dirty dog** A mean, dishonest person 3. **a dog's life** *infml.* A life of misery 4. **Let sleeping dogs lie** Don't bring up a problem that people seem to have forgotten about 5. **top dog** *infml.* The person on top, who has power —compare UNDERDOG 6. **treat someone like a dog** *infml.* To treat someone in a very bad way 7. **You can't teach an old dog new tricks.** An older person can't change his ways easily. 8. **hot dog** A cooked frankfurter usu. served on a bun 9. **lucky dog** A fortunate fellow

dog-ged (dɔg–əd) *adj.* Stubbornly determined —**doggedly** *adv.* —**doggedness** *n.*

dog-house (dɔg–haʊs) *n.* 1. A shelter for a dog 2. **in the doghouse** In trouble with someone; in a state of disgrace

dog-ma (dɔg–mə) *n.* A doctrine or body of doctrines formally proclaimed by a church

dog-mat-ic (dɔg–mæt–ɪk) *adj.* 1. Of or based on dogma 2. Forcing, or trying to force, one's opinions on others: *Don't be so dogmatic.*

dog-ma-tism (dɔg–mə–tɪz–əm/ **dag**–) *n.* Being dogmatic

dog-ma-tize (dɔg–mə–taɪz) *v.* **-tized, -tizing** To make dogmatic statements

dog-tired (dɔg taɪ–ərd/ dag) *adj.* Worn out; very tired

dog-wood (dɔg–wʊd/ **dag**–) *n.* An American tree with small white or pink flowers

doi-ly (dɔɪ–liʸ) *n.* **-lies** A small ornamental mat as of lace or paper

do-ing (duʷ–ɪŋ) *n.* 1. Sthg. that one has done: *This is the Lord's doing [our salvation] and it is marvelous in our eyes* (Psalm 118:23). 2. Hard work: *To complete this big job by sunset will take a lot of doing.* 3. **doings** *infml. pl.* Social activity: *There was a big doings at the Johnsons' house over the weekend.*

dol-drums (doʷl–drəmz) *n.* A sad state of mind; low spirits: *in the doldrums*

dole (doʷl) *n.* 1. A distribution, esp. of food, money, or clothing to the poor 2. A grant of government funds to the unemployed

dole *v.* **doled, doling** 1. To give as a charity 2. To give in small portions

dole-ful (doʷl–fəl) *adj.* Full of grief; very sad

doll (dɑl) *n.* 1. A toy in the shape of a human being, esp. of a baby 2. *infml.* An attractive and fashionable young lady 3. **doll up** *v. infml.* (a) To dress elegantly (b) To make more attractive

dol-lar (dɑl–ər) *n.* 1. The standard unit of money used in the US, Canada, and several other countries. Its sign is $ and it is worth 100 cents. 2. A piece of paper, a coin, etc. of this value

doll up (dɑl ʌp) *v. infml.* 1. To dress elegantly 2. To make more attractive

dol-ly (dɑl–iʸ) *n.* **-lies** 1. A doll 2. A small, wheeled apparatus used in moving heavy loads by hand

dol-phin (dɔl–fɪn) *n.* A sea animal like a porpoise but larger and having a beaklike snout

do-main (doʷ–meʸn) *n.* 1. A region under a single sovereign or government 2. An area of interest or knowledge

dome (doʷm) *n.* A roof resembling an inverted cup: *Many capitol buildings have domes.*

domed (doʷmd) *adj.* Covered with or shaped like a dome

do-mes-tic (də–mes–tɪk) *adj.* 1. Of the home or household or family affairs 2. Of animals, not wild 3. Of one's own country or one particular country; not foreign: *A domestic flight is one within the boundaries of a single country.* —**domestically** *adv.*

do-mes-ti-cate (də–mes–tə–keʸt) *v.* **-cated, -cating** To tame animals; to bring animals under control —com-pare TAME

dom-i-cile (dɑm–ə–saɪl/ doʷm–) *n.* A home; a permanent dwelling place

dom-i-nance (dɑm–ə–nəns) *n.* The fact or state of dominating —compare DOMINATION

dom-i-nant (dɑm–ə–nənt) *adj.* Dominating: *The castle was built in a dominant position on a hill overlooking the Rhine.*

dom-i-nate (dɑm–ə–neʸt) *v.* **-nated, -nating** 1. To have a commanding influence over 2. To have the most important place or position: *Athletics, not education, seems to dominate in that college.* 3. To rise or to be higher than; to tower over: *That huge cathedral dominated the scene.*

dom-i-na-tion (dɑm–ə–neʸ–ʃən) *n.* The act or fact of dominating or the state of being

dominated: *Bill's domination by his brother made him very angry.* —compare DOMI-NANCE

dom-i-neer (dɑm–ə–nɪər) v. To rule in an arrogant manner, showing no consideration for the feelings of others

dom-i-neer-ing (dɑm–ə–nɪər–ŋ) adj. *derog.* Arrogant; overbearing

do-min-ion (də–mɪn–yən) n. **1.** Authority to rule; control: *Tiberius Caesar held dominion over a large area.* **2.** Territory or people held in complete control by one person or government: *For he [God] has rescued us from the dominion of darkness [Satan's dominion] and brought us into the kingdom of the Son he loves [Jesus], in whom we have redemption, the forgiveness of sins* (Colossians 1:13,14). **3.** A self-governing nation of the British Commonwealth: *the Dominion of Canada*

dom-i-no (dɑm–ə–noʷ) n. **-noes** One of the pieces used in the game of dominoes, each one being marked with dots

do-nate (doʷ–neʸt/ doʷ–neʸt) v. **-nated, -nating** To give as a donation —see also DONOR

do-na-tion (doʷ–neʸ–ʃən) n. A gift; sthg. donated: *She made a donation of $1,000 to the orphanage.*

done (dʌn) v. Past part. of **do**

done adj. **1.** Completed: *The work is nearly done.* **2.** Cooked enough to eat: *Is the roast done yet?* **3. done for** Ruined or dead: *Another disaster like that and we're done for.* **4. done in** Extremely tired: *I'm completely done in!*

don-key (dɑŋ–kiʸ/ dʌŋ–/ dɒŋ–) n. **-keys** An animal similar to a horse, but smaller, used for carrying loads

de-nor (doʷ–nər) n. **1.** A person who gives or donates sthg. **2.** One who permits part of his/ her body to be put into someone else's body for medical purposes: *a blood donor*

don't (doʷnt) v. Short for **do not**: *I don't know him very well.*

do-nut (doʷ–nət) n. Variation of **doughnut**

doo-dle (duʷd–əl) v. **-dled, -dling** To draw in an aimless way

doom (duʷm) n. A terrible fate; death or ruin

doom v. To cause to experience or suffer sthg. unavoidable and unpleasant: *From the beginning, I felt that plan was doomed to failure.*

dooms-day (duʷmz–deʸ) n. The day of the final judgment at the end of this present age —see JUDGMENT DAY

door (dɔr) n. **1.** A movable flat surface that opens and closes the entrance to a building, room, vehicle, cabinet, etc. **2.** A means of obtaining sthg.: *This agreement opens the door to more trade and other benefits.* **3.** *fig.* A house; building: *My best friend lives only a few doors away./My brother sells books from door to door.*

door-knob (dɔr–nɑb) n. A knob which, when turned, releases the latch of a door

dope (doʷp) n. **1.** Any drug or drugs **2.** *infml.* Information: *I got all the dope about Hawaii from the travel agency.* **3.** A stupid person

dope v. **-doped, -doping** To give dope to someone or put dope in sthg.

dop-ey or **dop-y** (doʷp–iʸ) adj. **-ier, -iest** *infml.* **1.** A dullness of mind, caused by lack of sleep or by alcohol or drugs **2.** Stupid

dor-mant (dɔr–mənt) adj. Inactive: *a dormant volcano*

dor-mer (dɔr–mər) n. A small window that juts out from a sloping roof

dor-mi-to-ry (dɔr–mə–tɔr–iʸ) also **dorm** (dɔrm) *infml.* n. **-ries** A building where university students live, sleep, and study

dor-sal (dɔr–səl) adj. Pertaining to the back

dose (doʷs) n. The amount of medicine to be taken at one time —**dosage** n.

dos-si-er (dɑs–iʸ–eʸ) n. A collection of papers, documents, etc., relating to a particular person or subject

dot (dɑt) n. **1.** A small round mark: *The period at the end of a sentence is just a dot.* **2. on the dot** *infml.* At the exact time: *His plane arrived on schedule, right on the dot.*

dot v. **-tt- 1.** To mark with a dot: *Be sure to dot every "i" in "Mississippi."* **2.** To cover as if with dots: *The lake was dotted with sailboats.*

dot-age (doʷt–ɪdʒ) n. **1.** Feebleness of mind, due to old age **2.** Excessive affection

dote (doʷt) v. **doted, doting 1.** To lavish extreme fondness upon **2.** To be feeble minded due to old age

dou-ble (dʌ–bəl) adj. **1.** Two together: *double doors* **2.** Made for two: *a double bed* —**double** adv. *After that bump on the head, I am seeing*

double.

double n. **1.** Sthg. that is twice as much as another in size, value, or quantity **2.** A person who looks very much like another: *People say that he's my double, even though we're not related.* **3. on the double** *infml.* (esp. of soldiers) At a rate between walking and running

double predeterm. Twice: *The cost of food is double what it was ten years ago.*

double v. **-bled, -bling** To make, be, or become twice as much: *His income this year doubled last year's.*

double-talk (dʌ-bəl-tɔk) n. *infml.* Language that appears to be serious and have meaning but in fact is a mixture of sense and nonsense

doubt (daʊt) v. **1.** To be uncertain: *I doubt whether it's true.* **2.** To consider unlikely: *Jesus said to Thomas (who doubted that he had risen from the dead), "Stop doubting and believe"* (John 20:27). —**doubter** n.

doubt n. **1.** Uncertainty of belief or opinion: *Jesus appeared to his disciples after he had risen from the dead, and he said to them, "Why are you troubled, and why do doubts arise in your minds? Look at my hands and my feet [which had been pierced when he was crucified]. It is I myself! Touch me and see; a ghost does not have flesh and bones as you see I have"* (Luke 24:38,39). **2. in doubt** In a condition of uncertainty: *The whole matter is still in doubt.*

doubt-ful (daʊt-fəl) adj. **1.** Full of doubt; uncertain: *He was doubtful about accepting the new position in a distant city.* **2.** Not probable; unlikely: *It is doubtful that it will rain tonight.* —**doubtfully** adv.

doubt-less (daʊt-ləs) adv. **1.** Without doubt **2.** Probably —**doubtlessly** adv.

doubt-less adj. Free from doubt

douche (duʷʃ) n. **1.** Application of a stream of water in a cavity of the body for medicinal purposes **2.** The application of a douche **3.** An instrument for applying a douche

dough (doʷ) n. **1.** A mixture of flour and other ingredients, stiff enough to knead or roll **2.** *infml., esp. AmE.* Money

dough-nut (doʷ-nət) n. also **do-nut** A small, ring-shaped cake fried in deep fat, usu. covered with frosting

dour (daʊr) adj. **1.** Glum; sullen **2.** Harsh; stern

douse (daʊs) v. **doused, dousing 1.** To plunge into a liquid; to immerse **2.** To wet thoroughly; to drench **3.** To extinguish

dove (dʌv) n. **1.** A type of pigeon **2.** A person who is an advocate of peace at any cost

dove (doʷv) *esp. AmE.*, also **dived** (daɪvd) v. Past tense of **dive**

dow-a-ger (daʊ-ɪ-dʒər) n. **1.** A widow who has property or a title from her husband **2.** An elderly woman of dignified appearance

dow-dy (daʊ-diʸ) adj. Badly dressed; shabby; untidy

down (daʊn) adv. **1.** From a higher toward a lower place: *The man bent down to pick up the newspaper.* **2.** In a low place: *down at the bottom of the well* **3.** From an upright or raised position: *Please sit down.* **4.** Towards or in the south: *He's flying down to Rio.* **5.** Along with or away from the speaker: *Could you give me a lift down to the post office?* **6.** On paper; in writing: *Did you write down her phone number?* **7.** Showing a lower level or worse condition: *The temperature is down twenty degrees.* **8.** Showing less noise, strength, etc.: *Calm down./ Please turn the radio down.* **9.** From the past: *These jewels have been handed down in our family for 300 years.* **10.** So as to be less active: *Quiet down.* **11.** As a partial payment at the time of purchase: *He only paid $100 down on a new car.* **12. down under** *infml.* In or to Australia or New Zealand **13. come down with** To become sick with: *She came down with a cold.* **14. Down with (sthg.)** Stop; put an end to: *Down with drug abuse!* **15.** *infml., esp. AmE.* Finished; done: *Seven down and three to go!* (= *seven have been finished, and there are three more to be done.*)

down v. **1.** To defeat: *They downed the enemy.* **2.** To swallow: *He downed the medicine with one gulp.*

down adj. **1.** Sad: *She really feels down since her husband died.* **2.** *tech.* (esp. of computers) Not in operation: *The computer is down today.*

down prep. **1.** To or in a lower place than; downwards by way of: *He climbed down the ladder.* **2.** Along; to or at the far end of: *He*

looked down the road. **3.** In the direction of the current: *to go downstream*

down n. A covering of soft, fluffy feathers; the feathers —**downy, -ier, -iest** adj.

down-and-out (daʊn-ən-aʊt) adj. Completely destitute

down-cast (daʊn-kæst) adj. **1.** Dejected: *Why are you downcast, O my soul? Why so disturbed within me? Put your hope in God, for I will yet praise him, my Savior and my God* (Psalm 42:11). **2.** Directed down: *a downcast glance*

down-fall (daʊn-fɔl) n. A fall from prosperity or power, esp. from high rank; ruin: *Your sins have been your downfall* (Hosea 14:1).

down-grade (daʊn-greʸd) v. **-graded, -grading** To reduce to a lower grade, rank, or position —opposite UPGRADE

down-heart-ed (daʊn-hɑrt-əd) adj. In low spirits; sad

down pay-ment (daʊn peʸ-mənt) A part of the price paid at the time of purchase, with the rest to be paid later, usu. monthly

down-pour (daʊn-pɔr) n. A heavy rainfall

down-right (daʊn-raɪt) adv. infml. (esp. with sthg. bad) Thoroughly; completely: *She downright lied to me.* —**down-right** adj. *a downright thief*

down-stairs (daʊn-stɛərz) adj. On a lower floor

down-stairs adv. To a lower floor

down-stairs n. The lower floor of a building

down-stream (daʊn-striʸm) adj. In the direction of the current of a stream or river —**downstream** adv.

down-to-earth (daʊn-tuʷ-ərθ) adj. Practical and honest

down-town (daʊn-taʊn) adv. To, toward, or in the lower part of a town, esp. the main business district of the town —**downtown** adj.

downtown n. The downtown section of a city or town

down-trod-den (daʊn-trɑd-ən) adj. Treated badly by those in positions of power; kept in a humble, inferior position

down-ward (daʊn-wərd) adj., adv. Going down

dow-ry (daʊ-riʸ) n. **-ries** The money or property a wife brings to her husband at marriage

dox-ol-o-gy (dɑk-sɑl-ə-dʒiʸ) n. A hymn or verse in praise to God

doze (doʷz) v. **dozed, dozing** To sleep lightly

doz-en (dʌz-ən) abbr. **doz.** determ., n. **dozen** or **dozens** A group of 12: *a dozen eggs/ Eggs are 99 cents a dozen.*

Dr. Written abbr. Said as **doctor**

drab (dræb) adj. Uninteresting; dull: *a drab, colorless dress/ a drab speech*

draft (dræft) n. **1.** The first rough written form of anything: *Here's a first draft of my speech.* **2.** A written order for money to be paid by a bank, esp. from one bank to another —compare CHECK **3.** also **conscription** The system of compulsory military service **4.** **draught** BrE. A current of air flowing through a room, a chimney, etc.: *Don't sit in the draft; you'll catch a cold.*

draft v. **1.** To select for special duty **2.** To order someone into military service

draft-ee (dræf-tiʸ) n. A person who has been drafted into the armed force

drafts-man (dræfts-mən) n. **-men** One who draws or prepares plans for buildings, machinery, etc.

draft-y (dræf-tiʸ) adj. **-ier, -iest** Exposed to drafts of air —**draftiness** adj.

drag (dræg) v. **-gg- 1.** To pull sthg. with difficulty: *He was dragging a heavy log.* **2.** To move slowly: *Hurry up! Stop dragging.* **3.** To proceed in a slow, dull manner: *His speech dragged on and on.* **4.** To search the bottom of a lake or other body of water: *They dragged the lake in search of the missing fisherman.* **5.** **drag on** To last a long time: *The meeting dragged on all night.* **6.** **drag out (a)** To cause to last an unnecessarily long time: *They dragged out the meeting with long speeches.* **(b)** To force information out of someone: *The police dragged the truth out of the prisoner.* **7.** **drag sthg. up** infml. To keep bringing up a subject: *The senator's opponents keep dragging up his past mistakes.*

drag n. **1.** Sthg. or sbdy. that makes it harder to advance: *He felt that his family was a drag on his career.* **2.** infml. Sthg. dull and uninteresting: *The party was a drag, so we left early.*

3. *infml.* A puff on a cigarette

drag-net (dræg–net) n. **1.** A net used in dragging a body of water **2.** An organized widespread search for a criminal

drag-on (dræg–ən) n. **1.** Another name for Satan: *He [an angel] seized the dragon, that ancient serpent, who is the devil or Satan, and bound him for 1,000 years* (Revelations 20:2). —see SATAN **2.** An imaginary firebreathing animal

drag-on-fly (dræg–ən–flaɪ) n. Any of an order of insects with a long, slender body, large eyes, and four narrow wings. It lives near water and catches flies, mosquitoes, and other insects for food.

drain (dreʸn) v. **1.** To flow or cause to flow away gradually: *The rainwater drained off the hillside.* **2.** To exhaust physically or emotionally: *The old man's strength was draining away.* **3.** To become dry (as water or other liquid is removed): *They drained the swimming pool for the winter.*

drain n. **1.** A means of carrying waste water: *All the drains are stopped up.* **2.** Sthg. that empties or uses up: *All these medical bills are a drain on my bank account.* **3. down the drain** *infml.* Used wastefully: *The results of years of work went down the drain when the laboratory exploded.*

drain-age (dreʸ–nɪdʒ) n. A system or means for draining

drake (dreʸk) n. A male duck

dra-ma (drɑ–mə) n. **1.** A serious work of literature that can be acted **2.** The study of plays: *Which do you prefer: music or drama?* **3.** A number of exciting events: *Our vacation was full of drama.*

dra-mat-ic (drə–mæt–ɪk) adj. **1.** Of or related to the drama **2.** Exciting: *a dramatic moment when the movie star leaped from the bridge* —**dramatically** adv.

dram-a-tize also **-ise** *BrE.* (drɑ–mə–taɪz/dræ–) v. **-tized, -tizing 1.** To make whatever changes are necessary so that a book can be made into a play **2.** To present sthg. in a dramatic manner: *He always dramatizes everything. I wish he'd just give us the facts!* —**dram-a-tiz-a-tion** (drɑ–mə–tə–zeʸ–ʃən) n.

drank (dræŋk) v. Past tense of **drink**

drape (dreʸp) v. **draped, draping 1.** To cover or adorn sthg. with folds of cloth: *We draped the war memorial with the national flag.* **2.** To cause to hang or stretch out carelessly: *She draped herself across the couch.*

drape n. *AmE.* A heavy curtain arranged in loose folds —compare CURTAIN

drap-er-y (dreʸ–pər–iʸ) n. **-ies 1.** Cloth or a garment arranged in folds: *windows covered with drapery* **2.** *BrE.* Dry goods

dras-tic (dræs–tɪk) adj. Harsh, vigorous, and often violent or severe: *Drastic measures are required if we are going to improve our educational system.* —**drastically** adv.

draught (drɑft/dræft) n. *Chiefly British* for **draft**

draughts (drɑfts/dræfts) n. *Chiefly British* for the game of checkers

draw (drɔ) v. **drew** (druʷ), **drawn** (drɔn), **drawing 1.** To make a picture with a pencil or pen: *He drew a picture with colored pencils.* **2.** To cause to move by pulling: *The oxen drew the plow through the field./ He drew the curtains. (=opened or closed them)* **3.** To take or pull out: *She drew water from the well.* **4.** To withdraw funds: *John drew $100 from his savings account.* **5.** To take a breath in: *She drew a deep breath.* **6.** To produce or allow a current of air, esp. to make a fire burn better: *The chimney isn't drawing well.* **7.** To provoke: *Their gunfire drew the enemy's gunfire.* **8.** To cause to go in a certain direction: *She drew him aside.* **9.** To receive at random: *She drew the winning number.* **10.** To write a legal document: *He drew up his will.* **11.** Of money, business shares, etc., to earn: *My money is drawing interest in the bank.* **12.** To attract: *The New Year's Day parade always draws huge crowds.* **13. draw a conclusion** To come to a conviction; to decide: *After six attempts he drew the conclusion that he would never be able to climb that mountain.* **14. draw near** To approach: *Winter is drawing near./ Let us draw near to God with a sincere heart in full assurance of faith [in Christ Jesus, our Savior]* (Hebrews 10:22). **15. draw the line** To set a limit as to what one will do or not do **16. draw away (a)** To take or move sthg., usu. quickly: *He drew his hand away from the flame.* **(b)**

To get further and further ahead: *John was drawing farther and farther away from the other runners.* **17. draw back (a)** To move oneself away from: *The crowd drew back from the burning building.* **(b)** To be unwilling to consider or fulfill sthg.: *The company drew back from fulfilling its agreement.* —see DRAW-BACK **18. draw on/ upon sthg.** To make use of: *One has to draw on his imagination and experience.* **19. draw up** Of a vehicle, to get to a certain point and stop: *The car drew up to the front of the hotel.*

draw n. **1.** An act or example of drawing, esp. in a lottery: *On his first draw, he picked the winning number.* **2.** A result with neither side winning: *The game ended in a draw.* **3.** A person, group, or performance that attracts a paying public: *That new comedian is a big draw.*

draw-back (drɔ–bæk) n. A hindrance; a handicap: *The only drawback to the plan is that it costs too much.*

drawer (drɔr / drɔ–ər) n. A sliding boxlike compartment, as in a desk or chest of drawers

draw-ing (drɔ–ɪŋ) n. **1.** The art of representing objects with lines made with a pen, pencil, etc. **2.** A sketch, a plan, or figure made with lines drawn with pen or pencil, etc.

draw-ing card (drɔ–ɪŋ kɑrd) n. Sthg. that attracts attention or business

drawl (drɔl) v. To speak with drawn out or lengthened vowels, in a lazy manner

drawn (drɔn) v. Past part. of **draw**

dread (drɛd) v. To fear greatly: *I dread the thought of war.*

dread n. An extreme fear: *She has a dread of heights.*

dread-ful (drɛd–fəl) adj. **1.** Frightful; terrible **2.** *infml.* Very unpleasant; shocking; disgusting: *The movie (cinema) that we saw last night was so gory! It was dreadful!*

dread-ful-ly (drɛd–fəl–iʸ) adv. **1.** In a terrible way **2.** *polite* Extremely: *I'm dreadfully sorry.*

dream (driʸm) n. **1.** A series of mental images, thoughts, or emotions experienced during sleep **2.** Sthg. imagined and hopefully desired: *His dream was to live on an island in the South Pacific.* **3.** *fig.* Sthg. notable for beauty,

excellence, or enjoyable quality: *Their new house is a real dream.* —**dream-like** adj. —**dreamy** adj. **-ier, -iest**

dream v. **dreamed** (driʸmd/ drɛmt) *also* **dreamt** (drɛmt) *BrE.* **dreaming** (driʸm–ɪŋ) **1.** To have a dream about sthg.: *Do you dream at night?* **2.** *fig.* To think; consider: *I wouldn't dream of hurting the child.* **3. dream sthg. up** To think or imagine or make sthg. up: *He can always dream up a new excuse for not completing the assignment.*

dream-er (driʸm–ər) n. **1.** One who dreams **2.** Someone whose ideas or plans seem impractical

drear-y (drɪər–iʸ) adj. **-ier, -iest** Dull; gloomy: *dreary weather*

dredge (drɛdʒ) n. An apparatus for scraping earth, etc. from the bottom of a body of water

dredge v. **dredged, dredging** To bring up or clean out with a dredge

dredg-er (drɛdʒ–ər) n. A ship that deepens a channel, using a dredge

dregs (drɛgz) n. **1.** Bits of worthless matter that sink to the bottom of a liquid **2.** The worst part: *the dregs of society*

drench (drɛntʃ) v. To make or get soaking wet

dress (drɛs) v. **1.** To clothe oneself or put clothes on someone else: *Please dress the baby, Henry.* **2.** To provide clothing: *She dresses well on very little money.* **3.** To clean and put medicine and a protective covering on a wound **4. dress up (a)** To wear someone else's clothes for fun and pretense: *Little girls like dressing up in their mothers' clothes.* **(b)** To put on formal clothes: *She wanted to go to the school prom but didn't feel like dressing up.*

dress n. **1.** A woman's or girl's outer garment, generally of one piece **2.** Clothing, esp. the visible part of it —compare SKIRT

dress adj. **1.** Used for a dress: *dress material* **2.** Of clothing, suitable for a formal occasion: *a dress shirt/ suit*

dress-er (drɛs–ər) n. *AmE.* A chest of drawers, esp. for clothing

dress-ing (drɛs–ɪŋ) n. **1.** The act of a person who dresses: *Dressing is difficult for him since he hurt his back.* **2.** A bandage, ointment, etc.

for a wound **3**. A sauce for food, esp. a salad
4. *AmE.* Stuffing
dressing down n. A scolding
dress-y (dres-iʸ) adj. **-ier, -iest** Wearing stylish clothing
drew (druʷ) v. Past tense of **draw**
drib-ble (drib–əl) v. **-bled, -bling 1.** To cause to fall in small drops **2.** To let saliva run down the chin. In basketball, to move the ball forward with a series of bounces
drib-let (drib–lət) n. **1.** A small amount **2. in driblets** A little at a time
dried (draid) v. Past tense and part. of **dry**
dri-er (drar–ər) n. Dryer; a device for drying, esp. clothing, towels, sheets, etc.
drift (drift) n. **1.** A mass of snow or sand piled up by the wind: *a snow drift* **2.** The general meaning: *I didn't understand him. I couldn't even get the drift of what he was talking about.*
drift v. **1.** To float or be driven along by wind, waves, or currents: *They drifted out to sea.* **2.** To seemingly have no plans; no purpose in life: *She just drifts from job to job.* **3.** To pile up under the force of the wind or water: *The snow was drifting in great piles against the fence.*
drift-er (drif–tər) n. *derog.* A person who apparently has no purpose in life, but moves aimlessly about
drill (dril) v. **1.** To use a drill: *He drilled a hole in the board.* **2.** To train soldiers, students, etc. by means of drills: *Let's drill the students in spelling.*
drill n. **1.** A tool for boring holes **2.** Training and instruction in a subject, esp. by means of repetition **3.** Practice in dealing with an emergency: *a fire drill*
drink (driŋk) v. **drank** (dræŋk), **drunk** (drʌŋk), **drinking 1.** To swallow liquid **2.** To take in alcohol, esp. too much: *He drinks too much.* **3.** *spir.* Hearing and accepting the Word of God: *Jesus said, "Whoever drinks the water I give him will never thirst. Indeed, the water I give him will become in him a spring of water, welling up to eternal life"* (John 4:14).
drink n. **1.** A liquid suitable for drinking: *Milk is a healthful drink.* **2.** The act of drinking alcohol: *Some people think they need a drink every hour or two.*

drink-er (driŋk–ər) n. One who drinks too much alcohol: *a heavy drinker*
drip (drip) v. **-pp-** To fall in drops: *Water is dripping down from the roof.*
drip n. **1.** The action or sound of falling in drops: *All night I heard the drip, drip, drip of the water.* **2.** *infml.* A stupid or uninteresting person
drip-pings (drip–iŋz) n. Fat and juices that have dripped from roast meat
drive (draiv) v. **drove** (droʷv), **driven** (driv–ən), **driving** (draiv–iŋ) **1.** To guide and control a vehicle: *Can you drive my car to the airport?* **2.** To force to go: *The rancher was driving his cattle along the trail.* **3.** To provide the power for: *The engines drive the ship.* **4.** To force oneself or others to do sthg.: *Her pride drove her to do it.* **5.** To force to penetrate: *He drove the nail into the wood.* **6. drive sthg. home** To make sthg. unmistakably clear to someone **7. drive at sthg.** *infml.* To mean sthg. without actually saying it; hint: *What are you driving at? What do you mean?* **8. drive off sbdy./ sthg.** To force away or back; repel: *He drove off his attackers.* **9.** In baseball, to strike and propel (a ball) forcibly: *The batter drove the first pitch over the center field wall.*
drive n. **1.** A journey in a car: *It's a nice day for a drive.* **2.** A road, esp. one through a public park: *There's a beautiful and famous 17 mile drive near Monterey, California.* **3.** An act of hitting a ball forcefully: *Did you see the drive he hit over the center field fence?* **4.** A strong well-planned effort by a group of people for a particular purpose: *Our church is having a drive to raise funds for the earthquake victims.* **5.** An important natural need which must be fulfilled: *Hunger and thirst are among the strongest human drives.* **6.** Ambition: *He's intelligent but he won't succeed because he doesn't have much drive.*
driv-el (driv–əl) n. Silly talk; nonsense
driv-er (drai–vər) n. A person who drives
driz-zle (driz–əl) v. **-zled, -zling** To rain in small drops or very lightly —**driz-zly** adj.
droll (droʷl) adj. Quaintly amusing
droll n. A funny fellow; jester
drom-e-dar-y (drɑm–ə–dɛər–iʸ) n. **-ies** A camel with one hump

drone (dro^wn) v. **droned, droning 1.** To make a low humming sound **2.** To speak in a dull, boring voice

drone n. **1.** A low humming sound **2.** A dull, boring voice **3.** A male honeybee **4.** A lazy, idle person; a loafer **5.** A pilotless remote-control aircraft

drool (dru^wl) v. **1.** To let saliva flow from the mouth; to dribble **2.** To show gushing appreciation

droop (dru^wp) v. To bend or hang downwards through tiredness or weakness: *The flowers drooped./fig. His spirits drooped.* (=*he became sad*) —**droop** n. —**droopy** adj. **-ier, -iest**

drop (drɑp) n. **1.** A small, round mass of liquid: *a drop of water* **2.** Sthg. shaped like this, such as a piece of candy: *a lemon drop* **3.** A distance or movement straight down: *It was a long drop from the roof to the ground.* **4.** A fall: *a drop in temperature* **5. a drop in the bucket** A very small amount: *Surely the nations are like a drop in a bucket [to the Lord]... Before him all the nations are as nothing; they are regarded as nothing... and less than nothing* (Isaiah 40:15,17).

drop v. **-pp- 1.** To fall or let fall: *The olives dropped from the tree.* **2.** To lower: *Prices dropped last week.* **3.** To let someone out of a vehicle: *He dropped me off at the library.* **4.** To stop talking about sthg.: *Drop the subject.* **5.** To quit: *I had to drop two courses at the university this year.* (=*stop studying them*) **6.** To omit: *You drop the "o" when you combine "had" and "not" in "hadn't."* **7.** To visit informally: *Drop in and see us next time you're in town.* **8.** To get further behind by moving more slowly than the person or vehicle, etc. in front: *He started the race well, but soon dropped behind the others.* **9.** *infml.* To write a letter or note: *Drop me a note some time.* **10. drop dead** *infml.* (often used as an insult) To die suddenly

drop-let (drɑp–lət) n. A small drop

drops (drɑps) n. Liquid medicine to be taken drop by drop: *eye-drops*

dross (drɔs/drɑs) n. **1.** Refuse skimmed from molten metal **2.** Anything worthless

drought (draʊt) n. A long period of dry weather

drove (dro^wv) v. Past tense of **drive**

drown (draʊn) v. **1.** To die under water from suffocation **2.** To overpower with greater loudness: *The brass band drowned out our conversation.* **3.** To deaden (grief, etc.) with strong drink: *He tried to drown his sorrows with whiskey.* —**drowned** adj. *The drowned man's body washed ashore.*

drows-y (draʊ–ziʸ) adj. **-ier, -iest** Sleepy; half asleep —**drowsiness** n.

drub (drʌb) v. **-bb-** To defeat thoroughly

drub-bing (drʌb–ɪŋ) n. A severe defeat

drudge (drʌdʒ) v. **drudged, drudging** To do very dull or laborious work or menial work

drudge n. A person who does such work

drudg-er-y (drʌdʒ–ə–riʸ) n. Dull and laborious work

drug (drʌg) n. **1.** A substance used in medicines **2.** A substance one takes for pleasure or excitement, esp. one causing addiction: *Tobacco, alcohol, and cocaine are dangerous drugs.*

drug v. **-gg-** To add drugs or give drugs to someone, esp. so as to produce unconsciousness

drug-gist (drʌg–əst) n. A pharmacist; a dispenser of prescription drugs

drum (drʌm) n. **1.** A percussion instrument consisting of a skin stretched tight over a round frame and struck by hand or with a stick **2.** Sthg. that looks like such an instrument, esp. a part of a machine or a large container for liquids: *an oil drum*

drum v. **-mm- 1.** To play a drum or drums **2.** To make drum-like noises, esp. by continuous beating or striking: *He drummed on his desk with his fingers.* **3. drum into sbdy.** *infml.* To put an idea firmly into someone's mind by continuous repeating: *The government has been trying to drum it into people to not smoke or use drugs.* **4. drum up** *infml.* To get more of sthg. by continuous effort and by advertising: *We've got to drum up more business or we won't be in business very long.*

drum-mer (drʌm–ər) n. A person who plays a drum

drunk (drʌŋk) adj. Under the influence of alcohol: *The police charged him with being drunk and disorderly./ He's dead drunk.* (=*very*

drunk)/ *fig. He's drunk with power.* —compare SOBER

drunk v. Past part. of **drink**

drunk also **drunk-ard** (drʌŋ-kərd) n. A person who is habitually drunk

drunk-en-ness (drʌŋ-kən-əs) n. A state of being drunk: *Drunkenness is a sin that must be repented of. Those who practice such things "will not inherit the Kingdom of God"* (Galatians 5:21). NOTE: God hates the sin of drunkenness and all sins. But because of his great love and mercy he forgives those who repent of their sins and trust in Jesus for eternal life (Mark 1:15, Acts 16:31). —see JESUS, MAN, SIN

dry (draɪ) adj. **drier, driest 1.** Empty of water or other liquid; not wet: *The wells in the area are dry because of lack of rainfall this season.* **2.** Without rain or wetness: *dry weather* **3.** Not having natural moisture: *My skin is really dry from this weather.* **4.** Boring; uninteresting: *This is the driest book I have ever read.* —dryness n.

dry v. **dried, drying 1.** To make dry: *If you wash the dishes I'll dry them.* **2.** To cause food to be preserved through a process of removing the moisture: *dried peaches/ dried milk*

du-al (duʷ-əl) adj. **1.** Composed of two parts; double **2.** Having a double nature, character, or purpose NOTE: Do not confuse **dual** with **duel**.

dub (dʌb) v. **-bb- 1.** To name or nickname **2.** To add sound-effects to a film **3.** To provide a new sound-track for a film in order to change the language

du-bi-ous (duʷ-biʸ-əs) adj. **1.** Doubtful; skeptical **2.** Undecided; uncertain **3.** Questionable —dubiously adj.

duch-ess (dʌtʃ-əs) n. **1.** The wife or widow of a duke **2.** A woman with the same rank as a duke in her own right

du-chy (dʌtʃ-iʸ) n. **-chies** The land owned or ruled by a duke

duck (dʌk) **drake** *masc.* n. **1.** Any of various swimming birds which have a wide, flat beak, and short legs and necks, often kept for meat, eggs, and soft feathers (down): *Oh, look! There's a mother duck and her duckl-*

ings! **2. lame duck** *AmE.* A political official who will soon be replaced by someone newly elected

duck v. **1.** To lower one's head or move one's body quickly, esp. in order to escape a danger: *He ducked out of the way of the speeding car just in time.* **2.** To go or push under water: *He ducked his head down and swam under water.* **3.** *infml.* To try to escape difficulty or an unpleasant responsibility

duct (dʌkt) n. **1.** Any tube, pipe, or channel by which a fluid, gas, or glandular secretion, etc., is conveyed **2.** A tube in the body through which fluid passes: *tear ducts* **3.** A single enclosed runway for electric cables

duc-tile (dʌk-təl) adj. **1.** Capable of being drawn out into wire or otherwise being subjected to stress without breaking **2.** Easily molded or shaped **3.** Ready to obey; easily led

dud (dʌd) n. **1.** A bomb or shell that failed to explode **2.** *infml.* A worthless person or thing

dude (duʷd) n. **1.** A city person, esp. one vacationing on a ranch **2.** A man overly concerned with fashion and appearance

duds (dʌdz) n. *slang* Clothing

due (duʷ) adj. **1.** *fml.* Owed or owing: *The rent is due at the end of the month.* **2.** *fml.* Adequate; appropriate: *The talented musician is finally receiving the respect due him.* **3.** According to schedule; expected: *The Smith's baby is due in another two weeks.* **4. in due course/ time** According to the proper time

due adv. Directly; straight: *Just go due east about two miles and you'll reach our house.*

du-el (duʷ-əl) n. **1.** A fight between two people, usu. using pistols or swords **2.** Any contest between two individuals or groups

duel v. **-eled** or **-elled, -eling** or **-elling** To fight in a duel —duelist n. One who fights in a duel

dues (duʷz) n. Official charges for membership or other fees: *club dues/ union dues*

du-et (duʷ-ɛt) n. Music arranged for or performed by two persons —compare SOLO

due to prep. Resulting from; caused by: *His collapse was due to overwork.*

dug (dʌg) v. Past tense and part. of **dig**

dug-out (dʌg–aʊt) n. **1.** A boat made by hollowing out the trunk of a tree **2.** An underground shelter

duke (duʷk) n. **1.** A nobleman next in rank below a prince, ruler over a duchy **2. dukes** *infml*. Fists

dul-cet (dʌl–sət) adj. Sweet to the ear; melodious

dull (dʌl) adj. **1.** Not bright or shiny: *What dull, gloomy weather! I wish the sun would come out!* **2.** Lacking sharpness: *a dull knife* **3.** Mentally slow: *The teacher gave special help to the dull children in his class.* **4.** Uninteresting: *I like my new professor. His lectures are never dull.* —**dully** adv. —**dullness** n.

dull v. To make or become dull: *sthg. to dull the pain*

du-ly (duʷ–liʸ) adv. **1.** In a proper manner **2.** In due time

dumb (dʌm) adj. **1.** Not able to speak: *dumb animals/ The phone company provides special services for those who are deaf and dumb.* **2.** *infml*. Foolish: *That was a dumb mistake!* NOTE: We generally use the word **mute** when referring to persons who are unable to speak. —**dumbly** adv. —**dumbness** n.

dumb-bell (dʌm–bɛl) n. **1.** A bar with a weight at each end, used for exercising **2.** A stupid person

dumb-foun-ded (dʌm–faʊnd–əd) adj. Struck dumb with astonishment; amazed

dum-my (dʌm–iʸ) n. **1.** Sthg. that seems real but is not **2.** A model or a human being used to display clothing **3.** A stupid person

dump (dʌmp) v. To drop or unload sthg. in a careless manner: *Don't dump that junk in the street./ fig. After twenty-six years of friendship she dumped her best friend.*

dump n. **1.** A place for getting rid of things no longer wanted such as waste products: *We can haul this worn out old sofa to the city dump.* **2.** *derog. infml*. A dirty and disorderly or run-down place: *I hope you can move out of this dump soon.*

dump-ling (dʌmp–lɪŋ) n. A ball of dough filled with fruit, ground meat, etc. and steamed, baked or fried

dump-y (dʌm–piʸ) adj. Short and stocky

dunce (dʌns) n. Someone who is mentally slow

dune (duʷn) n. also **sand dune** A ridge or hill of sand piled up by the wind along the seashore or in the desert

dung (dʌŋ) n. Solid waste materials passed from the bowels by cows, horses, and other animals; animal manure

dun-ga-rees (dʌŋ–gə–riʸz/ dʌŋ–gə–riʸz) n. Blue denims; pants made of heavy cotton cloth

dun-geon (dʌn–dʒən) n. A dark underground prison

dunk (dʌŋk) v. To dip into liquid: *She dunked her donut into her coffee.*

du-o (duʷ–oʷ) n. **duos** pl. n. A pair of performers

du-o-de-num (duʷ–ə–diʸ–nəm/ duʷ–ɑd–ən–əm) n. The first part of the small intestine, immediately below the stomach

dupe (duʷp) n. One easily cheated

dupe v. **duped, duping** To deceive; to trick

du-pli-cate (duʷ–plə–kət) adj., n. Sthg. that is exactly like sthg. else: *My dress is an exact duplicate of yours in color, style, and material.*

du-pli-cate (duʷ–plə–keʸt) v. To copy sthg. exactly: *Can you duplicate this key for me, please?* —**duplication** (duʷ–plə–keʸ–ʃən) n.

du-pli-ca-tor (duʷ–plə–keʸt–ər) n. A machine that makes exact copies

du-pli-ci-ty (duʷ–plɪs–ə–tiʸ) n. **-ties** Deceitfulness; double dealing

dur-a-bil-i-ty (dʊr–ə–bɪl–ə–tiʸ/dyʊr–) n. Quality of lasting a long time

dur-a-ble (dʊr–ə–bəl/ dyʊr–) adj. Capable of lasting a long time: *My sister always buys durable clothing for her four active young sons.*

du-ra-tion (dʊ–reʸ–ʃən/dyʊ–) n. The period of time for which sthg. exists or lasts: *I hope this firewood lasts for the duration of the cold spell.*

du-ress (duʷ–rɛs) n. The use of force or threats in order to make someone do something

dur-ing (dʊr–ɪŋ/dyʊr–) prep. **1.** Throughout a length of time: *She skis almost every day during the winter.* **2.** At some point in a length of time: *It snowed during the night.*

dusk (dʌsk) n. The darker state of twilight

dust (dʌst) n. **1.** Very fine, dry pieces of waste or other matter: *The furniture was covered*

with dust when we returned from our vacation.
2. Finely powdered earth: *The strong winds blew clouds of dust across the fields.*

dust v. **1.** To remove the dust from: *When I was a child it was my job to dust the furniture.* **2.** To cover with fine powdery material: *The farmer dusted his crops with a chemical for killing insects.*

dust-er (dʌs–tər) n. **1.** A cloth or brush for dusting furniture **2.** A housecoat

dust-pan (dʌst–pæn) n. A pan into which dust is swept from the floor

dust-y (dʌs–ti^y) adj. **-ier, -iest** Covered or filled with dust

du-ti-a-ble (du^w–tɪ–ə–bəl) adj. Items on which duty must be paid

du-ti-ful (du^w–tɪ–fəl) adj. Showing proper respect, obedience, and responsibility —**dutifully** adv.

du-ty (du^w–ti^y) n. **-ties 1.** The responsibility one has because of a job or because he thinks it is right: *Fear God and keep his commandments, for this is the whole duty of man* (Ecclesiastes 12:13). NOTE: Man cannot be doing his duty or keeping God's commandments by his own effort. He can only be saved and have eternal life by the grace of God through faith in Jesus Christ our Savior. "For by grace are you saved through faith and that not of yourselves, it is a gift of God, not of works lest any man should boast" (Ephesians 2:8 KJV). —see JESUS **2.** A charge by the government, esp. on imported goods: *I had to pay a lot of duty on this camera in order to bring it into the country.* **3.** **heavy duty** (esp. of equipment) Capable of hard work or use: *heavy duty truck* **4. on/ off duty** (esp. of policemen, soldiers, nurses, etc.) Required/ not required to work: *When she is off duty, my friend often invites me to go to lunch with her.*

dwarf (dwɔrf) n. An undersized person, animal, or plant

dwarf v. **1.** To make seem small by contrast or distance **2.** To stunt

dwell (dwɛl) v. **dwelt** (dwɛlt) or **dwelled, dwelling 1.** *fml.* To live in a place: *The Smiths dwell in Canada near a lovely lake./ spir. Let the Word of Christ dwell in you richly* (Colossians 3:16). **2. dwell on/ upon sthg.** To continue to think, speak, or write about: *It's not healthy to dwell so much on your mistakes.*

dwel-ler (dwɛl–ər) n. One who lives in the stated place: *a prairie dweller*

dwell-ing (dwɛl–ŋ) n. *fml.* Any of various types of housing where people live: *This is a dwelling suitable for a king!*

dwin-dle (dwɪn–dəl) v. **-dled, -dling** To become gradually less

dye (daɪ) n. A vegetable or chemical substance, usu. liquid, used for coloring cloth and other things

dye v. **dyes, dyed, dyeing** To make a change in color by means of dye: *She dyed the curtains to match the carpet.*

dyed–in–the–wool (daɪd–ɪn–ðə–wʊl) adj. Very difficult to change: *John is a dyed-in-the-wool fisherman.*

dy-nam-ic (daɪ–næm–ɪk) adj. **1.** Of people, ideas, etc., full of power and activity or producing power and activity: *a dynamic teacher/ a dynamic program for feeding the hungry* **2.** *tech.* Concerning force or power that causes movement —opposite STATIC —**dynamically** adv.

dy-na-mite (daɪ–nə–maɪt) n. **1.** A powerful blasting explosive **2.** *infml.* A person or thing that will cause great shock, surprise, admiration, etc.: *This new product for washing clothes is dynamite!*

dynamite v. **-mited, -miting** To cause an explosion with dynamite

dy-na-mo (daɪ–nə–mo^w) n. **-mos** A small, compact generator producing electric current

dy-nas-ty (daɪ–nəs–ti^y) n. **-ties** A line of rulers all coming from the same family: *a dynasty of emperors*

dys-en-ter-y (dɪs–ən–tɛər–i^y) n. A painful disease marked by severe diarrhea with passage of blood and mucus

dys-tro-phy (dɪs–trə–fi^y) n. A condition causing progressive weakening of the muscles: *muscular dystrophy*

E, e (i^y) n. The fifth letter of the English alphabet

E. (i^y) *written abbr.* Said as: Eastern

each (i^ytʃ) determ., pron. Every one of two or more taken separately: *Each of you may have one apple.*

each adv. Apiece: *Candy bars are 40 cents each.*

ea-ger (i^y–gər) adj. Feeling keen interest or desire: *They were eager for the game to begin.* —**eagerly** adv. —**eagerness** n.

ea-gle (i^y–gəl) n. A large bird of prey with very good eyesight

eagle eyed (i^y–gəl aid) adj. Keen-sighted

ear (rər) n. **1.** One of the two organs of hearing, one on each side of the head: *spir. The eyes of the Lord are on the righteous and his ears are attentive to their prayer* (1 Peter 3:12). **2.** The ability to recognize slight differences in sound, esp. in music and languages: *He has an ear for languages.* **3. out on one's ear** *infml.* Thrown out of a place **4. play it by ear** *infml.* To act without making plans in advance **5. up to one's ears in** *infml.* Very involved in or very busy with: *I'm up to my ears in bills to pay.*

ear-ly (ɜr–li^y) adj. **-lier, -liest 1.** Arriving, happening, etc., sooner than expected; before the usual time: *The train is hardly ever early.* **2.** Happening near the beginning of a period of time: *She gets up early every morning.*

early adv. **-lier, -liest 1.** Before the expected time: *Our plane got in a little early.* **2.** Near the beginning of a period: *She takes a nap early in the afternoon./ Crocuses bloom early in the spring.*

earn (ɜm) v. **1.** To receive for work done: *He earned $1,000 this month at the factory.* **2.** To get sthg. that one deserves because of what one has done: *She earned the respect of the other workers because of her hard work.*

ear-nest (ɜm–əst) adj. Determined and sincere: *John made an earnest attempt to find a job, but did not get one.* —**earnest** n. *They began to work in earnest when the principal came in.* —**earnestly** adv.

earn-ings (ɜm–ɪŋz) n. Money that has been earned by working

earth (ɜrθ) n. **1.** The planet on which we live (the globe): *In the beginning God created the*

heavens and the earth (Genesis 1:1). **2.** All the people in the world: *The earth is the Lord's and everything in it* (Psalm 24:1). **3. soil** in which plants grow: *The tender plants broke through the warm earth.* —see LAND **4. down to earth** Simple, direct, and practical; saying what one thinks

earth-quake (ɜrθ–kwe^yk) n. A violent, shaking movement of the earth, often very destructive

earth-shak-ing (ɜrθ–ʃe^y–kɪŋ) adj. Having a violent effect on established arrangements, beliefs, etc.

ease (i^yz) v. **-eased, -easing 1.** To become or cause to become less severe: *Some aspirin might help to ease the pain.* **2.** To become less difficult or unpleasant: *The tension between the two families has eased.*

ease n. **1.** Freedom from difficulty: *He climbed over the fence with ease.* —compare EASILY **2.** The state of being comfortable and free from anxiety: *a life of ease* **3. ill at ease** Anxious **4. at ease** (used as a military command) To stand in a more relaxed manner, with feet apart

ea-sel (i^y–zəl) n. A folding frame for holding an artist's painting, blackboard, etc.

eas-i-ly (i^yz–ə–li^y) adv. **1.** With no difficulty: *I can easily get all this done by noon.* **2.** Without doubt: *She is easily the richest person in town.*

east (i^yst) n. **1.** The point of the horizon where the sun rises —compare EASTERN **2.** One of the four main compass points, on the right of a person facing north: *As far as the east is from the west, so far has he [God] removed our transgressions [sins] from us* (Psalm 103:12). **3.** The countries of Asia, esp. China and Japan: *living in the Far East* **4.** The eastern part of a country

east adv. Facing east: *Looking east, we can get a good view of the sunrise.*

Eas-ter (i^ys–tər) n. A festival in the Christian Church commemorating the resurrection of Jesus Christ. —see JESUS, RESURRECTION. NOTE: Christ's resurrection proved that he was who he claimed to be — true God and Savior of the world, with all power and authority in heaven and on earth (Romans 1:4; Matthew 28:18; John 14:9),

and that he "is coming again to receive all believers to himself, that where he is, they may be also" (John 14:3).

east-er-ly (i^yst–ər–li^y) adj. **1.** Toward the east **2.** Of a wind, from the east: *an easterly wind*

east-ern (i^yst–ərn) adj. Of or belonging to the part of the world or of a country that is located to the east

east-ward (i^yst–wərd) adj. Going towards the east: *an eastward trip*

eas-y (i^yz–i^y) adj. **-ier, -iest 1.** Not difficult: *Painting a picture was an easy task for John. He's an artist.* **2.** Comfortable and without anxiety: *He's enjoying the easy life since he retired.* **—easiness** n.

easy adv. **-ier, -iest 1.** Easily **2. easier said than done** More difficult to do than to talk about: *Finding a good used car is easier said than done.* **3. easy does it** *infml.* Do sthg. more slowly and more carefully **4. go easy on** (a) Be kinder to; don't punish him/ her too much: *Go easy on him; he didn't mean to do it.* (b) To use less of: *Go easy on sweets. You're gaining too much weight.* **5. take it/ things easy** Don't work too hard.

eat (i^yt) v. **ate** (e^yt), **eaten** (i^yt–ən), **eating 1.** To take food into the mouth, chew, and swallow it: *So whether you eat or drink or whatever you do, do it all for the glory of God* (1 Corinthians 10:31). **2.** To take food; have a meal: *Where are we going to eat tonight?* **3.** To damage or destroy sthg. as by chemical action: *The acid ate a hole in the carpet.* **4. eat one's words** To take back sthg. said earlier

eaves (i^yvz) n. The edge of a roof overhanging the walls

ebb (ɛb) n. **1.** The flow of water away from the shore; the going out of the tide **2. at a low ebb** To be in a low state of mind; unhappy: *Her enthusiasm seems to be at a low ebb.*

ebb v. **1.** To flow away from the shore **2.** To weaken: *Her strength slowly ebbed away.*

eb-o-ny (eb–ə–ni^y) n. A kind of dark, hard wood **—ebony** adj. **1.** Black as ebony **2.** Made of ebony

e-bul-lient (ɪ–bu^wl–yənt) adj. Lively and enthusiastic **—ebullience** n.

ec-cen-tric (ɪk–sɛn–trɪk) adj. Of a person,

strange, peculiar, unusual

eccentric n. A person with eccentric ideas, habits, etc. **—ec-cen-tric-i-ty** (ɛk–sɛn–trɪs–ət–i^y) n.

Ec-cle-si-as-tes (ɪ–kli^y–zi^y–æs–ti^yz) n. A book of the Old Testament reflecting on the futilities of life and our duties and obligations to God, traditionally ascribed to Solomon and written in his name **—see OLD TESTAMENT**

ec-cle-si-as-tic (ɪ–kli^y–zi^y–æs–tɪk) n. A clergyman in the Christian church

ec-cle-si-as-tic-al (ɪ–kli^y–zi^y–æs–tɪk–əl) adj. Having to do with the Christian church: *ecclesiastical law/ art*

ech-e-lon (ɛʃ–ə–lɑn) n. **1.** A group of people at a certain level, or of a particular grade, in a particular organization: *the upper/ lower echelons of society* **2.** A step-like arrangement, as of troops or aircraft **3.** A subdivision of a military force

ech-o (ɛk–o^w) n. **-oes** Repetition of a sound caused by a reflection of the sound waves from a wall, cliff, or other surface

echo v. **-oed, -oing 1.** To send back sound: *The cave was echoing with the shouts of the children.* **2.** To repeat: *She always echoed her husband's opinions.*

e-clipse (ɪ–klɪps/ i^y–) n. **1.** The disappearance from sight of all or part of a heavenly body, as of the moon when the earth is between it and the sun **2.** Loss of glory or brilliance

eclipse v. **-clipsed, -clipsing 1.** To cause an eclipse **2.** To do much better than: *Her success was eclipsed by that of her sister.*

e-col-o-gy (ɪ–kɑl–ə–dʒi^y) n. The study of plants and animals in relation to their natural surroundings **—ecological** (ɛ–kə–lɑdʒ–ɪ–kəl) adj. **—ecologically** adv. **—e-col-o-gist** (ɪ–kɑl–ə–dʒəst) n.

ec-o-nom-ic (ɛk–ə–nɑm–ɪk) adj. **1.** Connected with trade, industry, and money: *What is the economic state of our country compared to that of Germany?* **2.** Of or having to do with satisfying the needs of the people: *economic geography* **—compare ECONOMICAL**

ec-o-nom-i-cal (ɛk–ə–nɑm–ɪ–kəl/i^y–) adj. Not wasteful in the use of money, time, goods, etc.: *My small car is more economical than your*

large one. It uses less gasoline. —compare ECONOMIC —economically adv.

ec·o·nom·ics (ɛk–ə–**nɑm**–ɪks) n. pl. The science of the production and use of wealth by industry and government: *A country's economics are of concern to all governments.*

e·con·o·mist (ɪ–**kɑn**–ə–məst) n. A specialist in economics

e·con·o·mize also **-mise** *BrE.* (ɪ–**kɑn**–ə–maɪz) v. **-mized, -mizing** To save money, time, goods, etc. by avoiding waste

e·con·o·my (ɪ–**kɑn**–ə–mi*ʸ) n. **-mies 1.** The careful use of money, time, etc. —compare ECONOMICAL **2.** The operation of a country's money supply, industry, and trade

economy adj. Cheap: *I always buy soap in the large economy size to save money.*

ec·sta·sy (ɛk–stə–si*ʸ) n. **-sies** A feeling of intense delight

ec·stat·ic (ɛk–**stæt**–ɪk) adj. Causing or experiencing ecstasy —**ecstatically** adv.

ec·u·men·i·cal (ɛk–yə–**men**–ɪ–kəl) adj. Seeking worldwide Christian unity

ec·ze·ma (ɪg–zi*ʸ–mə) n. An itching skin inflammation

–ed (–d/–əd/–ɪd/–t) **1.** Past tense and past part. ending of regular verbs: *walked/talked/wanted/helped* **2.** Having, or characterized by: *A horse is a four-footed animal.*

ed·dy (ɛd–i*ʸ) n. **-dies** A current of water, air, etc. running against the main stream, causing a circular movement

e·del·weiss (e*ʸ–dəl–vaɪs) n. A kind of Alpine plant with white flowers

E·den (i*ʸd–ən) n. The beautiful garden where Adam and Eve lived before they disobeyed God; paradise

edge (ɛdʒ) n. **1.** The sharp cutting side of a blade, knife, tool, etc. **2.** The narrow part along the outside of sthg.: *the edge of the plate* **3. on edge** Nervous: *Everyone was on edge after the professor announced a major exam.*

edge v. **edged, edging 1.** To make an edge or border on sthg.: *a pillow edged with ruffles* **2.** To move sideways little by little: *Jane edged through the crowd to get closer to the front.*

ed·i·ble (ɛd–ə–bəl) adj. Eatable; fit to be eaten —opposite INEDIBLE

e·dict (i*ʸ–dɪkt) n. A proclamation made by a

public official; a decree

ed·i·fi·ca·tion (ɛd–ə–fə–**ke***ʸ–ʃən) n. Instruction, esp. of a moral or spiritual nature

ed·i·fice (ɛd–ə–fəs) n. A very large, fine building

ed·i·fy (ɛd–ə–faɪ) v. **-fied, -fying** *fml.* To instruct, esp. so as to encourage moral improvement: *This book is edifying. I learned a lot from it.*

ed·it (ɛd–ət) v. To prepare a piece of writing, a movie, etc. for printing or showing (by making corrections, improvements, etc.)

e·di·tion (ɪ–**dɪʃ**–ən) n. **1.** The total number of copies of one printing, esp. of a book: *a first edition* **2.** The form or style in which a book, movie, etc. appears: *Many books come in both hard cover and less expensive paperback editions.*

ed·i·tor (ɛd–ət–ər) n. A person who edits books, movies, etc.

ed·i·to·ri·al (ɛd–ə–**tɔr**–i*ʸ–əl) n. A part of a newspaper giving an opinion on a matter of public concern

ed·i·to·ri·al·ize (ɛd–ə–**tɔr**–i*ʸ–əl–aɪz) v. **-ized, -izing 1.** To express a view in the form of an editorial **2.** To introduce an opinion into the reporting of facts **3.** To express an opinion

ed·u·cate (ɛdʒ–ə–ke*ʸt) v. **-cated, -cating** To teach sbdy.; to train the character or mind of: *Moses was educated in all the wisdom of the Egyptians...* (Acts 7:22). —**educated** adj. *He was a well-educated man.*

ed·u·ca·tion (ɛdʒ–ə–**ke***ʸ–ʃən) n. **1.** Development of the mind and character: *One can continue getting an education well into his senior years.* **2.** A system of training and instruction, esp. for children and young people —**educational** adj.

ed·u·ca·tor (ɛdʒ–ə–ke*ʸt–ər) n. One who is professionally involved in education

eel (i*ʸl) n. A fish having a snake-like body

ee·rie (ɪər–i*ʸ) adj. **-rier, -riest** Causing a feeling of mystery and fear

ef·face (ɪ–fe*ʸs) v. **-faced, -facing 1.** To rub out; destroy the surface of **2. self-effacing** Making oneself inconspicuous

ef·fect (ɪ–fɛkt) v. *fml.* To bring sthg. about; have as a result: *He effected the rescue of several hostages.* —see AFFECT

effect n. **1.** An outcome: *Eating too many sweets can have a bad effect on one's health.* **2. in effect (a)** In operation; in use: *The new law will be in effect after midnight tomorrow.* **(b)** In actual practice: *In effect, the vice president of the company is running it. The president is out of the country.*

ef-fec-tive (ɪ–fɛk–tɪv) adj. **1.** Producing good results: *The prayer of a righteous man is powerful and effective* (James 5:16). **2.** Actual: *Although there is a president, the rebels are in effective control of the country.* —**effectively** adv. —**effectiveness** n.

ef-fects (ɪ–fɛkts) n. Personal belongings: *I have very few personal effects. I live quite simply.*

ef-fec-tu-al (ɪ–fɛk–tʃuʷ–əl) adj. Producing the outcome intended; able to do what is required

ef-fem-i-nate (ɪ–fɛm–ə–nət) adj. Of a man or his behavior, having characteristics considered usual in a woman; unmanly; womanish

ef-fer-vesce (ɛf–ər–vɛs) v. -vesced, -vescing **1.** To give off bubbles of gas; to fizz **2.** To act in a lively way —**effervescence** n. —**effervescent** adj.

ef-fi-ca-cious (ɛf–ə–keʸ–ʃəs) adj. Producing the desired result —**ef-fi-ca-cy** (ɛf–ə–kə–siʸ) n.

ef-fi-cient (ɪ–fɪʃ–ənt) adj. Able to work well, quickly, and without waste: *Ours is a very efficient, well-organized office./ The school needs to buy a more efficient copy machine.* —**efficiency** n. —**efficiently** adv.

ef-fi-gy (ɛf–ə–dʒiʸ) n. -gies A model of a person, made of stone, wood, etc.

ef-flo-resce (ɛf–lə–rɛs) v. -resced, -rescing **1.** To blossom or bloom **2.** *Chem.* To become powdery through evaporation of water **3.** To become covered with a powdery crust

ef-flo-res-cence (ɛf–lə–rɛs–əns) n. **1.** The act or season of flowering **2.** A fulfillment or culmination **3.** *Chem.* The act or process of efflorescing

ef-fort (ɛf–ərt) n. The use of much energy; a hard try: *He made an effort to be on time every morning./ It [salvation] does not... depend on man's effort, but on God's mercy* (Romans 9:16). *On the other hand, the Lord says, "Make every effort to live in peace with all men and be holy; without holiness no one will see the Lord"* (Hebrews 12:14). —see HOLY

ef-fron-ter-y (ɛ–frʌn–tə–riʸ) n. -ies Shameless insolence

ef-fu-sion (ɛ–fyuʷ–ʒən) n. **1.** A pouring forth **2.** An unrestrained outpouring of one's thoughts or feelings

ef-fu-sive (ɛ–fyuʷ–sɪv) adj. Expressing emotions in an unrestrained way

e.g. *written abbr.* Said as **for example**: *sports, e.g. baseball, swimming, and football*

egg (ɛg) n. **1.** An oval object with a hard shell, coming from a female bird, snake, etc., from which a baby animal comes (hatches): *There were two eggs in the robin's nest.* **2.** The contents of this, esp. from a hen, when eaten as food: *Many Americans eat eggs for breakfast.* **3.** In female mammals, the seed of life, which joins with the male seed (sperm) to produce a baby —see FERTILIZE

e-go (iʸ–goʷ) n. **1.** Personal pride: *His criticism really hurt my ego.* **2.** The self; the part of a person that is conscious and thinks

e-go-cen-tric (iʸ–goʷ–sɛn–trɪk) adj. Self-centered; thinking only about one's own interests

e-go-ism (iʸ–goʷ–ɪz–əm) n. The quality of thinking only about oneself; selfishness —**egoist** n.

e-go-tism (iʸ–gə–tɪz–əm) n. The habit of speaking too much about oneself; boastfulness —**egotist** n. —**egotistical** adj.

eight (eʸt) determ., n., pron. The number **8** —**eighth** determ., n., pron., adv.

eigh-teen (eʸ–tiʸn) determ., n., pron. The number 18 —**eighteenth** determ., n., pron., adv.

eight-y (eʸt–iʸ) determ., n., pron. -ies The number 80 —**eightieth** determ., n., pron., adv.

ei-ther (iʸ–ðər/ aɪ–ðər) determ., adj., conj., pron. **1.** One or the other of two: *You will have to choose either the yellow shirt or the green one. You can't have both.* **2.** One and the other (of two); each: *The two boys sat on either side of their father.* (=*one on each side*) —compare BOTH

either adv. (used with negative expressions)

Also; in addition: *I don't have any money, and my brother doesn't have any either.* (=*Both don't have any money.*)

e-ject (ɪ–dʒɛkt) v. To throw forcefully; expel; evict: *They were ejected from their house for not paying the rent.* —**ejection** n.

eke (iʸk) v. **eked, eking; eke out 1.** To make a living laboriously: *She was just barely eking out an existence.* **2.** To supplement or make a small amount go further

e-lab-o-rate (ɪ–læb–ə–rɑt) adj. Detailed; carefully worked out and with a large number of details: *an elaborate dinner* —**elaborately** adv.

e-lab-o-rate (ɪ–læb–ə–reʸt) v. **-rated, -rating** To state sthg. in detail: *Just give us the facts. You can elaborate on them later.* —**e-lab-o-ra-tion** (iʸ–læb–ə–reʸ–ʃən) n.

e-lapse (ɪ–læps) v. **-lapsed, -lapsing** Of time, to pass: *Several hours have elapsed since she went away.*

e-las-tic (ɪ–læs–tɪk) adj. Of material such as rubber, able to be stretched and then spring back into shape: *an elastic waistband* —**e-las-ti-ci-ty** (ɪ–læs–tɪs–ɪ–tiʸ) n.

e-lat-ed (ɪ–leʸ–təd) adj. Cheerful; full of pride and joy: *She was elated after winning the contest.*

el-bow (ɛl–boʷ) n. The joint where the arm bends, esp. the outer point of this

elbow v. To push one's way through with the elbows: *He elbowed his way through the crowded lobby.*

el-der (ɛl–dər) n. **1.** The older of two persons: *John is the elder of my two brothers.* **2.** Older persons: *Children should respect their elders.* **3.** A person having a respected official position: *a church elder/ village elder*

elder adj. Of people, older, esp. the older of two: *my elder brother* NOTE: **Elder** is used only of people, but **older** can be used of things, also. **Elder** can not be used in comparisons. *John is Mary's elder brother. John is older than (not elder than) Mary.*

el-der-ly (ɛl–dər–liʸ) adj. Of a person, nearing old age

el-dest (ɛl–dəst) adj., n. One who is the oldest of three or more: *The eldest of my four children is now in her twenties.*

e-lect (ɪ–lɛkt) v. **1.** To choose a person by voting: *The senior class elected John as their class president ?. fml.* To choose to do sthg. important: *My father elected to take early retirement so he could spend more time traveling.*

elect adj. Chosen, but not yet in office: *He is the president-elect.*

e-lec-tion (ɪ–lɛk–ʃən) n. The act of voting for representatives for a (political) position: *There is a Presidential election in the US every four years.*

e-lec-tion-eer (ɪ–lɛk–ʃən–ɪər) v. To try to get votes in an election

e-lec-tive (ɪ–lɛk–tɪv) adj. **1.** Concerning a course of study, freely chosen; not required: *John is taking four required courses in college and one elective.* **2.** Concerning a position to which a person is elected

e-lec-tor-ate (ɪ–lɛk–tər–ət) n. All those who have a right to vote in an election

e-lec-tric (ɪ–lɛk–trɪk) adj. **1.** Producing or powered by electricity: *an electric typewriter/ electric generator* **2.** *fig.* Thrilling; very exciting: *The effect of his speech was electric. The crowd went wild.* —**electrical** adj. —**electrically** adv.

e-lec-tri-cian (ɪ–lɛk–trɪʃ–ən) n. One whose job is to install and repair electrical equipment

e-lec-tric-i-ty (ɪ–lɛk–trɪs–ə–tiʸ) n. A form of energy used to produce heat, light, power, etc.

e-lec-tri-fy (ɪ–lɛk–trə–faɪ) v. **-fied, -fying 1.** To pass a current of electricity through sthg. **2.** To equip for the use of electric power: *Most farms in the country have been electrified by now.* **3.** To cause great excitement or surprise: *The actor's performance was electrifying.*

e-lec-tro-cute (ɪ–lɛk–trə–kyuʷt) v. **-cuted, -cuting 1.** To kill by passing electricity through the body **2.** To execute a criminal by electric shock

e-lec-trode (ɪ–lɛk–troʷd) n. Either of two points through which a current of electricity enters and leaves a battery, etc.

e-lec-tron (ɪ–lɛk–trɑn) n. A very small particle within an atom, having the smallest possible charge of electricity

e-lec-tron-ics (ɪ–lɛk–trɑn–ɪks) n. The branch of industry that makes products like comput-

ers, televisions, etc. —**electronic** adj. *an electronic organ/ an electronic typewriter*

el·e·gant (**εl**–ə–gənt) adj. Having grace, beauty, and dignity; stylish: *an elegant woman/ elegant house/ an elegant piece of jewelry* —**elegance** n. —**elegantly** adv.

el·e·ment (εl–ə–mənt) n. **1.** Any of about 100 simple substances that, alone or in combination, make up all substances; a substance that cannot be split into simpler substances: *Gold, silver, tin, and lead are elements.* **2.** A small quantity: *There was an element of truth in her story, but none of us thought she was telling the whole truth.* **3.** A necessary or characteristic part of a whole: *Respect for one another is one of the elements of a good marriage.* **4.** The part of an electrical device that gives off heat: *the heating element in a toaster* **5.** The forces of nature; the weather —**el·e·men·tal** (εl–ə–**ment**–əl) adj. —see COMPOUND

el·e·men·ta·ry (εl–ə–**men**–tə–ri^y) adj. **1.** Simple; easy; basic **2.** Dealing with the beginnings, esp. of education: *elementary education*

el·e·ments (εl–ə–mənts) n. **1.** The basic beginnings; the first steps **2.** *lit.* The forces of nature, esp. bad weather: *We knew he was out in the storm facing the elements alone.*

el·e·phant (εl–ə–fənt) n. **-phant** or **-phants** A huge, thick-skinned, almost hairless mammal, the largest four-footed animal in existence, with a long, flexible snout (called a trunk) and two ivory tusks growing out of the upper jaw

el·e·vate (εl–ə–ve^yt) v. **-vated, -vating 1.** To lift up; to raise **2.** To raise (a person) in position or rank **3.** To improve a person's mind; to uplift —**elevated** adj. *An elevated railway is one that is raised above the street on a framework so that the street is left free for other traffic.*

el·e·va·tion (εl–ə–ve^y–ʃən) n. **1.** Being elevated or raised in rank: *elevation to the rank of admiral* **2.** Height above sea level: *The elevation of Mexico City is about 7,000 feet.* **3.** A drawing of the side of a building: *the front elevation*

el·e·va·tor (εl–ə–ve^y–tər) *AmE.* n. A cage or compartment for raising persons, goods,

grain, etc. from one floor or level to another

e·lev·en (ɪ–lεv–ən) determ., n., pron. The number 11 —**eleventh** determ., n., pron., adv.

elf (εlf) n. **elves** An imaginary small being with magic powers

e·lic·it (ɪ–lɪs–ət) v. To succeed in getting or drawing out information, feelings, etc. from a person

el·i·gi·ble (εl–ə–dʒə–bəl) adj. **1.** Having the right to do or receive sthg.: *He is eligible to receive a presidential award for his excellent work in school.* **2.** Suitable: *John is eligible and he would make someone an excellent husband.* —opposite INELIGIBLE —**el·i·gi·bil·i·ty** (εl–ə–dʒə–bɪl–ət–i^y) n.

e·lim·i·nate (ɪ–lɪm–ə–ne^yt) v. **-nated, -nating** To get rid of: *to eliminate crime from our city* —**e·lim·i·na·tion** (ɪ–lɪm–ə–ne^y–ʃən) n.

e·lite (ɪ–li^yt) n. *often derog.* **1.** A group of people regarded as superior in some way and therefore favored **2.** A size of letters in typewriting, twelve letters per inch

elk (εlk) n. *pl.* **elk, elks 1.** A large deer of northern Europe and Asia **2.** A large North American deer with spreading antlers

el·lipse (ɪ–lɪps) n. A closed curve of oval shape

el·lip·sis (ɪ–lɪp–səs) n. **-ses** (–si^yz) **1.** The omission from a sentence of a word or words that would complete the construction **2.** Marks (...) to indicate the omission of one or more words

el·lip·ti·cal (ɪ–lɪp–tɪ–kəl) adj. **1.** Of or having the form of an ellipse **2.** Of or marked by grammatical ellipsis —**elliptically** adv.

elm (εlm) n. **1.** A tall shade tree with gradually spreading branches **2.** The hard, heavy wood of this tree

el·o·cu·tion (εl–ə–**kyu**^w–ʃən) n. The art of speaking clearly and effectively

e·lon·gate (ɪ–lɔŋ–ge^yt) v. **-gated, -gating** To make or become longer

e·lon·gat·ed (ɪ–lɔŋ–ge^yt–əd) adj. Length-ened; stretched out; long and narrow

e·lope (ɪ–lo^wp) v. **-loped, -loping** To run away secretly, esp. with a lover: *They eloped because her parents refused to give her permission to marry.*

embrace

el-o-quence (ɛl-ə-kwəns) adj. Ability to express ideas and opinions well, so that the hearers are impressed

el-o-quent (ɛl-ə-kwənt) adj. Having or showing eloquence: *a very eloquent speaker*

else (ɛls) adv. **1.** In addition; besides: *Who else (=in addition) should we invite?* **2.** Different; otherwise: *Someone else (=another person) will have to do the work. I'm too tired./ He must finish his report or else stay home and do it tonight.*

else-where (ɛls–wɛər) adv. In or to some other place: *The vacuum cleaner is not here. We'll have to look elsewhere.*

e-lu-ci-date (ɪ–luʷ–sə–deʸt) v. -dated, -dating To explain; make clear: *Please elucidate. I don't understand.*

e-lude (ɪ–luʷd) v. -luded, -luding **1.** To escape or avoid sthg. (or sbdy.) by a trick or cleverness **2.** To be too difficult to understand or remember

e-lu-sive (ɪ–luʷ–sɪv) adj. Hard to find, capture, or remember

e-ma-ci-at-ed (ɪ–meʸ–ʃiʸ–eʸt–əd) adj. Very thin and weak, esp. as a result of illness or lack of food —**e-ma-ci-a-tion** (ɪ–meʸ–ʃiʸ–eʸ–ʃən) n.

em-a-nate (ɛm–ə–neʸt) v. -nated, -nating To come out from some source: *Pleasant smells emanated from the kitchen.*

e-man-ci-pate (ɪ–mæn–sə–peʸt) v. -pated, -pating To set free from slavery or some other type of unfair control: *Women are being emancipated, little by little, from unfair social conditions.*

em-balm (ɪm–bam) v. To treat a dead body with spices or chemicals to prevent decay

em-bank-ment (ɪm–bæŋk–mənt) n. A long ridge of earth or a stone structure to keep a river from spreading or for supporting a road or railroad over low-lying places

em-bar-go (ɪm–bar–goʷ) n. -goes An official order forbidding commerce or other activity

embargo v. -goed, -going To put an embargo on sthg.

em-bark (ɪm–bark) v. **1.** To put or go on board a ship at the beginning of a journey **2.** To begin an undertaking: *He embarked on a new career.*

em-bar-rass (ɪm–bɛər–əs) v. To cause to feel ashamed, uncomfortable, or ill at ease: *I was embarrassed by his asking so many personal questions.* —**embarrassment** n. **embarrassing** adj.

em-bas-sy (ɛm–bə–siʸ) n. -sies **1.** An ambassador and his staff, sent by a government to live in a foreign country and keep good relations **2.** The ambassador's official headquarters

em-bed (ɪm–bɛd) v. -dd- To fix deeply (in sthg.): *The bullet was embedded in the wall.*

em-bel-lish (ɪm–bɛl–ɪʃ) v. **1.** To ornament; decorate; make more beautiful **2.** To improve a story, report, etc. by adding details that are entertaining but not necessarily true

em-ber (ɛm–bər) n. A piece of burning or glowing coal or wood

em-bez-zle (ɪm–bɛz–əl) v. -zled, -zling To steal money that is entrusted to one's care: *The bookkeeper was accused of embezzling thousands of dollars.*

em-bit-ter (ɪm–bɪt–ər) v. To make bitter and resentful: *He was embittered by his failure to get a promotion./ Fathers, do not embitter your children, or they will become discouraged* (Colossians 3:21).

em-bla-zon (ɪm–bleʸ–zən) v. **1.** To set out in bright colors or in some other very noticeable way **2.** To exalt

em-blem (ɛm–bləm) n. An object which is the sign of a school, idea, class of people, etc.: *The cross is an emblem of Christianity.* —compare SYMBOL

em-bod-y (ɪm–bad–iʸ) v. -ied, -ying **1.** To include: *Many new ideas are embodied in the latest model of this car.* **2.** To express in words, actions, etc.: *Many of his opinions are embodied in this magazine article.* —**embodiment** n.

em-boss (ɪm–bas/ ɪm–bɔs) v. To ornament with a raised design

em-brace (ɪm–breʸs) v. -braced, -bracing **1.** To take and hold one another in the arms as a sign of love: *The sisters embraced each other warmly.* **2.** *fml.* To include: *A course in English may embrace composition, grammar, and literature.* **3.** *fml.* To accept; become a believer in: *He embraced the Christian faith.* —**embrace** n.

a tender embrace

em-broi-der (ɪm–**brɔɪ**–dər) v. To do decorative stitching on cloth —**embroidery** n.

em-broil (ɪm–**brɔɪl**) v. To get a person into a quarrel or a difficult situation: *I don't want to get myself embroiled in their quarrel.*

em-bry-o (**ɛm**–bri^y–o^w) n. **1.** The young of any plant or animal in its first state before it is born **2.** Anything in its very early stage of development —**em-bry-on-ic** (ɛm–bri^y–**ɑn**–ɪk) adj.

e-mend (ɪ–**mɛnd**) v. To edit a text by removing flaws and errors —**e-men-da-tion** (i^y–mən–**de**^y–ʃən) n.

em-er-ald (**ɛm**–ər–əld) n. A bright green precious stone

e-merge (ɪ–**mɜrdʒ**) v. **-merged, -merging 1.** To come out **2.** To become known or clear

e-mer-gen-cy (ɪ–**mɜr**–dʒən–si^y) n. **-cies** A sudden and dangerous happening which must be dealt with quickly: *Dial 9-1-1 in an emergency.*

em-i-grate (**ɛm**–ə–gre^yt) v. **-grated, -grating** To leave one country in order to go and live in another —**emigrant** n. —**em-i-gra-tion** (ɛm–ə–**gre**^y–ʃən) n.

NOTE: **Migration** is to move from one country to another for a short period. *Some birds migrate south for the winter./ Farmers in Southern California hire a lot of migrant workers from Mexico.* **Emigration** is to leave one country to go and become a citizen of another. —compare IMMIGRATE

em-i-nent (**ɛm**–ə–nənt) adj. **1.** Distinguished; prominent; famous and admired: *an eminent senator* **2.** Conspicuous; evident **3.** Lofty; high —compare IMMINENT

e-mir (ɪ–**mɪər** / e^y–) n. A Muslim ruler in parts of Africa and Asia

e-mir-ate (**ɛm**–ər–ət) n. The position, lands, etc. of an emir

em-is-sar-y (**ɛm**–ə–sɛər–i^y) n. **-ies** One who is sent with a special message or to do a special work, esp. a secret agent

e-mit (ɪ–**mɪt**) v. **-tt-** To send or give out light, heat, fumes, etc. —**emission** n.

Em-man-u-el also **Im-man-u-el** (ɪ–**mæn**–yu^w–əl) n. **1.** A masculine name: "God with us" **2.** One of the names given to Jesus Christ in fulfillment of O.T. prophecy —see IMMANUEL

e-mo-tion (ɪ–**mo**^w–ʃən) n. **1.** Any of the strong feelings one may have: *Love, hatred, fear, and grief are only a few of the emotions.* **2.** Strength of feeling: *He spoke of his homeland with deep emotion.* —**emotionless** adj. —**emotionlessly** adv.

e-mo-tion-al (ɪ–**mo**^w–ʃən–əl) adj. **1.** Having strong or sensitive feelings: *It was an emotional meeting. We hadn't seen each other for twenty years.* —opposite UNEMOTIONAL **2.** Of music, literature, etc., showing or producing strong feelings **3.** Related to the emotions: *The child has severe emotional problems.* —**emotionally** adv.

em-pa-thy (**ɛm**–pə–θi^y) n. The ability to understand and share the feelings, experiences, etc. of someone else —**em-pathize** v.

em-per-or (**ɛm**–pər–ər) n. The head of an empire

em-pha-sis (**ɛm**–fə–səs) n. **-ses** (–si^yz) **1.** Special importance given to sthg.: *The university we attended put a lot of emphasis on sports.* **2.** Stress laid on part of a word or on a phrase

em-pha-size also **-sise** *BrE.* (**ɛm**–fə–saɪz) v. **-sized, -sizing** To put emphasis on sthg.

em-phat-ic (ɪm–**fæt**–ɪk) adj. Using or showing emphasis; expressing oneself with emphasis: *She stamped her foot to make her answer more emphatic.* —**emphatically** adv.

em-phy-se-ma (ɛm–fə–**si**^y–mə) n. A condition in which the air cells in the lungs lose their elasticity, causing difficulty in breathing

em-pire (**ɛm**–paɪ–ər) n. A group of countries or states under one government, usu. ruled by an emperor: *the British Empire*

em-pir-i-cal (ɪm–**pɪər**–ɪ–kəl) adj. **1.** Depending or based on experience or observation **2.** Subject to verification by observation or experiment

em-pir-i-cism (ɪm–**pɪər**–ə–sɪz–əm) n. **1.** The belief that knowledge is obtained only by direct experience through the physical senses **2.** Empirical method or procedure

em-ploy (ɪm–**plɔɪ**) v. **-ployed, -ploying** To use a person as a paid worker; hire a person for a job: *The company employs over 3,000 workers.*

em-ploy-ee (ɪm–plɔɪ–iʸ) n. A person who is employed

em-ploy-er (ɪm–plɔɪ–ər) n. A person or group that employs others

em-ploy-ment (ɪm–plɔɪ–mənt) n. The act of employing or state of being employed

em-por-i-um (ɛm–pɔr–iʸ–əm) n. **1.** A large retail store **2.** A center of commerce

em-pow-er (ɪm–paʊ–ər) v. *fml.* or *legal* To authorize; to give official permission to

em-press (ɛm–prəs) n. **1.** The female ruler of an empire **2.** The wife or widow of the emperor

emp-ty (ɛmp–tiʸ) adj. **1.** Having nothing in it: *an empty box* —opposite FULL **2.** Without meaning or purpose; unreal: *empty pleasure/ Let no one deceive you with empty words, for because of such things God's wrath comes on those who are disobedient* (Ephesians 5:6). —**emptiness** n.

empty n. **-ties** Sthg. that is empty, as a bottle, box, etc.

empty v. **-tied, -tying 1.** To become empty or cause sthg. to become empty: *I guess they were pretty hungry. They emptied their plates. (=ate all that was on them)* —compare FILL **2.** To take the contents of a container and put it somewhere else: *They emptied the truck into the warehouse.*

em-u-late (ɛm–yə–leʸt) v. **-lated, -lating** To try to do as well as someone else, esp. by imitating them: *He tried hard to emulate his older brother in sports and academic achievement.*

e-mul-si-fy (ɪ–mʌl–sə–faɪ) v. **-fied, -fying** To make into an emulsion

e-mul-sion (ɪ–mʌl–ʃən) n. **1.** A combination of two liquids that do not ordinarily mix, such as oil and water, in which tiny drops of one liquid are evenly distributed throughout the other **2.** A photosensitive material used for coating photographic film

–en (–ɛn/–n) suffix **1.** Forming verbs **(a)** (From adj.) To cause to be or become: *deepen* **(b)** (From nouns) Cause to have; gain: *strengthen* **2.** Used in the plural of some nouns: *oxen* **3.** Small: *kitten/chicken*

en– (ɛn–/ɪn–) prefix Forming transitive verbs **(a)** (From nouns) To cover or surround with; place into or upon: *encircle* **(b)** (From

nouns and adjectives) To make; cause to resemble: *enable* **(c)** (From verbs) Often used to form transitive verbs from intransitive verbs: *enact*

en-a-ble (ɪn–eʸ–bəl) v. **-bled, -bling** To make able; give the ability, means, or right: *His hearing aid enabled him to hear almost normally.*

en-act (ɪ–nækt) v. **1.** To act; perform **2.** To make a law

en-am-el (ɪ–næm–əl) n. **1.** A glass-like substance used for coating metal or pottery **2.** A kind of paint that dries hard and glossy **3.** The hard, outer covering of the teeth

en-am-or *AmE.* **en-am-our** *BrE.* (ɪ–næm–ər) v. To inflame with love

en-am-ored (ɪ–næm–ərd) adj. Fond: *He was enamored with the sound of his own voice.*

en-camp (ɪn–kæmp) v. To settle in a camp: *The angel of the Lord encamps around those who fear him, and he delivers them* (Psalm 34:7).

en-camp-ment (ɪn–kæmp–mənt) n. A camp

en-case (ɪn–keʸs) v. **-cased, -casing** To enclose in a case

–ence (–əns) suffix Forming nouns from adjectives ending in -ent: *violence*

en-chant (ɪn–tʃænt) v. **1.** To fill with intense delight **2.** To put under a magic spell —**enchanted** adj.

en-chant-ing (ɪn–tʃænt–ɪŋ) adj. Delightful: *an enchanting little village*

en-cir-cle (ɪn–sɜr–kəl) v. **-cled, -cling** To surround; form a circle around

en-close (ɪn–kloʷz) v. **-closed, -closing 1.** To shut in with a wall, fence, etc.: *Our porch is enclosed to keep out the rain.* **2.** To put inside sthg.: *I am enclosing a photo (with this letter).*

en-clo-sure (ɪn–kloʷ–ʒər) n. **1.** An enclosed piece of land or part of a building **2.** Sthg. that is put with sthg. else in a letter

en-com-pass (ɪn–kʌm–pəs) v. To surround; to encircle

en-core (ɑn–kɔr) n., interj. **1.** A call for repetition of a performance **2.** The song, dance, etc., performed in response to the call for it

en-coun-ter (ɪn–kaʊn–tər) v. To meet sthg. unexpectedly, esp. sthg. dangerous or unpleasant: *He encountered many difficulties along the way.* —**encounter** n. *a very unpleas-*

ant encounter

en-cour-age (ɪn-kɜr-ɪdʒ) v. -aged, -aging To give hope and support to someone; urge someone on: *His father encouraged him to become a doctor./ We urge you brothers, warn those who are idle, encourage the timid, help the weak, be patient with everyone* (1 Thessalonians 5:14). —opposite DISCOURAGE —**encouragement** n. *He received encouragement from his parents to start his own business.* —**encouraging** adj. —**encouragingly** adv.

en-croach (ɪn-kroʷtʃ) v. **1.** To intrude upon someone's territory or rights: *Do not... encroach on the fields of the fatherless* (Proverbs 23:10). **2.** To advance beyond the original or usual limits: *The sea encroached gradually upon the land.* —**encroachment** n.

en-cum-ber (ɪn-kʌm-bər) v. **1.** To weigh down; burden **2.** To hinder the function or activity of **3.** To burden with a legal claim, for example, as a mortgage —**encumbrance** n.

en-cy-clo-pe-di-a also **en-cy-clo-pae-di-a** (ɪn-saɪ-klə-piʸ-diʸ-ə) n. **1.** A work that contains information on all branches of knowledge **2.** A work that treats a single branch of knowledge in great detail —**encyclopedic** adj.

end (ɛnd) n. **1.** The last point or part of anything that has length: *the end of the street* **2.** The point in time at which sthg. is over: *the end of summer* **3.** *fml.* The aim or purpose of an action: *He should be able to gain his ends by hard work.* **4. at loose ends** *AmE.* **at a loose end** *BrE.* Restless because of having nothing to do **5. make ends meet** To have just enough income to meet one's needs **6. on end (a)** Continuously **(b)** In an upright position: *We had to stand the desk on end to get it through the office door.*

end v. To finish or cause to finish: *We expect the movie to end at ten o'clock.*

en-dan-ger (ɛn-deʸn-dʒər) v. To bring into danger —**endangered** adj.

en-dear (ɪn-dɪər) v. To cause someone or sthg. to become more dear to someone: *Her kindness endeared her to everyone.*

en-dear-ment (ɪn-dɪər-mənt) n. An expression of love

en-deav-or (ɛn-dɛv-ər) v. *AmE.* **endeavour** *BrE. fml.* To try; attempt: *We will endeavor to help you get through college.*

endeavor n. Effort: *Crossing the country 100 years ago was quite an endeavor.*

en-dem-ic (ɛn-dem-ɪk) adj. Restricted or peculiar to a particular place: *This disease is endemic in Africa.*

end-ing (ɛnd-ɪŋ) n. The end of a story, movie, play, etc.: *a dramatic ending* —opposite BEGINNING

en-dive (ɛn-daɪv) n. A type of plant with curly leaves, used in salads

end-less (ɛnd-ləs) adj. **1.** Having no end **2.** Extremely long or numerous **3.** Joined at the ends: *an endless chain*

en-dorse (ɪn-dɔrs) v. -dorsed, -dorsing **1.** To write one's name on the back of a check that has been made payable to him **2.** To express approval or support of

en-dow (ɪn-daʊ) v. **1.** To give a permanent income to: *The college was endowed by that great industrialist.* **2.** To provide or equip with a talent or quality: *She was endowed with great musical ability.* —**endowment** n.

en-dur-ance (ɪn-dʊər-əns/ -dyʊər-) n. Ability to last: *The winner of the race showed great endurance and strength.*

en-dure (ɪn-dʊər/ -dyʊər) v. -dured, -during **1.** To bear patiently; to tolerate pain, suffering, etc.: *I can't endure that noise a moment longer.* —see BEAR **2.** *fml.* To remain firm; to last: *Give thanks to the Lord for he is good. His love endures forever* (Psalm 136:1). —**endurable** adj. —**enduring** adj.

en-e-ma (ɛn-ə-mə) n. **1.** Injection of liquid into the rectum by means of a syringe, for medical purposes **2.** The liquid used for this purpose

en-e-my (ɛn-ə-miʸ) n. -mies **1.** A person who strongly dislikes another person: *The mayor has many friends, but he also has some enemies. (=some people dislike him)* **2.** Anyone or anything that is against sbdy. or sthg. or wants to harm them: *Your enemy, the devil, prowls around like a roaring lion, looking for someone to devour* (1 Peter 5:8). *Anyone who chooses to be a friend of the world is an enemy of God* (James 4:4). **3.** The army against whom one

is fighting

en-er-get-ic (ɛn–ər–dʒɛt–ɪk) adj. Full of energy: *an energetic person* —**energetically** adv

en-er-gy (ɛn–ər–dʒiʸ) n. -gies **1.** Vitality **2.** The capacity for vigorous activity: *Young people usually have more energy than the old.* **3.** Fuel and other resources used for the operation of machinery: *atomic/electric energy*

en-er-vate (ɛn–ər–veʸt) v. -vated, -vating To lessen the strength of —**enervation** n. —**enervator** n.

en-fold (ɛn–foʷld) v. **1.** To embrace **2.** To envelop

en-force (ɪn–fɔrs) v. -forced, -forcing To make happen or bring about by force: *The check point is to help the police enforce the drunk driving law.* —**enforceable** adj. —**enforcement** n.

en-gage (ɪn–geʸdʒ) v. -gaged, -gaging **1.** To arrange to hire sbdy. **2.** To keep busy with sthg.: *He is engaged in volunteer work among the homeless.* **3.** To cause to fit into or lock together; to mesh: *He engaged the gears and the heavy truck pulled forward.* **4.** *fml.* To attack: *They engaged the enemy (in battle).*

en-gaged (ɪn–geʸdʒd) adj. Having agreed to marry: *David is engaged to be married.*

en-gage-ment (ɪn–geʸdʒ–mənt) n. **1.** An agreement to marry someone: *Susan has broken off her engagement to Henry.* (=said she no longer wishes to marry him) **2.** An appointment to meet someone or to do sthg., esp. at a definite time: *He had to cancel his speaking engagement because of illness.*

en-gine (ɛn–dʒən) n. **1.** A machine which changes power from steam, oil, etc. into movement **2.** Also **locomotive** *fml.* A machine for pulling a railroad train

en-gi-neer (ɛn–dʒə–nɪər) n. **1.** A person who designs, builds and understands the making of machines, railroads, bridges, harbors, etc.: *My son plans to become an electrical engineer.* **2.** *AmE.* The driver of a railroad engine

engineer v. **1.** To plan, construct, and manage as an engineer: *That bridge is very well engineered.* **2.** To plan or accomplish by skill or by cunning means: *He had powerful enemies who engineered (=arranged) his defeat.*

en-gi-neer-ing (ɛn–dʒə–nɪər–ɪŋ) n. **1.** The science of making practical application of pure sciences such as physics, chemistry, etc. as in the construction of buildings, highways, bridges, etc. **2.** The work or profession of an engineer

Eng-lish (ɪŋ–glɪʃ) adj. Concerning England, its people, etc.: *the English countryside*

English n. **1.** The language of the UK, the US, etc. **2.** People of England

en-graft (ɪn–græft) v. **1.** To insert into a tree so as to cause to grow; graft **2.** To cause to take root, as an idea in the mind

en-grave (ɪn–greʸv) v. -graved, -graving **1.** To carve or cut a design or letters on wood, stone, or metal **2.** To print from such a surface **3.** To impress permanently: *The terrible tragedy was engraved on his mind.*

en-gross (ɪn–groʷs) v. To occupy completely, as the mind or one's attention: *The children were so engrossed in the TV program that I had to call them three times for dinner.*

en-gross-ing (ɪn–groʷs–ɪŋ) adj. Very, very interesting

en-gulf (ɪn–gʌlf) v. To surround or cause to disappear; to swallow up completely: *The plane was engulfed in the clouds.*

en-hance (ɪn–hæns) v. -hanced, -hancing To increase the attractiveness of other qualities: *The moonlight enhanced her beauty.* —**enhancement** n.

e-nig-ma (ɪ–nɪg–mə) n. A mysterious person or thing, difficult to understand

e-nig-ma-tic (ɛ–nɪg–mæt–ɪk) adj. Mysterious or puzzling

en-join (ɪn–dʒɔɪn) v. **1.** To order; to command **2.** In law, to prohibit; to restrain by an injunction

en-joy (ɪn–dʒɔɪ) v. -joyed, -joying **1.** To get pleasure from sthg. or someone **2.** *fml.* To possess or use sthg. as a benefit: *She enjoys the admiration of music lovers everywhere.* **3.** **enjoy oneself** To experience pleasure or happiness

en-joy-a-ble (ɪn–dʒɔɪ–ə–bəl) adj. Pleasant —**enjoyably** adv.

en-joy-ment (ɪn–dʒɔɪ–mənt) n. Pleasure; happiness: *Command those that are rich in this present world... to put their hope in God, who*

richly provides us with everything for our en-joyment (1 Timothy 6:17).

en-large (ɪn–lɑrdʒ) v. -larged, -larging To make larger: *We're enlarging our garden to grow more vegetables./ I'd like to have this photograph enlarged.* —**enlargement** n. *I'm sending Mother an enlargement of the baby's photograph.*

en-light-en (ɪn–lart–ən) v. 1. To give more information to someone 2. To furnish with spiritual understanding

en-list (ɪn–lɪst) v. 1. To enter the armed forces voluntarily 2. To obtain help, support, etc.

en-liv-en (ɪn–lar–vən) v. To make more lively, active, or cheerful

en-mi-ty (ɛn–mə–tiʸ) n. Unfriendliness; ill-will; hostility

e-nor-mi-ty (ɪ–nɔr–mə–tiʸ) n. -ties 1. The quality of being very large; huge size 2. Great wickedness 3. An outrageous act

e-nor-mous (ɪ–nɔr–məs) adj. 1. Great in size, number, or degree; huge 2. Exceedingly wicked —**enormously** adv.

e-nough (ɪ–nʌf) determ., pron. As much or as many as needed: *We have enough food for everyone.*

enough adv. 1. To the necessary degree: *warm enough/ fast enough/ big enough* 2. In a fairly acceptable way: *She does well enough in school to pass, but she could do much better if she studied harder.* 3. **sure enough** *infml.* As expected: *We believed the baby would be a girl, and sure enough it was.*

en-quire (ɪn–kwar–ər) v. -quired, -quiring A variation of **inquire**; to ask —**enquiry** n. Inquiry

en-rage (ɪn–reʸdʒ) v. -raged, -raging To make very angry; to fill with rage

en-rich (ɪn–rɪtʃ) v. 1. To make rich or richer: *Alaska was enriched by the discovery of gold.* 2. To improve the quality of sthg. by adding to it 3. *fig.* To improve one's own mind: *Reading good books can enrich your whole life.* —**enrichment** n. *Read the Bible for spiritual enrichment.*

en-roll (ɪn–roʷl) also enrol v. -ll- 1. To become a member of a society, club, institution, etc.: *He enrolled as a member of the club.* 2. To admit as a member —**enrollment** n.

en route (ɑn–ruʷt/ ɛn–raʊt) adv. On the way: *I met him at the station when he was en route to San Francisco.*

en-sconce (ɪn–skɑns) v. 1. To establish securely or comfortably 2. To shelter; hide

en-sem-ble (ɑn–sɑm–bəl) n. 1. A small group of musicians who perform together 2. A woman's outfit of harmonizing items: *Her hat, coat, and shoes made a beautiful ensemble.* 3. All the parts of a thing taken as a whole

en-sign (ɛn–sən) n. 1. An officer of the lowest rank in the navy 2. A flag on a ship, esp. one that shows what nation the ship belongs to

en-slave (ɪn–sleʸv) v. -slaved, -slaving 1. To make a slave of someone 2. To become a slave to sthg.

en-snare (ɪn–snɛər) v. -snared, -snaring To catch in a snare; to trap: *The evil deeds of a wicked man ensnare him; the cords of his sin hold him fast* (Proverbs 5:22).

en-sue (ɪn–suʷ) v. -sued, -suing To happen afterward or as a result of: *A panic ensued as a result of a bomb threat.*

en-sure (ɪn–ʃʊər) v. also insure *AmE.* -sured, -suring To make certain; to make sure: *You'd better make your reservations early to ensure yourself of a seat.*

–ent (–ənt) suffix, adj. and n. Equivalent of **–ant**

en-tail (ɪn–teʸl) v. To make necessary; to involve: *Writing a dictionary entails a lot of hard work.*

en-tan-gle (ɛn–tæŋ–gəl) v. -gled, -gling 1. To become twisted or tangled with sthg. else: *If they have escaped the corruption of the world by knowing our Lord and Savior Jesus Christ and are again entangled in it [the corruption] and overcome, they are worse off at the end than they were at the beginning* (2 Peter 2:20). 2. To be involved in sthg. complicated

en-ter (ɛn–tər) v. 1. To come or go into a place, room, etc.: *He entered the house.* 2. To become a member of a group: *to enter a university* 3. To record names, amounts of money, etc. in a book

en-ter-prise (ɛn–tər–praɪz) n. 1. A plan to do sthg. new or difficult, esp. if it requires boldness or courage 2. The qualities needed to attempt such an undertaking 3. A system

of organizing business: *I believe in private en-terprise rather than government control.* **4.** A business organization: *He's the head of a large enterprise that sells automobiles.*

en-ter-pris-ing (ɛn–tər–praɪz–ɪŋ) adj. Energetic; bold and vigorous in action

en-ter-tain (ɛn–tər–teᵞn) v. **1.** To receive and treat as a guest: *Do not forget to entertain strangers, for by so doing some people have entertained angels without knowing it* (Hebrews 13:2). **2.** To hold the attention of, so as to bring about pleasure; to amuse **3.** To provide food and drink for, give a party for, etc.: *Mr. and Mrs. Williams entertain often in their home.* **4.** To hold in the mind; to consider; think about: *Jesus said, "Why do you entertain evil thoughts in your hearts?"* (Matthew 9:4).

en-ter-tain-er (ɛn–tər–teᵞn–ər) n. A person who entertains professionally

en-ter-tain-ing (ɛn–tər–teᵞn–ɪŋ) adj. Amusing and interesting: *an entertaining story* —**entertainingly** adv.

en-ter-tain-ment (ɛn–tər–teᵞn–mənt) n. **1.** The act of entertaining people by providing food and drink, etc. **2.** Amusement for the general public: *The circus is an entertainment for people of all ages.*

en-thrall (ɪn–θrɔl) also **enthral** v. To fascinate; to hold the complete attention and interest of sbdy.: *The little boy was enthralled by the stories about people in other lands.*

en-throne (ɪn–θroʷn) v. **-throned, -throning 1.** To place on, or as if on, a throne: *He [God] sits enthroned above the circle of the earth* (Isaiah 40:22). **2.** To exalt

en-thuse (ɪn–θuʷz) v. **-thused, -thusing** To show a keen interest in; to show enthusiasm: *He was greatly enthused about taking a trip abroad.* NOTE: The word **enthuse** is disapproved by some careful users of English, so in formal writing it is best to avoid it. It is better to say that one is **enthusiastic** about sthg., rather than **enthused** about it.

en-thu-si-asm (ɪn–θuʷ–ziᵞ–æz–əm) n. **1.** Great or fervent interest or excitement **2.** A cause of keen or lively interest —**enthusiast** n. *an airplane enthusiast* —**en-thu-si-as-tic** (ɪn–θuʷ–ziᵞ–æs–tɪk) adj. —**enthusiastically** adv.

en-tice (ɛn–taɪs) v. **-ticed, -ticing** To tempt or persuade someone to do sthg., usu. wrong, usu. by offering a reward of sthg. pleasant: *If sinners entice you, do not give in to them* (Proverbs 1:10).

en-tire (ɪn–taɪ–ər) adj. Whole; complete: *She spent the entire day at the library./ The entire law [of God] is summed up in a single command: "Love your neighbor as yourself"* (Galatians 5:14). —**entirely** adv.

en-tire-ty (ɪn–taɪr–tiᵞ/ɪn–taɪ–ər–tiᵞ/ɪn–taɪ–rə–tiᵞ) n. The state of being entire or complete

en-ti-tle (ɪn–taɪ–təl) v. **-tled, -tling 1.** To give a title to a book, play, etc. **2.** To give someone the right to have or do sthg.

en-ti-ty (ɛn–tə–tiᵞ) n. **-ties** Sthg. that exists independently

en-to-mol-o-gy (ɛn–tə–mɑl–ə–dʒiᵞ) n. The study of insects

en-trails (ɛn–treᵞlz) n. The internal parts of an animal; the intestines

en-trance (ɛn–trəns) n., adj. **1.** An opening, gate, door, etc. by which one enters **2.** The act of entering: *She made her usual grand entrance.* **3.** The right of entering; admission: *entrance to the club*

en-trance (ɛn–træns) v. **-tranced, -trancing** To cause someone to be filled with great wonder and delight

en-tranc-ing (ɪn–træns–ɪŋ) adj. Charming

en-trant (ɛn–trənt) n. **1.** A person who enters **2.** A competitor in a contest

en-treat (ɪn–triᵞt) v. To ask or beg imploringly

en-trée or **en-tree** (ɑn–treᵞ) n. **1.** The main course of a meal **2.** The right or privilege of admission

en-trench (ɪn–trɛntʃ) v. **1.** To surround or defend with trenches **2.** To establish solidly —**entrenched** adj. Firmly established; difficult to remove

en-tre-pe-neur (ɑn–treᵞ–prə–nʊər) n. A person who organizes and manages a commercial undertaking, esp. one involving financial risk

en-tro-py (ɛn–trə–piᵞ) n. **1.** A measure of the amount of energy that is not available for work during a natural process **2.** The tendency of all systems, including the universe, to become increasingly disorderly; a

change inward and downward

en-trust (ɪn–**trʌst**) v. To charge with a trust or responsibility: *The Father [God the Father] judges no one, but has entrusted all judgment to the Son [Jesus], that all may honor the Son just as they honor the Father* (John 5:22). —see JESUS

en-try (**ɛn**–trɪ^y) n. -tries **1.** The act of entering **2.** A place for entering **3.** The act or result of recording on a list: *There were twenty-five entries on my list of students in this class.* **4.** A person or thing entered in a competition: *Which entry would you choose as the winner of the Beautiful Baby competition?* —see ENTRANCE

en-twine (ɪn–**twaɪn**) v. -twined, -twining To twist together

e-nu-mer-ate (ɪ–**nu**^w–mə–re^yt) v. -ated, -ating **1.** To name things one by one; to list **2.** To count

e-nun-ci-ate (ɪ–**nʌn**–si^y–e^yt) v. -ated, -ating **1.** To pronounce distinctly **2.** To state formally

en-vel-op (ɪn–**vɛl**–əp) v. To cover completely: *The ship was soon enveloped in the fog.*

en-ve-lope (**ɛn**–və–lo^wp/ **ɑn**–) n. The paper wrapper of a letter

en-vi-a-ble (**ɛn**–vi^y–ə–bəl) adj. Desirable enough to arouse envy —**enviably** adv.

en-vi-ous (**ɛn**–vi^y–əs) adj. Feeling, showing, or expressing envy: *Do not fret because of evil men or be envious of the wicked, for the evil man has no future hope, and the lamp of the wicked will be snuffed out* (Proverbs 24:19,20). —**enviously** adv. —see JEALOUS

en-vi-ron-ment (ɪn–**vaɪ**–rən–mənt) n. The natural surroundings or social conditions in which people live: *We must work to protect the environment.* (=the air, water, and land around us)/*an unhappy home environment* —**en-vi-ron-men-tal** (ɪn–vaɪ–rən–**mɛnt**–əl) adj.

en-vi-ron-men-tal-ist (ɪn–vaɪ–rən–**mɛnt**–əl–əst) n. A person who seeks to improve or protect the environment

en-vi-rons (ɪn–**vaɪ**–rənz) n. pl. The surroundings, esp. those around a city

en-vis-age (ɛn–**vɪz**–ɪdʒ) v. -visaged, -visaging **1.** To visualize **2.** To plan; expect

en-vi-sion (ɪn–**vɪ**–ʒən) v. To picture mentally

en-voy (**ɑn**–vɔɪ) n. A messenger, esp. one sent to deal with a foreign government

en-vy (**ɛn**–vi^y) n. A resentful feeling that a person has towards someone who has qualities or possessions that one would like for himself: *The acts of the sinful nature are obvious: sexual immorality, impurity... envy, drunkenness... and the like... Those who live like this will not inherit the kingdom of God* (Galatians 5:19-21). —compare JEALOUSY NOTE: Envy is a sin and God hates all sin. Even so, God is a God of love. He loves the sinner and he forgives those who repent of their sins and assures them of eternal life if they repent of their sins and put their trust in Jesus Christ (Mark 1:15; Acts 16:31).

envy v. -vied, -vying To feel or show envy: *Love is patient and kind. It does not envy. It does not boast...* (1 Corinthians 13:4).

en-zyme (**ɛn**–zaɪm) n. A substance produced in a living body which affects the speed of chemical changes without being changed itself

e-on (**i**^y–ən/ **i**^y–ɑn) n. An extremely long, indefinite period of time

e-phem-er-al (ɪ–**fɛm**–ər–əl) adj. Lasting a very short time

E-phe-sians (ɪ–**fi**^y–ʒənz) n. A book of the New Testament which is a letter from the Apostle Paul to the church at Ephesus, on the west coast of what is now Turkey. It is an exposition of God's glorious plan of salvation through faith in Jesus Christ and gives much instruction on living to the glory of God. It also says much about the unity of all believers. —see BIBLE, FAITH, GRACE, JESUS

ep-i– (**ɛp**–ə–/ –ɪ–) prefix Usu. means **upon**, **above**, or **over**: *epidermis*

ep-ic (**ɛp**–ɪk) adj. Of or relating to brave action and excitement; heroic

epic n. A long poem, usu. centered upon a hero or heroine, in which great achievements are narrated

ep-i-cure (**ɛp**–ɪ–kyu^wr) n. A person who has a refined taste in food, drink, and the arts —**ep-i-cu-re-an** (ɛp–ɪ–kyu^w–ri^y–ən) adj.

ep-i-dem-ic (ɛp–ə–**dɛm**–ɪk) n. An outbreak of a large number of cases of the same infec-

tious disease: *a flu epidemic*

epi-dem-ic adj. Spreading rapidly: *Drug use has become epidemic in many major cities of the world.*

ep-i-der-mis (ɛp–ə–dɜr–məs) n. The outer layer of the skin

ep-i-glot-tis (ɛp–ə–glɑt–ɪs) n. A leaf-shaped piece of skin that closes the windpipe during swallowing

ep-i-gram (ɛp–ə–græm) n. A short witty saying

ep-i-lep-sy (ɛp–ə–lɛp–siʸ) n. Any of various disorders of the brain marked by sudden attacks of uncontrolled violent movement and loss of consciousness

ep-i-lep-tic (ɛp–ə–lɛp–tɪk) adj., n. One who suffers from epilepsy

ep-i-logue (ɛp–ə–lɑg/ –lɔg) n. **1.** A concluding part added to a literary work **2.** A speech delivered by one of the actors or actresses at the end of a play

E-piph-a-ny (ɪ–pɪf–ə–niʸ) n. A Christian festival on January sixth, celebrating the visit of the wise men to the Baby Jesus

e-pis-co-pa-cy (ɪ–pɪs–kə–pə–siʸ) n. **1.** Government of the church by bishops **2.** Episcopate

e-pis-co-pal (ɪ–pɪs–kə–pəl) n. **1.** Of a bishop **2.** Based on or recognizing a governing order of bishops

e-pis-co-pate (ɪ–pɪs–kə–pət/ –peʸt) n. **1.** The office or term of a bishop **2.** The order or body of bishops

ep-i-sode (ɛp–ə–soʷd) n. **1.** An incident in a person's life or experience **2.** An incident that forms a unit in a narrative or dramatic work: *Tune in to this station next week at the same time for the next thrilling episode.*

e-pis-tle (ɪ–pɪs–əl) n. A letter, usu. long and important

Epistle n. Any of the letters written by the apostles of Jesus Christ during the first century A.D.: *The Epistle to the Romans is the first epistle in the New Testament.*

ep-i-taph (ɛp–ə–tæf) n. An inscription on a tomb or monument in memory of the dead

ep-i-thet (ɛp–ə–θɛt) n. **1.** A descriptive word or phrase, such as "the Great" in "Alexander the Great" **2.** A contemptuous word or phrase

e-pit-o-me (ɪ–pɪt–ə–miʸ) n. **1.** A typical or perfect example of a type: *He is the epitome of politeness.* **2.** A summary

e-pit-o-mize (ɪ–pɪt–ə–maɪz) v. **-mized, -mizing** To typify

ep-och (ɛp–ək) n. A period of historical time marked by certain important events or developments; an era: *The beginning of printing marked an epoch in the history of education.*

eq-ua-ble (ɛk–wə–bəl/ iʸk–) adj. **1.** Even; unvarying: *an equable climate, free from extreme temperatures* **2.** Even tempered NOTE: Do not confuse **equable** with **equability**

e-qual (iʸ–kwəl) adj. **1.** Of two or more, the same in size, amount, value, degree, etc.: *These two books are equal in length.* **2.** Of a person, having enough strength, ability, etc.: *Are you sure you are equal to this task?/ "To whom will you compare me? Or who is my equal?" says the Holy One. "Lift your eyes and look to the heavens: Who created all these? He who brings out the starry host one by one, and calls them each by name. Because of his great power and strength, not one of them is missing"* (Isaiah 40:25,26). —opposite UNEQUAL

equal v. **1.** To be the same as in size or number: *"2+4=6" means "2+4 equals or has the same value as 6."* **2.** To have as much of a certain quality (as): *It would be very difficult for anyone to equal her intelligence or her poise.*

e-qual-i-ty (iʸ–kwɑl–ə–tiʸ) n. **-ties** The state of being equal: *the equality of opportunity (=everyone having the same degree of opportunity to succeed, etc.)* —opposite INEQUALITY

e-qual-ize (iʸ–kwəl–aɪz) v. **-ized, -izing** To make equal in size or number —**e-qual-i-za-tion** (iʸ–kwə–lə–zeʸ–ʃən) n.

e-qual-ly (iʸ–kwə–liʸ) adv. **1.** As much; to the same degree: *These two cars are equally as expensive.* **2.** In equal parts: *They split the rent on their apartment equally between them.*

e-qua-nim-i-ty (iʸ–kwə–nɪm–ə–tiʸ/ ɛ–) n. Calmness of mind or temper: *He received the tragic news with equanimity.*

e-quate (ɪ–kweʸt) v. **-quated, -quating** To make two things equal or think of them as equal

e-qua-tion (ɪ–kweʸ–ʒən) n. **1.** Act of being

equal or state of being equal 2. *math.* Statement of equality between two expressions or quantities separated by the equal sign (=)

e-qua-tor (ɪ–kweʸ–tər/ iʸ–) n. An imaginary line, or one on a map, drawn around the earth halfway between its most northern and southern points (poles) —**e-qua-to-ri-al** (iʸ–kwə–tɔr–iʸ–əl) adj.

e-ques-tri-an (ɪ–kwɛs–triʸ–ən) adj. Of or pertaining to horseback riding —**equestrian** n. A horseback rider

e-qui-lat-er-al (iʸ–kwə–læt–ər–əl) adj. Having all sides equal: *an equilateral triangle*

e-qui-lib-ri-um (iʸ–kwə–lɪb–riʸ–əm) n. A state of balance between opposing forces, influences, or actions

e-qui-nox (iʸ–kwə–nɑks/ ɛ–) n. One of the two times in a year when every place on earth has day and night of equal length, namely March 21st and September 23rd

e-quip (ɪ–kwɪp) v. -pp- To supply sbdy. with what is necessary for doing sthg.: *The climbers were equipped with boots, ropes, etc. for mountain climbing./ All Scripture [the Bible] is God breathed and is useful for teaching, rebuking, correcting, and training in righteousness, so that the man of God may be thoroughly equipped for every good work* (2 Timothy 3:16,17).

e-quip-ment (ɪ–kwɪp–mənt) n. The things that are necessary for a particular activity: *camping equipment*

eq-ui-ta-ble (ɛk–wɪ–tə–bəl) adj. Just and fair; impartial

eq-ui-ty (ɛk–wə–tiʸ) n. Fairness; justice: *Say among the nations, "The Lord reigns." He will judge the peoples with equity* (Psalm 96:10).

e-quiv-a-lent (ɪ–kwɪv–ə–lənt) adj., n. **1.** The same; equal **2.** Almost equal in function or effect

e-quiv-o-cal (ɪ–kwɪv–ə–kəl) adj. **1.** Of words, having a double meaning that can be misunderstood **2.** Of behavior, questionable, suspicious

–er (–ər) n. suffix **1.** One who occupies himself with the stated activity: *singer/ builder* **2.** An instrument: *poker* **3.** Forming the comparative degree of adjectives and adverbs: *higher/ faster* **4.** Denoting repeated action: *glim-mer*

e-ra (ɪɜr–ə/ ɛ–rə) n. A period of time typified by some special feature

e-rad-i-cate (ɪ–ræd–ə–keʸt) v. -cated, -cating To get rid of; to remove all traces of: *We are trying to eradicate illiteracy, crime, and all kinds of pollution.*

e-rase (ɪ–reʸs) v. -rased, -rasing **1.** To rub out or remove, esp. pencil or chalk marks **2.** To wipe out a recorded signal from a magnetic tape **3.** To remove all traces of: *fig. He tried to erase the tragedy from his memory.*

e-ras-er (ɪ–reʸs–ər) n. Sthg. used to remove pencil or chalk marks

e-rect (ɪ–rɛkt) adj. Upright; standing straight up on end: *Stand erect!* —**erectly** adv. —**e-rectness** n.

erect v. **1.** *fml.* To build: *This monument was erected in honor of Abraham Lincoln.* **2.** To set upright: *The campers erected their tents down by the lake.* —**erection** n.

er-mine (ɜr–mən) n. **1.** An animal of the weasel family with brown fur that turns white in winter **2.** This white fur

e-rode (ɪ–roʷd) v. -roded, -roding To wear away gradually: *The waves eroded the sea shore.*

e-ro-sion (ɪ–roʷ–ʒən) n. **1.** Eroding; being eroded **2.** The natural process by which the earth's surface is worn away: *soil erosion/fig. We've seen a great amount of erosion of morality in recent years.*

e-ro-sive (ɪ–roʷ–sɪv) adj. Causing erosion

e-rot-ic (ɪ–rɑt–ɪk) adj. Of, or arousing, sexual love and desire

err (ɜr) v. *fml.* To make mistakes; do sthg. wrong: *To err is human./ It is better to err on the side of mercy. (=to be too merciful, rather than not merciful enough)*

er-rand (ɛr–ənd) n. A short trip to take care of some business, esp. for someone else: *I have a lot of errands to do today.*

er-rant (ɛr–ənt) adj. **1.** Erring or doing wrong **2.** Wandering in quest of adventure **3.** Moving aimlessly

er-rat-ic (ɪ–ræt–ɪk) adj. Inclined to be irregular or unpredictable; uneven in movement or quality: *The bus schedule is somewhat erratic.*

er-ro-ne-ous (ɪ–roʷ–niʸ–əs) adj. Wrong; mis-

taken; incorrect —**erroneously** adv.

er-ror (**er**-ər) n. A mistake; a thing done wrongly: *Who can discern his errors? Forgive my hidden faults* (Psalm 19:12). *Whoever turns a sinner from the error of his way will save him from death and cover over a multitude of sins* (James 5:20).

er-u-dite (**er**-yə-daɪt) adj. Having or showing great learning —**er-u-di-tion**(er-yə-**dɪ**-ʃən) n.

e-rupt (ɪ-**rʌpt**) v. **1.** To break out suddenly and violently: *The demonstration was peaceful for several days, but then violence erupted.* **2.** Of a volcano, to shoot out lava, etc.: *In 79 A.D. Mount Vesuvius erupted, and the ash and lava buried Pompeii and two other cities near Naples, Italy.* —**eruption** n.

–er-y (-ər-iy) n., suffix **1.** Place of business: *bakery* **2.** Quality; conduct: *bravery* **3.** A kind of goods: *millinery* **4.** State or condition: *slavery*

es-ca-late (**es**-kə-leyt) v. **-lated, -lating** To increase in intensity or extent: *The war escalated./ Prices are escalating.* —**es-ca-la-tion** (es-kə-**ley**-ʃən)

es-ca-la-tor (**es**-kə-ley-tər) n. A set of moving stairs in a department store, airport, etc.

es-ca-pade (**es**-kə-peyd) n. A reckless, mischievous adventure

es-cape (ɪs-**key**p) v. **-caped, -caping 1.** To get away: *They escaped from the burning house.* **2.** To stay out of the way of: *He escaped injury in the car accident because he was wearing a seat belt.* **3.** To be forgotten by: *The author's name escapes me.* (=*I've forgotten it) I'll think of it later.*

escape n. **1.** The act of escaping or fact of having escaped: *There has never been an escape from that prison.* **2.** Sth. that gives relief for a short time from unpleasant or dull reality: *Some people go to the movies or read novels as a means of escape (from reality).*

es-cap-ee (es-key-p-iy) n. One who has escaped, esp. from prison

es-carp-ment (es-**karp**-mənt) n. **1.** A long cliff **2.** A steep slope in front of a fortification

es-chew (es-tʃuw) v. To avoid; shun

es-cort (es-kɔrt) n. **1.** A man who accompanies a woman socially **2.** One or more persons, ships, or vehicles that accompany another (or others) in order to give guidance or protection, or to pay honor

es-cort (es-**kɔrt**) v. To accompany as an escort

es-crow (es-krow) n. A written agreement, such as a deed, put into the custody of a third party until certain conditions are met

e-soph-a-gus (ɪ-**saf**-ə-gəs) n. The muscular tube through which food passes from the back of the mouth to the stomach

es-o-ter-ic (es-ə-**tɛr**-ɪk) adj. Intended only for those who have a special interest or knowledge

es-pe-cial-ly (e-**spe**-ʃəl-iy) adv. **1.** Also **specially** BrE. To a very high degree: *I like New England, especially in the early fall.* **2.** In particular: *My mother made a quilt especially for me.*

es-pi-o-nage (es-piy-ə-naʒ) n. The act or practice of spying

es-pouse (es-**pauz**) v. **espoused, espousing 1.** To give support to a cause **2.** To marry; to give a woman in marriage

es-say (es-ey) n. A piece of writing, usu. short, on one subject, esp. as part of a course of study: *I had to write an essay about modern trends in language teaching.*

es-sence (es-əns) n. **1.** The basic or fundamental quality of a thing **2.** A substance extracted from another substance, retaining the special qualities of the original substance **3.** Perfume

es-sen-tial (ɪ-**sen**-ʃəl/-tʃəl) adj. **1.** Necessary: *Food and drink are essential to life.* **2.** Central; basic; most important: *The mayor gave the essential points of his plan for housing the homeless.* —**essential** n. *They only took a few essentials with them when they left the burning building.*

es-sen-tial-ly (ɪ-sen-ʃə-liy/-tʃə-) adv. In reality; basically: *This is essentially a very good plan.*

es-tab-lish (ɪs-**tæb**-lɪʃ) v. **1.** To set up or begin, esp. a company, school, etc.: *This company was established in 1923.* **2.** To settle securely in a position, esp. a favorable position: *He quickly established himself as the leader of the new organization.* **3.** To prove the truth of sth. **4.** To cause to be recognized and ac-

cepted: *The trial established his innocence once and for all.*

es-tab-lish-ment (ɪ–**stæb**–lɪʃ–mənt) n. **1.** The act of establishing or the condition of being established **2.** *fml.* A business firm: *The establishment next door sells drapery materials and carpets.*

es-tate (ɪs–**te**ʸt) n. **1.** A large piece of land in the country with a large house on it **2.** All of a person's possessions, esp. after his death **3.** A piece of land developed for building **4.** Social standing; condition or status of life: *Give thanks to the Lord... who remembered us in our low estate* (Psalm 136:1,23).

es-teem (ɪs–**ti**ʸm) v. *fml.* **1.** To place a high value on; to respect: *The Lord says, "This is the one I esteem: he who is humble and contrite in spirit, and trembles at my word"* (Isaiah 66:2). **2.** To believe sthg. to be: *I didn't esteem him to be very trustworthy.*

esteem n. Favorable regard; respect; admiration: *The old professor was held in high esteem.* —compare ESTIMATION

Es-ther (**es**–tər) n. A book of the Old Testament. It is the story of Queen Esther's deliverance of the Jews from the plot of Haman to destroy them all, and the establishment of the feast of Purim.

es-ti-mate (**es**–tə–meʸt) v. **-mated, -mating** To make an approximate calculation as to the amount, cost, size, etc. of sthg.: *I estimate that tree to be about 250 feet high.* —**es-ti-mate** (**es**–tə–mət) n. *We got three estimates on the cost before having the car repaired.*

es-ti-ma-tion (es–tə–meʸ–ʃən) n. Opinion: *In my estimation she's one of the best actresses to appear on the stage.*

es-trange (es–**tre**ʸndʒ) v. **estranged, estranging 1.** To alienate someone who was previously a friend **2.** To remove or disassociate oneself

es-tu-ar-y (es–tʃuʷ–εər–iʸ) n. **-ies** The wide mouth of a river where it meets the sea

etc. *abbr.* For et cet-er-a (et–**set**–ər–ə) adv. And so forth; and others, esp. of the same sort: *The library has many books about sports, hobbies, etc.*

etch (etʃ) v. **1.** To produce a design, image, etc. on copper or glass by the corrosive ac-

tion of acid **2.** To outline clearly or sharply

etch-ing (**etʃ**–iŋ) n. **1.** The act or art of etching designs or pictures **2.** A print made from an etched plate **3.** The design so produced

e-ter-nal (iʸ–**tɜr**–nəl) adj. Never ending; going on forever: *Now this is eternal life: that they might know you, the only true God, and Jesus Christ whom you have sent* (John 17:3). *Whoever believes in the Son [Jesus Christ] has eternal life* (John 3:36). —**eternally** adv.

e-ter-ni-ty (ɪ–**tɜr**–nə–tiʸ) n. **-ties** Time without end; all time: *Those who put their trust in Jesus will live and reign with him for all eternity* (John 17:3; 2 Timothy 2:12).

e-ther (iʸ–θər) n. A light, colorless liquid which is used medically to put people to sleep

eth-ic (**εθ**–ɪk) n. A system of moral principles or values: *the Christian ethic*

eth-i-cal (**εθ**–ɪ–kəl) adj. **1.** Having to do with right behavior, justice, or duty **2.** Right; just; honorable —opposite UNETHICAL —**ethically** adv.

eth-ics (**εθ**–ɪks) n. **1.** A system of moral principles **2.** The rules and standards governing the conduct of the members of a profession

eth-nic (**εθ**–nɪk) adj. Of or pertaining to a group of people of the same race or nationality, sharing common and distinctive cultural characteristics

eth-no- (εθ–nə/ –noʷ) Prefix Race; people; culture

eth-no-cen-tric (εθ–nə–**sen**–trɪk) adj. Believing in the superiority of one's own national culture —**eth-no-cen-tri-ci-ty** n. (εθ–nə–sen–**trɪ**–sɪ–tiʸ)

eth-nog-ra-phy (εθ–**nɑg**–rə–fiʸ) n. The scientific knowledge of races and people —**ethnographer** n. —**eth-no-graph-ic** (εθ–nə–**græf**–ɪk) adj.

eth-no-lo-gy (εθ–**nɑl**–ə–dʒiʸ) n. A branch of anthropology that treats of races of people, their origin, characteristics, etc.

e-thos (iʸ–θɑs) n. The character and beliefs peculiar to a particular culture or group

et-i-quette (et–ɪ–kət/ –kεt) n. The set of rules of proper behavior

et-y-mol-o-gy (et–ə–mɑl–ə–dʒiʸ) n. **-gies 1.** An account of the origin of a word and its

meaning 2. The study of words and their origins

eu-ca-lyp-tus (yuᵂ–kə–lɪp–təs) n. A type of large evergreen tree, native to Australia, that yields timber and aromatic medicinal oil

Eu-cha-rist (yuᵂ–kə–rəst) n. The religious ceremony of the Lord's Supper or Holy Communion practiced in the Christian church —see HOLY COMMUNION, JESUS CHRIST

eu-lo-gize (yuᵂ–lə–dʒaɪz) v. -gized, -gizing To praise highly, esp. in a eulogy

eu-lo-gy (yuᵂ–lə–dʒiʸ) n. -gies A speech or writing in honor of a person or thing, esp. one in honor of a dead person

eu-phe-mism (yuᵂ–fə–mɪz–əm) n. An inoffensive term substituted for an offensive one —**eu-phe-mis-tic** (yuᵂ–fə–mɪs–tɪk) adj.

eu-pho-ri-a (yuᵂ–fɔr–iʸ–ə) n. A feeling of great happiness —**euphoric** adj.

Eu-rope (yʊər–əp) n. A continent west of Asia and North of Africa (3,872,561 sq. miles)

Eu-ro-pe-an (yʊər–ə–piʸ–ən) n. 1. A person of European descent 2. A native or inhabitant of Europe —**European** adj.

eu-tha-na-sia (yuᵂ–θə–neʸ–ʒə) n. The painless putting to death of someone who is suffering from a painful and incurable disease

e-vac-u-ate (ɪ–væk–yuᵂ–eʸt) v. -ated, -ating To take all the people away from a place, esp. because of some kind of threat: *The area was evacuated because of a bomb threat.* —**e-vac-u-a-tion** (ɪ–væk–yuᵂ–eʸ–ʃən) n.

e-vac-u-ee (ɪ–væk–yuᵂ–iʸ) n. A person who has been evacuated

e-vade (ɪ–veʸd) v. -vaded, -vading 1. To avoid facing up to sthg. that one should do: *To evade paying one's taxes is called tax evasion.* 2. To escape from or keep out of the way of: *The prisoner evaded the police for several days.*

e-val-u-ate (ɪ–væl–yuᵂ–eʸt) v. -ated, -ating *fml.* To find out or state the value of sthg. —**e-val-u-a-tion** (ɪ–væl–yuᵂ–eʸ–ʃən) n.

e-van-gel-i-cal (ɛ–vən–dʒel–ɪ–kəl) adj., n. 1. Pertaining to the Christian Gospel (the Good News about our Savior Jesus Christ) 2. Pertaining to churches that believe in the importance of faith in Christ, holy living,

Bible study and prayer, rather than in religious ceremonies

e-van-gel-ism (iʸ–væn–dʒə–lɪz–əm) n. The zealous proclamation of the Good News about Jesus Christ, urging men and women to repent of their sins and put their trust in Jesus as their only Savior and to make him the Lord of their life —see JESUS, SAVIOR, GOSPEL

e-van-ge-list (ɪ–væn–dʒə–ləst) n. A person who travels from place to place preaching the Good News about Jesus, inviting people to accept Jesus as their Savior and live unto him who died for them and rose again —**e-van-ge-lis-tic** (ɪ–væn–dʒə–lɪst–ɪk) adj.

e-van-ge-lize (ɪ–væn–dʒə–laɪz) v. -lized, -lizing To spread the Good News about Jesus Christ in order to win people to Christ, that they may have eternal life

e-vap-o-rate (ɪ–væp–ə–reʸt) v. -rated, -rating To change into vapor and disappear: *The puddles of water left by the rain soon evaporated in the sun./fig. Hopes of reaching an agreement are beginning to evaporate. (=to disappear)* —**e-vap-o-ra-tion** (ɪ–væp–ə–reʸ–ʃən) n.

e-va-sion (ɪ–veʸ–ʒən) n. 1. An act or instance of evading 2. A trick or excuse used in evading

e-va-sive (ɪ–veʸ–sɪv) adj. 1. Having the purpose of evading 2. Not frank and direct; intentionally vague

eve (iʸv) n. 1. The evening before a festival: *Christmas Eve/ New Year's Eve* 2. The time just before an event: *The president died on the eve of victory. (=a few weeks before the victory was achieved, when victory was certain)*

Eve n. 1. A feminine name 2. In the Bible, the first woman that God created: *Adam named his wife Eve because she would become the mother of all the living* (Genesis 3:20). *Eve means "living."*

e-ven (iʸ–vən) adj. 1. Level, flat, smooth, and regular; forming a straight line: *The tabletop has to be even so things don't fall off.* 2. Of things that can be measured and compared, equal; being the same score for each side: *We came out even; two games apiece!* 3. A number that can be divided exactly by two: *Two, four, six, eight, etc. are even numbers.*

—**evenly** adv. *The toys were divided evenly among the children.*

even adv. **1.** (Used to make a statement stronger): *Even a fool is thought wise if he keeps silent* (Proverbs 17:28). **2.** (Used in making comparisons stronger): *It was hot yesterday, but it's even hotter today.* **3. even if** No matter if; though: *Even if we could afford it, we wouldn't buy a new car this year.* **4. even so** In spite of the fact that: *It's getting late. Even so, I have to finish my work before I leave.*

eve-ning (i^yv–nɪŋ) n. The part of the day between afternoon and night: *He goes to work in the morning and returns in the evening.*

evening gown (i^yv–nɪŋ gaʊn) n. A woman's long, formal dress, not to be confused with night gown, which is a woman's or girl's loose garment for sleeping in

e-vent (i^y–vɛnt) n. **1.** An incident; sthg. that happens, usu. sthg. important: *What were the chief events of 1989?* **2.** Any of the races, etc., arranged as part of a day's sports competition: *John is competing in three events: the 100-yard dash, the high jump, and the broad jump.* **3. in any event** Whatever happens **4. in the event of (sthg.)** In case sthg. happens: *In the event of an earthquake, we need to be prepared.*

e-vent-ful (i^y–vɛnt–fəl) adj. **1.** Full of events **2.** Important

e-ven-tu-al (i^y–vɛn–tʃuʷ–əl) adj. Coming at last: *The ever-increasing immorality in this nation will lead to its eventual self-destruction.* —**eventually** adv. *If we keep working, we will eventually finish the project.*

e-ven-tu-al-i-ty (i^y–vɛn–tʃuʷ–æl–ɪ–ti^y) n. -**ties** A likely or possible occurrence or outcome

ev-er (ɛv–ər) adv. **1.** Continuously: *My eyes are ever on the Lord* (Psalm 25:15). **2.** At any time: *Does he ever get angry?* **3.** Always: *He's been here ever since Monday./ The Lord is my refuge and strength, an ever present help in trouble* (Psalm 46:1). **4. hardly ever** Almost never: *He hardly ever goes out at night anymore.* **5. for ever and ever** For all eternity; never ending: *The Lord will reign for ever and ever* (Exodus 15:18). **6.** Increasingly: *The path of the righteous is like the first gleam of dawn, shining ever brighter...* (Proverbs 4:18) .

ev-er-last-ing (ɛv–ər–læs–tɪŋ) adj. or n. *fml.* Lasting forever; continual: *From everlasting to everlasting the Lord's love is with those who fear him* (Psalm 103:17).

ev-ery (ɛv–ri^y) determ. **1.** Each one of or all of a certain number: *I got up early every morning this week.* **2.** Each of an indefinite number or series: *She visits her father every day./ We have to make a house payment every month.* **3.** The most possible; as much as possible: *God exalted him [Jesus] to the highest place and gave him a name that is above every name, that at the name of Jesus every knee should bow... and every tongue confess that Jesus Christ is Lord, to the glory of God the Father* (Philippians 2:9-11). **4. every other** (of things that can be counted) The 1st, 3rd, 5th, etc. or the 2nd, 4th, 6th, etc.: *She does volunteer work at the hospital every other day.*

ev-ery-bod-y (ɛv–ri^y–bəd–i^y) also **everyone** (ɛv–ri^y–wən) pron. Every person: *Everybody gave her a nice birthday gift.*

ev-ery-one (ɛv–ri^y–wʌn) pron. Everybody: *Everyone in our office is invited to the party.*

ev-ery one (ɛv–ri^y wʌn) Each individual person or thing in a group, no exceptions: *Every one of the plants was infested with bugs.*

ev-ery-thing (ɛv–ri^y–θɪŋ) pron. (used with sing. verb) **1.** Each thing or all things: *The earth is the Lord's and everything in it* (Psalm 24:1). **2.** The most important thing: *My family means everything to me.*

ev-ery-where (ɛv–ri^y–wɛər) adv. In every place: *The eyes of the Lord are everywhere, keeping watch on the wicked and the good* (Proverbs 15:3).

e-vict (ɪ–vɪkt) v. To expel a tenant by legal process —**eviction** n.

ev-i-dence (ɛv–ə–dəns) n. **1.** Information that proves a statement, supports a belief, or makes a matter more clear: *The police are gathering evidence to help them prove who killed the bank clerk.* **2. in evidence** Capable of being seen and noticed: *Notices about the Beauty Pageant were in evidence everywhere.*

ev-i-dent (ɛv–ə–dənt) adj. Plainly to be seen, heard, understood, etc.; obvious because of evidence: *Let your gentleness be evident to all* (Philippians 4:5).

ev-i-dent-ly (ɛv–ə–dɛnt–liʸ) adv. Apparently: *Evidently he's been here. He left his business card on the table.*

e-vil (iʸ–vəl) adj. Very bad; wicked; sinful; harmful: *evil thoughts/ Out of men's hearts come evil thoughts...* (Mark 7:21). *Jesus Christ gave himself for our sins to rescue us from this present evil age* (Galations 1:4).

evil n. Great wickedness, difficulty, or tragedy: *The only thing necessary for evil to triumph is for good men to do nothing./ The fear of the Lord is to hate evil...* (Proverbs 8:13). *The face of the Lord is against those who do evil* (Psalm 34:16). —opposite GOOD

e-vince (ɪ–vɪns) v. -vinced, -vincing To indicate clearly or demonstrate: *The young lady evinced remarkable talent in music.* —evincible adj.

e-voke (ɪ–voʷk) v. -voked, -voking To summon or call forth; elicit: *The child's tears evoked sympathy.*

ev-o-lu-tion (ɛv–ə–luʷ–ʃən) n. 1. Development; a process of continual pro-gress: *the evolution of modern aircraft* 2. The unreasonable theory, held by many "scientists" and others, that our intricately designed and infinitely ordered universe developed all by itself out of chaos -- that certain unknown conditions in the primitive atmosphere and ocean acted upon certain mysterious chemicals to synthesize more complex chemicals which were able to reproduce themselves. These chemicals, whatever they were, supposedly constituted the original living systems from which all living organisms later evolved. NOTE: This is altogether contrary to the Word of God and to the first law of science (that nothing is now being created) and to the laws of thermodynamics. Creation, on the other hand, by an almighty, all-wise Creator, is a scientific theory that does fit all the facts of true science as well as God's revelation in the Holy Scriptures. There is not one shred of evidence that non-living substances were evolved into living organisms. The tremendous complexity and order of the world, its plants and animals, and the human body can only be explained by intelligent planning, not by a random process of chance variation and natural selection. Evolution at best is a re-ligious faith, not science. —see CREATION, GOD, THERMODYNAMICS —e-vo-lu-tion-ary (ɛv–ə–luʷ–ʃən–ɛər–iʸ) adj.

e-volve (ɪ–vɑlv) v. -volved, -volving To develop or work out gradually: *After many months of committee meetings, a workable plan evolved.*

ewe (yuʷ) n. A fully-grown female sheep

ex– (ɛks–) prefix 1. Former: *my ex-wife* 2. Out of: *the export of grain from the country* 3. Beyond: *exceeding*

ex-act (ɪg–zækt) adj. 1. Correct; precise: *The Son [Jesus Christ] is the radiance of God's glory and the exact representation of his being, sustaining all things by his powerful word* (Hebrews 1:3). 2. Marked by accuracy of small details of fact: *A good scientist is always exact in his work.*

ex-act-ing (ɪg–zæk–tɪŋ) adj. Demanding a lot of care and attention; painstaking: *an exacting piece of work*

ex-act-ly (ɪg–zækt–liʸ) adv. 1. (used with numbers and measures, and with "what," "where," "who," etc.) Precisely; with complete correctness: *Show me exactly how you want me to do this./ Measure exactly the right amount of medicine.* 2. (used for adding emphasis to an expression) Absolutely; just: *This painting is exactly what we want over the mantel in our home.*

ex-ag-ger-ate (ɪg–zædʒ–ə–reʸt) v. -ated, -ating To make sthg. seem to be, or describe it, as larger, better, worse, etc., than it really is: *They said that there were giants in the land and that we were like grasshoppers in comparison, but they were greatly exaggerating.* —exaggerated adj. —ex-ag-ger-a-tion (ɛg–zædʒ–ə–reʸ–ʃən) n.

ex-alt (ɛg–zɔlt) v. *fml.* 1. To give someone high praise 2. To make higher in rank: *God highly exalted him [Jesus Christ], that at the name of Jesus every knee should bow... and every tongue confess that Jesus Christ is Lord* (Philippians 2:9-11). *Righteousness exalts a nation* (Proverbs 14:34). *For everyone who exalts himself will be humbled, and he who humbles himself will be exalted* (Luke 14:11).

ex·am (ɪg–**zæm**) n. *infml.* Examination

ex·am·i·na·tion (ɪg–zæm–ə–**ne**ʸ–ʃən) n. **1.** Also **exam** An oral or written test of knowledge: *Did you pass your science examination?* **2.** An act of examining: *Before you go overseas to work you should have a complete medical examination.*

ex·am·ine (ɪg–**zæm**–ən) v. -ined, -ining **1.** To look at a person or thing carefully, to find out sthg.: *They examined the Scriptures every day to see if what Paul [an apostle of Jesus Christ] said was true* (Acts 17:11). **2.** To question a person, in order to find out sthg. or to measure knowledge as in a school, court, etc. —**examiner** n.

ex·am·ple (ɪg–**zæm**–pəl) n. **1.** An object, fact, event, etc. that demonstrates or represents a general rule: *This booklet is an example of what can be done today with modern printing equipment.* **2.** Behavior that is a pattern to be copied: *Set an example for the believers in speech, in life, in love and in purity* (1 Timothy 4:12). **3. for example** Also **e.g.** *abbr.* For instance; as an example: *The government is trying to deal with the worst problems in our society, for example, drug and alcohol abuse.*

ex·as·per·ate (ɪg–**zæs**–pə–reʸt) v. -ated, -ating To irritate or make angry: *Fathers, do not exasperate your children; instead, bring them up in the training and instruction of the Lord* (Ephesians 6:4).

ex·ca·vate (**ɛks**–kə–veʸt) v. -vated, -vating **1.** To make a hole or channel by digging **2.** To reveal or extract by digging: *They excavated many ancient cities.*

ex·ca·va·tion (ɛks–kə–**ve**ʸ–ʃən) n. A place that is being excavated

ex·ceed (ɪk–**si**ʸd) v. *fml.* **1.** To be more than: *The number of people in the room should not exceed 45.* **2.** To go beyond what is lawful, necessary, etc.: *If you exceed the speed limit (=go faster than is allowed), you may be stopped by the police and fined.*

ex·ceed·ing·ly (ɪk–**si**ʸd–ɪŋ–liʸ) adv. Very; extremely: *That new plane is exceedingly fast.*

ex·cel (ɛk–**sɛl**) v. *fml.* To be outstanding; to do or be better than: *Just as you excel in... faith, in speech, in knowledge... see that you also excel in this grace of giving* (2 Corinthians 8:7).

ex·cel·lent (**ɛks**–ə–lənt) adj. Unusually good; of very high quality: *If anything is excellent or praiseworthy, think about such things* (Philippians 4:8). —**excellence** n. —**excellently** adv.

ex·cept (ɛk–**sɛpt**) prep., conj. also **except for** Taking out or leaving out: *All the boys except Jim went home early.*

ex·cep·tion (ɛk–**sɛp**–ʃən) n. **1.** A case of not being included: *All the boys went home early, with the exception of Jim.* **2.** Sthg. that does not follow the general rule: *We usually have salad for lunch, but today we'll make an exception and have soup.* **3. take exception (to)** To object to: *I took exception to his rude remarks.*

ex·cep·tion·al (ɛk–sɛp–ʃən–əl) adj. Very unusual: *Their oldest child has exceptional ability in music.* —**exceptionally** adv. *He is exceptionally talented.*

ex·cerpt (**ɛk**–sərpt) n. An extract from a book, film, piece of music, etc.

ex·cess (ɛk–**sɛs**) n. **1.** The act of going beyond normal or suitable limits **2.** An abnormally large amount **3.** An outrageous act

ex·ces·sive (ɪk–**sɛs**–ɪv) adj. Beyond what is right and proper —**excessively** adv. *an excessively heavy drinker* —**excessiveness** n.

ex·change (ɪks–**tʃe**ʸndʒ) n. **1.** The giving and taking of one thing for another: *What good will it be for a man if he gains the whole world, yet forfeits his soul? Or what can a man give in exchange for his soul?* (Matthew 16:26). **2.** A place where people in business meet to buy and sell: *Business at the stock exchange has been very active this week.* **3.** A conversation or dispute: *an exchange of ideas* **4.** The act of exchanging the money of one country for that of another **5.** The difference between the value of money in different countries: *What is the rate of exchange between the American dollar and the British pound?*

exchange v. -changed, -changing To give sthg. and receive sthg. in return for it: *My sister and I like to exchange clothes. (=each gives the other her clothes)/They [foolish men] exchanged the glory of the immortal God for images made to look like mortal man and birds and animals and reptiles. They exchanged the truth about God for a lie, and worshiped and served*

created things rather than the Creator (Romans 1:22, 25) —exchangeable adj.

ex-cise (**ek**-saıs/ –saız) n. A tax on the manufacture, sale, or use of goods within a country

ex-cise (ık-**saız**) v. To remove by cutting out

ex-cit-a-ble (ık-**saıt**-ə-bəl) adj. Easily excited

ex-cite (ek-**saıt**) v. -cited, -citing To cause or awaken strong feelings of expectation, happiness, etc. in sbdy.: *The thought of going to the party excited the children.*

ex-cit-ed (ık-**saıt**-əd) adj. Having strong, pleasant feelings of happiness, expectation, etc.: *The excited children could hardly wait to go to the party.* —**excitedly** adv.

ex-cite-ment (ık-**saıt**-mənt) n. The state of being excited: *There was a lot of excitement when our team won the game.*

ex-cit-ing (ık-**saıt**-ıŋ) adj. Causing one to be excited: *an exciting trip*

ex-claim (ıks-**kle**ʸm) v. To call out, or say, suddenly and loudly: *Then my soul will rejoice in the Lord and delight in his salvation. My whole being will exclaim, "Who is like you, O Lord?"* (Psalm 35:9, 10). —**ex-clam-a-to-ry** (ıks-**klæm**-ə-tɔr-iʸ) adj.

ex-cla-ma-tion (ɛks-klə-**me**ʸ-ʃən) n. An expression of sudden strong feeling: *"Ouch!" is an exclamation expressing pain.*

ex-cla-ma-tion point (ɛks-klə-**me**ʸ-ʃən pɔınt) or **mark** (mɑrk) n. The punctuation mark (!) placed after an exclamation

ex-clude (ıks-**klu**ʷd) v. -cluded, -cluding 1. To purposely keep a person or thing from a place, group, or privilege: *Mary was excluded from the meeting.* 2. To omit 3. To leave out of consideration —**ex-clu-sion** (ıks-**klu**ʷ-ʒən) n.

ex-clud-ing (ıks-**klu**ʷd-ıŋ) prep. Not including: *The trip cost $50 excluding the cost of the gasoline.*

ex-clu-sive (ıks-**klu**ʷ-sıv) adj. 1. Leaving out; shutting out: *These two statements are mutually exclusive. That is, they cannot both be true.* 2. Open only to certain people: *an exclusive country club* 3. Given only to one individual or group: *He had an exclusive interview with the president.* 4. Fashionable and expensive: *an exclusive restaurant* —**exclusively** adv.

—**exclusiveness** n.

ex-com-mu-ni-cate (ɛks-kə-**myu**ʷ-nə-keʸt) v. -cated, -cating To expel from membership in the church —**ex-com-mun-i-ca-tion** (ɛks-kə-myu*ʷ*-nə-**ke**ʸ-ʃən) n.

ex-cre-ment (ɛks-krə-mənt) n. Waste matter discharged from the body, esp. feces

ex-crete (ıks-**kri**ʸt) v. -creted, -creting To expel waste matter from the body or tissues: *The sweat glands excrete sweat.*

ex-cre-tion (ɛks-**kri**ʸ-ʃən) n. 1. The act of excreting 2. That which is excreted

ex-cru-ci-at-ing (ıks-**kru**ʷ-ʃiʸ-eʸ-tıŋ) adj. Intensely painful —**excruciatingly** adv.

ex-cur-sion (ık-**skзr**-ʒən) n. 1. A short trip, returning to the starting place 2. A pleasure trip made by a number of people: *an excursion around Manhattan Island*

ex-cuse (ık-**skyu**ʷz) v. -cused, -cusing 1. To overlook a fault as unimportant: *Please excuse me. I didn't mean to knock over the vase.* 2. To grant freedom from a duty: *The coach excused me early from football practice so I could go to the dentist.* 3. **Excuse me** (a) A polite expression used to start speaking to a stranger, to ask to get past a person, or to disagree with sthg. sbdy. has said (b) Also **sorry** Polite expression used to ask to be forgiven for wrong behavior, esp. accidental behavior: *The lady who bumped my elbow said, "Excuse me."*

ex-cuse (ık-**skyu**ʷs) n. Sthg. offered as a reason for being forgiven for wrong behavior, whether the reason is true or not: *What was his excuse for making all those mistakes on the exam?/ Since the creation of the world, God's eternal power and divine nature have been clearly seen, being understood from what has been made, so that men are without excuse. (=That is, no one has any justifiable reason for not believing in God.)* (Romans 1:20). Compare **excuse** with **reason** and **pretext**: "His **reason** for staying home from work was that his car was broken down." (=it really was broken) "His **excuse** for staying home from work was that his car was broken down." (=it may or may not have been broken) "He stayed home from work on the **pretext** that his car was broken down." (=it

was not broken at all, and he had a different reason for staying home from work)

ex·e·cute (ɛk–sə–kyuᵂt) v. -cuted, -cuting **1.** To perform: *That dive from the ten meter platform was executed beautifully.* **2.** To carry out: *His orders were executed perfectly.* **3.** To put to death legally: *The convicted murderer was executed by the firing squad.* —**ex·e·cu·tion** (ɛk–sə–kyuᵂ–ʃən) n.

ex·ec·u·tive (ɪg–zɛk–yə–tɪv) adj. **1.** Related to the making and carrying out of decisions, esp. in business **2.** Having the power to put government decisions and laws into effect: *the executive branch of government*

executive n. **1.** A person in a managerial position **2.** The person or group in the executive position in a government: *The President of the US is the country's chief executive.*

ex·ec·u·tor (ɪg–zɛk–yə–tər) n. A person designated to execute the terms of a will

ex·em·pla·ry (ɪg–zɛm–plə–riʸ) adj. Worth following as an example: *an exemplary student*

ex·em·pli·fy (ɪg–zɛm–plə–faɪ) v. -fied, -fying To serve as an example: *This cathedral exemplifies the architecture of the 14th century.*

ex·empt (ɪg–zɛmpt) adj. Released from a duty, service, payment, etc. that is required of others: *John is exempt from military service.*

exempt v. To cause one to be exempt: *His blindness exempted him from military service.* —**exemption** n.

ex·er·cise (ɛk–sər–saɪz) n. **1.** Training or use of any part of the body or mind so as to strengthen and improve it: *Bodily exercise profits a little, but godliness is profitable for all things, having promise of the life that now is and of that which is to come* (1 Timothy 4:8). **2.** A group of questions or problems to be answered by a student for practice **3.** The use of a stated right: *the exercise of one's right of free speech*

exercise v. -cised, -cising **1.** To get exercise: *My husband exercises every morning before work.* **2.** fml. To use a power or right: *to exercise self-control*

ex·ert (ɪg–zɜrt) v. **1.** To use strength, skill, etc.: *He likes to exert his authority.* **2.** To force oneself to put forth some effort: *He really had to exert himself to finish the assignment by mid-*

night.

ex·er·tion (ɪg–zɜr–ʃən) n. **1.** The act of bringing forcefully into use: *the exertion of one's influence* **2.** A case of exerting; an effort: *The doctor says the heart patient must avoid all exertion.*

ex·hale (ɛks–heʸl) v. -haled, -haling To breathe out —opposite INHALE

ex·haust (ɪg–zɔst) v. **1.** To become extremely tired: *Running the marathon really exhausted him.* **2.** To use all of, or say all that can be said about sthg.: *We have nearly exhausted our food supply./We've completely exhausted the subject of last night's football game.*

exhaust n. also **exhaust pipe 1.** The pipe which lets out unwanted gas, steam, etc., from an engine **2.** The gas, steam, etc. which escapes through this pipe

ex·haust·ed (ɪg–zɔs–təd) adj. Completely worn out; very tired

ex·haus·tion (ɪg–zɔs–tʃən) n. The state of being extremely tired —**exhausting** adj.

ex·haus·tive (ɪg–zɔs–tɪv) adj. Detailed and thorough: *an exhaustive report/ an exhaustive search of the neighborhood*

ex·hib·it (ɪg–zɪb–ət) v. **1.** To show or display in public: *All the new cars were being exhibited at the auto show.* **2.** To show outwardly that one possesses a feeling, quality, etc.: *The parachutist exhibited a lot of anxiety when the time drew near for him to jump.*

exhibit n. **1.** Sthg. that is displayed esp. in a museum **2.** A public display of objects: *The whole class plans to attend the art exhibit next week at the school.*

ex·hi·bi·tion (ɛk–sə–bɪ–ʃən) n. An act of exhibiting

ex·hi·bi·tion·ist (ɛk–sə–bɪ–ʃən–ɪst) n. A person who behaves in a way designed to attract attention to himself, sometimes by indecent exposure

ex·hib·i·tor (ɪg–zɪb–ət–ər) n. A person or firm that exhibits

ex·hil·a·rate (ɪg–zɪl–ə–reʸt) v. -rated, -rating **1.** To invigorate **2.** To make cheerful —**ex·hil·a·ra·tion** (ɪg–zɪl–ə–reʸ–ʃən) n.

ex·hort (ɪg–zɔrt) v. fml. To urge or advise strongly and earnestly: *Do not rebuke an older man harshly, but exhort him as if he were*

your father (1 Timothy 5:1). —**ex-hor-ta-tion** (eg-zɔr-teᵞ-ʃən/ɛk-sɔr–) n.

ex-hume (ɪg-zyuʷm/ ɪks-ɦyuʷm) v. •**humed**, **-huming** To dig up sth. that has been buried, esp. a human body

ex-i-gen-cy (ɛk-sə-dʒən-siᵞ/ ɛk-sɪdʒ- ən–) n. **-cies 1.** Urgent needs **2.** Requirements

ex-i-gent (ɛk-sə-dʒənt) adj. Urgent

ex-ile (ɛg–zaɪl) n. **1.** Enforced removal or voluntary removal from one's native land **2.** One who has separated from his country

exile v. **exiled, exiling** To send someone into exile

ex-ist (ɪg–zɪst) v. **1.** To be sth. real or actual: *Without faith it is impossible to please God, because anyone who comes to him must believe that he exists and that he rewards those who earnestly seek him* (Hebrews 11:6). **2.** Of a person, to continue living, esp. with difficulty or with very little money: *The family can barely exist on the father's income.*

ex-is-tence (ɪg-zɪs-təns) n. **1.** The state of existing: *Cross-country railway travel in the US didn't come into existence until 1869.* **2.** Life; manner of living: *He led a miserable existence working in the mine day after day.* —**existent** adj.

ex-ist-ing (ɪg-zɪs-tɪŋ) adj. Present: *Young people find it hard to buy a house because of existing high interest rates.*

ex-it (ɛg-zət/ ɛk-sət) n. **1.** A way out of a building or off the freeway, etc. **2.** An act of leaving: *Be careful as you make your exit down the stairs.*

ex-o-dus (ɛk-sə-dəs) n. A departure of many people

Exodus The second book of the Bible which tells about the exodus of the Israelites from Egypt and of the giving of the Law (the Ten Commandments) on Mt. Sinai —see BIBLE

ex of-fi-ci-o (ɛks ə-fɪʃ-iᵞ-oʷ) adj., adv. Because of an office: *ex officio chairman*

ex-on-er-ate (ɪg-zɑn-ə-reᵞt) v. **-ated -ating** To declare free from blame

ex-or-bi-tant (ɪg-zɔr-bə-tənt) adj. Exceeding reasonable limits; excessive

ex-or-cism (ɛk-sɔr-sɪz-əm) n. The act of casting out demons: *Jesus and his disciples used exorcism in the casting out of demons* (Mark 6:13; Luke 4:31-37; Luke 10:17-20).

ex-or-cize (ɛk-sɔr-saɪz) v. **-cized, -cizing 1.** To drive out an evil spirit **2.** To free a person or place from evil spirits —**exorcist** n.

ex-ot-ic (ɪg-zɑt-ɪk) adj. **1.** Of plants, words, or fashions, introduced from abroad, not native **2.** Unusually attractive; colorful

ex-pand (ɪk-spænd) v. To make larger: *Some things expand when heated./ The company has expanded its operations in Hong Kong.* —opposite CONTRACT

ex-panse (ɪk-spæns) n. A broad extent, as of land or sea

ex-pan-sion (ɪk-spæn-ʃən) n. The action of expanding or state of being expanded: *the expansion of the university*

ex-pa-tri-ate (ɛks-peᵞ-triᵞ-ət) n. A person living outside his own country

ex-pect (ɪk-spɛkt) v. **1.** To believe that someone is coming or that sth. will happen: *The Son of Man [Jesus] will come at an hour when you do not expect him* (Matthew 24:44). **2.** To believe, hope, and think that someone is going to do sth.: *The train leaves at 8:30 so I'm expecting you to be at the station on time.* **3. to be expecting (a baby)** (of a woman) To be pregnant (=carrying a baby in her body): *His wife is expecting.*

ex-pec-ta-tion (ɛk-spɛk-teᵞ-ʃən) n. **1.** The condition of expecting: *We are looking forward to his arrival with great expectation.* **2.** Sth. that is expected: *His parents' expectations for him were quite high.*

ex-pe-di-ent (ɪk-spiᵞ-diᵞ-ənt) adj. Suited to the time and the occasion, but not always just and fair: *It is more expensive to buy sth. on the installment plan, making monthly payments, but sometimes it is also more expedient.* —**expediency** n. —**expediently** adv.

ex-pe-dite (ɛk-spə-daɪt) v. **-dited, -diting** To help or speed up the progress of; to perform business quickly: *What can be done to expedite the improvement of our transportation system?*

ex-pe-di-tion (ɛk-spə-dɪʃ-ən) n. **1.** A journey for a particular purpose: *an expedition to the South Pole* **2.** The people or ships making such a journey **3.** Promptness; speed

ex-pe-di-tion-ar-y (ɛk-spə-dɪʃ-ə-nɛər-iᵞ) adj.

Of or used in an expedition: *an expeditionary force*

ex-pe-di-tious (ɛk–spə–**dɪʃ**–əs) adj. Acting or done speedily and efficiently: *He was expeditious in his response to my request.* **—expeditiously** adv.

ex-pel (ɪk–**spɛl**) v. -ll- **1.** To put out officially from a school, club, etc.: *The school expelled him for his rebellious attitude.* **2.** *fml.* To push out from the body or from a container: *to expel smoke from the chimney* **—expulsion** n.

ex-pend (ɪk–**spɛnd**) v. To use or spend time, money, energy, etc.: *He expended all his energy on foolish pursuits.*

ex-pend-a-ble (ɪk–**spɛn**–də–bəl) adj. That which may be sacrificed for some worthy purpose

ex-pen-di-ture (ɪk–**spɛn**–dɪ–tʃər) n. **1.** The spending of money **2.** The amount spent

ex-pense (ɪk–**spɛns**) n. **1.** Any kind of cost — of money time, effort, etc.: *She spared no expense to give her children a good education.* —see COST **2. at someone's expense** With sbdy. paying the cost: *He went to Paris at his company's expense.*

ex-pen-sive (ɪk–**spɛn**–sɪv) adj. **1.** Costing more than the item is worth or the buyer is willing to pay: *These shoes are too expensive for me.* **2.** Involving a high cost of any kind, esp. of money: *The Apostle Paul writes, "I want women to dress modestly, with decency and propriety, not with braided hair or gold or pearls or expensive clothes, but with good deeds, appropriate for women who profess to worship God"* (1 Timothy 2:9,10). —opposite INEXPENSIVE **—expensively** adv.

ex-pe-ri-ence (ɪk–**spɪər**–iʸ–əns) n. **1.** The gaining of knowledge or skill from seeing and doing things: *Experience is the best teacher.* **2.** Sthg. that happens to a person that affects him in some way: *Being on the tenth floor during an earthquake was quite an experience.*

experience v. -enced, -encing To feel; to have the experience of: *We have experienced a lot of joy in meeting people of many different cultures.*

ex-pe-ri-enced (ɪk–**spɪər**–iʸ–ənst) adj. Having the stated knowledge, skill or experience: *an experienced airlines pilot* —opposite INEX-

PERIENCED

ex-per-i-ment (ɪk–**spɛər**–ə–mənt) n. **1.** A test; trial **2.** An operation carried out under controlled conditions for the purpose of testing a possible answer

experiment v. To make an experiment: *They experimented with new materials.* **—ex-per-i-men-ta-tion** (ɪk–spɛər–ə–mɛn–**teʸ**–ʃən) n.

ex-per-i-men-tal (ɪk–spɛər–ə–**mɛnt**–əl) adj. Concerning or used for experiments: *an experimental class* **—experimentally** adv.

ex-pert (ɛk–spərt) adj., n. A person who is skilled through training and practice: *She's an expert at teaching the deaf.* **—expertly** adv.

ex-per-tise (ɛk–spər–**tiʸ**z/ –tiʸs) n. Expert knowledge or skill in a particular field: *With her expertise in cooking they'd do well to open a restaurant.*

ex-pi-ate (ɛk–spiʸ–eʸt) v. **-ated, -ating** To atone for; make amends for

ex-pi-a-tion (ɛk–spiʸ–**eʸ**–ʃən) n. The covering or washing away of sins by a blood sacrifice: *The blood of Jesus Christ provides expiation for all sin. This expiation is called the Atonement.* —see JESUS, SIN, ATONEMENT

ex-pi-ra-tion (ɛk–spə–**reʸ**–ʃən) n. The end of sthg. which lasts for a period of time: *At the expiration of his term of office he will return to private life.*

ex-pire (ɛk–**spaɪ**–ər) v. **-pired, -piring 1.** Of sthg. which lasts for a period of time, to end: *Our subscription to that magazine expires next month.* **2.** To die

ex-plain (ɪk–**spleʸn**) v. **1.** To state the meaning of sthg.; make sthg. clear, by telling or by writing: *Paul... reasoned with them from the Scriptures, explaining and proving that the Christ had to suffer and rise from the dead* (Acts 17:3). **2.** To give the reason for: *Please explain why you are going to London.*

ex-pla-na-tion (ɛk–splə–**neʸ**–ʃən) n. An act of explaining: *He's giving an explanation of how to operate the new computer.*

ex-plan-a-tor-y (ɪk–**splæn**–ə–tɔr–iʸ) adj. Serving or intending to explain sthg.: *an explanatory note*

ex-ple-tive (ɛks–plə–tɪv) n. An exclamation, esp. a swear word

ex-pli-ca-ble (εks–plɪ–kə–bəl/ ɪks–plɪk–ə–bəl) adj. Able to be explained

ex-pli-cit (ɪk–splɪs–ət) adj. Stating sthg. in exact terms —explicitly adv.

ex-plode (ɪk–splo^wd) v. -ploded, -ploding 1. Esp. of a bomb or other explosive, to blow up or burst 2. Of a person, to suddenly burst out violently: *He exploded with an outburst of anger.* 3. A sudden increase: *The population of the tiny country exploded during the past decade.* 4. To destroy: *New scientific findings have exploded the old theory.*

ex-ploit (εk–splɔɪt) n. A bold or notable deed

ex-ploit (ɪk–splɔɪt) v. 1. To work or develop mines and other natural resources 2. To take full advantage of; to use workers to one's own advantage without regard for their needs —ex-ploi-ta-tion (ɪk–splɔɪ–te^y–ʃən) n.

ex-plore (ɪk–splɔr) v. -plored, -ploring 1. To travel into or through a place in order to learn about it: *Christopher Columbus, most famous of explorers, explored the Caribbean and the coast of South America between 1492 and 1502.* 2. To examine carefully: *to explore one's feelings* —ex-plor-a-tion (εk–splɔ–re^y–ʃən) n. —exploratory adj. *an exploratory operation to determine the cause and the seriousness of one's illness* —explorer n.

ex-plo-sion (ɪk–splo^w–ʒən) n. 1. A loud sound caused by sthg. exploding: *The explosion could be heard many miles away.* 2. A sudden increase: *explosion of the price of oil* 3. A sudden showing of strong feelings: *an explosion of laughter*

ex-plo-sive (ɪk–splo^w–sɪv) adj. Likely to explode: *Dynamite is explosive. Be careful how you handle it.*

explosive n. A substance that is likely to explode: *Be careful how you handle that dynamite. It's an explosive.*

ex-po-nent (ɪk–spo^w–nənt) n. 1. A person who is able to demonstrate skillfully a particular art or activity 2. A person who explains and supports a theory or belief

ex-port (ɪk–spɔrt/ εk–spɔrt) v. To send goods out of a country to be sold: *The United States exports cattle, dairy products, grains, chemicals, machinery, and many other manufactured goods.* —opposite IMPORT

ex-port (εk–spɔrt) n. 1. The act or business of exporting: *the export of grain* 2. Sthg. that is exported: *Oil is one of the chief exports of the Arab countries.* —opposite IMPORT —exportable adj.

ex-pose (ɪk–spo^wz) v. -posed, -posing 1. To make visible; to uncover: *After all the old paint and dirt were removed, the beautiful wood was exposed./ As a fighter pilot during the war, he was exposed to many dangers./ fig. to expose oneself to ridicule/ criticism* 2. To make known sthg. secret: *Have nothing to do with the fruitless deeds of darkness, but rather expose them* (Ephesians 5:11). 3. To uncover film to the light while taking a photograph

ex-po-si-tion (ɪk–spə–zɪ–ʃən) n. 1. *fml.* An act of explaining or making clear by giving details: *a full exposition of the dangers of smoking* 2. A large public exhibition of goods

ex-pos-i-tor (ɪk–spɑz–ə–tər) n. A person who explains or expounds sthg.

ex-pos-i-tor-y (ɪk–spɑz–ə–tɔr–i^y) adj. Serving to clarify or explain: *expository writing*

ex-pos-tu-late (ɪk–spɑs–tʃə–le^yt) v. -lated, -lating To make a friendly protest; to reason or argue with sbdy.

ex-po-sure (ɪk–spo^w–ʒər) n. 1. A state of being exposed: *Exposure of the skin to too much sun can cause cancer.* 2. An action of exposing: *The exposure of fraud in the company resulted in the arrest of two executives.* 3. The amount of film needed to take one photograph: *How many exposures are left on this roll of film?* —see EXPOSE

ex-pound (ɪk–spaʊnd) v. 1. To set forth or explain a view in detail 2. To explain or interpret

ex-press (ɪk–sprεs) v. To make known a feeling, opinion, or fact in words, actions, or in some other way: *The only thing that counts is faith expressing itself through love* (Galatians 5:6)./ *It's very important that we express our love to our children in words and in actions.*

express n. 1. Also express train A fast train that stops at few stations 2. A service or company for delivering goods quickly: *We sent the package by express.*

express adj. 1. Of a command, wish, etc.,

clearly stated and definite; explicit: *He gave the express command to sell all his property and give the money to charity.* **2.** Going or sent quickly: *an express train* **3.** Of a letter or package, sent faster and at a higher cost than usual: *express parcel*

ex-pres-sion (ɪk–sprɛ–ʃən) n. **1.** The act of expressing: *She sent her mother a beautiful card as an expression of her love.* **2.** The quality of showing feeling for the meaning when performing a song, play, etc.: *He read the poem with a lot of expression.* **3.** A word or phrase: *Use of the expression, "Shut up!" is very rude.* **4.** A look on a person's face that shows a mood or feeling: *a puzzled expression*

ex-pres-sive (ɪk–sprɛs–ɪv) adj. Showing feeling and meaning: *His art work is expressive of violent feelings against those who oppress the weak.* —**expressively** adv.

ex-press-ly (ɪk–sprɛs–liʸ) adv. Clearly and definitely: *I asked you expressly to be here at four o'clock.*

ex-pro-pri-ate (ɛks–proʷ–priʸ–eʸt) v. **-ated, -ating** To take property away from someone by official action, without the person's approval

ex-pul-sion (ɪk–spʌl–ʃən) n. **1.** The act of expelling **2.** The state of being expelled

ex-punge (ɪk–spʌndʒ) v. **-punged, -punging** To erase or wipe out

ex-qui-site (ɛks–kwɪz–ət/ ɪk–skwɪz–ət) adj. **1.** Having special beauty **2.** Having excellent discrimination —**exquisitely** adv. *exquisitely designed*

ex-tant (ɛk–stənt/ ɪk–stænt) adj. Still in existence

ex-tem-po-ra-ne-ous (ɪk–stɛm–pə–reʸ–niʸ–əs) adj. Spoken or done in haste without preparation

ex-tend (ɪk–stɛnd) v. **1.** Of space, land, or time, to reach or continue: *Our property extends to the edge of the driveway.* **2.** To make longer or larger: *They extended the railroad from the East Coast to the Midwest by 1860.* **3.** To stretch out a part of one's body to the limit: *The bird extended its wings in flight.* **4.** *fml.* To give or offer sthg.: *to extend friendship to someone*

ex-ten-sion (ɪk–stɛn–ʃən) n. **1.** The act of extending or the state of being extended: *the*

extension of the bird's wings **2.** A part which is added in order to extend sthg.: *We are building an extension onto our house.* **3.** Any of many lines which connect the telephone switchboard to the rooms or offices in a large building: *Extension four, seven, three, please.* (=4-7-3)

ex-ten-sive (ɪk–stɛn–sɪv) adj. **1.** Large in area: *extensive gardening* **2.** Large in scope; wide-ranging: *extensive knowledge* —**extensively** adv.

ex-tent (ɪk–stɛnt) n. **1.** The length or area to which sthg. reaches: *From the top of the hill I could see the full extent of the valley./fig. I was amazed at the extent of her talent.* **2.** To the degree stated: *He is correct to some extent.* (=partly)

ex-ten-u-ate (ɪk–stɛn–yuʷ–eʸt) v. **-ated, -ating** To excuse by minimizing the seriousness of —**ex-ten-u-a-tion** (ɪk–stɛn–yuʷ–eʸ–ʃən) n.

ex-te-ri-or (ɪk–stɪər–iʸ–ər) adj. Outside (esp. of places): *the exterior walls of the house* —opposite INTERIOR —compare EXTERNAL

exterior n. The outside; the outer appearance: *the exterior of the building*

ex-ter-mi-nate (ɪk–stɜr–mə–neʸt) v. **-nated, -nating** To destroy all the creatures or people in a place —**ex-term-i-na-tion** (ɛk–stɜr–mə–neʸ–ʃən) n.

ex-ter-nal (ɪk–stɜrn–əl) adj. On, of, from, or for the outside: *Put this cream on your skin; it's for external use only.* —opposite INTERNAL —compare EXTERIOR —**externally** adv.

ex-tinct (ɪk–stɪŋkt) adj. Out of existence: *The condor is a bird that is about to become extinct./ an extinct volcano* (=no longer active)

ex-tinc-tion (ɪk–stɪŋk–ʃən) n. **1.** Making or becoming extinct **2.** Extinguishing; being extinguished

ex-tin-guish (ɪk–stɪŋ–gwɪʃ) v. **1.** To put out a light or fire **2.** To put an end to: *Nothing could extinguish his faith in God.* —**extinguishable** adj.

ex-tol (ɪk–stoʷl) v. **-ll-** To praise enthusiastically: *I will extol the Lord at all times, his praise will always be on my lips* (Psalm 34:1).

ex-tort (ɪk–stɔrt) v. To obtain sthg. by force or threats

ex-tor-tion (ɪk–stɔr–ʃən) n. The act of extort-

ing (esp. money) —**extortioner** n. —**ex-tortionist** n.

ex-tra– (ɛk–strə–) prefix Beyond the scope, area, or limits of: *extracurricular/ extraterritorial/ extrasensory*

ex-tra (ɛk–strə) adj., adv. **1.** Additional; more than is usual or necessary: *an extra cup of sugar* **2.** In addition to the regular charge: *The restaurant charges extra for coffee.*

ex-tract (ɪk–strækt) v. To take or get out, often with difficulty: *to extract a tooth*

ex-tract (ɛk–strækt) n. **1.** A product obtained by extracting: *vanilla extract* **2.** A selected portion of a letter, book, play, etc.; an excerpt: *An extract from the book was printed in the magazine.*

ex-trac-tion (ɪk–stræk–ʃən) n. **1.** The act or an example of extracting: *the extraction of a tooth* **2.** Origin of a person's family; descent; lineage: *He is of Italian extraction. (=his ancestors came from Italy)*

ex-tra-cur-ric-u-lar (ɛk–strə–kə–rɪk–yə–lər) adj. Of or pertaining to student activites that are not a part of the curriculum

ex-tra-dite (ɛks–trə–daɪt) v. -dited, -diting **1.** To hand over a person accused or convicted of a crime to the country where the crime was committed **2.** To obtain such a person for trial or punishment —**ex-tra-di-tion** (ɛks–trə–dɪ–ʃən) n.

ex-tran-e-ous (ɪk–streʸn–iʸ–əs) adj. **1.** Of external origin **2.** Not belonging to sthg., or having nothing to do with the subject

ex-traor-di-nar-y (ɪk–strɔrd–ən–ɛər–iʸ/ ɛk–strə–ɔrd–) adj. Much more than what is usual or ordinary; exceptional; remarkable: *a man of extraordinary strength/ talent/wisdom* —**ex-traor-di-nar-i-ly** (ɪk–strɔrd–ən–ɛər–ə–liʸ/ ɛk–strə–ɔrd–) adv. *He has extraordinarily big ears.*

ex-trap-o-late (ɪk–stræp–ə–leʸt) v. -lated, -lating To infer unknown information from facts that are known

ex-tra-sen-so-ry (ɛks–trə–sen–sər–iʸ) n. Beyond the range of normal sense perception

ex-trav-a-gant (ɪk–stræv–ə–gənt) adj. *derog.* **1.** Spending too much, esp. of money: *my wife's extravagant spending* **2.** Of ideas, behavior, and the expression of feeling, going beyond what is reasonable or usual: *extrava-*

gant praise —**extravagance** n. *We should try to avoid extravagance when there are so many homeless people in the world with little to eat.* —**extravagantly** adv.

ex-trav-a-gan-za (ɛk–stræv–ə–gæn–zə) n. A lavish, spectacular theatrical production

ex-treme (ɪk–striʸm) adj. **1.** The furthest possible; concerning the very beginning or very end: *extreme depth of the ocean* **2.** Very great: *extreme heat/ cold* **3.** Drastic; severe: *Extreme measures were taken to curb the violence.*

extreme n. The greatest or utmost degree: *Sometimes she's very cheerful and sometimes she cries all the time. She goes from one extreme to the other./ The man who fears God will avoid all extremes* (Ecclesiastes 7:18).

ex-treme-ly (ɪk–striʸm–liʸ) adv. Very: *Please be extremely careful with my good dishes.*

ex-trem-ist (ɪk–striʸm–ɪst) n. A person with extreme views

ex-trem-i-ty (ɪk–strem–ə–tiʸ) n. -ties **1.** The farthest point or part **2.** The utmost degree **3.** Extreme danger or need **4.** An extreme or severe measure

ex-tri-cate (ɛk–strə–keʸt) v. -cated, -cating To set free: *It took the firemen three hours to extricate her from her demolished car.*

ex-tro-vert (ɛk–strə–vərt) n. A person who is more interested in others or in the surroundings than in self; a lively, sociable person —opposite INTROVERT

ex-u-ber-ant (ɪg–zuʷ–bər–ənt) adj. **1.** High spirited; very lively **2.** Growing profusely

ex-ude (ɪg–zuʷd/ ɪk–suʷd) v. exuded, exuding To give off or out in great amounts: *After all the hard work on such a hot day, he was exuding sweat./ fig. She simply exudes happiness.*

ex-ult (ɪg–zʌlt) v. To rejoice greatly —**ex-ul-ta-tion** (ɪg–zəl–teʸ–ʃən/ ɛk–səl–) n. NOTE: Do not confuse exult with exalt or exultation with exaltation.

eye (aɪ) n. **1.** The bodily organ of sight **2.** The iris of this organ: *She has blue eyes.* **3.** The part of the face around the eye: *He hit him and gave him a black eye.* **4.** The ability to see: *The eyes of the Lord are upon the righteous and his ears are attentive to their prayer* (1 Peter 3:12). *The eyes of the Lord are everywhere, keeping watch on the wicked and the good* (Pro

verbs 15:3). **5.** The hole in a needle through which the thread is passed **6.** A small metal piece into which a hook fits for fastening clothes **7. catch someone's eye** *infml.* To attract one's notice or attention: *That apple pie caught my eye.* **8. in the eyes of** In the opinion of **9. keep an eye on** To watch closely: *Please keep an eye on the baby for me.* **10. to fix one's eyes on** Pay rapt attention to; keep uppermost in your mind: *Let us fix our eyes on Jesus, the author and perfecter of our faith, who for the joy set before him endured the cross, scorning its shame, and sat down at the right hand of the throne of God* (Hebrews 12:2). **11. keep one's eyes open** To watch carefully (for) **12. see eye to eye (with)** To agree completely with someone: *She and I see eye to eye on this matter.*

eye-ball (aɪ-bɔl) n. The global part of the eye

eye-brow (aɪ-braʊ) n. The hair covering the bony ridge above the eye

eye-ful (aɪ-fʊl) n. **1.** A good look at **2.** A pleasing sight

eye-lash (aɪ-læʃ) n. One of the fringe hairs on the edge of each eyelid

eye-lid (aɪ-lɪd) n. Either of the movable folds of skin that close over the eyes

eye-o-pen-er (aɪ-oʷ-pən-ər) n. Sthg. startling that causes a person to see a truth that he never saw before

eye-sore (aɪ-sɔr) n. Sthg. ugly to look at

eye-wit-ness (aɪ-wɪt-nəs) n. A person who sees an event and can describe it: *We did not follow cleverly invented stories when we told you about the power and coming of our Lord Jesus Christ, but we were eyewitnesses of his majesty* (2 Peter 1:16).

E-ze-ki-el (ɪ-ziʸ-kiʸ-əl) n. A book of the Old Testament written by the Prophet Ezekiel during the 6th century B.C. —see BIBLE, OLD TESTAMENT

Ez-ra (ɛz-rə) n. **1.** A Jewish exile in Babylon during the sixth century BC who was of priestly descent **2.** A book of the Old Testament believed to have been written by Ezra, regarding the return of the Jews from their captivity in Babylon, the rebuilding of the temple, and the inauguration of social and religious reforms —see BIBLE, OLD TESTAMENT

F, f (ɛf) n. The sixth letter of the English alphabet

fa-ble (feʸ-bəl) n. **1.** A fictitious short story, esp. about animals, that teaches a lesson or truth **2.** A story about great people who never actually lived; legend; myth **3.** A falsehood —**fabled** adj. Legendary

fab-ric (fæb-rɪk) n. **1.** A type of cloth made of threads woven together **2.** The walls, floors, roof, etc., of a building; framework: *fig. the fabric (=framework) of society*

fab-ri-cate (fæb-rə-keʸt) v. **-cated, -cating 1.** To fashion or make; build **2.** To make up a story (=in order to deceive); to lie: *He quickly fabricated a story to cover up his absence from school.* —**fab-ri-ca-tion** (fæb-rə-keʸ-ʃən) n.

fab-u-lous (fæb-yə-ləs) adj. **1.** So great as to be unbelievable: *a fabulous treasure* **2.** *infml.* Wonderful; excellent: *We had a fabulous dinner.* —**fabulously** adv.

fa-cade (fə-sɑd) n. **1.** The front of a building **2.** A deceptive appearance

face (feʸs) n. **1.** The front part of the head **2.** Presence; favor: *Look to the Lord and his strength; seek his face always* (Psalm 105:4). *The face of the Lord is against those who do evil* (1 Peter 3:12). **3.** A facial expression: *He's making funny faces at me.* **4.** The surface of sthg.: *The hikers seem to have disappeared from the face of the earth.* **5.** Respect: *The new student didn't want to lose face in front of the class.*

face v. **faced, facing 1.** To have the front pointing towards: *Our living room faces the mountains.* **2.** To encounter; meet boldly: *All of us have to face difficult decisions at some time in our lives.* **3.** To cover sthg. with a layer of different material: *The collar of her red jacket was faced with black.* **4. face the music** To deal with the unpleasant circumstances resulting from one's own actions **5. face up to sthg.** To meet and deal with sthg., esp. sthg. difficult: *It's important for young people to learn to face up to reality.*

SPELLING NOTE:
Words having the sound /f/ may be spelled with **ph-**, like **philosopher**.

fac-et (fæs-ət)n. **1.** One side of a many-sided object, esp. a cut jewel **2.** *fml.* An aspect or view of a subject. *Many facets of this international problem must be taken into consideration.*

fa-ce-tious (fə-siʸ-ʃəs) adj. Intended to be funny, esp. at a time for being serious

fa-cial (feʸ-ʃəl) adj. Concerning the face

facial n. Beauty treatment for the face

fa-cil-i-tate (fə-sɪl-ə-teʸt) v. **-tated, -tating** *fml.* To make easy or less difficult

fa-cil-i-ties (fə-sɪl-ə-tiʸz) n. The buildings and equipment, etc. that can be used: *The city has excellent recreational facilities.*

fa-cil-i-ty (fə-sɪl-ə-tiʸ) n. **-ties 1.** *fml.* Ability to learn or do sthg. easily: *I'm gaining facility in the use of the computer.* **2.** A convenience: *An exercise room is a facility offered by some of the better hotels.* **3.** Sthg. set up for the stated purpose: *a housing facility/an office facility*

fa-cing (feʸ-sɪŋ) n. **1.** Sthg. used to cover the front to provide ornamentation or protection **2.** Lining near the edge of a garment

fac-sim-i-le (fæk-sɪm-ə-liʸ) n. An exact reproduction or copy

fact (fækt) n. **1.** An actual happening; sthg. that is known to be, or accepted as being, true: *It is a fact that George Washington was the first president of the United States.* **2.** The truth: *Is the story of William Tell fact or fiction?*

fac-tion (fæk-ʃən) n. **1.** A group of people within a political party, government, etc. working against other such groups or against the main body **2.** Partisan conflict within an organization or country

fac-tious (fæk-ʃəs) adj. Producing or tending to produce faction; causing dissension

fac-ti-tious (fæk-tɪʃ-əs) adj. Artificial; not natural: *factitious enthusiasm* —**factitiously** adj.

fac-tor (fæk-tər) n. **1.** Any one of the circumstances or elements which produce a result: *There are many factors to be considered before changing jobs.* **2.** A number which exactly divides into another: *Four is a factor of eight.* **3.** A person or company that finances the accounts of businesses

fac-to-ry (fæk-tə-riʸ) n. **-ries** A building or group of buildings in which goods are

made (manufactured)

fac-tu-al (fæk–t∫uʷ–əl) adj. Based on or containing facts —**factually** adv.

fac-ul-ty (fæk–əl–tiʸ) n. **-ties 1.** A natural power of the body or mind: *to be in possession of all one's faculties* **2.** A special aptitude: *He has the faculty to learn languages easily.* **3.** The whole teaching staff of a university or college

fad (fæd) n. A custom or style that many people are interested in for a short time; a passing fancy

fade (feʸd) v. **faded, fading 1.** To lose or cause to lose color, freshness, etc.: *I washed my new dress in hot water and the colors faded.* **2.** To lose strength: *Memories of her childhood faded as she grew older.* **3.** To disappear: *His dream of becoming a great musician has faded.*

fag (fæg) v. **-gg- 1.** To work very hard and become very tired **2. fagged out** *infml.* Very tired: *I'm completely fagged out after hiking all day.*

Fahr-en-heit (fɛər–ən–haɪt) n. A scale of temperature in which water freezes at 32° and boils at 212° —compare CENTIGRADE, CELSIUS

fail (feʸl) v. **1.** To be unsuccessful in sthg.: *Plans fail for lack of counsel, but with many advisors they succeed* (Proverbs 15:22). **2.** To give an unacceptable performance in an exam: *She failed the history exam.* —opposite PASS **3.** To miss performing sthg. that is expected: *The company failed to deliver the goods I ordered./Love never fails* (1 Corinthians 13:8). **4.** To cause disappointment: *We're counting on you. Don't fail us!* **5.** To be not enough for: *Words fail me.* **6.** To become weak: *Her strength has been failing ever since her operation.*

fail n. **1.** Failure **2. without fail** Absolutely; positively: *Be here at nine o'clock without fail.*

failure (feʸl–yər) n. **1.** Lack of success or instance of this: *The company finally succeeded after many failures.* **2.** A person, attempt, or thing that fails: *The new movie was a complete failure.* **3.** The state or instance of being unable to produce or perform what is expected or desired: *business failure*

faint (feʸnt) adj. **1.** Lacking strength: *Those who hope in the Lord will renew their strength...*

they will run and not grow weary, they will walk and not be faint* (Isaiah 40:31). **2.** Weak, dull, indistinct, etc.: *a faint sound of music in the distance/ faint-hearted (=lacking in courage)* **3.** Very small: *a faint hope/ infml. I don't have the faintest idea about the way this machine works.* —**faint** v. —**faint** n.

fair (fɛər) adj. **1.** Honest; just: *a fair judgment* —opposite UNFAIR **2.** Moderately good; average: *He has only a fair understanding of computers, but he's learning.* **3.** Clear and sunny weather **4.** Light in color, as of hair or skin **5.** Consistent with the rules: *a fair fight, no hitting below the belt, no kicking, etc.* **6.** Just; equitable: *Why should you always be first? It isn't fair.* **7. the fair sex** Women as a group —**fairness** n.

fair n. **1.** A show held once a year where farmers show their animals, produce, goods made by hand, etc. for judging: *a county/ state fair* **2.** A market for selling farm produce, usu. held regularly **3.** An exhibition of goods, advertising, etc.: *a trade fair*

fair-ly (fɛər–liʸ) adv. **1.** Honestly, justly, etc.: *This company always treats its customers fairly.* —opposite UNFAIRLY **2.** Moderately well: *Nancy plays the piano fairly well.* —see RATHER

fair-y (fɛər–iʸ) n. **-ies** An imaginary being supposed to have magical powers

fairy tale (fɛər–iʸ teʸl) n. **1.** A story about fairies, usu. for children **2.** A falsehood

faith (feʸθ) n. **1.** Strong belief; trust; confidence: *By grace [the unmerited love of God] you have been saved [from eternal punishment], through faith [in Jesus Christ]...* (Ephesians 2:8). *Without faith [in Jesus Christ] it is impossible to please God...* (Hebrews 11:6) *...a man is justified by faith [in Jesus] apart from observing the law* (Romans 3:28). **2.** Loyalty to one's promises or word of honor: *This company always acts in good faith; you can trust them.* **3.** A system of religious beliefs; religion: *the Christian faith*

faith-ful (feʸθ–fəl) adj. **1.** Loyal; firm in commitment: *...Be faithful [to Jesus], even to the point of death, and I [God] will give you the crown of life.* (Revelation 2:10). *...The Lord is faithful to all his promises and loving toward all*

he has made (Psalm 145:13). **2.** Accurate; true to the facts or to an original: *a faithful description of what happened* **3.** Loyal to one's husband or wife by having no sexual relationship with anyone else —**faithfulness** n.

faith-ful-ly (feʸθ–fə–liʸ) adv. **1.** With faith and loyalty: *He served the Lord faithfully.* **2.** Accurately; exactly: *I followed your instructions faithfully.*

faith-less (feʸθ–ləs) adj. **1.** Lacking faith in God **2.** Disloyal —**faithlessly** adv.

fake (feʸk) n. **1.** Sthg. that seems real but is not **2.** A person who tries to deceive others by pretending to be sthg. he is not

fake adj. Not genuine

fake v. **faked, faking 1.** To make sthg. that looks genuine, in order to deceive people **2.** To pretend: *He's not really sick; he's just faking it.*

fa-kir (feʸ–kər) n. **1.** A Muslim or Hindu who lives by begging, esp. one who performs feats of magic or endurance **2.** A member of any of the Muslim orders of monks who take vows of poverty and live in monasteries or as wandering friars

fal-con (fɔl–kən) n. A kind of hawk, having long, pointed wings, trained for hunting

fall (fɔl) v. **fell,** (fɛl), **fallen** (fɔ–lən), **falling 1.** To drop through the air: *He fell from the top of the tree./ Jesus said, "I saw Satan fall like lightning from heaven"* (Luke 10:18). **2.** To come down from an upright position suddenly: *She tripped and fell down the stairs.* **3.** To lose balance: *Don't put that lamp on that pillow. It will fall over.* **4.** To become lower in level, degree, pitch, quantity, etc.: *The temperature fell to below freezing.* **5.** To hang freely: *Her hair falls over her shoulders.* **6.** To take on an expression of sadness, disappointment, etc.: *His face fell when we told him the job had already been taken.* **7.** To die or be wounded in battle: *A memorial was erected in honor of those who had fallen in battle.* **8.** To suffer defeat, failure, etc.: *Cast your cares on the Lord, and he will sustain you; he will never let the righteous fall* (Psalm 55:22). **9.** To come or take place: *Her birthday falls on the same day as mine.* **10.** To pass into a new state or condition; become: *He fell asleep./to fall in*

love **11. fall flat** To fail to produce the desired result **12. fall short (a)** To have too little of sthg. **(b)** To fail in an attempt to reach a desired result, standard, etc.: *All have sinned and fall short of the glory of God* (Romans 3:23). **13. fall for sbdy./ sthg. (a)** To be deceived: *I was foolish enough to fall for the salesman's line.* **(b)** *infml.* To fall in love with: *They really fell for each other. They're getting married tomorrow.* **14. fall off** To become lower in number, quality, etc.: *Business has fallen off sharply this year.* **15. fall through** To fail to be completed: *Our business deal fell through.*

fall n. **1.** An act of falling: *She had a nasty fall and broke her leg.* **2.** Autumn; the season when trees drop their leaves **3.** Sthg. that falls or has fallen: *a fall of rocks* **4.** A decrease in quantity, price, demand, degree, etc.: *a fall in price* —opposite RISE **5.** A defeat or loss of greatness: *the fall of the Roman Empire* **6. The fall into sin** The Bible tells us that the first man and woman fell into sin. Since then all people (except Jesus) have been born with a sinful nature. We sin (break God's commandments) because we have a sinful nature.—see MAN, SIN, JESUS **7.** A waterfall

fal-la-cious (fə–leʸ–ʃəs) adj. Wrong; mistaken; showing faulty reasoning

fal-la-cy (fæl–ə–siʸ) n. **-cies** A wrong idea or belief; sthg. thought to be true but that is false; unsound arguing or reasoning

fal-li-ble (fæl–ə–bəl) adj. Capable of making mistakes: *Every human being is fallible.* —opposite INFALLIBLE *The Bible is the infallible Word of God.*

Fal-lo-pi-an tube (fə–loʷ–piʸ–ən tuʷb) n. Either of the two tubes carrying egg cells from the ovaries to the womb

fall-out (fɔl–aʊt) n. **1.** Radioactive debris from a nuclear explosion **2.** Incidental effect of a notable event

fal-low (fæl–oʷ) adj. **1.** Of land, plowed and left unseeded for a season or more **2.** Undeveloped or inactive

false (fɔls) adj. **1.** Untrue; incorrect: *false reports/What the newspaper printed was completely false./ God's law says, "You shall not*

give false testimony against your neighbor"
(Exodus 20:16). **2.** Unfaithful; disloyal:
Watch out for false prophets... (Matthew 7:15).
3. Artificial; not real: *false eyelashes* **4.** Made
so as to deceive: *a false passport/ A false balance is abomination [is hateful] to the Lord*
(Proverbs 11:1). **5. false alarm** A warning
sounded when there is no danger: *The police
received a false alarm; there was no bomb.*
—**falsely** adv.

false-hood (fɔls–hʊd) n. A lie

fal-set-to (fɔl–sɛt–oᵂ) n. **-tos** A high pitched
voice above one's natural range, esp. a
male voice

fal-si-fy (fɔl–sə–faɪ) v. **-fied, fying 1.** To alter
a document fraudulently **2.** To misrepresent the facts —**fal-si-fi-ca-tion** (fɔl–sə–fə–keᵞ–ʃən) n. —**falsifier** n.

fal-si-ty (fɔl–sət–iᵞ) n. **-ties 1.** A falsehood; a
lie **2.** An untruth

fal-ter (fɔl–tər) v. To stumble or fall

fame (feᵞm) n. The condition of being known
by many and well thought of: *He soon found
fame as a musician.* —**famed** adj. Famous: *Cleopatra was famed for her great beauty.*

fa-mil-i-al (fə–mɪl–yəl) adj. Concerning members of the family

fa-mil-iar (fə–mɪl–yər) adj. **1.** Well known; often seen or experienced; usual: *a familiar
path* **2.** Having a thorough knowledge of:
*He's very familiar with this part of town after
living here for sixty years.* —opposite UNFAMILIAR **3.** *derog.* Too friendly for the occasion; overly free: *He was thrown out of the restaurant for being too familiar with the waitress.*

fa-mil-i-ar-i-ty (fə–mɪl–ɪ–ɛər–ə–tiᵞ) n. **-ties 1.**
Thorough knowledge of a thing or subject
2. Friendly relationship **3.** Undue intimacy

fa-mil-iar-ize (fə–mɪl–yə–raɪz) v. **-ized, -izing
1.** To become well acquainted with sthg. **2.**
To bring sthg. into common knowledge or
use

fam-i-ly (fæm–ə–liᵞ) n. **-lies 1.** Any group of
people related by blood or marriage, esp.
parents and their children **2.** A group of
things related by common characteristics,
esp. animals, plants, etc.: *Dogs, foxes, and
wolves all belong to the same family of animals.*
3. A group of people bonded together by a
common faith: *All Christians are members of
the family of God because we are "all children of
God through faith in Christ Jesus"* (Galatians
3:26). **4.** A number of related languages: *the
Indo-European family of languages*

family adj. Suitable for children as well as
older people: *a family restaurant*

fam-ine (fæm–ən) n. An extreme lack of food:
*It is the children who suffer most in a famine.
Many children die during famines every year.*
—compare HUNGER

fam-ished (fæm–ɪʃt) adj. Extremely hungry

fa-mous (feᵞ–məs) adj. Very well known:
King Solomon was famous for his wisdom.
—**famously** adv.

fan (fæn) n. **1.** A hand-held, flat implement
for creating a cool breeze **2.** A series of
broad blades turned by a motor for the
same purpose

fan v. **-nn- 1.** To cause air to blow on sthg.
with a fan or as if with a fan: *The scout leader
fanned the dying embers with his hat and soon
had a blazing fire.* **2.** To spread out like a fan:
*The searchers fanned out to look for the lost
child.*

fan n. An eager follower or supporter, esp.
of a famous person or of a sport: *football fans*

fa-nat-ic (fə–næt–ɪk) adj., n. A person who is
overenthusiastic or eager about sthg.
—**fanatic** adj. —**fanaticism** n.

fan-ci-ful (fæn–siᵞ–fəl) adj. Inclined to have
fancies; imaginary

fan-cy (fæn–siᵞ) adj. **-cier, -ciest** Decorated or
brightly colored; not ordinary: *a fancy dress*

fancy n. **1.** The power of the mind to imagine: *the artist's fancy* **2.** Things imagined **3.**
Desire or liking for sthg.: *She took a fancy to
the dress in the store window immediately.*

fang (fæŋ) n. A tooth of a wild animal; the
poisonous tooth of a snake

fan-tas-tic (fæn–tæs–tɪk) adj. **1.** Imaginary; unreal; very strange, etc.: *fantastic dreams/ a
fantastic scheme* **2.** *infml.* Very, very good;
wonderful: *a fantastic wedding* —**fantastically** adv.

fan-ta-sy (fæn–tə–siᵞ) n. **-sies** An imaginary
scene; an idea not based on reality

far (far) adj. **farther** (far–ðər) or **further** (fɜr–ðər), **farthest** (far–ðəst) or **furthest** (fɜr–ðəst). **1.**

At a considerable distance: *This is the far-thest I have ever been from home.* **2.** Long: *a far journey* **3.** Being the more distant of two places: *Shall we camp here or on the far side of the lake?* **4. a far cry** Much different: *This is a far cry from former methods.*

far adv. **farther** or **further, farthest** or **fur-thest 1.** A long way: *We drove far up the coast.* **2.** Very much: *far prettier/far wiser* **3. so far (a)** Up to now: *So far I'm enjoying my job, but I've only been here two days.* **(b)** Up to a certain degree, distance, etc.: *She can only walk so far before she has to stop and rest./ to trust someone so far and no further* **4. far and wide** Everywhere **5. so far, so good** Things are successful up to now: *Our old car has made it half way home. So far, so good!* —see FURTHER

far-a-way (far-ə-we^y) adj. **1.** Distant in time, space, etc. **2.** Dreamy: *a faraway look in her eye*

farce (fars) n. **1.** Anything silly and useless **2.** A play with unlikely and ridiculous characters

fare (feər) n. **1.** The price charged for a person to ride on a train, bus, plane, etc. **2.** A paying passenger on a bus, train, etc. **3.** One's usual diet

fare v. **fared, faring** *fml.* To succeed: *How are you faring in your new job?*

fare-well (feər-wεl) n., adj., interj. Good-bye: *a farewell party*

far–fetched (far–fεtʃt) adj. Not very likely; improbable

far–flung (far–flʌŋ) adj. Widely extended

farm (farm) n. A plot of land, including its buildings, used for growing crops or raising animals: *a wheat farm*

farm v. To use land to grow crops, raise animals, etc.: *The Smiths have been farming this land for three generations.*

farm-er n. (far-mər) n. A person who uses land for growing crops, etc. —**farming** n.

far-off (far-ɔf) adj.. Remote

far-out (far-aʊt) adj. *slang* Excellent

far-sight-ed (far–saɪ-təd) adj. **1.** Foreseeing what is likely to happen and preparing for it; wise **2.** Seeing distant objects more clearly than nearby ones —**farsightedness** n.

far-ther (far-ðər) also **further** adv., adj. Com-parative of **far**; more distant: *We rode ten miles farther/further around the lake/ We'd bet-ter not carry this joke (=gag) any farther.* —see FURTHER

far-thest (far-ðəst) also **furthest** adv., adj. Su-perlative of **far**; most far: *This market is the farthest/ furthest from our house.* —see FUR-THEST

fas-ci-nate (fæs-ə-ne^yt) v. **-nated, -nating** To charm, attract, or interest irresistibly —**fas-ci-na-tion** (fæs-ə-ne^y-ʃen) n.

fas-ci-nat-ing (fæʃ-ə-ne^yt-ɱ) adj. Having great attraction or charm

fas-cism (fæʃ-ɪz-əm) n. A totalitarian govern-mental system led by a dictator emphasizing an aggressive nationalism and often racism —**fascist** adj., n.

fash-ion (fæʃ-ən) n. **1.** The style of dress that is popular at a certain time: *Bright colors are in fashion this season.* **2.** Manner or way of making or doing sthg.: *She speaks in an inter-esting fashion.* **3. after a fashion** To some ex-tent, but not well: *I play the piano after a fash-ion, but only for my own enjoyment.*

fashion v. To design or make sthg. —**fash-ionable** adj.

fast (fæst) adj. **-er, -est 1.** Moving quickly; swift; rapid: *a fast train* **2.** Adapted to rapid travel: *a fast freeway* **3.** Indicating a time ahead of the correct time: *The clock is ten minutes fast.* —compare SLOW **4.** Firmly fixed or fastened

fast adv. **1.** Swiftly: *Run fast./ Run faster.* **2.** Soundly; deeply: *He was fast asleep.* **3.** Tight-ly; securely: *stuck fast in the mud*

fast v. To go without food or certain kinds of food, esp. for religious reasons: *He fasted every Monday./ Jesus fasted for 40 days.*

fast n. An act or period of going without food

fas-ten (fæs-ən) v. **1.** To cause to become firm-ly fixed or joined: *He fastened his seat belt.* —opposite UNFASTEN **2.** *fig.* To fix or focus steadily: *He fastened his attention on the speak-er.*

fas-ten-er (fæs-ən-ər) n. Sthg. used to fasten things together

fast food n. Restaurant food prepared and served quickly

fas-tid-i-ous (fæs–tɪd–iʸ–əs) adj. Difficult to please

fast-ness (fæst–nəs) n. **1.** A state of being fast or firm **2.** A stronghold

fast–talk (fæst–tɔk) v. **-talked, -talking** To persuade, esp. by smooth, deceptive talk

fat (fæt) adj. **-tt- 1.** Fleshy; plump; overweight: *I'll have to go on a diet. I've gotten fat from sitting so much.* **2.** Thick; well-filled out; big: *We made a fat profit on the sale of our house.*

fat n. **1.** The greasy substance found under the skins of animals and in some plants **2.** This material used as food or in cooking: *This ground beef is 20% fat.* **3. the fat of the land** The best part **4. chew the fat** To have a casual, informal conversation **5. a fat chance** A very slight chance; not much chance at all

fa-tal (feʸt–əl) adj. **1.** Causing or resulting in death: *a fatal gun wound* **2.** Resulting in disaster: *a fatal mistake* —**fatally** adv. *fatally injured*

fa-tal-ism (feʸt–əl–ɪz–əm) n. The belief that fate controls everything and man cannot change it

fa-tal-ist (feʸ–təl–əst) n. One who accepts and submits to whatever happens, supposing it to be inevitable —**fa-tal-is-tic** (feʸ–təl–ɪs–tɪk) adj.

fate (feʸt) n. What the future holds for one —**fateful** adj.

fat-ed (feʸ– təd) adj. Controlled by fate

fat-head (fæt–hɛd) n. A stupid person

fa-ther (fɑð–ər) n. **1.** A male parent: *Fathers, do not embitter your children, or they will become discouraged. Instead, bring them up in the training and instruction of the Lord* (Colossians 3:21; Ephesians 6:4). **2.** God the Father Almighty, maker of heaven and earth and the entire universe and all therein: *Jesus said to his followers, "If you, then, though you are evil, know how to give good gifts to your children, how much more will your Father in heaven give good gifts to those who ask him!"* (Matthew 7:11). *Another time he said, "Do not be afraid, little flock [believers in Jesus], for your Father has been pleased to give you the kingdom [of heaven]"* (Luke 12:32). *Jesus taught his disciples to pray, "Our Father in heaven, hallowed*

be your name." (Matthew 6:9) *Jesus said, "...No one knows the Son except the Father, and no one knows the Father except the Son and those to whom the Son chooses to reveal him"* (Matthew 11:27). NOTE: God the Father is all-powerful, all-knowing, all-wise, and present everywhere all the time. He created all things out of nothing and he rules over all things. He is holy and just, and he is also a God of love. He loves us and all mankind so much that he sent his one and only Son, Jesus Christ, into the world to keep the Law perfectly for us, and then let wicked men nail him to a cross where he hung and suffered and died for us, to pay for all our sins with his own blood. God is the giver of every good gift and he wants only what is best for us in the present life and for all eternity. —see JESUS CHRIST —see also GOD

father–in–law (fɑð–ər–ən–lɔ) n. **fathers–in–law** The father of one's wife or husband

fath-om (fæð–əm) n. A nautical unit of length equal to six feet

fathom v. **1.** To measure the depth of **2.** To understand thoroughly

fath-om-less (fæð–əm–ləs) adj. Too difficult to understand

fa-tigue (fə–tiʸg) n. **1.** Weariness from exertion **2.** *mech.* The tendency of metals and other materials to break under repeated stress **3. fatigues** *pl.* Informal military dress

fat-ten (fæt–ən) v. To make or become fat

fat-ty (fæt–iʸ) adj. **-tier, -tiest** Like fat; containing fat —**fatty** n. A fat person

fat-u-ous (fætʃ–uʷ–əs) adj. Silly; foolish

fau-cet (fɔs–ət) n. *AmE.* also **tap** A device for controlling the flow of liquid from a pipe, barrel, etc.

fault (fɔlt) n. **1.** A mistake or imperfection: *In spite of his faults, all the children like him.* **2.** *tech.* In geology, a crack in the earth's surface **3.** Blame: *Which driver was at fault (=in the wrong) in the car accident?/ Do everything without complaining or arguing, so that you may become blameless and pure, children of God without fault in a crooked and depraved generation, in which you shine like stars in the universe as you hold out the word of life* (Philippians 2:14-16). —**faultless** adj.

fault-y (fȯl–tiʸ) adj. **-ier, -iest** Having faults: *a faulty light switch/ Every major decision you make will be faulty until you learn to see God's world as God sees it.*

fau-na (fȯ–nə) n. The animals of a region or country

fa-vor n. *AmE.* **favour** *BrE.* (feʸ–vər) **1.** An act of kindness: *I'd like to ask a favor of you. Would you let me borrow your typewriter for a few days?* **2.** Approval; good will: *Now is the time of God's favor, now is the day of salvation* (2 Corinthians 6:2). **3. in favor of** In agreement with: *Are you in favor of the new president's foreign policy?* **4. in one's favor** To one's advantage: *The score was six to four in favor of the home team.*

favor v. **1.** To treat with special favor: *The teacher favored the girls in her class over the boys.* **2.** To approve of a plan or idea: *Did your parents favor the idea of your going to work instead of to college?* **3.** To resemble: *The baby favors his grandfather.*

fav-or-a-ble *AmE.* **favourable** *BrE.* (feʸ–vər–ə–bəl) adj. *fml.* **1.** Helpful; pleasant: *favorable winds/ weather* **2.** Encouraging; promising: *First reports on the new product are favorable.* **3.** Advantageous: *One can get favorable interest rates at the bank now.* —opposite UNFAVORABLE —**favorably** adv. Compare **favorable** and **favorite**: Favorite is used in speaking of sthg. or sbdy. that is liked best. Favorable is used to talk about things, conditions, etc. that are advantageous or that show agreement, approval, etc.: *What's your favorite food?/ My boss gave a favorable report on my work.*

fa-vor-ite *AmE.* **favourite** *BrE.* (feʸ–vər–ət) n. Sthg. or someone that is liked more than all others: *The song they're playing on the radio is my favorite.* —**favorite** adj. *My favorite color is blue.*

fa-vor-it-ism (feʸ–vər–ə–tız–əm) n. Partiality; the unfair showing of favor toward one person or group over others: *If you show favoritism you sin and are convicted by the law as lawbreakers* (James 2:9). *Do nothing out of favoritism* (1 Timothy 5:21).

fawn (fȯn) n. **1.** A young deer **2.** Its color (a light yellow-brown)

fawn v. **1.** Of a dog, e.g., to try to win affection by crouching close to a person and licking him **2.** To try to win favor by a flattering manner

faze (feʸz) v. **fazed, fazing** To disturb: *The loss of his job didn't seem to faze him at all.*

fear (frər) n. **1.** The feeling caused by the nearness of danger or the possibility of sthg. bad happening: *I have a terrible fear of earthquakes.* **2.** Deep reverence: *The fear of the Lord is the beginning of wisdom...* (Psalm 111:10). *The fear of the Lord is to hate evil...* (Proverbs 8:13).

fear v. *fml.* **1.** To be afraid of: *Speaking to his followers, Jesus said, "Do not be afraid of [Don't fear] those who kill the body and after that can do no more... Fear him who, after the killing of the body, has power to throw you into hell. Yes, I tell you, fear him"* (Luke 12:4-5). *Jesus also told his followers (those who trust in him for eternal life): "Fear not,... it is your Father's good pleasure to give you the kingdom [of heaven]"* (Luke 12:32 RSV). **2.** To have a reverent awe of: *Let all the earth fear the Lord; let all the people of the world revere him* (Psalm 33:8).

fear-ful (frər–fəl) adj. **1.** *fml.* Having or showing fear: *After calming the violent storm at sea, Jesus said to his disciples, "Why are you fearful, O you of little faith?"* (Matthew 8:26 NKJV). —opposite FEARLESS **2.** Causing fear: *a fearful monster*

fear-some (frər–səm) adj. **1.** Causing fear **2.** Afraid; timid

fea-si-ble (fiʸz–ə–bəl) adj. **1.** Capable of being done **2.** Suitable **3.** Reasonable

feast (fiʸst) n. **1.** A splendid, elaborate, delicious meal **2.** A religious festival; a day kept in memory of a religious event: *Easter and Christmas are two important feasts for Christians.* **3.** *fig.* *...the cheerful heart has a continual feast* (Proverbs 15:15).

feast v. **1.** To eat and drink well; to partake of a feast: *They feasted on all their favorite foods.* **2.** *fig.* Gratify: *Just feast your eyes on those beautiful mountains.*

feat (fiʸt) n. An act notable for courage, skill, endurance, or ingenuity

feath-er (feᵭ–ər) n. **1.** One of the many light growths which cover a bird's body **2.** a

feather in one's cap Sthg. one has done for which he deserves honor: *Winning a medal in the Senior Olympics was quite a feather in her cap.*

feather v. 1. To cover or adorn with feathers 2. **to feather one's nest** To gain wealth for oneself, esp. by abusing a position of trust

fea-ture (fiˠ–tʃər) n. 1. A part, quality, or characteristic: *A good plot is an important feature in a story.* 2. One of the noticeable parts of the face: *The different features of one's face make up his appearance.* 3. A long newspaper article on a special topic: *a weekly feature on entertainment* 4. A full-length movie

feature v. **-tured, -turing** To give a prominent part to: *"Gone With The Wind" featured Clark Gable.*

Feb. Short for **February**

Feb-ru-ar-y (feb–ruˠ–ɛər–iˠ) also **Feb.** n. *written abbr.* The second month of the year

fe-ces (fiˠ–siˠz) n. Bodily waste discharged from the intestine

fe-cund (fiˠ–kənd/ fɛ–) adj. Fertile —**fe-cun-di-ty** (fɪ–kʌn–dɪ–tiˠ) n.

fed (fɛd) v. Past tense and part. of **feed**

fed up (fɛd ʌp) adj. *infml.* Unhappy, tired, bored, etc.: *I'm fed up with this job. I'm quitting!*

fed n. *infml.* A federal official

fed-er-al (fɛd–ər–əl) adj. 1. Of a system of government in which several states join for certain purposes such as foreign policy, but keep control over many of their affairs separately 2. In the US, concerning the central government of the federation rather than the individual states: *a federal law*

fed-er-al-ize (fɛd–ər–ə–laɪz/ fɛd–rə–laɪz) v. **-ized, -izing** 1. To unite in a federal organization 2. To bring under the control of the federal government

fed-er-ate (fɛd–ə–reˠt) v. **-ated, -ating** To unite in a federation

fed-er-a-tion (fɛd–ə–reˠ–ʃən) n. 1. A group of states joined into one government for deciding foreign affairs, defense, etc., but having each state in control of its own internal affairs 2. A similarly organized group of societies, organizations, etc.

fee (fiˠ) n. 1. A fixed charge 2. Money paid to a doctor, lawyer, etc. for professional services

fee-ble (fiˠ–bəl) adj. **-bler, -blest** Weak; having little strength: *a feeble old woman*

fee-ble-mind-ed (fiˠ–bəl–maɪn–dəd) adj. Mentally deficient —**feeblemindedness** n.

feed (fiˠd) v. **fed** (fɛd), **feeding** 1. To give food to a person or animal: *It's important to feed the baby nourishing food./ The Bible says, "If your enemy is hungry, feed him..."* (Romans 12:20). 2. To eat: *The sheep were feeding on the hillside.* 3. To move sthg. into a machine or opening to be processed: *Let's feed this information into the computer and see what answer it gives us.*

feed n. Food for animals: *feed for the hens*

feel (fiˠl) v. **felt** (fɛlt), **feeling** 1. To touch; to learn about sthg. by touching it or holding it in the hands: *The young child put her hands to her grandfather's face and felt his beard.* 2. To try to find sthg. by reaching with the fingers: *He felt for the door handle, opened it, and stepped into the light of day.* 3. To be aware of the touch or movement of: *I felt the soft, cool breeze against my skin.* 4. To be in the specified state because of a condition or event: *The family felt a great sense of loss when their baby died.* 5. To experience an emotion: *She felt happy./ I felt like a fool when I arrived two hours late./How does it feel to be famous?* 6. To have as an opinion: *She felt that moving to Chicago was a mistake.* 7. **feel like** To have a wish for; want: *Do you feel like walking?* 8. **feel for sbdy.** To be sorry for someone because of their suffering

feel n. 1. Act of feeling 2. **the feel** Sense of touch: *rough, wet, etc. to the feel* 3. **the feel** Sensation that sthg. gives when touching or being touched: *the feel of silk* 4. **get the feel of sthg.** Become familiar with doing sthg. 5. **have a feel for sthg.** Have an easy understanding of sthg. or an appreciation for it

feel-er (fiˠl–ər) n. 1. A long, slender organ in certain animals and insects, used for testing things by touch 2. A proposal put forth to test people's reactions

feel-ing (fiˠ–lɪŋ) n. 1. An awareness of sthg. felt: *a feeling of shame/ guilt/ hunger/ thirst/ joy, etc.* 2. A notion or belief, not based on

reason: *I have a feeling it might rain today even though there isn't a cloud in the sky.* **3.** The power to feel sensation: *She lost all feeling in her right hand.* **4.** An often indefinite state of mind: *a feeling of loneliness* **5.** Strong emotion, esp. anger, etc.: *When a large number of people lose their jobs, there's likely to be a lot of bad feeling against the management.* **6.** Emotion; sympathy and understanding: *to play the violin with great feeling*

feel-ings (fiʸ–lɪŋz) n. Emotions rather than intellect; sensations of love, hate, anger, happiness, greed, sympathy, etc.: *Some people get their feelings hurt rather easily./ Did John tell you about his feelings on the subject?*

feet (fiʸt) n. *pl.* of **foot**: *Your word [O Lord] is a lamp to my feet and a light for my path* (Psalm 119:105).

feign (feʸn) v. To pretend to feel or be: *He feigned illness.*

feint (feʸnt) n. A pretense; a move to put an enemy off his guard

feist-y (faɪst–iʸ) adj. **-ier, -iest** Full of nervous energy; ill-tempered

fe-lic-i-tate (fə–lɪs–ə–teʸt) v. **-tated, -tating** To congratulate —**fe-lic-i-ta-tion** (fə–lɪs–ə–teʸ–ʃən) n.

fe-line (fiʸ–laɪn) adj. Of or related to the cat family

fell (fɛl) v. Past tense of **fall**

fel-low (fɛl–oʷ) n. *infml.* A man: *All the fellows at my office are going to the game tomorrow.*

fel-low-ship (fɛl–oʷ–ʃɪp) n. **1.** A group or society sharing the same interest or aim: *The youth fellowship at church is having a special meeting.* **2.** Friendly relationship through sharing or doing sthg. together; companionship: *God, who has called you into fellowship with his Son Jesus Christ is faithful* (1 Corinthians 1:9). *If we walk in the light [spiritual light] as he [God] is in the light, we have fellowship with one another, and the blood of Jesus Christ his son purifies us from all sin* (1 John 1:7).

fe-lon (fɛ–lən) n. One who has committed a serious crime

fel-o-ny (fɛl–ə–niʸ) n. **-nies** A very serious crime, such as murder, kidnapping, burglary, armed robbery, etc., punishable by a very heavy sentence

felt (fɛlt) Past tense and part. of **feel**

felt n. Thick, firm cloth made of wool and fur, often mixed with other fibers: *felt slippers/felt hat*

fe-male (fiʸ–meʸl) adj., n. **1.** Of the sex that gives birth to young; a woman or a girl **2.** Of plants, producing fruit Compare **male** and **masculine, female** and **feminine. Female** and **male** are used when speaking about a creature's sex: *A female rabbit is called a doe.* **Feminine** and **masculine** are used to speak of typical qualities of the two human sexes: *a feminine voice*

fem-i-nine (fɛm–ə–nɪn) adj. **1.** Having the qualities typical of or suitable for a woman: *She wears very feminine dresses.* **2.** *Tech.* In grammar, a certain class of words: *"Lioness" is the feminine form of "lion."* —compare MASCULINE, NEUTER

fem-i-nism (fɛm–ə–nɪz–əm) n. Belief that women should be given every social freedom, privilege and opportunity enjoyed by men —**feminist** n.

fe-mur (fiʸ–mər) n. *pl.* **femurs** or **femora** (fɛm–ər–ə) Thighbone

fence (fɛns) n. **1.** A wooden or wire wall used to keep people or animals inside or out of a place **2. sit on the fence** *usu. derog.* To fail to decide between two sides in an argument

fen-cing (fɛn–sɪŋ) n. **1.** Material used in making fences **2.** Fences collectively **3.** A sport in which a sword is used for defence and to attack

fend (fɛnd) v. **1.** To resist **2. fend off** To act to protect oneself or avoid sthg. **3. fend for oneself** To get along by oneself

fend-er (fɛn–dər) n. The guard over the wheel of a car or bicycle

fer-ment (fər–mɛnt) v. **1.** To undergo fermentation: *fermented fruit juice* **2. (a)** To be in a state of political unrest **(b)** To cause this state: *The government's new policies only fermented further trouble.*

fer-ment (fɜr–mɛnt) n. The condition of political unrest: *a country in a state of ferment*

fer-men-ta-tion (fɜr–mən–teʸ–ʃən) n. The process of chemical change caused by the action of certain living substances such as

yeast: *The fermentation of milk is a step in the production of cheese.*

fern (fɜrn) n. A plant with large feathery fronds but no flowers or seeds

fe-ro-cious (fə-roʷ-ʃəs) adj. **1.** Fierce; savage **2.** Intense: *ferocious heat* —**ferociously** adv.

fer-ret (fɛər-ət) v. To search out by careful investigation

fer-ret n. **1.** A small weasel-like animal, related to the European polecat, often used for hunting rodents **2.** A black-footed weasel of the Western US

fer-rous (fɛər-əs) adj. Of, relating to, or containing iron

fer-ry (fɛər-iʸ) n. **-ries** A boat that carries people and/ or vehicles or other things across water: *We will take the ferry across the channel to the island.*

ferry v. To transport by boat

fer-tile (fɜr-təl) adj. **1.** Producing plenty; productive: *fertile soil* **2.** *fig.* Inventive: *a fertile imagination* **3.** Capable of reproducing: *fertile eggs* —opposite INFERTILE —compare STERILE —**fertility** n.

fer-til-ize also **-ise** *BrE.* (fɜr-təl-aɪz) v. **-ized, -izing 1.** To cause a plant, an egg, or a female animal to reproduce its young **2.** To spread fertilizer on land —**fer-til-i-za-tion** (fɜr-təl-ə-zeʸ-ʃən) n.

fer-til-iz-er (fɜr-təl-aɪ-zər) n. Chemical or natural substance that is added to land to make crops grow better —compare MANURE

fer-vent (fɜr-vənt) adj. **1.** Passionate; feeling or showing strong and warm feelings: *a fervent admirer* **2.** Extremely hot: *But the day of the Lord [return of Jesus] will come as a thief [unexpectedly]. The heavens will disappear with a roar; the elements will be destroyed by fire [with fervent heat, KJV], and the earth and everything in it will be laid bare... But we are looking forward to a new heaven and a new earth, the home of righteousness (2 Peter 3:10,13).* —**fervently** adv.

fer-vor (fɜr-vər) n. **1.** Intense heat **2.** A great warmth of feeling: *Never be lacking in zeal, but keep your spiritual fervor, serving the Lord* (Romans 12:11).

fes-tal (fɛs-təl) adj. Typical of a celebration; festive

fes-ter (fɛs-tər) v. To become infected

fes-ti-val (fɛs-tə-vəl) n. **1.** A day of feasting and/ or special observance, especially to mark a religious occasion **2.** A time of public gaiety and celebration **3.** A series of related cultural events: *a film festival* **4.** Revelry

fes-tive (fɛs-tɪv) adj. **1.** Of or suitable for a feast or festival **2.** Joyous or merry

fes-tiv-i-ty (fɛs-trɪv-ə-tiʸ) n. **-ties 1.** A festival **2.** Gladness and rejoicing **3.** *Pl.* Festive merrymaking

fes-toon (fɛs-tuʷn) n. Decorative garland draped between two points

festoon v. To decorate with or form into a festoon

fe-tal (fiʸ-təl) adj. Of or characteristic of a fetus

fetch (fɛtʃ) v. **1.** To go for sthg. and bring it back **2.** To cause to come

fet-id (fɛt-ɪd/ fiʸt-) adj. Having a foul odor

fet-ish (fɛt-ɪʃ) n. **1.** An object worshiped by primitive peoples who believe it to have magical powers or to be inhabited by a spirit **2.** Anything to which foolishly excessive respect or devotion is given

fet-ter (fɛt-ər) n. **1.** A chain put about the ankles of a person or animal to limit movement **2.** *Pl.* Anything checking freedom of expression or movement

fe-tus (fiʸt-əs) n. A young human, animal, or bird that has developed within the womb or the egg, but has not yet been born or hatched

feud (fyuʷd) n. A prolonged quarrel, usu. between two families, often leading to violence

feu-dal (fyuʷd-əl) adj. Of or like the feudal system

feu-dal system (fyuʷd-əl sɪs-təm) n. Of the system in which, in earlier times, certain services were given to the overlord by the tenants, in return for the use of his lands —**feudalism** n. —**feudalistic** adj.

fe-ver (fiʸ-vər) n. **1.** A higher than normal body temperature **2.** An illness in which the sufferer suddenly develops a much higher than normal body temperature

fe-ver-ish (fiʸ-vər-ɪʃ) adj. As if caused by fe-

ver: *The baby feels a little feverish.* —**feverishly** adv. *searching feverishly (=very quickly and excitedly) to find the missing man ey*

few (fyu^w) determ., pron., n. **1.** Not many; not enough: *Few people were willing to sacrifice their own comfort to help the homeless.* **2.** Not many, but at least some: *A few people offered to help.* **3. few and far between** Not frequent: *Vacations are few and far between.* **4. quite a few** A reasonable number: *There are quite a few stars out tonight.*

few-er (fyu^w–ər) adj. Comparative of **few** NOTE: **Fewer** is used with plural nouns and pronouns, while **less** is used with singular nouns and pronouns and is usu. applied in bulk: *fewer flowers, apples, bananas, etc., but less gasoline, sugar, flour, coffee, etc.*

fez (fɛz) n. **fezzes** A brimless felt cap with a tassel, worn chiefly by Muslim men in some countries

fi-an-cé (fiy–an–se^y/ fiy–an–se^y) n. A man to whom a woman is engaged: *Bob is Ann's fiancé.*

fi-an-cée (fiy–an–se^y/ fiy–an–se^y) fem. n. A woman to whom a man is engaged: *Ann is Bob's fiancée.*

fi-as-co (fiy–æs–ko^w) n. **-cos** or **-coes** A disastrous failure

fib (fɪb) v. **-bb-** To tell a lie —**fib** n. A lie

fi-ber (faɪ–bər) n. **1.** One of the thin threads that form many animal and plant growths: *coconut fiber/ muscle fiber* **2.** Material or substance formed from a mass of threads, such as cloth, rope, etc.: *This cloth is made of wool fiber.* **3.** A person's character: *She's a woman of great moral fiber.*

fi-brous (faɪ–brəs) adj. Like or made of fibers

fi-bro-sis (faɪ–bro^w–sɪs) n. The development in an organ of excess fibrous tissue

fick-le (fɪk–əl) adj. Changeable

fic-tion (fɪk–ʃən) n. **1.** A type of literature describing things that did not really happen **2.** A story that is false: *The TV story of the robbery was pure fiction.* —**fictional** adj. —compare FACT

fic-ti-tious (fɪk–tɪ–ʃəs) adj. Not true; imaginary; not real: *The story of Cinderella is fictitious./ The criminal gave a fictitious name.*

fid-dle (fɪd–əl) n. *infml.* **1.** A violin or any similar musical instrument **2. As fit as a fiddle** Completely healthy

fiddle v. **-dled, -dling** *infml.* **1.** To play the fiddle **2.** To spend time aimlessly and restlessly, esp. to play with sth. in the hands: *Quit fiddling around and get to work./ Stop fiddling with that knife. You might cut yourself!* —**fid-dler** (fɪd–lər) n.

fi-del-i-ty (fɪ–dɛl–ə–tiy/ faɪ–) n. **1.** *fml.* The quality or state of being faithful; loyalty: *fidelity to one's wife or husband* **2.** Accuracy of sth. copied or recorded, esp. in closeness of sound, facts, color, etc. to the original: *a high fidelity recording*

fidg-et (fɪdʒ–ət) v. To move about nervously —**fidgety** adj.

field (fiyld) n. **1.** A broad, level expanse of open land **2.** Land devoted to a particular crop: *a corn field* **3.** Land containing a specified natural resource: *an oil field* **4.** A background area, as on a flag: *white stars on a field of blue* **5.** An area in which a sports event takes place: *a football field* **6.** A battlefield **7.** A branch of knowledge or activity: *the field of medicine* **8.** A region or space in which the specified force is felt: *the moon's gravitational field*

field v. To catch or stop a ball in the game of baseball: *The first baseman fielded the ball.*

fiend (fiynd) n. **1.** Devil; evil spirit **2.** An extremely evil or cruel person **3.** A person who is very interested in the specified thing: *a dope fiend/ a fresh-air fiend* —**fiendish** adj.

fierce (fɪərs) adj. **1.** Wild and savage: *a fierce beast* **2.** Extremely severe or violent: *a fierce wind/The fighting was fierce.* **3.** Intense or ardent: *a fierce competitor* —**fiercely** adv. —**fierceness** n.

fi-er-y (faɪ–ər–iy) adj. **-ier, -iest 1.** Consisting of or containing fire **2.** Intensely hot **3.** Intensely impetuous or passionate

fi-es-ta (fiy–es–tə) n. **1.** A religious festival in Spanish-speaking countries **2.** A festival or celebration

fife (faɪf) n. A small shrill flute-like musical instrument

fif-teen (fɪf–tiy^n) determ., n., pron. The num-

ber 15 —**fifteenth** determ., n., pron., adv.
15th

fifth (fɪfθ) determ., n., pron., adv. 5th

fif-ty (fɪf–tiʸ) determ., n., pron. **-ties** The number 50

fif-ti-eth (fɪf–tiʸ–əθ) determ., n., pron., adv. 50th

fifty–fifty adj., adv. Shared equally: *We could go fifty-fifty on the rent if you'd like to share an apartment with me.* (=each would pay half)

fig (fɪg) n. **1.** A soft, pear-shaped fruit with many small seeds, often eaten dried **2.** The tree that bears this fruit

fig. *written abbr.* said as **figure** or **figurative**

fight (faɪt) v. **fought** (fɔt), **fighting 1.** To participate in battle: *Britain fought against Germany in World Wars I and II.* **2.** To prevent or oppose: *to fight crime/ a fire* **3.** To quarrel: *The two men had a fight ten years ago and haven't spoken to each other since.* **4.** To box or wrestle **5.** To make one's way, as if by combat: *We fought our way through the crowded streets.* —**fighter** n.

fight n. **1.** A battle; a combat: *The riot police were called to stop a fight.* **2.** A boxing match: *The fight only lasted two rounds.* **3.** A spiritual battle against the forces of evil: *Saint Paul says, "I have fought the good fight, I have finished the race, I have kept the faith. Now there is in store for me the crown of righteousness which the Lord, the righteous Judge will award to me on that day and not only to me, but also to all who have longed for his appearing"* (2 Timothy 4:7-8).

fig-ment (fɪg–mənt) n. Sthg. that one has imagined and that has no reality

fig-u-ra-tion (fɪg–yə–reʸ–ʃən) n. **1.** Form, shape or outline **2.** The act of shaping sthg.

fig-u-ra-tive (fɪg–yər–ə–tɪv) adj. Words used in some way to make a word picture: *In the expression, "screaming headlines," the word "screaming" is used in a figurative sense.* —**figuratively** adv. *Figuratively speaking, he's a tiger.*

fig-ure (fɪg–yər) n. **1.** The outline or form of sthg. as shown in art or as seen in reality: *A triangle is a figure with three sides and three angles.* **2.** A bodily shape or form considered from the point of view of attractiveness: *a*

slender figure **3.** An important person: *The mayor is an important figure in the community.* **4.** A number symbol, such as 0-9: *He has a salary in six figures.* **5.** A numbered illustration used in a book to explain sthg.: *Look at Figure 10 to see the population growth rate.* **6. figure of speech** A word or phrase having a figurative meaning: *"To fight like a tiger" is a figure of speech meaning to defend oneself or to attack fiercely.* —see FIGURATIVE

figure v. **-ured, -uring 1.** To consider; to regard: *We figured you must have been sick because you weren't at work today.* **2. That figures!** That makes sense **3. figure** sbdy./ sthg. **out** To try to understand: *I can't figure out why this machine doesn't work.*

fig-ure-head (fɪg–yər –hɛd) n. A person who is head or chief in name only

fig-u-rine (fɪg–yə–riʸn) n. A small carved or molded figure

fil-a-ment (fɪl–ə–mənt) n. A slender, thread-like object such as the thin wire in an electric light bulb

fil-bert (fɪl–bərt) n. An oblong edible nut

filch (fɪltʃ) v. To steal, esp. trifling things

file (faɪl) n. **1.** A metal tool with a rough edge, used for smoothing, shaping, or cutting hard surfaces **2.** A set of drawers, boxes, cases, etc. for storing papers in an office **3.** An organized collection of papers on a related subject: *Please bring me the file on Mrs. Jones.* **4.** A line of people one behind the other

file v. **filed, filing 1.** To use a file on sthg.: *to file until it is smooth* **2.** To put in the proper place in a file: *All this correspondence needs filing.* **3.** To register or record officially: *to file a report* **4.** To walk in a single row: *The circus elephants filed into the ring for their act.*

fil-i-al (fɪl–iʸ–əl/ –yəl) adj. Pertaining to or befitting a son or daughter

fil-i-bus-ter (fɪl–ə–bʌs–tər) n. The use of delaying tactics, esp. making long speeches, in a legislative assembly

fil-i-gree (fɪl–ə–griʸ) n. **1.** Delicate, lace-like ornamental work using gold, silver, or copper wire **2.** A pattern or design resembling such openwork

fill (fɪl) v. **1.** To make or become full: *He filled*

the tank with gasoline./ *The earth will be filled with the knowledge of the glory of the Lord as the waters cover the sea* (Habakkuk 2:14). *The earth is filled with your love, O Lord; teach me your decrees* (Psalm 119:64). *fig. The scent of roses filled the room.* **2.** To enter a position: *I'm sorry; the position of receptionist has been filled.* **3.** To fulfil; meet the requirements of: *This apartment fills my needs quite well.*

fill in 1. (a) fill sthg. in To supply whatever is needed to complete sthg.: *Fill in your name on the dotted line.* **(b) fill sthg. out** To complete by supplying whatever is needed: *to fill out an application form* **2. fill sbdy. in** To give the latest information: *Susan has already filled me in on what happened yesterday.* **3.** To substitute for someone: *The English teacher is absent today. Can you fill in for her?*

fil-ler (fĭl-ər) *n.* **1.** One that fills **2.** Sthg. added to another substance, as to increase bulk or weight **3.** A material used for filling cracks and holes in wood before painting

fil-let or **fil-et** (fĭ-lĕ^y) *n.* A piece of boneless meat or fish, esp. the tenderloin of beef

fill-ing (fĭl-m̥) *n.* **1.** Sthg. a dentist puts into a hole in a tooth **2.** A food mixture used to fill a pastry, sandwich, etc.

film (fĭlm) *n.* **1.** A roll or sheet of thin, flexible material on which one takes photographs or makes movies **2.** A thin skin of any material: *a sheet of plastic film* **3.** A thin covering or coating: *a film of ice over the pond* **4.** A motion picture: *Have you seen the new film?*

film *v.* To make a movie: *They were filming all day on Stage B.*

film-y (fĭlm-i^y) *adj.* **-ier, -iest 1.** Like a film **2.** Covered by or as if by a film; hazy

fil-ter (fĭl-tər) *n.* **1.** A device through which substances can be passed so as to separate out solids or impurities: *a water filter/ a coffee filter* **2.** A colored glass that changes light as it enters a camera

filter *v.* To pass through a filter: *All the impurities are filtered out as the water passes through the device./ fig. It didn't take long for news of his resignation to filter through to everyone in the company.*

filth (fĭlθ) *n.* **1.** Disgusting, very foul, dirt: *What filth! Why don't you clean this place up?*

2. Sthg. offensive or obscene: *Get rid of all moral filth and the evil that is so prevalent and humbly accept the word [of God]... which can save you* (James 1:21). **—filthiness** *n.* **— filthy** *adj.* **-ier, -iest**

fin (fĭn) *n.* **1.** A wing-like organ on the body of a fish, used for propulsion, steering, or balance **2.** Anything that looks or is used like a fin

fi-na-gle (fə-ney̆-gəl) *v.* **-gled, -gling 1.** To get sthg. by trickery or deceit **2.** To cheat or trick sbdy. **—finagler** *n.*

fi-nal (faɪ-nəl) *adj.* **1.** Last; coming at the end: *our final day at work* **2.** Decisive; sthg. that cannot or will not be changed: *The judge's decision is final.*

final *n.* **1.** The last and most important game in a series of games or a tournament: *the tennis finals* **2.** The last examination of an academic course: *I have to study tonight. We have finals this week.*(=final examinations)

fi-nal-e (fɪ-næl-i^y) *n.* The concluding part of a musical composition

fi-nal-ist (faɪ-nə-lɪst) *n.* A person who will take part in the finals, as in an athletic competition

fi-nal-ize (fam-əl-aɪz) *v.* **-ized, -izing** To put into final form

fi-nal-ly (faɪ-nəl-i^y) *adv.* At last: *After several long delays due to some very bad weather, his bus finally arrived at the station three hours late.*

fi-nance (faɪ-næns) *n.* **1.** The management of money **2.** Money, esp. provided by a bank or similar organization, to support an undertaking **3. finances** The amount of money available to a person, organization or government

finance *v.* **-nanced, -nancing** To provide money for a project, etc.: *Who is going to finance your new undertaking?*

fi-nan-cial (fɪ-næn-ʃəl) *adj.* Concerning money and finance: *The financial records have to be finished tonight.* **—fi-nancially** *adv.*

fin-an-cier (fɪn-æn-sɪər) *n.* A person who is engaged in financing businesses on a large scale

find (faɪnd) *v.* **found** (faʊnd), **finding 1.** To discover, esp. by searching, inquiry, or effort:

Did you find your keys yet?/ She found the answer on page 36. **2.** To learn or discover sthg. unexpectedly by chance, experience, etc.: *When we got to his house, we found he had already left./ This type of tree is found (=exists) only in West Africa.* **3.** *fml.* Of things, to arrive at naturally; reach: *Water always finds its level.* **4.** To obtain by effort: *How do you find time to read all those books?* **5.** To decide that sbdy. or sthg. has a particular quality: *We are finding our new home quite cozy.* **6.** To gain or regain the use of: *He found his voice again.* —opposite LOSE

find-ing (faɪnd–ɪŋ) n. **1.** Sthg. found **2.** The result of judicial proceeding or inquiry

fine (faɪn) n. An amount of money paid as a punishment for breaking a law, rule, etc.: *He had to pay a $50 fine.*

fine v. **fined, fining** To make someone pay a fine: *He was fined $50 for speeding.*

fine adj. **1.** Of high quality: *She gave a fine performance.* **2.** Very slender; thin: *fine hair/ a fine point* —see THIN **3.** Made of very small grains or pieces: *a fine powder* —opposite COARSE **4.** Of weather, bright and clear; not wet: *After raining all morning, the weather is fine now.* **5.** Healthy: *"How are you?" "Fine, thank you."* **6.** Delicate and carefully made: *fine silk* **7.** Terrible: *This is a fine mess you've gotten me into.*

fine also **finely** adv. **1.** Very thin: *finely sliced* **2.** Very well: *My car is working fine now.* **3.** Closely and delicately: *These instruments are very finely set.*

fine arts (faɪn ɑrts) n. Those arts such as painting, music, etc. that are more concerned with producing beautiful things than with useful things

fin-er-y (faɪn–ər–iʸ) n. Fine clothes or decorations

fi-nesse (fɪ–nɛs) n. Smoothness and tact in handling a delicate situation

fin-ger (fɪŋ–gər) n. **1.** One of the five digits (movable part with joints), at the end of each human hand **2.** The part of a glove that fits over a finger **3.** Sthg. that looks like a finger

finger v. **-ed, -ing** To handle or touch with the fingers

fin-ger-nail (fɪŋ–gər–neʸl) n. The hard transparent material at the end of each finger

fin-ger-print (fɪŋ–gər–prɪnt) n. Ink impression showing the lines on the inner surface of the tip of one's finger, used for identification

fin-ger-tip (fɪŋ–gər–tɪp) n. **1.** Extreme end of one's finger **2. have sthg. at one's fingertips** To be very familiar with sthg.

fin-ick-y (fɪn–ɪk–iʸ) adj. Excessively particular: *He's very finicky about what he eats.*

fin-ish (fɪn–ɪʃ) v. To reach the end or bring sthg. to an end; complete: *When do you expect to finish painting the house?*

finish n. **1.** The end or conclusion of sthg., esp. a race: *That was a close finish! (=the scores for the two teams were almost the same)* **2.** Having been properly finished with paint or polish: *This table has a nice finish on it.*

fin-ished (fɪn–ɪʃt) adj. Ended; completed; with nothing remaining to be done: *Just before Jesus died on the cross, he said: "It is finished," meaning that the work of redemption was finished; nothing else was necessary.*

fi-nite (faɪ–naɪt) adj. Limited: *Man's wisdom is finite.* —opposite INFINITE

fiord or **fjord** (fyɔrd) n. A long, narrow arm of the sea, bordered by steep cliffs

fir (fɜr) n. **1.** An evergreen tree that keeps its thin, sharp leaves (needles) in winter, and grows esp. in cold countries **2.** The wood of this tree

fire (faɪ–ər) n. **1.** Sthg. burning with flames: *He started a fire in the fireplace./ An arsonist set fire to the warehouse./ Some sparks from a brush fire landed on the roof, and the school caught fire.* **2.** Shooting by guns: *The soldiers were under fire (=being shot at) for five hours.* **3.** *fig.* Emotion: *His speech was full of fire.*

fire v. **fired, firing 1.** To shoot bullets: *The bank guard fired at the hold-up men three times.* **2.** To harden clay pots, dishes, etc. by baking in a kiln (oven) **3.** To cause someone to have strong feelings: *The team was fired with enthusiasm after the coach's pep talk.* **4.** *infml.* also **sack** *BrE.* To dismiss an employee from a job: *The store manager shouted, "Pick up your pay at the end of the week. You're fired!"*

fire-arm (faɪ–ər–ɑrm) n. *usu. pl.* A gun

fire-crack-er (faɪ–ər–kræk–ər) *AmE.* **-craker** *BrE.* n. A paper tube containing an explosive charge, used for making loud noises on special occasions

fire fight-er (faɪ–ər faɪt–ər) n. One whose job it is to put out fires

fire-fly (faɪ–ər–flaɪ) **-flies** n. A soft-bodied nocturnal beetle with luminous abdominal organs that produce flashing light

fire-man (faɪ–ər–mən) also **firefighter** n. **-men** A person whose job is to put out fires

fire-place (faɪ–ər–pleᵞs) n. A structure built to hold a fire, built of stone or brick, and when indoors, has a chimney to channel the smoke away

fire-trap (faɪ–ər–træp) n. A building which, because of its structure or age, is extremely dangerous in case of fire

fire-works (faɪ–ər–wɜrks) n. Combustible and explosive materials used for displaying a striking display of light and loud noises

firm (fɜrm) adj. **1.** Steady and strong; solid; hard: *I prefer a firm mattress to a soft one.* **2.** Unchanging; not yielding: *a firm belief in God* —**firmly** adv.

firm n. A business company —**firmness** n. *the firmness of the mattress/ the firmness of his action or decision*

fir-ma-ment (fɜr–mə–mənt) n. The sky

first (fɜrst) n., pron. **1.** The one before all the others: *He was one of the first to finish the exam.* **2. at first** In the beginning: *At first English was hard for me, but I'm doing much better now.*

first determ., adv. **1.** Before anyone or anything else: *I'd like to go to Hong Kong first, and then Manila.* **2.** For the first time: *This is my first trip to Paris.* **3.** In the beginning: *When the university first started, it was not very large.* **4. first and foremost** More than anything else: *He builds houses, but first and foremost he's a boat builder.*

first aid (fɜrst eᵞd) n. Emergency care or treatment given by an ordinary person to someone injured in an accident or suddenly taken ill: *I took a class in first aid so I could help accident victims.*

first class (fɜrst–klæs) n. **1.** The highest quality in a classification **2.** A class of mail that in-

cludes letters or other sealed matter: *How do you want to send this letter? First class costs a little more.* —**first-class** adj.

firth (fɜrθ) n. A long, narrow indentation of the sea coast

fis-cal (fɪs–kəl) adj. The financial year of a business, organization, government, etc., which is established without regard for the calendar year: *Our fiscal year is from July 1 to June 30.*

fish (fɪʃ) n. **fish** or **fishes** **1.** A cold-blooded animal which lives in water and uses its fins and tail to swim **2.** The flesh of this animal when used as food: *We had fish for dinner.*

fish v. **1.** To try to catch fish with hooks, nets, etc.: *I'm going trout fishing in the mountains.* **2.** *fig.* To seek sthg. in a roundabout way: *He's fishing for information.* —**fishing** n. *Fishing is a popular sport.*

fish-er-man (fɪʃ–ər–mən) n. A man who catches fish for a living or as a sport

fish-y (fɪʃ–iᵞ) adj. **-ier, -iest** **1.** Of or like a fish, esp. in taste or smell **2.** Seeming to be false: *His excuse sounded pretty fishy to me.*

fis-sion (fɪʃ–ən) n. **1.** The act of splitting into parts **2.** Cell division as a form of reproduction **3.** The splitting of an atom resulting in the release of large amounts of energy

fis-sure (fɪʃ–ər) n. **1.** A long deep crack in a rock or in the earth **2.** A groove between lobes or parts of an organ, as in the brain

fist (fɪst) n. The hand with the fingers closed tightly into the palm: *He pounded on the desk with his fist.*

fit (fɪt) v. **fitted** or **fit, fitting** **1.** To be the right size or shape: *This pencil doesn't fit in the box.* **2.** To make capable or qualified: *He worked hard to fit himself for this job.* **3.** To supply sthg. and fix it into place: *We'll have to have new handles fitted on the cupboard doors.* **4.** Succeed in finding time to see someone or to do sthg.: *I hope I can fit a visit to my mother into my schedule this week.*

fit n. **1.** The way in which sthg. fits: *a tight fit* **2.** A period of loss of control of one's self: *fig. Your father will have a fit (=be very angry) when he hears what you have done.* **3.** A sudden violent attack as of bodily disorder **4.** A

sudden outburst as of laughter: *She kept them in fits of laughter with her jokes.*

fit adj. **1.** Suitable for: *She certainly is fit for the job. She's had more than ten years experience./ Do as you think fit.* **2.** In good bodily condition: *He seems to be very fit. It looks as though he eats right and exercises regularly.*

fit-ness (fɪt–nəs) n. **1.** The state of being fit in body **2.** The quality of being suitable: *Her fitness for the position is evident.*

fit-ting (fɪt–ɪŋ) adj. *fml.* Suitable; appropriate: *It would be fitting to present him with a gift in gratitude for the way he has befriended all of us.*

fitting n. The action of trying on clothes that are being made for one, to see if they fit: *The bride will have a fitting for her gown on Friday.*

five (faɪv) determ., n., pron. The number 5

fix (fɪks) v. **1.** To repair or mend: *Mom, can you fix my shirt, please?* **2.** To fasten firmly to sthg.: *He fixed the stamp in the proper place.* **3.** To arrange: *If you want to meet him, I can fix it.* **4.** To cause the outcome of sthg. to be unfair: *The fight was fixed.* **5.** **fix on** To direct one's eyes, attention, etc. steadily at: *Let us fix our eyes on Jesus, the author and perfecter of our faith* (Hebrews 12:2). **6.** **fix the blame on (someone)** To assign the guilt to someone

fix n. **1.** A difficult or awkward position: *How did you get into such a terrible fix?* **2.** (used by drug-addicts) An injection (of the specified drug)

fixed (fɪkst) adj. Attached; not capable of being moved or changed: *We can't move this mirror. It's fixed to the wall.*

fix-ture (fɪks–tʃər) n. Sthg. fixed into a building and sold with it: *lighting fixtures*

fizz (fɪz) v. To make a hissing or sputtering sound

fizz n. **1.** A fizzing sound **2.** An effervescent drink, as soda water

fiz-zle (fɪz–əl) v. **-zled, -zling 1.** To fizz **2.** To fail after a good start; to come to nothing

fjord (fyɔrd) n. see fiord

flab (flæb) n. Soft body tissue; fat

flab-ber-gas-ted (flæb–ər–gæs–təd) adj. Very surprised; puzzled; overcome with bewilderment

flab-by (flæb–iʸ) adj. Loose and fat; not firm

flac-cid (flæs–əd/ flæk–səd) adj. Lacking firm-ness; weak

flag (flæg) n. A square or oblong piece of cloth, usu. with a pattern or picture on it, that can be fastened by one edge to a pole, often used as a symbol of a country, party. etc.

flag v. **flagged, flagging 1.** To mark with a flag **2.** To signal with a flag or as if with a flag **3.** *fig.* **flag sbdy./ sthg. down** To try to stop a vehicle by waving at the driver: *See if you can flag down a taxi.*

flag-el-late (flædʒ–ə–leʸt) v. **-lated, -lating** To punish by whipping —**flag-el-la-tion** (flædʒ–ə–leʸ–ʃən) n.

flag-on (flæg–ən) n. A large bottle, esp. with a handle, a spout, and a cover

fla-grant (fleʸ–grənt) adj. Especially bad and shocking; open and shameless: *flagrant violation of the rules or the law*

flair (fleər) n. A natural ability for doing sthg.: *She has a flair for writing.*

flak (flæk) n. **1.** Antiaircraft fire **2.** *infml.* Annoying opposition

flake (fleʸk) v. **flaked, flaking** To come off in flakes: *The paint is flaking (off).*

flake n. A light, thin chip: *snowflakes*

flam-boy-ant (flæm–bɔɪ–ənt) adj. **1.** Strikingly bold or brilliant **2.** Ornate; showy; intended to attract attention —**flamboyance** n. —**flamboyancy** n. —**flamboyantly** adv.

flame (fleʸm) n. **1.** A hot, bright light of sthg. burning: *A small flame burned in the lamp./ Our neighbor's house went up in flames before the firemen could arrive.* **2.** **old flame** A person with whom one was once in love: *She's an old flame of his.*

flam-ing (fleʸm–ɪŋ) adj. Bright: *She had flaming red hair.*

flam-ma-ble (flæm–ə–bəl) adj. Easily ignited; easily set aflame: *Gasoline (petrol) is highly flammable.* —opposite NONFLAMMABLE. NOTE: **Flammable** and **inflammable** are not opposites. They have the same meaning.

flan (flæn) n. A custard dessert

flange (flændʒ) n. A projecting rim or edge

flank (flæŋk) n. The side of an animal, person, building, or moving army: *a horse's flank*

flank v. To be placed beside: *a prisoner flanked by two policemen/ a fence flanked with roses*

flan·nel (flæn–əl) n. A type of soft, loosely woven, woolen cloth: *a flannel scarf*

flap (flæp) v. **-pp-** To move up and down or from side to side, usu. making a noise: *The curtains were flapping in the breeze.*

flap n. **1.** Anything broad or wide that hangs loosely, so as to cover an opening: *the flap of an envelope* **2.** The sound of flapping: *the flap of the awning in the wind*

flare (flɛər) v. **flared, flaring 1.** To burn brightly but uncertainly or for a short time **2.** To burst into intense emotion or activity: *Tempers flared./ Trouble may flare up during the night.*

flare n. **1.** A flaring flame: *the flare of the lantern as it was lighted* **2.** A blaze of light used as a signal **3.** The device that provides such a light: *When our ship began sinking, we sent out flares to attract attention.*

flash (flæʃ) n. **1.** A sudden, bright burst of light: *flashes of light from the fire/ the flash of diamonds in the candlelight* **2.** A brief news report, received by radio, telegraph, etc.: *A news flash from China says...* **3.** In photography, the method or device for taking photos in the dark **4. in a/ like a flash** Very quickly; immediately

flash v. **1.** To send out a brief light; shine for a moment: *The light flashed from the knife blade.* **2.** To cause to shine for a moment: *The policeman flashed a red light at the driver as a signal to stop.* **3.** To send a telegraph or radio message: *The news is flashed all over the country in just minutes.* **4.** To move very fast: *The train flashed past the station without stopping.*

flash-bulb (flæʃ–bəlb) n. An electric bulb that briefly gives off a bright light, used for taking photographs

flash-card (flæʃ–kɑrd) n. Any of a set of cards bearing words, pictures, numbers, etc. and shown briefly before a class for a quick response in a drill

flash-light (flæʃ–laɪt) n. **1.** *Esp. AmE.* A small, hand-held, battery-operated, electric light *BrE.* **torch 2.** A device for taking flash photographs

flash-y (flæʃ–iʸ) adj. **-ier, -iest** Showy; big and bright, but often of poor quality: *flashy jewelry* —**flashily** adv. *flashily dressed*

flask (flæsk) n. **1.** A glass bottle with a narrow neck, for holding liquids, esp. as used in a science laboratory **2.** A specially shaped bottle for carrying alcohol or other drinks in the pocket **3.** Also **thermos** A specially made bottle for keeping liquids either hot or cold

flat (flæt) adj. **-tt- 1.** Smooth and level; even: *The countryside was quite flat.* **2.** Having a broad, level surface, and not very thick or high: *a flat box* **3.** A tire without enough air in it **4.** Fixed: *a flat rate* **5.** Lacking taste; bland: *The food tasted flat.* **6.** Absolute: *a flat re-fusal*

flat adv. **1.** Completely: *flat broke* **2.** In music, lower than the correct pitch: *He keeps singing flat.* **3.** Exactly, implying an unexpectedly short time: *He ran 100 meters in 10 seconds flat.*

flat n. **1.** An apartment on one level **2.** A deflated tire: *We had a flat on the way home.* **3.** A stretch of low, level ground, esp. near water: *salt flats*

flat–foot-ed (flæt–fʊt–əd) adj. **1.** Having feet without normal raised arches **2. catch flat-footed** Take by surprise, esp. in an embarrassing situation

flat-ly (flæt–liʸ) adv. **1.** In a dull, level manner: *"It's no use trying," she said flatly.* **2.** Completely; firmly: *He flatly rejected the offer.*

flat-ten (flæt–ən) v. To make or become flat

flat-ter (flæt–ər) v. To praise someone too much or insincerely in order to gain favor for oneself: *Whoever flatters his neighbor is spreading a net for his feet* (Proverbs 29:5). *He who rebukes a man will in the end gain more favor than he who has a flattering tongue* (Proverbs 28:23).

flat-ter-y (flæt–ər–iʸ) n. **-ies** Excessive or insincere compliments

flaunt (flɔnt) v. To show off and attract attention to oneself

fla-vor v. *AmE.* **flavour** *BrE.* (fleʸ–vər) To give flavor to sthg. by adding spi-ces, herbs, etc.: *She flavored the cookies with coconut.* —**flavorless** adj.

fla-vor-ing (fleᵞ-vər-ɪŋ) n. also **flavor** *AmE*. n. Spices, herbs, etc. added to food to give or improve the taste: *I always put a little almond in my rice pudding for flavoring.*

flaw (flɔ) n. An imperfect part; defect; crack; fault: *a flaw in the glass/ a flaw in his character*

flaw-less (flɔ-ləs) adj. Without any flaws; perfect: *a flawless complexion/Every word of God is flawless* (Proverbs 30:5). *fig. a flawless performance* —**flawlessly** adv.

flax (flæks) n. A type of plant whose fibers are woven into linen cloth; grown also for its oily seeds

flay (fleᵞ) v. **1.** To strip off the skin or hide of **2.** To criticize severely

flea (fliᵞ) n. A small, jumping insect without wings that feeds on the blood of humans or animals

flea mar-ket (fliᵞ mɑr-kət) n. A usu. open-air market for selling used articles and antiques

fleck (flɛk) n. A small particle; a speck

flecked (flɛkt) adj. Marked with spots or specks

fledg-ling (flɛdʒ-lɪŋ) n. **1.** A young, inexperienced person **2.** A young bird that has just grown the feathers necessary to fly

flee (fliᵞ) v. **fled** (flɛd), **fleeing** *fml.* To escape by running or hurrying away: *They fled from the burning building./ Flee idolatry* (1 Corinthians 10:14). *Flee sexual immorality* (1 Corinthians 6:18). *Resist the devil and he will flee from you* (James 4:7).

fleece (fliᵞs) n. A sheep's coat of wool

fleet (fliᵞt) n. **1.** A number of ships, such as warships, under one command **2.** A group of trucks, buses, etc. under one control

fleet-ing (fliᵞt-ɪŋ) adj. Passing quickly

flesh (flɛʃ) n. **1.** The soft tissue of the body including fat and muscle, that covers the bones **2.** The body as distinguished from the mind or soul: *The spirit is willing but the flesh is weak* (Matthew 26:41 KJV). **3.** The soft, edible part of a fruit or vegetable **4.** **one's own flesh and blood** One's relatives; family: *They're my own flesh and blood and I love them dearly.* **5.** **in the flesh** In real life: *I've only seen his photographs. I'd love to meet him in the flesh.*

flesh-ly (flɛʃ-liᵞ) adj. **1.** Of the flesh **2.** Lascivious **3.** Worldly, not spiritual NOTE: Do not confuse **fleshly** with **fleshy**

flesh-y (flɛʃ-iᵞ) adj. **1.** Of or like flesh **2.** Having much flesh; plump NOTE: Do not confuse **fleshy** with **fleshly**

flew (fluʷ) v. Past tense of **fly**

flex (flɛks) v. **1.** To bend, esp. repeatedly **2.** To contract a muscle: *The weight lifter flexed his muscles.*

flex-i-ble (flɛk-sə-bəl) adj. **1.** Capable of being bent easily **2.** Capable of change in order to meet new needs, conditions, etc.: *You can visit my office almost anytime. My schedule is quite flexible.* —opposite INFLEXIBLE —compare RIGID —**flex-i-bil-i-ty** (flɛks-ə-bɪl-ə-tiᵞ) n.

flick (flɪk) n. A quick, sharp movement: *a flick of the wrist/ a flick of the switch* —**flick** v.

flick-er (flɪk-ər) v. To burn or move unsteadily: *The candle flickered in the wind.*

flicker n. **1.** A sudden, brief movement: *the flicker of an eyelid* **2.** A momentary stirring: *a flicker of interest*

fli-er (flar-ər) n. **1.** One who flies, esp. an aviator **2.** Sthg. like an express train that travels fast **3.** An advertising circular for mass distribution —also FLYER

flight (flart) n. **1.** An act of flying **2.** A trip made on a plane **3.** A group of birds, aircraft, etc. flying together **4.** The stairs between the floors of a building **5.** An act or instance of running away or escaping (fleeing): *The vandals took flight as soon as they heard the police siren.*

flight-y (flart-iᵞ) adj. **-ier, -iest 1.** Subject to flights of fancy or sudden changes of whim **2.** Not stable **3.** Always looking for amusement

flim-sy (flɪm-ziᵞ) adj. **-sier, -siest 1.** Light and thin: *flimsy curtains* **2.** Not strong enough for the purpose for which it is used: *a flimsy suitcase/fig. a flimsy argument/ excuse*

flinch (flɪntʃ) v. To move or shrink back from, as if from fear or pain

fling (flɪŋ) v. **flung** (flʌŋ), **flinging** To throw violently or hurriedly: *I don't like John's habit of flinging his clothes on the floor.*

fling n. A short, often wild period of satisfy-

ing one's own worldly desires; a period of uulr-in-lulgence

flint (flɪnt) n. A hard kind of stone that produces sparks when struck with steel and that breaks with sharp, cutting edges

flip (flɪp) n. A quick, light blow or movement that sends sthg. spinning into the air

flip v. **-pp-** 1. To toss sthg. into the air with a light quick movement: *to flip a coin* 2. To turn over: *to flip the pancakes* 3. To quickly turn the pages: *He flipped the pages of the book.* 4. Flick: *Flip the light switch on, please.* 5. To go crazy: *Joe really flipped.* 6. *infml.* **flip one's lid** *AmE.* To become angry

flip-pant (flɪp–ənt) adj. Frivolously shallow and disrespectful

flip-per (flɪp–ər) n. 1. A broad, flat limb, as of a seal, used for swimming 2. Either of a pair of flat rubber attachments worn on the feet as an aid in underwater diving and swimming

flirt (flɜrt) v. 1. To behave in a way that attracts the attention of a member of the opposite sex 2. To deal casually with sthg.: *He's been flirting with danger. (=not taking it seriously)*

flirt n. One given to flirting —**flir-ta-tion** (flər–te^y–ʃən) n. —**flir-ta-tious** (flər–te^y–ʃəs) adj.

flit (flɪt) v. **-tt-** To fly or move quickly or lightly: *She's always flitting around.*

fliv-ver (flɪv–ər) n. *infml.* An old, cheap car

float (flo^{w}t) v. To stay on or at the surface of liquid or be held in air without sinking: *The toy boat floated on the edge of the lake./ The balloon floated up and out of the stadium.*

float n. 1. A vehicle with a platform to carry an exhibit: *There were more than 60 beautiful floats in the Rose Parade last year.* 2. A piece of cork or other light object that floats, esp. used on a fishing net

flock (flɑk) n. 1. A group of birds, sheep, goats, etc. of the same kind 2. *infml.* A crowd of people 3. The group of people who regularly attend a church: *The pastor warned his flock against false prophets in the area.* 4. A group of people under the leadership of one person: *Jesus said to his disciples: "Do not be afraid, little flock, for your Father [God] has*

been pleased to give you the kingdom" (Luke 12:32).

flock v. To gather or move in a crowd: *People flocked to the stadium to see the football game.*

floe (flo^w) n. A flat mass of floating ice

flog (flɑg/ flɔg) v. **-gg-** To beat severely with a rod or whip —**flogging** n.

flood (flʌd) n. 1. The covering with water of a place that is usu. dry: *In the days of Noah, the whole world was destroyed by a flood because of people's wickedness. ...For 40 days the flood kept coming on the earth* (Genesis 7:11-24). 2. An abundant flow or outpouring: *There was a flood of cheap products on the market./a flood of complaints/ applications/ requests for information*

flood v. 1. To cause to be filled or covered with water: *The waters flooded the earth 150 days* (Genesis 7:24). 2. To arrive somewhere in large numbers: *Applications/ complaints/ requests for information flooded in.*

floor (flɔr) n. 1. The surface on which one stands indoors: *The children put on their slippers because the floor was cold.* 2. A level or story of a building: *Our apartment is on the tenth floor.*

floor v. 1. To cover with a floor or floor covering: *The kitchen was floored with plastic tiles.* 2. *infml.* To knock down: *The boxer floored his opponent in the first round.* 3. *fig.* Surprised; shocked: *The news of her resignation completely floored us. We hadn't expected anything like that.*

flop (flɑp) v. **-pp-** 1. To fall heavily or awkwardly 2. To move about in a clumsy way: *The fish flopped around in the boat.* 3. To fail

flop n. An utter failure: *His performance on the stage was a complete flop.*

flop-py (flɑp–i^y) adj. **-pier, -piest** 1. Tending to flop 2. Loose and flexible

flo-ra (flɔr–ə) n. **floras** or **florae** (–aɪ) Plants or plant life, esp. of a particular region

flo-ral (flɔr–əl) adj. Of flowers

flo-res-cence (flɔ–**res**–əns) n. Act, state, or period of flowering

flor-id (flɔr–əd) adj. 1. Of persons, highly colored; flushed 2. Too elaborately ornamented

flo-rist (flɔr–əst) n. A person who raises flow-

ers or keeps a store for selling flowers

floss (flɔs/flɑs) n. **1.** Fine silk thread used in embroidery **2.** A soft silken substance in the husks of certain plants **3.** Waste silk fibers

flo-til-la (floᵂ–tɪl–ə) n. **1.** A fleet of small vessels **2.** A small fleet

flounce (flaʊns) v. To move about in an exaggerated manner, esp. with impatience or anger

flounce n. **1.** A sudden, impatient movement of the body **2.** A wide strip of cloth, lace, etc. sewn to the edge of a garment: *a flounce on her skirt*

floun-der (flaʊn–dər) v. **1.** To move clumsily and with difficulty **2.** To make mistakes or become confused when trying to do sthg.

flour (flaʊ–ər) n. Grain, esp. wheat, ground fine and used for making bread, pastry, etc.

flour-ish (flɜr–ɪʃ) v. **1.** To grow well; thrive: *The family is flourishing.* **2.** To do well; succeed: *The company should flourish since you added the new products.* **3.** To wave sthg. in the hand in order to draw attention: *"My application has been accepted," she shouted, flourishing a letter.*

flourish n. A showy, dramatic action that draws attention: *She entered the room with a flourish.*

flour-ish-ing (flɜr–ɪʃ–ɪŋ) adj. Very good; profitable: *He had a flourishing business.*

flout (flaʊt) v. To disobey openly and scornfully

flow (floᵂ) v. **1.** To run or move freely as in a stream: *Blood was flowing from his wound.* **2.** To circulate, like blood through the body

flow n. **1.** A continuous outpouring: *a flow of ideas* **2.** A continuous movement: *a flow of traffic*

flow-chart (floᵂ–tʃɑrt) n. A diagram consisting of a set of symbols and connecting lines that show step-by-step progression through a procedure or system

flow-er (flaʊ–ər) n. **1.** A blossom; the part of a plant that produces seeds or fruit, often beautiful and colored, lasting only a short time **2.** A plant that is grown for its blossoms: *Roses are her favorite flowers./The Bible reminds us that "all men are like grass and all their glory is like the flowers of the field; the*

grass withers and the flowers fall, but the word of the Lord stands forever" (1 Peter 1:24,25).

flower v. **1.** To produce flowers; bloom **2.** To develop fully: *Her genius as an artist flowered early in life.*

flow-er-y (flaʊ–ər–iʸ) adj. **1.** Full of flowers **2.** Of language, full of ornamental phrases

flown (floᵂn) v. Past part. of **fly**

flu (fluᵂ) also **influenza** n. Any of several viral diseases like a bad cold but more serious

flub (flʌb) v. **-bb-** To bungle; to make a mistake

fluc-tu-ate (flʌk–tʃuᵂ–eʸt) v. **-ated, -ating 1.** To rise and fall or move back and forth **2.** To change from one state to another: *The price fluctuates between one hundred and two hundred dollars.* —**fluc-tu-a-tion** (flʌk–tʃuᵂ–eʸ–ʃən) n. *temperature fluctuations*

flue (fluᵂ) n. A pipe or passage for carrying away smoke, hot air, etc.

flu-en-cy (fluᵂ–ən–siʸ) n. The quality or state of being fluent

flu-ent (fluᵂ–ənt) adj. **1.** Capable of speaking or writing in an easy, smooth manner: *I admire people who are fluent in more than one language.* **2.** Speech, writing, etc. expressed smoothly, without effort or pause: *You need to speak fluent Spanish for this job.* —**fluently** adv.

fluff (flʌf) n. **1.** A soft, light-weight cluster of loosely gathered fibers of cotton, wool, etc. **2.** A mass of soft, fine feathers; down **3.** An error by an actor speaking lines

fluff v. **1.** To make (pillows, e.g.) soft by patting and shaking **2.** *infml.* To make an error in speaking one's lines

fluf-fy (flʌf–iʸ) adj. **-fier, -fiest** Having or being covered with a soft mass of fur or fibers

flu-id (fluᵂ–əd) n. A substance that flows, like a liquid or a gas

fluid adj. **1.** Capable of flowing, like liquids, air, gas, etc.; not solid **2.** *fig.* Not fixed; able to be changed: *The government's policy is still fluid on the matter.* —**flu-id-i-ty** (fluᵂ–ɪd–ət–iʸ) n.

fluke (fluᵂk) n. Sthg. that is accidentally successful

flung (flʌŋ) v. Past tense and part. of **fling**

flunk (flʌŋk) v. *AmE. infml.* **1.** To give a failing

grade to: *The teacher flunked me in music.* **2.** To receive a failing grade: *You'd better study for the finals or you'll flunk.*

flun-ky -kies, also **flun-key, -keys** (flʌŋk–iʸ) n. A person who performs menial tasks

flu-o-res-cence (fluɔr–ɛs–əns) n. **1.** The giving out of radiation, especially of visible light, by a substance during exposure to external radiation, as light or X-rays **2.** The radiation produced in this way —**fluorescent** adj.

fluor-i-date (fluɔr–ə–deʸt/flɔr–) v. **-dated, -dating** To add sodium fluoride to drinking water to prevent tooth decay —**flour-i-da-tion** (fluɔr–ə–deʸ–ʃən) n.

flu-o-ride (fluɔr–aɪd/ flɔ–raɪd) n. Chemical compound of fluorine

flu-o-rine (fluɔr–iʸn/ flɔ–riʸn) n. A chemical element, a pale yellow corrosive gas

flur-ry (flɜr–iʸ) n. **-ries 1.** A short, sudden rush of snow, rain, wind, etc. **2.** A commotion **3.** An outburst of nervous activity

flurry v. **-ried, -rying 1.** To fluster **2.** To come down as a flurry

flush (flʌʃ) adj. **1.** Exactly on the same level with an adjoining surface: *These two desks ought to be flush with each other.* **2.** Having plenty: *flush with cash*

flush v. To cause liquid to pour over or through, esp. to clean or wash out by a sudden flow: *The radiator on our car needs to be flushed out. It hasn't been cleaned for a long time.*

flush n. The act of cleaning with a sudden flow of water or other liquid

flus-ter (flʌs–tər) v. To cause to be nervous and confused

flute (fluʷt) n. A hollow pipe-like musical instrument —**flutist** n.

flut-ter (flʌt–ər) v. **1.** To flap the wings quickly without flying **2.** To fly by flapping the wings quickly: *There's a moth fluttering around the lamp.* **3.** To flap up and down or backwards and forwards: *The thin curtains fluttered at the window./ fig. The bride's mother fluttered about, getting ready for the wedding.*

flutter n. A fluttering movement: *a flutter of excitement*

flux (flʌks) n. A state of constant change: *The plans for our trip are still in a state of flux.*

fly (flaɪ) v. **flew** (fluʷ), **flown** (floʷn), **flying 1.** To pass through the air on wings: *A bird flew past the window.* **2. (a)** To pass through the air: *Some leaves flew past the window, blown by the wind.* **(b)** To cause an aircraft to move through the air: *My son flies his plane to San Francisco occasionally.* **3.** To travel by aircraft: *We plan to fly to Denver on Saturday.* **4.** To raise a flag: *The ship was flying a Norwegian flag.* **5.** To move quickly or suddenly: *The door flew open./This week has really flown by.* **6. fly the coop** To escape from; flee: *The prisoner has flown the coop.* (=*escaped*) **7. fly off the handle** To lose one's temper

fly n. **flies 1.** A type of small insect with two wings, esp. the housefly **2. fly in the ointment** A person or thing that spoils an otherwise perfect situation, occasion, etc.

fly-er (flaɪ–ər) n. One who flies, esp. an aviator —see FLIER

fly-ing (flaɪ–ŋ) adj. **1. a flying leap** A jump made after running a short distance: *He made a flying leap from one roof to the other.* **2. get off to a flying start** To do very well at the beginning **3. pass (a test, etc.) with flying colors** To pass with a very high score

flying n. Traveling by aircraft

F.M. (ɛf–ɛm) *abbr.* for **frequency modulation** A system of broadcasting in which the signal comes at a varying number of times per second

foal (foʷl) n. One of the young of an animal of the horse family

foam (foʷm) n. A light mass of fine bubbles on the surface of a liquid or on the seashore: *The waves lapping at the shore made a line of foam.*

foam v. To produce foam: *The sick dog was foaming at the mouth.* —**foamy** adj. **-ier, -iest**

fo-cal (foʷ–kəl) adj. Of or placed at a focus

fo-cus (foʷ–kəs) n. **-cuses** or **-ci** (–kiʸ) **1.** The point at which rays of light, waves of sound, etc. meet, or from which they seem to come **2.** The central point; center of interest: *The focus for the lesson was on verb phrases./ John's new car soon became the focus of everyone's attention.* **3.** The point or distance at which an object is seen most clearly by the eye or through a lens **4. in/ out of focus** Giv-

ing a blurry picture because the lens is placed at the wrong distance: *I'm having trouble getting the focus right. This picture won't be very clear.*

focus v. **-s-** or **-ss-** To adjust the focus: *Don't forget to focus the camera. We want this to be a good picture./fig.: All the attention was focused on the clowns in the center ring.*

fod-der (fɑd–ər) n. Coarse, dry food for livestock

foe (foʷ) n. An enemy

fog (fɑg/ fɔg) n. Fine drops of water close to or just above land or sea; a thick mist that is difficult to see through

fog v. **-gg-** To become covered with fog: *The windshield has fogged up and I can't see a thing!*

fog-gy (fɑg–iʸ/ fɔg–iʸ) adj. **-gier, -giest 1.** Not clear because of a covering of fog; very misty: *foggy weather/ a foggy day* **2. not have the foggiest (idea)** *infml.* Not to have any idea: *Where is your sister? I haven't the foggiest. I haven't seen her all day.*

fo gy, -gies or **fo-gey, -geys** (foʷ–giʸ) n. A person with old-fashioned ideas

foi-ble (fɔɪ–bəl) n. A personal weakness of character

foil (fɔɪl) v. **1.** To keep someone from doing sthg. **2.** To bring to nothing: *The Lord foils the plans of the nations* (Psalm 33:10).

foist (fɔɪst) v. To pass off sthg. worthless as genuine

fold (foʷld) v. **1.** To turn or bend sthg. and lay one part of it on the remaining part: *He folded the map.* **2.** To be capable of being bent in this way: *This table folds easily.* **3.** To cross: *She folded her arms (=crossed them over her chest) and stood glaring at me.* —opposite UNFOLD **4.** To fail; collapse: *His business folded.*

fold n. **1.** Part of sthg. that folds or hangs as if folded: *Her full velvet skirt hung to the floor in deep folds.* **2.** An enclosed, sheltered area in a field where sheep are kept for protection

fold-er (foʷl–dər) n. A folded cover for holding loose papers

fo-li-age (foʷ–lɪdʒ/foʷl–iʸ–ɪdʒ) n. The leaves of a tree or plant

folk (foʷk) also **folks** *AmE.* n. **1.** People from a

particular part of the country, or sharing a particular characteristic: *city folk/ the young folks* **2.** The persons of one's own family; esp. one's parents: *(pl. only) I'd like you to meet my folks.*

folk adj. Of the common people, typically reflecting their life-style: *folk dances/ music/ art*

folk-lore (foʷk–lɔr) n. The traditions, beliefs, customs, stories, etc. preserved among the common people

fol-li-cle (fɑl–ɪ–kəl) n. A very small sac or cavity in the body: *a hair follicle*

fol-low (fɑl–oʷ) v. **1.** To come or go after: *I know the way, so I'll go first and you follow (=following after) me.* **2.** To pursue: *The police were following the criminals.* **3.** To move along a certain course: *Follow this road to the end and you'll see my house.* **4.** To come next: *The letter X follows W in the English alphabet./The results were as follows. (=as will now be listed)* **5.** To imitate; copy: *Paul said, "Follow my example, as I follow the example of Christ"* (1 Corinthians 11:1). **6.** To listen carefully: *She followed the speaker with the greatest attention.* **7.** To understand: *I didn't quite follow what you said; could you repeat it please?* **8.** To accept as authority and act according to: *You need to follow the instructions on the bottle and take your medicine every four hours.* **9.** To think or believe like another: *Jesus said, "Whoever serves me must follow me"* (John 12:26). *Whoever follows me will never walk in darkness but will have the light of life* (John 8:12). **10.** To obey: *The Lord said to Moses: "You must obey my laws and... follow my decrees"* (Leviticus 18:4). **11.** To come into existence as a result or consequence of: *Surely goodness and mercy shall follow me all the days of my life, and I will dwell in the house of the Lord forever* (Psalm 23:6). **12. follow in someone's footsteps** To follow someone else's example in a business, profession, etc.: *John followed in his father's footsteps and became a teacher.* **13. follow sthg. through** To carry out fully and to the very end: *He followed through on his promise to pay her way through college.* **14. follow sthg. up (a)** To act further on sthg.: *Thank you for your suggestion. I'll certainly follow it up.* **(b)**

To take (an) additional action: *He followed up his letter with a phone call.* —**follow–up** n. *I'll make a follow-up phone call in noo if he received my letter.*

fol-low-er (fal–o^w–ər) n. **1.** One who comes, goes, or moves after another, along the same course **2.** One who obeys, worships and honors: *Be... followers of God, as dear children; and walk in love, as Christ also loved us and gave himself up for us as a fragrant offering and sacrifice to God* (Ephesians 5:1,2).

fol-low-ing (fal–o^w–iŋ) adj. What comes next: *He was here one day last week, but had to leave again the following day.*

following n. A group of followers; adherents: *The spiritual leader had quite a following.*

fol-ly (fal–i^y) n. -lies **1.** Lack of good sense **2.** A foolish act or idea **3.** An excessively costly or unprofitable undertaking

fo-ment (fo^w–ment) v. To stir up; instigate —**fo-men-ta-tion** (fo^w–men–te^y–ʃən)

fond (fand) adj. **1.** Loving; affectionate; tender: *to have fond memories/ She loves all her students, but she's especially fond of David.* **2.** Having a very strong liking for sthg.: *I'm very fond of chocolate.* **3.** Having tender but foolish feelings or hopes: *a fond belief/ fond hopes (=that may or may not come true)*

fon-dle (fan–dəl) v. -dled, -dling To touch or stroke lovingly

fond-ly (fand–li^y) adv. In a loving, caring way

font (fant) n. **1.** A basin in a church that holds the water used for baptizing people **2.** A source of abundance

food (fu^wd) n. **1.** That which living creatures eat or drink or which plants take in to give them strength and energy and help them to develop and grow: *We try to choose food that will give us a well-balanced diet./ plant food* **2.** Sthg. solid for eating, as distinguished from drink: *We have plenty of food but very little to drink.* **3.** Sthg. that supplies and nourishes: *fig. The professor's lectures always give us food for thought. (=ideas to think about)/ Jesus said, "Do not work for food that spoils, but for food that endures to eternal life which the Son of Man [Jesus] will give you"* (John 6:27). *He was referring to the word of God (spiritual food).*

fool (fu^wl) v. **1.** To deceive or trick: *Don't be fooled by what the salesman tells you about that car. It isn't nearly as good as he says.* **2. fool around** To behave stupidly or in a silly way: *Stop fooling around! This is serious business.* **3.** To tease or joke: *Your brother didn't mean it. He was only fooling.*

fool n. A stupid person; one lacking in judgment and understanding; one who can easily be deceived: *The fool has said in his heart, "There is no God"* (Psalm 14:1). *Fools make a mockery of sin* (Proverbs 14:9 KJV). *Fools despise wisdom and instruction* (Proverbs 1:7). *To the rich man who put his trust in his riches, God said, "You fool! This night your soul will be required of you; then whose will those things be which you have provided? So is he who lays up treasure for himself and is not rich toward God"* (Luke 12:20-21).

fool-ish (fu^wl–iʃ) adj. *derog.* Lacking good sense; stupid; laughable: *It was foolish of me to spend so much time in the hot sun. Now I have a sunburn./To those who were familiar with the prophecies of Jesus' resurrection, yet doubted, Jesus said, "O foolish ones, and slow of heart to believe all that the prophets have spoken!"* (Luke 24:25). —**foolishly** adv. —**foolishness** n.

fool-proof (fu^wl–pru^wf) adj. Sthg. so simple or reliable as to leave no opportunity for error, misuse, or failure: *a foolproof machine*

foot (fʊt) n. **feet** (fi^yt) **1.** The lowest part of the leg, below the ankle, on which a person or animal stands **2.** A measure of length equal to 12 inches: *Twelve inches make one foot./ The board is six feet long.* **3.** The base or lowest part of sthg.: *Our kitten likes to sleep at the foot of my bed./ the foot of the stairs* **4. get one's feet wet** To begin to get experience in sthg.: *Scott just started on this job. He hasn't had a chance to get his feet wet yet.* **5. get/ have cold feet** To lose courage and be afraid to do sthg.: *I got cold feet about making the trip when I found out we'd have to hike the last ten miles in the mud.* **6. have one foot in the grave** To be very old or weak; near death **7. on foot** Walking **8. put one's best foot forward** To make one's best effort in order to show oneself worthy **9. put one's foot down** *infml.* To take a firm stand on a particular matter **10.**

put one's foot in his/ her mouth *infml.* To say sthg. that offends, embarrasses, etc.

foot-age (fʊt–ɪdʒ) n. The length of sthg. expressed in feet, esp. in speaking of motion picture film used (as for a scene or subject)

foot-ball (fʊt–bɔl) n. 1. *AmE.* American football, a game played by two teams of 11 players each on a rectangular field, 100 yards in length, with goalposts at either end. The ball is in possession of one team at a time and is advanced by running and passing. Points are made by crossing the opponents' goal line, thus scoring a touchdown (six points) or by kicking the ball over a crossbar and between the goal posts, scoring a field goal (three points). 2. Any of several outdoor games for two teams in which a ball is kicked and/ or thrown in an attempt to score goals 3. A ball used in these games

foot-hill (fʊt–hɪl) n. A hill or low mountain at the base of a higher mountain or range of mountains

foot-hold (fʊt–hoʷld) n. 1. A secure spot where a foot can be placed to help one in climbing up or down 2. A secure position that provides a base for further advancement: *Don't give the devil a foothold* (Ephesians 4:27).

foot-ing (fʊt–ɪŋ) n. 1. A firm placing of the feet 2. A secure place for a person to stand on or room for placing the feet: *It was hard for the climbers to get a footing on the cliff.* 3. Basis; foundation: *fig. My brother's shoe repair business is now on a firm footing. (=has a good start, with enough money to support it)*

foot-loose (fʊt–luʷs) adj. Free from responsibilities and able to go wherever one pleases and do what one likes

foot-note (fʊt–noʷt) n. A note of reference, explanation, or comment at the bottom of a page in a book

foot-stool (fʊt–stuʷl) n. A low stool for supporting the feet: *The Lord says, "Heaven is my throne and the earth is my footstool"* (Isaiah 66:1).

for (fɔr) prep. 1. Used to indicate the recipient, the object, or the goal of an activity: *This gift is for you./ She made this sweater for the baby.* 2. Shows purpose or function: *We need*

a new car for driving to work. 3. Instead of; in behalf of: *Christ died for all* (2 Corinthians 5:15). 4. In favor of; in support or defense of: *If God is for us, who can be against us?* (Romans 8:31). 5. So as to reach a destination, aim, or purpose: *Father left for work.* 6. In order to catch, have, or get: *I'm going to the barber for a haircut.* 7. As part of or being made up of: *bacon and eggs for breakfast/Do you take me for a fool?* 8. Meaning; as a sign of: *What's the M for in your initials?/ Red is for "stop", green is for "go."* 9. Shows payment, price, or amount: *How much did you pay for your car?/Christ paid for our sins with his own blood* (1 Peter 1:18,19). 10. Shows amount of time or distance: *They'll be on vacation for two weeks./ After walking for six miles we were pretty tired.* 11. On the occasion of: *Will your children be home for Christmas?* 12. Because: *Repent, for the kingdom of heaven is near* (Matthew 3:2). 13. With regard to; in connection with: *Exercise is good for you.* 14. Considered as; considering: *For all his hard work, he didn't succeed very well.*

for-age (fɔr–ɪdʒ) n. 1. Food for horses or cattle 2. The seeking of such food

forage v. **-aged, -aging** 1. To search for provisions 2. To search about 3. To make a raid

for-ay (fɔr–eʸ) n. 1. A quick raid, usu. for plunder 2. A quick sudden attack

for-bear (fɔr–beər) v. **-bore** (–bɔr), **-borne** (–bɔrn), **-bearing** (–beər–ɪŋ) To refrain from doing sthg. that one has the right to do

for-bear-ance (fɔr–beər–əns) n. Patience; tolerance

for-bear-ing (fɔr–beər–ɪŋ) adj. Being patient or tolerant

for-bid (fər–bɪd) v. **-bade, -bad,** (–bæd), **bidden** (–bɪd–ən), or **-bid** (–bɪd), **-bidding** To command against doing sthg.: *The children were forbidden to play on the street.*

force (fɔrs) v. **forced, forcing** 1. To use physical power or strong influence on: *They forced me to sign the papers by threatening my family./ The thieves forced the lock and stole our TV. (=opened it by force)* 2. To produce by unwilling or unnatural effort: *a forced smile* 3. **force someone's hand** To make someone do what one wishes him to do before he or she

is ready to do it

force n. **1.** Power that can be felt: *The force of the wind caused the bridge to collapse.* **2.** Bodily power: *He had to use force to open the door.* **3.** Violence: *The mob resorted to force to obtain their demands.* **4.** Someone or sthg. that has a strong influence or power: *Our struggle is not against flesh and blood but against the spiritual forces of evil* (Ephesians 6:12). **5.** A physical power that cannot be seen or felt, but can be experienced: *The force of gravity pulls things toward the center of the earth.* **6.** A group of people trained for a special purpose, esp. fighting: *the police force/ military forces* **7. in force** In large numbers: *The riot squad came out in force because of the threat of violence.* **8. in force** Of a rule, law, etc., in effect

forced (fɔrst/ foʷrst) adj. Done or made because of necessity: *forced landing of a plane*

for-ceps (fɔr–sɛps) n. Tongs or pincers used by surgeons, dentists, etc. for gripping things

forc-i-ble (fɔr–sɛ–bəl) adj. **1.** Using bodily force **2.** Having power to influence the minds of others

ford (fɔrd) n. A shallow crossing place in a river

ford v. To cross a river on foot

fore– prefix Beforehand; in front

fore-arm (fɔr–ɑrm) n. The lower part of the arm between the wrist and the elbow

fore-bod-ing (fɔr–boʷd–ɪŋ) n. A feeling that sthg. evil is about to happen

fore-cast (fɔr–kæst) v. **-cast** or **-casted, casting** To predict what is going to happen, esp. because of information received: *Warm and partly cloudy weather has been forecast for tomorrow.* —compare PREDICT

forecast n. A prediction of future events, based on some kind of knowledge or judgment: *The economic forecast for this part of the country is rather grim.*

fore-close (fɔr–kloʷ z) v. **-closed, -closing** To take legal action to terminate a mortgage and take possession of mortgaged property —**foreclosure** n.

fore-fa-ther (fɔr–fɑ–ðər) n. Someone from whom the specified person is descended;

relative in the distant past; a male ancestor: *One of my forefathers was a Pony Express rider.*

fore-fin-ger (fɔr–fɪŋ–gər) n. The finger next to the thumb

fore-front (fɔr–frʌnt) n. Sthg. nearest the front; the foremost part or place

fore-go or **for-go** (fɔr–goʷ) v. To abstain from sthg.

fore-go-ing (fɔr–goʷ–ɪŋ) adj. Preceding

fore-gone (fɔr–gɔn) adj. Determined in advance: *Joan's getting the job was a foregone conclusion.*

fore-ground (fɔr–graʊnd) n. The part of a scene or picture nearest the viewer: *This is a picture of Mt. Shasta with our car in the foreground.* —compare BACKGROUND

fore-head (fɔr–hɛd/ fɑr–) n. The part of the face above the eyes and below the hairline

for-eign (fɔr–ən) adj. Of a country or nation other than one's own: *Carl speaks five foreign languages.*

for-eign-er (fɔr–ən–ər/ fɑr–) n. One who comes from or was born in another country —compare STRANGER

fore-know (fɔr–noʷ) v. To have previous knowledge of —**fore-know-ledge** n. (fɔr–knɑl–ɪdʒ)

fore-man (fɔr–mən) n. **-men** (–mɛn) A person in charge of a group of workers, as in a factory or on a ranch

fore-most (fɔr–moʷst/ foʷr–) adj. First in importance: *Man is God's foremost creature.*

fo-ren-sic (fə–rɛn–sɪk) adj. Related to or used in courts of law

fore-or-dain (fɔr–ɔr–deʸn) v. Arrange or determine beforehand

fore-run-ner (fɔr–rʌn–ər) n. A person or thing that prepares the way for, or is a sign of the coming of sbdy. or sthg. that follows: *John the Baptist was the forerunner of Jesus Christ.*

fore-see (fɔr–siʸ) v. **-saw** (–sɔ) **-seen** (–siʸn) **-seeing** To see or realize beforehand; expect: *We couldn't have foreseen the difficulties that would arise.*

fore-see-a-ble (fɔr–siʸ–ə–bəl) adj. That which can be foreseen: *We don't plan any trips abroad in the foreseeable future.* (=as far ahead in time as we can see)

fore-shad-ow (fɔr-ʃæd-oʷ) v. To give a hint or suggestion of sthg. beforehand

fore-sight (fɔr-saɪt/ foʷr-) n. **1.** The act or ability to foresee **2.** An act of looking forward **3.** Wise planning for the future: *He had enough foresight to store up plenty of firewood for the winter.* —compare HINDSIGHT

for-est (fɔr-əst) n. A thick growth of trees and underbrush on a large area of land: *the tropical forests of Africa*

fore-stall (fɔr-stɔl) v. To prevent or foil someone's plans by taking action first

for-est-a-tion (fɔr-ə-steʸ-ʃən) n. The planting of a forest

for-est-er (fɔr-ə-stər) n. **1.** A person trained in forestry **2.** A person in charge of a forest **3.** A person or animal that lives in the forest **4.** Any of several kinds of moths

for-est-ry (fɔr-əst-riʸ) n. **1.** The science of planting and caring for forests **2.** A systematic management of forests for the production of timber, conservation, etc.

fore-taste (fɔr-teʸst) n. An advance indication

foretaste v. **1.** To taste beforehand **2.** Anticipate

fore-tell (fɔr-tɛl) v. To forecast; to prophesy

fore-thought (fɔr-θɔt) n. Thoughtful provision before an undertaking

for-ev-er (fər-ɛv-ər/ fɔr-) also **for ever** adv. For all time; unending time; eternally: *The Lord is good and his love endures forever* (Psalm 100:5). *Jesus Christ is the same yesterday and today and forever* (Hebrews 13:8). *The word of the Lord stands forever* (1 Peter 1:25).

fore-word (fɔr-wɜrd) n. A short introductory statement in the front of a book, usu. by sbdy. other than the author

for-feit (fɔr-fət) v. To give up sthg. as a penalty for an offense: *They forfeited the game by not showing up to play it.*

forfeit n. Sthg. that has to be given up or paid as a penalty

forfeit adj. Paid or given up in this way

for-gave (fɔr-geʸv) v. Past tense of **forgive**

forge (fɔrdʒ) v. **forged, forging 1.** To make an imitation or copy of sthg. in order to deceive: *He was put in prison for forging a signature on a check.* **2.** To shape by heating and hammering: *He forged a horse shoe out of an iron bar.* **3.** To fashion or shape: *fig. The committee forged a new constitution for the organization.*

forg-er (fɔrdʒ-ər) n. A person who forges (=makes a copy or imitation of sthg. in order to deceive)

for-ger-y (fɔr-dʒər-iʸ) n. **-ies 1.** A result of the act of forging: *The painting was a forgery.* **2.** An action of forging: *He was arrested for forgery.*

for-get (fər-gɛt) v. **-got,** (-gɑt) **-gotten** (-gɑt-ən), **getting 1.** To fail to remember: *Don't forget to turn off the oven.* (=Remember to turn it off) **2.** To neglect: *Do not forget to entertain strangers, for by so doing some people have entertained angels without knowing it* (Hebrews 13:2). *Do not forget to do good and to share with others, for with such sacrifices God is pleased* (Hebrews 13:16). **3.** To stop thinking about: *Paul said, "One thing I do: forgetting what is behind and straining toward what is ahead"* (Philippians 3:13).

for-get-ful (fər-gɛt-fəl) adj. Having difficulty in remembering: *Some people become forgetful as they grow older, but others have no trouble at all in remembering.* —**forgetfully** adv. —**forgetfulness** n.

for-give (fɔr-gɪv) v. **-gave** (-geʸv), **-given** (-gɪv-ən), **-giving** (-gɪv-ɪŋ) To excuse for a fault or offense: *Please forgive me for forgetting your birthday./We must forgive those who sin or trespass against us./ Jesus tells us, "If you forgive men their trespasses, your heavenly Father also will forgive you. But if you do not forgive men their trespasses, neither will your Father forgive your trespasses"* (Matthew 6:14,15 RSV). *...if your brother [or anyone] sins, rebuke him, and if he repents, forgive him; and if he sins against you seven times in a day, and turns to you seven times, and says, "I repent," you must forgive him* (Luke 17:3-4 RSV).

for-give-ness (fər-gɪv-nəs) n. *fml.* The act of forgiving or state of being forgiven: *Repent [turn from your sins] and be baptized... in the name of Jesus Christ for the forgiveness of your sins...* (Acts 2:38).

for-giv-ing (fər-gɪv-ɪŋ) adj. Ready to forgive: *A Christian must have a forgiving nature, for God's Word teaches, "Be kind to one another,*

tenderhearted, forgiving one another, just as God in Christ also forgave you" (Ephesians 4:32 RSV).

for-go (fɔr-goʷ) v. **-went** (-wɛnt), **-gone** (-gɔn), **-going** To do without sth.

fork (fɔrk) n. **1.** A utensil with a handle at one end and several (usu. three or four) points at the other, for holding food and carrying it to the mouth **2.** A farm or gardening tool of similar shape, used esp. for digging or pitching hay **3.** A point where a road, stream, etc. divides into two or more branches: *When you come to the fork in the road, turn right to get to our house.*

fork v. **1.** Of a road, river, etc., to divide: *Watch for the place where the river forks, then go to the left.* **2. fork** sth. **up/ over** *infml.* To pay money unwillingly: *I didn't like having to fork over all that money for nothing.*

forked (fɔrkt) adj. **1.** Shaped like a fork: *a forked tail* **2.** Sth. that divides into two or more parts: *a forked trail*

for-lorn (fɔr-lɔrn/ fər-) adj. Left alone and unhappy

form (fɔrm) n. **1.** Shape; outward physical appearance: *a cake in the form of (=shaped like) a boat* **2.** The external appearance of a body, esp. of a person; figure **3.** A type; kind; sort: *different forms of questions* **4.** A printed or typed paper with spaces in which to answer questions and give other information: *Did you fill out your application form yet?* **5.** A mold: *a form for concrete* **6.** (in grammar) One of the ways in which a word is changed to show difference in use: *The plural form of "man" is "men."*

form v. **1.** To produce or give shape to sth.: *By faith we understand that the universe was formed at God's command, so that what is seen was not made out of what was visible* (Hebrews 11:3). **2.** To take a particular shape: *The teacher asked the children to draw lines in such a way as to form a square.* **3.** To cause to develop: *We would like to form a new corporation for the purpose of helping the homeless.* **4.** To cause to stand or move in a certain order: *The band formed a line and marched across the field.*

for-mal (fɔr-məl) adj. Ceremonial; following accepted behavior: *formal dress/a formal din-*

ner —**formally** adv. —opposite INFORMAL

for-mal-i-ty (fɔr-mæl-ə-tᶦ) n. **-ties 1.** An action required by law or custom: *to comply with all the legal formalities* **2.** Careful following of rules and accepted forms of behavior: *Please don't stand on formality. Just make yourself at home.* **3.** An established rule

for-mat (fɔr-mæt) n. The shape and size of sth., a book, for example

for-ma-tion (fɔr-meʸ-ʃən) n. **1.** The organizing and developing of sth.: *the formation of an educational program/ formation of character* **2.** An arrangement of a group of people, ships, etc.; order: *The planes flew in formation at the army air show.* **3.** Sth. that is formed; the way in which a thing is formed: *rock formations*

form-a-tive (fɔrm-ə-tɪv) adj. Having lasting influence in forming or developing: *the formative years of a child's life(=when his character is being developed)*

for-mer (fɔr-mər) adj. *fml.* Of an earlier time: *the former president*

former n. The first in order of two people, places, or things mentioned: *Jack and Bob are both running for office. Of the two choices I'd choose the former. (=Jack, who is the first mentioned)*

for-mer-ly (fɔr-mər-liʸ) adv. Previously; in earlier times: *Mr. Walters was formerly head of the police department.*

for-mi-da-ble (fɔr-məd-ə-bəl/ fɔr-mɪd-ə-bəl) adj. **1.** Inspiring fear or awe **2.** Difficult to do or overcome: *a formidable task*

for-mu-la (fɔrm-yuʷ-lə) n. **-las** or **-lae** (-laɪ) **1.** *tech.* A law, rule, fact, etc. expressed in a short way by means of a group of symbols, letters, numbers, etc.: *Do you know the chemical formula for water?* **2.** A list of ingredients or instructions for making sth. **3.** A milk mixture or substitute used for feeding a baby

for-mu-late (fɔrm-yə-leʸt) v. **-lated, -lating 1.** To express in a clear and exact form **2.** To devise: *They formulated a policy.* —**for-mu-la-tion** (fɔrm-yə-leʸ-ʃən) n.

for-ni-ca-tion (fɔr-nə-keʸ-ʃən) n. Sexual intercourse between a man and woman not married to each other NOTE: This is a grie-

vous sin (=transgression of God's law). *Out of the heart proceed evil thoughts, murders, adulteries, fornications, thefts...* (Matthew 15:19-20). *Now the works of the flesh are evident, which are adultery, fornication... those who practice such things will not inherit the kingdom of God* (Galatians 5:19,21). God hates sin. But he is a God of love. He loves the sinner and he forgives those who turn from their evil ways (repent) and trust in Jesus for eternal life (Mark 1:15; Acts 16:31). —see FORGIVENESS, JESUS, REPENTANCE, SIN

for-sake (fər-se^yk/ fɔr–) v. **-sook** (–sʊk) **-saken** (–se^yk–ən) **-saking** *fml.* To abandon or desert; give up entirely: *God has said, "I will never leave you nor forsake you"* (Deuteronomy 31:6).

fort (fɔrt) n. **1.** A strong or fortified place, usu. occupied only by troops **2.** A permanent army post **3. hold the fort** To look after things during someone's absence

for-te (fɔr-te^y) n., adv. **1.** A person's strong point **2.** (in music) Loudly

forth (fɔrθ) adv. **1.** Out from; forward: *Jesus cried with a loud voice: "Lazarus, come forth." And he who had been dead for four days, came forth (=out of the grave)* (John 11:43,44). **2. and so forth** Etc.; and other similar things

forth-com-ing (fɔrθ–kʌm–ŋ) adj. **1.** About to appear: *the forthcoming holidays* **2.** Readily available: *The funds will be forthcoming.*

forth-right (fɔrθ–raɪt) adj. **1.** Clear and honest in manner and approach: *a forthright answer* **2.** Going straight to the point: *a forthright appraisal of the problem*

for-ti-eth (fɔr–ti^y–əθ) determ., n., pron., adv. 40th

for-ti-fy (fɔr–tə–faɪ) v. **-fied, -fying** Strengthen against attack by building walls: *The old city was well fortified./fig.: You'd better fortify yourself with the facts before the meeting.*

for-ti-tude (fɔr–tə–tu^wd) n. Courage in bearing pain or trouble

fort-night (fɔrt–naɪt) n. *esp. BrE.* Two weeks —**fortnightly** adj., adv.

for-tress (fɔr–trəs) n. A large fort; place strengthened against attack: *The Lord is my rock, my fortress and my deliverer* (Psalm

18:2).

for-tu-i-tous (fɔr–tu^w–ə–təs) adj. Happening by chance —**fortuity** n.

for-tu-nate (fɔr–tʃə–nət) adj. Having or bringing some unexpected good; lucky: *We were fortunate in finding a parking place so near the store.* —opposite UNFORTUNATE

for-tu-nate-ly (fɔr–tʃə–nət–li^y) adv. By some good happening; luckily: *I left my books at home, but fortunately my brother brought them with him.*

for-tune (fɔr–tʃən) n. **1.** Events or changes, good or bad, that happen to a person: *The young man wondered what his fortune would be.* **2.** Riches; a large amount of money: *He made a fortune by the time he was thirty and lost it by the time he was forty.* **3.** Luck; fate; destiny —see FORTUNE-TELLER

for-tune–tell-er (fɔr–tʃən–tɛl–ər) n. A person who claims to be able to tell a person's future or destiny. NOTE: This is a sin against God's commandments. God hates sin, but he loves the sinner and wants all people to repent and believe the Gospel of Jesus Christ so that they may have eternal life. —see DIVINATION, JESUS

for-ty (fɔr–ti^y) determ., n., pron. **-ties** The number 40: *Four times ten is forty.*

for-um (fɔr–əm) n. **forums, fora** A place or meeting where a public discussion is held

for-ward (fɔr–wərd) adj. **1.** Towards the front or the future: *a forward movement* **2.** Ahead in development **3.** Too bold; lacking modesty

forward v. To direct letters, packages, etc. to a new address: *The post office forwarded our mail from our old address.*

forward also **forwards** (fɔr–wərdz) adv. **1.** Towards the front or end so as to make progress: *Buying the new computer was a big step forward for us.* **2.** Towards an earlier time: *The date of the trial has been moved forward from the 10th of April to the 20th of March.* **3.** Into a noticeable position: *The mayor stepped forward and began to speak.* —compare BACKWARDS

fos-sil (fɑs–əl) n. **1.** Remains of a prehistoric animal or plant preserved by being buried in the earth and now hard-ened like rock **2.** *infml. derog.* A person, esp. an old one, who

is unable to accept new ideas or adapt to new conditions

fos·sil·ize also **-ise** (**fɑs–ə–laɪz**) **-ized, -izing** v. To cause sthg. to become a fossil or like a fossil

fos·ter (**fɔs–tər**) v. **1.** To promote the growth or development **2.** To take care of and bring up a child that is not one's own

fought (fɔt) v. Past tense and part. of **fight**

foul (faʊl) adj. **1.** Having a bad smell and taste; impure: *foul water/ fig.: foulmouthed (=using bad language)* **2.** Of weather, rough or stormy

foul v. **1.** To make sthg. dirty or impure or block it with waste matter: *The oil spill fouled the beach for miles.* **2.** *fig.* To spoil an opportunity: *By being so stubborn he really fouled up his chances!* **3.** In sports, to commit a foul against: *The boxer hit his opponent below the belt and fouled him (=did sthg. against the rules).*

foul n. An act of breaking the rules

found (faʊnd) v. Past tense and part. of **find**: *Salvation is found in no one else [than Jesus], for there is no other name under heaven given among men by which we must be saved* (Acts 4:12).

found v. **1.** To begin to build sthg. large; establish: *The building is founded on solid earth./ This company was founded in 1923.* **2.** To start and support an institution, school, etc., esp. by supplying money: *The Smith family founded a hospital in our town.*

foun·da·tion (faʊn–de^y–ʃən) n. **1.** Supporting structure; base: *The workmen were pouring the foundation for the new house.* **2.** The act of starting the building of sthg. large: *Dr. Williams has been the head of the university ever since its foundation.* **3.** An organization established to give out money for certain special purposes: *The Kresge Foundation gives money for many worthy causes.* **4.** The basis on which a belief, custom, way of life, etc. stands: *The Christian Church's one foundation is Jesus Christ her Lord./ For no one can lay any foundation [for the Christian Church] other than the one already laid, which is Jesus Christ* (1 Corinthians 3:11). NOTE: The family is the foundation of society, the constitution is the foundation of the government, the ability to read is a foundation for further education, and the Bible is foundational for spiritual growth. Satan and evil people are striving to destroy these foundations in many lands. When the foundations are being destroyed, what can the righteous do? (Psalm 11:3). "All that is necessary for evil to triumph is for good men to do nothing." We must work and pray to strengthen these foundations.

found·er (faʊnd–ər) n. A person who founds or establishes sthg.: *William Cameron Townsend was the founder of the Summer Institute of Linguistics.*

found·ling (faʊnd–lɪŋ) n. A child abandoned by its parents

foun·tain (faʊn–tən) n. **1.** A spring of water that shoots into the air **2.** An artificial jet of water: *a drinking fountain* **3.** Source: *The fear of the Lord is a fountain of life* (Proverbs 14:27).

four (fɔr) determ., n., pron. The number **4**; one more than three

four·teen (fɔr–ti^yn) determ., n., pron. The number **14**; one more than 13

four·teenth (fɔr–ti^ynθ) determ., n., pron., adv. **14th**

fourth (fɔrθ) determ., n., pron., adv. **1. 4th**: *This is my fourth cup of coffee for the day.* **2.** AmE. Quarter: *I'll cut this apple into fourths so it's easier for you to eat.*

fowl (faʊl) n. **fowl** or **fowls** A bird of any kind, esp. a hen

fox (fɑks) n. **foxes** or **fox 1.** A mammal related to dogs and wolves but smaller, having reddish or grey fur and a long, bushy tail, said to have a clever and deceiving nature **2.** A clever, crafty person

fox v. To deceive through a clever trick; outwit —**foxy** adj. **-ier, -iest**

fox·hole (fɑks–ho^wl) n. A small hole dug by soldiers as shelter from enemy bullets

foy·er (fɔɪ–ər) n. An entrance hall or lobby

fra·cas (fre^y–kəs) n. A noisy quarrel or disturbance

frac·tion (fræk–ʃən) n. **1.** In mathematics, a part of a whole number: *"1/8," "3/4," and ".67" are all fractions.* **2.** A very small piece or

percentage: *Please move the table a fraction closer to the door.* —**fractional** adj.

frac-ture (fræk–tʃər) n. The act or result of breaking sthg., esp. a bone

fracture v. **-tured, -turing** To cause to break or crack: *He fractured his ankle when he jumped from the balcony.*

frag-ile (frædʒ–əl) adj. **1.** Easily broken; delicate: *Please handle these dishes carefully; they're fragile.* **2.** Frail in body or health: *a fragile old man* —**fra-gil-i-ty** (fræ–dʒɪl–ə–tiy) n.

frag-ment (fræg–mənt) n. A part broken off or incomplete: *A fragment of my tooth just broke off.*

frag-ment (fræg–mɛnt/ fræg–**mɛnt**) v. To break into small pieces: *fig. Reports from the disaster area were fragmented due to the lack of radio communication.* —**frag-men-ta-tion** (fræg–mən–tey–ʃən) n.

frag-men-tary (fræg–mən–tɛər–iy) adj. Not complete: *His account of the accident was fragmentary.*

fra-grant (frey–grənt) adj. A sweet or pleasant scent, esp. of flowers: *The lilacs gave off a fragrant aroma.* —**fra-grance** (frey–grəns) n.

frail (freyl) adj. **1.** Morally or physically weak **2.** Fragile

frail-ty (freyl–tiy) n. **-ties** The quality of being frail, physically or morally: *fig. One of his frailties is his stubbornness.*

frame (freym) v. **framed, framing 1.** To put a border or a solid, protecting edge around: *The young teacher had his diploma framed and hung on the wall.* **2.** To form words carefully; express: *The statements in the document were framed clearly.* **3.** *infml.* To make it appear that someone is guilty of a crime by means of false statements, evidence, etc.: *The man was framed by his fellow employees who had a grudge against him, and was sent to prison for a crime he didn't commit.*

frame n. **1.** The main part of a building, ship, bicycle, etc., which holds it together: *Most houses in California have wooden frames.* **2.** A solid border into which sthg. is fit or set: *a picture frame* **3. frame of mind** Mood; state or condition of one's mind or feelings: *She was in a troubled frame of mind.*

fran-chise (fræn–tʃaɪz) n. Authorization to

sell a company's goods or services in a particular area

frank (fræŋk) adj. Free and sincere expression; direct and honest: *If you want my frank opinion, I think you're making a big mistake.* —**frankness** n. —**frankly** adv.

frank-fur-ter (fræŋk–fər–tər) n. A seasoned sausage, usu. of beef or of beef and pork

frank-in-cense (fræŋk–ən–sɛns) n. A fragrant resin burned as incense

fran-tic (fræn–tɪk) adj. Very nervous; anxious; wildly excited, etc.: *The secretary was frantic about getting her report done in time.* —**frantically** adv.

fra-ter-nal (frə–tɜr–nəl) adj. Of a brother or brothers; brotherly or friendly

fra-ter-ni-ty (frə–tɜr–nə–tiy) n. **1.** A society of college men **2.** A group of people with common interests

frat-er-nize (fræt–ər–naɪz) v. **-nized, -nizing** To associate with others in a friendly way

frat-ri-cide (fræt–rə–saɪd) n. **1.** The murder of one's brother or sister **2.** One who has killed a brother or sister

fraud (frɔd) n. **1.** Deceitful behavior; dishonesty **2.** An impostor; a person who pretends to be someone or sthg. else: *He said he was raising money for a new orphanage, but fortunately we soon learned that he was a fraud.*

fraud-u-lent (frɔ–dʒə–lənt) adj. **1.** Deceitful or dishonest **2.** Obtained by fraud

fraught (frɔt) adj. Filled or loaded with; involving

fray (frey) n. **1.** A fight or scuffle **2.** A heated argument

fray v. **1.** To unravel, tear, or wear away by rubbing **2.** To strain or irritate: *frayed nerves*

freak (friyk) n. **1.** A living creature that is especially unusual or abnormal in form: *One of the new puppies is a freak; it was born with three ears.* **2.** A strange, unlikely happening: *a freak of nature* **3.** *infml.* A person who takes an exceptionally strong interest in the specified thing: *a health food freak*

freak adj. Unnatural; very unusual: *freak weather*

freck-le (frɛk–əl) n. A light brown spot on the skin

freckle v. **-led, -ling 1.** To mark with freckles

2. To become covered with freckles

free (fri^y) adj 1 Able to act as one chooses; at liberty; not bound or under control: *Many wars have been fought in the hope that the people would be free./ spir. Jesus said, "If you hold to my teaching..., you will know the truth, and the truth will set you free [from the bondage of sin]"* (John 8:31,32). 2. Not limited in any way, esp. by laws, rules or customs: *free speech (=able to express ideas and judgments in public)* 3. Without having to pay; costing nothing: *a free gift/ a free ticket to the movie* 4. Not taken up with work or duty: *Are you free this evening?* 5. Ready to spend money, give advice, etc.; generous: *He's a free spender.* 6. **free and easy** Without worries; cheerful: *a free and easy lifestyle*

–free (–fri^y) comb. form Free from; without: *It would be nice to have a trouble-free car./ My father has to be on a salt-free diet.*

free adv. 1. In a free manner: *Don't let that vicious criminal go free.* 2. Without charge: *Children under two years old are allowed to travel free on airplanes.* 3. Loose; unattached: *Two of the screws in this table have worked themselves free./ The dog got free from his leash.*

free v. freed , freeing 1. To set at liberty: *Free the hostages!/ Jesus loved us and freed us from our sins [by paying for our sins with his own blood]* (Revelations 1:5). 2. To cause someone or sthg. that is stuck or trapped to be loosened or moved: *The rescue team freed the trapped man from the crushed vehicle.* 3. To excuse someone from some kind of responsibility or duty

free-dom (fri^y–dəm) n. 1. The state of being free, not under control: *Where the Spirit of the Lord is, there is freedom* (2 Corinthians 3:17)./ *freedom from want/ freedom from fear/ freedom from the bondage of sin/ Live as free men. But do not use your freedom as a cover-up for evil; live as servants of God* (1 Peter 2:16). 2. The state of being able to do, say, think, or write as one wishes: *Two freedoms valued by most people are the freedom of speech and the freedom of religion.* —compare LIBERTY

free en-ter-prise (fri^y ɛnt–ər–praız) n. Business conducted by private individuals subject to free competition and the workings of sup-

ply and demand, with a minimum of government regulation

free-ly (fri^y–li^y) adv. 1. Willingly; readily: *All have sinned and fall short of the glory of God, and are justified freely by his grace [unmerited love] through the redemption that came by Christ Jesus* (Romans 3:23,24). —see JESUS CHRIST 2. Truthfully; without hiding anything: *It took courage for her to admit freely that she had disobeyed.* 3. Without any limitation on movement or action: *We were able to get about the city freely because of the excellent bus service.*

free-way (fri^y–we^y) n. *AmE.* for **expressway** A divided highway with no cross streets or traffic signals

free-will (fri^y–wıl) adj. Voluntary

freeze (fri^yz) v. froze (fro^wz), frozen (fro^w–zən) freezing 1. To harden into ice or a similar solid by loss of heat: *Water freezes at 32 degrees Fahrenheit.* 2. To become unable to function properly due to ice or very low temperatures: *The car radiator has frozen up.* 3. To be at or below 32 degrees Fahrenheit: *It's freezing in the area. I hope the orange crop won't be damaged.* 4. To preserve or be preserved by means of very low temperatures: *frozen vegetables* 5. To stop suddenly or become motionless, esp. with fear: *I froze, momentarily, at the sight of the snake.* 6. To fix prices or wages officially at a given level, usu. for a specified length of time

freeze n. 1. A period of weather during which temperatures are below freezing: *the big freeze of 1953* 2. An official fixing of prices or wages at a certain level: *a freeze on spending*

freez-er (fri^y–zər) n. A refrigerated compartment or container for preserving perishable goods

freight (fre^yt) n. 1. The carrying of goods by ships, aircraft, trains, and other means of transport: *We are sending your shipment by freight this week.* 2. Goods carried in this way: *This freight is frag-ile; handle with care.* —freight adj. *a freight train*

freight-er (fre^yt–ər) n. A ship for carrying freight

fre-net-ic (frı–nɛt–ık) adj. Frantic; frenzied

fren-zied (frɛn-ziᵞd) adj. In a state of frenzy

fren-zy (frɛn-ziᵞ) n. **-zies** Violent excitement

fre-quen-cy (friᵞ–kwən–siᵞ) n. **-cies 1.** The rate of occurrences of a specified event within a given period of time: *The frequency of violent crimes in this area is increasing alarmingly.* **2.** A rate at which a sound wave or radio wave vibrates: *a frequency of 200,000 cycles per second*

fre-quent (friᵞ–kwɛnt/ –kwənt) adj. Happening often: *Accidents are frequent along this stretch of highway.* —opposite INFRE-QUENT —**frequently** adv.

fre-quent (friᵞ–kwɛnt/ friᵞ–kwɛnt) v. To go to a place or be with someone often: *John frequents this restaurant because he loves the food here.*

fres-co (frɛs–koʷ) n. A picture painted on a wall while the plaster is still damp

fresh (frɛʃ) adj. **1.** Esp. of food, recently produced or prepared and in good condition: *fresh fish/ fresh flowers/ fresh berries* —compare STALE **2.** Of water, not sea water; not salty; drinkable **3.** Of air, pure and invigorating **4.** Fairly strong; brisk: *a fresh breeze* **5.** New and different: *We need to take a fresh look at this subject.* **6.** Recently added or supplied: *fresh news from the battle front* **7.** Clear and healthy: *a fresh complexion* **8.** *infml.* Too forward in speech or behavior, esp. with someone of the opposite sex: *That man is trying to get fresh with my sister.* —**freshly** adv. —**freshness** n.

fresh-en (frɛʃ–ən) v. To make or become fresh

fresh-et (frɛʃ–ət) n. A flood caused by melting snow or heavy rain

fresh-man (frɛʃ–mən) n. **freshmen** (–mɛn) A student in his or her first year at high school, college, or university

fret (frɛt) v. **-tt-** To worry or be dissatisfied about small and unnecessary things: *Do not fret — it only leads to evil* (Psalm 37:8).

fri-ar (frai–ər) n. A man who is a member of certain Roman Catholic religious orders that combine monastic life with work in the outside world

fric-tion (frɪk–ʃən) n. **1.** The rubbing of two surfaces together **2.** The force that tries to keep one surface from sliding over another

surface **3.** Disagreement between people caused by differences of opinion or sets of values

Fri-day (frai–diᵞ/ –deᵞ) n. The sixth day of the week —see also GOOD FRIDAY

friend (frɛnd) n. **1.** A person known well and liked, but not related **2. make friends (with)** To form a friendship or friendships: *We've made a lot of friends since we moved here two months ago./ Anyone who chooses to be a friend of the world [likes the pleasures of this world] becomes an enemy of God* (James 4:4). **3.** One who supports or favors sthg.: *a friend of the arts*

friend-ly (frɛnd–liᵞ) adj. **-lier, -liest** Acting like a friend —**friendliness** n.

friend-ship (frɛnd–ʃɪp) n. The sharing of a friendly relationship; the good feeling and behavior of friends toward each other: *I really value my friendship with Elaine. We have been friends since high school./ Friendship with the world [riches, fame, lust, pleasures of the world] is hatred toward God* (James 4:4).

frig-ate (frɪg–ət) n. A small warship

fright (frait) n. **1.** Sudden fear: *shaking with fright at the horrible sight* **2.** Sthg. ugly or shocking: *He looked a fright coming up out of that filthy pit.*

fright-en (frait–ən) v. To cause someone to be filled with fear

fright-ened (frait–ənd) adj. In a condition of fear; afraid: *Do not fear what they [unbelievers] fear; do not be frightened* (1 Peter 3:14). —see also AFRAID

fright-ful (frait–fəl) adj. **1.** Terrifying: *The destruction caused by the earthquake was a frightful scene.* **2.** Startling **3.** Extreme

frig-id (frɪdʒ–əd) adj. **1.** Extremely cold **2.** Having an abnormal dislike of sexual activity —compare IMPOTENT —**fri-gid-i-ty** (frɪ–dʒɪd–ɪ–tiᵞ) n.

frill (frɪl) n. **1.** A gathered or pleated strip of trimming attached at an edge **2.** An unnecessary extra

fringe (frɪndʒ) n. **1.** A decorative border made of hanging threads or strips on the edge of a curtain, tablecloth, garment, etc. **2.** The outer edge or part **3. fringe benefit** Benefit given to an employee in addition to wages:

The salary for this job is low, but the fringe benefits make up for it

fringe v. **fringed, fringing** To act as an edge or border: *Roses fringed the garden path.*

frisk (frɪsk) v. To search someone for concealed weapons

frisk·y (frɪsk–iʸ) adj. **-ier, -iest** Lively; playful

frit·ter (frɪt–ər) v. To reduce or squander little by little: *He frittered away all his money on junk and entertainment.*

frit·ter n. A small deep-fried cake, often containing fruit

fri·vol·i·ty (frɪv–ɑl–ə–tiʸ) n. **1.** The act or state of being frivolous **2.** A frivolous act or thing

friv·o·lous (frɪv–ə–ləs) adj. Not sensible or serious; foolish: *Her husband objected to her wasteful spending on frivolous items and refused to give her any more money.* —**frivolously** adv. —**frivolousness** n.

friz·zy (frɪz–iʸ) adj. Of hair, massed in small curls

fro (froʷ) adv. **to and fro** Back and forth

frock (frɑk) n. *becoming rare* A woman's or girl's dress

frog (frɔg/ frɑg) n. A small, green animal with no tail and long hind legs adapted for leaping, which lives in water and on land, and makes a deep, rough, croaking sound —compare TOAD

frol·ic (frɑl–ɪk) v. To play in a lively, cheerful way —**frolicsome** adj.

from (frʌm) prep. **1.** Indicating the starting place or time: *Maria is from Mexico and Heidi is from Holland./ Our office is open from nine to five./ We took the freeway from San Diego to Los Angeles.* **2.** Given, sent, or communicated by: *a gift from my friend* **3.** Out of: *Bricks are made from clay.* **4.** Indicates separation: *Deliver us from the evil one* (Matthew 6:13). **5.** Indicates difference: *This car is different from that one in many ways.* **6.** Shows distance: *That village is ten miles from here.* **7.** Because of: *suffering from heart disease* **8.** In contrast with: *knowing right from wrong*

frond (frɑnd) n. A leaf-like part of a fan or palm tree

front (frʌnt) n. **1.** The most forward position or part; farthest from the back **2.** Outward appearance or show: *He put on a cheerful front* (=tried to look happy), *but I know he was very lonely without his best friend.* **3.** The foremost line of an army, at which fighting takes place in time of war: *sent to the front* **4.** An organized and active political movement: *the People's Front* **5.** A line separating two masses of air of different temperature: *A cold front is moving in from the west tonight.* **6.** *infml.* Sthg. used as a cover for hiding the real nature of a secret or unlawful activity **7.** In or at the part facing forwards: *The front of our house faces west.* **8.** The most forward or important position: *As you enter the lecture hall, please take seats in the front.* **9.** In the presence of: *You'll have to sign this document in front of two witnesses if you want it to be legal.*

front adj. **1.** The side of a building that usu. contains the main entrance **2.** The forward part or surface: *the front cover of the book*

fron·tier (frʌn–tɪər) n. **1.** A border between two countries **2.** The border between the area of a country that is settled and the part that is not **3.** The outer limits of knowledge or achievement: *the frontiers of space*

frost (frɔst) n. **1.** Freezing temperature: *Frost has killed much of the orange crop this year.* **2.** A white, powdery covering of small ice crystals on a cold surface

frost v. **1.** To become covered with frost **2.** To make a sheet of glass impossible to see through by giving it a rough, frost-like surface: *frosted glass* **3.** To decorate a cake with frosting

frost·y (frɔst–iʸ) adj. **-ier, -iest** Very cold: *She gave me a frosty glass of ice tea./ a frosty day/ fig. a frosty welcome* (=not friendly)

froth (frɔθ) n. Foam

froth v. To cause froth; to foam

froth·y (frɔθ–iʸ) adj. **-ier, -iest** Of, like, or covered with froth; foamy

frown (fraʊn) v. **1.** To wrinkle the forehead as in anger or disapproval: *His mother frowned as she handed her his report card.* **2. frown on/ upon sthg.** To disapprove of sthg.: *The school frowns on anything that looks like cheating.* —**frown** n. *Father wore a frown as he worked. I could tell he was worried.*

froze (froʷz) v. Past tense of **freeze**

fro·zen (froʷ–zən) v. Past part. of **freeze**

fru-gal (fru^w-gəl) adj. **1.** Careful and economical **2.** Scanty; costing little: *a frugal meal*

fruit (fru^wt) n. **1.** The fleshy, seed-bearing part of a plant or tree, esp. considered as food: *Peaches, plums, and grapes are fruit.* **2.** The effect or result of sthg.: *The fruit of the Spirit [Holy Spirit] is love, joy, peace, patience, kindness, goodness, faithfulness, gentleness and self-control (Galatians 5:22,23)./ I hope your plans will bear fruit.* (=have successful results)

fruit-ful (fru^wt-fəl) adj. Successful; effective; producing fruit: *a fruitful business trip* —opposite FRUITLESS —**fruitfully** adv. —**fruitfulness** n.

fru-i-tion (fru^w-ɪʃ-ən) n. The fulfillment of hopes; results attained by work

fruit-less (fru^wt-ləs) adj. Not successful; not producing results: *My trip to the store was fruitless. They were out of bread./ Have nothing to do with the fruitless deeds of darkness, but rather expose them (Ephesians 5:11).* —opposite FRUITFUL

frus-trate (frʌs-tre^yt) v. **-trated, -trating 1.** To prevent someone from doing sthg.: *The game was called off, frustrating our team's attempt to win the championship.* **2.** To cause someone to be discouraged or disappointed: *Being stuck in traffic on the freeway frustrates me.* —**frus-tra-tion** (frə-stre^y-ʃən) n.

fry (fraɪ) v. **fried, frying** To cook in a pan or on a griddle in hot fat or oil —see COOK

fry n. pl. **fries** A serving of sthg. fried

fry-er also **fri-er** (fraɪ-ər) n. **1.** A deep pot used for deep-frying **2.** A young chicken suitable for frying

fuch-sia (fyu^w-ʃə) n. **1.** A plant of the evening primrose family, with drooping flowers, usu. red or pink **2.** A vivid reddish purple

fudge (fʌdʒ) n. A soft candy, made of milk, sugar, butter, and chocolate or other flavorings

fu-el (fyu^w-əl) n. Material that is burned to produce heat or power: *This stove uses either coal or wood as fuel.*

fuel v. To supply with fuel: *fig. The demonstration was fueled by student unrest.*

fu-gi-tive (fyu^w-dʒə-tɪv) n. A person who is running away or escaping from the police, etc.: *a fugitive from the war* —**fugitive** adj.

–ful (–fʊl) weak (–fəl/ –fl) suffix **1.** Used to form an adjective meaning **full of**: *beautiful* **2.** Used to form an adjective meaning accustomed **to**: *forgetful*

ful-crum (fʊl-krəm) n. The point on which a lever turns

ful-fill (fʊl-fɪl) v. **1.** To perform or carry out a responsibility, promise, prophecy, etc.: *After his resurrection, Jesus said, "Everything must be fulfilled that is written about me in the Law of Moses, the Prophets, and the Psalms [the books of the Old Testament]" (Luke 24:44).* —see OLD TESTAMENT, NEW TESTAMENT, JESUS **2.** To answer a need, demand or purpose: *"Meals on Wheels" fulfills an important need, esp. for elderly people who cannot drive to the store.*

ful-fill-ment (fʊl-fɪl-mənt) n. **1.** Success: *His dreams have come to fulfillment after many years of hard work.* **2.** The act of meeting the requirements: *Love does no harm to its neighbor. Therefore love is the fulfillment of the law* (Romans 13:10).

full (fʊl) adj. **1.** Completely filled: *This box is full; there's no more room./ The earth will be full of the knowledge of the Lord as the waters cover the sea (Isaiah 11:9).* **2.** Having great numbers or amounts of: *The hillside was full of wildflowers.* **3.** *infml.* Having eaten or drunk enough; satisfied: *I wouldn't care for any dessert, thank you. I'm full.* **4.** Complete, esp. in detail: *Please leave your full name and address with my secretary.* **5. in full** Completely: *Your wages will be paid in full at the end of the month.* **6.** Being at the highest or greatest degree: *You have our full support./ full speed*

full-ness (fʊl-nəs) n. Completion; condition of containing all that is wanted or needed or possible: *For God was pleased to have all his fullness dwell in him. For in Christ all the fullness of the Deity dwells in bodily form, and you have been given fullness in Christ, who is the head over every power and authority (Colossians 1:19; 2:9,10).*

ful-ly (fʊl-i^y) adv. **1.** Completely; thoroughly: *I don't think John is fully able to handle the job of vice president of the company.* **2.** Quite; at least: *It's fully a year since she promised to return in six months.*

fum-ble (fʌm-bəl) v. **-bled, -bling** To touch or handle sthg. awkwardly

fumes (fyuʷmz) n. A usu. irritating smoke, vapor or gas: *gasoline fumes*

fu-mi-gate (fyuʷ-mə-geʸt) v. **-gated, -gating** To treat with fumes in order to disinfect or destroy pests: *Our house had to be fumigated to get rid of termites.* **—fu-mi-ga-tion** (fyuʷ-mə-geʸ-ʃən) n.

fun (fʌn) n. **1.** Sthg. that provides enjoyment: *The children had lots of fun playing with their little dog.* **2.** Amusement; enjoyment; pleasure **3. in fun** As a joke; not meant to be taken seriously: *All the teasing was only in fun.* **4. make fun of** To tease or ridicule, often unkindly

func-tion (fʌŋk-ʃən) v. To be in action; work: *We'll have to repair the copy machine. It doesn't seem to be functioning well.* **—functional** adj.

function n. **1.** Purpose: *What's the function of this new gadget?* **2.** A large and important gathering of people

fund (fʌnd) n. **1.** A source of supply **2.** A supply of money set apart for a special purpose: *college fund*

fund v. To provide money for sthg.: *This research is being funded by the Schwan Foundation.*

fun-da-men-tal (fən-də-men-təl) adj. Basic; elemental; being at the base, from which all else develops: *fundamental rules/fundamental changes/ The fundamental difference between us is our stand on foreign policy.* **—fundamentally** adv.

fundamental n. That which is foundational; sthg. without which a thing or system or religion would not be what it is: *Accepting the Bible as the inspired and inerrant word of God is a fundamental of the Christian faith.*

fun-da-men-tal-ism (fən-də-men-təl-ɪz-əm) n. A Protestant religious movement emphasizing the literal infallibility of the Holy Scriptures, holding the Bible to be the sole historical and prophetic authority, fundamental to Christian life and teaching

fu-ner-al (fyuʷ-nər-əl) n. A ceremony of burying or burning a dead person, usu. religious: *When my grandfather died, many people came to his funeral.* **—funeral** adj. *a funeral service*

fun-gus (fʌŋ-gəs) n. **-gi** (–dʒiʸ /–giʸ) or **-guses** Any of those plants without leaves, flowers, or green coloring matter, growing on other plants or decaying matter, including molds, rusts, mildews, mushrooms, etc.

fun-nel (fʌn-əl) n. **1.** A tube or pipe that is wide and round at the top and narrow at the bottom, used for pouring liquids or powders into a narrow opening **2.** A metal chimney on a steam engine or steamship, for letting out smoke

funnel v. To cause to move through, or as if through, a funnel: *The sheep funneled through the gate and out onto the hillsides.*

fun-ny (fʌn-iʸ) adj. **-nier, -niest 1.** Amusing; causing laughter: *He's a funny person; he says and does the funniest things.* **2.** Strange; difficult to explain or understand: *The car is making a funny noise. I think there's sthg. wrong!*

funny adv. In a strange or amusing way: *Dan has been acting rather funny lately.*

fur (fɜr) n. **1.** The soft, thick, fine hair covering the bodies of some types of animals **2.** The hair-covered skin of certain animals, such as foxes, rabbits, mink, beavers, etc., used for clothing **3.** A garment made of one or more of these: *Are you going to wear your fur tonight? It's very cold out.* **—fur** adj. *a fur coat*

fur-bish (fɜr-bɪʃ) v. To polish, clean, or renovate

fu-ri-ous (fyʊ-riʸ-əs) adj. **1.** Very angry; fierce; violent: *I'd be furious, too, if some careless driver backed into my car.* **—see** ANGRY **2.** Wild; unrestrained: *a furious battle* **—furiously** adv. **—furiousness** n.

furl (fɜrl) v. To roll up

fur-long (fɜr-lɔŋ) n. One-eighth mile

fur-lough (fɜr-loʷ) n. A leave of abscence from duty, esp. that granted to soldiers, civil servants, and others in overseas work

furlough v. **1.** To grant a furlough to sbdy. **2.** To lay off from work

fur-nace (fɜr-nəs) n. An enclosed structure in which heat is produced

fur-nish (fɜr-nɪʃ) v. **1.** To supply what is needed; to equip **2.** To put furniture in a room, building, etc.

fur-ni-ture (fɜr-nɪ-tʃər) n. All large or quite large movable articles, such as beds, chairs, tables, etc., that are placed in a house, office, hotel, etc. to make it suitable for the specified purpose

fur-or *AmE.* **furore** *BrE.* (fyʊər-ər) n. **1.** An outburst of enthusiasm **2.** An uproar **3.** A popular craze

fur-ri-er (fɜr-iʸ-ər) n. A person who deals in furs

fur-row (fɜr-oʷ) n. **1.** A long narrow trench cut in the earth as by a plow **2.** A groove resembling this: *a furrow in his brow*

fur-ry (fɜr-iʸ) adj. **1.** Like fur **2.** Covered with fur

fur-ther (fɜr-ðər) adv., adj. **1.** Also **farther** More distant in time or space: *Who can throw the ball further/ farther, you or your brother?* **2.** In addition; more: *Are there any further questions?* NOTE: **Farther** and **farthest** may be used only when speaking of real places and distances: *My house is farther/further than your house.*

further v. To help sthg. advance; help to succeed: *He feels that he needs to further his education if he is to succeed.*

fur-ther-ance (fɜr-ðər-əns) n. Advancement; development; continuation: *working for the furtherance of peace*

fur-ther-more (fɜr-ðər-mɔr) adv. In addition; besides: *I'm too tired to finish this book, and furthermore, it's not very interesting.*

fur-thest (fɜr-ðəst) also **farthest** adv., adj. Superlative of **far**; most far

fur-tive (fɜr-tɪv) adj. Sly; sneaky

fu-ry (fyʊ-riʸ) n. -ries **1.** Very great anger; rage: *She flew into a fury because her parents wouldn't let her go to the party.* **2.** Extreme fierceness: *The fury of the storm leveled almost everything on the island.*

fuse (fyuʷz) n. **1.** An electric safety device in which metal melts and breaks the circuit when the current becomes too strong, thus preventing damage: *I blew a fuse when I turned on the coffee pot and the oven at the same time.* **2.** A string-like, flammable material that is lighted at one end to carry a flame to an explosive charge at the other end, causing it to blow up

fu-se-lage (fyuʷ-sə-lɑʒ/-lɑdʒ) n. The body of an airplane

fu-sion (fyuʷ-ʒən) n. **1.** The act or process of uniting different things into one, by melting, etc. **2.** The union of atomic nuclei to form heavier nuclei, usu. with energy being released: *nuclear fusion*

fuss (fʌs) n. **1.** Unnecessary excitement or activity **2.** A display of worry about sthg. unimportant **3.** A vigorous protest —**fuss** v. *Stop fussing about things that aren't important.*

fus-sy (fʌs-iʸ) adj. **1.** Often fussing **2.** Fastidious **3.** Full of unnecessary detail or decoration

fu-tile (fyuʷ-təl) adj. Useless: *The rescue workers made a futile attempt to save his life. They were just too late.* —**fu-til-i-ty** (fyuʷ-tɪl-ə-tiʸ) n.

fu-ture (fyuʷ-tʃər) adj., n. **1.** Time that will come after the present: *We can plan for the future, but only God really knows the future.* **2.** A person's life, or events in one's life, in time yet to come: *She's looking forward to a future in medicine. (=a career in medicine)* **3.** *infml.* Possibility of success: *There's no future in this job./ There is a future for the man of peace* (Psalm 37:37).

fuzz (fʌz) n. **1.** Fine hairs, fibers, or particles of down, wool, etc. **2. the fuzz** *slang* A policeman or the police

fuzz-y (fʌz-iʸ) adj. -ier, -iest **1.** Not clear; indistinct; blurred: *My eyes are failing. Everything looks kind of fuzzy./ fig.: Plans for the celebration are still fuzzy.* **2.** Of cloth, a garment, etc., having a furry or soft, hairy surface —**fuzziness** n.

-fy (-faɪ) v. suffix To make, cause, or form into: *liquify/ justify*

G, g (dʒiʸ) n. The seventh letter of the English alphabet

gab (gæb) v. **-bb-** To talk idly or thoughtlessly; to chatter

gab-ar-dine (gæb-ər-diʸn) n. A firm durable twilled fabric of worsted cotton, wool, or spun rayon

gab-by (gæb-iʸ) adj. **-bier, -biest** Very talkative

ga-ble (geʸ-bəl) n. The triangular area of wall at the end of a building with a pitched roof

Ga-bri-el (geʸ-briʸ-əl) n. The archangel who appeared to Daniel in Old Testament times and who appeared to Zacharias, announcing the miraculous birth of John the Baptist and to the Virgin Mary, announcing that she would give birth to Jesus, saying, "The Holy Spirit will come upon you, and the power of the Most High will overshadow you. So the Holy One to be born will be called the Son of God" (Luke 1:35). —see JESUS

gadg-et (gædʒ-ət) n. A usu. small tool for a special purpose: *Her kitchen is full of gadgets for mixing things, opening bottles and cans, etc.*

gag (gæg) v. **-gg- 1.** To prevent someone from speaking by putting sthg. into his/ her mouth **2.** To choke: *She gagged on a piece of meat.*

gag n. **1.** Sthg. put into the mouth to prevent a person from talking or crying out **2.** A joke **3.** A hoax or trick

gai-e-ty (geʸ-ə-tiʸ) n. **-ties 1.** Fun, happiness, enjoyment **2.** Merrymaking or festivity

gai-ly (geʸ-liʸ) adv. **1.** In a happy, cheerful manner **2.** Colorfully: *gaily dressed/decorated*

gain (geʸn) v. **1.** To obtain sthg. necessary or wanted: *A kindhearted woman gains respect* (Proverbs 11:16). *Whoever heeds correction gains understanding* (Proverbs 15:32). **2.** To make a profit **3.** To increase in momentum: *The car gained speed as it went down the hill.* **4.** To increase in time: *My watch gained ten minutes (by moving too fast) overnight.* **5.** To win: *Our team gained the victory.* **6.** To earn: *A man of lowly spirit gains honor* (Proverbs 29:23). **7.** To acquire gradually: *He gained strength after his operation.*

gain n. An increase in wealth, amount,

weight, etc.: *Godliness with contentment is great gain* (1 Timothy 6:6). —opposite LOSS

gain-ful (geʸn-fəl) adj. Profitable

gait (geʸt) n. **1.** A manner of walking or running **2.** One of the ways in which a horse steps or runs

gal (gæl) n. AmE. infml. A girl or woman

gal. abbr. for gallon

ga-la (geʸ-lə/ gæ-lə/ gɑ-lə) n., adj. A time of rejoicing and merrymaking: *a gala occasion*

Ga-la-tians (gə-leʸ-ʃəns) n. (in the New Testament) St. Paul's letter to the people of Galatia, in which he emphasizes the fact that "a man is not justified [in God's sight] by observing the law, but by faith in Jesus Christ" (Galatians 2:16). —see JESUS

gal-ax-y (gæl-ək-siʸ) n. **1.** Any of the innumerable, large groupings of stars, typically containing millions to hundreds of billions of stars: *Our sun and solar system are part of the galaxy called the Milky Way.* **2.** A large group of famous, beautiful, well-dressed, impressive people: *a galaxy of movie stars* **3.** A group of new, beautiful, impressive things: *a galaxy of cars at the Auto Show*

gale (geʸl) n. A very strong wind

gall (gɔl) n. **1.** A bitter, greenish liquid which is produced in the liver and stored in the gall bladder **2.** Sthg. that is bitter or distasteful **3.** Rude boldness; impudence; audacity: *How is it that you have the gall to call me your friend after the way you treated me yesterday?*

gal-lant (gæl-ənt) adj. **1.** Brave: *a gallant leader* **2.** Splendid looking: *a gallant old ship*

gal-lant (gəl-ɑnt) n. A man who is very polite and attentive to ladies

gal-lant-ry (gæl-ən-triʸ) n. **-ries** Bravery: *He won a medal for gallantry.*

gall bladder (gɔl blæd-ər) n. An organ of the body in which gall is stored, attached to the liver

gal-le-on (gæl-iʸ-ən/ -yən) n. A large Spanish sailing vessel of the 15th and 16th centuries

gal-ler-y (gæl-ər-iʸ) n. **1.** A large room or building in which paintings, statues, etc. are displayed: *an art gallery* **2.** An upper floor of seats in a theater, esp. the top floor **3.** A long narrow room: *a shooting gallery*

gal-ley (gæl-iʸ) n. **1.** A ship's kitchen **2.** A long,

low ship with one deck, moved by oars and sails, used esp. in ancient and medieval times

gal·ling (gɔl–ɪŋ) adj. Vexing; humiliating

gal·li·vant (gæl–ə–vænt/ gæl–ə–**vænt**) v. To go around to one place after another, amusing oneself: *When are you going to stop gallivanting around and get down to business?*

gal·lon (gæl–ən) n. A measure of liquid which equals 4 quarts or 8 pints

gal·lop (gæl–əp) n. The fastest pace of a horse

gallop v. Of a horse or a horse and rider, to go at the fastest speed: *The horses galloped around the track.*

gal·lows (gæl–oᵂz) n. A framework with a suspended noose for the hanging of criminals

gall·stone (gɔl–stoᵂn) n. A small hard mass that sometimes forms in the gall bladder

ga·lore (gə–lɔr) adj. (immed. after a noun) Plenty; a great abundance: *There are restaurants galore in this city.*

ga·losh·es (gə–lɑʃ–əz) n. Large rubber shoes worn over ordinary shoes in wet weather

gal·va·nize also -**nise** *BrE.* (gæl–və–naɪz) v. -**nized**, -**nizing 1.** To coat iron or steel with zinc to prevent rusting **2.** To stimulate as by an electric shock **3.** To startle into sudden activity: *The threat of losing their land galvanized the family into action.*

gam·ble (gæm–bəl) v. -**bled**, -**bling** To bet; wager; play a game for money or sthg. else of value: *He gambled away all his money in Las Vegas.*

gamble n. A risky undertaking: *The operation on her brain may not succeed. It's a gamble whether she will live through it.* —**gambler** n.

game (geᵞm) n. **1.** Amusement: *a game of checkers/chess* **2.** A sport: *A game of football/tennis/golf* —see also GAMES, RECREATION **3.** Wild animals that are hunted for food and as a sport

game adj. Brave: *It's a difficult and dangerous climb up that cliff. Who's game?*

games (geᵞmz) n. A particular set of games and sports competitions: *The Olympic Games are held every four years.*

gam·ma glob·u·lin (gæm–ə glɑb–yə–lɪn) n. A form of protein found in blood plasma containing antibodies effective against measles, infectious hepatitis, etc.

gam·ut (gæm–ət) n. **1.** The whole range of sound that a voice or instrument can make **2.** The whole extent of anything

gan·der (gæn–dər) n. A male goose

gang (gæŋ) n. **1.** A group of people working or associated together, esp. criminals or young delinquents: *There are fights between rival gangs every night in many large cities.* **2.** A group of friends: *It would be nice to see some of the old gang again.*

gan·gling (gæŋ–glɪŋ) adj. Tall, thin, and awkward looking

gang·plank (gæŋ–plæŋk) n. A movable platform used when boarding or leaving a ship

gan·grene (gæŋ–griᵞn/ gæŋ–**griᵞn**) n. The death and decay of body tissue, usu. caused by a blockage of blood supply to that part —**gan·gre·nous** (gæŋ–grə–nəs) adj.

gang·ster (gæŋ–stər) n. A member of a gang of criminals

gang·way (gæŋ–weᵞ) n. **1.** A passageway, as through an obstructed area **2.** A gangplank —**gangway** interj. Clear the way!

gaol (dʒeᵞl) n. *BrE.* Jail —**gaoler** n. Jailer

gap (gæp) n. **1.** An open space: *a gap in the fence* **2.** A pass through the mountains **3.** A lapse in time: *a time gap* **4.** A blank: *He tried to relate what had happened over the past few years, but there were many gaps in his story.*

gape (geᵞp) v. **gaped**, **gaping 1.** To stare with open mouth, as if in wonder or surprise: *What are you gaping at?* **2.** To be wide open

gape n. An open-mouthed stare

ga·rage (gə–rɑdʒ/ gə–**rɑʒ**) n. **1.** A small building, sometimes attached to a house, in which motor cars may be kept **2.** A place where cars can be repaired

garb (gɑrb) n. A mode of dress, esp. a distinctive way of dressing

garb v. To dress or clothe

gar·bage (gɑr–bɪdʒ) n. **1.** Food waste **2.** Waste material; rubbish

gar·ble (gɑr–bəl) v. -**bled**, -**bling** To distort so as to be misleading or unintelligible

gar·den (gɑrd–ən) n. **1.** A plot of land on which flowers and vegetables may be grown **2.** A public park with flowers, grass,

paths, and seats

garden v. To work in a garden, often as a hobby: *My mother enjoys gardening.* —**gardener** n.

gar-de-ni-a (gɑr–diᵧn–yə/ –diᵧ–niᵧ–ə) n. **1.** A tree or shrub with fragrant white or yellow flowers **2.** The flowers of this plant

gar-gle (gɑr–gəl) v. **-gled, -gling** To wash or rinse the inside of the throat with a soothing or germ-killing liquid

gar-goyle (gɑr–gɔil) n. A fancy, carved spout on a roof or eaves of a building, shaped in the form of a very ugly human or animal figure, used to carry rain water away from the edge of the building

gar-ish (geər–ıʃ/gær–) adj. Tasteless; gaudy; excessively ornate

gar-land (gɑr–lənd) n. Flowers or leaves woven or tied in a circle: *The girls on the island all wore garlands of flowers on their heads.*

gar-lic (gɑr–lık) n. An onion-like plant with a strong smell or taste, used in cooking

gar-ment (gɑr–mənt) n. An article of clothing: *Wash this garment carefully.*

gar-net (gɑr–nət) n. A dark red mineral used for fine jewelry

gar-nish (gɑr–nıʃ) v. To decorate (esp. food for the table)

garnish n. Sthg. used for garnishing

gar-ri-son (geər–ə–sən) n. **1.** Troops that are stationed at a fort or in a town to defend it **2.** The building or fort they occupy

garrison v. To furnish a town with troops to protect it: *They have garrisoned the city.*

gar-ru-lous (geər–ə–ləs/ geər–yə–ləs) adj. Fond of talking; habitually talking about unimportant things

gar-ter (gɑrt–ər) n. An elastic band for holding up a stocking

gar-ter snake (gɑrt–ər sneᵧk) n. A harmless small green or brown snake with three yellow or white stripes on its back from head to tail

gas (gæs) n. **gases 1.** A substance like air: *There are several kinds of gases in the air.* **2.** A substance of this type which is burned in many homes for heating and cooking **3.** *AmE.* Gasoline **4.** A poisonous or irritating gas used in warfare, etc.: *They used tear gas to break up*

the riot. **5.** A substance, usu. nitrous oxide, used by dentists as an anaesthetic

gas v. -ss- To poison with gas

gas-e-ous (gæ–ʃəs) adj. Of or like gas

gash (gæʃ) v. To make a deep cut in

gash n. A deep, open cut or wound: *How did you get that gash in your leg?*

gas-ket (gæs–kət) n. A flat sheet or ring of rubber (or other soft material) used for sealing a joint between metal surfaces in order to prevent gas, steam, or liquid from entering or escaping

gas-o-line (gæs–ə–liᵧn) n. *BrE.* **petrol** A liquid obtained from petroleum, used esp. as a fuel for motor vehicles: *How many miles does your car get per gallon of gasoline?*

gasp (gæsp) v. **1.** To struggle to get one's breath: *He came out of the water gasping for air.* **2.** To draw in the breath sharply, esp. because of surprise: *Lois gasped in surprise at the shocking news.*

gasp n. The sound made by suddenly breathing in, because of surprise or sudden pain: *a gasp of fear*

gas-sy (gæs–iᵧ) adj. **-sier, -siest** Full of or resembling gas

gas-tric (gæs–trık) adj. Of the stomach

gate (geᵧt) n. A movable barrier serving as a door in a wall or fence; a means of entrance or exit: *Please close the garden gate./ spir. Jesus said, "I am the gate [to eternal life]; whoever enters through me will be saved"* (John 10:9).

gate-way (geᵧt–weᵧ) n. **1.** That which gives access **2.** Entrance closed by a gate

gath-er (gæ–ðər) v. **1.** To come together in one place: *They gathered around the camp fire and sang several songs./ When the Son of Man [Jesus] comes in his glory, and all the angels with him... all the nations will be gathered before him* (Matthew 25:31,32). *And he will send his angels and gather his elect from the four winds, from the ends of the earth to the ends of the heavens* (Mark 13:27). **2.** To obtain or increase a little bit at a time: *The plane gathered speed as it went down the runway.* **3.** To collect: *He who gathers crops in summer is a wise son* (Proverbs 10:5).

gath-er-ing (gæ–ðər–ıŋ) n. **1.** A meeting **2.** A group: *There was quite a gathering at the scene*

of the accident.

gaud-y (gɔd–iʸ) adj. **-ier, -iest** Too brightly colored and/ or having too much decoration —**gaudily** adv. —**gaudiness** n.

gauge also **gage** *AmE.* (geʸdʒ) n. **1.** An instrument for measuring amount, size, etc., such as the amount of air in a tire or the amount of rainfall **2.** A standard measure of weight, fineness of textile, diameter of bullets, etc., to which objects can be compared

gauge v. **gauged, gauging 1.** To measure the size or quantity of sthg. **2.** To estimate or judge the worth or meaning of someone's actions

gaunt (gɔnt) adj. **1.** Thin and bony; haggard, as from great hunger; emaciated **2.** Bleak and desolate

gaunt-let (gɔnt–lət) n. **1.** Two rows of men armed with clubs, paddles, etc. to strike a man forced to run between them **2. run the gauntlet (a)** To undergo this punishment **(b)** To face an ordeal in which blows, criticism, etc. come from all sides at once **3. throw down the gauntlet** To challenge someone to a fight

gauze (gɔz) n. A thin fabric, sometimes used to cover wounds, or as a curtain material

gave (geʸv) v. Past tense of **give**

gav-el (gæv–əl) n. The mallet used by a presiding officer to signal for attention or order

gawk (gɔk) v. To stare stupidly

gawk-y (gɔk–iʸ) adj. **-ier, -iest** Of a person, looking awkward or clumsy

gay (geʸ) adj. **1.** Cheerful; happy **2.** Bright or attractive

gay n., adj. Homosexual

gaze (geʸz) v. **-gazed, -gazing** To look steadily at sthg. for quite some time: *She stood there gazing at the stars.*

gaze n. A steady look: *She turned her gaze from one fabulous sight to another.*

ga-ze-bo (gə–ziʸ–boʷ /–zeʸ–) n. *pl.* **-bos** or **-boes** A small open-sided roofed structure, often in a park or garden

ga-zelle (gə–zɛl) n. A small antelope known for its graceful movements and speed

ga-zette (gə–zɛt) n. **1.** A newspaper **2.** A government journal

gaz-et-teer (gæz–ə–tɪər) n. **1.** A geographical dictionary **2.** *Archaic* A journalist

gear (gɪər) n. **1.** A toothed wheel that interlocks with another toothed wheel, allowing power to be passed from one part to another, esp. from the engine of a car to its wheels: *He shifted [changed] gears to make the car go up the steep hill.* **2.** A mechanism that performs a specific function: *the steering gear/ the landing gear of an airplane* **3.** Things collected together for a particular purpose: *fishing gear*

gear v. **gear sthg. to sthg.** To cause one thing to depend on or be fixed in relation to sthg. else: *Education should be geared to people's needs and abilities.*

gear-shift (gɪər–ʃɪft) n. A lever for shifting from one gear to another, as in an automobile or truck

gear up To put into proper adjustment or working order

geese (giʸs) n. *pl.* of **goose**

Gei-ger counter (gaɪ–gər kaʊn–tər) n. A device for finding and measuring radioactivity

gel (dʒɛl) n. Semi-solid jelly-like material: *bath-gel*

gel v. **gelled, gelling** To change into a gel

gel-a-tin (dʒɛl–ə–tən) n. A clear, tasteless, jelly-like substance made from hooves, bones, skins, and connective tissues, used in food, glues, drugs, etc.

ge-lat-i-nous (dʒɛ–læt–ə–nəs) adj. Like jelly

gem (dʒɛm) n. **1.** A precious stone, esp. when cut into a particular shape **2.** *fig.* Someone or sthg. of special value: *She's a real gem.*

gem-stone (dʒɛm–stoʷn) n. A precious stone before it is cut and polished

gen-der (dʒɛn–dər) n. **1.** (in grammar) The class in which a noun or pronoun is placed — masculine, feminine, or neuter: *The German language has three genders.* **2.** A person's sex

gene (dʒiʸn) n. The basic unit of heredity, responsible for passing on certain characteristics from parents to their offspring —**genet-ic** (dʒə–nɛt–ɪk) adj.

ge-ne-al-o-gy (dʒiʸ–niʸ–al–ə–dʒiʸ) n. **-gies 1.** A history of families from generation to generation **2.** The science or study of family an-

cestries 3. A history or account of one's ancestry —ge-ne-a-log-i-cal (dʒiˠ–niˠ–ə–ladʒ-ɪ-
kəl) adj. —genealogically adv.

gen-er-a (dʒɛn–ər–ə) n. pl. of genus

gen-er-al (dʒɛn–ə–rəl) n. 1. An officer of very
high rank in an army or air force 2. in general, as a general rule Usually; in most cases:
*In general, people need about eight hours of
sleep every night.* —compare GENERALLY

general adj. 1. Concerning everybody or
most people: *the general feeling/opinion/
attitude* 2. Not limited to one subject: *general
education* 3. Not detailed; describing only
the main points: *Give me a general idea of
what it looks like.* 4. Chief; head of the department or agency: *Postmaster-general*

gen-er-al-i-ty (dʒɛn–ə–ræl–ə–tiˠ) n. -ties 1. The
quality of being general 2. A general statement, lacking in details

gen-er-al-ize also -ise BrE. (dʒɛn–ər–əl–aɪz) v.
-ized, -izing 1. To draw a general conclusion from particular instances 2. To speak in
generalities —gen-er-al-i-za-tion *also BrE.*
-sa-tion (dʒɛn–ər–əl–ɪ–zeˠ–ʃən) n.

gen-er-al-ly (dʒɛn–ə–rəl–iˠ) adv. 1. Usually:
We generally go to bed about 11 p.m. 2. By most
people: *The plan has generally been accepted.*

gen-er-ate (dʒɛn–ə–reˠt) v. -ated, -ating To
bring into existence; to produce: *This dyna-
mo generates a lot of electricity.*

gen-er-a-tion (dʒɛn–ə–reˠ–ʃən) n. 1. A single
stage in the descent of a family: *Here's a family photograph showing four generations — my
grandparents, my parents, myself and my son.*
2. All people of about the same age: *the
younger generation* 3. The act or action of
generating: *Falling water is used for the generation of electricity.*

gen-er-a-tor (dʒɛn–ə–reˠt–ər) n. 1. A machine
that generates electricity, gas, etc. 2. A person or thing that generates: *a generator of
fresh ideas*

ge-ner-ic (dʒə–neər–ɪk) adj. 1. Not specific;
general 2. Not protected by a trademark: *a
generic drug* 3. Of or relating to an entire ge-
nus or group

gen-er-ous (dʒɛn–ər–əs) adj. 1. Unselfish;
ready to give money, help, kindness, etc.: *A
generous man will prosper; he who refreshes
others will himself be refreshed* (Proverbs
11:25). *A generous man will himself be blessed,
for he shares his food with the hungry* (Proverbs 22:9). 2. Larger, kinder, than usual: *a
generous gift* —gen-er-os-i-ty (dʒɛn–ər–as–ə–
tiˠ) n. —gen-er-ous-ly (dʒɛn–ər–əs–liˠ) adv.

gen-e-sis (dʒɛn–ə–səs) n. geneses 1. The act or
mode of beginning 2. Origin

Gen-e-sis (dʒɛn–ə–səs) n. The first book of the
Bible, in which the story of the beginning of
the world is told, along with man's fall into
sin, the first promise of a Savior, the Great
Flood resulting from man's wickedness,
and which covered the whole earth, sparing only Noah and his family, the multipli-
cation of languages due to man's pride and
disobedience, the call of Abraham, further
promises of a Savior, and much more —see
OLD TESTAMENT, BIBLE

ge-net-ic (dʒə–nɛt–ɪk) adj. 1. Of or relating to
genetics or genes 2. Inherited: *a genetic defect*

ge-net-ics (dʒə–nɛt–ɪks) n. The scientific study
of heredity

ge-nial (dʒiˠ–nyəl) adj. 1. Kindly; pleasant;
cheerful: *a genial personality* 2. Mild; pleasant: *a genial climate* —ge-ni-al-i-ty (dʒiˠ–niˠ–
æl–ə–tiˠ) n. —genially adv.

ge-nie (dʒiˠ–niˠ) n. A mythical magical spirit
in Arab folklore capable of influencing
mankind for good or evil

gen-i-tal (dʒɛn–ə–təl) adj. Of or relating to reproduction or the sexual organs

gen-i-tals (dʒɛn–ə–təlz) n. pl. The external sex
organs of animals and people

gen-i-tive (dʒɛn–ə–tɪv) adj. Of the grammatical case showing possession or origin: *In the
sentence, "Mary's purse is on the table,"
"Mary's" is in the genitive case.*

genitive n. The possessive case

ge-nius (dʒiˠ–n–yəs/ dʒiˠ–niˠ–əs) n. 1. A person
having extraordinary intellectual power 2.
A special ability: *a genius for mathematics*

gen-o-cide (dʒɛn–ə–saɪd) n. The deliberate ex-
termination of a whole race of people

–gen-ous (–dʒə–nəs) suffix of adjectives 1.
Generating; yielding 2. Produced or generated by

gen-re (ʒan–reˠ) n. A kind or type as of works
of art, literature, etc.

gen-teel (dʒɛn–tiᵞl) adj. **1.** Polite and refined in manner **2.** Elegant; fashionable **3.** Trying to seem refined, but in an artificial way

Gen-tile (dʒɛn–taɪl) n. Anyone who is not a Jew: *He [God] redeemed us in order that the blessing given to Abraham might come to the Gentiles through Christ Jesus, so that by faith we might receive the promise of the Spirit* (Galatians 3:14). *...so that the Gentiles might glorify God for his mercy* (Romans 15:9). *...through the gospel [the Good News about Jesus] the Gentiles are heirs together with Israel, members together of one body, and sharers together in the promise in Christ Jesus* (Ephesians 3:6).

gen-tle (dʒɛn–təl) adj. **1.** Considerate; kind: *Be completely humble and gentle* (Ephesians 4:2). *Wives... your beauty should not come from outward adornment... Instead it should be that of your inner self, the unfading beauty of a gentle and quiet spirit, which is of great worth in God's sight* (1 Peter 3:3,4). **2.** Not rough or violent in manner or movement; soft: *a gentle breeze* **3.** Gradual: *a gentle slope* (=not steep) **4.** Easily managed or handled: *This horse is very gentle.* —**gentleness** n. *Writing to the Christians at Colosse, St.Paul says, "Clothe yourselves with compassion, kindness, humility, gentleness and patience"* (Colossians 3:12). —**gently** adv.

gen-tle-man (dʒɛn–təl–mən) n. -men **1.** A polite way of referring to men **2.** A polite man; one who behaves well towards others and who can be trusted to act honorably

gen-u-ine (dʒɛn–yə–wən) adj. **1.** Real; actually what it seems to be; not artificial: *This book cover is genuine leather.* —opposite FAKE **2.** Of people or feelings, sincere; frank, not pretended: *Writing to Christians, some of whom were suffering grief in all kinds of trials, the Apostle Peter says, "These [trials] have come so that your faith of greater worth than gold... may be proved genuine and may result in praise, glory and honor when Jesus Christ is revealed"* (1 Peter 1:6,7). —**genuinely** adv. —**genuineness** n.

ge-nus (dʒiᵞ–nəs) n. *pl.* **genera** (dʒɛn–ər–ə) **1.** A group of animals or plants with common characteristics, usu. containing several species **2.** *infml.* A kind or sort

ge-o- (dʒiᵞ–oʷ– /–ə–) prefix Earth; ground; soil: *geophysics*

ge-og-ra-pher (dʒiᵞ–ɑg–rə–fər) n. A person who is an expert in the studying and teaching of geography

ge-og-ra-phy (dʒiᵞ–ɑg–rə–fiᵞ) n. -phies The study of the countries of the world and of the people, cities, climate, physical features, crops, natural resources, industries, etc. —**ge-o-graph-ic** (dʒiᵞ–ə–græf–ɪk) adj. —**ge-o-graph-i-cal** (dʒiᵞ–ə–græ–fɪ–kəl) adj. —**geographically** adj.

ge-ol-o-gist (dʒiᵞ–ɑl–ə–dʒɪst) n. An expert in geology

ge-ol-o-gy (dʒiᵞ–ɑl–ə–dʒiᵞ) n. The scientific study of the earth's rocks and soil —**ge-o-log-ic** (dʒiᵞ–ə–lɑdʒ–ɪk) or **ge-o-log-i-cal** (dʒiᵞ–ə–lɑdʒ–ɪ–kəl) adj.

ge-om-e-try (dʒiᵞ–ɑm–ə–triᵞ) n. The branch of mathematics dealing with the relations, properties, and measurements of solids, surfaces, lines, and angles —**ge-o-met-ric** (dʒiᵞ–ə–mɛ–trɪk) adj. —**geometrical** adj. —**geometrically** adv.

ge-o-ther-mal (dʒiᵞ–oʷ–θɜr–məl) adj. Pertaining to heat produced inside the earth

ge-ra-ni-um (dʒə–reᵞ–niᵞ–əm) n. A garden plant, usu. having red or pink flowers

ger-bil (dʒɜr–bəl) n. A small desert rodent similar to a mouse but with long hind legs for leaping

ger-i-at-rics (dʒɛər–iᵞ–æt–rɪks) n. The branch of medicine that deals with the diseases and care of elderly people

germ (dʒɜrm) n. **1.** A very tiny living thing which cannot be seen but may live on food or in the body, causing disease —compare BACTERIA **2.** A beginning point, esp. of an idea

ger-mane (dʒɜr–meᵞn) adj. Relevant; of importance

ger-mi-cide (dʒɜr–mə–saɪd) n. A substance that kills germs

ger-mi-nate (dʒɜrm–ə–neᵞt) v. -nated, -nating Of a seed, to start growing; sprout —**ger-mi-na-tion** (dʒɜrm–ə–neᵞ–ʃən) n.

ger-on-tol-o-gist (dʒɛər–ən–tɑl–ə–dʒəst) n. An expert in gerontology

ger-on-tol-o-gy (dʒɛər–ən–tɑl–ə–dʒiᵞ) n. The

scientific study of the process of aging and of the special problems of old people

ger-und (dʒeər–ənd) n. The form of a verb ending in -ing when used as a noun: *My warning went unheeded.*

ges-ta-tion (dʒes–teʸ–ʃən) n. **1.** The process of carrying or being carried in the womb; pregnancy **2.** The time of this, from conception until birth

ges-tic-u-late (dʒes–tɪk–yə–leʸt) v. -lated, -lating To wave one's hands and arms about, e.g. when speaking or to express excitement or emotion

ges-ture (dʒes–tʃər) n. **1.** A movement of the head, hands, etc. to express a certain meaning, feeling, or emotion: *He uses a lot of gestures when he talks.* **2.** An action which is done to express one's feelings: *Mary baked us some cookies as a gesture of friendship.*

gesture v. -tured, -turing To make a gesture

get (get) v. **got** (gat), **got** or **gotten 1.** To receive: *I got a package from home.* **2.** To become: *It's getting hot in here.* **3.** To arrive: *When will he get here?* **4.** To cause to be in a certain condition: *I can't get the motor started.* **5.** To persuade: *Let's get Jim to join the club.* **6.** To hear: *I didn't get your name.* **7.** To communicate with: *I couldn't get him on the phone.* **8.** To receive as punishment: *He got a ten-year jail sentence.* **9.** To take vengeance on: *He got even with John.* **10.** To suffer: *Her arm got burned on the iron.* **11.** To be permitted: *We get to go to the game.* **12.** To prepare: *to get dinner* **13.** To catch an illness: *John got the mumps.* **14.** To understand: *Do you get what I mean?* **15.** To annoy: *Her rotten attitude really gets me.* **16.** To hit: *One shot got him in the leg.* **17.** To experience sthg.: *Jimmy got his hand stuck in the cookie jar.* **18.** To fetch: *Go get the ball.* **19.** To buy: *Go get some bread and milk.* **20.** To cause to move: *Get that cat out of here.* **21.** To have an obligation: *I've got to do it.* **22. get across** To make sthg. clear or understandable **23. get along (a)** Of people, to leave: *I have to be getting along now.* **(b)** To continue: *We can get along without your help.* **(c)** To have a friendly relationship: *How do you get along with your neighbors?* **24. get around (a)** To avoid: *How does he get around paying his taxes?* **(b)** To

move about: *How do you get around town without a car?* **25. get at** To reach: *Put that machine where the children can't get at it.* **26. get away** To escape: *The thief got away in a black car.* **27. get away with sthg.** To do sthg. bad and escape punishment: *He got away with murder.* **28. get back** To return: *When did you get back from your trip?* **29. get back at someone** To hurt someone in return for a wrong done to oneself: *Bill started an ugly rumor about Bob to get back at him for his insults.* **30. get by (a)** To exist; survive: *How can she get by on such a small income?* **(b)** To be acceptable, but just barely: *Your work will get by for now, but you must improve if you want to keep this job.* **31. get going** To start: *Get going, or you'll miss the bus.* **32. get into (a)** To enter: *They got into the car.* **(b)** To become involved: *How did I get into this mess?* **33. get off (a)** To quit work at the end of the day: *He gets off at five o'clock.* **(b)** Dismount: *He got off his bike.* **(c)** To leave a public vehicle: *He got off the bus.* **(d)** To receive less punishment than deserved or expected: *He should have been expelled but he got off with just a warning.* **34. get on (a)** To go aboard: *She got on the plane.* **(b)** To mount: *He got on the horse.* **(c)** To begin or continue: *Let's get on with the job.* **35. get out (a)** Exit; leave: *She got out of the car.* **(b)** To produce: *We got a lot of work out today.* **(c)** To gain from: *Why do you smoke? What do you get out of it?* **36. get out of (a)** To be excused from a responsibility: *How did she get out of that assignment?* **(b)** To escape: *He got out of jail.* **37. get onto (sbdy./ sthg.)** To find out about someone's deception: *He fooled people for years before they got onto him.* **38. get over (a)** To reach the end of: *He got over his illness sooner than expected?* **(b)** To cross: *How are we going to get over the stream?* **39. get over sbdy./ sthg.** To be surprised at: *I can't get over how much you've grown.* **40. get there** To make progress: *We're getting there.* **41. (a) get through** To make contact by telephone: *I tried to call you (on the phone), but I couldn't get through.* **(b)** To cause to be understood by (someone): *I can't get (it) through to him that he must train harder if he expects to win.* **(c)** To finish: *When will you get*

through with your work? (d) To come successfully to the end of: *We got through the storm with only minor damage.* (e) To pass (an examination): *I'll never get through this exam.* (f) To be approved: *This bill will never get through the senate.* 42. **get together** To have a discussion, meeting or party: *When can we get together?* 43. **get up** (a) To rise from bed: *He gets up every morning at six o'clock.* (b) To increase the amount of: *get up steam/speed*

get-a-way (gĕt–ə–weᵞ) n. An escape: *They made a quick getaway.*

get-to-geth-er (gĕt–tə–gĕ–ðər) n. A friendly, informal social gathering: *a friendly get-together of former classmates*

gey-ser (gaɪ–zər) n. An underground spring that produces and sends out hot water and steam: *There are 10,000 geysers in Yellowstone National Park in Wyoming.*

ghast-ly (gæst–liᵞ) adj. **-lier, -liest 1.** Very bad; ugly: *a ghastly mistake* **2.** Horrible: *a ghastly murder* **3.** Very upset: *I felt ghastly after our argument last night.* **4.** Very pale: *His face was a ghastly white as he stood there, petrified with fear.*

ghat (gŏt/ gät) n. **1.** In India, a stairway leading down to a river **2.** A mountain pass **3.** A range of mountains

ghee (giᵞ) n. In India, a butter-like substance, usu. made from buffalo milk

gher-kin (gɜr–kɪn) n. A small cucumber, esp. one used for pickling

ghet-to (gĕt–oᵂ) n. **-tos** A part of a city in which an ethnic or economically depressed minority group lives and is restricted by poverty, social pressures, etc.

ghost (goᵂst) n. **1.** The seat of life; the soul: *He gave up the ghost.* (=he died) **2.** The soul of a dead person believed by some to be living nearby, but in the unseen world, or even to appear in bodily form to living people from time to time: *When Jesus appeared to his disciples the first time after his resurrection, the disciples thought that they were seeing a ghost. But Jesus said to them, "It is I myself! Touch me and see; a ghost does not have flesh and bones, as you see me have"* (Luke 24:37,39). **3. a ghost of a chance** The slightest: *She hasn't a ghost of a chance of passing the final exam.*

ghost-ly (goᵂst–liᵞ) adj. Like a ghost, especially having a faint or uncertain color and shape

ghost-writer (goᵂst–raɪt–ər) n. A person who writes for another person and gives that person credit for it

ghoul (guᵂl) n. **1.** A person who robs graves and feeds on corpses **2.** One who takes pleasure in disgusting and revolting things —**ghoulish** adj.

GI (dʒiᵞ aɪ) n. **GIs** or **GI's** *Abbr.* for **government issue** An enlisted person in any of the US armed forces

gi-ant (dʒaɪ–ənt) n. **1.** A huge person with great strength: *Goliath was a giant, over nine feet tall.* **2.** A person of very great ability or importance: *Edison is a giant among inventors.* **3.** Very large: *a giant-sized problem/ headache/ape/shark*

gib-ber (dʒɪb–ər) v. To speak rapidly and unintelligibly

gib-ber-ish (dʒɪb–ər–ɪʃ) n. Rapid, unintelligible talk; nonsense

gib-bon (gɪb–ən) n. A small, slender ape of southern Asia and the East Indies

gibe (dʒaɪb) v. **gibed, gibing** To ridicule; to utter jeers or derisive remarks; to taunt —**gibe** n. A jeer

gid-dy (gɪd–iᵞ) adj. **-dier, -diest 1.** Silly; not serious **2.** Dizzy **3.** Causing dizziness —**giddily** adv. —**giddiness** n.

gift (gɪft) n. **1.** Sthg. given; a present: *The wages of sin is death, but the gift of God is eternal life through Jesus Christ our Lord* (Romans 6:23). **2.** A natural ability: *a gift of art/music/ writing/Every good and perfect gift is from above, coming down from [God] the Father...* (James 1:17).

gift-ed (gɪf–təd) adj. Having one or more special abilities (talents): *a gifted artist*

gi-gan-tic (dʒaɪ–gæn–tɪk) adj. Very large; huge

gig-gle (gɪ–gəl) v. **-gled, -gling** To laugh in a silly way —**giggle** n. *She has a funny giggle.*

gig-o-lo (dʒɪg–ə–loᵂ) n. A man who is paid by a woman to be her escort

Gi-la mon-ster (hiᵞ–lə mɑn–stər) n. A poisonous lizard of the southwestern US

gild (gɪld) v. **-gilded** or **gilt, gilding** To cover with gold or sthg. similar

gill (gɪl) n. **1.** One of the openings on the side of a fish's head through which it breathes

gill n. A liquid measure equal to 1/4 pint

gim-mick (gɪm–ɪk) n. A trick or device used for attracting notice or publicity or for raising funds: *Advertisers often use gimmicks to promote a firm's products.*

gin (dʒɪn) n. **1.** A colorless alcoholic liquor distilled from grain **2.** A machine for removing seeds from cotton fibers **3. gin rummy** A card game in which a player may win by matching all his cards or may end the game by placing his cards face up on the table for scoring

gin-ger (dʒɪn–dʒər) n. **1.** The hot-tasting root of a tropical plant **2.** The plant itself **3.** A light reddish color: *People call her 'Ginger' because of the color of her hair and because she is so lively.* **4.** Liveliness

gin-ger ale (dʒɪn–dʒər eʸl) n. A carbonated soft drink flavored with ginger

gin-ger-bread (dʒɪn–dʒər–brɛd) n. A cake flavored with ginger

gin-ger-ly (dʒɪn–dʒər–liʸ) adj., adv. Cautiously

ging-ham (gɪŋ–əm) n. A cotton fabric with a woven, often checked pattern

gin-gi-vi-tis (dʒɪn–dʒə–vaɪ–təs) n. Inflammation of the gums

gin-seng (dʒɪn–səŋ) n. **1.** A perennial plant of China and Korea **2.** The aromatic root of this plant, used in medicinal preparation

gi-raffe (dʒə–ræf) n. A long-necked, long-legged African animal with a tan coat and brown blotches

gird (gɜrd) v. To encircle or attach with a belt or metal band, e.g.: *The wooden crate was girded with steel bands.*

gird-er (gɜrd–ər) n. A beam that supports part of a building or a bridge

gir-dle (gɜr–dəl) n. **1.** A belt or cord that goes around sthg. (usu. the waist) **2.** A supporting undergarment worn over the waist and hips

girl (gɜrl) n. A young female person

girth (gɜrθ) n. **1.** The distance around sthg. **2.** The strap that holds a saddle on a horse

gist (dʒɪst) n. The main point or the general idea of sthg.: *Just give me the gist of what he said, no details.*

give (gɪv) v. **gave** (geʸv), **given** (gɪv–ən), **giving 1.** To cause someone to have or receive sthg.: *He gave her some flowers and a box of candy for her birthday./ God so loved the world that he gave his one and only Son that whoever believes in him will not perish but have eternal life* (John 3:16). *It is more blessed to give than to receive* (Acts 20:35). **2.** To allow to have: *Give him 24 hours and he'll be ready to go.* **3.** To do sthg. to someone or sthg.: *Give the car a push./ He gave her a kiss.* **4.** To produce: *Loud noise gives me a headache.* **5.** To supply with: *The sun gives light.* **6.** To devote oneself to doing sthg.: *He gives much of his time to entertaining the troops.* **7.** To perform publicly: *They gave a concert.* **8.** To pay: *How much did you give for that hat?* **9.** To allow sthg.: *to give permission* **10.** To say: *You shall not give false testimony* (Exodus 20:16). *Give thanks to the Lord, for he is good, for his mercy endures forever* (Psalm 136:1). **11.** To attribute or ascribe: *Let them give glory to the Lord* (Isaiah 42:12). **12.** To cause to believe sthg.: *I was given to understand that he was going on vacation.* **13.** To furnish or offer: *to give evidence* **14.** To impart: *to give advice* **15.** To hand to someone: *Can you give me a match?* **16.** To relinquish or sacrifice: *The Son of Man [Jesus] did not come to be served, but to serve, and to give his life as a ransom for many* (Matthew 20:28). **17. give one's word** To promise: *I give you my word, I'll pay you back tomorrow.* **18. give in** To yield: *Don't give in to him.* **19. give up (a)** To stop doing sthg.: *He gave up smoking.* **(b)** To stop trying to guess the answer: *I give up. What's the answer?* **(c)** To consider to be: *The soldiers that were missing in action were given up for dead.* **(d)** To surrender: *He gave himself up to the police.* **(e)** To quit trying: *She gave up in despair.*

giz-zard (gɪz–ərd) n. The second stomach of a bird, for crushing and grinding food

gla-cial (gleʸ–ʃəl) adj. **1.** Icy cold: *glacial winds* **2.** Of or from glaciers or other ice

gla-cier (gleʸ–ʃər) n. A large body of ice formed from the snow on mountains, which moves very slowly down a slope

glad (glæd) adj. **gladder, gladdest** Pleased and happy: *The Lord reigns; let the earth be*

glad (Psalm 97:1). —**gladness** n. *Serve the Lord with gladness* (Psalm 100:2).

glad-den (**glæd**–ən) v. To make glad

glade (gleᵞd) n. An open space in a forest

glad-i-a-tor (**glæd**–iᵞ–eᵞ–tər) n. In ancient Rome, a man who was compelled to fight other men or animals for the entertainment of the spectators

glad-i-o-lus (glæd–iᵞ–oʷ–ləs) n. -luses or -li (–liᵞ) A plant of the iris family having spikes of brightly colored flowers and sword-shaped leaves

glad-ly (**glæd**–liᵞ) adv. Happily; eagerly

glam-or or **gla-mour** (**glæm**–ər) n. Alluring charm; personal attractiveness

glam-or-ize (**glæm**–ər–aɪz) v. -ized, -izing To make glamorous —**glam-or-i-za-tion** (glæm–ər–ɪ–zeᵞ–ʃən) n.

glam-or-ous, -ourous (**glæm**–ər–əs) adj. Charming; beautiful; having glamour

glance (glæns) v. **glanced, glancing 1.** To give a quick look: *He glanced over his shoulder before changing lanes.* **2.** **glance off** To hit and bounce off: *The rock glanced off the wall.*

glance n. A quick look: *Would you at least take a glance at this report?*

gland (glænd) n. A cell or group of cells of the body which treat materials from the bloodstream to produce various liquid substances, such as saliva or sweat: *a sweat gland*

glan-du-lar (**glæn**–dʒə–lər) adj. Of or like a gland

glare (gleər) v. **glared, glaring 1.** To gaze fiercely at someone: *They just stood there glaring at each other.* **2.** To shine with a harsh light that hurts the eyes: *The sun glared all day.*

glare n. **1.** An angry stare **2.** A harsh, dazzling light: *The glare of the sun hurt my eyes.*

glar-ing (**gleər**–ŋ) adj. **1.** Too bright **2.** Very noticeable: *This composition has many glaring mistakes.* —**glaringly** adv.

glar-y (**gleər**–iᵞ) adj. -ier, -iest Dazzling; glaring

glass (glæs) n. **1.** A hard, brittle, usu. transparent material made from melted sand: *a glass bottle/window* **2.** A drinking vessel: *a glass of water*

glass-es (**glæs**–əz) n. A pair of lenses, usu. in a frame, and worn in front of the eyes to improve vision: *I wear glasses for reading and driving the car.*

glass-y (**glæs**–iᵞ) adj. -ier, -iest **1.** Smooth and shining, like glass: *The Coral Sea was glassy that day.* **2.** Of eyes, an expressionless, dull stare: *He had a glassy stare after he fell on his head.*

glau-co-ma (glɔ–koʷ–mə) n. A disease of the eye, characterized by increased pressure within the eyeball and gradual loss of vision

glaze (gleᵞz) v. **glazed, glazing 1.** To furnish with sheets of glass **2.** To put a smooth, glossy surface on bricks, etc. **3.** Of eyes, to become glassy and lifeless

glaze n. **1.** A smooth, glossy surface **2.** A thin coating of ice **3.** A thin, glossy coating on food

gla-zier (gleᵞ–ʒər) n. A person who fits windows with glass

gleam (gliᵞm) n **1** A beam or ray of soft light, esp. one that comes and goes: *the gleam of the fire* **2.** A faint trace: *a gleam of hope*

gleam v. To shine: *The furniture gleamed.*

glean (gliᵞn) v. **1.** To gather grain left by reapers **2.** To gather information, slowly and patiently —**gleaner** n.

glee (gliᵞ) n. A feeling of joy: *She danced with glee when she heard you were coming.* —**gleeful** adj. —**gleefully** adv.

glee club n. A chorus organized for singing, usu. short choral pieces

glen (glɛn) n. A long, narrow, secluded valley

glib (glɪb) adj. Speaking easily, but often without sincerity —**glibly** adv.

glide (glaɪd) v. **glided, gliding 1.** To move smoothly and seemingly without effort: *The skaters glided over the ice.* **2.** To descend at an easy angle with little or no engine power

glid-er (**glaɪd**–ər) n. **1.** A plane with no engine **2.** A porch seat suspended in a metal frame

glid-ing n. The sport of flying gliders

glim-mer (**glɪm**–ər) v. To give a faint or unsteady light

glimmer n. A small amount: *a glimmer of hope* —compare GLEAM

glimpse (glɪmps) n. A brief look at; an incom-

plete view of: *I just caught a glimpse of her, so I can't describe her very well.*

glint (glɪnt) n. A small, brief flash of light —**glint** v.

glis-ten (glɪs–ən) v. To shine like sthg. wet or polished; to sparkle

glitch (glɪtʃ) n. A minor defect in a machine or plan

glit-ter (glɪt–ər) v. To shine brightly with flashing points of light: *Stars glittered in the sky.* —**glitter** n. *the glitter of her diamond ring*

glit-ter-ing (glɪt–ər–ɪŋ) adj. Excellent; brilliant: *a glittering performance*

gloat (gloʷt) v. To be full of greedy or malicious delight: *Do not gloat when your enemy falls* (Proverbs 24:17). *Whoever gloats over disaster will not go un-punished* (Proverbs 17:5).

glob (glɑb) n. **1.** A drop or globule **2.** A rounded lump of sthg.

glob-al (gloʷ–bəl) adj. Of the whole earth; worldwide

globe (gloʷb) n. **1.** The earth **2.** An object in the shape of a ball, esp. one with a map of the earth on it **3.** Sthg. rounded or spherical

glob-u-lar (glɑb–yə–lər) adj. Shaped like a globe

glob-ule (glɑb–yuʷl) n. **1.** A small round body **2.** A small drop of a liquid

gloom (gluʷm) n. **1.** Semi-darkness: *He couldn't see much in the gloom.* **2.** Deep sadness; dejection: *News of the tragedy filled them with gloom.*

gloom-y (gluʷm–iʸ) adj. -ier, -iest **1.** Almost dark: *a gloomy day* **2.** Having little hope: *a gloomy outlook*

glo-ri-fy (glɔr–ɪ–faɪ/ gloʷr–) v. -fied, -fying **1.** To give glory, praise, honor, or adoration to: *Glorify the Lord with me; let us exalt his name together* (Psalm 34:3). *Jesus said, "Father, the time has come. Glorify your Son, that your Son may glorify you. Glorify me in your presence with the glory I had with you before the world began"* (John 17:1,5). **2.** To make sthg. seem more splendid than it is: *They tried to glorify their patio with all kinds of potted plants and other objects.*

glo-ri-ous (glɔ–riʸ–əs) adj. **1.** Possessing or deserving glory; praiseworthy: *Your saints will extol you, [O Lord]... so that all men may*

know... *of the glorious splendor of your kingdom* (Psalm 145:10-12). **2.** Resplendent; magnificent; beautiful: *We wait for... the glorious appearing of our great God and Savior Jesus Christ* (Titus 2:13). **3.** Delightful: *What a glorious day!*

glo-ry (glɔ–riʸ) n. **1.** Honor and praise rendered in worship: *Whatever you do, do all to the glory of God* (1 Corinthians 10:31). *Declare his glory among the nations, his marvelous deeds among all peoples* (Psalm 96:3). **2.** Sthg. that is worthy of praise: *All have sinned and fall short of the glory of God* (Romans 3:23). **3.** Majesty; splendor; radiance; magnificence: *The heavens declare the glory of God* (Psalm 19:1). *Jesus will come again with power and great glory* (Luke 21:27). *Jesus is the radiance of God's glory and the exact representation of his being* (Hebrews 1:3). *When the Chief Shepherd [Jesus] appears, you [pastors, shepherds of God's people] will receive the crown of glory that will never fade away* (1 Peter 5:4).

glory v. -ried, -rying To enjoy; to rejoice proudly; to exult: *I glory in Christ Jesus in my service to God* (Romans 15:17).

gloss (glɑs/ glɔs) n. **1.** The shine on a smooth surface **2.** In literary texts, an explanatory comment —see GLOSSARY

gloss v. **1.** To make glossy **2. gloss over** To cover up a mistake or fault

glos-sa-ry (glɑs–ə–riʸ) n. -ries A list of technical or special words with their definitions

gloss-y (glɔs–iʸ/ glɑs–) adj. -ier, -iest Having a surface that is shiny and smooth

glossy n. A photograph printed on smooth, glossy paper

glot-tis (glɑt–əs) n. *pl.* **glottises** The opening at the upper part of the larynx, between the vocal cords —**glottal** adj.

glove (glʌv) n. **1.** A covering for the hand, with separate parts for the thumb and each finger —compare MITTEN **2. fit like a glove** To fit perfectly **3. handle with kid gloves** To treat very gently

glow (gloʷ) v. **1.** To send out light and/or heat without flames or smoke: *The full moon was glowing over the lake.* **2.** To be bright or radiant: *glowing with enthusiasm*

glow n. **1.** The state of glowing: *the glow of*

sunset in the summer sky **2.** A warm feeling: *a glow of happiness*

glow-ing (gloᵂ–ıŋ) adj. **1.** That which glows **2.** Full of praise: *She gave a glowing report of the county fair.* —**glowingly** adv.

glu-cose (gluᵂ–koᵂs) n. **1.** A form of sugar found in fruit juice **2.** A thick syrup made from cornstarch and used as a sweetening agent

glue (gluᵂ) n. A substance used for sticking and holding things together

glue v. **glued, gluing** or **glueing** To stick or join with glue: *Billy glued the envelope shut.* / *fig. Their eyes were glued to the TV set.*

glu-ey (gluᵂ–iʸ) adj. **-ier, -iest** Like glue: *There's sthg. gluey on the table.*

glum (glʌm) adj. **glummer, glummest** Sad; dreary; gloomy: *Why does she look so glum?*

glu-ten (gluᵂt–ən) n. A tough, sticky mixture of protein obtained from wheat flour

glut-ton (glʌt–ən) n. **1.** A person who habitually eats too much: *Drunkards and gluttons become poor, and drowsiness clothes them in rags* (Proverbs 23:7). **2.** A person who is always eager for more of sthg. difficult or unpleasant: *She's a glutton for punishment.*

glut-ton-ous (glʌt–nəs/ –ən–əs) adj. Greedy for food

glut-ton-y n. **(glʌt–ən–iʸ)** The habit of eating and drinking too much: *Put a knife to your throat if you are given to gluttony* (Proverbs 23:2).

glyc-er-in (glıs–ər–ın) n. A thick, sweet, colorless liquid used in ointments and medicines and in the manufacture of explosives

gnarl (nɑrl) n. A knot on a tree

gnarled (nɑrld) adj. Of a tree or hands, covered with knobby lumps and misshapen

gnash (næʃ) v. To grind (as teeth) together in anger

gnat (næt) n. A small, biting fly

gnaw (nɔ) v. **1.** To bite or chew sthg. hard with a scraping movement: *Dogs like to gnaw bones.* **2.** To make a hole by gnawing at sthg.: *Mice have gnawed a hole in the wall.* **3.** *fig.* To cause physical or mental pain, as if by gnawing: *Something's gnawing at him.* (=*troubling or worrying him*)

gnaw-ing (nɔ–ıŋ) adj. Of a feeling, dull and persistent: *gnawing hunger/ anxiety*

gnu (mᵂ/nyuᵂ) n. A large African antelope having a mane and curved horns

go (goᵂ) v. **went (wɛnt), gone (gɔn/ gɑn), going** **1.** To leave or depart: *I have to go to work now.* **2.** To move: *The train is going down the track.* **3.** To do sthg.: *to go shopping* **4.** To lead to: *Where does this road go?* **5.** To belong: *Where do the dishes go?* **6.** To become: *He went blind./ The milk has gone sour.* **7.** To visit a place frequently: *He goes to school every day.* **8.** To be sent: *This letter must go out tonight.* **9.** To be destroyed or taken down: *This rotten old fence will have to go.* **10.** To be lost or used up: *All our money is gone.* **11.** To proceed: *The meeting was going badly.* **12.** To be in a certain state: *Millions of people are going hungry.* **13.** Of machines, to function *The clock isn't going.* **14.** To be sold: *That old lawn mower should go real cheap.* **15.** To become weakened or worn out: *His memory is going in his old age.* **16.** To make the specified sound. *Cows go "moo."* **17.** To fit: *This table won't go in the trunk of the car.* **18.** To harmonize: *Blue doesn't go very well with green.* **19.** To be allowable: *Anything goes.* **20.** To be used: *The money will go to help the flood victims.* **21.** To have a particular result: *Everything is going against him lately.* **22.** To have a certain tune or words: *How does that song go?* **23.** To last: *He won't go six rounds with Rocky (in boxing).* **24.** To pass: *Time sure goes fast.* **25.** To cease: *Long skirts have gone out of fashion.* **26.** To pay: *I'll go up to $50 on that bike.* **27. be going to** Shows the future intentions or probabilities: *It's probably going to rain. /God willing, I'm going to college next year.* **28. to go (a)** Time left or remaining before sthg. happens: *Only five days to go until my birthday.* **(b)** *AmE.* Of food, to be taken away from a restaurant and eaten elsewhere: *One hamburger and a Coke to go, please.* **29. go ahead** To begin or continue: *They have permission to go ahead with the new bridge construction.* **30. go along with** To support or agree with: *We'll go along with your plan for the time being.* **31. go around/ round (a)** To spread: *The flu is going around again.* **(b)** To spend time in public with someone: *Mary and John have*

been going around together for a long time. **(c)** To be enough for everyone: *Is there enough pie to go around, so that everyone gets a piece?* **32. go by (sthg.) (a)** To comply with: *to go by the rules* **(b)** To be called, esp. in addition to one's real name: *She goes by the name of "Ginger."* **(c)** Be guided by: *You can't go by what she says.* **33. go down (a)** To become lower or less: *Will prices ever go down again?* **(b)** To sink: *His ship went down in the North Atlantic.* **(c)** To deflate: *My tires have gone down overnight.* **34. go far (a)** To succeed: *With her brains and ambition she should go far.* **(b)** To satisfy many needs: *This food won't go far with such a large crowd to feed.* **35. go for** To like or be attracted by: *I don't go for that kind of music.* **36. go into (sthg.) (a)** To enter a profession: *He's going into journalism.* **(b)** To examine closely: *Let's not go into details.* **37. go off (a)** To shoot or explode: *The gun went off.* **(b)** To ring: *The alarm (clock) went off at 6 a.m.* **(c)** To succeed or fail: *The party didn't go off very well. (=was a failure)* **(d)** To cease functioning: *The air conditioner went off.* **(e)** To take away without permission: *Someone went off with my bike!* **38. go off sthg.** To stop doing sthg.: *I've gone off dessert until I lose ten pounds.* **39. go on (a)** To take place or happen: *What's going on tonight?* **(b)** To continue: *He went on talking for hours.* **(c)** To pass: *As the play went on, it got more interesting.* **(d)** To be put into operation: *When do the street lights go on?* **40. go out (a)** To leave the house, esp. for amusement: *He's gone out for some fresh air.* **(b)** To frequently spend time with someone of the opposite sex: *They've been going out together for ten months.* **(c)** To stop burning or shining: *The fire went out.* **41. go over sthg. (a)** To look at closely: *He went over my application form.* **(b)** To repeat: *I had better go over the instructions once again.* **42. go through (a)** To experience: *Mother has gone through six operations in two years.* **(b)** To pass through or be accepted by: *Do you think the new bill will go through the Senate?* **43. go through (with sthg.)** To finish sthg. that has been agreed upon: *He promised to fight the champ, but now he doesn't want to go through with it.* **44. go together** To match: *These socks*

don't go together. One is blue and one is brown. **45. go under (a)** To sink **(b)** To fail: *His business went under.* **46. go up (a)** To rise: *Prices keep going up and up.* **(b)** To be built: *How many tall buildings have gone up this year?* **(c)** To blow up or be destroyed by fire: *The school went up in flames.* **47. go with (sthg.) (a)** To match or suit: *Mary's blue shoes go with her dress.* **(b)** To be often found with; accompany: *Happiness doesn't necessarily go with fame and fortune.* **48. go without (sthg.)** Do without: *We're out of bread. We'll just have to go without it.* **49. go without saying:** To be obvious

goad (go^{w}d) n. **1.** A pointed stick for driving cattle **2.** Sthg. that stimulates a person to activity

goad v. To act as a stimulus to: *They goaded him into doing it.*

go–ahead (go^w–ə–hɛd) n. Permission to act: *We'll start construction of the new shopping mall, as soon as we get the go-ahead from the city council.*

goal (go^{w}l) n. **1.** Aim or purpose: *We make it our goal to please him [God]* (2 Corinthians 5:9). **2.** In games like soccer, football, and hockey, the place, usually between two posts (goalposts), where the ball or puck must go for a point to be scored —see FOOTBALL

goat (go^{w}t) n. A four-legged, cud-chewing animal which has horns and gives milk, related to the sheep

gob–ble (gɑb–əl) v. **-bled, -bling 1.** To eat quickly and greedily **2.** To take eagerly; grab: *He gobbled up all the land he could possibly buy.* **3.** To make a sound like a turkey

gob–let (gɑb–lət) n. A drinking glass with a long stem and a flat base

God (gɑd) n. The one supreme being, perfect in power, wisdom, and goodness, creator and ruler of the universe: *God created the entire universe and rules over it. He is eternal, without beginning and without end* (Psalm 90:2). NOTE: This God of the Bible is all-powerful (Luke 1:37), all-knowing (Psalm 147:5), and present everywhere (Psalm 139:7-12). He never changes (Malachi 3:6). He is holy (Isaiah 6:3) and just (always fair

and impartial, regardless of a person's race, color, age, sex, social standing, or anything else) (Isaiah 30:18). He is faithful, always keeping his promises (Psalm 145:13). He is gracious and compassionate, slow to anger and rich in love (Psalm 145:8). He is merciful (Deuteronomy 4:31), showing undeserved kindness, forgiving those who sin against him when they turn from their sins and seek his forgiveness (Psalm 103:12). He is good, and his love endures forever (Psalm 100:5). Although God hates sin (evil thoughts, words, and deeds and every transgression of his holy Law), he loved us sinners (you and me) so much that he sent his one and only Son (Jesus Christ) into the world to take our place under the Law and to live a sinless life for us (Galatians 4:4; 2 Corinthians 5:21), and then to pay for all of our sins with his holy, precious blood (1 Peter 1:18,19). On the third day he rose from the dead, just as he said he would (Luke 24:5-7). He showed himself to many people for 40 days (1 Corinthians 15:3-8; Acts 1:3). After giving them final instructions to tell everyone in the world about him, he returned to his heavenly throne (Luke 24:47-51) to prepare a place for all those who love him and put their trust in him for everlasting life (John 14:1-3). All of this is recorded in the Holy Bible, the Word of God, which holy men of God wrote as they were inspired by the Holy Spirit (2 Peter 1:21). The Holy Spirit also works faith in Jesus in the hearts of people by means of the spoken and written Word of God (1 Corinthians 12:3; Romans 10:17). And through that Word, he keeps us in the true faith and enables us to live holy lives to the glory of God (John 17:17). There is only one God. But he is a Triune God — Father, Son, and Holy Spirit, equal in every way. —see also FATHER, JESUS CHRIST, HOLY SPIRIT, CREED

god (gɑd) n. **god-dess** (gɑd–əs) *fem.* **1.** A being or object believed to have more than natural attributes and powers and believed to require man's worship: *But there is only one true God, and his first commandment is: "You shall have no other gods before me. You shall not make yourself an idol in the form of anything in heaven above or on earth beneath or in the water below. You shall not bow down to them and worship them"* (Exodus 20:3-5). *Nevertheless, there are many so-called gods* (1 Corinthians 8:4). *They have mouths, but they cannot speak, eyes but they cannot see; they have ears, but cannot hear, noses, but they cannot smell; they have hands, but they cannot feel, feet, but they cannot walk* (Psalm 115:5-7). *They are no gods at all* (Acts 19:26). *No wonder the writer of Psalm 16:4 says, "The sorrows of those who run after other gods will be increased."* **2.** Satan, the prince of devils, is also called the god of this age: *"The god of this age has blinded the minds of unbelievers so that they cannot see the light of the Gospel of Christ who is the image of God"* (2 Corinthians 4:4). —see GOD, FATHER, JESUS, HOLY SPIRIT, SATAN

god-child (gɑd–tʃhaɪld) n. *pl.* **–children** A child in relation to its godparent(s) —see GODPARENT

god-daugh-ter (gɑd–dɔ–tər) n. A female godchild —see GODPARENT, GODFATHER

god-fa-ther (gɑd–fɑ–ðər) n. **1.** A male godparent **2.** A powerful Mafia leader NOTE: This is a misnomer if there ever was one, an entirely wrong use of the word. A Mafia leader is anything but God-fearing. —see GODPARENT

God–fear-ing (gɑd–frər–ɱ) adj. Having reverence for God; devout: *All his family were devout and God-fearing* (Acts 10:2).

god-less (gɑd–ləs) adj. Not having belief in God; wicked: *Turn away from godless chatter* (1 Timothy 6:20). —**godless** n. *The joy of the godless lasts but a moment* (Job 20:5).

god-ly (gɑd–liʸ) adj. **-lier, -liest** Showing obedience to God by leading a holy life; devout; pious: *You ought to live holy and godly lives as you look forward to the day of God and speed its coming* (2 Peter 3:11). —**god-li-ness** (gɑd–liʸ–nəs) n. *Pursue righteousness, godliness, faith, love, endurance, and gentleness* (1 Timothy 6:11). *Godliness with contentment is great gain* (1 Timothy 6:6).

god-mo-ther (gɑd–mə–ðər) n. A female god-

parent

god-par-ent (gɑd–peər–ənt) n. **1.** A person who undertakes, when a child is baptized, to see that it is brought up in the faith **2.** A person who undertakes to act as sponsor or guardian of a child

god-send (gɑd–send) n. An unexpected and timely blessing

god-son (gɑd–sən) n. A male godchild —see GODPARENT

God-speed (gɑd–spiʸd) n. An expression of good wishes to a person starting a journey

go–get-ter (goʷ–get–ər) n. infml. A person who succeeds because he is very enterprising, aggressive, energetic, etc.

gog-gles (gɑg–əlz) n. Protective glasses set in a flexible frame for fitting snuggly against the face to protect one's eyes from wind, dust, etc.

go-ing (goʷ–ŋ) v. See go

goi-ter (gɔɪt–ər) n. Any abnormal enlargement of the thyroid gland

gold (goʷld) n. **1.** A precious, soft, yellow metal used for making coins, jewelry, etc.: *The price of gold today is $400 per ounce./A good name is more desirable than great riches; to be esteemed is better than silver or gold* (Proverbs 22:1). **2.** The color of this precious metal **3. as good as gold** Esp. of children, very well behaved

gold-en (goʷl–dən) adj. **1.** Of or like gold: *a golden crown* **2.** fig. Favorable; advantageous: *a golden opportunity*

gold-en-rod (goʷl–dən–rɑd) n. A North American herb with small yellow flowers

gold-finch (goʷld–fɪntʃ) n. A small North American bird that is mostly yellow

gold-fish (goʷld–fɪʃ) n. pl. **-fish** or **-fishes** A small, orange, fresh-water fish, often kept in aquariums and ponds

golf (gɑlf) n. A game played with a small ball and various clubs on a golf course having 9 or 18 holes, in which the players hit the balls into the holes, trying to do so with as few strokes as possible

gone (gɔn) v. Past part. of go —see GO

gong (gɔŋ/ gɑŋ) n. **1.** A disk or shallow bowl of metal that produces a resonant sound when struck **2.** Any bell similar in shape and sound

gon-or-rhe-a (gɑn–ə–riʸ–ə) n. An infectious disease of the genital organs, usu. communicated by sexual intercourse

goo (guʷ) n. infml. Any thick or sticky substance

good (gʊd) adj. **better** (bet–ər), **best** (best) **1.** Without defect; flawless: *God saw all that he had made, and it was very good* (Genesis 1:31). *For the Lord is good, and his love endures forever* (Psalm 100:5). **2.** Morally right: *Hate that which is evil; cling to that which is good* (Romans 12:9). **3.** Kind; helpful **4.** Pleasant; uplifting, encouraging: *A man finds joy in giving an apt reply — and how good is a timely word!* (Proverbs 15:23). **5.** Fertile; bountiful: *good land/a good crop* **6.** Honorable: *A good name [reputation] is more desirable than great riches* (Proverbs 22:1). **7.** Beneficial to health or character: *A cheerful heart is good medicine* (Proverbs 17:22). **8.** Skillful: *She's good at tennis.* —opposite BAD **9.** Enjoyable: *Did you have a good time?* **10.** Sufficient or ample: *a good salary* **11.** Complete; thorough: *He took a good look.* **12.** Much, considerable, etc.: *We waited a good while.* **13.** Skillfully or expertly done: *a really good job* **14.** Sensible: *a good reason* **15.** Well; healthy: *I don't feel very good today.* **16.** Attractive: *She has a good figure.* **17.** Not counterfeit: *good money* **18.** At least, or more than: *He lives a good ten miles from here.* **19. a good deal** A lot: *We're expecting a good deal of support for our new organization.* **20. as good as** Almost the same thing as: *This car is as good as new.*

good n. **1.** Beneficial: *Joseph told his brothers, "You intended to harm me [by selling me into slavery], but God intended it for good to accomplish what is now being done, the saving of many lives"* (Genesis 50:20). **2.** Morally right: *Anyone who knows the good he ought to do and doesn't do it, sins* (James 4:17). **3.** That which causes gain or improvement: *God disciplines us for our good* (Hebrews 12:10). *In all things God works for the good of those who love him* (Romans 8:28). *Nobody should seek his own good, but the good of others* (1 Corinthians 10:24). **4. for good** Forever: *We thought they'd come just for a visit, but it seems they're staying*

for good.

good–bye (gʊd–baɪ) interj. n. An expression used when leaving sbdy. or being left by sbdy.

Good Friday n. The Friday before Easter; the day Christ died for the sins of the world (He rose from the dead on Easter Sunday). NOTE: He was delivered [to death] for our offenses [sins] and raised again for our justification. Therefore, being justified by faith, we have peace with God through our Lord Jesus Christ (Romans 4:25-5:1). —see also JESUS CHRIST, EASTER

good-ness (gʊd–nəs) n. **1.** Excellence; virtue: *The fruit of the [Holy] Spirit is love, joy, peace, patience, kindness, goodness...* (Galatians 5:22). **2.** The best part, esp. of food; the part which is good for the health

goods (gʊdz) n. *pl.* Articles (food, clothing, towels, sheets, etc.) which can be bought or sold: *Department stores sell a variety of goods.*

goo-ey (guʷ–iʸ) adj. **gooier, gooiest** Sticky

goof (guʷf) n. **1.** A stupid person **2.** A mistake; blunder

goof v. To make a mistake

goof off v. To loaf; to spend time idly or foolishly; esp. to evade work

goof–off n. A person who evades work

goof-y (guʷf–iʸ) adj. **-ier, -iest** Stupid; silly

gook (gʊk/ guʷk) n. *infml.* Any gooey filth

goon (guʷn) n. A foolish person

goose (guʷs) n. *pl.* **geese 1.** A large, web-footed bird, related to swans and ducks, esp. a female goose as distinguished from a gander **2.** A foolish person

go-pher (goʷ–fər) n. Any of various short-tailed burrowing rodents of North America with pocket-like cheek pouches

gore (gor) v. **gored, goring** To pierce with a horn or tusk

gorge (gordʒ) n. A deep, narrow valley, usually made by a stream running through it

gorge v. **gorged, gorging** To fill oneself with food: *The hungry campers gorged themselves.*

gor-geous (gor–dʒəs) adj. Very beautiful; splendid; magnificent: *a gorgeous day* (=warm and bright)

go-ril-la (gə–rɪl–ə) n. A large, powerful African ape; the largest of the man-like monkeys

gor-y (gor–iʸ) adj. **-ier, -iest 1.** Covered with blood **2.** Involving bloodshed

gos-ling (gɑz–lɪŋ) n. A young goose

gos-pel (gɑs–pəl) n. Sthg. completely true: *You can take his word as gospel.*

Gospel (gɑs–pəl) n. **1.** The Good News about Jesus Christ who came into the world to save us sinners: *According to the Gospel he died for us and rose again that "whoever believes in him should not perish but have everlasting life"* (John 3:16). *By grace are you saved through faith [in Jesus], and that not of yourselves, it is the gift of God, not by works lest any man should boast* (Ephesians 2:8,9). *I am not ashamed of the Gospel, because it is the power of God for the salvation of everyone who believes...* (Romans 1:16). —see JESUS CHRIST, GRACE **2.** One of the four books of the New Testament (Matthew, Mark, Luke, and John) that tells about the life, death, and resurrection of Jesus Christ —see NEW TESTAMENT, BIBLE

gos-sa-mer (gɑs–ə–mər) n. **1.** Filmy gauze **2.** A very fine cobweb **3.** Any thin, filmy material

gos-sip (gɑs–əp) n. **1.** Talk about other people's affairs which is not always truthful and often spiteful: *Without wood a fire goes out; without gossip a quarrel dies down* (Proverbs 26:20). **2.** A person who listens to and passes on gossip: *A gossip betrays a confidence and separates close friends* (Proverbs 11:13; 16:28). —**gossip** v.

got (gɑt) v. **1.** Past tense and past part. of get **2.** To have: *He's got a lot of nerve/ courage/ money, etc.* **3.** Must: *I've got to go now or I'll be late to work.* NOTE: Numbers 2 and 3 above are not good grammar, but are in very common use.

got-ten (gɑt–ən) v. Past part. of get: *It has gotten a lot colder during the past hour.*

gouge (gaʊdʒ) n. **1.** A chisel with a rounded, hollow blade for cutting grooves in wood **2.** A hole or a groove made with, or as if with, a gouge

gouge v. **gouged, gouging 1.** To cut a hole or a groove in sthg. with a gouge **2.** To scoop or force out

gou·lash (gu^w–laʃ / –læʃ) n. A stew or thick soup of meat and vegetables, seasoned with paprika

gourd (gɔrd) n. **1.** A vine related to the pumpkin and squash that bears fruit with a hard rind **2.** The fruit of such a vine **3.** The dried, hollowed-out shell of such a fruit, often used as a drinking vessel or a dish

gour·met (gʊər–me^y) n. A person who knows a great deal about good food and drink

gov·ern (gʌv–əm) v. **1.** To rule a country, state, province, city, etc. and its people: *Pray for those in positions of leadership and authority, that they might govern justly and with diligence.* **2.** To control or determine: *The price of coffee is governed by the quantity which has been produced.*

gov·ern·ment (gʌv–ər–mənt/ gʌv–əm–mənt) n. **1.** The action, form, or method of ruling **2.** The people who rule: *The government is planning new tax increases.* —**gov·ern·men·tal** (gəv–ər–mɛn–təl) adj.

gov·er·nor (gʌv–ə–nər/ gʌv–nər) n. One who governs; a ruler, chief executive, or head of a political unit; (in the US) one who leads the administration of a state

gown (gaʊn) n. **1.** A loose, flowing garment, esp. a long dress, worn on formal occasions: *an evening gown* **2.** A loose outer garment worn esp. by judges, but also by professors for ceremonial occasions, etc.

grab (græb) v. **-bb-** To seize sthg. suddenly, esp. for a selfish reason; to snatch: *He grabbed her purse and ran./ fig. When she was offered a major role in a movie, she eagerly grabbed the opportunity.*

grab n. **1.** An attempt to seize sthg.: *The thief made a grab at her purse.* **2. up for grabs** Able to be taken by anyone: *All these books are up for grabs.*

grace (gre^ys) n. **1.** The unmerited favor of God; mercy: *It is by grace you have been saved, through faith [in Jesus Christ]* (Ephesians 2:8). *We are justified freely by his grace through the redemption that came through Christ Jesus* (Romans 3:24). —see JESUS, GOSPEL **2.** The application of Christ's righteousness to the sinner: *Where sin increased, grace increased all the more, so that, just as sin reigned in death,*

so also grace might reign through righteousness to bring eternal life through Jesus Christ our Lord (Romans 5:20,21). **3.** Eternal life; final salvation: *Set your hope fully on the grace to be given you when Jesus Christ is revealed* (1 Peter 1:13). **4.** Virtues proceeding from divine influence, such as faith, meekness, humility, patience, generosity: *See that you also excel in this grace of giving* (2 Corinthians 8:7). **5.** Spiritual power: *God is able to make all grace abound toward you, so that ... you will abound in every good work* (2 Corinthians 9:8). **6.** Gratitude: *Singing with grace in your hearts to the Lord* (Colossians 3:16). **7.** Privilege: *This grace was given to me, to preach to the Gentiles the unsearchable riches of Christ* (Ephesians 3:8). **8.** Kindness to say and do what is right: *Let your conversation be always full of grace... so that you may know how to answer everyone* (Colossians 4:6). **9.** A prayer before or after meals, giving thanks to God **10.** Beauty of form or movement: *to dance with grace* **11.** A delay allowed as a favor for payment, work, etc.: *The bill was due on the first of the month, but they gave us five days' grace.* **12.** A title used in speaking to or about a Duke, Duchess, or Archbishop: *Your Grace* **grace** v. To adorn; embellish: *My son, preserve sound judgment and discernment... they will be... an ornament to grace your neck* (Proverbs 3:21,22).

grace·ful (gre^ys–fəl) adj. **1.** Having or showing beauty of form or movement: *She's such a graceful skater.* **2.** Of speech and feeling, showing a sense of what is right or decent: *a graceful apology* —see GRACIOUS —**gracefully** adv.

grace·less (gre^ys–ləs) adj. **1.** Awkward **2.** Lacking in good manners; ungracious

gra·cious (gre^y–ʃəs) adj. **1.** Merciful; kind; forgiving: *The Lord is gracious and compassionate, slow to anger and rich in love* (Psalm 145:8). **2.** Showing qualities associated with good taste and breeding: *gracious living* —**graciously** adv. *She smiled graciously.*

Gracious! interj. An exclamation of surprise

grade (gre^yd) n. **1.** Rank or quality: *These eggs are grade AA.* **2.** A class in school: *She's in the third grade.* **3.** A mark showing the quality of

a student's schoolwork: *His grades were very good this semester — all A's and B's.* **4. make the grade** To succeed **5.** The degree of inclination of a slope: *The driver shifted into low gear to go up the steep grade.*

grade v. **graded, grading 1.** To sort according to size and quality **2.** To evaluate: *The teacher graded the papers.* **3.** To level or smooth the road: *This part of the road was graded last week.*

grad-u-al (græ–dʒuʷ–əl) adj. Happening slowly: *a gradual increase in the temperature* —**gradually** adv.

grad-u-ate (græ–dʒuʷ–ət) adj., n. **1.** *AmE.* A person who has received an academic degree or diploma: *She's a graduate of North High School.* **2.** Postgraduate; studies that are done at a university after one has received one's first degree: *He's a graduate student at a famous university.*

grad-u-ate (græ–dʒuʷ–eʸt) v. **-ated, -ating 1.** To complete an educational course and be granted an academic degree or diploma: *He graduated from college last June.* **2.** To arrange sthg. according to degree, amount, or quality (grade): *A thermometer is graduated in degrees.*

grad-u-a-tion (græ–dʒuʷ–eʸ–ʃən) n. **1.** The act of graduating **2.** A ceremony at which one receives a university degree or (in America) a high school diploma

graf-fi-to (grə–fiʸt–oʷ) n. *pl.* **-ti** (–tiʸ) Usu. used in the plural: **1.** Any design or scribble drawn on a wall or other surface **2.** *Archeo.* A pictograph scratched on an escarpment

graft (græft) v. **1.** To insert a shoot from one plant into another plant so that they join and grow: *Cultivated roses are often grown by being grafted onto the roots of wild roses.* **2.** To join skin from one part of the body onto, or into, another part of the same body: *The doctor treated her burns by grafting skin from her leg onto her back.* **3.** To get money dishonestly

graft n. **1.** A grafted plant **2.** The material (skin, for example) used in grafting **3.** Obtaining of money or advantage dishonestly **4.** The money obtained in this way

grain (greʸn) n. **1.** A seed of rice, wheat, or other cereal grass **2.** The gathered seeds

from such plants **3.** A small hard particle: *a grain of sand* **4.** *fig.* A tiny amount: *There's not a grain of truth in what he said.* **5.** The natural arrangement of the threads or fibers in wood, leather, etc.: *It's difficult to cut wood against the grain.*

gram (græm) n. A measure of weight equal to 1/1000 of a kilogram

gram-mar (græm–ər) n. **1.** The study of words and the rules for their formation, and of their relationships to each other in sentences **2.** The rules themselves **3.** A book that teaches these rules **4.** Speech or writing judged as good or bad according to these rules: *Her grammar is atrocious.* —**gram-mat-i-cal** (grə–mæt–ɪ–kəl) adj. —**grammatically** adv.

gram-mar-i-an (grə–mɛər–iʸ–ən) n. A specialist in grammar

grand (grænd) adj. **1.** Large and impressive in size or extent: *The Grand Canyon of Arizona is 217 miles long, four to 13 miles wide, and more than a mile deep.* **2.** Splendid in appearance: *a grand view of the ocean and islands* **3.** Most important; main: *the grand ballroom* **4.** Of the highest rank: *a grand duke* **5.** Very pleasant: *a grand party* **6.** Dignified; admirable **7.** Including everything: *the grand total*

grand n. **1.** A grand piano **2.** *slang* A thousand dollars: *That car costs twenty grand.*

grand-child (græn–tʃaɪld) n. **grandchildren** (græn–tʃɪl–drən) The child of one's son or daughter

grand-daugh-ter (græn–dɔt–ər) n. The daughter of one's son or daughter

gran-deur (græn–dʒər) n. Great beauty or power; splendor; magnificence; grandness

grand-fa-ther (græn–fɑ–ðər/ grænd–fɑ–ðər) n. The father of one's father or mother

gran-di-ose (græn–diʸ–oʷs) adj. **1.** Imposing; planned on a grand scale **2.** Trying to be grand; pompous

grand jury (grænd dʒʊr–iʸ) n. A jury appointed to study the facts of a case to determine whether sbdy. should be officially accused of a crime and put on trial

grand-ma (græn–mɑ/ græ–mɑ/ grænd–mɑ) n. *infml.* of grandmother

grand-moth-er (græn–mə–ðər/ grænd–mə–ðər)

n. The mother of one's father or mother

grand-pa (græn–pɑ/ græm–pɑ/ grænd–pɑ) n. *infml.* of **grandfather**

grand-par-ent (græn–peər–ənt) n. A parent of one's father or mother

grand-son (græn–sən/ grænd–sən) n. The son of one's son or daughter

grand-stand (grænd–stænd) n. A usu. roofed stand with rows of seats from which people watch sporting events

gran-ite (græn–ət) n. A hard, gray stone used for building

gran-ny or **gran-nie** (græn–iʸ) n. **-nies 1.** Grandmother **2.** Old woman **3.** A fussy person

gra-no-la (grə–noʷ–lə) n. A mixture of rolled oats, dried fruit, seeds, and other foods, used as a breakfast cereal, for snacks, etc.

grant (grænt) v. **1.** To give or allow: *May the Lord grant all your requests* (Psalm 20:5). *What the righteous desire will be granted* (Proverbs 10:24). **2.** To admit or agree that sthg. is true: *I grant you that this isn't the safest place to be at the moment.* **3. take sthg./sbdy. for granted (a)** To assume that sthg. is true: *I took it for granted that you would want to go to the game with me so I bought two tickets.* **(b)** To be so accustomed to sthg. that one no longer appreciates it: *He's so used to his wife doing things for him that he takes her for granted.*

grant n. Money granted, esp. a gift for a particular purpose: *a student grant*

gran-u-lar (græn–yə–lər) adj. Like grains or granules

gran-u-lat-ed (græn–yə–leʸt–əd) adj. Consisting of small grains or granules: *granulated sugar*

gran-ule (græn–yuʷl) n. A small grain

grape (greʸp) n. A small, round juicy fruit, usually a yellowish green or dark purple, which grows on a vine and is often used for making wine or raisins

grape-fruit (greʸp–fruʷt) n. **grapefruit** or **grapefruits** A large, round, yellow, edible citrus fruit

grape-vine (greʸp–vaɪn) n. **1.** The plant that bears grapes **2.** A way by which news is passed on unofficially

graph (græf) n. **1.** A drawing showing the re-

lationship between two sets of numbers **2.** Any drawing used to display numerical data: *a graph showing population growth/business profits*

–graph (græf) Suffix **1.** Sthg. written: *Paragraph* **2.** An instrument that writes or records: *Phonograph*

graph-ic (græf–ɪk) adj. **1.** Written, drawn, printed or engraved **2.** Of or relating to the arts of representation, decorating, and printing on flat surfaces: *the graphic arts* **3.** Clear and detailed: *a graphic description of the accident* —**graphically** adv.

graph-ite (græf–aɪt) n. A dark-gray natural form of carbon, used as lead in pencils and as a lubricant

–gra-phy (–grə–fiʸ) Suffix **1.** Manner of writing or representing: *Stenography* **2.** Science or study: *Geography*

grap-ple (græp–əl) v. **-pled, -pling 1.** To seize or hold firmly **2.** To struggle; wrestle **3.** To cope with: *She was grappling with many problems.*

grasp (græsp) v. **1.** To take or keep a firm hold of sthg. **2.** To understand: *Did you grasp what he was talking about?*

grasp n. **1.** A firm hold: *I kept the rope in my grasp.* **2.** Reach: *Stardom was within her grasp.* **3.** Understanding: *This subject is beyond my grasp.*

grasp-ing (græsp–ɪŋ) adj. *derog.* Eager for more, especially money

grass (græs) n. **1.** A common low-growing plant with green blades, grown in fields and eaten by animals **2.** Ground covered with grass; lawn; pasture: *Don't walk on the grass.* **3.** Any species of grass including corn, reeds, and bamboo **4.** *slang* Marijuana

grass-hop-per (græs–hɑp–ər) n. Any of numerous insects having two sets of wings and hind legs adapted for leaping, very destructive to vegetation

gras-sy (græs–iʸ) adj. **-sier, -siest** Covered with growing grass

grate (greʸt) n. The frame that holds the coal, wood, etc. in a fireplace

grate v. **grated, grating 1.** To rub sthg. on a rough surface so as to break it into small pieces: *Mother is grating the carrots on the*

grater. **2.** To make a very annoying, grinding sound by rubbing sthg. together: *He was grating his teeth.* **3.** To irritate: *grate on one's nerves*

grate-ful (gre^{y}t-fəl) adj. Thankful; showing thanks to another person: *Tom was grateful for Bob's help.* —opposite UNGRATEFUL —see also GRATITUDE —gratefully adv.

grat-er (gre^{y}t-ər) n. A device with a rough surface for grating food

grat-i-fy (græt-ə-faɪ) v. -fied, -fying To give pleasure to: *Clothe yourselves with the Lord Jesus Christ, and do not think about how to gratify the desires of the sinful nature* (Romans 13:14). *We were gratified when the little girl was rescued from the well.* —grat-i-fi-ca-tion (græt-ə-fə-ke^y-ʃən) n. —grat-i-fy-ing (græt-ə-faɪ-ɪŋ) adj. *a gratifying experience*

grat-ing (gre^{y}t-ɪŋ) adj. **1.** Harsh or scraping in sound; rasping **2.** Not pleasant; annoying: *a grating personality*

grat-ing n. An arrangement of bars or slats used as a cover or screen

gra-tis (græt-əs) adv., adj. Free; without charge or recompense

grat-i-tude (græt-ə-tu^{w}d) n. Being grateful; having kind feelings towards someone who has treated you kindly: *Let the word of Christ dwell in you richly... as you sing... with gratitude in your hearts to the Lord* (Colossians 3:16). —opposite INGRATITUDE

gra-tu-i-tous (grə-tu^w-ə-təs) adj. Done or provided without charge; free

gra-tu-i-ty (grə-tu^w-ə-ti^y) n. -ties A tip

grave (gre^{y}v) n. **1.** A hole in the ground where someone is to be buried **2.** The place in the ground where a dead person is buried: *Jesus said, "A time is coming and has now come when the dead [spir-itually dead] will hear the voice of the Son of God and those who hear will live. Do not be amazed at this, for a time is coming when all who are in their graves will hear his [Jesus'] voice and come out — those who have done good [those who trust in Jesus for salvation] will rise to live and those who have done evil will rise to be condemned"* (John 5:25,28,29). *Those who turn from their wicked ways and put their trust in Jesus for eternal life can say with the writer of Psalm 49, "God will*

redeem my soul from the grave; he will surely take me to himself" (Psalm 49:15). —see JESUS

grave adj. Serious or solemn: *He had a grave expression on his face when he heard the news./ The wounded man's condition is grave.* (=very, very serious) —gravely adv.

grav-el (græv-əl) n. Loose, rounded fragments of rock, used on the surface of roads or paths

grav-el-ly (græv-əl-i^y) adj. **1.** Containing much gravel **2.** Harsh; grating: *He has a gravelly voice.*

grav-en (gre^{y}v-ən) adj. Carved (A graven image is an idol. Making or worshiping a graven image is idolatry.): *God said, "You shall not make for yourself any graven image, or any likeness of anything that is in heaven above, or that is in the earth beneath, or that is in the water under the earth. You shall not bow down to them, nor serve them"* (Exodus 20:4,5). NOTE: God hates sin, but because of his great love and mercy he forgives the sins of those who turn from their wicked ways [repent] and put their trust in Jesus for eternal life. —see FORGIVENESS, JESUS, REPENT, SIN

grave-stone (gre^{y}v-sto^{w}n) n. A stone monument put over a grave, bearing the name of the person buried there, dates of birth and death, etc.

grave-yard (gre^{y}v-yard) n. A burial ground; cemetery; now more often called a **Memorial Park**

grav-i-tate (græv-ə-te^{y}t) v. -tated, -tating To be drawn toward sthg., as if by gravity

grav-i-ta-tion (græv-ə-te^y-ʃən) n. A natural force or attraction that draws bodies together —gravitational adj.

grav-i-ty (græv-ə-ti^y) n. **1.** The force that attracts objects to the earth and causes them to fall to the ground **2.** Seriousness of a situation: *the gravity of his illness*

gra-vy (gre^y-vi^y) n. **1.** The juice given off by meat when cooked **2.** The sauce made by thickening this juice with flour and seasoning

gray (gre^y) also **grey** adj. grayer, grayest A neutral color of black mixed with white; the

color of lead, ashes, rain clouds, etc.

graze (gro^yz) v grazed, grazing Of animals, to feed on grass: *The cattle are grazing in the field.*

graze v. **1.** To scrape or scratch in passing, esp. the skin: *The bullet grazed his shoulder.* **2.** To touch or rub lightly while passing: *Our car just grazed another as we passed on the narrow road.*

grease (gri^ys) n. **1.** Melted animal fat: *bacon grease* **2.** A thick, oily substance or lubricant: *This machinery needs some grease to make it run more smoothly.*

grease v. greased, greasing To put grease on: *If you grease the hinges, the door will open without squeaking.*

greas-y adj. -ier, -iest Covered with or containing grease: *greasy food*

great (gre^yt) adj. **1.** Of excellent quality or ability: *How awesome is the Lord most high, the great King over all the earth!* (Psalm 47:2). **2.** Important: *Jesus said to his followers, "Whoever wants to become great among you must be your servant"* (Matthew 20:26). *Whoever humbles himself like this little child is the greatest in the kingdom of heaven* (Matthew 18:4). **3.** Large in amount or degree: *a great loss/a great thrill* **4.** Unusually active in the stated way: *He's a great talker.* **5.** (before another adj. of size) Very: *a great big tree* **6.** Unusually good: *a great idea!/ Our new teacher is really great!* —**greatness** n. *Great is the Lord and most worthy of praise; his greatness no one can fathom [is beyond understanding]* (Psalm 145:3).

great-ly (gre^yt–li^y) adv. To a large degree; very much: *Great is the Lord, and greatly to be praised; and his greatness is unsearchable* (Psalm 145:3 KJV).

greed (gri^yd) n. *derog.* A selfish desire to obtain more than one needs or deserves, esp. more money or power: *Greed is a form of idolatry* (Colossians 3:5). NOTE: God detests the sin of greed, just as he hates all sin. But because of his great love and mercy he forgives those who truly repent (turn from their evil ways) and put their trust in Jesus for eternal life (Acts 2:38; Acts 16:31). —see JESUS, SIN, REPENT

greed-y (gri^yd–i^y) adj. -ier, -iest Full of greed: *No immoral, impure, or greedy person... has any inheritance in the Kingdom of Christ and of God* (Ephesians 5:5) —**greediness** n.

green (gri^yn) adj. -er, -est **1.** The usu. color of leaves and grass **2.** Lacking experience: *He's very green at this job.* **3.** green with envy Very jealous **4.** have a green thumb To be skillful in making plants grow well **5.** the green light Permission: *We'll begin construction of the new road as soon as we get the green light from the town council.*

green n. **1.** The color made by mixing yellow and blue: *She was dressed in green.* **2.** A smooth stretch of grass (a) for playing golf: *a putting green* (b) for general use of the public: *the village green* —**greenish** adj. —**greenness** n.

green-er-y (gri^yn–ər–i^y) n. Green leaves and plants

green-horn (gri^yn–hɔrn) n. An inexperienced person

green-house (gri^yn–haʊs) n. A glass structure for the growing of tender plants

green light (gri^yn laɪt) n. Permission: *The city council gave them the green light to proceed with their building plans.*

green thumb (gri^yn θʌm) n. A gift for making plants grow: *Mother has a green thumb.*

greet (gri^yt) v. **1.** To welcome: *Many friends were waiting at the airport to greet him.* **2.** To meet or receive in the specified way: *The speech was greeted by loud cheers/hisses/boos.*

greet-ing (gri^yt–ɪŋ) n. **1.** The act or the words used in greeting someone: *"Good morning," I said, but she didn't return the greeting.* **2.** A good wish: *Christmas greetings*

gre-gar-i-ous (grə–geər–i^y–əs) adj. **1.** Very sociable; liking to be with other people **2.** Tending to flock together

grem-lin (grem–lən) n. An imaginary, mischievous, invisible being

gre-nade (grə–ne^yd) n. A small bomb, thrown by hand or fired from a gun

grew (gru^w) v. Past tense of **grow**

grey (gre^y) *esp. BrE.* for **gray**

grid (grɪd) n. **1.** A grating —see GRATE **2.** A network of squares on maps, numbered for easy reference **3.** A network of wires in a

storage battery or a vacuum tube **4.** A system of electric power cables or gas-supply lines for distributing power evenly over a large area

grid-dle (grɪd–əl) n. A usu. circular metal plate for cooking flat cakes and other food

grid-iron (grɪd–aɪ–ərn) n. **1.** A grate for broiling food **2.** Sthg. that looks like a gridiron; a football field

grid-lock (grɪd–lɒk) n. Heavy traffic, preventing vehicles from moving

grief (griʸf) n. Great sorrow, esp. at the death of a loved person or the very bad behavior of a family member: *His wild behavior was a cause of grief to his parents./ Some people, eager for money, have wandered from the faith and pierced themselves with many griefs* (1 Timothy 6:10).

griev-ance (griʸ–vəns) n. A report of or cause for complaint, esp. of unjust treatment

grieve (griʸv) v. **grieved, grieving 1.** To feel grief; mourn: *She is still grieving over the death of her child.* **2.** To cause grief to; make very unhappy: *His use of drugs grieved his parents.*

griev-ous (griʸv–əs) adj. Very seriously harmful; causing grief, pain, or anguish: *grievous pain/ a grievous sin* —**grievously** adv.

grill (grɪl) n. A frame of metal bars which can be put over a fire for cooking purposes

grill v. To cook sthg. on a grill

grim (grɪm) adj. **-mm- 1.** Very serious and unsmiling in appearance: *a grim look* **2.** Sad, dismal, gloomy: *grim news of her son's death* **3.** Unpleasant: *grim weather* —**grimly** adv. —**grimness** n.

gri-mace (grɪm–əs) n. A facial expression showing disgust or disapproval

grime (graɪm) n. Dirt sticking to or embedded in a surface; accumulated dirtiness —**grimy** adj.

grin (grɪn) v. **-nn-** To smile broadly

grin n. The expression on one's face produced by grinning

grind (graɪnd) v. **ground** (graʊnd), **grinding 1.** To crush into tiny pieces or powder: *They ground the wheat to make flour.* **2.** To sharpen knives, scissors, etc. by rubbing (e.g. with a grindstone) **3.** To rub together; gnash: *to*

grind the teeth **4.** To rub sthg. into sthg. else: *The dirt was ground into the boy's trousers.* **5.** To move with difficulty or friction: *Stop grinding the gears.* **6.** *fig.* To oppress: *The tyrant ground the faces of his people into the dirt.* **7. grind to a halt** To come slowly or noisily to a stop

grind n. Boring, hard work: *To some people, any kind of study is a real grind.*

grind-er (graɪnd–ər) n. Someone or sthg. that grinds: *a knife grinder*

grind-stone (graɪnd–stoʷn) n. **1.** A wheel-shaped stone that turns, used for sharpening tools, knives, etc. **2. keep one's nose to the grindstone** To work hard continuously

grip (grɪp) v. **-pp-** To take a tight hold of: *The child gripped her mother's hand in fear.*

grip n. **1.** A tight, forceful hold: *The officer had a tight grip on the thief.* **2.** *fig.* Control: *He keeps a firm grip on his children.* **3.** The skill to do sthg.: *He has played poorly in several games this season. He seems to be losing his grip.*

gripe (graɪp) v. **griped, griping 1.** To complain; grumble **2.** To cause or suffer sharp pain in the bowels

gripe n. A complaint: *What's your gripe this time?*

grip-ping (grɪp–ɪŋ) adj. That which holds the attention: *a gripping story*

gris-ly (grɪz–liʸ) adj. Very unpleasant; causing horror or disgust: *the grisly job of recovering the dead bodies from the wreckage* NOTE: Do not confuse with **grizzly**

grist (grɪst) n. **1.** Grain that is to be ground **2.** Ground grain **3. grist for one's mill** Something appropriate or that can be used to one's advantage

gris-tle (grɪs–əl) n. Strands of tough tissue in meat —**gristly** adj.

grist-mill (grɪst–mɪl) n. A mill for grinding grain

grit (grɪt) n. **1.** Small pieces of hard material such as sand or stone **2.** *infml.* Determination; courage —**gritty** adj. **-tier, -tiest**

grit v. **-tt-** To hold the teeth closely together to keep from crying out in pain: *Though the operation on his leg was extremely painful, he gritted his teeth and bore the pain.*

grits (grɪts) n. Coarsely ground grain

griz·zle (grɪz–əl) n. **1.** Gray-haired **2.** Gray —**grizzled** adj. Streaked with gray

griz·zly (grɪz–liʸ) adj. **-zlier, -zliest** Grayish; streaked with gray NOTE: Do not confuse with **grisly**

griz·zly bear (grɪz–liʸ beər) n. A large ferocious bear of western North America

groan (groʷn) v. To make a deep, prolonged sound expressive of pain, grief, annoyance or disapproval: *The man who had been hit by a car lay groaning beside the road.* —**groan** n.

gro·cer (groʷ–sər) n. A storekeeper who sells food and household supplies such as matches and soap

gro·cer·y (groʷ–sər–iʸ/ groʷ–ʃriʸ) also **grocery store** n. **-ies 1.** A store where food and household supplies are sold **2. groceries** The goods sold by a grocer

grog·gy (grɑg–iʸ) adj. **-gier, -giest** Weak and unsteady, esp. after an illness —**grogginess** n.

groin (grɔɪn) n. **1.** The fold marking the juncture of abdomen and thigh **2.** This area of the body where the genitals are located

grom·met (grɑm–ət) n. **1.** A ring-shaped piece of firm material used to reinforce or protect an opening in a piece of material, leather, etc. **2.** A flexible loop that serves as a fastening, support, or reinforcement

groom (gruʷm) n. A man about to be married or just married —see BRIDEGROOM

groom v. **1.** Taking care of one's appearance by dressing neatly, keeping the hair tidy, etc. **2.** To prepare someone for a special position or occasion: *grooming him for an executive position* **3.** To clean and brush an animal

groove (gruʷv) n. **1.** A long narrow cut in the surface of sthg.: *The phonograph needle moves along the groove on a record.* **2.** A fixed routine

grope (groʷp) v. **groped, groping 1.** To search with the hands as if blind or in the dark: *I groped my way along the wall, trying to find the light switch.* **2.** To search uncertainly: *groping for an answer or for the right word*

gross (groʷs) adj. **1.** Impolite, rude; vulgar: *His gross behavior was shocking.* **2.** Inexcusable; outrageous: *gross negligence* **3.** Repulsively fat: *She was so gross she could hardly get*

through the door. **4.** Total, before any deductions: *Gross income is one's income before expenses are deducted.*

gross v. To earn as total profit before deductions: *The company grossed only $50,000 last year.* —compare NET

gross·ly (groʷs–liʸ) adv. Very (used esp. with things that are bad): *grossly underpaid*

gro·tesque (groʷ–tɛsk) adj. Fantastically ugly or absurd —**grotesquely** adv. —**grotesqueness** n.

grot·to (grɑt–oʷ) n. **-toes** or **-tos 1.** A picturesque cave **2.** An artificial cave-like structure

grouch (graʊtʃ) n. **1.** A habitually irritable or complaining person **2.** A bad-tempered complaint

ground (graʊnd) n. **1.** The surface of the earth; soil **2.** Land used for a particular purpose: *a playground* **3.** The foundation or basis for an argument, belief, or action: *There were no grounds for suspicion.* —see also GROUNDS

ground v. **1.** To prevent an aircraft or crew from flying: *This aircraft has been grounded.* **2.** To cause a ship to run ashore or be stuck in a seabed: *Several barges were grounded because of the unusually low water level in the river.* **3.** To base: *His argument was grounded on research and experience.* **4.** To be instructed in the basics: *He was well-grounded in the fundamentals of flying.* **5.** to give ground To retreat; to yield **6. to gain or lose ground** To gain or lose approval or acceptance: *It looked like Smith would get his party's nomination, but Johnson has been gaining ground rapidly.* **7. to run into the ground** To explain at unreasonable length **8. to get off the ground** To get started: *His business hasn't gotten off the ground yet.* **9. ground** *AmE.* **earth** *BrE.* To make an electrical device safer by connecting it to the ground with a wire **10.** Past tense and part. of grind

ground·hog (graʊnd–hɔg/ –hɑg) n. The woodchuck

ground·ing (graʊnd–ɪŋ) n. A thorough training in the main points which will enable further study or work on some subject: *a good grounding in English grammar*

ground·less (graʊnd–ləs) adj. Without good

reason: *groundless accusations* —**ground-lessly** adv.

grounds (graʊndz) n. **1.** An area of enclosed land surrounding a large house or an institution: *the hospital grounds* **2.** A reason: *We have grounds for believing he is guilty.* **3.** Solid particles that sink to the bottom of a liquid: *coffee grounds*

ground-work (graʊnd–wərk) n. Preliminary or basic work

group (gruʷp) n. **1.** A number of persons, animals, things, or organizations placed together or working together for a specific purpose: *There are many thousands of people groups in the world.* **2.** A number of commercial companies under one owner **3.** A trio or quartet or other small number of entertainers

group v. To form or gather into a group or groups: *Animals can be grouped into several types.*

grouse (graʊs) n. A bird with a plump body and brownish or grayish feathers, often hunted for food

grove (groʷv) n. A small group of trees: *an orange grove*

grov-el (grɑv–əl) v. **-eled** or **-elled, -eling** or **-elling 1.** To lie or move with the face down; crawl; cringe: *He was groveling in the dust.* **2.** To behave with a show of humility or shame

grow (groʷ) v. **grew** (gruʷ), **grown** (groʷn), **growing 1.** To develop; to increase in size by natural development: *Rice grows in warm climates.* **2.** Increase; expand: *My prayer is that you will "Grow in the grace and knowledge of our Lord and Savior Jesus Christ" (2 Peter 3:18). —see JESUS* **3.** To cause or to allow to grow: *Bob is growing a beard.* **4.** To become (gradually): *We are all growing older.*

grow-er (groʷ–ər) n. A person who grows plants: *a vegetable grower*

growl (graʊl) v. To make a deep, rough, threatening sound in the throat: *That dog growls at strangers.*

growl n. The sound made by growling

grown (groʷn) adj. **1.** Of full size or development; adult **2. grown-up** adj. Fully developed; adult: *She has a grown-up daughter who*

is a teacher.

grown-up n. Adult:*You children go outside and play and let the grown-ups have some time to themselves.*

growth (groʷθ) n. **1.** The process of growing and developing: *the growth of the population* **2.** Increase in numbers or amount: *a rapid growth in church membership* **3.** Sthg. that has grown: *a growth of grass*

grub (grʌb) n. **1.** Larva of an insect **2.** *colloq.* Food **3.** Drudge

grub v. **-bb- 1.** To dig up; root out of the ground **2.** To drudge or toil

grub-by (grʌb–iʸ) adj. **1.** Dirty; untidy **2.** Infested with grubs

grudge (grʌdʒ) n. A feeling of resentment; a bad feeling toward someone

grudg-ing-ly (grʌdʒ–ŋ–liʸ) adv. Reluctantly: *He grudgingly gave his approval because he had no other choice.*

gru-el-ing (gruʷ–ə–lŋ) adj. Very difficult and tiring; exhausting

grue-some (gruʷ–səm) adj. Filling one with horror or disgust; grisly; revolting: *the gruesome details of the murder*

gruff (grʌf) adj. **1.** Of the voice, low and harsh **2.** Rough in speech or manner —**gruffly** adv. —**gruffness** n.

grum-ble (grʌm–bəl) v. **-bled, -bling** To mutter in discontent; to complain, not loudly, but angrily: *Don't grumble against each other (James 5:9). Offer hospitality to one another without grumbling (1 Peter 4:9).*

grump-y (grʌm–piʸ) adj. Cross; bad-tempered: *The boss is a bit grumpy today.*

grunt (grʌnt) n. **1.** A deep, throaty sound made by pigs **2.** A similar sound made by people

grunt v. **1.** To make a sound similar to that made by a pig **2.** To say sthg. in a way that sounds like grunting: *He really didn't say anything. He just grunted his approval.*

guar-an-tee (gɛər–ən–tiʸ / gær–ən–tiʸ) n. **1.** A written agreement by the maker of an article to repair or replace that article if it is found imperfect within a pe-riod of time: *The washing machine has a one-year guarantee.* **2.** An agreement to be responsible for the fulfillment of someone else's promise, esp.

for paying a debt 3. Sthg. of value given to someone to keep until the owner has fulfilled a promise, esp. to pay. *He gave them the deed (proof of ownership) to his property as a guarantee that he would repay the money.* 4. Assurance: *Clear skies are no guarantee that the weather will be sunny tomorrow.*

guarantee v. -teed, -teeing 1. To give a promise of quality, payment, or fulfillment concerning sthg.: *The TV is guaranteed for one year.* 2. To promise that sthg. will certainly be so: *I guarantee that you'll enjoy the new facilities.*

guar-an-tor (gær–ən–tɔr/ –tər/ geər–) n. One who guarantees or gives a guaranty

guar-an-ty (gær–ən–ti^y/geər–) n. -ties 1. Assumption of responsibility for the payment of another's debt or for the performance of another person's obligation 2. That which is pledged as security —**guaranty** v. -tied, -tying To guarantee

guard (gɑrd) n. 1. A state of watchfulness or alertness for possible danger: *Soldiers are on guard at the gate./ Be on guard! Be alert! You do not know when that time [of the Lord's return] will come (Mark 13:33)./ fig. Set a guard over my mouth, O Lord; keep watch over the door of my lips [=don't let me speak in any sinful or hurtful way] (Psalm 141:3).* 2. A position for defense, especially in a fight: *He hit me when my guard was down. (=when I was not ready to defend myself)* 3. A soldier, policeman, or prison officer, who guards sbdy. or sthg. 4. A group of soldiers or police officers whose duty it is to guard sbdy. or sthg.: *The prisoner was brought in under armed guard.* 5. A device that covers and protects: *a mudguard over the chain of a bicycle*

guard v. 1. To watch over and protect; keep safe: *Don't be anxious about anything, but in everything, by prayer and petition, with thanksgiving, present your requests to God. And the peace of God which transcends all understanding will guard your hearts and your minds in Christ Jesus (Philippians 4:6,7).* 2. To watch (a prisoner) in order to prevent escape

guard-i-an (gɑrd–i^y–ən) n. Sbdy. who is legally responsible for the property of another person or of a child who cannot manage his

own affairs

guard-i-an an-gel (gɑrd–i^y–ən e^yn–dʒəl) n. A good angel who protects a person, esp. a child: *Jesus said, "See that you do not look down on one of these little ones. For I tell you that their angels in heaven always see the face of my Father in heaven" (Matthew 18:10). Are not all angels ministering spirits sent to serve those who will inherit salvation? (Hebrews 1:14).*

guard rail (gɑrd re^yl) n. A railing for guarding against danger or trespassing, esp. a railing along a highway to prevent cars from going off the road

gua-va (gwɑ–və) n. 1. A South American tree yielding a pear-shaped fruit used in jelly 2. Its fruit

gu-ber-na-to-ri-al (gu^w–bər–nə–tɔr–i^y–əl) adj. Pertaining to a governor or his office

guer-ril-la (gə–rɪl–ə) n. A member of an independent, unofficial fighting group which attacks in small groups, usu. unexpectedly: *guerrilla bands*

guess (gɛs) v. 1. To form an opinion or make a statement without knowing or considering all the facts: *You'll never guess who I saw at the store this morning.* 2. To think sthg. is likely: *I guess we'll go to Grandma's house for Christmas as usual, won't we?*

guess n. 1. An act of guessing: *If you don't know the answer, you can make a guess anyway.* 2. An opinion reached by guessing: *I didn't count how many people were at the party, but my guess is about eighty.*

guest (gɛst) n. 1. A person who is invited and stays in someone's home for a short time or has one or more meals there: *We enjoyed having the Andersons as guests in our home.* 2. A person who is invited out and whose meals, tickets, etc. are paid for: *The Johnsons are coming to the concert as our guests.* 3. A visiting participant as on a radio or TV program —**guest** adj. *guest room*

guess-work (gɛs–wərk) n. 1. The process of guessing 2. Sthg. based on a guess or guesses, as an opinion

guff (gʌf) n. 1. Insolent talk 2. Nonsense

guid-ance (gɑɪd–əns) n. Counseling; advice: *For lack of guidance a nation falls, but many ad-*

visors make victory sure (Proverbs 11:14).

guide (gaɪd) n. Sthg. or sbdy. that leads or shows the way, esp. to tourists: *Our guide did a good job of showing us the city.*

guide v. **guided, guiding** To act as a guide: *But when he, the Spirit of truth [the Holy Spirit] comes, he will guide you into all truth* (John 16:13). —**guided** adj. *We took the guided tour of the old castle.*

guide-lines (gaɪd–laɪnz) n. The main points of policy, conduct, or a course of action on sthg. that must be dealt with (esp. sthg. official)

guide-word (gaɪd–wɜrd) n. A word that appears at the top of a page in a dictionary, telling which is the first or last word on that page

guild (gɪld) n. An association of people who share the same interests, skills, profession, etc.

guile (gaɪl) n. The ability to deceive or trick people

guile-less (gaɪl–ləs) adj. Completely honest and sincere; without deceit

guil-o-tine (gɪl–ə–tiʸn/giʸ–) n. An apparatus for beheading a person by means of the fall of a heavy blade

guilt (gɪlt) n. **1.** The fact or state of having broken a law or a commandment of God: *I said, "I will confess my transgressions to the Lord" — and you [O Lord] forgave the guilt of my sin* (Psalm 32:5). —opposite INNOCENCE **2.** Blame or responsibility for sthg. wrong: *Guilt for the pollution in our environment lies with all of us who fail to take action to keep it clean.* **3.** The knowledge or belief, whether true or not, that one has done wrong; shame: *Johnny seems to feel a lot of false guilt because of his parents' divorce.* —**guiltless** adj.

guilt-y (gɪl–tiʸ) adj. **-ier, -iest 1.** Having broken a commandment of God or a state law or disobeyed a moral or social rule: *Whoever keeps the whole law [God's Commandments] and yet stumbles at just one point is guilty of breaking all of it* (James 2:10). —compare INNOCENT **2.** Suffering from a feeling of guilt: *I feel guilty about forgetting your birthday.* —**guiltiness** n.

guin-ea fowl (gɪn–iʸ faʊl) n. An African game bird having a dark gray plumage, raised for its flesh and eggs

guin-ea pig (gɪn–iʸ pɪg) n. **1.** A short-eared, short-legged, tailless rodent, often used in scientific experiments **2.** The subject of an experiment

guise (gaɪz) n. A pretense; an outward appearance put on in order to conceal the truth NOTE: Do not confuse **guise** with **disguise**

gui-tar (gɪ–tɑr) n. A musical instrument with six or more strings and with a wooden body like a violin but larger, played by plucking the strings with a pick or with the fingers

gulch (gʌltʃ) n. A ravine; a deep narrow valley formed by a stream

gulf (gʌlf) n. A large body of water partly enclosed by land: *the Gulf of Mexico*

gull (gʌl) n. A usu. white or gray long-winged, web-footed seabird

gul-li-ble (gʌl–ə–bəl) adj. Easily deceived, especially into a false belief: *She's pretty gullible to fall for his old tricks.*

gul-ly (gʌl–iʸ) n. **-lies** A small, narrow valley or ditch cut by a stream of water

gulp (gʌlp) v. **1.** To swallow eagerly and rapidly in large amounts **2.** To choke or gasp, as in nervousness or surprise

gulp n. **1.** An act of gulping **2.** A large mouthful

gum (gʌm) n. **1.** Either of the two areas of firm, pink flesh at the base of the teeth **2.** A glue-like substance which comes especially from the stems of some trees and bushes, used for sticking things together **3.** Chewing gum

gum v. **-mm- 1.** To stick sthg. to sthg. else with gum **2.** To become sticky or clogged with gum: *It won't work; it's all gummed up.*

gum-bo (gʌm–boʷ) n. A thick soup containing okra and chicken or seafood

gump-tion (gʌm–ʃən) n. **1.** Courage or spunk **2.** Initiative or resourcefulness

gun (gʌn) n. **1.** Any kind of firearm that sends shells or bullets from a metal tube (barrel) **2.** A device that forces out a substance through a tube: *a grease gun*

gun v. **-nn- 1.** To shoot sbdy. with a gun: *He gunned him down.* **2.** To feed gasoline to an engine quickly: *He gunned the engine and sped away.*

gung ho (gʌŋ hoʷ) adj. *infml.* Enthusiastic; eager

gunk (gʌngk) n. *infml.* Sticky, greasy, or slimy matter

gun-ner (gʌn–ər) n. A soldier, sailor, or airman who fires a gun, esp. a large gun

gun-ner-y (gʌn–ər–iʸ) **-ies** n. The art and science of constructing and managing guns, esp. large guns

gun-ny (gʌn–iʸ) **-nies** n. **1.** A coarse fabric made of jute or hemp **2.** Burlap

gun-ny sack (gʌn–iʸ sæk) n. A sack made of burlap

gun-sling-er (gʌn–slɪŋ–ər) n. A gunfighter, esp. of the old West

gun-smith (gʌn–smɪθ) n. A person who makes or repairs firearms

gup-py (gʌp–iʸ) **-pies** n. A small, freshwater fish, often kept in aquariums

gur-gle (gɜr–gəl) n. A low, bubbling sound

gurgle v. **-gled, -gling** To make this sound

gu-ru (guʷ–ruʷ) n. **1.** A Hindu spiritual teacher or head of a religious sect **2.** An influential and revered teacher

gush (gʌʃ) v. **1.** To flow or pour out in large quantities, suddenly and violently: *Blood gushed from his wound.* **2.** To talk with much emotion, esp. in an affected manner, without true feeling

gush n. A sudden flow of liquid: *a gush of oil when the pipe broke* —**gushing** adj. *a gushing spring*

gush-er (gʌʃ–ər) n. An oil well from which oil flows strongly without needing to be pumped

gust (gʌst) n. A sudden strong blast of wind: *a windy day with gusts up to 65 miles an hour* —**gusty** adj. **-ier, -iest**

gus-to (gʌs–toʷ) n. Eager enjoyment in doing sthg.: *He started his new job with great gusto.*

gut (gʌt) n. **1.** The lower part of the alimentary canal; the intestine **2. guts (a)** The bowels or

entrails **(b)** *infml.* Courage: *It took a lot of guts to jump into a net from the tenth floor window.* **3.** Strong cord made from animal intestines, used surgically and for violin or racket strings

gut v. **-tt-** To completely destroy the inside of a building, esp. by fire: *The fire gutted the old warehouse in minutes.*

gut feel-ing (gʌt fiʸl–ɪŋ) adj. A feeling based on emotions rather than on reason or thought: *a gut feeling that he shouldn't make that trip*

gut-less (gʌt–lɪs) adj. Lacking courage and determination

gut-ter (gʌt–ər) n. **1.** A small channel beside a street or a trough along the edge of a roof, to collect and carry away rainwater **2.** A slum area in a dirty part of a city: *After spending all his money on liquor and drugs, he ended up in the gutter.*

gut-tur-al (gʌt–ər–əl) adj. **1.** Throaty; harsh sounding **2.** Pronounced in the throat

guy (gaɪ) n. *esp. AmE.* A man; fellow: *a nice guy*

guz-zle (gʌz–əl) v. **-zled, -zling** To drink greedily and to excess —**guzzler** n.

gym (dʒɪm) n., adj. **1.** Gymnasium **2.** Physical education: *a gym class*

gym-na-si-um (dʒɪm–neʸ–ziʸ–əm) n. A room equipped for gymnastics and other sports

gym-nast (dʒɪm–nəst) n. A person who trains and is skilled in certain bodily exercises

gym-nas-tics (dʒɪm–næst–ɪks) n. Body-building exercises, esp. those performed with special apparatus in a gymnasium, often done in competition with others —**gymnastic** adj.

gy-ne-col-o-gy (gaɪ–nə–kɑl–ə–dʒiʸ) n. A branch of medicine dealing with the diseases and hygiene of women

gyp (dʒɪp) v. **-pp-** *slang* To cheat; swindle: *He gypped me out of $20.*

gy-rate (dʒaɪ–reʸt) v. **-rated, -rating** To spin round and round: *A spinning top gyrates.*

gy-ro-scope (dʒaɪ–rə–skoʷp) n. An apparatus in which a rapidly spinning wheel is used to keep steady the object in which it is fixed.

H, h (eʸtʃ) n. The eighth letter of the English alphabet

Hab-ak-kuk (hæb-ə-kək/ hə-bæk-ək) n. **1.** A Hebrew prophet of Judah in the seventh century B.C., who prophesied an imminent Chaldean invasion **2.** A prophetic book of the Old Testament written by the prophet whose name it bears —see BIBLE, OLD TESTAMENT

ha-be-as cor-pus (heʸ-biʸ-əs kɔr-pəs) A writ requiring a person to be brought before a judge or court as a protection against illegal imprisonment

hab-er-dash-er (hæb-ər-dæʃ-ər) n. A dealer in men's clothing —**haberdashery** n. A haberdasher's shop

hab-it (hæb-ət) n. Customary behavior that is done almost without thinking: *She has a habit of jogging two miles every morning before breakfast.* NOTE: People develop habits by doing the same thing over and over again over a long period of time. Some habits are good and some are bad. New Christians must guard against returning to bad habits of the past and develop good habits to replace the bad habits. A habit usually means sthg. done regularly by one person, and a custom usually means sthg. that has been done over a period of time by a whole society: *He has an annoying habit of leaving his books lying around the room./It is the custom to sing "Happy Birthday" at children's birthday parties.*

hab-it-a-ble (hæb-ət-ə-bəl) adj. Capable of being lived in —**hab-it-a-bil-i-ty** (hæb-ə-tə-bɪl-ə-tiʸ) n.

ha-bi-tant (hæb-ə-tənt) n. Inhabitant; resident

hab-i-tat (hæb-ə-tæt) n. The place or the kind of place where a particular animal or plant naturally occurs: *The Antarctic is the penguin's natural habitat.*

hab-i-ta-tion (hæ-bə-teʸ-ʃən) n. **1.** Occupancy; the act of living in (inhabiting): *a shack unfit for human habitation* **2.** A dwelling place **3.** Residence

ha-bit-u-al (hə-bɪtʃ-uʷ-əl) adj. **1.** Usual; customary: *She drank her habitual cup of coffee.* **2.** By habit: *He's a habitual drug user.* —**habitually** adv. *He's habitually late to work.*

ha-bit-u-ate (hə-bɪtʃ-uʷ-eʸt) v. **-ated, -ating** To accustom —**habituation** (hə-bɪtʃ-uʷ-eʸ-ʃən) n.

ha-ci-en-da (hɑ-siʸ-ɛn-də) n. **1.** A landed estate, esp. one for farming or ranching **2.** The main house on such an estate

hack (hæk) v. To cut up roughly or in uneven pieces; to chop: *They hacked a trail through the jungle.*

hack-ney (hæk-niʸ) n. **1.** A horse for ordinary riding or driving **2.** A carriage for hire

hack-neyed (hæk-niʸd) adj. Lacking in freshness or originality: *a hackneyed expression*

hack-saw (hæk-sɔ) n. A fine-toothed saw for cutting metal

had (hæd) v. **1.** Past tense and past part. of **have 2. to be had** *infml.* To be deceived or made a fool of: *I think you've been had! You could have bought the same camera for half the price.*

had-dock (hæd-ək) n. An ocean fish related to the cod, often used as food

Ha-des (heʸ-diʸz) n. **1.** Hades is the Greek word for grave, the place where all go after death. **2.** Hell: *Jesus said, "...I will build my church, and the gates of Hades [= all the evil forces of that infernal empire] will not overcome it"* (Matthew 16:18). —see HELL

hadn't (hæd-ənt/ hædnt) v. Short for **had not:** *They hadn't eaten supper yet, so we decided to go out.*

haem-or-rhage (hem-ə-rɪdʒ) n. Variation of hemorrhage

haft (hæft) n. A handle, esp. of a knife, sword, dagger, etc.

hag (hæg) n. **1.** A witch **2.** An ugly or evil looking old woman —**haggish** adj.

Hag-ga-i (hæg-iʸ-aɪ/**hæg**-aɪ) n. **1.** A Hebrew prophet who lived about 500 B.C. and who advocated that the Temple in Jerusalem be rebuilt **2.** A prophetic book of the Old Testament, written by the prophet Haggai about 500 B.C.

hag-gard (hæg-ərd) adj. An exhausted or emaciated appearance after an illness, lack of sleep, or great difficulty: *They really looked haggard after hacking their way through the jungle for several days.*

hag-gle (hæg-əl) v. **-gled, -gling** To argue

about prices or terms when buying sthg.

hail (he^yl) n. **1.** Rain drops which fall as little, hard balls of ice **2.** *fig.* A falling, showering, etc. in the manner of hail: *a hail of bullets*

hail v. To fall as hail in a shower

hail v. **1.** To call out a greeting to someone or to try to get their attention: *He missed the last bus, so he hailed a taxi.* **2.** To originate or come from: *Where do you hail from?*

hail-stone (he^yl-sto^wn) n. A pellet of hail

hail-storm (he^yl-storm) n. A storm with hail

hair (hɛər) n. **1.** A slender, thread-like growth from the skin of a person or animal: *There are hairs all over the couch where the dog was lying.* **2.** A mass of such growths, esp. on the head of persons: *Mary has very long, blond hair.* **3. get in someone's hair** *infml.* To annoy someone **4. let one's hair down** To act in a relaxed and informal manner: *Why don't you let your hair down and stop being so formal?* **5. make someone's hair stand on end** To make someone very afraid; terrify **6. split hairs** *derog.* To be overly concerned with minor differences, esp. in arguments

hair-cut (hɛər-kʌt) n. **1.** The act of cutting the hair **2.** The style in which the hair is cut or worn

hair-do (hɛər-du^w) n. *pl.* **-dos 1.** The style in which a woman's hair is cut, arranged, and worn **2.** The hair itself

hair-dress-er (hɛər-drɛs-ər) n. A person who arranges or cuts women's hair

hair-pin (hɛər-pɪn) n. A slender U-shaped piece of wire used to hold the hair in place —**hairpin** adj. Sharply curved: *a hairpin turn in the road*

hair-raising (hɛər-re^yz-ɪŋ) adj. A terrifying experience

hair-split-ter (hɛər-splɪt-ər) n. A person who makes fine or unnecessary distinctions —**hairsplitting** n., adj.

hair spray (hɛər spre^y) n. A spray used to keep one's hair in place

hair-style (hɛər-staɪl) n. A creative style of arranging the hair —**hair-stylist** n. --**hair-styling** n.

hair-y (hɛər-i^y) adj. **-ier, -iest** Covered with, or as if with, hair

haj-ji (hædʒ-i^y) n. **-jies** A Muslim who has made a pilgrimage to Mecca

hale (he^yl) adj. Free from disease or defect; very healthy: *hale and hearty*

half (hæf) n., pron. **halves** (hævz) **1.** The number 1/2 **2.** Either of two equal parts of sthg.; 1/2; 50% —**halfway** adj., adv.

half-baked (hæf-be^ykt) adj. **1.** Not thoroughly baked **2.** Not well-planned or trained

half-breed (hæf-bri^yd) n. The offspring of parents of two different races

half-cocked (hæf-kakt) adj. Acting rashly or without proper preparation

half dollar (hæf dal-ər) n. A coin of the US and Canada worth 50 cents

half-heart-ed (hæf-hart-əd) adj. Lacking interest; not very enthusiastic

half hour (hæf aʊr) n. Thirty minutes

half-mast (hæf-mæst) n. A point about half way up a mast (flagpole), to which a flag is lowered to show respect for a dead person

half-wit (hæf-wɪt) n. A feeble-minded person —**halfwitted** adj.

hal-i-but (hæl-ə-bət) n. *pl.* **-but** A large flatfish used as food

hal-i-to-sis (hæl-ə-to^w-səs) n. A condition of having breath that smells unpleasant

hall (hol) n. **1.** A large room in which activities, e.g. meetings or dances, can be held: *an assembly hall/a dance hall* **2.** The passage or corridor leading from the living room, e.g., to other rooms in the house **3.** In a college or university, a dormitory: *I live at Townsend Hall.* **4.** A large public building: *city hall*

hal-le-lu-jah (hæ-lə-lu^w-yə) also **halleluiah** or **alleluia** (a-lə-lu^w-yə) interj., n. An expression of praise, joy, and thanks to God: *I heard what sounded like the roar of a great multitude in heaven shouting: "Hallelujah! Salvation and glory and power belong to our God, for true and just are his judgments. Hallelujah! For our God Almighty reigns. Let us rejoice and be glad and give him glory"* (Revelation 19:1,2,6,7).

hall-mark (hol-mark) n. **1.** Any mark or proof of genuineness **2.** Any distinguishing feature

hal-low (hæl-o^w) v. **1.** To make holy or sacred **2.** To regard as holy; honor as sacred

hal-lowed (hæl–o^wd/ hæl–o^w–əd) adj. **1.** Made holy or sacred **2.** Honored as holy: *Our Father in heaven, hallowed be your name... (= may your name be honored as holy)* (Matthew 6:9). —see PRAYER

Hal-low-een, -e'en (hæl–ə–wi^yn/ hɑl–) n. The evening of October 31st, which is followed by All Saints Day, formerly called All Hallows: *Halloween is now a time when children play tricks on people and dress up in strange clothes.*

hal-lu-ci-nate (hə–lu^w–sə–ne^yt) v. **-nated, -nating** To have or cause to have a hallucination

hal-lu-ci-na-tion (hə–lu^w–sə–ne^y–ʃən) n. **1.** The illusion of hearing or seeing things that are not there, due usu. to the use of drugs or to disorder of the nervous system **2.** The thing heard or seen in this way

hall-way (hɔl–we^y) n. *AmE.* An entrance hall or corridor in a building

ha-lo (he^y–lo^w) n. **-los** or **-loes 1.** A ring of light shown around the head of a holy person in paintings **2.** A ring of light surrounding a luminous body such as the sun or moon

halt (hɔlt) v. To stop or cause to stop: *The guard halted, listened intently, and then moved on.*

halt n. A stop or pause: *The train came to a halt.*

hal-ter (hɔl–tər) n. **1.** A rope or strap for leading or restraining an animal **2.** A woman's garment worn above the waist and tied behind the neck and across the back **3.** A hangman's noose

halt-ing (hɔl–tɪŋ) adj. **1.** Walking slowly as if unsure of oneself **2.** Of speech, hesitating; faltering

halve (hæv) v. **halved, halving** To divide into halves

halves (hævz) n. *pl.* of the noun **half**

hal-yard (hæl–yərd) n. A rope for raising or lowering a sail or flag

ham (hæm) n. **1.** A cut of meat from a pig's thigh, preserved with special spices **2.** An actor, performer, speaker, etc. whose performance is showy and unnatural **3.** A person who receives and/ or sends radio messages using his/ her own radio

ham-burg-er (hæm–bərg–ər) n. **1.** Ground beef **2.** A sandwich consisting of a small flat cake of ground beef on a round roll

ham-let (hæm–lət) n. A small village

ham-mer (hæm–ər) n. **1.** A tool for driving nails into wood **2.** Sthg. like a hammer made to hit sthg. else, as in a piano, or part of a gun

hammer v. To strike sthg. with a hammer: *He hammered the nails in./fig. We hammered (=knocked hard) at the door, but nobody was at home.*

ham-mock (hæm–ək) n. A hanging bed of canvas or rope mesh, hung by cords at each end

ham-per (hæm–pər) v. To cause difficulty; to hinder: *The snow hampered our efforts to keep the traffic moving.*

hamper n. **1.** A large basket with a lid, used for carrying food and other items: *a picnic hamper* **2.** *AmE.* A large basket with a lid, in which dirty laundry is placed

ham-ster (hæm–stər) n. A rat-like rodent with pouches in its cheeks for carrying grain

ham-string (hæm–strɪŋ) n. One of the strong tendons behind the human knee

hamstring v. **-strung, -stringing 1.** To cripple by cutting the hamstrings **2.** To make a person powerless in some way: *We've been hamstrung by our lack of information.*

hand (hænd) n. **1.** The fingers and other movable parts at the end of the human arm **2.** A needle or pointer on a clock or machine: *Does your watch have a second hand?* **3.** A worker who uses his/ her hands, esp. a sailor: *All hands on deck! /fig. He's an old hand (=an experienced person) at this kind of work.* **4.** Applause: *Give the actors a big hand!* **5.** Help: *Could you give/ lend me a hand, please? I'll never get this job done alone.* **6.** Control: *The class is getting out of hand./My times [O Lord] are in your hands* (Psalm 31:15). **7. at hand (a)** *fml.* Nearby or near in time: *Jesus began to preach and to say, "Repent, for the kingdom of heaven is at hand"* (Matthew 4:17NKJV). **(b)** Within reach: *Please keep my phone number at hand in case you need to call me.* **8. right–hand man** A person who is someone's able assistant **9. the right hand of God** A position of

power, honor, and authority: *Christ Jesus... is at the right hand of God and is also interceding for us* (Romans 8:34). **10. have clean hands** Guiltless: *Who may stand in his [God's] holy place? He who has clean hands and a pure heart...* (Psalm 24:3,4). **11. firsthand** By direct experience: *My mother found out about it firsthand.* (=she saw it happen) **12. get the upper hand (of)** To get control over someone or sthg. difficult **13. on hand** Ready for use; present **14. on the other hand** (Used for comparing differences): *On the one hand this dress is more becoming to you, but on the other hand that one is more likely to stay in fashion.* **15. play into (someone's) hands** To give an advantage to one's opponent **16. time on one's hands** Not occupied; not too busy **17. wait on (sbdy.) hand and foot** To do everything for sbdy., not allowing them to help themselves

hand v. **1.** To give directly with the hand into someone else's hand: *Please hand me the hammer.* **2. (have to) hand it to (someone)** To (have to) acknowledge someone's success or high quality: *You have to hand it to him, he really got the job done quickly.* **3. hand sthg. down (a)** To give or leave to someone else, esp. someone younger or who came later: *When I was a child, my sister always handed her clothes down to me.* **(b)** *AmE.* To make a public statement about: *The judge will hand down the sentence tomorrow.* **4. hand sthg. in** To deliver; give by hand: *Please hand in your assignments at the end of the class.* **5. hand sbdy./ sthg. over** To place in someone else's care, control, etc.: *The robber shouted, "Hand over your money or I'll shoot."*

hand-bag (hænd–bæg/ hæn–bæg) also **purse, pocketbook** *AmE.* n. A small bag for a woman's money and personal items

hand-ball (hænd–bɔl) n. **1.** A game played by two or four players in which a ball is struck with the hands and hit against a wall **2.** The ball used in this game

hand-bill (hænd–bɪl) n. A printed advertisement distributed by hand

hand-book (hænd–bʊk) n. **1.** A small book giving information or directions **2.** An outline of some particular subject

hand-cuff (hænd–kʌf) n. One of a pair of metal rings connected by a short chain, fastened around a prisoner's wrists to keep him from using his hands

handcuff v. **1.** To put handcuffs on **2.** To prevent sbdy. from doing sthg.

hand-ful (hænd–fəl) n. *pl.* **handfuls 1.** As much as can be held in one hand **2.** A small number: *Only a handful of people came to the concert.* **3.** A person or thing hard to control: *That little boy is quite a handful.*

hand-i-cap (hæn–diᶌ–kæp) n. **1.** A disability or disadvantage that makes achievement unusually difficult: *Gloria is always cheerful in spite of her handicap of blindness.* **2.** In a race or other sport, an artificial advantage given to the weaker competitors or a disadvantage imposed on the stronger competitors, such as carrying more weight or running further than others

handicap v. **-pp- 1.** To cause a person to have a disadvantage: *Lack of education handicapped him badly.* **2.** Of a disability of mind or body, to keep someone from acting and living normally: *He is handicapped by blindness in one eye.*

hand-i-craft (hænd–iᶌ–kræft) n. A skill requiring careful use of the hands, such as quilting, ceramics, weaving, etc.

hand-i-work (hænd–iᶌ–wɜrk) n. **1.** Work done by hand **2.** Work performed by, or the result of the action of a particular person: *The heavens declare the glory of God and the firmament [sky] shows his handiwork* (Psalm 19:1KJV).

hand-ker-chief (hæŋ–kər–tʃəf/ –tʃiᶌf) n. **-chiefs** (–tʃəfs/ –tʃiᶌfs) A piece of cloth for various personal uses such as wiping the nose, drying the eyes, etc.

han-dle (hæn–dəl) n. **1.** A part of an object which is specially made for grasping it with the hand or for opening it **2. fly off the handle** To lose one's temper; to act out of extreme anger

handle v. **-dled, -dling 1. (a)** To feel with the hands **(b)** To move by hand: *Handle with care.* **2.** To deal with; control: *That teacher really knows how to handle children.* **3.** To use: *Are you sure you know how to handle an elec-*

tric knife?/A pastor or any man of God must be one "who correctly handles the word of truth" (2 Timothy 2:15).

han·dle·bars (hæn–dəl–barz) n. The bar above the front wheel of a bicycle or motorcycle, used for steering it

hand·out (hænd–aʊt) n. **1.** Sthg., such as food, clothes, etc., given to a beggar or as if to a beggar **2.** Information distributed, esp. a printed sheet: *Information about tomorrow's meeting is on the handout.*

hand·picked (hænd–pɪkt) adj. Carefully chosen

hand·shake (hænd–ʃeʸk) n. The shaking of the right hands by two people as a greeting, or as a gesture of agreement or congratulations

hand·some (hæn–səm) adj. **1.** Esp. of men, good-looking; attractive in appearance —see BEAUTIFUL **2.** Generous; plentiful: *a handsome profit* —**handsomely** adv.

hand·writ·ing (hænd–raɪt–ɪŋ) n. **1.** Writing done by hand **2.** The style of writing by a particular person: *Mary has unusual but beautiful handwriting.* **3. to see the handwriting on the wall** To foresee impending disaster, misfortune, etc. (Daniel 5:5-28).

hand·y (hænd–iʸ) adj. **-ier, -iest 1.** Convenient and useful: *A can opener is a handy tool.* **2.** Clever in using the hands **3.** *infml.* Nearby; at hand: *The shopping center is quite handy.* —**handily** adv.

hand·y·man (hænd–iʸ–mæn) n. A man hired to do miscellaneous small jobs

hang (hæŋ) v. **hung** (hʌŋ), **hanging 1.** To fasten or be fastened at the top with the lower part free: *to hang up your clothes* **2.** To fasten wallpaper on a wall: *We finished hanging the wallpaper in the hall in about two hours.* **3. hang around** *infml.* To stay in or near a place without purpose or activity: *The kids from my high school class used to hang around Bailey's Malt Shop when we had nothing to do.* **4. hang on (a)** To keep hold of: *Hang on to my hand. I'll help you up the cliff.* **(b)** To wait: *Hang on a minute. Mr. Smith is on another line right now.* **(c)** To continue doing sthg.: *Let's try to hang on a little longer. We're nearly finished with the job.* **5. hang onto sthg.** To try to

keep: *I hope I can hang onto this apartment. It would be hard to find another one.* **6. hang out** To spend much time in a place or with someone; to live in a place: *His grades have gone up since he started hanging out at the library.* **7. hang up (a)** To finish speaking on the telephone by putting the receiver back **(b) be hung up on** To be unwilling to change one's idea about sthg. —see also HANG-UP

hang (hæŋ) **hanged** (hæŋd) v. To (cause to) die, esp. in punishment for a crime, by suspending with a rope around the neck: *He was hanged for his crimes.*

hang n. **get the hang of sthg.** To learn how to do sthg. or how sthg. works

hang·ar (hæŋ–ər/ hæŋ–gər) n. A large building where planes are kept

hang·er (hæŋ–ər) n. also **coat hanger, clothes hanger** A device to fit inside or around a shirt, dress, etc. for hanging from a rod or hook

hang-glide (hæŋ–glaɪd) v. **-glided, -gliding** To fly through the air on a large kite —**hanggliding** n.

hang·ing (hæŋ–ɪŋ) n. Death by hanging

hang·man (hæŋ–mən) n. One whose job is to hang criminals

hang·out (hæŋ–aʊt) n. A place where one lives or spends a lot of time

hang·over (hæŋ–oʷ–vər) n. **1.** The sick feeling one has after drinking too much alcohol **2.** A condition remaining as a result of an earlier condition: *His tiredness is a hangover from the long hours he put in last week.*

hang-up (hæŋ–əp) n. A source of emotional or mental difficulty

hank (hæŋk) n. **1.** A coil or loop **2.** A specific length of coiled thread or yarn

han·ker (hæŋ–kər) v. To have a restless yearning to do sthg. —**hankering** n.

han·ky or **han·kie** (hæŋ–kiʸ) n. **-kies** *infml.* Handkerchief

han·ky-pan·ky (hæŋ–kiʸ pæŋ–kiʸ) n. **1.** Trickery or deception **2.** Illicit sexual behavior

Han·sen's disease (hæn–sənz dɪ–ziʸz) n. The disease of leprosy

han·som cab (hæn–səm kæb) n. A light two-wheeled covered carriage for two passen-

gers, pulled by one horse

Ha-nuk-kah (**hɑ**–nə–kə) or **Cha-nu-kah** (tʃɑ–nə–kə) n. An eight day Jewish holiday in memory of the rededication of the Temple of Jerusalem following its defilement by Antiochus of Syria

hap-haz-ard (hæp–hæz–ərd) adj. Happening in a disorderly and unplanned manner; aimless

hap-less (hæp–ləs) adj. Unfortunate

hap-pen (hæp–ən) v. **1.** To occur; take place: *When did the accident happen?* **2.** To take place by chance: *I just happened to be in the right place at the right time.* **3.** To come or go as if by chance: *He happened into the room where the robbers were hiding.*

hap-pen-ing (hæp–ən–ɱ) n. Sthg. that takes place

hap-pi-ly (hæp–ə–liʸ) adv. **1.** In a happy manner **2.** Luckily: *Happily, Mary is feeling much better now.*

hap-pi-ness (hæp–iʸ–nəs) n. The state of being happy

hap-py (hæp–iʸ) adj. **-pier, -piest 1.** Giving or feeling contentment and well-being: *a happy life/ A happy heart makes the face cheerful* (Proverbs 15:13). *Is anyone happy? Let him sing songs of praise* (James 5:13). —opposite UN-HAPPY **2.** Fitting; suitable: *a happy solution* **3.** *pol.* Pleased: *I'd be happy to help you .* **4.** Expressing joy: *Happy Birthday!*

hap-py-go-luck-y (hæp–iʸ–goʷ–lʌk–iʸ) adj. Carefree

ha-ra-ki-ri (hɛər–iʸ kɛər–iʸ/hɑr–iʸ kɑr–iʸ) Ritual suicide by disembowelment, formerly practiced by high ranking Japanese to avoid disgrace

ha-rangue (hə–ræŋ) v. To speak in an angry, scolding tone: *The teacher harangued the children for a long time about their bad behavior.*

har-ass (hə–ræs/ hær–əs) v. **1.** To annoy continually **2.** To make repeated attacks on (an enemy)

har-assed (hə–ræst/ hær–əst) adj. Tired and irritated by continual worry —**harassment** n.

har-bin-ger (hɑr–bɪn–dʒər) n. A person or thing that heralds the approach of sthg.

har-bor (hɑr–bər) n. **harbour** *BrE.* A part of a body of water which is sheltered from

rough waters so that ships are safe inside it

harbor v. **harbour** *BrE.* To give protection or shelter to: *He was charged with harboring a thief./ fig. He harbors (=keeps in his mind) a grudge against his former employer for firing him without good reason.*

hard (hɑrd) adj. **1.** Firm and stiff; not easily broken, bent, or penetrated: *hard metal* —opposite SOFT **2.** Difficult to do: *Ah, Sovereign Lord, you have made the heavens and the earth... Nothing is too hard for you* (Jeremiah 32:17). **3.** Difficult to answer: *All the questions on the exam were very hard.* —opposite EASY **4.** Requiring force of body or mind: *He worked hard in the hot sun all day./All hard work brings a profit, but mere talk leads only to poverty* (Proverbs 14:23). *fig. Have you taken a hard look at his plan? (=examined it very carefully)* **5.** Full of difficulty and trouble; not pleasant: *It's been a hard journey.* **6.** Showing no mercy; severe: *Don't be too hard on her; she's just learning the job.* **7.** Of water, containing minerals that prevent soap from mixing properly with the water **8.** Of a drug, being very harmful and capable of making one dependent (=addicted) in such a way that he/ she is ill without it

hard adv. **1.** With great effort or energy: *The wind is blowing hard./We thought long and hard before making the decision to move our office.* **2.** Heavily: *It's been snowing hard all day and the roads are blocked.* **3. be hard hit (by)** To suffer loss as a result of: *Los Angeles was hard hit by the earthquake.* **4. be hard put to do** sthg. To have great trouble in doing sthg. **5. hard at it** *infml.* Working with great energy: *He's hard at it preparing his report.* **6. take it hard** To suffer deeply: *She's taking the loss of her sister very hard.*

hard-and-fast (hɑrd–ən–fæst) adj. Strict; not to be violated: *Hard -and -fast rules*

hard-boiled (hɑrd–bɔɪld) adj. **1.** Of an egg, boiled until hard **2.** Of a person, tough, unsympathetic

hard-core (hɑrd–kɔr) adj. **1.** Uncompromising; unswerving **2.** Extremely bad, as in hardcore pornography **3.** Being of the most determined and dedicated members of a group

hard-en (hɑrd–ən) v. **1.** To become or make hard or firm: *The cement hard-ened./spir. Do not harden your hearts* (Hebrews 3:8). NOTE: **Harden** means "to make or become hard," but should only be used when hard means "firm and stiff," "unkind and severe," or "resistant to the truth of God's word." Otherwise, use **get harder**. Compare: *The snow hardened* (=became firm) *until ice was formed./The problems in my math book are getting harder.* (=becoming more difficult) *Living on one's income seems to be getting harder* (=becoming more troublesome) *for us.* **2. harden sbdy. to sthg.** To make or become less sensitive to sthg.: *I'm quite hardened to life on the ranch now.*

hard-head-ed (hɑrd–hed–əd) adj. **1.** Shrewd **2.** Unsentimental **3.** Stubborn, obstinate

hard-heart-ed (hɑrd–hɑrt–əd) adj. Unfeeling; showing no mercy: *Do not be hardhearted or tightfisted [stingy] toward your poor brother [fellowman]. Rather be openhanded and freely lend him whatever he needs* (Deuteronomy 15:7).

hard–line (hɑrd–lɑm) adj. Involving or advocating a persistently firm course of action

hard-ly (hɑrd–liʸ) adv. **1.** Almost not: *I could hardly hear the announcer on the radio./I hardly ever* (=almost never) *buy meat these days; it's too expensive.* **2.** Barely; only just: *We'd hardly started supper when the phone rang.* **3.** Certainly not; not at all: *This is hardly the best time to buy a bathing suit — it's the middle of winter.*

hard-ness (hɑrd–nəs) n. The quality or condition of being hard

hard-ship (hɑrd–ʃɪp) n. Severely difficult conditions of life: *The homeless must endure great hardships.*

hard up adj. Being in need, esp. of money: *My family was very hard up as a result of losing all our possessions in the fire.*

hard-ware (hɑrd–weər) n. **1.** Tools and household implements **2.** Parts which make up a computer —compare SOFTWARE

hard-wood (hɑrd–wʊd) n. The wood of various trees that have leaves and flowers rather than needles: *Oak, maple, teak, and mahogany are hardwoods.* —**hardwood** adj. *a hardwood floor*

hard-y (hɑrd–iʸ) adj. **-ier, -iest 1.** Of people or animals, strong; able to bear hardship **2.** Of plants, able to live through the winter above ground —**hardiness** n.

hare (heər) n. An animal similar to a rabbit, but larger

hare-brained (heər–breʸnd) adj. Stupid; foolish; reckless

hare-lip (heər–lɪp) n. A split in the upper lip at birth, like that of a hare

har-em (heər–əm) n. **1.** The women of a Muslim household **2.** Their living quarters

hark (hɑrk) v. To listen; pay close attention

har-le-quin (hɑr–lə–kwɪn) n. **1.** A character in comic theater, usu. masked and in a costume of many colors, in a pantomime **2.** A clown

har-lot (hɑr–lət) n. Prostitute

harm (hɑrm) n. **1.** Damage; wrong: *Love does no harm to its neighbor. Therefore, love is the fulfillment of the law* (Romans 13:10). **2. out of harm's way** Safe from danger —**harmful** adj.

harm v. To damage; to hurt: *There was a severe earthquake yesterday, but our house was not harmed by it.*

harm-less (hɑrm–ləs) adj. Unable or unwilling to cause harm: *The dog barks a lot, but he's quite harmless.* —**harmlessly** adv.

har-mon-i-ca (hɑr–mɑn–ɪ–kə) n. A small, musical, wind instrument played by passing it along the lips while blowing air out or sucking it in

har-mo-nize (hɑr–mə–nɑɪz) v. **-nized, -nizing** BrE. **-nise 1.** To sing or play music in harmony **2.** To be or cause to be in agreement in style, color, etc. with each other or sthg. else: *Her green scarf doesn't harmonize very well with her blue blouse.*

har-mo-ny (hɑr–mə–niʸ) n. **-nies 1.** Notes of music combined together in a way that is pleasing to the ear **2.** A state of agreement; peacefulness: *The Bible says, "Live in harmony with one another"* (Romans 12:16). —compare DISCORD —**har-mo-ni-ous** (hɑr–moʷ–niʸ–əs) adj. —**harmoniously** adv.

har-ness (hɑr–nəs) n. **1.** The leather bands and other gear used to control a horse or hitch it to a cart **2.** Any fastening resembling this,

such as that for attaching a parachute to its wearer

harness v. **1.** (a) To put a harness on (b) To attach by means of a harness **2.** To control and use natural forces to produce useful power: *The Colorado River has been harnessed to produce electricity.*

harp (harp) n. A large, musical instrument with strings running from the top to the bottom of an open, three-cornered frame, played by plucking or stroking with the fingers

har-poon (har–pu^wn) n. A barbed spear fastened to a rope, used for hunting large fish or whales

harpoon v. To strike with a harpoon

harsh (harʃ) adj. **1.** Disagreeable in causing pain to the senses: *A gentle answer turns away wrath, but a harsh word stirs up anger* (Proverbs 15:1). —opposite SOFT **2.** Of people, punishments, etc., showing cruelty —harshness n. —harshly adv.

har-vest (har–vəst) n. **1.** The gathering of the crops **2.** The season when crops are picked: *God said, "As long as the earth endures, seed-time and harvest... will never cease"* (Genesis 8:22). *He who gathers crops in summer is a wise son, but he who sleeps during harvest is a disgraceful son* (Proverbs 10:5). **3.** The amount of crops gathered: *a good/large harvest* **4.** *fig.* The amount of souls to be brought into the kingdom of God through the preaching of the Good News about Jesus Christ: *Jesus said, "The harvest is plentiful but the workers are few. Ask the Lord of the harvest, therefore, to send out workers into his harvest field [= the world]"* (Matthew 9:37,38). **5.** The outcome or consequence of any effort or series of events: *No discipline seems pleasant at the time, but painful. Later on, however, it produces a harvest of righteousness and peace for those who have been trained by it* (Hebrews 12:11). *Let us not become weary in doing good, for at the proper time we will reap a harvest if we do not give up* (Galatians 6:9).

harvest v. To gather a crop —compare REAP

has (hæz) v. 3rd person singular present tense of **have**

hash (hæʃ) n. **1.** Chopped meat, mixed with potatoes, and browned **2.** A hodgepodge; a haphazard mixture

hash v. **1.** To chop into small pieces **2.** To discuss; talk about: *They stayed up late, hashing over their plans.*

hasn't (hæz–ənt/ hæznt) v. Short for **has not**: *Hasn't he finished yet?*

hasp (hæsp) n. A hinged, metal fastener for a box or door, which fits over a hook and is made secure with a padlock

has-sock (hæs–ək) n. **1.** A thick cushion used as a footstool or to sit on **2.** A cushion on which to kneel in prayer

haste (he^yst) n. Quick movement or action: *Do you see a man who speaks in haste? There is more hope for a fool than for him* (Proverbs 29:20).

has-ten (he^ys–ən) v. To cause to happen faster: *She hastened to finish her homework./I will hasten and not delay to obey your commands [O Lord]* (Psalm 119:60).

hast-y (he^y–sti^y) adj. -ier, -iest **1.** Done quickly **2.** Too quick in speaking, acting, or deciding sthg., often with a bad result: *Do not be hasty in your heart to utter anything before God. God is in heaven and you are on earth, so let your words be few* (Ecclesiastes 5:2). —hastily adv. —hastiness n.

hat (hæt) n. **1.** A covering worn on top of the head, usually having a shaped crown and a brim —compare CAP **2. at the drop of a hat** Ready upon the slightest suggestion: *He'd start a fight at the drop of a hat.* **3. pass the hat around** To collect money, esp. for a worthy purpose **4. take one's hat off to (someone)** To show admiration for someone for their actions **5. talking through one's hat** Talking foolishly **6. keep (sthg.) under one's hat** To keep secret **7. throw one's hat in the ring** To enter a campaign for a political office, promotion, etc.

hatch (hætʃ) v. **1.** Of an egg, to break, so the young bird can get out: *Six eggs have hatched already.* **2.** Of a young bird, to break out of the shell: *Three baby robins have hatched.* **3.** To devise or originate: *They hatched a plan to begin a new company.*

hatch n. A small door or opening, as in the deck of a ship or in an airplane

hatch-e-ry (hætʃ–ər–iʸ) n. -ries A place where eggs, esp. of fish and poultry, are hatched

hatch-et (hætʃ–ət) n. A small, short-handled ax

hate (heʸt) n. A strong feeling of dislike: *The villain's eyes were full of hate.* —opposite LOVE

hate v. **hated, hating 1.** To dislike sbdy. or sthg.: *I hate getting up in the morning.* **2.** To dislike strongly: *The two enemies hated each other./The fear of the Lord is to hate evil* (Proverbs 8:13). *Whoever hates his brother is a murderer and you know that no murderer has eternal life abiding in him* (1 John 3:15). *You [God] love righteousness and hate wickedness* (Psalm 45:7). —opposite LOVE

hate-ful (heʸt–fəl) adj. Very unpleasant; very bad: *That was a hateful thing to do to him.* —hatefully adv.

ha-tred (heʸ–trəd) n. Great dislike; hate: *Hatred stirs up dissension* (Proverbs 10:12). *Don't you know that friendship with the world (=its sinful pleasures) is hatred toward God?* (James 4:4). —op-posite LOVE

haugh-ty (hɔt–iʸ) adj. **-tier, -tiest** Proud of oneself and looking down on other people: *Pride goes before destruction, a haughty spirit before a fall* (Proverbs 16:18). *There are six things the Lord hates, seven that are detestable to him: haughty eyes, a lying tongue...* (Proverbs 6:17). —haughtily adv. —haughtiness n.

haul (hɔl) v. **1.** To pull hard: *They hauled a truckload of logs home from the forest.* **2.** To force to appear, esp. in court: *Jane was hauled before the court for child abuse.*

haul n. **1.** The act of hauling or the distance hauled: *It's a long haul to town from our ranch.* **2.** (a) The amount of fish caught at one time (b) The amount gotten, esp. stolen goods: *The jewel thieves got quite a haul.*

haunch (hɔntʃ/ hɑntʃ) n. **1.** The fleshy part of the body about the hip **2.** The hip **3.** The hind quarter of an animal **4.** The leg and loin of an animal, used for food

haunt (hɔnt/ hɑnt) v. **1.** Said esp. of a ghost, to visit: *A friendly ghost is said to haunt the old house.* **2.** To visit a place frequently **3.** To linger in the mind of someone: *I was haunted by*
his last words to me.

haunt n. A place where someone goes often: *The museum of natural history was one of the man's favorite haunts.*

haunt-ing (hɔnt–ŋ/ hɑnt–ŋ) adj. Remaining in one's thoughts: *a haunting memory* —hauntingly adv.

have (v/ əv/ həv/ hæv) v. Used as a helping verb with another verb **1.** Used with the past participle to form the perfect tenses of verbs: *I have seen him many times at the library.* **2. have got to** Must: *I have got to finish this report by tomorrow or fail the course*

Present tense, singular:
I **have**, I've; You **have**, you've; He/ She/ It **has**; He's/ She's/ It's;

Present tense, plural:
We **have**, We've; You **have**, You've; They **have**, They've

Past tense, singular:
I **had**, I'd; You **had**, You'd; He/ She/ It **had**, He'd/ She'd/ It'd

Past tense plural: We **had**, We'd; You **had**, You'd; They **had**, They'd

Past participle: **had**

Present participle: **having**

Negative short forms:
haven't, hasn't, hadn't

have v. **had, having 1.** To own or possess: *I have a new bike.* **2.** To obtain or receive: *Have a piece of birthday cake!* **3.** To experience or enjoy: *Have fun at the party!* **4.** To be under obligation to: *We have to get to work now.* **5.** To ask sbdy. to one's home: *We're having some friends (over) for dinner tonight.* **6.** To contain: *The house has three bedrooms.* **7.** To allow; permit: *The company can't have you late for work every morning.* **8.** To cause sthg. to be done or to happen: *I had my car repaired.* **9.** To show a quality: *Lord, have mercy upon us.* **10.** To be engaged in: *We had a long talk.* **11.** To be cheated: *We've been had.* **12.** To give birth to: *She had a baby boy.* **13. have to do with** To have a connection with: *Her job has sthg. to do with keeping medical records.*

ha-ven (heʸ–vən) n. A place of calm and safety; a refuge

have-n't (hæv–ənt) v. Short for **have not**: *We haven't sent your order yet.*

hav-oc (hæv–ək) n. Widespread damage; great disorder

hawk (hɔk) n. **1.** A bird of prey (= one that catches other birds and small animals for food) **2.** A person who favors a war or a war-like policy

hawk v. To sell goods on the street or from door to door

haw-thorn (hɔ–θɔrn) n. A thorny tree or shrub that has white or red flowers, and red berries in the autumn

hay (heʸ) n. **1.** Grass, clover, etc. which has been cut and dried, esp. for cattle food **2.** infml. **hit the hay** To go to bed **3.** infml. **make hay while the sun shines** To seize opportunities before they disappear

hay fe-ver (heʸ fiʸ–vər) n. An acute allergy, sthg. like a bad cold, but caused by breathing in pollen dust from certain plants

hay-wire (heʸ–wair/ –wai–ər) n. Badly disorganized; out of control: *Everything seems to have gone haywire with our plans.*

haz-ard (hæz–ərd) n. A danger: *Smoking is a health hazard.* —**hazardous** (hæz–ər–dəs) adj.

hazard v. To risk: *He hazarded all his money in the attempt to save the business.*

haze (heʸz) n. A light mist or smoke

ha-zel (heʸ–zəl) n. **1.** A small tree bearing an edible nut **2.** A light golden brown color

haz-y (heʸ–ziʸ) adj. -ier, -iest **1.** Rather misty or cloudy: *It's too hazy to see the mountains today.* **2.** Uncertain: *He was rather hazy about what we should do next.* **3.** Vague; indistinct —**hazily** adv. —**haziness** n.

he (hiʸ) pron. (Used as the subject of a sentence) **1.** That male person or animal already mentioned: *John said he was going to the store.* **2.** A person of unspecified sex: *He who hesitates is lost.*

he n. A male person or animal: *Is your dog a he or a she?*

head (hɛd) n. **1.** The top part of the body of a human or an animal which contains the eyes, ears, nose, etc. and the brain **2.** The end of a bed, sofa, etc. where this part rests: *at the head of the bed* **3.** A person's mind or brain: *I can't get into my head how to work this machine.* **4.** A leader of a government, company, etc.: *heads of state/ government/Christ is*

the head of the church... (Ephesians 5:23). *You [Christians] have been given fullness in Christ, who is the head over every power and authority* (Colossians 2:10). **5.** The top or front part of sthg.; the most important part: *at the head of the table* **6. (a)** A person in the phrase "per head": *The buffet luncheon will cost $5.50 per head.* **(b)** Used in counting certain farm animals: *four head of cattle* **7. above/over someone's head** Too difficult for someone to understand **8. bring sthg. to a head** To bring an event or a discussion to reach a point where sthg. must be done or decided **9. go to someone's head (a)** To cause someone to be over-excited or intoxicated **(b)** To cause someone to become too conceited **10. have one's head in the clouds** To be unrealistic or impractical **11. head over heels (a)** Turning over in the air head first **(b)** Very; completely: *head over heels in love* **12. keep one's head** To remain calm: *Keep your head in all situations* (2 Timothy 4:5). **13. lose one's head** To act hastily and often wrongly because of being afraid, angry, confused, etc. **14. not being able to make heads or tails of** To be unable to understand **15. bury one's head in the sand** To refuse to face a difficulty **16. have sthg. hanging over one's head** To feel the threat of sthg. bad about to happen

head v. **1.** To be the leader: *The high school band headed the parade down Main Street.* **2.** To be in charge of: *Who heads the committee?* **3.** To move or cause to move in a certain direction: *The team was heading home after their victory.* **4. head for** To go to or move towards: *We're heading for California.*

head-ache (hɛd–eʸk) n. **1.** A pain in the head **2.** A problem causing worry

head-ing (hɛd–ŋ) n. The title written at the top of each part of a piece of writing

head-light (hɛd–lait) n. also **headlamp** (hɛd–læmp) A powerful light mounted on the front of a vehicle, usually one of a pair

head-line (hɛd–lain) n. **1.** The heading printed in large letters above a newspaper story or article **2.** usu. pl. A main point of the news, as read on radio or television: *The big storm made headlines all over the country.*

head-long (hɛd-lɔŋ) adv. **1.** With the head first **2.** Rashly; without thought or delay, often foolishly

head-man (hɛd-mæn) n. -men pl. The highest ranking man in a tribe or in a business organization

head-mas-ter (hɛd-mæs-tər/ hɛd-mæs-tər) **head-mis-tress** (hɛd-mɪs-trɪs/ hɛd-mɪs-trɪs) fem. n. The teacher heading the staff of a private school AmE. Principal

head-on (hɛd-ɑn/ -ɔn) adj. With the front end getting hit squarely: He was killed in a head-on collision with a truck.

head-quart-ers (hɛd-kwɔr-tərz) n. The place from which an organization or military force is controlled NOTE: This word can also be treated as singular: The company's headquarters is in Los Angeles.

head start n. An advantage gained at the beginning of a race or an event: a ten-minute head start

head-strong (hɛd-strɔŋ) adj. Self-willed and obstinate; stubborn

head-way (hɛd-weʸ) n. Progress: Our boat could make little headway against the wind.

head wind (hɛd wɪnd) n. A wind blowing towards one

heal (hiʸl) v. **1.** To cause to become healthy: Jesus healed every disease and sickness among the people (Matthew 4:23). **2.** To cause to become productive: If my people, who are called by my name, will humble themselves and pray and seek my face and turn from their wicked ways, then I will hear from heaven and will forgive their sin and will heal their land (2 Chronicles 7:14). **3.** spir. To cause to become spiritually healthy: But he [Jesus] was pierced for our transgressions, he was crushed for our iniquities; the punishment that brought us peace was upon him, and by his wounds we are healed... The Lord laid on him the iniquity of us all (Isaiah 53:5,6). Jesus went around doing good and healing all who were under the power of the devil (Acts 10:38). **4.** To comfort the afflicted: He [God] heals the brokenhearted... (Psalm 147:3). —healer n.

health (hɛlθ) n. **1.** The state of being well: As long as I keep my health, I'll be happy./ Do not be wise in your own eyes; fear the Lord and shun evil. This will bring health to your body (Proverbs 3:8). —opposite SICKNESS **2.** The state of being well or ill: in poor health/ in good health

health-ful (hɛlθ-fəl) adj. Good for one's health: Milk is a healthful drink.

health-y (hɛl-θiʸ) adj. -ier, -iest **1.** Strong and usually in good health: It is not the healthy who need a doctor, but the sick (Mark 2:17). **2.** Producing or showing good health: healthy living/fig. The children have a healthy attitude toward school. —opposite UNHEALTHY

heap (hiʸp) n. A large number of things in a pile: The bedding and dirty clothes lay in a heap on the floor.

heap v. **1.** To pile up in large amounts: He heaped his plate full of meat and vegetables. **2.** To put or throw in a heap: He heaped his clothes on the bed.

hear (hɪər) v. **heard** (hɑrd), **hearing 1.** To receive and understand sounds by using the ears: Please turn the radio down! I can't hear what you're saying. **2.** To know or receive news or information about sbdy. or sthg.: Jesus said to the unbelievers, "He who belongs to God hears what God says. The reason you do not hear is that you do not belong to God" (John 8:47). Blessed are they that hear the Word of God and keep it (Luke 11:28). **3.** To listen for a particular purpose esp. to a case in court: The judge heard the case. **4. wouldn't hear of it** Will not allow: I won't hear of your buying me such an expensive gift.

heard (hɑrd) v. Past tense and past part. of hear

hear-ing (hɪər-ɪŋ) n. **1.** The sense by which one hears sound: Her hearing is very good for an eighty-year-old./Faith comes by hearing...the word of Christ (Romans 10:17). **2.** The distance at which sthg. can be heard: Stay within hearing. I'll call you for supper soon. **3.** Law A trial of a case before a judge

hear-say (hɪər-seʸ) n. Things heard in rumors or gossip, and not necessarily true

hearse (hɑrs) n. A car which is used to carry a body in a coffin to the funeral

heart (hɑrt) n. **1.** The organ inside the chest which maintains the flow of blood through the body by regular contractions **2.** This or-

gan when thought of as the emotional center of a person: *out of the kindness of his heart/ You shall love the Lord your God with all your heart* (Matthew 22:37). *Create in me a pure heart, O Lord* (Psalm 51:10). *Blessed are the pure in heart, for they shall see God* (Matthew 5:8). **3.** The central or inner part of anything: *Let's get to the heart of the matter.* **4.** Courage: *Don't lose heart; keep on trying!* **5.** A playing card with one or more heart-shaped figures printed on it in red: *the Queen of Hearts* **6. after one's own heart** Of exactly the type one likes: *He's a man after my own heart.* **7. break someone's heart** To cause someone great unhappiness **8. by heart** By memory: *to know by heart* **9. set one's heart on (doing) sthg.** To want sthg. very much **10. take (sthg.) to heart** To feel deeply and take action about a matter **11. eat one's heart out** To be very worried or troubled **12. wear one's heart on one's sleeve** To show one's feelings instead of hiding them

heart-ache (hɑrt–eʸk) n. Mental pain and anguish; feelings of deep sorrow

heart at-tack (hɑrt ə–tæk) n. Sudden failure of the heart to work properly, often causing death: *He died of a heart attack.*

heart-break-ing (hɑrt–breʸk–ɪŋ) adj. Causing great sorrow —**heartbreakingly** adv.

heart-burn (hɑrt–bɜrn) n. An unpleasant burning in the chest, caused by indigestion

heart-en (hɑrt–ən) v. To encourage; cheer up: *He was heartened by her letter.* —opposite DISHEARTEN

hearth (hɑrθ) n. The floor of a fireplace, usu. of stone or brick

heart-i-ly (hɑrt–əl–iʸ) adv. With energy, appetite, etc.: *They laughed heartily.*

heart-less (hɑrt–ləs) adj. Cruel; very unkind

heart-rend-ing (hɑrt–rɛnd–ɪŋ) adj. That which causes feelings of sorrow or deep pity: *heartrending screams of pain*

heart–to–heart adj. Of a discussion, open and sincere, usu. private: *The two men had a heart-to-heart talk and settled their differences.*—**heart–to–heart** n.

heart-warm-ing (hɑrt–wɔr–mɪŋ) adj. Giving a feeling of pleasure, esp. because of a kindness done: *It was heartwarming to see so many*

people willing to help.

heart-y (hɑrt–iʸ) adj. **-ier, -iest 1.** Very friendly: *a hearty handshake* **2.** Healthy (esp. in the phrase "hale and hearty") **3.** Of meals, large: *a hearty meal* —**heartiness** n.

heat (hiʸt) n. **1.** The quality or quantity of being hot **2.** Hot weather: *When will this heat ever let up?*

heat v. To make or become warm or hot: *Your supper is cold; I'll heat it (up) again.*

heat-ed (hiʸt–əd) adj. **1.** Having been made warm or hot: *The water in the pool is heated.* **2.** Angry or excited: *a heated debate* —**heatedly** adv.

heat-er (hiʸt–ər) n. An apparatus for heating air or water, such as those which burn gas, oil, or electricity for producing heat

hea-then (hiʸ–ðən) n. pl. **-then** or **-thens** A person who does not acknowledge the God of the Bible: *Why did the heathen rage... against the Lord and against His anointed [Christ]?* (Psalm 2:1,2; Acts 4:25).

heath-er (hɛð–ər) n. An evergreen plant with small purple, pink, or white bell-shaped flowers

heave (hiʸv) v. **heaved, heaving 1.** To raise or lift with effort **2.** To lift and throw with force or violence: *He heaved a brick through my window.* **3.** To utter laboriously or painfully: *He heaved a sigh of relief.* **4.** To haul or pull on a rope or cable, etc. **5.** To vomit: *He heaved up everything he had eaten for supper.*

heave n. **1.** The act or effort of heaving: *Let's give this boulder another heave and see if we can move it.* **2.** The throwing of sthg. heavy: *He threw that heavy luggage onto the truck with one big heave.*

heav-en (hɛv–ən) n. **1.** usu. pl. The sky: *He looked up into the heavens.* **2.** usu. pl. The universe; the stars of the universe: *In the beginning God created the heavens and the earth* (Genesis 1:1). *The heavens declare the glory of God* (Psalm 19:1). **3.** The place where God and the holy angels are and where all believers in Jesus will be: *Jesus told his followers, "Rejoice that your names are written in heaven"* (Luke 10:20). *There is rejoicing in heaven... in the presence of the angels of God over one sinner who repents* (Luke 15:7,10).

heav-en-ly (hɛv–ən–li^y) adj. **1.** Refers to the place where God and the holy angels are and where all believers in Jesus will be: *St. Paul wrote: "The Lord will rescue me from every evil attack and will bring me safely to his heavenly kingdom"* (2 Timothy 4:18). **2.** *infml.* Wonderful: *What a heavenly day!* **3. heavenly bodies** The sun, moon, and stars

heav-i-ly (hɛv–ə–li^y) adv. To a large degree: *India is a heavily populated country*

heav-y (hɛv–i^y) adj. **-ier, -iest 1.** Of a weight that makes carrying, moving, or lifting difficult: *These books are too heavy for me. Would you carry some of them, please?* **2.** Of a certain weight, not necessarily a great weight: *How heavy is the baby now?* **3.** Unusual force or amount: *heavy snowfall/heavy traffic during the rush hour* **4.** Difficult to read and understand: *This philosophy text is heavy reading.* **5.** Difficult or slow movement: *heavy movements* **6.** Hard to do and causing tiredness: *a heavy day at work* **7.** Of food, rather difficult to digest **8.** Dense: *a heavy mist* **9.** Of the seas, stormy **10.** Unhappy: *with a heavy heart* —**heavily** adv.

He-brew (hi^y–bru^w) n. **1.** A member of a Semitic people in ancient Palestine **2.** Their language; a modern form of this used in Israel

He-brews (hi^y–bru^wz) n. A book of the New Testament which is a letter written primarily to Hebrew Christians. The chief doctrinal purpose of the writer was to show the pre-eminence of Christ and the glory of the Christian age as compared to that of the Old Testament

heck-le (hɛk–əl) v. **-led, -ling** To harass a (speaker, performer, etc.) with unfriendly questions or gibes —**heckler** n.

hec-tare (hɛk–tər) n. A unit of area equal to 2.471 acres.

hec-tic (hɛk–tɪk) adj. Full of excitement and confused, rapid movement: *a hectic day*

hec-to- (hɛk–to^w/–tə) Prefix meaning "hundred" as in hectometer

hec-to-me-ter (hɛk–tə–mi^yt–ər) n. 100 meters

he'd (hi^yd) v. **1.** Short for he would: *He'd rather go to the mountains than to the beach.* **2.** Short for he had: *He'd better finish his report before he leaves for the weekend.*

hedge (hɛdʒ) n. **1.** A line of bushes or small trees planted close together and dividing one yard or field from another **2.** A barrier **3.** Sthg. which protects from possible loss, damage, etc.: *The young couple bought a house as a hedge against inflation.* (=protection against their money losing its value)

hedge v. **hedged, hedging 1.** To enclose an area with a hedge **2.** To refuse to answer directly: *Stop hedging and tell me. Did you finish your assignment or not?*

he-do-nism (hi^yd–ən–ɪz–əm) n. **1.** The doctrine that pleasure is the chief good in life **2.** A way of life based on this belief —**hedonist** n. —**hedonistic** (hi^yd–ən–ɪs–tɪk) adj.

heed (hi^yd) v. *fml.* To give attention to: *It is better to heed a wise man's rebuke than to listen to the song of fools* (Ecclesiastes 7:5). *Whoever heeds instruction gains understanding* (Proverbs 15:32).

heed n. *fml.* Attention; notice: *He gave no heed to my warning.* —**heedless** adj.

heel (hi^yl) n. **1.** The back part of the foot **2.** The part of a shoe, sock, etc. which covers this part of the foot, esp. the raised part of a shoe **3.** *infml.* An unpleasant man who treats others badly **4. at/ on one's heels** Right behind: *The police followed (hot) on the heels of the thieves.*

heft-y (hɛf–ti^y) adj. **-ier, -iest** Big and/ or powerful: *a hefty football player*

heif-er (hɛf–ər) n. A young cow which has not yet given birth to a calf

height (haɪt) n. **1.** The distance from the top to the bottom: *With a height of 1,454 feet, the Sears Tower in Chicago is the tallest building in the world./What is your height?* (=how tall are you?)**2.** A fixed or measured distance above another given point: *The window is at a height of ten feet above the ground.* **3.** A high position or place: *We looked down from a great height to the town below.* **4.** The highest degree: *It's the height of stupidity to give an answer before you hear the question.* **5.** The greatest point: *at the height of his career*

height-en (haɪt–ən) v. To make or become greater in degree: *As she drew near home, her excitement heightened.*

hei-nous (he^y–nəs) adj. Hateful or shockingly

evil —heinously adv. —heinousness n.

heir (εər), heiress (εər–əs) fem. n. The one who
has the lawful right to receive the title or
property of an older member of the family
who dies: *My two brothers and I are heirs to
our parents' property./God sent his Son... to redeem those under the law, that we [believers in
Jesus] might receive the full rights of sons.
...and since you are a son, God has made you
also an heir [of salvation]* (Galatians 4:4-5,7).
—see JESUS

heir-loom (εər–lu^wm) n. A possession valued
by family members, passed down from
generation to generation

held (hεld) v. Past tense and past part. of
hold

hel-i-cop-ter (hεl–ɪ–kɑp–tər) also chopper,
copter *infml.* n. An aircraft which is lifted
and made to fly by a set of large, fast-
turning, metal blades fixed on top of it

he-li-um (hi^y–li^y–əm) n. A colorless gas that is
lighter than air, will not burn, and is used
in inflating airships and balloons

hell (hεl) n. The place or state of eternal punishment for the wicked after death. NOTE:
In the Old Testament, the Prophet Daniel
tells us, "Multitudes who sleep in the dust
of the earth will awake; some to everlasting
life; others to everlasting shame and contempt" (Daniel 12:2). In the New Testament, our Savior speaks of eternal fire, saying to those on his left on Judgement Day,
"Depart from me, you who are cursed, into
the eternal fire prepared for the devil and
his angels" (Matthew 25:41). And these
shall go into everlasting punishment (Matthew 25:41). The damned in hell are forever
rejected and banished from the blissful
presence of God. Their suffering is intensified by the fact that they are aware of the
bliss of the saints in heaven (Luke 13:28).
Because of being utterly forsaken by God,
there is no relief from the torment of hell;
even a drop of water is denied the rich man
in the parable (Luke 16:23-25); from hell
there is no escape; to the suffering there is
no end, for it is an everlasting punishment
in an unquenchable fire (Mark 9:43-48). In
hell there is no hope. All people are sinners

(Romans 3:10) and deserve everlasting
punishment in hell. The wages of sin is
(eternal) death (Romans 6:23). But God
doesn't want anyone to perish (2 Peter 3:9).
God so loved the world that he gave his one
and only Son (to suffer and die for our
sins), that whoever believes in him shall not
perish but have eternal life. For God did not
send his Son into the world to condemn the
world, but to save the world through him.
Whoever believes in him is not condemned,
but whoever does not believe stands condemned already, because he has not believed in the name of God's one and only
Son (John 3;16-18). Whoever believes and is
baptized will be saved, but whoever does
not believe will be condemned (to eternal
punishment in hell) (Mark 16:16). Repent,
therefore, and put your trust in Jesus for
eternal life, for there is no condemnation
for those who are in Christ Jesus (Romans
8:1). —see JESUS —compare HEAVEN

he'll (hi^yl) v. 1. Short for he will 2. Short for he
shall

hel-lo (hε–lo^w/ hε–lo^w) interj. 1. The usual
word of greeting 2. The usual word for answering the phone: *Hello, this is Mrs. Jones.*

helm (hεlm) n. 1. A lever or wheel for steering
a ship 2. A position of control: *There's a new
man at the helm of this company.*

hel-met (hεl–mət) n. A type of cap worn by
soldiers, miners, motorcyclists, etc. for protecting the head

help (hεlp) v. 1. To assist someone who needs
sthg. done for them; aid: *Please help me move
this desk. I can't do it alone.* 2. To improve: *An
aspirin should help your headache.* 3. To avoid;
prevent; change: *I can't help feeling as I do.*
(=*I can't change it*)

help n. 1. Assistance; aid: *I'm going to need
some help with this project.* 2. Sthg. or sbdy.
that helps: *God is our refuge and strength, an
ever present help in trouble* (Psalm 46:1). 3.
AmE. Workers, esp. housekeepers: *Were you
able to find good help?* 4 Help! A call for help
in time of danger or need: *Help! I'm drowning!*

help-ful (hεlp–fəl) adj. Useful; willing to help
—opposite UNHELPFUL —helpfully adv.

n.

help-ing (help-ɪŋ) n. A portion of food

help-less (help-ləs) adj. Without the ability to act or to look after oneself: *a helpless invalid* —**helplessly** adv. —**helplessness** n.

hel-ter-skel-ter (hel-tər-skel-tər) adv. In hurried confusion and disorder

hem (hem) n. The edge of a piece of cloth when turned under and sewn down, esp. the lower edge of a skirt or dress

hem v. -mm- 1. To put a hem on sthg. 2. Enclose or surround: *We were hemmed in by the storm, and there was no way out.*

hem-i- (hem-ɪ-/ -ə-/ -iʸ-) Prefix meaning "half"

hem-i-sphere (hem-ə-sfɪər) n. 1. One of two halves of a sphere (an object which is round like a ball) 2. A half of the earth, esp. the northern or southern half above or below the equator, or the eastern or western half

hem-lock (hem-lak) n. 1. A poisonous herb 2. A poisonous drink made from this herb 3. An evergreen tree of the pine family

he-mo-glo-bin (hiʸ-mə-gloʷ-bɪn) n. The red coloring matter in the blood that serves to carry oxygen to the tissues

he-mo-phil-i-a (hiʸ-mə-fɪl-iʸ-ə) n. A usu. inherited tendency to severe, prolonged bleeding

hem-or-rhage (hem-ə-rɪdʒ) n. A large discharge of blood from the blood vessels

hem-or-rhoid (hem-ə-rɔɪd) n. *usu. pl.* A swollen blood vessel in the rectum

hemp (hemp) n. 1. A plant from which coarse fibers are obtained for making rope and cloth 2. A narcotic made from this plant

hen (hen) n. 1. The female chicken, often kept for its eggs 2. The female of any of several types of bird

hence (hens) adv. 1. From this time: *a week hence (= a week from now)* 2. For this reason: *I fell down the stairs yesterday; hence the bruises.*

hence-forth (hens-fɔrθ/ hens-fɔrθ) adv. From now on; in the future: *Henceforth I expect you to be in class on time.*

hench-man (hentʃ-mən) n. 1. A trusted follower 2. A political follower whose support is chiefly for personal advantage

hep-a-ti-tis (hep-ə-tar-tɪs) n. A disease of the liver

hep-ta-gon (hep-tə-gan) n. A seven-sided figure

her (hər) Possessive form of **she** 1. Of that female person or animal already mentioned: *Ann put her books on her desk.* 2. (Used of things, esp. vehicles or countries, that are thought of as female): *The ship let down her anchor.*

her (ər/ hər) pron. Object form of **she**: *John told Nancy that he loved her.*

her-ald (heər-əld) n. 1. A person who carries and reads important notices 2. Sthg. that is a sign of future events

herald v. 1. To announce loudly 2. To be a sign of: *The return of the swallows heralded the beginning of spring.*

herb (ərb) n. Any of various plants which are used to make medicine or to improve the taste of food —compare SPICE —**herbal** adj. *an herbal tea* —**her-ba-ceous** (hər-beʸ-ʃəs/ ər-) adj.

herb-age (ər-bɪdʒ) n. Herbs collectively

herb-al-ist (ərb-əl-ɪst) n. One who sells herbs used in cooking or medicine

her-bi-vore (hər-bə-vɔr/ ər-) n. A plant- eating animal

her-biv-o-rous (hər-bɪv-ə-rəs/ ər-) adj. Feeding entirely on plants or parts of plants: *Rabbits are herbivorous animals.*

herd (hərd) n. 1. A group of animals (of the same kind) which live and feed together: *a herd of cattle* 2. comb. form Someone who looks after a group of animals: *herdsman/ shepherd* 3. *derog.* People, thought of as acting or thinking in a mass: *to follow the herd*

herd v. To group together as if in a herd: *They herded the cattle into the corral.*

here (hɪər) adv. 1. In, at, to, or from this place: *My brother lives here./They're coming over here./My office is two miles from here.* 2. On this point: *We'll work with you here.* 3. (Used for drawing attention to someone or sthg.): *Here's our bus. (≈I can see the bus coming)* —compare THERE 4. **here and there** (a) In one place or another (b) From time to time 5. **Here goes!** *infml.* (Used as an interjection to express lack of confidence when trying sthg., esp. new or difficult): *I've never tried*

skiing before. Here goes! **6. Here you are** Here's what you want. **7. neither here nor there** Unimportant or irrelevant

here-af-ter (hɪər–æf–tər) adv. In the future

here-by (hɪər–baɪ) adv. By this means: *Opening the letter, John read, "You are hereby notified that you are to appear in court on April 18th."*

he-red-i-tary (hə–red–ə–teər–iʸ) adj. That which can be or is passed down from parent to child: *Is musical ability hereditary?*

he-red-i-ty (hə–red–ə–tiʸ) n. The passing on of qualities (appearance, intelligence, etc.) from parent to child in the cells of the body: *Does a child's artistic ability depend on heredity?*

here-in (hɪər–ɪn) adv. In this (piece of writing)

here's (hɪərz) Contraction of **here is**

her-e-sy (heər–ə–siʸ) n. **-sies** Holding to a religious belief that is against the accepted teachings of the church

her-e-tic (heər–ɛ–tɪk) n. A person who is guilty of a heresy —**he-ret-i-cal** (hə–ret–ɪk–əl) adj.

her-it-age (heər–ə–tɪdʒ) n. **1.** Sthg. that comes or belongs to a person by reason of birth **2.** Sthg. that is passed down over many years within a family or nation: *Our country has a rich artistic heritage. (=pictures and beautiful buildings)*

her-mit (hɜr–mət) n. One who lives in solitude, esp. for religious reasons

her-ni-a (hɜr–niʸ–ə) n. A rupture, esp. one caused by a part of the bowel being pushed through a weak point of the muscle wall of the abdomen

he-ro (hɪər–oʷ/hiʸ–roʷ) **-roes, heroine** (her–ə–wən) *fem.* n. **1.** A person remembered or admired for an act of, or qualities of, bravery, strength, or goodness **2.** The most important character in a story, drama, poem, etc.

he-ro-ic (hɪ–roʷ–ɪk) adj. **1.** Showing the qualities of a hero: *a heroic rescue* **2.** Concerned with heroes: *heroic movies* —**heroically** adv.

her-o-in (her–ə–wən) n. An addictive narcotic derived from morphine

her-o-ine (her–ə–wən) **1.** A female hero **2.** The principal female character in a story

her-o-ism (heər–oʷ–ɪz–əm) n. Great courage: *She showed great heroism in her battle against cancer*

her-on (heər–ən) n. A bird with a long neck, long legs, and a long bill and large wings

her-ring (heər–ɪŋ) n. A fish of the North Atlantic Ocean, caught for food, usu. canned, pickled, or smoked

hers (hɜrz) pron. Possessive form of **she** Of that female person or animal already mentioned: *Is this Mary's book? Yes, it's hers.*

her-self (hər–self) pron. **1.** (As the object of a verb, or after a preposition, when the same female is both the performer of the action and the receiver of the action): *She dressed herself./She bought herself a new bicycle.* **2.** (Used to make "she", or the name of a female person or animal, stronger): *Mary wrote the story herself.*

he's (hiʸz) v. **1.** Short for **he is**: *He's going to become a doctor./He's coming for a visit.* **2.** Short for **he has**: *He's often visited us before.*

hes-i-tant (hez–ə–tənt) adj. Inclined to hesitate; showing uncertainty in making decisions: *He's very hesitant about investing a large amount of money in this venture.* —**hesitantly** adv. —**hes-i-tan-cy** (hez–ə–tən–siʸ) also **hesitance** n.

hes-i-tate (hez–ə–teʸt) v. **-tated, -tating 1.** To pause during or before an action: *He hesitated before entering the car.* **2.** pol. To be unwilling or uncertain about doing sthg.: *I hesitate to ask you, but may I borrow your car tonight?* —**hesitating** adj. —**hesitatingly** adv. —**hes-i-ta-tion** (hez–ə–teʸ–ʃən) n.

het-er-o- (het–ər–ə–) prefix Other; different

het-er-o-dox (het–ər–ə–daks) adj. Not conforming to accepted standards or beliefs —opposite ORTHODOX

het-er-o-ge-ne-ous (het–ər–ə–dʒiʸ–niʸ–əs) adj. Made up of different kinds; varied in composition: *Los Angeles is a heterogeneous city, with more than 140 languages being spoken in the homes of the school children.*

het-er-o-sex-u-al (het–ər–ə–sek–ʃuʷ–wəl) adj. A person who is attracted to people of the other sex —opposite HOMOSEXUAL

hex-a-gon (heks–ə–gɑn) n. A figure with six sides

hey (he^y) interj. A word used to show surprise or attract attention

hey-day (he^y-de^y) n. A period of greatest strength, fame, prosperity, etc.: *In his heyday, he was the best baseball player in the world.*

hi (haɪ) interj. *infml.* Hello

hi-a-tus (haɪ-e^y-təs) n. **-tuses** or **-tus** *pl.* A break or gap where sthg. is missing

hi-ber-nate (haɪ-bər-ne^{y}t) v. **-nated, -nating** To pass the winter in a sleep-like state: *Bears hibernate.* —**hi-ber-na-tion** (haɪ-bər-ne^y-ʃən) n. —**hi-ber-na-tor** (haɪ-bər-ne^{y}t-ər) n.

hi-bis-cus (haɪ-bɪs-kəs) n. A cultivated plant having large, showy flowers

hic-cough See hiccup

hic-cup also **hiccough** (hɪk-əp) n. A sudden, involuntary stopping of the breath with a sharp, gulp-like sound, often occurring at short intervals: *She laughed so much she got the hiccups./ John got the hiccups from eating and drinking too much too quickly.*

hick (hɪk) n. *AmE. infml.* An awkward, inexperienced person

hick adj. Not sophisticated: *a hick town*

hick-o-ry (hɪk-ə-ri^y) n. The wood of a type of tree of North America that provides hard wood and produces nuts

hid (hɪd) v. Past tense of **hide**

hid-den (hɪd-ən) v. Past tense and past part. of **hide**

hide (haɪd) v. **hid** (hɪd), **hidden** (hɪd-ən) or **hid, hiding** (haɪd-ɪŋ) **1.** To put or keep sthg. or sbdy. or oneself out of sight: *I'll hide under the bed./She hid her jewelry in the refrigerator.* **2.** To make or keep secret: *She managed to hide her guilt from the police for several months.* **3.** To store: *In whom [Christ] are hidden all the treasures of wisdom and knowledge* (Colossians 2:3). **4. go into hiding** To be hidden: *The escaped convict went into hiding in order to escape the police.* **5. hidden in one's heart** Kept; memorized: *I have hidden your word in my heart [O Lord], that I might not sin against you* (Psalm 119:11).

hide n. The skin of an animal, esp. when removed to be used for leather

hide-a-way (haɪd-ə-we^y) n. A place that one can use to hide from others; a place that is difficult to find

hid-e-ous (hɪd-i^y-əs) adj. Very ugly; frightful: *She looks hideous in all that make-up.*

hide-out (haɪd-aʊt) n. A place where one can safely hide

hi-er-ar-chy (haɪ-ə-rɑr-ki^y) n. **1.** A system with grades of authority or status from the lowest to the highest: *He quickly climbed up the hierarchy to become the president of the company.* **2.** The group of people in any organization who control that organization —**hi-er-ar-chi-cal** (haɪ-ər-ɑr-kɪ-kəl) adj.

hi-er-o-glyph-ic (haɪ-ər-ə-glɪf-ɪk) n. **1.** A symbol in a pictographic script **2.** A symbol that is difficult to decipher

hi-fi (haɪ-faɪ) n. High fidelity (=very sensitive) equipment for reproducing recorded sound: *This record will sound great on your hi-fi.* —**hi-fi** adj.

high (haɪ) adj. **1.** Reaching upward to some great distance, esp. a large distance above ground: *a high building* **2.** At a point well above the ground or floor or above what is usual: *I can't reach the top shelf; it's too high for me.* **3.** Great: *the high cost of living/a high rate of speed* **4.** Worthy of admiration: *high ideals* **5.** Of or concerning people of great wealth or rank: *high officials* **6.** Of time, at the most important or mid-point of: *It's high time for us to leave.* **7.** *infml.* (a) Drunk (b) Under the effects of drugs NOTE: People are **tall** rather than **high**. Buildings that are narrow, as well as high, are also **tall**:. *a tall man/ a tall spire/ a high wall*

high adv. **1.** To or at a high place in position or level of movements or sound: *The bird soared high above the mountain top./ As high as the heavens are above the earth, so great is his [God's] love for those who fear him* (Psalm 103:11). —opposite LOW **2. high and dry** *infml.* Without help; left to care for oneself: *He left me high and dry with no food and no money.* **3. high and low** Everywhere: *We looked high and low for the umbrella.*

high n. **1.** A high level; the highest point: *The crime rate in the city has reached a new high.* —opposite LOW **2.** *infml.* A state of great excitement produced (as if) by a drug **3.** A high place, esp. heaven (only in the phrase **on high**): *Though the Lord is on high, he looks*

upon the lowly, but the proud he knows from *afar* (Psalm 138:6). **4. the Most High** The one true God, creator and ruler of the universe: *For you, O Lord, are the Most High over all the earth* (Psalm 97:9).

high-ball (hai-bɔl) n. Whiskey or other liquor mixed with water, soda, or ginger ale

high-brow (hai-brav) n. A person of intellectual interests and tastes —**high-brow** adj. Of or characteristic of a highbrow

high-chair (hai-tʃeər) n. A baby's chair, mounted on long legs and having an attached tray

high–class (hai-klæs) adj. Of high quality: *This is a high-class restaurant.*

high-fa-lu-tin (hai-fə-luʷ-tən) adj. *infml.* Pompous; pretentious; too showy or grand: *She's too highfalutin to speak to her employees when she meets them on the street.*

high fi-del-i-ty (hai fə-**del**-ə-ti⁀y) n. also **hi-fi** The reproduction of sound with a high degree of faithfulness to the original

high–hand-ed (hai-**hæn**-dəd) adj. *derog.* Using power or authority without considering the opinions or wishes of others —**high-handedly** adv.

high-lan-der (hai-lən-dər) n. An inhabitant of the highlands

high-lands (hai-ləndz) n. *pl.* Mountainous land or land at a higher elevation: *We live in the highlands.*

high-light (hai-lait) n. An important detail or event which stands out from the rest: *one of the highlights of his career*

high-ly (hai-li⁀y) adv. **1.** Very; to a high degree: *highly respected/ highly trained* **2.** Very well: *She speaks highly of her employer.*

high–mind-ed (hai-maind-əd) adj. Having or showing good or noble ideals, principles, etc.: *The young man was so high-minded that he was horrified at the corruption in politics.* —**highmindedness** n.

high-ness (hai-nəs) n. **1.** The quality or state of being high **2.** A title of a prince or princess: *Your highness*

high–pres-sure (hai-prɛ-ʃər) adj. **1.** Having or using air, water, etc. at high pressure **2.** Using very aggressive sales techniques: *a high-pressure salesman* —**high pressure** v. *He high-*

pressured me into buying it when I really didn't want it.

high–strung (hai-strʌŋ) also **highly-strung** adj. Nervous; excitable

high-way (hai-we⁀y) n. *esp. AmE.* A broad main road used esp. by traffic going from one town to another

hi-jack (hai-dʒæk) v. To take over the control of a vehicle or aircraft by force of arms, often for political aims —**hi-jack** n. —**hijacker** n. —**hijacking** n.

hike (haik) n. A long walk in the country, for pleasure or exercise

hike v. **hiked, hiking** To go on a hike —**hiker** n. —**hiking** n.

hi-lar-i-ous (hi-**leər**-i⁀y-əs/ –lær–) adj. Causing laughter: *a hilarious joke* —**hi-lariously** adv.

hi-lar-i-ty (hi-**leər**-ə-ti⁀y) n. Cheerfulness expressed in noisy laughter

hill (hil) n. **1.** A raised, usu. rounded part of the earth's surface, not as high as a mountain **2.** The slope of a road or path —**hilly** adj. **-ier, -iest**

hilt (hilt) n. **1.** The handle of a sword or dagger **2. to the hilt** Completely or fully

him (him) pron. Object form of **he**: *Mary told her husband that she loved him.*

him-self (him-**self**) pron. **1.** (Used as the object of a verb, or after a preposition, when the same male is both the performer and the receiver of the action): *He hit himself on the finger with the hammer.* **2.** (Used to make "he", or the name of a male person or animal, stronger): *He himself went to the mayor's office.*

hind (haind) adj. Belonging to the back part: *The dog's hind legs.*

hin-der (hin-dər) v. To prevent someone from doing sthg.: *Jesus said, "Let the little children come to me, and do not hinder them, for the kingdom of God belongs to such as these"* (Matthew 19:14).

hin-drance (hin-drəns) n. Sthg. or sbdy. that hinders: *If you can't help us with this work, please don't be a hindrance by getting in the way.*

Hin-du (hin-duʷ) n. One whose religion is Hinduism

Hin-du-ism (hɪn–duʷ–ɪz–əm) n. The chief religion of India, notable esp. for its social ranks (Caste System), its many gods, and the belief that after death one returns to earth in another form (reincarnation)

hinge (hɪndʒ) n. A metal part which joins two objects together and allows the first to swing freely, such as when joining a door to a frame

hinge v. **hinged, hinging 1.** To fix (sthg.) on hinges **2. hinge on/ upon sthg.** Depend on: *Our buying the house hinges on our getting a loan from the bank.*

hint (hɪnt) n. **1.** A small or indirect suggestion: *But among you [Christians] there must not even be a hint of sexual immorality, or of any kind of impurity, or of greed* (Ephesians 5:3). **2.** A slight sign: *There was a hint of fear in her question.* **3. take a hint** To understand a suggestion and act upon it: *I made several remarks about being hungry, but she didn't offer me anything to eat; she just couldn't take a hint.* **4.** Useful advice: *helpful hints*

hint v. To suggest indirectly: *She hinted that she was interested in a job at our company.*

hin-ter-land (hɪn–tər–lænd) n. The region lying inland from the coast

hip (hɪp) n. The part of either side of the human body where the bone of a person's leg is joined to the trunk: *She put her hands on her hips and glared at me.*

hip-po-pot-a-mus (hɪp–ə–pɑt–ə–məs) n. **-mus-es** or **-mi** A large African animal with a thick hairless body, living in and near rivers

hire (haɪr/ haɪ–ər) v. **hired, hiring 1.** To obtain the services of someone for a time, for payment: *The fruit is picked by hired laborers.* **2. hire sbdy. out** To give one's own or another's services for payment: *My brother and I hired ourselves out to a fruit grower for the summer.*

hire n. The payment for being hired: *to work for hire*

hire-ling (haɪr–lɪŋ) n. A person who works for someone else, just for money

his (hɪz) pron. Possessive form of **he 1.** Of that male person or animal already mentioned: *John cleaned his room.* **2.** Of that person being

spoken about: *Is this John's car? No, his is in the garage for repairs.*

hiss (hɪs) v. **1.** Of snakes, geese, people, etc., to make a sound like that of the letter **s** when prolonged **2.** To express disapproval by making this sound —**hiss** n.

his-to-ri-an (hɪ–stɔr–iʸ–ən/ –stoʷr–) n. A person who is an expert on history

his-tor-ic (hɪ–stɔr–ɪk) adj. Famous or important in history: *a historic discovery* —see HISTORY

his-tor-i-cal (hɪ–stɔr–ɪ–kəl) adj. **1.** Of or relating to history as a study: *historical research* **2.** Representing a fact of history: *Is it a historical fact (=is it true) that Lincoln once lived in this house?* —see HISTORY —**historically** adv.

his-to-ry (hɪs–tə–riʸ) n. **-ries 1.** The study of events in the past, esp. events concerning the rulers and government of a country, the social and trade conditions, etc.: *I enjoyed studying history in high school.* **2.** A (written) account of past events: *a history of our country* **3.** A set of events concerning a place or person: *Mr. Brown's medical history* **4. make history** To do sthg. important which will be recorded and remembered

hit (hɪt) v. **hit, hitting 1.** To deliver a blow to; strike: *He hit the table (with his hand).* **2.** To (cause to) strike sthg. with force: *The car hit the side of the bridge.* **3.** *infml.* To reach: *We hit Los Angeles just as the traffic began to get heavy./I love to hear her sing; she hits all the high notes so easily.* **4. hit it off** *infml.* To have a good relationship: *It's great to see the team hitting it off so well together.* **5. hit the roof** also **hit the ceiling** *AmE. infml.* To become very angry **6. hit the nail on the head** To be exactly right (in saying sthg.) **7. hit someone where it hurts (most)** To attack someone through his/ her weaknesses **8. hit the bottle** *infml.* To start a habit of drinking too much alcohol **9. hit the hay/ sack** *infml.* To go to bed **10. hit the road** *esp. AmE.* To leave **11. hit the brakes** *AmE.* To use the brakes suddenly to stop a vehicle **12. hit on/ upon sthg.** To find out by chance or have a good idea about: *I think we've hit on the answer to our difficulty.*

hit n. **1.** A blow: *That timely two-base hit won the game for us.* **2.** A blow successfully striking sthg. aimed at: *a direct hit on an enemy ship* —opposite MISS **3.** A recorded song, performance, etc. that is very successful: *The movie was one of the biggest hits of all time.* **4.** A very good impression: *You made a hit with my dad; he thinks you're great.*

hitch (hɪtʃ) v. To fasten by hooking a rope, metal part, etc. over another object: *He hitched the horse to the cart and drove away.*

hitch n. A connection between a vehicle or implement and a detachable source of power: *a trailer hitch*

hitch-hike (hɪtʃ–haɪk) v. **-hiked, -hiking** To travel by getting free rides from passing vehicles —**hitchhiker** n.

hith-er (hɪð–ər) adv. *old use* To this place: *Come hither.*

hith-er-to (hɪð–ər–tuʷ) adv. Until now: *Hitherto I've never missed a day of work due to illness.*

hive (haɪv) n. **1.** A box for housing honey bees **2.** A colony of bees **3.** Anyplace swarming with busy occupants: *This office is a real hive (or beehive) of activity.*

hives (haɪvz) n. A skin disease with itchy red patches, caused by an allergic reaction

hoard (hɔrd/ hoʷrd) v. To store secretly in large amounts

hoard n. A hidden accumulation —**hoarder** n.

hoarse (hɔrs) adj. Of a person or voice, rough and harsh-sounding, as when a person has a cold —**hoarsely** adv. —**hoarseness** n.

hoar-y (hoʷr–iʸ/hɔr–) adj. **-ier, -iest 1.** White or gray with age **2.** Ancient

hoax (hoʷks) n. A trick, esp. one which makes someone believe a lie and take action upon that belief: *Everyone was asked to leave the plane after a passenger claimed he had a bomb, but it was just a hoax.* —**hoax** v.

hob-ble (hab–əl) v. **-bled, -bling** To walk with difficulty, because of being lame or very tired after a long hike, for example

hob-by (hab–iʸ) n. **-bies** An activity which a person enjoys doing in his free time: *His hobby is collecting rare stamps.*

hob-nob (hab–nab) v. **-bb-** To be on very friendly terms with

ho-bo (hoʷ–boʷ) n. **-boes** A tramp; a wanderer who has no regular work

hock (hak) v. To pawn sthg.: *I hocked my watch and camera for $50.*

hock n. The condition of having been pawned: *Now I want to get my camera out of hock.*

hock-ey (hak–iʸ) n. **1. ice hockey** A game played on ice in which two opposing teams use curved sticks to try to drive a puck (a hard rubber disk) into the opponent's goal **2. field hockey** A type of hockey played on foot on a grass field, using a ball instead of a puck

ho-cus-po-cus (hoʷ–kəs–poʷ–kəs) n. **1.** Meaningless incantation used by magicians **2.** Trickery; deception

hod (had) n. **1.** A long-handled trough for carrying bricks or mortar **2.** A scuttle or bucket for holding coal

hodge-podge (hadʒ–padʒ) n. A haphazard mixture

hoe (hoʷ) n. A long-handled garden tool used esp. for removing weeds

hoe v. **hoed, hoeing** To use a hoe

hog (hɔg/ hag) n. **hogs or hog 1.** Esp. *AmE.* A pig, esp. a full-grown domesticated one —compare BOAR, SOW **2.** A gluttonous, greedy, or dirty person **3. go whole hog** *infml.* To do sthg. thoroughly

hog v. *infml.* To take and keep all or most of sthg. for oneself: *Drivers who hog the road are stupid, inconsiderate, selfish, and a threat to everyone they encounter.*

hoist (hɔɪst) v. To raise or haul up: *We hoisted the flag./The men hoisted cargo onto the ship.*

hoist n. **1.** An upward push **2.** An apparatus for lifting heavy goods

hold (hoʷld) v. **held** (hɛld)**, holding 1.** To have and keep in one's possession, esp. in one's hand: *He was holding a knife in his hand.* **2.** To put or keep a part of the body in the stated position: *She held her hand over her head.* **3.** To keep a person or thing between parts of the body or between parts of a tool: *She held the baby in her arms./The pipe was held by a vise.* **4.** To keep back or control: *The police held the crowd back.* **5.** To contain: *How much water does the jar hold?* **6.** To have and keep a job or

position: *He has held nearly every public office in this city.* **7.** To attract and keep: *His speech held their attention.* **8.** To make sthg. happen: *They held the meeting in the conference room.* **9.** To keep in the stated position or condition: *fig. He held himself aloof.* **10.** *infml.* To express one's belief (that); consider: *I hold (the belief) that there is only one God and Savior of the world.* **11.** To be or remain in a certain state; continue: *What he said still holds.* (=is true)/ *The bridge failed to hold and crashed into the canyon below.* **12. Hold it!** Stay in that position! **13. hold one's breath** To stop breathing out of fear or expectation **14. be left holding the bag** *AmE.* To have to be responsible for doing sthg. which sbdy. else has started and left unfinished **15. hold one's own** To stand firm even when attacked **16. hold the line** To wait on the telephone **17. hold sthg. against sbdy.** To allow sthg. bad that sbdy. has done to have an effect on one's feelings about this person: *We shouldn't hold his prison record against him.* **18. hold back (a)** To cause to stay in control: *We built banks of earth to hold back the rising flood waters.* **(b)** To prevent the development of: *Lack of training holds many young people back from a successful career.* **(c)** To keep sthg. secret: *Please don't hold anything back; we need to know the whole story in order to help you.* **19. hold down (a)** To keep (esp. a job): *How long have you held down this job?* **(b)** To maintain at a low level: *to hold interest rates down* **20. hold forth** To speak at length: *Our professor knows his subject very well. He could hold forth for hours.* **21. hold out for** To demand sthg. and wait firmly in order to get it: *The employees are still holding out for better working conditions.* **22. hold over** To continue beyond a specified time: *The movie has been held over for three weeks already.* **23. hold to** To insist that someone does what he said he would do: *He promised to finish the job for $2,000, and we should hold him to it.* **24. hold together** To cause to remain united: *I hope we can hold our team together for the season.* **25. hold up (a)** To delay: *The opening of school has been held up because of the teachers' strike.* **(b)** To rob: *The robbers held up the stage coach.* **(c)** To use

as an example: *Abraham Lincoln is often held up as a model of honesty.* **26. hold with** To agree with: *I don't hold with letting children do as they please.*

hold n. **1.** The act of holding; grip: *Get a good hold on the rope, and we'll let you down.* **2.** Sthg. which can be held onto, esp. in climbing: *The climber was able to get a hold on the rocks and climb up the steep cliff.* **3.** The part of a ship (below deck) where cargo is stored **4. no holds barred** Any method allowed

hold-er (ho^wl–dər) n. **1.** One who has control of or who possesses a place, a position, or money: *the holder of a title* **2.** A device which holds sthg.: *a match holder*

hold-up (ho^wld–əp) n. **1.** A delay: *a traffic hold-up* **2.** Also **stickup** *infml.* An attempt to rob sbdy. by threatening them with a gun

hole (ho^wl) n. **1.** An empty space within sthg. solid: *He's digging a hole in the back yard./ There's a hole in my shoe.* **2.** The home of a small animal: *a gopher hole* **3.** In golf, a small, hollow, cup-like pit into which the ball must be hit **4.** *derog.* A small unpleasant place: *His apartment is just a hole in the wall.* **5. poke holes in sthg.** To criticize sthg., esp. when it is not really faulty

hol-i-day (hɑl–ə–de^y) n. **1.** A day of rest from work (often originally of religious or historical importance) **2.** *BrE.* for vacation

ho-li-ness (ho^w–li^y–nəs) n. The state or quality of being holy; purity or integrity of moral character (Applied to the Supreme Being, holiness denotes perfect purity, one of his essential attributes): *"Who is like you— majestic in holiness?"* (Exodus 15:11). —see HOLY

hol-low (hɑl–o^w) adj. **1.** Solid on the outside, but having an empty space inside: *This house is not very well made; the walls are hollow. /fig. hollow (=insincere) promises* **2.** Of sound, ringing, like the sound made when one beats on an empty container: *We were frightened by the hollow sound of footsteps in the empty building.*

hol-ly (hɑl–i^y) n. A type of evergreen bush with prickly leaves and red berries

hol-ly-hock (hɑl–i^y–hɑk) n. A tall plant with showy flowers of various colors

hol-o-caust (hɑl-ə-kɔst) n. **1.** Great or total destruction, esp. by fire. **2.** Holocaust The mass murder of the Jews, carried out by the Nazi government of Germany

hol-ster (hoʷl-stər) n. A leather case for a pistol, attached to a belt

ho-ly (hoʷ-liʸ) adj. **-lier, -liest 1.** Sacred; spiritually pure; godly: *God is perfectly holy and righteous./God commands his people to be holy. "Be holy in all you do; for it is written [in God's Word]: 'Be holy, because I am holy'"* (1 Peter 1:16). **2.** Consecrated; declared holy by religious use or set aside for religious use: *You are standing on holy ground* (Exodus 3:5). *From infancy you have known the Holy Scriptures, which are able to make you wise for salvation through faith in Christ Jesus* (2 Timothy 3:15). *Remember the Sabbath day by keeping it holy* (Exodus 20:8).

Ho-ly Ghost (hoʷ-liʸ goʷst) n. —see Holy Spirit

Ho-ly Scrip-ture (hoʷ-liʸ skrɪp-tʃer) n. The Word of God as recorded in the Old and New Testaments of the Holy Bible, given by inspiration of the Holy Spirit NOTE: The Old Testament gives prophecies concerning the Savior. The New Testament (49 - 96 A.D.) tells us about Jesus Christ, who fulfilled these prophecies. ...*the Holy Scriptures, which are able to make you wise for salvation through faith which is in Christ Jesus* (1 Timothy 3:15).

Ho-ly Spir-it (hoʷ-liʸ spɪr-ɪt) n. The Holy Bible teaches that there is only one true God, but that he is a Triune (three-in-one) God — Father, Son, and Holy Spirit. NOTE: All are equal in power, glory, and in every way. All are equally worthy of our worship and praise. All are eternal, without beginning and without end. All took part in the creation of heaven and earth and all things. The Holy Spirit is also called the Spirit of Truth (John 14:17). It is the Holy Spirit who inspired holy men of God to write the Holy Scriptures (the Bible), both the Old and the New Testaments, over a period of 1600 years, from about 1500 years before the birth of Christ to about 100 years after his birth: *Holy men of God spoke as they were*

moved by the Holy Spirit (2 Peter 1:21 NKJV). It is the Holy Spirit who gives us the saving knowledge of Jesus Christ, so that we trust in him, rejoice and take comfort in the assurance of our salvation through faith in him (Jesus). The Holy Spirit also enables Christians to live a holy life to the glory of God. The Holy Spirit also gives various gifts to Christians to help them glorify God, serve Christ, and minister to their fellow men. Those who are filled with the Holy Spirit also bear the fruit of the Spirit, namely, "love, joy, peace, patience, kindness, goodness, faithfulness, gentleness, and self control" (Galatians 5:22). This work of the Holy Spirit is necessary, for "no one can say, 'Jesus is Lord' except by the Holy Spirit" (1 Corinthians 12:3). "The natural man [unbeliever] receives not the things of the Spirit of God, for they are foolishness to him, neither can he know them, because they [the things of God] are spiritually discerned [can only be understood through the power of the Holy Spirit]" (1 Corinthians 2:14). The Holy Spirit dwells in those who believe in Jesus. "The world cannot accept him [the Spirit of Truth], because it neither sees him nor knows him. But you know him, for he lives with you and will be in you" (John 14:17). The Holy Spirit is given in answer to prayer. "If you then, though you are evil, know how to give good gifts to your children, how much more will your Father in heaven give the Holy Spirit to those who ask him!" (Luke 11:13).

hom-age (ɑm-ɪdʒ/ hɑm-ɪdʒ) n. Special honor or respect shown or expressed publicly

home (hoʷm) n. **1.** The place where a person lives, esp. with his family: *Where do you live? I was born in Hong Kong, but now my home is in Los Angeles./God blesses the home of the righteous* (Proverbs 3:33). *Jesus replied: "If anyone loves me, he will obey my teaching. My Father will love him, and we will come to him and make our home with him"* (John 14:23). **2.** A place where a plant or animal is most common: *China is the home of the panda.* **3.** A place that provides care and shelter for the handicapped, elderly, orphans, and others

who do not live with a family: *a nursing home* **4. be/ feel at home** To be comfortable and relaxed because one is on familiar ground: *Do you feel at home working in the kitchen?* **5. make oneself at home** To behave in a relaxed manner as though at home —**homeless** adj.

home adv. To or at one's home: *I usually get home from work at about six.*

home adj. **1.** Having to do with a home, base of operations, or origin: *Where is your home town? Mine's in the East./The home office is expanding rapidly and starting branches in three new cities.* **2.** Within the country; not foreign: *home government* **3.** Made or done in a home or as if in a home: *home baking* **4.** Working, playing, or happening in a home area: *The team has won all their home games this year.*

home-com-ing (ho^wm–kəm–ᵑ) n. **1.** A return home after a long absence **2.** In many colleges, an annual celebration for visiting alumni

home-land (ho^wm–lænd) n. One's native land

home-ly (ho^wm–li^y) adj. -lier, -liest **1.** Not good looking; plain **2.** Typical of home life

home-mak-er (ho^wm–me^y–kər) n. One in charge of managing one's own home, as a housewife

home-sick (ho^wm–sɪk) adj. A longing to be at home when away from it —**homesickness** n.

home-stead (ho^wm–stɛd) n. **1.** A house, esp. the main house on a farm, with the land and buildings that go with it **2.** Land given by the government to a family that settles on it

home-work (ho^wm–wɜrk) n. **1.** Work, such as schoolwork, done at home **2.** Work of a preparatory nature

hom-i-cide (**ham**–ə–saɪd/ ho^wm–ə–) n. The killing of one person by another

hom-i-ny (ham–ə–ni^y) n. Kernels of corn, hulled and boiled as food, at times ground into a coarse white meal called hominy grits.

ho-mo- (ho^w–mə/ ha–mə) comb. form Same: *A homophone is a word pronounced the same as another word, but having a different meaning.*

ho-mo-ge-ne-ous (ho^w–mə–dʒi^y–ni^y–əs) adj. **1.**

Of the same or similar kind **2.** Of uniform structure —**ho-mo-ge-ne-i-ty** (ho^w–mə–dʒə–**ni^y**–ə–ti^y) n. —**homogeneously** adv.

ho-mog-e-nize (ho^w–**madʒ**–ə–naɪz/ hə–) v. **-nized, -nizing 1.** To make homogeneous **2.** To reduce the particles (e.g., in milk) to uniform size and distribute them evenly throughout the liquid: *In homogenized milk, there is no cream on top because the fat is broken up and distributed all through the liquid.*

hom-o-graph (ham–ə–græf/ ho^wm–ə–) n. One of two or more words spelled the same but pronounced differently, as **wind** (wɪnd) in "The wind blew."and **wind** (waɪnd) in "Wind up the clock."

ho-mo-nym (ham–ə–nɪm/ ho^wm–ə–) n. One of two or more words spelled and pronounced alike but different in meaning: *We played a game of pool, and then went swimming in the pool. These two pool's are homonyms.*

ho-mo-phone (ham–ə–fo^wn/ ho^wm–ə) n. One of two or more words (as **do, due,** and **dew**) pronounced alike but different in meaning and spelling

Ho-mo sa-pi-ens (ho^w–mo^w se^y–pi^y–ənz/ sæp–i^y–ənz) n. Man; mankind

ho-mo-sex-u-al (ho^w–mə–sek–ʃu^w–əl) adj., n. Of or being a person sexually attracted to others of the same sex: *"Neither the sexually immoral nor idola-ters nor adulterers nor male prostitutes nor homosexual offenders nor thieves nor the greedy... will inherit the kingdom of God." "And that is what some of you were. But you were washed, you were sanctified, you were justified in the name of the Lord Jesus Christ and by the Spirit of our God"* (1 Corinthians 6:9-11). NOTE: This is a grievous sin for which Sodom and Gomorrah and other cities were destroyed by God. God is perfectly holy and he detests all sin, including the sin of homosexuality. But he is also a God of love and mercy, and he forgives those who truly repent (turn from their wicked ways) and put their trust in Jesus for forgiveness of sins and for eternal life (Mark 1:15; Acts 16:31; Romans 3:23-24; Romans 6:23). —see FORGIVENESS, JESUS, SIN, REPENTANCE

hone (ho^wn) n. A kind of stone for

sharpening a cutting instrument —**hone** v. honed, honing To sharpen

hon-est (**ɑn**–əst) adj. **1.** Of people, worthy of being trusted; truthful: *A truthful witness gives honest testimony* (Proverbs 12:17). **2.** Of actions, appearance, etc., having the qualities of truthfulness and sincerity: *an honest answer* —opposite DISHONEST

hon-est-ly (**ɑn**–əst–liʸ) adv. **1.** In a trustworthy manner —opposite DISHONESTLY **2.** Truthfully: *She honestly believed what her friend told her.*

hon-es-ty (**ɑn**–əs–tiʸ) n. The quality of being honest —opposite DISHONESTY

hon-ey (**hʌn**–iʸ) n. **-eys 1.** The sweet, thick, syrupy substance produced by bees from the nectar of flowers **2.** Sweetness; pleasantness **3.** *AmE.* Darling

hon-ey-bee (**hʌn**–iʸ–biʸ) n. A bee that makes honey

hon-ey-comb (**hʌn**–iʸ–koʷm) n. A network of waxed cells in which bees store honey

hon-ey-combed (**hʌn**–iʸ–koʷmd) adj. Having holes like the cells in an empty honeycomb

hon-ey-moon (**hʌn**–iʸ–muʷn) n. A vacation taken by a newly married couple —**honeymoon** v. *The couple honeymooned in Hawaii.* —**honeymooner** n.

hon-ey-suck-le (**hʌn**–iʸ–sʌk–əl) n. A climbing vine with sweet-smelling flowers

honk (hɑŋk/ hɔŋk) v. To make a sound similar to that of a goose or to sound a car horn: *A flock of geese flew overhead honking noisily./He honked the horn angrily as the truck pulled out in front of him, narrowly missing his front fender.* —**honk** n.

hon-or *AmE.* **honour** *BrE.* (**ɑn**–ər) n. **1.** An expression of great respect: *The Lord bestows favor and honor; no good thing does he withhold from those whose walk is blameless* (Psalm 84:11). —opposite DISHONOR **2.** High standards of character, making one worthy of respect by others: *upholding the honor of one's country* **3.** Sthg. that brings pride or pleasure: *It was an honor for him to be asked to lead the parade.* **4.** A title of respect for a holder of a high office: *Your Honor* **5. on one's honor** Under a moral obligation to do sthg.: *The students were on their honor to complete the ex-*amination without cheating.

honor *AmE.* **honour** *BrE.* v. **1.** To respect: *Honor your father and your mother* (Exodus 20:12). *Honor God with your body* (1 Corinthians 6:20). *[God] the Father judges no one, but has entrusted all judgment to the Son, that all may honor the Son just as they honor the Father. He who does not honor the Son does not honor the Father who sent him* (John 5:22,23). **2.** To keep an agreement or promise, esp. an agreement to make a payment: *I intend to honor our agreement, even though you have already broken your part of it.*

hon-or-a-ble *AmE.* **honourable** *BrE.* (**ɑn**–ər–ə–bəl) adj. Showing honor or worthy of honor —opposite DISHONORABLE —compare HONORARY —**honorably** adv.

Hon-or-a-ble *AmE.* **Honourable** *BrE.* (**ɑn**–ər–ə–bəl) adj. A title given to judges and certain other official people, including Members of the British Parliament

hon-o-ra-ri-um (ɑn–ə–**rer**–iʸ–əm) n. **1.** Payment for services for which there is no set fee **2.** A fee for professional services

hon-or-ar-y (**ɑn**–ə–rɛər–iʸ) adj. **1.** Of a rank, a university degree, etc., given as an honor: *awarded an honorary doctorate* **2.** Of an office or position held, unpaid; voluntary: *She's the honorary chairman of the committee.* —compare HONORABLE

hood (hʊd) n. **1.** A covering for the head and neck, often fastened to a coat so it can hang down in the back or be removed **2.** *AmE.* The movable metal covering of an automobile engine **3.** Short for **hoodlum**

hood-lum (**huʷd**–ləm) n. **1.** A gangster or a thug **2.** A wild, destructive youth

hood-wink (**hʊd**–wɪŋk) v. To deceive; to cheat sbdy.

hoo-ey (**huʷ**–iʸ) n. *Slang and interj.* Nonsense

hoof (hʊf/ huʷf) n. *pl.* **hooves** (hʊvz/ huʷvz) The hard part of the foot of a horse, deer, cow, etc.

hook (hʊk) n. **1.** A curved piece of wire, plastic, etc. for catching sthg. on or hanging things on: *a fish hook/a cup hook* **2. be/ get off the hook** To be freed from a responsibility or get out of a difficult situation **3. by hook or by crook** By any way possible **4. hook,**

line, and sinker Altogether: *Little Mary swallowed her brother's tall stories hook, line, and sinker.* (= *she believed them all*)

hook v. **1.** To catch with a hook or as if with a hook: *to hook a fish* **2.** To fasten with a hook or hang on a hook: *Hook the two chains together.* **3. hook up** To connect to a supply of water, electricity, etc.: *We need to get the heater hooked up. It's getting cold in here.*

hooked (hʊkt) adj. **1.** Similar to a hook in shape: *a hooked beak* **2.** *infml.* **(a)** De-pendent on drugs **(b)** Very fond of a thing, food, activity, etc.: *She's hooked on chocolate ice cream.* —compare ADDICTED TO

hoo-li-gan (huʷ-lɪ-gən) n. A ruffian; a rowdy person who causes trouble by fighting, breaking things, etc.

hoop (huʷp) n. A circular band of wood, metal, etc. around a barrel or used as a child's toy

hoot (huʷt) n. **1.** The sound made by an owl **2.** A shout of contempt **3. not give a hoot** Not to care at all: *I don't give a hoot who wins the game.*

hoot v. To make a hoot: *The owl hooted./When he began his speech, they all (the audience) hooted at him.*

hooves (hʊvz/ huʷvz) n. *pl.* of hoof

hop (hɑp) v. **-pp- 1. (a)** Of people, to move by jumping on one leg **(b)** Of small creatures, to move by jumping: *The rabbit hopped along the path.* **2.** *infml.* To get onto, into, or out of quickly: *She hopped onto her bicycle and rode off.* **3. hopping mad** Very angry

hop n. **1.** An act of hopping or jumping **2.** *infml.* A distance traveled by a plane: *It's quite a hop from San Francisco to New York.*

hope (hoʷp) v. **hoped, hoping 1.** To trust, to rely (on): *Those who hope in the Lord will renew their strength* (Isaiah 40:31). **2.** To wish and expect, though the thing wished for seems unlikely: *After this dry weather, everyone hopes for rain.* NOTE: Compare **hope** and **wish**: We use the word **hope** to speak of a desire that is possible and may or may not be likely. We use **wish** to speak about any desire, whether possible or not and whether likely or not.: *"I wish it would stop raining." "He hopes to become a doctor."*

hope n. **1.** A person or thing that may be trusted or relied on to bring success: *The Bible says: "We [believers] wait for the blessed hope — the glorious appearing of our great God and Savior Jesus Christ, who gave himself for us to redeem us from all wickedness and to purify for himself a people that are his very own, eager to do what is good"* (Titus 2:13,14). **2.** Trust that sthg. will happen as one expects: *Those without Christ are... without hope and without God in the world* (Ephesians 2:12). *The Apostle Paul, writing to Pastor Timothy, says, "Command those who are rich...not to be arrogant nor to put their hope in wealth which is so uncertain, but to put their hope in God, who richly provides us with everything for our enjoyment"* (1 Timothy 6:17).

hope-ful (hoʷp-fəl) adj. Having hope or being a cause for hope: *We're hopeful that you get the job you applied for./The signs of his complete recovery are hopeful.* —**hopefully** adv. —**hopefulness** n.

hope-less (hoʷp-ləs) adj. **1.** Without hope: *John's condition is hopeless. There's no hope he will ever be able to walk.* **2.** *infml.* Completely useless: *Mary is hopeless as a secretary. She can't even spell her own name.* —**hopelessly** adv.

horde (hɔrd) n. A great number or large crowd: *Hordes of insects gathered around the lantern.*

ho-ri-zon (hə-raɪ-zən) n. **1.** The line where the sky seems to meet the earth or sea **2.** The limit of what one can see or understand

hor-i-zon-tal (hɔr-ə-zɑn-təl) adj. Level; in a position parallel to the horizon: *Be sure to keep this box in a horizontal position.* —compare VERTICAL —**horizontally** adv.

hor-mone (hɔr-moʷn) n. Any of several substances produced by glands of the body, which are carried to other organs or tissues where they influence growth, development, etc.

horn (hɔrn) n. **1.** A hard growth found on the top of the heads of cattle, sheep, and goats **2.** Sthg. made of this material or shaped like a horn: *My comb is made of horn.* **3.** A device, as in a car, which sounds a warning **4.** A musical instrument made of a long metal

tube, usually bent several times and played by blowing: *The horn I played in high school was a tuba.*

hor-net (hor–nət) n. A large, stinging insect, related to the wasp

hor-o-scope (hor–ə–sko^wp) n. In astrology, a diagram of the heavens showing the relative position of planets and the twelve signs of the zodiac, for use in (supposedly) foretelling events in a person's life. NOTE: Relying on the horoscope to let us know when to do anything is a sinful practice, totally contrary to the Word of God, and it is totally unreliable, for God alone knows the future. God hates this and all sin, but he is also a God of love and mercy and forgiveness. If we truly repent of our sins and put our trust in Jesus for our salvation, we shall have eternal life. —see JESUS, SIN, REPENT, FORGIVENESS, ASTROLOGY

hor-ren-dous (ho–rɛn–dəs/hə–) adj. Dreadful; horrible

hor-ri-ble (hor–ə–bəl/ har–) adj. 1. Very bad, terrible; causing horror: *a horrible tragedy* 2. *infml.* Cruel, disagreeable, or ugly: *Selling drugs to children is a horrible crime!* —**horribly** adv.

hor-rid (hor–ɪd/ har–) adj. 1. Horrible 2. Very unpleasant;

hor-ri-fy (hor–ə–faɪ/ har–) v. -fied, -fying To cause to feel horror: *We were horrified to hear that war had been declared.*

hor-ror (hor–ər/ har–) n. A very bad feeling of shock, fear, and distaste: *The child's mother cried out in horror as she saw him fall from the roof.*

horse (hors) n. 1. A large, four-legged animal with hooves and a mane, used for carrying people and goods and for pulling heavy things 2. A padded block on legs used for vaulting or jumping: *a vaulting horse* 3. **Hold your horses!** Don't be in too big a hurry to do or decide sthg. 4. **put the cart before the horse** To do or put things in the wrong order 5. **saw horse** A frame used by carpenters to support boards, etc.

horse-back (hors–bæk) n. A horse's back **horseback** adv. Mounted on a horse

horse-play (hors–ple^y) n. Rough, boisterous fun: *Stop that horseplay and get to work.*

horse-pow-er (hors–paʊ–ər) n. A unit of power equal to that required to lift 33,000 pounds one foot in one minute, or 550 foot-pounds per second

horse-rad-ish (hors–ræd–ɪʃ) n. 1. A plant cultivated for its pungent root 2. A condiment made by grinding this root

hor-ta-to-ry (hor–tə–tɔr–i^y) adj. Urging to some course of good conduct or action *also* **hortative** adj.

hor-ti-cul-ture (hor–tə–kʌl–tʃər) n. The science of raising fruits, vegetables, flowers, and ornamental plants —**hor-ticulturist** n.

Ho-san-na (ho^w–zæn–ə) n., interj. A word from the Hebrew language meaning **save now**. The early Christian church adopted this cry of acclamation and adoration into its worship.

hose (ho^wz) n. **hose** or **hoses** 1. A flexible rubber or plastic tube used for passing water and other liquids from place to place 2. Stockings or socks

Ho-se-a (ho^w–ze^y–ə) n. 1. A prophet of Israel in the eighth century B.C., a contemporary of the Prophets Isaiah and Micah 2. An Old Testament book written by the Prophet Hosea. His message was addressed to the Northern Kingdom of Israel which had fallen into idolatry. It is a call to repentance and contains promises of future blessings. —see BIBLE, OLD TESTAMENT

ho-sier-y (ho^w–ʒər–i^y) n. Socks, stockings, etc.

hos-pice (has–pəs) n. 1. A hospital for dying people 2. A shelter for the very poor and homeless

hos-pi-ta-ble (has–pɪt–ə–bəl/has–pɪt–ə–bəl) adj. Showing generous and cordial reception of guests, feeding them, etc. —opposite IN-HOSPITABLE —**hospitably** adv. —see HOSPITALITY

hos-pi-tal (has–pɪt–əl) n. A place where sick or injured people stay and have treatment

hos-pi-tal-i-ty (has–pə–tæl–ə–ti^y) n. Friendly and generous reception and entertainment of guests: *Share with God's people who are in need. Practice hospitality* (Romans 12:13). *Offer hospitality to one another without grum-*

bling (1 Peter 4:9).

hos-pi-tal-ize (hɑs–pɪt–əl–aɪz) v. **-ized, izing** To send or admit a patient to a hospital: *My father has been hospitalized with a stroke.*

host (hoʷst) n. **1.** One who receives or entertains guests **2.** One who provides facilities for an event or function **3.** A person who introduces guests or other performers, such as those on a TV show: *My friend has just been asked to be the host on the new TV show.* **4.** A large number; a multitude **5.** An army

hos-tage (hɑs–tɪdʒ) n. A person held by an enemy to try to force the other side to do what the enemy wants: *The hijacker of the airliner was holding 75 hostages — 70 passengers and five crew members — and demanding $100,000.*

hos-tel (hɑs–təl) n. A supervised lodging place for young people

host-ess (hoʷs–təs) n. **1.** A female host **2.** A flight attendant

hos-tile (hɑs–təl) adj. **1.** Not friendly; showing opposition: *The sinful mind is hostile toward God* (Romans 8:7). **2.** Of or relating to an enemy

hos-til-i-ty (hɑs–tɪl–ə–tiʸ) n. **1.** The state of being unfriendly or at war **2.** *pl.* **hos-tilities** Acts of fighting in war

hot (hɑt) adj. **hotter, hottest 1.** Having or causing a great deal of heat: *This cup is too hot to hold.* **2.** Having a sharp, burning taste: *This sauce is really hot. You put in too much pepper.* **3. hot–blooded** Excitable; quick to show strong feelings **4. hot air** Empty talk or ideas, esp. boasting: *He's full of hot air.* **5. hot under the collar** Angry and ready to argue or fight **6. not so hot** *infml.* Not as good as expected **7. in hot water** In trouble: *I'm really in hot water with my boss.*

hot-bed (hɑt–bɛd) n. An environment favoring the rapid growth of sthg., esp. sthg. bad: *a hotbed of crime and violence*

hot dog (hɑt dɔg/ dɑg) n. A frankfurter alone or a frankfurter served in a bread roll

ho-tel (hoʷ–tɛl) n. A building where lodging and usually meals and personal services are provided for the public

hot-house (hɑt–haʊs) n. A heated house, usu. with a glass roof and sides, for growing plants that need a consistently warm temperature; a greenhouse

hot-ly (hɑt–liʸ) adv. **1.** Angrily and forcefully: *hotly debated* **2.** Eagerly and with great interest: *He was hotly pursued by his many eager fans.*

hot plate (hɑt pleʸt) n. A simple, portable appliance on which food can be cooked

hound (haʊnd) n. A hunting dog, esp. a foxhound

hound v. To pursue continually and relentlessly: *I better do this work as soon as possible or my boss will keep hounding me about it.*

hour (aʊr/ aʊ–ər) n. **1.** Any of the 24 equal parts into which a whole day is divided: *Every day has 24 hours and ev-ery hour has 60 minutes.* **2.** A particular time of day when a new such period starts: *You'll find the news on this station every hour on the hour.* (=exactly at 1 o'clock, 2 o'clock, etc.) **3.** A particular point or period of time: *in her hour of need* **4. the eleventh hour** At the last possible moment **5.** An indefinite point in time: *The Son of Man [Jesus] will come at an hour when you do not expect him* (Luke 12:40).

hour-glass (aʊr–glæs) n. A device that measures time by passing sand from one glass container into a lower one through a narrow tube

hour-ly (aʊr–liʸ/ aʊ–ər–liʸ) adv. Happening or done every hour

house (haʊs) n. **houses** (haʊ–zəz) **1. (a)** A building that serves as a place for people to live **(b)** The people in such a building: *The sirens awakened the whole house.* **2.** A building for a particular use: *a schoolhouse/a birdhouse* **3.** A place of worship: *Let us go to the house of the Lord* (Psalm 122:1). *My house will be called a house of prayer for all nations* (Mark 11:17). **4.** A legislative body: *The House of Representatives* **5.** A theater, or the people in it: *The movie played to a full house.*

house-hold (haʊs–hoʷld) n. All the people who live together in a house, esp. a family: *Believe in the Lord Jesus, and you will be saved — you and your household* (Acts 16:31).

house-keep-er (haʊs–kiʸ–pər) n. One paid to run or manage a home

house-maid (haʊs–meʸd) n. A female hired for

housework

house-moth-er (haus–mʌð–ər) n. A woman in charge of a residence, esp. for young women

House of Commons (haus əv kɑm–ənz) n. Lower house of the British or Canadian Parliament

House of Lords (haus əv lɔrdz) n. Upper, non-elective house of the British Parliament

House of Representatives (haus əv rep–rɪ–zent–ət–ɪvz) n. Lower house of the US Congress, and of many states and some countries

house-wares (haus–weərz) n. Kitchen utensils, glassware and other household equipment

house-warm-ing (haus–wɔr–mɪŋ) n. A party to celebrate a family's occupancy of a new house

house-wife (haus–waɪf) n. A married woman who manages her own household, esp. as her principle occupation

hous-ing (hau–zɪŋ) n. 1. Lodging or shelter 2. An act of providing lodging or shelter 3. Anything that covers or protects

hov-el (hʌv–əl/ hɑv–) n. A small, dirty, wretched dwelling

hov-er (hʌv–ər) v. 1. Of birds and certain aircraft, to remain in the air in one place: *A helicopter hovered overhead.* 2. Of people, to stay in or around one place: *It was hard to concentrate on my studies with all those people hovering around me.*

hov-er-craft (hʌv–ər–kræft) n. A vehicle that is capable of moving over land or water while supported on a cushion of air made by jet engines

how (hau) adv. 1. (a) In questions about what way sthg. is done: *How do you want your egg cooked?* (b) In questions about health: *How are you feeling?* (c) In questions about amount or number: *How many cups of coffee do we need?* 2. Used in certain expressions of feeling: *How wonderful to see you!/How sweet it is!* 3. **How come?** *infml.* Why?: *How come we didn't get any mail today?* 4. **How do you do?** Polite greeting 5. **How are you?** (a) A question used to ask about the state of someone's health (b) A phrase used as a greeting when meeting again a person already

known: *How are you? Fine, thanks. How are you?*

how conj. The way or manner in which: *I remember how it rained.*

how-ev-er (hau–ev–ər) conj. In whatever way: *However you decorate the cake it'll be fine with me.*

however adv. In spite of this: *I'm on a diet. However, I'll take a small dish of ice cream.*

how-it-zer (hau–ɪt–sər) n. A short cannon that throws shells at a high angle

howl (haul) v. 1. To make a long, loud call like that of a dog or wolf 2. To cry loudly

hub (hʌb) n. 1. The central part of a wheel, propeller, fan, etc. 2. The center of activity or importance

hub-bub (hʌb–əb) n. 1. A loud, confused noise, as of many voices 2. Uproar; turmoil

hub-cap (hʌb–kæp) n. A removable metal covering over the center of a wheel of a motor vehicle

huck-ster (hʌk–stər) n. A person who sells small items in the street or from door to door

hud-dle (hʌd–əl) n. 1. A closely packed group 2. A meeting; a conference

huddle v. **-dled, -dling** 1. To crowd together 2. To confer

hue (hyuʷ) n. A color, as distinct from white, gray, or black

hue and cry (hyuʷ–n–kraɪ) n. A public clamor or protest: *There was a great hue and cry against the proposed new taxes.*

huff (hʌf) n. A state of bad temper: *She left in a huff because I didn't agree with her.* —**huffy** adj.

huff v. To puff or blow

hug (hʌg) v. **-gg-** 1. To press tightly in the arms, esp. as a sign of love 2. To stay close to sthg. as one follows along the edge of it: *The road hugged the river.*

hug n. The act of hugging: *Guests at the reunion were giving hugs to friends they hadn't seen for many years.*

huge (hyuʷdʒ) adj. **huger, hugest** Very large: *a huge crowd/a huge success* —**hugely** adv.

hulk (hʌlk) n. 1. An old ship, unfit for use 2. Anything big and clumsy

hulk-ing (hʌl–kɪŋ) adj. Big and clumsy

hull (hʌl) n. **1.** The body or framework of a ship **2.** The outer covering of a rocket or missile **3.** The husk, shell, or outer covering of a seed or fruit, as of a nut
hull v. To remove the hull of a grain, nut, etc.
hul-la-ba-loo (hʌl-ə-bə-luᵂ) n. An uproar; tumult; noisy disturbance
hum (hʌm) v. **-mm- 1.** Esp. of bees, to make a continuous buzzing sound **2.** Of people, to make an m-m-m-m sound continuously, esp. as a way of singing music with closed lips: *humming a pleasant tune* **3.** Of work being carried out, to work rapidly and efficiently: *Things are humming right along.*
hu-man (hyuᵂ-mən/ yuᵂ) n. Also **human being** A person (man, woman, or child), not an animal
human adj. **1.** Of or concerning human beings: *the human voice* **2.** Showing the feelings which are considered normal for people, esp. kindness: *His response to my appeal was quite human. He really wanted to help.*
hu-mane (hyuᵂ-meʸn/ yuᵂ) adj. Showing compassion, sympathy, and the other qualities of a civilized person —op-posite INHUMANE
hu-man-ism (hyuᵂ-mən-ɪz-əm/ yuᵂ) n. Any system of thought in which human interests and values are taken to be of primary importance, esp. as opposed to spiritual values; a philosophy that declares, "no deity will save us, we must save ourselves": *Humanism teaches (contrary to the Word of God) that man is basically good, and that his goals should be self-actualization, self-determination, and self-indulgence.* NOTE: Humanism teaches that, since there is no life after death (contrary to Scripture), it is in man's best interest to find the "good life" here and now. Humanists advocate sexual activity and promiscuity for the young, as well as the old. They advocate free use of pornography and drugs and endorse prostitution, homosexuality, and abortion on demand in the name of human rights. They are hostile to Christianity and morality. Humanists hold a religious theory that permits them to explain man's origin without

God, thus leaving man unaccountable to God. In spite of scientific evidence to the contrary, they insist that man is the highest form of primate, that he evolved from lower forms of life, which is altogether contrary to the Scriptural teaching that God created man in his own image (Genesis 1:27). They will not permit creation to be given equal time in our so-called "free public schools" in the US. Humanists foster the unscientific religious belief that there is not now, and never has been, either a Supreme Being, or a personal God, who is interested in the affairs of man. The Bible clearly warns us against the teachings of humanism, saying: "See to it that no one takes you captive through hollow and deceptive philosophy, which depends on human tradition and the basic principles of this world rather than on Christ" (Colossians 2:8). "Turn away from godless chatter and the opposing ideas of what is falsely called knowledge, which some have professed and in so doing have wandered from the faith" (1 Timothy 6:20).
—**humanist** n. —**humanistic** adj.
hu-man-i-tar-i-an (hyuᵂ-mæn-ə-teər-iʸ-ən/ yuᵂ) n., adj. A person concerned with the improvement of people's lives through better living conditions, fair treatment, etc.
—**humanitarianism** n.
hu-man-i-ties (hyuᵂ-mæn-ə-tiʸz/ yuᵂ) n. Subjects of study concerned with human culture, esp. literature, language, history and philosophy
hu-man-i-ty (hyuᵂ-mæn-ə-tiʸ/ yuᵂ)) n. **1.** Human beings collectively **2.** The quality or state of being human or humane; kindheartedness
hu-man-ize (hyuᵂ-mən-aɪz/ yuᵂ) v. **-ized, -izing** To make human or humane
hu-man-kind (hyuᵂ-mən-kaɪnd) n. Mankind
hu-man-ly (hyuᵂ-mən-liʸ/ yuᵂ) adv. Within the capacity of humans: *It's not humanly possible to fly.*
hum-ble (hʌm-bəl) adj. **-bler, -blest 1.** Not proud or haughty; having or showing a modest estimate of one's own importance: *Be completely humble and gentle* (Ephesians 4:2). —compare PROUD **2.** Lowly; unimpor-

tant: *a humble job* —**humble** n. *God opposes the proud but gives grace to the humble* (James 4:6). —**humbly** adv. *And what does the Lord require of you? To act justly and to love mercy and to walk humbly with your God* (Micah 6:8).

humble v. **-bled, -bling** To lower the position of oneself or another: *Everyone who exalts himself will be humbled, and he who humbles himself will be exalted* (Luke 18:14). *Whoever humbles himself like this little child is the greatest in the kingdom of heaven* (Matthew 18:4). *Your attitude should be the same as that of Christ Jesus, who, being in very nature God, ...made himself nothing, taking the very nature of a servant, being made in human likeness. And... he humbled himself and became obedient to death even death on a cross [that he might pay for our sins with his own blood]. Therefore, God exalted him to the highest place and gave him the name that is above every name, that at the name of Jesus every knee should bow, in heaven and on earth and under the earth, and every tongue confess that Jesus Christ is Lord, to the glory of God the Father* (Philippians 2:5-11). —see JESUS

hu-mid (hyu^w–məd/ **yu^w**) adj. Of air and weather, moist, esp. to the point of being uncomfortable; damp: *This hot, humid weather is hard on the elderly.*

hu-mid-i-fy (hyu^w–mɪd–ə–faɪ/ yu^w) v. **-fied, -fying** To cause to become humid

hu-mid-i-ty (hyu^w–mɪd–ə–ti^y/ yu^w) n. A degree of water vapor contained in the air; dampness: *The heat is made worse in summer by the high humidity.*

hu-mil-i-ate (hyu^w–mɪl–i^y–e^{y}t/ yu^w) v. **-ated, -ating** To make someone feel ashamed or look foolish in front of other people: *Mrs. Brown felt humiliated because of her son's bad behavior at the dinner table.* —**hu-mil-i-a-tion** (hyu^w–mɪl–i^y–e^y–ʃən/ yu^w) n.

hu-mil-i-ty (hyu^w–mɪl–ə–ti^y/ yu^w) n. The quality of being humble: *With humility comes wisdom* (Proverbs 11:2). *Humility comes before honor* (Proverbs 15:33). *Humility and the fear of the Lord bring wealth and honor and life* (Proverbs 22:4). *Clothe yourselves with humility toward one another, because "God opposes*

the proud but gives grace to the humble" (1 Peter 5:5).

hum-ming-bird (hʌm–ɱ–bərd) n. A very small, brightly colored American bird whose rapidly moving wings make a humming sound

hu-mor (hyu^w–mər/ yu^w) *AmE.* humour *BrE.* n. **1.** The ability to see things as amusing: *He has a great sense of humor.* **2.** The quality of being able to amuse others: *His humor is very clever.* **3.** Mood: *He's in a good humor today.*

hu-mor v. To soothe or calm someone by acceptance of wishes, behavior, etc., whether one agrees or not: *Maybe if you humor him, he'll stop making such unreasonable demands.*

hu-mor-ist (hyu^{w}m–ə–rɪst/ yu^w) n. **1.** A person who can bring out the amusing side of things **2.** A person who writes or tells amusing stories, jokes, etc.

hu-mor-ous (hyu^{w}m–ə–rəs/ yu^w) adj. Funny; comical: *a humorous incident/TV show* —**humorously** adv.

hump (hʌmp) n. **1.** A round, raised part, esp. on the back of a camel **2.** A deformity of a similar shape on the back of a person **3.** A round, raised mound of earth

hu-mus (hyu^w–məs/ yu^w) n. Rich soil resulting from the decay of plants, leaves, etc.

hunch (hʌntʃ) n. An idea concerning a future event based more on feeling than on reason: *He had a hunch that his team would win the game, and he was right.*

hunch v. **1.** To assume or cause to assume a crooked position: *She hunched her shoulders and pulled her coat about her.* **2.** To thrust oneself forward

hunch-back (hʌntʃ–bæk) n. **1.** Humpback **2.** A person with a humpback

hun-dred (hʌn–drəd) determ., n., pron. **-dred** or **-dreds** The number 100: *10 X 10 = 100 (ten times ten equals one hundred)* —**hundredth** (hʌn–drədθ) n., pron., adv.

hung (hʌŋ) v. Past tense and past part. of **hang**

hun-ger (hʌŋ–gər) n., v. **1.** The desire or need for food **2.** A desire or need: *spir. Blessed are those who hunger and thirst for righteousness, for they will be filled* (Matthew 5:6). **3.** Prolonged lack of food: *World hunger is one of*

the problems that must be faced in the years to come.

hun·gry (**hʌŋ**–gri^y) adj. -grier, -griest **1.** Feeling or showing the need for food: *If your enemy is hungry, give him food* (Proverbs 25:21). **2.** Hunger for emotional, spiritual, or other needs: *spir. Jesus declared, "I am the bread of life. He who comes to me will never go hungry, and he who believes in me will never be thirsty"* (John 6:35). —**hungrily** adv.

hunk (hʌŋk) n. A large piece; a chunk

hunt (hʌnt) v. **1.** To try to catch and/or kill animals and birds for food or for sport **2.** To look for: *I have hunted all over town for a good place to buy shoes.*

hunt n. An act of hunting: *a treasure hunt/a fox hunt* —**hunter** n.

hur·dle (hɜr–dəl) n. **1.** A frame for jumping over in a race **2.** A difficulty to be overcome

hurdle v. -dled, -dling **1.** To run a hur·dle race **2.** To jump over various obstacles: *He had to hurdle several trash cans and boxes as he chased the thief down the alley.*

hurl (hɜrl) v. To throw forcefully: *The rock was hurled from a passing car./fig. She kept hurling insults at me for no reason.*

hur·rah (hə–rɔ / –rɑ) interj. A word used as a shout of praise or joy

hur·ri·cane (hɜr–ə–ke^yn) n. A tropical storm with winds of 74 miles per hour or greater, usu. accompanied by rain, thunder, and lightning

hur·ried (hɜr–i^yd) adj. Done rapidly, and usu. poorly: *hurried note* —**hurriedly** adv.

hur·ry (hɜr–i^y) v. -ried, -rying **1.** To be quick in action or to cause someone else to be quick: *If you hurry too much, you are likely to fall.* **2.** To send or bring quickly: *Relief supplies were hurried to the scene of the earthquake.*

hurry n. **1.** Rapid activity **2.** Need for quick action: *What's the hurry? We don't need to get these letters out today.* **3. in a hurry** (a) Hastily: *You'd better get dressed in a hurry. Your friend is waiting.* (b) Eager: *She was sure in a hurry to take that job.*

hurt (hɜrt) v. **hurt, hurting 1.** To injure a part of the body: *She was badly hurt in the car accident.* **2.** To have or cause a feeling of pain: *That was a nasty fall. Does your arm hurt?/fig.*

to hurt someone's feelings —**hurtful** adj. *Nasty remarks about people can be more hurtful than physical abuse.*

hur·tle (hɜr–təl) v. -tled, -tling **1.** To move very quickly, often violently: *The car hurtled down the mountainside.* **2.** To hurl; fling

hus·band (hʌz–bənd) n. The man to whom a woman is married: *Husbands, love your wives, just as Christ loved the church and gave himself for her...* (Ephesians 5:25).

hush (hʌʃ) v., interj. (often a command) Be still: *Hush, I don't want to hear another word out of you.*

hush n. A silence, esp. a peaceful one: *There is a hush in the air.*

husk (hʌsk) n. The dry outer covering of some seeds and grains

hus·ky (hʌs–ki^y) adj. -kier, -kiest **1.** Big and strong **2.** Of the voice, rough; hoarse

husky n. -kies A heavy-coated dog of the arctic region of North America, used to pull sledges

hus·sy (hʌs–i^y) n. -sies **1.** A badly behaved or mischievous girl **2.** A sexually immoral woman

hus·tle (hʌs–əl) v. -tled, -tling **1.** To (cause to) hurry: *You'd better hustle off to work.* **2.** To persuade someone to do sthg. without giving it careful consideration: *Don't try to hustle me into making such an important decision.*

hustle n. Hurried activity, esp. in the phrase, "hustle and bustle"

hus·tler (hʌs–lər) n. **1.** Someone who hustles **2.** *AmE.* A prostitute

hut (hʌt) n. A small building, usu. made of wood, esp. one used for living in temporarily; a shack —compare SHED

hutch (hʌtʃ) n. **1.** A chest or compartment for storage **2.** Shack; shanty

hy·a·cinth (haɪ–ə–smθ) n. A plant of the lily family, cultivated for its fragrant, bell-shaped flowers

hy·ae·na (haɪ–i^y–nə) n. see **hyena**

hy·brid (haɪ–brɪd) n. **1.** The offspring of two animals or plants of different breeds or species: *A mule is a hybrid of a male donkey and a female horse.* **2.** Anything derived from mixed sources

hy-dran-gea (hɪn–dreˠn–dʒə /–dræn–/–dʒiˠ–ə) n. Any of a genus of small shrubs or trees with large clusters of showy flowers in delicate colors

hy-drant (haɪr–drənt) n. **1.** Also fire hydrant A main water pipe in the street from which water is drawn for putting out a fire **2.** A water pipe outside a house or building from which one may draw water —compare FAUCET

hy-drau-lic (haɪr–drɔ–lɪk) adj. Operated or moved by the pressure of water or other liquids: *hydraulic power*

hy-drau-lics (haɪr–drɔ–lɪks) n. A branch of science which studies the use of water to produce power

hy-dro– (haɪr–droˠ/–drə) prefix Water

hy-dro-e-lec-tric (haɪr–droˠ–ɪ–lɛk–trɪk) adj. Using water power to produce electricity —**hy-dro-e-lec-tric-i-ty** (haɪr–droˠ–ɪ–lɛk–trɪs–ɪ–tiˠ) n. —**hydroelectrically** adv.

hy-dro-gen (haɪr–drə–dʒən) n. A gas that is without color or smell, that is lighter than air and that burns easily

hydrogen bomb (haɪr–drə–dʒən bɑm) n. An extremely powerful bomb in which the explosion is caused by turning hydrogen into helium at a very high temperature

hy-dro-pho-bi-a (haɪr–drə–foˠ–biˠ–ə) n. **1.** Rabies, esp. in humans: *He developed hydrophobia from the bite of a rabid dog.* **2.** The abnormal fear of water and of drinking

hy-e-na (haɪr–iˠ–nə) n. A carnivorous, dog-like animal native to Africa and Asia with a howl that sounds like laughter

hy-giene (haɪr–dʒiˠn) n. **1.** The study and practice of how to maintain good health **2.** General cleanliness

hy-gien-ic (haɪr–dʒɛn–ɪk/ haɪr–dʒiˠ–ɛn–ɪk) adj. Causing or keeping good health —**hygienically** adv.

hy-grom-e-ter (haɪr–grɑm–ət–ər) n. An instrument for measuring atmospheric moisture

hymn (hɪm) n. A song of praise, especially to God, usually one adapted for singing by the congregation in a Christian church service: *Speak to one another with psalms, hymns and spiritual songs* (Ephesians 5:19).

hym-nal (hɪm–nəl) n. A book of hymns

hype (haɪp) n. **1.** *slang* Hypodermic **2.** *slang* A narcotics addict **3.** A deception **4.** *slang* A statement to promote sales

hy-per– (haɪr–pər–) comb. form More than normal, excessive: *hyperactive/hypersensitive/hypercritical*

hy-per-bo-le (haɪr–pɜr–ho–liˠ) n. A gross exaggeration in speech or writing in order to express a particular effect: *"The shot that killed President Kennedy was heard around the world," is a hyperbole.*

hy-per-ten-sion (haɪr–pər–tɛn–ʃən) n. Abnormally high blood pressure

hy-phen (haɪr–fən) n. A short written or printed line (-) used to join words together or to break them into syllables

hy-phen-ate (haɪr–fə–neˠt) v. **-ated, -ating** To join with a hyphen —**hyphenation** n.

hyp-no-sis (hɪp–noˠ–səs) n. A sleep-like state caused by the action of another person who can then make the hypnotized person obey his commands

hyp-not-ic (hɪp–nɑt–ɪk) adj. **1.** Inducing sleep **2.** Concerning hypnosis or hypnotism

hyp-no-tism (hɪp–nə–tɪz–əm) n. The act or practice of hypnotizing someone

hyp-no-tize (hɪp–nə–taɪz) v. **-tized, -tizing** To cause hypnosis in someone

hy-po– (haɪr–poˠ– /–pə–) Also before vowels **hyp–** comb. form **1.** Under; below **2.** Less than normal **3.** Denoting a lack or deficiency in

hy-po-chon-dri-a (haɪr–pə–kɑn–driˠ–ə) n. The state of worrying too much about one's health

hy-po-chon-dri-ac (haɪr–pə–kɑn–driˠ–æk) n. One who constantly worries about his health: *Her husband suffers from hypochondria. He's a hypochondriac.*

hy-poc-ri-sy (hɪ–pɑk–rə–siˠ) n. **-sies** The act or practice of pretending to be what one is not, esp. to be better than one is: *Rid yourselves of all malice and all deceit, hypocrisy, envy, and slander of every kind* (1 Peter 2:1).

hyp-o-crite (hɪp–ə–krɪt) n. A person who pretends to be what he is not; one who practices hypocrisy: *When you pray, do not be like the hypocrites, for they love to pray standing in the synagogues and on the street corners to be seen*

by *men* (Matthew 6:5). —**hyp·o·crit·i·cal** (hɪp–ə–**krɪt**–ɪ–kəl) adj.

hy·po·der·mic (haɪ–pə–**dər**–mɪk) adj., n. A means or instrument used for injecting a drug under the skin

hy·pot·e·nuse (haɪ–**pɑt**–ə–nuʷs) n. The longest side of a right-angled triangle

hy·poth·e·sis (haɪ–**pɑθ**–ə–səs) n., *pl.* -eses Sthg. that is assumed to be true, and on which an argument may be based

hy·po·thet·i·cal (haɪ–pə–**θet**–ɪ–kəl) adj. Thought to be true, but not yet proved to be true or known to have happened —**hypo·**thetically adv.

hys·ter·i·a (hɪs–**teər**–iʸ–ə) n. **1.** Uncontrollable fear or emotion **2.** A condition of extreme nervous excitement in which the sufferer may laugh or cry uncontrollably and show other strange behavior

hys·ter·i·cal (hɪs–**teər**–ɪ·kəl) adv. **1.** Showing hysteria **2.** Expressing feelings in an uncontrolled manner **3.** *AmE. infml.* Extremely funny: *The show was hysterical. You'd like it.*

hys·ter·ics (hɪs–**teər**–ɪks) n. A fit of uncontrollable laughter or crying

I, i (aɪ) n. **1.** The ninth letter of the English alphabet **2.** The Roman numeral (number) for 1 (one)

I (aɪ) pron. The person who is speaking (used as the subject of the sentence): *I will meet you at the station./ My brother and I will meet you at the station.* NOTE: Never say, "He will meet my brother and I." Rather say, "He will meet my brother and me." Never say, "between you and I" or "for you and I". Rather say "between/for you and me." Following a preposition, always use the objective form "me" rather than the subjective form "I."

–i-an (–iʸ–ən) suffix adj. **1.** Of or belonging to: *Oregonian* **2.** Resembling: *reptilian*

–i-an (–iʸ–ən) suffix n. **1.** One that is of or relating to: *American/ Bostonian* **2.** An expert in: *electrician*

i-bex (aɪ–bɛks) n. A wild mountain goat

i-bis (aɪ–bəs) n. A large heron-like wading bird

–i-ble (–ə–bəl) suffix Variation of **–able**

–ic (–ɪk) suffix adj. **1.** Of, pertaining to, or characteristic of: *ironic/ historic/angelic* **2.** Having or taking a valence higher than in corresponding **–ous** compounds: *ferric iron* **3.** Made up of: *runic*

ice (aɪs) n. **1.** Water which has frozen solid **2.** A frozen dessert made of fruit juice **3. break the ice** To be the first to do sthg. or to try to become friends with someone previously not known **4. cut no ice (with someone)** To have little influence on someone; to be unconvincing **5. on thin ice** In a dangerous position **6. keep sthg. on ice** To save for later consideration: *Let's keep your plan on ice just in case our other plans don't work out.*

ice-berg (aɪs–bɜrg) n. A huge mass of floating ice broken off from a glacier, very dangerous to ships

ice cream (aɪs–kriʸm) n. A frozen dessert, usu. containing milk or other fat products, sugar, eggs and flavoring —**ice–cream** adj. *an*

SPELLING NOTE:
Words having the sound /aɪ/ may be spelled with **e-**, as in **eye**, or with **ai-**, as in **aisle**.

ice-cream cone

ich-thy-ol-o-gy (ɪk–θiʸ–ɑl–ə–dʒiʸ) n. The branch of zoology that deals with the study of fish

i-ci-cle (aɪ–sɪ–kəl) n. A long hanging piece of ice formed by the freezing of dripping water

ic-ing (aɪ–sɪŋ) n. also **frosting** A mixture of powdered sugar and liquid, used to cover and decorate cakes

i-con or **i-kon** (aɪ–kɑn) n. **1.** An image, figure, or representation **2.** In the Orthodox Eastern Church, a picture or carving of a holy person, itself regarded as sacred

i-con-o-clast (aɪ–**kɑn**–ə–klæst) n. **1.** A person who attacks popular beliefs or established customs **2.** Formerly, a person who destroyed sacred images —**iconoclasm** n. —**i-con-o-clas-tic** (aɪ–kɑn–ə–**klæs**–tɪk) adj.

i-cy (aɪ–siʸ) adj. **-cier, -ciest 1.** Very cold; thoroughly chilled: *She served us tall glasses of icy lemonade./My feet are icy.* **2.** Unfriendly: *an icy welcome* **3.** Covered with ice: *Don't slip on the icy steps.*

ID (aɪ diʸ) abbr. for **identification**

I'd (aɪd) **1.** Short for **I would:** *I'd like to go.* **2.** Short for **I had:** *I'd better go.*

i-de-a (aɪ–diʸ–ə) n. **1.** A mental picture: *I have a fairly good idea of what she looks like.* **2.** A belief or opinion: *His ideas and mine don't always agree.* **3.** A plan formed by thinking: *Maybe if we all work together we can come up with an idea for raising the money.*

i-deal (aɪ–diʸl/ aɪ–diʸ–əl) adj. Satisfying one's idea of what is perfect: *This tool is ideal for the job I have in mind.*

ideal n. **1.** A person or thing thought of as a perfect example: *Miss Jones is my ideal of a good teacher.* **2.** usu. pl. A standard of perfection: *St. Paul was a man of high ideals, like every Christian should be.* —**ideally** adv.

i-de-al-ist (aɪ–diʸ–ə–ləst) n. A person who has high ideals, esp. one who tries in an unrealistic way to achieve these —**idealism** n. —**i-de-al-is-tic** (aɪ–diʸ–ə–lɪs–tɪk) adj. —**idealistically** adv.

i-de-al-ize (aɪ–diʸ–ə–laɪz) v. **-ized, -izing** To regard or represent as perfect —**i-de-al-i-za-tion** (aɪ–diʸ–ə–lɪ–zeʸ–ʃən) n.

i-den-ti-cal (aɪ-dɛn-tɪ-kəl) adj. **1.** Alike in every detail: *Our dresses are identical. I wonder if we bought them at the same store.* **2.** The same: *This is the identical table we sat at last time we came to this restaurant.* —**identically** adv.

i-den-ti-fi-ca-tion (aɪ-dɛn-tə-fɪ-keʸ-ʃən) n. **1.** The act of identifying or the state of being identified **2.** Means of proving who one is: *His passport and driver's license were his means of identification.*

i-den-ti-fy (aɪ-dɛn-tə-faɪ) v.-**fied, -fying 1.** To prove or show who or what sbdy./ sthg. is; to recognize as being a specified person or thing: *I identified him by the scar on his left cheek.* **2.** To associate or connect someone with someone else, or one thing with another: *One cannot identify riches with happiness.* **3.** To associate very closely in feeling or interest: *She is too closely identified with comedy to be taken seriously.* **4.** To regard oneself as sharing the characteristics or the fortunes of someone else: *He identifies himself with the football hero in the film.*

i-den-ti-ty (aɪ-dɛn-tɪ-tiʸ) n. -**ties 1.** The distinguishing character or personality of an individual **2.** The quality or condition of being exactly like sthg. else

i-de-ol-o-gy (aɪ-diʸ-al-ə-dʒiʸ/ ɪd-iʸ-) n. -**gies 1.** The body of ideas characteristic of a particular person, group, or culture **2.** The ideas that form the basis for a political or economic theory, etc. —**i-de-o-log-i-cal** (aɪ-diʸ-ə-ladʒ-ɪ-kəl) —**ideologically** adv.

id-i-o-cy (ɪd-iʸ-ə-siʸ) n. -**cies 1.** The state of being an idiot **2.** Extreme stupidity **3.** Stupid behavior

id-i-o-lect (ɪd-iʸ-ə-lɛkt) n. The total amount of a language that any one person knows and uses

id-i-om (ɪd-iʸ-əm) n. **1.** A phrase that means sthg. different from the meaning of the individual words: *To be "hot under the collar" is an English idiom meaning "very angry."* **2.** The language used by a particular people or group: *the idiom of the Middle Westerner* —**id-i-o-mat-ic** (ɪd-iʸ-ə-mæt-ɪk) adj. *"To kill two birds with one stone" is an idiomatic expression.*

id-i-o-syn-cra-sy (ɪd-iʸ-ə-sɪŋ-krə-siʸ) n. -**sies**

A person's own way of thinking or doing things which is different from others

id-i-ot (ɪd-iʸ-ət) n. **1.** A mentally deficient person who is permanently incapable of rational conduct **2.** *infml.* A very stupid person

id-i-ot-ic (ɪd-iʸ-at-ɪk) adj. Stupid: *Intentionally going the wrong way on a one-way street was an idiotic thing to do.* —**idiotically** adv.

i-dle (aɪ-dəl) adj. -**dler, -dlest 1.** Not employed; inactive: *He found a job after being idle for six months.* **2.** Avoiding work; lazy: *In the name of the Lord Jesus Christ, we command you, brothers [fellow Christians], to keep away from every brother who is idle and does not live according to the teaching you received from us. If a man will not work [= is too lazy to work], he shall not eat* (2 Thessalonians 3:6,10). **3.** Not effective; having no result: *idle gossip/ rumors/ threats/ Jesus said, "Every idle word that men shall speak, they shall give account thereof in the day of judgment"* (Matthew 12:36). —**idleness** n. —**idly** adv.

i-dle v. -**dled, -dling 1.** To waste time; do nothing: *idling the day away* **2.** Of an engine, to run slowly without doing work

i-dler (aɪd-lər) n. One who idles away his time

i-dol (aɪ-dəl) n. **1.** An image or anything that is worshiped as a god or instead of the one true God: *The one and only true God says, "You shall not make for yourself an idol in the form of anything in heaven above or on the earth beneath or in the waters below. You shall not bow down to them or worship them"* (Exodus 20:4,5). *We know that an idol is nothing in the world, and that there is no God but one* (1 Corinthians 8:4). **2.** An object or a person of passionate devotion: *That popular singer is his idol.*

i-dol-a-ter (aɪ-dal-ə-tər) n. **1.** A worshiper of idols: *The Bible says, "Neither the sexually immoral nor idolaters... will inherit the kingdom of God"* (1 Corinthians 6:9,10). **2.** A greedy person: *No... greedy person — such a man is an idolater — has any inheritance in the kingdom of God* (Ephesians 5:5).

i-dol-a-try (aɪ-dal-ə-triʸ) n. **1.** The worship of idols, a sin against the first commandment:

Rebellion is like the sin of divination and arrogance like the evil of idolatry (1 Samuel 15:23). —see IDOL **2**. Greed: *Greed... is idolatry* (Colossians 3:5). —**idolatrous** adj. NOTE: God detests the sin of idolatry and all sin. But because of his great love and mercy, he forgives the sins of those who repent and trust in Jesus Christ for eternal life (Acts 2:38; John 3:16).

i-dol-ize also **-ise** *BrE.* (aɪ-də-laɪz) v. **-ized -izing** To treat like an idol: *She idolizes her baby sister.*

i-dyl-lic (aɪ-dɪl-ɪk) adj. Simple and delightful: *an idyllic setting for a country cottage*

i.e. (aɪ-iᵞ) *abbr.* That is.

if (ɪf) conj. **1**. On condition that: *I'll bake a cake if you'll make some coffee.* **2**. Even though: *I'm going to finish this job if it takes all night.* **3**. Whether or not: *I don't know if I can come to class tonight.* **4**. In the event that: *If I don't start now, I'll be late.* **5**. Granted that: *If what you say is true, what can we do about it?* **6**. Used to introduce a clause indicating a wish: *If only he had arrived at the station five minutes earlier!* **7**. Used when giving advice: *If I were you, I'd leave now.*

ig-loo (ɪg-luʷ) n. An Eskimo dome-shaped hut made of blocks of packed snow

ig-nite (ɪg-naɪt) v. **-nited, -niting** To set fire to sthg. or to start to burn

ig-ni-tion (ɪg-nɪʃ-ən) n. **1**. Igniting; being ignited **2**. The mechanism that provides the spark for igniting the fuel in an internal combustion engine

ig-no-ble (ɪg-noʷ-bəl) adj. Of low character or aims —**ig-no-bil-i-ty** (ɪg-noʷ-bɪl-ə-tiᵞ) n.

ig-no-min-i-ous (ɪg-nə-mɪn-iᵞ-əs) adj. **1**. Marked by disgrace or dishonor **2**. Deserving of contempt or shame

ig-no-min-y (ɪg-nə-mɪn-iᵞ) n. Public disgrace; shame

ig-no-ra-mus (ɪg-nə-reᵞ-məs) n. An exceedingly stupid person

ig-no-rance (ɪg-nə-rəns) n. Lack of knowledge: *And these times of ignorance [concerning God's Divine Nature] God overlooked, but now commands all men everywhere to repent* (Acts 17:30).

ig-no-rant (ɪg-nə-rənt) adj. Lacking knowledge: *There are some who are ignorant of God — I say this to your shame* (1 Corinthians 15:34).

ig-nore (ɪg-nɔr/ɪg-noʷr) v. **-nored, -noring** To refuse to take notice of; to pay no attention; disregard: *He who ignores discipline despises himself, but whoever heeds correction gains understanding* (Proverbs 15:32). *How shall we escape if we ignore such a great salvation [as that which we have through faith in Jesus Christ our Savior]?* (Hebrews 2:3).

i-gua-na (ɪ-gwɑn-ə) n. A large green lizard of tropical America

–ile (–aɪl/–əl) suffix Of, like, or pertaining to: *infantile*

ilk (ɪlk) n. Kind; sort; class

ill (ɪl) adj. **1**. Not healthy; sick **2**. Bad; harmful; unfavorable: *ill health/ an ill wind* **3**. **ill-tempered** Having a bad temper; irritable: *Better to live in a desert than with a quarrelsome and ill-tempered wife* (Proverbs 21:19).

ill adv. **1**. Poorly; badly; unpleasantly: *We were ill-advised* (=not wise) *to go out in such weather./ an ill-fated* (unsuccessful) *business venture* **2**. Scarcely; not easily: *ill-suited for the job* **3**. **ill at ease** Uncomfortable; embarrassed: *Mary was ill at ease giving a party for the first time.* **4**. **ill-gotten** Wrongfully obtained: *Ill-gotten treasures are of no value* (Prov-erbs 10:2).

I'll (aɪl) v. **1**. Short for **I will 2**. Short for **I shall**

il-le-gal (ɪ-liᵞ-gəl) adj. Not legal; unlawful —**illegally** adv.

il-le-gal-i-ty (ɪl-liᵞ-gæl-ə-tiᵞ) n. State or act of being against the law

il-leg-i-ble (ɪ-lɛdʒ-ə-bəl) adj. Not legible; sthg. that cannot be read: *Her signature is illegible.*

il-le-git-i-mate (ɪl-ɪ-dʒɪt-ə-mət) adj. **1**. Born to parents who are not married to each other: *an illegitimate child* **2**. Not permitted by law or by the rules: *an illegitimate medical practice*

ill–got-ten (ɪl-gɑt-ən) adj. Obtained by evil or unlawful means: *Such is the end of all who go after ill-gotten gain; it takes away the lives of those who get it* (Prov-erbs 1:19).

il-lic-it (ɪ-lɪs-ət) adj. Not permitted; against a law or rule

il-lit-er-ate (ɪ-lɪt-ə-rət) adj., n. 1. Not literate 2. One who is unable to read and write: *There are hundreds of millions of illiterates throughout the world because no one ever taught them to read.* —illiteracy n.

ill-ness (ɪl-nəs) n. Sickness; a disease; state of poor health:

il-log-i-cal (ɪ-lɑdʒ-ɪ-kəl) adj. Not logical; contrary to good sense; senseless

ill-tem-pered (ɪl-tɛm-pərd) adj. Irritable: *Better to live in a desert than with a quarrelsome and ill-tempered wife* (Prov-erbs 21:19).

il-lu-mi-nate (ɪ-luʷ-mə-neʸt) v. -nated, -nating 1. To supply with light: *I saw an angel coming down from heaven... and the earth was illuminated by his splendor* (Revelation 18:1). 2. To place bright lights on sthg. for a special occasion 3. To enable to understand; enlighten

il-lu-mi-nat-ing (ɪ-luʷ-mə-neʸt-ɪŋ) adj. Helping to make clear

il-lu-mi-na-tion (ɪ-luʷ-mə-neʸ-ʃən) n. Illuminating or being illuminated

il-lu-sion (ɪ-luʷ-ʒən) n. 1. Sthg. that deceives because it gives a false idea or belief; sthg. that seems real but is not: *I didn't really see water on the sidewalk; it was only an optical illusion.* 2. An idea or belief that seems true but is not: *The poor man has illusions of grandeur; he thinks he's rich./He has no illusions about his ability to sing. He knows he's not very good.*

il-lu-so-ry (ɪl-uʷs-ə-riʸ) adj. Deceptive

il-lus-trate (ɪl-ə-streʸt) v. -trated, -trating 1. To draw or paint pictures or add pictures to sthg. that has been written: *The magazine was beautifully illustrated.* 2. To explain the meaning of sthg. by giving examples: *The story of the Good Samaritan in the Bible illustrates what it means to be a good neighbor.*

il-lus-tra-tion (ɪl-ə-streʸ-ʃən) n. 1. A picture, diagram, etc., esp. in a book: *Children especially like books that have colorful illustrations.* 2. An example which demonstrates and explains sthg.: *The speaker gave many illustrations of what it means to be brave.*

il-lus-tra-tive (ɪ-lʌs-trə-tɪv) adj. Being or acting as an example in order to make sthg. clearer: *an illustrative diagram*

il-lus-tra-tor (ɪl-əs-treʸt-ər) n. An artist who

draws and paints pictures, esp. for a book

il-lus-tri-ous (ɪ-lʌs-triʸ-əs) adj. Famous; celebrated; known for one's great works: *an illustrious career*

I'm (aɪm) Short for I am

im- (ɪm-) prefix Not (used before b- and p-): *impolite/ impossible/ imbalance*

im-age (ɪm-ɪdʒ) n. 1. A likeness of a person or thing: *He [Jesus Christ] is the image of the invisible God* (Colossians 1:15). 2. A mental picture; impression; idea 3. The impression that a person, company, etc. give to others: *It's important for a new company to develop a good public image from the start.* 4. A likeness of a god or person, made to be worshiped, esp. one carved out of wood or stone: *All who worship images are put to shame* (Psalm 97:7). —compare IDOL, IDOLATRY 5. A personification: *He is the image of health.*

image of God n. (ɪm-ɪdʒ əv gɑd) n. Likeness of God: *We are told in the first chapter of the Bible that the first man and woman were created in the image of God* (Genesis 1:27). NOTE: This image of God consisted in the blissful knowledge of God (Colossians 3:10) and in perfect righteousness and true holiness of life (Ephesians 4:24). NOTE: Our first parents knew the will of God and were fully able to conform to it in thought, word, and deed. But they were also given freedom to sin against God by transgressing his commandment. This original state of innocence came to an abrupt end when the first man and woman (Adam and Eve) yielded to temptation and fell into sin by transgressing the one and only commandment that God had given them. By this disobedience, the man and woman consciously set themselves in opposition to God, and thus severed that spiritual union and communion with their Maker. The immediate result was the loss of the image of God. Man was no longer holy. He had exchanged fellowship with God for fellowship with the devil, for "He that commits sin is of the devil" (1 John 3:8). The happiness and bliss of Paradise were lost, and depravity, misery, and death were the result. Since that time, all people have

been born, not in the image of God, but in the image of Adam. Man is by nature sinful (Psalm 51:5). His holy relationship to God has ceased. He no longer has a reverential fear of God. He no longer trusts God. He is spiritually dead (Ephesians 2:1) and an enemy of God (Romans 8:7). Having lost the image of God, man is by nature selfish, pitiless, and cruel. There have been many other dire consequences of the fall into sin and loss of the image of God, such as physical weakness, pain, sorrow, death, (Genesis 3:16-19) and eternal damnation (Romans 5:12; 6:23). Never in this life will man attain that state of perfection which Adam and Eve had before they fell into sin. But a beginning of its restoration is made, when man is justified by faith in Jesus Christ, who came into the world to save sinners (1 Timothy 1:15), suffered and died for us on Calvary's cross, rose again from the dead, and returned to his heavenly throne to prepare a place for those who put their trust in him for eternal life (John 3:16). The knowledge of Jesus fills the believer's heart with joy and happiness, and this, in turn, moves him to forsake the ways of sin and to walk in the paths of righteousness. Because of the old Adam (the old sinful nature), this restoration of the image of God will never be perfect in this life. For this reason the Apostle Paul admonishes believers to "put on the new self, which is being renewed in knowledge in the image of its Creator," (Colossians 3:10) and "to put on the new self, created to be like God in true right-eousness and holiness" (Ephesians 4:24). The image of God, however, will be restored completely in heaven where "we shall be like him (God), for we shall see him as he is" (1 John 3:2). —see JESUS, MAN, ORIGINAL SIN, SIN

im-age-ry (ɪm–ɪdʒ–riʸ) n. The use of figures of speech in poetry, stories, etc.

i-mag-i-na-ble (ɪ–mædʒ–ə–nə–bəl) adj. That which can be imagined; conceivable: *He tried every way imaginable to save the patient, but nothing could save her.*

i-mag-i-nar-y (ɪ–mædʒ–ə–nɛər–iʸ) adj. Not

real; existing only in the imagination: *Her troubles were only imaginary.*

i-mag-i-na-tion (ɪ–mædʒ–ə–neʸ–ʃən) n. **1.** The act or power to form a mental image of sthg. not present to the senses (sight, smell, touch, etc.) or not previously known or experienced **2.** Creative ability **3.** The mind: *He's not really sick; it's all in his imagination.* —**i-mag-i-na-tive** (ɪ–mædʒ–ə–nə–tɪv) adj. *The author of mystery novels has to be very imaginative.*

i-mag-ine (ɪ–mædʒ–ɪn) v. **-ined, -ining 1.** To form a mental picture or idea: *Can you imagine a city where the streets are paved with gold and where trees bear fruit all the time, and where there is no sickness or pain or hunger or thirst or sorrow or death? That is what heaven is like, but the glory and splendor and majesty of heaven is really beyond our imagination./ [God] is able to do immeasurably more than all we ask or imagine...* (Ephesians 3:20). **2.** To form an idea about sthg., esp. a wrong idea or one for which there is no proof: *I imagine all my friends will come to the reunion but I haven't heard from any of them.*

i-mam (ɪ–mɑm) n. **1.** A recognized Muslim religious leader **2.** The prayer leader in a mosque

im-bal-ance (ɪm–bæl–əns) n. The state or condition of lacking balance: *The imbalance in his diet led to some serious health problems.*

im-be-cile (ɪm–bə–səl) n. **1.** A person lacking the capacity to develop beyond the mental age of seven or eight years **2.** A stupid person —**im-be-cil-ic** (ɪm–bə–sɪl–ɪk) adj. —**imbecility** n.

im-bibe (ɪm–baɪb) v. **-bibed, -bibing** To drink or take in liquid, esp. alcohol

im-bue (ɪm–byuʷ) v. **-bued, -buing** To fill or inspire the mind: *He was imbued with feelings of sympathy*

im-i-tate (ɪm–ə–teʸt) v. **-tated, -tating 1.** To copy the behavior, appearance, speech, etc., of a person: *James can imitate his father's speech perfectly.* —com-pare IMPERSONATE **2.** To look like; resemble —**im-i-ta-tive** (ɪm–ə–teʸ–tɪv) adj.

im-i-ta-tion (ɪm–ə–teʸ–ʃən) n. The act or result of imitating (imitate): *Her diamond is an imi-*

tation. —imitation adj.

im-i-ta-tor (ɪm-ə-teᵞ-tər) n. A person who copies the speech, actions, dress, etc. of someone else; a mimic: *Be imitators of God... and live a life of love, just as Christ loved us and gave himself up for us...* (Ephesians 5:1,2).

im-mac-u-late (ɪ-mæk-yə-lət) adj. 1. Free from sin or error; pure 2. Spotlessly clean: *an immaculate white uniform* —immaculately adv.

im-ma-nent (ɪm-ə-nənt) adj. 1. Living or operating within; inherent 2. Said of God, present throughout the universe

Im-man-u-el (ɪ-mæn-yuʷ-əl) n. 1. A masculine name 2. A name meaning "God with us," given by the prophet, Isaiah, to the Messiah who was to be born of a virgin (Isaiah 7:14), fulfilled in Jesus Christ our Savior (Matthew 1:23). —see JESUS CHRIST

im-ma-te-ri-al (ɪm-ə-tɪər-iᵞ-əl) adj. 1. Unimportant 2. Not consisting of matter; spiritual

im-ma-ture (ɪm-ə-tʃʊər/ -tʊər/ -tyʊər) adj. 1. Not mature, developed, or perfected 2. Childish; silly —immaturely adv. —immaturity n.

im-meas-ur-a-ble (ɪ-mɛʒ-ər-ə-bəl) adj. 1. Not capable of being measured 2. Indefinitely extensive; limitless

im-me-di-a-cy (ɪ-miᵞ-diᵞ-ə-siᵞ) n. Urgency or nearness of sthg.; importance

im-me-di-ate (ɪ-miᵞ-diᵞ-ət) adj. 1. Happening, done, or needed at once: *Your immediate reply would be appreciated.* 2. Very close in time, space, or relationship: *my immediate family/ the immediate future*

im-me-di-ate-ly (ɪ-miᵞ-diᵞ-ət-liᵞ) adv. At once: *Please come immediately. Your father is very ill.*

im-me-mo-ri-al (ɪm-ə-mɔr-iᵞ-əl) adj. From a time beyond anyone's memory or written records: *Wars have been fought since time immemorial.*

im-mense (ɪ-mɛns) adj. Very large; huge

im-mense-ly (ɪ-mɛns-liᵞ) adv. Very much: *I appreciated your gift immensely.* —immensity n. *The immensity of the task of taking the census in such a large country as China is difficult*

to imagine.

im-merse (ɪ-mɜrs) v. -mersed, -mersing 1. To put under water so as to be completely covered 2. *fig.* To be very busy or very occupied or absorbed with sthg.: *John was so immersed in his studies that he didn't see me come in.* —im-mer-sion (ɪ-mɜr-ʒən) n.

im-mi-grant (ɪm-ə-grənt) n. A person who comes into a new country to make his home there —opposite EMIGRANT

im-mi-grate (ɪm-ə-greᵞt) v. -grated, -grating To come into a country to make one's home there —opposite EMIGRATE —im-mi-gra-tion (ɪm-ə-greᵞ-ʃən) n.

im-mi-nence (ɪm-ə-nəns) n. The nearness of sthg. that is about to happen: *They decided to call off their picnic because of the imminence of rain.*

im-mi-nent (ɪm-ə-nənt) adj. Likely to happen very soon: *imminent attack* —compare EMINENT, IMPENDING —imminently adv.

im-mo-bile (ɪ-moʷ-bəl) adj. 1. Incapable of being moved 2. Motionless —im-mo-bil-i-ty (ɪ-moʷ-bɪl-ə-tiᵞ) n.

im-mo-bi-lize (ɪ-moʷ-bə-laɪz) v. -lized, -lizing 1. To make incapable of being moved 2. To make impossible to move or to mobilize, such as army troops

im-mod-er-ate (ɪ-mɑd-ə-rət) adj. Lacking in moderation; excessive

im-mod-est (ɪ-mɑd-əst) adj. 1. Lacking in modesty; indecent 2. Conceited —immodesty n. —immodestly adv.

im-mor-al (ɪ-mɔr-əl) adj. Not moral; sinful, esp. in sexual matters: *No immoral, impure or greedy person... has any inheritance in the kingdom of Christ and of God* (Ephesians 5:5). —immorally adv.

im-mor-al-i-ty (ɪ-mə-ræl-ə-tiᵞ) n. -ties The state or quality of being immoral: *God is perfectly holy and he hates immorality and every sin, but because of his great love and mercy he forgives all who repent of their sins and put their trust in Jesus for eternal life* (Mark 1:15; Romans 6:23). —see FORGIVENESS, JESUS,

im-mor-tal (ɪ-mɔr-təl) adj. Not mortal; not subject to death; continuing for ever: *The human soul is immortal. It will never die. It will*

live forever in perfect bliss with Jesus in heaven or suffer forever in hell (Matthew 25:34,41,46; Luke 16:22-26; John 3:16,36).

im-mor-tal-i-ty (ɪ-mɔr-tǽl-ə-tiʸ) n. Unending existence: *Christ Jesus destroyed death [by rising from the dead] and has brought life and immortality to light through the gospel* (2 Timothy 1:10). —see GOSPEL, JESUS CHRIST

im-mov-a-ble (ɪ-muʷv-ə-bəl) adj. **1.** Firmly fixed; unable to be moved **2.** Unyielding: *Once he gets it in his mind to do sthg., he is immovable. He will not change his mind, no matter what.* —**im-mov-a-bil-i-ty** (ɪ-muʷv-ə-bɪl-ə-tiʸ) n.

im-mune (ɪ-myuʷn) adj. **1.** Exempt **2.** Resistant, esp. to a particular disease **3.** Protected from: *immune from punishment* —**immunity** n.

im-mu-nize *AME.* -**nise** *BrE.* (ɪm-yə-naɪz) v. -**nized, -nizing** To make someone safe against a disease by an injection of a vaccine: *Most of us have been immunized against smallpox.* —**im-mu-ni-za-tion** (ɪm-yə-nə-zeʸ-ʃən) n.

im-mu-ta-ble (ɪ-myuʷ-tə-bəl) adj. Unchangeable

imp (ɪmp) n. **1.** A mischievous child **2.** A small demon

im-pact (ɪm-pækt) n. **1.** A collision; the force of sthg. hitting another object: *The speeding car hit the wall with quite an impact.* **2.** The effect or impression of one thing on another: *the impact of TV on the younger generation*

im-pair (ɪm-peər) v. To diminish; weaken; lessen; damage: *I hope his injury doesn't impair his sight.*

im-pa-la (ɪm-pǽl-ə) n. An African antelope known for its ability to leap

im-pale (ɪm-peʸl) v. -**paled, -paling** To pierce with a sharpened stake through the body, as for torture or punishment

im-part (ɪm-pɑrt) v. **1.** To make known **2.** To give a share of: *A teacher's duty is not only to impart knowledge.*

im-par-tial (ɪm-pɑr-ʃəl) adj. Fair; giving equal favor to all concerned: *Wisdom that comes from heaven is... impartial and sincere* (James 3:17). —**impartially** adv. —**im-par-ti-al-i-ty** (ɪm-pɑr-ʃiʸ-æl-ə-tiʸ) n.

im-passe (ɪm-pæs/ ɪm-pæs) n. **1.** A position from which there is no escape **2.** A road or way that has no outlet

im-pas-sioned (ɪm-pæʃ-ənd) adj. Full of passion and fervor: *an impassioned plea for help for the homeless*

im-pa-tient (ɪm-peʸ-ʃənt) adj. Lacking patience; not able to deal calmly with people or things or to wait for sbdy. or sthg.

im-peach (ɪm-piʸtʃ) v. To bring charges of a serious crime against a public official, esp. a crime against the state —**impeachable** adj. —**impeachment** n.

im-pec-ca-ble (ɪm-pɛk-ə-bəl) adj. **1.** Without fault **2.** Not liable to sin —**im-pec-ca-bil-i-ty** (ɪm-pɛk-ə-bɪl-ə-tiʸ) n. —**impeccably** adv.

im-pe-cu-ni-ous (ɪm-pɪ-kyuʷ-niʸ-əs) adj. Having very little or no money —**impecuniously** adv. —**impecuniousness** n.

im-ped-ance (ɪm-piʸd-əns) n. The total opposition to alternating current by an electric current

im-pede (ɪm-piʸd) v. -**peded, -peding** To hinder in speed or progress

im-ped-i-ment (ɪm-pɛd-ə-mənt) n. Sthg. that impedes, esp. a speech disorder

im-pel (ɪm-pɛl) v. -**ll**- To urge or force someone to do sthg.

im-pend-ing (ɪm-pɛnd-ɪŋ) adj. About to happen: *the impending elections*

im-pen-e-tra-ble (ɪm-pɛn-ə-trə-bəl) adj. **1.** Unable to be penetrated, entered, or passed through: *an impenetrable fortress* **2.** Impossible to understand: *an impenetrable difficulty*

im-pen-i-tent (ɪm-pɛn-ə-tənt) adj. Not penitent; not sorry for one's sins

im-per. *abbr.* for imperative

im-per-a-tive (ɪm-pɛr-ə-tɪv) adj. **1.** Which must be done: *It's imperative that we go now, or we'll miss our plane.* **2.** The form of a verb that expresses a command: *"Drink your milk!" is an imperative sentence.* —**imperatively** adv.

im-per-cep-ti-ble (ɪm-pər-sɛp-tə-bəl) adj. Not perceived by or affecting the senses —**im-per-cep-ti-bil-i-ty** (ɪm-pər-sɛp-tə-bɪl-ə-tiʸ) n.

im-per-cep-tive (ɪm-pər-sɛp-tɪv) adj. Lacking perception —**imperceptiveness** n.

im-perf. *abbr.* for imperfect

im-per-fect (ɪm–pɜr–fɪkt) adj. Having defects; not perfect; faulty —**imperfectly** adv. —**im-per-fec-tion** (ɪm–pər–fɛk–ʃən) n.

imperfect n. *tech.* The verb tense which shows incomplete action in the past: *In "They were working in the field" the verb "were working" is in the imperfect.* —see also PERFECT.

im-pe-ri-al (ɪm–pɪər–iʸ–əl) adj. Of an empire or an emperor

im-pe-ri-al-ism (ɪm–pɪər–iʸ–əl-ɪz–əm) n. The policy of having or extending control over the territory of other nations —**imperialist** n.

im-per-il (ɪm–pɛər–əl) v. -iled, -iling or -lled, -illing To cause to be in danger: *When there is a war, famine, or other disaster the lives of many children are imperilled.*

im-pe-ri-ous (ɪm–pɪər–iʸ–əs) adj. 1. Commandingly arrogant; domineering 2. Urgent or imperative

im-per-ish-a-ble (ɪm–pɛər–ɪʃ–ə–bəl) adj. Not perishable; enduring forever

im-per-ma-nent (ɪm–pɜr–mə–nənt) adj. Not permanent

im-per-me-a-ble (ɪm–pɜr–miʸ–ə–bəl) adj. Not able to be penetrated, esp. by a liquid: *Clay is impermeable by water.* —**im-per-me-a-bil-i-ty** (ɪm–pɜr–miʸ–ə–bɪl–ət–iʸ) n. —**impermeably** adv.

im-per-son-al (ɪm–pɜr–sən–əl) adj. 1. Not influenced by personal feelings 2. Not referring to any particular person

im-per-son-ate (ɪm–pɜr–sən–eʸt) v. -ated, -ating To pretend to be another person as entertainment or as a fraud: *He is very good at impersonating politicians and movie stars.* —**im-per-son-a-tion** (ɪm–pɜr–sən–eʸ–ʃən) n. —**impersonator** n.

im-per-ti-nent (ɪm–pɜr–tɪ–nənt) adj. Rude; insolent; not showing proper respect

im-per-turb-a-ble (ɪm–pər–tɜr–bə–bəl) adj. Incapable of being perturbed or agitated

im-per-vi-ous (ɪm–pɜr–viʸ–əs) adj. 1. Impenetrable; incapable of being passed through 2. Not affected or influenced by

im-pe-ti-go (ɪm–pə–taɪ–goʷ) n. A contagious skin disease

im-pet-u-ous (ɪm–pɛtʃ–uʷ–əs) adj. Acting in a hasty manner and without thinking: *Peter was often quite impetuous.* —**im-pet-u-os-i-ty** (ɪm–pɛtʃ–uʷ–ɑs–ə–tiʸ) n. —**impetuously** adv.

im-pe-tus (ɪm–pə–təs) n. -tuses 1. A moving or motivating force: *The new treaty gave impetus for trade between the two countries.* 2. The force of sth. moving

im-pi-e-ty (ɪm–paɪ–ə–tiʸ) n. -ties Lack of reverence

im-pinge (ɪm–pɪndʒ) v. -pinged, -ping-ing 1. To have an effect or impact 2. To make steady inroads; encroach; infringe 3. To come into contact: *The sound impinged upon her ears.* —**impingement** n.

im-pi-ous (ɪm–piʸ–əs/ ɪm–paɪ–əs) adj. Not pious; not showing any respect for God; wicked —**impiously** adv.

imp-ish (ɪmp–ɪʃ) adj. 1. Of or like an imp 2. Mischievous

im-pla-ca-ble (ɪm–plæk–ə–bəl) adj. Not able to be calmed or satisfied: *She was so very angry that she could not be placated. She was implacable.* —**im-pla-ca-bil-i-ty** (ɪm–plæk–ə–bɪl–ət–tiʸ) n.

im-plant (ɪm–plænt) v. 1. To plant or put (an idea, etc.) in someone's mind 2. To put sth. permanently into a human body: *The surgeon implanted a pace-maker in the heart patient's chest.*

im-plant (ɪm–plænt) n. Sth. implanted in someone's body —**im-plan-ta-tion** (ɪm–plæn–teʸ–ʃən) n.

im-plau-si-ble (ɪm–plɔ–zə–bəl) adj. Difficult to believe; not plausible

im-ple-ment (ɪm–plə–mənt) v. To put into practice: *It will be difficult to implement the new plan because of lack of funds.*

implement n. A tool; instrument; utensil

im-pli-cate (ɪm–plə–keʸt) v. -cated, -cating 1. To imply or indicate that someone is involved in sth., esp. a crime: *The senator's enemies tried without success to implicate him in the conspiracy.* 2. To involve

im-pli-ca-tion (ɪm–plɪ–keʸ–ʃən) n. 1. The act of expressing indirectly: *The news reporter did not accuse the professor of any wrongdoing, but he made some very damaging implications about him.* 2. A suggestion not expressed but understood

im-plic-it (ɪm–plɪs–ət) adj. **1.** Implied rather than expressly stated **2.** Essentially a part or condition of sthg. **3.** Unreserved; unquestioning: *implicit obedience*

im-plore (ɪm–plɔr) v. **-plored, -ploring** To beg someone to do sthg.; to entreat: *Implore God to be gracious to us* (Malachi 1:9). *After reminding the Corinthians that "God was reconciling the world to himself in Christ, not counting men's sins against them," the Apostle Paul continued by saying, "We implore you on Christ's behalf: Be reconciled to God. God made him who had no sin to be sin [a sin offering] for us, so that in him we might become the righteousness of God in him"* (2 Corinthians 5:19-21). —see JESUS CHRIST

im-ply (ɪm–plaɪ) v. **-plied, -plying** To suggest indirectly; hint: *Bill didn't receive an invitation, but he implied that he would like to come to the party.*

im-po-lite (ɪm–pə–laɪt) adj. Not polite; rude

im-pon-der-a-ble (ɪm–pɑn–dər–ə–bəl) adj. Having an influence or importance which is impossible to be measured or explained

imponderable n. Sthg. that has an importance or influence which is impossible to measure: *The rate of inflation for the coming decade is one of the great imponderables of our time.*

im-port (ɪm–pɔrt/ ɪm–pɔrt) v. To bring in from another country or from an outside source: *The US imports many products from the Far East.* —compare EXPORT

im-port (ɪm–pɔrt) n. **1.** Sthg. brought into a country from another country: *imports from the Orient* **2.** The act of importing —**im-por-ta-tion** (ɪm–pɔr–teʸ–ʃən) n.

im-por-tance (ɪm–pɔr–təns) n. **1.** Being important **2.** The reason sthg. or someone is considered important: *The importance of exercise and proper diet in maintaining good health is well known.*

im-por-tant (ɪm–pɔr–tənt) adj. Of great effect, value, significance, concern, etc: *It's nice to be important, but it's more important to be nice./ When asked which was the most important commandment, Jesus replied, "The most important one is... 'Love the Lord your God with all your heart and with all your soul and*

with all your mind and with all your strength.' The second is this: 'Love your neighbor as yourself'" (Mark 12:29-31). —opposite UNIMPORTANT adv. —**importantly** adv.

im-por-tu-nate (ɪm–pɔrtʃ–ə–nət) adj. Repeatedly asking; persistent in solicitation

im-por-tune (ɪm–pɔr–tyuʷn/ –tuʷn/ –pɔr–tʃen) v. **-tuned, -tuning** To keep asking for sthg. persistently and urgently

im-pose (ɪm–poʷz) v. **-posed, -posing 1.** To place or put: *The government has imposed a new tax on alcohol.* **2.** To inflict: *The increase in taxes has imposed a great strain on our resources.* **3.** To force to be accepted: *He tried to impose his ideas on the rest of the group.* **4.** To take unfair advantage of: *We don't want to impose on your hospitality.*

im-pos-ing (ɪm–poʷz–ɪŋ) adj. Impressive because of power, dignity, large size, etc.: *an imposing personality*

im-po-si-tion (ɪm–pə–zɪ–ʃən) n. **1.** An act of imposing **2.** An unfair demand; a burden: *It was no imposition to help that little old lady.*

im-pos-si-ble (ɪm–pɑs–ə–bəl) adj. **1.** That cannot exist or be done; not possible: *Nothing is impossible with God* (Luke 1:37). *Without faith [in Jesus] it is impossible to please God* (Hebrews 11:6). **2.** Difficult to bear; hopeless; very unpleasant: *He finds fault with everything; he's impossible to work with.* —**im-pos-si-bil-i-ty** (ɪm–pɑs–ə–bɪl–ə–tiʸ) n.

im-pos-tor also **imposter** (ɪm–pɑs–tər) n. One who pretends to be someone else, or to be sthg. he is not, in order to deceive someone

im-po-tent (ɪm–pə–tənt) adj. **1.** Lacking power to take action; helpless: *The local police force seems impotent in dealing with drugs.* **2.** Of a man who is unable to perform the sex act —opposite POTENT —**impotence** n. —**impotently** adv.

im-pound (ɪm–paʊnd) v. To take and hold in legal custody: *The police have the power to impound your car if you leave it parked here.*

im-pov-er-ish (ɪm–pɑv–ə–rɪʃ) v. **1.** To cause to become poor: *Because of his gambling and drinking, he was impoverished.* **2.** To exhaust the natural strength or fertility of: *The soil was impoverished.*

im-prac-ti-ca-ble (ɪm–præk–tɪ–kə–bəl) adj. Not

able to be put into practice; not practicable

im-prac-ti-cal (ɪm–**præk**–tɪ–kəl) adj. Unwise; not practical —**im-prac-ti-cal-i-ty** (ɪm–præk–tɪ–**kæl**–ət–iʸ) n.

im-preg-na-ble (ɪm–**preg**–nə–bəl) adj. Safe against attack; not able to be captured or overcome by force: *an impregnable fortress*

im-preg-nate (ɪm–**preg**–neʸt) v. -nated, -nating **1.** To make pregnant **2.** To cause to be infused as with a substance **3.** To permeate, as with ideas

im-pre-sa-ri-o (ɪm–prə–**sar**–iʸ–oʷ) n. The organizer or manager of a play, opera, ballet, concert, etc.

im-press (ɪm–**pres**) v. **1.** To cause sbdy. to feel admiration and respect: *I was impressed with his new book.* **2.** To fix the importance of sthg. on someone's mind: *God said, "These commandments that I give you today are to be upon your hearts. Impress them on your children"* (Deuteronomy 6:6,7).

im-pres-sion (ɪm–**preʃ**–ən) n. **1.** The idea, image or feeling one has of a person or thing: *Most people want to make a good impression on others, esp. on their teacher, boss, or someone else who is famous or important./ You never get a second chance to make a "first" impression.* **2.** A mark left by pressing an object into a surface: *The car tires left an impression in the wet sand.* **3. under the impression** To think (that sthg. is true): *He was still under the impression that the world was flat.*

im-pres-sion-a-ble (ɪm–**preʃ**–ən–ə–bəl) adj. Easy to influence or affect: *impressionable child*

im-pres-sion-ism (ɪm–**preʃ**–ə–nɪz–əm) n. A form of art that attempts to convey general impressions rather than reality —**impressionist** n.

im-pres-sive (ɪm–**pres**–ɪv) adj. Causing admiration; making a marked impression: *an impressive demonstration* —**impressively** adv.

im-print (ɪm–**prɪnt**) v. **1.** To print or press a mark on a surface **2.** *fig.* Impress: *Every detail is imprinted on my mind as if it happened yesterday.* —**imprint** (ɪm–**prɪnt**) n.

im-pris-on (ɪm–**prɪz**–ən) v. To put in prison or in a state as if in prison: *He felt imprisoned on that tiny island without a boat.* —**impris-**

onment n.

im-prob-a-ble (ɪm–**prab**–ə–bəl) adj. Unlikely to be true or correct —**im-prob-a-bil-i-ty** (ɪm–prab–ə–bɪl–ə–tiʸ) n.

im-promp-tu (ɪm–**pramp**–tuʷ) adj., adv. Said or done without previous preparation: *an impromptu speech*

im-prop-er (ɪm–**prap**–ər) adj. Not proper; not suitable: *Among you there must not even be a hint of sexual immorality, or any kind of impurity, or of greed, because these things are improper for God's holy people* (Ephesians 5:3,4). —**improperly** adv.

im-pro-pri-e-ty (ɪm–prə–**praɪ**–ət–iʸ) n. -ties **1.** Sthg. which is improper **2.** An improper act or expression

im-prove (ɪm–**pruʷv**) v. -proved, -proving To make or become better: *She was trying very hard to improve her appearance.*

im-prove-ment (ɪm–**pruʷv**–mənt) n. The act or process of improving: *Has his work shown any improvement during the past month?*

im-prov-i-dent (ɪm–**prav**–ə–dənt) adj. Lacking foresight; taking no thought for future needs; wasteful

im-pro-vise (ɪm–prə–vaɪz) v. -vised, -vising **1.** To devise or provide from whatever material is available, esp. in response to an immediate need **2.** To compose and perform without previous preparation

im-pru-dent (ɪm–**pruʷd**–ənt) adj. Lacking in judgment

im-pu-dence (ɪm–pyuʷ–dəns) n. A contemptuous lack of regard for others

im-pu-dent (ɪm–pyuʷ–dənt) adj. Offensively bold

im-pugn (ɪm–**pyuʷn**) v. To express doubts about the truth or honesty of; to try to discredit: *We do not impugn their motives, but we question the wisdom of their decision.*

im-pulse (ɪm–pʌls) n. **1.** A sudden urge to do sthg.: *a sudden impulse to go and buy a new bike* **2.** A force that starts sthg. in motion; the motion produced by such a force: *an electrical impulse*

im-pul-sive (ɪm–**pʌl**–sɪv) adj. Having a tendency to act suddenly without thinking about the consequences —**impulsively** adv. —**impulsiveness** n.

im-pu-ni-ty (ɪm–**pyu**ʷ–nət–iʸ) n. Freedom from injury or punishment: *He behaved badly with impunity since he knew he wouldn't be punished.*

im-pure (ɪm–pyʊər) adj. **1.** Not pure; morally bad, esp. with regard to sexual habits: *No immoral, impure, or greedy person...has any inheritance in the kingdom of Christ and of God* (Ephesians 5:5). **2.** Not clean; contaminated: *impure water* **3.** Mixed with sthg. else of poorer quality: *an impure chemical*

im-pu-ri-ty (ɪm–pyʊər–ə–tiʸ) n. -ties **1.** A substance mixed with sthg. else so that it is not pure **2.** The state or act of not being pure: *Put to death whatever belongs to your earthly nature; sexual immorality, impurity, lust ... Because of these things, the wrath of God is coming* (Colossians 3:5). —opposite PURITY. NOTE: God detests sexual impurity and all sin, but because of his great love and mercy he forgives those who repent and put their trust in Jesus for eternal life (Mark 1:15; Romans 10: 8,9).

im-pute (ɪm–pyuʷt) v. -puted, -puting **1.** To attribute (a fault or sin) to a person; to blame or charge: *Blessed is the man to whom the Lord shall not impute sin* (Psalm 32:2; Romans 4:8 NKJV). *God was in Christ reconciling the world to himself, not imputing [charging] their sins to them, and has committed to us the word of reconciliation* (2 Corinthians 5:19). **2.** To ascribe goodness to a person as coming from another: *David (in Psalm 32:1) describes the blessedness of the man to whom God imputes righteousness apart from works, (saying): "Blessed are those whose lawless deeds are forgiven, and whose sins are covered"* (Romans 4:6-8).

in (ɪn) prep. **1.** Used to show physical surroundings: *in a house/car/boat* **2.** Used when speaking of time: *in the future/ in March/ in 1776/ in a few days/ in the morning/ in an hour (but "on" Monday "at" 8 o'clock)* **3.** Used to indicate a condition: *in a rage/ in charge of/ in a hurry/ in love/ in trouble* **4.** Towards: *in the west/ in the right direction* **5.** Shows employment: *He's in construction./ She's in the film industry.* **6.** Wearing: *the girl in the pink hat/ the man in the gray suit* **7.** With: *written in ink*

8. Used to show how sthg. happens: *in public (=publicly)/ in secret (=secretly)* **9.** Shows how sthg. is arranged or divided: *in groups of four/ in a square/ in large numbers*

in adv. **1.** To move to or toward the inside: *The children opened the door and walked in./ Come in!* **2.** At home or at a place of work, etc.; present: *Tom is not in, but we expect him soon.* **3.** From many people, sources, or directions: *Do you have your report in?/ The votes are all in and Mr. Smith has won the election.* **4.** In control or in power: *The new government is in. (=elected)* **5.** Currently fashionable: *Costume jewelry is in.* **6.** Of the tide, close to the coast; high: *The tide is in.* **7.** Within: *locked in* **8. in for** To be about to experience sthg. (esp. sthg. bad): *If your report card is too bad, you'll be in for a scolding from your father.* **9. in on** Having a knowledge of or a share in: *Jim and Al were in on the joke. (=knew about it)* **10. day in and day out; year in and year out** Continuing day after day, year after year, etc., without changing —opposite OUT (for 2, 4, 5, and 6)

in– (ɪn–) prefix Before certain words, "in" means "not" as in inaccessible, inability, inaccurate, inattentive, incapable, incurable, indecent, indecisive, indefinite, indigestible, indiscreet, indivisible, ineffective, inefficient, ineligible, inequality, inestimable, inexpensive. NOTE: "In" at the beginning of a word doesn't always mean "not." Compare, for example: **industry, infant, inferior, initial.**

in-a-bil-i-ty (ɪn–ə–bɪl–ə–tiʸ) n. Lack of power or capability

in ab-sen-ti-a (ɪn æb–sɛn–tʃə) adv. During one's absence

in-ac-ces-si-ble (ɪn–ɪk–sɛs–ə–bəl) adj. Not accessible; unapproachable —**in-ac-ces-si-bil-i-ty** (ɪn–ɪk–sɛs–ə–bɪl–ə–tiʸ) n. —**inaccessibly** adv.

in-ac-ti-vate (ɪn–æk–tɪ–veʸt) v. -vated, -vating To make inactive

in-ad-e-quate (ɪn–æd–ɪ–kwət) adj. Not adequate or sufficient

in-ad-ver-tent (ɪn–əd–vɜrt–ənt) adj. Not intentional —**inadvertence** n.—**inadvertently** adv.

in·al·ien·a·ble (ɪn–e^yl–yə–nə–bəl) adj. Unalienable; which cannot be legally or justly alienated or transferred to another: *All men have certain natural rights which are inalienable.*

in·ane (ɪn–e^yn) adj. Silly or meaningless

in·an·i·mate (ɪn–æn–ə–mət) adj. **1.** Not living: *A rock is an inanimate object.* **2.** Lacking energy or vitality: *an inanimate conversation*

in·ar·tic·u·late (ɪn–ɑr–tɪk–yə–lət) adj. **1.** Not able to speak effectively **2.** Not fully expressed or expressible

in·as·much as (ɪn–əz–mʌtʃ əz) conj. In view of the fact that; since; because

in·au·di·ble (ɪn–ɔd–ə–bəl) adj. Not audible; incapable of being heard —**inaudibly** adv.

in·au·gu·ral (ɪn–ɔ–gyə–rəl) adj. **1.** Of an inauguration **2.** Marking the beginning of a new venture

in·au·gu·rate (ɪn–ɔ–gyə–re^yt) v. **-rated, -rating** **1.** To begin formally **2.** To induct into office with a formal ceremony —**in·au·gu·ra·tion** (ɪn–ɔ–gyə–re^y–ʃən) n.

in·aus·pi·cious (ɪn–ɔ–spɪʃ–əs) adj. Unfavorable; having signs that indicate that future success is unlikely —**inauspiciously** adv.

in·born (ɪn–bɔrn) adj. Existing from birth; natural: *an inborn mechanical ability*

in·bred (ɪn–brɛd) adj. **1.** Natural; innate: *an inbred sense of duty* **2.** Produced by inbreeding

in·breed·ing (ɪn–bri^yd–ɪŋ) v. Breeding among closely related people or animals

Inc. (ɪŋk) *AmE. abbr.* for **incorporated** (ɪn–kɔr–pər–e^y–təd): *R.C. Law and Co., Inc.*

in·cal·cu·la·ble (ɪn–kæl–kyə–lə–bəl) adj. **1.** Too large or too great to be calculated **2.** Uncertain

in·can·des·cent (ɪn–kən–dɛs–ənt) adj. **1.** Glowing or white with heat **2.** Brilliant; intensely bright —**incandescence** n.

in·ca·pac·i·tate (ɪn–kə–pæs–ə–te^yt) v. **-tated, -tating** To cause someone to be unable to do sthg.; to disable: *She was incapacitated by a severe form of arthritis.*

in·car·cer·ate (ɪn–kɑr–sə–re^yt) v. **-ated, -ating** To put in prison

in·car·nate (ɪn–kɑr–nət) v. **-nated, -nating** **1.** To endow with a human body; to become flesh **2.** To give actual form to **3.** To be the embodiment of

in·car·na·tion (ɪn–kɑr–ne^y–ʃen) n. The act of becoming flesh, esp. when Christ became a man as well as God, when he was born on earth —see JESUS

in·cen·di·a·ry (ɪn–sɛn–di^y–ɛər–i^y) adj. **1.** Intended for setting on fire: *an incendiary bomb* **2.** Tending to cause a public disturbance or violence: *an incendiary speech*

in·cense (ɪn–sɛns) n. Material that is burned, giving off a sweet smell, used esp. in religious services

in·cense (ɪn–sɛns) v. **-censed, -censing** To cause great anger: *The crowd was incensed at his insulting remarks.*

in·cen·tive (ɪn–sɛn–tɪv) n. Sthg. that encourages one to greater activity: *No matter how hard he worked, he received the same wages, so there was little incentive to work harder.*

in·cep·tion (ɪn–sɛp–ʃən) n. The beginning of sthg.: *He's been president of the organization since its inception.*

in·ces·sant (ɪn–sɛs–ənt) adj. Unending; never stopping: *incessant complaining* —**incessantly** adv.

in·cest (ɪn–sɛst) n. A sexual relationship between people who are too closely related to marry, as between brother and sister: *Incest is a grievous sin in the sight of God* (Leviticus 18:6-19; Deuteronomy 27:20,22). NOTE: God is perfectly holy and righteous. He detests sexual perversion and every sin. But because of his great love and mercy, he forgives those who truly repent (turn from their wicked ways) and put their trust in Jesus for eternal life (Romans 6:23; Acts 2:38; 16:31). —see FORGIVENESS, JESUS

inch (ɪntʃ) n. A measure of length equal to 1/12 of a foot (about 2.5 centimeters)

inch v. To move slowly, carefully, and with difficulty: *The traffic was so bad that cars were just inching their way along the highway.*

in·cho·ate (ɪn–ko^w–ət) adj. Just begun and thus not fully formed

in·ci·dence (ɪn–sɪ–dəns) n. The rate of happening or having an effect: *There's a high incidence of fatal accidents on this highway.*

in·ci·dent (ɪn–sɪ–dənt) n. An event or happening

in·ci·den·tal (ın–sı–dɛn–təl) adj., n. **1.** Sthg. happening at the same time as sthg. more important **2.** Sthg. unimportant; of a minor or casual nature: *incidental expenses*

in·ci·den·tal·ly (ın–sı–dɛn–tə–liʸ) adv. Used when adding sthg., usu. of minor importance, to what was said before: *Thank you for the delicious dinner. Incidentally, apple pie is my favorite dessert.*

in·cin·er·ate (ın–sın–ə–reʸt) v. **-ated, -ating** To burn to ashes

in·cin·er·a·tor (ın–sın–ər–eʸt–ər) n. A furnace for burning waste

in·cip·i·ent (ın–sıp–iʸ–ənt) adj. Beginning to exist

in·cise (ın–saız) v. **-cised, -cising** To cut into; carve; engrave

in·ci·sion (ın–sıʒ–ən) n. A cut, esp. a surgical one

in·ci·sive (ın–saı–sıv) adj. **1.** Cutting; penetrating **2.** Acute; clear-cut: *incisive remarks*

in·ci·sor (ın–saı–zər) n. One of the four front teeth in the upper or lower jaw

in·cite (ın–saıt) v. **-cited, -citing** To try to stir someone to strong feelings or action: *His violent speech incited a riot.*

in·clem·ent (ın–klɛm–ənt) adj. **1.** Severe; stormy: *inclement weather* **2.** Unmerciful: *an inclement judge*

in·cli·na·tion (ın–klə–neʸ–ʃən) n. **1.** A tendency or liking for sthg.: *The Lord saw how great man's wickedness on earth had become, and that every inclination of the thought of his heart was only evil all the time* (Genesis 6:5). NOTE: Because of man's inclination to evil, God destroyed the earth with a great flood, saving only Noah and his family, just eight people. That was many thousands of years ago. Because of our evil nature, people today are also inclined to do evil. Unless we turn from evil and trust in Jesus for our salvation, we will perish in our sins. But God doesn't want anyone to perish. He loves us and sent his Son into the world to save sinners. —see JESUS. **2.** An act of bowing or bending the head: *an inclination of the head* **3.** *fml.* A slope or slight hill

in·cline (ın–klaın) n. A slope: *a sharp incline*

in·cline (ın–klaın) v. **-clined, -clining 1.** To lean toward an opinion or course of conduct; to have a tendency toward **2.** To cause to lean or slope

in·clined (ın–klaınd) adj. Having a tendency; likely

in·clude (ın–kluʷd) v. **-cluded, -cluding 1.** To have sbdy./ sthg. as part of a whole; contain in addition to other parts: *The price includes tax.* —opposite EXCLUDE **2.** To put with sthg. else: *My list of things to do includes a trip to the hospital to visit my friend.*

in·clu·sion (ın–kluʷ–ʒən) n. The state of being included

in·clu·sive (ın–kluʷ–sıv) adj. Containing or including many things or everything —**inclusively** adv.

in·cog·ni·to (ın–kɑg–niʸ–toʷ) adj., adv. With one's identity concealed: *The famous actor was traveling incognito, so as not to be hounded by the press and autograph seekers.*

in·co·her·ent (ın–koʷ–hıər–ənt) adj. **1.** Of one's speech, not coherent; unconnected; rambling **2.** Of a person, speaking in this way: *She became quite incoherent in the later stages of her illness.* —**incoherently** adv.

in·com·bus·ti·ble (ın–kəm–bʌs–tə–bəl) adj. Not able to be burned by fire

in·come (ın–kəm) n. Money received by someone regularly as payment for work or as interest from investments: *Whoever loves wealth is never satisfied with his income* (Ecclesiastes 5:10).

in·com·ing (ın–kəm–ıŋ) adj. **1.** Approaching: *an incoming train* **2.** Recently elected or appointed: *the incoming president*

in·com·pa·ra·ble (ın–kɑm–prə–bəl/ –pər–ə–bəl) adj. Too good, great, etc. to be compared with other things of the same type; having no equal; extremely great: *The incomparable riches of his [God's] grace, expressed in his kindness to us in Christ Jesus* (Ephesians 2:7-9). —**in·com·pa·ra·bil·i·ty** n. (ın–kɑm–prə–bıl–ət–iʸ/–pər–ə–bıl–et–iʸ) n. —**incomparably** adv.

in·com·pat·i·ble (ın–kəm–pæt–ə–bəl) adj. Not compatible; not capable or not suited for association: *Although married, they are quite incompatible. They don't agree on anything.*

in·com·pe·tent (ın–kɑm–pə–tənt) adj. **1.** Not

competent; lacking sufficient skill, knowledge, strength, or ability 2. Not legally qualified —incompetence n.

in·com·plete (ɪn–kəm–pliᵞt) adj. Not complete —incompletely adv. —in·completeness n.

in·com·pre·hen·si·ble (ɪn–kam–priᵞ–hɛn–sə–bəl) adj. Not understandable; beyond comprehension

in·con·ceiv·a·ble (ɪn–kən–siᵞv–ə–bəl) adj. Not conceivable; sthg. too strange to be believed: *It is inconceivable that people will ever live on the moon.* —in·conceivably adv.

in·con·clu·sive (ɪn–kən–kluʷ–sɪv) adj. Not conclusive; not leading to a definite decision: *We don't know if he's guilty or not. The evidence is inconclusive.* —**inconclusively** adv. —inconclusiveness n.

in·con·gru·ous (ɪn–kaŋ–gruʷ–əs) adj. Unsuitable or out of place; odd; not consistent with or suitable to the surroundings: *Wearing tennis shoes with a beautiful evening gown would be completely incongruous.* —in·congru·i·ty (ɪn–kaŋ–gruʷ–ə–tiᵞ) n.

in·con·se·quen·tial (ɪn–kan–sə–kwɛn–ʃəl) adj. Of no importance

in·con·sid·er·a·ble (ɪn–kən–sɪd–ər–ə–bəl) adj. Not very much; small in size or value: *The cost of one airmail stamp is inconsiderable in view of the time saved.*

in·con·sid·er·ate (ɪn–kən–sɪd–ər–ət) adj. Not considerate; not thinking of other people's feelings or rights; thoughtless: *My roommate is very inconsiderate, always talking or playing the radio loudly while I'm trying to study.* —inconsiderately adv. —inconsiderateness n.

in·con·sis·tent (ɪn–kən–sɪs–tənt) adj. 1. Not consistent; contradictory in some way: *One day he says one thing, and the next day he says just the opposite. He's very inconsistent.* 2. Likely to change: *The weather in this area is very inconsistent.* —inconsistently adv.

in·con·sol·a·ble (ɪn–kən–soʷl–ə–bəl) adj. Unable to be comforted: *She suffered inconsolable grief when her baby died.* —inconsolably adv.

in·con·spic·u·ous (ɪn–kən–spɪk–yuʷ–əs) adj. Not conspicuous; not noticeable; not easily seen: *The secret service agents tried to be as in-*

conspicuous as possible. —inconspicuously adv. —inconspicuousness n.

in·con·ti·nent (ɪn–kant–ən–ənt) adj. 1. unable to control one's bladder or bowels 2. Lacking self-control, esp. in sexual matters

in·con·tro·vert·i·ble (ɪn–kan–trə–vɜrt–ə–bəl) adj. So obvious and certain that it cannot be disputed

in·con·ven·ience n. (ɪn–kən–viᵞn–yəns) Trouble; difficulty: *The lack of electricity due to the storm caused a lot of inconvenience.*

inconvenience v. -ienced, -iencing To cause slight difficulty: *I'm sorry to inconvenience you, but I'd really appreciate your help.*

in·con·ven·ient (ɪn–kən–viᵞn–yənt) adj. Not convenient; not suitable; awkward; difficult: *It would be very inconvenient for me to attend the meeting on Tuesday, but I'll try to come anyway.*

in·cor·po·rate (ɪn–kɔr–pə–reᵞt) v. -rated, -rating 1. To form into a corporation 2. To unite; to combine; include: *We'll try to incorporate your suggestions into the plan.* —incorporation n.

in·cor·po·rat·ed (ɪn–kɔr–pər–eᵞ–təd) adj. abbr. **Inc.** Formed into a legal corporation

in·cor·rect (ɪn–kə–rɛkt) adj. 1. Not correct; wrong; erroneous 2. Improper —incorrectly adv. —incorrectness n.

in·cor·ri·gi·ble (ɪn–kɔr–ɪ–dʒə–bəl) adj. Incapable of being corrected or reformed: *She's an incorrigible gossip.* —in·cor·ri·gi·bil·i·ty (ɪn–kɔr–idʒ–ə–bɪl–ə–tiᵞ) n.

in·cor·rupt·i·ble (ɪn–kə–rʌp–tə–bəl) adj. 1. That which will not decay: *Writing to the Christians in Corinth, St. Paul says, "We [believers in Jesus] shall not all sleep [die], but we shall all be changed — in a moment... at the last trumpet. For the trumpet will sound, and the dead [in Christ] will be raised incorruptible, and we shall be changed"* (1 Corinthians 15:51,52). 2. Not able to be corrupted morally, as by a bribe

in·crease (ɪn–kriᵞs/ ɪn–kriᵞs) v. -creased, -creasing To grow; to make or become larger in size or quantity: *The population of many cities is increasing rapidly./ May the Lord make your love increase and overflow for each other and for everyone else* (1 Thessalonians 3:12).

—opposite DECREASE

in-crease (m–kri^ys/ m–kri^ys) n. The result of growing or increasing in numbers or strength: *Because of the increase of wickedness [in the last days], the love of many will grow cold, but he who stands firm to the end [in his faith in Jesus] will be saved* (Matthew 24:12).

in-creas-ing-ly (m–kri^y–sɪŋ–li^y) adv. Constantly growing in amount or degree: *Traffic is increasingly heavy on this freeway.*

in-cred-i-ble (m–krɛd–ə–bəl) adj. 1. Unbelievable 2. Amazing; unbelievably good: *Why should any of you consider it incredible that God raises the dead?* (Acts 26:8). *It's incredible, but it's absolutely true.* —see RESURRECTION —in-cred-i-bil-i-ty (m–krɛd–ə–bɪl–ə–ti^y) n. —incredibly adv.

in-cred-u-lous (m–krɛdʒ–ə–ləs) adj. Expressing disbelief: *an incredulous look*

in-cre-ment (m–krə–mənt) n. An increase; an added amount: *Your salary will be $20,000 to start, with annual increments of $500.*

in-crim-i-nate (m–krɪm–ə–ne^yt) v. -nated, -nating To make it seem that a person has committed a crime or other act of misconduct, or has somehow been involved in one: *He was incriminated by a letter he had written to a friend.*

in-cu-ba-tor (ɪŋ–kyə–be^y–tər) n. 1. An apparatus for hatching eggs by artificial warmth 2. An apparatus in which babies, born prematurely, can be kept in constant controlled heat and supplied with oxygen

in-cul-cate (m–kʌl–ke^yt) v. -cated, -cating To implant (ideas or habits) in someone by persistent urging: *She inculcated good manners into her children.*

in-cul-pa-ble (m–kʌl–pə–bəl) adj. Blameless

in-cum-bent (m–kʌm–bənt) adj. 1. Holding the specified office: *the incumbent governor* 2. Forming an obligation or duty: *It is incumbent on you to warn people of the risk they are taking.*

in-cur (m–kɜr) v. -rr- To bring upon oneself (sthg. unpleasant): *He incurred a lot of debts during his term as governor.*

in-cur-a-ble (m–kyʊər–ə–bəl) adj. Unable to be cured: *She is suffering from an incurable disease.*

in-cur-sion (m–kɜr–ʒən) n. 1. A brief invasion; raid 2. Inconvenient invasion of someone's time or privacy

in-debt-ed (m–dɛt–əd) adj. 1. Owing money 2. To be obligated to someone; to be very grateful for help given: *I'm indebted to all of you who helped me win this election.* —indebtedness n.

in-de-cent (m–di^y–sənt) adj. Not decent, morally offensive: *Men also abandoned natural relations with women and were inflamed with lust for one another. Men committed indecent acts with other men, and received in themselves the due penalty for their perversion* (Romans 1:27). —indecency n. -cies —indecently adv. *indecently dressed* NOTE: God detests sexual perversion and all sin (Ephesians 5:3-5). But because of his great love and mercy, he forgives the sins of those who truly repent (turn from their evil deeds) and put their trust in Jesus for eternal life (Acts 2:38; 16:31; Romans 6:23; John 3:16). —see JESUS

in-de-ci-sion (m–dɪ–sɪʒ–ən) n. The state of not being able to decide; hesitation

in-deed (m–di^yd) adv. 1. Definitely; certainly; yes: *Did you hear the scream? Indeed I did.* 2. Used to make the meaning stronger: *very pretty indeed*

in-de-fat-i-ga-ble (m–dɪ–fæt–ɪ–gə–bəl) adj. Untiring

in-de-fen-si-ble (m–dɪ–fɛn–sə–bəl) adj. 1. Not justifiable or excusable 2. Not capable of being defended against attack

in-de-fin-a-ble (m–dɪ–fai–nə–bəl) adj. Not easily described or defined or put into words

in-def-i-nite (m–dɛf–ə–nət) adj. Not definite; unclear; not fixed or set: *His travel plans are rather indefinite.*

in-def-i-nite-ly (m–dɛf–ə–nət–li^y) adv. Having no fixed limit or amount: *She'll be teaching overseas indefinitely.*

in-del-i-ble (m–dɛl–ə–bəl) adj. Unable to be erased: *indelible ink* —indelibly adv. *The experience was indelibly printed on his mind. He could never forget it.*

in-del-i-cate (m–dɛl–ɪ–kət) adj. 1. Not subtle 2. Offensive to decency —indelicacy n.

in-dem-ni-fy (ɪn-dɛm-nə-faɪ) v. -fied, -fying
1. To compensate for damage or loss sustained **2.** To give security against future damage or loss

in-dem-ni-ty (ɪn-dɛm-nə-tiʸ) n. -ties **1.** Security against loss or damage **2.** Payment for loss or damage

in-dent (ɪn-dɛnt) v. To start a line of print farther from the margin than other lines: *We usually indent the first line of each paragraph.* —indentation n.

in-de-pend-ence (ɪn-dɪ-pɛn-dəns) n. The state of being independent; freedom: *Nigeria gained its independence from Britain in 1960.*

in-de-pend-ent (ɪn-dɪ-pɛn-dənt) adj. **1.** Self-governing: *Ghana became independ-ent in 1957.* **2.** Not requiring other things or people: *My 80 year old mother is very independent and lives alone.* **3.** Not easily influenced: *an independent mind* **4.** Not belonging to any particular political party: *an independent voter* —opposite DEPENDENT —independently adv.

in-de-scrib-a-ble (ɪn-dɪ-skraɪ-bə-bəl) adj. Unable to be described because it is too great, too beautiful, too bad, etc: *an indescribable mess/ indescribable splendor* —indescribably adv. *indescribably beautiful*

in-de-struc-ti-ble (ɪn-dɪ-strʌk-tə-bəl) adj. Unable to be destroyed —in-de-struc-ti-bil-i-ty (ɪn-dɪ-strʌkt-ə-bɪl-ə-tiʸ) n. —indestructibly adv.

in-de-ter-mi-nate (ɪn-dɪ-tɜr-mə-nət) adj. **1.** Not definite as to extent **2.** Not clear or precise

in-dex (ɪn-dɛks) n. -dexes or -dices (-də-siʸz) An alphabetical list of people, places, subjects, etc., mentioned in a book and telling on what pages they can be found

In-di-an (ɪn-diʸ-ən) n., adj. **1.** A native or an inhabitant of India or of the East Indies **2.** Also **American Indian, Native American, Amerindian** A person belonging to or connected with any of the original peoples of America except the Eskimos

in-dic. *abbr.* for **indicative**

in-di-cate (ɪn-də-keʸt) v. -cated, -cating **1.** To draw attention to, esp. by pointing: *He pointed at the map, indicating where he would be traveling.* **2.** To show by a sign: *He nodded his head, indicating that he agreed with me.* **3.** To signal with the hand, lights, etc. to show the direction in which one is turning in a vehicle: *Her signal indicates that she wants to turn left.* —in-di-ca-tion (ɪn-də-keʸ-ʃən) n. *His running away was taken as an indication of his guilt.*

in-dic-a-tive (ɪn-dɪk-ə-tɪv) adj. Indicating or suggesting sthg.: *Her willingness to apologize was indicative of a humble spirit.*

in-di-ca-tor (ɪn-də-keʸ-tər) n. **1.** A needle or pointer that indicates speed, quantity, of other measurement **2.** Any of the automobile lights that flash to show which way it will turn.

in-di-ces (ɪn-də-siʸz) n. *pl.* of index

in-di-ci-a (ɪn-dɪʃ-ə) n. Envelope markings substituted for postage stamps

in-dict (ɪn-daɪt) v. To charge formally with an offense: *He was indicted for armed robbery.* —indictment n.

in-dif-fer-ent (ɪn-dɪf-ə-rənt) adj. **1.** Showing no interest or concern: *Those people were indifferent to the suffering of their neighbors. They did nothing to help.* **2.** Of no importance, one way or the other: *He is not interested in baseball. He doesn't care who wins. He's indifferent.* —indifference n.

in-dig-e-nous (ɪn-dɪdʒ-ə-nəs) adj. Originating in and belonging to a place: *Kangaroos are indigenous to Australia.* —indigenously adv.

in-di-gent (ɪn-dɪ-dʒənt) adj. Lacking the necessities of life; poor —indigence n.

in-di-gest-i-ble (ɪn-daɪ-dʒɛs-tə-bəl) adj. Not easily digested

in-di-ges-tion (ɪn-də-dʒɛs-tʃən) n. **1.** Inability to digest food **2.** Discomfort caused by the lack of ability to digest food

in-dig-nant (ɪn-dɪg-nənt) adj. Angry, usu. because of some harm that has been done to oneself or others

in-dig-na-tion (ɪn-dɪg-neʸ-ʃən) n. Anger aroused by sthg. unfair, unworthy, or mean

in-dig-ni-ty (ɪn-dɪg-nə-tiʸ) n. -ties An offense against personal dignity or self-respect; humiliating treatment, causing a person to feel shame

in-di-rect (ɪn-də-rɛkt) adj. Not going in a

straight line; not directly connected: *We had to take an indirect flight because there were no direct routes to such a small town.* —opposite DIRECT —**indirectly** adv.

in-dis-creet (ɪn-dɪ-skri�validʸt) adj. Not discreet; lacking tact or caution in what one says and does: *His indiscreet remarks about my friend really upset me.*

in-dis-cre-tion (ɪn-dɪ-skreʃ-ən) n. **1.** The state or quality of being indiscreet **2.** An indiscreet act, remark, etc.

in-dis-crim-i-nate (ɪn-dɪ-skrɪm-ə-nət) adj. Not discriminating; not choosing carefully; acting without careful judgment: *indiscriminate in his choice of friends*

in-dis-pen-sa-ble (ɪn-dɪ-spen-sə-bəl) adj. Necessary for a person to have; too important for one to get along without: *Clean air is indispensable to good health.* —**in-di-spen-sa-bil-i-ty** (ɪn-dɪ-spen-sə-bɪl-ə-tiʸ) n. —**indispensably** adv..

in-dis-posed (ɪn-dɪs-poᵂzd) adj. **1.** Slightly ill **2.** Not inclined or willing to do sthg.

in-dis-put-a-ble (ɪn-dɪs-pyuᵂt-ə-bəl) adj. Not able to be denied; certainly true

in-dis-tinct (ɪn-dɪ-stɪŋkt) adj. Not distinct; not able to be seen, heard, or understood clearly

in-dis-tin-guish-a-ble (ɪn-dɪ-stɪŋ-gwɪ-ʃə-bəl) adj. Not able to be distinguished from others or from each other

in-di-vid-u-al (ɪn-də-vɪdʒ-ə-wəl) adj. **1.** Intended for one person: *an individual serving* **2.** Separate; distinct: *Each individual snowflake is different.* —**individually** adv. Separately: *He dealt with each person individually.*

individual n. **1.** A single human being: *The rights of the individual are very important in a free society.* **2.** A particular person: *He's a very bad-tempered individual.*

in-di-vid-u-al-ist (ɪn-də-vɪ-dʒə-wəl-əst) n. One who shows a great amount of independence in thought or action —**individualism** n. —**in-di-vid-u-al-is-tic** (ɪn-də-vɪ-dʒə-wəl-ɪst –ɪk)

in-di-vid-u-al-i-ty (ɪn-də-vɪ-djə-wæl-ə-tiʸ) n. **-ties** The characteristics which make someone or sthg. different from all others: *Each of our seven children has his own distinct individ-*

uality.

in-di-vis-i-ble (ɪn-də-vɪz-ə-bəl) adj. Not able to be separated or divided into parts —**in-di-vis-i-bil-i-ty** (ɪn-də-vɪz-ə-bɪl-ə-tiʸ) n. —**indivisibly** adv.

Indo– (ɪn-doᵂ–) comb. form Of India: *Indo-European languages*

in-doc-tri-nate (ɪn-dɑk-trə-neʸt) v. **-nated, -nating** To teach; to instruct in the fundamentals; to fill a person's mind with particular ideas or doctrines

in-do-lent (ɪn-də-lənt) adj. Lazy: *an indolent good-for-nothing*

in-dom-i-ta-ble (ɪn-dɑm-ə-tə-bəl) adj. Unconquerable: *indomitable courage*

in-door (ɪn-dɔr) adj. Happening, done, used, etc. inside a building: *indoor swimming pool* —opposite OUTDOOR

in-doors (ɪn-dɔrz/ ɪn-dɔrz) adv. Into a building or already inside it: *All the children went indoors when it started to rain.* —opposite OUTDOORS

in-du-bi-ta-ble (ɪn-duᵂ-bə-tə-bəl) adj. That cannot be doubted —**indubitably** adv.

in-duce (ɪn-duᵂs) v. **-duced, -ducing 1.** To persuade or influence: *Nothing could induce me to go there again.* **2.** To stimulate the occurrence of: *induce childbirth* **3.** To infer by considering specific facts **4.** To cause or bring about a feeling: *Too much food induces sleepiness.* —**inducement** n. *The offer of a higher salary was quite an inducement for him to accept a position in a distant land.*

in-duct (ɪn-dʌkt) v. **1.** To install into office **2.** To receive a draftee formally into the armed forces

in-duc-tee (ɪn-dək-tiʸ/ ɪn-dʌk-tiʸ) n. A person inducted into the armed forces

in-duc-tion (ɪn-dʌk-ʃən) n. **1.** Installation of a person into office **2.** The act of enlisting a draftee into military service **3.** A process of reasoning from a part to a whole; from the specific to the general **4.** A conclusion reached by this process

in-dulge (ɪn-dʌldʒ) v. **-dulged, -dulging 1.** To gratify a desire for: *Many Americans indulge in too many sweets.* **2.** To yield to the desire: *She indulged the sick child.*

in-dul-gence (ɪn-dʌl-dʒəns) n. The act of al-

lowing someone to do or have what they want: *Because of their mother's indulgence the children became very spoiled.*

in-dul-gent (ɪn-dʌl-dʒənt) adj. Not strict; showing indulgence

in-dus-tri-al (ɪn-dʌs-triʸ-əl) adj. 1. Relating to industry and the people who work in it 2. Highly engaged in industry: *Japan is an industrial nation.* —com-pare INDUSTRIOUS —industrialist n. —industrially adv.

in-dus-tri-al-ize (ɪn-dʌs-triʸ-ə-laɪz) -ized, -izing v. To develop industrially —in-dus-tri-al-i-za-tion (ɪn-dʌs-triʸ-əl-ə-zeʸ-ʃən) n.

in-dus-tri-ous (ɪn-dʌs-triʸ-əs) adj. Hardworking: *The Japanese are very industrious people. (=hard-working)* —compare INDUSTRIAL —industriously adv.

in-dus-try (ɪn-dəs-triʸ) n. -tries 1. A particular branch of manufacture: *the automobile/aircraft/film industry* 2. Manufacturing activity in general: *Where would this country be without the support of industry?*

in-e-bri-ate (ɪn-iʸ-briʸ-eʸt) v. -ated, -ating To intoxicate —inebriated adj. Drunk; intoxicated

in-ed-i-ble (ɪn-ɛd-ə-bəl) adj. Not eatable

in-ef-fa-ble (ɪn-ɛf-ə-bəl) adj. Too overwhelming to describe

in-ef-fec-tive (ɪn-ɪ-fɛk-tɪv) adj. 1. Not effective 2. Incompetent

in-ef-fec-tu-al (ɪn-ə-fɛk-tʃə-wəl) adj. 1. Not having the intended effect 2. Powerless —ineffectually adv.

in-ef-fi-cient (ɪn-ɪ-fɪʃ-ənt) adj. Not efficient; not able to produce good results because of not working well: *an inefficient system*

in-el-i-gi-ble (ɪn-ɛl-ɪ-dʒə-bəl) adj. Not eligible; not having the necessary qualifications: *Mary is ineligible to vote because she failed to register.*

in-ept (ɪn-ɛpt) adj. 1. Inappropriate or unsuitable: *an inept reply* 2. Lacking skill or competence: *an inept secretary* 3. Foolish; absurd

in-e-qual-i-ty (ɪn-ɪ-kwɑl-ə-tiʸ) n. -ties The condition of being unequal

in-ert (ɪn-ɜrt) adj. 1. Unable to move or act 2. Moving or acting slowly 3. *tech.* Not reacting chemically with other substances

in-er-tia (ɪ-nɜr-ʃə) n. 1. The tendency of a person or thing to remain at rest or to continue on a direct course unless acted upon by an outside force 2. Resist-ance to action, motion, or change

in-es-ti-ma-ble (ɪn-ɛs-tə-mə-bəl) adj. Too great to be measured or estimated

in-ev-i-ta-ble (ɪn-ɛv-ə-tə-bəl) adj. Unpreventable; that cannot be kept from happening: *Death and taxes are inevitable.* —inevitability (ɪn-ɛv-ə-tə-bɪl-ə-tiʸ) n. —inevitably adv.

in-ex-cus-a-ble (ɪn-ɪk-skyuʷ-zə-bəl) adj. Not excusable; unpardonable: *There's no excuse for your behavior last night. It was inexcusable.*

in-ex-haust-i-ble (ɪn-ɪg-zɔs-tə-bəl) adj. That can never be used up: *an inexhaustible supply* —inexhaustibly adv.

in-ex-o-ra-ble (ɪn-ɛks-ə-rə-bəl) adj. Not capable of being persuaded; unyielding; relentless; unalterable: *The inexorable march of time.*

in-ex-pe-di-ent (ɪn-ɪk-spiʸ-diʸ-ənt) adj. Not serving a useful purpose; not suitable or wise —inexpediency n.

in-ex-pe-ri-ence (ɪn-ɪk-spɪər-iʸ-əns) n. Lack of knowledge of the ways of the world

in-ex-pli-ca-ble (ɪn-ɪks-plɪ-kə-bəl) adj. Not able to be explained or understood

in-ex-plic-it (ɪn-ɪk-splɪs-ət) adj. Vague; indefinite; general

in-ex-press-i-ble (ɪn-ɪk-sprɛs-ə-bəl) adj. Too great or too wonderful to be expressed in words: *Though you [Christians] have not seen him [Jesus], you love him; and even though you do not see him now, you believe in him and are filled with an inexpressible and glorious joy, for you are receiving the goal of your faith, the salvation of your souls* (1 Peter 1:8,9).

in-ex-tri-ca-ble (ɪn-ɛks-trɪ-kəl-bəl) adj. 1. Not capable of being untied or disentangled 2. Too complex or intricate to solve

in-fal-li-ble (ɪn-fæl-ə-bəl) adj. 1. Of people, not fallible; not capable of making a mistake or doing anything bad: *No one even comes close to being infallible; God alone is infallible.* 2. Of things, without error: *Christians are convinced that the Holy Bible is the infallible Word of God.* —in-fal-li-bil-i-ty (ɪn-fæl-ə-bɪl-ə-tiʸ) n. *the infallibility of the Bible, the*

infinitive

Word of God

in·fa·mous (**ɪn** fə məs) adj 1 Famous for wicked behavior 2. Deserving or producing infamy

in·fa·my (ɪn-fə-miᵉ) n. -mies 1. Dishonor; disgrace 2. The state of being infamous 3. An infamous act

in·fan·cy (ɪn-fən-siᵉ) n. -cies 1. Early childhood 2. An early period of exist-ence: *Our new travel agency is still in its infancy.*

in·fant (ɪn-fənt) n. A baby; a very young child: *Stop thinking like children. In regard to evil be infants, but in your thinking be adults* (1 Corinthians 14:20).

in·fan·ti·cide (ɪn-fænt-ə-saɪd) n. 1. The murder of an infant 2. One who murders an infant

in·fan·tile (ɪn-fən-taɪl) adj. Like or relating to small children: *infantile behavior*

in·fan·tile pa·ral·y·sis (ɪn-fən-taɪl pə-ræl-ə-sɪs) n. Same as **poliomyelitis**

in·fan·try (ɪn-fən-triᵉ) n. Soldiers who fight on foot

in·fat·u·at·ed (ɪn-fætʃ-ə-weᵉ-təd) adj. Filled with a strong, but usu. foolish, feeling of love for someone —**in·fat·u·a·tion** (ɪn-fætʃ-ə-weᵉ-ʃən) n.

in·fect (ɪn-fɛkt) v. 1. To cause disease in someone by introducing germs 2. To affect with one's feelings or beliefs, esp. in a harmful way

in·fec·tion (ɪn-fɛk-ʃən) n. The result of being infected, or the act of infecting: *He is suffering from a kidney infection.*

in·fec·tious (ɪn-fɛk-ʃəs) adj. Concerning a disease that can spread by infection, esp. in the air: *Colds are infectious.* —compare CONTAGIOUS

in·fer (ɪn-fɜr) v. -rr- To reach an opinion from facts or reasoning; to reach a conclusion or a decision from sthg. known or assumed —compare IMPLY NOTE: Compare "infer" and "imply": The speaker or writer **implies** sthg., and the listener or reader **infers** it. *His remarks implied (=suggested indirectly) that he would soon resign. I inferred from his remarks that he would soon resign.*

in·fer·ence (ɪn-fə-rəns) n. 1. Process or act of inferring 2. That which is inferred

in·fe·ri·or (ɪn-frər-iᵉ-ər) adj. Lower in value or quality: *Copper is inferior to gold in value.* —opposite SUPERIOR —**in·te·ri·or·i·ty** (ɪn-frər-iᵉ-or-ə-tiᵉ) n.

in·fer·nal (ɪn-fɜr-nəl) adj. 1. Very bad; extremely annoying: *Stop that infernal racket.* 2. Hellish; fiendish: *infernal flames/ infernal schemes* 3. Damnable —**infernally** adv.

in·fer·no (ɪn-fɜr-noʷ) n. -nos A place or state that resembles hell

in·fer·tile (ɪn-fɜr-təl) adj. 1. Not fertile; not able to reproduce young 2. Of land, unable to grow plants —**in·fer·til·i·ty** (ɪn-fər-tɪl-ə-tiᵉ) n.

in·fest (ɪn-fɛst) v. To cause trouble by being present continuously and in large numbers: *The room was infested with ants.* —**in·fes·ta·tion** (ɪn-fɛs-teᵉ-ʃən) n.

in·fi·del (ɪn-fə-dəl) n. 1. One who rejects all religious beliefs; an unbeliever 2. One who rejects a particular religion, esp. Christianity or Islam: *If anyone does not provide for his own, and especially for those of his own household, he has denied the faith, and is worse than an infidel* (1 Timothy 5:8 KJV, NKJV).

in·fi·del·i·ty (ɪn-fə-dɛl-ə-tiᵉ) n. -ties Lack of loyalty; unfaithfulness, especially to one's marriage partner

in·field (ɪn-fiᵉld) n. 1. In baseball, the space within base lines 2. The infielders collectively

in·field·er (ɪn-fiᵉl-dər) n. In baseball, one positioned in the infield

in·fil·trate (ɪn-fɪl-treᵉt/ ɪn-fɪl-treᵉt) v. -trated, -trating 1. To enter or join a group or society, esp. stealthily and with an unfriendly purpose: *troops infiltrating enemy lines* 2. To pass through by filtering; penetrate: *No light can infiltrate the depths of the ocean.* —**infiltrator** n. —**in·fil·tra·tion** (ɪn-fɪl-treᵉ-ʃən) n.

in·fi·nite (ɪn-fə-nət) adj. Not finite; without limit or end: *Great is our Lord and mighty in power, his understanding is infinite* (Psalm 147:5).

in·fin·i·tes·i·mal (ɪn-fɪn-ə-tɛs-ə-məl) n. Immeasurably small

in·fin·i·tive (ɪn-fɪn-ə-tɪv) n., adj. A verb form having the characteristics of both verb and

noun and, in English, usu. being used with "to." NOTE: In the sentence, "To err is human; to forgive is divine," both "err" and "forgive" are infinitives.

in-fin-i-ty (ɪn-fɪn-ə-ti^y) n. -ties Unlimited time or space

in-firm (ɪn-fɜrm) adj. *fml.* Feeble; weak in body or mind —infirmity n. -ties

in-fir-ma-ry (ɪn-fɜr-mə-ri^y) n. -ries A hospital or room for caring for the ill or injured

in-fir-mi-ty (ɪn-fɜr-mə-ti^y) n. -ties 1. Physical illness 2. Weakness; frailty: *Jesus healed all the sick in fulfillment of the Scriptures, "He took up our infirmities and carried our diseases"* (Isaiah 53:4).

in-flame (ɪn-fle^ym) v. -flamed, -flaming 1. To set on fire 2. To excite or arouse someone to excessive or unnatural feelings or action: *Men... were inflamed with lust for one another... and committed indecent acts with other men, and received in themselves the due penalty for their perversion* (Romans 1:27). NOTE: God is holy and he detests sexual perversion and all sin (Ephesians 5:3-5). But because of his great love and mercy, he forgives the sins of those who truly repent and turn from their wicked ways and put their trust in Jesus for eternal life (Acts 2:38; 16:31; Romans 6:23; John 3:16-18,36).

in-flamed (ɪn-fle^ymd) adj. Swollen and sore because hurt or diseased

in-flam-ma-ble (ɪn-flæm-ə-bəl) adj. Also **flammable**, esp. *AmE.* Easily set on fire: *Gasoline is highly inflammable.* —opposite NONFLAMMABLE —compare INFLAMMATORY

in-flam-ma-tion (ɪn-flə-me^y-ʃən) n. Swelling and soreness in part of the body, often red and hot to the touch or itchy

in-flam-ma-to-ry (ɪn-flæm-ə-tɔr-i^y) adj. 1. Tending to arouse anger, disorder or violence: *an inflammatory speech* 2. Causing or accompanied by inflammation: *an inflammatory disease*

in-flate (ɪn-fle^yt) v. -flated, -flating 1. To fill with air, gas, etc. 2. To puff up: *inflated with pride* 3. To expand or increase abnormally: *The government's action has caused the cost of living to be greatly inflated.*

in-flat-ed (ɪn-fle^y-təd) adj. 1. Filled with air: *an inflated balloon* 2. Exaggerated: *an inflated opinion of oneself/ inflated style of writing*

in-fla-tion (ɪn-fle^y-ʃən) n. An abnormal and undesirable rise in prices because of an increasing supply of money, credit, etc.: *The cost of living is barely keeping up with the rate of inflation.* (=the rate of increase in prices) —opposite DEFLATION —inflationary adj.

in-flect (ɪn-flɛkt) v. 1. *Gram.* To change the ending or form of a word to show its grammatical function in a sentence: *Most English verbs are inflected with "-ed" in the past tense./ The word "child" inflects differently in the plural than the word "boy".* 2. To make the voice higher or lower in speaking: *By inflecting the voice more, a person is better able to hold the attention of the audience.*

in-flec-tion (ɪn-flɛk-ʃən) n. 1. *Gram.* (a) Inflecting (b) A suffix used to inflect a word: *In the word "shortest," "-est" is an inflection meaning "most".* 2. The rise and fall of the voice in speaking

in-flex-i-ble (ɪn-flɛk-sə-bəl) adj. Not flexible; not capable of being bent, influenced, or changed: *All library books must be returned within the two week period. The rules are inflexible.* —in-flex-i-bil-i-ty (ɪn-flɛk-sə-bɪl-ə-ti^y) n. —inflexibly adv.

in-flict (ɪn-flɪkt) v. To force sthg. unpleasant on someone: *Our team inflicted a crushing defeat on the opposing team.*

in-flu-ence (ɪn-flu^w-əns) n. 1. The power to produce an effect on one's mind or to get results from someone without using apparent force or authority: *She used her influence to get me into the meeting.* 2. A person with this power: *He's a good/bad influence in school.* 3. The power to cause an effect indirectly: *He was driving under the influence of alcohol when he had the accident.*

influence v. -enced, -encing To have an effect on; to cause sbdy. or sthg. to think or behave in a certain way: *His speech influenced many people to vote for his candidate.*

in-flu-en-tial (ɪn-flu^w-ɛn-ʃəl) adj. Having much influence: *He's a very influential person.*

in-flu-en-za (ɪn-flu^w-ɛn-zə) n. also **flu** An

acute and very contagious virus disease marked by fever, aches and pains and respiratory inflammation

in-flux (ɪn–flʌks) n. A flowing in, esp. in large numbers

in-form (ɪn–fɔrm) v. To tell; to give knowledge to: *The policeman informed the suspected thief of his legal rights before arresting him.*

in-for-mal (ɪn–fɔr–məl) adj. Not formal; casual; without ceremony: *an informal meeting/ informal dress* —**in-for-mal-i-ty** (ɪn–fɔr–mæl–ə–tiʸ) n.

in-for-mant (ɪn–fɔr–mənt) n. A person who provides information

in-for-ma-tion (ɪn–fər–meʸ–ʃən) n. Knowledge of the facts: *Please send information about job opportunities.*

in-form-a-tive (ɪn–fɔr–mə–tɪv) adj. That gives useful information: *an informative magazine article*

in-formed (ɪn–fɔrmd) adj. Educated; having the information: *well-informed*

in-form-er (ɪn–fɔr–mər) n. One who gives incriminating information to the police or other authorities

in-fra– (ɪn–frə–) Prefix Below; beneath

in-fra-red (ɪn–frə–red) n. Rays of heat with wavelengths longer than that of visible light

in-fre-quent (ɪn–friʸ–kwənt) adj. Not often; rare

in-fringe (ɪn–frɪndʒ) v. -fringed, -fringing To break a rule or regulation or interfere with a person's freedom or his rights; violate: *to infringe on the rights of others* —**infringement** n. *Robbery is an infringement of the law.*

in-fu-ri-ate (ɪn–fyʊr–iʸ–eʸt) v. -ated, -ating To make very, very angry: *He was infuriated when he heard what his opponent had done.*

in-fuse (ɪn–fyuʷz) v. -fused, -fusing 1. To instill a principle or a quality: *infused with courage* 2. To inspire; animate 3. To soak tea or another substance in hot water in order to make a liquid of a certain flavor, a medicine, etc.

in-gen-ious (ɪn–dʒiʸn–yəs) adj. 1. Clever, resourceful, original, inventive: *an ingenious person* 2. Made or done in a clever, original way: *an ingenious device*

in-ge-nu-i-ty (ɪn–dʒə–nuʷ–ə–tiʸ) n. -ties Cleverness in making or arranging things

in-gest (ɪn–dʒest) v. To put or receive into the stomach —**ingestion** n.

in-glo-ri-ous (ɪn–glɔr–iʸ–əs) adj. 1. Humble or ordinary: *From an inglorious beginning in the slums, he became the greatest composer of the century.* 2. Shameful: *He met an inglorious death in a drunken brawl.*

in-got (ɪŋ–gət) n. A mass of metal cast into a mold

in-grained (ɪn–greʸnd/ –ɪn–) adj. Deep-seated; firmly fixed: *ingrained beauty of character*

in-grate (ɪn–greʸt) n. An ungrateful person

in-gra-ti-ate (ɪn–greʸ–ʃiʸ–eʸt) v. -ated, -ating To get oneself liked or approved by sbdy.: *Bill tried to ingratiate himself with his boss.*

in-grat-i-tude (ɪn–græt–ə–tuʷd) n. Ungratefulness; lack of gratitude

in-gre-di-ent (ɪn–griʸ–diʸ–ənt) n. One of the substances that makes up a mixture: *This product is made entirely of pure and natural ingredients..*

in-grown (ɪn–groʷn) adj. 1. Growing within 2. Grown into adjacent flesh: *an ingrown toenail*

in-hab-it (ɪn–hæb–ət) v. To live in: *He who fashioned and made the earth... formed it to be inhabited* (Isaiah 45:18). —**inhabitable** adj. Able to be inhabited

in-hab-i-tant (ɪn–hæb–ə–tənt) n. A person or animal that lives in a particular place

in-hal-ant (ɪn–heʸ–lənt) n. 1. Used for inhaling 2. Medicine to be inhaled

in-hale (ɪn–heʸl) v. -haled, -haling To breathe in; to draw air into the lungs —opposite EXHALE

in-hal-er (ɪn–heʸ–lər) n. An apparatus for inhaling medicated vapors

in-here (ɪn–hɪər) v. -hered, -hering To be inherent; belong

in-her-ent (ɪn–hɪər–ənt) adj. An essential characteristic: *Hard work is inherent for success.* —**inherently** adv.

in-her-it (ɪn–heər–ət) v. To receive money, property, a title, etc. left by someone who has died: *Blessed are the meek for they shall inherit the earth* (Matthew 5:5). *The wicked will not inherit the kingdom of God* (1 Corinthians

6:9).

in-her-i-tance (ɪn–**heər**–ɪ–təns) n. The action of inheriting: *In his great mercy he [God] has given us new birth into a living hope through the resurrection of Jesus Christ from the dead and into an inheritance that can never perish... kept in heaven for you...* (1 Peter 1:3,4).

in-hib-it (ɪn–**hɪb**–ət) v. **1.** To prohibit; forbid **2.** To hold in check; restrain: *He was not the least bit inhibited; he did whatever he wanted to do.*

in-hi-bi-tion (ɪn–hɪ–**bɪʃ**–ən) n. A condition or feeling that hinders someone from doing sthg.: *She had no inhibitions about expressing her views on any subject, whether anyone agreed with her or not.*

in-hib-i-tor (ɪn–**hɪb**–ət–ər) n. A substance added to another to retard or stop a chemical action

in-hos-pi-ta-ble (ɪn–has–**pɪt**–ə–bəl/ ɪn–**has**–pɪt–ə–bəl) adj. **1.** Unfriendly; not welcoming strangers **2.** Barren: *Greenland is an inhospitable land.*

in-hu-man (ɪn–**hyu**ʷ–mən) adj. Brutal; cruel; savage; barbarian; lacking normal human qualities of kindness, sympathy, etc. —**in-hu-man-i-ty** (ɪn–huʷ–**mæn**–ə–tiʸ) n.

in-hu-mane (ɪn–huʷ–**me**ʸn) adj. Cruel; brutal

in-im-i-cal (ɪ–**nɪm**–ɪ–kəl) adj. **1.** Hostile; unfriendly **2.** Harmful —**inimically** adv.

in-im-i-ta-ble (ɪ–**nɪm**–ə–tə–bəl) adj. Not capable of being imitated; too good to be copied by anyone, esp. with the same high quality

in-iq-ui-ty (ɪn–**ɪk**–wət–iʸ) n. **-ties** Sin; wickedness; transgression of God's commandments: *But he [Jesus] was pierced for our transgressions [when he was nailed to the cross], he was crushed for our iniquities; the punishment that brought us peace [with God] was upon him, and by his wounds we are healed. We all, like sheep, have gone astray, each of us has turned to his own way; and the Lord laid on him the iniquity of us all* (Isaiah 53:5,6).

in-i-tial (ɪ–**nɪʃ**–əl) adj. Of or relating to the beginning: *the initial stage of a disease* —**initially** adv. *Initially we had planned to go to a movie, but later we decided to stay at home and watch TV.*

initial n. A capital letter at the beginning of a name: *Fred Smith's initials are F.S.*

initial v. To sign one's initials, usu. to show agreement: *He initialed the agreement in three places.*

in-i-ti-ate (ɪ–**nɪʃ**–iʸ–eʸt) v. **-ated, -ating 1.** To put sthg. into operation: *The university will initiate the new courses in the next quarter.* **2.** To instruct someone in the first principles of sthg. **3.** To introduce someone into membership in a club or group, esp. with a special ceremony —**in-i-ti-a-tion** (ɪ–nɪʃ–iʸ–**e**ʸ–ʃən) n.

in-i-ti-a-tive (ɪ–**nɪʃ**–iʸ–ə–tɪv) n. **1.** The action of taking the first step; responsibility for originating sthg.: *He took the initiative in organizing the new agency.* **2.** Power and ability to make decisions and take action without help from anyone else

in-ject (ɪn–**dʒɛkt**) v. To force liquid into someone's body with a special needle (syringe): *The child was injected with an antibiotic to prevent infection.*

in-jec-tion (ɪn–**dʒɛk**–ʃən) n. The act of injecting: *an injection of antibiotics*

in-ju-di-cious (ɪn–dʒuʷ–**dɪʃ**–əs) adj. Unwise

in-junc-tion (ɪn–**dʒʌŋk**–ʃən) n. An order forbidding an action or commanding that sthg. should be done: *An injunction was issued by the court forbidding him from taking the child from its mother.*

in-jure (ɪn–**dʒər**) v. **-jured, -juring 1.** To hurt a living thing physically: *Many people were seriously injured in the earthquake.* **2.** To offend someone; to hurt someone's feelings: *injured pride* —**injurious** (ɪn–**dʒʊər**–iʸ–əs) adj. *Being even a few pounds overweight can be injurious to one's health.*

in-ju-ry (ɪn–**dʒə**– riʸ) n. **-ries** Physical harm to a living thing: *He suffered serious injuries from his fall.* —compare WOUND (wuʷnd)

in-jus-tice (ɪn–**dʒʌs**–təs) n. Unfairness; a wrong; a violation of a person's rights: *Now let the fear of the Lord be upon you. Judge carefully, for with the Lord our God there is no injustice or partiality or bribery* (2 Chronicles 19:7).

ink (ɪŋk) n. **1.** Colored liquid used esp. for writing and drawing **2.** Sticky colored paste used for printing: *printer's ink*

ink v. To put ink on: *They inked the press.*

ink-ling (ɪŋk-lɪŋ) n. A hint; suggestion

in-laid (ɪn-le^yd) adj. Decorated or made with a design set in the surface

in-land (ɪn-lənd) adj. Of or relating to the interior of a country

inland (ɪn-lænd/ ɪn-lənd) adv. Towards the interior of the country: *The group traveled inland on horseback.*

in-law (ɪn-lɔw) n. Relative by marriage: *mother-in-law/father-in-law*, etc.

in-lay (ɪn-le^y) n. A kind of decoration made by fitting pieces of different shapes and colors into a background

inlay (ɪn-le^y) v. —see INLAID

in-let (ɪn-lɛt/ ɪn-lət) n. 1. A narrow strip of water extending from a sea, lake, etc., into the land or between islands 2. An opening, entrance, or passage —inlet adj. *inlet hose*

in-mate (ɪn-me^yt) n. A person who lives in the same institution as others, esp. in an asylum or a prison

in me-mo-ri-am (ɪn mə–mɔr–i^y–əm) prep. + n. In memory of a person who has died

in-most (ɪn-mo^wst) adj. 1. Situated farthest within 2. Most intimate

inn (ɪn) n. A small hotel, esp. one in the country or along the highway

in-nate (ɪn-e^yt) adj. Inborn; natural; belonging to a person as a part of his nature —innately adv.

in-ner (ɪn-ər) adj. 1. Inside; located farther within 2. More intimate: *inner emotions* 3. inner circle A small exclusive group who control or influence —opposite OUTER

in-ner-most (ɪn-ər-mo^wst) adj. The farthest inward

in-ner-vate (ɪn-ɜr-ve^yt) v. -vated, -vating To stimulate NOTE: Do not confuse with enervate

in-ning (ɪn-ɪŋ) n. 1. A division of a baseball game in which each team has a turn at bat 2. innings In the game of cricket, a unit of play in which each team has a turn at bat

in-no-cent (ɪn-ə-sənt) adj. Guiltless: *Be wise about what is good and innocent about what is evil* (Romans 16:19). —opposite GUILTY —innocently adv. —innocence n.

in-noc-u-ous (ɪ-nɑk-yu^w-əs) adj. 1. Harmless

2. Lacking impact; inoffensive

in-no-vate (ɪn-ə-ve^yt) v. -vated, -vating To introduce sthg. new, or as new

in-no-va-tion (ɪn-ə-ve^y-ʃən) n. The introduction of sthg. new: *There have been many innovations in the 20th century, esp. in the fields of travel and communications.* —in-no-va-tive (ɪn-ə-ve^y-tɪv) adj. —innovator n.

in-nu-en-do (ɪn-yu^w-ɛn-do^w) n. -does or -dos An unpleasant insinuation

in-nu-mer-a-ble (ɪ-nu^w-mər-ə-bəl) adj. Too many to be counted

in-oc-u-late (ɪ-nɑk-yə-le^yt) v. -lated, -lating To treat an animal or person with vaccines or serums, esp. in order to protect from a disease —in-oc-u-la-tion (ɪ-nɑk-yə-le^y-ʃən) n.

in-op-er-a-ble (ɪn-ɑp-ər-ə-bəl) adj. Not operable; not suitable for surgery: *She has an inoperable kind of cancer.*

in-op-er-a-tive (ɪn-ɑp-ə-rə-tɪv) adj. Not working or functioning: *My car is inoperative.*

in-op-por-tune (ɪn-ɑp-ər-tu^wn) adj. Happening at the wrong time; not convenient

in-or-di-nate (ɪn-ɔr-də-nət) adj. 1. Beyond reasonable limits; excessive: *He has an inordinate affection for her.* 2. Not regulated; disorderly

in-or-gan-ic (ɪn-ɔr-gæn-ɪk) adj. Of mineral origin; not organic: *Rocks are inorganic.*

in-pa-tient (ɪn-pe^y-ʃənt) n. A patient staying in a hospital for treatment NOTE: Do not confuse with impatient

in-put (ɪn-pʊt) n. 1. Contribution to, or participation in, a common effort: *We appreciate your input.* (=we value your comments and suggestions) 2. Energy or power put into a machine or system 3. Information put into a data processing system

in-quest (ɪn-kwɛst) n. A legal or judicial inquiry or investigation

in-quire (ɪn-kwaɪ-ər) v. -quired, -quiring 1. To ask about: *He inquired about her health.* 2. To search for the truth: *Should not a people inquire of their God?* (Isaiah 8:19). —inquirer n.

in-quir-y (ɪn-kwɪ-ri^y) n. -ies 1. The act of inquiring 2. An investigation: *The government is making inquiries into the dangers of smoking.*

in-qui-si-tion (ɪn-kwə-zɪʃ-ən) n. A careful questioning or investigation

in-quis-i-tive (ɪn–**kwɪz**–ə–tɪv) adj. Questioning; trying to find out too many details about other people's affairs: *Don't be so inquisitive.*

in-road (ɪn–roʷd) n. **1.** An invasion; a raid: *inroads into enemy territory* **2. make inroads** To gradually use up more and more of sthg.: *Hospital bills made deep inroads into his savings account.*

in-sane (ɪn–seʸn) adj. Not sane; mad; mentally ill —**insanely** adv. *He was insanely jealous of his wife.*

in-san-i-ty (ɪn–**sæn**–ə–tiʸ) n. Madness; the state of being insane: *fig. Driving at that speed on the icy highway would be pure insanity.*

in-sa-tia-ble (ɪn–seʸ–ʃə–bəl) adj. Unable to satisfy: *an insatiable appetite*

in-scribe (ɪn–skraɪb) v. **-scribed, -scribing** To write, print, or engrave sthg. on or in a surface: *The names of those who died in battle were inscribed on the plaque.* —**in-scrip-tion** (ɪn–skrɪp–ʃən) n.

in-scru-ta-ble (ɪn–skruʷ–tə–bəl) adj. Of people and their acts, difficult to understand; mysterious

in-seam (ɪn–siʸm) n. The seam from the crotch to the bottom on the inside of a trouser leg

in-sect (ɪn–sɛkt) n. A type of small creature having no bones, a hard outer covering, six legs, and a body divided into three parts: *Ants, spiders, flies, beetles, wasps, and mosquitoes are insects.*

in-sec-ti-cide (ɪn–sɛk–tə–saɪd) n. A chemical substance used to kill insects

in-se-cure (ɪn–sɪ–kyuər) adj. **1.** Unsure of oneself; lacking confidence **2.** Not safe or firmly fixed —**insecurely** adv. —**insecurity** n.

in-sem-i-nate (ɪn–sɛm–ə–neʸt) v. **1** To sow seeds in, esp. to introduce semen into the genital tract of a female, either naturally or by artificial means **2.** To implant ideas into the mind

in-sen-si-ble (ɪn–sɛn–sə–bəl) adj. **1.** Not conscious: *knocked insensible by a falling branch* **2.** Unmindful; unaware: *insensible to the danger* **3.** Not able to feel: *insensible to pain* **4.** Too small or gradual to be noticed

in-sen-si-tive (ɪn–sɛn–sə–tɪv) adj. **1.** Not realizing or caring how other people feel, and therefore likely to offend them: *It was insensitive of you to mention her husband's failure to keep his job.* **2.** Not able to have the feeling that is normally expected when one meets a certain experience: *insensitive to cold*

in-sep-a-ra-ble (ɪn–sɛp–ə–rə–bəl) adj. Not separable; incapable of being separated: *inseparable friends/Rights and responsibilities are often inseparable.*

in-sert (ɪn–sɜrt) v. To put sthg. inside another thing: *He inserted the letter into the envelope.*

in-sert (ɪn–sərt) n. A thing inserted: *The envelope contained several inserts.*

in-ser-tion (ɪn–sɜr–ʃən) n. The act of inserting, or the thing inserted

in-set (ɪn–sɛt) v. To set into sthg.; insert

in-set (ɪn–sɛt) n. Sthg. set in, e.g. a piece of material set into a garment or a smaller picture, map, etc. set within the border of a larger one

in-side (ɪn–saɪd/ ɪn–) n. The area within; an inner side or surface; interior: *Let's paint the inside of this room.* —opposite OUTSIDE

inside (ɪn–saɪd) prep. **1.** Within the specified time or distance: *He'll come back inside a month.* **2.** Into: *He's getting inside the car.*

inside (ɪn–saɪd) adv. **1.** Within: *Mary's getting into the car. Joan is already inside.*. **2.** Indoors: *The children are playing inside.*

inside (ɪn–saɪd) adj. **1.** Secret; known only to people with special privileges: *inside information* **2. inside out (a)** Having the inside part/s on the outside: *He was wearing his shirt inside out.* **(b)** Thoroughly; completely: *He knows this town/ this subject inside out.* —opposite OUTSIDE

in-sid-i-ous (ɪn–sɪd–iʸ–əs) adj. Spreading or acting gradually and unnoticed but with harmful effects: *an insidious disease* —**insidiously** adv. *She had insidiously wormed her way into the supervisor's affections.*

in-sight (ɪn–saɪt) n. The ability to see and understand clearly the inner nature of things: *Traveling helps to broaden one's insights into the way other people live./I have more insight than all my teachers, for I meditate on your statutes [God's word] (Psalm 119:99).*

in-sig-ni-a (ɪn–sɪg–niʸ–ə) n. A distinguishing

in-sig-ni-a (m–sɪg–niˠ–ə) n. A distinguishing sign, esp. of office, rank, honor; a badge or emblem

in-sig-nif-i-cant (m–sɪg–nɪf–ə–kənt) adj. Not significant; lacking in value or importance

in-sin-cere (m–sm–sɪər) adj. Not sincere, hypocritical —**insincerely** adv. —**in-sin-cer-i-ty** (m–sm–sɛər–ət–iˠ) n.

in-sin-u-ate (m–sm–yuᵂ–eˠt) v. -ated, -ating To suggest sthg. unpleasant in an indirect manner: *an insinuating remark* —**in-sin-u-a-tion** (m–sm–yuᵂ–eˠ–ʃən) n.

in-sip-id (m–sɪp–əd) adj. 1. Having almost no taste: *insipid food* 2. Lacking in interest or vigor; dull: *insipid colors/an insipid remark*

in-sist (m–sɪst) v. 1. To declare firmly: *He insisted that he was right.* 2. To demand vehemently and persistently: *He insisted that we begin immediately.*

in-sis-tence (m–sɪs–təns) n. The act of insisting

in-sis-tent (m–sɪs–tənt) adj. 1. Insisting or making demands again and again: *Mother was insistent on my taking an umbrella.* 2. Requiring a response: *the insistent sound of the alarm clock*

in-so-lent (m–sə–lənt) adj. Insulting; disrespectful; extremely rude: *insolent remarks*

in-sol-u-ble (m–sɑl–yə–bəl) adj. 1. Having no solution: *an insoluble riddle/ mystery* 2. Sthg. that cannot be easily dissolved: *insoluble in water*

in-sol-vent (m–sɑl–vənt) adj. Unable to pay one's debts —**insolvency** n.

in-som-ni-a (m–sɑm–niˠ–ə) n. Habitual sleeplessness

in-spect (m–spɛkt) v. 1. To look at carefully; examine critically 2. To make an official visit to examine and judge the quality of sthg.

in-spec-tion (m–spɛk–ʃən) n. The act of inspecting or the state of being inspected: *an inspection of the hospital equipment*

in-spec-tor (m–spɛk–tər) n. An official who inspects: *a customs inspector*

in-spi-ra-tion (m–spə–reˠ–ʃən) n. 1. The act of drawing air into the lungs 2. A divine influence upon human beings, as that resulting in the writing of the Holy Scriptures: *All Scripture [the Holy Bible] is given by inspira-*

tion of God (2 Timothy 3:16). 3. Any stimulus to creative thought or action 4. An inspiring agent or influence: *His music was a real inspiration to me.* —**inspirational** adj.

in-spire (m–spaɪ–ər) v. -spired, -spiring 1. To draw air into the lungs; to inhale 2. To encourage or stimulate someone to some creative effort: *His courage and determination inspired me to greater efforts.* 3. To influence, move or guide by divine inspiration: *His best music was inspired by his love for our Savior Jesus Christ.* —**inspired** adj. *She paints like a woman inspired.* —**inspiring** adj.

in-sta-bil-i-ty (m–stə–bɪl–ə–tiˠ) adj. -ties Lack of firmness or stability; unsteadiness, esp. of character

in-stall (m–stɔl) v. 1. To place someone in an official position, esp. with a formal ceremony: *The new teacher will be installed today.* 2. To fix sthg (machinery, equipment) in a place ready for use: *They're installing a new air conditioner.* 3. To settle in a certain place, condition, or state: *Lassie, my pet dog, installed herself at the foot of my bed and refused to move.* —**in-stal-la-tion** (m–stə–leˠ–ʃən) n.

in-stall-ment (m–stɔl–mənt) AmE. n. 1. One of the parts into which a debt is divided for payment: *The installment on my car is $87.19 per month.* 2. One of several parts of a book, play, or television show which appears regularly until the story is completed

in-stance (m–stəns) n. 1. A single case or example 2. An occasion 3. **for instance** For example

in-stant (m–stənt) n. A moment or point of time: *The instant I saw him I knew that we were in trouble.*

instant adj. 1. Immediate: *instant change* 2. Of food, capable of being quickly prepared for use: *instant coffee/ tea/ cocoa/ rice* —**instantly** adv.

in-stan-ta-ne-ous (m–stən–teˠ–niˠ–əs) adj. Done or occurring in an instant without delay: *His car was hit by a train and his death was instantaneous.* —**instantaneously** adv.

in-stead (m–stɛd) adv. 1. In place of sthg.: *We're out of coffee, so I'll have tea instead.* 2. **instead of** As a substitute for: *I should be at the office instead of sitting here watching TV.*

in-step (ɪn-stɛp) n. Arched middle part of the human foot

in-sti-gate (ɪn-stə-geʸt) v. -gated, -gating To start sthg. happening; to goad or urge forward; incite —**in-sti-ga-tion** (ɪn-stə-geʸ-ʃən) n. —**instigator** n. *Bob was really the instigator of this movement.*

in-still (ɪn-stɪl) v. -ll- To cause sbdy. to acquire a particular quality: *He instilled in his children a sense of responsibility.* —**instillation** n.

in-stinct (ɪn-stɪŋkt) n. **1.** The natural, unlearned force in people and animals which causes them to behave in certain ways: *Birds build nests by instinct, without being taught.* **2.** Behavior originating below the conscious level **3.** A natural talent or ability —**instinctive** (ɪn-stɪŋk-tɪv) adj.—**instinctively** adv.

in-sti-tute (ɪn-stə-tuʷt) n. **1.** A society or association formed for a specific purpose: *a language institute* **2.** An educational institution: *a Bible institute*

institute v. -tuted, -tuting To establish a society, actions in law, a school, etc.: *Submit yourselves for the Lord's sake to every authority instituted among men: whether to the king, as the supreme authority, or to governors...* (1 Peter 2:13).

in-sti-tu-tion (ɪn-stə-tuʷ-ʃən) n. **1.** An organization such as a hospital, school, prison, etc. that provides education, medical treatment, protection, correction, etc. **2.** A very old well-established habit, custom, etc.: *Marriage, the oldest institution in history, was instituted by God himself in the beginning of time.* **3.** The action of instituting sthg.: *the institution of a new library* —**institutional** adj.

in-sti-tu-tion-al-ize (ɪn-stə-tuʷ-ʃən-əl-aɪz) v. -ized, -izing **1.** To make sthg. into an institution **2.** To place someone in an institution **3.** To become accustomed to living in an institution —**in-sti-tu-tion-al-i-za-tion** (ɪn-stə-tuʷ-ʃən-əl-ə-zeʸ-ʃən) n.

in-struct (ɪn-strʌkt) v. **1.** To give knowledge; teach; educate: *Instruct a wise man and he will be wiser still* (Proverbs 9:9). **2.** To order: *He was instructed to sound the alarm at the first hint of smoke.*

in-struc-tion (ɪn-strʌk-ʃən) n. **1.** The act or action of instructing; teaching: *Fathers, do not exasperate your children; instead, bring them up in the training and instruction of the Lord* (Ephesians 6:4). **2.** Directions on how to do sthg.: *an instruction book* —**instructional** adj. —**instructive** adj.

in-struc-tor (ɪn-strʌk-tər) n. One who teaches an activity: *a swimming instructor*

in-stru-ment (ɪn-strə-mənt) n. **1.** A tool or implement, esp. one used for delicate work **2.** Any of the various devices used to produce music, such as a piano, violin, trumpet, etc. **3.** Any of the various devices used to indicate position, direction, measurement, etc.: *There are many instruments on the instrument panel of an airplane.*

in-stru-men-tal (ɪn-strə-mɛn-təl) adj. **1.** Helpful: *He was instrumental in finding a replacement for the professor who retired.* **2.** Music for instruments, not voices: *an instrumental arrangement* —**instrumentalist** n.

in-sub-or-di-nate (ɪn-sə-bor-də-nət) adj. Unwilling to submit to authority; rebellious —**in-sub-or-di-na-tion** (ɪn-sə-bor-də-neʸ-ʃən) n.

in-sub-stan-tial (ɪn-səb-stæn-ʃəl) adj. **1.** Not actually existing; imaginary **2.** Weak, not well founded; inadequate; not convincing: *insubstantial evidence*

in-suf-fer-a-ble (ɪn-sʌf-ər-ə-bəl) adj. **1.** Not able to be endured; unbearable **2.** Unbearably conceited or arrogant

in-suf-fi-cient (ɪn-sə-fɪʃ-ənt) adj. Not sufficient; not enough

in-su-late (ɪn-sə-leʸt) v. -lated, -lating **1.** To cover (sthg.) so as to prevent the passage or leakage of unseen forces such as electricity, heat, or sound: *Our house is well insulated, which saves us money on heating and air conditioning.* **2.** To protect a person from ordinary experiences: *My parents tried to insulate me from many of the problems that my friends had to face.* —**insulator** n.

in-su-la-tion (ɪn-sə-leʸ-ʃən) n. **1.** The act of insulating or the state of being insulated **2.** Any material used to insulate

in-sul-in (ɪn-sə-lən) n. A hormone secreted by the pancreas, used in the treatment and control of diabetes

control of diabetes

in-sult (ɪn-sʌlt) v. To treat or speak to some-one with scorn or great disrespect; to say or do sth. that hurts or intends to hurt the feelings of someone: *If you are insulted be-cause of the name of Christ [because you are a Christian], you are blessed, for the Spirit of glo-ry and of God rests on you* (1Peter 4:14).

in-sult (ɪn-səlt) n. Speech or action that in-sults: *Whoever corrects a mocker invites insult* (Proverbs 9:7). *A prudent man overlooks an insult* (Proverbs 12:16).

in-su-per-a-ble (ɪn-suʷ-pə-rə-bəl) Unable to be overcome

in-sur-ance (ɪn-ʃʊər-əns) n. **1.** An agreement with a company that they will pay you money if sth. of yours is lost or damaged: *life/ health/ car/ fire insurance/ an insurance policy* **2.** Money that is paid (a) by an insu-rance company as a result of such a con-tract, or (b) to an insurance company in or-der to make or keep such a contract

in-sure (ɪn-ʃʊər) v. **-sured, -suring 1.** To ar-range with a company that they will pay you money if sth. of yours is lost or dam-aged: *My house is insured against fire.* **2.** Esp. *AmE* for **ensure** —**insurable** adj.

in-sur-gent (ɪn-sɜr-dʒənt) n. **1.** A person who revolts against established authority; a re-bel **2.** One who acts contrary to the policies of his political party —**insurgence** n. —**insurgency** n. —**insurgent** adj.

in-sur-mount-a-ble (ɪn-sər-**maʊn**-tə-bəl) adj. Too large or difficult to be dealt with —**insurmountably** adv.

in-sur-rec-tion (ɪn-sə-**rek**-ʃən) n. The act of rising up against the people who are in power, such as a government; rebellion

in-tact (ɪn-tækt) adj. Undamaged; complete

in-tan-gi-ble (ɪn-tæn-dʒə-bəl) adj. **1.** Not able to be felt by touch **2.** Difficult to define or describe; not clear

in-te-ger (ɪn-tɪ-dʒər) n. A whole number as distinguished from a fraction

in-te-gral (ɪn-tə-grəl) adj. Essential to the completeness of sth.: *Arms and legs are inte-gral parts of the human body.*

in-te-grate (ɪn-tə-greʸt) v. **-grated, -grating 1.** To join to sth. else so as to form a whole; to

unite **2.** To join with members of other eth-nic groups to do this: *Some people seem to in-tegrate into the culture of a new land much more quickly than others.* —opposite SEGRE-GATE —**in-te-gra-tion** (ɪn-tə-**greʸ**-ʃən) n.

in-te-grat-ed (ɪn-tə-greʸ-təd) adj. With the various parts fitting well together: *an inte-grated personality/ an integrated school with children of different races and social classes*

in-teg-ri-ty (ɪn-**teg**-rə-tiʸ) n. **1.** Strength and firmness of character; utter sincerity and honesty: *The man of integrity walks securely* (Proverbs 10:9). *Right-eousness guards the man of integrity, but wickedness overthrows the sinner* (Prov-erbs 13:6). **2.** A state of being undivided; completeness

in-tel-lect (ɪn-tə-lekt) n. **1.** The ability to think, reason, and learn **2.** A person of great intel-lectual ability —see INTELLIGENT

in-tel-lec-tu-al (ɪn-tə-**lek**-tʃə-wəl) adj. **1.** Con-cerning the intellect —compare SPIRITUAL **2.** Showing unusual ability to reason and use the intellect **3.** Interested in learning, thinking, and judging ideas rather than in feelings

intellectual n. A person who is engaged in work that requires the creative use of the intellect; one who lives by using his/her mind —**intellectually** adv.

in-tel-li-gence (ɪn-**tel**-ə-dʒəns) n. **1.** Ability to acquire and apply knowledge **2.** Superior powers of the mind: *The Lord says: "These people come near to me with their mouth and honor me with their lips, but their hearts are far from me. Their worship of me is made up only of rules taught by men. Therefore... the wisdom of the wise will perish, the intelligence of the intel-ligent will vanish"* (Isaiah 29:13,14). **3.** Infor-mation gathered, esp. about an enemy country

in-tel-li-gent (ɪn-**tel**-ə-dʒənt) adj. Having or showing intelligence; having or showing an alert mind; bright, perceptive, clever —**intelligently** adv. NOTE: Compare **intel-ligent** and **intellectual**. Any person with a quick and clever mind is **intelligent**, but an **intellectual** is one who is well-educated and interested in or able to deal with things of the mind. *My five-year-old grandson is very*

tellectual.

in-tel-li-gi-ble (ɪn–**tɛl**–ə–dʒə–bəl) adj. Able to be understood —opposite UNINTELLIGI-BLE

in-tem-per-ance (ɪn–**tɛm**–pər–əns) n. **1.** Habitual or excessive drinking of liquor **2.** Lack of moderation, esp. in satisfying an appetite or passion —**intemperate** adj.

in-tend (ɪn–**tɛnd**) v. **1.** To plan; to mean to do sthg.: *Joseph said to his brothers, "You intended to harm me, but God intended it for good to accomplish... the saving of many lives."* **2.** To mean to be: *The money in the bank was intended for my son's college education, but we had to use it for his hospital bill.* **3.** To design for a specified use or for the future: *I intend that you shall take over the business.* —**intended** adj.

in-tense (ɪn–**tɛns**) adj. **1.** An extreme degree: *intense heat/intense pain* **2.** Feeling deeply: *She has very intense feelings about the suffering in her country.* —**intensely** adv.

in-ten-si-fy (ɪn–**tɛn**–sə–faɪ) v. **-fied, -fying** To become more intense; increase; strengthen: *Scientists have intensified their search for a cure for that disease.* —**in-ten-si-fi-ca-tion** (ɪn–tɛn–sə–fə–**keʸ**–ʃən) n.

in-ten-si-ty (ɪn–**tɛn**–sə–tiʸ) n. **-ties 1.** The quality or state of being intense **2.** Degree of strength, force, or energy

in-ten-sive (ɪn–**tɛn**–sɪv) adj. Marked by special effort: *My daughter works in the intensive care unit at the hospital, taking care of the seriously ill patients.* —**intensively** adv.

in-tent (ɪn–**tɛnt**) n. **1.** Purpose; aim; intention: *He entered the building with intent to steal.* **2. to all intents (and purposes)** In all important respects

intent adj. Having or showing fixed attention: *an intent expression* —**intently** adv. *She watched the movie intently.*

in-ten-tion (ɪn–**tɛn**–ʃən) n. That which one plans or determines to do: *His intentions were to help but he only got in the way.*

in-ten-tion-al (ɪn–**tɛn**–ʃən–əl) adj. Not by accident; done on purpose —opposite UNIN-TENTIONAL —**intentionally** adv.

in-ter– (ɪn–tər–) prefix Between, among, or together: *intermarry/ intertwine/ interlock*

in-ter (ɪn–**tɜr**) v. **-rr-** To bury a dead person: *He was interred at Forest Lawn Memorial Park.* —**interment** n.

in-ter-act (ɪn–tər–**ækt**) v. Of two or more persons or things, to act together or have some effect on each other —**in-teraction** n. *The interaction of the two kinds of medicine had a very bad effect on him.*

in-ter-cede (ɪn–tər–**siʸd**) v. **-ceded, -ced-ing** To plead or make a request in behalf of another or others: *Christ Jesus... who was raised to life — is at the right hand of God and is also interceding for us* (Romans 8:34). *And he who searches our hearts knows the mind of the Spirit, because the Spirit intercedes for the saints in accordance with God's will* (Romans 8:27).

in-ter-cept (ɪn–tər–**sɛpt**) v. **1.** To stop sthg. (a person or thing moving from one place to another) before it reaches its destination: *The drug shipment was intercepted by the police.* **2.** To gain possession of an opponent's pass in American football —**interception** n. —**interceptor** n.

in-ter-ces-sion (ɪn–tər–**sɛʃ**–ən) n. Prayer or petition in behalf of others: *I urge... that requests, prayers, intercession and thanksgiving be made for everyone* (1 Timothy 2:1). *Christians are to intercede [make intercession] for other Christians and for non-Christians.*

in-ter-ces-sor (ɪn–tər–**sɛs**–ər) n. One who intercedes —**intercessory** adj.

in-ter-change (ɪn–tər–**tʃeʸ**ndʒ) n. **1.** The act or action of exchanging; putting each (of two things) in the other's place **2.** To make an exchange of; to give and receive: *an interchange of ideas* **3.** A highway intersection

in-ter-change-a-ble (ɪn–tər–**tʃeʸ**ndʒ–ə–bəl) adj. Able to be interchanged; able to be used in place of each other

in-ter-com (ɪn–tər–**kɑm**) n. An intercommunication system by which a person can talk to other people nearby, as used in an office building; a telephone system within a building

in-ter-con-ti-nen-tal (ɪn–tər–kɑn–tə–**nɛn**–təl) adj. Connecting or carried on between two continents: *an intercontinental airline/ Intercontinental missiles can be fired from one continent to another.*

nent to another.

in-ter-course (ˈɪn-tər-kɔrs) n. **1.** Any dealings or communications between people or between two countries **2. sexual intercourse** An intimate physical relationship between a man and woman, involving the sex organs NOTE: Sexual intercourse outside of marriage is a detestable sin in God's sight. And the wages of sin is eternal death (Romans 6:23). But because of God's great love and mercy, he forgives those who truly repent (turn from their wicked ways) and put their trust in Jesus for eternal life (Acts 2:38; 16:31; John 3:16). —see JESUS

in-ter-est (ɪn-trəst/ ɪn-tə-rəst) n. **1.** A feeling of curiosity or concern about sthg.; readiness to give attention **2.** The thing in which one takes pleasure: *Music is one of his many interests.* **3.** Benefit; welfare: *Each of you should look not only to your own interests, but also to the interests of others* (Philippians 2:4). **4.** Money charged for the use of money: *The interest rate on our mobile home loan is 11%.*

interest v. **1.** To arouse the attention or concern of: *The topic of travel interests my wife and me.* **2.** To persuade or influence someone to buy or accept sthg.: *The salesman tried to interest us in buying a waterbed.*

in-ter-est-ed (ɪn-trəst-əd/ ɪn-tər-əst-əd) adj. Concerned; having or taking an interest: *an interested onlooker*

in-ter-est-ing (ɪn-trəst-ɪŋ/ ɪn-tər-əst-ɪŋ) adj. Holding the attention: *an interesting story/ idea*

in-ter-fere (ɪn-tər-fɪər) v. **-fered, -fering 1.** To get in the way of another; hinder the action of another **2.** To take action in someone else's affairs without their approval

in-ter-fer-ence (ɪn-tər-fɪər-əns) n. An act of interfering

in-ter-ga-lac-tic (ɪn-tər-gə-læk-tɪk) adj. Of or existing in the space between galaxies

in-ter-im (ɪn-tər-əm) n. The time between two events —**interim** adj.

in-te-ri-or (ɪn-tɪər-iʸ-ər) adj., n. **1.** Inside; indoors: *The interior walls of our house are covered with oak paneling.* **2.** Inland: *We will be teaching in the interior of China, about three hundred miles from the coast.* —opposite EX-TERIOR

in-ter-ject (ɪn-tər-dʒɛkt) v. To say sthg. that interrupts what sbdy. else is saying, or what one is saying himself

in-ter-jec-tion (ɪn-tər-dʒɛk-ʃən) n. **1.** A word or words of exclamation: *"Ooh!," "Ouch!" and "Oh my!" are interjections.* **2.** The act of interjecting sthg .

in-ter-lock (ɪn-tər-lɑk) v. To lock with one another; to fit together: *The pieces of a jigsaw puzzle interlock.*

in-ter-lope (ɪn-tər-loʷp) v. **-loped, -loping 1.** To encroach on the rights of others **2.** To intrude; interfere —**interloper** n.

in-ter-lude (ɪn-tər-luʷd) n. **1.** A period of time between activities **2.** Sthg., esp. music, performed during the time between parts of a play, film, concert, etc.

in-ter-mar-ry (ɪn-tər-mɛər-iʸ/ -mær-iʸ) v. **-ried, -rying 1.** To marry within a group **2.** To marry someone from another group or race: *God's Word commands us not to intermarry with unbelievers: Do not intermarry with them* (Deuteronomy 7:3).

in-ter-me-di-ar-y (ɪn-tər-miʸ-diʸ-ɛər-iʸ) n. **-ies** A mediator; a go-between; a person who acts as a means of communication between two other persons, groups of people, etc., esp. in order to bring them into agreement

in-ter-me-di-ate (ɪn-tər-miʸ-diʸ-ət) adj. Between two extremes; in between; halfway: *an intermediate book (=between beginning and advanced levels)*

in-ter-mez-zo (ɪn-tər-mɛt-soʷ/ -mɛd-zoʷ) n. **1.** A short musical composition between main divisions of a longer musical work **2.** A short independent musical composition

in-ter-mi-na-ble (ɪn-tɜr-mə-nə-bəl) adj. Continuing for a long time, usu. too long: *His speech was very boring and seemed interminable.*

in-ter-min-gle (ɪn-tər-mɪŋ-gəl) v. To mix or mingle

in-ter-mis-sion (ɪn-tər-mɪʃ-ən) n. A period of time between parts of a movie, concert, etc.

in-ter-mit-tent (ɪn-tər-mɪt-ənt) adj. Not constant; happening with breaks in between: *intermittent showers*

in-tern (ɪn-tɜrn) n. An advanced student or

cal experience: *medical intern*

in-tern (ɪn–tɜm) v. To serve as an intern —**internship** n.

in-tern (ɪn–tɜrn/ ɪn–təm) v. To hold sbdy. from the enemy side as a prisoner while a war is going on —**internment** (ɪn–tɜrn–mənt) n.

in-ter-nal (ɪn–tɜr–nəl) adj. **1.** Within the body: *internal injuries* **2.** Inside a country; not foreign; relating to the domestic affairs of a country: *internal trade* —opposite EXTERNAL —**internally** adv.

in-ter-na-tion-al (ɪn–tər–næʃ–ə–nəl) adj. Affecting two or more nations or nationalities: *international trade* —**internationally** adv.

in-ter-ne-cine (ɪn–tər–nɛs–iʸn/–neʸs–iʸn/ –ən/ ɪn–tɜr–nə–seʸn/–sən/mt–ər–nə–seʸn) adj. **1.** Mutually destructive **2.** Pertaining to conflict within a group

in-tern-ee (ɪn–tər–niʸ) n. A person who is interned, as a prisoner of war

in-tern-ist (ɪn–tər–nəst) n. A physician who specializes in internal medicine, as distinguished from a surgeon

in-ter-plan-e-tar-y (ɪn–tər–plæn–ə–tɛər–iʸ) adj. Within our own solar system, being or occurring between planets

in-ter-play (ɪnt–ər–pleʸ) n. The action of two or more things upon each other

in-ter-po-late (ɪn–tər–pə–leʸt) v. **-lated, -lating** **1.** To alter by the insertion of new or false material **2.** To insert into a text or into a conversation

in-ter-pose (ɪn–tər–poʷz) v. **-posed, -posing** **1.** To interrupt or add (e.g., a remark) to a conversation, quarrel, etc. **2.** To put forward sthg. that prevents or interferes with some action: *The judge interposed his authority to keep certain questions from being asked of the witness.*

in-ter-pret (ɪn–tɜr–prət) v. **1.** To put one language into the words of another language, usu. by speaking —compare TRANSLATE **2.** To explain or bring out the intended meaning of sthg. —**interpreter** n.

in-ter-pre-ta-tion (ɪn–tər–prə–teʸ–ʃən) n. The act or the result of interpreting

in-ter-ro-gate (ɪn–tɛər–ə–geʸt) v. To question formally for the purpose of getting specific information: *He was interrogated at the police station.* —**in-ter-ro-ga-tion** (ɪn–tɛər–ə–geʸ–ʃən) n.

in-ter-rog-a-tive (ɪn–tə–rɑg–ə–tɪv) adj. In the nature of a question: *An interrogative sentence is one that asks a question.*

in-ter-rupt (ɪn–tə–rʌpt) v. **1.** To speak or cause some sort of disturbance that stops or hinders the flow of speech of sbdy. **2.** To break the flow of sthg. meant to be continuous —**in-ter-rup-tion** (ɪn–tə–rʌp–ʃən) n.

in-ter-sect (ɪn–tər–sɛkt) v. To cut across each other: *The two highways intersect five miles east of town.*

in-ter-sec-tion (ɪn–tər–sɛk–ʃən)n. **1.** The act of intersecting **2.** A place where two or more roads cross: *I'll meet you at the coffee shop at the intersection of 5th and Broadway.*

in-ter-sperse (ɪnt–ər–spɜrs) v. **-spersed, -spersing** To scatter sthg. between or among other things: *Her speech was interspersed with jokes.*

in-ter-state (ɪn–tər–steʸt) adj. Of, between, or connecting two or more states: *interstate commerce*

in-ter-state (ɪn–tər–steʸt) n. A highway connecting two or more states, esp. in the US

in-ter-val (ɪn–tər–vəl) n. **1.** Time between events: *There was a long interval between the two races.* **2.** BrE. for **intermission** **3.** Space between two or more objects **4. at intervals** Happening regularly after equal periods of time or appearing after equal spaces: *These trees need to be planted at intervals of twenty feet or more.*

in-ter-vene (ɪn–tər–viʸn) v. **-vened, -ven-ing** **1.** To interrupt sthg. in such a way as to hinder or prevent sthg. bad from happening: *The police intervened to stop the riot.* **2.** To happen between times or events —**in-ter-ven-tion** (ɪn–tər–vɛn–ʃən) n.

in-ter-view (ɪn–tər–vyuʷ) n. **1.** A meeting in which a writer or reporter asks questions to obtain information from a person **2.** A meeting where a person is asked questions to decide whether he/she can qualify for a job **interview** v. To ask questions of someone in an interview: *She was interviewed by several reporters.* —**interviewer** n.

in-tes-tine (ɪn-tɛs-tən) n. The long tube in the body which carries food from the stomach —compare BOWELS —**intestinal** adj.

in-ti-ma-cy (ɪn-tə-mə-siʸ) n. **1.** The state of being intimate **2.** Close friendship or relationship

in-ti-mate (ɪn-tə-mət) adj. **1.** Marked by closeness in relationship; familiarity: *intimate friends* **2.** Personal and private: *an intimate diary* **3.** Detailed; marked by very close relationship or study: *an intimate knowledge of the law* **4.** Close in sexual relationship: *Her husband accused her of being intimate with another man.* —**intimately** adv.

in-ti-mate (ɪn-tə-meʸt) v. **-mated, -mating** To make known indirectly; imply subtly; suggest: *George intimated that he and Donna would be married soon.* —**in-ti-ma-tion** (ɪn-tə-meʸ-ʃən) n.

in-tim-i-date (ɪn-tɪm-ə-deʸt) **-dated, -dating** To frighten someone in order to get them to do what is wanted, esp. by threatening them with violence: *They threatened to ruin his business if he didn't comply with their wishes, but he would not be intimidated.*

in-to (ɪn-tə/ɪn-tuʷ) prep. **1.** To the inside: *He put the letter into the envelope./He got into the car.* **2.** So as to be changed to: *translated into Hindi* **3.** Against: *He ran into a tree with his bicycle.* **4.** Used when dividing one number by another: *Two into ten equals five.* **5.** To get involved in: *He got into trouble./My brother got into real estate after his retirement.*

in-tol-er-a-ble (ɪn-tɑl-ə-rə-bəl) adj. Unbearable; not able to be endured

in-tol-er-ant (ɪn-tɑl-ə-rənt) adj. Unwilling to put up with people of different races, religions, political beliefs, ideas, etc. —**intolerance** n. —**intolerantly** adv.

in-to-na-tion (ɪn-tə-neʸ-ʃən) n. In speech, the rising and falling pitch of the voice: *He spoke monotonously, with very little intonation.*

in-tox-i-cate (ɪn-tɑk-sə-keʸt) v. **-cated, -cating** To make drunk

in-tra- (ɪn-trə-) Prefix Within; inside, as in **intravenous**

in-trac-ta-ble (ɪn-træk-tə-bəl) adj. Obstinate; not easily controlled

in-tra-mur-al (ɪn-trə-myʊr-əl) adj. Existing or carried on within a school or other institution

in-tran-si-gent (ɪn-træn-sə-dʒənt) adj. Refusing to come to any agreement; uncompromising; stubborn —**intransigence** n.

in-tran-si-tive (ɪn-træn-sə-tɪv) n., adj. Of a verb that has a subject but not an object: *In the sentence, "We can hear," the word "hear" is an intransitive verb because it has no object.*

in-tra-state (ɪn-trə-steʸt) adj. Within the boundaries of a state

in-tra-ve-nous (ɪn-trə-viʸ-nəs) adj. Being within or entering by way of a vein (a blood vessel carrying blood back to the heart) —**intravenously** adv. *He couldn't eat, so they had to feed him intravenously.*

in-trep-id (ɪn-trɛp-əd) adj. Of a person, fearless; brave

in-tri-ca-cy (ɪn-trɪ-kə-siʸ) n. **-cies 1.** The quality of being intricate **2.** Sthg. intricate

in-tri-cate (ɪn-trə-kət) adj. **1.** Complicated; having many detailed parts: *an intricate design* **2.** Difficult to follow, understand, or solve

in-trigue (ɪn-triʸg) v. **-trigued, -triguing 1.** To interest greatly; fascinate: *This mystery novel intrigues me.* **2.** To make a secret plan; to plot or scheme

in-trigue (ɪn-triʸg / ɪn-triʸg) n. **1.** The act of plotting or scheming: *political intrigue* **2.** A secret love affair

in-trigu-ing (ɪn-triʸ-gɪŋ) adj. Very interesting; amusing; curious

in-trin-sic (ɪn-trɪn-sɪk/ -zɪk) adj. Belonging to the essential nature of a thing: *Her necklace was made of glass, not diamonds, so it had very little intrinsic worth.*

in-tro-duce (ɪn-trə-duʷs) v. **-duced, -ducing 1.** To make people known to each other by name for the first time: *Would you please introduce me to your friend? I'd like to get to know her.* **2.** To bring into use for the first time: *They introduced a new game at the party.* **3.** To present a plan and recommend it **4.** To inform of sthg. for the first time **5.** To produce the first part of sthg., esp. to suggest or explain the main part: *The first chapter of the book introduces the main characters.*

in-tro-duc-tion (ɪn-trə-dʌk-ʃən) n. **1.** The act

of introducing people to each other or the state of being introduced 2. An explanation at the beginning of a book or speech 3. A book or a course of study that gives one a basic knowledge of the subject before going on to advanced studies: *An Introduction to Biology* —**introductory** adj. *They had an introductory offer on the new product. They were selling it at a very low price.*

in-tro-spec-tion (ın–trə–spek–ʃən) n. Self-examination; the examination of one's own thoughts, feelings, etc. —**introspect** v. —**introspective** adj. —**introspectively** adv.

in-tro-vert (**ın**–trə–vɜrt) n. A person whose interest is more in himself than in his environment or in other people

in-trude (ın–tru^wd) v. -**truded, -truding** To enter or force one's way in where not wanted —**intruder** n.

in-tru-sion (ın–tru^w–ʒən) n. The act of intruding: *Pardon the intrusion, but there's sthg. you need to know.*

in-tu-i-tion (ın–tu^w–ıʃ–ən) n. The power of knowing or understanding sthg. immediately without reasoning or being taught

in-tu-i-tive (ın–tu^w–ət–ıv) adj. Having or showing intuition

in-ure (ın–yʊər) v. -**ured, -uring** To become accustomed to sthg. such as pain, heat, etc.

in-vade (ın–ve^yd) v. -**vaded, -vading** 1. To enter by force into a country or island to take control of it 2. To enter in large numbers: *Students invade the resort town of Palm Springs every year at spring break.* 3. To enter into and disturb or harm: *Germs invaded his bloodstream.* —**invader** n.

in-va-lid (ın–və–ləd) n. A person who is disabled by illness or injury: *She's been an invalid since her accident five years ago.*

in-val-id (ın–**væl**–əd) adj. Not valid; falsely based; unjustified: *an invalid passport* —**in-va-lid-i-ty** (ın–və–lıd–ə–ti^y) n.

in-val-i-date (ın–**væl**–ə–de^yt) v. -**dated, -dating** To make invalid, esp. to weaken and make valueless —opposite VALIDATE —**in-val-i-da-tion** (ın–væl–ə–**de**^y–ʃən) n.

in-val-u-a-ble (ın–**væl**–yə–bəl/ –**væl**–yu^w–ə–bəl) adj. 1. Too valuable to be measured; priceless 2. Greatly appreciated: *Thanks so much for your invaluable suggestions.*

in-var-i-a-ble (ın–**veər**–i^y–ə–bəl) adj. Constant; unchanging —**invariably** adv. Always

in-va-sion (ın–ve^y–ʒən) n. 1. An act of invading 2. The entrance or spread of sthg. usu. harmful —see INVADE

in-vec-tive (ın–**vɛk**–tıv) adj. Characterized by vehement denunciation; abusive

invective n. Words of hate or scorn

in-veigh (ın–ve^y) v. To protest vehe-mently

in-vei-gle (ın–**ve**^y–gəl/ –**vi**^y–) v. -**gled, -gling** To coax sbdy. into doing sthg.: *The little girl could inveigle her father into doing almost anything for her.*

in-vent (ın–**vɛnt**) v. 1. To make, design, or produce for the first time: *Thomas Edison invented the phonograph in 1877.* 2. To make up or think of sthg. unreal or untrue: *Can't you invent a better story than that?* NOTE: The word "discover" refers to finding sthg. that existed before but was not known, such as a place or a fact. "Invent" refers to making sthg. that did not exist before, such as a machine or a method

in-ven-tion (ın–**vɛn**–tʃən) n. 1. The act of inventing 2. Sthg. invented: *The computer was a remarkable invention.*

in-ven-tive (ın–**vɛnt**–ıv) adj. Capable of inventing: *an inventive mind* —**inventively** adv. —**inventiveness** n. —**inventor** n.

in-ven-to-ry (ın–vən–tɔr–i^y) n. -**ries** A list of all the goods in a store, business, etc.

in-verse (ın–**vɜrs**) adj. Opposite in order

in-vert (ın–**vɜrt**) v. Turn upside down or reverse the order of

in-ver-te-brate (ın–**vɜr**–tə–brət/ –bre^yt) n. Not having a backbone: *Insects are invertebrates.*

in-vest (ın–**vɛst**) v. 1. To use money to buy shares, property, or other things that will increase in value to make more money: *He invested in a large piece of property near the new airport.* 2. To make use of one's time, effort, etc. for future benefits or advantages, esp. in a way that involves some sacrifice: *He invested a lot of time in preparing himself for his profession.* —**investment** n.

in-ves-ti-gate (ın–vɛs–tə–ge^yt) v. -**gated, -gating** To examine carefully and systematically, inquiring about the character of peo-

ple and the reasons for sthg., etc. —in-ves-ti-ga-tion n. investigator n

in-ves-ti-ture (m–**vɛs**-tə–t∫ər/ –t∫yʊər) n. A ceremony giving the robes of high rank or office to sbdy.

in-vet-er-ate (m–**vɛt**-ə–rət) adj. Firmly fixed in a habit: *an inveterate gambler*

in-vid-i-ous (m–**vɪd**-iʸ–əs) adj. Likely to cause ill-will or envy: *the invidious task of judging the baby competition*

in-vig-or-ate (m–**vɪg**-ə–reʸt) v. -ated, -ating To give vigor or vitality to; to animate

in-vin-ci-ble (m–**vɪn**-sə–bəl) adj. Unconquerable—in-vin-ci-bil-i-ty (m–vɪn-sə–**bɪl**-ə–tiʸ) n.

in-vi-o-la-ble (m–**vaɪ**-ə–lə–bəl) adj. Safe from violation: *Freedom of speech should be an inviolable right.*

in-vis-i-ble (m–**vɪz**-ə–bəl) adj. Not visible; incapable of being seen: *He [Jesus] is the image of the invisible God. By him all things were created; things in heaven and on earth, visible and invisible...* (Colossians 1:15,16).

in-vi-ta-tion (m–və–**teʸ**–∫ən) n. The act of inviting

in-vite (m–**vaɪt**) v. -vited, -viting 1. To request the presence or participation of someone: *They invited me to dinner.* 2. To provoke: *He's inviting trouble by making those inflammatory speeches.*

in-vit-ing (m–**vaɪt**-ɪŋ) adj. Attractive; tempting: *That apple pie looks very inviting.* —opposite UNINVITING

in-vo-ca-tion (m–voʷ–**keʸ**–∫ən) n. 1. The act of appealing to a higher authority 2. A prayer used in invoking

in-voice (m–**vɔɪs**) n. A detailed list of goods shipped or service rendered, with an account of all costs

invoice v. -voiced, -voicing To make or send an invoice

in-voke (m–**voʷk**) v. -voked, -voking 1. To call upon God in prayer 2. To call for the help or protection of: *to invoke the law* 3. To resort to: *The president invoked his veto power.*

in-vol-un-tar-y (m–**vɑl**-ən–tɛər–iʸ) adj. 1. Not done by the control of the will 2. Not done by choice 3. Unintentional

in-volve (m–**vɑlv**) v. -volved, -volving 1. To become a participant: *Don't get involved in*

too many jobs at the same time. 2. To have as a part of itself: *This job involves a lot of travel.* —involvement n.

in-volved (m–**vɑlvd**) adj. 1. Difficult to understand; complex 2. Connected in relationships and activities with others, esp. in a close personal way: *They are very involved with their family.*

in-vul-ner-a-ble (m–**vʌl**–nər–ə–bəl) adj. That cannot be successfully attacked

in-ward (m–**wərd**) adj. 1. Towards the inside 2. Of the inner being: *inward happiness* —opposite OUTWARD —inwardly adv.

i-o-dine, -din (**aɪ**-ə–dam/ –dɪn) n. A nonmetallic element used in medicine, photography, and analysis

i-on (**iʸ**–ən/iʸ–ɑn) n. An electrically charged atom or group of atoms

i-on-o-sphere (aɪ–**ɑn**–ə–sfɪər) n. The outer part of the earth's atmosphere, from about 25 miles out, extending to the highests parts of the atmosphere

i-o-ta (aɪ–**oʷt**-ə) n. (only used in negatives) A very, very small amount: *not an iota of truth in it*

ir– (**ɪr**) A prefix meaning "not" before many adjectives that begin with "r" such as irrational, irreconcilable, irrefutable, irregular, irresistible, irresponsible

i-ras-ci-ble (ɪr–**æs**-ə–bəl/ iʸ–**ræs**–) adj. Easily excited to anger; irritable

i-rate (aɪ–**reʸ**t) adj. Angry

ire (**aɪr**/ **aɪ**–ər) n. Anger; wrath

ir-i-des-cent (ɪr–ə–**dɛs**–ənt) adj. Shining or glittering with the colors of the rainbow

i-ris (**aɪ**-rəs) n. 1. The colored part around the pupil of the eye 2. A tall flower with sword-shaped leaves and white, yellow, or purple flowers

irk (**ɜrk**) v. To be tiresome; to annoy; trouble

irk-some (**ɜrk**-səm) adj. Annoying; tiresome

i-ron (**aɪ**-ərn) n. 1. A very common and the most frequently used of all metals that is a simple substance (element), esp. used in the making of steel 2. A flat-bottomed appliance with a handle, used when heated to press clothing and other fabrics

iron adj. 1. Of or relating to iron 2. Having a very strong character; unyielding: *an iron*

man

iron v. **1.** To make clothes smooth with an iron **2. iron sthg. out** To remove the difficulty or solve it: *to iron out the misunderstandings*

i-ron-clad (aɪ–ərn–klæd) adj. **1.** Covered with iron **2.** Strict; rigid: An ironclad rule

i-ron-ic (aɪ–ron–ɪk) or **ironical** adj. **1.** Of, related to, or marked by irony **2.** Given to irony —**ironically** adv.

i-ro-ny (aɪ–rə–niʸ / aɪ–ər–niʸ) n. **1.** A sarcastic or humorous use of words to express the opposite of what one really means **2.** A result or ending which is just the opposite of what was expected

ir-ra-di-ate (ɪ–reʸ–diʸ–eʸt) v. -ated, -ating **1.** To shed light upon **2.** To enlighten **3.** To expose to radiation

ir-ra-tion-al (ɪ–ræʃ–ən–əl) adj. **1.** Incapable of reasoning: *irrational beasts* **2.** Not based on reason: *irrational fears* —**ir-ra-tion-al-i-ty** (ɪ–ræʃ–ən–æl–ət–iʸ) n. —**irrationally** adv.

ir-rec-on-cil-a-ble (ɪ–rɛk–ən–saɪ–lə–bəl) adj. Not willing or ready to be reconciled; incapable of being brought into harmony or adjustment: *They could never agree; their views were irreconcilable.*

ir-re-deem-a-ble (ɪ–iʸ–diʸm–ə–bəl) adj. **1.** Of paper money, not exchangeable for coins **2.** Incapable of being redeemed, that is, bought back or paid off NOTE: All people everywhere are in need of redemption, since all have sinned (broken God's laws) and fall short of the glory of God (Romans 3:23). But no one, not even the worst criminal, is irredeemable. For we are justified freely by his [God's] grace through the redemption which is in Christ Jesus (Romans 3:24). For the wages of sin is death, but the gift of God is eternal life through Jesus Christ our Lord (Romans 6:23). We were not redeemed with perishable things such as silver or gold, but with the precious blood of Christ (1 Peter 1:18-19). —see JESUS, SIN, REDEEMER, REDEMPTION, GRACE

ir-re-duc-i-ble (ɪ–ɪ–dyuʷ–sə–bəl) adj. Not able to be reduced

ir-ref-u-ta-ble (ɪ–rɛf–yə–tə–bəl/ɪ–ɪ–fyuʷ–tə–bəl) adj. Too strong to be refuted or disproved: *The resurrection of Jesus Christ is an irrefutable fact of history. Many people saw him, talked with him, ate with him, etc. during the 40 days between his resurrection and his ascension into heaven. Because of this irrefutable fact, which assured them that Jesus was who he claimed to be, true God and Savior of the world, thousands of believers laid down their lives for the sake of the Gospel, the Good News that because he lives, we shall live also, forever and ever with him in heaven.* —**irrefutably** adv.

ir-reg-u-lar (ɪ–rɛg–yə–lər) adj. **1.** Of shape, not regular; uneven; not level; having different sizes and shapes **2.** Of time, not scheduled **3.** Not conforming to the rules of grammar: The verb "walk, walked, walked" is regular, but "go, went, gone" is irregular.

ir-rel-e-vant (ɪ–rɛl–ə–vənt) adj. Not relevant; beside the point; not having any connection with sthg. else; not applicable

ir-re-li-gious (ɪ–ɪ–lɪdʒ–əs) adj. **1.** Showing a lack of religion **2.** Showing hostility toward religion

ir-re-me-di-a-ble (ɪ–ɪ–miʸ–diʸ–ə–bəl) adj. Unable to be cured or repaired

ir-re-mov-a-ble (ɪ–ɪ–muʷv–ə–bəl) adj. That cannot be removed, such as a stain

ir-rep-ar-a-ble (ɪ–ɛp–ər–ə–bəl) adj. Not able to be repaired

ir-re-place-a-ble (ɪ–ɪ–pleʸ–sə–bəl) adj. Too good or too rare to be replaced if lost or stolen

ir-re-press-i-ble (ɪ–ɪ–prɛs–ə–bəl) adj. Not able to be subdued or repressed: *irrespressible cheerfulness*

ir-re-proach-a-ble (ɪ–ɪ–proʷ–tʃə–bəl) adj. Free from reproach or blame; innocent; faultless: *Since an overseer [pastor] is entrusted with God's work, he must be blameless [irreproachable]* (Titus 1:7).

ir-re-sist-i-ble (ɪ–ɪ–zɪs–tə–bəl) adj. Too strong, tempting, or delightful to be resisted

ir-res-o-lute (ɪ–ɛz–ə–luʷt) adj. Not firmly resolved or determined —**irresolutely** adv.

ir-re-spec-tive of (ɪ–ɪ–spɛk–tɪv ʌv) adj. + prep. Without regard to

ir-re-spon-si-ble (ɪ–ɪ–span–sə–bəl) adj. Hav-

ir-re-spon-si-ble (ɪr-ɪ-**spɑn**-sə-bəl) adj. Having no sense of responsibility; thoughtless —**ir-re-spon-si-bil-i-ty** (ɪr-ɪ-spɑn-sə-**bɪl**-ət-iʸ) n. —**irresponsibly** adv.

ir-re-triev-a-ble (ɪr-ɪ-**triʸ**-və-bəl) adj. That cannot be recovered or corrected —**irretrievably** adv.

ir-rev-er-ent (ɪr-**ɛv**-ər-ənt) adj. Showing no respect or reverence, esp. for sacred things: *It is irreverent to talk loudly in church.*

ir-re-vers-i-ble (ɪr-ɪ-**vɜr**-sə-bəl) adj. Incapable of being reversed or changed

ir-re-voc-a-ble (ɪr-**ɛv**-ə-kə-bəl) adj. That cannot be changed: *an irrevocable decision* —**irrevocably** adv.

ir-ri-gate (ɪr-ə-**geʸ**t) v. -**gated,** -**gating** To supply water to dry land, esp. by artificial means —**ir-ri-ga-tion** (ɪr-ə-**geʸ**-ʃən) n.

ir-ri-ta-ble (ɪr-ɪ-tə-bəl) adj. Easily made angry —**ir-ri-ta-bil-i-ty** (ɪr-ə-tə-**bɪl**-ət-iʸ) n. —**irritably** adv.

ir-ri-tant (ɪr-ə-tənt) n. A substance that irritates —**irritant** adj.

ir-ri-tate (ɪr-ə-teʸt) v. -**tated,** -**tating 1.** To make angry **2.** To cause pain and soreness: *Smoke irritates my eyes.*

ir-ri-ta-ting (ɪr-ə-teʸt-ɪŋ) adj. Tending to annoy: *He has an irritating voice*

ir-ri-ta-tion (ɪr-ə-**teʸ**-ʃən) n. The process of irritating or the condition of being irritated

is (ɪz) v. Third person singular., present tense of **be**

I-sa-iah (aɪ-**zeʸ**-ə) n. **1.** A book of the Old Testament attributed to the 8th century B.C. prophet, Isaiah, especially rich in Messianic references, prophecies fulfilled by our Lord and Savior Jesus Christ some 700 years later **2.** The prophet, Isaiah, generally regarded as the greatest of the Old Testament prophets because he is preeminently the prophet of redemption, and because many of the passages in his book are among the finest in literature. The name Isaiah means "Salvation of Jehovah."

Is-lam (ɪs-lɑm/ ɪs-**lɑm**/ ɪz-) n. **1.** The religious faith of Muslims **2.** The civilization built on this faith **3.** An Arabic word meaning "Submission to the will of God."

is-land (aɪ-lənd) n. **1.** Land that is completely surrounded by water: *Greenland is an island.* **2. traffic island** *also* **safety island** *AmE.* A raised place in the middle of the street where people can wait for traffic to pass

isle (aɪl) n. A little island

is-n't (ɪz-ənt) v. Short for **is not**

i-so- (aɪ-sə-/ **aɪ**-soʷ-) Prefix Equal

i-so-bar (**aɪ**-sə-bɑr) n. A line on a map connecting points where the barometric pressure is the same

i-so-late (aɪ-sə-leʸt) v. -**lated,** -**lating** To be separated from others: *Several towns have been isolated by the floods.* —**i-so-la-tion** (aɪ-sə-**leʸ**-ʃən) n. *Mary didn't like living in such isolation -- so far from town.*

i-so-la-ted (aɪ-sə-leʸt-əd) adj. **1.** Standing alone: *an isolated farmhouse* **2.** The only one of its kind: *an isolated case*

i-so-met-ric (aɪ-sə-**me**-trɪk) or **i-so-met-ri-cal** (aɪ-sə-**me**-trɪ-kəl) adj. **1.** Having equality of measure **2.** Pertaining to isometrics

i-so-met-rics (aɪ-sə-**me**-trɪks) n. An exercise in which one muscle is employed against another or against an immovable object

i-sos-ce-les (aɪ-**sɑs**-ə-liʸz) adj. Of a triangle, having two sides of equal length

i-so-therm (**aɪ**-sə-θɜrm) n. A line on a map connecting places having the same temperature

Is-ra-el (ɪz-riʸ-ɛl/ -reʸ-ɛl) n. **1.** A masculine name **2.** Jacob, grandson of Abraham **3.** Ancient land of the Hebrews at the southeast end of the Mediterranean **4.** The country between the Mediterranean Sea and the country of Jordan established in 1948 **5.** The Jewish people, as descendants of Israel

is-sue (ɪʃ-uʷ) n. **1.** The act of coming out or bringing sthg. out: *the issue of the new stamp* **2.** A discharge as of blood from the body **3.** A point of debate or controversy: *What will be the main issues of this debate?*

issue v. -**sued,** -**suing 1.** To bring out sthg. (esp. sthg. printed): *The government is issuing some new stamps.* **2.** To supply or provide officially: *Our passports were issued in New Orleans.* **3.** To flow out: *Blood issued from his wounds.*

isth-mus (ɪs-məs) n. A narrow strip of land which connects two larger land surfaces: *the*

Isthmus of Panama

it (ɪt) pron. **1.** Used (as subject or object) to refer to a human being whose sex is unknown, to an animal, to a plant or any nonliving thing, or to an idea or other abstraction: *Who is it? (in response to a knock on the door)/ Whose idea was it?/Whose book is it?* **2.** Used in statements in the normal subject or object position to indicate that there is a longer subject or object, esp. in statements about weather, time, or distance: *It's raining./ It's Friday./What time is it?/It's your turn to drive.* **3.** Used with the verb **be** to make part of a sentence more emphatic: *It was Bill who told me. (=Bill told me, not Tom)/It was just an hour ago that I heard the news. (=I just heard the news an hour ago, not a bit earlier)* **4.** Used to refer to a general situation or state of affairs: *I can't help it. I don't know what to do about it.*

i-tal-ics (ɪ–tæl–ɪks/ aɪ–tæl–ɪks) n. A style of printing with sloping letters: *This sentence is printed in italics.* —**italic** adj.

itch (ɪtʃ) v. **1.** To feel a sensation on the skin which makes one want to scratch: *My arm itches where the mosquito bit me.* **2.** *fig.* To have a restless desire to do sthg.: *I'm itching to visit my old friends again.* —**itch** n. —**itchy** adj. **-ier, -iest**

i-tem (aɪt–əm) n. **1.** A single thing on a list **2. a news item** A short news article in a newspaper or magazine

i-tem-ize (aɪt–ə–maɪz) v. **-ized, -izing** To list item by item: *I need a list of repairs. Please itemize them.*

i-tin-er-ant (aɪ–tɪn–ər–ənt) adj. Traveling from place to place: *an itinerant preacher*

i-tin-er-ar-y (aɪ–tɪn–ə–rɛər–iʸ) n. **1.** A plan of a journey **2.** Route **3.** Record of a journey

it'll (ɪt–əl) v. Short for **it will**

its (ɪts) determ. Possessive form of it: *The dog wagged its tail.*

it's (ɪts) Short for **1. it is:** *It's Friday./It's cloudy.* **2. it has:** *It's been raining all day.*

it-self (ɪt–sɛlf) pron. **1.** Used reflexively, for emphasis as the object of a verb or of a preposition, when the person or the thing that does the action is also the object of the action: *The dog was limping because it had hurt itself on the hind leg.* **2.** Used to make "it," or the name of a thing or creature, stronger: *The book itself is very boring; I don't think they should make a movie of it.*

–i-ty (ət–iʸ) suffix State or quality: *vulgarity*

I've (aɪv) Short for **I have:** *I've lived here a long time.*

i-vo-ry (aɪ–vər–iʸ) n. **-ries 1.** The hard creamy-white material of which elephants' tusks are made **2.** A creamy-white color: *Print the letter on ivory. (=ivory colored paper)*

i-vy (aɪ–viʸ) n. **-vies** Any of various climbing plants with shiny evergreen leaves

–ize (–aɪz) *AmE.* **–ise** *BrE.* suffix **1. (a)** To cause to become; make into: *dramatize* **(b)** To cause to conform to or resemble: *Anglicize/ Romanize* **(c)** To treat as: *idolize* **2. (a)** To affect with: *magnetize* **(b)** To subject to: *terrorize* **3.** To treat according to: *pasteurize* **4.** To become or become like: *fossilize* **5.** To perform, engage in, or produce: *scandalize*

J, j (dʒeʸ) n. The 10th letter of the English alphabet

jab (dʒæb) v. **-bb-** To poke or push with a pointed object: *She jabbed herself in the foot.*

jab n. A sudden rough blow

jab-ber (dʒæb-ər) v. To talk fast and not clearly: *She's jabbering about sthg., but I can't understand her.*

jack (dʒæk) n. A device for raising sthg. heavy off the ground, esp. a car

jack v. To lift sthg. with a jack: *We had to jack up the wheel to change a tire.*

jack-al (dʒæk-əl) n. A dog-like wild animal of Asia and Africa and southeastern Europe.

jack-ass (dʒæk-æs) n. **1.** A male donkey **2.** *Infml.* A stupid person

jack-et (dʒæk-ət) n. A short coat with sleeves

jack-pot (dʒæk-pɑt) n. **1.** In games of chance, a fund of prize money that keeps increasing until it is won **2.** *infml.* **hit the jackpot (a)** To win the biggest possible prize **(b)** To achieve a major success

jade (dʒeʸd) n. A precious stone (usu. green) used for making jewelry and ornaments

jad-ed (dʒeʸd-əd) adj. Worn out; exhausted; dulled by over-indulgence

jag (dʒæg) n. **1.** A sharp, projecting point **2.** *slang* A period of uncontrollable activity: *a crying jag* **3.** *slang* A drinking bout; spree

jag-ged (dʒæg-əd) adj. Having a rough, uneven, often sharp, edge

jag-uar (dʒæg-wɑr/ –uʷ–ɑr) n. A large, ferocious, leopard-like cat of tropical America

jail (dʒeʸl) n. A prison or place of punishment for criminals

jail-er, jail-or (dʒeʸ-lər) n. One who is in charge of a prison or prisoners

Jain (dʒeʸn) n. An adherent of Jainism

Jain-ism (dʒeʸn-ɪz–əm) n. A religion of India originating in the sixth century B.C. and teaching liberation of the soul by right knowledge, right faith, and right conduct

ja-lop-y (dʒə-lɑp–iʸ) n. **-ies** A battered, worn-out car

SPELLING NOTE:
Words having the sound /dʒ/ may be spelled with **g-**, like **gentle.**

---

jam (dʒæm) v. **-mm- 1.** To force sthg. tightly into a space: *She had jammed her suitcase so full she could hardly get it shut.* **2.** To push hard and suddenly: *The bus driver jammed on the brakes and everyone flew forward.* **3.** To become unworkable because sthg. is stuck: *The ship is jammed in the ice and can't move.* **4.** To make radio messages difficult to hear by broadcasting at the same time

jam n. **1.** Crowding together of people or things so that movement is difficult or impossible: *a traffic jam* **2.** A preserve made by boiling fruit with sugar, used esp. as a spread on bread —compare JELLY **3. get into/be in a jam** *infml.* Get into/ be in trouble

jam-bo-ree (dʒæm-bə-riʸ) n. **1.** Any noisy merrymaking **2.** A national or international gathering, as of Boy Scouts

James (dʒeʸmz) n. **1.** One of the inspired books of the New Testament in which the writer stresses the point that "faith without works is dead," that if we have faith in Jesus Christ, we will, out of love for him, do good works **2.** The Apostle James, author of the above named book —see BIBLE, NEW TESTAMENT

jan-gle (dʒæŋ-gəl) v. **-gled, -gling 1.** To make a harsh, unpleasant ringing sound **2.** To upset or irritate

jan-i-tor (dʒæn-ə-tər) n. *AmE.* caretaker *BrE.* Custodian; a person who is employed to take care of a building, doing the cleaning and making repairs

Jan-u-ar-y (dʒæn-yə-wɛər-iʸ/ –yuʷ–) n. **-ies** also **Jan.** *written abbr.* The first month of the year

jar (dʒɑr) v. **-rr-** To give a sudden or painful shock to sbdy. or sthg.: *Falling on the sidewalk really jarred my back.*

jar n. **1.** Sthg. that causes a sudden or painful shock **2.** A short-necked, wide-mouthed container made of glass, stone, clay, etc.: *The cookie jar is empty.* **3.** The contents of such a container: *a jar of peaches*

jar-gon (dʒɑr-gən) n. Language that is difficult to understand except by members of a particular group: *medical jargon*

jas-per (dʒæs-pər) n. An opaque variety of

quartz, usu. red, yellow, or brown

jaun-dice (dʒɔn–dəs) n. **1.** A diseased condition of the liver, characterized by yellowness of skin and eyeballs **2.** An embittered state of mind

jaundice v. **-diced, -dicing 1.** To affect with jaundice **2.** To make bitter or biased —**jaundiced** adj.

jaunt (dʒɔnt) n. A short, usu. pleasurable journey

jav-e-lin (dʒæv–lən/ dʒæv–ə–lən) n. A light spear, esp. one used in an athletic event

jaw (dʒɔ) n. Either of the two bony parts of the face which contain the teeth: *He hit me in the jaw and knocked a tooth loose.*

jay (dʒeʸ) n. A brightly colored bird of the crow family

jay-walk (dʒeʸ–wɔk) v. To cross the street recklessly, violating traffic regulations or signals

jazz (dʒæz) n. **1.** Music having a strong, characteristic rhythm, originated by black Americans, usu. with each musician of the band doing some free playing **2. all that jazz** *slang* Additional, related items

jazz v. **1.** To quicken; speed up **2. to jazz up** To make more exciting

jeal-ous (dʒɛl–əs) adj. **1.** Showing fear or resentment of possible rivals in love or affection: *a jealous husband* **2.** Showing resentment over someone else's belongings, achievements, etc.; envious: *She's jealous of her sister's new car.* **3.** Possessive; wanting to keep what one has: *jealous of her career* —**jealously** adv.

jeal-ous-y (dʒɛl–ə–siʸ) n. **-ies** Jealous feeling: *The acts of the sinful nature are obvious: sexual immorality... idolatry... hatred, discord, jealousy, fits of rage, selfish ambition... Those who live like this will not inherit the kingdom of God* (Galatians 5:20,21). NOTE: God detests jealousy and all sin, but because of his great love and mercy he forgives the sins of those who repent (turn from their evil ways) and put their trust in Jesus for eternal life (Acts 2:38; 16:31).

jeans (dʒiʸnz) n. Pants made of a strong, cotton cloth for informal wear

jeep (dʒiʸp) n. A small, durable, four-wheel

drive motor vehicle, used esp. by the armed forces or for traveling over rough ground

jeer (dʒɪər) v. To speak or shout at sbdy. with derision or mockery —**jeer** n.

Je-ho-vah (dʒə–hoʷ–və) n. The name of God most frequently used in the Hebrew Scriptures, but commonly represented in English versions by "Lord"

jel-ly (dʒɛl–iʸ) n. **-lies 1.** A spread for bread made out of fruit juice strained and then boiled with sugar, so as to become clear —compare JAM **2.** Any jelly-like substance that is between a liquid and a solid state

jeop-ard-ize, also **-ise** *BrE.* (dʒɛp–ər–daɪz) v. **-ized, -izing** *fml.* To put in possible danger: *Failing to arrive on time could jeopardize your job.*

jeop-ar-dy (dʒɛp–ərd–iʸ) n. **-dies** Danger: *His careless spending has put the future of the company in jeopardy.*

Jer-e-mi-ah (dʒɛər–ə–maɪ–ə) n. The Old Testament book containing the prophecies of the seventh century B.C. Hebrew prophet, Jeremiah —see BIBLE, OLD TESTAMENT

jerk (dʒɜrk) v. **1.** To pull quickly and suddenly: *The impatient rider jerked the reins and the horse came to a sudden stop.* **2.** To move with a short, sudden action or a series of such actions: *The old car jerked along the rough, country road.*

jerk n. **1.** A short, sudden pull or movement **2.** *AmE. derog. infml.* A stupid or foolish person: *He's a real jerk! He stepped on my foot and didn't even say he was sorry.*

jerk-y (dʒɜrk–iʸ) adj. **-ier, -iest** With sudden starts and stops

jerk-y n. Meat, esp. beef, cut into strips and dried in the sun

jer-sey (dʒɜr–ziʸ) n. **-seys** A close-fitting, knitted garment, often worn over a shirt or blouse

jest (dʒɛst) n. **1.** Sthg. said or done to provoke laughter; a joke **2.** Playfulness; fun

jest v. **1.** To make amusing remarks **2.** To speak or act playfully

Jesus Christ (dʒiʸ–zəs kraɪst/ –zəz) n. True God and Savior of the world (1 John 5:20; Colossians 2:9) who came down from heaven to take our place [the place of all of us

sinners] under the law and keep the law perfectly for us and then to pay for all our sins with his own blood (1 John 1:9). NOTE: On the 3rd day he rose again from the dead (Luke 24:5-7). After appearing to his followers for forty days (Acts 1:3; 1 Corinthians 15:3-8), proving that he really was alive, and giving them final instructions, he returned to heaven to prepare a place for those who believe in him (John 14:3) and to rule over all things (Hebrews 1:3; Matthew 28:18). Before he returned to his heavenly throne, he promised that he would come again with power and great glory (Matthew 24:30) to judge the living and the dead (Acts 10:42). Those who believe in him will enjoy all the glory and splendor of heaven with Jesus for ever and ever (John 3:16). Those who reject Jesus and trust in their own "good deeds" or in their idols or anything else will be judged accordingly and found wanting. They will be cast into eternal flames prepared for the devil and his angels (Matthew 25:41) to suffer for ever and ever (2 Thessalonians 1:9; Revelation 21:8). Tragically, many perish needlessly, for anyone, no matter how wicked, can be saved if he will just turn from his evil ways and trust in Jesus. Whoever believes in him will not perish, but have eternal life (John 3:16). If you confess with your mouth, "Jesus is Lord," and believe in your heart that God has raised him from the dead, you will be saved (Romans 10:9,13). —see GOD, MAN, SIN, SAVIOR, REDEEMER

jet (dʒɛt) n. **1.** A strong, narrow stream of liquid, steam, gas, or flame shooting out of a small hole: *a jet of water from the fireman's hose* **2.** The narrow opening from which this comes: *She lit the gas jet on the oven.* **3.** A jet airplane: *We often travel by jet.* **4.** A hard coal-like mineral used in making jewelry **5.** A deep, lustrous black

jet adj. **1.** Made of jet **2.** Black like jet

jet v. **1.** To shoot out like liquid in a fast stream **2.** To travel or convey by jet plane

jet-ty (dʒɛt-iʸ) n. **-ties 1.** A structure projecting into a body of water to influence the current or protect a harbor or shoreline **2.** A wharf; pier

Jew (dʒuʷ) n. **1.** An Israelite **2.** One whose religion is Judaism: *I have declared to both Jews and Greeks that they must turn to God in repentance and have faith in our Lord Jesus* (Acts 20:21). —**Jewish** adj. —see JUDAISM

jew-el (dʒuʷ-əl) n. **1.** A precious stone **2.** An ornament set with one or more of these and worn on clothes or on the body **3.** *spir.* Lips *that speak knowledge are a rare jewel* (Proverbs 20:15).

jew-el-er *AmE.* **jeweller** *BrE.* (dʒuʷ-ə-lər) n. A person who makes, repairs, or deals in jewelry

jew-el-ry *AmE.* **jew-el-ler-y** *BrE.* (dʒuʷ-əl-riʸ) n. Jewels: *Wives... your beauty should not come from outward adornment, such as braided hair and the wearing of gold jewelry and fine clothes. Instead, it should be that of your inner self, the unfading beauty of a gentle and quiet spirit, which is of great worth in God's sight* (1 Peter 3:3,4).

jibe (dʒaɪb) v. **jibed, jibing** *infml.* To fit or agree with: *Your information doesn't jibe with mine.* NOTE: Do not confuse jibe with gibe.

jif-fy (dʒɪf-iʸ) n. **-fies** *infml.* A moment; a very short time: *I'll have it fixed in a jiffy.*

jig (dʒɪg) n. **1.** A rapid, springy dance, often in triple time **2.** A guiding tool; template

jig v. To dance or play music in jig time

jig-gle (dʒɪg-əl) v. **-gled, -gling** To move with quick little jerks from side to side or up and down: *Stop jiggling and sit still for a while.* —**jiggle** n. —**jiggly** adj.

jig-saw (dʒɪg-sɔ) n. A saw with a narrow blade, used to cut curves or irregular lines

jig-saw puz-zle (dʒɪg-sɔ pʌz-əl) n. A picture cut into irregular pieces that can be fitted together again

ji-had (dʒɪ-hɑd) n. A holy war undertaken by Muslims

jin-gle (dʒɪŋ-gəl) v. **-gled, -gling** To make or cause to make a tinkling or ringing metallic sound: *She jingled the doorbell impatiently, but nobody answered.*

jingle n. **1.** A repeated clinking sound as of coins or light metal objects striking against each other **2.** A simple, repetitious rhyme or tune, usually of poor quality, especially as a

radio or TV advertisement: *an advertising jingle*

jinx (dʒɪŋks) *n*. Sthg. that is thought to bring bad luck: *He thought someone had put a jinx on his car because it was always breaking down.*

jinx *v. infml.* To bring bad luck to

jit-ters (dʒɪt-ərz) *n*. Extreme nervousness: *I always get the jitters before I have to give a speech.* —**jittery** *adj.*

jive (dʒaɪv) *n*. **1.** Swing music or dancing performed to it **2.** Deceptive or foolish talk

job (dʒab) *n*. **1.** Regular paid position: *Did you find a job yet? They're looking for people at the bank.* **2.** A task; a piece of work: *When you finish that job you can sweep the floor.* **3.** Sthg. difficult to do: *Just getting a chance to talk to the mayor on the phone was quite a job.*

Job (dʒoʷb) *n*. **1.** One of the books of the Old Testament, universally recognized as superb literature. NOTE: The book is named after its principal character who lived in the land of Uz, evidently somewhere south of Damascus and east of Palestine. The book of Job centers around the perplexing question of why the righteous suffer and how their suffering can be reconciled with the infinite goodness and holiness of God. **2.** Job, the man NOTE: Job is known for his great patience. Even in the midst of great suffering he could say, "I know that my Redeemer lives, and that in the end he will stand upon the earth. And after my skin has been destroyed, yet in my flesh I will see God. I myself will see him with my own eyes — I, and not another" (Job 19:25-27). Although Job had lost ten children, 7,000 sheep, 3,000 camels, 500 yoke of oxen, and 500 donkeys, he said,"Naked I came from my mother's womb, and naked I will depart. The Lord gave and the Lord has taken away; may the name of the Lord be praised" (Job 1:21-22). The Lord blessed the latter part of Job's life more than the first. He gave him twice as much as he had before (Job 42:10). —see BIBLE, OLD TESTAMENT

jock-ey (dʒak-iʸ) *n*. **-eys** A person who rides a horse, esp. as a professional in a race

jockey (for position) *v*. **-eyed, -eying** To ma-

neuver for a favorable position: *It seems like everyone in this company is jockeying for a better administrative position.*

joc-u-lar (dʒak–yə–lər) *adj*. Funny; joking

Jo-el (dʒoʷ–əl) *n*. A book of the Old Testament by the Hebrew prophet, Joel. The key thought is national repentance and its blessings. —see BIBLE, OLD TESTAMENT

jog (dʒag) *v*. **-gg- 1.** To move slowly and unsteadily, esp. up and down: *The wagon jogged along the country road.* **2.** To run slowly and steadily for a time: *My son jogs six miles every morning.* **3. jog someone's memory** To remind someone of sthg.

jog *n*. A slow, steady run

jog-gle (dʒag–əl) *v*. **-gled, -gling** To shake slightly

joggle *n*. A slight shake or jolt

John (dʒan) *n*. **1.** One of the four Gospels of the New Testament which emphasizes the love of God, and was written "that you [the reader] may believe that Jesus is the Christ, the Son of God, and that by believing you may have life in his name" (John 20:31). —see BIBLE, NEW TESTAMENT **2.** The Apostle John, the author of the Gospel that bears his name, and of I, II, and III John and Relevation in the New Testament

join (dʒɔɪn) *v*. **1.** To fasten one thing to another; connect with; unite: *These two pipes are joined. I can't get them apart./two people joined in marriage* **2.** To do sthg. together with: *Two more couples would like to join us on the tour of the city.* **3.** To become a member or employee of: *My son has joined the air force.* **4. join forces with** To work together for a common purpose

joint (dʒɔɪnt) *n*. **1.** A place or point at which two or more parts of the same thing come together: *Be sure the boards are fastened well at the joint.* **2.** A place where bones are joined together: *elbow joint* **3.** A low-class public place, esp. one where people go for amusement

joint *adj*. Shared, held, or done by two or more people: *joint ownership* —**jointly** *adv.*

joist (dʒɔɪst) *n*. One of the beams on which the floor is laid or to which the ceiling is fastened

joke (dʒoʷk) n. **1.** Sthg. said or done to cause laughter or amusement: *He's very good at telling jokes. Everyone laughs at them.* **2.** **play a joke on someone** Trick sbdy. in order to make other people laugh at him —**jokingly** adv.

joke v. **joked, joking** v. To tell jokes: *But among you [Christians], there must not be...foolish talk or coarse [vulgar] joking, which are out of place, but rather thanksgiving* (Ephesians 5: 3,4).

jo-ker (dʒoʷ-kər) n. **1.** One who tells or plays jokes **2.** A playing card, used in certain games as the highest ranking card or as a wild card

jol-ly (dʒal–iʸ) adj. **-lier, -liest** Merry; happy; cheerful; lively: *a jolly fellow*

jolt (dʒoʷlt) v. **1.** To cause to move in jerks: *The car jolted along the rough road.* **2.** To shock: *Getting fired from my job jolted me into going back to school for more training.* —**jolt** n.

Jo-nah (dʒoʷ–nə) n. A book of the Old Testament containing the story of the eighth or ninth century Hebrew prophet, Jonah —see BIBLE, OLD TESTAMENT

Josh-u-ua (dʒaʃ–yuʷ–ə) n. A book of the Old Testament bearing the name of the Israelite leader, Joshua —see BIBLE, OLD TESTAMENT

jos-tle (dʒas–əl) v. **-tled, -tling** To push roughly: *We were jostled by the people on the crowded bus.*

jot (dʒat) v. **-tt-** To make a quick written note, esp. without preparation: *Jot the phone number down before you forget it.*

jot n. The smallest bit or particle; iota

jour-nal (dʒɜr–nəl) n. **1.** A diary **2.** A magazine, esp. one that deals seriously with special subjects: *She's reading the Journal of Linguistics.*

jour-nal-ism (dʒɜr–nəl–ɪz–əm) n. The profession of collecting, writing, editing, and publishing material for newspapers, magazines, radio, or TV —**jour-nal-is-tic** (dʒər–nəl–ɪs–tɪk) adj.

journ-al-ist (dʒɜr–nəl–əst) n. A person whose profession is journalism

jour-ney (dʒɜr–niʸ) v.**-neyed, -neying** To travel over or through; to go on a trip: *They jour-*

neyed across the Sahara by camel caravan.

journey n. **-neys** A trip of some distance: *Did you have a good journey?*

jo-vi-al (dʒoʷ–viʸ–əl) adj. Cheerful and good humored; friendly: *a jovial laugh* —**jovially** adv.

jowl (dʒaʊl/ dʒoʷl) n. **1.** The lower jaw and flesh around it **2.** The cheek

joy (dʒɔɪ) n. **1.** A feeling of delight, happiness, gladness, a source of pleasure: *My children are a great joy to me./ She was filled with joy when she won the prize.* **2.** The greatest joy, which is also a lasting joy, a fruit of the Holy Spirit: *The fruit of the Spirit is love, joy, peace...* (Galatians 5:22). *The joy of the Lord is your strength* (Nehemiah 8:10). *When an angel announced the birth of Jesus to the shepherds in the field, he said, "Do not be afraid, I bring you good news of great joy that will be for all people. Today... a Savior has been born to you; he is Christ the Lord"* (Luke 2:11). *There is rejoicing [joy] in the presence of the angels of God over one sinner who repents* (Luke 15:10). *St. John wrote: "I have no greater joy than to hear that my children are walking in the truth"* (3 John 4).

joy-ful (dʒɔɪ–fəl) adj. Filled with joy; showing or causing joy: *a joyful celebration/ Be joyful always, pray continuously...* (1 Thessalonians 5:16-17). —**joyfully** adv.

joy-ous (dʒɔɪ–əs) adj. Filled with or causing joy: *a joyous feeling* —**joyously** adv.

ju-bi-lant (dʒuʷ–bə–lənt) adj. Full of or showing great joy, esp. following a success: *Shout for joy to the Lord, all the earth, burst into jubilant song with music* (Psalm 98:4). —**ju-bilantly** adv. —**ju-bi-la-tion** (dʒuʷ–bə–leʸ–ʃən) n.

ju-bi-lee (dʒuʷ–bə–liʸ) n. A celebration, esp. to mark or remember some event: *The firm celebrated its golden jubilee (50th anniversary).*

Ju-da-ism (dʒuʷ–də–ɪz–əm) **1.** A religion developed among the ancient Hebrews and characterized by belief in one God who has revealed himself to Abraham, Moses, and the Hebrew prophets and by a religious life in accordance with the Old Testament Scriptures and the Talmud **2.** The cultural, social, and religious beliefs and practices of

the Jews 3. Jews collectively

Ju-das (dʒuʷ–dəs) n. Judas Iscariot, the disciple who betrayed Jesus for thirty pieces of silver as prophesied by Zechariah about 500 years earlier (Zechariah 11: 12).

Jude (dʒuʷd) n. A book of the New Testament written by the Apostle Jude —see BIBLE, NEW TESTAMENT

judge (dʒʌdʒ) v. **judged, judging 1.** To form or give an opinion about sbdy. or sthg. whether he, she, or it is right or wrong, or guilty or innocent of a sin or crime **2.** To evaluate another person's actions: *We are not to judge motives. Jesus said, "Do not judge, or you will be judged"* (Matthew 7:1). *Jesus warns his followers to "Stop judging by mere appearances, and make a right judgment"* (=do not be hypocritical or self-righteous in your judgment) (John 7:24). **3.** To make a decision, as in a beauty contest or figure skating contest, for example **4.** To guess or estimate, as in judging distance or speed —opposite MISJUDGE

judge n. **1.** A public official who hears and decides cases before a court of law **2.** God is the judge of all the earth: *Jesus is the One whom God appointed as judge of the living and dead. All the prophets testify about him that everyone who believes in him receives forgiveness of sins through his name* (Acts 10:42, 43). *Saint Paul wrote, "I have kept the faith [in Jesus]. Now there is in store for me the crown of righteousness which the Lord, the right-eous Judge will award to me on that day — and not only to me, but also to all who have longed for his appearance"* (2 Timothy 4:8). **3.** One appointed to make a decision in a contest **4.** A person who is qualified by his knowledge and experience to give valuable opinions: *He's a good judge of music.*

Judg-es (dʒʌdʒ–əz) n. A book of the Old Testament which contains a history of the Jewish people —see BIBLE, OLD TESTAMENT

judg-ment, or judge-ment (dʒʌdʒ–mənt) n. **1.** An official decision of a judge or court of law: *The court has still to pass judgment in the case./ It is appointed unto men once to die, but after this the judgment* (Hebrews 9:27 KJV). **2.** An opinion about sthg.: *I respect your judg-*

ment in this. **3.** The ability to judge wisely; good sense: *good/ poor judgment*

Judg-ment Day (dʒʌdʒ–mənt deʸ) n. The day when God will judge all people: *For we must all appear before the judgment seat of Christ [on that day]* (2 Corinthians 5:10).

ju-di-cial (dʒuʷ–dɪʃ–əl) adj. Of a court of law, a judge, or of his/ her judgment NOTE: A judicial decision is one made by a judge. A judicious decision is a wise decision made by anyone. —**judicially** adv.

ju-di-ci-ar-y (dʒuʷ–dɪʃ–iʸ–ɛər–iʸ) n. **-ies** The judges of a country taken as a whole —**judiciary** adj.

ju-di-cious (dʒuʷ–dɪʃ–əs) adj. Having or showing good sense; wise; prudent —**judiciously** adv.

ju-do (dʒuʷ–doʷ) n. A Japanese form of wrestling

jug (dʒʌg) n. also **pitcher,** *AmE.* A deep pot with a handle and a lip for pouring liquids

jug-gle (dʒʌg–əl) v. **-gled, -gling 1.** To throw several objects in the air, catch them and throw them up again and again, keeping one or more in the air at the same time **2.** To keep changing the arrangement of sthg. for a particular purpose, esp. to deceive someone: *I'll have to juggle my schedule to be able to come to the meeting, but I'll be there./The company's bookkeeper went to prison for juggling the accounts.*

jug-gler (dʒʌg–lər) n. A person who can do juggling tricks

jug-u-lar (dʒʌg-yuʷ–lər) n. One of the two large veins on either side of the neck bringing the blood back from the head

juice (dʒuʷs) n. **1.** The liquid made from fruit, vegetables, or meat: *tomato juice* **2.** The liquid in the stomach or certain other parts of the body that helps people and animals to digest food **3.** *infml.* Anything that produces power, esp. electricity: *The lights won't work. There's no juice.*

juic-y (dʒuʷ–siʸ) adj. **-ier, -iest** Having a lot of juice: *a juicy grapefruit*

ju-jit-su (dʒuʷ–dʒɪt–suʷ) n. A Japanese method of wrestling

Ju-ly (dʒuʷ–laɪ/ dʒə–laɪ) n. **-lies** The seventh month of the year

jum-ble (dʒʌm–bəl) v. -bled, -bling To mix or throw together without order

jum-ble n. A confused mixture

jump (dʒʌmp) v. **1.** To move quickly into the air by the force of one's legs; spring: *Can you imagine someone jumping over a bar almost eight feet above the ground?* **2.** To make a quick, sudden, movement of shock or surprise: *She jumped when the phone rang.* **3.** Of prices and quantities, to increase suddenly and sharply: *The price of houses jumped 27% in our city last year.* **4. jump the gun** To do sthg. too soon, before the proper time **5. jump at sthg.** To accept eagerly: *Who wouldn't jump at the chance to see Europe, especially with all expenses paid?*

jump n. An act of jumping

jum-per (dʒʌm–pər) n. **1.** A person or thing that jumps **2.** A parachutist **3.** A sleeveless dress, usu. worn over a blouse **4.** A loose jacket

jump-y (dʒʌm–piʸ) adj. -ier, -iest Nervous; anxious: *I was a little jumpy about speaking before the entire class.*

junc-tion (dʒʌŋk–ʃən) n. A place where two or more things join or meet: *When you reach the junction, turn to the left.*

junc-ture (dʒʌŋk–tʃər) n. *fml.* A point in time, esp. a turning point: *At this juncture in our lives, we need to make some wise decisions.*

June (dʒuʷn) n. The sixth month of the year

jun-gle (dʒʌŋ–gəl) n. **1.** An area of tropical land, covered with trees and bushes too thick to walk through easily **2.** *fig.* A place of ruthless competition or struggle for survival: *the jungle of the business world with its fierce competition*

jun-ior (dʒuʷn–yər) *written abbr.* Jr. adj. **1.** Younger, esp. when used to distinguish the son from the father of the same name: *Bill Smith, Jr.* **2.** Of or for younger persons: *junior dresses* **3.** Of lower rank or position: *a junior executive* —compare SENIOR

junior n. **1.** A younger person **2.** A less important person **3.** *AmE.* A student in the third year of a high school or university

jun-ior col-lege (dʒuʷn–yər kɑl–ɪdʒ) n. (in the US) A school of higher education at which a student can complete the first two years

of a university education

ju-ni-per (dʒuʷ–nə–pər) n. A type of evergreen shrub with berries and prickly leaves

junk (dʒʌŋk) n. *infml.* **1.** Rubbish; trash; useless things: *Take that junk to the city dump.* **2.** Scrap materials that can be converted into sthg. useful

junk food (dʒʌŋk fuʷd) n. *infml.* Food eaten as a snack and thought to have little value to one's health

jun-kie (dʒʌŋ–kiʸ) or **jun-ky** n. -kies A person who is addicted to drugs, esp. heroin

Ju-pi-ter (dʒuʷ–pə–tər) n. The largest planet in our solar system

ju-ris-dic-tion (dʒʊər–əs–dɪk–ʃən) n. **1.** Legal power or authority **2.** The district over which a judge, court, etc. has power

ju-ris-pru-dence (dʒʊər–əs–pruʷ–dəns) n. The study or knowledge of law

ju-rist (dʒʊər–ɪst) n. *fml.* An expert in law

ju-ror (dʒʊər–ər) n. also **ju-ry-man** (dʒʊər–iʸ–mən) *masc.*, **ju-ry-wom-an** (–wʊm–ən) *fem.* One who serves on a jury

ju-ry (dʒʊr–iʸ) n. -ries **1.** A group of usu. twelve people chosen to listen to the facts in a court of law and decide on the guilt or innocence of the accused: *The jury has reached a verdict of "not guilty."* **2.** The group of judges in a competition: *the jury of the Miss Universe competition*

just (dʒʌst) adj. Honorable and fair; righteous: *Oh praise the greatness of our God, his works are perfect, all his ways are just. A faithful God who does no wrong, upright and just is he* (Deuteronomy 32:3,4). *Jesus said, "My judgment is just"* (John 5:30). *If we confess our sins, he [God] is faithful and just to forgive us our sins and purify us from all unrighteousness* (1 John 1:9). *To do what is right and just is more acceptable to the Lord than sacrifice* (Proverbs 21:3).

just adv. **1.** Exactly at that time or place; exactly as: *The tire blew out just as I drove into my garage.* **2.** Only a little; almost not: *The rain started just after lunch./ He got home just in time for dinner.* **3.** Only: *I'm not sick; I just need some sleep./ Do sthg. to help; don't just stand there.*

just about (dʒʌst ə–baʊt) adv. Almost: *We have*

just about finished all the coffee. We'll have to buy some more.

jus-tice (dʒʌs–təs) n. **1.** Right and fair behavior or treatment: *Blessed are they who maintain justice who constantly do what is right* (Psalm 106:3). *He [Jesus] will reign... over his Kingdom, establishing it with justice and righteousness* (Isaiah 9:7). —opposite INJUSTICE **2.** The law and its action or power: *a court of justice* **3.** *AmE.* A judge of a law court **4. do justice to someone/ do someone justice** To treat someone fairly

jus-ti-fi-a-ble (dʒʌs–tə–faɪ–ə–bəl) adj. That can be justified —opposite UNJUSTIFIABLE —**justifiably** adv.

jus-ti-fi-ca-tion (dʒʌs–tə–fə–keʸ–ʃən) n. The act of justifying a person, declaring him free from blame: *He [Jesus] was delivered over to death for our sins and was raised again for our justification* (Romans 4:25). *For just as one trespass [by the first man, Adam] resulted in the death and condemnation of all mankind, so also one act of righteousness [Christ's suffering and death on the cross to pay for our sins] resulted in justification and eternal life for all people [who put their trust in him rather than in their own good deeds or righteous acts]. For just as through the disobedience of one man [Adam] many were made sinners, so also through the obedience of one man [Jesus] many [all who put their trust in him] will be made righteous* (Romans 5:18-19).

jus-ti-fy (dʒʌs–tə–faɪ) v. **-fied, -fying 1.** To declare free from blame: *For all have sinned and fall short of the glory of God, and are justified freely by his grace through the redemption that comes by Christ Jesus* (Romans 3:23,24). *We maintain that a man is justified by faith apart from observing the law. There is only one God, who will justify the circumcised by faith and the uncircumcised through that same faith* (Romans 3:30). *To the man who does not work but trusts God who justifies the wicked [who turn from their sins and trust in Jesus], his faith is credited as righteousness* (Romans 4:5). **2.** To be or give a good reason for: *How can you justify your rude behavior?* —**justified** (dʒʌs–tə–faɪd) adj.: *This kind of cruel behavior is never justified.*

jut (dʒʌt) v. **-tt-** To stick out; project

jute (dʒuʷt) n. A strong fiber used for making coarse sacks, burlap, rope etc.

ju-ve-nile (dʒuʷ–və–naɪl) n. A young person **juvenile** adj. Of, like, by, or for young people: *juvenile books*

jux-ta-pose (dʒʌk–stə–poʷz) v. To place side by side; put close together —**jux-ta-po-si-tion** (dʒʌk–stə–pə–zɪʃ–ən) n.

K,k (ke^y) n. The 11th letter of the English alphabet

kale (ke^yl) n. A cabbage-like plant having loose, curled leaves that do not form a head

ka·lei·do·scope (kə–lai–də–sko^wp) n. **1.** A tube, with an eyepiece at one end, containing loose bits of colored glass or plastic which cause changing patterns to be reflected in two or more mirrors as the tube is turned **2.** Constantly and quickly changing patterns: *The bazaar was a kaleidoscope of strange and exciting events.*

kan·ga·roo (kæŋ–gə–ru^w) n. **-roos** A large, leaping animal of Australia with powerful hind legs and a long, thick tail

kan·ga·roo court (kæŋ–gə–ru^w kɔrt) n. A court or an illegal, self-appointed tribunal characterized by irresponsible, perverted, or irregular procedures

ka·o·lin (ke^y–ə–lən) n. A fine white clay used in making porcelain and in medicine

ka·pok (ke^y–pak) n. The cotton-like substance that covers the seeds of a tropical tree, used for stuffing cushions, etc.

kar·at (kɛər–ət) n. A unit for expressing proportion of gold in an alloy equal to 1/24th part pure gold: *12 karat gold is 50% pure gold.* –see CARAT

ka·ra·te (kə–rat–i^y) n. An art of self-defense in which an attacker is disabled by crippling kicks and punches

kar·ma (kar–mə) n. In Hinduism and Buddhism, both of which teach a continual series of reincarnations, the belief that whatever one does in this life and whatever he did in previous lives, decides his fate in the next life. NOTE: This belief is altogether contrary to the Word of God which says: "Man is destined to die once, and after that to face judgment" (Hebrews 9:27). There is no such thing as reincarnation, and there is no such thing as karma. Jesus Christ came into the world to save sinners (1 Timothy 1:15). He

SPELLING NOTE:
Words having the sound /k/ may be spelled with c-, like cat, or qu-, like quit.

died for our sins and rose again (2 Corinthians 5:15). He paid for all of our sins with His own blood (1 Peter 1.18, 19). If we repent of our sins [turn from our wicked ways] and put our trust in Jesus, we shall not perish [and we shall not return to earth in another form] but we shall have eternal life with Jesus Christ in paradise (John 3:16). But those who do not believe in Jesus — their place will be in the fiery lake of burning sulfur (Revelation 21:8). But God doesn't want anyone to perish. He wants all people ev-erywhere to come to the knowledge of the truth about his Son Jesus Christ, believe in him and have eternal life. —see JESUS

kay·ak (kar–æk) n. **1.** A canoe with a deck that fits tightly around the waist of the paddler **2.** A similarly styled, portable boat used in the US

ke·bab or **ke·bob** (kə–bab) n. Small pieces of meat and/or vegetables cooked and often served on a skewer

keel (ki^yl) n. The long supporting piece of a ship's frame that lies lengthwise along the bottom

keel o·ver (ki^yl o^w–vər) v. + adv. To fall over suddenly; to faint or collapse: *When she heard the tragic news about her son's accident, she keeled over on the kitchen floor.*

keen (ki^yn) adj. **1.** Mentally alert: *a keen mind* **2.** Strong; acute: *a keen sense of hearing* **3.** Highly developed; active: *a keen interest* **4.** Having a fine, sharp edge or point: *a keen knife* **5.** Enthusiastic: *keen on skiing* —**keenly** adv. —**keenness** n.

keep (ki^yp) v. **kept** (kɛpt), **keeping 1.** To have possession of sthg.: *I'll keep this for you until you need it.* **2.** To save: *Shall I keep this junk or throw it away?* **3.** To fulfill: *God keeps his promises.* **4.** Hold: *How long will you keep us in suspense?* **5.** Prevent:*He is able to keep you from falling* (Jude 24). **6.** To know a secret without telling: *Can you keep a secret?* **7.** To write and preserve regular written records: *She kept a diary.* **8.** To take care of and provide for: *Mary kept Sue's children while Sue was in the hospital.* **9.** Guard; protect: *The Lord will keep you from all harm! O Lord, keep your*

servant also from willful sins (Psalm 19:13).
10. Obey; apply: *Blessed are they who hear the Word of God and keep it* (Luke 11:28). **11.** Remember: *Keep them [God's words] within your heart* (Proverbs 4:21). **12.** Maintain: *Keep your spiritual fervor, serving the Lord* (Romans 12:11). *Keep yourself pure* (1 Timothy 5:22). **13. keep from** Avoid: *Keep corrupt talk from your lips* (Proverbs 4:24). **14. keep off** To stay; remain: *Keep off the grass.* **15. keep up (a)** To continue: *Keep up the good work.* **(b)** To maintain in good condition **(c)** To maintain the pace; not lag behind **16. keep someone company** To remain with someone **17. keep sbdy./ sthg. down (a)** To control; prevent from growing, advancing, succeeding, etc. **(b)** To treat people, a nation, etc. like slaves; oppress

keep-er (ki^y–pər) n. One who guards, protects, or cares for: *storekeeper/gatekeeper/ Am I my brother's keeper?* (Genesis 4:9). *Yes, you are your brother's keeper.*

keep-ing (ki^y–pɪŋ) n. **1.** Care or custody: *You may leave your car with me for safe keeping.* (*=to be guarded carefully*) **2. in keeping with** In harmony or agreement with: *Produce fruit [good deeds] in keeping with repentance* (Matthew 3:8).

keg (kɛg) n. A small cask or barrel

kelp (kɛlp) n. A kind of seaweed

ken-nel (kɛn–əl) n. **1.** A house for one or more dogs **2.** A place where dogs are bred, trained or boarded

kept (kɛpt) v. Past tense and past part. of **keep**

ker-chief (kɜr–tʃɪf) n. **1.** A cloth worn about the head or around the neck **2.** A handkerchief

ker-nel (kɜr–nəl) n. **1.** The inner, usu. edible (eatable) part of a cereal plant **2.** The important or essential part of sthg. said: *a kernel of truth in his remarks*

ker-o-sene, -sine (kɛər–ə–si^yn/ kɛər–ə–si^yn) A thin oil made from petroleum, coal, etc., used in lamps for light and burned for heat

ketch-up (kɛtʃ–əp) n. Any of the various sauces for meat, etc., made from tomatoes, onions, and spices

ket-tle (kɛt–əl) n. A metal pot for boiling liq-

uids, esp. a teakettle that has a lid, a handle, and a spout for pouring

key (ki^y) n. **keys 1.** A notched metallic instrument that one puts into a keyhole and turns, to lock or unlock a door, start or stop a car engine, etc. **2.** Sthg. that helps you to understand: *a key to the grammar exercises* **3.** Any of the parts of a typewriter or musical instrument that are pressed with the fingers to operate it: *typewriter keys* **4.** A set of answers to a test **5.** A set of related musical notes based on a particular note: *a song in the key of C* **6.** A crucial fact: *The Lord... will be a sure foundation... a rich store of salvation and wisdom and knowledge; the fear of the Lord is the key to this treasure* (Isaiah 33:5,6). *Then he [Jesus] placed his right hand on me and said, "Do not be afraid. I am the First and the Last. I am the Living One; I was dead, and behold I am alive for ever and ever! And I hold the keys of death and Hades"* (Revelation 1:18).

key adj. Very important; essential for success: *As president of the company he holds one of the key offices.*

key-board (ki^y–bord) n. The set of keys on a musical instrument or machine: *the keyboard of a computer/piano*

key-hole (ki^y–ho^wl) n. The hole in a lock into which a key fits

kg. n. *written abbr.*, said as **kilogram/s** (kɪl–ə–græm/z) 1,000 grams; a basic metric unit of mass and weight equal to about 2.2 pounds

kha-ki (kæ–ki^y) n. **1.** A light yellowish-brown color **2.** Cloth of this color, esp. a military uniform —**khaki** adj.

kib-butz (kɪ–bu^wts/ –buts) n. *pl.* **-but-zim** (–bu^w–tsi^ym) A collective farming community in Israel

kib-itz (kɪb–əts/kɪb–ɪts) v. To give unsolicited advice, as a spectator at a card game

kick (kɪk) v. **1.** To strike with the foot: *The boys kicked the football back and forth.* **2.** To move the feet and legs as if to strike a blow: *The children were kicking and splashing in the water.* **3.** *fig.* **kick sbdy. around** To treat someone badly **4. kick off** To begin a football game **5. kick sbdy. out (a)** To remove sbdy. from a place, esp. violently **(b)** To dismiss sbdy. from a job

kick n. **1.** An act of kicking: *He gave the door a little kick and it flew right open.* **2.** *fig.* Excitement; a thrill: *She gets a kick out of riding on a roller coaster.*

kid (kɪd) n. **1.** A young goat **2.** Leather made from its skin **3.** *infml.* A child or young person: *college kids/How many kids are there in your family?* **4. kid brother/ sister** adj. *AmE. infml.* A younger brother or sister

kid v. **-dd-** *infml.* To tease; to deceive as a joke: *I wouldn't kid you. It really is raining outside.*

kid-nap (kɪd–næp) v. **-p-** or **-pp-** To seize someone and hold them against his/ her will in order to demand money or sthg. else for his/ her safe return —**kidnapper** or **kidnaper** n.

kid-ney (kɪd–niⁱ) n. **-neys** Either of a pair of human or animal organs that remove waste products from the blood

kill (kɪl) v. **1.** To cause death; deprive of life: *Many people are killed in car accidents every year./ fig. My feet are killing me! (=hurting very much)* **2.** To put an end to: *to kill one's chances of promotion* **3. kill time** To make free time pass as pleasantly as possible by finding sthg. to do **4. kill two birds with one stone** To get two good results from a single action NOTE: **Kill** is a general word meaning to cause anything to die. **Murder** is used to speak of killing a person on purpose, which is a sin against one of God's commandments. "You shall not kill" (Exodus 20:13 NKJV). Even to hate someone is murder in God's sight. "Whoever hates his brother [anyone] is a murderer, and... no murderer has eternal life..." (1 John 3:15). **Assassinate** is used to speak of killing an important political figure, and **massacre** of killing large numbers of people at one time. To **execute** is to put to death legally.

kill-er (kɪl–ər) n. A person, animal, or thing that kills: *The police have caught the killer./ Heart disease and cancer are major killers.*

kill-ing (kɪl–ɪŋ) n. **make a killing** To have a sudden, great financial success

kill-joy (kɪl–dʒɔɪ) n. A person who lessens the joy of others

kiln (kɪl/ kɪln) n. A large furnace or oven for baking pottery, bricks, etc. or for drying grain, etc.

kil-o-gram, also **-gramme** *BrE.* (kɪl–ə–græm) n. also **kilo** (kiⁱ–loʷ) 1,000 grams (approx. 2.2 pounds)

kil-o-me-ter *AmE.* **-tre** *BrE.* (kil–lɑm–ə–tər/ kɪ–lə–miⁱ–tər) n. 1,000 meters

kil-o-watt (kɪl–ə–wɑt) n. 1,000 watts

kilt (kɪlt) n. A pleated skirt traditionally worn by men in the Scottish Highlands

kil-ter (kɪl–tər) n. *infml.* Good condition: *out of kilter (not in working order)*

ki-mo-no (kə–moʷ–nə/ –noʷ) n. **1.** A loose Japanese robe, fastened with a sash **2.** A woman's loose dressing gown

kin (kɪn) n. One's relatives: *Who is your next of kin? (=Who is the one most closely related to you?)*

kind (kaɪnd) n. **1.** A group whose members share certain qualities; type; sort: *We sell all kinds of toys.* **2.** Essential quality or character: *Are you the kind of person that God wants you to be?* **3. kind of** *infml. esp. AmE.* Rather; sort of: *I'm kind of busy right now. Can you call later?*

kind adj. Helpful, considerate, showing interest in the happiness or feelings of others: *Be kind and compassionate to one another, forgiving one another, just as in Christ God forgave you* (Ephesians 4:32). *Blessed is he who is kind to the needy* (Proverbs 14:21). *Love is patient, love is kind...* (1 Corinthians 13:4). —opposite UNKIND

kin-der-gar-ten (kɪn–dər–gɑr–tən/ –gɑr–dən) n. A school or class for very young children, which they attend before entering grade school

kin-dle (kɪn–dəl) v. **-dled, -dling 1.** To set or catch on fire: *Would you please kindle the fire in the fireplace?* **2.** To arouse or excite

kin-dling (kɪn–dlɪŋ) n. Material for lighting a fire, esp. dry wood, leaves, etc.

kind-ly (kaɪnd–liⁱ) adj. **-lier, -liest** Pleasant in manner or appearance; friendly —**kindliness** n.

kindly adv. **1.** In a kind manner: *The teacher spoke kindly to the children.* —opposite UNKINDLY **2.** Please: *Would you kindly type this letter for me?* **3. not take kindly to** Not accept

easily or willingly: *I don't think Bill would take kindly to your suggestion.*

kind-ness (kaınd–nəs) n. The act or quality of being kind: *When the kindness and love of God our Savior appeared, he saved us not because of righteous things we had done, but because of his mercy* (Titus 3:4).

kin-dred (kın–drəd) n. **1.** A group of related persons **2.** A person's relatives

kindred adj. **1.** Having a common source; related **2.** Similar: *Hunting and fishing are kindred sports.*

ki-net-ic (kı–net–ık) adj. Of, relating to, or produced by motion

kin-folk or **kinsfolk (kın**–fo^wk) n. Members of one's family —**kinship** n.

king (kıŋ) n. **1.** The male ruler of a country, usually inheriting the position and ruling for life **2.** The person, animal, or thing regarded as most important in some way: *the king of beasts*

King of kings (kıŋ əv kıŋz) n. Jesus Christ: *Jesus Christ is "King of kings and Lord of lords"* (1 Timothy 6:15), *for he has all power and authority in heaven and on earth* (Matthew 28:18), *and he sustains all things by his powerful Word* (Hebrews 1:3). NOTE: Jesus' kingdom is not of this world (John 18:36). His kingship and his kingdom are far greater than that of any earthly ruler, for "all kings will bow down to him, and all nations will serve him," (Psalm 72:11) and "his kingdom will never end" (Luke 1:33). —see KINGDOM OF GOD and JESUS CHRIST

king-dom (kıŋ–dəm) n. A country ruled over by a king or queen

King-dom of God (kıŋ–dəm əv gad) n. It is customary to make a distinction between the kingdom of power, the kingdom of grace, and the kingdom of glory. **(a)** The **kingdom of power** includes the entire universe and extends to ev-ery living thing. NOTE: God controls the forces of nature and the destiny of nations. Without his will, not one small bird falls to the ground, nor one hair from our head. "For God is the King of all the earth" (Psalm 47:7). **(b)** The **kingdom of grace** does not include all creation but only those who have been born

again through the preaching of the gospel [Good News] of the kingdom. NOTE: Only true believers in Jesus Christ are citizens in this kingdom. This kingdom is governed solely by God's Word (John 18:37). This kingdom has proved itself stronger than the kingdoms of this world. Many mighty empires have come and gone, but the kingdom of Christ has continued and flourished in spite of bloody persecutions, ridicule, disrupting heresies, and science, falsely so-called, and it will continue until the Lord's return. It is called the kingdom of grace because it is the promise of divine grace (the unmerited love of God) that wins people for this kingdom. It is the acceptance of this grace by faith that makes them citizens of this kingdom. It is the rule of Christ in the hearts of the believers. **(c)** The **kingdom of glory** is not on earth but in heaven, where Christ himself shall have all glory (Luke 24:26; John 17:5,24), and where those who have been faithful to him unto death shall likewise be crowned with glory and honor (Philippians 3:21; Romans 8:18). NOTE: The souls of the believers enter this kingdom of glory at the time of their death (Luke 23:43). After the resurrection, their bodies shall inherit the kingdom prepared for them (Matthew 25:34). Christ rules the kingdom of power for the benefit of his kingdom of grace. The world continues for no other purpose than this, that sinners might repent and believe the gospel and enter the kingdom of grace. The chief purpose of the kingdom of grace is to win and prepare men for the kingdom of glory.

king-ly (kıŋ–li^y) adj. **-lier, -liest** Like or suitable to a king

Kings (kıŋz) n. Either of two historical books of the Old Testament —see BIBLE, OLD TESTAMENT

kink (kıŋk) n. **1.** A tight curl or twist of hair, rope, etc. **2.** A painful muscle spasm **3.** A slight flaw, as in a plan or system

kin-ship (kın–ʃıp) n. **1.** Family relationship **2.** A strong connection or similarity between persons or things: *He felt a strong kinship with other musicians*

kins-man (kınz–mən) n. A male blood relative

ki-osk (ki⸱ōsk / kiⱽ **ask**) n. An open circular pavilion used as a bandstand, newsstand, etc.

kiss (kıs) v. To touch with the lips as a sign of love or in greeting or farewell

kiss n. An act of kissing: *The little girl gave her mother a good night kiss.*

kit (kıt) n. **1.** A set of articles for personal use: *a shaving kit/a sewing kit* **2.** A box or a bag for a set of articles or tools to be used for a particular purpose **3.** A set of parts or materials to be assembled

kitch-en (kıtʃ–ən) n. A room or building used for preparing and cooking meals

kite (kaıt) n. **1.** Any of various birds of the hawk family, with long narrow wings and, usually, a forked tail **2.** A light frame covered with paper or cloth, held by a long string and flown in the air

kit-ten (kıt–ən) n. A young cat

kit-ty (kıt–iⱽ) n. **-ties 1.** A kitten **2.** A reserve of money for some particular purpose

klep-to-ma-ni-a (klɛp–tə–meⱽ–niⱽ–ə) n. An uncontrollable urge to steal —**kleptomaniac** n.

km. *written abbr.* said as **kilometer/s** (kı-**lam**-ə-tər/ kıl-ə-miⱽ-tər) n. 1,000 meters (about six-tenths of a mile)

knack (næk) n. Some special skill or ability: *She has a knack for learning languages.*

knead (niⱽd) v. To mix and work dough, clay, etc. into a pliable mass by folding over, pressing, and squeezing, usu. with the hands

knee (niⱽ) n. **1.** The middle joint of the leg, between the lower leg and the thigh: *At the name of Jesus every knee should bow, in heaven and on earth and under the earth, and every tongue confess that Jesus Christ is Lord, to the glory of God the Father* (Philippians 2:10,11). **2.** The part of a garment that covers the knee

knee v. **kneed, kneeing** To strike with the knee

kneel (niⱽl) v. **knelt** (nɛlt) or **kneeling** To go down on one or both knees; remain on the knee(s): *He knelt to pray./Let us kneel before the Lord, our Maker* (Psalm 95:6).

knew (nuⱽ/ nyuⱽ) v. Past tense of **know:** *Jesus knew their thoughts* (Matthew 12:25). *He also said, "If you really knew me, you would know my Father as well"* (John 14:7).

knick-knack or **nick-nack** (nık–næk) n. A small ornament of any type, usu. of little value

knife (naıf) n. **knives** (naıvz) A cutting or stabbing instrument with a sharp blade, single-edged or double-edged, set in a handle, used as a tool or weapon

knife v. **knifed, knifing** To cut or stab with a knife, used as a weapon: *Last night he was knifed and robbed on his way to the store.*

knight (naıt) n. **1.** In the Middle Ages, one of noble birth, trained to use arms **2.** A man to whom the king or queen has given a rank of honor, having the title **Sir** used before the first name **3.** A piece used in chess

knit (nıt) v. **knitted** or **knit, knitting 1.** To make things to wear by intertwining yarn or thread in a series of connected loops by means of long needles **2.** To join closely: *The broken bones in his arm have knit together well.*

knit-ting (nıt–ŋ) n. Sth. being knitted: *Do you have a bag for your knitting?*

knives (naıvz) n. *pl.* of **knife**

knob (nab) n. **1.** A round lump on the surface of sthg. **2.** A round handle or control button: *I can't turn down the volume on the TV. The knob has come off.*

knock (nak) v. **1.** To strike a sharp blow, esp. making a noise when doing so: *to knock at the door* **2.** To hit or strike sthg., esp. causing it to fall: *He knocked over a small table as he entered the room.* **3.** *infml.* To find fault with; say critical things about sbdy.: *Stop knocking the senator; he's doing the best he can.* **4. knock down (a)** To destroy sthg. by means of striking it repeatedly: *Those old buildings ought to be knocked down.* **(b)** To reduce a price: *The rent was knocked down to $600 per month.* **5. knock off** *infml.* **(a)** To stop doing sthg.: *I have to knock off work early today to go to the bank.* **(b)** To deduct from a total payment: *Because you are such a good customer I'll knock off $50 from the price.* **6. knock out (a)** To cause sleep or unconsciousness: *The blow on the head knocked him out.* **(b)** In boxing, to cause

one's opponent to lose consciousness or be unable to get up before a count of ten (c) To cause to fall from competition: *Our team fought hard, but they were knocked out of the competition in the last game of the series.*

knock n. **1.** A sharp blow **2.** The sound of pounding: *a loud knock on the door* **3.** *fig.* A piece of bad luck or trouble: *He's had quite a few hard knocks lately.*

knock-out (nɑk–aʊt) n. **1.** In boxing, a blow that knocks the other fighter unconscious or knocks him down so that he is unable to get up before the count of ten: *He won by a knockout in the 3rd round.* **2.** *infml.* Sbdy. or sthg. sensationally attractive, causing great admiration: *She's really a knockout in her new dress.*

knoll (noʷl) n. A small round hill or mound

knot (nɑt) n. **1.** A fastening made by tying together pieces of string, rope, wire, etc.: *He tied it with a square knot.* **2.** (a) A hard lump on a tree where a branch grows out (b) A cross section of such a lump appearing as cross-grained in a board or log **3.** One nautical mile per hour, equal to 1.15 miles per hour on land

knot-ty (nɑt–iʸ) adj. **-tier, -tiest** Having one or more knots: *This pine board has too many knots in it. It's too knotty./fig. This is a knotty problem.* (=complicated)

know (noʷ) v. **knew (nuʷ/ nyuʷ), known (noʷn), knowing 1.** To have information firmly secured in the mind or memory: *Writing to Timothy, the Apostle Paul says, "From infancy you have known the Holy Scriptures which are able to make you wise for salvation through faith in Christ Jesus"* (2 Timothy 3:15). **2.** To be capable of: *to know how to swim* **3.** To be able to distinguish: *to know right from wrong, left from right, etc.* **4.** To be well acquainted with someone: *I've known Stanley for years.* **5.** To be able to recognize: *Jesus said, "If you hold to my teaching, you are really my disciples. Then you will know the truth and the truth will set you free"* (John 8:31, 32). **6.** To have experienced: *I know that my Redeemer [Jesus] lives* (Job 19:25). *Search me, O God, and know my heart* (Psalm 139:23). *Lord, you know everyone's heart* (Acts 1:24).

We know that in all things God works for the good of those who love him (Romans 8:28). *I write these things to you who believe in the name of the Son of God, so that you may know that you have eternal life* (1 John 5:13).

knowl-edge (nɑl–ɪdʒ) n. **1.** The state or fact of knowing: *In Christ are hidden all the treasures of wisdom and knowledge* (Colossians 2:3). *The fear of the Lord is the beginning of knowledge* (Proverbs 1:7). *The Lord gives wisdom and from his mouth come knowledge and understanding* (Proverbs 2:6). *Lips that speak knowledge are a rare jewel* (Proverbs 20:15). **2.** Learning: *a knowledge of Latin* **3.** Familiarity with, gained through experience or study: *a good knowledge of this part of the country* —**knowl-edge-a-ble (nɑl–ɪdʒ–ə–bəl)** adj.

known (noʷn) adj. **1.** Also **well-known**; Generally recognized: *He's a known thief.* **2.**

known as (a) Generally recognized as: *He's known as the author of two best sellers.* (b) Publicly called; named: *Hong Kong, known as the Gateway to the Orient, is a thriving, busy city.*

known v. Past part. of **know**

knuck-le (nʌk–əl) n. A finger joint, esp. one that connects the finger to the rest of the hand

knuck-le down (nʌk–əl daʊn) v. + adv. **-led, -ling** *infml.* To work very hard and seriously: *We really have to knuckle down if we expect to finish this job by Friday.*

knuck-le un-der (nʌk–əl ʌn–dər) v.+ adv. To yield to pressure; to admit defeat; give in

ko-a-la (koʷ–ɑ–lə) n. A sluggish, gray, furry animal of Australia, also called **koala bear**

Ko-ran (kə–rɑn/ koʷ–rɑn) n. The sacred book of the Muslims, written in Arabic, believed to contain the revelations made to Mohammed by Allah

ko-sher (koʷ–ʃər) adj. Pure and clean according to Jewish law

kow-tow (kaʊ–taʊ/ koʷ–) v. **1.** To touch the forehead to the ground while kneeling, as an act of worship or reverence **2.** To treat with too much respect

ku-dos (kuʷ–dɑz/ –doʷz) n. Honor and glory; credit

kung fu (kʊŋ fuʷ / guʷŋ fuʷ) n. A form of self-defense developed in China

kw *written abbr.*, said as **ki-lo-watt/s** (kɪl-ə—   wɑt/s) n.

L, l (εl) n. **1.** The 12th letter of the English alphabet **2.** The Roman numeral (number) for **50**

lab (læb) n. *Infml.* for **laboratory**

la·bel (leʸ–bəl) n. A piece of paper, cloth, etc. stuck or tied to sthg. to identify its owner or its contents

label v. **-beled, -beling** or **-belled, -belling 1.** To fasten a label on sthg.: *The teacher labeled the boxes.* **2.** To consider, call, or classify: *He was labeled a liberal by his enemies.*

la·bi·al (leʸ–biʸ–əl) adj. Of the lips

la·bor *AmE.* **la·bour** *BrE.* (leʸ–bər) n. **1.** Hard work, esp. physical work **2.** Workmen on the job: *The company is having labor problems.* **3.** The act of giving birth: *She was in labor for two days before the baby was born.*

labor v. To move or act with difficulty; struggle: *He labored up the stairs with several pieces of luggage.*

lab·o·ra·to·ry (læb–rə–tor–iʸ) *AmE.* (lə–bor–ə–triʸ) *BrE.* n. A room or building for scientific research and experiments

la·bored (leʸ–bərd) adj. Made or done with great effort; strained

la·bor·er (leʸ–bər–ər) n. A person employed to do unskilled manual work

la·bo·ri·ous (lə–bor–iʸ–əs) adj. Needing much effort and perseverance —**laboriously** adv.

lab·y·rinth (læb–ə–rɪnθ) n. A place filled with confusing, intricate passageways; a maze

lace (leʸs) v. **laced, lacing** To draw together or fasten with a lace

lace n. **1.** A string or cord for fastening shoes, etc. **2.** Delicate net-like decorative fabric

lac·er·ate (læs–ə–reʸt) v. **-ated, -ating 1.** To injure (flesh) by tearing: *Her face was badly lacerated from the car accident.* **2.** To hurt one's feelings —**lac·er·a·tion** (læs–ə–reʸ–ʃən) n.

lack (læk) v. To not have enough of sthg.: *If any of you lacks wisdom, he should ask God who gives generously* (James 1:5).

lack n. Absence or need: *For the lack of guidance a nation falls* (Proverbs 11:14). *Plans fail for lack of counsel* (Proverbs 15:22).

lack·a·dai·si·cal (læk–ə–deʸ–zɪ–kəl) adj. Lacking enthusiasm: *a lackadaisical attitude*

lack·ey (læk–iʸ) n. **-eys 1.** A male servant. **2.** One who acts like a slave

lack·lus·ter (læk–ləs–tər) adj. Dull: A *lackluster performance*

la·con·ic (lə–kon–ɪk) adj. Terse; not talkative —**laconically** adv.

lac·quer (læk–ər) n. A hard, glossy varnish

lac·tate (læk–teʸt) v. **-tated, -tating** To secrete milk —**lac·ta·tion** (læk–teʸ–ʃən) n.

lac·te·al (læk–tiʸ–əl) adj. Consisting of, producing, or resembling milk

lac·tic (læk–tɪk) adj. Of or obtained from milk

lactic acid (læk–tɪk æs–əd) n. A yellowish or clear syrupy liquid occurring in sour milk

lac·tose (læk–toʷs) n. Sugar present in milk

lad (læd) n. A boy; youth

lad·der (læd–ər) n. A structure for climbing up or down, usu. consisting of two parallel sidepieces joined by equally spaced cross-pieces

lad·en (leʸd–ən) adj. Heavily loaded: *The vines were laden with grapes.*

la·dle (leʸ–dəl) n. A long-handled cup-like spoon for taking up and conveying liquids —**ladle** v. **-dled, -dling**

la·dy (leʸ–diʸ) n. **-dies 1.** A woman, esp. one of refinement and good manners **2.** A polite name for an adult member of the feminine sex

lag (læg) v. **-gg-** To move slowly and fall behind; to fail to keep pace: *Tom is always lagging behind the others./ Production is lagging this year.*

lag n. **1.** A slowing down or falling behind **2.** The amount by which one falls behind

lag·gard (læg–ərd) n. One who lags behind

la·goon (lə–guʷn) n. The area of shallow salt water separated from the sea by sand dunes or enclosed by a circular coral reef

laid (leʸd) v. Past tense and part. of **lay**

lain (leʸn) v. Past part. of **lie**

lair (leər) n. **1.** The den of a wild beast **2.** A hideout, as of criminals

lais·sez–faire (lε–seʸ–feər/–zeʸ–/ leʸ–) n. Noninterference in economic affairs, esp. by the government

la·i·ty (leʸ–ət–iʸ) n. **-ties 1.** The people of a church who are not clergy **2.** People not initiated into a particular discipline: *Some medical doctors find it difficult to communicate*

with the laity.

luke (loᵛḵ) n. A large inland body of water: *Some lakes are natural; some are man-made.*

la-ma (lɑ–mə) n. A Buddhist monk of Tibet or Mongolia

La-ma-ism (lɑ–mə–ɪz–əm) n. The Bud-dhism of Tibet and Mongolia

lamb (læm) n. **1.** A young sheep **2.** The meat of a young sheep

Lamb of God (læm əv gɑd) n. Jesus Christ: *Je-sus Christ is called, "The Lamb of God who takes away the sin of the world"* (John 1:29). NOTE: Before Jesus came into the world, it was required that lambs be offered as a burnt sacrifice for the sins of the people. One lamb was offered every morning and one every evening (Exodus 29:38,39). These lambs were to be without spot and without blemish — perfect. Jesus is called the Lamb of God because He was perfectly righteous and holy — sinless. His sacrifice on the cross paid for all the sins of all people for all time (Hebrews 10:14). His blood cleanses us from all sin (1 John 1:7). He truly is the Lamb of God who takes away the sin of the world. "Whoever believes in him shall not perish but have everlasting life" (John 3:16).

lam-baste (læm-beᵛst/ –bæst) v. -basted, -basting **1.** To beat soundly **2.** To scold or denounce severely

lame (leᵛm) adj. **1.** Not able to walk very well because of some weakness in the leg or foot **2.** Difficult to believe; weak: *He gave a lame excuse for being late.*

lame-brain (leᵛm–breᵛn) n. A stupid person

la-ment (lə–mɛnt) v. **1.** To mourn aloud **2.** To feel or express regret

la-men-ta-ble (lə–mɛn–tə–bəl/ læm–ən–tə–bəl) adj. Regrettable

lam-en-ta-tion (læm–ən–teᵛ–ʃən) n. Lament-ing; expression of grief

Lam-en-ta-tions (læm–ən–teᵛ–ʃənz) n. One of the 39 books of the Old Testament. It was written by the Prophet Jeremiah near the end of the 6th century B. C. as if for a na-tional funeral, portraying the capture and destruction of Jerusalem because of the sins of her people.

lam-i-nate (læm–ə–neᵛt) v. -nated, -nat-ing **1.** To roll or press into a thin sheet **2.** To separ-ate into thin layers **3.** To build by joining several layers together

lamp (læmp) n. A device for giving light, us-ing kerosene, gas, or electricity: *(fig.) Your word [O Lord] is a lamp to my feet and a light for my path* (Psalm 119:105).

lam-poon (læm–puᵂn) n. Violent criticism of a person (in writing)

lance (læns) n. A weapon with a long shaft or handle of wood, a spearhead and often a small flag: *He carried a lance and shield as he rode into battle*

lance v. -lanced, -lancing To cut open (e.g., a boil) with a knife

lanc-er (læn–sər) n. A cavalry soldier armed with a lance

land (lænd) n. **1.** The solid part of the earth's surface **2.** A political division such as a country or nation **3.** An expanse of the earth's surface having common characteris-tics: *grassland /arid land* **4.** Earth; soil: *He who works his land will have abundant food, but he who chases fantasies lacks judgement* (Pro-verbs 12:11). NOTE: The earth's surface when compared with the sea is the **land,** but when compared with the sky it is the **earth.** The substance in which plants grow is the **ground, earth,** or **soil.**

land v. **1.** To come to, or put on land: *The plane landed in Dallas.* **2.** To settle or come to rest: *The bird landed on the fence.* **3.** To bring to some point or condition: *His remarks landed him in some serious trouble.*

land-ing (læn–dɪŋ) n. **1.** The act of bringing an aircraft to land: *The plane's landing was very difficult due to the bad weather.* **2.** A place where people and goods are landed, esp. from a ship **3.** The level part of a staircase between flights of steps

land-la-dy (lænd–leᵛ–diᵛ) n. -dies *masc.* **land-lord 1.** A woman who leases land, houses, apartments, etc. to tenants **2.** A woman who operates a rooming house or inn

land-locked (lænd–lɑkt) adj. Enclosed by land; having no seaport: *Bolivia is a land-locked country.*

land-lord (lænd–lɔrd) n. *fem.* **land-la-dy** (lænd–

le^y–di^y) -dies A person from whom someone rents a house, apartment, office, land, etc.

land-lub-ber (lænd–lʌb–ər) n. **1.** One who has had little experience at sea **2.** A seaman's term of contempt

land-mark (lænd–mɑrk) n. **1.** An easily recognizable object, such as a large rock or a tall tree, by which one can know his position **2.** An event that marks a turning point in history or in a person's life: *The discovery of America was a landmark in history.* **3.** A building of unusual historical interest

land-scape (lænd–ske^yp) n. **1.** A wide view of scenery on land **2.** A picture of such a scene

landscape v. -scaped, -scaping To beautify the land around houses, office buildings, etc. by adding trees and other plants

land-slide (lænd–slaɪd) n. **1.** A sudden fall of earth or rocks down a slope **2.** An overwhelming number of votes for one political party or candidate in an election: *He won by a landslide.*

lane (le^yn) n. **1.** A narrow road or street **2.** A part of the name of a street in town: *Melody Lane* **3.** A division of a wide road for one line of traffic: *The new freeway has four lanes in each direction.* **4.** A regular course taken by ships in crossing the ocean: *We saw very few ships on our voyage since we were not on a regular shipping lane.*

lan-guage (læŋ–gwɪdʒ) n. **1.** Communication between human beings by means of using speech and hearing: *In the beginning of time, "the whole world had one language..."* (Genesis 11:1). **2.** The speech of a particular people or nation: *She speaks three foreign languages quite well.* **3.** A manner of speaking — good or bad: *Rid yourselves of all such things as... filthy language...* (Colossians 3:8).

lan-guid (læŋ–gwɪd) adj. **1.** Weak **2.** Sluggish in character or disposition **3.** Slow

lan-guish (læŋ–gwɪʃ) v. **1.** To become weak or feeble **2.** To be or become weak because of unfulfilled longings **3.** To pass through a period of discomfort and mental anguish: *He languished in prison for several years.* —languishing adj.

lan-guor (læŋ–gər) n. **1.** Lack of vigor or vitality; weariness **2.** A lack of interest; indifference

lank-y (læŋ–ki^y) adj. -ier, -iest Ungracefully tall and thin

lan-o-lin (læn–əl–ən) n. A fatty substance obtained from sheep's wool, used in ointments

lan-tern (læn–tərn) n. A container, usu. of glass and metal, and usu. portable, that encloses the flame of a light: *a kerosene lantern*

lap (læp) n. **1.** The front part of a seated person between the waist and the knees: *He was holding his grandchild on his lap.* **2.** The act or sound of splashing: *the lap of the water against the bow of the ship* **3.** A single circuit of a race

lap v. -pp- **1.** To take up liquids with quick movements of the tongue: *The cat quickly lapped up the milk.* **2.** To ripple or splash with soft sounds: *The waves lapped against the shore.* **3.** In racing, to be one or more laps ahead of another person in a race around a track

la-pel (lə–pɛl) n. The front of a coat, jacket, etc. that is folded back to form an extension of the collar

lap-i-dar-y (læp–ə–dɛər–i^y) -ies **1.** A workman who cuts, polishes, or engraves precious gems **2.** The art of such a workman **3.** An expert who collects precious gems

lapse (læps) n. **1.** A small mistake or failure: *a lapse of memory* **2.** A passing of time: *After a lapse of several minutes, he finally answered my question.*

lapse v. lapsed, lapsing **1.** To sink or slip gradually: *to lapse into silence* **2.** To cease to exist: *Her insurance policy had lapsed and was not renewed.*

lar-ce-ny (lɑr–sə–ni^y) n. -nies An act of stealing; robbery; theft

lard (lɑrd) n. The melted fat of hogs, esp. the internal fat of the abdomen, used in cooking

lar-der (lɑr–dər) n. **1.** A room or place where food is kept **2.** A supply of food

large (lɑrdʒ) adj. **1.** Great in size or amount; big: *a large country with a very large population* —opposite SMALL **2.** at large (a) Esp. of dangerous people, free; uncontrolled (b) As a whole; altogether: *The country at large is*

experiencing some bad times economically.

large·ly (lardʒ–liy) adv. **1.** Chiefly; mostly: *Saudi Arabia is largely desert.* **2.** To a great extent: *Her success was due largely to her determination.*

lar·i·at (lɛər–iy–ət) n. A rope with a noose, used to catch and tether livestock; a lasso

lark (lark) n. **1.** Any of several small sandy-brown songbirds, esp. the skylark **2.** A playful adventurous action **3.** An amusing incident

lark v. To play around lightheartedly

lark·spur (lark–spər) n. A plant with tall stalks and clusters of pink, blue, or white flowers

lar·va (lar–və) n. *pl.* **-vae** (–viy) An insect in the first stage of its life after coming out of the egg

lar·yn·gi·tis (lær–n–dʒaɪ–təs) n. Inflammation of the larynx, which makes it difficult to speak loudly

lar·ynx (lær–ŋks) n. *pl.* **larynges** (lə–rɪn–dʒiyz) or **larynxes** The upper part of the windpipe, containing the voice box

la·sa·gna (lə–zan–yə) n. **1.** Broad, flat noodles **2.** Lasagna noodles baked with a sauce, usu. of tomatoes, cheese, and meat

las·civ·i·ous (lə–sɪv–iy–əs) adj. **1.** Expressing lust or lewdness **2.** Arousing sexual desires

las·civ·i·ous·ness (lə–sɪv–iy–əs–nəs) n. Filthy, lewd conduct: *Now the works of the flesh are manifest... adultery, fornication, uncleanness, lasciviousness... and such like. They which do such things shall not inherit the kingdom of God* (Galatians 5:19-21 KJV). NOTE: God is perfectly holy and he detests all sin, but he is also a God of love and mercy and he forgives all who repent of their sins and put their trust in Jesus for eternal life (Mark 1:15; Acts 16:31). —see FORGIVENESS, JESUS

la·ser (ley–zər) n. A device that generates an intense and highly concentrated beam of light: *laser beams*

lash (læʃ) n. **1.** An eyelash **2.** A stroke with a whip: *St. Paul received 39 lashes on several occasions* (2 Corinthians 11:24). **3.** A thin piece of rope or cord, esp. of a whip

lash v. **1.** To strike with a lash **2.** To make a sudden or restless move, esp. of a tail: *The tiger's tail lashed angrily.* **3.** To fasten with ropes or cords: *During the storm, everything on deck had to be lashed down.*

las·si·tude (læs–ə–tuwd) n. Lack of energy; weariness

las·so (læs–ow/ læ–suw) n. **-sos** or **-soes** A rope with a running noose, used for catching cattle

last (læst) n. **1.** Sthg. final; the person or thing after all the others: *the last of the customers* **2. at long last** After a long wait: *At long last they heard the voices of the rescue party.*

last determ., adv. **1.** After everything else: *Mary arrived last./ There will be terrible times in the last days* (2 Timothy 3:1). **2.** Most recent: *They have lived there for the last six years.*

last v. **1.** To continue in existence: *The storm lasted all night.* **2.** To remain in good condition: *This cheap radio won't last a year.*

last·ing (læs–tŋ) adj. Continuing for a long time: *She made a lasting impression on the audience.*

last·ly (læst–liy) adv. After everything else; finally: *Lastly, I'd like to thank ev-eryone who made this meeting a success.*

last straw (læst strɔ) n. The last of a sequence of troubles or annoyances that result in an emotional breakdown, loss of patience, etc.

Last Sup·per (læst sʌp–ər) n. The last supper eaten by Jesus with his disciples before the Crucifixion —see JESUS

latch (lætʃ) n. **1.** A small bar fastening a door or gate, lifted from its catch by a lever **2.** A spring lock that catches when the door is closed

latch v. To fasten or be fastened with a latch: *Be sure to latch the door when you leave.*

latch·et (lætʃ–ət) n. A strap for fastening a shoe or sandal to one's foot

late (leyt) adj. **1.** After the expected time: *The plane was 20 minutes late.* **2.** Toward the end of the day or season, etc.: *It began to rain in the late afternoon.* **3.** Happening a short time ago: *Did you hear the late news?* **4.** Of a person, having died recently: *Her late husband was a doctor.* —**lateness** n.

late adv. **1.** After the expected time: *She was 15 minutes late for her appointment.* **2.** At or

until an advanced time: *They always go to bed late.*

late-ly (leʸt–liʸ) adv. Recently: *Have you seen John lately?*

la-tent (leʸ–tənt) adj. In existence but not yet noticeable; hidden; undeveloped, but capable of becoming developed: *latent ability*

lat-er (leʸt–ər) adv. Compar. of late Afterward; subsequently: *He hasn't arrived yet, but surely he will be here later.*

lat-er-al (læt–ə–rəl) adj. Of, at, to, or from the side

la-tex (leʸ–tɛks) n. -texes or -tices The milky juice of plants, esp. the rubber tree

lath (læθ) n. **laths** A thin, narrow strip of wood

lathe (leʸð) n. A machine for turning and shaping articles of wood or metal

lath-er (læð–ər) n. A mixture of soap and water, for example: *He put some lather on his face and began to shave.*

Lat-in A-mer-i-ca (læt–ən ə–mɛər–ɪ–kə) n. The Spanish and Portuguese speaking countries of Central and South America —**Latin American** adj.

lat-i-tude (læt–ə–tuʷd) n. **1.** The distance north or south of the equator, measured in degrees —compare LONGITUDE **2.** Freedom of action or expression, etc.: *His new job allows him more latitude than his old job did.*

la-trine (lə–triʸn) n. A toilet, esp. one for use by a large number of people as in a military camp

lat-ter (læt–ər) adj. At or near the end, later: *He mentioned you in the latter part of his speech.*

latter n. The second of two people or things just mentioned: *The only apparent difference between Mary and Alice is that the latter is a little bit taller.*

lat-tice (læt–əs) n. A structure of crossed wooden or metal strips with open spaces between them, used as a support for climbing plants, a screen, etc.

laud (lɔd) v. To praise highly

laud-a-ble (lɔd–ə–bəl) adj. Praiseworthy

laud-a-to-ry (lɔd–ə–tɔr–iʸ) adj. Relating to, or expressing, high praise

laugh (læf) v. **1.** To express joy or mirth by making explosive sounds with the voice, usually with smiling: *It was so funny that I couldn't stop laughing.* **2.** To ridicule or make a mockery of sthg. or sbdy.: *They laughed at the Word of God that people must repent of their sins and put their trust in Jesus for eternal life.* (=*That is, they made a mockery of their sins and of the Word of God.*)

laugh (læf) n. **1.** An act of laughing: *She has a silly laugh.* **2.** A joke: *That's a laugh!*

laugh-a-ble (læf–ə–bəl) adj. Causing laughter; funny; foolish

laugh-ing-stock (læf–ŋ stɑk) n. A person or thing that is made the object of ridicule

laugh-ter (læf–tər) n. The act or sound of laughing

launch (lɔntʃ) v. **1.** To float a newly constructed boat or ship **2.** To send forth forcefully: *They launched a rocket.* **3.** To start; to put a plan into action: *The company launched a huge advertising campaign.*

laun-der (lɔn–dər) v. To wash clothes, sheets, etc.

laun-dry (lɔn–driʸ) n. -dries **1.** A place where laundering is done **2.** Clothes, towels, sheets, etc., that need washing or that have just been washed

lau-re-ate (lɔr–iʸ–ət) adj. **1.** Crowned with a laurel as a mark of honor **2.** Worthy of honor —**laureate** n. A person who has been honored in a particular field

laur-el (lɔr–əl) n. **1.** A small evergreen tree **2.** The foliage of this tree, esp. when woven into a wreath and used as an emblem of victory or distinction **3.** A wreath of laurel foliage **4. laurels** pl. Honor won **5. rest on one's laurels** To maintain one's reputation because of past successes without actually doing anything more: *This company used to be good, but they've been resting on their laurels for the past ten years.*

la-va (læ–və/ lɑ–və) n. Molten rock, thrown out by a volcano, becoming solid as it cools

lav-a-to-ry (læv–ə–tɔr–iʸ) n. -ries **1.** A washbowl with its fixtures **2.** A room equipped with washbowls and usually toilets, esp. one for public use

lav-en-der (læv–ən–dər) n. **1.** A plant with small, sweet-smelling pale purple flowers

2. A pale bluish-purple

lav-ish (læv–ɪʃ) v. To spend or give very freely: *In him [Jesus] we have redemption through his blood, the forgiveness of sins, in accordance with the riches of God's grace that he lavished on us with all wisdom and understanding* (Ephesians 1:8).

lavish adj. Very, very generous

law (lɔ) n. **1.** A rule, esp. an established or permanent rule, prescribed by the supreme power of a state to its subjects **2.** The whole body of such rules **3.** Trial in court to determine what is just and right **4.** The profession of a lawyer **5.** The science that deals with laws and their interpretation and application **6.** A rule or principle stating that sthg. always works in the same way under the same conditions: *the law of gravitation* **7.** A rule or principle of construction or procedure **8. natural knowledge of God's Law** The natural knowledge of God's will (the Moral Law) inscribed on man's heart when God created him (Colossians 3:10). NOTE: When the first man and woman (Adam and Eve) disobeyed God, their knowledge of his Law was obscured but not totally lost. To this day, all people have by nature some knowledge of God's Law, according to which their conscience judges their deeds and words (Romans 2:14,15). This innate knowledge of the Law is far from perfect, but it is sufficient to convict one of his sinfulness and of his guilt before God (Romans 1:32; 3:19,20). In no other way can we explain the efforts of people worldwide to atone for their sins by all manner of sacrifices. **9. The Revealed Law of God** Whether the natural Law written in man's heart was amplified by any revealed law between the time of Adam and Moses, we do not know. But on Mt. Sinai, the natural Law was amplified and codified in the Ten Commandments by God himself, and recorded by Moses in the 15th century B.C. (Exodus 20: 2-17; Deuteronomy 5:6-22) and is binding on all people (Galatians 3:10). NOTE: Obedience to the Moral Law is not optional, but is mandatory, and must be perfect (Matthew 5:48). Before the fall into sin in the Garden of Eden, man not only knew the will of God, but was able to keep it perfectly. But since the fall, unregenerate man can not keep the Law of God at all. "There is not a righteous man on earth who does what is right and never sins" (Ecclesiastes 7:20). Though outwardly a person may comply with certain demands of the Law, he cannot keep the Law in the right spirit, which is love to God. Man is by nature opposed to God (Romans 8:7). Therefore, he does not keep the commandments for God's sake, but for his own sake, from fear of punishment or from selfishness and self-righteousness. Lacking the proper motive, it is impossible for natural man to keep the Law as God wants it kept. Even Christians cannot keep the Law perfectly. The Apostle Paul confessed that he was not perfect, but was striving after a more perfect fulfilling of the Law (Romans 7:14,23). The best of Christians will have to admit many transgressions (1 John 1:8,9), and each transgression renders him guilty of transgressing the whole Law (James 2:10). The Law carries with it the threat of eternal punishment: "The soul who sins will die" (Ezekiel 18:20; Romans 6:23). The purpose of the Law is not to save man. "No one will be declared righteous in his (God's) sight by observing the law" (Romans 3:20). "All who rely on observing the Law are under a curse, for it is written, 'Cursed is everyone who does not continue to do everything written in the Book of the Law.' Clearly, no one is justified before God by the law" (Galatians 3:10,11). The chief purpose of the Law is to convict man of his sinfulness and lost condition and of his need for a Savior. The Law was our schoolmaster to bring us to Christ, that we might be justified by faith (Galatians 3:24 KJV). Jesus Christ came into the world to save sinners (1 Timothy 1:15). He kept the Law perfectly for us (2 Corinthians 5:21; Hebrews 4:15; 1 Peter 2:22), and he suffered all the punishment that we deserve when he suffered and died on the cross (Isaiah 53:5; 1 Peter 2:24). His blood cleanses us from all sin (1 John 1:7). Chris-

tians know that they cannot earn salvation by keeping the Law. They put their trust completely in Jesus for salvation. However, they use the Law as a guide , that they may be the kind of people God wants them to be, doing that which is truly good and pleasing in his sight, not out of any fear of punishment, not out of any hope of reward, but solely out of love for God, who loved the world so much that he gave his one and only Son (Jesus), that whoever believes in him. shall not perish but have eternal life (John 3:16): *A man is justified by faith [in Jesus Christ] apart from observing the law* (Romans 3:28)./ *The Bible says, "Cursed is everyone who does not continue to do everything written in the Book of the Law."* But Christ redeemed us from the curse of the law by becoming a curse for us, for it is written: *"Cursed is everyone who is hung on a tree"* (Galatians 3:10,13). In other words, Christ paid for all our sins against God's holy Law by dying on the cross (made out of a tree). He paid for all our sins with his own blood. Then he rose again from the dead. —see JESUS CHRIST, TEN COMMANDMENTS 10.The Old Testament: In John 10:34, Jesus refers to a passage in the Psalms, a poetic book, saying, *"Is it not written in the Law...?"* 11. The first five books of the Bible, the Pentateuch, which are largely historical and also prophetic: *Jesus said, "Everything must be fulfilled that is written about me in the Law of Moses, the Prophets and the Psalms"* (Luke 24:44).

law-ful (lɔ–fəl) adj. 1. Permitted by law: *It is not lawful to have more than one wife.* 2. Recognized by or established by law: *These newcomers are lawful citizens.* —opposite UNLAWFUL —**lawfully** adv.

lawn (lɔn) n. A piece of ground covered with closely cut grass

law-suit (lɔ–suʷt) n. A case in court

law-yer (lɔ–yər) n. One whose work it is to know about laws and advise and help others concerning the law; an attorney

lax (læks) adj. 1. Careless or not strict in discipline or morals 2. Lacking in control —**laxness** n.

lax-a-tive (læk–sə–tɪv) n. A medicine (or sthg. else you may eat or drink) that causes the bowels to empty easily, relieving constipation —**laxative** adj.

lay (leʸ) v. **laid** (leʸd), **laying** 1. To put sthg. down so as to rest in a horizontal position: *Lay the book on the table./ Men are laying a new carpet in the living room.* 2. To set in proper order or position: *The bricklayers are laying the bricks very quickly.* 3. To sacrifice or give up: *Jesus Christ laid down his life for us, and we ought to lay down our lives for our brothers* (1 John 3:16). 4. To produce eggs: *The chickens aren't laying many eggs these days.* 5. To make a claim or charge against someone in an official way: *The police have laid many charges against him.* NOTE: Do not confuse **lay, laid, laid** with **lie, lay, lain.** *I will lie down on the bed./ Last night I lay in bed for six hours without a wink of sleep./ On some occasions I have lain in bed for eight hours without sleeping./ I will lay the book on the table./ I laid my pen there already./ I have laid my coat on the bed.*

lay adj. 1. A lay person is one who is any member of the church except the pastor 2. A non-professional person

lay v. Past tense of lie: *I lay down on the couch last night and fell asleep.*

lay-er (leʸ–ər) n. 1. A single thickness, coating, or sheet of some material laid over a surface: *They put down a layer of crushed rock before paving the road.* 2. A hen: *This hen is a poor layer; she lays few eggs.* 3. A person who lays things, putting them in place: *a bricklayer*

lay-ette (leʸ–ɛt) n. A complete outfit for a newborn baby including clothing, bedding, etc.

lay-man (leʸ–mən) n. **-men** (–mən) A person who is not a pastor or other ordained person in the church

lay-off (leʸ–ɔf) n. The dismissal of employees temporarily, due to a lack of work or lack of funds: *There was a large layoff of employees by the auto factory.*

lay off v. (usu. past tense) To dismiss from employment: *About one-third of the employees were laid off last week.*

lay-out (leʸ–aʊt) n. 1. Arrangement of a town, garden, etc. 2. A drawing or plan of a building or a piece of literature, etc.

Laz-a-rus (lǽz–ə–rəs) n. **1.** A masculine name **2.** The brother of Mary and Martha whom Jesus raised from the dead after he had been dead for four days (John 11:17-44). —see JESUS, RESURRECTION

la-zy (leʸ–ziʸ) adj. **-zier, -ziest 1.** Disliking and avoiding work or other activity: *Lazy hands make a poor man* (Proverbs 10:4). **2.** Encouraging inactivity: *a lazy summer afternoon* **3.** Sluggish; moving slowly: *a lazy river* —**lazily** adv. —**laziness** n.

leach (liʸtʃ) v. **1.** To cause water to filter through sthg. **2.** To pass water through sthg. to remove soluble substances: *The minerals had been leached from the soil because of so much rain.*

lead (liʸd) v. **led** (lɛd), **leading 1.** To guide or direct someone or sthg. in a certain direction, by going first or by holding their hand, holding by a rope, etc.: *The horses were led into the yard./ If a blind man leads a blind man, both will fall into a pit* (Matthew 15:14). **2.** To be the means of going through an area to a certain place: *This road leads to the castle./ Jesus said, "I am the way [that leads to eternal life]... No one comes to the Father except through me"* (John 14:6). **3.** To influence someone to do or not to do sthg.: *Those who lead many to righteousness [will shine] like the stars for ever and ever* (Daniel 12:3). *Lead us not into temptation* (Matthew 6:13). **4.** To direct, control, or govern: *The general led his troops into battle.* **5.** To be winning in sports or in a game or contest: *North High (School) was leading South High 7 to 3 at half time.* **6.** To live; pursue: *He led a hectic life.* **7. lead up to sthg.** To be an introduction to: *With his kind words, he was leading up to a request for a day off.*

lead n. **1.** The front place or position: *North High was in the lead at half time.* **2.** The distance or number of points by which a person or team (or thing, etc.) is ahead of another: *Central High had a lead of 17 points.* **3.** A piece of evidence or a clue that may help discover or settle sthg.: *The police have several leads concerning the identity of the thief.* **4.** A leading part in a play or motion picture: *Who plays the lead in that new film?* **5.** The state of being first: *Who has the lead in scientific research?*

lead (lɛd) n. **1.** A soft, heavy, grayish metal that is easily bent and shaped, and used esp. in pipes, batteries, and solder **2.** A black substance (a kind of carbon) used in pencils: *I need a soft lead pencil to make a dark line.*

lead-er (liʸd–ər) n. **1.** A person who is in front or goes first: *The leader of the race was at least 100 yards ahead of the runner in second place.* **2.** A person who guides or directs a group or a movement: *an orchestra leader/ the leader of the protest/of the rebellion/of a new political party* —**leadership** n.

lead-ing (liʸ–dɪŋ) adj. **1.** Chief or most important **2.** Directing or guiding

lead-ing light (liʸ–dɪŋ laɪt) n. An important or influential person in a community, church, etc.

leaf (liʸf) n. **leaves** (liʸvz) **1.** A usu. flat and green outgrowth of a plant stem **2.** A sheet of paper, esp. a page in a book **3.** Part of a table top that may be folded up or down to make the table bigger or smaller

leaf-let (liʸf–lət) n. A small sheet of printed matter; pamphlet

league (liʸg) n. **1.** An association or an alliance working together for a common cause **2.** A number of teams that play games among themselves in competition: *the National Football League* **3. in league with** Working together, often secretly or for a bad purpose

lea-guer (liʸ–gər) n. A member of a league

leak (liʸk) n. **1.** A crack or a hole, made by accident, which allows fluid, gas, light, etc. to enter or escape **2.** The liquid or gas that passes through a leak **3.** An accidental or intentional spreading of news that ought to be secret

leak v. **1.** To let a liquid or gas in or out of a crack or small hole: *The milk carton leaks.* **2.** To make known information that should be kept secret: *The senator leaked the news to the press.* —**leak-age** (liʸ–kɪdʒ) n.

leak-y (liʸ–kiʸ) adj. **-ier, -iest** Letting liquid leak in or out: *a leaky faucet*

lean (liʸn) v. **leaned** or **leant, leaning 1.** To slope to one side; not to be upright: *The tow-*

er of Pisa (in Italy) leans so much that it is amazing that it doesn't fall down. **2.** To bend at the waist: *Bill leaned forward to hear her better.* **3.** To rest oneself or sthg. against sthg. else: *He leaned the ladder against the house.* **4. lean on** To trust or depend on: *Trust in the Lord with all your heart and lean not on your own understanding* (Proverbs 3:5).

lean adj. **1.** Very thin; not fat: *He is tall and lean.* **2.** Not containing much fat: *lean meat* **3.** Not producing much: *It was a lean year for some businesses.* **—leanness** n.

lean-ing (liᵞ–nɪŋ) n. A liking or a preference: *She has a leaning toward classical music.*

leap (liᵞp) v **leaped** or **leapt, leaping 1.** To jump: *He leaped from the second story window.* **2.** To jump over: *The dog leaped over the wall and ran away.*

leap n. **1.** A jump **2.** The distance leaped: *A leap of 29 feet would break the long jump record.*

leap year (liᵞp yɪər) n. A year that has 366 days, occurring every fourth year, February 29th being the extra day

learn (lɜrn) v. **learned** also *BrE.* **learnt, learning 1.** To gain knowledge, understanding, or skill by study or experience: *Mary is learning how to swim.* **2.** To memorize: *Learn these rules.* **3.** To become informed of: *Mrs. Brown learned that her son survived the plane crash.* NOTE: For the past tense and past participle **learned** is the usual *AmE.* form but **learned** and **learnt** are equally common in *BrE.* **—learner** n.

learn-ed (lɜr–nəd) adj. Having or showing much knowledge: *The professor is a very learned man.*

learn-ing (lɜr–nɪŋ) n. Knowledge: *Let the wise listen and add to their learning* (Proverbs 1:5).

lease (liᵞs) n. A written agreement giving the use of a car, house, building, piece of land, etc., on payment of rent: *a four-year lease*

lease v. **leased, leasing** To give or acquire a car, house, etc. in this way: *He never buys a car; he leases them.*

leash (liᵞʃ) n. A length of chain or strip of leather, etc. for leading or restraining an animal: *Some dogs should be kept on a leash.*

least (liᵞst) adj. Superl. of **little 1.** That which is the smallest that exists or is the smallest possible: *the least number of errors* **2.** Lowest in importance

least adv. **1.** Superl. of **little**; in the smallest or lowest degree: *the least expensive* **2. least of all** Especially not: *I don't want to talk to anyone right now. Least of all that scatterbrain!*

least determ., pron. Superl. of **little 1.** The smallest number or amount: *The one that costs the least is not necessarily the best buy.* **2. at least (a)** As much or more than: *This car gets at least 30 miles per gallon of gas.* **(b)** If nothing else: *This car doesn't look very good, but at least it runs well.*

leath-er (lɛð–ər) n. The skin of an animal prepared for use as clothing, wallets, etc.: *a leather jacket*

leath-er-y (lɛð–ə–riᵞ) adj. Like leather: *leathery meat*

leave (liᵞv) v. **left, leaving 1.** To go away (from): *God has said, "Never will I leave you; never will I forsake you"* (Hebrews 13:5). *Mary is leaving for the Orient tomorrow.* **2.** To let sthg. remain behind after going away: *Jim left this note for you and said he'd call you later.* **3.** To fail to take or to bring sthg.: *He left his hat behind.* **4.** To put in one's will for someone to inherit: *He left everything to his wife when he died.* **5.** To entrust to someone's care while absent: *He left his car when he went overseas.* **6.** To allow or remain for someone else to do: *Leave that job for the experts.*

leave n. In the navy, a period of time away from duty, like an army furlough or a civilian vacation: *The naval officers had a 30-day leave.*

leav-en (lɛv–ən) n. **1.** A small piece of fermenting dough set aside to be used for producing fermentation of a fresh batch of dough **2.** *Spiritual* A good or evil person or teaching that influences the whole group: *A little leaven leavens the whole lump. Purge out, therefore, the old leaven [of wickedness]. Let us keep the feast, not with old leaven [of mistaken ideas], neither with the leaven of malice or wickedness; but with the unleavened [bread] of sincerity and truth* (1 Corinthians 5:6-8).

leaven v. **1.** To make batter or dough rise be-

fore or during baking by means of a leaven-ing agent 1. To spread through, causing a gradual change: *A little leaven leavens the whole lump.*

leav-en-ing (lɛv-ən-ɪŋ) n. 1. A substance such as baking powder or yeast, used to make baked goods rise by the formation of carbon dioxide in the batter or dough 2. Any influence spreading through sthg. and working on it to bring about a gradual change

leaves (liʸvz) n. *pl.* of leaf

lech-er (lɛtʃ-ər) n. A man who is always thinking about and looking for sexual pleasure —lecherous adj.

lech-er-y (lɛtʃ-ər-iʸ) n. Unrestrained, excessive indulgence of sexual desires; gross sensuality

lec-tern (lɛk-tərn) n. A stand with a slanted top to hold a book, used in churches and by lecturers

lec-ture (lɛk-tʃər) n. -tured, -turing 1. A speech given to a class or other audience, esp. as a method of instruction 2. A long, solemn scolding: *The teacher gave the children a long lecture about running in the hall.*

lecture v. The action of lecturing: *She lectured them for 15 minutes about running in the hall.* —lec-tur-er n. (lɛk-tʃər-ər) n.

led (lɛd) v. Past tense and past part. of lead

ledge (lɛdʒ) n. A narrow shelf or sthg. that sticks out like a shelf: *They rested on a ledge, half way up the mountain.*

ledg-er (lɛdʒ-ər) n. The chief book of accounts, recording money going in and out of a business

lee (liʸ) n. The side away from the wind; the sheltered side

leech (liʸtʃ) n. 1. A small blood-sucking worm usu. living in water 2. *Fig.* A person who persistently tries to get money, food, etc. from other people without doing anything to earn it

leek (liʸk) n. A vegetable resembling a long onion but having a milder flavor

leer (lɪər) n. A sly, sideways look, esp. one expressing sexual desire —leer v.

lee-ward (liʸ-wərd) n. Direction toward which the wind blows —leeward adj. On or to the side sheltered from the wind —leeward adv. Toward the lee

lee-way (liʸ-weʸ) n. 1. The sideways drift of a ship or plane due to the wind 2. The amount of freedom a person has to move or change: *This itinerary gives us a lot of leeway for sight-seeing.*

left (lɛft) adj. 1. The side of the body that usually contains the heart; on the west side if you are facing north 2. On or in the direction of one's left side: *In England people drive on the left side of the road.* —opposite RIGHT

left n. 1. The left side or direction: *Keep to the left when driving in England.* 2. The most radical, socialist, or communist parties or party members

left v. Past tense and past part. of leave

left-hand (lɛft-hænd) adj. 1. Of or on the left 2. Turning from right to left: *He made a left-hand turn.*

left-ist (lɛft-əst) n. A person whose political position is radical or liberal

left-o-vers (lɛft-oʷ-vərz) n. Food remaining after a meal, esp. that which is saved for a future meal: *We're having leftovers for dinner.*

left wing (lɛft wɪŋ) n. Supporters of a more extreme form of socialism than other members of their party or group —left-wing adj.

leg (lɛg) n. 1. One of the limbs on which a person or an animal walks 2. The part of a garment that covers the leg 3. One of the supports on which a piece of furniture stands 4. One part of a journey: *The last leg of our cross-country journey was from Pittsburgh to New York.* 5. on one's last legs (a) Very, very tired (b) Nearly worn out 6. pull someone's leg A joking attempt to make sbdy. believe sthg. that is not true 7. stretch one's legs To take a walk after sitting a long time 8. he hasn't a leg to stand on (a) No excuse for one's behavior (b) No justification for one's request

leg-a-cy (lɛg-ə-siʸ) n. *pl.* -cies 1. Inheritance 2. Sthg. left behind by someone who had one's job, house, etc. previously 3. Sthg. passed down to people from predecessors or from earlier events: *the cultural legacy of the Renaissance*

le-gal (li^y–gəl) adj. **1.** Allowed by law; lawful —opposite ILLEGAL **2.** Concerning or using the law: *He took legal action to stop the new construction.* —**le-gal-i-ty** (lɪ–gæl–ə–ti^y) n. —**legally** adv.

le-gal-ism (li^y–gəl–ɪz–əm) n. Strict adherence to the law, esp. to the letter rather than the spirit

le-gal-ize or **-ise** (li^y–gə–laɪz) v. **-ized, -izing** To make legal —**le-gal-i-za-tion** (li^y–gə–lə–ze^y–ʃən) n.

le-ga-tion (lɪ–ge^y–ʃən) n. **1.** A diplomatic minister and his or her staff in a foreign mission **2.** Their official headquarters

leg-end (lɛdʒ–ənd) n. **1.** A story handed down from one generation to another but probably not true **2.** A notable person whose deeds are much talked about in his own time **3.** Wording on a map explaining the symbols used **4.** Words that accompany a picture or an illustration

leg-en-dar-y (lɛdʒ–ən–dɛər–i^y) adj. **1.** Of, based on, or presented in legends; fabled; mythical; fanciful; imaginary: *King Arthur is a legendary figure.* **2.** Famous; familiar to all: *Babe Ruth performed legendary feats as a home run hitter.*

leg-i-ble (lɛdʒ–ə–bəl) adj. Handwriting or print that is easy to read —opposite ILLEGIBLE —**leg-i-bil-i-ty** n. (lɛdʒ–ə–bɪl–ə–ti^y) —**legibly** adv. *Please write legibly.*

le-gion (li^y–dʒən) n. **1.** In ancient Rome, a body of 3,000 to 6,000 soldiers **2.** A large group of people

leg-is-late (lɛdʒ–əs–le^yt) v. **-lated, -lating** To make or enact laws

leg-is-la-tion (lɛdʒ–əs–le^y–ʃən) n. **1.** The act of making laws **2.** Laws made by a legislative body

leg-is-la-tive (lɛdʒ–əs–le^y–tɪv) adj. **1.** Concerning making of laws **2.** Having the authority and responsibility to make laws —**legislatively** adv.

leg-is-la-tor (lɛdʒ–əs–le^yt–ər) n. A member of a legislative body; a lawmaker

leg-is-la-ture (lɛdʒ–əs–le^y–tʃər) n. An organized body of persons who have the power to make and to change laws

le-git-i-ma-cy (lə–dʒɪt–ə–mə–si^y) n. The quality or state of being legitimate

le-git-i-mate (lə–dʒɪt–ə–mət) adj. **1.** In accordance with the law or the rules **2.** Of a child, born of parents who are lawfully married to each other —op-posite ILLEGITIMATE **3.** Reasonable; logical; justifiable: *She had a legitimate excuse for being absent.* —**legitimately** adv.

le-git-i-ma-tize (lə–dʒɪt–ə–mə–taɪz) v. **-tized, -tizing** Same as legitimize

le-git-i-mize (lə–dʒɪt–ə–maɪz) v. **-mized, -mizing** To make or declare legitimate —**le-git-i-mi-za-tion** (lə–dʒɪt–ə–mə–ze^y–ʃən) n.

leg-ume (lɛg–yu^wm/ lɪ–gyu^wm) n. **1.** Any of a large family of herbs, shrubs, and trees, including peas and beans **2.** The pod and beans of some members of this family, used for food

le-gu-mi-nous (lɪ–gyu^w–mə–nəs) adj. Having the nature of, or bearing a legume or legumes

lei (le^y /le^y– i^y) n. In Hawaii, a wreath of flowers and leaves, usu. worn around the neck

lei-sure (li^y–ʒər/ lɛ–ʒər) n. **1.** Time when one is free from work or other responsibilities; free time: *He lives a life of leisure.* **2. at leisure (a)** Not busy **(b)** Not rushed

lei-sure-ly (li^y–ʒər–li^y/ lɛ–) adj. Done without haste: *a leisurely stroll through the garden*

lem-on (lɛm–ən) n. **1.** A yellow citrus fruit **2.** Sthg. unsatisfactory: *This car is a real lemon; it's always breaking down.*

lem-on-ade (lɛm–ə–ne^yd) n. A drink made from fresh lemons with sugar and water added

le-mur (li^y–mər) n. A monkey-like animal that lives in Madagascar and is active at night

lend (lɛnd) v. **lent** (lɛnt), **lending** **1.** To let someone use sthg. for a limited time: *They [the righteous] are always generous and lend freely* (Psalm 37:26). *He who is kind to the poor lends to the Lord* (Proverbs 19:17). **2.** To add: *The flowers lent color to the display.* —compare BORROW, LOAN

length (lɛŋkθ) n. **1.** The distance from one end of sthg. to the other end or of the longest side of sthg.: *The length of the swimming pool is 100 feet; it is 100 feet long.* **2.** Extent of time:

The fear of the Lord adds length to life (Proverbs 10:27). —compare BREADTH **3.** A piece of sth.: *a length of string* **4.** In racing, the measurement from one end to the other of a boat, car, horse, etc.: *Silver Streak won by three lengths.*

length-en (lɛŋk–θən/ lɛŋ–θən) v. To make or become longer —opposite SHORTEN

length-y (lɛŋ–θiʸ) adj. **-ier, -iest** Too long: *a lengthy speech* —**lengthiness** n.

le-ni-ent (liʸ–niʸ–ənt/ liʸ–nyənt) adj. Merciful in judgment; punishing only lightly: *Our courts are much too lenient with vicious criminals.* —compare STRICT —**lenience** also **leniency** n.

lens (lɛnz) n. **1.** A piece of glass or plastic, curved on one or both sides, used to make eye-glasses, cameras, microscopes, etc.: *I need new lenses for my glasses./ The camera lens is dirty.* **2.** A part of the eye, behind the pupil

lent (lɛnt) v. Past tense and past part. of lend

Lent (lɛnt) n. The 40 days before Easter during which many Christians fast —see EASTER

len-til (lɛnt–əl) n. The seed of a pod-bearing plant, used in soup

leop-ard (lɛp–ərd) n. **leopardess** *fem.* A large, fierce, cat-like animal, yellowish with black spots, found in Africa and southern Asia

le-o-tard (liʸ–ə–tard) or **leotards** (liʸ–ə–tardz) n. A one-piece, tight-fitting garment, worn by dancers, acrobats, etc.

lep-er (lɛp–ər) n. A person who has leprosy

lep-ro-sy (lɛp–rə–siʸ) n. A contagious skin disease, causing serious and permanent damage to the body, including loss of fingers, toes, etc. —**leprous** adj.

les-bi-an (lɛz–biʸ–ən) adj., n. A woman who is sexually attracted to other women, a sin, referred to in Scripture as a shameful lust (Romans 1: 26). —**lesbianism** n. —compare HOMOSEXUAL. NOTE: God is holy, and He detests all sin, but because of his great love and mercy, he forgives those who repent of their sins and put their trust in Jesus for eternal life. —see FORGIVENESS, JESUS, MAN

le-sion (liʸ–ʒən) n. **1.** Injury; wound **2.** A harmful change in the tissue of a bodily organ, tending to result in impairment or loss of function: *a lesion of the right lung*

-less (–ləs) suffix Lacking: *sleepless/ worthless*

less (lɛs) adv. **1.** To a smaller degree: *less crowded/ less fortunate* **2.** Smaller in rank or importance: *This job is less important than my last job.* —opposite MORE

less determ., pron. **1.** A smaller amount: *They drink less coffee now./ It's less than a mile to my house.* **2. nonetheless** Nevertheless; anyway: *I know I can't afford it, but I want to buy it nonetheless.* NOTE: When speaking of countable things, use **fewer;** when speaking of uncountable things, use **less.** *fewer men/ cars/flowers/apples, etc.; less sugar/ coffee/ salt/ flour, etc.*

les-see (lɛ–siʸ) n. A person to whom property is leased

less-en (lɛs–ən) v. To become less in size, importance, appearance, etc.

less-er (lɛs–ər) adj. *fml.* Smaller; not so much or so great: *the lesser number* —**lesser** adv. *a lesser-known author*

les-son (lɛs–ən) n. **1.** A passage from the Holy Scriptures, read in a service of worship **2.** A reading or exercise taught to or learned by a pupil, esp. in school: *a music lesson* **3.** The period of time a pupil or class studies a subject: *Each English lesson lasts 50 minutes.* **4.** An experience from which one should learn: *His car accident taught him a lesson. He'll be more careful in the future.*

les-sor (lɛs–ər/ lɛs–ɔr) n. A person who leases property of another; a landlord

lest (lɛst) conj. For fear that: *The thief ran, lest he should be caught.*

let (lɛt) v. **let, letting 1.** To allow someone to do sth.: *Jesus said, "Let the little children come to me, and do not hinder them, for the kingdom of God belongs to such as these"* (Mark 10:14). **2.** To allow sth. to happen: *He let a whole month go by before answering my letter.* **3.** To cause to: *I will let you know as soon as possible.* **4.** Used in the imperative to give orders or suggestions: *Come, let us sing for joy to the Lord; let us shout aloud to the Rock of our salvation. Let us come before him with thanksgiving* (Psalm 95:1-2). **5. let alone** Not to mention: *There's not even room for her, let*

alone the children. **6. let someone alone** To stop annoying someone: *Let her alone. Why are you always teasing your sister?* **7. let go** To stop holding onto someone or sthg.: *Let go of my arm! You're hurting me.* **8. let oneself go: (a)** To relax; behave more freely **(b)** To pay less attention to one's personal appearance than usual: *Since the tragedy in his family, he's just let himself go.* **9. let someone know** To inform someone: *Let them know when you're coming.* **10.** Used when making a suggestion that includes the one spoken to: *Let's go!* **11. let well enough alone** *AmE.* To allow things to remain as they are for fear of making matters worse **12. let sthg. out** To express; utter: *She let out a scream when she saw the snake.* **13. let out** To end: *What time does the movie let out?* **14. let up** To lessen or stop: *I wish the rain would let up.* **15. let-down** Disappointment: *He thought he would get a big promotion, so it was a real let-down when he didn't get it.*

le-thal (liˠ–θəl) adj. Causing or able to cause death

leth-ar-gy (lɛθ–ər–dʒiˠ) n. Extreme lack of energy or vitality —**le-thar-gic** (lɪ–θɑr–dʒɪk) adj. Unnaturally drowsy; sluggish

let-ter (lɛt–ər) n. **1.** A message, usu. written or printed by hand or typewritten, and usu. sent in an envelope **2.** One of the signs in writing or printing, such as A, B, C, etc. that represents a speech sound: *There are 26 letters in the English alphabet.* **3.** The literal meaning of an agreement, law, etc., rather than the intended meaning: *Unfortunately, they felt bound by the letter of the law, rather than by the spirit of the law.*

let-ter-head (lɛt–ər–hɛd) n. **1.** A piece of stationery with the name and address of an organization **2.** The heading at the top of such a piece of stationery

let-tuce (lɛt–əs) n. A garden plant with large, pale green leaves, used in salads and on some sandwiches

leu-ke-mi-a (luʷ–kiˠ–miˠ–ə) n. Cancer affecting white blood cells

lev-ee (lɛv–iˠ) n. **1.** A bank built to keep a river from overflowing **2.** A landing place for boats

lev-el (lɛv–əl) n. **1.** A position of height: *Denver is a mile above sea level./ His car is on the sixth level of the parking lot.* **2.** Quality: *The level of his work has improved rapidly.* **3.** A device for establishing a horizontal line or surface **4.** Amount, size or number: *The workmen have been told that they must increase their production level.* **5. on the level** *infml.* Honest; honestly

lev-el adj. **1.** Horizontal; even **2. on a level with** Equal to: *He's on a level with the best musicians in the country.* **3. level-headed** Having good sense: *He is level-headed and can think quickly in an emergency.* **4. one's level best** *infml.* One's very best effort

lev-er (lɛv–ər) n. **1.** A bar or other device, which turns about a fixed point, in order to lift sthg. heavy or to force sthg. open **2.** A handle used to operate or control a machine: *Pull the lever to start the machine.*

lev-er-age (lɛv–rɪdʒ/ lɛv–ə–rɪdʒ) n. **1.** The action or mechanical effect of a lever **2.** Power or influence in obtaining a result: *He has a lot of leverage with certain politicians.*

le-vi-a-than (lə–vaɪ–ə–θən) n. **1.** A sea monster **2.** Anything of immense size

lev-i-tate (lɛv–ə–teˠt) v. **-tated, -tating** To rise or float in the air, esp. by means of supernatural power

lev-i-ta-tion (lɛv–ə–teˠ–ʃən) n. The illusion of raising a body in the air without support: *The magician gave an example of levitation by making his assistant float in the air.*

Le-vit-i-cus (lə–vɪt–ɪ–kəs) n. The third book in the Bible, containing the laws and ritual relating to priests and Levites —see BIBLE, OLD TESTAMENT

lev-i-ty (lɛv–ə–tiˠ) n. Lack of proper seriousness or respect; frivolity

lev-y (lɛv–iˠ) v. **-ied, -ying** To impose or collect a tax, tariff or other fee

lev-y n. **-ies 1.** An imposing or collecting, as of a tax **2.** The amount collected **3.** The conscription of troops **4.** The troops conscripted

lewd (luʷd) adj. Sexually impure; lustful; thinking about sex in a sinful manner —**lewdly** adv. —**lewdness** n. *Out of men's hearts come evil thoughts, sexual immorality...,*

lewdness... All these evils come from inside and make a man unclean (Mark 7:21-23). NOTE: God hates the sin of lewdness and all sin, but because of his great love and mercy, he forgives the sins of those who repent (turn from their wicked ways) and put their trust in Jesus for eternal life (Acts 2:38;16:31). —see JESUS, SIN, FORGIVENESS

lex-i-cal (**lek**-sɪ-kəl) adj. **1.** Pertaining to the words of a language, as contrasted with its grammar **2.** Of a lexicon

lex-i-cog-ra-phy (lek-sə-**kag**-rə-fiⁱ) n. **1.** The editing or making of a dictionary **2.** The principles or procedures followed in making a dictionary

lex-i-cog-ra-pher (lek-sə-**kag**-rə-fər) n. A maker of dictionaries

lex-i-con (**lek**-sə-kən/ -kan) n. **1.** A dictionary, esp. of an ancient language **2.** The vocabulary of a particular language or field of study

li-a-bil-i-ty (laɪ-ə-**bɪl**-ə-tiⁱ) n. -ties **1.** The condition of being legally liable; responsible: *He accepted liability for the damages to my car.* **2.** A debt or obligation **3.** Sthg. which is a nuisance or more of a disadvantage than an advantage: *This old car is a real liability.* —opposite ASSET

li-a-ble (**laɪ**-ə-bəl) adj. **1.** Tending to have, to get, or to suffer from: *This road is liable to get flooded every time it rains.* **2.** Possibly or probably about to happen: *John is liable to call on the phone any minute now.* **3.** Responsible: *He is liable for his son's debts.*

li-ai-son (liⁱ-**eⁱ**-zan/ liⁱ-ə-zan) n. **1.** A close bond; a working relationship **2.** Communication, esp. between parts of an armed force **3.** An illicit sexual relationship

li-ar (**laɪ**-ər) n. A person who tells lies: *Jesus said, "He [the devil] is a liar and the father of lies"* (John 8:44). *Who is the liar? It is the man that denies that Jesus is the Christ* (1 John 2:22). *If anyone says, "I love God," yet hates his brother, he is a liar. For anyone who does not love his brother, whom he has seen, cannot love God whom he has not seen* (1 John 4:20). *Anyone who does not believe God has made him out to be a liar, because he has not believed the testimony God has given about His Son* (1 John

5:10). NOTE: Lying is a sin and God hates sin, but he is also a God of love and forgiveness. Those who repent and trust in Jesus for salvation will have eternal life. —see JESUS, SIN, FORGIVENESS

lib (lɪb) n. *infml.* Liberation (esp. in the phrase **women's lib**)

li-ba-tion (laɪ-**beⁱ**-ʃən) n. **1.** The ritual of pouring out wine or oil as a sacrifice to a god **2.** The liquid that is poured out **3.** Used humorously, an alcoholic drink or the act of drinking

li-bel (**laɪ**-bəl) n. Sthg. written that is harmful to someone else's reputation: *He sued the newspaper for libel.*

li-bel-ous (**laɪ**-bəl-əs) adj. **1.** Of the nature of, or involving, a libel **2.** Given to writing and publishing libels

lib-er-al (**lɪb**-ə-rəl) adj. **1.** Generous: *He was very liberal with his money.* **2.** Tolerant; willing to respect the ideas and feelings of others **3.** Favoring civil liberties, democratic reforms, and the use of public resources to promote social progress **4.** In Christian doctrine, concerning persons or beliefs that do not follow traditional beliefs —see LIBERALISM **5.** An education that is not specialized or technical, aiming rather at general culture and wide possibilities for self-expression **6.** Lacking moral restraint; licentious **7.** Not literal; loose: *a liberal interpretation*

liberal n. **1.** A person who is not strict in the observance of orthodox, traditional, or established forms or ways **2.** A member or supporter of a liberal political party **3.** An advocate of liberalism, esp. in individual rights **4.** In Christianity, a person who accepts the ideas of liberalism which casts doubt on basic Christian doctrines, such as the deity of Jesus Christ and the divine inspiration of the Bible

liberal arts (**lɪb**-ər-əl arts) n. The subjects of an academic college course, such as literature, history, philosophy, languages, survey courses of the sciences, etc. that provide the student with a broad cultural background rather than any specific professional background

lib-er-al-ism (lɪb-ər-əl-ɪz-əm) n. **1.** In Christianity, the view that tries to explain traditional Christian beliefs in new ways. It is sometimes called modernism. Liberalism casts doubts on many basic Christian doctrines, such as the teachings that the Scriptures contain no errors and that Jesus Christ is true God. It says that the Bible must be judged by reason and science. **2.** A political philosophy based on belief in what some consider progress, the essential goodness of man, and the autonomy of the individual and standing for the protection of political and civil liberties

lib-er-al-i-ty (lɪb-ə-ræl-ət-iʸ) n. Generosity

liberally (lɪb-ə-rə-liʸ) adv. Generously

lib-er-ate (lɪb-ə-reʸt) v. **-ated, -ating** *fml.* To set free from control or confinement: *The hostages were liberated by the army.* —**liberation** n. —**liberator** n.

lib-er-ty (lɪb-ər-tiʸ) n. **-ties 1.** The condition of being free from restriction or control; freedom; the right to act as one chooses **2.** The permission or opportunity to do or use sthg. **3. take liberties (a)** To behave too familiarly toward a person **(b)** To interpret facts too freely, making changes that should not be made: *They took many liberties with the original story when producing the movie.* **4.** Authorized leave from naval duty: *The sailors were on liberty from Friday night until Monday morning.* —compare FREEDOM

li-brar-i-an (laɪ-brɛər-iʸ-ən) n. A person who is in charge of, or who assists in a library

li-brar-y (laɪ-brɛər-iʸ) n. **-ies 1.** A building or room that contains books, periodicals, etc., that may be used in that building or borrowed and taken from the building **2.** A collection of books, periodicals, etc.

lice (laɪs) n. *pl.* of **louse**

li-cense (laɪ-səns) n. **1.** An official printed form showing that permission has been given to do or to own sthg., usu. for a payment: *a driver's license/a fishing license* **2.** Too much freedom of action, speech, etc.: *Godless men... change the grace of God into a license for immorality and deny Jesus Christ our only Sovereign and Lord* (Jude 4).

license v. **-censed, -censing** To give official permission to do sthg.

li-cen-tious (laɪ-sen-tʃəs) Morally unrestrained; immoral; lewd; lascivious —**licentiously** adv. —**licentiousness** n. *Let us walk [behave] properly, as in the day, not in revelry and drunkenness, not in licentiousness... But put on the Lord Jesus Christ, and make no provision for the flesh, to fulfill its lusts* (Romans 13:13,14). NOTE: God is holy and he hates all sin, but because of his great love and mercy, he forgives the sins of those who come to him in true repentance and put their trust in Jesus for eternal life (Romans 6:23; John 3:16; Mark 1:15).

li-chen (liʸ-kən) n. A large group of moss-like plants that grow on rocks, trees, and other hard surfaces

lick (lɪk) v. **1.** To move the tongue across a surface in order to wet, clean, or taste it: *The dog licked my hand./ We licked a lot of stamps for our Christmas mailing.* **2.** To play lightly over: *Waves licked the shore.* **3.** *infml.* To defeat: *Our team really licked their team, 25 to 3.*

lick n. **1.** The act of licking **2.** A small quantity: *He doesn't have a lick of sense.* **3. a lick and a promise** A hasty careless effort: *He gave his room a lick and a promise. (=He cleaned it only a little.)*

lic-o-rice (lɪk-ə-rɪʃ / lɪk-rɪʃ) n. **1.** The sweet-tasting dried root of a European plant **2.** The black substance obtained from this root, used in medicine and candy **3.** Candy flavored with licorice

lid (lɪd) n. **1.** The removable cover of a pot, box, or other container **2.** Eyelid

lie (laɪ) v. **lay** (leʸ), **lain** (leʸn), **lying** (laɪ-ɪŋ) **1.** To be in a horizontal position on a surface: *The dog is lying on the floor.* **2.** To be in the specified position; be situated: *Our town lies at the foot of the mountains.* **3.** To remain in the specified condition or position: *The printing presses have lain idle since the print shop fire last month.*

lie v. **lied, lying** To tell a lie: *God hates a lying tongue* (Proverbs 6:16,17). *Do not steal. Do not lie. Do not deceive one another* (Leviticus 19:11). NOTE: God hates the sin of lying and all sin, but because of his great love

and mercy, he forgives the sins of those who repent (turn from their wicked ways) and put their trust in Jesus for eternal life (Acts 2:38; 16:31). —see JESUS

lie n. An untrue statement purposely made in order to deceive someone

lien (li'n) n. A legal claim against some property until a debt is paid

lieu (lu^w) n. **in lieu of** Instead of

lieu-ten-ant (lu^w–tɛn–ənt) n. An officer in the armed forces

life (laif) n. **lives** (laivz) **1.** Physical life or existence; the ability to function and grow that distinguishes human beings, animals, and plants from rocks, minerals, water, etc.: *And the Lord God formed man from the dust of the ground and breathed into his nostrils the breath of life, and man became a living being* (Genesis 2:7). **2.** Spiritual life: *Jesus said, "Whoever hears my word and believes him who sent me... has crossed over from death to life"* (John 5:24). **3.** Eternal life: *The gift of God is eternal life through Jesus Christ our Lord* (Romans 6:23). *For God so loved the world that he gave his one and only Son, that whoever believes in him shall not perish but have eternal life* (John 3:16). **4.** The period during which one is alive: *I have lived in California all my life.* **5.** A person: *Several lives were lost (=people died) in the flood.* **6.** Activity, movement: *There were signs of life this morning.* **7.** Sbdy. who is stimulating, adding interest or enjoyment or activity in a group: *Bob was the life of the party.*

life-guard (laif–gard) n. An expert swimmer employed to rescue bathers at public swimming pools or beaches

lift (lift) v. **1.** To raise, elevate; bring from a lower to a higher level: *These bags are too heavy to lift.* **2.** To disappear: *The fog lifted.* **3.** To bring a ban, blockade, e.g., to an end: *The curfew was lifted.* **4.** *infml.* To steal small articles —see SHOPLIFT **5.** To rise: *The blimp lifted into the air.*

lift n. **1.** The act of lifting **2.** A free ride in a vehicle: *Can you give me a lift into town?* **3.** *BrE.* for elevator **4.** *infml.* A good feeling: *It really gave me a lift to see my old friends again.* **5.** Assistance of any kind: *Can you give me a lift with this piano? (=help me move it)* **6.** A device for lifting

lig-a-ment (lig–ə–mənt) n. One of the strong bands of tough fibrous tissue that joins bones or holds some part of the body in position

light (lait) n. **1.** The brightness given by the sun, a flame, a lamp, etc. that makes vision possible: *I can't read in this bad light.* **2.** Sthg. that produces light: *Dim the car lights when in the city or following closely behind another car.* **3.** Public knowledge: *Some new information has come to light about last week's fire.* **4.** The way in which sbdy. or sthg. is regarded: *Young people and elderly people often see things in a different light.* **5.** Spiritual light: *Jesus said, "I am the light of the world. Whoever follows me shall not walk in darkness, but will have the light of life [spiritual life]"* (John 8:12). *He also said to his followers, "You are the light of the world. Let your light so shine before men, that they may see your good works and glorify your Father who is in heaven"* (Matthew 5:14,16). **6.** The Word of God: *Your Word is a lamp to my feet and a light for my path* (Psalm 119:105).

light v. **lit** or **lighted**, **lighting 1.** To cause sthg. to catch fire: *He lit the fire in the fireplace.* **2.** To cause to give out light: *The room was lit only by candles.* **3.** To cause to become bright with excitement: *His eyes really lit up when he saw her.*

light adj. **1.** Easy to see in: *The kitchen is the lightest room in this house.* **2.** Pale in color; not dark: *light green* **3.** Not very heavy: *She is so light, she only weighs 90 pounds.* **4.** Not requiring much concentration: *light reading* **5.** Not much: *a light meal* **6.** Not severe: *a light rain* **7.** Of sleep, not deep or sound: *He's a light sleeper. The slightest noise will wake him up.* **8. make light of** To treat as of little importance

light adv. **1.** Lightly **2.** Without much luggage: *I always travel light.*

light-en (lait–ən) v. **1.** To make or become brighter —compare DARKEN **2.** To make or become less heavy: *We have to lighten the load before we cross that weakened bridge.* **3.** To make or become less troubled

light-head-ed (lait–hed–əd) adj. **1.** Frivolous;

giddy **2.** Dizzy or delirious

light-heart-ed (laɪt–**hɑrt**–əd) adj. Cheerful; happy; free from care

light-house (laɪt–haʊs) n. A tower or similar structure with a powerful beacon light, at or near a dangerous place, to serve as a warning or a guide for ships

light-ly (laɪt–liʸ) adv. **1.** Gently: *He pressed lightly on the brake.* **2.** To a small degree: *lightly toasted* **3.** Without serious consideration: *He didn't take those insults lightly.* **4.** Without proper respect

light-ness (laɪt–nəs) n. **1.** A state of being light in weight **2.** A state of being light in color; paleness **3.** Lack of seriousness

light-ning (laɪt–nɪŋ) n. **1.** A powerful flash of light in the sky, usu. followed by thunder **2.** Very fast: *Jesus said, "I saw Satan fall like lightning from heaven"* (Luke 10:18).

light-year (laɪt–yɪər) n. The distance travelled by light in one year, about five trillion, eight hundred seventy-eight billion miles (5,878,000,000,000 miles)

lig-nite (lɪg–naɪt) n. A soft, brownish-black coal

lik-a-ble also **like-a-ble** (laɪ–kə–bəl) adj. Pleasant, easy to like

like (laɪk) v. **liked, liking 1.** To be fond of: *I like tea.* **2.** To want: *I'd like to see you.* NOTE: When **like** means *to be fond of,* it is used alone: when it means *to want,* it is used with *would.* Compare: *I like milk, but I would not like any right now.* —opposite DISLIKE

like prep. **1.** Similar; the same kind or in the same way: *We know that when he [God] appears, we shall be like him, for we shall see him as he is* (1 John 3:2)./ *He was like a son to me./ Do not answer a fool according to his folly, or you will be like him yourself* (Proverbs 26:4). **2.** Typical of: *It was just like her to be late. She's always late.* —opposite UNLIKE

like conj. *infml.* **1.** In the same way as: *Tell it like it is.* (=*tell the whole truth; don't exaggerate, and don't omit any important details*) **2.** As if: *He drives like he owns the road.*

like-li-hood (laɪk–liʸ–hʊd) n. Probability; the chance of sthg. happening

like-ly (laɪk–liʸ) adj. **-lier, -liest 1.** Probable; expected: *Is it likely to rain?* **2.** Apparently capable of doing well: *Jim was voted the most likely to succeed.*

likely adv. Probably: *He is likely to come by bus.*

lik-en (laɪk–ən) v. To compare with: *Our little group can be likened to one big happy family.*

like-ness (laɪk–nəs) n. Resemblance: *a family likeness*

like-wise (laɪk–waɪz) adv. Similarly: *Tom took off his coat and Bob did likewise.*

li-lac (laɪ–lək/ –læk/ –lɑk) n. A shrub with clusters of fragrant purplish or white flowers

lilac adj. Of pale purple color

lilt (lɪlt) n. **1.** A gay, lively song or tune **2.** A rhythmical swing, flow, or cadence

lil-y (lɪl–iʸ) n. **-ies** A tall plant with showy, often trumpet-shaped flowers

lily of the valley n. *pl.* **lilies of the valley** A plant with a slender cluster of white bell-shaped flowers

li-ma bean (laɪ–mə biʸn) n. **1.** A plant cultivated for its flat, edible, pale green seeds **2.** The seed of the lima bean

limb (lɪm) n. **1.** A large tree branch **2.** An arm or leg of a person, a leg of an animal, or a wing of a bird **3.** **out on a limb** In a dangerous situation

lim-ber (lɪm–bər) adj. Flexible; capable of bending easily; agile

limber v. To make or become limber: *They were limbering up before running the race.*

lim-bo (lɪm–boʷ) n. A condition of prolonged uncertainty: *Plans were completed last year, but the whole project has been in limbo since then.*

lime (laɪm) n. **1.** A white substance obtained by heating limestone or shells until they crumble to powder, used in making cement and in fertilizer **2.** A small lemon-shaped, greenish-yellow citrus fruit

lime-ade (laɪm–eʸd) n. A beverage made from lime juice, sugar, and water

lime-light (laɪm–laɪt) n. The center of public attention: *She's been in the limelight for 40 years.*

lim-er-ick (lɪm–ər–ɪk) n. A light or humorous poem of five lines

lime-stone (laɪm–stoʷn) n. Stone consisting

essentially of calcium carbonate, used in building

lim-it (lɪm–ət) n. **1.** The point, edge, or line beyond which sbdy. or sthg. cannot or may not go: *I can walk about 20 miles. That's my limit.* **2.** A prescribed maximum or minimum: *the speed limit* **3. off limits** Where one is not allowed

limit v. To keep below or at a certain point or amount: *We must limit our spending.*

lim-i-ta-tion (lɪm–ə–te^y–ʃən) n. **1.** The conditions of being limited **2.** A weakness which limits one's actions: *I know my limitations; I can't swim that channel.*

lim-it-ed (lɪm–ə–təd) adj. **1.** Small in amount, strength, endurance, efficiency, etc. and not able to improve: *Her capacity for learning is quite limited.* —opposite UNLIMITED **2.** Also **Ltd.** (of a company) *Dawson, Brown, and Co., Ltd.*

lim-ou-sine (lɪm–ə–zi^yn/ lɪm–ə–zi^yn) n. **1.** A large, luxurious automobile **2.** A small bus used to carry passengers to and from airports, etc.

limp (lɪmp) v. To walk lamely, favoring one leg: *He twisted his ankle badly, but he got up and limped away.*

limp n. The act of limping: *He walks with a limp.*

limp adj. **1.** Lacking strength: *Her leg went limp, and she fell down.* **2.** Not stiff: *These plants haven't been watered lately and the leaves are limp.* —**limply** adv. —**limpness** n.

lim-pid (lɪm–pəd) adj. Esp. of liquid, clear; transparent

lin-den (lɪn–dən) n. A shade tree with heart-shaped leaves and clustered yellow flowers

line (laɪn) n. **1.** A thin mark with length but no width: *She drew straight lines across the page.* **2.** A stripe that acts as a border or as a place to start or finish: *Jim was first to cross the finish line.* **3.** A row: *a line of people waiting to buy tickets* **4.** A length of rope, cord, or wire: *a clothes line* **5.** An electric power transmission cable **6.** A railway track: *the main line from Kansas City to Los Angeles* **7.** A system of transportation, esp. a company owning that system: *an airline/a shipping line* **8.** A direction: *You're standing in my line of*

vision. **9.** A business, profession, occupation, etc.: *What's your line (of work or business)?* **10.** A telephone connection: *I tried to call you but the line was busy.* **11.** A type of goods: *a new line of shoes* **12.** People following one another in time, esp. a family: *He comes from a long line of preachers.* **13.** An official point of view; policy: *the party line.* **14. draw the line (at)** To state the limit that one is willing to go: *He said he'd do almost anything for money, but that he would draw the line at doing anything dishonest.* **15. in line for** Being considered for sthg. and likely to get it: *He's in line for a big promotion.* **16. in line with** In accordance with: *That isn't in line with the company policy.* **17. out of line (a)** Not in a straight line **(b)** Not in agreement **(c)** Disobedient

line v. **lined, lining 1.** To form lines: *Trees lined the riverbank./ Crowds lined the street to see the parade.* **2.** To cover on the inside: *She lined the box with newspaper.* **3.** To put a lining in: *She lined her coat with silk.*

lin-e-age (lɪn–i^y–ɪdʒ) n. Ancestry; family

lin-e-al (lɪn–i^y–əl) adj. **1.** Of or composed of lines **2.** In the direct line of descent

lin-e-ar (lɪn–i^y–ər) adj **1.** Of or relating to lines **2.** In respect to length only **3.** Of a style of art in which line is more emphasized than color, design, etc.

lin-er (laɪ–nər) n. **1.** Commercial ships or airplanes **2.** One that makes lines **3.** A baseball line drive **4.** Sthg. used as a lining

lin-en (lɪn–ən) n. **1.** Thread or cloth made from flax **2.** Household articles such as sheets and towels, made from linen or other fabrics —**linen** adj.

lin-ger (lɪŋ–gər) v. **1.** To wait; to delay going: *They lingered in the hall, looking at the pictures.* **2.** To be slow to go away: *The smell of the fire lingered for days.*

lin-ge-rie (lɑn–dʒə–re^y) n. Underclothes for women

lin-gua fran-ca (lɪŋ–gwə fræn–kə) n. Any language used amongst peoples of different nations to communicate with each other

lin-guist (lɪŋ–gwəst) n. **1.** One who speaks several languages fluently **2.** A specialist in historical, comparative, descriptive, or geographical linguistics

lin-guis-tic (lɪŋ-**gwɪs**-tɪk) adj. Of languages

linguistics (lɪŋ-**gwɪs**-tɪks) n. **1.** The science of languages, including phonology, morphology, syntax, and semantics, usu. subdivided into descriptive, historical, comparative, and geographical linguistics **2.** The study of the structure, development, etc. of a particular language and of its relationship to other languages

lin-i-ment (lɪn-ə-mənt) n. A kind of thin, usu. oily ointment, for rubbing into the skin, esp. to help soreness and stiffness of the joints

lin-ing (laɪ-nɪŋ) n. A piece of material covering the inner surface of sthg.

link (lɪŋk) n. **1.** Sthg. which connects two other parts: *There is definitely a link between smoking and lung cancer.* **2.** Any of the series of rings or loops of a chain: *A chain is no stronger than its weakest link.* **3.** A section of sthg. resembling a chain: *a link of sausage* **4.** Anything serving to connect: *a link with the past*

link v. To connect: *This railroad links all the major cities on the east coast.*

link-age (lɪŋ-kɪdʒ) n. **1.** A linking or being linked **2.** The fact or way of being connected

links (lɪŋks) n. **1.** A golf course **2.** A stretch of rolling, sandy land, esp. along a seashore

li-no-le-um (lɪ-noʷ-liʸ-əm) n. A hard, smooth, washable floor covering

lin-seed (lɪn-siʸd) n. The seed of the flax plant

linseed oil (lɪn-siʸd ɔɪl) n. A yellowish oil pressed from linseed, used in making paints, printing inks, and linoleum

lint (lɪnt) n. **1.** Cotton fiber used to make yarn **2.** The waste cotton that remains after ginning **3.** Bits of thread, ravelings, or fluff from cloth or yarn

lin-tel (lɪn-təl) n. The horizontal beam or stone above a window or door to support the weight above it

li-on (laɪ-ən) **lioness** (laɪ-ən-əs) *fem.* n. **1.** A large, powerful mammal of the cat family which lives mainly in Africa **2.** A person of great courage or strength **3.** the lion's share (of) The biggest share

lip (lɪp) n. **1.** One of the two fleshy folds forming the edges of the mouth and important

in speech: *His [God's] praise will always be on my lips* (Psalm 34:1). **2.** The tip of a pouring spout: *the lip of the pitcher* **3.** give/ pay lip service to To agree in words, but not in fact: *These people honor me with their lips, but their hearts are far from me* (Matthew 15:8).

lip-stick (lɪp-stɪk) n. A stick of coloring for the lips, usu. a shade of red or pink

liq-ue-fy (lɪk-wə-faɪ) v. **-fied, -fying** To cause to become liquid

li-queur (lɪ-kɜr) n. A sweet, strongly flavored alcoholic liquor

liq-uid (lɪk-wəd) n. A substance that is not solid or gas, which flows and has no fixed shape: *Water is a liquid.*

liquid adj. Flowing freely like water: *liquid gold/oxygen*

liq-ui-date (lɪk-wə-deʸt) v. **-dated, -dating 1.** To pay off a debt **2.** To settle the accounts of a bankrupt business firm by apportioning assets and debts **3.** To get rid of; kill: *All the dictator's opponents have been liquidated.* —**liq-ui-da-tion** (lɪk-wə-deʸ-ʃən) n.

liq-uor (lɪk-ər) n. A strong alcoholic drink, esp. one made by distillation, such as whiskey or rum

lisp (lɪsp) v. To speak with /s/ sounds that are not clear, making the /s/ sound like a /th/ —**lisp** n. *He speaks with a lisp.*

list (lɪst) n. A series of names, words, numbers, etc., set in order: *a shopping list*

list v. To make a list: *He listed all the groceries he had to buy.*

lis-ten (lɪs-ən) v. **1.** To make an effort to hear sthg.; to pay attention: *Everyone should be quick to listen, slow to speak, and slow to become angry* (James 1:19). *A wise man listens to advice* (Proverbs 12:15). **2.** listen for To pay attention so as to be sure of hearing: *The radioman was listening for distress signals.*

lis-ten-er (lɪs-ən-ər) n. One who listens

list-ing (lɪs-tɪŋ) n. **1.** The act of making a list **2.** An entry in a list, as in a telephone directory

list-less (lɪst-ləs) adj. Weary; without energy or interests; seeming too tired to care about anything —**listlessness** n.

lit (lɪt) v. Past tense and past part. of **light**

lit-a-ny (lɪt-ə-niʸ) n. **-nies** A prayer consisting

of a series of invocations with responses

lit-er *AmL.* ll-uv *D: I.* (li**ᵛ** tər) n. A metric unit of capacity equal to 1.0567 liquid quarts or .908 dry quarts

lit-er-a-cy (lɪt–ə–rə–si**ʸ**) n. The ability to read and write: *The rate of adult literacy in many countries is very low. Much work is needed.* —opposite ILLITERACY

lit-er-al (lɪt–ə–rəl) adj. **1.** Exact: *Give me a literal account of what happened.* **2.** Word for word, with no explanations or exaggerations and nothing added by the imagination: *a literal, word for word translation*

lit-er-al-ly (lɪt–ər–ə–li**ʸ**) adv. **1.** Exactly: *He did literally nothing all day.* **2.** Used to intensify an adjective: *He was literally blue with cold.* **3.** Word for word: *to translate literally* **4.** According to the words and not the intention: *When he said, "Lend me your ears," he didn't mean that literally. He meant, "Listen to me."*

lit-er-ar-y (lɪt–ə–rɛər–i**ʸ**) adj. **1.** Concerning literature or the writing of books **2.** A person knowledgeable about books: *He's one of my literary friends.*

lit-er-ate (lɪt–ər–ət) adj. **1.** Able to read and write: *Less than 50% of the people are literate in some countries.* —opposite ILLITERATE **2.** Well-educated

lit-er-a-ture (lɪt–ə–rə–tʃər) n. **1.** Written works which are of artistic value **2.** Printed material, esp. giving information: *Have you any literature on travel in India?*

lith– (lɪθ–) or **litho-** (lɪθ–o**ʷ**–) Prefix Stone **–lith** (–lɪθ) Suffix Stone: *monolith*

lithe (laɪθ) adj. Flexible; limber; bending easily

lith-i-um (lɪθ–i**ʸ**–əm) n. A silver-white metallic element, the lightest metal known

lith-o-graph (lɪθ–ə–græf) n. A print made by lithography

lithograph v. To produce by lithography —**li-thog-ra-pher** (lɪ–θɑg–rə–fər) n.

li-thog-ra-phy (lɪ–θɑg–rə–fi**ʸ**) n. The process of printing from a smooth surface, such as a metal plate, treated so that ink adheres only to the design to be printed

li-thol-o-gy (lɪ–θɑl–ə–dʒi**ʸ**) n. The scientific study of rocks

lith-o-sphere (lɪθ–ə–sfɪər) n. The earth's crust

lit-i-gate (lɪt–ə–ge**ʸ**t) v. **-gated, -gating 1.** To bring to court in a lawsuit **2.** To engage in a lawsuit —**lit-i-ga-tion** (lɪt ə **ɡo**ᵛ ʃən) n

lit-mus (lɪt–məs) n. A blue coloring matter that turns red in an acid solution and back to blue in an alkali solution

litmus paper (lɪt–məs pe**ʸ**–pər) n. Paper that is treated with litmus, used to indicate whether a solution is acidic or alkaline

li-tre (li**ʸ**–tər) n. British for liter

lit-ter (lɪt–ər) n. **1.** Things thrown away; rubbish; trash scattered in an untidy way: *Put your litter in that trash can over there.* **2.** A number of young animals born to the same mother at the same time: *Our cat had a litter of six kittens.*

litter v. To scatter untidily: *Don't litter the highway by throwing things out of the car window.*

lit-ter-bug (lɪt–ər–bʌg) n. One who litters the highway or public places

lit-tle (lɪt–əl) adj. **-tler, -tlest 1.** Small: *She's little for her age.* **2.** Young: *Jesus said, "Let the little children come to me, and do not hinder them, for the kingdom of God belongs to such as these... anyone who will not receive the kingdom of God like a little child [=with childlike faith] will never enter it"* (Mark 10:14, 15). **3.** Short: *I'll only be here a little while./ My uncle is too little to qualify for the police force.* **4.** Not important: *I didn't think she'd be so upset about such a little thing.*

little adv. **less, least 1.** Not much: *He sleeps very little.* **2.** Not at all: *Little did they know what difficulties lay ahead.* **3.** Rather: *I was a little annoyed with them.* **4. little by little** Gradually

little pron. **less, least** Small quantity: *I understood little of what he said.*

little n. Not much: *Better the little that the righteous have than the wealth of many wicked* (Psalm 37:16).

lit-ur-gy (lɪt–ər–dʒi**ʸ**) n. **-gies** The prescribed form of a religious worship service, esp. in the Christian church —**li-tur-gi-cal** (lɪ–tɜr–dʒɪ–kəl) adj. —**li-turgically** adv.

liv-a-ble also **live-a-ble** (lɪv–ə–bəl) adj. **1.** Suitable to live in; habitable **2.** Endurable

live (lɪv) v. **lived, living 1.** To be alive physi-

cally; have life: *One of God's commandments is: "Honor your father and your mother, so that you may live long in the land the Lord your God is giving you"* (Exodus 20:12). **2.** To be alive spiritually: *The righteous will live by faith* (Romans 1:17). *Saint Paul said, "I no longer live, but Christ lives in me"* (Galatians 2:20). **3.** To have eternal life: *Jesus said to his disciples, "Because I live, you shall also live"* (John 14:19). *Jesus also said, "Whoever lives and believes in me will never die"* (John 11:25). **4.** To reside; to dwell: *Where do you live?* —see LIFE, JESUS

live (laɪv) adj. **1.** Alive; living; not dead **2.** Charged for explosion: *live ammunition* **3.** Carrying electrical current: *a live wire* **4.** Not extinct: *a live volcano* **5.** Of immediate or present interest: *a live issue* **6.** Having resilience or elasticity: *a live rubber ball* **7.** Involving a performance or appearance in person, rather than a filmed or recorded one: *It was not a recorded show; it was a live broadcast.*

live-li-hood (laɪv–liʸ–hʊd) n. The way in which one earns a living: *What is his means of livelihood?*

live-li-ness (laɪv–liʸ–nəs) n. A lively condition; vigor

live-ly (laɪv–liʸ) adj. **-lier, -liest 1.** Full of life; active; vigorous: *a lively performance* **2.** Vivid; intense: *lively colors* **3.** Exciting; animated: *a lively debate* **4.** Moving quickly and lightly, as a dance **5.** Having great resilience: *a lively ball*

liv-en (laɪ–vən) v. To make or become lively or livelier

liv-er (lɪv–ər) n. A large glandular organ of the body which produces bile and cleans the blood

liv-er-y sta-ble (lɪv–ər–iʸ steʸ–bəl) n. A stable where horses and vehicles are cared for or let out for hire

lives (laɪvz) n. pl. of **life**: *More than a hundred lives were lost in the plane crash.*

live-stock (laɪv–stɑk) n. Domestic animals raised for use or profit

live wire (laɪv waɪr) n. **1.** A wire carrying an electric current **2.** *Slang* An extremely energetic person

liv-id (lɪv–əd) adj. **1.** Bluish-gray in color **2.** Ashen or pale, as from anger

liv-ing (lɪv–ɪŋ) adj. **1.** Alive: *The Lord God formed man from the dust of the ground and breathed into his nostrils the breath of life, and man became a living being* (Genesis 2:7). **2.** Existing; in use: *The Word of God is living and active...* (Hebrews 4:12). **3.** Vivid: *living color* **4. living water** The Word of God which gives spiritual and eternal life: *Jesus, who is the way, the truth, and the life* (John 14:6) *told the woman: "If you knew the gift of God and who it is that asks you for a drink, you would have asked him and he would have given you living water. Everyone who drinks this water [from the well] will be thirsty again, but whoever drinks the water I give him will never thirst [spiritually]. Indeed, the water I give him will become in him a spring of water welling up to eternal life"* (John 4: 10-14).

living n. **1.** Alive now: *God is not the God of the dead but of the living* (Matthew 22:32). *Why do you look for the living among the dead? He [Jesus] is not here; he has risen!* (Luke 24:5,6). **2.** Earnings with which one buys the necessities of life: *How do you make a living?* **3. standard of living** A standard one enjoys with regard to the necessities, comforts and luxuries of life (food, drink, etc.): *The cost of living increased by ten per cent last year.*

liv-ing room (lɪv–ɪŋ ruʷm) n. A room used by a family for various shared and social activities: *After dinner we sat in the living room and talked for hours.*

liz-ard (lɪz–ərd) n. A reptile having an elongated body and a long tapering tail

lla-ma (lɑ–mə) n. A wooly, South American animal resembling a camel, but smaller and without a hump, used as a beast of burden and raised for its meat, milk, and wool

lo (loʷ) Interj. Behold! Look!

load (loʷd) n. **1.** Sthg. carried or to be carried, esp. sthg. heavy: *a load of rocks* **2.** The quantity that can be carried, as on a truck: *a two-ton load* **3.** *Infml.* **loads of,** also **a load of** A lot of: *We had loads of fun at the beach./ He had loads of work to do.*

load v. **1.** To put a load in or on sthg.; to fill with goods; to receive a cargo: *They loaded the ship with iron ore.* **2.** To put a roll of film

into a camera **3.** To put bullets into a gun: *He loaded his rifle.*

load-ed (lo^wd–əd) adj. **1.** Full, carrying a load: *The truck was fully loaded.* **2.** Very rich: *He's so loaded he could buy the international airport.* **3.** Drunk: *He got loaded and then passed out on the floor.* **4. a loaded question** One that is worded unfairly **5. load the dice** To take unfair advantage of someone: *He didn't have a chance; the dice were loaded against him.*

loaf (lo^wf) n. **loaves** (lo^wvz) Bread shaped and baked in one piece

loaf v. To waste time, esp. by not working when one should: *Stop loafing and get to work.*

loaf-er (lo^w–fər) n. **1.** One who loafs **2.** *AmE.* A lightweight shoe

loam (lo^wm) n. Rich, fertile earth in which decaying and decayed plants are mixed with clay and sand

loan (lo^wn) n. **1.** Sthg. which is lent; sthg. to be returned or paid back: *That money was a loan, not a gift.* **2.** The act of lending: *I gave him the loan of my bicycle until tonight.*

loan v. To lend: *Will you loan me your pen?*

loath (lo^wθ) adj. Unwilling; reluctant

loathe (lo^wð) v. **loathed, loathing** To feel intense hatred and disgust for

loath-ing (lo^wð–ıŋ) n. Intense disgust

loath-some (lo^wð–səm) n. Sthg. extremely unpleasant; disgusting; horrible: *a loathsome disease*

loaves (lo^wvz) n. *pl.* of **loaf**

lob (lɑb) v. **-bb-** To hit the ball in a high arc: *He lobbed the ball over the net.*

lo-bar (lo^w–bər/ lo^w–bɑr) adj. Pertaining to a lobe

lo-bar pneu-mo-nia (lo^w–bər nu^w–**mo**^w**n**–yə) n. Acute pneumonia, involving a lobe or lobes of the lungs

lob-by (lɑb–i^y) n. **-bies 1.** An entrance or a waiting room in a hotel, an apartment building, or a theater **2.** A group of people who try to influence the government in a certain way

lob-by v. **-bied, -bying** To try to persuade one or more legislators (members of lawmaking bodies) to vote for or against a certain measure

lob-by-ist (lɑb–i^y–ıst) n. One who lobbies

lobe (lo^wb) n. **1.** Any rounded or projected part, as the fleshy lower part of the ear **2.** A part of an organ, marked off by a fissure or connective tissue

lob-ster (lɑb–stər) n. A kind of shell fish with long claws, used for food

lo-cal (lo^w–kəl) adj. **1.** Of or in the place where one lives or is visiting: *the local weather forecast* **2.** Concerning a particular part: *a local infection* —**locally** adv.

local n. **1.** A bus or a train that makes all the stops: *Take the Local to 14th Street. Don't take the Express.* **2.** A person living in a particular place: *I don't know how often the buses stop here. Let's ask one of the locals.*

lo-cale (lo^w–kæl) n. A locality, esp. with reference to events connected with it

lo-cal-i-ty (lo^w–**kæl**–ə–ti^y) n. **-ties** A particular place, situation, or location

lo-cal-ize (lo^w–kə–laız) v. **-ized, -izing** To limit to a small area: *to localize the pain*

lo-cate (lo^w–ke^yt) v. **-cated, -cating 1.** To determine the position of: *We located the bank and post office right away, but we haven't found the library yet.* **2.** To establish residence or a business in a certain place: *to locate one's home in the country* **3.** To find by searching: *Did you locate the source of the trouble?*

lo-ca-tion (lo^w–ke^y–ʃən) n. **1.** A situation or position: *He asked about the location of our house.* **2.** A site away from a motion picture studio where scenes for a movie are being filmed

lo-ca-tor (lo^w–ke^yt–ər) n. **1.** A person who fixes boundaries **2.** A filing card that shows the location of personnel, etc. **3.** A device for locating airborne aircraft

lo-ci (lo^w–si^y/–ki^y/–kaı) n. *pl.* of **locus**

loc. cit. *abbr.* In the place cited

lock (lɑk) n. **1.** A device for closing and fastening sthg. by means of a key or a combination: *He bought a new lock for his bike.* **2.** A stretch of water closed off by gates, esp. on a canal, so that the water level can be raised or lowered **3.** A curl of hair: *The child has curly locks.* **4. lock, stock and barrel** Completely

lock v. **1.** To fasten or become fastened with a

lock: *Be sure to lock your bike whenever you leave it anywhere out of your sight.* **2.** To put in jail: *They locked up the suspect.* **3.** To embrace tightly: *locked in each other's arms* **4.** To be entangled in a struggle: *locked in battle*

lock-er (lɑk–ər) n. A small, usu. metal closet for keeping articles locked up, esp. at a school where there is one for each pupil, or in a sports building where clothes may be kept

lock-et (lɑk–ət) n. A small, ornamental case made of silver or gold, etc. for holding a picture of sbdy. or a lock of hair, usu. worn around the neck on a chain

lock-jaw (lɑk–dʒɔ) n. A form of tetanus in which the jaws lock together

lo-co-mo-tion (loʷ–kə–moʷ–ʃən) n. The act or power of motion

lo-co-mo-tive (loʷ–kə–moʷ–tɪv) n. A self-propelled engine that moves railroad cars

lo-cus (loʷ–kəs) n. **lo-ci** (loʷ–siʸ/–kiʸ/–kaɪ) Place; locality; site

lo-cust (loʷ–kəst) n. **1.** Any of various large grasshoppers, esp. a type that travels in destructive swarms, destroying crops by eating them **2.** Cicada **3.** A tree with feather-like leaves, fragrant white flowers, and hard durable wood

lo-cu-tion (loʷ–kyuʷ–ʃən) n. **1.** A particular style of speech **2.** Phraseology **3.** Regional expressions

lode (loʷd) n. A vein of metal ore

lode-stone (loʷd–stoʷn) n. **1.** A magnetic stone that attracts iron and steel **2.** Sthg. that attracts

lodge (lɑdʒ) v. **lodged, lodging 1.** To stay, for a short time, usu. paying rent: *We lodged at Paradise Inn last night.* **2.** To settle or become fixed firmly in a position: *A bone lodged in his throat.* **3.** To complain officially: *He lodged a complaint with the store manager.*

lodge n. **1.** A cottage or cabin, often rustic, used as a temporary shelter **2.** A resort hotel for hunters, skiers, etc.

lodg-er (lɑdʒ–ər) n. A person who pays rent to stay in somebody's house or in a furnished lodge; a roomer

lodg-ing (lɑdʒ–ɪŋ) n. A place to stay for payment

loft (lɔft/lɑft) n. **1.** A room under the roof of a barn where hay is stored **2.** An attic **3.** A gallery in a church or hall: *a choir loft*

loft-y (lɔf–tiʸ) adj. **-ier, -iest 1. (a)** Exalted; noble; an unusually high quality of thinking, etc.: *lofty goals* **(b)** Arrogant; a feeling of superiority; showing belief of being better than other people: *a lofty attitude* **2.** Of imposing height; towering: *lofty mountain peaks*

log (lɔg/ lɑg) n. **1.** A trunk, or a section of a trunk, of a fallen or felled tree: *Many early settlers built their houses out of logs./As a boy Abraham Lincoln lived in a cabin made of logs.* **2.** An official written record of a journey: *The captain described the storm in the ship's log.* **3. sleep like a log** To sleep deeply without moving

lo-gan-ber-ry (loʷ–gən–bɛər–iʸ) n. **1.** A plant that is a cross between a red raspberry and a blackberry **2.** It's fruit

log-a-rithm (lɔg–ə–rɪð–əm/ lɑg–) n. The power to which a base number must be raised to equal a given number

log-ger (lɔg–ər/ lɑg–) n. One whose job is felling trees and getting them to the lumber mill; a lumberjack

log-ging (lɔg–ɪŋ/lɑg–) n. The work of cutting down trees, sawing them into logs, and removing them from the forest

log-ic (lɑdʒ–ɪk) n. **1.** The study and art of reasoning correctly **2.** Correctness of reasoning: *There's no logic in spending money on liquor, tobacco, and other useless and harmful things.*

log-i-cal (lɑdʒ–ɪ–kəl) adj. **1.** Thinking or acting in accordance with the rules and science of logic: *a logical conclusion* **2.** Having or showing good reasoning; sensible —opposite ILLOGICAL —compare REASONABLE —**logically** adv.

lo-gi-cian (loʷ–dʒɪʃ–ən) n. One skilled in logic

lo-gis-tics (loʷ–dʒɪs–tɪks) n. The procurement, maintenance, and transportation of personnel, materiel, etc.

lo-go (loʷ–goʷ) n. An identifying symbol used as a trademark

loin (lɔɪn) n. *usu. pl.* **1.** The part of the sides and back between the lower ribs and the

hipbone 2. A cut of meat from this region of an animal

loin-cloth (lɔɪn–klɔθ) n. A cloth worn around the loins, as by some people in the tropics

loi-ter (lɔɪt–ər) v. 1. To linger aimlessly in a public place 2. To move in a slow, idle manner

lone (loʷn) adj. Without other people: *the lone ranger* —see ALONE

lone-ly (loʷn–liʸ) adj. -lier, -liest 1. Alone and unhappy; lacking and wanting companionship: *a lonely child, without any friends* 2. Of a place, far away from busy places: *a lonely cottage in the country* —loneliness n.

lon-er (loʷ–nər) n. One who avoids others

lone-some (loʷn–səm) adj. Lonely; sad because of being alone: *Though surrounded by people, he was very lonesome, because he didn't know anyone there.* —see ALONE

long (lɔŋ) adj. 1. Not short; having considerable length: *The cathedral was 600 feet long.* 2. For a great period of time: *Mary and Jane had a long conversation.* 3. Having a specified length or duration: *a yard long/an hour long* 4. Seeming to be of greater length or duration of time than usual: *This trip gets longer every time I make it./ This has been a very long day.* —opposite SHORT

long adv. 1. A great period of time: *That happened long before you were born./ Have you been waiting long?* 2. **as long as:** (a) Provided that; if: *You children may go out, as long as you promise to be back before dark.* (b) While; inasmuch as; since: *As long as you're here, why not stay a few days?* 3. **no longer** Not any more: *He no longer lives here.* 4. **So long!** *infml.* Goodbye!

long n. 1. A long time: *We'll be there before long. (=soon)* 2. **the long and the short of it** A story, etc. told in few words; a summary

long v. To desire very much; to yearn: *She longed to see her friend again.*

lon-gev-i-ty (lɑn–dʒɛv–ə–tiʸ /lɔn–) n. 1. A long duration of life 2. The length of life

long-ing (lɔŋ–ɪŋ) n., adj. Showing a feeling of wanting sthg.: *Hope deferred makes the heart sick, but a longing fulfilled is a tree of life* (Proverbs 13:12). —longingly adv.

lon-gi-tude (lɑn–dʒə–tuʷd) n. The distance measured in degrees, east or west of the Greenwich meridian (near London): *Los Angeles is approximately 120 degrees west longitude.* —lon-gi-tu-di-nal (lɑn–dʒə–tuʷd–ən–əl) adj.

long-shore-man (lɔŋ–ʃɔr–mən) n. A person whose job is loading and unloading ships

long shot (lɔŋ–ʃɑt) n. 1. Anything thought to have little chance of success 2. **not by a long shot** By no means

long–stand-ing (lɔŋ–stæn–dɪŋ) adj. Of long duration; extending over a long period of time

long–suf-fer-ing (lɔŋ–sʌf–ər–ɪŋ) n. Long and patient endurance —long–suffering adj.

long-term (lɔŋ–tɜrm) adj. Covering or extending to a long period of time

look (lʊk) v. 1. To turn the eyes so as to see, examine, or find sthg.: *You are looking at this dictionary./ Man looks at the outward appearance [of a person] but God looks at the heart* (1 Samuel 16:7). 2. To appear a certain way (ill, well, etc.) *Mom looks tired./ John looks like his father.* 3. To see and notice carefully: *Now look what you've done!* 4. **look as if/ look like** To seem probable: *It looks like rain.* 5. **look after sbdy./sthg.** To take care of: *Religion that God our Father accepts as pure and faultless is this: To look after orphans and widows in their distress and to keep oneself from being polluted by the world* (James 1:27). 6. **look at (a)** To watch; to regard; judge: *He looks at things differently, now that he's in charge.* **(b)** To consider: *I wouldn't look at such a small offer.* **(c)** To think about and be warned: *Look at Mr. Smith: he died of lung cancer at the age of 49.* 7. **look down on** To despise; to have a low opinion of: *Jesus said, "See that you do not look down on one of these little ones. [=children who believe in Jesus] For I tell you that their angels in heaven always see the face of my Father in heaven"* (Matthew 18:10,11). —compare LOOK UP TO 8. **look for** To search; to try to find 9. **look forward to sthg.** To wait with pleasure for sthg. to happen: *I'm looking forward to seeing you.* 10. **look into sthg.** To inspect or investigate closely: *We're looking into the cause of her death.* 11. **look on (a)** To watch sthg. but not participate **(b)** To re-

gard: *I've lived with my aunt since I was five years old, and I look on her as my mother.* **12. look upon sbdy./ sthg.** To regard: *I look on/ upon him as a friend.* **13. look out** To be careful; take care; watch (for): *Look out! You'll hit that car!* —see also LOOKOUT **14. look sthg. over** To examine quickly —compare OVERLOOK **15. look up (a)** To get better; improve: *Things are looking up.* **(b) look sthg. up** To find information in a book: *Look up the word in the dictionary.* **(c) look sbdy. up** To visit when in the same area: *Look me up next time you're in town.* **16. look up to sbdy.** To respect —compare LOOK DOWN ON

look (lʊk) n. **1.** An act of looking: *He gave me a dirty look. (=looked angrily at me)* **2.** An expression on the face: *A cheerful look brings joy to the heart* (Proverbs 15:30). *God hates a proud look* (Proverbs 6:16,17 KJV). **3.** An appearance: *He has the look of a winner.*

look-out (lʊk–aʊt) n. **1.** A careful watching for sbdy. or sthg. **2.** A place for keeping watch **3.** A person engaged in keeping watch

looks (lʊks) n. Appearance: *By the looks of things, no one is home.*

loom (luːm) n. A machine in which thread is woven into fabric

loom v. **1.** To come into view as a large, indistinct, often threatening image: *The shape of a huge ship loomed up through the fog.* **2.** To appear imminent and usu. threatening: *A storm was looming on the horizon.*

loon (luːn) n. Any of several northern diving birds

loon-y (luː**n**–iʸ) adj. **-ier, -iest** *Slang* Lunatic; crazy

loop (luːp) n. **1.** A circular shape made by a piece of rope, string, etc. when curved back on itself: *The loop of rope makes a handle for the package.* **2.** A roughly oval, closed or nearly closed, turn or figure: *a loop in the road* **3.** A flying stunt in which a plane makes a vertical circle

loop-hole (luː**p**–hoʷl) n. A way of avoiding a rule, the terms of a contract, etc., esp. one provided by vague and careless wording

loose (luːˢs) adj. **1.** Not tied or fastened down or penned in; free from control: *The horse broke loose and ran away.* **2.** Not firmly fixed;

not tight: *The buttons on my shirt are loose.* **3.** Of clothes, not fitting tightly: *She lost a lot of weight. Now all her clothes are loose.* **4.** Lewd; unchaste: *a loose woman/ loose morals* **5.** Not tight; slack: *The clothes line is too loose.* **6. at loose ends** Having nothing to do **7. on the loose** n. Free from control, esp. of law: *A convicted murderer is on the loose.* —**loosely** adv.

loos-en (luːˢs–ən) v. To make or become loose; set free; unfasten: *He loosened his tie.*

loose ends (luːs ɛndz) n. *pl.* **1.** Unsettled details **2. at loose ends** Not knowing what to do

loose–leaf (luːˢs–liʸf) adj. Having removable leaves held by clasps or rings, as in a loose-leaf notebook

loot (luːt) n. Goods stolen by thieves in time of disaster or social unrest

loot v. To take loot from: *Following the earthquake, crowds of people looted the stores.*

loot-er (luːᵗt–ər) n. Someone who takes advantage of other people's misfortune and steals whatever possessions he may have left: *The police warned: "Looters will be shot on sight!"*

lop (lɑp) v. **-pp-** To cut off: *They lopped off several branches from the tree.*

lope (loʷp) v. To move along easily with long strides or an easy canter

lop-sid-ed (lɑp–saɪd–əd) adj. Unevenly balanced

lo-qua-cious (loʷ–**kweʸ**–ʃəs) adj. Very talkative

lord (lɔrd) n. **1.** A ruler or master **2.** A nobleman

lord v. **lord it over (someone)** *derog.* To behave like a lord, or like the master of someone

Lord (lɔrd) n. **1.** God; Jesus: *Believe in the Lord Jesus and you will be saved — you and your household* (Acts 16:31). *If you confess with your mouth, "Jesus is Lord," and believe in your heart that God raised him from the dead, you will be saved (=you will have eternal life)* (Romans 10:9). *He [Jesus] is the King of kings and Lord of lords* (Revelations 19:16). —see JESUS **2.** A title of certain official people, esp. in Britain

Lord's Prayer (lɔrdz prɛər) n. The prayer that

our Lord Jesus Christ taught us to pray, beginning with the words, "Our Father."
—see PRAYER, JESUS, LORD

lore (lɔr) n. A body of knowledge of a traditional or popular nature: *Bird lore*

lor-ry (lɔr–iʸ) n. **-ries 1.** Any of various trucks running on rails **2.** *BrE.* Motortruck

lose (luʷz) v. **lost** (lɔst), **losing 1.** To come to be without sthg. because of misplacing it: *I lost my keys.* **2.** To fail to keep or maintain sthg.: *I've lost interest in professional sports.* **3.** To fail to win, gain, or obtain sthg.: *We lost the game.* **4.** To come to be without sthg. due to a disaster: *We lost everything when our house burned down.* **5.** To have less than previously: *He lost a lot of weight./ The contractor lost money on that last job.* **6.** To waste: *He lost no time in getting his wife to the hospital.* **7.** To no longer see, hear or understand: *I've lost sight of him.* **8.** Of a watch or clock, to work too slowly: *My watch loses two minutes a day.*
—opposite GAIN **9. lose heart** To become discouraged

los-er (luʷ–zər) n. **1.** A person who has been defeated **2. a born loser** One who always loses —opposite WINNER

losing (luʷ–zɪŋ) adj. **1.** Involving loss **2.** Involved in loss

loss (lɔs) n. **1.** The act or instance of losing possession of sthg.: *Did you report the loss of your bicycle to the police?/ Saint Paul said, "I consider everything a loss compared to the surpassing greatness of knowing Christ Jesus my Lord, for whose sake I have lost all things"* (Philippians 3:8). **2.** A person who dies or leaves a job, position, or community: *His death was a great loss to the literary world.* **3.** A thing or amount of money that is lost or stolen **4.** Failure to make a profit: *His business suffered a loss last year.* **5. at a loss** Too surprised or confused to speak: *I was at a loss for words.*

lost (lɔst) v. Past tense and past part. of **lose**

lost adj. **1.** That which cannot be found **2.** No longer possessed: *a lost opportunity* **3.** Unable to find one's way: *I was lost in the fog.* **4.** Not able to find one's way spiritually: *For the Son of Man [Jesus] came to seek and to save what was lost [=all people, who were lost in sins, not knowing the way of salvation, for no*

one comes to God the Father but through faith in Jesus] (Luke 19:10) (John 14:6). **5.** Destroyed; killed: *1,500 lives were lost when the Titanic hit an iceberg and sank in the North Atlantic in 1912.*

lot (lɑt) n. A large amount: *a lot of friends/ money/courage*

lot n. **1.** An area of land used for building or for parking cars: *a parking lot* **2.** pl. **lots** Objects of various sizes or having different marks, used in making a decision: *They drew lots to determine who should go first.*

lo-tion (loʷ–ʃən) n. A liquid cosmetic or medicine to be applied to the skin

lot-ter-y (lɑt–ə–riʸ) n. **-ies** A drawing of lots in which prizes are given to the winning names or numbers, picked by chance

lo-tus (loʷt–əs) n. **1.** A kind of tropical water lily **2.** A mythical fruit represented as inducing a state of lazy and luxurious dreaminess

loud (lɑʊd) adj. **1.** Not quiet; noisy; having or producing a great volume of sound **2.** Too brightly colored: *loud clothing/ wallpaper/ curtains* —**loudly** adv. —**loudness** n.

lounge (lɑʊndʒ) v. **lounged, lounging** To stand, sit, or lie in a lazy, relaxed way

lounge n. **1.** A comfortable room for sitting in, as in a hotel or theater **2.** A long couch

louse (lɑʊs) n. pl. **lice** (lɑɪs) **1.** Any of an order of small, wingless insects that suck blood **2.** *fig. slang* A mean, contemptible person

louse v. **loused, lousing** *slang* To bungle; work or perform inefficiently: *You loused up that job once. Don't louse it up again.*

lous-y (lɑʊ–ziʸ) adj. **-ier, -iest 1.** Very bad **2.** Full of lice **3.** Amply supplied: *lousy with money*

lou-ver (luʷ–vər) n. Slanted strips of slats that cover an opening so as to admit air but exclude rain

lov-a-ble or **love-a-ble** (lʌv–ə–bəl) adj. Having qualities that attract love

love (lʌv) n. **1.** A strong feeling of affection and concern for a person, such as a mother's love for her children **2.** An emotional, romantic feeling toward a member of the opposite sex **3.** A strong feeling of friendship for a member of the same sex: *Greater*

love has no one than this, that one lay down his life for his friends (John 15:13). **4.** A strong interest and enjoyment in sthg.: *a love for music/ art/ travel/ sports, etc.* **5.** The love of God for sinful mankind, love which no one deserves: *This is love: not that we loved God, but that he loved us and sent his Son as an atoning sacrifice for our sins* (1 John 4:10). *God is love* (1 John 4:8). *Love does no harm to its neighbor. Therefore, love is the fulfillment of the law* (Romans 13:10). *Love is patient, love is kind. It does not envy, it does not boast, it is not proud. It is not rude, it is not self-seeking, it is not easily angered, it keeps no record of wrongs. Love does not delight in evil, but rejoices with the truth. It always protects, always trusts, always hopes, always perseveres. Love never fails* (1 Corinthians 13:4-8).

love v. **loved, loving 1.** To cherish: *I love my wife and children very much.* **2.** To feel a passion, devotion, or tenderness for: *For God so loved the world [the people in the world] that he gave his One and Only Son [to die for us and pay for all our sins with his own blood] that whoever believes in him [puts his trust in him for salvation] will have everlasting life* (John 3:16). *The two greatest commandments are: "Love the Lord your God with all your heart and with all your soul and with all your mind, and love your neighbor [everyone] as [you love] yourself"* (Matthew 22:37,39). **3.** To take pleasure in: *She loves playing the piano.* —opposite HATE

love-less (lʌv–ləs) adj. **1.** Not loved **2.** Not giving love

love-ly (lʌv–liʸ) adj. **-lier, -liest 1.** Beautiful; that which one loves or likes: *a lovely view of the ocean* **2.** Enjoyable; delightful; very pleasant: *a lovely girl/ a lovely home* —**loveliness** n.

lov-er (lʌv–ər) n. **1.** Someone who loves another **2.** A person who is fond or devoted to sthg.: *an art lover* **3. lovers** A couple in love with each other

lov-ing (lʌv–ɪŋ) adj. Showing or feeling love: *The Lord is righteous in all his ways and loving toward all he has made* (Psalm 145:17). —**lovingly** adv.

low (loʷ) adj. **1.** Having little height; not far above the ground or floor: *a low ceiling/*

bridge/ shelf **2.** Small in degree, worth, amount, etc: *a low price/ temperature* **3.** Lacking in strength or spirit; weak or unhappy: *She's still feeling rather low after her long illness.* **4.** Having only a small amount of a particular substance: *low fat milk* **5.** Not loud: *Turn the radio lower.* **6.** Of a musical note, deep: *She can't sing those low notes.* **7.** Near the bottom in position or rank: *low caste* **8.** A gear used for a slow speed: *You have to shift into low gear to go up a steep hill.* —opposite HIGH

low (loʷ) adv. **1.** In, at, or to a low place or position: *Aim lower.* **2.** Near the ground or floor; not high **3.** In music, in or with low notes: *Basses sing lower than tenors.* —opposite HIGH **4.** Quietly: *Turn the TV lower, please.*

low (loʷ) n. A point, price, degree, etc., that is below normal: *Profits have reached an all-time low this month.* —opposite HIGH

low-down (loʷ–daʊn) n. *Infml.* The whole truth; all of the important information: *Give us the lowdown on the recent talks between management and labor.*

low-down adj. Mean; contemptible: *Tripping that blind man was a dirty, rotten, lowdown thing to do.*

low-er (loʷ–ər) adj. In, on, at, or near the bottom part of sthg.: *The cups are on one of the lower shelves.* —opposite UPPER

low-er v. **1.** To let sthg. descend by its own weight: *They lowered the cargo into the hold of the ship.* **2.** To reduce in value, volume, amount, or degree: *Please lower your voice in the library.* **3.** To move or let down: *We lowered the sails.* —opposite RAISE **4.** To degrade oneself: *I wouldn't lower myself to do such a shameful thing.*

lower class (loʷ–ər klæs) n. Often *derog.* A social class comprising the laboring and very poor people

low-key (loʷ–kiʸ) adj. Low intensity

low-ly (loʷ–liʸ) adj. **1.** In a low position, manner, or degree **2.** Not proud; humble —**lowliness** n. —**lowly** adv.

low profile (loʷ proʷ–faɪl) adj. Inconspicuous posture, stance, or lifestyle

loy-al (lɔɪ–əl) adj. Faithful; true to one's

friends, group, country, and religious convictions a loyal supporter —opposite DIS-
LOYAL —loyalty n. -ties

loz-enge (lɑz–ənʤ) n. **1.** A small medicated
candy **2.** A diamond shaped figure

Lt. *Abbr.* Lieutenant

Ltd. *Abbr.* Limited

lu-au (luᵂ–aʊ) n. A lavish Hawaiian feast

lube (luᵂb) n. **1.** *infml.* Lubricant **2.** An application of a lubricant, as to an automobile

lu-bri-cant (luᵂ–brə–kənt) n. A substance such
as grease or machine oil which helps moving parts (of a machine, e.g.) to move more
easily

lu-bri-cate (luᵂ–brə–keʸt) v. also **lube** *infml.*
-cated, -cating To make smooth and able to
move easily by adding a lubricant —**lu-bri-
ca-tion** (luᵂ–brə–keʸ–ʃən) n. —**lubricator** n.

lu-cerne (luᵂ–sɜrn) n. A type of plant used for
feeding cattle; alfalfa

lu-cid (luᵂ–səd) adj. **1.** Shining **2.** Clear mind-
ed **3.** Easily understood —**lu-cid-i-ty** (luᵂ–
sɪd–ə–tiʸ) or **lucidness** n. —**lucidly** adv.

Lu-ci-fer (luᵂ–sə–fər) n. Satan; the Devil, who
was cast out of heaven for leading a revolt
of the angels: *How are you fallen from heaven,
O Lucifer, son of the morning! ...For you have
said in your heart, "I will exalt my throne above
the stars of God... I will be like the most High."
Yet you shall be brought down to hell, to the
sides of the pit* (Isaiah 14:12-15). —see SA-
TAN

luck (lʌk) n. The force that seems to operate
for good or bad in a person's life; chance;
fortune: *Winning in that game takes no brains;
it's just plain luck.*

luck-y (lʌk–iʸ) adj. **-ier, -iest** Having good
luck —opposite UNLUCKY —**luckily** adv.
Luckily she had the winning number.

lu-cra-tive (luᵂ–krə–tɪv) adj. Producing
wealth; profitable

lu-cre (luᵂ–kər) n. Money

lu-di-crous (luᵂ–dɪ–krəs) adj. Causing laughter because of its foolish absurdity

lug (lʌg) v. **-gg-** To drag, pull, or carry laboriously: *He's been lugging those heavy suitcases
around all day.*

lug-gage (lʌg–ɪʤ) n. The suitcases, briefcases,
bags, boxes, etc. of a traveller; baggage: *We*

checked four pieces of luggage to Nairobi.

Luke (luᵂk) n. **1.** A fellow worker with St.
Paul and author of two of the books of the
New Testament — The Gospel According
to St. Luke which tells about the life and
teachings and the suffering, death, resurrection, and ascension into heaven of our
Lord and Savior Jesus Christ, and the Book
of the Acts of the Apostles, which tells
about the early Christian Church, from the
ascension of Jesus into heaven to the imprisonment of St. Paul in Rome during the
reign of Nero some 30 years later **2.** The
Gospel [Good News about Jesus Christ]
written by St. Luke

luke-warm (luᵂk–wɑrm) adj. **1.** Of liquid, neither cold nor hot **2.** *fig.* Showing hardly any
interest

lull (lʌl) v. To cause to sleep, rest or become
less active: *The motion of the train soon lulled
me to sleep.*

lull n. A period of quietness or less activity

lull-a-by (lʌ–lə–baɪ) n. **-bies** A pleasant song
used to lull a child to sleep

lum-ba-go (ləm–beʸ–goᵂ) n. Pain in the lower
back

lum-bar (lʌm–bər/ –bɑr) adj. Of or in the lower part of the back

lum-ber (lʌm–bər) n. Timber sawed into
planks, boards, etc.

lumber v. To move clumsily, in a heavy,
awkward manner

lu-mi-nar-y (luᵂ–mə–nɛər–iʸ) n. **-ies 1.** A person of eminence **2.** Source of light

lu-mi-nous (luᵂ–mə–nəs) adj. Giving out light
—**luminously** adv.

lump (lʌmp) n. A mass of sthg. solid with no
particular shape: *a lump of clay*

lump adj. **lump sum** An amount of money
given all at once, not in monthly payments:
*We can save money by paying for things in one
lump sum rather than making monthly payments and paying a lot of interest.*

lump v. To group people or things together,
treating them all the same

lump-y (lʌm–piʸ) adj. **-ier, -iest** Having lumps:
a lumpy bed

lu-na-cy (luᵂ–nə–siʸ) n. **-cies 1.** Insanity **2.** Irresponsible or reckless conduct

lu-nar (luʷ–nər) adj. 1. Of the moon 2. Round or crescent-shaped like the moon 3. Measured by the revolutions of the moon: *a lunar month*

lu-na-tic (luʷ–nə–tɪk) n. An insane person

lunatic adj. 1. Insane 2. For the insane 3. Extremely wild and foolish

lunch (lʌntʃ) also luncheon (lʌntʃ–ən) n. A meal eaten at noon (midday)

lunch-room (lʌntʃ–ruʷm) n. A place set aside for eating lunch

lung (lʌŋ) n. Either of two breathing organs, in the chest of man or certain animals, that draw in air and bring it into contact with the blood

lunge (lʌndʒ) v. lunged, lunging To make a sudden, strong or violent movement forward: *The attacker lunged at his victim with a knife.*

lunge n. A movement of this sort: *He made a lunge at her.*

lu-pine *AmE.* lu-pin *BrE.* (luʷ–pɪn) n. A garden plant with tall spikes of flowers, bearing seeds in pods

lurch (lɜrtʃ) v. To move suddenly, without warning: *The train lurched forward, throwing many people to the floor.*

lurch n. 1. A sudden, uncontrolled movement: *The train gave a lurch forward.* 2. leave someone in a lurch An uncomfortable, often embarrassing or desperate situation; a predicament: *The groom left his bride-to-be waiting at the church. He left her in a lurch, and no one has seen him since.*

lure (lʊər) n. 1. Sthg. very attractive or tempting: *the lure of gold* 2. A bait or decoy to attract wild animals or fish so that they can be caught

lure v. lured, luring To entice; to attract by promise of pleasure or gain: *He was lured from one firm to the other by a much higher salary.*

lu-rid (lʊər–əd) adj. 1. Gruesome and revolting 2. Startlingly sensational 3. Wildly red

lurk (lɜrk) v. To be hidden, while waiting to attack: *The two thieves lurked behind the bushes.*

lus-cious (lʌʃ–əs) adj. Richly sweet in taste or smell: *luscious fruit*

lush (lʌʃ) adj. Of plants, esp. grass, green and plentiful in growth: *lush meadows* —lush-ness n.

lust (lʌst) n. 1. Excessive sexual desire: *Put to death... whatever belongs to your earthly nature: sexual immorality, impurity, lust... Because of these things the wrath of God is coming* (Colossians 3:5,6). NOTE: God hates sin, but because of his great love and mercy, he forgives the sins of those who truly repent and turn from their wicked ways and put their trust in Jesus for eternal life (Acts 2:38; Acts 16:31: Romans 6:23). 2. An intense desire for power: *The president of that organization has a lust for power.* —lustful adj. —lusty adj.

lus-ter *AmE.* lus-tre *BrE.* (lʌs–tər) n. Brilliance or radiance: *Her hair had a brilliant luster.* —lustrous adj. *She had lustrous black hair.*

lust-y (lʌs–tiʸ) adj. -ier, -iest Strong and healthy; robust; vigorous

lute (luʷt) n. A stringed musical instrument, much in use in the 16th and 17th centuries

lux-u-ri-ant (ləg–ʒɜr–iʸ–ənt) adj. Abundant and healthy in growth: *Luxuriant forests covered the hills.* —luxuriance n. —luxuriantly adv.

lux-u-ry (lʌk–ʃə–riʸ / lʌg–ʒə–riʸ) n. -ries 1. Sthg. not necessary that provides comfort and enjoyment 2. The enjoyment of sumptuous living: *We shouldn't be spending money on luxuries when so many people in the world don't even have food to eat.* —lux-u-ri-ous (ləg–ʒɜr–iʸ–əs) adj. —luxuriously adj.

–ly (–liʸ) suffix, adv. In a specified way: *quickly/softly*

–ly (–liʸ) suffix, adj. 1. Characteristic of, or resembling: *brotherly* 2. Recurring at regular intervals: *weekly/yearly*

lye (laɪ) n. Any white, alkaline substance used for washing and in making soap

ly-ce-um (laɪ–siʸ–əm) n. 1. A hall for public lectures or discussions 2. An association providing public lectures, concerts, etc.

ly-ing (laɪ–ŋ) v. Present part. of lie; telling lies —lying adj. *The Lord detests lying lips* (Proverbs 12:22). NOTE: Lying is a sin, and God hates sin. But the true God is also a God of love and mercy and forgiveness. If

we truly repent of all our sins and put our trust in Jesus for our salvation, we shall have eternal life (Romans 3:23; 6:23, John 3:16). —see JESUS

lymph (lımpf) n. A colorless fluid in the body, consisting chiefly of blood plasma and white blood cells, circulating in thin-walled tubes called **lymph glands**

lym-pha-tic (lım–fæt–ık) adj. **1.** Pertaining to or carrying lymph **2.** Sluggish

lymph node (lımpf noᵂd) n. Any of the small compact masses lying in groups along the lymphatic vessels and producing typical lymph cells

lynch (lıntʃ) v. To attack and hang or otherwise kill sbdy. suspected of a crime, without giving him a fair trial

lynx (lıŋks) n. **lynxes** or **lynx** A spotted wild animal of the cat family, noted for its keen sight

lyre (lıər) n. A small stringed instrument similar to the harp, used by the ancient Greeks to accompany singers and reciters

lyr-ic (lır–ık) adj. **1.** Suitable for singing; melodic **2.** Expressing direct and usu. strong personal emotion

lyr-ic n. **1.** A lyric poem **2.** pl. The words of a popular song —**lyrical** adj. —**ly-rically** adv.lord

lyr-i-cist (lır–ə–səst) n. One who writes words for songs

M, m (ɛm) n. **1.** The 13th letter of the English alphabet **2.** The Roman numeral (number) for 1,000

ma'am (mæm) n. **1.** A short form of **madam 2.** A polite way of addressing a woman

ma·ca·bre (mə–kɑb–ər) adj. **1.** Pertaining to or symbolizing death **2.** Grim; gruesome

mac·ad·am (mə–kæd–əm) n. A road surface made of crushed stone compacted with tar or asphalt

mac·a·ro·ni (mæk–ə–roʷ–niʸ) n. A paste of wheat flour pressed (usu.) into hollow tubes and dried, prepared for eating by boiling

mac·a·roon (mæk–ə–ruʷn) n. A small, sweet cookie, made of ground coconut or almonds, egg whites, and sugar

ma·caw (mə–kɔ) n. A large, brightly-colored tropical American parrot

ma·chet·e (mə–ʃɛt–iʸ) n. A broad heavy knife used as a cutting tool and also as a weapon, esp. in Latin America, the West Indies, and Africa

mach·i·na·tion (mæk–ə–neʸ–ʃən) n. An evil plot or scheme

ma·chine (mə–ʃiʸn) n. A man-made instrument or device which uses power (such as electricity) to do some kind of work: *a washing machine*

ma·chin·er·y (mə–ʃiʸn–ər–iʸ) n. **-ies 1.** Machines in general **2.** The working parts of a mechanism **3.** The operation of a system or organization: *The machinery of government works slowly.*

ma·chin·ist (mə–ʃiʸn–nəst) n. **1.** One who makes or repairs machines **2.** One who operates machines or machine tools

mack·er·el (mæk–ə–rəl) n. An edible sea fish

mack·i·naw (mæk–ə–nɔ) n. **1.** A short coat made of heavy woolen cloth **2.** A thick woolen blanket

mack·in·tosh (mæk–ən–tɑʃ) n. A waterproof coat

mac·ra·mé (mæk–rə–meʸ) n. A heavy, coarse lace or fringe made by knotting twine or cord in decorative patterns, used for wall hangings, hangers for flower pots, etc.

mac·ro– (mæk–roʷ) *Prefix* Large; large-scale

ma·cro·cosm (mæk–rə–kɑz–əm) n. **1.** The universe **2.** Any large complete structure containing smaller structures —**ma·cro·cos·mic** (mæk–rə–kɑz–mɪk) adj.

ma·cron (meʸk–rɑn) n. A short horizontal line placed over a vowel to show that it is pronounced as a long vowel or diphthong: *In some dictionaries, the "a" in "apron" would have a macron over it* (ā).

mad (mæd) adj. **-dd- 1.** Crazy; insane; ill in the mind: *She went mad after the loss of her family in a tragic accident.* **2.** *infml.* Angry: *I was mad at him for his insulting remarks.* **3.** Filled with enthusiasm: *She's mad about ice skating.* **4. drive sbdy. mad** To annoy sbdy. very much **5. like mad** *infml.* Very fast, loud etc.; furiously: *working/driving/yelling like mad*

mad·am (mæd–əm) n. **mes·dames** (meʸ–dɑm) *pl.* **1.** A polite form of address to a woman, esp. one in an official position and when addressing a woman in a business letter **2.** The mistress of a household **3.** A woman in charge of a brothel

mad·ame (mə–dæm/mæ–) n. **mes·dames** (meʸ–dɑm/ –dæm) *pl.* **1.** French title equivalent to Mrs. **2.** A title used in English as a title of respect for a distinguished woman or for any foreign married woman

mad·den (mæd–ən) v. To make angry

mad·den·ing (mæd–nɪŋ) adj. *infml.* Very annoying

made (meʸd) v. Past tense and part. of **make:** *The Lord made the heavens* (Psalm 96:5). *The sea is his and he made it* (Psalm 95:5). *I praise you (God) because I am fearfully and wonderfully made* (Psalm 139:14).

ma·de·moi·selle (mæd–ə–mə–zɛl/ mæm–zɛl) n. A French title meaning Miss

mad·ly (mæd–liʸ) adv. **1.** In an insane manner: *madly intent on destroying his enemies* **2.** *infml.* Very, very much; intensely: *madly in love*

mad·ness (mæd–nəs) n. **1.** Insanity; lunacy **2.** Great anger; fury **3.** Wild excitement **4.** Great folly

maes·tro (maɪs–troʷ) n. **1.** A great musical composer, conductor, or teacher **2.** A master of any art

mag·a·zine (mæg–ə–ziʸn) n. **1.** A publication, usu. with a paper cover and often illustrat-

ed, appearing at regular intervals (weekly or monthly), and containing articles and stories by various writers, usu. on a special subject for a certain group of people: *a sports magazine* **2.** A storehouse or room where arms and bullets (cartridges) are placed before firing **3.** A compartment for cartridges in or on a gun

ma‧gen‧ta (mə–dʒent–ə) n., adj. A purplish red

mag‧ic (mædʒ–ɪk) n. **1.** The art or practice of using supernatural forces; the use of charms, spells, and rituals in seeking or pretending to control events; sorcery (This is forbidden by God's Word.): *This is what the Sovereign Lord says, "I am against your magic charms..."* (Ezekiel 13:20). —see also SORCERY, DIVINATION, WITCHCRAFT. NOTE: God hates this sinful practice and all sin, but because of his great love and mercy he forgives those who truly repent and put their trust in Jesus for eternal life (Mark 1:15; Acts 16:31; 1 John 1:9). —see JESUS **2.** A type of entertainment such as sleight of hand, producing unexpected objects by tricks **3.** A charming quality or influence: *the magic of love* —**magic** adj. *the magic touch*

mag‧i‧cal (mædʒ–ɪ–kəl) adj. Of strange power, mystery, or charm —**magically** adv.

ma‧gi‧cian (mə–dʒɪʃ–ən) n. A person who practices magic

mag‧is‧trate (mædʒ–ə–streyt) n. A civil officer with power to administer the law

mag‧ne‧si‧um (mæg–niy–ziy–əm) n. A light, silver-white, metallic chemical element that is fairly hard, used in many alloys

mag‧net (mæg–nət) n. A piece of iron or steel that can attract other (metal) objects towards it, and which points north and south when suspended

mag‧net‧ic (mæg–net–ɪk) adj. **1.** Of, or relating to a magnet **2.** Possessing power to attract: *He has a magnetic personality.* (=He attracts people to himself.)

mag‧ne‧tize (mæg–nə–taɪz) v. -tized, -tizing To give magnetic properties to: *You can magnetize a piece of iron by passing an electric current around it.* —**mag‧ne‧tism** (mæg–nə–tɪz–əm) n.

mag‧ni‧fi‧ca‧tion (mæg–nə–fə–key–ʃən) n. **1.** The act or power of magnifying or being magnified: *The telescope has a magnification of 100.* (=It makes a thing look 100 times larger than it actually is.) **2.** A magnified image or representation

mag‧nif‧i‧cent (mæg–nɪf–ə–sənt) adj. Great, splendid: *[God is] wonderful in counsel and magnificent in wisdom* (Isaiah 28:29). / *The wedding was a magnificent occasion.* —**magnificence** n. —**magnificently** adv.

mag‧ni‧fy (mæg–nə–faɪ) v. -fied, -fying **1.** To make sthg. appear larger than it really is, as a microscope does **2.** To exaggerate: *She magnifies all her troubles.* **3.** To praise (old use): *O magnify the Lord with me, and let us exalt his name together* (Psalm 34:3).

mag‧ni‧fy‧ing glass (mæg–nə–faɪ–ɪŋ glæs) n. A lens that makes things look bigger

mag‧ni‧tude (mæg–nə–tuwd) n. *fml.* **1.** Greatness of size: *a star of great magnitude* **2.** Importance: *a decision of great magnitude*

mag‧no‧lia (mæg–nowl–yə) n. A type of tree with large, white or purplish sweet-scented flowers

mag‧pie (mæg–paɪ) n. -pies A black and white bird with a long tail, related to the crow and jay

ma‧hog‧a‧ny (mə–hɑg–ə–niy) n. -nies A tropical tree with reddish wood, used in making furniture

maid (meyd) n. **1.** An unmarried woman, esp. a young one **2.** A female servant: *a housemaid*

maid‧en (meyd–ən) adj. **1.** Of a woman who is not married: *my maiden aunt* **2.** First: *The ship is making its maiden voyage.*

maid‧en name (meyd–ən neym) n. The family name of a woman before marriage

maid of hon‧or (meyd ʌv ɑn–ər) n. *pl.* **maids of honor** An unmarried woman who is the chief attendant of the bride at a wedding

mail (meyl) n. **1.** The postal system: *Airmail is faster than surface mail.* **2.** Letters and anything else sent by the postal system

mail v. To put a letter, etc. in a mailbox or take it to the post office for sending

mail‧box (meyl–bɑks) n. **1.** A public place for collecting mail: *There's a mailbox on the cor-*

ner. **2.** A box at or near one's dwelling for collecting mail

mail-man (me^yl–mæn) also **postman** n. -men A person employed to deliver the mail

maim (me^ym) v. To injure a person badly, so that part of the body can no longer be used

main (me^yn) n. A chief pipe, channel, or cable in a public system that supplies water, gas, or electricity

main adj. Chief; most important: *Fifth Avenue is one of the main streets in this town.*

main-land (me^yn–lænd/–lənd) n. A country or continent without its adjacent islands: *Sri Lanka is not a part of the Asian mainland.* —**mainlander** n.

main-ly (me^yn–li^y) adv. Chiefly: *His money comes mainly from business interests.*

main-mast (me^yn–mæst) n. The principal mast of a sailing vessel

main-stay (me^yn–ste^y) n. **1.** A rope or wire supporting the mainmast of a ship **2.** The main support: *Loyal friends were his mainstay in times of trouble.*

main-tain (me^yn–te^yn) v. **1.** To keep in existence: *Blessed are they who maintain justice* (Psalm 106:3). **2.** To provide for; to support financially: *to maintain a family* **3.** To keep in repair: *The house is well-maintained.* **4.** To continue to argue or believe: *Some people still maintain that the earth is flat.*

main-te-nance (me^yn–tə–nəns) n. The act of maintaining

maize (me^yz) n. Corn

majestic adj. (mə–dʒəs–tɪk) Having or showing majesty: *The voice of the Lord is majestic* (Psalm 29:4).

maj-es-ty (mædʒ–ə–sti^y) n. -ties Greatness and dignity, as of a king or queen: *After he [Jesus Christ] had provided purification for sins, he sat down at the right hand of the Majesty in heaven* (Hebrews 1:3).

Ma-gi (mæ–dʒaɪ) n. The wise men from the East who came to worship the infant Jesus in Bethlehem (Matthew 2:1-12) , born to be King of Kings and Savior of the world —see JESUS

ma-jor (me^y–dʒər) adj. **1.** Greater in size, number, or importance: *The house needed major repairs after the storm.* **2.** Serious: *Brain sur-*

gery is a major operation. **3.** Notable or conspicuous in effect: *a major improvement* —opposite MINOR

major n. **1.** An officer of middle rank in military service **2.** A course of study in which one is specializing at a college or university: *She is a music major in college.*

ma-jor-i-ty (mə–dʒɔr–ə–ti^y) n. -ties **1.** More than half of the total, esp. of people: *The majority of voters are against any tax increases.* **2.** The difference between a greater and a smaller number: *Tom won the election for class president by a majority of 12 votes.*

make (me^yk) v. **made, making 1.** To create, form, shape: *God told Abraham, "I will make you into a great nation"* (Genesis 12:2). **2.** To fashion: *She's making a dress.* **3.** To produce: *That old car makes a lot of noise.* **4.** Cause to be: *Overeating made him fat.* **5.** To cause sbdy. to do sthg.: *The pain made him cry out.* **6.** To earn (money): *He makes a lot of money.* **7.** To result in: *Six and two make eight.* **8.** To arrange ready for use: *He made the bed this morning.* **9.** To set a time and date: *He made an appointment to see the doctor at 10 a.m. on Tuesday.* **10.** To formulate in the mind: *to make plans* **11.** To conclude: *She didn't know what to make of it.* **12.** To perform: *He made a wonderful speech.* **13.** To have the qualities of: *This purse will make a good gift for my sister.* **14.** To arrive at: *We barely made it to the station in time for Bob to catch the train.* **15.** *infml.* To ensure the success of: *The good news made my day.* **16.** To draw up a legal document or contract: *He made his will.* **17.** To establish: *They made a new law.* **18.** To serve as: *This book makes good reading.* **19. make believe** To pretend: *The children are making believe that they are grown up.* **20. make do** To manage to get along with what is available **21. make good** To succeed; to carry out successfully: *He made good in the big city.* **22. make room** To clear a space for sthg. or someone **23. make up (a)** To invent a story or excuse, often in order to deceive: *I don't believe your story; you're just making it up.* **(b)** To apply cosmetics to change or improve one's appearance: *The clown is making himself up for his next performance.* **(c)** To become friends again after a

fight or a quarrel: *Let's shake hands and make up.* **24. make up one's mind** To decide **25. make up for** sthg. To compensate for sthg.: *They drove fast to make up for the lost time.*

make n. The origin of manufacture; a brand: *What make is your car? Is it a Ford, Volvo, Honda, or what?*

make–be·lieve (**me**ʸ**k**-biʸ-liʸv) n. A pretense: *The child lives in a world of make-believe.* —**make–believe** adj.

mak·er (**me**ʸ**k**-ər) n. A person or firm that makes sthg.: *Our help is in the name of the Lord, the Maker of heaven and earth* (Psalm 124:8)./ *My father is a cabinet maker.*

make-shift (**me**ʸ**k**-ʃɪft) adj. A temporary substitute, used for a time for lack of sthg. better

make-up (**me**ʸ**k**-əp) n. **1.** Cosmetics worn on the face **2.** The combination of qualities (in a person's character)

mak·ings (**me**ʸ**k**-ɪŋz) n. The essential qualities for becoming: *He has the makings of a great leader.*

mal– (mæl–) prefix **1.** Badly; poorly: *He is maladjusted.* **2.** Insufficient: *malnutrition*

Mal·a·chi (**mæl**-ə-kaɪ) n. The last book of the Old Testament and the last of the Minor Prophets, written about 455 B.C. It presents a graphic picture of the times, showing that great reforms were needed to prepare the way for the coming Messiah. —see BIBLE, OLD TESTAMENT

mal·ad·just·ed (mæl-ə-dʒʌs-təd) adj. Of a person, not well-adjusted to his own circumstances

mal·a·dy (**mæl**-əd-iʸ) n. -dies An illness; a disease

ma·laise (mə-leʸz/ mæ-) n. A feeling of illness or mental uneasiness

ma·lar·i·a (mə-lɛər-iʸ-ə) n. An infectious disease characterized by cycles of chills, fever, and sweating, caused by a bite of an infected mosquito —**malarial** adj.

ma·lar·key (mə-lɑr-kiʸ) n. *infml.* Nonsense

mal·con·tent (mæl-kən-tɛnt) adj. Discontented

male (meʸl) adj., n. The sex that does not give birth to young —opposite FEMALE

mal·e·fac·tor (**mæl**-ə-fæk-tər) n. A criminal; an evil-doer

ma·lev·o·lent (mə-lɛv-ə-lənt) adj. Wishing harm to others —**malevolence** n. —**malevolently** adv.

mal·fea·sance (mæl-fiʸ-zəns) n. An unlawful act; evildoing; esp. official misconduct: *malfeasance of office*

mal·for·ma·tion (mæl-fɔr-meʸ-ʃən) n. Faulty formation —**mal-formed** (mæl-fɔrmd) adj.

mal·func·tion (mæl-fʌŋk-ʃən) n. Faulty functioning

mal·ice (**mæl**-əs) n. **1.** The desire to hurt other people or to see others suffer: *Rid yourself of all malice and all deceit...* (1 Peter 2:1). **2. bear malice** Spite; to feel dislike for sbdy. continually

ma·li·cious (mə-lɪʃ-əs) adj. Feeling, showing, or caused by malice: *a malicious lie* —**maliciously** adv.

ma·lign (mə-laɪn) v. To say unpleasant and untrue things about sbdy.: *He viciously maligned that innocent person.*

malign adj. **1.** Harmful **2.** Showing malice

ma·lig·nant (mə-lɪg-nənt) adj. **1.** Feeling or showing great ill-will **2.** *tech.* Of a disease or condition, serious enough to cause death if not prevented: *a malignant growth (tumor) on the body* —**malignancy** n. —**malignantly** adv.

mall (mɔl) n. A shopping center

mal·lard (**mæl**-ərd) n. A kind of wild duck

mal·le·a·ble (**mæl**-iʸ-ə-bəl) adj. **1.** Of metal, able to be hammered or pressed into shape **2.** Of people, easy to influence

mal·let (**mæl**-ət) n. **1.** A kind of wooden hammer **2.** A similar hammer with a long handle, used in playing certain games such as croquet or polo

mal·nour·ished (mæl-**nɜr**-ɪʃt) adj. Poorly nourished

mal·nu·tri·tion (mæl-nuʷ-trɪʃ-ən) n. Bad health resulting from lack of food, or the wrong kind of food —see NUTRITION

mal·prac·tice (mæl-**præk**-təs) n. Wrongdoing

malt (mɔlt) n. Barley or other grain prepared for making beer or whiskey

malt·ed milk (mɔl-təd mɪlk) n. A drink made from dried milk and malt

mal·treat (mæl-triʸt) v. *fml.* To treat badly

—maltreatment n.

ma-ma or **mam-ma** (mɑ–mə) n. *infml.* Mother

mam-mal (mæm–əl) n. Animal of the type which nourish their young with milk

man (mæn) n. *pl.* **men** (mɛn) **1.** A human being, esp. an adult male **2. mankind** All human beings, male or female, young or old NOTE: In this sense, man is God's foremost visible creature. Man was created in the image of God (Genesis 1:26), that is, with a perfectly holy and righteous nature (Colossians 3:10). He knew God perfectly and was perfectly happy in such knowledge. Man was created to worship, serve, and glorify God (Matthew 4:10). But God did not want mankind to worship, praise, and glorify him because he had no other choice. So God gave the man a free will, so that he could disobey God if he chose to do so. God gave the man just one command — not to eat of the tree of the Knowledge of Good and Evil which was in the middle of the Garden of Eden where man was placed. God warned the man that in the day that he ate the fruit of that tree he would surely die (Genesis 2:16,17). By that God meant that man would lose the image of God with which he was created, and he would die spiritually. He would also begin to die physically. If man had not disobeyed God, he would have lived forever in perfect peace and harmony with God and there would never have been any suffering in the world. For some time the first man and woman obeyed God, but then one day they yielded to temptation and ate the forbidden fruit (Genesis 3:6). After that, they no longer looked forward to talking with God. They were afraid of God, and they tried to hide from him (Genesis 3:8). Adam, the first man, blamed his wife, Eve, for his sin; he even blamed God who had given him a wife. Now the man no longer had a holy and righteous nature. He had a sinful nature. And because he had a sinful nature, his children were born, not in the "image of God" with a holy nature, but in the image of their earthly father, that is, with a sinful nature. Ever since that time, all people have been born with a sinful nature (Psalm 51:5; 58:3), and since they are born with a sinful and evil nature, they continually do evil things. "Every inclination of his heart is evil from childhood" (Genesis 8:21). They lie, cheat, fight, steal, and kill. Their hearts are filled with envy and greed, jealousy and hate (Jeremiah 17:9). Man is by nature selfish, seeking only to gratify the desires of his own sinful flesh. If he does anything good in the eyes of men, it is to gain favor with them or to gain their confidence, or he does it with the hope of earning favor with God and to gain eternal life or a more noble position in the life hereafter. When man fell into sin, he was broken and ruined in the fall. Just like a broken egg, there was nothing that the man could do to put himself back together again and make himself right with God, that is, to gain God's favor. No matter how good the man tried to be, no matter how much he prayed or how much he punished himself or how much money he gave or how many animals he sacrificed, he could not gain God's favor and earn eternal life. Just as it would take a miracle (a supernatural act) to put a broken egg back together again and make it perfect, so it would also take a miracle to put fallen and broken man back together again spiritually and make him right with God. God is perfect and heaven (God's dwelling place) is perfect. God cannot allow anyone into heaven unless he is perfect. God would have to become a man and live a perfect life in this world in man's place, as man's substitute. And since man could not pay for his own sins with his own sinful blood (or anything else) (Psalm 49:7), God would have to pay for man's sin with his own blood. In order to do this, God would have to become a man. So God did become a man, and that's who Jesus Christ is (John 1:1-3,14). But centuries passed before the birth of Jesus took place. Meanwhile, those who put their faith in the promised Savior were assured of everlasting life. Today people are saved through faith in Jesus Christ, who came into the world to save sinners (1 Timothy

1:15), paid for our sins with his own suffering and death on the cross (1 Peter 1:18,19; Acts 20:28), rose from the dead on the third day (Luke 24: 5,6), and then, after 40 days, returned to heaven (Luke 24:51) to prepare a place for all those who put their trust in him for eternal life (John 14:1-3). In short, man cannot be saved and have eternal life by his own good works, because he is by nature evil and corrupt and even dead in sin (Ephesians 2:1). There is nothing man can do to save himself (Romans 3:20). Man can only be saved through faith in his Savior Jesus Christ (Acts 4:12). Without faith in Christ, it is impossible to please God (Hebrews 11:6). But when man has faith in Jesus Christ, he does good works and lives his life to the glory of God, not to earn salvation or anything else, but simply to show his love for God in appreciation of all that God has done for us (John 14:15,23). —see JESUS

man-a-cle (mæn–ɪ–kəl) n. *often pl.* **1.** A device for shackling the hands; handcuff **2.** Sthg. that confines or restrains

manacle v. -cled, -cling To restrain with, or as with, manacles

man-age (mæn–ɪdʒ) v. -aged, -aging **1.** To be in control or in charge of: *A man of God must be able to manage his own household well* (1 Timothy 3:4). **2.** To be able to cope with a problem: *His car broke down, but he still managed to get to work on time.*

man-age-a-ble (mæn–ɪdʒ–ə–bəl) adj. Possible to manage or control —opposite UNMANAGEABLE

man-age-ment (mæn–ɪdʒ–mənt) n. **1.** The art or practice of managing sthg. **2.** The people in charge of a business, industry, etc.: *This restaurant is under new management.*

man-ag-er (mæn–ɪdʒ–ər) n. One who manages; one who directs the affairs of a business or a sports team, a singer, etc.

man-da-rin (mæn–də–rən) n. **1.** A small, sweet orange with a thin, loose peel **2.** Mandarin The main language of modern China **3.** Formerly, a high ranking government official in China

man-date (mæn–deʸt) n. Authority given to sbdy. to perform a certain task

mandate v. -dated, -dating To give or assign by a mandate

man-da-to-ry (mæn–də–tɔr–iʸ) adj. Compulsory; obligatory

man-di-ble (mæn–də–bəl) n. **1.** In insects, etc., mouthparts used for seizing and biting **2.** Either part of a bird's beak **3.** A jaw, esp. the lower jaw

man-do-lin (mæn–də–lɪn/ mæn–də–lən) n. A musical instrument with a pear-shaped body and metal strings

mane (meʸn) n. The long hair on a lion's or horse's neck

ma-neu-ver (mə–nuʷ–vər) v. **1.** To move a thing's course or position carefully: *He maneuvered the car down the narrow street.* **2.** To guide skillfully or craftily: *She maneuvered the conversation to the subject dearest to her heart.*

maneuver n. **1.** A planned and controlled movement of ships, troops, etc. **2.** A skillful or crafty proceeding: *That was quite a maneuver by the chairman to get the delegates to vote his way.* **3.** maneuvers *pl.* Large scale exercises of troops, warships, etc. —**maneuverable** adj.

mange (meʸndʒ) n. A skin disease of animals, accompanied by scabs and loss of hair

man-ger (meʸn–dʒər) n. A trough or open box in which feed is placed for livestock

man-gle (mæŋ–gəl) n. A machine for pressing and smoothing cloth, esp. flat pieces, between heated rollers

mangle v. -gled, -gling **1.** To batter, hack, or cut; to crush: *The car was badly mangled when it was hit by a freight train.* **2.** To press cloth in a mangle

man-go (mæŋ–goʷ) n. -gos or -goes **1.** A tropical fruit with yellowish flesh **2.** The tree that bears this fruit

man-grove (mæn–groʷv/ mæŋ–) n. A tropical tree that has many roots growing above the ground

man-gy (meʸn–dʒiʸ) adj. -gier, -giest **1.** Having the mange: *a mangy dog* **2.** Shabby and dirty: *a mangy old blanket*

man-han-dle (mæn–hæn–dəl) v. -handled, -handling **1.** To treat roughly **2.** To move

sthg. by human effort alone

man·hole (mæn–ho^wl) n. A hole through which an underground structure (a sewer, e.g.) can be entered

man·hood (mæn–hʊd) n. The condition of being a man

ma·ni·a (me^y–ni^y–ə) n. **1.** A mental disorder characterized by excessive physical activity and emotional excitement **2.** An intense enthusiasm; craze: *a mania for skydiving*

ma·ni·ac (me^y–ni^y–æk) n. **1.** An insane person; a lunatic: *a dangerous sex maniac* **2.** A wild, thoughtless person —**ma·ni·a·cal** adj. (mə–naɪ–ə–kəl)

man·ic–de·pres·sive (mæn–ɪk–di^y–pres–ɪv) adj. Characterized by alternating periods of excitement and depression

manic–depressive n. A person who suffers from this disorder

man·i·cure (mæn–ə–kyʊər) n. A treatment for the care of the hands and fingernails

manicure v. -cured, -curing **1.** To give a manicure **2.** To trim closely

man·i·cur·ist (mæn–ə–kyʊər–əst) n. A person who cares for the hands and fingernails

man·i·fest (mæn–ə–fɛst) adj. Clearly apparent to the sight or understanding; obvious —**manifestly** adv.

manifest v. To show plainly —**man·i·fes·ta·tion** (mæn–ə–fɛs–te^y–ʃən) n.

man·i·fes·to (mæn–ə–fɛs–to^w) n. A public declaration of principles and policy

man·i·fold (mæn–ə–fo^wld) adj. **1.** Of many and different kinds **2.** Having many features and forms

manifold n. A pipe with several openings for making many connections

man·i·kin or **man·ni·kin** (mæn–ɪ–kən) n. **1.** A little man; a dwarf **2.** A dummy for displaying clothes in a store; a mannequin

ma·nip·u·late (mə–nɪp–yə–le^yt) v. -lated, -lating **1.** To arrange or influence sthg. craftily **2.** To manage or use sthg. skillfully —**manipulator** n. —**manipulative** adj. —**ma·nip·u·la·tion** (mə–nɪp–yu^w–le^y–ʃən) n.

man·kind (mæn–kaɪnd) n. **1.** All human males; the male sex **2.** The human race, both men and women —see MAN

man·ly (mæn–li^y) adj. -lier, -liest Having the qualities expected of a man, such as strength, courage, etc. —**manliness** n.

man·na (mæn–ə) n. **1.** Food miraculously supplied every morning to the Isra-elites throughout their entire 40 years in the wilderness (Exodus 16:31; Joshua 5:12) **2.** Sthg. of value that comes one's way

man·ne·quin (mæn–ɪ–kən) n. **1.** A form representing the human body, used to display clothing in stores **2.** A dressmaker's or tailor's model of the human body **3.** A woman who models clothing

man·ner (mæn–ər) n. **1.** The way of doing sthg.: *Please fold the sheets in this manner.* **2.** A personal way of behaving: *He has a very frank and sincere manner.* **3.** Kind; sort: *Jesus healed every manner of disease and sickness among the people* (Matthew 4:23).

man·ners (mæn–ərz) n. **1.** Socially proper behavior: *Children should be taught good manners.* **2.** –**mannered** Having a certain type of manners: *well/ill-man-nered*

ma·noeu·vre (mə–nu^w–vər) n. *BrE. for* ma-neu-ver

man·or (mæn–ər) n. **1.** The land and buildings belonging to a lord in the Middle Ages. Part of the land was set aside for peasants who farmed the land and paid the lord by doing jobs for him and giving him part of their crops. **2.** Any large estate **3.** The large main house on an estate

man·sion (mæn–tʃən) n. A large, luxurious house

man·slaugh·ter (mæn–slɔt–ər) n. The unlawful killing of a human being without express or implied malice

man·tel (mæn–təl) n. A structure of wood or marble, etc. above and around a fireplace

man·tis (mænt–əs) n. -tises, -tes (–ti^yz) A large insect similar to a grasshopper that seizes and feeds on other insects. It is often called a praying mantis because it holds its front legs folded up as if praying.

man·tle (mæn–təl) n. **1.** A cloak or loose-fitting garment **2.** A covering **3.** A piece of thin, transparent material around the light in a gas or paraffin (kerosene) lamp

man·u·al (mæn–yu^w–əl) adj. Pertaining to use of the hands: *Manual labor can be very hard*

and tiring. —**manually** adv.

manual n. A book of instructions on how to do sthg., esp. how to operate and maintain a machine

man-u-fac-ture (mæn–yə–fæk–tʃər) v. **-tured, -turing** To make or produce things by machinery, esp. in large quantities —**manufacturer** n.

ma-nure (mə–**nyur**) n. Waste matter from animals which is used to fertilize soil and produce better crops —compare FERTILIZER

man-u-script (mæn–yə–skrɪpt) n. **1.** The handwritten or typed material for a book, etc., usu. prepared for printing **2.** A book or document written by hand

man-y (mɛn–iʸ) more, most adj., pron. A large but indefinite number

map (mæp) n. A drawing or plan showing the shape and position of countries, towns, rivers, lakes, mountains, roads, etc.: *When traveling in a strange land, it is important to have a road map.*

ma-ple (meʸ–pəl) n. One of several kinds of trees, some of which yield a type of sugar that is often used for syrup

mar (mɑr) **-rr-** v. To spoil or damage: *That ugly old house mars the beauty of the neighborhood.*

mar-a-thon (mær–ə–θən) n. **1.** A foot race of 26 miles, 385 yards (42 km., 195 m.) The world record is: 2 hr., 6 m., 50 s. **2.** Any test or contest of endurance

marathon adj. Very long: *a marathon speech lasting for hours*

ma-raud (mə–rɔd) v. To rove about in search of plunder —**marauder** n. —**marauding** adj. *a marauding band of thieves*

mar-ble (mɑr–bəl) n. **1.** A hard kind of stone usu. having an irregular pattern of colors, used esp. in sculpture and for building **2.** A small hard ball of colored glass used to play a children's game

march (mɑrtʃ) v. **1.** To walk with a regular step, usu. keeping pace with others, like a soldier: *The soldiers marched 20 miles yesterday.* **2.** To go on steadily: *Time marches on.*

march n. **1.** The act of marching: *We went on a long march.* **2.** A piece of music for marching in rhythm to: *John Philip Sousa wrote many*

marches.

March n. The third month of the year

mare (mɛər) n. A female horse or donkey

mar-ga-rine (mɑr–dʒə–rən/ –riʸn) n. A food made mainly from vegetable fats, used instead of butter on bread or in baking

mar-gin (mɑr–dʒən) n. **1.** A blank space around a page of writing or print: *He wrote notes in the margin of his book.* **2.** An extra amount allowed, above what is needed: *a margin of safety* **3.** In business, the amount of profit: *a high margin of profit*

mar-gin-al (mɑr–dʒən–əl) adj. An insignificant amount: *The improvement in his work is marginal.* —**marginally** adv.

mar-i-gold (mær–ɪ–goʷld/ mɛər–) n. A kind of plant related to daisies, with yellow, orange, or reddish flowers

mar-i-jua-na (mær–ə–**wɑ**–nə/ mɛər–) n. The dried leaves, stems, etc. of the hemp plant, used to make a hallucinogenic drug, esp. in the form of cigarettes

ma-rine (mə–riʸn) adj. **1.** Of the sea **2.** Of ships and sea trade

marine n. **1.** A member of a marine military force, esp. a member of the Marine Corps **2.** Naval or merchant ships: *the merchant marine*

mar-i-ner (mær–ə–nər/ mɛər–) n. A sailor or seaman

mar-i-o-nette (mær–iʸ–ə–nɛt/ mɛər–) n. A small puppet or doll that can be moved with wire or strings from above, making it seem to be alive

mar-i-tal (mær–ə–təl/ mɛər–) adj. Of or concerning marriage: *Jesus said, "Anyone who divorces his wife, except for marital unfaithfulness, and marries another woman, commits adultery"* (Matthew 19:9).

mar-i-time (mær–ə–taɪm/ mɛər–) adj. **1.** Concerning the sea, shipping, etc.: *a great maritime power* (=with a strong navy) **2.** Living or existing near the sea: *a maritime nation*

mark (mɑrk) n. **1.** A spot, scratch, tear, etc. that spoils the natural color or appearance of sthg.: *His muddy shoes left ugly marks on the carpet./ fig. His years in prison have left their mark on him.* **2.** A visible impression on a surface: *The police followed the marks that the*

car had left in the mud. **3.** A letter or figure indicating a person's grade on a test: *Lisa had a mark of 98 on her mid-term exam.* **4.** made his **mark** Had a great influence **5.** An indication of where sthg. is located: *That mark on the map shows where our house is located.*

mark v. **1.** To show; to be a sign of: *"'X' marks the spot where the treasure is buried."* **2.** To make a mark on, or to receive a mark, in a way that spoils the appearance: *That hot cup has marked the table.* **3.** To give grades to: *I have 30 examination papers to mark.* **4. Mark my word!** Take note of what I say and remember it **5. mark sthg. down/up** To lower/raise the price of goods in a store **6. mark off sthg.** To draw lines around (an area): *They marked off the football field with white chalk.*

Mark (mɑrk) n. **1.** A masculine name **2.** The author of the second Gospel in the New Testament which tells of the life, teachings, death, and resurrection of Jesus Christ —see JESUS CHRIST

marked (mɑrkt) adj. Noticeable: *He showed a marked interest in learning foreign languages.*

mark-er (mɑrk–ər) n. **1.** Sthg. used for making marks **2.** An object which marks a place

mar-ket (mɑr–kət) n. **1.** A place where people buy and sell goods **2.** A gathering of people to buy and sell on certain days: *The village market is on Saturday.* **3.** An area or country where there is a demand for goods **4.** Demands for goods: *There's not much of a market for fur coats in a tropical country.*

market v. To offer for sale: *It does no good to produce anything for a profit if it isn't successfully marketed.* —**marketable** adj.

mar-ket-ing (mɑr–kət–ɪŋ) n. The processes by which anything can be sold

mark-ing (mɑr–kɪŋ) n. A mark or marks: *The snake had red and yellow markings.*

mar-ma-lade (mɑr–mə–leʸd) n. A kind of jam made from citrus fruit, esp. oranges

mar-mot (mɑr–mət) n. A burrowing animal with short legs and brownish fur

ma-roon (mə–ruʷn) n. A brownish red color

maroon adj. Brownish red

maroon v. To leave abandoned, isolated, or helpless

mar-quis (mɑr–kwɪs/ mɑr–kiʸ) n. -quises or

-**quis** (–kiʸz) A nobleman ranking below a duke and above an earl or count

mar-riage (mær–ɪdʒ/ meər–) n. **1.** The ceremony by which a man and woman become husband and wife: *The mar-riage took place in St. John's Church.* **2.** The state of being married: *God instituted marriage and intended for a man and woman to remain married as long as they both should live./ At the resurrection people will neither marry nor be given in marriage; they will be like the angels in heaven* (Matthew 22:30). —see MARITAL

mar-riage-a-ble (mær–ɪ–dʒə–bəl/ meər–) adj. Old enough or eligible for mar-riage

mar-ried (mær–iʸd/ meər–) adj. **1.** Having a wife or husband: *a married man/woman/fig. He's married to his work. (=he gives it all his attention)* **2.** Of the state of marriage: *married life*

mar-row (mær–oʷ/ meər–) n. **1.** A soft substance that fills the hollow, central part of most bones **2.** The inmost or important part: *He was shocked to the marrow by her actions.*

mar-ry (mær–iʸ/ meər–) v. -ried, -rying **1.** To take a person as husband or wife: *They've been married for 50 years.* **2.** To perform the marriage ceremony: *The pastor married them in the wedding chapel.*

Mars (mɑrz) n. The seventh largest planet in the solar system and fourth in distance from the sun

marsh (mɑrʃ) n. Low-lying, watery ground —**marshy** adj.

mar-shal (mɑr–ʃəl) n. **1.** An officer of high rank **2.** An administrative officer of a federal court **3.** An official whose responsibility it is to arrange for certain public events or ceremonies

marshal v. **1.** To arrange in proper order **2.** To cause to assemble **3.** To usher

marsh-mal-low (mɑrʃ–mɛl–oʷ/ –mɑl–oʷ) n. A light, creamy confection made from corn syrup, sugar, albumen, and gelatin

mar-su-pi-al (mɑr–suʷ–piʸ–əl) n. Any of a large group of (mostly Australian) mammals which bear young that are nourished in a pouch on the abdomen of the female: *The kangaroo is a marsupial.*

mart (mɑrt) n. A market; shopping center

mar-ten (mɑr–tən) n. **1.** A slender animal like a weasel **2.** The valuable fur of this animal

mar-tial (mɑr–ʃəl) adj. **1.** Of or pertaining to war **2.** Pertaining to military life

mar-tial law (mɑr–ʃəl lɔ) n. Rule by military authorities imposed on a civilian population during an emergency

mar-tin (mɑrt–ən) n. A bird with dark feathers and forked tail, related to the swallow

mar-tyr (mɑr–tər) n. **1.** A person who dies rather than renounce his religion **2.** One who makes a great sacrifice for the sake of principle —mar-tyr-dom (mɑr–tər–dəm) n.

mar-vel (mɑr–vəl) v. -veled, -veling or -velled, -velling To be filled with wonder, surprise, etc.

marvel n. That which excites wonder: *This child violinist is a real marvel.*

mar-vel-ous (mɑrv–ə–ləs) adj. Wonderful; splendid: *Declare his [God's] glory among the nations, his marvelous deeds among all peoples* (Psalm 96:3). —marvelously adv.

Marx-ism (mɑrk–sɪz–əm) n. The system of economic, political, and social doctrines developed by Carl Marx (1818-83) and his co-worker, Friedrich Engels and their followers, the system on which Communism is based, and which explains the changes in history according to the struggle between the different social classes: *Marxism is atheistic, denying the existence of God, often persecuting those who believe in God regardless of their religious persuasion.* —Marxist n., adj. —see COMMUNISM

Mary (meər–iʸ) n. The Virgin Mary, mother of our Lord and Savior Jesus Christ according to his human nature. He was conceived by the Holy Spirit and thus, unlike all others, born without sin. —see JESUS , CREED

mas-car-a (mæs–kær–ə/ –keər–) n. A cosmetic for darkening the eyelashes

mas-cot (mæs–kɑt) n. A person or thing believed to bring good luck

mas-cu-line (mæs–kyə–lən) adj. **1.** Characteristics suitable for a man: *a masculine voice* **2.** *tech.* (in grammar) Of a certain class of words: *"Actor," "bull," "rooster," and "buck" are masculine forms.* —compare FEMININE —mas-cu-lin-i-ty (mæs–kyə–lɪn–ə–tiʸ) n.

mash (mæʃ) v. To crush into a soft substance: *She's mashing the potatoes with her fork.*

mask (mæsk) n. A covering for the face to hide or protect it: *The burglar was wearing a mask./ The soldiers were wearing gas masks./ fig. He often comes to our house under a mask of friendship.* (=pretending to be a friend)

mask v. To cover with a mask; hide: *fig. She tried to mask her feelings by smiling, but it was obvious that she was really very unhappy.*

ma-son (meʸ–sən) n. A person who works with stone or similar material such as brick or concrete

ma-son-ry (meʸ–sən–riʸ) n. **1.** Sthg. constructed with the materials used by a mason **2.** The art, work, or trade of a mason

mas-quer-ade (mæs–kə–reʸd) n. **1.** A party where people wear masks **2.** Sthg. pretended

masquerade v. -aded, -ading To pretend to be: *Satan himself masquerades as an angel of light* (=pretends to be holy). *It is not surprising, then, if his servants masquerade as servants of righteousness* (2 Corinthians 11:14,15).

mass (mæs) n. **1.** A large solid lump: *a solid mass of rock* **2.** A large quantity, gathered together: *masses of people* **3.** In science, the amount of matter in a body **4. the masses** The common people **5. Mass** In some Christian churches, the celebration of the Lord's last supper with his disciples; the celebration of the Eucharist or Holy Communion

mass v. *lit.* To gather or form into large numbers: *Dark clouds were massing on the horizon.*

mass adj. Of or for a great number of people: *mass evangelism*

mas-sa-cre (mæs–ə–kər) n. An unnecessary killing of large numbers of people who cannot defend themselves

massacre v. -cred, -cring **1.** To kill a large number of people **2.** *fig.* To defeat another team badly: *Their team was much better than ours, and we were massacred 49 to 0.*

mas-sage (mə–sɑʒ/ –sɑdʒ) v. -saged, -saging A treatment of the body by pressing and rubbing one's hands on it to aid circulation or to relax the muscles

mass-es (mæs–əz) n. *pl.* The lower or poorer

classes in society: *The king was loved because he showed concern for the masses.*

mas-sive (**mæs**-ɪv) adj. Very big; strong and powerful: *massive walls around the prison* —**massively** adv.

mass me-di-a (mæs mi⁷-di⁷-ə) n. Radio, television, and newspapers which give news and opinions to large numbers of people

mass pro-duce (mæs prə–du^ws) v. **-duced, -ducing** To manufacture large numbers of the same article by standardized processes —**mass pro-duc-tion** (mæs prə–dʌk–ʃən) n.

mast (mæst) n. **1.** A long, upright pole that supports a ship's sails **2.** Any upright pole: *Flags were flying at half-mast.*

mas-ter (**mæs**-tər) n. **1.** God: *You know that you also have a Master in heaven* (Colossians 4:1). **2.** A man who controls people or things: *Masters, provide your slaves with what is right and fair* (Colossians 4:1). **3.** Money or sin, or anything that controls a person: *No one can serve two masters. You cannot serve God and money* (Matthew 6:24). *For sin shall not be your master* (Romans 6:14). **4.** The male head of a household **5.** The captain of a merchant ship **6.** *BrE.* Male teacher **7.** The male owner of a dog **8.** A person of great skill in art or work with the hands: *This painting is the work of a master.*

master adj. Chief; most important: *the master bedroom*

master v. To gain control over or learn thoroughly: *It takes years to master a new language.*

mas-ter-ful (**mæs**-tər–fəl) adj. **1.** Having an ability to control others **2.** Showing mastery or skill: *a masterful artist* —**masterfully** adv.

mas-ter key (**mæs**-tər ki⁷) n. A key that opens all the locks in a building

mas-ter-ly (**mæs**-tər–li⁷) adv. Worthy of a master; very skillful: *His handling of the problem was indeed masterly.*

mas-ter-mind (**mæs**-tər–maɪnd) n. A person who plans and controls an undertaking or scheme

mastermind v. To plan: *Who masterminded the bank robbery?*

mas-ter-piece (**mæs**-tər–pi⁷s) n. **1.** Any production of masterful skill **2.** The best artistic

work a person has done

Mas-ter's (**mæs**-tərz) n. A Master of Arts or Master of Science degree: *He has his Master's in geology.*

mas-ter stroke (**mæs**-tər stro^wk) n. A very clever thing to do

mas-ter-y (**mæs**-tər–i⁷) n. Control over: *Since Christ was raised from the dead, he cannot die again; death no longer has mastery over him* (Romans 6:9)./*The enemy had complete mastery of the seas. No ships could get through.*

mas-ti-cate (**mæs**-tə–ke⁷t) v. **-cated, -cat-ing** To chew—**mas-ti-ca-tion** (mæs-tə–**ke**⁷–ʃən) n.

mas-tiff (**mæs**-təf) n. A large, strong dog with short hair and square jaws

mas-toid (**mæs**-tɔɪd) n. A part of a bone behind the ear

mas-toid-i-tis (mæs-tɔɪd–aɪt–əs) n. Inflammation of the mastoid

mat (mæt) n. **1.** A piece of strong material, often rubber or fabric, used as a floor covering; a doormat **2.** A small pad or piece of material placed under a cup, glass, or hot object to protect the table or other surface on which it stands **3.** A thick pad on the floor for the protection of wrestlers or gymnasts **4.** A piece of cardboard used to form a border around a picture

match (mætʃ) n. **1.** A short piece of wood (a match stick) or cardboard with a substance at the tip which ignites when struck against a rough surface **2.** A game or sports event in which individuals or teams compete: *a tennis match* **3.** A person who is equal or better in ability than another: *I'm no match for him when it comes to weight lifting.* (=*he's much stronger than I am*) **4.** A set of things that are like or suitable to each other: *Your skirt and jacket are a perfect match.* **5.** A partner in marriage

match v. **1.** To be equal or suitable: *Your socks don't match.* **2.** To be equal to: *He tried to match John's record, but he couldn't.* **3.** To place in opposition: *Our team was matched against the best team in the West.*

match-less (**mætʃ**-ləs) adj. *fml.* That which has no equal in quality

mate (me⁷t) n. **1.** A fellow student or someone

on the same team: *a classmate/teammate* 2. A husband or wife 3. The officer of a merchant vessel, ranking below the captain: *first mate/ second mate* 4. One of a pair of mated animals

mate v. **mated, mating** To couple in marriage or for producing young

ma-te-ri-al (mə-tɪər-iᵞ-əl) n. 1. Anything from which sthg. is or may be made: *Rubber is a widely used material.* 2. Cloth; fabric: *curtain material* 3. Facts from which a written work may be produced: *He's collecting material for a magazine article he's writing.*

material adj. 1. Formed or consisting of substances that are able to be seen or felt: *The storm did a lot of material damage.* (=to buildings, property, etc.) 2. Concerning the body rather than the mind or soul: *Our material needs are food, shelter, and clothing.* —**materially** adv.

ma-te-ri-al-ism (mə-tɪər-iᵞ-əl-ɪz-əm) n. *esp. derog.* Emphasis on material objects and needs with little or no interest in spiritual values —**ma-te-ri-al-is-tic** (mə-tɪər-iᵞ-ə-lɪs-tɪk) adj.

ma-te-ri-al-ize (mə-tɪər-iᵞ-ə-laɪz) v. **-ized, -izing** 1. To take on bodily form: *The shape of a monster materialized out of the shadows.* 2. To become actual fact: *His hopes never materialized.*

ma-ter-nal (mə-tɜr-nəl) adj. 1. Motherly 2. Related through a mother: *My mother's father is my maternal grandfather.* —see also PATERNAL —**maternally** adv.

ma-ter-ni-ty (mə-tɜr-nə-tiᵞ) adj., n. 1. Motherhood or the physical condition of becoming a mother 2. A hospital facility for the care of women before and during childbirth and for the care of newborn babies: *a maternity ward* 3. Of or for women having or about to have a baby: *a maternity dress*

math (mæθ) n. *infml.* Mathematics

math-e-ma-tics (mæθ-ə-mæt-ɪks) also **math** n. (*pl. form, used as sing.*) *infml.* The branch of knowledge dealing with measurements, numbers, and quantities —compare ARITHMETIC —**mathematical** adj. —**mathematically** adv. —**math-e-ma-ti-cian** (mæθ-ə-mə-tɪʃ-ən) n.

mat-i-nee (mæt-ə-neᵞ) n. Afternoon perfor-

mance of a play or movie

mat-ins (mæt-ənz) n. Morning prayers or worship service in certain churches

ma-tri-arch (meᵞ-triᵞ-ɑrk) n. A woman who is the head and ruler of her family or of a tribe —**matriarchy** n.

mat-ri-cide (mæ-trə-saɪd) n. 1. The killing of one's own mother 2. The person who kills his or her own mother

ma-tric-u-late (mə-trɪk-yə-leᵞt) v. **-lated, -lating** To enroll in a group, esp. a college or university

mat-ri-mo-ny (mæ-trə-moᵂ-niᵞ) n. The state of being married —**mat-ri-mo-ni-al** (mæ-trə-moᵂ-niᵞ-əl) adj.

ma-trix (meᵞ-trɪks) n. **-trixes** or **-trices** 1. A mold in which sthg. is cast or shaped 2. A place in which a thing is developed

ma-tron (meᵞ-trən) n. 1. A married woman, esp. one who is older and dignified 2. A woman in charge of housekeeping or nursing in a school, hostel, etc. 3. A woman attendant in a prison

matt or **mat** or **matte** (mæt) adj. Of a painting or photograph, having a dull surface without gloss or shine

mat-ter (mæt-ər) n. 1. That which occupies space in the world as opposed to spirit, mind, or qualities 2. A specific kind of substance: *organic matter* 3. A subject to which one gives attention: *an important matter for consideration* 4. Trouble or cause of pain, malfunction, etc.: *What's the matter with Susan. Why is she crying?/ What's the matter with the radio? Why isn't it working?* 5. Written material: *reading matter* 6. A quantity: *a matter of twenty years* 7. The content of a book or speech: *subject matter* 8. A situation or problem being considered: *a serious matter* 9. Discharge from the body; pus 10. **a matter of life or death** Sthg. that could result in death if swift action isn't taken 11. **a matter of opinion** Sthg. about which different people may have different opinions or views 12. **mind over matter** A strong will conquering bodily weakness 13. **a matter of course** Sthg. that one expects to happen 14. **for that matter** As far as that is concerned 15. **no matter** It makes no difference: *We'll have to*

finish the job, no matter how long it takes.

matter v. To be important: *It doesn't matter if I miss my bus. There'll be another one soon.*

mat-ter-of-fact (mæt–ər əv fækt) adj. Sticking to the facts; not imaginative or fanciful: *a matter-of-fact account of the accident*

Mat-thew (mæθ–yuᵂ) n. **1.** One of the twelve apostles of Jesus Christ and author of the book in the New Testament that bears his name **2.** The first of the four Gospels in the New Testament. It is an account of the life and teachings of Jesus Christ, his suffering and death on the cross for our sins, and of his resurrection, all in fulfillment of the Old Testament prophecies —see JESUS CHRIST

mat-ting (mæt–m̩) n. **1.** Mats **2.** Material for making these

mat-tress (mæt–rəs) n. A large pad used as a bed, consisting of a case of heavy cloth that contains foam rubber, cotton, straw, or some other suitable substance

ma-tu-ra-tion (mætʃ–ə–reʸ–ʃən) n. The process of becoming mature

ma-ture (mə–tʃʊər) adj. **1.** Fully grown and developed **2.** Typical of an older person; sensible **3.** Ripe, as fruit, or fully aged, as cheese or wine, etc. —opposite IMMA-TURE —**maturely** adv.

mature v. -tured, -turing To (cause to) bring to maturity or completion: *He matured quickly during the war.*

ma-tu-ri-ty (mə–tʃʊər–ət–iʸ) n. **1.** A state of ripeness or full development **2.** The condition of being completed or ready —opposite IMMATURITY

maud-lin (mɔd–lən) adj. Sentimental in a silly or tearful way, esp. from drunk-enness

maul (mɔl) v. **1.** To hurt by tearing the flesh: *The hunter was mauled by a leopard.* **2.** To handle roughly or in an unwelcome way

mau-so-le-um (mɔ–sə–liʸ–əm/ mɔ–zə–) n. A building, usu. made of stone, with places for entombment of the dead above the ground, named after Mausolus, ruler of Caria in Asia Minor in the 4th century B.C., whose tomb was one of the seven wonders of the ancient world

mauve (moᵂv/ mɔv) adj. A pale shade of purple in color

mav-er-ick (mæv–ə–rık) n. **1.** A nonconform-ist; someone who takes an independent stand, different from others in the group **2.** An unbranded calf or other young animal

max-im (mæk–səm) n. A general truth or rule of conduct, as in "Waste not; want not."

max-i-mum (mæk–sə–məm) n. -ma or -mums The largest possible quantity or degree: *This lamp will give you the maximum of light.*

maximum adj. **1.** An upper limit allowable by law: *a maximum speed limit* **2.** The highest or most for a given period: *Today's maxi-mum temperature was 85 degrees.* —opposite MINIMUM

may (meʸ) v. **1.** Might possibly: *He may come or he may not.* **2.** To have permission to: *You may sit down now.*

May (meʸ) n. The fifth month of the year

may-be (meʸ–biʸ) adv. Perhaps: *Maybe it will rain today.*

May-day (meʸ–deʸ) n. An international radio signal of distress

may-flow-er (meʸ–flaʊ–ər) n. Any of several flowering plants that bloom in the spring

may-hem (meʸ–hɛm) n. **1.** Violent action **2.** The crime of maiming or mutilating a per-son so as to make him defenseless

may-on-naise (meʸ–ə–neʸz/ meʸ–ə–neʸz) n. A creamy sauce made with egg yolks, oil, and vinegar or lemon juice, often used in sand-wiches and salads

may-or (meʸ–ər) n. The head of a city or other municipality —**mayoral** adj.

maze (meʸz) n. **1.** A series of winding paths, deliberately laid out in such a way as to make it difficult to find one's way out **2.** Sthg. complicated and confusing: *a maze of regulations*

M.D. *abbr.* for **Doctor of Medicine:** *Joan Smith, M.D.*

me (miʸ) pron. Objective case of I: *Can you hear me?*

mead-ow (mɛd–oᵂ) n. A grassland

mead-ow-lark (mɛd–oᵂ–lɑrk) n. Any of sever-al American songbirds

mea-ger (miʸ–gər) adj. Scanty in amount; not enough: *a meager income/harvest* —**meagerly** adv.

meal (miʸl) n. **1.** An occasion when food is

eaten: *Most people in America eat three meals a day.* 2. The food itself: *a delicious meal*

meal n. 1. Coarsely ground edible grain 2. Any substance resembling this —**mealy** adj. **-ier, -iest**

mean (miᵞn) adj. 1. Very unkind; cruel: *He was mean to his children, beating them often and for no good reason.* 2. Vicious: *That's a mean dog; it has bitten several people.* 3. Of low social position: *a man of mean birth*

mean v. **meant, meaning** 1. To represent: *The green light means "Go."* 2. Intend: *She said "Monday," but she meant "Sunday."* 3. To be a sign of: *Those dark clouds mean rain.* 4. To be of specified importance: *Her work means everything to her.* 5. To be serious about sthg.: *I wasn't joking; I really meant it.* 6. To be determined to do sthg.: *I said I'd help you, and I meant it.* 7. Of words, to be equivalent in the same or in another language: *"Casa" in Spanish means "house" in English.*

me-an-der (miᵞ–æn–dər) v. 1. Of a stream, to follow a winding course, flowing slowly and gently 2. To wander in a leisurely way

mean-ing (miᵞ–nɪŋ) n. 1. That which is meant; the idea which is intended to be understood: *Many words have more than one meaning.* 2. Importance: *She says life has no meaning for her since her husband died.*

mean-ing-ful (miᵞ–nɪŋ–fəl) adj. Of importance; significant —**meaningfully** adv.

mean-ness (miᵞn–nəs) n. 1. Being selfish in small things; stingy 2. Being cruel or unkind; having a mean nature; spiteful: *He is known for his meanness. He is always doing mean things like pulling the cat's tail or ears or doing worse things than that.*

means (miᵞnz) n. 1. A way of doing sthg.: *The fastest means of travel is by plane.* 2. Money necessary to live on; income: *She hasn't the means to quit working.* 3. **a man of means** A rich man 4. **by all means** Certainly 5. **by means of** By using: *She couldn't walk but she got around well by means of a wheelchair.* 6. **by no means** Not at all: *I'm by no means happy with your decision.*

meant (mɛnt) v. Past tense and part. of **mean**

mean-time (miᵞn–taɪm) n. The intervening time; the time between two events

mean-while (miᵞn–waɪl) adv. Meantime; during this time; in the same period of time

mea-sles (miᵞ–zəlz) n. An infectious disease affecting children and sometimes adults, in which the sufferer has a fever and small red spots on the face and body

mea-sly (miᵞz–liᵞ) adj. **-slier, -sliest** *infml.* A very small amount

meas-ur-a-ble (mɛʒ–ə–rə–bəl) adj. Able to be measured: *We haven't had any measurable rainfall in months.*

meas-ur-a-bly (mɛʒ–ə–rə–bliᵞ) adv. Significantly: *Your work has improved measurably this year.*

meas-ure (mɛʒ–ər) n. 1. The size or quantity of sthg., found by measuring 2. Extent or amount: *a measure of success* 3. An instrument used for finding amount, length, weight, etc.: *a tape measure* 4. An action taken as a means to an end: *The administration has promised to take measures to help the unemployed.* 5. **for good measure** Sthg. extra: *After he weighed the peanuts, he put another handful in the sack for good measure.*

measure v. **-ured, -uring** 1. To find the size of sthg.: *He measured the length and width of the room.* 2. To show or record time, size, weight, temperature, etc.: *A clock measures time.* 3. To be of a certain size: *The living room measures 14 by 20 feet.* 4. To choose with care: *He measured his words.* 5. **measure up (a)** To be the equal of: *His work doesn't measure up to his brother's.* **(b)** To have the necessary qualifications: *He didn't measure up to our standards.*

meas-ure-ment (mɛʒ–ər–mənt) n. 1. The process of measuring or being measured 2. A length, height, width, depth, etc. found by measuring

meat (miᵞt) n. 1. Animal flesh as food 2. The edible, inner part of sthg., such as a nut 3. Valuable matter: *He gave an interesting talk, but there wasn't much meat in it.* —**meaty** adj.

me-cha-nic (mɪ–kæn–ɪk) n. A person skilled in repairing machinery: *an auto mechanic*

me-cha-ni-cal (mɪ–kæn–ɪ–kəl) adj. 1. Having to do with machinery or tools 2. Caused, operated, or produced by machinery 3. Done as if by machine; automatic: *a very mechanical*

recitation —mechanically adv.

me-cha-nics (mɪ‿kæn–ɪks) n. **1.** A branch of science that deals with energy and forces and their effect on objects **2.** The study and art of making machinery **3.** the mechanics of The way sthg. works: *the mechanics of government*

mech-a-nism (mɛk–ə–nɪz–əm) n. **1.** The arrangement of connected parts in a machine and the action they have: *My watch doesn't work. Sthg.'s wrong with the mechanism.* **2.** Any system of parts working together

mech-a-nize (mɛk–ə–naɪz) *also* -nise v. -nized, -nizing To use machines instead of using the effort of human beings or animals: *Mechanized farming can produce more crops with fewer people.* —mech-a-ni-za-tion (mɛk–ə–nə–zeʸ–ʃən) n.

med-al (mɛd–əl) n. A flat piece of metal, often in the shape of a coin, usu. with words and/or a picture on it, issued in commemoration of an event or person, or given a person for an act of bravery or for special achievement: *He won seven gold medals in swimming at the Olympics Games.*

med-dle (mɛd–əl) v. -dled, -dling To involve oneself in sthg. which is not one's concern; to interfere —meddler n. —meddlesome adj. *a meddlesome person, always giving unwanted advice*

me-di-a (miʸ–diʸ–ə) n. *pl.* the media The newspapers, television and radio; mass media: *The media controls the news and influences large numbers of people.*

me-di-ate (miʸ–diʸ–eʸt) v. -ated, -ating To act as an intermediary between two or more people (as in settling a dispute); to act as a peacemaker —me-di-a-tion (miʸ–diʸ–eʸ–ʃən) n.

me-di-a-tor (miʸ–diʸ–eʸt–ər) n. One who acts as a peacemaker between two or more people, as in settling a dispute: *There is one God and one mediator between God and men, the man Christ Jesus, who gave himself as a ransom for all men* (1 Timothy 2:5,6). —see JESUS

med-ic (mɛd–ɪk) n. **1.** *slang* A medical student **2.** A doctor or intern

Med-i-caid (mɛd–ɪ–keʸd) n. A public health program in the US through which certain medical and hospital expenses of people with low incomes or no income, are paid from State and Federal funds

med-i-cal (mɛd–ɪ–kəl) adj. **1.** Of or concerning medicine and the work of doctors and nurses **2.** The treatment of disease by medicine rather than surgery —medically adv.

Med-i-care (mɛd–ɪ–kɛər) n. A national health program in the US through which certain medical and hospital expenses of the elderly are paid for from Federal, esp. Social Security, funds

med-i-cate (mɛd–ɪ–keʸt) v. **1.** To treat with medicine **2.** To add a medicinal substance to sthg.

med-i-ca-ted (mɛd–ɪ–keʸt–əd) adj. Mixed with a healing or disinfecting substance: *medicated shampoo*

med-i-ca-tion (mɛd–ɪ–keʸ–ʃən) n. A medical substance, esp. a drug: *It is better to sleep naturally, without taking medication.*

me-dic-i-nal (mə–dɪs–ə–nəl) adj. Of or having the properties of medicine —compare MEDICAL —medicinally adv.

med-i-cine (mɛd–ə–sən) n. **1.** A substance to treat disease **2.** The science of diagnosing, treating, curing, and preventing disease **3.** *fig.* Anything that helps a person feel better: *A cheerful heart is good medicine* (Proverbs 17:22).

med-i-cine man (mɛd–ə–sən mæn) n. A person believed by North American Indians to be possessed with supernatural powers of curing diseases and controlling spirits; shaman; witch doctor

me-di-e-val or me-di-ae-val (miʸ–diʸ–iʸ–vəl/ mɛd–/ miʸ–diʸ–vəl) adj. Of, relating to, or characteristic of the Middle Ages, the period of European history from about 500 to 1500 A.D. —me-di-e-val-ism (miʸ–diʸ–iʸ–vəl–ɪz–əm)/mɛd–/ miʸ–diʸ–vəl–ɪz–əm) n.

me-di-o-cre (miʸ–diʸ–oʷ–kər) adj. Of only ordinary quality or ability —me-di-oc-ri-ty n. (miʸ–diʸ–ɑ–krə–tiʸ)

med-i-tate (mɛd–ə–teʸt) v. -tated -tating To fix and keep the attention on one matter; to think deeply and in quietness, contemplatively, esp. for religious reasons: *Blessed is the man (whose) delight is in the law of the Lord*

and on his law meditates day and night (Psalm 1:1-2). Meditate on it [God's word] day and night, so that you may be careful to do everything written in it. Then you will be prosperous and successful (Joshua 1:8). **2.** To plan in one's mind

med-i-ta-tion (mɛd–ə–teʸ–ʃən) n. The act or result of meditating: May the words of my mouth and the meditation of my heart be pleasing in your sight, O Lord... (Psalm 19:14).

med-i-ta-tive (mɛd–ə–teʸ–tɪv) adj. Thoughtful; showing deep thought —meditatively adv.

me-di-um (miʸ–diʸ–əm) n. pl. -dia or -diums **1.** A method for giving information such as TV: Television is a medium used for informing, entertaining, and teaching people. **2.** A substance, like air, in which things exist, or through which a force travels; surroundings: Air is a medium through which sound travels. **3.** A middle position: a happy medium between talking all the time and not talking at all **4.** A person through whom spirits of dead persons are said to speak NOTE: This practice is condemned by the Holy Word of God (Leviticus 20:27). God hates sin, but he is also a God of love and mercy and forgiveness, and if we truly repent of this and all our sins and put our trust in Jesus, we shall have everlasting life (Romans 6:23; John 3:16). —see JESUS

medium adj. Middle or average in size, amount, value, etc.: a medium-sized car/shirt, etc.

med-ley (mɛd–liʸ) n. pl. **medleys 1.** A musical composition made up of a series of songs: a medley of Jerome Kern songs **2.** A confused mixture; a hodgepodge

meek (miʸk) adj. Having a patient, gentle disposition; yielding to others' actions and opinions: Jesus said, "Blessed are the meek, for they will inherit the earth" (Matthew 5:5). —meekly adv. —meekness n.

meet (miʸt) v. met, meeting **1.** To come into face to face contact with a person that one already knows, by chance or arrangement: We just happened to meet at the mall. **2.** To be introduced to sbdy. for the first time: I'd like you to meet Miss Jones. **3.** To join: The two roads meet about a mile south of here. **4.** To ex-

perience: He met his death in a tragic bicycle accident. **5.** To respond: His speech was met with cheers and excitement. **6.** To be equal to, or satisfy: Did the opera meet your expectations? **7. make ends meet** To use one's money wisely in order to pay one's bills, esp. when one's income is small

meet n. Gathering of people for sports events: a track meet

meet-ing (miʸt–ɪŋ) n. **1.** A gathering of people for discussion or for another purpose: There will be a meeting of the senior class this afternoon at two o'clock. **2.** A face-to-face coming together of two or more people, by chance or arrangement: The meeting between the two old friends was a joyful experience.

me-ga- (mɛg–ə–) prefix **1.** Large or great, as in "megalith" **2.** One million, as in "megacycle"

meg-a-lith (mɛg–ə–lɪθ) n. One of the huge stones used in the building of prehistoric monuments

meg-a-lo-ma-ni-a (mɛg–ə–loʷ–meʸ–niʸ–ə) n. A mental disorder in which a person believes himself to be more important or more powerful than he really is —megalomaniac n.

meg-a-lop-o-lis (mɛg–ə–lɔp–ə–ləs) n. **1.** A very large city **2.** The very densely populated area around one or more cities

meg-a-phone (mɛg–ə–foʷn) n. A cone-shaped device used to intensify and/or direct one's voice

meg-a-ton (mɛg–ə–tʌn) n. A unit of explosive power equal to a million tons of TNT

mel-an-chol-y (mɛl–ən–kɑ–liʸ) n. Excessive gloom; sadness over a long period of time, for no particular reason

melancholy adj. **1.** Gloomy and depressed **2.** Suggesting or promoting sadness: a melancholy day

me-lee (meʸ–leʸ / meʸ–leʸ) n. **1.** A confused hand-to-hand fight among a large number of people; a brawl **2.** Confusion or turmoil

mel-low (mɛl–oʷ) adj. **1.** Sweet and ripe or mature, having become pleasant or agreeable with age **2.** Of colors and surfaces, rich, warm, and soft in quality **3.** Of people, made gentle and sympathetic through maturity or experience

mellow v. To (cause to) become more mellow with the passing of time

me·lo·di·ous (mə-lo͞w-diʸ-əs) adj. Tuneful; full of melody —**melodiously** adv.

mel·o·dra·ma (mɛl-ə-dram-ə/ -dræm-) n. **1.** A play full of suspense in a sensational and emotional style **2.** A situation in real life resembling this —**mel·o·dra·mat·ic** (mɛl-ə-drə-mæt-ɪk) adj.

mel·o·dy (mɛl-ə-diʸ) n. **-dies 1.** Sweet music; tunefulness: *But be filled with the Spirit, speaking to one another in psalms, hymns, and spiritual songs, singing and making melody in your heart to the Lord* (Ephesians 5:18,19 NKJV). **2.** The main part in a piece of harmonized music

mel·on (mɛl-ən) n. A large round or oval fruit, such as watermelon or cantaloupe, with a firm skin and juicy flesh which can be eaten

melt (mɛlt) v. **1.** To cause a solid to become liquid by heating: *The snow melted.* **2.** To (cause to) become mild, tender, or gentle: *Her sweet smile melted his heart.* **3. melt away** To disappear: *The opposition melted away when they realized that they had very little support.*

melt·ing pot (mɛlt-ŋ-pɑt) n. **1.** A place where there is a mixture of people from many different nations: *Los Angeles is a melting pot; 137 languages are spoken in its homes.* **2.** A container in which metals can be melted

mem·ber (mɛm-bər) n. **1.** A person belonging to a family, church, political party, society, club, or other group **2.** A part of a person: *Our fingers and toes, arms and legs, are members of our bodies.*

mem·ber·ship (mɛm-bər-ʃɪp) n. **1.** The state of being a member: *He has membership in several organizations.* **2.** All the members of a club, church, society, etc.: *The total membership of this society is 550.*

mem·brane (mɛm-breʸn) n. Thin, flexible, skin-like tissue, esp. that which covers or lines the organs or other structures in animals or plants

me·men·to (mə-mɛn-to͞w) n. Anything that serves as a reminder of the past; a souvenir

mem·o (mɛm-o͞w) n. *pl.* **memos** A memorandum

mem·oir (mɛm-wɑr) n. A written account of the events one has lived through, esp. of an important public figure: *The ex-president is writing his memoirs.*

mem·o·ra·ble (mɛm-ə-rə-bəl) adj. Special in some way; worth remembering: *a memorable occasion* —**memorably** adv.

mem·o·ran·dum (mɛm-ə-ræn-dəm) n. *pl.* **-dums** or **-da 1.** A written reminder **2.** An informal written note

me·mo·ri·al (mə-mɔr-iʸ-əl) n. **1.** An object, such as a stone monument, or an institution or custom established in memory of a person or event: *The Golden Spike Memorial commemorates the completion of the first transcontinental railroad in 1869.* **2.** A statement presented to a legislative body as the reason for a request or petition

Me·mo·ri·al Day (mə-mɔr-iʸ-əl deʸ) n. (in the US) A holiday at the end of May commemorating those who were killed in active military service

mem·o·rize_AmE._ also **-rise** _BrE._ (mɛm-ə-raiz) v. **-rized, -rizing** To commit sthg. to memory; to learn and remember: *Have you memorized the English alphabet?* —**mem·o·ri·za·tion** (mɛm-ə-rə-zeʸ-ʃən) n.

mem·o·ry (mɛm-ə-riʸ) n. **-ries 1.** An ability to remember: *He has an excellent memory for names and faces.* **2.** A thing remembered: *She had fond memories of her childhood.* **3.** The length of time over which a person's memory extends: *There have been two world wars within my father's memory.* **4.** The part of the computer in which information (data) is stored until wanted

men (mɛn) n. *pl.* of **man**: *God wants all men to be saved and come to a knowledge of the truth [about Jesus Christ our Savior]* (1 Timothy 2:4). —see MAN

men·ace (mɛn-əs) n. Sthg. threatening: *Drunk drivers are a menace on our highways.*

men·ace v. **-aced, -acing** To threaten

men·ac·ing (mɛn-əs-ŋ) adj. Threatening: *Those dark clouds look menacing.* —**menacingly** adv.

me·nag·er·ie (mə-nædʒ-ə-riʸ) n. **1.** A collection of wild animals kept in cages for exhi-

bition **2.** The place where these animals are kept

mend (mɛnd) v. **1.** To fix or repair sthg.: *I'll mend that shirt.* **2.** To regain one's health: *He's mending nicely after his surgery.* **3. mend one's ways** To change one's attitude and way of living for the better; to improve one's behavior

mend n. **1.** A part that has been mended **2. on the mend** Getting better after illness or injury

me·ni·al (miʸ–niʸ–əl) adj. Of a job, degrading; unskilled: *Cleaning the latrine is a menial task.* —**menially** adv.

men·o·pause (mɛn–ə–pɔz) n. The time in life when a woman's menstrual periods cease

men·strual (mɛn–strəl/ –struʷ–əl) adj. Concerning a woman's menstruation period

men·stru·ate (mɛn–struʷ–eʸt) v. **-ated, -ating** To experience the discharge of blood from the uterus that normally occurs among women between puberty and middle age at approximately monthly intervals; to have a menstrual period —**men·stru·a·tion** (mɛn–struʷ–eʸ–ʃən) n.

-ment (–mənt) Suffix **1.** The product, means, or act of: *entertainment* **2.** The state of being: *amazement*

men·tal (mɛn–təl) adj. **1.** Of the mind: *mental powers* —compare PHYSICAL **2.** Done only in the mind, without the help of writing: *mental arithmetic* **3.** Having to do with disorders of the mind: *a mental hospital/patient* —**mentally** adv.

men·tal·i·ty (mɛn–tæl–ə–tiʸ) n. **-ties 1.** A person's mental ability **2.** Way of thinking: *That man has a child's mentality.*

men·tion (mɛn–tʃən) v. **1.** To speak of briefly; to remark: *He mentioned his interest in travel.* **2. don't mention it** There's no need for thanks. I'm glad I could help.

mention n. **1.** The act of mentioning: *There was no mention of the fire in the newspaper.* **2.** Formal recognition as a reward: *He didn't win, but he did get honorable mention.*

men·tor (mɛn–tɔr/ –tər) n. A trusted advisor

men·u (mɛn–yuʷ) n. *pl.* **menus.** A list of the dishes or foods available for a meal, as in a restaurant

me·ow (miʸ–aʊ) n. The sound made by a cat or kitten

meow v. To make the sound of a cat or kitten

mer·ce·nar·y (mɜr–sə–nɛər–iʸ) n. **-ies** A professional soldier who fights for any country or group that pays him, not for his own country

mercenary adj. *derog.* Working merely for money or other reward; grasping

mer·chan·dise (mɜr–tʃən–daɪz) n. Goods for sale, esp. manufactured goods

mer·chant (mɜr–tʃənt) n. **1.** One who buys and sells goods for profit, esp. in large quantities **2.** A storekeeper or retailer

merchant adj. Used for trade or commerce: *a merchant ship*

mer·chant ma·rine (mɜr–tʃənt mə–riʸn) n. **1.** The ships of a nation, used in trade, not in war **2.** The men who work on those ships

mer·ci·ful (mɜr–sɪ–fəl) adj. Showing mercy; willing to forgive instead of punishing; loving, kind, and compassionate; tenderhearted: *The Lord our God is merciful and forgiving* (Daniel 9:9). *Jesus said, "Blessed are the merciful, for they will be shown mercy"* (Matthew 5:7). *Be merciful as your Father [in heaven] is merciful* (Luke 6:36). —**mercifully** adv.

mer·ci·less (mɜr–sɪ–ləs) adj. Having no mercy; without pity —**mercilessly** adv.

mer·cu·ry (mɜr–kyə–riʸ) n. **-ries 1.** A heavy, silvery, normally liquid, metallic element, used in thermometers and barometers **2. Mercury** The second smallest of the nine planets in our solar system and the one nearest to the sun

mer·cy (mɜr–siʸ) n. **-cies** Willingness to forgive, not to punish: *But when the kindness and the love of God our Savior appeared, he saved us, not because of righteous things we had done, but because of his mercy* (Titus 3:5). *The Apostle Paul tells us, "I was shown mercy so that in me, the worst of sinners, Christ Jesus might display his unlimited patience as an example for those who would believe on him and receive eternal life"* (1 Timothy 1:16). —see JESUS

mere (mɪər) adj. **1.** Nothing more than: *He won the election by a mere three votes.* **2.** The least; smallest: *The merest delay really tries his*

patience.

mere-ly (mɪər–li^y) adv. Only: *He merely wants to know the facts.*

merge (mɜrdʒ) v. **merged, merging 1.** To unite or come into a whole: *One color merged into the other.* **2.** To join together to become one: *The two societies merged.*

merg-er (mɜrdʒ–ər) n. The joining together of two or more companies or firms

me-rid-i-an (mə–rɪd–i^y–ən) n. A half circle along the earth's surface from the North Pole to the South Pole; a line of longitude

me-ringue (mə–ræŋ) n. Egg whites and sugar, beaten well and baked, used as a topping for pies: *Lemon meringue pie is his favorite.*

mer-it (mɛər–ət) n. **1.** The quality of deserving to be praised: *There's no merit in passing the examination if you cheated.* **2.** A feature or quality that deserves praise: *Judge it on its own merits (=on its own qualities).*

mer-i-to-ri-ous (mɛər–ə–tɔr–i^y–əs) adj. Having merit; deserving praise

mer-maid (mɜr–me^yd) n. A legendary sea creature with a female body and a fish's tail

mer-ri-ment (mɛər–ɪ–mənt) n. Laughter; fun; gaiety

mer-ry (mɛər–i^y) adj. **-rier, -riest 1.** Cheerful; full of mirth and laughter: *A merry heart makes a cheerful countenance [face]* (Proverbs 15:13KJV). **—merrily** adv.

mesh (mɛʃ) n. **1.** The fabric of a net **2.** One of the openings between the threads or cords of a net **3.** A network **4.** Working contacts as in the teeth of gears

mesh v. To fit together properly: *The teeth on these gears don't mesh (=don't fit together the way they should).*

mess (mɛs) n. **1.** An untidy or disgusting sight; disorder; confusion: *This room's a mess.* **2.** A place to eat for members of the armed forces **3.** Trouble: *You're in a real mess now that you've been caught cheating.*

mess v. To make or let become untidy: *Don't mess up your room again.*

mes-sage (mɛs–ɪdʒ) n. **1.** A piece of information, spoken or written, passed from one person to another: *Leave a message for her at the front desk (of the hotel).* **2.** The central idea: *What's the message of this book?* **3. get the**

message: *infml.* To understand what is wanted or meant

mes-sen-ger (mɛs–ən–dʒər) n. A person who delivers a message

Mes-si-ah (mə–saɪ–ə) n. Hebrew for the Greek word Christ, both meaning "anointed." Jesus Christ is the true Messiah, that is, the promised Savior of the world. —see JESUS CHRIST NOTE: There are many false messiahs, (false Christs) who claim to be deliverers from political bondage, etc., but they are deceivers. Whatever success they might enjoy is only temporary. Jesus Christ, however is the true God, the Savior of the world, who delivers us from the power of sin and the devil and gives us everlasting life. He is true God who alone could and did live a perfectly holy (sinless) life for us (as our substitute); he alone could pay the price (suffer all the punishment that we deserve) with his own blood when he suffered and died for us on the cross. He proved to be the true Messiah when he rose again from the dead on the third day, as he foretold (Romans 1:4) (Luke 24: 44-48). —see JESUS

mess-y (mɛs–i^y) adj. **-ier, -iest** Not neat; untidy; dirty: *a messy job/room/desk* **—messily** adv. **—messiness** n.

met (mɛt) v. Past tense and past part. of **meet**

me-tab-o-lism (mə–tæb–ə–lɪz–əm) n. The physical and chemical processes carried on within living things in order to maintain life; the process by which food is built into living material or used to supply energy **—met-a-bol-ic** (mɛt–ə–bɑl–ɪk) adj.

met-al (mɛt–əl) n. Any mineral substance which can be shaped by pressure and used for passing an electric current: *Copper and silver are both metals.*

me-tal-lic (mə–tæl–ɪk) adj. Of or like metal: *a metallic sound*

met-a-mor-phose (mɛt–ə–mɔr–fo^wz/–fo^ws) v. **-phosed, -phosing** To change or be changed in form or character

met-a-mor-pho-sis (mɛt–ə–mɔr–fə–səs) n. pl. **-pho-ses 1.** Change from one form to another by any means **2.** Complete transformation of character, purpose, circumstances,

etc. **3.** *Biological* Any marked change in the form and structure of an animal in its development from embryo to adult: *By metamorphosis a caterpillar is changed into a butterfly.* —**metamorphic** adj.

met-a-phor (mɛt–ə–fɔr) n. A word or phrase that describes one thing by stating another thing with which it can be compared, without using the words "as" or "like": *In the sentence, "He's a tiger on the football field," the word "tiger" is a metaphor, suggesting that the football player is fierce, like a tiger.*

me-te-or (mi�material–tiᵧ–ər) n. A small mass moving rapidly through space, becoming very bright when it enters the earth's atmosphere; a falling or shooting star

me-te-or-ite (miᵧ–tiᵧ–ə–raɪt) n. A meteor that falls to the earth in the form of a piece of rock

me-te-or-ol-o-gy (miᵧ–tiᵧ–ə–ral–ə–dʒiᵧ) n. The science that deals with the atmosphere, esp. with weather forecasting —**meteorologist** n. —**me-te-o-ro-log-i-cal** (miᵧt–iᵧ–ə–rə–ladʒ–ɪ–kəl) adj.

me-ter (miᵧ–tər) n. **1.** An instrument or device that measures the amount: *a gas meter/a parking meter* **2.** The fundamental unit of length in the metric system equal to 39.37 inches

-meter (–mə–tər/ –miᵧ–tər) comb. form A suffix meaning (a) An instrument for measuring: *speedometer* (spiᵧ–dam–ə–tər) (b) A linear measure: *centimeter* (sɛn–tə–miᵧ–tər)

meth-od (mɛθ–əd) n. An orderly way of doing sthg. —**me-thod-i-cal** (mə–θad–ɪ–kəl) adj. —**methodically** adv.

meth-od-ol-o-gy (mɛθ–ə–dal–ə–dʒiᵧ) n. **-gies** A set of methods used for the study of a particular subject, as in education or science —**meth-od-o-log-i-cal** (mɛθ–ə–də–ladʒ–ɪ–kəl) adj. —**methodologically** adv.

me-tic-u-lous (mə–tɪk–yə–ləs) adj. Extremely careful, giving close attention to every little detail: *He takes meticulous care of his car.* —**meticulously** adv.

me-tre (miᵧt–ər) *BrE.* for **meter**

met-ric (mɛt–rɪk) adj. Of or relating to the meter, esp. to the system of measurement based on the meter and kilogram

me-trop-o-lis (mə–trap–ə–ləs) n. A major city or the capital city of a country

met-ro-pol-i-tan (mɛ–trə–pal–ə–tən) adj. Of or like a big city with its suburbs: *The New York metropolitan area includes parts of New Jersey and Connecticut.*

met-tle (mɛt–əl) adj. Courage and fortitude: *He showed his mettle by continuing the race with a sore ankle.*

mez-za-nine (mɛz–ə–niᵧn/ mɛz–ə–niᵧn) n. **1.** A low-ceilinged story between two main stories of a building **2.** The lowest balcony or the lowest part of such a balcony in a theater

Mi-cah (maɪ–kə) n. **1.** A Hebrew prophet of the eighth century B.C. **2.** The book containing his prophecies, one of which is that the promised Messiah would be born in Bethlehem (Micah 5:2). Jesus, of course, fulfilled this prophecy (Matthew 2:1-6; Luke 2:4-7). —see JESUS, BIBLE, OLD TESTAMENT

mice (maɪs) n. *pl.* of **mouse**

mi-cro- (maɪ–kroʷ–) prefix Very small

mi-crobe (maɪ–kroʷb) n. A microscopic organism; a living creature so small that it cannot be seen without a microscope; esp. one that causes disease

mi-cro-bi-ol-o-gy (maɪ–kroʷ–baɪ–al–ə–dʒiᵧ) n. A branch of biology dealing esp. with microscopic forms of life —**mi-cro-bi-o-log-i-cal** (maɪ–kroʷ–baɪ–ə–ladʒ–ɪ–kəl) adj. —**microbiologically** adv.

mi-cro-chip (maɪ–kroʷ–tʃɪp) n. A very small piece of silicon or similar material carrying a complex electrical circuit

mi-cro-cosm (maɪ–krə–kaz–əm) n. A representative version on a small scale: *The misery in their family was a microcosm of the misery to be found in the whole country.*

mi-cro-com-put-er (maɪ–kroʷ–kəm–pyuʷt –ər) n. A very small computer

mi-cro-fiche (maɪ–kroʷ–fiᵧʃ) n. A sheet of microfilm: *The documents were stored on microfiche.*

mi-cro-film (maɪ–krə–fɪlm) n. Film on which extremely small photographs are stored, esp. of documents, printed matter, etc.

mi-cro-or-gan-ism (maɪ–kroʷ–ɔr–gən–ɪz–əm) n. An organism so small that it cannot be seen

without the aid of a microscope

mi-cro-phone (**mai**–krə–fo^{w}n) n. An instrument for making sounds louder or one used for changing sound waves into electrical waves in broadcasting or recording sound (as in radios, telephones, tape recorders, etc.): *Speak into the microphone so people can hear you better.*

mi-cro-scope (**mai**–krə–sko^{w}p) n. An instrument that causes objects too small to be seen by the eye to appear larger, so they can be examined

mi-cro-scop-ic (mai–krə–**skap**–ık) adj. Too small to be seen without a microscope

mi-cro-wave (**mai**–krə–we^{y}v) n. 1. An electromagnetic wave of extremely high frequency, used in sending radio messages, in radar, and also in cooking 2. **microwave oven** n. A type of oven that cooks food very quickly, using microwaves

mid– (mıd–) adj., prefix Placed or coming in the middle

mid-day (mıd–de^y /mıd–de^y) n. Noon

mid-dle (mıd–əl) adj. In or nearly in the center: *The knives and forks are in the middle drawer.*

middle n. The central part, point, or position: *We live in the middle of the country.*

mid-dle-aged (mıd–əl–e^{y}dʒd) adj. The period of life between youth and old age, approximately between the ages of 40 and 60

Mid-dle Ages (mıd–əl–**e^y**–dʒəs) n. A period in European history from about A.D. 500 to 1500

mid-dle class (mıd–əl klæs) n., adj. A social class between the lower/working class and upper class, including professional and business people

mid-dle school (mıd–əl sku^{w}l) n. A school that usu. includes grades five through eight

mid-get (mıdʒ–ət) n. A person who is fully developed but has not grown to normal height

midget adj. Very small, compared with others of the same kind: *midget autos*

mid-land (mıd–lənd) adj. Of the middle or central part of the country

mid-night (mıd–naıt) n. Twelve o'clock at night

midst (mıdst) n. 1. Among or in the center of: *He was in the midst of the crowd.* 2. **in our midst** Among us

mid-way (mıd–we^y/ mıd–**we^y**) adv., adj. In the middle; halfway

midway (mıd–we^y) n. A place at a fair or carnival for games and entertainment

might (maıt) v. (shows a possibility) *He might come, but it is not likely.*

might n. Power; strength: *He tried with all his might, but he couldn't lift the heavy load./ Not by [human] might nor by power, but by my Spirit, says the Lord* (Zechariah 4:6).

might-y (**mai**–i^y) adj. **-ier, -iest 1.** Having great power or strength; very great: *Be strong in the Lord and in his mighty power* (Ephesians 6:10). *Great is our Lord and mighty in power* (Psalm 147:5). **2. high and mighty** derog. Showing too much pride and a feeling of one's own importance —**mightily** adv.

might've (**mait**–əv) v. Contraction of **might have**

mi-graine (**mai**–gre^{y}n) n. A severe, recurrent headache, usu. confined to one side of the head, often accompanied by nausea and with disorder of the eyesight

mi-grant (**mai**–grənt) n. A person, bird, etc., that migrates: *Germany employs many migrant workers from Turkey./ The swallows are migrant birds that return to Capistrano every year on March 19th.*

mi-grate (**mai**–gre^{y}t) v. **-grated, -grating 1.** Of birds and fish, to travel regularly from one part of the world to another, at certain times of the year **2.** To move from one region or country to settle in another: *Some tribes migrate with their cattle in search of fresh grass.* —**mi-gra-to-ry** (**mai**–grə–tɔr–i^y) adj.

mi-gra-tion (mai–**gre^y**–ʃən) n. The act of migrating

mild (maıld) adj. **1.** Not severe or extreme: *a mild winter* **2.** Not bitter or strong: *a mild flavor* **3.** Gentle: *He has a mild nature.* **4.** Not harsh; not causing much discomfort at all; slight: *Many vicious criminals are given milder punishment than they deserve.* —**mildness** n.

mil-dew (**mıl**–du^w) n. A fungus that forms a white coating on things exposed to moisture

mildew v. To become coated with mildew

mild·ly (maɪld–li^y) adv. 1. In a mild manner: *She complained loudly to the store manager, but he answered her mildly.* 2. Slightly: *He was only mildly interested in the story.*

mile (maɪl) n. A distance of 1,609.34 meters or 1,760 yards

mile·age (maɪ–lɪdʒ) n. 1. The distance traveled, measured in miles: *What mileage does your car get per gallon of gasoline?* 2. *infml.* An amount of use: *He gets a lot of mileage out of his family name.*

mile·stone (maɪl–sto^wn) n. 1. A stone set up on the side of the road to show the number of miles to the next town or the town designated 2. An important event in history or in someone's life: *The invention of the steam engine was a milestone in world history.*

mi·lieu (mi^yl–yu^w) n. pl. -lieus or lieux Environment, surroundings

mil·i·tant (mɪl–ə–tənt) adj. Having or expressing a readiness to fight or use force; vigorously active and aggressive: *A few militant people in the crowd started throwing stones at the police.*

militant n. A militant person: *All of this uproar has been caused by just a few militants.*

mil·i·tar·y (mɪl–ə–tɛər–i^y) adj. Having to do with the armed forces

mi·li·tia (mə–lɪʃ–ə) n. A group of citizens who are trained to fight or keep order in times of emergency

milk (mɪlk) n. 1. A white liquid produced by human or animal females for feeding their young 2. The milk of cows used as food for human beings 3. A whitish liquid or juice obtained from certain plants and trees: *coconut milk*

milk v. 1. To take milk from a cow, goat, or other animal 2. To drain strength, information, or wealth from: *Some politicians milk the public.*

milk shake (mɪlk ʃe^yk) n. A drink of milk, ice cream and flavoring shaken together

milk·y (mɪlk–i^y) adj. -ier, -iest 1. Like milk in appearance 2. Having milk in it

Milk·y Way (mɪlk–i^y we^y) n. The large group of stars that our planet and sun belong to, seen on clear nights as a band of hazy light stretching across the sky

mill (mɪl) n. 1. (A building containing) a large machine for crushing grain into flour 2. A factory or workshop: *a paper mill*

mil·len·ni·um (mə–len–i^y–əm) n. -nia or -niums A period of 1,000 years

mill·er (mɪl–ər) n. One who owns or operates a mill, esp. a grain mill

mil·let (mɪl–ət) n. 1. A cereal grass cultivated in Asia and Europe and used as food 2. The white seeds of this plant

mil·li– (mɪl–li^y–/ –lə–) prefix One-thousandth of a specified unit

mil·li·gram (mɪl–ə–græm) n. One-thousandth of a gram

mil·li·me·ter (mɪl–ə–mi^y–tər) n. One-thousandth of a meter

mil·li·ner (mɪl–ə–nər) n. A person who makes and/or sells women's hats

mil·li·ner·y (mɪl–ə–nɛər–i^y) n. 1. Women's hats sold in a shop 2. The business of a milliner

mil·lion (mɪl–yən) n., pron. million or millions The number 1,000,000 —mil·lionth n., pron., adv., determ.

mil·lion·aire (mɪl–yə–nɛər) n. millionairess (mɪl–yə–nɛər–əs) *fem.* A person who has 1,000,000 dollars, pounds, francs, etc. or more

mill·stone (mɪl–sto^wn) n. One of a pair of large, round, flat stones used to grind grain

mime (maɪm) n. 1. An actor, comedian, etc. who acts in pantomime, using actions rather than words to show meaning 2. A performance by a mime or mimes

mime v. mimed, miming To play a part with gestures and usu. without words —compare MIMIC

mim·e·o·graph (mɪm–i^y–ə–græf) n. A machine that makes exact copies by using a stencil

mimeograph v. To copy exactly by using a mimeograph machine

mim·ic (mɪm–ɪk) n. A person who is clever at mimicking another person's speech, manners, etc. esp., in a way that causes laughter

mimic v. mimicked, mimicking 1. To imitate the ways or the speech of another person playfully or for entertainment 2. To resemble closely

mince (mɪns) v. minced, mincing To cut or chop into very small pieces

mince-meat (mɪns-miᵞt) n. A mixture of finely chopped fruit, spices, and sometimes meat, used as a pie filling

mind (maɪnd) n. 1. The part in a human being that reasons, understands, etc. 2. A person's way of thinking, attitude; feeling: *Do not conform any longer to the pattern of this world, but be transformed by the renewing of your mind* (Romans 12:2). *Love the Lord your God with all your heart and with all your soul and with all your mind. This is the first and greatest commandment* (Matthew 22:37,38). *God searches minds and hearts* (Psalm 7:9). 3. Memory: *We had met before, but I couldn't call her name to mind.* 4. Attention: *Set your minds on things above, not on earthly things* (Colossians 3:2). 5. Intention: *Nothing was further from my mind.* 6. Determination: *When Bill sets his mind on doing sthg., nothing can stop him.* 7. Opinion: *My wife and I are of the same mind on almost everything.* (=we both think the same about it) 8. A person considered for his/her ability to think well: *She's among the best minds (=most intelligent people) in the country.*

mind v. 1. To take care of; to look after: *Our neighbor is minding our dog while we're out of town.* 2. To care or object: *Would you mind if I close the window?* 3. To obey: *The boy was told to mind his Aunt Jane while his mother went shopping.* 4. never mind Don't worry; it's okay; it doesn't matter

mine (maɪn) pron. Possessive form of I: *That book is mine./ That's your hat, and this one is mine.*

mine n. 1. A hole or a network of underground holes from which gold and other minerals are dug 2. A kind of bomb placed in or on the ground, or in the sea, ready to explode when sthg. touches it or passes near it 3. An abundant resource: *The professor is a mine of information.*

mine v. mined, mining 1. To dig or work in a mine: *mining for gold* 2. To obtain by digging from a mine: *Coal is mined in West Virginia.* 3. To put explosive mines in strategic places, on land or in the water: *The entrance to the harbor has been mined so that no enemy ships can enter it.*

min-er (maɪn-ər) n. Sbdy. who works in a mine —compare MINOR

min-er-al (mɪn-ə-rəl) n. 1. An inorganic substance, such as stone, coal, salt, etc., that occurs naturally in the earth, esp. one obtained for man's use 2. Any substance that is neither animal nor vegetable

mineral adj. Of or containing minerals

min-gle (mɪŋ-gəl) v. -gled, -gling To mix or associate, as with a crowd: *The movie star often left his mansion and mingled with the people at the amusement park.*

min-i- (mɪn-iᵞ-/ -ə-) n. prefix *infml.* Very small compared with others of its type: *He drives a minibus.*

min-i-a-ture (mɪn-iᵞ-ə-tʃər/ mɪn-ə-tʃər) n. A very small representation of anything

min-i-mal (mɪn-ə-məl) adj. A very small amount, degree, or size —minimally adv.

min-i-mize (mɪn-ə-maɪz) v. -mized, -mizing To reduce to the smallest possible degree: *We can minimize the hazards of the highway by observing the rules of the road.* —opposite MAXIMIZE

min-i-mum (mɪn-ə-məm) n. -ma or -mums The least, or the smallest possible, quantity, number, or degree: *He couldn't buy a house because he didn't have the minimum required for the down payment.*

min-ing (maɪ-nɪŋ) n. The industry or action of taking minerals out of the ground by digging: *West Virginia is a coal mining state.*

min-is-ter (mɪn-ə-stər) n. 1. A clergyman; the religious leader in Christian churches 2. In some countries, a politician who is a member of the government and is in charge of a government department: *the Minister of Education*

minister v. To serve: *Christ came into the world, not to be ministered to [not to be served] but to minister and give his life as a ransom for many* (Matthew 20:28 KJV).

min-is-te-ri-al (mɪn-ə-stɪər-iᵞ-əl) adj. Of a minister: *As part of his ministerial duties, he often travelled abroad.*

min-is-try (mɪn-ə-striᵞ) n. -tries 1. The profession or functions of a clergyman or church

leader **2.** A government department under the direction of a minister: *the Ministry of Finance*

mink (mɪŋk) n. **1.** A small weasel-like animal **2.** The valuable brown fur of this animal: *a mink coat*

min-now (mɪn–ow) n. **-nows, -now** A very small fish, often used as bait

mi-nor (maɪ–nər) adj. Less quantity, importance, or extent: *The young actress was given a minor role in the new film.* —see MAJOR

minor n. One who is under legal age, which is 18 in the US —compare MINER

mi-nor-i-ty (mə–nɔr–ə–tiʸ) n. **-ties 1.** A number that is less than half the total **2.** A small part of a population, different from others in race, religion, etc. —compare MAJORITY

min-ster (mɪn–stər) n. **1.** The church of a monastery **2.** A large church or cathedral

mint (mɪnt) n. **1.** Any of several aromatic herbs, as spearmint and peppermint, used in preparing drinks, making chewing gum, etc. **2.** A peppermint flavored candy **3.** A place where coins and bank notes are made by the government **4.** *infml.* A large amount (esp. of money): *He made a mint in the insurance business.* **5. in mint condition** In perfect condition, esp. when speaking of coins, stamps, etc., that people collect as a hobby

mint v. To make coins

min-u-et (mɪn–yə–wet) n. **1.** A slow, graceful dance with short steps **2.** A piece of music to accompany this dance

mi-nus (maɪ–nəs) prep. **1.** Used to show subtraction; made less by the stated amount: *12 minus 4 equals 8.* **2.** The specified number of degrees (Celsius) below the freezing point of water: *The temperature was minus 5 degrees.* **3.** Without: *I'm minus my car today.* —opposite PLUS

mi-nus-cule (mɪn–əs–kyuʷl) adj. Very, very small

min-ute (mɪn–ət) n. **1.** One sixtieth (1/60th) of an hour: *The plane arrived just five minutes late.* **2.** A unit of angular measure equal to 1/60th of a degree: *The exact measurement of this angle is 45 degrees 15 minutes (45'15").*/ *Hong Kong is 22 degrees and 17 minutes north of the equator.* **3.** *pl.* An official record of the business discussed and transacted at a meeting or conference: *At the beginning of the meeting, the secretary read the minutes of the previous meeting.*

mi-nute (maɪ–nuʷt) adj. **1.** Exceedingly small: *The printing in this contract is so minute that it's almost impossible to read.* **2.** Of little importance: *minute details* —**minutely** adv.

mir-a-cle (mɪr–ɪ–kəl) n. An event that appears unexplainable by the laws of nature and so is held to be supernatural: *Jesus worked many miracles such as healing all kinds of sickness and raising the dead.*

mi-rac-u-lous (mɪ–ræk–yə–ləs) adj. Like a miracle: *Nicodemus said to Jesus, "No one could perform the miraculous signs that you are doing if God were not with him"* (John 3:2). NOTE: Jesus' birth was miraculous, since he was conceived by the Holy Spirit and born of a virgin. He performed all kinds of miracles during his short earthly ministry. He gave sight to the blind, hearing to the deaf and speech to the dumb. He healed the lame, the paralyzed and the lepers. He cast devils out of people and raised the dead. He calmed storms, walked on water, and fed 5,000 people with just five loaves of bread and two small fish. Last of all, he rose from the dead and by so doing he conquered sin, death, and the devil for us. Those who put their trust in him will also be raised from the dead. He said, "I have come down from heaven not to do my will but to do the will of him who sent me. And this is the will of him who sent me ... that everyone who looks to the Son and believes in him shall have eternal life, and I will raise him up at the last day" (John 6:38-40). —see JESUS, VIRGIN BIRTH, JUDGMENT, RESURRECTION —**miraculously** adv.

mi-rage (mɪ–rɑʒ) n. A strange effect of hot air conditions in which objects, esp. sheets of water, seem to appear on the desert or on a hot road: *He thought he saw a lake in the middle of the desert, but it was only a mirage.*

mir-ror (mɪr–ər) n. A piece of glass, or other shiny surface that reflects images that fall on it

mirror v. To show, as in a mirror: *fig. The elec-*

tion results mirrored public opinion.

mirth (mɜrθ) n. Gaiety accompanied by laughter

mis– (mɪs–) prefix **1.** Bad, badly; wrong; wrongly: *misapply, misbehave, miscalculate, misconduct, misdirect, misguided, misjudge, mislead, misrepresent, misunderstand, etc.* **2.** Failure; lack: *misfire/miscarriage*

mis·ap·pro·pri·ate (mɪs–ə–proᵂ–priʸ–eʸt) v. **ated, -ating** To take dishonestly, esp. for one's own use: *The lawyer had misappropriated the funds entrusted to him.* —**mis·ap·pro·pri·a·tion** (mɪs–ə–proᵂ–priʸ–eʸ–ʃən) n.

mis·be·have (mɪs–bɪ–heʸv) v. **-haved, -having** To behave badly —**misbehavior** n.

misc. *abbr.* for miscellaneous

mis·cal·cu·late (mɪs–kæl–kyə–leʸt) v. **-lated, -lating** To misjudge; to calculate wrongly

mis·car·ry (mɪs–kɛər–riʸ) v. **-ried, -rying 1.** To give birth to a fetus before it can survive, esp. before the proper time of birth **2.** To be unsuccessful; to go wrong **3.** To fail to do justice —**mis·car·riage** (mɪs–kær–rɪdʒ) n.

mis·cel·la·ne·ous (mɪs–ə–leʸ–niʸ–əs) adj. **1.** Of several different kinds **2.** Dealing with a variety of subjects —**miscellaneously** adv.

mis·chief (mɪs–tʃɪf) n. Bad, but not seriously bad, conduct (esp. of children): *This little boy is always getting into mischief.*

mis·chie·vous (mɪs–tʃə–vəs) adj. **1.** Playful, teasing, or troublesome: *Most children are mischievous at times.* **2.** Causing harm or injury —**mischievously** adv.

mis·con·ceive (mɪs–kən–siʸv) v. To interpret incorrectly —**mis·con·cep·tion** (mɪs–kən–sɛp–ʃən) n.

mis·con·duct (mɪs–kɑn–dəkt) n. Bad behavior

mis·con·strue (mɪs–kən–struᵂ) v. **-strued, -struing** To place wrong meaning on sthg.: *He misconstrues everything I say or do.*

mis·count (mɪs–kaʊnt) v. To make a mistake in counting —**miscount** n.

mis·deed (mɪs–diʸd) n. A wrong or improper act; a crime

mis·de·mean·or (mɪs–dɪ–miʸ–nər) n. **1.** A bad or improper act that is not very serious **2.** A crime that is less serious than robbery, murder, etc., which are felonies —compare FELONY

mi·ser (maɪ–zər) n. *derog.* A person who hates spending money and lives in poor circumstances in order to store up wealth —**miserly** adj.

mis·er·a·ble (mɪz–ər–ə–bəl) adj. **1.** Very unhappy; wretched: *He's cold and hungry. No wonder he's feeling so miserable.* **2.** Very bad: *What miserable weather!* —**miserably** adv. *He failed miserably.*

mis·er·y (mɪz–ə–riʸ) n. **1.** Great pain and suffering of body **2.** A great feeling of unhappiness: *Her child died and, to add to her misery, her husband had a stroke.*

mis·fire (mɪs–faɪ–ər) v. **-fired, -firing 1.** Of a gun, to fail to go off correctly **2.** Of a plan, joke, etc., to fail to have the intended effect

mis·fit (mɪs–fɪt) n. **1.** A poor fit **2.** A person who does not fit well into his social surroundings, or who is not suitable for the job he holds

mis·for·tune (mɪs–fɔr–tʃən) n. Adversity; hardship; an unfortunate event; a missed opportunity

mis·giv·ing (mɪs–gɪv–ɪŋ) n. A feeling of doubt or distrust: *He has misgivings about loaning his car to anyone.*

mis·guide (mɪs–gaɪd) v. To act from, or show, mistaken beliefs or motives —**misguided** adj.

mis·hap (mɪs–hæp) n. An accident

mish·mash (mɪʃ–mæʃ) n. A confused mixture or collection of things

mis·in·form (mɪs–ɪn–fɔrm) v. To give false information to sbdy. —**mis·in·for·ma·tion** (mɪs–ɪn–fər–meʸ–ʃən) n.

mis·lead (mɪs–liʸd) v. **-led** (–lɛd)**, -leading 1.** To lead sbdy. astray; to lead in the wrong direction **2.** To deceive **3.** To lead into error

mis·lead·ing (mɪs–liʸd–ɪŋ) adj. Causing a mistake

mis·no·mer (mɪs–noᵂ–mər) n. A name wrongly applied to sthg.: *The name, "Holy Roman Empire" was a misnomer, for it was neither holy nor Roman.*

mis·place (mɪs–pleʸs) v. **-placed, -placing** To put sthg. in the wrong place

mis·print (mɪs–prɪnt) n. A mistake in printing

mis·pro·nounce (mɪs–prə–naʊns) v. To pronounce in an incorrect way

mis-quote (mɪs–kwoᵂt) v. **-quoted, -quoting** To make a mistake in quoting someone

mis-rep-re-sent (mɪs–rɛp–rɪ–zɛnt) v. To represent falsely or misleadingly —**mis-rep-re-sen-ta-tion** (mɪs–rɛp–rɪ–zɛn-teᵞ–ʃən) n.

miss (mɪs) v. **1.** To fail to hit, catch, find, or otherwise make contact with: *He missed the bus.* **2.** To be unhappy because of the absence or loss of a loved one: *She misses her son who has joined the navy.* **3.** To discover the loss of sthg.: *I didn't miss my passport until I got to the airport and couldn't find it in my purse.* **4.** To fail to hear or understand: *I fell asleep and I missed the main point of his speech.* **5. miss the boat** *infml.* To miss an opportunity by acting too slowly

miss n. A failure to hit or succeed: *We almost got hit by a truck. It was a near miss.*

miss n. **1. (a) Miss** A title of courtesy, used before the name of an unmarried woman: *Have you met Miss Jones?* **(b)** A word used in speaking to an unmarried woman: *Miss, could you please tell me where there's a good restaurant?* **2.** An unmarried woman or girl

mis-sile (mɪs–əl) n. **1.** A weapon or an object that is fired from a gun or a bow, etc. **2.** A rocket-powered weapon carrying an explosive charge: *a ground-to-air missile*

miss-ing (mɪs–ɪŋ) adj. **1.** Lost; not in the proper or expected place: *My keys are missing.* **2.** Absent: *He's always missing when you need him the most.* **3.** Someone whose whereabouts are unknown: *She has been listed as a missing person for more than a year.* **4.** Of a soldier, absent after a battle but not known to be dead: *missing in action*

mis-sion (mɪʃ–ən) n. **1.** Any group of people who are sent abroad for a specific purpose **2.** The duty or purpose for which these people are sent: *The soldiers' mission was to blow up the railroad track.* **3.** A body of missionaries or their ministry: *The African Inland Mission* **4.** A place where a particular form of religion is taught, spiritual counseling given, etc.: *People come to the mission for education, Christian literature, spiritual counseling, medical treatment, etc.* **5.** The particular work for which one believes oneself to have been sent into the world: *Her mission in life seems*

to be helping the blind.

mis-sion-ar-y (mɪʃ–ə–nɛər–iᵞ) n. **-ies** A person who is sent, usu. to another country or to a different ethnic group in his own country, to teach and spread his faith there and/or help people physically: *a medical missionary*

mis-spell (mɪs–spɛl) v. To make a mistake in spelling

mist (mɪst) n. A mass of very small drops of water floating in the air, near or reaching to the ground: *The valley was covered in mist./ A fine mist sprayed into the air.*

mist v. To make or become covered with mist

mis-take (mə–steᵞk) v. **mistook** (–stʊk), **mistaken, mistaking** To be wrong about sthg.: *She speaks so softly, I mistook what she said.*

mistake n. **1.** An error or blunder: *She wanted the bus to Westlake, but she got on the bus to Westwood by mistake.* **2.** A wrong judgment or idea: *I thought the man could be trusted, but that was a big mistake.* —see ERROR

mis-taken (mə–steᵞk–ən) adj. Incorrect; wrong: *I thought I saw her, but I was mistaken.* —**mistakenly** adv.

Mis-ter (mɪs–tər) n. *abbr.* **Mr. 1.** A title for a man **2.** A title used when addressing certain men in official positions: *Mr. Chairman*

mis-tle-toe (mɪs–əl–toᵂ) n. A parasitic shrub with yellowish-green leaves and waxy white berries, used as a Christmas decoration

mis-took (mɪ–stʊk) v. Past tense of **mistake**

mis-treat (mɪs–triᵞt) v. To treat cruelly

mis-tress (mɪs–trəs) n. **1.** A woman who is in a position of authority or control **2.** A female head of a household **3.** A female teacher **4.** A woman who has habitual sex relations with a man to whom she is not married

mis-trust (mɪs–trʌst) n. A lack of trust or confidence —**mistrust** v. *He mistrusts all politicians* —**mistrustful** adj.

mist-y (mɪs–tiᵞ) adj. **-ier, -iest** Full of or covered with mist: *Her eyes were misty with tears.*

mis-un-der-stand (mɪs–ʌn–dər–stænd) v. **-stood, -standing** To not understand

mis-un-der-stand-ing (mɪs–ʌn–dər–stæn–dɪŋ) n. **1.** A failure to understand or agree about

directions or instructions **2.** An argument or quarrel

mis-un-der-stood (mɪs-ʌn-dər-stʊd) v. Past tense of **misunderstand**

mis-use (mɪs-yuᵂz) v. **-used, -using** To use in a bad way; to abuse

mite (maɪt) n. **1.** A very small contribution or offering **2.** A tiny person or child **3.** A small spider-like insect that may be found in food and may carry disease

mit-i-gate (mɪt-ə-geʸt) v. **-gated, -gating 1.** To make or become less severe or intense **2.** **mitigating circumstances** Facts that partially excuse wrongdoing —**mit-i-ga-tion** (mɪt-ə-geʸ-ʃən) n. —**mitigator** n. —**mitigative** adj.

mitt (mɪt) n. **1.** A strong covering for the hand (glove) worn by a baseball player **2.** Mitten

mit-ten (mɪt-ən) n. A covering for the hand that has one section for the thumb and another for all four fingers

mix (mɪks) v. **1.** To combine in such a way that the parts cannot easily be separated one from another: *You can't mix oil and water./ She put flour, eggs, milk, and sugar into a bowl and mixed them all together.* **2.** Of a person, to enjoy being in the company of others: *He's a friendly person who mixes well with all kinds of people.* **3. mixed up (a)** Confused: *They are all mixed up; they don't know what they're doing.* **(b)** Connected with someone or sthg. bad: *He seems to be mixed up in some dishonest business.* **4. mix sbdy. up** To mistake: *It's easy to mix Melody up with her sister Joy, since they are twins.*

mix n. **1.** Commercially packaged blend of dry ingredients for easy preparation of a food: *cake mix* **2.** A group of different people or things: *a strange mix of people on the committee*

mixed (mɪkst) adj. **1.** Different kinds: *I have mixed emotions about the plan. In some ways I like it; in other ways I don't.* **2.** Of or for both sexes: *a mixed class/audience*

mix-er (mɪk-sər) n. **1.** A mechanical device in which substances are mixed: *a food mixer/ a cement mixer* **2.** A sociable person

mix-ture (mɪks-tʃər) n. **1.** Sthg. produced by mixing **2.** A combination of things, ingredients, or qualities

mix-up (mɪks-əp) n. *infml.* A confused situation; a muddle, due to lack of planning: *There was a mix-up at the station and some of our group got on the wrong train.*

mne-mon-ic (nɪ-mɑn-ɪk) n. Sthg. (often a rhyme) that helps the memory

moan (moᵂn) n. A prolonged, low, mournful sound, usu. indicating suffering or grief

moan v. **1.** To make the sound of a moan **2.** *derog.* To complain: *What is she moaning about? She has no reason to complain.* —**moaner** n.

moat (moᵂt) n. A wide, deep ditch, usu. filled with water, dug around castles and towns during the Middle Ages to protect them from enemies

mob (mɑb) n. **1.** Often *derog.* A large, disorderly crowd of people: *An angry mob gathered outside the jail.* **2.** *derog.* The common people: *The government feared mob rule.* **3.** A group of criminals

mob v. **-bb-** To gather around in great numbers, either to attack or to admire: *The famous singer was mobbed when he got off the train.*

mo-bile (moᵂ-bəl/ -biʸl/ -baɪl) adj. Movable; not fixed in one position: *He's more mobile now that he has a bicycle.* —**mo-bil-i-ty** (moᵂ-bɪl-ə-tiʸ)n.

mo-bile home (moᵂ-bəl hoᵂm) A home which is able to be moved more easily than a regular house, but not as mobile as a house trailer

mo-bi-lize (moᵂ-bə-laɪz) v. **-lized, -lizing 1.** To assemble for a particular service: *They are mobilizing all the prayer support they can get for their new endeavor.* **2.** To assemble troops for service, to prepare for war, or for some other emergency: *They are mobilizing the troops to help with the war on drugs.* —**mo-bi-li-za-tion, -sation** (moᵂ-bə-lə-zeʸ-ʃən) n.

mobs-ter (mɑb-stər) n. A member of a mob; a gangster

moc-ca-sin (mɑk-ə-sən) n. A soft leather shoe that has no heel, first worn by North American Indians

mock (mɑk) v. To laugh at or make fun of: *Fools mock at making amends for sin* (Proverbs

14:9). *Do not be deceived: God cannot be mocked. A man reaps what he sows* (Galatians 6:7).

mock adj. Not real or true; pretending to be sthg. real: *The marine training exercises ended with a mock battle.*

mock-er (mɑk–ər) n. One who treats another person or the Word of God with contempt or ridicule: *Blessed is the man who does not ... sit in the seat of mockers [esp. those who mock God and make a mockery of sin]. But his delight is in the law of the Lord and on his law he meditates day and night* (Psalm 1:1-2). *Drive out the mocker and out goes strife; quarrels and insults are ended* (Proverbs 22:10).

mock-er-y (mɑk–ə–riʸ) n. -ies 1. Ridicule; contempt 2. A ridiculous or unsatisfactory imitation: *The court trial was a mockery of justice.*

mock-ing-bird (mɑk–ɪŋ–bɜrd) n. A gray and white American songbird that often imitates the songs of other birds

mode (moʷd) n. *fml.* 1. The way in which a thing is done: *She suddenly became rich and changed her whole mode of life.* 2. The current fashion

mod-el (mɑd–əl) n. 1. A small, three-dimensional representation of sthg.: *a model of the village* 2. A person, esp. a young woman employed to display clothes in a shop or fashion show by wearing them 3. A person employed to pose for an artist or photographer 4. A person, place, or thing regarded as excellent and thus worthy to be copied: *The city of Tyre was once said to be a model of perfection* (Ezekiel 28:12). *We worked night and day ... in order to make ourselves a model for you to follow* (2 Thessalonians 3:9). 5. A design or style of vehicle, furniture, computer, etc., made by a particular manufacturer: *Chrysler has produced two new models this year.*

model v. To wear a garment as a model: *Ann is modeling a beautiful blue dress.*

mod-er-ate (mɑd–ə–rət) adj. 1. Of middle degree: *a moderate rate of speed.* 2. Not extreme; not favoring political or social ideas that are different from those of most people: *He held a moderate position on most issues.*

moderate n. A person whose opinions are moderate

mod-er-ate (mɑd–ə–reʸt) v. -ated, -ating 1. To lessen the intensity of 2. To act as a moderator

mod-er-a-tion (mɑd–ə–reʸ–ʃən) n. 1. The practice of not going to extremes; self-control 2. in moderation Within sensible limits: *Some people claim that smoking in moderation isn't harmful to one's health, but they are only fooling themselves.*

mod-er-a-tor (mɑd–ə–reʸt–ər) n. One who presides over an assembly, meeting, or discussion

mod-ern (mɑd–ərn) adj. Of the present time, or of the recent past: *This is a very modern office with all the latest equipment.*

mod-ern-ize (mɑd–ər–naɪz) v. -ized, -izing To make modern; to adapt to modern ideas —**mod-ern-i-za-tion** (mɑd–ər–nə–zeʸ–ʃən) n.

mod-est (mɑd–əst) adj. 1. Not exaggerating one's own achievements or abilities; not boastful: *She's very modest about her success.* 2. Rather shy; not putting oneself forward 3. Small: *There's been a modest rise in prices this year.* 4. Esp. of a woman or her clothes, not indecent; not showing anything that is improper: *...that the women adorn themselves in modest apparel, with propriety and moderation...* (1 Timothy 2:9NKJV). —**modestly** adv. *I also want women to dress modestly, with decency and propriety...* (1 Timothy 2:9).

mod-es-ty n. (mɑd–əs–tiʸ) The state or fact of being modest

mod-i-fi-er (mɑd–ə–taɪ–ər) n. A word or group of words that limits or adds to the meaning of another word or group of words NOTE: A modifier can be an adjective, adverb, or noun. In the sentences "She lives in that yellow house," "Run faster," and "We had a class reunion," the words "yellow," "faster," and "class" are modifiers.

mod-i-fy (mɑd–ə–faɪ) v. -fied, -fying 1. To make partial changes in: *The plane has been modified so that it can land and take off in a shorter distance.* 2. To make less severe or harsh 3. *Gram.* To describe: *Adjectives modify nouns.* —**mod-i-fi-ca-tion** (mɑd–ə–fə–keʸ–ʃən) n.

mod-ish (moᵂ-dɪʃ) adj. Fashionable

mod-u-late (madʒ-ə-leʸt) v. -lated, -lating To vary the tone, pitch, frequency, etc. —**mod-u-la-tion** (madʒ-ə-leʸ-ʃən) n.

mod-ule (madʒ-uᵂl) n. The separate parts of a spacecraft, each being used for a special job or jobs

Mo-ham-med-an-ism (moᵂ-hæm-əd-ən-ɪz-əm) n. —see ISLAM

moist (mɔɪst) adj. Slightly wet; damp —**moistly** adv. —**moistness** n.

mois-ten (mɔɪ-sən) v. To dampen or make slightly wet

mois-ture (mɔɪs-tʃər) n. Slight wetness; water or other liquids, in small quantities or in the form of steam or mist: *There is hardly any moisture in the desert air.*

mo-lar (moᵂ-lər) n. Any of the teeth in the back of the mouth, used for grinding food in chewing

mo-las-ses (mə-læs-əz) n. A thick, sweet syrup that is produced when sugar cane is made into sugar

mold (moᵂld) n. A container into which some soft substance is poured, so that when the substance becomes cool and hard, it takes the shape of the mold

mold v. To form sthg. solid, using a mold

mold n. *BrE.* **mould** A soft, furry, greenish growth on bread, cheese, etc. or on objects that have been left for a long time in warm moist air

mold-ing (moᵂl-dɪŋ) n. 1. The act of giving shape to sthg., esp. to a soft substance 2. An ornamental edge or band of wood, esp. at the top or bottom of a wall, etc.

mold-y (moᵂl-diʸ) adj. -ier, -iest Covered with mold: *The old house smells moldy.* —**moldiness** n.

mole (moᵂl) n. 1. A small, permanent, brown spot on the human skin 2. A small, burrowing animal with tiny eyes, hidden ears, and soft fur 3. **make a mountain out of a mole hill** To make a big issue of some little problem or difficulty

mol-e-cule (mal-ə-kyuᵂl) n. The smallest unit into which any substance can be divided without a change in its own chemical nature —**mo-lec-u-lar** (mə-lɛk-yə-lər) adj.

mo-lest (mə-lɛst/ moᵂ-) v. 1. To annoy or torment 2. To attack (esp. a woman or a child) sexually —**mo-les-ta-tion** (moᵂ-lɛs-teʸ-ʃən) n.

mol-li-fy (mal-ə-faɪ) v. -fied, -fying To soothe the anger of: *He tried to mollify his wife by bringing her some flowers.* —**mol-li-fi-ca-tion** (mal-ə-fɪ-keʸ-ʃən) n.

mol-lusk (mal-əsk) n. One of a large group of animals that have a soft body and usu. live in water. Some mollusks such as snails, clams, and oysters have shells. Others such as octopuses and squids have no outer shell.

molt (moᵂlt) v. To shed an outer covering such as hair, feathers, or skin

mol-ten (moᵂl-tən) adj. Of metal or rock, melted; turned to liquid by very intense heat: *Molten lava flowed down the hill.*

mom (mam) n. *infml.* (used esp. by children) Mother

mo-ment (moᵂ-mənt) n. 1. A very short period of time: *Truthful lips endure forever, but a lying tongue lasts only a moment* (Proverbs 12:19). 2. A particular point in time

mo-men-tar-y (moᵂ-mən-tɛər-iʸ) adj. Lasting for a very short time —**mo-men-tar-i-ly** (moᵂ-mən-tɛər-ə-liʸ) adv.

mo-men-tous (moᵂ-mɛn-təs) adj. Of very great importance

mo-men-tum (moᵂ-mɛn-təm) n. -tums, -ta The force of a moving body: *As the car rolled down the hill, it gathered momentum.* (=moved faster and faster)

mom-my (mam-iʸ) n. -mies *infml.* (usu. used by small children) Mother

mon- (man-) prefix Variation of **mono-**

mon-arch (man-ark) n. A hereditary sovereign; a king or queen, emperor or empress

mon-ar-chy (man-ər-kiʸ) n. -chies A country ruled by a monarch; government by a monarch

mon-as-ter-y (man-ə-stɛər-iʸ) n. -ies The dwelling place of a community of monks —**mon-as-ter-i-al** (man-ə-stɪər-iʸ-əl) adj. —see MONK

mo-nas-tic (mə-næs-tɪk) adj. Of or characteristic of monks or monasteries

mo-nas-ti-cism (mə-næs-tə-sɪz-əm) n. The

monastic system or mode of life

Mon-day (mʌn–di^y / –de^y) n. The second day of any week; the day after Sunday

mon-e-tar-y (mɑn–ə–tɛər–i^y) adj. **1.** Of a country's money: *our monetary system* **2.** Of or involving money: *the monetary value*

mon-ey (mʌn–i^y) n. Coins or paper notes with their value printed on them, given and taken in buying and selling: *The love of money is the root of all kinds of evil. Some people, eager for money, have wandered from the faith and pierced themselves with many griefs* (1 Timothy 6:10).

mon-goose (mɑŋ–gu^ws) n. **-gooses** A weasel-like tropical animal that can attack and kill poisonous snakes

mon-grel (mɑŋ–grəl) n. **1.** A dog of no definable breed **2.** An animal or plant of mixed breed

mongrel adj. Of mixed origin or character

mon-i-tor (mɑn–ə–tər) n. **1.** A student chosen to help the teacher in various ways **2.** The part of the electrical apparatus, such as a computer, that has a screen on which pictures or information appear **3.** A receiver, loudspeaker, or other apparatus used to check radio or television broadcasts for quality of transmission, frequency, etc.

monitor v. To watch, listen to, or examine; to keep check on sthg., esp. a radio or television broadcast: *They monitored the enemy's radio broadcasts to try to find out their plans.*

monk (mʌŋk) n. One of a male religious group who lives apart from the world in a monastery; a member of a monastic order within any religion

mon-key (mʌŋ–ki^y) n. **-keys 1.** A long-tailed, active, tree-climbing animal, belonging to that class of animals most like a man **2.** *infml.* A mischievous child

monkey v. *infml.* To meddle or tamper with sthg.: *Don't monkey with that.*

mo-no- (mɑ–no^w–/–nə–) prefix Alone; single; one: *A monorail is a (train traveling on) a single track./ A monoplane is one with a single wing on each side.*

mo-no (mɑ–no^w) n. *AmE. infml.* for mononucleosis

mon-o-cle (mɑn–ɪ–kəl) n. An eyeglass for one eye

mo-nog-a-my (mə–nɑg–ə–mi^y) n. The state of having only one wife or husband at a time —compare BIGAMY, POLYGAMY

mon-o-gram (mɑn–ə–græm) n. Two or more letters combined in a single design

mon-o-graph (mɑn–ə–græf) n. A scholarly book or article on a specific and usu. limited subject

mon-o-lith (mɑn–ə–lıθ) n. **1.** A large block of stone used in architecture or sculpture **2.** A pillar made from one huge piece of stone and standing by itself **3.** A large organization that acts as a powerful unit

mon-o-lith-ic (mɑn–ə–lıθ–ık) n. **1.** Consisting of one or more monoliths **2.** Like a monolith in being single and massive: *a monolithic organization*

mon-o-logue (mɑn–ə–lɔg) n. A long speech by a single speaker

mon-o-nu-cle-o-sis (mɑn–o^w–nu^w–kli^y–o^w–sıs) n. An infectious disease with swelling of the lymph glands

mo-nop-o-lize *AmE.* also **-ise** *BrE.* (mə–nɑp–ə–laız) v. **-lized, -lizing** To take exclusive control or use of: *These two huge companies monopolize the soap industry./ fig. The naughty child monopolized the teacher's attention.* —**mo-nop-o-li-za-tion** (mə–nɑp–ə–lə–ze^y–ʃən) n. *She is known for her monopolization of every conversation.*

mo-nop-o-ly (mə–nɑp–ə–li^y) n. **-lies 1.** The right or the power, not shared by others, to produce sthg., provide a service, or sell sthg.; complete control **2.** Sthg. controlled in this way: *A university education should not be the monopoly of the rich.*

mon-o-rail (mɑn–ə–re^yl) n. **1.** A single rail on which railway cars are run, or from which they are suspended **2.** The railroad using this system

mon-o-syl-la-ble (mɑn–ə–sıl–ə–bəl) n. A word of one syllable —**mon-o-syl-la-bic** (mɑn–ə–sə–læb–ık) adj.

mon-o-the-ism (mɑn–ə–θi^y–ız–əm) n. The doctrine or belief that there is only one God, which, of course, is true —see GOD —**monotheist** n. —**mon-o-the-is-tic** (mɑn–ə–θi^y–ıs–tık) adj.

mon-o-tone (mɑn–ə–toͫn) n. Sbdy. who speaks or sings continually on the same note: *It's tiresome listening to him; he's such a monotone.*

mo-not-o-nous (mə–nɑt–ə–nəs) adj. Having a tiresome, uninteresting repetition or lack of variety: *My job on the assembly line at the factory is monotonous.* —**monotonously** adv.

mo-not-o-ny (mə–nɑt–ə–niʸ) n. A lack of variety; wearisome sameness

mon-ox-ide (mə–nɑk–saɪd) n. A chemical compound whose molecules contain one atom of oxygen combined with one or more other atoms: *carbon monoxide*

mon-sieur (mə–ʃɜr) n. A French title for a man; Mr.; sir

mon-soon (mɑn–suʷn) n. 1. A seasonal wind of the Indian Ocean and southern Asia, blowing in the summer from the southwest and in the winter from the northeast 2. The summer monsoon that brings heavy rains

mon-ster (mɑn–stər) n. 1. A creature, imaginary or real, that is unusual in size and/or shape, often hideous and frightening 2. An animal or thing of unusually great size or strange form: *That gorilla is a real monster, the biggest one I've ever seen.* 3. An extremely wicked person 4. A menace; a terror: *That kid is a little monster, wrecking everything in sight.*

mon-stros-i-ty (mɑn–strɑ–sə–tiʸ) n. **-ties** 1. That which is monstrous 2. Sthg. made or built in such a way that it is, or is considered, very ugly: *That new office building is a monstrosity!*

mon-strous (mɑn–strəs) adj. 1. Unusual in size or shape 2. Very bad; shocking: *His behavior in class was monstrous.*

month (mʌnθ) n. 1. Any of the 12 parts into which the calendar year is divided 2. A period of about 30 days

month-ly (mʌnθ–liʸ) adj. Happening, appearing, etc. every month or once a month: *a monthly meeting/magazine*

mon-u-ment (mɑn–yə–mənt) n. 1. A building, pillar, statue, etc. erected to the memory of a person or event: *The Washington Monument was erected in 1848 in Washington D.C.* 2. A natural feature or area of special interest set aside by the government as public

property: *Death Valley in California and Nevada is the largest national monument in the United States, covering more than two million acres.*

mon-u-men-tal (mɑn–yə–ment–əl) adj. 1. Very large, and of great and lasting worth: *The artist spent years on his monumental painting, which is 195 feet long and 45 feet high.* 2. Of or serving as a monument

moo (muʷ) n. The sound a cow makes

moo v. **mooed, mooing** To make such a sound

mood (muʷd) n. 1. A state of a person's feelings or temper: *He's in a good/bad mood today.* 2. The right state of mind for a particular activity: *She was very upset, and in no mood for fun and games.*

mood-y (muʷd–iʸ) adj. **-ier, -iest** *derog.* 1. Given to gloomy moods 2. Exhibiting various moods, but often bad-tempered, angry, displeased, or unhappy

moon (muʷn) n. 1. The body which orbits the earth approx. once each month (actually 29.5 days) and reflects the light of the sun 2. This body as it appears at a particular time: *a full moon* 3. A body that revolves around a planet other than the earth: *The planet Saturn has many moons.* 4. **once in a blue moon** Once in a very long time

moon-beam (muʷn–biʸm) n. A ray of moonlight

moon-light (muʷn–laɪt) n. The light of the moon NOTE: Do not confuse "moonlight" with "moonshine."

moonlight v. To hold a second job in addition to a regular one, usu. working at night

moon-lit (muʷn–lɪt) adj. Lighted by the moon: *a moonlit night*

moon-shine (muʷn–ʃaɪn) n. Intoxicating liquor, usu. illegally made NOTE: Do not confuse "moonshine" with "moonlight"

moon-struck (muʷn–strʌk) adj. 1. Romantically sentimental 2. Slightly mad; mentally unbalanced, supposedly due to the influence of the moon

moor (muʌr) n. *BrE.* An open area of land, covered with rough grass or bushes, not farmed because of its poor soil

moor v. To fasten a boat or ship to land or

the bottom of the sea, by means of ropes, chains, an anchor, etc.

moor-ing (mʊər-ɪŋ) n. **1.** A place where boats and ships can be moored **2.** That which can secure a ship or boat or other object, such as a cable

moose (muʷs) n. A large, heavily built animal of the deer family found in the northern US and Canada, the male of which has huge antlers

moot (muʷt) adj. **1.** Open to discussion **2.** So hypothetical as to be meaningless: *a moot point*

mop (mɒp) n. **1.** A bunch of short pieces of coarse yarn or a sponge at the end of a handle, used for washing floors **2.** A thick head of hair

mop v. **-pp- 1.** To clean or wipe, as if with a mop: *She mopped the floor.* **2.** To make dry by rubbing or wiping with sthg. dry

mope (moʷp) v. **moped, moping 1.** To feel very unhappy and pity oneself: *Stop moping!* **2. mope about/around** To wander around in an unhappy and listless mood: *He's been moping around the house all day.*

mo-ped (moʷ-pɛd) n. A motorized bicycle

mo-raine (mə-reʸn) n. A mass of earth, stones, etc. carried along and deposited by a glacier

mor-al (mɔr-əl) adj. **1.** Having to do with right and wrong behavior and character: *Get rid of all moral filth and the evil that is so prevalent, and humbly accept the Word of God [the Good News about Jesus Christ] which can save you* (James 1:21). **2.** Behaving exactly according to what is considered by society to be good or acceptable **3. moral support** Encouragement, but no financial or physical assistance **4. moral victory** Defeat that is in some ways as satisfying as victory, esp. when the principles that one is fighting for are shown to be right —morally adv.

moral n. **1.** The lesson or teaching contained or implied in a story or poem **2. morals** pl. Rules or habits of conduct

mo-rale (mə-ræl) n. The state of mind of a person, team, army, etc., esp. with reference to pride, courage, hope, zeal, and determination: *Even though our team was beaten*

badly, their morale is still high.

mor-al-ist (mɔr-ə-ləst) n. One who concerns himself/herself with regulating the morals of other people —**mor-al-is-tic** (mɔr-ə-lɪs-tɪk) adj. —moralistically adv.

mo-ral-i-ty (mə-ræl-ə-tiʸ) n. **1.** Rightness or pureness of behavior: *One often wonders if there's any morality in politics.* —opposite IMMORALITY **2.** Virtuous conduct; right or good behavior: *As to morality, he was above reproach.*

mor-a-to-ri-um (mɔr-ə-tɔr-iʸ-əm) n. **-riums** or **-ria** A suspension of activities

mor-bid (mɔr-bəd) adj. **1.** Unwholesome; gruesome **2.** Showing an unusual interest in gloomy and gruesome things

more (mɔr/ moʷr) determ., adj. **1.** Comparative of **many, much 2.** A greater amount: *There are more cars on this road than on any other.* **3.** An additional amount: *Have some more rice!* **4. any more** Any longer: *He doesn't work here any more.* **5. more and more** Increasingly **6. more or less** Approximately; perhaps a little more, perhaps a little less **7.** Used to show that things get larger, smaller, etc., together: *The more he gets, the more he wants.* —opposite LESS, FEWER

more adv. **1.** (used to show the comparative of many adjectives and adverbs): *She's more intelligent than I, and she finishes her work more quickly than I.* **2.** To a greater degree: *I exercise more now than I used to.* **3.** Again: *Please play that song once more.*

more-o-ver (mɔr-oʷ-vər) adv. *fml.* In addition; besides what has been said: *The price is too high, and moreover, the bike is in need of repairs.*

morgue (mɔrg) n. A place where dead bodies of people are kept until they are identified and claimed by relatives or released for burial —compare MORTUARY

morn-ing (mɔr-nɪŋ) n. The first part of the day, until noon

morn-ing-glo-ry (mɔrn-ɪŋ-glɔr-iʸ) n. **-glories** A climbing vine with showy, trumpet-shaped flowers that usu. close in the afternoons

mor-on (mɔr-ɑn) n. **1.** A mentally retarded person with a mental age of between eight

and twelve years, able to do routine work under supervision 2. Loosely, a stupid person —mo-ron-ic (mə-**ran**-ık) adj. —moron-ically adv.

mo-rose (mə-**ro**ʷs) adj. Bad tempered; gloomy; having a sullen disposition

mor-phine (mor-fiʸn) n. A drug made from opium, used for relieving pain

mor-sel (**mor**-səl) n. A tiny piece of food

mor-tal (**mort**-əl) adj., n. 1. A human being (as compared with God or an angel); that which must die: *And if the Spirit of him who raised Jesus from the dead is living in you, he who raised Christ from the dead will also give life to your mortal bodies through his Spirit, who lives in you* (Romans 8:11). —opposite IMMORTAL 2. Causing death: *a mortal wound* 3. Very great (in degree): *in mortal danger*

mor-tal-i-ty (mor-**tæl**-ə-tiʸ) n. -ties 1. The condition of being mortal; perishable; esp. the nature of man, who is going to die eventually: *God's word tells us that we will all be changed in a flash, in the twinkling of an eye, at the last trumpet. For the trumpet will sound, the dead will be raised imperishable, and we will be changed. For the perishable must clothe itself with the imperishable, and the mortal with immortality. When the perishable has been clothed with the imperishable, and the mortal with immortality, then the saying that is written will come true: "Death has been swallowed up in victory." He [God] gives us the victory (over death) through our Lord Jesus Christ* (1 Corinthians 15:51-54,57). —see JESUS CHRIST, RESURRECTION 2. infant mortality The rate at which deaths of babies occur

mor-tal-ly adv. In such a way that causes death: *mortally wounded*

mor-tar (**mort**-ər) n. A mixture of lime or cement with sand and water, used for joining bricks or stones

mortar v. To plaster or join together with mortar (bricks, stones, etc.)

mortar n. 1. A bowl-shaped vessel in which substances are crushed with a pestle 2. A short cannon used for firing shells at a high angle

mort-gage (**mor**-gıdʒ) n. A sum of money lent through a legal agreement, esp. for buying a house (which the borrower must give up if he fails to repay the loan)

mortgage v. To offer buildings or land as security for money borrowed: *They mortgaged their house to pay off their other debts.*

mor-tu-ar-y (mor-tʃə-weər-iʸ) n. -ies A place where a dead body is kept until the time of the funeral —compare MORGUE

mo-sa-ic (moʷ-**ze**ʸ-ık) n. A pattern or picture made by placing together small pieces of different colored glass, stone, etc.

Mo-sa-ic Law (moʷ-zeʸ-ık lɔ) n. The code of civil and religious laws contained in the Pentateuch (the first five books of the Bible) and attributed to Moses —see LAW

Mo-ses (**mo**ʷ-zəz/ -zəs) n. The deliverer, leader, lawgiver, and prophet of Israel in the 15th century B.C. NOTE: God called Moses to lead the people of Israel out of slavery in Egypt. He led them first to Mt. Sinai where God made a covenant with them. God gave his law to Moses, and Moses gave it to the people. Thus, the books of the law, the Torah, are called the Law of Moses. Moses, by divine inspiration, wrote about the creation of the world, the fall into sin, the promise of a Savior, the wickedness of succeeding generations, the Great Flood which destroyed all mankind except Noah and his family, the confusion of languages at the Tower of Babel and subsequent scattering of the various language groups, the call of Abram (Abraham) and the history of Israel down to and including his own lifetime. He also prophesied of Jesus. Fifteen hundred years later, Jesus, speaking to the Jewish leaders who claimed to be followers of Moses, said, "If you believed Moses, you would believe me, for he wrote about me. But since you do not believe what he wrote, how are you going to believe what I say?" (John 5:46,47).

mo-sey (**mo**ʷ-ziʸ) v. -seyed, -seying To walk in a leisurely, unhurried manner

Mos-lem (**maz**-ləm) n., adj. —see MUSLIM

mosque (mask) n. A Muslim place of worship

mos-qui-to (məs-**ki**ʸ-toʷ) n. -toes Any of a

class of small flying insects that prick the skin and then suck the blood, and that are in some cases carriers of serious diseases

moss (mɔs) n. A type of small, green or yellow, flowerless plant that grows in a furry mass in damp places, on tree trunks, etc. —**mossy** adj.

most (moʷst) adj. Superl. of **much, many** 1. The majority of: *most men* 2. Greatest in quantity, extent, or degree: *the most money/ ability*

most adv. Superl. of **much** 1. To the greatest degree: *The most beautiful house in town.* 2. *fml.* Very: *a most unusual day*

most determ., pron. Superl. of **many, much** 1. The greatest number or amount: *We all ate a lot at the party, but John ate the most.* 2. The greatest part: *Most of the students speak English.* 3. **at the most** Not more than; if not less: *She's at the most only 15 years old.* 4. **make the most of** To get the best advantage from: *We only have one day in New York, so let's make the most of it, and see as much as we can.* 5. **for the most part** Mainly: *Summers in California, for the most part, are very dry.*

most-ly (moʷst–liʸ) adv. Mainly; most of the time; in most cases: *I get books mostly from the library, rather than buying them at the bookstore.*

mo-tel (moʷ–tɛl) n. A hotel esp. for motorists, which provides lodging and parking

moth (mɔθ) n. pl. **moths** (mɔðz) 1. A winged insect related to the butterfly, which flies mainly at night 2. The smaller members of the same family of insects, which eat holes in clothing

moth-ball (mɔθ–bɔl) n. A small ball made of a strong-smelling substance, used for keeping moths away from clothes

moth-er (mʌð–ər) n. 1. A female parent: *Honor your father and your mother — which is the first commandment with a promise — that it may go well with you and that you may enjoy long life on the earth* (Ephesians 6:2). 2. **one's mother country** The country where one was born and raised

moth-er-hood (mʌð–ər–hʊd) n. The condition of being a mother

moth-er-in-law (mʌð–ər-ɪn-lɔ) n. The mother

of a person's husband or wife

moth-er-ly (mʌð–ər–liʸ) adj. Of or like a mother; loving and protective

moth-er-of-pearl (mʌð–ər-əv-pɜrl) n. The hard, smooth lining of the shell of the pearl oyster, used in making buttons and ornaments

Moth-er's Day (mʌð–ərz deʸ) A holiday celebrated in the US on the second Sunday in May in honor of mothers

mo-tion (moʷ–ʃən) n. 1. The act or manner of moving 2. A particular movement or way of moving: *He made a motion with his hand.* 3. A proposal formally put before a meeting

motion v. To direct someone by a movement, usu. with the hand: *He motioned to the waitress to bring more coffee.*

mo-tion-less (moʷ–ʃən–ləs) adj. Not moving

mo-tion pic-ture (moʷ–ʃən pɪk–tʃər) A series of pictures projected so quickly upon a screen that the people and objects in the pictures seem to be moving; moving picture; a cinema film

mo-ti-vate (moʷt–ə–veʸt) v. **-vated, vating** To cause someone to act in a certain way: *His crime was motivated by greed.*

mo-ti-va-tion (moʷt–ə–veʸ–ʃən) n. The act or state of being motivated

mo-tive (moʷ–tɪv) n. That which causes a person to act or do sthg.; a reason: *The Lord searches every heart and understands every motive behind the thoughts* (1 Chronicles 28:9). *Motives are weighed by the Lord* (Proverbs 16:2).

mo-tor (moʷt–ər) n. A machine, usu. a gasoline (petrol) engine or an electrical device that brings about motion or does work: *Most washing machines have electric motors.*

motor adj. 1. Driven by an engine: *a motorboat/a motor scooter* 2. Having to do with vehicles driven by an engine, esp. those used on roads: *the motor industry*

mo-tor-bike (moʷt–ər–baɪk) n. A small light motorcycle

mo-tor-boat (moʷt–ər–boʷt) n. A boat that moves by the power of a motor

mo-tor-cy-cle (moʷt–ər–saɪ–kəl) n. Sthg. like a bicycle but much heavier and driven by an engine

motorcycle v. **-cycled, -cycling** To ride on a motorcycle: *They motorcycled all over the country.* —**motorcyclist** n.

mo·tor·ist (moᵂt-ə-rəst) n. A person who drives a car

mot·to (mɑt-oᵂ) n. **-tos** or **-toes** A short sentence or a phrase expressing a rule of conduct, principle, etc.; a maxim: *"Honesty is the best policy" is a good motto.* —compare SLOGAN

mound (mavnd) n. **1.** A heap of earth, stones, debris, etc., natural or artificial **2.** *fig.* Any kind of pile or heap: *There's a mound of papers on my desk.* **3.** A small hill

mount (mavnt) n. A mountain or a hill: *Mount Ararat*

mount v. **1.** To get on a horse —opposite DIS-MOUNT **2.** To rise in level or increase in amount: *His debts continued to mount.* **3.** To set, fix, or secure in or on a support or frame: *He mounted the photograph on some paper.* **4.** To prepare and begin (an offensive): *The army is getting ready to mount an attack on the island.* **5.** To set or raise into position: *A large gun was mounted on the stern of the ship.*

moun·tain (mavnt-ən) n. A landmass higher than a hill: *In the Rocky Mountains many peaks are over 14,000 ft. high.*

moun·tain·eer (mavnt-ən-ıər) n. A person who climbs mountains as a sport or profession

moun·tain·ous (mavnt-ən-əs) adj. Full of or containing mountains: *mountainous country*

mourn (mɔrn) v. To feel and/or show grief, esp. for the death of sbdy. or because of our sins: *Jesus said, "Blessed are those who mourn [concerning their sins] for they will be comforted"* (Matthew 5:4; James 4:8-10).

mourn·ful (mɔrn-fəl) adj. Causing, feeling, or expressing sorrow or sadness —**mournfully** adv.

mourn·ing (mɔr-nɪŋ) n. The expression of grief, esp. for a death: *The woman was in mourning for her dead husband./ In heaven "there will be no more death or mourning or crying or pain..."* (Revelation 21:4).

mouse (mavs) n. *pl.* **mice** (maıs) **1.** A small, furry, long-tailed animal, usu. brownish-gray, that lives in houses and in fields; a ro-

dent **2.** A hand-operated device for controlling the pointer on the screen of a computer

mous·tache (mʌs-tæʃ/ məs-tæʃ) n. *BrE.* for mustache

mous·y (mav-siʸ) adj. **-ier, -iest 1.** Having a dull, brownish-gray color **2.** Unattractive; drab

mouth (mavθ) n. **1.** The opening at which food is taken into the body and through which a person or animal speaks or makes sounds: *If you confess with your mouth, "Jesus is Lord," and believe in your heart that God raised him from the dead, you will be saved [have eternal life]* (Romans 10:9). **2.** Representative of a whole person: *We have many mouths to feed.* **3.** An opening, entrance, or way out: *the mouth of a river (where it joins the sea)/the mouth of a cave* **4. down in the mouth** Not cheerful; in low spirits

mov·a·ble or **move·a·ble** (muᵂv-ə-bəl) adj. Able to be moved

move (muᵂv) v. **moved, moving 1.** To change place or position: *He moved from one end of the bench to the other.* **2.** To change one's place of residence: *He's moving to New York.* **3.** To rouse or affect one's feeling: *He was moved by the inspiring music.* **4.** To be in movement; running, going: *Don't get off the bus while it's still moving.* **5.** To advance; to progress; get nearer to an end: *Work on the new bridge is moving ahead nicely now.* **6.** Offer a proposal on which arguments for and against are heard, and a decision taken, esp. by voting: *I move that we support this new proposal.*

move n. **1.** An act of moving; movement: *If you make a move, I'll shoot.* **2.** A turn of play in a game such as checkers or chess: *That was a good move.*

move·ment (muᵂv-mənt) n. **1.** An act of moving or being moved: *Movement can be painful when you've hurt your back.* **2.** A group of people who make united efforts for a particular purpose: *the anti-war movement*

mov·er (muᵂ-vər) n. **1.** One who moves **2.** A person or company in the business of moving furniture, etc. from one residence or office to another **3.** *slang* A person who makes progress

mov·ie (muᵂ-viʸ) n. A motion picture; cinema

mov-ing (mu^wv–ıŋ) adj. 1. Causing strong feelings: *The story was so moving that she cried all night.* 2. Parts that move; not fixed: *Be sure to oil the moving part of this machine.*

mow (mo^w) v. mowed, mowed or mown, mowing 1. To cut grass etc. with a mower 2. mow sbdy. down To kill in great numbers: *A man went crazy with his machine gun and mowed down twenty-two people in a restaurant.*

mow-er (mo^w–ər) n. A machine for cutting grass: *a lawn mower*

mown (mo^wn) v. Past part. of mow

mpg *abbr.* for miles per gallon (esp. of gasoline)

mph *abbr.* for miles per hour: *The speed limit on that street was 35 mph.*

Mr. *abbr.* for mister (mıs–tər) n. *pl.* Messrs. (mes–ərz) 1. A title for a man who has no other title 2. A title used when addressing certain men in official positions: *Mr. Chairman*

Mrs. (mıs–əz) n. *pl.* Mes-dames (me^y–dæm/ –dam) *abbr.* for mistress, now used as a title for a married woman (*pl. abbr.* Mmes.)

much (mʌtʃ) determ., pron. more, most 1. Great in quantity, amount, extent, or degree: *There's too much to do, and not much time to do it.* 2. Sthg. significant or important: *not much of a leader*

much adv. 1. To a great degree or extent: *much easier* 2. Almost: *much the same*

muck (mʌk) n. 1. Filth; dung; mud; rubbish 2. Slanderous remarks or writings

muck up (mʌk ʌp) v. To make a mess of

muck-y (mʌk–i^y) adj. 1. Very dirty 2. Obscene

mu-cous (myu^w–kəs) adj. Of, like, or covered with mucus

mu-cous mem-brane (myu^w–kəs mem–bre^yn) Moist skin that lines the nose, mouth, and certain internal organs

mu-cus (myu^w–kəs) n. The slimy fluid from the nose, etc. that moistens and protects

mud (mʌd) n. 1. Wet, sticky, soft earth 2. one's name is mud One is badly spoken of 3. *fig.* Sin: *God lifted me out of the slimy pit, out of the mud and mire [sins]* (Psalm 40:2).

mud-dle (mʌd–əl) n. A state of confusion and disorder

mud-dled (mʌd–əld) adj. Confused

muez-zin (myu–ez–ın/ mwez–ın) n. A Muslim crier who summons the faithful to prayer, usu. from a minaret

muff (mʌf) n. A tube-shaped cover often made of fur, for keeping the hands warm

muff v. 1. In some games, to fail to catch a ball 2. To miss an opportunity

muf-fin (mʌf–ən) n. A small, cup-shaped bread, often eaten hot with butter

muf-fle (mʌf–əl) v. -fled, -fling 1. To wrap in a shawl, etc., esp. to keep warm 2. To wrap with sthg. to deaden the sound

muf-fler (mʌf–lər) n. 1. A scarf worn around the neck 2. A device for reducing the noise of a gasoline engine

mug (mʌg) n. 1. A type of cup, usu. with a flat bottom and straight sides and a handle 2. *derog. infml.* The face of a person: *a mug shot* (=a picture of a person's face) 3. *slang* A person: *OK you mugs, get to work.*

mug v. -gg- To rob with violence —mugger n. —mugging n.

mug-gy (mʌg–i^y) adj. -gier, -giest Warm and very humid weather

Mu-ham-mad (mu–hæm–əd) n. A.D. 570-632 Founder of Islam

Mu-ham-mad-an n. (mu–hæm–əd–ən) A follower of Muhammad; a Muslim —see IS-LAM

mu-lat-to (mə–la–to^w/ –læ–) n. -toes 1. A person who has one white and one black parent 2. A person of mixed Caucasian and Negro ancestry

mul-ber-ry (mʌl–beər–i^y) n. 1. A type of tree with broad, dark green leaves on which silkworms feed 2. Its wood 3. Its edible fruit

mulch (mʌltʃ) n. Compost, peat, straw, etc. laid on the ground around plants in order to keep the soil moist, to protect the plants' roots, etc. —mulch v.

mule (myu^wl) n. The animal which is the offspring of a male donkey and a female horse (mare)

mull (mʌl) v. To ponder; think sthg. over

mul-lah (mu–lə/ ma–) n. A Muslim who is learned in Islamic theology and sacred law

mul-ti- (mʌl–ti^y–) prefix Many; much NOTE:

In forming compounds *multi-* is usually joined to the following word or element without using a space or hyphen. But if the second element begins with "i," it is separated with a hyphen, as in *multi-infectious*

mul-ti-fac-et-ed (məl–tɪ–fæs–ət–əd) adj. Having many facets or aspects

mul-ti-far-i-ous (məl–tə–fɛər–iʸ–əs) adj. Having great variety; very diverse

mul-ti-ple (mʌl–tə–pəl) adj. Having or affecting many parts, individuals, elements, etc.: *The driver received multiple injuries.*

multiple n. A number that contains a smaller number an exact number of times: *6 x 7 = 42 so 42 is a multiple of 6.*

mul-ti-ple scler-o-sis (mʌl–tə–pəl sklə–roʷ–səs) n. A chronic disease of the nervous system characterized by speech defects, loss of muscle coordination, etc.

mul-ti-pli-ca-tion (mʌl–tə–plə–keʸ–ʃən) n . The act of adding a number to itself a particular number of times

mul-ti-pli-ci-ty (mʌl–tə–plɪ–sə–tiʸ) n. A large number or great variety: *a multiplicity of ideas*

mul-ti-ply (mʌl–tə–plaɪ) v. -plied, -plying 1. To add a number to itself a particular number of times: *6 multiplied by 6 is 36.* 2. To increase: *By getting a better education he multiplied his chances for success.*

mul-ti-tude (mʌl–tə–tuʷd) n. *fml.* A large number: *Love each other deeply, because love covers over a multitude of sins* (1 Peter 4:8). *There before me was a great multitude that no one could count, from every nation, tribe, people, and language, standing before the throne [of God in heaven] and before the Lamb [Jesus Christ, the Lamb of God, who takes away the sin of the world]* (Revelation 7:9). —see also LAMB OF GOD

mum (mʌm) adj. Silent; not speaking

mum-ble (mʌm–bəl) v. -bled, -bling To speak unclearly: *Stop mumbling and speak clearly.*

mum-my (mʌm–iʸ) n. A dead body preserved from decay in the manner of the ancient Egyptians

mumps (mʌmps) n. An infectious disease marked by fever and swelling, esp. of the glands around the neck and mouth

munch (mʌntʃ) v. To chew with a crunching sound: *munching on an apple*

mun-dane (mən–deʸn/ mʌn–deʸn) adj. 1. Ordinary; routine; unexciting 2. Of or relating to the world

mu-nic-i-pal (myuʷ–nɪs–ə–pəl) adj. 1. Of or pertaining to a town or city 2. Having local self-government

mu-nic-i-pal-i-ty (myuʷ–nɪs–ə–pæl–ə–tiʸ) n. A political unit, as a city or town, incorporated for local self-government

mu-nif-i-cent (myuʷ–nɪf–ə–sənt) adj. Very, very generous —**munificence** n. —**munificently** adv.

mu-ni-tion (myuʷ–nɪ–ʃən) n. Ammunition and all other necessary war material

mu-ral (myʊər–əl) n. A painting which is painted on the wall

mur-der (mɜr–dər) n. The sin of killing a human being intentionally —**murder** adj. *murder victim*

murder v. 1. To kill unlawfully, and intentionally, which is a sin against God's law: *You shall not murder* (Exodus 20:13). 2. To ruin language, music, etc. by using or performing it badly: *He really murdered that song!* —**murderer** n.

mur-der-ous (mɜr–dər–əs) adj. Of, like, or suggesting murder: *murderous intentions* —**murderously** adv.

murk (mɜrk) n. Darkness

murk-y (mɜrk–iʸ) adj. Dark and gloomy

mur-mur (mɜr–mər) n. 1. A muttered complaint 2. A soft, indistinct and often continuous sound

murmur v. 1. To mumble or mutter a complaint; to grumble: *Writing to the Christians at Philippi, St. Paul writes, "Do all things without murmuring and disputing, that you may become blameless and harmless, children of God without fault in the midst of a crooked and perverse generation, among whom you shine as lights in the world, holding fast the word of life [the Good News about Jesus Christ]..."* (Philippians 2:14-16 NKJV). 2. To make a low, indistinct sound

mus-cle (mʌs–əl) n. 1. One of the bundles of fibers in the body which, by contracting or relaxing, cause movement of the body 2.

Strength; power: *military/political muscle*

mus-cu-lar (MAS–kyə–lər) adj. **1.** Concerning the muscles: *a muscular disease* **2.** Having powerful muscles: *muscular arms/ legs*

mus-cu-lar dys-tro-phy (MAS–kyə–lər dɪs–trə–fiʸ) n. A chronic, noncontagious disease in which the muscles are gradually wasted

muse (myuʷz) v. **mused, musing** To think about sthg., usu. without serious concentration

mu-se-um (myuʷ–ziʸ–əm) n. A building where objects are on display and shown to the public because of their historic, cultural, scientific, or artistic interest: *The Museum of Natural History*

mush (mʌʃ) n. **1.** A thick porridge made by boiling meal, esp. cornmeal, in water or milk **2.** Any thick, soft, yielding mass

mush-room (mʌʃ–ruʷm) n. An edible fungus with a stem and domed cap, noted for its rapid growth

mushroom v. **1.** To grow rapidly: *Restaurants are mushrooming near the new sports arena.* **2.** To rise and spread in the shape of a mushroom

mush-y (mʌʃ–iʸ) adj. **-ier, -iest 1.** Like mush **2.** Affectionate or passionate in a maudlin fashion

mu-sic (myuʷ–zɪk) n. **1.** Vocal or instrumental sounds having rhythm, melody, or harmony: *Sing and make music in your heart to the Lord; always giving thanks to God the Father for everything in the name of our Lord Jesus Christ* (Ephesians 5:19-20). **2.** The art of doing this: *She enjoys playing sacred music* **3.** An agreeable sound or good news: *What you just told me is music to my ears.* **4. face the music** To admit to responsibility for sthg. and accept the result, esp. rebuke or punishment

mu-si-cal (myuʷ–zɪ–kəl) adj. **1.** Of or relating to music or musicians: *musical instruments* **2.** Having the pleasing tonal qualities of music **3.** Skilled in and/or fond of music: *a very musical child*

musical n. A play or film that includes singing and sometimes dancing

mu-si-cian (myuʷ–zɪ–ʃən) n. A person who plays one or more musical instruments, or

who writes music

mus-ket (mʌs–kət) n. An old gun with a long barrel, in use before the invention of the rifle

mus-ket-eer (mʌs–kə–tɪər) n. A soldier armed with a musket

musk-rat (mʌsk–ræt) n. **1.** A North American animal that lives in or near water, having thick brown fur **2.** The fur of this animal

Mus-lim (mʌz–ləm/ mʊz–/ mʊs–) also **Moslem** (mɑz–ləm) n. also **Mohammadan** or **Muhammadan** adj. A person who believes in the Islamic faith, founded by Muhammad in the seventh century A.D.

Muslim adj. Of or pertaining to Islam

mus-lin (mʌz–lən) n. A very fine, thin, cotton material

muss (mʌs) v. To put into disorder: *Don't muss up my hair*

muss n. Disorder; a mess: *Your room is a dreadful muss.*

mus-sel (mʌs–əl) n. A mollusk having two hinged parts to its shell: *The shells of freshwater mussels are used to make buttons.*

must (mʌst) v. neg. short form **mustn't** (mʌs–ənt) **1.** To be necessary: *We must eat to stay alive.* **2.** To be likely or certain to: *This must be the place he said to meet him, but where is he?*

mus-tache (mʌs–tæʃ/ mə–stæʃ) n. *AmE.* Hair growing above the upper lip

mus-tang (mʌs–tæŋ) n. A wild horse of the American plains

mus-tard (mʌs–tərd) n. A type of seasoning, yellow in color, with a hot taste, made from the seeds of the mustard plant

mus-ter (mʌs–tər) v. **1.** To gather or collect: *The troops were mustered for an attack.* **2.** To gather courage, energy, etc.: *He mustered his courage.*

must-y (mʌs–tiʸ) adj. **-ier, -iest** Having a stale or moldy odor

mu-ta-tion (myuʷ–teʸ–ʃən) n. An alteration or change, as in nature, form, or quality

mute (myuʷt) n. A person who is unable to speak

mu-ti-late (myuʷt–əl–eʸt) v. **-lated, -lating** To have a part of the body removed, or to be badly cut up or mangled: *She was mutilated*

in the accident and now has only one leg. —**mu-ti-la-tion** (myuʷ–tə–leʸ–ʃən) n.

mu-ti-neer (myuʷ–tə–nɪər) n. One who takes part in a mutiny —**mu-ti-nous** (myuʷ–tə–nəs) adj.

mu-ti-ny (myuʷ–tən–iʸ) n. Open rebellion against constituted authority, esp. by military personnel against their superior officers

mutt (mʌt) n. *AmE. infml.* A mongrel dog, of no particular breed

mut-ter (mʌt–ər) v. To speak angry or complaining words in a low voice; to grumble: *What are you muttering about?*

mut-ton (mʌt–ən) n. The meat from a sheep

mu-tu-al (myuʷ–tʃuʷ–əl) adj. **1.** Given to each by the other: *Let us therefore make every effort to do what leads to peace and to mutual edification* (Romans 14:19). **2.** Common to two or more people: *a mutual friend/a mutual interest* —**mutually** adv.

muz-zle (mʌz–əl) n. **1.** The front part of an animal's head, including its snout, jaws, and mouth **2.** A covering around the animal's mouth to keep it from biting **3.** The front end of the barrel of a gun

muzzle v. **-zled, -zling** To put a muzzle on an animal: *fig. Sometimes, those who know the truth have been muzzled (=kept silent) by those in power.*

my (maɪ) possessive pron., adj. Belonging to me: *This is my book.*

myr-i-ad (mɪər–iʸ–əd) adj., n. A very great, but indefinite number: *Then as I looked I heard the voices of countless angels. These were all round the throne [of God]... Myriads upon myriads there were, thousands upon thousands...* (Revelation 5:11NEB).

myr-tle (mɜrt–əl) n. **1.** A vine with shiny evergreen leaves and blue flowers, also called a periwinkle **2.** A shrub with evergreen leaves, white or pinkish flowers, and blackish berries

my-self (maɪ–self) pron. **1.** (used reflexively) *I hurt myself.* **2.** (used for emphasis) *I myself will be there.*

mys-te-ri-ous (mɪ–stɪər–iʸ–ɔs) adj. Not easily understood; full of mystery —**mysteriously** adv.

mys-ter-y (mɪs–tər–iʸ) n. Sthg. that cannot be, or has not been explained

mys-tic (mɪs–tɪk) n. A person who practices mysticism

mys-ti-cal (mɪs–tɪ–kəl) adj. Concerning mysticism

mys-ti-cism (mɪs–tə–sɪz–əm) n. **1.** The attempt to gain union with God and a knowledge of real truth through prayer and meditation **2.** The belief in a direct, intimate union of the soul with God through contemplation without reference to God's Holy Word. This belief is anti-Scriptural, for the Scriptures plainly teach that "He that is of God, hears God's word" (John 8:47).

mys-ti-fy (mɪs–tə–faɪ) v. **-fied, -fying** To bewilder, puzzle, make someone wonder: *We are completely mystified by his disappearance.* —**mys-ti-fi-ca-tion** (mɪs–tə–fə–keʸ–ʃən) n.

myth (mɪθ) n. A false story or idea which may be widely believed; sthg. imagined or untrue

myth-i-cal (mɪθ–ə–kəl) adj. Of a myth; imagined; invented; never having existed

my-thol-o-gy (mɪ–θɑl–ə–dʒiʸ) n. **-gies 1.** A body of myths and esp. those dealing with the imaginary gods and heroes of a people **2.** A body of beliefs about the origin and history of a people **3.** The study of myths —**myth-o-log-i-cal** adj. (mɪθ–ə–lɑdʒ–ɪ–kəl)

narcotic

N, n (ɛn) n. The 14th letter of the English alphabet

N *abbr.* for North(ern)

nab (næb) v. **-bb- 1.** To seize and arrest **2.** To grab

na-dir (ne^y–dɪər) n. **1.** The point in the heavens directly beneath the observer, that is, directly over the head of sbdy. on the opposite side of the earth **2.** *Fig.* The lowest point; time of the greatest depression; despair

nag (næg) v. **-gg- 1.** To annoy by constant scolding **2.** To hurt continuously: *a nagging toothache*

nag n. **1.** *derog.* A person who nags **2.** An old horse that is in bad condition

Na-hum (ne^y–həm) n. One of the books of the Minor Prophets in the Old Testament, written by the prophet Nahum during the seventh century B.C. —see BIBLE, OLD TESTAMENT

nail (ne^yl) n. **1.** A thin piece of metal for hammering into pieces of wood, usu. to hold them together **2.** Fingernail, toenail **3. hard as nails** *infml.* A person without any tender feelings **4. hit the nail on the head** *infml.* To do or say exactly the right thing

nail v. **1.** To fasten as with a nail or nails **2. nail down** To make a definite agreement or set a definite price, etc.: *Before they repair the roof, nail them down to a definite price.* (=make them tell you how much it will cost)

na-ive (nɑ–i^yv) adj. **1.** Simple in thought, manner, or speech **2.** Inexperienced and lacking knowledge of the world —**naively** adv.

na-ked (ne^y–kəd) adj. **1.** Without clothing **2.** Uncovered: *a naked window* **3.** Without addition, disguise, or embellishment: *the naked truth* **4. with a naked eye** Without the help of a microscope or any other instrument to help one see: *Bacteria are too small to be seen with the naked eye.*

nam-by–pam-by (næm–bi^y–pæm–bi^y). adj. (usu. of boys and men) Weak; without strength of character

---

SPELLING NOTE:
Words having the sound /n/ may be spelled with **kn-**, like **knee**, or **pn-**, like **pneumonia**.

---

name (ne^ym) n. **1.** A word or words by which a person, animal, class, concept or thing is known: *" and you are to give him the name Jesus, because he will save his people from their sins"* (Matthew 1:21). *God exalted him (Jesus) to the highest place and gave him the name that is above every name, that at the name of Jesus every knee should bow... and every tongue confess that Jesus Christ is Lord, to the glory of God the Father* (Philippians 2:9-11). **2.** Reputation; the opinion that others have of a person: *A good name [reputation] is more desirable than great riches; to be esteemed is better than silver or gold* (Proverbs 22:1).

name-less (ne^ym–ləs) adj. **1.** Having no name **2.** Unknown by name **3.** Anonymous; unidentified: *The donor wants to remain nameless.*

name-ly (ne^ym–li^y) adv. That is to say: *Only one person can save us from our sins, namely, Jesus.*

name-sake (ne^ym–se^yk) n. One having the same name as another

nap (næp) n. **1.** A short sleep **2.** The downy or hairy surface of cloth, leather, etc.

nap v. **-pp-** To sleep a short time; doze: *John was caught napping on the job.*

na-palm (ne^y–pɑm) n. Petrol in jellied form, used in making fire bombs

nape (ne^yp) n. The back of the neck

naph-tha (næf–θə) n. A kind of clear liquid that readily catches fire, obtained from coal tar and petrol

nap-kin (næp–kən) n. A piece of cloth or paper used while eating to protect one's clothes and for cleaning one's hands and lips

nar-cis-sism (nɑr–sə–sɪz–əm) n. **1.** A tendency to self-worship **2.** Love of or sexual desire for one's own body

nar-cis-sus (nɑr–sɪs–əs) n. **-cis-sus** or **-cis-sus-es** or **-cis-si** Any of a group of flowers including daffodils, esp. the kind with heavily scented single white flowers

nar-co-sis (nɑr–ko^w–səs) n. A state of unconsciousness produced by a drug

nar-cot-ic (nɑr–kɑt–ɪk) n. *often plural* A drug that dulls the senses and causes sleep, but in large amounts is harmful and habit-

forming —**narcotic** adj.

nar-rate (nær–eʸt/ neər–) v. -rated, -rating *fml.* To give an account or commentary; describe an event or events: *The film was narrated by a famous movie star.* —**nar-ra-tion** (nə–reʸ–ʃən) n. —**nar-ra-tor** (nær–eʸt–ər/ neər–) n.

nar-ra-tive (nær–ə–tɪv/neər–) n. A spoken or written story

nar-row (nær–oʷ/ neər–) adj. **1.** Small from side to side; not wide —opposite BROAD, WIDE **2.** Limited; restricted **3.** Just barely successful: *We won the game by a narrow margin.* **4.** Rigid; not flexible: *He has a very narrow view on things, since he has led a rather sheltered life.* —**narrowly** adv. Barely —**narrowness** n.

narrow v. To become narrower; decrease in width: *The highway narrows to two lanes when you approach the ridge, so be very careful.*

nar-row–mind-ed (nær–oʷ–maɪnd–əd/neər–) adj. Unwilling to respect the opinions of others; bigoted

na-sal (neʸ–zəl) adj. **1.** Of or pertaining to the nose: *a nasal infection* **2.** Sounded through the nose

na-sal-ize (neʸ–zəl–aɪz) v. -ized, -izing To give a nasal sound —**na-sal-i-za-tion** (neʸ–zə–lə–zeʸ–ʃən) n.

na-stur-tium (nə–stər–ʃəm) n. A garden plant with red, yellow, or orange flowers

nas-ty (næs–tiʸ) adj. -tier, -tiest **1.** Disgustingly dirty; filthy: *a nasty habit* **2.** Malicious; spiteful: *a nasty temper* **3.** Unpleasant or threatening: *nasty weather* **4.** Horrible; bloody: *a nasty accident.* **5.** Morally wicked; obscene; evil: *a nasty mind* —**nastily** adv. —**nastiness** n.

na-tal (neʸt–əl) adj. Of or pertaining to one's birth

na-tion (neʸ–ʃən) n. **1.** A large number of people organized under a single government: *Blessed is the nation whose God is the Lord* (Psalm 33:12). *Righteousness exalts a nation, but sin is a disgrace to any people* (Proverbs 14:34). **2.** A group of people with the same race and language: *There are several American Indian nations in the western United States./ All nations will be blessed through him [Jesus]* (Psalm 72:17).

na-tion-al (næʃ–ən–əl) adj. Concerning or belonging to a nation: *a national holiday*

national n. A person belonging to a nation: *Turkish nationals in Germany*

na-tion-al-ism (næʃ–ən–əl–ɪz–əm) **1.** The desire to bring the people of a nation together under their own government **2.** Devotion to the interests of one's own nation —**nationalist** adj. —**na-tion-al-is-tic** (næʃ–ən–əl–ɪs–tɪk) adj.

na-tion-al-i-ty (næʃ–ən–æl–ə–tiʸ) n. -ties Membership in a particular nation: *She lives in India but has American nationality.*

na-tion-al-ize (næʃ–ə–nə–laɪz) v. -ized, -izing Of a central government, to take control of a business, industry, etc. for the state —**na-tion-al-i-za-tion** (næʃ–ə–nə–lə–zeʸ–ʃən) n.

na-tive (neʸ–tɪv) adj. **1.** Born in a certain place: *a native Californian* **2.** Belonging to a person from birth or early childhood: *her native language* **3.** Growing naturally in a certain place: *Palm trees are native to West Africa.* **4.** Inborn; innate; not learned: *native ability*

native n. Someone who was born in a specified place: *He's a native of Japan/India/Ghana.*

na-tiv-i-ty (nə–tɪv–ə–tiʸ) n. **1.** Birth, esp. with reference to time, place, etc. **2. the Nativity** The birth of Jesus Christ: *Christians celebrate the Nativity at Christmas time.* —see JESUS CHRIST

nat-u-ral (nætʃ–ə–rəl) adj. **1.** Determined by nature or birth: *natural ability* **2.** Of or relating to nature: *the natural mineral wealth of a country* **3.** Not artificial: *That's her natural hair color.*

natural n. Sbdy. well suited to a job and certain to succeed: *As a jockey, he's a natural.*

nat-u-ral gas (nætʃ–ə–rəl gæs) n. Gas suitable for burning, found underground or under the sea

nat-u-ral his-to-ry (nætʃ–ə–rəl hɪs–tə–riʸ) n. The study of plants, animals, and rocks

nat-u-ral-ist (nætʃ–ə–rəl–əst) n. A person who studies plants and animals, esp. in the field

nat-u-ral-ize (nætʃ–ə–rə–laɪz) v. -ized, -izing **1.** To confer the rights and privileges of a citizen on sbdy. from another country: *a naturalized citizen* **2.** To introduce animals or plants into a region and cause them to flourish there as if native to that place

—nat·u·ral·i·za·tion (næt∫–ə–rə–lə–ze^y–∫ən) n.

nat·u·ral·ly (næt∫–ə–rə–li^y / næt∫–ər–li^y) adv **1.** Of course: *Naturally, I didn't want to risk driving in a storm like that.* **2.** By nature: *He is naturally comical.* **3.** In a relaxed way: *Although he was very nervous, he behaved quite naturally.*

nat·u·ral re·sourc·es (næt∫–ə–rəl ri^y–sɔrs–əz/ –zɔrs–) n. *pl.* The land, forests, mineral wealth, etc., that a country possesses

nat·u·ral sci·ence (næt∫–ə–rəl saɪ–əns) n. Biology, chemistry, and physics —compare SOCIAL SCIENCE

nat·u·ral se·lec·tion (næt∫–ə–rəl sə–lɛk–∫ən) n. A process in nature resulting in the survival of only those forms of plant and animal life that have characteristics that enable them to adapt to their environment

na·ture (ne^y–t∫ər) n. **1.** Everything in the world that exists by nature, independently of human beings, such as earth and rocks, streams, the weather, plants and animals **2.** The basic qualities or characteristics of God, people, or animals: *God's invisible qualities — his eternal power and divine nature — have been clearly seen, being understood from what has been made (sun, moon, stars, earth, etc.) so that men are without excuse* (Romans 1:20). *On the other hand, all people are by nature sinful and unclean./ St. Paul wrote: "I know that nothing good lives in me, that is, in my sinful nature"* (Romans 7:18). *He also said, "Those who live according to the sinful nature have their minds set on what that nature desires." Those who live by the sinful nature cannot please God* (Romans 8:5,8). *Those who belong to Jesus Christ have crucified (put to death) the sinful nature with its passions and desires* (Galatians 5:24). **3.** Qualities that make one person different from another; character: *She has a very jealous nature.* **4.** A type; sort: *The meeting was very solemn in nature.* **5. second nature** A long-established habit that has become part of one's character: *Tom has been flying for so many years that it is second nature to him now.*

–natured (–ne^y–t∫ərd) comb. form Having the stated nature or personality: *good-natured*

naught (nɔt/ nɑt) n. Nothing: *His hopes came to naught when he learned of his terminal illness.*

naugh·ty (nɔt–i^y/ nɑt–) adj. -tier, -tiest **1.** Esp. of children, not nice, disobedient **2.** Sexually immoral

nau·se·a (nɔ–zi^y–ə/ nɔ–ʒə) n. **1.** Sickness of the stomach with a desire to vomit **2.** Extreme disgust

nau·se·ate (nɔ–zi^y–e^{y}t) v. -ated, -ating To feel sick, and like vomiting: *His disgusting behavior nauseated me.* —nau·se·ous (nɔ–zi^y–əs/ nɔ–∫əs) adj.

nau·ti·cal (nɔt–ɪ–kəl) adj. **1.** Concerning ships, sailors, and seamanship **2. nautical mile** A measurement of distance used at sea, equal to one-sixtieth of a degree at the earth's equator, or 1,853.24 meters or 6,076.103 feet

na·val (ne^y–vəl) adj. **1.** Of, involved in, or having a navy **2.** Of or pertaining to ships

nave (ne^{y}v) n. The long central part of a church

na·vel (ne^y–vəl) n. A depression in the middle of the abdomen which marks the point of attachment of the fetus to the mother

nav·i·ga·ble (næv–ɪ–gə–bəl) adj. Of water, deep and wide enough to allow ships to navigate safely —nav·i·ga·bil·i·ty (næv–ɪ–gə–bɪl–ət–i^y) n.

nav·i·gate (næv–ə–ge^{y}t) v. -gated, -gating To steer or direct the course of a ship or aircraft

nav·i·ga·tion (næv–ə–ge^y–∫ən) n. The act or practice of navigating

nav·i·ga·tor (næv–ə–ge^{y}t–ər) n. A person who navigates a ship or aircraft

na·vy (ne^y–vi^y) n. -vies **1.** A nation's fighting ships **2.** The men serving on these —see NAVAL

nay (ne^y) adv. **1.** A "no" vote **2. the nays** Those who vote "no"

near (nɪər) adj. Not far; close in time or distance: *In the near future we hope to move to Portland to be closer to our children.* —nearness n.

near adv. or prep. Not far from: *We live near a beautiful park.*

near v. To draw close: *He jumped into the boat as it neared the dock.*

near·by (nɪər–baɪ) adv. Not far away

—**nearby** adj.

near-ly (nɪər–li^y) adv. Almost: *It's nearly midnight.*

near-ness (nɪər–nəs) n. The state or condition of being near

near-sight-ed (nɪər–saɪt–əd) adj. Not able to see things that are far away as clearly as things that are near

neat (ni^yt) adj. **1.** Orderly and clean; tidy; showing care in appearance: *She keeps her room neat and tidy.* **2.** Clever and effective: *a neat trick* **3.** Very pleasant: *a really neat vacation* —**neatly** adv. —**neatness** n.

neb-u-la (**neb**–yə–lə) n. **-las** or **-lae** (–laɪ) Any of many vast cloud-like masses of gas or dust among the stars

neb-u-lous (neb–yə–ləs) adj. **1.** Confusedly hazy or vague **2.** Of or resembling a nebula or nebulae

nec-es-sar-i-ly (nɛs–ə–**sɛər**–ə–li^y) adv. Of necessity; as a necessary consequence; unavoidably: *Food that tastes good isn't necessarily good for you.*

nec-es-sary (**nɛs**–ə–sɛər–i^y) adj. **1.** Absolutely essential; sthg. one must have: *Water is necessary for life.* **2.** Required: *A passport is necessary in order to travel to another country.*

ne-ces-si-tate (nə–**sɛs**–ə–te^yt) v. To cause to be necessary

ne-ces-si-ty (nə–**sɛs**–ə–ti^y) n. **-ties 1.** Sthg. that is needed or necessary: *Food, water, and air are absolute necessities.* **2.** A requirement: *For this job, a knowledge of French is a necessity.*

neck (nɛk) n. **1.** The part of the body between the body and the head **2.** The part of an article of clothing that covers that part of the body: *The neck of this shirt is dirty.* **3.** Sthg. like a neck in shape or position: *the neck of a bottle* **4. stick one's neck out** *infml.* To take a risk **5. neck of the woods** *infml. esp. AmE.* An area of the country

neck-er-chief (nɛk–ər–tʃɪf/–tʃi^yf) n. **neckerchiefs** A cloth or scarf worn around the neck

neck-lace (**nɛk**–ləs) n. An ornamental chain or string of beads, pearls, precious stones, etc., or a chain of gold, silver, etc. worn around the neck

neck-tie (**nɛk**–taɪ) *AmE.* also **tie** n. A band of cloth worn around the neck and tied in a knot at the front

nec-ro-man-cy (**nɛk**–rə–mæn–si^y) n. The art or practice of communicating with the dead through use of magic in order to learn about the future, a practice which is strictly forbidden by God's Law which says, "Let no one be found among you who. . . practices divination or sorcery. . .or who consults the dead. Anyone who does these things is detestable to the Lord" (Deuteronomy 18:11). NOTE: God hates this and all sin, but he is also a God of love and mercy and forgiveness. If we truly repent of our sins and put our trust in Jesus Christ, we will have everlasting life. —see JESUS

nec-tar (**nɛk**–tər) n. **1.** A sweet liquid that bees collect from flowers to make honey **2.** A delicious drink

nec-tar-ine (nɛk–tə–**ri^yn**) n. A smooth-skinned variety of peach

née or **nee** (ne^y) adj. Born; used to state a woman's name before she was married: *Mrs. Betty Smith, nee Rogers*

need (ni^yd) n. **1.** Sthg. necessary that one must have: *Food, shelter, and clothing are basic needs./ St Paul wrote to the Christians saying, "My God will meet all your needs according to His glorious riches in Christ Jesus"* (Philippians 4:19). **2.** An obligation: *There's no need for you to pay me anything.* **3.** Sthg. required or wanted: *The hotel staff (workers) will attend to all your needs.* **4.** Poverty: *If anyone has material possessions and sees his brother in need, but has no pity on him, how can the love of God be in him.?* (1 John 3:17).

need v. To desire or require sthg. for a useful purpose; lack: *Babies need milk.*

nee-dle (**ni^yd**–əl) n. **1.** A long pointed piece of steel with an eye (hole) at one end for thread, used in sewing **2.** A longer piece of steel used in working with a threadlike piece of wool: *knitting needles* **3.** A similar object used for giving injections: *A hypodermic needle is hollow so that the substance injected can flow through it.* **4.** In a compass, the pointer which always points to the north **5.** The pointer in a gauge that indicates the amount of fuel, the speed, the altitude, etc.:

We have to stop soon and get some gas. The needle is almost on "empty." **6.** In a record player, the very small pointed jewel or piece of metal which picks up the sound recorded on a record; a stylus **7.** The thin, sharp-pointed leaf of a pine or fir tree

needle v. **-dled, -dling** *infml.* To repeatedly tease or annoy sbdy.: *The other kids were always needling Tommy about his being so fat.*

need-less (niᵞd–ləs) adj. Not needed, unnecessary

need-n't (niᵞd–ənt) A contraction of "need not"

need-y (niᵞ–diᵞ) n. Those who are in need; the poor: *The Lord hears the needy...* (Psalm 69:33). *Blessed is he who is kind to the needy* (Proverbs 14:21). —**needy** adj.

ne-far-i-ous (nɪ–fɛər–iᵞ–əs) adj. Extremely wicked

neg-a-tive (neg–ə–tɪv) adj. **1.** Saying or meaning "no" —opposite AFFIRMATIVE **2.** Expecting to fail: *a negative attitude* **3.** Not indicating the presence of a particular disease, organism, etc.: *The test for bacteria was negative."* (=none were found)

negative n. **1.** A word, statement, or expression meaning "no": *The answer to my question was in the negative.* **2.** A photograph image on transparent film showing naturally dark areas as light, and light areas as dark —opposite POSITIVE —**negatively** adv.

neg-lect (nɪ–glɛkt) v. **1.** To fail to give proper attention to: *He neglected his wife and his children because of his work.* **2.** To fail to do sthg. because of indifference or forgetfulness or carelessness: *He neglected to lock the door when he left home for the weekend.* —**neglectful** adj.

neg-li-gee (neg–lə–ʒeᵞ / neg–lə–ʒeᵞ) n. A woman's light, flimsy dressing gown

neg-li-gence (neg–lɪ–dʒəns) n. Carelessness: *The driver's negligence was the cause of a tragic accident.*

neg-li-gent (neg–lɪ–dʒənt) adj. Careless —**negligently** adv.

neg-li-gi-ble (neg–lɪ–dʒə–bəl) adj. Very small; not worth mentioning; unimportant: *The damage from the accident was negligible.*

ne-go-ti-a-ble (nɪ–goᵂ–ʃiᵞ–ə–bəl) adj. **1.** That

which can be settled or changed by negotiation **2.** That which can be exchanged for money **3.** Capable of being negotiated: *This road is not negotiable (not passable) during the rainy season.*

ne-go-ti-ate (nɪ–goᵂ–ʃiᵞ–eᵞt) v. **-ated, -ating 1.** To talk to another person or group in order to reach an agreement **2.** To arrange by conferring: *They negotiated a contract.* **3.** To go safely through, around, over, etc.: *The car failed to negotiate the curve and crashed into a tree.* —**ne-go-ti-a-tion** (nɪ–goᵂ–ʃiᵞ–eᵞ–ʃən) n.

Ne-gro (niᵞ–groᵂ) n. **-groes** A member of the black race of mankind, distinguished from other races by characteristic physical features —**Negro** adj.

Ne-groid (niᵞ–grɔɪd) adj. Of, pertaining to, or belonging to a major ethnic division of mankind characterized by skin color ranging from brown to almost black, and having distinctive physical features

Ne-he-mi-ah (niᵞ–hə–maɪ–ə) n. A book of the Old Testament attributed to the 5th century B.C. Hebrew statesman, Nehemiah —see BIBLE

neigh (neᵞ) n. The long, high-pitched sound made by a horse —**neigh** v.

neigh-bor (neᵞ–bər) n. **1.** A person who lives near or next to another: *my next-door neighbor* **2.** Often used in speaking of the bordering country: *Mexico is a neighbor of the US.* **3.** Anyone who is kind to someone else can be said to be a good neighbor: *Love your neighbor as yourself. Love does no harm to its neighbor. Therefore love is the fulfillment of the law* (Romans 13:9,10).

neigh-bor-hood (neᵞ–bər–hʊd) n. **1.** A small area with distinctive characteristics: *the quietest neighborhood in town* **2.** Vicinity: *I lost my wallet somewhere in this neighborhood.* **3.** An approximate amount: *The temperature is somewhere in the neighborhood of 95 degrees Fahrenheit.*

neigh-bor-ing (neᵞ–bə–rɪŋ) adj. Near or close by: *Los Angeles and Hollywood are neighboring cities.*

neigh-bor-ly (neᵞ–bər–liᵞ) adj. Friendly, like a good neighbor

nei-ther (niᵞ–ðər / naɪ–ðər) pron. Not either;

not one or the other: *Neither of the two roads is very good.*

neither conj. **1.** Used with **nor** to mark two negative alternatives: *They had neither seen us nor heard of us.* **2.** Nor: *He doesn't have a car and neither do I (=nor do I).*

nem-e-sis (nɛm–ə–səs) n. **-ses** (–siʸz) **1.** A strong and stubborn opponent **2.** An instrument of vengeance **3.** Punishment that is sure to follow wrongdoing

ne-o- (niʸ–oʷ–) prefix New; recent

ne-on (niʸ–ɑn) n. A gaseous, colorless chemical used in electric lamps —**neon** adj. *a neon sign*

ne-o-phyte (niʸ–ə–faɪt) n. **1.** A recent convert **2.** Any beginner

neph-ew (nɛf–yuʷ) n. A son of a brother or sister, brother-in-law, or sister-in-law —compare NIECE

nep-o-tism (nɛp–ə–tɪz–əm) n. Favoritism shown on the basis of family relationship, as in business or politics

Nep-tune (nɛp–tuʷn) n. The fourth largest planet in our solar system and eighth farthest from the sun

nerve (nɑrv) n. **1.** Any of the cords that carry messages between all parts of the body and the brain: *He is in great pain because of a pinched nerve.* **2.** Courage: *He didn't have the nerve to jump.* **3.** *derog.* Rudeness: *She had a lot of nerve telling me to lose weight when she is at least 50 pounds overweight herself.*

nerves pl. The condition of being too easily excited or upset: *She's a bundle of nerves. She needs a lot of pills to calm her nerves.*

nerve–rack-ing (nɑrv–ræk–ɪŋ) adj. Extremely disturbing or frightening: *Driving on that narrow, winding mountain road in the rain was nerve-racking.*

ner-vous (nɛr–vəs) adj. **1.** Of or related to the nervous system: *a nervous disorder* **2.** Afraid; worried: *My mother is too nervous to drive a car.* —**nervousness** n.

–ness (–nəs) suffix (of nouns) State or quality of being: *goodness*

nest (nɛst) n. **1.** A structure of twigs, grass, mud, etc. formed by a bird as a place to lay eggs and rear its young **2.** The home of certain other animals or insects **3.** A warm and comfortable place

nest v. **1.** To build or occupy a nest **2.** To fit compactly together or within one another

nest egg (nɛst ɛg) n. A large amount of money put aside for future use

nes-tle (nɛs–əl) v. **-tled, -tling 1.** To lie snugly or comfortably: *The village was nestled among the hills.* **2.** To press closely and affectionately: *She nestled her head on her father's shoulder.*

net (nɛt) n. **1.** A loose, open fabric made of string, cord, thread or finer material, knotted together, used for catching fish, birds, butterflies, etc. **2.** Any fabric made like this: *A hair net is sometimes used to keep the hair in place.* **3.** An open fabric made of cord, strung between two posts to divide the two halves of a volleyball, tennis, or badminton court **4.** An enclosure at the back of the goal in soccer, hockey, etc.

net v. **-tt- 1.** To catch, as in a net: *They netted 153 fish.* **2.** To gain as a profit: *The sale netted a huge profit for the company.* —compare GROSS

net also **nett** adj. **1.** The amount of money remaining after all expenses have been paid **2.** The weight of sthg., not including the weight of the container —compare GROSS

neth-er (nɛð–ər) adj. Lower or under

net-tle (nɛt–əl) n. A type of plant having hairs that sting sharply

net-tle v. **-tled, -tling** To make angry; to provoke

net-work (nɛt–wərk) n. **1.** A large system of roads, railroads, lines, etc. that cross or meet one another: *a vast network of interstate highways* **2.** *fig.* A widespread association: *a network of business associates throughout the country* **3.** A group of radio or television stations in different places using many of the same broadcasts: *the ABC radio network*

neu-ral (nʊr–əl) adj. Of or related to the nervous system

neu-ral-gia (nʊ–ræl–dʒə) n. Acute pain that follows the course of a nerve —**neuralgic** adj.

neu-ri-tis (nʊ–raɪt–əs) n. pl. **-ritises** or **-ri-ti-des** (–rɪt–ə–diʸz) Inflammation of a nerve —**neurit-ic** (nʊ–rɪt–ɪk) adj.

neu-rol-o-gy (nʊ–rɑl–ə–dʒiʸ) n. The scientific

study of the nervous system —neu-ro-log-i-
cal (ⁿⁱ ᵃ **lədn** ɪ-kɔl) adj. —**neurologically**
adv. —**neu-rol-o-gist** (nʊ-**ral**-ə-dʒəst) n.

neu-ron (nʊ-ran) n. A nerve cell with all its
processes

neu-ro-sis (nʊ-roʷ-səs) n. -**ses** (-siʸz) A functional nervous disorder, marked by strong
unreasonable fears and ideas about the outside world

neu-rot-ic (nʊ-**rat**-ɪk) adj. Of, related to, or affected by neurosis

neu-ter (**nuʷ**-tər) adj. **1.** In some languages, of
the gender that is neither masculine or feminine: *In German, "das buch" (the book) is neuter.* **2.** Without sex

neuter v. To make an animal unable to father
or to bear any young: *The cat has been neu-
tered.*

neu-tral (**nuʷ**-trəl) adj. **1.** Not taking sides in a
quarrel or war: *Switzerland was neutral in
both World Wars.* **2.** Of color, not strong or
definite: *Gray and beige are neutral colors.*

neu-tral-i-ty (nuʷ-**træl**-ə-tiʸ) n. -**ties** The state
of being neutral, esp. in time of war

neu-tral-ize (**nuʷ**-trəl-aɪz) v. -**ized, -izing** To
cause or to have no effect: *Higher costs of living and higher taxes have neutralized our increase in wages.* —**neu-tral-i-za-tion** n. (nuʷ-
trə-lə-zeʸ-ʃən)

neu-tron (**nuʷ**-tran) n. A small particle in the
nucleus of any atom except one of hydro-
gen. It has an electric charge and is a little
larger than a proton.

nev-er (**nɛv**-ər) adv. Not ever: *Keep yourselves
free from the love of money and be content with
what you have, because God has said, "Never
will I leave you; never will I forsake you"* (Hebrews 13:5).

nev-er-the-less (nɛv-ər-ðə-**lɛs**) adv. In spite
of that: *It may rain before the game begins; nevertheless we're going.*

new (nuʷ) adj. **1.** Not old; recent: *We have a
new address.* **2.** Only recently found: *the discovery of a new island* **3.** Having been in the
stated position only a short time: *If anyone is
in Christ (has faith in him as Savior), he is a
new creation; the old has gone, the new has
come!* (2 Corinthians 5:17). **4.** Different: *to
learn a new language* **5.** Just beginning to be

used, etc.; fresh: *They've gone to California to
start a new life.*

New Age Movement (nuʷ ᵉʸdʒ mmʷv-mənt) n.
A loosely knit group of individuals and organizations that fundamentally believe that
persons will all evolve into God and
achieve a global unity that will transcend
religious, racial, cultural, and political ide-
ologies. It is a "conscious revolution" that is
preparing people to recognize and receive
the coming world ruler, whom the Bible
calls the Antichrist. New Agers believe in
the oneness of all life and in themselves as a
part of the Universal Self or Consciousness.
The "god" of the New Age Movement is
the pantheistic god of ancient paganism.
Like Hinduism, the New Age Movement
claims to embrace all beliefs, all reli-gions,
on the premise that all is one, but its basic
underlying philosophy represents a carefully calculated undermining of Christian
beliefs. The New Age Movement fits the
description of the Antichrist's religion — a
rejection of the God of the Bible and the
declaration that self is God. New Agers reject the Biblical teaching of salvation by
God's grace through faith in Jesus Christ
who paid for all of our sins by his suffering
and death on the cross (Ephesians 2:8,9;
John 3:16; Romans 6:23). They believe that
salvation is earned and that reincarnation is
a vital part of the process of salvation. Astrology, which claims that one's personality
and destiny depend on the date and location of his or her birth in relation to certain
heavenly bodies, also plays an important
role in the New Age beliefs. —see GOD, JE-
SUS CHRIST, ASTROLOGY, REINCAR-
NATION, ANTICHRIST

new-born (nuʷ-bɔrn) adj. **1.** Just recently born
2. Renewed: *newborn zeal and determination*

new-com-er (nuʷ-kəm-ər) n. One who has recently arrived in a place: *a newcomer to the
city*

new-fan-gled (nuʷ-**fæŋ**-gəld) adj. Something
new that is not regarded as good

new-ly (**nuʷ**-liʸ) adv. Recently: *a newly established business*

new-ly-wed (nuʷ-liʸ-wɛd) n. *usu. pl.* A man or

woman very recently married —**newlywed** adj.

news (nu^wz) n. **1.** Current events, esp. those reported in newspapers and on radio and television **2.** Any new information: *That's news to me. This is the first I've heard of it.*

news-cast (nu^wz–kæst) n. A radio or TV program that broadcasts the news

news-pa-per (nu^wz–pe^y–pər) n. A paper printed and sold, usu. daily or weekly, with news, advertisements, etc.

New Test-a-ment (nu^w tɛs–tə–mənt) n. The part of the Bible that tells about the life, death, resurrection, and ascension into heaven of our Lord and Savior Jesus Christ — and of his promised return. It was written by eyewitnesses who were so convinced that Jesus was all that he claimed to be — true God and Savior of the world — that they endured all kinds of hardship and persecution and laid down their lives proclaiming the good news about Jesus. One of the writers of the New Testament, the Apostle John, referring to his own writings said, "These (things) are written that you may believe that Jesus is the Christ, the Son of God, and that by believing you may have life in his name" (John 20:31). —see JESUS

New World (nu^w wɜrld) n. North, Central, and South America; the Western Hemisphere

New Year's Day n. (nu^w yɪərz de^y) In Western countries, January 1st

New Year's Eve n. (nu^w yɪərz i^yv) In Western countries, Dec. 31st

next (nɛkst) adj. **1.** Immediately following or preceding; nearest; with nothing coming between: *"O" is the next letter after "N."* **2.** Closest in space or position: *Tom sits next to Bob in class, just across the aisle.*

next adv. **1.** Just afterwards: *What will they think of next?* **2.** The first after someone or sthg. else: *He was next in line at the grocery store.* **3. next to (a)** Close beside: *He is sitting next to Ann.* **(b)** Almost: *He earns next to nothing.*

next of kin (nɛkst əv kɪn) n. The person most closely related to someone

nib (nɪb) n. **1.** The bill or beak of a bird **2.** Originally, the sharpened end of a quill pen **3.** The projecting end of anything; point

nib-ble (nɪb–əl) v. -bled, -bling **1.** To bite gently and repeatedly **2.** To take small or hesitant bites: *He doesn't eat much; but he nibbles a lot.* —**nibbler** n.

nice (naɪs) adj. **nicer, nicest** Good; pleasant: *How nice to see you again!/ It's nice to be important, but it's more important to be nice.* —**niceness** n.

nice-ly (naɪs–li^y) adv. Very well: *Mother is doing nicely after her operation.*

niche (nɪtʃ) n. **1.** A recess in a wall for a statue or other decorative object **2. find a niche for oneself** To find a job, position, or activity specially suited to one's abilities or character

nick (nɪk) n. **1.** A small accidental cut **2. in the nick of time** Just barely in time: *We got to the station just in the nick of time to catch the train.*

nick v. To make or cut a nick in: *We nicked the new table when moving it through the narrow doorway.*

nick-el (nɪk–əl) n. **1.** A hard silver-white metal that is a simple substance (ELEMENT) and is used in the production of alloys **2.** In the US and Canada, a five-cent piece made of copper and nickel

nick-name (nɪk–ne^ym) n. A name used informally instead of someone's real name: *General Eisenhower's nickname was "Ike."*

nickname v. -**named, -naming** To give someone a nickname

nic-o-tine (nɪk–ə–ti^yn) n. A poisonous chemical found in tobacco

niece (ni^ys) n. The daughter of one's brother or sister, brother-in-law or sister-in-law —compare NEPHEW

nif-ty (nɪf–ti^y) adj. -**tier, -tiest** *infml.* Very good; stylish; clever

nig-gard (nɪg–ərd) n. A very stingy person —**niggardly** adj.

nigh (naɪ) adj., adv., prep. Near

night (naɪt) n. **1.** The period from sunset to sunrise, esp. the dark hours: *God made... the sun to govern the day... the moon and stars to govern the night* (Psalm 136:7-9). **2.** A period of misery and gloom **3.** Spiritual darkness: *Jesus said, "The night is coming when no one can work"* (John 9:4).

night-gown (naɪt–gaʊn) n. A woman's loose fitting garment, made to be worn in bed. NOTE: Do not confuse *nightgown* with *evening gown* which may be worn to a party, banquet, etc.

night-in-gale (naɪt–ən–geᵞl) n. A small, migratory bird, noted for its melodious songs, esp. at night

night-ly (naɪt–liᵞ) adj. Taking place, done, or used every night

night-mare (naɪt–mɛər) n. A terrible, frightening dream: *fig. Driving through that snowstorm was a nightmare.*

night-mar-ish (naɪt–mɛər–ɪʃ) adj. Very frightening: *a nightmarish experience*

ni-hil-ism (naɪ–ə–lɪz–əm) n. 1. Total rejection of moral judgments or value statements 2. Absolute destructiveness of the world at large and of oneself

nil (nɪl) n. Nothing; zero

nim-ble (nɪm–bəl) adj. -bler, -blest Agile; able to move quickly —nimbleness n. —nimbly adv.

nim-bus (nɪm–bəs) n. A formless, dark-gray cloud layer

nin-com-poop (nɪn–kəm–puʷp) n. A foolish or stupid person

nine (naɪn) determ., n., pron., adj. The number between eight and ten; the number 9

nine-teen (naɪn–tiᵞn) n. determ., pron. The number 19

nine-teenth (naɪn–tiᵞnθ) determ., n., adv. pron. The last of 19 things; 19th

nine-ti-eth (naɪn–tiᵞ–əθ) determ., adj., n. pron. The last of 90 things; 90th

nine-ty (naɪn–tiᵞ) determ., n. or pron. -ties The number 90

nin-ny (nɪn–iᵞ) n. A fool

ninth (naɪnθ) determ., n., pron., adv. The last of nine (persons, things, etc.): *He was ninth in line.*

nip (nɪp) v. -pp- 1. To seize and pinch or bite: *The dog nipped the thief's leg.* 2. **nip in the bud** To prevent sthg. at an early stage of its development, so as to keep from succeeding

nip (nɪp) n. 1. A sharp coldness in the weather: *There's a nip in the air this morning; winter is coming.* 2. A sip of liquor: *a nip of brandy*

nip-ple (nɪp–əl) n. 1. The pointed part of the breast from which a baby may suck milk 2. *AmE.* The piece of rubber shaped like this on the baby's bottle

nip-py (nɪp–iᵞ) adj. -pier, -piest Chilly: *a nippy winter morning*

nir-va-na (nɪər–vɑn–ə) n. In Hindu and Buddhist teaching, the state of perfect bliss obtained when the soul is freed from all suffering and absorbed into the supreme spirit

nit-pick-ing (nɪt–pɪk–ɪŋ) adj. Paying too much attention to minor details —nit-pick v.

ni-trate (naɪ–treᵞt) n. Any of several substances formed from nitric acid, often used as fertilizer: *Sodium nitrate and potassium nitrate are used as fertilizers.*

nit-ric ac-id (naɪ–trɪk æs–əd) n. A corrosive liquid containing nitrogen, used in making dyes, explosives, and fertilizers

ni-tro-gen (naɪ–trə–dʒən) n. A gas that is a simple substance (ELEMENT), without color or smell that forms about four-fifths of the earth's air, used in the manufacture of ammonia, nitric acid, etc.

ni-tro-glyc-er-in, -ine (naɪ–trə–glɪs–ə–rən) n. A powerful liquid explosive used in making dynamite and in medicine

nit-wit (nɪt–wɪt) n. A silly, stupid person

no (noʷ) determ., adv. Not so; used to express refusal, denial, or disagreement: *No, it's not raining.* —opposite YES

no adj. 1. Not at all: *He's no expert.* 2. Not any: *There's no coffee in the jar.* 3. Hardly any: *in no time*

no n. nos or noes A negative vote

No. Written *abbr.*, said as 1. north; northern 2. Also **no.** *pl.* nos. Said as number/s

No-ah (noʷ–ə) n. The righteous patriarch who built the ark (vessel) in which he and his family (eight people) and animals of every species survived the great flood that covered the entire earth because of the wickedness of mankind, the ark coming to rest near the top of Mt. Ararat (Genesis 6-9)

no-bil-i-ty (noʷ–bɪl–ət–iᵞ) n. 1. In some countries, dukes and earls; people of the highest social class 2. The quality or state of being noble

no-ble (noʷ–bəl) adj. -bler, -blest 1. Of high moral quality; deserving praise; honorable;

unselfish: *A wife of noble character is her husband's crown* (Proverbs 12:4). *Whatever is true, whatever is noble..., think about such things* (Philippians 4:8). —opposite IGNOBLE 2. Of or belonging to a high titled rank: *a man of noble birth*

no·ble·man (no^w–bəl–mən) -men n. A man of noble birth, position, or title

no·ble·wo·man (no^w–bəl–wʊm–ən) -wom-en (–wɪm–ən) n. A woman of noble birth, position, or title

no·bly (no^w–bli^y) adv. In a way deserving of praise: *He worked nobly for the cause of justice.*

no·bod·y (no^w–bəd–i^y) n., pron. -ies 1. No person; no one; not anybody: *There's nobody home.* 2. A person of no importance: *He says he wants to be important. He's tired of being a nobody.*

noc·tur·nal (nɑk–tɜrn–əl) adj. 1. Of or in the night 2. Active in the night: *nocturnal animals*

noc·turne (nɑk–tɜrn) n. A work of art dealing with night, esp. a dreamy musical composition

noc·u·ous (nɑk–yə–wəs) adj. Likely to cause injury; harmful

nod (nɑd) v. To bend one's head forward and down to show agreement or from drowsiness: *She nodded her head in agreement with the plan./ John nodded off (to sleep) momentarily and didn't hear what was said.* —nod n. *fig.* We waited for Bob to give his nod of approval.

node (no^{w}d) n. 1. A knot, knob, or swelling 2. That part, or joint, of a stem from which a leaf starts to grow

nod·ule (nɑdʒ–u^{w}l) n. 1. A small knot or irregular, rounded lump 2. A small knot or joint on a stem or root

noise (nɔɪz) n. Unwanted sound: *There's so much noise outside, I can hardly hear you.*

noise·less (nɔɪz–ləs) adj. With little or no noise; very quiet —noiselessly adv.

nois·y (nɔɪ–zi^y) adj. -ier, -iest 1. Making noise: *a noisy car* 2. Full of noise: *a noisy street* —nois-i-ly (nɔɪ–zə–li^y) adv.

no·mad (no^w–mæd) n. A member of a group of people who have no permanent home and move from place to place, esp. to find grass for their animals —no-mad-ic (no^w–mæd–ɪk) adj.

no·men·cla·ture (no^w–mən–kle^y–tʃər) n. A system of naming things, esp. in art or science

nom·i·nal (nɑm–ən–əl) adj. 1. In name only; not in reality: *He is only a nominal member of the church. He seldom attends a church service.* 2. Regarding an amount of money, very small; insignificant; negligible: *It was sold at a nominal price.* —nominally adv.

nom·i·nate (nɑm–ə–ne^{y}t) v. -nated, -nating To suggest or name someone for possible election to a specific office or position: *I nominated Mary Smith for secretary.* —nominator n.

nom·i·na·tion (nɑm–ə–ne^y–ʃən) n. The act or result of nominating or being nominated: *Who will get the nomination for governor?*

nom·i·na·tive (nɑm–ə–nə–tɪv) adj. Of, relating to, or belonging to the grammatical case that usu. indicates the subject of a verb —nominative case n.

nom·i·nee (nɑm–ə–ni^y) n. A person who has been nominated

non– (nɑn–) prefix Used with many words to change their meanings to the opposite, as in **nonexistent, nonfat, nonfiction, nonstop,** etc. NOTE: In forming compounds, *non-* is normally joined to the following element without a space or hyphen. However, if the second element begins with a capital letter, it is separated with a hyphen: *non-English*

non·ab·sor·bent (nɑn–əb–zɔr–bənt) adj. Not absorbent

non·cha·lant (nɑn–ʃə–lɑnt) adj. Calm and showing little or no interest —nonchalance n. —nonchalantly adv.

non·com·mit·tal (nɑn–kə–mɪt–əl) adj. 1. Not revealing one's opinion or purpose 2. Unwilling to commit oneself

non·com·mu·ni·ca·ble (nɑn–kə–myu^w–nɪ–kə–bəl) adj. Not communicable

non·con·form·ist (nɑn–kən–fɔr–məst) n. One who does not conform to accepted customs, beliefs, or practices —nonconformity n.

non·con·ta·gious (nɑn–kən–te^y–dʒəs) adj. Not contagious

non·de·script (nɑn–dɪ–skrɪpt) adj. Difficult to describe; of no special class

none (nʌn) pron. Not any; not one

non-ef-fec-tive (nɑn-ɪ-fɛk-tɪv) adj. Not effective

none-the-less (nən-ðə-lɛs) adv. In spite of that; nevertheless

non-fic-tion (nɑn-fɪk-ʃən) n. Literary works other than fiction

non-plus (nɑn-plʌs) v. -plused or -plussed, -plusing or -plussing To bewilder; perplex

non-poi-son-ous (nɑn-pɔɪz-nəs/ –ən-əs) adj. Not poisonous

non-sense (nɑn-sɛns) n. Foolishness; foolish words, actions, etc. —**non-sen-si-cal** (nɑn-sɛn-sɪ-kəl) adj.

non se-qui-tur (nɑn sɛk-wət-ər) n. A statement that does not follow logically from what preceded it

noo-dle (nuʷd-əl) n. usu. pl. A long thin strip made from a flour, water, and egg paste, boiled until soft and eaten in soups, with meat, etc.

nook (nʊk) n. **1.** A small corner, esp. in a room: a breakfast nook next to the kitchen or in one corner of the kitchen **2.** A sheltered and secluded (private) place: a shady nook in a garden

noon (nuʷn) n. Midday; 12 o'clock in the daytime

no one (noʷ wən) n., pron. Nobody

noose (nuʷs) n. A ring formed in a rope which, by means of a slipknot, closes more tightly as it is pulled

nor (nɔr) conj. And not; likewise not: Neither you nor anyone else can do it.

norm (nɔrm) n. A standard, model, or pattern for a group

nor-mal (nɔr-məl) adj. **1.** Average; usual; that which is expected: The temperature has been above normal this summer. **2.** Of average intelligence and development **3.** Free from any physical or emotional disorder —**normalcy** n.

nor-mal-ize (nɔr-mə-laɪz) v. -ized, -izing To make normal, esp. in relations between countries; to once again have friendly relations: The two countries tried to normalize relations after the war. —**nor-mal-i-za-tion** (nɔr-mə-lə-zeʸ-ʃən) n.

nor-mal-ly (nɔr-mə-liʸ) adv. **1.** In the usual way: She was behaving normally despite her crushing defeat. **2.** Ordinarily: I normally get up at dawn, but I slept late this morning.

north (nɔrθ) n. The direction to the left of someone facing the rising sun

north adj. **1.** Toward or at the north: the north door **2.** Of a wind, coming from this direction: a cold north wind

north adv. Towards the north: Niger is north of Nigeria. —**north-ern** (nɔr-ðərn) adj. Kano is in northern Nigeria.

north-east (nɔrθ-iʸst) adj. **1.** The point on the compass which is half way between north and east: Cairo is in the northeastern part of Egypt. **2.** Of a wind, coming from this direction —**north-easterly** adv. traveling in a northeasterly direction —**northeastern** adj.

north-er-ly (nɔr-ðər-liʸ) adv. Toward the north: The plane was flying in a northerly direction.

north-ern-er (nɔr-ðər-nər) n. Someone who lives in the north or was born and raised in the north

north-ern-most (nɔr-ðərn-moʷst) adj. Farthest north

North Pole (nɔrθ-poʷl) n. The northernmost point on the earth's surface

north-ward (nɔrθ-wərd) adj. Towards the north —**northward** adv.

north-west (nɔrθ-wɛst) n. The direction midway between north and west

northwest adj. **1.** Toward or at the northwest **2.** Of a wind, coming from this direction —**northwest** adv. flying northwest —**northwestern** adj. Morocco is in the northwestern part of Africa. —**northwesterly** adj.

nose (noʷz) n. **1.** The part of the face above the mouth which is the organ of smell and through which air is breathed **2.** infml. This organ regarded as having the ability to perceive or discover things as if by the sense of smell: He has a nose for news./ Stop poking your nose into other people's business! **3.** Sthg. resembling a nose, as the forward end of an airplane

nose v. nosed, nosing **1.** To move ahead slowly or carefully: He nosed the car slowly into the traffic. **2.** infml. To try to find out sthg., esp. sthg. that does not concern oneself; to search: I found her nosing around in

my desk.

nose cone (no^wz ko^wn) n. The front end of a rocket or missile

nose-dive (no^wz–daɪv) v. **-dived, -diving** (Of an aircraft) **1.** To fall suddenly with the nose pointing straight down **2.** *fig.* To fall sharply: *Sales have nosedived this year.*

nos-tal-gia (nɑ– stæl–dʒə) n. A longing for sthg. in the past: *He was filled with nostalgia when he heard his favorite old songs.* —**nostalgic** adj.

nos-tril (nɑs–trəl) n. Either of the two external openings at the end of the nose, through which one breathes

nos-y, nos-ey (no^w–zi^y) adj. Prying; taking too much interest in other people's affairs: *I wouldn't want her working for me; she's too nosey.*

not (nɑt) adv. **1.** In no way; to no degree: *I'm not hungry.* **2.** Used in place of a whole expression: *Will it snow? I hope not.* (=I hope it won't snow.) **3. not at all** (an answer when someone thanks you for sthg.) You're welcome: *Thanks for the ride. Not at all. It was my pleasure.*

no-ta-ble (no^wt–ə–bəl) adj. Remarkable; worthy of notice: *a notable achievement*

notable n. A person of distinction

no-ta-bly (no^wt–ə–bli^y) adv. Noticeably; especially; particularly: *Many of the board members were absent, notably the treasurer.*

no-ta-rize (no^wt–ə–raɪz) v. **-rized, -rizing** To acknowledge and make legally authentic as a notary public

no-ta-ry (no^wt–ə–ri^y) *also* **notary public** (no^wt–ə–ri^y pʌb–lɪk) n. A person with legal power to witness the signing of written statements and make them official

no-ta-tion (no^w–te^y–ʃən) n. **1.** Annotation; note **2.** A system of signs or symbols that represent numbers, musical notes, etc.

notch (nɑtʃ) n. **1.** A V-shaped cut in a surface or edge: *He cut a notch in the tree with an axe.* **2.** *infml.* A degree: *He's a notch above the rest in his class.*

notch v. **1.** To make a notch in **2.** *infml.* To record a victory: *Our team notched (up) its tenth consecutive victory.*

note (no^wt) v. **noted, noting** To take notice; to

pay attention and remember: *Please note that this library book must be returned tomorrow.*

note n. **1.** A written record or reminder: *She takes good notes in class.* **2.** A short letter, usu. informal: *She left a note for her husband when she went to the store.* **3.** A written sign representing a single musical sound of a particular degree of highness or lowness: *He can't sing the high notes.* **4.** A quality of voice: *There was a note of anger in her voice.* **5.** A promise to pay money: *a promissory note* **6. of note** *fml.* Famous: *an actor of some note*

note-book (no^wt–bʊk) n. A small book with blank pages in which to make notes

not-ed (no^wt–əd) adj. Famous: *a noted author*

note-wor-thy (no^wt–wɜr–ði^y) adj. Remarkable

noth-ing (nʌθ–ɪŋ) pron. **1.** Not anything; no thing: *Ah Sovereign Lord,... Nothing is too hard for you* (Jeremiah 32:17). **2.** Sthg. unimportant: *She means nothing to me.*

nothing n. A person or thing that has no value: *Her husband is a real nothing; he hasn't worked a day in his life.*

no-tice (no^wt–əs) n. **1.** An announcement made or shown publicly: *He placed the notice on the bulletin board.* **2.** Attention: *He took no notice of her.* **3.** A review; a statement of opinion, esp. in a newspaper, regarding a new play, movie, book, etc.: *The new stage show got favorable notices in the newspapers.*

notice v. **-ticed, -ticing** To be aware of, esp. by seeing: *He noticed that she was wearing a new dress.*

no-tice-a-ble (no^wt–ə–sə–bəl) adj. Sthg. that can be noticed or observed: *a noticeable drop in the temperature* —**noticeably** adv. *Bob was noticeably saddened by the news.*

no-ti-fi-a-ble (no^wt–ə–faɪ–ə–bəl) adj. That must be reported to health authorities

no-ti-fy (no^wt–ə–faɪ) v. **-fied, -fying** To give notice formally: *The police notified the Smiths of their son's accident.* —**no-ti-fi-ca-tion** (no^wt–ə–fə–ke^y–ʃən) n.

no-tion (no^w–ʃən) n. **1.** A sudden idea: *She had a notion to sing.* **2.** A picture in the mind of what sthg. is or what it looks like or how it works, etc. **3. notions** Small, useful items such as needles, pins, thread, buttons, etc.

no-to-ri-e-ty (no^wt–ə–raɪ–ət–i^y) n. **-ties** The

state of being notorious

no-to-ri-ous (no^w-tor-i^y-əs) adj. *derog.* Widely known and disapproved of or deplored. *a notorious pornographer*

not-with-stand-ing (nɑt–wɪθ–stæn–dɪŋ) prep. In spite of

nought (nɔt/ nɑt) adj. *variation of* naught Nothing

nought n. In British English, **nought** is commonly used when referring to the figure 0 as a part of a number: *Ten thousand is a 1 followed by four noughts.*

noun (naʊn) n. A word that is the name of a person, place, thing, quality, action, etc., and can be used as the subject or object of a verb: *Nouns are marked "n." in this dictionary.*

nour-ish (nɜr–ɪʃ) v. **1.** To feed; to cause to stay alive or grow by giving food, water, etc. **2.** *fig. The lips of the righteous nourish many* (Proverbs 10:21).

nour-ish-ing (nɜr–ɪʃ–ɪŋ) adj. Giving the body what is necessary for good health and growth

nour-ish-ment (nɜr–ɪʃ–mənt) n. Sthg. that nourishes; food

no-va (no^w–və) n. A star that suddenly becomes much brighter for a short time

nov-el (nɑv–əl) n. A long written story dealing with people and events: *"Ben Hur" was a great novel.*

novel adj. New; not like anything known before: *a novel idea*

nov-el-ist (nɑv–ə–lɪst) n. A writer of novels

nov-el-ty (nɑv–əl–ti^y) n. -ties **1.** The state or quality of being novel **2.** Sthg. unusual: *She hardly ever goes to a ball game, so it was a novelty for her to go to the game with me last night.* **3.** A small, cheap, manufactured article

No-vem-ber (no^w–vem–bər) n. *abbr.* **Nov.** The 11th month of the year

nov-ice (nɑv–ɪs) n. A beginner; a person who is inexperienced and untrained

now (naʊ) adv. **1.** At this time; at present: *Now is the time of God's favor, now is the day of salvation* (2 Corinthians 6:2). **2. now that** conj. Because, since: *I can go out, now that it has stopped raining.* **3. now and then** Sometimes

now-a-days (naʊ-ə-de^{y}z) adv. At the present time, in contrast with the past

no-where (no^w–weər/ –hweər) adv. Not anywhere: *My keys were nowhere to be found.*

nox-ious (nɑk [ʃəs) adj. Harmful; poisonous

noz-zle (nɑz–əl) n. A spout fitted to the end of a hose, e.g., to direct and control the stream of liquid or gas coming out

NT *Abbr. for* **New Testament** of the Bible

nth (enθ) adj. **1.** The latest in a long se-ries: *For the nth time, you can't go out tonight.* **2. to the nth degree** In a very extreme way: *She's fussy to the nth degree.*

nu-ance (nu^w–ɑns/nyu^w–ɑns/nu^w–ɑns) n. A subtle difference in meaning, feeling, etc.

nub (nʌb) n. **1.** The central point of a problem or matter **2.** A small lump or projection

nu-cle-ar (nu^w–kli^y–ər) adj. **1.** Of, concerning, or being a nucleus: *A father, mother, and children make up a nuclear family.* **2.** Of, relating to, or using the nucleus of an atom: *nuclear energy*

nu-cle-us (nu^w–kli^y–əs) n. *pl.* nu-cle-i (nu^w–kli^y–aɪ) also **nucleuses 1.** The central part around which sthg. collects or from which sthg. grows; core: *These 500 books are the nucleus of a new library.* **2.** The part of a plant or animal cell that controls its development **3.** The central part of an atom, comprising almost all the atomic mass

nude (nu^{w}d/ nyu^{w}d) adj. Bare, naked, unclothed —**nude** n.

nudge (nʌdʒ) v. **nudged, nudging** To touch or push with, esp. with the elbow, often to get attention

nud-ism (nu^{w}d–ɪz–əm) n. The practice of going nude, esp. in mixed groups, at special secluded places —**nudist** n.

nu-di-ty (nu^w–də–ti^y) n. The quality or state of being nude

nug-get (nʌg–ət) n. A lump of a precious metal, found in the earth: *a gold nugget*

nui-sance (nu^{w}s–əns) n. Someone or sthg. that annoys or causes trouble: *That bee is getting to be a real nuisance.*

null (nʌl) adj. **1.** Having no legal or binding force **2.** Amounting to nothing **3. null and void** Without legal force

nul-li-fy (nʌl–ə–faɪ) -fied, -fying v. *fml.* **1.** To make useless or ineffective; undo **2.** To deprive of legal force or effect —**nul-li-fi-ca-**

tion (nəl–ə–fə–**ke**ʸ–ʃən) n.

numb (nʌm) adj. **1.** Having no sensation; without feeling: *My hands are numb from the cold weather.* **2.** *fig.* Paralyzed with fear or from shock; unable to move: *We were all numb from the shocking news of his death.* —**numbly** adv. —**numbness** n.

numb v. To cause to feel nothing; make numb

num-ber (nʌm–bər) n. **1.** A specific quantity **2.** A written sign representing a quantity: *The number fifteen comes after the number fourteen.* **3.** Several: *A number of visitors came today.* **4.** A piece of popular music

number v. **1.** To give a number to: *Number your papers from 1 to 25.* **2.** To reach as a total: *Attendance at the football game numbered about 95,000.* **3.** Included; counted: *He [Jesus] was numbered with the transgressors. For he bore the sin of many, and made intercession for the transgressors* (Isaiah 53:12). NOTE: Jesus was the sinless Son of God, but he allowed himself to be numbered with the transgressors (as prophesied 700 years earlier by Isaiah). He suffered and was crucified to pay for all our sins, as also prophesied by Isaiah and others. On the third day he rose again from the dead, also as prophesied by himself and others. —see JESUS CHRIST, LAMB OF GOD, CREED

num-ber-less (nʌm–bər–ləs) adj. Too many to count

Numbers (nʌm–bərz) n. The fourth book of the Old Testament Scriptures, containing the history of Israel during the forty years they spent in the wilderness due to unbelief. It continues where the book of Exodus leaves off. It deals with the failure of God's people in the face of every divine provision for their welfare and success. The book is significant in warning against the dangers of unbelief. —see BIBLE, NEW TESTAMENT, MOSES

nu-mer-al (nuʷ–mə–rəl) n. A figure used to express a number: *I, V, and X are Roman numerals; 1, 2, 3, and 4 are Arabic numerals.*

nu-mer-ate (nuʷ–mə–reʸt) v. -ated, -ating To count

nu-mer-a-tor (nuʷ–mə–reʸt–ər) n. The number above or to the left of a line in a fraction: *In the fraction 7/8, seven is the numerator.*

nu-mer-i-cal (nuʷ–mɛər–ɪ–kəl) adj. **1.** Using or consisting of numbers **2. in numerical order** Following in order one, two, three, four, etc.

nu-mer-i-cal-ly (nuʷ–mɛər–ɪ–kə–liʸ) adv. **1.** In or by means of numbers **2.** In size or amount: *Their army is numerically stronger than ours.*

nu-mer-ous (nuʷm–ə–rəs) adj. Many: *His mistakes are too numerous to mention.* —**numerously** adv.

num-skull (nʌm–skʌl) n. A stupid person

nun (nʌn) n. A member of a female religious group that lives together in a convent

nun-ner-y (nʌn–ər–iʸ) n. A residence for a group of nuns

nup-tial (nʌp–ʃəl/ –tʃel) adj. **1.** Of marriage or a wedding **2.** Having to do with mating

nurse (nɜrs) n. **1.** A person who is trained to take care of sick, injured, and infirm, esp. as directed by a doctor **2.** A person, usu. a woman, who takes care of young children

nurse, nursed, nursing v. **1.** To take care of someone as a nurse: *She nursed him back to health.* **2.** To feed a baby milk from the breast: *She was nursing her newborn child.* **3.** To promote the growth and development of: *She was nursing her tomato plants.* **4.** To take steps to cure: *He nursed his injured dog back to health.* **5.** To preserve or prolong deliberately: *Stop nursing your jealous feelings, or they will destroy you.*

nurs-er-y (nɜrs–ə–riʸ) -ies n. **1.** A place where small children are cared for while their parents are at work **2.** A place where young plants are grown **3.** Sthg. that fosters, breeds, or develops

nurs-ing (nɜrs–ɪŋ) n. The job of a nurse

nurs-ing home (nɜrs–ɪŋ hoʷm) n. A residence where old or sick people are cared for by nurses

nur-ture (nɜr–tʃər) n. **1.** That which nourishes; food **2.** Training, education: *Fathers, provoke not your children to wrath, but bring them up in the nurture of the Lord.* (Ephesians 6:4 KJV).

nurture v. -tured, -turing To give food and

care to: *nurtured by loving parents*

nut (nʌt) n. **1.** A dry fruit consisting of a seed surrounded by a hard shell: *a walnut* **2.** A small piece of metal with a round hole through it, for screwing onto the end of a bolt to hold pieces of wood or metal together **3.** *infml.* A crazy or eccentric person who behaves strangely: *He's some kind of nut.* **4.** *infml.* A person with an unusually strong interest of the stated kind: *She's a health food nut.* **5. a tough nut to crack** *infml.* A difficult problem to deal with

nut-meg (nʌt–mɛg) n. The hard seed of a tropical tree, used as a spice when ground and grated

nu-tri-ent (nuᵂ–triʸ–ənt) n. Sthg. that nourishes; food

nu-tri-tion (nuᵂ–trɪʃ–ən) n. **1.** The process by which food is changed into tissue in living organisms **2.** That which nourishes: *Good nutrition is necessary for good health.*

nu-tri-tious (nuᵂ–trɪʃ–əs) adj. Valuable to the body as food; nourishing

nuts (nʌts) n. **1.** *pl.* of nut **2.** *infml.* Enthusiastic: *He's nuts about football.* **3.** *infml.* Crazy: *He must be nuts to do a stupid thing like that.* —**nuts** adj.

nut-shell (nʌt–ʃɛl) n. **1.** The shell of a nut **2.** In just a few words; a brief summary

nut-ty (nʌt–iʸ) adj. **-tier, tiest 1.** Tasting like nuts **2.** Containing nuts: *a nutty cake* **3.** *infml.* Mad; crazy

nuz-zle (nʌz–əl) v. **-zled, -zling** To rub or push in a gentle way with the nose or snout

ny-lon (naɪ–lɑn) n. A strong man-made material made into clothing, rope, and many products

ny-lons (naɪ–lɑnz) n. Women's nylon stockings: *a pair of nylons*

nymph (nɪmf) n. **1.** In Greek or Roman mythology, a minor goddess living in rivers, trees, hills, etc. **2.** Esp. in poetry, a young woman, esp. a beautiful one **3.** A young insect that has a similar form to the adult

O O, o (o^w) n. **1.** The 15th letter of the English alphabet **2.** In speech, zero: 305 (three, o, five) **3.** O symbol Oxygen

oak (o^wk) n. A large tree which grows acorns and is valued for its timber

oar (ɔr) n. A long pole with a wide flat blade, used for rowing a boat

o-a-sis (o^w–e^y–səs) n. **oases** (o^w–e^y–si^yz) A fertile area in a desert

oath (o^wθ) n. **oaths** (o^wðz/ o^wθs) **1.** A solemn appeal to God, esp. in a court of law, to witness the truthfulness of one's testimony —compare VOW **2.** A casual use of the name of God in anger or to give emphasis: Jesus told the multitude, "It was said to the people long ago, 'Do not break your oath, but keep the oaths you have made to the Lord.' But I tell you, Do not swear at all: either by heaven, for it is God's throne; or by the earth, for it is his footstool... Simply let your 'Yes' be 'Yes,' and your 'No,' 'No'; anything beyond this comes from the evil one" (Matthew 5:33-37).

oat-meal (o^wt–mi^yl) n. **1.** Meal made by grinding oat grains **2.** A cooked cereal made from this

oats (o^wts) n. A hardy cereal plant that grows in cool climates and provides food for people and animals

ob- (ab–/əb–) prefix Also **o-** before **-m** as in omit; **oc-** before **-c** as in occur; **of-** as in offend; and **op-** as in oppress **1.** Toward; to; facing: obverse **2.** Against; in opposition to: object **3.** Over; upon: obliterate **4.** Completely: obdurate

O-ba-di-ah (o^w–bə–daɪ–ə) n. **1.** A masculine name **2.** The Old Testament prophet who lived in the 9th century B.C. **3.** The short prophecy of Obadiah against the Edomites, descendants of Esau, who participated with other foreign powers in the devastation of Israel, that Edom would be destroyed

ob-du-rate (ab–dyə–rət) adj. Stubborn; resistant; unyielding —**obduracy** n.

o-be-di-ent (o^w–bi^yd–i^y–ənt) adj. Obeying or willing to obey; doing what one is ordered to do: We take captive every thought to make it obedient to Christ (2 Corinthians 10:5). We are to be obedient in all God has commanded, even as Jesus humbled himself and became obedient to death — even death on a cross (Philippians 2:8). —opposite DISOBEDIENT —**obedience** n. —**obediently** adv.

o-bei-sance (o^w–bi^y–səns/ o^w–be^y–) n. **1.** A gesture, such as a bow, showing high respect for sbdy. **2.** Reverence; homage

ob-e-lisk (ab–ə–lɪsk) n. A four-sided pillar that tapers near the top and ends in a pyramid, usu. built in honor of a person or event

o-bese (o^w–bi^ys) adj. Very fat —**o-be-si-ty** (o^w–bi^y–sət–i^y) n.

o-bey (o^w–be^y) v. To follow the commands of; to do what one is asked or ordered to do: We ought to obey God rather than men (Acts 5:29). To obey [God] is better than making sacrifices [of animals or crops] in order to please God (1 Samuel 15:22). Jesus said to his followers, "If you love me you will obey what I command (John 14:15). Children, obey your parents in the Lord (Ephesians 6:1).

o-bit-u-ar-y (ə–bɪtʃ–ə–wear–i^y) n. **-ies** A formal notice of a person's death, esp. in a newspaper, usu. with a short account of the person's life

ob-ject (ab–dʒɪkt) n. **1.** Sthg. that can be seen or touched **2.** Purpose: The object of his visit was to start a new school. **3.** gram. A noun, noun phrase, or pronoun that receives the action of a verb or follows a preposition: In the sentence, Ann offered Bob a cup of coffee, "Bob" is the indirect object of the verb, and "cup of coffee" is the direct object. In the sentence, Tom is in the house, "house" is the object of the preposition "in." **4.** A thing or person toward which or to whom thought or action is directed: The little child was the object of her affection.

ob-ject (əb–dʒɛkt) v. **1.** To dislike; to be against: Most non-smokers object to smoking. **2.** To present an opposing argument

ob-jec-tion (əb–dʒɛk–ʃən) n. **1.** A statement or feeling of disapproval **2.** A reason or cause for objecting

ob-jec-tion-a-ble (ab–dʒɛk–ʃən–ə–bəl) adj. Unpleasant; offensive; causing disapproval

ob-jec-tive (əb–dʒɛk–tɪv) adj. **1.** Not influenced by personal feelings or prejudice; fair **2.** Existing outside the mind; real

objective n. Aim or purpose of a plan: *Our objective is freedom for all.*

ob-la-tion (ə–ble^y–ʃən) n. Any religious or solemn offering

ob-li-gate (ɑb–lə–ge^{y}t) v. -gated, -gating To make sbdy. feel it necessary to do sthg.: *He felt obligated to visit his sick uncle.*

ob-li-ga-tion (ɑb–lə–**ge**^{y}–ʃən) n. A duty; necessity: *We are all under obligation to help others who are in need, esp. members of our own family.*

ob-lig-a-to-ry (ə–blɪg–ə–tɔr–i^y) adj. Sthg. that must be done; compulsory: *Military service is obligatory in some countries.*

o-blige (ə–blaɪdʒ) v. -bliged, -bliging 1. To compel sbdy. to do sthg.: *I'll be obliged to report you to the principal if you do that again.* 2. Help: *Could you oblige me by giving me a ride into town?*

o-blig-ing (ə–blaɪ–dʒɪŋ) adj. 1. Kind and eager to help: *a very obliging person* 2. **Much obliged!** An expression of gratitude; "Thank you!"

ob-lique (o^w–bli^{y}k) adj. 1. Deviating from the perpendicular or horizontal 2. Sloping; slanting 3. Not direct or straightforward in meaning, expression, etc.: *an oblique remark*

oblique v. -liqued, -liquing To slant; to deviate from the perpendicular or horizontal

ob-lit-er-ate (ə–blɪt–ə–re^{y}t) v. -ated, -ating 1. To destroy completely; to wipe out 2. To remove from memory

ob-liv-i-on (ə–blɪv–i^y–ən) n. 1. The state of being completely forgotten 2. The state of forgetting

ob-liv-i-ous (ə–blɪv–i^y–əs) adj. Completely unaware; not noticing: *He was oblivious to what was happening around him.* —**obliviously** adv. —**obliviousness** n.

ob-long (ɑb–lɔŋ) adj. Having a shape that is longer than it is wide, with opposite sides parallel

ob-nox-ious (ɑb–nɑk–ʃəs) adj. Highly disagreeable; offensive —**obnoxiously** adv. —**obnoxiousness** n.

o-boe (o^w–bo^w) n. A woodwind musical instrument

ob-scene (ɑb–si^{y}n) adj. 1. Sexually indecent; nasty; disgusting; offensive; lewd 2. Intended to cause sexual excitement or lust: *There ought to be stricter laws against the publication and circulation of this disgusting obscene literature and these nasty obscene films.* —**ob-scen-i-ty** (ɑb–sɛn–ət–i^y) n. -ties *But among you [Christians] there must not be even a hint of sexual immorality, or of any kind of impurity ... nor should there be obscenity* (Ephesians 5:3,4).

ob-scure (ɑb–skyʊər) adj. -scurer, -scurest 1. Not easily understood 2. Not famous: *an obscure artist* —**obscurely** adv. —**obscurity** n. -ties

obscure v. -scured, -scuring To hide; to make less clear: *My view was obscured by the smoke.*

ob-se-qui-ous (ɑb–si^y–kwi^y–əs) adj. Trying to win favor by being too attentive, too humble, or too ready to agree

ob-serv-ance (əb–zɜr–vəns) n. 1. The act of observing a law: *the observance of the speed limit* 2. The keeping or celebrating of a holiday or other ritual occasion

ob-ser-vant (əb–zɜr–vənt) adj. Watchful; quick to observe

ob-ser-va-tion (ɑb–zər–ve^y–ʃən) n. 1. The act of noticing 2. Ability to notice things 3. Sthg. that has been observed 4. **under observation** Being carefully observed for a period of time: *Mother is in the hospital under observation* (=to determine the cause of her illness).

ob-ser-va-to-ry (əb–zɜr–və–tɔr–i^y) n. -ries A place from which astronomers observe the sun, moon, stars, etc.

ob-serve (əb–zɜrv) v. -served, -serving 1. To perceive; to notice: *He was observed coming out of the church.* 2. To obey: *Jesus told his disciples (followers), "Go and make disciples of all nations; baptizing them in the name of the Father and of the Son and of the Holy Spirit, teaching them to observe [obey] everything I have commanded you"* (Matthew 28:19-20).

ob-serv-er (əb–zɜrv–ər) n. 1. One who sees or observes 2. One who is sent to listen to, but not take part in, a conference, etc.

ob-sess (əb–sɛs) v. To fill the mind completely: *He's obsessed with baseball and can't think or talk about anything else.*

ob-ses-sion (əb–sɛʃ–ən) n. A feeling or an idea from which the mind cannot get away;

to be obsessed

ob-ses-sive (əb–sɛs–ɪv) adj. Of or like an obsession —obsessively adv.

ob-so-les-cent (ab–sə–lɛs–ənt) adj. Going out of date —obsolescence n.

ob-so-lete (ab–sə–liᵞt/ ab–sə–liᵞt) adj. Out of date; no longer used

ob-sta-cle (ab–stɪ–kəl) n. A hindrance; sthg. that gets in the way and prevents progress

ob-ste-tri-cian (ab–stə–trɪʃ–ən) n. A doctor who specializes in obstetrics

ob-stet-rics (ab–stɛ–trɪks) n. A branch of medicine that deals with helping women before, during, and after childbirth

ob-sti-nate (ab–stə–nət) adj. Stubborn; not willing to change one's opinion; not yielding

ob-strep-er-ous (əb–strɛp–ə–rəs) adj. Noisy; unruly

ob-struct (əb–strʌkt) v. 1. To block; keep from passing 2. To hold back: *to obstruct justice* —obstruction n. *the obstruction of justice* — obstructive adj. —obstructively adv.

ob-tain (əb–teᵞn) v. To get: *A good man obtains favor from the Lord, but the Lord condemns a crafty man* (Proverbs 12:2). —obtainable adj.

ob-trude (əb–truᵂd) v. -truded, -truding 1. To thrust out 2. To thrust oneself forward when not wanted 3. To thrust sthg. unwanted on sbdy.

ob-tru-sive adj. (əb–truᵂ–sɪv) Too noticeable; impudent —obtrusion n.

ob-tuse (əb–tuᵂs/ ab–) adj. 1. Not sharp intellectually; dull; stupid 2. An angle between 90 and 180 degrees

ob-vi-ate (ab–viᵞ–eᵞt) v. -ated, -ating To remove, prevent, or get around an obstacle, difficulty, etc.

ob-vi-ous (ab–viᵞ–əs) adj. Clear; easily seen or understood: *The acts of the sinful nature are obvious: sexual immorality, impurity and debauchery, idolatry and witchcraft, hatred, discord, jealousy, fits of rage, selfish ambition ...* (Galatians 5:19-20). NOTE: While all of these sins and all other sins are detestable to the Lord, and although the wages of sin is eternal death, even so, God loves us and he forgives us our sins if we repent and put our trust in Jesus for eternal life (Mark 1:15;

Romans 6:23). —see SIN, REPENT, FORGIVENESS, JESUS

ob-vi-ous-ly (ab–viᵞ–əs–liᵞ) adv. Clearly; plainly

oc-ca-sion (ə–keᵞ–ʒən) n. 1. The time of an event: *And pray in the Spirit on all occasions with all kinds of prayers and requests* (Ephesians 6:18). 2. A special event: *The opening of a new school is always a great occasion.* 3. **on occasion** From time to time

oc-ca-sion-al (ə–keᵞʒ–ən–əl) adj. Happening from time to time; not often and not very regularly: *We get an occasional letter from her.* —occasionally adv.

Oc-ci-dent (ak–sə–dənt) n. The countries of the West, that is, Europe and the Americas

Oc-ci-den-tal (ak–sə–dɛnt–əl) n. A person from the Occident —occidental adj. Of or from the Occident

oc-cult (ə–kʌlt/ a–) adj. 1. Of or pertaining to various magical arts and practices that depend on evil, supernatural powers 2. Beyond human understanding; mysterious 3. Secret; revealed only to the initiated —see DEMON, DEMONIC, SATAN, SATANIC, OCCULTISM

occult n. Occult studies or practices: *He's making a study of witchcraft, astrology, and the occult, all things which are condemned in the Holy Scriptures.*

oc-cult-ism (ə–kʌl–tɪz–əm) n. An attempt to bring hidden and mysterious powers under human control; the practice of knowing and using evil spiritual powers. Witchcraft, divination, and sorcery are types of occultism. These practices are strongly forbidden by the Holy Scriptures: *Let no one be found among you who sacrifices his son or daughter in the fire, who practices divination or sorcery, interprets omens, engages in witchcraft, or casts spells, or who is a medium or spiritist or who consults the dead. Anyone who does these things is detestable to the Lord* (Deuteronomy 18:10-12; 2 Chronicles 33:1-6). NOTE: While all of these sins and all other sins are detestable to the Lord, and although the wages of sin is eternal death, even so, God loves us and he forgives us our sins if we repent and put our trust in Jesus for eternal

life (Mark 1:15; Romans 6:23; John 3:16).

oc·cu·pan·cy (ak–yə–pən–si^y) n. **1.** The act of taking and/or holding possession **2.** The condition of being occupied: *Occupancy of this restaurant by more than 68 people is prohibited.*

oc·cu·pant (ak–yə–pənt) n. One who occupies a seat or a room or residence; a resident

oc·cu·pa·tion (ak–yə–pe^y–ʃən) n. **1.** Type of work; job; employment: *His occupation is boat building.* —see JOB **2.** Taking possession of: *The people detested the occupation of their country by a foreign power.*

oc·cu·pa·tion·al (ak–yə–pe^y–ʃən–əl) adj. Concerning an occupation: *an occupational hazard*

oc·cu·pi·er (ak–yə–paɪ–ər) n. One who has possession (of a house, e.g.)

oc·cu·py (ak–yə–paɪ) v. -pied, -pying **1.** To take or hold possession of: *All the seats in the theater were occupied.* **2.** To fill a certain space: *His books occupied several shelves.* **3.** To take up a certain amount of time: *Most of his time is occupied in writing a book.* **4.** To take possession of an enemy's country, town, region, etc.: *Their country was occupied by foreign troops.*

oc·cur (ə–kɜr) v. -rr- **1.** To happen: *Most accidents occur at home or near home.* **2.** To appear or be found: *Fish occur in most waters.* **3.** To come to remembrance: *When I was half way to the airport, it occurred to me that I had forgotten my plane tickets.* —occurrence n.

o·cean (o^w–ʃən) n. **1.** The salt water that covers about 72% of the earth's surface **2.** Often capitalized as part of a name of one of these great bodies of water: *The Pacific Ocean is the largest of all oceans.* —o·ce·an·ic (o^w–ʃi^y–æn–ɪk) adj.

oc·e·lot (as–ə–lat) n. A wild cat of Mexico and Central and South America having a yellowish coat spotted with black

o·cher *AmE.* **o·chre** *BrE.* (o^w–kər) n. **1.** A kind of fine pale yellow or red clay, used as a pigment in paints **2.** The color of ocher; esp. dark yellow

o'clock (ə–klak) adv. **1.** Used in stating the time, referring to a particular hour: *It's ten o'clock.* **2.** Used for indicating position or direction as if on a clock dial

Oct. *abbr.* for October

oct-, octa-, octo- (akt–/ ak–tə–) Prefix meaning eight

oc·ta·gon (ak–tə–gan) n. A geometric figure having eight sides and eight angles

oc·tave (ak–tɪv) n. In music, a series or stretch of eight notes, as from one C to the next C above it

oc·tet (ak–tɛt) n. **1.** A musical composition for eight singers or musicians **2.** A group of eight singers or instrumentalists **3.** Any group of eight

Oc·to·ber (ak–to^w–bər) n. *abbr.* Oct. The tenth month of the year

oc·to·ge·nar·i·an (ak–tə–dʒə–nɛər–i^y–ən) n. A person between 80 and 90 years of age

oc·to·pus (ak–tə–pəs) n. -puses or -pi (paɪ) Any of the various sea mollusks having eight long arms, each having two rows of suckers for seizing and holding prey

odd (ad) adj. **1.** Strange: *odd behavior* **2.** Belonging to a pair or set of which the others are missing: *an odd glove* **3.** Of a number that cannot be divided exactly by two: *One, three, five, seven, and nine are odd numbers.* —opposite EVEN **4.** Not regular; different kinds of: *He does odd jobs now and then; he has no regular work.* —oddly adv.

odd·ball (ad–bol) n. Any peculiar or eccentric person

odd·i·ty (ad–ət–i^y) n. -ties **1.** One that is odd **2.** The quality or state of being odd

odds (adz) n. **1.** The probability that a certain thing will happen; chances: *The odds are that it will be hot again tomorrow.* **2. at odds with** In disagreement or in conflict with **3. odds and ends** n. Miscellaneous items, usu. small and without much value: *There are a few odds and ends left in the garage./fig. a few odds and ends of business to discuss* **4. odds-on** Having a better than even chance to win: *He's the odds-on favorite to win the race/election.*

ode (o^wd) n. A long poem, usu. characterized by a feeling and style of exaltation

o·di·ous (o^w–di^y–əs) adj. Exciting hate or disgust; offensive

o·dor (o^w–dər) n. A scent or smell, esp. an un-

pleasant one —opposite ODORLESS —**o-dored** (o**ᵂ**–dərd) adj.

of (ʌv) prep. **1.** Belonging to: *the leg of the chair* **2.** Consisting of: *a bouquet of flowers* **3.** Containing: *a glass of milk* **4.** Owing to; due to; because of: *He died of cancer.* **5.** Shows a part or amount: *all of us* **6.** Named: *the city of Rome* **7.** About; concerning: *stories of adventure* **8.** In relation to: *the Queen of Sheba* **9.** Having: *acres of wild flowers* **10.** Shows what sbdy. or sthg. is or does: *the singing of the birds* **11.** (Used in dates): *the 25th of August* **12.** Shows position: *the end of the line/ the middle of the road/ south of London* **13.** Set aside for: *a day of rest* **14.** On the part of: *It was nice of you to say that.* **15.** From: *within a mile of the river* **16.** So as to be separated from: *He was robbed of an opportunity.* **17.** By or coming from: *the music of Jerome Kern* **18.** Before or until: *It's five minutes of eight.* **19.** Having particular qualities: *a man of wisdom* **20.** Shows relationship: *a member of the family/club/gang*

off (ɔf) adv. **1.** Away from a certain place: *He got on his bike and rode off.* **2.** To get, go, or fall down from: *He always rides the bus to work and gets off at Main Street.* **3.** Not in operation: *Turn the radio off.* **4.** Cancelled: *Due to the rain, the game has been called off./ The deal is off.* **5.** Away from one's work or duty: *He has the day off.* **6.** To remove from its place: *Take off your hat.* **7.** Discount: *ten percent off* **8.** At a distance in future time: *My birthday is just two weeks off.* **9.** To start: *They're off to the mountains.* **10. well off** Not rich, but having a comfortable income **11. off and on** From time to time; sometimes

off prep. **1.** Not on; away from: *Keep off the grass.* **2.** Near: *off the coast of Spain / off Broadway* **3.** So as to be no longer attached: *Cut a branch off that tree.* **4.** Disengaged: *He's off duty now.* **5.** Refraining from: *He's off drugs* **6.** At the expense of: *He lives off his relatives.*

off adj. **1.** Not as good as usual: *Our usually good team had an off day and they were beaten badly.* **2.** Slack; slow: *Sales are down during the off season.*

of-fal (ɔ–fəl) n. **1.** The parts of an animal unfit for use as food **2.** Certain internal parts of an animal, such as the heart and liver, that are eaten

off-beat (ɔf –biᵞt) adj. Unusual

off–col-or (ɔf–kʌl–ər) adj. **1.** Varying from the usu. or standard color **2.** Not proper; in rather poor taste; risque: *an off-color joke*

of-fend (ə–fɛnd) v. **1.** To sin; transgress **2.** To make angry; to hurt sbdy.'s feelings: *An offended brother is more unyielding than a fortified city...* (Proverbs 18:19). **3.** To be unpleasant or disagreeable: *Cigarette smoke offends me.* —**of-fender** n.

of-fense *AmE.* **offence***BrE.* (ə–fɛns) n. **1.** A wrong; crime; sin: *Jesus Christ was delivered for our offenses [sins] and raised again [from the dead] for our justification* (Romans 4:25 KJV). **2.** A cause for hurt feelings

of-fen-sive (ə–fɛn–sɪv) adj. **1.** Unpleasant; disagreeable —opposite INOFFENSIVE **2.** Attacking or used for attacking: *offensive weapons* —opposite DEFENSIVE —**offensiveness** n.

offensive n. **1.** An aggressive movement or attack **2.** The position or attitude of attack

of-fer (ɔf–ər) v. **1.** To present for acceptance or refusal: *Unlike other high priests, he [Jesus] does not need to offer sacrifices day after day, first for his own sins, and then for the sins of the people. He sacrificed for their sins once for all when he offered himself [when he died on the cross to pay for our sins]* (Hebrews 7:27). **2.** To express willingness to do sthg.: *Mary offered to help.* **3.** To put up: *to offer resistance*

offer n. **1.** The act or an instance of offering sthg.: *Thanks for your offer to help.* **2.** Sthg. offered: *Ann made me an offer of $500 for my car.*

of-fer-ing (ɔf–ə–rɪŋ) n. Sthg. offered, esp. to God

of-fer-to-ry (ɔf–ər–tɔr–iᵞ) n. **1.** That part of Holy Communion in which the Eucharistic bread and wine are offered to God **2.** The collection of money during the church service **3.** The prayers, anthem, or music offered during this part of the service

off-hand (ɔf–hænd) adj. Casual or careless; disrespectful: *an offhand remark*

offhand adv. Without previous preparation or thought: *Just offhand, I'd say that car isn't worth much.*

of-fice (ɔf–əs) n. **1.** A place of business **2.** Any

post or position of authority **3.** A position of responsibility, esp. in government: *Our political party has been in office for three years.*

of-fi-cer (ɔf-ə-sər) n. **1.** In the armed forces, a person in a position of authority and command **2.** A policeman **3.** A person who holds a position of some responsibility: *She's a loan officer at the bank.*

of-fi-cial (ə-fɪʃ-əl) n. **1.** A person who holds an office **2.** A referee in a sport

official adj. **1.** Done or confirmed by people in authority: *an official decision* **2.** Supported by authority: *English is an official language in many countries.*

of-fi-cial-ly (ə-fɪʃ-ə-liʸ) adv. **1.** As or because of being an official: *As ambassador he attended the ceremony officially.* **2.** Formally: *The library was officially opened yesterday, though people had been using it for several days.* **3.** According to what is announced publicly: *Officially the diplomat was on a vacation overseas, but actually he was there on some important business.*

of-fi-ci-ate (ə-fɪʃ-iʸ-eʸt) v. **-ated, -ating** **1.** To act or serve as a priest or minister **2.** To perform the duties or functions of any office

of-fi-cious (ə-fɪʃ-əs) adj. *derog.* Fond of interfering, esp. in a pompous way; too eager to give advice

off-ing (ɔf-ɪŋ) n. Likely to appear or happen soon; not far away: *The smell coming from the kitchen told them that a delicious meal was in the offing.*

off-set (ɔf-sɛt) v. **-set, -setting** To balance or make up for sthg. else: *The increase in my salary was more than offset by the increase in the cost of living.* —**off-set** (ɔf-sɛt) n.

off-shoot (ɔf-ʃuʷt) n. **1.** A shoot that branches out from the main stem of a plant **2.** Sthg. that comes from a main source: *an offshoot of an international industry*

off-spring (ɔf-sprɪŋ) n. Child or children; descendants: *God said to Abraham, "Through your offspring all peoples on earth will be blessed"* (Acts 3:25).

oft (ɔft) adv. (in poetry) Often

of-ten (ɔf-ən/ ɔf-tən) adv. **1.** Frequently: *How often do you sing and make music in your hearts to the Lord? How often do you give thanks to God? The Bible says, "Sing and make music in your heart to the Lord, always giving thanks to God the Father for everything, in the name of our Lord Jesus Christ"* (Ephesians 5:19-20). **2. as often as not** Quite often **3. every so often** Sometimes; occasionally **4. more often than not** Most of the time

o-gle (oʷ-gel/ ɑ-) v. **ogled, ogling** To look or stare at (esp. a woman) in a way that suggests sexual interest

o-gre (oʷ-gər) n. **1.** In legends and fairy tales, a cruel giant who eats people **2.** *Fig.* A frightening and cruel person

oh (oʷ) interj. An expression of surprise, admiration, dismay, fear, etc.

ohm (oʷm) n. A unit of electrical resistance

oil (ɔil) n. A fatty or greasy liquid substance from animals, plants, or minerals, used for fuel, lighting, medicine, making machines run easily, for cooking, etc.: *corn oil/motor oil*

oil v. To put oil into or onto: *The machinery will run better if it is oiled.*

oil-y (ɔɪ-liʸ) adj. **-ier, -iest** **1.** Of or like oil: *an oily liquid* **2.** Covered with or containing oil: *an oily rag*

oint-ment (ɔmt-mənt) n. A greasy substance, often medicated, to be rubbed on the skin

o-kay, OK (oʷ-keʸ) adv. *infml.* **1.** All right: *The TV works okay now.* **2.** Giving or asking for permission: *Is it okay to borrow your bike? Okay, but bring it back in an hour.* —**okay, OK** adj. *The TV is okay now.*

okay v. **okayed, okaying** *infml.* To approve: *Has the boss okayed your request for a day off next week?*

okay n. *infml.* Approval; permission: *I got the OK to go home at noon today.*

o-kra (oʷ-krə) n. **1.** A tall plant with edible green pods **2.** The pods of this plant, used esp. in soup

old (oʷld) adj. **1.** Having lived or existed for a long time: *My mother is quite old.* **2.** Made long ago; not new: *The pyramids of Egypt are thousands of years old.* **3.** Having been in use for a long time: *an old car* **4.** Having had a relationship for a long time: *They were still quite young, but they were old friends.* **5.** Known for a long time: *Don't tell me the same*

old joke again! **6.** Former: *He got his old job back.* NOTE: **Old** is a general word for age, but **elderly** is a polite way of saying **old** when speaking of people: *an "old" building/ an "elderly" woman*

old-en (oᵂl–dən) adj. Of an earlier time when things were quite different than they are now

old–fash-ioned (oᵂld–fæʃ–ənd) adj. Out-dated

Old Tes-ta-ment (oᵂld tɛs–tə–mənt) n. The part of the Bible that was written before the birth of Christ NOTE: The Old Testament was written by more than 20 authors over a period of about 1,100 years, from 1500 to 400 B.C. (=Before Christ). It tells about the creation of the world and all things, man's fall into sin, the promise of a Savior, many prophecies concerning him and concerning Israel and other nations. It gives the history of Israel and her neighbors. The Old Testament contains the Ten Commandments and several poetic books including Psalms and Proverbs. The Old Testament was given by inspiration of God. God spoke directly to men and told them what to write. Like the New Testament, the Old Testament Scriptures "are able to make one wise for salvation through faith in Christ Jesus" (2 Timothy 3:15). —see BIBLE, NEW TESTAMENT

o-le-o-mar-ga-rine (oᵂ–liʸ–oᵂ–mɑrdʒ–ə–rən) n. A food made as a substitute for butter

ol-ive (ɑl–ɪv) n. **1.** A small oily fruit native to southern Europe and the Middle East, important for its fruit and for its edible oil **2.** The evergreen tree that bears this fruit **3. olive green** The dull green color of the unripe olive

olive oil (ɑl–ɪv ɔɪl) n. A yellowish oil pressed from olives, used in cooking, in salad dressings, and in making soap

O-lym-pic Games (oᵂ–lɪm–pɪk geʸmz/ ə–) n. A sports competition held every four years for competitors from all over the world

om-e-let or **om-e-lette** (ɑm–ə–lət/ ɑm–lət) n. Eggs beaten together and cooked in a frying pan, often served folded around a filling: *A cheese omelet, please.*

o-men (oᵂ–mən) n. A sign of a future event: *a good/bad omen*

om-i-nous (ɑm–ə–nəs) adj. Threatening: *ominous black clouds* —**ominously** adv.

o-mis-sion (oᵂ–mɪʃ–ən) n. **1.** The act of omitting or leaving sthg. out or undone: *He's annoyed about the omission of his name on the program.* **2.** Sthg. that has been left out or left undone: *There are sins of omission as well as sins of commission. When we fail to do good, we are guilty of a sin of omission. Anyone, then, who knows the good he ought to do and doesn't do it, sins* (James 4:17).

o-mit (oᵂ–mɪt) v. **-tt- 1.** To leave sthg. out; either on purpose or by mistake: To leave undone; not do: *The Lord spoke to Jeremiah saying, "Speak to all the people and tell them everything I command you; do not omit a word"* (Jeremiah 26:2). **2.** To leave sthg. undone: *He omitted to tell me of the change in the date of the meeting.*

om-ni– (ɑm–niʸ–) comb. form All; everywhere; totally

om-ni-bus (ɑm–niʸ–bʌs) n. **-buses** A large motor vehicle for passengers; a bus

om-nip-o-tent (ɑm–nɪp–ə–tənt) adj. All-powerful: *God is omnipotent* (Genesis 1:1; Psalm 115:3; Luke 1:37; Ephesians 3:20). —**omnipotence** n.

om-ni-pres-ent (ɑm–nɪ–prɛz–ənt) adj. Present everywhere: *God is omnipresent* (Proverbs 15:3; Psalm 139:1-4; Jeremiah 23:24). —**omnipresence** n.

om-ni-scient (ɑm–nɪʃ–ənt) adj. All-knowing; knowing everything: *God is omniscient* (1 John 3:20: Psalm 147:5; Hebrews 4:13). —**omniscience** n.

om-niv-o-rous (ɑm–nɪv–ə–rəs) adj. **1.** Of animals that eat both plants and animals **2.** *Fig.* Reading all types of books; watching all kinds of TV, etc.: *an omnivorous reader*

on (ɑn/ ɔn) prep. **1.** Used to indicate: **(a)** Location: *on the waterfront* **(b)** Resting upon: *the book on the desk* **(c)** Connection with: *a ring on her finger* **(d)** Direction: *on my left* **(e)** Contents; subject matter: *a book on astronomy* **(f)** Purpose: *traveling on business* **(g)** Attachment to: *a picture on the wall* **(h)** Covering: *a rug on the floor* **(i)** Touching: *a fly on the ceiling* **(j)** Supported by: *standing on one foot* **2.** Used

with days, dates and times: *on Tuesday/on July 1st/on time* 3. By means of: *on foot/on a bicycle/talking on the phone* 4. In the state of: *on fire/on sale/on vacation* 5. Working for; belonging to: *to serve on a committee* 6. Receiving or taking: *He's on drugs.* 7. Near or beside: *a town on the Mississippi River* 8. Toward: *The army marched on the town* 9. When; during: *On investigation I found that he was innocent.*

on adv. 1. Continuously: *He drove on and on, all day and all night.* 2. Forward: *If any letters come for me, send them on to me at my brother's address.* 3. To put in place: *Put your shoes on.* 4. **head on** Front to front: *The two cars crashed head on.* 5. So as to function: *Turn the light on.* —opposite OFF 6. Happening or going to happen: *The play-off games will be on T.V.*

on adj. 1. Not cancelled; going to happen: *Is the party still on tonight?* 2. Working, functioning: *Is the television on?* 3. In progress: *The game is still on.*

once (wʌns) adv. 1. One time only: *I met her only once.* 2. Formerly: *We once were neighbors, but no longer.* 3. **all at once** Suddenly 4. **At once (a)** Immediately: *Do it at once!* **(b)** At the same time; together: *Don't all speak at once!* 5. **just for once** For this one time only: *For once he arrived on time.* 6. **once (and) for all** For the last time: *But he [Jesus] appeared once for all... to do away with sin by the sacrifice of himself. Just as man is destined to die once, and after that to face judgment, so Christ was sacrificed once to take away the sins of many people; and he will appear a second time, not to bear sin, but to bring salvation to those who are waiting for him (Hebrews 9:26-28). We have been made holy through the sacrifice of the body of Jesus Christ once for all (Hebrews 10:10).* 7. **once in a while** Now and then; sometimes 8. **once more (a)** One more time **(b)** Once again; now again as before: *Tom's back home once more.* 9. **once upon a time** At some time in the past

once n. One time only: *just once*

once conj. As soon as: *Once you have learned it you will never forget it.*

on-com-ing (ɑn–kəm–ɪŋ/ ɔn–) adj. Coming towards one: *oncoming cars*

one (wʌn) determ. 1. A single person or thing: *one book/ desk/pen* 2. An unspecified person, thing, or date: *I met her one day last year.* 3. The same: *In the beginning of time, the whole earth was of one language, and of one speech* (Genesis 11:1 KJV). 4. The number 1: *Only one person*

one n. A single person or thing: *I want that one./ one after the other/ one by one*

one pron. **ones** pl. 1. A single person mentioned: *John saw Jesus coming toward him and said, "Look, the Lamb of God who takes away the sin of the world! This is the one I meant when I said, 'A man who comes after me has surpassed me because he was before me."* (John 1:26-30). 2. Anyone; no one: *There is no one right-eous, not even one; there is no one who does good, not even one* (Romans 3: 10,12). 3. **ones** Persons or things: *I want to be with my loved ones for Christmas./ These books are the ones I want to keep.*

one another (wʌn ə–nʌ–ðər) pron. Each other: *Jesus told his followers, "Love one another. By this shall all men know that you are my disciples, if you love one another"* (John 13:34,35).

on-er-ous (ɑn–ə–rəs/ oʷn–) adj. Difficult to bear or do: *an onerous task*

one-self (wʌn–sɛlf) pron. A person's own self, used **(a)** Reflexively: *It is good to forget oneself and help others who are less fortunate.* **(b)** For emphasis: *One must take the initiative oneself.*

on-go-ing (ɔn–goʷ–ɪŋ) adj. Continuing; currently going on; progressing

on-ion (ʌn–yən) n. A strong-smelling vegetable used in cooking or eaten raw

on-look-er (ɔn–lʊk–ər) n. A spectator; one who sees sthg. happening without participating in it

on-ly (oʷn–liʸ) adj. 1. One of a kind: *Ann is an only child.* 2. Solely; exclusively: *The only thing that counts is faith [in Jesus] expressing itself in love* (Galatians 5:6)./ *We've only* (used as adj.) *one life, it will soon be past; only* (used as adv.) *what's done for Christ will last.*

only adv. 1. No more than: *It only costs $2.* 2. Not longer ago than: *I saw her only yesterday.*

only conj. But; except that: *He wants to come with us, only he can't.*

on-rush (ɔn–rʌʃ/ ɑn–) n. A strong movement

forward

on-set (ɔn–sɛt/ **an**–) n. The beginning

on-slaught (ɔn–slɔt/ **an**–) n. A violent assault

on-to (ɔn–tuʷ/ **an**–) prep. On top of; upon

o-nus (oʷ–nəs) n. onuses The duty or responsibility of doing sthg.; obligation

on-ward (ɔn–wərd) adj. Directed or moving forward in space or time: *the onward march of time* —**onward** adv.

on-yx (ɑn–ɪks) n. A type of precious stone with layers of different colors in it

oo-dles (uʷd–əlz) n. A great quantity

ooh (uʷ) interj. An expression of surprise, anger, or pain

oomph (ʊmf) n. **1.** Attractiveness **2.** Energy; enthusiasm: *He has a lot of oomph!*

ooze (uʷz) v. **oozed, oozing 1.** To flow out slowly: *The syrup oozed out of the bottle.* **2.** To exude moisture **3.** To show one's feelings freely: *He oozed confidence.*

ooze n. Mud at the bottom of a river, lake, etc.

o-pal (oʷ–pəl) n. A type of bluish-white precious stone, with flecks of various colors

o-paque (oʷ–peʸk) adj. **1.** Not able to be seen through **2.** Not clear; not easily understood —**opaquely** adv.

o-pen (oʷ–pən) adj. **1.** Not closed or blocked: *The eyes of the Lord are on the righteous and his ears are open to their prayers* (1 Peter 3:12 NKJV). **2.** Not fenced in; not enclosed: *an open field* **3.** Not covered or concealed: *an open ditch* **4.** Not fastened: *an open coat* **5.** Available; not taken: *Is that job still open?* **6.** Not concealing any bad feelings or misgivings or anything else; honest: *Let's be open with each other.* **7.** Ready for business: *The store isn't open yet.* **8.** Competition that anyone can enter: *an open golf tournament*

o-pen v. **1.** To (cause to) become open: *O Lord, open my lips and my mouth will declare your praise* (Psalm 51:15). **2.** To unfold or spread out: *Open your books to page 40.* **3.** To start: *The story opens with a plane crash.* **4.** To make usable: *They've opened the mountain road again after removing the fallen rocks.* **5. to open fire** To start shooting

o-pen-er (oʷ–pə–nər) n. A device that opens sthg.: *a bottle opener*

open-hand-ed (oʷ–pən–hæn–dəd) adj. Generous: *There will always be poor people in the land. Therefore, I command you to be openhanded toward your brother and toward the poor and needy in the land* (Deuteronomy 15:11).

o-pen-ing (oʷp–ə–nɪŋ) n. **1.** The beginning of sthg.: *the opening of a new shopping mall* **2.** A hole or a gap: *an opening in the garden wall* **3.** An opportunity: *job openings* **4.** In chess, the first few moves

o-pen-ly (oʷ–pən–liʸ) adv. Frankly; publicly; not secretly: *The subject was discussed openly on television.* —**openness** n.

op-en-mind-ed (oʷ–pən–**mam**–dəd) adj. Free from prejudices; willing to consider new ideas, etc. —compare BROADMINDED —**open-mindedly** adv.

op-er-a (ɑp–ər–ə/ **ɑp**–rə) n. A sort of drama set to music, in which many or all of the words are sung —**op-er-at-ic** (ɑp–ə–ræt–ɪk) adj.

op-er-a-ble (ɑp–ər–ə–bəl) adj. **1.** Capable of being operated on surgically **2.** Practicable: *This plan looks operable.*

op-er-ate (ɑp–ə–reʸt) v. **-ated, -ating 1.** To function effectively; to work: *The washing machine isn't operating properly.* **2.** To cause sthg. to function: *My father operates heavy machinery at the factory.* **3.** To perform surgery: *Dr. Smith operates on several patients every day at the hospital.*

op-er-a-tion (ɑp–ə–reʸ–ʃən) n. **1.** The act or process of operating; performance: *The operation of heavy equipment can be difficult and dangerous at times.* **2.** A method of operating: *a rescue operation* **3.** The removal or repair of certain diseased or injured parts of the body by surgery: *a kidney operation* **4.** A military action; movement: *the army's operations in Western Europe.*

op-er-a-tion-al (ɑp–ə–reʸ–ʃən–əl) adj. **1.** Ready to use **2.** Maintenance: *Operational expenses of an automobile are becoming extremely high.*

op-er-a-tive (ɑp–ə–rə–tɪv) adj. **1.** Moving or working efficiently: *That old equipment is no longer operative.* **2.** Being in operation or in force: *The airport is operative again after the snowstorm.*

op-er-a-tor (ɑp–ə–reʸ–tər) n. **1.** A person who works a machine, mechanism, etc., esp. one

who operates a telephone switchboard **2.** One who operates a commercial or industrial establishment

op-er-et-ta (ɑp–ə–rɛt–e) n. A play with music and singing

oph-thal-mol-o-gy (ɑf–θæl–mɑl–ə–dʒiʸ /ɑp–) n. The science dealing with the structure, function, and diseases of the eye —**ophthalmologist** n.

o-pi-ate (oʷ–piʸ–ət) n. **1.** A drug containing opium, used to make a person sleep **2.** Anything that dulls the mind or feelings

o-pin-ion (ə–pɪn–yən) n. **1.** What a person thinks or believes: *A fool finds no pleasure in understanding, but delights in airing his own opinions* (Proverbs 18:2). **2.** Professional judgment or advice: *I asked for a second opinion from another doctor as to whether I should have the operation or not.*

o-pin-ion-at-ed (ə–pɪn–yən–eʸt–əd) adj. Having very strong opinions which one is unwilling to change

o-pi-um (oʷ–piʸ–əm) n. An addictive narcotic drug that is the dried juice of a poppy

o-pos-sum (ə–pɑs–əm) n. A furry animal that lives mostly in trees. The female carries her young in a pouch. Also called a **possum**

op-po-nent (ə–poʷ–nənt) n. **1.** A person or group that opposes another in a political battle or in a war **2.** An individual or group that competes with others in a game or sporting event

op-por-tune (ɑp–ər–tuʷn) adj. **1.** Suitable **2.** Occurring at a favorable time

op-por-tun-ism (ɑp–ər–tuʷn–ɪz–əm) n. Taking advantage of every opportunity of success, esp. at someone else's expense

op-por-tu-ni-ty (ɑp–ər–tuʷn–ɪ–tiʸ) n. -ties **1.** A favorable time or occasion for a certain purpose: *Be wise in the way you act toward outsiders [unbelievers]; make the most of every opportunity [to share your faith in Christ with them]* (Colossians 4:5). —see CHANCE **2.** A chance for advancement or progress

op-pose (ə–poʷz) v. -posed, -posing To act against: *God opposes the proud, but gives grace to the humble* (James 4:6).

op-pos-ing (ə–poʷz–ɪŋ) adj. Opposite; hostile; contrary: *Turn away from godless chatter and*

the opposing ideas of what is falsely called knowledge [or science] (1 Timothy 6:20).

op-po-site (ɑp–ə–zət) adj. **1.** Situated on the other side: *Jim and Bill were on opposite sides of the room.* **2.** Differing as much as possible: *Red and green are opposite colors.*

opposite n. A person or thing that is opposite or contrary: *Mary is just the opposite from her sister.*

opposite or **opposite to** prep. Facing; across from: *The house opposite ours is for sale.*

op-po-si-tion (ɑp–ə–zɪʃ–ən) n. **1.** The act of opposing **2.** Antagonism or hostility **3.** A person or group that opposes, protests, and criticizes **4.** The major political party that is opposed to the party in power

op-press (ə–prɛs) v. To rule by harsh and unjust use of power and authority: *Do not oppress an alien [stranger] ...* (Exodus 23:9). *He who oppresses the poor, shows contempt for their Maker [God]* (Proverbs 14:31).

op-pres-sion (ə–prɛʃ–ən) n. **1.** The unjustly harsh exercise of authority and power **2.** The condition of oppressing or being oppressed **3.** The feeling of being oppressed mentally or physically

op-pres-sive (ə–prɛs–ɪv) adj. **1.** Unjustly harsh: *an oppressive government* **2.** Causing discomfort: *oppressive heat and humidity* **3.** Causing illness or sadness —**oppressively** adv. —**oppressiveness** n.

op-pres-sor (ə–prɛs–ər) n. A person (or group) that oppresses

op-pro-bri-um (ə–proʷ–briʸ–əm) n. **1.** A great or public disgrace **2.** Sth. that brings great disgrace —**opprobrious** adj. Disgraceful

opt (ɑpt) v. To choose; decide

op-tic (ɑp–tɪk) adj. Pertaining to the eyes or vision: *the optic nerve*

op-ti-cal (ɑp–tɪ–kəl) adj. Having to do with the sense of sight or with what one sees: *A microscope is an optical instrument./ The two lines seem to be the same length, but they aren't. It's an optical illusion.* —**optically** adv.

op-ti-cian (ɑp–tɪʃ–ən) n. One who makes and sells spectacles and optical instruments

op-tics (ɑp–tɪks) n. pl. The branch of physical science that deals with light and vision

op-ti-mism (ɑp–tə–mɪz–əm) n. The habit of

taking a bright, hopeful view of things —opposite PESSIMISM —**op-ti-mis-tic** (ɑp-tə–**mıs**–tık) adj.

op-ti-mum (ɑp–tə–məm) adj. Best; most favorable: *optimum conditions for growth*

op-tion (ɑp–ʃən) n. **1.** The power or freedom to choose: *They are renting the house, with an option to buy it.* **2.** Sthg. that may be chosen: *We have two options: either to reduce spending or get an extra job and increase our income.* — **op-tional** adj. —opposite OBLIGATORY, COMPULSORY —**optionally** adv.

op-tom-e-try (ɑp–tɑm–ə–triʸ) n. The profession of measuring vision and prescribing corrective lenses to compensate for visual defects —**optometrist** n.

op-u-lent (ɑp–yə–lənt) adj. **1.** Very wealthy **2.** Plentiful; abundant: *the opulent growth of tropical plants* —**opulence** n.

o-pus (oʷ–pəs) pl. **op-e-ra** (oʷ–pə–rə/ ɑp–rə) or **o-pus-es** n. A literary or musical work or composition

or (ɔr) conj. **1.** Used in a list of possibilities: *Who shall separate us from the love of Christ? Shall trouble or hardship or persecution or famine or nakedness or danger or sword? ... No, in all these things we are more than conquerors through him who loved us. For I am convinced that neither life nor death ... nor anything else in all creation, will be able to separate us from the love of God that is in Christ Jesus our Lord* (Romans 8:35-39). **2.** Otherwise: *I better go now, or I'll be late.* **3. or so** About; approximately: *I'll be ready in a minute or so.*

–or (–ər) suffix Used to form nouns showing action or occupation: *elevator/inventor*

o-ra-cle (ɔr–ə–kəl) n. **1.** A message from God, esp. one given to an Old Testament prophet **2.** A message given by a false prophet or as if by a false god **3.** In ancient Greece, a shrine for the worship of a false god who was believed to tell the future

o-ral (ɔr–əl) adj. **1.** Spoken, not written: *an oral report* **2.** Done or taken by mouth —**orally** adv.

or-ange (ɔr–ınʤ/ –ənʤ) n. **1.** A round, reddish-yellow citrus fruit with a thick peel, valued for its juice **2.** The evergreen tree bearing this fruit **3.** The reddish-yellow col-

or of an orange: *The school colors were blue and orange.*

orange adj. **1.** Reddish-yellow in color **2.** Flavored like an orange: *orange soda*

o-rang-u-tan (ə–ræŋ–ə–tæn) n. A large ape that has long arms and shaggy, reddish-brown hair

or-a-tion (ɔ–reʸ–ʃən) n. A long formal speech, esp. at a ceremony

or-a-tor (ɔr–ət–ər) n. **1.** A person who makes an oration **2.** One who is good at making public speeches

or-a-to-ri-o (ɔr–ə–tɔr–iʸ–oʷ) n. A sacred story set to music, performed by soloists, choir, and usu. an orchestra

or-a-to-ry (ɔr–ə–tɔr–iʸ) n. **-ries 1.** The art of public speaking **2.** Eloquent speech —**or-a-tor-i-cal** (ɔr–ə–tɔr–ı–kəl) adj.

orb (ɔrb) n. Anything in the shape of a ball; a sphere

or-bit (ɔr–bət) n. The path of sthg. moving around the earth or other heavenly body: *The earth's orbit around the sun takes approximately 365 days.*

orbit v. To move in an orbit: *Spacecraft orbit the earth in about one and a half hours.*

or-chard (ɔr–tʃərd) n. A piece of land where fruit trees grow

or-ches-tra (ɔr–kəs–trə) n. A large group of musicians who perform together —**or-ches-tral** (ɔr–kɛs–trəl)adj.

or-ches-trate (ɔr–kə–streʸt) v. **-trated, -trating 1.** To arrange a piece of music for an orchestra to play **2.** To carefully (and sometimes unfairly) arrange things in order to bring about a desired result

or-chid (ɔr–kəd) n. **1.** A plant with brightly colored or unusually shaped flowers, grown in warm climates **2.** A light purple color

or-dain (ɔr–deʸn) v. **1.** To install as a minister or priest: *The seminary graduates were ordained into the ministry.* **2.** To destine or predestine: *All the days ordained for me were written in your book [O Lord] before one of them came to be* (Psalm 139:16). **3.** To order or command formally: *The king ordained that the prisoner should be set free.*

or-deal (ɔr–diʸl) n. A difficult or painful ex-

perience that tests one's character or power of endurance

or-der (ɔr–dər) n. **1.** The systematic way in which things are arranged in relation to each other: *The names in a telephone book are in alphabetical order.* **2.** The condition in which things are arranged: *This room is a mess. Get busy and put things in order.* —opposite DISORDER **3.** A specific rule, law, or authoritative direction: *Be back by ten o'clock; that's an order./ He [Jesus] even gives orders to evil spirits, and they obey him* (Mark 1:27). **4.** Control: *That teacher has difficulty keeping order in her classroom.* **5.** A request to supply goods: *You can place an order by mail or over the telephone, using your charge card.* **6.** A printed paper obtained from a post office or bank, etc. which allows the holder to receive the designated amount of money: *a money order* **7.** A body or society of persons who lead a holy life of service according to a particular set of religious rules **8.** A quantity of food asked for in a restaurant: *an order of French fries* **9. in order to, in order that** So that; for the purpose of: *John flew instead of driving his car in order to save time.* **10. made to order** Made esp. for a particular person's body or to meet his particular needs **11. out of order (a)** Not working properly: *This vending machine is out of order.* **(b)** Not following the rules of a formal meeting: *Your motion is out of order. There's another motion on the floor./ Robert's Rules of Order*

or-der v. **1.** To give an order; command: *The general has ordered an attack.* **2.** To request sthg. to be brought in return for payment: *John ordered bacon, eggs, and toast for breakfast.*

or-der-ly (ɔr–dər–liʸ) adj. **1.** Well-arranged **2.** Neat; tidy: *an orderly person* **3.** Well-behaved: *The crowd at the concert was very orderly.* —opposite DISORDERLY —**orderly** adv.

orderly n. **-lies 1.** A soldier who assists a superior officer **2.** A hospital attendant who does general work

or-din-al num-ber (ɔrd–ən–əl nʌm–bər) A number that shows position in a series: *First, second, and third are ordinal numbers.*

or-di-nance (ɔrd–ən–əns) n. **1.** A law made by

government authority **2.** An authoritative decree; a required ceremony

or-di-nar-i-ly (ɔr dɪ nɛr–ə–liʸ) adv. **1.** In a normal, ordinary way **2.** Usually: *Ordinarily, he works eight hours a day.*

or-di-nar-y (ɔr–də–nɛər–iʸ) adj. Common; not unusual

or-di-na-tion (ɔrd–ən–eʸ–ʃən) n. The act of ordaining a minister or a priest

ore (ɔr) n. Rock or earth from which a metal is obtained

or-gan (ɔr–gən) n. **1.** A part of an animal or plant that has a special purpose: *The liver is an organ which we can't live without.* **2. (a)** A large musical instrument similar to a piano, in which air is forced through sets of pipes, producing a characteristic sound **(b)** Any of various instruments producing similar sounds **3.** An agency that is part of a larger organization: *Parliament is the main organ of government in Britain.*

or-gan-dy or **or-gan-die** (ɔr–gən–diʸ) n. A very sheer, crisp cotton fabric used for dresses, curtains, etc.

or-gan-ic (ɔr–gæn–ɪk) adj. **1.** Of or concerning the organs of the body **2.** Food grown without the use of artificial fertilizers: *Some people will only eat organic food.* **3.** Found in, or produced by living things: *All organic compounds contain carbon.*

or-gan-ism (ɔr–gə–nɪz–əm) n. A living person, animal, or plant

or-gan-ist (ɔr–gə–nəst) n. A person who plays an organ

or-gan-i-za-tion also **-sation** BrE. (ɔr–gə–nə–zeʸ–ʃən) n. **1.** A group of people with a special purpose **2.** The act of organizing: *Efficiency depends on the organization of one's work.* **3.** The state of being organized —**organizational** adj. —**organizationally** adv.

or-ga-nize (ɔr–gə–naɪz) v. **-nized, -nizing 1.** To arrange in an orderly or systematic way: *He spent the day organizing the papers in his filing cabinets.* **2.** To make arrangements for: *She organized the bridal shower.* **3.** To form an association of like-minded people for a special purpose: *They organized a new association for helping the blind.* —**organizer** n.

or-ga-nized (ɔr-gə-naɪzd) adj. **-nised** Arranged into a system that works well —opposite DISORGANIZED

or-gasm (ɔr-gæz-əm) n. The climax of sexual excitement

or-gy (ɔr-dʒiʸ) n. **-gies 1.** A wild drunken party or revelry **2.** Over-indulgence in one or more activities

o-ri-ent (ɔr-iʸ-ənt) n. **1.** *Poet.* The east **2. The Orient** The East or Asia, esp. the Far East

o-ri-ent (ɔr-iʸ-ənt) *AmE.* **o-ri-en-tate** (ɔr-iʸ-ən-teʸt) *BrE.* v. **1.** To give direction or guidance to: *I need time to get oriented when I go to a new place.* **2.** To make familiar or acquainted with a situation —**o-ri-en-ta-tion** (ɔr-iʸ-ən-teʸ-ʃən) n. *People need some orientation before going to another country.*

O-ri-en-tal (ɔr-iʸ-ɛnt-əl) n. A member of one of the peoples native to the Orient

Oriental adj. Of or having to do with the Orient: *Oriental features/art/carpets*

or-i-fice (ɔr-ə-fəs) n. An opening

or-i-gin (ɔr-ə-dʒən) n. **1.** The point, source, or cause from which a thing has its beginning: *For prophecy [Holy Scripture] never had its origin in the will of man, but men spoke from God as they were carried along by the Holy Spirit* (2 Peter 1:21). **2.** Parents and ancestors: *a person of humble origin*

o-rig-i-nal (ə-rɪdʒ-ə-nəl) adj. **1.** New; different; unlike others: *an original idea/painting* —opposite UNORIGINAL **2.** The first: *The original owner of the house was Paul Revere.*

o-rig-i-nal-i-ty (ə-rɪdʒ-ə-næl-ə-tiʸ) n. The quality of being original: *Her painting shows great originality.*

o-rig-i-nal-ly (ə-rɪdʒ-ə-nə-liʸ) adv. In the beginning: *Her family originally came from Norway.*

original sin (ə-rɪdʒ-ə-nəl sɪn) n. The sinful nature that all of us are born with as a result of Adam's disobedience in the Garden of Eden which led to spiritual death. NOTE: Since Adam's first sin, all people are born in sin and are by nature self-centered, seeking constantly to satisfy their own selfish interests. They find it easy to disobey God. They do nothing to glorify God and thus to serve the purpose for which they were

created. But Jesus Christ came into the world to save sinners from their original sin and all actual sins of thought, word, deed, and omission. He led a perfectly holy life for us, and he paid for all our sins on the cross. "He was delivered over to death for our sins, and raised again for our justification" (Romans 4:25). "For as in Adam all die, so in Christ all will be made alive" (1 Corinthians 15:22). This new life is the work of the Holy Spirit, through the Word of God. "If anyone is in Christ [trusting in him for eternal life], he is a new creation" (2 Corinthians 5:17). He loves God and wants to serve, obey, and glorify him. However, original sin clings to us through life. By faith in Christ we are freed from sin's guilt and punishment; but the corruption itself remains, as St. Paul himself experienced (Romans 7:14-24) and as every Christian still experiences. By faith Christians will, with the aid of the Holy Spirit, constantly strive to suppress the Old Adam, the old sinful nature (Ephesians 4:22; Galatians 5:24), but in this life they will never succeed in totally destroying him. He, the Old Adam, will not be destroyed until redemption is final and complete at the resurrection. —see MAN, SIN, DEPRAVITY, JESUS CHRIST, CREED

o-rig-i-nate (ə-rɪdʒ-ə-neʸt) v. **-nated, -nating** To begin: *This flight originated in Tokyo.* —**originator** n.

o-ri-ole (ɔr-iʸ-oʷl/ -əl) n. Any of the North American songbirds of which the male has bright yellow or orange and black plumage

or-na-ment (ɔr-nə-mənt) n. Sthg. that decorates or adorns; sthg. thought to be beautiful rather than useful

or-na-men-tal (ɔr-nə-mɛn-təl) adj. **1.** Serving as an ornament **2.** *often derog.* Perhaps beautiful, but not necessary —**ornamentally** adv.

or-nate (ɔr-neʸt) adj. Excessively ornamented; overly decorative

or-ni-thol-o-gy (ɔr-nə-θɑl-ə-dʒiʸ) n. A branch of zoology dealing with birds —**ornithologist** n.

or-phan (ɔr-fən) n. A person (esp. a child)

whose parents are dead: *Religion that God our Father accepts as pure and faultless is this: to look after orphans and widows in their distress and to keep oneself from being polluted by the world* (James 1:27).

orphan v. To cause to become an orphan

or-phan-age (orf-ə-nıdʒ) n. A home for orphans

or-tho- (or-θoʷ-) prefix **1.** Straight; in line **2.** At right angles; perpendicular **3.** Correct; proper **4.** *medical* The correction of irregularities, deformities, etc.: *orthopedics*

or-tho-don-tics (or-θə-dɑn-tıks) n. A branch of dentistry that deals with preventing and correcting irregularities in the position of the teeth and jaws

or-tho-don-tist (or-θə-dɑn-təst) n. A specialist in orthodontics

or-tho-dox (or-θə-dɑks) adj. **1.** Having beliefs, opinions, etc. that are generally or officially accepted **2.** *esp. in religion* Following the older, more traditional, beliefs and practices: *Orthodox Christians accept all the basic creeds or beliefs of Christianity.* —see CREED —**orthodoxy** n.

or-thog-ra-phy (or-θɑg-rə-fiʸ) n. **1.** The art of spelling according to accepted usage **2.** The part of grammar that deals with letters and spelling —**or-tho-graph-ic** (or-θə-græf-ık) adj.

or-tho-pe-dics (or-θə-piʸd-ıks) n. The branch of medicine that deals with diseases and injuries to the bones, straightening the bones, etc.: *Dr. Jones specializes in orthopedics.*

-o-ry (-oʷ-riʸ/-ɔ-riʸ/-ə-riʸ) suffix (of nouns) A place or instrument for performing the action of the main element: *dormitory*

-ory suffix (of adj.) Related to; resembling: *auditory*

os-cil-late (ɑs-ə-leʸt) v. **-lated, -lating 1.** To swing back and forth like the pendulum of a clock **2.** To vary or move between two points: *Radio waves oscillate./ fig. He oscillated between two opinions.* —**os-cil-la-tion** (ɑs-ə-leʸ-ʃən) n.

os-mo-sis (ɑz-moʷ-səs/ ɑs-) n. **1.** The diffusion of a liquid through a semipermeable membrane resulting in the equalization of concentrations of the liquid on each side **2.**

A gradual process of assimilation or absorption that resembles osmosis

os-prey (ɑs-preʸ) n. A type of hawk that eats fish

os-ten-si-ble (ɑs-tɛn-sə-bəl) adj. Apparent, stated or claimed, but not necessarily true: *Illness was the ostensible reason for his absence, but in fact he just didn't want to attend the meeting.* —**os-tensibly** adv.

os-ten-ta-tious (ɑs-tɛn-teʸ-ʃəs) adj. Doing sthg. in such a way as to be seen by other people in order to impress them: *an ostentatious style of living* —**osten-tation** n.

os-te-op-a-thy (ɑs-tiʸ-ap-ə-θiʸ) n. A system of healing that emphasizes manipulation (as of joints) but does not exclude use of medicine and surgery —**os-te-o-path** (ɑs-tiʸ-ə-pæθ) n. —**os-te-o-path-ic** (ɑs-tiʸ-ə-pæθ-ık) adj.

os-tra-cize (ɑs-trə-saız) v. **-cized, -cizing** To shut out or exclude from society or from a particular group: *The villagers ostracized him because he had broken one of their taboos.* —**ostracism** n.

os-trich (ɑs-tırtʃ / ɔs-) n. A large bird of Africa and Arabia that runs fast but cannot fly, the largest of all birds

oth-er (ʌð-ər) determ. **1.** The remaining one of two or more persons or things: *They live on the other side of the street.* **2.** More of the same kind: *Jane and two other girls* **3.** Additional: *I have no other shoes./ God is one and there is no other but him* (Mark 12:32). **4.** Alternate; second: *We play golf every other day.*

other pron. **1.** People or things that are different or in addition to those already mentioned: *These pencils are broken. Do you have any others?/ Each loved the other.* **2.** (Used with the or a possessive determ.) The remaining persons or things in a group: *Mary went home; the others stayed for the party.*

oth-er-wise (ʌð-ər-waız) adv. **1.** In a different way: *We'll get there by car or otherwise.* **2.** In all other ways: *The meat was tough; otherwise the meal was very good.* **3.** Or else; if not: *I must leave now. Otherwise, I'll miss the bus.* **4.** Other than supposed: *Everyone thought he was innocent, but the evidence proved otherwise.* —**otherwise** adj.

ot-ter (ɑt–ər) n. **1.** An animal that has thick dark brown fur and webbed feet, living in or near the water **2.** The fur of this animal

ot-to-man (ɑt–ə–mən) n. **1.** A sofa without arms or back **2.** A cushioned footstool or a low seat

ouch (aʊtʃ) interj. An expression of sudden pain

ought (ɔt) v. **1.** Used to show a moral obligation or duty: *We ought to obey God rather than men* (Acts 5:29)./ *She ought to take better care of her children.* **2.** Used to show that sthg. can be expected: *It ought to be hot at this time of the year.*

oughtn't (ɔt–ənt) Contraction of **ought not**

ounce (aʊns) *written abbr.* **oz** n. **1.** A measure of weight equal to 1/16 of a pound; approx. 28 grams **2.** A small amount: *He hasn't an ounce of sense.*

our (aʊ–ər/ ɑr) determ., poss. pron. Form of **we,** the people who are speaking; belonging to us: *But he [Jesus] was pierced for our transgressions [sins], he was crushed for our iniquities; the punishment that brought us peace [with God] was upon him, and by his wounds we are healed. The Lord has laid on him the iniquity of us all* (Isaiah 53: 5,6).

ours (aʊ–ərz/ ɑrz) pron. Form of **we,** the people who are speaking; belonging to us: *He [Jesus Christ] is the atoning sacrifice for our sins, and not only for ours but also for the sins of the whole world* (1 John 2:2).

our-selves (aʊ–ər–selvz/ ɑr–selvz) pron. **1.** Used as the object of a verb when the people who are speaking do the action and are also the objects of the action: *If we claim to be without sin, we deceive ourselves and the truth is not in us. If we confess our sins, he [Jesus] is faithful and just and will forgive us our sins and purify us from all unrighteousness* (1 John 1: 8,9). **2.** Used to make "we" stronger; *We built the house ourselves.* **3.** Without help: *We'll have to do this job ourselves.*

–ous (–əs) suffix (of adj.) **1.** Full of; having: *dangerous/ courageous* **2.** *chem.* Having a lower valence than indicated by -ic: *nitrous oxide*

oust (aʊst) v. To force out: *The dictator was ousted from office.*

oust-er (aʊs–tər) n. Eviction; expulsion

out (aʊt) adv. **1.** Outside: *Open the door and let the dog out.* **2.** Away from home or the usual place: *They went out to eat.* **3.** In the open: *The sun came out from behind a cloud.* **4.** No longer fashionable: *Short skirts are out this year.* **5.** Of a fire or light, extinguished; no longer burning: *The fire has gone out.* **6.** Completely: *I'm worn out.* **7.** Impossible: *Visiting Tom is out; he left for Alaska yesterday.*

out adj. **1.** External (usu. in comb. form): *outpost/ outpatient* **2.** Turned off; extinguished: *The fire is out.* **3.** In baseball, not safe: *The batter was out at first base.*

out prep. **1.** Through to the outside: *out the door* **2.** Along the way of: *He backed the car out the driveway.*

out n. **1.** In baseball, the failure of the batter or runner to reach base safely **2.** In tennis or squash, a service or return that lands out of bounds **3. on the outs** *infml.* (a) On unfriendly terms (b) Of a prisoner, living outside the institution

out-age (aʊt–ɪdʒ) n. A period during which a power supply is not functioning: *After the storm there was a power outage.*

out–and–out (aʊt–ən–aʊt) adj. **1.** Complete: *an out-and-out lie* **2.** Not concealed or disguised

out-break (aʊt–breʸk) n. A sudden beginning of sthg. bad: *an outbreak of measles*

out-burst (aʊt–bɜrst) n. A sudden, often violent display of emotion or activity

out-cast (aʊt–kæst) n. One who has been excluded from society

out-class (aʊt–klæs) v. To surpass decisively: *Our team was completely outclassed by the visiting team, and we lost the game 49 to 0.*

out-come (aʊt–kəm) n. Result: *It is time for judgment to begin with the family of God; and if it begins with us, what will the outcome be for those who do not obey the gospel of God?* (1 Peter 4:17).

out-cry (aʊt–kraɪ) n. **-cries** A strong public protest: *If more isn't done about crime in this city, there'll be a great outcry by its law-abiding citizens.*

out-dat-ed (aʊt–deʸt–əd) adj. No longer in use

out-do (aʊt–duʷ) v. **-did, -done, -doing, -does** To be better in performance: *They outdid us*

in production.

out-door (aʊt–dɔr) adj. Located in, done in, or suited to the open air: *an outdoor activity*

out-doors (aʊt–dɔrz) adv. also **out–of–doors** Outside of a house or other building: *The children are playing outdoors.*

out-doors n. The open air; not in a building: *He loved to be in the great outdoors, esp. in the mountains.*

out-er (aʊt–ər) adj. Farther from the middle: *the outer walls* —opposite INNER

out-field (aʊt–fiʸld) n. In baseball: **(a)** The space beyond the infield **(b)** The three outfielders as a group

out-field-er (aʊt–fiʸld–ər) n. In baseball, any of the three players whose positions are in the outfield

out-fit (aʊt–fɪt) n. **1.** Clothing or equipment for a special purpose **2.** *infml.* A group of people who work together

out-flank (aʊt–flæŋk) v. To get around the flank of (an opposing armed force); to gain a tactical advantage

out-fox (aʊt–fɑks) v. To outsmart

out-go (aʊt–goᵂ) n. **-goes** Sthg. that goes out, esp. money

out-go-ing (aʊt–goᵂ–ŋ) adj. **1.** Departing; leaving office, esp. a political office: *the outgoing congressman* —opposite INCOMING **2.** Friendly; sociable; eager to mix socially with others

out-grow (aʊt–groᵂ) v. **-grew, -grown 1.** To grow too large for sthg.: *Children are always outgrowing their clothes.* **2.** To grow too mature for: *He finally outgrew his childish ideas.* **3.** To surpass in growth: *Tommy outgrew his older brother.*

out-growth (aʊt–groᵂθ) n. **1.** Sthg. that grows out of sthg. else **2.** A result or consequence

out-guess (aʊt–gɛs) v. **1.** To outdo in forethought **2.** To guess correctly the actions of an opponent, e.g.

out-house (aʊt–haʊs) n. A toilet housed in a small outdoor structure

out-ing (aʊt–ŋ) n. **1.** An excursion **2.** A walk outdoors

out-land-ish (aʊt–læn–dɪʃ) adj. Very strange; ridiculous: *What an outlandish hat!*

out-last (aʊt–læst) v. To endure longer than

out-law (aʊt–lɔ) n. A criminal who has not been caught by the police

outlaw v. To make unlawful. *That kind of activity ought to be outlawed.*

out-let (aʊt–lɛt/ –lət) n. **1.** A passage by which sthg. (usu. a liquid or a gas) is let out **2.** A fixture into which the cord of an electric appliance may be plugged **3.** A market for goods **4.** A means of expression or of releasing energy: *Playing football was an outlet for his energy.* —opposite INLET

out-line (aʊt–laɪn) n. **1.** The line showing the outer edge of sthg.: *He drew the outline of her face first, then he drew the eyes, nose, etc.* **2.** The main ideas or facts; a brief description: *an outline of his speech*

out-line v. **-lined, -lining 1.** To make an outline of: *The new director outlined his plans for the organization's future.* **2.** To give a brief description

out-live (aʊt–lɪv) v. **-lived, -living** To live longer than

out-look (aʊt–lʊk) n. **1.** That which is likely to happen **2.** One's general view of the future: *His outlook for the future was quite hopeful.*

out-ly-ing (aʊt–laɪ–ŋ) adj. At considerable distance from the center: *an outlying province*

out-ma-neu-ver (aʊt–mə–nuᵂ–vər) v. To overcome by more skillful maneuvering

out-mo-ded (aʊt–moᵂ–dəd) adj. No longer fashionable

out-num-ber (aʊt–nʌm–bər) v. To be more numerous: *How precious to me are your thoughts, O God! How vast is the sum of them! Were I to count them, they would outnumber the grains of sand* (Psalm 139:17,18).

out of (aʊt əv) prep. **1.** From within to the outside: *He walked out of the room.* **2.** From among: *Two out of three people choose this brand of coffee.* **3.** Lacking: *We're out of bread.* **4.** Because of: *I came out of curiosity.* **5.** From (a certain material): *made out of oak*

out-pa-tient (aʊt–peʸ–ʃənt) n. A sick or injured person who goes to a hospital or clinic for treatment while continuing to live at home

out-post (aʊt–poᵂst) n. **1.** Troops stationed at a distance from the main unit of military

forces **2.** The fort or station occupied by such troops **3.** Any outlying settlement

out-put (aʊt–pʊt) n. **1.** The goods produced by a machine, factory, etc.: *an output of 10,000 cars a year* **2.** The amount of work done by a person

out-rage (aʊt–reʸdʒ) n. **1.** An act of extreme viciousness **2.** An act extremely offensive to decency or morality **3.** Resentful anger

outrage v. **-raged, -raging 1.** To inflict violence upon someone **2.** To rape **3.** To produce anger

out-ra-geous (aʊt–reʸ–dʒəs) adj. Extremely offensive

out-rig-ger (aʊt–rɪg–ər) n. A long, narrow float attached to the side of a canoe to keep the canoe from turning over

out-right (aʊt–raɪt) adv. **1.** Completely: *He's been paying for that car for four years. Now he owns it outright.* **2.** Openly: *I told him outright what I thought.*

outright adj. Complete; entire: *an outright loss*

out-set (aʊt–sɛt) n. The beginning: *The explorers knew the hardships they would have to face from the outset.*

out-side (aʊt–saɪd/ aʊt–saɪd) n. **1.** Any place or area not inside: *We enjoyed the picnic in the outside.* **2.** Elsewhere: *We can't do it ourselves; we need help from the outside.*

outside adj. **1.** Away from the edge of a road: *If you want to drive fast, use the outside lane.* **2.** Exterior: *We need to paint the outside walls.* —opposite INSIDE

outside of (aʊt–saɪd əv) prep. Except for: *Outside of Jim, no one available qualifies for the job.*

out-sid-er (aʊt–saɪd–ər) n. Sbdy. who is not accepted as a member of a social group —compare INSIDER

out-skirts (aʊt–skɜrts) n. pl. Esp. of a town, the outer areas: *The train wreck was on the outskirts of Mexico City.*

out-spo-ken (aʊt–spoʷ–kən) adj. Expressing frankly what is thought or felt

out-spread (aʊt–sprɛd) adj. Spread out; extended: *She ran to meet him with outspread arms.*

out-stand-ing (aʊt–stæn–dɪŋ) adj. **1.** Excellent **2.** Not yet paid: *Let no debt remain outstand-*

ing, except the continuing debt to love one another (Romans 13:8).

out-stretched (aʊt–strɛtʃt) adj. Stretched out to full length: *This is what the Lord Almighty says: "With my great power and outstretched arm I made the earth and its people and the animals that are on it ..."* (Jeremiah 27:4,5).

out-strip (aʊt–strɪp) v. **-pp- 1.** To leave behind; outrun **2.** To do better than; to surpass

out-vote (aʊt–voʷt) v. **-voted, -voting** To defeat by a greater number of votes

out-ward (aʊt–wərd) also **out-wards** adj. The outside: *Man looks at the outward appearance (of a person) but God looks at the heart* (1 Samuel 16:7). —opposite INWARD —**outward** adv.

out-ward-ly (aʊt–wərd–liʸ) adv. **1.** Seeming to be, but probably not: *Outwardly he appeared calm, but he was really very nervous.* **2.** Physically: *Though outwardly we are wasting away, yet inwardly we [who know the Lord] are being renewed day by day* (2 Corinthians 4:16).

out-weigh (aʊt–weʸ) v. To be more important than: *For our light and momentary troubles are achieving for us [who know the Lord Jesus] an eternal glory that far outweighs them all [everything else]* (2 Corinthians 4:17).

out-wit (aʊt–wɪt) v. **-tt-** To get the better of someone by superior cleverness

out-worn (aʊt–wɔrn) adj. Of an idea, custom, etc., no longer useful or used

o-va (oʷ–və) n. pl. of **ovum**

o-val (oʷ–vəl) adj. Egg-shaped —**oval** n.

o-va-ry (oʷv–ə–riʸ) n **-ries** One of the pair of female reproductive glands that produces ova (eggs)

o-va-tion (oʷ–veʸ–ʃən) n. Enthusiastic and prolonged applause

ov-en (ʌv–ən) n. An enclosed chamber for baking, heating, or drying

o-ver (oʷ–vər) prep. **1.** Above: *He held his hand over his head.* **2.** On the other side: *He lives over there, across the street.* **3.** In excess of; more than: *He is over six feet tall.* **4.** In many parts of; everywhere in: *Toys were scattered all over the floor./ They traveled all over Europe.* **5.** Commanding; in control of: *He ruled over a large kingdom.* **6.** During: *They held a meeting over dinner.* **7.** By means of: *I don't want to*

tell you over the telephone. **8.** About; concerning: *They quarreled over money.*

over adv. **1.** From an upright position: *The lamp fell over.* **2.** Across an open space: *The plane flew over about an hour ago.* **3.** Across the edge: *The car came to a cliff and went over.* **4.** To a different opinion or allegiance: *They tried to win him over.* **5.** To a different person: *Mr. Smith had to sign over the car that Mr. Smith bought from him.* **6.** So that the opposite side is shown: *Turn the page over.* **7.** So as to be completely covered: *It's too dirty to clean. Let's paint it over.* **8.** Thoroughly; carefully: *Think it over.* **9. over and over** Repeatedly: *I've told him over and over again not to do it.* **10.** During: *You can stay over at our house tonight.* **11.** Too much: *Don't be overanxious about it.* **12.** Again: *I failed my driving test, so I'm going to take it over (again) next week.* **13.** More than: *I have $100, but the car repairs will be a little over.* **14.** Remaining: *There are three cookies for each of us, and one left over.*

over adj. Finished; ended: *The war is over.*

o-ver-all (oᵂ–və–rɔl) adj. From end to end: *the overall measurements of the ship*

overall adv. Generally: *Overall, the cost of living is increasing.*

o-ver-alls (oᵂ–və–rɔlz) n. Loose fitting work trousers often fastened over the shoulders and worn over other clothes

o-ver-awe (oᵂ–və–rɔ) v. **-awed, -awing** To be overcome with awe; to make silent by fear or amazement: *We were overawed by the beauty of the waterfall at sunset.*

o-ver-bear-ing (oᵂ–vər–beər–ŋ) adj. Too sure that one is right; frequently telling other people what to do without regard for their ideas or feelings —**overbearing** adv. *Since an overseer is entrusted with God's work, he must be blameless — not overbearing, not quick-tempered ...* (Titus 1:7).

o-ver-board (oᵂ–vər–bord) adv. **1.** Over the side of a ship or boat into the water **2. go overboard** To go to extremes because of too much enthusiasm

o-ver-cast (oᵂ–vər–kæst) adj. Cloudy: *an overcast sky/day*

o-ver-charge (oᵂ–vər–tʃardʒ) v. **-charged, -charging** To charge sbdy. too much: *They*

overcharged us for the dinner at the restaurant.

o-ver-coat (oᵂ–vər–koᵂt) n. A long, heavy, warm coat worn over all other clothing, esp. in cold weather

o-ver-come (oᵂ–vər–kʌm) v. **-came, -come, -coming 1.** To defeat or conquer: *Do not be overcome by evil, but overcome evil with good* (Romans 12:21). *Who is it that overcomes the world? Only he who believes that Jesus is the Son of God* (1 John 5:5). **2.** Usu. of feelings, defeated by exhaustion, emotion, etc.: *He was overcome by grief.*

o-ver-crowd (oᵂ–vər–kraʊd) v. To put too many people or things in one place: *Overcrowding a building can be very dangerous, especially in case of fire.*

o-ver-do (oᵂ–vər–du) v. **-did, -done, -doing** To do too much: *Grandpa is working too hard. I'm afraid he's overdoing it.*

o-ver-done (oᵂ–vər–dʌn) adj. Cooked too long

o-ver-dose (oᵂ–vər–doᵂs) n. Too great an amount, esp. of a drug: *He died by taking an overdose.*

o-ver-draw (oᵂ–vər–drɔ) v. **-drew, -drawn, -drawing** To withdraw more money from a bank than one has in his account

o-ver-due (oᵂ–vər–duᵂ) adj. **1.** Later than expected: *The train is 15 minutes overdue.* **2.** Not paid on time: *This bill is long overdue.* **3.** Not returned on time: *These books are overdue at the library.*

o-ver-flow (oᵂ–vər–floᵂ) v. To flow over the edges: *The river overflowed its banks./fig. May the Lord make your love increase and overflow for each other and for everyone else ...* (1 Thessalonians 3:12).

overflow (oᵂ–vər–floᵂ) n. **1.** More than expected: *We were not expecting to fill the auditorium, but there was an overflow of about 50 people.* **2.** Sthg. that overflows: *Bring a bucket to catch the overflow from this pipe.*

o-ver-grown (oᵂ–vər–groᵂn) adj. Covered with unwanted plants: *The garden was overgrown with weeds.*

o-ver-hand (oᵂ–vər–hænd) adj. With the hand moving above the shoulder: *an overhand pitch*

o-ver-hang (oᵂ–vər–hæŋ) v. **-hung, -hanging** To hang over sthg.: *Vines were overhanging*

the garden wall.

o-ver-hang (oᵂ–vər–hæŋ) n. *The roof of the house had an overhang of four feet because of so much rain in that part of the country.* NOTE: Do not confuse **overhang** with **hangover**

o-ver-haul (oᵂ–vər–hɔl) v. To repair: *My car needs to be completely overhauled.* —**o-verhaul** n.

o-ver-head (oᵂ–vər–hɛd) adj. Above one's head: *Electricity carried by overhead wires.*

o-ver-head (oᵂ–vər–hɛd) adv. Above one's head: *The birds were flying overhead.*

o-ver-head (oᵂ–vər–hɛd) n. The cost of operating a business: *Their office is in Manhattan, so their overhead is very high.*

o-ver-hear (oᵂ–vər–hɪər) v. **-heard, -hear-ing** To hear what others are saying without their knowledge: *I overheard them talking about me.*

o-ver-joyed (oᵂ–vər–dʒɔɪd) adj. Full of joy: *The disciples were overjoyed when they saw the Lord [after his resurrection]* (John 20:20).

o-ver-land (oᵂ–vər–lænd) adv. Across or by land; not by sea or air

o-ver-lap (oᵂ–vər–læp) v. **-pp-** To partly cover sthg.: *Every shingle on the roof is overlapped by the one above it.*

overlap (oᵂ–vər–læp) n. The amount by which two or more things overlap each other

o-ver-load (oᵂ–vər–loᵂd) v. **1.** To load too heavily **2.** To cause a machine to work too hard and use too much electricity: *Don't overload the electrical system by using too many machines.*

o-ver-load (oᵂ–vər–loᵂd) n. Too great a load

o-ver-look (oᵂ–vər–lʊk) v. **1.** To have a view of sthg. from above: *Our living room overlooks the ocean.* **2.** To look at but not see; forgive: *A man's wisdom gives him patience; it is to his glory to overlook an offense* (Proverbs 19:11).

o-ver-ly (oᵂ–vər–liʸ) adv. Excessively: *I'm not overly interested in opera.*

o-ver-night (oᵂ–vər–naɪt) adj. During the night: *an overnight trip*

overnight adv. Suddenly: *He became famous overnight.*

o-ver-pass (oᵂ–vər–pæs) n. A place where one road passes over another by means of a kind of bridge

o-ver-pow-er (oᵂ–vər–paʊ–ər) v. **1.** To overcome by superior force: *Their team simply overpowered us.* **2.** To overwhelm: *overpowered by the terrible smell*

o-ver-rate (oᵂ–vər–reʸt) v. **-rated, -rating** To put too high a value on sthg.: *I think that movie has been overrated; it isn't really very good.*

o-ver-rule (oᵂ–vər–ruʷl) v. **-ruled, -ruling** To decide against or cancel an earlier judgment or request: *The judge overruled the lawyer's objection.*

o-ver-run (oᵂ–vər–rʌn) v. **-ran, -run, -running 1.** To spread over an area, often causing harm: *The resort area was overrun with tourists.* **2.** To infest: *The house was overrun by ants.*

ov-er-seas (oᵂ–vər–siʸz) adv. Across or beyond the sea —**overseas** adj.

o-ver-see (oᵂ–vər–siʸ) v. To direct work or workers as a supervisor

o-ver-se-er (oᵂ–vər–siʸ–ər) n. One who oversees or supervises

o-ver-shad-ow (oᵂ–vər–ʃæd–oᵂ) v. **1.** To surpass in importance and make others appear less important: *He was a good ball player, but he was completely overshadowed by Babe Ruth and Lou Gehrig, who were superstars that year.* **2.** To cast a shadow

o-ver-shoe (oᵂ–vər–ʃuʷ) n. A shoe or boot worn over another shoe to keep the foot warm and/or dry, often made of rubber or plastic

o-ver-sight (oᵂ–vər–saɪt) n. A failure (unintentional) to notice or do sthg.: *The mistake was simply due to an oversight.* —see ERROR

o-ver-state (oᵂ–vər–steʸt) v. **-stated, -stating** To exaggerate: *She overstated her case.*

o-ver-step (oᵂ–vər–stɛp) v. **-pp-** To go beyond: *He overstepped his authority by ordering all that equipment.*

o-vert (oᵂ–vɜrt) adj. Not hidden or secret; said or done openly —**overtly** adv. Openly; publicly: *His objections were never overtly stated.*

o-ver-take (oᵂ–vər–teʸk) v. **-took** (-tʊk), **-taken** (-teʸ–kən) **-taking** To catch up with: *The police car overtook the robbers' car, even though they were driving extremely fast.* NOTE: Do not confuse with **take over.** *Overtake that car.*

(=Pass it) Take over that car. (=Take control of it.)

o-ver-throw (oʷ–vər–θroʷ) v. -threw, -thrown, -throwing **1.** To bring about the downfall **2.** To overturn **3.** To remove from official power

o-ver-time (oʷ–vər–taɪm) n. **1.** Time spent working beyond the usual number of hours **2.** The money paid for this extra time: *He made $50 overtime last week.*

o-ver-tones (oʷ–vər–toʷnz) n. *pl.* Suggestions; hints; an additional meaning to what is actually said or written: *Although he did not specifically mention the government, his speech was full of revolutionary overtones.*

o-ver-ture (oʷ–vər–tʃər) n. **1.** A proposal or offer intended to start discussions: *The government is making overtures of peace.* **2.** An orchestral introduction to an extended musical work

o-ver-turn (oʷ–vər–tɜrn) v. To turn over; capsize: *Their boat overturned in the middle of the lake.*

o-ver-view (oʷ–vər–vyuʷ) n. A broad survey or review of a subject

o-ver-weight (oʷ–vər–weʸt) adj. **1.** Heavier than is usual or allowed: *Your suitcase is five pounds overweight.* **2.** Of people, too heavy; fat

o-ver-whelm (oʷ–vər–wɛlm/ –hwɛlm) v. **1.** To defeat due to a much greater force **2.** Of feelings, to overcome completely and usu. suddenly: *When Jesus healed the deaf and dumb man, people were overwhelmed with amazement* (Mark 7:37).

o-ver-whelm-ing (oʷ–vər–wɛlm–ɪŋ/ –hwɛlm–) adj. Decisive; great: *The president won the election by an overwhelming majority.* —**overwhelmingly** adv.

o-ver-work (oʷ–vər–wɜrk) v. To work or make sbdy. work too hard —**overwork** n. *Not many people die from overwork.*

o-vip-a-rous (oʷ–vɪp–ə–rəs) adj. Of fish, birds, reptiles, etc., producing eggs that hatch outside the body

o-vum (oʷ–vəm) n. *pl.* **o-va** (oʷ–və) The egg from which the young of people and animals develop: *The ovum is fertilized by the sperm of the male.*

owe (oʷ) v. **owed, owing 1.** To be under an obligation to pay: *He owes (me) $20.* **2.** To have a duty to render: *We owe allegiance to the flag.* **3.** To feel grateful toward another or others for what they have done for us personally or for mankind in general: *We owe our parents a lot.*

ow-ing (oʷ–ɪŋ) adj. An amount still to be paid: *How much is owing to you?*

ow-ing to prep. Because of: *Owing to a flat tire, we were late to the meeting.*

owl (aʊl) n. A large night bird with a large head, large eyes, and a hooked beak, said to be very wise

own (oʷn) determ. Belonging to oneself or itself: *This is my own book.*

own pron. **1.** Belonging to oneself or itself: *This book is my own.* **2.** **on one's own** Without help: *I can't help you anymore; you're on your own.* **3.** **holding one's own** Keeping pace; not losing ground; not losing strength

own v. **1.** To possess sthg.; to have as one's own property: *Who owns this house?* **2.** **own up** To confess; to admit that one is guilty: *When they questioned him about starting the rumors, he owned up to it. (=admitted he was the one who did it)*

own-er (oʷ–nər) n. A person who owns sthg., esp. by lawful right —**ownership** n.

ox (ɑks) n. **oxen** (ɑk–sən) **1.** A bovine mammal **2.** An adult castrated male of the common domestic ox

ox-ide (ɑk–saɪd) n. A compound of oxygen with another element: *iron oxide*

ox-i-dize (ɑk–sə–daɪz) v. -dized, -dizing **1.** To combine or cause to combine **2.** To coat with an oxide **3.** To make or become rusty

ox-y-gen (ɑk–sɪ–dʒən) n. A colorless, odorless, tasteless gas present in the air and in water

oys-ter (ɔɪ–stər) n. A type of shellfish which is edible and from which pearls are obtained

oz (aʊnz) *written abbr.* said as: **Ounce** or **ounces**

o-zone (oʷ–zoʷn) n. **1.** A type of oxygen **2.** Fresh air

P, p (pi^y) n. The 16th letter of the English alphabet

pace (pe^ys) n. **1.** A single step: *He took two paces forward.* **2.** Speed of movement: *running at a fast pace* **3. Set the pace** To lead the way, setting or determining the speed of an event: *John set the pace for most of the race, but was passed by two other runners just before crossing the finish line.*

pace v. **paced, pacing 1.** To walk back and forth slowly: *Bob paced the floor nervously, waiting for word from the doctor concerning his wife.* **2.** To measure by taking steps of an equal and known length

pach-y-derm (pæk–ɪ–dɜrm) n. Any of certain thick-skinned, hoofed animals, esp. an elephant, hippopotamus, or rhinoceros —**pach-y-der-mous** (pæk–ɪ–dɜrm–əs) adj. —**pach-y-der-ma-tous** (pæk–ɪ–dɜrm–ə–təs) adj.

pa-cif-ic (pə–sɪf–ɪk) adj. **1.** Peaceful **2.** Tending or leading to peace or conciliation

Pa-cif-ic Ocean (pə–sɪf–ɪk o^w–ʃən) n. The world's largest ocean, between Asia and the Americas

pac-i-fy (pæs–ə–faɪ) v. **-fied, -fying** To make calm or peaceful: *They pacified the crying baby by rocking it and humming a lullaby.*

pack (pæk) n. **1.** A group of things wrapped together for easy handling, esp. for carrying on the back **2.** A group of wild animals that hunt together **3.** A group or a bunch; a lot: *a pack of lies/a pack of thieves* **4.** A complete set of cards used in playing a game **5.** *also* **packet** A small package; a number of small things tied or put together into a small box, case, or bag

pack v. **1.** To put things, esp. one's belongings, into a suitcase or a box or other container for traveling or storing **2.** To cover or surround closely with a protective material: *They packed some paper around the dishes in the box so they wouldn't break.* **3. pack in** *infml.* To attract in large numbers: *That new play at the theater is really packing them in.*

pack-age (pæk–ɪdʒ) n. Sthg. wrapped in paper or placed in a box and tied or fastened for easy carrying or mailing: *Take this package to the post office.*

package v. **-aged, -aging** To place in or tie up as a package: *Books are packaged in the shipping department.*

packed (pækt) adj. Full of people; crowded

pack-er (pæk–ər) n. A person who packs things

pack-et (pæk–ət) n. A small package

pack-ing (pæk–ɪŋ) n. Material used in packing

pact (pækt) n. A solemn agreement: *a peace pact between the two nations*

pad (pæd) n. **1.** Sthg. made or filled with a soft material used to protect sthg., make it more comfortable, etc. **2.** A number of sheets of paper fastened together, used for writing letters, etc.: *a writing pad*

pad v. **-dd-** To fill with soft material in order to protect, shape, or make more comfortable: *Jimmy padded his puppy's bed with a soft blanket./fig. He made his speech longer by padding it with a few jokes.*

pad-ding (pæd–ɪŋ) n. Material used to pad sthg.

pad-dle (pæd–əl) n. **1.** A short pole with a wide flat blade at one or both ends, used for moving and guiding a small boat through the water (Unlike an oar, it is not fastened in position on the side of the boat.) **2.** An implement used for mixing or stirring **3.** A specially shaped wooden stick used for hitting the ball in table tennis —compare RACKET

paddle v. **-dled, -dling** To move a small light boat, esp. a canoe, through water, using one or more paddles

pad-dock (pæd–ək/ –ɪk) n. A fenced field where horses graze and exercise

pad-dy (pæd–i^y) n. **-dies** A flooded field where rice is grown

pad-lock (pæd–lɑk) n. A movable lock that can be used to lock gates, bicycles, etc.

padlock v. To fasten with, or as if with, a padlock

pa-gan (pe^y–gən) n. **1.** One who worships many gods or no god at all, rather than the one and only true God as revealed in the Bible: *The sacrifices of pagans are offered to demons, not to God...* (1 Corinthians 10:20). **2.** An irreligious person —**pagan** adj.

page (pe^ydʒ) n. **1.** One side of a sheet of paper in a book, newspaper, etc. **2.** One employed to run errands or to deliver messages, as in a hotel

page v. **paged, paging** To call aloud for sbdy., esp. over a loudspeaker (in an airport, a hotel, hospital, etc.)

pag-eant (pædʒ–ənt) n. An elaborate public spectacle, usu. out of doors, esp. one in which there is a procession of people and/or historical scenes are enacted —**pageantry** n.

pa-go-da (pə–go^wd–ə) n. A religious building in China and Eastern Asia, usu. a tall tower with several stories, each having an overhanging roof, commonly built over a sacred relic or as a work of devotion

paid (pe^yd) v. Past tense and part. of **pay**

pail (pe^yl) n. A bucket used for carrying liquids: *a milk pail*

pain (pe^yn) n. **1.** Suffering or distress of body or mind **2. pains** pl. Trouble; effort: *The teacher took great pains to make sure that we all understood.*

pain v. To cause to feel pain in the mind or body; hurt: *It pained him to see his child suffer.*

pained (pe^ynd) adj. Showing that one's feelings have been hurt or that he is displeased with a person, a decision, etc.: *After they had quarreled, there was a pained silence between them.*

pain-ful (pe^yn–fʊl) adj. **1.** Feeling or causing pain: *a painful cut on his left arm/ painful memories* **2.** Requiring effort: *a long, painful trip* —**painfully** adv. —**painfulness** n.

pain-less (pe^yn–ləs) adj. Causing no pain —**painlessly** adv.

pains-tak-ing (pe^ynz–te^y–kɪŋ) adj. Very careful

paint (pe^ynt) n. A liquid coloring substance that can be spread on a surface to make it a certain color

paint v. **1.** To put paint on a surface: *He painted the walls a light blue.* **2.** To use paint to make a picture of sbdy. or sthg.: *He paints beautiful landscapes.*

paint-er (pe^ynt–ər) n. **1.** One whose job is painting houses, rooms, etc. **2.** A person who paints pictures; an artist: *a portrait painter*

paint-ing (pe^ynt–ɪŋ) n. **1.** The art or practice of painting pictures **2.** A picture made in this way

pair (pɛər) n. **pairs** or **pair 1.** Sthg. made up of two parts that are alike and are joined and used together: *a pair of pants/scissors/pliers* **2.** Two things that are alike and are usu. used together: *a pair of shoes/gloves* **3.** Two people closely associated, esp. a married or engaged couple: *The happy pair will go to Switzerland after their wedding.*

pair v. To make into a pair: *Helen was paired with my sister in the tennis match.*

pa-ja-mas pl. (pə–dʒɑm–əz/ –dʒæm–) **pyjamas** BrE. n. A loose-fitting pair of pants and shirt used for sleeping

pal (pæl) n. *infml.* A close friend

pal-ace (pæl–əs) n. **1.** A large and splendid house, esp. where a king or queen officially lives **2.** *fig.* Any large or splendid residence; mansion: *Their beautiful house is a palace compared with ours!*

pal-at-a-ble (pæl–ət–ə–bəl) adj. **1.** Agreeable to the taste **2.** Pleasing to the mind or sensibilities

pal-ate (pæl–ət) n. The roof of the mouth

pa-la-tial (pə–le^y–ʃəl) adj. **1.** Like a palace; spacious and splendid **2.** Of or related to a palace

pa-la-ver (pə–læv–ər/ –lɑv–) n. Fuss or bother, often with a lot of talking

pale (pe^yl) adj. **1.** Of a person's face, having less than the usual amount of color **2.** Not bright; faint: *pale blue* —**pale-ness** n.

pale v. **paled, paling** To become pale, weaker, or less important: *Our other troubles paled when we learned of the enemy's attack on our coastline.*

pal-e-o- (pe^y–liy–ə/ –o^w) AmE. **pal-ae-o** BrE.. A prefix meaning very old, ancient times

pal-e-o-lith-ic AmE. **pal-ae-o-lith-ic** BrE. (pe^y–liy–ə–lɪθ–ɪk) adj. Of the early Stone Age when men used stone tools

pal-e-on-to-lo-gy AmE. **pal-ae-on-to-lo-gy** BrE. (pe^y–liy–ən–tɑl–ə–dʒiy) n. The study of fossils as a guide to the history of life on earth

pal-ette (pæl–ət) n. A thin board with a hole for the thumb at one end, used by an artist

for mixing his paints

pal-i-sade (pæl–ə–se^{y}d) n. **1.** A line of lofty, steep cliffs, usu. along a river **2.** A high fence made of stakes, forming a defensive barrier

pall (pɔl) n. **1.** A covering of dark cloth for a coffin **2.** AmE. A coffin **3.** Sthg. that produces a gloomy effect

pall-bear-er (pɔl–bɛər–ər) n. One who helps to carry the coffin at a funeral

pal-lid (pæl–əd) adj. **1.** Unusually pale in complexion **2.** Lifeless; lacking in vitality

pal-lor (pæl–ər) n. The state of being pale or pallid; paleness

palm (pɑm/ pɑlm) n. **1.** A tall tropical tree having a mass of large leaves at its top: *a date palm/a coconut palm* **2.** The inner surface of the hand between the base of the fingers and the wrist

pal-met-to (pæl–mɛt–o^w/ pɑl–) n. **-tos** or **-toes** A palm tree with leaves shaped like fans

palm-ist (pɑm–əst/ pɑl–məst) n. One who claims to tell fortunes by the lines on one's hand NOTE: This is a sinful practice in God's sight. God hates sin, but he is also a God of love and mercy and forgiveness. If we truly repent of our sins and put our trust in Jesus, we will have eternal life (Romans 6:23). —see JESUS

palm-ist-ry (pɑm–ə–stri^y/ pɑl–məst–ri^y) n. The telling of fortunes by reading the markings on one's hand —see PALMIST

palm off (pɑm ɔf/ pɑlm ɔf) v. To give with the intention of cheating

Palm Sun-day (pɑm sʌn–di^y/ pɑlm/ sʌn–de^y) n. The Sunday before Easter (Resurrection Day), commemorating (=in memory of) Christ's triumphal entry into Jerusalem (John 12:12-15). —see JESUS CHRIST, EASTER

palm-y (pɑ–mi^y/ pɑl–) adj. **-ier, -iest 1.** Abounding in palm trees **2.** Prosperous or glorious

pal-o-mi-no (pæl–ə–mi^{y}n–o^w) n. A horse with a light tan color and a whitish mane and tail

pal-pa-ble (pæl–pə–bəl) adj. **1.** Able to be touched or felt **2.** Easily noticed; obvious

pal-pi-tate (pæl–pə–te^{y}t) n. **-tated, -tating 1.** To

pulsate with unusual rapidity, as of the heart **2.** To quiver or throb —**pal-pi-ta-tion** (pæl–pə–te^y–ʃən) n.

pal-sy (pɔl–zi^y) n. **-sies** Any of the various forms of paralysis: *cerebral palsy*

pal-try (pɔl–tri^y) adj. **-trier, triest 1.** Extremely small **2.** Worthless **3.** Contemptible

pam-per (pæm–pər) v. To show too much attention to sbdy.; to coddle: *They always pampered their children.*

pam-phlet (pæm–flət) n. A small booklet with paper covers which usu. deals with some matter of public interest

pan– (pæn–) Comb. form meaning "all" or "whole," as in Pan-American, a term which includes all of America or all Americans, North and South

pan (pæn) n. **1.** A metal container, usu. with a long handle and sometimes with a lid, used in cooking **2.** Any similar vessel —see also BEDPAN, DUSTPAN, FRYING PAN, SAUCEPAN

pan v. **-nn-** To wash in a pan: *They were panning for gold.*

pan-a-ce-a (pæn–ə–si^y–ə) n. Sthg. that is said or believed to cure all ills or troubles

pan-cake (pæn–ke^{y}k) n. A thin, soft, flat cake made of flour, milk, eggs, etc., cooked in a flat pan and eaten hot, esp. for breakfast

pan-cre-as (pæn–kri^y–əs/ pæŋ–) n. A gland near the stomach that discharges digestive juices into the intestine and insulin into the blood

pan-da (pæn–də) n. A bear-like animal with black and white fur, originally from China

pan-dem-ic (pæn–dɛm–ɪk) adj. Of a disease, e.g., occurring over a wide area and affecting a large number of people

pan-de-mo-ni-um (pæn–də–mo^w–ni^y–əm) n. Wild and noisy disorder

pan-der (pæn–dər) v. To be over-anxious to give way to other people's wishes

pane (pe^{y}n) n. A single sheet of glass for use in a frame, esp. of a window

pan-el (pæn–əl) n. **1.** A four-sided division of the surface of a door, wall, etc., different in some way from the surface around it **2.** An instrument panel (board) on which controls or instruments are fastened **3.** A group of

persons gathered together for public dis-cussion or to decide sthg

pan-e-list (pæn–ə–ləst) n. A member of a panel

pang (pæŋ) n. A sudden sharp pain: *pangs of hunger / pangs of conscience*

pan-han-dle (pæn–hæn–dəl) n. A long narrow strip of a larger territory: *the Texas Panhandle*

panhandle v. **-dled, -dling** To beg in the street

pan-han-dler (pæn–hænd–lər) n. A beggar

pan-ic (pæn–ɪk) n. A state of sudden uncontrollable fear or terror: *There was a lot of panic during the earthquake.*

panic v. **-icked, -icking** To feel or cause to feel panic: *The crowd panicked when the shooting began.*

pan-ic–strick-en (pæn–ɪk–strɪk–ən) n. Filled with terror

pan-o-ply (pæn–ə–pliʸ) n. All the splendid and magnificent dress, equipment, etc. associated with a particular event

pan-o-ram-a (pæn–ə–ræm–ə) n. **1.** An unobstructed view of a wide area **2.** A continuously changing scene or series of events

pan-sy (pæn–ziʸ) n. **-sies** A small plant of the violet family with wide, flat velvety flowers

pant (pænt) v. To take quick short breaths, as after exertion

pant n. A short quick breath

pan-the-ism (pæn–θiʸ–ɪz–əm) n. **1.** The unscriptural belief that God is not a personality, but that all laws, forces, manifestations, etc. existing in the universe are God **2.** The worship or toleration of worship of all gods of various cults NOTE: The Bible (God's Word) clearly teaches that there is only one God and that we are to worship and serve only him (Matthew 4:4). —**pantheist** n. —**pan-the-ist-ic** (pæn–θiʸ–ɪs–tɪk) adj.

pan-ther (pæn–θər) n. A large wild black leopard; a cougar

pan-ties (pæn–tiʸz) or **pan-ty** also **pants** n. A woman's or a child's underpants

pan-to-mime (pænt–ə–maɪm) n. *also* **mime** A play in which the performers express themselves by gestures, rather than with words

pantomime v. **-mimed, -miming** To act or express oneself in pantomime, without words

pan-try (pæn–triʸ) n. **-tries** A small room with shelves, where dishes, food, etc., are kept, usu. near the kitchen

pants (pænts) n. **1.** A pair of trousers **2.** A pair of underpants

pant-suit (pænt–suʷt) n. A woman's suit, usu. with jacket and pants of matching material

pa-pa (pɑp–ə) n. *infml.* Father

pa-pa-cy (peʸ–pə–siʸ) n. **-cies 1.** The position or authority of the pope, the head of the Roman Catholic Church **2.** The term of a pope's time in office **3.** The system of church government by the popes

pa-pal (peʸ–pəl) n. Of the pope or papacy

pa-pa-ya (pə–paɪ–ə) n. A large, sweet yellow fruit of a tropical tree

pa-per (peʸ–pər) n. **1.** Material made in the form of sheets from very thin threads of wood or cloth, used for writing, covering packages, walls, etc. **2.** *infml.* A newspaper

paper v. To cover a wall with wallpaper

pa-per-boy (peʸ–pər–bɔɪ) n. A boy who delivers newspapers

pa-per–mâ-ché (peʸ–pər–mə–ʃeʸ) n. Molded paper pulp used for making trays, ornaments, boxes, etc.

pa-poose (pæ–puʷs) n. A North American Indian baby

pap-ri-ka (pə–priʸ–kə/ pæ–) n. A red sauce with a mild taste, made from powdered sweet red peppers

pa-py-rus (pə–paɪ–rəs) **-ruses** or **-ri** (–riʸ) n. A type of reed from which people used to make paper

par (pɑr) n. **1.** The same level or nearly the same level: *This history course is on a par with that one.* **2.** In golf, the number of strokes a player should take to hit the ball into a hole **3. below par** *infml.* Not in the usual or average condition (of health, activity, etc.): *He's not feeling up to par today.*

pa-ra- (pæ–rə–/ peər–ə–) or **par–** prefix **1.** Beside; along with: *paramedic* **2.** Beyond; aside from: *paradox* **3.** Shelter or protection from: *parasol*

par-a-ble (pær–ə–bəl/ peər–) n. A short simple story which teaches a moral or religious les-

son

par-a-chute (pær-ə-ʃuᵂt/ **peər**-) n. An umbrella-like device made of strong fabric, fastened to persons or objects dropped from aircraft in order to make them fall slowly —**parachute** v.

par-a-chut-ist (pær-ə-ʃuᵂt-əst/ peər-) n. A person who drops from an aircraft using a parachute

pa-rade (pə-reᵞd) n. **1.** A large public procession for the purpose of being viewed by a crowd, usually of a festive nature: *The beautiful Rose Parade is held every News Year's Day in Pasadena, California.* **2.** A military ceremony that involves the formation and marching of troops

parade v. -raded, -rading **1.** To march in, or as if in, a parade: *The circus performers paraded through the town.* **2.** *Often derog.* To show in order to gain admiration: *She was parading her new clothes in front of her friends.*

par-a-digm (pær-ə-daım/ peər-) n. An example showing a certain pattern

par-a-dise (pær-ə-daıs/ –daız/ **peər**-) n. **1.** Heaven **2.** Where God and the holy angels are, and where all believers in Jesus Christ will spend eternity: *Jesus told the thief on the cross, who repented of his sins, "Today you will be with me in paradise"* (Luke 23:43). —see HEAVEN **3.** A place of perfect happiness: *fig. This country is a sportsman's paradise.*

par-a-dox (pær-ə-daks/ **peər**-) n. **1.** A statement that appears to contradict itself or be contrary to common sense, but which may be true **2.** A person or situation displaying an apparently contradictory nature —**par-a-dox-i-cal** adj. (pær-ə-daks-ı-kəl/ peər-) —**paradoxically** adv.

par-af-fin (pær-ə-fən/ peər-) n. **1.** A white waxy substance obtained from petroleum, used in making candles **2.** *BrE.* for kerosene

par-a-gon (pær-ə-gɑn/-gən/ peər-) n. A perfect model to copy: *a paragon of virtue*

par-a-graph (pær-ə-græf/ peər-) n. A division of a piece of writing that has one or more sentences, of which the first word starts a new line

par-a-keet (pær-ə-kiᵞt/ peər-) n. A type of small, long-tailed parrot

par-al-lel (pær-ə-lɛl/ peər-) adj. Lines or rows running side by side but never getting nearer or further away from each other: *The railroad tracks run parallel to each other.*

parallel v. To equal: *No one has paralleled his success as a film star.*

par-al-lel-o-gram (pær-ə-lɛl-ə-græm/ peər-) n. A flat four-sided figure, the opposite sides of which are equal and parallel

par-al-y-sis (pə-ræl-ə-səs) n. -ses (–siᵞz) A loss of feeling in and control of the muscles

par-a-lyt-ic (pær-ə-lıt-ık/ peər-) adj. **1.** Of a person suffering from paralysis **2.** Causing paralysis —**paralytic** n.

par-a-lyze (pær-ə-laız/ **peər**-) v. -lyse, *BrE.* -lyzed, -lyzing **1.** To make the body muscles unable to move **2.** To bring things to a halt: *The strike paralyzed train service.* **3. paralyzed with fear** Unable to move because of fear

par-a-med-ic (pær-ə-**med**-ık/ peər-) n. One who is trained to provide emergency medical treatment or to assist medical professionals

par-a-mount (pær-ə-maunt/ **peər**-) adj. Chief in importance or rank

par-a-noi-a (pær-ə-**nɔı**-ə/ peər-) n. A disease of the mind that causes a person to think that people are trying to abuse or persecute him or causes him to have delusions of grandeur

par-a-noid (pær-ə-nɔıd/ peər-) adj. Of a person suffering from paranoia

par-a-pet (pær-ə-pət/ -pɛt/ **peər**-) n. A low wall on a bridge or balcony to keep a person from falling off

par-a-pher-na-li-a (pær-ə-fər-neᵞl-yə/ –fə-neᵞl-yə/ peər-) n. A number of articles needed for a specific job or activity: *The baseball catcher has to wear a lot of protective paraphernalia.*

par-a-phrase (pær-ə-freᵞz/ **peər**-) v. -phrased, -phrasing To rewrite or retell sthg. in words that are easier to understand

par-a-ple-gic (pær-ə-pliᵞ-dʒık/ peər-) n. Sbdy. who is suffering from paralysis of the lower part of the body —**paraplegia** n.

par-a-site (pær-ə-saıt/ peər-) n. **1.** A plant or animal that lives on or in another and gets its nourishment from it **2.** A useless person

who gets his support from others without doing anything for them in return

par-a-sol (pær-ə-sɒl/ -sɔl/ **peǝr**-) n. A small umbrella for protection from the sun

par-a-troops (pær-ə-truʷps/ **peǝr**-) n. Troops that are trained to attack an enemy position by dropping from aircraft, using parachutes —**paratrooper** n.

par-cel (par-səl) n. 1. A package 2. A distinct portion or tract of land 3. **part and parcel** An important part that cannot be separated from the whole

parch (partʃ) v. 1. To make very dry with intense heat 2. To make thirsty: *I'm parched! Do you have anything to drink?*

parch-ment (partʃ-mənt) n. The skin of a sheep or goat, prepared as a material to write on

par-don (pard-ən) v. 1. To forgive; excuse: *Pardon me, I didn't mean to interrupt.* 2. To give an official pardon, releasing a prisoner from the penalty of his offense: *The governor pardoned the criminal.*

pardon n. 1. An act or example of forgiveness 2. An action of a court or governor or other ruler, forgiving a person for an unlawful act, and giving freedom from punishment 3. **I beg your pardon** *polite:* Excuse me; I'm sorry: *I beg your pardon. I didn't mean to shut the door in your face.* 4. **pardon me** *infml.* A polite way to make a request: *Pardon me, would you please repeat that telephone number?*

par-don-a-ble (par-dən-ə-bəl) adj. That which can be pardoned: *a pardonable mistake* —opposite UNPARDONABLE

pare (peǝr) v. **-pared**, **-paring** To trim by cutting away the edges of; to cut away the outer covering of sthg.: *to pare an apple*

par-ent (pær-ənt/ **peǝr**-) n. 1. The father or mother of a person or animal: *Children, obey your parents in everything, for this pleases the Lord* (Colossians 3:20). 2. The source or cause of sthg.; origin: *a parent organization*

par-ent-age (pær-ən-tɪdʒ/ **peǝr**-) n. Ancestry; descent from parents

pa-ren-tal (pə-rent-əl) adj. Of parents

pa-ren-the-sis (pə-ren-θə-səs) n. **-ses** (-siʸz) 1. *usu. pl.* Either of a pair of small curved lines

( ), used in writing to enclose added information 2. An added explanation or thought enclosed in this way —**par-en-thet ic** (pær-ən-θet-ɪk/ **peǝr**-) or —**parenthetical** adj. —**parenthetically** adv.

pa-ri-ah (pə-raɪ-ə) n. 1. A social outcast 2. In India, a person of no caste or of very low caste

par-ish (pær-ɪʃ/ **peǝr**-) n. 1. The members of the congregation of any church 2. An administrative district of various churches, esp. a part of a diocese, under the charge of a priest or minister 3. A civil division equivalent to a county

pa-rish-ion-er (pə-rɪʃ-ə-nər) n. A member of a particular church parish or congregation

par-i-ty (pær-ət-iʸ/ **peǝr**-) n. The state of being equal

park (park) n. A large, usu. grassy piece of land in a town, used by the public for picnics, recreation, or rest

park v. To stop a car or other vehicle and leave it in a certain place for a time: *Don't park the car by a red curb.*

par-ka (par-kə) n. A warm jacket with a hood, often lined with fur

park-ing (park-ɪŋ) n. The leaving of a vehicle in a certain place for a period of time: *She's a good driver, but parallel parking (between two other cars) is difficult for her.*

par-lia-ment (par-lə-mənt) n. 1. The people who are wholly or partly elected by the citizens of a country to make laws 2. In the United Kingdom, the main law-making body of the country —**par-lia-men-ta-ry** (par-lə-men-tə-riʸ) adj.

par-lia-men-tar-i-an (par-lə-men-teǝr-iʸ-ən) n. An expert in parliamentary procedure, whose duty it is to see that business is conducted according to the rules

par-lor *AmE.* **par-lour** *BrE.* (par-lər) n. 1. (now rare) A room in a private home set aside for the entertainment of visitors 2. A business establishment: *a beauty parlor/an ice cream parlor*

pa-ro-chi-al (pə-roʷ-kiʸ-əl) adj. 1. Of or pertaining to a church parish 2. Narrow in scope; local; showing interest in a limited area only

par-o-dy (pær-əd-i^y/ pɛər-) n. -dies 1. An amusing imitation of a serious author's style; comic imitation 2. Sthg. done so badly that it seems to be an intentional mockery of what it ought to be: *The trial was a parody of justice.*

pa-role (pə-ro^wl) n. The release of a prisoner before his term has expired, on condition of good behavior

par-rot (pær-ət/ pɛər-) n. A tropical bird, with a curved beak, brightly colored feathers, and the ability to learn to talk

par-ry (pær-i^y/ pɛər-) v. -ried, -rying 1. To turn aside or ward off a blow by using one's weapon or an arm or hand 2. To avoid having to answer

Par-see (par-si^y) A member of a religious sect in India whose ancestors originally came from Persia; a believer in Zoroastrianism — **Parsiism** or **Parsism** —see ZOROASTRIANISM

par-si-mo-ny (par-sə-mo^wn-i^y) n. Excessive carefulness in spending money or using resources; stinginess; meanness —**par-si-mo-ni-ous** (par-sə-**mo^w**-ni^y-əs) adj. —**parsimoniously** adv.

pars-ley (par-sli^y) n. A plant with feathery leaves that are used to flavor or decorate food

pars-nip (par-snɪp) n. A long, whitish plant root with a rather strong taste, eaten as a vegetable

par-son (pars-ən) n. A clergyman in charge of a church

par-son-age (pars-ən-ɪdʒ) n. The official residence, provided by the church, for its parson or pastor

part (part) n. 1. A piece which is less than a whole: *Which part of the town do you live in?* 2. Any of the pieces into which sthg. is divided: *Cut the cake into eight equal parts.* 3. A necessary piece of a machine or other equipment: *They sell all kinds of parts for all kinds of cars.* 4. A share in some activity: *Did you take part in the demonstration?* 5. The words spoken by a character acted by an actor in a play: *In our next production, I will take the part of a detective.* 6. A side or position in an argument: *He always takes his brother's part.* 7. A

line on the head made when hair is separated by combing 8. **for my part** As far as I'm concerned 9. **for the most part** *fml.* Mostly; most of the time: *For the most part she is a well-behaved child.* 10. **in part** Partially; partly: *She agreed that she was in part responsible for the accident.* 11. **on the part of sbdy.** By sbdy.: *It was a mistake on your part to sign that petition before reading it.*

part v. 1. To put or keep apart by coming between: *She tried to part the fighting children.* 2. To separate hair on the head by combing on each side of a line: *He parted his hair on the left.* 3. **part company** To end a relationship with sbdy.: *They were friends for years, but now they've parted company.* 4. **part with sthg.** To give up, esp. unwillingly: *It's difficult to part with one's lifelong friends.*

part adj. A portion: *He's part English and part Norwegian.*

par-take (par-te^yk/ pər-) v. -took, -taken, -taking 1. To take part in; participate: *Don't partake in other men's sins* (1 Timothy 5:22). 2. To eat or drink, esp. sthg. offered: *You can safely partake of this food.*

par-tak-en Past part. of **partake**

par-tial (par-ʃəl) adj. 1. Not complete: *a partial answer* 2. Favoring one person or group more than another, esp. in a way that is unfair —opposite IMPARTIAL 3. Having a strong liking for: *I'm very partial to apple pie.*

par-ti-al-i-ty (par-ʃi^y-æl-ə-ti^y/par-ʃæl-ə-ti^y) n. The quality or fact of being partial; biased; showing favoritism —opposite IMPARTIALITY

par-tial-ly (par-ʃəl-i^y) adv. 1. Not completely; partly: *I am partially to blame for the accident.* 2. In a partial way

par-tic-i-pant (par-tɪs-ə-pənt) n. One who participates in a particular event: *He was a participant in the Olympic games.*

par-tic-i-pate (par-tɪs-ə-pe^yt) v. -pated, -pating To take part or have a share in an activity or event —**par-tic-i-pa-tion** (par-tɪs-ə-pe^y-ʃən) n. —**par-tic-i-pa-tor** (par-tɪs-ə-pe^yt-ər) n.

par-ti-cip-i-al (par-tə-sɪp-i^y-əl) adj. Of or containing a participle: *a participial phrase*

par-ti-ci-ple (par-tə-sɪp-əl) n. *Gram.* Either of

two forms of a verb, ending in **-ing**. (pres.
[____], or ___ed, -en, etc (past part.) and used
(a) in verb phrases: "She is writing" or "She
has written." or **(b)** used as an adjective: "a
written report"

par-ti-cle (part–ɪ–kəl) n. **1.** A very small piece
of matter: *dust particles floating in the sunlight* **2.** A very small amount: *There wasn't a
particle of truth in what he said.*

par-tic-u-lar (pər–tɪk–yə–lər) adj. **1.** Relating to
one person or thing rather than others; special: *I thought the third paragraph would be of
particular interest to you.* **2.** Single and different from others; of a certain sort: *I didn't appreciate that particular remark.* **3.** Showing too
much concern in small matters; hard to
please: *He's very particular about his food.* **4.**
in particular Especially

par-tic-u-lar-ly (pər–tɪk–yə–lər–liʸ) adv. Especially; in a way that is special and different
from others: *He was happy to see all of us, particularly his brother whom he hadn't seen for
years.*

par-tic-u-lars (pər–tɪk–yə–lərz) n. *pl.* The details

part-ing (part–ŋ) n. Departure

parting adj. Done at the time of leaving: *a
parting kiss*

par-ti-san (part–ə–zən/ –sən) **1.** A strong supporter of a political party, group, or plan **2.**
A member of an armed resistance movement in a country occupied by enemy forces; sbdy. who fights in secret against an enemy that has conquered his country

par-ti-tion (par–tɪʃ–ən/ pər–) n. **1.** Sthg. that divides; a light, often temporary, wall be-
tween rooms **2.** The act of dividing; the state
of being divided: *the partition of India*

partition v. To divide: *They partitioned the
room off with a curtain.*

part-ly (part–liʸ) adv. To some extent but not
entirely: *I was exhausted; partly from the trip
and partly from the meal.*

part-ner (part–nər) n. **1.** A person associated
with another in some common activity, as
in dancing, playing tennis, etc. **2.** Any of the
owners of a business, who share the profits
and losses **3.** A spouse: *a marriage partner*

part-ner-ship (part–nər–ʃɪp) n. **1.** The state of

being a partner, esp. in business: *We've enjoyed a long partnership in this business.* **2.** A
business owned by two or more people

par-took (par–tʊk) v. Past tense of **partake**

par-tridge (par–trɪdʒ) n. A bird with a plump
body and brownish feathers, often hunted
as game

par-ty (part–iʸ) n. **-ties 1.** A gathering of people, usu. by invitation, for food and amusement: *a birthday party* **2.** A group of people
doing sthg. together: *This table is for a party
of four./The search party found the missing
child.* **3.** A political group organized to promote and support its principles and candidates: *The two major political parties in the
United States are the Republican Party and the
Democratic Party.* **4.** A person or a group involved in a legal proceeding **5.** A participant: *I refuse to be a party to their argument.*

pass (pæs) v. **1.** To move beyond a person or
place: *I passed your house on my way to work.*
2. To go forward: *The road was blocked by a
fallen tree so we couldn't pass.* **3.** To hand over
or deliver: *Please pass the salt!* **4.** In various
sports, to relay or transfer a ball to a member of one's own team **5.** To spend time: *He
passed the time by reading a book.* **6.** To approve or sanction; enact: *Congress finally
passed the much disputed bill.* **7.** To succeed in
an examination: *She passed her driving test on
her first try.* —opposite FAIL **8.** To come to
an end: Jesus said, *"Heaven and earth will
pass away, but my words will never pass away"*
(Matthew 24:35). **9. pass away** Esp. of a person, to die: *She passed away in her sleep last
night.* **10. pass for** To be mistakenly accepted
as: *She could pass for a much younger woman.*
11. pass out (a) To faint **(b)** Hand out sthg.;
distribute **12. pass sthg. up** To let go; to
miss an opportunity: *Don't pass up a chance
like that.* **13. come to pass** To occur; happen
14. bring to pass To cause sthg. to happen
15. pass over To disregard or ignore **16.**
pass up To reject, as an opportunity

pass n. **1.** A way by which one may go
through, esp. over a range of mountains:
*The Khyber Pass is a famous 35 mile mountain
pass in eastern Afghanistan near the Pakistan
border.* **2.** An act of moving past: *The plane*

made a few passes over the airport. **3.** A free ticket or permit **4.** A successful result in an examination —opposite FAIL **5.** An act of passing a ball: *a fifty yard pass*

pass-a-ble (pæs–ə–bəl) adj. **1.** Acceptable; not bad: *His English compositions are not the best in the class, but they are passable.* **2.** Of a road or river, fit to be used, crossed, etc.: *This road is rough but it's passable.* —opposite IMPASSABLE

pas-sage (pæs–ɪdʒ) n. **1.** A way or channel through which a person or thing may pass **2.** A hall or corridor between apartments in a building **3.** A journey, esp. by sea: *We hope to arrange passage on the ship next month.* **4.** The action of going across, by, over, or through: *The bridge is not strong enough to allow the passage of heavy vehicles.*

pas-sen-ger (pæs–ən–dʒər) n. A person, not the driver, traveling in a public or private vehicle

pas-ser-by (pæs–ər–baɪ/ pæs–ər–baɪ) n. One who passes by, usu. casually

pass-ing (pæs–ɪŋ) adj. **1.** Moving or going by: *We sat there counting the cars on the passing train.* **2.** Not lasting very long: *He didn't even give the matter a passing thought.*

pas-sion (pæʃ–ən) n. Strong, deep, often uncontrollable feelings, esp. of love, hatred, or anger: *Those who belong to Christ Jesus have crucified the sinful nature with its passions and desires* (Galatians 5:24).

Pas-sion n. The sufferings of Jesus Christ, esp. after the Last Supper and while on the cross where he suffered and died for our sins —see JESUS CHRIST

pas-sion-ate (pæʃ–ə–nət) adj. **1.** Capable or inclined toward strong passion; excitable: *a passionate person* **2.** Expressing or characterized by passion; ardent: *a passionate speech* **3.** Strong or vehement, as a feeling or emotion —**passionately** adv.

pas-sive (pæs–ɪv) adj. **1.** Not active **2.** *Gram.* (of a verb) Expressing an action that was done to the subject of a sentence: *"Was written" is a passive verb in "This book was written by Moses."*

passive voice (pæs–ɪv vɔɪs) A form of a verb that shows that the subject of the sentence

is the receiver of the action expressed by the verb: *In the sentence, "The bank was robbed," the verb form "was robbed" is in the passive voice.*

Pass-o-ver (pæs–oʷ–vər) n. An annual Jewish holiday in memory of their escape from Egyptian bondage and the sparing of their first-born children when a destroying angel passed over the homes of the Hebrews and killed the first-born in every Egyptian home (Exodus 12:1-30). This occurred in the 15th century B. C.

pass-port (pæs–pɔrt) n. A small official booklet that proves the nationality of a person, and is used esp. when entering a foreign country

pass-word (pæs–wərd) n. A secret word or phrase that identifies a person and allows him or her to enter a certain place

past (pæst) adj. **1.** Of time, much earlier than the present: *In the past God spoke to our forefathers through the prophets at many times and in various ways, but in these last days he has spoken to us by his Son [Jesus]* (Hebrews 1:1,2). —opposite FUTURE **2.** A little earlier than the present; up until the time of speaking: *I haven't been feeling very well for the past few days.* **3.** Finished; ended: *Spring is past and summer has come.* **4.** Former; not any longer: *She's a past president of the club.*

past prep. **1. (a)** Farther than: *The hospital is about a mile past the school.* **(b)** Beyond: *We drove past the house.* **2.** Beyond in time or age: *It's half past three./ She's past (=older than) eighty.* —**past** adv. *A whole year went past before we saw them again.*

pas-ta (pɑs–tə) n. A dough used in making spaghetti, macaroni, etc.

paste (peʸst) n. **1.** A sticky substance used for sticking paper together or onto other surfaces **2.** Any soft wet mixture that is easily shaped or spread: *toothpaste* **3.** A food made by crushing solid foods into a smooth soft mass: *We need a can of tomato paste to make the sauce.*

pas-tel (pæs–tɛl) n. **1.** A color having a soft, subdued shade **2.** A stick of chalk-like coloring matter **3.** A picture drawn with such a stick

pas-teur-ize (pæs–tʃə–raɪz) v. -ized, -izing To expose (milk e.g.) to a high temperature in a certain way in order to destroy bacteria —**pas-teu-ri-za-tion** (pæs–tʃə–rə–zeʸ–ʃən) n.

pas-time (pæs–taɪm) n. A hobby; a spare-time interest

pas-tor (pæs–tər) n. A Christian religious leader in charge of a church and its members: *It was he [Christ] who gave some to be apostles, some to be prophets, some to be evangelists, and some to be pastors and teachers* (Ephesians 4:11).

pas-to-ral (pæs–tə–rəl) adj. **1.** Of or belonging to shepherds **2.** Of or pertaining to rural life **3.** Concerning the pastor of a church or his duties **4.** Pertaining to letters written by St. Paul, the Apostle, to Pastors Timothy and Titus: *pastoral letters or epistles*

past par-ti-ci-ple (pæst pɑrt–ə–sɪp–əl) In grammar, a form of a verb that expresses time gone by or a former state or action: *In the sentence, "She has worked hard all day, " the word "worked" is a past participle.*

pas-tra-mi (pə–strɑm–iʸ) n. A highly seasoned smoked beef prepared esp. from shoulder cuts

past-ry (peʸs–triʸ) n. -ries Sweet baked foods, usu. made with a crust of dough, as pies, tarts, etc.

past tense (pæst tɛns) In grammar, a verb tense that expresses an action that happened or a condition that existed in time gone by: *In the sentence, "He wrote ten letters today," the word "wrote" is in the past tense.*

pas-ture (pæs–tʃər) n. Grassy land where cattle feed

pat (pæt) n. **1.** A light friendly touch with the hand: *She gave her daughter a pat on the shoulder.* **2.** A small shaped mass of butter **3. pat on the back** *infml.* An expression of praise or satisfaction for sthg. done

pat v. -tt- **1.** To tap gently or lovingly with the hand: *He patted him on the back for a job well done.* **2.** To tap lightly: *The boy patted the dog on the head.*

pat adv. **1.** Firm; steadfast: *He stood pat and would not change his mind.* **2. down pat** To have memorized: *He has his part in the play down pat.*

patch (pætʃ) n. **1.** A piece of material used to cover a hole or a damaged place: *He had a patch on the knee of his pants.* **2.** An area that is different from the area around it: *There will be a few patches of fog near the coast.* **3.** A small piece of ground, esp. as used for growing vegetables: *a cabbage patch*

patch v. **1.** To put a patch on a hole esp. on a garment **2. patch sthg. up (a)** To mend with patches: *to patch up an old coat/fig. The doctor patched up the soldier and sent him home.* **(b)** To make up and become friends again: *They patched up their quarrel and are best friends again.*

patch-work (pætʃ–wərk) n. **1.** Pieces of cloth of various shapes and colors sewn together **2.** Anything like this

patch-y (pætʃ–iʸ) adj. -ier, -iest Made up of patches: *patchy fog*

pate (peʸt) n. The top of the head

pa-tel-la (pə–tɛl–ə) n. Kneecap

pat-ent (pæt–ənt) also **patented** (pæt–ən–təd) adj. Protected by a patent from being copied or sold by people who have no right to do so

patent n. **1.** The exclusive right granted by the government to an inventor to make or sell a new invention for a certain number of years **2.** An official document conferring such a right **3.** An invention protected by this right

pa-ter-nal (pə–tɜrn–əl) adj. **1.** Of, like, or received from a father: *paternal love* **2.** Related to a person through the father's side of the family: *my paternal grandmother (=my father's mother)* **3.** *derog.* Protecting the people like a father but allowing them no freedom —**paternally** adv. —compare MATERNAL

pa-ter-nal-ism (pə–tɜrn–əl–ɪz–əm) n. *Derog.* The paternal way of ruling a country, controlling a company, etc. —**pa-ter-nal-is-tic** (pə–tɜr–nəl–ɪs–tɪk) adj.

path (pæθ) n. **1.** Also **pathway** A trail or way made by people walking over the ground: *a path through the forest* **2.** An open space made to allow forward movement: *The police cleared a path through the crowd.* **3.** Direction: *Your word [O, Lord] is a lamp to my feet and a light for my path* (Psalm 119:105). *He*

guides me in paths of righteousness (Psalm 23:6).

pa·thet·ic (pə–θet–ɪk) adj. **1.** Causing a feeling of pity: *the child's pathetic cries of hunger* **2.** *derog.* Worthless; hopelessly unsuccessful: *She's a pathetic cook!* —**pathetically** adv.

path·o·log·i·cal (pæθ–ə–lɑdʒ–i–kəl) adj. **1.** Of or concerning pathology **2.** Caused by disease, esp. of the mind **3.** Unreasonable; caused solely by the imagination: *a pathological fear of darkness* —**pathologically** adv.

pa·thol·o·gist (pæ–θɑl–ə–dʒəst/ pə–) n. An expert in pathology

pa·thol·o·gy (pæ–θɑl–ə–dʒiʸ/ pə–) n. **-gies** The study of disease

pa·thos (peʸ–θɑs) n. The quality in sthg. seen or experienced that arouses pity

pa·tience (peʸ–ʃəns) n. The quality of being patient: *The fruit of the Spirit is love, joy, peace, patience...* (Galatians 5:22). *As God's chosen people, ... clothe yourselves with compassion, kindness, humility, gentleness, and patience* (Colossians 3:12). *I was shown mercy so that in me, the worst of sinners, Christ Jesus might display his unlimited patience as an example for those who would believe on him and receive eternal life* (1 Timothy 1:16). —opposite IMPATIENCE

pa·tient (peʸ–ʃənt) adj. Able to bear long waiting, or anything unpleasant, calmly and without complaining: *Love is patient and kind* (1 Corinthians 13:4). *Be patient, bearing with one another in love* (Ephesians 4:2). *He [God] is patient with you, not wanting anyone to perish, but everyone to come to repentance* (2 Peter 3:9). —opposite IMPATIENT —**patiently** adv.

patient n. A person receiving medical treatment from a doctor and/or in a hospital

pa·ti·o (pæt–iʸ–oʷ) n. **-os 1.** An open inner court **2.** A paved area adjoining a house, used for parties, barbecues, etc.

pa·tri·arch (peʸ–triʸ–ɑrk) n. **1.** The male head of a family or tribe **2.** An old, highly-respected man **3.** A chief bishop in the Eastern Orthodox Church —**pa·tri·ar·chal** (peʸ–triʸ–ɑr–kəl) adj. Ruled by a patriarch

pa·tri·ot (peʸ–triʸ–ət) n. One who loves his country

pa·tri·o·tism (peʸ–triʸ–ə–tɪz–əm) n. Love of and loyalty to one's country —**pa·tri·ot·ic** (peʸ–triʸ–ɑt–ɪk) adj.

pa·trol (pə–troʷl) v. **-ll-** To keep guard or watch by going back and forth (on foot, in a vehicle, or on a ship): *Soldiers patrolled the streets./ Naval ships patrolled the coastline.*

patrol n. The act of keeping guard in this way: *My brother is on patrol tonight.*

pa·trol·man (pə–troʷl–mən) n. A policeman who patrols a particular area

pa·tron (peʸ–trən) n. **1.** A regular customer of a shop **2.** A person who supports an artist, musician, writer, etc.: *He's a patron of the arts.*

pa·tron·age (pæ–trə–nɪdʒ/ peʸ–) n. The support given by a patron: *The store owner thanked his customers for their pa·tronage.*

pa·tron·ize (pæ–trə–naɪz/ peʸ–) v. **-ized, -izing 1.** To be a patron **2.** To act nicely toward other people, but in a way that shows that one feels that he is better or more important than others

pat·ter (pæt–ər) n. **1.** The sound of sthg. striking a hard surface: *the patter of rain on the window* **2.** Fast talk, esp. that of a persuasive salesman, or that of a comedian —**patter** v.

pat·tern (pæt–əm) n. **1.** A model or a guide for making sthg.: *a dress pattern* **2.** A regularly repeated arrangement of lines, shapes, etc.: *I like the way the dress is made, but I don't like the pattern on the material.* **3.** The way in which sthg. happens or develops: *The illness is not following its usual pattern.* **4.** A habitual way of doing things: *Do not conform any longer to the [sinful] pattern of this world, but be transformed by the renewing of your mind* (Romans 12:2).

pat·ty (pæt–iʸ) n. **-ties 1.** A small, usu. round, flat cake of chopped meat: *a hamburger patty* **2.** A small round flat piece of candy: *a peppermint patty*

pau·ci·ty (pɔ–sət–iʸ) n. Smallness of number or quantity

Paul (pɔl) n. **1.** A masculine name **2.** The Apostle Paul (Saint Paul), missionary to the Gentiles in the first century, author of thirteen Epistles (letters) of the New Testament, emphasizing the deity of Jesus Christ

and salvation by grace through faith in Jesus without the deeds of the Law, but also stressing the fact that Christians are to live holy lives to the glory of God, out of appreciation for all that God has done and continues to do for them.

paunch (pɒntʃ / pɑntʃ) n. A fat stomach

pau-per (pɔ-pər) n. A very poor person

pause (pɔz) n. A short but noticeable break in activity or speech

pause v. **paused, pausing** To stop for a short time before continuing: *She paused to pour a cup of coffee, then continued sewing.*

pave (peᵞv) v. **paved, paving 1.** To cover a path, road, or other area with a surface of concrete: *They are going to pave the tennis court today.* **2.** *fig.* **pave the way** Make possible: *This zoning change will pave the way for the new housing project.*

pave-ment (peᵞv-mənt) n. The hard paved surface of a street

pa-vil-ion (pə-vɪl-yən) n. **1.** A large, usu. open-sided building, used for shelter, pleasure, etc. **2.** A fancy or elaborate tent **3.** A building that houses an exhibition at a fair **4.** Any of the separate or connected parts of a group of related buildings, such as a part of a hospital

paw (pɔ) n. An animal's foot that has nails or claws

paw v. Of an animal, to touch or try to touch with a paw: *The horse was pawing impatiently at the ground.*

pawn (pɒn) v. To leave sthg. of value with a pawnbroker as a promise that one will repay the money one has borrowed

pawn-bro-ker (pɒn-broᵂ-kər) n. One who loans money in exchange for pawned articles

pawn-shop (pɒn-ʃap) n. A pawnbroker's place of business

pay (peᵞ) v. **paid** (peᵞd) **paying 1.** To give money to sbdy. in return for work done, goods purchased, etc. **2.** To be profitable or worth the effort: *Crime doesn't pay.* **3.** To suffer for some bad action: *He had to pay a lot for his mistake.* **4.** To do, make, or say: *pay a visit/ pay a compliment* **5.** To give one's attention: *Pay attention and listen to the sayings of the*

wise (Proverbs 22:17).

pay n. Wages; salary; reward; punishment

pay-a-ble (peᵞ-ə-bəl) adj. That which may or must be paid: *Your check should be made payable to "Pasadena Shoe Store, Inc."* (=this name should be written on the check)

pay-ee (peᵞ-iᵞ) n. The person to whom money is to be paid

pay-ment (peᵞ-mənt) n. **1.** The act of paying: *He made the final payment on his car./No man can redeem the life of another or give to God a ransom for him — the ransom for a life is costly, no payment is ever enough* (Psalm 49:7,8). *Only God could make sufficient payment for our sin, and he did, "For God so loved the world that he gave his one and only Son [Jesus Christ who paid for our sins with his own blood] that whoever believes in him shall not perish but have eternal life"* (John 3:16). **2.** An amount of money to be paid: *monthly payment for rent*

pay-roll (peᵞ-roᵂl) n. **1.** A list of all the employees and the amount of salary that each one is to be paid **2.** The total amount of money paid to employees at one time

pea (piᵞ) n. A round green seed, eaten as a vegetable

peace (piᵞs) n. **1.** A condition or period in which there is no war **2.** A state of freedom from disorder within a country, with the citizens living according to the law **3.** Calmness; quietness; freedom from anxiety: *The fruit of the [Holy] Spirit is love, joy, peace...* (Galatians 5:22). *There can be no peace with God until a person knows and accepts Jesus Christ, the Prince of Peace, as his personal Savior from sin: Therefore, being justified by faith [in Jesus] we have peace with God through our Lord Jesus Christ* (Romans 5:1). *Apart from Jesus there can be no peace between man and God, for "without faith [in Jesus] it is impossible to please God..."* (Hebrews 11:6). —see JESUS CHRIST

peace-a-ble (piᵞs-ə-bəl) adj. Not liking to argue, quarrel, or fight —**peaceably** adv.

peace-ful (piᵞs-fəl) adj. **1.** Quiet; untroubled: *It's so peaceful in the country.* **2.** Liking peace: *a peaceful nation* —**peace-ful-ly** adv.

peace-mak-er (piᵞs-meᵞ-kər) n. One who makes peace between others: *Jesus said,*

"Blessed are the peacemakers for they will be called sons of God" (Matthew 5:9).

peace pipe (piʸs paɪp) n. A pipe smoked by North American Indians in ceremonies as a sign or pledge of peace

peach (piʸtʃ) n. **1.** A round fruit with yellowish-red skin and sweet juicy flesh **2.** The orange-pink color of this fruit

pea-cock (piʸ–kɑk) n. The male of the peafowl. Its beautiful blue or green tail feathers can be spread out like a large fan.

pea-fowl (piʸ–faʊl) n. A large bird related to the pheasants

pea-hen (piʸ–hɛn) n. The female of the peafowl

peak (piʸk) n. **1.** A pointed mountain top: *Some mountain peaks are covered with snow all year.* **2.** The highest point or level: *Sales have reached a new peak.*

peak v. To reach a peak: *Sales have now peaked, and will probably decline after Christmas.*

peal (piʸl) n. **1.** A ringing of bells **2.** A loud, long sound or number of sounds one after the other: *peals of laughter/thunder*

peal v. To ring out or sound loudly: *Thunder pealed through the valley.*

pea-nut (piʸ–nət) n. A type of edible nut that looks rather like a pea and which grows in a shell under the ground: *Peanuts are one of the most common nuts eaten in America.*

pea-nut but-ter (piʸ–nət bʌt–ər) n. A substance made of crushed peanuts, usu. eaten on bread

pear (pɛər) n. A sweet juicy fruit, narrow at the stem end and wide at the other end

pearl (pɜrl) n. **1.** A smooth, hard, often rounded, lustrous white mass formed in the shell of oysters and valued as a gem: *Jesus said, "The kingdom of heaven is like a merchant looking for fine pearls. When he found one [pearl] of great value, he ... sold everything he had and bought it* (Matthew 13:45,46). **2.** The color of this; silvery white **3.** *fig.* Sthg. precious: *pearls of wisdom*

pearl-y (pɜr–liʸ) adj. **-ier, -iest** Like pearls: *pearly teeth*

peas-ant (pɛz–ənt) n. A person who lives and works on the land, esp. in a poor, primitive, or underdeveloped area

peas-ant-ry (pɛz–ən–triʸ) n. Peasants as a group

peat (piʸt) n. A rich soil made up of decaying plants, used as a fertilizer or as a fuel when dried

peb-ble (pɛb–əl) n. A small, usu. smooth stone

pe-can (pɪ–kɑn/ piʸ–kæn) n. **1.** A kind of nut found in North America **2.** The tree that bears this nut

pec-ca-ry (pɛk–ə–riʸ) n. **-ries** A type of wild pig-like animal found in Central and South American

peck (pɛk) v. **1.** Of birds, to strike at sthg. with the beak: *That woodpecker has been pecking at that tree for a long time.* **2.** *infml.* To kiss in a hurry or without much feeling

peck n. **1.** A stroke or mark made by pecking **2.** *infml.* A hurried kiss: *He gave his wife a peck on the check and ran to catch the bus.* **3.** A dry measure equal to eight quarts or approx. nine litres

pec-to-ral (pɛk–tə–rəl) adj. Of the chest or breast

pe-cu-liar (pɪ–kyuʷl–yər) adj. **1.** Strange; unusual: *This milk has a peculiar taste; do you think it's all right?* **2.** Belonging only to a particular person, place, etc.: *This style of cooking is peculiar to the South.*

pe-cu-li-ar-i-ty (pɪ–kyuʷ–liʸ–ær–ə–tiʸ/–ɛər–) n. **-ties 1.** The quality of being peculiar **2.** Different: *One of the peculiarities of his behavior is the strange hours he keeps.*

pe-cu-ni-ar-y (pɪ–kyuʷ–niʸ–ɛər–iʸ) n. Of or pertaining to money

ped-a-gogue (pɛd–ə–gɑg) n. A teacher

ped-a-go-gy (pɛd–ə–goʷ–dʒiʸ/–gɑdʒ–) n. The art or profession of teaching —**ped-a-gog-ic** (pɛd–ə–gɑdʒ–ɪk/–goʷdʒ–) or **pedagogical** adj. —**pedagogically** adv.

ped-al (pɛd–əl) n. A lever which is part of a machine and can be pressed with the foot in order to control the working of the machine: *One of the pedals came off her bicycle.*

pedal -ll- v. To move (esp. a bicycle) along by the use of pedals

ped-ant (pɛd–ənt) n. **1.** One who makes a great show of his knowledge **2.** One who

attaches too much importance to details or to rules —pe-dan-tic (pɪ dænt-ɪk) adj.

ped-ant-ry (pɛd–ən–triʸ) n. Too much emphasis on formal rules or detail

ped-dle (pɛd–əl) v. -dled, -dling To try to sell things by going from house to house

ped-dler (pɛd–lər) n. also **pedlar** A person who peddles

ped-es-tal (pɛd–əs–təl) n. **1.** The base on which a pillar or statue stands **2. put/ set sbdy. on a pedestal (a)** To consider sbdy. better than oneself or others **(b)** To treat sbdy. with too much respect: *She put her husband on a pedestal.*

pe-des-tri-an (pə–dɛs–triʸ–ən) n. A person on foot; a walker: *Pedestrians should use the pedestrian crosswalk when crossing the street in the city.* —**pedestrian** adj.

pe-di-a-tri-cian (piʸd–iʸ–ə–trɪʃ–ən) n. A doctor who specializes in pediatrics

pe-di-at-rics (piʸd–iʸ–æ–trɪks) n. The science dealing with the diseases and medical care of children

ped-i-gree (pɛd–ə–griʸ) n. **1.** An ancestral line **2.** A genealogical record, esp. of purebred animals **3.** Distinguished ancestry

peek (piʸk) v. To look at sthg. quickly: *He just had time to peek into the room before the door closed.*

peek n. A quick look: *I only caught a peek of her before she disappeared in the crowd.*

peel (piʸl) v. **1.** To remove the outer covering from a fruit or vegetable: *He peeled the oranges/bananas/potatoes.* **2.** To come off, esp. in small pieces: *My skin peels when I've been sunburned.*

peel n. The outer covering, esp. of fruit and vegetables that one usu. peels before eating: *orange peels*

peep (piʸp) v. To look quickly and secretly

peep n. A feeble, shrill sound, as that made by a young bird: *fig. I don't want to hear a peep (even the smallest sound) out of you.*

peer (pɪər) n. An equal in age, rank, or quality: *The opinion of his peers (his peer group) is more important to him than that of his parents.*

peer v. To look very intently or carefully, esp. as if not able to see well: *She peered into the darkness, trying to see what was making that noise.*

peer-less (pɪər–ləs) adj. Without an equal; better than any other

peeve (piʸv) v. **peeved, peeving** To annoy

peeve n. Sthg. that annoys one: *What is your pet peeve?*

pee-vish (piʸ–vɪʃ) adj. Ill-tempered; easily annoyed by little things —**peevishly** adv. —**peevishness** n.

peg (pɛg) n. **1.** A short piece of wood, metal, etc., on which to hang sthg. **2.** A piece of wood or metal with which to fasten sthg.: *He hammered the ten pegs into the ground, and tied the ropes onto them.* **3. clothes peg** A wooden or plastic clip for holding clothes, towels, etc. to a rope while drying **4. square peg in a round hole** A person who is not suited to the position or group in which he/ she is placed **5. take sbdy. down a peg** To make a proud person more humble: *He thought he was pretty smart until he failed the final exam. That took him down a peg.*

peg (pɛg) v. **-gg- 1.** To fasten with a peg **2.** To fix or hold at a certain level

pe-jo-ra-tive (pɪ–dʒɔr–ət–ɪv) adj. Having or giving a derogatory meaning or sense; showing dislike; disapproval: *a pejorative remark* —**pejoratively** adv.

Pe-kin-ese or **Pe-king-ese** (piʸ–kən–iʸz/ –kəŋ–) n. A small dog with short legs, long hair, and a flat nose, originally from China

pel-i-can (pɛl–ɪ–kən) n. A large water bird with a large beak for catching fish and a large pouch for storing it

pel-let (pɛl–ət) n. **1.** A small ball of soft material: *The children threw paper pellets at each other.* **2.** A small ball of metal, made to be fired from a gun

pell–mell (pɛl–mɛl) adv. **1.** In a hurrying, disorderly manner: *The boys ran pell-mell down the hall.* **2.** In a confused or jumbled manner; untidily: *The books were scattered pell-mell over the floor.*

pelt (pɛlt) v. To throw sthg. at sbdy. repeatedly: *The children pelted each other with snowballs.*

pelt n. The untreated skin of an animal with the fur left on it

pel-vis (pɛl–vəs) n. **-vises** or **-ves** (–viʸz) The

framework of bone around the body below the waist —**pelvic** adj.

pen (pɛn) n. **1.** An instrument for writing or drawing with ink: *a ballpoint pen/ a felt-tip pen* **2.** A piece of land enclosed by a fence, esp. for keeping animals in

pen v. **-nn- 1.** To write: *He penned a few lines of poetry.* **2.** To shut animals in a pen

pe-nal (piᵞn–əl) adj. Of , related to, or used for punishment: *a penal colony*

pe-nal-ize (pen–əl–laɪz/ piᵞn–) **-ised** BrE. v. **-ized, -izing** To put a penalty on: *Their team was penalized for unnecessary roughness.*

pen-al-ty (pɛn–əl–tiᵞ) n. **-ties 1.** The punishment for breaking a law, rule, or agreement in law: *She has paid the penalty for her crimes.* **2.** In sports, a disadvantage suffered by a player or team for breaking a rule: *Our team received penalties totaling 35 yards during the first half.*

pen-ance (pɛn–əns) n. Punishment that a person suffers willingly to show that he is sorry for his sins. NOTE: Acts of penance are done under the direction of a priest after confession. Some people believe that doing acts of penance gains favor with God. Evangelical Christians do not believe in penance. They believe that God through Jesus Christ forgives and restores those who confess their sins. This full and free forgiveness makes penance unnecessary. Evangelicals believe in repentance for sin, not penance. They also believe that forgiven people will live in a new way, that they will, out of love for God, keep his commandments and do all they can to glorify him. —see REPENT

pence (pɛns) BrE. plural for penny

pen-chant (pɛn–tʃənt) n. A strong liking: *a penchant for Chinese food*

pen-cil (pɛn–səl) n. **1.** A narrow pointed instrument, usu. wooden, containing a thin stick of graphite or similar substance for writing or drawing **2. eyebrow pencil** Used for darkening the eyebrows

pen-dant (pɛn–dənt) n. A hanging ornament

pen-dent (pɛn–dənt) adj. **1.** Hanging from sthg. **2.** Remaining undecided

pend-ing (pɛnd–ɪŋ) prep. Until: *This matter must wait, pending the decision of the board of directors.*

pending adj. Waiting to be answered or decided or done: *pending correspondence*

pen-du-lum (pen–dʒə–ləm) n. A swinging weight like that which operates the mechanism of a clock

pen-e-trate (pen–ə–treᵞt) v. **-trated, -trating 1.** To enter, cut, or force a way into or through sthg.: *The forest was too dense to penetrate./ The word of God [the Bible] is living and active. Sharper than any double-edged sword, it penetrates even to dividing soul and spirit...; it judges the thoughts and attitudes of the heart* (Hebrews 4:12). **2.** To understand: *to penetrate the mystery of the atom* —see also IMPENETRABLE —**pen-e-tra-tion** (pen–ə–treᵞ–ʃən) n.

pen-e-trat-ing (pen–ə–treᵞt–ɪŋ) adj. **1.** Of the eye, a question, etc., sharp and searching **2.** Of a person, the mind, etc., able to understand clearly and deeply **3.** Of sounds, sharp and loud: *a penetrating voice*

pen-guin (pen–gwɪn/ peŋ–) n. A large flightless black and white bird of the Antarctic

pen-i-cil-lin (pen–ə–sɪl–ən) n. A kind of antibiotic medicine that destroys many harmful bacteria in people and animals

pen-in-su-la (pə–nɪn–sə–lə) n. A piece of land almost completely surrounded by water: *Italy is a peninsula.* —**peninsular** adj.

pe-nis (piᵞ–nɪs) n. **-nises** or **-nes** (–niᵞz) The male sexual organ of humans and many animals

pen-i-tent (pen–ə–tənt) adj. Feeling or showing sorrow for having sinned (broken one of God's commandments), with the determination not to do so again —opposite IMPENITENT —see also SIN, REPENT —**penitence** n. —**penitently** adv.

pen-i-ten-tia-ry (pen–ə–tenʃ–ə–riᵞ) n. **-ries** A state or federal prison, esp. in the US

pen-man-ship (pen–mən–ʃɪp) n. The art, skill, or style of handwriting

pen-nant (pen–ənt) n. A small flag, usu. in the shape of a narrow triangle, used by schools or on ships for signaling

pen-ni-less (pen–ɪ–ləs) adj. Having no money whatsoever

pen-ny (pen–iᵞ) n. **pennies** In the US and Can-

ada, a coin worth one cent or 1/100th of a dollar

pen-sion (**pen**–tʃən) n. Money paid regularly by a government or a company to an individual or his family, given when certain conditions such as age or length of service have been fulfilled

pen-sive (**pen**–sɪv) adj. Thinking deeply about sthg.

pen-ta-gon (**pɛn**–ə–gɑn) n. A flat figure with five sides and five angles

Pen-te-cost (**pɛnt**–ə–kɔst) n. A Christian festival occurring on the 7th Sunday after Easter to celebrate the outpouring of the Holy Spirit upon the followers of Jesus Christ in Jerusalem — the 50th day after the resurrection of Jesus Christ —see EASTER

pent-house (**pɛnt**–haʊs) n. A luxurious residence at the top of a building

pent-up (**pɛnt**–ʌp) adj. **1.** Shut in **2.** Kept from being expressed openly: *pent-up anger*

pen-u-ry (**pɛn**–yə–riʸ) n. Extreme poverty

pe-o-ny (piʸ–ə–niʸ) n. The large white, pink, or red flower of a garden plant

peo-ple (piʸ–pəl) n. **1.** Persons in general: *The angel said to them, "I bring you good news of great joy that will be for all the people. Today ... a Savior has been born to you; he is Christ the Lord"* (Luke 2:10,11). **2.** A race; nation: *Righteousness exalts a nation, but sin is a disgrace to any people* (Proverbs 14:34). **3.** The persons from whom one is descended and to whom one is related: *His people have lived in this valley for over 200 years.* **4.** God's people: *God said, "If my people who are called by my name, will humble themselves and pray and seek my face and turn from their wicked ways, then I will hear from heaven and will forgive their sins and will heal their land"* (2 Chronicles 7:14). —see PERSON

pep (pɛp) n. Energy; vigor

pep-per (**pɛp**–ər) n. **1.** A hot-tasting powder made from the dried berries of certain plants, used to season food **2.** Any of several hollow fruits containing many seeds, used as a food, either raw, cooked or pickled —**peppery** adj.

pepper v. **1.** To add or give the taste of pepper to food **2.** To hit over and over again, esp. with shots or with small but annoying things: *fig. The news media peppered him with questions for nearly an hour.* **3.** To sprinkle here and there: *a speech peppered with jokes*

pep-per-mint (**pɛp**–ər–mɪnt) n. **1.** A mint plant with a special strong taste, used in adding flavor to candy, chewing gum, medicine, etc. **2.** also **mint** A candy with this taste

pep talk (**pɛp** tɔk) n. A brief, vigorous talk intended to inspire confidence or enthusiasm

per (pər/ pər) prep. Each: *My car gets 30 miles per gallon (of gasoline).*

per-am-bu-late (pə–**ram**–byə–leʸt) v. -lated, -lating To walk about; stroll

per-am-bu-la-tor (pə–**ram**–byə–leʸt–ər) n. *British* A baby carriage

per cap-i-ta (pər **kæp**–ət–ə) prep. + n. For each person

per-ceive (pər–siʸv) v. -ceived, -ceiving *fml.* **1.** To be aware of sthg. by means of the sense of sight, hearing, touch, smell, or taste **2.** To understand: *O Lord, you have searched me and you know me. You know when I sit and when I rise; you perceive my thoughts from afar* (Psalm 139:1,2). —**perceivable** adj.

per-cent (pər–**sɛnt**) n. One part in a hundred: *In the US and Canada, one penny is one percent (1%) of a dollar and a nickel is five percent (5%) of a dollar./fig. I am 100 percent (totally) in agreement with you.* —**percent** adv. —**percentage** n.

per-cep-ti-ble (pər–**sɛp**–tə–bəl) adj. Noticeable; able to be perceived: *The radio signals were very weak; barely perceptible.* —**perceptibly** adv. —opposite IMPERCEPTIBLE

per-cep-tion (pər–**sɛp**–ʃən) n. **1.** The ability to understand or perceive **2.** The result or effect of perceiving

per-cep-tive (pər–**sɛp**–tɪv) adj. To be quick to notice and understand

perch (pərtʃ) n. **1.** A horizontal pole where a bird rests **2.** A high place where a person might be: *From our perch on top of the cliff we could see the whole valley.* **3.** A small, freshwater fish used as food

perch v. **1.** Of a bird, to come to rest after flying: *The bird perched on the fence.* **2.** To cause to go into the stated position: *She perched herself in front of the television set.*

per-co-late (pər–kə–le^yt) v. -lated, -lating **1.** To filter or cause to filter, esp. through small holes **2.** To prepare coffee in a percolator —**per-co-la-tion** (pər–kə–le^y–ʃən) n.

per-co-la-tor (pər–kə–le^yt–ər) n. A pot in which coffee is made

per-cus-sion (pər–kʌʃ–ən) n. **1.** A striking together of two hard objects **2.** Musical instruments that are played by striking them: *Drums are a type of percussion instrument.* —**percussionist** n.

per-di-tion (pər–dɪʃ–ən) n. Eternal damnation

per-emp-to-ry (pə–rɛmp–tə–ri^y) adj. **1.** Leaving no opportunity for denial or refusal **2.** Dictatorial **3.** Absolute or final

pe-ren-ni-al (pə–rɛn–i^y–əl) adj. **1.** Lasting a long time; constantly recurring: *a perennial problem* **2.** Of a plant, living for several years

per-fect (pər–fɪkt) adj. **1.** Of the very best possible kind, degree, or standard: *The weather during our vacation was perfect. / As for God, his way is perfect; the word of the Lord is flawless* (Psalm 18:30). **2.** Complete, with nothing missing, spoiled, etc.: *She's 75, but she still has a perfect set of teeth.* **3.** Suitable and satisfying in every way: *This house is perfect for our large family.* **4.** *Often infml.* Total: *a perfect stranger* **5.** Complete, without any defect; regarding human behavior, sinless: *No one on earth is perfect, but God demands that we be perfect. Jesus said, "Be perfect, even as your Father in heaven is perfect"* (Matthew 5:48). NOTE: Jesus is the only one who ever lived a perfect, holy, and sinless life. All the rest of us are sinners (Romans 3:23) and the wages of sin is death (Romans 6:23). But Christ Jesus came into the world to save sinners. He suffered and died for us on the cross. He died for all ... and rose again (2 Corinthians 5:15). His blood purifies us from all sin (1 John 1:7). *By one sacrifice he has made perfect those who are being made holy* (Hebrews 10:14).

perfect (pər–fɛkt) v. To make perfect

per-fec-tion (pər–fɛk–ʃən) n. **1.** The state or quality of being perfect: *Our prayer is for your perfection* (2 Corinthians 13:9). *Aim for perfection ... be of one mind, live in peace. And the God of peace will be with you* (2 Corinthi-

ans 13:11). —**op-posite** IMPERFECTION **2.** The act of developing completely or making perfect: *The perfection of this new medical treatment may take several years.*

per-fec-tion-ist (pər–fɛk–ʃə–nəst) n. *Often derog.* A person who is not satisfied with anything other than perfection

per-fect-ly (pər–fɪkt–li^y) adv. In a perfect way: *She speaks Arabic perfectly.*—**op-posite** IMPERFECTLY

per-fid-i-ous (pər–fɪd–i^y–əs) adj. Disloyal; treacherous

per-fo-rate (pər–fə–re^yt) v. -rated, -rating To make a series of tiny holes so that parts can be torn off easily: *The sheet of stamps was perforated.* —**per-fo-ra-tion** (pər–fə–re^y–ʃən) n.

per-form (pər–fɔrm) v. **1.** To do: *Which doctor performed the operation?* **2.** To act, sing, or play a musical instrument, esp. before an audience **3.** To work or carry out an activity in the specified way: *This car performs badly, esp. on hills.*

per-for-mance (pər–fɔr–məns) n. **1.** The action of performing, or an action performed: *Our team's performance has been excellent this year.* **2.** Of people or machines, the ability to do sthg., esp. sthg. needing skill: *This car's performance should be better after a tune-up.*

per-form-er (pər–fɔr–mər) n. A person who performs, esp. an actor or a musician

per-fume (pər–fyu^wm/ pər–fyu^wm) n. A sweet-smelling liquid, often made from flowers, for use esp. on a woman's face, wrists, and body: *fig. A good name [reputation] is better than fine perfume* (Ecclesiastes 7:1).

per-func-to-ry (pər–fʌŋk–tə–ri^y) adj. Done hastily and without care

per-haps (pər–hæps) adv. Maybe; possibly

pe-ri- (pɛər–ə–/ –i^y–) Comb. form **1.** Around, about, encircling, enclosing **2.** Near

per-il (pɛər–əl) n. Danger, esp. of being harmed or killed: *He [God] has delivered us from such a deadly peril, and he will deliver us* (2 Corinthians 1:10).

per-il-ous (pɛər–ə–ləs) adj. Dangerous; risky: *In the last days perilous times shall come. For men shall be lovers of themselves, lovers of money, boasters, proud, blasphemers, disobedient to parents, unthankful, unholy, unloving, unfor-*

giving, slanderers, without self-control, brutal, despisers of good, traitors... (2 Timothy 3:1-4 NKJV). —**perilously** adv.

pe-rim-e-ter (pə-rɪm-ə-tər) n. **1.** The boundary line around any closed flat figure **2.** The length of this boundary: *The perimeter of a two inch square is eight inches.*

pe-ri-od (pɪər-iʸ-əd) n. **1.** A portion or division of time with a beginning and an end, but not always of measured length: *long periods of draught* **2.** A long stretch of history: *the Victorian period of English history* **3.** A division of a school day; lesson: *a history period* **4.** A point (.) marking the end of a sentence or a shortened form of a word; *BrE.* A full stop

pe-ri-od-ic (pɪər-iʸ-ɑd-ɪk) adj. Happening occasionally, usu. at regular times: *periodic attacks of fever* —**periodically** adv.

pe-ri-od-i-cal (pɪər-iʸ-ɑd-ɪ-kəl) n. A magazine which appears at regular intervals, usu. weekly or monthly

pe-riph-er-al (pə-rɪf-ə-rəl) adj. **1.** Of or on the periphery **2.** Relatively unimportant

pe-riph-er-y (pə-rɪf-ə-riʸ) n. **1.** An outer boundary or edge **2.** A line surrounding sthg.

per-i-scope (peər-ə-skoʷp) n. A tube containing mirrors, through which a person can look and see things that are above him, esp. useful for one in a submarine to see what is on the surface of the water

per-ish (peər-ɪʃ) v. **1.** To die, esp. in a terrible or sudden way; be completely destroyed: *Thousands of people perished in the earthquake.* **2.** To suffer eternal separation from God in the flames of hell, prepared for the devil and his angels: *Jesus said, "Unless you repent, you too will perish"* (Luke 13:5). *God is patient with you, not wanting anyone to perish, but everyone to come to repentance* (2 Peter 3:9), *For God so loved the world that he gave his one and only Son, that whoever believes in him shall not perish but have eternal life* (John 3:16).

per-ish-a-ble (peər-ɪʃ-ə-bəl) adj. **1.** Decaying quickly **2.** Of anything that will not last: *For you know that it was not with perishable things such as silver or gold that you were redeemed ... but with the precious blood of Christ* (1 Peter

1:18,19). —**perishable** n. —opposite NON-PERISHABLE

per-i-win-kle (peər-ɪ-wɪŋ-kəl) n. **1.** A vine with evergreen leaves and blue flowers **2.** A small sea snail sometimes eaten as food

per-jure (pɜr-dʒər) v. **-jured, -juring** To intentionally lie in a court of law after taking an oath to tell the truth, the whole truth, and nothing but the truth

per-jur-er (pɜr-dʒər-ər) n. One who perjures himself by lying in a court of law

per-ju-ry (pɜrdʒ-ə-riʸ) n. The act of perjuring oneself: *He was sent to prison for perjury.*

perk (pɜrk) n. Short for **perquisite**

perk up (pɜrk ʌp) v. + adv. To become more cheerful and/ or enthusiastic

perk-y (pɜr-kiʸ) adj. **-ier, -iest 1.** Cheerful; full of life and interest **2.** Spirited and self-assured

perm (pɜrm) n. Short for **permanent wave**

per-ma-nence (pɜr-mə-nəns) n. The state of being permanent

per-ma-nent (pɜr-mə-nənt) adj. Lasting or intended to last for a long time or forever —compare TEMPORARY —**permanently** adv.

per-me-a-ble (pɜr-miʸ-ə-bəl) adj. Capable of being permeated

per-me-ate (pɜr-miʸ-eʸt) v. **-ated, -ating** To pass through or into every part of sthg.

per-mis-si-ble (pər-mɪs-ə-bəl) adj. Allowable; permitted

per-mis-sion (pər-mɪʃ-ən) n. A written or spoken agreement that sbdy. may do sthg.

per-mis-sive (pər-mɪs-ɪv) adj. Allowing a lot, usu. too much freedom, esp. in sexual or moral matters: *Society has become too permissive.* —**permissiveness** n.

per-mit (pər-mɪt) v. **-tt- 1.** To allow: *Smoking is not permitted on this flight.* **2.** To make it possible for a specified thing to happen: *I will come in June if my health permits.*

per-mit (pɜr-mɪt/ pər-mɪt) n. An official written statement giving one the right to do sthg.: *a learner's permit for driving the car*

per-ni-cious (pər-nɪʃ-əs) adj. **1.** Having the power to injure or destroy; deadly **2.** Wicked; malicious —**perniciously** adv. —**perniciousness** n.

per-ox-ide (pə–rɑk–saɪd) n. also **hydrogen peroxide** A chemical sometimes used for bleaching hair and for cleansing wounds

per-pen-dic-u-lar (pər–pən–dɪk–yə–lər) adj. **1.** Vertical; being at a right angle with the horizon: *The flag pole should be perpendicular to the ground.* **2.** At an angle of 90 degrees to another line or surface: *Main Street and Sixth Avenue are perpendicular to each other.*

per-pe-trate (pɜr–pə–treʸt) v. -trated, -trating To do sthg. bad; to be guilty of —**per-petrator** n.

per-pet-u-al (pər–petʃ–uʷ–əl) adj. **1.** Lasting a long time; not ceasing: *perpetual motion* **2.** Frequent; often repeated: *perpetual quarreling* —**perpetually** adv.

per-pet-u-ate (pər–petʃ–ə–weʸt) v. -ated, -ating To cause to be continued or remembered: *His book will perpetuate his memory.*

per-pe-tu-i-ty (pər–pə–tuʷ–ə–tiʸ) n. **1.** The state or character of being perpetual **2.** Endless

per-plex (pər–plɛks) v. To puzzle or confuse sbdy.: *He was perplexed by her accusation.*

per-plex-ing (pər–plɛks–ɪŋ) adj. Confusing: *a perplexing situation*

per-plex-i-ty (pər–plɛks–ə–tiʸ) n. The state of being perplexed

per-qui-site (pɜr–kwə–zət) n. Money, goods, or other benefits received in addition to one's salary, for work done: *The perquisites included use of a company car.*

per-se-cute (pɜr–sɪ–kyuʷt) v. -cuted, -cuting To treat cruelly; cause to suffer (esp. for religious or political beliefs): *Blessed are those who are persecuted because of righteousness, for theirs is the kingdom of heaven* (Matthew 5:10). *Love your enemies and pray for those who persecute you, that you may be sons of your Father in heaven* (Matthew 5:44,45). —**per-se-cu-tion** (pɜr–sɪ–kyuʷ–ʃən) n. —**per-secutor** n.

per-se-ver-ance (pər–sə–vɪər–əns) n. Continual steady effort made to fulfill some purpose: *The testing of your faith develops perseverance. Perseverance must finish its work so that you may be mature and complete, not lacking anything* (James 1:3-4).

per-se-vere (pər–sə–vɪər) v. -vered, -vering To continue firmly in spite of difficulties: *Blessed is the man who perseveres under trial,* *because when he has stood the test, he will receive the crown of life that God has promised to those who love him* (James 1:12). —**per-severing** adj.

per-sim-mon (pər–sɪm–ən) n. **1.** An orange-red fruit which is good to eat only when fully ripe **2.** The tree that bears this fruit

per-sist (pər–sɪst) v. **1.** To continue firmly (and perhaps unreasonably) in spite of opposition or warning: *If you persist in breaking the law, you will go to prison.* **2.** To continue to exist: *The cold weather will persist for the rest of the week.*

per-sis-tent (pər–sɪs–tənt) adj. often derog. **1.** Continuing in a habit or course of action, in spite of opposition or warning **2.** Continuing to exist for a long time: *a persistent cough* —**persistence** n. —**persistently** adv.

per-snick-e-ty (pər–snɪk–ət–iʸ) adj. infml. Fussy; fastidious

per-son (pɜrs–ən) n. **1.** A human being **2.** The living body of a human being **3.** The personality of a human being; self **4.** Gram. Any of three groups of pronouns with corresponding verb inflections that distinguish between the speaker (first person), the one spoken to (second person), and the individual or thing spoken about (third person)

per-son-a-ble (pɜr–sən–ə–bəl) adj. Attractive in appearance or character: *a personable young man*

per-son-al (pɜr–sən–əl) adj. **1.** Belonging to a particular person, or for his use; private: *Here are Jane's personal effects.* (=belongings) **2.** Done or made directly by a particular person, not by a representative: *The president made a personal visit to the disaster area.* **3.** Of the body or appearance: *Personal cleanliness is important for health.*

per-son-al-i-ty (pɜr–sə–næl–ə–tiʸ) n. -ties The whole nature or character of a particular person; all of a person's characteristics

per-son-al-ly (pɜr–sən–əl–iʸ) adv. **1.** In one's own opinion: *Personally, I prefer cherry pie.* **2.** Doing sthg. for oneself, not letting anyone else do it for him: *The president visited the disaster area personally.*

personal pronoun (pɜr–sən–əl proʷ–naʊn) In grammar, a pronoun that indicates the per-

son speaking, the person spoken to, or the person or thing spoken about

per-son-i-fi-ca-tion (pər–sɑn–ə–fə–**ke**ʸ–ʃən) n. **1.** An idea, quality, etc. spoken of as if it were a person **2.** A perfect example of sthg.: *Solomon was the personification of wisdom.*

per-son-i-fy (pər–**sɑn**–ə–faɪ) v. **-fied, -fying 1.** To speak of an idea or quality as if it were a person **2.** To be a perfect example: *Jesus personifies love and forgiveness and patience.*

per-son-nel (pər–sə–**nɛl**) n. All the people employed by a company, in the armed forces, etc.: *New personnel are needed for the highway department.*

per-spec-tive (pər–**spɛk**–tɪv) n. **1.** A point of view **2.** In drawing or painting, a sense of depth or distance, like that in real life **3.** The way in which a matter is judged, so that background, future or possible problems, etc., are taken into consideration: *We have to look at the problem in its proper perspective.* **4.** A view, esp. one stretching far into the distance: *fig. a proper perspective of our country's history*

per-spi-ca-cious (pər–spə–**ke**ʸ–ʃəs) n. Having keen mental perception —**per-spi-cac-i-ty** (pər–spə–**kæs**–ət–iʸ) n.

per-spi-cu-i-ty (pər–spə–**kyu**ʷ–ət–iʸ) n. Clearness in expressing one's thoughts

per-spire (pər–spaɪr/ –spaɪ–ər) v. **-spired, -spiring** To lose moisture through the skin when hot; to sweat —**per-spi-ra-tion** (pər–spə–**re**ʸ–ʃən) n.

per-suade (pər–**swe**ʸd) v. **-suaded, -suading** To convince sbdy. to do sthg. by reasoning, arguing, begging, etc.: *Try to persuade him to come with us.*

per-suad-ed (pər–**swe**ʸ**d**–əd) adj. Certain; convinced: *Abraham did not waver through unbelief ... being fully persuaded that God had power to do what he had promised* (Romans 4:20,21).

per-sua-sion (pər–**swe**ʸ–ʒən) n. **1.** The act of persuading **2.** The ability to influence others **3.** A group holding a particular belief: *People of many political persuasions attended the meeting.*

per-sua-sive (pər–**swe**ʸ–sɪv) adj. Having the power to influence others to believe or do what one wishes: *a persuasive speech* —**per-**

suasively adv. —**persuasiveness** n.

pert (pərt) adj. **1.** Lively; energetic **2.** Impudently bold **3.** Trim and stylish

per-tain (pər–**te**ʸn) v. To belong; to have to do with: *instructions pertaining to the job*

per-ti-na-cious (pərt–ən–**e**ʸ–ʃəs) n. Holding strongly to an idea; obstinate; stubbornly persistent —**per-ti-nac-i-ty** (pərt–ən–**æs**–ə–tiʸ) n.

per-ti-nent (**pərt**–ən–ənt) adj. Connected with the subject spoken about

per-turb (pər–**tɜrb**) v. To disturb greatly; to make anxious or uneasy

per-tur-ba-tion (pər–tər–**be**ʸ–ʃən) n. Great worry; anxiety

pe-ruse (pə–**ru**ʷz) v. **-rused, -rusing 1.** To read carefully **2.** To examine —**pe-rus-al** (pə–**ru**ʷz–əl) n.

per-vade (pər–**ve**ʸd) v. **-vaded, -vading** Of smells, ideas, feelings, etc., to spread through every part of; to permeate

per-va-sive (pər–**ve**ʸ–sɪv) adj. Widespread: *the pervasive influence of television* —**pervasively** adv.

per-verse (pər–**vɜrs**) adj. **1.** Purposely continuing in what one knows to be wrong or unreasonable: *a perverse child* **2.** Obstinately persisting in an error or a fault

per-ver-sion (pər–**vɜr**–ʒən) n. **1.** The action of perverting **2.** A perverted form of what is true, reasonable, considered to be natural, etc.: *Men committed indecent acts with other men and received in themselves the due penalty for their perversion...* (Romans 1:27). NOTE: God hates perversion and all sin, but because of his great love and mercy he forgives those who truly repent (turn from their wicked ways) and put their trust in Jesus for eternal life (Acts 2:38; 16:31; Romans 6:23). —see JESUS

per-vert (pər–**vɜrt**) v. **1.** To lead astray; to corrupt; to turn sbdy. away from what is right and natural, esp. in relation to sexual habits **2.** To use for a bad purpose: *Scientific knowledge is often perverted to help cause destruction and war. / To pervert the cause of justice is to prevent justice being done. / A wicked man accepts a bribe to pervert the course of justice* (Proverbs 17:23).

pervert (pər–vərt) n. *derog.* A person whose sexual behavior is different from what is natural

pes-ky (pes–ki[y]) adj. Annoying; causing trouble: *a pesky fly*

pes-si-mism (pes–ə–mɪz–əm) n. The habit of expecting the worst possible outcome, that whatever happens will be very bad —opposite OPTIMISM —**pessimist** n.

pes-si-mis-tic (pes–ə–mɪs–tɪk) adj. Showing pessimism —**pessimistically** adv.

pest (pest) n. **1.** A usu. small animal or insect that is harmful or destructive **2.** *infml.* A troublesome person or thing; a nuisance

pes-ter (**pes**–tər) v. To annoy sbdy. continually, esp. with demands or requests: *The children kept pestering the tourists for money.*

pes-ti-cide (pes–tə–saɪd) n. A chemical substance that kills animal pests

pes-ti-lence (**pes**–tə–ləns) n. A deadly, infectious, rapidly-spreading disease

pes-ti-lent (pes–tə–lənt) adj. **1.** Producing or tending to produce pestilence **2.** Destructive to life **3.** Injurious to peace or morals

pes-tle (**pes**–əl/ pes–təl) n. An implement used to crush or pulverize substances in a kind of bowl (mortar)

pet (pet) n. **1.** A tame animal, such as a cat or dog, kept in the home as a companion **2.** A person (esp. a child) specially favored above others: *She is the teacher's pet.*

pet v. **-tt- 1.** To touch kindly with the hands, showing love: *Tommy was petting the dog.* **2.** *infml.* To fondle

pet adj. Favorite; chief: *my pet peeve*

pet-al (pet–əl) n. Any of the leaf-like parts of a flower

Pe-ter (pi[y]–tər) n. **1.** A masculine name **2.** **Saint Peter** One of the twelve Apostles chosen by our Lord and Savior Jesus Christ, and the author of two books of the New Testament **3.** Either of the two books written by the Apostle Peter , an eye-witness of the resurrection and ascension of our Lord Jesus Christ. NOTE: First Peter was written primarily to encourage Christians who were being persecuted. Second Peter warns against false teachers, esp. those who deny the Second Coming of Jesus.

peter out (pi[y]–tər aʊt) v. To become too tired to do anything; to dwindle away to nothing

pe-tite (pə–ti[y]t) adj. Of a small and trim figure: *a petite woman*

pe-ti-tion (pə–tɪʃ–ən) n. **1.** A solemn request **2.** A request or demand signed by many people and sent to a governmental or other authority

petition v. To make a petition or request: *The people petitioned the government to be allowed to return to their homeland.*

pet-ri-fy (pe–trə–faɪ) v. **-fied, -fying 1.** To convert organic material, such as wood, into a substance of stony character **2.** To paralyze with fear: *He was so petrified with fear that he couldn't even move.*

pet-rol (pe–trəl) n. *BrE.* Gasoline *AmE.* A liquid obtained from petroleum, used as fuel for motor cars, airplanes, boats, etc.

pe-tro-le-um (pə–tro[w]–li[y]–əm) n. Oil in its raw, unrefined form, which is found below the earth's surface, and used to produce petrol (gasoline), kerosene, and various chemical substances

pet-ti-coat (pet–i[y]–ko[w]t) n. A woman's slip or underskirt

pet-ty (pet–i[y]) adj. **-tier, -tiest 1.** Unimportant; small; trivial: *Our difficulties seem petty when compared to those of people who are starving to death.* **2.** *derog.* Narrow-minded **3.** Mean, spiteful **4.** Having a comparatively low rank or position —**pettiness** n.

petty cash (pet–i[y] kæʃ) n. Money used for small, everyday expenses in an office, etc.

petty officer (pet–i[y] ɔf–ə–sər) n. Any of a class of non-commissioned officers in the navy

pet-u-lant (petʃ–ə–lənt) adj. Showing sudden, impatient irritation, esp. over some small annoyance —**petulance** n. —**petulantly** adv.

pe-tu-nia (pɪ–tu[w]n–yə) n. A plant with white, red, or purple funnel-shaped flowers

pew (pyu[w]) n. A long seat for people to sit on in church

pew-ter (pyu[w]t–ər) n. **1.** A metal alloy in which tin is the chief constituent **2.** Articles made of this

pey-o-te (pe[y]–o[w]t–i[y]) n. **1.** A hallucinatory drug obtained from a spineless cactus **2.**

This cactus

phan-tom (**fæn** təm) n. Sthg apparently seen, heard, or sensed, but having no physical reality; a ghost

Phar-aoh (fɛər-o^w/ fe^yr-/ fær–) n. The title of the rulers of ancient Egypt

Phar-i-see (fær-ə-si^y/ fɛər–) n. **1.** A member of an ancient Jewish sect that emphasized strict observance of the moral and ceremonial law **2.** A sanctimonious hypocritical person —**phar-i-sa-ic** (fær-ə-se^y–ık/ fɛər–) or **-ical** (fær-ə-se^y–ı–kəl/ fɛər–) adj. —**pharisaically** adv.

phar-ma-ceu-ti-cal (far-mə-**su^w**t-ı-kəl) adj. Connected with the making of medicine: *a pharmaceutical company*

phar-ma-cist (far-mə-səst) n. Also **druggist, chemist** *fml.* A person who prepares and sells medicine

phar-ma-col-o-gy (far-mə-**kal**-ə-dʒi^y) n. The scientific study of drugs and their effects —**pharmacologist** n.

phar-ma-cy (**far**-mə-si^y) n. **-cies** Drug store *AmE.* Chemist's shop *BrE.* A store where medicines are sold

phar-yn-gi-tis (fær-ən-**dʒart**-əs/ fɛər–) n. Inflammation of the mucous membrane of the pharynx

phar-ynx (**fær**-ŋks/ fɛər–) n. *pl.* **pharynxes** or **phar-yn-ges** (fə-rın-dʒi^yz) The back of the throat behind the tonsils

phase (fe^yz) n. **1.** One of a series of changes in the shape or appearance of sthg.: *the phases of the moon* **2.** A stage of development

Ph.D. (pi^y–e^yʧ–di^y) n. *abbr.* Doctor of Philosophy, an advanced university degree

pheas-ant (**fez**-ənt) n. **1.** A long-tailed game bird with bright feathers **2.** The flesh of this bird as food

phe-nom-e-na (fə-**nam**-ə-nə) n. A plural of the noun **phenomenon**

phe-nom-e-nal (fə-**nam**-ən-əl) adj. Very unusual; hardly believable; extraordinary

phe-nom-e-non (fə-**nam**-ə-nan/ –nən) **-nons** or **-na** (–nə) n. **1.** A fact or event perceived by the senses: *Snow is a common phenomenon in winter.* **2.** An unusual occurrence; a wonder: *Magnetic attraction is an interesting phenomenon.*

phi-lan-der (fə-**læn**-dər) v. Of a man, to make love without serious intentions, frivolously or casually —**philanderer** n.

phil-an-throp-ic (fıl-ən-**θrap**-ık) adj. **1.** Benevolent **2.** Concerned with human welfare and the reduction of suffering

phi-lan-thro-pist (fə-**læn**-θrə-pəst) n. One who is philanthropic, kind and helpful to the poor and needy, making generous gifts of money

phi-lan-thro-py (fə-**læn**-θrə-pi^y) n. Love of mankind; benevolence

phi-lat-e-ly (fə-**læt**-əl-i^y) n. The collection and study of postage stamps —**philatelist** n.

Phi-le-mon (fə-**li^y**-mən/ far–) n. A book of the New Testament, written by St. Paul to Philemon concerning his slave, Onesimus, who was returning to him

Phi-lip-pi-ans (fə-**lıp**-i^y–ənz) n. One of the letters of the New Testament, written by the Apostle Paul, the central message of which is Jesus Christ, true God and Savior of the world, at whose name every knee shall bow and every tongue confess that he [Jesus] is Lord, to the glory of God the Father —see JESUS, BIBLE, NEW TESTAMENT

phil-o-den-dron (fıl-ə-**den**-drən) n. A climbing plant with glossy evergreen leaves

phi-lol-o-gy (fə-**lal**-ə-dʒi^y) n. The study of words and their history —**philologist** n. —**phil-o-log-i-cal** (fıl-ə-**ladʒ**-ı-kəl) adj.

phi-los-o-pher (fə-**las**-ə-fər) n. **1.** A person who studies (and sometimes teaches) philosophy **2.** A person who has formed a philosophy

phil-o-soph-ic (fıl-ə-**saf**-ık) or **phil-o-soph-i-cal** (fıl-ə-**saf**-ı-kəl) adj. **1.** Accepting difficulty or unhappiness with calmness and quiet courage **2.** Of or concerning philosophy

phi-los-o-phy (fə-**las**-ə-fi^y) n. **-phies 1.** The study of the nature and meaning of existence, reality, knowledge, goodness, etc. **2.** Any of various systems of thought having this as its base: *The Bible warns, "See to it that no one takes you captive through hollow and deceptive philosophy, which depends on human tradition and the basic principles of this world rather than on Christ"* (Colossians 2:8).

phlegm (flɛm) n. The thick, jelly-like substance (mucus) produced in the nose and throat when one has a cold

phleg-mat-ic (flɛg–mæt–ɪk) adj. Calm; unexcitable

phlox (flɑks) n. A plant with clusters of purple, reddish, or white flowers

pho-bi-a (foᵂ–biʸ–ə) n. A strong and lasting unusual fear of sthg.

phone (foᵂn) n. A telephone

phone v. **phoned, phoning** To make a telephone call: *He phoned to say he'll be home by six p.m.* —see TELEPHONE

pho-neme (foᵂ–niʸm) n. Any one of the set of distinctive speech sounds in a language that distinguish one word from another: *In English, the "s" in "sip" and the "z" in "zip" are two separate phonemes.*

pho-net-ic (fə–nɛt–ɪk) adj. 1. Concerning the sounds of human speech 2. Using signs to represent the actual sounds of speech: *This dictionary uses a phonetic alphabet as a guide to pronunciation.* 3. **phonetics** (a) The study of speech sounds and their production (b) The system of sounds in a particular language —**phonetically** adv.

phon-ics (fɑn–ɪks) n. *pl.* 1. The study of sound 2. The use of elementary phonetics in the teaching of reading

pho-no-graph (foᵂ–nə–græf) n. A record player

pho-nol-o-gy (fə–nɑl–ə–dʒiʸ) n. 1. The science of speech sounds including esp. the history and theory of sound changes in two or more related languages 2. The system of sounds in a particular language, esp. at a given point in history

pho-ny (foᵂ–niʸ) **pho-ney** adj. **-nier, -niest** *derog.* Pretended; false —**phony, -nies** or **phoney , -neys** n.

phos-phate (fɑs–feʸt) n. A fertilizer containing phosphorus compounds

phos-pho-rus (fɑs–fə–rəs) n. A poisonous wax-like substance that gives out a faint light and catches fire easily

pho-to (foᵂt–oᵂ) n. **-tos** *infml.* Photograph

pho-to-cop-i-er (foᵂ–toᵂ–kɑp–iʸ–ər/ (foᵂ–tə–) n. A machine that makes photocopies

pho-to-cop-y (foᵂ–toᵂ–kɑp–iʸ/ foᵂ–tə–) n. A photographic copy of a letter, drawing, etc. —**photocopy** v. **-ied, -ying** *He photocopied several pages of the book.*

pho-to-gen-ic (foᵂ–tə–dʒɛn–ɪk) adj. Of a good subject for photography; looking good when photographed: *She is very photogenic*

pho-to-graph (foᵂt–ə–græf) Also **photo** n. A picture taken by photography

pho-to-graph v. To take a photograph

pho-tog-ra-pher (fə–tɑg–rə–fər) n. A person who takes photographs, esp. as a business or an art

pho-to-graph-ic (foᵂt–ə–græf–ɪk) adj. Concerning, gotten by, or used in producing photographs —**photographically** adv.

pho-tog-ra-phy (fə–tɑg–rə–fiʸ) n. The art of taking pictures by means of a cam-era and film sensitive to light

pho-to-syn-the-sis (foᵂt–oᵂ–sɪn–θə–səs) n. The process by which chlorophyll-containing cells in green plants use the energy of light to synthesize carbohydrates from carbon dioxide and water —**pho-to-syn-the-size** (foᵂt–oᵂ–sɪn–θə–saɪz) v. —**pho-to-syn-thet-ic** (foᵂt–oᵂ–sɪn–θɛt–ɪk) adj. —**photosynthetically** adv.

phrase (freʸz) n. **phrased, phrasing** 1. *Gram.* A small group of words forming part of a sentence: *"Singing in the rain" is a phrase.* —compare SENTENCE, CLAUSE 2. A short expression, esp. one that is clever and very suited to what is meant

phra-se-ol-o-gy (freʸ–ziʸ–ɑl–ə–dʒiʸ) n. The choice and arrangement of words

phys-ic (fɪz–ɪk) n. A laxative

phys-i-cal (fɪz–ɪ–kəl) adj. 1. Of or concerning material things, as opposed to things of the mind or spirit —compare MENTAL 2. Of or concerning the body: *Physical training is of some value, but godliness has value for all things, holding promise for both the present life and the life to come* (1 Timothy 4:8). —compare BODILY 3. Concerning the natural formation of the earth's surface: *physical geography* 4. Of the branch that is connected with physics: *physical chemistry*

phys-i-cal-ly (fɪz–ɪ–kə–liʸ) adv. 1. According to the laws of nature: *It's physically impossible to travel faster than the speed of light.* 2.

With regard to the body: *The old man is still physically fit.*

phy·si·cal sci·ence (fɪz–ɪ–kəl saɪ–əns) The sciences, such as physics, chemistry, astronomy, geology, etc. that deal primarily with nonliving materials

phy·si·cal ther·a·py (fɪz–ɪ–kəl θɛər–ə–piʸ) n. The treatment of disability, injury, and disease by external physical means —**physical therapist** n.

phy·si·cian (fə–zɪʃ–ən) n. A doctor, esp. one who treats disease with medicines (as opposed to a surgeon, who performs operations)

phys·i·cist (fɪz–ə–səst) n. A person who studies physics

phys·ics (fɪz–ɪks) n. The science which includes the study of heat, light, sound, electricity, magnetism, etc.

phys·i·ol·o·gy (fɪz–iʸ–ɑl–ə–dʒiʸ) n. The study of the way in which living bodies function, e.g. blood-circulation, breathing, digestion of food, etc. —**physiologist** n.

phy·sique (fə–ziʸk) n. A person's muscular build and physical development: *That weight-lifter has a powerful physique.*

pi (paɪ) n. A letter of the Greek alphabet used as a mathematical symbol representing the ratio of the circumference of a circle to its diameter: *Pi equals 3.14159. Pi times the diameter of a circle equals the circumference.*

pi·an·ist (piʸ–æn–əst/ piʸ–ə–nəst) n. A piano player

pi·a·no (piʸ–æn–oʷ) n. -nos A large musical instrument, played by pressing narrow black or white bars (keys) which cause small hammers to hit wire strings

pic·co·lo (pɪk–ə–loʷ) n. A small flute, sounding an octave higher than an ordinary flute

pick (pɪk) v. **1.** To choose: *We picked a beautiful day for a picnic.* **2.** To pull or break off a part of a plant: *She picked some flowers.* **3.** To take up or remove little by little: *He picked the meat from the bone.* **4.** To bring about intentionally: *He picked a fight with John.* **5.** To lift sthg. with the hands or fingers: *Pick up your clothes.* **6.** To play a stringed instrument by quickly pulling the strings **7.** To steal from

someone's pocket: *A thief picked my pocket and got my wallet.* **8. to pick holes in** To find fault with **9. pick on** To tease or abuse: *Stop picking on your sister.* **10. pick over** To select the best of **11. pick up (a)** To give sbdy. a ride: *You can pick me up at eight o'clock.* **(b)** To catch sbdy.: *The police picked him up at the airport.* **(c)** To succeed in seeing or hearing: *He picked up a station 8,000 miles away on short-wave radio.* **(d)** To improve: *Business is picking up.* **(e)** To go faster: *His car is picking up speed.* **12. pick a lock** To open it without a key, using a piece of wire or pointed tool **13. pick someone's brains** To get information from sbdy.

pick n. **1.** The best selection: *the pick of the crop* **2.** A sharp pointed instrument: *an ice pick* **3.** Pick-ax

pick·ax (pɪk–æks) n. A tool consisting of a curved iron bar with one or both ends pointed, mounted at right angles to its handle, used for breaking up hard ground

pick·er (pɪk–ər) n. A person or instrument that picks cotton, corn, fruit, or other crops: *The fruit pickers have gone on strike.*

pick·et (pɪk–ət) n. **1.** A strong pointed stick placed with others to make a fence **2.** A person placed in front of a store or factory, e.g., to keep people, esp. other workers, from entering during a strike

pick·le (pɪk–əl) n. **1.** Food, esp. a cucumber, preserved in vinegar or brine **2.** Vinegar or brine used for this **3.** *infml.* A mess; an unpleasant situation: *I'm really in a pickle now.*

pickle v. -led, -ling To preserve food in vinegar or brine: *Mother is pickling the cucumbers.* —**pickled** adj. *slang* Drunk

pick·pock·et (pɪk–pɑk–ət) n. One who steals from pockets or purses

pick·up (pɪk–əp) n. **1.** The act or process of picking up: *a pickup in business* **2.** The process of gaining speed **3.** A small open truck **4.** *infml.* An acquaintance met informally

pic·nic (pɪk–nɪk) n. A very informal meal eaten in the open air, usu. at a park or at the beach or in the mountains

picnic v. **picnicked, picnicking 1.** To go on a picnic **2.** To eat in picnic fashion

pic·to·ri·al (pɪk–tɔr–iʸ–əl) adj. Having many

pictures

pic-ture (pɪk–t∫ər) n. **1.** A painting or drawing **2.** A photograph **3.** A perfect example: *That little girl is a picture of health.* **4.** A movie: *There's a good picture on TV tonight.* **5.** Whatever is seen on the TV set: *I can't get a clear picture on this set.* **6.** An image in the mind: *This book gives a very clear picture of what life is like in India.*

pic-ture v. **-tured, -turing 1.** To imagine: *I can't picture myself doing that.* **2.** To illustrate in a particular way: *He pictured the president as a much younger man than he is.*

pic-tur-esque (pɪk–t∫ə–resk) adj. **1.** Pretty; charming; interesting: *a picturesque village* **2.** Of language, clear, strong, and descriptive

pid-dling (pɪd–lɪŋ/ –lən) adj. Small and unimportant

pid-gin (pɪdʒ–ən) n. A language which is a mixture of two or more other languages, used by people who do not speak each other's language

pie (paɪ) n. A baked pastry shell, often filled with fruit, and often covered with a crust: *an apple pie*

piece (piʸs) n. **1.** A single thing or example of sthg.: *a piece of paper* **2.** A distinct portion of sthg.: *a piece of pie* **3.** One of a set of sthg.: *a three piece suit* **4.** An example of sthg.: *This watch is a masterful piece of work.* **5.** A coin: *a $5 gold piece* **6. a piece of cake** Sthg. easy to do **7. give sbdy. a piece of one's mind** To angrily tell sbdy. what one thinks of him/her or scold severely **8. in one piece** Undamaged or unharmed, esp. after an accident

piece-meal (piʸs–miʸl) adj. Little by little, one part at a time —**piecemeal** adv.

pier (pɪər) n. **1.** A structure built out into the sea to serve as a breakwater, a, dock or an amusement park **2.** A pillar or arch supporting a bridge or similar structure

pierce (pɪərs) v. **pierced, piercing** To make a hole in; to go into or through: *Jesus' hands, feet, and side were pierced on the cross, just as was prophesied hundreds of years before* (Psalm 22:16; Zechariah 12:10; John 19:34,37; Revelation 1:7). *fig. The bright light pierced the darkness./Misery pierced her heart.*

pierc-ing (pɪər–sɪŋ) adj. **1.** Loud; shrill: *a piercing scream* **2.** Of wind or cold weather, sharp; intense: *a piercing wind* **3.** Looking at sthg. intently: *piercing eyes*

pi-e-ty (paɪ–ə–tiʸ) n. A deep devotion and reverence for God

pif-fle (pɪf–əl) n., interj. Nonsense

pig (pɪg) n. **1.** A farm animal whose flesh is eaten as ham, pork, and bacon **2.** *infml.* A dirty or greedy person: *You pig, you've eaten the whole cake!*

pi-geon (pɪdʒ–ən) n. A quiet, light gray, short-legged bird of the dove family

pig-head-ed (pɪg–hed–əd) adj. Very stubborn

pig-ment (pɪg–mənt) n. **1.** Coloring matter that is mixed with oil, water, etc. to make paint **2.** Natural coloring matter in leaves, skin, etc. —**pig-men-ta-tion** (pɪg–mən–teʸ–∫ən) n.

pig-my (pɪg–miʸ) n. Variation of **pygmy**

pig-tail (pɪg–teʸl) n. Long hair worn in a braid hanging at the back of the head

pike (paɪk) n. *AmE. infml.* for **turnpike**

pike n. A voracious freshwater fish that eats other fish

pile (paɪl) n. **1.** A heap: *a pile of sand* **2.** A lot: *I have piles of work to do.* **3.** A lot of money: *She made a pile from the sale of her property.* **4.** A heavy vertical structure of wood, concrete, steel, etc. used as a support for a bridge or building, etc. **5.** Cut or uncut loops on the surface of a fabric, esp. a carpet

pile v. **piled, piling 1.** To make a pile: *He piled the books on the desk, one on top of the other.* **2.** To load or fill: *They piled the little cart high with watermelons.* **3.** *infml.* To come in or go out in a disorderly way: *I opened my car door and six people piled in.*

pile driv-er (paɪl draɪ–vər) n. A machine for hammering piles into the ground

piles (paɪlz) n. *pl.* Hemorrhoids

pile-up (paɪl–əp) n. A traffic accident involving a number of vehicles

pil-fer (pɪl–fər) v. To steal small items or in small quantities —**pilferage**

pil-grim (pɪl–grəm) n. **1.** One who journeys in foreign lands **2.** A person who travels to a holy place as an act of religious devotion

pil-grim-age (pɪl–grə–mɪdʒ) n. **1.** A journey a person makes to a holy place **2.** A long jour-

ney or search

pill (pɪl) n. **1.** A small pellet or tablet of medication to be swallowed whole **2. the pill** A pill to be taken regularly by women as a means of birth control **3. bitter pill** Humiliation

pil-lar (pɪl–ər) n. **1.** A tall, upright, usu. round post used as a support or as an ornament **2.** Sthg. in the shape of this: *a pillar of smoke* **3.** An important worker or supporter of a cause: *He has been a pillar in this church for 30 years.*

pillar–box (pɪl–ər–baks) n. *BrE.* Postbox or mailbox; a round pillar-shaped box in the street into which letters are placed for mailing

pil-lion (pɪl–yən) n. A passenger's seat on a motorcycle, behind the driver

pil-lo-ry (pɪl–ə–ri^y) n. -ries A wooden frame with holes for head and hands, in which wrongdoers were formerly locked in a standing position in a public square as a form of punishment

pil-low (pɪl–o^w) n. A cloth case stuffed with sthg. soft and used as a cushion for the head during sleep

pil-low-case (pɪl–o^w–ke^ys/ –ə–) n. A washable cloth covering for a pillow

pi-lot (par–lət) n. **1.** A person who flies an aircraft **2.** A person who is familiar with a certain stretch of water and who guides the ships that use it —**pilot** v. *He piloted the ship into Sydney harbor.*

pilot adj. Serving as a trial for sthg.: *a pilot project*

pilot light n. (par–lət laɪt) A small gas flame that is kept burning at all times, used for lighting larger gas burners when the gas in them is turned on

pi-men-to or **pi-mien-to** (pɪ–men–to^w) n. -tos A red pepper with a mild taste, often used to stuff olives or to add color and flavor to foods

pimp (pɪmp) n. A man who solicits customers for a prostitute or brothel

pim-per-nel (pɪm–pər–nɛl) n. An herb having small white, scarlet, or purplish flowers

pim-ple (pɪm–pəl) n. A small inflamed spot on the skin —**pimply** adj.

pin (pɪn) n. **1.** A short, thin piece of metal used for fastening things together **2.** A thin piece of metal, pointed at one end, having an ornament at the other end, used as a form of jewelry **3. clothes pin** A short piece of wood or plastic used to hold clothes, towels, etc. to the clothesline while they dry **4. hairpin** A pin used to keep one's hair in place **5. rolling pin** A cylindrical device rolled over dough to flatten it

pin v. -nn- **1.** To fasten with a pin or pins: *She pinned a flower on her dress.* **2.** To hold a person down: *The fallen tree pinned George to the ground.* **3. pin down** v. To make sbdy. give a definite answer: *I can't pin him down to a definite date.* **4. pin one's hopes on** To rely on: *We're pinning our hopes on Ted Smith to win several races in the track meet today.* **5. pin sthg. on sbdy.** To accuse sbdy. of sthg.: *You can't pin that robbery on me. I can prove I wasn't there.*

pin-a-fore (pɪn–ə–fɔr) n. A loose garment, resembling an apron, worn over a dress to keep it clean

pi-ña-ta (pi^y–nya–tə) n. A colorfully decorated container filled with candy and hung from the ceiling. NOTE: In many countries it is a Christmas tradition for a child to be blindfolded and given a stick to try to hit and break open the piñata.

pin-cers (pɪn–sərz) n. **1.** A tool for gripping things tightly **2.** The claws of lobsters, crabs, etc.

pinch (pɪntʃ) v. **1.** To press the skin tightly together between two hard surfaces or between two fingers, intentionally or accidentally **2.** To cause pain by being too tight: *These shoes are too tight. They pinch.*

pinch n. **1.** The act of pinching: *He gave her a pinch.* **2.** An amount that can be picked up between the thumb and forefinger: *a pinch of salt* **3. in a pinch** If necessary **4. feel the pinch** To be in difficulty due to a lack of money

pin-cush-ion (pɪn–kʊʃ–ən) n. A small, firm cushion in which pins and needles are stuck when not in use

pine (paɪn) n. **1.** A tall evergreen tree with needle-shaped leaves growing in clusters **2.**

The soft wood of this tree, used in building

pine v. **pined, pining 1.** To lose strength slowly through illness or grief: *She is pining away since her husband died.* **2.** To feel an intense longing

pine-apple (paɪn–æp–əl) n. A large juicy tropical fruit with a mass of stiff leaves on top

ping (pɪŋ) v. To make a sharp ringing sound —**ping** n.

Ping–Pong (pɪŋ–paŋ) n. *trademark* for table tennis

pin-ion (pɪn–yən) n. **1.** A bird's wing **2.** A small cogwheel that engages or is engaged by a larger cogwheel or a rack (a bar with teeth)

pinion v. **1.** To restrain or immobilize by binding the wings or arms **2.** To fix in one place

pink (pɪŋk) n., adj. **1.** Pale red **2. in the pink** In good health; very well

pink-ish (pɪŋ–kɪʃ) adj. Somewhat pink

pin-na-cle (pɪn–ə–kəl) n. **1.** A tall thin spire built on the roof of a church, castle, etc. **2.** A high pointed rock or mountain **3.** The highest degree: *the pinnacle of success*

pi-ñon (pɪn–yoʷn/–yən/–yɑn/pɪn–**yoʷn**) n. A kind of pine tree of western North America, the seeds of which are eaten

pinpoint (pɪn–pɔɪnt) v. To show exactly: *He pinpointed his destination on the map.*

pint (paɪnt) A measure for liquids equal to half a quart

pin-to (pɪn–toʷ) n. A horse with spots or other markings that are not regular

pi-o-neer (paɪ–ə–nɪər) n. **1.** One of the first settlers in a new and unknown land **2.** A person who does sthg. first and so leads the way for others: *a pioneer in the field of heart transplants*

pi-ous (paɪ–əs) adj. Having or showing strong religious feelings, reverence for God, etc.

pipe (paɪp) n. **1.** A tube, usu. made of metal or earthenware, through which water, gas, etc. can flow **2.** A small tube with a bowl at one end in which tobacco is smoked **3.** A simple tube-like musical instrument, played by blowing **4.** Any of the tube-like parts through which air is forced in an or-

gan: *a pipe organ*

pipe v. **piped, piping 1.** To convey water, gas, oil, etc. through a pipe: *Water is piped to the city from the reservoir.* **2.** To play music on a pipe: *He piped a cheerful tune.* **3. pipe down** *infml.* Stop talking; be quiet **4. pipe up** *infml.* To begin talking; to complain

pipe dream (paɪp driʸm) n. An idea that can only be imagined and which would be impossible to carry out

pipe-line (paɪp–laɪn) n. **1.** A series of pipes used to carry water, oil, natural gas, etc. over long distances **2.** A direct, often confidential channel for information

pip-er (paɪ–pər) n. A person who plays pipes, esp. bagpipes

pip-ing (paɪ–pɪŋ) n. **1.** Pipes collectively, or a system of pipes **2.** The sound of music or pipes **3. piping hot** Very hot

pi-ra-cy (paɪ–rə–siʸ) n. **1.** Robbery at sea **2.** The unauthorized reproduction or use of a copyrighted book, patented invention, etc.

pi-ra-nha (pə–ræn–yə/ –rɑn–) n. A small, extremely voracious South American fish, schools of which have been known to attack and devour people

pi-rate (paɪ–rət) n. **1.** (esp. in former times) A person who attacks and robs ships at sea **2.** The ship used for this **3.** A person who uses another person's material without legal right, such as publishing sbdy. else's book as his own

pir-ou-ette (pɪər–ə–**wet**) n. A full turn of the body on the tip of the toe or on the ball of the foot —**pirouette** v. **-etted, -etting**

pis-ta-chi-o (pə–stæʃ–iʸ–oʷ/ –stɑʃ–) n. **1.** A small tree of the cashew family **2.** Its edible greenish seed (**pistachio nut**) **3.** The flavor of this nut **4.** A light yellow-green color

pis-til (pɪs–təl) n. The female part of a flower

pis-tol (pɪs–təl) n. A small gun

pis-ton (pɪs–tən) n. A sliding disk or cylinder fitting closely inside a tube in which it moves up and down by pressure or explosion and gives movement to other parts of an engine or a pump

pit (pɪt) n. **1.** A large hole in the ground **2.** A place where materials are dug out: *a gravel pit* **3.** A place beside a motor race track for

repairing and refueling race cars **4.** A sunken area at the front of a theater where the orchestra sits: *the orchestra pit* **5.** A sunken area in a garage floor, from which mechanics can work on the underside of the car **6.**The single, hard-shelled seed of certain fruits, such as a peach, plum, or apricot; a stone **7. the pits** *slang* The worst imaginable

pit v. **-tt- 1.** To make depressions or scars in: *The windshield was pitted by gravel on the country road.* **2.** To place in competition against one another **3.**To extract pits or stones from fruit

pitch (pɪtʃ) n. **1.** A dark, thick, sticky substance that sets hard, used for caulking seams of ships, roofing, paving, etc. **2.** In baseball, a ball thrown by the pitcher to the batter: *The batter swung at the first pitch but missed.* **3.** The steepness of a slope: *The roof had a steep pitch.* **4.** The degree of highness or lowness of a musical note **5.** A salesman's persuasive talk: *a sales pitch*

pitch v. **1.** To throw sthg., as a pitcher throwing a baseball to the batter **2.** To throw horseshoes **3.** To erect a tent or make camp **4.** Of a ship or vehicle, to plunge up and down, back and forth alternately **5.** To remove sbdy. from a place forcefully: *We pitched those troublemakers out of the club.* **6.** **pitch in** To start to eat or work eagerly

pitch–black (pɪtʃ–blæk) *also* **pitch–dark** (pɪtʃ–dark) adj. As black as can be; total darkness

pitch-blende (pɪtʃ–blɛnd) n. A mineral ore that yields uranium and radium

pitch-er (pɪtʃ–ər) n. **1.** The baseball player who throws the ball to the batter **2.** A container for holding and pouring liquids: *a water pitcher*

pitch-fork (pɪtʃ–fɔrk) n. A large, long-handled fork for lifting and pitching hay

pit-e-ous (pɪt–iʸ–əs) adj. Causing or intending to cause pity: *a piteous cry*

pit-fall (pɪt–fɔl) n. An unexpected danger or difficulty: *There are many pitfalls in English spelling, esp. for foreign students.*

pith (pɪθ) n. **1.** The spongy tissue in the stem of certain plants **2.** A white material just under the skin of oranges and other citrus fruit **3.** The essential part: *the pith of an argu-*

ment

pith-y (prθ–iʸ) adj. **-ier, -iest 1.** Like pith; containing much pith: *This orange juice is quite pithy.* **2.** Brief and full of meaning: *pithy comments* **—pithiness** n.

pit-i-a-ble (pɪt–iʸ–ə–bəl) adj. Worthy of pity

pit-i-ful (pɪt–iʸ–fəl) adj. **1.** Very sad; causing pity **2.** So inferior or insignificant as to cause contempt: *a pitiful attempt*

pit-i-less (pɪt–iʸ–ləs) adj. Showing no pity; without mercy

pits (pɪts) n. *Slang* An extremely unpleasant thing or person

pit-tance (pɪt–əns) n. A very small amount

pit-y (pɪt–iʸ) n. **1.** Sorrow aroused by the misfortune of another **2.** A cause of sorrow or regret: *What a pity that she couldn't be here.*

piv-ot (pɪv–ət) n. A fixed central point on which sthg. turns

pivot v. To turn on, or as if on, a pivot **—pivotal** adj.

piz-za (piʸt–sə) n. A baked dish consisting of a pie-like crust, usu. covered with a spiced mixture of tomatoes and cheese

plac-ard (plæk–ərd/–ard) n. A notice printed on some stiff material (usu. wood or cardboard) and carried or hung in a public place

pla-cate (pleʸ–keʸt/ plæk–eʸt) v. **-cated, -cating** To cause sbdy. to stop feeling angry; to appease by making some concessions

place (pleʸs) n. **1.** A particular portion of space: *This is the place where they buried the treasure.* **2.** Any part or spot on a body or surface: *Show me the place where it hurts.* **3.** A position or situation: *I lost my place in line.* **4.** A region or area: *The desert is a dry place.* **5.** A short street **6.** A building set aside for a specific purpose: *a place of worship* **7.** A residence or house: *Let's have the meeting at my place.* **8.** A seat for a person in a theater: *I'm afraid sbdy. has taken my place.* **9.** A position on a team, office staff, etc.: *He took my place on the football team when I got injured.*

place v. **placed, placing 1.** To put in a particular position: *He placed it on the table.* **2.** To arrange for: *He placed an order.* **3.** To finish in the specified position: *He placed second in the marathon.* **4.** To remember: *Her face is familiar*

but I can't place where we met.

pla-ce-bo (plə–**si**ʸ–boʷ) n. **-bos** or **-boes** A substance that has no medicinal value but given to a patient who thinks he is sick

place-ment (**ple**ʸ**s**–mənt) n. **1.** The act of placing or the state of being placed **2.** Location or arrangement **3.** The act of an employment office in filling a position

pla-cen-ta (plə–**sen**–tə) n. **-tas** or **-tae** (–tiʸ) An organ that connects the fetus to the uterus and through which the embryo obtains nourishment

plac-id (**plæs**–əd) adj. Pleasantly calm and peaceful

pla-gia-rize (**ple**ʸ–dʒə–raɪz) v. **-rized, -rizing** To steal the ideas, story, song, etc. from sbdy. and pretend that it is one's own original work —**pla-gia-rism** (**ple**ʸ–dʒə–rɪz–əm) n.

plague (**ple**ʸg) n. **1.** An epidemic disease that claims the lives of many: *The Bubonic Plague (1348-50 A.D.) wiped out one-third of the population of Europe.* **2.** Any widespread affliction or evil: *a plague of rats* **3.** Any cause of relentless disturbance

plague v. **plagued, plaguing** To annoy by a repeated action: *The president was plagued with questions from the news media.*

plaid (plæd) n. **1.** A long piece of cloth worn over the shoulder, often with a special colored pattern **2.** This pattern itself: *She's wearing a plaid skirt.*

plain (**ple**ʸn) n. A large area of flat land: *We drove all day to cross the Great Plains of North America.*

plain adj. **1.** Clear; obvious: *It's very plain that you don't want to go.* **2.** Without lines or any decoration: *plain paper* **3.** Straightforward: *plain talk* **4.** Ordinary; homey in manner **5.** Not pretty: *a rather plain girl*

plain-ly (**ple**ʸn–liʸ) adv. Obviously: *She's plainly mistaken.*

plain-tiff (**ple**ʸn–tɪf) n. A person who brings a charge against sbdy. in court

plain-tive (**ple**ʸn–tɪv) adj. Sounding sad or sorrowful: *a plaintive tune*

plan (plæn) n. **1.** An idea of how to do sthg.; a method of achieving sthg., thought out in advance: *There is no wisdom, no insight, no plan that can succeed against the Lord* (Pro-

verbs 21:30). *Plans fail for lack of counsel, but with many advisors they succeed* (Proverbs 15:22). *"No plan of yours [O Lord] can be thwarted"* (Job 42:2). **2.** A drawing showing the relative size and position of the parts of sthg.: *the floor plan of a house* **3.** A map of a city or district, esp. one showing where businesses, factories, etc. may be located in the future

plan v. **-nn- 1.** To intend: *We plan to go to Paris in April.* **2.** To decide how sthg. is to be done: *We have to plan very carefully if we are to succeed.* **3.** To design a building

plane (**ple**ʸn) n. **1.** A tool with a blade used for making wood smooth **2.** In geometry, a flat or level surface **3.** *infml.* Airplane **4.** Standard or level of thought, development, etc.: *We didn't agree, but we kept the discussion on a friendly plane.*

plan-et (**plæn**–ət) n. One of the heavenly bodies moving around the sun: *The earth is a planet.*

plan-e-tar-i-um (plæn–ə–**teər**–iʸ–əm) n. A large room with a domed ceiling on which lights are projected to show the position of the stars and planets at any given time

plank (plæŋk) n. **1.** A long flat piece of timber **2.** One of the fundamental principles of a political party

plank-ton (**plæŋk**–tən) n. Tiny plant and animal organisms, generally microscopic, that float on the surface of fresh or salt water, used as food by fish

plan-ner (**plæn**–ər) n. Sbdy. who makes plans: *a city planner*

plant (plænt) n. **1.** A living organism that has stems, leaves, and roots and usu. grows in the ground **2.** A factory or its machinery and equipment

plant v. **1.** To put sthg. into the ground so it will grow **2.** *fig.* To put an idea or suggestion into someone's mind **3.** To put down heavily: *He planted himself between the two who were arguing.*

plan-tain (**plæn**–tən) n. **1.** A tropical banana plant having a coarse fruit, eaten as a cooked vegetable **2.** This fruit

plantain n. A plant like a weed with clusters of small green or whitish flowers

plan-ta-tion (plæn–te^y–ʃən) n. A large piece of land for growing certain crops, such as cotton, rubber, tea, sugar, etc.

plan-ter (plænt–ər/ plæn–tər) n. The owner of a plantation

plaque (plæk) n. 1. A thin flat plate or tablet, usu. metal, intended as an ornament on a wall 2. An inscribed commemorative tablet, as on a monument 3. An accumulation of bacteria that forms on the teeth

plas-ma (plæz–mə) n. The liquid part of blood in which cells are suspended

plas-ter (plæs–tər) n. 1. A substance that may be put on walls to form a hard, smooth surface 2. A similar quick-drying substance that may be used for mending broken arms and legs, making models, etc.

plaster v. 1. To put plaster on: *They plastered the walls.* 2. To apply hair oil, e.g., thickly: *He plastered his hair with hair cream.* —plasterer n.

plas-tered (plæs–tərd) adj. *infml.* Intoxicated

plas-tic (plæs–tık) n. A light-weight man-made material produced chemically, which can be made into different shapes when soft and which keeps its shape when hard: *forks made of plastic*

plastic adj. 1. Made of plastic: *plastic spoons* 2. Capable of being molded or shaped 3. *slang* Superficial: *a plastic society*

plas-tic-i-ty (plæ–stıs–ət–i^y) n. The state or quality of being plastic

plate (ple^yt) n. 1. A shallow, usu. circular dish from which food is eaten 2. A plateful: *a plate of spaghetti* 3. A flat piece of metal: *The ship was made of steel plates.* 4. A piece of metal with numbers and/or letters on it: *a license plate* 5. A sheet of glass: *a plate of glass in the window* 6. The part of a denture that conforms to the mouth and contains the teeth 7. A full-page illustration in a book

plate v. plated, plating To cover with a thin layer of gold or silver —plated adj. *gold-plated*

pla-teau (plæ–to^w) n. -teaux or -teaus 1. An area of land that is higher than the land around it, at least on one side 2. Any period of little or no growth or of decline

plat-form (plæt–fɔrm) n. 1. A level surface raised above the surrounding ground or floor, esp. one from which a speaker addresses an audience 2. A raised area at a train station from which passengers can board the train 3. The policy or program of a political party

plat-ing (ple^yt–ıŋ) n. A coating of silver or gold, etc.

plat-i-num (plæt–ən–əm) n. A heavy, silver-white metallic element that will not tarnish, used esp. in jewelry

plat-i-tude (plæt–ə–tu^wd) n. A flat, dull, or trite remark

pla-ton-ic (plə–tɑn–ık/ ple^y–) adj. Free from sexual desire, esp. in the relationship between a man and a woman

pla-toon (plə–tu^wn) n. 1. A military unit consisting of two or more squads 2. Any similar group

plat-ter (plæt–ər) n. A large shallow dish, usu. oval in shape, used for serving food, esp. meat

plat-y-pus (plæt–ı–pəs/ –pʊs) n. A furry water animal of Australia, one of the few mammals that lays eggs. It has webbed feet and a bill like that of a duck

plau-dit (plɔ–dət) n. A demonstration of approval, usu. by applause

plau-si-ble (plɔ–zə–bəl) adj. 1. Of a statement, seeming to be true or reasonable, but not proved 2. Of a person, skilled in making statements that seem to be true but may not be

play (ple^y) v. 1. Do things for pleasure or amusement as children do: *Tommy is playing in the back yard.* 2. To take part in a sport: *He plays football.* 3. To act: *He played the part of Romeo.* 4. To perform: *She plays the piano.* 5. To plan and carry out for one's own amusement: *He played a dirty trick on me.* 6. To make a move in a game; to take one's turn: *It's your play.* 7. To cause a radio or record player to produce sound: *He was playing his phonograph records.* 8. play it safe To be cautious 9. play it by ear To act as things develop rather than plan in advance 10. play one's cards right To make the most of the opportunities and not make any mistakes 11. to play along with To cooperate, but

unenthusiastically **12. play around** To behave irresponsibly **13. play down** To minimize the importance **14. play up** To emphasize or publicize **15. play up to** To try to gain one's favor **16. played out** Exhausted **17. play into someone's hands** To do sthg. unknowingly that gives the other person an advantage **18. play with fire** To take risks **19. play havoc** To cause a lot of damage

play n. **1.** Recreation; amusement: *All work and no play makes Johnny a dull boy.* **2.** A drama: *Shakespeare wrote many plays.* **3.** A move or action in a game: *The first baseman made a great play.* **4.** Freedom of movement: *The steering wheel had a lot of play in it.* **5.** A pun: *a play on words*

play-a-ble (ple^y-ə-bəl) adj. Fit to be played with or on: *Because of the rain, the football field was not playable.*

play-boy (ple^y-bɔɪ) n. A man who spends his time chiefly in finding enjoyment for himself

play-er (ple^y-ər) n. **1.** One who participates in a sport or game **2.** A performer on a musical instrument **3.** An actor

play-ful (ple^y-fəl) adj. **1.** Liking to play: *a playful kitten* **2.** In a mood for fun; not serious —**playfully** adv.

play-ground (ple^y-graʊnd) n. An area in which children can play in a park, at school, etc.

play-mate (ple^y-me^yt) n. A child's companion in play

play-off (ple^y-ɔf) n. A game or series of games to determine a championship

play-wright (ple^y-raɪt) n. A person who writes plays

pla-za (plɑ-zə/ plæz-ə) n. A public square or open space in town

plea (pli^y) v. **1.** A prisoner's answer to a charge: *a plea of not guilty* **2.** An urgent request: *a plea for blood-donors* **3.** An excuse

plead v. **pleaded** or **pled, pleading 1.** To answer a criminal charge: *How do you plead, guilty or not guilty?* **2.** To make an urgent request: *He pleaded with her not to jump.* **3.** To give as an excuse: *He pleaded ignorance of the law.*

pleas-ant (plɛz-ənt) adj. **1.** Sthg. that gives pleasure; nice; enjoyable: *a pleasant day/ taste/view* **2.** Friendly: *a pleasant smile* —**pleasantly** adv. —**pleasantness** n.

please (pli^yz) v. **pleased, pleasing 1.** To give pleasure or satisfaction: *The Lord detests the sacrifice of the wicked, but the prayer of the upright pleases him* (Proverbs 15:8). **2.** To choose: *Our God is in heaven; he does whatever pleases him* (Psalm 115:3).

please adv. A word used with a request in order to be polite: *Please pass the salt.*

pleased (pli^yzd) adj. Satisfied; happy: *Do not forget to do good and to share with others, for with such sacrifices God is pleased* (Hebrews 13:16).

pleas-ing (pli^y-zɪŋ) adj. Satisfying; attractive; enjoyable: *When a man's ways are pleasing to the Lord, he makes even his enemies live at peace with him* (Proverbs 16:7).

plea-sure (plɛʒ-ər) n. Sthg. that gives enjoyment: *She gets much pleasure out of playing the piano./ "As surely as I live," declares the sovereign Lord, "I take no pleasure in the death of the wicked, but rather that they turn from their wicked ways and live"* (Ezekiel 33:11). —**pleasur-a-ble** (plɛʒ-ə-rə-bəl) adj.

pleat (pli^yt) n. A fold in cloth, pressed or sewn in: *a skirt with pleats* —**pleated** adj. *a pleated skirt*

ple-be-ian (plɪ-bi^y-yən) n. One who is common or crude —**plebeian** adj. Common; vulgar

pleb-i-scite (plɛb-ə-saɪt) n. A vote of all the people in the city, state, country, etc. on a particular matter

pled (plɛd) Past tense and part. of **plead**

pledge (plɛdʒ) n. **1.** A formal promise **2.** A sign or token: *They exchanged rings as a pledge of their love.* **3.** Sthg. left with sbdy. as security until money borrowed is repaid

pledge v. **pledged, pledging 1.** To promise solemnly: *I pledge allegiance to my Lord and Savior Jesus Christ...* **2.** To bind by, or as if by, a pledge **3.** To deposit as security

ple-na-ry (pli^y-nə-ri^y/ plɛn-ə-) adj. **1.** Full; complete **2.** Attended by everyone who should be present

plen-te-ous (plɛnt-i^y-əs) adj. Plentiful

plen-ti-ful (plɛnt-ɪ-fəl) adj. Abundant; exist-

ing in large amounts

plen-ty (plɛnt–iʸ) n. **1.** Enough; sufficient **2.** A large amount

pleth-o-ra (plɛθ–ə–rə) n. Superabundance; more than enough

pleu-ri-sy (plʊr–ə–siʸ) n. An illness in which the covering of the lung becomes inflamed, causing severe pain in the chest or sides

pli-a-ble (plaɪ–ə–bəl) adj. **1.** Flexible; easily bent or shaped **2.** Easily influenced or persuaded

pli-ers (plaɪ–ərz) n. A tool used for gripping, bending or cutting wire, etc.

plight (plaɪt) n. A condition of difficulty

plight v. To promise by a solemn pledge

plod (plɑd) v. **-dd- 1.** To walk laboriously: *The tired old man plodded along the path.* **2.** To work slowly but usu. thoroughly: *He just keeps plodding along, but he gets the job done, and he does it well.*

plod-der (plɑd–ər) n. Sbdy. who works slowly but usu. thoroughly

plop (plɑp) n. A sound similar to the sound of a drop of water falling into a liquid

plop v. **-pp- 1.** To fall with this sound: *The sugar cube plopped into her teacup.* **2.** To allow one's body to fall heavily, as when sitting down: *Mary plopped into the chair next to mine.*

plot (plɑt) n. **1.** A plan, esp. for doing sthg. unlawful or evil **2.** The main events on which a story or movie is based **3.** A piece of land for building or growing things

plot v. **-tt-** To plan to do sthg., esp. sthg. evil or unlawful

plow (plaʊ) AmE. **plough** (plaʊ) BrE. n. **1.** A type of farm tool pulled through the top layer of soil to turn it over, drawn by a tractor or by draft animals **2.** An implement resembling a plow

plow v. **1.** To turn up earth with a plow **2.** To clear snow from a road or driveway, etc. **3.** To proceed laboriously: *He plowed his way through the work that had piled up on his desk during his absence.* **4.** To force a way: *The steamboat plowed its way up the river.*

ploy (plɔɪ) n. A cunning maneuver to gain an advantage

pluck (plʌk) v. **1.** To pull out hair or feathers **2.**

To pick flowers or fruit **3.** To sound the strings of a musical instrument by pulling at them with the fingers or a pick: *Pluck us out a tune on your guitar/banjo.*

pluck n. **1.** Courage: *That daring leap took a lot of pluck.* **2.** The act of plucking

plug (plʌg) n. **1.** Sthg. used to stop up a hole **2.** A device with metal pins to be fitted into an outlet to make an electrical connection **3.** A spark plug for an engine **4.** A piece of favorable publicity for a commercial product: *He gave my new book a plug on the radio.* **5.** slang An old worn-out horse

plug v. **-gg- 1.** To stop up a hole with sthg.: *He plugged up the hole in the boat to stop it from leaking.* **2.** To make an electrical connection: *She plugged in the electric heater.* **3.** To mention favorably: *They've been plugging that book on TV for months.*

plum (plʌm) n. **1.** A round fruit with smooth skin and a single flat seed **2.** The tree that bears this fruit **3.** A deep purple

plum-age (pluʷ–mɪdʒ) n. The feathers of a bird

plumb (plʌm) n. **1.** A small piece of lead suspended on a string or cord (plumb line), used to determine water depth **2.** A similar device used to ascertain a true vertical line

plumb adj., adv. **1.** Exactly straight up and down: *This wall isn't plumb. It slants slightly to the left.* **2.** slang Utter; complete: *plumb crazy*

plumb v. **1.** To test the angle of sthg. with a plumb line **2.** To ascertain the depth of sthg.

plumb-er (plʌm–ər) n. A person whose job it is to install and repair water pipes, fixtures, etc.

plumb-ing (plʌm–ɪŋ) n. **1.** The pipes, fixtures, etc. of a water system **2.** The work done by a plumber

plume (pluʷm) n. **1.** A large decorative feather, esp. a long fluffy one: *She wore a plume in her hat.* **2.** A column of smoke, blowing snow, etc.

plum-met (plʌm–ət) v. To fall or drop swiftly: *The rocks plummeted to the bottom of the canyon.*

plump (plʌmp) adj. Well filled out and rounded in form; pleasantly fat: *plump cheeks*

plun-der (plʌn–dər) v. To rob by force, esp. in

time of war: *The soldiers plundered the city.*

plunder n. The goods stolen by force

plunge (plʌndʒ) v. **plunged, plunging 1.** To throw oneself forcefully into a substance or place: *He plunged into the pool./They plunged into the room, breaking down the door.* **2.** To enter suddenly into an activity: *He plunged into his work with renewed interest.* **3.** To descend steeply and suddenly: *The car plunged down the cliff.* **4.** To push sthg. suddenly: *He plunged his knife into the attacking beast.* **5.** To cause sthg. to happen suddenly: *He plunged the room into darkness by the flip of a switch.* **6.** Of the neckline of a dress, to become lower: *Necklines have plunged this year.*

plunge n. **1.** The act of plunging: *He took a plunge into the river.* **2. take the plunge** To do sthg. determinedly after a long delay due to uncertainty

plung-er (plʌn–dʒər) n. A rubber cup at the end of a long handle, used to unblock pipes by means of suction

plunk (plʌŋk) v. **1.** To put down heavily: *She plunked herself down on the couch.* **2.** To pluck the strings of a musical instrument

plunk n. The sound or act of plunking

plu-per-fect (pluʷ–pɜr–fɪkt) adj. *Gram.* Past perfect tense: *In the sentence, "He had lived in New York before coming to St. Louis," the words "had lived" are in the pluperfect tense.* — **pluperfect** n.

plu-ral (plʊr–əl) n. *Gram.* The form of a word that expresses more than one: *"Geese" is the plural of "goose."*

plu-ral-i-ty (plʊ–ræl–ət–iʸ) n. **-ties 1.** The state of being plural **2.** In an election in which there are three or more candidates the number of votes received by the leading candidate in excess of those received by the next candidate

plus (plʌs) prep. **1.** Increased by; in addition to: *Three plus four equals seven.* **2. plus sign** A sign (+) showing that two or more numbers are to be added together, or that a number is greater than zero

plus adj. And above: *The senior citizens are all 80 plus.*

plush (plʌʃ) adj. Luxurious: *a plush hotel*

Plu-to (pluʷt–oʷ) n. The planet that is farthest from the sun in our solar system

plu-toc-ra-cy (pluʷ–tɒk–rə–siʸ) **-cies** n. **1.** Government by the wealthy **2.** A ruling class of wealthy people —**plu-to-crat** (pluʷ–tə–kræt) n. —**plu-to-crat-ic** (pluʷ–tə–kræt–ɪk) adj.

plu-to-ni-um (pluʷ–toʷ–niʸ–əm) n. A radioactive silver-white metal, used to produce atomic energy

ply (plaɪ) v. **plied, plying 1.** Of ships, buses, etc., to travel regularly between two places: *This ship plies between San Francisco and Manila.* **2.** To work regularly at a trade: *The newsboy plies his trade at that busy corner.*

ply-wood (plaɪ–wʊd) n. A building material made by gluing several thin sheets of wood together

p.m. (piʸ ɛm) *abbr. for* post meridiem (=after midday) Used to express the time between twelve noon and twelve midnight: *Five p.m. is five o'clock in the afternoon.*

pneu-mat-ic (nʊ–mæt–ɪk) adj. **1.** Of or containing air, gases, or wind **2.** Operating by compressed air: *a pneumatic pump* **3.** Filled with compressed air, as a tire

pneu-mo-nia (nʊ–moʷ–nyə) n. Acute inflammation of one or both lungs caused by bacterial or viral infection

P.O. *abbr. for* post office

poach (poʷtʃ) v. **1.** To cook an egg, removed from its shell, in boiling water or in a poacher **2.** To cook fish, e.g., by simmering it in a small amount of liquid **3.** To trespass on another's property in order to fish or hunt **4.** To take fish or game illegally from private property or water

poacher (poʷtʃ–ər) n. A person who poaches

pock-et (pɒk–ət) n. **1.** A small bag-like part sewn onto a garment for holding money, keys, and other small articles **2.** A pouch-like compartment in a suitcase or on a car door, etc. **3.** One of the six pouches in the corners and sides of a pool table into which the balls are driven **4.** An isolated group: *small pockets of resistance*

pocket adj. Of a size suitable for carrying in one's pocket: *a pocket radio*

pocket v. **1.** To put in one's pocket or to keep for oneself: *He pocketed the money.* **2.** To take for oneself dishonestly: *He pocketed the mon-*

ey that was intended for the orphans. **3.** To send a ball into one of the pockets of a pool table: *He pocketed the eight ball.*

pock-et-book (pɑk–ət–bʊk) n. **1.** A purse or handbag **2.** A paperback book, small enough to be carried in one's pocket

pock-mark (pɑk–mɑrk) n. A scar or small hole left in the skin by smallpox, etc.

pod (pɑd) n. A long narrow seed case like that of a bean or pea, that splits open when ripe

podg-y (pɑdʒ–iʸ) adj. Short and fat

po-di-um (poʷ–diʸ–əm) n. -diums or -dia **1.** A platform for an orchestra conductor **2.** A lectern

po-em (poʷ–əm) n. A composition in verse, esp. one expressing deep feelings or noble thoughts

poet (poʷ–ət) n. A person who writes poetry

po-et-ic (poʷ–ɛt–ɪk) also **poetical** adj. Of or like poetry —**poetically** adv.

po-et-ry (poʷ–ə–triʸ) n. **1.** The art of a poet **2.** Poems in general: *a book of poetry* **3.** A graceful quality that pleases the mind as poetry does: *That ice skater is poetry in motion.*

poi-gnant (pɔɪ–nyənt) adj. Arousing sympathy; deeply moving to the feelings; keenly felt: *poignant grief*

poin-ci-an-a (pɔɪn–siʸ–æn–ə) n. A shrub or small tree having showy orange or scarlet flowers

poin-set-ti-a (pɔɪn–sɛt–iʸ–ə/ –sɛt–ə–) n. A tropical plant with showy bright red leaves that look like petals, often used for Christmas decorations

point (pɔɪnt) n. **1.** A sharp end: *She pricked herself with the point of a needle.* **2.** A dot: *a decimal point/Three, point, five percent = 3.5% or three and one-half percent* **3.** A place: *The bus stops at five points along this road.* **4.** A particular act, instance, or thought: *Whoever keeps the whole law [of God] and yet stumbles at just one point is guilty of breaking all of it* (James 2:10). **5.** A scoring system used in deciding who is the winner in certain games and sports: *Our team won the game by 3 points.* **6.** A degree of temperature: *Heat the water till it reaches its boiling point.* **7.** A single particular idea, fact, or part of an argument or statement: *There were three major points in his speech.* **8.** A piece of land with a sharp end that stretches out to the sea: *Point Loma is in San Diego.* **9.** An exact moment: *The chairman accused John of lying, and at that point, John got up and stormed out of the room.* **10.** A mark of character: *Patience is not her strong point.* **11.** Purpose; use: *There's not much point in putting on clean clothes if you're going to work on the car.* **12. at the point of** Just before: *at the point of death/Be faithful [to Christ], even to the point of death, and I [Christ] will give you the crown of life* (Revelation 2:10). **13. beside the point** Not related to the subject being discussed **14. point of no return** A point in doing sthg. at which one has to decide whether to stop or go on, because if one continues, one will not be able to go back **15. point of order** A matter connected with the proper running of an official meeting **16. point of view** A way of thinking about sthg. or looking at various issues: *The rich and the poor see things from different points of view.* **17.** A division on a compass: *People came from all points: north, northeast, northwest, etc.*

point v. **1.** To hold out a finger or a stick, etc., to show direction or position **2.** To aim: *He pointed his gun at the target.* **3. point the finger at** To accuse or blame sbdy. **4. point out** To call attention to; to indicate: *He pointed out her mistake./He pointed her out in the crowd.*

point–blank (pɔɪnt–blæŋk) adv. **1.** Of the firing of a gun, from a very close position **2.** Of speaking, very direct and forceful: *She told him point-blank that he wasn't wanted there.* —**point-blank** adj.

point-ed (pɔɪnt–əd) adj. **1.** Having a point **2.** Being to the point; direct: *a pointed question*

point-er (pɔɪnt–ər) n. **1.** Sbdy. or sthg. that points; an indicator: *The pointer on the gasoline gauge is stuck.* **2.** A hint or tip: *Let me give you a few pointers on how to do that.* **3.** A large short-haired hunting dog

point-less (pɔɪnt–ləs) adj. Meaningless

point of view (pɔɪnt əv vyuʷ) n. The way sbdy. thinks about sthg.

poise (pɔɪz) v. **poised, poising** To balance: *He*

was poised on the diving board.

poise n. **1.** Gracefulness; control of bodily movement: *Good poise is important for a figure skater or dancer.* **2.** Self-confidence

poised (pɔɪzd) adj. **1.** In a state of tension and ready for action: *The two nations were poised for war.* **2.** Remaining in a state of balance: *The car was poised on the edge of a cliff.* **3.** Self-controlled

poi-son (pɔɪz–ən) n. **1.** A substance which, through chemical action, can injure or kill **2.** An evil and deadly influence on someone's behavior, mind, etc.: *No man can tame the tongue. It is a restless evil, full of deadly poison* (James 3:8).

poison v. **-ed, -ing 1.** To injure or kill with poison **2.** To treat or taint with poison **3.** To corrupt: *Those filthy books poisoned his mind.*

poison ivy (pɔɪz–ən aɪ–viʸ) A shrub having white berries and pointed leaves in clusters of three, causing a skin irritation if touched

poi-son-ous (pɔɪz–ən–əs) adj. Containing or having the effects of poison: *fig. poisonous ideas*

poke (poʷk) v. **poked, poking 1.** To thrust with a finger or a stick: *Poke the fire and stir it up.* **2.** To push a pointed thing into sbdy. or sthg.: *She nearly poked me (in the eye) with her elbow.* **3.** To hit or jab: *Stop poking me!* **4.** To thrust forward; protrude: *He poked his head through the open window.* **5.** To move slowly: *The children were just poking along on their way to school.* **6.** To hit: *He poked him in the nose.* **7.** To search: *He poked around in the attic, looking for some old photos.* **8. to poke one's nose into sthg.** To pry into other people's private affairs; to intrude

poke n. **1.** The act of poking or jabbing: *Give him a poke and wake him up.*

po-ker (poʷ–kər) n. A stiff metal rod for stirring a fire

pok-y (poʷ–kiʸ) adj. **-ier, -iest 1.** Slow in movement: *Hurry up! Don't be so poky.* **2.** Small and cramped; uncomfortable: *a poky little house*

poky n. *slang* A jail

po-lar (poʷ–lər) adj. **1.** Of or near the North or South Pole **2.** Either of the opposite ends of a magnet

polar bear (poʷ–lər bɛər) n. A large white bear that lives near the North Pole

po-lar-i-ty (poʷ–lær–ət–iʸ / –lɛar–) n. **-ties 1.** Having two opposite poles, as in a magnet or storage battery **2.** The presence of two opposite qualities, opinions, or tendencies

po-lar-i-za-tion (poʷ–lə–ɪə–zeʸ–ʃən) n. A division of groups or forces into two extreme, opposing positions or points of view

po-lar-ize (poʷ–lər–aɪz) v. **-zed, -izing** To cause or to be in a state of polarization

pole (poʷl) n. **1.** A long, round stick or post: *telephone poles* **2.** Either end of an imaginary straight line around which a solid round mass turns: *the North Pole and the South Pole* **3.** Either of the points at the ends of a magnet **4.** Either of the two points at which wires may be fixed onto a battery: *the negative pole and the positive pole*

pole-cat (poʷl–kæt) n. **1.** A European mammal of the weasel family, able to spray a liquid having a very unpleasant smell **2.** A skunk

po-lem-ic (pə–lɛm–ɪk) n. **1.** A verbal attack on a belief or opinion **2. polemics** The art or practice of argumentation

polemic adj. **1.** Argumentative **2.** Controversial

pole vault (poʷl vɔlt) n. A sport in which a person uses a long pole to vault over a crossbar

po-lice (pə–liʸs) n. Men and women whose duty it is to protect people and property and enforce the law

police v. **policed, policing** To keep order by using, or as if by using, police

po-lice-man (pə–liʸs–mən) n. **-men** (–mən) A male police officer

po-lice-wo-man (pə–liʸs–wʊ–mən) n. **-wo-men** (–wɪ–mən) A female police officer

pol-i-cy (pɑl–ə–siʸ) n. **-cies 1.** A planned or agreed course of action based on a particular principle; a plan that guides the actions taken by a person or group: *It's against government policy to trade with that country.* **2.** A document setting forth the details of an agreement with an insurance company: *a health insurance policy*

po-li-o (poʷ–liʸ–oʷ) n. A serious infectious

pomegranate

disease that occurs mainly in children and in its acute form attacks the central nervous system causing paralysis (loss of power to move certain muscles) and often death —see PARALYSIS

pol-ish (pɑl–ɪʃ) v. **1.** To make or become smooth and glossy by rubbing **2.** To improve a speech or piece of writing: *He was polishing up the speech that he was to deliver that evening.*

polish n. **1.** A substance used to make sthg. smooth and glossy: *furniture polish* **2.** A smooth shiny surface produced by rubbing

po-lite (pə–laɪt) adj. Courteous; having good manners, being considerate of others; using correct social behavior —opposite IMPOLITE —**politely** adv.

po-lit-i-cal (pə–lɪt–ɪ–kəl) adj. **1.** Of or concerning politics or government: *What political party do you support?* **2.** Having an organized system of government: *What kind of political system does that country have?* —**politically** adv.

pol-i-ti-cian (pɑl–ə–tɪʃ–ən) n. One who is engaged in politics, esp. professionally

pol-i-tics (pɑl–ə–tɪks) n. **1.** The science or art of governing a country **2.** The activities and policies of those who control or seek to control a government **3.** The activities or practices of anyone who seeks any position of power or advantage

pol-ka (po^wl–kə) n. A lively dance for couples

pol-ka dots (po^wl–kə dɑts) n. Round dots, evenly spaced, to form a pattern on cloth —**polka–dot** adj. *a polka-dot dress*

poll (po^wl) n. **1.** The voting at an election **2.** The total number of votes cast **3.** The place where votes are cast and counted **4.** A survey of public opinion on a certain subject

poll v. **1.** To receive a specified number of votes **2.** To cast a vote

pol-len (pɑl–ən) n. The fine yellow powder inside a flower which fertilizes other flowers when it is carried to them

pol-li-nate (pɑl–ə–ne^yt) v. **-nated, -nating** To cause a plant to produce seeds by supplying it pollen: *Insects pollinate the flowers.* —**pol-li-na-tion** (pɑl–ə–ne^y–ʃən) n.

pol-li-wog (pɑl–i^y–wɑg) n. A tadpole; another form of the word **pollywog**

pol-lu-tant (pə–lu^wt–ənt) n. Anything that pollutes

pol-lute (pə–lu^wt) v. **-luted, -luting 1.** To make air, water, etc. dangerously impure or unfit for use; to contaminate: *Factory waste products have polluted the river.* **2.** To corrupt: *His teachings polluted the students' minds. /...keep oneself from being polluted by the [sinful] world* (James 1:27).

pol-lu-tion (pə–lu^w–ʃən) n. **1.** The act of polluting **2.** A substance that pollutes: *There's so much pollution in the air that it's difficult to breathe.*

pol-ly-wog (pɑl–i^y–wɑg) n. Another form of the word **polliwog**

po-lo (po^w–lo^w) n. A sport played by two teams of horseback riders who hit a wooden ball with mallets. Each team tries to hit the ball into the other team's goal.

pol-ter-geist (po^wl–tər–gaɪst) n. A kind of ghost supposed to be responsible for throwing objects around the room and making strange noises

pol-y– (pɑl–i^y–) *prefix* Many; several; much

po-ly-an-dry (pɑ–li^y–æn–dri^y) n. Having more than one husband at the same time

pol-y-es-ter (pɑ–li^y–ɛs–tər) n. A complex ester used in making fibers and plastics

po-lyg-a-my (pə–lɪg–ə–mi^y) n. Having more than one wife at the same time —**po-lygamist** n.

pol-y-glot (pɑl–i^y–glɑt) adj. **1.** Speaking or writing many languages **2.** Containing many languages: *a polyglot dictionary*

polyglot n. A person who speaks many languages

pol-y-gon (pɑl–i^y–gɑn) n. A many-sided geometric figure, usu. having five sides or more

pol-y-tech-nic (pɑl–ɪ–tɛk–nɪk) n. An institution giving instruction in many subjects, esp. technical ones and industrial arts

pol-y-the-ism (pɑl–ɪ–θi^y–ɪz–əm) n. The belief in and worship of more than one god —**polytheist** n. —**pol-y-the-is-tic** (pɑl–ɪ–θi^y–ɪs–tɪk) adj.

po-me-gran-ate (pɑm–ə–græn–ət) n. **1.** A fruit with a tough reddish rind and tart red pulp

surrounding many small seeds **2.** The shrub
or small tree that bears it

pomp (pamp) n. **1.** Magnificent display;
splendor **2.** Pretentious or excessive display

pomp-ous (pam–pəs) adj. Self-important in
manner or speech

pon-cho (pan–tʃoʷ) n. A blanket-like cloak
with a hole in the center for the head, often
worn as a raincoat

pond (pand) n. A still body of water, smaller
than a lake

pon-der (pan–dər) v. To spend time in consid-
ering sthg.: *Great are the works of the Lord.
They are pondered by all who delight in them*
(Psalm 111:2).

pon-der-ous (pan–də–rəs) adj. **1.** Slow and
awkward because of size and weight **2.** A
difficult style of writing; dull —**ponder-
ously** adv.

pon-tiff (pant–ɪf) n. In the Roman Catholic
Church, a bishop, esp. the pope

pon-tif-i-cal (pan–tɪf–ɪ–kəl) adj. **1.** Concerning
or belonging to the pontiff **2.** Pompous in
speech

pon-tif-i-cate (pan–tɪf–ə–keʸt) v. **-cated,
-cating** To speak in a pompous manner

pon-toon (pan–tuʷn) n. **1.** A kind of flat-
bottomed boat **2.** One of a number of hollow cylinders used to support a temporary
floating bridge

po-ny (poʷ–niʸ) n. **-nies** A small horse

poo-dle (puʷd–əl) n. Any of a breed of active,
intelligent dogs with thick, curly hair

pool (puʷl) n. **1.** A swimming pool **2.** A small
body of still water, esp. one that is naturally
formed: *After the rain, there were pools of water on the way to school.* **3.** A small amount of
any liquid on a surface: *The victim was lying
in a pool of blood.* **4.** A supply of money,
goods, workers, etc., which may be used by
a number of people: *Some of us have formed a
car pool and ride to work together.* **5.** Any of
the various games played on a pool table

pool v. To combine; share: *If we pool our resources, we can buy more equipment and get
more done than if each of us buys all of his own
equipment.*

poor (pʊər) adj. **1.** Having very little money:
The family was so poor they had almost nothing

to eat. / *For you know the grace of our Lord Jesus
Christ, that though he was rich [enjoying all the
glory and riches and splendor of heaven] yet for
your sakes he became poor, so that you through
his poverty might become rich [eternally rich in
heaven]* (2 Corinthians 8:9). —see JESUS
—opposite RICH **2.** Below the usual standard or amount: *in poor health / a poor crop* **3.**
Deserving or causing pity: *The poor old woman had lost both her sons in the war.* —**poor** n.
*He who oppresses the poor shows contempt for
their Maker, but whoever is kind to the needy
honors God* (Proverbs 14:31).

poor-ly (pʊər–liʸ) adv. Badly; not well: *poorly
dressed / paid*

pop (pap) v. **-pp- 1.** To make a sharp explosive
sound: *The balloon popped when I stuck a pin
in it.* **2.** To stop briefly to see sbdy.: *I've just
popped in to return your book.* **3.** To leap or
spring: *A small frog popped out from under the
rock.*

pop n. *infml.* **1.** Papa; father **2.** A familiar term
of address for an old man **3.** Soda pop; a
kind of fizzy, flavored soft drink

pop-corn (pap–kɔrn) n. Grains of corn that
burst when heated, usu. eaten with salt and
butter

pope (poʷp) n. The head of the Roman Catholic Church

pop-lar (pap–lər) n. **1.** A tall, narrow fast
growing tree having soft wood and leaves
shaped like a triangle **2.** Its wood

pop-py (pap–iʸ) n. **-pies** Any of a variety of
plants that have cup-shaped red, violet, orange, or yellow flowers, one kind of which
yields opium

pop-py-cock (pap–iʸ–kak) n. Nonsense

pop-u-lace (pap–yə–ləs) n. The common people

pop-u-lar (pap–yə–lər) adj. Favored by many
people; well liked: *She's very popular with her
pupils.* —opposite UNPOPULAR

pop-u-lar-i-ty (pap–yə–lær–ə–tiʸ / –lɛər–) n. The
quality or state of being well liked, favored,
or admired —opposite UNPOPULARITY

pop-u-lar-ize (pap–yə–lə–raɪz) v. **-ized, -izing**
To make or become popular

pop-u-lar-ly (pap–yə–lər–liʸ) adv. Generally;
by most people: *It is popularly believed that*

smoking is dangerous to one's health.

pop-u-late (**pɑp**-yə-leʸt) v. lated, -lating To settle or live in a particular area; to inhabit: *This place is populated with people from nearly every country on earth.*

pop-u-la-tion (pɑp-yə-leʸ-ʃən) n. The number of people living in a particular city, state, country, etc.

pop-u-lous (**pɑp**-yə-ləs) adj. Having many inhabitants

por-ce-lain (pɔr-sə-lən) n. A glazed ceramic ware; a kind of fine china, produced by baking a clay mixture

porch (pɔrtʃ/ poʷrtʃ) n. An addition to a house, built out from any of the walls, having a floor and sometimes a roof but no outside walls

por-cu-pine (pɔr-kyə-paɪn) n. One of the largest kinds of gnawing animals, covered with long, sharp spines called quills

pore (pɔr/ poʷr) n. A tiny opening (esp. in the skin) through which liquids (esp. sweat) may pass

pore v. **pored, poring** To examine sthg. with great care and attention

pork (pɔrk/ poʷrk) n. Meat from pigs: *a pork chop* —compare BACON, HAM

por-nog-ra-pher (pɔr-nɑg-rə-fər) n. One who produces pornography

por-nog-ra-phy (pɔr-nɑg-rə-fiʸ) n. The ungodly, immoral treatment of sexual subjects in writing and pictures, produced by men of depraved minds, in a way that is intended to arouse sexual excitement NOTE: The Bible says, But among you there must not be even a hint of sexual immorality, or any kind of impurity... for these are improper for God's holy people (Ephesians 5:3). Do not think about how to gratify the desires of the sinful nature (Romans 13:13). No immoral, impure or greedy person... has any inheritance in the kingdom of Christ and of God (Ephesians 5:5). God is perfectly holy and he detests all sin. But because of his great love and mercy, he forgives sinners who truly repent of their sins and put their trust in Jesus for eternal life (Mark 1:15; Acts 2:38; Romans 6:23; John 3:16). —see JESUS

por-ous (pɔr-əs/ poʷr-) adj. Full of pores, allowing liquid to pass through slowly

por-poise (pɔr-pəs/ poʷr) n 1. A playful sea mammal resembling a whale, having a blunt, rounded snout 2. Any of several dolphins

por-ridge (pɔr-ɪdʒ) n. A food made from oatmeal boiled in water or milk

port (pɔrt/ poʷrt-) n. 1. Harbor: *The ship came into port.* 2. A town with a harbor: *Singapore is one of the world's busiest ports.*

port adj. The left side of a ship or aircraft as one faces forward

por-ta-ble (pɔrt-ə-bəl/ poʷrt-) adj. That which can be carried or moved: *a portable typewriter/radio*

por-tal (pɔrt-əl) n. An entrance, door, or gate, esp. one that is imposing

por-tend (pɔr-tɛnd) v. To be a warning of; to foreshadow

por-tent (pɔr-tɛnt) n. A significant sign of sthg. to come —**por-ten-tous** (pɔr-tɛnt-əs) adj.

por-ter (pɔrt-ər/ poʷrt-) n. 1. A person who is hired to carry baggage, as at a railway station 2. An attendant on a passenger train

port-fo-li-o (pɔrt-foʷ-liʸ-oʷ/poʷrt-) n. 1. A case for carrying important papers, drawings, etc. 2. The contents of such a case 3. The post or job of a government minister

port-hole (pɔrt-hoʷl/ poʷrt-) n. A small, usu. round window on a ship

por-ti-co (pɔrt-ɪ-koʷ) n. A porch or a walk with a roof held up by columns

por-tion (pɔr-ʃən/ poʷr-) n. 1. A part: *He read the first portion of the book.* 2. A share: *His portion of the profit was $1,000.* 3. A quantity of food for one person as served in a restaurant

port-ly (pɔrt-liʸ) adj. -lier, -liest Round and fat: *a portly old gentleman*

por-trait (pɔr-trət/ pɔr-treʸt/ poʷr-) n. 1. A painting, drawing, or photograph of a real person: *He painted a portrait of our family.* 2. A written description of a place: *I read "A Portrait of India" with great interest.*

por-tray (pɔr-treʸ/ poʷr-) v. -trayed, -traying 1. To represent sbdy. or sthg. in painting, in a book, etc., according to one's own ideas or

to produce a certain effect: *Her book portrays her father as a very wise man.* **2.** To act the part of a particular character in a play —**portrayal** n. *The actor's portrayal of Abraham Lincoln was excellent.*

pose (po^wz) v. **-posed, -posing 1.** To sit or stand in a particular position, esp. for a painting or photograph: *Our class posed for a photograph.* **2.** To offer for consideration: *This new offer poses many opportunities.* **3. pose as somebody** To pretend to be: *The spy posed as a naval officer.*

po-si-tion (pə-zɪʃ-ən) n. **1.** The place where sbdy. or sthg. is located: *See if you can find the ship's position on this map.* **2.** A person's place or rank in relation to others in a group, company, class, etc.: *She holds an important position at the university.* **3.** A set of circumstances: *Tom said he would like to help but he was not in a position to do so.* **4.** The way or manner in which sbdy. sits, stands, etc.: *The riveter had to work in a rather awkward position.*

position v. To place in the stated position: *He positioned himself right in front of the window.*

pos-i-tive (paz-ə-tiv) adj. **1.** Allowing no room for doubt: *We are positive that the world is round.* **2.** Of a medical test, showing signs of disease —opposite NEGATIVE

pos-i-tive-ly (paz-ə-tiv-li^y/ paz-ə-trv-li^y) adv. **1.** Unquestionably; absolutely: *He said positively that he would pay the bill.* **2.** (used to add force to a statement) Absolutely: *The sunset was positively beautiful!*

pos-se (pas-i^y) n. A body of persons called by a sheriff to assist in preserving the peace, usu. in an emergency

pos-sess (pə-zɛs) v. **1.** To own: *Millions of poor people possess only the clothes they are wearing.* **2.** To influence: *What possessed you to say such a terrible thing as that?*

pos-sessed (po^w-zɛst) adj. Wildly mad, as if controlled by an evil spirit: *As Jesus was getting into the boat, the man who had been demon-possessed begged to go with him. Jesus [who had cast the demons out of him], did not let him, but said, "Go home to your family and tell them how much the Lord has done for you, and how he has had mercy on you"* (Mark 5:18,19).

pos-ses-sion (pə-zɛʃ-ən) n. Ownership: *Be on your guard against all kinds of greed; a man's life does not consist in the abundance of his possessions* (Luke 12:15). *If anyone has material possessions and sees his brother in need but has no pity on him, how can the love of God be in him?* (1 John 3:17).

pos-ses-sive (pə-zɛs-ɪv) adj. **1.** *derog.* Having a strong desire to dominate or control another person **2.** Unwilling to share sthg. that one owns or someone's attention with other people **3.** (In grammar, a word that shows ownership or connection): *"His" and "Our" are possessive adjectives.*

pos-si-bil-i-ty (pas-ə-bɪl-ət-i^y) n. **-ties** The condition of being possible: *There's a strong possibility that it will rain today.*

pos-si-ble (pas-ə-bəl) adj. **1.** That which can exist, happen, or be done: *With God all things are possible* (Matthew 19:26). *If it is possible, as far as it depends on you, live at peace with everyone* (Romans 12:18). —opposite IMPOSSIBLE **2.** That which may or may not happen: *It is possible that I'll go there tomorrow, but it is not likely.*

pos-si-bly (pas-ə-bli^y) adv. **1.** In accordance with what is possible: *You can't possibly walk 20 miles in an hour.* **2.** Perhaps: *Will you be here tomorrow? Possibly.*

pos-sum (pas-əm) n. **1.** *infml.* for **opossum 2. play possum** To pretend to be asleep or unaware of what is happening, since the possum pretends to be dead when danger is near

post– (po^wst-) comb. form After: *postgraduate/ post-mortem/ postwar*

post (po^wst) n. **1.** A strong upright pole, usu. made of wood: *a fence post* **2.** The starting post or winning post in a race, esp. a horse race **3.** A place where a soldier is on guard duty: *The sentry is at his post.* **4.** A place where trading is carried on, esp. a place on the frontier: *a trading post* **5.** A place occupied by soldiers, esp. on the frontier: *a military post* **6.** A position of paid employment

post v. **1.** To make public by fixing to a wall, bulletin board, or other noticeable place: *The notice was posted on the bulletin board.* **2.**

To place or station: *The sentries were posted all around the fort.* **3.** To mail: *I posted the letter yesterday.* **4.** In bookkeeping, to carry an entry from an auxiliary book to a more formal one **5. keep sbdy. posted** To keep sbdy. informed

post-age (po^wst–ɪdʒ) n. The charge for mailing a letter or package: *The postage for this package is $3.50.* —**postage** adj. *a postage stamp*

post-al (po^ws–təl) adj. Connected with the public letter service: *postal service*

post-card (po^wst–kɑrd) n. A card on which a message may be sent by post, often having a picture on one side

post-date (po^wst–de^yt) v. -dated, -dating **1.** To fix a date later than the actual date **2.** To follow in time

post-er (po^w–stər) n. A large notice, often with pictures, posted in a public place

pos-te-ri-or (pɑ–stɪər–i^y–ər) n. **1.** Situated in the rear **2.** The buttocks

pos-ter-i-ty (pɑ–stɛər–ət–i^y) n. People coming afterwards; future generations

post-grad-u-ate (po^wst–**grædʒ**–ə–wət) adj. Of or relating to studies beyond the bachelor's degree —**postgraduate** n.

post-haste (po^wst–**he^yst**) adv. Urgently; in a great hurry

post-hu-mous (pɑs–tʃə–məs) adj. Happening after a person's death —**posthumously** adv. *Mrs. Smith accepted the medal that was awarded to her heroic husband posthumously.*

post-lude (po^wst–lu^wd) n. A piece of organ music played at the end of a church service

post-man (po^wst–mən) n. -men A mailman; a person who works for the postal service

post-mark (po^wst–mɑrk) n. An official mark stamped on a letter or package, usually over the postage stamp, to indicate when and from where it was sent —**postmark** v. *The letter was postmarked London.*

post-mas-ter (po^wst–mæs–tər) n. The person officially in charge of a post office

post-mor-tem (po^wst–**mort**–əm) n. An examination of a dead body to determine the cause of death

post-na-sal (po^wst–ne^y–zəl) adj. At the back of the nose

post-na-tal (po^wst–ne^yt–əl) adj. Occurring immediately after birth or giving birth

post of-fice (po^wst–ɔf–ɪs) n. A building or office that handles the mail, sells stamps, etc.

post-pone (po^wst–po^wn) v. -poned, -poning To delay; put off to a later date: *The baseball game was postponed because of rain.* —**postponement** n.

post-script (po^wst–skrɪpt) n. A short note at the end of a letter, after one's signature

pos-tu-late (pɑs–tʃə–le^yt) v. -lated, -lating To assume to be true, esp. as a basis for reasoning

pos-ture (pɑs–tʃər) n. **1.** The general way of holding the body: *Sbdy. who models dresses must have good posture.* **2.** A fixed bodily position: *She was photographed in various postures: sitting, standing, etc.*

post-war (po^wst–wɔr) adj. Occurring after a war

po-sy (po^w–zi^y) n. -sies **1.** A flower **2.** A bunch of flowers

pot (pɑt) n. **1.** A round vessel made of metal, glass, clay, etc., used as a container for liquids or solids, esp. for cooking: *a soup pot* **2.** The amount a pot will hold: *A pot of tea, please.* **3.** *infml.* Marijuana **4. go to pot** *infml.* To become ruined or worthless, esp. from lack of care

pot-ash (pɑt–æʃ) n. Potassium carbonate, esp. the form obtained from wood ashes, used in making soap, fertilizers, etc.

po-tas-si-um (pə–tæs–i^y–əm) n. A soft, silver-white, easily melted metallic element

po-ta-to (pə–te^yt–o^w) n. -toes A root vegetable with a thin brown skin, that is cooked and served in many ways

po-tent (po^wt–ənt) adj. **1.** Physically powerful **2.** Having great authority **3.** Having a strong influence on one's mind: *a potent argument* **4.** Of a drug, liquor, etc., having a strong chemical effect —**potency** n. —see also IMPOTENT

po-ten-tate (po^wt–ən–te^yt) n. A ruler with absolute power

po-ten-tial (pə–tɛn–ʃəl) adj. Capable of coming into existence or of being developed: *Your child is a potential writer.* —**potential** n. *He has great potential.* —**potentially** adv.

po-ten-ti-al-i-ty (pə–tən–tʃi^y–**æl**–ət–i^y) n. Possi-

bility; sthg. that may develop

pot-head (pɑt–hɛd) n. *infml.* A person who uses marijuana frequently

pot-hole (pɑt–hoʷl) n. A hole in the surface of a road

po-tion (poʷ–ʃən) n. A liquid for drinking as a medicine or drug, or as a magic charm

pot-luck (pɑt–lʌk) n. Whatever food is available; a meal available to a guest for whom no special preparation has been made

pot-pour-ri (poʷ–pu–riʸ) 1. A scented mixture of dried petals and spices 2. A literary or musical medley 3. A miscellaneous collection

pot-shot (pɑt–ʃɑt) n. 1. A carelessly aimed shot 2. A shot taken at an animal at close range 3. A critical remark made casually: *She takes potshots at everything I suggest.*

pot-ter (pɑt–ər) n. 1. A person who makes pots, dishes, etc., out of baked clay, esp. by hand 2. *fig.* Yes, Lord, you are our Father. We are the clay, you are the potter; we are all the work of your hands (Isaiah 64:8).

pot-ter-y (pɑt–ər–iʸ) n. -ies 1. The work of a potter 2. Objects made out of baked clay

pot-ty (pɑt–iʸ) n. -ties A child's toilet

pouch (pɑʊtʃ) n. 1. A small bag for carrying pipe tobacco or, formerly, gun powder 2. The pocket of skin in which the young of certain animals (kangaroos, opossums, e.g.) are carried

poul-ter-er (poʷl–tər–ər) n. A dealer in poultry

poul-tice (poʷl–təs) n. A wet, sticky kind of dressing spread on a bandage and placed on inflamed areas of skin

poul-try (poʷl–triʸ) n. Farmyard birds such as hens, ducks, etc., kept for supplying eggs and meat

pounce (pɑʊns) v. -pounced, -pouncing To spring suddenly upon sthg.: *The lion pounced on its prey.*

pound (pɑʊnd) n. 1. A standard measure of weight equal to 16 ounces (.454 kilograms): *Apples are sold by the pound.* 2. The standard monetary (money) unit of the United Kingdom equal to 100 pence 3. A standard monetary unit of various other countries 4. A public enclosure where stray animals are kept

pound v. 1. To beat to a powder or a pulp by striking repeatedly with a heavy object: *She pounded the yams in a mortar.* 2. To strike or beat repeatedly: *The waves pounded against the shore./fig. Her heart was pounding when the car slid out of control on the ice.*

pour (pɔɔr/poʷr) v. 1. To cause to flow: *Shall I pour you another cup of tea?* 2. To rain hard: *It's pouring down.* 3. **pour out** To give freely, in abundance: *God said, "I will pour out my Spirit on all people ... and everyone who calls on the name of the Lord will be saved"* (Joel 2:28,32). *God has poured out his love into our hearts by the Holy Spirit whom he has given us [believers in Jesus]* (Romans 5:5).

pout (pɑʊt) v. To show childish displeasure by pushing out one's lips while looking sullen

pov-er-ty (pɑv–ərt–iʸ) n. The state of being very poor: *For you know the grace of our Lord Jesus Christ, that though he was rich [enjoying all the riches and glory and splendor of heaven], yet for your sakes he became poor [for a time here on earth] that you through his poverty might be rich [infinitely and eternally rich]* (2 Corinthians 8:9).

P.O.W. n. *abbr.* Prisoner of war

pow-der (pɑʊ–dər) n. 1. A substance in the form of very fine dry particles: *milk powder* 2. A type of cosmetic: *face powder* 3. Gun powder

powder v. To put powder on: *Mary powdered her nose.*

powdered (pɑʊ–dərd) adj. Produced in the form of powder: *powdered milk*

pow-der-y (pɑʊ–dər–iʸ) adj. 1. Like powder 2. Covered with powder

pow-er (pɑʊ–ər) n. 1. The ability to act effectively: *God made the world by his power* (Jeremiah 10:12). *By his power God raised the Lord [Jesus] from the dead, and he will raise us also* (1 Corinthians 6:14). 2. Force; strength: *a nation's sea power* (=the strength of its navy)/*At the end of this present age [very soon], "All the nations of the earth ... will see the Son of Man [Jesus] coming on the clouds of the sky, with power and great glory"*(Matthew 24:30). *I am not ashamed of the Gospel [the Good News*

about Jesus Christ] because it is the power of God for the salvation of everyone who believes (Romans 1:16). *...you [believers] have been given fullness in Christ who is the head over every power and authority* (Colossians 2:10). **3.** Force that may be used for doing work, driving a machine, or producing electricity: *Mills used to depend on wind power or water power.* **4.** Authority; right to act, given by law or official position: *The police have been given special powers to deal with the drug traffic./After Jesus rose from the dead, he told his disciples, "All power is given unto me in heaven and in earth"* (Matthew 28:18 KJV). *Just before Jesus returned to heaven, he told his disciples: "You will receive power when the Holy Spirit comes on you; and you will be my witnesses ... to the ends of the earth"* (Acts 1:8). **5.** A person, group, nation, etc., that has influence or control: *The world powers must try to avoid war.* **6.** In mathematics, the number of times that a number is to be multiplied by itself: *Five to the third power means 5 x 5 x 5, which equals 125.* **7. power of attorney** A signed, official paper giving the right to act: *He has the power of attorney to act for his father.*

power v. To supply with power (esp. mechanical power): *This golf cart is powered by electricity.*

pow-er-ful (pau–ər–fəl) adj. **1.** Having great power; very strong: *The Son [Jesus Christ] is the radiance of God's glory and the exact representation of his being, sustaining all things by his powerful word* (Hebrews 1:3). **2.** Having a strong effect: *The prayer of a righteous man is powerful* (James 5:16). —**powerfully** adv. *He's very powerfully built.* (=has a big strong body)

pow-er-less (pau–ər–ləs) adj. Helpless; without strength or power; not able to resist or help

powers (pau–ərz) n. Rulers, authorities, kingdoms: *Be strong in the Lord and in his mighty power ... so you can take your stand against the devil's schemes. For our struggle is not against flesh and blood, but against... powers of this dark world...* (Ephesians 6:10-12). *And having disarmed the powers and authorities, he [Christ] made a public spectacle of them, trium-*

phing over them by the cross (Colossians 2:15).

prac-ti-ca-ble (præk–tɪ–kə–bəl) adj. Capable of being carried out or executed: *His plan for irrigating the Sahara desert is not very practicable.* —opposite IMPRACTICABLE

prac-ti-cal (præk–tɪ–kəl) adj. **1.** Concerned with actual experience and facts, rather than with ideas: *She has studied accounting but has not had much practical experience.* **2.** Useful; effective or convenient in actual use: *Your invention is very clever, but it isn't very practical.* **3.** Sensible: *We've got to be practical and not spend our hard-earned money on things we don't need.* —opposite IMPRACTICAL

prac-ti-cal-ly (præk–tɪ–kə–liʸ) adv. Nearly; almost: *Our vacation is practically over; there's only one day left.*

prac-ti-cal nurse (præk–tɪ–kəl nərs) n. A person who has completed a practical nurses training program and is licensed by the state to provide routine patient care under the supervision of a registered nurse or physician

prac-tice AmE. **-ise** BrE. (præk–təs) n. **1.** Repeated performance or exercise in order to acquire or perfect a skill: *It takes a lot of practice to play the piano well.* **2.** The actual doing of sthg.: *Jesus said, "Everyone who hears these words of mine and puts them into practice is like a wise man who built his house on the rock"* (Matthew 7:24). **3.** Sthg. that is regularly or habitually done: *It's his practice to get up at six a.m. and exercise for 20 minutes.* —see HABIT **4.** An act that is often repeated, in a fixed manner or with ceremony: *religious practices* **5.** The business of a doctor or lawyer: *Dr. Smith has followed the practice of medicine for 30 years.*

prac-tice also **-tise** v. **-ticed, -ticing 1.** To do or perform repeatedly in order to gain or perfect a skill: *If you want to play the harp well, you must practice, practice, practice.* **2.** To do anything habitually: *God says, "No one who practices deceit will dwell in my house; no one who speaks falsely will stand in my presence"* (Psalm 101:7). *Practice hospitality* (Romans 12:13). **3.** To do the work of a doctor or lawyer: *She practices law.* **4. practice what you**

preach To carry out or apply; to do yourself what you are always telling others to do

prac-ti-tion-er (præk–tʃ–ə–nər) n. A person who works in a profession, such as a medical doctor who does not specialize in any particular field of medicine: *a general practitioner*

prag-mat-ic (præg–mæt–ɪk) adj. Concerned with facts or actual occurrences, rather than with ideas or theories; practical —**pragmatically** adv.

prai-rie (prɛər–iʸ) n. A wide tract of level or almost level land covered by grass but with very few trees

prairie dog (prɛər–iʸ–dɔg) n. A brownish, furry animal related to the woodchuck

prairie schooner (prɛər–iʸ skuʷ–nər) n. A large wagon covered by canvas; a covered wagon used by North American pioneers traveling across the prairies

praise (preʸz) v. **praised, praising 1.** To speak favorably and with admiration **2.** To offer thanks and honor to God; to glorify him, often in song in a church service: *I praise you [O Lord] because I am fearfully and wonderfully made* (Psalms 139:14). *Praise the Lord, O my soul, and forget not all his benefits. He forgives all my sins and heals all my diseases* (Psalms 103:2,3).

praise n. **1.** The expression of admiration: *His new book is receiving a lot of praise.* **2.** Glory; worship: *Sing praises to God, sing praises; sing praises to our King, sing praises. For God is the King of all the earth; sing to him a psalm of praise* (Psalm 47:6,7).

praise-wor-thy (preʸz–wər–ðiʸ) adj. Deserving praise: *If anything is excellent or praiseworthy, think about such things* (Philippians 4:8).

pram (præm) n. also **per-am-bu-la-tor** n. *BrE.* Baby carriage

prance (præns) v. **pranced, prancing 1.** To move about in a lively or spirited manner **2.** To spring from the hind legs: *a prancing horse*

prank (præŋk) n. A playful or mischievous trick

prat-tle (præt–əl) v. **-tled, -tling** To chatter meaninglessly in a simpleminded way —**prattle** n.

prawn (prɔn) n. Any of several shellfish resembling a large shrimp

pray (preʸ) v. **prayed, praying** To bring our requests before God with our hearts and lips and offer praise and thanksgiving to him: *Jesus said, "This is how you should pray: Our Father in heaven, hallowed [holy] be your name, your kingdom come, your will be done on earth as it is in heaven. Give us today our daily bread. Forgive us our debts as we also forgive our debtors. And lead us not into temptation, but deliver us from the evil one"* (Matthew 6:9-13). *Pray in the Spirit on all occasions with all kinds of prayers and requests* (Ephesians 6:18). *Pray continuously* (1 Thessalonians 5:17). —compare ASK, CALL

prayer (prɛər) n. An act of worship by which we offer up praise and thanksgiving to God and bring our requests before him: *The Lord is far from the wicked, but he hears the prayers of the righteous* (Proverbs 15:29). *Do not be anxious about anything, but in everything, by prayer and petition, with thanksgiving, present your requests to God* (Philippians 4:6). *I urge, then, first of all, that requests, prayers, intercession and thanksgiving be made for everyone — for kings and all those in authority ...* (1 Timothy 2:1,2). *For the eyes of the Lord are on the righteous and his ears are attentive to their prayers* (1 Peter 3:12). *Jesus told his followers: "... whatever you ask for in prayer, believe that you have received it, and it will be yours. And when you stand praying, if you hold anything against anyone, forgive him, so that your Father in heaven may forgive you your sins"* (Mark 11:24,25). *Jesus also said, "Anyone who has faith in me... may ask me for anything in my name, and I will do it"* (John 14:12-14). —**prayerful** adj.

pray-ing man-tis (preʸ–ɪŋ mæn–təs) n. **-tises** or **-tes** (–tiʸz) —see mantis

pre– (priʸ–) A prefix meaning "before" or "beforehand" in such words as: prearrange, precondition, precook, predate, preheat, prepay, preschool, preview, prewar, but <u>not</u> in such words as **preach, precious, precise, prefer, press,** and **pretty**

preach (priʸtʃ) v. To deliver a spiritual message (called a sermon), based on the Holy

Scriptures, esp. as a part of a worship service in church: *After Jesus rose from the dead, he told his disciples to go into all the world and preach the Gospel (the Good News about Jesus) to all creation* (Mark 16:15). —**preacher** n.

pre-am-ble (pri^y–æm–bəl) n. A statement at the beginning of a document, giving the reason for it and its purpose

pre-ar-range (pri^y–ə–re^yndʒ) n. **-ranged, -ranging** To arrange beforehand

pre-car-i-ous (prɪ–keər–i^y–əs) adj. Not safe; risky —**precariously** adv.

pre-cau-tion (prɪ–kɔ–ʃən) n. An action taken beforehand in order to prevent or avoid anything unpleasant —**precautionary** adj.

pre-cede (pri^y–si^yd) v. **-ceded, -ceding** To come, go, or happen before sthg. else: *She preceded him into the room.*

prec-e-dence (prɛs–əd–əns) n. The right to a particular place before others, esp. because of importance: *Studying must take precedence over sports.*

prec-e-dent (prɛs–əd–ənt) n. Sthg. said or done that may serve to authorize, justify, or encourage similar words or acts in the future: *If you let these criminals go unpunished, it will set a precedent, and this kind of crime will increase more and more.*

pre-ced-ing (prɪ–si^yd–ɪŋ) adj. Happening just before; previous

pre-cept (pri^y–sɛpt) n. A command; a rule of conduct: *The fear of the Lord is the beginning of wisdom; all who follow his precepts have good understanding* (Psalm 111:10).

pre-cinct (pri^y–sɪŋkt) n. **1.** A subdivision of a city or town for voting or police purposes **2.** An area that surrounds an important building or group of buildings **3.** A limited area **4. precincts** pl. Neighborhood

pre-cious (prɛʃ–əs) adj. Of great value or worth: *a precious jewel/ Wisdom is more precious than rubies* (Proverbs 8:11). *It was not with perishable things such as silver and gold that you were redeemed... but with the precious blood of Christ...* (1 Peter 1:18,19). —see JESUS

prec-i-pice (prɛs–ə–pəs) n. A very steep, almost upright cliff

pre-cip-i-tate (prɪ–sɪp–ə–te^yt) v. **-tated, -tating**

1. To make sthg. happen sooner: *The president's assassination precipitated the war.* **2.** To cause to happen suddenly: *His treacherous acts precipitated the overthrow of his country.* **3.** To condense and fall as rain or snow **4.** *chem.* To cause a solid substance to separate from a liquid

precipitate (prɪ–sɪp–ə–tət) adj. **1.** Moving forward, rapidly and recklessly **2.** Occurring suddenly and unexpectedly

precipitate (prɪ–sɪp–ə–tət/ –te^yt) n. The substance that settles at the bottom of a liquid

pre-cip-i-ta-tion (prɪ–sɪp–ə–te^y–ʃən) n. **1.** Rain, snow, hail **2.** Abrupt or impulsive haste **3.** *chem.* The forming of a precipitate

pre-cip-i-tous (prɪ–sɪp–ə–təs) adj. Very steep

pré-cis (pre^y–si^y) n. *pl.* **-cis** (–si^yz) A summary of a piece of writing

pre-cise (prɪ–saɪs) adj. **1.** Exact **2.** Careful to be accurate in every detail: *An engineer must be precise.*

pre-cise-ly (prɪ–saɪs–li^y) adv. Exactly

pre-ci-sion (prɪ–sɪʒ–ən) n. Exactness

precision adj. Used for measuring or producing exact (precise) results: *precision instruments*

pre-clude (prɪ–klu^wd) v. **-cluded, -clud-ing** To prevent; to exclude the possibility of

pre-co-cious (prɪ–ko^w–ʃəs) adj. Usu. of children, advanced or well-developed —**precociously** adv. —**precociousness** n.

pre-con-ceive (pri^y–kən–si^yv) v. **-ceived, -ceiving** To form an idea about sthg. before it happens

pre-con-ceived (pri^y–kən–si^yvd) adj. Of an idea, notion, opinion, formed in advance without much knowledge or experience: *a preconceived notion*

pre-con-cep-tion (pri^y–kən–sɛp–ʃən) n. An idea or opinion that one has about sthg. without any actual knowledge of it

pred-a-tor (prɛd–ə–tər)/ –tɔr) n. An animal that attacks and kills other animals for food

pred-a-to-ry (prɛd–ə–tɔr–i^y) adj. **1.** Living by attacking and eating other animals **2.** *fig., derog.* Of humans, cheating or robbing others and seizing their property

pred-e-ces-sor (prɛd–ə–sɛs–ər) n. Sbdy. who has held an official position before sbdy.

else: *The new mayor is a better speaker than his predecessor.*

pre-des-ti-na-tion (priᵞ–dɛs–tɪ–neᵞ–ʃən) n. The belief that God has determined in advance everything that will ever happen

pre-des-tine (priᵞ–dɛs–tɪn) v. -tined, -tining To decide or decree beforehand: *For those God foreknew he also predestined to be conformed to the image of his Son* (Romans 8:29). *In love he [God] predestined us to be adopted as his sons through Jesus Christ ... to the praise of his glorious grace, which he has freely given us in the One he loves* (Ephesians 1:5,6).

pre-dic-a-ment (prɪ–dɪk–ə–mənt) n. An unpleasant situation in which one must make a difficult decision

pred-i-cate (prɛd–ɪ–kət) n. *gram.* The part of a sentence that makes a statement about the subject

pred-i-cate (prɛd–ɪ–keᵞt) v. -cated, -cating To found or base: *His argument was predicated on sound reasoning and experience.*

pre-dict (prɪ–dɪkt) v. To tell in advance what is going to happen, based on knowledge, experience, reason, etc.; to forecast; prophesy: *Can you predict what the weather will be like a month from today?*

pre-dict-a-ble (prɪ–dɪk–tə–bəl) adj. That which can be predicted: *His anger was predictable.* —opposite UNPREDICTABLE

pre-dic-tion (prɪ–dɪk–ʃən) n. Sthg. predicted; the act of predicting

pre-di-lec-tion (priᵞd–əl–ɛk–ʃən) n. A preference; a liking for sthg.

pre-dis-pose (priᵞd–ɪs–poʷz) v. 1. Influence sbdy. in a specific way in advance 2. To make susceptible or liable —**pre-dis-po-si-tion** (priᵞ–dɪs–pə–zɪʃ–ən) n.

pre-dom-i-nant (prɪ–dɑm–ə–nənt) adj. Most powerful, noticeable or important: *English is the predominant language in the United States.* —predominance adj.

pre-dom-i-nant-ly (prɪ–dɑm–ə–nənt–liᵞ) adv. Mainly: *Australia is predominantly English-speaking.*

pre-dom-i-nate (prɪ–dɑm–ə–neyt) v. -nated, -nating To be greater or greatest in numbers, power, effect, etc.

pre-em-i-nent (priᵞ–ɛm–ə–nənt) adj. Above all

others; having supremacy —**preeminence** n. *And he [Christ] is the head of the body, the church, who is the beginning, the firstborn from the dead, that in all things, he may have the preeminence* (Colossians 1:18KJV). —**preeminently** adv. *preeminently successful.*

pre-empt (priᵞ–ɛmpt) v. 1. To take possession of sthg. for oneself before others can 2. To replace or cancel a scheduled program on radio or TV with or without notice —**preemption** n. —**preemptive** adj. —**preemptively** adv.

pre-fab-ri-cate (priᵞ–fæb–rə–keᵞt) v. -cated, -cating To manufacture standardized sections of a house, building, etc. in a factory, for quick assembly at the building site —**prefabricated** adj. —**pre-fab-ri-ca-tion** (priᵞ–fæb–rə–keᵞ–ʃən) n.

pref-ace (prɛf–əs) n. A brief introduction to a book or speech

preface v. -faced, -facing To introduce with a preface: *She prefaced her speech by telling us sthg. about her own experience.*

pre-fer (prɪ–fɜr) v. -rr- 1. To like better: *I prefer rice to potatoes.* 2. **to prefer charges** To bring a charge against a person according to law

pref-er-a-ble (prɛf–ə–rə–bəl) adj. More desirable —preferably adv.

pref-er-ence (prɛf–ə–rəns) n. Choice; liking for one thing rather than another: *Chocolate ice cream is his preference.*

pref-er-en-tial (prɛf–ər–ɛn–ʃəl) adj. Showing or giving preference: *He received preferential treatment.*

pre-fix (priᵞ–fɪks) n. *gram.* An affix that is placed at the beginning of a word: *In the word "refill," "re-" is a prefix that means "again." The word "refill" means "fill again."* —prefix v. —compare SUFFIX

preg-nan-cy (prɛg–nən–siᵞ) n. -cies The condition of being pregnant

preg-nant (prɛg–nənt) adj. 1. A woman or female animal having a developing child or young in the womb 2. Full of meaning: *a pregnant suggestion*

pre-his-tor-ic (priᵞ–hɪs–tɔr–ɪk) adj. Belonging to a time before history was written down

prej-u-dice (prɛdʒ–ə–dəs) n. An opinion or feeling for or esp. against sbdy. without

reason or knowledge: *What a wonderful world it would be if there were no racial prejudice or any other kind of prejudice.* —**prejudiced** adj. —**pre-ju-di-cial** (prɛdʒ-ə-dɪʃ-əl) adj. Damaging; harmful

prejudice v. -diced, -dicing v. To cause sbdy. to have opinions or feelings of prejudice against others: *Unfortunately, some people try to prejudice others against people of another creed, race, or social standing.*

pre-lim-i-nar-y (prɪ-lɪm-ə-nɛər-iʸ) n. -ies Sthg. that precedes or introduces the main business or event: *After the usual preliminaries, the meeting began.*

preliminary adj. Coming before or preparing for the main event: *The chairman made a few preliminary remarks before introducing the main speaker.*

pre-lude (preʸl-uʷd/ prɛl–) n. **1.** An action or event that precedes sthg. more important and acts as an introduction to it **2.** A short piece of music that introduces the main theme of a large musical work

pre-mar-i-tal (priʸ-mɛær-ə-təl/ –mær–) adj. Occurring or existing before marriage

pre-ma-ture (priʸ-mə-tʃʊər) adj. Developing or happening before proper time: *The baby was five weeks premature. (=born five weeks earlier than expected)* —**prematurely** adv.

pre-med-i-tate (priʸ-mɛd-ə-teʸt) v. -tated, -tating To plan or plot in advance —**pre-med-i-ta-tion** (priʸ-mɛd-ə-teʸ-ʃən) n.

pre-mier (prɪ-mɪər) adj. First in position or importance: *the country's premier medical school*

premier n. A prime minister

pre-miere (prɪ-mɪər) n. A first public presentation as of a play or movie

prem-ise (prɛm-əs) n. A proposition or an assumption on which a conclusion is formed or an argument is based

prem-is-es (prɛm-əs-əz) n. A building and the area of land belonging to it: *the school premises*

pre-mi-um (priʸ-miʸ-əm) n. **1.** An amount paid, usu. monthly or quarterly, for an insurance policy **2.** An unusually high value: *He put a premium on hard work.* **3. at a premium** Rare or difficult to obtain, and therefore worth more than usual: *Tickets to the championship game were at a premium.*

pre-mo-ni-tion (priʸ-mə-nɪʃ-ən/ prɛm–) n. A feeling that sthg. (usu. unpleasant) is going to happen; a forewarning

pre-na-tal (priʸ-neʸt-əl) adj. Existing before birth: *Women who are pregnant should have regular prenatal examinations.*

pre-oc-cu-pa-tion (priʸ-ɑk-yə-peʸ-ʃən) n. Complete absorption of the mind

pre-oc-cu-pied (priʸ-ɑk-yə-paɪd) adj. Having one's thoughts totally on sthg., so much so that he hears or sees little around him except what his attention is focused on: *He was so preoccupied with the football game that he didn't hear a word I said.*

pre-oc-cu-py (priʸ-ɑk-yə-paɪ) v. -pied, -pying To fill the thoughts of sbdy. so completely that he gives little or no attention to other matters

prep-a-ra-tion (prɛp-ə-reʸ-ʃən) n.The act of preparing or the state of being prepared

pre-par-a-to-ry (prɪ-pɛær-ə-tɔr-iʸ/ prɛp-ə-rə-tɔr-iʸ) adj. Serving or designed to prepare or introduce

pre-pare (prɪ-pɛər) v. -pared, -paring **1.** To get ready; make ready: *Jesus told his followers, "I am going there [to heaven] to prepare a place for you. And if I go and prepare a place for you, I will come back and take you to be with me that you also may be where I am"* (John 14:2,3). **2.** To put oneself in readiness for a new situation or condition: *He prepared himself for defeat.*

pre-pared (prɪ-pɛərd) adj. **1.** Gotten ready in advance: *The principal read a prepared statement.* —opposite UNPREPARED **2.** Willing: *I'm not prepared to listen to your poor excuses.*

pre-par-ed-ness (prɪ-pɛər-əd-nəs) n. The state of being prepared, esp. for war

pre-pay (priʸ-peʸ) v. -paid, -paying To pay for sthg. in advance

pre-pon-der-ance (prɪ-pɑn-dər-əns) n. A greater number, weight, or strength: *There was a preponderance of children at the picnic.* —**preponderant** adj. —**preponderantly** adv.

prep-o-si-tion (prɛp-ə-zɪʃ-ən) n. A word used before a noun or pronoun to show position (at school; in town) or time (on Sunday; at

ten o'clock) or means (by train)

prep-o-si-tion-al (prep–ə–**zɪʃ**–ən–əl) adj. Having a preposition; functioning as a preposition: *"In the boat" and "on the roof" are prepositional phrases.*

pre-pos-ter-ous (prɪ–**pɑs**–tə–rəs) adj. Contrary to reason; absurd

pre-req-ui-site (pri^y–**rek**–wə–zət) n. Sthg. required beforehand: *Spanish I is a prerequisite to Spanish II; Biology is a prerequisite to Botany.*

pre-rog-a-tive (prɪ–**rɑg**–ət–ɪv) n. An exclusive or special right or privilege: *They say it's a woman's prerogative to change her mind.*

pre-scribe (prɪ–**skraɪb**) v. -scribed, -scribing 1. To order the use of sthg. as a remedy: *The doctor prescribed complete rest for his condition.* 2. To set down a rule or guidelines: *What penalties are prescribed for this offense?*

pre-scrip-tion (prɪ–**skrɪp**–ʃən) n. 1. The act of prescribing 2. A written order for the preparation and use of a medicine 3. The medicine that is prescribed 4. *fig.* A recommendation: *What's your prescription for a happy marriage?*

pres-ence (**prez**–əns) n. 1. The state or fact of being present: *Blessed are those who have learned to acclaim you, who walk in the light of your presence, O Lord* (Psalm 89:15). —opposite ABSENCE 2. An impressive personal appearance and manner that has a strong effect on others

pres-ent (**prez**–ənt) adj. 1. Being here or in the place mentioned or understood: *The entire class was present every day last week. No one was absent.* 2. Existing now: *God is our refuge and strength, an ever present help in trouble* (Psalm 46:1). 3. at present Now; at this time

present n. A gift: *They unwrapped their wedding presents.*

pre-sent (prɪ–**zent**) v. 1. To give sthg. to sbdy., esp. on a formal occasion: *He presented the winner with a gold medal.* 2. To introduce: *May I present our chairman, Mr. John Smith?* 3. To bring before the public: *The local theater is presenting "Hamlet" this week.* 4. Concerning non-material things, to be the cause of: *The illness of our chairman presents quite a problem.* 5. To offer for consideration or

bring to someone's attention: *The committee will present its recommendations on Tuesday.* 6. To express: *She presents her case very clearly.*

pre-sent-a-ble (prɪ–**zent**–ə–bəl) adj. In a condition fit to be shown in public: *She had just been splattered with mud, and wasn't very presentable.*

pres-en-ta-tion (pri^y–zən–**te**^y–ʃən) n. 1. The act of presenting sthg.: *The presentation of awards will take place Saturday evening at seven o'clock.* 2. The way in which sthg. is said, shown, or explained: *His presentation of the subject was very interesting.*

pres-ent-ly (**prez**–ənt–li^y) adv. 1. Very soon: *He will be here presently.* 2. *AmE.* At present; right now: *Presently she's living in New York.*

pres-ent par-ti-ci-ple (**pre**–zənt **part**–ə–sɪp–əl) n. In grammar, a form of the verb that ends in -ing and shows an action or condition that is happening or exists at present

pres-ent tense (**pre**–zənt **tens**) n. In grammar, a verb tense that expresses an action or condition that exists now

pres-er-va-tion (prez–ər–**ve**^y–ʃən) n. The act of preserving

pre-serv-a-tive (prɪ–**zɜr**–və–tɪv) n. A substance that can be used to preserve foods —**preservative** adj.

pre-serve (prɪ–**zɜrv**) v. -served, -serving 1. To keep sthg. from destruction: *The city council voted to preserve the old court house.* 2. To keep sbdy. or sthg. alive and safe from injury: *O Lord, you preserve both man and beast. How priceless is your unfailing love!* (Psalm 36:6,7). 3. To cause a condition to continue unchanged: *It is the duty of the police to preserve public order.* 4. To keep sthg., esp. food, in good condition for a long time by some special treatment: *preserved fruit* —compare CONSERVE

pre-serve n. 1. A type of jam, made from fruit and sugar boiled together, for spreading on bread 2. Land or water where game animals and birds, etc. are protected: *a game preserve* 3. A kind of activity, interest, etc. reserved only for a particular person

pre-side (prɪ–**zaɪd**) v. -sided, -siding To be in charge, esp. to act as chairperson: *The president presided over the meeting.*

pres-i-den-cy (prɛz–ə–dən–siʸ) n. -cies The office of the president: *George Washington was elected two times to the presidency of the US.*

pres-i-dent (prɛz–əd–ənt/ –ent) n. **1.** The chief executive of a republic, as in the United States **2.** The chief officer of a bank, college, company, society, etc. **3.** One who is appointed or elected to preside —**pres-i-den-tial** (prɛz–ə–dɛn–tʃəl) adj. *a presidential election*

press (prɛs) v. **1.** To push firmly: *Press that button to ring the door bell.* **2.** To apply force on sthg. in order to crush it, pack it tightly, or get juice out of it: *The grapes were pressed to extract the juice.* **3.** To give clothes a smooth surface and a sharp fold by using a hot iron: *I took my suit to the cleaners to be cleaned and pressed.* **4.** To try to force sbdy. to do sthg.: *They kept pressing me for an answer.* **5.** To crowd: *The crowd pressed in on him.* **6.** To hold firmly as a sign of friendship or affection: *He pressed her hand warmly in his.* **7.** To continue: *They pressed onward with their urgent work.* **8. time is pressing** Time is running out; there isn't much time left

press n. **1.** An act of pushing firmly against sthg.: *The child was encouraged by the press of the teacher's hand on his shoulder.* **2.** Newspapers in general: *It was reported in the press.* **3.** The people who work on newspapers and magazines; journalists **4.** A printing machine **5.** A business for printing (and sometimes also for selling) books, magazines, etc.: *The University Press* **6.** A crowd: *There was a terrible press in the lobby of the theater.* **7.** The condition of smoothness of a garment after pressing with a hot iron **8.** A device or machine used for pressing

pressed (prɛst) adj. Having very little of sthg.: *I'm pressed for time right now; I'll call you later.*

press-ing (prɛs–ŋ) adj. Urgent; demanding immediate attention: *Pressing business matters keep me working late at night.*

pres-sure (prɛʃ–ər) n. **1.** The amount of force exerted by pressing: *Apply pressure against that wound to stop the bleeding.* **2.** Stress or strain: *Jim is suffering from the pressure of the*

work. **3.** Strong persuasion; forcible influence: *The director was under pressure to resign.* **4.** The strength of this force: *These containers will burst at high pressures.* **5.** The weight of the air in the atmosphere: *Low (air) pressure often brings rain.*

pressure v. -sured, -suring To (try to) force sbdy. to do sthg.: *They pressured him into resigning.*

pres-sur-ize also *BrE.* -ise (prɛʃ–ə–raɪz) v. -ized, -izing **1.** To keep the air pressure in an airplane about the same as the air pressure at ground level **2.** *BrE.* To force sbdy. to do sthg.: *He was pressurized to resign as president of the company.*

pres-tige (prɛ–stiʸʒ) n. Respect or admiration for sbdy. or sthg. because of rank, proven high quality, etc.: *Oxford and Cambridge Universities have a lot of prestige.*

pres-ti-gious (prɛ–stɪdʒ–əs) adj. Having or bringing prestige

pre-sum-a-ble (prɪ–zuʷ–mə–bəl) adj. Able to be presumed —**presumably** adv.

pre-sume (prɪ–zuʷm) v. -sumed, -suming **1.** To believe sthg. to be true without proof; to assume: *From the way he talked, I presumed that he was the boss.* **2.** *fml.* To dare to do sthg. which one has no right or qualification to do: *Are you presuming to tell me how to run my business?*

pre-sump-tion (prɪ–zʌmp–ʃən) n. **1.** An act of supposing: *Jane remarried on the presumption that her first husband was dead.* **2.** A presumptuous attitude; unsuitable boldness toward another person: *She strongly objected to his presumption that she would go to such a place with him.*

pre-sump-tu-ous (prɪ–zʌmp–tʃəs/ –tʃə–wəs) adj. *derog.* Behaving with impudent boldness because of an exalted opinion of oneself: *It was presumptuous of you to ask for an invitation to the party.* —**presumptuously** adv.

pre-sup-pose (priʸ–sə–poʷz) v. -posed, -posing **1.** To take for granted; to assume to be true beforehand **2.** To require sthg. as a condition; to imply

pre-tend (prɪ–tɛnd) v. **1.** To make believe; to imagine sthg. to be true: *Children often pre-*

tend to be grown up. **2.** To give an appearance that sthg. is true when it is not; to deceive: *He pretended to be sick, so he wouldn't have to go to school.*

pre-tend-er (prɪ–tɛn–dər) n. One who pretends to be sbdy. else, esp. one who lays claim to sthg. such as the title of king

pre-tense *AmE.* **pre-tence** *BrE.* (priᵞ–tɛns/ prɪ–tɛns) n. The act of pretending; a false appearance, intended to deceive: *He's really not happy about his dismissal; it's only a pretense.*

pre-ten-sion (prɪ–tɛn–ʃən/ tʃən) n. **1.** A claim to possess skills or qualities, etc. that one does not have **2.** Self-importance

pre-ten-tious (prɪ–tɛn–ʃəs/ –tʃəs) adj. Showy; pretending or claiming to be important: *a pretentious home* —op-posite UNPRETEN-TIOUS —**pretentiously** adv.

pre-text (priᵞ–tɛkst) n. A reason given in order to conceal the real reason: *He went there under the pretext that he wanted to see Mr. Smith, but he really wanted to see his daughter.*

pret-ty (prɪt–iᵞ) adj. **-tier, -tiest 1.** (usually used with women, girls, things, or views, not with men or boys) Pleasing to look at, listen to, etc., but not beautiful: *She gets prettier every day.* —see BEAUTIFUL **2.** Often used ironically, meaning just the opposite of what is said: *This is a pretty mess you've gotten us into.* **3. sitting pretty** *infml.* In a favorable position

pretty adv. Rather; quite: *pretty good/bad/hot/ cold*

pret-zel (prɛt–səl) n. A crisp, dry biscuit, usu. shaped like a knot or stick, salted on the outside

pre-vail (prɪ–veᵞl) v. **1.** To triumph; to win mastery: *Justice has prevailed; the guilty man has been punished.* **2.** To prove superior in power or influence: *Many are the plans in a man's heart, but it is the Lord's purpose that prevails* (Proverbs 19:21). **3.** To continue to exist: *A belief in magic still prevails among some people groups.* **4.** To urge successfully: *We prevailed upon her to sing one more song.*

pre-vail-ing (prɪ–veᵞl–lɪŋ) adj. **1.** (Of a wind that blows over an area most of the time): *the prevailing westerly winds* **2.** Most com-

mon or general: *the prevailing fashion*

prev-a-lent (prɛv–ə–lənt) adj. *fml.* Common; widespread: *Lung cancer is prevalent among heavy smokers.* —**prevalence** n.

pre-var-i-cate (prɪ–vær–ə–keᵞt/ –veər–) v. **-cated, -cating** To lie; to speak falsely with deliberate intent —**pre-var-i-ca-tion** (prɪ–vær–ə–keᵞ–ʃən) n. —**pre-var-i-ca-tor** (prɪ–vær–ə–keᵞt–ər/ –veər–) n.

pre-vent (prɪ–vɛnt) v. To keep sbdy. or sthg. from doing sthg.: *We must do all we can to prevent this deadly disease from spreading.*

pre-vent-a-ble (prɪ–vɛnt–ə–bəl) adj. *Most accidents are preventable.*

pre-ven-tion (prɪ–vɛn–tʃən) n. The act of preventing: *An ounce of prevention is worth a pound of cure.*

pre-ven-tive (prɪ–vɛnt–ɪv) adj. Intended to prevent sthg., esp. illness: *Boiling your drinking water is a preventive measure that one can take to keep from getting certain diseases.*

pre-view (priᵞ–vyuʷ) v. To view or show in advance of public presentation

preview n. **1.** An advance showing or viewing **2.** A showing of small parts from a motion picture advertised for future appearance

pre-vi-ous (priᵞ–viᵞ–əs) adj. Occurring or existing before sthg. else: *Have you had any previous experience in this kind of work?*

pre-vi-ous-ly (priᵞ–viᵞ–əs–liᵞ) adv. Before; earlier:*Where did you live previously, before moving to New York City?*

prey (preᵞ) n. **1.** An animal that is hunted or caught for food **2.** A victim **3.** The action or habit of preying upon other animals: *A tiger is a beast of prey.*

prey on/upon (preᵞ ɔn/ə–pɔn) v. **1.** Of an animal, to hunt and eat as prey: *The hawk preys upon smaller birds.* **2.** Of sorrow, troubles, etc., to have a harmful effect; to disturb: *This problem has been preying on my mind for weeks.*

price (praɪs) n. **1.** The amount of money that one must pay to buy sthg.: *What's the price of this coat?* **2.** The cost at which sthg. is obtained: *You are not your own. You were bought at a price [with the precious blood of Christ]. Therefore, glorify God with your body* (1 Corin-

thians 6:20)./ *Isn't loss of your health too high a price to pay for the pleasure of smoking?*

price v. **priced, pricing 1.** To fix the price on sthg.: *That printer has priced himself right out of the market by charging such high prices.* **2.** To mark goods in a store with the price

price-less (prai–sləs) adj. Of worth too great to be calculated: *O Lord...How priceless is your unfailing love!* (Psalm 36:7).

prick (prik) v. **1.** To stab or puncture lightly: *Jean pricked herself with a pin.* **2.** To affect sharply with a mental or emotional pang: *She felt badly that she hadn't been more generous and more helpful. Her conscience pricked her.*

prick n. **1.** The sensation of being pricked: *She felt a sharp prick from a cactus thorn.* **2.** A mark or small wound made by sthg. with a sharp point

prick-ly (prik–li^y) adj. **-lier, -liest 1.** Having small sharp thorns or points **2.** Stinging; pricking; tingling

pride (praid) n. **1.** Proper and justified self-respect: *Teachers ought to take pride in their work.* **2.** Self-respect: *You hurt his pride by laughing at him.* **3.** The most valuable one of its kind: *This painting is the pride of my collection. It's my pride and joy.* (=it is greatly valued) **4.** Too high an opinion of one's importance or superiority: *A man's pride brings him low* (Proverbs 29:23)./ *Pride goes before destruction* (Proverbs 16:18)./ *Out of the heart of men proceed evil thoughts, adulteries, fornications, murder, thefts ... pride, foolishness. All these evils come from within and defile a man* (Mark 7:21,22 KJV)./ *God says, "I hate pride and arrogance"* (Proverbs 8:13). NOTE: God hates pride and all sin, but because of his great love and mercy he forgives those who truly repent (turn from their evil ways) and put their trust in Jesus for eternal life (Acts 2:38; 16:31; Romans 6:23). —see JESUS

pride v. To take pleasure and satisfaction with oneself about sthg.,: *He prides himself on his artistic ability.*

priest (pri^yst) n. **1.** In the Christian Church, esp. in the Roman Catholic Church, a specially-trained person, usu. a man, who performs various religious duties or ceremo-

nies for a group of worshipers NOTE: In Protestant churches the usual word for a specially-trained person who performs various religious duties, the spiritual leader, is "pastor" or "minister." The term "chaplain" is also used, esp. for a minister who is responsible for the spiritual needs of a large organization, such as a university, hospital, or the armed forces. —see JESUS 2. In Old Testament times, before the birth of Jesus Christ, a priest who was responsible for making animal sacrifices "for his own sins as well as for the sins of the people" (Hebrews 5:3). NOTE: We don't need such priests anymore, since Jesus Christ made the supreme sacrifice. He paid for all our sins with his own blood. He is the only one who ever lived who could do this, since he was without sin, perfectly righteous and holy. *Therefore, since we have a great high priest who has gone through the heavens, Jesus the Son of God, let us hold firmly to the faith we profess. For we do not have a high priest who is unable to sympathize with our weaknesses, but we have one who has been tempted in every way, just as we are, yet was without sin. Let us then approach the throne of grace with confidence [pray directly to God without going through an earthly priest], so that we may receive mercy and find grace to help us in our time of need* (Hebrews 4:14-16). Because Jesus lives forever, he has a permanent priesthood. Therefore he is able to save completely those who come to God through him, because he always lives to intercede [pray] for them. Such a high priest meets our need — one who is holy, blameless, pure, set apart from sinners, exalted above the heavens. Unlike the other high priests, he does not need to offer sacrifices day after day, first for his own sins, and then for the sins of the people. He sacrificed for their sins once for all when he offered himself (Hebrews 7:24-27). Day after day every priest stands and performs his religious duties; again and again he offers the same sacrifices, which can never take away sins. But when this priest [Jesus] had offered for all time one sacrifice for sins, he

sat down at the right hand of God ... because by one sacrifice he has made perfect forever those who are being made holy (Hebrews 10:11,12,14).

priest-hood (prīʸst–hʊd) n. **1.** The position or rank of a priest **2.** Priests as a group **3.** All the believers in Jesus Christ: *Writing to Christians in general, the Apostle Peter said, "... you are a chosen people, a royal priesthood ... that you may declare the praises of him who called you out of [spiritual] darkness into his wonderful light"* (1 Peter 2:9). NOTE: As the priesthood of Christ, they are to witness to him (share their faith with others) (Acts 1:8), teach his word (Matthew 28:19), rebuke sin and error (Luke 17:3), encourage and comfort (2 Corinthians 2:7; 1 Thessalonians 4:18), pray and intercede for others (James 5:16).

prig (prĭg) n. A self-righteous person; one who demands exaggerated correctness, esp. in behavior

prim (prĭm) adj. Stiffly formal and precise in manner or appearance, disliking anything he or she considers rough or improper

pri-ma-cy (prī–mə–siʸ) n. The state or condition of being first or supreme

pri-ma don-na (prĭ–mə dän–ə) n. **1.** The principal female singer, as in an opera **2.** An extremely sensitive, vain, and undisciplined person

pri-mal (prī–məl) adj. **1.** Original; primitive **2.** First in importance

pri-mar-i-ly (prī–mɛər–ə–liʸ) adv. Mainly; chiefly; in the first place: *His failure was primarily due to his laziness.*

pri-ma-ry (prī–mɛər–iʸ) adj. **1.** First or most important: *Our primary purpose in life is to glorify God* (1 Corinthians 10:31). **2.** Of the first level or stage of sthg.; of the first three or four years of elementary school: *a primary school* —compare ELEMENTARY, SECONDARY

primary n. **-ries** The first stage of an election, in which voters of each party nominate their candidates

pri-ma-ry col-or (prī–mɛər–iʸ kʌl–ər) n. Any of three colors (red, yellow, and blue) from which all other colors can be made by mixing

pri-mate (prī–meʸt) n. **1.** A bishop of highest rank in a country **2.** One of a group of mammals that includes monkeys and apes

prime (prīm) adj. **1.** First in time or significance: *a matter of prime importance* **2.** Of the very best quality: *a prime cut of beef* **3. prime time** The hours considered best for television, when most people are able to watch TV, from 8 to 11 p.m.

prime n. **1.** The most active time or successful period of time in a person's life or in his career **2.** A number that cannot be divided by any other number except by itself, such as 19, 23, 31, 37, etc.

prime v. **primed, priming 1.** To prepare for operation, as by pouring water into a pump **2.** To prepare for painting by covering a surface with an undercoat **3.** To prepare with information; instruct beforehand: *He was well primed with the facts before the convention.*

prime min-is-ter (prīm mĭn–ə–stər) n. The chief executive of a parliamentary government

prim-er (prīm–ər) n. A substance spread over the surface of wood before the main painting

primer (prĭm–ər) *AmE.* (prīm–ər) *BrE.* n. A small book for teaching people to read

pri-me-val also **-mae-** (prī–miʸ–vəl) adj. Concerning the earliest period of the earth's existence: *primeval forests*

prim-i-tive (prĭm–ət–ĭv) adj. **1.** Of or belonging to the earliest times: *primitive tools made of stones and animal bones* **2.** Simple and roughly made: *We were living in a rather primitive hut in the mountains.* —**primitively** adv.

pri-mor-di-al (prī–mord–iʸ–əl) adj. **1.** Original; existing from the beginning **2.** Earliest formed; primitive

primp (prĭmp) v. To dress, adorn, or arrange in a finicky manner: *She primps for hours before a date.*

prim-rose (prĭm–roʷz) n. A plant with clusters of flowers of various colors, usu. pale yellow

primrose path (prĭm–roʷz pæθ) **1.** A path of

ease and pleasure, esp. sensual pleasure 2. The path of least resistance

prince (prɪns) n. 1. A male member of the royal family, esp. a son of the king 2. A person of high standing: *a prince among poets* 3. A very nice person: *He's a prince of a fellow.*

prin-cess (prɪn–sɛs) n. 1. The daughter of a king or queen, or other near relative 2. The wife of a prince

Prince of Peace (prɪns əv piᵞs) n. Jesus is called the Prince of Peace: *God spoke through the Prophet Isaiah, saying: "For to us a child is born, to us a son is given ... And he will be called Wonderful Counselor, Mighty God, Everlasting Father, Prince of Peace"* (Isaiah 9:6). NOTE: After Jesus rose from the dead and returned to heaven, Peter and the other apostles (disciples of Jesus) told the religious leaders: *"The God of our fathers raised Jesus from the dead — whom you had killed by hanging him on a tree. God exalted him to his own right hand as Prince and Savior"* (Acts 5:29-31).

prin-ci-pal (prɪn–sə–pəl) adj. Most important: *The principal character in the story was a naval officer.*

principal n. 1. The chief officer of a high school or elementary school and some other educational institutions 2. A sum of money lent, on which interest is paid 3. A leading performer in a play, group of musicians, etc. —compare PRINCIPLE

prin-ci-pal-i-ty (prɪn–sə–pæl–ət–iᵞ) n. -ties The territory, jurisdiction, or position of a prince

prin-ci-pal-ly (prɪn–sə–pliᵞ) adv. Chiefly; mostly: *I am principally concerned with teaching English as a second language.*

prin-ci-ple (prɪn–sə–pəl) n. 1. A general truth, rule, or law: *the principles of education* 2. The theory by which a machine works: *the principle of the jet engine* 3. **principles** A rule or code of conduct: *It's against my principles to borrow money.* 4. **in principle** In general, but not necessarily in detail: *We agreed with his plan in principle, but we weren't in agreement with all the details* 5. **on principle** Because of fundamental beliefs and moral standards: *See to it that no one takes you captive through*

hollow and deceptive philosophy, which depends on human tradition and the basic principles of this world rather than on Christ (Colossians 2:8). —compare PRINCIPAL

print (prɪnt) v. 1. To produce lettering on a book, newspaper, magazine, etc. by applying inked type to paper by means of a printing press, rubber stamp, or some similar way 2. To write in unjoined letters like those used in this book 3. To produce a photograph from a photographic negative or transparency

print n. 1. A mark left where sthg. was pressed against a surface: *footprints in the mud* 2. Words in printed form: *I can't read the small print without my glasses.* 3. A printed picture or photograph 4. A printed fabric

print-er (prɪnt–ər) n. 1. Sbdy. who is in the printing business, printing books, tracts, etc. 2. The part of a computer that prints letters, printouts, etc., stored in the computer's memory

print-ing (prɪnt–ɪŋ) n. The act or art of printing: *The invention of printing by movable type in the 15th century was an exceedingly important event in the history of education.*

pri-or (praɪ–ər) adj. 1. Earlier, previous: *I missed the party because of a prior commitment.* 2. Coming first in importance: *Mrs. Smith quit her job because her family needed her and they had a prior claim on her life.* 3. **prior to** Before: *Prior to teaching in this country, he taught in Spain.*

pri-or n. 1. The superior ranking next to an abbot of a monastery 2. The superior of a house or group of houses of any of various religious communities

pri-or-ess (praɪ–ə–rəs) n. A nun corresponding in rank to a prior

pri-or-i-ty (praɪ–ɔr–ət–iᵞ) n. -ties 1. Sthg. that is more important than other items of consideration: *Top priority should be given to knowing and worshiping the true God and serving him. Jesus said, "Seek first the kingdom of God and his righteousness, and all these [material] things will be added unto you..."* (Matthew 6:33). 2. The right to be first: *The badly wounded should have top priority for medical attention.*

pri-o-ry (praɪ-ə-riᵞ) n. -ries A building where monks or nuns live

prism (prɪz-əm) n. 1. A solid geometric shape having ends that are similar, equal, and parallel 2. A transparent solid object with three rectangular sides and two ends that are triangular. When a ray of light passes through it, the prism breaks the ray up into the colors of the rainbow

pris-on (prɪz-ən) n. 1. A large building where criminals are kept locked up; a jail 2. Any place where people are held against their will

pris-on-er (prɪz-ən-ər) n. 1. Sbdy. under arrest or locked up in a jail 2. A captured enemy soldier or anyone held in captivity

pris-tine (prɪs-tiᵞn/prɪs-tiᵞn) adj. In the original or unspoiled state

pri-va-cy (praɪ-və-siᵞ) n. The quality or state of being away from others; seclusion

pri-vate (praɪ-vət) adj. 1. Sthg. intended only for one's personal use 2. Not connected with or paid for by the government or any public funds: *a private school* 3. Having nothing to do with one's business; unofficial: *The boss is on a private visit to Washington.* 4. A soldier of the lowest rank

pri-vate-ly (praɪ-vət-liᵞ) adv. Alone: *I'd like to speak to you privately.*

pri-va-tion (praɪ-veᵞ-ʃən) n. 1. Loss or lack of sthg, esp. of the necessities of life 2. An act of depriving or state of being deprived

priv-i-lege (prɪv-ə-lɪdʒ) n. 1. A special right granted to one person or a small group of people: *In countries where there are only a few schools, people are more likely to realize what a privilege it is to go to school.* 2. A special favor; sthg. that gives one great pleasure: *He felt that it was a great privilege to meet the famous actress.* —privileged adj.

priv-y (prɪv-iᵞ) adj. 1. Secret 2. Private 3. Sharing secret knowledge

privy n. -ies A toilet, esp. one in an outhouse

prize (praɪz) n. 1. An award given as a symbol of victory or superiority 2. Sthg. striven for or worth striving for: *Do you not know that in a race, all the runners run, but only one gets the prize? Run in such a way as to get the prize* (1 Corinthians 9:24). 3. Sthg. of value that can be won in a lottery or game of chance

prize v. **prized, prizing** To value highly: *He prized my friendship above everything.*

prize adj. 1. Given as a prize: *prize money* 2. Treasured or highly valuable: *prize horses* 3. Worthy of a prize: *a prize photograph*

pro– (proᵂ–) Prefix 1. In front of: *protection* 2. To the front: *proceed* 3. Instead or in place of: *pronoun* 4. Before in place, time, rank, etc.: *prologue*

pro (proᵂ) n. 1. In favor of 2. **pros and cons** Arguments for and against sthg.: *Let's hear all the pros and cons of the matter before making a decision.*

pro n. pl. **pros** *infml.* for PROFESSIONAL: *pro football/basketball/golf*

prob-a-bil-i-ty (prɑb-ə-bɪl-ət-iᵞ) n. -ties Likelihood: *There's little probability of snow in Cairo or Bombay.* —opposite IMPROBABILITY

prob-a-ble (prɑb-ə-bəl) adj. 1. Likely; apparently true 2. Sthg. that is likely to happen: *It is possible that our team could win today, but it doesn't seem probable.* —opposite IMPROBABLE —**probably** adv. *John will probably be late; he usually is.*

pro-bate (proᵂ-beᵞt) n. The legal determination of the validity of a will

probate v. **-bated, -bating** To establish a will by probate as authentic and valid

pro-ba-tion (proᵂ-beᵞ-ʃən) n. 1. A trial period in which a person's fitness, as for membership, is tested 2. A system by which a criminal is released under the supervision of a probation officer

pro-ba-tion-er (proᵂ-beᵞ-ʃən-ər) n. One on probation

probe (proᵂb) n. 1. A careful and thorough search for the truth; a penetrating inquiry into a matter 2. An instrument for examining a cavity, such as a wound 3. An information-gathering device sent into outer space

probe v. **probed, probing** 1. To examine with a probe 2. To investigate thoroughly

pro-bi-ty (proᵂ-bət-iᵞ) n. Honesty; integrity

prob-lem (prɑb-ləm) n. 1. A matter that is difficult to deal with, that needs attention and thought: *The pollution problem in this area is getting worse.* 2. A question for considera-

tion or for which an answer is needed: *The boy can do simple problems in addition, but has more difficulty with subtraction.*

prob-lem-at-ic (prɑb–lə–mæt–ɪk) adj. **1.** Doubtful; uncertain **2.** Puzzling

pro-bos-cis (prə–bɑs–əs) n. **1.** An elephant's trunk or the long flexible snout of certain other animals **2.** Elongated mouth parts of certain insects **3.** *Slang* Nose

pro-ce-dure (prə–siᵞ–dʒər) n. A method of doing sthg.: *They followed the usual procedure in conducting the meeting./parliamentary procedure* —**procedural** adj.

pro-ceed (prə–siᵞd/ proʷ–) v. **1.** To begin an action: *They finally got their building permit and proceeded with the construction.* **2.** To continue: *After a brief stop for lunch, we proceeded on our journey.* **3.** To follow a course of action: *He didn't know how to proceed* **4.** To result: *Fear often proceeds from ignorance* **5.** **proceed against** To take legal action

proceedings n. (prə–siᵞd–ɪŋz/ proʷ–) n. *pl.* **1.** The things said and done at a meeting of a society, etc. **2.** An action taken in law

pro-ceeds (proʷ–siᵞdz) n. Money gained from the sale of sthg.: *The proceeds from the bake sale were donated to an orphanage.*

proc-ess (prɑs–ɛs) n. **1.** Natural actions over which man has little control: *the process of breathing* **2.** Actions performed intentionally in order to reach some result: *the process of learning to read* **3.** A method of manufacturing or packaging sthg.: *It seems that they are always finding a better process for packaging food products.* **4.** A course of action: *The trailer company is now in the process of moving to another city.* **5.** A method or series of operations used in manufacturing goods —compare PROCEDURE

process v. To treat by a particular process: *Has your film been processed yet?*

processed (prɑs–ɛst) adj. Treated in a special way: *processed cheese*

pro-ces-sion (prə–sɛʃ–ən/ proʷ–) n. **1.** A line of people, vehicles, etc., moving forward in an orderly way: *a funeral procession* **2.** A continuous onward movement: *Thanks be to God who always leads us in triumphal procession in Christ and through us spreads everywhere the fragrance of the knowledge of him* (2 Corinthians 2:14).

pro-ces-sion-al (prə–sɛʃ–ən–əl/ proʷ–) adj. Having to do with a solemn religious procession

pro-claim (proʷ–kleᵞm) v. **1.** *fml.* To make known publicly: *A new national holiday was proclaimed.* **2.** *lit.* To show clearly: *The heavens declare the glory of God; the skies proclaim the work of his hands* (Psalm 19:1).

pro-cla-ma-tion (prɑk–lə–meᵞ–ʃən) n. An official, sometimes ceremonial, public announcement

pro-cliv-i-ty (prə–klɪv–ət–iᵞ/ proʷ–) n. **-ties** A strong habitual inclination or tendency, esp. to do sthg. bad

pro-cras-ti-nate (prə–kræs–tə–neᵞt/ proʷ–) v. **-nated, -nating** To habitually put off doing sthg. until a future time —**procrastination** n. —**procrastinator** n.

pro-cre-ate (proʷ–kriᵞ–eᵞt) v. **-ated, -ating** To reproduce; to produce offspring

pro-cure (proʷ–kyʊər) v. **-cured, -curing** *fml.* **1.** To obtain by effort; to acquire **2.** To bring about; effect

prod (prɑd) v. **-dd- 1.** To jab or poke with a pointed instrument **2.** To rouse to action; stir

prod n. **1.** A pointed instrument **2.** A poke or a jab

prod-i-gal (prɑd–ɪ–gəl) adj. Recklessly wasteful

prodigal n. A recklessly wasteful person

pro-di-gious (prə–dɪdʒ–əs) adj. **1.** Enormous **2.** Marvelous

prod-i-gy (prɑd–ə–dʒiᵞ) n. **-gies 1.** A person, esp. a child, who has exceptional talent **2.** Sthg. extraordinary

pro-duce (prə–duʷs/ proʷ–) v. **-duced, -ducing 1.** To grow: *Burma produces much rice.* **2.** To make or manufacture: *This company produces automobiles.* **3.** To show or offer for examination or consideration: *Can you produce any proof of your citizenship?* **4.** To cause: *Suffering produces perseverance* (Romans 5:3). **5.** To prepare for public viewing or reading: *The film was poorly produced.* —see PRODUCTION

produce (proʷ–duʷs/ prɑ–) n. Sthg. produced

by farming: *You'll find the oranges in the produce department.*

pro-du-cer (prə–duʷ–sər/ proʷ–duʷ–sər) n. **1.** A person or company that produces foods or goods **2.** A person who produces a play, or movie, radio or TV show, etc., but is not responsible for directing the actors —compare DIRECTOR

prod-uct (prɑd–əkt) n. **1.** Sthg. produced by growth or from the ground: *Fruit and vegetables are important products of California.* **2.** Sthg. manufactured: *This firm produces plastic products.* **3.** Sthg. that is produced as a result of thought, will, planning, conditions, etc.: *Criminals are often the product of ungodly homes.* **4.** In mathematics, the number gotten by multiplying two or more numbers: *The product of 5 multiplied by 3 is 15.*

pro-duc-tion (prə–dʌk–ʃən) n. **1.** The act or process of producing sthg.: *The production of the film cost $10 million.* **2.** The amount produced: *Auto production is down this year.* **3.** The act of producing a play, movie, or broadcast: *This production of "The Glory of Easter" is better than the one I saw last year.*

pro-duc-tive (prə–dʌk–tɪv/proʷ–) adj. **1.** That which produces well or much: *He's a very productive person; he gets a lot done.* **2.** That which gets results: *The meeting was not very productive.* —**pro-duc-tiv-i-ty** (proʷ–dək–tɪv–ə–tiʸ/ prə–) n.

Prof. (prɑf) *abbr.* Professor (prə–fɛs–ər) n.

pro-fane (proʷ–feʸn/ prə–) adj. **1.** Having or showing disrespect for God or for holy things **2.** Nonreligious; secular **3.** Vulgar —**profane** n. *You must distinguish between the holy and the profane* (Leviticus 10:10).

profane v. To treat sthg. that is holy with disrespect: *One of God's commandments is: "Do not swear falsely by my name and so profane the name of your God"* (Leviticus 19:12).

pro-fan-i-ty (proʷ–fæn–ət–iʸ) n. **-ties 1.** Lack of respect for God **2.** Profane language or its use; swear words: *He smashed his finger and let out a string of profanities.* —compare BLASPHEMY

pro-fess (prə–fɛs/ proʷ–) v. **1.** To declare plainly: *She professed to be a Christian.* **2.** To claim (often falsely): *I don't profess to know much*

about nuclear physics. —**pro-fessed** adj.

pro-fes-sion (prə–fɛʃ–ən) n. **1.** A form of employment that is respected in society and is possible only after many years of training (such as law, medicine, teaching, and clergy): *He is a doctor by profession.* **2.** All the people in a particular profession: *the teaching profession* **3.** *fml.* A declaration of one's beliefs: *a profession of faith* —see CREED

pro-fes-sion-al (prə–fɛʃ–ən–əl) adj. **1.** One who works in one of the professions: *A doctor is a professional person.* **2.** Giving evidence of the training of a member of a profession: *She danced with professional skill.* **3.** Sbdy. who is paid for doing what others do for pleasure: *a professional tennis player* —**professional** n. *You can't be a professional and compete in the Olympic Games.* —**professionally** adv. *She now skates professionally.*

pro-fes-sor (prə–fɛs–ər) n. A teacher in a university department or college

prof-fer (prɑf–ər) v. To offer

proffer n. An offer

pro-fi-cient (prə–fɪʃ–ənt) adj. Very skilled and competent: *proficient in typing.* —**proficiently** adv. —**proficiency** n.

pro-file (proʷ–faɪl) n. **1.** A side view, esp. of a person's head **2.** A brief description of a person's life and character **3. keep a low profile** Try to avoid drawing attention to oneself

prof-it (prɑ–fət) n. **1.** Money gained by business activity —opposite LOSS **2.** Advantage gained from some action: *All hard work brings a profit* (Proverbs 14:23).

profit v. To be of use or advantage to sbdy. or sthg.: *For what shall it profit a man, if he shall gain the whole world, and lose his own soul?* (Mark 8:36 KJV).

prof-it-a-ble (prɑf–ət–ə–bəl) adj. Useful; resulting in gain: *For bodily exercise profits a little, but godliness is profitable for all things, having promise of the life that now is and of that which is to come* (1 Timothy 4:8 NKJV). —opposite UNPROFITABLE —**profitably** adv.

prof-li-gate (prɑf–lə–gət/ –geʸt) adj. **1.** Wicked; shameless; immoral **2.** Outrageously wasteful in the spending of money —**profligate**

n

pro-found (prə–taʊnd/ proᵂ–) adj. 1. Marked by intellectual depth or insight; absolute; complete: *His [God's] wisdom is profound, his power is vast* (Job 9:4). 2. Having, showing, or using thorough knowledge and deep understanding: *How great is your work, O Lord, how profound your thoughts* (Psalms 92:5). 3. Deeply felt; intense: *profound sympathy* —**pro-fun-di-ty** (proᵂ–fʌn–də–tiʸ) n.

pro-fuse (proᵂ–fyuᵂs/ prə–) adj. Done freely and abundantly: *He was profuse in his expression of thanks.* —**profusely** adv. *He apologized profusely.*

pro-fu-sion (prə–fyuᵂ–ʒən) n. Great abundance: *a profusion of wild flowers*

pro-geni-tor (proᵂ–dʒɛn–ət–ər) n. An ancestor

pro-ge-ny (prɑdʒ–ə–niʸ) n. Children; descendants

prog-no-sis (prɑg–noᵂ–səs) n. Prediction, esp. as to the outcome of a disease

prog-nos-tic (prɑg–nɑs–tɪk) adj. 1. Pertaining to prognosis 2. Omen or sign 3. Prediction

prog-nos-ti-cate (prɑg–nɑs–tə–keʸt) v. -cated, -cating 1. To predict 2. To make a forecast —**prog-nos-ti-ca-tion** (prɑg–nɑs–tə–keʸ–ʃen) n. —**prognosticator** n.

pro-gram (proᵂ–græm/ –grəm) *AmE.* **programme** *BrE.* n. 1. A booklet or paper giving the details of performers or things to be performed at an entertainment, ceremony, etc. 2. A complete show or performance: *What's your favorite radio program?* 3. A plan of action: *a new political program* 4. Coded instructions for a computer

pro-gram *AmE.* **programme** *BrE.* (proᵂ–græm) v. 1. To plan or arrange: *The sprinkling system for watering the lawn is programmed to start working at six a.m.* 2. To supply a computer with a plan of the operations to be performed: *Do you know how to program a computer?*

pro-gram-mer also **programer** (proᵂ–græm–ər) n. A person who prepares a program for a computer

pro-gress (prɑg–rəs/ –rɛs) n. 1. A forward movement; advance: *the progress of civilization* 2. A gradual improvement: *The students are making good progress.*

progress (prə–grɛs) v. 1. To advance: *The building is progressing according to schedule.* 2. To improve: *Ann is progressing nicely after her surgery.*

pro-gres-sion (prə–grɛʃ–yən) n. 1. Movement forward 2. Succession, as of events

pro-gres-sive (prə–grɛs–ɪv) adj. 1. Moving forward, esp. by stages 2. Favoring new ideas, methods, equipment, uses, etc.: *This firm is very progressive; it uses the most modern systems and equipment.* 3. Promoting or favoring political reform 4. Continuously spreading or increasing in severity: *the progressive deterioration of his health* —**progressively** adv. *Things got progressively worse/better.*

pro-hib-it (proᵂ–hɪb–ət) v. 1. To forbid by authority: *Smoking is prohibited in this building.* 2. To prevent: *His small size prohibits his becoming a policeman.*

pro-hi-bi-tion (proᵂ–ə–bɪʃ–ən) n. 1. The act of prohibiting 2. *fml.* An order by law, forbidding sthg. 3. **Prohibition** In the US, the time from 1920 to 1933 during which a national law forbade the making or sale of alcoholic drinks

pro-hib-i-tive (proᵂ–hɪb–ət–ɪv) adj. Preventing the use, misuse, or sale of sthg.: *The price of houses is prohibitive for most people these days.*

proj-ect (prɑdʒ–ɛkt/ –ɪkt) n. A proposal of sthg. to be done; a plan; a scheme: *Writing a dictionary is a big project.*

pro-ject (prə–dʒɛkt) v. 1. To extend outward from a surface: *A sharp rock projected from the sea.* 2. To cause sound or light to be directed somewhere: *The pictures were projected on the screen.* 3. Plan ahead: *A new dictionary has been projected.*

pro-jec-tile (prə–dʒɛk–təl) n. An object that can be thrown or shot through the air or through space: *A bullet is a projectile.*

pro-jec-tion (prə–dʒɛk–ʃən) n. 1. The act of projecting 2. Sthg. that has been projected 3. An estimate of future trends (growth, decline, etc.) based on the study of present ones

pro-jec-tion-ist (prə–dʒɛk–ʃən–əst) n. A person who operates a movie projector in a theater

pro-jec-tor (prə–dʒɛk–tər) n. A device for pro-

jecting pictures on a screen: *a movie/slide/ filmstrip/overhead projector*

pro-le-tar-i-an (pro^w–lə–tɛər–i^y–ən) n. A member of the proletariat

pro-le-tar-i-at (pro^w–lə–tɛər–i^y–ət) n. The class of workers who have to work for wages, esp. unskilled workers

pro-lif-er-ate (prə–lɪf–ə–re^{y}t/ pro^w–) v. **-ated, -ating** To increase very rapidly; multiply

pro-lif-ic (prə–lɪf–ɪk/ pro^w–) adj. **1.** Producing much fruit or offspring **2.** Producing much art, many books, etc.: *a prolific writer*

pro-log (pro^w–lɔg/ –lɑg) also **prologue** n. **1.** An introduction to a poem or play **2.** Sthg. that serves as an introduction to sthg. else

pro-long (prə–lɔŋ) v. To extend; lengthen; make longer: *They prolonged their vacation another three days.* —**prolonged** adj. *a prolonged absence*

prom-e-nade (prɑm–ə–ne^{y}d/ –nɑd) n. **1.** A slow, easy walk for pleasure or recreation **2.** A place for taking such a walk

prom-e-nade v. **-naded, -nading** To go for a stroll: *We promenaded through the park.*

prom-i-nent (prɑm–ə–nənt) adj. **1.** Well-known; distinguished: *a prominent politician* **2.** Noticeable; easily seen: *His nose was rather prominent.* —**prominently** adv. —**prominence** n. *He is gaining prominence as a writer.*

pro-mis-cu-ous (prə–mɪs–kyə–wəs) adj. Engaging in sexual intercourse indiscriminately with more than one partner NOTE: This is contrary to the will of God who commanded us not to commit adultery (Exodus 20:14). Jesus Christ, our Savior, said that whoever even looks at a woman lustfully has already committed adultery with her in his heart (Matthew 5:28). —see ADULTERY —**pro-mis-cu-it-y** (prɑ–mɪ–skyu^w–ə–ti^y) n. —**pro-mis-cu-ous-ly** (prə–mɪs–kyu^w–əs–li^y) adv. —**pro-mis-cu-ous-ness** (prə–mɪs–kyu^w–əs–nəs) n.

prom-ise (prɑm–ɪs) n. **1.** A pledge to do or not to do sthg. specific: *If you make a promise, you should keep it; you should not break a promise.* NOTE: Jesus promised his followers that he would never leave them nor forsake them (Hebrews 13:5) and that he was going away (to heaven) to prepare a place for them, and that he would come again, that they may be where he is (John 14:3). *The Lord is faithful to all his promises, and loving toward all he has made* (Psalm 145:13). *[The Apostle] Peter replied, "Repent and be baptized, every one of you, in the name of Jesus Christ so that your sins may be forgiven. And you will receive the gift of the Holy Spirit. The promise is for you and your children and for all who are far off — for all whom the Lord our God will call"* (Acts 2:38,39). **2.** Signs of future success: *My son is showing great promise as a student at the university.*

promise v. **-ised, -ising 1.** To give as-surance or a pledge to do or give sthg. or that sthg. will be done: *He promised to return my book by Tuesday.* **2.** To offer hope for sthg.: *Those clouds promise rain.*

prom-is-ing (prɑm–ə–sɪŋ) adj. Likely to succeed; full of promise —opposite UNPROMISING

pro-mon-to-ry (prɑm–ən–tɔr–i^y) n. **-ries** A high piece of land or rock that juts out into a body of water

pro-mote (prə–mo^{w}t) v. **-moted, -moting 1.** To raise or be raised to a higher position or rank: *The seasoned naval officer was promoted to the rank of admiral.* —opposite DEMOTE **2.** To contribute to the growth or prosperity of sthg.: *How can we best promote the sale of this new book?*

pro-mot-er (prə–mo^{w}t–ər) n. A person who promotes, esp. one who takes the first steps in starting an activity or enterprise

pro-mo-tion (prə–mo^w–ʃən) n. **1.** An advancement in rank or position: *The naval officer received a promotion; he is now a captain.* —opposite DEMOTION **2.** An effort to help sthg. succeed (esp. publicly): *Our sales promotions haven't been very successful this year.* **3.** The encouragement of a cause: *the promotion of world peace*

prompt (prɑmpt) v. **1.** To induce to action: *We constantly pray for you, that our God may count you worthy of his calling, and that by his power, he may fulfill every good purpose of yours and every act prompted by your faith* (2 Thessalonians 1:11). **2.** To remind an actor of the next words in a speech

prompt Adj. Done or given without delay: *He was always prompt in paying his bills*

prompt-er (prampt–ər) n. Sbdy. who prompts actors who forget their words

prompt-ly (prampt–li^y) adv. At the appointed time; exactly: *The performance will start promptly at seven o'clock.* promptness n.

prom-ul-gate (pram–əl–ge^yt) v. -gated, -gating To make known to the public; to proclaim —pro-mul-ga-tion (pram–əl–ge^y–ʃən) n.

prone (pro^wn) adj. 1. Likely to experience; inclined to experience sthg. unpleasant: *He's accident prone* 2. Lying flat, esp. face downward: *in a prone position*

prong (praŋ/ prɔŋ) n. 1. One of the sharp points of a fork: *Most forks have four prongs.* 2. Any pointed projected part

pro-noun (pro^w–navn) n. Gram. A word that is used in place of a noun or a noun phrase: *Instead of saying, "The girl is smiling," you can use a pronoun and say, "She is smiling."*

pro-nounce (prə–navns) v. -nounced, -nouncing 1. To utter the sound of a word or part of a word: *The word "sign is pronounced "sam" The "g" is not pronounced.* 2. To announce officially: *At the end of the wedding ceremony, the pastor said, "I now pronounce you man and wife."*

pro-nun-ci-a-tion (prə–nən–si^y–e^y–ʃən) n. The way sthg. is pronounced: *The correct pronunciation of "naive" is* /na–i^yv/.

proof (pru^wf) n. 1. Evidence or information which shows that sthg. is true: *For he [God] has set a day when he will judge the world with justice by the man he has appointed. He has given proof of this to all men by raising him [Jesus] from the dead.* (Acts 17:31). 2. A test or trial: *A soldier's courage is put to the proof in battle.* 3. A trial copy made of sthg. printed, so that mistakes can be corrected before the printing is done* —see PROVE

–proof (–pru^wf) comb. form Giving protection against sthg. harmful or unwanted: *a waterproof coat / a soundproof room*

proof-read (pru^wf–ri^yd) v. proof-read (–rεd), proof-read (–rεd) To read over and correct mistakes in printed or written material

prop (prap) n. 1. A support 2. Any small article that is used on the stage in the acting of a play 3. *Abbr.* for propeller

prop v. -pp- To hold sthg. in an upright position; to keep sthg. from falling or closing: *The gate was propped open. / We propped up the sagging roof.*

prop-a-gan-da (prap–ə–gæn–də) n. 1. The information and ideas methodically spread in order to promote or hurt a cause, a group, or a nation, etc. 2. The activity of spreading such ideas and information —prop-a-gan-dist (prap–ə–gæn–dəst) n. —prop-a-gan-dize (prap–ə–gæn–daɪz) v. -ized, -izing

prop-a-gate (prap–ə–ge^yt) v. -gated, -gating 1. To increase in number by natural reproducing: *Plants usually propagate by means of seeds.* 2. To cause to spread and influence a large number of people: *The group started its own newspaper to propagate its ideas.*

pro-pel (prə–pel) v. -ll- To drive or push forward; to give an onward movement to: *A sail boat is propelled by the wind.*

pro-pel-ler (prə–pel–ər) n. A revolving device with two or more blades for propelling a ship or aircraft, to which it is fixed

pro-pen-si-ty (prə–pen–sət–i^y) n. -ties A natural tendency or inclination toward a particular kind of behavior: *a propensity to laziness*

prop-er (prap–ər) adj. 1. Right; suitable; correct: *Show proper respect for everyone* (1 Peter 2:17). 2. Complete and thorough: *Have you made a proper investigation.* 3. **in the city proper** Not including the suburbs —opposite IMPROPER

proper noun (prap–ər navn) A name of a particular person, place, or thing: *Mary, China, and Toyota are proper nouns.*

prop-er-ly (prap–ər–li^y) adv. 1. Correctly: *He didn't pronounce my name properly* 2. Thoroughly: *I don't have time to do this job properly.*

prop-er-ty (prap–ərt–i^y) n. -ties 1. Land or buildings or both together: *Property in this city is becoming more valuable.* 2. Possession of any kind: *The stolen property was hidden in the thief's car.* 3. A quality that belongs naturally to sthg.: *Some plants have healing properties.*

proph-e-cy (praf–ə–si^y) n. -cies 1. The foretelling of what is to come 2. A statement telling

sthg. that is to happen in the future NOTE: There are hundreds of prophecies in the Bible concerning Jesus Christ, all of which have been fulfilled or soon will be. There are also many prophecies about various nations: prophecies concerning the last days, the end of the world, and the second coming of Christ: *No prophecy of Scripture came about by the prophet's own interpretation. For prophecy never had its origin in the will of man, but men spoke from God as they were carried along by the Holy Spirit* (2 Peter 1:20,21).

proph-e-sy (prɑf–ə–saɪ) v. -sied, -sying **1.** To speak by divine inspiration: *In the last days, God says, "I will pour out my Spirit on all people. Your sons and daughters will prophesy"* (Acts 2:17). **2.** To predict; foretell —see PROPHET, PROPHECY

proph-et (prɑf–ət) n. **1.** One who speaks for God **2.** One who foretells future events: *The Prophet Isaiah, who lived 700 years before Christ was born (700 B.C.), prophesied many things about Christ, including: "We all, like sheep, have gone astray, each of us has turned to his own way; and the Lord has laid on him (Christ) the iniquity of us all"* (Isaiah 53:6). NOTE: This prophecy was fulfilled when Jesus Christ suffered and died for us on the cross and paid for all our sins with his own blood. Then he rose from the dead as prophesied by David (1000 B.C.), when he wrote, "You [God] will not abandon me [Christ] to the grave, nor will you let your Holy One see decay" (Psalm 16:10). St. Paul said, "I am saying nothing beyond what the prophets and Moses said would happen — that the Christ would suffer, and, as the first to rise from the dead, would proclaim light to his own people and to the Gentiles [nations]" (Acts 26:22,23).

pro-phet-ic (prə–fɛt–ɪk) adj. **1.** Correctly foretelling future events: *Her words proved to be prophetic.* **2.** Like a prophet —**prophetically** adv.

pro-pin-qui-ty (prə–pɪŋ–kwət–iʸ) n. **1.** Nearness in place or time **2.** Nearness of relation

pro-pi-ti-ate (prə–pɪʃ–iʸ–eʸt) v. -ated, -ating To win or gain the favor or the forgiveness of; to conciliate; to appease; to placate: *Some*

people make animal sacrifices, and even human sacrifices, to propitiate their gods. Such sacrifices are of no value at all, but, praise God, neither is any kind of sacrifice necessary to propitiate the wrath of God. NOTE: The one true God sent his only Son, Jesus Christ, into the world to be the atoning sacrifice (the propitiation) for the sins of the world (1 John 2:2), "that whoever believes in him should not perish but have eternal life" (John 3:16). This was necessary because all people are sinners (Romans 3:23), and sin separates people from God. It offends his Holiness. The justice of God must be satisfied to provide reconciliation. His anger against sin must be propitiated. No one else could do this for us. Jesus is the only one who could do it. So he became a man and suffered and died for us on the cross. The death of Jesus Christ fully atoned for the sins of all people and fully propitiated the wrath of God, as proved by his resurrection three days later (Romans 1:4). God himself provided the sacrifice that his justice demanded. He offered his only Son as the atoning sacrifice (propitiation) for sin. This shows that God, who is holy and just, is also loving and forgiving. In this is love, not that we loved God, but that he loved us and sent his Son to be the propitiation for our sins (1 John 4:10). —see PROPITIATION, JESUS, ATONEMENT

pro-pi-ti-a-tion (prə–pɪʃ–iʸ–eʸ–ʃən) n. The atoning sacrifice for sins: *If anyone sins, we have an Advocate with the Father, Jesus Christ the righteous. And he himself is the propitiation for our sins, and not for ours only but also for the whole world* (1 John 2:2 NKJV). —see PROPITIATE, ATONEMENT, JESUS

pro-pi-tious (prə–pɪʃ–əs) adj. **1.** Favorably disposed: *God is propitious.* **2.** Presenting favorable conditions

pro-po-nent (prə–poʷ–nənt/ proʷ–) n. One who argues in favor of sthg.

pro-por-tion (prə–pɔr–ʃən) n. **1.** The correct relationship, esp. in size, between different parts of a whole: *This picture isn't in proportion; the dog is larger than the house.* **2.** The compared relationship between two things

in regard to size, importance, etc.: *The proportion of men and women in this school is not equal; men outnumber the women two to one.* **3.** A part or share: *What proportion of your income do you spend on food?* —**proportional** adj. —**proportionate** adj.

pro-pos-al (prə-po^w-zəl) n. **1.** Sthg. proposed or suggested: *peace proposals* **2.** An offer of marriage

pro-pose (prə-po^wz) v. -**posed**, -**posing 1.** To suggest sthg. for consideration: *I propose that we start the meeting earlier next time.* **2.** To make an offer of marriage: *John proposed to Mary last night, and she accepted his proposal.* **3.** To intend: *John proposed to spend the summer helping his father in his business.*

prop-o-si-tion (prɑp-ə-zɪʃ-ən) n. **1.** Sthg. proposed for consideration **2.** A thing or situation that must be dealt with **3.** An indecent proposal; a request for sexual relations

proposition v. To suggest having sexual relations with sbdy. to whom one is not married: *He tried to proposition her.* —see SIN, ADULTERY

pro-pri-e-tor (prə-praɪ-ət-ər) n. An owner, as of a business or patent

pro-pri-e-ty (prə-praɪ-ət-i^y) n. The standard of what is socially acceptable in conduct and speech: *I also want women to dress modestly, with decency and propriety...* (1 Timothy 2:9).

pro-pul-sion (prə-pʌl-ʃən) n. **1.** The act of propelling or the state of being propelled **2.** A propelling force: *jet propulsion*

pro-sa-ic (pro^w-ze^y-ɪk) adj. **1.** Pertaining to or resembling prose **2.** Dull; uninteresting

pro-scribe (pro^w-skraɪb) v. -**scribed**, -**scribing 1.** To condemn as dangerous: *Doctors have declared this drug to be dangerous and have proscribed its use.* **2.** To forbid by law

prose (pro^wz) n. Ordinary spoken or written language, not in verse form

pros-e-cute (prɑs-ə-kyu^wt) v. -**cuted**, -**cuting 1.** To bring a criminal charge against sbdy. in a court of law: *He was prosecuted for murder.* **2.** To conduct or carry on

pros-e-cu-tion (prɑs-ə-kyu^w-ʃən) n. **1.** The act of prosecuting or being prosecuted by law **2.** The people who bring a criminal charge

against sbdy. in court —compare DEFENSE

pros-pect (prɑs-pɛkt) n. **1.** Reasonable hope of sthg. good happening: *The prospect of the righteous is joy, but the hopes of the wicked come to nothing* (Proverbs 10:28). **2.** A possibility or likelihood: *Sad to say, there is always the prospect of war in some part of the world.* **3.** A potential buyer or customer: *We haven't sold our house yet, but we have several good prospects.*

prospect v. To explore an area in order to find gold, silver, oil, etc. —**prospector** n.

pro-spec-tive (prə-spɛk-tɪv) adj. Expected; probable; intended: *Mr. Smith is a prospective buyer for the house.*

pro-spec-tus (prə-spɛk-təs/ prɑ-) n. **1.** A booklet giving information about a school, organization, etc. **2.** A printed document describing the chief features of an investment or business enterprise

pros-per (prɑs-pər) v. To become successful: *He who trusts the Lord will prosper* (Proverbs 28:25). *Blessed is the man who does not walk in the counsel of the wicked... But his delight is in the law of the Lord, and on his law he meditates day and night ... Whatever he does prospers* (Psalm 1:1-3).

pros-per-i-ty (prɑs-pɛər-ə-ti^y) v. Success, esp. in money matters: *Blessed are all who fear the Lord, who walk in his ways. You will eat the fruit of your labor; blessings and prosperity will be yours* (Psalm 128:1-2).

pros-per-ous (prɑs-pə-rəs) adj. Successful; rich: *Do not let this Book of the Law [the word of God] depart from your mouth; meditate on it day and night so that you may be careful to do everything written in it. Then you will be prosperous and successful* (Joshua 1:8).

pros-tate (prɑs-te^yt) n. A gland around the neck of the bladder in males, also called **prostate gland** —**pros-tat-ic** (prɑ-stæt-ɪk) adj.

pros-ti-tute (prɑs-tə-tu^wt) n. One who performs sexual acts with others for pay, a detestable sin against God's holy law —see PROSTITUTION

pros-ti-tute v. -**tuted**, -**tuting 1.** To hire oneself as a prostitute **2.** To put to a dishonorable use, for money: *He prostituted his talents on worthless work.*

pros-ti-tu-tion (prɑs–tə–tu^w–ʃən) n. The act or practice of prostituting, or the fact of being prostituted, esp. the trade of a prostitute NOTE: Prostitution is a detestable sin in God's sight, and the wages of sin is eternal death. But because of God's great love and mercy, he forgives all those who truly repent of their sins and put their trust in Jesus for eternal life (Mark 1:15; Acts 2:38; Acts 16:31). —see FORGIVENESS, JESUS

pros-trate (prɑs–tre^yt) adj. **1.** Lying flat, esp. face downward **2.** Overcome; exhausted

prostrate v. **-trated, -trating** To cast oneself face downward on the ground or floor in humility or adoration

pro-tag-o-nist (pro^w–tæg–ə–nəst) n. **1.** The leading character of a drama or novel **2.** A leader of a movement or cause

pro-tect (prə–tekt) v. To keep safe; to guard or defend from danger: *He raised his hand to protect his eyes from the sun./ Jesus prayed for his disciples saying, "Holy Father, protect them by the power of your name ... protect them from the evil one"* (John 17:11,15).

pro-tec-tion (prə–tek–ʃən) n. **1.** The act of protecting or state of being protected: *This strong lock will give us protection against burglary.* **2.** A person or thing that protects: *This high wall will give us protection from the wind.*

pro-tec-tive (prə–tek–tɪv) adj. **1.** That which gives protection: *protective clothing* **2.** Wishing to protect: *protective parents*

pro-tec-tor (prə–tek–tər) n. A guardian; defender

pro-tec-tor-ate (prə–tek–tə–rət) n. A country that is partly governed and defended by another one

pro-té-gé (pro^w–tə–ʒe^y) n. A man who is helped in his career by an important or influential person

pro-té-gée (pro^w–tə–ʒe^y) n. A female protégé

pro-tein (pro^w–ti^yn) n. Any of many substances present in such foods as meat, eggs, and milk, that help to build up the body and keep it healthy

pro-test (pro^w–test) n. **1.** A complaint or strong expression of disagreement: *The home team strongly disagreed with the ruling of the referees, so they played the game under protest.* **2.** An organized public demonstration of disapproval

pro-test (pro^w–test/ pro^w–test) v. **1.** To express strong objection to sthg., esp. publicly: *A large crowd had gathered and were protesting the ruling of the court.* **2.** To state or declare definitely, esp. against opposition: *She protested that she was nowhere near the scene of the crime.* —**protester** n.

prot-es-tant (prɑt–əs–tənt) n. A member of a part of the Christian church that separated from the Roman Catholic Church in the 16th century —**protestant** adj. —**Protestantism** n.

pro-tes-ta-tion (prɑt–əs–te^y–ʃən) n. A protest; a solemn declaration

pro-to-col (pro^wt–ə–kɔl) n. **1.** A formal code of etiquette for affairs of state with regard to one's rank or status **2.** The original draft of an agreement in preparation for a treaty

pro-ton (pro^w–tɑn) n. A particle having a positive electrical charge forming part of the nucleus of an atom or all of the nucleus of a hydrogen atom

pro-to-plasm (pro^wt–ə–plæz–əm) n. A colorless, jelly-like substance which is the chief material in all living cells

pro-to-type (pro^wt–ə–tɑɪp) n. The original model from which anything is copied

pro-to-zo-an (pro^wt–ə–zo^w–ən) n. One of a large group of microscopic animals consisting of only one cell: *Amebas are protozoans.*

pro-tract (pro^w–trækt) v. To draw out or lengthen in time —**pro-trac-tion** (pro^w–træk–ʃən) n.

pro-trac-tor (pro^w–trækt–ər) n. An instrument having a graduated arc for measuring and drawing angles on paper

pro-trude (pro^w–tru^wd) v. **-truded, -truding** To stick out or thrust forward —**pro-tru-sion** (pro^w–tru^w–ʒən) n. —**protrusive** adj.

pro-tu-ber-ance (pro^w–tu^w–bə–rəns) n. A thing that protrudes —**pro-tu-ber-ant** (pro^w–tu^w–bə–rənt) adj.

proud (prɑʊd) adj. **1.** Having and showing self-respect: *too proud to beg* **2.** *derog.* Haughty; having too high an opinion of oneself: *God opposes the proud, but gives grace [favor] to the humble* (James 4:6). **3.** Having or ex-

pressing personal satisfaction and pleasure in sthg.: *Our basketball team is proud of its record this year.* **4.** Splendid; noble; grand: *The military parade was a proud sight.*

prove (pruᵂv) v. **proved, proved** or **proven 1.** To show to be true: *Jesus asked the crowd, "Can any of you prove me guilty of sin?"* (John 8:46). *Of course, they could not. He was tempted in every way, just as we are — yet without sin* (Hebrews 4:15). **2.** To show in the course of time and experience to be of the quality stated: *Paul preached that they should repent and turn to God and prove their repentance by their deeds* (Acts 26:20).

prov-en (pruᵂ–vən) adj. That which has been tested and shown to be true: *a man of proven ability* —opposite UNPROVEN

prov-en-der (prɑv–ən–dər) n. Food, esp. for horses and cattle

prov-erb (prɑv–ɜrb) n. A short well-known saying usu. in popular language: *"The fear of the Lord is the beginning of wisdom,"* (Proverbs 9:10) *is a proverb./ "The fear of the Lord is to hate evil,"* (Proverbs 8:13) *is another proverb.* —see PROVERBS, BIBLE, OLD TESTAMENT

pro-ver-bi-al (prə–vɜr–biʸ–əl) adj. **1.** Concerning or like a proverb **2.** Well-known; widely spoken of: *The slyness of the fox is proverbial.*

Prov-erbs (prɑv–ɜrbz) n. One of the books of the Old Testament Scriptures, written about 1,000 years before the birth of Christ by King Solomon and others to give moral instruction, esp. to young people —see BIBLE, OLD TESTAMENT

pro-vide (prə–vaɪd) v. **-vided, -viding** To supply sthg. needed or useful: *After he [Jesus] provided purification for sins, he sat down at the right hand of the Majesty in heaven* (Hebrews 1:3). *If anyone does not provide for his relatives, and especially for his immediate family, he has denied the faith and is worse than an unbeliever* (1 Timothy 5:18).

pro-vid-ed (prə–vaɪd–əd) conj. On condition that: *I will go, provided (that) you come with me.*

prov-i-dence (prɑv–əd–əns) n. A special event showing God's care (often in the phrase **divine providence**): *It seemed like providence*

that the doctor happened to be passing just at the time of the accident

prov-i-dent (prɑv–əd–ənt) adj. Providing for future needs

prov-i-den-tial (prɑv–ə–den–tʃəl) adj. **1.** Determined by Divine Providence **2.** Happening just when needed: *It was providential that you came along just when you did.*

prov-ince (prɑv–əns) n. One of the main divisions of some countries that forms a separate whole for purposes of government administration: *How many provinces are there in China?*

pro-vin-cial (prə–vɪn–tʃəl) adj. **1.** Of a province or the provinces **2.** A narrow-minded or unsophisticated person

pro-vi-sion (prə–vɪʒ–ən) n. **1.** The act of providing: *The provision of a new school has been a real blessing to the community.* **2.** Preparation for future needs: *Put on the Lord Jesus Christ, and make no provision for the flesh, to fulfill its lusts* (Romans 13:14). **3.** *usu. pl.* Supplies: *They had provisions on board the ship for 500 passengers for two weeks.* **4.** A condition in an agreement or law

pro-vi-sion-al (prə–vɪʒ–ən–əl) adj. Provided for a temporary need —com-pare TEMPORARY —**provisionally** adv.

pro-vi-so (prə–viʸ–zoᵂ) n. **-sos** or **-soes** A clause in a contract or statute by which a condition is introduced

prov-o-ca-tion (prɑv–ə–keʸ–ʃən) n. **1.** An act of provoking or being provoked **2.** Sthg. that provokes anger or retaliation

pro-voc-a-tive (prə–vɑk–ə–tɪv) adj. **1.** Arousing or likely to arouse interest, anger, or sexual desire: *a very provocative dress* **2.** Deliberately annoying

pro-voke (prə–voᵂk) v. **-voked, -voking 1.** To make angry: *That dog is vicious when provoked.* **2.** To cause: *His jokes provoked much laughter.*

pro-vok-ing (prə–voᵂk–ɪŋ) adj. Annoying

prow (prɑv) n. The pointed front part of a ship or boat

prow-ess (prɑv–əs) n. Unusual ability or skill

prowl (prɑvl) v. To move about quietly trying not to be seen or heard: *Be self-controlled and alert. Your enemy the devil prowls around like a*

roaring lion looking for someone to devour (1 Peter 5:8).

prowl n. An act of prowling: *on the prowl*

prowl-er (pravl–ər) n. A person who prowls: *Call the police. There's a prowler in the back-yard.*

prox-im-i-ty (prɑk–sim–ət-i^y) n. **1.** Nearness **2.** Neighborhood

prox-y (prɑk–si^y) n. -ies A person having the right to act for or represent another person, esp. as a voter at an election: *He voted by proxy.*

prude (pru^{w}d) n. A very modest person, esp. one who dislikes any mention of sex —**prudish** adj.

pru-dence (pru^w–dəns) n. Caution in practical matters, esp. one's personal affairs: *A fool spurns his father's discipline, but whoever heeds correction shows prudence* (Proverbs 15:5).

pru-dent (pru^w–dənt) adj. Sensible; careful: *A simple man believes anything, but a prudent man gives thought to his steps* (Proverbs 14:15). *A prudent man sees danger and takes refuge, but the simple keep going and suffer for it* (Proverbs 22:3). —opposite IMPRUDENT

pru-den-tial (pru^w–den–tʃəl) adj. Showing or involving prudence

prune (pru^{w}n) n. A dried plum

prune v. **pruned, pruning 1.** To trim by cutting away dead branches or excessive growth of a tree or bush **2.** To shorten and improve a speech or a book, etc., by removing unimportant parts

pru-ri-ent (prʊər-i^y–ənt) adj. Showing too much interest in sex; tending to have or cause lustful thoughts

pry (praɪ) v. **pried, prying 1.** To try to find out sthg. that is secret, esp. about sbdy. else's personal affairs: *Stop asking so many personal questions and prying into other people's business.* **2.** To force out or open by leverage: *I lost my key to the door, so I pried the window open.* **3.** To get with difficulty: *The police tried to pry the truth out of the suspect.*

psalm (sɑm/ sɑlm) n. A song or poem in praise of God, esp. one of the collection of Psalms in the Bible: *Speak to one another with psalms, hymns and spiritual songs. Sing and make music in your heart to the Lord, always giving thanks to God the Father for everything, in the name of our Lord Jesus Christ* (Ephesians 5:19-20).

Psalms (sɑmz/ sɑlmz) n. A book of the Old Testament containing 150 spiritual songs and poems used by the church in worship and devotional exercises. The predominant themes are prayer and praise, but they cover a great variety of religious experiences. They are quoted more frequently in the New Testament than any other book except Isaiah. Many of them contain references to Jesus Christ. Nearly half of the Psalms have been attributed to King David who lived more than 1,000 years before the birth of Christ. —see BIBLE, OLD TESTAMENT

pseudo–(su^w–do^w–) prefix False

pseu-do-nym (su^w–də–nɪm) n. A fictitious name, often used by authors to conceal their identity

pseu-do-sci-en-tif-ic (su^w–do^w–saɪ–ən–tɪf-ɪk) adj. Pretending to be scientific

pso-ri-a-sis (sə–raɪ–ə–səs) n. A skin disease causing red scaly patches

psych (saɪk) v. **1.** To intimidate or frighten psychologically: *They psyched out the competition.* **2.** To treat by psychoanalysis

psy-che (saɪ–ki^y) n. **1.** The human soul or spirit **2.** The human mind

psy-che-del-ic (saɪ–kə–del–ɪk) adj. Of or producing hallucinations and similar experiences

psy-chi-a-trist (saɪ–kaɪ–ə–trəst) n. A doctor trained in psychiatry

psy-chi-a-try (saɪ–kaɪ–ə–tri^y) n. The study and treatment of mental disorders —**psy-chi-at-ric** (saɪ–ki^y–æ-trɪk) adj. *a psychiatric hospital*

psy-chic (saɪ–kɪk) adj. **1.** Of or relating to the psyche **2.** Lying outside the sphere of physical science **3.** Sensitive to supernatural forces

psychic n. A person apparently susceptible to psychic influences; a medium

psy-cho-an-a-lyze (saɪ–ko^w–æn–ə–laɪz) v. -lyzed, -lyzing To treat sbdy. who is suffering from a mental illness by discussing events of his/ her past life which may have caused it —**psy-cho-a-nal-y-sis** (saɪ–ko^w–ə–

næl-ə-səs) n.

psy-chol-o-gist (saɪ-**kɑl**-ə dʒɔɒt) n. A person who is trained in psychology

psy-chol-o-gy (saɪ-kɑl-ə-dʒiᵍ) n. -gies **1.** The study or science of the mind and how it works **2.** *infml.* The mind and character of a particular person or group —**psy-cho-log-i-cal** (saɪ-kə-**lɑdʒ**-ɪ-kəl) adj. —**psychologically** adv.

psy-cho-path (saɪ-kə-pæθ) n. A mentally ill or unstable person —**psychopathic** adj.

psy-cho-sis (saɪ-koʷ-səs) n. *pl.* **-choses** (-koʷ-siᵍz) A mental disorder characterized by defective or lost contact with reality

psy-cho-so-mat-ic (saɪ-koʷ-sə-**mæt**-ɪk) adj. Of or concerning the relationship between mind and body: *A psychosomatic illness is one caused by a mental state./His stomach trouble is psychosomatic.*

psy-cho-ther-a-py (saɪ-koʷ-**θɛər**-ə-piᵍ) n. The treatment of disease by psychological means

psy-chot-ic (saɪ-**kɑt**-ɪk) adj. A person suffering from a psychosis

ptar-mi-gan (tɑr-mɪ-gən) n. A mountain-dwelling bird of the grouse family that turns white in winter

pter-o-dac-tyl (tɛər-ə-**dɑk**-təl) n. An extinct flying lizard that had wings of skin up to twenty feet in length

pto-maine (toʷ-meᵍn/toʷ-meᵍn) n. **1.** A chemical substance, often poisonous, formed by bacteria in decaying matter **2. ptomaine poisoning** An intestinal disorder caused by eating contaminated food

pub (pʌb) n. *Chiefly British* Short for Public House, an establishment where alcoholic beverages are sold and consumed; a bar

pu-ber-ty (pyuʷ-bərt-iᵍ) n. The stage in a person's life when his/her reproductive organs are in the process of becoming mature and he/she becomes capable of producing children

pub-lic (pʌb-lɪk) adj. **1.** Concerning people in general; not privately owned: *We have a new public library in this little town.* **2.** Known to all or to most people: *News of the president's death was not made public for nearly a week.* **3. public opinion** The attitude of people in general

public n. **1.** People in general: *The American public is interested in baseball.* **2.** A group that is interested in a particular person: *She tries to please the public by singing the songs that they request.* **3. in public** In the presence of other people —opposite IN PRIVATE

pub-li-ca-tion (pʌb-lə-**keᵍ**-ʃən) n. **1.** The act or process of publishing: *The first successful publication of a daily newspaper in the US was in 1784.* **2.** A published work, such as a book or magazine

pub-lic-i-ty (pʌ-**blɪs**-ət-iᵍ) n. **1.** Advertising; information given to attract public attention: *The new film received a lot of publicity.* **2.** The business of bringing sbdy. or sthg. to favorable public notice, esp. for purposes of gain

pub-li-cize (pʌb-lə-saɪz) v. **-cized, -cizing** To bring to public notice or attention

pub-lish (pʌb-lɪʃ) v. **1.** To produce literature, information, musical scores, art, etc., for sale to the public **2.** To make known generally: *News of their engagement was published in all the papers.*

pub-lish-er (pʌb-lɪʃ-ər) n. A person or company whose business is to publish books, newspapers, etc.

pub-lish-ing (pʌb-lɪʃ-ɱ) n. The business of publishing books, etc.

puck (pʌk) n. A hard rubber disk used in playing ice hockey

puck-er (pʌk-ər) v. To come together in small wrinkles or bulges: *to pucker one's lips*

pud-ding (pʊd-ɱ) n. A soft and creamy dessert: *Do you prefer chocolate or vanilla pudding?*

pud-dle (pʌd-əl) n. A very small pool of usu. muddy water, lying in a hollow place in the ground: *Why do the children like playing in those mud puddles?*

pudg-y (pʌdʒ-iᵍ) adj. **-ier, -iest** Short and fat

pueb-lo (pwɛb-loʷ) n. An American Indian village of the southwest made up of flat-roofed stone and adobe buildings

puff (pʌf) n. **1.** A short, forceful discharge of air or smoke: *a puff of wind* **2.** A small pad for applying cosmetic powder: *a powder puff* **3.** A light, flaky pastry, often filled with cus-

tard or cream: *a cream puff*

puff v. **1.** To blow in small gusts repeatedly **2.** To breathe forcefully and rapidly; to pant **3.** To send out little clouds of smoke: *The train puffed into the station.* **4. puff up (a)** To swell: *His ankle puffed up after he sprained it.* **(b)** To fill with pride or conceit

puf·fin (pʌf–ən) n. A type of seabird with a plump body, black and white feathers, and a short, thick, brightly-colored beak

puf·fy (pʌf–iʸ) adj. **-fier, -fiest** Swollen —**puffiness** n.

pug (pʌg) n. A small dog with short hair and a flat nose

pu·gi·list (pyuʷ–dʒə–ləst) n. A professional boxer —**pugilism** n.—**pu·gil·is·tic** (pyuʷ–dʒə–lɪs–tɪk) adj.

pug·na·cious (pəg–neʸ–ʃəs) adj. Excessively inclined to argue or fight —**pugnaciously** adv.

pug nose (pʌg noʷz) n. A short, flattish turned-up nose —**pug-nosed** adj.

puke (pyuʷk) v. **puked, puking** *infml.* To vomit —**puke** n.

pul·chri·tude (pʌl–krə–tyuʷd) n. Physical beauty

pull (pʊl) v. **1.** To use force to cause sthg. to move toward oneself or after oneself: *The boy was pulling his wagon. / The locomotive was pulling 110 freight cars.* **2.** To draw towards oneself in order to cause a device to operate: *To fire the gun, pull the trigger.* **3.** To attract: *The amusement park pulled in huge crowds.* **4.** To extract or dislodge: *He pulled the nail out of the board.* **5.** To attempt or perform: *He pulled a robbery.* **6.** To bring out (of a pocket, e.g.): *He pulled a gun on me.* **7.** To stretch or pull a muscle **8. pull a fast one (on)** *infml.* To act unfairly in order to get an advantage over sbdy. **9. pull away** Esp. of a road vehicle, to start to move off: *He jumped onto the bus just as it was pulling away.* **10. pull in** To arrive at a station: *The train pulled in about five minutes late.* **11. pull sthg. in** *infml.* To earn money: *He's pulling in quite a bit in his new job.* **12. pull off (a)** *infml.* To succeed in doing sthg. difficult: *That stunt looked impossible, but she pulled it off.* **(b)** To drive a vehicle onto the side of the road: *He*

pulled off to the side of the road because he had a flat tire. **13. pull out (a)** To leave a station: *The train pulled out of the station.* **(b)** To quit, resign: *Tom saw that the agency would be ruined, so he pulled out.* **14. pull over** To direct or move one's vehicle to one side of the road **15. pull through** To come through a difficult sickness successfully **16. pull together (a)** To work together for a common cause **(b)** To control one's own emotions: *Stop acting like a baby! Pull yourself together.* **17. pull up** To come to a stop: *A taxi cab pulled up in front of the house.*

pull n. **1.** An act of pulling: *Give the rope a pull.* **2.** *infml.* Special influence: *John has a lot of pull with his boss, since he is his brother-in-law.*

pul·let (pʊl–ət) n. A young domestic hen

pul·ley (pʊl–iʸ) n. **-leys** Any device consisting of a wheel with a grooved rim over which a rope or chain can be moved, used for lifting things

pul·mo·nar·y (pʊl–mə–neər–iʸ) adj. Of or relating to the lungs

pulp (pʌlp) n. **1.** The soft juicy or fleshy part of a fruit or vegetable **2.** A soft moist mass **3.** Material used in making paper

pul·pit (pʊl–pɪt/–pət) n. The raised platform or enclosure from which the pastor addresses the worshipers in a church

pulp·y (pʌl–piʸ) adj. **-ier, -iest** Like pulp; containing much pulp

pul·sate (pʌl–seʸt) v. **-sated, -sating 1.** To expand and contract rhythmically **2.** To vibrate; to quiver

pulse (pʌls) n. **1.** The regular throbbing of blood in the main blood vessels, as caused by the contractions of the heart **2.** Edible seeds, such as beans and peas, that grow in pods

pulse v. **pulsed, pulsing** To beat steadily, as the heart does: *He could feel the blood pulsing through his body.*

pul·ver·ize also **-ise** (pʌl–vər–aɪz) v. **-ized, -izing 1.** To crush into a fine powder or dust **2.** *infml.* To defeat thoroughly: *The home team pulverized the visiting team 59 to 0.*

pu·ma (pyuʷ–mə) n. A mountain lion

pum·ice (pʌm–əs) n. A light, porous kind of

lava used for smoothing skin and rubbing away stains

pum-mel (pʌm–əl) v. **-meled, -meling** or **-melled, -melling** To beat again and again, esp. with the fists

pump (pʌmp) n. A device for transferring a liquid or gas from a source or container through pipes or tubes to another container: *a water pump/a gasoline pump*

pump v. **1.** To empty or fill with a liquid or gas by means of a pump: *Al pumped up his bicycle tire.* **2.** *infml.* To question sbdy. persistently to obtain information

pump-kin (pʌmp–kɪn/**pʌm**–kɪn/ **pʌŋ**-kɪn) n. **1.** A large, round, yellowish-orange, gourd-like fruit with many seeds, growing on a vine on the ground **2.** The vine of the gourd family on which this fruit grows

pun (pʌn) A humorous use of a word, which depends on two interpretations of the meaning: *He made the following pun: "Seven days without food make one weak."*

punch (pʌntʃ) v. **1.** To hit sbdy. or sthg. hard with the closed hand (fist) **2.** To make a hole in sthg., using a punch: *He punched three holes inside of each page of his report and put them into a notebook.*

punch n. **1.** A steel tool for cutting holes: *a paper punch* **2.** A drink made from fruit juice, spices, sugar, water, etc.

punch–drunk (pʌntʃ–drʌŋk) adj. **1.** Stupefied from being severely or repeatedly punched **2.** Dazed or bewildered

punch-y (pʌn–tʃiʸ) adj. **1.** Punch-drunk **2.** Of a writing style, forceful

punc-til-i-ous (pʌŋk–tɪl–iʸ–əs) adj. Very strict or exact in the observance of all formalities of behavior

punc-tu-al (pʌŋk–tʃə–wəl) adj. Not tardy; arriving or doing sthg. at the right time: *She's never punctual; she's always late.* —**punc-tu-al-i-ty** (pəŋk–tʃuʷ–æl–ə–tiʸ) n.

punc-tu-ate (pʌŋk–tʃə–weʸt) v. **-ated, -ating 1.** To divide written material into sentences, phrases, etc., by the use of periods (full stops), commas, and other punctuation marks **2.** To interrupt repeatedly: *The football game was punctuated by penalties.*

punc-tu-a-tion (pʌŋk–tʃuʷ–eʸ–ʃən) n. The

marks used in punctuating a piece of writing: *Commas and periods (full stops) are punctuation marks.*

punc-ture (pʌŋk–tʃər) n. **1.** A small hole in a tire or sthg. similar **2.** A small hole in another surface, such as the skin

puncture v. **-tured, -turing** To make or get a puncture: *A sharp rock punctured my bicycle tire./ Tom has a punctured lung.*

pun-dit (pʌn–dɪt) n. *sometimes derog.* An expert

pun-gent (pʌn–dʒənt) adj. Strong and sharp in taste or smell

pun-ish (pʌn–ɪʃ) v. **1.** To cause sbdy. to suffer for his/her sins or misdeeds: *People should be punished for reckless driving./God is just; he will pay back trouble to those who trouble you. ... This will happen when the Lord Jesus is revealed from heaven in blazing fire with his powerful angels. He will punish those who do not know God and who do not obey the gospel of our Lord Jesus Christ. They will be punished with everlasting destruction and shut out from the presence of the Lord ...* (2 Thessalonians 1:6-9). **2.** To deal roughly with (an opponent), esp. by taking advantage of a weakness

pun-ish-a-ble (pʌn–ɪʃ–ə–bəl) adj. That which may be punished by law

pun-ish-ing (pʌn–ɪʃ–ɪŋ) adj. *infml.* Sthg. that makes a person very tired and weak: *a long, punishing trip over very rough roads*

pun-ish-ment (pʌn–ɪʃ–mənt) n. **1.** The act of punishing or condition of being punished: *But he [Jesus] was pierced for our transgressions...the punishment that brought us peace [with God] was upon him, and by his wounds we are healed* (Isaiah 53:5). —see JESUS **2.** The way in which a person is punished

pu-ni-tive (pyuʷ–nə–tɪv) adj. Giving punishment or suffering: *Punitive measures will be taken against offenders.*

punk (pʌŋk) adj. Very poor; inferior

punk n. **1.** A young, inexperienced person **2.** A thug; a young ruffian **3.** A movement among certain young people, in the US and Britain, who are opposed to the values of money-based society and who express this esp. in loud often violent music (punk rock)

punt (pʌnt) v. To kick a football that has been dropped from the hands before it touches

the ground

punt n. A kick of this kind

pu-ny (pyuᵂ–niʸ) adj. -nier, -niest *derog.* Small and weak

pup (pʌp) n. **1.** A young dog (puppy) **2.** A young seal or otter

pu-pa (pyuᵂ–pə) n. -pas or -pae (–piʸ / –paɪ) An insect during a resting stage while it is changing from a larva into an adult, protected by an outer covering such as a cocoon

pu-pil (pyuᵂ–pəl) n. A person, esp. a child, who is being taught

pupil n. The round black opening in the middle of the eye which allows light to enter

pup-pet (pʌp–ət) n. **1.** A doll, made of wood or cloth, made to move by strings or wires or by a person's hand placed inside the body of the doll **2.** often *derog.* Not independent, but controlled by sbdy. else: *a puppet government*

pup-pe-teer (pʌp–ə–tɪər) n. A person who performs with puppets

pup-py (pʌp–iʸ) also **pup**, n. -pies A young dog

pur-chase (pɜr–tʃəs) v. To buy: *With your blood you [Jesus] purchased men for God from every tribe and language and people and nation* (Revelation 5:9). —see JESUS

purchase n. An act of buying: *She made several purchases in the department store.*

pur-chas-er (pɜr–tʃəs–ər) n. A buyer

pur-dah (pɜrd–ə) n. The seclusion of women from public observation among Muslims and some Hindus, esp. in India

pure (pyʊər) adj. **1.** Not mixed with any other substance, esp. dirt or anything harmful: *pure water for drinking* **2.** Mor-ally clean: *Blessed are the pure in heart, for they shall see God* (Matthew 5:8). *How can a young man keep his way pure? By living according to your [God's] word* (Psalm 119:9). **3.** *infml.* Complete; only: *By pure chance they met on the subway in New York.*

pure-bred (pyʊər–brɛd) adj. Having ancestors that are all of the same breed: *purebred horses and dogs*

pure-ly (pyʊər–liʸ) adv. Wholly; entirely: *I did it purely out of love and respect for my parents.*

pur-ga-tive (pɜr–gət–ɪv) adj. A medicine that clears waste matter out of the body

purge (pɜrdʒ) v. **purged, purging 1.** To clean or purify, esp. from sin, guilt, or defilement **2.** To get rid of an unwanted person in a government, political party, etc., by unjust or forceful means **3.** To clear waste matter from the bowels by means of a laxative

purge n. **1.** The act, process, or result of purging: *a purge of disloyal army officers* **2.** Sthg. that purges

pu-ri-fy (pyʊər–ə–faɪ) v. -fied, -fying **1.** To make pure physically: *In some cities we must do sthg. soon to purify the air.* **2.** To make pure spiritually: *If we walk in the light [of God's word], as he is in the light, we have fellowship with one another, and the blood of Jesus Christ, his Son, purifies us from all sin* (1 John 1:7). —**pur-i-fi-ca-tion** (pyʊər–ə–fə–keʸ–ʃən) n.

Pu-rim (pyʊər–əm) n. A Jewish holiday celebrated in February or March in commemoration of the deliverance of the Jews from the massacre plotted by Haman (Esther 7-9)

Pu-ri-tan (pyʊər–ət–ən) A member of the Anglican Church of England in the 16th and 17th centuries who wanted to purify the church and be free from governmental control

pu-ri-ty (pyʊər–ət–iʸ) n. The quality or state of being pure: *St. Paul wrote to Timothy, saying, "Treat... older women as mothers, and younger women as sisters, with absolute purity"* (1 Timothy 5:1-2). —opposite IMPURITY

pur-ple (pɜr–pəl) adj. n. A dark color made of a mixture of red and blue

pur-plish (pɜr–pə–lɪʃ) adj. Somewhat purple

pur-pose (pɜr–pəs) n. **1.** An intention or plan; a reason for an action: *It is fine to be zealous, provided the purpose is good* (Galatians 4:18). **2.** Use: *Don't waste your money; put it to some good purpose./I don't have a pen, but a pencil will serve the purpose.* —**purposeful** adj. —**purposeless** adj. —**purposely** adv.

purr (pɜr) n. The soft vibrant sound like that made by a contented cat —**purr** v. **purred, purring** *fig. The rebuilt engine purred like a kit-*

purse (pɔrs) n. **1.** A small leather or plastic bag used, esp. by women, for carrying money and other small articles **2.** Wealth or resources **3.** Money offered as a gift or as a prize

pur-sue (pər–su^w) v. -sued, -suing **1.** To follow in an effort to overtake or capture; to chase: *The police were pursuing the criminals.* **2.** To strive to gain or accomplish: *The Lord detests the way of the wicked, but he loves those who pursue righteousness* (Proverbs 15:9). *He who pursues righteousness and love finds life, prosperity, and honor* (Proverbs 21:21). **3.** To continue steadily with; be busy with: *He is pursuing his studies at the university./to pursue a hobby* —**pursuer** n.

pur-suit (pər–su^wt) n. **1.** The act of pursuing sbdy.: *The police were in pursuit of the escaped convicts.* **2.** To go after; to seek sthg. intangible: *the pursuit of happiness* **3.** Any activity to which sbdy. gives his time: *One of his favorite pursuits is collecting rare books.*

pus (pʌs) n. A thick yellowish liquid that forms in infected wounds, etc.

push (pʊʃ) v. **1.** To use pressure in order to move sbdy. or sthg. away from oneself or itself **2.** To make one's way by doing this: *He pushed his way through the crowd.* **3.** To continually urge sbdy. to do sthg.: *My parents are pushing me to go to college.* **4.** *infml.* To promote a product or a cause: *The company is pushing its new product (=advertising it widely)*

push n. An act of pushing: *They gave the car a push to get it started.*

push-er (pʊʃ–ər) n. *infml.* One who sells unlawful drugs

push-y (pʊʃ–i^y) also **pushing** adj. -ier, -iest Offensively forward or aggressive; too active and forceful in getting things done

put (pʊt) v. **put, putting 1.** To place, lay, or set sthg. in a stated place: *Put the book on the table.* **2.** To fix: *I'm putting new locks on all the doors.* **3.** To say or express: *It's cold outside, to put it mildly./That's one way of putting (saying) it.* **4.** To submit or present a question: *The reporter put many questions to the governor.* **5. put aside** To save, usu. for a

special purpose: *He's putting aside some money each month for a new suit.* **6. put away** *infml.* To place sbdy. in a prison or in a hospital for insane people **7. put sbdy. or sthg. down (a)** To control; defeat: *They put down the rebellion.* **(b)** *infml.* To make sbdy. feel humble: *She really put him down when she called him a lazy bum.* **(c)** To make a down payment: *He put down $1,000 on the new car as a down payment, and he has to pay $220 a month for five years.* **8. put forward (a)** To offer: *May I put your name forward as a possible candidate?* **(b)** To cause to show a later time: *Put your watches forward one hour.* **9. put in (a)** To make or send a request or claim: *If the goods were damaged, you can put in a claim at the customer service center.* **(b)** To spend time doing sthg.: *He put in 12 hours at the office yesterday.* **10. put in for sthg.** To make a formal request for; apply for: *They've put in for a raise (in salary).* **11. put sthg. into (a)** To add to: *Put more effort into your studies!* **(b)** To enter a port: *The ship put into Singapore for repairs.* **12. put off (a)** To move to a later date; delay: *He had to put off his visit for another month.* **(b)** To make excuses to sbdy. in order to avoid a duty: *We put him off by assuring him that we'd pay the bill next month.* **13. put on (a)** To cover part of the body with clothing: *She put on her hat.* **(b)** *infml.* To give the appearance of feeling sthg.: *He's not really sick; he's just putting on.* **(c)** To increase: *She put on weight.* **(d)** To perform a play, show, etc. on a stage: *They put on a variety show.* **14. put out (a)** To make stop burning: *He put out the fire.* **(b) put sbdy. out** To annoy: *She was very put out by his disgusting behavior.* **(c) put sthg. out** To broadcast or print: *The department will put out an official statement next week.* **(d) put oneself out** To take trouble: *She never puts herself out to help anyone.* **15. put sthg. over** To make clear: *He couldn't put over his ideas very well.* **16. put through (a)** To connect by telephone: *Operator, can you put me through to this number?* **(b)** To complete a piece of business successfully **17. put sbdy. through** To cause to experience: *You put her through a lot of anguish.* **18. put to (a)** To test by using

the stated means: *We put the matter to a vote.*
(b) To cause to be in a certain place: *She put the child to bed.* (c) **be hard put to do sthg.** To find it difficult to (do sthg.): *We were hard put to find a parking place near the stadium.* **19. put together (a)** To form; make a group of: *He wanted to put a new agency together.* (b) Combined: *Her share was more than all the others' put together.* (c) To combine ideas: *They put their heads together to plan for the year ahead.* **20. put up (a)** To raise: *to put up a tent* (b) To put in a public place: *put up a notice* (c) To provide food and lodging for: *We can put you up for the night.* (d) To offer or make, esp. in a struggle: *He didn't even put up a fight!* (e) To offer for sale: *They have put their house up for sale.* **21. put up. up to sthg.** To suggest doing sthg.: *Who put you up to this nonsense?* **22. put up with sbdy/sthg.** To suffer without complaining; to tolerate: *I won't put up with his nonsense any longer.*

pu·tre·fy (pyu^w–trə–faɪ) v. -fied, -fying To make or become rotten —**pu·tre·fac·tion** (pyu^w–trə–fæk–ʃən) n.

pu·trid (pyu^w–trəd) adj. **1.** Rotten; decayed **2.** Vile; corrupt

putt (pʌt) v. To strike a golf ball lightly

put·ter (pʌt–ər) n. **1.** A golf club used for putting **2.** A person who putts in golf

put·ter v. To occupy oneself aimlessly: *Bill was just puttering around in the garage.*

put·ty (pʌt–i^y) n. A soft oily paste, used esp. in fixing glass to window frames

puzzle (pʌz–əl) n. **1.** Sthg. that a person cannot understand or explain **2.** A game or toy in which parts must be fitted together correctly, mainly for entertainment: *a crossword puzzle/a jigsaw puzzle*

puz·zle v. -zled, -zling To bewilder mentally: *The disease puzzled the doctors.*

puz·zled (pʌz–əld) adj. Bewildered; confused: *a puzzled look on his face*

pyg·my (pɪg–mi^y) n. -mies A member of a race of small people in equatorial Africa

py·lon (paɪ–lɑn) n. **1.** A tower for supporting electric power cables **2.** A guide post at an airport

py·or·rhea (paɪ–ə–ri^y–ə) n. A disease that causes the formation of pus in the gums and loosening of the teeth

pyr·a·mid (pɪər–ə–mɪd) n. **1.** A solid figure with a flat, square base and four triangular sides that slope upwards to meet at a point **2.** A huge stone structure in the shape of this, used formerly as the burial place of a king, esp. in Egypt

pyre (paɪ–ər/ paɪr) n. A pile of wood on which a dead body is ceremonially burned

py·rite (paɪ–raɪt) n. A brass-yellow mineral that is a compound of sulfur and iron

py·ro·ma·ni·a (paɪ–ro^w–me^y–ni^y–ə) n. An irresistible impulse to start fires —**pyromaniac** n.

py·thon (paɪ–θɑn) n. A large non-poisonous snake that kills its prey by crushing it

Q Q, q (kyu^w) n. The 17th letter of the English alphabet

quack (kwæk) v. To make the noise that ducks make

quack (kwæk) n. 1. Sbdy. dishonestly claiming to be a medical doctor: *That so-called doctor is a quack.* 2. The sound made by a duck

quad (kwɑd) n. Short for **quadrangle**

quad-ran-gle (kwɑd–ræŋ–gəl) 1. A geometrical figure having four sides and four angles: *A square is a quadrangle, but not all quadrangles are square.* 2. A four-sided courtyard or enclosure, esp. in a college or a university

quad-rant (kwɑd–rənt) n. 1. One-fourth of the circumference or area of a circle 2. An instrument used formerly in navigation, astronomy, etc., for measuring heights

qua-dren-ni-al (kwɑ–dren–i^y–əl) adj. 1. Lasting four years 2. Occurring every fourth year

quad-ri– (kwɑd–rə) comb. form 1. Four 2. Fourth 3. Square

quad-ri-lat-er-al (kwɑd–rə–læt–ər–əl) n. A figure with four sides: *Squares and rectangles are quadrilaterals.* —**quadrilateral** adj.

quad-ri-ple-gic (kwɑd–rə–pli^y–dʒɪk) n. A person suffering from a paralysis of both arms and both legs —**quadriplegic** adj.

quad-ru-ped (kwɑd–rə–pɛd) n. An animal that has four feet or four paws or hoofs: *Horses, cows, and pigs are quadrupeds.*

qua-dru-ple (kwɑ–drʌp–əl/ kwɑd–ru^w–pəl) v. **-pled, -pling** To multiply by four; increase fourfold: *The population of the world will quadruple during the 20th century.*

quadruple adj. Four times as much: *Rainfall this month is quadruple the amount we had last year.*

quag-mire (kwæg–maɪ–ər) n. Wet, boggy ground

quail (kwe^{y}l) n. A short-winged, stout-bodied game bird, highly regarded as food

quaint (kwe^{y}nt) adj. 1. Unusual in character or appearance 2. Attractive, esp. because of its age: *a quaint old bakery shop* —**quaintly** adv. —**quaintness** n.

quake (kwe^{y}k) v. **quaked, quaking** To shake; tremble, usu. from cold or fear: *to quake with fear*

quake n. Short for **earthquake**

qual-i-fi-ca-tion (kwɑl–ə–fə–ke^y–ʃən) n. 1. A skill or achievement that makes a person suitable or fit for a particular job or position 2. A limitation or restriction: *a statement with these qualifications...*

qual-i-fied (kwɑl–ə–faɪd) adj. 1. Having suitable training, ability, or experience for a certain purpose: *He's a qualified English teacher.* 2. Limited or restricted in some way

qual-i-fy (kwɑl–ə–faɪ) v. **-fied, -fying** 1. To fit by training, skill, or ability for a special purpose: *Mary has finished the course which qualifies her to teach first aid.* 2. To lessen the force of a statement by adding sthg. not so strong: *I'd like to qualify that statement.*

qual-i-ty (kwɑl–ə–ti^y) n. **-ties** 1. Peculiar and essential feature or characteristic: *For since the creation of the world, God's invisible qualities — his eternal power and divine nature — have been clearly seen, being understood from what has been made* (Romans 1:20). 2. Sthg. characteristic of a person or object: *For if you possess these qualities (faith, goodness, knowledge, self-control, perseverance, godliness, brotherly kindness, love) in increasing measure, they will keep you from being ineffective and unproductive in your knowledge of our Lord Jesus Christ* (2 Peter 1:5-8).

qualm (kwɑm/kwɑlm/kwɔm) n. 1. A feeling of anxiety; a misgiving; a pang of conscience 2. A sudden feeling of sickness or faintness

quan-da-ry (kwɑn–də–ri^y) n. **-ries** A feeling of uncertainty; perplexity; not knowing what to do

quan-ti-ta-tive (kwɑn–tə–te^y–tɪv) adj. Having to do with quantity, not quality

quan-ti-ty (kwɑn–tə–ti^y) **-ties** n. 1. Number or amount: *We need to know how many guests are coming so we will know the quantity of food to order.* 2. A large amount: *I usually buy a quantity of flour at a time because I do a lot of baking.* **3. an unknown quantity** Sbdy. or sthg. untried so that the true worth is not yet known: *I've never used this brand of shampoo before; it's an unknown quantity./ "X" represents the unknown quantity in this equation.*

quar-an-tine (kwɔr–ən–ti^{y}n/ kwɑr) n. A period of time when a person or animal with an infectious disease is kept separate from oth-

ers to prevent the spread of the disease

quarantine, v. **-tined, -tining** To put under quarantine

quar-rel (kwɔr-əl/ kwɑr-) n. **1.** An angry argument **2.** A reason for complaint

quarrel v. To disagree violently or have an angry argument: *He who loves to quarrel loves sin* (Proverbs 17:19) *Every fool is quick to quarrel.* (Proverbs 20:3).

quar-rel-some (kwɔr-əl-səm/ kwɑr-) adj. Likely to quarrel: *Better to live on a corner of the roof than to share a house with a quarrelsome wife* (Proverbs 21:9).

quar-ry (kwɔr-iʸ/ kwɑr-) n. **-ries 1.** An open hole in the earth where rock, slate, or limestone is excavated (=dug out and removed) **2.** An intended prey or victim being hunted **3.** Sthg. that is sought or pursued

quarry v. **-ried, -rying** To dig out sand, stone, etc. and remove it

quart (kwɔrt) n. A measure for liquids which equals two pints or one-fourth of a gallon

quar-ter (kwɔrt-ər) n. **1.** A fourth part; one-fourth part of a whole: *a quarter of a pound of candy* **2.** In telling time, fifteen minutes before or past the hour: *It's a quarter past six* (6:15). **3.** A period of three months of the year, used for making payments of taxes, interest, etc.: *We have to pay our fire insurance each quarter.* **4.** In the U.S. and Canada, a coin worth 25 cents (one-fourth of a dollar) **5.** A person or group of people from whom sthg. comes: *Help came for the earthquake victims from all quarters.* **6.** An area of a town, often the area where certain people live: *the French quarter*

quar-ter-back (kwɔrt-ər-bæk) n. In football, the player who directs the offense and usu. passes the ball

quar-ter-ly (kwɔrt-ər-liʸ) adj. Happening or produced every three months (four times a year) —**quarterly** adv.

quar-tet (kwɔr-tɛt) n. **1.** A group of four players or singers **2.** A piece of music written for performance by four people

quartz (kwɔrts) n. A hard metal substance used in making very exact watches and clocks

quartz-ite (kwɔrt-saɪt) n. A granular rock

consisting of quartz in interlocking grains

qua-sar (kweʸ-zɑr) n. A star-like object that gives out light and radio waves

qua-si- (kwɑ-ziʸ/ kweʸ-ziʸ) comb. form Resembling or seeming to be: *quasi-scientific*

qua-train (kwɑ-treʸn/kwɑ-treʸn) n. A stanza or poem of four lines

quay (kiʸ) n. A solid landing place, often built of stone, where ships can load and unload

quea-sy (kwiʸ-ziʸ) adj. **-sier, -siest 1.** A feeling of nausea **2.** Uneasy or uncomfortable

queen (kwiʸn) n. **1. (a)** A female ruler of a country, usu. one who inherits the position: *The queen of Sheba heard about the fame of Solomon.* **(b)** The wife of a king **2.** The female winner in a competition: *Kathy was homecoming queen at her college.* **3.** A fertile female insect, that produces eggs: *the queen bee*

queen-ly (kwiʸn-liʸ) adj. **-lier, -liest** Majestic; like, or suitable for, a queen

queer (kwɪər) adj. Strange, esp. in an unpleasant way; odd: *It's queer the children showed up at school today. This is Saturday!*

queer n. *derog.* A male homosexual

quell (kwɛl) v. To put a stop to; suppress: *The general quelled the rebellion.*

quench (kwɛntʃ) v. **1.** To satisfy one's thirst by drinking **2.** To put out, as a fire: *They quenched the fire by throwing water on it.*

quer-u-lous (kwɛər-yə-ləs/ -ə-) adj. **1.** Complaining **2.** Fretful

que-ry (kwɪər-iʸ) v. **-ried, -rying 1.** To ask sbdy. a question **2.** To express a doubt about —**query** n. **-ries** A question

quest (kwɛst) n. An act of searching; an attempt to find: *He continued his quest for knowledge by going to graduate school.* /*in quest of adventure/gold/happiness*

ques-tion (kwɛs-tʃən) n. **1.** A sentence or phrase that requests an answer: *Janice asked a question and the teacher answered her.* **2.** A difficulty or matter to be solved: *It's a question of finding enough money and manpower to do it.* **3.** An expression of doubt: *There was some question regarding his ability.* **4. call (sthg.) into question** To raise doubts about sbdy. or sthg.: *The need for building the new prison was called into question.* **5. in question**

Being considered *His honesty was never in question; only his ability to handle the job.* **6. out of the question** Absolutely not!: *You can't borrow the car tonight; it's out of the question.* **7. no question about it** No doubt about it

ques-tion (kwɛs–tʃən) v. **1.** To ask someone sthg.: *The police questioned him for an hour.* **2.** To raise doubts about: *I would never question her motive for doing it.*

ques-tion-a-ble (kwɛs–tʃə–nə–bəl) adj. Doubtful: *Whether he should attend such a meeting or not was questionable.* **—questionably** adv.

ques-tion-ing (kwɛs–tʃən–ɪŋ) adj. Seeming to ask a question: *He gave his wife a questioning look.*

questioning n. An act of asking many questions: *She underwent a severe questioning by the police.* **—questioningly** adv.

ques-tion mark (kwɛs–tʃən mɑrk) n. In writing, the mark (?) put after a question

ques-tion-naire (kwɛs–tʃə–neər) n. A form with a set of questions to be answered in order to provide information

quet-zal (kɛt–sɑl/ –sæl) n. A bird of Central America with bright green and red feathers

queue (kyuʷ) n. *BrE.* A line of people waiting to move, get on a vehicle, or to enter a building

queue v. **queued, queuing** *BrE.* To form a line to wait for sthg.: *The customers at the Post Office queued (up).*

quib-ble (kwɪb–əl) v. **-bled, -bling** To argue about unimportant matters: *Don't quibble over a few cents; it isn't important.* **—quibble** n. **—quibbling** adj. or n.

quick (kwɪk) adj. **1.** Fast; soon finished: *a quick snack* **2. quick–tempered** Easily angered: *A quick-tempered man does foolish things* (Proverbs 14:17). **—quickly** adv. **—quickness** n.

quick-en (kwɪk–ən) v. To speed up; to cause to become faster

quick-sand (kwɪk–sænd) n. A deep bed of water-soaked sand that swallows up anything upon it

quick-sil-ver (kwɪk–sɪl–vər) n. Mercury

quid (kwɪd) n. *BrE.* A pound sterling, or a sovereign

qui-es-cent (kwɪ–ɛs–ənt) adj. In a state of inac-

tion; quiet; still **—quiescence** n.

qui-et (kwaɪ–ət) adj. **1.** With little or no noise: *a quiet motor* **—opposite** LOUD **2.** Gentle; mild· *Make it your ambition to lead a quiet life* (1 Thessalonians 4:11). **3.** Not active: *a quiet breeze /a quiet day at the office* **4.** Secluded: *a quiet nook* **5.** Not showy; modest: *quiet conduct* **—quietly** adv. **—quietness** n. *The fruit of righteousness will be peace; the effect of righteousness will be quietness and confidence forever* (Isaiah 32:17).

quiet n. State of being quiet; stillness: *Better a dry crust with peace and quiet than a house full of feasting with strife* (Proverbs 17:1).

quiet v. To become or cause to become quiet: *The horses in the corral quieted down.*

quill (kwɪl) n. **1.** One of the long straight flight feathers or tail feathers of a bird **2.** Sthg. made from a quill, such as a pen **3.** One of the long sharp spines of a porcupine

quilt (kwɪlt) n. A padded covering for a bed made of two layers of fabric, often decorative

quilt v. To make quilts **—quilted** adj.

qui-nine (kwaɪ–naɪn) n. A bitter white substance used esp. in treating malaria

quint (kwɪnt) n. Short for **quintuplet**

quin-tes-sence (kwɪn–tɛs–əns) n. **1.** The most important part of anything **2.** The purest form or part of anything **—quin-tes-sen-tial** (kwɪnt–ə–sɛn–tʃəl) adj.

quin-tet (kwɪn–tɛt) n. **1.** A group of five, esp. of five musicians **2.** A musical composition for five instruments or voices

quin-tu-ple (kwɪn–tʌp–əl/ –tuʷp–) v. To make or become five times as great

quin-tu-plet (kwɪn–tʌp–lut/ –tuʷp–) n. **1.** A group of five of a kind **2.** One of five offspring born at the same time

quip (kwɪp) v. **-pp-** To make a clever remark **—quip** n.

quire (kwaɪr) n. A set of 24 or sometimes 25 sheets of paper of the same size and quality

quirk (kwɜrk) n. **1.** A strange happening or accident: *By some strange quirk the man who lives across the street went to the same high school as I did fifty years ago.* **2.** A strange type of behavior: *Mr. Brown has many unusual quirks in his character.* **3.** A sudden twist or

turn

quit (kwɪt) v. **quit, quitting** To stop doing sthg.: *I'm quitting work for the day.*

quite (kwaɪt) adv. **1.** Entirely; perfectly: *The cake isn't quite done; it has to bake another five minutes.* **2.** To some extent; rather: *She sings quite well, but her sister sings better.*

quit-ter (kwɪt–ər) n. One who gives up easily: *He's a quitter; he never finishes anything he starts.*

quiv-er (kwɪv–ər) v. To shake or vibrate slightly

quiv-er n. **1.** A case for holding arrows **2.** The act or action of quivering

quix-ot-ic (kwɪk–sɑt–ɪk) adj. Having noble but unrealistic aims which cannot be carried out

quiz (kwɪz) n. **-zz-** A short oral or written test: *We had three quizzes this week.*

quiz v. **-zz-** To ask questions of: *We were quizzed on the places we'd visited in China.*

quiz-zi-cal (kwɪz–ɪ–kəl) adj. **1.** Done in a questioning way **2.** Gently amusing or teasing

quo-rum (kwɔr–əm) n. The number of members, of a board of directors, e.g., without whom an official meeting cannot be conducted: *We couldn't vote for new officers because we didn't have a quorum.*

quo-ta (kwoᵂt–ə) n. **1.** A part or share to be given or received by each member of a group **2.** The maximum number allowed

quot-a-ble (kwoᵂt–ə–bəl) adj. Worthy of being quoted

quo-ta-tion (kwoᵂ–teʸ–ʃən) n. **1.** The act or process of quoting **2.** A sentence quoted from literature **3.** The estimation of the cost of a piece of work: *I need to get a quotation for repairs on the car.*

quotation mark (kwoᵂ–teʸ–ʃən mɑrk) n. Either of a pair of marks (" ") (' ') placed at the beginning and end of words quoted

quote (kwoᵂt) v. **quoted, quoting 1.** To repeat the words of a person exactly as they were spoken or written **2.** To state a price for sthg.

quote n. A quotation

quo-tient (kwoᵂ–ʃənt) n. The result obtained by dividing one number into another: *If fifty is divided by five, the quotient is ten.*

R R, r (ɑr) n. 1. The 18th letter of the English alphabet 2. The three R's Reading, writing, and arithmetic: *A child's formal education begins with the three R's.*

rab-bi (ræb–aɪ) n. -bis 1. The ordained spiritual leader of a Jewish congregation 2. Formerly, a person authorized to interpret Jewish law

rab-bit (ræb–ət) n. A common small furry animal with long ears that lives in a hole in the ground

rab-ble (ræb–əl) n. A disorderly crowd

rab-ble–rous-er (ræb–əl–rauz–ər) n. A person who stirs up the prejudices of the public

rab-id (ræb–əd) adj. 1. Afflicted with rabies 2. Over zealous; fanatical

ra-bies (reʸ–biʸz) n. A deadly virus disease transmitted by the bite of an infected animal

rac-coon (ræ–kuʷn/ –rə) n. 1. A nocturnal North American animal having grayish-brown fur and a bushy tail with black rings 2. The fur of this animal

race (reʸs) n. 1. A competition of speed: *During the Olympics, several races, such as running and swimming, are held.* 2. One of the subdivisions of mankind, each with different physical characteristics, such as skin color, hair, etc.: *The Indians who inhabit North America are members of the red race.* 3. A group of people with the same ancestry, language, customs, etc.: *the Anglo-Saxon race* 4. the human race People in general

race v. raced, racing 1. To compete in a race: *The three boys raced to see which one could run the fastest.* 2. To go very fast: *The ambulance raced the injured man to the hospital.* 3. To cause an animal or vehicle to run a race: *I am going to race my horse against twenty others at the racetrack tomorrow.* 4. Of an engine, to run too fast: *My car needs repair, because the motor races even though I don't put my foot on the gas pedal.*

ra-cial (reʸ–ʃəl) adj. 1. Pertaining to or based on race: *racial characteristics* 2. Occurring be-

SPELLING NOTE:
Words with the sound /r/ may be spelled **wr-**, like **wrote**.

tween races: *racial discrimination* —**racially** adv.

rac-ism (reʸ–sɪz–əm) n. Also **racialism** *derog.* Practices based on the belief that one race is superior to the others; racial discrimination, segregation, etc. —**racist** adj. —**racist** n.

rack (ræk) n. 1. A pole or bar, often with hooks, to hang things on: *coat/towel rack* 2. A framework for holding things: *luggage rack/ magazine rack* 3. A bar with teeth on one face, for gearing with a pinion or worm gear

rack v. 1. To cause to feel great pain or distress: *Following the accident, she was racked with pain for several hours.* 2. To stretch or strain: *He racked his brain for an answer.*

rack-et, also **racq-uet** (ræk–ət) n. A paddle with a long handle connected to a round or oval frame with a network of strings, used for hitting the ball in tennis, badminton, etc.

racket n. 1. *infml.* A loud, on-going noise: *The children were making such a racket we couldn't talk.* 2. *infml.* A dishonest business: *The police caught the men who were running the racket.*

rack-et-eer (ræk–ə–tɪər) n. Person who runs a racket

ra-dar (reʸ–dɑr) n. A method of showing the position of solid objects by receiving radio waves on a screen: *In spite of the fog, the airplane was located by radar.*

ra-di-ance (reʸd–iʸ–əns) n. The quality of being radiant: *The Son [Jesus] is the radiance of God's glory and exact representation of his being...* (Hebrews 1:3).

ra-di-ant (reʸd–iʸ–ənt) adj. 1. Sending out rays of light or heat; shining: *the radiant sun* 2. Showing love and happiness: *The bride's face was radiant./Those who look to him [Jesus] are radiant* (Psalm 34:5). 3. *tech.* Carried by rays of light or heat: *radiant heat* —**radiantly** adv.

ra-di-ate (reʸd–iʸ–eʸt) v. -ated, -ating To send out light or heat: **(a)** *The heat radiated by the burning house forced everyone to move back.* **(b)** *fig. The bride and groom radiated happiness.*

ra-di-a-tion (reʸd–iʸ–eʸ–ʃən) n. 1. The act or process of radiating 2. *Physics* **(a)** The emission and movement of waves, atomic parti-

cles, etc. through space or other media (b) The waves or particles that are emitted

ra·di·a·tor (re^y–di^y–e^y–tər) n. **1.** A device having pipes with steam or hot water flowing through them, used for heating rooms: *On a cold winter day, it feels good to stand in front of a radiator.* **2.** In a motor vehicle, any device which cools the engine: *The car was overheating, because the radiator needed repair.*

rad·i·cal (ræd–ɪ–kəl) adj. **1.** Basic; thorough; complete: *The invention of the automobile made a radical change in methods of transportation.* **2.** In politics, favoring thorough and complete change: *The next election will show which the voters prefer — a radical approach or a conservative one.* —**radically** adv.

radical n. A person in favor of basic and thorough social and political changes: *The radicals won the last election, but I think the conservatives will win the next one.*

ra·di·i (re^yd–i^y–aɪ) n. *pl.* of **radius**

ra·di·o (re^yd–i^y–o^w) n. **-os 1.** Communication by sending and receiving sounds through the air without wires: *The ship used its radio to communicate with the other ship nearby.* **2.** A receiving set for sounds sent through the air: *He heard the news on the radio.*

radio v. **-oed, -oing** To send a message by radio: *The police car radioed for help.*

ra·di·o ac·tive (re^yd–i^y–o^w–æk–tɪv) adj. Giving off rays that are often dangerous but which can be used in medicine —**ra·di·o·ac·tiv·i·ty** (re^yd–i^y–o^w–æk–tɪv–ət–i^y) n.

ra·di·ol·o·gy (re^yd–i^y–ɑl–ə–dʒi^y) n. The science of dealing with x-rays or rays from radioactive substances

ra·di·o·man (re^yd–i^y–o^w–mæn) n. A person who operates a radio or repairs radio equipment

ra·di·o·ther·a·py (re^yd–i^y–o^w–θɛər–ə–pi^y) n. The treatment of diseases by means of x-rays and radioactive substances

rad·ish (ræd–ɪʃ) n. A small vegetable with a red or white root which is eaten raw, usu. in salads

ra·di·um (re^yd–i^y–əm) n. A white, radio-active metal used in treating cancer

ra·di·us (re^yd–i^y–əs) n. **-dii** (–di^y–aɪ) **1.** A straight line from the center of a circle or sphere to its edge or surface —com·pare DIAMETER **2.** A circular area measured by its radius: *That post office serves a rural area within a 20-mile radius of the town.*

raf·fia (ræf–i^y–ə) n. Fiber from the stalks of leaves of a palm tree, used esp. for making baskets and hats

raf·fle (ræf–əl) n. A lottery in which a prize is won by one of the persons buying chances

raffle v. **-fled, -fling** To sell in a raffle

raft (ræft) n. **1.** A flat floating structure, made of wood, empty barrels, etc.: *The two boys floated down the river on a raft.* **2. life raft** A small rubber boat which can be filled with air, carried by planes and ships to save lives in case of emergency

raf·ter (ræf–tər) n. One of the sloping beams that support a roof

rag (ræg) n. **1.** Old torn piece of cloth: *She cleaned the kitchen floor with an old rag./The prophet Isaiah says, "All of us have become like one who is unclean, and all our righteous acts are like filthy rags"* (Isaiah 64:6). **2.** Old worn-out clothing (*pl.*): *The poor little boy was dressed in rags.* **3.** *infml. derog.* A newspaper of low quality: *Don't waste your time by reading that rag!* **4. glad rags** *infml.* Best clothes

rag·a·muf·fin (ræg–ə–mʌf–ən) n. A rag-ged, dirty person

rage (re^ydʒ) n. **1.** Uncontrolled anger; fury: *He flew into a rage when they accused him of cheating.* —see ANGRY **2. all the rage** *infml.* Sthg. fashionable: *Miniskirts were all the rage in the US in the 1960's.*

rage v. **raged, raging 1.** To be very angry/furious: *He raged at the cook for burning the steak.* **2.** To act with violent force: *The battle raged for two days./The storm raged all night.*

rag·ged (ræg–əd) adj. **1.** Worn out and torn: *a ragged pair of pants.* **2.** Wearing torn and worn out clothes: *A ragged beggar asked for money.* —**raggedly** adv. —**raggedness** n.

raid (re^yd) n. **1.** A sudden attack on the enemy: *The Germans flew several air raids over London during the second World War./ fig. He was hungry at midnight, so he made a raid on the refrigerator to get sthg. to eat.* **2.** A sudden visit by police to search for criminals, guns, etc.: *The police discovered a lot of stolen goods*

when they made a raid on the old house. —**raid** v.

raid-er (reʸd–ər) *n.* A person who makes a raid

rail (reʸl) *n.* **1.** A fixed bar, esp. for protection: *The old lady put her hand on the rail as she went down the steps./He stood at the ship's rail, looking back, as it left the port.* **2.** One of the two steel bars forming the track on which a train runs **3. by rail** By train: *Send my shipment by rail.*

rail-ing (reʸ–lɪŋ) *n.* A fence or protective barrier: *They built a railing around the flat roof to keep people from falling off.*

rail-road (reʸl–roʷd) *n.* **1.** A track with rails for trains to run on **2.** A system, including train engines, stations, track, etc., and its administration: *He has worked for the railroad for forty years.*

railroad *v.* To rush sbdy./sthg. unfairly: *Its proponents railroaded the bill through Congress before anyone had had time to consider it carefully.*

railway (reʸl–weʸ) *n.* **1.** Railroad, esp. operating in a small area or with light equipment **2.** Any track with rails for guiding wheels

rain (reʸn) *n.* **1.** Water falling from the clouds: *The rain fell for two days, causing flooding./He [God] sends rain on the righteous and the unrighteous* (Matthew 5:45). *Because of man's wickedness, God destroyed the earth and every living thing, except those with Noah on the ark [large boat]. "Rain fell on the earth 40 days and 40 nights"* (Genesis 7:12). **2.** A heavy fall of sthg. other than water: *A rain of ashes from the burning building fell on nearby houses.* —see WEATHER —**rain** v.

rain-bow (reʸn–boʷ) *n.* An arch of many colors that sometimes forms in the sky opposite the sun during or after rain: *After the great flood that destroyed the whole earth and all mankind, except for Noah and his family, God established a covenant [made a promise] that he would never again destroy the earth by means of a flood. God said to Noah, "I have set my rainbow in the clouds, and it will be a sign of the covenant between me and the earth. Whenever the rainbow appears in the clouds, I will remember the everlasting covenant between*

God and all living creatures..." (Genesis 9:13,16).

rain-coat (reʸn–koʷt) *n.* A waterproof coat for keeping one dry in rainy weather

rain-fall (reʸn–fɔl) *n.* The total amount of water that falls in the form of rain, sleet or snow on a particular area during a certain length of time

rain-y (reʸ–niʸ) *adj.* **-ier, -iest 1.** Marked by continuing rain: *It was a rainy day, so the children played indoors.* **2. for a rainy day** *fig.* For an emergency: *It is wise to save some money while you can for a rainy day, when things are not going well.*

raise (reʸz) *v.* **raised, raising 1.** To lift; push or move sthg. up: *She raised the glass to her lips to take a drink./He [Jesus] was delivered over to death for our sins, and was raised to life for our justification* (Romans 4:25). *If you confess with your mouth, "Jesus is Lord," and believe in your heart that God raised him from the dead, you will be saved [you will have everlasting life]* (Romans 10:9). **2.** To increase in amount, degree, etc.: *Our landlord is going to raise our rent next month./The heater quickly raised the temperature in the room.* **3.** To gather sthg. together: *The group raised money to buy a gift for the director.* **4.** To produce, take care of, etc.: *My father was a farmer and raised corn and wheat; my uncle was a rancher and raised horses./My grandmother raised a family of eight children.* **5.** To speak of: *We need to raise the question of when our meetings will be held next year.* **6.** To cause feelings: *The police report raised our hopes that the lost child would be found.* —see RISE

raise (reʸz) *n. AmE.* **rise (raɪz)** *BrE.* An increase in wages: *The management gave everyone a 10% raise in salary last month.*

rai-sin (reʸz–ən) *n.* A sweet dried grape

ra-jah or **ra-ja (rɑ–dʒə)** *n.* An Indian prince

rake (reʸk) *n.* A long-handled garden tool with a row of metal teeth at the end: *He used the rake to rid the lawn of dead leaves.*

rake *v.* **raked, raking 1.** To gather with a rake: *He raked up some hay for the horses.* **2. rake sthg. in** *infml.* To make a lot of money: *His business is so good right now that he is raking in $100,000 a month.*

ral·ly (ræl–iʸ) v. -lied, -lying 1. To come to-gether for a purpose: *All the members of the class rallied behind their teacher to keep him from losing his job as the result of false charges made against him.* 2. To get well from illness or recover from bad news: *After a month in the hospital, he had rallied enough so that he could go home.* —**rally** n. *The class members held a rally in support of their teacher.*

ram (ræm) v. -mm- 1. To run into sthg. with great force: *The brakes on his car didn't work and he rammed into the car in front of him.* 2. To force into place; stuff: *He rammed everything for the trip into one suitcase.*

ram n. A male sheep

Ram·a·dan (ræm–ə–dɑn) n. The ninth month of the Muslim year, during which no food or drink may be taken between sunrise and sunset

ram·ble (ræm–bəl) v. -bled, -bling 1. To roam about, walk, or stroll having no special goal: *The two friends rambled through the gardens as they talked.* 2. To speak in a confused way: *The old soldier rambled on and on about his war experiences.* —**rambler** n. —**rambling** adj.

ram·i·fi·ca·tion (ræm–ə–fə–keʸ–ʃən) n. 1. Result; consequence 2. The act or process of ramifying

ram·i·fy (ræm–ə–faɪ) v. -fied, -fying To divide and spread out into branches, or as into branches

ramp (ræmp) n. 1. A sloping surface joining two levels, esp. for use of wheeled vehicles: *This hospital has ramps so that patients in wheelchairs may move from one floor to another.* 2. *AmE.* A sloping road for driving onto or off of a highway, expressway, or freeway

ram·page (ræm–peʸdʒ) v. -paged, -pag·ing To rush about violently or angrily: *It was a night of terror, when angry mobs rampaged through the streets breaking into shops and looting.*

ram·pant (ræm–pənt) adj. Spreading un-checked; beyond control, esp. crime, disease, etc.: *Before mosquito control was established, yellow fever was rampant in Panama.* —**rampantly** adv.

ram·part (ræm–part) n. An embankment of earth built to protect a fort or a city; a pro-tective barrier

ram·rod (ræm–rad) n. 1. A rod that is used to push or ram ammunition into the barrel of a gun that is loaded from the muzzle 2. A rod for cleaning the barrel of a firearm

ram·shack·le (ræm–ʃæk–əl) adj. Poorly made or falling to pieces

ran (ræn) v. Past tense of **run**

ranch (ræntʃ) n. A large farm for raising sheep, cattle, or horses, esp. in the western US: *That ranch employs ten cowboys to look after the cattle.*

ranch·er (ræntʃ–ər) n. A person who owns or works on a ranch

ran·cid (ræn–səd) adj. Of oily food or its smell or taste, not fresh: *This butter is rancid.*

ran·cor *AmE.* **ran·cour** *BrE.* (ræŋ–kər) n. Bitter enmity; hatred —**rancorous** adj.

ran·dom (ræn–dəm) adj. 1. Having no pattern; without any plan: *As the police were shooting at the robbers, a random bullet hit a man standing nearby.* 2. **at random (a)** Aimlessly; by chance **(b)** In a haphazard way —**random** n.

rang (ræŋ) v. Past tense of **ring**

range (reʸndʒ) n. 1. A row, line, or series, esp. of mountains: *You can see the mountain range in the distance.* 2. A limited area, usu. with a target, for practicing shooting, etc.: *a firing range/a golf range/archery range* 3. In western US, a wide area of grassy land where cattle, sheep, etc., may roam and feed 4. The distance at which a person can see or hear: *He can't hear me, because he is out of the range of my voice.* 5. The maximum distance that a gun, etc., can fire: *What is the range of that missile?* 6. The extent of variation: *The temperature range in that place may be as great as 40 degrees in one day./The price range of houses in this town is from $25,000 to $100,000.* 7. A variety of objects of the same kind: *That store carries a wide range of sporting goods.* 8. A large kitchen stove

range v. ranged, ranging 1. To indicate varia-tion within set limits: *The ages of the students ranged from 18 to 24.* 2. To wander; move over a wide area: *Deer range through the woods of the northern part of the US./Our dis-cussion ranged over a variety of subjects.*

rang-er (re^yn–dʒər) n. (in North America) **(a)** A person who guards national forests and parks **(b)** A guard on horseback in a rural area

rank (ræŋk) n. **1.** An official position, esp. in the military: *In twenty years, he rose from the rank of lieutenant to the rank of general.* **2.** Social position or class: *The bank president was included in the upper ranks of society in the town.* **3. rank and file** The ordinary people in a group, in the army, etc., not the leaders or officers

rank v. To be put in a position or class: *This university ranks as one of the best in the country.*

rank adj. Unpleasant in smell or taste

rank-ing (ræŋ–kŋ) adj. **1.** Having a high position; foremost **2.** Taking precedence over others

rank-le (ræŋ–kəl) v. **-led, -ling** To cause lasting annoyance, bitterness, etc.

ran-sack (ræn-sæk/ ræn-sæk) v. **1.** To search thoroughly: *She ransacked her purse for the keys.* **2.** To search and rob: *The thief ransacked the house in search of silver and gold.*

ran-som (ræn-səm) n. A sum of money paid for freeing a prisoner or hostage: *The guerrillas are demanding a $10,000 ransom for the release of the prisoner./For there is one God and one mediator between God and men, the man Christ Jesus, who gave himself as a ransom for all men* (1 Timothy 2:6). —see JESUS **—ransom** v.

rant (rænt) v. To speak wildly and loudly: *He ranted on and on about the evils of our society.*

rap (ræp) n. **1.** A quick light knock: *They heard a soft rap on the door.* **2.** *infml.* A conversation

rap v. **-pp-** To hit quickly and lightly: *The teacher rapped on her desk to get her students' attention.*

ra-pa-cious (rə-pe^y-ʃəs) adj. **1.** Greedy; grasping **2.** Plundering **3.** Predatory

rape (re^yp) v. **raped, raping** To have sex with a person against his or her will

rape n. The act and crime of raping

rap-ist (re^y-pəst) n. A man who has committed rape

rap-id (ræp–əd) adj. Quick; fast: *They made a rapid visit to the new factory.* **—ra-pid-i-ty** (rə-pɪd–ət–i^y) n. **—rapidly** adv. *He walked rapidly across the campus.*

rapid n. *usu. pl.* A place in a river where the water flows very fast, usu. over rocks: *It is difficult to ride a boat over the rapids in this river.*

rap-port (rə-por/ ræ–) n. Harmony of relation; agreement and understanding

rap-proche-ment (ræp-ro^wʃ–mɑⁿ/ræp-ro^wʃ-mɑⁿ) n. Renewal of friendly relations, esp. between nations

rapt (ræpt) adj. Deeply interested; enraptured: *She listened to the speaker with rapt attention.*

rap-ture (ræp–tʃər) n. **1.** The state of being carried away with deep emotion; ecstatic joy **2.** An expression of great joy

rare (reər) adj. **1.** Not common; not often found: *He had to pay a high price for that rare book./Lips that speak knowledge are a rare jewel* (Proverbs 20:15). **2.** Thin, esp. air at high altitudes: *They had difficulty breathing at the top of the mountain because of the rare air.* **3.** Lightly-cooked meat: *I like steak rare, but my wife likes it well done.* **—rarely** adv. **—compare** SCARCELY

ra-re-fy (reər-ə-faɪ) v. **-fied, -fying 1.** To make rare or less dense **2.** To refine or purify **3.** To become thin or less dense

rar-ing (reər–ŋ) adj. *infml.* Very eager: *He was raring to get started on the new job.*

rar-i-ty (reər-ə-ti^y) n. **-ties** Something rare; uncommon

ras-cal (ræs-kəl) n. **1.** A mean, dishonest person: *The police caught the rascal who had stolen money from the poor old lady.* **2.** A naughty child: *That little rascal has taken my glasses!*

rash (ræʃ) adj. Foolish; too hasty: *a rash action* **—rashly** adv.

rash n. **1.** Redness or small red spots on the skin, caused by illness or allergy: *It's such a hot day that the baby has developed a heat rash.* **2.** *fig.* A large number of sthg. in a short time; outbreak: *There has been a rash of brush fires during this hot, dry weather.*

rasp (ræsp) v. **1.** To scrape or rub with or as if with a rough instrument **2.** To make a grating sound **3.** To irritate

rasp n. **1.** A coarse file **2.** Any similar tool **3.** A

harsh, grating noise

rasp-ber-ry (ræz–bɛər–i⁽ʸ⁾) n. -ries A soft sweet red berry which grows on a bush

rat (ræt) n. 1. A small long-tailed animal similar to but larger than a mouse 2. *infml.* A person who betrays or deserts others: *That rat has not only left us but has also taken all our money!* 3. **smell a rat** *infml.* To guess that sthg. is wrong: *She said she stayed home that night, but I smell a rat because I saw her in the park about 8:00 p.m.*

rat v. *slang* To betray one's associates

ratch-et (rætʃ–ət) n. 1. A device consisting of a toothed wheel with a catch that fits between the teeth allowing movement in only one direction 2. **ratchet wheel** The wheel that forms part of this device

rate (reʸt) n. 1. Amount of sthg. compared to some other amount: *The airplane flew at the rate of 500 miles an hour.* 2. **the birth rate** The number of babies born each year: *The birth rate in this city increased by ten per cent during the past year.* 3. A charge or payment based on a fixed scale: *The rate for electricity has not gone up for the past three years.* 4. Of certain quality (with first as best): *In the show we saw last night, I thought the music was first-rate, but the acting was only second-rate.* 5. **at any rate** In any case; whatever may happen/has happened: *At any rate, he got to work on time, even though the bus broke down on the way.* 6. **at this/that rate** If the situation continues as it is now: *At this rate we won't be able to finish this assignment today.* 7. **rate of exchange** The relative value between the money of two countries: *What is the rate of exchange between the British pound and the American dollar today?*

rate (reʸt) v. **rated, rating** To consider; regard; set the value of: *John rates Bob as one of his best friends.* —**rating** n.

rath-er (ræ♭–ər) adv. 1. To some extent; quite: *It was a rather difficult lesson./Those trees are rather tall.* 2. **would rather** Prefer: *Would you rather have tea or coffee?* 3. Instead of: *He'll telephone rather than write a letter.*

rat-i-fy (ræt–ə–faɪ) v. **-fied, -fying** To approve officially and formally —**rat-i-fi-ca-tion** (ræt–ə–fə–keʸ–ʃən) n.

rat-ing (reʸt–ɪŋ) n. 1. Classification according to grade or rank 2. The credit standing of an individual or firm 3. A percentage indicating the number of listeners to or viewers of a particular radio or TV program

ra-tio (reʸ–ʃiʸ–oʷ/ –ʃoʷ) n. **-tios** The amount of one thing compared to another: *There is a ratio of five teachers to 250 students in this school; that is, each teacher has fifty students.* —compare PROPORTION

ra-tion (ræʃ–ən/ reʸ–ʃən) n. A limited amount of food, gasoline, etc., allowed to one person for a fixed period of time, during a war or other time of short supply: *During the war, the meat ration was two pounds per person per week.* —**ration** v.

ra-tio-nal (ræʃ–ə–nəl) adj. 1. Able to reason: *Is it true that men are more rational and women are more emotional?* 2. Sensible; logical; reasonable: *Is there a rational explanation for her fears?* —opposite IRRATIONAL —**ra-tion-al-i-ty** (ræʃ–ə–næl–ət–i⁽ʸ⁾) n. —**rationally** adv.

ra-tion-ale (ræʃ–ə–næl) n. *fml.* The basic reason(s): *The rationale behind their moving the factory is that costs are lower in the new location.*

ra-tio-nal-ize (ræʃ–ən–əl–aɪz) also -**ise** *BrE.* v. -**ized, -izing** To cause an action, attitude, etc., to seem reasonable: *He rationalized taking money from the office by saying he planned to put it back.* —**ra-tio-nal-i-za-tion** (ræʃ–ən-əl-ə-zeʸ–ʃən) n.

rat race (ræt reʸs) n. Strenuous and generally competitive activity: *After this year-long rat race, I need a vacation.*

rat-tan (ræ–tæn/rə–) n. 1. The long tough flexible stem of various tropical palm trees, used in making wickerwork 2. The palm itself

rat-tle (ræt–əl) v. -**tled, -tling** 1. To make a series of short, sharp sounds: *The cook was rattling the dishes as she prepared dinner./The old car rattled along the bumpy road.* 2. *infml.* To get upset or nervous: *She got so rattled that she even forgot her own name!* 3. **rattle sthg. off** To speak quickly and easily, usu. from memory: *He rattled off the names of his cousins.* 4. **rattle on/away** To talk rapidly and continuously: *She rattled on about her trip*

abroad, but no one was really listening to her.

rat-tle n. 1. The sound of rattling: *His car needed repair, because there was a rattle in the motor.* 2. A toy or instrument that makes a rattling noise: *The baby shook the rattle.*

rat-tle-brain (ræt–əl–breʸn) n. An emptyheaded, talkative person

rat-tle-snake n. (ræt–əl–sneʸk) A poisonous snake with a rattle at the end of its tail

rat-tle-trap n. (ræt–əl–træp) Sthg. rickety and noisy; full of rattles: *That old car is a real rattle trap.*

rat-trap (ræt–træp) n. 1. A trap for catching rats 2. An old run-down, filthy place

rat-ty (ræt–iʸ) adj. -tier, -tiest 1. Full of rats 2. Wretched; shabby

rau-cous (rɔ–kəs) adj. 1. Harsh; hoarse 2. Rowdy or disorderly —**raucously** adv.

raun-chy (rɔn–tʃiʸ) adj. -chier, -chiest 1. Dirty; nasty; filthy 2. Obscene or smutty

rav-age (ræv–ɪdʒ) v. -aged, -aging 1. To ruin: *The crops were ravaged by the hail-storm.* 2. To cause violent destruction as by an invading army —**ravage** n. *the ravages of war*

rave (reʸv) v. raved, raving 1. To speak wildly and usu. loudly: *He raved at the man who had tried to cheat him.* 2. **rave about sbdy./sthg.** *infml.* To speak about very favorably: *They raved about the excellent new play they had just seen.*

—**raving** adj. —**raving** adv. *He's raving mad.*

rav-el (ræv–əl) v. -eled or -elled, -eling or -elling 1. To become tangled and knotted 2. To become unwoven 3. To draw out the threads of (a woven fabric) 4. To cause to become untwisted

ra-ven (reʸ–vən) n. A large black bird of the crow family, having a loud, harsh call

rav-en-ing (ræv–ə–nɪŋ) adj. Greedy for prey

rav-en-ous (ræv–ə–nəs) adj. Violently voracious or hungry: *a ravenous beast/a ravenous appetite*

ra-vine (rə–viʸn) n. A deep gorge or gully, esp. one made by a river or stream

rav-ish (ræv–ɪʃ) v. 1. To fill with delight 2. To rape

rav-ish-ing (ræv–ɪʃ–ɪŋ) adj. Very beautiful; enchanting

raw (rɔ) adj. 1. Not cooked: *raw vegetables* 2. In the natural state; not yet manufactured: *raw cotton* 3. **raw materials** Natural substances used in manufacturing: *Iron ore is the basic raw material used in making steel.* 4. **raw deal** *infml.* Unfair treatment

ray (reʸ) n. 1. A beam of light or heat: *The sun's rays came through the crack in the old wall./fig. a ray (=a little bit) of hope* 2. One of the lines radiating out from a center point

ray-on (reʸ–ɑn) n. 1. A synthetic fiber made from cellulose 2. Cloth made from such fibers

raze (reʸz) v. razed, razing 1. To demolish, as a building 2. To scrape or shave off

ra-zor (reʸ–zər) n. A sharp, sometimes electric, instrument for removing hair from the skin: *He shaves his face with an electric razor every morning.*

razz (ræz) v. To heckle; deride

Rd. (roʷd) *written abbr.* Said as **road**

re– (riʸ–) prefix Again; anew: *readjust/ reaffirm/reappear/ rearm/rearrange*

reach (riʸtʃ) v. 1. To go as far as; arrive at: *They reached London on Tuesday.* 2. To stretch one's hand out or up for some purpose: *I reached up and replaced the light bulb in the ceiling.* 3. To touch sthg. by stretching out a hand: *Can you reach those cherries on the lower branch?*

reach n. 1. The distance that one can touch; the length of one's arm: *He likes to keep paper and pencil within reach./Mrs. Brown has a longer reach than her little girl.* 2. **within/out of reach** *The goal he had set for himself was within his reach./Keep that bottle of poison out of the children's reach.*

re-act (riʸ–ækt) v. To act in response; to change as a result of someone else's action: *He reacted to the good news by shouting for joy.*

re-ac-tion (riʸ–æk–ʃən) n. 1. Responsive action or attitude 2. A trend toward an earlier social, political, or economic policy or condition 3. The response of a muscle, nerve, etc. to a stimulus 4. *Med.* Response, esp. adverse, to a drug or serum: *The doctor observed the patient's reaction to a skin test for TB.*

re-ac-tion-ar-y (riʸ–æk–ʃə–neər–iʸ) n. -ies One who favors political or social reaction

reactionary adj. Pertaining to or favoring reaction

re-ac-tor (rĭᵞ–ǽk–tər) n. A device in which atoms are split under controlled conditions, resulting in heat used to generate electricity and radioactive substances

read (rĭᵞd) v. read (rɛd) reading (rĭᵞd–ĭŋ) **1.** To understand printed or written words or drawings: *Have you ever read the Bible daily?/ Can you read music/a map?* **2.** To get the stated information from print or writing: *I read about God's love for us.* **3.** To record and show measurements: *The thermometer reads 41 degrees.* **4.** To understand another person's thoughts: *You yourselves are our letter, written on our hearts, known and read by everybody* (2 Corinthians 3:2). —**readable** adj.

read-er (rĭᵞd–ər) n. **1.** A person who reads **2.** A book for children learning to read or others learning a foreign language

read-i-ly (rɛd–əl–ĭᵞ) adv. **1.** Willingly **2.** Without difficulty: *Fresh fruit can be bought readily anywhere in town.*

read-i-ness (rɛd–ĭᵞ–nəs) n. **1.** Willingness or eagerness **2.** The state of being ready or prepared

read-ing (rĭᵞd–ĭŋ) n. **1.** The act or practice of reading **2.** A measurement on a thermometer, dial, etc.: *The temperature reading was 25 degrees.* **3.** Sthg. to read: *These magazines are good reading for those interested in sports.*

reading adj. For reading: *a reading lamp/ reading glasses*

re-ad-just (rĭᵞ–ə–dʒʌst) v. To adjust again **(a)** Put back into the right position: *I need to readjust this lamp so that it shines on my book.* **(b)** Change to fit a different situation: *When he returned from a year's study in France, my son had to readjust to life in the US.* —**readjustment** n.

read-y (rɛd–ĭᵞ) adj. -ier, -iest **1.** Prepared to do sthg.; in condition to be used, eaten, etc.: *Dinner is ready. Please come and eat!* **2.** Willing: *Jane is always ready to help.*

re-al (rĭᵞl) adj. Actually existing; not imitation; genuine: *Is that real silver?*

real adv. *infml.* Very: *I'm real glad that you're here.*

real estate (rĭᵞl ə–steᵞt) n. **1.** Property in land and buildings **2.** Buildings and land to be bought or sold

re-al-ism (rĭᵞ–ə–lĭz–əm) n. **1.** Behavior based on facts, not on feelings **2.** True and faithful portrayal of nature and of people by means of art or literature —**realist** n. —**re-al-is-tic** (rĭᵞ–ə–lĭs–tĭk) adj. —**realistically** adv.

re-al-i-ty (rĭᵞ–ǽl–ə–tĭᵞ) n. -ties **1.** The quality or state of being real; truth: *The fruit on the table looked good enough to eat, but in reality it was artificial.* **2.** Sthg. real: *Their dream of owning a house became a reality.*

re-al-ize (rĭᵞ–ə–laɪz) also **-ise** *BrE.* v. **-ized, -izing 1.** To understand fully and accept as a fact: *We suddenly realized we had gone too far, so we had to turn around and go back.* **2.** To make real; fulfill a hope or goal: *She realized her dream of becoming a doctor.* **3.** *fml.* To make a profit by selling property: *By selling the business, they realized a profit of $10,000.* —**re-al-i-za-tion** (rĭᵞ–ə–lə–zeᵞ–ʃən) n.

re-al-ly (rĭᵞ–ə–lĭᵞ / rĭᵞ–lĭᵞ) adv. **1.** Actually: *I really don't know.* **2.** Very: *That's a really beautiful dress!*

realm (rɛlm) n. **1.** A kingdom: *Praise be to the God and Father of our Lord Jesus Christ, who has blessed us in the heavenly realms with every spiritual blessing in Christ* (Ephesians 1:3). **2.** Area of interest or activity: *the realm of economics*

re-al-tor (rĭᵞ–əl–tər) n. *AmE.* Real estate agent

ream (rĭᵞm) n. **1.** A measure for sheets of paper, variously 480, 500, or 516 sheets **2.** *infml.* A large quantity of writing: *She has written reams but never had anything published.*

reap (rĭᵞp) v. To cut and gather grain: *It's time to reap the wheat./ fig. to reap a reward/a profit/ Do not be deceived: God cannot be mocked. A man reaps what he sows. The one who sows to please his sinful nature, from that nature will reap destruction; the one who sows to please the Spirit, from the Spirit will reap eternal life* (Galatians 6:7,8). —compare HARVEST —opposite SOW

reap-er (rĭᵞ–pər) n. A person or machine that reaps

re-ap-pear (rĭᵞ–ə–pɪər) v. To appear again

rear (rɪər) v. **1.** To care for children until fully

grown: *Johnny's grandmother reared him after his parents died* ?. Of a four-legged animal, to raise itself up on the back legs: *The horse reared and threw the rider off.* **3.** To lift up; raise: *The snake suddenly reared its head./fig. An obstacle has just reared its ugly head.*

rear n. **1.** The back: *She rents a room at the rear of the building.* —compare FRONT **2.** *euph.* The part of the body on which one sits; buttocks **3. bring up the rear** To be last, as in a procession: *The children marched up the stairs to go to bed, the smallest one bringing up the rear.*

rea-son (ri^{y}z–ən) n. **1.** Purpose; cause; explanation or excuse: *The reason he arrived late was that he got lost on the way.* **2.** The power to think, understand, and decide: *My reason tells me that we should leave now before things get worse.* **3. listen to reason** To be persuaded by good advice **4. anything within reason** Anything reasonable, sensible, or needed: *She'll do anything within reason for money, but she won't steal.* **5. it stands to reason** Obviously; most people would agree: *It stands to reason that the car will not run without gasoline.*

reason v. **1.** To use one's power to think: *The prophet Isaiah writes: "Come now, let us reason together... Though your sins are like scarlet, they shall be as white as snow..."* (Isaiah 1:18). *This was a prophecy of Jesus, who suffered and died on the cross for our sins: "The blood of Jesus ... purifies us from all sin"* (1 John 1:7). —see JESUS **2.** To think about and decide: *He reasoned that because his book was not where he had left it, someone else must have taken it.* —**reasoned** adj. —**reasoning** n.

rea-son-a-ble (ri^{y}z–ən–ə–bəl) adj. **1.** Ready to use reason: *Carrying an umbrella when the weather is rainy is a reasonable thing to do.* —opposite UNREASONABLE —compare LOGICAL **2.** Esp. of prices, fair; not too expensive: *This store charges reasonable prices.* —**reasonableness** n. —**reasonably** adv.

re-as-sure (ri^y–ə–ʃʊər) v. **-sured, -suring** To take away a person's doubts or fears —**reassurance** n.

re-bate (ri^y–be^{y}t) n. A partial refund of a payment: *The manufacturer gave us a $50 rebate*

when we bought our new refrigerator. —compare DISCOUNT

re-bel (ri–bɛl) v. **-ll-** To fight against people in power, esp. the government: *The students rebelled against the school authorities.* —**re-bel-lious** (ri–bɛl–yəs) adj.

reb-el (rɛb–əl) n. A person who rebels

re-bel-lion (ri–bɛl–yən) n. A violent attack, usu. unsuccessful, against the government or other authority: *The government forces were able to stop the rebellion led by the army captain.* —com-pare REVOLUTION

re-birth (ri^y–bərθ/ ri^y–bərθ) n. A renewal of life; revival: *the rebirth of learning*

re-born (ri^y–bɔrn) adj. Revived; *fig.* born again: *His hope of victory was reborn.*

re-bound (ri^y–baʊnd) v. To bounce back: *The ball hit the window but rebounded without breaking it.* —**rebound** (ri^y–baʊnd) n.

re-buff (ri–bʌf) n. A blunt rejection or refusal —**rebuff** v.

re-build (ri^y–bɪld) v. **-built (–bɪlt), -building** To build again: *Their house was blown down by the hurricane, but they immediately started to rebuild it.*

re-buke (ri^y–byu^{w}k) v. **-buked, -buking** To speak strongly to, usu. because of wrongdoing: *Rebuke a wise man and he will love you* (Proverbs 9:8). *If your brother sins, rebuke him, and if he repents, forgive him* (Luke 17:3). *Jesus rebuked his disciples for their lack of faith and their stubborn refusal to believe those who had seen him after he had risen from the dead* (Mark 16:14). —**rebuke** n.

re-but (ri–bʌt) v. To deny sthg. that has been said —**rebuttal** n.

re-cal-ci-trant (ri–kæl–sə–trənt) adj. Stubborn; disobedient —**recalcitrance** n.

re-call (ri–kɔl) v. **1.** To bring to memory: *I met that man last week, but I can't recall his name.* **2.** To call for the return of sbdy./ sthg.: *The manufacturer recalled the cars that had unsafe brakes.*

re-call (ri^y–kɔl) n. **1.** A command to return: *The recall of the ambassador was a surprise.* **2. total recall** The ability to remember sthg. learned or experienced

re-cant (ri–kænt) v. **1.** To take back what one has said **2.** To reject publicly one's beliefs

—**re·can·ta·tion** (riᵞ–kæn–teᵞ–ʃən) n.

re·cap (riᵞ–kæp) Short for **recapitulation** or **recapitulate**

re·ca·pit·u·late (riᵞ–kə–pɪtʃ–ə–leᵞt) v. **-lated, -lating** To repeat the main points of sthg. that has been said: *The sports announcer recapitulated all the scoring immediately after the game.* —**re·ca·pit·u·la·tion** (riᵞ–kə–pɪtʃ–ə–leᵞ–ʃən) n.

re·cap·ture (riᵞ–kæp–tʃər) v. **-tured, -turing 1.** To capture someone or some animal that has escaped or sthg. that had been taken by the enemy **2.** To experience again: *Visiting her home town, she recaptured the joys of her youth.*

re·cede (rɪ–siᵞd) v. **-ceded, -ceding 1.** To move back or away from: *His hair receded quite a bit when he was between 50 and 60 years old.* **2.** To become less or smaller; go down: *The water receded after the flood.*

re·ceipt (rɪ–siᵞt) n. **1.** A written acknowledgement that sthg. (money or goods) has been received **2. receipts** Income received from a business: *The director reported that receipts had increased in the past year.*

re·ceive (rɪ–siᵞv) v. **-ceived, -ceiving 1.** To get; to be given sthg.: *Did you receive my letter?/It is more blessed to give than to receive* (Acts 20:35). *All the prophets testify about him [Jesus] that everyone who believes in him receives forgiveness of sins through his name* (Acts 10:43). **2.** To admit as a visitor or member; welcome: *We always received visitors warmly into our home.*

re·ceiv·er (rɪ–siᵞ–vər) n. **1.** The part of a telephone that receives the sound and is held to one's ear **2.** On an American football team, one who receives (catches) the football when it is passed (thrown) to him **3.** A radio or television set

re·cent (riᵞs–ənt) adj. Happening a short time ago: *Recent events show that the new president is able to handle the situation.* —**recently** adv.

re·cep·ta·cle (rɪ–sep–tɪ–kəl) n. A container; an object to retain or hold things

re·cep·tion (rɪ–sep–ʃən) n. **1.** An act of receiving or being received; welcome: *The new director got a friendly reception from the office employees.* **2.** A large formal social occasion

to welcome sbdy.: *a wedding reception* **3.** BrE. for **reception desk 4.** The receiving of radio or television signals: *Radio reception isn't very good tonight.*

re·cep·tion·ist (rɪ–sep–ʃən–ɪst) n. An employee who receives people arriving at a hotel, a doctor's office, etc.

re·cep·tive (rɪ–sep–tɪv) adj. Ready to consider new ideas, suggestions, etc.: *a receptive mind/student*

re·cess (riᵞ–ses) n. **1.** A period of time taken out of the work day or year for rest: *Congress is in recess for the summer./In our school, the children have their morning recess from 10:15 to 10:30.* **2.** A space set back in the wall of a room to allow for shelves, cupboards, etc.

re·ces·sion (rɪ–seʃ–ən) n. **1.** A temporary period of reduced business activity: *The recession caused a decrease in employment.* **2.** The act of receding **3.** A departing procession, as the choir at the close of a church service —**recessional** n.

re·ci·pe (res–ə–piᵞ) n. A set of instructions for cooking or baking sthg.: *She followed her friend's recipe for making chocolate cake./fig. They have a fine recipe for a happy marriage.*

re·cip·i·ent (rɪ–sɪp–iᵞ–ənt) n. One who, or that which receives

re·cip·ro·cal (rɪ–sɪp–rə–kəl) adj. Mutual; both given and received: *their reciprocal affection* —**reciprocally** adv.

re·cip·ro·cate (rɪ–sɪp–rə–keᵞt) v. **-cated, -cating** To feel or do the same in return: *They gave us gifts and we reciprocated by giving gifts to them.*

rec·i·proc·i·ty (res–ə–prɑs–ət–iᵞ) n. **-ties** Principle or practice of mutual exchange, esp. granting privileges in exchange for privileges granted

re·cit·al (rɪ–saɪt–əl) n. **1.** A public delivery (speech) of sthg. memorized **2.** A telling over in detail, or that which is told **3.** A concert given by an individual musician or dancer, or by a troupe of dancers **4.** A public display of talent and skill by music or dance pupils

re·cite (rɪ–saɪt) v. **-cited, -citing 1.** To repeat from memory sthg. that one has learned,

esp. publicly: *The child recited the poem correctly.* **2.** To tell in detail, esp. to give a list of: *He recited the names of the guests who were coming to the party.* —**rec-i-ta-tion** (rɛs–ə–te^y–ʃən) n.

reck-less (rɛk–ləs) adj. Of a person or behavior, too quick; not caring about danger to oneself or others: *reckless driving/ Reckless words pierce like a sword, but the tongue of the wise brings healing* (Proverbs 12:18). *A wise man fears the Lord and shuns evil, but a fool is hotheaded and reckless* (Proverbs 14:16). —**recklessness** n.

reck-on (rɛk–ən) v. **1.** To consider that sthg. is as stated; regard: *He is reckoned among the finest musicians of our time.* **2.** *infml.* To suppose: *I reckon I'll finish my work by supper time.* **3.** To calculate time, price, age, etc.: *My rent is reckoned from the 15th of the month.* **4. reckon with (a)** To have to face possible bad results: *If you hurt that child, you'll have his father to reckon with.* **(b) to be reckoned with** To be considered seriously as a possible opponent, competitor, danger, etc.: *Earthquakes are sthg. to be reckoned with in California.*

reck-on-ing (rɛk–ə–nɪŋ) n. **1.** The act or result of calculating: *By my reckoning, we should arrive home in about two hours.* **2. day of reckoning** The time when one will be punished for a mistake or wrongdoing

re-claim (rɪ–kle^ym) v. **1.** To have possession of sthg. returned to one: *Our car was reclaimed by the finance company when we couldn't make the monthly payments.* **2.** To make suitable for use: *They are reclaiming land from the sea.* **3.** To make a waste product into sthg. useful: *to reclaim paper from old magazines and newspapers/ aluminum from soda cans*

re-cline (rɪ^y–klaɪm) v. **-clined, -clining** To lie back or down, esp. for rest during the day: *She likes to recline on the sofa in the afternoon.*

rec-luse (rɛk–lu^ws/rɪ–klu^ws) n. A person who lives alone and avoids other people

rec-og-ni-tion (rɛk–ɪg–nɪʃ–ən) n. The act of recognizing: *He received recognition for his act of bravery.*

rec-og-nize (rɛk–ɪg–naɪz) *AmE.* Also **-nise** *BrE.* v. **-nized, -nizing 1.** To be able to identify sthg. or sbdy. one has seen before: *He recognized his cousin even though he had not seen her for ten years.* **2.** To accept as being lawful or genuine, or as having value: *This is how you can recognize the Spirit of God: Every spirit that acknowledges that Jesus Christ has come in the flesh is from God, but every spirit that does not acknowledge Jesus is not from God* (1 John 4:2). **3.** To see sthg. as true; realize: *Because I recognized that his facts were correct, I changed my opinion on the subject.* **4.** To show official appreciation for: *On his retirement, the company recognized his long years of service by giving him a gold watch.* —**recognizable** adj. —**recognizably** adv.

rec-ol-lect (rɛk–ə–lɛkt) v. To remember —**recollection** n.

rec-om-mend (rɛk–ə–mɛnd) v. **1.** To have and communicate a favorable opinion of; praise: *I was glad to recommend Mary for the job.* **2.** To advise or suggest: *If you're in a hurry, I recommend that you go by plane rather than by train.* **3.** To make sbdy. or sthg. pleasing or attractive: *This house has nothing to recommend it except its good location.* —**rec-om-men-da-tion** (rɛk–ə–mən–de^y–ʃən) n.

re-com-mit (rɪ^y–kə–mɪt) v. **-tt- 1.** To commit again **2.** To refer back to a committee, as a bill —**recommittal** n.

rec-om-pense (rɛk–əm–pɛns) v. **-pensed, -pensing** n. To pay money to or reward a person for damages suffered, etc.

recompense n. A repayment or reward

rec-on-cile (rɛk–ən–saɪl) v. **-ciled, -ciling 1.** To make peace between persons or groups: *God was reconciling the world to himself in Christ, not counting men's sins against them ... We implore you on Christ's behalf: Be reconciled to God. God made him who knew no sin to be sin for us, so that in him we might become the righteousness of God* (2 Corinthians 5:19-21). **2.** To find agreement between opposing points of view: *After long discussions, the management and the union reconciled their differences and the strike was settled.* —**rec-on-cil-a-ble** (rɛk–ən–saɪl–ə–bəl) adj.

rec-on-cil-i-a-tion (rɛk–ən–sɪl–i^y–e^y–ʃən) n. The act of reconciling; peace-making: *God was reconciling the world to himself in Christ,*

not counting men's sins against them. And he has committed to us the message of reconciliation (2 Corinthians 5:19).

re·con·di·tion (riʸ–kən–dɪ–ʃən) v. To repair and put back into working order, usu. using new parts: *After the mechanic reconditioned the car, it ran like new.*

re·con·nais·sance (n–kɑn–ə–səns/ –zəns) n. A survey or close examination of an area, esp. for obtaining useful information regarding enemy troops

re·con·noi·ter (riʸ–kə–nɔɪt–ər) v. To make a reconnaissance

re·con·sid·er (riʸ–kən–sɪd–ər) v. To consider again; think again with the possibility of changing one's mind: *We asked him to reconsider his decision to leave, so he stayed for another month.* —**re·con·sid·er·a·tion** (riʸ–kən–sɪd–ə–reʸ–ʃən) n.

re·con·sti·tute (riʸ–kɑn–stə–tuʷt) v. **-tuted, -tuting** To restore to its original form

re·con·struct (riʸ–kən–strʌkt) v. To rebuild sthg. after it has been damaged or destroyed: *The town had to be reconstructed after the earthquake.* —**recon·struction** n.

re·cord (riʸ–kɔrd) v. **1.** To write down information for future reference: *She recorded the events of the day, so that the information could be used later.* **2.** To preserve sounds to be heard again: *Beethoven's Fifth Symphony has been recorded by several orchestras.* **3.** To preserve a television program so that it can be seen again **4.** To show a measurement: *The thermometer recorded a temperature of 35 degrees.*

rec·ord (rek–ərd) n. **1.** A written statement of information: *We kept a record of our expenses on the trip.* **2.** The facts about someone's past actions: *If you, O Lord, kept a record of sins, O Lord, who would stand? But with you there is forgiveness* (Psalm 130:3,4). **3.** The best or worst yet done: *The temperature set a record here yesterday of 125 degrees.* **4.** A flat round piece of plastic on which sound is preserved: *Have you heard the record of Bing Crosby singing "White Christmas"?* **5. off the record** *infml.* Not intended to be made public: *He told me off the record that the president was dying of cancer.* **6. on record** Information

kept for future use: *This is the hottest summer on record.*

record adj. The best ever done: *They finished the job in record time thanks to the new machinery.*

re·cord·er (n–kɔrd–ər) n. **1.** Sbdy. or sthg. that records: *a tape recorder* **2.** A flute with eight finger holes and a mouthpiece resembling a whistle

re·cord·ing (n–kɔrd–ŋ) n. Recorded sounds of a performance, speech, etc.: *Many recordings have been made of that song.*

re·count (riʸ–kɑʊnt) v. To count again

re·count (n–kɑʊnt) v. To tell a story

re·count (riʸ–kɑʊnt) n. A second count: *The candidate who lost the election demanded a recount.*

re·coup (n–kuʷp) v. To recover expenses, losses, etc.

re·course (riʸ–kɔrs) n. **1.** A turning to sbdy. or sthg. for protection or assistance **2.** A source of assistance

re·cov·er (n–kʌv–ər) v. **1.** To regain possession of sthg. lost or taken away: *He was glad to recover the wallet that he had left at the restaurant.* **2.** To return to good health, strength, ability, etc.: *He has not recovered the use of his leg since the accident last year.* —**recoverable** adj. —**recovery** n.

re·cov·er (riʸ–kʌv–ər) v. To put a new cover on: *Do you know how to recover a sofa? This one is getting worn.*

re·cov·er·y (riʸ–kʌv–ər–iʸ) n. **1.** A return to good health **2.** The act of getting back sthg. that was lost or stolen

re·cre·ate (riʸ–kriʸ–eʸt) v. **-ated, -ating** To create again; make again: *Visiting my home town after an absence of thirty years helped me recreate in my mind the scenes of my childhood.*

rec·re·a·tion (rek–riʸ–eʸ–ʃən) n. A form of amusement; enjoyable activities (as contrasted to work): *His favorite form of recreation is playing golf.* NOTE: A **sport** is a physical activity usu. played in a special area and following fixed rules. A **game** is a form of physical or mental activity or a competition played according to rules. Golf, **tennis**, chess, and cards are all games. Golf and tennis are also sports. A **hobby** is a pleasurable

activity that people usu. do on their own, not in order to compete and not as a part of their regular work. Collecting coins, quilting, and writing poetry, etc. are hobbies. Sports, games, and **hobbies** are all types of recreation. —**recreational** adj.

re-crim-i-nate (riᵞ–krɪm–ə–neᵞt) v. -**nated, -nating** To bring a countercharge against an accuser

re-crim-i-na-tion (rɪ–krɪm–ə–neᵞ–ʃən) n. An accusation made by sbdy. who himself is accused —**re-crim-i-na-to-ry** (rɪ–krɪm–ə–nə–tɔr–iᵞ) adj.

re-cruit (rɪ–kruʷt) n. **1.** A newly enlisted or drafted member of the armed forces **2.** A new member of any organization

recruit v. **1.** To enlist someone for military service **2.** To engage or hire new members, employees, etc.

rec-tan-gle (rɛk–tæŋ–gəl) n. tech. A figure with four sides and four right angles —compare SQUARE —**rect-an-gu-lar** (rɛk–tæŋ–gyə–lər) adj.

rec-ti-fy (rɛk–tə–faɪ) v. -**fied, -fying** fml. To make right; correct: *The bank was able to rectify its mistake in my account.* —**rec-ti-fi-ca-tion** (rɛk–tə–fə–keᵞ–ʃən) n.

rec-ti-tude (rɛk–tə–tuʷd) n. **1.** Moral integrity; rightness of conduct **2.** Correctness of judgment

rec-tor (rɛk–tər) n. **1.** In some churches, a clergyman in charge of a parish **2.** The head of certain universities, colleges, and schools —**rectorate** n. —**rec-to-ri-al** (rɛk–tɔr–iᵞ–əl) adj.

rec-to-ry (rɛk–tə–riᵞ) n. -**ries** A rector's residence

rec-tum (rɛk–təm) n. -**tums,** or **-ta** The lower part of the large intestine

re-cu-per-ate (rɪ–kuʷ–pə–reᵞt) v. -**ated, -ating** To recover good health: *It took me a long time to recuperate after my surgery last year.* —**re-cu-per-a-tion** (rɪ–kuʷ–pə–reᵞ–ʃən) n.

re-cur (rɪ–kɜr) v. -**rr-** To occur again, or more than once

re-cur-rence (rɪ–kɜr–əns) n. The act of happening again —**recurrent** adj.

re-cy-cle (riᵞ–saɪ–kəl) v. -**cled, -cling** To treat a used substance so that further use is possi-

ble: *recycle aluminum cans*

red (rɛd) adj. -**dd-** **1.** Of the color of fresh blood: *a red pencil* **2.** Of hair, a reddish-brown color —**redness** n.

red n. **1.** Red color: *Red is my favorite color for some things.* **2. in the red** In debt: *Our company has operated in the red for the past three months, and we need to increase our sales.* —opposite IN THE BLACK **3. see red** To become very angry: *I saw red when I learned I had been falsely accused of cheating.*

red–blood-ed (rɛd–blʌd–əd) adj. Of a person, bold and strong: *a red-blooded young man*

red car-pet (rɛd kɑr–pət) n. A welcome or greeting to a guest, marked by special ceremony: *They rolled out the red carpet for the visiting king and queen.* —**red–carpet** adj. *red-carpet treatment*

Red Cross (rɛd krɔs) n. An international organization that looks after sick and suffering people, esp. after disasters

red-dish (rɛd–ɪʃ) adj. Somewhat red

re-deem (rɪ–diᵞm) v. **1.** To set someone free by paying a ransom; buy the freedom of: *to redeem someone from sin/Christ redeemed us from the curse of the law by becoming a curse for us, for it is written, "Cursed is everyone who is hung on a tree"* (Galatians 3:13). **2.** To buy back sthg. pawned or mortgaged: *I must redeem my gold ring which I left at the pawn shop.* **3.** To carry out; fulfill **4. redeeming feature** A single good point in a person or thing that makes up for the bad points: *Her one redeeming feature is her willing spirit.* —**redeemable** adj.

re-deem-er (rɪ–diᵞm–ər) n. **1.** One who redeems or ransoms **2.** The Savior of the world, Jesus Christ, who paid for all our sins with his own blood —see REDEEM, JESUS, SAVIOR

re-demp-tion (rɪ–dɛmp–ʃən) n. The act of redeeming or being redeemed: *All have sinned and fall short of the glory of God, and are justified freely by his grace [unmerited love] through the redemption that came by Jesus Christ* (Romans 3:23-24).

red-hand-ed (rɛd–hæn–dəd) adj. In the act of doing sthg. wrong: *The police caught the burglar red-handed.*

red-let-ter (rɛd–lɛt–ər) adj. An especially important day

red light (rɛd laɪt) n. **1.** A signal to stop **2.** A danger signal

re-draw (riʸ–drɔ) v. **-drew, -drawn** To draw again

red tape (rɛd teʸp) n. Excessive formality and routine required before official action can be taken

re-duce (rɪ–duʷs) v. **-duced, -ducing 1.** To make smaller in number, price, degree, etc.: *We decided to buy the house after the seller reduced the price ten per cent.* —compare INCREASE **2.** *infml.* Of a person, to lose weight: *She is dieting in order to reduce.* —**reducible** adj.

re-duc-tion (rɪ–dʌk–ʃən) n. **1.** The act of reducing or being reduced: *reduction in price* **2.** The amount by which sthg. is reduced: *The store made a big reduction in its prices.* —compare INCREASE

re-dun-dan-cy (rɪ–dʌn–dən–siʸ) n. **-cies 1.** The quality or state of being redundant; unnecessary repetition **2.** An instance of such repetition

re-dun-dant (rɪ–dʌn–dənt) adj. **1.** Being more than is required; superfluous **2.** No longer needed

red-wood (rɛd–wʊd) n. A very tall evergreen tree in Northern California that often reaches a height of 300 feet

reed (riʸd) n. **1.** The straight stalk of any of the various grasses that grow in swampy places **2.** Any of the plants themselves **3.** A musical instrument made from the stalk of such a plant

reef (riʸf) n. A ridge of rocks or, esp. coral, near the surface of the water

reek (riʸk) n. A strong unpleasant smell

reek v. To smell strongly: *He reeked of tobacco/ whiskey.*

reel (riʸl) n. A round device on which a length of thread, wire, film, fishing line, etc., is wound

reel v. **1.** To pull in by using a reel: *When he caught a shark, he needed help reeling it into the boat.* **2.** To move or seem to move unsteadily: *After being shot, the man reeled and then fell to the ground.*

re-e-lect (riʸ–ə–lɛkt) v. To elect again: *The governor was reelected to serve another four years.*

re-en-try (riʸ–ɛn–triʸ) n. **1.** An act of entering again **2.** The return to earth's atmosphere of a rocket or artificial satellite

re-fec-to-ry (rɪ–fɛk–tə–riʸ) n. A dining hall in a college or monastery

re-fer (rɪ–fɜr) v. **-rr- 1.** To mention; speak or write about: *In her letter describing her stay in New York, she referred to her visit with Uncle Bill.* **2.** To look up information: *You may refer to the encyclopedia for information about that country.* **3.** To concern; apply to: *The new regulation does not refer to bicycles.* **4.** To send a person to someone else for a decision or action: *The receptionist referred the customer to the sales manager.*

ref-er-ee (rɛf–ə–riʸ) n. **1.** A person responsible for making sure the rules are kept in football, basketball, and other games **2.** A person who is asked to help bring about a decision in a disagreement —**referee** v.

ref-er-ence (rɛf–ə–rəns/ rɛf–rəns) n. **1.** An act of referring to sthg. in speaking or writing: *In our discussion about travel, George made several references to his recent trip abroad.* **2.** A book, passage, etc. referred to as a source for information: *An encyclopedia can be used for reference on many subjects.* **3. (a)** A written statement about a person's character, ability, etc.: *Professor Smith wrote an excellent reference for his student who was applying for a job.* **(b)** *AmE.* A person who provides such a statement: *When he applied for the job, the student gave the names of three businessmen as references.* **4. in/with reference to** Concerning

ref-er-ence book (rɛf–ə–rəns/ rɛf–rəns bʊk) n. A written source of information, for example, a dictionary or encyclopedia

ref-er-en-dum (rɛf–ə–rɛn–dəm) n. **-dums, -da 1.** The referring of a question to the people of a county, state, or country, etc. for direct decision by a general vote **2.** A vote taken in this way

re-fill (riʸ–fɪl) v. To fill again

re-fill (riʸ–fɪl) n. **1.** A second or later filling: *Give her your cup for a refill (of coffee).* **2.** A replacement for sthg. used up: *I need a refill for my pen.*

re-fine (rı–faın) v. **-fined, -fining** To improve the quality of, to make pure. *Sugar cane is refined to make sugar.*

re-fined (rı–faınd) adj. **1.** Improved; made pure: *Only refined oil can be used in an engine.* **2.** Of a person, behavior, etc., having or showing education and good manners: *Dr. Parker was a refined gentleman, both in his actions and in his speech.* —**refinement** n.

re-fin-er-y (rı–faın–ə–riʸ) n. **-ies** Buildings and equipment used for refining

re-fin-ish (riʸ–fın–ıʃ) v. To give a new finish to, as wood or furniture

re-flect (rı–flɛkt) v. **1.** To send back heat, light, sound, or an image: *The mirror reflected the light from the candle.* **2.** To give an expression of: *His comments reflect his opinion on the subject.* **3.** To think carefully; consider: *The wise teacher reflected quietly on the problem, and then offered a solution.* —**reflection** n.

re-flec-tor (rı–flɛk–tər) n. A surface that reflects light or heat: *On the back of his bicycle, there is a red reflector.*

re-flex (riʸ–flɛks) n. A bodily movement that is made in response to some outside influence: *The doctor tested her reflexes by tapping her knee with a hammer.* —**reflex** adj. *When there's a sudden bright light, we close our eyes; it's a reflex action.*

re-flex-ive (rı–flɛk–sıv) adj. Of a word or phrase, referring back to the subject of the verb, in which the action of the verb is performed upon its subject: *"I hurt myself."* In the foregoing sentence, *"myself"* is a reflexive pronoun.

re-form (rı–fɔrm) v. **1.** To improve; do or become right: *The thief promised to reform, saying that he would never steal again.* **2.** To improve social or political conditions, etc.: *The government passed new laws to reform the tax system.*

reform n. An action that improves conditions, removes injustice, etc.: *a reform of the prison system*

ref-or-ma-tion (rɛf–ər–meʸ–ʃən) n. **1.** The act of reforming or being reformed, esp. morally **2. Reformation** The 16th century movement within the Christian church in Europe which led to the establishment of Protestant churches

re-for-ma-to-ry (rı–fɔr–mə–tɔr–iʸ) n. **-ries** An institution for young people who have broken the law

reformatory adj. Tending to or aiming at reformation

re-form-er (rı–fɔr–mər) n. A person who leads reform efforts

re-fract (rı–frækt) v. To change the direction of, as a ray of light

re-frac-tion (rı–fræk–ʃən) n. The bending of a ray of light, heat, or sound in passing from one medium into another

re-frac-to-ry (rı–fræk–tə–riʸ) adj. **1.** Unruly; disobedient **2.** Difficult to melt, reduce, or corrode

re-frain (rı–freʸn) v. To keep from doing sthg.: *They were asked to refrain from making noise after 11:00 in the evening.*

refrain n. A part of a song that is repeated, esp. at the end of each verse: *The soloist sang the verse and everyone joined in singing the refrain.*

re-fresh (rı–frɛʃ) v. **1.** To make fresh again: *A cold drink of water will refresh a person on a hot day./A generous man will prosper; he who refreshes others will himself be refreshed* (Proverbs 11:25). **2.** To help bring back to mind: *She read the recipe again to refresh her memory before making the bread.*

re-fresh-ing (rı–frɛʃ–ıŋ) adj. **1.** Giving a feeling of comfort and new strength: *A refreshing breeze came up in the afternoon which made us all feel cooler.* **2.** Welcome and interesting because of being new and unusual: *It's refreshing to view the work of young artists.* —**refreshingly** adv.

re-fresh-ment (rı–frɛʃ–mənt) n. **1.** Being refreshed **2. refreshments** pl. Drinks and a small amount of food served at a meeting, after a concert, etc.

re-frig-er-ate (rı–frıdʒ–ə–reʸt) v. **-ated, -ating** To keep food, drinks, etc., cold, in a large appliance usu. run by electricity: *It is necessary to refrigerate milk to keep it fresh.* —**re-frig-er-a-tion** (rı–frıdʒ–ə–reʸ–ʃən) n.

re-frig-er-a-tor (rı–frıdʒ–ə–reʸt–ər) n. Also **fridge** *BrE.* A large appliance, usu. run by electricity, used for preserving food and

drinks at a low temperature, and including a small unit kept at a temperature below freezing for ice and frozen foods

ref-uge (ref–yu^{w}dʒ) n. A place that gives protection from danger: *God is our refuge and strength, an ever present help in trouble* (Psalm 46:1).

re-fugee (ref–yʊ–dʒiʸ) n. A person who has been forced to leave his or her country for political reasons or because of a war

re-fund (ri–fʌnd) v. To give money back; repay: *The store refunded her money when she returned the dress that was too small for her.* —**refund** (riʸ–fənd) n.

re-fur-bish (ri–fɜr–bɪʃ) v. To restore to a clean or bright appearance again; to renovate; redecorate

re-fuse (ri–fyu^{w}z) v. **-fused, -fusing** To show or say that one is unwilling to accept or do or give sthg.: *The doctor kindly refused to accept payment for his treatment of the poor widow's sick child.* —opposite ACCEPT —**refusal** n.

re-fuse (ref–yu^{w}s/ –yu^{w}z) n. Garbage; rubbish: *Refuse from the restaurant's kitchen is thrown out every day.*

re-fute (ri–fyu^{w}t) v. To prove sthg. that has been said or written to be wrong —**ref-u-ta-tion** (ref–yu^w–teʸ–ʃən) n.

re-gain (ri–geʸn) v. **1.** To get back: *He regained his health.* **2.** To get back to; to reach: *After several hours in the water, he regained the shore.*

re-gal (riʸ–gəl) adj. Royal; kingly

re-ga-li-a (ri–geʸl–yə/ ri–geʸ–liʸ–ə) n. **1.** The symbols and emblems of kingship, such as a crown, scepter, etc. **2.** Rights and privileges belonging to a king

re-gard (ri–gɑrd) n. **1.** Respect; good opinion of someone: *The people of the town had high regard for their mayor.* **2.** Respectful thought; consideration: *They showed no regard for their neighbors when they played loud music at midnight.* **3.** regards Greetings; good wishes: *Give my best regards to your family.*

regard v. To consider in the stated way: *The students regarded their professor as a fine teacher as well as a good friend.*

re-gard-less (ri–gɑrd–ləs) adv. In spite of; no matter what might happen: *Regardless of the*

danger, the two boys started to climb the cliff.

re-gen-cy (riʸ–dʒən–siʸ) n. Rule by a regent

re-gen-er-ate (ri–dʒen–ə–reʸt) v. **-ated, -ating 1.** To make new and good again; to reproduce **2.** To change the heart and affections from natural enmity to the love of God —**regenerated** adj.

re-gen-er-ate (ri–dʒen–ə–rət) adj. **1.** Reproduced **2.** Born anew; renewed spir-itually

re-gen-er-a-tion (ri–dʒen–ə–reʸ–ʃən) n. New birth by the grace of God; that change by which the will and natural enmity of man to God and his law are subdued, and a principle of supreme love to God and his law are implanted in the heart: *When the kindness and love of God our Savior toward man appeared, not by works of righteousness which we have done, but according to his [God's] mercy he saved us, by the washing of regeneration and renewing of the Holy Spirit, whom he poured out on us abundantly through Jesus Christ our Savior* (Titus 3:4-6 NKJV). —see JESUS

re-gent (riʸ–dʒənt) n. One who governs in place of a king or queen

re-gime (reʸ–ʒiʸm/ ri–ʒiʸm) n. A type of government: *That country was under a military regime until the new president was elected.*

reg-i-men (redʒ–ə–mən/ redʒ–) n. A set of rules regarding diet, exercise, etc. aimed at improving one's health

reg-i-ment (redʒ–ə–mənt) n. A large body of soldiers commanded by a colonel, usu. made up of several battalions —**reg-i-men-tal** (redʒ–ə–men–təl) adj.

regiment v. To control people firmly: *The prisoners were strictly regimented in their daily activities.* —**reg-i-men-ta-tion** (redʒ–ə–mən-teʸ–ʃən) n.

re-gion (riʸ–dʒən) n. A part of a larger area: *Desert covers much of the southwestern region of the United States.*

re-gion-al (riʸ–dʒən–əl)adj. Of or pertaining to a particular region, as of a country —**regionally** adv.

reg-i-ster (redʒ–əs–tər) v. **1.** To record in an official list or record: *His parents registered their new baby's birth at the city hall.* **2.** To write a person's name on a list, usu. when

doing sthg. for the first time: *Mr. and Mrs. White registered at the hotel on their arrival./ All students must register before attending classes at the university.* **3.** To show on an instrument or dial: *The thermometer registers 35 degrees.*

register n. A written record

reg-i-stered mail (redʒ-ə-stərd meʸl) *AmE.*, **registered post** *BrE.* n. A postal service which, for a fee, records the sending of a letter or package to protect it against loss

reg-i-stered nurse (redʒ-ə-stərd nərs) n. also **RN** (in the US) A trained nurse who has passed the state registration exam

reg-is-trar (redʒ-ə-strɑr) n. A person who keeps registrations and records, esp. in a university or college

reg-is-tra-tion (redʒ-ə-streʸ-ʃən) n. The act of registering

reg-is-try (redʒ-ə-striʸ) n. **-tries** A place where records are kept

re-gress (rɪ-gres) v. To return to a previous less desirable condition —compare PRO-GRESS —**regression** n.

re-gret (rɪ-gret) v. **-tt-** To be sorry; to be sad: *If you sell your car, you'll regret it, because you need a car for your work.* —**regret** n. —**regretful** adj. —**regretfully** adv.

re-gret-ta-ble (rɪ-gret-ə-bəl) adj. To be regretted: *a regrettable accident that could have been prevented with more careful driving* —**regrettably** adv.

reg-u-lar (reg-yə-lər) adj. **1.** Happening again and again, at the same intervals: *In the quiet room, she could hear the regular breathing of the sleeping child.* **2.** Normal; usual: *She bought the regular size box of cereal, not the large./We had a substitute teacher today, because our regular teacher was sick.* **3.** Paid, full-time employment: *I am looking for a regular job, not a temporary or part-time one.* —opposite IR-REGULAR —**regular** n. **regularly** adv.

reg-u-lar-i-ty (reg-yə-lær-ə-tiʸ/ -leər-) n. The state of being regular: *The bell rang with regularity at noon every day.*

reg-u-late (reg-yə-leʸt) v. **-lated, -lating 1.** To adjust, esp. related to time or quantity: *Please regulate this watch so that it will keep correct time.* **2.** To make rules; to keep sthg.

within limits: *Traffic lights regulate the flow of traffic at an intersection.*

reg-u-la-tion (reg-yə-leʸ-ʃən) n. **1.** The act or process of regulating **2.** A law or rule by which sthg. is regulated: *traffic regulations*

reg-u-la-tor (reg-yə-leʸt-ər) n. A person or thing that regulates

re-gur-gi-tate (riʸ-gɜr-dʒə-teʸt) v. **-tated, -tating** To bring partly digested food back from the stomach into the mouth

re-ha-bil-i-tate (riʸ-hə-bɪl-ə-teʸt) v. **-tated, -tating 1.** To restore to a condition of good health and the ability to work: *He was an alcoholic for years and unable to hold a job, but now he has been rehabilitated.* **2.** To restore sthg. to good condition: *He rehabilitates old houses, making them fit to live in again.*

re-hash (riʸ-hæʃ) v. To use old material (as in writing) in a new form: *He keeps rehashing the same old story.* —**re-hash** (riʸ-hæʃ) n.

re-hearse (riʸ-hɜrs) v. **-hearsed, -hears-ing** To repeat sthg. in private before presenting it in public: *The musicians rehearsed the symphony many times before they gave the concert.* —**rehearsal** n.

reign (reʸn) v. **1.** To rule as a sovereign: *God reigns over the nations* (Psalm 47:8). **2.** To hold sway; prevail or predominate: *Do not let sin reign in your mortal body, so that you obey its evil desires* (Romans 6:12). —**reign** n.

re-im-burse (riʸ-ɪm-bɜrs) v. To pay back to sbdy. the exact amount of expenses incurred

rein (reʸn) n. **1.** A long narrow leather strap attached to the bridle for controlling a horse **2. give (free) rein to** To release control: *The art teacher gave free rein to her students to develop their individual artistic talents.* **3. keep a tight rein on** To keep firm control: *If anyone considers himself religious and yet does not keep a tight rein on his tongue, he deceives himself and his religion is worthless* (James 1:26).

re-in-car-nate (riʸ-ɪn-kɑr-neʸt) v. Bring a soul back after death, in another body

re-in-car-na-tion (riʸ-ɪn-kɑr-neʸ-ʃən) n. The rebirth of the soul in successive bodies; the belief in such rebirth NOTE: This belief is completely contrary to the Word of God

which says, "Man is destined to die once, and after that to face judgment" (Hebrews 9:27). The Bible teaches that we must be born again, but that rebirth is a spiritual rebirth that takes place during this present lifetime when one comes to faith in his Savior Jesus Christ through the power of the Holy Spirit. "Unless a man is born again [spiritually], he cannot see the kingdom of God" (John 3:3). On the other hand, "Whoever believes in him [Jesus] shall not perish but have eternal life" (John 3:16). "Whoever believes in him is not condemned, but whoever does not believe stands condemned already because he has not believed in the name of God's one and only Son. Whoever believes in the Son has eternal life, but whoever rejects the Son will not see life, for God's wrath remains on him" (John 3:17-18, 36). —reincarnate v. -nated, nating

rein-deer (reʸn–dɪər) n. A deer with large antlers in both sexes, found in Arctic regions where it is domesticated and used as a beast of burden and as a source of meat, milk, and leather

re-in-force (riy–ɪn–fɔrs) v. -forced, -forcing To make stronger by adding extra support to —reinforcement n.

re-in-state (riy–ɪn–steyt) v. -stated, -stating To restore, or be restored, to a position formerly held: *He was dismissed from his job as a bookkeeper, but reinstated when proven innocent of charges of stealing.*

re-it-er-ate (riy–ɪt–ə–reyt) v. -ated, -ating To repeat many times: *The workers reiterated their demands for better working conditions.*

re-ject (rɪ–dʒɛkt) v. To refuse sthg.: *Whoever believes in the Son [Jesus] has eternal life, but whoever rejects the Son will not see life, for God's wrath remains on him* (John 3:36). —rejection n.

re-joice (rɪ–dʒɔɪs) v. -joiced, -joicing To feel or show much happiness: *Rejoice in the Lord always. I will say it again: "Rejoice!"* (Philippians 4:4). *There is rejoicing in the presence of the angels of God over one sinner who repents* (Luke 15:10).

re-join-der (rɪ–dʒɔɪn–dər) n. An answer to a reply

re-ju-ve-nate (riy–dʒuw–və–neyt) v. -nated, -nating To restore to youthful vigor, appearance, etc.: *The clear, fresh mountain air will rejuvenate you.* —re-ju-ve-na-tion (riy–dʒuw–və–ney–ʃən) n.

re-lapse (riy–læps/ rɪ–læps) n. The act of falling back into a former state, esp. into an illness after a partial recovery: *My mother was recovering, but now she has had a relapse.*

relapse v. -lapsed, -lapsing To suffer a relapse; to fall back into a former state of bad health, after a partial recovery

re-late (rɪ–leyt) v. -lated, -lating 1. To tell a story or report at length: *He related all that had happened to him in Alaska.* 2. relate to To have a relationship with someone: *Dr. Johnson relates well to his patients.*

re-lat-ed (rɪ–ley–təd) adj. 1. Connected: *The course covered the related subjects of hotel management and resort management.* 2. Of the same family or kind: *Those two men are related. They are brothers.* —opposite UNRELATED

re-la-tion (riy–ley–ʃən) n. 1. A recounting or telling 2. An account given 3. Manner of being related 4. A person connected with others by blood or marriage; relative 5. relations Contact; communication: *Diplomatic relations were broken between the two countries after the violence at the border.* 6. in relation to Regarding; with reference to

re-la-tion-ship (riy–ley–ʃən–ʃɪp) n. 1. Connection: *There is a good relationship between the teachers and students in that school; they get along well with each other.* 2. Family: *What relationship is there between John and you? He's my brother.*

rel-a-tive (rɛl–ət–ɪv) also relation n. Family; people connected by blood or by marriage: *We are having a family reunion next month, and hope to see about thirty relatives — aunts, uncles, and cousins — as well as our immediate family consisting of my father, mother, one brother, and two sisters./ The Bible says, "If anyone doesn't provide for his relatives, and especially for his immediate family, he has denied the faith and is worse than an unbeliever"* (1 Timothy 5:8).

relative adj. Comparative: *There is relative*

hope in that situation now as compared to a year ago. —**re·lat·ive·ly** adv.

re·lax (rɪ–lǽks) v. **1.** To become less tense; to rest: *After a hard day's work, it is good to come home and relax.* —com·pare TENSE **2.** To become less tight, stiff, etc.: *Do not relax the tension on the rope; keep it tight!* **3.** To make less harsh: *On week nights, the children had to go to bed by 8:00; but on weekends, their parents relaxed the rules and they could stay up until 10:00.* —**re·lax·a·tion** (riʸ–lǽk–seʸ–ʃən) n.

re·lay (riʸ–leʸ) n. **1.** A team effort in which one member does his part, then the next takes over, and then the next, etc.: *In the past, messages were sent by a relay of runners, each man running as fast as possible to a pre-arranged stopping place, where another runner took the message and carried it on.* **2. relay race** A race between teams in which each individual covers a specified part of the course: *A relay race will be held tomorrow at the university; teams of four swimmers will compete, each man swimming one length of the pool.* —**relay** (riʸ–leʸ / rɪ–leʸ) v.

re·lease (riʸ–liʸs) v. **-leased, -leasing 1.** To set free; permit to come out: *They released the prisoner after he had completed his ten-year sentence.* **2.** To let sthg. be made public for the first time: *That new movie was released in several theaters across the country a week ago./ The company released the story about its new president for publication in the newspapers the following day.* —**release** n.

rel·e·gate (rɛl–ə–geʸt) v. **-gated, -gating** To assign to a lower position: *The local baseball team has been relegated to a lower division, from AAA to AA.*

re·lent (rɪ–lɛnt) v. To become less severe

re·lent·less (rɪ–lɛnt–ləs) adj. **1.** Not relenting; harsh; severe; pitiless **2.** Persistent

rel·e·vant (rɛl–ə–vənt) adj. Connected with the subject: *The professor helped us by adding some relevant information to our discussion.* —opposite IRRELEVANT —**relevance** n.

re·li·a·ble (rɪ–laɪ–ə–bəl) adj. Trustworthy; dependable: *That textbook is a reliable source of information.* —opposite UNRELIABLE —**re·li·a·bil·i·ty** (rɪ–laɪ–ə–bɪl–ət–iʸ) n. —**re·li·a·bly**

(rɪ–laɪ–ə–bliʸ) adv.

re·li·ance (rɪ–laɪ–əns) n. The act of relying on: *Their reliance on outside help limited their independence.* —**reliant** adj.

rel·ic (rɛl–ɪk) n. **1.** Sthg. that has survived from the past **2.** An object, having interest because of its age or association in the past, esp. an item as·sociated with a holy person or place

re·lief (rɪ–liʸf) n. **1.** The stopping of anxiety, fear, or pain: *It was a great relief to the parents to find their lost child.* **2.** Aid given to people in need: *The Red Cross provided relief for the people who lost their homes in the fire.* **3.** A person or group taking over a duty from another: *The nurse could not leave the hospital until her relief arrived to take her place.*

re·lieve (rɪ–liʸv) v. **-lieved, -lieving 1.** To lessen or reduce pain or anxiety **2.** To release from a duty or position: *The guard was relieved of his duty at midnight.* —**relieved** adj.

re·li·gion (rɪ–lɪdʒ–ən) n. A system of belief in and worship of one or more gods NOTE: There are basically only two religions in the world. Most religions teach that man can be saved and have eternal life by being good and attending religious ceremonies and services. Christianity, on the other hand, teaches that all people are sinners and cannot do anything to save themselves, that God became a man (Jesus Christ) and took our place under the law, and kept the law perfectly for us (as our substitute), then died on the cross to pay for our sins with his own blood. The blood of Jesus, his Son, purifies us from all sin (1 John 1:7). He died and was buried, but rose from the dead on the third day. Christians put their trust in Jesus for forgiveness of sins and for everlasting life. They want to live holy lives, however, out of love and appreciation for what Jesus has done for them. As Jesus said, If you love me, you will obey what I command (John 14:15). —see JESUS

re·li·gious (rɪ–lɪdʒ–əs) adj. Concerning religion, esp. obeying the rules very carefully: *If anyone considers himself religious and yet does not keep a tight rein on his tongue, he deceives himself and his religion is worthless* (James

1:26). —religiously adv.

re·lin·quish (rɪ-lɪŋ-kwɪʃ) v. **1.** To give up or surrender a possession or a right **2.** To let go

rel·ish (rɛl-ɪʃ) n. **1.** Sthg. taken with food to give it flavor **2.** Enjoyment **3.** A pleasing or enjoyable quality

relish v. To enjoy sthg.: *He relished the idea of a vacation in Hawaii.*

re·luc·tant (rɪ-lʌk-tənt) adj. **1.** Not willing **2.** Struggling in opposition: *He was reluctant to go out in the storm, but he had to do it.*

re·ly on/upon (rɪ-laɪ) v. **-lied, -lying** To trust; to depend on: *This happened that we might not rely on ourselves but on God, who raises the dead* (2 Corinthians 1:9).

re·main (rɪ-meʸn) v. **1.** To stay or be left behind: *The younger son remained at home when the older son moved to another city to work.* **2.** To continue to be: *Jesus told his disciples: "Remain in me, and I will remain in you. No branch can bear fruit by itself; it must remain in the vine. Neither can you bear fruit [do good deeds, pleasing to God] unless you remain in me. I am the vine; you are the branches. If a man remains in me and I in him, he will bear much fruit; apart from me you can do nothing. If you remain in me and my words remain in you, ask whatever you wish, and it will be given to you"* (John 15:4,5,7). —see STAY

re·main·der (rɪ-meʸn-dər) n. What is left behind: *Some people left the meeting early, but the remainder stayed to continue the discussion.*

re·mains (rɪ-meʸnz) n. **1.** Parts which remain **2.** A dead body: *His remains lay in the casket during the funeral.*

re·mark (rɪ-mɑrk) v. To comment: *In reporting on his trip, he remarked that the weather was especially pleasant.*

remark n. A spoken or written comment: *In praising the young man for his fine work, his employer also made a remark about his neat appearance.*

re·mark·a·ble (riʸ-mɑr-kə-bəl) adj. Worth noting (sthg. usu. very good); unusual: *He did a remarkable job of writing that book in such a short time.* —**remarkably** adv.

re·me·di·al (rɪ-miʸd-iʸ-əl) adj. Improving; providing a remedy: *The child took a remedial*

reading course to improve his ability to read.

rem·e·dy (rɛm-əd-iʸ) v. **-died, -dying** To correct a situation or make it right: *They called a meeting to find a way to remedy the problem.* —**remedy** n.

re·mem·ber (rɪ-mɛm-bər) v. To hold the memory of; recall: *I've lost my hat; I can't remember where I left it.* / *God says, "I, even I, am he who blots out your transgressions, for my own sake, and remembers your sins no more"* (Isaiah 43:25). —opposite FORGET

re·mem·brance (rɪ-mɛm-brəns) n. **1.** The act of remembering, esp. sbdy. who has died: *A monument was built in remembrance of those killed on the battlefield.* **2.** Sthg. kept as a reminder: *She kept the old photograph as a remembrance of her grandmother.*

re·mind (rɪ-maɪnd) v. **1.** To bring back to the mind: *These mountains remind me of my home back in Colorado.* **2.** To cause sbdy. to remember: *Please remind me of my dental appointment tomorrow at nine o'clock.*

re·mind·er (rɪ-maɪnd-ər) n. A note or letter to remind sbdy. of sthg.

rem·i·nisce (rɛm-ə-nɪs) v. **-nisced, -niscing** To think or talk pleasantly about the past —**reminiscence** n.

rem·i·nis·cent (rɛm-ə-nɪs-ənt) adj. That which reminds one of sthg.: *These buildings are reminiscent of Old Granada.*

re·miss (rɪ-mɪs) adj. Careless; negligent in carrying out one's duty

re·mis·sion (rɪ-mɪʃ-ən) n. **1.** God's pardon or forgiveness of sins: *To him [Jesus Christ] give all the prophets witness that, through his name, whoever believes in him will receive remission of sins* (Acts 10:43KJV). **2.** The remitting of a debt or penalty; the shortening of a convict's prison sentence because of his good behavior **3.** A period of improvement in an illness: *The cancer has gone into remission; at present, there is no trace of it in his body.*

re·mit (rɪ-mɪt) v. **-tt- 1.** To send money: *He received a statement for the books he had ordered by mail asking him to remit $12.95 in payment.* **2. (a)** To cancel a penalty or punishment **(b)** To pardon; forgive

re·mit·tance (rɪ-mɪt-əns) n. Sum of money remitted

rem-nant (**rem**–nənt) n. **1.** A part that remains, esp. a small group of people: *The remnant of the army retreated after the defeat.* **2.** A small piece of cloth left over from a larger piece and sold at a lower price: *At the store, she found enough cloth among the remnants to make a skirt.*

re-mon-strate (rɪ–**man**–stre^yt) v. **-strated, -strating 1.** To protest; object **2.** To present reasons in complaint or argument —**re-mon-strance** (rɪ–**man**–strəns) n.

re-morse (rɪ–**mors**) n. A deep feeling of sorrow and guilt for wrongdoing —**re-morseful** adj. —**remorsefully** adv.

re-mote (rɪ–**mo**^wt) adj. **1.** Far away; at a distance: *We went camping in a remote place in the mountains, far from any town.* **2.** Widely separated; distant **3.** Small or slight: *His plane will arrive so late, there is only a remote chance he will get to the meeting on time.* —**remoteness** n.

re-mote-ly (rɪ–**mo**^wt–li^y) adv. To a very small extent: *Because he has never studied medicine, he isn't remotely qualified to be a doctor.*

re-mov-al (rɪ–**mu**^w–vəl) n. **1.** A change of place or site **2.** Dismissal: *His removal from office was unexpected.*

re-move (rɪ–**mu**^wv) v. **-moved, -moving 1.** To take away; take off: *Did you remove my pen from my desk?/ He removed his coat after entering the house.* **2.** *fml.* To dismiss: *That teacher must be removed from her position, as she is not doing a good job.* **3. removed from** Separated from: *For as high as the heavens are above the earth, so great is his [God's] love for those who fear him; as far as the east is from the west, so far has he removed our transgressions from us* (Psalm 103:11, 12). —**removable** adj.

re-mov-er (rɪ–**mu**^wv–ər) n. A chemical that takes off the substance mentioned: *wax remover*

re-mu-ner-ate (rɪ–**myu**^w–nə–re^yt) v. **-ated, -ating** To pay or reward sbdy. for his work or services —**re-mu-ner-a-tion** (rɪ–**myu**^w–nə–re^y–ʃən) n.

re-mu-ner-a-tive (rɪ–**myu**^w–nə–rə–tɪv) adj. Profitable

Ren-ais-sance (rɛn–ə–**sans**/ –zans/ rɛn–ə–**sans**/ –zans) n. The vigorous revival of learning and art in Europe between the 14th and 17th centuries

rend (rɛnd) v. To tear

ren-der (**ren**–dər) v. **1.** To give; provide: *for services rendered* **2.** To give as expected: *to render obedience* **3.** To translate: *rendered into English* **4.** To cause to be: *The ship was rendered seaworthy.* **5.** To perform: *He rendered an invaluable service.* **6.** To represent as in a painting

ren-dez-vous (ran–də–vu^w/–de^y–) n. **1.** An agreement to meet at a certain time and place **2.** The place of the meeting **3.** The meeting itself

rendezvous v. **-voused** (–vu^wd) **-vousing** (–vu^w–ɱ) To bring or come together at a rendezvous: *The ships rendezvoused off the coast of Casablanca.*

ren-di-tion (ren–**dɪʃ**–ən) n. A performance of a piece of music or a role in a play: *the most beautiful rendition of that song*

ren-e-gade (**ren**–ɪ–ge^yd) n. **1.** One who deserts a cause or set of beliefs **2.** A traitor; deserter

re-new (rɪ–**nu**^w) v. **1.** To make like new; refresh: *Her vacation renewed her health./Those who hope in the Lord will renew their strength* (Isaiah 40:31). *Turn my eyes away from worthless things, [O Lord]; renew my life according to your word* (Psalm 119:37). **2.** To bring up to date: *Once a year, I must renew my driver's license.* **3.** To begin to do again: *The next day, they renewed their efforts to climb to the top of the mountain.* —**renewal, renewing** n. *Do not conform any longer to the pattern of this world, but be transformed by the renewing of your mind* (Romans 12:2). —**renewable** adj.

re-nounce (rɪ–**naʊns**) v. **-nounced, -nouncing** More *fml.* than **give up 1.** To give up, esp. a claim or a right: *He renounced his right to retire at age 65 in order to keep on working as long as possible.* **2.** Give up formally: *He who conceals his sins does not prosper, but whoever confesses and renounces them finds mercy* (Proverbs 28:13).

ren-o-vate (**ren**–ə–ve^yt) v. **-vated, -vating** To put sthg. back into good condition, esp. after extensive repairs

re-nown (rɪ–**naʊn**) n. Fame: *an artist of great renown* —**re-nowned** (rɪ–**naʊnd**) adj. *a renowned*

inventor

rent (rɛnt) n. Money paid regularly for the use of sthg. owned by someone else: *The rent on the house was $500 per month, and the rent on the car amounted to $135 per week.*

rent v. To pay for the use or occupation of a house, telephone, car, etc.: *They rented a house on Main Street.*

rent-al (rɛnt–əl) n. **1.** Amount of money paid as rent: *Rentals are high in this area due to the housing shortage.* **2.** Rented housing —**rental** adj.

re-nun-ci-a-tion (rɪ–nʌn–siʸ–eʸ–ʃən) n. A case of renouncing —see RENOUNCE

re-or-gan-ize (riʸ–or–gə–naɪz) v. -ized, -izing To organize again or in a new way —**re-or-ga-ni-za-tion** (riʸ–org–ə–nə–zeʸ–ʃən) n.

rep (rɛp) n. Short for representative

re-paid (riʸ–peʸd) v. Past tense and past part. of repay

re-pair (rɪ–peər) v. To put sthg. broken or worn out into good condition: *The mechanic repaired my car so that it ran well again./He took his shoes to the shoemaker to be repaired.* —**repair** n. *My car was in good repair after the mechanic worked on it.*

rep-a-ra-tion (rɛp–ə–reʸ–ʃən) n. **1.** The making of amends for injury or wrong done **2. reparations** Compensation for war damages, demanded by the victor of the defeated enemy

re-pa-tri-ate (riʸ–peʸ–triʸ–eʸt) v. -ated, -ating To send or bring sbdy. back to his own country

re-pay (riʸ–peʸ) v. -paid, -paying **1.** To pay back: *Here is $10 to repay you for the money I borrowed last week.* **2.** Do sthg. in return: *How can I repay the Lord for all his goodness to me?* (Psalm 116:12). —**re-payment** n.

re-peal (rɪ–piʸl) v. Of a law, to withdraw officially; revoke or annul

re-peat (rɪ–piʸt) v. To say or do again one or more times: *Please repeat your name; I didn't understand you.*

repeat n. A performance or program given again, esp. on television —**repeated** adj. —**repeatedly** adv.

re-pel (rɪ–pɛl) v. -ll- **1.** To drive away or back, usu. by force: *The soldiers were able to repel*

the attack of the rebels. **2.** To cause dislike or disgust: *The visitors were repelled by the filthy conditions in the prison.*

re-pel-lent (rɪ–pel–ənt) adj. Causing dislike: *A repellent odor came from the garbage dump.*

repellent n. A substance that keeps sthg., esp. insects, away: *They used ant repellent to keep ants out of the house.*

re-pent (rɪ–pɛnt) v. To be sorry for one's sins and determined not to sin again: *Jesus said, "Repent, for the kingdom of heaven is near"* (Matthew 4:17). *Jesus also said, "Unless you repent you too will all perish [in your sins]"* (Luke 13:3). *The Apostle Peter said, "Repent and be baptized, every one of you, in the name of Jesus Christ so that your sins may be forgiven. And you will receive the gift of the Holy Spirit"* (Acts 2:38). —see JESUS, REPENTANCE, SIN

re-pent-ance (rɪ–pɛnt–əns) n. A genuine sorrow toward God on account of sin and an extreme dislike of sin, followed by the actual forsaking of it and humble surrender to the will and service of God: *He [God] is patient with you, not wanting anyone to perish, but everyone to come to repentance* (2 Peter 3:9). *He [Jesus] told them, "This is what is written: The Christ will suffer and rise from the dead on the third day, and repentance and forgiveness of sins will be preached in his name to all nations"* (Luke 24:46,47).

re-per-cus-sion (riʸ–pər–kʌʃ–ən) n. (*usu. pl.*) Result; effect: *The assassination of the president had serious repercussions.*

rep-er-toire (rɛp–ər–twɑr/ –twɔr) n. **1.** A list of songs, jokes, stories, plays, etc. that a performer or company is prepared to perform **2.** The total number of skills, techniques, etc., existing in a particular field

rep-er-to-ry (rɛp–ər–tɔr–iʸ) n. -ries **1.** A collection or stock of anything **2.** Repertoire

rep-e-ti-tion (rɛp–ə–tɪʃ–ən) n. The act of repeating: *His speech was a repetition of the one he gave a week ago.*

rep-e-ti-tious (rɛp–ə–tɪʃ–əs) also **repetitive** (rɪ–pet–ət–ɪv) adj. Repeated too many times: *A repetitious speaker is difficult to listen to.*

re-place (rɪ–pleʸs) v. -placed, -placing **1.** To put a thing back in its right place: *After washing*

and drying the dishes, he replaced them in the cupboard. 2. To take the place of sbdy./ sthg.: *When Mr. Smith retired, Mr. Jones replaced him and carried on his work.* —replacement n. —replaceable adj.

re-plen-ish (rɪ–plɛn–ɪʃ) v. To fill up again

re-plete (rɪ–pliᵞt) adj. 1. Abundantly filled 2. Stuffed with food and drink

rep-li-ca (rɛp–lɪ–kə) n. Any close copy or reproduction of a work of art, architecture, e.g.

re-ply (rɪ–plaɪ) v. -plied, -plying To answer: *This letter is urgent.We must reply immediately.* —see ANSWER —reply n.

re-port (rɪ–port) n. 1. A statement, written or spoken, usu. with details, of an event, experience, etc.: *The boy gave a long report to his parents on everything that had happened at school that day.* 2. Information that may not be true; a rumor: *A report was spread that the president had been killed, but later it was learned that he had only been injured./Do not spread false reports* (Exodus 23:1). —**reportedly** adv. *They reportedly arrived early, but we haven't seen them yet.*

report v. 1. To make a report 2. To present oneself for work or duty: *He has to report for guard duty at 7:00 each morning.* 3. To complain about someone: *They will report the man for attempted robbery.* 4. To tell sthg. to authorities: *To report a fire, you must call the fire department.*

re-port-er (rɪ–port–ər) n. A person who gathers and writes news for the newspaper, radio, etc.: *Bob Jones is a reporter for the local newspaper.* —compare JOURNALIST

re-pose (rɪ–poʷz) n. Rest; sleep

repose v. -posed, -posing 1. To rest 2. To place trust in a person

re-po-si-tion (riᵞ–pə–zɪʃ–ən) v. To take up a new position: *They repositioned the troops on higher ground.*

re-pos-i-to-ry (rɪ–pɑz–ə–tɔr–iᵞ) n. 1. A place for the storing and safekeeping of goods 2. A person in whom one confides

re-pos-sess (riᵞ–pə–zɛs) v. To take or have possession of sthg. again; regain possession of, esp. in default of payment

rep-re-hend (rɛp–rɪ–hɛnd) v. To show sharp

disapproval of; to rebuke —**reprehension** n.

rep-re-hen-si-ble (rɛp–rɪ–hɛn–sə–bəl) adj. Deserving to be blamed or censured

rep-re-sent (rɛp–rɪ–zɛnt) v. 1. To serve as a sign or picture of; stand for; depict: *The blue lines on the map represent rivers.* 2. To act officially in place of another person or group of people: *Because he was too busy himself, the president asked the vice-president to represent him at the conference.* 3. To describe (perhaps falsely) as having certain qualities: *He represents himself as a member of the British royal family, but no one here knows him.*

rep-re-sen-ta-tion (rɛp–riᵞ–zɛn–teᵞ–ʃən) n. 1. The act of representing or state of being represented: *The Son [Jesus] is the radiance of God's glory and the exact representation of his being, sustaining all things by his powerful word* (Hebrews 1:3). 2. A thing, such as a picture, statue, etc., that represents sbdy./ sthg.: *That statue of a father, mother, and child is a representation of family life.*

rep-re-sen-ta-tive (rɛp–riᵞ–zɛnt–ət–ɪv) adj. 1. Typical; serving as an example: *This dress is representative of the new spring fashions.* —opposite UNREPRESENTATIVE 2. **representative government** Government carried on by elected people

representative n. A person who represents another person or a group of persons: *The president sent his secretary to the meeting as his representative ./In the US, representatives from each state are elected to serve a two-year term in the House of Representatives in Washington, D.C.*

re-press (rɪ–prɛs) v. 1. To keep under control 2. To put down, by force, as a rebellion 3. To subdue painful thoughts from the conscious mind and force them into the subconscious

re-pres-sive (rɪ–prɛs–ɪv) adj. Severe and cruel: *repressive police measures*

re-prieve (rɪ–priᵞv) n. 1. An official suspension of the death sentence of a prisoner 2. To relieve for a time from trouble, pain, or danger

reprieve v. -prieved, -prieving To give a reprieve

rep·ri·mand (rɛp–rə–mænd) v. To rebuke officially and severely

reprimand n. A severe rebuke

re·print (riʸ–prɪnt) v. To print again; to print more copies

re·print (riʸ–prɪnt) n. A new impression of a printed work; a copy

re·pri·sal (rɪ–praɪ–zəl) n. Retaliation for an injury with intent to inflict at least as much damage in return

re·proach (rɪ–proʷtʃ) n. Blame; disgrace; discredit: *Now the overseer [in the church] must be above reproach, the husband of but one wife, temperate, self-controlled, respectable, hospitable, able to teach...* (1 Timothy 3:2).

reproach v. To rebuke; censure: *He was reproached for his disgraceful behavior.*

rep·ro·bate (rɛp–rə–beʸt) adj. **1.** Very immoral; abandoned to sin; lost to virtue and religion: *They profess that they know God, but in works deny him, being abominable and disobedient and to every good work reprobate* (Titus 1:16KJV). **2.** Abandoned to error or in apostasy: *men opposed to the truth, men of reprobate minds* (2 Timothy 3:8). **3.** Not of standard purity or fineness; disallowed; rejected: *reprobate silver*

reprobate n. A person abandoned to sin

rep·ro·ba·tion (rɛp–rə–beʸ–ʃən) n. Strong disapproval; condemnation

re·pro·duce (riʸ–prə–duʷs) v. -duced, -ducing **1.** To make a copy of sthg. **2.** To have offspring —**re·pro·duc·tion** (riʸ–prə–dʌk–ʃən) n.

re·proof (rɪ–pruʷf) n. A scolding; criticism for a fault

re·prove (rɪ–pruʷv) v. -proved, -proving To scold for wrongdoing: *The teacher reproved the two girls for talking during class.*

rep·tile (rɛp–taɪl/ –təl) n. Any of a group of creeping, cold-blooded animals such as snakes, lizards, alligators, and crocodiles

re·pub·lic (rɪ–pʌb–lɪk) n. A nation, usu. governed by elected representatives, whose head of state is a president rather than a king or queen

re·pub·li·can (rɪ–pʌb–lɪ–kən) adj. Of, like, or advocating, a republic

republican n. **1.** A person advocating a republican form of government **2.** A member of the Republican Party, one of the two main political parties in the US —see also DEMOCRAT

re·pu·di·ate (rɪ–pyuʷ–diʸ–eʸt) v. -ated, -ating **1.** To refuse to acknowledge as one's own **2.** To refuse to recognize, acknowledge, or accept —**re·pu·di·a·tion** (rɪ–pyuʷd-i-eʸ–ʃən) n.

re·pug·nant (rɪ–pʌg–nənt) adj. Hateful; disgusting: *The idea of accepting a bribe was repugnant to him.* —**repugnance** n.

re·pulse (rɪ–pʌls) v. -pulsed, -pulsing **1.** To repel; to drive back an enemy: *The enemy attack was repulsed.* **2.** To refuse to accept: *His offer to help was rudely repulsed.* —**repulse** n.

re·pul·sion (rɪ–pʌl–ʃən) n. Strong dislike; disgust

re·pul·sive (rɪ–pʌl–sɪv) adj. Causing a feeling of loathing or aversion: *a repulsive smell/ sight*

rep·u·ta·ble (rɛp–yət–ə–bəl) adj. Respectable; having a good reputation: *a reputable construction firm*

rep·u·ta·tion (rɛp–yuʷ–teʸ–ʃən/ –yə–) n. **1.** The opinion other people hold about sbdy. or sthg.: *That restaurant has a bad reputation, because its food is poor and the cost is high./ Dr. Black has a fine reputation as a doctor.* —compare CHARACTER, CHARACTERISTICS **2. live up to one's reputation** To act as other people expect a person to do: *He lived up to his reputation as an excellent salesman by selling more than anyone else in the office over the past three months.*

re·pute (rɪ–pyuʷt) n. Reputation: *a house of ill repute*

repute v. To believe; consider

re·put·ed (rɪ–pyuʷ–təd) adj. Considered: *reputed to be the best violinist in the country*

re·quest (rɪ–kwɛst) n. **1.** The act of asking for (more formal than **ask for**): *The workman made a request for new tools.* **2.** Sthg. asked for: *Do not be anxious about anything, but in everything, by prayer and petition, with thanksgiving, present your requests to God* (Philippians 4:6). —**request** v.

re·qui·em (rɛk–wiʸ–əm) n. **1.** A hymn or mass sung for the dead **2.** The music for this

re·quire (rɪ–kwaɪ–ər) v. -quired, -quiring **1.** To need (more formal than **need**): *Babies require*

milk to grow. 2. To demand; insist upon: *And what does the Lord require of you? To act justly and to love mercy and to walk humbly with your God* (Micah 6:8).

re-quire-ment (rɪ–kwaɪ–ər–mənt) n. **1.** Sthg. required **2. meet the requirements** To do or be all that is required: *Because Miss Martin met all the requirements, she was hired as the new secretary.*

req-ui-site (rɛk–wə–zət) adj. n. Required; necessary: *the requiste funds for starting a new business*

req-ui-si-tion (rɛk–wə–zɪʃ–ən) n. An official demand, esp. by the army for the use of property: *Their farm was under requisition as a base of operation for the army.* —**requisition** v. *The army requisitioned the farm and all their horses.*

re-quit-al (rɪ–kwaɪt–əl) n. Adequate return for good or evil; compensation; reward

re-quite (rɪ–kwaɪt) v. **-quited, -quiting 1.** To repay; to give back in return **2.** To make retaliation for; to avenge

re-scind (rɪ–sɪnd) v. To cancel; revoke

res-cue (rɛs–kyuʷ) v. **-cued, -cuing** To save from harm or danger: *[Jesus Christ] gave himself for our sins to rescue us from the present evil age...* (Galatians 1:4). *For he [God] has rescued us from the dominion of darkness and brought us into the kingdom of the Son he loves, in whom we have redemption, the forgiveness of sins* (Colossians 1:13,14).

rescue n. An act of rescuing: *John came to her rescue.* —**rescuer** n.

re-search (rɪ–sɜrtʃ / riʸ–sərtʃ) n. Careful study of a subject so as to find new facts: *Thanks to past research, it is now possible to send people to the moon.* —**research** v.

re-sem-ble (rɪ–zɛm–bəl) v. **-bled, -bling** To look like; to be similar to: *It is easy to see that they are father and son; the son resembles his father.* —**resemblance** n.

re-sent (rɪ–zɛnt) v. To feel angry, esp. at sthg. unfair: *He still resents the way his parents raised him, because his younger brother got a good education but he did not.* —**resentful** adj. —**resentfully** adv. —**resentment** n.

res-er-va-tion (rɛz–ər–veʸ–ʃən) n. **1.** Doubt; uncertainty: *We had reservations about visit-*

ing Alaska in the winter because of the cold weather. **2.** In the US, land set apart for American Indians to live on **3.** *AmE.* also **booking** *BrE.* Asking in advance that a hotel, ship, restaurant, etc., hold a place: *I am writing today to make a reservation for a room at the hotel where we plan to stay next month.*

re-serve (rɪ–zɜrv) v. **-served, -serving 1.** *AmE.* **to book** *BrE.* To make a reservation: *We called to reserve a table for four at the restaurant this evening.* **2.** To hold for a special purpose: *That car is reserved for the president; no one else may use it.*

reserve n. **1.** A supply of sthg. for future use: *During the hurricane season, it is wise to keep a reserve of food and water on hand.* **2.** A military force, in addition to the regular army, navy, etc., for use only if needed: *The outbreak of war caused the government to call out the reserves.* **3.** An area of land set apart for a special purpose: *They took a trip to Kenya to visit the wild animal reserve.* **4. in reserve** Kept on hand for use if needed: *We keep candles in reserve in case the electricity is shut off.*

re-served (rɪ–zɜrvd) adj. **1.** Slow to show feelings or express opinions **2.** Saved or held for sbdy.: *reserved tickets*

res-er-voir (rɛz–ərv–wɑr / –rɛz–ərv–wɔr) n. A large place for storing water, usu. a manmade lake, for a city or other community

re-side (rɪ–zaɪd) v. **-sided, -siding** To live in a place: *Their home is in New York, but they reside in Florida during the winter.*

res-i-dence (rɛz–əd–əns) n. **1.** A house or the place where one lives: *His permanent residence is in Paris, but his summer residence is on the Riviera.* —see HOUSE **2. in residence** *The king is in residence in his summer palace during July and August.*

res-i-den-cy (rɛz–əd–ən–siʸ) n. **-cies 1.** A usu. official place of residence **2. (a)** A period of advanced training in a medical specialty at a hospital **(b)** The tenure or position of a doctor during this period **3.** Official residence of certain diplomatic agents

res-i-dent (rɛz–əd–ənt) n. A person who lives in a place, not a visitor: *In order to vote, a person must be an American citizen who has been a resident of the given state for a year.* —**resident**

adj. —opposite NON-RESIDENT

res-i-den-tial (rɛz–ə–**dɛn**–ʃəl) adj. An urban area containing housing rather than offices, factories, etc.: *My friends live in an apartment in a quiet residential neighborhood.*

re-sid-u-al (rɪ–**zɪdʒ**–yuʷ–əl/ rɪ–**zɪdʒ**–yəl) adj. Remaining

res-i-due (**rɛz**–ə–duʷ) n. That which is left over

re-sign (rɪ–**zam**) v. **1.** To give up or leave a job or position: *She resigned her job as waitress, because she was offered a better job as manager of a different restaurant.* **2. resign oneself to** To accept sthg. unpleasant calmly and patiently: *They resigned themselves to staying at home during their vacation, because the trip they had planned was too expensive.* —**res-ig-na-tion** (rɛz–ɪg–**neʸ**–ʃən) n.

re-signed (rɪ–**zamd**) adj. Accepting sthg. unpleasant calmly and patiently: *People who live in big cities are resigned to traffic problems.* —**re-sign-ed-ly** (rɪ–**zaɪ**–nəd–liʸ) adv.

re-sil-i-ent (rɪ–**zɪl**–yənt) adj. **1.** Of an object, readily recovering its original shape after being twisted, bent, etc. **2.** Of a person, readily recovering from misfortune, hurt, etc. —**resilience** n.

res-in (**rɛz**–ən) n. A yellowish or brownish sticky substance that oozes from pine trees and certain other plants, used in making varnishes, lacquers, plastics and many other products

re-sist (rɪ–**zɪst**) v. **1.** To oppose; fight against: *The soldiers resisted the attack by rebel forces./ Submit yourselves, then, to God. Resist the devil, and he will flee from you* (James 4:7). **2.** To remain unchanged or undamaged by: *This metal resists rust.* **3.** To keep from doing sthg., usu. tempting: *The children could hardly resist eating the cake their mother had just baked.* —**resistible** adj. —opposite IRRESISTIBLE

re-sis-tance (rɪ–**zɪs**–təns) n. **1.** An act of resisting, opposing: *The army put up strong resistance to the enemy's attack.* **2.** Ability to be unchanged or unharmed by: *Vaccination gives the body resistance to smallpox.* —**resistant** adj. —**resistor** n.

res-o-lute (**rɛz**–ə–luʷt) adj. Of a person, firm;

having or showing determination in purpose

res-o-lu-tion (rɛz–ə–**luʷ**–ʃən) n. **1.** Determination; being resolute **2.** A firm decision to do sthg.: *He made a resolution not to drink or smoke anymore.* **3.** A proposal passed by a meeting: *The board of directors passed a resolution to...* **4.** A solution: *the resolution of a question/problem*

re-solve (rɪ–**zɑlv**) v. **-solved, -solving 1.** To find a solution to a difficulty: *The disagreement was resolved when they accepted the advice of their good friend.* **2.** To make a firm decision: *He resolved never to smoke cigarettes again.* **3.** fml. To agree on and pass (at a group meeting) a rule or regulation: *At its annual meeting, the board resolved that the financial report for the year be accepted.*

res-o-nant (**rɛz**–ə–nənt) adj. **1.** Continuing to resound; echoing **2.** Intensifying sound —**resonance** n.

re-sort (rɪ–**zɔrt**) n. **1.** A place for recreation and vacation: *They spent their two-week vacation at a seaside resort.* **2.** The act of resorting to **3. last resort** Sthg. done when there is no other choice: *As a last resort, the poor farmer sold his only cow to buy food for his family.* **4. resort to** To turn to (often sthg. bad) because of great need: *Because he had no money, he resorted to begging.*

re-sound (rɪ–**zaʊnd**) v. **1.** To sound loudly: *The music from the radio in the living room resounded throughout the house.* **2.** To be full of sound; echo: *The auditorium resounded with applause after the excellent concert.*

re-sound-ing (rɪ–**zaʊnd**–ɪŋ) adj. **1.** Of a sound, loud; echoing: *Resounding thunder broke the silence, and the rain started to pour down.* **2.** Great: *Our football team won a resounding victory over the opposing team.* —**resoundingly** adv.

re-source (**riʸ**–sɔrs) n. A source of supply, usu. in large quantity: *An encyclopedia is a good resource for all kinds of information./The US has many natural resources, such as coal, water, and oil.*

re-source-ful (rɪ–**sɔrs**–fəl) adj. Capable of handling difficult situations: *She is a resourceful young woman who has a full-time job*

and also takes care of her husband and three children. —resourcefully adv. —resourcefulness n.

re-spect (rɪ-spɛkt) n. **1.** Admiration; high regard: *He had a lot of respect for his teacher./ Show proper respect to everyone ...* (1 Peter 2:17). —opposite DISRESPECT —compare SELF-RESPECT **2.** An act of giving attention to: *He drives his car as fast as he likes, with no respect for the speed limit.* **3.** A particular detail; point: *The new nurse has had good experience, but in some respects is not as well qualified as the previous one.* **4. respects** Polite greetings: *Please give my respects to your father.* **5. with respect to** *fml.* Concerning; with reference to: *With respect to the conference, please send me your report within a week.*

respect v. **1.** To feel high regard for; to honor: *Each of you must respect his mother and father ...* (Leviticus 19:3). **2.** To pay attention to: *Everyone should respect the laws of his country.* —respectful adj. —opposite DISRESPECTFUL —respectfully adv.

re-spect-a-ble (rɪ-spɛk-tə-bəl) adj. **1.** Holding standards acceptable to society: *He put on a tie and jacket to look respectable at the business luncheon.* **2.** Fairly large: *When my daughter married, her husband hardly made enough money for them to live on, but now he has a respectable income.* —re-spect-a-bil-i-ty (rɪ-spɛk-tə-bɪl-ət-iʸ) n. —respectably adv.

re-spec-tive (rɪ-spɛk-tɪv) adj. Of or for each one; individual: *After the convention, the delegates went back to their respective cities.* —respectively adv.

res-pi-ra-tion (rɛs-pə-reʸ-ʃən) n. *fml.* Breathing: *His heart problems made respiration difficult for him when walking fast or climbing steps.*

res-pi-ra-tor (rɛs-pə-reʸt-ər) n. **1.** A device worn over the nose and mouth to filter the air before it is inhaled **2.** A device for giving artificial respiration

res-pi-ra-to-ry (rɛs-pə-rə-tor-iʸ) adj. Having to do with breathing: *a respiratory disease*

re-spire (rɪ-spaɪr) v. -spired, -spiring To breathe; to inhale and exhale successfully

res-pite (rɛs-pət) n. A short period of rest

re-splen-dent (rɪ-splɛn-dənt) adj. Splendid; gorgeous; shining brilliantly

re-spond (rɪ-spɑnd) v. **1.** To answer (more formal than **answer**): *Please respond (to this letter) immediately.* **2.** To act in reply; to react: *She responded to his threat by running away from him.* —respondent n.

re-sponse (rɪ-spɑns) n. An answer or reply —responsive adj. —opposite UNRESPONSIVE —responsively adv.

re-spon-si-ble (rɪ-spɑn-sə-bəl) adj. **1.** Liable to be called to account for; to be blamed if things go wrong: *The treasurer is responsible for keeping the financial records.* **2.** Trustworthy; reliable: *They are responsible people, and will take good care of your house while you are away.* —opposite IRRESPONSIBLE **3.** Being the cause or source of: *The waitress was responsible for breaking the cup. (=she broke it)/ Who is responsible for these beautiful flowers on the table? (=who put them there?)* —re-spon-si-bil-i-ty (rɪ-spɑn-sə-bɪl-ət-iʸ) n. —re-spon-si-bly (rɪ-spɑn-sə-bliʸ) adv.

rest (rɛst) n. **1.** A time of not working or participating in activity: *He worked in the garden for two hours, and then took a rest before starting the next job./The children had been playing all morning, so they needed a rest before lunch.* **2.** A support for sthg.: *a foot rest/a book rest* **3.** Freedom from worry; being at peace: *[Jesus said,] "Come to me all you who are weary and burdened [with guilt and trying to earn salvation], and I will give you rest. Take my yoke upon you and learn from me, for I am gentle and humble in heart, and you will find rest for your souls"* (Matthew 11:28,29). —restful adj. —opposite RESTLESS —restfully adv. **4.** The remainder; the part that is left: *He has only one shirt today, because the rest are at the laundry./They ate most of the ice cream, and put the rest in the freezer.*

rest v. **1.** To take a rest; to lie down or sit quietly for a short time: *He rested after playing the game of tennis./Please sit down here and rest for a while.* **2.** To lean on or against: *He rested the ladder against the wall.* **3.** Remain without change or further action: *They decided to let the problem rest, as they could not agree about a solution.* **4. lay to rest** To bury:

After her death, her body was laid to rest in the grave beside her husband's. **5. rest assured** To be sure, certain: *You can rest assured that there will be enough rice for all of us, as the harvest was excellent this year.*

res-tau-rant (rɛs–tə–rənt/ –tə–rɑnt) n. A public place where meals are bought and eaten: *The Smiths went to a restaurant for dinner, instead of eating at home.*

rest-ful (rɛst–fəl) adj. Peaceful —**restfully** adv.

res-ti-tu-tion (rɛs–tə–tuʷ–ʃən) n. **1.** The act of returning sthg. to its rightful owner or original state: *A thief must certainly make restitution* (Exodus 22:3). **2.** The act of making good or rendering an equivalent for injury or loss

res-tive (rɛs–tɪv) adj. Restless; unruly

rest-less (rɛst–ləs) adj. Unable to rest; unceasingly active: *He is very restless; always busy doing sthg. or going somewhere.*

re-store (rɪ–stɔr) v. **-stored, -storing** To give or bring back to the original condition or place: *The police found the stolen car and restored it to its owner./ After many repairs and the replacement of old fixtures, the old house was restored to good condition./Restore to me the joy of your salvation [O Lord]* (Psalm 51:12). —**res-to-ra-tion** (rɛs–tə–reʸ–ʃən) n. —**re-stor-a-tive** (rɪ–stɔr–ət–ɪv) adj.

re-strain (rɪ–streʸn) v. To control; hold back; prevent: *He was so angry his friends had to restrain him from hitting the man who had insulted him.* —**restraint** n. —**restrained** adj.

re-strict (rɪ–strɪkt) v. To limit; keep within limits: *The right to vote is restricted to citizens of the country./This city has restricted the height of new buildings to ten stories.* —**restriction** n. —**restricted** or **restrictive** adj. —**restrictively** adv.

rest room (rɛst ruʷm) n. *AmE.* A public toilet in a hotel, restaurant, airport, etc.

re-struc-ture (riʸ–strʌk–tʃər) v. To build or structure again

re-sult (rɪ–zʌlt) n. **1.** Consequences of an action or event: *His victory in the tennis match was the result of much training and practice.* **2. (a) as a result** Therefore **(b) as a result of** Because of **3. results** The news of a person's or

team's success or failure: *We heard the results of the baseball game on the radio./ Your examination results will be available tomorrow.*

result v. To occur as a result —**resultant** adj.

re-sume (rɪ–zuʷm) v.**-sumed, -suming 1.** To begin sthg. again after stopping: *They resumed their work after lunch.* **2.** To return to the original place: *He resumed his seat after introducing the speaker.* —**re-sump-tion** (rɪ–zʌmp–ʃən) n.

re-su-mé (rɛz–ə–meʸ) n. **1.** Summary **2.** A short written statement of someone's education and past employment, used esp. when applying for a new job

re-sup-ply (riʸ–sə–plaɪ) v. **-plied, -plying** To supply again

re-sur-face (riʸ–sɜr–fəs) v. **-faced, -facing 1.** To provide with a new surface **2.** To come up again to the surface (of the water) **3.** To show up again

re-sur-gence (rɪ–sɜr–dʒəns) n. A revival after defeat, destruction, or disappearance —**resurgent** adj.

res-ur-rec-tion (rɛz–ə–rɛk–ʃən) n. **1.** In Christian belief, the rising of Christ from the grave: *He [Jesus Christ] was declared with power to be the Son of God by his resurrection from the dead ...* (Romans 1:4). *Jesus said..., "I am the resurrection and the life. He who believes in me will live, even though he dies; and whoever lives and believes in me will never die..."* (John 11:25,26). *Praise be to the God and Father of our Lord Jesus Christ! In his great mercy he has given us new birth into a living hope through the resurrection of Jesus Christ from the dead* (1 Peter 1:3). **2.** The act of bringing an old custom, practice, etc., back into use —**resurrect** v.

re-sus-ci-tate (rɪ–sʌs–ə–teʸt) v. **-tated, -tating** To bring or come back from apparent death or unconsciousness —**re-sus-i-ta-tion** (rɪ–sʌs–ə–teʸ–ʃən) n.

re-sus-ci-ta-tor (rɪ–sʌs–ə–teʸt–ər) n. **1.** A person or thing that resuscitates **2.** A respiratory machine that supplies oxygen (or a mixture of oxygen and carbon dioxide) to a person's lungs to restore respiration

re-tail (riʸ–teʸl) n. The sale of articles directly to a store's customers for their use, not for

resale —compare WHOLESALE

re-tail-er (ri^y–tu^wl̩ ər) n. A person who sells at retail

re-tain (ri–te^yn) v. To keep; hold in place or condition; remember: *Mrs. Jones retained her family home even though her husband had died and her children had moved away./John is a fine student; he retains facts easily.* —see also RETENTION

re-tain-er (ri–te^y–nər) n. A fee paid in advance to secure the services of a professional person

re-take (ri^y–te^yk) v. **-took** (–tʊk), **-taken, -taking 1.** To take again: *The enemy troops retook the important town.* **2.** To photograph again, esp. a scene for a film: *They had to retake the scene ten times before the director approved it.*

retake n. (ri^y–te^yk) A scene that has been photographed again

re-tal-i-ate (ri–tæl–i^y–e^yt) v. **-ated, -ating** To strike back, physically or verbally; to get even; to pay back evil with evil: *The Bible tells us not to retaliate, but to overcome evil with good* (Romans 12:21). *When they hurled their insults at him [Jesus], he did not retaliate; when he suffered, he made no threats. He himself bore our sins in his body on the tree [the wooden cross], so that we might die to sins and live for righteousness; by his wounds we have been healed* (1 Peter 2:23,24).

re-tard (ri–tɑrd) v. To delay; hinder: *The snow-fall retarded the work on the new road.*

re-tard-a-tion (ri–tɑr–de^y–ʃən) n. **1.** An act or instance of retarding **2.** The extent to which sthg. is retarded **3.** An abnormal slowness of thought or action **4.** Slowness in development or progress

re-tard-ed (ri–tɑrd–əd) adj. Of a person, having less mental development than others: *Retarded children need special love and attention.*

re-ten-tion (ri–tɛn–tʃən) n. The act of retaining

re-ten-tive (ri–tɛnt–ɪv) adj. To retain things, esp. in the mind: *a retentive memory*

ret-i-cent (rɛt–ə–sənt) adj. Quiet; not revealing one's thoughts or feelings readily

ret-i-na (rɛt–nə/ –ə–nə) n. **-nas** or **-nae** (–ni^y/ –naɪ) A light-sensitive membrane at the back of the eyeball, that receives the image

ret-i-nue (rɛt–ə–nu^w) n. A number of attendants accompanying an important person

re-tire (ri–taɪ–ər) v. **-tired, -tiring 1.** To stop working in business, a profession, etc., because of age: *Miss Black retired at age 65, after working as a secretary for forty years.* **2.** To go away for rest or quiet: *After the campaign, the newly-elected senator retired to his country home to rest.* **3.** *fml.* To go to bed

re-tir-ee (ri–taɪ–ri^y) n. A retired person

re-tire-ment (ri–taɪ–ər–mənt) n. The act of stopping work because of age: *His retirement took effect on June 30.* —**re-tired** adj.

re-tir-ing (ri–taɪr–ɪŋ) adj. Of a person, shy: *She has a quiet, retiring personality, and avoids crowds.*

re-tort (ri–tɔrt) v. To give a quick, usu. angry or witty reply —**retort** n.

re-trace (ri^y–tre^ys) v. **-traced, -tracing** To trace backward; to go back to where one started, following the same path or route: *to retrace one's steps* —**retraceable** adj.

re-tract (ri–trækt) v. **1.** To pull sthg. back or in **2.** To withdraw a statement as wrong or unjustified —**retractable** adj. —**retraction** n.

re-treat (ri–tri^yt) v. To draw back; go back, esp. in the face of opposition: *The enemy troops forced the soldiers to retreat.*

retreat n. **1.** The act of retreating: *When the police arrived, the thieves made a fast retreat.* **2.** A place where one can go for peace and safety **3.** A period of time for quiet and meditation, esp. religious study and prayer: *Pastor Martin spent a week in retreat at Lake Arrowhead.*

re-trench (ri–trentʃ) v. To economize; cut back; curtail

ret-ri-bu-tion (rɛ–trə–byu^w–ʃən) n. Punishment that is deserved —**re-trib-u-tive** (ri–trɪb–yət–ɪv) adj.

re-trieve (ri–tri^yv) v. **-trieved, -trieving** To find or recover; to get back

ret-ro-ac-tive (rɛ–tro^w–æk–tɪv) adj. Made effective as of a prior date

ret-ro-grade (rɛ–trə–gre^yd) adj. **1.** Going backward **2.** Going from a better to a worse stage

ret-ro-gress (rɛ–trə–grɛs) v. **1.** To go back-

wards **2.** To get worse **—retrogression** n. **—retrogressive** adj.

ret·ro·spect (rɛ–trə–spɛkt) n. The act of looking back to events or opportunities of the past **—ret·ro·spec·tion** (rɛ–trə–spɛk–ʃən) n. **—ret·ro·spec·tive** (rɛ–trə–spɛk–tɪv) adj.

re·turn (rɪ–tɜrn) v. **1.** To come or go back to a place: *Mr. Turner returned home on Friday after a week's absence on business.* **2.** To give, put, or send sthg. back: *I'll return your pen to you after I finish writing this letter.* **3.** To do or say sthg. in reply to what has been done or said to oneself; repay: *He complimented her on her fine work, and she returned the compliment by praising his work.*

return n. **1.** The act of coming or going back: *His return to the office after his vacation was last Monday.* **2.** The act of giving, putting, or sending sthg. back **3.** A gain or profit: *Thanks to good weather, the farmer's return from his wheat was excellent.* **4. tax return** A written report of one's income, made to the government for tax purposes **5. return ticket** *BrE.* A ticket for going on a trip and coming back again —see also ROUND-TRIP TICKET *AmE.* **6. by return mail** *AmE.* **by return (of post)** *BrE.* Immediate reply to a letter or request for information **7. in return (for)** As payment or reward for: *We invited them to dinner in return for their lending us their car.*

re·un·ion (riʸ–yuʷn–yən) n. **1.** The state of being together after a separation: *It was a happy reunion for the husband and wife who had been separated for a year while he was studying overseas.* **2.** A gathering of former classmates or other former friends: *The 50th reunion of the class of 1939 was held in 1989.*

re·u·nite (riʸ–yuʷ–naɪt) v. **-nited, -niting** To come or join together again: *After completing a year's military service, the young men were reunited with their families.*

re·us·a·ble (riʸ–yuʷ–zə–bəl) adj. Able to be used again

re·vamp (riʸ–væmp) v. To make over; to renovate

re·veal (rɪ–viʸl) v. **1.** To show sthg. hidden; to allow to be seen: *The coming of daylight revealed that the two ships had sailed away dur-*

ing the night. **2.** To make known hidden or secret information: *We hope that the investigation will reveal the cause of the airplane crash.*

re·veal·ing (rɪ–viʸl–ɪŋ) adj. Allowing facts to be seen or known

rev·cil·le (rɛv–ə–liʸ) n. A bugle call at daybreak (or earlier) to awaken soldiers

rev·el (rɛv–əl) v. **reveled** or **revelled, reveling** or **revelling 1. revelled in** Took delight in: *He revelled in his new-found freedom.* **2.** To engage in wild, noisy festivities

rev·e·la·tion (rɛv–ə–leʸ–ʃən) n. **1.** The making known of sthg. that was secret or hidden: *I had not seen my cousin in twenty years, so it was a revelation to me to learn that she had been married for ten years.* **2.** Making known a divine truth **3. Revelation** The last book of the New Testament in the Christian Bible, which reveals much about the end of this present age, just before the return of Jesus Christ. —see BIBLE, NEW TESTAMENT

rev·el·ry (rɛv–əl–riʸ) n. Unrestrained, wild, noisy festivities

re·venge (rɪ–vɛndʒ) n. Injury done to others in return for harm done to oneself or another: *He took revenge on the man who murdered his sister by killing him./Do not take revenge, my friends, but leave room for God's wrath, for it is written: "It is mine to avenge; I will repay," says the Lord* (Romans 12:19).

rev·e·nue (rɛv–ə–nuʷ) n. Income, esp. that which is received by the government in the form of taxes

re·ver·ber·ate (rɪ–vɜr–bə–reʸt) v. **-ated, -ating 1.** To resound or echo back and forth; to echo repeatedly **2.** To reflect or be reflected

re·vere (rɪ–vɪər) v. **-vered, -vering** *fml.* To deeply respect and honor: *Let all the earth fear the Lord; let all the people of the world revere him* (Psalm 33:8).

rev·er·ence (rɛv–ə–rəns / rɛv–rəns) n. A feeling of deep respect: *[Husbands and wives,] submit to one another out of reverence for Christ* (Ephesians 5:21).

Rev·er·end (rɛv–ə–rənd / rɛv–rənd) adj. A title of respect for a clergyman *abbr.* **Rev.:** *The Rev. John Wilson will lead our church service this Sunday.*

rev-er-ent (rev-ə-rənt/ rev-rənt) adj. Feeling or showing reverence. Live your lines as strangers here [on earth] in reverent fear (1 Peter 1:17). —reverently adv. —opposite IRREVERENCE, IRREVERENT, IRREVERENTLY

rev-er-ie (rev-ə-ri^y) n. -ies A state of pleasant, dreamy thoughts

re-ver-sal (ri-vɜr-səl) n. The act of being reversed, esp. financial or legal: He feared a reversal of his financial situation.

re-verse (ri-vɜrs) v. -versed, -versing 1. Move backwards; turn in the opposite direction: They realized they were going the wrong way, so they had to reverse their steps and start over again. 2. To set aside a judgment: The higher court reversed the judge's decision, and the guilty man was declared innocent. 3. T o change the order or position: Usually, Mary goes first and Elizabeth second, but today we will reverse the order. 4. reverse the charges also call collect To telephone someone, having the cost paid by the person receiving the call

reverse n. 1. The opposite: The response to the new book was the reverse of what we thought it would be. 2. in reverse Of motor vehicles, changing gears so that the vehicle will move backward: I put the car in reverse to back it out of the garage.

reverse adj. In reverse order

re-vers-i-ble (ri-vɜr-sə-bəl) adj. Usable on either side: This raincoat is reversible; one side for rainy weather, and the other for dry weather.

re-vert (ri-vɜrt) v. 1. To return to a former practice, condition, subject of conversation, etc.: She stopped smoking for a week, but then reverted to her old habit of smoking a pack of cigarettes a day. 2. Of property, ownership to go back to the previous owner: When the British lease expires in 1997, Hong Kong will revert to China. —reversion n.

re-view (ri-vyu^w) v. 1. To consider and examine again, esp. in order to come to a decision: The university is reviewing its entrance requirements. 2. To evaluate and write a report on a new play, book, etc., for a newspaper or magazine: The history professor was asked to review the new book on African history.

3. To go over again, esp. study again, lessons already learned: The teacher told the students to review for the exam the next day. 4. To make a formal inspection of military forces: The president reviewed the troops on the national holiday.

review n. 1. An act of reconsidering or re-examining, esp. renewed study of material already learned 2. A survey or report of past events or a subject 3. (a) A published critical report of a movie, play, etc. (b) A periodical or a section of a periodical containing such reports 4. A formal military inspection of troops, a ship, etc.

re-view-er (ri-vyu^w-ər) n. One who reviews books, films, plays, etc.

re-vile (ri-vail) v. -viled, -viling To curse; to use abusive language

re-vise (ri-vaiz) v. -vised, -vising 1. To examine sthg. written in order to make corrections and improvements: This report needs to be revised before you hand it in; it has many errors. 2. To change sthg. because of new information or further thought: The author was asked to revise his book because it had gotten out-of-date. 3. BrE. To review a lesson —revision (ri-vɪʒ-ən) n.

re-vi-tal-ize also -ise BrE. (ri^y-vait-əl-aiz) v. -ized, -izing To give new life or vigor —revi-tal-i-za-tion (ri^y-vait-əl-ə-ze^y-ʃən) n.

re-viv-al (ri-vai-vəl) n. 1. The act of reviving; renewal: There is a revival of interest in movies made in the 1930s. 2. A new performance of an old play from the past 3. (a) An increase of interest in Christianity (b) Special church services intended to bring this about: They held a four-day revival at their church last month.

re-viv-al-ist (ri-vaiv-ə-ləst) n. A preacher or leader in a religious revival movement

re-vive (ri-vaiv) v. -vived, -viving 1. To bring back to good health or consciousness: When I am hot and tired, a cold shower revives me. 2. To come back into use again: They recently revived a show which was written in the 1920s.

re-voke (ri-vo^wk) v. -voked, -voking To withdraw permission; change a law or decision; cancel: The police revoked his driver's license, because he had had too many accidents.

re-volt (rɪ-voᵂlt) v. **1.** To fight against those in power: *The army revolted against the dictator.* —see also REBEL 2. To shock and disgust, sometimes to the point of illness: *They were revolted by the sight of the dead bodies lying in the street after the shooting.*

revolt n. A fight against those in power: *The lieutenant led the revolt against the temporary military government.* —see also REBELLION

re-volt-ing (rɪ-voᵂlt-ɪŋ) adj. Disgusting: *A revolting smell came from the filthy house.*

rev-o-lu-tion (rɛv-ə-luᵂ-ʃən) n. **1.** Change in government and society brought about by military force: *The American Revolution resulted in the winning of freedom from England and the establishment of a new country, the United States of America.* —compare REBELLION 2. A complete or drastic change in conditions, ways of thinking or acting, etc.: *The Industrial Revolution in Europe in the 19th century was brought about by the use of machines to do what had been done by hand in the past.* **3.** A complete turn around a fixed point: *The revolution of the earth around the sun takes place each year.* **4.** Also **rev** *infml.* Of a machine, one complete circular movement or turn around a central point, as of a wheel: *a speed of 100 revolutions per minute* —see also REVOLVE

rev-o-lu-tion-ar-y (rɛv-ə-luᵂ-ʃə-nɛər-iʸ) adj. **1.** Related to a revolution: *George Washington was a revolutionary general during the American Revolution.* **2.** Causing complete change: *The use of computers has made revolutionary changes in modern office procedures.*

revolutionary n. **-aries** A person who leads or takes part in a revolution

rev-o-lu-tion-ize (rɛv-ə-luᵂ-ʃə-naɪz) v. **-ized, -zing** To make a complete change: *In this century, the invention of the automobile has revolutionized travel.*

re-volve (rɪ-vɑlv) v. **-volved, -volving 1.** To turn around a central point: *The moon revolves around the earth.* **2.** To be centered on: *Mrs. Lee's life revolves around her family.* —**revolving** adj. *a revolving door*

re-volv-er (rɪ-vɑl-vər) n. A small type of firearm; a handgun; a pistol

re-vue (rɪ-vyuᵂ) n. A theatrical show consist-

ing of songs, jokes, dances, and skits, esp. about contemporary people and events

re-vul-sion (rɪ-vʌl-ʃən) n. A feeling of disgust; great dislike

re-ward (rɪ-wɔrd) n. **1.** Sthg. received as a result of obedience or good service: *The ordinances of the Lord are sure and altogether righteous. In keeping them there is great reward* (Psalm 19:9,11)./*She told the sick old woman, "Your thanks are reward enough for the care I have given you; you don't need to pay me."* **2.** Money received for special information or service: *The man offered a $10 reward for the return of his lost dog.* —**reward** v.

re-ward-ing (rɪ-wɔrd-ɪŋ) adj. Satisfying; enjoyable because a person has given good service: *The doctor found it very rewarding to work in the clinic where the patients were too poor to pay.* —opposite UNREWARDING

re-write (riʸ-raɪt) v. **-wrote, -written 1.** To write again **2.** To write in a different form **3.** To write news submitted by a reporter to be included in a newspaper

rhap-so-dy (ræp-sə-diʸ) n. **1.** A musical composition of irregular form **2.** An expression of great praise and excitement, in speech or writing

rhe-o-stat (riʸ-ə-stæt) n. An adjustable resistor used for controlling the current in a circuit (as for dimming lights)

rhet-o-ric (ret-ə-rɪk) n. **1.** The study of speaking or writing effectively **2.** *derog.* Speech that sounds good, but is often insincere: *A politician's speech is often just a lot of rhetoric.* —**rhe-tor-i-cal** (rɪ-tɔr-ɪ-kəl) adj.

rhe-tor-i-cal question (rɪ-tɔr-ɪ-kəl kwɛs-tʃən) n. A question that is asked only for effect, not expecting an answer

rheu-mat-ic fe-ver (ruᵂ-mæt-ɪk fiʸ-vər) n. An infectious disease, accompanied by fever, usu. affecting children, characterized by inflammation around the joints and of the heart valves

rheu-ma-tism (ruᵂ-mə-tɪz-əm) n. A painful disorder, with stiffness and inflammation in the joints or muscles

rhine-stone (raɪn-stoᵂn) n. An imitation diamond

rhi-noc-er-os (raɪ-nɑs-ə-rəs) also **rhino** (raɪn-

o^w) n. A large plant-eating mammal of Africa and Asia, with one or two horns on its snout and a very thick hide

rho-do-den-dron (ro^w–də–den–drən) n. An evergreen plant with large bright pink, purple, or white flowers

rhom-bus (ram–bəs) n. A geometrical figure having four equal sides and angles which are not right angles

rhu-barb (ru^w–barb) n. **1.** A plant that has thick reddish leafstalks, eaten in pies or as stewed fruit **2.** A heated argument or quarrel

rhyme (raim) n. **1.** A word that has the same final sound as another: *"Right" and "fight" are rhymes.* **2.** A poem or verse using rhymes at the end of the lines **3. without rhyme or reason** Nonsense; disorder: *These library books have been put back on the shelf without rhyme or reason, and I can't find the one I want.*

rhyme v. **rhymed, rhyming** To use words that have the same final sound: *"Rain" rhymes with "plane".*

rhythm (rið–əm) n. A repeated pattern of events, sounds in speech or music, or movements in dancing, etc., sometimes regular and other times varied: *A farmer must follow the rhythm of the seasons in planting his crops./The rhythm of the drum beats became louder and faster as time went on.* —**rhyth-mic** (rið–mik) adj. —**rhythmically** adv.

rib (rib) n. **1.** One of the bones inside the chest of a person or animal **2.** One of a grouping of long narrow pieces of wood or metal similar to the bones in the chest: *During the rainstorm, the wind broke one of the ribs of my umbrella.*

rib-ald (ri–bəld/ ri–bɔld/ rai–bɔld) adj. Rude; vulgar

rib-bon (rib–ən) n. **1.** A long narrow strip of cloth used for decorating clothing, tying hair, etc.: *She wore a pink ribbon in her hair.* **2. typewriter ribbon** An inked strip of cloth, usu. black, for printing typewritten letters on paper

:e (rais) n. **1.** A cereal plant grown in well-watered ground in a warm place **2.** The seeds of this plant, which are cooked and eaten as a staple food, esp. in the Orient

and Africa: *Mr. and Mrs. Park enjoy chicken and rice for dinner, and their children like rice for dessert.*

rich (ritʃ) adj. **1.** Owning a lot of money and possessions: *For you know the grace of our Lord Jesus Christ, that though he was rich [enjoying all the riches and glory and splendor of heaven], yet for your sakes he became poor [while fulfilling the law for us and suffering and dying on the cross to pay for our sins], so that you through his poverty might become rich [eternally rich]* (2 Corinthians 8:9). —opposite POOR **2.** Containing a lot of sthg.: *Carrots are rich in vitamin A./ Saudi Arabia is rich in oil.* **3.** Of clothes, furniture, etc., expensive and beautiful: *The queen wore a gown of rich satin.* **4.** Of food, containing a lot of fat, eggs, etc.: *I am on a diet and cannot eat such a rich cake.* **5.** Of land, fertile: *Rich soil produces good crops.* **6.** Of sounds or colors, full, deep, strong: *The color of her dress was a rich purple.* —**richly** adv. —**richness** n.

rich-es (ritʃ–əz) n. Wealth

rick-ets (rik–əts) n. A disease of children characterized by softening of the bones, resulting from a lack of vitamin D

rick-et-y (rik–ət–i^y) adj. Likely to fall apart or collapse: *a rickety old chair*

ric-o-chet (rik–ə–ʃe^y) v. **-cheted** (–ʃe^yd), **-cheting** (–ʃe^y–ŋ) Of a bullet or stone, etc., to glance off sthg. and change directions: *The bullet ricocheted off the car.*

rid (rid) v. **rid** or **ridded, ridden 1.** To free sbdy./sthg from sbdy./sthg.; remove: *Therefore, rid yourselves of all malice and all deceit, hypocrisy, envy, and slander of every kind* (1 Peter 2:1). **2. get rid of** To throw/give away sthg.; to make sbdy./sthg. go away: *We must clean this room and get rid of the trash./They used poison to get rid of the rats.*

rid-den (rid–ən) v. The past part. of the verb **ride**: *Have you ever ridden in an airplane?*

rid-dle (rid–əl) n. **-dled, -dling 1.** A problem or puzzling question to be answered by guessing: *Question: "What has four legs but cannot walk?" Answer: "A table".* **2.** A puzzling person, situation, etc.: *Richard's personality is a riddle to me; I can't understand him.* **3. riddle sbdy./sthg. with sthg.** v. **-dled,**

ride

-dling To fill with holes: *This old wool blanket is riddled with moth holes.*

ride (raɪd) v. **rode** (roʷd), **ridden** (rɪd–ən), **riding 1.** To sit on and control the movement of a horse or other animal, a bicycle, etc., in order to travel; —compare DRIVE (a car, bus, etc.): *I wondered whether to ride my bicycle or drive my car to work today.* **2.** To sit in a moving vehicle as a passenger, not the driver: *The children rode in the back seat of the car.* **3.** *infml.* **let sthg. ride** To let sthg. remain as it is; do nothing about a situation: *They worked for hours to try to repair the broken pipeline without success, and finally decided to let it ride until the next day.*

ride n. **1.** Traveling on an animal, in a vehicle, etc. —compare DRIVE **(a)** For pleasure or business: *It's a beautiful afternoon; let's go for a ride in the car!* **(b)** For the convenience of another: *Could you give me a ride to work today? My car is being repaired.* **2. take sbdy. for a ride** *infml.* **(a)** To cheat someone **(b)** To take someone for a ride in a car for the purpose of killing him, as gangsters do

rid-er (raɪd–ər) n. A person who rides, esp. on a horse

ridge (rɪdʒ) n. **1.** The edge or line where two sloping surfaces meet: *The birds sat on the ridge of the roof.* **2.** A long narrow surface, such as at the top of a hill or mountain: *The sun set slowly behind the mountain ridge.*

rid-i-cule (rɪd–ə–kyuʷl) v. To make fun of; laugh at unkindly; mock: *The teacher told the children they must not ridicule the little blind girl.* —ridicule n.

ri-dic-u-lous (rɪ–dɪk–yə–ləs) adj. **1.** Funny; silly: *The children all laughed at the ridiculous tricks of the clown.* **2.** Impossible; absurd: *What a ridiculous idea! An apple tree can never produce oranges!* —ridiculously adv.

rife (raɪf) adj. Prevalent; widespread

riff-raff (rɪf–ræf) n. Worthless, disreputable people

ri-fle (raɪ–fəl) n. A long-barreled gun that is fired from the shoulder

ri-fle v. **-fled, -fling** To look carefully through sthg. for the purpose of stealing: *The thief rifled the drawers and stole the valuable jewelry.*

rift (rɪft) n. **1.** A split or crack in the ground **2.**

A disagreement between friends

rig (rɪg) v. **-gg-** To arrange in advance for a dishonest result: *The politicians in power rigged the election so that their candidate would win.*

right (raɪt) adj. **1.** On the side of the body, or a thing, towards the east when a person faces north: *He fell and broke his right leg.* —opposite LEFT **2.** Correct; good: *The precepts [rules] of the Lord are right, giving joy to the heart* (Psalm 19:8). —opposite WRONG **3. right side up** Top side up: *Keep your glass right side up, or the water will spill out.* —opposite UPSIDE DOWN **4. at the right hand of God** Having all power and authority in heaven and on earth: *He [God] raised him [Jesus] from the dead and seated him at his right hand in the heavenly realms, far above all rule and authority, power and dominion, and every title that can be given, not only in the present age but also in the one to come* (Ephesians 1:20-21). *After he [Jesus] had provided purification for sins, he sat down at the right hand of the Majesty in heaven* (Hebrews 1:3).

right n. **1.** The side of the body, or a thing, towards the east when a person faces north: *In England you must drive your car on the left, but in the US, on the right.* —opposite LEFT **2. in the right** Being good, correct, just —opposite IN THE WRONG **3.** Sthg. a person is allowed to have or do: *Everyone ought to have a right to free speech.* —see also RIGHTS **4. in one's own right** Because of one's own ability, work, etc., not depending on anyone else: *John graduated from the university with high honors in his own right, not because he was the son of the president.*

right adv. **1.** Towards the right: *To get to the bank, walk north two blocks, turn right and walk east one block.* —opposite LEFT **2.** Exactly; directly: *Stand right there so I can take your picture./While I was sitting under the apple tree, an apple fell right on my head./Continue on this road, and you'll come right to the school.* **3.** Immediately: *Wait a minute! He's coming right now./I'll meet you right after lunch.* **4.** Correctly: *This engine isn't running right. Can you repair it?* —opposite WRONG **5.** Yes; I agree: *He's working today, isn't he?*

Right! He's at his office today. **6. right away** At once, in a minute: *The train is leaving right away; we have to hurry to catch it.* **7. right on!** *infml.* An expression used to show agreement and encourage a speaker

right angle (rart æŋ–gəl) n. An angle formed by two perpendicular lines, making an angle of 90 degrees: *The corners of this page are right angles.*

righ-teous (rar–tʃəs) adj. Morally good; just: *The Lord our God is righteous in everything he does...* (Daniel 9:14). *He saved us, not because of righteous things we had done, but because of his mercy* (Titus 3:5). *For Christ died for sins once for our sins, the righteous one for the unrighteous, to bring us to God. He was put to death in the flesh but made alive in spirit* (1 Peter 3:18NET). **—righteously** adv. **—righteousness** n.

right-ful (rart–fəl) adj. Lawful; correct: *The lost sheep was found and returned to its rightful owner.* **—rightfully** adv.

right-ly (rart–liʸ) adv. **1.** Correctly; justly: *He was rightly punished for having stolen the watch.* **2. rightly or wrongly** Thinking or acting in a certain way, whether or not correctly: *They believed, rightly or wrongly, that their son should attend the university.*

right of way (rart əv weʸ) n. **rights of way** In traffic, the rules which say which vehicle (on land) or ship (on water) may go first: *Where a road crosses a railway track, a train has the right of way over a car.*

rights (rarts) n. **1.** Legal or moral justice or fairness in political, social, and economic matters, etc.: *The struggle for women's rights has continued for a long time.* **2. by rights** Properly or correctly; in justice: *By rights, Mr. Green should be made president of the company, not Mr. White.* **3. within one's rights** Not beyond what is legal: *She was within her rights when she demanded an investigation into the matter.*

rig-id (rɪdʒ–əd) adj. **1.** Stiff; difficult to bend: *We need two rigid poles to hold up this tent.* **2.** Strict; unchanging: *The school teacher used rigid discipline with the children.* **—rigidly** adv.

rig-ma-role (rɪg–ə–mə–roʷl/ rɪg–mə–roʷl) n. **1.** A long, rambling sentence **2.** A complicated and formal procedure

rig-or (rɪg or) n. *also* **rigour** *BrE.* **1.** Harshness; severity: *The rigor of his punishment seemed too great for the crime he had committed.* **2.** Severe conditions, *usu. pl.*: *The scientists spent a year at the North Pole in spite of the rigors of life in the Arctic.* **—rigorous** adj. **—rigorously** adv.

rig-or mor-tis (rɪg–ər mort–əs) n. Muscular stiffening after death

rile (rail) v. **riled, riling** To anger; irritate

rim (rɪm) n. Edge or border, esp. on sthg. circular: *The rim of this cup has a crack; let's not use it./To put on a new tire, you must first remove the old one from the rim of the wheel.* **—rim** v. **—rimmed** (rɪmd) adj. **—opposite** RIMLESS

rind (raɪnd/ raɪn) n. A thick, firm covering, esp. the peelings of melons and citrus fruit. Some cheeses also have rinds.

ring (rɪŋ) n. **1.** A small circle of gold, silver, etc., worn on a finger: *When they were married, he placed a gold wedding ring on her finger.* **2.** A circle, of any size, of things or people: *Sometimes, there's a ring around the moon./To play the game, the children first drew a ring on the ground.* **3.** An enclosed place where performances or exhibitions are held: *circus ring/boxing ring* **4.** A group working together dishonestly for their own profit: *The police have just caught the men in the smuggling ring.* **5.** The sound of a bell: *The ring of the alarm clock woke him up.* **6. run rings around sbdy.** To do sthg. much better than someone else: *John can run rings around his friends when it comes to playing tennis.*

ring v. **rang** (ræŋ), **rung** (rʌŋ), **ringing 1.** To make the sound of a bell: *The church bells rang to announce the beginning of the service.* **2.** *BrE.* To telephone sbdy.: *I'll ring you up tomorrow.* **3.** To sound a bell as a signal that one wants sthg.: *He rang for the maid.* **4.** To sound continually in the ears: *The loud explosion made his ears ring for several hours.* **5.** To draw a ring around sthg. **6. ring a bell** *fig. infml.* To have seen or heard before but not to remember exactly: *His name rings a bell, but I'm not sure I know him.*

ring-lead-er (rɪŋ-liʸd–ər) n. The leader of a group, esp. an unlawful one

ring-let (rɪŋ-lət) n. A lock of hair; a curl

ring-mas-ter (rɪŋ-mæs-tər) n. A leader of circus ring performances

ring-worm (rɪŋ-wərm) n. A skin disease causing circular red patches

rink (rɪŋk) n. An enclosed area with a smooth surface of ice for ice skating, or of wood for roller skating

rinse (rɪns) v. **rinsed, rinsing 1.** To use clean water to remove the soap when washing clothes, dishes, etc.: *After washing the shirt in soapy water, she rinsed it twice.* **2.** To use clean water to remove dirt, etc.: *He rinsed the mud off his shoes before entering the house.* —**rinse** n.

ri-ot (raɪ-ət) n. **1.** Violent public disturbance by a crowd of people: *The police had to be called when the fight between the two opposing groups turned into a riot.* **2.** *infml.* A very funny, successful person, thing, or event: *The new play was a riot; I laughed during the entire performance!* —**riotous** adj. —**riotously** adv.

riot v. To take part in a violent public disturbance: *The prisoners rioted against the bad conditions in the prison.*

ri-ot-er (raɪ-ət–ər) n. A person who takes part in a riot

rip (rɪp) v. **-pp- 1.** To tear or make a hole in cloth, paper, etc.: *He ripped his pants when climbing over the fence./She ripped open the envelope and took out the letter.* **2.** To tear open violently: *The violent wind ripped off the roof of the house.* **3. rip into sbdy.** To attack violently with words: *He ripped into his wife when he learned she had been lying to him.* **4. rip off** *infml.* To cheat or steal from sbdy.: *He ripped us off by charging us double what the watch was worth.* —**rip-off** n.

rip n. A tear in cloth or paper: *She sewed up the rip in her dress.*

ripe (raɪp) adj. **1.** Of fruit, vegetables, and grains, ready to be eaten or gathered in: *Those apples are ripe, so we can pick them now.* —opposite UNRIPE **2.** Of cheese, having a good flavor because it has been kept for the right length of time **3.** Ready for; the right time for: *The revolution succeeded because the time was ripe for the overthrow of the corrupt and cruel dictator.* —**ripe-ness** n.

rip-en (raɪp–ən) v. To become or cause to become ripe

rip-ple (rɪp–əl) n. **1.** A small wave on the surface of water, esp. a lake or pond: *He watched the ripples spread out in circles around the place where he had dropped the stone into the quiet water of the lake.* **2.** A gentle sound of flowing water: *In the silence of the night, they could hear the ripple of the nearby stream.* —**ripple** v.

rise (raɪz) v. **rose** (roʷz), **risen** (rɪz–ən), **rising** (raɪz–ɪŋ) **1.** To move up; become higher: *The heavy rains caused the flood waters to rise./ Because of his hard work, he rose to a responsible position in the company.* —opposite FALL **2.** Of the sun and moon, to come up in the east: *The sun rose at 6:30 this morning.* —opposite SET **3.** *fml.* To get up from a bed, chair, etc.: *He rose from his chair to welcome his guests.* **4.** To expand because of yeast in bread, rolls, etc.: *She waited for the bread to rise before putting it in the oven to bake.* **5. rise again** also **rise from the dead** To come back to life after being dead: *Jesus told his disciples that he must suffer many things and "that he must be killed and after three days rise again."* *This prophecy was fulfilled* (Mark 8:31). *Jesus died for all, that those who live should live no longer for themselves but for him who died for them and rose again* (2 Corinthians 5:15 NKJV). —see JESUS, RESURRECTION **6. rise to the occasion** To be able to handle a serious situation: *I was proud of my son, because when the manager became ill suddenly, he rose to the occasion and took charge of the office for two weeks.*

NOTE: Do not confuse RISE, which means to go up, and RAISE, which means to lift sthg. or sbdy.: *They rose from their seats around the table, and raised their glasses for a toast to the new president.* ARISE can mean the same as RISE, but this is very formal: *What time do you arise in the morning?* More often it is used to mean "to come into being": *Accidents arise when people are careless.* **7. rise (up) against** To rebel against; protest: *In the French Revolution, the poor people rose*

up against the king.

rise n. **1.** The act of rising; an increase; *There will be a ten per cent rise in the price of cars next year.* **2.** BrE. An increase or raise in salary or wages **3.** The beginning and growth in power of a movement, etc.: *the rise of the Roman Empire* **4.** **give rise to** To cause sthg. to happen, esp. sthg. bad: *Unhealthy working conditions give rise to illness among the workers.*

ris-en (rız–ən) v. Past part. of the verb **rise:** *Jesus Christ has risen from the dead.*

risk (rısk) n. **1.** Possible danger: *If you try to cross the river when it is flooded, you take the risk of drowning.* **2.** In insurance, a person or thing that is a danger: *He is a poor risk for car insurance, because he has already had three accidents this year.* —**risk** v. —**risky** adj.

ris-qué (rı–skeᵞ) adj. Bordering on indecency; suggestive; daring

rite (raıt) n. A formal ceremony or act with a set pattern, usu. religious: *baptism rites*

rit-u-al (rıtʃ–uʷ–əl) n. **1.** All the rites or ceremonies used, esp. in public worship: *The rituals of the Catholic Church have been used for many years.* **2.** A set pattern of action: *The old soldier goes through the ritual of polishing his boots every day even though he is now retired.* —**ritual** adj. —**ritually** adv. —**ritualist** n. —**rit-u-al-is-tic** (rıtʃ–uʷ–əl–ıs–tık) adj.

ritz-y (rıt–siᵞ) adj. Smart; luxurious; elegant

ri-val (raı–vəl) n. A person who competes with another, esp. who wants the same thing as another: *Bob and Bill were rivals for my sister; but she loved only Bob, and she married him last week.* —**rival** v. —**rival** adj.

ri-val-ry (raı–vəl–riᵞ) n. -**ries** Competition; a situation where there are rivals: *There has been rivalry between the two football teams for many years; each year they compete with each other.*

riv-er (rıv–ər) n. Natural flowing water that runs between banks into a lake, another river, or the sea: *The Amazon River and the Mississippi River are among the largest rivers of the world.* —compare STREAM

riv-et (rıv–ət) n. A metal pin or bolt used to hold metal plates, etc. together by pushing it through a hole and hammering the flat

end of it into a head

riv-et v. **1.** To fasten with a rivet **2.** To fasten firmly **3.** *fig.* To hold one's attention firmly; *His eyes seemed riveted to the TV set.*

riv-u-let (rıv–yə–lət) n. A small stream

R.N. or **RN** abbr. for **registered nurse:** *Mary Smith, R.N.*

roach (roʷtʃ) n. A cockroach

road (roʷd) n. **1.** A prepared open way for the passage of vehicles **2.** *fig.* A way to achieve success, riches, etc.

road-run-ner (roʷd–rʌn–ər) n. A bird of southwestern North America that runs fast. It has a long tail and brownish, streaked feathers

road-way (roʷd–weᵞ) n. A road over which vehicles travel

roam (roʷm) v. To wander; to move freely through an area or from place to place: *Deer roam through the woods in the northern part of the country.*

roar (rɔr) v. **1.** To make loud deep sounds: *When a lion roars, the sound is frightening./The motorcycle roared along the highway.* **2.** To laugh loudly: *The audience roared as he told one funny joke after another.* —**roar** n.

roar-ing (rɔr–ıŋ) adj. **1.** Enraged: *Be self-controlled and alert. Your enemy the devil prowls around like a roaring lion looking for someone to devour* (1 Peter 5:8). **2.** *infml.* Extremely good; very successful: *That new store is doing a roaring business.*

roaring adv. Exceedingly: *He is roaring drunk.*

roast (roʷst) v. To cook over an open fire; bake in an oven, usu. meat or poultry: *She roasted the chicken in the oven for an hour.*

roast n. A large piece of meat which will be or has been roasted

rob (rɑb) v. -**bb**- To steal; take sthg. without permission, esp. by force: *Two armed men robbed the bank.*

rob-ber (rɑb–ər)n. A person who steals, usu. by force —see THIEF

rob-ber-y (rɑb–ə–riᵞ) n. -**ies 1.** Stealing; taking someone's property without permission: *For I, the Lord, love justice; I hate robbery and iniquity* (Isaiah 61:8). **2. highway robbery** also **daylight robbery** BrE. *infml.* Charging a

price that is too high: *Five dollars for a loaf of bread! That's highway robbery!*

robe (ro^wb) n. A long loose garment for **(a)** Informal use: *a bath robe* **(b)** Official occasions: *The judge was wearing a black robe.*

robe v. *fml.* To put on a robe

rob-in (rɑb–ən) n. A common North American bird with a grayish-black back and a dull-red breast

ro-bot (ro^w–bət/ –bɑt) n. **1.** A man-like machine **2.** One who works mechanically, without seeming to get tired **3.** Any device that works automatically or is operated by remote control

ro-bust (ro^w–bəst/ ro^w–bʌst) adj. Very healthy; strong; rugged

rock (rɑk) v. **1.** To move continually back and forth or from side to side: *The mother gently rocked the cradle until the baby fell asleep./The storm caused the small boat to rock violently.* **2.** *infml.* To shock and surprise: *The news of the assassination of the king rocked the nation.*

rock n. **1.** The hard land surface of the earth: *In New York City, the skyscrapers are built on the solid rock of Manhattan Island./Therefore everyone who hears these words of mine [Jesus'] and puts them into practice is like a wise man who built his house on the rock* (Matthew 7:24). **2.** A large piece of this hard surface, usu. larger than a stone: *The angry crowd picked up rocks and threw them at the car, breaking the windows.* **3. on the rocks** *infml.* **(a)** Undiluted alcoholic beverages served over ice cubes: *He ordered whiskey on the rocks.* **(b)** In serious difficulty; about to end: *Because of the falling demand for his product, his business was on the rocks./The Browns fought constantly. Their marriage was on the rocks.* —**rocky** adj.

rock-er (rɑk–ər) n. **1.** One of the curved pieces of wood or metal which support a rocking chair, rocking horse, or cradle **2.** Rocking chair: *The old lady enjoyed sitting in the rocker, quietly rocking back and forth.*

rock-et (rɑk–ət) n. A tube-shaped device filled with fuel which, when fired, drives the device into the air, used for fireworks, missiles, spacecraft, etc.

rocket v. *infml.* To increase quickly: *The unex-*

pected frost damaged the orange crop, and the price of oranges rocketed in the markets.

rock-et-ry (rɑk–ə–tri^y) n. The science of rocket design, construction, and flight

rock 'n' roll (rɑk–ən–ro^wl) n. Modern dance music with a strong, heavy beat, esp. popular with young people

rock-y (rɑk–i^y) adj. **-ier, -iest 1.** Having rocks **2.** Having difficulty; unstable: *a rocky marriage*

rod (rɑd) n. A long straight thin stick or pole made of wood, metal, or plastic: *fishing rod/lightning rod/He who spares the rod hates his son, but he who loves him is careful to discipline him* (Proverbs 13:24).

rode (ro^wd) v. Past tense of **ride**

ro-dent (ro^wd–ənt) n. Any of various related mammals such as mice, rats, squirrels, or beavers, that have large incisors for gnawing or nibbling

ro-de-o (ro^w–di^y–o^w/ro^w–de^y–o^w) n. **1.** A competition featuring cowboy skills, such as riding bucking broncos, roping of calves, etc. **2.** A roundup; the driving together of cattle to be inspected, branded, etc.

roe (ro^w) n. **roes** Fish eggs

rogue (ro^wg) n. **1.** A very dishonest person **2.** A playfully mischievous person

ro-guish (ro^w–gɪʃ) adj. Fond of playing tricks; playfully mischievous: *a roguish fellow/smile*

role (ro^wl) n. **1.** An actor's part in a play, etc.: *Mary played the role of Juliet in the new stage production.* **2.** A person's part in real life: *She played the role of housewife while her children were growing up, even though she had been trained as a nurse.*

roll (ro^wl) n. **1.** A piece of flat paper or cloth that has been turned over and over on itself to form a cylinder: *At the supermarket, she bought a roll of paper towels.* **2.** Bread, usu. in the shape of a cube or a ball, for one person: *At the restaurant, they serve assorted rolls with their dinners.* **3. call the roll** To read a list of names aloud to find out if everyone is present: *The teacher called the roll before beginning the lesson.*

roll v. **1.** To move by turning over and over or round and round: *The ball rolled down the hill.* **2.** To move along on wheels: *After the*

plane landed, it rolled up to the terminal. **3.** To form into a cylinder or tube: *They rolled up the carpet in order to polish the floor.* **4.** Of a boat, to move from side to side with the movement of the waves **5.** To flatten with a roller or rolling pin: *She rolled the dough flat with the rolling pin before cutting out the cookies.* **6.** To make a long deep sound: *The sound of thunder rolled across the hills.*

roll-er (ro^w–lər) n. **1.** A straight cylinder of wood, metal, plastic, etc., that rolls and is used for flattening, printing, crushing, etc.: *At the printing press, ink is first put on the rollers and then the paper is printed.* **2.** A rod used for rolling sthg. up: *In the classroom, there is a big chart on a roller on the wall./She puts her hair on rollers to make it curly.* **3.** Small wheels that make it easy to move heavy objects: *The big suitcase had rollers on the bottom so it could be pulled along the floor.*

roll-er coast-er (ro^w–lər ko^ws–tər) n. A thrilling kind of train ride in an amusement park, with many steep descents and sharp turns

roll-er skate (ro^w–lər ske^yt) n. One of a pair of sets of four small wheels attached to the soles of shoes or boots for gliding across the pavement and other hard surfaces

roller skate v. **skated, skating** To glide across a hard surface on a pair of skates having four small wheels attached to the soles of the shoes or boots

rol-lick (rɑl–ɪk) v. To play or behave in a lively, joyous manner; romp

roll-ing (ro^wl–ɪŋ) adj. Of land, having gentle slopes: *The rolling farm land was ready for the crops to be planted.*

ro-ly-po-ly (ro^w–li^y–po^w–li^y) adj. Short and fat

ro-mance (ro^w–mæns) n. **1.** Love relationship between a man and woman, esp. before marriage: *Robert and Martha are having a beautiful romance, and they hope to marry in June.* **2.** A love story, usu. more exciting, beautiful, and dramatic than in real life: *The story about Romeo and Juliet was one of the most famous romances ever written.* —**romantic** adj. —**romantically** adv.

Ro-man num-er-als (ro^w–mən nu^wm–ər–əlz) n. A numbering system based on that of the ancient Romans, in which letters stand for numbers: I = 1, II = 2, III = 3, IV = 4, V = 5, VI =6, VII = 7, VIII = 8, IX = 9, X = 10, L = 50, C =100, D = 500, M = 1000

Ro-mans (ro^w–məns) n. A letter written by St. Paul to the Christians of Rome, emphasizing "salvation through faith in Jesus Christ without the deeds of the law," and included in the New Testament —see JESUS, NEW TESTAMENT

ro-man-tic (ro^w–mænt–ɪk) adj. **1.** Of or having to do with romance **2.** Full of adventure or heroism **3.** Suitable or proper for love and romance: *romantic music* **4.** Full of ideas about romance and adventure

romp (rɑmp) v. **1.** To play in a lively and boisterous manner: *Children, stop romping around and sit down.* **2.** To win without much effort: *Our team really got romped (beaten badly) by North High.*

roof (rʊf/ ru^wf) n. **roofs** **1.** Top covering of a house or other building, vehicle, etc.: *When the rain comes down hard, we can hear it falling on the roof.* —compare CEILING **2.** A home: *In our home, my grandfather, my aunt, my parents, and my two brothers and I all live under the same roof.* **3. go through/ hit/ raise the roof** *infml.* To get angry or excited: *He hit the roof when he learned that the man had stolen his car and crashed it against a tree.* **4. roof of the mouth** The upper inside of the mouth; palate

roof v. To put a roof on: *They started roofing the house this morning.*

roof-ing (rʊf–ɪŋ/ ru^wf–ɪŋ) n. Material used for making a roof

rook (rʊk) n. **1.** A chess piece that can move vertically or horizontally over any number of unoccupied squares **2.** A swindler —**rook** v. To swindle; cheat

rook-ie (rʊk–i^y) n. Any raw recruit, as a new member of the police force

room (ru^wm) n. **1.** A part of a house or other building, separated from others by walls and usu. a door: *living room/ dining room/ bedroom* **2.** A need for: *room for improvement* **3.** Space for sthg.: *There's room to put the sofa along that wall.* **4. double room** In a hotel, one room for two persons **5. room and board** Sleeping accommodations and meals

—see PLACE

room v. **1.** To live in a rented room **2.** To provide room/s for sbdy.

room-mate (ruʷm–meʸt) n. One who occupies a room with another

room-y (ruʷm–iʸ) adj. **-ier, -iest** Spacious: *a roomy car*

roost (ruʷst) v. Of a bird, to settle and sleep for the night —**roost** n.

roost-er (ruʷs–tər) n. A fully-grown male chicken

root (ruʷt/ rʊt) n. **1.** The part of a plant that grows under the ground **2.** The part of a tooth, hair, etc., that cannot be seen above the surface **3.** The origin; source; cause: *The love of money is the root of all kinds of evil...* (1 Timothy 6:10). **4. roots** *fig. His roots are in California where he was born, but now he lives in New York.*

root v. **1.** To send out roots or a root **2.** To become or cause to become thoroughly implanted **3.** To remove by the roots or as if by the roots **4.** To turn up or dig in the earth as if with the snout **5. root for** To applaud or lend support to sbdy. or sthg.

root-ed (ruʷt–əd/ rʊt–əd) adj. Fixed (as if by roots): *St. Paul, writing to Christians in Colosse, said: "Continue to live in him [Jesus], rooted and built up in him, strengthened in the faith..."* (Colossians 2:6,7).

rope (roʷp) n. **1.** Strong thick cord: *The boat was tied to the dock with a rope.* —compare STRING **2. know the ropes** *infml.* To be very familiar with the details, rules, operations, etc., of sthg.: *John has worked here 20 years, and he really knows the ropes.*

rope v. **roped, roping 1.** To fasten sthg. with a rope **2.** To catch and tie up an animal with a rope; lasso: *rope a calf* **3. rope in** *infml.* To persuade someone to do sthg.: *We've roped him into joining us on the picnic tomorrow.*

rose (roʷz) n. **1.** A sweet-smelling flower of various colors, with thorns on its stem **2.** A color between deep pink and purplish red **3. a bed of roses** *infml.* A comfortable situation: *Repairing a roof in the hot summer sun is no bed of roses!*

rose adj. **1.** Of the color rose **2.** Of or relating to a rose **3.** Flavored, scented, or colored like a rose

rose v. Past tense of **rise**

rose-mar-y (roʷz–mɛər–iʸ) n. An evergreen plant of the mint family that yields a fragrant oil used in perfumes, cooking, etc.

Rosh Ha-sha-na (roʷʃ hə–ʃoʷ–nə/ roʃ/ –ʃɑn–ə) n. The Jewish New Year, observed as a religious holiday in September or October

ros-ter (rɑs–tər) n. A list of persons or groups: *His name was on page 220 of the clergy roster.*

ros-trum (rɑs–trəm) n. **-trums** or **-tra** (–trə) n. A raised platform from which public speeches are made

ros-y (roʷ–ziʸ) adj. **-ier, -iest 1.** Pink or pinkish-red **2.** Having a fresh, healthy redness **3.** Cheerful; optimistic —**rosily** adv. —**rosiness** n.

rot (rɑt) v. **-tt-** To decay due to natural causes: *The apples on the ground under the tree have rotted; they must be thrown away./ fig. A heart at peace gives life to the body, but envy rots the bones* (Proverbs 14:30). —**rot** n.

ro-ta-ry (roʷt–ə–riʸ) adj. **1.** Turning around on an axis, as a wheel on an axle **2.** Having a part or parts that rotate

rotary n. **-ries 1.** A rotary machine **2.** A traffic circle

ro-tate (roʷ–teʸt) v. **-tated, -tating 1.** To move in circles around a fixed point: *The earth rotates on its axis and also revolves around the sun.* **2.** To take turns or change in regular succession: *Most farmers try to rotate their crops in such a way as to produce the best crops.*

ro-ta-tion (roʷ–teʸ–ʃən) n. **1.** The action of rotating or being rotated **2.** One complete movement of this kind: *Each rotation of the earth takes 24 hours.*

rote (roʷt) n. **by rote** The use of memory, usu. with little understanding

rot-or (roʷt–ər) n. The revolving part of a machine

rot-ten (rɑt–ən) adj. **1.** Containing rot; decayed: *The rotten wood in the beams supporting the roof had to be replaced.* **2.** *slang* Bad; unkind: *Stealing from a poor old lady is a rotten thing to do!* —**rot-tenness** n.

ro-tund (roʷ–tʌnd/ roʷ–tʌnd) adj. Round; plump

ro-tun-da (roʷ–tʌn–də) n. A round building,

hall, or room, esp. one with a dome

rouge (ru^wʒ) n. A red cosmetic for coloring the cheeks

rough (rʌf) adj. **1.** Having an irregular surface; not level or smooth: *The rough path made walking difficult.* **2.** Rude; violent: *The man was too rough with the little boy, and he hurt him.* **3.** Difficult; uncomfortable: *The mountain climbers had a rough time trying to reach the top of the mountain.* **4.** Stormy: *rough weather/seas/winds* **5.** Incomplete; preliminary: *He had the editor read the rough draft of his article before he wrote the final version.* **6.** Approximate: *I'd make a rough guess and say there were 500 people at the game.* **7. be rough on sbdy.** *infml.* Unpleasant; unlucky: *It was rough on him to have to drop out of school because of his father's illness.*

rough adv. In a somewhat violent way (physically): *Don't play so rough; you'll hurt your baby sister.* —**roughly** adv.

rough-age (rʌf–ɪdʒ) n. Coarse food that stimulates the activity of the intestines

rough-ly (rʌf–li^y) adv. **1.** In a rough way: *He was angry and spoke roughly to her.* **2.** Approximately: *There were roughly 500 people at the game.*

rough-neck (rʌf–nɛk) n. Rowdy, tough

rou-lette (ru^w–lɛt) n. A game of chance in which players bet on the space on a rotating wheel at which a small, spinning ball will come to rest when the wheel stops turning

round (raʊnd) adj. **1.** Circular and flat: *a round, flat tray* **2.** Shaped like a ball or sphere: *a round stone/The earth is round.* **3.** Of persons, somewhat fat and curved: *a round face/round cheeks* **4. in round figures** Approximate; numbers that have zeros in them: *In round figures, that stadium seats 50,000 people.* **5. round trip** In travel, going to a place and returning: *They bought round-trip tickets on the plane for their vacation in Switzerland.* —see also BrE. RETURN TICKET

round adv. **1.** also **around** Going in a circle: *The hands on the clock keep going round.* **2.** Throughout a period of time: *Pine trees stay green all year round.* **3.** On all sides; in a circle: *A crowd was gathered round to listen to the speaker.*

round prep. Around: *He drove the car round the track at top speed.*

round n. **1.** A series of events: *The diplomats held a continual round of talks until the problem was settled.* **2.** A regular series of visits: *Dr. Nelson made the rounds of his patients at the hospital each morning.* **3.** A unit of action in a contest or game: *a round of golf/The champion won the boxing match by a knockout in the third round.* **4.** One single shot from a gun or shots from several guns at the same time: *They heard only one round, and then silence.*

round-a-bout (raʊn–də–baʊt) adj. Indirect

round-up (raʊn–dəp) n. **1.** The gathering together of cattle on the range **2.** The men and horses taking part in a roundup **3.** The gathering together of scattered persons or things —**round up** v.

rouse (raʊz) v. **roused, rousing 1.** To wake up from sleep **2.** To stir people to anger; to stimulate

rous-ing (raʊ–zɪŋ) adj. Making people excited: *a rousing cheer*

roust-a-bout (raʊ–stə–baʊt) n. A transient worker; one who does heavy, unskilled labor

rout (raʊt) n. **1.** A disorderly flight, as of an army **2.** A complete defeat

rout v. **1.** To defeat utterly **2.** To search haphazardly **3.** To gouge out, as wood or metal

route (raʊt/ ru^wt) n. **1.** The way taken from one place to another: *He took the quickest route from his home to his office.* **2.** A fixed territory or course covered: *My son has a paper route.*

route v. **routed, routing** To fix the route of: *They routed the traffic around the construction area.*

rou-tine (ru^w–ti^yn) n. The regular fixed way of doing things; customary procedure: *daily routine/office routine*

routine adj. Regular; ordinary: *routine duties/questions* —**routinely** adv.

rove (ro^wv) v. **roved, roving** To wander around, without a definite destination: *On vacation they just roved through the hills and woodlands.*

rov-er (ro^w–vər) n. A wanderer

row (ro^w) v. To move the oars of a boat: *They rowed the boat across the river.* —**row** n. *go for a row on the lake*

row n. **1.** A straight line of people or things side by side: *The street was lined with a row of palm trees./The class stood in three rows for the photograph.* **2.** A line of seats across a theater, auditorium, etc.

row (rao) n. *infml.* **1.** A noisy quarrel, sometimes violent: *Mr. Black and his wife had a row about his coming home late at night.* **2.** A loud noise: *Those cats are making an awful row! Can you stop them?*

row-dy (rao-di^y) adj. **-dier, -diest** Rough and disorderly

rowdy n. A quarrelsome, disorderly person

roy-al (rɔɪ-əl) adj. Connected with a king or queen: *the royal crown/Speaking to fellow-believers in Jesus, Peter wrote, "But you are a chosen people, a royal priesthood... that you may declare the praises of him who called you out of darkness into his wonderful light"* (1 Peter 2:9). —**royally** adv.

roy-al-ty (rɔɪ-əl-ti^y) n. **-ties 1.** Members of a royal family **2.** A payment of proceeds made to an author, inventor, landowner: *The composer continues to receive royalties on his music whenever it is played, even though he is now retired.*

RPM *abbr.* for **Revolutions per minute**

RSVP or **r.s.v.p.** (ɑr ɛs vi^y pi^y) *abbr.* for **please reply**

rub (rʌb) v. **-bb- 1.** To move one thing with pressure on the surface of another: *She rubbed the table with polish until it shone./The cat rubbed against my legs.* **2. rub sbdy. the wrong way** *infml.* To annoy sbdy.; irritate sbdy.: *She doesn't know why she doesn't like him! He just rubs her the wrong way!* **3. rub sthg. in** To move one thing with pressure into the surface of another: *She rubbed the hand cream into her skin.* **4. rub it in** *infml.* To keep reminding sbdy. of a failure: *I know our baseball team lost the game! Don't rub it in!*

rub n. The act of rubbing

rub-ber (rʌb-ər) n. **1.** An elastic substance made from the sap of a tropical tree, now usu. produced chemically, used to make tires, balls, pencil erasers, etc. **2.** A low-cut overshoe: *He wore rubbers over his shoes to keep his feet dry when walking in the rain.* —**rubber** adj.

rub-ber band (rʌb-ər bænd) n. A loop of rubber to hold papers, etc. together: *He put a rubber band around the envelopes to keep them together.*

rub-ber ce-ment (rʌb-ər sɪ-mɛnt) n. A kind of glue

rub-ber-neck (rʌb-ər-nɛk) n. A gaping sightseer; an inquisitive person —**rubbernecker** n.

rubberneck v. **1.** To look about or stare with great curiosity **2.** To go on a sightseeing tour

rub-ber stamp (rʌb-ər stæmp) n. **1.** A device for stamping the date or other information on a surface **2.** A person who automatically approves whatever a person or group proposes

rubber–stamp v. To approve automatically without careful consideration

rub-ber-y (rʌb-ər-i^y) adj. *often derog.* Like rubber: *rubbery meat*

rub-bish (rʌb-ɪʃ) n. **1.** Trash: *Let's clean the house, and throw out this rubbish.* **2.** Nonsense; worthless talk: *That book is rubbish; don't read it!* —**rubbishy** adj.

rub-ble (rʌb-əl) n. **1.** Rough pieces of broken stone **2.** Broken pieces of anything, esp. in a large mass: *After the tornado, our house was a pile of rubble.*

ru-bel-la (ru^w-bɛl-ə) n. German measles

ru-be-o-la (ru^w-bi^y-o^w-lə) n. Measles

ru-bi-cund (ru^w-bɪ-kənd) adj. Ruddy, reddish

ru-ble (ru^w-bəl) n. The standard unit of money in Russia

ru-bric (ru^w-brɪk) n. Words put as a heading or a note of explanation as to how sthg. is to be done

ru-by (ru^w-bi^y) n. **-bies** A deep red precious stone: *Wisdom is more precious than rubies, and nothing you desire can compare with her* (Proverbs 8:11).

ruby adj. The color of a ruby

ruck-us (rʌk-əs) n. Noisy confusion; uproar; disturbance

rud-der (rʌd-ər) n. A flat piece of wood, met-

al, etc., below the water at the back of a boat or ship that can be moved from side to side to steer it; a similar object at the back of an aircraft

rud-dy (rʌd–iʸ) adj. **-dier, -diest** Having a healthy pink or reddish color

rude (ruʷd) adj. **ruder, rudest 1.** Not polite or courteous: *It's rude to interrupt others when they are talking.* **2.** Roughly made; simple: *They built a rude cabin in the woods.* **3.** Surprising; sudden: *It was a rude awakening for him to learn his assistant had been stealing from him.* —**rudely** adv. —**rudeness** n.

ru-di-ment (ruʷ–də–mənt) n. *usu. pl.* **1.** The fundamental element, principle, or skill **2.** Any undeveloped form of sthg.

ru-di-men-ta-ry (ruʷ–də–men–tər–iʸ) adj. Of knowledge, simple; that which is learned first: *a rudimentary knowledge of astronomy*

rue (ruʷ) v. **rued, ruing** To repent or regret

rue-ful (ruʷ–fəl) adj. **1.** Pitiable **2.** Regretful; sorrowful: *a rueful expression*

ruff (rʌf) n. **1.** A pleated frill worn around the neck **2.** A frill-like band of feathers or hair on a bird or animal's neck

ruf-fi-an (rʌf–iʸ–ən) n. A rough, lawless person

ruf-fle (rʌf–əl) v. **-fled, -fling 1.** To erect the feathers, as a bird in anger: *The chicken ruffled its feathers.* **2.** To destroy the smoothness of sthg. **3.** To gather fabric into a ruffle **4.** To become disturbed or irritated

ruffle n. **1.** A strip of frilled fabric, used for trimming or decorating **2.** Disturbance or irritation **3.** A ripple

rug (rʌg) n. **1.** A thick floor covering, made of wool, nylon, etc., smaller than a carpet: *We've just bought a small rug to put in front of the fireplace.* **2. sweep sthg. under the rug** To try to hide sthg. bad

rug-by (rʌg–biʸ) n. A British form of football that developed from soccer

rug-ged (rʌg–əd) adj. Rough; uneven; often rocky: *rugged mountains* —**ruggedly** adv. —**ruggedness** n.

ru-in (ruʷ–ən) n. **1.** Destruction; collapse; serious damage: *Wise men store up knowledge, but the mouth of a fool invites ruin* (Proverbs 10:14). **2.** A ruined building: *The old castle is now only a ruin.* **3. in ruins** In a damaged condition: *After the storm, the house was in ruins.*

ruin v. **1.** To destroy completely; damage seriously: *Jesus knew their thoughts and said to them, "Every kingdom divided against itself will be ruined, and every city or household divided against itself will not stand"* (Matthew 12:25). **2.** To cause financial collapse; loss of money: *Many businessmen were ruined by the stock market crash of 1929.* —**ru-in-ous** (ruʷ–ən–əs) adj. —**ruinously** adv.

rule (ruʷl) n. **1.** A regulation, order, or principle which governs behavior: *...and whatever other commandments there might be, are summed up in this one rule: "Love your neighbor as yourself"* (Romans 13:9). **2.** Custom; the usual way that sthg. happens: *I make it a rule to wash my hands before eating.* **3.** Governing power: *...[God] raised him [Jesus] from the dead and seated him at his right hand in the heavenly realms, far above all rule and authority, power and dominion ...* (Ephesians 1:20,21). **4.** Strip of wood, metal, etc., used to measure: *a slide rule* **5. as a rule** Usually; generally: *As a rule, I get up at six o'clock in the morning.*

rule v. **ruled, ruling 1.** To govern; have authority over: *Direct my footsteps according to your word, [O Lord]; let no sin rule over me* (Psalm 119:133). *Let the peace of Christ rule in your hearts...* (Colossians 3:15). **2.** To give a decision as an authority: *The judge ruled that the thief must spend ten years in prison.*

rul-er (ruʷ–lər) n. **1.** A person who governs: *God, the blessed and only Ruler, the King of kings and Lord of lords...* (1 Timothy 6:15). **2.** A narrow flat piece of wood, metal, etc., with straight edges, marked with inches or centimeters, for use in measuring or drawing straight lines: *an 18-inch ruler*

rul-ing (ruʷ–lɪŋ) adj. Governing: *the ruling powers*

rul-ing n. An official decision made by a judge or other person in authority

rum (rʌm) n. A strong alcoholic drink made from the sugar cane plant

rum-ble (rʌm–bəl) v. **-bled, -bling** To make a low, heavy, continuous sound: *The thunder rumbled in the distance as the storm ap-*

proached./The old bus rumbled along the bumpy road. —**rumble** n.

ru-mi-nant (ru^w–mə–nənt) n. An animal that chews the cud

ru-mi-nate (ru^w–mə–ne^yt) v. -nated, -nating 1. To chew the cud 2. To meditate; to ponder —**ru-mi-na-tion** (ru^w–mə–**ne^y**–ʃən) n. Deep thought

rum-mage (rʌm–ɪdʒ) v. -maged, -maging To look through things in order to find sthg.: *We rummaged through our old papers trying to find our marriage certificate.*

rum-mage sale (rʌm–ɪdʒ se^yl) n. A sale of used items, usu. to raise money for charity

rum-my (rʌm–i^y) n. 1. Any of several card games played by two or more people with two sets (decks) of cards 2. *slang* A drunkard

ru-mor also **ru-mour** *BrE.* (ru^w–mər) n. Reports or statements that may not be true, passed from person to person; gossip: *Speaking of his own return to earth and the end of the present age, Jesus told his disciples, "You will hear of wars and rumors of wars, but see to it that you are not alarmed. Such things must happen, but the end is still to come"* (Matthew 24:6).

rump (rʌmp) n. The rounded upper part of an animal just above the back legs

rum-ple (rʌm–pəl) v. -pled, -pling To make untidy; to crease

rum-pus (rʌm–pəs) n. A noisy disturbance

run (rʌn) v. ran (ræn), running 1. Of people, animals, and some birds, to move the feet faster than walking: *The little boy ran home when his mother called him./But those who hope in the Lord will renew their strength... they will run and not grow weary, they will walk and not be faint* (Isaiah 40:31). 2. To compete in a race: *Peter will run in the one-mile race tomorrow.* 3. To move quickly through: *An idea ran through his mind./She ran a comb through her hair.* 4. Of machines, to work or operate: *My new sewing machine runs very well.* 5. To be located; to extend: *The railway track runs beside the river.* 6. Of public transportation, to move on a schedule: *That bus runs ev-ery 15 minutes.* 7. To flow: *The Amazon River runs through the jungles of Brazil.* 8. To pour out liquid: *She ran the water to fill the bathtub.* 9.

Compete for an elected office: *He's going to run for senator in next year's election.* 10. To continue performances, etc.: *That play has been running in New York for two years.* 11. *infml.* To take sbdy./sthg., or go, on a short trip in a vehicle: *I'm going to run to the bank.* 12. To manage; to own and be in charge of: *He runs a restaurant, and his wife runs a beauty shop.* 13. To send out a fluid: *Her nose is running.* 14. To tear or ravel: *Her stockings ran.* 15. To have or suffer: *She's running a fever.* 16. To pass into a certain condition: *He ran into debt.* 17. To thrust or chase: *The police ran him out of the country.* 18. **run short** (a) To use up the supply of sthg.: *They ran short of wood and couldn't finish the construction.* (b) also **run low** To have less than enough: *We're running short/low on bread; be sure to buy some more when you go to the grocery store.* 19. **run sbdy. down** (a) To hit and knock down a person, animal, or smaller object with one's vehicle (b) To say bad things about sbdy./sthg. (c) To chase and catch sbdy. 20. **run down** (a) Of a clock or battery, to lose power and stop working (b) Of facts, to look for and find the needed information 21. **run into** (a) To hit sthg. with one's vehicle (b) To fall into debt, difficulty, etc. 22. **run into sbdy.** To meet a friend unexpectedly on the street, in a shop, etc.

run (rʌn) n. 1. An act or period of running on foot: *He goes for a two-mile run every morning.* 2. A short trip, esp. by train: *It's a four-hour run from New York to Washington, D.C.* 3. A continuous series of performances of a play, show, etc.: *That play had a two-week run in Boston.* 4. A continuous series of similar events: *There's been a run of thefts in the neighborhood recently.* 5. In baseball, a point scored by a player reaching home plate safely 6. A rip in a stocking caused by stitches coming undone 7. **a (good) run for one's money** *infml.* (a) A lot of opposition in a competition (b) Reward, enjoyment, etc. for money spent or effort made 8. **in the long run** In the end: *Completing your schooling may not seem important to you now, but in the long run, you will be glad you did.* 9. **on the run** Trying to escape: *The thief had to stay on*

the run to keep from being caught by the police.

run-a-round (rʌn o–raʊnd) n. A series of evasive or deceptive actions, esp. in response to a request

run-a-way (rʌn–ə–we^y) n. 1. A person or animal that runs away 2. The act of running away or being out of control

runaway adj. 1. Accomplished by eloping: *a runaway marriage* 2. Winning by a long margin: *a runaway victory for the horse* 3. Subject to uncontrolled changes: *runaway inflation*

run-down (rʌn–daʊn) n. A point-by-point report or summary: *He gave her a rundown on all they discussed at the meeting.*

run-down (rʌn–daʊn) adj. 1. Of a person, in poor health; tired: *I have been working too hard lately and feel run-down.* 2. Of things, in poor condition; worn out: *We have just bought a run-down old house that will need a lot of repairs before we can live in it.*

rung (rʌŋ) n. A round crosspiece that forms one of the steps of a ladder

rung v. Past part. of **ring**

run-in (rʌn–ɪn) n. *infml.* A quarrel

run-ner (rʌn–ər) n. 1. A person who runs 2. (a) A long narrow rug, esp. for a hallway or stairs (b) A long narrow piece of cloth to cover the length of a table

runner-up (rʌn–ər–ʌp/ rʌn–ər–ʌp) n. **runners-up** also **runner-ups** The person or team that finishes second in a race or competition

run-ning (rʌn–ɪŋ) n. 1. The act of moving fast, flowing, etc. 2. **in/out of the running** With some/no possibility of winning: *Charles won the primary election so he is still in the running for senator.*

running adj. 1. Of water, flowing: *This house has hot and cold running water in the bathroom and kitchen.* 2. Continuous; on-going: *He gave a running commentary on the baseball game.* 3. Used for running, or having to do with running: *running shoes/a running start* 4. Giving out liquid: *a running faucet/sore* 5. **in (good) running order** Of a machine, working properly

run-ny (rʌn–i^y) adj. **-nier, -niest** Tending to discharge: *a runny nose*

run-off (rʌn–ɔf) n. 1. The rainfall that drains off 2. A final deciding contest or vote

run-of-the-mill (rʌn–əv–ðə–mɪl) adj. Ordinary; average

runt (rʌnt) n. A small person or animal that has not grown fully

run-way (rʌn–we^y) n. The part of an airport where airplanes take off and land

ru-pee (ru^w–pi^y) n. The standard coin of India, Pakistan, and Sri Lanka

rup-ture (rʌp–tʃər) n. 1. The act of breaking or bursting: *The extreme cold caused a rupture in the pipeline.* 2. A tearing of the wall of the stomach; a hernia

rupture v. **-tured, -turing** 1. To cause a rupture: *He ruptured himself lifting that heavy trunk.* 2. To break or tear: *She ruptured a blood vessel.*

ru-ral (rʊr–əl) adj. Of or concerning the countryside; not of the city: *They liked quiet rural life better than busy city life.* —compare URBAN

ruse (ru^ws) n. A trick; a cunning plan

rush (rʌʃ) v. 1. To hurry; act quickly: *Don't rush! We are early for our appointment.* 2. To attack suddenly: *The police rushed the door and broke into the house before the robbers could escape.*

rush n. 1. Any of a variety of plants having small greenish flowers, and stems and leaves which are often used for making mats, baskets, etc. 2. A sudden quick action: *There was a rush for the doors when the fire alarm sounded.* 3. Hurry; haste: *I'm in a rush! I can't stop to talk!* 4. A period of special activity: *To avoid the Christmas rush, let's buy our presents in October.* —**rush** adj. *a rush order/job*

rush hour (rʌʃ aʊr) n. In and around a city, the time before and after offices open or close when many people are going to work or going home

rus-set (rʌs–ət) n. Reddish brown

rust (rʌst) n. 1. The reddish brown coating formed on iron and some other metals due to contact with water or air: *Do not store up for yourselves treasures on earth, where moth and rust destroy, and where thieves break in and steal. But store up for yourselves treasures in heaven, where moth and rust do not destroy, and where thieves do not break in and steal. For*

where your treasure is, there your heart will be also (Matthew 6:19-21). **2.** The color of this: *a rust-colored blouse* —**rust** v.

rus-tic (ʀʌs–tɪk) adj. **1.** Typical of country life; suitable for the country: *a kind of rustic charm* **2.** Simple and rough

rustic n. **1.** A rural person **2.** A crude, coarse, or simple person

rus-ti-cate (ʀʌs–tɪ–keʸt) v. **-cated, -cating** To go to or to live in the country

rus-tle (ʀʌs–əl) v. **-tled, -tling 1.** To make a dry, light sound when moved or rubbed together: *the rustling of the leaves in the breeze* **2.** To cause these sounds by movement: *Stop rustling those papers.* **3.** To steal cattle or horses that are loose in open country **4. rustle up** To find a supply of sthg. or prepare sthg. quickly: *We need to rustle up a few volunteers to help at the rummage sale.* —**rustling** n.

rustle n. The sound of rustling: *We heard the rustle of the wind in the trees.*

rus-tler (ʀʌs–lər) n. One who rustles cattle

rust-y (ʀʌs–tiʸ) adj. **-ier, -iest 1.** Affected with rust: *a rusty old metal box* **2.** Almost forgotten: *My French is pretty rusty, and I need to study it again before going to France this summer.*

rut (ʀʌt) n. **1.** A deep narrow track made by a wheel, esp. in soft ground: *Be careful driving your car on this dirt road so that you don't get stuck in the big ruts made by trucks.* **2. be in/ get into a rut** To be, live, or work in a fixed and boring way of life: *You're getting into a rut by staying home all day; you need to get out and do sthg. different.*

Ruth (ruʷθ) n. **1.** A Moabite woman who went with Naomi to Bethlehem and became an ancestor of David and of Jesus Christ **2.** A short book in the Old Testament, containing the story of Ruth —see BIBLE, OLD TESTAMENT

ruth-less (ruʷθ–ləs) adj. Cruel; without mercy or pity: *They [godless men] are senseless, faithless, heartless, ruthless* (Romans 1:31). —**ruthlessly** adv.

rye (raɪ) n. A cereal plant, the grain of which is used for making flour: *rye bread*

S, s (ɛs,z,s,əz) n. The 19th letter of the English alphabet
S or **S.** *Written abbr. for* **1.** South **2.** Southern

Sab·bath (sæb–əθ) n. The day which God appointed to be observed by the Jews as a day of rest and worship. NOTE: This was formerly on the seventh day of the week (Saturday), the day on which God rested from the work of creation; and this day is still observed by the Jews and some Christians. But the Christian church very early began, and still continues, to observe the first day of the week, in commemoration of the resurrection of Jesus Christ on that day. Hence it is often called the Lord's Day, but some refer to it (Sunday) as the Sabbath.

sa·ber *AmE.* **sa·bre** *BrE.* (seʸ–bər) n. A heavy sword with a curved blade

sa·ble (seʸ–bəl) n. **1.** An animal of Asia and northern Europe, related to the mink and weasel, having soft, dark fur that is very valuable **2.** This fur **3.** The color black

sab·o·tage (sæb–ə–tɑʒ) n. The damaging of machinery or materials or the disruption of work by dissatisfied workers or hostile agents
sabotage v. **-taged, -taging 1.** To commit sabotage on **2.** To destroy or render useless

sab·o·teur (sæb–ə–tɜr) n. A person who commits sabotage

sac (sæk) n. A bag-like part in an animal or plant, often containing a liquid

sac·cha·rin (sæk–ə–rən) n. A synthetic sugar substitute

sa·cer·do·tal (sæs–ər–doʷt–əl) adj. Priestly; of priests or the priesthood

sa·chet (sæ–ʃeʸ) n. **1.** A small bag (to hold handkerchiefs, etc.) **2.** A small sealed bag for holding sthg. in a liquid or powdered form

sack (sæk) n. **1.** A bag of strong, usu. brown, paper, used for carrying groceries, one's lunch, etc. **2.** Often a bag of strong cloth

SPELLING NOTE:
Words having the sound /s/ may be spelled with **c-**, as in **city**, or **ps-**, like **psychologist**.

used for storing or moving flour, sugar, grain, etc. **3. hit the sack** *infml.* To go to bed
sack v. **1.** To put sthg. into a sack **2.** *infml.* To dismiss from a job

sack·cloth (sæk–klɔθ) n. **1.** Coarse cloth for making sacks **2.** A garment made from this, worn as a sign of repentance

sac·ra·ment (sæk–rə–mənt) n. An outward and visible sign of inward and spiritual grace, more specifically a solemn religious ceremony instituted by Jesus Christ, the head of the Christian Church, to be observed by his followers, by which their special relation to him is created or strengthened and their obligations to him renewed and ratified. These sacraments are Baptism and the Lord's Supper, also called Communion, Holy Communion, or the Eucharist —**sac·ra·men·tal** (sæk–rə–ment–əl) adj.

sa·cred (seʸ–krəd) adj. **1.** Sthg. dedicated to, or set apart for worship **2.** Made or declared holy **3.** Religious in nature or use; holy by connection with God: *sacred music/art/ writings*

sac·ri·fice (sæk–rə–faɪs) n. **1.** Sthg. offered to God or a god, esp. an animal killed in a ceremony NOTE: Animal sacrifices were commanded by God in Old Testament times. Jesus Christ made the supreme sacrifice for us, paying for all our sins with his own blood when he suffered and died for us on the cross: *He [Jesus] is the atoning sacrifice for our sins...* (1 John 2:2). *...He [Jesus] has appeared once for all... to do away with sin by the sacrifice of himself* (Hebrews 9:26). *...By one sacrifice he has made perfect forever those who are being made holy* (Hebrews 10:14). **2.** The giving up of sthg. of value, esp. for a particular purpose: *She made a lot of sacrifices to get an education./Paul wrote to the Christians in Rome saying, "I urge you, brothers, in view of God's mercy, to offer your bodies as living sacrifices, holy and pleasing to God — which is your spiritual worship"* (Romans 12:1). —see JESUS —also LAMB OF GOD

sacrifice v. To make an offering of sthg. valuable as a sacrifice: *...He [Jesus] sacrificed for their sins [and ours] once for all when he offered himself [on the cross]* (Hebrews 7:27). *Just as*

man is destined to die once, and after that to face judgment, so Christ was sacrificed once to take away the sins of many people... (Hebrews 9:27,28). —see JESUS, LAMB OF GOD

sac·ri·fi·cial (sæk–rə–fɪʃ–əl) adj. Of or like a sacrifice: *a sacrificial gift* —**sacrificially** adv.

sac·ri·lege (sæk–rə–lɪdʒ) n. The using of a holy object in a disrespectful way

sac·ris·ty (sæk–rə–sti^y) n. -ties The place in a church where sacred vessels, etc. are kept

sac·ro·sanct (sæk–ro^w–sæŋkt) adj. Very sacred, not to be violated or damaged

sad (sæd) adj. -dd- **1.** Unhappy; showing or causing grief or sorrow: *News that my best friend is moving away makes me very sad.* **2.** Worthy of blame; bad: *The old house was in a sad state of repair.* —**sadly** adv. —**sadness** n. *There was a note of sadness in his farewell speech.*

sad·den (sæd–ən) v. To become sad or cause sbdy. to become sad: *Saying good-bye to old friends always saddens me.*

sad·dle (sæd–əl) n. **1.** A seat made to fit on the back of a horse, camel, or other animal for riding, usu. made of leather **2.** A similar seat for a bicycle, motorcycle, etc.

saddle v. -dled, -dling **1.** To place a saddle on **2.** To give sbdy. an unpleasant task, responsibility, etc.

sad·ism (sæd–ɪz–əm/ se^yd–) n. **1.** Sexual satisfaction by causing physical pain to others **2.** Any enjoyment in being cruel —**sadist** n.

sa·dis·tic (sə–dɪs–tɪk/ se^y–) adj. Taking pleasure in seeing others suffer —**sadistically** adv.

sa·fa·ri (sə–far–i^y) n. -ris An expedition for hunting or exploring, esp. in Eastern Africa

safe (se^yf) adj. **safer, safest 1.** Protected from harm and danger; not threatened: *Fear of man will prove to be a snare [trap], but whoever trusts in the Lord is kept safe* (Proverbs 29:25). **2.** Not harmed: *We were glad to find our little boy safe after the night in the cold.* **3.** Not likely to cause or lead to danger or harm: *This is a safe place for storing your valuables.* —opposite UNSAFE **4.** Not likely to result in risk or disagreement: *It's safe to say that the war on drugs will be with us for quite some time.* **5. play it safe** To take no risk —**safely** adv.

safe n. A strong box with a lock used for protecting valuable things from thieves, fire, etc.

safe·guard (se^yf–gɑrd) n. Anything that gives protection or security —**safeguard** v.

safe·ty (se^yf–ti^y) n. -ties The state or condition of being safe: *We are all concerned about the safety of our loved ones.*

safety pin (se^yf–ti^y pɪn) n. A pin with a guard protecting the point to prevent it from coming loose or pricking the user

saf·flow·er (sæf–lau–er) n. A thistle-like plant with large orange-red flowers, yielding a red dye used in rouge and seeds from which a cooking oil is extracted

saf·fron (sæf–rən) n. **1.** The orange-colored stigmas of a kind of crocus, used for coloring and flavoring food **2.** This yellowish orange color

sag (sæg) v. -gg- To droop or bend downwards, esp. from the usual or correct position: *The mattress sagged after being used for so many years./fig. Her spirits sagged (=she became less happy) when her parents told her she could not go on the trip.*

sag n. A downward curving or sinking: *a sag in the roof of the old house*

sa·ga (sɑg–ə/ sæg–) n. A tale of heroic exploits

sa·ga·cious (sə–ge^y–ʃəs/ sɪ–) adj. Having keen mental discernment and sound judgment —**sagaciously** adv. —**sa·ga·ci·ty** (sə–gæs–ət–i^y) n.

sage (se^ydʒ) n. **1.** A wise man **2.** A type of herb with grayish green leaves which are used for flavoring

sage·brush (se^ydʒ brʌʃ) n. A type of bush having a sage-like odor, that grows in dry areas of western North America

sa·go (se^y–go^w) n. -gos A white sticky substance obtained from the pith of a certain palm tree, often used in puddings

sa·gua·ro (sə–gwɑr–o^w/ –ə) n. A giant cactus found in the southwestern US and Mexico

said (sɛd) v. Past tense and past part. of **say**

sail (se^yl) n. A sheet of strong cloth fixed in position on a ship or a boat to catch the wind and drive the boat through the water

sail v. **1.** To travel on the water on a boat or a

ship (with or without sails): *My ship sails at midnight.* **2.** To control or direct a ship: *The captain sailed the ship skillfully between the islands.*

sail-boat (seʸl–boʷt) n. A boat propelled by one or more sails

sail-ing (seʸ–lɪŋ) n. **1.** The act of controlling the course of a ship **2.** The sport of riding in or directing a small sailboat

sail-or (seʸ–lər) n. **1.** One who sails **2.** A member of a ship's crew **3.** A seaman in the navy

saint (seʸnt) n. **1.** A person officially recognized by the Christian church, after the person's death, as especially holy and worthy **2.** *infml.* An especially unselfish or patient person: *He must be a saint to put up with her constant nagging and complaining.* **3.** The word "saint" as used in the Bible, refers to any true believer in Jesus Christ, made holy by the blood of Christ which cleanses us from all sins: *Paul, an apostle of Christ Jesus by the will of God, to the saints in Ephesus, the faithful in Christ Jesus...* (Ephesians 1:1). Saint *abbr.* St. n. A title before a saint's name: *St. Paul and St. John each wrote several books of the New Testament.*

saint-ly (seʸnt–liʸ) adj. **-lier, -liest** Very holy, kind, gentle, forgiving, unselfish: *a saintly mother/He was the saintliest person I've ever met.*

sake (seʸk) n. **1. for the sake of (a)** For the benefit of sbdy. or out of love for sbdy.: *The Bible says, "Submit yourselves for the Lord's sake to every authority instituted among men..."* (1 Peter 2:13). **(b)** In order to get or keep sthg.: *He's working so hard for the sake of the money to go to college.* **2. for goodness sake** *infml.* Used as an exclamation before or after a command or request: *For goodness sake, stop crying and tell me what's wrong!*

sa-laam (sə–lɑm) n. A greeting in Islamic countries

sa-la-cious (sə–leʸ–ʃəs) adj. Lustful; lewd

sal-ad (sæl–əd) n. A mixture of vegetables or fruits served cold, sometimes with other foods added: *a pasta salad/a tossed green salad*

salad dressing (sæl–əd drɛs–ɪŋ) n. A kind of sauce, cooked or uncooked, for putting on salads

sal-a-man-der (sæl–ə–mæn–dər) n. A reptile that looks like a lizard

sa-la-mi (sə–lɑm–iʸ) n. A highly seasoned sausage of pork and beef

sal-a-ried (sael–ə–riʸd) adj. Receiving a salary

sal-a-ry (sael–ə–riʸ) n. **-ries** Fixed regular monthly payment for work, esp. to someone in a profession

sale (seʸl) n. **1.** Act of selling sthg.; transfer of ownership and title from one person to another in exchange for money: *The sale of our mobile home took over a year.* **2.** A selling of goods at lower prices than usual: *I always buy extra groceries when there is a sale.* **3.** The total amount sold: *Sales of his new book are beyond his expectations.* **4. FOR SALE** Intended to be sold, esp. by a private owner: *Our neighbors have just put a "FOR SALE" sign on their house.*

sales (seʸlz) adj. Of, related to, or used for selling: *the salesroom/the sales department*

sales-clerk (seʸlz–klɜrk) n. A person who sells items in a store

sales-lady (seʸlz–leʸd–iʸ) n. A woman who sells things

sales-man (seʸlz–mən) n. A man who sells things in a store or outside a store, or to outside customers

sales-man-ship (seʸlz–mən–ʃɪp) n. The principles and techniques of selling

sales tax (seʸlz tæks) n. Tax paid by a customer in addition to the ordinary sale price of an article

sa-li-ent (seʸ–lyənt/ seʸ–liʸ–ənt) adj. Prominent; noticeable: *the salient points of a speech*

sa-line (seʸ–liʸn/ –m) adj. Salty —**sa-lin-i-ty** (sə–lɪn–ət–iʸ) n.

sa-li-va (sə–laɪ–və) n. The natural liquid produced in the mouth to help one chew and digest food

sal-i-var-y (sæl–ə–vɛər–iʸ) adj. Of or producing saliva

sal-i-vate (sæl–ə–veʸt) v. **-vated, -vating** To produce saliva —**sal-i-va-tion** (sæl–ə–veʸ–ʃən) n.

sal-low (sæl–oʷ) adj. Yellowish in color or complexion

sal·ly (sæl–i^y) n. -lies **1.** A brief excursion **2.** A witty remark **3.** A sudden rush forward in attack —**sally** v. -lied, -lying

salm·on (sæm–ən) n. **1.** A large fish with pinkish flesh eaten as food **2.** The flesh of this fish **3.** The color of the flesh of this fish

sa·lon (sə–lɑn) n. A stylish business establishment or shop: *a fashion salon*

sa·loon (sə–lu^wn) n. **1.** A place where alcoholic drinks may be bought and drunk; a bar; a tavern **2.** A large public room, as on a passenger ship

salt (sɔlt) n. **1.** A very common white substance with many uses, esp. for flavoring and preserving foods; sodium chloride: *table salt/The soup has too much salt.* **2.** *tech.* A chemical compound formed by the combining of an acid and a base or metal **3.** **old salt** An experienced sailor **4.** **rub salt in someone's wounds** To make a painful experience even worse **5.** **the salt of the earth** People who have a wholesome influence on society: *Jesus said to His followers, "You are the salt of the earth"* (Matthew 5:13). **6.** **take sthg. with a grain/ pinch of salt** To accept a statement as probably not true **7.** **worth one's salt** *infml.* Worthy of respect or one's pay

salt v. To apply salt to sthg.: *You may salt the meat either before or after roasting it.*

salt adj. Containing, full of, tasting of, or preserved with salt: *a salt lake/salt pork*

salt·y (sɔl–ti^y) adj. -ier, -iest Of, containing, or tasting of salt —**saltiness** n.

sa·lu·bri·ous (sə–lu^w–bri^y–əs) adj. Favorable to health, as fresh air or mild climate —**salubriously** adv.

sal·u·tar·y (sæl–yə–tɛər–i^y) adj. Conducive to some beneficial purpose

sal·u·ta·tion (sæl–yə–te^y–ʃən) n. A greeting

sa·lu·ta·to·ri·an (sə–lu^wt–ə–tɔr–i^y–ən) n. A student in some schools and colleges who gives a welcoming address at commencement exercises

sa·lute (sə–lu^wt) n. **1.** A military gesture of recognition, such as **(a)** A raising of the right hand to the forehead **(b)** A ceremonial firing of guns, lowering of flags, etc. **2.** A greeting

salute v. **saluted, saluting 1.** To show respect to a superior officer by a formal position of hand, rifle, or sword: *He saluted his commanding officer.* **2.** To greet politely, esp. with words or a gesture: *He saluted his friends as they entered the room.*

sal·vage (sæl–vɪdʒ) v. **-vaged, -vaging** To save goods or property from loss or damage, esp. a damaged ship from the sea: *They recently salvaged a ship that had been at the bottom of the sea for centuries./We were able to salvage most of our belongings after the flood.*

salvage n. **1.** The act of rescuing things from destruction, esp. of saving a damaged ship or its goods from the sea **2.** Property that is salvaged: *We collect glass, paper, and aluminum for salvage.*

sal·va·tion (sæl–ve^y–ʃən) n. **1.** Esp. in the Christian religion, the saving of a person's soul from sin and its consequences; the state of being saved from sin: *God did not appoint us to suffer wrath but to receive salvation through our Lord Jesus Christ* (1 Thessalonians 5:9). *Salvation is found in no one else for there is no other name under heaven given to men by which we must be saved* (Acts 4:12). *The Holy Scriptures are able to make you wise for salvation through faith in Christ Jesus* (2 Timothy 3:15). **2.** *fml.* Way of avoiding loss, ruin, or failure: *The man of the house has lost his job. The only salvation for his family is the charity of his neighbors.*

salve (sæv) n. A medicinal ointment for putting on a cut, insect bite, etc.

salve v. **salved, salving** To make less painful; soothe: *Apologizing may salve your conscience but the vase you broke cannot be repaired.*

sal·vo (sæl–vo^w) n. **-vos** or **-voes** Multiple bursts of gunfire, often in salute

Sa·mar·i·tan (sə–mær–ə–tən/ –mɛər–) n. **Good Samaritan** One who helps someone in need, esp. a total stranger

same (se^ym) adj. **1.** Being the one referred to; not different: *We have lived in the same house for eight years.* **2.** Completely alike; identical; equal: *My twin sister's dress is exactly the same as mine.*

same pron. **1.** The same person, thing, idea, etc.: *Jesus Christ is the same yesterday and to-*

day and forever (Hebrews 13:8)./ *Is his understanding of the job the same as yours?* **2. Same to you!** *infml.* Used in answer to a greeting or a wish, sometimes an angry wish: *"Happy New Year." "Same to you!"/ "I wish you'd stop being so rude!" "Same to you!" (=I wish you would, too!)*

sam·pan (sæm–pæn) n. A small, flat-bottomed boat of the Far East

sam·ple (sæm–pəl) n. A small part that represents the whole thing: *This is a sample of the cloth I plan to use for my new suit.* —**sample** adj.

sample v. -pled, -pling To take and examine in order to judge the quality of sthg., esp. by tasting a sample: *The judges sampled the cakes before choosing the winner in the baking contest.*

sam·pler (sæm–plər) n. **1.** A person who samples **2.** An embroidered cloth serving to show a beginner's skill in nee-dlework

Sam·u·el (sæm–yə–wəl) n. **1.** A masculine name **2.** The last of the judges of Israel and a great prophet (1170-1060 B.C.) **3.** One of the two historical books of the Old Testament. NOTE: First Samuel starts with the birth of Samuel and ends with the death of Saul, the first king of Israel. Second Samuel is about the reign of David, the second king of Israel. Two important verses of Samuel are: "To obey [God] is better than sacrifice" (1 Samuel 15:22) and "Man looks at the outward appearance [of a person] but the Lord looks at the heart" (1 Samuel 16:7). —see BIBLE, OLD TESTAMENT

san·a·to·ri·um (sæn–ə–tɔr–iʸ–əm) n. -riums or -ria An institution for the treatment of chronic disorders, such as alcoholism, mental illness, or for inva-lids; also **san·i·ta·ri·um** (sæn–ə–tɛər–iʸ–əm)

sanc·ti·fi·ca·tion (sæŋk–tə–fə–keʸ–ʃən) n. The act of making holy; in an evangelical sense, the act of God's grace, through the power of the Holy Spirit, by which the affections of men are pu-rified or alienated from sin and the world, and exalted to a supreme love of God: *God has from the beginning chosen you to salvation through sanctification of the Spirit and belief of the truth* (2 Thessaloni-

ans 2:13).

sanc·ti·fy (sæŋk–tə–faɪ) v. -fied, -fying *fml.* **1.** To make holy; purify: *Jesus said to Paul, "I am sending you to open their eyes and turn them from darkness to light, and from the power of Satan to God, so that they may receive forgiveness of sins and a place among those who are sanctified by faith in me"* (Acts 26:18). *Jesus prayed, "Sanctify them [my followers] by the truth; your word is truth. As you sent me into the world, I have sent them into the world. For them I sanctified myself, that they too may be truly sanctified"* (John 17:17-19). **2.** To reserve for sacred use; consecrate

sanc·ti·mo·ni·ous (sæŋk–tə–moʷ–niʸ–əs) adj. Making a show of righteousness —**sanctimoniously** adv.

sanc·ti·mo·ny (sæŋk–tə–moʷ–niʸ) n. Hypocritical piety or righteousness

sanc·tion (sæŋk–ʃən) n. **1.** Permission or approval for an action or change: *The president of the company acts only with the sanction of his board of directors.* **2.** A measure taken against a person or country that has broken a law or rule: *political sanctions* **3.** A reason or reasons that force people to obey rules or standards: *Fear of prison is a sanction against crime.*

sanction v. *fml.* To grant acceptance, approval, or permission: *The church would not sanction his second marriage.*

sanc·ti·ty (sæŋk–tət–iʸ) n. **1.** Holiness; sacredness **2.** The state of being formally binding upon one: *the sanctity of mar-riage*

sanc·tu·ar·y (sæŋk–tʃuʷ–ɛər–iʸ) n. -ies **1.** A sacred place, the holiest part of a temple, the part of a chancel containing the altar **2.** A place of protection or refuge: *a bird sanctuary*

sanc·tum (sæŋk–təm) n. **1.** A holy place **2.** A person's private room

sand (sænd) n. Fine loose pieces of rock that have been worn down, found on beaches and in deserts, used for making cement, glass, etc.

sand v. **1.** To smooth or polish sthg. by rubbing with sandpaper, etc. **2.** To sprinkle or cover with sand: *The icy sidewalks were sanded so people wouldn't fall.*

san-dal (sæn–dəl) n. A type of light open-sided shoe

san-dal-wood (sæn–dəl–wʊd) n. A kind of scented wood from a tropical tree

sand-bag (sænd–bæg) n. A bag filled with sand, used for fortification or for protection against floodwaters, etc.

sand-bar (sænd–bɑr) n. A ridge of sand formed in a river or harbor by tides or currents

sand-blast (sænd–blæst) v. To clean with sand that is blown by compressed air or steam, used to clean hard surfaces

sand dune (sænd duʷn) n. A ridge of sand blown up by the wind

sand-lot (sænd–lɑt) n. A vacant lot, esp. when used for unorganized sports

sand-man (sænd–mæn) n. A fictitious character who supposedly makes children sleepy at bedtime

sand-pa-per (sænd–peʸ–pər) n. A strong paper, coated with sand or other abrasive substance, used for smoothing or polishing —sandpaper v.

sand-pi-per (sænd–paɪ–pər) n. A shore bird, having a slender bill and a piping call

sand-stone (sænd–stoʷn) n. A rock formed of compressed sand

sand-wich (sænd–wɪtʃ/ sæn–) n. **1.** Two pieces of bread with meat, cheese, or other food between them **2.** Sthg. resembling this arrangement

sandwich v. To insert sthg. between two other things

sand-y (sæn–diʸ) adj. -ier, -iest **1.** Like sand or full of sand **2.** Of hair, etc., yellowish brown

sane (seʸn) adj. **1.** Having a healthy mind; not crazy: —opposite INSANE **2.** Showing good judgment; sensible: *a sane decision* —saneness n.

sang (sæŋ) v. Past tense of sing

san-guine (sæŋ–gwən) adj. Hopeful; optimistic

san-i-tar-i-um (sæn–ə–**tɛər**–iʸ–əm) n. -tariums or -taria An establishment for the treatment of chronic diseases, such as tuberculosis, and for convalescents

san-i-tar-y (sæn–ə–tɛər–iʸ) adj. **1.** Of or concerning the protecting of health, esp. the treatment or removal of dirt, waste, etc. **2.** Free from dirt or other dangers to health: *Conditions in a res-taurant ought to be sanitary.*

san-i-ta-tion (sæn–ə–teʸ–ʃən) n. Systems that protect public health, esp. by the removal and treatment of waste

san-i-tize (sæn–ə–taɪz) v. -tized, -tizing To make sanitary

san-i-ty (sæn–ət–iʸ) n. Soundness of mind

sank (sæŋk) v. Past tense of sink

sap (sæp) n. **1.** The watery juice in trees and other plants **2.** *Infml.* A stupid person

sap v. **sapped, sapping** To weaken a person physically: *The heat and humidity really sapped our strength.*

sa-pi-ent (seʸ–piʸ–ənt) adj. Wise and discerning —sapience n. —sapiently adv.

sap-ling (sæp–lɪŋ) n. A young tree

sap-phire (sæf–aɪr) n. **1.** A hard, deep blue precious stone **2.** The color of this stone

sap-py (sæp–iʸ) adj. -pier, -piest **1.** Full of sap **2.** Silly

sar-casm (sɑr–kæz–əm) n. Using expressions which clearly mean the opposite of what is said; a cutting or contemptuous remark

sar-cas-tic (sɑr–kæs–tɪk) adj. Of or using sarcasm: *a sarcastic joke* —sarcastically adv.

sar-dine (sɑr–diʸn) n. A young herring or similar small fish, often canned as food

sar-don-ic (sɑr–dɑn–ɪk) adj. Scornful; derisive; sarcastic —sardonically adv.

sa-ri (sɑr–iʸ) n. -ris An outer garment worn by women in India, consisting of a long piece of cotton or silk cloth worn around the body

sa-rong (sə–rɔŋ/ –rɑŋ) n. A loose-fitting skirt-like garment worn by both men and women on many South Pacific islands

sash (sæʃ) n. **1.** An ornamental band worn over the shoulder or around the waist **2.** A window or door frame in which panes of glass are set

sass (sæs) v. To talk back; talk disrespectfully

sass n. Impudent back talk

sas-sa-fras (sæs–ə–fræs) n. **1.** A North American tree with bark used in medicine and perfume **2.** The bark of this tree

sas-sy (sæs–iʸ) adj. -sier, -siest Impudent

sat (sæt) v. Past tense and past part. of sit

Sa-tan (seɪ't ən) n. The prince of devils It is Satan's intention to destroy the work of God, esp. mankind, but he will not succeed./The God of Peace will soon crush Satan under your feet (Romans 16:20). —see DEVIL, LUCIFER

sa-tan-ic (sə-tæn-ɪk/ seʸ–) adj. Of or like Satan; very evil or wicked; fiendish. Also **satanical** —satanically adv.

satch-el (sætʃ–əl) n. A small bag for carrying school books, etc.

sate (seʸt) v. sated, sating To satisfy fully or give more than enough; to satiate

sat-el-lite (sæt–əl-aɪt) n. 1. A natural body or man-made device which moves around a larger one: The moon is a satellite which moves around the earth./A communications satellite relays telephone messages and radio and TV signals back to the earth. 2. A country controlled by a more powerful neighboring one

sa-ti-ate (seʸ–ʃiʸ–eʸt) v. -ated, -ating To fill or gratify excessively —sa-ti-a-tion (seʸ–ʃiʸ–eʸ–ʃən) n.

sat-in (sæt–ən) n. Silk cloth that is shiny and smooth on one side —satin adj.

sa-tire (sæ–taɪr) n. 1. The use of sarcasm or irony to expose foolishness or vice 2. A literary work in which such use is made —sa-tir-i-cal (sə-tɪər-ɪ-kəl) adj. —satirically adv.—sat-i-rist (sæt–ə-rəst) n.

sat-i-rize (sæt–ə-raɪz) v. -rized, -rizing To attack with satire

sat-is-fac-tion (sæt-ɪs-fæk-ʃən) 1. Feeling of contentment or pleasure: Doing a job well gives me a feeling of satisfaction. —opposite DISSATISFACTION 2. Fulfillment of a requirement, need, desire, etc. 3. Condition of being convinced: proved to my satisfaction (= I am fully persuaded) 4. Adequate response to a complaint or revenge for an insult: We demand satisfaction for the damages to our car.

sat-is-fac-tor-y (sæt–əs-fæk-tə-riʸ) adj. Giving satisfaction —sat-is-fac-tor-i-ly (sæt–əs-fæk-tə-rə-liʸ)

sat-is-fy (sæt–əs-faɪ) v. -fied, -fying 1. To please someone by meeting their needs: He [God] satisfies my desire with good things (Psalm 103:5). —opposite DISSATISFY 2. To meet certain requirements: You must satisfy the language requirements before you are accepted at this college. 3. To give sbdy. proof; convince: I'm satisfied that he is innocent.

sat-is-fy-ing (sæt–əs-faɪ-ɪŋ) adj. Giving contentment: a satisfying meal/job

sat-u-rate (sætʃ–ə-reʸt) v. -rated, -rating 1. To soak thoroughly or completely: Saturate a cloth in cold water and apply it to the injury. 2. To fill completely: They saturated the market with computers —sat-u-ra-tion (sætʃ–ə-reʸ-ʃən) n.

sat-u-rat-ed (sætʃ–ə-reʸt–əd) adj. Not capable of holding any more of a substance: After the heavy rainfall the ground was saturated.

Sat-ur-day (sæt–ər-diʸ / -deʸ) n. The seventh and last day of the week; the day before Sunday

Sat-urn (sæt–ərn) n. The second largest planet in our solar system

sat-ur-nine (sæt–ər-naɪn) adj. Of a person or his looks, having a gloomy, forbidding appearance

sauce (sɔs) n. A somewhat thick, usu. cooked liquid added to food to improve the flavor: spaghetti sauce/tartar sauce

sauce-pan (sɔs–pæn) n. A cooking pan with a long handle and usu. a lid

sau-cer (sɔ–sər) n. A small plate with edges curving up, designed for carrying or holding a cup

sau-cy (sɑs–iʸ/sɔs–) adj. -cier, -ciest Impudent

sau-er-kraut (sɑʊ–ər-krɑʊt) n. Shredded cabbage fermented in brine

sau-na (sɑʊ–nə/sɔ–) n. 1. A steam bath, the steam resulting from water thrown on hot stones 2. A dry heat bath 3. A room used for such a bath

saun-ter (sɔnt–ər/ sɑnt–) v. To stroll

sau-sage (sɔ–sɪdʒ) n. Minced and highly seasoned meat (as pork) usu. encased in a tubular casing

sau-té v. sautéed, sautéing To fry in a small amount of fat

sauté n. A dish prepared by frying in a small amount of fat

sav-age (sæv–ɪdʒ) adj. 1. Wild, untamed: a savage river 2. derog. At an early stage of civilization: savage tribes 3. Cruel, fierce; hostile: a

savage dog/savage criticism

savage n. **1.** An uncivilized person: *The people in that place were savages.* **2.** A cruel, hostile person: *I hope the police catch the savage that murdered those children in New York.*

sav-age-ry (sǽv–ɪdʒ–ə–riʸ) n. **-ries** Savage behavior: *the brutal savageries of war*

sa-van-na or **sa-van-nah** (sə–vǽn–ə) n. A grassland with scattered trees

save (seʸv) v. **saved, saving 1.** To rescue from danger **2.** To preserve or guard from loss or destruction **3.** To redeem from sin: *He [Jesus] will save his people from their sins* (Matthew 1:21). *Jesus Christ came into the world to save sinners* (1 Timothy 1:15). *Believe in the Lord Jesus Christ, and you will be saved* (Acts 16:31). *It is by grace [unmerited love of God] you have been saved* (Ephesians 2:8). *God wants all men to be saved and come to the knowledge of the truth [about Jesus Christ, our Savior]* (1 Timothy 2:4). **4.** To put aside (esp. money) for later use: *We're saving (up) for our children's education./ Grandmother saved her strength for the big family reunion.* **5.** To make it unnecessary for sbdy. to do, make, or spend sthg., etc.: *Will you do some research in the library for me? It'll save (me) a lot of time.* **6. save one's breath** To keep quiet because it is useless to talk to someone about a particular subject: *Save your breath; you'll never convince him to see a doctor.*

save n. In soccer, an action by the goalkeeper which keeps the opponents from scoring a goal

sav-er (seʸ–vər) n. **1.** Sthg. that avoids loss or waste: *My new car is a real fuel-saver.* **2.** A person who saves money

sav-ings (seʸ–vɪŋz) n. Money saved up, esp. in the bank

sav-ings ac-count (seʸ–vɪŋz ə–kaʊnt) n. A sum of money deposited in a bank and drawing interest

Sav-ior *AmE.* **Saviour** *BrE.* (seʸv–yər) n. One who saves someone else; refers especially to Jesus Christ who came unto the world to save sinners: *When Jesus was born, an angel of the Lord appeared to shepherds in the field and said to them, "...I bring you good news of great joy that will be for all people. Today ... a Savior*

has been born to you; he is Christ the Lord" (Luke 2:10,11). —see JESUS

sav-or *AmE.* **sav-our** *BrE.* (seʸ–vər) n. **1.** A characteristic taste or flavor **2.** A specific quality

savor v. **1.** To taste with enjoyment **2.** To have a specified taste, smell, or quality

sa-vor-y (seʸ–vər–iʸ) adj. **-ier, -iest** Having an appetizing taste or smell

sav-vy (sǽv–iʸ) n. *Slang* Understanding —**savvy** v. **-vied, -vying**

saw (sɔ) n. A hand or power-driven tool with a long blade and a sharp edge for cutting wood or metal

saw v. **sawed, sawed** also **sawn 1.** To cut sthg. with a saw: *He sawed the tree down.* **2.** To make a movement backwards and forwards as if cutting with a saw: *She sawed at the piece of frozen meat with her knife.*

saw v. Past tense of **see**

saw-dust (sɔ–dʌst) n. Small particles of wood produced in sawing

saw-horse (sɔ–hɔrs) n. A frame for holding wood while it is sawed

saw-mill (sɔ–mɪl) n. A place where logs are sawed into planks, boards, etc.

saw-yer (sɔ–yər) n. A person who saws, esp. as an occupation

sax-o-phone (sǽk–sə–foʷn) n. A musical wind instrument that has a sharply curved metal body, a reed in the mouthpiece and keys on the body

say (seʸ) v. **said** (sɛd) **saying** (seʸ–ɪŋ) **1.** To express in words: *Say what you mean.* **2.** Allege; assume to be: *People say that he's rich.* **3.** To show or indicate: *My watch says it's six o'clock.* **4.** To state positively: *No one can say exactly when the Lord will return, but we know it will be soon.* **5. it goes without saying** It is very obvious that: *It goes without saying that you are welcome to visit us any time.* **6. that is to say** Stated in other words **7. You don't say so!** An expression of surprise, esp. disbelief **8. You said it!** I agree strongly!: *"It's hot today." "You said it!"*

say-ing (seʸ–ɪŋ) n. A well-known phrase, proverb, etc.: *As the saying goes, "A penny saved is a penny earned."*

says (sɛz) v. Pres. tense, 2nd person sing. of

say

scab (skæb) n. A protective crust formed over a sore

scab-bard (skæb–ərd) n. A sword sheath

scab-by (skæb–i^y) adj. **-bier, -biest** Covered with scabs

sca-bies (ske^y–bi^{y}z) n. A kind of itchy skin disease

scaf-fold (skæf–əld) n. A temporary platform for materials and workers on a building

scald (skɔld) v. **1.** To burn with hot liquid or steam **2.** To heat, esp. milk, almost to the boiling point **3.** To clean with boiling water

scald-ing (skɔl–dɪŋ) adj. Hot enough to scald —**scalding** adv. *Steam from the kettle was scalding hot.*

scale (ske^{y}l) n. **1.** A standard of measurement or comparison: *an equal pay scale for men and women* **2.** A series of marks, esp. numbers, at regular fixed distances, used for measuring: *a ruler with one scale in inches and the other in centimeters* **3.** The measurements of a map, model, plan, etc. compared with the actual size of the country or object represented: *a scale of one fourth inch to the foot* **4.** Relative size, extent, etc.: *entertaining on a grand scale* **5.** A series of musical notes in upward or downward order: *The little girl was practicing her scales on the piano.* **6.** (a) Either pan of a balance, used in weighing an object by comparing it with a known weight: *The Lord abhors [hates] dishonest scales* (Proverbs 11:1). (b) Any weighing machine **7.** A small thin flake or layer on the skin of a fish, snake, etc. **8.** A thin coating that forms on the inside of hot water pipes, pots in which water is boiled, etc.

scale v. **scaled, scaling 1.** To climb up: *They scaled the mountain.* **2.** To increase or reduce sthg., esp. by a fixed rate: *We're going to scale down our production in the next few years.*

scal-lion (skæl–yən) n. An onion without the large round bulb

scal-lop (skæl–əp) n. **1.** A sea animal with a soft body and a double shell that is shaped like a fan **2.** One of a series of curves that form a fancy border

scal-ly-wag (skæl–ə–wæg) n. A rogue

scalp (skælp) n. The skin on the top of the hu-

man head and the hair rooted in it

scal-pel (skæl–pəl) n. A small, sharp surgical knife

scal-y (ske^y–li^y) adj. **-ier, -iest** Covered with scales

scamp (skæmp) n. A rascal; mischievous person

scam-per (skæm–pər) v. To run quickly

scan (skæn) v. **-nn- 1.** To examine very carefully, esp. in search of sthg.: *He scanned the map for the street where his friend lived.* **2.** To go over quickly without careful reading: *I scanned several books last night.* **3.** To obtain an image by using a scanner

scan n. An act of scanning, esp. in search of sthg.: *a brain scan*

scan-dal (skæn–dəl) n. **1.** Sthg. disgraceful which causes public disapproval **2.** True or false talk or gossip about someone's misdeeds: *Stop repeating scandal about our friends!*

scan-dal-ize (skæn–də–laɪz) v. To shock; horrify

scan-dal-ous (skæn–də–ləs) adj. Of behavior, shameful; disgraceful —**scandalously** adv.

scan-ner (skæn–ər) n. A machine which uses a computer to get an image, esp. one used by doctors for getting a picture of body parts

scant (skænt) adj. Not very much: *She paid scant attention to her mother's warnings.*

scant-y (skænt–i^y) adj. **-ier, -iest** Very little; not enough: *scanty clothing*

scape-goat (ske^{y}p–go^{w}t) n. A person who takes the blame for the wrongdoing of others

scap-u-la (skæp–yə–lə) n. The shoulder blade

scar (skɑr) n. **1.** A mark left on the skin following the healing of a wound, cut, etc. **2.** Feelings of guilt, sadness, etc. left after a bad experience

scar v. **-rr-** To leave a scar as a result of a wound, cut, etc.: *Her face was scarred by burns from the fire.*

scarce (skɛərs) adj. Not much or many; rare; difficult to find: *After the freeze, fruit will be scarce and prices will go up.*

scarce-ly (skɛərs–li^y) adv. Hardly; almost none: *There is scarcely any food in the refrigerator. We'd better go shopping.*

scar-ci-ty (skɛər–sət–i^y) n. **-ties** A shortage; a

state of being scarce: *a scarcity of food*

scare (skɛər) v. **scared, scaring 1.** To frighten: *Don't be scared; it's only the wind.* **2.** To cause sbdy. or sthg. to go away by making them afraid: *Animals were scared away by the fire.*

scare n. A sudden frightened feeling: *What a scare I got when I heard a rustling sound in the dark!*

scare-crow (skɛər-kroʷ) n. A figure of a person dressed in old clothes, set in a field to scare crows and other birds away from the crops

scarf (skɑrf) n. **scarfs** or **scarves** A piece of cloth worn around the neck, head, or shoulders for protection against the cold or for decoration

scar-let (scɑr-lət) adj. A bright red color

scarlet fever (scɑr-lət fiʸ-vər) n. An acute contagious disease occurring esp. among children and characterized by a scarlet skin eruption and a high fever

scar-y (skɛər-iʸ) adj. **-ier, -iest** Causing fear

scathe (skeʸð) v. **scathed, scathing** To criticize severely

scath-ing (skeʸ-ðiŋ) adj. Bitterly severe; scorching

scat-ter (skæt-ər) v. **1.** To cause a group, mob, flock, herd, etc. to separate widely: *When the police arrived, the mob scattered in all directions.* **2.** To throw sthg. in different directions in order to spread widely: *to scatter seed on the ground*

scat-ter-brain (skæt-ər-breʸn) n. A person who is incapable of serious thought

scav-enge (skæv-əndʒ) v. **-enged, -enging 1.** To cleanse from filth **2.** To collect (sthg. usable) from discarded material **3.** To search, esp. for food

scav-en-ger (skæv-ən-dʒər) n. **1.** A person who searches through rubbish to find sthg. edible or usable **2.** An animal that feeds on dead or decaying matter

scene (siʸn) n. **1.** A division of a play, opera, TV show, etc. **2.** A view of a place, real or imaginary: *She took a picture of the beautiful scene.* **3.** The actual place where sthg. happens: *The thief returned to the scene of the crime.* **4.** A violent quarrel or show of anger in public: *We were all embarrassed when he*

made such a scene in the restaurant.* **5.** A sphere of given activity: *the drug scene* **6. behind the scenes** Not seen or known about by the public **7. set the scene** To prepare for, esp. to help cause sthg.: *The assassination of the president set the scene for a major conflict between the two nations.*

scen-er-y (siʸn-ə-riʸ) n. **-ies 1.** The furniture, woodwork, and painted backgrounds used on a theater stage **2.** A picturesque view of the surrounding country

sce-nic (siʸ-nɪk) adj. Of or concerning the natural surroundings, esp. in beautiful and open country

scent (sɛnt) n. **1.** A smell as left by a hunted animal: *The dogs picked up the scent of the rabbit.* **2.** An especially pleasant smell: *There was a scent of orange blossoms in the air.* **3.** A perfume

scent v. **1.** To detect as if by smelling: *to scent danger* **2.** To fill with odor

scep-ter *AmE.* **scep-tre** *BrE.* (sɛp-tər) n. A rod or staff held by a monarch as a symbol of authority

sched-ule (skɛdʒ-uʷl/ skɛdʒ-əl) *AmE.* (ʃedʒ-əl/ ʃedʒ-uʷl)*BrE.* n. **1.** A timetable **2.** A production plan: *Production is right on schedule.*

schedule v. **-uled, -uling 1.** To arrange future plans for a certain time: *The meeting is scheduled for next Monday at two o'clock.* **2.** To place a flight, train, etc. into a regular prearranged timetable: *Flight 303 is scheduled to arrive at six p.m.*

scheme (skiʸm) n. **1.** A plan; a systematic arrangement: *a scheme for making cars that run on waste materials* **2.** A clever but dishonest plan: *a scheme to smuggle drugs into the country/ The Lord hates a heart that devises wicked schemes* (Prov-erbs 6:16,18).

scheme v. **schemed, scheming** To make secret, dishonest plans; plot —**schemer** n.

schism (sɪz-əm/ skɪz-) n. A division or split between opposing factions due to disagreement

schiz-o-phre-ni-a (skɪt-sə-friʸ-niʸ-ə) n. A mental illness characterized by withdrawal from reality and personality deterioration —**schiz-o-phren-ic** (skɪt-sə-frɛn-ɪk) adj.

schol-ar (skɑl-ər) n. A person with deep

knowledge of an academic subject; a learned person

schol-ar-ly (skɑl–ər–li^y) adj. Showing or having great knowledge, high intelligence, and a love of accuracy

schol-ar-ship (skɑl–ər–ʃɪp) n. **1.** Money given to worthy students so that they can continue their education **2.** Knowledge or learning in a particular field of study

scho-las-tic (skə–læs–tɪk) adj. Pertaining to schools, scholars or education —**scholastically** adv.

school (sku^wl) n. **1.** An institution for the education of children: *an elementary school* **2.** An institution for teaching a particular subject: *drama school* **3.** The teachers and students at such a school **4.** A department of a university concerned with a particular area of study **5.** Activity or experience that supplies training: *the school of experience* **6.** A group of people with the same ideas, methods, etc. on a particular subject: *different schools of thought* **7.** A large number of fish, whales, etc. swimming together

school v. To teach, train, discipline, or control: *well-schooled in good manners*

school-ing (sku^wl–ɪŋ) n. Education: *Where did he get his schooling?*

schoon-er (sku^w–nər) n. A sailing vessel having two or more masts

schwa (ʃwɑ) n. **1.** The neutral, uncolored, central vowel sound of most unstressed syllables in English; sound of "a" in "ago" **2.** The symbol (ə) used for this sound

sci-at-ic (saɪ–æt–ɪk) adj. Of the hip

sci-at-i-ca (saɪ–æt–ɪ–kə) n. A pain in the hip and the back of the thigh

sci-ence (saɪ–əns) n. **1.** Knowledge that depends on observation and experimentation **2.** A branch of such knowledge, esp. **(a)** A study leading to a particular branch of knowledge, such as physics, biology, chemistry, etc. **(b)** Any subject which may be studied exactly: *police science* —see also SOCIAL SCIENCE

sci-en-tif-ic (saɪ–ən–tɪf–ɪk) adj. Relating to science: *scientific method/knowledge/studies* NOTE: There are some things that are called scientific but are not scientific at all.

Evolution for example, is not a scientific fact or even a theory. It is a very dangerous teaching, for it denies the existence of an almighty, all-wise God, who created all things. The Bible warns us about being deceived by such false science. The Apostle Paul wrote to Pastor Timothy warning him to avoid "...opposition of sciences falsely so-called" (1 Timothy 6:20 KJV).

sci-en-tist (saɪ–ən–tɪst) n. A person who works in a science, esp. the natural sciences (physics, chemistry, or biology)

scin-til-late (sɪn–tə–le^yt) v. **-lated, -lating 1.** To show brilliance in wit **2.** To sparkle

scin-til-lat-ing (sɪn–tə–le^yt–ɪŋ) adj. Brilliant and witty: *a scintillating discussion or performance* —**scin-til-la-tion** (sɪn–tə–le^y–ʃən) n.

scis-sors (sɪz–ərz) n. A cutting implement of two blades joined by a pin that allows the cutting edges to be opened and closed: *There are many kinds of scissors for cutting hair, fingernails, paper, cloth, etc.*

scoff (skɔf/ skɑf) v. To express scorn; to mock; ridicule; to make fun of sbdy. or sthg. taught

scoffer (skɔf–ər/ skɑf–) n. One who scoffs NOTE: The Bible warns us about scoffers who will appear in the last days, shortly before the return of Jesus: *In the last days scoffers will come, scoffing and following their own evil desires. They will say, "Where is this 'coming' he promised?"* (2 Peter 3:3,4). Some of these scoffers are even teaching in public schools. God's holy word, the Bible, warns us very plainly not to sit at the feet of such people to be taught by them, saying, Blessed is the man [or child] who does not walk in the counsel of the wicked... or sit in the seat of mockers (scoffers) (Psalm 1:1). —see also SCIENCE

scold (sko^wld) v. To speak in an angry way, esp. to blame or rebuke: *His mother scolded him for staying out so late at night.* —**scolding** n. *She gave him a lengthy scolding.*

scone (sko^wn/skɑn) n. A kind of small plain cake

scoop (sku^wp) n. **1.** Any of the several kinds of instruments such as a spoon or shovel used for digging out or lifting up loose material,

water, etc.: *Two scoops of vanilla ice cream, please.* **2.** A news item that one newspaper prints before others do

scoop v. **1.** To take sthg. up or out with a scoop or as with a scoop **2.** To make a news report before another newspaper does

scoot (sku^wt) v. To go quickly: *I've got to scoot.*

scoot-er (sku^wt–ər) n. **1.** Also **motor scooter** A small, light motorcycle, with small wheels and a low seat **2.** A kind of two-wheeled child's vehicle pushed along by the foot

scope (sko^wp) n. The limits or extent of the subject dealt with: *outside the scope of this dictionary*

scorch (skərtʃ) v. To burn slightly; singe

scorch-ing (skər–tʃɪŋ) adj. Very hot: *Let's get out of this scorching heat.*

score (skər) n. **1.** The number of points, goals etc., made by a person or team in a game, sport, examination, etc.: *He got a high score on the final exam.* **2. (a)** A written copy of a piece of music that shows what each instrument is to play or each voice to sing **(b)** The music for a movie, play, etc. **3.** A wrong done against one in the past; grudge: *They were trying to settle an old score with each other.* **4.** Twenty: *Four score and seven = 87.* **5. scores of** A large number

score v. **scored, scoring 1.** To make points, goals, etc., in a sport, game, test, etc.: *Our footfall team scored 17 points in the final quarter.* **2.** To compose or arrange a piece of music for one or more performers in a movie, play, etc.

score-board (skər–bərd) n. A large board on which the score is shown as a game is being played

scor-er (skər–ər) n. **1.** A person who keeps a record of points scored **2.** A player who makes points in a game, competition, etc.

scorn (skərn) n. Strong contempt; angry disrespect: *He was filled with scorn for his enemies.* —**scornful** adj. —**scornfully** adv.

scorn v. **1.** To refuse proudly: *She scorned our invitation.* **2.** To feel or show scorn for

scor-pi-on (skər–pi^y–ən) n. A small animal that has a narrow body and a long tail with a stinger that carries poison

scot–free (skɑt–fri^y) adj. Free from harm or punishment

scoun-drel (skaʊn–drəl) n. A rascal; a worthless person

scour (skaʊr) v. **1.** To clean or polish by hard rubbing **2.** To clean or dig out, esp. by force of water **3.** To search: *They scoured the countryside all night for the lost child.* **4.** To pass quickly over: *We scoured all the drawers of the filing cabinet looking for the misplaced letter.*

scourge (skɜrdʒ) n. **1.** Sthg. that causes great suffering, esp. widespread: *the scourge of famine* **2.** A whip made of leather thongs

scourge v. **1.** To whip; to flog **2.** To punish severely

scout (skaʊt) v. **1.** To go looking in various places for sthg.: *He scouted around for a good place to camp for the night.* **2.** To inspect or observe to get information

scout n. **1.** A soldier, ship or aircraft sent out to look for information about the enemy's position, strength, etc. **2.** A member of either of two organizations — the Boy Scouts or the Girl Scouts **3. talent scout** One who searches for talent for sports organizations or for the entertainment industry

scout-mas-ter (skaʊt–mæs–tər) n. An adult who leads a troop of Boy Scouts

scow (skaʊ) n. A flat-bottomed boat

scowl (skaʊl) v. To look at with an angry, threatening expression

scowl n. An angry, threatening frown

scrag-gly (skræg–li^y) adj. **-glier, -gliest** Rough and uneven, as in appearance

scram (skræm) v. **-mm-** To get out or away quickly

scram-ble (skræm–bəl) v. **-bled, -bling** v. **1.** To crawl or climb quickly and with difficulty, esp. over a rough or steep surface: *We scrambled up the cliff.* **2.** To struggle or compete with others in a disorderly way: *People scrambled for shelter when it began to rain.* **3.** To beat the white and yellow parts of eggs together while cooking them: *Mother was scrambling the eggs.* **4.** To mix together without order: *The man was so drunk that his words were all scrambled.*

scramble n. **1.** An act of crawling or climbing over a rough surface: *It was quite a scramble up the river bank, but we made it.* **2.** An eager

and disorderly struggle: *a scramble for seats on the bus*

scrap (skræp) n. **1.** A small piece: *a scrap of cloth* **2. scraps** Pieces of food left over at a meal: *There's no need to throw the scraps away; they can be frozen and used in soup later in the week.* **3.** Material not suitable for its original purpose but which may still have some value: *scrap iron* **4.** *infml.* A fight or quarrel, not too serious: *The ball players had a scrap on the field, but nobody was hurt.*

scrap v. **-pp- 1.** To discard; get rid of; to throw away; abandon: *The fire forced them to scrap all their plans.* **2.** *infml.* To quarrel or fight: *What are the boys scrapping about this time?*

scrap-book (skræp-bʊk) n. A book having blank pages for keeping a collection of photographs, newspaper articles, etc.

scrape (skreᵧp) v. **scraped, scraping 1.** To remove mud, paint, grease, etc. from a surface by repeated rubbing or by pulling an edge firmly across it: *I scraped the paint off the wall.* **2.** To rub roughly: *Johnny scraped (=hurt) his knees and elbows when he fell on the street.* **3.** To just barely manage to do sthg.: *He just barely scraped through last month after losing his job.* **4.** To gather enough of sthg. (esp. money) with difficulty, by putting small amounts together: *Somehow she managed to scrape together enough money to buy a car.*

scrape n. **1.** An act of scraping **2.** An injury made by scraping

scratch (skrætʃ) v. **1.** To draw or pull a sharp point across a surface **2.** To mark by doing this **3.** To scrape or rub a part of the body lightly to stop itching, esp. with the fingernails **4.** To withdraw from competition; to cancel: *Three runners were disqualified and had to be scratched from their events.* **5. scratch the surface** To deal with a subject for only a short time; to make a mere beginning: *I've only scratched the surface in my required reading.*

scratch n. **1.** A mark, cut, or sore place made by scratching: *She got a big scratch on her arm when she fell.* **2.** A sound made by scratching

scratch-y (skrætʃ-iᵧ) adj. **-ier, -iest 1.** Damaged

by scratches **2.** Of clothing, rough, and prickly: *I can't wear wool clothing, because it's too scratchy.* —**scratchiness** n.

scrawl (skrɔl) v. To write or draw in a scribbling, illegible manner

scrawn-y (skrɔ-niᵧ) adj. **-ier, -iest** Skinny; thin; bony

scream (skriᵧm) v. To utter a loud, shrill, piercing cry caused by fear, pain, or excitement: *The girls on the roller coaster were screaming during the entire ride. / Mary screamed when a man stepped out of the shadows.*

scream n. **1.** A sudden loud shrill cry: *She let out a scream that could be heard all over the neighborhood.* **2.** *infml.* A very funny person: *He is really a scream.*

screech (skriᵧtʃ) v. To make a harsh, shrill and sudden sound; shriek —**screech** n.

screen (skriᵧn) n. **1.** An upright fixed or movable frame used for dividing a room, as a protection, etc.: *a fireplace screen* **2.** A device used on windows and some outside doors to let air in but keep insects out: *a window screen* **3.** A sieve for sifting unwanted material from what is wanted: *They used a screen to separate the sand from the gravel.* **4.** A surface on which pictures are shown (as in the movies or on TV): *Do you have a screen? We'd like to see the slides from our vacation trip.*

screen v. **1.** To shelter or protect sthg. from light, wind, heat, etc.: *This room is screened from the afternoon sun by the tree in the front yard.* **2.** To conceal with, or as if with, a screen: *A tall fence screens our house and yard from view.* **3.** To examine people to see whether they are loyal, suitable for a job, etc. or to determine if they have health problems

screw (skruʷ) n. A type of metal fastener similar to a nail but having a winding groove or ridge (called a thread) on its surface so that it holds firmly when fastened into sthg. by turning

screw v. **1.** To fasten or tighten with one or more screws: *The shelves are screwed to the wall.* **2.** To turn or tighten sthg.: *Please screw this lid on the jar tightly.*

screw-driv-er (skruʷ-draɪ-vər) n. A tool for

turning screws

screw-y (skru^w–i^y) adj. Crazy; eccentric

scrib-ble (skrıb–əl) v. **-bled, -bling** To write carelessly or make meaningless marks: *He scribbled his name on the bottom of the page.* **scribble** n. Careless writing; meaningless marks: *I can't read this letter; it's nothing but a bunch of scribbles.*

scribe (skraıb) n. **1.** One who served in ancient Palestine as a copyist and teacher **2.** A person whose business it is to copy written material **3.** (Facetiously) An author

scrim-mage (skrɪm–ɪdʒ) n. **1.** The play between two football teams, starting with the snap of the ball **2.** Practice play between squads of the same team —**scrimmage** v. **-maged, -maging**

scrimp (skrɪmp) v. To use great economy; to be very frugal

script (skrɪpt) n. **1.** The system of letters used in writing a language; alphabet: *Devanagari script* **2.** Writing done by hand or as if by hand, esp. with the letters or words joined; cursive writing **3.** Text of a speech, play, broadcast, etc.

Scrip-tur-al (skrɪp–tʃər–əl) adj. Based on the Holy Scriptures, the Bible, the Word of God

Scrip-ture (skrɪp–tʃər) n. Holy writings; the Bible: *The Holy Scriptures are able to make you wise for salvation through faith in Jesus Christ* (2 Timothy 3:15). *And beginning with Moses [the first five books of the Bible, written by Moses] and all the Prophets, he [Jesus] explained to them what was said in all the Scriptures concerning himself* (Luke 24:27). —see BIBLE, OLD TESTAMENT, NEW TESTAMENT

scroll (skro^{w}l) n. A roll of paper or parchment used for writing a document

scrooge (skru^{w}dʒ) n. A miserly, stingy person

scro-tum (skro^{w}t–əm) n. **scrotums** or **scrota** A pouch which contains the testes in most mammals

scrounge (skraʊndʒ) v. **scrounged, scrounging 1.** To collect by, or as if by, foraging **2. scrounge around** To search about in a haphazard fashion

scrub (skrʌb) v. **-bb-** To clean sthg. thoroughly by hard rubbing, esp. with a stiff brush and soap and water

scrub n. **1.** An act of scrubbing: *Your hands are dirty; give them a good scrub.* **2.** Land covered with low-growing bushes and short trees

scruff (skrʌf) n. The back of the neck

scruff-y (skrʌf–i^y) adj. **-ier, -iest** Shabby; untidy

scrump-tious (skrʌmp–ʃəs) adj. Delightful; delicious: *What a scrumptious meal!*

scru-ple (skru^w–pəl) n. **1.** A moral or ethical consideration **2.** A very small quantity

scru-pu-lous (skru^w–pyə–ləs) adj. **1.** Showing or having scruples **2.** Conscientiously careful; painstaking; exacting —**scrupulously** adv.

scru-ti-nize (skru^{w}t–ən–aız) v. **-nized, -nizing** To examine very carefully; inspect in detail

scru-ti-ny (skru^{w}t–ən–i^y) n. **-nies** A careful examination

scu-ba (sku^w–bə) n. A device used for breathing under water

scuba diving (sku^w–bə daı–vɪŋ) n. A sport of underwater swimming with the aid of scuba gear

scuff (skʌf) v. To make a mark or scrape on the smooth surface of sthg.: *His shoes were badly scuffed and in need of shining.*

scuf-fle (skʌf–əl) v. **-fled, -fling** To struggle briefly with disorder and confusion, but usu. not seriously —**scuffle** n.

scul-ler-y (skʌl–ə–ri^y) n. A room where cooking utensils are cleaned and kept

sculp (skʌlp) or **sculpt** (skʌlpt) v. To sculpture

sculp-tor (skʌlp–tər) n. An artist who carves or molds figures, designs, etc. in wood, stone, clay, etc.

sculp-ture (skʌlp–tʃər) n. The art of the sculptor

scum (skʌm) n. **1.** A thin layer of impure material on the surface of a liquid **2.** *derog.* People considered to be evil or worthless: *scum of the earth* (=the worst people in the world) —**scummy** adj. **-mier, -miest**

scur-ril-ous (skɜr–ə–ləs) adj. Grossly abusive; obscene; vulgar —**scurrilously** adv.

scur-ry (skɜr–i^y) v. **-ried, -rying** To hurry; scamper

scur-vy (skɜr–vi^y) n. A vitamin deficiency disease marked by spongy gums and loosened teeth

scut-tle (skʌt–əl) v. **-tled, -tling 1.** To sink a ship intentionally by letting water in through holes in the hull **2.** To abandon or destroy plans

scuttle n. A small opening, with a cover, in the hull or deck of a ship

scuttle n. A pail for carrying coal

scut-tle-butt (skʌt–əl–bət) n. Gossip

scythe (saið) n. An implement for cutting grain or grass by hand

SE written abbr. said as **southeast(ern)**

sea (siʸ) n. **1.** The body of salty water that covers much of the earth's surface; ocean; the waters of the earth as distinguished from the land **2.** A large body of salty water, smaller than an ocean, more or less surrounded by land: *the Red Sea/the Black Sea* **3.** A large mass or quantity likened to a sea: *The actor looked out from the stage onto a sea of faces.* **4.** Movement of waves: *heavy seas* **5. at sea** infml. At a loss; bewildered; not understanding: *He felt completely at sea in a strange new land and a strange new job.*

sea-bird (siʸ–bərd) n. A bird living near the sea

sea-board (siʸ–bord) n. A region bordering the seacoast —**seaboard** adj.

sea-coast (siʸ–koʷst) n. The land bordering a sea or ocean

sea dog (siʸ dɒg/dɑg) n. **1.** An old sailor **2.** A pirate

sea-far-er (siʸ–fɛər–ər) n. A traveler on the sea, esp. a sailor —**seafaring** adj.

sea-food (siʸ–fuʷd) n. Any fish or shellfish eaten as food

sea-go-ing (siʸ–goʷ–ŋ) adj. Built for crossing the ocean: *a seagoing ship*

sea-gull (siʸ–gʌl) n. A large, long-winged seabird with usu. white or gray and black feathers

sea horse (siʸ hɔrs) n. A small fish that has a head resembling that of a horse

seal (siʸl) n. **1.** The official mark of a government, company, etc., put on some formal and official document: *The king put his seal on the letter.* **2.** Anything that joins tightly or closes up completely **3.** A piece of sticky paper with a design or picture on it: *a Christmas seal* **4.** A large fish-eating animal with flippers that lives near the sea

seal v. **1.** To fix sthg. onto **2.** To fasten or close with a seal or a tight cover or band of sthg.: *The jars of jelly must be tightly sealed./a sealed envelope* **3.** To make legally binding: *to seal a bargain* **4. sealed lips** Able to keep a secret: *My lips are sealed. I won't tell anyone.*

seal-ant (siʸ–lənt) n. A substance used for sealing, waterproofing, stopping leaks, etc.

sea lev-el (siʸ lɛv–əl) n. The level of the surface of the sea: *The highest mountain peak is about 29,000 feet above sea level.*

sea li-on (siʸ laɪ–ən) n. A large type of seal, the male of which has a mane

seam (siʸm) n. **1.** A line formed by the sewing together of two pieces of cloth, leather, etc. **2.** A narrow layer of mineral in the earth: *a seam of coal between the layers of rock*

sea-man (siʸ–mən) n. **-men 1.** One who assists in the handling of ships; a mar-iner **2.** An enlisted man in the navy, ranking next below a petty officer third class

sea-man-ship (siʸ–mən–ʃip) n. Skill in the navigation and maintenance of a ship

seam-stress (siʸm–strəs) n. A woman whose occupation is sewing

seam-y (siʸ–miʸ) n. **-ier, -iest 1.** Unpleasant **2.** Degraded; squalid—**seaminess** n.

sé-ance (seʸ–ɑns) n. A meeting in which a spiritualist tries to communicate with the dead NOTE: This practice is clearly forbidden by God's Word, the Holy Bible, which says, "Let no one be found among you who...is a medium or spiritist or who consults the dead. Anyone who does these things is detestable to the Lord" (Deuteronomy 18:9-12).

sea-plane (siʸ–pleʸn) n. An airplane that can land and take off from water

sea-port (siʸ–port) n. A harbor for seagoing vessels

sear (sɪər) v. **1.** To burn the surface **2.** To scorch **3.** To dry up or wither **4.** To become callous, insensitive: *In the latter times some will depart from the faith...speaking lies in hypocrisy, having their conscience seared with a hot iron* (1 Timothy 4: 1-2).

search (sɜrtʃ) v. To look at, examine, or go over thoroughly to try to find sbdy. or

sthg.: *The whole town was out searching the woods for the lost child./I the Lord search the heart and examine the mind* (Jeremiah 17:10)./*The police searched the thief for the stolen goods but found nothing.*

search n. An act of searching: *a long search for the missing woman*

searching (**sɜr–tʃɪŋ**) adj. Keen and thorough, seeking to find the truth: *The policeman asked the accused man many searching questions.*

sea-scape (si^y–ske^yp) n. A picture of a scene of the ocean or sea

sea-shore (si^y–ʃor) n. The land next to the sea

sea-sick-ness (si^y–sɪk–nəs) n. Nausea and dizziness from the rolling of the ship —**seasick** adj.

sea-son (si^yz–ən) n. **1.** One of the four divisions of the year (summer, winter, autumn, spring) **2.** A special period: *the Easter season/the rainy season/the football season* **3. in season** Of food, available in large amounts because it is the time they are usually ready for eating: *Fruit and vegetables are cheapest in season.*

season v. **1.** To add salt, pepper, spice, etc. to a food to give it special flavor **2.** Of wood, to be prepared for use by gradual drying: *well-seasoned oak*

sea-son-a-ble (si^yz–ən–ə–bəl) adj. Suitable for the time of year: *seasonable temperatures* —**seasonably** adv.

sea-son-al (si^yz–ən–əl) adj. Taking place in one particular season only: *a seasonal job picking fruit*

sea-soned (si^yz–ənd) adj. Having much experience in the stated activity: *a seasoned politician*

sea-son-ing (si^yz–ən–ɪŋ) n. Sthg. (as salt, pepper, and spices) added to food to give it more flavor

seat (si^yt) n. **1.** A thing made or used for sitting: *We only have seats for six people.* **2.** The part of a chair, couch, etc. on which one sits: *Sthg. is spilled on the seat of the chair.* **3.** A position as a member of an official body: *He won a seat in Senate in the latest election.* **4.** A place where a particular activity is carried on: *Oxford is a famous university and seat of learning.*

seat v. **1.** To cause sbdy. or oneself to sit: *The man and his wife were seated next to each other.* **2.** To have room for a certain number of people: *This room seats 400 people.* —see SIT

sea ur-chin (si^y ɜr–tʃən) n. A type of small sea creature with a spiny shell

sea-weed (si^y wi^yd) n. Any of many kinds of plants growing in the sea

sea-wor-thy (si^y–wɜr–ði^y) adj. Of a ship, in good enough condition to go to sea

se-cede (sɪ–si^yd) v. **-ceded, -ceding** *Fml.* To withdraw officially from membership in an organization, state, etc., esp. because of disagreement —**se-ces-sion** (sɪ–sɛʃ–ən) n.

se-clude (sɪ–klu^wd) v. **-cluded, cluding** To shut off by oneself: *He secluded himself from the rest of society.*

se-clud-ed (sɪ–klu^wd–əd) adj. Of a place, very quiet and private

se-clu-sion (sɪ–klu^w–ʒən) n. The state of secluding or being secluded

sec-ond (sɛk–ənd) adv. Next after, following the first in time, place, etc.: *My brother is a fast runner, but he usually comes in second.* —**second** adj.

second n. **1.** A length of time equal to 1/60 of a minute **2.** A measure of an angle equal to 1/60 of a minute or 1/3600 of a degree: *The ship was exactly 10 degrees, 15 minutes and 30 seconds north of the equator.* **3.** The one that is next after the first: *second in line*

second v. To support a formal suggestion already made at a meeting so that argument or voting may follow: *I second the motion.*

sec-ond-ar-y (sɛk–ən–dɛər–i^y) adj. **1.** Of education, coming after primary or elementary school **2.** Second in rank, value, or importance **3.** Belonging to a second or later stage of development

se-cret (si^y–krət) n. **1.** Sthg. kept from the knowledge of others: *A trustworthy man keeps a secret* (Proverbs 11:13). **2.** Unexplained mystery: *What is the secret for your delicious apple pie?* —**se-cre-cy** (si^y–krə–si^y) n. **-cies**

secret adj. Hidden; concealed: *"Can anyone hide in secret places so that I cannot see him?" declares the Lord. "Do not I fill heaven and earth?" declares the Lord* (Jeremiah 23:24).

—secretly adv.

sec-re-tai-i-al (sɛk-rə-tɛər-iʸ-əl) adj. Concerning the work of a secretary: *secretarial work*

sec-re-tar-y (sek-rə-tɛər-iʸ) n. -ies 1. An employee in an office, usu. working for another person, preparing letters, filing, arranging meetings, etc.: *A good secretary is an asset to any office.* 2. A high-ranking government officer, as (a) (US) a non-elected director of a large department: *Secretary of State* (b) (Brit.) a minister: *The Home/Foreign Secretary* 3. An officer of an organization who deals with its business affairs, records, official letters, etc.

se-crete (sɪ-kriʸt/siʸ-) v. -creted, -creting 1. To produce and discharge a secretion:*The liver secretes bile..* 2. To hide or conceal

se-cre-tion (sɪ-kriʸ-ʃən) n. 1. An act of secreting 2. The fluid secreted: *Bile is a secretion of the liver.*

se-cre-tive (siʸ-krət-ɪv/sɪ-kriʸt-ɪv) adj. Tending to keep secrets or to act secretly

sect (sɛkt) n. A group of people who hold certain views, esp. in religious matters deviating from a generally accepted tradition

sec-tar-i-an (sɛk-tɛər-iʸ-ən) adj. 1. Of or belonging to a sect 2. Narrowly limited in interest or scope —sectarianism n. —opposite NON-SECTARIAN

sec-tion (sɛk-ʃən) n. 1. A part or division: *This section of the freeway has a lot of traffic.* 2. A picture, diagram, etc. of sthg. as if it were cut from top to bottom and looked at from the side 3. In medicine, a thin slice of sthg. to be examined under a microscope

section v. To separate into sections: *They sectioned off part of the room for special guests.*

sec-tor (sɛk-tər) n. 1. A separate part or section 2. A part of a circle lying between two straight lines drawn from the center to the circumference

sec-u-lar (sɛk-yə-lər) adj. 1. Worldly; not spiritual or religious 2. Not bound by monastic vows —secularism n. —secularist n. —sec-u-lar-is-tic (sɛk-yə-lər-ɪs-tɪk) adj. —sec-u-lar-ly (sɛk-yə-lər-liʸ) adv.

se-cu-lar-ize (sɛk-yə-lə-raɪz) v. -ized, -izing 1. To make secular 2. To transfer from ecclesiastical to secular (worldly) use, posses-

sion, or control

se-cure (sɪ-kyʊər) adj. 1. Safe; protected from harm and fear 2. Firmly fixed or fastened: *The locks are all secure.* 3. Confident, without doubts or fears —opposite INSECURE —securely adv.

secure v. -cured, -curing 1. To make safe: *They secured the windows as the storm began.* 2. To obtain, esp. as the result of effort: *He has secured himself a good job.*

se-cu-ri-ty (sə-kyʊər-ət-iʸ) n. 1. Safety: *My family's security is very important to me.* 2. Sthg. which protects: *These jewels are my security against hardship.* 3. Valuable property that can be used to guarantee that one will pay back borrowed money, keep a promise, etc.: *His land was used as security to borrow the money.* —compare GUARANTEE 4. Measures taken to prevent lawbreaking, violence, etc.: *Security in this building is very strict.*

se-dan (sɪ-dæn) n. 1. An enclosed automobile seating four to seven passengers 2. A covered chair borne on poles by two men

se-date (sɪ-deʸt) v. -dated, -dating To calm or treat with a sedative —sedation n.

se-date adj. 1. Calm; serious; dignified 2. Undisturbed by passion or excitement —sedateness n.

sed-a-tive (sɛd-ət-ɪv) n. Serving or tending to relieve tension, esp. to allay nervousness

sed-en-tar-y (sɛd-ən-tɛər-iʸ) adj. Of a job, requiring little physical activity

sed-i-ment (sɛd-ə-mənt) n. 1. The material that settles to the bottom of a liquid 2. Sand, rocks, and other material deposited by a river —sed-i-men-tar-y (sɛd-ə-ment-ə-riʸ) adj. —sed-i-men-ta-tion (sɛd-ə-mən-teʸ-ʃən) n.

se-di-tion (sɪ-dɪʃ-ən) n. Incitement to revolt against lawful authority—seditious n.

se-duce (sɪ-duʷs) v. -duced, -ducing 1. To tempt sbdy. (esp. a young person without sexual experience) to have sex with one 2. To persuade sbdy. to do sthg. wrong by offering some type of reward; entice: —seducer n. —se-duc-tion (sɪ-dʌk-ʃən) n.

see (siʸ) v. saw, seen 1. To have sight: *It was so dark he could hardly see anything.* 2. To be-

come aware of by using the eyes; notice, examine, or recognize by looking: *He looked out the window and saw a car driving up.* **3.** To experience: *She has seen a great deal of sorrow in her life.* **4.** To understand: *I don't think he saw the point of my joke.* **5.** To find out or discover sthg.: *I'll see where the rest want to go for dinner.* **6.** To make sure; tend to: *See that you lock the doors when you leave.* **7.** To visit, call upon, meet, or spend time with: *We will come and see you when we get a chance.* **8.** To do sthg. with sbdy.: *I'll see you to the door.* **9.** **see things** To imagine that one sees sthg.: *I must be seeing things. I thought I saw a man flying.* **10.** **see sbdy. off** To go to the airport or station with sbdy. to say good-bye: *We will see our children off at the airport.* **11.** **see sbdy. or sthg. through (a)** To take part in or support to the end **(b)** Not to be deceived: *He saw through her evil scheme.* **12.** **see to** To attend to: *She always sees to it that we all get enough to eat.* —compare LOOK, WATCH

seed (si�assets'd) n. **1.** The part of some plants from which a new plant of the same kind can grow **2.** Spiritual food; the Word of God: *For you have been born again [born spiritually], not of perishable seed, but of imperishable, through the living and enduring word of God* (1 Peter 1:23). **3.** The beginning from which anything grows: *seeds of rebellion* —**seedless** adj.

seed v. **1.** Of a plant, to produce seed **2.** To sow seeds

seed-ling (si�250'd-lɪŋ) n. A new young plant grown from a seed

seed-y (si�250'd-i�250) adj. **-ier, -iest 1.** Abounding in seeds **2.** *Infml.* Shabby; run-down —**seed-iness** n.

see-ing (si�250-ɪŋ) conj. Since, considering, in view of the fact that

seek (si�250k) v. **sought** (sɔt), **seeking 1.** To look for earnestly; try to find or get sthg.: *Seek first the kingdom of God and his righteousness...* (Matthew 6:33 KJV). **2.** To request: *You should seek medical help for your cough.* **3.** To attempt: *We sought to raise funds for a new university, but we failed.* —**seeker** n.

seem (si�250m) v. To give the impression or appearance of being or doing sthg.: *She seems (to be) nervous about sthg./It seems (as if) they are very good friends.*

seem-ing (si�250m-ɪŋ) adj. Appearing to be true or evident —**seemingly** adv.

seen (si�250n) v. Past part. of **see**

seep (si�250p) v. Of liquid, to flow slowly and in small amounts through a substance: *Water had seeped into the boat from a small crack in the bottom.* —**seep-age** n. (si�250-pɪdʒ) n.

se-er (si�250-ər) n. A person who foretells future events

seer-suck-er (sɪər-sʌk-ər) n. A light fabric of cotton or rayon

seethe (si�250ð) v. **seethed, seething 1.** Of a liquid, to bubble and move about as if boiling **2.** To be greatly excited or angry: *to be seething with rage*

seg-ment (seg-mənt) n. Any of the parts into which sthg. may be divided —**seg-men-ta-tion** (seg-mən-te�250-ʃən) n.

seg-re-gate (seg-rɪ-ge�250t) v. **-gated, -gating** To separate a person or group from others: *He went to a school where boys and girls were segregated.* —**seg-re-ga-tion** (seg-rɪ-ge�250-ʃən) n. —opposite INTEGRATION

se-gre-ga-tion-ist (seg-rɪ-ge�250-ʃə-nəst) n. A person who favors or practices segregation, esp. racial segregation

seis-mic (saɪz-mɪk) adj. Of, resembling, or caused by an earthquake

seis-mo-graph (saɪz-mə-græf) n. An instrument for measuring vibrations of the earth —**seis-mog-ra-pher** (saɪz-mɒg-rə-fər) n. —**seis-mo-graph-ic** (saɪz-mə-græf-ɪk) adj. —**seis-mog-ra-phy** (saɪz-mɒg-rə-fi�250) n.

seize (si�250z) v. **seized, seizing 1.** To take hold of suddenly and forcefully; grab: *The thief seized my purse.* **2.** To take control of officially or forcefully: *The shipment of drugs was seized by the police.* **3.** *fig.* To take advantage: *Seize the opportunity.*

sei-zure (si�250-ʒər) n. **1.** The act of seizing by force or legal authority **2.** A sudden attack as of a disease

sel-dom (sel-dəm) adv. Not often; rarely: *She seldom eats sweets because she is dieting.*

se-lect (sə-lekt) v. To choose from two or more items according to one's preference

select adj. **1.** Carefully chosen, esp. as the best out of a larger group: *select passages*

from the book **2.** Of an organization, limited to certain members: *a select group of top musical artists*

se-lec-tion (sə–lɛk–ʃən) n. **1.** The act of selecting, or a thing selected **2.** A number of things from which to choose: *They have a fine selection of clothing in that store.*

se-lec-tive (sə–lɛk–tɪv) adj. **1.** Tending to choose carefully **2.** Concerning only specially chosen articles; not general

self (sɛlf) n. **selves** (sɛlvz) **1.** One's own nature, character, abilities, etc.; personality: *One's concept of self is greatly influenced by the attitudes in the home.* **2.** A particular part of one's mental or physical nature: *She's back to her old self following an intensive treatment.*

self–as-ser-tive (sɛlf–ə–sɜrt–ɪv) adj. Expressing one's opinions and demands confidently

self–as-sured (sɛlf–ə–ʃʊərd) adj. Confident; trusting in one's own strength or ability

self–cen-tered (sɛlf–sɛnt–ərd) adj. Selfish; concerned only with one's own affairs

self–con-scious (sɛlf–kɑn–ʃəs) adj. Too aware of one's own faults and therefore embarrassed in the company of others

self–contained (sɛlf–kən–teʸnd) adj. Having within itself everything needed

self–controlled (sɛlf–kən–troʷld) adj. Able to control one's own behavior: *For the grace of God that brings salvation ... teaches us to say "No" to ungodliness and worldly passion, and to live self-controlled, upright and godly lives* (Titus 2:12).

self–de-ni-al (sɛlf–dɪ–naɪ–əl) n. The practice of not allowing oneself pleasures

self–dis-ci-line (sɛlf–dɪs–ə–plɪn) n. The training of one's self in order to produce self-control or a particular skill

self–ef-fac-ing (sɛlf–ə–feʸs–ŋ) adj. Keeping oneself in the background, as in humility

self–es-teem (sɛlf–ə–stiʸm) n. A good opinion of one's own character and abilities

self–im-por-tant (sɛlf–ɪm–pɔr–tənt) adj. Thinking too highly of oneself, of one's own worth

self–im-posed (sɛlf–ɪm–poʷzd) adj. Of a duty or task, imposed on oneself: *a self-imposed diet*

self–in-dul-gent (sɛlf–ɪn–dʌl–dʒənt) adj. Too ready to satisfy one's own inclinations and desires

self–in-ter-est (sɛlf–ɪn–tər–əst) n. A selfish desire to satisfy only one's personal interests

self–ish (sɛl–fɪʃ) adj. Concerned first with one's own advantage without care for others —opposite UNSELFISH —**selfishly** adv. —**selfishness** n. *"The love of money is the root of all kinds of evil,"* (1 Timothy 6:10) *but selfishness and pride are really at the root of every evil thought and deed or failure to do good.*

self–less (sɛlf–ləs) adj. Thinking more of others' needs than of one's own; completely unselfish —**selflessly** adv. —**selflessness** n.

self–pos-sessed (sɛlf–pə–zɛst) adj. Composed; self-assured; confident

self–re-spect (sɛlf–riʸ–spɛkt) n. Proper respect for oneself and concern for one's own character and reputation

self–righ-teous (sɛlf–raɪ–tʃəs) adj. *derog.* Showing too much pride in one's own rightness or goodness —**self–righteously** adv. —**self–righteousness** n.

self–sac-ri-fice (sɛlf–sæk–rə–faɪs) n. The giving up or willingness to give up one's own pleasure or interests in favor of others or of a more worthy purpose: *Jesus Christ is the supreme example of self-sacrifice. He said, "I lay down my life for the sheep [his followers] ... I lay down my life only to take it again. No one takes it from Me, but I lay it down of my own accord"* (John 10:15-18). *He [Jesus] is the atoning sacrifice for our sins, and not only for ours, but also for the sins of the whole world* (1 John 2:2). —**self–sacrificing** adj. —see also JESUS CHRIST, LAMB OF GOD

self–sat-is-fied (sɛlf–sæt–əs–faɪd) adj. Overly pleased with oneself; smug; complacent —**self–sat-is-fac-tion** (sɛlf–sæt–ɪs–fæk–ʃən) n.

self–seek-ing (sɛlf–siʸ–kŋ) adj. Working only for one's own advantage; seeking only one's own personal welfare: *Love ... is not self-seeking* (1 Corinthians 13:5).

self–serv-ice (sɛlf–sɜr–vɪs) n. The serving of oneself, as at a restaurant or gasoline station, and paying at a cashier's desk, usu. upon leaving —**self–service** adj.

self–serv-ing (sɛlf–sɜr–vŋ) adj. Tending to

advance oneself, often at the expense of others

self–suf–fi–cient (sɛlf-sə-**fɪʃ**-ənt) adj. Needing no help or support from anyone else

self–willed (sɛlf-**wɪld**) adj. Determined to have one's own way

sell (sɛl) v. **sold** (so**ʷ**ld) **selling 1.** To exchange property or goods for money: *They sell just about everything in this department store.* **2.** To be sold: *The house on the corner is selling for $200,000.* **3.** To make people want to buy: *The high quality of this product sells it.* **4.** *infml.* To convince someone to accept an idea, product, etc.: *I'm sold on the idea of pure water, but I'm not convinced your product is the best.*

sell–er (sɛl-ər) n. **1.** A salesperson **2.** An item that is sold in the manner specified: *This old-fashioned can opener is a poor seller. (=not many have been sold)*

se–man–tic (sɪ-**mænt**-ɪk) n. The study of word meanings and changes

sem–a–phore (sɛm-ə-fɔr) n. A form of signaling, usu. with flags held in each hand, with arms held in different positions for each letter of the alphabet

sem–blance (**sɛm**-bləns) n. An outward, often false, appearance

se–men (si**ʸ**-mən) n. The fluid produced in the male reproductive organs

se–mes–ter (sə-**mɛs**-tər) n. One of the periods into which the school year is divided at many US schools

sem–i– (sɛm-ɪ-/ sɛm-aɪ-) prefix **1.** Precisely half of: *semiannual* **2.** Partial; incomplete: *a semiprecious stone* **3.** Having some of the characteristics of: *semiskilled/ semiclassical music*

sem–i–an–nu–al (sɛm-i**ʸ**-**æn**-yə-wəl) adj. **1.** Occurring or published twice each year **2.** Lasting half a year —**semiannually** adv.

sem–i–cir–cle (sɛm-i**ʸ**-sər-kəl) n. Half a circle

sem–i–co–lon (sɛm-i**ʸ**-ko**ʷ**-lən) n. A punctuation mark (;) used to separate different parts of a list and independent parts of a sentence

sem–i–fi–nal (sɛm-i**ʸ**-fam-əl) adj. Next before the last in competition

semifinal n. A semifinal contest

sem–i–nar (sɛm-ə-nɑr) n. **1.** A group of students engaged in advanced study **2.** Any group meeting to consider or discuss a certain topic, usu. concerned with their occupation

sem–i–nar–y (sɛm-ə-nɛər-i**ʸ**) n. **-ies** An educational institution, esp. one that gives theological training

sem–i–pre–cious (sɛm-ɪ-**prɛʃ**-əs) adj. Gems not as valuable as precious stones

sen–ate (sɛn-ət) n. **1.** The upper house of the two law-making bodies in some countries such as the US —compare CONGRESS **2.** The governing body at some universities, usu. composed of the principal or representative members of the faculty

sen–a–tor (sɛn-ət-ər) n. A member of Senate

send (sɛnd) v. **sent, sending 1.** To cause to go: *They sent their children to school.* **2.** To cause to be in a specified state: *The strange and comical sight sent the audience into fits of laughter.* **3.** To cause to move suddenly and uncontrollably: *The sudden wind sent things flying everywhere.* **4.** To transmit messages: *The radio station sent programs into many countries.*

se–nile (si**ʸ**n-aɪl) adj. **1.**Weakened by old age, esp. in mental faculties **2.** Of or belonging to old age or aged persons —**se–nil–i–ty** (sɪ-**nɪl**-ət-i**ʸ**) n.

se–nior (si**ʸ**-nyər) n. **1.** A person who is older or higher in rank or authority than another **2.** A student in the final year of high school or university

se–nior–i–ty (si**ʸ**n-yɔr-ət-i**ʸ**) n. The condition of being higher in rank or age

sen–sa–tion (sɛn-se**ʸ**-ʃən) n. **1.** The ability to feel through any of the five senses of touch, sight, hearing, taste, or smell: *Cold temperatures can cause a loss of sensation in the fingers and toes.* **2.** A general feeling in one's mind or body as a result of sthg. that happens: *a sensation of warmth/ dizziness/ security* **3.** A state of great excitement or interest or the cause of this: *The discovery of gold caused a great sensation./That new singer is quite a sensation on Broadway (=in a theater there).*

sen–sa–tion–al (sɛn-se**ʸ**-ʃən-əl) adj. **1.** Causing or intended to cause excitement and inter-

est: *a sensational account of the murder* **2.** Extremely good or exciting —**sensationally** adv.

sense (sɛns) n. **1.** One of the five powers by which we feel or notice sthg. (sight, hearing, taste, smell, touch) **2.** A general feeling, esp. one that's hard to explain: *a sense that someone was watching him* **3.** An ability to understand or appreciate: *a sense of humor* **4.** Ability to understand and make reasonable judgments about sthg.: *a sense of values/a successful man with good business sense/Come back to your senses as you ought, and stop sinning* (1 Corinthians 15:34). —see SENSIBLE **5.** Good understanding and judgment, esp. in practical matters: *She has more sense than to spend all her money on clothes and jewelry when she needs it for her education.* **6. in a sense** Partly: *Your criticism is correct in a sense, but let me tell you my side of it.* **7. make sense (a)** To be clear in meaning: *What he said didn't make sense.* **(b)** To be reasonable or wise: *Buying a bathing suit in the winter makes sense if the price is very low and you've found exactly the style you want.*

sense v. **sensed, sensing** To feel or realize sthg. without being told: *We sensed his disapproval.*

sen-si-ble (sɛn–sə–bəl) adj. Suitable and practical; having or showing good judgment —**sen-si-bil-i-ty** (sɛn–sə–bɪl–ət–iʸ) n.

sen-si-tive (sɛn–sət–ɪv) adj. **1.** Responding quickly to the effect of sthg.: *sensitive to heat/change* **2.** Showing perceptive feelings or judgment (=seeing and understanding the situation): *She's a very sensitive person, easily offended./She's very sensitive to the needs of others.* —opposite INSENSITIVE —**sensitively** adv. —**sen-si-tiv-i-ty** (sɛn–sə–tɪv–ət–iʸ) n.

sen-si-tize (sɛn–sə–taɪz) v. **-tized, tizing** To make sensitive

sen-so-ry (sɛns–ə–riʸ) adj. Of the bodily senses

sen-su-al (sɛn–ʃuʷ–əl) adj. **1.** Of the body and the senses as distinguished from the intellect or mind **2. (a)** Connected or preoccupied with bodily or sexual pleasures **(b)** Full of lust; lewd; licentious

sen-su-ous (sɛn–ʃuʷ–əs) adj. **1.** Appealing to, or derived from the senses **2.** Keenly appreciative of and aroused by beauty, refinement, or luxury

sent (sɛnt) v. Past tense and past part. of **send**

sen-tence (sɛnt–əns) n. **1.** In grammar, a group of words forming a statement, command, exclamation, or question, usu. containing a subject and a verb, and (in writing) beginning with a capital letter and ending with a period, question mark, etc.: *She's singing again./How beautifully she sings!/Who sang at church yesterday?* —compare CLAUSE, PHRASE **2.** A statement of the punishment for a criminal found guilty in court: *The sentence was twenty years in the state penitentiary (prison).*

sentence v. **-tenced, -tencing** To state the punishment for sbdy.: *The court sentenced the man to six months of community service and a fine of $500.*

sen-ti-ment (sɛnt–ə–mənt) n. **1.** A show of feeling or emotion, often excessive **2.** A thought or judgement, influenced by feeling: *My sentiments, exactly!*

sen-ti-men-tal (sɛnt–ə–mɛnt–əl) adj. **1.** Resulting from tender feelings rather than reasonable or practical thinking: *The rocking chair isn't very attractive, but we keep it for sentimental reasons. It belonged to my grandfather.* **2.** Showing too much feeling or emotion —**sentimentally** adv. —**sen-ti-men-tal-i-ty** (sɛnt–ə–mɛn–tæl–ət–iʸ) n.

sen-ti-nel (sɛnt–ən–əl) n. A soldier on guard

sen-try (sɛn–triʸ) n. A soldier stationed at a place to stand guard

se-pal (siʸ–pəl) n. One of the leaf-like parts of a flower

sep-a-ra-ble (sɛp–ə–rə–bəl) adj. Able to be separated

sep-a-rate (sɛp–ə–reʸt) v. **-rated, -rating 1.** To move or keep apart: *St. Paul wrote: "For I am convinced that neither death nor life ... nor any powers ... nor anything else in all creation, will be able to separate us from the love of God which is in Christ Jesus our Lord"* (Romans 8:38,39). **2.** To be kept apart by sthg. that makes a division between: *The two towns are separated by a river.* **3.** To cause to come apart or di-

vide into parts: *Please separate the orange and divide it between the two children.* **4.** Of a husband and wife, to stop living together, esp. by a formal agreement

separate (sɛp–ə–rət) adj. **1.** Different or distinct: *They made three separate trips to the store for groceries.* **2.** Individual; not shared: *We have separate living quarters.* **3.** Apart: *The history books should be separate from the science books on the shelf.* —**separately** adv.

sep-a-ra-tion (sɛp–ə–re^y–ʃən) n. **1.** Dividing or coming apart **2.** A state of existing apart: *The separation from his parents was difficult for the child.* **3.** A formal agreement between a husband and wife to live apart, but not to end the marriage —compare DIVORCE

sep-a-rat-ist (sɛp–ə–rət–əst) n. A person who separates or advocates separation, esp. from a religious or political body

sep-a-ra-tive (sɛp–ə–re^{y}t–ɪv/ –rət–) adj. **1.** Tending to separate **2.** Causing separation

sept– (sɛpt–) Prefix meaning **seven**

Sep-tem-ber (sɛp–tɛm–bər) also **Sept.** *written abbr.* n. The ninth month of the year

sep-tic (sɛp–tɪk) adj. Putrid; full of germs

septic tank (sɛp–tɪk tæŋk) n. A tank in which sewage is partially purified

sep-tu-a-ge-nar-i-an (sɛp–tyu^w–ə–dʒə–nɛər–i^y–ən) n. A person between seventy and seventy-nine years old

sep-ul-cher *AmE.* **sep-ul-chre** *BrE.* (sɛp–əl–kər) n. A tomb

se-quel (si^y–kwəl) n. **1.** A story that is a continuation of an earlier story **2.** A result; a consequence

se-quence (si^y–kwəns) n. **1.** The order of events, esp. following one another in time: *Try to remember these historical events in their correct sequence.* **2.** An order of succession; arrangement **3.** A related or continuous series

se-ques-ter (sɪ–kwɛs–tər) v. **1.** To cause to withdraw into obscurity **2.** To confiscate; appropriate **3.** To segregate, as a jury during a trial

se-quin (si^y–kwən) n. A small shiny disk used to ornament a dress

se-quoi-a (sɪ–kwɔɪ–ə) n. A giant, coniferous, redwood tree

ser-aph (sɛər–əf) n. **seraphs** or **seraphim** A member of the highest order of angels —**se-raph-ic** (sə–ræf–ɪk) adj.

ser-e-nade (sɛər–ə–ne^{y}d) n. Music suitable to be played or sung at night, esp. under a lady's window

serenade v. To sing or play a serenade

ser-en-dip-i-ty (sɛr–ən–dɪp–ət–i^y) n. Making desirable discoveries accidentally

se-rene (sə–ri^{y}n) adj. Very calm; completely at peace: *a serene sky* —**serenely** adv. —**sereneness** n.

se-ren-i-ty (sə–rɛn–ət–i^y) n. **-ties** The quality or state of being serene; calmness; tranquility: *God give me the serenity to accept the things I cannot change, the courage to change the things I can, and the wisdom to know the difference.*

serf (sɑrf) n. A person bound in service to a landowner, bought and sold with the land he worked

serf-dom (sɑrf–dəm) n. Slavery

serge (sɑrdʒ) n. A strong twilled fabric, used esp. for clothing

ser-geant (sɑr–dʒənt) n. **1.** A non-commissioned officer ranking just above a corporal in the US Army **2.** A police officer

se-ri-al (sɪər–i^y–əl) adj. **1.** Of, relating to, or arranged in a series: *serial order* **2.** Appearing in successive parts that follow regularly: *a serial story*

serial n. A work appearing (as in a magazine or on television) in parts and at intervals

serial number (sɪər–i^y–əl nʌm–bər) n. A number indicating place in a series and used as a means of identification

se-ries (sɪər–i^{y}z) n. **series** A number of things, events, etc. of the same kind, coming one after another in order: *A television/ radio series (=a series of shows on television/ radio)/a series of job interviews/the world series (=a series of baseball games to determine the championship)*

se-ri-ous (sɪər–i^y–əs) adj. **1.** Thoughtful and solemn; not to be taken lightly: *The lack of rain for nearly a year has created a very serious problem.* **2.** Important because of possible danger or harm: *The fire caused some very serious damage.* **3.** Important because of the kind of topic, idea, etc.; needing thoughtful

study: *a serious business* —**seriousness** n.

se-ri-ous-ly (sɪər-i^y-əə li^y) adv 1. In an earnest manner: *John doesn't play around; he takes his work seriously.* 2. **take sbdy./ sthg. seriously** To treat as important and worthy of respectful treatment

ser-mon (sɜr–mən) n. A talk on a moral or religious subject, usu. by a clergyman in a place of worship

ser-pent (sɜr–pənt) n. A snake

ser-pen-tine (sɜr–pən–ti^yn/ –taɪn) adj. Like a serpent

ser-rat-ed (sə–re^yt–əd/ sɛər–e^yt–əd) adj. Having notches or teeth like a saw

se-rum (sɪər–əm) n. 1. The fluid part of the blood that helps fight disease 2. Fluid from the blood of an immunized animal

serv-ant (sɜr–vənt) n. 1. A person paid to work for another in the other's house, often receiving food and lodging in addition to wages 2. *fml.* A person who serves the needs or purposes of another, esp. one who serves out of devotion: *A politician should be a servant of the people./Jesus said to his disciples, "Whoever wants to become great among you must be your servant ... just as the Son of Man [Jesus] did not come to be served, but to serve and to give his life as a ransom for many"* (Matthew 20:26,28).

serve (sɜrv) v. **served, serving** 1. To work as a servant: *George served the family faithfully for twenty years.* 2. To render obedience and worship to God: *Jesus said, "It is written, 'Worship the Lord your God, and serve him only!'"* (Matthew 4:10). *Serve the Lord with gladness* (Psalm 100:2). 3. To help one another: *Serve one another in love* (Galatians 5:13). 4. To be suitable for a particular purpose: *We are out of coffee; will some hot tea serve the purpose?* 5. To offer food or drink: *I will serve dinner before they leave.* 6. By a person who will wait on a customer in a store: *How may I serve you?* 7. To spend a designated amount of time in prison: *He served time in prison for armed robbery.* 8. In tennis, volleyball, etc., to begin play by hitting the ball to the opponent 9. To deliver an official order [subpoena] to sbdy. to appear in court

ser-vice (sɜr–vəs) n. 1. Attention given to buyers in a store or to guests in a hotel, restaurant, etc,: *The service in this res-taurant is excellent.* 2. Act of serving God. *Jesus replied, "No one who puts his hand to the plow [begins to serve] and looks back [wishing to go back to whatever he was doing before] is fit for service in the kingdom of God"* (Luke 9:62). 3. Work done for someone; a helpful act: *Our secretary has given us valuable service.* 4. Duty done for someone: *He received a medal for his service to the country during wartime.* 5. The repair and maintenance of a machine: *He took the computer in for service.* 6. A person, company, or organization doing useful work or supplying a need: *Is there any train service to Badger Creek?* 7. A religious ceremony of public worship or the fixed form of worship used: *an Easter Sunrise Service/ Some churches have a more informal service than others.* 8. A department of the government: *the Diplomatic Service* 9. A business or job that supplies the needs of the public rather than producing goods: *telephone/ medical/postal service* 10. **at your service** Ready to help: *If you need any help, I am at your service.* 11. **of service** Useful and helpful: *Her children could be of more service to her.*

service adj. Relating to or used by people working in a place, esp. servants in a house: *a service entrance*

service v. **-iced, -icing** To repair or maintain in order to keep in good condition: *I have to get the car serviced.*

ser-vice-a-ble (sɜr–və–sə–bəl) adj. That can be used, esp. for a long time under hard use: *a very serviceable set of tires/a serviceable pair of jeans*

ser-vice-man (sɜr–vɪs–mæn/ –mən) n. **-men** 1. A member of the military 2. A person whose occupation is to service and repair equipment

service station (sɜr–vɪs ste^y–ʃən) n. A place equipped for servicing automobiles

ser-vi-ette (sɜr–vi^y–ɛt) *BrE.* A table napkin

ser-vile (sɜr–vɪl/ –vaɪl) adj. 1. Slavishly obedient 2. Of or for slaves —**servilely** adv. —**servil-i-ty** (sɜr–vɪl–ət–i^y) n.

serv-ing (sɜr–vɪŋ) n. A single portion of food or drink

ser-vi-tude (sɜr–və–tuᵂd) n. **1.** Slavery of any kind **2.** Compulsory punishment for criminals

ses-a-me (sɛs–ə–miʸ) n. An herb with seeds used for oil and flavoring

ses-sion (sɛʃ–ən) n. **1.** A formal meeting or series of meetings of an organization, esp. a law-making body or court: *the next session of Congress/The Congress is now in session.* (=*meeting for business*) **2.** One of the parts of the year when classes are held at a university: *the fall session* **3.** A single meeting or period of time used esp. by a group for a particular activity: *a planning session*

set (sɛt) v. **set, setting 1.** To put sth. down or in a certain place: *Set that box of groceries on the table.* **2.** To be or to give: *Set an example for the believers in speech, in life, in love, in faith and in purity* (1 Timothy 4:12). **3.** To put into order for use: *to set the table* (=*put the plates, glasses, etc. on it.*)/*She set pots of flowers on the porch.* **4.** To fix, establish, or determine the cost, time, standard, number, etc.: *The time has been set for 8:00 a.m./to set a speed record* **5.** To fix firmly a part of the face or body, esp. to show one's feelings: *He set his jaw in determination./ spir. Set your hearts on things above where Christ is seated at the right hand of God. Set your minds on things above, not on earthly things* (Colossians 3:1,2). **6.** Esp. of the sun, to go down out of sight: *In the summer the sun sets late.* **7.** To start: *His actions have set me thinking.* **8.** To describe a specified time and place for the action in a movie, play, book, etc.: *The novel is set in 20th-century Africa.* **9.** To compose music for words: *to set a poem to music* **10.** To fix sth. firmly into a surface; *I'd like this sapphire set in a gold necklace.* **11.** To put a broken bone or limb into place and keep it in a fixed position so that it will mend **12.** Of a liquid, paste, jelly, etc., to become firm **13.** To arrange wet hair so that it will give the desired style when dry **14. all set** Ready **15.** To distinguish: *Her humble attitude sets her apart* (=*makes her clearly different*) *from other women.* **16. set foot in/ on** To come into/onto; visit: *We are not allowed to set foot on her property.* **17. set fire/ set a match to** To start a fire

18. set the pace To fix the rate for others to follow **19. set right** To cause to be correct, just, healthy, etc. **20. set back (a)** To place at a distance from sth.: *a building set back from the street* **(b)** To make late: *The bad weather will set back our building plans by three weeks.* **(c)** *infml.* To cost a specified amount of money: *This ticket only set me back five dollars.* **21. set in** To begin: *Winter set in earlier than usual this year./You need to see a doctor about that wound before infection sets in.* **22. set forth/ off/out** To start a trip: *My friend set off on a trip across the country.* **23. set sth. off (a)** To cause an explosion: *Be careful! The explosives could be set off at any time.* **(b)** To cause sudden anxious activity: *The angry speech by one man set off a riot.* **24. set sth. up (a)** To put up into position: *The children set up a stand to sell lemonade.* **(b)** To found an organization, business, etc.: *They set up an organization to help the homeless.*

set n. **1.** A group of similar things that belong together in some way: *a set of dishes* **2.** A device for receiving television or radio signals: *a television set* **3.** The furniture, scenery, etc. for a play, movie, etc.: *stage set* **4.** A series of six or more games in a tennis match

set adj. **1.** Specified; fixed; arranged: *She takes medicine at set hours each day.* **2.** Fixed in a position that does not move: *a set expression/a set policy* **3.** Firmly intending; determined: *He's set on making a trip to London.* **4.** Ready; prepared: *We are all set to go on a picnic.*

set-back (sɛt–bæk) n. A return to a less favorable position: *She recovered quickly after her operation, but then she had a sudden setback.*

set-tee (sɛ–tiʸ) n. A kind of sofa

set-ter (sɛt–ər) n. A hunting dog

set-ting (sɛt–ɱ) n. **1.** The action of sbdy. or sth. that sets: *the setting of the date for a wedding* **2.** The way or position in which a machine or device is set: *This dryer has two settings, hot and cold.* **3.** Environment; surroundings; background: *The beautiful mountains and pine trees were an ideal setting for the country cabin.*

set-tle (sɛt–əl) **-tled, -tling 1.** To go and live somewhere: *My ancestors settled in Boston.* **2.** To place so as to be and remain comforta-

ble: *The mother settled the baby in the crib.* **3.** To go downwards: *The huge plane settled on the landing strip.* (=came down and landed)/ *The tea leaves settled in the bottom of the cup./ The dust settled after the wind storm.* **4.** To make or become calm, etc.: *After the children settle down, we will watch a movie.* **5.** To make a final decision: *That settles it; we'll begin tomorrow!* **6. settle down (a)** To get into a comfortable position **(b)** To establish a home **(c)** To become comfortable in a way of life, a job, etc. **7. settle for sthg.** To accept sthg. that is seen as not quite satisfactory: *Why settle for second best when the ultimate and very best is within your immediate reach?*

set-tled (sɛt–əld) adj. Not likely to change; fixed

set-tle-ment (sɛt–əl–mənt) n. **1.** A small village **2.** The movement of a large number of people into a new area: *the settlement of the West* **3.** An agreement or decision that settles an argument, question, etc.: *the settlement of a court case* **4.** An act of paying a bill, claim, etc.: *insurance settlement*

set-tler (sɛt–lər/ –əl–ər) n. One who settles in a new country or new area with few people: *He was one of the early settlers in Australia.*

set-up (sɛt–ʌp) n. **1.** A system or plan of operation **2.** An arrangement of machinery, equipment, etc. **3.** A task or contest deliberately made easy **4.** An opponent easy to defeat

sev-en (sɛv–ən) determ., n., pron. The number 7 —**seventh** determ., n., pron.

sev-en seas (sɛv–ən siʸz) n. All the navigable waters of the world

sev-en-teen (sɛv–ən–tiʸn) determ., n., pron. The number 17 —**seventeenth** determ., n., pron., adv.

sev-en-ty (sɛv–ən–tiʸ) determ., n., pron. The number 70 —**seventieth** determ., n., pron.

sev-er (sɛv–ər) v. To cut or break; to divide, esp. into two parts: *a severed limb*

sev-er-al (sɛv–ə–rəl) determ., pron. Some, but not many; more than two, but less than many

several Adj. Various, different, respective: *The boys went their several ways.*

se-vere (sə–vɪər) adj. **1.** Serious: *a severe illness* **2.** Harsh; stern; strict; unkind in treatment: *a severe judge/severe disciplinary measures* **3.** Very bad; intensely painful: *a severe toothache* —**severely** adv. —**se-ver-i-ty** (sə–vɛər–ət–iʸ) n. -**ties**

sew (soʷ) v. **sewed, sewn, sewing 1.** To join or fasten cloth, leather, etc. together by stitches made with thread; make or mend with needle and thread: *Mother is sewing a new dress.* **2. sew sthg. up (a)** To close or mend by sewing **(b)** *infml.* To get control of: *He's sure to get the job; he has it sewed up.* —**sewing** n.

sew-age (suʷ–ɪdʒ) n. Waste matter from factories, towns, human beings, etc. that is carried away in sewers

sew-er (suʷ–ər) n. A large underground passage or pipe for carrying away water and waste material

sex (sɛks) n. **1.** The condition of being male or female **2.** Either of the two divisions of creatures — male or female: *Is it true that the female is the weaker sex?* **3.** The sum of activities, attitudes, relationships, etc. involved in the bodily system of reproduction: *a movie with a lot of sex in it* **4.** Sexual intercourse; a relationship between a man and a woman involving the union of the parts of the body involved in reproducing young: *Sex without marriage is a sin against God's holy commandment: "You shall not commit adultery"* (Exodus 20:14).

sex-a-ge-nar-i-an (sɛk–sə–dʒɪ–nɛər–iʸ–ən) n. A person between sixty and sixty-nine years of age

sex-tant (sɛks–tənt) n. An instrument for measuring angular distance between stars in determining latitude and longitude at sea

sex-ton (sɛks–tən) n. An official who takes care of church property

sex-tu-ple (sɛks–tuʷ–pəl/ –tʌ–) adj. **1.** Consisting of six parts **2.** Being six times as great

sextuple v. -**pled, -pling** To make six times as much or six times as many

sex-u-al (sɛk–ʃuʷ–əl) adj. Concerning sex or the sexes —**sexually** adv. —**sex-u-al-i-ty** (sɛk–ʃə–wæl–ət–iʸ) n.

sex-y (sek–si^y) adj. **-ier, -iest** Arousing, or intending to arouse, sexual desire or interest

shab-by (ʃæb–i^y) adj. **-bier, -biest** Threadbare, worn-out clothing: *a shabby pair of jeans*

shack (ʃæk) n. A small roughly built house; hut

shack-le (ʃæk–əl) n. Chains fastening the arms or legs of prisoners

shackle v. **shackled, shackling 1.** To fasten with a chain **2.** To hold back; prevent; hinder

shade (ʃe^{y}d) n. **1.** A place where heat, direct sunlight, etc. are blocked, causing it to be cooler and darker **2.** Sthg. that blocks out light or its full brightness: *a window shade* **3.** A slight difference in color: *a lighter/ brighter shade of green* **4.** A slight difference in sthg.: *What are the shades of meaning between "small" and "tiny"?*

shade v. **shaded, shading 1.** To block out direct light or heat: *She shaded the baby from the sun with her umbrella.* **2.** To make parts of a picture darker

shad-ow (ʃæd–o^w) n. **1.** A patch of partial darkness where direct light, esp. sunlight, is blocked: *As the sun set, the shadows became longer.* **2.** A least bit: *not a shadow of truth in his criticism*

shadow v. **1.** To shade or darken **2.** To follow sbdy. closely and watch him, esp. secretly: *The police were shadowing someone they suspected of being a spy.*

shad-y (ʃe^{y}d–i^y) adj. **-ier, -iest 1.** Shaded from the light or heat **2.** *derog.* Dishonest: *a shady character*

shaft (ʃæft) n. **1.** Anything long and straight **2.** The long rod on which the head of an arrow or spear is fixed **3.** A bar or rod which turns, with a belt or wheel turning around it, to pass power through a machine: *the drive shaft of a car* **4.** A long narrow space, usu. up and down or sloping: *an elevator shaft*

shag-gy (ʃæg–i^y) adj. **-gier, -giest** Consisting of or covered with long, unruly, rough hair: *a shaggy old dog* —**shag-giness** n.

shake (ʃe^{y}k) v. **shook** (ʃʊk), **shaken** (ʃe^{y}k–ən), **shaking 1.** To move quickly up and down or from side to side: *When the building began*

to shake I knew we were having an earthquake./ She was so nervous her hands were shaking. **2.** To grasp and hold someone's right hand briefly in one's own, as a sign of greeting, good-bye, or agreement: *Let's shake hands on our new business partnership.* **3.** To disturb the mind or feelings; upset: *David said about him [Jesus]: "I saw the Lord always before me. Because he is at my right hand, I will not be shaken"* (Acts 2:25). **4.** To wave: *He shook his fist in anger.* **5. shake sthg. off** To get rid of sbdy./sthg. that is unwanted: *The thief tried to shake off his pursuers.* **6. shake sthg. up (a)** To bring about changes, as in an organization: *The new management has really shaken up the company. Many changes have been made.* **(b)** To mix by shaking **7. shake one's head** To move one's head from side to side quickly, indicating "No" NOTE: Moving one's head up and down quickly (nodding) indicates "Yes."

shake n. An act of shaking: *I gave the rug a good shake to get the dirt out.*

shake-down (ʃe^{y}k–daʊn) n. **1.** A thorough search **2.** *Infml.* Extortion of money

shake-up (ʃe^{y}k–ʌp) n. Extensive change or reorganization: *There has been a major company shake-up with ten people losing their jobs*

shak-y (ʃe^{y}k–i^y) adj **-ier, -iest 1.** Shaking or trembling from nervousness, weakness, unsteadiness, etc. **2.** Not steady or firm; not reliable: *a shaky government/shaky promises* —**shakiness** n.

shale (ʃe^{y}l) n. A rock formed from clay that easily breaks into layers

shall (ʃæl) v. **1.** Used to form the future tense of other verbs when the subject is **I** or **we**: *I shall return./We shall both be here next week.* **2.** Used with **you, he, she, it,** and **they** to show a promise, law, or command: *You shall not steal* (Exodus 20: 15). *It shall be unlawful to carry firearms.* **3.** Used esp. with **I** and **we** in questions or offers in which the hearer must decide: *Shall I lock the door?* —see also SHOULD, WILL In modern speech, in the first two meanings, we use "will" much more often than "shall", but "shall" is always used in the third meaning: *I'll (I will) see you tomorrow./You'll (you will) be glad to*

see the movie./Shall I shut the door?

shal·low (ʃæl–oʷ) adj. 1. Having little depth; not far from top to bottom: *He will be safe at the shallow end of the swimming pool.* 2. Not thinking or capable of serious thought; superficial: *a shallow thinker*

sha·lom (ʃɑ–loʷm/ʃə–) interj. Peace! A conventional Hebrew greeting or farewell

sham (ʃæm) n. A thing, feeling, etc. that is not what it pretends to be

sha·man (ʃɑm–ən/ ʃeʸ–mən) n. A medicine man who uses magic for the purpose of curing the sick, influencing spirits for good or evil, controlling events, etc.

sha·man·ism (ʃɑm–ən–ɪz–əm/ ʃeʸ–mən–) n. A religion of northern Asia and North America characterized by a belief in an unseen world of demons and ancestral spirits who must be appeased, and will only respond to shamans

sham·bles (ʃæm–bəlz) n. *infml.* A mess; confused disorder: *After the earthquake the office was a shambles.*

shame (ʃeʸm) n. 1. The painful feeling caused by one's own guilt, wrongness, or failure or that of a close friend, relative, etc.: *He who ignores discipline comes to poverty and shame* (Proverbs 13:18). 2. Dishonor; disgrace: *Let us fix our eyes on Jesus ... who for the joy set before him, endured the cross, scorning its shame, and sat down at the right hand of God* (Hebrews 12:2). —see JESUS, RIGHT HAND OF GOD 3. A state of affairs that ought not to be; a pity: *What a shame that your luggage never got on the plane with you.* 4. **put someone or sthg. to shame** To be greatly better than sbdy. else in sthg.: *The wise [worldly wise] will be put to shame; they will be dismayed and trapped. Since they have rejected the word of the Lord, what kind of wisdom do they have?* (Jeremiah 8:9).

shame v. **shamed, shaming** To bring dishonor upon sbdy.; to disgrace: *He shamed his family by his drunkenness and irresponsibility.*

shame·ful (ʃeʸm–fəl) adj. Causing shame; deserving blame because of guilt: *Nothing impure will ever enter it [heaven], nor will anyone who does what is shameful or deceitful, but only those whose names are written in the Lamb's book of life* (Revelation 21:27).

shame·less (ʃeʸm–ləs) adj. 1. Not feeling or able to feel shame: *a shameless liar* 2. Done without shame; indecent: *shameless acts of cruelty* —**shamelessly** adv.

sham·poo (ʃæm–puʷ) n. -poos 1. A soapy, liquid product used for washing hair, cleaning carpets, etc. 2. An act of shampooing sthg.

shampoo v. -pooed, -pooing To clean by washing with shampoo

sham·rock (ʃæm–rɑk) n. A plant having a bright green leaf divided into three parts, the national emblem of Ireland

shank (ʃæŋk) n. 1. The part of the leg between the knee and ankle 2. A similar part of an animal's leg 3. A cut of meat from the upper or lower part of an animal's leg 4. Any part like a leg 5. A long narrow part of sthg.; a shaft

shan·ty (ʃæn–tiʸ) n. A small, roughly made dwelling

shape (ʃeʸp) n. 1. Appearance: *a cookie in the shape of a star* 2. *infml.* Condition; state: *Exercising and eating right help me to stay in shape. (=keep a good physical condition)/ Our car should be in good shape after getting all that work done on it.* 3. Bodily contour apart from the head and face 4. **take shape** To begin to be like the finished product

shape v. **shaped, shaping** 1. To form in a particular shape: *to shape the wet clay on the potter's wheel* 2. To have a great influence on: *to shape one's career* 3. To develop in a certain way: *How are your vacation plans shaping up?*

shape·less (ʃeʸp–ləs) adj. 1. Having no definite shape 2. Not shapely

shape·ly (ʃeʸp–liʸ) adj. -lier, -liest Having a pleasing shape —**shapeliness** n.

share (ʃeər) n. 1. A portion belonging to one person or group: *If you want a share of the pay, you'll have to do your share of the work.* 2. Any of the equal parts into which the capital stock of a company or corporation is divided

share v. **shared, sharing** 1. To use, pay, have, etc., a part of sthg. with others: *There's only one typewriter; we'll have to share.* 2. To divide and give out in shares: *Do not forget to do*

good and to share with others, for with such sacrifices God is pleased (Hebrews 13:16).

shark (ʃɑrk) n. **1.** Any of various types of ocean fish, some of which are large and dangerous **2.** *infml.* A person who loans out money at very high rates or gets money from people in other dishonest ways

sharp (ʃɑrp) adj. **1.** Having a fine edge or point for cutting: *a sharp needle/shears* **2.** Keen and sensitive: *a sharp eye/a sharp person* **3.** Piercing, producing a sensation like that of cutting, biting, or stinging: *a sharp pain in the chest* **4.** Making a quick change in direction: *a sharp curve in the road* **5.** Well-defined in shape or detail; distinct: *a sharp outline* **6.** Of words, intended to cause pain: *a sharp criticism* **7.** Intense: *a sharp pain* **8.** *Slang.* Attractive or stylish **9.** In music **(a)** raised half a tone in pitch **(b)** above the correct pitch

sharp adv. Precisely at the stated time: *The service starts at eleven o'clock sharp.*

sharp-en (ʃɑr-pən) v. **1.** To become or cause to become sharp: *He sharpens knives, saws, and other tools for a living.* **2.** *fig.* Sharpening of the intellect: *As iron sharpens iron, so one man sharpens another* (Proverbs 27:17).

sharp-en-er (ʃɑrp-ə-nər) n. A machine or tool for sharpening

shat-ter (ʃæt-ər) v. To break suddenly and forcefully into tiny pieces; smash: *The baseball shattered the window./ fig. to shatter someone's hopes*

shave (ʃeʸv) v. **shaved, shaving 1.** To cut hair off the face with a razor **2.** To cut or scrape off very thin pieces from a surface

shave n. **1.** An act or result of shaving **2. a close shave** *infml.* A very narrow escape

shav-en (ʃeʸ-vən) adj. Having been shaved: *He always looks neat and clean-shaven.*

shav-er (ʃeʸ-vər) n. **1.** A tool for shaving, esp. an electric razor **2. a little shaver** a boy; a youngster

shav-ing (ʃeʸ-vɪŋ) n. **1.** The act of closely cutting off hair with a razor **2.** A very thin piece of wood, cut from a surface with a sharp blade: *The floor of the carpenter shop was covered with shavings.*

shawl (ʃɔl) n. A loose cloth covering for the head and shoulders

she (ʃiʸ) pron. Used as the subject of a sentence **1.** The female person or animal mentioned, seen, heard, etc. earlier and being talked about now: *Mary was here a minute ago. Where is she now?* **2.** Used of certain things, esp. countries and certain vehicles: *When we boarded the ship, she was just ready to sail.*

sheaf (ʃiʸf) n. *Pl.* **sheaves** Stalks of cut grain bound together; a bundle

shear (ʃɪr) v. **sheared, shorn** (ʃɔrn) To clip or cut with a sharp instrument

shears (ʃɪərz) n. **1.** Large scissors **2.** Any of various heavier cutting tools similar to scissors: *gardening shears*

sheath (ʃiʸθ) n. **1.** A case for a sword or dagger **2.** A long close-fitting covering

sheathe (ʃiʸð) v. **sheathed, sheathing** To put into a sheath

shed (ʃɛd) n. A lightly-built building, usu. for storing things, sheltering animals, or as a workshop: *a wood shed*

shed v. **shed, shedding 1.** To cause or allow to flow out: *to shed tears/to shed blood* **2.** Of a plant or animal, to come off naturally: *Flowers shed their petals.* **3.** To cast off: *to shed one's coat*

sheen (ʃiʸn) n. Shining brightness; gloss

sheep (ʃiʸp) n. **1.** A grass-eating animal with a thick wool coat, that is kept for its wool and its meat **2.** Those who believe in Jesus Christ as their Savior and Lord are sometimes called "sheep", and Jesus is called the "Good Shepherd": *Jesus said, "I am the good Shepherd. The good Shepherd lays down his life for the sheep. My sheep hear my voice and I know them, and they follow Me. I give them eternal life, and they shall never perish; no one can snatch them out of My hand"* (John 10:11,27,28). —see SHEPHERD **3. black sheep** A person regarded as a failure by other members of his group: *My cousin is the black sheep of the family.*

sheep-dog (ʃiʸp-dɔg) n. A dog trained to help a shepherd watch and tend sheep

sheep-fold (ʃiʸp-foʷld) n. An enclosure for sheep

sheep-ish (ʃiʸ-pɪʃ) adj. Embarrassed, as if one had done sthg. wrong —**sheepishly** adv.

sheer (ʃɪər) adj. 1. Complete; not mixed with anything else: *sheer nonsense* 2. Very steep; almost straight up and down: *a sheer drop of fifty feet* 3. Very thin, light, and almost transparent: *sheer nylon curtains*

sheet (ʃiʸt) n. 1. A large piece of cloth used on a bed 2. A piece of paper for writing or printing on, usu. in a standard size: *I'll need two sheets of paper for this letter.* 3. A broad thin piece of sthg.: *a sheet of plywood/metal*

sheet-ing (ʃiʸt–ɪŋ) n. 1. Fabric used to make bed sheets 2. Material used to cover sthg.

sheik or sheikh (ʃeʸk/ ʃiʸk) n. 1. An Arab chief 2. A wealthy or prominent Arab

shelf (ʃɛlf) n. shelves (ʃɛlvz) 1. Material, usu. wood or metal, fixed horizontally to hold books, dishes, and other articles: *book shelves* 2. Sthg. like a shelf 3. on the shelf Inactive or useless

shell (ʃɛl) n. 1. A hard outer covering of eggs, nuts, some seeds and fruits, some animals, etc.: *The squirrel cracked the shell of the nut open with its teeth.* 2. A metal case filled with an explosive, designed to be fired from a gun

shell v. 1. To take the shells from eggs, nuts, etc. 2. To fire shells: *The enemy lines were shelled heavily.*

shel-lac (ʃə–læk) n. A liquid that hardens to a smooth, shiny finish when applied to wood, metal, etc.

shel-lac or shel-lack v. 1. To coat or treat with shellac 2. *Infml.* To defeat decisively

shel-ter (ʃɛl–tər) n. 1. Some type of protection, esp. from the weather: *to find shelter from a storm* 2. A building or enclosure built for protection: *a shelter for cattle*

shelter v. To provide with shelter: *After the flood, homeless people were sheltered in the school gymnasium.*

shel-tered (ʃɛl–tərd) adj. Kept away from harm, risk, or the world's problems: *She had a very sheltered life as she was growing up.*

shelve (ʃɛlv) v. shelved, shelving 1. To put or arrange on shelves 2. To set aside until a later time; delay: *They decided to shelve their plans for a trip around the world until their children finished college.*

shelves (ʃɛlvz) n. *pl.* of shelf

shelv-ing (ʃɛl–vɪŋ) n. Material for shelves

shep-herd (ʃɛp–ərd) n. 1. One who takes care of sheep 2. Jesus is called the Good Shepherd since he leads and feeds (spiritually) and protects his sheep (those who believe in him and put their trust in him for eternal life) (John 10:11,14, 27,28). —see SHEEP

shepherd v. To watch over carefully; to guide: *The tourists were shepherded around by two guides.*

sher-bet (ʃɜr–bət) n. *AmE.* A sweet, fruit-flavored frozen dessert *BrE.* A fizzy drink

sher-iff (ʃɛr–əf) n. In the US, the chief law-enforcement official in a county

she's (ʃiʸz) Contraction of (a) she is: *She's sick.* (b) she has: *She's been here before.*

shield (ʃiʸld) n. 1. A broad piece of metal, wood, etc. carried by soldiers on the fore-arm (in former times) as a protection from arrows, etc. 2. A means of defense; protection: *He [God] is a shield to those who take refuge in him* (Proverbs 30:5). 3. shield of faith Faith in Jesus Christ our Savior which comes by hearing and reading the Bible: *Take up the shield of faith with which you can extinguish all the flaming arrows [lies and temptations] of the evil one [Satan]* (Ephesians 6:16).

shield v. To protect or defend someone or sthg. from harm or danger: *She hid her friend to shield her from her pursuers./She shielded her eyes from the sun.*

shift (ʃɪft) v. 1. To change or move from one position or direction to another: *The load on the truck shifted, causing it to throw the truck out of balance./You're always trying to shift the blame on me!* 2. shift for oneself To take care of oneself without help from others 3. shift gears To change the gear of the engine of a vehicle: *He shifted gears to go up the hill.*

shift n. 1. A change in place, nature, direction, etc.: *a shift in policy/fashion* 2. A group of workers who work for a certain period: *the night shift*

shift-less (ʃɪft–ləs) adj. Having no set plan or purpose; lazy

shift-y (ʃɪf–tiʸ) adj. -ier, -iest Appearing to be dishonest; not to be trusted

shim-mer (ʃɪm–ər) v. To shine faintly with

flickering light

shimmer n. A faint gleam or shine

shim-my (ʃɪm–iʸ) n. A vibration, esp. in the front wheels of a motor vehicle

shin (ʃɪn) n. The front part of the leg from the knee to the ankle

shin v. -nn- To climb (as a rope or pole) by gripping alternately with hands and legs

shine (ʃaɪn) v. shone (ʃoʷn), shining 1. To give out or reflect light; look bright: *The sun is shining brightly./ spir. The Son of Man [Jesus] will send out his angels, and they will weed out ... everything that causes sin and all who do evil... Then the righteous will shine like the sun in the kingdom of their Father* (Matthew 13:41,43). 2. To direct a flashlight, etc.: *Shine your light on the path so we can see.*

shine n. 1. Brightness; shining quality: *The newly waxed floors had a beautiful shine.* 2. An act of making sth. bright by polishing: *Your father's shoes need a shine.* 3. **come rain or come shine** Whatever happens: *We're going on vacation; rain or shine.*

shine (ʃaɪn) v. shined (ʃaɪnd), shining To rub sth. until it is bright: *Please shine your shoes before going to church.*

shin-gle (ʃɪŋ–gəl) n. A small flat piece of wood, asbestos, etc. laid with others in rows to cover a roof or wall

shingle v. -gled, -gling To cover with shingles

shingles (ʃɪŋ–gəlz) n. A type of infectious disease causing a painful rash

shin-ny (ʃɪn–iʸ) n. A simple kind of hockey played on ice with skates, or without skates on the street or in a field

shin-y (ʃaɪn–iʸ) adj. -ier, -iest Glossy; polished; bright: *a shiny new dime*

ship (ʃɪp) n. 1. A large sea-going vessel for carrying people or goods on the sea 2. An aircraft or spacecraft

ship v. shipped, shipping 1. To take or place on board a ship 2. To send or cause to be transported by any carrier: *The cattle were shipped by rail.*

ship-ment (ʃɪp–mənt) n. 1. A load of items shipped together 2. The act of shipping goods

ship-per (ʃɪp–ər) n. A dealer who arranges for goods to be shipped

ship-ping (ʃɪp–ɪŋ) n. 1. The act or business of transporting goods: *the business of shipping* 2. Ships collectively, esp. those of a country or port 3. The sending and delivery of sth. by any carrier: *There was a $75 charge for shipping.*

shirk (ʃɜrk) v. To avoid or get out of doing work —shirker n.

shirt (ʃɜrt) n. A kind of garment worn by men on the upper part of the body, usu. of light cloth with a collar and sleeves, buttoning down the front

shiv-er (ʃɪv–ər) v. To shake or tremble, esp. from cold or fear: *We all sat in the cold building shivering.*

shiver n. A feeling of shivering: *That strange noise sent shivers up and down my spine.*

shoal (ʃoʷl) n. 1. A place in a river, lake, etc. where the water is shallow 2. A sand bar that makes the water shallow

shoal n. A large number: *a shoal of fish*

shock (ʃak) n. 1. A violent blow as from a crash, earthquake, or explosion: *The shock of the earthquake was felt for hundreds of miles.* 2. The condition caused by an unexpected and usu. very unpleasant happening: *It was a great shock for us when our baby died.* 3. The sudden jolt of electricity passing through the body 4. A condition of extreme weakness after illness or other physical damage to the body: *She went into shock as a result of losing so much blood in the accident.*

shock v. To cause a feeling of disgust, angry surprise, etc.: *I was shocked by her behavior.*

shod (ʃad) v. Past tense and past part. of shoe: *The blacksmith shod the horse.*

shod-dy (ʃad–iʸ) adj. -dier, -diest 1. Of material, inferior or imitation 2. Mean: *shoddy treatment; a shoddy trick*

shoe (ʃuʷ) n. Outer covering for a person's foot, usu. with a stiff base (sole) and a firm support (heel) under the heel of the foot

shoe-lace (ʃuʷ–leʸs) n. A lace or string for fastening a shoe

shone (ʃoʷn) v. Past tense and part. of shine

shoo (ʃuʷ) interj. An expression used to scare birds or chickens away

shoo v. shooed, shooing To scare or drive

away

shook (ʃʊk) v. Past tense of **shake**

shoot (ʃuʷt) v. **shot** (ʃɑt), **shooting 1.** To fire a weapon: *They shot their way out of prison.* **2.** To hit, wound, or kill with a gun, arrow, or other weapon: *He shot a lion.* **3.** To flow or come out forcefully and quickly: *The pipe burst and water shot out.* **4.** To go fast: *He shot past me to the finish line.* **5.** To take a photograph or make a movie: *She shot a lot of pictures for her photography class.*

shoot-ing star (ʃuʷt–ŋ star) n. A meteor as seen when it enters the earth's atmosphere

shop (ʃɑp) n. **1.** A store **2.** A place for making or repairing things; a workshop: *My brother operates a shoe repair shop.* **3. set up shop** To go into a business: *He's set up shop as a cabinetmaker in Lagos.*

shop v. **-pp-** To visit stores in order to buy sthg.: *We went shopping for new furniture today.* —**shopper** n.

shop-lift-er (ʃɑp–lɪf–tər) n. One who steals goods from a shop

shore (ʃɔr) n. The land along the edge of a large body of water

shorn (ʃɔrn) v. Past part. of **shear**

short (ʃɔrt) adj. **1.** Measuring little from one end to the other: *A straight line is the shortest distance between two points.* **2.** Continuing only a little time: *a short visit of ten minutes* **3.** Not very tall: *I'm short but my brother is even shorter.* **4.** Not having much or enough of sthg.: *I'm short of money this month.* **5. for short** As a short way of saying the same name: *Her real name is "Susan," but everyone calls her "Sue" for short.* **6. In short** To put sthg. into a few words **7. fall short** To fail to measure up to that which is expected or required: *All have sinned and fall short of the glory of God, and are justified freely by his grace through the redemption that came by Christ Jesus* (Romans 3:23,24).

short-age (ʃɔrt–ɪdʒ) n. A lack

short cake (ʃɔrt keʸk) n. A kind of sponge cake covered or filled with berries or other fruit: *Let's have some strawberry short cake.*

short circuit (ʃɔrt sɜr–kət) n. A faulty electrical connection that usu. puts the power supply out of operation

short–circuit v. To cause a short circuit

short-com-ing (ʃɔrt–kʌm–ŋ) n. Fault; defect: *He has a lot of shortcomings, but I still like him.*

short-cut (ʃɔrt–kʌt) n. **1.** A quicker, easier way or route **2.** Any method that saves time or energy

short-en (ʃɔrt–ən) v. To make or become shorter

short-en-ing (ʃɔrt–ən–ŋ) n. A fat such as butter used to make pastry crisp or flaky

short-hand (ʃɔrt–hænd) n. A method of rapid handwriting using simple strokes in place of letters, phrases, etc.

short-hand-ed (ʃɔrt–**hæn**–dəd) adj. Not having enough workers

short-lived (ʃɔrt–laɪvd) adj. Lasting only for a little while

short-ly (ʃɔrt–liʸ) adv. Soon

shorts (ʃɔrts) n. **1.** Pants ending at or above the knees, worn in playing games or in hot weather **2.** *AmE.* Men's underpants

short-sight-ed (ʃɔrt–saɪt–əd) adj. **1.** Lacking in foresight **2.** Near sighted; not able to see very far —**shortsightedness** n.

short-stop (ʃɔrt–stɑp) n. In baseball, a player who covers the area between second and third base

short-wave (ʃɔrt–weʸv) n. A radio wave used for long distance transmission or reception

shot (ʃɑt) v. Past tense and part. of **shoot**

shot n. **1.** An act of firing a weapon: *We heard three shots.* **2.** A throw or stroke in a game intended to win a point **3.** A marksman: *He's really a good shot.* **4.** An effort: *I'll give it my best shot.* **5.** Launch of a spacecraft or rocket: *the first space-shot this year* **6.** A metal ball (sphere) that is thrown for distance in the shot put **7.** Tiny non-explosive metal balls for shooting from some kinds of guns **8.** A photograph or a short continuous action in a movie: *a good shot of my dog chasing his tail* **9.** An injection: *a yellow fever shot* **10.** *infml.* The taking of an illegal drug into the bloodstream through a needle **11. big shot** *derog.* An important person **12. like a shot** *infml.* Rapidly and eagerly: *He went out of here like a shot.* **13. shot in the arm** *infml.* Sthg. that brings one back to a better, more active condition **14. a shot in the dark** *infml.* A wild

guess

shot-gun (ʃɑt–gʌn) n. A double barreled shoulder weapon with a small bore, used to fire small shot at short range

shot put (ʃɑt pʊt) n. A field event in which an iron ball is propelled with an overhand thrust from the shoulder

should (ʃʊd) v. **1. (a)** Ought to: *You should be more careful.* **(b)** To show that sthg. is expected to happen: *We should finish this work soon.* **2.** Happen to: *Should anyone come to the door, don't open it!*

shoul-der (ʃoʷl–dər) n. **1.** The part of a person's body at each side of the neck where the arms are connected **2.** The part of a garment covering this

shoulder v. **1.** To thrust or push with the shoulders **2.** To take upon the shoulder **3.** *fig.* To take responsibility

shoulder blade (ʃoʷl–dər bleʸd) n. The scapula; the short, triangular bone at the back of the shoulder

shouldn't (ʃʊd–ənt) v. Contraction of **should not**

should've (ʃʊd–əv) v. Contraction of **should have**

shout (ʃaʊt) v. Speak or call out very loudly: *Shout for joy to the Lord with gladness; come before him with joyful songs* (Psalm 100:1).

shout. n. A loud cry or call: *a shout of joy*

shove (ʃʌv) n. A strong push: *We gave the car a shove to get it started.* —**shove** v. *He shoved his way through the crowd.*

shov-el (ʃʌv–əl) n. **1.** A usu. long-handled tool with a broad blade with curved edges for lifting and moving loose material —compare SPADE **2.** Part of a large earth-moving machine for digging and moving loose material

shovel v. **-eled** or **elled**, **-eling** or **elling** To take up and throw with a shovel: *He shoveled the snow from the driveway.*

show (ʃoʷ) v. **showed, showed** or **shown, showing 1.** To allow or cause sbdy./sthg. to be seen: *Can you show me where we are on this map?* **2.** To be visible: *Don't worry about that hole in your sock. It won't show.* **3.** To guide: *May I show you to the nursery?* **4.** To instruct: *Will you show me how to work this math prob-*

lem? **5.** Used esp. of a movie: *There's a good movie showing at the theater tonight.* **6.** To reveal or express a quality or emotion: *This is how God showed his love among us: He sent his one and only Son into the world that we might live through him. This is love: not that we loved God, but that he loved us and sent his Son as an atoning sacrifice for our sins* (1 John 4:9,10). **7. show one's face** To appear in public: *I didn't feel I could show my face after I lost my wallet with all the club's money.* **8. show off** To behave so as to try to get people to admire one's appearance, abilities, etc.: *He doesn't have many friends because he likes to show off.* **9. show up (a)** Cause to be seen: *This bright light really shows up the dust on the furniture.* **(b)** To arrive or be present somewhere: *How many showed up for the meeting?*

show n. **1.** Any type of public entertainment, esp. a performance in a theater or on radio or television: *There are not very many educational shows on television.* **2.** A public display of things, for example, new products, things in a competition, etc.; exhibition: *an automobile show* **3.** A demonstrative display: *a show of strength* **4.** A thing done to give a certain impression, often a false one; outward appearance: *She tries to appear very efficient, but it's only a show.*

show-down (ʃoʷ–daʊn) n. A confrontation

show-er (ʃaʊ–ər) n. **1.** A brief fall of rain or snow: *a spring shower* **2. (a)** A bath taken by standing under running water **(b)** A small room with an apparatus for this **3.** A party given on some occasion, usu. by a woman's friends, who bring appropriate gifts: *a baby shower/ wedding shower*

shower v. **1.** To pour down rain, snow, etc., in showers **2.** To give many presents: *She was showered with gifts.* **3.** To take a shower

shown (ʃoʷn) v. Past part. of **show**

show-off (ʃoʷ–ɔf) n. A person who tries to impress others with his talents, possessions, etc.

show-y (ʃoʷ–iʸ) adj. **-ier, -iest** Too colorful, bright, exaggerated, etc.

shrap-nel (ʃræp–nəl) n. **1.** An artillery shell containing pieces of metal that are scattered when the shell explodes **2.** The pieces that it

scatters

shred (ʃrɛd) n. A small narrow strip torn or roughly cut off: *His shoe was torn to shreds.*

shred v. -dd- To cut or tear into shreds —**shredder** n.

shrew (ʃruʷ) n. 1. A small, mouse-like animal with a long nose 2. A nagging woman

shrewd (ʃruʷd) adj. 1. Clever in judgment and dealings: *a shrewd businessman* 2. Well thought out and likely to be correct: *a shrewd decision* —**shrewdly** adv.

shriek (ʃriʸk) n. A sharp, shrill cry; screech

shriek v. To make such a cry

shrill (ʃrɪl) adj. Of a sound or voice, high in tone; piercing

shrimp (ʃrɪmp) n. **shrimp or shrimps** 1. Any of a large number of small, slender, long-tailed sea creatures, many of which are highly valued for food 2. *derog.* A small person

shrine (ʃraɪn) n. 1. A place or object held sacred for its associations 2. The tomb of a saint

shrink (ʃrɪŋk) v. **shrank, shrunk or shrunken, shrinking** 1. To become smaller, esp. from moisture, heat, or cold: *fig. The number of car sales has shrunk in recent months.* 2. To move back and away from sbdy./sthg.: *The nervous dog shrank into a corner.*

shrink n. *infml. Humor* for **psychiatrist**

shriv-el (ʃrɪv-əl) v. To dry out, shrink and draw into wrinkles; wither

shroud (ʃraʊd) n. 1. The cloth around a dead body 2. Anything that covers: *a shroud of mist*

shroud v. To cover, as with a shroud: *His disappearance was shrouded in mystery*

shrub (ʃrʌb) n. A plant, lower than a tree and usu. having smaller branches

shrub-ber-y (ʃrʌb-ə-riʸ) n. 1. An area planted with shrubs 2. Shrubs collectively

shrug (ʃrʌg) v. -gg- To draw up one's shoulders as if expressing doubt or indifference

shrunk-en (ʃrʌŋk-ən) v. Past part. of **shrink**

shud-der (ʃʌd-ər) v. To tremble from fear, cold, or disgust: *He shuddered at the sight of the accident./ fig. He shuddered at the thought of such cruelty to animals.* —**shudder** n.

shuf-fle (ʃʌf-əl) v. -fled, -fling 1. To change the order of playing cards: *Go ahead and shuffle the cards; we're ready for the game to start.* 2. To walk slowly or without lifting one's feet completely off the ground: *The tired old man shuffled across the room.*

shuf-fle-board (ʃʌf-əl-bɔrd) n. A game in which players use long-handled cues to push wooden disks into scoring areas on a smooth surface

shun (ʃʌn) v. -nn- To stay away from: *Do not be wise in your own eyes; fear the Lord and shun evil* (Proverbs 3:7). *To shun evil is understanding* (Job 28:28).

shunt (ʃʌnt) v. 1. To move a train from one track to another 2. To move (e.g. a child) from one place to another: *The poor child was always being shunted off to one neighbor or another.* 3. To divert blood or other fluid from one part of the body to another by a surgical shunt

shunt n. 1. A mechanism for turning sthg. aside, such as a railway switch 2. A conductor joining two points in an electrical circuit 3. A surgical passage created to divert blood or other fluid from one part of the body to another

shush (ʃʌʃ) interj. Be quiet!

shut (ʃʌt) v. **shut, shutting** 1. To move a door, window, lid, etc. so that it covers an opening; to close: *Shut the window, please./ What [God] opens, no one can shut and what he shuts, no one can open* (Revelation 3:7). 2. To cause to stop operating, esp. temporarily; shut down: *The business had to shut down when they lost the lease to the property.* —opposite OPEN 3. **shut off** (a) To cause to stop in flow or operation, usu. by turning a handle or pressing a button (b) To keep sbdy./sthg. away from sthg.: *His deafness shuts him off from many activities that others enjoy.* 4. **shut up** *infml.* Be quiet; stop talking: *Shut up! We're trying to listen to the news.*

shut-ter (ʃʌt-ər) n. 1. A moveable wooden or metal cover that can be closed in front of a window to keep out light or thieves 2. A part of a camera which opens for a very short time to let light come through the lens and fall on the film

shut-tle (ʃʌt-əl) n. A regular service back and

forth by air, bus, etc.: *There is a shuttle (bus service) between the town center and the train station.*

shuttle v. -tled, -tling To move back and forth often or regularly: *This airline shuttles passengers from New York to Washington.*

shy (ʃaɪ) adj. **shyer** or **shier, shyest** or **shiest 1.** Bashful; not bold; retiring or nervous in the company of others **2.** Of animals, unwilling to be seen by or be near people **3. camera shy** Not liking to be photographed —**shyly** adv. —**shyness** n.

shy v. **shied, shying** To turn aside or hold back; avoid sthg. unpleasant: *She has always shied away from close friendships.*

shy-ster (ʃaɪ-stər) n. *Infml.* A dishonest lawyer

sib-ling (sɪb-lɪŋ) n. A brother or sister

sick (sɪk) adj. **1.** Not healthy; ill —see DISEASE **2.** Tired of sthg.: *I'm sick of listening to his same old stories.* **3. (a)** Deeply distressed; upset **(b)** Disgusted: *Hope deferred makes the heart sick, but a longing fulfilled is a tree of life* (Proverbs 13:12). **4.** Feeling ill, like vomiting, from the stated kind of travel: *carsick/ seasick*

sick-en (sɪk-ən) v. **1. {a)** To make or become distressed or disgusted **(b)** To nauseate (=make one feel like vomiting) **2.** To begin to be ill; show signs of a disease

sick-le (sɪk-əl) n. A curved blade for cutting grain, hay, etc.

sick-ly (sɪk-liʸ) adj. **-lier, -liest 1.** Often weak and unhealthy: *a sickly child* **2.** Causing a feeling of sickness: *a sickly smell*

side (saɪd) n. **1.** A vertical surface of sthg.: *Most buildings have four sides.* **2.** Any of the lines or flat surfaces that limit or form the boundary of sthg.: *A triangle has three sides.* **3.** Off the edge of: *We pulled off the side of the road.* **4.** Either surface of a thin flat object: *Write on both sides of the paper.* **5.** A place or area set off by a real or imaginary line: *Mary lives on the other side of the river.* **6.** The right or left part of the body: *The whole left side of my head hurts.* **7.** The space next to sbdy.: *He saved her a seat by his side.* **8.** A point of view to be considered, usu. in opposition to another: *Jesus said, "Everyone on the side of the*

truth listens to me"* (John 18:37). **9.** A team or a political party: *Whose side are you on? (=which side do you want to win?)* **10.** A slope: *a hillside/mountainside* **11.** A set of relatives: *He takes after his father's side of the family.* **12. on the side** In addition: *She's a waitress, but she makes a little money on the side by baby sitting.*

side adj. **1.** On, at, in, from the side: *the side window* **2.** In addition to the main or regular thing: *Some pills have harmful side effects.*

side v. **sided, siding** To support one person or group in a quarrel with someone else

side-burns (saɪd-bɜrnz) n. Short hair on a man's face in front of the ears

side-ef-fect (saɪd-ə-fɛkt) n. An additional, often bad, effect of a drug

side-kick (saɪd-kɪk) n. A partner or special friend

side-track (saɪd-træk) v. To leave one subject or activity to follow another one

side-walk (saɪd-wɔk) n. A paved surface at the side of a street or road

side-ways (saɪd-weʸz) adv. **1.** With one side forward **2.** Toward or from one side **3.** Directed to one side —**sideways** adj.

siege (siʸdʒ) n. The surrounding of a town, fort, etc. to block its supplies and force it to surrender: *The city was under siege for ten months before falling to the enemy.*

si-er-ra (siʸ-ɛər-ə) n. A range of mountains with jagged peaks

si-es-ta (siʸ-ɛs-tə) n. A short rest, esp. one taken in the afternoon

sieve (sɪv) n. A container with a meshed wire bottom for separating solid materials from liquid

sieve v. **sieved, sieving** To put through a sieve

sift (sɪft) v. **1.** To put sthg. through a screen: *Mother sifted the flour.* **2.** To examine closely: *He sifted through a pile of papers in search of his tickets.*

sigh (saɪ) n. A long deep-sounding breath, showing tiredness, sadness, longing, etc.: *We all heaved (=made) a sigh of relief when the storm was over.* —**sigh** v. *He sighed when he realized how much further he had to walk.*

sight (saɪt) n. **1.** The act or power of seeing **2.**

In one's view: *He never lets that child out of sight.* 3. Sthg. that one sees familiar sights on the way to work 4. Sthg. attractive to see: *There are many interesting sights in nearly every country.* 5. Sthg. laughable: *What a sight you were when you fell in the mud.*

sight v. To see sthg., esp. after looking for it for a long time: *The crew shouted when they sighted land.*

sign (sam) n. 1. A board or metal plate giving information, a warning, etc. 2. A mark that has meaning (such as +, @, #); a symbol 3. A gesture: *He put his hand to his ear as a sign that she should talk louder.* 4. Evidence that shows the presence or coming of sthg. else: *The return of the swallows to Capistrano are one of the signs that spring is here.*

sign v. 1. To write one's name on a letter, document, check, etc.: *The checks need to be signed by you.* 2. **to sign up (a)** To join an organization or make an agreement to do sthg. **(b)** To engage for work by making a legal contract: *The football team has signed up four new players for this season.*

sig-nal (sɪg–nəl) n. 1. A sound, light, gesture, etc., giving a command, warning or other message: *a railway signal* 2. Waves sent by radio or television

signal v. **-naled or nalled, naling or nalling** 1. To make signals: *The policeman signaled the driver to stop.* 2. To send a message by means of signals: *The signalman on our ship signaled another ship in the harbor, requesting information.*

sig-nal-ize (sɪg–nə–laız) v. **-ized, -izing** 1. To make conspicuous 2. To indicate particularly—**sig-nal-i-za-tion** (sɪg–nə–lə–zeʸ–ʃən) n.

sig-na-to-ry (sɪg–nə–tɔr–iʸ) n. One who signs an agreement

sig-na-ture (sɪg–nə–tʃər) n. A person's name written by himself or herself at the end of a letter, on a check, etc.

sig-nif-i-cance (sɪg–nɪf–ə–kəns) n. Importance; meaning; value: *a decision of great significance* —opposite INSIGNIFICANCE

sig-nif-i-cant (sɪg–nɪf–ə–kənt) adj. 1. Very important: *a significant change in the patient's condition* —opposite INSIGNIFICANT 2. Suggesting a particular idea; having a spe-

cial meaning: *a significant glance* —significantly adv.

sig-ni-fy (sɪg–nə–faı) v. **-fied, -fying** 1. To indicate; to mean: *That pin on the map signifies a school.* 2. To express by an action: *She signified her approval by nodding her head.*

sign post (sam poʷst) n. A post bearing a sign

Sikh (siʸk) n. A member of a monotheistic religious sect in India, founded in the 16th century

si-lage (saı–lɪdʒ) n. Fodder preserved in a silo

si-lence (saı–ləns) n. Quietness; stillness; absence of sound

silence v. **-lenced, -lencing** 1. To make silent 2. To fail to mention

si-lenc-er (saı–lən–sər) n. A device for deadening the sound of a firearm

si-lent (saı–lənt) adj. 1. Not speaking: *Even a fool is thought wise if he keeps silent* (Proverbs 17:28). 2. Quiet: *the silent hours of the night* 3. Concerning a letter in a word, not pronounced: *In the word "knee" the "k" is silent.* —silently adv.

sil-hou-ette (sɪl–ə–wɛt) n. 1. The outline of sthg., usually filled in with a solid color 2. An outline

silhouette v. **-etted, -etting** To cause an object to be seen as a silhouette: *The church on the hill was silhouetted against the setting sun.*

sil-i-ca (sɪl–ɪ–kə) n. A hard, glassy mineral found in a variety of forms including quartz, sand, opal, etc.

silica gel (sɪl–ɪ–kə dʒɛl) n. A highly absorbent form of silica used as a drying agent

silk (sɪlk) n. Very fine, soft fibers produced by a kind of insect (silkworm) and made into cloth

silk-worm (sɪlk wɜrm) n. The caterpillar that produces a cocoon of fine, shiny fiber used to make silk thread and cloth

silk-y (sɪl–kiʸ) adj. **-ier, -iest** Like silk; soft, smooth, or shiny: *She has the silkiest hair!*

sill (sɪl) n. The ledge of wood, stone, etc. at the base of an opening or frame, esp. a windowsill

sil-ly (sɪl–iʸ) adj. **-lier, -liest** Not sensible; often laughably foolish

si-lo (saı–loʷ) n. A tall, round structure in which food for farm animals is stored

silt (sɪlt) n. Sand or mud left behind by flowing water

sil-ver (sɪl–vər) n. A whitish precious metal used esp. in jewelry, coins, and table utensils: *"It was not with perishable things such as silver or gold that you were redeemed ... but with the precious blood of Christ, a lamb without blemish or defect"* (1 Peter 1:18, 19).

silver adj. **1.** Made of silver **2.** Like silver in color: *a silver-haired lady*

silver-ware (sɪl–vər–wɛər) n. Knives, forks, spoons, etc., made of silver

sil-ver-y (sɪlv–ə–riʸ) adj. Like silver in one way or another, esp. in shine or color: *the silvery moon*

sim-i-lar (sɪm–ə–lər) adj. Almost the same; like or alike: *His opinions are similar to mine.* —similarly adv.

sim-i-lar-i-ty (sɪm–ə–lɛər–ə–tiʸ) n. **-ties** The quality of being alike: *The two sisters are as different as night and day; there's no similarity between them.*

sim-i-le (sɪm–ə–liʸ) n. An expression using "like" or "as" in which one thing is likened to another that is well known, such as "bright as day" or "He runs like a rabbit."

sim-mer (sɪm–ər) v. To cook gently, just below or just at the boiling point

sim-per (sɪm–pər) v. **1.** To smile in a silly manner **2.** To say with a simper

sim-ple (sɪm–pəl) adj. **1.** Not fancy or decorated; plain **2.** Not complicated or involved: *simple instructions* **3.** Of the ordinary kind: *A hammer is a simple tool.* **4.** Pure: *the simple facts*

sim-ple-ton (sɪm–pəl–tən) n. A stupid person

sim-plic-i-ty (sɪm–plɪs–ət–iʸ) n. The state of being simple

sim-pli-fi-ca-tion (sɪm–plə–fə–keʸ–ʃən) n. **1.** An act of making simpler **2.** A simpler form

sim-pli-fied (sɪm–plə–faɪd) adj. Made less complicated

sim-pli-fy (sɪm–plə–faɪ) v. **-fied, -fying** To make easier

sim-plis-tic (sɪm–plɪs–tɪk) adj. Tending to over-simplify

sim-ply (sɪm–pliʸ) adv. **1.** In a simple manner: *On the frontier, people live very simply.* **2.** Only: *I don't like my job; I do it simply to make*

a living. **3.** Absolutely: *She's simply beautiful.*

sim-u-late (sɪm–yə–leʸt) v. **-lated, -lating** To cause sthg. to appear to be the case: *This machine simulates the take-off and landing of an airplane.* —simulator n. —simulative adj.

sim-u-la-ted (sɪm–yə–leʸt–əd) adj. Having the appearance of

sim-u-la-tion (sɪm–yə–leʸ–ʃən) n. **1.** Sthg. made to resemble sthg. else **2.** Act of simulating

si-mul-ta-ne-ous (saɪ–məl–teʸ–niʸ–əs) adj. Occurring at the same time —simultaneously adv.

sin (sɪn) n. The transgression of God's Law (1 John 3:4) by thought, word, deed or omission; wickedness; evil; iniquity. NOTE: Every departure from God's Law is sin, whether this be great or small, known or unknown, intended or accidental. On the other hand, only what is at variance with the word of God is sin. The transgression of man-made laws and rules may not be regarded as sin, unless by so doing we also transgress a commandment of God. If we transgress the laws of the government, we sin against God, for he has commanded us to submit to every authority instituted among men (1 Peter 2:13). To disobey parents is also a sin against God, for he says, "Children, obey your parents in everything" (Colossians 3:20). We also sin when we do sthg. against our own conscience (Romans 14:23) and when we cause or encourage sbdy. else to sin against his conscience by doing sthg. that he or she thinks is wrong, even though it is not forbidden by God's Law (1 Corinthians 8:9-13). However, when people ask us to do anything that is contrary to the word of God, then it is not a sin if we disobey them, but we are being loyal to God, for "we must obey God rather than men" (Acts 5:29). The external cause of sin is the devil who "has been sinning from the beginning" (1 John 3:8) and who is called "a liar and the father of lies" (John 8:44). He is the driving force in the children of unbelief, and is tempting Christians to do evil (1 Peter 5:8,9). The internal cause of sin is the heart of man. "Out of the

heart come evil thoughts, murder, adultery, sexual immorality, theft, false testimony, slander" (Matthew 15:19) "greed, malice, deceit, lewdness, envy, arrogance, and folly. All these evils come from inside and make a man unclean" (Mark 7:21-23). Sexual immorality includes incest (sexual relations with close relatives) (Leviticus 18:6-16; 20: 11,12, 19-21), adultery (sexual relations with another person's husband or wife) (Leviticus 20:10), fornication (sexual relations with anyone other than one's own wife or husband) (Ephesians 5:3), homosexuality (sex with a person of the same sex) (Leviticus 18:22; 20:13), bestiality (sex acts with an animal) (Leviticus 20:15,16), or even the desire for such immoral activity (Matthew 5:28). Other sins include idolatry (Exodus 20:3-5), blasphemy (Exodus 20:7), failure to keep the holy day holy (Ex. 20:8), disobedience to parents (Ex. 20:12), the withholding of justice (Deuteronomy 27:19), divination (Leviticus 19:6), sorcery (Leviticus 19:6), witchcraft (Deuteronomy 18:10), consulting mediums or spiritists (Leviticus 19:31), debauchery, hatred, discord, jealousy, fits of rage, selfish ambition, dissensions, factions, drunkenness, orgies (Galatians 5:19-21), obscenity, foolish talk, coarse joking (Ephesians 5:4), lying (Proverbs 12:22), cheating (Proverbs 11:1), and bribery (Proverbs 17:23). Obviously we are all sinners, as the Bible says we are (Romans 3:23; Ecclesiastes 7:20), and the wages of sin (what we deserve) is death (Romans 6:23). All of us are by nature "dead in transgressions and sins" (Ephesians 2:1) and therefore unable to do anything to save ourselves from eternal damnation. "By observing the law no one will be justified" (Galatians 2:16) . But God doesn't want anyone to perish in his sins (Ezekiel 33:11; 2 Peter 3:9). Despite the fact that God hates sin, he loves people so much that he sent his one and only Son into the world to keep the Law for us and to suffer all the punishment that we deserve by his innocent suffering and death on Calvary's cross.

"He was pierced for our transgressions, he was crushed for our iniquities; the punishment that brought us peace [with God] was upon him, and by his wounds we are healed... the Lord laid on him the iniquity of us all" (Isaiah 53: 5,6). "For God so loved the world that He gave his one and only Son, that whoever believes in Him should not perish but have eternal life" (John 3:16). "The wages of sin is death, but the Gift of God is eternal life in Christ Jesus our Lord" (Romans 6:23). The worst possible sin, then, is to reject Jesus as our Savior, for there is no other way to eternal life (John 14:6; Acts 4:12). "Repent, and be baptized, every one of you, in the name of Jesus Christ so that your sins may be forgiven. And you will receive the gift of the Holy Spirit. The promise is for you and your children and for all who are far off — for all whom the Lord our God will call" (Acts 2:38,39). "If you confess with your mouth, 'Jesus is Lord,' and believe in your heart that God raised him from the dead, you will be saved" (Romans 10:9). —see COMMANDMENTS, SINFUL, SINNER, ORIGINAL SIN, LAW, IMAGE OF GOD, MAN, JESUS, SAVIOR, GRACE, GOSPEL —sin v. sinned, sinning

since (sms) adv. **1.** From that time onward; between then and now: *has lived there ever since* **2.** Before the present time: *long since forgotten* **3.** After a time in the past: *They've since moved away from here.*

since prep. From or in a period after a specified time in the past: *since yesterday afternoon*

since conj. **1.** At a time in the past after or later than another event: *Ever since he graduated he's held two jobs.* **2.** Because of the fact that: *Since my bicycle is broken, I'll have to walk.*

sin-cere (sm–sɪər) adj. Honest; without deceit or dishonesty —sincerely adv.

sin-cer-i-ty (sm–sɛr–ət–iʸ) n. Honesty

sin-ew (sm–yuʷ) n. **1.** A strong cord made of tissue that joins a muscle to a bone; a tendon **2.** Strength; energy **3.** Anything supplying strength

sin-ew-y (sm–yuʷ–iʸ) adj. Of meat, tough and stringy, having too many sinews

sin-ful (sm–fəl) adj. Full of sin; wicked; evil. The Bible, God's holy word, tells us that all people born since the fall of Adam have been born with a sinful nature: *"Surely I have been a sinner from birth, sinful from the time my mother conceived me"* (Psalms 51:5). *"Even from birth the wicked go astray; from the womb they are wayward and speak lies"* (Psalms 58:3). Saint Paul, author of 13 of the 27 books of the New Testament, writes: *"I know that nothing good lives in me, that is, in my sinful nature"* (Romans 7:18). *"The sinful mind is hostile to God. It does not submit to God's law, nor can it do so. Those controlled by the sinful nature cannot please God"* (Romans 8:7, 8). *"The acts of the sinful nature are obvious: sexual immorality, impurity and debauchery; idolatry and witchcraft, hatred, discord, jealousy, fits of rage, selfish ambition, dissensions, factions and envy, drunkenness, orgies, and the like... Those who live like this will not inherit the kingdom of God"* (Gal. 5:19-21). NOTE: But *"Christ Jesus came into the world to save sinners..."* (1 Timothy 1:15). *"God sent his Son, born of a woman, born under the law, to redeem those under the law"* (Galatians 4:4,5). *"He has been tempted in every way, just as we are — yet was without sin"* (Hebrews 4:15). *"He committed no sin, and no deceit was found in his mouth"* (1 Peter 2:22). Nevertheless, *"He himself bore our sins in his body on the tree"* [the cross on which he was crucified] (1 Peter 2:24). *"God made him who had no sin to be sin* [a sin offering] *for us, so that in him we might become the righteousness of God"* (2 Corinthians 5:21). *"He was delivered over to death for our sins and was raised to life for our justification"* (Romans 4:25). *"Whoever believes in him shall not perish but have eternal life"* (John 3:16). *"For the wages of sin is death, but the gift of God is eternal life in Christ Jesus our Lord"* (Romans 6:23). —see also MAN, SIN, SINNER, ORIGINAL SIN, LAW, JESUS, SAVIOR, CREED

sing (sm) v. **sang** (sæŋ) **sung** (sʌŋ) **singing** To produce music, song, etc. with the voice: *Sing praises to God, sing praises; sing praises to our King, sing praises* (Psalm 47:6). *Sing and make music in your heart to the Lord, always giving thanks to God the Father for everything in the name of our Lord Jesus Christ* (Ephesians 5:19,20).

singe (smdʒ) v. **singed, singeing** To burn slightly on the surface; to scorch

sin-gle (sm–gəl) adj. 1. Only one: *The entire law is summed up in a single commandment: "Love your neighbor as yourself"* (Galatians 5:14). 2. Not married: *Three married couples and two single ladies went with us on the trip.*

sin-gle-hand-ed (sm–gəl–hæn–dəd) adj. Accomplishing sthg. without the help of others

sin-gle-mind-ed (sm–gəl–maɪn–dəd) adj. Having a single purpose

sin-gles (sm–gəlz) n. A tennis match with one player against one —compare DOUBLES

sin-gly (sm–gliʸ) adv. One by one: *Some people came singly, others in groups.*

sin-gu-lar (sm–gyə–lər) adj. 1. *gram.* A word or form representing only one thing: *The noun "goose" is singular; it is the singular form of "geese."* —compare PLURAL 2. Unusual; extraordinary; rare: *a woman of singular intelligence* —**singularly** adv.

sin-is-ter (sm–ə–stər) adj. Suggesting, or warning of, evil

sink (sm̩k) v. **sank** (sæŋk) **sunk** (sʌŋk) **sinking** 1. To go down below the surface of the water: *A block of wood won't sink; it floats.* 2. To go below the surface of anything: *He was sinking in the mud.* 3. To go down in strength, value, etc.: *He's sinking (=losing strength) fast. He probably won't live much longer.* 4. **sink in** (a) To penetrate one's mind; be fully understood (b) To be absorbed: *The rain water on the path will soon sink in.*

sink n. 1. A basin in a kitchen, usu. with a drainpipe and a piped water supply 2. A lavatory or washbasin, esp. a basin for washing the hands and face

sin-ner (sm–ər) n. A person who is guilty of sin: *All people are by nature sinful and unclean, transgressing God's holy laws, falling far short of glorifying God as they were created to do* (Romans 3:24). *The prophet Isaiah tells us that*

*even the most righteous things we do are like
filthy rags* (Isaiah 64:6). *There is not a righteous
man on earth who does what is right and
never sins* (Ecclesiastes 7:20). *But thanks be to
God, Jesus Christ came into the world to save
sinners* (1 Timothy 1:15). *While we were still
sinners, Christ died for us* (Romans 5:8). *If we
claim to be without sin, we deceive ourselves
and the truth is not in us. If we confess our sins,
he [God] is faithful and just and will forgive us
our sins and purify us from all unrighteousness*
(1 John 1:9). —see SIN, SINFUL, JESUS

sin-u-ous (sɪn–yuʷ–əs) adj. **1.** Bending in and
out; winding: *Snakes move in a sinuous manner.* **2.** Graceful and bending easily: *a sinuous dance*

si-nus (saɪ–nəs) n. Any of the hollow cavities
in the skull that connect with the nasal passages

sip (sɪp) v. **-pp-** To drink only a little at a time:
She sipped her tea slowly.

sip n. A tiny amount of a drink

si-phon (saɪ–fən) n. A bent tube used for
drawing off liquid from one container into
another

siphon v. To draw off through a siphon: *The
thieves siphoned the gasoline out of my car.*

sir (sər) n. **1.** A respectful or formal way to
address a man: *Thank you, sir.* **2. Sir** A title
used before the name of a knight or baronet
3. Used at the beginning of a formal letter:
Dear Sir

si-ren (saɪ–rən) n. A device for making a loud
warning sound, used on police cars, etc.

sir-loin (sər–lɔɪn) n. Beef cut from the upper
part of the back

sis-al (saɪ–səl/–zəl/ sɪs–əl) n. A kind of fiber
made from a tropical plant, used in making
ropes, etc.

sis-sy (sɪs–iʸ) n. **-sies 1.** An effeminate boy or
man **2.** A cowardly person

sis-ter (sɪs–tər) n. **1.** A female relative with the
same parents: *Mary is my sister.* **2.** A member
of a women's religious group or community, a nun: *Sister Mary Ann*

sister adj. Of things considered female: *a sister ship* **—sisterly** adv.

sister–in–law (sɪs–tər–m–lɔ) n. **1.** The sister of
one's spouse **2.** The wife of one's brother **3.**
The wife of one's spouse's brother

sit (sɪt) v. **sat** (sæt), **sitting 1.** To rest on the upper
legs and buttocks: *He was sitting at his
desk.* **2.** To go into this position; to take a
seat: *Please sit down and make yourself comfortable.* **3.** To perch: *birds sitting on a branch* **4.**
To be an official member: *He sits on several
committees.*

site (saɪt) n. **1.** The place where some activity
takes place or has taken place: *a camp site* **2.**
A place where a building, school, mall, etc.
once stood, now stands, or is to be built: *a
building site*

sit-ter (sɪt–ər) n. **1.** A person who is seated **2.**
One who poses for a portrait **3.** A baby sitter **4.** A hen sitting on eggs

sit-u-ate (sɪtʃ–ʊ–eʸt) v. **-ated, -ating** To place,
locate, position

sit-u-ated (sɪtʃ–yuʷ–eʸ–təd) adj. Located

sit-u-a-tion (sɪtʃ–ʊ–eʸ–ʃən) n. **1.** A set of circumstances **2.** A location or site **3.** A place of
employment

six (sɪks) determ., n., pron. The number 6

six-teen (sɪks–tiʸn) determ., n., pron. The
number 16

six-teenth (sɪks–tiʸnθ) determ., n., pron., adv.
16th

sixth (sɪksθ) determ., n., pron., adv. 6th

six-ti-eth (sɪks–tiʸ–əθ) determ., n., pron., adv.
60th

six-ty (sɪks–tiʸ) determ., n., pron. The number
60

siz-a-ble or **size-a-ble** (saɪz–ə–bəl) adj. Quite
large

size (saɪz) n. **1.** Dimensions; bigness or smallness: *What's the size of the Pacific Ocean?/
What size shirt do you wear?* **2. the size of it**
The facts about it; the way it is

size v. **sized, sizing 1.** To arrange according
to size **2. size up** To make an estimate or
judgment: *Before we could begin, we had to
size up the situation.*

siz-zle (sɪz–əl) v. **zled, zling 1.** To make the
hissing sound of food cooking in hot fat **2.**
To be very hot **3.** To be very angry

skate (skeʸt) n. **1.** A blade-like metal runner
fixed to the sole of a shoe, used for gliding
(skating) over the ice; an ice skate **2.** Roller
skate

skate v. **skated, skating** To move on skates —**skater** n.

ske-dad-dle (skɪ–dǽd–əl) v. **-dled, -dling** *Slang* To go away quickly

skein (skeʸn) n. A coil of thread or yarn loosely tied

skel-e-ton (skɛl–ə–tən) n. **1.** The bony framework of a person or animal not including the flesh **2.** The framework of a building **3.** A small number of employees, just enough to keep a business going, as during a holiday

skep-tic (skɛp–tɪk) n. **1.** One who habitually doubts, questions, or disagrees **2.** One inclined to skepticism in religious matters

skep-ti-cal (skɛp–tɪ–kəl) adj. Having doubts; distrustful —**skeptically** adv. —**skep-ti-cism** (skɛp–tə–sɪz–əm) n.

sketch (skɛtʃ) n. **1.** A hasty or undetailed drawing: *Here's a rough sketch of my house.* **2.** A brief outline, as of a book to be completed **3.** A brief account of sthg.: *The speaker gave us a sketch of life in the 1890's.*

sketch-y (skɛtʃ–iʸ) **-ier, -iest** adj. Not very thorough: *a sketchy knowledge of the subject*

skew (skyuʷ) adj. Slanting; not straight —**skew** v. To turn or twist around

skew-er (skyuʷ–ər) n. A long pin of wood or metal for holding meat together while roasting

skewer v. To fix or fasten with a skewer or sthg. similar

ski (skiʸ) n. **skis 1.** One of a pair of long thin narrow pieces of wood, plastic, or metal, fastened to a boot and used for gliding over the snow **2.** Similar equipment for traveling over the water, pulled by a boat —see WATER SKI

ski v. **skied, skiing** To go on skis

skid (skɪd) v. **-dd- 1.** To slide without rotating **2.** To slip sideways out of control: *The car skidded on the ice.*

skid n. An act of skidding

skiff (skɪf) n. A small, light boat

skill (skɪl) n. **1.** Ability to use one's knowledge effectively in doing sthg. **2.** Developed or acquired ability

skilled (skɪld) adj. Having or requiring skill —opposite UNSKILLED

skil-let (skɪl–ət) n. A frying pan

skill-ful (skɪl–fəl) adj. Having or showing great skill —**skillfully** adv.

skim (skɪm) v. **1.** To remove sthg. from the surface of a liquid **2.** To read quickly, missing some parts, to get the main ideas; scan **3.** To move swiftly and smoothly over a surface: *The skaters skimmed across the ice.*

skimp (skɪmp) v. **1.** To spend too little money **2.** To give insufficient funds, effort, or attention to sthg.

skimp-y (skɪm–piʸ) adj. **-ier, -iest** Not being enough: *a skimpy bathing suit* —**skimpily** adv.

skin (skɪn) n. **1.** The outer layer of a human or animal body: *Babies have smooth skin.* **2.** A thin outer layer, as on a fruit **3. get under someone's skin** *infml.* To annoy sbdy.

skin v. **-nn-** To remove the skin from

skin div-ing (skɪn daɪv–ɪŋ) n. Swimming under water for long periods of time with the aid of flippers, a mask, and equipment that allows one to breathe

skin-flint (skɪn–flɪnt) n. A stingy person

skin-ny (skɪn–iʸ) adj. **-nier, -niest** Very thin; without much flesh —see THIN

skip (skɪp) v. **-pp- 1.** To go along with a hop on each foot in turn: *The little girl skipped along happily.* **2.** To jump over a rope that is being passed repeatedly beneath one's feet: *Skipping rope is good exercise.* **3.** To miss sthg.: *I skipped lunch today.* **4.** To pass over; omit: *He skipped the boring parts of the book.*

skip n. A light, quick, stepping and jumping movement

skip-per (skɪp–ər) n. The master of a ship

skir-mish (skɜr–mɪʃ) n. A minor conflict in war

skirt (skɜrt) n. A garment or part of a garment that hangs below the waist

skirt v. **1.** To go around the outside of: *The road skirted the city.* **2.** To avoid: *Her speech skirted the main issues.*

skit (skɪt) n. **1.** A short comic play **2.** A short dramatic play, often by amateurs

skit-tish (skɪt–ɪʃ) adj. **1.** Restless; nervous **2.** Coy; timid **3.** Fearful **4.** Of horses, easily frightened —**skittishly** adv. —**skittishness** n.

skull (skʌl) n. **1.** The bony case that encloses the brain **2.** The head

skunk (skʌŋk) n. **1.** A small, bushy-tailed, black and white North American mammal, able to spray a bad smelling liquid from glands near its tail **2.** A contemptible person

sky (skaɪ) n. **skies** The region of the clouds or upper air; the space above the earth: *The heavens declare the glory of God; the skies proclaim the work of his hands* (Psalm 19:1).

sky-diving (skaɪ–daɪv–ɪŋ) n. The sport of parachute jumping with delayed opening of the parachute —**skydive** v. **-dived, -diving** —**skydiver** n.

sky-lark (skaɪ–lɑrk) n. A bird that sings while hovering high overhead

sky-light (skaɪ–laɪt) n. A window in the roof that lets in daylight

sky-line (skaɪ–laɪn) n. The horizon; outline of buildings, trees, etc. against the sky

sky-rocket (skaɪ–rɑk–ət) n. A kind of fireworks; a rocket that goes high into the air and explodes

skyrocket v. To rise rapidly in fame, fortune, or cost of living

sky-scrap-er (skaɪ–skreʸ–pər) n. A very tall building

slab (slæb) n. A broad, flat, rather thick piece of stone, metal, food, etc.: *The church was built on a cement slab.*

slack (slæk) adj. **1.** Careless, negligent, slow: *One who is slack in his work is brother to one who destroys* (Proverbs 18:9). **2.** Weak: *slack gun controls* **3.** Not busy: *a slack period for the tourist business right now* **4.** Of a rope, wire, etc., not tight

slack v. **1.** To be slow, lazy, or careless in work **2.** To reduce in amount, speed, effort, or tightness: *This business always slacks off at this time of the year.*

slack n. Sth. that hangs loose: *take up the slack*

slack-en (slæk–ən) v. **1.** To make or become looser **2.** To make or become less active

slacks (slæks) n. Trousers, esp. for casual wear

slag (slæg) n. Residue from metal smelting

slain (sleʸn) v. Past part. of slay

slake (sleʸk) v. **slaked, slaking 1.** To quench

or appease **2.** To mix (lime) with water, forming slaked lime

sla-lom (slɑl–əm) v. To ski in a zigzag course between obstacles —**slalom** n.

slam (slæm) v. **-mm- 1.** To shut a door, lid, etc. loudly and forcefully: *He slammed the door shut angrily.* **2.** To put sth. down with a loud noise: *She slammed the books down on her desk.* —**slam** n.

slan-der (slæn–dər) n. A false report made maliciously with the intention of damaging a person's reputation, usu. an oral statement: *Do not go about spreading slander among your people* (Leviticus 19:16). *Whoever spreads slander is a fool* (Proverbs 10:18).

slander v. To harm sbdy. by making a false statement: *Remind the people... to slander no one* (Titus 3:2). —**slanderous** adj.

slang (slæŋ) n. Words and phrases used informally in everyday speech and writing and not for formal or polite use: *"Kick the bucket" is a slang expression for "die."*

slant (slænt) v. **1.** To be or lie at an angle; to slope: *The walls in this old house slant a little bit.* (=they are not straight up and down) **2.** To report the news or give a talk in such a way as to give favor to a certain point of view or influence a particular group: *His talk was slanted to appeal to the young.*

slant n. A slope: *That roof has a steep slant to it.*

slap (slæp) n. A quick blow with the flat part of the hand: *She gave him a slap on the back.*

slap v. **-pp- 1.** To strike with the flat part of the hand: *She slapped his face.* **2.** To do sth. carelessly: *They quickly slapped the sandwiches together.*

slap-hap-py (slæp–hæp–iʸ) adj. **-pier, -piest** Cheerfully irresponsible; carefree

slap-stick (slæp–stɪk) n. Comedy based on visual jokes, pillow fighting, pie throwing, etc.

slash (slæʃ) v. **1.** To cut with sweeping strokes: *They slashed his tires.* **2.** To reduce prices sharply: *They slashed prices on everything in the store.*

slash n.**1.** A long cut **2.** A big reduction in prices: *This is the biggest slash in prices I've ever seen.*

slat (slæt) n. A thin, narrow strip of wood or

metal; lath

slate (sle^{y}t) n. **1.** Rock that splits into plates **2.** A thin plate of this rock or similar material used for roofing or a writing table **3.** A list of candidates **4. a clean slate** A good record

slate v. **slated, slating 1.** Set down for nomination **2.** To schedule: *a meeting slated for Monday evening*

slaugh-ter (slɔt–ər) n. **1.** The butchering of animals for market **2.** The killing of many people or animals cruelly; a massacre

slaughter v. **1.** To kill animals for food **2.** To brutally kill large numbers of people **3.** *infml.* To defeat another team severely

slave (sle^{y}v) n. **1.** A person owned by another and forced to work for him **2.** Sbdy. completely in the control of another person or thing: *Writing to fellow Christians in Rome, the Apostle Paul wrote: "Thanks be to God that, though you used to be slaves to sin..., you have been set free from sin and have become slaves to righteousness. But now that you have been set free from sin and have become slaves to God, the benefit you reap leads to holiness, and the result is eternal life"* (Romans 6:16-18,22).

slave v. **slaved, slaving** To work hard, like a slave: *I've been slaving away all week at this job.*

slav-er-y (sle^{y}v–ə–ri^y) n. **1.** The system of owning slaves **2.** The condition of being a slave

slav-ish (sle^y–vɪʃ) adj. **1.** Showing complete dependence on others **2.** Copied very closely from sthg. else: *a slavish translation* —**slavishly** adv.

slay (sle^y) v. **slew** (slu^w), **slain** (sle^{y}n), **slaying** To kill —**slayer** n.

slea-zy (sli^y–zi^y) adj. **-zier, -ziest 1.** Thin; flimsy, as cloth **2.** Of a place, dirty and not respectable

sled (slɛd) n. A vehicle with long, narrow strips of wood or metal instead of wheels, for travelling over ice or snow

sledge (slɛdʒ) n. *BrE.* for **sled**

sledge ham-mer (slɛdʒ hæm–ər) n. A large heavy hammer with a long handle, used for breaking large rocks or driving posts into the ground, etc.

sleek (sli^{y}k) adj. **1.** Smooth and glossy **2.** Well-styled: *a sleek sports car*

sleep (sli^{y}p) v. **slept** (slɛpt) **1.** To rest with the eyes closed and in a state of natural unconsciousness: *I will lie down and sleep in peace, for you alone, O Lord, make me dwell in safety* (Psalm 4:8). **2.** *euph.* To be dead: *Multitudes who sleep in the dust of the earth will awake: some to everlasting life; others to shame and everlasting contempt. Those who are wise will shine like the brightness of the heavens, and those who lead many to righteousness, like the stars for ever and ever* (Daniel 12:2,3). —see DEATH, LIFE, RIGHTEOUSNESS

sleep n. A natural periodic condition of rest characterized by unconsciousness: *He [the Lord] grants sleep to those he loves* (Psalm 127:2).

sleep-er (sli^y–pər) n. **1.** A person that is asleep **2.** A railway car with beds

sleep-y (sli^y–pi^y) adj. **-ier, -iest 1.** Tired and ready for sleep **2.** Inactive or slow-moving: *a sleepy little village* —**sleepily** adv. —**sleepiness** n.

sleet (sli^{y}t) n. Partly frozen rain —**sleety** adj. **-ier, -iest**

sleeve (sli^{y}v) n. A part of a garment covering an arm —**sleeveless** adj.

sleigh (sle^y) n. A vehicle on runners that slides along over the snow, pulled by a horse

sleight–of–hand (slaɪt–əv–**hænd**) n. Skill and quickness of hand in performing card tricks, etc.

slen-der (slɛn–dər) n. **1.** Thin; slim: *a slender woman* **2.** Slight: *His chances of winning are very slender.*

slen-der-ize (slɛn–də–raɪz) v. **-ized, -izing** To make oneself thinner by eating less, exercising, etc.

slept (slɛpt) v. Past tense & part. of **sleep**

sleuth (slu^{w}θ) n. *Infml.* A detective

slice (slaɪs) n. **1.** A thin piece cut from sthg.: *a slice of cheese* **2.** A portion or share: *a slice of pie*

slice v. **sliced, slicing 1.** To cut into slices **2.** To cut with a knife: *Ann accidentally cut her finger while slicing tomatoes.* —**slicer** n.

slick (slɪk) adj. **1.** Very smooth; slippery: *Be careful, the streets are very slick after the rain.* **2.**

Clever

slick n. A smooth patch of water covered with a film of oil

slide (slaid) v. slid (slid), sliding 1. To move or cause to move over a surface, while keeping continual contact: *He slid the heavy box across the floor.* 2. To glide 3. To slip or skid: *My car hit a patch of ice and slid off the road.* 4. In baseball, to drop down and skid into a base: *Henry slid into second base.* 5. To move quietly or secretly: *He slid past the window without being seen.*

slide n. 1. A slipping movement over a surface 2. An apparatus for sliding down: *a playground slide* 3. A sudden fall of rocks or mud down a hill: *a rock slide/a mud slide* 4. A small transparent photograph for projection onto a screen 5. A small glass plate on which objects are placed to be examined under a microscope

slight (slait) v. To treat without proper respect, or as if unimportant

slight adj. 1. Very little: *a slight breeze* 2. Thin and delicate; weak-looking: *a slight old lady*

slight-ly (slait–liʸ) adv. 1. A little bit: *slightly worried* 2. Slenderly: *She was slightly built.*

slim (slim) adj. 1. Esp. of people, attractively thin 2. Concerning probability, very slight: *His chance of winning is quite slim.*

slime (slaim) n. Slippery mud or other matter that is soft, sticky and part liquid

slim-y (slaim–iʸ) adj. -ier, -iest 1. Covered with slime 2. Like slime 3. Oily, greasy 4. Disgusting, repulsive: *He's a slimy character.*

sling (sliŋ) v. slung (slʌŋ), slinging To throw forcibly: *He slung a rope over a branch of the tree.*

sling n. 1. A band of cloth looped around the neck to support an injured arm or hand 2. A weapon made of a looped strap with which a stone is hurled 3. An apparatus of ropes or chains for lifting heavy objects

slink (sliŋk) v. slunk, slinking To sneak away; move stealthily

slip (slip) v. -pp- 1. To slide along or cause to slide along smoothly 2. To slide and fall: *Ann slipped and fell on the ice.* 3. To move quietly and unnoticed: *Jane slipped into the back row unnoticed.* 4. To put on a garment: *She slipped into her bathrobe.*

slip n. 1. A small piece of paper 2. A sudden mishap: *a slip on the ice* 3. A small mistake: *a slip of the tongue* 4. An undergarment worn under a dress; a petticoat 5. A pillowcase 6. An escape: *The police caught the criminal, but he gave them the slip.* 7. A shoot or twig from a plant, for planting or grafting 8. A long, narrow piece of paper for a record: *a deposit slip* 9. A sloping platform next to water, used for building and launching ships 10. A ship's berth between two piers

slip-knot (slip–nat) n. A knot made with a loop so that it can slip

slip-page (slip–idʒ) n. An act or amount of slipping

slip-per (slip–ər) n. A light shoe with the top made of soft material, usu. worn indoors

slip-per-y (slip–ə–riʸ) adj. -ier, -iest 1. Difficult to hold on to, stand on, or drive on without slipping: *The roads were too slippery for her to drive on.* 2. Infml. Sly; dishonest: *a very slippery fellow*

slip-shod (slip–ʃad) adj. Untidy; careless

slip-up (slip–əp) n. A mistake; oversight —slip up (slip ʌp) v.

slit (slit) n. A narrow cut or opening

slit v. slit, slit-ting To make a long cut

slith-er (slið–ər) v. To glide along a surface with a snake-like movement —slithery adj.

sliv-er (sliv–ər) n. A small, thin, sharp piece of wood, glass, etc.: *He had a sliver in his finger.*

slob (slab) n. An untidy person

slob-ber (slab–ər) v. 1. To let saliva or food dribble from the mouth: *Babies slobber a lot.* 2. To express emotion in an exaggerated way

slog (slag) v. To work or plod on steadily, esp. against difficult circumstances

slo-gan (sloʷ–gən) n. A word or phrase expressing the spirit or aim of a group or a cause —compare MOTTO

sloop (sluʷp) n. A boat with one mast

slop (slap) v. -pp- To spill: *Some water slopped over the side onto the floor.*

slop n. 1. Liquid spilled or splashed 2. Unappetizing watery food or soup: *I don't want any of that slop.*

slope (sloʷp) n. A surface that is not flat: *a ski*

slope

slope v. **-sloped, -sloping** To be at an angle: *The road slopes very steeply at this point.*

slop-py (slɑp-iʸ) adj. **-pier, -piest 1.** Careless or dirty-looking: *a sloppy person* **2.** Poorly done: *a sloppy job of ironing* —**sloppily** adv. —**sloppiness** n.

slosh (slɑʃ) v. To splash

slot (slɑt) n. **1.** A straight narrow opening as in a vending machine or telephone: *Put your coins in the slot.* **2.** A position in a list, schedule, etc.: *The six o'clock slot on television is filled with a news broadcast.*

sloth (slɔθ) n. A very slow-moving animal that lives in trees in South America

sloth-ful (slɔθ-fəl) adj. Lazy

slouch (slaʊtʃ) v. To sit or move in an unattractive way, with head hanging and shoulders rounded

slough (sluʷ /slaʊ) n. A bog or marsh

slov-en-ly (slʌv-ən-liʸ) adj. **-lier, -liest** Careless; untidy

slow (sloʷ) adj. **1.** Not fast; not hasty or hurrying: *a slow train* —opposite FAST **2.** Dull in mind **3.** Of a clock, showing a time earlier than the correct time: *This clock is ten minutes slow.*

slow v. To become slower: *We slowed down as we approached the corner.*

slow or **slowly** adv. Not fast or hurrying: *I had to drive slow (slowly) because of the fog.*

sludge (slʌdʒ) n. Mud; ooze; sediment

slug (slʌg) n. **1.** A slimy animal similar to a land snail **2.** A bullet **3.** A metal disk **4.** *Infml.* A drink of liquor **5.** A heavy blow

slug v. **-gg-** To strike heavily

slug-gish (slʌg-ɪʃ) adj. Moving slowly: not very active: *a sluggish stream / I feel rather sluggish on a hot, humid day.* —**sluggish** adv. —**sluggishness** n.

sluice (sluʷs) n. **1.** An artificial water passage having a gate to regulate the flow **2.** A stream of water issuing through a floodgate **3.** The water held back by such a gate **4.** A tilted trough for washing gold ore, carrying logs, etc.

sluice v. **sluiced, sluicing 1.** To clean out with a strong flow of water **2.** To transport (as logs) in a sluice **3.** To draw off through a

sluice

slum (slʌm) n. **1.** An area of the city with poor, overcrowded living conditions and dirty unrepaired buildings **2.** *infml.* A very messy place

slum v. **-mm-** To visit a slum, esp. out of curiosity

slum-ber (slʌm-bər) v. **1.** To sleep; doze **2.** To be in a sluggish state

slumber n. Sleep

slump (slʌmp) v. **1.** To sink down suddenly; collapse: *The old man slumped into his bed.* **2.** To decrease in number or strength: *Our income slumped during the summer months.*

slump n. **1.** A time of seriously bad business conditions —compare RECESSION **2.** A period of poor performance, losing several consecutive games, e.g.: *The team has lost ten consecutive games. They're in a terrible slump.*

slung (slʌŋ) v. Past tense of **sling**

slunk (slʌŋk) v. Past tense of **slink**

slur (slər) v. **-rr- 1.** To pronounce indistinctly **2.** To play or sing notes in a smoothly connected way **3.** To pass lightly over sthg. in order to avoid dealing with it **4.** To speak ill of

slur n. **1.** An injury unfairly done to a person's reputation **2.** A damaging or insulting remark or suggestion **3.** An act of slurring of words **4.** A smooth connection between (musical) notes

slurp (slərp) v. To make a noisy, sucking sound in eating or drinking —**slurp** n.

slush (slʌʃ) n. **1.** Partly melted snow **2.** Soft mud **3.** Silly, sentimental talk or writing —**slushy** adj. **-ier, -iest**

slut (slʌt) n. **1.** A slovenly woman **2.** A prostitute

sly (slaɪ) adj. **slier** or **slyer, sliest** or **slyest 1.** Crafty; deceiving: *a sly old fox* **2. on the sly** Secretly —**slyly** adv. —**slyness** n.

smack (smæk) v. **1.** To slap sbdy. **2. smack one's lips** *infml.* To bring one's lips together with a sharp noise, as a sign of an eager appetite or having enjoyed some good food: *He smacked his lips when he saw the good dinner that his wife had prepared.*

smack n. **1.** A slap **2.** A hard hit **3.** A loud kiss

smack adv. *infml.* **1.** Directly: *She wasn't look-*

ing where she was going and ran smack into the door. **2.** **smack-dab** (used to emphasize smack): *She ran smack-dab into the door.*

small (smol) adj. **1.** Little; less than average —opposite LARGE **2.** A limited size, esp. of a business **3.** Doing things on a small scale: *a small farmer (=He has a small farm.)* **4.** Of the letters of the alphabet, not capitals: *Most of the letters on this page are small letters.* —opposite CAPITAL —**small** adv.

small n. A part smaller or narrower than the rest: *the small of the back*

small-pox (smol–poks) n. A contagious virus disease marked by fever and rash that leaves scars (pocks)

smart (smart) adj. **1.** Clever; intelligent **2.** In good style; fashionable: *a smart business suit* **3.** **play it smart** *infml.* To be clever; plan wisely: *He played it smart and took traveler's checks instead of cash on the trip.* —**smartly** adv. —**smartness** n.

smart v. **1.** To feel a stinging pain: *My eyes are smarting because of the smoke.* **2.** To feel offended or insulted: *She was smarting because of bad things said about her.*

smash (smæʃ) v. **1.** To break into pieces **2.** To hit or drive with force against sthg. hard; crash: *He smashed his car into a tree.*

smash n. **1.** A strong or heavy blow **2.** The sound of sthg. breaking: *They heard the smash of the glass when the pitcher fell to the floor.* **3.** **smash hit** *infml.* A very popular new play, song, movie, etc.

smat-ter-ing (smæt–ə–rıŋ) n. A very slight knowledge (of a subject)

smear (smıər) n. **1.** A dirty, greasy mark **2.** Unkind words intended to harm another person's reputation: *Those ugly remarks were meant as a smear against an honest man.* **3.** **smear campaign** A planned attack on the reputation of another person, esp. in politics

smear v. **1.** To cover with sthg. sticky or greasy: *His hands were smeared with grease.* **2.** To make a sticky or greasy mark: *Don't touch that printed page yet; the ink will smear.*

smell (smɛl) v. **smelled** or **smelt**, **smelling 1.** Using the sense of the nose: *When I smell onions, my eyes start to water.* **2.** To notice sthg.

because of its odor: *I can smell gas; there must be a leak.* **3.** To have a special smell: *Roses smell sweet.* **4.** To have a bad smell; to stink: *The meat has started to smell.*

smell n. **1.** The sense of being aware of things through one's nose: *a good sense of smell* **2.** The quality that is noticed by using this sense: *Roses have a sweet smell.* **3.** The act of using this power or sense: *Have a smell of this perfume*

smelt (smɛlt) n. A small, silvery fish found in northern waters

smelt v. To melt ore in order to separate the metal

smelt-er (smɛl–tər) n. **1.** One who smelts **2.** An establishment for smelting

smile (smaıl) v. **smiled, smiling** To have a happy look on one's face, with the corners of the mouth turned up: *Smile and the whole world smiles with you. Cry and you cry alone.* —**smile** n. *There are smiles that make us happy; there are smiles that make us blue (sad).*

smirch (smɜrtʃ) v. **1.** To make dirty or stained **2.** To bring disgrace on sbdy. —**smirch** n.

smirk (smɜrk) v. To smile in a foolish or self-satisfied way

smite (smaıt) v. **smote** (smoᵂt), **smitten** (smıt–ən) **1.** To strike hard **2.** To have a sudden, powerful effect: *His conscience smote him because he had treated his wife badly.*

smith (smıθ) n. A person who works with metal: *a blacksmith/silversmith*

smith-er-eens (smıð–ə–riᵞnz) n. *infml.* Very tiny pieces: *The vase was smashed to smithereens.*

smock (smak) n. A loose garment worn over other clothes for protection

smog (smag/ smɔg) n. A mixture of fog and smoke which is found in many large cities

smoke (smoᵂk) n. **1.** The cloudy-looking vapor given off when sthg. burns, esp. wood or coal: *Smoke from the forest fire could be seen from many miles away.* **2.** *infml.* The act of smoking cigarettes, etc.: *During the intermission, they went out for a smoke.* **3.** **go up in smoke (a)** Completely destroyed by fire **(b)** *fig.* Destroyed suddenly and completely: *All of his plans went up in smoke.* —opposite SMOKELESS —**smoky** adj.

smoke v. **smoked, smoking 1.** To draw smoke in and out from cigarettes, etc.: *He is smoking a pipe.* **2.** To give off smoke: *The fire is still smoking, even though there are no more flames.* **3.** To preserve certain foods in smoke, or give them a smoky flavor: *to smoke a ham*

smoke-screen (smo^wk–skri^yn) n. Anything meant to confuse or mislead

smoke-stack (smo^wk–stæk) n. A chimney or funnel through which smoke and gases are discharged

smol-der *AmE.* **smoul-der** *BrE.* (smo^wl–dər) v. **1.** To burn slowly with smoke but no flame **2.** *fig.* To burn inwardly with concealed anger and jealousy

smooch (smu^wtʃ) v. *slang* To engage in kissing and caressing

smooth (smu^wð) adj. **1.** Having a flat surface, with no bumps or cracks; not rough: *a smooth road* **2.** Steady, or without shaking or bumping; without sudden changes or interruptions: *a smooth flight* **3.** Of a liquid mixture, with no lumps or small pieces: *smooth peanut butter* **4.** *infml.* Too polite in manner; deceitful: *He has smooth manners, but he's a liar and a thief.*

smooth v. To make smooth —**smoothly** adv. —**smoothness** n.

smor-gas-bord (smor–gəs–bord) n. A luncheon or supper buffet with many foods

smote (smo^wt) v. Past tense of **smite**

smoth-er (smʌð–ər) v. **1.** To cause death from lack of air; suffocate: *He murdered her by smothering her with a pillow.* **2.** To completely cover: *ice cream smothered with strawberries*

smudge (smʌdʒ) n. A dirty spot or mark: *He made a smudge on the wall with his dirty hand.* —**smudge** v. —**smudgy** adj.

smug (smʌg) adj. **-gg-** Self-satisfied; too well pleased with oneself —**smugly** adv. —**smugness** n.

smug-gle (smʌg–əl) v. **-gled, -gling 1.** To take sth./sbdy. across an international border illegally: *Criminals try to smuggle drugs from Mexico into the US.* **2.** To take sth./sbdy. in or out of a place illegally: *His friends smuggled a knife into the prison for him.*

smug-gler (smʌg–lər) n. A person who smug-gles —**smuggling** n.

smut (smʌt) n. **1.** A spot of dirt or soot **2.** *infml.* Indecent or obscene language or action: *That book is smut; don't read it!* —**smutty** adj.

snack (snæk) n. A small amount of food, esp. sth. eaten between meals

snag (snæg) n. **1.** An unexpected difficulty or problem: *The new program ran into some snags, and we had to make some changes.* **2.** A thread pulled out of place in cloth, esp. in a stocking: *She got a snag in her stocking.* —**snag** v.

snail (sne^yl) n. **1.** A small crawling animal that has a soft body and a hard shell, and lives in gardens or water **2. snail's pace** Very slow movement: *Construction on that new house is moving ahead at a snail's pace. It should have been done months ago.*

snake (sne^yk) n. A cold-blooded animal with a long body and no legs, which moves by sliding along the ground, and is sometimes poisonous

snake v. To move like a snake

snap (snæp) v. **-pp- 1.** Of an animal, to (try to) close the teeth quickly: *The dog snapped at her but didn't bite her.* **2.** To break off suddenly with a sharp dry sound: *He snapped the small branch off the tree.* **3.** To make a sharp dry sound: *She snapped the lid back on the box.* **4.** To speak quickly and sharply: *"I don't want to see you!" he snapped.* **5.** *Infml.* To photograph quickly: *He snapped a photo while she wasn't looking.* **6. snap one's fingers** To make a snapping sound by moving the middle finger against the thumb: *She snapped her fingers to get his attention.* **7. snap out of it** *infml.* To recover quickly from an illness or an unhappy state of mind

snap n. **1.** An act or sound of snapping **2.** A small two-part metal fastener for clothing, in which one part fits into the other with a snapping sound: *She sewed an extra snap on the neckline of her dress to make sure it would stay closed.* **3. It's a snap!** It's sth. easy to do

snap adj. Done in haste and without much thought: *a snap judgment*

snap-dra-gon (snæp–dræg–ən) n. A garden plant with long spikes of showy flowers, which, when the sides are pressed, opens

and closes like the mouth of a dragon

snap·py (snæp iᵛ) adj. **-pier, -piest 1.** Lively; interesting: *a snappy party* **2.** Quick; fast: *Make it snappy!* (=Hurry up!)

snap·shot (snæp-ʃɑt) n. An informal photograph taken on a simple camera: *He took many snapshots during the birthday party.*

snare (snɛər) n. **1.** A trap made with a noose of string, wire, etc., for catching an animal **2.** A temptation or danger: *Fear of man will prove to be a snare, but whoever trusts in the Lord is kept safe* (Proverbs 29:25).

snare v. **snared, snaring** To catch with a snare

snarl (snɑrl) v. **1.** Of a dog, wolf, etc., to make an angry sound while showing the teeth:*The dog snarled at the stranger.* **2.** *fig.* Of a person, to speak in an angry voice **3.** To cause to become confused; tangled: *The traffic was snarled so badly that nothing was moving.*

snarl n. An angry growl

snatch (snætʃ) v. To take suddenly; grab: *The thief snatched the woman's purse and ran away.* —**snatcher** n.

snatch n. The act of snatching sthg.

sneak (sniᵞk) v. **sneaked** or **snuck, sneaking** To move or take silently and secretly: *She sneaked out of the house without her parents seeing her.*

sneak n. A deceitful person —**sneaky** adj.

sneer (snɪər) v. **1.** To raise the top lip on one side in a kind of smile that expresses scorn **2.** To show contempt for sthg. by such an expression or by scornful words —**sneer** n.

sneeze (sniᵞz) v. **sneezed, sneezing** To force air suddenly and with no control out of the nose and mouth: *He was so cold that he started to sneeze.*

snick·er (snɪk-ər) v. To giggle or laugh disrespectfully, esp. at someone's misfortune

sniff (snɪf) v. To draw air into the nose in quick short breaths, esp. with a soft sound, usu. to smell sthg.: *The dog sniffed the meat before eating it.* —**sniff** n.

snif·fle (snɪf-əl) also **snuf-fle** v. **-fled, -fling** To draw air into the nose in short breaths, usu. noisily, when one is crying or has a cold: *The little girl was sniffling because she had lost her doll.*

snig·ger (snɪg-ər) v. To laugh quietly in an unpleasant way at another's misfortune

snip (snɪp) v. **-pp-** To make a small cut with scissors: *After sewing the button on, she snipped the thread.* —**snip** n.

snipe (snaɪp) v. **sniped, sniping** To shoot at sbdy. from a hidden position, usu. from a long distance —**sniper** n.

snitch (snɪtʃ) v. **1.** To steal, usu. small things **2.** To give information about sbdy. to the police

snitch n. A person who snitches

sniv·el (snɪv-əl) v. **1.** To have a runny nose, due to a cold **2.** To whine or complain tearfully

snob (snɑb) n. A person who seeks association with people of a higher social standing than himself and looks down on people that he considers inferior —**snobbish** adv. —**snobbishness** n.

snob·ber·y (snɑb-ə-riᵞ) n. The behavior of a snob

snood (snuʷd) n. A kind of net worn by women on the back of the head to hold the hair in place

snook·er (snʊk-ər) n. A kind of game like pool, played with 15 red balls and six other balls, having various point values

snoop (snuʷp) v. To look into other people's property or activities secretively; to pry: *He snooped into her handbag while she wasn't looking.* —**snoopy** adj. **-ier, -iest**

snoop or **snooper** n. A person who snoops

snoot (snuʷt) n. *Slang* Nose

snooze (snuʷz) v. **snoozed, snoozing** To take a short nap; doze

snooze n. A short nap

snore (snɔr) v. **snored, snoring** To make a loud noise through the nose and mouth while sleeping —**snore** n.

snor·er (snɔr-ər) n. A person who snores

snor·kel (snɔr-kəl) n. **1.** A tube or tubes which extend above the surface of the water, through which air is brought into a submerged submarine **2.** A similar device that enables an underwater swimmer to breathe

snort (snɔrt) v. **1.** To force air noisily through the nostrils as horses do **2.** To make such a

noise to express disapproval or anger

snort n. **1.** The sound of snorting **2.** *Slang* A drink of liquor

snot (snɑt) n. Mucus of the nose

snot-ty (snɑt–iʸ) adj. **-tier, -tiest** Like or covered with snot

snow (snoʷ) n. **1.** Small white flakes that fall from the clouds instead of rain if the temperature is below freezing: *Snow has been falling for two hours.* **2.** The accumulation of snow on the ground: *The snow is two feet deep.*

snow v. **1.** To fall as snow: *It's been snowing for two hours.* **2.** *AmE. infml.* To persuade sbdy. deceptively: *He tried to snow her with his kindness, but she was not deceived.*

snowed un-der (snoʷd ʌn–dər) adj. Having more work to do than one can possibly deal with in the time given

snow-y (snoʷ–iʸ) adj. **-ier, iest** Abounding in snow

snub (snʌb) v. **-bb-** To treat or speak to sbdy. in a scornful way

snub n. An act of snubbing; an insult

snub adj. Short and slightly turned up at the end: *snub nosed*

snuff (snʌf) v. **1.** To extinguish **2.** To snort or sniff

snuff n. Powdered tobacco

snug (snʌg) adj. **-gg- 1.** Comfortable and protected from the cold; cozy: *It's a cold night, but the children are snug in their beds.* **2.** Of clothes, close-fitting: *This sweater is too snug; I need a larger size.* —**snugly** adv. —**snugness** n.

snug-gle (snʌg–əl) v. **-gled, -gling** To curl up comfortably; nestle: *Susie snuggled up in her mother's lap and fell asleep.*

so (soʷ) adv. **1.** To such a degree; to this extent: *She was so short that she couldn't reach the top shelf.* **2.** Likewise: *Whatever you wish that men would do to you, do so to them* (Matthew 7:12 RSV). **3.** Used instead of sthg. already said: *Peter is a good student, but even so* (=even though that is true) *he failed the test.* **4.** Also: *I liked the book, and so did my wife.* **5.** In this manner: *I was putting the children to bed, and while so engaged, the telephone rang.* **6. and so on/ forth** And other things of the

same type: *He bought the things he needed for school — paper, pen, notebook, and so forth.* **7. So long!** *infml.* To say good-bye for a short absence

so adj. True: *He said he'd be there, but it wasn't so, because he didn't come.*

so conj. **1.** As a consequence; therefore: *It was raining, so I took my umbrella.* **2.** In order that: *Mr. Martin gave his wife some money so (that) she could buy a new dress.*

soak (soʷk) v. **1.** To put sthg. into water or other liquid, esp. for a certain length of time: *She soaked the dirty clothes for fifteen minutes, and then she washed them.* **2.** Of a liquid, to enter into cloth, paper, etc.: *The rain soaked her dress; she didn't have an umbrella.* —**soak** n. —**soaked** (soʷkt) adj.

soap (soʷp) n. **1.** A cleansing substance made from fat or oil combined with an alkali **2. bar/ cake of soap** Soap in a solid form, usu. used for washing oneself **3. soap powder** Soap in powdered form, usu. used for washing dishes or clothes **4. liquid soap** Soap in liquid form, usu. used for washing one's hands or for washing dishes or clothes —**soap** v. —**soapy** adj. **-ier, -iest**

soar (sor) v. **1.** To fly high into the sky: *The plane soared into the air.* **2.** *fig.* To rise high: *The price of coffee soared last year.*

sob (sɑb) v. **-bb-** To cry loudly and in short bursts: *She sobbed when she heard about the accident.* —**sob** n.

so-ber (soʷ–bər) adj. **1.** Reasonable, thoughtful, or serious: *The judge said he would give the problem some sober thought.* **2.** Not drunk —**sober** v. —**soberly** adv.

so-bri-e-ty (sə–braɪ–ət–iʸ / soʷ–) n. The state of being sober

soc-cer (sɑk–ər) n. *also BrE.* **football** A game played on a field between two teams of eleven players using a round ball which is kicked but not touched with the hands

so-cia-ble (soʷ–ʃə–bəl) adj. Friendly: *He is a sociable man who enjoys spending time with his friends.* —opposite UNSOCIABLE —**so-cia-bil-i-ty** (soʷ–ʃə–bɪl–ət–iʸ) n.

so-cial (soʷ–ʃəl) adj. **1.** Concerning human relationships between people and society: *Mr. Brown's work put him in contact with social*

groups, not political or economic groups. **2.** Concerning groups that are separated by their place within society: *Farmers and ambassadors belong to different social classes.* **3.** Concerning activities shared with and enjoyed by friends: *They had a busy social life, going to parties, dances, and having a good time with their friends.* —**socially** adv.

so-cial-ism (soʷ–ʃə–lɪz–əm) n. A theory of social organization based on government ownership, management, or control of means of production and exchange of goods —**socialist** n., adj.

so-cial-ize (soʷ–ʃə–laɪz) v. **-ized, -izing** To participate in social activities as friends: *Mr. Smith and Miss Green are business associates only, and do not socialize with each other.*

social science (soʷ–ʃəl saɪ–əns) also **social studies** n. The study of the relationships between people and society: *Anthropology, psychology, sociology, history, etc., are social sciences.*

so-ci-e-ty (sə–saɪ–ət–iʸ) n. **-ties 1.** All people in general and their relationships with each other: *Illegal drugs are a danger to society.* **2.** A group of people who share customs, laws, etc.: *American society* **3.** A group of people who join together because of common interests, etc.: *music society* **4. high society** The rich and fashionable people in a city or area

so-ci-ol-o-gy (soʷ–siʸ–al–ə–dʒiʸ) n. The science which studies the development and organization of human society —compare ANTHROPOLOGY —**so-ci-o-log-i-cal** (soʷ–siʸ–ə–ladʒ–ə–kəl) adj. —**so-ci-ol-o-gist** (soʷ–siʸ–al–ə–dʒəst) n.

sock (sak) n. A cloth covering for the foot and ankle, and sometimes the lower part of the leg, worn inside a shoe; a short stocking: *He put on his shoes and socks.*

sock-et (sak–ət) n. An opening or hollow place that forms a holder for sthg.: *electric socket*

sod (sad) n. A piece of earth with grass growing on it

so-da (soʷd–ə) n. **1.** One of several substances containing sodium, used in washing clothes, baking, etc. **2. soda water** Water charged with carbon dioxide **3.** *AmE.* also

pop A sweet cold drink made with soda water and flavoring: *orange soda*

so-dal-i-ty (soʷ–dæl–ət–iʸ) n. **-ties 1.** A fellowship whose members do not span the whole age-spectrum of the normal human community **2.** An association or brotherhood **3.** A lay organization for evangelistic, devotional or charitable activity: *The men's Bible class, the ABC Mission Society, and the Rotary Club are examples of sodalities.*

sod-den (sad–ən) adj. Soaked thoroughly

so-di-um (soʷd–iʸ–əm) n. A soft silver-white metal that is a simple substance (an element) from which many substances are formed, including common salt (**sodium chloride**)

sod-om-y (sad–ə–miʸ) n. Unnatural sexual relations with a member of the same sex, esp. between male persons or between a human being and an animal, detestable sins for which the city of Sodom was destroyed in the days of Abraham (Genesis 19:24; Leviticus 20:13,15,16). NOTE: God hates sex perversion and all sin, but because of his great love and mercy, he forgives those who repent of their sins and put their trust in Jesus for eternal life (Mark 1:15; Acts 2:38; Acts 16:31). —see JESUS, FORGIVENESS

so-fa (soʷ–fə) n. A wide comfortable seat with a back and arms, and large enough for two or three people to sit on: *We'll put the sofa in the living room.*

soft (sɔft) adj. **1.** Not hard; changing shape under pressure; *a soft pillow / a soft bed* **2.** Smooth and pleasant to the touch; not rough: *A rabbit has soft fur.* **3.** Restful to the eyes; not harsh: *soft lighting / soft yellow* **4.** Not loud or harsh: *soft music* **5.** *infml.* Easy; weak: *Don't be too soft with your children, or you will spoil them.* **6.** Of a beverage, not alcoholic: *This restaurant has only soft drinks; no wine, beer, or hard liquor.* **7.** Of water, having low mineral content so that soap dissolves easily: *Soft water is better than hard water for washing clothes.* **8. have a soft spot for** To have a special liking for: *She has a soft spot in her heart for her youngest niece.* —**softly** adv. —**softness** n.

soft-ball (sɔft–bɔl) n. **1.** A game like baseball

but on a smaller diamond (playing field) and a softer ball **2.** The ball used

soft–boiled (sɔft–bɔıld) adj. Of an egg, boiled only a short time so that the yoke is still soft

soft drink (sɔft drıŋk) n. A non-alcoholic beverage, esp. one that is carbonated

sof-ten (sɔ–fən) v. To make or grow softer

sof-ten-er (sɔf-ə-nər) n. A compound added to water to make it softer or to make the clothes washed in it softer and fluffier

soft goods (sɔft gʊdz) n. Goods that last a relatively short time, such as textile products

soft-head-ed (sɔft–hed–əd) adj. Stupid or foolish

soft-heart-ed (sɔft–hɑrt–əd) adj. Kind and generous

soft-ped-al (sɔft–ped–əl) v. -aled or -alled, -aling or -alling **1.** To make less emphatic or less conspicuous; to tone down **2.** To soften the tone of a musical instrument by use of a special pedal

soft touch (sɔft tʌtʃ) adj. A person who is easily persuaded, esp. to give or loan money

soft-ware (sɔft–weər) n. The programs, data, routines, etc. for a digital computer

soft-wood (sɔft–wʊd) n. The wood of a conebearing tree: *Pine is a softwood.*

soft-y (sɔf–tiʸ) adj. -ies **1.** A person who is unusually sentimental or trusting **2.** One who lacks physical stamina

sog-gy (sɑg–iʸ / sɔg–) adj. -gier, -giest Wet and soft

soil (sɔıl) n. **1.** The upper layer of the earth in which plants grow; ground **2.** A country or region: *African soil*

soil v. To make dirty: *The clothes were badly soiled.*

so-journ (soʷ–dʒɔrn) v. To stay for a time

sojourn n. A short stay

sol-ace (sɑl–əs) n. Sthg. that makes pain or sorrow easier to bear; comfort

solace v. -aced, -acing To give solace to; to console

so-lar (soʷ–lər) adj. **1.** Concerning the sun **2.** **solar system** The sun together with the earth and other planets that move around it

so-lar-i-um (soʷ–lær–iʸ–əm/ –leər–) n. **1.** A glass-enclosed room or porch **2.** An area

having overhead sun lamps

sold (soʷld) v. Past tense and part. of sell

sol-der (sɑd–ər) n. Melted metal used for joining metal surfaces

solder v. To join with solder

sol-dier (soʷl–dʒər) n. A person in the army, esp. one who is not an officer —**soldiery** n.

sole (soʷl) n. **1.** The undersurface of one's foot **2.** The part of a shoe covering this part of the foot, but not including the heel: *The soles of his shoes needed repair, but not the heels.* **3.** A kind of fish valued as food

sole v. **soled, soling** To put a new sole on a shoe

sole adj. **1.** Only; single: *the sole survivor of the plane crash* **2.** Restricted to one person or group: *the sole rights*

sole-ly (soʷ–liʸ) adv. Only

sol-emn (sɑl–əm) adj. **1.** Serious; grave: *The judge spoke in a solemn voice.* **2.** Very formal, with dignity: *The inauguration of the new president was a solemn event.* —**solemnly** adv.

so-lem-ni-ty (sə–lem–nət–iʸ) n. -ties **1.** The state of being solemn **2.** A solemn ceremony

sol-em-nize (sɑl–əm–naız) also -nise BrE. v. -nized, -nizing To perform a special religious ceremony, esp. a wedding

so-lic-it (sə–lıs–ət) v. **1.** To ask for money, help, etc.; to beg **2.** To approach with a request or plea: *to solicit votes* **3.** Of a prostitute, to make an immoral sexual offer, esp. in a public place

so-lic-i-tor (sə–lıs–ə–tər) n. **1.** AmE. A person who goes from door to door to sell or solicit **2.** A law officer of a city or town **3.** BrE. A lawyer who advises clients on legal matters and prepares legal documents

so-lic-i-tous (sə–lıs–ət–əs) adj. Anxious about a person's welfare and comfort

sol-id (sɑl–əd) adj. **1.** Hard; firm; not yielding to pressure; not liquid: *solid rock* **2.** Not hollow: *solid chocolate candy* **3.** Of good quality (a) Of things, well made and strong: *a solid old chair* (b) Of people, honest and dependable: *a solid citizen* **4.** Of time, continuous: *It rained for one solid week.* **5.** Without breaks; united: *a solid line* **6.** Made of one material: *This ring is solid gold.* —**so-lid-i-ty** (sə–lıd–ə–tiʸ) n. —**sol-id-ly** (sɑl–əd–liʸ) adv.

solid n **1** An object that is hard, firm, and does not flow: *When water freezes it becomes a solid.* **2.** An object with length, width, and height: *A cube is a solid.* **3.** *usu. pl.* Of food, not liquid: *The baby can't eat solids yet.*

sol-i-dar-i-ty (sɑl–ə–**dær**–ət–iʸ / –**deər**–) n. **-ties** Unity of purpose

so-lid-i-fy (sə–**lɪd**–ə–faɪ) v. To make or become solid

so-lil-o-quize (sə–**lɪl**–ə–kwaɪz) v. **-quized, -quizing** To talk to oneself

so-lil-o-quy (sə–**lɪl**–ə–kwiʸ) n. **-quies** A speech to oneself, esp. on stage

sol-i-taire (**sɑl**–ə–tɛər) n. **1.** A card game played by just one person **2.** A single gem, as a diamond, set alone

sol-i-tar-y (**sɑl**–ə–tɛər–iʸ) adj. **1.** Alone; without companions **2.** Single: *a solitary example* **3.** Lonely: *a solitary place*

sol-i-tude (**sɑl**–ə–tuʷd) n. The state of being alone

so-lo (**soʷ**–loʷ) n. **-los** A musical piece for one person to play or sing: *a violin solo*

solo adj. Done by one person: *The student pilot made his first solo flight.* —**solo** adv.

solo v. **soloed, soloing** To perform alone

so-lo-ist (**soʷ**–loʷ–əst) n. A person who sings or plays a solo

sol-stice (**sɑl**–stəs / **soʷl**–/ sɔl–) n. The time of the year when the sun is farthest from the equator, June 22 and December 22

sol-u-ble (**sɑl**–yə–bəl) adj. **1.** Of solid substances, able to be dissolved: *Sugar is soluble in coffee.* **2.** Of problems, troubles, etc., able to be solved —opposite INSOLUBLE

so-lu-tion (sə–**luʷ**–ʃən) n. **1.** The way or process of solving a difficulty or problem **2.** The answer found: *We must find a solution to the problem.* **3.** A liquid with a solid substance or a gas dissolved in it: *a salt solution*

solve (sɑlv / sɔlv) v. **solved, solving** To find a solution to a problem, difficulty, mystery, etc. —**solvable** adj.

sol-vent (**sɑl**–vənt / sɔl–) adj. Able to pay all that is owed —opposite INSOLVENT —**solvency** n.

sol-vent n. A liquid capable of dissolving a solid substance

som-ber *AmE.* **som-bre** *BrE.* (**sɑm**–bər) adj. **1.** Gloomy; sad **2.** Serious; grave

som-bre-ro (səm–**breər**–oʷ /sɑm–) n. A kind of broad-brimmed hat

some (sʌm) determ., adj. **1.** A part; not all: *Have some grapes.* **2.** An indefinite number: *Some people have been camping here.* **3.** An unknown: *He must have had some reason for doing that.* **4.** A considerable number: *That happened some years ago.* **5.** About; approximately: *He waited some twenty minutes.* **6.** Worthy of notice: *That was some storm!*

some pron. **1.** A small amount: *I don't have much money, but I do have some.* **2.** Certain ones, not known or specified: *Some agree with you and some do not.*

some adv. **1.** To some extent: *That's going some!* **2.** Approximately: *We first met some twenty or thirty years ago.*

some-bod-y (**sʌm**–bəd–iʸ) also **some-one** (**sʌm**–wən) pron. An unknown person: *Somebody is knocking on the door.*

some-day (**sʌm**–deʸ) adv. At an indefinite future time: *I hope we meet again someday.*

some-how (**sʌm**–haʊ) also **some-way** (**sʌm**–weʸ) adv. In some unknown way: *Our car broke down, but we'll get there somehow.*

some-one (**sʌm**–wən) pron. Some person

some-place (**sʌm**–pleʸs) n. Somewhere; some unknown or unnamed place

som-er-sault (**sʌm**–ər–sɔlt) n. A leap or roll in which a person turns completely over forward or backward bringing the feet over the head and landing on the feet

some-thing (**sʌm**–θɪŋ) pron. **1.** An unknown thing: *There's sthg. wrong with this water; it doesn't taste good.* **2.** An act or a thing that is better than nothing: *I have a dollar. It isn't much, but at least it's sthg.* **3.** **something like** (a) Similar to: *A pen is something like a pencil.* (b) *infml.* Approximately: *Something like 80,000 people attended the football game.* **4.** **have something to do with** Be related to or connected with: *That movie has sthg. to do with World War II.*

some-time (**sʌm**–taɪm) adv. At an indefinite or unknown time: *We'll go there sometime next year.*

some-times (**sʌm**–taɪmz) adv. From time to time; occasionally: *Sometimes I drive; some-*

times I take the bus.

some-what (sʌm–wət) adv. To some degree; rather: *That book is somewhat long.*

some-where (sʌm–wɛər) also **some-place** (sʌm–pleʸs) adv. In or to an unknown place: *He left his hat somewhere, and now he can't find it.*

som-nam-bu-lism (sɑm–næm–byə–lɪz–əm) n. Walking or otherwise active while one is asleep —**somnambulist** n.

som-no-lent (sɑm–nə–lənt) adj. Sleepy —**somnolence** n.

son (sʌn) n. A person's male child: *Mr. and Mrs. Nelson have two sons.*

so-nar (soʷ–nɑr) n. A device for detecting objects under water by sound

so-na-ta (sə–nɑt–ə) n. A musical composition for one or two instruments, usu. with three or four movements

song (sɔŋ) n. **1.** Music with words for singing: *The soloist sang a beautiful song.* **2.** The act of singing: *At dawn, the birds broke into song.*

Song of Solomon (sɔŋ əv sɑl–ə–mən) One of the prophetic books of the Old Testament, written by King Solomon who also wrote many of the Proverbs and Ecclesiastes. Song of Solomon is regarded by many as a spiritual allegory, representing the holy affections existing between God and his chosen people or Jesus Christ and his church. It is an oriental poem which can only be properly interpreted by a mature spiritual mind. —see BIBLE, OLD TESTAMENT

son-ic (sɑn–ɪk) adj. Of sound waves

son-in-law (sʌn–ɪn–lɔ) n. **sons-in-law** The husband of a person's daughter

son-net (sɑn–ət) n. A poem of 14 lines

Son of God/ Son of Man (sʌn əv gɑd/mæn) Jesus Christ is the Son of God and Son of Man who came into the world to save sinners, died for our sins, and rose again. —see JESUS CHRIST

so-no-rous (sə–noʷr–əs/ –nɔr–/ sɑn–ə–rəs) adj. **1.** Giving out sound when struck **2.** Rich in sound; resonant

soon (suʷn) adv. **1.** In a short time: *I'll be ready soon.* **2. sooner or later** At a future time; at some indefinite time: *We'll get there sooner or later.*

soot (sʊt) n. The black powder left after the burning of coal, etc. —**sooty** adj. **-ier, -iest**

soothe (suʷð) v. **soothed, soothing 1.** To calm sbdy. down: *The baby's mother soothed his crying.* **2.** To reduce pain: *The medicine soothed her pain.* —**soothingly** adv.

sooth-say-er (suʷθ–seʸ–ər) n. One who supposedly foretells future events without divine inspiration. NOTE: This is a sin and is strictly forbidden by the Word of God. It is sinful to pretend to foretell the future, and it is sinful to inquire of a so-called soothsayer or fortune-teller. —see FORTUNE-TELLER, DIVINATION —**soothsaying** n.

sop (sɑp) n. **1.** A piece of solid food, like bread, for dipping in liquid food **2.** Sthg. given to pacify or quiet someone, or as a bribe

sop v. **-pp- 1.** To dip or soak in liquid food **2.** To take up liquid by absorption: *Sop up that milk you spilled on the floor.*

so-phism (sɑf–ɪz–əm) n. A clever but specious argument, lacking real merit

so-phist (sɑf–əst) n. One who reasons cleverly, but in a way that is often faulty

so-phis-tic (sə–fɪs–tɪk) adj. Of or pertaining to sophists or sophistry

so-phis-ti-cate (sə–fɪs–tə–keʸt) v. **-cated, -cating 1.** To make worldly wise **2.** To bring to a more developed or refined form

so-phis-ti-cat-ed (sə–fɪs–tə–keʸt–əd) adj. **1.** Having a good deal of experience in social life and behavior; having refined tastes; cultured: *a sophisticated lady* **2.** Highly developed; elaborate; produced with a high degree of skill: *sophisticated machinery* —**sophis-ti-ca-tion** (sə–fɪs–tə–keʸ–ʃən) n.

soph-ist-ry (sɑf–ə–striʸ) n. **-ries** The use or practice of sophisms

soph-o-more (sɑf–ə–mɔr/ –sɑf–mɔr) n. In the US, a student in the second year of high school or university

sop-ping (sɑp–ŋ) adj. Very wet; drenched —**sopping** adv.

sop-py (sɑp–iʸ) adj. **-pier, -piest 1.** Very wet; rainy: *soppy weather* **2.** Sentimental; maudlin; too full of tender feelings

so-pra-no (sə–præn–oʷ/–prɑn–oʷ) n. **-nos 1.** A voice of the highest range **2.** A singer with

such a voice **3.** The music intended for such a voice

sor-cer-er (sɔrs–ə–rər) n. One who practices sorcery

sor-cer-y (sɔrs–ə–riʸ) n. *pl.* **-ies** An attempt to use evil, supernatural powers to influence people and events, using magic charms, drugs, and spells to try to produce evil results. NOTE: This practice is detestable in God's sight (Deuteronomy 18:10-12). In Biblical times there was even the death penalty for one who practiced sorcery (Exodus 22:18). Though God hates sin, because of his great love and mercy he forgives those who repent [turn from their sins] and put their trust in Jesus for eternal life (Acts 2:38; 16:31; Romans 6:23). —see FORGIVENESS, JESUS

sor-did (sɔrd–əd) adj. **1.** Not very pleasant or admirable; shameful; vile; base: *a sordid person* **2.** Very dirty; filthy: *a sordid neighborhood*

sore (sɔr) adj. **1.** Hurting; aching: *a sore throat* **2.** Causing anger or offense: *Don't talk politics with George; that's a sore point with him.* **3.** *infml. AmE.* Mad; angry: *He got sore when he was wrongfully accused of cheating.*

sore n. A sore spot on the body

sore-ly (sɔr–liʸ) adv. Desperately: *Those starving children are sorely in need of food.*

sore-ness (sɔr–nəs) n. A painful feeling

so-ror-i-ty (sə–rɔr–ət–iʸ) n. **-ties** A women's organization with chapters at colleges and universities

sor-row (sɑr–oʷ) n. **1.** Suffering or distress due to loss, illness, or injury of a loved one, or other hardship or adversity **2.** The anguish suffered by Christians over the fact that members of their own family and of their own race, as well as others, do not know Jesus Christ, their Savior: *In his letter to fellow Christians in Rome, the Apostle Paul wrote: "I have great sorrow and anguish in my heart. For I could wish that I myself were cursed and cut off from Christ for the sake of my brothers, those of my own race, the people of Israel"* (Romans 9:2,3). **3.** The expression of sadness **4. godly sorrow** Sorrow over our own sins: *Godly sorrow brings repentance that leads to salvation and leaves no regret, but worldly sor-row brings death* (2 Corinthians 7:10). —see REPENTANCE —**sorrow** v. —**sorrowful** adj. —**sorrowfully** adv.

sor-ry (sɑr–iʸ) adj. **-rier, -riest 1.** Sad; feeling sorrow: *They were sorry to hear of her illness.* **2.** Used to express an apology: *I'm sorry! I didn't mean to hurt you.* **3.** Used to refuse sthg. politely or to disagree: *I'm sorry, but no smoking is allowed in this room.* **4.** *fml.* Poor; bad; pitiful: *The refugees who have just arrived are in a sorry state.* **5. be/ feel sorry for** To feel sympathy towards: *I'm sorry to hear of your mother's illness.* **6.** A sincere feeling of regret for having grieved God with sinful thoughts and conduct: *Christians are sorry for their sins, because they know that their sins are offensive to God who loves us so much that he gave his one and only Son (to suffer and die for their sins), that whoever believes in him should not perish but have everlasting life* (John 3:16).

sort (sɔrt) n. **1.** A kind or type of person or thing: *What sort of food do you like?* —see KIND **2. a good/ bad sort** *infml.* A good/bad person **3. sort of** *infml.* Rather: *I'm sort of tired. I'd better go to bed early tonight.* **4. of sorts** Of a poor or inferior kind: *They served us a meal of sorts, but we're still hungry.* **5. out of sorts** Not feeling well; feeling annoyed

sort v. To put things in order, alphabetically, or by kind, type, etc.: *His secretary sorted the letters by date.*

SOS (ɛs–oʷ–ɛs) n. An internationally recognized call for help or rescue

so-so (soʷ–soʷ) adj. Mediocre; neither very good nor very bad

souf-flé (suʷ–fleʸ) n. A light, baked dish made fluffy with beaten egg whites combined with egg yolks

sought (sɔt) v. Past tense and part. of **seek**

soul (soʷl) n. The part of a person that is the real person, not one's body which is just a house for one's soul: *God will redeem my soul from the grave, he will surely take me to himself* (Psalm 49:15). *Jesus told the thief on the cross [who repented of his sins and trusted in Jesus for eternal life], "Today you will be with me in paradise [heaven]"* (Luke 23:43). *Jesus also asked, "What good will it be for a man if he*

gains the whole world, yet forfeits [loses] his soul?" (Matthew 16:26). NOTE: The Bible clearly teaches, and Christians firmly believe, that when a Christian dies, his soul goes immediately to heaven to be with Jesus and the holy angels and all other believers forever and ever, and that an unbeliever's soul goes to hell (a place of eternal torment) to remain there forever and ever. —compare JUDGMENT DAY, RESURRECTION

sound (saʊnd) n. **1.** Sthg. that can be heard through the ears: the sound of music **2.** An idea; an impression; a thought: From the sound of his voice, the situation is serious. **3.** A narrow body of water that usu. connects two larger areas of water, and wider than a strait: Seattle is on Puget Sound.

sound v. **1.** To seem; to make a particular impression: It sounds like a good idea. **2.** To make a sound: The driver sounded his horn. **3.** To signal: Sound the alarm! **4.** To pronounce: In the word, "numb," the "b" is not sounded.

sound adj. **1.** Healthy; in good condition: For a man of his age, he's in sound health and sound mind. **2.** Solid; firm; strong: Their business is running on a sound financial basis. —opposite UNSOUND **3.** Reliable; dependable: sound advice **4.** Of sleep, deep and undisturbed: The child was sound asleep. —soundly adv.

sound-ing (saʊn–dɪŋ) n. An act of measuring water depth

sound-less (saʊnd–ləs) adj. Making no noise; silent

sound-proof (saʊnd–pruʷf) adj. Resistant to the penetration of sound: Is your room soundproof?

soup (suʷp) n. A liquid food containing small cooked pieces of meat, fish, or vegetables, and usu. served hot: She made chicken soup for lunch.

souped up (suʷpt ʌp) adj. Having the power increased: a souped up motor

soup-spoon (suʷp–spuʷn) n. A spoon for eating soup, larger than a teaspoon

soup-y (suʷp–iʸ) adj. -ier, -iest **1.** Having the consistency of soup **2.** Densely foggy

sour (saʊ–ər/ saʊr) adj. **1.** Not sweet to taste: Green apples taste sour. **2.** Unpleasant to taste

because a food has started to spoil: sour milk **3.** fig. Of a person, unpleasant because of unhappy experiences: Hardships have made him sour on life. —sourly adv.

sour v. To make or become sour: This hot weather has soured the milk.

source (sɔrs) n. **1.** A place or point of origin: What was the source of information for that news report? **2.** A spring or other place where a stream begins: Lake Itasca is the source of the Mississippi River.

souse (saʊs) v. **soused, sousing 1.** To plunge into liquid **2.** To drench **3.** To pickle

souse n. **1.** A drunkard **2.** Brine **3.** A soaking in a liquid

south (saʊθ) n. **1.** One of the four main points of the compass, on the left of a person facing the setting sun —opposite NORTH **2.** The southern part of a country **3.** The states in the southeastern part of the US that were part of the Confederacy during the Civil War

south adj. **1.** Situated toward or at the south **2.** Coming from the south —south adv.

south-east (saʊ–θiʸst) n. The point or direction halfway between south and east

south-east adj. **1.** Situated toward or at the southeast **2.** Coming from the southeast

south-east-er-ly (saʊ–θiʸ–stər–liʸ) adj. **1.** Of the wind, from the southeast **2.** Toward the southeast —southeasterly adv.

south-east-ern (saʊ–θiʸ–stərn) adj. Of, from, or situated in the southeast —southeastern adv.

south-east-ward (saʊ–θiʸs–twərd) adj. Toward the southeast —southeastward adv.

south-er-ly (sʌð–ər–liʸ) adj. **1.** In or toward the south **2.** Of the wind, coming from the south: a southerly breeze —southerly adv.

south-ern (sʌð–ərn) adj. Of or in the south

south-ern-er (sʌð–ər–nər) n. Someone who lives in the south or is from the south

south-ern-most (sʌð–ərn–moʷst) adj. The place that is the farthest south

South Pole (saʊθ poʷl) n. The southernmost point on earth

south-ward (saʊθ–wərd) adj. Toward the south: a southward journey

south-west (saʊθ–wɛst) n. The point or direc-

tion halfway between south and west

south-west (savθ–wɛst) adj. **1.** Situated in or toward the southwest **2.** Coming from the southwest

south-west-er-ly (savθ–wɛst–ər–liʸ) adj. **1.** Of the wind, from the southwest **2.** Toward the southwest —**southwesterly** adv.

south-west-ern (savθ–wɛst–ərn) adj. Of, from, or situated in the southwest —**southwestern** adv.

south-west-ward (savθ–wɛst–wərd) adj. Toward the southwest —**southwestward** adv.

sou-ve-nir (suʷ–və–nıər) n. Sthg. kept as a reminder of an event, trip, place, etc.: *We bought many post cards as souvenirs of the places we visited in Europe.*

sov-er-eign (sav–ə–rən/sav–rən) n. A king, queen, or emperor having unlimited power to rule a nation: *Godless men... deny Jesus Christ our only Sov-ereign and Lord* (Jude 4).

sovereign adj. **1.** Governing a country; ruling: *sovereign power* NOTE: A sovereign king or nation is not controlled by any other person or nation. Only God is sovereign in the full sense. "The Most High is sovereign over the kingdoms of men and gives them to anyone he wishes" (Daniel 4:32). All other powers are limited in some way. God is sovereign in his acts of creation and redemption. His sovereignty was shown in the life, death, and resurrection of Jesus. The power of God can be limited only if God places limits on himself. He did this when he created man and gave him freedom. God does not force people to serve him. *"They [false prophets and false teachers] will secretly introduce destructive heresies, even denying the sovereign Lord who bought them [with his own blood on Calvary's cross] — bringing swift destruction on themselves"* (2 Peter 2:1). **2.** Of a country, independent: *a sovereign state* —**sovereignty** n.

sow (sav) n. An adult female **pig** —compare HOG

sow (soʷ) v. **sowed, sown or sowed, sowing 1.** To plant seeds in the ground: *Farmers sow seeds in the spring and reap the crops in the fall.* **2.** To spread abroad; disseminate: *fig. Peace-*makers who sow in peace raise a harvest of righteousness (James 3:18)./A man reaps what he sows. The one who sows to please his sinful nature, from that nature will reap destruction; the one who sows to please the Spirit, from that Spirit will reap eternal life* (Galatians 6:7). —compare REAP

soy (sɔɪ) n. A dark, salty Chinese sauce made from soybeans fermented in brine

soy-bean (sɔɪ–biʸn) n. A kind of bean, rich in protein, from which an edible oil and flour are obtained

spa (spɑ) n. A mineral spring; a resort where people go to bathe in a natural spring

space (speʸs) n. **1.** An area that can be measured in length, width, height or depth: *Is there enough space on that shelf for all these books?* —see also ROOM **2.** The unlimited expanse which surrounds all people and things: *Above the surface of the ocean, there is nothing but open space.* **3.** What is beyond the earth's air, in which the other planets, stars, etc., move: *outer space*

space v. **spaced, spacing** To separate things or people by spaces: *They spaced the soldiers ten feet apart.*

space-craft (speʸs–kræft) n. A vehicle that can travel through outer space

spa-cious (speʸ–ʃəs) adj. Big in extent; roomy: *That wealthy family lives in a spacious house on a hill.*

spade (speʸd) n. **1.** A long-handled tool with a blade at one end for digging into the ground **2. call a spade a spade** *infml.* To speak plainly and clearly: *Let's call a spade a spade; you cheated on your exam.* —**spade** v.

spa-ghet-ti (spə–gɛt–iʸ) n. An Italian food made of a dough of wheat flour and formed into long sticks, which soften when boiled: *We ordered spaghetti and meatballs for dinner.*

span (spæn) n. **1.** A period of time **2.** The distance between the supports of a bridge or arch: *That bridge crosses the bay in three spans.*

span v. **-nn-** To measure or extend across

span-gle (spæŋ–gəl) n. A small sparkling piece of metal used as an ornament

spangle v. **-gled, -gling** To adorn with spangles —**spangled** adj.

spank (spæŋk) v. To hit with the palm of the

hand, esp. on the buttocks, in punishment: *The mother spanked her little girl for disobeying her.* —spanking n.

span-ner (spæn–ər) BrE. for wrench

spar (spɑr) n. 1. A pole, as a mast or boom, supporting the sail on a ship 2. A structure supporting the ribs of an airplane wing

spar v. -rr- To box with jabbing or feinting movements, landing few heavy blows, as in an exhibition or practice

spare (speər) v. spared, sparing 1. To part with; to set aside sthg./ sbdy. for someone else: *Brother, can you spare a dime?/ Can you spare a few minutes to read this report./ He [God] who did not spare his own Son, but gave him up for us all — how will he not also, along with him, graciously give us all things?* (Romans 8:32). —see JESUS 2. To keep from harming or killing: *Although his car was demolished, his life was spared.* 3. To save sbdy. from annoyance: *I'll spare you the details, and just tell you that our team won the game.*

spare adj. 1. Kept as an extra thing in case of need: *spare parts for the car* 2. spare time Time during the day when a person is not working; leisure time: *Here's a good book you can read in your spare time.*

spare n. An extra object kept in case of need: *One tire on my car was flat, so I took it off and put on the spare.*

spar-ing (speər–ɪŋ) adj. Not generous or wasteful; frugal; not giving or spending freely: *The righteous give without sparing* (Proverbs 21:26).

spark (spɑrk) n. 1. A burning bit of wood, paper, etc., thrown off by a fire: *Sparks from the burning trees near our house set fire to our roof.* 2. A brief flash of fire produced by (a) striking hard metal or stones together, or (b) electric current passing through the air 3. fig. A small amount of a particular quality: *a spark of interest*

spark v. 1. To set off sparks 2. To set off a burst of activity

spar-kle (spɑr–kəl) v. -kled, -kling 1. To give out repeated brief flashes of light: *The splashing water sparkled in the sunlight.* 2. fig. To become lively: *The child's eyes sparkled with excitement when he saw the Christmas*

tree.

spark-ling (spɑrk–lɪŋ) adj. Of water, soft drinks, etc., giving off bubbles of gas: *sparkling water*

spar-row (spær–oʷ/speər–) n. A small brownish bird, common in many parts of the world

sparse (spɑrs) adj. Thinly scattered; not crowded: *Vegetation is sparse in the desert.* —sparsely adv. —sparseness or —spar-si-ty (spɑr –sə–tiʸ) n.

spasm (spæz–əm) n. 1. A sudden involuntary contraction of muscles; a jerk 2. A sudden violent activity, feeling, etc.: *a spasm of coughing*

spas-mod-ic (spæz–mɑd–ɪk) adj. 1. Consisting of sudden, short periods of activity 2. Happening now and then, but not regularly

spas-tic (spæs–tɪk) n. A person suffering from brain damage that causes extreme muscle spasms and/or muscular paralysis —spastic adj.

spat (spæt) n. A short, relatively unimportant quarrel

spat v. To quarrel briefly

spa-tial (speʸ–ʃəl) adj. Having to do with space

spat-ter (spæt–ər) v. 1. To scatter or fall in small drops 2. To splash with drops: *Her dress was spattered with muddy water.*

spatter n. A splash or splashes

spat-u-la (spætʃ–ə–lə) n. A kind of utensil with a broad, blunt, flexible blade, used for blending foods, mixing drugs, spreading plaster, etc.

spawn (spɔn/ spɑn) n. 1. The eggs of fish or frogs, etc.: *frog-spawn* 2. derog. Offspring

spawn v. 1. To deposit spawn; to produce from spawn: *Salmon swim upriver to spawn.* 2. To generate, esp. in large numbers: *One good idea can spawn many activities.*

spay (speʸ) v. To remove the ovaries of an animal

speak (spiʸk) v. spoke (spoʷk), spoken (spoʷ–kən), speaking 1. To use one's voice to say things; talk; tell: *She spoke to him about the problem.* 2. To be able to communicate in another language: *He speaks three languages: English, Dutch, and German.* 3. To give a

speech: *The senator spoke to the convention about his plans.* **4.** To show feelings, thoughts, ideas, etc., without words: *Actions speak louder than words.* **5. speak out** To say boldly what one thinks **6. speak up** To talk louder

speak-er (spi^yk–ər) n. **1.** One who speaks **2.** The presiding officer of a legislative body **3.** A loudspeaker

spear (spɪər) n. A weapon with a sharp point at one end of a long pole which is held in the hand and thrown

spear v. To pierce sthg. or take hold of sthg. with a spear or sthg. similar: *He speared a piece of fruit with his fork.*

spear-head (spɪər–hɛd) n. **1.** The metal point on a spear **2.** A person or group that leads an attack, usu. on a problem of public interest —**spearhead** v. *Major Smith was chosen to spearhead the attack.*

spear-mint (spɪər–mɪnt) n. A common mint plant whose leaves are used for flavoring

spe-cial (spɛʃ–əl) adj. **1.** Unusual; different from the ordinary: *There's a special tool just for that repair job.* **2.** Not regular: *They're running a special train today, in addition to the scheduled trains.* —**specially** adv.

special n. Sthg. that is not regularly scheduled, esp. a television program: *They're showing a Christmas special on TV on Christmas Day.*

spe-cial-ist (spɛʃ–əl–əst) n. A person who specializes —**specialization** n.

spe-cial-ize (spɛʃ–ə–laɪz) v. **-ized, -izing** To study or work in one particular field of interest: *Dr. Brown decided to specialize in heart disease.*

spe-cial-ty (spɛʃ–əl–tiʸ) n. **-ties 1.** A particular field of work or study: *That artist's specialty is painting rural scenes.* **2.** A unique product or service of high quality: *Fine steaks are the specialty of this restaurant.*

spe-cies (spiʸ–ʃiʸz/spiʸ–siʸz) n. **-cies** A group of related plants or animals that can breed together

spe-cif-ic (spɪ–sɪf–ɪk) adj. **1.** Definite; exact: *Please be specific when you order: give us the size, style, color, and number.* **2.** Related to one particular purpose, use, etc.: *Give this pack-*

age to the specific person whose name is on the address, not to anyone else. —**specifically** adv.

spec-i-fi-ca-tion (spɛs–ə–fə–keʸ–ʃən) n. **1.** Usu. pl. Detailed description, including measurements and other necessary information, usu. for making sthg.: *Please make this desk according to my specifications; otherwise, I cannot use it.* **2.** Sthg. that is specified

spec-i-fy (spɛs–ə–faɪ) v. **-fied, -fying** To mention or name specifically

spec-i-men (spɛs–ə–mən) n. **1.** One of sthg. used as an example of a group or class: *They collected one specimen of each kind of plant they found in the valley.* **2.** An amount of sthg. to be tested, etc.: *The nurse took a specimen of his blood before he saw the doctor.*

spe-cious (spiʸ–ʃəs) adj. Apparently good or right, but without merit

speck (spɛk) n. A small spot or a tiny bit of dirt: *There's a speck of dirt on this shirt.*

speck-le (spɛk–əl) v. **-led, -ling** To mark with specks —**speckle** n. A speck

spec-ta-cle (spɛk–tɪ–kəl) n. **1.** An impressive public show: *The 100th anniversary celebration was a magnificent spectacle.* **2.** A funny or embarrassing sight: *He made an awful spectacle of himself by wearing old shoes and a dirty suit to the formal reception.* **3. spectacles** Eyeglasses

spec-tac-u-lar (spɛk–tæk–yə–lər) adj. Impressive and different, usu. beautiful: *a spectacular sunset/a spectacular performance* —**spectacularly** adv.

spectacular n. A grand public entertainment, esp. a television show

spec-ta-tor (spɛk–teʸt–ər) n. A person who sees or watches a public event or sport, but does not take part: *Hundreds of spectators stood on both sides of the street to watch the parade.*

spec-ter (spɛk–tər) n. **1.** A ghost **2.** A haunting fear of future trouble: *The specter of defeat loomed over the team.*

spec-trum (spɛk–trəm) n. **-tra** or **-trums 1.** An entire range of related qualities or ideas, etc. **2.** A band of colors as seen in a rainbow **3.** A similar band of waves of sound

spec-u-late (spɛk–yə–leʸt) v. **-lated, -lating 1.** To guess; think about a subject without

enough facts to make a decision or conclusion: *We can only speculate about what we will be doing 30 years from now.* **2.** To buy and sell shares of stock, land, etc., taking a risk on whether or not they will be sold at a profit: *Mr. Richman made a lot of money speculating in oil shares.*

spec-u-la-tor (spɛk–yə–leᵞt–ər) n. A person who speculates —**spec-u-la-tion** (spɛk–yə–leᵞ–ʃən) n.

speech (spiᵞtʃ) n. **1.** The act of speaking: *Animals do not have the power of speech.* **2.** A special manner of speaking, esp. a dialect or accent: *I can tell he is from Canada by his speech.* **3.** A formal talk given to a group of people: *The governor made a speech at the convention last night.*

speed (spiᵞd) n. Rate of movement or action: *at the speed of light / He drove at a speed of 30 miles per hour in the city.*

speed v. **sped** or **speeded, speeding 1.** To go fast; to rush: *The ambulance sped the injured man to the hospital.* **2.** To go faster than the speed limit: *He was going 50 miles per hour in a 30 mile per hour zone, and was given a ticket for speeding.* —**speeder** n. —**speedily** adv. —**speedy** adj.

speed-om-e-ter (spiᵞ–dɑm–ət–ər) n. An instrument for measuring the speed of a vehicle: *He looked at his speedometer and was surprised to see he was driving 70 miles per hour.*

speed-up (spiᵞd–əp) v. An increase in speed

speed-y (spiᵞd–iᵞ) adj. **-ier, -iest** Fast; rapid

spell (spɛl) v. **spelled** or **spelt, spelling 1.** To pronounce or write the letters in a word: *How do you spell your name? It's spelled M-A-R-T-I-N.* **2.** *fml.* To mean; imply: *The freezing temperatures spelled disaster for the orange crop.* **3. spell out** To describe in detail; specify: *Please spell out your plans for me, so that I can carry them out exactly.* —**speller** n.

spell n. A short period of time: *We had a hot spell for a week last spring.*

spell n. **1.** A word or phrase supposed to have magical power **2.** Any irresistible influence

spell-bind (spɛl–baɪmd) v. **-bound, -binding** To make spellbound

spell-bind-er (spɛl–baɪm–dər) n. A speaker

who holds his or her audience spellbound

spell-bound (spɛl–baʊnd) adj. Enchanted or fascinated by, or as if by a spell

spell-er (spɛl–ər) n. **1.** One who spells words **2.** A textbook to teach spelling

spell-ing (spɛl–ɪŋ) n. **1.** The manner in which words are spelled **2.** A group of letters representing a word **3.** The act of making words from letters in an accepted way: *Children study spelling in school.*

spend (spɛnd) v. **spent, spending 1.** To give out money to buy sthg.; to pay: *How much do you spend each week to buy food at the supermarket?* **2.** To pass time: *How much time do you spend in prayer each day? Most of us do not spend enough time in prayer, esp. since Jesus promised his followers, "You may ask me for anything in my name, and I will do it" (John 14:14).* **3.** *fml.* To use up; consume; exhaust: *His strength was spent after he tried to climb the mountain.* —**spender** n.

spend-thrift (spɛnd–θrɪft) n. A person who spends his or her money wastefully

spent (spɛnt) Past tense and past part. of **spend**

spent adj. **1.** Drained of energy; exhausted **2.** Already used: *spent bullets*

sperm (spɜrm) n. **1.** The male fertilizing fluid; semen **2.** A male reproductive cell

spew (spyuʷ) v. **1.** To vomit; throw up **2.** To cast out forcefully in a stream: *The pipe broke and water came spewing out.*

sphere (sfɪər) n. **1.** A solid round ball: *The planet earth is a sphere.* **2.** A field of existence, action, etc.: *Dr. Harper's main sphere of activity is in heart disease.* —**spher-i-cal** (sfɪər–ə–kəl / sfɛər–) adj.

spice (spaɪs) n. **1.** A product, such as pepper, which comes from certain plants used to add special flavor to food **2.** *fig.* Sthg./sbdy. which adds special interest or excitement: *She was the spice of the party last night.* —**spice** v. —**spicy** adj.

spick–and–span (spɪk–ən–spæn) adj. Clean and tidy

spi-der (spaɪd–ər) n. A small eight-legged animal (not an insect) which spins a web in which to catch insects

spi-der mon-key (spaɪd–ər mʌŋ–kiᵞ) n. A South

American monkey with long, slender limbs and a long tail with which it can grasp and hold on

spike (spaɪk) n. **1.** A sharp projecting point; a pointed piece of metal **2. spikes** Shoes fitted with spikes, worn by runners, baseball players, etc.,

spike v. **spiked, spiking 1.** To pierce or fasten with a spike **2.** To add alcohol to a drink **3.** In volleyball, to hit the ball almost straight down

spill (spɪl) v. **spilled** or **spilt, spilling 1.** Of a liquid, to cause to run out, and of a solid substance, to spread out, accidentally out of its container: *His hand hit the glass accidentally, and the water was spilled on the table.* **2.** *fig.* To spread beyond bounds: *The spectators spilled out of the stadium after the baseball game.* **3. spill the beans** *infml.* To reveal a secret

spill n. **1.** Sthg. spilled: *She wiped up the spill with a rag.* **2.** An accidental fall: *The child tripped over a rock and took a nasty spill.*

spil-lage (spɪl-ɪdʒ) n. **1.** An act of spilling **2.** That which is spilled

spin (spɪn) v. **spun** (spʌn), **spinning 1.** To twist raw cotton into thread, or wool into yarn: *In the past, women used to spin thread at home; now it is done in factories.* **2.** To turn around quickly; whirl: *He spun around when he heard the noise behind him.* **3.** Of a spider, to produce a web

spin n. **1.** The act of spinning: *The accident sent the car into a spin.* **2.** A short ride for pleasure: *It was such a nice afternoon that they went for a spin in the country.*

spin-ach (spɪn-ɪtʃ) n. A type of plant whose leaves are eaten as a vegetable

spi-nal (spaɪn-əl) adj. Of or relating to the spine

spin-dle (spɪn-dəl) n. **1.** A slender rod on which thread is twisted or wound in spinning **2.** A pin that revolves or on which sthg. else revolves

spin-dly (spɪn-dliʸ) adj. **-dlier, -dliest** Being long or tall and thin, and usu. frail

spine (spaɪn) n. **1.** Backbone; the series of connected bones going down the center of the back of humans and of many animals **2.** The

enclosed end of a book, where its title can be seen —**spinal** adj. *spinal column*

spine-less (spaɪn-ləs) adj. **1.** Having no backbone **2.** Lacking determination or strength of character **3.** Cowardly

spin-ster (spɪn-stər) n. A woman beyond the usu. age of marrying and still unmarried

spin-y (spaɪ-niʸ) adj. **1.** Having spines **2.** Abounding with obstacles

spi-ral (spaɪ-rəl) n. A winding and gradually widening coil: *The spring in a watch is a spiral.*

spiral adj. Coiled; coiling: *a spiral staircase*

spiral v. **spiraled** or **spiralled, spiraling** or **spiralling** To move in a spiral: *The flaming airplane spiraled to the earth.*

spire (spaɪ-ər) n. A tall narrow spear-like structure on top of a building, esp. as on a church; steeple

spir-it (spɪr-ət) n. **1.** A term used in the Bible for purely spiritual beings, or for the spiritual, immortal part of man: *Create in me a pure heart, O God, and renew a steadfast spirit within me* (Psalm 51:10). *The spirit [of man] returns to God who gave it* (Ecclesiastes 12:7). *Jesus' last words on the cross, before he died, were, "Father, into your hands I commit my spirit"* (Luke 23:46). *God is a spirit and they that worship him must worship him in spirit and in truth* (John 4:24). *Repent and be baptized, every one of you, in the name of Jesus Christ for the forgiveness of your sins, and you will receive the gift of the Holy Spirit* (Acts 2:38). —see HOLY SPIRIT **2.** A ghost: *They say that old house is haunted and has evil spirits in it.* **3.** The unique quality or mood of sthg.: *the spirit of the times* **4.** A non-physical force that unites people: *The coach inspires the players with a wonderful team spirit.* **5.** Attitude; intention: *She sat down as a spectator and did not enter into the spirit of the party.* **6.** The basic meaning of a law, rule, etc., as opposed to the literal meaning: *It is helpful to live by the spirit of the law, not the letter of the law.*

spir-it-ed (spɪr-ət-əd) adj. Animated; lively

spir-it-ism (spɪr-ət-ɪz-əm) n. Often referred to erroneously as spiritualism, the belief that living persons can receive messages

from dead people, usually sent through a person with special spiritual powers, called a medium: *The Bible, the holy word of God, says, "Let no one be found among you who... practices divination or sorcery, interprets omens, engages in witchcraft, or casts spells, or who is a medium or spiritist or who consults the dead. Anyone who does these things is detestable to the Lord"* (Deuteronomy 18:9-12). *Do not turn to mediums or seek out spirits, for you will be defiled by them* (Leviticus 19:31). *I will set my face against the person who turns to mediums and spiritists to prostitute himself by following them* (Leviticus 20:6). NOTE: It is the clear testimony of the Holy Scriptures, the Bible, that spiritism is the masquerading of demonic forces, who pretend to be departed spirits with the intent of deceiving, through the power of Satan, those who are foolish enough to believe the testimony of demons in preference to the authority of the word of God himself. Spiritism is altogether contrary to the word of God and is detestable in His sight (Leviticus 20:6). But because of his great love and mercy, he forgives the sins of all those who truly repent of their sins and put their trust in Jesus for eternal life (Acts 2:38; 16:31; Romans 6:23). —see JESUS —spiritists n.

spir-it-less (spɪər–ət–ləs) adj. Lacking enthusiasm

spi-rits (spɪər–əts) n. **1.** A person's state of mind; mood: *Mary is in good spirits today, because she has just learned that she passed her exams.* **2.** Strong alcoholic beverages; hard liquor

spir-it-u-al (spɪər–ɪ–tʃuʷ–əl) adj. Of the human spirit; not physical and not mental: *Keep your spiritual fervor, serving the Lord* (Romans 12:11). *The Bible says, "Offer your bodies as living sacrifices, holy and pleasing to God — this is your spiritual act of worship"* (Romans 12:1). *Speak to one another with psalms, hymns and spiritual songs* (Ephesians 5:19). —**spiritually** adv. *The man without the Spirit does not accept the things that come from the Spirit of God, for they are foolishness to him, and he cannot understand them, because they are spiritually discerned* (1 Corinthians 2:14).

spir-it-u-al-ism n. —see SPIRITISM

spir-it-u-al-i-ty (spɪər–ɪ–tʃuʷ–æl–ət–iʸ) n. -ties The state of being concerned with the soul

spir-it-u-al-ize (spɪər–ɪ–tʃuʷ–ə–laɪz) v. -ized, -izing **1.** To make spiritual **2.** To give a spiritual sense or meaning —**spir-it-u-al-i-za-tion** (spɪər–ɪ–tʃuʷ–ə–lə–zeʸ–ʃən) n.

spir-it-u-ous (spɪər–ɪ–tʃuʷ–əs) adj. Containing alcohol

spit (spɪt) v. spit or spat (spæt), spitting To eject sthg. from the mouth: *As his mother tried to feed him, the little boy spit the food out of his mouth.*

spit n. The liquid in the mouth; saliva

spite (spaɪt) n. **1.** Ill will towards sbdy. with a desire to hurt or annoy: *She took my books when I needed to study for exams, not because she needed them but just out of spite.* **2. in spite of** Regardless of; even though sthg. has happened: *In spite of the cold, he didn't wear a coat.* —**spiteful** adj. —**spitefully** adv.

spit-fire (spɪt–faɪr) adj. A quick-tem-pered person

spit-tle (spɪt–əl) n. Spit; saliva

spit-toon (spɪ–tuʷn) n. A receptacle for spitting into

splash (splæʃ) v. **1.** Of a liquid, to fall or hit with a sound: *The water from the fountain splashed into the pool below it.* **2.** To cause to splatter about, esp. with force, making a slapping sound: *The children splashed happily in the shallow water at the edge of the lake.* **3.** To cover with drops of liquid: *When I spilled my coffee, some of it splashed on my skirt.* —**splash** n.

splat-ter (splæt–ər) v. To splash noisily

splatter n. A noisy, splashing sound

spleen (spliʸn) n. An organ at the left of the stomach that produces lymph cells and destroys worn-out red blood cells

splen-did (splen–dəd) adj. **1.** Magnificent; glorious: *Come and look at the splendid sunset!* **2.** *infml.* Excellent; very good: *The mechanic did a splendid job of repairing our car.* —**splendidly** adv.

splen-dor *AmE.* n. **-our** *BrE.* (splen–dər) n. Glorious beauty: *Worship the Lord in the splendor of his holiness* (Psalm 29:2). *Yours, O Lord, is the greatness and the power and the glory and*

the majesty and the splendor, for everything in heaven and earth is yours (1 Chronicles 29:11).

splice (splaɪs) v. **spliced, splicing 1.** To unite two pieces of film or tape, end to end **2.** To join (two ropes) by weaving strands together **3.** To unite timbers by overlapping and binding their ends

splice n. A joint made by splicing

splin-ter (splɪnt–ər) n. **1.** A small thin sharp piece broken off a bigger piece, esp. wood: *He got a splinter in his hand when he rubbed it against the rough piece of wood.* **2. splinter group** A small group that has broken away from a larger one —**splinter** v.

split (splɪt) v. **split, splitting 1.** To divide lengthwise, esp. wood with an ax: *He split the logs in half with his ax.* **2.** To open a thin crack or slit: *His pants split when he bent over.* **3.** To divide a large group into smaller groups, often one opposing the other: *The political party split into two groups, conservative and liberal.* **4.** To share among two or more people: *Let's invite Mary to lunch, and you and I can split the cost.* **5. split up (a)** Of a couple, to be separated: *John and Mary have split up and are getting a divorce.* **(b)** Of a group of people or things, to be divided up or separated: *After the conference, the group split up, and everyone went home.* —**split** n.

splotch (splɒtʃ) n. A large, irregular spot or blotch

splotch v. To mark or be marked with splotches

splurge (splɜrdʒ) n. An ostentatious display, esp. of wealth

splurge v. **splurged, splurging** To spend money extravagantly

splut-ter (splʌt–ər) v. To speak rapidly and confusedly

splutter n. The act or sound of spluttering

spoil (spɔɪl) v. **spoiled** or **spoilt, spoiling 1.** To rot or decay; become bad, esp. food: *Don't eat that meat; it has spoiled from being on the table for two days.* **2.** To damage, ruin, harm, esp. relationships: *We were having a good time at the party until two men spoiled it by starting a fight.* **3.** To treat a child with indulgence or lack of discipline: *Bobby's mother is spoiling him by letting him do anything he*

wants to do.

spoil n. *usu. pl.* Objects taken as a result of victory in battle, or by thieves: *The soldiers divided the spoils — clothing, jewelry, household goods — among themselves after they conquered the town.*

spoil-er (spɔɪ–lər) n. A person or thing that spoils

spoke (spoʷk) n. One of the rods which connect the center to the outer rim of a wheel, as on a bicycle, cart, etc.

spoke v. Past tense of **speak**

spo-ken (spoʷ–kən) v. Past part. of **speak**

spokes-man (spoʷks–mən) n. One who speaks in behalf of another —**spokeswoman** *fem.* n.

sponge (spʌndʒ) n. **1.** A simple sea animal with a skeleton full of small holes **2. (a)** A piece of this animal, which takes up water easily and releases it when squeezed, used for washing the body or other things: *He used a sponge to wash his car.* **(b)** A man-made product similar to the natural one

sponge v. **sponged, sponging 1.** To wash or wipe with a sponge: *She sponged up the spilled water.* **2. sponge off/ on** *infml.* To take advantage of someone's kindness or hospitality rather than earn one's own living: *Our cousins came for a weekend visit, but they have stayed and sponged off us for the past two months.*

spong-er (spʌndʒ–ər) n. A person who sponges off others, living at their expense

spon-sor (spɑn–sər) n. **1.** A person who accepts responsibility for another person, such as a student or a foreigner who wishes to immigrate: *My uncle acted as a sponsor for my father when he came to the US thirty years ago.* **2.** A person or group which plans and initiates some action: *Our senator is the sponsor of a new bill in the legislature.* **3.** A godmother or godfather **4.** A business organization which pays for a radio or television show, usu. in return for advertising during the show —**sponsor-ship** n. —**sponsor** v.

spon-ta-ne-ous (spɑn–teʸ–niʸ–yəs) adj. Without advance preparation or planning; done freely and naturally: *Her spontaneous reaction to his beautiful gift was to give him a big*

hug. —**spontaneously** adv.

spoof (spuʷf) n. **1.** A playful joke; a prank **2.** Deception

spoof v. **1.** To fool by a hoax **2.** To mock in a good-humored way

spook (spuʷk) n. A ghost or specter

spook-y (spuʷ-kiʸ) adj. **-ier, -iest** Scary; causing fright or alarm

spool (spuʷl) n. A small cylinder, usu. of wood, on which thread is wound, or a larger cylinder for photographic film, wire, etc.

spoon (spuʷn) n. A small utensil used for eating, together with a knife and fork; or a larger one for mixing and serving food

spoon-fed (spuʷn–fɛd) v. **1.** Fed with a spoon **2.** Coddled; pampered

spoor (spʊɑr/ spoʷ–ər/ spɔ–ər) n. The track or scent left by an animal

spo-rad-ic (spə–ræd–ɪk) adj. **1.** Occurring infrequently **2.** Irregular; happening now and then —**sporadically** adv.

spore (spoʷ–ər/ spɔər) n. One of the tiny reproductive cells of certain plants like ferns and fungi

sport (spɔrt) n. **1.** A physical activity done for pleasure or as a profession, such as swimming, golf, or tennis **2.** A game played by two teams, for pleasure or as a profession, such as baseball, football, or basketball —see RECREATION **3.** A person who remains cheerful in spite of a defeat or of being the victim of a bad joke: *She was a good sport about losing the tennis match.* —**sports** adj. *the sports page of the newspaper*

sport-ive (spɔrt–ɪv) adj. **1.** Fond of sport or play **2.** Done in sport or fun

sports-man (spɔrts–mən) n. **-men 1.** A man who engages in a sport, esp. in an open-air sport **2.** A person who plays fair and is a good loser —**sportswoman** *fem.* n.

sports-man-like (spɔrts–mən–laɪk) adj. Behaving generously and fairly

sports-man-ship (spɔrts–mən–ʃɪp) n. Behavior befitting a sportsman or sportswoman

sport-y (spɔrt–iʸ) adj. **-ier, -iest 1.** Befitting a sportsman or sportswoman **2.** Flashy or showy, as in clothing

spot (spɑt) n. **1.** An area on cloth or other surface which is a different color from the main surface **2.** A small dirty area on cloth, a rug, a clean floor, etc.: *There's a spot of grease on your shirt.* **3.** A special place or location: *This is one of my favorite spots for a vacation.* **4. on the spot (a)** A place where the action is: *He's a wonderful assistant; he is always on the spot when I need him.* **(b)** In a difficult situation: *He's on the spot; the police found stolen goods in his house.* **5. spot–check** To make a check or test for sthg., not of everyone or everything but of just a few here and there: *The police were making spot checks of the cars going across the border, looking for smuggled goods.* **6. hit the spot** *infml.* To be just the right thing to fill a need, esp. thirst or hunger: *A glass of cold water really hits the spot on a hot day.*

spot v. **-tt- 1.** To find sbdy./ sthg. with the eyes, esp. in a crowd, at a distance, or partly hidden: *She spotted her sister among the many passengers coming off the ship.* **2.** To make spots on sthg.: *The dirty water spotted her skirt as she walked on the muddy road.*

spot-less (spɑt–ləs) adj. Completely clean

spot-light (spɑt–laɪt) n. **1.** A very bright light that is focused on a particular person, object, or area, as on a stage **2.** Public notice: *That actress has been in the spotlight ever since her first movie forty years ago.*

spot-ter (spɑt–ər) n. **1.** One who watches for approaching airplanes **2.** One who locates enemy targets

spot-ty (spɑt–iʸ) adj. **-tier, -tiest 1.** Uneven in quality **2.** Covered with spots

spouse (spaʊs) n. A husband or wife

spout (spaʊt) n. An opening through which liquid comes out

spout v. **1.** To discharge forcibly in a jet or stream **2.** To state sthg. lengthily, esp. in a pompous manner: *He's always spouting off. He thinks he knows everything.*

sprain (spreʸn) v. To wrench or twist the muscles or tendons of a joint without breaking the bones of the joint: *He sprained his ankle when he fell down the steps.* —**sprain** n.

sprang (spræŋ) v. Past tense of **spring**

sprawl (sprɔl) v. **1.** To sit, stand, or fall with the arms and legs spread out widely and carelessly **2.** Of a city, to spread out in an ir-

regular or straggling way

spray (spre^y) n. **1.** A fine mist of small drops of water, blown by the wind, esp. from the sea, a waterfall, etc.: *Waves crashed on the shore, and we all got wet from the spray.* **2.** Tiny drops of liquid forced out under pressure: *We need some insect spray to kill the bugs in the house.* —**spray** v.

spray gun (spre^y gʌn) n. A device for spraying paints or insecticides

spread (sprɛd) v. **spread, spreading 1.** To extend over; to cover with: *He spread peanut butter on the bread.* **2.** To open or stretch out: *She spread the tablecloth on the table.* **3.** To cover a large period of time: *The construction will be completed this year, but the costs will be spread over five years.* **4.** To expand; distribute: *Branches of our local bank are now spread throughout the state.* **5.** To make information widely known: *They spread the news through the radio, television, and newspapers.*

spread n. **1.** A cloth cover for a bed **2.** A food, like butter, to be spread on bread or crackers **3.** An expanse **4.** The act or process of spreading **5.** A prominent display in a newspaper or magazine

spree (spri^y) n. **1.** Any period of unrestrained spending: *a shopping spree* **2.** A period of heavy drinking or fun and frolic

sprig (sprɪg) n. A shoot or sprout of a plant

spright-ly (spraɪt-li^y) adj. **-lier, -liest** Vivacious; lively —**sprightliness** n.

spring (sprɪŋ) v. **sprang** (spræŋ), **sprung** (sprʌŋ), **springing 1.** To jump; leap; move suddenly: *He sprang to his feet when the queen entered the room.* **2.** To appear suddenly: *After the rain, the warm sun caused the plants to spring up.* **3.** To be closed or opened suddenly: *The trap sprang shut when the mouse touched the bait.* **4.** To surprise sbdy. by doing sthg. unexpected: *Her friends sprang a party for her without telling her in advance.* **5. spring a leak** To develop a leak, as in the bottom of a boat, barrel, or other container

spring n. **1.** The act of springing: *The lion made a spring and caught the deer.* **2.** A movement similar to this: *He walked with a spring in his step.* **3.** A coil of wire or metal which goes back to its original form after being

pushed or pulled: *a bed spring* **4.** A place in the ground where water comes up naturally: *This stream flows from the spring in those rocks.* **5.** The season of the year between winter and summer, March to June in the northern hemisphere

spring-board (sprɪŋ–bord) n. **1.** A springy board from which divers may dive **2.** A starting point

spring-fever (sprɪŋ–fi^y–vər) n. A lazy or restless feeling often associated with the coming of spring

spring-time (sprɪŋ–taɪm) n. The season of spring

spring up (sprɪŋ ʌp) v. **sprang up** (spræŋ ʌp), **sprung up** (sprʌŋ ʌp) To develop or appear suddenly: *Towns in Southern California seem to spring up over night.*

spring-y (sprɪŋ–i^y) adj. **-ier, -iest** Able to spring back easily after being stretched or squeezed

sprin-kle (sprɪŋ–kəl) v. **-kled, -kling 1.** Of rain, to fall lightly **2.** Of seeds, etc., to scatter lightly: *He sprinkled some grass seed on the lawn.*

sprink-ler (sprɪŋ–klər) n. A device for sprinkling water, usu. attached to a hose for use outside, or attached to a ceiling for use inside in case of fire

sprint (sprɪnt) v. To run at full speed, esp. over a short distance

sprint n. A run of this kind: *a 100-meter sprint*

sprock-et (sprɑk–ət) n. **1.** A projection, as on the rim of a wheel, that engages with the links of a chain to make sthg. move **2.** A wheel bearing such projections; sprocket wheel: *a bicycle sprocket*

sprout (spraʊt) v. **1.** To begin to grow or appear: *The trees are sprouting new leaves.* **2.** To cause to spring up as a growth

sprout n. A new shoot or bud: *bean sprouts*

spruce (spru^{w}s) n. **1.** An evergreen tree of the pine family, having short, needle-shaped leaves **2.** The wood of these trees

spruce adj. Neat and trim

spruce v. **spruced, sprucing** To make oneself neat and trim: *He's sprucing himself (up) for the party.*

sprung (sprʌŋ) v. Past part. of **spring**

spry (spraɪ) adj. Active or lively, said esp. of older people: *He's 95 years old, and quite spry for his age.*

spume (spyuᵂm) n. Froth; foam

spun (spʌn) v. Past tense and part. of **spin**

spunk (spʌŋk) n. Courage; mettle

spunk-y (spʌŋk–iʸ) adj. -ier, -iest Courageous; spirited

spur (spɜr) n. **1.** A pointed object on the heel of a rider's boot, used to urge a horse to run faster **2.** Sthg. that urges to action; an incentive: *News of his heroic effort will be a spur to others to follow his example.* **3.** A ridge extending sideways from a mountain **4.** A branch of a railroad track **5. on the spur of the moment** Without preparation or planning; hastily; impulsively

spur v. -rr- **1.** To prick (a horse) with spurs **2.** To urge to greater action

spu-ri-ous (spyʊr–iʸ–əs) adj. **1.** Not genuine; false **2.** Bad in reasoning; wrong —**spuriously** adv.

spurn (spɜrn) v. To reject with disdain; scorn: *She spurned his offer to help.*

spurred (spɜrd) adj. Having spurs; fitted with spurs

spurt (spɜrt) v. **1.** To gush; to send out (a liquid) suddenly: *Blood spurted from the wound.* **2.** To increase one's speed suddenly

spurt n. **1.** A sudden gush **2.** A sudden increase in speed or activity

sput-ter (spʌt–ər) v. **1.** To speak hastily in a confused, explosive manner **2.** To spit out drops of saliva, as when talking excitedly **3.** To make sharp, sizzling or spitting sounds, as wood burning, bacon frying in a pan, etc.

spy (spaɪ) n. **spies** A person who watches and obtains information in secret, esp. one paid by a government to get information from an enemy —**spy** v. **spied, spying**

squab-ble (skwab–əl) n. A petty quarrel

squabble v. -bled, -bling To engage in such a quarrel: *What are you kids squabbling about?*

squad (skwad) n. **1.** A small organized group of military personnel **2.** A small group engaged in a common effort

squad car (skwad kar) n. *AmE.* A police patrol car connected with headquarters by radio/ telephone

squad-ron (skwad–rən) n. In the military, any of several units of persons, vessels, and/ or aircraft

squal-id (skwal–əd) adj. **1.** Filthy and repulsive **2.** Wretched and degrading

squall (skwɔl) n. A sudden, violent gust of wind, often bringing rain or snow

squal-or (skwal–ər) n. The quality or condition of being squalid; filth and wretchedness

squan-der (skwan–dər) v. To spend foolishly; use wastefully

square (skwɛər) n. **1.** A rectangle with four equal sides **2.** The result obtained when a number is multiplied by itself: *The square of 5 is 25.* **3.** A four-sided open area with buildings surrounding it; a plaza: *There's a fountain in the middle of the public square in that town.*

square adj. **1.** Having four equal sides and four right angles: *Four people can sit comfortably at a square table.* **2.** Measured by multiplying the width by the length: *This room has an area of 120 square feet.* (=10 feet wide by 12 feet long) **3. square deal** Honest and fair treatment or business transaction: *We always take our car to Smith's Garage for repair, because he gives us a square deal.* **4. square meal** A complete meal: *His wife makes sure he eats three square meals a day.* —**squarely** adv. —**squareness** n

square v. **squared, squaring 1.** To make a square form: *He squared the corners of the piece of wood.* **2. squared paper** Paper that is marked into small squares: *He drew a graph on the squared paper.* **3.** To multiply a number by itself: *5 squared equals 25.* **4.** To be consistent with: *His report of the accident squares with mine, I'm happy to say.* **5.** To settle or pay (an account, etc.): *He squared his accounts yesterday; he no longer owes them any money.*

squash (skwaʃ/skwɔʃ) v. **1.** To be forced into a flat shape: *He sat on my hat and squashed it.* **2.** To suppress

squash n. **1.** The act or sound of squashing **2.** A game played with a ball and rackets on a four-walled court **3.** The fruit of any of the various gourd-like plants, used as a vegeta-

ble 4. Its plant 5. *BrE.* A beverage, of which one ingredient is a fruit juice

squash-y (**skwɑʃ**–iʸ / **skwɔʃ**–) adj. **-ier, -iest** Soft and moist; muddy

squat (**skwɑt**) v. **-tt- 1.** To sit with one's legs drawn fully up under the body **2.** To settle on a piece of land without title or payment

squat n. **1.** The act of squatting **2.** A squatting position

squat-ter (**skwɑt**–ər) n. Sbdy. who lives on a piece of land or in an otherwise empty building without permission

squat-ty (**skwɑt**–iʸ) adj. Short and thick

squaw (**skwɔ**) n. A North American Indian woman, esp. a wife

squeak (**skwiʸk**) v. To make a thin, high, short sound: *That hinge squeaks. Put some oil on it.* —**squeak** n. —**squeaky** adj.

squeal (**skwiʸl**) v. **1.** To make a long, shrill cry: *the squealing of children on the playground* **2.** To betray a secret; become an informer

squeam-ish (**skwiʸ**–mɪʃ) adj. **1.** Having a digestive system that is easily upset; easily nauseated **2.** Easily shocked or offended; prudish **3.** Oversensitive

squee-gee (**skwiʸ**–dʒiʸ) n. An implement for wiping liquid off a surface

squeeze (**skwiʸz**) v. **squeezed, squeezing 1.** To press together by force: *Four people squeezed into the back seat of the car.* **2.** To force liquid out by pressure: *She squeezed some oranges to make orange juice.* **3.** To hold or press on all sides: *She gently squeezed my hand as she said good night.* —**squeeze** n.

squelch (**skwɛltʃ**) v. To force into silence or inactivity

squid (**skwɪd**) n. A sea animal related to the octopus, but having ten arms surrounding the mouth

squint (**skwɪnt**) v. **1.** To look with half closed eyes, as into a bright light **2.** To look or glance sideways **3.** To be cross-eyed

squint n. **1.** The act of squinting **2.** *infml.* A quick glance

squire (**skwaɪr**) n. **1.** In the Middle Ages a young man of noble birth who served as an attendant to a knight **2.** An English country gentleman

squirm (**skwɜrm**) v. To twist the body about like a worm, as from discomfort or nervousness

squir-rel (**skwɜr**–əl) n. **1.** A small, tree-climbing animal with a bushy tail **2.** Its fur

squirt (**skwɜrt**) v. **1.** To force liquid out in a thin stream: *While I was squeezing a lemon, some juice squirted in my eye.* **2.** To hit with a strong stream of liquid: *Firemen squirted water onto the burning house.*

squirt n. **1.** A thin stream of liquid forced out of a hose or other container **2.** *infml.* A small or young person, esp. one who thinks he knows everything or is an annoying person: *That little squirt is getting to be a pest.*

Sr. *Written abbr.* Said as **Senior** (**siʸn**–yər)

stab (**stæb**) v. **-bb-** To pierce with a pointed weapon: *The woman was stabbed to death.*

stab n. **1.** A wound made with a pointed weapon **2.** A sudden painful feeling **3.** *fig.* An attempt: *I'll take /make a stab at it.*

stab-bing (**stæb**–ŋ) adj. Esp. of pain, sharp and sudden

sta-bil-i-ty (**stə**–**bɪl**–ət–iʸ) n. The state of being stable; steadiness: *the stability of their marriage* —opposite INSTABILITY

sta-bi-lize also **-lise** *BrE.* (**steʸ**–bə–laɪz) v. **-lized, -lizing** To make steady

sta-ble (**steʸ**–bəl) adj. Steady; firm; not easily moved, upset, or changed: *a stable government*

sta-ble n. A building for keeping and feeding horses

stable v. **-bled, -bling** To put in a stable

stac-ca-to (**stə**–**kɑt**–oʷ) n. **1.** Of speech sounds, sharp and separate, like the sound of tapping **2.** In music, with each note sounded separately and clearly

stack (**stæk**) n. **1.** An orderly pile, esp. one arranged in layers: *a stack of papers/ books* **2.** *infml.* A large amount: *stacks of letters to write*

stack v. **1.** To make into a neat pile; arrange in a stack: *The lumber was stacked neatly beside the wall.* **2.** *infml.* To arrange playing cards in a dishonest way: *They accused him of cheating by stacking the deck (of cards).* **3. stack up** *infml.* **(a)** To compare: *How does this year's income stack up against the previous year's?* **(b)** To be as a result or condition: *I*

wonder how things will stack up this weekend.

sta-di-um (steᵛd–iᵛ–əm) n. **-diums** or **-dia** (–diᵛ–ə) A large sports arena, usu. oval or U-shaped with rows of seats, often all the way around the stadium: *Some stadiums hold 100,000 people or more.*

staff (stæf) n. **1.** The group of workers who do the work of an organization **2.** The body of assistants to an executive **3.** A thick pole used as a support or as a mark of authority: *a flagstaff* **4.** Sthg. that sustains: *Bread is the staff of life.* **5.** The five horizontal lines on which music is written

staff v. To provide with staff; provide the workers: *The office was staffed with some brilliant people.*

stag (stæg) n. **1.** A male deer that is fully grown **2. stag party** A party for men only

stage (steᵛdʒ) n. **1.** Platform or area on which plays are performed in a theater **2.** The theater, or the job of being an actor: *She chose the stage for her career.* **3.** A period or step in the development of sthg.: *The cancer is still in its early stages.* **4.** A part of a journey: *We made the trip in easy stages, stopping often along the way.*

stage-coach (steᵛdʒ–koʷtʃ) n. A horse-drawn vehicle used for carrying passengers in former times

stag-ger (stæg–ər) v. **1.** To move unsteadily on one's feet: *The drunk man staggered down the street.* **2.** To arrange things so that they don't come at the same time: *We staggered our vacations.* **3.** To affect strongly; overwhelm: *The need for literacy workers staggers the imagination.*

stag-ger-ing (stæg–ər–ɱ) adj. Tremendous: *The need for literacy workers is staggering.*

stag-nant (stæg–nənt) adj. **1.** Standing still; not flowing, as of water or air **2.** Bad-smelling; foul from standing, as water **3.** Sluggish; not moving very well: *Business is stagnant.*

stag-nate (stæg–neᵛt) v. **-nated, -nating** v. To become stagnant —**stagnation** n.

staid (steᵛd) adj. **1.** Sober, sedate **2.** Set in one's ways

stain (steᵛn) v. **1.** To change the color of sthg. in a way that is difficult to remove: *The baby's clothes were stained from the formula.* **2.**

To darken, using chemicals: *We stained the woodwork a dark brown.*

stain n. **1.** A stained place or area: *How did you get those grass stains on your pants?* **2.** A chemical for darkening wood, etc. **3.** Sthg. shameful in one's character or reputation

stair (stɛər) n. **1.** A step in a set of stairs **2.** All of the steps in a series going from one level to another, esp. in a building

stair-case (stɛər–keᵛs) n. A flight of steps and its supporting framework and railing

stair-way (stɛər–weᵛ) n. One or more sets of stairs with connected landings

stair-well (stɛər–wɛl) n. A vertical shaft in which stairs are located

stake (steᵛk) n. **1.** A pointed piece of wood or metal for driving into the ground as a marker or for support **2.** Sthg. wagered or risked **3.** A share in a business enterprise **4.** In former times, a pole to which a person was bound and executed by burning: *Joan of Arc was burned at the stake.*

stake v. **staked, staking 1.** To mark an area of ground with stakes: *We staked off one end of the field.* **2. stake out** *infml.* To watch secretly: *The police have been staking out the house for several days now.*

stake-out (steᵛk–aʊt) n. A close watch by police of an area or a person suspected of criminal activity

sta-lac-tite (stə–læk–taɪt) n. A calcium deposit hanging from the roof of a cavern, formed by the dripping of water that contains minerals

sta-lag-mite (stə–læg–maɪt) n. A mineral deposit pointing upward from the floor of a cave or cavern, formed by water containing minerals, dripping from above

stale (steᵛl) adj. **1.** No longer fresh: *stale bread* **2.** Lacking in originality: *a stale joke*

stale-mate (steᵛl–meᵛt) n. **1.** In chess, a position when a player cannot make a move without putting his king in check **2.** Any deadlock

stalemate v. **-mated, -mating** To bring to a stalemate

stalk (stɔk) n. The main part of a plant, supporting its leaves, etc.: *a stalk of corn*

stalk v. **1.** To approach stealthily, quietly and

unseen **2.** To walk stiffly and proudly —**stalker** n.

stall (stɔl) v. **1.** To delay: *Stop stalling and give me an answer.* **2.** Of an engine, to stop because of insufficient power or speed: *Our motor stalled on the hill.*

stall n. **1.** An enclosure for one animal in a barn or stable **2.** A booth where articles may be displayed for sale in a street, market, etc.

stal-lion (stæl–yən) n. A fully grown male horse

stal-wart (stɔl–wərt) adj. **1.** Strong; robust **2.** Determined **3.** Brave; courageous

sta-men (steʸ–mən) n. One of the thread-like pollen-bearing spikes in the middle of a flower

stam-i-na (stæm–ə–nə) n. Capacity to withstand hardship; vitality

stam-mer (stæm–ər) v. To hesitate or stumble in speaking

stamp (stæmp) v. **1.** To put one's foot down firmly and noisily: *He stamped out of the room angrily.* **2.** To mark by pressing: *I stamped the embroidery pattern onto the towel with a hot iron.* **3.** To stick a stamp onto an envelope: *Be sure to stamp those letters before mailing them.* **4. stamp sthg. out** To eliminate sthg. completely: *That epidemic disease has been stamped out.*

stamp n. **1. postage stamp** A small piece of paper with an official design on it for sticking onto a piece of mail **2.** A mark made by an instrument: *When does the stamp say your book is due?* **3.** An instrument for making a stamp mark: *a rubber stamp*

stam-pede (stæm–piʸd) n. **1.** A sudden rush of a herd of frightened animals **2.** A rush of people under a sudden common impulse: *The school bell rang for recess, and there was a stampede for the door.*

stampede v. **-peded, -peding 1.** To take part or cause to take part in a stampede: *The gunfire stampeded the cattle.* **2.** To force a person into a hasty action or decision: *Don't be stampeded into buying a car that you don't like.*

stance (stæns) n. **1.** A person's position or manner of standing, esp. in playing a game **2.** One's point of view **3.** Attitude

stanch (stɔntʃ/ stantʃ) v. To stop or check the flow of blood, as from a wound

stan-chion (stæn–tʃən) n. An isolated upright structural support

stand (stænd) v. **stood** (stʊd), **standing 1.** To be on one's feet, not sitting or lying down: *There was no room in the theater, so I had to stand.* **2.** To rise to one's feet: *He stood up when the captain entered the room.* **3.** To be on one's guard: *Stand firm in the faith [in Jesus]* (1 Corinthians 16:13). **4.** To be in height: *The building stands taller than any other building in the world.* **5.** To rest or remain upright on a base: *Few houses were left standing after the earthquake.* **6.** To be in a particular state: *If you, O Lord, kept a record of sins, O Lord, who could stand? But with you there is forgiveness* (Psalm 130:3). —see FORGIVENESS **7.** To remain stationary or inactive: *The car has been standing idle for months.* **8.** To continue to exist: *Every city or household divided against itself will not stand* (Matthew 12:25). **9.** To bear: *She can't stand the sight of blood.* **10. to know how one stands** To know how one person feels about another: *How do you stand with the boss? Does he like you?* **11. stand a chance** To have a chance: *He doesn't stand a chance of winning that race.* **12. to stand on one's own two feet** To be able to think or do sthg. independently **13. it stands to reason** It is clear/ obvious **14. to stand trial** To be tried in court **15. to stand by (a)** To support and encourage; be loyal to: *Jesus said to his disciples, "You are those who have stood by me in my trials"* (Luke 22:28). **(b)** To remain inactive: *How can you stand by and let your company take advantage of you?* **(c)** To be ready: *Stand by to receive my telephone call.* **16. stand for (a)** To mean; to be a short form of: *"COD" stands for "CASH ON DELIVERY"* **(b)** To believe in or have as a principle; to support: *Before we vote for or against her, we should find out what she stands for.* **(c)** To tolerate; put up with: *I won't stand for his physical abuse.* **17. stand out (a)** To be easily seen: *Tom is so tall that he stands out above everyone.* **(b)** To be much better or the best: *Among baseball players, Babe Ruth stood out as one of the best.* **18. stand up (a)** To re-

main in good condition: *These tires have stood up under some very rough use.* **(b)** To be accepted as true: *The accusations you've made will never stand up in court.* **19. stand up for sbdy./ sthg.** To defend against attack: *They said they were just standing up for their rights!*

stand (stænd) n. **1.** A position or attitude taken: *What is his stand on this issue?* **2.** The place occupied by a person giving testimony in court **3.** A strong effort of defense: *In February, 1916, the French Army made a stand at Verdun.* **4.** A small place, often outdoors, for selling things: *a fruit stand/ a newsstand* **5.** A stop on a performance tour: *a one-night stand* **6.** The place where spectators sit to watch a sporting event; bleachers; grandstand

stan-dard (stæn–dərd) n. **1.** The required level of quality: *His work was rejected as being below standard.* **2.** The average quality: *Her standard of work is very high.* **3.** The basis to which the value of a monetary system is related: *the gold standard* **4.** A distinctive flag: *the royal standard* **5.** Sthg. fixed as a rule for measuring weight, value, etc.: *The government has an official standard for the purity of silver.*

standard adj. **1.** Ordinary; regular; not rare: *These screws come in six standard sizes.* **2.** Generally recognized as au-thoritative: *This is one of the standard books on the subject.*

stan-dard-ize (stæn–dərd–aɪz) v. **-ized, -izing** To make or adapt to a fixed standard: *a standardized test for all schools* —**stan-dard-i-za-tion** (stæn–dərd–ə–zeʸ–ʃən) n.

standard of living (stæn–dərd əv lɪv–ŋ) n. The degree of wealth and comfort enjoyed by a person, nation, etc.

stand-by (stænd–baɪ) n. **1.** A reliable supporter **2.** A substitute

stand-in (stænd–ɪn) n. A substitute person

stand-ing (stæn–dɪŋ) adj. Remaining; permanent; kept in use or force: *a standing invitation to visit them anytime we are in the area*

standing n. **1.** One's social position or reputation: *a diplomat of high standing* **2.** Length of time sthg. has existed; duration: *friends of long standing*

stand-off (stænd–ɔf) n. A draw or tie in a game

stand-off-ish (stænd–ɔf–ɪʃ) adj. Unfriendly; aloof in manner

stand-out (stænd–aʊt) n. A remarkable person or thing

stand-point (stænd–pɔɪnt) n. A point of view

stand-still (stænd–stɪl) n. A complete halt

stank (stæŋk) v. Past tense of **stink**

stan-za (stæn–zə) n. A group of lines, often rhymed, forming a subdivision of a poem

sta-ple (steʸ–pəl) n. **1.** A small piece of metal or wire driven into papers, etc. and clenched to fasten them **2.** A U-shaped piece of wire for holding sthg. in place

staple v. **-pled, -pling** To secure with one or more staples —**sta-pler** (steʸ–plər) n.

staple n. **1.** A chief or main item of diet: *Rice is a staple in many countries.* **2.** A chief product of trade or industry: *Paper is one of the staples of Sweden.*

star (stɑr) n. **1.** A brightly-burning heav-enly body that is visible as an apparently fixed point of light: *He [God] determines the number of stars and calls them each by name* (Psalm 147:4). **2.** A five or more pointed figure, e.g., for wearing as a mark of office, rank, etc., or as a sign to show quality **3.** A famous performer: *a movie star*

star v. **-rr- 1.** To mark with one or more stars **2.** To appear as a main performer: *an old movie starring Mary Pickford*

star-board (stɑr–bərd) n. The right-hand side of a ship when a passenger is looking forward

starch (stɑrtʃ) n. **1.** A white tasteless substance that is stored in plants such as rice, beans, corn, potatoes, and is used in adhesives, laundering, etc. **2.** A product made from this for stiffening cloth

starch v. To stiffen or treat with starch: *My wife starches my uniform.*

starch-y (stɑr–tʃiʸ) adj. **-ier, -iest 1.** Having a lot of starch: *starchy food* **2.** *Infml.* Stiff and unfriendly; stiffly correct and formal: *a very starchy person*

star-dom (stɑr–dəm) n. The state of being a famous performer

stare (steər) v. **stared, staring** To look at sthg. with a fixed gaze, as in amazement, fear,

etc.: *It's not polite to stare at people.* —**stare** n.

star-fish (stɑr-fiʃ) n. A star-shaped marine animal having five or more arms

stark (stɑrk) adj. **1.** Complete: *stark nonsense* **2.** Bare; harsh: *a stark, rocky landscape* **3.** Desolate; cheerless: *stark prison conditions* **4.** Sharply evident: *in stark contrast* —**stark** adv. *stark naked*

star-ling (stɑr-lɪŋ) n. A dark brown or greenish-black European bird related to the crows

star-ry (stɑr-i^y) adj. **-rier, -riest** Filled with stars: *starry winter sky*

star-ry–eyed (stɑr-i^y–aɪd) adj. **1.** Having eyes shining with happiness **2.** Too naive and idealistic

start (stɑrt) v. **1.** To begin: *It started to rain just as he started to go home.* **2.** To get sthg. (a machine, e.g.) going: *He started the motor.* **3.** To leave from a particular place: *The train starts in Bombay and goes to Delhi.*

start (stɑrt) n. **1.** The beginning of an activity; journey; performance, etc. **2.** A sudden uncontrolled jerking movement of the body, as in fear or surprise: *I woke with a start.*

start-er (stɑrt-ər) n. **1.** A person who gives the signal for a race to begin **2.** A device for starting an engine

star-tle (stɑrt–əl) v. **-tled, -tling** To give a shock or surprise to

starve (stɑrv) v. **starved, starving 1.** To die or suffer from lack of food **2.** *Infml.* To be very hungry: *When can we eat? I'm starving!* —**star-va-tion** (stɑr-ve^y-ʃən) n.

stash (stæʃ) v. To hide or conceal (money, etc.) for future use

state (ste^{y}t) n. **1.** The condition in which a person or thing is: *He inquired about her state of health.* **2.** A country or an organized community forming a part of a federal republic: *The US has 50 states.* **3.** Ceremonial dignity and splendor connected with high-level government: *The queen was in her robes of state.* **4.** lie in state Said of a dead body that has been put in a public place so that people may honor it

state v. **stated, stating 1.** *fml.* To express or put into words: *She states the reason for her opposition in the paper she wrote.* **2.** To fix or specify: *Theater tickets must be used on the date stated.*

stat-ed (ste^{y}t əd) adj. Fixed or determined: *Trains run at stated intervals from this station.*

state-ly (ste^{y}t–li^y) adj. **-lier, -liest** Dignified; imposing; grand: *a stately old gentleman*

state-ment (ste^{y}t–mənt) n. **1.** The act of stating **2.** Sthg. that is stated: *The Prime Minister will make an official statement tomorrow regarding the crisis.* **3.** A list showing how much money a person has, owes, etc.: *We get a statement from the bank every month.*

states-man (ste^{y}ts–mən) n. **-men** A man skilled and prominent in government —**statesmanship** n.

stat-ic (stæt–ɪk) adj. Not moving or changing; stationary: *Weather conditions will remain static for the week.*

static n. Atmospheric conditions causing poor radio reception: *I couldn't hear the program last night because of all the static.*

sta-tion (ste^y–ʃən) n. **1.** A building on a railroad or bus line, with a ticket office and waiting rooms, where passengers or goods are picked up or let off; a depot **2.** A building that is a center for a particular service: *a police/fire/gasoline station* **3.** A company equipped for radio or television transmission: *a radio station* **4.** A small military base: *a naval station*

station v. To put in a certain place for a purpose: *Guards were stationed around the camp.*

sta-tion-ar-y (ste^y–ʃə–neər–i^y) adj. Standing, not moving

sta-tion-er-y (ste^y–ʃə–neər–i^y) n. Writing paper, envelopes, etc.

sta-tis-tic (stə–tɪs–tɪk) n. A numeral fact or datum

stat-is-ti-cian (stæt–ə–stɪʃ–ən) n. An expert in statistics

sta-tis-tics (stə–tɪs–tɪks) n. **1.** Numerical facts about people, business conditions, the weather, etc.: *These statistics show the population growth rate.* **2.** The science of collecting and classifying such facts in order to show their significance —**statistical** adj. —**statistically** adv.

stat-ue (stætʃ–u^w) n. An image, esp. of a person or animal, carved in stone or wood, or

cast in bronze

stat-u-esque (stætʃ-u^w-**ɛsk**) adj. Like a statue in size, dignity or stillness

stat-ure (stætʃ-ər) n. **1.** The natural height of one's body **2.** Greatness attained by ability or achievement

sta-tus (ste^yt-əs/ stæt–) n. **1.** A person's social, legal, or professional position in relation to others **2.** High rank or position in society

status quo (ste^yt-əs kwo^w/ stæt–) n. The existing state of affairs

stat-ute (stætʃ-u^wt) n. **1.** An established rule; formal regulation: *The statutes of the Lord are trustworthy, making wise the simple* (Psalm 19:7). *Blessed are they who keep his statutes and seek him with all their heart* (Psalm 119:2). **2.** A law passed by a legislative body **3.** One of the rules of an institution

stat-u-to-ry (stætʃ-ə-tɔr-i^y) adj. **1.** Prescribed or authorized by statute **2.** Legally punishable, as an offense

staunch (stɔntʃ) adj. **1.** Extremely loyal: *a staunch supporter of the political party* **2.** Strong or well-built

stave (ste^yv) n. One of the strips of wood making the side of a barrel or tub

stave v. **staved** or **stove, staving 1.** To crush or break in the staves of **2. stave off** To prevent

stay (ste^y) v. **1.** To remain; to continue to be in a place or in the presence of sbdy. else **2.** To be a visitor or guest: *Our son is staying with us for one week.* **3.** To continue: *He stayed in the race, though he was far behind.*

stay n. **1.** A usu. limited time of remaining in a place: *a short stay in the hospital* **2.** A suspension of a judicial proceeding: *The prisoner was given a stay of execution.* (=the execution was not carried out)

stead (stɛd) n. **1.** The place of a person or thing as occupied by a substitute: *Shall I go in your stead?* **2. stand in good stead** To be useful to

stead-fast (stɛd–fæst) adj. **1.** Faithful; loyal: *Create in me a pure heart, O God, and renew a steadfast spirit within me* (Psalm 51:10). *You (Lord) will keep in perfect peace, him whose mind is steadfast, because he trusts in you* (Isaiah 26:3). **2.** Fixed, unwavering, steady

stead-y (stɛd-i^y) adj. **-ier, -iest 1.** Firm, not moving or changing: *as steady as the Rock of Gibralter* **2.** Developing evenly; regular: *steady industrial growth* —op-posite UN-STEADY **3.** Ongoing; continuing: *a steady job* —steadily adv. —steadiness n.

steady v. **-ied, -ying** To make or become steady: *He stumbled but managed to steady himself.*

steak (ste^yk) n. A slice of meat, esp. beef, typically cut thick and across the muscle grain

steal (sti^yl) v. **stole** (sto^wl), **stolen** (sto^w–lən), **stealing 1.** To take what belongs to another without any right or permission, a sin against one of God's Ten Commandments: *You shall not steal* (Exodus 20:15). *Jesus said, "Do not store up for yourselves treasures on earth ... where thieves break in and steal"* (Matthew 6:19). **2.** To move stealthily: *Tom stole out of the room without anyone knowing it.* —see SIN, SAVIOR

stealth (stɛlθ) n. The quality or habit of acting secretly —stealthily adv.

steam (sti^ym) n. **1.** Water in the state of a gas, produced by boiling **2.** Water vapor when used under pressure to produce power or heat: *an engine run by steam* —steamy adj.

steam v. **1.** To pass off as vapor **2.** To travel by steam power: *The ship steamed into the harbor.* **3.** To use steam for unsticking sthg.: *to steam open a letter*

steam-er (sti^y–mər) n. A ship driven by steam

steam-roll-er (sti^ym–ro^w–lər) n. A steam-driven engine with wide, heavy wheels, used to flatten surfaces

steam-ship (sti^ym–ʃɪp) n. A large, sea-going vessel, driven by steam

steam-y (sti^y–mi^y) adj. **1.** Of or like steam **2.** Covered or filled with steam **3.** Giving off steam

steed (sti^yd) n. A horse, esp. a spirited one

steel (sti^yl) n. **1.** A tough alloy of iron, containing some carbon and sometimes other metals **2.** A quality suggestive of steel: *nerves of steel* (=strong nerves)

steep (sti^yp) adj. **1.** Having a very sharp slope: *a steep hill* **2.** *Infml.* Too much: *He's asking $50 for his old bike, which I think is a little steep.*

stee-ple (sti^y–pəl) n. A tall tapering structure

built on top of a church tower

steer (stɪər) n. A young male of domestic cattle, castrated and raised for its beef

steer v. **1.** To control the course of a ship or vehicle **2. to steer clear** To stay away from; avoid

steg-o-sau-rus (stɛg–ə–sɔr–əs) n. **-ri** (–ri^y) A large, plant-eating dinosaur that had a row of large, upright, bony plates down the center of its back and tail

stel-lar (stəl–ər) adj. **1.** Of or pertaining to stars **2.** Resembling a star

stem (stɛm) n. **1.** The main body or stalk of a plant **2.** The relatively slender growth supporting the fruit, flower, or leaf of a plant **3.** Anything like a stem, such as the stem of a goblet or smoker's pipe **4.** The bow or front end of a boat **5.** The form of a word to which inflectional endings are added

stem (stɛm) v. **-mm- 1.** To stop: *He tried to stem the flow of blood from the wound.* **2.** To start; to spring from: *Hatred often stems from envy.*

stench (stɛntʃ) n. A very strong bad smell

sten-cil (stɛn–səl) n. A piece of paper or metal in which letters or patterns have been cut

stencil v. **-l-** *AmE.* **-ll-** *BrE.* To make copies of sthg., using a stencil

ste-nog-ra-phy (stə–nɑg–rə–fi^y) n. The art of writing in shorthand —**stenographer** n.

step (stɛp) n. **1.** The act of putting one foot in front of the other in order to walk: *The baby took three steps today.* **2.** The distance passed over in making such a motion: *Our house is just a few steps from the corner.* **3.** One of the parts of a stairway or ladder on which one stands **4.** An act, esp. in a set of actions: *Our first step must be to draw the plans.* **5.** A particular movement of the feet as in dancing **6. step by step** Gradually **7. watch one's step** *Infml.* To be careful

step v. **-pp- 1.** To put one foot down usu. in front of the other, in order to walk: *He stepped off the distance from one end of the field to the other.* **2.** To walk: *She'll be right back; she just stepped into the phone booth over there.* **3. step aside** To give one's place to another **4. step down** To resign: *He stepped down from his position as president of the organization.* **5. step in** To get involved in an argument,

plan, etc. with other people by saying or doing sthg. **6. step up** To increase the amount of sthg.: *They are stepping up production.*

step-bro-ther (stɛp–brʌð–ər) n. Son of one's step-parent by a former marriage

step-child (stɛp–tʃaɪld) n. A child of one's husband or wife by a former marriage

step-daugh-ter (stɛp–dɔt–ər) n. The daughter of one's spouse by a former marriage

step-father (stɛp–fɑð–ər) n. The husband of one's re-married mother

step-lad-der (stɛp–læd–ər) n. A light, portable set of steps in a hinged frame

step-mother (stɛp–mʌð–ər) n. The wife of one's re-married father

step-par-ent (stɛp–pɛər–ənt) n. The husband or wife of one's mother or father by a subsequent marriage

steppe (stɛp) n. A dry, grass-covered land in regions of wide temperature range, esp. in SE Europe and Asia

step-ping-stone (stɛp–ɪŋ–sto^wn) n. **1.** A stone raised above the water or mud used for crossing on **2.** Anything that helps one advance

step-sis-ter (stɛp–sɪs–tər) n. The daughter of one's step-parent by a former marriage

step-son (stɛp–sən) n. The son of one's spouse by a former marriage

ster-e-o (stɛər–i^y–o^w) n. A record player that gives out sound from two places by means of two loudspeakers

ster-e-o-phon-ic (stɛər–i^y–ə–fɑn–ɪk) n. A system of sound reproduction in which two channels present different sounds

ster-e-o-type (stɛər–i^y–ə–taɪp) n. A fixed pattern that represents a type of person or event: *He's the stereotype of an army sergeant.*

stereotype v. **typed, typing** To think of a thing or person as an example of a general type: *The actor was becoming stereotyped as a villain.*

ster-ile (stɛər–əl) adj. **1.** Of living things, unable to reproduce —compare FERTILE **2.** Free from all germs and bacteria: *a sterile operating table* —**ste-ril-i-ty** (stə–rɪl–ət–i^y) n.

ster-i-lize also **-lise** *BrE.* (stɛər–ə–laɪz) v. **-lized, -lizing** To make sterile: *We sterilized*

the water by boiling it to make it safe to drink.
—**ster-il-i-za-tion** n. (stɛər-ə-lə-**ze**ʸ-ʃən)

ster-ling (stɜr-lɪŋ) n. **1.** Of standard quality for silver, containing 92.5 percent pure silver **2.** Knives, forks, spoons, etc., made of sterling silver

sterling adj. Genuine; excellent; reliable: *a man of sterling character*

sterling n. British money, esp. the pound as the standard British unit of money in international trade

stern (stɜrn) adj. **1.** Severe; firm; strict in one's attitude toward the behavior of others: *The teacher's stern frown frightened the children.* **2.** Stout; sturdy: *a stern resolution*

stern n. The back end of a boat or ship —**sternness** n.

ster-num (stɜr-nəm) n. **-nums** or **-na** The breastbone

ster-oid (stɜr-ɔɪd/ **stɛər**-) n. Any of a group of organic compounds that includes certain hormones and other bodily secretions. NOTE: Steroids are naturally found in the human body, but may be taken in pill form or by injection. This practice may be harmful.

steth-o-scope (stɛθ-ə-skoʷp) n. An instrument used by doctors to listen to the beat of the heart, the breathing, etc.

ste-ve-dore (stiʸv-ə-dɔr) n. A person who loads and unloads ships

stew (stuʷ) n. A dish of meat and vegetables, cooked together and served with gravy

stew v. To cook by boiling slowly

stew-ard (stuʷ-ərd) n. **1.** A man who serves on a large estate to manage domestic concerns, such as collecting rent, handling accounts, directing servants, etc. **2.** A man who serves passengers on a ship or plane; a male flight attendant **3.** A Christian who serves the Lord faithfully. NOTE: Christians are sometimes called stew-ards in the New Testament since they are stewards of the grace of God. They care for the Gospel (the Good News about Jesus) that has been given to them. They are stewards of the gifts that God gives to the Church.

stew-ard-ess (stuʷ-ərd-əs) n. A woman steward, esp. one who waits on passengers on

an airplane; a female flight attendant

stew-ard-ship (stuʷ-ərd-ʃɪp) n. The act of fulfilling the duties of a steward

stick (stɪk) n. **1.** A long, thin part of a tree or branch **2.** A slender piece of wood used for a special purpose: *He needs to use a walking stick until his leg heals completely.* **3.** A thin piece of any material: *a stick of chewing gum*

stick v. **stuck** (stʌk), **sticking 1.** To pierce with a pointed instrument **2.** To fasten; attach with a sticky substance: *Stick your return address label on this letter.* **3.** To become or remain fastened: *This window sticks. I can't open it.* **4.** *Infml.* To put: *He stuck his clothes in the closet.* **5.** To give someone an unpleasant responsibility: *We got stuck with paying the bill.* **6. stick around** To stay or wait in a place **7. stick by** To continue to give one's support: *to stick by a friend* **8. stick out (a)** To extend out from the rest: *He stuck his tongue out.* **(b)** To be quite evident **9. stick to sthg.** To keep on; hold fast: *She sticks to a job until it is finished.* **10. stick together** To stay loyal to each other: *My brother and I stick together, especially in times of trouble.* **11. stick up for** To defend someone by words or actions **12. stick with** To continue to work at: *He really didn't like his job, but he stuck with it.*

stick-er (stɪk-ər) n. A gummed label

stick-ler (stɪk-lər) n. A person who attaches a great deal of importance to a matter: *He's a stickler for details.*

stick-y (stɪk-iʸ) adj. **-ier, -iest 1.** Covered with glue or sthg. like glue **2.** Difficult: *a sticky problem* **3.** Of weather, hot and humid —**stickiness** n.

stiff (stɪf) adj. **1.** Rigid; not easily bent **2.** Firm, thick, not easily stirred: *Whip the cream until it is stiff.* **3.** Difficult: *a stiff examination* **4.** Painful from unusual exercise: *stiff muscles* **5.** Strong: *a stiff breeze* **6.** Formal, not friendly: *a stiff smile*

stiff adv. **1.** *Infml.* **bored stiff** Very, very bored from dull talk or a dull performance **2. scared stiff** Very, very fright-ened

stiff-en (stɪf-ən) v. To make or become stiff: *The jelly will stiffen as it cools.* —**stiffness** n.

stiff-en-ing (stɪf-ə-nɪŋ) n. Material used to stiffen sthg.: *His collar has some stiff-ening in*

it.

stiff-ly (stɪf-liʸ) adv. A stiff manner or way of doing sthg.: *He bowed stiffly.*

stiff-necked (stɪf-nɛkt) adj. Stubborn; unyielding

sti-fle (staɪ-fəl) v. **-fled, -fling 1.** To prevent or be prevented from breathing easily because of bad air: *I'm stifling in this heat.* **2.** To extinguish flames: *He stifled the fire by throwing a wet blanket over it.* **3.** To keep back; suppress: *Our plans were stifled.*

stif-ling (staɪ-flɪŋ) adj. So hot and stuffy that breathing is difficult: *This heat is stifling.*

stig-ma (stɪg-mə) n. **-mas** or **-mata 1.** A mark of disgrace or shame: *These days there is little stigma attached to being mentally ill.* **2.** The part of a pistil (of a flower) that receives the pollen in pollination

stig-ma-tize (stɪg-mə-taɪz) v. **-tized, -tizing 1.** To characterize or mark with disgrace **2.** To mark with a stigma

still (stɪl) adj. **1.** Not moving: *Please stand still while I brush your hair./ He [Jesus] got up, rebuked the wind and said to the waves, "Quiet! Be still!" Then the wind died down and it was completely calm* (Mark 4:39). **2.** Silent: *Be still before the Lord and wait patiently for him* (Psalm 37:7).

still v. To make calm: *The mother stilled the crying baby by rocking him gently in her arms.*

still n. Quietness: *in the still of the night*

still adv. **1.** At a time later than expected: *Are you still here?* **2.** Even so; in spite of that: *I know it's snowing outside, but I still have to go.* **3.** In a greater amount or degree: *It's hot now, but it will be still hotter this afternoon.*

still-born (stɪl-bɔrn) n. Born dead

stilts (stɪlts) n. **1.** A pair of poles for walking, each pole having a step for the foot, so a person can walk while raised above the ground **2.** Poles fixed under a house to support it, esp. if it is built over water or on a hillside

stilt-ed (stɪl-təd) adj. Formal; pompous; unnatural: *He writes in a rather stilted English.*

stim-u-lant (stɪm-yə-lənt) n. Sthg. that makes a person more alert or a part of his body more active: *Tea and coffee are stimulants.*

stim-u-late (stɪm-yə-leʸt) v. **-lated, -lating 1.** To rouse or make a person more alert: *Peter said, "I have written [my letters] ... to stimulate you to wholesome thinking"* (2 Peter 3:1). **2.** To encourage: *She was stimulated by the good news.*

stim-u-lat-ing (stɪm-yə-leʸt-ɪŋ) adj. Rousing; very interesting: *a very stimulating speech.* —**stim-u-la-tion** (stɪm-yə-leʸ-ʃən) n.

stim-u-lus (stɪm-yə-ləs) n. pl. **stim-u-li** (stɪm-yə-laɪ/ -liʸ) Sthg. that causes a reaction in a living thing: *Light is the stimulus that causes a flower to open.*

sting (stɪŋ) n. **1.** A sharp-pointed part of an insect used for wounding and often injecting poison **2.** A part of some plants that can prick and inject an irritating fluid into the wound **3.** A sharp pain caused by a plant or insect: *The sting of a scorpion is very painful.*

sting v. To pierce with a sting, or to cause pain like that of a sting: *I was stung by a bumblebee.*

sting-er (stɪŋ-ər) n. An insect or animal part that is used for stinging

sting-ray (stɪŋ-reʸ) n. A fish that has a flat body and a long tail with a stinger containing poison

stin-gy (stɪn-dʒiʸ) adj. **-gier, -giest** *Infml.* Not generous; unwilling to give: *A stingy man is eager to get rich and is unaware that poverty awaits him* (Proverbs 28:22).

stink (stɪŋk) v. **stank** (stæŋk), **stunk** (stʌŋk), **stinking** To have a very bad smell: *The meat stinks./ fig. The whole rotten business stinks (of corruption).*

stink n. A very bad smell: *What a stink!/ fig. If you sack that man (fire him), he will make quite a stink (=cause a lot of trouble).*

stint (stɪnt) n. A fixed amount of work or duty: *He did a stint in the army.*

sti-pend (staɪ-pɛnd/ -pənd) n. A fixed sum of money paid periodically for services or to defray expenses

stip-u-late (stɪp-yə-leʸt) v. **-lated, -lating** To make a special demand for sthg. as a condition in an agreement: *She stipulated that the contract was only to be in effect for 30 days.* —**stip-u-la-tion** (stɪp-yə-leʸ-ʃən) n.

stir (stɜr) v. **-rr- 1.** To move around and mix (esp. a liquid) with a spoon or other utensil

2. To move from one position to another, esp. when done often: *Some people stir around a lot in their sleep.* **3.** To arouse people's feelings: *A gentle answer turns away wrath, but a harsh word stirs up anger* (Proverbs 15:1)./ *A hot-tempered man stirs up dissension [violent quarrelling]* (Proverbs 15:18).

stir-ring (stɜr-ŋ) n., adj. Exciting: *a stirring story*

stir-rups (stɜr-əps) n. A pair of metal loops with flat bottoms, hanging from a horse's saddle, to support the rider's feet.

stitch (stɪtʃ) n. **1.** A single movement of a threaded needle in and out of fabric (in sewing) or tissue (in surgery) **2.** A particular method of arranging the thread or yarn: *cross-stitch/purl stitch* **3.** The piece of thread or wool left in place after the completion of such a movement. **3. in stitches** Laughing uncontrollably

stitch v. To sew; to join or close with stitches

stock (stɑk) n. **1.** An amount of sthg. available for use **2.** Goods in a shop or warehouse **3.** The animals on a farm; livestock **4.** The capital (money) that a corporation raises through the sale of shares **5.** A wooden part of a thing serving as its support, frame, or handle: *the stock of a rifle* **6.** A group having a common origin; family: *He comes from good stock.* **7.** The broth made from boiled meat or fish, used in preparing soup, gravy, or sauces **8.** The raw material from which sthg. is made **9.** The trunk or main stem of a tree **10.** A type or breed of plant or animal

stock v. **1.** To provide stock: *We stocked the kitchen shelves with food.* **2.** To keep regularly for sale: *The toy store stocks all kinds of toys.*

stock adj. **1.** In common use: *a stock answer* **2.** Kept on hand regularly for use or sale: *stock sizes of shirts*

stock-ade (stɑ-keʸd) n. **1.** A defensive barrier consisting of strong posts fixed upright in the ground **2.** A military prison

stock-bro-ker (stɑk–broʷ–kər) n. A person who buys and sells stocks and bonds for others

stock-car (stɑk–kɑr) n. An automobile of standard make, modified for racing

stock exchange (stɑk ɛks–tʃeʸndʒ) n. A place where stocks and bonds are bought and sold

stock-hold-er (stɑk–hoʷl–dər) n. One who owns stock in a company

stock-ing (stɑk–ŋ) n. A close-fitting knitted covering for the foot and leg

stock mar-ket (stɑk mɑr–kət) n. **1.** Stock exchange **2.** A market for stocks

stock-pile (stɑk–paɪl) v. **-piled, -piling** To build up a large supply

stockpile n. A reserve supply

stock-y (stɑk–iʸ) adj. **-ier, -iest** Solidly built and usually short —**stockily** adv. *He was stockily built.*

stock-yard (stɑk–yɑrd) n. A large, enclosed yard in which livestock is kept before being slaughtered or shipped elsewhere

stodg-y (stɑdʒ–iʸ) adj. **-ier, -iest 1.** Lacking excitement; dull **2.** Pompous; stuffy

sto-ic (stoʷ–ɪk) also **sto-i-cal** (stoʷ–ɪk–əl) n. A person seemingly indifferent to or unaffected by pleasure or pain. —**stoically** adv.

sto-i-cism (stoʷ–ə–sɪz–əm) n. The bearing of pain patiently

stoke (stoʷk) v. **stoked, stoking 1.** To stir up a fire **2.** To tend and supply fuel to a furnace

stole (stoʷl) v. Past tense of **steal**

stole n. **1.** A long, narrow band worn around the neck by some clergymen **2.** A long, wide scarf or similar covering worn by women

sto-len (stoʷ–lən) v. Past part. of **steal**

stol-id (stɑl–əd) adj. Not easily aroused or excited

stom-ach (stʌm–ək/ –ɪk) n. **1.** The large muscular bag in the body where food is received and is partly digested before it is passed on to the intestines **2.** The part of the body containing the stomach; abdomen: *He hit me in the stomach.* **3.** Liking: *I have no stomach for killing harmless creatures.*

stomach v. Endure: *I can't stomach these insults much longer.*

stom-ach-ache (stʌm–ək–eʸk) n. A pain in the stomach

stomp (stɑmp/ stɔmp) v. To stamp with the foot; tread heavily and noisily

stone (stoʷn) n. **1.** The material of which rocks are composed; a piece of rock **2.** A type of rock: *limestone* **3.** A precious stone; gem: *Dia-*

monds and rubies are precious stones. **4.** The hard seed of some fruits, such as cherries, peaches, and plums **5. leave no stone unturned** Do everything possible **6. a stone's throw away** A very short distance

stone (sto^wn) v. **stoned, stoning 1.** To throw stones at someone, esp. as a punishment: *People once were to be stoned to death for murder, adultery, and many other sins.* **2.** To remove the seeds or stones from fruit

stoned (sto^wnd) adj. **1.** Under the influence of drugs **2.** Very drunk

ston-y or **stoney** (sto^w–ni^y) adj. **-ier, -iest 1.** Containing stones or covered with stones: *stony ground* **2.** Cruel; unmerciful: *stony heart*

stood (stʊd) v. Past tense and part. of **stand**

stooge (stu^wdʒ) n. A person used by another to do a (usu. unpleasant) job

stool (stu^wl) n. **1.** A seat without a back or arms **2.** *fml. and tech.* Solid waste matter passed from the body

stool pigeon (stu^wl pɪ–dʒən) n. An informer

stoop (stu^wp) v. **1.** To bend forward and down: *She stooped over to pick up a coin on the floor.* **2.** To lower oneself morally and do a very wicked thing: *We should never stoop so low as to lie or cheat.*

stoop n. A forward bend of the head and shoulders: *My aunt walks with a stoop.*

stop (stɑp) v. **-pp- 1.** Cease doing anything: *Stop and consider God's wonders* (Job 37:14). **2.** End: *Stop doing wrong* (Isaiah 1:16). *Stop trusting in man* (Isaiah 2:22). **3.** To prevent: *You can't stop the rain from falling.* **4.** To close a hole or opening by filling it: *Sthg. is stopping (up) the pipe.* **5.** To stay somewhere for a short time: *She stopped at the bank for a few minutes.* **6.** To prevent from being given or paid: *The bank stopped payment on his check.*

stop n. **1.** An act of stopping or the state of being stopped: *We made several stops along the way for food, gasoline, etc.* **2.** A place where buses stop for passengers: *a bus stop* **3.** An object which holds a door open or shut: *a doorstop* **4.** A device that controls the pitch of a musical instrument

stop-page (stɑp–ɪdʒ) n. A blockage; obstruction; the act or state of being stopped

stop-per (stɑp–ər) n. A plug or cork for clos-

ing a bottle or drain

stop-watch (stɑp–wɑtʃ) n. A watch that can be stopped or started at any instant, indicating fractions of seconds, used in timing races and contests

stor-age (stɔr–ɪdʒ) n. **1.** The act of storing goods **2.** The condition of being stored **3.** A place for storing **4.** The cost of storing

store (stɔr) n. **1.** A building where goods are regularly kept and sold: *a grocery store* **2.** A supply for future use: *Squirrels make a store of nuts for the winter.* **3. in store** Coming in the future: *There's trouble in store for her.*

store v. **stored, storing** To save for future use: *We stored food in the pantry.*

store-house (stɔr–haʊs) n. A building where goods or supplies are stored

store-keep-er (stɔr–ki^y–pər) n. Someone who runs a retail shop

store-room (stɔr–ru^wm) n. A room where supplies are stored

stork (stɔrk) n. A large, long-legged wading bird with a long neck and a long bill

storm (stɔrm) n. **1.** A sudden burst of bad weather, esp. with heavy rain, lightning, thunder, fierce wind, etc.: *He [Jesus] rebuked the wind and the raging waters; the storm subsided, and all was calm* (Luke 8:24). **2.** A show of anger: *a storm of protest*

storm v. **1.** To attack with violence: *They stormed the city.* **2.** To show violent anger: *He stormed into the room, smashing things.*

storm-y (stɔr–mi^y) adj. **-ier, -iest 1.** Having storms; likely to have storms; troubled by storms: *stormy weather* **2.** Violent: *a stormy argument*

sto-ry (stɔr–i^y) n. **-ries 1.** An account of an event, or series of events, real or imagined **2.** A lie: *Don't tell stories.*

sto-ry *AmE.* **sto-rey** *BrE.* (stɔr–i^y) n. **stories** or **storeys** A floor or level of a house or other building: *The house she lives in has two stories.*

stout (staʊt) adj. **1.** Strongly built **2.** Brave; bold **3.** Fat

stout-heart-ed (staʊt–hɑrt–əd) adj. Brave; courageous

stove (sto^wv) n. An apparatus using wood, coal, gas, electricity, etc. for cooking and heating: *Most stoves in America use electricity*

or gas.

stow (stoᵂ) v. **1.** To pack: *Cargo was stowed in the ship's hold.* **2.** To fill by packing

stow-a-way (stoᵂ-ə-weʸ) n. A person who hides on a ship or vehicle to get a free ride

strad-dle (stræd-əl) v. -dled, -dling **1.** To sit or stand with the legs on either side of sthg. **2.** Have a leg on each side of a horse, bicycle, etc. **3.** To appear to favor both sides of an issue

strag-gle (stræg-əl) v. -gled, -gling **1.** To stray from or lag behind the main body **2.** To wander about —**straggler** n.

strag-gly (stræg-liʸ) adj. Growing or spreading out in an untidy way: *straggly hair*

straight (streʸt) adj. **1.** Without a bend or curve: *straight, not a curved line* **2.** Properly positioned: *Your tie isn't straight.* **3.** Correct: *Just to set the record straight, this is what really happened.* **4.** Serious: *It was difficult to keep a straight face when he fell in the mud.* **5.** *Infml.* for **heterosexual 6.** Continuous: *nine straight wins* **7.** Honest and upright; holy: *They [some people] have left the straight way and wandered off to follow the way of Balaam ... who loved the wages of wickedness* (2 Peter 2:15).

straight adv. **1.** In a straight line: *She can't drive straight.* **2.** Directly: *Go straight to your room!*

straight-en (streʸt-ən) v. **1.** To make or become straight, level, or neat: *He straightened the picture on the wall.* **2. straighten things out** To remove the confusion or difficulties

straight-for-ward (streʸt-fɔr-wərd) adj. Going about things in a very direct way

strain (streʸn) v. **1.** To separate a liquid from a solid by pouring through the fine holes of a sieve (a strainer) or other filtering agent **2.** To pull, draw, or stretch tight **3.** To make a great effort: *I had to strain my ears to hear what was said.* **4.** To damage a part of the body: *I strained a muscle in my leg.* **5.** *fig.* To force beyond acceptable limits: *Don't strain my patience.*

strain n. **1.** Excessive tension: *The cable broke under the strain.* **2.** A condition that tests the powers, esp. of mind and body: *The intensive study put a great strain on him.* **3.** Bodily injury from excessive tension **4. under a**

strain Suffering from emotional stress or pressure: *She's under a great strain at the moment because of all the illness in the family.*

strained (streʸnd) adj. **1.** Unnatural; forced: *a strained smile* **2.** Tired; nervous: *He seems strained after the meeting.*

strain-er (streʸ-nər) n. A device for separating solids from liquids, such as a sieve (sɪv) or a filter

strait (streʸt) n. **1.** A narrow passage of water connecting two larger bodies of water: *The Strait of Gibraltar* **2. straits** A position of perplexity or distress: *He's in desperate financial straits now that he has lost his job.*

strait-jack-et or **straight-jack-et** (streʸt dʒæk-ət) n. A garment of strong material used to bind one's body, to restrain a violent criminal or patient

strait-laced or **straight-laced** (streʸt-leʸsd) adj. Strict in the observance of moral or religious laws

strand (strænd) n. **1.** A length of sthg. soft and fine: *a strand of hair/thread* **2.** One of the fibers twisted together into a cord, rope, or cable

strand v. To bring into or be left in a difficult or helpless position

strand-ed (stræn-dəd) adj. Left in a helpless position or situation: *The stranded sailor was alone on a desert island.*

strange (streʸndʒ) adj. **1.** Unfamiliar; not previously known: *This is a strange country to me. I've never been here before.* **2.** Different: *That's a strange looking animal.* **3.** Uncomfortable or peculiar: *I have a strange feeling that we're being followed.* —**strangely** adv. *He's been acting very strangely of late.*

strang-er (streʸn-dʒər) n. **1.** A person with whom one is unacquainted: *The children were told never to talk to strangers.* **2.** A person in an unfamiliar place **3.** A foreigner, newcomer, or outsider: *Do not forget to entertain strangers, for by so doing some people have entertained angels without knowing it* (Hebrews 13:2).

stran-gle (stræŋ-gəl) v. -gled, -gling To kill by pressing on the throat to stop the breath

stran-gu-late (stræŋ-gyə-leʸt) v. -lated, -lating To become so constricted as to stop circulation —**stran-gu-la-tion** (stræŋ-gyə-leʸ-ʃən) n.

strap (stræp) n. A long, narrow strip of leather or other material, used esp. for holding sthg. together, fastening, or wrapping: *a watch strap*

strap v. -pp- 1. To fasten with a strap 2. To whip with a strap

strap-less (stræp–ləs) adj. Having no straps, esp. having no shoulder straps

strapped (stræpt) adj. *infml.* Without money

strap-ping (stræp–ɪŋ) adj. Large, husky, strong

stra-ta (stræt–ə/ streᶦt–ə) n. *pl.* of stratum

strat-a-gem (stræt–ə–dʒəm) n. A trick in war to deceive an enemy

strat-e-gy (stræt–ə–dʒiᶦ) n. -gies 1. The art of planning a campaign or large military operation 2. The art of managing an affair cleverly 3. Any plan of action —stra-te-gic (strə–tiᶦ–dʒɪk) also strategical adj. —strategically adv.

strat-i-fy (stræt–ə–faɪ) v. -fied, -fying To form or arrange in separate levels or strata —stratified adj. *stratified rock* —strat-i-fi-ca-tion (stræt–ə–fə–keᶦ–ʃən) n.

strat-o-sphere (stræt–ə–sfɪər) n. A portion of the earth's atmosphere about seven to thirty-seven miles above the earth's surface

stra-tum (stræt–əm/ streᶦt–əm) n. *pl.* -ta (–tə) 1. A natural or artificial layer or thickness 2. A band of rock of a particular kind

stra-tus (streᶦt–əs/ stræt–) n. -ti (–tiᶦ) A continuous horizontal sheet of cloud

straw (strɔ) n. 1. Stalks of grain, such as wheat, after threshing 2. A thin paper or plastic tube for sucking up liquids, etc.

straw-ber-ry (strɔ–beər–iᶦ) n. -ries 1. An edible, juicy, red fruit which grows on a low creeping vine 2. The plant bearing this fruit

stray (streᶦ) v. strayed, straying 1. To wander beyond established limits 2. To lose one's way 3. To wander about or meander; go astray

stray n. A lost animal

stray adj. 1. Lost from home: *stray dogs* 2. Happening by chance: *A man on the sidewalk was hit by a stray bullet.*

streak (striᶦk) n. 1. A line or mark of different color or texture than its background: *streaks of gray in her hair* 2. A tendency: *He has a mean streak in him.* 3. **a winning/ losing streak** Consecutive wins or losses

streak v. 1. To move swiftly: *The train streaked by.* 2. To cover with streaks: *a shirt streaked with dirt*

streak-y (striᶦ–kiᶦ) adj. -ier, -iest Having streaks: *streaky mirror*

stream (striᶦm) n. 1. A small river; a brook 2. A flow of water, air, or light: *a stream of water from the garden hose* 3. A flow of people or things: *a stream of traffic/people* 4. A current of public opinion: *It takes courage to go against the stream.*

stream v. To pour forth or issue in a stream; pour out: *fig. They streamed out of the sport's arena.*

stream-bed (striᶦm–bed) n. The channel occupied or formerly occupied by a stream

stream-er (striᶦ–mər) n. 1. A long, narrow ribbon-like flag 2. A long ribbon on a dress or hat 3. A newspaper headline that runs across the entire page

stream-line (striᶦm–laɪn) n. Any shape designed to offer a minimum of resistance to the wind —streamlined adj. *a streamlined car*

streamline v. -lined, -lining 1. To design with a streamlined shape 2. To make more simple or efficient

street (striᶦt) n. A road in a city or town that usu. has houses or other buildings on one or both sides: *I live on Maple Street.* —see AVENUE, BOULEVARD

street-car (striᶦt–kɑr) *AmE.* tram *BrE.* n. A public vehicle for many passengers, that runs along a metal track, and is usu. driven by electricity

strength (strɛŋθ) n. 1. Power in general, or a source of power: *God is our refuge and strength, an ever-present help in trouble* (Psalm 46:1). *Those who hope in the Lord will renew their strength. They will run and not grow weary, they will walk and not be faint* (Isaiah 40:31). 2. Moral courage or power: *The joy of the Lord is your strength* (Nehemiah 8:10). 3. Numerical force: *They came in strength (=a lot of them came) to see the big event.*

strength-en (strɛŋk–θən) v. To make or become stronger; give strength to: *Strengthen me according to your word [O Lord]* (Psalm

119:28). *May our Lord Jesus Christ himself and God our Father ... strengthen you in every good deed and word* (2 Thessalonians 2:16,17).

stren·u·ous (strɛn-yuʷ-əs) adj. Requiring great effort, energy, or exertion

strep throat (strɛp θroʷt) n. A throat infection caused by streptococci, characterized by fever and inflamed tonsils

strep·to·coc·cus (strɛp-tə-kɑk-əs) n. -coc·ci (-kɑk-iʸ) Any of various bacteria that occur in pairs or chains and are often a cause of disease

strep·to·my·cin (strɛp-tə-mai-sən) n. An antibiotic used esp. to combat tuberculosis

stress (strɛs) n. **1.** Importance or emphasis placed upon sthg.: *He puts too much stress on dressing neatly.* **2.** Pressure or mental anguish caused by difficulties in life: *He's under a lot of stress because of all the added responsibilities and extra work given to him recently.* **3.** Force of weight caused by sthg. heavy. *The heavily loaded trucks put too much stress on the bridge.* **4.** In speaking, the force or emphasis placed on particular syllables or words: *In "harmony," the stress is placed on "har."*

stress v. To emphasize; give importance to: *She stressed the fastening of seat belts, even for short trips.*

stretch (strɛtʃ) v. **1.** To draw out to greater length, or too far, or from one point to another: *He stretched the rubber band as far as it would go./ fig. He stretches my patience.* **2.** To straighten oneself to full length: *He stretched out on the couch.* **3.** To exaggerate: *He is always stretching the truth.* **4.** To extend or put forth: *He stretched out his hand.* **5.** To cause to make do or make last: *By eating less, maybe we can make this money stretch until we get paid again.* **6.** To flex one's muscles **7.** To prolong: *They stretched out their vacation from two weeks to three.*

stretch n. **1.** An act of stretching **2.** The ability to increase in length or width: *These socks have a lot of stretch.* **3.** A level area of land or water **4.** A continuous period of time: *On our way to China, we flew for a stretch of 17 hours without stopping.*

stretch·er (strɛtʃ-ər) n. A framework on which a disabled person can be carried

strew (struʷ) v. **strewed, strewn** (struʷn) **strewing** To scatter: *Trash was strewn all over the place.*

strick·en (strɪk-ən) adj. **1.** Wounded **2.** Afflicted with illness, misfortune, or sorrow: *poverty-stricken*

strict (strɪkt) adj. **1.** Observing or enforcing rules exactly: *She is a very strict teacher.* **2.** Complete; absolute: *strict loyalty/strict secrecy* —**strictly** adv.

stric·ture (strɪk-tʃər) n. **1.** An abnormal narrowing of a bodily passage **2.** An unfavorable remark or criticism

stride (straɪd) n. **1.** A long, measured step **2.** The space passed over by such a step **3.** A step forward; progress: *We made great strides today toward reaching our goal.*

stride v. **strode** (stroʷd), **strid·den** (strɪd-ən) **striding** To walk with long steps: *He strode angrily out of the room*

strid·den (strɪd-ən) v. Past part. of **stride**

stri·dent (straɪd-ənt) adj. Having a shrill or harsh sound or effect —**stridently** adv.

strife (straɪf) n. Trouble between people; conflict; struggle; quarreling: *strife between the two countries*

strike (straɪk) v. **struck** (strʌk), **striking** (straɪk-ɪŋ) **1.** To hit with force: *The bullet struck his helmet.* **2.** To knock: *He struck his head against a low hanging branch.* **3.** To put into action by hitting: *She struck a match and lit a fire.* **4.** To stop working because of a disagreement: *The union struck for better working conditions.* **5.** Finding sthg., esp. a mineral, under the earth: *They struck oil on my property.* **6. strike it rich** To win or inherit a lot of money; to become wealthy or wealthier, esp. suddenly

strike (straɪk) n. **1.** A period of time during which no work is done due to a disagreement, e.g., over pay or working conditions **2.** Success in finding sthg. esp. a mineral in the earth: *an oil strike* **3.** In baseball, a pitched ball that is in the strike zone or is swung at and not hit fair

strike·out (straɪ-kaʊt) n. An out made in baseball when a batter is charged with three strikes

strike out v, struck out In baseball, to be charged with three strikes or to be credited with a strikeout: *That batter struck out twice last night. That pitcher strikes out about ten batters in every game he pitches.*

strik-er (strai–kər) n. A person on strike

strik-ing (strai–kɪŋ) adj. That which attracts attention or interest: *a woman of striking beauty and charm* —strikingly adv.

string (strɪŋ) n. 1. A thin cord 2. A tightly stretched thin length of gut, wire, etc. used on a musical instrument, such as a violin, to give sound 3. no strings attached With no special conditions

string v. strung (strʌŋ), stringing 1. To put strings on a musical instrument 2. To thread beads on a string 3. *fig.* To string phrases/words together 4. High strung also highly strung *infml.*Very sensitive; easily excited, etc. 5. string sbdy. along *infml.* To give sbdy. hope of receiving sthg., with no intention of giving it to him: *He will never get the job they promised him; they're just stringing him along.*

string bean (strɪŋ–biᵞn) n. A green bean with long green pods which are eaten as food

stringed (strɪŋd) adj. Having strings: *The violin is a stringed instrument.*

strin-gent (strɪn–dʒənt) adj. Severe; strict —stringency n. —stringently adv.

string-er (strɪŋ–ər) n. A long, horizontal member in a framed structure or a bridge

string-y (strɪŋ–iᵞ) adj. -ier, -iest Like string: *Celery is quite stringy.*

strip (strɪp) v. -pp- 1. To remove the covering or parts of: *They stripped the wrecked car of everything that was worth taking.* 2. To remove one's clothing: *The nurse asked her to strip to the waist.*

strip n. A narrow piece of sthg.: *a strip of material*

stripe (straɪp) n. A line or band of color, among one or more other colors: *The flag has red and white stripes.* —striped adj. *a pinstriped suit*

stripe v. striped, striping To make stripes on sthg.

strive (straɪv) v. strove, (stroʷv), striven (strɪv–ən) or strived (straɪvd), striving (straɪv–ɪŋ) To struggle physically, morally, mentally, emotionally, etc.: *Paul said, "I strive always to keep my conscience clean before God and man"* (Acts 24:16).

stroke (stroʷk) n. 1. A blow; an impact 2. A sudden illness in the brain which can cause loss of the power to move, speak clearly, etc. 3. A single movement as made in swimming: *Bill won the event by just one stroke.* 4. A single movement or mark as made by a pen or brush: *fig. With a stroke of the pen, he signed away all his possessions.* 5. An inspired idea: *a stroke of genius*

stroke v. stroked, stroking To pass the hand over gently: *Stroke the cat very gently.*

stroll (stroʷl) v. To walk slowly, esp. for pleasure

strol-ler (stroʷl–ər) n. 1. A person who strolls 2. A light, often collapsible carriage in which a small child may sit upright

strong (strɔŋ) adj. stronger (strɔŋ–gər), strongest (strɔŋ–gəst) 1. Physically powerful 2. Healthy 3. Spiritually strong; firm in the faith, able to withstand all the crafty schemes of Satan and all the spiritual forces of evil: *Be strong in the Lord and in his mighty power. Put on the full armor of God [truth, righteousness, the gospel of peace, the shield of faith, the helmet of salvation, and the sword of the spirit, all of which are the word of God or are dependent upon his word]* (Ephesians 6:10-17). —see JESUS, BIBLE —strongly adv.

strong-arm (strɔŋ–arm) adj. Having or using unnecessary force: *strongarm tactics*

strong-hold (strɔŋ–hoʷld) n. 1. A strongly fortified place 2. An area where a certain religion, political party, etc. is strong

strop (strɔp) n. A strap for sharpening a razor

strop v. stropped, stropping To sharpen a razor on a strop

strove (stroʷv) v. Past tense of strive

struck (strʌk) v. Past tense and part. of strike

struc-tur-al (strʌk–tʃər–əl) adj. Of or concerning structure, esp. of a building —structurally adv. *Is this building structurally sound?*

struc-ture (strʌk–tʃər) n. 1. Sthg. consisting of many parts that are put together in a particular way: *the structure of the human body* 2. The way in which the parts are put together

to form a whole **3.** Sthg. constructed, as a building or a bridge: *The Sears Building in Chicago is the tallest structure in the world.*

structure v. **-tured, -turing** To organize (esp. ideas) into a whole form: *to structure one's education*

stru-del (stru^w–dəl) n. A pastry made of thin sheets of dough rolled up with a filling (usu. fruit or cheese) and baked

strug-gle (strʌg–əl) v. **-gled, -gling 1.** To make strenuous efforts against opposition **2.** To proceed with great effort

struggle n. A violent fight or bodily effort: *Our struggle is not against flesh and blood, but ... against the spiritual forces of evil* (Ephesians 6:12).

strum (strʌm) v. **-mm-** To play a stringed instrument casually or without skill

strung (strʌŋ) v. Past tense and part. of **string**

strut (strʌt) v. **-tt-** To walk in a proud way, trying to look important

strych-nine (strik–nam/ –nən/ –ni^yn) n. A very poisonous substance sometimes used in medicine as a stimulant

stub (stʌb) n. **1.** The short, blunt, remaining end of sthg. **2.** The piece of a check or receipt retained as a record **3.** The part of a ticket returned as a voucher of payment

stub v. **-bb-** To hurt one's toe by striking it against sthg. hard

stub-ble (stʌb–əl) n. The stumps of herbs and esp. grasses left in the soil after harvest

stub-born (stʌb–ərn) adj. **1.** Having a strong will; unwilling to yield: *He's too stubborn to take advice from anybody.* **2.** Firm; determined **3.** Not easily controlled or remedied: *a stubborn cold* —**stubbornly** adv. —**stubbornness** n.

stub-by (stʌb–i^y) adj. Short, blunt, and thick, like a stub

stuc-co (stʌk–o^w) n. **-cos** or **-coes** Plaster for coating exterior walls

stuck (stʌk) adj. **1.** Not able to move or be moved; fixed in place: *The window's stuck; I can't open it.* **2.** Unable to solve sthg.: *Can you help me figure this out? I'm stuck.* **3.** Fastened by sticky material: *Some chewing gum is stuck on that chair.*

stuck v. Past tense and part. of **stick**

stuck–up (stʌk–ʌp) adj. Snobbishly conceited

stud (stʌd) n. **1.** A male animal, esp a horse, kept for breeding **2.** One of a number of upright beams in a wall to which laths, paneling or siding is fastened **3.** A button-like object used to fasten men's formal shirts **4.** A small knob or nail head projecting from a surface as an ornament

stud-ded (stʌd–əd) adj. Covered or adorned with: *a star-studded sky*

stu-dent (stu^wd–ənt) n. **1.** A pupil; a person who is studying at a place of education or training **2.** A person with a specified interest: *a student of anthropology*

stu-di-o (stu^w–di^y–o^w) n. **-os 1.** The workroom of an artist, photographer, etc. **2.** A room or rooms where radio and TV programs are broadcast or recorded **3.** A place where motion pictures are filmed

stu-di-ous (stu^wd–i^y–əs) adj. **1.** Wanting to study; studying hard **2.** *fml.* Careful: *studious avoidance of anything unpleasant* —**studiously** adv.

stud-y (stʌd–i^y) n. **-ies 1.** The use of the mind to gain knowledge **2.** The act or process of learning about sthg. **3.** A room used for studying **4.** A branch of learning; subject

study v. **studied, studying 1.** To apply the mind to learning a subject: *He is studying English.* **2.** To look at or examine carefully: *He studied the road map carefully.*

stuff (stʌf) n. **1.** *infml.* The material of which sthg. is made: *What is this stuff?* **2.** Many different things: *Throw all that stuff in this box.*

stuff v. **1.** To pack full; to push (a substance) into a container or to fill with a substance: *See if you can stuff another blanket into that box.* **2.** To put stuffing inside a chicken **3.** To overeat: *He eats like a pig. He really stuffs himself.* **4. do one's stuff** *infml.* To do what one is able and expected to do

stuff-ing (stʌf–ɪŋ) n. **1.** Anything used as a filling for a cushion, pillow, etc.: *We used feathers as stuffing.* **2.** Special food (a seasoned mixture) placed inside a bird or piece of meat before cooking

stuff-y (stʌf–i^y) adj. **-ier, -iest 1.** Of a room, badly ventilated; having air which is not fresh **2.** Of ideas, dull, old-fashioned, etc.

—**stuffiness** n.

stul-ti-fy (stʌl-tə-taɪ) v. **-fled, -fying 1.** To make appear foolish or ridiculous **2.** To make futile or ineffectual —**stul-ti-fi-ca-tion** (stʌl-tə-fə-keʸ-ʃən) n.

stum-ble (stʌm-bəl) v. **-bled, -bling 1.** To trip in walking: *The baby stumbled and fell.* **2.** To walk unsteadily: *The drunk man stumbled along the street.* **3.** To make mistakes or hesitate in speech: *He stumbled several times in his pronunciation of people's names.* **4.** *spir.* To fall into sin: *Great peace have they who love your law [O Lord], and nothing can make them stumble* (Psalm 119:165).

stum-bling block (stʌm–blɪŋ blɑk) adj. An obstacle or hindrance to progress

stump (stʌmp) n. Anything that remains after the rest of it has been cut down, cut off, or worn down: *a tree stump*

stump v. **1.** To walk heavily: *He stumped angrily out of the room.* **2.** *infml.* To cause a person to be unable to answer; to puzzle or baffle: *The question completely stumped her; she didn't know the answer.*

stump-y (stʌm–piʸ) adj. **-ier, -iest** Short and thick

stun (stʌn) v. **-nn- 1.** To render dazed or senseless by a blow on the head **2.** To shock greatly; to stupefy: *We were all stunned by the news of his tragic death.*

stung (stʌŋ) v. Past and past part. of sting

stunk (stʌŋk) v. Past part. of stink

stun-ning (stʌn–ŋ) adj. *Infml.* Very attractive; impressive; beautiful

stunt (stʌnt) v. To prevent full growth or development: *Inadequate food could stunt the child's growth.*

stunt n. **1.** A spectacular feat displaying unusual skill and daring **2. publicity stunt** An action which gains attention: *The so-called feud between the two actresses was just a publicity stunt.*

stu-pe-fy (stuʷ–pə–faɪ) v. **-fied, -fying** To make dull or numb as if by drugs; to make unable to think

stu-pen-dous (stuʷ–pen–dəs) adj. Tremendous; very great

stu-pid (stuʷ–pəd) adj. Not intelligent or clever: *a stupid person/a stupid idea* —**stupidly**

adv. —**stu-pid-i-ty** n. (stuʷ–pɪd–ət–iʸ)

stu-por (stuʷ–pər) n. A state in which one cannot use the senses: *a drunken stupor*

stur-dy (stɜrd–iʸ) adj. **-dier, -diest** Strong and solid: *a sturdy suitcase*

stur-geon (stɜr–dʒən) n. A large food fish valued as a source of caviar.

stut-ter (stʌt–ər) v. To speak with involuntary hesitations and repetitions of sounds —compare STAMMER —**stutter** n.

sty, stye (staɪ) **sties, styes** n. **1.** An inflamed swelling on the eyelid **2.** A pen for pigs **3.** Any filthy place

style (staɪl) n. **1.** Fashion, esp. in clothing **2.** A way of speaking or writing **3.** Type, sort, kind, esp. of goods: *They sell every style of lamp in this store.* **4.** A hair style **5.** A fashionable manner or mode: *a dinner party in grand style*

style v. **styled, styling** To arrange or design: *Her hair is carefully styled.*

styl-er (staɪ–lər) n. **1.** An electrical appliance for setting or styling the hair **2.** A person who does hair styling

styl-ish (staɪ–lɪʃ) adj. Fashionable —**stylishly** adv. —**stylishness** n.

styl-ist (staɪ–ləst) n. A master of styles, esp. in writing or speaking —**sty-lis-tic** (staɪ–lɪs–tɪk) adj. —**stylistically** adv.

styl-ize (staɪl–aɪz) v. **-ized, -izing** To conform or restrict to a particular style

sty-lus (staɪ–ləs) n. **-luses** or **-li** (–liʸ) **1.** A sharp pointed instrument for writing or engraving **2.** A phonograph needle

sty-mie (staɪ–miʸ) v. **-mied, -mieing** or **-mying** To block; thwart

suave (swɑv) adj. Smooth-mannered; pleasant; elegant, polite and agreeable, esp. in a sincere way —**suavely** adv.

sub– (sʌb–) prefix **1.** Under or beneath: *submarine (an underwater ship); subway (an underground railroad, etc.)* **2.** Secondary: *the subplot in a play* **3.** Less than: *Subtropical/ substandard*

sub-con-scious (səb–kɑn–tʃəs) adj. Of the thoughts and feelings of the mind, of which the person himself is not aware

subconscious n. Mental activities just below the level of consciousness

sub·con·tract (sʌb–kɑn–trækt) n. A contract that assigns part of the obligations of an original contract to another firm or party

sub·cul·ture (sʌb–kəl–tʃər) n. A smaller cultural group within a larger cultural group

sub·cu·ta·ne·ous (səb–kyuʷ–teʸ–niʸ–əs) adj. Just beneath the skin —**subcutaneously** adv.

sub·di·vide (sʌb–də–vaɪd) v. To divide into several parts, esp. to divide a tract of land into building lots

sub·due (səb–duʷd) v. **-dued, -duing 1.** To conquer an enemy **2.** To keep under control, esp. a desire to do sthg. **3.** To make quieter

sub·dued (səb–duʷd) adj. **1.** Soft; reduced in strength of light or sound, etc.: *subdued lighting/a subdued voice* **2.** Unnaturally quiet in behavior: *He was quite subdued after hearing how badly he lost the election.*

sub·ject (sʌb–dʒɪkt) n. **1.** The person or thing being discussed or considered: *Don't change the subject; answer the question.* **2.** A course or area of study: *What is your favorite subject in school?* **3.** Sthg. represented in art: *The subject of the painting is the "Sinking of the Titanic."* **4.** A person who is under the rule of a monarch, or a member of a nation that has a monarchy **5.** *Gram.* A word, phrase, or clause in a sentence that denotes the doer of the action (Bob spoke to me), the receiver of the action in passive construction (Bob was hit by a stray bullet), or that which is described or identified (Bob is six feet tall). In each of the above sentences, "Bob" is the subject.

subject adj. **1.** Under the power or authority of someone else; not independent **2.** Likely or tending to have: *The prices are subject to change.*

subject (sʌb–dʒekt) v. **1.** To bring a person or country under control **2.** To cause (a person or thing) to suffer: *He was subjected to all kinds of ridicule.* —**subjection** n.

sub·jec·tive (səb–dʒek–tɪv) adj. **1.** Influenced by personal feelings, resulting from one's own thoughts, emotions, interests, etc., unaffected by the outside world; not objective or impartial: *You must try not to be subjective if you are on a jury in a court of law.* —see also

OBJECTIVE **2.** *Gram.* Of or designating the subject of a verb —**subjectively** adv. —**sub·jec·tiv·i·ty** (səb–dʒek–tɪv–ət–iʸ) n.

sub·ju·gate (sʌb–dʒɪ–geʸt) v. **-gated, -gating** To conquer; subdue; to bring a country into subjection

sub·junc·tive (səb–dʒʌŋk–tɪv) adj. Of the form of a verb used in expressing what is imagined, wished, or possible, such as "were" in "If I were you."

sub·let (sʌb–lɛt) v. **-let, -letting 1.** To rent all or part (of a leased property) to another **2.** To rent (a property) from a lessee **3.** To subcontract

sub·li·mate (sʌb–lə–meʸt) v. **-mated, -mating 1.** To express certain urges, esp. sexual ones, in constructive, socially acceptable ways **2.** To convert a substance from a solid state to a gas by heating it, then allowing it to cool and become solid again, in order to purify it

sub·lime (sə–blaɪm) adj. **1.** Of the most exalted, noble, or impressive kind **2.** Lofty in thought, expression, or manner

sub·lim·i·nal (səb–lɪm–ən–əl) adj. Being perceived or affecting the mind without one being aware of it

sub·ma·rine (sʌb–mə–riʸn/ səb–mə–riʸn) n. A ship that can travel under water

submarine adj. Under the surface of the water

sub·merge (səb–mɜrdʒ) v. **-merged, -merging** To go under the surface of water

sub·mis·sion (səb–mɪʃ–ən) n. The acceptance of someone else's authority: *her submission to her husband's wishes*

sub·mis·sive (səb–mɪs–ɪv) adj. Gentle and willing to obey orders: *Wisdom that comes from heaven is first of all pure, then peace-loving, considerate, submissive, full of mercy, and good fruit [deeds], impartial and sincere* (James 3:17). —**submissiveness** n.

sub·mit (səb–mɪt) v. **-tt- 1.** To surrender or yield (oneself) to the will or authority of another; agree to obey: *God opposes the proud but gives grace to the humble. Submit yourselves, then, to God* (James 4:6,7). *Submit to one another out of reverence for Christ* (Ephesians 5:21). **2.** To offer a plan, bid, etc. for

consideration

sub-nor-mal (sʌb-nɔr-ıᴜəl) adj. 1. Less than normal 2. Below the normal standard of intelligence

sub-o-ce-an-ic (sʌb-oʷ-ʃiʸ-æn-ɪk) adj. Situated or occurring on or beneath the ocean floor

sub-or-di-nate (sə-bɔrd-ən-ət) adj. 1. Of lesser importance or rank 2. Working under the authority or control of another person

subordinate n. A person in a subordinate position

subordinate (sə-bɔrd-ən-eʸt) v. -nated, -nating 1. To make subordinate 2. To treat as of lesser importance than sthg. else —**sub-or-di-na-tion** (sə-bɔrd-ən-eʸ-ʃən) n.

sub-or-di-nate clause (sə-bɔrd-ən-ət klɔz) n. A clause that modifies the principal clause in a sentence, as "since summer arrived" in "It has been very hot since summer arrived."

sub-orn (sə-bɔrn) v. 1. To incite secretly; to instigate 2. To induce to commit perjury —**sub-or-na-tion** (sʌb-ɔr-neʸ-ʃən) n.

sub-poe-na (sə-piʸ-nə) n. A written order to appear in a court of law

subpoena v. -naed, -naing To summon with a subpoena

sub-scribe (səb-skraɪb) v. -scribed, -scribing 1. To promise to accept and pay for a newspaper, magazine, etc. 2. To give one's assent or approval; to support a notion, belief, policy, etc. 3. To promise to give money to a charity or other cause: He subscribes to a lot of charities. —**subscriber** n.

sub-scrip-tion (səb-skrɪp-ʃən) n. 1. An act of subscribing 2. The amount of money given regularly in order to receive a magazine, newspaper, etc.

sub-se-quent (sʌb-sə-kwənt) adj. Following after; succeeding; later

sub-ser-vi-ent (səb-sɜr-viʸ-ənt) adj. Respectful or slave-like

sub-side (səb-saɪd) v. -sided, -siding 1. Sink to a lower level 2. Become less active; die down

sub-sid-i-ar-y (səb-sɪd-iʸ-ɛər-iʸ) adj. 1. Furnishing aid or support 2. Owned or controlled by a parent organization 3. Of or relating to a subsidy

subsidiary n. -ies One that is subsidiary, esp. a company controlled by another company

sub-si-dize (sʌb-sə-daɪz) v. -dized, -dizing To aid or assist with a money grant

sub-si-dy (sʌb-sə-diʸ) n. A grant or contribution of money, esp. one made by a government

sub-sist (səb-sɪst) v. To stay alive by means of

sub-sis-tence (səb-sɪs-təns) n. 1. Existence 2. Means of maintaining life: Their subsistence comes from the sea, that is, they fish for a living.

sub-stance (sʌb-stəns) n. 1. A material that can be seen or felt: Glue is a sticky substance 2. The main argument or general meaning of a speech, etc. 3. Wealth: a man of substance

sub-stan-tial (səb-stæn-tʃəl) adj. 1. Solid or strong: a substantial table 2. Important; of considerable size or value: a substantial sum of money —**substantially** adv.

sub-stan-ti-ate (səb-stæn-tʃiʸ-eʸt) v. -ated, -ating To give facts that are able to prove or support a claim

sub-sti-tute (sʌb-stə-tuʷt) n. A person or thing used or acting instead of another: There is no substitute for a man's soul nor for the word of God.

substitute v. -tuted, -tuting 1. To put a person or thing in, to take the place of sbdy. or sthg. else: We're out of potatoes, so we substituted rice. 2. To serve as a substitute: If you can't attend the meeting yourself, please find someone to substitute for you. —**sub-sti-tu-tion** (səb-stə-tuʷ-ʃən) n.

sub-ter-fuge (sʌb-tər-fyuʷdʒ) n. A cunning trick to get out of a difficulty, blame or failure

sub-ter-ra-ne-an (səb-tə-reʸ-niʸ-ən) adj. Lying or being underground

sub-ti-tle (sʌb-taɪt-əl) n. 1. A secondary title, as of a book 2. A translation of a foreign language at the bottom of a television or motion picture screen

sub-tle (sʌt-əl) adj. subtler, subtlest 1. Delicate; refined; hardly noticeable: a subtle difference in meaning 2. Clever or cunning; shrewd: a subtle way of making us spend more money —**subtleness** n.

sub·tle·ty (sʌt–əl–tiʸ) n. -ties The quality of being subtle

subt·ly (sʌt–liʸ) adv. In a subtle way

sub·to·tal (sʌb–toʷt–əl) n. The total of part of a group of figures

subtotal v. -taled or -talled, -taling or -talling To add up part of a group of figures

sub·tract (səb–trækt) v. To take away or deduct, as one number from another: *If you subtract 3 from 7, you'll have 4 left.* / *God says, "Do not add to what I command you and do not subtract from it, but keep the commands of the Lord your God ..."* (Deuteronomy 4:2). —**subtraction** n.

sub·trop·i·cal (səb–trɑp–ɪ–kəl) adj. Bordering on the tropics

sub·urb (sʌb–ərb) n. **1.** An outlying part of a city; a small community adjacent to a city **2. suburbs** A residential area adjacent to a city —**sub·ur·ban** (sə–bɜr–bən) adj., n.

sub·ver·sive (səb–vɜr–sɪv) adj. Likely to destroy or overthrow school authorities, a government, etc.

sub·vert (səb–vɜrt) v. To overthrow or ruin completely

sub·way (sʌb–weʸ) n. **1.** An underground passage, as for pedestrians, under a busy street **2.** AmE. An underground railroad system in the city Also **underground** BrE.

suc·ceed (sək–siʸd) v. **1.** To accomplish sthg. attempted; to do well: *Plans fail for lack of counsel, but with many advisors they succeed* (Proverbs 15:22). *Commit to the Lord whatever you do, and your plans will succeed* (Proverbs 16:3). —opposite FAIL **2.** To be the next to take a position or rank after: *Mr. Johnson succeeded Miss Brown as our teacher.*

suc·cess (sək–sɛs) n. **1.** The achievement of sthg. attempted: *As long as [the king] sought the Lord, God gave him success* (2 Chronicles 26:5). **2.** A person or thing that succeeds

suc·cess·ful (sək–sɛs–fəl) adj. Having succeeded; having reached one's goal: *a successful doctor* —opposite UNSUCCESSFUL —**successfully** adv.

suc·ces·sion (sək–sɛʃ–ən) n. **1.** A number of things following one after another: *a succession of victories* **2.** The act or process of following in order **3.** The act or right of suc-

ceeding someone in a position, esp. the act or right of succeeding to a title or a throne

suc·ces·sive (sək–sɛs–ɪv) adj. Coming one after the other —**successively** adv.

suc·ces·sor (sək–sɛs–ər) n. A person or thing that comes after another and takes the place of sbdy./sthg.

suc·cinct (sək–sɪŋkt) adj. Brief; concise; clearly expressed in few words

suc·cor (sʌk–ər) n. Help given in time of need

succor v. To give help in time of need

suc·co·tash (sʌk–ə–tæʃ) n. A cooked dish of corn and lima beans

suc·cu·lent (sʌk–yə–lənt) adj. Juicy and delicious —**succulence** n.

suc·cumb (sə–kʌm) v. To give up; to die

such (sʌtʃ) adj. **1.** Similar, of the same kind: *dogs and cats and all such animals* **2.** So much; so great: *Don't be such a pessimist.* **3.** Of a previously mentioned kind: *Such hard workers are not easy to find.* **4.** Used for emphasis: *It's such a hot day!*

such as (sʌtʃ æz) pron. The same kind: *Jesus said, "Let the little children come to me ... for the kingdom of God belongs to such as these"* (Mark 10:14).

suck (sʌk) v. **1.** To draw liquid into the mouth **2.** A similar action: *The girl was sucking her thumb.* **3.** To eat sthg. by holding it in the mouth and melting it: *sucking a cough drop* **4.** To pull or draw in a particular direction with a sucking action: *The vacuum cleaner sucked up all the dirt from the carpet.*

suck·er (sʌk–ər) n. **1.** A person or thing that sucks **2.** A disc, usu. of rubber that sticks to a surface by suction, used for fastening things to a wall **3.** infml. A gullible person who is easily cheated **4.** A shoot growing from an underground stem or root

suck·le (sʌk–əl) v. -led, -ling **1.** To nurse at the breast or udder **2.** To nourish or bring up

suck·ling (sʌk–lɪŋ) n. An infant or young animal that suckles

suc·tion (sʌk–ʃən) n. **1.** The act of sucking **2.** The act or process of drawing sthg. (as liquid or dust) into a space (as in a vacuum cleaner) by partially exhausting the air in the space

sud-den (sʌd–ən) adj. 1. Happening quickly and unexpectedly: *a sudden gust of wind* 2. Abrupt, steep: *a sudden descent to the sea* 3. Hasty: *a sudden decision* 4. Made or brought about in a short time: *a sudden cure* 5. all of a sudden Unexpectedly —suddenly adv. —suddenness n.

suds (sʌdz) n. The bubbles or foam formed by soap when mixed with water

sue (suʷ) v. sued, suing 1. To start a law case against sbdy.: *He's suing the company for a million dollars.* 2. To ask or beg for sth.

suede (sweʸd) n. Soft leather with a rough surface

su-et (suʷ–ət) n. The hard fat about the loins and kidneys in beef, mutton, etc. used in cooking

suf-fer (sʌf–ər) v. 1. To endure pain, misery or difficulty: *He suffered terribly following his surgery./This is what is written: "The Christ will suffer and rise from the dead on the third day"* (Luke 24:46). *We see Jesus ... crowned with glory and honor because he suffered death, so that by the grace of God he might taste death for everyone* (Hebrews 2:9). 2. To undergo a painful experience: *The army suffered heavy losses. Many were killed in battle.* 3. To become worse; lessen in quality: *He drank a lot of liquor; consequently his work suffered more and more.*

suf-fer-ance (sʌf–ə–rəns) n. Allowance or toleration for sth. not really wanted

suf-fer-er (sʌf–ər–ər) n. One who suffers, esp. from a stated illness

suf-fer-ing (sʌf–ə–rɪŋ) n. An experience of pain or difficulty: *St Paul said, "We rejoice in our sufferings, because we know that suffering produces perseverance..."* (Romans 5:3). *Rejoice that you participate in the sufferings of Christ, so that you may be overjoyed when his glory is revealed* (1 Peter 4:13; Matthew 5:10-12).

suf-fice (sə–faɪs) v. -ficed, -ficing To be enough

suf-fi-cien-cy (sə–fɪʃ–ən–siʸ) n. A supply which is enough —opposite INSUFFICIEN-CY

suf-fi-cient (sə–fɪʃ–ənt) adj. Enough: *Is $20 sufficient for a new hat?* —opposite INSUFFI-CIENT

suf-fix (sʌf–ɪks) n. *Gram.* A letter or combination of letters added at the end of a word to make a new word (such as -ful added to "help" to make "helpful") or as an inflection (such as -ing added to "teach" to make "teaching") —com-pare PREFIX

suf-fo-cate (sʌf–ə–keʸt) v. -cated, -cating 1. To die because of a lack of air 2. To suppress or stifle —suf-fo-ca-tion n. (sʌf–ə–keʸ–ʃən)

suf-frage (sʌf–rɪdʒ) n. 1. The right to vote 2. The vote

sug-ar (ʃʊg–ər) n. A sweet, usu. white substance obtained from plants, esp. sugar cane and sugar beets, used in cooking and for sweetening tea, coffee, etc.

sug-ar-y (ʃʊg–ə–riʸ) adj. 1. Tasting like or resembling sugar 2. Deceitfully sweet: *His sugary talk was only to deceive her into giving him some money.*

sug-gest (səg–dʒest) v. 1. To call forth an idea or possibility: *Her smile suggested that she appreciated his remarks.* 2. To propose a plan or theory to be accepted or rejected

sug-gest-i-ble (səg–dʒes–tə–bəl) adj. Easily influenced

sug-ges-tion (səg–dʒes–tʃən) n. 1. Sth. suggested 2. The act of suggesting: *It was her husband's suggestion that she quit her job.* 3. A slight trace: *There was just a faint suggestion of anger in her voice.*

sug-ges-tive (səg–dʒes–tɪv) adj. 1. Conveying a suggestion 2. Tending to convey an indecent or improper meaning: *suggestive remarks and glances*

su-i-ci-dal (suʷ–ə–saɪd–əl) adj. 1. Inclined to suicide 2. Extremely dangerous: *He was driving at a suicidal speed.*

su-i-cide (suʷ–ə–saɪd) n. The act of killing oneself intentionally; to commit suicide

suit (suʷt) n. 1. A set of clothing to be worn together, esp. a jacket and trousers or skirt 2. Clothing for a special purpose: *a diving suit* 3. Any of the four sets of playing cards that make up a deck 4. A court proceeding to recover a right or claim

suit v. 1. To satisfy; to meet the demands or needs of: *It's a small car, but it will suit our needs.* 2. To look right with: *That style doesn't*

suit her. **3.** To be fit for: *He wasn't suited for this kind of work.* **4. suit oneself** *infml.* To do as one pleases: *You can come with us or stay at home. Suit yourself.*

suit-a-ble (suᵂt–ə–bəl) adj. **1.** Right or appropriate for a given job or occasion **2.** Convenient: *Is the time of the meeting suitable to you?* —**suit-a-bil-i-ty** n. (suᵂt–ə–**bıl**–ət–iʸ)

suit-case (suᵂt–keʸs) n. A usu. rectangular and flat piece of luggage; a traveling case for carrying clothes

suite (swiʸt) n. **1.** A set of rooms, esp. in a hotel **2.** A set of furniture: *a living room suite* **3.** A set of musical pieces or extracts: *The Nutcracker Suite*

suit-or (suᵂt–ər) n. **1.** A man who is courting a woman **2.** A person bringing a law suit

sul-fur (sʌl–fər) n. *AmE.* **sul-phur** *BrE.* A light yellow, non-metallic element found in the earth, used in matches, gunpowder, etc.

sul-fu-ric (səl–**fyʊər**–ık) adj. Containing sulfur

sul-fur-ous (sʌl–fə–rəs) adj. **1.** Of or like sulfur **2.** Containing sulfur

sulk (sʌlk) v. To show anger or resentment by being silent

sulk-y (sʌl–kiʸ) adj. **-ier, -iest** Sulking or tending to sulk

sul-len (sʌl–ən) adj. **1.** Showing resentment in a gloomy and silent way **2.** Gloomy or dismal: *a sullen sky*

sul-ly (sʌl–iʸ) v. **-lied, -lying** To make less pure

sul-phur (sʌl–fər) n. Sulfur

sul-tan (sʌlt–ən) n. A ruler in certain Muslim countries

sul-tan-a (səl–tæn–ə) n. The status of the mother, wife, sister, or daughter of the sultan

sul-tan-ate (sʌlt–ən–ət/ –eʸt) n. **1.** The office, dignity, or power of a sultan **2.** A state or country governed by a sultan

sul-try (sʌl–triʸ) adj. **-trier, -triest 1.** Very hot and humid **2.** Sensual

sum (sʌm) n. **1.** The result obtained by addition: *The sum of 3 plus 6 is 9.* **2.** An amount of money: *I had to spend a large sum of money on car repairs this month.* **3.** An arithmetic problem **4.** The general meaning of sthg. written

or said; a summary

sum up (sʌm ʌp) v. **1.** To summarize **2.** To add together

sum-ma-rize (sʌm–ə–raız) v. **-rized, -rizing** To make or give a summary

sum-ma-ry (sʌm–ə–riʸ) n. A brief account giving the main points —**sum-mar-i-ly** (sə–**mɛər**–ə–liʸ) adv.

sum-ma-tion (sə–**meʸ**–ʃən) n. **1.** The act or process of summing up **2.** Final arguments in a law case

sum-mer (sʌm–ər) n. The season between spring and autumn when the sun is hot —**summery** adj. *a summery suit*

sum-mer-time (sʌm–ər–taım) n. The summer season

sum-mit (sʌm–ət) n. **1.** The highest point of a mountain, mountain pass, etc. **2.** A meeting between heads of state: *The President is attending the summit (meeting) in Geneva.*

sum-mon (sʌm–ən) v. **1.** To call together, to convene **2.** To send for; to request to appear **3.** To give an official order to appear in court **4. summon sthg. up** To call forth, rouse; draw (a quality) out of oneself, esp. with an effort: *She summoned up all her courage to make her first parachute jump.*

sum-mons (sʌm–ənz) n. pl. **-monses** An order to appear in a court of law

sump-tu-ous (sʌmp–tʃuᵂ–əs) adj. Expensive and splendid —**sumptuously** adv. —**sumptuousness** n.

sun (sʌn) n. **1.** The burning star in the sky, around which the earth and other planets revolve, and from which they receive light and heat **2.** The light and heat of the sun: *He's working out there in that hot sun.*

sun v. **-nn-** To place (oneself) in the sunlight: *She was sunning herself by the swimming pool.*

sun-bath (sʌn–bæθ) n. Exposure of one's body to the sun

sun-bathe (sʌn–beʸð) v. **-bathed, -bathing** To take a sun bath, sitting or lying in the sun to get a suntan

sun-beam (sʌn–biʸm) n. A beam or ray of sunlight

sun-burn (sʌn–bərn) n. An inflammation or blistering of the skin caused by overexposure to the sunlight —**sunburned** or **sun-**

burnt adj.

sun-burst (sʌn–bərst) n. **1.** A burst of sunlight **2.** An ornament resembling the sun with rays going out in all directions

sun-dae (sʌn–di^y / –de^y) n. Ice cream served with topping

Sun-day (sʌn–di^y / –de^y) n. The first day of the week and the day of Christian worship, since it is the day of the week on which Christ rose from the dead

Sunday school (sʌn–di^y sku^{w}l/–de^y) n. Christian teaching for children, and often for adults, on Sunday

sun-di-al (sʌn–daɪl / –dar–əl) n. An instrument for telling time by the shadow cast by a pointer on a sunny day

sun-dries (sʌn–dri^{y}z) n. *pl.* Various small items not named individually

sun-dry (sʌn–dri^y) adj. Various; several

sun-flow-er (sʌn–flav–ər) n. A large yellow flower that bears seeds used to make cooking oil

sung (sʌŋ) v. Past part. of sing

sun-glass-es (sʌn–glæs–əs) n. Eyeglasses with colored lenses to protect the eyes from the glare of the sun

sunk (sʌŋk) v. Past tense and past part. of sink

sunk-en (sʌŋ–kən) adj. **1.** That which has been sunk **2.** Having fallen lower than the surrounding surface: *sunken eyes* **3.** Below the surrounding level: *a sunken garden*

sun-lamp (sʌn–læmp) n. A lamp that gives off ultraviolet rays for therapeutic purposes

sun-light (sʌn–laɪt) n. The sunshine

sun-lit (sʌn–lɪt) adj. Lighted by the sun

sun-ny (sʌn–i^y) adj. -nier, -niest **1.** Not cloudy: *a bright sunny day* **2.** Cheerful: *a sunny smile*

sun-rise (sʌn–raɪz) n. The time when the sun first appears on the eastern horizon in the morning

sun-set (sʌn–sɛt) n. The time when the sun disappears below the western horizon and night begins

sun-shine (sʌn–ʃaɪn) n. Sunlight —**sunshiny** adj.

sun-spot (sʌn–spɑt) n. One of the dark spots that appear on the sun's surface from time to time

sun-stroke (sʌn–stro^{w}k) n. Illness caused by too much exposure to the sun

sun-tan (sʌn–tæn) n. The brownness of the skin caused by exposure to sunlight

sun-up (sʌn–əp) n. Sunrise

sup (sʌp) v. -pp- **1.** To eat or drink in small mouthfuls **2.** To eat one's evening meal

su-per (su^w–pər) adj. *infml.* **1.** Very fine; excellent **2.** Extreme; excessive

su-per– (su^w–pər–) prefix Very; beyond; above; too

su-per-an-nu-at-ed (su^w–pər–æn–yu^w–e^{y}t–əd) adj. **1.** Retired because of age or infirmity **2.** Too old for use or service **3.** Antiquated or obsolete

su-perb (sʊ–pərb) adj. Magnificent; excellent: *a superb view*

su-per-charge (su^w–pər–tʃɑrdʒ) v. To increase the power of an engine by using a device that supplies air or fuel at more than normal pressure

su-per-cil-i-ous (su^w–pər–sɪl–i^y–əs) adj. Haughty and scornful; having an air of superiority —**superciliously** adj.

su-per–du-per (su^w–pər–du^w–pər) adj. Excellent; superb

su-per–er-o-ga-tion (su^w–pə–rɛər–ə–ge^y–ʃən) n. The doing of more than is required —**super-e-rog-a-to-ry** (su^w–pə–rə–rɑg–ə–tɔr–i^y) adj.

su-per-fi-cial (su^w–pər–fɪʃ–əl) adj. **1.** On, or affecting the surface only: *a superficial flesh wound* **2.** Not thorough: *He has only a superficial knowledge of the subject.* **3.** *derog.* Of a person, not capable of deep thought or feeling: *a superficial person*

su-per-flu-i-ty (su^w–pər–flu^w–ət–i^y) n. A superfluous amount

su-per-flu-ous (sʊ–pər–flu^w–əs) adj. More than necessary —**superfluously** adv.

su-per-hu-man (su^w–pər–hyu^w–mən) adj. **1.** Beyond ordinary human power or ability **2.** Higher than humanity; divine

su-per-im-pose (su^w–pər–ɪm–po^{w}z) v. -posed, -posing To place or add sthg. on top of sthg. else

su-per-in-tend (su^w–pər–ɪn–tɛnd) v. To supervise; direct

su-per-in-ten-dent (su^w–pər–ɪn–tɛn–dənt) n.

superior

One who supervises a work crew, a school, a hospital, etc.: *the superintendent of education*

su-pe-ri-or (sʊ-pɪər-iʸ-ər) adj. **1.** Of higher rank: *Who is your superior officer?* **2.** Of high quality: *a superior product* —opposite IN-FERIOR —**su-pe-ri-or-i-ty** (sə-pɪər-iʸ-ɔr-ə-tiʸ) n.

superior n. A person of higher rank

su-per-la-tive (sʊ-pər-lə-tɪv) adj. The highest degree of comparison of an adjective or adverb: *"Big" becomes "biggest" in the superlative and "short" becomes "shortest."*

su-per-mar-ket (suʷ-pər-mɑr-kət) n. A large retail store selling mostly food in which customers wait on themselves, putting items in shopping carts and wheeling them to the check-out stand where they are paid for

su-per-nat-u-ral (suʷ-pər-nætʃ-ə-rəl) adj. Powers and events that cannot be explained through human or natural causes NOTE: Many things are called supernatural simply because people do not understand them. Sometimes magic is described as supernatural. Sometimes the word is used to describe the works of evil. Properly speaking, supernatural should only refer to God. Only the acts of God are beyond nature. All powers other than God are created ones. Thus, they are natural. God alone is supernatural. —**supernaturalism** n.

su-per-scribe (suʷ-pər-skraɪb) v. **-scribed, -scribing** To write or engrave on the outside or top of —**superscription** n.

su-per-script (suʷ-pər-skrɪpt) n. A small letter, number, or symbol written or printed high on a line of text

su-per-sede (suʷ-pər-siʸd) v. **-seded, -seding** To take the place of someone or sthg.: *These methods are being superseded by more modern ones.*

su-per-son-ic (suʷ-pər-sɑn-ɪk) adj. Faster than the speed of sound

su-per-sti-tion (suʷ-pər-stɪʃ-ən) n. A belief about why things happen, not based on reason. NOTE: Superstitions result from fear of the unknown, or from lack of knowledge.

su-per-sti-tious (suʷ-pər-stɪʃ-əs) adj. Strongly influenced by superstition —**superstitiously** adv.

su-per-struc-ture (suʷ-pər-strʌk-tʃər) **1.** Any construction above the main deck of a ship **2.** The part of a building above its foundation

su-per-vise (suʷ-pər-vaɪz) v. **-vised, -vising** To direct, control, or be in charge of

su-per-vi-sion (suʷ-pər-vɪʒ-ən) n. Oversight; direction: *She will be under supervision the first few weeks of her new job.*

su-per-vi-sor (suʷ-pər-vaɪ-zər) n. One who supervises —**su-per-vi-so-ry** (suʷ-pər-vaɪ-zə-riʸ) adj. *He works in a supervisory capacity.*

su-pine (sʊ-piʸn/ suʷ-piʸn) adj. **1.** Lying on the back with face upward **2.** Sluggish

sup-per (sʌp-ər) n. The evening meal

sup-plant (sə-plænt) v. **1.** To take the place of, esp. by force or scheming **2.** To replace one thing with sthg. else

sup-ple (sʌp-əl) adj. **1.** Able to bend easily without damage **2.** Limber: *a supple dancer* **3.** Showing mental adaptability

sup-ple-ment (sʌp-lə-mənt) n. **1.** Sthg. that supplies a want or makes an addition **2.** A continuation (as of a book) with corrections or additional material: *a supplement to the dictionary*

supplement v. To add to; to fill up the deficiencies of —**sup-ple-men-tal** (sʌp-lə-mənt-əl) adj. —**sup-ple-men-ta-ry** (sʌp-lə-mənt-ə-riʸ) adj.

sup-pli-ant (sʌp-liʸ-ənt) n. A person asking humbly for sthg. —**suppliant** adj.

sup-pli-cant (sʌp-lɪ-kənt) n. A suppliant

sup-pli-cate (sʌp-lə-keʸt) v. To make a humble entreaty, esp. to pray earnestly to God —**sup-pli-ca-tion** n. (səp-lə-keʸ-ʃən) *St. Paul says in his letter to Timothy: "I exhort therefore, that, first of all, supplications, prayers, intercessions, and giving of thanks be made for all men; For kings and for all that are in authority; that we may lead a quiet and peaceable life in all godliness and honesty"* (1 Timothy 2:1,2KJV).

sup-pli-er (sə-plaɪ-ər) n. A person or company that supplies goods

sup-plies (sə-plaɪz) n. *pl.* Provisions for a group of people over a period of time, kept

in storage and distributed when needed

sup-ply (sə–plaɪ) v. **plied, -plying 1.** To give sthg. that is needed: *Paul wrote to the Christians in Philippi: "My God shall supply all your need according to his riches in glory by Christ Jesus"* (Philippians 4:19). **2.** To furnish; provide sthg. for use: *Everyone in the military is supplied with a uniform.*

supply n. **-plies 1.** The providing of what is needed: *the water supply* **2.** An amount of sthg. provided or available: *a large supply of firewood*

sup-port (sə–pɔrt) v. **1.** To hold in position; to keep from falling; to bear the weight of: *Will that bridge support such a heavy truck?* **2.** To provide with food, shelter, and clothing: *He has a wife and eight children to support.* **3.** To approve of and encourage: *Do you support the workers' demand for shorter hours and more pay?* **4.** To be loyal to: *Which team do you support?*

support n. **1.** Necessary money to live on: *His part-time job was his family's only means of support.* **2.** Sthg. that holds sthg. in position: *One of the supports of the bridge collapsed.* —**supportive** adj.

sup-port-er (sə–pɔrt–ər) n. A person who loyally supports a team or activity, defends a principle (such as equal rights), a charity or other worthy cause: *He's been a supporter of this cause for years.*

sup-pose (sə–poʷz) v. **-posed, -posing 1.** To think probable: *I suppose he's in school right now.* **2.** To accept as true; believe: *It was commonly supposed that he was dead.* **3.** To be expected to do sthg.: *I'm supposed to walk two miles every day.*

suppose or **supposing** conj. Accepting as true: *Suppose the bridge is washed out, what will we do?*

sup-posed (sə–poʷzd) adj. Believed to exist or have certain identity; accepted as fact: *His supposed illness was just an excuse to stay home.*

sup-pos-ed-ly (sə–poʷ–zəd–liʸ) adv. According to supposition

sup-pos-ing (sə–poʷz–ɱ) conj. If: *Supposing it rains, what shall we do?*

sup-po-si-tion (sʌp–ə–zɪʃ–ən) n. What is sup-

posed: *This rumor is based on supposition, not on fact.*

sup-pos-i-to-ry (sə–pɑz–ə–tɔr–iʸ) n. A solid medicinal substance placed in the rectum, vagina or urethra and left to melt

sup-press (sə–pres) v. **1.** To put down by authority or force: *The riot was quickly suppressed by the police.* **2.** To prevent from being known or seen: *He suppressed his feelings of anger./to suppress the truth/The wrath of God is being revealed from heaven against all the godlessness and wickedness of men who suppress the truth by their wickedness* (Romans 1:18). —**suppression** n. —**suppressible** adj.

sup-pres-sant (sə–pres–ənt) n. A drug or other agent that tends to suppress rather than to eliminate sthg. undesirable

sup-pres-sor (sə–pres–ər) n. A person or thing that suppresses

su-prem-a-cy (sʊ–prem–ə–siʸ) n. **-cies** The state of being supreme: *All things were created by him [Jesus] and for him ... He is before all things, and in him all things hold together. And he is the head of the body, the Church; he is the beginning and the firstborn from among the dead, so that in everything he might have the supremacy* (Colossians 1:16,17).

su-preme (sʊ–priʸm) adj. **1.** Highest in authority, rank, etc.: *the supreme ruler of a vast kingdom* **2.** Most important: *Wisdom is supreme; therefore get wisdom* (Proverbs 4:7).

Su-preme Court (sʊ–priʸm kɔrt) n. The highest court of the US and of most states in the US

sur- (sɜr–) prefix Above; over: *surcharge/ surplus*

sur-charge (sɜr–tʃɑrdʒ) n. **1.** An excessive fee **2.** An excessive burden **3.** Sthg. officially printed on a postage stamp to give it new value or use

surcharge v. **-charged, -charging 1.** To fill to excess; to overload **2.** To print or write a surcharge on

sure (ʃʊər) adj. **1.** Certain; having no doubt **2.** Certain to do sthg.: *Be sure to keep the commands of the Lord* (Deuteronomy 6:17). **3. sure of oneself** Confident; believing in one's own abilities

sure-fire (ʃʊər–faɪr) adj. Certain to perform as expected

sure-foot-ed (ʃʊər-fʊt-əd) adj. Not likely to slip or stumble

sure-ly (ʃʊər-liʸ) adv. 1. Certainly; without doubt 2. With confidence or assur-ance

surf (sɜrf) n. The white water (foam) formed by waves when they break on the shore, etc.

surf v. To ride over breaking waves near the shore, esp. using a surfboard —surfer n.

sur-face (sɜr-fəs) n. 1. The outer part of sthg.: *the surface of the apple* 2. The top of a body of water or other liquid: *He swims under water more than on the surface.* 3. Qualities of sbdy./sthg. that are easily seen: *On the surface she seemed very calm, but she was as nervous as everyone else.*

surface v. -faced, -facing 1. To come to the top of water or other liquid: *The submarine surfaced.* 2. To cover a road, floor, etc. with a hard material

surface adj. Of mail, sent by land and sea, not airmail: *Sending this book by surface mail will take longer than airmail, but it will cost less.*

surf-board (sɜrf-bɔrd) n. A long, narrow board on which a person can stand to ride the waves

sur-feit (sɜr-fət) n. 1. Excessive amount; too much 2. Excessive indulgence (as in food and drink)

sur-feit v. To feed, drink, or indulge in sthg. excessively

surf-ing (sɜr-fɪŋ) n. The sport of riding on a surfboard

surge (sɜrdʒ) n. 1. A sudden increase of current in an electrical circuit 2. A strong wave-like forward movement 3. A sudden, powerful increase, as in emotion

surge v. surged, surging To rise suddenly or strongly

sur-geon (sɜr-dʒən) n. A physician who specializes in surgery

sur-ger-y (sɜrdʒ-ə-riʸ) n. -ies 1. A branch of medicine concerned with the correction of physical defects, the repair of injuries, and the treatment of disease, esp. by operation 2. Work done by a surgeon

sur-gi-cal (sɜr-dʒɪ-kəl) adj. Relating to, or associated with surgeons or surgery

sur-ly (sɜr-liʸ) adj. Bad-tempered or rude

sur-mise (sər-maɪz) v. -mised, -mising To guess or suppose

sur-mount (sər-maʊnt) v. To overcome or deal with problems, etc. successfully

sur-name (sɜr-neʸm) n. One's family name: *Tom Jones' surname is Jones.*

sur-pass (sər-pæs) v. To do or be better than sbdy./sthg.: *And I pray that you ... may have power ... to grasp how wide and long and high and deep is the love of Christ ... this love that surpasses knowledge ... that you may be filled to the measure of all the fullness of God* (Ephesians 3:17, 18).

sur-plice (sɜr-pləs) n. A loose white gown worn by clergymen, etc.

sur-plus (sɜr-pləs) n. Amount left over after using all that is needed or wanted: *We will have no surplus of food at the picnic; there will hardly be enough.* —opposite DEFICIT —surplus adj.

sur-prise (sər-praɪz/ sə-praɪz) n. 1. Sudden and unexpected event 2. The feeling or emotion caused by a sudden and unexpected event

surprise v. -prised, -prising 1. To cause sbdy. to feel surprise 2. To come up on (a person, an enemy, etc.) suddenly and without warning —surprising adj. —surprisingly adv.

sur-re-al-ism (sə-riʸ-ə-lɪz-əm) n. A modern movement in art and literature that tries to express what is in the subconscious mind by showing objects and events as seen in dreams —surrealist n. —sur-re-al-is-tic (sə-riʸ-ə-lɪs-tɪk) adj.

sur-ren-der (sə-rɛn-dər) v. 1. To yield to the power of another 2. To give up possession of sthg.: *The Apostle Paul said: "If I give all I possess to the poor and surrender my body to the flames, but have not love, I gain nothing"* (1 Corinthians 13:3). 3. To give oneself up, as to an emotion: *Unfortunately, many have surrendered to their craving for drugs.*

surrender n. The act of surrendering

sur-rep-ti-tious (sər-ep-tɪʃ-əs) adj. Done or acting secretly —surreptitiously adv.

sur-ro-gate (sɜr-ə-geʸt/ -gət) n. 1. A person appointed to act as a substitute or deputy 2.

In some states in the US, a judicial officer who presides in a probate court

sur-round (sə–raʊnd) v. To be in position on every side; encircle: *For surely, O Lord, you bless the righteous; you surround them with your favor as with a shield* (Psalm 5:12). *Many are the woes of the wicked, but the Lord's unfailing love surrounds the man who trusts in him* (Psalm 32:10).

sur-round-ings (sə–raʊnd–ɪŋz) n. All the objects, conditions, etc. that are around a place or person, esp. as they affect the quality of life: *As a child he had very uncomfortable surroundings.*

sur-tax (sɜr–tæks) n. An extra tax on sthg. already taxed

sur-veil-lance (sər–veʸ–ləns) n. A watch kept over a person or group, esp. over a suspect or prisoner

sur-vey (sər–veʸ) v. -veyed, -veying 1. To look at sbdy./ sthg. in general and from a distance: *to survey the countryside* 2. To investigate the opinions, ideas, etc. of sbdy., esp. by asking them questions: *They surveyed the city and found that eighty percent of the people had TV's.* 3. To make and record careful measurements of a piece of land, etc.

sur-vey (sɜr–veʸ) n. 1. A wide, general view: *A survey of English literature* 2. An examination of some land, esp. for a possible buyer 3. A plan or map of surveyed land

sur-vey-or (sər–veʸ–ər) n. A person whose job is to survey land

sur-viv-al (sər–vaɪ–vəl) n. 1. The state of continuing to survive: *Her survival was a real miracle.* 2. A person, thing, custom, etc. that has continued to exist from an earlier time: *That song is a survival from the 60's.*

sur-vive (sər–vaɪv) v. -vived, -viving 1. To continue to live in spite of an event that nearly caused death: *The children survived the accident in which their parents were killed.* 2. To continue to exist: *This custom has survived for centuries.*

sur-viv-or (sər–vaɪ–vər) n. A person who has continued to live after an event which brought him near death, or which caused other people to die

sus-cep-ti-ble (sə–sɛp–tə–bəl) adj. 1. Especial-

ly liable to be affected by: *Mary is susceptible to colds* 2. Of such a nature as to permit; *words susceptible of being misunderstood* 3. Easily affected emotionally —**sus-cep-ti-bil-i-ty** (sə–sɛp–tə–bɪl–ət–iʸ) n.

sus-pect (sə–spɛkt) v. 1. To believe to be true; to regard as probable 2. To distrust or doubt: *We suspected their motives.* 3. To believe sbdy. to be guilty without proof

sus-pect (sʌs–pɛkt) n. A person who is suspected, esp. of having committed a crime —see also SUSPICION

sus-pend (sə–spɛnd) v. 1. To hang from above, esp. so as to be free on all sides except at the point of support: *He [God] spreads out the northern skies over empty space; he suspends the earth over nothing* (Job 26:7). 2. To hold in liquid or air without falling or sinking: *dust suspended in the air* 3. To postpone or stop for a period of time: *to suspend judgment* 4. To bar temporarily from a privilege, usu. because of bad conduct: *The two boys were suspended from school.* —see SUSPENSION

sus-pend-er (sə–spɛn–dər) n. One of two supporting straps that pass over the shoulders and are fastened to the trousers

sus-pense (sə–spɛns) n. A state of uncertainty about what will happen: *Everyone was kept in suspense waiting for the judge to announce the winner.*

sus-pen-sion (sə–spɛn–tʃən) n. 1. The act of suspending; the state or period of being suspended 2. Sthg. suspended 3. A device by which sthg. is suspended 4. The mixture of a fluid with solid particles that do not sink, but remain suspended 5. In a motor vehicle, the system of springs, etc. supporting the frame on the axles

sus-pen-so-ry (sə–spɛns–ə–riʸ) adj. 1. Suspended 2. Fitted or serving to suspend sthg. 3. Temporarily leaving sthg. undetermined

sus-pi-cion (sə–spɪʃ–ən) n. 1. (a) The act of suspecting or state of being suspected: *He's under suspicion of arson.* (b) Mistrust: *He seems to have a great deal of suspicion of everyone.* 2. (a) A feeling about someone's guilt: *I have a suspicion (=I suspect) that he's not telling the truth.* (b) A belief about someone's guilt, with some basis for judgment: *We*

have our suspicions about who did this terrible thing.

sus·pi·cious (sə-spɪʃ-əs) adj. **1.** Having or showing suspicion; not trusting: *She is suspicious of strangers.* **2.** Causing suspicion: *a suspicious remark* —**suspiciously** adv. —see also SUSPECT

sus·tain (sə-steⁱn) v. **1.** To cause to remain strong: *A light breakfast will not sustain you until noon.* **2.** To maintain over a long period: *Our efforts must be sustained or we will fail.* **3.** To experience or suffer pain, losses, etc.: *The army, though victorious, sustained heavy losses.* **4.** To endure or withstand: *to sustain hardship* **5.** To affirm the validity or justice of: *The judge sustained the lawyer's objection.*

sus·te·nance (sʌs-tə-nəns) n. **1.** Food; nourishment **2.** A supplying with the necessities of life **3.** Sthg. that sustains or supports

su·ture (suʷ-tʃər) n. **1.** A line along which two parts are joined by, or as if by, sewing **2.** Material for sewing a wound together

su·zer·ain (suʷz-ə-rən/ -ə-reⁱn) n. **1.** A feudal lord **2.** A nation that has political control over another nation —**suzerainty** n.

swab (swɑb) v. **-bb-** To mop

swab n. **1.** A mop **2.** A wad of absorbent material, esp. for cleansing or applying medicine **3.** *Infml.* A sailor

swad·dling clothes (swɑd-lɪŋ kloʷz/ kloʷðz) n. Bands of cloth wrapped around an infant

swag·ger (swæg-ər) v. **1.** To walk with a conceited strut **2.** To boast or brag

swal·low (swɑl-oʷ) v. **1.** To cause food or drink to move from the throat to the stomach **2.** To use the muscles of the throat in making this same movement, esp. as a sign of nervousness **3.** *infml.* To accept as true: *to swallow a story* (=to believe it without doubting)

swallow n. **1.** An act of swallowing **2.** A small, long-winged migratory bird with a forked tail

swam (swæm) v. Past tense of **swim**

swa·mi (swɑm-iⁱ) n. A Hindu ascetic or religious teacher

swamp (swɑmp) v. **1.** To fill (a boat) with water, esp. causing it to sink **2.** Be over-

whelmed: *The postal service is always swamped with work during the Christmas season.*

swamp n. Wet, marshy ground

swan (swɑn) n. A large water bird that is usually white and has a long, slender neck and webbed feet

swank (swæŋk) adj. Dashing smartness as in dress or appearance —**swanky** adj.

swan song (swɑn sɔŋ) n. The last work, act, or achievement of a person

swap (swɑp) v. **-pp-** *infml.* To trade or exchange goods, positions, etc.: *Bob and I swapped jobs.*

swap n. An exchange: *It was a good swap; we both got what we wanted.*

swarm (swɔrm) n. **1.** A large number of insects or other organisms, esp. when on the move **2.** A large group of persons or animals

swarm v. **1.** To move in mass: *As the alarm sounded, children came swarming out of the building.* **2.** To be overrun: *The place was swarming with insects/ tourists, etc.*

swarth·y (swɔr-ðiⁱ/ −θiⁱ) adj. **-ier, -iest** Dark in complexion or color

swat (swɑt) v. **-tt-** To hit hard with a flat object, esp. in trying to kill an insect

swat n. An act of swatting

swath (swɑθ) n. **1.** The space covered by the stroke of a scythe or the cut of a mowing machine **2.** The section or strip so cut **3.** The grass or grain cut or thrown together in a line

sway (sweⁱ) v. **swayed, swaying 1.** To move or cause to move back and forth with a swinging motion: *The flowers swayed in the breeze.* **2.** To influence or change someone's opinions, ideas, etc.: *He was a powerful speaker and easily swayed the audience.*

sway n. **1.** A swaying movement: *The constant sway of the ship made him seasick.* **2.** A controlling influence: *educators under the sway of humanistic teaching*

swear (sweər) v. **swore** (swɔr), **sworn** (swɔrn), **swearing 1.** To curse, using the name of God or other sacred things without respect, as in anger, surprise, etc. This is a sin against God's holy commandment. "You shall not

misuse the name of the Lord your God" (Exodus 20:7). 2. To appeal to God as a witness of one's words: *Jesus said, "Do not swear at all; either by heaven, for it is God's throne; or by the earth, for it is God's footstool. Simply let your "Yes" be "Yes," and your "No","No". Anything beyond this comes from the evil one"* (Matthew 5:34-37). NOTE: This prohibition of swearing does not refer to official oaths, but to private conduct. The Christian should live a pure, holy, and honest life that, to those who live in the community and know him, his "Yes" and "No" are equivalent to an oath. His "Yes" and "No" are oath enough. 3. To take or cause to take an oath, as in a court of law. Taking an oath in court, swearing "to tell the truth, the whole truth, and nothing but the truth," was not prohibited by Jesus. He allowed himself to be placed under oath by the high priest (Matthew 26:63-64). 4. **swear sbdy. in** To cause to take an oath of loyalty at the official entrance into a position, office, etc.: *The President has to be sworn in publicly.* 5. **swear off** To renounce; give up: *He swore off smoking and drinking.*

sweat (swɛt) n. 1. Perspiration; the moisture which comes out through the skin to cool the body: *I was covered with sweat after doing my exercises.* 2. *fig.* An anxious, fearful state

sweat-er (swɛt–ər) n. A garment, often made of wool, worn over the upper part of the body to keep warm

sweat-y (swɛt–iʸ) adj. **-ier, -iest** 1. Covered, or smelly and damp with sweat: *a sweaty T-shirt* 2. Very hot, causing one to sweat: *sweaty work*

sweep (swiʸp) v. **swept** (swɛpt), **sweeping** 1. To clean a floor, sidewalk, etc. with a brush or broom: *She swept the floor.* 2. To move quickly and forcefully: *The youth swept through the doors./A disease is sweeping the country. (=be-coming more and more widespread)* 3. **sweep someone off his/her feet** (a) To overwhelm sbdy. with an emotion, esp. love (b) To persuade someone thoroughly

sweep-er (swiʸp–ər) n. Sbdy./ sthg. that sweeps: *a carpet sweeper*

sweep-ing (swiʸp–ɪŋ) adj. 1. Very great, very many: *sweeping reforms* 2. Too broad and general: *a sweeping accusation*

sweet (swiʸt) adj. 1. Tasting like sugar: *The cake is too sweet for me.* 2. Agreeable to the senses: *sweet taste/the sweet smell of orange blossoms* 3. Attractive and charming: *What a sweet little baby!* 4. Pleasant or attractive in manner: *a sweet smile/personality* —**sweetly** adv. —**sweetness** n.

sweet n. Sthg. that is sweet or contains sugar; candy

sweet corn (swiʸt kɔrn) n. A type of corn with kernels that are sweet and juicy when young

sweet-en (swiʸt–ən) v. To make sweet or sweeter: *The lemonade needs to be sweet-ened. (=it needs sugar)*

sweet-en-er (swiʸt–nər/ –ən–ər) n. A substance used to make food and drink taste sweet, esp. as a substitute for sugar

sweet-heart (swiʸt–hɑrt) n. 1. One who is loved by another 2. A lovable person

sweet pea (swiʸt piʸ) n. An annual climbing plant having sweet smelling flowers

sweet potato (swiʸt pə–teʸt–oʷ) n. A plant having a sweet, orange root that is cooked and eaten as a vegetable

sweet-talk (swiʸt–tɔk) n. Flattery

sweet tooth (swiʸt tuʷθ) n. A liking and craving for candy and other sweet food

swell (swɛl) v. **swelled, swollen** (swoʷ–lən) or **swelled, swelling** 1. To grow big or become bigger: *the crowd swelled* 2. To puff up: *Her ankle swelled (up) after twisting it.* 3. To fill or become filled with an emotion: *swelled with pride*

swell n. 1. A swollen part 2. A long wave that moves continuously without breaking

swell adj. *infml.* Very good: *That's swell./ You're looking swell./He's a swell guy.*

swell-head (swɛl–hɛd) n. A conceited person; one who has an exaggerated opinion of himself

swell-ing (swɛl–ɪŋ) n. Sthg. that is swollen: *Has the swelling of your ankle gone down?*

swel-ter (swɛl–tər) v. To suffer from oppressive heat —**sweltering** adj. *sweltering heat*

swept (swɛpt) v. Past tense and part. of

sweep

swerve (swɜrv) v. **swerved, swerving** To turn suddenly to one side

swift (swɪft) adj. Fast; quick in action: *a swift current* —**swiftly** adv. —**swiftness** n.

swig (swɪg) n. A large swallow, esp. of liquor; a gulp

swim (swɪm) v. **swam** (swæm), **swum** (swʌm), **swimming 1.** To move through the water by using the arms and legs or fins and tail **2.** *fig.* To seem to move round and round because of dizziness or an overwhelming amount of work: *Her head was swimming.*

swim n. An act of swimming: *Who wants to go for a swim?* —**swimmer** n.

swin-dle (swɪn-dəl) v. To cheat; defraud —**swindler** (swɪnd-lər) n.

swine (swaɪn) n. *pl.* **swine 1.** Any of the hoofed mammals of the family that includes pigs or hogs **2.** *infml.* A mean or greedy person

swing (swɪŋ) v. **swung** (swʌŋ), **swinging 1.** To (cause to) move to and fro (forwards and backwards): *swinging on the schoolyard swing* **2.** To turn quickly: *He swung around and twisted his ankle in his haste.* **3.** To sway or cause to sway back and forth: *The lamp was swinging from the ceiling.* **4.** To march or walk with free swaying movements: *He swung his arms vigorously as he walked.*

swing n. **1.** An act of swinging: *He took a swing at him.* (= *tried to hit him*). **2.** A seat suspended by ropes or chains, on which one moves backwards and forwards **3.** A large turnaround or change: *There's been a big swing in public opinion since the election.* **4.** A type of music played, esp. by a large band and marked by a steady, lively rhythm, simple harmony, and a basic melody: *Benny Goodman was called the "King of Swing."* **5. in full swing** At the most active part: *The party was in full swing.*

swipe (swaɪp) n. *infml.* A sweeping stroke: *He took two swipes at the ball and missed both times.*

swipe v. **swiped, swiping 1.** *infml.* To strike with a swipe **2.** *slang* To steal, esp. by snatching: *He swiped the old lady's purse.*

swirl (swɜrl) v. To rotate or spin as if in a whirlpool

swirl n. A whirling or circular motion or shape, etc.: *swirls of dust*

swish (swɪʃ) n. A hissing sound: *the swish of the horse's tail*

swish v. To (cause to) make a hissing sound: *The basketball swished through the net (without hitting the rim that held it).*

switch (swɪtʃ) n. **1.** A device for starting or stopping an electric current **2.** A complete shift or change in opinion, methods, or policy, etc.: *a switch of support from one political party to another* **3.** A small thin stick **4.** A device for causing a train to turn from one railroad line to another

switch v. **1.** To cause to turn on: *She switched on the lights.* **2.** To cause to change: *They switched jobs.*

switch-board (swɪtʃ-bɔrd) n. An apparatus with equipment for making telephone connections

swiv-el (swɪv-əl) n. A fastening that allows the thing fastened on it to turn freely —**swivel** adj. *a swivel chair*

swivel v. **-eled , -eling** or **-elled, -elling** To turn on a swivel: *She swivelled her chair around.*

swol-len (swoᵂ-lən) v. Past part. of **swell**

swoon (swuᵂn) v. To faint

swoon n. An act of fainting: *Some cold water will bring her out of her swoon.*

swoop (swuᵂp) v. **1.** To descend or pounce quickly, like a hawk, on its prey: *The gull swooped down and caught a fish.* **2.** *fig.* To make a sudden attack: *The police swooped down on the criminals.*

swoop n. **1.** An act of swooping **2. at one fell swoop** In a single movement or action: *The new manager got rid of several unwanted employees in one fell swoop.*

sword (sɔrd) n. **1.** A weapon with a long steel blade, that is sharp on one or both edges, used esp. in former times **2. to cross swords with** To oppose, esp. in argument

swore (swɔr) v. Past tense of **swear**

sworn (swɔrn) v. Past part. of **swear**

swum (swʌm) v. Past part. of **swim**

swung (swʌŋ) v. Past tense and part. of **swing**

syc-a-more (sɪk-ə-mɔr) n. **1.** A North American shade tree with smooth bark that is easy to flake off **2.** A European and Asian maple tree

syc-o-phant (sɪk-ə-fənt) n. A self-seeking servile flatterer —**sycophancy** n.

syl-lab-i-cate (sə-læb-ə-keʸt) v. **-cated, -cating** To syllabify —**syllabication** or **syllabification** (sə-læb-ə-fə-keʸ-ʃən) n.

syl-lab-i-fy (sə-læb-ə-faɪ) v. **-fied, -fy-ing** To divide or form into syllables

syl-la-ble (sɪl-ə-bəl) n. A unit of spoken language consisting of an uninterrupted utterance and forming either a whole word, as "cow", or a commonly recognized division of a word, as "cow" in "cowboy," or "sym" in "symbol"

syl-la-bus (sɪl-ə-bəs) n. pl. **-buses** or **-bi** (-baɪ/ -biʸ)An outline of the subjects that are included in a course of study

syl-lo-gism (sɪl-ə-dʒɪz-əm) n. A type of deductive argument consisting of two premises by which a conclusion is supported

sym-bi-o-sis (sɪm-biʸ-oʷ-səs) n. The living together of two dissimilar organisms, esp. when mutually beneficial

sym-bol (sɪm-bəl) n. **1.** Sthg. that stands for or represents a person, idea, etc.: *The cross is a symbol for Christianity.* **2.** A letter, figure, or sign that expresses a sound, a number, or a chemical substance: *"O" is the symbol for oxygen.* —**sym-bol-ic** (sɪm-bɑl-ɪk) also —**symbolical** adj.

sym-bol-ize (sɪm-bə-laɪz) v. **-ized, -izing** To be a symbol of; stand for; represent: *The dove symbolizes peace.*

sym-me-try (sɪm-ə-triʸ) n. **-tries** Correspondence in size, shape, and position of parts that are on opposite sides of a dividing line —**sym-met-ri-cal** (sə-mɛ-trɪ-kəl) adj. *The two sides of a person's face are almost symmetrical.* —**symme-trically** adv.

sym-pa-thet-ic (sɪm-pə-θɛt-ɪk) adj. Having or showing kind feelings toward other people; compassionate: *Live in harmony with one another; be sympathetic, love as brothers, be compassionate and humble* (1 Peter 3:8).

sym-pa-thize (sɪm-pə-θaɪz) v. **-thized, -thiz-ing 1.**To feel compassion; to express or feel sympathy **2.** To share in a feeling or feelings —**sympathizer** n.

sym-pa-thy (sɪm-pə-θiʸ) n. **-thies 1.** A sharing of another person's sorrow or trouble; compassion **2.** Agreement in feeling; understanding of the feelings of others

sym-pho-ny (sɪm-fə-niʸ) n. **-nies 1.** Harmony of sounds **2.** An elaborate musical composition for an orchestra, usu. having four parts (movements) —**sym-phon-ic** (sɪm-fɑn-ɪk) adj.

sym-po-si-um (sɪm-poʷ-ziʸ-əm) n. pl. **-posiums** or **-posia** (-poʷ-ziʸ-ə) n. A meeting for discussion of a particular subject

symp-tom (sɪmp-təm) n. An outward sign or indication of an inward, often bad, condition: *A fever is a symptom of illness.* —**symptom-at-ic** (sɪmp-tə-mæt-ɪk) adj.

syn-a-gogue (sɪn-ə-gɑg) n. **1.** A Jewish congregation **2.** The house of worship of a Jewish congregation

syn-chro-nize (sɪŋ-krə-naɪz/ sɪn-) v. **-nized, -nizing 1.** To move and take place at the same rate and exactly together: *The sound on the film must synchronize with the action.* **2.** To make agree in time: *We must synchronize our watches.*

syn-co-pate (sɪŋ-kə-peʸt) v. **-pated, -pating** To change the beat in music by putting the accent on notes not usually accented —**syn-co-pa-tion** (sɪŋ-kə-peʸ-ʃən) n.

syn-di-cate (sɪn-dɪ-kət) n. **1.** A group of persons who combine to carry out a financial or industrial undertaking **2.** A group of newspapers under the same management

syn-di-cate (sɪn-də-keʸt) v. **-cated, -cating 1.** To combine into or manage a syndicate **2.** To publish through a syndicate

syn-drome (sɪn-droʷm) n. A group of symptoms that together are characteristic of a specific disease

syn-er-gism (sɪn-ər-dʒɪz-əm) n. The joint action of agents that when taken together increase each other's effectiveness

syn-od (sɪn-əd) n. **1.** An assembly of church officials or delegates **2.** A church governing body **3.** A regional or national organization of congregations —**syn-od-i-cal** (sə-nɑd-ɪ-kəl) or —**syn-od-ic** (sə-nɑd-ɪk) adj.

syn·o·nym (sm–ə–nɪm) n. One of two or more words in the same language which have the same or nearly the same meaning: *"Little" and "small" are synonyms.*

syn·on·y·mous (sə–nɑn–ə–məs) adj. Having the same meaning or almost the same meaning:*"Big" is synonymous with "large."*

syn·op·sis (sə–nɑp–səs) n. -ses A condensed statement or outline; a summary

syn·tax (sm–tæks) n. Sentence structure; the way in which the words and phrases of a sentence are arranged to show how they relate to each other

syn·the·sis (sm–θə–səs) n. A combination of parts or elements into a whole: *Plastics are produced by a synthesis of various chemicals.*

syn·the·size (sm–θə–saɪz) v. -sized, -sizing 1. To combine into a new complex product 2. To produce by combining separate elements

syn·the·siz·er (sm–θə–saɪ–zər) n. 1. A person or thing that synthesizes 2. An electronic device that produces a variety of sounds by generating electric waves and combining them

syn·thet·ic (sm–θɛt–ɪk) adj. 1. Produced artificially, esp. by chemical means 2. Not genuine —**synthetically** adv.

syph·i·lis (sɪf–ə–ləs) n. A destructive, contagious venereal disease, affecting almost any body organ —**syph·i·lit·ic** (sɪf–ə–lɪt–ɪk) adj.

sy·ringe (sə–rɪndʒ) n. A device used for injecting liquids into or withdrawing them from the body

syr·up (sɪər–əp/ sɜr–) n. 1. A thick, sticky solution of sugar and water, often flavored 2. Concentrated juice of a fruit or plant

syr·up·y (sɪər–əp–iʸ/ sɜr–) adj. 1. Like or containing syrup 2. Too sweet; sentimental

sys·tem (sɪs–təm) n. 1. A set of things or parts forming a whole: *the nervous system* 2. An ordered group of facts, principles, beliefs, methods, etc.: *different systems of government* 3. An orderly way of doing things: *You have to develop a system if you're going to succeed.*

sys·tem·at·ic (sɪs–tə–mæt–ɪk) adj. According to a system; thorough: *a systematic search of the entire area* —**systematically** adv.

sys·tem·a·tize (sɪs–tə–mə–taɪz) v. -tized, -tizing To make into a system; arrange methodically

T, t (ti^y) n. **1.** The 20th letter of the English alphabet **2. to a T** *infml.* Exactly; perfectly: *The shoes fit her to a T.*

tab (tæb) n **1.** A short projected loop, flap, or tag (usu. paper or cloth) by which sthg. is gripped or which tells what sthg. is **2.** esp. *AmE. infml.* A bill **3. keep tabs/a tab on** *infml.* To watch closely: *Keep tabs on your spending.*

tab v. **-bb-** To label or designate

tab-er-na-cle (tæb–ər–næk–əl) n. **1.** The portable sanctuary carried by the Jews during their wanderings in the wilderness for forty years after their Exodus from Egypt (Exodus 25:8,9) **2.** A house of worship for a large congregation **3.** The receptacle for the consecrated elements of the Eucharist

ta-ble (te^y–bəl) n. **1.** A piece of furniture with a flat top supported by one or more legs **2.** A statement of facts and figures set out in columns: *an airplane timetable*

table v. **-bled, -bling 1.** To postpone consideration of a matter until a future meeting **2.** To put facts, figures, information, etc. into the form of a table

tab-leau (tæb–lo^w/tæ–blo^w) n. **-leaux** or **-leaus 1.** A silent and motionless group of people, props, etc. arranged to represent a scene **2.** A dramatic or picturesque scene

ta-ble-spoon (te^y–bəl–spu^{w}n) n. A spoon equal in size to three teaspoons, used esp. for serving

tab-let (tæb–lət) n. **1.** A small round solid piece of medicine; a pill: *an aspirin tablet* **2.** A writing pad consisting of sheets of paper glued together at one edge **3.** A flat block, esp. of stone or metal, with words cut into it: *When the Lord finished speaking to Moses... he gave him the two tablets of the Testimony [the Ten Commandments], the tablets of stone inscribed [written] by the finger of God* (Exodus 31:18). **4.** *spir. God says, "My son, keep my words and store up my commands within you [memorize them] ... write them on the tablet of your heart"* (Proverbs 7:1,3).

ta-ble-ware (te^y–bəl–wɛər) n. Dishes, utensils, etc. used for dining

tab-loid (tæb–lɔɪd) n. **1.** A newspaper printed on sheets that are half the size of those of larger newspapers **2.** Such a newspaper containing sensational news

ta-boo (tə–bu^w) n. **1.** The practice of setting things apart as forbidden for general use, as among certain primitive people **2.** A ban in any society against the use of anything

tab-u-lar (tæb–yə–lər) adj. Of or arranged in a table

tab-u-late (tæb–yə–le^{y}t) v. **-lated, -lating** To arrange in a table or a list —**tab-u-la-tion** (tæb–yə–le^y–ʃən) n.

tab-u-lat-or (tæb–yə–le^{y}t–ər) n. **1.** A person or thing that tabulates facts or figures **2.** A device on a typewriter for advancing to one or more set positions

tac-it (tæs–ət) adj. **1.** Not spoken **2.** Implied by actions or statements

tac-i-turn (tæs–ə–tərn) adj. Habitually silent or uncommunicative

tack (tæk) n. A short nail with a sharp point and flat head: *He hammered a tack into the wall to hang a calendar.*

tack v. To fasten to a solid surface with a tack: *He tacked a note to the bulletin board.*

tack-le (tæk–əl) n. **1.** In football or rugby, an act of stopping, or trying to stop, an opponent who has the ball **2.** The equipment used in a sport or occupation, esp. in fishing: *Be sure to bring your fishing tackle.* **3.** The ropes, rigging, etc. of a ship, used for working a ship's sails, raising heavy loads, etc.

tackle v. **-led, -ling 1.** To try to deal with a difficult situation: *How can I tackle this problem?* **2.** In football, to seize and stop an opponent and throw him to the ground

tack-y (tæk–i^y) adj. **-ier, -iest 1.** Of paint or varnish, slightly sticky, not quite dry **2.** Shabby

tact (tækt) n. Skill in dealing with people so as to say the right thing at the right time and not offend anyone —**tactful** adj. —**tactfully** adv. —**tactless** adj.

tac-tic (tæk–tɪk) n. A method of achieving one's goal

tac-tile (tæk–təl) adj. Of or having the sense of touch

tad-pole (tæd–po^{w}l) n. The larva of a frog or toad, which lives in water and has gills and

a long tail

taf·fe·ta (tæf–ət–ə) n. A stiff silk or synthetic lustrous fabric

taf·fy (tæf–i^y) n. A chewy, sticky candy made from boiled brown sugar or molasses

tag (tæg) n. **1.** A small piece of paper or other material fixed to sthg. to give information about it: *a name/price tag* **2.** A children's game in which one player chases and tries to touch the others

tag v. **-gg- 1.** To fasten a tag to sthg. **2.** *infml.* To follow a person closely and continually: *That boy is always tagging along behind his brother.*

tail (te^yl) n. **1.** The movable long growth at the back of an animal's body: *a dog's tail* **2.** Sthg. that resembles an animal's tail **3.** The rear or hindmost part: *the tail of the plane* **4.** **tails** **(a)** A formal evening costume worn by men **(b)** The side of a coin that does not have the head of a ruler on it

tail v. *infml.* To follow closely behind someone: *The police have been tailing the suspect for days.*

tail·gate (te^yl–ge^yt) n. A door or gate at the rear of a vehicle that can be let down

tailgate v. **-gated, -gating** To follow too closely behind another vehicle

tai·lor (te^y–lər) n. A person who makes, repairs, and alters garments, esp. for men

tailor v. **1.** To make an outer garment by cutting and sewing cloth, esp. to fit a particular person **2.** *fig.* To make to fit a particular need, purpose, etc.: *We can tailor our insurance to meet your needs.*

tai·lor–made (te^y–lər–me^yd) adj. **1.** Made by a tailor **2.** Anything suitable for a particular person, situation, etc.

tail·spin (te^yl–spin) n. **1.** The uncontrolled descent of an airplane in a spiral path **2.** *Fig.* A sudden mental or emotional upheaval

taint (te^ynt) v. **1.** To affect or become affected with sthg. bad **2.** To corrupt

take (te^yk) v. **took** (tʊk), **tak·en** (te^y–kən), **tak·ing 1.** To get or lay hold of: *He took the book from the shelf.* **2.** To use: *He takes the bus to school.* **3.** To occupy: *She took a seat.* **4.** To accept: *She took the seat I offered her.* **5.** To grab; seize: *They took the money and ran.* **6.** To hold

with the hands: *He took her arm and led her down the aisle.* **7.** To remove from someone's possession by mistake: *Who took my hat?* **8.** To remove intentionally: *Jesus is "the Lamb of God who takes away the sin of the world"* (John 1:29). —see JESUS, LAMB OF GOD **9.** To make a photograph: *He took my picture.* **10.** To inhale: *He took a deep breath.* **11.** To copy, making a few changes: *This play was taken from a book by Mark Twain.* **12.** To remove from a place: *After Jesus had spoken to them [his disciples], he was taken up into heaven* (Mark 16:19). **13.** To require, need: *It takes courage to do a thing like that.* **14.** To write down; record: *She took notes in class. /The nurse took my temperature.* **15.** To suppose; assume that: *I took his smile to mean that he agreed.* **16.** To act toward in a stated way: *I always take your advice seriously.* **17.** To do; perform; put into effect: *He took an oath in court./ He took a step forward* **18.** To cause to become: *He was taken ill and nearly died.* **19.** To eat or drink: *She took a bite out of an apple and took a sip of tea.* **20.** To endure: *He can't take criticism.* **21.** To commit oneself to the study of: *He took a course in music.* **22.** To allow to come in: *I was a stranger and you took me in.* **23.** To select or choose: *I'll take the one in the middle.* **24.** To charm or captivate: *She took him captive with her smile.* **25.** To subtract: *Nine take away five equals four.* **26.** To assume upon oneself: *He took full responsibility for her safety.* **27.** **take after (a)** To resemble: *Mary takes after her mother; she's always cheerful.* **(b)** *AmE.* To chase **28.** **take back (a)** To admit that one was wrong in what one said: *I'm sorry I was rude; I take back what I said.* **(b)** To agree to receive sthg. or sbdy. back: *The salesperson promised to take the shirt back if it didn't fit.* **29.** **take care** Be careful **30.** **take effect** To begin; to go into effect **31.** **take exception** To object to or take offense at **32.** **take for granted (a)** To accept sthg. as fact without questioning it: *I just took it for granted that you'd be there.* **(b)** To treat a person without consideration or kindness: *He never thanks you for your help; he just takes you for granted.* **33.** **take in (a)** To view: *His eyes took in the whole scene.* **(b)** To include: *Greater*

London takes in Middlesex. (c) To make clothes smaller: *She lost a lot of weight, so she had to take in all her clothes.* (d) To deceive or cheat: *Many people are taken in every day by swindlers and false advertising.* (e) To give shelter: *I was a stran-ger and you took me in.* 34. take off (a) To remove: *Take your coat off.* (b) To rise into the air: *The plane took off.* (c) To leave: *He took off for the beach (in his car).* (d) To rest from one's usual job: *I'm taking a day off.* 35. take over (a) To gain control or assume responsibility for: *When Mr. Green retired, his son took over the business.* (b) To do sthg. after sbdy. else stops doing it: *I drove the first hundred miles, then John took over.* 36. take to (a) To like: *John took to Mary as soon as they met.* (b) To begin doing a lot: *Allen has taken to drinking lately.* 37. take up (a) To begin to do; interest oneself in: *Ruth took up playing the piano.* (b) To fill: *His books took up a lot of space.* (c) To continue: *We'll take up our story where we left off yesterday.* (d) To complain or to ask about: *I'll take up this matter with the principal.* (e) To accept an offer: *I'll take you up on your offer of a job.* (f) To make clothes shorter: *She took up the hem in her dress.* (g) taken up with Very busy with: *He can't help you now; he's too taken up with his own problems.*

take-off (te^yk–ɔf) n. 1. The beginning of an airplane flight: *a smooth takeoff* 2. *infml.* An amusing copy of someone's behavior: *an amusing takeoff on a famous movie star* —see also TAKE OFF

take-o-ver (te^y–ko^w–vər) n. An act of gaining control, esp. of a business, company, or government: *a military takeover* —see also TAKE OVER

tale (te^yl) n. 1. A story: *A Tale of Two Cities* 2. A false story or gossip: *Have nothing to do with godless myths or old wives' tales; rather, train yourself to be godly* (1 Timothy 4:7).

tal-ent (tæl–ənt) n. A special ability or skill: *Tom has a lot of musical talent.*

tal-ent-ed (tæl–ənt–təd) adj. Skilled; gifted

tal-is-man (tæl–ə–smən) n. An object that is supposed to ward off evil and bring good luck; a charm

talk (tɔk) v. 1. To speak: *We talked for hours.* 2.

To gossip: *We shouldn't be seen together so much. People will talk.* 3. To express thoughts as if by speech: *People who are unable to speak can still talk by using the sign language.* 4. To discuss: *Let's talk business.* 5. To persuade: *He talked me into it.* 6. talk back to sbdy. To reply in a disrespectful way 7. talk down to sbdy. Speaking to sbdy. in a way that makes the speaker seem more important than the one to whom he is speaking 8. talk sbdy. out of sthg. To persuade sbdy. not to do sthg.: *She talked him out of seeking revenge.* 9. talk one's way out of To escape from trouble by talking 10. talk sthg. over To discuss thoroughly

talk n. 1. A conversation or discussion: *The Prime Ministers were having talks about economic problems.* 2. An informal speech: *The doctor gave a talk on preventive medicine.* 3. A particular manner of talking: *baby talk* 4. Empty or meaningless speech: *His threats were just talk. He won't do anything.*

talk-a-tive (tɔ–kə–tɪv) adj. Liking to talk a lot

tall (tɔl) adj. 1. Used when speaking of people or thin, narrow things such as buildings or trees, not short; having a greater than average height 2. Having the stated height: *He (Goliath) was over nine feet tall* (1 Samuel 17:4). —see HIGH

tal-low (tæl–o^w) n. Solid animal fats

Tal-mud (tæl–məd/ tɑl–məd) n. A collection of ancient Rabbinical writings that constitute the basis of religious authority of orthodox Judaism —**Tal-mu-dic** (tɑl–mu^wd–ɪk) adj.

tam-a-ble or **tame-a-ble** (te^y–mə–bəl) adj. Able to be tamed

ta-ma-le (tə–mɑl–i^y) n. A Mexican dish of ground meat and red pepper rolled in cornmeal dough

tam-bou-rine (tæm–bə–ri^yn) n. A percussion instrument consisting of a small hoop with parchment stretched over one side and jingling metal disks in slots around the hoop

tame (te^ym) adj. 1. Not fierce or wild; domesticated: *Cows are usually tame animals.* 2. *infml.* Dull; unexciting: *a tame football game*

tame v. tamed, taming To train sthg., esp. a wild animal, to be gentle: *All kinds of animals... are being trained and have been trained*

by man, but no man can tame the tongue. It is a restless evil, full of deadly poison (James 3:7,8). **—tamer** n. *a lion tamer*

tamp (tæmp) v. To pack down by repeated light blows

tam-per (tæm–pər) v. To interfere or meddle with sth. in such a way as to damage it: *The car crash was no accident; the brakes had been tampered with.*

tam-pon (tæm–pɑn) n. A plug of cotton for insertion into a body cavity, wound, etc. chiefly for stopping bleeding

tan (tæn) v. **-nn- 1.** To change an animal skin into leather **2.** To make or become brown, esp. by sunlight: *Mary was tanning herself in the sun.* **3.** *infml.* A beating or thrashing: *I'll tan your hide.*

tan n. **1.** A yellowish brown color: *He's wearing a tan shirt.* **2.** Suntan

tan-dem (tæn–dəm) n. A long bicycle with two seats and two sets of pedals, one behind the other

tandem adj. **1.** Consisting of things arranged one behind the other **2.** Working in conjunction with each other

tandem adv. Usu. of two people riding on a bicycle, one behind the other: *They rode tandem.*

tang (tæŋ) n. A strong or sharp taste, flavor, or smell **—tangy** adj. **-ier, -iest**

tan-ge-lo (tæn–dʒɛ–loʷ) n. **1.** A hybrid between a tangerine and a grapefruit **2.** Its fruit

tan-gent (tæn–dʒənt) n. **1.** A straight line that touches the outside of a curve but does not intersect it **2. go off on a tangent** Any sudden change of direction from the subject under discussion or the matter at hand **—tangent** adj.

tan-ger-ine (tæn–dʒɚ–riʸn/ tæn–dʒɚ–riʸn) n. A citrus fruit with dark orange skin

tan-gi-ble (tæn–dʒə–bəl) adj. **1.** Able to be felt by touching **2.** Real, definite **—tangibly** adv. **—tan-gi-bil-i-ty** (tæn–dʒə–bɪl–ə–tiʸ) n.

tan-gle (tæŋ–gəl) v. **-gled, -gling 1.**To twist or become twisted into a confused mass: *This string is so tangled that I'll never get it straightened out.* **—opposite UNTANGLE 2.** To entangle **3.** To be involved in a conflict: *The*

criminals tangled with the police.

tangle n. A confused mass of hair, thread, etc. **—tangled** adj.

tangle with (tæŋ–gəl wɪθ) v. To become involved in a fight or quarrel

tan-go (tæŋ–goʷ) n. **-gos** A dance of Spanish-American origin

tango v. To perform this dance

tank (tæŋk) n. **1.** A large container for holding liquid or gas **2.** A large, heavy, armored vehicle that has a gun and moves on caterpillar tracks

tank-ard (tæŋ–kərd) n. A tall, one-handled drinking vessel

tank-er (tæŋ–kər) n. A ship, aircraft, or truck built for carrying oil or other liquid in bulk

tan-ner (tæn–ər) n. A person who tans hides into leather

tan-ner-y (tæn–ə–riʸ) n. **-ies** A place where hides are tanned into leather

tan-nin (tæn–ən) n. Any of various substances of plant origin used in tanning and dyeing

tan-ta-lize (tænt–əl–aɪz) v. **-lized, -lizing** To torment someone by presenting sth. desirable to the view but continually keeping it out of reach **—tantalizing** adj.

tan-ta-mount (tænt–ə–maʊnt) adj. Equal to; equivalent in effect or meaning: *The general's request was tantamount to a command.*

tan-trum (tæn–trəm) n. A sudden burst of bad temper

Tao-ism (daʊ–ɪz–əm/ taʊ–) n. A religion developed from a Chinese mystic philosophy and Buddhist religion, emphasizing freedom from desire, effortless action and simplicity **—Taoist** adj., n.

tap (tæp) n. **1.** A light knock: *She felt a light tap on her shoulder.* **2.** A device for letting out liquid or gas from a pipe, etc.; a faucet **3.** A device put on a telephone to listen secretly to phone conversations **4. on tap (a)** Of beer, from a barrel **(b)** Ready for use when needed

tap v. **-pp- 1.** To strike gently or knock lightly: *He was nervously tapping on the table.* **2.** To draw liquid from a barrel **3.** To use or draw from: *to tap the country's natural resources* **4.** To listen to (telephone conversations)

through a secret telephone connection

tap danc·ing (tæp dɑːn–sɪŋ) v. Dancing in which the dancer beats time to the music with his or her feet, wearing special shoes

tape (te^yp) n. **1.** A narrow strip of paper, plastic, etc. used for sticking materials together: *adhesive tape* **2.** A narrow strip or band of cloth used for tying, etc. **3.** A piece of cloth, string, or sthg. similar, stretched above the finish line on a race track **4. (a)** A magnetic band on which sound can be recorded **(b)** A length of magnetic tape on which sound has been recorded

tape (te^yp) v. **taped, taping 1.** To fasten or tie a package, etc. with tape **2.** To measure with a tape measure

tape meas·ure (te^yp mɛʒ–ər) n. A length of plastic, cloth, or metal tape, marked with centimeters or inches for measuring

ta·per (te^y–pər) v. **1.** To make or become gradually narrower toward one end **2.** To decrease gradually

taper n. **1.** A slender candle **2.** A gradual decrease in thickness or width of a long object

tape-record (te^yp–rɪ–kɔrd) v. To record (sound) on tape by using a tape re·corder

tape re·cord·er (te^yp rɪ–kɔrd–ər) n. An electric machine for recording and playing back sound on magnetic tape

tap·es·try (tæp–ə–stri^y) n. **-tries** A heavy woven decorative fabric with a pictorial design

tape-worm (te^yp–wɜrm) n. A long flatworm that lives in the intestines

tap·i·o·ca (tæp–i^y–o^w–kə) n. A starchy food substance obtained from cassava and used in puddings

ta·pir (te^y–pər) n. A large tropical animal that looks like a pig but has a very long, flexible snout

tar (tɑr) n. A black substance, thick and sticky when hot, but hard when cold, used esp. for making and repairing roads

tar v. **tarred, tarring** To coat with tar

ta·ran·tu·la (tə–ræntʃ–ə–lə) n. A large, hairy, poisonous spider

tar·dy (tɑrd–i^y) adj. **-dier, -diest 1.** *AmE.* Late **2.** Slow in acting or happening —**tardily** adv. —**tardiness** n.

tar·get (tɑr–gət) n. **1.** Anything to aim at or shoot at with darts, arrows, bullets, etc., esp. a round board with circles on it, used in shooting practice **2.** An object of ridicule or attack: *Fred was the target of much ridicule.* **3.** A goal or object which one desires or strives to reach: *June 15th is our target for completing this task.*

tar·iff (tær–ɪf/ teər–) n. **1.** A list of prices **2.** A list of taxes to be paid on goods brought into a country

tar·nish (tɑr–nɪʃ) v. **1.** Of metals, to become dull or discolored **2.** *fig.* To spoil one's reputation

tar·pau·lin (tɑr–pə–lən/ tɑr–pɔ–lən) n. Waterproof canvas used to cover and protect things

tar·ry (tær–i^y/ teər–) v. **-ried, -rying** To delay or be late; linger

tar·ry (tɑr–i^y) adj. **-rier, -riest** Like tar

tart (tɑrt) n. A small pie containing jam, fruit, etc.

tart adj. **1.** Of taste, sharp **2.** Sarcastic

tar·tan (tɑrt–ən) n. A plaid design on woolen cloth

tar·tar (tɑrt–ər) n. A hard yellowish deposit that forms on the teeth

tar·tar sauce (tɑrt–ər sɔs) n. Mayonnaise mixed with chopped onion, pickles, etc. and served as a sauce with fish

task (tæsk) n. **1.** A set piece of work to be done; duty: *the task of mowing the lawn* **2.** A difficult or tedious undertaking **3. take sbdy. to task** To scold sbdy. severely

task force (tæsk fɔrs) n. A group of people, esp. a military force, gathered together with the purpose of performing a specific task

task-mas·ter (tæsk–mæs–tər) n. One who sets and supervises tasks

tas·sel (tæs–əl/ tɑs–) n. **1.** A bunch of loose threads or cords bound together at one end and hanging free at the other, used as an ornament on curtains, clothing, etc. **2.** Sthg. resembling this, such as the head of a corn plant

taste (te^yst) v. **tasted, tasting 1.** To try to determine the flavor of (food or drink) by taking a small quantity into the mouth **2.** To eat or drink, esp. in small quantities; to sample **3.** To have a certain taste: *This milk tastes sour.*

4. *fig.* To experience for the first time: *Taste and see that the Lord is good; blessed is the man who takes refuge in him* (Psalm 34:8). *[Jesus] suffered death, so that by the grace of God he might taste death for everyone* (Hebrews 2:9). —see JESUS

taste n. **1.** The sense that distinguishes between the salty, sweet, sour, and bitter qualities of sthg. placed in the mouth: *Sugar has a sweet taste.* **2.** A small quantity of food or drink: *I had a taste of the milk to see if it was sour or not.* **3.** *fig.* A short experience: *The escaped convict had just a taste of freedom before he was caught.* **4.** The ability to enjoy and judge beauty, art, music, etc.: *She has good taste in music.*

taste-ful (te^{y}st–fəl) adj. **1.** Conforming to taste **2.** Possessing good taste

taste-less (te^{y}st–ləs) adj. **1.** Lacking flavor **2.** Having or showing poor taste regarding style of clothing, furniture, music, etc.

tast-y (te^y–sti^y) adj. **-ier, -iest** Having a pleasant flavor: *a tasty meal*

tat-tered (tæt–ərd) adj. Ragged: *a tattered old coat*

tat-ters (tæt–ərz) n. Torn and ragged clothing

tat-tle (tæt–əl) v. **1.** To reveal the secrets of another **2.** To chatter idly

tattle-tale (tæt–əl–te^{y}l) n. One who reveals the secrets of another

tat-too (tæ–tu^w) n. **-toos 1.** A permanent mark or design made on the skin, esp. by the process of pricking and staining with an indelible pigment **2.** A call made (by bugle or drumming) to summon soldiers and sailors at night **3.** A continuous beating or drumming

taught (tɔt) v. Past tense & part. of teach

taunt (tɔnt) v. To try to provoke with scornful remarks or criticism

taunt n. A taunting remark

taut (tɔt) adj. **1.** Not slack; stretched tightly **2.** Showing signs of anxiety: *a taut expression on her face*

tau-ten (tɔt–ən) v. To make or become tight

tav-ern (tæv–ərn) n. An inn; a place licensed to sell liquor to be drunk on the premises

taw-dry (tɔd–ri^y/tɑd–) adj. **-drier, -driest** Showy and cheap; lacking good taste

taw-ny (tɔ–ni^y) adj. **-nier, -niest** Tan colored; brownish yellow

tax (tæks) n. A sum of money imposed on incomes, property, and sales, for the support of the government: *A new tax was imposed to help earthquake victims.*

tax v. **1.** To charge a tax on: *Tobacco is heavily taxed.* **2.** To strain or burden: *His constant complaining was taxing my patience.* —**taxable** adj.

tax-a-tion (tæk–se^y–ʃən) n. The act of taxing; money raised from taxes: *We must increase taxation if we are to spend more on education.*

tax-i (tæk–si^y) n. **-is** or **-ies** also **cab** or **taxicab** An automobile and driver that can be hired

tax-i v. **-ied, -iing** or **-ying** Of a plane, to move along on the ground before taking off and after landing

tax-i-der-my (tæk–sə–dər–mi^y) n. The art of preparing, stuffing, and mounting skins of animals

tax-on-o-my (tæk–sɑn–ə–mi^y) n. The classification, esp. of animals and plants according to natural relationships

TB *abbr.* Tuberculosis

tbsp. *abbr.* Tablespoon or tablespoons

tea (ti^y) n. **1. (a)** A shrub with evergreen leaves which grows mostly in China, Japan, India, and Sri Lanka **(b)** The dried leaves of this bush grown in Asia **(c)** The drink made by pouring boiling water onto these leaves **2.** A small meal, usu. served in the afternoon with a cup of tea **3.** A beverage similar to tea: *herb tea* **4.** one's cup of tea *infml.* The kind of thing one likes a lot: *Chess is his cup of tea.*

teach (ti^{y}tʃ) v. **taught** (tɔt), **teaching** To impart knowledge or skill, directly, or indirectly by example: *Jesus said, "Anyone who breaks one of the least of these [God's] commandments and teaches others to do the same will be called least in the kingdom of heaven, but whoever practices and teaches these commands will be called great in the kingdom of heaven"* (Matthew 5:19). —**teachable** adj. —**teachableness** n. —**teachability** n. —compare LEARN

teach-er (ti^y–tʃər) n. A person who teaches, esp. as a profession: *I have more insight than*

all my teachers, for I meditate upon your statutes [the word of God] (Psalm 119:99).

teach-ing (ti^y–tʃɪŋ) n. **1.** The work of a teacher **2.** Sthg. that is taught: *Jesus said, "If anyone loves me, he will obey my teaching"* (John 14:23).

teak (ti^yk) n. A kind of tree or its very hard wood, used for making furniture

tea-ket-tle (ti^y–kɛt–əl) n. A covered kettle with a handle and spout, for boiling water

team (ti^ym) n. **1.** A group of people who work, play, or act together **2.** Two or more animals pulling the same vehicle: *a team of oxen or horses*

team-ster (ti^ym–stər) n. One who drives a team or a motor truck, esp. as an occupation

tea-pot (ti^y–pɑt) n. A vessel with a spout, for brewing and serving tea

tear (tɛər) v. **tore** (tɔr), **torn** (tɔrn), **tearing 1.** To pull apart or into pieces by force: *How did you tear your shirt?* **2.** To remove by force: *A tornado ripped through our area, tearing the whole neighborhood apart.* **3.** To pull or snatch violently: *The thief tore her purse right out of her hand.* **4.** To rebuke angrily: *His brother really tore into him for wrecking his car.* **5.** To become torn: *This paper tears easily.* **6.** To move with great speed: *He jumped on his bike and tore down the street.* **7. tear sthg. down** To knock sthg. down; destroy: *They tore down the old buildings to make room for a new shopping mall.* **8. tear sthg. up** To destroy completely by tearing: *He angrily tore up her letter.*

tear n. A torn place in a piece of cloth or paper

tear (tɪər) n. A drop of liquid that flows from the eye during sadness or pain: *God will wipe away every tear from their [the followers of Jesus] eyes* (Revelation 7:17).

tear-ful (tɪər–fəl) adj. Weeping or likely to weep —**tearfully** adv.

tease (ti^yz) v. **teased, teasing 1.** To annoy persistently, esp. in fun, by tantalizing **2.** To make fun of someone by laughing at him and saying unkind things about him

teas-er (ti^y–zər) n. *infml.* **1.** Also **tease** A person who likes to tease **2.** A difficult question

tea-spoon (ti^y–spu^wn) n. **1.** A small spoon used for stirring tea, coffee, etc. **2.** A measurement used in cooking

teat (ti^yt/tɪt) n. A nipple on an udder or breast

tech-ni-cal (tɛk–nə–kəl) adj. **1.** Of or pertaining to a particular science, profession, or trade: *This nuclear physics book is too technical.* **2.** Of or related to a particular subject, esp. a scientific one: *technical training* —**technically** adv.

tech-ni-cal-i-ty (tɛk–nə–kæl–ə–ti^y) n. **-ties** A small detail or rule

tech-ni-cian (tɛk–nɪʃ–ən) n. A skilled worker in a technical field or process

tech-nique (tɛk–ni^yk) n. The way in which a skilled process is carried out: *different artistic techniques*

tech-nol-o-gy (tɛk–nɑl–ə–dʒi^y) n. **-gies 1.** The scientific study of mechanical arts and applied sciences **2.** The practical application of these subjects in industry —**tech-no-log-i-cal** (tɛk–nə–lɑdʒ–ɪ–kəl) adj. *The development of the steam engine was a great technological advance.* —**technologically** adv.

te-di-ous (ti^yd–i^y–əs) adj. Long and boring; tiresome —**tediously** adv.

tee (ti^y) n. **1.** A peg from which a golf ball is driven **2.** A starting place

tee v. **teed, teeing 1.** To place the ball on a tee **2. tee off (a)** To hit a golf ball off the tee **(b)** *Slang* To make or become irritated or disgusted

teem (ti^ym) v. To be present in large numbers: *The air was teeming with various kinds of insects.*

teen-age (ti^y–ne^ydʒ) adj. Of, for, or being a teenager: *teenage fashions*

teen-ag-er (ti^y–ne^ydʒ–ər) n. A young person of between 13 and 19 years old

teens (ti^ynz) n. The period of one's life from age 13 to 19

tee-ter (ti^yt–ər) v. To stand or move unsteadily

teeth (ti^yθ) n. *Pl.* of **tooth**

teethe (ti^yð) v. **teethed, teething** Of babies, to grow teeth

tee-to-tal-er (ti^y–to^wt–əl–ər) n. A person who abstains totally from the drinking of alcoholic beverages

tel-, tele-, or **telo-** comb. form **1.** At or over a

distance 2. Of or by television: *telecast*

tel-e-cast (tɛl–ə–kæst) v. -cast or -casted, -casting To broadcast by television

tel-e-gram (tɛl–ə–græm) n. A message sent by telegraph

tel-e-graph (tɛl–ə–græf) n. A method of sending messages along wire by electric signals

telegraph v. To send by telegraph: *We telegraphed the news to her.*

te-lep-a-thy (tə–lɛp–ə–θiʸ) n. Supposed communication between two minds without the use of sight, hearing, or other bodily senses

tel-e-phone (tɛl–ə–foʷn) n. also **phone** 1. A system by which sound (esp. speech) can be transmitted over long distances by wire or radio 2. An instrument used for this purpose, with a mouthpiece and a receiver, and a bell to indicate an incoming call: *Some people do almost all their business by telephone.*

telephone also **phone** *infml.* v. -phoned, -phoning To speak to (someone) by telephone: *When I was in Singapore, I telephoned my wife in Los Angeles.*

tel-e-pho-to (tɛl–ə–foʷ–toʷ) adj. Of a camera lens which gives a large image of a distant object

tel-e-scope (tɛl–ə–skoʷp) n. A long tube-shaped instrument equipped with lenses for viewing distant objects, esp. celestial bodies

tel-e-scope v. -scoped, -scoping To push or be pushed together so that one thing slides inside another

tel-e-scop-ic (tɛl–ə–skɑp–ɪk) adj. 1. Of or relating to a telescope 2. Seen only by a telescope 3. Able to discern objects at a distance 4. Made of parts that slide over one another to make the whole thing shorter

tel-e-vise (tɛl–ə–vaɪz) v. -vised, -vising To broadcast by television: *The football game was televised.*

tel-e-vi-sion (tɛl–ə–vɪʒ–ən) also **TV** *AmE.* also **telly** *BrE. infml.* n. 1. The sending and receiving of images of objects, with accompanying sound by electronic means 2. The news, movies, sporting events, etc. shown in this way 3. Also **television set** The receiving apparatus used in this process

tell (tɛl) v. **told** (toʷld), **telling** 1. To express by speech or writing 2. To show, make known: *This green light tells us we can go now.* 3. To recognize; know: *It was so dark I couldn't tell it was you.* 4. To be noticeable; have an effect: *In the last days of the campaign, his tiredness began to tell on him.* 5. **all told** Altogether; when all have been counted 6. **tell the time** To read the time from a clock or watch 7. **tell off** To rebuke severely 8. **there's no telling** It's impossible to know 9. **you can never tell** Who knows for sure? One can not be sure about sth.

tell-er (tɛl–ər) n. 1. A person employed by a bank to receive and pay out money over the counter 2. A person who counts votes at an election

tell-ing (tɛl–ŋ) adj. 1. Having force or effect: *a telling argument* 2. Sthg. that shows one's feeling or opinions: *a telling remark*

tell-tale (tɛl–teʸl) adj. Revealing; betraying

te-mer-i-ty (tə–mɛər–ət–iʸ) n. Boldness

tem-per (tɛm–pər) n. 1. A state of mind or feelings 2. An angry state of mind: *Better a patient man than a warrior, a man who controls his temper than one who takes a city* (Proverbs 16:32). 3. **keep one's temper** To stay calm 4. **lose one's temper** To become angry

temper v. 1. *tech.* To give strength or toughness to (steel, e.g.) by heating and then cooling it 2. *fml.* To make less severe: *justice tempered with mercy*

tem-per-a-ment (tɛm–pə–rə–mənt) n. A person's nature or usual way of acting: *an easygoing temperament*

tem-per-a-men-tal (tɛm–pə–rə–mɛn–təl) adj. Excessively irritable or sensitive; having fits of excitable or moody behavior: *He was so temperamental that no one would work with him.* —temperamentally adv.

tem-per-ance (tɛm–pə–rəns/ tɛm–prəns) n. Habitual moderation in the indulgence of appetites or passions, esp. total abstinence from drinking alcoholic beverages

tem-per-ate (tɛm–pə–rət/ tɛm–prət) adj. 1. Practicing or showing self-control: *temperate behavior* 2. Free from very high or very low temperatures: *a temperate climate*

Temperate Zone (tɛm–pə–rət zoʷn/ tɛm–prət)

n. The region between the Tropic of Cancer and the Arctic Circle or between the Tropic of Capricorn and the Antarctic Circle, where most of the world's inhabitants dwell

tem·per·a·ture (tɛm–pə–rə–tʃər) n. **1.** A measure of the warmth or coldness of the air or water of any body or object: *Seventy degrees Fahrenheit is a comfortable temperature for most people.* **2. to have or run a temperature** To have a higher than normal body temperature, due to illness or fever **3. take someone's temperature** To measure the temperature of someone's body with a thermometer

tem·pered (tɛm–pərd) adj. **1.** Having a certain temper or disposition **2.** Lessened or mitigated

tem·per tan·trum (tɛm–pər tæn–trəm) n. A sudden burst of bad temper

tem·pest (tɛm–pəst) n. A violent storm, esp. one accompanied by hail, rain, or snow —**tem·pes·tu·ous** (tɛm–pɛs–tʃuʷ–əs) adj. *a tempestuous wind/ fig. a tempestuous meeting*

tem·plate or **tem·plet** (tɛm–plət) n. A pattern used as a guide in mechanical work

tem·ple (tɛm–pəl) n. **1.** A building erected in honor of the true God or in honor of some imaginary deity and used as a place of worship. The most celebrated and magnificent temple erected to the true God was that of Solomon in Jerusalem about 1,000 B.C. (1 Chronicles 6:10), rebuilt under the supervision of Zerubbabel and Jeshua about 520 B.C. (Ezra 3:8-9), enlarged and beautified by Herod the Great, beginning about 20 B.C. (John 2:20). Among the most celebrated of the ancient pagan temples were those of Diana (Artemis) at Ephesus (Acts 19:27) and Jupiter at Thebes. The tabernacle at Shiloh was referred to as a temple long before Solomon's temple was built. **2.** A church; an edifice erected among Christians as a place of worship **3.** Heaven: *The Lord is in his holy temple; the Lord is on his heavenly throne* (Psalm 11:4). **4.** The body of Jesus: *Jesus told the Jews, "Destroy this temple and I will raise it again in three days." But the temple he spoke of was his own body* (John

2:19,20). **5.** Anyone filled with the Holy Spirit: *Writing to Christians, Paul said, "Don't you know that you yourselves are God's temple and that God's spirit lives in you? If anyone destroys God's temple, God will destroy him; for God's temple is sacred, and you are that temple* (1 Corinthians 3:16,17). *We are the temple of the living God* (2 Corinthians 6:16). **6.** The whole Christian Church; the family of God (Ephesians 2:19-22). **7.** God himself: *I did not see a temple in the city (the New Jerusalem), because the Lord God Almighty and the Lamb (Jesus Christ) are its temple* (Revelation 21:22). **8.** Wherever God is: *The God who made the world and everything in it is the Lord of heaven and earth and does not live in temples built by hands* (Acts 17:24).

tem·ple n. One of the flat places on each side of the forehead

tem·po (tɛm–poʷ) n. **-pos** or **-pi** (piʸ) **1.** The speed at which a piece of music is played or sung **2.** The speed or rate of any activity: *the fast tempo of the city*

tem·po·ral (tɛm–pə–rəl) adj. **1.** Of or relating to this present world; worldly, not sacred **2.** Of or pertaining to time as opposed to space

tem·po·rar·y (tɛm–pə–rɜər–iʸ) adj. Lasting only for a limited time; not permanent —**tem·po·rar·i·ly** (tɛm–pə–rɛər–ə–liʸ) adv.

tem·po·rize (tɛm–pə–raɪz) v. **-rized, -rizing 1.** To adapt one's actions to the time or to the dominant opinion; compromise **2.** To draw out matters so as to gain time —**temporizer** n.

tempt (tɛmpt) v. **1.** To try to persuade sbdy. to do sthg. sinful: *When tempted, no one should say, "God is tempting me." For God cannot be tempted by evil, nor does he tempt anyone; but each one is tempted when by his own evil desire, he is dragged away and enticed* (James 1:13,14). *[Jesus Christ] has been tempted in every way, just as we are — yet was without sin* (Hebrews 4:15). **2.** To attract: *The hot weather tempted us to go swimming.*

temp·ta·tion (tɛmp–teʸ–ʃən) n. **1.** The act of tempting or the state of being tempted: *the temptation to cheat on the examination* **2.** Sthg. that attracts or tempts: *the temptation of the*

big city/ Pray so that you will not fall into temptation (Matthew 26:41). *No temptation has seized you except what is common to man. And God is faithful; he will not let you be tempted beyond what you can bear. But when you are tempted, he will also provide a way out, so that you can stand up under it* (1 Corinthians 10:13).

ten (tɛn) determ., n., pron. The number 10

ten-a-ble (tɛn–ə–bəl) adj. Capable of being upheld or defended: *a tenable argument*

te-na-cious (tə–ney–ʃəs) adj. **1.** Unyielding; holding firmly to one's convictions: *tenacious of his rights* **2.** Sticking firmly together or to an object or surface **3.** Retentive: *a tenacious memory* —**tenaciously** adv. —**te-nac-i-ty** (tə–næs–ət–iy) n.

ten-an-cy (tɛn–ən–siy) n. **-cies 1.** The use of land or buildings by a tenant **2.** The period of time during which a tenant has this use

ten-ant (tɛn–ənt) n. One who rents or leases a house, apartment, etc. from a landlord

Ten Com-mand-ments (kə–mænd–mənts) n. *pl.* The moral law of God given through Moses (Exodus 20:3-17) nearly 1500 years B.C. [Before Christ] and intended for all people for all time. NOTE: No one can keep the Ten Commandments perfectly, so no one can earn his own salvation through keeping the law (Psalm 53:3). Jesus alone has kept the commandments perfectly, and he did it for us (Hebrews 4:15). Then he suffered and died on the cross to pay for our sins (1 Peter 3:18 and Isaiah 53:6), then rose from the dead on the third day (2 Corinthians 5:15). By the grace [unmerited love] of God, we are saved and have eternal life through faith in Jesus our Lord without the deeds of the law (Ephesians 2:8,9). But out of love for Jesus we keep his commandments, as he said, "If you love me, you will obey what I command" (John 14:15). —see SIN, LAW, COMMANDMENTS, JESUS, SAVIOR, BIBLE

tend (tɛnd) v. **1.** To be likely to do sthg.; have a tendency: *It tends to get very hot in Texas in July.* **2.** To take care of; look after: *shepherds tending their sheep*

ten-den-cy (tɛn–dən–siy) n. **-cies** An inclination to think or behave in a certain way: *a tendency to sleep late*

ten-der (tɛn–dər) adj. **1.** Soft; easy to chew: *tender meat* —opposite TOUGH **2.** Sensitive or sore: *His wound is still tender.* **3.** Loving; sympathetic: *a tender heart* **4.** *lit.* Young; inexperienced: *a tender child* —**tenderly** adv. —**tenderness** n.

ten-der n. **1.** A person who takes care of sthg. **2.** A ship that services one or more larger ships **3.** A railroad car attached to a locomotive, carrying fuel and water **4.** A formal offer or proposal made for acceptance, esp. a bid for a contract; a statement of the price one would charge for doing a job **5.** Also **legal tender** Sthg. (as money) that may be offered in payment

tender v. *fml.* To offer; present: *The director tendered his resignation.*

ten-der-heart-ed (tɛn–dər–**hart**–əd) adj. Compassionate; easily moved to love, pity, or sorrow: *Be kind to one another, tenderhearted, forgiving one another, just as God in Christ also has forgiven you* (Ephesians 4:32).

ten-don (tɛn–dən) n. A band of tough, fibrous tissue that connects a muscle to a bone; sinew

ten-dril (tɛn–drəl) n. A thin curling part of a plant serving to attach itself to a support

ten-e-ment (tɛn–ə–mənt) n. A dwelling divided into separate apartments for rent to families; apartments which meet only minimal standards of comfort and safety

ten-et (tɛn–ət) n. One of the principles or doctrines held in common by members of an organized group

ten-nis (tɛn–əs) n. A usu. outdoor game played with rackets and a small, light ball by two players or two pairs on a level court divided by a low net

ten-or (tɛn–ər) n. **1.** The highest, normal male singing voice **2.** A singer with this high voice **3.** A musical part written for this **4.** A musical instrument with approximately the range of a tenor voice **5.** The general routine of sthg. **6.** The general idea or meaning of sthg.: *the tenor of his speech*

tense (tɛns) n. Any of the forms of a verb that indicate the time of the action as past,

present, or future: *"He is"* is present tense. *"He was"* is past tense, and *"He will be"* is future tense.

tense adj. **tenser, tensest 1.** Stretched tight: *tense muscles* **2.** Nervous; anxious: *a tense moment before the race began* —**tensely** adv.

tense v. **-tensed, -tensing** To make or become tense —compare RELAX

ten-sion (tɛn–tʃən) n. **1.** The act of stretching or the condition of being stretched tight **2.** Mental strain; nervous anxiety, worry, or pressure **3.** Any strained relationship, as between governments **4.** Electric power: *high tension wires*

ten-si-ty (tɛn–sət–iʸ) n. The state of being tense; tension

tent (tɛnt) n. A movable shelter made of canvas or other material supported by poles and ropes: *The campers pitched (=put up) their tent.*

ten-ta-cle (tɛnt–ɪ–kəl) n. A long, thin flexible part of some animals, used for feeling, handling, or grasping: *The eight arms of an octopus are tentacles.*

ten-ta-tive (tɛnt–ət–ɪv) adj. Not final or definite; not fully worked out or developed

tenth (tɛnθ) determ., n., pron. **10th**

ten-u-ous (tɛn–yuʷ–əs) adj. **1.** Thin; slim; delicate; unsubstantial **2.** Having slight density

ten-ure (tɛn–yər) n. **1.** Permanent status granted an employee, usually after a period of several years: *He has tenure at the university.* **2.** A holding of office or property or other accommodations, or the state of being held **3.** The term during which a thing is held

te-pee (tiʸ–piʸ) n. A cone-shaped tent made by stretching animal hides or tree bark over tall poles, a common form of shelter for some North American Indians

tep-id (tɛp–əd) adj. Lukewarm

term (tɜrm) n. **1.** An expression, esp. one used in a particular activity, profession, etc. *a medical term* **2.** An unspecified period of time: *a prison term* **3.** One of the three periods of time into which the school or university year is divided —compare SEMESTER **4.** A fixed period of time: *The president is elected for a four-year term.* —see TERMS

term v. To designate by means of a term; to

call: *This music is termed "Jazz."*

ter-mi-nal (tɜrm–ən–əl) n. **1.** A building containing the arrival and departure areas at an airport **2.** A bus or railroad station usu. in the center of town, esp. for passengers going to or arriving from an airport **3.** A point at which connections can be made to an electric system (circuit) or messages passed to or from a computer

terminal adj. **1.** Pertaining to an illness that will cause death: *a terminal disease* **2.** Of or at the end of sthg. —**terminally** adv.

ter-mi-nate (tɜr–mə–neʸt) v. **-nated, -nating** To bring to an end: *to terminate a contract* —**ter-mi-na-tion** (tɜr–mə–neʸ–ʃən) n.

ter-mi-nol-o-gy (tɜr–mə–nɑl–ə–dʒiʸ) n. **-gies** Terms and expressions used in a particular science or profession: *medical terminology*

ter-min-us (tɜr–mə–nəs) n. **-uses** or **-i 1.** Final point **2.** Either end of a railroad line

ter-mite (tɜr–maɪt) n. An ant-like tropical insect that feeds on wood

terms (tɜrmz) n. **1.** The provision or conditions of a contract **2.** Conditions of payment, prices, etc. **3.** Mutual relationship: *We are on good terms with our neighbors.* **4. come to terms with** To accept (sthg. unpleasant): *He had to come to terms with the fact that he had an incurable disease.* **5. in no uncertain terms** Clearly and usu. angrily: *He told me in no uncertain terms to go away.* **6. in terms of** With regard to: *In terms of property, we don't have much.* **7. on speaking terms** Friendly enough to speak: *After their argument, they were on speaking terms again.*

tern (tɜrn) n. A small sea gull

ter-race (tɛər–əs) n. **1.** A raised level of earth, which is one of a series, on the side of a hill, used to prevent erosion and for growing crops **2.** A nearly level strip of land with a sharp descent along the edge of a river, lake, or sea **3.** An outside balcony **4.** An open area, often paved, adjacent to a house, often used as an outdoor living area

terrace v. **-raced, -racing** To form into a terrace: *They are terracing the hillside.*

ter-rain (tə–reʸn) n. A tract of land considered with its physical features: *mountainous terrain*

ter-ra-pin (tɛər-ə-pən/ tær-) n. A kind of small turtle that lives in fresh water or at the edge of the sea

ter-rar-i-um (tə-rɛər-iʸ-əm) n. A glass enclosure for growing small plants

ter-res-tri-al (tə-res-triʸ-əl) adj. 1. Of or related to the earth 2. Living on land rather than in the water 3. Earthly or worldly

ter-ri-ble (tɛər-ə-bəl) adj. 1. Causing fear; dreadful: *There will be terrible times in the last days [just before the Lord's return]* (2 Timothy 3:1). 2. Very severe: *a terrible flood* 3. *infml.* Very bad: *a terrible actor* —terribly adv.

ter-ri-er (tɛər-iʸ-ər) n. Any of several species of small, energetic dogs, originally bred to hunt small animals

ter-rif-ic (tə-rɪf-ɪk) adj. *infml.* 1. Very good; marvelous; enjoyable: *a terrific party* 2. Powerful: *a terrific explosion*

ter-ri-fy (tɛər-ə-faɪ) v. -fied, -fying To fill with terror or fear: *Snakes terrify me.*

ter-ri-to-ri-al (tɛər-ə-tɔr-iʸ-əl) adj. Of, belonging to a territory

ter-ri-to-ry (tɛər-ə-tɔr-iʸ) n. -ries 1. An area of land, esp. ruled by one government: *Northwest Territory* 2. An area regarded by a person, animal, group, etc., as belonging to it alone: *The salesman regarded this entire county as his own territory.*

ter-ror (tɛər-ər) n. 1. Extreme fear: *When justice is done it brings joy to the righteous but terror to evildoers* (Proverbs 21:15). 2. *infml.* An annoying person: *That child is a real terror!*

ter-ror-ism (tɛər-ər-ɪz-əm) n. The use of violence to obtain political demands

ter-ror-ist (tɛər-ər-əst) n. Sbdy. who uses violence to obtain political demands: *Terrorists were responsible for the bomb explosion.* —terrorist adj.

ter-ror-ize also -ise BrE. (tɛər-ər-aɪz) v. -ized, -izing To fill someone with terror

terse (tɜrs) adj. Using few words —tersely adv. —terseness n.

ter-ti-ar-y (tɜr-ʃiʸ-ɛər-iʸ/ -ʃər-iʸ) adj. Third in place, degree, or rank

test (tɛst) n. 1. A number of questions or problems designed to measure one's knowledge or aptitude; a short examination 2. A practical examination or trial; sthg. done to find out if a thing is good, durable, efficient, etc.: *a blood test* —tester n.

test v. 1. To examine: *The students were tested on their knowledge of English.* 2. To subject to an examination to determine certain characteristics: *Man is tested by the praise he receives* (Proverbs 27:21). 3. To search by means of tests: *The Lord tests the heart* (Proverbs 17:3). 4. To show or develop specific qualities under trial: *The testing of your faith develops perseverance* (James 1:3).

tes-ta-ment (tɛs-tə-mənt) n. 1. *fml.* A will (esp. in the phrase, last will and testament) 2. A written statement of one's beliefs —see also OLD TESTAMENT, NEW TESTAMENT

tes-tate (tɛs-teʸt) adj. Having made and left a valid will

tes-ti-fy (tɛs-tə-faɪ) v. -fied, -fying To make a solemn statement; bear witness: *All the prophets testify about him [Jesus] that everyone who believes in him receives forgiveness of sins through his name* (Acts 10:43).

tes-ti-mo-ni-al (tɛs-tə-moʷ-niʸ-əl) n. 1. A formal written statement of a person's character, ability, etc. 2. Sthg. given or done to show thanks

tes-ti-mo-ny (tɛs-tə-moʷ-niʸ) n. -nies A formal statement or affirmation of a fact, as made by a witness in a court of law: *One of God's Ten Commandments is: "You shall not give false testimony against your neighbor"* (Exodus 20:16).

test tube (tɛst tuʷb) n. A thin tube of glass that is closed at one end, used for laboratory experiments

tet-a-nus (tɛt-ən-əs) n. An acute, often deadly, bacterial disease in which the muscles become extremely stiff, caused by germs that enter the body through a wound

teth-er (tɛð-ər) n. A length of rope or chain used as a leash to keep an animal in a certain area

tether v. To fasten with a length of rope or chain

text (tɛkst) n. 1. The words in a book, rather than pictures: *Children's books usually have more pictures than text.* 2. The actual or original words of an author 3. A passage from the Bible, esp. when used as the basis of a

sermon: *He preached on a text from the Gospel of St. Mark.* —**tex-tu-al** (**tɛks**–tʃyu″–əl) adj. Of or in a text

text-book (tɛkst–bʊk) n. A book used for the instruction of a particular subject

tex-tile (tɛk–staɪl/ **tɛks**–təl) n. Any cloth or fabric made by weaving: *cotton textiles*

tex-ture (tɛks–tʃər) n. 1. The degree of smoothness or roughness of a surface, as felt by touch 2. The structure, composition, or appearance of sthg., such as the surface of a painting

than (ðæn/ ðən) conj. or prep. 1. (Used to show a comparison between what precedes and what follows): *Mary is older than I am./ The train arrived later than usual.* 2 **other than** Except for: *His eyesight is poor; other than that, he is in excellent physical condition.*

thank (θæŋk) v. To express gratitude; give thanks to: *Give thanks to the Lord, for he is good; his love endures forever* (Psalm 118:1).

thank-ful (**θæŋk**–fəl) adj. Grateful: *Let us be thankful, and so worship God acceptably with reverence and awe* (Hebrews 12:28). —**thankfully** adv. —**thankfulness** n.

thank-less (θæŋ–kləs) adj. 1. Ungrateful 2. Not rewarded with thanks: *a thankless job* —**thanklessly** adv. —**thanklessness** n.

thanks (θæŋks) n. Words expressing gratefulness: *Give thanks to the Lord, for he is good, his love endures forever* (Psalm 107:1). *Be joyful always, pray continually, give thanks in all circumstances, for this is God's will for you in Christ Jesus* (1 Thessalonians 5:16-18).

thanks-giv-ing (θæŋks–**gɪv**–ɱ) n. An expression of gratefulness, esp. to God: *Let us come before him [God] with thanksgiving* (Psalm 95:2). *Do not be anxious about anything but in everything, by prayer and petition, with thanksgiving, present your requests to God* (Philippians 4:6).

Thanksgiving also **Thanksgiving Day** n. A holiday in the US and Canada, on which God is thanked for a year of success and blessings, usu. marked with a feast

thank you also **thanks** *infml.* (**θæŋk**–yuʷ) interj. Used politely to mean "I am grateful to you": *Thank you for all your help.* NOTE: If one is offered sthg. that one does not want,

he/she replies *"No, thank you."*

that (ðæt) determ , pron. those (ðoʷz) 1. Used to point out a person or a thing: *that woman over there* 2. The one farthest away or first mentioned: *This is an oak tree; that one over there is an elm.* 3. Referring to sthg. mentioned earlier in the conversation: *After that, we went to the theater.* 4. The one or ones: *Those who arrive late will probably have to stand; all the seats will have been taken.* 5. **that is (to say)** In other words 6. **that's that** That settles the matter: *You can't go, and that's that.* —compare THIS

that conj. 1. Introduces various kinds of clauses. It can often be omitted: *It's true (that) she's lonely./ I believe (that) we've met before.* 2. Used as a subject meaning "who" or "which": *Did you see the letter that (which) came today?* 3. To this purpose; in order that: *He shouted that all might hear.* 4. So as to have the following result: *He is so badly injured that he can't be moved.* 5. Because: *We are so glad that you came.*

that adj. **those** 1. The ones now mentioned, indicated or understood: *That boy is my brother.* 2. Being the one farthest away: *Do you want this chair or that one.*

that adv. *infml.* So; as much as that: *I don't like her that much.*

thatch (θætʃ) n. 1. Roof covering made of straw, reeds, etc., arranged so as to shed water 2. Any material used for this purpose **thatch** v. To cover with thatch —**thatched** adj. *Our house has a thatched roof.*

that's (ðæts) Contraction of **(a)** that is: *That's where I live.* **(b)** that has: *That's got to be the one!*

thaw (θɔ) v. 1. To melt or cause to melt: *The snow is thawing.* 2. Of a person, to become friendlier, less formal, etc. —**thaw** n. *There was a thaw in the spring.* (= a warmer period when snow and ice melted)

the (ðʌ/ ðə) before a consonant, (ðiʸ) before a vowel Def. art. , determ. 1. Used before singular and plural nouns when it should be obvious who or which one is meant: *The sky is clear.* 2. Used as part of some names, esp. rivers, seas, oceans, and mountains: *The Nile/The Ganges/The Andes/The Red Sea/The*

Pacific Ocean **3.** Used before an adjective to make it into a noun: *the elderly* (=elderly people) **4.** Used before names of musical instruments: *Ann plays the violin.* **5.** Used after a preposition and before a unit of measure; each: *Bananas are sold by the pound./ He is paid by the hour./ My car gets twenty five miles to the gallon (of gasoline).* **6.** Used with superlatives to show that a person or thing is more of sthg. than any other: *He is the kindest man I know.* **7.** Used with comparative adjectives to show that a person or thing is better or worse: *Mary has been on a diet and looks all the better for it.* **8.** Used before the plural of 20, 30, 40, etc., to show a decade: *A lot of changes took place in the 60's (=from 1960 to 1970)* **9.** Used before a singular noun to refer to all members of a group: *The panther is a wild animal./ The French are said to be good cooks.*

the adv. **1.** To that extent: *The more he eats, the more he wants./ The more you do for him, the more he expects.* **2.** Showing that sthg. or someone is more than any other: *Of all our children, Daniel is the tallest.*

the-a-ter *AmE.* also **theatre** esp. *BrE.* (θiᵞ–ət–ər) n. **1.** A building where plays or operas are performed or where motion pictures are shown **2.** The work of people who write or act in plays **3.** A scene of important military events: *He fought in the South Pacific theater of war during World War II.* **4.** *BrE.* An operating room in a hospital

the-at-ri-cal (θiᵞ–æ–tɪɪ–kəl) adj. **1.** Of or for the theater **2.** Concerning behavior, showy; not natural: *He's too theatrical.* —**theatrically** adv.

thee (ðiᵞ) pron. (old English) You: *Whosoever shall smite thee on the right cheek, turn to him the other also* (Matthew 5:39 KJV). *Jesus told the paralytic man, "Son, be of good cheer, thy (your) sins be forgiven thee* (Matthew 9:2 KJV).

theft (θeft) n. The act of stealing

their (ðeər) determ. Possessive form of **they** Of or relating to them or themselves: *They put on their coats.*

theirs (ðeərz) pron. Possessive form of **they** Of those people, animals, or things already mentioned: *I locked my bike and they locked*

theirs.

them (ðem) pron. Objective form of **they**: *Have you seen my shoes? I can't find them.*

theme (θiᵞm) n. **1.** A subject to be discussed or developed in speech or writing **2.** A brief composition, esp. one written as an exercise as part of a course of instruction **3.** A melody on which a piece of music is based

them-selves (ðem–selvz) pron. **1.** Used as the object of a verb or preposition when people, animals, etc. are the object of the actions they perform: *The ladies are enjoying themselves.* **2.** Used to emphasize **they, them** or the name of the people or things referred to: *They did all that work themselves.*

then (ðen) adv. **1.** At that time: *We'll see you then.* **2.** Next; afterwards: *I'm going to the bank, then to the post office.* **3.** In that case; therefore: *If you want to quit, then quit.* **4.** Besides; and also: *Be sure to invite Mary to dinner, and then, of course, there's Bob also.* **5. but then** However: *He lost the election, but then no one expected him to win.*

then adj. At that time in the past: *the then principal of the school*

thence (ðens) adv. **1.** From that place or time **2.** Therefore; from that fact

thence-forth (ðens–fɔrθ) adv. From that time onward

the-oc-ra-cy (θiᵞ–ak–rə–siᵞ) n. **-cies 1.** A government in which God is recognized as the supreme civil ruler, directly or through a priestly order **2.** A state under such a form of government —**the-o-crat-ic** (θiᵞ–ə–kræt–ɪk) adj. —**theocratically** adv.

the-o-lo-gian (θiᵞ–ə–loʷ–dʒən) n. A person who has studied theology —**the-o-og-i-cal** (θiᵞ–ə–ladʒ–ɪ–kəl) adj. —**theo-logically** adv.

the-ol-o-gy (θiᵞ–al–ə–dʒiᵞ) n. **1.** The study of the nature of God and religious truth **2.** An organized body of beliefs concerning God and man's relationship to God

the-o-rem (θiᵞ–ə–rəm) n. **1.** A mathematical statement to be proved by a chain of reasoning **2.** A rule in algebra, esp. one expressed as a formula

the-o-ret-i-cal (θiᵞ–ə–ret–ɪ–kəl) adj. Based on theory, not on practice or experience —**theoretically** adv.

the-o-rist (θiʸ-ə-rəst) n. A person who theorizes

the-o-rize (θiʸ-ə-raiz) v. -rized, -rizing To form theories

the-o-ry (θiʸ-ə-riʸ /θiʸ-riʸ) n. -ries 1. An explanation which one believes to be true, but which has not been proved or tested 2. The general principles of a science or art as opposed to its practice: *The plans seem to be good in theory, but will they work in practice?* —the-o-ret-i-cal (θiʸ-ə-ret-ɪ-kəl) adj. —theoretically adv. *Theoretically, it's his job, but he really doesn't do it.*

the-os-o-phy (θiʸ-**as**-ə-fiʸ) n. **1.** Teaching about God and the world, based on mystical insight **2.** The teachings of a modern movement originating in the US in 1875 and following chiefly Buddhist and Brahmanic theories, esp. of pantheistic evolution and reincarnation —the-o-soph-i-cal (θiʸ-ə-**saf**-ɪ-kəl) adj. —theosophically adv.

ther-a-peu-tic (θɛər-ə-**pyu**ʷt-ɪk) adj. Having healing or curative powers —therapeutically adv.

ther-a-pist (**θɛər**-ə-pəst) n. One who gives therapeutic treatment: *a speech therapist*

ther-a-py (**θɛər**-ə-piʸ) n. The treatment of illnesses or disability, esp. without operations: *occupational therapy*

there (ðɛər) adv. **1.** To, at, or in that place: *He lives over there.* —opposite HERE **2.** At that point: *I drove to Portland and stopped there.* **3.** Used for drawing attention to someone or sthg.: *There's that song again.* **4.** then and there or there and then At that time and place: *Right then and there he started a fight.*

there pron. Used to show that someone or sthg. exists or happens: *There are birds in the trees./ There's a church on the corner.*

there-a-bouts also thereabout (ðɛər-ə-**bavts** / ðɛər-ə-**bavts**) *AmE.* adv. Approximately: *He's 70 years old or thereabouts.*

there-af-ter (ðɛər-**æf**-tər) adv. *fml.* After that; afterwards; from that time on

there-by (ðɛər-**baɪ**) adv. By that means: *Desire...the milk of the word [God's Word], that you may grow thereby* (1 Peter 2:2).

there-fore (**ðɛər**-fɔr) adv. For that reason: *After his resurrection, Jesus said to his disciples:*

"All authority in heaven and on earth has been given to me. Therefore, go and make disciples of all nations" (Matthew 28:18,19).

there-in (ðɛər-**ɪn**) adv. **1.** In that place: *Turn from these vanities unto the living God who made heaven and earth, and the sea, and all things that are therein* (Acts 14:15KJV). **2.** In that respect: *The Gospel of Jesus Christ... is the power of God unto salvation to every one that believeth. For therein is the righteousness of God revealed* (Romans 1:16,17KJV).

there-of (ðɛər-**ʌv**) adv. *fml.* or *law* Of that; of it: *The earth is the Lord's and the fullness thereof* (Psalm 24:1 KJV).

there-on (ðɛər-**ɑn**/ -**an**) adv. **1.** On that or it **2.** thereupon

there's (ðɛərz) Contraction of (a) There is:*There's my house.* (b) there has: *There's got to be a better way of doing this.*

there-to-fore (ðɛər-tuʷ-fɔr/ -tə-) adv. Before or until that time

there-up-on (ðɛər-ə-pɔn/ -pan) adv. **1.** Immediately **2.** Because of that

there-with (ðɛər-**wɪθ**) adv. With that or it; thereupon; immediately afterward

there-with-al (ðɛər-wɪð-ɔl) adv. **1.** In addition **2.** With that or it

therm (θɜrm) n. Any of several units of quantity of heat

ther-mal (θɜr-məl) adj. **1.** Of or caused by heat or temperature **2.** Knitted with air space between layers, so as to keep cold air out: *thermal underwear*

ther-mo- (θɜr-moʷ-) or therm- comb. form Heat

ther-mo-dy-nam-ics (θɜr-moʷ-daɪ-**næm**-ɪks) n. A branch of physics dealing with the relations between heat and other forms of energy. According to the first law of thermodynamics, processes change matter and energy from one form to others, but the total quantity of energy in the universe always remains the same. According to the second law, orderly things become disordered, new things get old and break down, and living things age and wear out. This is one of the most constant laws of nature, found everywhere in the universe. Every energy system in the universe wears out.

Stars burn out, galaxies fly apart, energy becomes less and less useful through time. Everything in our physical universe is running down. The first law of thermodynamics speaks of a total creation originally completed, and now sustained by God's power. The second law speaks of the curse of decay and death, brought on by man's sin, and causing a degeneration in everything. Creationism, the Biblical teaching that God created all things, is in complete harmony with the Laws of Science. Evolution, the belief and teaching that life progressed from one-celled organisms to its highest state, the human being, by a series of biological changes taking place over millions of years, is completely contrary to the Laws of Science. Those who insist on teaching evolution as a fact or even as a reasonable theory are not good scientists, and they are willfully ignorant of the truth of God's Word. They "refuse to love the truth and so be saved. For this reason God sends them a powerful delusion, so they will believe the lie and so that all will be condemned who have not believed the truth but have delighted in wickedness" (2 Thessalonians 2:10-12). —see CREATION, EVOLUTION

ther-mom-e-ter (θər–**mɑm**–ət–ər) n. An instrument for measuring temperature

ther-mo-nu-cle-ar (θər–mo^w–**nu**^w–kli^y–ər) adj. **1.** Of or derived from the fusion of atomic nuclei at high temperatures **2.** Of or involving hydrogen bombs

ther-mos bot-tle (**θɜr**–məs **bɑt**–əl) n. *trademark* A vacuum flask, having a double wall enclosing a vacuum, used for keeping liquids hot or cold

ther-mo-stat (**θɜr**–mə–stæt) n. A device that automatically regulates temperature-controlling equipment, such as air conditioners and furnaces

the-sau-rus (θɪ–**sɔr**–əs) n. **1.** A book of information about a particular field or set of concepts, esp. a book of words and their synonyms **2.** A treasury or storehouse **3.** A categorized index of terms for use in information retrieval

these (ði^yz) determ., pron. *Pl.* of **this**

the-sis (**θi**^y–səs) n. *pl.* **-ses** (si^yz) **1.** An idea or point of view advanced and maintained by argument **2.** A long written essay or treatise resulting from original academic research for a university degree

Thes-sa-lo-ni-ans (θɛs–ə–lo^w–**ni**^y–ənz) n. Either of the two books of the New Testament which were letters written by the Apostle Paul to the Christians of Thessalonica, in Macedonia (Northern Greece). Paul praised them for their faithfulness in the face of persecution. He reminded them of the call of God to holy living, and that God was faithful to sanctify them completely. He also wrote about the Second Coming of our Lord and Savior Jesus Christ.

they (ðe^y) pron. (used as the subject of a sentence) **1.** Those people, animals or things already mentioned: *John and Mary are here; they want to talk to you./ Take these books to the library; they are overdue.* **2.** People; everyone: *They say prices will increase.*

they'd (ðe^yd) Short for **1.** They had: *If only they'd been here.* **2.** They would: *They'd like to talk to you.*

they'll (ðe^yl) Short for **1.** They will **2.** They shall

they're (ðe^yr) Short for **They are**

they've (ðe^yv) Short for **They have**

thick (θɪk) adj. **1.** Not thin: *The ice was thick on the windshield this morning.* **2.** Having a certain distance between sides: *The dust was an inch thick.* **3.** Of liquid not flowing easily: *thick syrup* **4.** Filled with: *The air was thick with dust.* **5.** Closely packed together; dense: *The traffic is very thick at 5 p.m.* **6.** Stupid or stubborn: *He was very thick headed.* **7. thick-skinned** Not easily hurt by criticism or insults

thick adv. *The trees grew thickest near the river.* —**thickly** adv. —**thickness** n.

thick n. **1. in the thick of** In the place or time of greatest activity: *in the thick of the battle* **2. through thick and thin** Through both good and bad times

thick-en (**θɪk**–ən) v. **1.** To make or become thick or thicker: *Add some flour to thicken the soup.* **2.** *fig.* **the plot thickened** The story became more complicated

thick-et (θɪk–ət) n. Dense shrubbery

thief (θiᶠf) n. thieves A person who steals: *This is a sin against God's holy commandment: You shall not steal* (Exodus 20:15). *God's word also says: Whoever is partner with a thief hates his own soul* (Proverbs 29:24 KJV). NOTE: God hates sin, and the wages of sin is death (Romans 6:23), but because of his great mercy, he forgives those who truly repent of their sins and put their trust in Jesus for eternal life (Mark 1:15; Acts 2:38; 16:31; Romans 3:23,24; 6:23; John 3:16). —see SIN, LAW, MAN, FORGIVENESS, JESUS

thigh (θaɪ) n. The part of the leg between the knee and the hip

thim-ble (θɪm–bəl) n. A kind of metal or plastic cap to protect the finger and push the needle while sewing

thin (θɪn) adj. -nn- 1. Not thick; having a short distance between opposite surfaces: *on thin ice* 2. Slim; not fat: *She was very thin after her long illness.* 3. Of a liquid, watery: *thin soup* 4. Not dense: *His hair is getting very thin.* 5. thin-skinned Very sensitive; easily hurt by criticism or insults —thinly adv. *a thinly populated area* —thinness n. —compare SLENDER, SLIM, SKINNY, NARROW, FINE

thin v. -nn- To make or become thin or less dense; to make or become thin or thinner

thine (ðaɪn) pron. A possessive form of you

thing (θɪŋ) n. 1. Any material object; an object that is not living: *Every house is built by someone, but he that built all things is God* (Hebrews 3:4). *For by him [Jesus] all things were created: things in heaven and on earth ... all things were created by him and for him. He is before all things and in him all things hold together* (Colossians 1:16,17). 2. A remark, subject, or idea 3. An act; deed: *Attempt great things for God; expect great things from God./ Is any thing too hard for the Lord?* (Genesis 18:14). 4. A creature, person, animal, etc.: *There wasn't a living thing in the room.* 5. *infml.* Sthg. nec-essary or desirable

things (θɪŋz) n. 1. One's clothing and other personal belongings: *Pack your things. We're going.* 2. The general state of affairs: *Things are getting worse and worse.* 3. to hear or see things To hear or see things which do not exist; have hallucinations

think (θɪŋk) v. thought (θɔt), thinking 1. To use the power of reason; use the mind to form opinions: *For as he [anyone] thinks in his heart, so is he* (Proverbs 23:7 NKJV). *[God] is able to do exceedingly abundantly [far more] above all that we ask or think* (Ephesians 3:20 NKJV). 2. To believe; consider: *People used to think that the world was flat.* 3. To remember: *I couldn't think of her name.* 4. To expect: *I think it will rain.* 5. To direct the mind in a particular way: *Whatever is true... noble... right... pure...lovely... admirable... excellent... praiseworthy, think about such things* (Philippians 4:8). 6. To ponder: *All day long I've been thinking about what you said.* 7. To have an opinion: *What do you think of/about this plan?* 8. think better of To decide against 9. think nothing of To regard as usual or easy: *He thinks nothing of working twelve hours a day.* 10. think nothing of it There's no need to thank me; it was my pleasure to help. 11. think through *AmE.* To consider carefully and in detail 12. think up To devise or invent (esp. an idea): *to think up an excuse* 13. think over To consider carefully —thinkable adj. —thinker n. *John is a deep thinker.*

think-ing (θɪŋk–ɪŋ) n. 1. The act of using one's mind to produce thoughts 2. Opinion; judgment: *What's your thinking on this matter?*

thin-ner (θɪn–ər) n. A liquid added, esp. to paint, to make it spread more easily

third (θɜrd) determ., adv., n., pron. 3rd

thirst (θɜrst) n. 1. The desire to drink sthg.: *After not drinking anything all day he had a great thirst.* 2. A strong desire for anything: *He had a great thirst for adventure.*

thirst v. 1. To be thirsty 2. To crave; yearn for: *Blessed are those who hunger and thirst for righteousness, for they will be filled* (Matthew 5:6).

thirst-y (θɜr–stiᵞ) adj. -ier, -iest 1. Feeling or causing thirst: *Eating salty food makes one thirsty./ Jesus said, "I was thirsty and you gave me sthg. to drink... whatever you did for one of the least of these brothers of mine, you did it for me"* (Matthew 25:35,40). 2. Having a strong desire for: *He was thirsty for power,*

—**thirstily** adv.

thir-teen (θɚr–ti^yn) determ., n., pron. The number 13

thirteenth (θɚr–ti^ynθ) determ., n., pron., adv. 13th

thir-ti-eth (θɚr–ti^y–əθ) determ., n., pron., adv. 30th

thir-ty (θɚr–ti^y) determ., n., pron. -ties The number 30

this (ðɪs) determ., pron. **these** The person or thing present, nearby, or just mentioned: *Where did you get this book? (=the one in my hand)/ I saw Mrs. Jones this morning. (=earlier today)* —opposite THAT

this (ðɪs) adv. To such an extent: *I've never been this happy before.*

this-tle (θɪs–əl) n. A type of prickly plant

thith-er (θɪð–ər) adv. To that place

thong (θɔŋ/ θɑŋ) n. **1.** A piece of leather used to fasten sthg. **2.** The long thin part of a whip

tho-rax (θɔr–æks) n. **1.** The part of the body of an animal or human between the neck and the abdomen **2.** The middle part of an insect's body

thorn (θɔrn) n. **1.** A hard, sharp point sticking out from the stem of certain plants: *Rose bushes have thorns.* **2. thorn in one's flesh/ side** A continual cause of annoyance

thorn-y (θɔrn–i^y) adj. -ier, -iest *fig.* Difficult: *a thorny question* —**thorniness** n.

thor-ough (θɚr–o^w) adj. Complete and careful: *a thorough search* —**thoroughly** adv. —**thoroughness** n.

thor-ough-bred (θɚr–ə–brɛd) adj. **1.** Pure bred, as a horse or dog; pedigreed **2.** Thoroughly trained, educated, cultured, etc.; well-bred **3.** Excellent; first-rate

thoroughbred n. **1.** Any of a breed of race-horses developed by crossing English mares with Arabian stallions **2.** A cultured, well-bred person

thor-ough-fare (θɚr–ə–fɛər/ –fær) n. An unobstructed public street

those (ðo^wz) determ., pron. Plural of **that**

thou (ðaʊ) pron. (Old use) You; the second person singular in the nominative case; the person to whom one is speaking: *Thou shalt (=you shall) worship the Lord thy (=your) God,*

and him only shalt thou (=shall you) serve (Matthew 4:10KJV).

though (ðo^w) conj. **1.** In spite of the fact that; even if: *God is our refuge and strength, an ever present help in trouble. Therefore we will not fear, though the earth give way and the mountains fall into the heart of the sea* (Psalm 46:1,2). **2. as though** As if; like: *He behaves as though he were rich.*

though adv. However; despite the fact that: *It's hard work. I enjoy it, though.*

thought (θɔt) n. **1.** The act or manner of thinking: *Let the wicked forsake his way and the evil man his thoughts. Let him turn to the Lord, and he will have mercy on him. "For my thoughts are not your thoughts, neither are my ways your ways," declares the Lord* (Isaiah 55:7,8). **2.** An idea or opinion: *What are your thoughts on the subject?* **3.** Intention: *I had no thought of hurting you.* **4. second thought** A change of mind or opinion: *On second thought, I'd like to sell my car.*

thought v. Past tense & part. of **think**: *When I was a child... I thought like a child* (1 Corinthians 13:11).

thought-ful (θɔt–fəl) adj. **1.** Thinking deeply **2.** Considerate of other people's needs and feelings —**thoughtfully** adv. —**thoughtfulness** n.

thought-less (θɔt–ləs) adj. Careless; showing lack of consideration for others —**thoughtlessly** adv. —**thoughtlessness** n.

thou-sand (θaʊz–ənd) determ., n., pron. -sand or -sands The cardinal number 1,000, equal to 10 x 100 —**thousandth** determ., n., pron., adv. 1000th

thrash (θræʃ) v. **1.** To beat with a whip: *The thief was thrashed unmercifully.* **2.** To defeat thoroughly: *Our team was thrashed, 98 to 44.* **3.** To move wildly about: *The fish thrashed around in the net.*

thread (θrɛd) n. **1.** A very thin cord of any material, such as cotton, nylon, or silk, used in sewing or weaving **2.** A ridge around the outside of a screw **3. hanging by a thread** In great danger of losing sthg.: *His life is just hanging by a thread.*

thread v. **1.** To pass a thread through a needle **2.** To make one's way through a

crowd or a narrow place: *The bicycle rider threaded his way through the traffic.*

thread-bare (**θrɛd**–beər/ –bær) adj. Shabby; worn

threat (θrɛt) n. **1.** A warning that one intends to hurt or punish someone: *When they hurled their insults at him [Jesus], he did not retaliate; when he suffered, he made no threats. He himself bore our sins on the tree [the cross of Calvary]* (1 Peter 2:23). **2.** A warning of possible danger: *The dark clouds brought a threat of rain.*

threat-en (θrɛt–ən) v. **1.** To express or be a threat to: *Many lives are threatened ev-ery day by vicious criminals.* **2.** To give warning of sthg. bad: *Insects threatened to destroy the entire crop.*

three (θriʸ) determ., adj., n., pron. The cardinal number 3 —see also THIRD

thresh (θrɛʃ) v. To beat cereal plants in order to remove the grain or seeds —**thresher** n.

thresh-old (θrɛʃ–oʷld) n. **1.** A piece of wood or stone fixed beneath the doorway forming the entrance to a house **2.** The beginning; outset: *Our company is on the threshold of a major new advance.*

threw (θruʷ) v. Past tense of **throw**

thrice (θraɪs) adv. Three times

thrift (θrɪft) n. Careful and wise use of money and goods

thrift-y (θrɪf–tiʸ) adj. -ier, -iest Careful about spending

thrill (θrɪl) n. A strong feeling of excitement, pleasure, or fear

thrill v. To feel or cause to feel excitement

thrill-er (θrɪl–ər) n. A book, play, or motion picture that tells a very exciting story —**thrilling** adj. —**thrillingly** adv.

thrive (θraɪv) v. **throve** (θroʷv) or **thrived, thrived** or **thriven** (θrɪv–ən), **thriving** To grow or do well; be successful: *When the righteous thrive, the people rejoice; when the wicked rule, the people groan* (Proverbs 29:2).

throat (θroʷt) n. **1.** The passage from the back of the mouth down inside the neck **2.** The front of the neck **3. force sthg. down sbdy's throat** To force someone to hear sthg. against his will **4. jump down sbdy's throat** To attack sbdy. verbally in a violent way

before he has a chance to explain sthg. he said or did or is accused of

throat-y (θroʷt–iʸ) adj. -ier, -iest Coming from the back of the throat; guttural: *She has a very throaty voice for a woman.*

throb (θrɑb) v. -bb- **1.** To beat more strongly and rapidly than usual: *My heart was throbbing with excitement.* **2.** To beat or vibrate rhythmically: *The machinery was throbbing.* —**throb** n.

throe (θroʷ) n. **1.** Pang or spasm **2.** A hard or painful struggle

throm-bo-sis (θrɑm–boʷ–səs) n. -boses The formation or presence of a clot in a blood vessel during life —**throm-bot-ic** (θrɑm–bɑt–ɪk) adj.

throne (θroʷn) n. **1.** The chair occupied by a king or queen on ceremonial occasions: *God is seated on his holy throne* (Psalm 47:8). *This is what the Lord says, "Heaven is my throne and the earth is my footstool"* (Isaiah 66:1). *Jesus also said, "To him who overcomes [through faith in me], I will give the right to sit with me on my throne, just as I overcame and sat down with my Father on his throne"* (Revelation 3:21). **2.** The rank or office of a king or queen

throng (θrɑŋ/ θrɔŋ) v. **1.** To move in a crowd **2.** To crowd; fill: *Thousands of people thronged into the stadium.*

throng n. A crowd: *A huge throng gathered on the hillside to listen to Jesus.*

throt-tle (θrɑt–əl) v. -tled, -tling **1.** To choke; strangle **2.** To suppress **3.** To obstruct the flow(of fuel) to an engine

throttle n. A valve that controls the flow of fuel to an engine

through (θruʷ) prep. **1.** In one side and out the other: *The river flows right through the middle of town./ She pushed her way through the crowd.* **2.** By way of: *She climbed through the window.* **3.** Because of: *He lost all he had through gambling.* **4.** Past: *He drove through a red light. (=a traffic light that means, "Stop")* **5.** To the end of: *She isn't expected to live through the night.* **6.** Up to and including: *Open Monday through Friday, from nine a.m. to six p.m.* **7.** From end to end or from side to side: *We drove through Spain.*

through adv. **1.** In one side and out the other:

There was an accident in the tunnel, but somehow John got through. **2.** All the way from beginning to end: *Does this bus go right through to Los Angeles?* **3.** Connected by telephone: *Can you put me through to Mr. Wong?* **4.** Finished: *Aren't you through eating yet?* **5. through and through** Completely; in every way: *He was a soldier through and through.*

through adj. Going all the way from one end to the other: *The sign says, "NOT A THROUGH STREET."*

through-out (θru^w–aʊt) adv. **1.** Everywhere; all over **2.** From beginning to end —**throughout** prep. *We traveled throughout Europe./ The trees stay green throughout the year.*

throw (θro^w) v. **threw** (θru^w), **thrown**(θro^wn), **throwing 1.** To send sthg. through the air, esp. with a forward motion of the hand and arm: *Don't throw rocks.* **2.** To move suddenly: *The threat of war has thrown the country into a state of panic.* **3.** To cause to fall off: *He was thrown from his horse.* **4.** To move a handle or switch to turn sthg. on or off: *He threw a switch and started the machinery.* **5. throw a fit** To lose one's temper **6. throw oneself into** To work very busily at **7. throw out (a)** To refuse to accept: *They threw out my suggestions.* **(b)** To force someone to leave: *The manager threw him out for causing a disturb-ance.* **8. throw together** To make hastily: *She threw the meal together.* **9. throw-up (a)** To vomit **(b)** To build hastily: *They threw up all those houses in a few months.*

throw n. **1.** An act of throwing **2.** The distance to which sthg. is thrown: *His discus throw of 243 feet was almost a world record throw.*

throw-back (θro^w–bæk) n. Reversion to an earlier type or condition

thru (θru^w) adv., adj., prep. *AmE. infml.* Through

thrush (θrʌʃ) n. One of a family of singing birds that includes bluebirds and robins

thrust (θrʌst) v. **thrust, thrusting 1.** To push or drive with force; shove: *We thrust our way through the crowd.* **2.** To stab or pierce —**thrust** n. *the thrust (=force) of an engine*

thud (θʌd) n. A dull sound like sthg. heavy falling to the ground: *He fell with a thud.*

thud v. **-dd-** To make a thud; to fall with a thud: *He thudded down the stairs.*

thug (θʌg) n. A violent criminal

thumb (θʌm) n. **1.** The short thick finger, set apart from the other four **2.** The part of a glove that covers the thumb **3. stick out like a sore thumb** Very noticeable and seeming out of place **4. thumbs up** An expression of a wish for success **5. under sbdy's thumb** *infml.* Under someone's control or influence

thumb v. *infml.* To ask for a free ride from passing motorists by holding out one's thumb; to hitchhike: *He thumbed rides all the way across the country.*

thumb-nail (θʌm–ne^yl) n. The nail (hard flat piece) on the thumb

thumbnail adj. Short: *a thumbnail biographical sketch (=a short account of one's life)*

thumb-tack (θʌm–tæk) n. A short nail with a flat head that can be pushed into a bulletin board, etc. with one's thumb, to hold a picture, poster, notice, etc. in place

thump (θʌmp) v. To hit or stomp with a heavy blow: *He's always thumping (=walking with a heavy step) around upstairs.*

thump n. A heavy blow

thun-der (θʌn–dər) n. **1.** The loud sound following a flash of lightning **2.** A similar sound: *the thunder of distant guns* —**thunderous** adj. *fig. thunderous (=very loud) applause* —**thunderously** adv.

thunder v. **1.** To produce thunder: *The children are afraid when it thunders./ fig. The guns thundered in the distance.* **2.** To shout loudly: *"Come here!" he thundered.*

thun-der-bolt (θʌn–dər–bo^wlt) n. Lightning accompanied by thunder

thun-der-cloud (θʌn–dər–claʊd) n. An electrically charged cloud that produces lightning and thunder

thun-der-storm (θʌn–dər–stɔrm) n. A storm with lightning and thunder

thun-der-struck (θʌn–dər–strək) adj. Astonished; struck with amazement

Thurs-day (θɜrz–di^y / –de^y) also **Thurs.** *written abbr.* The fifth day of the week

thus (ðʌs) adv. **1.** As a result: *He ran the mile in three minutes and 47 seconds, thus breaking the world record at that time.* **2.** In this manner:

The new equipment will speed up production, thus cutting operational expenses. **3. thus far** Up until now

thwart (θwɑrt/ θwɔrt) v. To prevent from taking place; to frustrate: *Our plans were thwarted by the enemy./I know [O Lord] that you can do all things; no plan of yours can be thwarted* (Job 42:2).

thy (ðaɪ) determ. (Old use) Possessive form of **thou**; your; belonging to you (thee): *Thy kingdom come [O Lord]; Thy will be done on earth as it is in heaven* (Matthew 6:10 KJV).

thyme (taɪm/ θaɪm) n. Any of the herbs of the mint family, used as seasoning

thy-roid gland (θaɪ–rɔɪd glænd) n. A large gland in the front of the neck which influences the rate at which energy is used in the body

ti-ar-a (tiᶕ–ɑr–ə/ –eɑr–) n. **1.** A three-tiered crown **2.** A woman's crown-like headdress of jewels or flowers

tib-i-a (tɪb–iᶕ–ə) n. The shinbone; the larger of the two bones between the knee and the ankle

tic (tɪk) n. A recurrent muscle spasm

tick (tɪk) n. **1.** A slight, sharp, recurring click or beat, as that of a clock **2.** A light mark used to check off or call attention to an item **3.** Any of a variety of tiny blood-sucking insects, some of which transmit diseases **4.** Outer covering of a mattress or pillow

tick v. **1.** Of a clock or watch, to make a regularly repeated short clicking sound **2.** To mark or check with a tick

tick-et (tɪk–ət) n. **1.** A printed piece of paper which shows that a person has paid for entrance into a theater or stadium, a journey on a bus, plane, or train, etc. **2.** A summons, esp. for a traffic violation: *a ticket for speeding* **3.** A list of candidates endorsed by a political party

ticket v. To provide with a ticket

tick-le (tɪk–əl) v. **-led, -ling 1.** To touch someone's body lightly to cause laughter **2.** To give or feel a tingling sensation on the skin **3.** To amuse

tickle n. An act or feeling of tickling

tick-lish (tɪk–lɪʃ) adj. **1.** Sensitive to tickling **2.** Of a problem, etc., difficult: *a ticklish ques-*tion

tid-bit (tɪd–bɪt) n. A choice bit of food, news or gossip

tide (taɪd) n. **1.** The regular rising and falling of the surface of the ocean **2.** Sth. that fluctuates like the tides of the sea: *the tide of public opinion* **3. tide someone over** To help someone through a difficult period, usu. by loaning him money: *I loaned him some money to tide him over until pay day.*

tid-ings (taɪd–ɪŋz) n. News

ti-dy (taɪd–iᶕ) adj. **-dier, -diest 1.** Neat; clean; well arranged: *a tidy room/person* **2.** *infml.* Quite large: *a tidy income*

tidy v. **-died, -dying** To make neat: *The only time she tidies up the house is when she expects visitors.* —**tidily** adv. —**tidiness** n.

tie (taɪ) n. **1.** Also **necktie** *AmE.* A band of cloth worn around the neck and tied in front **2.** A cord, rope, etc., used for fastening sth. **3.** Sth. that unites: *family ties* **4.** An equal score in a game or contest **5.** *AmE.* Any of the row of heavy pieces of wood supporting a railroad track

tie v. **-tied, -tying 1.** To fasten or be fastened with a rope, cord, string, etc.: *He tied his shoelaces* **2.** To make a knot: *To tie a knot* **3.** To score the same number of points in a game or contest, finish a race at the same time, or jump or throw sthg. the same distance as another: *Bill and Jim tied for first place.* **4. tie down (a)** To limit one's freedom: *Al feels too tied down by his new job.* **(b)** To force a person to make a definite decision or state sthg. clearly: *They tied him down to a definite "Yes" or "No" answer.* **5. tied up** Very busy: *Mr. Smith can't see you right now; he's all tied up (=in an important meeting and can't leave it).* **6. sthg. is tied up** Unable to be used: *Jones doesn't have much money in the bank; it's all tied up in real estate.*

tier (tɪər) n. Any of a number of levels of seats, rising one behind or above another, as in a sports arena: *He was sitting in the front row of the upper tier.*

tiff (tɪf) n. A petty, minor quarrel

ti-ger (taɪ–gər) **tigress** (taɪ–grəs) *fem.* n. A large, fierce, tawny, black-striped, flesh-eating Asian mammal related to the cat

tight (taɪt) adj. **1.** Fitting usu. too closely: *My shoes are too tight./ This drawer is too tight; I can't open it.* **2.** Leaving little extra time: *a tight schedule* **3.** Firmly stretched, drawn, or set: *a tight knot* **4.** Difficult to obtain: *tight money* **5.** Intoxicated **6.** Stingy **7.** Difficult to deal with or get out of: *a tight spot* **8.** Closely contested: *a tight race (for the nomination)*

tight adv. **1.** Securely, firmly: *He held her tight.* **2.** Soundly: *Sleep tight* **3. sit tight** Don't make any changes —**tightly** adv. —**tightness** n.

tight-en (taɪt–ən) v. **1.** To make or become tighter **2.** To take firmer action against: *The government is tightening up (on) drug abuse.*

tight-fist-ed (taɪt–fɪs–təd) adj. Stingy

tight-lipped (taɪt–lɪpt) adj. **1.** Not talkative; close-mouthed **2.** Having the lips pressed tightly together

tight-rope (taɪt–roʷp) n. A tightly stretched rope on which acrobats perform

tights (taɪts) n. A tight fitting garment covering the legs and lower part of the body, worn by acrobats, dancers, etc.

tight-wad (taɪt–wɑd) n. A stingy person

tile (taɪl) n. A thin slab of baked clay or other material used for covering roofs, walls, floors, etc.

tile v. **tiled, tiling** To put tile on a roof, floor, etc.

till (tɪl) prep., conj. Until

till n. A drawer where money is kept in a store

till v. (old use) To cultivate the ground

till-age (tɪl–ɪdʒ) n. Land cultivation

til-ler (tɪl–ər) n. A lever for turning a rudder for steering a boat

tilt (tɪlt) v. To move or cause to move into a sloping or slanting position: *He tilted his chair backwards.*

tilt n. **1.** A slanting position: *The table is at a slight tilt.* **2. at full tilt** At full speed

tim-ber (tɪm–bər) n. **1.** Wood, esp. for building **2.** Trees suitable for this **3.** A wooden beam

tim-bered (tɪm–bərd) adj. **1.** Made of timbers **2.** Wooded; covered with trees **3.** Having exposed timbers

tim-ber-line (tɪm–bər–laɪm) n. The line above or beyond which trees do not grow, as on mountains or in polar regions

tim-bre (tæm–bər/tɪm–) n. The characteristic quality of sound that distinguishes one voice or musical instrument from another or one vowel sound from another

tim-brel (tɪm–brəl) n. An ancient type of tambourine

time (taɪm) n. **1.** All the minutes, days, months, and years of the past, present, and future **2.** A period between two events or for the completion of an action: *Learning English takes quite a long time.* **3.** A system of measuring time: *Pacific Standard Time* **4.** The period in which an action is completed: *World record time for running the marathon is 2 hours, 7 minutes and 12 seconds.* **5.** A particular point in the day stated in hours, minutes, and sometimes seconds: *What time is it? The time is exactly 11:15 p.m.* **6.** A particular moment or occasion: *Now is the time of God's favor, now is the day of salvation* (2 Corinthians 6:2). *Christ was sacrificed once to take away the sins of many people, and he will appear a second time... to bring salvation to those who are waiting for him* (Hebrews 9:28). **7.** The rate of speed of a piece of music **8. ahead of one's time** Having ideas that are too advanced for the period in which one lives **9. for the time being** For a limited period **10. from time to time** Occasionally **11. time after time** Repeatedly

time v. **timed, timing 1.** To measure or record the speed or duration of sthg.: *He was timed at 3:58 (three minutes and fifty-eight seconds) for the one mile run.* **2.** To set the time at which sthg. is to happen: *The sprinkling system was timed to start at six a.m.* **3.** To choose the proper moment for: *He timed his jump just right in order to catch the ball before it went over the fence.* **4.** To set the measure or rhythm of, as in music

time bomb (taɪm bɑm) n. A bomb that can be set to explode at a particular time

time clock (taɪm klɑk) n. An apparatus that records the arrival and departure time of employees

time de-pos-it (taɪm dɪ–pɑz–ət) n. A bank deposit that cannot be withdrawn before a specified date

time-hon-ored (taɪm ɑn–ərd) adj. Honored be-

time-less (taɪḿ–ləś) adj. **1.** Endless **2.** Unaffected by time —**timelessly** adv. —**timelessness** n.

time-ly (taɪm–liʸ) adj. **-lier, -liest** Occurring at just the right time; well-timed

time-out (taɪm–aʊt) n. also **time out** A period of suspended play during a game

time-piece (taɪm–piʸs) n. A clock or watch

tim-er (taɪ–mər) n. Sbdy. or sthg. that records time

times (taɪmz) prep. Multiplied by: *Four times six equals twenty-four is also written: 4 x 6 = 24.*

times n. **1.** The present time: *You are my God. My times are in your hands* (Psalm 31:14,15). **2.** Occasions on which sthg. is or was done: *I usually eat three times a day.* **3. at times** Occasionally; sometimes **4. behind the times** Not up-to-date; old-fashioned **5. for old times' sake** Because of the good times we had in the past

time-ta-ble (taɪm–teʸ–bəl) n. *BrE.* Schedule

tim-id (tɪm–əd) adj. Shy; fearful; lacking courage: *Encourage the timid, help the weak* (1 Thessalonians 5:14). —**ti-mid-i-ty** (u–mɪd–ə–tiʸ) n. —**timidly** adv.

tim-ing (taɪm–ŋ) n. The regulation of occurrence, pace, etc., to achieve the most desirable effects: *Trapeze artists must have perfect timing.*

tim-o-rous (tɪm–ə–rəs) adj. Fearful; timid

Tim-o-thy (tɪm–ə–θiʸ) n. Either of the two letters of the New Testament, written by the Apostle Paul to young Pastor Timothy. They contain instructions regarding the daily life of the local church, rules for Christian worship, and rules for church leaders. They also contain warnings against heresies (false teachings) in the church.

tin (tɪm) n. **1.** A soft silvery-white kind of metal that is a simple substance (element), used to cover metal objects with a protective surface **2.** *BrE.* Tin can for canned goods

tin adj. Made of tin: *a tin can*

tin v. **tinned, tinning 1.** To plate or coat with tin **2.** *BrE.* To preserve or pack in tins

tinc-ture (tɪŋk–tʃər) n. **1.** A substance that colors or dyes **2.** A solution of a drug or other substance in alcohol: *tincture of iodine* **3.** A slight trace

tin-der (tɪn–dər) n. *fml.* Dry material easily set on fire

tine (taɪm) n. A slender projecting part, pointed at the end; a prong

tinge (tɪndʒ) n. A slight amount: *a tinge of pink/ a tinge of resentment in her voice*

tin-gle (tɪŋ–gəl) v. **-gled, -gling** To feel a slight prickly sensation: *She was tingling with excitement*

tingle n. A slight prickly sensation —**tingly** adj.

tin-ker (tɪŋ–kər) v. To try unskillfully to fix sthg. or make it work better: *Don't tinker with my radio.*

tin-kle (tɪŋ–kəl) v. **-kled, -kling** To (cause to) make a light sound like the ringing of small bells: *The bell tinkled as he opened the shop door.* —**tinkle** n. *the tinkle of glasses*

tin-ny (tɪn–iʸ) adj. **-nier, -niest 1.** Of or containing tin **2.** Resembling tin; cheap **3.** Having a thin metallic sound

tin-sel (tɪn–səl) n. A sparkling, glittering substance used for decoration

tint (tɪnt) n. **1.** A pale shade of a color **2.** Any of the various shades of a color

tint v. To give a tint to: *She had her hair tinted red.*

ti-ny (taɪ–niʸ) adj. **-nier, -niest** Very, very small

tip (tɪp) n. **1.** The somewhat pointed end of sthg.: *the tip of one's fingers* **2.** A helpful piece of advice: *Mother gave her some tips on cooking.* **3.** A small gift of money for services rendered: *He gave the waitress a 15% tip.*

tip v. **-pp- 1.** To give a small gratuity to: *He tipped the taxi driver generously for his helpfulness.* **2.** To overturn or upset: *The car spun half way around and tipped over.* **3.** To (cause to) fall over: *He leaned back too far and his chair tipped over.* **4.** To raise or touch the brim of one's hat as a greeting **5.** In baseball, to hit the ball slightly, almost missing it: *The batter swung hard at the ball but just barely tipped it.*

tip off (tɪp–ɔf) v. To give secret information or a warning to: *The police were tipped off regarding the bank robbery, and the robbers were caught in the act.* —**tip-off** n.

tip-per (tɪp–ər) n. One who leaves a gratuity for services rendered: *He's a good tipper; he always leaves at least 15%.*

tip-sy (tɪp–siʸ) adj. Slightly drunk

tip-toe (tɪp–toʷ) n. The tip of the toe ; the ends of the toes

tiptoe v. **-toed, toeing** To walk stealthily or cautiously on the tip of one's toes

tip-top (tɪp–tɑp) adj. **1.** The highest point **2.** At the highest point of excellence

ti-rade (tai–reʸd/tai–reʸd) n. A prolonged speech of condemnation; a lengthy scolding

tire (tai–ər) v. **tired, tiring** To make or become weary: *Never tire of doing what is right* (2 Thessalonians 3:13).

tire *AmE.* **tyre** *BrE.* n. A thick rubber cushion, usu. filled with compressed air, that fits around the outside edge of a wheel, esp. on a motor vehicle or bicycle

tired (tai–ərd/ taird) adj. **1.** Weary; fatigued; needing to rest or sleep: *The Lord is the ever-lasting God, the Creator of the ends of the earth. He will not grow tired or weary* (Isaiah 40:28). **2.** No longer interested in; bored; annoyed with: *I'm tired of hearing that same old joke over and over again.* —**tiredly** adv. —**tiredness** n.

tire-less (tai–ər–ləs) adj. Never getting tired: *a tireless worker* —**tirelessly** adv.

tire-some (tai–ər–səm) adj. Tedious: *a tiresome job*

tis-sue (tɪʃ–uʷ) n. **1.** A soft, absorbent paper **2.** A substance of which the organs of the body are made: *muscle tissue*

ti-tan (tai–ən) n. A person of gigantic size or strength —**ti-tan-ic** (tai–tæn–ɪk) adj.

tithe (taið) n. A tenth part of one's income, esp. when donated to the church: *Since God gives us life and salvation and all that we possess, it is only fitting that we should return to him at least ten percent of what he has entrusted to us. In the book of Malachi, God speaks through his prophet saying: "Will a man rob God? Yet you rob me...in tithes and offerings... Bring the whole tithe into the storehouse...Test me in this, and see if I will not throw open the floodgates of heaven and pour out so much blessing that you will not have room enough for*

it" (Malachi 3:8-10).

tit-il-late (tɪt–əl–eʸt) v. **-lated, -lating 1.** To tickle **2.** To excite pleasurably —**tit-il-la-tion** (tɪt–əl–eʸ–ʃən) n.

ti-tle (tait–əl) n. **1.** A name given to a book, play, painting, song, etc. **2.** A word put before a person's name to show rank, honor, or profession: *Mr. Jones/ Dr. Smith/ Captain Cook* **3.** *tech.* The lawful right to ownership or possession: *Do you have the title to this land?*

title v. **-tled, -tling** *AmE.* To give a title to a book, movie, etc.

ti-tled (tait–əld) adj. Having a noble title, such as "Lord"

tit-mouse (tɪt–maʊs) n. **tit-mice** (tɪt–mais) Any of numerous small, long-tailed songbirds

tit-tle (tɪt–əl) n. A very small particle

tit-tle-tat-tle (tɪt–əl–tæt–əl) n. **1.** Idle talk **2.** Gossip

tit-u-lar (tɪtʃ–ə–lər) adj. **1.** Of, or having the nature of a title **2.** Having a title **3.** Existing only in title; in name only: *He is the titular head of the organization.*

Ti-tus (tait–əs) n. A book of the New Testament which was a letter written by the Apostle Paul to his disciple Titus, who was a leader of the churches of Crete. It contains rules for daily Christian living and qualifications for church leaders such as bishops, elders, and deacons. It speaks of "our great God and Savior Jesus Christ, who gave himself for us to redeem us from all wickedness and to purify for himself a people that are his very own, eager to do what is good" (Titus 2:13-14). Paul reminds Titus [and us] that "having been justified by his grace [God's undeserved love for us] we might become heirs, having the hope of eternal life (Titus 3:7).

tiz-zy (tɪz–iʸ) n. **to be or get into a tizzy** To be or become very nervous or upset: *She gets into a tizzy whenever we have unexpected guests for dinner.*

TNT (tiʸ–ɛn–tiʸ) n. A highly explosive substance used in military shells and in blasting

to (tuʷ/ tə) prep. **1.** In the direction of; towards: *the road to Monterey* **2.** As far as: *Bill*

went to Portland. 3. In contact with: *cheek to cheek* 4. In front of: *face to face* 5. Until: *They work from nine a.m. to five p.m.* 6. In relation with: *parallel to the coast* 7. Before: *ten minutes to five* 8. In connection with: *the key to the car* 9. For the attention of: *He's writing a letter to his mother.* 10. Touching: *stuck to the wall* 11. Concerning or regarding: *He was deaf to their cries for help.* 12. Used before a verb to indicate the infinitive: *I'd like to see you.* 13. Consisting in: *four quarts to the gallon* 14. Showing the indirect object in a phrase: *He who gives to the poor will lack nothing, but he who closes his eyes to them receives many curses* (Proverbs 28: 27) 15. In accord with: *It was not to my liking.* 16. As compared with: *a score of eight to six* 17. For or of: *the button to your shirt* 18. Resulting in: *frozen to death* 19. In recognition of: *a monument to their bravery* 20. Used to express addition: *Four added to six equals ten.* 21. Involved in: *That's all there is to it.* 22. By: *known to everyone*

to (tuᵂ) adv. 1. **come to** To regain consciousness: *The challenger was knocked out in the first round (of a boxing match) and didn't come to for ten minutes.* 2. **close to/near to** *The Lord is near to all who call on him, to all who call on him in truth* (Psalm 145:18).

toad (toᵂd) n. A tailless, jumping amphibious animal similar to a frog but having no teeth in the upper jaw and entering the water only for breeding purposes

toad-stool (toᵂd–stuᵂl) n. A mushroom, esp. a poisonous one

to-and-fro (tuᵂ–ən–froᵂ) adj. Backwards and forwards or from side to side —**to and fro** adv. *Bill walked to and fro in the waiting room at the hospital while waiting to hear of his wife's condition.*

toast (toᵂst) n. 1. Bread that has been made brown and crisp by heating 2. The act of drinking to someone's success and happiness

toast v. 1. To make bread brown and crisp by placing it close to heat 2. To drink and wish someone success and happiness

toast-er (toᵂ–stər) n. An electric appliance for toasting bread

toast-mas-ter (toᵂst–mæs–tər) n. Master of ceremonies; a person at a banquet who proposes toasts, introduces speakers, etc.

to-bac-co (tə–bæk–oᵂ) n. -cos or -coes 1. A plant native to tropical America, having broad leaves, used chiefly for smoking 2. The leaves of this plant, processed for use in cigarettes, cigars, pipes, etc. NOTE: The smoking of tobacco is a major cause of throat and lung cancer and emphysema (a lung condition that causes difficulty in breathing)

to-bog-gan (tə–bɑg–ən) n. A flat-bottomed sled, now used to coast down a prepared slope

toboggan v. To descend swiftly on a toboggan

to-day (tə–deʸ) adv., n. 1. This present day: *One of the men who was crucified [nailed to a cross] next to Jesus said, "Jesus, remember me when you come into your kingdom." Jesus answered him, "I tell you the truth, today you will be with me in paradise [heaven]"* (Luke 23:42,43). 2. This present time; these days: *People travel more today than ever before.*

tod-dle (tɑd–əl) v. To walk with unsteady steps as a small child just learning to walk

tod-dler (tɑd–lər) n. A small child

to-do (tə–duᵂ) n. A fuss; stir; commotion: *She's always making a big to-do about nothing.*

toe (toᵂ) n. 1. One of the parts (five in humans) at the end of each foot 2. The part of a shoe or stocking that covers this part of the foot

toe v. **toed, toeing** 1. To touch or kick with the toe 2. *infml.* **toe the line** To obey orders

toe-nail (toᵂ–neʸl) n. The hard flat piece that covers the front of each toe

to-ga (toᵂ–gə) n. A loose outer garment worn by ancient Roman citizens

to-geth-er (tə–geð–ər) adv. 1. Into one group: *People gathered together.* 2. With one another: *We went to school together.* 3. At the same time: *Let's all go together.* 4. So as to be joined or united: *He glued the two pieces of wood together.* 5. **together with** In addition to: *He gave her some flowers and candy, together with a nice birthday card.* 6. **get one's act together** *infml.* To arrange things in an orderly way; to work in a way that has good results 7. As

a joint action: *Together we were able to do it.*

toil (tɔil) v. **1.** To work hard and long **2.** To proceed with laborious effort and pain

toil n. **1.** Laborious effort **2.** Drudgery

toi-let (tɔɪ–lət) n. **1.** A large bowl with a seat, connected to a drain pipe, used for getting rid of the body's waste matter **2.** A room with this

toilet paper (tɔɪ–lət peᵞ–pər) n. Thin, soft tissue for cleaning oneself after using the toilet

toi-let-ry (tɔɪ–lə–triᵞ) n. **-ries** An article or cosmetic used in dressing or grooming

toi-let wa-ter (tɔɪ–lət wɑt–ər) n. Scented water for use on the skin after bathing or shaving, not as strong smelling as perfume

to-ken (toᵂ–kən) n. **1.** A sign, symbol, or evidence of sthg.: *She wore his ring as a token of their friendship.* **2.** A piece of metal or plastic in the shape of a coin used instead of money: *a bus token* **3. by the same token (a)** In proof of this **(b)** Similarly **4. in token of** *Please accept this small gift in token of our appreciation.*

token adj. Minimal: *Token resistance*

to-ken-ism (toᵂ–kən–ız–əm) n. The practice or policy of making only a token effort

told (toᵂld) v. Past tense & part. of **tell**

tol-er-a-ble (tɑl–ə–rə–bəl) adj. **1.** Capable of being tolerated; endurable **2.** Fairly good: *The weather is tolerable at this time of year.*

tol-er-ance (tɑl–ə–rəns) n. **1.** The ability to be fair and understanding of other people's views, etc., that are different from one's own: *racial/religious tolerance* **2.** The ability to resist the effects of medications, drugs, etc.: *a tolerance for quinine*

tol-er-ant (tɑl–ə–rənt) adj. Showing or practicing tolerance; to bear or endure

tol-er-ate (tɑl–ə–reᵞt) v. **-ated, -ating** To allow, bear, endure sthg. one does not like: *We should tolerate other people's opinions and ways of doing things, but we should not tolerate wickedness./ Your eyes [O Lord] are too pure to look on evil; you cannot tolerate wrong* (Habakkuk 1:13). **—tol-er-a-tion** (tɑl–ə–reᵞ–ʃən) n.

toll (toᵂl) n. **1.** A fixed tax charged for use of a road or bridge **2.** A charge for a service, such as a long-distance phone call **3.** The

amount or extent of loss or destruction: *The death toll from automobile accidents in the US is about 50,000 per year.*

toll v. To ring a bell slowly at regular intervals

toll n. The act or sound of tolling a bell

toll-gate (toᵂl–geᵞt) n. A gate at which a toll must be paid for the use of a road or bridge, etc.

tom-a-hawk (tɑm–ɪ–hɔk) n. A light ax used formerly by North American Indians as a weapon and a tool

to-ma-to (tə–meᵞt–oᵂ / –mɑt–) n. **-toes 1.** A soft red fruit used in salads or eaten as a vegetable **2.** The plant on which this fruit grows

tomb (tuᵂm) n. **1.** A place of burial; a grave **2.** A monument, tombstone, etc. commemorating the dead

tom-boy (tɑm–bɔi) n. A girl who prefers boyish activities and clothing

tomb-stone (tuᵂm–stoᵂn) n. Gravestone

tom-fool-er-y (tɑm–fuᵂl–ə–riᵞ) n. Stupid or foolish behavior

to-mor-row (tə–mɑr–oᵂ/–mɔr–oᵂ) adv., n. **1.** The day following today **2.** In the future: *Don't boast about tomorrow, for you do not know what a day may bring forth* (Proverbs 27:1). *Jesus said, "Seek first his kingdom [the kingdom of God] and his righteousness, and all these things [food, shelter, and clothing] will be given to you as well. Therefore, do not worry about tomorrow"* (Matthew 6:33,34).

ton (tʌn) n. **tons** or **ton 1.** A measurement of weight equal in the US to 2,000 pounds (a short ton) and in Britain to 2,240 pounds (a long ton) **2.** Also **metric ton** A measurement of weight equal to one thousand kilograms **3.** *infml.* A very large amount: *I have tons of work to do.*

tone (toᵂn) n. **1.** A sound of definite pitch, quality, or strength **2.** A particular quality of the voice; manner of expression: *Don't speak to your mother in that tone of voice.* **3.** A tint or shade of a color: *The car was a two-tone brown.* **4.** The general quality: *His comical opening speech set the tone for the evening.* **5.** A fixed distance between musical notes on a scale **—tonal** adj.

tone (toᵂn) v. **toned, toning 1.** To give tone to

2. To modify in tone 3. **tone down** To reduce the violence or force of. *Tone down your language; stop swearing.*

tongs (taŋz/ tɔŋz) n. An implement used for grasping, lifting, or holding objects

tongue (tʌŋ) n. 1. The freely moving organ in the mouth, used as an organ of taste and (in humans) in producing speech: *Before a word is on my tongue, you know it completely, O Lord* (Psalm 139:4). *God exalted him [Jesus] to the highest place... that at the name of Jesus every knee should bow... and every tongue confess that Jesus Christ is Lord, to the glory of God the Father* (Philippians 2:9-11). 2. An object shaped like a tongue such as the piece of material under the laces in a shoe 3. A spoken language: *My native tongue is English.* 4. **hold one's tongue** To be quiet

tongue–lash (tʌŋ–læʃ) v. To scold severely

tongue–tied (tʌŋ–taɪd) adj. Unable to speak, as from surprise or shyness

tongue twist-er (tʌŋ twɪs–tər) n. A phrase or sentence difficult to pronounce rapidly

ton-ic (tan–ɪk) n. Sthg. that increases health or strength: *The doctor gave him a special tonic (=medicine).* —**tonic** adj.

to-night (tə–naɪt) adv., n. This present night, or the one after today

ton-nage (tʌn–ɪdʒ) n. 1. The capacity of a merchant vessel, expressed in tons 2. The total amount of shipping of a country or a port 3. The total weight of anything expressed in tons

ton-sil (tan–səl) n. One of two oval organs at the back of the throat

ton-sil-lec-to-my (tan–sə–lɛk–tə–miʸ) n. **-mies** The surgical operation of removing the tonsils

ton-sil-li-tis (tan–sə–laɪt–əs) n. Inflammation of the tonsils

ton-so-ri-al (tan–sɔr–iʸ–el) adj. Pertaining to a barber or to his or her work

ton-sure (tan–tʃər) n. 1. The rite of shaving the head of a person becoming a priest or monk 2. The part of the head so shaven

too (tuʷ) adv. 1. More than enough: *The water is too cold, and I'm too tired to go swimming.* 2. Also: *She sings beautifully, and she plays the piano well, too.*

took (tʊk) v. Past tense of **take**

tool (tuʷl) n. 1. Any instrument such as a hammer, saw, screwdriver, etc., for doing a special job 2. Anything used to accomplish a definite purpose: *We believe this dictionary will be a helpful tool in learning the English language.*

tool v. To equip with tools: *We're getting tooled up for the new job.*

toot (tuʷt) v. To sound a horn or whistle in short blasts —**toot** n. An act or sound of tooting

tooth (tuʷθ) n. **teeth** (tiʸθ) 1. One of the small bony objects in the mouth, used for biting and chewing 2. Any of the pointed parts of a comb or a saw 3. **sweet tooth** A liking for candy and other sweet foods 4. **tooth and nail** With all one's resources and energy: *They fought tooth and nail to save the flood victims.* —see also TEETH

top (tap) n. 1. The highest part: *the top of the hill* 2. The upper surface: *the top deck* 3. The highest position or rank: *He has always been at the top of his class.* 4. A cover or lid: *Be sure to open this box at the top.* 5. **at top speed** As fast as one can possibly go 6. A kind of spinning toy 7. **off the top of one's head** Without much thought 8. **on top of** *infml.* In control of 9. **on top of** In addition to: *His wife died, and on top of that his car was stolen.* 10. **on top of the world** Very happy

top adj. First or best: *our top priority/our top salesman*

top v. **-pp-** 1. To form a top for: *pie topped with ice cream* 2. To be more than: *Sales this year have already topped our sales for all of last year.* 3. **top off** *AmE.* To complete; conclude: *Let's top off the meal with some apple pie ala mode.*

to-paz (toʷ–pæz) n. A type of precious stone of various colors, usu. yellow or brownish

top-ic (tap–ɪk) n. A subject spoken or written about

top-i-cal (tap–ɪ–kəl) adj. 1. Dealing with matters of current or local interest 2. Of or arranged by topics —**topically** adv.

to-pog-ra-phy (tə–pag–rə–fiʸ) n. 1. The science of describing or mapping the physical features of an area, such as mountains, rivers, lakes, etc. 2. These physical features —**to-**

po-graph-i-cal (tɑp–ə–**græf**–ɪ–kəl) adj.

top-ping (tɑp–ɱ) n. Sthg. to put on top of other food: *ice cream with chocolate topping*

top-ple (tɑp–əl) v. **-pled, -pling 1.** To fall **2.** To overthrow a government

top-sy-tur-vy (tɑp–siʸ–tɜr–viʸ) adj., adv. In a state of confusion

To-rah (tɔr–ə) n. **1. (a)** The Pentateuch, the first five books of the Old Testament, written about 1450 B.C.; the Books of Moses **(b)** A large handwritten scroll containing this, used in a synagogue **2.** The entire body of Jewish Law

torch (tɔrtʃ) n. **1.** *BrE.* A flashlight; a small hand-held light with a switch and an electric battery **2.** *AmE.* for **blowtorch 3.** (old use) Burning material tied to a stick and carried to give light **4. carry a torch for** To be in love with someone, esp. with one who is not aware of the other person's existence or doesn't care

tore (tɔr) v. Past tense of **tear**

tor-e-a-dor (tɔr–iʸ–ə–dɔr) n. A bullfighter

tor-ment (tɔr–mɛnt) n. Great physical or mental suffering or pain: *In hell, where he was in torment... (he said) "I am in agony in this fire"* (Luke 16:23,24).

torment (tɔr–mɛnt) v. **1.** To treat cruelly and cause great suffering **2.** To worry greatly **3.** To tease or annoy: *That child is always tormenting his sister.* **—tor-mentor** n.

torn (tɔrn) v. Past part. of **tear**

tor-na-do (tɔr–**neʸ**d–oʷ) n. **-does** or **-dos** A very violent, destructive whirling wind accompanied by a funnel-shaped cloud that moves over a narrow path

tor-pe-do (tɔr–**piʸ**d–oʷ) n. A cigar-shaped type of missile fired by ships and planes designed to explode on contact with, or in the vicinity of a target

torpedo v. **-doed, -doing** To attack or destroy with, or as with, a torpedo: *The submarine torpedoed three enemy ships in a single day.*

tor-pid (tɔr–pəd) adj. **1.** Slow; sluggish **2.** Lacking vigor **—tor-pid-i-ty** (tɔr–**pɪd**–ə–tiʸ) n. **—torpidly** adv.

torque (tɔrk) n. A force that causes rotation **—torque** v. **torqued, torquing**

tor-rent (tɔr–ənt) n. **1.** A rapid, violently flowing stream of water **2.** A heavy downpour of rain: *The rain fell in torrents.*

tor-ren-tial (tɔ–**rɛn**–tʃəl/ tə–) adj. **1.** Relating to or having the character of a torrent: *torrential rain* **2.** Resembling a torrent in violence or rapidity

tor-rid (tɔr–əd/ **tɑr**–) adj. **1.** Very hot and dry: *torrid weather* **2.** Intensely passionate: *torrid love scenes* **—torridly** adv.

tor-sion (tɔr–ʃən) n. **1.** Twisting **2.** A twisted state **3.** Stress by twisting **—torsional** adj. **—torsionally** adv.

tor-so (tɔr–soʷ) n. The trunk of the human body

tor-ti-lla (tɔr–**tiʸ**–yə) n. A round thin cake of unleavened cornmeal or wheat flour, baked on a sheet of iron or a slab of stone, usu. eaten with a topping of ground meat and cheese

tor-toise (tɔrt–əs) n. A turtle, esp. a land turtle

tor-tu-ous (tɔr–tʃuʷ–əs) adj. **1.** Full of twists and turns **2.** Not direct; devious

tor-ture (tɔr–tʃər) n. **1.** The infliction of severe pain, done out of cruelty or to get information **2.** Severe pain: *Driving on these rough, rocky roads is torture.*

tor-ture v. **-tured, -turing** To cause great suffering to a person or animal out of cruelty, as a punishment, or to obtain information **—torturer** n.

toss (tɔs/ tɑs) v. **1.** To throw lightly: *He tossed the ball to his little sister.* **2.** To move restlessly or turbulently: *The boat was tossed around in the stormy sea.* **3.** To mix lightly: *to toss a salad* **4.** To fling or lift with a sudden motion: *She tossed her head angrily.* **5.** To twist and turn repeatedly: *He tossed restlessly all night, unable to sleep.* **6.** To flip a coin to decide sthg.

toss n. **1.** A flip of a coin **2.** A rapid lift, as of the head

toss-up (tɔs–ʌp) n. *infml.* An even chance: *Who will win the basketball game? It looks like a toss-up to me.*

tot (tɑt) n. A very small child

to-tal (toʷt–əl) adj. Entire; complete; whole: *the total population* **—totally** adv. *I totally agree with you.*

total n. The sum of two or more numbers when added: *Add these numbers and give me*

the total.

to-tal v. **totaled, totaling** *AmE.* **totalled, totalling** *BrE.* To add up to: *His debts totaled more than five thousand dollars.*

to-tal-i-tar-i-an (toᵂ–tæl–ə–teər–iʸ–ən) adj. A political system in which one political group controls everything and does not allow an opposition party to exist

to-tal-i-ty n. (toᵂ–tæl–ət–tiʸ) n. Completeness

tote (toᵂt) v. **toted, toting** To carry

to-tem (toᵂt–əm) n. **1.** An animal, plant, or object serving as an emblem of a family or clan and often as a reminder of its ancestry **2.** A carved or painted representation of such an animal, plant, or object

to-tem pole (toᵂ–təm poᵂl) n. A pole that is carved with a series of totems and is erected in front of some of the houses of some Northwest American Indians

tot-ter (tɑt–ər) v. **1.** To walk unsteadily **2.** To rock or shake as if about to collapse

tou-can (tuᵂ–kɑn/ –kæn) n. A brilliantly colored South American bird with a large bill

touch (tʌtʃ) v. **1.** To be or come into contact **2.** To tap or nudge lightly **3.** To feel with a part of the body, esp. the hands or fingers **4.** To make use of: *He never touches tobacco.* **5.** To mention briefly: *In his talk he touched on many subjects.* **6.** To feel pity: *We were all greatly touched by her tragic story.* **7.** To compare equally with: *No one in our school can touch Bob Smith in athletic ability.* —**touchable** adj.

touch n. **1.** One of the five senses, the others being sight, hearing, smell, and taste **2.** The sense by which a material object is known to be hot, cold, hard, soft, smooth, rough, wet, dry, esp. by feeling with the fingers **3.** A light stroke or tap: *He felt the touch of her hand on his shoulder.* **4.** Communication: *I'm trying to get in touch with the governor.* **5.** A small amount: *This food needs a touch of salt.* **6.** A slight added detail that improves or completes sthg.: *She's just putting the finishing touches on her report.* **7.** Skill: *The piano player had a delicate touch.* **8.** Awareness or understanding: *He's out of touch with reality.* **9.** A mild onset of an illness: *a touch of the flu* **10. keep in touch** Write or call from time to

time **11. losing his touch** To be losing one's skill or ability

touch and go (tʌtʃ ən goᵂ) adj. Risky; uncertain

touch-down (tʌtʃ–daʊn) n. **1.** In American football, a play scoring six points made by carrying or catching the ball beyond the opponent's goal line **2.** Of an aircraft or spacecraft, the moment of landing

tou-ché (tuᵂ–ʃeʸ) **1.** A fencing score **2.** An acknowledgement that one's opponent has made a hit in fencing or a valid accusation or criticism in a discussion

touched (tʌtʃt) adj. **1.** Moved: *I was very touched by their kind remarks.* **2.** *infml.* Slightly crazy: *He's a little touched in the head.*

touch-ing (tʌtʃ–ɪŋ) adj. Affecting the emotions, rousing kindly feelings or sympathy or pity

touch-y (tʌtʃ–iʸ) adj. **-ier, -iest** Easily offended; too sensitive —**touchily** adv. —**touchiness** n.

tough (tʌf) adj. **1.** Of persons or animals, strong; durable; able to withstand hardship —opposite WEAK **2.** Difficult to cut or chew: *tough meat* —opposite TENDER **3.** Difficult to do: *a tough assignment* **4.** Unyielding or stubborn: *tough opposition* **5.** Strict and determined, as a policy: *The government is getting tough in its war on drugs.* **6.** *infml.* Hard; unpleasant: *Tough luck!* —**toughly** adv. —**toughness** n.

tough n. *infml.* A rough, violent person

tough-en (tʌf–ən) v. To make or become tough

tou-pee (tuᵂ–peʸ) n. A wig; an artificial patch of hair to wear over a place where hair no longer grows

tour (tʊər) n. **1.** A journey during which one visits several places **2.** A short trip to or through a place: *We went on a guided tour of the palace.* **3.** A period of duty at a single place or job, esp. overseas

tour v. To make a tour

tour-ism (tʊər–ɪz–əm) n. **1.** The activities of tourists and those who provide services for them **2.** The practice of traveling for pleasure

tour-ist (tʊər–əst) n. A person traveling for

pleasure

tour-na-ment (tɜr–nə–mənt/ tʊər–) n. A championship series of games or athletic contests, played until the most skillful wins: *a golf tournament*

tour-ni-quet (tɜr–nɪ–kət/ tʊər–) n. A device like a bandage twisted tight with a stick to stop the flow of blood

tou-sle (taʊ–zəl) v. **-sled, -sling** To make (hair) untidy by ruffling; muss

tout (taʊt) v. **1.** To praise or publicize loudly **2.** To give a tip or to solicit bets on a racehorse —**tout** n.

tow (toʷ) v. To pull sthg. along by a rope or chain

tow n. An act of towing or the state of being towed

to-ward (tɔrd/ toʷrd) also **towards** prep. **1.** In the direction of: *She was walking toward home.* **2.** Not long before: *Toward the end of the trip, we had a flat tire.* **3.** Regarding: *his attitude toward his wife* **4.** As a contribution to: *He gave $500 toward his son's tuition.*

to-wel (taʊ–əl) n. A piece of cloth or paper used for wiping or drying

tow-er (taʊ–ər) n. A tall structure either standing alone or built upon a larger structure: *The Eiffel Tower*

tow-er v. To be very tall in relation to the surroundings: *The Empire State Building still towers over most of the city of New York.*

tow-er-ing (taʊ–ər–ŋ) adj. **1.** Lofty **2.** Excessive

tow-head (toʷ–hɛd) n. A person with light blond hair —**towheaded** adj.

town (taʊn) n. **1.** A large number of houses and other buildings where people live and work, larger than a village and smaller than a city —compare CITY, VILLAGE **2.** The business district of such a place: *We drove into town to go to a movie.* **3.** The people who live in the town: *The whole town is talking about the Jones boy.* **4. go to town** To do sthg. lavishly or with great enthusiasm in order to succeed

town-ship (taʊn–ʃɪp) n. **1.** An administrative division of a county with varying powers of government **2.** A division of land approximately six miles square

tox-ic (tɑk–sɪk) adj. **1.** Poisonous **2.** Caused by a poison

tox-in (tɑk–sən) n. A naturally occurring poison produced by animals, plants, bacteria, etc.

toy (tɔɪ) n. **1.** A thing to play with, esp. for a child **2.** An object intended for amusement rather than serious use

toy adj. Serving as a toy: *a toy car*

toy v. **1.** To handle sthg. idly: *The little boy was toying with his food.* **2.** To lightly consider sthg.: *He toyed with the idea of sailing a small boat around the world.*

trace (treʸs) v. **traced, tracing 1.** To copy by following lines seen through transparent paper (tracing paper) **2.** To follow the course of history or development of sthg.: *He has traced his family's history back to the 12th century.* —**trace-able** adj.

trace n. **1.** A mark or some kind of evidence showing that someone or sthg. has been present in a place: *The search party found no trace of the missing child.* **2.** A tiny amount: *traces of poison in his blood*

tra-che-a (treʸ–kiʸ–ə) n. **-che-as** or **-che-ae** (–kiʸ–iʸ/ –kiʸ–aɪ) The tube that carries air to and from the lungs

track (træk) n. **1.** Marks left by a person, animal, or vehicle: *It was easy to follow the car tracks in the mud.* **2.** The iron lines on which a train travels **3.** A course prepared for racing **4.** A course of action taken: *I think you're on the right track in your investigation* **5.** Athletic competition: *John is out for track. He's a good runner.* **6.** A section of a long-playing phonograph record or tape **7. one-track mind** *infml.* Unable to think, or not wanting to think about anything else; always focusing on one pet subject **8. off the beaten track** An out-of-the-way place, not often visited

track v. **1.** To follow the track of sbdy. or sthg.: *The hunters were tracking a wolf.* **2. track sthg. down** To find sthg. by searching even when there are no tracks or any clues: *I finally tracked down a copy of that rare book I've been looking for.* —**tracker** n.

track and field (træk ænd fiʸld) n. Athletic events performed on a running track and an adjacent field

track meet (træk miʸt) n. A sports competition

with a number of running events, high jumping, long jumping, pole vaulting, etc.

tract (trækt) n. A short pamphlet, esp. about a religious or moral subject

tract n. **1.** A stretch of land without precise boundaries **2.** A defined piece of land: *a garden tract* **3.** A system of body parts or organs serving a special purpose: *the digestive tract*

trac-ta-ble (**træk**-tə-bəl) adj. Easily led or controlled; docile

trac-tion (**træk**-ʃən) n. **1.** The act of drawing or pulling, or condition of being drawn or pulled **2.** Adhesive friction, as of a wheel on a track **3.** The pulling power of a railroad engine

trac-tor (**træk**-tər) n. A motor vehicle with large wheels and thick tires, or belt-like metal tracks, used for pulling farm machinery or other heavy equipment

trade (tre^{y}d) n. **1.** The act or process of buying and selling goods **2.** An exchange of one thing for another **3.** A particular business: *He works in the tourist trade.* **4.** An occupation, esp. one needing special skills: *He's a mechanic by trade.*

trade v. **traded, trading 1.** To carry on trade: *Our country trades with several other countries.* **2.** To buy, sell, or exchange: *Tom traded his pocket knife for a baseball.* **3. trade sthg. in** To give in partial payment for sthg. new or newer: *We traded in our old car for a newer one.*

trade-mark (tre^{y}d-mɑrk) n. A mark, wording, or symbol to distinguish a product from that of a competitor

trad-er (tre^{y}d-ər) n. A person who buys and sells goods for a living

trade-wind (tre^{y}d-wɪnd) n. A wind that blows toward the equator, from the southwest or from the northeast

tra-di-tion (trə-dɪʃ-ən) n. **1.** The passing down of a culture (opinions, beliefs, practices, customs etc.) from one generation to another, esp. orally **2.** An opinion, belief, custom, etc., passed down in this way: *See to it that no one takes you captive through... deceptive philosophy which depends on human tradition and the basic principles of this world rather than on Christ* (Colossians 2:8). **—traditional**

adj. *the traditional Thanksgiving dinner* **—traditionally** adv.

traf-fic (**træf**-ɪk) n. **1.** The movement of vehicles, planes, or pedestrians within a certain place or from one place to another **2.** The quantity or the rate of such movement **3.** Buying and selling some commodity, esp. sthg. illegal: *the illegal traffic in drugs*

traffic v. **-ficked, -ficking** To carry on traffic, esp. illegally

trag-e-dy (**trædʒ**-əd-i^y) n. **-dies 1.** A very terrible, disastrous event: *The worst tragedy in the world is not knowing Christ our Savior who alone is the way to eternal life* (John 14:6; Acts 4:12). **2.** A serious drama that ends sadly: *Shakespeare wrote many tragedies.*

trag-ic (**trædʒ**-ɪk) adj. Causing or likely to cause suffering, sorrow, or death: *a tragic accident/decision* **—tragically** adv.

trail (tre^{y}l) v. **1.** To draw or drag along behind: *The queen's robe was trailing (along) behind her.* **2.** To follow the tracks of: *The police trailed the escaped convicts to a cabin in the woods.* **3.** To follow slowly; lag behind: *The tired hikers trailed along behind the others.* **4.** To be losing in a contest: *At halftime, our team was trailing by a score of 14 to 6.*

trail n. **1.** A path across rough country: *The Oregon Trail* **2.** A trace or mark that has been left by someone or sthg. that has passed along: *a trail of blood* **3.** A stream of dust, smoke, etc., behind sthg. moving: *The car left a long trail of dust behind it.* **4.** A marked path through the woods

trail-er (tre^y-lər) n. **1.** A vehicle pulled by another vehicle: *The car was pulling a trailer loaded with furniture.* **2.** A vehicle that is equipped to serve as a dwelling or an office wherever it is parked: *a house trailer* **3.** A creeping plant, such as ivy

train (tre^{y}n) n. **1.** Several connected railroad cars pulled by an engine **2.** A part of a long gown that trails behind the wearer **3.** A succession of connected ideas: *a train of thought* **4.** A file of people, animals or vehicles traveling together **5.** A series of events

train v. **1.** To educate: *Train a child in the way he should go and when he is old he will not turn from it* (Proverbs 22:6). **2.** To make or be-

come proficient with specialized instruction and practice: *Train yourself to be godly [which] has value for all things, holding promise for both the present life and the life to come* (1 Timothy 4:7,8KJV). **3.** To coach in some mode of behavior or performance: *He has trained many animals for the circus.* **4.** To direct the growth of a plant —**trainable** adj. —**trainer** n.

train-ee (tre^y–ni^y) n. A person who is being trained for a particular purpose: *The new waitress is a trainee.*

train-ing (tre^y–nɪŋ) n. **1.** The act of being trained: *Fathers, do not exasperate your children; instead, bring them up in the training and instruction of the Lord* (Ephesians 6:4). **2.** Preparation for a sport: *Spring training for baseball begins in early March.*

traipse (tre^yps) v. To wander; tramp

trait (tre^yt) n. A particular quality of a person's character: *Enthusiasm is one of her best traits.*

trai-tor (tre^yt–ər) n. **1.** One who is disloyal, esp. to his/her own country **2.** One who commits treason —**traitorous** adj.

tra-jec-to-ry (trə–dʒek–tə–ri^y) -ries n. Path of an object moving through space, as a bullet

tram (træm) n. **1.** *Chiefly British* A streetcar **2.** A box-like car running on a railway in a mine or logging camp —see TRAMWAY

tram-mel (træm–əl) n. **1.** A kind of dragnet for catching fish **2.** *Usu. pl.* Anything that hinders movement

trammel v. -ll- To hinder

tramp (træmp) v. **1.** To walk or step heavily **2.** To walk about or through: *We tramped through the woods all day.*

tramp n. **1.** A person who has no home or job and who wanders about on foot, and usu. lives by begging **2.** The sound of heavy footsteps: *the tramp, tramp, tramp of the soldiers' feet along the highway* **3.** A long walk, esp. in the country: *They went for a tramp through the woods.* **4.** esp. *AmE.* A sexually immoral woman; a prostitute **5.** A ship that does not follow a regular course but takes cargo to any port: *A tramp loaded with cargo steamed into port.*

tram-ple (træm–pəl) v. -pled, -pling **1.** To step heavily with the feet so as to injure or destroy; crush **2.** To treat disrespectfully, cruelly, or ruthlessly: *Many trample on the feelings of others.*

tram-po-line (træm–pə–li^yn) n. A horizontal framework across which a piece of canvas is stretched, attached by springs, for gymnasts, etc. to jump on

tram-way (træm–we^y) n. **1.** The rails for a tram **2.** An aerial passenger or freight car suspended from a cable —see TRAM

trance (træns) n. **1.** A daze; stupor **2.** A sleeplike or half-conscious condition

tran-quil (træŋ–kwəl/ træn–) adj. Quiet, peaceful; free from agitation or disturbance

tran-quil-ize also -**quillize** *AmE.* also -**ise** *BrE.* (træŋ–kwə–laɪz/træn–) v. -ized, -izing To make calm

tran-quil-iz-er also -**quillizer** *AmE.* also -**liser** *BrE.* (træŋ–kwə–laɪ–zər/træn–) A drug to calm the nerves or cause sleep

tran-quil-li-ty or **tranquility** (træn–kwɪl–ət–i^y/ træn–) n. Peacefulness

trans- (trænz–/ træns–) prefix **1.** Across; crossing: *transcontinental* **2.** Change: *transfer*

trans-act (træns–ækt/trænz–) v. To carry out or conduct business

trans-ac-tion (træns–æk–ʃən/ trænz–) n. **1.** The act or process of transacting **2.** Some business transacted

tran-scend (træn–send) v. **1.** To rise above the limits of **2.** To surpass; exceed: *Do not be anxious about anything, but in everything, by prayer and petition, with thanksgiving, present your requests to God. And the peace of God, which transcends all understanding, will guard your hearts and your minds in Christ Jesus* (Philippians 4:6,7). —see JESUS

tran-scen-den-tal (træns–ɛn–dent–əl) adj. Going beyond normal human experience or knowledge

tran-scen-den-tal-ism (træns–ɛn–dent–əl–ɪz–əm) n. The belief that knowledge of reality is derived from intuitive sources rather than objective experiences

tran-scen-den-tal med-i-ta-tion (træns–ɛn–dent–əl mɛd–ə–te^y–ʃən) n. A spiritual practice or yoga which was first introduced to the Western World as a religious exercise or

philosophy NOTE: Later TM was promoted as a scientifically sound, nonreligious psychological exercise designed to relieve stress, and to enable the advanced practitioner to participate in astral projection (his soul leaving his body) in levitation. TM concentrates on those Hindu scriptures which present a pantheistic view of God, claiming that one can lose his own personality in the oneness of God. This, of course, takes away from the unique and separate personality of God. TM ignores Jesus Christ almost completely. It is clear from his neglect of Jesus Christ and from his world view that Maharishi Mahesh Yogi, the founder of TM, does not consider Jesus Christ to be the unique Son of God who was manifest in the flesh to destroy the works of the devil and to save fallen mankind. Christians, of course, will have nothing to do with this kind of meditation, but will read and meditate day and night upon the word of God which makes us wise unto salvation through faith in Christ Jesus and is useful for teaching, rebuking, correcting and training in righteousness, that the man of God may be thoroughly equipped for every good work (Psalm 1:1-3; Romans 1:16; 2 Timothy 3:16,17). —see JESUS

trans-con-ti-nen-tal (træns–kɑnt–ən–ɛnt–əl) adj. Crossing a continent

tran-scribe (træns–**kraɪb**) v. 1. (a) To write or type a copy of sthg. (b) To write out fully, as from notes 2. To adapt (a musical composition) for a particular instrument or group of instruments 3. To record sthg. for broadcasting at a later date

tran-script (**træns**–krɪpt) n. 1. A written, typed, or printed copy 2. An official copy, esp. of a student's educational record

tran-scrip-tion (træns–krɪp–ʃən) n. 1. The act or process of transcribing 2. Sthg. transcribed, esp. (a) An adaptation of a musical composition (b) A recorded radio or television program

tran-sect (træns–ɛkt) v. To cut across —**transection** n.

tran-sept (**træns**–ɛpt) n. In a cross-shaped church, either of the two arms that lie at right angles to the nave (where most of the congregation sits)

trans-fer (**træns**–fɚ/ trænɔ̍–**far**) v. -rr- **1.** To (cause to) move from one place, job, vehicle, etc., to another: *John transferred from one bus to another at the corner of Sixth and Main.* **2.** To give the ownership of (property) to someone else **3.** To print or copy from one surface to another by contact —**transferable** adj.

transfer n. **1.** The act of transferring: *He wants a transfer to another team.* **2.** A ticket which allows a passenger on a bus or other public conveyance to continue his journey on another route: *Ask for a transfer when you get on the bus.*

trans-fig-ure (træns–**fɪg**–yɚ) v. **-ured, -uring** To change in appearance, and make glorious: *a face transfigured with joy/ Jesus was transfigured before them [Peter, James, and John]: "His face shone like the sun, and his clothes became as white as the light." And a voice from the cloud said, "This is my Son, whom I love; with him I am well pleased. Listen to him!"* (Matthew 17:2-5). —**trans-fig-u-ra-tion** (træns–fɪg–yə–**reʸ**–ʃən) n.

trans-fix (træns–**fɪks**) v. **1.** Impale; fasten **2.** To cause (sbdy.) to be unable to move **3.** To make a person motionless with fear or astonishment

trans-form (træns–**fɔrm**) v. **1.** To change completely in form, appearance, or nature: *Do not conform any longer to the pattern of this world, but be transformed by the renewing of your mind* (Romans 12:2). **2.** To transform heat into power —**trans-for-ma-tion** (træns–fɚ–**meʸ**–ʃen) n.

trans-form-er (træns–**fɔr**–mɚ) n. A device used for transferring electric energy from one circuit to another

trans-fuse (træns–**fyuʷz**) v. **-fused, -fusing 1.** To transfer liquid from one vessel into another **2.** To administer a transfusion **3.** To permeate

trans-fu-sion (træns–**fyuʷ**–ʒən) n. The direct injection of the blood of one person into the body of another: *He lost a lot of blood and had a transfusion after the accident.*

trans-gress (træns–**grɛs**/ trænz–) v. To go be-

yond the limits imposed by a law or commandment; to break the law

trans·gres·sion (træns–**greʃ**–ən/ trænz–) n. An act of breaking or going against: *Sin is the transgression of the law [God's Law]* (1 John 3:4). *You [all of us] were dead in your transgressions and sins* (Ephesians 2:1). *But God, who is rich in mercy, made us alive with Christ even when we were dead in transgressions. It is by grace [the unmerited love of God] you have been saved* (Ephesians 2:5). *For he [Jesus] was pierced [nailed to a cross] for our transgressions* (Isaiah 53:5). *He was delivered over to death for our sins [transgressions] and was raised to life for our justification* (Romans 4:25). *Blessed are they whose transgressions are forgiven, whose sins are covered. Blessed is the man whose sin the Lord will never count against him [because of his faith in Jesus Christ]* (Romans 4:7,8). *For the wages of sin is death, but the gift of God is eternal life through Jesus Christ our Lord* (Romans 6:23). *As far as the east is from the west, so far has he removed our transgressions from us* (Psalm 103:12). —see also TRANSGRESSOR, SIN, INIQUITY, TRESPASS

trans·gres·sor (træns–**gres**–ər/ trænz–) n. A sinner; one who transgresses God's Law: *He [Jesus] bore the sin of many [paid for our sins with his own blood], and made intercession for the transgressors [all of us]* (Isaiah 53:12). —see JESUS

tran·sient (træntʃ–ənt/ træn–siʸ–ənt) adj. **1.** Passing by quickly with time **2.** Staying only a short time: *transient workers*

transient n. One that is transient, esp. a person staying only one night at a hotel or motel —**transiency** n.

tran·sis·tor (trænz–**ɪs**–tər/ træns–) n. **1.** A device used for amplification, switching, etc. **2.** A radio equipped with transistors

tran·sit (træns–ət/ trænz–) n. **1.** A passing through, across, or over **2.** Conveyance of persons or things from one place to another, esp. by a local public conveyance **3.** A surveyor's instrument for measuring angles

tran·si·tion (træns–**ɪʃ**–ən/ trænz–) n. An instance of changing from one subject to another, or from one form, state, or place to

another —**transitional** adj.

tran·si·tive (**træn**–sə–tɪv) adj. Being or using a verb that requires a direct object to complete its meaning

tran·si·to·ry (træns–ə–tɔr–iʸ/ trænz–) adj. Existing only briefly

trans·late (træns–**leʸ**t/ trænz–) v. **-lated, -lating** To change (speech or writing) from one language into another —**trans·la·tion** (træns–**leʸ**–ʃən/ trænz–) n. —**translator** n.

trans·lit·er·ate (træns–lɪt–ə–reʸt) v. **-ated, -ating** To substitute words or letters of one language for those of another —**trans·lit·er·a·tion** (træns–lɪt–ə–**reʸ**–ʃən) n.

trans·lu·cent (træns–**luʷs**–ənt) adj. Allowing light to pass through, but not allowing a clear view of any object: *translucent glass*

trans·mi·grate (træns–**maɪ**–greʸt) v. **-grated, -grating 1.** To supposedly become incarnate in a different body, as the soul. This does not happen. —see TRANSMIGRATION OF THE SOUL **2.** To migrate

trans·mi·gra·tion (træns–maɪ–**greʸ**–ʃən) n.

transmigration of the soul The passing of a person's soul into another body after his death NOTE: This cannot happen, and this is altogether contrary to the word of God which says: "Man is destined to die once, and after that to face judgment" (Hebrews 9:27). Or as Jesus told the repentant thief on the cross: "Today you will be with Me in paradise" (Luke 23:43). —see SOUL and the note under REINCARNATION

trans·mis·sion (træns–**mɪʃ**–ən/ trænz–) n. **1.** The act or process of transmitting **2.** Sthg. broadcast by television or radio **3.** The part of an automobile, truck, etc. that transmits motive force from the engine to the wheels

trans·mit (træns–**mɪt**/ trænz–) v. **-tt- 1.** To send out (electric signals, messages, news, etc.); to broadcast **2.** To cause to spread, as an infection, from one person, place, or thing to another: *to transmit a disease* **3.** To impart, as by heredity

trans·mit·ter (træns–**mɪt**–ər/ trænz–) n. **1.** An electrical or electronic device that originates radio or television signals: *a radio transmitter* **2.** Someone or sthg. that transmits

trans-mute (træns–**myu**ᵂt/ trænz–) v. -muted, -mutlng To cause a thing to change in form, nature, or substance —**transmutable** adj. —**trans-mu-ta-tion** (træns–myuᵂ–teʸ–ʃən) n.

tran-som (**træn**–səm) n. 1. A small window above a door or other window2. The cross-piece that separates a door or a window from the window above it

trans-par-en-cy (træns–**pær**–ən–siʸ/–**peər**–) n. -cies 1. A photographic slide, esp. on film as distinct from glass 2. The state of being transparent

trans-par-ent (træns–**pær**–ənt/ –**peər**–) adj. 1. Permitting light to pass through, so that what is on one side can be seen from the other side: *Most glass is transparent.* 2. So sheer in texture that light can pass through: *The curtains were transparent.* 3. Easily seen to be true or false: *a transparent excuse* 4. Candid or frank: *a transparent style of writing*

tran-spire (træns–**pai**–ər) v. -spired, -spiring 1. To take place; occur 2. To become gradually known 3. To pass out moisture, odor, etc. as through pores of the skin

trans-plant (træns–**plænt**) v. 1. To remove a plant from one place and plant it in another place 2. To transfer an organ, tissue, etc. from one part of the body to another part or from one person to another 3. To bring a family from one part of the country or from another country for resettlement in a new land

transplant (**træns**–plænt) n. 1. The act or process of transplanting 2. Sthg. transplanted: *a heart transplant*

trans-port (træns–**port**) v. To carry people or goods from one place to another —**trans-portable** adj.

transport (**træns**–port) n. A ship used to transport troops

trans-por-ta-tion (træns–pər–teʸ–ʃən) n. 1. The act of transporting or of being transported: *The transportation of goods by air is very expensive.* 2. A means of carrying passengers or goods from one place to another: *public transportation* 3. The business of transporting goods or passengers

trans-port-er (træns–port–ər) n. A vehicle on which a number of cars can be transported

trans-pose (træns–**po**ᵂz) v. -posed, -posing 1. To cause two or more things to change places 2. To put a piece of music into a different key

trans-verse (træns–**vɜrs**/ trænz–) adj. Lying or placed across sthg.; set crosswise

trap (træp) n. 1. A device for catching and holding animals: *a mouse trap* 2. Any plan by which a person may be captured unawares: *The police set a trap for criminals./ We pray that those who don't know Jesus as their Savior from sin, death and the devil will come to the knowledge of the truth about Jesus, put their trust in him, and escape the trap of the devil, who has taken them captive to do his will* (2 Timothy 2:26).

trap v. -pp- To catch in a trap or by a trick

trap-door (**træp**–dor) n. A hinged or sliding door in a floor or ceiling

tra-peze (træ–**pi**ʸz/ trə–) n. A short horizontal bar suspended by two parallel ropes, used for acrobatic stunts

trap-e-zoid (**træp**–ə–zɔid) n. A four-sided figure that has two sides parallel: *A rectangle is a trapezoid, but not all trapezoids are rectangles.*

trap-per (**træp**–ər) n. A person who traps wild animals, esp. for their fur

trap-pings (**træp**–ŋs) n. 1. Articles of equipment or dress, esp. of an ornamental nature 2. An ornamental covering for a horse

trash (træʃ) n. 1. Sthg. of little worth; rubbish 2. A contemptible person

trash-y adj. -ier, -iest Cheap or worthless expressions or ideas: *trashy books*

trau-ma (trau–mə/ trɔ–) n. -mas, -mata 1. An emotional shock that has a damaging and lasting effect on mental life 2. A bodily injury produced by sudden force —**trau-mat-ic** (trə–**mæt**–ik) adj. —**trau-ma-tize** (**trau**–mə–taiz) v.

tra-vail (trə–veʸl/ træv–eʸl) n. 1. Agony; anguish 2. Strenuous exertion

travail v. 1. To toil 2. To be in labor of childbirth

trav-el (**træv**–əl) v. -l- *AmE.* -ll- *BrE.* 1. To make a journey: *He has traveled all over the world by air, land, and sea.* 2. To pass or go through a place: *Sound travels at the rate of about 1,100*

feet per second at sea level.

travel n. The act of traveling: *This modern age is an age of travel.*

trav-el-er *AmE.* **traveller** *BrE.* (træv–ə–lər) n. A person on a journey

tra-verse (trə–vərs/ træ–vərs) v. **-versed, -versing 1.** To pass through; penetrate **2.** To go or travel across or over **3.** To move forward and backward over: *Many lights traversed the night sky in search of enemy planes.*

tra-verse (træ–vərs) n. Sthg. that lies across sthg. else, as a beam or crosspiece

trav-es-ty (træv–ə–sti^y) n. **-ties** A miserable imitation; a mockery: *Innocent people were sent to jail; the guilty were declared innocent. What a travesty of justice!*

trawl (trɔl) v. To draw a large net behind a fishing boat

trawl v. To fish with a trawl

trawl-er (trɔ–lər) n. **1.** A boat used in trawling **2.** A person who fishes by trawling

tray (tre^y) n. A flat receptacle with a low rim used to carry, hold, or display food or other items

treach-er-ous (tretʃ–ə–rəs) adj. **1.** Disloyal; deceitful; betraying or likely to betray **2.** Dangerous: *treacherous mountain roads* —**treacherously** adv.

treach-er-y (tretʃ–ə–ri^y) n. **-ies** Disloyalty; deceit; the act of betraying those who trusted one —compare TREASON

tread (tred) v. **trod, trodden** or **trod, treading 1.** To walk on again and again, so as to make a path: *The cattle had trodden a path to the barn.* **2.** To walk on, over, or along: *Every day he trod the same path to school.* **3.** To press with the feet; to trample **4. tread water** To keep oneself afloat in an upright position by moving the arms and legs

tread n. **1.** A mark made by, or as if by, treading **2.** The manner or sound of walking **3.** The raised pattern on an automobile or bicycle tire **4.** The flat part of a stair on which one places his foot

trea-dle (tred–əl) n. A lever pressed by the foot to operate a machine: *the treadle of a sewing machine*

tread-mill (tred–mɪl) n. **1.** A mechanism that rotates when people or animals walk on it

2. A monotonous routine or unrewarding effort

trea-son (tri^y–zən) n. An act of disloyalty to one's own country (by giving away or selling its secrets to the enemy or by trying to overthrow it, e.g.)

treas-ure (treʒ–ər) n. **1.** Wealth in the form of gold, silver, jewels, etc.: *Jesus said, "Do not store up for yourselves treasures on earth, where moth and rust destroy and where thieves break in and steal. But store up for yourselves treasures in heaven... For where your treasure is, there your heart will be also"* (Matthew 6:19-21). *Jesus told a rich young man, "If you want to be perfect, go, sell your possessions and give to the poor, and you will have treasure in heaven. Then come, follow me"* (Matthew 19:21). **2.** A very valuable object: *the nation's art treasures/ The Apostle Paul wrote, "My purpose is that... they may know... Christ, in whom are hidden all the treasures of wisdom and knowledge"* (Colossians 2:2-3).

treasure v. **-ured, -uring** To value; cherish; to keep or regard as precious: *He treasured the memory of his children when they were young.*

treas-ur-er (treʒ–ər–ər) n. An officer entrusted with the receipt, care, and disbursement of the funds belonging to a club, organization, etc.

treas-ur-y (treʒ–ə–ri^y) n. **-ies 1.** A place in which stores of wealth are kept **2.** A collection of valuable things: *The library is a treasury of valuable information.* **3.** A government department in charge of finances

treat (tri^yt) v. **1.** To act or behave towards: *Husbands, be considerate as you live with your wives, and treat them with respect* (1 Peter 3:7). **2.** To regard in the specified manner: *He treated them as inferiors.* **3.** To handle: *These dishes are breakable. Treat them gently.* **4.** To give medical or surgical treatment: *to treat a disease* **5.** To buy or give someone sthg. special: *Let's treat ourselves to a vacation on the seashore.* **6.** To pay for the food or entertainment: *He treated them all to a chicken dinner.* **7.** To subject sthg. to chemical or physical action

treat n. **1.** Sthg. that gives pleasure: *A vacation in the South Pacific would be a real treat.* **2.** An

entertainment designed to do this: *The circus was a real treat.* **3.** The treating of others to sthg. at one's own expense: *This time the treat is on me.*

treat-a-ble (tri^{y}t-ə-bəl) adj. Of a disease, able to be treated

trea-tise (tri^{y}t-əs) n. A systematic exposition of a subject in writing

treat-ment (tri^{y}t-mənt) n. The manner or method of treating someone or sthg.: *a new treatment for cancer*

trea-ty (tri^{y}t-i^y) n. **-ties** A formal agreement made between countries

tre-ble (treb-əl) n. **1.** Triple **2.** Of music, having, or performing the highest part, voice, or range **3.** High pitched

treble n. **1.** A treble voice, singer, or instrument **2.** The upper range of a musical instrument or voice

treble v. **-bled, -bling** To make or become three times as big: *They trebled their money on the sale of their house. (=they sold it for three times what they paid for it.)*

tree (tri^y) n. The largest kind of plant, having a thick wooden trunk, branches and leaves, and often, edible fruit: *The tallest trees in the world are the giant redwood trees in California, one of which is 362 feet high.* **—treeless** adj.

trek (trek) n. A long, difficult journey, esp. one made on foot

trek v. **-kk-** To make one's way with great difficulty

trel-lis (trel-əs) n. A wooden framework used esp. as a support for climbing plants

trem-ble (trem-bəl) v. **-bled, -bling 1.** To shake involuntarily, as with cold **2.** To be troubled with anxiety or concern: *I tremble to think what will happen.* **3.** To quiver and shake due to awe and astonishment at the great size or force of sthg.: *God says, "This is the one I esteem: he who is humble and contrite in spirit and who trembles at my word"* (Isaiah 66:2).

tre-men-dous (tri-men-dəs) adj. **1.** Extremely great in size, amount, or degree: *traveling at a tremendous speed/ a tremendous explosion* **2.** Wonderful: *a tremendous performance* **—tremendously** adv. *tremendously important*

trem-or (trem-ər) n. **1.** A quick, shaking

movement: *an earth tremor (=small earthquake)* **2.** An involuntary trembling motion in the body or voice: *a tremor of fear*

trem-u-lous (trem-yə-ləs) adj. **1.** Characterized by trembling **2.** Fearful **—tremulously** adv. **—tremulousness** n.

trench (trentʃ) n. **1.** A long narrow hole cut in the ground; a ditch **2.** A ditch protected by walls of earth and used by soldiers as protection

tren-chant (tren-tʃənt) adj. **1.** Going deep; hurting: *a trenchant remark* **2.** Vigorous or effective **3.** Clearly defined

trend (trend) n. **1.** A general direction; tendency: *the trend of events* **2.** The current style or preference

trep-i-da-tion (trep-ə-de^y-ʃən) n. A state of fear and anxiety; nervous agitation

tres-pass (tres-pæs/ –pəs) n. **1.** An offense or sin; a transgression of God's Law: *Jesus taught us to pray to our heavenly Father, "Forgive us our debts as we also have forgiven our debtors. For if you forgive men their trespasses, your heavenly Father also will forgive you; but if you do not forgive men their trespasses, neither will your Father forgive your trespasses"* (Matthew 6:12,14-15RSV). **2.** An infringement upon the privacy or attention of another **3.** An invasion of the property right of another without his consent **—trespass** n. **—trespasser** n.

tri– (traɪ–) comb. form **1.** Three: *tricycle* **2. (a)** Occurring at intervals of three months, years. etc.: *trimonthly* **(b)** Occurring three times during a year, month, etc.: *triweekly*

tri-al (traɪ-əl) n. **1.** The fact or state of being tried by suffering, temptation, etc.: *The Apostle James says, "Consider it pure joy, my brothers [fellow Christians], whenever you face trials of many kinds, because... the testing of your faith develops perseverance"* (James 1:2,3). **2.** The formal hearing and judging of a person or a case in a court of law: *He's on trial for attempted murder.* **3.** A person or thing that causes worry or trouble and tries one's patience: *That child is a trial to his parents.*

trial adj. Testing: *We brought the TV home for a trial period of ten days.*

tri-an-gle (trai–æŋ–gəl) n. **1.** A figure having three straight sides and three angles **2.** A three-sided metal musical instrument played by striking with a rod —**tri-an-gu-lar** (trai–**æŋ**–gyə–lər)

tribe (traib) n. A group of people comprising several villages and sharing the same ancestry, language, and culture, under the leadership of a chief or chiefs: *There are thousands of such tribes in the world, speaking thousands of languages./ After this I looked and there before me [in heaven] was a great multitude that no one could count, from every nation, tribe, people and language standing before the throne and before the Lamb [Jesus Christ, the Lamb of God who takes away the sin of the world]* (Revelation 7:9). —**tribal** adj. —**tribalism** n.

trib-u-la-tion (trib–yə–le**y**–ʃən) n. Great hardship and sorrow; grief; suffering

tri-bu-nal (trai–byu**w**–nəl) n. **1.** The seat of a judge **2.** A court of justice **3.** Sthg. that decides or determines: *the tribunal of public opinion*

trib-une (trib–yu**w**n) n. **1.** A defender of the people **2.** In ancient Rome, an official elected to protect the rights of the common people

trib-u-tar-y (trib–yə–tɛər–i**y**) n. **-ies** A stream or river that flows into a larger stream or river and contributes to it: *The Amazon River has many, many tributaries.*

trib-ute (trib–yu**w**t) n. **1.** Sthg. done to show gratitude, admiration or respect for sbdy.: *We pay tribute to him for his years of outstanding service.* **2.** Payment that one country or ruler was formerly made to pay to a more powerful one **3.** An indication of the effectiveness of sthg.: *His great success is a tribute to his good training and hard work.*

tri-cen-ten-ni-al (trai–sɛn–tɛn–i**y**–əl) n. A 300th anniversary or its celebration

tri-ceps (trai–sɛps) n. **-cepses** The muscle on the back of the upper arm whose action straightens the elbow

tri-cer-a-tops (trai–sɛər–ə–taps) n. A dinosaur with a very large head, a big horn above each eye and a smaller one on the nose, a bony collar around the neck, and a powerful tail

trich-i-no-sis (trik–ə–no**w**–səs) n. A disease caused by eating undercooked infected pork

trick (trik) n. **1.** A clever act intended to entertain: *magic tricks* **2.** A special skill: *the tricks of the trade* **3.** A practical joke; a prank: *People like to play tricks on others, esp. on April Fool's Day.* **4. do the trick** infml. To serve the purpose: *This ointment should do the trick.* (=heal the rash, e.g.)

trick adj. **1.** Meant to deceive: *trick photography* **2.** Full of hidden meaning or difficulties: *a trick question*

trick v. To cheat someone: *They tricked us into paying the bill twice.*

trick-er-y (trik–ə–ri**y**) n. Deception by tricks

trick-le (trik–əl) v. **-led, -ling** To flow in small amounts: *Tears trickled down her cheeks.*

trickle n. *fig.* A small number or amount: *only a trickle of customers today*

trick-ster (trik–stər) n. A person who deceives or cheats others

trick-y (trik–i**y**) adj. **-ier, -iest 1.** Of work or a situation, difficult to handle or deal with; a delicate problem: *a tricky situation* **2.** Clever and deceitful; sly: *a tricky politician* —**trickiness** n.

tri-cy-cle (trai–sik–əl) n. Sthg. like a bicycle but with three wheels, one in front and two in the back, propelled by pedals

tried (traid) adj. Tested: *a tried and proven method*

tried v. Past tense & part. of **try**

tri-en-ni-al (trai–ɛn–i**y**–əl) adj. **1.** Occurring every three years **2.** Lasting three years —**triennially** adv.

tri-fle (trai–fəl) n. **1.** Sthg. of little value or importance: *Why waste money on such trifles?* **2.** A small amount: *It rained just a trifle.*

trifle v. **-fled, -fling 1.** To treat sthg. as if it were valueless **2.** To play with sthg.: *Stop trifling with that TV dial.* **3.** To act with little respect toward sbdy.: *Captain Smith is not a man to be trifled with.*

tri-fling (trai–fliŋ) adj. **1.** Insignificant **2.** Frivolous **3.** Trivial

trig-ger (trig–ər) n. The small lever on a gun which, when pulled with the finger, causes

a bullet to be fired

trigger v. To start a chain of events: *Wage increases trigger higher prices and vice versa.*

trig-o-nom-e-try (trɪg–ə–nɑm–ə–triʸ) n. Mathematics of the properties of triangles

tri-lat-er-al (traɪ–læt–ə–rəl) adj. Having three sides or three participants

tri-lin-gual (traɪ–lɪŋ–gwəl) adj. Speaking or using three languages

trill (trɪl) n. **1.** A fluttering sound; a sound sung or spoken in a quivering way **2.** In music, the rapid alternation of two tones either a whole or a half tone apart —**trill** v.

tril-lion (trɪl–yən) n. **1.** In the US and France, a million times a million; 1,000,000,000,000 **2.** 1,000,000,000,000,000,000 in Britain and Germany

tril-o-gy (trɪl–ə–dʒiʸ) n. **-gies** A group of three related literary or operatic works

trim (trɪm) v. **-mm- 1.** To make neat or tidy by cutting: *He trimmed the hedges.* **2.** To decorate: *We trimmed the Christmas tree.* **3.** To reduce: *They trimmed the prices on everything in the store.*

trim adj. **-mm-** Tidy, neat in appearance: *a trim figure/garden*

trim n. An act of cutting: *He told the barber just to give him (his hair) a trim.*

trim-ming (trɪm–ɪŋ) n. **1.** Sthg. that trims, ornaments, or completes: *the trimmings on the cake* **2.** Parts removed by trimming: *What shall I do with the trimmings from this hedge?* **3.** Defeat: *Our football team took a real trimming from North High.*

Trin-i-tar-i-an (trɪn–ə–teər–iʸ–ən) adj. A person who believes in the doctrine of the Trinity

Trin-i-ty (trɪn–ət–iʸ) n. The unity of God the Father, God the Son, and God the Holy Spirit in one Godhead —see also GOD, FATHER, SON, JESUS, HOLY SPIRIT, CREED

trin-ket (trɪŋ–kət) n. A small ornament of little value

tri-o (triʸ–oʷ) n. **-os** A group of three people, esp. musicians

trip (trɪp) v. **-pp- 1.** To catch one's foot on sthg., causing one to stumble: *He tripped over a rock and fell.* **2.** To cause someone to make a mistake: *The lawyer tripped up the witness by asking confusing questions.*

trip n. **1.** A journey: *a business/pleasure trip* **2.** A fall; act of tripping **3.** An intense visionary experience undergone by a person who has taken a drug, such as LSD

tri-par-tite (traɪ–pɑr–taɪt) adj. Of or concerning three countries, governments, etc.

tripe (traɪp) n. **1.** Parts of the stomach of a cow or sheep, used as food **2.** Sthg. worthless; nonsense: *Don't listen to such tripe.*

tri-ple (trɪp–əl) v. **-pled, -pling 1.** To make or become three times as great: *The population of the world has more than tripled since 1900.* **2.** In baseball, hitting the ball so that the batter is able to reach third base safely: *Snyder tripled in the 9th inning, driving in the winning runs.*

triple n. In baseball, a hit that enables the batter to reach third base safely

triple adj. **1.** Consisting of three parts **2.** Three times as many: *a triple dose of medicine* (=3 times the amount prescribed)

trip-let (trɪp–lət) n. **1.** One of three children or three animals born of the same mother at the same time **2.** A group of three rhyming lines in a poem

trip-li-cate (trɪp–lɪ–kət) adj. Made in three identical copies

tri-pod (traɪ–pɑd) n. A stand with three legs, esp. for a camera

tri-sect (traɪ–sɛkt/ traɪ–sɛkt) v. To divide into three parts

trite (traɪt) adj. Sthg. that has been said so often in the same way that it has lost its effectiveness: *a trite remark*

tri-umph (traɪ–əmpf) v. To be victorious; win; prevail: *Mercy triumphs over judgment* (James 2:13).

triumph n. A complete victory or success: *a triumph over the enemy* —**tri-um-phant** (traɪ–əm–fənt) adj. *a triumphant army* —**triumphantly** adv.

tri-um-phal (traɪ–ʌm–fəl) adj. Of, related to, or marking a triumph: *Thanks be to God who always leads us in triumphal procession in Christ and through us spreads everywhere the fragrance of the knowledge of him* (2 Corinthians 2:14).

tri-um-vi-rate (traɪ–ʌm–və–rət) n. A group of

three who govern

tri-une (trai–u^wn) adj. One in three: *The Christian God is a triune God, one God in three persons, God the Father, God the Son, and God the Holy Spirit.* —see TRINITY, GOD, JESUS, HOLY SPIRIT

triv-i-a (trɪv–i^y–ə) n. Insignificant or useless things; trifles

triv-i-al (trɪv–i^y–əl) adj. 1. Of little importance 2. Commonplace —**triv-i-al-i-ty** (trɪv–i^y–æl–ət–ti^y) n.

triv-i-um (trɪv–i^y–əm) n. In ancient Rome, the three liberal arts of grammar, rhetoric, and logic

trod (trɑd) v. Past tense & part. of tread

trod-den (trɑd–ən) v. Past part. of tread

troll (tro^wl) n. A mythical cave-dweller

troll v. 1. To sing in a loud, full voice 2. To sing the parts of a song in succession, as a round 3. To fish with a moving line, as from a moving boat

trol-ley (trɑl–i^y) n. 1. A device that carries current from a wire to an electrically driven vehicle 2. *AmE.* A trolley car; streetcar; a vehicle that runs on tracks, powered by electricity from overhead wires 3. A wheeled vehicle or basket that operates on an overhead track 4. *BrE.* A small cart for carrying things, such as in a supermarket; a shopping cart 5. *BrE.* A small cart used in homes, etc. for serving tea, food, etc.

trolley car (trɑl–i^y kar) n. A streetcar propelled electrically by current received by means of a trolley

trom-bone (trɑm–bo^wn/ trɑm–bo^wn) n. A type of brass musical wind instrument which is played by sliding a tube in and out

tromp (trɑmp) v. 1. To stamp with the foot 2. To defeat badly

troop (tru^wp) n. 1. A group of people or animals 2. **troops** A group of soldiers or police 3. A unit of boy or girl scouts under a leader

troop v. To move together in a group: *They all trooped into the assembly hall.*

troop-er (tru^w–pər) n. 1. An enlisted cavalryman 2. A member of the state police force NOTE: Do not confuse **trooper** with **trouper**.

tro-phy (tro^w–fi^y) n. -phies Anything taken or won in a battle, in a competition or in a hunting expedition, esp. when preserved as a memento

trop-ic (trɑp–ɪk) n. One of the two imaginary parallel lines of latitude drawn around the world approx. 23 1/2 degrees north of the equator (the **tropic of Cancer**) and 23 1/2 degrees south of the equator (the **tropic of Capricorn**)

trop-i-cal (trɑp–ɪ–kəl) adj. 1. Of, related to, or living in the tropics 2. Very hot: *tropical weather*

trop-ics (trɑp–ɪks) n. The hot area between the tropic of Cancer and the tropic of Capricorn —see TROPIC

trop-o-sphere (tro^wp–ə–sfɪər/ trɑp–) n. The portion of the atmosphere that is below the stratosphere and extends outward about seven miles above the earth's surface — **trop-o-spher-ic** (tro^wp–ə–sfɪər–ɪk/ trɑp–) adj.

trot (trɑt) v. **-tt-** 1. Of a horse, to run with short, high steps 2. Of humans, to run slowly with short steps

trot n. 1. A moderately fast gait of a four-footed animal, as a horse 2. A jogging gait of a man, between a walk and a run

trou-ba-dour (tru^w–bə–dɔr) n. One of a class of poet-musicians in northern Italy and southern France during the 11th, 12th, and 13th centuries

trou-ble (trʌb–əl) v. **-bled, -bling** 1. To worry, disturb, agitate someone: *You look upset; what's troubling you?* 2. To put someone to an inconvenience: *I'm sorry to trouble you, but can you help me with this?* 3. To cause pain: *He's been troubled with bad eyes for years.*

trouble n. 1. A difficulty, worry, anxiety, annoyance, etc.: *God is our refuge and strength, an ever-present help in trouble* (Psalm 46:1). 2. Danger, risk; a difficult or dangerous state of affairs: *God says, "Call upon me in the day of trouble. I will deliver you and you shall honor me"* (Psalm 50:15). 3. An inconvenience; effort: *Thanks for taking the trouble to help me.* 4. Political unrest: *a lot of trouble in that country* 5. A shortcoming; a fault: *The trouble with you is, you're lazy.* 6. An illness: *heart trouble*

trou-ble-mak-er (trʌb–əl–me^y–kər) n. One

who causes trouble

trou-ble-shoot-er (trʌb–əl–ʃuᵂt ər) n. **1.** A skilled worker who is hired to locate and repair damaged machinery and equipment **2.** An expert in resolving disputes and problems

trou-ble-some (trʌb–əl–səm) adj. Causing trouble or anxiety

trough (trɔf) n. **1.** A long, shallow, boxlike container, esp. for water or feed for livestock **2.** A gutter along the eaves of a house

trounce (travns) v. **trounced, trouncing** To defeat severely

troupe (truᵂp) n. A company of actors or acrobats

troup-er (truᵂ–pər) n. **1.** A member of a theatrical troupe **2.** A hard-working colleague, esp. one who has been doing a particular job for a long time

trou-sers (trav–zərz) n. pl. An outer garment that extends from the waist to the ankle or sometimes only to the knee, covering each leg separately, worn esp. by males; pants

trous-seau (truᵂ–soᵂ) n. **-seaux** (–soᵂz) The personal outfit of a bride

trout (travt) n. A freshwater fish of the salmon family

trow-el (trav–əl) n. **1.** A small garden tool for digging **2.** A tool with a flat blade for spreading mortar, plaster, etc.

tru-ant (truᵂ–ənt) n. **1.** A child who stays away from school without permission **2.** Anyone who shirks his duty

truce (truᵂs) n. A temporary halt in warfare by agreement of both sides

truck (trʌk) n. **1.** also **lorry** BrE. A large motor vehicle for transporting goods **2.** A two-wheeled device for carrying heavy objects by hand **3.** An open container with wheels for carrying goods: coal trucks —**trucker** n.

tru-cu-lent (trʌk–yə–lənt) adj. Fierce; pugnacious; always ready to quarrel or fight —**truculence** n. —**truculently** adv.

trudge (trʌdʒ) v. **trudged, trudging** To walk or march with great effort, laboriously

true (truᵂ) adj. **truer, truest 1.** In accordance with the facts; actual: This is life eternal: That they may know you, the only true God, and Jesus Christ, whom you have sent (John 17:3).

We know also that the Son of God has come and has given us understanding, so that we may know him who is true, and we are in him who is true, even in his Son Jesus Christ. He is the true God and eternal life (1 John 5:20). **2.** Real; sincere: True worshipers will worship [God] the Father in spirit and truth (John 4:23). **3.** Faithful; loyal: a true friend **4.** Exact: a true copy

true blue n. One marked by unswerving loyalty —**true-blue** adj.

tru-ism (truᵂ–ız–əm) n. A self-evident, obvious truth

tru-ly (truᵂ–liʸ) adv. Sincerely; honestly; genuinely

trump (trʌmp) n. In some card games, any card of the suit declared higher than other suits

trump v. To defeat another card by playing a card of the trump suit: He trumped my ace of spades with a heart.

trumped-up (trʌmpt–əp) adj. Fraudulent; false

trum-pet (trʌm–pət) n. **1.** A brass wind instrument with a bright ringing tone, played by pressing three buttons in various combinations **2.** Sthg. resembling the sound of a trumpet: the trumpet of an elephant

trumpet v. **1.** To blow a trumpet **2.** To call or proclaim loudly —**trumpeter** n.

trun-cate (trʌŋ–keʸt/ trʌn–) v. **-cated, -cating** To shorten by cutting off the top or end

truncate adj. Truncated; having the ends square or even

trun-cat-ed (trʌŋ–keʸt–əd) adj. **1.** Cut short; curtailed **2.** Lacking an expected or normal element at the beginning or end

trun-dle (trʌn–dəl) v. To move along on a wheel or wheels

trun-dle bed (trʌn–dəl bed) n. A low bed on wheels that may be pushed under another bed when not in use

trunk (trʌŋk) n. **1.** The thick main stem of a tree **2.** AmE. also **boot** BrE. A large compartment in an automobile, usually in the rear, for carrying luggage, a spare tire, etc. **3.** A large box in which clothes or belongings are stored or packed for travel **4.** The human body apart from the head and limbs (arms and legs) **5.** The very long nose of an

elephant

trunks (trʌŋks) n. A short trouser-like garment worn by men, esp. for swimming

truss (trʌs) v. **1.** To tie, bind, or fasten **2.** To brace or support; strengthen

truss n. **1.** Supporting framework **2.** Hernia brace

trust (trʌst) n. **1.** Firm reliance; confident belief; faith: *Do not put your trust in princes, in mortal men, who cannot save* (Psalm 146:3). **2.** Responsibility: *a position of trust* **3.** Care; custody: *After their parents' death, the children were put in their grandparents' trust.* **4.** Sthg. entrusted to sbdy. to be cared for in the interest of another: *money held in trust for a child*

trust v. **1.** To have faith in; to believe in the honesty and worth of: *Trust in the Lord with all your heart and lean not on your own understanding* (Proverbs 3:5). *It is better to take refuge in the Lord than to trust in man* (Psalm 118:8). **2.** To hope: *I trust you enjoyed yourself.*

trus-tee (trʌs–tiʸ) n. **1.** One of a body of persons appointed to administer the affairs of an organization **2.** A person who holds the title to property for the benefit of another **3.** A country charged with the supervision of a trust territory

trus-tee-ship (trʌs–tiʸ–ʃɪp) n. **1.** The office or function of a trustee **2.** Supervisory control by one or more nations over a trust territory

trust-ful (trʌst–fəl) also **trusting** adj. Full of trust; confiding; sometimes too ready to trust others —**trustfully** adv. —**trustfulness** n.

trust ter-ri-to-ry (trʌst tɛər–ə–tɔr–iʸ) n. A territory under the administrative control of a country designated by the United Nations

trust-wor-thy (trəst–wɜr–ðiʸ) adj. Worthy of trust; dependable: *Here is a trustworthy saying that deserves full acceptance: "Christ Jesus came into the world to save sinners"* (1 Timothy 1:15). —**trustworthiness** n.

trust-y (trʌs–tiʸ) adj. **-ier, -iest** Faithful; dependable

trusty n. A prisoner to whom special privileges are granted for continuous good behavior

truth (truʷθ) n. **truths** (truʷðz/truʷθs) **1.** That which is true; the true facts: *Jesus said, "I am the way, the truth and the life, no one comes to the Father but by me"* (John 14:6). *He also said, "If you hold to my teaching you are really my disciples. Then you will know the truth, and the truth will set you free"* (John 8:31,32). **2.** The quality of being true **3.** A fact or principle accepted as true **4. in truth** In fact; really

truth-ful (truʷθ–fəl) adj. **1.** True: *a truthful account of what happened* **2.** A person who habitually tells the truth: *God is truthful* (John 3:33). *Truthful lips endure forever, but a lying tongue lasts only a moment* (Proverbs 12:19). —**truthfully** adv. —**truthfulness** n.

try (traɪ) v. **tried, trying 1.** To attempt to do sthg.: *Always try to be kind to each other and to everyone else* (1 Thessalonians 5:15). *We are not trying to please men but God* (1 Thessalonians 2:4). **2.** To test the limits of: *You're trying my patience.* **3.** To investigate: *Try all the doors and windows to make sure they are locked.* **4.** To examine a person who is thought to be guilty in a court of law: *He was tried for grand theft.*

try n. **tries** An attempt: *It was a good try, but it was unsuccessful.*

try-ing (traɪ–ŋ) adj. Exasperating; irksome; hard to endure: *a trying experience*

try-out (traɪ–aʊt) n. A trial or test of fitness, strength, or skill

tset-se fly (tsɛt–siʸ flaɪ) n. A blood-sucking African fly that can transmit sleeping sickness to humans and animals

T–shirt, tee shirt (tiʸ–ʃɜrt) n. A tight-fitting, collarless, short-sleeved garment for the upper body

tsp. *abbr.* of teaspoon

T-square (tiʸ–skwɛər) n. A T-shaped instrument used in mechanical and architectural drawing for drawing parallel lines and right angles

tub (tʌb) n. **1.** A large round open container for washing clothes, etc. **2.** *AmE.* Bathtub

tu-ba (tuʷ–bə) n. A large brass wind instrument that produces low notes

tub-by (tʌb–iʸ) adj. **-bier, -biest** Short and fat

tube (tuʷb) n. **1.** A hollow, cylinder-shaped

object, like a pipe, made of metal, glass, rubber, plastic, etc., through which liquid may pass 2. A small soft container from which sthg. may be squeezed: *a tube of toothpaste*

tu·ber (tu^w–bər) n. An oblong or rounded outgrowth of an underground stem, such as a potato

tu·ber·cu·lo·sis (tə–bər–kyə–lo^w–səs) n. An infectious disease, usu. affecting the lungs

tub·ing (tu^w–bɪŋ) n. Metal, plastic, etc., in the form of a tube

tu·bu·lar (tu^w–byə–lər) adj. 1. Of or shaped like a tube 2. Made with tubes

tuck (tʌk) v. 1. To gather (cloth) together into a fold 2. To put into a desired position: *He tucked his shirt in. (=into his trousers)* 3. To cover or wrap snuggly: *The little girl's mother tucked her snuggly into bed.*

–tude (–tu^{w}d) Suffix equivalent to **–ness**: *multitude*

Tues·day (tu^{w}z–di^y/ –de^y) n. The third day of the week

tuft (tʌft) n. 1. A small bunch of grass, feathers, or hair growing close together 2. A cluster of cut threads used as a decorative finish

tuft v. 1. To furnish or decorate with tufts 2. To arrange into tufts —**tufted** adj.

tug (tʌg) v. **-gg-** To pull steadily with force: *He tugged at the door but it wouldn't open.*

tug n. A sudden strong pull

tug-boat (tʌg–bo^{w}t) n. A small but powerful boat used for towing larger ships

tu·i·tion (tu^w–ɪ–ʃən) n. 1. The charge to students for instruction, esp. at a university or private school 2. The instruction itself

tu·lip (tu^w–ləp) n. A plant with bright, cup-shaped flowers, grown from a bulb

tum·ble (tʌm–bəl) v. **-bled, -bling** 1. To fall or roll end over end, helplessly: *The child tripped and tumbled down the stairs.* 2. To perform gymnastic feats, such as somersaults, flips, vaults, etc. 3. To decline or fall suddenly: *prices tumbled* 4. To spill or roll out in disorder: *The children tumbled out of bed.* 5. To fall into ruin

tumble n. A fall

tum·bler (tʌm–blər) n. 1. A drinking glass without a stem 2. An acrobat 3. A part of a

lock that, when lifted by a key, allows the bolt to move

tum·my (tʌm–i^y) n. **-mies** *infml.* Stomach

tu·mor *AmE.* **tumour** *BrE.* (tu^w–mər) n. An abnormal or diseased swelling or growth in any part of the body —**tumorous** adj.

tu·mult (tu^w–məlt) n. 1. Noisy commotion of a crowd 2. Turbulent emotional or mental disturbance

tu·mul·tu·ous (tə–mʌl–tʃu^w–əs) adj. 1. Full of tumult 2. Highly agitated: *a tumultuous storm*

tu·na (tu^w–nə) n. *pl.* **tuna** or **tunas** A large sea fish, used for food

tun·dra (tʌn–drə/ tʊn–) n. A vast treeless plain of the northern arctic regions

tune (tu^{w}n) n. 1. An arrangement of musical sounds; a melody: *He was humming a happy tune.* 2. **in/out of tune (a)** At/not at the correct musical level (pitch): *The piano is out of tune.* **(b)** In/not in agreement with: *His ideas are not in tune with ours.* 3. **change one's tune** To change one's opinions, attitudes, etc.

tune (tu^{w}n) v. **tuned, tuning** 1. To bring a musical instrument into harmony; to set at the proper musical level (pitch): *He's tuning the piano.* 2. To put an engine in good working order: *He's tuning (up) his engine.* —see TUNE UP 3. **tune in** To set a radio to receive broadcasts from a particular station: *He missed the program he wanted to hear, because he wasn't tuned in to the right station. /fig.* In touch with what others are thinking and saying: *A politician must be tuned in to popular feelings about various issues if he expects to be successful.*

tune·ful (tu^{w}n–fəl) adj. Having a pleasing tune —**tunefully** adv. —**tunefulness** n.

tune·less (tu^{w}n–ləs) adj. Without musical quality —**tunelessly** adv.

tun·er (tu^w–nər) n. 1. A person or thing that tunes: *a piano tuner* 2. The part of a radio or television set that one uses to select the desired station or channel

tune-up (tu^{w}n–əp) n. An adjustment, as of a motor, to improve performance

tung·sten (tʌŋ–stən) n. A rare metallic element having a high melting point, used in

electric-light filaments, alloys, etc.

tu-nic (tu^w–nık/ tyu^w–) **1.** A loose, gown-like garment **2.** A woman's blouse-like garment, usu. hip length

tun-nel (tʌn–əl) n. **1.** A passageway, as for cars, trains, etc., underground or underwater, through or under a hill, river, town, etc. **2.** A horizontal passageway in a mine

tunnel v. **-ll-** or **-l-** To make a tunnel: *The prisoners tunneled under the wall and escaped.*

tur-ban (tɜr–bən) n. **1.** A man's headdress consisting of a long cloth wound around the head **2.** Any similar head covering

tur-bid (tɜr–bəd) adj. **1.** Muddy **2.** Disordered or confused

tur-bine (tɜr–bən/ –bi^yn) n. A machine or motor driven by a wheel which is turned by a current of water, steam, air, or gas

tur-bu-lence (tɜr–byə–ləns) n. **1.** The state of being turbulent **2.** In the atmosphere, irregular movement of the air currents, esp. when affecting the flight of aircraft

tur-bu-lent (tɜr–byə–lənt) adj. Causing violence or disturbance; uncontrolled; stormy: *turbulent weather*

tu-reen (tʊ–ri^yn) n. A deep dish with a lid from which soup, vegetables, etc. are served

turf (tɜrf) n. **1.** The upper level of the soil bound by grass and roots into a close mat; sod **2.** An artificial substitute for this, as on some athletic fields **3.** A track or course for horse racing

tur-gid (tɜr–dʒɪd) adj. **1.** Pompous and difficult to follow; boring: *a turgid article about ancient law* **2.** Swollen; bloated

tur-key (tɜr–ki^y) n. **-keys** A type of large farmyard bird, bred for its meat which is used as food, esp. at Christmas and Thanksgiving

tur-moil (tɜr–mɔɪl) n. An extremely confused and troubled condition: *After the tornado, the whole town was in turmoil./ Better a little with the fear of the Lord than great wealth with turmoil* (Proverbs 15:16).

turn (tɜrn) v. **1.** To rotate or revolve: *The wheel turned slowly./ The earth turns on its axis.* **2.** To bend around or go part way around (not a complete circle): *The car turned the corner./ She turned the key in the lock./ He turned his head and looked over his shoulder.* **3.** To cause to change direction: *fig. Turn from evil and do good* (Psalm 34:14). *Train a child in the way he should go, and when he is old, he will not turn from it* (Proverbs 22:6). *Turn to me and be saved, all you ends of the earth; for I am God, and there is no other* (Isaiah 45:22). *Repent then, and turn to God, so that your sins may be wiped out* (Acts 3:19). **4.** To fold: *He turned the corner of the page down so that he could find his place.* **5.** To cause to become different: *In 50 years my home town has turned from a small village into a large city.* **6.** To become: *The milk turned sour./ My father turned 65 (years of age) last month.* **7.** To wrench: *She turned her ankle.* **8.** To transfer: *They turned the work over to Bill.* **9. turn loose** To let a person or thing go: *They turned her loose when the real thief was found.* **10. turn one's stomach** To make one feel sick **11. turn over a new leaf** To abandon one's previous bad behavior **12. turn the tables** To change a situation in one's favor **13. turn against** To become hostile **14. turn away (a)** To refuse to look at someone or sthg. **(b)** To refuse entrance to sbdy.: *We were turned away from the fancy restaurant because we were not properly dressed.* **15. turn back** To cause to go back the same direction that one has just come from: *The army made us civilians turn back because of the danger up ahead.* **16. turn down (a)** To lower the volume: *Please turn down that radio; it's too loud.* **(b)** To refuse: *He turned down the offer.* **17. turn in (a)** *infml.* To go to bed **(b)** To deliver to the police: *He turned in his own brother for setting the fire.* **18. turn off (a)** To stop the flow of water, electricity, gas, etc.: *Turn off the lights.* **(b)** To leave one road and get onto another: *We turned off the main road and took the scenic route.* **(c)** To annoy: *That kind of "music" really turns me off.* **19. turn on (a)** To cause water, gas, electricity, etc. to flow **(b)** To attack suddenly: *I thought he was my friend, but he turned on me and caused me a lot of grief.* **(c)** *infml.* To excite someone sexually **20. turn out (a)** To turn off: *Turn out the light.* **(b)** To gather for a game, meeting, banquet, etc.: *More than 90,000 people turned out for the football game.* **(c)** To produce: *This factory*

turns out thousands of new trucks every day.
(d) To prove different: *His statements turned out to be false.* **21. turn over (a)** To transfer. *They turned the task over to John.* **(b)** Of an engine, to run at a low speed: *It's just barely turning over.* **(c)** To think about; ponder: *He was turning the idea over in his mind.* **22. turn to (a)** To go to someone for help: *I know I can always turn to God for help, for he promised, "I will never leave you nor forsake you."* **(b)** To find the designated page: *Turn to page 77.* **23. turn up (a)** To discover sthg. new: *to turn up new information* **(b)** To find sthg. that was lost: *The missing bag turned up at the wrong airport.* **(c)** To shorten: *She turned up the hem of her dress.* **(d)** To arrive: *She turns up late for everything.* **(e)** To increase the loudness, heat, etc., by using controls: *Turn up the heat, it's cold in here.*

turn n. **1.** The act of turning: *One complete turn of the minute hand on the clock equals one hour.* **2.** A change of direction: *He made a sharp turn to the left at Broadway.* **3.** A change in one's physical condition: *Your father's condition has taken a turn for the better.* **4.** A point of change in time: *the turn of the century* **5.** A rightful change or duty to do sthg.: *It's my turn to drive.*

turn-coat (tɜrn–koʷt) n. A traitor; renegade

tur-nip (tɜr–nəp) n. **1.** A type of plant with a large round root, usu. white with some purple **2.** This root used as food

turn-out (tɜrn–aʊt) n. The number of people who attend a meeting, ball game, etc.: *a turnout of 700 people for the banquet* —compare TURN OUT

turn-o-ver (tɜrn–oʷ–vər) n. The total amount of sales made by a firm over a certain period of time: *a turnover of $5,000 a week* —compare TURN OVER

turn-pike (tɜrn–paɪk) n. In the US, a road on which a toll is paid

turn-stile (tɜrn–staɪl) n. A gate which turns, allowing only one person to pass at a time

turn-ta-ble (tɜrn–teʸ–bəl) n. A rotating disk on which a phonograph record rests

tur-pen-tine (tɜr–pən–taɪn) n. A type of thin oil obtained from certain trees, used for thinning paint, cleaning paint brushes, etc.

tur-pi-tude (tɜr–pə–tuʷd) n. Shameful wickedness; depravity

tur-quoise (tɜr–kɔɪz) n. **1.** A kind of bluish-green precious stone **2.** Its color

tur-ret (tɜr–ət) n. **1.** A small tower on a building **2.** A gun enclosure

tur-tle (tɜrt–əl) n. **turtles** or **turtle** A four-footed, slow-moving kind of reptile, with a soft body covered with a hard shell —compare TORTOISE

tusk (tʌsk) n. A very long pointed tooth, as of an elephant or walrus, extending out of the mouth

tus-sle (tʌs–əl) n. A scuffle; struggle

tus-sle v. **-sled, -sling** To take part in a tussle

tu-te-lage (tuʷt–əl–ɪdʒ/tyuʷt–) n. **1.** Guardianship **2.** Instruction

tu-te-lar-y (tuʷt–əl–ɛər–iʸ/ tyuʷt–) adj. Serving as a guardian: *a tutelary power*

tu-tor (tuʷ–tər) n. A private instructor, esp. one who gives additional or remedial instruction

tu-tor v. To act as a tutor; to teach

tu-to-ri-al (tuʷ–tɔr–iʸ–əl) adj. Of or related to a tutor and his duties

tux-e-do (tʌk–siʸ–doʷ) n. **-dos** or **-does 1.** A usu. blue or blackish-blue dinner-jacket **2.** Semiformal evening clothes for men

TV (tiʸ–viʸ) abbr. for television

twang (twæŋ) n. **1.** A sharp ringing sound like that made by a wire when plucked **2.** A harsh, nasal sound in speech —**twang** v.

tweed (twiʸd) n. A coarse woolen cloth

tweez-ers (twiʸ–zərs) n. A small metal tool with two joined arms, esp. used for pulling out hairs and picking up small objects

twelfth (twɛlfθ) adj. **1.** One of 12 equal parts **2.** The one following the eleventh in a series; **12th** —**twelfth** n.

twelve (twɛlv) determ., n., pron. The number **12**

twen-ti-eth (twɛn–tiʸ–əθ) determ., n., pron., adv. **1.** One of twenty equal parts **2.** The one following the nineteenth in a series; **20th**

twen-ty (twɛn–tiʸ) determ., n., pron. **-ties** The number **20**

twice (twaɪs) predeterm., adv. Two times

twid-dle (twɪd–əl) v. **1.** Play idly with sthg. **2.**

Twirl idly

twig (twɪg) n. A small stem of a tree branch

twi-light (twaɪ-laɪt) n. The dim light between sunset and night

twill (twɪl) n. Woven cloth with parallel, diagonal lines or ribs

twin (twɪn) n. 1. One of two children or animals born of the same mother at the same time 2. Either of two people or things closely connected or very much like each other: *Minneapolis and St. Paul are called the twin cities.*

twine (twaɪn) n. A strong kind of cord or string made by twisting threads together

twine v. **twined, twining** To twist; wind: *The stems twined around the tree trunk.*

twinge (twɪndʒ) n. A sudden sharp physical or emotional pain: *fig. a twinge of conscience*

twin-kle (twɪŋ-kəl) v. **-kled, -kling** 1. To shine with an unsteady or flickering light: *Stars twinkled in the sky.* 2. Of the eyes, to seem to shine or sparkle with delight: *Her eyes twinkled.*

twinkle n. A sparkle of merriment in one's eye: *a twinkle in his eye*

twin-kling (twɪŋ-klɪŋ) n. **in the twinkling of an eye** A very short moment: *We will not all sleep [die], but we will all be changed — in a flash, in the twinkling of an eye, at the last trumpet. For the trumpet will sound, the dead will be raised imperishable, and we will be changed* (1 Corinthians 15:51,52). —see PERISHABLE, JUDGMENT DAY

twirl (twɜrl) v. To turn around and around quickly; spin

twirl n. A spin: *Give that toy top a twirl.*

twist (twɪst) v. 1. To wind: *He twisted two or more threads so as to make a single strand.* 2. To wrench or sprain: *I twisted my ankle and it really hurts.* 3. To coil: *Vines twisted around the flagpole.* 4. To turn or open by turning: *He twisted off the bottle cap.* 5. To distort the meaning: *Do not accept a bribe, for a bribe blinds those who see and twists the words of the righteous* (Exodus 23:8). 6. To break sthg. off by turning: *He twisted off the dead branch.* 7. To move in a winding course: *The road twisted its way through the mountains.* 8. **to twist one's arm** *fig.* To persuade someone to do sthg.

twist n. 1. An act of twisting 2. A bend: *a road with a lot of twists in it* 3. An unexpected change or development: *a strange twist of events* —**twisty** adj. **-ier, -iest** *a twisty road*

twitch (twɪtʃ) v. To move or cause to move jerkily: *The rabbit's nose twitched.*

twitch n. A sudden involuntary muscular movement: *His thumb gave a sudden twitch.*

twit-ter (twɪt-ər) v. 1. To make a series of light, chirping sounds 2. To talk rapidly in a nervous way

two (tuʷ) determ., n., pron. **twos** 1. The number 2: *One plus one equals two.* —compare SECOND 2. **in two** Into two parts: *Cut the board in two.*

two-faced (tuʷ-feʸst) adj. Deceitful; insincere

two-time (tuʷ-taɪm) v. **-timed, -timing** *infml.* To be disloyal to (one's husband, wife, or lover): *She was two-timing (him), and he never knew it.*

ty-coon (taɪ-kuʷn) n. A rich industrialist or businessman

ty-ing (taɪ-ɪŋ) v. Pres. part. of **tie**

tyke (taɪk) n. A small child

type (taɪp) n. 1. A particular kind, class, or group: *What type of house would you prefer to live in?* 2. (in printing) (a) One of the small blocks of metal with the shapes of letters on them, used in printing (b) Such blocks of metal collectively 3. Printed words: *a line of type*

type v. **typed, typing** To write (sthg.) with a typewriter: *She types 70 words per minute.*

type-set (taɪp-set) v. **-set, -setting** To set type in proper order for printing —**typesetter** n.

type-write (taɪp-raɪt) v. **-wrote, -written, -writing** To write with a typewriter

type-writ-er (taɪp-raɪt-ər) n. A machine that prints letters by means of keys which are struck with the fingers

ty-phoid (taɪ-fɔɪd) n. An infectious disease caused by germs in infected food or drinking water, marked by fever, diarrhea, prostration, and intestinal inflammation

ty-phoon (taɪ-fuʷn) n. A violent storm of wind and rain in the region of the Philippines or the China Sea

ty-phus (taɪ-fəs) n. A dangerous disease car-

ried by lice and marked by high fever, stupor and delirium, intense headache and a dark red rash

typ·i·cal (tɪp–ɪ–kəl) adj. Showing the traits or characteristics peculiar to a certain kind, group, or category: *typical July weather* —**typically** adv. *typically American*

typ·i·fy (tɪp–ə–faɪ) v. -fied, -fying To serve as a typical example of: *Vandalism at sporting events and rock concerts, etc., typifies the modern disregard for law and order.*

typ·ist (taɪ–pəst) n. A person who types, esp. one employed to do so

ty·po (taɪ–poᵂ) n. *infml.* A typographical error

ty·pog·ra·pher (taɪ–pɑg–rə–fər) n. A person engaged in typography

ty·po·graph·i·cal er·ror (taɪ–pə–**græf**–ɪ–kəl ɛər–ər) adj. An error in typing or typesetting

ty·pog·ra·phy (taɪ–pɑg–rə–fiʸ) n. **1.** The art or process of printing with type **2.** The general appearance of printed matter

ty·ran·nic (tə–**ræn**–ɪk/taɪ–) or **ty·ran·ni·cal** (tə–**ræn**–ɪ–kəl/taɪ–) adj. Like a tyrant; obtaining obedience by force or threats

tyrannically (tə–**ræn**–ɪ–kə–lɪʸ) adv. Cruelly and unjustly

tyr·an·nize (tɪər–ə–naɪz) v. To rule harshly

ty·ran·no·sau·rus (tə–ræn–ə–sɔr–əs) n. A large meat-eating dinosaur that walked upright on its two hind legs and had two front legs like arms

tyr·an·ny (tɪər–ə–niʸ) n. The rule of a tyrant

ty·rant (taɪ–rənt) n. A cruel, unjust, oppressive ruler, esp. one who has gained power by force

tyre (taɪ–ər) n. *BrE.* **tire** *AmE.* A thick rubber cover around an automobile or cycle wheel

ty·ro (taɪ–roᵂ) n. A novice; beginner

tzar (zɑr/ tsɑr) n. **Czar 1.** A former emperor of Russia **2.** Any person in a high position of power

U, u (yu^w) n. The 21st letter of the English alphabet

u-biq-ui-tous (yu^w–**bɪk**–wət–əs) adj. Existing everywhere at the same time; omnipresent

U–boat (yu^w–bo^wt) n. A German submarine

ud-der (**ʌd**–ər) n. The downward-hanging bag-like organ of cows and certain other animals, with protruding teats from which milk can be drawn

ug-ly (**ʌg**–li^y) adj. -lier, -liest **1.** Unpleasant to the sight: *an ugly person/animal/building/ picture, etc.* **2.** Disagreeable or unpleasant: *an ugly attitude/ ugly behavior* —opposite BEAUTIFUL —**ugliness** n.

UK (yu^w–ke^y) n. *abbr.* for **United Kingdom** Great Britain and Northern Ireland

u-ku-le-le (yu^w–kə–le^y–li^y) n. A small guitar-like instrument with four strings, popularized in Hawaii

ul-cer (**ʌl**–sər) n. A break or rough place on the skin or inside the body: *a stomach ulcer*

ul-cer-a-ted (**ʌl**–sə–re^yt–əd) adj. Having an ulcer or ulcers

ul-te-ri-or (əl–tɪər–i^y–ər) **1.** Intentionally hidden: *ulterior motives* **2.** More remote: *ulterior considerations* **3.** Lying on the farther side: *ulterior regions*

ul-ti-mate (**ʌl**–tə–mət) adj. **1.** Final; last in a series: *The ultimate responsibility lies with the president.* **2.** Basic; fundamental: *the ultimate cause* —**ultimately** adv.

ul-ti-ma-tum (əl–tə–me^yt–əm) n. -tums or -ta (–tə) A final demand, esp. one whose rejection will bring about an end of negotiations

ul-tra (**ʌl**–trə) adj. Extreme

ul-tra– (**ʌl**–trə–) comb. form **1.** On the other side of; beyond: *ultrasonic/ultraviolet rays* **2.** Extremely; excessively: *ultraconservative/ ultramodern*

ul-tra-ma-rine (əl–trə–mə–ri^yn) n. A very bright, deep blue color —**ultramarine** adj.

ul-tra-son-ic (əl–trə–**sɑn**–ɪk) adj. Sound wave frequencies beyond the limits of human audibility

ul-tra-vi-o-let rays (əl–trə–**vaɪ**–ə–lət re^yz) adj. Invisible light rays present in sunlight and the light from sun lamps, used for healing, forming vitamins, and as sterilizers and disinfectants

um-ber (**ʌm**–bər) n. **1.** A mineral used as a brown or reddish brown pigment **2.** A dark, reddish brown color —**umber** adj.

um-bil-i-cal (əm–**bɪl**–ɪ–kəl) adj. **1.** Pertaining to the umbilicus or the umbilical cord **2.** Referring to or situated near the navel

umbilical cord (əm–**bɪl**–ɪ–kəl kɔrd) n. The cord that connects the fetus with the placenta of the mother and transmits nourishment from the mother

um-bil-i-cus (əm–bə–**laɪ**–kəs/əm–**bɪl**–ɪ–kəs) n. -cuses The navel; depression in the middle of the abdomen, marking the spot where the cord was attached

um-brage (**ʌm**–brɪdʒ) n. A feeling of offence

um-brel-la (əm–**brel**–ə) n. **1.** A folding frame covered with cloth and having a handle, used for protection against the weather **2.** Sthg. which protects, such as a protecting power or organization: *under the umbrella of the government*

um-pire (**ʌm**–paɪr) n. An official judge in charge of a game, esp. baseball —see REFEREE

ump-teen (**ʌmp**–ti^yn) determ., pron. *infml.* A large, indefinite number —**umpteenth** n., determ.

un– (**ʌn**–; *unstressed also* ən–) Prefix **1.** Not: *unafraid/ unfair* **2.** Opposite of: *un-American* **3.** Reversing an action: *untie/ uncover* **4.** Removal or depriving: *undress/ unclog* **5.** Release from: *unleash/ unhand* NOTE: **un-** is not a prefix in words like: **uncle, uniform, unity, unique, universal, university.**

un-a-bashed (ən–ə–**bæʃt**) adj. Not embarrassed —**un-a-bash-ed-ly** (ən–ə–**bæʃ**–əd–li^y) adv.

un-a-ble (ən–e^y–bəl) adj. Not able; lacking the power, knowledge, time, resources, or whatever is required

un-a-bridged (ən–ə–**brɪdʒd**) adj. Not shortened: *An unabridged English dictionary is several inches thick.*

un-ac-cept-a-ble (ən–ɪk–**sep**–tə–blə/–**æk**–) adj. Not acceptable; not pleasing; not welcome

un-ac-count-a-ble (ən–ə–**kaʊnt**–ə–bəl) adj. Unexplainable; odd

un-ac-cus-tomed (ən–ə–**kʌs**–təmd) adj. **1.** Not

accustomed 2. Unusual or unfamiliar

un-a-dul-ter-at-ed (ən-ə-dʌl-tə-reʸt-əd) adj.
Pure; not mixed with anything

un-af-fect-ed (ən-ə-fɛk-təd) adj. Natural; sincere; genuine

un-al-ien-a-ble (ən-eʸl-yə-nə-bəl/ən-eʸ-liʸ-ən-ə-bəl) adj. *Archaic* Inalienable; that cannot be alienated; that may not be transferred, as unalienable rights —**unalienably** adv.

u-nan-i-mous (yuʷ-næn-ə-məs) adj. With all the people agreeing: *The vote was unanimous.* —**u-na-nim-i-ty** (yuʷ-nə-nɪm-ət-iʸ) n.

un-ap-proach-a-ble (ən-ə-proʷ-tʃə-bəl) adj. **1.** Sbdy. who is difficult to talk to; one who doesn't encourage friendliness **2.** Inaccessible

un-armed (ən-ɑrmd) adj. Without weapons

un-as-sail-a-ble (ən-ə-seʸ-lə-bəl) adj. **1.** Not open to attack **2.** Not subject to denial or dispute

un-as-sum-ing (ən-ə-suʷ-mɪŋ) adj. Not pretentious; modest; not showing any desire to be noticed

un-at-tached (ən-ə-tætʃt) adj. **1.** Not attached **2.** Not engaged or married

un-au-tho-rized (ən-ɔ-θə-raɪzd) adj. Not authorized; not warranted by proper authority; not duly commissioned

un-a-void-a-ble (ən-ə-vɔɪd-ə-bəl) adj. Incapable of being avoided; inevitable

un-a-ware (ən-ə-wɛər) adj. Not knowing; ignorant

un-a-wares (ən-ə-wɛərz) adv. **1.** Without knowing or being aware; unintentionally **2.** By surprise or without warning

un-bal-anced (ən-bæl-ənst) adj. **1.** Not properly balanced **2.** Mentally disordered; not quite sane **3.** In bookkeeping, not adjusted so that credits and debits correspond

un-bear-a-ble (ən-bɛər-ə-bəl) adj. Not bearable or tolerable

un-be-com-ing (ən-bɪ-kʌm-ɪŋ) adj. Not attractive; unsuitable; improper

un-be-lief (ən-bɪ-liʸf) n. **1.** Habitual lack of belief, esp. in God **2.** In the New Testament, disbelief of the Gospel or Good News about Jesus as Savior and of the doctrines he taught; distrust of God's promises and faithfulness

un-be-liev-a-ble (ən-bə-liʸ-və-bəl) adj. Impossible to believe —**unbelievably** adv.

un-be-liev-er (ən-bɪ-liʸ-vər) n. Those who do not believe in sthg. or in sbdy., esp. those who do not believe the Bible and its teaching about salvation through faith in Jesus Christ

un-bend-ing (ən-ben-dɪŋ) adj. Unwilling to change opinions, decisions, etc.

un-bi-ased (ən-baɪ-əst) adj. Not prejudiced; free from bias

un-bib-li-cal (ən-bɪb-lɪ-kəl) adj. Not taught in the Bible

un-bound-ed (ən-baʊn-dəd) adj. Not limited; very great: *unbounded energy or enthusiasm*

un-bri-dled (ən-braɪd-əld) adj. Uncontrolled: *unbridled passion*

un-brok-en (ən-broʷ-kən) adj. **1.** Not broken **2.** Uninterrupted **3.** Not tamed

un-bur-den (ən-bər-dən) v. To tell one's secrets or problems freely

un-called-for (ən-kɔld-fɔr) adj. Not deserved; not justified: *His rude behavior was completely uncalled-for.*

un-can-ny (ən-kæn-iʸ) adj. **-nier, -niest** Mysterious; beyond what is normal or usual

un-cer-e-mo-ni-ous (ən-sɛər-ə-moʷ-niʸ-əs) adj. **1.** Informal: *She received an unceremonious but very warm and friendly welcome.* **2.** Rude; abrupt; discourteous —**unceremoniously** adv.

un-cer-tain (ən-sɜrt-ən) adj. **1.** Not definitely known: *It is uncertain what the weather will be like next Friday.* **2.** Not precisely determined: *He was uncertain what he would do if he lost his job.* **3.** Not dependable: *Whether he will keep his promises or not is uncertain.* **4.** Not definitely fixed: *They announced their engagement but were still uncertain about their wedding date.*

un-cer-tain-ty (ən-sɜrt-ən-tiʸ) n. **-ties 1.** The state of being uncertain **2.** Sthg. uncertain

un-chap-er-oned (ən-ʃæp-ə-roʷnd) adj. Not accompanied by a chaperone

un-char-i-ta-ble (ən-tʃær-ə-tə-bəl/ –tʃɛər-) adj. Not fair in judging others

un-chart-ed (ən-tʃɑrt-əd) adj. Not shown on a map or chart

un·chris·tian (ən–krɪs–tʃən) adj. **1.** Not of the Christian faith which teaches that man is saved by grace [the unmerited love of God] through faith in Jesus Christ apart from the deeds of the law (John 3:16; Romans 3:28). **2.** Contrary to Christian precepts: *Christians, as well as unbelievers, are often guilty of unchristian thoughts and deeds.* NOTE: Christians, however, repent of their sinful thoughts, words, and deeds and put their trust in Jesus for forgiveness and salvation. The Apostle Paul wrote: "What a wretched man I am! Who shall rescue me..? Thanks be to God — through Jesus Christ our Lord! Therefore, there is now no condemnation for those who are in Christ Jesus (Romans 7:24,25 and 8:1). The main difference between Christians and non-Chris-tians is that while striving to be obedient to all that God has commanded, Christians do not trust in their own works of righteousness for eternal life, but put their trust in Jesus Christ who came into the world to save sinners, died for us, rose again, and returned to heaven to prepare a place for us. —see JESUS, CHRIST, CREED, CHRISTIANITY, HOLINESS, RIGHTEOUSNESS

un·churched (ən–tʃɜrtʃt) adj. **1.** Having no church membership **2.** Excluded from a church

un·cle (ʌŋ–kəl) n. The brother of one's father or mother, or husband of one's aunt

un·clean (ən–kliʸn) adj. Dirty; impure

un·clear (ən–klɪər) adj. Not clear; indistinct; confusing; not understandable

un·clog (ən–klɑg) v. **-gg-** To remove an obstruction from

un·coil (ən–kɔɪl) v. To unwind

un·com·mon (ən–kɑm–ən) adj. Not common; strange

un·com·mu·ni·ca·tive (ən–kə–myuʷ–nə–keʸt–ɪv/ –nɪ–kət–ɪv) adj. Not talkative; not inclined to give information

un·com·pro·mis·ing (ən–kɑm–prе–maɪ–zɪŋ) adj. Not willing to give in or make concessions to others; unyielding; inflexible

un·con·di·tion·al (ən–kən–dɪʃ–ən–əl) adj. Not limited by conditions —**unconditionally** adv.

un·con·scio·na·ble (ən–kɑn–tʃə–nə–bəl/–ʃə–) adj. **1.** Not guided by conscience **2.** More than is reasonable: *unconscionable demands*

un·con·scious (ən–kɑn–tʃəs/–ʃəs) adj. **1.** Temporarily devoid of consciousness **2.** Not consciously realized or done; unintentional —**unconsciously** adv.

un·con·sti·tu·tion·al (ən–kɑn–stə–tuʷʃ–ən–əl) adj. In violation of, or contrary to the constitution

un·con·ven·tion·al (ən–kən–vɛn–tʃən–əl/ –ʃən–) adj. Not ordinary —**un·con·ven·tion·al·i·ty** (ən–kən–vɛn–tʃə–næl–ət–iʸ/–ʃə–) n.

un·cou·ple (ən–kʌp–əl) v. **-pled, -pling** To disconnect; unfasten

un·couth (ən–kuʷθ) adj. **1.** Ill-mannered; rough; crude **2.** Clumsy, awkward

unc·tion (ʌŋk–ʃen) n. **1.** An act of anointing, esp. as a medical treatment or a religious rite **2.** The oil used in anointing **3.** Sthg. soothing or comforting **4.** Hypocrisy; affected sincerity

unc·tu·ous (ʌŋk–tʃuʷ–əs) adj. **1.** Like an oil or ointment in texture **2.** In speech and manner, too smooth and oily; insincere; false or affected emotion

un·daunt·ed (ən–dɔnt–əd) adj. Fearless; not discouraged

un·de·ni·a·ble (ən–dɪ–naɪ–ə–bəl) adj. Clearly and certainly true —**unde·niably** adv.

un·der (ʌn–dər) adv. **1.** In or to a lower place: *The children jumped out of the boat just as it went under.* (=below the surface of the water) **2.** So as to be less than: *Children are admitted free, that is, those who are six and under.* (=below the age of six)

under prep. **1.** Directly beneath; covered by: *The children were playing under a tree.* **2.** Below; less than: *children under six* (=below the age of six) —opposite OVER **3.** Belonging to the stated class: *"French" comes under "Foreign Languages" in the college catalog.* **4.** Ruled by: *The country prospered under him (his leadership.)* **5.** Supervised by: *The foreman had fifty men under him.* **6.** Receiving the effect of: *under attack/under the influence of alcohol* **7.** Less than: *under two tons* **8.** In the process of: *The road is under repair.* **9.** Propelled by: *The*

damaged ship sailed into the harbor under its own power. 10. In accordance with: *under the law* 11. Inferior to: *No one under a colonel is permitted in here.* 12. **under age** Too young, esp. in law for certain activities such as voting, driving a car, etc. 13. **under cover (of)** Hidden or sheltered by: *They escaped under cover of darkness.* —com-pare BELOW, BE-NEATH

un-der-brush (ʌn–dər–brʌʃ) n. Low-growing plants amongst trees

un-der-coat (ʌn–dər–koʷt) n. 1. A rustproof seal applied to the underside of a vehicle 2. A coat of paint applied before applying the finishing coat

un-der-cov-er (ən–dər–kʌv–ər) adj. Done in secret, as a spy: *He's an undercover agent for his country.*

un-der-cur-rent (ʌn–dər–kɜr–ənt) n. 1. A current, as of water or air, that flows beneath another current 2. A hidden tendency, attitude, or feeling

un-der-cut (ən–dər–kʌt) v. -cut, -cutting 1. To cut under 2. To sell at a lower price than a competitor 3. To cut away a lower portion of sthg. 4. In sports, to hit a ball so as to give it a backspin 5. To destroy the effectiveness of —**un-der-cut** (ʌn–dər–kət) n.

un-der-dog (ʌn–dər–dɔg) n. A person or team that is not expected to win an election, athletic competition, etc.

un-der-foot (ən–dər–fʊt) adj. In the way: *He's always underfoot.*

un-der-gird (ən–dər–gɜrd) v. 1. To strengthen or brace from the bottom side 2. To give support to sbdy. in some way, morally, spiritually, financially, etc.: *His ministry was undergirded with much prayer and financial support.*

un-der-go (ən–dər–goʷ) v. -went, -gone, -going To go through; experience, esp. with difficulty: *She has just undergone surgery on her knee.*

un-der-grad-u-ate (ən–dər–grædʒ–ə–wət) n. A university student who has not yet taken his first degree

un-der-ground (ʌn–dər–graʊnd) n. 1. The entire region beneath the surface of the earth 2. An underground train; a subway: *He took*

the underground from the airport to downtown London. 3. A secret movement organized in a country to overthrow the government in power or the enemy forces of occupation

underground (ʌn–dər–graʊnd) adj. 1. Under the surface of the ground: *an underground cable* 2. Secret: *an underground political movement*

underground (ʌn–dər–graʊnd) adv. 1. Under the surface of the ground: *Gophers live underground.* 2. Into hiding: *The escaped convicts had to go underground.*

un-der-hand (ʌn–dər–hænd) also **underhanded** adj. In a tricky, dishonest way: *I don't trust him. He handled the deal in a very underhanded way.*

un-der-lie (ən–dər–laɪ) v. -lay (-leʸ), -lain (-leʸn), -lying 1. To be beneath 2. To be the hidden cause or source of

un-der-line (ʌn–dər–laɪn) also **underscore** v. -lined, -lining 1. To mark one or more words with a line underneath, esp. to show added force 2. To emphasize: *I would like to underline the need for greater enforcement of the law.*

un-der-ling (ʌn–dər–lɪŋ) n. A person of lower rank; one who must obey orders; a subordinate

un-der-ly-ing (ən–dər–laɪ–ɪŋ) adj. Basic; fundamental

un-der-mine (ʌn–dər–maɪn) v. -mined, -mining 1. To weaken sthg. from beneath by removing support: *The bridge is not safe because it was undermined by the recent floods.* 2. *fig.* To gradually weaken one's health, confidence, etc.: *His morale was undermined by her constant complaining.*

un-der-neath (ən–dər–niʸθ) prep., adv. Under; below: *Write your address underneath your name.*

un-der-pass (ʌn–dər–pæs) n. A road or a path that goes under another road or path

un-der-pay (ən–dər–peʸ) v. -paid (-peʸd), -paying To pay someone less than he is worth

un-der-priv-i-leged (ən–dər–prɪv–ə–lɪdʒd) adj. Not having normal privileges or living conditions

un-der-rate (ən–dər–reʸt) v. -rated, -rating To

underestimate: *Smith is perhaps the most un-derrated player in the entire league.*

un-der-score (ən–dər–**skor**) v. **-scored, -scoring** To underline

un-der-signed (ʌn–dər–**samd**) n. The person or persons whose names are written at the bottom of a letter or document

un-der-slung (ʌn–dər–**sləŋ**) adj. Of a vehicle chassis, hanging lower than the axles

un-der-staffed (ən–dər–**stæft**) adj. Having too small a staff for the amount of work to be done

un-der-stand (ən–dər–**stænd**) v. **-stood -standing 1.** To perceive the meaning, nature, or importance of sthg.: *Do you understand what the author is trying to say?* **2.** To know or feel closely the character or nature of a person, idea, etc.: *The fear of the Lord is the beginning of wisdom, and the knowledge of the Holy One [God] is understanding* (Proverbs 9:10). *By faith we understand that the universe was formed at God's command, so that what is seen was not made out of what was visible* (Hebrews 11:3). **3.** To take as the meaning even though it was not actually expressed: *Since there is no maid service, we understand that everyone must clean his own room.* **4.** *fml.* To have come to know a fact: *We understand that you're interested in buying our house.* —**understandable** adj. —**understandably** adv.

un-der-stand-ing (ən–dər–**stæn-dɪŋ**) n. **1.** The act or power of perceiving the truth and making judgments: *My understanding of the situation is that both of you are at fault in this matter.* **2.** Sympathy: *Nurse Ann Smith always treats her patients with understanding.* **3.** A private, friendly, agreement: *They have an understanding about whose job it is to do the grocery shopping.*

un-der-state (ən–dər–**ste^y t**) v. **-stated, -stating 1.** To state too weakly or less emphatically than one should **2.** To say less than the full truth about sthg.

un-der-stood (ən–dər–**stʊd**) adj. **1.** Agreed upon: *understood limits* **2.** Thoroughly known; comprehended **3.** Implied; not verbally expressed: *the understood meaning of her smile*

un-der-stood v. Past tense and past part. of **understand**

un-der-stud-y (ʌn–dər–**stʌd**–i^y) n. **-ies** An actor who studies an important part in a play in order to be able to play that part in case of an emergency

un-der-take (ən–dər–**te^y k**) v. **-took** (**-tʊk**), **-taken, -taking 1.** To begin; set about working: *She undertook the task with zeal and determination.* **2.** To promise or agree to do sthg.: *He undertook to pay off his debts by the end of the year.*

un-der-tak-er (ʌn–dər–**te^y** –kər) n. A person whose business it is to arrange for burial or cremation of the dead and to oversee funerals; a mortician

un-der-tak-ing (ən–dər–**te^y** –kɪŋ) n. A big project or piece of work: *Collecting funds for a new hospital was quite an undertaking.*

un-der-the-count-er (ʌn–dər–ðə–**kaʊnt**–ər) adj. Illegal: *an under-the-counter business transaction*

un-der-tone (ʌn–dər–**to^w n**) n. **1.** A subdued voice or whisper **2.** A soft or subdued shade of a color **3.** A subdued or partly concealed emotional quality: *undertones of discontent*

un-der-tow (ʌn–dər–**to^w**) n. **1.** A strong current below the surface of the water, moving in the opposite direction from the current on the surface **2.** The backward flow from waves breaking on the beach

un-der-way (ən–dər–**we^y**) adv. In pro-gress

un-der-wear (ʌn–dər–**wɛər**) n. Garments worn underneath one's outer garments

un-der-world (ʌn–dər–**wərld**) n. The criminal world

un-der-write (ʌn–dər–**wraɪt**/ ʌn–dər–**wraɪt**) v. **1.** To write under or at the end of sthg., esp. to endorse a document **2.** To sign an insurance policy, thus guaranteeing payment **3.** To subscribe to; to agree **4.** To assume financial responsibility for sthg. or sbdy.

un-do (ən–**du^w**) v. **-did, -done, -doing** Third pers. sing. present tense **undoes 1.** To unfasten sthg. that is tied or wrapped **2.** To cause sthg. to be of no effect, as if it had never been done: *One fire can undo in minutes what took months or even years to write or construct.*

un-do-ing (ən–duᵂ–ŋ) n. The cause of ruin: *A fool's mouth is his undoing* (Proverbs 18·7)

un-done (ən–dʌn) adj. Not finished: *I don't want to go to bed and leave all that work undone.*

un-dress (ən–drɛs) v. 1. To take one's clothes off; disrobe 2. To take the clothes off of sbdy.: *John undressed the baby and gave him a bath.*

un-due (ən–duᵂ) adj. 1. Not yet due or payable 2. Too much; excessive: *undue caution* 3. Not appropriate or suitable

un-du-late (ʌn–dʒə–leʸt) v. -lated, -lating 1. To have a wave-like motion or appearance 2. To rise or fall in pitch or volume

un-du-lat-ing (ʌn–dʒə–leʸt–ŋ) adj. Wave-like; having a wave-like appearance: *undulating hills*

un-du-ly (ən–duᵂ–liʸ) adv. Excessively *He was unduly worried.*

un-earth (ən–ɜrθ) v. To dig up

un-earth-ly (ən–ɜrθ–liʸ) adv. 1. Supernatural; not of this world 2. Weird; strange; ghostly; 3. *Infml.* Outlandish; ridiculous: *to rise at an unearthly hour*

un-eas-y (ən–iʸ–ziʸ) adj. -ier, -iest Uncomfortable, esp. because of pain or worry: *He was uneasy about flying with an inexperienced pilot.* —**uneasiness** n.

un-e-quiv-o-cal (ən–ɪ–kwɪv–ə–kəl) adj. Totally clear in meaning

un-err-ing (ən–eɜr–ŋ) adj. Never making a mistake; always right

un-e-ven (ən–iʸ–vən) 1. Not smooth or level 2. Not all of the same quality

un-ex-pect-ed (ən–ɪk–spɛk–təd) adj. Not expected; sudden

un-ex-plain-a-ble (ən–ɪk–**spleʸ**–nə–bəl) adj. Not possible to explain

un-ex-plained (ən–ɪk–**spleʸ**nd) adj. Not explained

un-fail-ing (ən–feʸ–lŋ) adj. Not failing or likely to fail, esp. sthg. good; continuing on forever: *The eyes of the Lord are on those who fear him, on those whose hope is in his unfailing love* (Psalm 33:18). *Put your hope in the Lord, for with the Lord is unfailing love, and with him is full redemption* (Psalm 130:7). —see LOVE, REDEMPTION, REDEEMER

un-fair (ən–fɛər) adj. Not fair; unjust

un-faith-ful (ən–feʸθ–fəl) adj. 1. Not faithful; disloyal 2. Adulterous; not faithful to one's marriage partner, esp. having sexual relations with another person 3. Not accurate or complete —**unfaithfulness** n. *Jesus said, "Anyone who divorces his wife, except for marital unfaithfulness, and marries another woman commits adultery"* (Matthew 19:9).

un-fea-si-ble (ən–fiʸ–zə–bəl) adj. Not feasible; impracticable

un-feel-ing (ən–fiʸ–lŋ) adj. Hard-hearted; not kind or compassionate

un-feigned (ən–feʸnd) adj. Sincere; real

un-fin-ished (ən–fɪn–ɪʃt) adj. 1. Not finished; incomplete 2. Having no paint or special surface treatment, as wood

un-fit (ən–fɪt) adj. 1. Not suitable; not good enough 2. Not as vigorous (physically or mentally) as one could be

un-flag-ging (ən–flæg–ŋ) adj. Not tiring or losing strength

un-flinch-ing (ən–flɪn–tʃŋ) adj. Steadfast; not drawing back from difficulty, danger, or pain

un-fold (ən–foᵂld) v. 1. To open from a folded position; to spread or straighten out: *He unfolded the map and spread it out on the table.* 2. To make or become clear, gradually: *The reasons behind his strange behavior began to unfold as he told us of his lonely childhood.*

un-fore-seen (ən–fɔr–siʸn) adj. Unexpected

un-for-tu-nate (ən–fɔrtʃ–ə–nət) adj. 1. Not successful; not prosperous: *an unfortunate venture* 2. Causing bad effects 3. To be deplored: *an unfortunate situation/ experience* —**unfortunately** adv. —**unfortunateness** n.

unfortunate n. An unfortunate person

un-found-ed (ən–faᵘn–dəd) adj. Not supported by facts; lacking a basis: *The rumor that he wanted to resign was completely unfounded.*

un-furl (ən–fɜrl) v. To unfold a flag, sail, etc.

un-gain-ly (ən–geʸn–liʸ) adj. -lier, -liest Awkward

un-god-ly (ən–**gɑd**–liʸ) adj. -lier, liest 1. Not revering God 2. Sinful; wicked: *When we were still powerless [to please God or save ourselves from eternal death], Christ died for the ungodly* (Romans 5:6).

un-gra-cious (ən–greʸ–ʃəs) adj. **1.** Lacking courtesy; not polite; rude **2.** Unpleasant; disagreeable

un-guent (əŋ–gwənt/ ʌn–/ʌn–dʒənt) n. A healing ointment for sores, burns, scrapes, etc.

un-hand (ən–hænd) v. To let go; release

un-hap-py (ən–hæp–iʸ) adj. **-pier, -piest 1.** Not happy or cheerful; sad **2.** Unfortunate **3.** Unsuitable

un-health-y (ən–hel–θiʸ) adj. **-ier, -iest 1.** Not in good health **2.** Harmful to good health **3.** Morally harmful

un-heard-of (ən–hərd–əv) adj. **1.** Never heard of **2.** Never known or done before **3.** Outrageous; shocking

un-hinge (ən–hɪndʒ) v. **-hinged, -hing-ing 1.** To take a door off its hinges **2.** To remove the hinges from **3.** *Fig.* To separate from sthg.; detach **4.** *Fig.* To make imbalanced or disordered; to upset, as one's mind: *He became completely unhinged when he heard of the tragedy.*

un-ho-ly (ən–hoʸ–liʸ) adj. **-lier, -liest 1.** Not hallowed or sacred **2.** Wicked; immoral: *The law [God's moral law] is made not for good men, but for lawbreakers and rebels, the ungodly and sinful, the unholy and irreligious...* (1 Timothy 1:9).

u-ni- (yuʷ–nə-) comb. form One or only one: *unicameral*

u-ni-cam-er-al (yuʷ–nə—kæm–ə–rəl) adj. Of or consisting of a single legislative body

u-ni-cel-lu-lar (yuʷ–nə–sel–yə–lər) adj. Consisting of a single cell

u-ni-corn (yuʷ–nə–kɔrn) n. A mythical creature resembling a horse, having a single horn in the middle of its forehead

u-ni-form (yuʷ–nə–fɔrm) adj. **1.** Having the same form, appearance, or quality as others of its kind **2.** The same at all times or in all places —**un-i-form-i-ty** (yuʷ–nə–fɔr–mət–iʸ) n.

uniform n. Clothing of distinctive design, worn by all who are in the same branch of military service or work for the same company

u-ni-fy (yuʷ–nə–faɪ) v. **-fied, -fying** To make into one unit or whole: *The arrival of the new coach helped to unify the team.* —**un-i-fi-ca-**tion (yuʷ–nə–fə–keʸ–ʃən) n.

u-ni-lat-er-al (yuʷ–nɪ–læt–ər–əl) adj. Done by only one person, group, or nation —compare BILATERAL

un-im-peach-a-ble (ən–ɪm–piʸ–tʃə–bəl) adj. Blameless; not to be called into question; so trustworthy that it cannot be doubted: *of unimpeachable character*

un-im-por-tant (ən–ɪm–pɔrt–ənt) adj. Not important; not significant

un-in-hib-it-ed (ən–ɪn–hɪb–ə–təd) adj. **1.** Not inhibited or restricted **2.** Not restrained as by social pressure; expressing feelings freely and without embarrassment

un-in-spi-ra-tion-al (ən–ɪn–spə–reʸ–ʃən–əl) adj. Commonplace; dull; without imagination or inspiration

un-ion (yuʷ–nyən) n. **1.** The act of uniting or the process of being united **2.** The state of being united in marriage: *a marriage union* **3.** A group of countries or states joined together: *The United States is a union of fifty states.* **4.** An organization or club having a common purpose: *a labor union*

un-ion-ize (yuʷ–nyə–naɪz) v. **-ized, -izing** Organized into a labor union

u-nique (yuʷ–niʸk) adj. **1.** Having none exactly like it: *I was amazed to learn that every snowflake is unique. There are never any two snowflakes alike.* **2.** *infml.* Very unusual: *Their house is rather unique. I don't think I've ever seen another one like it.* —**uniquely** adv. —**uniqueness** n.

u-ni-son (yuʷ–nə–sən) n. **1.** Harmony **2. in unison (a)** In perfect agreement **(b)** Uttering the same words or producing the same musical note at the same time: *singing in unison.*

u-nit (yuʷ–nət) n. **1. (a)** The least whole number; one **(b)** Any whole number from 0 to 9; the number occupying the position immediately to the left of the decimal point in the Arabic system of numerals **2.** A single thing within a group or class: *This apartment building has twelve units (=twelve separate apartments)* **3.** An amount or quantity taken as a standard of measurement: *The foot is a unit for measuring length.* **4.** A piece of furniture, equipment, etc., designed so that other pieces can be added to it: *a storage unit*

u-nite (yu^w–naɪt) v. **-nited, -niting 1.** To join into one. *The original thirteen colonies united to form the United States of America.* **2.** To act together for a common purpose: *The people of the neighborhood united to stamp out crime.*

u-nit-ed (yu^w–naɪt–əd) adj. **1.** In harmony or agreement: *a united, loving fellowship* **2.** With everyone concerned agreeing on the same aim: *a united effort* **3.** Organized into a political union: *the United Nations* —**unitedly** adv.

U-nit-ed States (yu^w–naɪt–əd ste^yts) n. A large country of 50 states, located in North America, except for Hawaii which is in the Pacific Ocean

u-ni-ty (yu^w–nət–i^y) n. **-ties** A quality or state of being united: *May the God who gives endurance and encouragement give you a spirit of unity among yourselves as you follow Christ Jesus* (Romans 15:5).

u-ni-ver-sal (yu^w–nə–vɜr–səl) adj. **1.** Sthg. that affects all people everywhere: *English may become a universal language.* **2.** Unlimited: *All people everywhere are sinners in need of a Savior* (Romans 3:23-24). *That is a universal truth.* —**universally** adv. —**un-i-ver-sal-i-ty** (yu^w–nə–vər–sæl–ət–i^y) n.

U-ni-ver-sal-ist (yu^w–nə–vɜr–sə–ləst) n. A member of a denomination, officially merged with the Unitarians in 1961, that emphasizes the universal fatherhood of God and the final salvation of all people. NOTE: This, of course, is altogether contrary to the Bible, the Holy Word of God, which teaches that no one comes to the Father (and thus eternal life) but through faith in Jesus Christ who died for us and rose again (John 14:6; Acts 4:12; 1 John 5:12).

u-ni-verse (yu^w–nə–vərs) n. All space and everything that exists in it: *By faith we understand that the universe was formed at God's command, so that what is seen was not made out of what was visible* (Hebrews 11:3).

u-ni-ver-si-ty (yu^w–nə–vɜr–sət–i^y) n. **-ties 1.** An institution of learning at the highest level, where teaching and research are done and degrees are given **2.** The physical plant for such an institution

un-just (ən–dʒʌst) adj. Unfair; characterized by injustice —**unjustly** adv.

un-jus-ti-fi-a-ble (ən–dʒəs–tə–faɪ–ə–bəl/ ən–dʒʌs–tə–faɪ–ə–bəl) adj. That cannot be justified; not right; not defensible

un-jus-ti-fi-a-bly (ən–dʒəs–tə–faɪ–ə–bli^y/ən–dʒʌs–tə–faɪ–ə–bli^y) adv. In a manner that cannot be justified

un-jus-ti-fied (ən–dʒəs–tə–faɪd/ ən–dʒʌs–tə–faɪd) adj. **1.** Unwarranted **2.** Not brought into a state of justification theologically; still subject to the penalty of sin —see JUSTIFICATION

un-kempt (ən–kɛmpt) adj. **1.** Not neat or tidy **2.** Esp. of the hair, uncombed

un-kind (ən–kaɪnd) adj. Unsympathetic; cruel

un-know-ing (ən–no^w–ɪŋ) adj. Not knowing; ignorant —**unknowingly** adv.

un-known (ən–no^wn) adj. Unfamiliar

un-law-ful (ən–lɔ–fəl) adj. **1.** Not lawful; illegal **2.** Illegitimate —**unlawfully** adv.

un-lead-ed (ən–lɛd–əd) adj. Not treated or mixed with lead or lead compounds

un-leash (ən–li^yʃ) v. To release from or as from a leash; to let go

un-less (ən–lɛs) conj. Except; only on the condition that: *Don't come unless I call you first.*

un-let-tered (ən–lɛt–ərd) adj. Not educated; illiterate

un-like (ən–laɪk) prep. **1.** Different from: *She's quite unlike her sister.* **2.** Unusual for: *It's unlike him to be late to a meeting.* **3.** Different from: *His attitude is unlike that of his brother.*

un-like adj. **1.** Not like **2.** Unequal

un-like-ly (ən–laɪk–li^y) adv. **-lier, -liest** Not likely; not probable; unpromising

un-lim-it-ed (ən–lɪm–ət–əd) adj. Not restricted; infinite

un-load (ən–lo^wd) v. **1.** To remove the load or cargo from **2.** To relieve or be relieved of sthg. burdensome **3.** To withdraw a charge of ammunition from: *He unloaded his gun.*

un-loose (ən–lu^ws) v. **-loosed, -loosing** To set free; to untie

un-loos-en (ən–lu^ws–ən) v. To unloose

un-lov-ing (ən–lʌv–ɪŋ) adj. Not showing or expressing love

un-luck-y (ən–lʌk–i^y) adj. **-ier, -iest** Unfortunate

un-man-ly (ən–mæn–li^y) adj. Weak; cowardly

un-mask (ən–mæsk) v. To reveal or expose

un-matched (ən–mætʃt) adj. Without an equal

un-men-tion-a-ble (ən–mentʃ–ə–nə–bəl) adj. Unfit to be noticed or talked about; indecent; scandalous

un-mer-ci-ful (ən–mɜr–sɪ–fəl) adj. 1. Merciless; cruel 2. Extreme; excessive —**unmercifully** adv.

un-mis-tak-a-ble (ən–mə–steʸ–kə–bəl) adj. Obvious

un-mit-i-gat-ed (ən–mɪt–ə–geʸt–əd) adj. 1. Not softened or lessened 2. Absolute: *He's an unmitigated liar*

un-moved (ən–muʷvd) adj. 1. Not feeling pity or other emotion 2. Not upset; calm

un-nat-u-ral (ən–nætʃ–ə–rəl) adj. Contrary to nature or natural instincts —**unnaturally** adv.

un-nec-es-sar-i-ly (ən–nɛs–ə–sɛər–ə–liʸ) adj. 1. Not by necessity 2. To an unnec-essary degree

un-nec-es-sar-y (ən–nɛs–ə–sɛər–iʸ) adj. Not required

un-nerve (ən–nɜrv) v. -nerved, -nerving To cause to lose courage or determination: *The recent accident was unnerving.*

un-ob-tru-sive (ən–əb–truʷ–sɪv) adj. Not very obvious or noticeable: *a quiet unobtrusive girl*

un-oc-cu-pied (ən–ɑk–yə–paɪd) adj. 1. Not busy; unemployed 2. Empty; vacant

un-pack (ən–pæk) v. To open (luggage) and remove the contents

un-pal-at-a-ble (ən–pæl–ət–ə–bəl) adj. 1. Not agreeable to the taste 2. Not pleasant to do: *an unpalatable task*

un-par-al-leled (ən–pɛər–ə–lɛld/ –pær–) adj. Never yet equaled

un-pleas-ant (ən–plɛz–ənt) adj. Disagreeable ; not pleasant —**unpleasantly** adv. —**unpleasantness** n.

un-plug (ən–plʌg) v. -gg- 1. To unclog 2. To remove (a plug) from a receptacle 3. To disconnect from an electric circuit by removing a plug: *Please unplug the radio.*

un-pop-u-lar (ən–pɑp–yə–lər) adj. Generally disliked or unaccepted

un-prec-e-dent-ed (ən–prɛs–ə–dɛnt–əd) adj. Being without precedent; never before heard of

un-pre-ten-tious (ən–prɪ–tɛn–tʃəs/–ʃəs) adj. Modest; not showy or affected

un-prin-ci-pled (ən–prɪn–sə–pəld) adj. Without moral principles; unscrupulous

un-ques-tion-a-ble (ən–kwɛʃ–tʃən–ə–bəl/ –kwɛs–) adj. Completely certain; that cannot be doubted

un-rav-el (ən–ræv–əl) v. -eled, -eling or -elled, -elling 1. To disentangle 2. To solve

un-read (ən–rɛd) adj. 1. Unlearned; uninformed 2. Not yet read

un-re-al (ən–riʸ–əl) adj. 1. Not real or actual 2. Imaginary —**un-re-al-i-ty** (ən–riʸ–æl–ət–iʸ) n.

un-rea-son-a-ble (ən–riʸz–ən–ə–bəl) adj. Contrary to reason; absurd

un-re-lent-ing (ən–rɪ–lɛnt–ɪŋ) adj. Not letting up; not softening or weakening: *a week of unrelenting cold* —**unrelenting** adv.

un-re-li-a-ble (ən–rɪ–laɪ–ə–bəl) adj. Not dependable

un-re-mit-ting (ən–rɪ–mɪt–ɪŋ) adj. Unceasing; continuous; persevering —**unremittingly** adv.

un-re-solved (ən–rɪ–zɑlvd) adj. 1. Not resolved; not determined 2. Not solved; not clear

un-rest (ən–rɛst/ ʌn–) n. Disturbed conditions, esp. socially: *Political unrest followed the elections.*

un-re-strained (ən–rɪ–streʸnd) adj. 1. Uncontrolled 2. Spontaneous

un-right-eous (ən–raɪ–tʃəs) adj. Not righteous; unjust; wicked: *Christ died for sins once for all, the righteous for the unrighteous, to bring you to God* (1 Peter 3:18). —see SIN

un-ri-valed *AmE.* -ll- *BrE.* (ən–raɪ–vəld) adj. Unequaled

un-ruf-fled (ən–rʌf–əld) adj. 1. Not upset; calm 2. Not ruffled: *unruffled feathers*

un-ru-ly (ən–ruʷ–liʸ) adj. -lier, -liest Wild in behavior; not easily controlled: *unruly crowd* —**unruliness** n.

un-sat-is-fac-to-ry (ən–sæt–əs–fæk–tə–riʸ) adj. Not giving satisfaction —**unsatisfactorily** adv.

un-sat-u-rat-ed (ən–sætʃ–ə–reʸt–əd) adj. 1. Having the power to dissolve or absorb

more of sthg. **2.** Capable of uniting with additional elements

un·sa·vor·y (ən–se^yv–ə–ri^y) adj. **1.** Tasteless **2.** Unpleasant to the taste or smell **3.** Morally offensive; disgusting

un·scathed (ən–ske^yŏd) adj. Unharmed

un·scrip·tur·al (ən–skrɪp–tʃə–rəl) adj. Not taught in the Holy Scriptures, the Bible

un·scru·pu·lous (ən–skru^w–pyu^w–ləs) adj. Without principles; not concerned about the welfare of others: *an unscrupulous drug dealer* —opposite SCRUPULOUS —**unscrupulously** adv. —**unscrupulousness** n.

un·seat (ən–si^yt) v. **1.** To remove from a seat, esp. a political seat **2.** To throw from a saddle (of a horse, e.g.)

un·seem·ly (ən–si^ym–li^y) adj. -lier, -liest Not proper; indecent

un·self·ish (ən–sɛl–fɪʃ) adj. Not selfish —**unselfishly** adv. —**unselfishness** n.

un·set·tle (ən–sɛt–əl) v. -tled, -tling To disrupt; upset; disturb; confuse

un·sheathe (ən–ʃi^yŏ) v. To draw from a sheath, as a sword

un·sight·ly (ən–saɪt–li^y) adj. Not pleasing to the sight; ugly —**unsightliness** n.

un·skilled (ən–skɪld) adj. **1.** Having no technical training or skill **2.** Not requiring any special training or skill

un·skill·ful (ən–skɪl–fəl) adj. Not skillful or proficient —**unskillfully** adv.

un·so·phis·ti·cat·ed (ən–sə–fɪs–tə–ke^yt–əd) adj. **1.** Not worldly wise **2.** Without sophistication **3.** Simple

un·sound (ən–saʊnd) adj. **1.** Not healthy or strong: *The department of streets and roads declared the old bridge unsound and unsafe for travel.* **2.** Lacking a firm base in fact: *His thinking was unsound in this regard.*

un·spar·ing (ən–spɛər–ɪŋ) adj. **1.** Not merciful; hard and ruthless **2.** Holding nothing back, esp. money or help —**unsparingly** adv.

un·speak·a·ble (ən–spi^y–kə–bəl) adj. Beyond what can be expressed in words

un·spo·ken (ən–spo^w–kən) adj. Unsaid; not expressed: *an unspoken desire*

un·stud·ied (ən–stʌd–i^yd) adj. Natural; not forced

un·sung (ən–sʌŋ) adj. **1.** Obscure; unknown:

unsung heroes **2.** Not sung

un·sus·pec·ting (ən–sə–spɛkt–ɪŋ) adj. **1.** Not aware of coming danger **2.** Having no suspicion

un·swerv·ing (ən–swɜr–vɪŋ) adj. Firm in purpose

un·ten·a·ble (ən–tɛn–ə–bəl) adj. Of a belief or argument, that cannot be defended

un·think·a·ble (ən–θɪŋ–kə–bəl) adj. Not reasonable, desirable, or likely to happen; out of the question

un·til (ən–tɪl) also till prep., conj. Up to the time that: *We don't plan to leave until morning.*

un·time·ly (ən–taɪm–li^y) adj. *fml.* **1.** Happening before the proper time **2.** Not suitable for the occasion: *an untimely remark* —**untimeliness** n.

un·to (ʌn–tu^w) prep. To

un·told (ən–to^wld) adj. **1.** Too great or numerous to be counted; without limit: *untold suffering* **2.** Not told or related: *Her side of the story remained untold.*

un·touch·a·ble (ən–tʌtʃ–ə–bəl) adj. **1.** Not to be touched **2.** Out of reach

Untouchable n. A member of the lowest Hindu caste, with whom physical contact is considered defiling by Hindus of higher castes

un·tram·meled (ən–træm–əld) *AmE.* **un·trammelled** *BrE.* adj. Not hampered: *His life was untrammeled by responsibilities.*

un·true (ən–tru^w) adj. **1.** Not true; false **2.** Unfaithful

un·truth·ful (ən–tru^wθ–fəl) adj. Not containing or telling the truth

un·u·su·al (ən–yu^wʒ–ə–wəl) adj. Not common; rare —**unusually** adv.

un·var·nished (ən–vɑr–nɪʃt) adj. **1.** Having no covering or varnish **2.** Having no embellishment; plain; straightforward: *the unvarnished truth*

un·veil (ən–ve^yl) v. To remove a veil: *They unveiled the memorial that had been presented to the school.*

un·war·rant·ed (ən–wɔr–ən–təd) adj. Having no reason or justification; groundless: *an unwarranted scolding*

un·wield·y (ən–wi^yl–di^y) adj. -ier, -iest Not

easily managed or moved because of size, weight, shape, etc.: *an unwieldy piece of furniture* —**unwieldily** adv. —**unwieldiness** n.

un-wit-ting (ən-wɪt-ɪŋ) adj. Not knowing or intended; unaware —**unwittingly** adv.

un-wor-thy (ən-wɜr-ðiy) adj. **1.** Not worthy or deserving **2.** Not suitable or proper

up (ʌp) adv. **1.** In a high place: *The plane was flying 39,000 feet up and we could see the clouds below.* **2.** From below towards a higher position or level; away from the floor, the ground, or the bottom: *We climbed up to the top of the mountain to watch the sunrise.* **3.** Into an upright or raised position: *Don't just sit there! Get up and help us!* **4.** Towards or in the north: *We like it here in Naples, but we are going up to Rome tomorrow.* **5.** Out of bed: *What time do you get up in the morning?* **6.** Higher, better, or improved in some way: *The price of houses has gone up by 27% this year.* **7.** Completely used: *Time's up! We'll have to leave now!* **8.** Greater in volume, strength, activity, etc.: *I wish our neighbors wouldn't turn their radio up so high.* **9.** Towards the speaker: *The beggar came up and asked me for $20.* **10.** Into parts or pieces: *to cut up an apple* **11.** Tightly: *Tie up that thief.* **12.** So as to be together: *Do not store up for yourselves treasures on earth... but store up for yourselves treasures in heaven...* (Matthew 6:19-20). **13.** On top: *right side up* **14. up against** Facing or having to face or deal with a serious problem: *Jim is up against it now. He bought a new house and car and then lost his job.*

up adj. **1.** Moving upward or directed upward: *Take the up escalator to the third floor.* **2. up and about** Out of bed: *Mr. Smith is up and about today after his long illness.* **3.** *infml.* **What's up?** What's going on? **4. up to (a)** Doing sthg., esp. sthg. bad: *I wonder what he's up to.* **(b)** Capable of: *John really isn't up to such strenuous work yet.* **(c)** Responsible for: *If it were up to me to decide, I'd say, "Let's go."*

up prep. **1.** To or into a higher place: *He climbed up the ladder.* **2.** Along; in a direction toward the end of: *The bank is just two blocks up the street.* **3.** Against the current of a river:

Rowing the boat up the river was difficult. —opposite DOWN

up v. **-pp-** *infml.* **1.** To cause to increase: *The university has just upped the graduation requirements.* **2.** To stand up or act with determination: *She up and slapped him.*

up-and-coming (əp-ən-kʌm-ɪŋ) adj. Progressing well, esp. in a profession: *an up-and-coming artist*

up-braid (əp-breyd) v. *fml.* To scold

up-bring-ing (ʌp-brɪŋ-ɪŋ) n. The way in which a child is cared for and trained: *The kind of upbringing a child has is very important.* —see also BRING UP

up-com-ing (ʌp-kəm-ɪŋ) adj. To happen soon —compare UP-AND-COMING

up-date (ʌp-deyt) v. **-dated, -dating** To make or bring up-to-date

up-end (əp-ɛnd) v. **1.** To put sthg. on its end: *We had to upend the sofa to get it into the living room.* **2.** Overthrow or overturn

up-grade (ʌp-greyd) v. **-graded, -grading** To raise to a higher standard

upgrade n. An incline leading uphill

up-heav-al (əp-hiyv-əl) n. **1.** A sudden heaving upward **2.** A great change or disturbance

up-hold (əp-howld) v. **-held** (-hɛld) **-holding 1.** To give support to: *The Lord upholds the righteous* (Psalm 37:17). **2.** To declare to be right; confirm: *The decision of the lower court was upheld by the judge.* **3.** To maintain: *The old traditions are still upheld in this school.* —**upholder** n.

up-hol-ster (əp-howl-stər) v. To put a fabric, stuffing, springs, etc. on furniture: *He upholsters furniture for a living.* —**upholsterer** n. —**upholstery** n. *He's in the upholstery business.*

up-keep (ʌp-kiyp) n. The cost and the work of keeping sthg. in good condition: *The upkeep of our car is expensive.*

up-lands (ʌp-ləndz/ -lændz) n. A hilly or mountainous region: *We live in the uplands.*

up-lift (ʌp-lɪft) v. To improve, esp. spiritually, socially, or intellectually: *We all felt uplifted by the music.* —**uplift** (ʌp-lɪft) n.

up-on (ə-pɒn/-pɑn) prep. On: *Upon hearing the news everyone cheered loudly.*

up-per (ʌp–ər) adj. 1. Higher in position or rank: *the upper grades in school/the upper floor of a building* 2. **upper hand** Control

upper class (ʌp–ər klæs) n. 1. In the US, a social class whose members are rich 2. In Europe, a small class whose members belong to a few very rich families, usu. old and sometimes noble —see also MIDDLE CLASS, WORKING CLASS —**upper–class** adj. *This store has an upper–class group of customers.*

up-per-most (ʌp–ər–moᵂst) adj. In or into the highest: *of uppermost importance* —**uppermost** adv.

up-pish (ʌp–ɪʃ) adj. Arrogant

up-pi-ty (ʌp–ət–iʸ) adj. Arrogant; snobbish

up-right (ʌp–raɪt) adj. 1. Standing straight up; erect; vertical: *Place the books in an upright position, please.* 2. A person of the highest moral character: *A faithful God who does no wrong, upright and just is he* (Deuteronomy 32:4). *The Lord is righteous, he loves justice; upright men will see his face* (Psalm 11:7). —**upright** adv. Not bent; straight up

up-ris-ing (ʌp–raɪ–zɪŋ) n. A rebellion or revolt

up-roar (ʌp–rɔr) n. An outbreak of confused, noisy activity, often with violence

up-roar-i-ous (əp–rɔr–iʸ–əs) adj. Very noisy with loud laughter

up-root (əp–ruᵂt/ –rʊt) v. 1. To pull up by the roots or as if by the roots 2. *fig.* To move a family to a distant place after living in one place for a long time: *Being uprooted and moved about the country is difficult for children.*

ups and downs (ʌps ən daʊnz) n. Good times, followed by bad times: *She's certainly had a life full of ups and downs.*

up-set (əp–sɛt) v. -set, -setting 1. To knock sthg. over: *He upset his cup of coffee on the new carpet.* 2. To cause distress: *Losing her job upset Janice badly.* 3. To cause a slight physical illness, esp. of the stomach: *Heavy fried foods can upset one's stomach.*

up-set (ʌp–sɛt/ əp–sɛt) adj. 1. Distressed or disturbed: *He was really upset about failing the exam.* 2. A slight physical illness: *The baby had an upset stomach.*

up-set (ʌp–sɛt) n. 1. Slight physical pain: *stom-ach upset* 2. The defeat of a person or team that was expected to win: *It was quite an upset when our team beat the league champs.*

up-shot (ʌp–ʃat) n. The result or outcome: *The upshot of our meeting was that two new men were added to the staff.*

up-stairs (əp–stɛərz) adj. Up the stairs; to or on the upper floors of a building: *an upstairs apartment* —**upstairs** adv.

up-start (ʌp–start) n. *derog.* A person who has risen quickly to prominence, wealth, or power, esp. one who is arrogant

up-tight (əp–taɪt) adj. Uneasy; anxious; tense; nervous

up-ward (ʌp–wərd) adj. Directed or moving toward a higher place: *We took the upward bend in the road.*

upward Also upwards adv. 1. Going up: *Tom climbed upward along the trail.* 2. With a particular side facing up: *He lay on the grass, face upwards, watching the clouds drifting by.*

u-ra-ni-um (yʊ–reʸ–niʸ–əm) n. A heavy, radioactive, metallic element, used in nuclear weapons

ur-ban (ɜr–bən) adj. Of, in, or comprising cities: *urban life/traffic* —compare RURAL —**ur-ban-ize** (ɜr–bən–aɪz) v. -ized, -izing —**ur-ban-i-za-tion** (ər–bən–ɪ–zeʸ–ʃən) n.

ur-bane (ɜr–beʸn) adj. Polite in a smooth way; suave

ur-chin (ɜr–tʃən) n. A small boy, esp. a dirty, ragged one

urge (ɜrdʒ) v. urged, urging 1. To encourage: *They urged him onward, deeper into the jungle.* 2. To strongly persuade: *Many friends urged her to go to college.*

urge n. A strong desire or need: *He has a strong urge to become an airplane pilot.*

ur-gent (ɜr–dʒənt) adj. Very important; requiring immediate attention: *an urgent phone call for you from the hospital* —**urgency** n. —**urgently** adv.

u-ri-nal (yʊr–ən–əl) n. A receptacle in a public lavatory for men to urinate into

u-ri-nar-y (yʊr–ə–nɛər–iʸ) adj. Of or relating to urine or its production or excretion: *a urinary infection*

u-ri-nate (yʊr–ə–neʸt) v. -nated, -nating To discharge urine

u-rine (yʊr–ɪn) n. Human and animal liquid waste that passes from the body

urn (ɜrn) n. **1.** A large container with a tap, used for making coffee or tea **2.** A vase for holding the ashes of a cremated person

us (ʌs) pron. Object form of **we**: *They invited us to dinner.*

us-a-ble also **use-a-ble** (yu^w–zə–bəl) adj. Capable of being used

us-age (yu^w–sɪdʒ) n. **1.** The act or manner of using sthg. **2.** The actual way in which language or words and phrases are used

use (yu^ws) n. **1.** The act of using or the state of being used: *Hopefully, the use of force will not be necessary.* **2.** The purpose for which sthg. may be used: *This little gadget has many uses.* **3.** The ability to use: *He lost the use of his left hand when it got smashed.* **4.** Advantage: *What's the use of saying anything? He won't listen anyhow.*

use (yu^wz) v. **used, using 1.** To put into action or service **2.** To consume or take regularly, as drugs **3.** To act with regard to sbdy. or sthg.: *use cruelly* **4. to be used to** To be accustomed to **5. used** Secondhand: *a used car* **6. used to** Showing that sthg. happened regularly or always in the past: *I used to live in Los Angeles.*

used adj. **1.** Second-hand; owned by another person previously: *used furniture* **2.** Accustomed: *I'm not used to getting up so early.*

use-ful (yu^ws–fəl) adj. **1.** Capable of being used **2.** Helpful: *A pencil sharpener is a useful tool.* —**usefulness**

use-less (yu^ws–ləs) adj. Having or being of no use —**uselessly** adv. —**uselessness** n.

ush-er (ʌʃ–ər) n. **usherette** *fem.* n. A person who shows people to their seats as in a theater or at a church wedding

usher v. To bring in: *fig. Spring often ushers in rainstorms.*

usu. adv. *written abbr.* for **usually**

u-su-al (yu^wʒ–ə–wəl) adj. **1.** Happening as the normal thing; customary: *Our office will be open at the usual hours, nine to five daily.* **2. as usual** As generally has happened before: *We'll meet at ten o'clock, as usual.*

u-su-al-ly (yu^wʒ–ə–wəl–i^y / yu^wʒ–wəl–i^y / yu^wʒ–li^y) adv. Generally: *We usually go to bed before midnight.*

u-surp (yu^w–sɜrp) v. To seize power illegally: *The younger brother tried to usurp his brother's throne.* —**usurper** n. —**u-sur-pa-tion** (yu^w–sər–pe^y–ʃən) n.

u-su-ry (yu^wʒ–ə–ri^y) n. The practice of lending money at a high rate of interest

u-ten-sil (yu^w–tɛn–səl) n. An instrument or container for domestic use: *pots and pans and other kitchen utensils*

u-ter-us (yu^wt–ə–rəs) n. **-i** (–aɪ) or **-uses** (əs–əz) *tech.* The womb; the organ of the female mammal in which the young are developed and protected before birth

u-til-i-ty (yu^w–tɪl–ət–i^y) n. **-ties 1.** The degree of fitness for some use **2.** Any useful public service, such as gas, water, or electricity

u-til-ize (yu^wt–əl–aɪz) v. **-ized, -izing** To make use of; to use: *Your abilities will be fully utilized in this job.* —**utilizable** adj. —**u-til-i-za-tion** (yu^wt–əl–ə–ze^y–ʃən) n.

ut-most (ʌt–mo^wst) also **ut-ter-most** adj. Best; greatest: *This job is of the utmost importance. I'll do my best to help you.*

ut-ter (ʌt–ər) adj. Complete: *Our trip was an utter disaster. Everything went wrong.* —**utterly** adv.

utter v. **1.** To express in words **2.** To express in any way

ut-ter-ance (ʌt–ə–rəns) n. **1.** An act of expressing sthg. **2.** Sthg. that is spoken

U–turn (yu^w–tɜrn) n. Act of turning a car around so as to go back in the direction one came from

u-vu-la (yu^w–vyə–lə) n. **-las** or **-lae** (–li^y / –laɪ) The small piece of flesh hanging at the back of the palate, at the back of the mouth

V, **v** (vi�406) n. **1.** The 22nd letter of the English alphabet **2.** The Roman Numeral (number) for 5 (five) **3.** V written abbr. said as verb (vɜrb)

va-can-cy (ve�API–kən–siᶜ) n. **-cies 1.** An apartment, hotel room, etc. that is not occupied **2.** An unfilled position or job in an office, industry, etc. **3.** The state of being vacant; emptiness

va-cant (veᶜ–kənt) adj. **1.** Not occupied; not being used **2.** Of a job, not presently filled **3.** Showing no thought or interest: *a vacant stare* —**vacantly** adv.

va-cate (veᶜ–keᶜt) v. **-cated, -cating** To move out of: *We must vacate our apartment by the end of the month.*

va-ca-tion (veᶜ–keᶜ–ʃən) n. A period of rest or freedom from one's regular work or study —**vacation** v. *We vacationed at the lake this year.*

vac-ci-nate (væk–sə–neᶜt) v. **-nated, -nating** To protect someone against disease, such as smallpox, by putting vaccine into his body —**vac-ci-na-tion** (væk–sə–neᶜ–ʃən) n.

vac-cine (væk–siᶜn) n. A substance made from the germs that cause smallpox, and given to a person or animal to prevent him from catching that disease —compare SERUM

vac-il-late (væs–ə–leᶜt) v. **-lated, -lating** To be continually changing back and forth from one opinion or feeling to another —**vac-il-la-tion** (væs–ə–leᶜ–ʃən) n.

vac-u-ous (væk–yuᵂ–əs) adj. **1.** Lacking in ideas or intelligence **2.** Containing a vacuum —**vacuously** adv. —**vacuousness** n.

vac-u-um (væk–yuᵂ–əm) n. **1.** A space from which (almost) all air and gas has been removed **2.** An emptiness: *Her husband's death left a vacuum in her life.*

vacuum v. To clean a floor, etc., using a vacuum cleaner

vac-u-um cleaner (væk–yuᵂ–əm kliᶜ–nər) n. An electrical appliance that cleans surfaces by means of suction

vag-a-bond (væg–ə–bɑnd) n. One who wanders from place to place with no visible means of support; a tramp

va-gar-y (veᶜ–gə–riᶜ) n. **-ies 1.** An unpredicta-

ble or erratic action **2.** A wild idea

va-gi-na (və–dʒaɪ–nə) n. **-nae** or **-nas** In the female of humans and other mammals, the passage that leads from the outer sex organ to the womb —**vag-i-nal** (vædʒ–ən–əl) adj.

va-grant (veᶜ–grənt) n. **1.** A person who wanders about, having no settled home; a vagabond; a tramp —compare VAGABOND **2.** A person, such as a drunkard, who is a public nuisance

vagrant adj. Wandering; roving: *a vagrant life* —**vagrancy** n.

vague (veᶜg) adj. **1.** Not clearly seen, described, or understood: *I have only a vague idea of what he's talking about* **2.** Not clearly expressing oneself: *His directions to the station were very vague.* —**vaguely** adv. —**vagueness** n.

vain (veᶜn) adj. **1.** Conceited; full of self-admiration; thinking too highly of one's appearance, abilities, etc. **2.** Without result; useless **3.** **in vain (a)** Uselessly; without success: *Your labor in the Lord is not in vain* (1 Corinthians 15:58). *Unless the Lord builds the house, its builders labor in vain. Unless the Lord watches over the city, the watchmen stand guard in vain* (Psalm 127:1-2). **(b)** Irreverently; disrespectfully: *You shall not take the name of the Lord your God in vain* (Exodus 20:7KJV).

vain-glo-ry (veᶜn–gloᵂ–riᶜ/–glɔr–iᶜ) n. Extreme vanity; boastfulness —**vain-glor-i-ous** (veᶜn–gloᵂ–riᶜ–əs) adj.

va-lance (væl–əns) n. **1.** A short curtain placed across the top of a window **2.** A short drapery hanging from an edge, as from the frame of a bed NOTE: Don't confuse **valance** with **valence**.

vale (veᶜl) n. *Chiefly poetic* A valley

val-e-dic-to-ri-an (væl–ə–dɪk–tɔr–iᶜ–ən) n. The highest ranking member of a graduating class, giving a valedictory speech at a graduation ceremony

val-e-dic-to-ry (væl–ə–dɪk–tə–riᶜ) n. A farewell speech, usu. given in college by the highest ranking member of the graduating class —**valediction** n.

va-lence (veᶜ–ləns) n. The capacity of an atom to combine with another or others NOTE:

Don't confuse **valence** with **valance**.

val-en-tine (**væl**–ən–taın) n. **1.** A greeting card sent to a sweetheart or friend on Saint Valentine's Day (February 14th) **2.** A sweetheart: *Will you be my valentine?*

va-let (**væl**–ət/ væ–le^y) n. **1.** A man's personal servant who takes care of his clothes, etc. **2.** An employee, as of a hotel, who provides laundry service, cleaning and pressing, etc.

val-iant (**væl**–yənt) adj. **1.** Brave; courageous **2.** Heroic —**valiantly** adv.

val-id (**væl**–əd) adj. **1.** Acceptable: *He had a valid excuse for being late to work, since he had a serious accident that morning.* **2.** Legally binding or effective: *a valid passport* —opposite INVALID —**va-lid-i-ty** (və–**lıd**–ət–i^y) n.

val-i-date (**væl**–ə–de^{y}t) v. **-dated, -dating** To make valid: *Get your parking ticket validated in the store, so you won't have to pay for parking in their parking lot.* —opposite INVALI-DATED —**val-i-da-tion** (væl–ı–**de**^{y}–ʃən) n.

va-lise (və–**li**^{y}s) n. A small suitcase

val-ley (**væl**–i^y) n. **-leys** The stretch of flat, low land between hills or mountains, often with a river running through it

val-or *AmE.* **val-our** *BrE.* (**væl**–ər) n. *Fml.* Great bravery, esp. in battle —**valorous** adj. —**valorously** adv.

val-u-a-ble (**væl**–yə–wə–bəl) adj. **1.** Worth a lot of money: *This property is very valuable.* **2.** Very useful: *Thanks for the valuable advice.* **3.** **valuables** Things such as pieces of jewelry that are worth a lot of money

val-u-ate (**væl**–yu^w–e^{y}t) v. **-ated, -ating** To set a value on —**valuator** n.

val-u-a-tion (væl–yu^w–**e**^{y}–ʃən) n. The estimated or determined market value of sthg.

val-ue (**væl**–yu^w) n. **1.** Worth; importance: *This street map will be of great value to you in finding your way around the city.* **2.** Purchasing power: *The value of the dollar has fallen in recent months.* **3.** A bargain: *We got a 50% discount; that's real value.* **4.** **values** Sthg. regarded as desirable or right, as a belief or moral precept

value v. **valued, valuing** **1.** To calculate the worth of sthg.: *He valued the house at $95,000.* **2.** To consider to be of great worth:

Some people value fame and fortune above everything else, but the Bible says, "What is highly valued among men is detestable in God's sight" (Luke 16:15).

val-ue-less (**væl**–yu^w–ləs) adj. Without worth

valve (vælv) n. **1.** A device that temporarily closes a passage or that permits the flow of liquid, air, or gas in one direction only **2.** A small flap that controls the flow of blood in the body

val-vu-lar (**væl**–vyə–lər) adj. Having the form or function of a valve

vamp (væmp) n. An unscrupulous, seductive woman who exploits or ruins the men she seduces

vamp v. To seduce or try to seduce a man by using feminine charms

vamp n. **1.** The upper part of a boot or shoe **2.** Sthg. added to give an old thing a new appearance **3.** Musically, a simple, improvised accompaniment

vamp v. **1.** To provide with a vamp **2.** To repair or patch **3.** To improvise a musical accompaniment

vam-pire (**væm**–paı–ər) n. **1.** A mythical corpse who rises at night to suck the blood of the living **2.** A person who preys ruthlessly upon others **3.** A tropical American bat that feeds on the blood of animals and sometimes people —**vampirish** adj. —**vampirism** n.

van (væn) n. **1.** A large closed truck for carrying furniture and other supplies and equipment: *a moving van* **2.** A small enclosed truck for carrying goods and people, often equipped with sleeping, dining, and other facilities —compare TRUCK

van-dal (**væn**–dəl) n. A person who intentionally destroys public or private property: *Vandals broke into the house and sprayed red paint all over everything.*

van-dal-ism (**væn**–dəl–ız–əm) n. The willful destruction of other people's property

van-dal-ize (**væn**–dəl–aız) v. **-ized, -izing** To damage or destroy by vandalism

vane (ve^{y}n) n. **1.** A flat piece of metal, strip of cloth, etc. placed up high to move in the wind and show which direction the wind is blowing; weather vane **2.** The blade of a

windmill or propeller that makes it possible to use the force of wind or water as the driving power

van-guard (væn-gard) n. **1.** The part of an army going in front of the main body **2.** The leading group in a movement

va-nil-la (və-nɪl-ə) n. A flavoring substance obtained from the pods of a tropical plant —**vanilla** adj.

van-ish (væn-ɪʃ) n. **1.** To disappear; to go out of sight: *The plane streaked across the sky and soon vanished.* **2.** To cease to exist; to become extinct: *Many kinds of animals have vanished from the face of the earth.*

van-i-ty (væn-ət-i^y) n. Too much pride in one's personal appearance or accomplishments

van-quish (væŋ-kwɪʃ/væn-) v. To defeat completely

van-tage point (vænt-ɪdʒ pɔmt) n. A position which gives one an advantage or a clear view

va-pid (væp-əd) adj. Dull; uninteresting

va-por *AmE.* **va-pour** *BrE.* (ve^y-pər) n. **1.** Fine particles of matter, as fog, suspended in the air **2.** A substance in a gaseous state that is a liquid or solid at normal temperatures **3.** *fig.* Sthg. that is worthless or not long lasting: *What is your life? It is even a vapor that appears for a little time and then vanishes away* (James 4:14 NKJV).

va-por-ize (ve^y-pə-raɪz) n. -ized, -izing To change into vapor —**vaporizer** n.

var-i-a-ble (veər-i^y-ə-bəl/ vær-) adj. **1.** Changeable; likely to vary or change **2.** Capable of being varied or changed **3.** Inconsistent —**var-i-a-bil-i-ty** (veər-i^y-ə-bɪl-ə-ti^y/ vær-) n. —**var-i-a-bly** (veər-i^y-ə-bli^y/vær-) adv. —see VARY

var-i-ance (veər-i^y-əns/vær-) n. **1.** Discrepancy **2.** Difference **3. at variance** Of people, disagreeing, conflicting, or in a state of discord

var-i-ant (veər-i^y-ənt/vær-) adj. Differing from sthg. or from a standard: *"Colour" is a variant spelling of "color."*

var-i-a-tion (veər-i^y-e^y-ʃən/vær-) n. A varying; a change: *In the desert there are great variations of temperature.*

var-i-cose (veər-ə-ko^ws/vær-) adj. Abnormally swollen: *varicose veins*

var-ied (veər-i^yd/vær-) adj. **1.** Different: *Opinions on the subject were varied.* **2.** Not staying the same: *a varied life*

var-i-e-gate (veər-i^y-ə-ge^yt/vær-) v. -gated, -gating **1.** To make varied in appearance, esp. by adding various colors **2.** To give variety to —**variegated** adj. *variegated thread*

va-ri-e-ty (və-raɪ-ə-ti^y) n. -ties **1.** Of many different kinds, conditions, or activities: *My job at the factory lacks variety. I do the same things all the time.* **2.** A mixed collection: *This box contains a variety of tools.* **3.** A sort or kind: *How many varieties of breakfast cereal are there?* **4. variety show** A show including singing, dancing, comedy, and various kinds of entertainment: *a variety show*

var-i-ous (veər-i^y-əs/vær-) adj. **1.** Different: *various ways of cooking potatoes* **2.** Several; a number of: *In the last days, shortly before our Lord's return, "there will be famines and earthquakes in various places"* (Matthew 24:7). —see DIFFERENT —**variously** adv. *The oldest living things on earth are some trees in California, variously estimated to be 4,400 to 4,600 years old.*

var-mint (var-mənt) n. **1.** A mischievous or discreditable person **2.** An objectionable animal or insect

var-nish (var-nɪʃ) n. **1.** A liquid preparation that gives wood a clear, shiny surface: *This table needs a coat of varnish.* **2.** The shiny appearance produced by using this substance: *Hot cups will spoil the varnish on a table.*

varnish v. To cover with varnish: *I varnished that desk today.* —compare LACQUER

var-si-ty (var-sə-ti^y) n. -ties **1.** The main team that represents a university, college, or school in some competition, esp. an athletic one **2.** *BrE.* A university

var-y (veər-i^y/vær-) v. -ried, -rying **1.** To change in form, appearance, substance, or nature; modify: *She varies her diet quite often.* **2.** Differ: *Opinions vary on this subject.*

vas-cu-lar (væs-kyə-lər) adj. Consisting of vessels or ducts for conveying blood or sap in an organism —**vascularly** adv.

vase (ve^ys) n. A jar of glass, pottery, etc., used

as a decoration or to put cut flowers in

va-sec-to-my (və–**sɛk**–tə–mi^y) n. **-mies** Surgical removal of all or part of each of the ducts through which semen passes, esp. as a means of birth control

vas-sal (**væs**–əl) n. A humble servant or subordinate in feudal times

vast (væst) adj. Very large; great in size or amount: *How precious to me are your thoughts, O God! How vast is the sum of them* (Psalm 139:17). —**vastness** n.

vast-ly (**væst**–li^y) adv. Very greatly: *His opinions are vastly different from ours.*

vat (væt) n. A large tank or tub for storing or holding liquids

vaude-ville (**vɔd**–vɪl/vɔd–ə–vɪl) n. A stage show consisting of mixed specialty acts such as singing, dancing, comic skits, etc.; a variety show

vault (vɔlt) n. **1.** An arched roof as in many churches **2.** An underground storage room **3.** A strongly built chamber for keeping money and valuable articles **4.** A burial chamber **5.** A jump made by pole vaulting: *The world pole vault record is nearly 20 feet.*

vault v. To jump over sthg. using a pole to gain more height: *to pole vault*

VCR (vi^y–si^y–ɑr) n. *abbr.* for **videocassette recorder**

VD (vi^y–di^y) n. *abbr.* for **venereal disease**

V–Day (vi^y–de^y) n. A day of final victory

veal (vi^{y}l) n. The meat of a young calf

vec-tor (**vɛk**–tər) n. **1.** A quantity possessing both magnitude and direction **2.** An organism that transmits a disease-producing microorganism

Veda (ve^{y}d–ə) n. Any of four ancient sacred books of Hinduism, consisting of psalms, chants, etc. —**Vedic** adj.

Ve-dan-ta (ve^y–**dɑnt**–ə/ –**dænt**–) n. The chief Indian philosophy that forms the basis of Hinduism —**Vedantic** adj.

veer (vɪər) v. To change direction, turn, or swing around

veg-e-ta-ble (**vɛdʒ**–tə–bəl/**vɛdʒ**–ət-ə–bəl) n. A plant, or part of a plant other than a fruit, that is used for food: *Beans and peas are vegetables.*

veg-e-tar-i-an (vɛdʒ–ə–**tɛər**–i^y–ən) n. A person

who doesn't eat meat

veg-e-tate (**vɛdʒ**–ə–te^{y}t) v. **-tated, -tating 1.** To grow as a plant does **2.** To lead a dull, aimless life

veg-e-ta-tion (vɛdʒ–ə–te^y–ʃən) n. Plants in general: *the beautiful vegetation of the tropical forest*

veg-e-ta-tive (**vɛdʒ**–ə–te^{y}t–ɪv) adj. **1.** Of vegetations **2.** Concerned with growth and development, rather than sexual reproduction **3.** Living a monotonous, uneventful life

ve-he-ment (vi^y–ə–mənt) adj. Forceful or violent: *a vehement wind/temper* —**vehemence** —**vehemency** n. —**vehemently** adv.

ve-hi-cle (vi^y–hɪk–əl/vi^y–ə–kəl) n. **1.** A means of transportation, esp. sthg. having a motor and wheels **2.** *fml.* A means of communication, such as television or radio —**ve-hic-u-lar** (vi^y–**hɪk**–yə–lər) adj.

veil (ve^{y}l) n. **1.** A covering of fine cloth or netting worn esp. by women to shade or hide the face, sometimes for religious reasons **2.** Sthg. that covers or hides sthg. else: *Even to this day when Moses is read, a veil covers their hearts, but whenever anyone turns to the Lord [Jesus], the veil is taken away* (2 Corinthians 3:15,16). —see JESUS, GOSPEL

veil v. To cover with a veil

veiled (ve^{y}ld) adj. **1.** Wearing a veil **2.** Hidden: *veiled threats*

vein (ve^{y}n) n. **1.** Any of the tubes carrying blood from various parts of the body to the heart —compare ARTERY **2.** One of a system of thin lines which runs in a pattern through leaves and the wings of certain insects **3.** A thin layer of mineral in a rock: *a vein of silver* —compare SEAM **4.** A manner or mood: *speaking in a serious vein*

veld, veldt (vɛlt/ fɛlt) n. An open grassland, esp. in southern Africa

vel-lum (**vɛl**–əm) n. **1.** A fine parchment made of lambskin, calfskin, etc. used for bookbinding and for a fine writing surface **2.** Paper or cloth that looks like this

ve-loc-i-pede (və–**lɑs**–ə–pi^{y}d) n. An early type of bicycle or tricycle

ve-loc-i-ty (və–**lɑs**–ət-i^y) n. **-ties** Speed in a given direction: *The velocity of sound is generally placed at 1,088 feet per second at sea level at*

32 degrees F.

ve-lour (və-lʊər) n. A heavy cloth similar to velvet

vel-vet (vɛl-vət) n. A type of cloth, esp. of silk or nylon, having a soft, furry surface

vel-vet-een (vɛl-və-tiᵞn) Fabric, usu. cotton, having a short pile, in imitation of velvet

vel-vet-y (vɛl-vət-iᵞ) adj. Like velvet; very soft

ve-nal (viᵞn-əl) adj. 1. Open to bribery 2. Influenced by bribery —**ve-nal-i-ty** (vɪ-næl-ət-iᵞ) n. —**venally** adv.

vend (vɛnd) v. To sell, esp. by peddling on the street or from door to door —**vendible** adj.

ven-det-ta (vɛn-dɛt-ə) n. A prolonged, bitter feud

vend-ing ma-chine (vɛnd-ɪŋ mə-ʃiᵞn) n. A coin-operated machine from which drinks, candy, stamps, and other small articles can be obtained

ven-dor or **ven-der** (vɛn-dər) n. A seller of small articles that can be carried around or pushed on a cart: *a fruit vendor*

ve-neer (və-nɪər) n. 1. A thin layer of fine wood used in covering the surface of cheaper wood or in making plywood 2. A deceptive outward appearance

ven-er-a-ble (vɛn-ər-ə-bəl) adj. Commanding respect because of great age or associated dignity

ven-er-ate (vɛn-ə-reᵞt) v. To respect or honor greatly

ven-er-a-tion (vɛn-ə-reᵞ-ʃən) n. Great respect

ve-ner-e-al (və-nɪər-iᵞ-əl) adj. Of or relating to sexual intercourse or to diseases transmitted by it

venereal disease (və-nɪər-iᵞ-əl dɪz-iᵞz) n. A contagious disease (as gonorrhea or syphilis) that is typically acquired through sexual intercourse

ve-ne-tian blind (və-niᵞ-ʃən blamd) n. A blind for windows, formed of thin horizontal slats that may be raised and lowered and set at a desired angle to regulate the amount of light admitted

ven-geance (vɛn-dʒəns) n. 1. Retaliation for a wrong or injury to oneself, one's family, etc.: *Repay no one evil for evil. Do not avenge*

yourselves, but rather give place to wrath; for it is written, "Vengeance is mine, I will repay says the Lord." Therefore, if your enemy is hungry, feed him; if he thirsts, give him a drink... Do not be overcome by evil, but overcome evil with good* (Romans 12:17,19-21KJV). —see REVENGE 2. **with a vengeance** *infml.* With greater force than usual

venge-ful (vɛndʒ-fəl) adj. An intense desire to punish a person for the harm he/she has done to oneself —**vengefully** adv.

ve-ni-al (viᵞ-niᵞ-əl / -nyəl) adj. Of sin, capable of being forgiven; pardonable NOTE: All sins are detestable in God's sight, and we must repent of every sin of thought word, or deed. On the other hand, no sin is so great that it cannot be forgiven by God. He is a God of love and mercy and forgiveness. If we truly repent of every sin (the breaking of God's commandments) and put our trust in Jesus for salvation, we shall have eternal life. For the wages of sin is death, but the gift of God is eternal life through Jesus Christ our Lord (Romans 6:23). —**ve-ni-al-i-ty** (viᵞ-niᵞ-æl-ət-iᵞ) n.

ven-i-son (vɛn-ə-sən) n. The flesh of deer, used for food

ven-om (vɛn-əm) n. 1. The poisonous fluid secreted by certain snakes, scorpions, etc., injected into a victim by biting or stinging 2. Great hatred

ven-om-ous (vɛn-əm-əs) adj. 1. Poisonous 2. Full of bitter feeling or hatred

ven-ous (viᵞ-nəs) adj. Of or pertaining to veins

vent (vɛnt) v. To express one's rage or other strong feelings in some way

vent n. 1. An opening, serving as an outlet for air, smoke, or fumes 2. **give vent to** To express a strong feeling, idea, etc. freely

ven-ti-late (vɛnt-əl-eᵞt) v. **-lated, -lating** To allow fresh air to enter a room, etc. —**ven-ti-la-tion** (vɛnt-ə-leᵞ-ʃən) n.

ven-ti-la-tor (vɛnt-əl-eᵞt-ər) n. A device for bringing fresh air (into a room, etc.)

ven-tri-cle (vɛn-trɪ-kəl) n. 1. One of the two chambers of the heart that pumps blood into the arteries by contraction 2. Any cavity or chamber in an organ of the body

—ven-tric-u-lar (vɛn–trɪk–yə–lər) adj.

ven-tril-o-quist (vɛn–trɪl–ə–kwəst) n. An entertainer who produces voice sounds that seem to come from a source other than himself —ventriloquism n.

ven-ture (vɛn–tʃər) v. -tured, -turing 1. To go somewhere or do sthg. that involves some risk 2. To dare; to take the risk of saying sthg. that may be opposed or be considered insulting or foolish

ven-ture n. An undertaking, esp. a business enterprise, involving some risk: *a business venture* NOTE: **Venture** suggests some risk to one's life or possessions. An **adventure** is an exciting experience, which may or may not be dangerous.

ven-ture-some (vɛn–tʃər–səm) adj. Ready to take risks; daring —ven-turesomely adv. —venturesomeness n.

ven-tur-ous (vɛntʃ–ə–rəs) adj. Venturesome —venturously adv. —venturousness n.

ven-ue (vɛn–yuʷ) n. 1. The place where a crime is committed or a cause of legal action takes place 2. The county or political division from which a jury must be summoned and in which the trial must be held 3. **change of venue** The changing of the place of a trial

Ve-nus (viʸ–nəs) n. The sixth largest of the nine planets in our solar system

ve-ra-cious (və–reʸ–ʃəs) adj. 1. Habitually speaking the truth 2. True or factual

ve-rac-i-ty (və–ræs–ə–tiʸ) n. -ties Conformity to truth or fact

ve-ran-da (və–ræn–də) n. A kind of covered porch or balcony with a roof extending beyond the main building

verb (vɜrb) n. A word or phrase that tells what someone or sthg. is, does, or experiences: *In the sentence, "He caught a fish," "caught" is the verb.*

ver-bal (vɜr–bəl) adj. 1. Consisting of spoken words; not written: *a verbal agreement* 2. Having to do with words and their use: *verbal skill*

ver-bal-ize also -ise (vɜr–bə–laɪz) v. -ized, -izing To express sthg. in words

ver-bal-ly (vɜr–bə–liʸ) adv. In or by speech, not writing

ver-ba-tim (vər–beʸt–əm) adj. Word for word; exactly as written or spoken: *After hearing the speech once, he repeated it verbatim.*

ver-bi-age (vɜr–biʸ–ɪdʒ) n. An abundance of useless words

ver-bose (vər–boʷs) adj. Using too many words

ver-dant (vɜrd–ənt) adj. Green with vegetation

ver-dict (vɜr–dɪkt) n. 1. The official decision made by a jury in a court of law, following a trial 2. *infml.* A person's opinion on a matter

ver-di-gris (vɜrd–ə–griʸs/–grɪs/–grəs/–griʸ) n. The green or greenish blue deposit found on exposed copper, bronze, or brass surfaces

verge (vɜrdʒ) n. The edge, border or brink: *He was on the verge of a nervous breakdown.* —verge v.

ver-i-fy (vɛər–ə–faɪ) v. -fied, -fying To prove the truth of —ver-i-fi-a-ble (vɛər–ə–faɪ–ə–bəl) adj. —ver-i-fi-ca-tion (vɛər–ə–fə–keʸ–ʃən) n.

ver-i-si-mil-i-tude (vɛər–ə–sə–mɪl–ə–tuʷd) n. Appearance of truth

ver-i-ta-ble (vɛər–ət–ə–bəl) adj. Real; rightly named: *a veritable thief*

ver-i-ty (vɛər–ət–iʸ) n. -ties Truth

ver-mi-cel-li (vɜr–mə–tʃɛl–iʸ/–sɛl–) n. A pasta thinner than spaghetti

ver-mil-ion or ver-mil-lion (vər–mɪl–yən) n. A bright red pigment —vermilion adj.

ver-min (vɜr–mən) n. *pl.* vermin 1. Objectionable small insects, as lice or fleas, that are difficult to control 2. Birds and mammals that prey on game 3. An offensive person

ver-nac-u-lar (vər–næk–yə–lər) n. The native spoken language of a country or region —vernacular adj.

ver-nal (vɜr–nəl) adj. Of or occurring in the season of spring —vernally adv.

ver-sa-tile (vɜr–sət–əl) adj. 1. Having many different skills or abilities: *a versatile performer* 2. Having many different uses: *versatile material*

verse (vɜrs) n. 1. Writing in the form of poetry 2. A number of lines grouped together which form one part of a poem or song:

Most hymns have only three or four verses, some have six or eight or more. 3. A short division of a chapter of the Bible: *In the Gospel of St. John, chapter three has 36 verses. The 16th verse is probably the best known verse in the Bible.*

versed (vɜrst) adj. Possessing a thorough knowledge of a subject: *He is well versed in the Holy Scriptures.*

ver-sion (vɜr-ʒən) n. 1. One person's account of an event: *The two witnesses gave different versions of how the accident happened.* 2. A translation: *The King James Version of the Bible first appeared in 1611.*

ver-sus (vɜr-səs) prep. also *abbr.* **vs.** *AmE. or v. BrE.* Against: *The boxing match tonight is Leonard versus (vs.) Doran.*

ver-te-bra (vɜrt-ə-brə) n. **-brae** (breʸ) One of the small hollow bones that form the spine

ver-te-brate (vɜrt-ə-brət/-breʸt) n. Having a spinal column

ver-tex (vɜr-tɛks) n. **-texes** or **-tices** (-ə-səs) Apex; summit; zenith

ver-ti-cal (vɜr-tɪ-kəl) adj. Upright, standing at right angles to the earth's surface: *The walls of the house should be vertical.* —compare HORIZONTAL —**vertically** adv.

ver-ti-go (vɜrt-ɪ-goʷ) n. **-tigoes** or **ver-tig-i-nes** (vɜr-tɪdʒ-ə-niʸz) A feeling of great dizziness, unsteadiness, or sickness caused usu. by looking down from a high place

ver-y (vɛər-iʸ) adv. 1. To a great degree: *It's very hot today.* 2. Used with words like "same", "own", "first", and "last" to make them stronger: *That's the very last time I'll try that.*

very adj. Actual; used for giving force to an expression: *This is the very pen that was used to sign the treaty.*

ves-pers (vɛs-pərz) n. In the Christian church, the evening service

ves-sel (vɛs-əl) n. 1. A ship or large boat: *a fishing vessel* 2. A container, such as a glass, pot, pan, etc., used esp. for holding liquids: *a drinking vessel* 3. **blood vessel** An artery or vein

vest (vɛst) n. 1. A man's close-fitting, sleeveless garment worn under a suit coat 2. *BrE.* An undershirt

vest v. 1. To give authority or power to 2. To clothe, esp. with ecclesiastical vestments

vest-ed in-ter-est (vɛst-əd ɪnt-ə-rəst) n. An interest in which a person does sthg. or promotes some scheme or product, because one gains advantage from it

ves-ti-bule (vɛs-tə-byuʷl) n. An entrance hall or lobby of a building

ves-tige (vɛs-tɪdʒ) n. 1. A small remaining bit of what once existed 2. A very small amount: *a vestige of truth* —**ves-ti-gi-al** (vɛ-stɪdʒ-iʸ-əl) adj.

vest-ment (vɛst-mənt) n. A ceremonial robe or other garment, esp. one worn by the clergy or choir members at a religious service

ves-try (vɛs-triʸ) n. **-tries** 1. A room in a church where vestments are kept 2. In some churches, a similar room used as a chapel

vet (vɛt) n. *abbr.* 1. A veteran 2. A veterinarian

vetch (vɛtʃ) n. A type of plant of the pea family

vet-er-an (vɛt-ər-ən) n. 1. A person who has served in the armed forces, esp. during a war: *My father is a veteran of World War II.* 2. Anyone with many years of experience in an occupation or office: *a veteran at teaching* —**veteran** adj.

vet-er-i-nar-i-an (vɛt-ə-rən-ɛər-iʸ-ən) n. A person who practices veterinary medicine or surgery

vet-er-i-nar-y (vɛt-ə-rən-ɛər-iʸ) adj. Having to do with the medical treatment of sick and injured animals

ve-to (viʸt-oʷ) n. **-toes** 1. An authoritative rejection of sthg. that has been proposed 2. The right to make such a rejection

veto v. **-toed, -toing** To prevent or forbid some action; refuse to allow sthg.: *The senate's proposal to increase taxes was vetoed by the President.*

vex (vɛks) v. To annoy or irritate someone

vexation (vɛk-seʸ-ʃən) n. 1. Being vexed; a state of irritation 2. Sthg. that causes this

vi-a (viʸ-ə/ vaɪ-ə) prep. By way of: *We drove to Chicago from New Orleans via Memphis.*

vi-a-ble (vaɪ-ə-bəl) adj. 1. Workable; practicable; able to succeed in operation: *a viable plan* 2. Of a fetus, able to survive after birth 3. Of plants, able to live and grow —**vi-a-**

bil-i-ty (vaɪ-ə-bɪl-ət-iʸ) n. —**viably** adv.

vi-a-duct (vaɪ-ə-dəkt) n. A long, high, bridge-like structure that carries a road or railroad line across a valley

vi-al (vaɪ-əl) n. A small bottle, esp. for liquid medicine

vibes (vaɪbz) n. pl. **1.** Vibraphone **2.** slang also called **vibrations** General emotional feelings that one has from another person or a place

vi-brant (vaɪ-brənt) adj. **1.** Full of energy; thrilling; exciting **2.** Of color or light, pleasantly bright and strong —**vibrantly** adv.

vi-bra-phone (vaɪ-brə-foʷn) n. A musical percussion instrument resembling the marimba, with metal bars played with mallets, but having electrically powered resonators

vi-brate (vaɪ-breʸt) v. To shake or cause to shake continuously and rapidly; tremble —**vibrator** n.

vi-bra-tion (vaɪ-breʸ-ʃən) n. A continuous shaky movement: We live next to a railroad track, and there's a lot of vibration whenever a train goes by.

vic-ar (vɪk-ər) n. **1.** One authorized to perform functions instead of another; a substitute **2.** In some churches, an advanced seminary student or recent graduate under supervised practical training **3.** In the Church of England, a parish priest **4.** In the Protestant Episcopal Church, a member of the clergy whose charge is a chapel in a parish **5.** In the Roman Catholic Church, an official representing the pope or a bishop

vic-ar-age (vɪk-ə-rɪdʒ) n. **1.** The term of service as a vicar (2 above) **2.** A vicar's residence

vi-car-i-ous (vaɪ-keər-iʸ-əs/-kær-) adj. **1.** Filling the place of another person **2.** Done or suffered on behalf of another person **3.** Experienced by the imagination through watching or reading about other people and places, etc.: He gets vicarious pleasure by watching movies, travel films, etc. on TV. —**vicariously** adv.

vice (vaɪs) n. **1.** Great wickedness; grossly immoral conduct, esp. in sexual practices, use of harmful drugs, etc. **2.** infml. A bad habit

vice adj. Acting or having the authority to act as a deputy or substitute for another:

vice president

vice n. also **vise** A kind of tool with two jaws for gripping objects firmly

vice pres-i-dent (vaɪs prez-əd-ənt) n. The person next in rank to the president, who presides at a meeting if the president is absent

vice-roy (vaɪs-rɔɪ) n. A person governing a colony or province as the sov-ereign's representative

vi-ce ver-sa (vaɪs vɜr-sə) adj. Conversely; the opposite of what was just stated

vi-cin-i-ty (və-sɪn-ət-iʸ) n. -**ties** Nearness; the surroundings; neighborhood

vi-cious (vɪʃ-əs) adj. **1.** Malicious; spiteful; cruel; wicked; likely to attack and cause harm **2.** vicious circle A set of events in which cause and effect follow each other in a circular pattern: Workers demand more pay, which causes prices of goods to increase, which makes it necessary for workers to demand more pay. It's a vicious circle. —**viciously** adv. —**viciousness** n.

vi-cis-si-tude (və-sɪs-ə-tuʷd) n. **1.** The quality or state of being changeable **2.** An event that occurs by chance, favorable or unfavorable

vic-tim (vɪk-təm) n. Someone who suffers as a result of other people's actions, or of an accident, illness, etc.: Ninety-five people were killed in the plane crash, but the victims' names have not yet been released.

vic-tim-ize also -**ise** BrE. (vɪk-tə-maɪz) -**ized**, -**izing** To cause someone to suffer in an undeserved way: He claims he was victimized by his fellow workers because he did not go along with their demands for more pay. —**vic-tim-i-za-tion** (vɪk-tə-mə-zeʸ-ʃən) n.

vic-tor (vɪk-tər) n. The winner in a battle, race, game or other contest or struggle

Vic-to-ri-an (vɪk-tɔr-iʸ-ən) adj. **1.** Belonging to or characteristic of the reign of Queen Victoria in England (1837-1901) **2.** Prudish

vic-to-ri-ous (vɪk-tɔr-iʸ-əs) adj. Having gained the victory —**victoriously** adj.

vic-to-ry (vɪk-tə-riʸ) n. -**ries** An act of winning or state of having won a battle or any kind of struggle: Death has been swallowed up in victory... The sting of death is sin, and the power of sin is the law. But thanks be to God! He gives us the victory [over sin and death]

through our Lord Jesus Christ (1 Corinthians 15:54,56,57). *This is the victory that has overcome the world [the temptations of the world], even our faith... he who believes that Jesus is the Son of God* (1 John 5:4,5). —opposite DEFEAT

vic-tu-al (vɪt–əl) n. **1.** Food **2. victuals** provisions

vid-e-o (vɪd–iʸ–oʷ) adj. **1.** Used in TV in the showing of pictures, not having to do with the sound or audio portion **2.** Using videotape: *a video recording*

video n. also **vid-e-o-cas-sette re-cord-er** (vɪd–iʸ–oʷ–kə–sɛt n–kɔrd–ər) An instrument which uses videotape to record pictures and sound

vid-e-o-tape (vɪd–iʸ–oʷ–teʸp) n. Magnetic tape on which television pictures and sound are recorded

videotape v. **-taped, -taping** To make a recording of a TV show on videotape

vie (vaɪ) v. **-vied, -vying** To compete: *They are vying for the championship.*

view (vyuʷ) n. **1.** A sight; that which can be seen from a particular place: *Our view from the mountain lodge was fantastic.* **2.** An opinion, belief, idea, etc., about sthg.: *Your views on education are interesting.* **3. in view of** Considering; taking into account: *In view of the circumstances, the judge gave him a light sentence.* **4. take a dim/ poor view of** *infml.* To think negatively **5. viewpoint (a)** A place from which a scene is viewed **(b)** One's way of considering things **6. with a view to** With the intention of

view v. **1.** To examine thoroughly: *Several committee members are viewing the situation.* **2.** To regard: *He viewed the situation with joyful anticipation.*

view-er (vyuʷ–ər) n. A person watching sthg. on TV or at a movie theater

view-point (vyuʷ–pɔɪnt) n. Opinion

vig-il (vɪdʒ–əl) n. **1.** A religious observance formerly held on the night before a religious feast **2.** The day before a religious feast observed as a day of spiritual preparation **3.** A period of watchfulness that is kept through the night

vig-i-lant (vɪdʒ–ə–lənt) adj. Continually on watch: *A vigilant military force helps keep the peace.* —**vigilance** n. —**vigilantly** adv.

vi-gi-lan-te (vɪdʒ–ə–læɛnt–iʸ) n. A member of a group that takes it upon itself to restore and keep order in a community, as in pioneer days in the US

vi-gnette (vɪn–yet) n. **1.** A short literary sketch **2.** A design used at the beginning or end of a chapter or on the title page **3.** An engraving or photograph that is shaded off gradually at the edges

vig-or *AmE.* **vigour** *BrE.* (vɪg–ər) n. Strength of body or mind; energy; vi-tality

vig-or-ous (vɪg–ər–əs) adj. Full of mental or physical vigor —**vigorously** adv. *The new director attacked the problem vigorously.*

vile (vaɪl) adj. **1.** Very bad; evil; cheap and low: *What a vile man to steal from his own mother.* **2.** *Fml.* Very bad; not pleasant: *We look for the Savior, the Lord Jesus Christ; who shall change our vile body that it may be fashioned like unto his glorious body* (Philippians 3:20, 21 KJV).

vil-i-fy (vɪl–ə–faɪ) v. **-fied, -fying 1.** To say bad things about someone; slander; malign; abuse **2.** To degrade —**vil-i-fi-ca-tion** (vɪl–ə–fə–keʸ–ʃən) n.

vil-la (vɪl–ə) n. A large, luxurious country house or estate

vil-lage (vɪl–ɪdʒ) n. **1.** A group of houses and usu. a few other buildings, such as a church, school, and one or more stores, in a rural area **2.** The people who live in a village, collectively: *It seems as though the whole village has gone to Mr. Smith's funeral.*

vil-lag-er (vɪl–ɪdʒ–ər) n. One who lives in a village

vil-lain (vɪl–ən) n. **1.** A very wicked man **2.** Such a man represented as a leading character in a novel or play —opposite HERO —**villainous** adj.

vil-lain-y (vɪl–ən–iʸ) n. **-ies 1.** Extreme wickedness **2.** A villainous act

vim (vɪm) n. Vitality and energy

vin-di-cate (vɪn–də–keʸt) v. **-cated, -cating** To clear from accusation or suspicion; to prove blameless —**vin-di-ca-tion** (vɪn–də–keʸ–ʃən) n.

vin-dic-tive (vɪn–dɪk–tɪv) adj. Strongly in-

clined toward revenge; desiring to harm someone who has harmed oneself —**vindictively** adv. —**vindictiveness** n.

vine (vaɪn) n. **1.** Any creeping or climbing plant, such as ivy **2.** A plant that produces grapes (juicy green or yellow or purple fruit.) —see GRAPES **3.** *fig.* Jesus compared himself with the vine and his followers with branches: *He said, "I am the vine, you are the branches. If a man remains in me [through faith in him] and I in him [through his word], he will bear much fruit [good deeds to the glory of God]; apart from me you can do nothing... If you remain in me, and my words remain in you, ask whatever you wish and it will be given you"*(John 15:5,7).

vin-e-gar (vɪn-ɪ-gər) n. A sour liquid made usu. from sour wine, used to flavor or preserve food

vin-e-gar-y (vɪn-ɪ-gə-riʸ) adj. **1.** Like vinegar, esp. in taste **2.** Of a person, having a disagreeable character

vine-yard (vɪn-yərd) n. Land planted with vines for growing grapes

vin-tage (vɪnt-ɪdʒ) n. **1.** The wine from a particular year or crop **2.** The annual produce of a grape harvest, esp. regarding the wine produced **3.** The date or period when sthg. was produced

vintage adj. Of high quality, esp. of a past year —**vintage year** A year in which the wine is of high quality

vi-nyl (vaɪn-əl) n. Any of various tough plastics used instead of wood, rubber, leather, etc.

vi-o-la (viʸ-oʷ-lə) n. A stringed musical instrument, somewhat larger than a violin and with a lower pitch

vi-o-late (vaɪ-ə-leʸt) v. -lated, -lating **1.** To break a law or regulation, whether intentionally or not **2.** To disregard a promise or an oath **3.** To disturb rudely or improperly: *to violate a grave* **4.** To rape —**vi-o-la-tion** (vaɪ-ə-leʸ-ʃən) n. *Gary received a ticket for a traffic violation.*

vi-o-lence (vaɪ-ə-ləns) n. **1.** Very strong force: *The storm struck with great violence.* **2.** Use of bodily force to kill, hurt, or damage: *Far too much violence is shown on the TV screen. It*

only leads to more violence in the homes and in our streets.

vi-o-lent (vaɪ-ə-lənt) adj. Done with great force: *He has a violent temper./ She suffered a violent death* —**violently** adv.

vi-o-let (vaɪ-ə-lət) n. **1.** A small plant with dark purplish-blue flowers **2.** A bluish purple color

vi-o-lin (vaɪ-ə-lɪn) n. A type of musical instrument with four strings, played by drawing a bow across the strings —**violinist** n.

VIP (viʸ-aɪ-piʸ) n. A very important person having great influence or fame

vi-per (vaɪ-pər) n. A small poisonous snake

vi-ral (vaɪ-rəl) adj. Of or relating to a virus

vir-gin (vɜr-dʒən) n. A person who has never had sexual relations with a member of the opposite sex: *Jesus Christ was conceived by the Holy Spirit and born of the Virgin Mary. This took place to fulfill what the Lord had said (700 years earlier) through the Prophet. The virgin will be with child and will give birth to a son, and they will call him Immanuel (Isaiah 7:14). Immanuel means, "God with us."* —see JESUS

virgin adj. **1.** Without sexual experience **2.** Fresh; unspoiled; unused: *a virgin forest*

vir-gin-i-ty (vɜr-dʒɪn-ət-iʸ) n. The state of being a virgin

Vir-gin Mar-y (vɜr-dʒɪn meər-iʸ) n. In the Christian religion, Mary, the mother of Jesus Christ NOTE: Jesus is the true God and eternal life (1 John 5:20), the Creator and Sustainer of the universe (Hebrews 1:2,3; Colossians 1:16,17). Thus, according to his divine nature, he had no mother. But in order to save us from our sins, he had to become a man and to suffer all the temptations of man, yet without sin. Then he had to suffer all the punishment that we deserve. He had to pay for our sins with his own blood. He had to become a man in order to do this, and to become a true man, he had to have a human mother. But he had to be born of a virgin, so as not to be born with a sinful nature like everyone else. He had to be conceived by the Holy Spirit to be born without sin and to live a perfectly holy life as our substitute, and then to pay the price

of the sins of the world with his holy, precious, divine blood. There was no other way that we could be saved from the power of sin, death and the devil and have eternal life (Acts 4:12). —see JESUS, GOD, VIRGIN, CREED

vir-ile (vɪər–əl) adj. **1.** Having the nature, powers, qualities, etc. of a man **2.** Masterful; forceful —**vi-ril-i-ty** (və–rɪl–ə–tiᵞ) adj.

vi-rol-o-gy (vaɪ–rɑl–ə–dʒiᵞ) n. The scientific study of viruses —**virologist** n. —**vi-ro-log-i-cal** (vaɪ–rə–lɑdʒ–ɪ–kəl) adj.

vir-tu-al (vɜr–tʃuʷ–əl) adj. Practically what is stated; in fact, but not in name: *The flight was a virtual sell-out (=almost every ticket was sold).*

vir-tu-al-ly (vɜr–tʃuʷ–ə–liᵞ) adv. Practically; almost; very nearly: *Because the king was so weak, his sister was virtually the ruler of the country.*

vir-tue (vɜr–tʃuʷ) n. **1.** Goodness, morality, nobleness, and worth of character: *Add to your faith [in Jesus] virtue, and to virtue, knowledge.* —opposite VICE **2.** Any good quality or characteristic: *Among her many virtues are loyalty, cour-age, and honesty.* **3.** Advantage: *One of the virtues of that car is its low mileage.* **4. by virtue of** As a result of; because of: *He was only allowed to attend this banquet by virtue of the fact that he is related to the host.*

vir-tu-o-so (vɜr–tʃuʷ–oʷ–soʷ) n. A person who excels in sthg., esp. in singing or in playing a musical instrument —**vir-tu-o-si-ty** (vɜr–tʃuʷ–wɑs–ət–iᵞ) n. **-ties**

vir-tu-ous (vɜr–tʃuʷ–əs) adj. Morally good, noble, just: *A virtuous woman is a crown to her husband* (Proverbs 12:4 KJV). —**vir-tuousness** n.

vir-u-lent (vɪər–yə–lənt) adj. **1.** Of a disease, highly infectious; spreading rapidly; deadly **2.** Poisonous; noxious **3.** Strongly and bitterly hostile

vi-rus (vaɪ–rəs) n. A living thing even smaller than bacteria which causes various infectious diseases, such as mumps and chicken pox: *The common cold is a virus.* —compare GERM

vi-sa (viᵞ–sə/–zə) n. A mark put on one's passport by the authorities of a country, to show that one may enter and travel in that country

vis-age (vɪz–ɪdʒ) n. **1.** Face or countenance **2.** Appearance; aspect

vis-a-vis (viᵞz–ə–viᵞ) prep. *fml.* **1.** Face to face with; opposite **2.** With regard to; when compared to

vis-cer-a (vɪs–ə–rə) n. Soft interior organs, as lungs —**visceral** adj.

vis-cid (vɪs–əd) adj. Sticky; glue-like —**vis-cid-i-ty** (vɪs–ɪd–ət–iᵞ) n.

vis-cose (vɪs–koʷs/ –koʷz) n. A gelatinous substance used in making cellophane and rayon

vis-cos-i-ty (vɪs–kɑs–ət–iᵞ) n. **1.** Stickiness **2.** Internal frictional resistance of a fluid by forces causing it to flow **3.** A measure of a fluid's resistance to flowing

vis-count (vaɪ–kaʊnt) n. A nobleman ranking between an earl or a count and a baron

vis-cous (vɪs–kəs) adj. **1.** Having the sticky consistency of glue **2.** Having or characterized by viscosity

vise (vaɪs) n. A tool with metal jaws, for holding an object firmly in place so that it can be worked on

vis-i-bil-i-ty (vɪz–ə–bɪl–ət–iᵞ) n. The degree of clearness with which objects can be seen: *The fog was so thick that visibility was less than 10 feet.*

vis-i-ble (vɪz–ə–bəl) adj. Capable of being seen; noticeable to the eye: *Everything exposed by the light becomes visible, for it is light that makes everything visible* (Ephesians 5:13). —opposite INVISIBLE

vi-sion (vɪʒ–ən) n. **1.** The sense of sight; the ability to see: *His vision is 20/20 (=perfectly normal)* **2.** Wisdom in understanding what lies in the future: *Where there is no vision, the people perish* (Proverbs 29:18 KJV). **3.** A mental representation of objects, scenes, etc. as in a spiritual revelation or dream: *She had a vision in which angels appeared before her.* **4.** Sthg. vividly imagined: *He had visions of grandeur.*

vi-sion-ar-y (vɪʒ–ə–nɛər–iᵞ) n. **1.** A person who sees visions; a prophet **2.** A person with unusual foresight **3.** A person whose ideas are

often too idealistic, or considered to be so

vis-it (vɪz–ət) v. **1.** To go and spend time with a friend for social reasons **2.** To go and spend time in a place: *While in Europe they visited Spain and Portugal.* **3.** To go and see someone in a professional capacity or for business reasons: *He visited the dentist.* **4.** To go to a place in order to inspect and evaluate it: *The prisons were visited by government officials.* **5.** To go to a place in order to make use of it: *He visits the library frequently.*

visit n. The act or an instance of visiting: *He pays a visit to his mother in the hospital nearly every day./ He paid a visit to the museum.*

vis-i-ta-tion (vɪz–ə–te^y–ʃən) n. A formal visit by someone in charge

vis-i-tor (vɪz–ət–ər) n. A person who visits

vi-sor (vaɪ–zər) n. **1.** The projecting front brim of a cap, for shading the eyes **2.** An adjustable flap above an automobile windshield that can be lowered to protect one's eyes from glare when driving toward the sun

vis-ta (vɪs–tə) n. A distant view, esp. through or along an avenue or opening

vi-su-al (vɪʒ–u^w–əl) adj. Based on or connected with seeing: *Visual aids are a great help in teaching.* —**visually** adv.

vi-su-al-ize (vɪʒ–u^w–ə–laɪz) v. **-ized, -izing** To form a clear picture of sthg. or someone in the mind; to form a mental image; envision —**vi-su-al-i-za-tion** (vɪʒ–u^w–ə–lə–ze^y–ʃən) n.

vi-tal (vaɪt–əl) adj. **1.** Necessary to life; of the greatest importance: **2.** Vigorous; energetic; full of life and strength: *His leadership was considered vital to the success of the campaign.* **3. vital statistics** Certain official records, esp. of births, marriages and deaths

vi-tal-i-ty (vaɪ–tæl–ət–i^y) n. Lively forcefulness: *He has a lot of experience, but his leadership lacks vitality.*

vi-tal-ize (vaɪt–əl–aɪz) v. **-ized, -izing 1.** To fill or endow with life **2.** To invigorate or energize

vi-tal-ly (vaɪt–əl–i^y) adv. In the highest possible degree; extremely: *Your attendance at the meeting is vitally important. Many major decisions will be made.*

vi-ta-min (vaɪt–ə–mən) n. Any one of several organic substances essential in small quan-

tities to good health, found in foods and also produced synthetically: *Lack of vitamin A results in night blindness.*

vi-ti-ate (vɪʃ–i^y–e^yt) v. **-ated, -ating 1.** To contaminate; pollute **2.** To invalidate; render ineffective or worthless —**vi-ti-a-tion** (vɪʃ–i^y–e^y–ʃən) n.

vit-re-ous (vɪ–triy–əs) adj. Like glass

vi-tri-fy (vɪ–trə–faɪ) v. **-fied, -fying** To change into glass or a glassy substance —**vit-ri-fi-ca-tion** (vɪ–trə–fə–ke^y–ʃən) n.

vit-ri-ol (vɪ–triy–əl) n. **1.** Sulphuric acid **2.** A sulphate of any of various metals, as iron or zinc **3.** Sthg. very biting, corrosive, or caustic

vit-ri-ol-ic (vɪ–triy–ɑl–ɪk) adj. **1.** Sharp; caustic; sarcastic **2.** Derived from or pertaining to vitriol

vi-tu-per-ate (vaɪ–tu^w–pə–re^yt) v. To blame abusively; berate; scold —**vi-tu-per-a-tion** (vaɪ–tu^w–pe–re^y–ʃən) n.

vi-va (vi^y–və) interj. "Long live sbdy./sthg.!" (Used to express good will)

vi-va-cious (və–ve^y–ʃəs/ vaɪ–) adj. Lively in temper or conduct: *a vivacious person* —**vivaciousness** n.

vi-vac-i-ty (və–væs–ə–ti^y) n. The quality or state of being vivacious

vi-var-i-um (vaɪ–veər–i^y–əm) n. **-ia** or **-iums** An enclosure for keeping, raising, and observing animals and plants indoors

viv-id (vɪv–əd) adj. **1.** Strikingly bright or intense, as color **2.** Presenting lifelike freshness or spirit **3.** Producing sharp clear pictures in the mind: *He has a vivid imagination.* —**vividly** adv.

viv-i-fy (vɪv–ə–faɪ) v. **-fied, -fying 1.** To animate **2.** To make vivid —**viv-i-fi-ca-tion** (vɪv–ə–fə–ke^y–ʃən) n.

vi-vip-a-rous (vaɪ–vɪp–ə–rəs) adj. **1.** Producing offspring from within the body rather than from eggs **2.** Producing seeds that germinate on a plant —**viviparously** adv.

viv-i-sec-tion (vɪv–ə–sek–ʃən) n. **1.** The cutting of or operating on a living animal **2.** Animal experimentation

vix-en (vɪk–sən) n. **1.** A female fox **2.** An ill-tempered woman

viz. or **viz** (vɪz) adv. Namely: *Three games are*

played in this school, viz. *football, basketball, and baseball.* NOTE: In reading aloud, the word *namely* is usually spoken where *viz.* is written.

vi-zier (və–zɪər) n. A high official in certain Muslim countries; minister of state

vi-zor (vaɪ–zər) *Var.* of visor

vo-cab-u-lar-y (voᵂ–kæb–yə–lɛər–iʸ) n. -ies 1. All the words of a language 2. The stock of words known by a particular person, or used in a particular kind of work, etc.: *Our baby has a vocabulary of about six words.* 3. A list of words, usu. in alphabetical order and with their meanings, less complete than a dictionary

vo-cal (voᵂ–kəl) adj. 1. Related to or produced by or for the voice 2. Expressing oneself freely out loud in words; talkative: *She was very vocal.* —**vocally** adv.

vo-cal-ist (voᵂ–kə–ləst) n. A singer

vo-cal-ize (voᵂ–kə–laɪz) v. -ized, -izing To give vocal expression to —**vo-cal-i-za-tion** (voᵂ–kəl-ə–zeʸ–ʃən) n.

vo-ca-tion (voᵂ–keʸ–ʃən) n. 1. Any occupation regularly followed for a living 2. A particular fitness, calling or ability for a certain kind of work, esp. of a worthy kind 3. A feeling that one is called by God to a certain career or occupation

vo-ca-tion-al (voᵂ–keʸ–ʃən–əl) adj. Preparing for a particular kind of work: *He went to vocational school to learn to be a mechanic.*

vo-cif-er-ous (voᵂ–sɪf–ə–rəs) adj. Making a loud or noisy outcry; clamorous; noisy in expressing one's feelings

vod-ka (vɑd–kə) n. An alcoholic beverage made from potatoes or grains

vogue (voᵂg) n. The fashion at a particular time: *Long skirts were the vogue for women many years ago, but not today.*

voice (vɔɪs) n. 1. The sound(s) made by people when speaking and singing: *Jesus said, "I tell you the truth, a time is coming and has now come when the dead [spiritually] will hear the voice of the Son of God and those who hear will live [eternally]"* (John 5:25). 2. A silent expression or declaration: *The heavens declare the glory of God; the skies proclaim the work of his hands. Their [the sun, moon and stars] voice* goes out into all the earth (Psalm 19:1,4). 3. An opinion: *The entire crowd was of one voice; they all said the same thing.* 4. Any of the vocal parts in a musical score: *soprano/alto/tenor/bass voices* 5. The form of the verb which shows whether the subject of a sentence acts (active voice) or is acted upon (passive voice)

voice v. **voiced, voicing** Give an opinion esp. forcefully: *The chairman voiced the feeling of the entire board of directors in no uncertain terms.*

voiced (vɔɪst) adj. Spoken; expressed

voice-less (vɔɪs–ləs) adj. Mute; silent

void (vɔɪd) adj. 1. Empty; lacking: *That argument is completely void of sense.* 2. Not valid; having no value or effect *This document is void; it's not binding.* —see also NULL and VOID

void n. 1. An empty space, esp. the large space surrounding our world and beyond the stars 2. Emptiness: *The loss of their only child left a painful void in the parents' lives.*

vol. *abbr.* for vol-ume (vɑl–yəm/ –yuᵂm)

vol-a-tile (vɑl–ət–əl/ –ə–taɪl) adj. 1. Of a liquid, evaporating quickly 2. Of a person, changing quickly from one mood or interest to another

vol-ca-no (vɔl–keʸ–noᵂ) n. -noes or -nos A mountain, usu. cone-shaped, with a large opening (crater) at the top through which melting rock (lava), steam, gases, etc., have been thrown up from inside the earth with explosive force: *An active volcano is one that may erupt at any time. An extinct volcano is one that is no longer able to erupt.* —**vol-ca-nic** (vɔl–kæn–ɪk) adj. *volcanic activity*

vole (voᵂl) n. Any of several kinds of small rodents, including the water rat

vo-li-tion (voᵂ–lɪʃ–ən) n. 1. An act of willing, choosing, or deciding 2. The power or capability of choosing 3. A conscious choice; decision

vol-ley (vɑl–iʸ) n. -leys 1. A flight of missiles, as bullets or arrows 2. A simultaneous discharge of a number of weapons 3. A pouring forth of many things at the same time: *a volley of insults*

volley v. 1. To discharge in a volley 2. In ten-

nis, to return the ball before it touches the ground

vol-ley-ball (val-i^y-bɔl) n. **1.** A game in which two teams try to hit an inflated ball over a high net before it touches the ground **2.** The ball used

volt (vo^{w}lt) n. A standard unit used for measuring the force of electricity —compare AMP

volt-age (vo^{w}l-tɪdʒ) n. Electrical force measured in volts

vol-ta-ic (val-te^y-ɪk/ vo^{w}l-) adj. Pertaining to electricity produced by chemical action, as in a cell

vol-u-ble (val-yə-bəl) adj. With a great flow of words; talkative

vol-ume (val-yəm/ -yu^{w}m) n. **1.** A book, esp. one of a set **2.** The amount of space that a 3-dimensional object occupies or contains: *A box 12 inches high, 12 inches wide, and 12 inches long has a volume of one cubic foot or 1,728 cubic inches.* **3.** Intensity of sound; loudness: *Your radio is too loud. Would you mind turning the volume down, please?* **4.** Amount: *The volume of air travel has increased every year.*

vo-lu-mi-nous (və-lu^w-mə-nəs) adj. **1.** Having great volume, fullness, size or number **2.** Filling or capable of filling volumes: *a voluminous report*

vol-un-tar-y (val-ən-tɛar-i^y) adj. **1.** Acting or done willingly, not under compulsion, and not for pay: *In times of disaster, a lot of voluntary aid is given to the victims.* —compare COMPULSORY **2.** Controlled or supported by people who give their money, services, etc., freely: *Many voluntary organizations sent food and other supplies to the flood victims.* —**vol-un-tar-i-ly (val-ən-tɛr-ə-li^y)** adv. *He confessed to the theft voluntarily. No one forced him to.*

vol-un-teer (val-ən-tɪər) n. **1.** A person who offers to perform a task voluntarily: *Many volunteers gave their time in helping the fire victims.* **2.** A person who enrolls for military service voluntarily

volunteer v. **1.** To help or offer to help voluntarily: *Bill volunteered to drive me to the airport.* **2.** To offer to join the armed forces of one's own free will **3.** To tell sthg. without

being asked: *Jim volunteered the news that he lost his job.*

vo-lup-tu-ar-y (və-lʌp-tʃu^w-ɛar-i^y) n. A person whose life is devoted to luxury and sensual pleasure

vo-lup-tu-ous (və-lʌp-tʃu^w-əs) adj. **1.** Fond of luxury and sumptuous living **2.** Of a woman, arousing the sensual appetites —**voluptuously** adv. —**voluptuousness** n.

vom-it (vam-ət) v. To eject (throw up) the contents of the stomach through the mouth

vomit n. The matter ejected in vomiting

voo-doo (vu^w-du^w) n. A form of religion based on witchcraft and magical rites, practiced by some people in the West Indies and America. This is altogether contrary to the Word of God and detestable in his sight (Deuteronomy 18:10; Galatians 5:20). —see WITCHCRAFT

vo-ra-cious (vɔ-re^y-ʃəs/və-) adj. Very greedy; difficult to satisfy: *Bill has a voracious appetite./fig. Tom is a voracious reader.* —**vo-rac-i-ty (vɔ-ræs-ət-i^y)** n.

vor-tex (vɔr-tɛks) n. **-texes** or **-tices (vɔrt-ə-səz)** A whirlpool; a whirlwind —**vor-ti-cal (vɔrt-ɪ-kəl)** adj.

vo-ta-ry (vo^{w}t-ə-ri^y) n. **1.** One consecrated by a vow to some service, esp. to a religious work **2.** One devoted to any pursuit

vote (vo^{w}t) n. **1. (a)** A choice or opinion of a person or a group of persons expressed by ballot, spoken word, or raised hand **(b)** The ballot, word or gesture used to express a choice or opinion **2.** The decision reached by voting **3.** The whole number of such choices made by a particular group of people: *In El Paso, Texas the Spanish vote is very important.* **4.** The right to vote in political elections: *In the US, women got the vote in the Nineteenth Amendment.* **5. vote of thanks** A public expression of thanks: *The team gave Mr. Elliot a vote of thanks for his outstanding help as their coach.*

vote v. **voted, voting 1.** To cast a vote: *Every good citizen should vote in every election.* **2.** To agree, by a vote, to provide sthg.: *The city council voted a large sum of money for low-income housing.* **3.** *infml.* To express a general opinion: *The banquet was voted a big success.*

vo-tive (vo^wt–ɪv) adj. Performed or given in fulfillment of a vow or in gratitude or devotion

vouch (vaʊtʃ) v. **1.** To give a personal guarantee or assurance **2.** To support as being true or valid

vouch-er (vaʊ–tʃər) n. **1.** A record of an expense paid **2.** A person who vouches for someone or to the truth or validity of sthg.

vow (vaʊ) n. A solemn oath: *All the men took/ made a vow of faithfulness to their cause./ I will fulfill my vows to the Lord* (Psalm 116:14). *This is what the Lord commands: "When a man makes a vow to the Lord or takes an oath to obligate himself by a pledge, he must not break his word but must do everything he said* (Numbers 30:1,2).

vow v. To declare or swear solemnly that one will do sthg.; to take an oath —see OATH

vow-el (vaʊ–əl) n. **1.** A speech sound in which the breath is let out without obstructing the flow of air from the lungs **2.** A letter as **a, e, i, o, u,** and sometimes **y,** representing such a sound: —com-pare CONSONANT, DIPHTHONG

voy-age (vɔɪ–ɪdʒ) n. **1.** A long journey by water from one place or country to another **2.** A journey through space

V.P. Vice President

vs. 1. Verse **2.** Versus

vul-can-ize (vʌl–kə–naɪz) v. **-ized, -izing** To treat rubber under heat with sulfur to make it more durable

vul-gar (vʌl–gər) adj. **1.** Lacking good taste or manners **2.** Indecent or obscene **3.** A vernacular, esp. as distinguished from a classical language **4.** Of or belonging to the common people as opposed to the intellectual people —**vulgarly** adv. —**vulgarness** n.

vul-gar-i-an (vəl–gær–i^y–ən/ –geər–) n. A person who has vulgar tastes or manners

vul-gar-ism (vʌl–gə–rɪz–əm) n. **1.** A vulgar word or phrase **2.** Vulgar behavior; vulgarity

vul-gar-i-ty (vəl–geər–ət–i^y/–gær–) n. **-ties** The quality of being vulgar

vul-gar-ize (vʌl–gə–raɪz) v. **-ized, -izing 1.** To make vulgar or coarse **2.** To make sthg. easier to understand

vul-ner-a-ble (vʌln–ə–rə–bəl/vʌl–nər–bəl) adj. **1.** Easily harmed or attacked: *The poorly armed ship was vulnerable to enemy attack.* **2.** Sensitive; easily hurt in body or feelings —**vul-ner-a-bil-i-ty** (vəl–nər–ə–bɪl–ət–i^y) adj.

vul-ture (vʌl–tʃər) n. **1.** Any of the several large birds of prey that feed on dead animals **2.** *fig.* An excessively greedy person

vy-ing (vaɪ–ɱ) v. Present part. of **vie**

W, w (dʌb–əl–yuᵂ) n. The 23rd letter of the English alphabet **W** (dʌb–əl–yuᵂ) *Written abbr.* Said as: (a) West(ern) (b) Watt

wack-y (wæk–iʸ) adj. **-ier, -iest** *AmE. infml.* Silly or absurd

wad (wɑd) n. **1.** A small mass or lump of sthg., such as pieces of paper pressed together: *a wad of paper/tobacco/chewing gum* **2.** A thick soft mass of material used for filling an empty space, hole, etc. **3.** A roll of paper money: *He pulled out a wad of $20 bills and paid cash for the new furniture.*

wad-dle (wɑd–əl) v. **-dled, -dling** To walk like a duck, taking short steps and moving the body from side to side

wade (weʸd) v. **waded, wading 1.** To walk through shallow water: *We waded across the shallow stream.* **2. wade through sthg.** *fig. infml.* To get through a difficult job, reading assignment, etc.

wa-fer (weʸ–fər) n. **1.** A flat cookie, cracker, or piece of candy, usu. round or square **2.** A small, thin, round piece of unleavened bread used in the Christian service of Holy Communion

waf-fle (wɑf–əl) n. A thin crisp cake made of pancake batter, baked in a special hinged griddle with a pattern of small squares (waffle iron), usu. served hot with butter and syrup

waft (wɑft/ wæft) v. To float gently through the air —**waft** n. A slight breeze; a puff

wag (wæg) v. **-gg-** To move back and forth or up and down, esp. with quick movements: *The happy dog wagged its tail.* —**wag** n.

wage (weʸdʒ) n. **1.** *usu. pl.* Money earned for work done, usu. paid daily or weekly: *The worker deserves his wages* (1 Timothy 5:18). **2.** Reward or payment: *The wages of sin is death, but the gift of God is eternal life in Christ Jesus our Lord* (Romans 6:23).

wage v. **waged, waging** *fml.* To carry on a fight of some kind: *The government is waging war on illegal drugs.*

wa-ger (weʸ–dʒər) v. *fml.* To bet: *He wagered $10 that the home team would win.* —**wager** n.

wag-on *AmE.* **wag-gon** *BrE.* (wæg–ən) n. **1.** A long, strong, four-wheeled cart, usu. pulled by horses or oxen **2.** A similar but much smaller cart used as a toy and pulled by a child

waif (weʸf) n. A homeless and helpless person, esp. a child

wail (weʸl) v. **1.** To give a long loud cry expressing pain or grief: *The mother wailed for hours at the death of her child.* **2.** A similar sound made by sthg. else: *The wind wailed through the trees.* —**wail** n.

waist (weʸst) n. The part of the human body between the ribs and the hips

waist-line (weʸst–laɪn) n. The narrowest part of the waist

wait (weʸt) v. **1.** To remain and take no action until sthg. happens or sbdy. comes: *You turned to God from idols to serve the living and true God, and to wait for his Son from heaven, whom he raised from the dead* (1 Thessalonians 1:9, 10). *We wait for the blessed hope — the glorious appearing of our great God and Savior, Jesus Christ, who gave himself for us to redeem us from all wickedness* (Titus 2:13, 14). **2. wait on tables** To serve food and drinks to customers in a restaurant

wait n. **1.** An act or time of waiting: *They'll have a long wait between trains.* **2. lie in wait (for someone)** To remain hidden until time to attack

wait-er (weʸt–ər) **wait-ress** (weʸ–trəs) *fem.* n. A person who serves food and drinks to customers in a restaurant

waive (weʸv) v. **waived, waiving** To surrender (give up) a claim or right willingly

waiv-er (weʸ–vər) n. **1.** The intentional surrendering of a claim or right **2.** A document stating such surrender of a right

wake (weʸk) v. **woke** or **waked, waked or woken, waking 1.** To stop sleeping: *She woke up this morning at six o'clock.* **2. wake up** *fig. infml.* Attention! Please listen!

wake n. A vigil over a dead person on the night before the burial

wake n. **1.** The track left behind a ship as it moves through the water: *The boat left its wake on the smooth water.* **2.** *fig.* **in the wake of** After; following; as the result of: *There was destruction and disorder in the wake of the riot.*

wake-ful (we^yk–fəl) adj. Not sleeping; alert

wak-en (we^y–kən) v. *fml.* To cause to wake: *He was wakened by the telephone.*

wak-ing (we^y–kiŋ) adj. Being awake: *waking hours*

walk (wɔk) v. **1.** Of people and animals, to go on foot: *The children walk to school every day.* **2.** *spir.* To exist or go through life: *Jesus said, "I am the light of the world. Whoever follows me will never walk in darkness, but will have the light of life* (John 8:12). **3.** To take an animal for a walk: *She walks her dog three times a day.* **4.** To accompany sbdy. on foot, usu. to a stated destination: *He'll walk us home.* —compare STROLL, MARCH

walk n. **1.** The act of walking in an unhurried way: *Let's go for a walk in the woods.* **2.** A short distance on foot: *The park is just a five-minute walk from our house.* **3.** A path or trail for walking: *This park has a beautiful walk beside the lake.*

walk-er (wɔ–kər) n. A frame used to support one in walking

walk-ie–talk-ie (wɔ–ki^y–tɔ–ki^y) n. A portable two-way radio-telephone set

wall (wɔl) n. **1.** One of the four sides of a building or a room **2.** An upright structure built of bricks, stones, etc., to enclose an area for safety or protection: *There's a high brick wall around the prison.*

wal-la-by (wɑl–ə–bi^y) n. **-bies** A small to medium-sized kangaroo

wal-let (wɑl–ət) n. A small flat folding case, usu. of leather, for carrying paper money, identification cards, etc., in the pocket —compare PURSE

wall-flow-er (wɔl–flɑu–ər) n. A person who stands on the sidelines during a social activity

wal-lop (wɑl–əp) v. To hit someone or sthg. with force: *The batter (in baseball) really walloped that ball.* —**wallop** n. *He gave the ball quite a wallop.*

wal-low (wɑl–o^w/–ə) v. **1.** To roll in the mud **2.** To live self-indulgently

wall-pa-per (wɔl–pe^y–pər) n. A decorative paper for covering walls in rooms

wallpaper v. To put wallpaper on a wall

wal-nut (wɔl–nət) n. **1.** An edible nut with a round hard wrinkled shell **2.** The tree that grows these nuts **3.** The wood of this tree, which is often used for making furniture

wal-rus (wɔl–rəs/wɑl–) n. A large type of sea animal, related to the seals, having two flippers and two large tusks

waltz (wɔlts) n. A type of slow ballroom dance for couples

waltz v. **1.** To dance a waltz **2.** To move cheerfully or with confidence: *He waltzed into the room and told us about his big promotion.*

wan (wɑn) adj. Pale and sickly looking

wand (wɑnd) n. **1.** A long slender rod waved by a magician or (in fairy tales) by a fairy **2.** A rod symbolic of authority or of an office

wan-der (wɑn–dər) v. **1.** To go or walk about aimlessly: *wander through the woods.* **2.** *fig.* To have one's thoughts or attention move away from the main subject: *Her thoughts wandered from the lecture to her wedding plans./ Some people, eager for money, have wandered from the faith [saving faith in Jesus] and pierced themselves with many griefs* (1 Timothy 6:10). —**wanderer** n.

wan-der-lust (wɑn–dər–ləst) n. A desire to travel; restlessness

wane (we^yn) v. **waned, waning** Of the moon, to become less visible after being full: *The moon waxes and wanes each month.* —opposite WAX

wane n. **1.** The act or process of waning **2. on the wane** Becoming smaller, weaker, or less

wan-gle (wæŋ–gəl) v. **-gled, -gling** To obtain by devious means; manipulate

want (wɑnt) v. **1.** To desire sthg.; to wish for: *I'm hungry and want sthg. to eat./ What does God want? God wants all men [all people] to be saved and to come to a knowledge of the truth [about Jesus Christ]* (1 Timothy 2:4). **2.** To lack sthg.: *The Lord is my shepherd; I shall not want.* (=will never lack anything I really need) (Psalm 23:1KJV) **3.** Esp. of the police, to chase or look for: *That man is wanted by the police for robbery.* **4.** To need: *The socks want mending.* **5.** Ought: *You want to get that cough taken care of right away.* **6.** To need or demand the presence of: *He wasn't wanted in the afternoon, so he left at 1:00 o'clock.*

want n. **1.** Lack or need of sthg.: *The beggar must walk for want of a horse.* **2.** Extreme lack of the necessary things of life: *After the war, many people lived in terrible want.* **3. wants** Desires; things needed: *Their wants are many and are rarely satisfied.*

want ad (want æd) n. *esp. AmE.* A short advertisement in a newspaper or other publication saying that someone wants a job, a car, an apartment to rent, etc., or that one wishes to buy, sell, or trade sthg.

want-ing (want–ıŋ) adj. *fml.* To be lacking in good qualities such as honesty, integrity, compassion, etc.: *God spoke to the king through handwriting on the wall that said: "You have been weighed on the scales and found wanting"* (=he didn't measure up to what a king should be) (Daniel 5:27).

wan-ton (wont–ən/want–ən) adj. **1.** Without reason: *wanton cruelty* **2.** Immoral: *a wanton woman*

war (wɔr) n. **1.** Armed fighting between countries or between groups within a country —compare BATTLE **2.** A fight between opposing forces or against a particular thing: *the war on drugs*

war v. **-rr-** To engage in or direct a war: *Abstain from sinful desires, which war against your soul* (1 Peter 2:11).

war-ble (wɔr–bəl) v. To sing in a trembling voice as some birds do: *Birds were warbling in the trees.*

ward (wɔrd) n. **1.** A division of a prison or a hospital: *the maternity ward* **2.** One of the areas into which a town or city is divided esp. for political purposes: *Mr. Nelson represents our ward on the council.* **3.** A person, esp. a child, who is under the legal protection of a person other than his parents or of a law court: *She is a ward of the court.* —compare GUARDIAN

war-den (wɔrd–ən) n. **1.** A person who is in charge of a place and the people in it: *the warden of a prison* **2.** An official in charge of a certain division of government: *A game warden sees that rules concerning hunting and fishing are obeyed.*

ward-robe (wɔrd–rowᵇb) n. **1.** A large movable closet in which one hangs up clothes **2.** A collection of clothing, esp. for one person: *She bought a new spring wardrobe.*

ware-house (weər–haʊs) n. **-houses (–haʊz–əz)** A large building for storing things, usu. temporarily

wares (weərz) n. Articles for sale by a store or peddler

war-fare (wɔr–feər) n. **1.** The act of waging war; armed battle: *guerrilla warfare* **2.** *fig.* A struggle or conflict: *verbal warfare between the two candidates*

war-head (wɔr–hɛd) n. Explosive part of a bomb or missile

warm (wɔrm) adj. **1.** At a high temperature but not hot and not cold: *a warm spring day* **2.** Of clothing or coverings, able to keep the cold out: *a warm coat* **3.** Friendly or affectionate feelings: *warm greetings* **4.** Enthusiastic; strong; excited: *warm support* **5.** Of sounds, colors, etc., pleasant or cheerful: *Red is a warm color./ John has a warm voice.* **6.** Esp. in games, close to finding sthg. hidden or close to guessing the answer to a question, etc.: *No, that's not the answer, but you're getting warm.* —opposite COOL —**warmly** adv. *They shook hands warmly.* —**warmness** n.

warm v. **1.** To make or become warm: *They rubbed their hands together to warm them.* **2. warm up (a)** To make or become warm: *Warm up the food before you serve it.* **(b)** To prepare for action: *The musicians are warming up, and the concert is about to begin./ We need to warm up the car engine on cold mornings.* —**warm–up** n. *After a brief warm-up, the players were ready for the game to begin.*

warm-heart-ed (wɔrm–hart–əd) adj. Showing kind and friendly feelings —opposite COLDHEARTED —**warmheartedness** n.

war-mong-er (wɔr–maŋ–gər) n. One who favors or incites war

warmth (wɔrmθ) n. The state of being warm: *the warmth of the sun/the warmth of her smile*

warn (wɔrn) v. **1.** To inform sbdy. in advance that sthg. bad will happen: *The weather forecast warned them that a hurricane was coming.* **2.** Tell sbdy. how to prevent sthg. bad: *She warned the children not to play on the street.*

warning n. Admonishment

warp (wɔrp) n. **1.** A twist or bend that causes

sthg. to be out of shape: *There's a warp in this board.* **2.** In weaving, threads running along the length of cloth —compare WOOF

warp v. **1.** To turn or twist out of shape: *The door was warped by all the rain.* **2.** *fig.* To cause to think in a twisted or wrong way: *His war experiences had warped his mind.*

war-rant (wɔr–ənt/wɑr–) n. Any written authorization, esp. giving the police the right to take a certain action: *a search warrant/a warrant for someone's arrest*

war-rant v. To give justification for: *The child's behavior wasn't bad enough to warrant such severe punishment.*

war-ran-ty (wɔr–ən–tiʸ/wɑr–) n. **-ties** A written guarantee: *We offer a five-year warranty on this car. If anything breaks, we'll fix it.*

war-ri-or (wɔr–iʸ–ər/wɑr–) n. *fml.* A fighting man; a soldier

war-ship (wɔr–ʃɪp) n. A ship used for battle

wart (wɔrt) n. A small hard abnormal growth on the skin, esp. of the hands

war-y (wɛər–iʸ/wær–) adj. **-ier, -iest** Cautious; on guard against danger: *Our youngest daughter is a little wary of strangers.* —**warily** adv. —**wariness** n.

was (wʌz) v. Past tense of **be**, 1st and 3rd person singular: *I/he/she/it was*

wash (wɔʃ) v. **1.** To clean with water or other liquid, usu. with soap: *Wash the dishes/dirty clothes/car.* **2.** To clean oneself or a part of one's body with water or other liquid, usu. with soap: *His mother told him to wash before dinner.* **3.** To be able to be cleansed with soap and water without damage: *I'm afraid this woolen dress won't wash well.* **4.** To flow over sthg. again and again: *The waves washed over the rocks.* **5.** To cause to be carried by water or other liquid: *Some of the ship's wreckage washed ashore.* **6. wash one's hands of** *fig. infml.* To refuse to take responsibility for: *I wash my hands of the whole crazy idea.*

wash n. **1.** The act of washing or being washed: *I gave the car a wash yesterday.* **2.** Clothes to be washed, or being washed; laundry: *You should put your dirty shirts in the wash.* **3.** *(often in compound words)* The liquid with which sthg. is washed: *mouthwash*

washed out (wɔʃt–aʊt) adj. **1.** Faded by washing **2.** Very, very tired: *After working all day and all night she was all washed out.*

washed up (wɔʃt əp) adj. *infml.* Finished; having no further opportunity for success: *As a tennis player, he's all washed up.*

wash-er (wɔʃ–ər) n. **1.** A machine that washes: *Put the dishes in the dishwasher.* **2.** A small ring of metal, rubber, etc., placed between two pipes to seal the connection

wash-ing (wɔʃ–ŋ) n. Things washed or to be washed

wash-ing ma-chine (wɔʃ–ŋ mə–ʃiʸn) n. A household appliance for washing clothes

wash-out (wɔʃ–aʊt) n. *infml.* A failure; one who fails in a training program or course of study

wash-room (wɔʃ–ruʷm) n. A lavatory; a room equipped with washing and toilet facilities

was-n't (wʌz–ənt) Short for **was not**

wasp (wɑsp/ wɔsp) n. A winged, stinging insect

wast-age (weʸ–stɪdʒ) n. Loss by use; waste

waste (weʸst) n. **1.** Bad or wrong use of material things or time: *Let's eat this fruit before it spoils. We don't want it to go to waste.* **2.** Damaged, harmful, or unwanted material: *Poisonous waste in the water makes it unfit to drink.* **3.** Rubbish; sthg. to be thrown away **4.** An unused or useless area of land: *Nothing will grow in the Arctic wastes.* —**waste** adj. *wasteland/wastepaper basket*

waste v. **wasted, wasting 1.** To use in the wrong way: *I've wasted a lot of time on foolish things.* **2.** To lose strength slowly: *The Apostle Paul, writing to fellow Christians, said: "Though outwardly [physically] we are wasting away, yet inwardly [spiritually] we are being renewed day by day. For our light and momentary troubles are achieving for us an eternal glory that far outweighs them all"* (2 Corinthians 4:16, 17).

waste-bas-ket (weʸst–bæs–kət) n. Also **wastepaper basket** A container for waste paper and other waste

waste-ful (weʸst–fəl) adj. Using more than is needed; causing waste: *wasteful spending* —**wastefully** adv. —**wastefulness** n.

waste-land (weʸst–lənd/ –lænd) n. A barren

region

watch (watʃ) v. **1.** To look at some activity: *He's watching television.* **2.** To be on guard: *Watch and pray so that you will not fall into temptation* (Matthew 26:41). **3.** To take care of: *His grandmother watched Bobby while his mother went shopping./ The Lord watches over all who love him* (Psalm 145:20). **4.** To pay careful attention to: *Watch me. I'll show you how to do it.* **5. Watch it/out!** *infml.* Be careful! Pay attention!: *Watch out! Don't step in that hole!* —**watcher** n.

watch n. **1.** A small clock that can be worn, usu. on the wrist, or carried: *a pocket watch/ My watch has stopped.* **2.** One or more people guarding a place or a person: *The police kept a watch on the house all night long.* **3.** A period (usu. four hours) during which a part of a ship's crew remains on watchful duty: *the first watch* **4.** To put careful attention on: *We are keeping a close watch on that country's foreign policy.*

watch-ful (watʃ-fəl) adj. Watching or observing closely: *He kept a watchful eye out for any houses for sale in the area.* —**watchfully** adv. —**watchfulness** n.

watch-man (watʃ-mən) n. -men A guard, esp. of a building or several buildings: *The night watchman caught a man trying to steal our television set.*

watch-word (watʃ-wərd) n. **1.** A password **2.** A slogan; motto

wa-ter (wɔt-ər/ wat-ər) n. **1.** The colorless, tasteless, odorless liquid, which falls from clouds as rain, and which is essential to life on earth: *She said she was thirsty and wanted a drink of water./ People usually cannot survive more than three days without a drink of water.* **2.** *spir.* The Bible which produces faith in Jesus and gives spiritual and eternal life: *Jesus told the woman at the well, "Everyone who drinks this water will be thirsty again, but whoever drinks the water I give him will never thirst. Indeed, the water I give him will become in him a spring of water welling up to eternal life.* (John 4:13,14). **3. above water** *fig. infml.* Out of debt: *It's hard to keep our heads above water since Mary lost her job.* **4. in hot water** *fig. infml.* In trouble: *We'll get into hot water with*

Mom for eating this cake. **5. throw cold water on** *fig. infml.* To discourage; point out difficulties, etc.

water v. **1.** To pour or sprinkle water on: *It's very dry; we'd better water the lawn.* **2.** Of the eyes, to form tears: *My eyes are watering because of the cold wind.* **3.** Of the mouth, to form saliva: *The smell of my favorite food cooking made my mouth water.*

wa-ter-bed (wat-ər-bɛd) n. A bed whose mattress is a vinyl bag filled with water

wa-ter clos-et (wat-ər klɔz-ət) n. A toilet which is emptied (flushed) by a flow of water

wa-ter-col-or (wat-ər-kəl-ər) n. **1.** Artists' paint in which the pigment is diluted with water (not oil) **2.** A picture painted with paints of this kind

wa-ter-course (wat-ər-kɔrs) n. **1.** A stream of water **2.** A channel for water

wa-ter-cress (wat-ər-krɛs) n. A small type of plant found beside streams, used in salads, etc.

wa-ter-fall (wat-ər-fɔl) n. The water of a stream falling from a higher level to a lower level, sometimes over rocks: *The largest waterfall in North America is Niagara Falls.*

wa-ter-front (wat-ər-frənt) n. Land on the edge of a body of water

water lil-y (wat-ər lɪl-iʸ) n. -ies **1.** A water plant having large floating leaves and showy, fragrant flowers **2.** Its flower

water line (wat-ər lam) n. **1.** The line on the hull of a boat or ship that shows where the water level reaches **2.** A line corresponding to the height to which water has risen or may rise

wa-ter-logged (wat-ər-lɔgd/-lagd) adj. Thoroughly filled or soaked with water

wa-ter-main (wat-ər meʸn) n. A large main pipe for carrying water in a system

wa-ter-mark (wat-ər-mark) n. **1.** A mark showing the extent to which water rises **2.** A mark or design impressed on paper which is visible when held up to the light

wa-ter-mel-on (wat-ər-mɛl-ən) n. A large round or oblong fruit with a hard thick shell, juicy red flesh, and many black seeds

wa-ter moc-ca-sin (wat-ər mak-ə-sən) n. A

poisonous snake of southern United States

wa-ter po-lo (wɑt–ər pŏ^w–lŏ^w) n. A water sport played by two teams of swimmers who push or throw an inflated ball toward the opponent's goal

wa-ter-proof (wɑt–ər–pru^wf) adj. Not allowing water to go through: *I hope your coat is waterproof, because it's raining heavily outside.*

wa-ter-shed (wɑt–ər–ʃed) n. **1.** A line of high land where streams on one side flow into one river or sea and streams on the other side flow into another **2.** A turning point in the course of events **3.** A region drained by a river or river system

wa-ter-ski (wɑt–ər–ski^y) v. **-skied, -skiing** To glide over water on water skis, while being towed by a motor boat

water ski n. Either of a pair of flat boards on which a person stands in order to ski on water

wa-ter ta-ble (wɑt–ər te^y–bəl) n. The depth below which the ground is saturated with water

wa-ter-tight (wɑt–ər–taɪt) adj. **1.** So tight that water cannot pass through it **2.** So well planned that no fault can be found: *a watertight alibi*

wa-ter-works (wɑt–ər wɜrks) **1.** A system of reservoirs, pumps, pipes, etc. used in bringing water to an urban area **2.** A pumping station in such a system, with its machinery, filters, etc.

wa-ter-y (wɑt–ə–ri^y) adj. **1.** Of or pertaining to water: *When the ship sank, many went to a watery grave.* **2.** Containing too much water: *This soup is too watery.* **3.** Tearful: *watery eyes* **4.** Resembling water in appearance **5.** Weak: *a watery piece of writing/a watery speech*

watt (wɑt) n. A unit of electrical power

watt-age (wɑt–ɪdʒ) n. Electric power measured in watts

wat-tle (wɑt–əl) n. **1.** Twigs and branches interwoven, used for fences, etc. **2.** A red, fleshy skin hanging from the throat of certain fowl, as the turkey

wave (we^yv) v. **waved, waving 1.** To move one's hand, or sthg. held in the hand, back and forth, esp. as a greeting: *The children waved good-bye to their grandparents.* **2.** To

move in the air, usu. blown by the wind, back and forth or up and down: *Her silk scarf was waving in the wind.* **3.** To form straight hair into curves: *She had her hair waved at the beauty shop yesterday.* —**wavy** adj. *She has wavy blond hair.*

wave n. **1.** The motion of the hand, or sthg. held in the hand, in waving: *He gave us a friendly wave as he drove by.* **2.** Movement along the surface of a body of water: *Without warning, a furious storm came up on the lake so that the waves swept over the boat [that Jesus and his disciples were in]. But ... Jesus rebuked the winds and the waves, and it was completely calm. The men were amazed and asked: "What kind of man is this? Even the winds and the waves obey him!"* (Matthew 8:24-27). **3.** A curved arrangement of the hair: *My little girl has natural waves in her hair.* **4.** A sudden emotion or increase in activity, esp. bad activity: *We've had a recent wave of burglaries in our neighborhood.* **5.** A movement in which some kinds of energy, such as light and sound, flow: *sound waves*

wa-ver (we^y–vər) v. To be unsteady; to hesitate, esp. about making a decision: *He wavered between the two jobs, but decided to take the one closest to home.*

wax (wæks) n. **1.** The sticky, fatty substance of which bees make their cells; beeswax **2.** The sticky, yellowish substance formed in the ears **3.** Any of various soft sticky substances that melt easily, used for various purposes such as candles and polishes: *Use wax to polish the table.*

wax v. **1.** To apply wax: *He's waxing the car.* **2.** To increase or become more visible, esp. the moon as it changes from a new moon to a full moon —see also WANE

wax-en (wæk–sən) adj. Made of wax or like wax

wax-y (wæk–si^y) adj. **-ier, -iest** Like wax —**waxiness** n.

way (we^y) n. **1.** The route, path, etc., to take in order to arrive at one's destination: *I hope this is the way to the post office./ Jesus answered, "I am the way, the truth, and the life. No one comes to the Father except through me"* (John 14:6). **2.** A method: *He taught me his way of re-*

membering names and faces. **3.** A direction: *Which way is it to the bank?* **4.** The distance to be traveled to reach a place: *a long way to the beach* **5.** Time: *My birthday is a long way off.* **6.** A person's course of life: *Commit your way to the Lord; trust in him, and he will do this: He will make your righteousness shine like the dawn* (Psalm 37:5,6). *Train a child in the way he should go, and when he is old he will not turn from it* (Proverbs 22:6). **7.** A characteristic: *The Lord is righteous in all his ways* (Psalm 145:17). **8.** A particular aspect of sthg.: *In some ways, I agree with you.* **9.** Manner: *She spoke in a kindly way.* **10.** A talent or skill: *She has a way with children.* **11.** A state or condition: *Things are in a bad way.* **12. by the way** (used to introduce a new subject in the speech) Incidentally; in addition **13. by way of** By going through: *We went to Hong Kong by way of Manila.* **14. get one's own way** To do or get what one wants **15. give way** To yield: *They would not give way, no matter how we pleaded.* **16. in the way** An obstacle or hindrance: *He's always in the way.* **17. on the way** Going from one place to another: *He's on his way home.* **18. under way** Moving forward: *The meeting got under way at nine a.m.*

way adv. Far: *That movie was made way back in 1932./ We're way ahead of others in our class.*

way-far-er (we^y–fɛər–ər/ –fær–) n. A traveler, usu. on foot

way-lay (we^y–le^y) v. **-laid, -laying** To lie in wait for sbdy., usu. to talk to or to rob

ways (we^yz) n. pl. Habits or customs: *"My thoughts are not your thoughts, neither are your ways my ways," declares the Lord. "As the heavens are higher than the earth, so are my ways higher than your ways and my thoughts than your thoughts..."* (Isaiah 55:8,9).

–ways (–we^yz) comb. form Used to form adverbs showing direction or manner: *sideways/lengthways*

way-side (we^y–saɪd) n. By the side of the road or path

way-ward (we^y–wərd) adj. Childishly self-willed; not obedient or easily controlled

W.C. *Abbr.* Water closet; toilet

we (wi^y) pron. (used as the subject of a sentence) The people who are speaking; the speaker and one or more others: *Shall we (=you and I) go now?*

weak (wi^yk) adj. **1.** Not strong; feeble: *I still feel weak after my illness./ Defend the cause of the weak and fatherless; maintain the rights of the poor and oppressed* (Psalms 82:3). **2.** Not strong in character: *The teacher is so weak (in disciplining) that the students do whatever they want.*

weak-en (wi^y–kən) v. To cause to become weak: *The illness weakened her heart.* —opposite STRENGTHEN

weak-kneed (wi^yk–ni^yd) adj. Cowardly

weak-ling (wi^y–klɪŋ) n. A person lacking strength in body or character

weak-ly (wi^yk–li^y) adv. **-lier, -liest** Feebly: *She smiled weakly at my feeble joke.*

weak-mind-ed (wi^yk–maɪn–dəd) adj. **1.** Feeble-minded **2.** Indecisive

weak-ness (wi^yk–nəs) n. **1.** The state of being weak, esp. in mind, body, or character **2.** A fault; weak part: *Alcoholism is more than a weakness; it's a sin.* —opposite STRENGTH **3.** A strong liking, esp. for sthg. which is bad for one: *Alice has a weakness for chocolate.*

wealth (wɛlθ) n. **1.** A large amount of money and possessions: *Remember the Lord your God, for it is he who gives you the ability to produce wealth* (Deuteronomy 8:18). *Honor the Lord with your wealth. Then your barns will be filled to overflowing* (Proverbs 3:9-10). *Humility and the fear of the Lord bring wealth and honor and life* (Proverbs 22:4). *Command those who are rich in this present world not to be arrogant nor to put their hope in wealth, which is so uncertain, but to put their hope in God, who richly provides us with everything for our enjoyment. Command them to do good, to be rich in good deeds, and to be generous and willing to share. In this way they will heap up treasures for themselves as a firm foundation for the coming age, so that they may take hold of life that is truly life* (1 Tim. 6:17-19). **2.** A large number or amount: *A wealth of material*

wealth-y (wɛl–θi^y) adj. **-ier, -iest** Of a person, rich

wean (wi^yn) v. **1.** To make a child or young animal accustomed to food other than its mother's milk **2.** To cause a person to give

up sthg. gradually, such as a bad habit

weap-on (wɛp–ən) n. A tool for harming or killing: *They had guns, bombs, knives, and other weapons.*

wear (wɛər) v. **wore** (wɔr), **worn** (wɔrn), **wearing 1.** To have on the body, as clothing, jewelry, makeup, glasses, or a hearing aid: *My brother wears glasses.* **2.** To keep in a particular way: *How does she wear her hair?* **3.** To have a particular expression on the face: *She wore a pleasant smile.* **4.** To endure continued use; to last: *This material wears well; it doesn't wear out for a long time.* **5.** To become exhausted: *I'm all worn out after working hard all day.* **6. wear off** To become less and less until it disappears: *The effect of the medicine is wearing off.* **7. wear on (a)** To pass slowly: *The days wore on until school started again.* **(b) wear on sbdy.** To have a negative effect on: *The heat really wears on elderly people.* **8. wear out (a)** To use sthg. until it is no longer usable: *These shoes are worn out.* **(b) wear sbdy. out** To tire greatly: *Do not wear yourself out to get rich* (Proverbs 23:4).

wear n. **1.** Clothing: *Children's wear is on the second floor.* **2.** Damage from ordinary use: *These shoes have seen a lot of wear.*

wear-ing (wɛər–ɪŋ) adj. Fatiguing

wea-ri-some (wɪər–iʸ–səm) adj. Causing fatigue; making one feel tired and bored: *a wearisome day on the job*

wea-ry (wɪər–iʸ) adj. **-rier, -riest 1.** Tired: *Let us not grow weary while doing good, for in due season we shall reap if we do not lose heart* (Galatians 6:9 NKJV). *Those who hope in the Lord will renew their strength... they will run and not grow weary* (Isaiah 40:31). **2.** Bored —**wearily** adv. —**weariness** n.

weary v. To make or become tired

wea-sel (wiʸ–zəl) n. **1.** A type of small flesh-eating animal with a long slender body **2.** A sneaky, treacherous person

weath-er (wɛð–ər) n. **1.** The condition of the atmosphere with respect to wind, rain, sunshine, snow, etc.: *We've been having beautiful weather lately.* **2. under the weather** Not very well: *He's feeling a bit under the weather today, so he didn't go to school.*

weather v. To bear up against difficulties

with success: *Many houses were damaged during the hurricane, but we weathered the storm quite well.*

weath-er-beat-en (wɛð–ər–biʸt–ən) adj. Worn by exposure to weather

weath-er-man (wɛð–ər–mæn) n. Weather forecaster; meteorologist

weath-er-proof (wɛð–ər–pruʷf) adj. Capable of withstanding rain, snow, etc.

weath-er vane (wɛð–ər veʸn) n. A vane that indicates wind direction

weave (wiʸv) v. **wove** (woʷv), **woven** (woʷ–vən), **weaving 1.** To produce a textile by interlacing threads or yarns, esp. in a loom **2.** To form by interlacing strands, strips, twigs, etc.: *She's weaving a basket.*

weave n. The method of weaving in and out, and the pattern formed by this: *The scarf was made with a loose weave.*

weave v. **weaved, weaving** To move along, turning in and out: *The car was weaving in and out through the traffic.*

weav-er (wiʸ–vər) n. A person who weaves cloth

web (wɛb) n. **1.** The network of threads spun by a spider to trap insects **2.** Any complex network: *a web of highways* **3.** Anything artfully contrived into a trap: *She was tangled in her own web of deceit.* **4.** Skin filling the spaces between the toes of birds such as ducks

webbed (wɛbd) adj. Having a skin-like substance between the toes, as on a duck's foot: *webbed feet*

web-bing (wɛb–ɪŋ) n. Strong bands of woven fabric used in upholstery, belts, etc.

web-foot-ed (wɛb–fʊt–əd) adj. Having the toes joined by a web

wed (wɛd) v. **wedded, or wed, wedding 1.** To marry **2.** To join closely

we'd (wiʸd) Short for **(a)** we had **(b)** we would

wed-ding (wɛd–ɪŋ) n. A marriage ceremony —compare MARRIAGE

wedge (wɛdʒ) n. **1.** A V-shaped piece of metal, used to split wood **2.** A V-shaped piece of wood, e.g., for holding a door open **3.** Sthg. shaped like this: *a wedge of pie/cake*

wedge v. **wedged, wedging 1.** To force apart or split, as with a wedge **2.** To fix firmly

with a wedge: *Wedge the door open, please.* **3.** To crowd or squeeze into a small space: *We all sat wedged into one narrow seat.*

wed-lock (wɛd–lɒk) n. The state of being married

Wednes-day (wɛnz–di^y/ –de^y) also **Wed.** *written abbr.* n. The fourth day of the week

wee (wi^y) adj. **1.** Very small **2.** Very early: *the wee hours of the morning*

weed (wi^{y}d) n. Any unwanted wild plant

weed v. **1.** To remove weeds: *to weed the dandelions out of the lawn* **2. weed out** To get rid of sthg. or sbdy. not wanted: *He weeded out all the old magazines.*

weed-y (wi^{y}d–i^y) adj. **-ier, -iest** Abounding in weeds

week (wi^{y}k) n. **1.** A period of seven days and nights, esp. from Sunday to Saturday **2. work week** The period of time during which one goes to work: *She puts in a 40-hour work week.*

week-day (wi^{y}k–de^y) n. A day of the week other than Saturday or Sunday: *Children only go to school on weekdays.*

week-end (wi^{y}k–end) n. Saturday and Sunday

week-ly (wi^{y}k–li^y) adj. Once a week or every week —**weekly** adv.

weekly n. **-lies** A magazine or newspaper which comes once a week

weep (wi^{y}p) v. **wept** (wɛpt), **weeping** To cry

wee-vil (wi^y–vəl) n. A small beetle, destructive to cotton, grain, etc.

weigh (we^y) v. **1.** To find the weight of, esp. with a scale: *to weigh the baby* **2.** To have a certain weight: *The baby weighs eight pounds.* **3.** To think about or consider carefully: *All a man's ways seem right to him, but the Lord weighs the heart* (Proverbs 21:2). **4. weigh sbdy./sthg. down** To place a heavy load on sbdy./sthg.: *I was weighed down with shopping bags./fig. weighed down with worry/An anxious heart weighs a man down, but a kind word cheers him up* (Proverbs 12:25).

weight (we^{y}t) n. **1.** The heaviness of sthg.: *light in weight* **2.** A piece of metal of a standard heaviness, used on a balance or scale in weighing: *The Lord abhors [hates] dishonest scales, but accurate weights are his delight* (Proverbs 11:1). **3.** A usu. heavy object, esp. one

used for holding sthg. down: *a paperweight* **4.** Importance: *Since he became a senator, his opinion carries a lot of weight.* **5. throw one's weight around** To take advantage of one's position by giving orders to others

weight-y (we^{y}t–i^y) adj. **-ier, -iest** Important and serious

weir (wæər/ wɛər/ wɪər) n. **1.** A dam across a small stream **2.** A fence in a stream or channel to catch fish

weird (wɪərd) adj. **1.** Strange; unnatural **2.** *infml.* Unusual and not sensible or acceptable: *People laughed at his weird ideas.*

wel-come (wɛl–kəm) v. **-comed, -coming** To meet or greet, esp. in a friendly way: *The students welcomed the teacher back after her vacation.*

welcome adj. **1.** Gladly received: *You are always welcome at our house.* **2.** Freely and willingly permitted: *You're welcome to use the library anytime.* **3. You're welcome** A polite expression when thanked for sthg.: *"Thank you!" "You're welcome."*

welcome n. A greeting or receiving of an arriving person: *We were given a warm (friendly) welcome when we arrived.*

weld (wɛld) v. **1.** (a) To join pieces of metal by hammering together, esp. after rendering them soft by heat (b) To become joined in this way **2.** To bring into close association: *welded together in friendship*

weld n. A union or joint made by welding

wel-fare (wɛl–fɛər) n. **1.** Well-being **2.** The system of government money paid to people without jobs, the ill, or the poor in the US

well (wɛl) n. **1.** A shaft dug in the ground in order to obtain water or oil from beneath the earth's surface **2.** A spring serving as a source of water: *an artesian well* **3.** An enclosed space in a building, a space resembling the shaft of a well, containing an elevator or staircase: *a stairwell*

well v. To rise up and pour forth: *fig. Pity for the sick welled up in her heart.*

well adv. **bet-ter** (bɛt–ər), **best** (bɛst) **1.** In a good way: *She sings very well.* —op-posite BADLY **2.** Thoroughly: *Dry it well before you put it away.* **3.** Very much: *The price is well over what I want to pay.* **4.** Justifiably: *One may*

well *ask*.,. **5. as well (a)** Also: *I have a room at the hotel and my friend has one as well.* **(b)** Without a good result: *She might as well have kept quiet.* **6. as well as** In addition to: *I'm learning German as well as English.* **7. pretty well** Almost: *The painting is pretty well finished.* **8. Well done!** (said when someone has been successful): *You played that beautifully. Well done!*

well interj. Used for showing surprise, doubt, or for a pause in speech: *Well, what a surprise!*

well adj. **bet-ter, best 1.** Healthy: *I'm not feeling well.* **2.** All right: *Is everything well with you, today?*

we'll (wi^yl) v. Short for **(a)** we will **(b)** we shall

well–be-ing (wɛl–bi^y–ŋ) n. State of being well, happy, etc.

well–bred (wɛl–brɛd) adj. Well brought up; well-mannered

well disposed (wɛl–dɪs–po^wzd) adj. Having favorable feelings toward a person, plan, etc.

well–done (wɛl–dʌn) adj. **1.** Performed well **2.** Of food, esp. meat, cooked for a longer period of time —opposite RARE

well–fixed (wɛl–fɪkst) adj. Wealthy

well–found-ed (wɛl–faʊn–dəd) adj. Based on facts

well–groomed (wɛl–gru^wmd) adj. Neat and clean in one's personal appearance

well–ground-ed (wɛl–graʊn–dəd) adj. **1.** Well trained in the basics **2.** Well-founded

well–heeled (wɛl–hi^yld) adj. Wealthy

well–nigh (wɛl–naɪ) adv. Almost

well–off (wɛl–ɔf) adj. **1.** In fortunate circumstances: *He should have kept his old job. He didn't know when he was well-off.* **2.** Prosperous: *My aunt and uncle are not millionaires, but they are quite well-off.*

well–read (wɛl–rɛd) adj. Knowledgeable

well–round-ed (wɛl–raʊn–dəd) adj. **1.** Of a person, having developed many abilities **2.** Varied and complete **3.** Complete and well-expressed

well–to-do (wɛl–tu^w–du^w) adj. Fairly rich

welt (wɛlt) n. **1.** A raised mark on the skin **2.** A firm edging or band, as on a garment

wel-ter (wɛl–tər) v. **1.** To roll; to wallow: *wel-*

tering in his own blood **2.** Of a ship, to be tossed to and fro on the waves

wend (wɛnd) v. To proceed

went (wɛnt) v. Past tense of **go**

wept (wɛpt) v. Past tense and past part. of **weep**

were (wɜr) v. Past tense of **be**

weren't (wɜrnt) Negative short form for **were not**

we're (wɪər) Short for **we are**

were-wolf or **wer-wolf** (wɪər–wʊlf/ wɛər–/ wɜr–) n. In folklore, a person transformed into a wolf

west (wɛst) n. One of the four main points of the compass, which is on the left of a person facing north: *The sun sets in the west./ The farthest star in the east is millions of light years from the farthest star in the west, but God says, "As far as the east is from the west, so far has he [God] removed our transgressions from us"* (Psalms 103:12). NOTE: He did this through his Son Jesus Christ who was pierced (nailed to a cross) for our transgression, (for) the Lord laid on him the iniquity (sin) of us all (Isaiah 53:5). —see JESUS

West (wɛst) n. **1.** The western part of the world, esp. western Europe and the US **2.** The part of a country that is farther west than the rest **3.** In the US, the part of the country west of the Mississippi River

west-er-ly (wɛs–tər–li^y) adj. **1.** Towards or in the west **2.** Of a wind, coming from the west: *a strong westerly wind*

west-ern (wɛs–tərn) adj. Of or belonging to the west part of the world or of a country: *the Western world*

western n. A movie or story about life in the western part of the US, esp. in the 1800's

West-ern-er (wɛs–tər–nər) n. *AmE.* Someone who lives in or comes from the West

west-ern-ize (wɛs–tər–naɪz) v. **-ized, -izing** To give western characteristics to —**west-ern-i-za-tion** (wɛs–tər–nə–ze^y–ʃən) n.

west-ward (wɛst–wərd) adj. Going towards the west

wet (wɛt) adj. **-tt- 1.** Not dry: *It stopped raining but the grass is still wet.* **2.** Rainy weather: *It's too wet to play baseball.* **3. wet blanket** *derog.* A person who lessens the joy of others, keeps

them from enjoying themselves, etc.
—**wetness** n.

wet v. **wet** or **wetted, wetting 1.** To cause to be wet: *Wet the cloth and clean the table with it.* **2. all wet** *infml.* Wrong: *He's all wet.* **3. wet behind the ears** Inexperienced **4. wet one's whistle** *infml.* Get a drink

we've (wiᵛv) Short for **we have**

whack (hwæk/wæk) v. To hit with a noisy blow: *He got whacked on the head.*

whack n. **1.** The noise made by a hard blow **2. out of whack** *AmE.* Not working properly: *My camera is out of whack.*

whale (hweᵛl/weᵛl) n. **1.** A huge air-breathing mammal that lives in the ocean and looks like a fish **2. whale of a time** *infml.* A very enjoyable social occasion

whal-ing (hweᵛl–ŋ/weᵛl–ŋ) n. The hunting of whales

wharf (hwɔrf/wɔrf) n. **wharfs** or **wharves** A landing place or pier where ships can be tied up for loading or unloading —compare DOCK

what (hwʌt/wʌt) predeterm., determ., or pron. **1.** Used in questions about an unknown person, place, thing, event, etc.: *What's your name?/ What are you reading?* **2.** The thing or things that: *I know what you mean.* **3.** Shows surprise: *What a story!* **4. what for?** *infml.* Why?: *What are you doing that for?*

what-ev-er (hwət–**ɛv**–ər/wət–**ɛv**–ər) also **what-so-ev-er** determ. or pron. **1.** Anything at all that: *I'll take whatever job I can find./ ...whatever you do, do it all for the glory of God* (1 Corinthians 10:31). **2.** No matter what: *Whatever anyone says, he'll go ahead with his plans anyway.*

whatever pron. **1.** Other similar things: *I need lots of things for my apartment, a table, chairs, ...whatever.* **2.** (Showing surprise) What?: *Look at that strange animal! Whatever is it?*

whatever also **whatsoever** adj. At all: *He has no sense whatever.*

what's (hwʌts/wʌts) Contraction of **what is:** *What's that?*

what-so-ev-er (hwət–soʷ–**ɛv**–ər/wət–soʷ–**ɛv**–ər) pron., adj. Whatever

wheat (hwiᵛt/wiᵛt) n. A cereal grain that yields a fine white flour, the most common grain used in bread products in temperate regions

wheat germ (hwiᵛt–dʒɜrm/ wiᵛt–) n. The embryo of the wheat kernel, used as a source of vitamins

whee-dle (hwiᵛ–dəl/wiᵛ–) v. **-dled, -dling 1.** To try to persuade by flattery **2.** To obtain by coaxing: *He wheedles things out of his mother nearly every day.*

wheel (hwiᵛl/wiᵛl) n. **1.** A circular rim and a hub connected by spokes or a disk, capable of rotating on an axis, as in making vehicles move, driving machinery, etc.: *Bicycles have two wheels.* **2.** An instrument having a wheel as its distinguishing characteristic **3.** **–wheeler** A vehicle with the stated number of wheels: *an eighteen-wheeler*

wheel v. **1.** To roll sthg. on an object that has wheels: *The nurse wheeled the patient down the hall in a wheel chair.* **2.** To turn suddenly: *The thief suddenly wheeled around and shot at the pursuing policeman.*

wheel-bar-row (hwiᵛl–bær–oʷ/wiᵛl–/–beər–) n. A light vehicle with one wheel and two handles, used for carrying small loads

wheel-chair (hwiᵛl–tʃeər/wiᵛl–) n. A chair with two large wheels, used by invalids for moving about

wheeze (hwiᵛz/wiᵛz–) v. **wheezed, wheezing** To breathe with difficulty and a whistling sound

wheez-y (hwiᵛz–iᵛ/wiᵛz–) adj. Afflicted by or characterized by wheezing

whelp (hwɛlp/wɛlp) n. **1.** A puppy; cub **2.** An ill-bred boy or young man

when (hwɛn/wɛn) adv., conj., or pron. **1.** At what time?; at the time that: *When will we eat? We'll eat when the food is ready.* **2.** Since; considering that: *I can't help you when you won't tell me what's wrong./ Why do you want a new car when the old one is in such good condition?*

whence (hwɛns/wɛns) conj., adv. From what source or place

when-ev-er (hwɛn–ɛv–ər/wɛn–) adv., conj. At whatever time: *We can go whenever you like.*

where (hweər/weər) adv., conj. In or to what place?: *Where are you going?/ Where did you*

park the car?

where pron. **1.** The place in which: *He lives two miles from where he works.* **2** The point at which: *That's where you're wrong.*

where-a-bouts (hwɛɚr-ə-baʊts/wɛɚr–) n. The place where someone or sthg. is: *The missing plane's whereabouts is still unknown.*

where-as (hwɛɚr–æz/wɛɚr–) conj. **1.** Because of; inasmuch as: *Whereas the cost of living has gone up five per cent this past year, therefore be it resolved that...* **2.** While on the contrary: *They wanted to go to the mountains, whereas the rest of us wanted to go to the beach.*

where-by (hwɛɚr–baɪ/wɛɚr–) adj. *fml.* By which: *That was the means whereby he made his escape.*

where-in (hwɛɚr–ɪn/wɛɚr–) adv. **1.** In what: *Wherein is he mistaken?* **2.** In which: *a marriage wherein there is perfect harmony*

wher-ev-er (hwɛr–ɛv–ɚr/wɛr–) adv., conj. **1.** To, in, or at whatever place: *Wherever you go, I'll go with you.* **2.** (showing surprise) To or at what place?: *Wherever have you been?*

where-with-al (hwɛɚr–wɪð–ɑl/wɛɚr–) n. The necessary means or resources, esp. money

whet (hwɛt/wɛt) v. **-tt- 1.** To sharpen by friction **2.** To stimulate one's appetite, for food or adventure, e.g.

wheth-er (hwɛð–ɚr/wɛð–) conj. **1.** If it is true that: *He asked me whether I liked the movie (or not).* **2.** In either case: *I'll go, whether it rains or not.*

whew (hwɪuʷ/wɪuʷ/hyuʷ) interj. An exclamation of dismay, relief, or amazement

which (hwɪtʃ/wɪtʃ) determ., pron. **1.** (used in questions, when a choice is to be made) What one or ones: *Which dress should I wear tonight?* **2.** The thing designated; that: *Did you see the book which I brought home from the library yesterday?*

which-ev-er (hwɪtʃ–ɛv–ɚr/wɪtʃ–) determ., pron. **1.** Whatever one or ones: *Take whichever one you like.* **2.** No matter which: *You will like this ice cream, whichever flavor you choose.*

whiff (hwɪf/wɪf) n. **1.** A slight gust of air: *a whiff of fresh air* **2.** A gust of odor: *I got a whiff of her perfume as she passed by.*

while (hwaɪl/waɪl) n. **1.** A period of time: *You'll have to wait a while, the doctor is very*

busy. **2.** **worth one's while** Worth one's time and trouble: *Visiting the museum will be worth your while.* —see also WORTH WHILE

while conj. **1.** During the time that: *They watched our house while we were away.* **2.** Although; whereas: *Their house is very large, while ours is quite small.*

whim (hwɪm/wɪm) n. A sudden impulse

whim-per (hwɪm–pɚr/wɪm–) n. **1.** To cry softly, with a whining sound **2.** To speak in a weak, trembling voice

whimper n. A cry of this kind

whim-si-cal (hwɪm–zɪ–kəl/wɪm–) adj. **1.** Given to fanciful notions **2.** Impulsive and playful **3.** Full of or proceeding from whimsy —whimsically adv.

whim-sy (hwɪm–ziʸ/wɪm–) n. **-sies 1.** Playful humor **2.** An odd or fanciful notion

whine (hwaɪn/waɪn) v. **whined, whining 1.** To make a long, high complaining cry, like that of a child or a dog **2.** To complain in an unnecessarily sad voice, in a petty or feeble way

whin-ny (hwɪn–iʸ/wɪn–) v. **-nied, -nying** Of a horse, to neigh, esp. in a low gentle way

whinny n. **-nies** A neigh

whip (hwɪp/wɪp) n. **1.** A long piece of rope or leather lash fastened to a handle, used for whipping (beating) **2.** A dessert made of beaten eggs and other foods whipped together. **3.** A member of a legislative body who is responsible for the discipline and attendance of members of his/her party and looks after party needs

whip v. **-pp- 1.** To strike or urge on with a whip **2.** To move sthg. quickly and fiercely: *He whipped a knife out of his pocket.* **3.** To beat cream, eggs, etc. into a froth: *whipped cream* **4.** To defeat: *Their team whipped us badly.* **5.** **whip sthg. up (a)** To cause feelings to rise; excite: *They're whipping up support for the new children's hospital.* **(b)** To make sthg. quickly: *She whipped up a meal.*

whip-lash (hwɪp–læʃ/wɪp–) n. The lash of a whip

whip-lash injury (hwɪp–læʃ ɪndʒ–ə–riʸ/wɪp–) n. An injury to the neck caused by a sudden jolting, as being hit from the rear in an automobile accident

whip·per·snap·per (hwɪp–ər–snæp–ər/wɪp–) n. A pretentious but insignificant person, esp. a young one

whip·pet (hwɪp–ət/wɪp–) n. A small, swift breed of dog

whip·ping (hwɪp–ɪŋ/wɪp–) n. A beating, esp. as a punishment

whirl (hwɜrl/wɜrl) v. To move around in circles very fast

whirl n. **1.** A dizzy or confused state: *Too many things are happening all at once. My head's in a whirl.* **2.** Very fast, confused movement or activity: *a whirl of social activity*

whirl·pool (hwɜrl–puᵂl/wɜrl–) n. A current of water, whirling in a circle, often drawing floating objects toward its center

whirl·wind (hwɜrl–wɪnd/wɜrl–) n. A mass of air whirling violently around a central point: *A tornado is a violent and destructive whirlwind.*

whisk (hwɪsk/wɪsk) v. **1.** To move quickly with a light sweeping movement: *The horse whisked its tail to chase away the flies.* **2.** To convey or go rapidly: *As soon as he completed his speech, he was whisked off to the airport.* **3.** To beat eggs, cream, etc. into a froth, esp. with a whisk

whisk n. **1.** A whisking movement **2.** An instrument for beating eggs **3.** Strips of straw tied to a handle, used to whisk flies away **4.** **whisk broom** A short handled broom for brushing clothes, etc.

whisk·er (hwɪs–kər/wɪs–) n. **1.** One of the long, hair-like bristles growing near the mouth of a cat and certain other animals **2.** *infml.* A very short distance: *He came within a whisker of getting hit by that bullet.* **3** **whiskers** *pl.* Hair growing on a man's face, esp. on the cheek and chin —compare BEARD

whis·key (hwɪs–kiʸ/wɪs–) n. -keys A strong alcoholic drink, distilled from a fermented mash of corn, barley, or other grains NOTE: The spelling "whiskey" is used for Irish and American products, "whisky" for Scotch and Canadian.

whis·per (hwɪs–pər/wɪs–) n. **1.** A low, soft, breathy voice: *He spoke in a whisper./ "Whispers in the Dark" was once a popular romantic*

song. **2.** A soft, swishing kind of sound, as the wind blowing through tall grass or through pine trees: *the whisper of the breeze in the trees*

whisper v. **1.** To speak in a whisper: *He whispered in her ear.* **2.** To make a soft sound by moving gently in the wind: *leaves whispering in the breeze*

whis·tle (hwɪs–əl/wɪs–) n. **1.** A device for producing a shrill sound by forcing air through a narrow opening **2.** The sound produced by a whistle: *If you're in trouble just give a little whistle (=let me know), and I'll be there.* **3.** The high shrill sound made by forcing breath through the teeth or through puckered lips

whis·tle v. -tled, -tling **1.** To make a shrill sound by forcing air through the teeth or through puckered lips **2.** To produce (music) by doing this: *He whistled a popular tune.*

white (hwaɪt/waɪt) adj. **whiter, whitest 1.** The color of snow and milk **2.** Having light-colored skin, being of European descent: *a white man*

white n. **1.** The color which is opposite of black **2.** A person of a pale-skinned race: *There were both whites and blacks in our class.* **3.** The part of an egg which is colorless, but white after cooking **4.** Of the eye, the part surrounding the pupil and iris: *The whites of her eyes are bloodshot.*

white elephant (hwaɪt ɛl–ə–fənt/waɪt) n. An object that requires much maintenance but has little value

whit·en (hwaɪt–ən/waɪt–) v. To make white or whiter: *This soap with bleach will whiten your clothes.*

white slave (hwaɪt sleʸv/waɪt) n. A woman enticed or forced into or held in prostitution for the profit of others

white slavery (hwaɪt sleʸv–ə–riʸ/waɪt) n. Enforced prostitution

white·wash (hwaɪt–wɔʃ/waɪt–) n. **1.** A mixture of slaked lime and water, used for whitening walls, fences, etc. **2.** *Slang* A covering up of errors, defects, sinful actions, etc. **3.** A failure to score in a game

whitewash v. **1.** To put whitewash on a wall, etc. **2.** To try to hide someone's crime,

mistake, or faults

whith-er (**hwɪð–ər/wɪð–**) adv. or conj. **1.** To which place, point, condition, etc. **2.** To whatever place, point, condition, etc.; wherever

whit-ing (**hwaɪt–ɪŋ/waɪt–**) n. **1.** Powdered white chalk **2.** An edible fish

whit-ish (**hwaɪt–ɪʃ/waɪt–**) adj. Somewhat white

Whit-sun-tide (**hwɪt–sən–taɪd/wɪt–**) n. The feast or season of Pentecost, so called because in the early Christian church, those who had been newly baptized appeared at church between Easter and Pentecost in white garments —see PENTECOST

whit-tle (**hwɪt–əl/wɪt–**) v. **-tled, -tling** To cut or shape with a knife

whiz or **whizz** (**hwɪz/wɪz**) v. **-zz- 1.** To make a hissing sound like an arrow flying through the air **2.** To move rapidly: *He whizzed her to the hospital immediately after the accident.*

whiz kid (**hwɪz kɪd/wɪz**) n. An extremely intelligent or successful young person

who (**huʷ**) pron. **1.** (Used in questions) What person or people?: *Who's that man across the street?* **2.** The person referred to: *The man who wrote this letter is a college professor.* **3.** Used, when preceded by a comma, to add more information about a person or people: *This is my brother, who lives in Detroit.*

who'd (**huʷd**) Short for **(a)** who had **(b)** who would

who-ev-er (**huʷ–ɛv–ər**) pron. **1.** Anybody, without exception: *God so loved the world that he gave his one and only Son, that whoever believes in him shall not perish but have eternal life* (John 3:16). *Whoever believes in the Son has eternal life, but whoever rejects the Son will not see life, for God's wrath remains on him* (John 3:36). **2.** No matter who: *Whoever it is, I don't have time to see them/him right now.*

whole (**hoʷl**) adj. **1.** Entire; complete; total: *the whole truth* **2.** Not broken; in one piece: *She swallowed it whole.*

whole n. **1.** Including everyone and/or everything; complete: *I can't speak for the group as a whole. Every member must speak for himself.* **2.** The sum of the parts: *Two halves make a whole.* **3. on the whole** Generally

speaking; taking all things into consideration: *Some parts of this town are not so nice, but on the whole it is a good place to live.*

whole-heart-ed (**hoʷl–hart–əd**) adj. Sincere and enthusiastic —**wholeheartedly** adv.

whole-sale (**hoʷl–seʸl**) n. The business of selling goods in large quantity, usu. to store-keepers for resale —compare RETAIL

wholesale adj. **1.** Of or concerned with selling in large quantities, esp. for resale in smaller quantities **2.** In large, unlimited numbers: *a wholesale rush from the burning building* —**wholesale** adv.

whole-sal-er (**hoʷl–seʸl–ər**) n. A person who buys and sells wholesale goods

whole-some (**hoʷl–səm**) adj. **1.** Promoting mental, spiritual, or physical health: *wholesome advice* **2.** Good in effect, esp. morally: *St. Peter wrote two letters to Christians to stimulate them to wholesome thinking* (2 Peter 3:1). **3.** Prudent: *a wholesome respect for the law* —**wholesomeness** n.

whole wheat (**hoʷl hwiʸt/wiʸt**) n. Made from the entire wheat grain

who'll (**huʷl**) Short for **who will**

whol-ly (**hoʷl–liʸ**) adv. **1.** Completely; totally **2.** Solely; exclusively: *He was wholly to blame for the accident.*

whom (**huʷm**) pron. The object form of **who,** used esp. in formal speech or writing: *With whom were you speaking?/To whom it may concern* —see WHO

whom-ev-er (**huʷm–ɛv–ər**) pron. Objective case of **whoever**

whoop (**huʷp/hwuʷp**) n. **1.** A loud cry or shout of excitement: *The fans of the winning team are giving loud whoops over there (on their side of the football field).* **2.** A noisy sound made when breathing in after coughing when one has the whooping cough

whoop-ing cough (**huʷ–pɪŋ kɔf/hwuʷp–**) n. An infectious disease with violent bouts of coughing followed by a whoop when the breath is drawn in again

whop-per (**hwap–ər/wap–**) n. **1.** Anything big **2.** A big lie

whop-ping (**hwap–ɪŋ/wap–**) adj. *infml.* Uncommonly large

whore (**hɔr**) n. A prostitute

who's (hu^{w}z) Short for **(a)** who is: *Who's that?* **(b)** who has: *Who's been sitting in my chair?*

whose (hu^{w}z) determ., pron. **1.** Belonging to which person?: *Whose car is this?* **2.** Of whom: *That's the man whose car was stolen.* **3.** Of which: *a painting whose artist is unknown*

why (hwaɪ/waɪ) adv., conj., interj. **1.** For what reason?: *Why did you say that?* **2.** For which: *Now we know the reason why he said it.*

wick (wɪk) n. A loosely bound bundle of soft fibers that draw up oil or wax to be burned in a candle, oil lamp, or stove

wick-ed (wɪk–əd) adj. Morally very bad; evil; sinful: *The Lord detests the sacrifices [and the way and the thoughts] of the wicked* (Proverbs 15:8,9,26). *Nevertheless, the Lord says,"If my people who are called by my name, will humble themselves and pray and seek my face and turn from their wicked ways, then will I hear from heaven and will forgive their sin and will heal their land"* (2 Chronicles 7:14). NOTE: I take no pleasure in the death of the wicked [declares the Sovereign Lord], but rather that they turn from their ways and live (Ezekiel 33:11). Because of God's great love and mercy, he forgives the wicked who truly repent of their wicked ways, envy, greed, jealousy, and hatred — all their sins — and put their trust in Jesus for eternal life (Mark 1:15; Acts 16:31; Romans 3:23-24; 6:23; John 3:16). —**wickedly** adv. —**wickedness** n. —see WICKEDNESS, SIN, FORGIVENESS, JESUS
NOTE: **Wicked** and **evil** are very strong words for people or acts that are seriously morally wrong. Disobedient children are usually called **naughty** or **mischievous**.

wick-ed-ness (wɪk–əd–nəs) n. Sin, evil; extreme immorality: *You, Lord, love righteousness and hate wickedness* (Psalm 45:7). *We [disciples of Jesus] wait for the blessed hope – the glorious appearing of our great God and Savior, Jesus Christ, who gave himself for us [when he suffered and died on the cross] to redeem us from all wickedness and to purify for himself a people that are his very own, eager to do what is good* (Titus 2:13-14). NOTE: Though the Lord hates wickedness, he takes no pleasure in the death of the wicked

(Ezekiel 33:11). He doesn't want anyone to perish in his sins; rather that all should come to repentance and to the knowledge of the truth about Jesus, who came into the world to save sinners, that they may not perish but have eternal life (Ezekiel 33:11 2 Peter 3:9; 2 Timothy 2:4; 1 Timothy 1:15; John 3:16; Romans 3:23; 6:23). —see WICKED, SIN, MAN, LAW, JESUS, FORGIVENESS

wick-er (wɪk–ər) n. **1.** A slender pliant twig **2.** Wickerwork

wicker adj. Made of wicker

wick-er-work (wɪk–ər–wərk) n. Anything made of wicker

wick-et (wɪk–ət) n. **1.** A small door or gate, usu. within a larger one, for use when the larger one is closed **2.** A small window, as in a ticket office **3.** In cricket, either of the two frameworks at which the bowler aims the ball **4.** In croquet, any of the hoops through which the ball must be hit

wide (waɪd) adj. **wider, widest 1.** The distance from one side to the other: *How wide is Lake Victoria?* **2.** Not narrow; broad **3.** Completely; fully: *Her eyes were wide open.* **4.** Not limited; extensive: *a wide range of experience* **5.** Astray: *The bullet went wide of the target.* **6.** Great in extent: *I pray that you ... may have power, together with all the saints [believers in Jesus], to grasp how wide and long and high and deep is the love of Christ and to know this love that surpasses knowledge — that you may be filled to the measure of all the fullness of God* (Ephesians 3:17-19). —compare NARROW —**wide** adv. *He opened his eyes wide*

wide-a-wake (waɪd–ə–we^{y}k) adj. Fully awake; alert

wide-ly (waɪd–li^y) adv. **1.** Extensively **2.** Fully open **3.** Away from the mark

wid-en (waɪd–ən) v. To make wider; broaden

wide-spread (waɪd–sprɛd) adj. Spread over a large area or among many

wid-ow (wɪd–o^w) n. A woman whose husband has died and who has not married again

wid-ow-er (wɪd–o^w–ər) n. A man whose wife has died and who has not married again

width (wɪdθ) n **1.** The distance from side to

side; breadth **2.** A piece of material of the full width, as it was woven: *We need four widths of curtain material.*

wield (wiᵞld) v. **1.** To use or handle, esp. effectively: *to wield a weapon* **2.** To influence the action of: *He wields a lot of power in the government.*

wie-ner (wiᵞ–nər) n. Hot dog; frankfurter

wife (waɪf) n. **wives** (waɪvz) The woman to whom a man is married: *Wives, submit to your husbands as to the Lord ... Husbands, love your wives just as Christ loved the Church and gave himself up for her [when he died on the cross to pay for all our sins]. In this same way, husbands ought to love their wives as their own bodies* (Ephesians 5:22,25,28). *Each one of you must love his wife as he loves himself, and the wife must respect her husband* (Ephesians 5:33).

wig (wɪg) n. A covering of artificial hair worn on the head as an adornment, to conceal baldness, or as part of a costume: *The actress wore a black wig over her blond hair.*

wig-gle (wɪg–əl) v. **-gled, -gling** To move in short irregular movements, esp. from side to side: *He wiggled his way through the small opening.* —**wiggle** n. —**wiggler** n.

wig-gly (wɪg–liᵞ) adj. **-glier, -gliest 1.** Tending to wiggle: *a wiggly worm* **2.** Wavy: *a wiggly line* —**wiggly** adv.

wig-wam (wɪg–wɑm) n. An American Indian dwelling, typically having an arched framework covered by bark or hides

wild (waɪld) adj. **1.** Living in a natural state or condition; not tame or cultivated: *wild animals/flowers* **2.** Not civilized; savage: *wild tribes* **3.** Showing strong feelings, esp. of anger: *He went wild with rage.* **4.** Violent; fierce: *a wild wind* **5.** Lack of serious thought: *a wild guess* (=*because no facts are known*) **6.** Having a great liking for; very enthusiastic: *She's wild about tennis* **7.** Sinful; reckless: *The foolish son squandered his wealth in wild living.* **8.** Wide of the mark or target: *a wild shot/pitch* **9.** Crazy: *wild ideas* **10.** Rash: *a wild hope*

wild-cat (waɪld–kæt) n. **1.** A small or medium-sized kind of wild cat, as the lynx or ocelot **2.** Financially risky **3.** A strike not supported by union officials **4.** A quick-tempered, hard-fighting person **5.** A well drilled for oil or gas in a region not known to be productive

wild-cat v. **-tt-** To drill for oil or gas in a region not known to be productive

wild-cat adj. **1.** Not sound or safe: *a wildcat plan* **2.** Initiated by a group of workers without official approval: *a wildcat strike*

wil-der-ness (wɪl–dər–nəs) n. An area of uninhabited and uncultivated land

wild-fire (waɪld–faɪ–ər) n. **1.** A destructive, hard to extinguish fire **2. like wildfire** With great rapidity

wild–goose chase (waɪld–gu**ʷ**s tʃeᵞs) n. Pursuit of the unattainable

wile (waɪl) n. Cunning deception; trickery

wile v. **wiled, wiling** To lure; entice

wil-ful see **will-ful** adj.

will (wɪl) v. **would 1.** Used to show the future: *Do you think it will snow tomorrow?* **2.** To be willing: *I will go to work tomorrow, no matter how bad I feel.* **3.** Used when making a request: *Will you please turn the radio down?* **4.** Shows what is to be expected: *Accidents will happen.* **5.** Shows customary action: *She will sit and read for hours at a time.* **6.** Is able to: *This car will hold six people.* —see also WOULD, SHALL

will n. **1.** The power to choose or decide: *He was forced to do it against his will.* **2.** Desire and determination to make things happen: *the will to live* **3.** What is wished or intended (by the stated person): *In the prayer that Jesus taught us, we pray that God's will be done* (Matthew 6:10). *It is God's will that we should be holy* (1 Thessalonians 4:3). *Be joyful always; pray continually; giving thanks in all circumstances, for this is God's will for you in Christ Jesus* (1 Thessalonians 5:16-18). —see JESUS **4.** The written wishes of a person in regard to sharing his property among other people after his death: *Have you made your will yet?* **5. at will** As one desires **6. -willed** Having a certain kind of will: *a strong-willed man*

will v. **willed, willing 1.** To desire and intend to happen: *[God] will have all men to be saved [have everlasting life] and come to the knowledge of the truth [about our Savior Jesus*

Christ] (1 Timothy 2:4). **2.** To leave possessions or money in a will to be given after one's death: *My grandfather willed me his watch.*

will-ful *AmE.* **wil-ful** *BrE.* (wɪl–fəl) adj. **1.** Done deliberately or intentionally: *willful disobedience* **2.** Stubborn; obstinate; inclined to impose one's will on others; determined to have one's own way: *a willful child*

will-ing (wɪl–ɪŋ) adj. Ready to agree: *God is not willing that any should perish, but that all should come to repentance* (2 Peter 3:9 KJV). —**willingly** adv. —**will-ing-ness** n.

wil-low (wɪl–oʷ) n. **1.** A tree which grows near water, with long thin branches **2.** The wood of a willow tree

wil-low-y (wɪl–oʷ–iʸ) adj. Tall and graceful

will-pow-er (wɪl–paʊ–ər) n. The power or determination to do sthg.: *He doesn't have the willpower to stop smoking, though he knows that smoking causes lung cancer.*

wil-ly-nil-ly (wɪl–iʸ–nɪl–iʸ) adj. Without decisiveness; uncertain

willy-nilly adv. Willingly or unwillingly

wilt (wɪlt) v. Of a plant, to droop; to become less fresh: *The flowers are wilting for lack of water.*

wi-ly (waɪ–liʸ) adj. **-lier, -liest** Sly; cunning

wimp (wɪmp) n. *AmE. infml. derog.* A person, esp. a man, lacking strength of character

win (wɪn) v. **won** (wʌn), **winning 1.** To be the best or first in a struggle, competition, election, or a race: *Who won the game?* **2.** To be awarded sthg. as the result of success in a competition: *She won a gold medal.* **3.** To gain: *He that wins souls [for Christ] is wise* (Proverbs 11:30). *Make it your ambition to lead a quiet life, to mind your own business and to work with your hands... so that your daily life may win the respect of outsiders [and everyone]* (1 Thessalonians 4:11,12).

win n. A victory or success: *nine wins and only two defeats*

wince (wɪns) v. **winced, wincing** To shrink back; flinch

wince n. An act of wincing

winch (wɪntʃ) n. **1.** A machine consisting of a horizontal drum on which a rope or chain is wound, used for hoisting **2.** The crank or handle of a revolving machine, as a grindstone

wind (wɪnd) n. **1.** Strongly moving air: *a fierce wind* —compare BREEZE **2. four winds** All directions; all the world: *When Jesus returns to earth, "he will send his angels with a loud trumpet call, and they will gather his elect from the four winds, from one end of the heavens to the other"* (Matthew 24:31). **3.** Breath: *The fall knocked the wind out of him.* **4. get wind of** *infml.* To hear about sthg. accidentally or otherwise: *If anyone gets wind of our plans, we'll be in trouble.* **5. second wind (a)** A steady breathing regained during exercise which had at first made one breathless **(b)** Ability to try hard again **6. in the wind** About to happen

wind v. **winded** (wɪnd–əd), **winding** (wɪnd–ɪŋ) To cause to be breathless: *He was winded from the long climb.*

wind (waɪnd) v. **wound** (waʊnd), **winding** (waɪnd–ɪŋ) **1.** To wrap around several times: *She wound some cloth around his injured arm.* **2.** To tighten the spring of a clock or watch by turning sthg.: *I don't have to wind my watch, it's self-winding.* **3.** To open or shut sthg. by turning: *Please wind down the car window.* **4.** To twist and turn: *The road winds its way through the mountains.*

wind-bag (wɪnd–bæg) n. *slang* An idly talkative person

wind-ed (wɪnd–əd) adj. Out of breath

wind-fall (wɪnd–fɔl) n. **1.** An unexpected gain, profit, or gift **2.** Sthg. such as ripening fruit brought down by the wind

wind-ing (waɪn–dɪŋ) adj. Having a twisting, turning shape: *a winding stream*

wind-lass (wɪnd–ləs) n. A type of winch operated by a crank, used esp. for raising an anchor

wind-mill (wɪnd–mɪl) n. A mill worked by the action of wind on projecting blades that radiate from a central shaft, used for pumping water, generating electricity, grinding grain, etc.

win-dow (wɪn–doʷ) n. An opening, usu. of glass, esp. in the wall of a building or in a car, bus, train, or plane to let in air and light and so that people can see out

win-dow–shop-ping (wɪn–doᵂ–ʃɑp–ɪŋ) v. Looking at merchandise in store windows without necessarily planning to buy anything

wind-pipe (wɪnd–paɪp) n. The tube that forms an air passage from the throat to the lungs

wind-shield (wɪnd–ʃiʸld) *AmE.* **wind-screen** (wɪnd–skriʸn) *BrE.* n. The transparent sheet of glass or other material that forms a shield in front of the occupants of a vehicle

wind-sock (wɪnd–sak) A tube-like piece of material attached to a high pole for indicating the direction and speed of wind at an airport

wind-y (wɪn–diʸ) adj. **-ier, -iest 1.** With much wind: *a windy day* **2.** Exposed to the wind: *high on a windy hill* **3.** *derog.* A person who talks a lot

wine (waɪn) n. An alcoholic drink made from grapes or other fruit: *Wine is a mocker and beer a brawler; whoever is led astray by them is not wise* (Proverbs 20:1) *Do not get drunk on wine, which leads to debauchery. Instead, be filled with the Spirit. Speak to one another with psalms, hymns and spiritual songs. Sing and make music to the Lord, always giving thanks to God the Father for everything, in the name of the Lord Jesus Christ* (Ephesians 5:18-20).

win-er-y (waɪn–ə–riʸ) adj. A place where wine is made

wing (wɪŋ) n. **1.** One of a pair of projecting parts by which a bird or bat or insect is able to fly **2.** A corresponding part of a non-flying bird or insect: *Ostriches have wings but they don't fly.* **3.** One of the parts standing out from the side of a plane which supports it in flight **4.** A section built out to the side of a large building: *the west wing of the hospital* **5.** A section of a political party or of politics in general **6. under someone's wing** Being protected, helped, etc. by someone: *He took some of the new students under his wing.*

wing v. To fly quickly and gracefully: *The eagle winged its way across the valley.*

winged (wɪŋd) adj. Having wings

wings (wɪŋz) n. The sides of the stage, where an actor is hidden from view

wink (wɪŋk) v. To close and open one eye rapidly, usu. as a signal between people: *He winked at her and she knew he had only been joking.*

wink n. **1.** A winking movement: *He gave me a wink.* **2.** A brief period of sleep; a nap: *I didn't sleep a wink last night.*

win-ner (wɪn–ər) n. A person or animal that wins —opposite LOSER

win-ning (wɪn–ɪŋ) adj. **1.** Successful in competition: *the winning entry* **2.** Attractive: *a winning smile*

win-nings (wɪn–ɪŋz) n. Sthg. won, esp. money

win-now (wɪn–oᵂ) v. **1.** To separate the grain from the chaff **2.** To get rid of sthg. unwanted; to sift

win-some (wɪn–səm) adj. Pleasant; causing joy or pleasure: *a winsome personality*

win-ter (wɪn–tər) n. The coldest period of the year, between autumn and spring

win-ter-ize (wɪn–tər–aɪz) v. **-ized, -izing** To put sthg. in condition for winter

win-try (wɪn–triʸ) adj. **-trier, -triest** Like winter, esp. cold or snowy

wipe (waɪp) v. **wiped, wiping 1.** To clean or dry by rubbing, esp. with a cloth: *Wipe your shoes on the mat.* **2.** To remove sthg. by doing this: *In heaven [God] will wipe every tear from their eyes. There will be no more death or mourning or crying or pain* (Revelation 21:4). **3. wipe sbdy./sthg. out (a)** To destroy: *The tornado wiped out the entire village:* **(b)** To beat badly: *The home basketball team wiped out their opponent, 99 to 46!*

wip-er (waɪ–pər) n. Windshield wiper

wire (waɪ–ər) n **1.** A thread-like length of metal, but often thicker and heavier: *a wire fence* **2.** A piece of wire used to carry electric current **3.** A long cable used in telegraph or telephone systems **4.** *AmE.* A telegram or cablegram: *Send me a wire when you get there.* **5. to get one's wires crossed** To become confused **6. under the wire** Just barely in time

wire v. **wired, wiring 1.** To provide or equip with wire, esp. in an electrical system: *He wired the house.* **2.** To bind or strengthen with wire: *He wired it together.* **3.** To send a telegram to: *He wired me about my mother's illness.*

wire-tap (waɪr–tæp) n. A concealed device connected to a telephone in order to listen

to or record messages

wiretap v. -pp- To connect or use a wiretap

wir-ing (waɪr-ŋ) n. A system of wires, esp. one for distributing electricity throughout a building

wir-y (waɪr-iʸ) adj. -ier, -iest Lean but tough and sinewy; like wire

wis-dom (wɪz-dəm) n. The quality of being wise: *God gave Solomon wisdom* (1 Kings 4:29). *The fear of the Lord is the beginning of wisdom* (Psalm 111:10). *The Lord gives wisdom and from his mouth come knowledge and understanding* (Proverbs 2:6). *Wisdom is supreme; therefore get wisdom* (Proverbs 4:7). *In Christ are hidden all the treasures of wisdom and knowledge* (Colossians 2:3). *Wisdom that comes from above [heaven] is first of all pure; then peace-loving, considerate, submissive, full of mercy and good fruit [deeds], impartial and sincere* (James 3:17).

wise (waɪz) adj. **wiser, wisest** Having or showing good sense; the ability to understand what happens and decide on the right action: *The Holy Scriptures [the Bible] are able to make you wise for salvation through faith in Christ Jesus* (2 Timothy 3:15). —see WISDOM *He that wins souls [to Christ] is wise* (Proverbs 11:30). *The statutes [rules, laws] of the Lord are trustworthy, making wise the simple* (Psalm 19:7). *Rebuke a wise man and he will love you. Instruct a wise man and he will be wiser still* (Proverbs 9:8,9). —**wisely** adv.

wise-acre (waɪ-zeʸ-kər) n. A person who claims to know everything

wise-crack (waɪz-kræk) n. A clever or flippant remark

wish (wɪʃ) v. **1.** To want; have a desire; long for; crave: *Jesus said, "If you remain in me [through faith] and my words remain in you, ask whatever you wish, and it will be given you"* (John 15:7). **2.** To form or express a wish concerning someone or sthg.: *We wish you a Merry Christmas.* **3.** To request by expressing a desire: *I wish you would turn the radio down.* —see HOPE

wish n. A desire: *It's his wish to travel around the world.*

wish-ful (wɪʃ-fəl) adj. Desirous; hopeful

wishful thinking (wɪʃ-fəl θɪŋk-ŋ) n. Basing one's beliefs on false hopes rather than on known facts

wish-y–wash-y (wɪʃ-iʸ-wɔʃ-iʸ/-wɑʃ-) adj. **1.** Lacking in strength or decisiveness **2.** Thin and weak, as a liquid —**wishy–washiness** n.

wisp (wɪsp) n. **1.** A person or thing that is small and delicate: *a mere wisp of a girl* **2.** A small bundle, as of straw **3.** A small tuft, as of hair **4.** A thin puff, as of smoke

wis-ter-i-a (wɪs-tɪər-iʸ-ə) n. A climbing shrub having showy clusters of flowers

wist-ful (wɪst-fəl) adj. Feeling or showing a vague, unsatisfied yearning —**wistfully** adv. —**wistfulness** n.

wit (wɪt) n. **1.** The ability to say things in a clever and amusing way **2.** Intelligence **3. at one's wits' end** Totally confused; perplexed; too worried by difficulties to know what to do next **4. keep one's wits about one** To stay calm and able to act sensibly; not to panic: *You need to keep your wits about you when driving in all this traffic.* **5.** –**witted** Having the stated type of ability or understanding: *quick-witted (=clever)/ dim-witted (=stupid)* —**witty** adj.

witch (wɪtʃ) n. **1.** A woman who practices witchcraft **2.** A vicious, ugly, old woman; an old hag

witch-craft (wɪtʃ-kræft) n. Black magic; sorcery; the practice of magic to make bad things happen: *The acts of the sinful nature are obvious: sexual immorality... idolatry, witchcraft, hatred, discord, jealousy... selfish ambition... those who live like this will not inherit the Kingdom of God* (Galatians 5:19-21). NOTE: God hates the sin of witchcraft and all sin, but because of his great love and mercy, he forgives those who truly repent (turn from their wicked ways) and put their trust in Jesus for eternal life (Acts 2:38; 16:31; Romans 6:23-24; John 3:16). —see JESUS

witch doc-tor (wɪtʃ dɑk-tər) n. A medicine man or shaman among some primitive peoples or tribes; in African tribes, one believed to have magical powers to cure illnesses —see SHAMAN, MEDICINE MAN

with (wıθ) prep. **1.** In the presence of: *I was walking with my father.* **2.** Having. *a man with a beard* **3.** By means of: *He cut it with a knife.* **4.** Containing: *tea with sugar* **5.** In support of; in favor of: *Jesus said, "He who is not with me is against me"* (Matthew 12:30). **6.** In the same direction as: *drifting with the current* **7.** At the same time as: *He got up with the sun. (=at sunrise)* **8.** Used in comparisons: *His strength is great compared with mine.* **9.** Used with the idea of covering: *He was covered with dust./ She was overwhelmed with work.* **10.** Against: *Stop fighting with each other.* **11.** Shows separation from: *He didn't want to part with her.* **12.** As a result: *She was shaking with fright.* **13.** Because of: *Singing with joy* **14.** Concerning; in the case of: *God is patient with us.* **15.** In the opinion of: *His argument carried much weight with the judges.* **16.** As well as: *He can play football with the best of them.* **17.** In spite of: *With all her wealth, she still lives very simply.* **18.** Used in exclamations expressing a wish or command: *On with the show. (=let the show continue)./ Off to bed with you! (=Go to bed!)*

with-draw (wıθ–drɔ) v. **-drew** (druʷ), **-drawn**, **-drawing 1.** To move away or back: *The army withdrew to a more strategic position.* **2.** To take away or back: *He withdrew $50 from his checking account.* —compare DEPOSIT **3.** Not to take part in: *He withdrew from the presidential race. (=chose not to be a candidate)*

with-draw-al (wıθ–drɔ–əl) n. The act of withdrawing or state of being withdrawn

with-drawn (wıθ–drɔn) adj. Shy, retiring; quiet and concerned with one's own thoughts

with-er (wıŏ–ər) v. To dry up and shrink, as flowers: *The grass withers and the flowers fall, but the word of the Lord stands forever* (1 Peter 1:24).

with-hold (wıθ–hoʷld) v. **-held**, **-holding** To refuse to give: *No good thing does he [God] withhold from those whose walk is blameless* (Psalm 84:11).

with-in (wıŏ–ın/wıθ–) adv., prep. **1.** *fml.* Inside: *Office For Rent. Inquire Within.* **2.** Not more than: *It will be dark within two hours.*

with-out (wıŏ–aʊt/wıθ–) adv., prep. **1.** Not

having: *Without faith [in Jesus] it is impossible to please him [God]* (Hebrews 11:6 KJV). **2.** (To indicate the lack or absence of sthg.): *Pray without ceasing* (1 Thessalonians 5:17 KJV).

with-stand (wıθ–stænd) v. **-stood** (stʊd), **-standing** To resist: *Take up the whole armor of God, that you may be able to withstand [the temptations of Satan] in the evil day* (Ephesians 6:13). NOTE: The whole armor of God is the word of God plus faith and righteousness which are dependent upon God's Word and our attitude toward it. Faith comes from hearing the message, and the message is heard through the word of Christ (Romans 10:17). Abraham believed God [the Word of God], and it was credited to him as righteousness (Romans 4:3).

wit-less (wıt–ləs) adj. Foolish

wit-ness (wıt–nəs) n. **1.** A person who is present when sthg. happens, esp. one who is able to give an account of what took place: *Jesus told them [his disciples], "This is what is written: The Christ will suffer and rise from the dead on the third day, and repentance and forgiveness of sins will be preached in his name to all nations... You are witnesses of these things"* (Luke 24:47,48). **2.** A person who tells what he saw happen: *Jesus said to his disciples, "You will receive power when the Holy Spirit comes on you; and you will be my witnesses ... to the ends of the earth"* (Acts 1:8). **3.** A person who signs an official paper to show that he has seen someone else sign it **4.** A sign or proof of: *The success of the organization bears witness to good planning.*

witness v. **1.** To be present at the time of an event and see it: *Did anybody witness the robbery?* **2.** To be a witness to the signing of a document, esp. by also signing the document oneself: *He witnessed the signing of the treaty/will.*

wit-ti-cism (wıt–ə–sız–əm) n. A clever remark

wit-ting-ly (wıt–ıŋ–liʸ) adv. Knowingly; aware; intentionally

wit-ty (wıt–iʸ) adj. **-tier**, **-tiest** Full of wit —**wittily** adv. —**wittiness** n.

wives (waıvz) n. *Pl.* of wife

wiz-ard (wız–ərd) n. **1.** A man who is sup-

posed to have magic powers —compare WITCH **2.** *infml.* A person who has unusual skill or ability: *He's a wizard at chess.*

wk. *Abbr.* Week

wkly *Abbr.* Weekly

wob-ble (**wɑb–əl**) v. **-bled, -bling** To move or stand unsteadily; to rock from side to side

woe (**wo͏ʷ**) n. Great sorrow, grief, or misery: *Woe to the world because of the things that cause people to sin! Such things must come, but woe to the man through whom they come* (Matthew 18:7).

woe-be-gone (**wo͏ʷ–bɪ–gɔn**) adj. Looking unhappy

woe-ful (**wo͏ʷ–fəl**) adj. **1.** Very sad **2.** Making one sad: *a woeful lack of compassion* —**woefully** adv.

wok (**wɑk**) n. A bowl-shaped pot used in cooking Chinese food

woke (**wo͏ʷk**) v. Past tense of **wake**

wolf (**wʊlf**) n. **wolves** (**wʊlvz**) A wild animal of the dog family which hunts other animals in a group: *a pack of wolves*

wol-ver-ine (**wʊl–və–ri͏ʸn**) n. A North American flesh-eating mammal noted for its strength and cunning

wolves *Pl.* of **wolf**

wom-an (**wʊm–ən**) n. **women** (**wɪm–ən**) A female of the human race grown to adult years: *Who can find a virtuous woman for her price is far above rubies?* (Proverbs 31:10KJV). *A virtuous woman is a crown to her husband* (Proverbs 12:4KJV).

wom-an-ly (**wʊm–ən–li͏ʸ**) adj. Having the qualities suitable to a woman

womb (**wu͏ʷm**) n. **1.** Uterus **2.** A place where sthg. is generated or developed

wom-bat (**wɑm–bæt**) n. An Australian burrowing animal resembling a small bear

won (**wʌn**) v. Past tense and past part. of **win**

won-der (**wʌn–dər**) v. **1.** To be curious or in doubt: *I wonder when he will return.* **2.** To feel amazement: *I wonder how he can show his face around here after the shameful things he did.*

won-der n. **1.** A feeling of awe or admiration: *We were filled with wonder at the sight of the great waterfall.* **2.** A wonderful act or producer of such acts: *The heavens praise your wonders, O Lord* (Psalm 89:5). **3. it's a wonder**

(that) It's surprising: *It's a wonder he survived such a terrible accident.*

won-der-ful (**wʌn–dər–fəl**) adj. Full of wonder; amazing; marvelous: *Give thanks to the Lord: make known among the nations what he has done... Tell of all his wonderful works* (1 Chronicles 16:8). *He [Jesus] shall be called Wonderful Counselor, Mighty God, Everlasting Father, Prince of Peace* (Isaiah 9:6).

won-drous (**wʌn–drəs**) adj. Wonderful; marvelous —**wondrously** adv.

wont (**wo͏ʷnt**) adj. Accustomed to doing sthg.

wont n. Habit

won't (**wo͏ʷnt**) v. Short for **will not**: *I won't do it.*

woo (**wu͏ʷ**) v. **wooed 1.** To try to win the love of someone **2.** To try to gain success, support, etc.

wood (**wʊd**) n. The hard part of a tree, esp. when cut for use in building or for fuel

wood-chuck (**wʊd–tʃʌk**) n. A marmot of eastern North America, having a chunky body and brown, bristly coat; also called a **ground hog**

wood-ed (**wʊd–əd**) adj. Covered with growing trees

wood-en (**wʊd–ən**) adj. **1.** Made of wood **2.** Stiff and unnatural: *a wooden translation* **3.** Clumsy; awkward

wood-land (**wʊd–lənd**) n. Land covered with trees

wood-peck-er (**wʊd–pɛk–ər**) n. A type of bird that pecks holes in the bark of trees in search of insects

woods (**wʊdz**) n. **1.** A place where trees grow, smaller than a forest **2. out of the woods** Clear of danger or difficulty

wood-wind (**wʊd–wɪnd**) n. Any of the wind instruments of an orchestra made of wood, as an oboe, clarinet, flute, etc.

wood-y (**wʊd–i͏ʸ**) adj. **-ier, -iest 1.** Consisting of or containing wood **2.** Like wood: *This fruit has a woody texture. It's not juicy.*

wooer (**wu͏ʷ–ər**) n. One who woos

wool (**wʊl**) n. **1.** The soft, thick, and often curly hair of some animals, esp. sheep, used to make yarn, cloth, and clothing **2.** The thread or cloth made from this **3.** Soft material from plants, such as cotton before it is

spun: *cotton wool* **4. pull the wool over someone's eyes** To trick someone or hide the facts from him/ her

wool-ly (wʊl–iʸ) adj. **-lier, -liest 1.** Covered with wool or wool-like hair **2.** Like wool —**woolliness** n.

woo-zy (wuʷ–ziʸ) adj. **-zier, -ziest** Dizzy; dazed —**wooziness** n.

word (wɜrd) n. **1.** One or more sounds expressing an idea, object, or action, etc. and forming one of the basic elements of speech **2.** This represented by letters or symbols: **3.** The Holy Bible: *Man does not live on bread alone, but on every word that comes from the mouth of God* (Matthew 4:4). *Blessed are those who hear the word of God and keep it* (Luke 11:28). *Faith comes by hearing the message, and the message is heard by the word of Christ* (Romans 10:17). *Let the word of Christ dwell in you richly* (Colossians 3:16). **4.** A short conversation: *Can I have a word with you?* **5.** A brief message: *An anxious heart weighs a man down, but a kind word cheers him up* (Proverbs 12:25). **6.** News: *My brother sent word that he had survived the accident.* **7.** A solemn promise: *He gave his word that he would never do it again.* **8.** An order: *When I give the word, start the music.* **9.** A rumor: *Word has it that he will soon resign.* **10.** A quarrel: *They had a few words.*

Word (wɜrd) n. Refers to Jesus Christ: *In the beginning was the word and the word was with God, and the word was God. He was with God in the beginning. Through him all things were made; without him nothing was made that has been made. The word became flesh and lived for a while among us. We have seen his glory, the glory of the one and only Son who came from the Father full of grace and truth* (John 1:1-3,14).

wore (wɔr) v. Past tense of **wear**

work (wɜrk) n. **1.** Physical or mental effort or exertion, esp. with a special purpose: *There are many kinds of work: construction, industrial, clerical, medical, agricultural, mechanical, to mention but a few./If a man will not work, he shall not eat* (2 Thessalonians 3:10). **2.** Righteous deeds: *The work of God is this: to believe in the One [Jesus] he has sent [to be the Savior*

of the world] (John 6:29). *By grace you have been saved through faith — and this not from yourselves, it is the gift of God, not of works, so that no one can boast* (Ephesians 2:8,9). *Not by works of righteousness that we have done, but according to his [God's] mercy, he saved us [from the eternal punishment we all deserve]* (Titus 3:5). **3. a work of art** An object produced by painting, writing, etc.: *the works of Shakespeare (=plays and poems)* —see also WORKS

work v. **1.** To be active or use effort or power: *She's been working in the garden all day./This machine works by electricity.* **2.** To be employed: *My father works in a factory.* **3.** To function in the proper way: *Does this light work?* **4.** To reach a position or condition by small movements: *He gradually worked his way to the front of the crowd.* **5.** To produce: *I think a long vacation would work wonders for your health.*

work-er (wɜrk–ər) n. **1.** A person who works **2.** A hard worker: *Bob is a real worker; he gets more done than anyone else.*

work-man (wɜrk–mən) n. **-men** A man who works with his hands, esp. in a particular skill or trade: *The workmen are hard at work on the drainage system.*

work-man-ship (wɜrk–mən–ʃɪp) n. Skill in making things: *Look at the workmanship in this old table. /spir. For we [Christians] are God's workmanship, created in Christ Jesus to do good works, which God prepared in advance for us to do* (Ephesians 2:10).

work-out (wɜrk–aʊt) n. *infml.* A period of bodily exercise and training

works (wɜrks) n. **1.** The moving parts of a machine **2.** An industrial place of work: *boat works*

work-shop (wɜrk–ʃɑp) n. **1.** A room or building where things are produced, repairs are made, etc. **2.** A class of students or professionals meeting to study some subject: *a management workshop*

world (wɜrld) n. **1.** The earth and everything in it: *God says, "The world is mine and all that is in it"* (Psalm 50:12). *Jesus prayed, "And now, Father, glorify me in your presence with the glory I had with you before the world began"*

(John 17:5). **2.** The people in the world: *For God so loved the world that he gave his one and only Son, that whoever believes in him shall not perish but have eternal life* (John 3:16). **3.** The evils of this world; pleasures of this world; money and the things money can buy: *Do not love the world or anything in the world. If anyone loves the world, the love of the Father is not in him. For everything in the world — the cravings of sinful man, the lust of his eyes, and the boasting of what he has and does — comes not from the Father but from the world* (1 John 2:15,16). *What good will it be for a man if he gains the whole world, yet forfeits his soul?* (Matthew 16:26). *Seek first the kingdom of God and His righteousness* (Matthew 6:33). *Set your minds on things above, not on earthly things* (Colossians 3:2). **4.** A particular part of the earth or of life on earth: *the New World* (=*the western hemisphere*) **5.** A particular area of human interest or activity: *the world of football* **6.** A very great amount: *The fresh air and sunshine did him a world of good.* **7. a world beater** A person or thing that surpasses all others of like kind

world-ly (wɜrld–liʸ) adj. **-lier, -liest 1.** Of the material world: *The fire destroyed all my worldly possessions.* **2.** Concerned with the ways of society, esp. social advantage; not spiritual —**worldliness** n.

world-wide (wɜrld–waɪd) adj. Extended or spread throughout the world —**worldwide** adv.

worm (wɜrm) n. **1.** Any of the long, slender, soft-bodied legless creeping animals, such as earthworms, roundworms, tapeworms, etc. **2.** *fig.* A worthless, contemptible person

worm v. **1.** To move or advance like a worm: *He wormed himself through the crowd.* **2.** *fig.* To advance politically, socially, etc. by devious means: *He wormed his way into a top position in the company.*

worm-wood (wɜrm–wʊd) n. **1.** A type of plant with a bitter taste, formerly used as a remedy for worms, now used mostly in making absinthe, a green, bitter liqueur **2.** Sthg. bitter or grievous

worn (wɔrn) v. Past part. of **wear**

worn–out (wɔrn–aʊt) adj. **1.** Used until no longer fit for use: *worn-out shoes* **2.** Very tired; unable to work anymore: *After fighting the forest fire all day, the worn-out men were happy to see help arrive.*

wor-ried (wɜr–iʸd) adj. Tormented with disturbing thoughts; overly concerned

wor-ri-some (wɜr–iʸ–səm) adj. Causing worry or anxiety

wor-ry (wɜr–iʸ) v. **-ried, -rying** To be or cause to be overly concerned or anxious; to torment oneself with disturbing thoughts: *Jesus said, "Do not worry about your life, what you will eat or drink, or about your body, what you will wear. Who of you by worrying can add a single hour to his life? But seek first the kingdom of God and his righteousness, and all these things will be given to you as well. Therefore, do not worry about tomorrow, for tomorrow will worry about itself. Each day has enough trouble of its own"* (Matthew 6:25,27,33,34).

worse (wɜrs) adj. **1.** Comparative of **bad** or **ill**; bad or ill in a greater degree **2.** More unfavorable or injurious **3.** In poorer health or condition —opposite BETTER

worse adv. Comparative of **ill** or **bad 1.** In a poorer or less respectable way: *You're behaving worse than an animal.* **2.** More painful: *My head hurts worse than before.*

worse n. A poorer condition: *The sick man took a turn for the worse.*

wors-en (wɜrs–ən) v. To become worse: *The patient's condition worsened during the night.*

wor-ship (wɜr–ʃɪp) n. **1.** The act of showing great reverence, honor, respect, etc., esp. to God or a god: *Come, let us bow down in worship* (Psalm 95:6). **2.** A religious service: *We attended early worship.* **3.** *BrE.* A title of honor in addressing a magistrate or mayor (usu. preceded by "Your" or "His" or "Her"

worship v. **-shiped, -shiping** or **-shipped, -shipping 1.** To show great reverence: *God is spirit, and his worshipers must worship in spirit and in truth* (John 4:23,24). **2.** To attend a church service: *We should worship regularly.* —**worshiper** n.

worst (wɜrst) adj. Superl. of **ill** or **bad**; the most corrupt, bad, or evil; the most painful, unpleasant, etc.: *This is the worst fire around here in many years.*

worst adv. Superl. of ill or of **bad** or **badly; to the greatest degree of "bad":** *She is the worst-dressed actress in Hollywood.* —compare BEST

worst n. The one that is worst; the greatest degree of "bad": *I've heard a lot of bad music, but this is the worst.*

wor-sted (wʊs–təd/ wɜr–stəd) n. A fabric made from finely twisted wool yarn

worth (wɜrθ) prep. 1. Equal in value to: *This house is worth $125,000./ A wife of noble character, who can find? She is worth far more than rubies* (Proverbs 31:10). 2. Deserving: *The Apostle Paul wrote to fellow Christians in Rome saying, "Our present sufferings are not worth comparing with the glory that will be revealed in us [in heaven]"* (Romans 8:18).

worth n. Value: *These old coins are of little or no worth.*

worth-less (wɜrθ–ləs) adj. 1. Of no value: *Wealth is worthless in the day of wrath* (Proverbs 11:4). 2. Contemptible

worth-while (wɜrθ–waɪl) adj. Worth doing; worth the trouble taken

wor-thy (wɜr–ðiʸ) adj. -thier, -thiest 1. Having worth or merit: *We pray ... that you may live a life worthy of the Lord and may please him in every way* (Colossians 1:10). 2. Deserving: *Great is the Lord and most worthy of praise* (1 Chronicles 16:25). 3. –worthy (a) Fit or safe to travel in or on: *Is this boat seaworthy?* (b) Deserving: *praiseworthy* —**worthily** adv. —**worthiness** n.

would (wʊd) v. 1. Past tense and past part. of **will:** *I would have done it yesterday if I could.* 2. Used as an auxiliary to express (a) Preference: *I would rather go swimming than hiking on a day like this.* (b) A wish or intent: *I would put an end to crime if I could.* (c) Habitual action: *They would meet often for lunch.* (d) A possibility: *He said it would rain today.* (e) A probability: *He would have won the race if he hadn't tripped.* (f) A request: *Would you close the window, please?* 3. Used instead of **will** with a past tense verb: *They finally found someone who would (=who was willing to) take the job.*

would-be (wʊd–biʸ) adj. Desiring, professing, or intended to be

wouldn't (wʊd–ənt) v. Contraction of **would not**

would've (wʊd–əv) Contraction of **would have:** *I would've gone if I could have.*

wound (wuʷnd) n. 1. An injury in which the skin is broken, esp. when caused by a weapon 2. An injury to one's feelings or reputation: *a wound to his pride*

wound v. To inflict a wound: *The shot wounded him in the shoulder.* NOTE: People get **wounded** in war or fighting and **injured** in accidents. Both words are more serious than **hurt:** *Tom was seriously wounded by an enemy bullet. John was badly injured in a car accident. I hurt my knee when I fell down.*

wound (waʊnd) v. Past tense and past part. of **wind** (waɪnd)

wove (woʷv) v. Past tense of **weave**

wo-ven (woʷ–vən) v. Past part. of **weave**

wow (waʊ) interj. An exclamation of surprise, amazement, or pleasure

wow v. To gain an enthusiastic response from: *The dancer hoped to wow the audience with his performance.*

wow n. An extraordinary success

wrack (ræk) n. Seaweed cast up on the shore

wraith (reʸθ) n. **wraiths** (reʸθs/reʸðz) An apparition of a living person, supposed to be a sign that he will die soon

wran-gle (ræŋ–gəl) v. -gled, -gling 1. To have a noisy, angry argument or quarrel 2. To herd cattle or horses in the western US —**wrangler** n.

wrangle n. A noisy, angry argument

wrap (ræp) v. -pp- 1. To cover by folding sthg. around: *They were busy wrapping Christmas presents.* 2. **wrap up (a)** To wear warm clothing: *We need to wrap up well in cold weather.* (b) *infml.* To complete a meeting or business deal: *Let's try to wrap up this meeting by five o'clock.* 3. **wrapped up in** Giving complete attention to: *He's so wrapped up in his work, he is ruining his marriage.*

wrap-per (ræp–ər) n. Paper used as a cover for sthg.: *a gum wrapper*

wrap-ping (ræp–ɪŋ) n. Sthg. used to wrap sthg. in

wrap-up (ræp–əp) n. 1. Summary; conclusion 2. Final event

wrath (ræθ) n. Violent rage; fury: *God did not appoint us to suffer wrath but to receive salvation through our Lord Jesus Christ* (1 Thessalonians 5:9). —**wrathful** adj. —**wrathfully** adv.

wreak (riᵛk) v. To inflict: *to wreak vengeance on someone*

wreath (riᵛθ) n. **wreaths** (riᵛðz/riᵛθs) **1.** A usu. circular garland of flowers or leaves, given at a funeral **2.** Sthg. similar placed on someone's shoulders or head after his or her victory

wreck (rɛk) v. **1.** To destroy accidentally, as by a collision: *The ship was wrecked on the rocks.* **2.** To tear down or take apart: *They wrecked the old apartment buildings that were dangerous to live in.* **3.** To bring to a state of ruin: *All our plans were wrecked because of the company's failure.*

wreck n. **1.** The remains of sthg., as a ship lost at sea or (partly) destroyed on rocks **2.** A person or thing in the state of ruin: *He's a nervous wreck after his tragic experience.*

wreck-age (rɛk–ɪdʒ) n. The remains of sthg. wrecked

wreck-er (rɛk–ər) n. **1.** A person or thing that demolishes **2.** A tow truck

wren (rɛn) n. A very small, usu. brown, songbird

wrench (rɛntʃ) v. **1.** To pull hard with a twisting motion: *He wrenched the doorknob off the locked door.* **2.** To twist and damage a part of the body: *She wrenched her ankle.*

wrench n. **1.** *AmE.* A tool for gripping and turning a bolt or a nut **2.** A sudden violent twist **3.** A painful twist, as of an ankle **4.** Sudden and sharp emotional strain

wrest (rɛst) v. To take away by force: *The policeman wrested the gun from the terrorist.*

wres-tle (rɛs–əl) v. **-tled, -tling 1.** To fight by attempting to throw one's opponent to the ground **2.** To struggle to solve or master sthg.: *to wrestle with a problem* —**wrestler** n.

wretch (rɛtʃ) n. **1.** A miserable, pitiable person **2.** A worthless or contemptible person

wretch-ed (rɛtʃ–əd) adj. **1.** Very bad; hateful: *a wretched person* **2.** Miserable: *wretched weather*

wrig-gle (rɪg–əl) n. **-gled, -gling** To move with a short twisting movement: *The worm wriggled its way across the path.* —**wriggle** n. A wriggling move-ment —**wriggler** n.

-wright (–raɪt) comb. form Someone who writes or makes something: *a playwright, a shipwright, a wheelwright*

wring (rɪŋ) v. **wrung** (rʌŋ), **wringing 1.** To twist and squeeze in order to remove liquid: *She wrung out the clothes by hand.* **2.** To twist a neck in order to cause death: *He wrung the chicken's neck.* **3.** *fig.* To squeeze sthg. like a confession out of someone: *The police wrung the truth out of him.* **4. wringing wet** Very wet

wring-er (rɪŋ–ər) n. An old-fashioned machine with two rollers between which clothes are squeezed to remove water

wrin-kle (rɪŋ–kəl) n. **1.** A small crease, as in some cloth or one's skin: *There were several wrinkles in his coat./ His face had very few wrinkles for a man his age.* **2.** A slight problem: *This is basically a good plan but there are a few wrinkles to be ironed out.* (=some slight details to be corrected or improved)

wrin-kle v. **-kled, -kling** To cause to form into lines or folds: *He wrinkled up his nose at the bad suggestion.*

wrist (rɪst) n. The joint by which the hand is joined to the arm

writ (rɪt) n. A document by which sbdy. is summoned or required to do sthg.

write (raɪt) v. **wrote** (roʷt), **written** (rɪt–ən) **1.** To form letters, symbols, or characters on a surface with an implement such as a pen or pencil **2.** To put into writing: *She's writing a letter to her mother.* **3.** To work as a writer by profession: *She has written many books.*

writ-er (raɪt–ər) n. A person who writes, esp. as a profession

writhe (raɪð) v. **writhed, writhing 1.** To twist one's body about, as in pain **2** To suffer because of great shame or embarrassment: *writhing under the vicious verbal attack on his character* **3.** To wriggle: *the writhing snakes*

writ-ing (raɪt–ɪŋ) n. **1.** The activity of writing, esp. books: *Writing is his profession.* **2.** Handwriting: *I can't read the doctor's writing.*

writ-ten (rɪt–ən) v. Past part. of **write**

wrong (rɔŋ) adj. **1.** Not correct: *He drove off in*

the wrong direction. **2.** Of a person, mistaken: *I disagree. I think you are wrong about that.* **3.** Evil; against moral standards: *It is altogether wrong to show favoritism to people because of their race or color.* **4.** Of a person, not suitable: *He is the wrong person for this job.* **5.** Out of order; not working properly: *There's sthg. wrong with the phone.*

wrong adv. Incorrectly or badly: *I think I spelled her name wrong./ You've done this assignment wrong. You'll have to do it over again.*

wrong n. **1.** Sthg. that is wrong: *Hatred stirs up dissension; but love covers over all wrongs* (Proverbs 10:12). *It [love] is not easily angered, it keeps no record of wrongs* (1 Corinthians 13:5). *Do not follow the crowd in doing wrong* (Exodus 23:2). *It is unthinkable that God would do wrong* (Job 34:12). *Make sure that nobody pays back wrong for wrong, but always be kind to each other and to everyone else* (1 Thessalonians 5:15). **2.** The condition or state of being mistaken: *in the wrong*

wrong v. To treat someone unjustly: *You wronged him by accusing him of such a terrible thing.*

wrong-do-ing (rɔŋ–duʷ–ŋ) n. Sin: *All wrong-doing is sin* (1 John 5:17). —**wrongdoer** n.

wrong-ful (rɔŋ–fəl) adj. Not lawful or fair —**wrongfully** adv. *wrongfully accused*

wrong-ly (rɔŋ–liʸ) adv. Incorrectly: *The letter was wrongly addressed.*

wrote (roʷt) v. Past tense of **write**

wrought (rɔt) adj. Beaten out or shaped by hammering

wrought v. (old use) Made, esp. by hand: *This ironwork was wrought by the local blacksmith.*

wrought iron (rɔt aɪ–ərn) n. A type of iron containing only small amounts of other materials, which rusts less and welds more easily than steel

wrought up (rɔt ʌp) adj. Very excited or perturbed

wrung (rʌŋ) v. Past tense and past part. of **wring**

wry (raɪ) adj. **wrier, wriest 1.** Twisted into an expression of disgust or disappointment: *a wry grin* **2.** Bitterly ironic: *wry humor* **3.** Twisted or bent out of shape —**wryness** n.

wt. *abbr.* Weight

WW I *abbr.* World War I

WW II *abbr.* World War II

X, x (ɛks) n. **1.** The 24th letter of the English alphabet **2.** The Roman Numeral (number) for **10**

X chro-mo-some (ɛks kro^w–mə–so^{w}m) n. One of the tiny rods or threads in animal and plant cells that carries genes producing female characteristics

xe-no-pho-bi-a (zɛn-ə–fo^w–bi^y–ə) n. A strong dislike or distrust of foreigners —**xeno-phobic** adj.

Xe-rox (zɪər–ɑks/ zi^y–) n. *trademark* **1.** Process for making photographic copies of sthg. printed or written, on a special electric copying machine **2.** A copy made in this way —**Xerox** v.

X-mas n. *infml.* Short for **Christmas**, the Christian festival (celebrated December 25th) commemorating the birth of Jesus Christ who came into the world to save sin-ners, died for our sins and rose again —see JESUS CHRIST

X-rat-ed (ɛks–re^y–təd) adj. A rating used in the US for immoral movies that are not allowed for children under 17

X-ray (ɛks–re^y) n. **1.** A powerful unseen beam of light which can pass through substances which are solid, and which is used esp. for photographing medical conditions inside the body **2.** A photograph taken with an X-ray machine

X-ray v. To photograph, examine, or treat by means of X-rays: *They x-rayed his back to see if it was broken.*

xy-lo-phone (zaɪ–lə–fo^{w}n) n. A musical instrument consisting of a set of flat wooden bars of various lengths which produce different musical notes when struck with small wooden hammers

Y, y (waɪ) n. The 25th letter of the English alphabet

yacht (yɑt) n. **1.** A light sailing-boat, esp. one built for racing **2.** A large vessel used for pleasure, often motor-driven

yacht-ing (yɑt–ɪŋ) n. The act, practice, or sport of sailing or racing in a yacht

Yah-weh (yɑ–weᵉ/–veᵉ) n. The ancient Hebrew name for God, corresponding to Jehovah

yak (yæk) n. A long-haired type of ox found in Tibet

yak v. **-ked, -king** infml. To talk continuously: She never stops yakking.

yam (yæm) n. **1.** A tropical climbing plant, the root of which is eaten as a vegetable and used as a staple food **2.** A sweet potato

yank (yæŋk) v. To give a sudden, sharp pull: She yanked the dress off the hanger.

yank n. A strong, sudden pull; a jerk

Yan-kee (yæŋ–kiᵉ) also **Yank** n. **1.** An inhabitant of the United States of America **2.** An inhabitant of the northeastern states in the US.

yap (yæp) v. **-pp- 1.** Esp. of dogs, to bark: The neighbors' dog kept yapping all night long. **2.** To talk noisily and foolishly; gab: What are you yapping about? —**yap** n.

yard (yɑrd) n. **1.** A unit of length that is 0.9144 meters; three feet; 36 inches **2.** An enclosed or partly enclosed area near or around a building or group of buildings **3.** An enclosed area used for a special purpose or business: a railroad yard/ lumber yard/ brickyard

yard-age (yɑrd–ɪdʒ) n. Amount in yards

yard goods (yɑrd gʊdz) n. Materials, such as cloth, sold by the yard

yard-stick (yɑrd stɪk) n. **1.** A measuring stick one yard (36 inches) long **2.** A standard for making a judgment or comparison: Honesty is a reliable yardstick of character.

yarn (yɑrn) n. **1.** Wool, cotton, etc., spun into thread **2.** One of the threads of a rope **3.** A

SPELLING NOTE:
Words having the sound /y/ may be spelled with **u-**, like in **use**, or **eu-**, like in European.

story, esp. a long unlikely one

yawn (yɔn/yɑn) v. **1.** Unintentionally to open the mouth wide and breathe in deeply, as when tired or bored **2.** Of large holes, to be wide open: a yawning cavern —**yawn** n.

Y chro-mo-some (waɪ kroʷ–mə–soʷm) n. One of the tiny rods or threads in animal and plant cells that carries genes that produce male characteristics

yd. written abbr. for yard or yards

ye (yiᵉ) pron. Old use for you

yea (yeᵉ) adv. **1.** Yes, used in voting **2.** More than this: He's a good man, yea, even a great one.

yeah (yɛə) adv. infml. Yes (Also used in oral voting)

year (yɪər) n. **1.** A period of 365.25 days required for one revolution of the earth around the sun, divided into 12 months beginning on January 1st and ending on December 31st **2.** Any period of 365 days: She's worked here for three years. **3.** A period of time other than a calendar year: In this university, the school year lasts nine months, ending in May.

year-ling (yɪər–lɪŋ) n. An animal between one and two years old

year-ly (yɪər–liᵉ) adj. Every year or once each year: Workers in our company can expect a yearly raise in pay. —**yearly** adv.

yearn (yɜrn) v. To be filled with great longing or desire

yearn-ing (yɜrn–ɪŋ) n. An eager longing

yeast (yiᵉst) n. A form of very small plant life which causes fermentation, used in brewing beer and to make the dough rise in the baking of bread —**yeasty** adj.

yell (yɛl) v. To shout loudly: Stop yelling. I can hear you.

yell n. **1.** A shout **2.** A cheer used, esp. to encourage an athletic team

yel-low (yɛl–oʷ) adj. **1.** One of the three primary colors; the color of butter or egg yolk or ripe lemons: Yellow and red paint mixed together produces orange; blue mixed with yellow produces green. **2.** Of a person, cowardly: He runs away when there's any danger; he's yellow. —**yellow** n.

yellow fever (yɛl–oʷ fiᵉ–vər) n. An acute in-

fectious fever, chiefly in the tropics, transmitted by a mosquito and characterized by yellowness of the skin, vomiting, etc.

yel-low-ish (yɛl–oʷ–ɪʃ) adj. Somewhat yellow

yellow jacket (yɛl–oʷ dʒæk–ət) n. A wasp with a black abdomen spotted or banded with yellow

yelp (yɛlp) v. To utter a sharp, quick, shrill cry: *The frightened dog yelped and ran away.* —**yelp** n. *The dog let out a yelp.*

yen (yɛn) n. **1.** A unit of money in Japan **2.** A longing; a yearning

yen v. To have a longing for sbdy. or sthg.

yeo-man (yoʷ–mən) n. **1.** A petty officer in the US Navy, having chiefly clerical duties **2.** In Britain, a farmer who cultivates his own land **3.** Formerly, an attendant or official in a royal household

yeoman adj. **1.** Staunch, valiant: *yeoman service* **2.** Of or pertaining to a yeoman

yes (yɛs) adv. **1.** An expression of agreement; it is so; the statement is correct **2.** What you request or command will be done

yes n. An affirmative reply

ye-shi-va or **yesh-i-va** (yə–ʃiʸ–və) n. **1.** A Jewish day school providing religious and secular instruction **2.** A seminary for rabbinical students

yes–man (yɛs–mæn) n. A person who endorses uncritically every opinion or proposal of a superior

yes-ter-day (yɛs–tər–deʸ/–diʸ) n. **1.** The day before today **2.** Only a short time ago **3.** In the past: *Jesus Christ is the same yesterday and today and forever* (Hebrews 13:8).

yet (yɛt) adv. **1.** By now; by this time: *Has he arrived yet?* **2.** Before it is over; before the matter is decided: *He may win yet.* **3. yet another** Another one in addition

yet conj. **1.** But; nevertheless: *They were surrounded, yet they would not surrender.*

yield (yiʸld) v. **1.** To surrender; give up: *They yielded to his demands.* **2.** To produce a crop: *How many bushels of corn will this field yield this year?* **3.** Of traffic, to allow other traffic to have the right of way **4.** To allow another to speak first, as in a debate

yield n. The amount yielded or produced; the quantity obtained

yip (yɪp) v. **-pp-** To bark sharply

yip n. A sharp bark

yip-pee (yɪp–iʸ) interj. An exclamation of excitement, success, etc.

yo-del (yoʷ–dəl) v. To sing, switching frequently from an ordinary to a high-pitched voice and back again —**yodeler** or **yodeller** n. One who yodels

yo-ga (yoʷ–gə) n. **1.** A Hindu system of meditation and self-control designed to produce mystical experience and spiritual insight **2.** A system of physical exercises and breathing control

yo-gi (yoʷ–giʸ) n. A devotee of yoga

yo-gurt or **yo-ghurt** (yoʷ–gərt) n. A food prepared from milk that has been thickened by the action of certain bacteria

yoke (yoʷk) n. **1.** A wooden frame joining oxen when pulling a plow, cart, etc. **2.** A pair, as of oxen **3.** Sthg. that joins together **4.** A frame placed across the shoulders for carrying a pail or other load at each end **5.** Slavery; dominion: *It is for freedom that Christ has set us free. Stand firm, then, and do not let yourselves be burdened again by a yoke of slavery* (Galatians 5:1).

yoke v. **yoked, yoking 1.** To put a yoke on **2.** To attach an ox or other draft animal to a plow **3.** To join, esp. to marry: *Do not be yoked together with unbelievers. For what do righteousness and wickedness have in common? Or what fellowship can light have with darkness?* (2 Corinthians 6:14).

yo-kel (yoʷ–kəl) n. A country man or boy, used insultingly

yolk (yoʷk) n. The yellow part of an egg

Yom Kip-pur (yɑm kɪp–ər/ –kɪ–puər) (from *yom* "day" + *kippur* "atonement") A Jewish holiday observed in September or October with fasting and prayer, as a day of atonement

yon (yɑn) adv. Yonder

yon-der (yɑn–dər) adv. At or to that place: *He lives over yonder.*

yonder adj. **1.** More distant: *the yonder side of the mountain* **2.** Being at a distance within view: *yonder hills*

yore (yɔr) n. Former times

you (yuʷ) pron. **1.** The person or persons

spoken or written to; used as the *sing.* or *pl.* subject or object of a verb: *You are loved./God loves you.* **2.** A person; anyone, everyone: *You never can tell.*

you'd (yuᵂd) Contraction of **(a) you had (b) you would**

you'll (yuᵂl) Contraction of **(a) you will (b) you shall**

young (yʌŋ) adj. **younger** (yʌŋ-gər), **youngest** (yʌŋ-gəst) **1.** In early life **2.** In the early stage of development **3.** Concerning or characteristic of young people

young n. The offspring of animals

young-ster (yʌŋ-stər) n. A young person; a child

your (yɔr/ yər) adj., determ. Possessive form of **you 1.** Of or relating to you: *your father/ your school* (=the school you attend) **2.** Belonging to you: *your hand/your book*

you're (yuər/yɔr/yər) Contraction of **you are**

yours (yɔrz/ yərz) pron. Possessive form of **you;** the one or ones belonging to you: *Is this book yours?*

your-self (yɔr-sɛlf/ yər-sɛlf) pron. **-selves** (-sɛlvz) **1.** Used as the object of a verb or after a preposition, when the person spoken of causes an action and is also affected by the same action: *Be careful, you'll hurt your-self./Are you all enjoying yourselves?* **2.** Used to make you stronger: *You yourself can do it./ You and Ann will have to finish the work (by) yourselves.*

youth (yuᵂθ) n. **youths** (yuᵂðz/ yuᵂθs) **1.** The period of life between childhood and maturity **2.** A young person, esp, a young male **3.** Young people considered as a group: *the youth of today*

youth-ful (yuᵂθ-fəl) adj. **1.** Of or having the qualities typical of youth: *youthful energy* **2.** Young or seeming young: *She's a youthful sixty-five.* **3.** Fresh; vigorous **—youthfully** adv. **—youthfulness** n.

you've (yuᵂv) Contraction of **you have**

yowl (yaʊl) n. A distressed howl, as of an animal

yowl v. To utter a yowl

yo-yo (yoᵂ–yoᵂ) n. A type of toy consisting of a small reel which spins up and down on a string

yr. *Abbr.* Year

yrs. *Abbr.* Years

yuc-ca (yʌk–ə) n. A plant having white bell-like flowers and stiff spiky leaves

yule-tide (yuᵂl–taɪd) n. Christmas: *Yuletide greetings (on a Christmas card)* **—see** CHRISTMAS

Z, z (ziᵞ) n. The 26th and last letter of the English alphabet

za-ny (zeᵞ–niᵞ) adj. **-nier, -niest** Crazy; clown-like

zap (zæp) v. **-pp- 1.** *Slang* To kill, shoot, or attack, esp. with sudden speed

zeal (ziᵞl) n. Eagerness; enthusiasm: *Never be lacking in zeal, but keep your spiritual fervor, serving the Lord* (Romans 12:11).

zeal-ot (zɛl–ət) n. One who shows zeal, esp. to a fanatic extent

zeal-ous (zɛl–əs) adj. Very eager; enthusiastic: *Do not let your heart envy sinners, but always be zealous for the fear of the Lord* (Proverbs 23:17). *It is fine to be zealous, provided the purpose is good...* (Galatians 4:18). **—zealously** adv. **—zealousness** n.

ze-bra (ziᵞ–brə) n. An African wild animal of the horse family having a body covered with black and white stripes

ze-bu (ziᵞ–buʷ) n. A domesticated Asiatic bovine animal having a large hump over the shoulders

Zech-a-ri-ah (zɛk–ə–raɪ–ə) n. **1.** A masculine name **2.** An Old Testament prophet who joined the prophet Haggai in arousing the Jews to rebuild the temple at Jerusalem in the 6th century B. C. His prophecies included the coming of the Messiah (Jesus) and the dawning of a brighter day for the Jewish people. **3.** The book of the Old Testament that he wrote and which bears his name

zed (zɛd) *British* The letter Z or z

Zen (zɛn) n. A Japanese Buddhist sect that teaches self-discipline, meditation, and attainment of enlightenment through direct intuitive insight

ze-na-na (zə–nɑn–ə) n. In India, the part of the house in which the women in a high-caste family were formerly secluded

ze-nith (ziᵞ–nəθ) n. **1.** The point of the heavens which is exactly overhead **2.** The highest point of achievement, hope, etc.: *at the zenith of his career*

Zeph-a-ni-ah (zɛf–ə–naɪ–ə) n. **1.** A masculine name **2.** An Old Testament prophet who prophesied during the reign of Josiah, king of Judah, during the 7th century B. C. **3.** The book of the Old Testament, written by the prophet Zephaniah, announcing the coming judgment on the sinful people of Judah because of their corruption and spiritual blindness, and sounding a call to repentance. He also foretells the future glory of Israel, when Jehovah will deliver his people, and cause them to become famous throughout the earth.

zeph-yr (zɛf–ər) n. A gentle breeze

ze-ro (ziᵞ–roʷ) n. **-ros** or **-roes 1.** Nothing, or the sign "0" that stands for it **2.** The point between (+) and (-) on a scale **3.** Temperature, pressure, etc. that corresponds to zero on a scale: *On the Centigrade scale water freezes at zero degrees and it was five below zero last night.* NOTE: The symbol "0" is often pronounced "oh" (oʷ), esp. in giving an address or a phone number: *I live at Five Oh Nine (=509) East Main Street.*

zest (zɛst) n. Eagerness; great enjoyment: *His zest for life is amazing in sbdy. who is nearly eighty years old.*

zig-zag (zɪg–zæg) n. A line that turns sharply right, then left, then right again, and so on **—zigzag** v. **-gg-** *The road zigzagged up the mountainside.*

zilch (zɪltʃ) n. Zero or nothing

zil-lion (zɪl–yən) adj. An extremely high number: *There must be a zillion grains of sand in the Sahara Desert.*

zinc (zɪŋk) n. A bluish-white metal that is a simple substance (element) used in the production of other metals and to cover wires, sheets, etc. to protect them against rust

zing (zɪŋ) n. **1.** A sharp, high-pitched humming noise **2.** Energy; vitality

zing v. To move with zing

zin-ni-a (zɪn–iᵞ–ə/zɪn–yə/ziᵞn–yə) n. A daisy-like plant with bright colored flowers

zip (zɪp) v. **-pp- 1.** To open or close with or as with a zipper: *He zipped up his jacket and pulled the collar around his ears.* —opposite UNZIP **2.** To move at a very high speed:

zip n. **1.** A short, sharp sound like that of a bullet going through the air **2.** Vim, vigor, vitality, energy

zip code (zɪp koʷd) n. *AmE.* postcode *BrE.* A number that identifies each postal delivery area and enables mail to be delivered more quickly

zip-per (zɪp–ər) n. Also zip fastener *BrE.* A fastener made of two rows of metal or plastic teeth on a cloth tape with a sliding piece that draws them together, used for fastening clothes, bags, etc.

zip-py (zɪp–iʸ) adj. -pier, -piest Energetic; snappy; peppy

zith-er (zɪð–ər/zɪθ–) n. A stringed musical instrument played by plucking

zo-di-ac (zoʷd–iʸ–æk) n. 1. A somewhat imaginary belt in the heavens within which the sun, moon, and planets seem to travel and which is divided into twelve equal parts (signs of the zodiac) 2. A circular diagram of these signs, esp. used in astrology by people who believe in the influence of the stars upon people's lives NOTE: Use of the signs of the zodiac to tell the future is condemned by God: "Let no one be found among you who ... practices divination or sorcery ... (Deuteronomy 18:10.) Genesis 1:14 indicates that these were made by God and depict Christian life: "And God said, 'Let there be lights in the expanse of the sky to separate the day from the night, and let them serve as signs to mark seasons and days and years, and let them be lights in the expanse of the sky to give light on the earth.'" Only God knows the future: "Can you bind the beautiful Pleiades? Can you loose the cords of Orion? Can you bring forth the constellations in their seasons or lead out the Bear with its cubs? Do you know the laws of the heavens? Can you set up God's dominion over the earth?(Job 38:31-33) Even though the practice of astrology is sinful, God will also forgive this and all sins to those who repent and put their trust in Jesus as their Savior. —see ASTROLOGY

zom-bie (zɑm–biʸ) n. 1. A corpse supposedly reactivated by sorcery, but still dead 2. A person said to resemble this, who seems to have no mind or will 3. The snake god worshiped in voodoo ceremonies 4. A strong cocktail made from rum, several fruit juices, and liqueur

zone (zoʷn) n. An area or division with a particular feature or use: *time zone*

zone v. zoned, zoning To divide into zones: *This area is zoned for apartments only.* —zoning n.

zoo (zuʷ) n. A place where many kinds of wild animals are kept for exhibition and study

zo-ol-o-gist (zoʷ–ɑl–ə–dʒəst) n. One who studies animal life

zo-ol-o-gy (zoʷ–ɑl–ə–dʒiʸ) n. A science that deals with animal life

zoom (zuʷm) v. 1. Of an aircraft, to climb quickly upwards for a short time 2. *infml.* To drive very fast: *The police car zoomed past in pursuit of the robbers.* 3. Of a movie camera, to make a distant person or object look nearer without moving the camera, by use of a zoom lens: *The camera zoomed in on the bride's face.*

Zo-ro-as-tri-an-ism (zoʷ–roʷ–æs–triʸ–ən–ɪz–əm) n. The religion founded by Zoroaster in Persia about 600 B.C. It recognizes two creative powers, one good and one evil, includes the belief in life after death, and teaches the final triumph of good over evil. NOTE: Like all man-made religions it is a religion of salvation by good works and knows nothing of the grace of our Lord and Savior Jesus Christ

zuc-chi-ni (zʊ–kiʸ–niʸ) n. -ni or -nis A summer squash with smooth, cylindrical, dark green fruits

zwie-back (swiʸ–bæk/swaɪ–/zwiʸ–/–bɑk) n. A kind of bread thickly sliced and toasted until it is very dry

zy-mur-gy (zaɪ–mər–dʒiʸ) n. The branch of applied chemistry that deals with the use of fermentation in brewing

THE GRAMMATICAL SYSTEM OF ENGLISH

In this section we will examine the general pattern of English grammar. Later we will look at some of the points that are likely to cause problems for those who are learning English as a second or foreign language.

MAJOR GRAMMATICAL FEATURES OF ENGLISH

In English, each word or phrase in a sentence has a definite role in the message of that sentence. We generally speak of two kinds of words: content words and function words. Content words are nouns, verbs, adjectives, and adverbs. Function words are words that show relationships, but have no specific meaning of their own.

There are seven major grammatical features in English that show us what the role of a word is. These features help to establish the meaning of the sentence.

I. Inflection of <u>content</u> words (Parts of words added to other words according to grammatical rules):

    A. Plural of nouns: rat<u>s</u>, dog<u>s</u>, boss<u>es</u>

    B. Possessive of nouns: rat<u>'s</u>, dog<u>'s</u>, boss<u>'s</u>

    C. Third person singular of verbs: walk<u>s</u>, open<u>s</u>, bounce<u>s</u>
The -s suffix is used in forming the plural and the possessive of nouns and the third person singular of verbs. The pronunciation rule is as follows:
    When a noun or verb ends in one of the sounds called sibilants /s, z, ʃ, ʒ, tʃ, dʒ/ the -s suffix is pronounced /əz/. Ex: roses (roʷz-əz)
    When a noun or verb ends in a voiceless sound that is not a sibilant, it is pronounced /s/. Ex: hats (hæts)
    When a noun or verb ends in a voiced sound that is not a sibilant, it is pronounced /z/. Ex: drives (draɪvz)
    Irregular nouns do not form their plurals using the -s suffix although they do form their possessives this way.

    D. Past tense of verbs: talk<u>ed</u>, open<u>ed</u>, point<u>ed</u>

    E. Past participle of verbs: walk<u>ed</u>, spok<u>en</u>, ben<u>t</u>
The -ed suffix signals the past tense and the past participle of regular verbs. The pronunciation rule is as follows:
    When a verb ends in the sound /d/ or /t/, the -ed suffix is pronounced /əd/. Ex: wanted (**wɑnt**-əd)
    When a verb ends in a voiced sound other than /d/, the -ed is pronounced /d/. Ex: begged (bɛgd)
    When a verb ends in a voiceless sound other than /t/, the -ed is pronounced /t/. Ex: looked (lʊkt)

    F. Present participle of verbs: walk<u>ing</u>, sing<u>ing</u>
The present participle of a verb becomes the progressive verb phrase when

combined with the auxiliary verb "be". It may be used as either a noun or an adjective. Ex: <u>Walking</u> is good exercise./ The mother picked up her <u>crying</u> baby.

G. Comparative of adjectives and adverbs: happi<u>er</u>, fast<u>er</u>

H. Superlative of adjectives and adverbs: happi<u>est</u>, fast<u>est</u>
Adjectives and adverbs of more than two syllables generally form the comparatives and superlatives by using "more" and "most" rather than -er and -est. Ex: small, small<u>er</u>, small<u>est</u>/ beautiful, <u>more</u> beautiful, <u>most</u> beautiful

II. Function words
Function words like "a", "for", "and", and "which" form the framework of the sentence. The most common function words are:
A. Articles. Ex: a, an, the

B. Prepositions. Ex: on, in, at, to

C. Auxiliary verbs. Ex: be, do, have, can, may

D. Coordinating conjunctions. Ex: and, or

E. Indefinite pronouns. Ex: some, any

F. Reflexives. Ex: himself, myself

G. Interjections. Ex: Oh!, Help!

H. Personal pronouns. Ex: she, I

I. Subordinating conjunctions. Ex: because, if

J. Interrogative pronouns. Ex: <u>Who</u> is that man?

K. Relative pronouns. Ex: The boy <u>who</u> threw the ball is a good player.

L. Complementizers. Ex: <u>That</u> John came early did not surprise us.

Function words receive their meaning from the use they have in the sentence. There are few of them and they are used frequently. Words such as "the," "in,"and the auxiliary verbs "be," "do," "may," etc. occur many times on every page in English. They are usually unstressed in spoken language which makes them hard for the non-English speaker to identify.

III. Word order
English word order is relatively fixed and differences in word order often signal differences in meaning and grammatical function. A change in word order often causes other changes in the structure of the sentence.

IV. Derivation (The way in which the basic units of meaning are put together to

form words)

Knowledge of the prefixes and suffixes is a great help in increasing one's vocabulary in English. The various prefixes and suffixes also help identify the functional or grammatical use of a word.

The language learner also has to learn to distinguish between suffixes and prefixes and syllables that only look like suffixes or prefixes. Ex: disgraceful = disgrace + ful, not dis + graceful

V. Concord or agreement

Concord occurs in:

A. The agreement of the subject with the verb in the present tense. Ex: He walks to school./ We walk to school.

B. The agreement of singular and plural forms of demonstrative pronouns with the nouns they modify. Ex: this cup/ these cups

C. The agreement of the relative pronoun with the noun it represents. Ex: the woman who/ the cup which

VI. Government

Different functions in a clause govern (cause changes in) the forms of words (such as pronouns). Personal pronouns change according to their use as a subject, object, possessive, or reflexive. Ex: He is reading a book./ The dog bit him.

VII. Stress and intonation

Stress and intonation are features of sound, but they are also important in grammar. Ex: Will you permit us to go?/ We need a permit to go. (The change in stress indicates that the word "permit" in the first example is a verb while the word "permit" in the second example is a noun.)

SYNTACTICAL ARRANGEMENTS

It is impossible to cover all the various grammatical arrangements of English sentences here. The native speaker of English knows what is a grammatical sentence and what is not. A person who is learning English has to gain that same type of knowledge.

The same thought or information can be expressed by several quite different sentences. However, sentences that seem quite similar can also be very different in meaning.

I. Sentences

A. A sentence consists of a subject and a predicate. In modern linguistics, we speak of a noun phrase (NP) and a verb phrase (VP).

B. A sentence may be simple or it may be complex. Ex: The dog chased the cat./ The dog with the droopy ears chased the cat that belonged to the lady who lives up the street in the house with the green shutters.

C. The complex sentence may be thought of as a number of simple sentences

joined together. This will make it easier for the student to understand a complex sentence and to create sentences of his/her own.

D. In English there are five basic simple sentence types:

Type of Verb	Sentence pattern
BE	NOUN + BE + NOUN (Those men are teachers.) NOUN + BE + ADJECTIVE (The pencil is blue.) NOUN + BE + ADVERB (The book is there.)
INTRANSITIVE VERB	NOUN + INTRANSITIVE VERB (They live near the office.)
TRANSITIVE VERB	NOUN + TRANSITIVE VERB + NOUN (They drink milk.) NOUN^1 + TRANSITIVE VERB + NOUN^2 + NOUN^3 (He bought his wife a gift.) NOUN^1 + TRANSITIVE VERB + NOUN^2 + NOUN^2 (The club elected Mary president.)
LINKING VERB	NOUN + LINKING VERB + ADJECTIVE (She looks beautiful.) NOUN^1 + LINKING VERB + NOUN^1 (John became a doctor.)
MODAL AUXILIARY	A modal auxiliary may precede the verb in any of the patterns above. (The books might be there.) (He could buy his wife a gift.)

E. Another feature of word order in sentences is a process of changing the word order, called _transformation._ By changing word order, a sentence can be changed from a sentence to a negative statement, a question, a negative question, etc.

The following examples of transformations illustrate how we can begin with simple components (parts) of sentences and put them together to form quite complex sentences:

1. NOUN + BE + NOUN

(Affirmative) Statement:	Those men are teachers.
Negative Statement:	Those men are not teachers.
(Affirmative) Question:	Are those men teachers?
Negative Question:	Aren't those men teachers?
Tag Questions:	Those men are teachers, aren't they?
"Or" Questions:	Are those men teachers or doctors?
	Aren't those men teachers or doctors?
Question-Word Questions:	Who are those men?
	Where are those men?

2. NOUN + transitive VERB + NOUN

Statement:	They drink milk.
Negative Statement:	They don't drink milk.
Question:	Do they drink milk?
Negative Question:	Don't they drink milk?
Tag Questions:	They drink milk, don't they?
	They don't drink milk, do they?
"Or" Questions:	Do they drink milk or coffee?
	Don't they drink milk or coffee?
Question-Word Questions:	What do they drink?
	When do they drink milk?

3. PASSIVE TRANSFORMATIONS (Passive transformations may be made from sentences with transitive verbs. The receiver of the action is the subject, and a form of BE is used with the past participle of the main verb. The doer of the action, if expressed, follows the preposition "by.")
Ex: (Active: Bill drank the milk.)

Passive:

Statement:	The table was built by Bill.
Negative Statement:	The table wasn't built by Bill.
Question:	Was the table built by Bill?
Tag Questions:	The table was built by Bill, wasn't it?
	The table wasn't built by Bill, was it?
"Or" Questions:	Was the table built by Bill or Ray?
	Wasn't the table built by Bill or Ray?
Question-Word Questions:	When was the table built?
	Why was the table built?

II. Negative and interrogative sentences
    A. As shown in the examples of transformations above, negative sentences and questions are closely related.
    1. Verb phrases with "be," "have," or any modal are made negative by adding "not."
    2. Questions are formed by inverting the order of the subject and the auxiliaries, "be," "have," or the modal.
    3. Where a verb phrase has no auxiliary, "do" must be added in order to form a question or a negative. This form of "do" carries the tense and person, receives the particle "not," and is inverted with the subject to form the question. Ex: I like swimming. Do you like swimming? Mary doesn't like it.

    B. Tag questions also demonstrate the relationship between negative forms and interrogative forms. Ex: John doesn't sing very well, does he?

III. Other types of sentences
    A. Requests or commands Ex: Open your books.
    B. "It" and "there" sentences Ex: It's five o'clock. There's a pen on the table.
    C. Exclamations Ex: How pretty she is!

D, Ellipsis Ex: How pretty!

IV. Combining sentences

A. The conjunctions "and," "or, "and "but" are commonly used for joining simple sentences, depending on the speaker's intended meaning.

    1. In some cases, the <u>order</u> of the clauses may be important. Ex: He has an old car and keeps it in good repair. (Here the second clause is a result of the first.)

    2. Use of the correct verb form and of the connecting words, "and...too," "and...so,""and...not...either," "and...neither," and "but...not" in connected statements may be difficult for learners of English. The chart illustrates a few basic principles.

FIRST STATEMENT	SECOND STATEMENT
AFFIRMATIVE Mary speaks Russian, He can swim, Mary speaks Russian, He can swim,	*AFFIRMATIVE* **and** John does **too.** **and** she can **too.** *or* **and so** does John. **and so** can she.
NEGATIVE Mary doesn't speak Russian, He can't swim, Mary doesn't speak Russian, He can't swim,	*NEGATIVE* **and** John doesn't either. **and** she can't either. *or* **and neither** does John. **and neither** can she.
AFFIRMATIVE Mary speaks Russian, He can swim, *NEGATIVE* Mary doesn't speak Russian, He can't swim,	*NEGATIVE* **but** John **doesn't.** **but** she **can't.** *AFFIRMATIVE* **but** John does. **but** she can.

B. Elements within sentences may also be conjoined. Ex: Bill went to the party <u>and</u> Mary went to the party. Bill <u>and</u> Mary went to the party.

V. Embedded sentences (small sentences within larger sentences) may be of three basic types:

A. Relative clauses - the introductory word, a relative pronoun, refers to a noun phrase in the main clause. Ex: The child <u>who is sick</u> went to bed early(subject). The lady <u>whom you met</u> is my piano teacher (object).

B. Adverbial clauses - introduced by such words as "because," "if," etc. They differ from relative clauses in 2 ways:

    1. They are introduced by words that show a relationship in meaning between the two clauses, as well as function as introductory words. Ex: We will have a picnic <u>if it doesn't rain.</u>

    2. They may be placed either before or after the main clause. Ex: He didn't go out <u>because it was raining.</u> <u>Because it was raining</u>, he didn't go out.

C. Clauses functioning as noun phrases, which take the place of subjects, objects, and objects of prepositions. Ex: He said <u>whatever he pleased.</u> (Direct ob-

ject)

VI. The noun phrase

A. The noun phrase may be simple (Ex: The boy) or complex (Ex: The boy who likes to swim) and it may be used as a subject (Ex: <u>The boy</u> ate the apple.) or as an object (Ex: The dog bit <u>the boy</u>). The form of the noun phrase does not change except in the case of personal pronouns. Ex: Mary gave <u>Beth</u> the book. Mary gave <u>her</u> the book. <u>Mary</u> gave Beth the book. <u>She</u> gave Beth the book.

B. A difficult problem for the learner of English is the choice of the article to be used (or not used). See: SPECIAL HELPS, *"Articles in the English Language."*

VII. Order of modifiers (adjectives and adverbs)

Both adjectives and adverbs appear in a very definite order in the sentence, as shown in the following diagram.

Ex: (They live in) <u>the</u>   <u>first two</u>   <u>red</u>   <u>brick</u>   HOUSES   <u>on the block</u>.

1. Noun Determiner	2. Order and Quantity	INTEN-SIFIER (Adverb)	3. Descrip-tion	4. Classifi-cation	NOUN BEING MODIFIED	5. Miscel-laneous

VIII. Verb phrases

A. The verb phrase is what we have commonly called the predicate of the sentence. It may be composed of:

1. The verb alone Ex: <u>eat</u>
2. Main verb + an auxiliary (helping) verb Ex: <u>has eaten</u>
3. Verb (or verb + auxiliary) + a noun phrase Ex: <u>has eaten an apple</u>

The following rule shows the order in arranging auxiliaries within a verb phrase:

$$\text{tense} + (\text{modal}) + (\text{HAVE} + \text{-}en)\ (\text{BE} + \text{-}ing) + \text{MV}$$

The MODAL can be any modal auxiliary such as "may," "can," "must," or "should." -*en* represents the <u>past participle</u> of the verb and -*ing* the <u>present participle</u>. MV is the <u>main verb</u>. The parenthesis indicate <u>optional choices</u>. The inflectional suffixes are added to the MV to form the selected <u>participle</u>. Except when making a command or request, <u>tense</u> is either <u>past</u> or <u>present</u>.

Ex:

<u>might</u>	<u>have</u>	<u>been</u>	<u>walk</u>	-ing
modal	HAVE	BE + participle (-*en*)	main verb	present participle

B. The verb forms are a very important part of learning English. The student must not only learn the forms, but how and when to use them, and the differences in meaning. Ex: "He remembered to go" and "He remembered going" have different meanings while "He likes to swim" and "He likes swimming" have quite similar meanings.

C. Modal auxiliaries are particularly difficult for non-native speakers of English because they differ from other auxiliaries in three ways:

1. The form of the modal is different from other verbs in that modals do not use the **-s** ending in the 3rd person (Ex: He can, He may, etc.) and the modal is

followed by the simple form of the main verb instead of the -ing or the past participle form (Ex: "is looking", but "can look"). Modals cannot occur as infinitives or past participles.

2. The meanings of modal forms are different from other verbs, especially in regard to tense. Some modals refer to the future or to something that will probably happen while others refer to permission, ability, or the need for something. Ex: Jim will sing (future). Jim can sing (ability).

3. Students must learn modals in the same way they learn vocabulary, by relating meaning to context. A great deal of practice is necessary.

D. Additional information about the formation of verb phrases will be given under SPECIAL HELPS, *"The English Verb."*

IX. Phrasal verbs

A. Phrasal verbs also cause non-native speakers great difficulty. The meaning of the complete verb is different from the sum of the 2 parts. Ex: He looked up the number in the phone book. He looked it up. (Many of these are given in the All Nations dictionary.) Compare: He looked up at the sky (verb + preposition).

B. Some phrasal verbs can be separated as in the above example. Others cannot. Ex: She looked into the matter. She looked into it.

C. Phrasal verbs need to be differentiated from verbs followed by prepositions. Ex: Wait for the girl. (The preposition always precedes its object.)

SPECIAL HELPS
FOR LEARNERS OF ENGLISH

THE ENGLISH VERB

The following is a linguistic study of all English verbs other than "be," "have," and "do." Since inflections for the verb forms are related to the sound system of English, the learner should focus on the oral forms before going on to the written spellings of them.

I. In all cases, the -ing form of the verb differs from the simple form only by the addition of -ing.

II. The -s form, used with the present tense, singular, third person, may be pronounced in one of three ways:

A. - [s] when the final element of the simple form is voiceless and is not sibilant or palatal /s,z,ʃ,ʒ, tʃ, dʒ/. Ex: pats (pæts)

B. - [z] when the final element of the simple form is voiced and is not sibilant or palatal. Ex: pads (pædz)

C. - [əz] when the final element of the simple form is sibilant or palatal. Ex: misses (mɪs–əz)

Apart from <u>Be</u>, <u>Have</u>, and <u>Do</u>, there is only one verb in English which is irregular in the -s form: the verb <u>say</u> is pronounced [sɛz] in this form. (Forms for <u>Be</u>, <u>Have</u>, and <u>Do</u> are given under the entry in the All Nations dictionary.)

III. Past tense and past participle forms are divided into four main categories, each with two or more sub-categories:

A. - [t] or [d] in final position. Ex: walked (wɔkt)

1. Voiceless [t]: like, liked, liked (laɪk, laɪkt, laɪkt)

2. Voiced [d]: love, loved, loved; stay, stayed, stayed (lʌv, lʌvd, lʌvd; steʸ, steʸd, steʸd)

3. Voiced [d] preceded by the vowel [ə]: hate, hated (heʸt, **heʸt**–əd)

4. In England, <u>smell, smelt, smelled</u> (in America, <u>smelled</u>); also <u>burnt</u>, <u>learnt</u>, <u>spelt</u>, <u>spilt</u>, <u>spoilt</u>, and <u>dwelt</u> in alternation with the final [d] sound. (smɛlt-smɛld; spɔɪlt-spɔɪld; etc.)

5. Verbs whose simple forms end in a <u>voiced</u> [d] while the past tenses and the past participle forms end in a <u>voiceless</u> [t]. Ex: bend, bent, bent (bɛnd, bɛnt, bɛnt) Others in the category: <u>build</u>, <u>lend</u>, <u>send</u>, <u>spend</u>, <u>rend</u>, <u>gird</u>

6. Past tense and past participle are the <u>same as the simple form</u>: <u>hit</u>, <u>spread</u>, <u>bet</u>, <u>burst</u>, <u>cast</u>, <u>cost</u>, <u>cut</u>, <u>hit</u>, <u>hurt</u>, <u>let</u>, <u>put</u>, <u>quit</u>, <u>set</u>, <u>shut</u>, <u>slit</u>, <u>split</u>, <u>thrust</u>, <u>upset</u>

B. - [n] in final position. Ex: eat, ate, eaten (iʸt , eʸt, iʸt–ən)

1. Small group with past tense form having a [t and d] and the past participle having a final [n]. Ex: sew, sewed, sewn (soʷ, soʷd, soʷn) Also: sow, show, hew

2. One verb. Ex: beat, beat, beaten (biʸt, biʸt, biʸt–ən)

C. - vowel change. Ex: run, ran, run (rʌn, ræn, rʌn)

1. vowel change only

a) drink, drank, drunk (-ɪ-, -æ-, -ʌ-)

b) Past tense and past participle are identical, but differ from the simple forms. (12 patterns here) Ex: win, won, won (-ɪ-, -ʌ-, -ʌ-)

c) Past participle is the same as the simple form but the past tense form is different. Ex: come, came, come (-ʌ-, -eʸ-, -ʌ-)

2. Vowel change and [t] or [d]. Ex: keep, kept, kept (t) on end (kiʸp, kɛpt, kɛpt)

3. Vowel change and [n].

a) Three distinct vowels are involved: ride, rode, ridden (raɪd, roʷd, **rɪd**–ən) Also: drive, rise, strive, write, smite

b) Vowels of the past tense and the past participle are identical but differ from those of the simple forms. Ex: steal, stole, stolen (stiʸl, stoʷl, **stoʷl**–ən)

c) Vowel of the past participle is the same as that of the simple form, but different from the past form. Ex: see, saw, seen (siʸ, sɔ, siʸn)

d) Only one verb has the feature of vowel change plus [n] in the past participle, with only the addition of [t] or [d] in the past tense: swell, swelled, swollen (swɛl, swɛld, **swoʷ**–lən)

4. - loss of final consonant. Ex: make, make, made (meʸk, meʸk, meʸd) (al-

ways occurring with [t] or [d], and, except for one verb, vowel change):

a) There is only one verb in which there is no vowel change: make, made, made (meᵏk, meʸd, meʸd)

b) The past tense and past participle forms end in [t] even though the preceding sound is a vowel. Ex: bring, brought, brought (brɪŋ, brɔt, brɔt)

c) Exceptions (The next to the last consonant is lost instead of the last): stand, stood, stood (stænd, stʊd, stʊd) Also: understand, understood, understood

5. Suppletion (The past tense and past participle forms are both entirely new forms): The only verb in English where there is suppletion is **go**: go, went, gone (goʷ, wɛnt, gɔn)

PREPOSITIONS

I. Introduction

Prepositions may be a source of great difficulty for learners of English as a second or foreign language. Information that is signaled by prepositions in English may be signaled by an inflection of the noun or article in other languages. In some languages, *post*-positions may be used rather than *pre*-positions. Another problem is that prepositions may not match up well with the translations into other languages. Examples: English *to* = German *zu*; English *at* = German *an* (or *in* or *bei*); but: English "John is *at* home" = German "Johann ist *zu* Hause."

II. Basic Uses of Prepositions

A. A preposition shows a relationship between its object and other words in a sentence.

B. A preposition may be one word (e.g.: **in, on, by, of,** etc.) or in the form of a phrase that functions as a single unit (e.g.: **in back of, on top of, at the bottom of,** etc.).

C. Prepositions may express the following relationships: Place, position, direction, time, manner, and agent.
Ex:
The book is **on** the table. (place or position)
The dog ran **toward** the boy. (direction)
Class begins **at** ten o'clock. (time)
The team will travel **by** train. (manner)
This book was written **by** my favorite author.(agent)

1. Prepositions that show place or position: **at, to, from, in, on, by, beside, near, against, over, under, beneath, underneath, on top of, behind, in back of, in front of, up, down, across, around, through, between, among, inside, outside, after, before, above, below, at the top of, at the bottom of, at the head of**

Compare the uses of in, on, and at in the following situations:

a) IN-ON In general, in means "beneath the surface" and on means "touching the surface." Ex: I have $10 in my pocket. I have a hat on my head.

b) ON-AT In an address, on is used with the name of the street; at, with the house number plus the name of the street. Ex: Mary lives on Main Street. She lives at 4370 Main Street.

d) AT-IN In referring to location, at usually indicates a specific location; in, a location within a building, city, etc. Ex: We'll meet you at the office. Mother is in the kitchen.

In is also used in referring to a location within a country. Ex: The Smiths are traveling in Mexico.

In is ordinarily used in referring to cities. Ex: We live in Denver, Colorado.

At is sometimes used in referring to the arrival of a train, bus, etc. Ex: Our plane will arrive at Los Angeles at 10:00 A.M.

2. Prepositions of <u>direction</u>: **into, out of, toward, by way of**

Compare the uses of in and into in the following situations:

In usually refers to place or position. Ex: He is in the library this afternoon.

Into generally refers to motion or action, although in may be used interchangeably with into in situations of this kind. Ex: He went into (in) the library just now.

3. Prepositions of <u>time</u>: **at, by, in, on, for, during, since, after, before, until, (till), at the beginning of, at the end of, in the middle of**

Compare the uses of on, in, for, during, and since in the following situations:

a) ON-IN In giving dates, on is used before days of the week or before months plus the day of the month; in before months not followed by the day, and before numbers indicating the year. Ex: The new store will open on Saturday. We'll take our vacation in June this year.

b) FOR-DURING-SINCE In expressions of time, for refers to a period of time, often stated in number of hours, days, etc. and in such expressions as for a little while, for a few minutes, etc. Ex: He worked for two hours. During also refers to a period of time. Ex: It must have rained during the night.

In many cases for refers to something more or less continuous, during to something intermittent. For is followed by the indefinite article, during, by the definite article. Ex: I swam for an hour (I swam continuously for an hour.) I swam during the summer (At some time, but not continuously.)

Since refers to a time that extends from a point in the past to the present, or to another point in the past. Ex: I have been at work since eight A.M.

c) ON TIME - IN TIME on time means "on schedule"; in time means before an appointed time. Ex: I always get to work on time. I got to work in time to read the mail before our meeting.

d) FROM...TO - FROM...UNTIL These mean about the same and are usually interchangeable. Only from...to is used in referring to place or position. Ex: We drove from Denver to Phoenix this week.

e) AROUND - ABOUT Both expressions are used to indicate approximate time.

4. Prepositions of <u>manner</u>: **by, on, in, with, like**

5. Some other types of prepositions are as follows:

a) <u>Agent</u>: **by, with** Ex: He locked the door with his key.

b) <u>Accompaniment</u>: **with** Ex: Will you go with me to the mall?

c) <u>Purpose</u>: **for** Ex: Here's a broom for sweeping the floor.

d) <u>Association</u>: **of** Ex: The leg **of** the table is broken.
e) <u>Measure</u>: **of, by** Ex: Bread is sold **by** the loaf.
f) <u>Similarity</u>: **like** Ex: The baby looks like his father.
g) <u>In the capacity of</u>: **as** Ex: Mr. Smith is serving **as** our new director.

ARTICLES IN THE ENGLISH LANGUAGE

I. Introduction

All English nouns must be classified as either proper (Ex: Mary Jones, New York City, Saturn) or common (Ex: apple, dog, city). In English, as in all languages, proper nouns, personal nouns, and possessive determiners are definite because they refer to specific persons or things.

In addition, all English common nouns must be classified as either mass (Ex: water, literature, clothing) or count (Ex: a beverage, a book, a dress). It is this distinction between mass and count nouns that accounts for differences in the article used. Because what is countable in one language may be a mass noun in another language, and because there may be a shift from count to mass or mass to count on certain nouns, the learner will have considerable difficulty.

II. General Principles of Article Usage

The way that <u>definite</u> and <u>indefinite</u> articles are used depends on the context, that is, how familiar the speaker/writer is and how familiar the listener/reader is with the noun being mentioned. In general, the English <u>definite article</u> is used in the first reference to a noun (topical position) while the <u>indefinite article</u> is used in later references to the same noun (comment position).

<u>DEFINITE ARTICLE</u>: **the**

In English, the main use of **the** is to single out or identify a specific or particular person or thing.

<u>INDEFINITE ARTICLE</u>: **a/an** Use **a** before words beginning with a consonant <u>sound</u> (Ex: **a** <u>b</u>ook, **a** <u>ch</u>air, **a** <u>h</u>otel, **a** <u>u</u>niversity); **an,** before words beginning with a vowel <u>sound</u> (e.g. **an** <u>a</u>pple, **an** <u>e</u>gg, **an** <u>h</u>our, **an** <u>o</u>nion).

Functions of the indefinite article are as follows:
1. To introduce to the listener a noun that is singled out or identified for the speaker but not for the listener. Ex: "I watched a good movie on T.V. last night."
2. To show that the noun is not identified for either the speaker or the listener. Ex: "Mr. Jones bought a new car."
3. To refer to a noun that is not identified to the speaker but is assumed to be known to the listener. Ex: "Miss Smith, I understand you have sent a letter to the editor."

III. Mass-count Distinction

Some English nouns are essentially mass nouns (Ex: rice) while others are essentially count (Ex: girl). Ex:

COUNT
a. The girl was playing tennis.
b. A girl was playing tennis.
c. The girls were playing tennis.
d. Some girls were playing tennis.
e. Girls usually like to get new clothes.

MASS
a. We are having rice for dinner.
b. Some rice was left in the pot.
c. The rice was prepared just the way I like it.

Some mass nouns may also be used as count nouns. Such a noun, when used with an article, denotes "an instance of" the noun given, and it functions like a count noun. Ex: (Mass) **"Crime** is a serious problem in our major cities." (Count) "The **crimes** of robbery and murder are very serious."

Other regular shifts from mass to count are those where the count noun denotes "a kind/type of" or "a unit/serving of." Ex: (Mass) "I usually have **coffee** with my breakfast." (Count) "I'd like **a coffee**, please."(Meaning a cup of coffee).

IV. Articles With Singular Count Nouns

A. An article is used with a *singular count noun* (a noun that stands for a person or thing that can be counted as a single unit or item). It is either **a book** or **the book, an apple** or **the apple**,etc. In a few situations, **a** or **an** means almost the same as the number **one**. Ex: "We'll need a chair or two." (*or* "We'll need **one** or two chairs.") More often **a** or **an** has the meaning of **one** in the sense of one unit or thing. In situations of this kind, **one** cannot be substituted for **a** or **an** without changing the meaning.Ex: "John has **a** black suit."(*but* "John has only **one** black suit.")

B. The main use of **the** is to point out a specific person or thing. Before a singular countable noun, **the** has the same meaning as the demonstrative **that**, although **that** is more emphatic in pointing something out. Ex: "Did you give **the** rose to Mary?"/ "Did you give **that** rose to Mary?

C. In the above example, the speaker has in mind a specific *rose* and he assumes that the listener also has in mind the same *rose*. If necessary, the speaker might identify the rose by adding a qualifying word, phrase, or clause. Ex: "**the** rose **that is on her desk**"; "I ate **the** apple **that was on the plate.**"

D. Sometimes an *indefinite* article is used to identify the noun and then there is a shift to the *definite* article after the specific identity has been established. Examples: "There is **a** map of China on the wall. Can you find Beijing on **the** map?"; "**A** boy and **a** girl where sitting on a bench at the bus stop. **The** girl was waiting for the bus to the library and **the** boy was waiting for the bus to the shopping center."

V. Articles With Plural Count Nouns

A. Because a plural countable noun refers to more than one person or thing, the *indefinite* article *cannot* be used. It is either **pens** or **the pens; oranges** or **the**

oranges, etc.

B. An article is not used before a plural noun that refers to persons or things in general or as a group, e.g. "**Teachers** are needed in every part of the world."

C. **The** singles out specific or particular persons or things. Used with a plural countable noun, **the** has the same meaning as **those**, although **those** is more emphatic. Compare: "Please give Mary **the** flowers."/ "Please give Mary **those** flowers."

VI. Articles With Non-count Nouns

The article is omitted with the following types of nouns, which are considered non-countable:

A. *Mass nouns,* such as **water, air, coffee, oxygen,** etc.: "The balloon is filled with **air**."

1. Indefinite adjectives, such as **some, any, much,** etc. may be used with *mass nouns* to indicate indefinite quantity: "Do you want **some coffee?**"

2. To indicate a definite amount of a *mass noun,* a countable unit of measure may be used. Compare: "I'd like some ice cream." "I'd like a dish of ice cream, please."

B. *Abstract nouns,* such as **honesty, law, life, truth, beauty, democracy,** etc.: "**Crime** does not pay."; "What is **truth?**"

C. Names of general areas of subject matter, such as **history, art, science, economics, English:** "She is taking courses in **English, mathematics,** and **history.** (If the name of an area of subject matter is used as a modifier, it may be preceded by an article: "She is studying **the French language.**")

D. Names of recreational activities or sports: "My grandsons all play **soccer.**" *but* "He is playing in **the soccer game** this afternoon."

VII. Some Specific Uses of the Definite Article

A. **The** is generally used with names of things that are automatically singled out because of their obvious identification. Ex:"I'm going to **the** store/beach/library." (People in each locality would refer to many things in this way).

B. **The** is also used on a universal scale. Ex: "**the** moon/equator/north"

C. Monuments, places considered unique, etc., may be thought of in the same way. Ex: **the** White House, **the** Taj Mahal

D. **The** is used in some expressions of time. Ex: "in **the** morning"

E. **The** is used when **first, second,** etc., precede a noun. Ex:"**the** first chapter." No article is used when **one, two,** etc. follow a noun. Ex: "Chapter One"

FORMING THE PLURAL OF NOUNS

I. Most nouns, except those ending in *s, z, ch, sh,* and some that end in *o,* and *y,* form the plural by adding **-s**. Ex: book - book<u>s</u>

II. Most nouns ending in *s, z, ch,* and *sh* form the plural by adding **-es**. Ex: dish - dish<u>es</u>

III. Words that end in *y,* preceded by a consonant, form the plural by changing the *y* to *i* and adding **-es**. Ex: baby - bab<u>ies</u>

IV. Words ending in *y* preceded by a vowel, form the plural by simply adding **-s**. Ex: boy - boy<u>s</u>

V. Nouns ending in *o,* preceded by a vowel, form the plural by adding **-s**. Ex: radio - radio<u>s</u>

VI. Nouns ending in *o* preceded by a consonant, form the plural by adding **-es**. Ex: hero - hero<u>es</u>

VII. Nouns referring to music and ending in *o* preceded by a consonant, form the plural by simply adding **-s**. Ex: piano - piano<u>s</u>

VIII. Some nouns follow none of the above rules, but form the noun in an unusual way. Ex: child - children; mouse - mice

IX. Compound nouns form the plural from the main word. Ex: mother-in-law - mother<u>s</u>-in-law

X. When a solid compound ends in *ful,* the plural is formed at the end of the solid compound and not within the word. Ex: spoonful - spoonful<u>s</u>

XI. Nouns taken from another language form their plurals as they would in the original language. Ex: datum - data

A FEW HELPFUL SPELLING RULES

I. IE and EI
    A. The *e* usually precedes the *i* when it follows *c*. Ex: rec<u>ei</u>ve

    B. The *e* usually follows the *i* when it follows any letter other than *c*. Ex: th<u>ie</u>f

    C. There are a few exceptions that must be learned, since they do not follow any rule. Ex: n<u>ei</u>ther; l<u>ei</u>sure; w<u>ei</u>rd; s<u>ei</u>ze

    D. When the sound is not (i^y), and especially if it is (e^y), the *e* precedes the *i*. Ex: sl<u>ei</u>gh; v<u>ei</u>l

BASIC PUNCTUATION RULES

I. The period
 A. A period is used at the end of statements and commands or requests. Ex: Mary is reading a book.
 B. A period is used after initials or abbreviations. Ex: Mr. R. K. Black

II. The question mark
 A. A question mark is used at the end of all <u>direct</u> questions. Ex: Where do you live?
 B. A question mark is not used after an <u>indirect</u> question. Ex: She asked where I lived.

III. The exclamation point is used after words, expressions, or sentences to show strong feeling or to emphasize the sentence. Ex: Help! Thief!

IV. The comma
 A. A comma is used between two long main clauses that are joined by *and, but, or, nor,* or *for.* Ex: I enjoy watching good movies, but I don't think there's a good one showing this weekend.
 B. When a modifying clause precedes the main clause, it is usually followed by a comma. Ex: When she arrived at work, it was already past nine o'clock.
 C. When a modifying clause follows the main clause, a comma is not used. Ex: It was after nine o'clock when she arrived.
 D. Clauses that modify nouns, but are not necessary for clarification or iden-tification of the noun modified, are set off by commas. Ex: My brother, whom you met, is planning to visit us this week. ("Whom you met" is not necessary for iden-tifying my brother.)
 E. An appositive (word, phrase, or clause that is used to explain or describe another noun) is set off by commas when it merely adds information about the noun it modifies. Ex: John, **my brother,** lives in another state.
 F. An appositive that only serves to identify the noun modified is not set off by commas. Ex: My brother **John** lives in another state.
 G. Side remarks that interrupt the main idea are set off by commas. Ex: By the way, what time does the bus arrive?
 H. If the words **yes, no, well,** etc. introduce a sentence, they are set off by commas. Ex: Yes, I want to come to your party.
 I. Names in direct address are set off by commas. Ex: **John,** do you hear me?
 J. A direct quotation is set off by commas. Ex: John said, "Yes, I hear you."
 K. Commas are used to separate items in a date. Ex: Today is August 24th, 1992.
 L. A comma is used to separate the city from the state and the state from the country. Ex: I was born in Sterling, Johnson County, Nebraska.

V. The semicolon
 A. A semicolon is used before the following conjunctions when they join two main clauses: **then, thus, furthermore, moreover, consequently, besides, there-fore, still, otherwise, however, nevertheless.** (A comma often follows the con-junction.) Ex: He is an important person; however, he is also required to follow

the rules.

B. Sometimes a semicolon is used to join two closely related main clauses. Ex: Mary is a doctor; her brother is a dentist.

VI. The colon

A. A colon is used to introduce a word, sentence, or list in a formal way. Ex: My address is as follows: 123 East Street; Sterling, Nebraska.

B. A colon follows the greeting in a business letter. Ex: Dear Mr. Smith:

C. A colon is used in telling time. Ex: It is 6:15 P.M.

VII. Quotation Marks

A. Quotation marks are placed at the beginning and end of the direct words of a speaker. Ex: "Where are you going?" she asked.

B. If a quotation is interrupted, an extra set of quotation marks is used. Ex: "Excuse me," he said. "I'd like to go with you."

C. Quotation marks are not used with an indirect quotation. Ex: She asked me where I was going.

D. Titles of poems, short stories, musical compositions, and articles are enclosed in quotation marks. Ex: Every school child has read "Rip Van Winkle."

E. When one quotation is placed inside another quotation, the outside quotation will be shown by *double* quotation marks and the inside quotation by *single* quotation marks. Ex: The teacher said, "Children, be sure to finish reading 'Rip Van Winkle' by class time tomorrow."

F. When a quotation has two or more paragraphs, quotation marks are placed at the *beginning* of each paragraph and at the *end* of the last one.

Ex: The teacher read, "Hudson Taylor was sick for much of his life, but he depended on God for His strength and direction.

" Famine and disease swept through China, where he worked. He lost his wife, Maria, and their third child to cholera. He fell and for a time was paralyzed from spinal injury.

" Yet, in spite of all this trouble, Hudson Taylor was one of God's greatest warriors. With much prayer and faith, he started the China Inland Mission."

G. Following are some notes on using quotation marks with other punctuation:

1. Quotation marks are placed *outside* the comma and the period. Ex: "I'm going to the store," she said. / She said, "I'm going to the store."

2. Quotation marks are placed *inside* the semicolon and the colon. Ex: The students read "Rip Van Winkle"; however, they really wanted to go out for recess.

3. Quotation marks are placed *outside* the question mark and the exclamation point when the question mark or exclamation point belong to the quoted matter only. Ex: The policeman shouted, "Stop!"

4. Quotation marks are placed *inside* the question mark and the exclamation point when the question mark or exclamation point belongs to the whole sentence or clause that contains the quoted matter. Ex: Shall we sing "America The Beautiful"?

VIII. The apostrophe

A. An apostrophe is used in contractions to show that letters have been omit-

ted Ex: Don't go. It's early yet.

    B. An apostrophe followed by **s** ('s) is added to singular nouns and to plural nouns that do not end in **s** to form the possessive. Ex: This is Mary's book and that is mine.

    C. An apostrophe only (') is added to plural nouns that end in **s** or **es** to form the possessive. Ex: The teachers' lunchroom is closed today.

    D. An apostrophe is used with the indefinite pronouns: **one, other, somebody, nobody, anyone, someone,** etc. to show possession. Ex: Somebody's coat is lying on the floor.

    E. An apostrophe followed by **s** ('s) is added to form the plural of numbers or letters. Ex: How many **s's** are in the word "Mississippi"?

IX. Parentheses may be used to set off remarks, comments, explanations, etc. that interrupt the main thought. Ex: If it doesn't rain (and I hope it doesn't) we'll all go to the beach.

X. Brackets may be used to show comment or questions added to quoted material by someone other than the author. Ex: Acquitting the guilty and condemning the innocent — the Lord detests [hates] them both (Proverbs 17:15).

XI. Ellipsis (three dots) is used to indicate omission in quoted material. (If the omission occurs at the end of the sentence, a period is added.) Ex: "I think...that is...I don't know...," he faltered and then stopped speaking.

XII. The dash

    A. The dash is used to indicate an interruption in the expression of an idea or to give an afterthought. Ex: I'll finish this report—at long last—by noon tomorrow.

    B. A dash is sometimes used in place of a comma to give special emphasis. Ex: He gave us statistics on the country—population, average income, the literacy rate, etc.

XIII. Underlining

    A. Titles of magazines, newspapers, and books are underlined in handwriting and typewriting, but italicized in printing. Ex: (Handwritten or typed) Did you read the article about Bill and Sarah in the <u>Denver Post</u>? / (Printed) Did you read the article about Bill and Sarah in the *Denver Post*?

    B. Foreign phrases and emphasized words are underlined in handwriting or typewriting, but italicized in print. Ex: (Handwritten or typed) He said <u>what?</u>/ (Printed) He said *what*?

XIV. Capitalization

    A. Every sentence begins with a capital letter. Ex: The book is on the shelf.

    B. The first person singular pronoun (I) is always capitalized. Ex: My husband doesn't like watermelon, but **I** do.

    C. Proper names of people, countries, cities, streets, buildings, etc. begin with capital letters. Ex: My friend, John, comes from Spain.

    D. Names of languages and adjectives of nationality begin with capital letters. Ex: John speaks Spanish very well.

E. Names of college or university courses, other than languages, are capitalized when the official title of the course is given, but not when speaking of the subject in a general way. Ex: I'm taking History 101 this semester./ I don't enjoy studying history.

F. The names of the days of the week, holidays, and the names of the months are capitalized. Ex: My birthday is on Tuesday, March 12th.

G. Names of the seasons are usually not capitalized. Ex: I enjoy spring more than fall.

H. **East, West, North,** and **South** are capitalized only when they refer to a section of the country. Ex: Mary is from the South.

I. Names of religions and deities are written with a capital letter. Ex: She is a Christian and she believes that Jesus is the only way of salvation.

J. Prepositions, articles, conjunctions, and auxiliary verbs are not capitalized in a title unless they begin the sentence. Ex: The name of the book is *Gilberto and the Wind.*

K. Professional titles used with the name of a person are capitalized. Ex: My appointment was with Dr. Martin, but I saw another doctor instead.

XV. Numerals

A. In general, numbers that can be stated in only one or two words are spelled out while other numbers are usually shown in figures. Ex: The book cost twenty-one dollars./ There are 835 pages in the book.

B. The number at the beginning of a sentence is spelled out. Ex: Two hundred and twenty-five people came to the party.

C. Use figures for dates, pages, dimensions, decimals, percentages, measures, exact amounts of money, designations of time followed by A.M. of P.M., and addresses. Ex: 5475 Jennifer Lane

D. Spell out ordinal numbers where possible. Ex: Third Avenue

E. Be consistent in the treatment of numbers, especially in the same sentence or paragraph.

XVI. Abbreviations

A. Abbreviate the following titles and forms of address, even in formal usage: **Mr., Mrs., Ms., Dr., Mme., Mlle, M.** Ex: Mr. Smith

B. Abbreviate titles of the clergy, government officials, officers in organizations, and military personnel only when the title is followed by a first name or initials as well as the surname. Ex: Gen. Robert E. Lee/ *but* General Lee

C. **Jr.** and **Sr.** following a name. These abbreviations should be used only when a first name or initial is included. Ex: Paul Smith, Sr.

D. **Esq.** following a name. This abbreviation should not be used with any other title. Ex: John Hollingsworth, Esq.

E. Academic degrees are abbreviated. Ex: B.A. (Bachelor of Arts)

F. The terms used to describe businesses are abbreviated. Ex: Bill's Plumbing, Inc.

G. The names of states, territories, or possessions that immediately follow the name of a city, mountain, or other identifiable geographic location, are abbreviated except in formal writing. Ex: Denver, Colo.

H. Certain Latin expressions are abbreviated. Ex: i.e. (*id est*), that is

I. The following are not abbreviated:

1. Names of countries except U.S.S.R. (Union of Soviet Socialist Republics)

2. U.S. (United States) except when used before the name of an American ship or in tables, footnotes, etc.

3. The words **street, avenue, boulevard, drive,** etc., except when space is limited or brevity is required.

4. The days of the week and months of the year except in the most informal situations or tables.

5. Weights and measures except in lists of items, technical writing, etc.

XVII. Division of words

A. The division of a word at the end of a line should be avoided if possible. If it is necessary to divide a word, the divisions given in the dictionary should be followed.

B. Do not divide a word so that only one letter stands alone at the end or the beginning of a line.

C. Do not divide a one-syllable word ending in **-ed**.

D. Avoid the division of a word that carries only two letters over to the next line.

E. If a hyphenated word must be broken, divide the word where the hyphen already stands. Ex: mother-   or   mother-in-
        in-law   law

WEIGHTS AND MEASURES

LINEAR MEASURE

12 inches	=1 foot
3 feet	=1 yard
5.5 yards	=1 rod
40 rods	=1 furlong
8 furlongs (5280 feet)	=1 statute mile

MARINER'S MEASURE

6 feet	=1 fathom
1000 fathoms (approx.)	=1 nautical mile
3 nautical miles	=1 league

SQUARE MEASURE

144 square miles	=1 square foot
9 square feet	=1 square yard
30.25 square yards	=1 square rod
160 square rods	=1 acre
640 square acres	=1 square mile

CUBIC MEASURE

1728 cubic inches	=1 cubic foot
27 cubic feet	=1 cubic yard

SURVEYOR'S MEASURE

7.92 inches	=1 link
100 links	=1 chain

LIQUID MEASURE

4 gills	=1 pint
2 pints	=1 quart
4 quarts	=1 gallon
31.5 gallons	=1 barrel
2 barrels	=1 hogshead

APOTHECARIES' FLUID MEASURE

60 minims	=1 fluid dram
8 fluid drams	=1 fluid ounce
16 fluid ounces	=1 pint
2 pints	=1 quart
4 quarts	=1 gallon

DRY MEASURE

2 pints	=1 quart
8 quarts	=1 peck
4 pecks	=1 bushel

WOOD MEASURE

16 cubic feet	=1 cord foot
8 cord feet	=1cord

TIME MEASURE

60 seconds	=1 minute
60 minutes	=1 hour
24 hours	=1 day
7 days	=1 week
4 weeks (28 to 31 days)	=1 month
12 months (365-366 days)	=1 year
100 years	=1 century

ANGULAR AND CIRCULAR MEASURE

60 seconds	=1 minute
60 minutes	=1 degree
90 degrees	=1 right angle
180 degrees	=1 straight angle
360 degrees	=1 circle

TROY MEASURE

24 grains	=1 pennyweight
20 pennyweights	=1 ounce
12 ounces	=1 pound

AVOIRDUPOIS WEIGHT

27 11/32 grains	=1 dram
16 drams	=1 ounce
16 ounces	=1 pound
100 pounds	=1 short hundred-weight
20 short hundred-weight	=1 short ton

APOTHECARIES' WEIGHT

20 grains	=1 scruple
3 scruples	=1 dram
8 drams	=1 ounce
12 ounces	=1 pound

LINEAR MEASURE

10 millimeters	≈1 centimeter
10 centimeters	≈1 decimeter
10 decimeters	≈1 meter
10 meters	≈1 decameter
10 decameters	≈1 hectometer
10 hectometers	≈1 kilometer

LIQUID MEASURE

10 milliliters	≈1 centiliter
10 centiliters	≈1 deciliter
10 deciliters	≈1 liter
10 liters	≈1 decaliter
10 decaliters	≈1 hectoliter
10 hectoliters	≈1 kiloliter

SQUARE MEASURE

100 sq. millimeters	=1 sq. centimeter
100 sq. centimeters	=1 sq. decimeter
100 sq. decimeters	=1 sq. meter
100 sq. meters	=1 sq. decameter
100 sq. decameters	=1 sq. hectometer
100 sq. hectometers	=1 sq. kilometer

WEIGHTS

10 milligrams	≈1 centigram
10 centigrams	≈1 decigram
10 decigrams	≈1 gram
10 grams	≈1 decagram
10 decagrams	≈1 hectogram
10 hectograms	≈1 kilogram
100 kilograms	≈1 quintal
10 quintals	≈1 ton

CUBIC MEASURE

1000 cu. millimeters	=1 cu. centimeter
1000 cu. centimeters	=1 cu. decimeter
1000 cu. decimeters	=1 cu. meter

METRIC AND U.S. EQUIVALENTS

LINEAR MEASURE

U.S. Unit	Metric Unit
1 inch =	25.4 millimeters
	2.54 centimeters
1 foot =	30.48 centimeters
	3.048 decimeters
	0.3048 meter
1 yard =	0.9144 meter
1 mile =	1609.3 meters
	1.6093 kilometers
0.03937 inch =	1 millimeter
0.3937 inch =	1 centimeter
3.937 inches =	1 decimeter
39.37 inches =	1 meter
3.2808 feet =	1 meter
1.0936 yards =	1 meter

U.S. Unit	Metric Unit
3280.8 feet	= 1 kilometer
1093.6 yards	≈ 1 kilometer
0.62137 mile	= 1 kilometer

WEIGHTS

U.S. Unit	Metric Unit
1 grain	= 0.064799 gram
1 avoirdupois ounce	= 28.350 grams
1 troy ounce	= 31.103 grams
1 avoirdupois pound	= 0.45359 kilogram
1 troy pound	= 0.37324 kilogram
1 short ton	= 907.18 kilograms or 0.90718 metric ton

LIQUID MEASURE

U.S. Unit	Metric Unit
1 fluid ounce	= 29.573 milliliters
1 quart	= 9.4635 deciliters or 0.94635 liter
1 gallon	= 3.7854 liters
0.033814 fluid ounce	= 1 milliliter
1.0567 quarts	= 1 liter
0.26417 gallon	= 1 liter